# Encyclopedia of Social Work

19th
Edition

NASW PRESS

National Association of Social Workers
Washington, DC

*Executive Editor* Linda Beebe
*Managing Editor* Nancy A. Winchester
*Senior Editor* Fran Pflieger
*Editorial Secretary* Sarah Lowman

*Copy Editors*
Wendy Almeleh
Stephen D. Pazdan
Laurel J. Rumpl
Kendall W. Sterling

Samuel Allen Annette Hansen
Ida Audeh K. Hyde Loomis
Donna L. Brodsky Jack C. Neal
Greg Edmondson Chhaya M. Rao
Kathleen A. Elinskas Stephanie Selice

Wolf Publications, Inc.

*Proofreaders*
Susan J. Harris
Editorial Experts, Inc. Vivian Mason
Marcie Fenster Stella D. Matalas
Louise Goines

*Indexer*
Bernice Eisen

*Word Processor*
Donna Rambler



**Library of Congress Cataloging-in-Publication Data**
Encyclopedia of social work. 19th edition, 1995
Washington, DC, National Association of Social Workers.
v. 25 cm.
Decennial, 1977–
The 18th updated with a supplement, 1990
Continues: Social work year book.
ISSN 0071-0237 = Encyclopedia of social work.

Social service—Yearbooks. I. National Association of Social Workers.
II. Supplement to the Encyclopedia of social work.
DNLM: HV 35 E56

HV35.S6 361′.003 30-30948
ISBN 0-87101-255-3 hardcover MARC-S
0-87101-256-1 softcover
0-87101-258-8 CD-ROM

Printed in the United States of America
Cover and interior design by Quinn Information Design

# Editorial Board

# Contents

## Appendixes



(Full index appears in all three volumes.)

# Preface

The preparation of the 19th edition of the *Encyclopedia of Social Work* was begun in 1991 and completed in late 1994. The editorial board, appointed by NASW president Barbara White and with supplemental appointments by NASW president Ann Abbott, worked diligently to produce a publication that will be of value to a range of individuals inside and outside the social work profession. The product of our efforts builds on the foundations laid by previous editions, yet it reflects societal issues and concerns, as well as professional considerations, that represent a different context from that in which previous editions were produced.

This edition is the 19th in a series that began in 1929. From that year until 1960, the *Social Work Year Book* was published, first at two-year and later at three-year intervals. Each edition of the *Year Book* contained a section of topical articles accompanied by a Directory of National Social Agencies. From 1929 to 1949, 10 editions of the *Social Work Year Book* were published by the Russell Sage Foundation. The American Association of Social Workers (AASW) published the 11th and 12th editions of the *Year Book* in 1951 and 1954. In 1955 AASW and six other professional organizations merged to form the National Association of Social Workers, which continued to publish the *Year Book* at three-year intervals until 1960, at which time a special committee chaired by Robert Morris was appointed to evaluate the nature and use of the publication. Morris's committee recommended that the publication be enlarged and become an encyclopedia. The first edition to be titled the *Encyclopedia of Social Work* was published in 1965, and it was the first edition to include two volumes. Subsequent editions were published in 1971, 1977, and 1987. Because of the lag between the 17th and 18th editions, a one-volume supplement was published in 1983–84. A second supplement was published in 1990 between the 18th edition and the current edition. The current edition, the 19th, is the first to include three volumes, as well as the first to be published in electronic CD-ROM form.

In determining what to include in the 19th edition, the editorial board was cognizant of what John B. Turner, editor-in-chief of the 17th edition, stated in his introduction: "The encyclopedia should reflect social work as it is in a particular era and not what it ought to be." With Dr. Turner's admonition in mind, the editorial board made a conscious decision not to attempt to use a particular theoretical or conceptual framework for the selection of topics. Instead, previous editions were reviewed to determine which of the topics they included continued to be relevant. The board also consulted various contemporary journals to ascertain topics of current relevance and invited various NASW committees and practice specialty groups to identify topics they believed should be included. Finally, the board members drew on their own considerable professional experience in identifying topics for inclusion.

In deciding on content areas, the editorial board gave careful consideration to recent events and social shifts that have had and are having a major influence on the profession. In all, a total of 290 entries were commissioned. In some topical areas, decisions were made to include somewhat longer "overview" articles, with a number of shorter entries on specific aspects of the particular topic area. The number of biographies was expanded, and particular efforts were made to include more entries on women and people of color who had a significant impact on social work and social welfare. As in previous editions, the editorial board adhered to the basic criterion that an individual must be deceased to be considered for inclusion in the biography section.

One of the most significant changes in this edition is the increased attention to diversity and the social work response to the ugliness of racism, homophobia, sexism, and other "isms" such as age discrimination. The editorial board determined that populations would not be grouped under umbrellas as had been done in previous editions. Instead, they commissioned entries on people of different national origins, thereby more than doubling the number of entries related to people of color. The editorial board also paid particular attention to increasing the diversity of authors. For the first time, more than half of the authors are female, compared to 30 percent in the 17th edition and 44 percent in the 18th edition. In this edition, nearly 25 percent of the authors are people of color, compared to 16 percent in the 18th edition (data are not available for the 17th edition). Whereas only two entries in the 18th edition related to sexual orientation, the 19th edition contains eight such entries. Further, this edition contains double the number of entries from the previous edition related to both women and aging. Also, throughout the entire 19th edition, there is greater emphasis on multicultural competency.

Unfortunately, although there have been significant changes throughout the world, language has not kept pace with those changes. For example, use of the word "minority" to describe nonwhite populations has been the subject of debate within and outside the profession. Many people find this usage pejorative and inaccurate. The 1993 NASW Delegate Assembly instructed NASW to study the issue and propose a different term to the 1996 assembly. NASW'S National Committee on Minority Affairs voted in April 1994 to request the Board of Directors to approve a new name—National Committee on Racial and Ethnic Diversity—and the Board did so in June 1994. The *Encyclopedia* editorial board agreed to try to avoid using the term "minority" in the context of describing people of color whenever possible, and we selected several terms to head related Reader's Guides, including National Origin Groups, People of Color, Racial and Ethnic Groups, and Special Populations.

As the entries went through the process of review and copyediting, they were scrutinized for language that might inappropriately label the people being discussed. For example, readers generally will see "elderly people" or "elders," not "the elderly." Or "people with disabilities" or "handicapping conditions," not "the handicapped." The words "homosexual" and "poor" are used as adjectives, not nouns. The editorial board recognizes that eliminating pejorative language will not resolve issues of hatred and discrimination, but we believe doing so models fair and equitable treatment.

Developing a comprehensive publication that covers a profession such as social work is an arduous task. At the outset, the editorial board concluded that readers of this *Encyclopedia* should be able to gain a comprehensive and exhaustive, yet objective, overview of the profession. There was great concern that this *Encyclopedia* present information in a user-friendly manner. Thus, it was decided that entries should be ordered alphabetically, with tables of contents in each volume, and that there should be numerous Reader's Guides to maximize the accessibility of information about specific topics.

## Acknowledgments

An enterprise as complex as the development of this *Encyclopedia* could not possibly be accomplished without the efforts of many people. All the members of the editorial board served in a voluntary capacity, without remuneration. Most were appointed by NASW president Barbara White in the late summer of 1991. Later, two additional members were appointed by NASW president Ann Abbott to assist with the heavy workload. Members of the editorial board include Drs. Diane Bernard, Diana DiNitto, Patricia Ewalt, Michael Frumkin, Alejandro Garcia, Jesse Harris, June Gary Hopps, Martha Ozawa, Rosemary Sarri, Elfriede Schlesinger, Fredrick Seidl, and Constance Williams. Each of these individuals devoted a tremendous amount of time to the process of identifying and contacting potential authors, reviewing outlines, editing entries, and contributing to the overall process in a variety of other important ways.

The work of developing topics, identifying and working with authors, and editing manuscripts was divided among the various members of the editorial board. Associate editor-in-chief June Gary Hopps assumed overall responsibility for entries related to social work direct practice, in addition to her more general editorial responsibilities. The responsibility for entries on social problems and social policy was shared by Diana DiNitto and Martha Ozawa. Diane Bernard and Alejandro Garcia shared responsibility for entries related to special populations. Patricia Ewalt had responsibility for entries related to mental health until she assumed the editorship of *Social Work.* At that point, Elfriede Schlesinger was added to the board and assumed responsibility for mental health entries. Jesse Harris was responsible for health entries, Rosemary Sarri for corrections and criminal justice entries, and Constance Williams for entries related to families and children. Fredrick Seidl was responsible for entries related to research and served as editor for the biography section. Michael Frumkin was responsible for entries related to professional associations, as well as a number of entries that were grouped under the category of miscellaneous. The editor-in-chief assumed responsibility for entries related to management, as well as a number of miscellaneous entries.

Dr. June Gary Hopps served very ably as associate editor-in-chief. I want to express my gratitude to her and to each of my colleagues on the editorial board. This is a special collection of individuals, and it was a real privilege to work with them. Few will know how much effort these people gave to this project.

The NASW staff support for this effort was excellent. Those staff members who were directly involved in the process of producing the 19th edition of the *Encyclopedia* repeatedly went far beyond the call of duty to support the editorial board and ensure that the publication would be of the highest quality and be produced in a timely manner. In particular, I want to recognize the efforts of several NASW Press staff members who made this *Encyclopedia* a reality. Linda Beebe, NASW's director of communications, had the overall managerial responsibility for this project. She was in constant communication with both the associate editor-in-chief and myself, as well as with the other members of the editorial board. In addition, she read and commented on every manuscript during the production process. Her contributions to the success of this effort cannot be overstated. Nancy Winchester, NASW's editorial services director, managed all the staff involved in the development and production of the *Encyclopedia* and handled the numerous editorial and production issues associated with this massive project. She also read most of the manuscripts. Fran Pflieger, senior editor for the *Encyclopedia,* functioned as project manager. She dealt directly with the authors, copyeditors, and proofreaders who were involved with the project, and she also performed senior editor reviews of the manuscripts. Sarah Lowman, editorial secretary for the *Encyclopedia,* maintained accurate records, logged in manuscripts and reviews, handled correspondence with authors, followed up on late submissions and reviews, made arrangements for editorial board meetings, and performed other important functions too numerous to list here. Stephen Pazdan, NASW staff editor, provided essential production support as staff readied the publication for press. Finally, Marie Flowers, administrator for NASW's Communications Department, provided logistical support during the early meetings of the editorial board, and she and her staff provided back-up support to the staff who were directly involved with the *Encyclopedia.*

Each member of the staff team involved with the production of this *Encyclopedia* consistently performed in an exemplary manner throughout the life of the project. They maintained a sense of humor in the face of the stresses coming from missed deadlines, revised time frames, and the like. I am deeply indebted to each of them for their competence and their commitment to this project. I know the other members of the editorial board join me in expressing our gratitude to these individuals. Without them, this project would not have been completed.

Richard L. Edwards
Editor-in-Chief
October 1994

# How to Use the Encyclopedia

For the 19th edition of the *Encyclopedia of Social Work,* the editorial board sought to collect the most current scholarly analyses of practice and research. Reflecting the breadth of the diverse social work profession, this edition also includes more-comprehensive entries than previous editions. The net effect is that this edition is more than 30 percent larger than the 18th edition, which was the largest collection when it was published in 1987. (See Table 1 for a comparison of the 18th and 19th editions.) The objective in assembling this substantial body of knowledge was to make it as easy to use as possible. Consequently, we have provided many different tools to help readers locate the references they seek.

## Content

Attempting to develop the most comprehensive reference possible, the editorial board did not restrict authors to specific page limits; instead, the board sought the most information provided in the most succinct fashion possible. Consequently, entries are longer than those in previous editions.

The editorial board also commissioned longer overview entries in major areas. Some overviews stand alone as the single exhaustive entry on the subject; others integrate a topic for which there are several other entries.

All of the entries are new, and several areas of interest are covered in much greater depth than in previous editions. Among the topics with greatly enhanced content are

- Corrections and Justice
- Cultural Competence
- Direct Practice
- HIV/AIDS
- International Social Work
- Management
- Racial and Ethnic Groups
- Research
- Sexual Orientation

TABLE 1
**Comparison of 18th and 19th Editions**

| 18th Edition | 19th Edition |
|---|---|
| 221 Entries | 290 Entries |
| 99 Biographies | 142 Biographies |
| 22 Reader's Guides | 80 Reader's Guides |
| 2 Volumes | 3 Volumes |
| Casebound | Paperback, casebound, and CD-ROM |

Just as the editorial board increased the diversity of the content, members also sought to increase the diversity of authors. (Table 2 demonstrates the changes in diversity of authors from the 18th to 19th edition.)

## Organization

The print version, which consists of 290 full entries and 142 biographies, is published in three volumes:

| | |
|---|---|
| Volume I | A–E |
| Volume II | F–O |
| Volume III | P–Y and biographies |

Each volume contains a full table of contents and an index to make it easier for you to find the entries.

Entries have been placed in alphabetic order, word by word; colons within a title precipitate a secondary sort. The following example illustrates the pattern:

Asian Americans Overview
Asian Americans: Chinese
Asian Americans: Japanese
Asian Americans: Southeast Asians
Asian Indians

The volumes are paginated consecutively to make it easier to find entries and to ensure that citations are not confusing. The indexes are paginated separately, starting on page I-1, so that they do not interfere with the pagination of entries.

## Search Tools

Readers may simply open a volume and turn to the appropriate place in the alphabet to find the information they seek. We have also incorporated several tools to help you find a specific topic or a set of related topics.

TABLE 2
**Comparison of Authors, 18th and 19th Editions**

| | 18th Edition | | 19th Edition | |
|---|---|---|---|---|
| | Number | Percent | Number | Percent |
| Total Authors | 261 | 100 | 344 | 100 |
| Men | 146 | 56 | 162 | 47 |
| Women | 115 | 44 | 182 | 53 |
| White | 219 | 84 | 261 | 76 |
| Other Racial or Ethnic Group | 42 | 16 | 83 | 24 |

**Detailed Table of Contents**
At the beginning of each volume, there is a complete table of contents for the full encyclopedia. Entry titles, stated as simply and descriptively as possible, are listed in alphabetic order, and the names of authors and the opening page number are given.

**Subject Cross-References**
Although we have attempted to place entries where readers might be most likely to look, many terms might be used interchangeably. Over 100 subject cross-references were inserted to help readers find the entries quickly. Some examples:

**Native Americans**
*See* American Indians

**Refugees**
*See* Displaced People

**Comprehensive Indexes**
The highly detailed, yet easy-to-follow, indexes are your best source for people, organizations, federal legislation, and places. Browsing through the index will lead you to a wide range of key topics. The index also includes cross-references (such as *OAA.* See Old Age Assistance—Title I) and "see also" references (such as *Prisons.* See also Community-Based Corrections; Family-Based Corrections).

**Reader's Guides**
Freestanding cross-reference boxes will help you locate entries on related topics. Altogether, 80 Reader's Guides are interspersed with entries in alphabetic order. These Reader's Guides list the pertinent entries related to the subject. For example:

READER'S GUIDE

**HIV/AIDS**

*The following entries contain information on this general topic:*

HIV/AIDS Overview
HIV/AIDS: Direct Practice
HIV/AIDS: Men
HIV/AIDS: Pediatric
HIV/AIDS: Women

We have attempted to provide as many ways to find a subject as possible. For example, you will find entries related to people of color in several Reader's Guides:

Cultural Competence
National Origin Groups
People of Color
Racial and Ethnic Groups
Special Populations

A full listing of Reader's Guides appears at the end of this section.

**For Further Information**
Another way to find related entries is to review the cross-references listed at the end of each entry. For example, the "Aid to Families with Dependent Children" entry includes the following:

**For further information see**
Child Support; Families: Demographic Shifts; Federal Social Legislation from 1961 to 1994; Hunger, Nutrition, and Food Programs; Income Security Overview; Jobs and Earnings; JOBS Program; Poverty; Social Planning; Social Security; Social Welfare Policy; Unemployment Compensation and Workers' Compensation; Welfare Employment Programs: Evaluation.

**Key Words**
Authors have supplied two to five key words or key word phrases that most succinctly describe the content of the entry. You may use these to search for other entries in the index. In the CD-ROM version, this field will lead the searcher to all entries that include the same key word or key word phrase.

## Authors

Identifying the scholars who wrote the entries in the 19th edition is easy. The author is listed with the title of the entry in the table of contents, and there is a byline immediately following the entry title in the text. At the end of each entry, you will find the author's position and address as they were at the time the *Encyclopedia* was published. Appendix 10 contains an alphabetic list of all authors.

## Bibliographic Information

Because of the number of entries and the extensive reference and reading lists for them, this edition provides perhaps the most comprehensive bibliographic database extant in social work. The reference style is the author–date citation style used in all NASW Press publications. References are listed immediately following each entry.

Most entries also include a "Further Reading" list. The materials in these listings, although not specifically mentioned in the text of the entry, provide additional helpful information on the topic.

## Biographies

The 19th edition, like previous ones, includes biographical information on people who had a major impact on the profession during their lives. In addition to the 99 people profiled in the 18th edition, the biography section, which immediately follows the "Youth Services" entry in Volume 3, includes another 43 people. These individuals, all of whom are deceased, are recognized for their significant contributions.

Not all of the people whose biographies appear are social workers, but the work they did during their lives influenced social work significantly or made a major difference in the delivery of social services. The editorial board was particularly concerned about adding people from many racial and ethnic groups.

## Statistics

Previous editions have included a specific section devoted to statistics, generally within the body of the *Encyclopedia*. Concerned that a statistics section would not serve readers well for the life of an edition, the editorial board of the 18th edition commissioned a separate volume of statistical tables, charts, and graphs.

In 1992 the NASW Press released Leon Ginsberg's *Social Work Almanac*, which is a full book of data related to social services. Rather than duplicate this effort, the editorial board of the 19th edition requested that Ginsberg update the volume; the 2nd edition of the *Social Work Almanac* is being published simultaneously with the *Encyclopedia*. In addition, the editorial board requested that authors include more figures and graphs than have been used in previous editions, particularly for trend data.

## Conclusion

This reference has been three years in development. Many people—the editorial board, 344 authors, and staff—have collaborated to create an encyclopedia that presents the richness, the vitality, and the depth of social work knowledge. We hope that it will be useful to scholars, practitioners, and students as they continue to expand the knowledge base of the profession.

Linda Beebe
Executive Editor

# Reader's Guides

Abuse and Neglect
Adolescents
Adults
African Americans
Aging
AIDS/HIV
Asian Americans
Assessment
Budgeting
Child Abuse
Children and Youths
Clinical Social Work
Community
Computer Use
Courts and Corrections
Crisis Intervention
Cultural Competence
Death and Dying
Direct Practice
Disabilities
Education
Employment
Ethics
Families
Feminist Practice
Fields of Practice
Finances
Foster Care
Fundraising
Gay Men
Gerontology
Group Work
Health
Hispanics/Latinos
History
HIV/AIDS
Homelessness
Homosexuality
Immigrants
Income Security
Information Systems
International Issues
Justice
Legal Issues
Legal Regulation
Legislation
Lesbians
Management
Medical Care
Men
Mental Health
National Origin Groups
Needs Assessments
Parenting
People of Color
Planning
Poverty
Professional Associations
Public Assistance
Public Policy
Public Social Services
Racial and Ethnic Groups
Regulation of Social Work
Research
Residential Care
Sexuality
Social Services Delivery
Social Supports
Social Welfare
Social Work Education
Social Work Profession
Special Populations
Staff Development
Substance Abuse
Third-Party Payments
Treatment Approaches
Vendorship
Violence
Welfare
Women

# Introduction

**Richard L. Edwards, Editor-in-Chief**

In compiling the 19th edition of the *Encyclopedia of Social Work,* the editorial board was cognizant that the social work profession, like any other profession, is influenced by the times in which it is practiced. Perhaps as Leon Ginsberg suggested in his introduction to the 18th edition of the *Encyclopedia,* social work may be even more influenced by the times than many other professions. With this in mind, the editorial board, in identifying topics for inclusion, gave careful consideration to recent events and social shifts that have had and are having a major influence on the profession.

## Technology

One area in which the shifts have had a direct impact on the production of this reference work, as well as on the profession, is technology. In the interval since the 18th edition of the *Encyclopedia* was published, there have been major changes in technology, especially communications technology. Today fax machines and cellular phones are everyday tools—we now fax overseas often with far less effort or concern than we formerly expended to make long-distance phone calls. Nearly all authors now use electronic literature searches and computers with fast, powerful, user-friendly word-processing systems. Laptops and other miniature computers travel with professionals. Social work practitioners interact with various databases, and computer literacy has become a prerequisite for most forms of social work practice. The 19th edition contains more entries on technology than previous editions. It also is the first edition to be produced in electronic form, as well as in print.

## Global View

The world has changed dramatically since the 18th edition of the *Encyclopedia* was published in 1987. The Berlin Wall has been torn down, and East and West Germany have been reunited, despite a series of traumas and economic upheavals. The Union of Soviet Socialist Republics has broken up, totalitarian governments in Central and Eastern Europe have fallen, and many former communist-dominated countries are now allies of the United States. There has been an end to apartheid in South Africa, and Nelson Mandela has gone from being a prisoner of the state to his nation's president. And there is a new government in Palestine that is now struggling with a range of domestic issues, from producing postage stamps and a postal system to creating laws to govern virtually all aspects of the nation's activities.

Certainly, despite changes in the world political order, the world is not yet at peace. In little more than a decade, the United States has used military force in Granada, Panama, and the Persian Gulf and has participated in a United Nations peacekeeping mission in Somalia in which the lives of American military personnel were lost. As this was being written, there were ongoing armed conflicts in such places as Bosnia, Rwanda, and Chechnya, to mention just three. Large numbers of residents of Haiti and Cuba have risked their lives in homemade rafts and leaky boats to cross the waters from their homelands to the United States. The United States threatened a military invasion of Haiti, which was averted by a last-minute diplomatic effort led by former president Jimmy Carter; U.S. troops did occupy Haiti on a "peacekeeping" mission.

In Russia, organized crime seems to have replaced the KGB. In the United States, some children are afraid to go to school because so many of their classmates carry and use weapons. Violence has become increasingly prevalent in American society, and the most dangerous place in the country is in the home because of the very high rates of spousal and child abuse.

In some quarters, at least, there has been a growing sensitivity to and appreciation for diversity in terms of race, ethnicity, gender, and sexual orientation. This appreciation may be due in part to a growing awareness of the interconnectedness of the global village in which we live. Or it may partly be the result of the fact that in many parts of the world and of the United States, white people or Caucasians do not constitute a majority of the population. Unfortunately, there also has been an increase in public expressions of racism and homophobia and a concomitant increase in the violent acting out of these hatreds.

Just as there have been geopolitical shifts, there have been major economic shifts. The reduced value of the dollar is just one indication that the United States is no longer the dominant economy it once was. There have been other shifts as well. When the 18th edition of the *Encyclopedia* was being developed, Japan was exerting its economic power on the world stage. Today, Japan is experiencing its own economic woes.

As the world has changed, so has the role of the social work profession. Since the fall of communism, social workers from the United States and Western Europe have been involved in the former communist countries, assisting them in creating their own social work professional organizations and education programs. Social workers are also involved in importing technology from other countries to use in the United States.

Since the publication of the 18th edition of this *Encyclopedia,* the world has come to grips with a new health crisis, one which has reached epidemic proportions in some places. Little was known about HIV/AIDS when the 18th edition was being developed, and there was only one paragraph in one entry (Homosexuals: Male) that mentioned the disease. Today, however, we know a great deal about HIV infection, and the current edition includes five entries addressing this critical health care problem.

The world around us has changed profoundly in the past several years, and changed in ways that most of us had not dreamed of in 1987 when the previous edition of the *Encyclopedia* was published. The rapid changes in the world have heightened awareness that we live in a global village and that countries around the globe are interdependent. This awareness is echoed in this edition of the *Encyclopedia,* not only in the increased number of entries that specifically address international topics, but also in the content interwoven into many entries, whether it's child labor or bioethics.

## U.S. Policy

When work on the 18th edition of the *Encyclopedia* was begun, Ronald Reagan had been president for three years. He had already dismantled many social services programs and had significantly cut the budgets of many others. Many social workers were concerned about their own futures, in addition to the well-being of their clients and their profession. Thus, the work on that edition occurred in an era of great uncertainty over what would be the nature of the profession in the years immediately following publication. By the time work on the 18th edition had been completed, Reagan had been reelected.

The major development of the 19th edition, on the other hand, occurred in the midst of a different type of uncertainty about social policies and programs. Development spanned the last year of the administration of President George Bush, who had largely carried on the social policy thrust of the Reagan administration, through the first year-and-a-half or so of the Clinton administration.

### Clinton Administration

By the time of the 1992 presidential election, the social work profession had become increasingly politically active. The NASW political action committee, Political Action for Candidate Election (PACE), actively supported the Clinton candidacy. Social workers helped elect Bill Clinton, who was seen as a moderate, and hoped that he would reverse many of the policy decisions of the previous two administrations. He started out well, in the view of many social workers, by reversing the gag rule on abortion and signing into law the Family and Medical Leave Act.

However, after more than a year-and-a-half in office, it is clear that Clinton is a centrist with a propensity for compromise. The policies he has put forth have tended to be less progressive than many social workers would like. Even though NASW has had great access to the White House since Clinton took office and even though both the president and First Lady Hillary Rodham Clinton seem to greatly respect the opinions of social workers, many social workers have found themselves in disagreement with at least some major aspects of the president's proposals on health care, welfare reform, and crime. Ironically, the National Rifle Association aired commercials opposing the 1994 crime bill, labeling it "soft on crime" and warning that a call to 911 would elicit a "social worker, rather than a police officer," while NASW declined to support the bill because of its harsh punitive provisions.

### 1994 General Elections

The 1992 elections had been termed the Year of the Woman as voters elected women, Democrats, and advocates of social programs in record numbers. Two short years later, the mood and votes of the country had changed dramatically. Some newspaper headlines described 1994 as the Year of the Man or the Year of the Angry Man, because men, particularly white men, cast deciding votes in large numbers. In a masterful political stroke, the Republican Party put forth a "Contract with America" that defined what would have been state or regional electoral politics in national terms and cast the election as a referendum on the Clinton presidency. As a result, dozens of Democrats, many of whom had had popular support in their own states, were defeated.

The election resulted in some historic changes as Republicans gained their first majority in the House of Representatives in 40 years. Speaker of the House Thomas S. Foley of Washington became the first sitting speaker to be defeated since 1862. Going into the election, the Democrats held a 56 to 44 majority in the Senate; when the election was over, the ratio had changed to 47 to 53 as the Republicans gained the majority they had held during the first six years of Reagan's presidency and lost in 1986. Republicans also made significant gains in state elections, particularly for governor's seats. After a giant leap in 1992, the numbers of women and people of color in Congress remained unchanged.

Exit polls showed the largest gender gap since 1982, when exit polls began looking at gender. Whereas 54 percent of male voters voted Republican in contests for the House of Representatives and 46 percent voted Democrat, 46 percent of female voters cast their votes for Republicans and 54 percent for Democrats. People who identified themselves as born-again or Evangelical Christians accounted for more than 25 percent of voters, and they cast their votes 3 to 2 for Republican candidates. The National Rifle Association had mounted a vigorous campaign against Democrats who had supported the Brady handgun bill and the crime bill's ban on assault weapons; their supporters constituted even a larger share of the voters than Evangelical Christians and voted more overwhelmingly Republican.

Political analysts offered a variety of reasons for the historic shift in power. Senator Phil Gramm of Texas, chairman of the National Republican Senatorial Committee, declared, "This isn't an anti-incumbent vote, it's an anti-Democratic vote." It appeared that ideology was more of a force than incumbency, and the key factor seemed to be competency in government. Outgoing chairman of the Democratic National Committee David Wilhelm noted that Democrats paid the price for failing "to govern with discipline or unity." Voters expressed some conflicting views: For example, term limits were widely supported even though voters by a 3 to 1 margin indicated in exit polls that they thought it was more important to have experienced people than to put new people in office. Voters urged "Get government out of our lives," yet they supported more prisons and more-stringent laws related to crime. Although the election may not have signaled a solid move to the far right, it was clear that the average voter was more concerned about reducing taxes and improving life for the middle class than about reducing poverty or achieving other more altruistic goals.

One of the key issues of concern to supporters of social programs was that of Proposition 187 in California. The measure, which voters approved by a vote of 59 percent to 41 percent, would deny illegal immigrants virtually all access to public social services. Voters were polarized along racial lines: White voters approved the proposition by a wide margin, whereas Latino voters rejected it by 3 to 1 and Asian Americans and black voters rejected it by a lower margin. As this introduction was written, numerous groups were preparing lawsuits to challenge Proposition 187 and lead to a U.S. Supreme Court decision, which they hope will uphold immigrants' rights.

**Outcome for Social Programs**

In January 1995 the newly constituted Congress will be grappling with major legislation at the same time it puts together a new Republican leadership. In November 1994, House Republicans were promising to introduce the following legislation in the first 100 days of the new Congress:

1. *Fiscal Responsibility Act.* This constitutional amendment would require a balanced budget by the year 2002.
2. *Taking Back Our Streets Act.* Proponents call for stronger "truth-in-sentencing" and death penalty provisions, as well as cuts in social spending from the 1994 crime bill.
3. *Personal Responsibility Act.* The bill would provide no welfare to unwed mothers and would cut off most welfare after two years.
4. *Family Reinforcement Act.* Provisions would include stronger policing of child-support payments, tougher child pornography laws, and tax credits for elderly dependents.
5. *American Dream Restoration Act.* The bill would provide a $500-per-child tax credit, repeal the marriage tax penalty, and expand individual retirement accounts.
6. *National Security Restoration Act.* Proponents call for no U.S. troops under the control of the United Nations as well as a restoration of essential national security funding.
7. *The Senior Citizens Fairness Act.* This bill would raise the social security earnings limit and repeal the 1993 tax boosts on higher-income recipients of social security.
8. *Job Creation and Wage Enhancement Act.* In addition to creating small-business incentives, the bill would cut the capital gains tax by 50 percent.
9. *Common Sense Legal Reform Act.* The bill would reform product liability laws and limit punitive damages.
10. *Citizen Legislature Act.* The House would vote on limiting House members to three terms and senators to two terms.

If the bills are introduced and work their way through Congress, provisions no doubt will change many times. Reforming welfare and dealing with health care are likely to be among the issues, and the likelihood of passing progressive legislation appears to be lower than it was before the 1994 elections. The debates on major issues such as welfare reform are likely to be rancorous and filled with potentially explosive tensions.

## Evolving Roles for Social Workers

Since the 18th edition of the *Encyclopedia* was published, the roles social workers play have continued to evolve. Social workers have become increasingly involved in a wider array of settings, including those under the auspices of public, nonprofit, and for-profit organizations. New forms of practice, such as managed care, have come into being. And, of course, the trend toward private or independent practice has continued.

### Public Policy

Perhaps nowhere is the evolution in social work roles more clear than in the public policy arena. Social work educators and public and nonprofit executives find that they must work with local, state, and federal legislators; legislative committees; and appointed officials to protect and expand their programs. Social workers are becoming increasingly effective advocates for their clients, as well as for issues that affect the social work profession. Both NASW and the Council on Social Work Education (CSWE) have become more sophisticated in their public policy efforts. One measure of this increased sophistication is the fact that NASW has tripled its national legislative staff since 1985. Furthermore, NASW has increased the effectiveness of lobbying efforts at the state and local levels, and the organization now has paid staff in every one of its chapters. Since the 18th edition of the *Encyclopedia* was published, the social work profession has achieved legal regulation in every one of the states, and there has been a significant increase in the number of states that permit social workers to receive third-party reimbursement for their services.

Social workers also have become more involved in actual policy-making. In recent years, more and more social workers have run for and been elected to public offices and more have been appointed to high-level policy-making positions. In the Clinton administration, for example, there are seven social workers who hold positions as undersecretaries for various federal agencies; there never was more than one social worker in such a high-level position in any previous administration. When Mary Ann Mahaffey looked at social workers in public office in 1979, she found 51; NASW found 113 in 1991 and 165 in 1993. In addition, social workers increasingly can be found on the personal staffs of individual legislators or on committee staffs at both the federal and state levels.

### Other Practice Roles

There are increased numbers of social workers in high-level management positions throughout the public and nonprofit sectors. In addition, the nonprofit sector, which Peter Drucker has labeled the "third sector," has been experiencing dramatic growth both in the United States and elsewhere. There has been tremendous growth in purchase of service arrangements, whereby public agencies contract with nonprofit organizations to provide mandated services. Cognizant of these changes, the editorial board has included a number of entries that relate to nonprofit organizations. It also decided to use the term "management" rather than "administration" throughout the 19th edition. This decision was based primarily on two factors: First, the term "administration" has pretty much fallen from use in the general literature about organizations; second, the term "manager" conveys a much more proactive leadership role than does "administrator," which conveys a more reactive stance.

In recent years there has been a growing interest in family preservation and family-based services. This trend can be described as a kind of national movement that has caught the attention of many state legislatures, as well as a number of national and regional foundations. The increasing amount of funding available to support the development of family-based services is having an impact on social work education and on practice.

## Knowledge Development

Throughout much of its history, the social work profession was characterized by the fact that its knowledge base was heavily borrowed from other professions. As a consequence, social work tended to produce fewer researchers and research studies, as well as fewer outlets for their research. However, over the past few years, there has been an increased emphasis on the need for social work research of all kinds. Policymakers have recognized the need for research that addresses social functioning, and social work researchers have recognized that they have generally not been successful in obtaining major funding for their research.

In response to concerns about funding for social work research, the National Institute on Mental Health funded a special Task Force on

Social Work Research in the early 1990s. The task force ultimately produced a major report outlining strategies for increasing social work research, which led to the establishment of the Institute for the Advancement of Social Work Research. The institute is being funded by the social work practice community, represented by NASW, and the education community, represented by CSWE, the National Association of Deans and Directors of Social Work Programs, the Group for the Advancement of Graduate Education, and the Association of Baccalaureate Program Directors. In 1994 the NASW Press separated *Social Work Research & Abstracts*. The separation occurred 18 years after the research section was added to the existing *Abstracts for Social Workers* in 1977; at that time the journals had been combined because NASW did not believe there would be a sufficient audience to support a stand-alone research journal. As a reflection of the greater interest in social work research, this edition of the *Encyclopedia* includes more than double the number of entries related to research and research methodologies. It seems fitting that the *Encyclopedia of Social Work*, which is the reference that contains the general knowledge base of the profession, should devote more attention to methods of building the knowledge base.

## Conclusion

The years following the publication of this *Encyclopedia* are likely to be tumultuous ones for social workers, other human services professionals, and the world at large. There are many political and economic uncertainties, and people around the globe are struggling to learn to cope with the reverberations that now rapidly occur worldwide whenever there is a major shift anywhere in the world. There are great dichotomies at work in the world: On the one hand, for example, world powers have come to peaceful terms; on the other, there has been an increase in racism and hatred and in hostility to people who need help.

In the United States, a new Congress takes office in 1995 with many of its members believing they have been elected with a mandate to reduce government, decrease services, and increase punitive actions not only for criminals, but for people whose only crime is to be poor and needy. A general spirit of frustration, even mean-spiritedness, seems to pervade the general society. If social work is to fulfill its mission of improving the quality of life, social workers will need all of the political and management skills they have been acquiring as a profession. Further, they will need to continue to enhance their knowledge base, developing an evermore sophisticated approach to demonstrating the need for and efficacy of social work services.

**Richard L. Edwards, PhD, ACSW,** is dean, School of Social Work, University of North Carolina at Chapel Hill, 223 East Franklin Street, Chapel Hill, NC 27599.

## Abbott, Edith

*See* Biographies section, Volume 3

## Abbott, Grace

*See* Biographies section, Volume 3

## Abernathy, Ralph David

*See* Biographies section, Volume 3

# Abortion

**Josefina Figueira-McDonough**

The war on abortion has dominated political life in the United States since the late 1970s. It has all the characteristics of a religious conflict between antagonists with mutually exclusive absolute goals, with no ground for compromise. Centered on the status of the fetus (attribution of personhood), the conflict has led to dramatic public confrontations staged by Operation Rescue and pro-choice activists that have fueled journalistic sensationalism. The belief that a candidate's position on abortion determines electoral outcomes adds to the perception that the issue is a central one.

A closer analysis shows that this overall perception is distorted. First, opinion research has revealed that the supporters of extreme positions are a minority and that most Americans favor a middle-of-the-road position that would allow for compromise. Second, the media's attention to dramatic instances of confrontation between extreme groups has magnified the presumed number of activists and the proportion of the general public that they represent. Third, in a pluralistic democracy elections are won by small percentages. Groups with extreme positions on the abortion controversy may vote in blocs and thereby determine the results in a close election. It is inaccurate to conclude, however, that the majority of the supporters of a given candidate share that candidate's position on abortion or that the position constitutes the basis of their support. Fourth, research on abortion has demonstrated that the issue stands as a strong symbol for a "way of life." During a period of rapid change in sexual mores and family organization, the intensity of the abortion debate crystallizes the beliefs of groups in different structural positions about interpretations of life that are less threatening or less constraining.

In an effort to frame the abortion issue in the United States in a different manner from the perceptions constructed by the media, this entry gives a historical overview of the treatment of abortion in the United States and the conditions that led to the Supreme Court decision in *Roe v. Wade* (1973). This overview is followed by a summary of the results of public opinion surveys on abortion and a discussion of the profiles of respondents who support different positions on the topic.

### Historical Evolution

Throughout most of the history of Western Christianity, abortion in the early period of pregnancy, though verbally chastised, was legally ignored. The idea that abortion was criminal emerged in the United States fewer than 100 years ago. Until the first half of the 19th century, abortion—defined as the intentional termination of gestation during pregnancy—was not regulated and thus was legal. The practice was monitored in line with the tradition of British common law, as interpreted by local courts. Abortion before "quickening" (when the movement of the fetus can be felt, around five months of pregnancy, indicating that the fetus has the semblance of separate existence), was not controlled.

Policies that emerged during the first half of the 19th century were concerned mainly with public safety and hence addressed the use of dangerous poisons and practices. Moral considerations were not included as rationales for these policies (Chilman, 1987; Luker, 1984; Mohr, 1978). Major changes in abortion policy appeared in the second half of the 19th century, and by 1900, legislation criminalizing abortion was established throughout the nation. These changes started around 1860 and peaked in 1880, so that the earlier policy on abortion was reversed in the span of two decades.

Historians agree that two factors were decisive in the speedy evolution of abortion policy: (1) the crusade by physicians against abortion and (2) fears inspired by the dramatic lowering of the fertility rate in the United States from 1840 to 1850. The objective of university-trained physicians who fought against the proliferation of "healers" during the 19th century was to control the domain of health care and to exclude these so-called Indian doctors through regulations that would constrain the legitimacy of their activities (Mohr, 1978; Petchesky, 1984). Abortion became a favorite arena in this process, mostly through legislation that forbade it in the name of public safety (Larson, 1977; Rothstein, 1972).

It was only during the 1870s that the morality of the procedure gained attention, as physicians unsuccessfully tried to form alliances with the Protestant churches. The Roman Catholic Church, following Pope Pius IX's enactment of the first doctrinal prohibition of all abortions, offered its support in 1869. But the organized medical profession considered an alliance with the Catholic Church marginal to its interests at that time (Grisez, 1970). From the outset, policy forbidding abortion clearly served to consolidate medical professionalism, and most legislation incorporated clauses that allowed for "therapeutic exceptions" when the life of the mother was in danger.

The country's fertility rate was halved from 1840 to 1850, from 7.04 to 3.56 children per family (Luker, 1984). Demographers have shown that declines in fertility are strongly associated with changes in economic organization and the structure of work. In the passage from a predominantly rural–agricultural to an urban–industrial society, the need for large families decreases, and children move from being productive assets to dependent consumers. These transformations affected the United States at a time when the child mortality rate was decreasing. Because these changes were more visible among the better-off, elite populations became increasingly concerned with the numeric imbalance between the classes. By 1840 abortion services had spread considerably, and legislation began to address the flagrant commercialization of abortion and its link to diminished fertility (Petchesky, 1984).

Prodded, then, by the physicians' crusade and the perceived demographic threat, new policies initially mirrored the medical profession's preoccupation with the consequences to health of services provided by unregulated and presumably incompetent abortionists. Subsequent legislation took on moral overtones, evident, for example, in the passage of the Comstock Law of 1873, a federal law that opened the way to the prohibition of abortion and the advertising and distribution of contraceptives as practices related to pornography.

To these two factors that facilitated the establishment of antiabortion legislation can be added a third: the first feminist movement. At the time, feminists held that abortion degraded women and that its practice was the costly result of the failure of sexual restraint by men, whether husbands or lovers (Mohr, 1978; Petchesky, 1984).

By 1900, when most antiabortion legislation was in place, antiseptic techniques had resolved concerns about public safety, the medical profession was securely entrenched, and the threat of demographic imbalance had disappeared. Still, the legislation was firmly in place, affecting abortion in two ways. First, the only recourse that lower-class women, especially unwed girls, had to deal with unwanted pregnancy was illegal, nonmedical abortions that entailed a high risk of illness or death. Second, better-off married women with access to family physicians made extensive use of "therapeutic exception" clauses. The best statistics available for the period of antiabortion legislation indicate that in the 1930s more than half a million abortions were performed each year (Taussig, 1936) and that in 1950 (Niswander, 1967), 90 percent of premarital pregnancies ended in abortion and 22 percent of married women had abortions.

Examination of the development of antiabortion legislation reveals several key facts:

- Antiabortion legislation in the United States surfaced during a short period in the second half of the 19th century and stood out as an aberration against long-term traditional approaches to the issue.
- The reversal of traditional abortion policies can be traced first to the stake of physicians in the

professionalization of medicine. Legislative rationales first emphasized public safety and then demographic trends; only later did legislation reflect moral concerns tied to pornography. At this stage the role of the Catholic Church, with doctrine from the Vatican formulae of 1869 that forbade all abortions, was peripheral. Also, the feminist movement supported the doctors' crusade, interpreting abortion as the result of the sexual exploitation of women.

- All but six states included "therapeutic exception" clauses in their antiabortion legislation that were aimed at in effect permitting abortions to save the lives of mothers and thus treating the rights of mothers as superior to those of their fetuses.

As the treatment of abortion evolved, certain traditionally held values, such as the differentiation between early and later abortions, disappeared, and the priority given to the life of the mother over the fetus was reaffirmed. The issue of the moral status of the fetus was not addressed. The rise in attempts to control women's sexuality by removing access to abortion was plain in the Comstock Law and, from a different angle, through the feminist perspective on the issue (Petchesky, 1984).

## *Roe v. Wade*

### Antecedents

The contemporary debate on abortion has centered largely on whether to reverse, maintain, or extend the Supreme Court's 1973 decision in *Roe v. Wade.* Little attention has been given to the antecedents of this judicial policy. Some commentary from antiabortion groups has depicted the Supreme Court's decision as an expression of judicial totalitarianism that occurred in a social vacuum. In fact, however, a series of cumulative pressures led to it.

Throughout the 20th century, but particularly in the 1960s, one-third of the states modified their abortion laws to permit a wide array of exceptions. New York, for example, adopted a policy of abortion on demand. Regional diversity created instances of discrimination based on residence that affected mostly poor women, who were less able to travel to states where they could get fully assisted legalized abortion. By 1960, the number of illegal abortions performed each year was estimated at more than 1 million (New York State, 1968).

Worries about overpopulation reemerged in the early 1950s, as did an ecological agenda of zero population growth. Presidents Truman and Eisenhower promoted U.S. participation in the World Planned Parenthood Organization, and Presidents Kennedy and Johnson gave federal support to research on contraception. In line with this national shift in popular support, Connecticut's anticontraception law was struck down by the Supreme Court.

Physicians completely reversed their position. By 1967, 87 percent of physicians supported abortion. Cumbersome boards that supervised decisions on abortion limited professional autonomy (Cohen, 1967). Medical data demonstrated that abortion in the first trimester was safer for the mother than was delivery, refuting the original argument about public safety (Tietze, 1968). The women's movement also reversed itself, strongly defending the idea that women alone had the right to decide what happened to their bodies and, as moral adults, to make responsible life commitments (Petchesky, 1984). Finally, a concern for the quality of life, prompted by the Thalidomide disaster, in which many pregnant women who took the medicine to help them sleep gave birth to children with serious defects, expanded the abortion issue beyond preservation or nonpreservation of the fetus's life to considerations of the type of life that would be preserved (Luker, 1984; Mohr, 1978).

### Supreme Court Decision

It was within this context that the Supreme Court made its decision on *Roe v. Wade* in 1973. As judicial policy, the decision was reached not through successive state referenda, but by way of constitutional interpretation. Undeniably, constitutional interpretations reflect the historical circumstances under which they are made. Arguments against the Supreme Court's decision often point out the judicial policy is antidemocratic and that the right to privacy on which the decision was based is an inferred, not a de facto, constitutional right (Glendon, 1987). Arguments in support of the Court's decision stress that judicial policy has been important in cases of discrimination (Ely, 1980); that the right to privacy had precedents in other decisions; and that the right to religious freedom, guaranteed by the separation of church and state, would have given a strong constitutional basis to the decision (Wenz, 1992).

What is more important is the analysis of the policy in relation to legal and social traditions in the United States before the antiabortion period and new elements that have been incorporated in it. Contrary to antiabortion legislation, the Roe decision is sensitive to the traditional perspective regarding the stages of development of the fetus. Abortion during the first trimester gives priority to the interests of the mother and can be thought of as abortion on demand. Abortion in the second trimester is regulated to protect the mother's health; requires a physician's approval; and attributes increasing rights to the fetus by requiring the presentation of reasonable cause to justify the termination of pregnancy. In the third trimester, following quickening, the state assumes a more direct role in protecting the fetus (Dworkin, 1989). Compelling reasons must be given before abortion is permitted. In simple terms, the fetus's interest is protected unless the pregnancy is a serious threat to the mother's health and survival.

According to current policy, the rights of the fetus increase as it develops but, as in the past, the life of the fetus is not valued equally with the life of the mother. Replacement of the concept of quickening by the notion of the fetus's viability and the shift of concern for the mother's safety to the second trimester are consequences more of the improvements in medical technology than of the rejection of earlier conceptualizations of the problem. So, on the whole, the Roe decision was consistent with the older tradition of regulating abortion prevalent until the mid-19th century.

### Sequelae of Roe v. Wade

The Supreme Court's later rulings regarding the involvement of husbands, parents, and physicians in women's decision to have abortions, above and beyond the stipulations of the policy, were supportive of women's autonomy. However, some rulings had the effect of clearly restricting access to abortion. The 1980 *Harris v. McRae* decision opened the door to the enactment of the Hyde Amendment of 1982, which relieved the federal government of its obligation to provide funds through Medicaid to cover abortions for low-income women.

The Supreme Court's ruling on *Webster v. Reproductive Health Services* (1989) returned a good part of the decision making to the states and, to a certain extent, re-created the regional variation that the Roe decision had attempted to resolve. The outcome of this ruling, as expected, was the proliferation of local bills in 44 state legislatures (Wattleton, 1990).

An awareness that the selection of Supreme Court justices during the antiabortion Reagan and Bush administrations had contributed to this outcome fueled the legislative initiatives behind the Freedom of Choice bill introduced in Congress in 1993. It appears that antiabortion forces are attempting to reverse the Roe decision by challenging its constitutionality and hoping that enough Supreme Court justices will vote in their favor, whereas pro-choice activists are trying to advance their goals through the legislative branch under the pro-choice Clinton administration.

## Public Opinion on Abortion

Despite the fierce polemics of extremist groups that have called for the criminalization of abortion or abortion on demand, studies of public opinion since the 1970s have documented majority support for the type of compromise represented by the Roe decision. The results of surveys from 1972 onward (Burtchael, 1982; Cook, Jelen, & Wilcox, 1993; Figueira-McDonough, 1990; Granberg & Granberg, 1980; Rodman, Sarvis, & Walker, 1987; Sachett, 1985) have consistently shown that most Americans support a situational approach to abortion, that is, that abortion should be permitted under specific circumstances. Only a small minority (estimates range from 8 percent to 13 percent) want to make all abortions illegal and take the position that the fetus is a person and that abortion amounts to murder (Dworkin, 1993; Figueira-McDonough, 1990). Although proponents of abortion on demand, regardless of the stage of development of the fetus, are more numerous than opponents of abortion (estimates range from 36 percent to 40 percent), their numbers lag behind supporters of conditional abortion (around 50 percent). There is evidence of some regional variation, but the overall pattern is the same. A 1989 survey of Louisiana residents at the time of the Webster decision indicated that all the extreme groups added up to only 42 percent and that the middle group constituted a clear majority (58 percent) (Cook et al., 1992).

Americans show great consistency regarding the morality and timing of abortion. Evidence from a variety of polls (for example, Henslow & Martine, 1982; Opinion Roundup, 1989) indicates that most people view abortion with moral distaste but support its legality. Disapproval of abortion increases steadily with the development of the fetus, reflecting the old criterion tied to quickening and the stringent regulations set by the Supreme Court for abortions in the third trimester. In fact, 90 percent of abortions in the United States take place in the first trimester, with fewer than 1 percent occurring in the third trimester (Tietze & Henshaw, 1986).

Analysts have attempted to identify the profiles of respondents who support different positions on abortion. Luker's (1984) conclusion from her study of abortion activists was substantiated for the general population: The abortion issue connotes a worldview and mirrors the positions of different groups in their efforts to cope with social change, especially the reorganization of the family and of gender roles. The attitudes of respondents who embrace a pro-life position have been found to be significantly more traditional with regard to gender roles and more conservative with respect to the government's role in leveling social differences than the attitudes of those supporting choice. Gender, by itself, and a commitment to humanitarian values are not indicators of a respondent's view of abortion. The most powerful correlates of opinion on abortion are religiosity and education. Regardless of denominational affiliation (Catholics equal Protestants in their support for abortion), the greater the activity in church affairs and the less educated a person is, the more likely that person is to hold a pro-life position and to oppose legalized abortion (see, for example, Callahan & Callahan, 1984; Cook et al., 1992; Figueira-McDonough, 1987, 1989a; Luker, 1984).

Opinions on abortion are shaped by people's experiences and perceptions of how, given their resources, certain changes will improve or jeopardize the meaning of their lives. The research summarized here confirms that perceptions of the outcome of social change are symbolically bound with the issue of abortion; indicators of fear of change or conservatism are associated with an antiabortion position.

In summary, public opinion surveys regularly show that most Americans hold positions that are in line with the Supreme Court's decision in *Roe v. Wade*. They also reveal that most Americans have moral reservations about abortion, but overwhelmingly support its legality. The majority opinion is consonant with the long history of ambivalence regarding the status of the fetus and a tolerance of abortion during the early stages of pregnancy. Only a small minority holds that the fetus and the mother are equals. Rather, most Americans view the fetus as a "would-be person" and oppose abortion on demand, but they do not support Pope Pius XII's 1951 declaration that full personhood starts at conception and that therapeutic exceptions are inadmissible (Byrnes & Segers, 1992). Hence, focusing the debate exclusively on the belief or absence of belief in the personhood of the fetus does not appear to capture adequately the concerns of the American public. It reflects, instead, the concerns of a minority who are committed to particular religious beliefs (Wenz, 1992).

In a formulation of the fetus–personhood debate, Dworkin (1993) observed that what most Americans express in abortion-related opinion surveys is that we share an ideal that human life in all forms is sacred, but that as a people, we disagree about the source and character of that sacred value and, therefore, about which decisions respect or desecrate it. Individuals still need to make their own decisions about abortion according to their religious and philosophical perspectives. These interpretations cannot be handed down by the government, certainly not in a nontheocratic, heterogeneous, pluralistic society. The state may, however, set conditions that reflect the consensus about the gravity of such decisions.

## The Abortion Controversy and Social Work

Abortion stands at the juncture of a variety of social systems connecting gender relations, heterosexual experiences, reproduction, family, economics, and law (Lamanna, 1984). This being so, the issue cannot be defined as a taboo zone for the social work profession. Social work is, by definition, targeted at facilitating problem solving and conflict resolution at the individual, interpersonal, organizational, and societal level; the abortion controversy touches on all these dimensions. As professionals, social workers are trained to adhere, in their interventions, to certain professional values. Hence, although social workers, like all people, base their personal decisions on values derived from their religious, cultural, and family experiences, as professionals they are trained not to impose these values on their clients. This point is especially important inasmuch as professional relationships reflect power over clients (see, for example, Callahan, 1991).

It has been argued that the values of self-determination and social justice distinguish social work from other helping professions and that these values can be conceptualized as interdependent (Figueira-McDonough, 1993; Wakefield, 1988). In other words, without access to basic goods (distributive justice), one cannot truly speak of freedom of choice (self-determination). Therefore, regardless of individual preferences, what is important for social workers is how they can facilitate women's self-determination with regard to reproductive decisions and to what extent they can ensure their clients' access to resources to support their clients' choices.

### Direct Practice and Self-Determination

Self-determination, a basic value in social work that dominates all direct practice regardless of theories or methods, is rooted in the belief in the autonomy and dignity of the individual (NASW, 1994). The norm takes for granted that individuals have the capacity to define their goals and choose the means to achieve them. This norm, a centerpiece not only of social work but of liberal societies in general, gives priority to individualism and pluralist systems that recognize cultural heterogeneity. Adherence to this principle is indispensable to professional intervention regarding reproductive behavior.

Hull (1990) pointed out that ethical issues in reproduction have to be looked at from four different perspectives: individual, group, professional, and societal. The professional ethic is defined in terms of self-determination in interpersonal practice, and the other ethical issues refer to the individual client and the group of which she is a part. Thus, in helping the client to decide whether to proceed with her pregnancy, the social worker should focus on the woman's definition of her situation, her interpretation of self-interest, and her values. This perspective should guide the consideration of both personal and contextual alternatives without the superimposition of the social worker's own beliefs.

Indeed, to impose one's beliefs on the client, as Callahan (1991) suggested, is contrary to professional social work principles, even though it is acceptable in volunteer work. The objective of professional intervention should be to help in the deliberation and reflection of the client's values, self-interest, and available supports so that a reflexive, rather than an impulsive or submissive, decision is made. This objective is particularly important in working with women because women, especially poor and young women, often experience barriers to self-determination (MacKinnon, 1984). In addition, because reproductive decisions are tied to an area of conflicting values, intervention should be client-centered, nonjudgmental, and nondirective. Moreover, given that the decision has implications for the group context in which the client lives, this context should be taken into consideration. As Joffe (1986) noted in her study of family planning, the client must ultimately decide how much weight should be given to the group context.

The nature of the abortion decision falls into what Litwak and Figueira (1970) termed nonuniform problems—that is, problems that cannot be handled in a standardized fashion and that do not benefit from the treatment of experts. Beyond the commitment to self-determination, certain approaches may offer some advantages in dealing with nonuniform problems (Figueira-McDonough, 1989b). Contextual approaches, for example, focus on changing circumstances that prevent the client from making autonomous decisions. These approaches were developed in radical social work and feminist attempts to raise the client's awareness of structural barriers and to reduce negative self-attributions.

Participation in self-help groups can also foster a client's empowerment because the sharing of similar experiences and feelings counteracts self-attributions of deviance and inferiority. The reciprocity informal help groups promote enhances self-esteem, which, in turn, increases the capacity for self-determination. Self-help groups may, in addition, offer alternative support resources to the natural groups to which the client belongs, expanding options as the client tries to make a difficult decision (Burden & Gottlieb, 1987; Joffe, 1986). Cox (1977) defined "nurturing the natural," an expression he coined, as a professional activity targeted at the development of the caring capabilities of natural systems (such as families and communities). Arguing that most of these systems have bonds that professionals cannot replace, Cox proposed that it would be most effective to develop the systems' caring capabilities through a process of "adding value," rather than dealing with shortcomings by undervaluing the systems. The strength of this approach is directly related to the promotion of group support at the time a woman decides on the future of her pregnancy.

**Policy Practice and Social Justice**

Social justice, another major value guiding the social work profession, is directly linked to policy practice (Figueira-McDonough, 1993). As a professional value, social justice is concerned with the distribution of and access to different rights for the vulnerable populations that social workers serve. With regard to abortion, the major concern is the assessment of the fairness of existing policies. Three such policies regulating abortion clearly discriminate against some women as a function of these women's powerless status: the Hyde amendment, the Webster decision, and parental consent policies.

The Hyde Amendment of 1976 discriminates against destitute women because it prevents their access to medically safe abortions. The Webster ruling opened the door to further class discrimination. Banning abortions from public hospitals and clinics disproportionately affects the populations that depend on such institutions for their health care, namely, the poor. Furthermore, the freedom given to the states in regulating abortion carries with it the seeds of residential discrimination; that is, access to abortion becomes a function not only of the state a women resides in but of the woman's ability to gain access to abortion in other states.

Parental consent laws discriminate against females on the basis of age. The popularity of such legislation, even among pro-choice supporters, appears to reflect support for greater parental control, rather than a concern with the conflict of rights involved in abortion. The protective argument, as an extension of parental authority in medical decisions, should be relevant only in cases when either alternative—to bear a child or to terminate pregnancy—would endanger the life of the pregnant girl. In addition, contrary to laws regarding other parental rights, the legislation granting parents control of their daughters' decision to abort a pregnancy has not established the responsibilities that parents should incur by assuming this power. Should parents be obligated, for example, to provide psychological treatment in instances of postabortion trauma? Should they automatically assume responsibility for the care of the grandchild whose birth they willed?

With regard to the four social work methods of policy practice—legislative advocacy, reform through litigation, social action, and analysis of the implementation of policy—proposed by Figueira-McDonough (1993), national abortion policy is an outcome of reform through litigation and exemplifies judicial policy, whereas the Freedom of Choice bill, introduced into Congress in 1993 would make abortion policy open to tactics of legislative advocacy. Considering the three discriminatory instances of abortion policy, what options do social workers have to rectify discrimination against poor and young women?

The theory behind the Hyde amendment embraces equal treatment in terms of passive rights. In other words, the liberal state is obliged to treat all citizens equally. It gives them equal freedom of action but it is not committed to compensatory equality. Equal opportunity in this view means that although the poor are not forbidden to have abortions within the legal conditions set by the Supreme Court, the state is under no obligation to contribute to their ability to have abortions by way of Medicaid subsidies. Goodin (1985) argued that passive rights have no meaning because they are discriminatory in a stratified society. Affirmative action legislation, for example, accepts Goodin's logic in its commitment to rectify racial and gender inequities. The courts, however, have been reluctant to enforce compensatory laws for the poor, largely because compensatory rights cannot be derived readily from a constitution conceived within a capitalist framework. So, legislative advocacy may be a more fruitful path. Although poor people are not a powerful constituency that could affect the political process, women are increasingly so. To the extent that nonpro-life women are willing to resolve their differences (Clymer, 1993), the chances of extending access to abortion to poor women through the Freedom of Choice bill are likely to be high.

In contrast, a reversal of the Webster decision seems more feasible through litigation because of the antecedents of the Roe decision, especially the anticipated consequences of regional discrimination and the denial of public facilities for carrying out legal health-related interventions. In such instances, a strong test case might throw open the question of the constitutional basis of the Webster decision and the supremacy of states in barring access to a basic right with constitutional precedents.

Options for equalizing access to abortion among minors are more complex, in part because they place two strongly held American values in conflict: the family ethic and individual autonomy. Recent legislation has reflected this ambivalence. The 1976 and 1979 *Bellotti v. Baird* decisions exemplify the Supreme Court's efforts to conciliate these two values. In the 1976 decision the court held that states may not give parents of unmarried minors a blanket veto over abortions sought by their daughters. The 1979 decision held that a state may not require parental consent for a minor's abortion unless the young woman is allowed the opportunity to show the court that she is mature enough to make her own decisions or that an abortion is in her best interests.

Nevertheless, as Glendon (1987) suggested, this dilemma could be resolved by supportive implementation strategies. Comparing the resistance of the United States to enforce a waiting period before abortion is permitted against the routine adoption of limited delay in France, Glendon acknowledged that the intent of the use of such periods differs in each case. In the bills proposed in the United States, this period is seen as a mechanism for dissuading women from undergoing abortions. In France the waiting period is used to share information about the supports available for any final decision. Rather than assuming a "parents know best" attitude or neglecting family resources, the institution of counseling units to help orient and protect minors in different circumstances might be a better alternative in that it would be more responsive to the various needs of this population than would the enforcement of either–or solutions (Joffe, 1986).

## Conclusion

A review of policies on abortion indicates that, rather than being at odds with history, the Roe decision is consistent with earlier regulations. An important element of abortion policy is the acknowledgment of the distinctive status of the fetus depending on its development.

Although the absolute attribution of personhood from conception is a dramatic and emotional platform for the Right-to-Life movement, the concept lacks the scientific, historical, and cultural basis of moral universalism. Such a belief, although very important in private life should not be imposed publicly, much less in a profession that abides by self-determination.

On the other hand, proponents of abortion-on-demand tend to present their position as a matter of free choice, implying a choice that is morally neutral. In fact, however, abortion is a morally conflicting choice, in which the woman weighs the potential for creating a life for which she will be responsible against other responsibilities to herself and others. The morality of the decision depends on individual circumstances. For the social worker committed to self-determination the goal is to help pregnant women make reflexive decisions that consider their values, their supportive environments, and the viable options for the future. It is important to bear in mind that many pregnancies are unchosen and therefore the abortion choice can be viewed as a coerced one. That is, a painful choice taking place in a context not freely chosen. To promote women's full agency in future pregnancies social workers need to help them gain greater self-determination within loving and sexual relationships (Ruether, 1994).

The social justice value is central for social work activities in redressing inequities at the policy level. There is evidence that judicial decisions implemented after the Roe decision do in fact allow discrimination by socioeconomic level, age, and residence. For example, at present only a few states offer Medicaid-covered abortions whereas two-thirds of the fee-for-service insurance plans routinely cover abortions. These inequities will either be erased or worsened depending on the type of health security bill Congress eventually passes. The several bills being discussed at this time handle abortion services differently and threats by the National Abortion and Reproductive Rights Action League and by the United States Catholic Conference to support or oppose them indicate the rebirth of mutually exclusive agendas.

For social workers the health legislation has the potential to redress long-standing inequalities. Because 40 million Americans have no health care and another 30 million have coverage that is inadequate to meet their basic health care needs, the goals of universal and comprehensive care are central to redressing this injustice. The issue of comprehensive care is most relevant in terms of inclusion and exclusion of abortion services. A national health care program that does not include comprehensive reproductive care discriminates against women and therefore cannot claim to offer universal coverage.

## References


Bellotti v. Baird, 428 U.S. 132 (1976).

Bellotti v. Baird, 443 U.S. 623 (1979).

Burden, D. S., & Gottlieb, N. (Eds.) (1987). *The woman client.* New York: Tavistock.

Burtchael, J. T. (1982). *Rachel weeping and other essays on abortion.* Kansas City, MO: Andrenos & McNeal.

Byrnes, T. A., & Segers, M. C. (1992). *The Catholic Church and the politics of abortion.* Boulder, CO: Westview Press.

Callahan, S. (1991). Counseling abortion alternatives: Can it be value free? *America, 165,* 110–113.

Callahan, S., & Callahan, D. (1984). *Abortion: Understanding differences.* New York: Plenum Press.

Chilman, C. (1987). Reproduction norms and social control. In J. Figueira-McDonough & R. Sarri (Eds.), *The trapped woman: Catch 22 in deviance and control* (pp. 34–53). Newbury Park, CA: Sage Publications.

Clymer, A. (1993, April 2). Abortion rights supporters are split on U.S. measures. *New York Times,* p. A13.

Cohen, L. M. (1967). Abortion and the doctor's dilemma. *Modern Medicine, 24,* 12–32.

Cook, E. A., Jelen, T. G., & Wilcox, C. (1992). *Between two absolutes: Public opinion and the politics of abortion.* Boulder, CO: Westview Press.

Cox, I. (1977, June). *Nurturing the natural.* Paper presented at the Conference on Issues of Human Service Organizations. Racine, WI.

Dworkin, R. (1989, June 29). The great abortion case. *New York Review of Books,* pp. 49–53.

Dworkin, R. (1993). *Life's dominion: An argument about abortion, euthanasia and individual freedom.* New York: Alfred A. Knopf.

Ely, J. (1980). *Democracy and distrust: A theory of judicial review.* Cambridge, MA: Harvard University Press.

Figueira-McDonough, J. (1987). To protect and to control: An inquiry into the correlates of opinions on abortion. In J. Figueira-McDonough & R. C. Sarri (Eds.), *The trapped woman: Catch-22 in deviance and control* (pp. 53–80). Newbury Park, CA: Sage Publications.

Figueira-McDonough, J. (1989a). Men and women as interest groups in the abortion debate. *Women's Studies International Forum, 12,* 539–550.

Figueira-McDonough, J. (1989b, May 11). *New directions in social work: Keeping faith with old goals.* Paper presented at the Conference on Social Work in the Year 2000, Universidad Pontificia de Comillas. Madrid.

Figueira-McDonough, J. (1990). Abortion: Ambiguous criteria and confusing policies. *Affilia, 5*(4), 27–54.

Figueira-McDonough, J. (1993). Policy practice: The neglected side of social work intervention. *Social Work, 38,* 178–188.

Glendon, M. A. (1987). *Abortion and divorce in western law: American failures, European challenges.* Cambridge, MA: Harvard University Press.

Goodin, R. E. (1985). *Protecting the vulnerable.* Chicago: University of Chicago Press.

Granberg, D., & Granberg, B. (1980). Abortion attitudes, 1965–1980: Trends and determinants. *Family Planning Perspectives, 12,* 250–261.

Grisez, G. (1970). *Abortion: The myths, the realities and the arguments.* New York: Corpus Books.

Harris v. McRae, 448 U.S. 297 (1980).

Henslow, S. K., & Martine, G. (1982). Abortion and the public opinion polls: Morality and legality. *Family Planning Perspectives, 14,* 53–60.

Hull, R. T. (1990). *Ethical issues: The new reproductive technologies.* Belmont, CA: Wadsworth.

Hyde Amendment of 1982. P.L. 97-377, 96 Stat. 1894.

Joffe, C. (1986). *The regulation of sexuality: Experiences of family planning workers.* Philadelphia: Temple University Press.

Lamanna, M. A. (1984). Social science and ethical issues: The policy implications of pool data on abortion. In S. Callahan & D. Callahan (Eds.), *Abortion: Understanding the differences* (pp. 1–23). New York: Plenum Press.

Larson, R. (1977). *The rise of professionalism: A sociological analysis.* Berkeley: University of California Press.

Litwak, E., & Figueira, J. (1970). Technological innovation and ideal forms of family structure in an industrial democratic society. In R. Hill & R. König (Eds.), *Families east and west.* Paris: Mouton.

Luker, K. (1984). *Abortion and the politics of motherhood.* Berkeley: University of California Press.

MacKinnon, C. (1984). Roe v. Wade: A study in male ideology. In J. Garfield (Ed.), *Abortion: Moral and legal perspectives* (pp. 45–53). Amherst: University of Massachusetts Press.

Mohr, J. C. (1978). *Abortion in America: The origins and evolution of national policy.* New York: Oxford University Press.

National Association of Social Workers. (1994). *NASW code of ethics.* Washington, DC: Author.

New York State. (1968, March). *Report of the governor's commission appointed to review New York State's abortion law.* Albany, NY: Government Reports.

Niswander, K. R. (1967). Medical abortion practices in the United States. In D. T. Smith (Ed.), *Abortion and the law* (pp. 37–38). Cleveland.

Opinion Roundup. (1989, May–June). Abortion rights and wrongs. *Public Opinion,* pp. 35–38.

Petchesky, J. P. (1984). *Abortion and women's choice: The state, sexuality, and reproductive freedom.* Boston: Northeastern University Press.

Rodman, H., Sarvis, B., & Walker, B. J. (1987). *The abortion question.* New York: Columbia University Press.

Roe v. Wade, 410 U.S. 113 (1973).

Rothstein, W. (1972). *American physicians in the nineteenth century: From sects to science.* Baltimore, MD: Johns Hopkins University Press.

Ruether, R. R. (1994). Refections on the word "free" in free choice. *Conscience, 15*(2), 2–3.

Sachett, V. (1985, April–May). Between pro-life and pro-choice. *Public Opinion,* pp. 53–55.

Taussig, F. J. (1936). *Abortion, spontaneous and induced: Medical and social aspects.* St. Louis: St. Louis Press.

Tietze, C. (1968). Therapeutic abortions in the United States. *American Journal of Obstetrics and Gynecology, 101,* 784–787.

Tietze, C., & Henshaw, S. (1986). *Induced abortion: A world view* (6th ed.). Washington, DC: Allen Guttmacher Institute.

Wakefield, D. C. (1988). Psychotherapy, distributive justice, and social work. *Social Service Review, 62,* 189–211.

Wattleton, F. (1990, April). Editorial. *Newsletter of the Planned Parenthood Association of America,* p. 1.

*Webster v. Reproductive Health Services,* 109 U.S. 3040 (1989).

Wenz, P. Z. (1992). *Abortion rights as religious freedom.* Philadelphia: Temple University Press.

## Further Reading

Christofer, E. (1987). *Sexuality and birth control in community work.* London: Tavistock.

Colker, R. (1992). *Abortion and dialogue: Pro-choice, pro-life and American law.* Bloomington: Indiana University Press.

Conover, P. J. (1983). *Feminism and the new right: Conflict over the American family.* New York: Praeger.

Druker, D. (1990). *Abortion decisions of the Supreme Court, 1973–1989.* Jefferson, NC: McFarland & Co.

Feinman, C. (Ed.). (1992). *The criminalization of a woman's body.* New York: Haworth Press.

Fried, M. G. (1990). *From abortion to reproductive freedom: Transforming a movement.* Boston: Southend Press.

Greenberg, P. (1989). *State abortion laws and the Webster decision.* Denver: National Conference of State Legislatures.

Olasky, M. (1988). *The press and abortion.* Hillsdale, NJ: L. Erlbaum Associates.

Rodman, H., Lewis, S. H., & Griffith, S. B. (1984). *The sexual rights of adolescents: Competence, vulnerability and parental control.* New York: Columbia University Press.

Sheeran, P. J. (1987). *Women, society, the state and abortion: A structural analysis.* New York: Praeger.

**Josefina Figueira-McDonough, PhD,** is professor, Arizona State University, School of Social Work, Tempe, AZ 85287.

**For further information see**

Adolescent Pregnancy; Adoption; Advocacy; Bioethical Issues; Civil Rights; Ethics and Values; Family Planning; Federal Social Legislation from 1961 to 1994; Policy Practice; Social Workers in Politics; Women Overview.

**Key Words**

| | |
|---|---|
| abortion | reproductive freedom |
| family planning | women's health care |

READER'S GUIDE

**Abuse and Neglect**

*The following entries contain information on this general topic:*

Child Abuse and Neglect Overview
Child Abuse and Neglect: Direct Practice
Domestic Violence
Domestic Violence: Legal Issues
Elder Abuse

## Accounting

*See* Financial Management

## Adams, Frankie

*See* Biographies section, Volume 3

## Addams, Jane

*See* Biographies section, Volume 3

## Addiction

*See* Substance Abuse *(Reader's Guide)*

## Adjudication

*See* Professional Conduct

# Adolescence Overview

**Diane de Anda**

The concept of adolescence, a period in the life cycle between childhood and adulthood, was introduced by Hall (1904) at the beginning of the 20th century. Although Hall considered adolescence to extend from the age of 12 years to between 22 and 25 years, most researchers and theorists consider the adolescent age span to be from 12 to 18 years. Adolescence has also been divided into phases or age groupings, most typically preadolescence; early adolescence; middle adolescence, or adolescence proper; and late adolescence (Blos, 1941, 1979; Dunphy, 1963; Sullivan, 1953).

Although menarche (the onset of menstruation) serves as a fairly clear biological marker for the entry of girls into adolescence, no similar clear-cut criterion exists for boys. Moreover, although all cultures formally or informally recognize puberty—"the biological and physiological changes associated with sexual maturation" (Muuss, 1962, p. 5)—adolescence appears to be a phenomenon primarily of postindustrial societies.

The criteria that can indicate the end of adolescence are even less clear. Consider the lack of uniformity in laws discriminating between the status of minors and the status of adults for activities ranging from voting to marriage to alcohol consumption.

### Demographics

According to 1990 census data, adolescents constitute 11.2 percent of the U.S. population (U.S. Bureau of the Census, 1992), a decrease of 3 percent from 1980. The distribution of this population by age, gender, and ethnicity is shown in Table 1.

Males account for a slightly larger percentage (51.2 percent) of the adolescent population than do females (48.8 percent), a difference found across all ethnic groups. White adolescents make up 69.4 percent of the adolescent population (a decrease from 79.8 percent in 1980). The percentage by ethnic group for the remaining adolescent cohorts are as follows: African American, 15.0 percent; Hispanic, 11.6 percent; Asian/Pacific Islander, 3.3 percent; Native American, 1.0 percent; and other, 5.4 percent.

### Biological Development

The development of primary and secondary sexual characteristics during adolescence is the result of endocrine changes that produce changes in hormone levels. Although the growth rate during infancy proceeds at a more accelerated rate, the

TABLE 1
**Adolescent Population by Age, Gender, and Ethnicity, 1990**

| | All Persons | | | | | | | | |
|---|---|---|---|---|---|---|---|---|---|
| Age (yr) | Total | Male | Female | White | African American | Hispanic | Asian or Pacific Islander | Native American | Other |
| 12 | 3,423,450 | 1,752,999 | 1,670,451 | 2,377,773 | 519,424 | 397,566 | 108,190 | 37,420 | 181,893 |
| 13 | 3,339,000 | 1,706,417 | 1,632,583 | 2,311,109 | 505,268 | 393,120 | 109,012 | 37,047 | 180,629 |
| 14 | 3,243,107 | 1,662,245 | 1,580,862 | 2,244,557 | 488,452 | 382,405 | 107,944 | 35,728 | 177,475 |
| 15 | 3,321,609 | 1,705,780 | 1,615,829 | 2,303,102 | 499,514 | 387,038 | 112,663 | 35,740 | 179,800 |
| 16 | 3,304,890 | 1,697,995 | 1,606,895 | 2,280,559 | 504,009 | 385,257 | 115,477 | 35,886 | 179,670 |
| 17 | 3,410,062 | 1,758,400 | 1,651,662 | 2,348,737 | 522,291 | 402,212 | 117,717 | 35,945 | 188,936 |
| 18 | 3,641,238 | 1,862,377 | 1,778,861 | 2,525,629 | 545,985 | 426,930 | 125,310 | 35,798 | 203,098 |
| 19 | 4,076,216 | 2,078,146 | 1,998,070 | 2,886,674 | 586,694 | 452,520 | 132,594 | 37,147 | 217,038 |

SOURCE: U.S. Bureau of the Census. (1992). *1990 census of population (Vol. 1): Characteristics of the population*. Washington, DC: U.S. Government Printing Office.

magnitude and rate of change experienced during puberty is more significant, because the adolescent is more cognizant of the changes (Tanner, 1972). The sequence of development is considered universal; however, individual timetables for the various stages differ, and the areas of development may not be synchronous (Peterson & Taylor, 1980).

Since the late 19th century (and especially since the 1930s and 1940s), physical maturation has continued to occur earlier with each successive generation. This "secular trend" is particularly evident in the earlier onset of menarche and in the increases in the rate of growth and full adult stature. At the beginning of the century in the United States, the average age of menarche was slightly over 14 years; by midcentury it was less than 13 years (Tanner, 1962). Among the factors hypothesized to explain this phenomenon are improvements in health and nutrition, as well as the "hybrid vigor" hypothesis, which attributes the changes to the intermarriage of various groups resulting from greater social mobility (Muuss, 1970).

Among the most dramatic of the physical changes during adolescence is the height spurt. Girls generally experience their major increase in height at about age 12, or approximately two years earlier than boys. However, there is great individual variation, so the range for girls is 10½ to 14 years and for boys, 12½ to 15 years.

Changes also occur in weight; girls develop increased subcutaneous fatty tissue, and boys usually become heavier than girls. Although the hips and shoulders become wider in both boys and girls, boys' shoulders become wider than their hips, and girls' hips become wider than their shoulders. Changes in skin texture and oiliness take place, along with gradual changes in the timbre and pitch of the voices of both boys and girls (Faust, 1977; Peterson & Taylor, 1980; Tanner 1972).

Early physical maturation generally has a positive effect on boys: Boys who mature early are rated as more relaxed and poised, higher in self-esteem, less dependent, and more attractive to and popular with their peers than those who mature later (Clausen, 1975; Jones, 1965; Mussen & Jones, 1957; Peskin, 1967; Petersen, 1987; Simmons & Blyth, 1987). Girls seem to have the opposite experience: Early maturation appears to result in negative evaluations, including feelings of isolation, submissive behavior, and less popularity with and leadership of their peers (Clausen, 1975; Jones & Mussen, 1958; Peskin, 1973; Simmons & Blyth, 1987; Weatherley, 1964). In any case, research indicates that the individual's idiosyncratic range of physical development and its degree of synchronicity with cultural norms has an impact on overall development.

Although research in the biological aspects of adolescent development is straightforward, the literature on other aspects of adolescent development is characterized by controversy and conflicting viewpoints. Theorists and researchers agree that during adolescence, notable development occurs in a number of areas. These researchers differ, however, about the following aspects of adolescence:

- whether the development is continuous or discontinuous with the preceding and following stages in the life cycle
- whether the period of adolescence is one of turmoil and stress or is relatively uneventful
- whether it is critical for adolescents to experience or resolve specific developmental tasks or issues during this time

- whether internal or environmental factors have a more significant influence on the experiences and outcome of adolescent development
- whether there are specific adolescent responses (such as coping or defense mechanisms) to internal and external changes.

For example, Hall (1904) often referred to as the "father" of the psychology of adolescence, viewed adolescence as a discontinuous experience, a period qualitatively and quantitatively different from both childhood and adulthood. This discontinuity, along with the great physical changes that adolescents experience, caused Hall to label the period as one of *sturm und drang* (literally, storm and stress). Hall's biogenetic approach posited that adolescence was a "recapitulation" of one stage of human evolution—a turbulent time for the species and, therefore, for the individual.

## Psychological Development

### Psychosexual Theories

Psychoanalytic theorists have posited a different recapitulation theory. Specifically, they see the developmental processes of adolescence as a recapitulation of earlier infantile stages of development through the reexperiencing of either oedipal or preoedipal conflicts (Blos, 1941, 1979; A. Freud, 1948; S. Freud, 1924/1973).

The physiological changes that bring about sexual–reproductive maturation are considered to usher in the genital stage, which disturbs the psychological equilibrium achieved during the latency period (S. Freud, 1924/1973). The sheer "quantity of the instinctual impulses" (A. Freud, 1948, p. 164) is thought of as rekindling a conflict over dominance between the ego and the id, the latter of which has predominated and matured during the latency period. The ego is conceptualized as torn between the impulses and demands of the id and the restrictions of the superego (A. Freud, 1948). Consequently, adolescence is viewed as a period of stress and turmoil and as discontinuous with other phases in the life cycle.

According to psychosexual theorists, two tasks must be accomplished during adolescence if psychological maturity is to be attained: (1) detachment from the opposite-sex parent as an incestuous love object and (2) establishment of a nonantagonistic, nondominated relationship with the same-sex parent. This process of detachment may result in negativism and hostility toward parents and other authority figures for a time. S. Freud (1924/1973) believed that this process is seldom completed ideally.

Blos (1941, 1979) modified traditional psychoanalytic theory, stressing the importance of the "cultural milieu and social stratum" (Blos, 1941, p. 7) in personality formation and positing a reciprocal influence between the individual and the environment. Although he insisted that adolescent development must be considered in the context of a particular culture and the family's "unique version of the culture" (Blos, 1941, p. 260), he—like his psychoanalytic predecessors—saw adolescence as a transitional period that involves a recapitulation of earlier familial patterns of interaction. However, he considered this process to be qualitatively different from earlier developmental experiences because of the significant maturation of the ego (ego supremacy and ego differentiation) during the latency period (Blos, 1941). This ego development allows the adolescent in most cases to resolve the oedipal conflicts and the component infantile dependencies (Blos, 1979).

According to Blos (1979), the second individuation process during adolescence requires a "normative regression in the service of development" (p. 153); that is, only in adolescence is regression an essential and normal process. Although normal, this regression still produces turmoil, volatile behavior, and anxiety that, if they become unmanageable, may result in the use of various defense mechanisms such as withdrawal and secrecy, fantasy, temporary compulsive habit formation, compensation, intellectualization, rationalization, projection, and changes in the ego ideal (Blos, 1941).

Chodorow (1974, 1978) reinterpreted the individuation process, challenging the male gender bias of earlier formulations. According to Chodorow, because the male's first love object—the mother—is of the opposite sex, separation and individuation are critical to male gender identity and development but not to the progress of female identity development.

### Psychosocial Theories

Psychosocial theories of adolescence, although based on Sigmund Freud's psychosexual conceptualization of development, emphasize the impact of the sociocultural context on individual development. Erikson (1963, 1968) viewed development as proceeding through a sequence of stages, each of which is characterized by a specific crisis. Not only are the crises of each stage produced by internal mechanisms, they are also the result of the interaction between the individual and the social environment, which makes cultural demands in the form of social expectations, norms, and values.

Erikson (1968) thought of identity formation as a process that continues throughout one's life, but he believed that identity "has its normative crisis in adolescence" (p. 23). Like the psychosexual theorists, Erikson described adolescence as a time of turmoil and stress, but he considered the turmoil the result of an "identity crisis" rather than the result of a conflict between the ego and the id. Furthermore, he viewed adolescence as a necessary and productive period during which the adolescent experiments with and works to consolidate his or her personal, occupational, and ideological identity. This identity is formed through the individual's psychological integration as well as through the social environment, which serves critical functions during this process. In the search for self-definition, conflict arises between the adolescent and his or her parents as a necessary movement toward establishing the adolescent's own view of self, of the world, and of his or her place in that world.

Erikson's conceptualization has been criticized for its gender bias, as he generalized changes in the life cycle from a male model of development (Chodorow, 1974, 1978; Gilligan, 1979). Gilligan noted that individuation and separation from the mother are accepted as critical for the development of gender identity among males, but she proposed the opposite dynamic for females: "Femininity is defined through attachment" to the mother (p. 434). According to Gilligan, "male gender identity will be threatened by intimacy while female gender identity will be threatened by individuation" (p. 434). Erikson (1968) viewed separation as a healthy sign of progressive development and attachment as a problem. However, Chodorow (1974, 1978) and Gilligan (1979) proposed that, in the course of female development, intimacy may more appropriately precede separation or at least be fused with identity formation.

**Social Learning Theory**

Social learning theorists describe adolescence as a period of development that, for the majority of individuals, proceeds from childhood with great continuity in behavior, interpersonal relationships, and self-evaluation (Bandura & Walters, 1963). The behavioral and social learning principles that apply in infancy and childhood remain the same, with the possible expansion of sources of reinforcement in the environment, a greater number and variety of models, and an expanded capacity for self-regulated behavior.

The process of socialization includes the development of behavioral repertoires through differential reinforcement, stimulus-and-response generalization, higher-order conditioning, modeling, and rule learning (Bandura, 1969; Gagne, 1970). *Differential reinforcement* refers to the process whereby behavior that is reinforced increases in frequency, and behavior that is punished or placed on extinction (ignored) decreases. For example, adolescents shape each other's social behaviors by positively responding to specific mannerisms, dress, and the latest slang terms and by ostracizing or ridiculing behaviors that do not meet the norms of their peers. *Response generalization* involves the production of behaviors (responses) that have properties similar to the response that has been reinforced. Through stimulus generalization, the adolescent is likely to respond with the same repertoire of responses to other peers he or she perceives as being similar to those from whom he or she received reinforcement. In *higher-order conditioning,* certain individuals, environments, objects, words, symbols, and the like become positive or negative stimuli for the individual and result in specific responses because they are associated with positive or negative events.

*Modeling* is a mode of imitative or vicarious learning that involves the observation, coding, and retention of a set of behaviors for their performance at a later time. It is a particularly efficient method for learning complex behaviors such as interpersonal skills. Furthermore, modeled behaviors are more readily learned in situations for which the individual has no previous repertoire of responses. The adolescent also combines behaviors of various models into novel responses or abstracts a "rule" that allows him or her to act as the model would act in a novel situation for which specific responses have not been observed (Mehrabian, 1970). Hence, as one moves from childhood into adolescence and is exposed to a greater number and variety of models, one's potential behavioral repertoire increases substantially.

Finally, as an individual progresses through childhood into adolescence and adulthood, an increase in self-regulatory behavior, most notably self-evaluation and self-reinforcement, is noted (Bandura, 1969). Self-reinforcement is generally established through modeling as the observer evaluates and reinforces his or her performance using the same criteria as the model. Over time, the responses become independent of the original learning experience and are generalized to other situations. Although self-evaluation and reinforcement can be independent of social norms, they often correspond.

Bandura and Walters (1963) noted that empirical research has not borne out the claim that adolescence constitutes a sudden and drastic change from childhood, particularly in parent–child relations. They indicated that the pattern instead appears to be one of gradual socialization toward independence by means of a gradual change in reinforcement conditions.

## Cognitive Development

According to Piagetian theory, cognitive development consists of the progression through stages of quantitatively and qualitatively more complex thought processes and structures. Piaget and Inhelder (1958) emphasized the discontinuity between the concrete operational thinking of the child and the qualitatively different formal operations of the adolescent. Piaget (1972) viewed the progression from concrete to formal operations as the product of individual "spontaneous and endogenous factors" (p. 7) and experiences in the environment that stimulate intellectual growth.

Formal operational thought is characterized by hypotheticodeductive reasoning: Because the adolescent's thinking is no longer tied to concrete objects, he or she is able to construct possibilities, to manipulate and reflect on mental constructs, and to assess probabilities. According to Piaget and Inhelder (1958), this new capacity enables the adolescent to "analyze his [or her] own thinking and construct theories" (p. 340). The adolescent's thinking is no longer tied to trial and error but can generate hypotheses regarding all the possible relations among the various factors in solving a problem. Moreover, the adolescent systematically tests alternative hypotheses, varying one factor at a time while holding all other factors constant (Piaget & Inhelder, 1958).

Cognitive development also is conceptualized as a process of *decentering,* which involves the reduction of egocentric thought that thereby allows for the generation and testing of hypotheses. Formal operations progress through transitional stages (generally from age 11 to 14) in which the operations of formal thought are confounded by the adolescent's egocentrism. Elkind (1967, 1974, 1978) believed that this results in the phenomenon he called the *imaginary audience;* that is, the adolescent feels as though his or her actions and appearance are constantly being scrutinized by others. Elkind (1978) believed that this egocentrism may explain the feelings of self-consciousness that prevail during adolescence and "a good deal of adolescent boorishness, loudness, and faddish dress" (p. 387).

Also demonstrative of cognitive egocentrism is the complementary development of the *personal fable* (Elkind, 1967, 1974, 1978; Inhelder & Piaget, 1978), which involves viewing one's thoughts and feelings as unique experiences, often ones that should be saved for posterity (in diaries or poetry). Feelings of invulnerability accompany this perception and have been linked to such adolescent problems as the failure to use contraceptives and other risk-taking behavior (Elkind, 1967). This cognitive egocentrism also results in projecting one's preoccupation with and plans for the future onto the society as a whole and viewing oneself in a messianic role (Inhelder & Piaget, 1978). Primarily because of reality testing and the sharing of perceptions and experiences with peers, the egocentrism of early adolescence gives way to full formal operations by age 15 or 16 (Elkind, 1978; Inhelder & Piaget, 1978).

## Moral Development

Moral development is incorporated in psychoanalytic theory through the development of a conscience in childhood and such conceptualizations as the "reexternalization" of the superego in adolescence (Settlage, 1972), which consists of a conscious appraisal, challenging, and discarding of values and an incorporation into the superego of reappraised ideals and values that are no longer mirrors of parental values (Hoffman, 1980). Erikson (1970) described the adolescent in the process of identity development as moving from the specific moral learnings of childhood to the pursuit of a moral ideology that facilitates identity formation.

Piaget (1965) formulated a simple two-stage dichotomous model moving from moral realism to subjectivism. In the first stage, *moral realism,* the child judges the moral value (rightness or wrongness) of an act by the magnitude of the damage or injury or by simple conformity to stated rules, irrespective of intention. In the second or autonomous stage, *subjectivism,* intention becomes the foremost consideration in judging the moral value of an act; the subjective nature of rules and the concept of rules by mutual consent are recognized.

It is only with the attainment of formal operations in adolescence that the individual has the capacity for developing postconventional morality, recognizing individual and cultural differences as well as universal principles. Although Kohlberg and Gilligan (1975) proposed that many adolescents regress to an instrumental level of moral development, Turiel (1974) described the extreme relativism of the adolescent as a transitional phase. With attainment of formal operations and the recognition of differences in perspectives, the adolescent questions the rigid law-and-order morality of the conventional stage and rejects the imposition of moral codes and values on the individual. The adolescent's extreme relativism results from the rejection of conventional criteria for moral judgment, which temporarily leaves the adolescent with the sense that no basis exists for objectively verifying values.

Hoffman (1980) proposed that the development of empathy and its transformation during cognitive maturation provide the fundamental basis for moral development. As a result of cognitive development, the adolescent begins not only to conceptualize others as distinct but also to project the self into another's experiences beyond the immediate concrete situation and, therefore, to respond with empathic distress and "a more reciprocal feeling of concern for the victim" (Hoffman, 1980, p. 311). Moreover, this empathic distress can also be transformed into feelings of guilt if the victim's distress leads to self-blame with respect to one's action or inaction. Finally, one's empathic distress, sense of guilt, and impetus to relieve the distress perceived in another are viewed as the significant motivational components for moral action.

In social learning theory, moral values, judgments, and behaviors are viewed as being dependent on a variety of environmental factors, such as the long- and short-term consequences, the setting, the type of act, and the characteristics of the victim. Moral development involves a process of learning through direct instruction (rule learning), reinforcement contingencies, modeling, and evaluative feedback. By exposure to diverse situations and models, one learns which factors are important to consider in various situations when moral judgments are required (Bandura, 1977; Rosenthal & Zimmerman, 1978).

## Social Development

The adolescent's social development is closely related to psychological development, particularly identity formation and the need for intimacy. Sullivan (1953) viewed interpersonal relations as central to one's individual identity. He posited three stages of adolescent development that are distinguished by different needs and expressions of interpersonal intimacy: preadolescence, early adolescence, and late adolescence. Preadolescence is characterized by the need for intimacy expressed through strong relationships, usually with people of the same sex. These relationships differ from those of childhood in their exclusivity and extent of personal intimacy, as evidenced by disclosure of one's secret thoughts, feelings, and aspirations.

The stage of early adolescence is ushered in by the physiological changes of puberty and the concomitant appearance of the lust dynamism (Sullivan, 1953). *Lust*—a psychological rather than a moralistic construct—refers to genital drives that impel the individual toward sexual satisfaction. This new integrating dynamism results in the shift to intimate relationships with people of the opposite (or the same) sex, patterned, to some degree, after preadolescent same-sex relationships.

According to Sullivan (1953), a person enters late adolescence when he or she "discovers what he [she] likes in the way of genital behavior and how to fit it into the rest of life" (p. 297). By late adolescence, Sullivan claimed, most adolescents have established heterosexuality as their preferred mode of sexual relationships and continue to develop and expand their interpersonal skills. Intimacy is the core of what Sullivan (1953) described as the mature person; it involves "a very lively sensitivity to the needs of the other and to the interpersonal security or absence of anxiety in the other" (p. 310).

Although little research has been conducted on sex differences in the development of friendships, Coleman's (1980) review of the literature pointed out that the need for friendships changes, and the greatest need for friendships (especially for girls) occurs during middle adolescence. It is during middle adolescence that the dread of rejection and the lack of social confidence take their toll. Moreover, girls experience more feelings of anxiety about friendships than do boys, probably because the socialization of girls places greater emphasis on the fulfillment of emotional needs through relationships. In contrast, boys tend to be socialized to seek relationships that are focused on actions (Douvan & Adelson, 1966).

Bandura (1964) and others indicated that increased peer interaction does not usually result in a simultaneous shifting away from parental relationships and values. A number of studies (Bandura, 1964; Bandura & Walters, 1963; Hess & Goldblatt, 1957; Maxwell, Connor, & Walters, 1961; Meissner, 1965; Offer, 1967; Offer, Sabshin, & Marcus, 1965) found that adolescents and parents hold positive views of one another. With increasing age, an adolescent's decisions and values rely less on either parents or peers and reflect his or her own views (Gardner & Thompson, 1963).

## Sexual Development

Sexual development is the result of the interaction of intrapsychic, sociocultural, and biological factors. The physiological changes initiated in puberty influence the individual in a social context (Miller & Simon, 1980) and by way of personal evaluation of the meaning and significance of these changes.

Gender identity and gender role expectations form the foundation of the young adolescent's sexual identity "since the sexual and social scenarios of the society are organized around norms for gender-appropriate behavior" (Miller & Simon, 1980, p. 383). Particularly in early adolescence, motivations for sociosexual behavior may be nonerotic, impelled instead by what are considered gender-appropriate behaviors in the specific social context (Miller & Simon, 1980).

With the onset of puberty, the adolescent must add a sexual dimension to his or her gender identity. According to Miller and Simon (1980), the progress of psychosexual development and concomitant sexual behavior depend on two factors and their interaction: "the intrapsychic history and life of the individual" and "the interpersonal requirements of social life" (p. 388)—that is, the social context. The intrapsychic life of the individual refers to idiosyncratic values that result in the eroticizing of events, attributes, relationships, and so forth. Interpersonal "scripts" are less idiosyncratic, because they reflect present social expectations and constraints, which vary with time and the individual's reference group (Gagnon, 1974; Gordon & Gilgun, 1987; Miller & Simon, 1980). Hence, majority and minority adolescent cohorts may have significantly different interpersonal scripts.

When there is congruence between intrapsychic and interpersonal factors, sexual identity formation proceeds smoothly. When these two factors are discordant, the adolescent must choose to risk either alienation from others or a sense of self-betrayal. Particularly vulnerable in this regard are individuals whose intrapsychic content is homoerotic but who feel constrained by sociocultural norms and demands (Miller & Simon, 1980).

## Characteristic Problems of Adolescence

### Runaway and Homeless Youths

Runaway youths are those "under the age of eighteen who are away from home at least overnight without parent or caretaker permission" (U.S. Department of Health and Human Services [DHHS], 1983). Homeless youths are a subpopulation of this group who have no parent, parental figure, or institutional caretakers.

The number of runaway youths has increased at an alarming rate, from an estimated 733,000 in 1975 to a continuing estimate in the 1980s and 1990s of as many as 1.3 million to 1.5 million per year (DHHS, 1983; National Network of Runaway and Youth Services, 1991a). Moreover, the percentage of homeless youth within this population has appeared to increase; most of these youths are from economically disadvantaged families who are no longer able to support them (Zide & Cherry, 1992).

The Runaway and Homeless Youth Act of 1974 provided grants and technical assistance for agencies to develop and support community-based programs to deal with the immediate needs of runaway youth (including shelter, counseling, and aftercare services) and to encourage a reunion of the youths with their families by working toward resolving problems in these families and strengthening familial relationships. In keeping with this goal, a survey of 151 youth shelters found that 61 percent of the youths served returned home, 26 percent were provided with placements, and 13 percent returned to the streets or to other unstable living situations (National Network of Runaway and Youth Services, 1991a).

However, it appears that youth shelters serve a relatively small percentage of the runaway and homeless adolescent population. For example, according to data collected by the U.S. General Accounting Office (GAO) (1989), 44,274 youths (9,179 of whom were classified as homeless) were provided with residential services by federally funded shelters between October 1985 and June 1988. A survey of community-based runaway and homeless youth centers conducted in the summer of 1990 by the National Network of Runaway and Youth Services (1991b) found that 404,279 youths were provided with both residential and nonresidential services by the 178 agencies who responded. The majority (54 percent) of those served were 15 to 17 years old; however, a notably large proportion (38 percent) were quite young (14 years of age or younger). Similar rates were found in a survey conducted by the Family and Youth Services Bureau (FYSB) (1990), with 42 percent of those served being 14 years of age or younger and 56 percent being 15 to 16 years of age. Findings of various surveys of runaway and homeless shelters concur with regard to gender differences, with the percentage of females served higher than the percentage of males (National Network of Runaway and Youth Services, 1991b; FYSB, 1990; GAO, 1989). Finally, a 1989 survey of 151 agencies indicated that they had not been able to provide shelter for 10,769 youths in need (National Network of Runaway and Youth Services, 1991a).

Runaway youths are a particularly at-risk population, having high rates of victimization from robbery, assault, and rape (Simons & Whitbeck, 1991; Whitbeck & Simons, 1990); greater engagement in criminal activities such as shoplifting, robbery, prostitution, pornography, and drug sales (Whitbeck & Simons, 1990; Zide & Cherry, 1992); and greater exposure to sexually transmitted diseases and human immunodeficiency virus (HIV) (Athey, 1991; Kalinski, Rubinson, Lawrence, & Levy, 1990). A two-year study of 2,667 youths seeking shelter at Covenant House in New York City found a 5 percent HIV seropositive rate (Athey, 1991).

Although various typologies have been suggested for classifying and understanding runaway youths, three major types of runaways have emerged (Zide & Cherry, 1992):

1. those adolescents, usually from a fairly well-functioning family system, "running to" or in search of some form of adventure or excitement
2. those "running from" a dysfunctional family system, which might include a substance-abusing parent and physical or sexual abuse, which has been found to occur with higher rates within the runaway population (Angenet & de Man, 1989; Caton, 1986; Janus, Burgess, & McCormack, 1987; Whitbeck & Simons, 1990).
3. those "thrown out" by their families, often after a history of conflict with the family and problems in the school and the community.

Zide and Cherry (1992) added a fourth group they labeled "forsaken," representing adolescents, usually social isolates with low self-esteem, who have been abandoned to their own resources for survival owing to the inability of the family to continue to provide support.

**HIV/AIDS**

Through June 1994, 1,768 cases of acquired immune deficiency syndrome (AIDS) in adolescents ages 13 to 19 were reported to the Centers for Disease Control and Prevention. The majority of cases (1,203) were in males, with the largest number occurring in white adolescent males (570), followed by African American (368) and Hispanic (239) youths. Fourteen cases among Asian/Pacific Islander youths and twelve cases among Native American/Alaska Native adolescents were also reported. In cases occurring in females (565), African American adolescents predominated (358), followed by their white (113) and Hispanic (91) cohorts. The two primary modes of transmission for AIDS in male adolescents were transfusion for hemophilia or other coagulation disorders (531 [44 percent]) and homosexual contact (446 [37 percent]). For females, heterosexual contact (292 [52 percent]) was the main mode of transmission, particularly contact with an intravenous drug user (105 [19 percent]) (DHHS, 1994).

Although the number of adolescent AIDS cases appears low (1 percent or less of reported U.S. cases), the increase since 1988 is noteworthy:

| | *Males* | *Females* | *Total* |
|---|---|---|---|
| December 1988 | 276 | 59 | 335 |
| December 1990 | 472 | 157 | 629 |
| December 1992 | 671 | 275 | 946 |

Approximately 300 additional AIDS cases were reported for each two-year period from 1988 to 1990 and from 1990 to 1992. However, between December 1992 and June 1994, 804 additional cases were reported, an 84 percent increase overall with a 79 percent (532) increase for males and a 119 percent (308) increase for females (DHHS, 1989a, 1991, 1994). Moreover, given the long latency period for AIDS, these figures probably do not indicate the incidence of HIV infection within this age group, as an unknown number of the 15,204 AIDS cases reported for the 20-to-24-year-old age group may have resulted from infection during adolescence (Brooks-Gunn, Boyer, & Hein, 1988; DHHS, 1994; Schwarez & Rutherford, 1989).

In addition, researchers cite a number of indicators of high risk for HIV infection in the adolescent population. In surveys of adolescents, rates of condom use have varied from as low as 2.1 percent to 38 percent (Boyer & Kegeles, 1991). Twenty-five percent of those with sexually transmitted diseases are adolescents (Boyer & Kegeles, 1991), and this age group has the highest percentage of sexually active individuals with gonorrhea, syphilis, cytomegalovirus, or chlamydial cervicitis or who have been hospitalized for pelvic inflammatory disease (Bell & Hein, 1984). These facts signify that adolescents are not using methods that would also protect them from HIV infection. In fact, in a study of users of sexually transmitted disease clinics, the HIV-seropositive rate for 15- to 19-year-olds was 22 per 1,000, in contrast to a rate of 3.7 per 1,000 for 20- to 24-year-olds (Quinn et al., 1988). Similar evidence is offered by the low rates of contraceptive use among adolescents, especially for barrier methods of contraception (Boyer & Kegeles, 1991; Strunin & Hingson, 1987). Furthermore, the risk increases with the trend for sexual activity to begin at earlier ages (Boyer & Kegeles, 1991; Zelnik & Shah, 1983) and when substance use and abuse are involved (Boyer & Kegeles, 1991; Strunin & Hingson, 1992).

Factors related to cognitive development, such as adolescent egocentrism and the concomitant sense of personal invulnerability (Elkind, 1967,

1974, 1978), along with the lack of achievement of formal operations, contribute to an underestimation of risk and failure to engage in preventive behaviors. For example, in a study by Reuben, Hein, and Drucker (1988), adolescents engaging in the highest-risk behaviors perceived their risk of HIV infection to be low. This risk-taking behavior is reinforced by the fact that most HIV-infected adolescents are asymptomatic until they are adults (Brooks-Gunn et al., 1988).

Finally, homeless youths are considered a population that is particularly at risk as a result of their high rate of intravenous drug use (Yates, MacKenzie, Pennbridge, & Cohen, 1986) and greater risk of sexual transmission via rape, survival sex, and prostitution.

The following factors should be considered when planning prevention programs for adolescents:

- the extent of knowledge regarding HIV transmission
- the sense of personal vulnerability and degree of egocentrism
- acceptance of one's sexuality and communication abilities in this area
- social norms regarding risk perception and the costs–benefits of condom use
- the contribution of substance use and abuse.

Furthermore, if programs are to be effective, they must encourage exploration of attitudes and open discussion of feelings, concerns, and experiences; increase problem-solving abilities and feelings of control; and be sensitive to differences in cultural values, religious beliefs, and social norms (Boyer & Kegeles, 1991; Brooks-Gunn et al., 1988).

**Pregnancy**

The pregnancy rate for adolescents has continued to rise since the 1970s, from 13.5 per 1,000 in 1972 to 15.9 per 1,000 in 1980 and 17.4 per 1,000 in 1989 for females 14 years old or younger, and from 64.1 per 1,000 in 1972 to 72.5 per 1,000 in 1980 and 74.9 per 1,000 in 1989 for 15- to 17-year-olds. The 1989 live birthrate for the adolescent population was a little less than half the pregnancy rate (7.1 per 1,000 for those 14 or less and 36.4 per 1,000 for 15- to 17-year-olds) and is partially accounted for by the legal abortion rates (8.1 per 1,000 for those 14 or younger and 28.4 per 1,000 for 15- to 17-year-olds) (Henshaw, 1993). In actual figures, this amounted to 400,660 pregnancies among adolescent females 17 or younger in 1989, with 192,530, or 48.1 percent, resulting in a live birth and 154,200, or 38.5 percent, ending with a legal abortion. It is important to note that these figures apply only to one year, and the number of adolescent mothers 17 and younger at any given time would require adding in the number of underage females who had given birth in previous years and who had not yet attained majority. For example, of the 145,044 females 17 and younger who gave birth in 1988, 76,464 were still 17 or younger in 1989 (DHHS, 1989b). In addition, in 1988, 111,061 adolescent males 19 years of age or younger became fathers (DHHS, 1989b). These combined figures indicate a substantial population of adolescent parents and offspring in need of ongoing support services, particularly because fewer than 10 percent of adolescent parents place their infants for adoption (Henshaw, 1993).

Ethnic differences are evident in the pregnancy and live birth rates. For example, in 1991, the pregnancy rate for white adolescents 15 to 17 years of age was 23.3 per 1,000, in contrast to the rate for Hispanic adolescents (70.6 per 1,000) and African American adolescents (86.1 per 1,000) (National Center for Health Statistics, 1993). In 1990, 20 percent of the first births in the white population were to adolescents, while 40 percent of the first births in the African American population were to adolescents (Henshaw, 1993). The birthrate among Hispanic adolescents is also significant, because Hispanics have the highest overall fertility rate in the nation (89.6 per 1,000, compared with 60.0 per 1,000 for white women and 86.8 per 1,000 for African Americans), and one in five of these births is to an adolescent (National Center for Health Statistics, 1993; Ventura, 1982; Ventura & Heuser, 1981). These differential rates of pregnancy and motherhood indicate that we may need to develop a variety of prevention efforts and prenatal and postpartum support services to meet the needs of culturally different populations.

**Drug Abuse**

Trends in adolescent drug use show an increase from the mid-1970s to 1982, followed by a slow but steady reduction in the use of illegal substances (Oetting & Beauvais, 1990). Data from the National Household Survey on Drug Abuse (DHHS, 1993) show that the percentage of adolescents using any illegal substance dropped consistently between 1988 and 1992, with current user percentage ranging from 6.1 percent to 11.7 percent in a sample of 3,672 males and 3,582 females (see Table 2). Gender differences are noteworthy, with male rates higher for marijuana use and female rates slightly higher for hallucinogen and cocaine use. In the past, Hispanic adolescents have generally reported drug use rates similar to but slightly lower than those reported by white adolescents (Oetting &

TABLE 2

**Estimated Use of Illegal Drugs in 12- to 17-Year-Olds (Percentages)**

| When Used | Any Illegal Drug | Marijuana | Hallucinogens | Cocaine |
|---|---|---|---|---|
| Ever | | | | |
| Total | 16.5 | 10.6 | 2.6 | 1.7 |
| Male | 15.3 | 11.6 | 2.4 | 1.6 |
| Female | 16.6 | 9.6 | 2.9 | 1.8 |
| White | 16.9 | 10.8 | 3.2 | 1.7 |
| African American | 15.1 | 9.1 | 0.2 | 0.8 |
| Hispanic | 17.6 | 11.9 | 2.8 | 3.6 |
| Previous year | | | | |
| Total | 11.7 | 8.1 | 1.9 | 1.1 |
| Male | 11.0 | 8.7 | 1.8 | 1.0 |
| Female | 12.5 | 7.5 | 1.9 | 1.2 |
| White | 12.1 | 8.4 | 2.3 | 1.0 |
| African American | 9.9 | 5.9 | 0.1 | 0.4 |
| Hispanic | 12.7 | 9.0 | 2.0 | 2.8 |
| Previous month | | | | |
| Total | 6.1 | 4,.0 | 0.6 | 0.3 |
| Male | 5.7 | 4.6 | 0.6 | 0.2 |
| Female | 6.5 | 3.0 | 0.5 | 0.3 |
| White | 6.1 | 4.1 | 0.6 | 0.1 |
| African American | 6.1 | 3.4 | — | 0.2 |
| Hispanic | 7.1 | 4.8 | 0.9 | 1.2 |

SOURCE: U.S. Department of Health and Human Services. (1993). *National household survey on drug abuse*. Washington, DC: Substance Abuse and Mental Health Service Administration.

Beauvais, 1990); however, the rates for Hispanic youths in the 1992 Household survey are higher than those for their white and African American cohorts. Oetting and Beauvais (1990), in their review of various sources of data, found that Native American youths on reservations have the highest substance abuse rates. They hypothesize that substance abuse rates for youths of color may be substantially higher among economically disadvantaged youths than surveys indicate, because this population has often been excluded in sampling procedures.

Another consistent pattern is the increase with age in the use of all illicit substances, except inhalants, with the highest use reported among high school seniors. In the 1986 National Senior Survey, 52 percent of white high school seniors and 41 percent of African American high school seniors reported having *ever* used marijuana. In the Annual Drug and Alcohol Survey conducted in 1988, 45 percent of white adolescents reported *ever* using marijuana, with a comparable rate (45 percent) for Hispanics and the highest rate for Native American youths living on reservations (78 percent) (Oetting & Beauvais, 1990). Although the lower rates for younger age groups could have reduced the average rates for the adolescent population as a whole, there does appear to be some discrepancy between these figures and those reported on the National Household Survey (DHHS, 1993).

Inhalant use is most prevalent among young adolescents, equaling (1988 Annual Drug and Alcohol Survey) or surpassing (1986 National Adolescent Student Health Survey) the use of marijuana as the most frequently used drug (Oetting & Beauvais, 1990), possibly because inhalants are more readily accessible. Ethnic differences in the use of inhalants are somewhat equivocal, with earlier studies by Padilla, Padilla, Morales, Olmeda, and Ramirez (1977) reporting use among Latino adolescents to be 14 times that of their cohorts followed by a notable reduction in inhalant use in the same population two years later (Perez, Padilla, Ramirez, & Rodriguez, 1979). Furthermore, data from the 1988 Annual Drug and Alcohol Survey indicate that only a small percentage of high school seniors have *ever* used inhalants, with the lowest rates for Mexican American youths (12 percent), compared with 14 percent for white seniors and 17 percent for Native American youths on reservations. In the 1988 National Senior Survey, 8 percent of African American seniors and 17 percent of white seniors reported using inhalants.

Frequent users of marijuana and multiple drug users have been identified as a subset of the population, manifesting personality characteristics indicative of psychological disturbance (Shedler & Block, 1990). However, some researchers view marijuana use as normative behavior in American adolescents, given developmental issues and social norms, as long as such use remains infrequent and experimental (Newcomb & Bentler, 1988; Shedler & Block, 1990).

Much of the research in this area examines the influence of environmental and interpersonal factors on drug use and abuse. A number of researchers have confirmed the influence of peer use and attitudes toward use along with susceptibility to peer pressure as the most significant factors affecting substance use and abuse (Barnea, Teichman, & Rahav, 1992; Dielman, Butchart, Shope, & Miller, 1991; McGee, 1992). Conflicting findings have been reported regarding the impact of parental behavior and attitudes on drug use, with some studies indicating both direct and indirect effects (Barnea et al., 1992; Dielman et al.,

1991) and other results indicating no significant relationship (McGee, 1992).

Barnea et al. (1992) concluded that "drug use emerges as a complex behavior such that no single factor should be singled out as the critical one" (p. 198). Dielman et al. (1991) concurred, adding that the adolescent population is not homogeneous, so that different weights must be assigned to different factors based on this heterogeneity. This complexity may also help explain the lack of consistency in the findings of various surveys of adolescent drug use.

TABLE 3
**Alcohol Use Among 12- to 17-Year-Olds (Percentages)**

| Year | Lifetime | Previous Year | Previous Month |
|---|---|---|---|
| 1988 | 50.2 | 44.5 | 25.2 |
| 1990 | 48.2 | 41.0 | 24.5 |
| 1991 | 46.4 | 40.3 | 20.3 |
| 1992 | 39.3 | 32.6 | 15.7 |

SOURCE: U.S. Department of Health and Human Services. (1993). *National household survey on drug abuse*. Washington, DC: Substance Abuse and Mental Health Service Administration.

**Alcohol Abuse**

Alcohol is the drug of choice and the drug most frequently abused by the adolescent population (Newcomb & Bentler, 1986). As with drug use, according to the National Household Survey on Drug Abuse (DHHS, 1993), alcohol use decreased among 12- to 17-year-olds between 1988 and 1992 (Table 3).

Ethnic differences have been noted for alcohol abuse, with rates consistently highest for Native American adolescents, followed by white adolescents (Barnes & Welte, 1986b; Lee & Di Climante, 1985). In a survey of 27,335 seventh- through 12th-grade students in New York State, Barnes and Welte (1986b) found that rates for both the average amount of alcohol consumed per day and the frequency of intoxication per month were highest among Native American youths (0.94 ounces consumed per day and intoxicated 6.3 times per month) followed by whites (0.58 ounces per day, 4.7 times per month), Hispanics (0.54 ounces per day, 4.2 times per month), Asian Americans (0.66 ounces per day, 3.5 times per month), African Americans (0.30 ounces per day, 2.6 times per month), and West Indians (0.32 ounces per day, 2.6 times per month). Interestingly, however, Native American youths had the highest number of alcohol-related social problems per month, followed by their Hispanic and African American cohorts, whereas white students reported the fewest alcohol-related social problems. Moreover, a strong relationship was found between alcohol-related social problems and school misconduct, especially for males. The overall alcohol abuse rate for 10th through 12th graders was 39 percent. The authors cautioned, however, that alcohol use and abuse rates in New York State have frequently been found to be higher than in the country as a whole (Barnes & Welte, 1986a, 1986b).

Problem drinking involves "frequent drinking to the point of drunkenness or intoxication" or drinking that results in "negative social consequences and that compromises role obligations and interpersonal relations" (Jessor, 1985, p. 75). One-fourth of male adolescents and one-sixth of female adolescents who drink seem to be problem drinkers (Jessor, 1985). Drinking alcoholic beverages is illegal for adolescents; in 1992, 79,521 youths were arrested for violating liquor laws, and 11,939 were arrested for drunkenness. Although these numbers are substantial, they represent a 25 percent drop in arrests from 1988 figures (Federal Bureau of Investigation, 1992).

Adolescents who abuse alcohol appear to engage in a syndrome of deviant behavior that includes delinquent behavior and drug use (Barnes & Welte, 1986a; Jessor, 1985; Newcomb & McGee, 1989). However, 50 percent of the males and 75 percent of the females who were problem drinkers as adolescents no longer were problem drinkers as young adults (Jessor, 1985).

**Suicide**

Suicide continues to rank third (11.0 per 100,000) among the leading causes of death for adolescents after accidents (40.3 per 100,000) and homicides (19.6 per 100,000) (National Center for Health Statistics, 1993). However, the suicide rates may actually be higher than those reported, as an unknown percentage of the deaths reported as accidents might actually be suicides.

Suicide rates differ by gender, with the rate for males 15 to 19 years of age (32.8 per 100,000) notably higher than that for females of the same age (5.5 per 100,000). Rates also differ by ethnicity, with rates higher for white adolescents than their African American cohorts of the same gender. In 1991, the rate per 100,000 for white males was 19.1 (1,351 cases); for African American males, 12.2 (164 cases); and for white females, 4.2 (277 cases). The rate for African American females, with only 19 cases, was below calculable levels (National Center for Health Statistics, 1993). Moreover, for the first three groups, the rates have shown a noteworthy increase. For example, the 1986 rates were 15.1 for white males, 6.5 for African American males, and 3.5 for white females (National Center for Health Statistics, 1987). This appears to be a continuing trend, as the suicide rates for 15- to 19-year-olds doubled between 1961 and 1975 and tripled between 1956 and 1975 (Holinger & Offer, 1982).

National suicide rates have not been calculated for adolescents in other ethnic groups. Although comparable national figures are not available for Hispanic youths, suicide data for 1976 through 1980 are available from a comparative study of white and Hispanic populations in five southwestern states. When the rates for all age groups are combined, the white population has a rate approximately double that of the Hispanic population. However, the rates are remarkably similar when the adolescent populations are compared: white males, 18.5; Hispanic males, 14.8; white females, 5.2; Hispanic females, 3.4 (Smith, Mercy, & Warren, 1985).

The available morbidity statistics do not account for the even greater number of attempted, but unsuccessful, suicides. A number of authors claim that those who attempt suicide make up a larger proportion of the youth population than do their counterparts in the adult population and that the ratio of suicide attempts to actual suicides may be as high as 50 to 1 (Peck, 1982) or 150 to 1 (Tishler, McKenry, & Morgan, 1981). Various proportions of those sampled in anonymous surveys of adolescent high school students have reported attempting suicide: 8.4 percent in a midwest study (K. Smith & Crawford, 1986), 9 percent in a study in New York City (Harkavy-Friedman, Asnis, Boeck, & Di Fiore, 1987), and 13 percent in a study conducted in California (Ross, 1985).

The gender ratio for suicide attempts is the reverse of that for completed suicides, with females attempting suicide two to three times more often than males (Harkavy-Friedman et al., 1987; Holinger, 1978; Peck, 1982; Spirito, Brown, Overholser, & Fritz, 1989; Toolan, 1975).

Although the use of firearms accounts for the highest percentage of completed suicides, the great majority of suicide attempters use drug overdose as their method (Hawton, 1986; Spirito, Stark, Fristad, Hart, & Owens-Stively, 1987).

Youthful suicide attempters consistently have been found to be from families with higher rates of conflict and dysfunction, divorce, separation, and parental death, particularly at an early age (Hawton, 1982; Spirito et al., 1989). Physical abuse and a family history of violence and suicide also are characteristic of suicide attempters (Christoffel, Marcus, Sagerman, & Bennett, 1988; Green, 1978; Kerfort, 1979; Levin & Schonberg, 1987; Tishler et al., 1981). A high incidence of drug abuse has been noted in this population (Christoffel et al., 1988; McKenry, Tishler, & Kelley, 1983; Schrieber & Johnson, 1986; Withers & Kaplan, 1987). As in adult populations, depression has been diagnosed in a significant portion of suicide attempters (Bettes & Walker, 1986; Christoffel et al., 1988; Reuben, Boeck, & Kurzon, 1987; Robbins & Alessi, 1985; Withers & Kaplan, 1987).

Most suicide attempts occur after a "major disruption of a personal relationship," either parental or romantic (Hawton, 1982, p. 501). The prognosis for unsuccessful suicide attempters is generally good, with only 10 percent repeating the suicide attempt (Hawton, 1982); this statistic indicates that many suicide attempts are extreme and atypical responses to a crisis. However, because only about half of adolescent suicide attempters receive some type of professional treatment (Kienhorst, Wolters, Diekstra, & Otte, 1987), a substantial portion of this population continues to attempt to deal on their own with the factors that precipitated their crisis.

A significant number of adolescents have not attempted suicide, but have experienced suicidal ideation. According to Peck (1982), as many as 10 percent to 20 percent of the youths in the United States may contemplate suicide at any one time. Recent studies have found suicidal ideation to have been experienced by approximately 60 percent of the adolescents sampled (Harkavy-Friedman et al., 1987; Smith & Crawford, 1986). These figures point to the need for crisis services such as walk-in facilities and suicide telephone help lines for this population, particularly services adolescents can identify as geared specifically to their needs (de Anda & Smith, 1993).

**Crime and Victimization**

Reports from 7,937 law enforcement agencies indicated that 1,621,796 persons under the age of 18 were arrested in 1992, an increase of 11.5 percent over the 1988 figures. Although the number of males (1,245,637) was substantially higher than the number of females (376,159) arrested, the percentage increase over 1988 figures was greater for females (16.6 percent) than for males (10.0 percent). This trend was also apparent with regard to violent crime (murder, forcible rape, robbery, and aggravated assault): 80,627 males were arrested, an increase of 45.4 percent; 11,561 females were arrested, an increase of 63.0 percent. Ethnic differences were also evident, as 70.0 percent of those arrested were white adolescents (including Hispanic and white non-Hispanic youths), and 27.3 percent were African American adolescents. White adolescents were arrested for 71.5 percent of property crimes, compared with 25.6 percent for African American adolescents. The percentage of those arrested for violent crimes, however, was equally divided between the two groups (49.1 percent each) (FBI, 1992). Between 1980 and 1990, juvenile arrest rates increased differentially, with a notably larger increase among white adolescents (43.8 percent) than among African American adolescents (19.2 percent) (FBI, 1991).

Crimes against property accounted for the largest number of arrests (503,724, an increase of 7.6 percent), followed by larceny/theft (333,906, an increase of 8.5 percent), running away (127,873, an increase of 12.9 percent), other assaults (123,253, an increase of 49.1 percent), vandalism (102,015, an increase of 27.9 percent), burglary (99,667, an increase of 1.5 percent), disorderly conduct (93,929, an increase of 24.4 percent), violent crime (92,188, an increase of 47.4 percent) and weapons violations (39,872, an increase of 66.0 percent), representing the greatest increase in arrests over 1988 rates (FBI, 1992). The 1990s have seen a 79 percent increase in the frequency with which guns are used by juveniles in committing murder, with three-fourths of all murders by adolescents committed with a firearm (FBI, 1991). However, arrests for substance abuse decreased in all categories: drug abuse violations (down 9.9 percent), liquor law violations (down 24.4 percent), and drunkenness (down 25.6 percent) (FBI, 1992).

Dramatic ethnic and gender differences also are evident in victimization rates. Although the 1991 homicide rate per 100,000 for white adolescent males 15 to 19 years of age was 14.4, the rate for their African American cohorts was 134.6. The homicide rate for white adolescent females was 5.5, compared with 15.6 for African American females, a rate even higher than that for white adolescent males (K. Lipkind, National Center for Health Statistics, personal communication, December 1993).

Adolescents 16 to 19 years of age had the highest rates of victimization for crimes of violence of all people age 12 and over. The rate for 16- to 19-year-old males was 94.7 per 1,000, followed by 92.2 per 1,000 for 12- to 15-year-olds and 78.4 per 1,000 for 20- to 24-year-olds. Females 16 to 18 years of age had a rate of 53.8 per 1,000, followed by 48.5 per 1,000 for 20- to 24-year-olds and 44.1 per 1,000 for 12- to 15-year-olds (National Crimes Victimization Survey, 1992).

### School Leavers

The term "school leavers," rather than the more pejorative term "dropout," is being used more frequently to refer to youths who leave school before graduating from high school. Since the 1980s, the percentage of students who leave school before graduation has varied significantly by ethnic group, with the rates for white students declining from 11.4 percent in 1982 to 8.9 percent in 1991. Rates for African American students also declined, from 18.4 percent in 1982 to 13.6 percent in 1991. In direct contrast, the percentage of school leavers among Hispanic students increased from 31.7 percent in 1982 to 35.3 percent in 1991. However, it appears that Hispanics may complete their education at a later time: 82 percent of the Hispanic students in the class of 1982 had completed their high school education by 1986. Finally, gender differences occur only among Hispanic students, with the rate higher for males (39.2 percent) than females (31.1 percent) (U.S. Department of Education, 1992a).

There appears to be a direct relationship between years of school completed and employability, with overall unemployment rates among 16- to 19-year-olds of 36.5 percent for those completing eight years or less of schooling, 21.6 percent for those with one to three years of high school, and 11 percent for high school graduates (U.S. Department of Education, 1992b). The employment consequences of failing to complete high school vary by ethnic group, with unemployment rates for 16- to 19-year-olds who leave school of 19.3 percent for white students and 28.1 percent and 39.4 percent, respectively, for their Hispanic and African American cohorts (U.S. Department of Education, 1992b). Moreover, of those employed, two-thirds held jobs paying the minimum wage, with 80 percent holding unskilled positions, compared with 20 percent of those with high school diplomas (Muha & Cole, 1991). Despite these figures, Tanner's (1990) survey of 162 school leavers indicated that they maintained higher career aspirations, with 40 percent of females reporting a preference for professional occupations and 60 percent of males preferring a skilled occupation or professional career.

Reasons for leaving school as reported in surveys of high school leavers include both school-related problems, such as irrelevance of the curriculum, lack of interest in school, dissatisfaction with teachers, and discipline problems (Bearden, Spencer, & Moracco, 1989; Jordan, 1984; Peng, Takai, & Fetters, 1983; Pittman, 1986; Rumberger, 1983), and non-school-related problems such as financial need, pregnancy and marriage, and family problems (Harris, 1983; Peng et al., 1983; Tanner, 1990; Tidwell, 1988; Valles & Oddy, 1984). Failure to complete high school appears to be more frequent among students with low socioeconomic status (Rumberger, 1983; Rumberger, Ghatak, Poulos, Ritter, & Dornbusch, 1990); those from single-parent families (Amato, 1987; Fine, 1990; Krein & Beller, 1988; McLanahan, 1985), with the attendant financial stressors (Shaw, 1982; Tidwell, 1988); and those with poor academic achievement including poor grades and grade retention (Larsen & Shertzer, 1987; Rumberger, 1983; Tidwell, 1988). Discrimination and insensitivity to the needs of culturally different students have also been found to contribute to the high attrition rates among students of color (Bearden et al., 1989; Beck & Muia, 1980; National Commission on Secondary Education for Hispanics, 1984; Pittman, 1986). Svec (1987) concluded that a multicontributory model must be used to understand the unique complex of factors that increase student's risk for leaving school before graduation and that advocacy at the individual, institutional, and policy levels is needed to deal with the problem.

## Conclusion

It is important to recognize that the foregoing issues and problems of adolescent populations often do not exist in isolation, but interact with and exacerbate one another. For example, depressed youths are at higher risk of suicide, and drug abuse has been found to be particularly high among suicide attempters and completers (Christoffel et al., 1988; Kandel & Davies, 1982; Schrieber & Johnson, 1986; Withers & Kaplan, 1987). Substance abuse has also been identified as one element of a syndrome of delinquent behaviors (Jessor, 1985), and poverty has been linked to higher school-leaving and youth unemployment rates. However, Offer and Sabshin (1984) found that only 20 percent of adolescents consider adolescence to be a severely stressful period.

To address the needs of adolescent populations, social work practitioners and policymakers must take a multipronged approach. Furthermore, they must overlay their analyses of these problems with a keen recognition of developmental processes and of how developmental factors interact with environmental and cultural factors to alter or exacerbate problems.

The absence of significant studies of the development of minority and poor adolescents is a particular problem. Given that these are the populations whom social workers primarily serve, serious questions should be raised about whether existing models of practice can be validly generalized to these populations. Offer and Sabshin (1984), for example, hypothesized that the number of normal adolescent growth patterns would increase if research samples were expanded to include subjects from different cultures and socioeconomic statuses. Given the broader sociocultural context of the mainstream culture with which adolescents of color must deal, it is possible that their experience with adolescence may have significant conflict. However, there is evidence that identification with one's primary culture positively enhances the developmental process, particularly with respect to self-esteem (Zimbardo, 1971). The application of theories or principles that address the impact of various sociocultural factors on an individual's behavior, values, and beliefs holds the most promise and is most consonant with the practice of social work, which views the individual within his or her psychosociocultural context. Meanwhile, the deficiencies of the literature on adolescence must be dealt with so that developmental guidelines that are applicable in a pluralistic society can be established.

## References


Amato, P. R. (1987). Family processes in one parent, stepparent, and intact families: The child's point of view. *Journal of Marriage and the Family, 49,* 327–337.

Angenet, H., & de Man, A. (1989). Running away: Perspectives on causation. *Journal of Social Behavior and Personality, 4,* 377–388.

Athey, J. (1991). HIV infection and homeless adolescents. *Child Welfare, 70,* 517–528.

Bandura, A. (1964). The stormy decade: Fact or fiction? *Psychology in the Schools, 1,* 224–231.

Bandura, A. (1969). *Principles of behavior modification*. New York: Holt, Rinehart & Winston.

Bandura, A. (1977). *Social learning theory.* Englewood Cliffs, NJ: Prentice Hall.

Bandura, A., & Walters, R. M. (1963). *Social learning and personality development*. New York: Holt, Rinehart & Winston.

Barnea, Z., Teichman, M., & Rahav, G. (1992). Personality, cognitive, and interpersonal factors in adolescent substance abuse: A longitudinal test of an integrative model. *Journal of Youth and Adolescence, 21*(2), 187–201.

Barnes, G. M., & Welte, J. W. (1986a). Adolescent alcohol abuse: Subgroup differences and relationships to other problem behaviors. *Journal of Adolescent Research, 1*(1), 79–94.

Barnes, G. M., & Welte, J. W. (1986b). Patterns and predictors of alcohol use among 7–12th grade students in New York state. *Journal of Studies on Alcohol, 47*(1), 53–62.

Bearden, L., Spencer, W., & Moracco, J. (1989). A study of high school dropouts. *School Counselor, 37,* 112–119.

Beck, L., & Muia, J. (1980). The portrait of a tragedy: Research findings on the dropout. *High School Journal, 64,* 65–72.

Bell, T., & Hein, K. (1984). The adolescent and sexually transmitted diseases. In K. Holmes, P. A. Mardh, P. S. Sparling, & P. J. Wiesner (Eds.), *Sexually transmitted diseases* (pp. 73–84). New York: McGraw-Hill.

Bettes, B. A., & Walker, E. (1986). Symptoms associated with suicidal behavior in childhood and adolescence. *Journal of Abnormal Child Psychology, 14,* 591–604.

Blos, P. (1941). *The adolescent personality*. New York: D. Appleton-Century.

Blos, P. (1979). *The adolescent passage: Developmental issues*. New York: International Universities Press.

Boyer, C., & Kegeles, S. (1991). AIDS risk and prevention among adolescents. *Social Science and Medicine, 33*(1), 11–23.

Brooks-Gunn, J., Boyer, C., & Hein, K. (1988). Preventing HIV infection and AIDS in children and adolescents. *American Psychologist, 43,* 958–964.

Caton, C. L. (1986). The homeless experience in adolescent years. *New Directions for Mental Health Services, 30,* 63–70.

Chodorow, N. (1974). Family structure and feminine personality. In M. Rosoldo & L. Lamphere (Eds.), *Women, culture and society*. Stanford, CA: Stanford University Press.

Chodorow, N. (1978). *The reproduction of mothering*. Berkeley: University of California Press.

Christoffel, K. K., Marcus, D., Sagerman, S., & Bennett, S. (1988). Adolescent suicide and suicide attempts: A population study. *Pediatric Emergency Care, 4,* 32–40.

Clausen, J. A. (1975). The social meaning of differential physical and sexual maturation. In S. E. Gragastin & G. E. Elder, Jr. (Eds.), *Adolescence in the life cycle: Psychological change and social context* (pp. 24–47). New York: John Wiley & Sons.

Coleman, J. C. (1980). Friendship and the peer group in adolescence. In J. Adelson (Ed.), *Handbook of adolescent psychology*. New York: John Wiley & Sons.

de Anda, D., & Smith, M. (1993). Differences among adolescent, young adult and adult callers of suicide helplines. *Social Work, 38,* 421–428.

Dielman, T. E., Butchart, B. A., Shope, J. T., & Miller, M. (1991). Environmental correlates of adolescent substance use and misuse: Implications for prevention programs. *International Journal of the Addictions, 25*(7A & 7B), 855–880.

Douvan, E., & Adelson, J. (1966). *The adolescent experience*. New York: John Wiley & Sons.

Dunphy, D. S. (1963). The social structure of urban adolescent peer groups. *Sociometry, 26,* 230–246.

Elkind, D. (1967). Egocentrism in adolescence. *Child Development, 38,* 1025–1034.

Elkind, D. (1974). *Children and adolescents: Interpretive essays on Jean Piaget* (2nd ed.). New York: Oxford University Press.

Elkind, D. (1978). Egocentrism in adolescence. In J. K. Gardner (Ed.), *Readings in developmental psychology* (2nd ed.). Boston: Little, Brown.

Erikson, E. H. (1963). *Childhood and society* (2nd ed.). New York: W. W. Norton.

Erikson, E. H. (1968). *Identity, youth and crisis*. New York: W. W. Norton.

Erikson, E. H. (1970). Reflections on the dissent of contemporary youth. *International Journal of Psychoanalysis, 51,* 11–22.

Family and Youth Services Bureau. (1990). *Annual report to the Congress on runaway and homeless youth program, fiscal year 1989*. Washington, DC: U.S. Government Printing Office.

Faust, M. S. (1977). Somatic development of adolescent girls. *Monographs of the Society for Research in Child Development, 42*(1), 1–89.

Federal Bureau of Investigation. (1991). *Uniform crime reports for the United States, 1991*. Washington, DC: Author.

Federal Bureau of Investigation. (1992). *Uniform crime reports for the United States, 1992*. Washington, DC: Author.

Fine, M. (1990). *Framing dropouts: Notes on the politics of an urban public high school*. New York: State University of New York Press.

Freud, A. (1948). *The ego and the mechanisms of defense* (C. Baines, Trans.). New York: International Universities Press.

Freud, S. (1973). *A general introduction to psychoanalysis*. New York: Pocket Books. (Original work published 1924)

Gagne, R. (1970). *The conditions of learning*. New York: Holt, Rinehart & Winston.

Gagnon, J. H. (1974). Scripts and the coordination of sexual conduct. In J. K. Cole & R. Deinstbrier (Eds.), *Nebraska symposium on motivation* (Vol. 21). Lincoln: University of Nebraska Press.

Gardner, E. F., & Thompson, G. G. (1963). *Investigation and measurement of the social values governing interpersonal relations among adolescent youth and their teachers*. Washington, DC: U.S. Government Printing Office.

Gilligan, C. (1979). Woman's place in man's life cycle. *Harvard Educational Review, 49*(4), 431–446.

Gordon, S., & Gilgun, J. F. (1987). Adolescent sexuality. In V. B. Van Husselt & M. Hersen (Eds.), *Handbook of adolescent psychology*. New York: Pergamon.

Green, A. H. (1978). Self-destructive behavior in battered children. *American Journal of Psychiatry, 135,* 579–582.

Hall, G. S. (1904). *Adolescence: Its psychology and its relations to physiology, anthropology, sociology, sex, crime, religion, and education* (Vols. 1 & 2). New York: D. Appleton-Century.

Harkavy-Friedman, J. M., Asnis, G. M., Boeck, M., & Di Fiori, J. (1987). Prevalence of specific suicidal behaviors in a high school sample. *American Journal of Psychiatry, 144,* 1203–1206.

Harris, L. (1983). Role of trauma in the lives of high school dropouts. *Social Work in Education, 5,* 77–88.

Hawton, K. (1982). Annotation: Suicide in American children and adolescents. *Journal of Child Psychiatry, 3*(4), 497–503.

Hawton, K. (1986). *Suicide and attempted suicide among children and adolescents*. Beverly Hills, CA: Sage Publications.

Henshaw, S. K. (1993). *U.S. teenage pregnancy statistics.* New York: Allan Guttmacher Institute.

Hess, R. D., & Goldblatt, I. (1957). The status of adolescents in American society: A problem in social identity. *Child Development, 28,* 459–468.

Hoffman, M. L. (1980). Moral development in adolescence. In J. Adelson (Ed.), *Handbook of adolescent psychology* (pp. 293–343). New York: John Wiley & Sons.

Holinger, P. C. (1978). Adolescent suicide: An epidemiological study of recent trends. *American Journal of Psychiatry, 135,* 754–756.

Holinger, P. C., & Offer, D. (1982). Prediction of adolescent suicide: A population model. *American Journal of Psychiatry, 139,* 302–307.

Inhelder, B., & Piaget, J. (1978). Adolescent thinking. In J. K. Gardner (Ed.), *Readings in developmental psychology*. Boston: Little, Brown.

Janus, M. D., Burgess, A. W., & McCormack, A. (1987). Histories of sexual abuse in adolescent male runaways. *Adolescence, 22,* 405–417.

Jessor, R. (1985). Adolescent problem drinking: Psychosocial aspects and developmental outcomes. *Alcohol, Drugs and Driving, Abstracts and Reviews, 1*(1–2), 69–91.

Jones, M. C. (1965). Psychological correlates of somatic development. *Child Development, 36,* 899–911.

Jones, M. C., & Mussen, D. H. (1958). Self-conceptions, motivations, and interpersonal attitudes of early- and late-maturing girls. *Child Development, 29,* 491–501.

Jordan, D. (1984). *The cry for help unheard: Dropout interviews*. ERIC Document Reproduction Service No. ED 248 413.

Kalinski, E. M., Rubinson, L., Lawrence, L., & Levy, S. (1990). AIDS, runaways, and self-efficacy. *Family Community Health, 13*(1), 65–72.

Kandel, D. B., & Davies, M. (1982). Epidemiology of depressive mood in adolescents: An empirical study. *Archives of General Psychiatry, 39,* 1205–1212.

Kerfort, M. (1979). Self-poisoning by children and adolescents. *Social Work Today, 10,* 9–11.

Kienhorst, C.W.M., Wolters, W.H.G., Diekstra, R.F.W., & Otte, E. (1987). A study of the frequency of suicidal behavior in children aged 5–14. *Journal of Child Psychology & Psychiatry, 28,* 153–165.

Kohlberg, L., & Gilligan, E. C. (1975). The adolescent as a philosopher: The discovery of self in a postconventional world. In J. Conger (Ed.), *Contemporary issues in adolescent development* (pp. 414-443). New York: Harper & Row.

Krein, S. F., & Beller, A. H. (1988). Educational attainment of children from single parent families: Differences by exposure, gender, and race. *Demography*, *25*, 221–234.

Larsen, P., & Shertzer, B. (1987 January). The high school dropout: Everybody's problem? *School Counselor,* 163–169.

Lee, G. P., & Di Climante, C. C. (1985). Age at onset versus duration of problem drinking on alcohol use inventory. *Journal of Studies on Alcohol, 46,* 398–402.

Levin, L., & Schonberg, K. (1987). Familial violence among adolescents who attempted suicide. *Society of Adolescent Medicine*, abstract, p. 10.

Maxwell, P. H., Conner, R., & Walters, J. (1961). Family members' perceptions of parent role performance. *Merrill-Palmer Quarterly, 7,* 31–37.

McGee, Z. (1992). Social class differences in parental and peer influences on adolescent drug use. *Deviant Behavior, 13,* 349–372.

McKenry, P. C., Tishler, C., & Kelley, C. (1983). The role of drugs in adolescent suicide attempts. *Suicide and Life-Threatening Behavior, 13*(3), 166–175.

McLanahan, S. S. (1985). Family structure and the intergenerational transmission of poverty. *American Journal of Sociology, 90,* 873–901.

Mehrabian, A. (1970). *The tactics of social influence*. Englewood Cliffs, NJ: Prentice Hall.

Meissner, W. W. (1965). Parental interaction of the adolescent boy. *Journal of Genetic Psychology, 107,* 225–233.

Miller, Y., & Simon, W. (1980). The development of sexuality in adolescence. In J. Adelson (Ed.), *Handbook of adolescent psychology* (pp. 383–407). New York: John Wiley & Sons.

Muha, D., & Cole, C. (1991, December–January). Dropout prevention and group counseling: A review of the literature. *High School Journal,* pp. 76–80.

Mussen, P. H., & Jones, M. C. (1957). Self-conceptions, motivations, and interpersonal attitudes of late- and early-maturing boys. *Child Development, 28,* 243–256.

Muuss, E. (1962). *Theories of adolescent development*. New York: Random House.

Muuss, E. (1970). Adolescent development and the secular trend. *Adolescence, 5,* 267–286.

National Center for Health Statistics. (1987). Washington, DC: U.S. Department of Health and Human Services, Public Health Service, Centers for Disease Control.

National Center for Health Statistics. (1993). Unpublished data. Washington, DC: U.S. Department of Health and Human Services, Public Health Service, Centers for Disease Control and Prevention.

National Commission on Secondary Education for Hispanics. (1984). *Make something happen*. Washington, DC: Hispanic Policy Development.

National Crimes Victimization Survey. (1992). *Criminal victimization in the U.S., 1990*. Washington, DC: Congressional Information Service.

National Network of Runaway and Youth Services. (1991a). *Fact sheet.* Washington, DC: Author.

National Network of Runaway and Youth Services. (1991b). *To whom do they belong? Runaway, homeless and other youth in high-risk situations in the 1990's.* Washington, DC: Author.

Newcomb, M. D., & Bentler, P. (1986). Frequency and sequence of drug use: A longitudinal study from early adolescence to young adulthood. *Journal of Drug Education, 16,* 101–120.

Newcomb, M. D., & Bentler, P. (1988). *Consequences of adolescent drug use: Impact on the lives of young adults*. Newbury Park, CA: Sage Publications.

Newcomb, M. D., & McGee, L. (1989). Adolescent alcohol use and other delinquent behaviors. *Criminal Justice and Behavior, 16*(3), 345–369.

Oetting, E. R., & Beauvais, F. (1990). Adolescent drug use: Findings of national and local surveys. *Journal of Consulting and Clinical Psychology, 58*(4), 385–394.

Offer, D. (1967). Normal adolescents: Interview strategy and selected results. *Archives of General Psychiatry, 17,* 285–290.

Offer, D., & Sabshin, M. (1984). *Normality and the life cycle: A critical integration*. New York: Basic Books.

Offer, D., Sabshin, M., & Marcus, I. (1965). Clinical evaluation of normal adolescents. *American Journal of Psychiatry, 21,* 864–872.

Padilla, E. R., Padilla, A. M., Morales, A. P., Olmeda, E. L., & Ramirez, R. (1977). *Inhalant, marijuana, and alcohol abuse among barrio children and adolescents* (Occasional Paper No. 4). Los Angeles: University of California, Spanish Speaking Mental Health Research Center.

Peck, M. (1982). Youth suicide. *Death Education, 6,* 29–47.

Peng, S. S., Takai, R. T., & Fetters, W. B. (1983). *High school dropouts: Preliminary results from the High School and Beyond Survey*. Paper presented at the annual meeting of the American Educational Research Association, Montreal.

Perez, R., Padilla, A. M., Ramirez, R., & Rodriguez, M. (1979). *Correlates and changes over time in drug and alcohol use within a barrio population* (Occasional Paper No. 9). Los Angeles: University of California, Spanish Speaking Mental Health Research Center.

Peskin, H. (1967). Pubertal onset and ego functioning. *Journal of Abnormal Psychology, 72,* 1–15.

Peskin, H. (1973). Influence of the developmental schedule of puberty on learning and ego development. *Journal of Youth and Adolescence, 2,* 273–290.

Petersen, L. L. (1987). Change in variables related to smoking from childhood to late adolescence: An eight-year longitudinal study of a cohort of elementary school students. *Canadian Journal of Public Health, 77*(Suppl. 1), 33–39.

Peterson, A. C., & Taylor, B. (1980). The biological approach to adolescence. In J. Adelson (Ed.), *Handbook of adolescent psychology*, New York: John Wiley & Sons.

Piaget, J. (1965). *The moral judgment of the child.* New York: Free Press.

Piaget, J. (1972). Intellectual evolution from adolescence to adulthood. *Human Development, 15*(1), 1–12.

Piaget, J., & Inhelder, B. (1958). *The growth of logical thinking from childhood to adolescence*. (A. Parsons & S. Seagrin, Trans.). New York: Basic Books.

Pittman, R. (1986, October–November). Importance of personal, social factors as potential means for reducing high school dropout rate. *High School Journal*, pp. 7–13.

Quinn, T. C., Glasser, D., Cannon, R. O., Matuszak, D. L., Dunning, R. W., Kline, R. L., Campbell, C. H., Israel, E., Fanci, A. S., & Hook, E. W. (1988). Human immunodeficiency virus infection among patients attending clinics for sexually transmitted diseases. *New England Journal of Medicine, 318,* 197–203.

Reuben, N., Boeck, M., & Kurzon, M. (1987). *Relations between suicidal intent, depression, and disposition in adolescent suicide attempters.* Paper presented at the Annual Conference for the Society of Adolescent Medicine, Seattle.

Reuben, N., Hein, K., & Drucker, E. (1988). *The relationship of high risk behaviors to AIDS knowledge in adolescent high school students*. Paper presented at the Annual Conference for the Society for Adolescent Medicine, New York.

Robbins, D. R., & Alessi, N. E. (1985). Depressive symptoms and suicidal behavior in adolescents. *American Journal of Psychiatry, 90*(4), 588–592.

Rosenthal, T. L., & Zimmerman, B. J. (1978). *Social learning and cognition*. New York: Academic Press.

Ross, C. P. (1985). Teaching children the fact of life and death: Suicide prevention in the schools. In M. L. Peck, N. L. Farberow, & R. E. Litman (Eds.), *Youth suicide* (pp. 147–169). New York: Springer.

Rumberger, R. (1983). Dropping out of high school: The influence of race, sex, and family background. *American Educational Research Journal, 20*(2), 199–220.

Rumberger, R., Ghatak, R., Poulos, G., Ritter, P., & Dornbusch, S. (1990). Family influences on dropout behavior in one California high school. *Sociology of Education, 63,* 283–298.

Runaway and Homeless Youth Act of 1974. P.L. 93-415, 88 Stat. 1129.

Schrieber, T. J., & Johnson, R. L. (1986). The evaluation and treatment of adolescent overdoses in an adolescent medical service. *Journal of the National Medical Association, 78,* 101–108.

Schwarez, S., & Rutherford, G. (1989). Acquired immunodeficiency syndrome in infants, children, and adolescents. *The Journal of Drug Issues, 19*(1), 75–92.

Settlage, C. F. (1972). Cultural values and the superego in late adolescence. *Psychoanalytic Study of the Child, 27,* 57–73.

Shaw, L. B. (1982). High school completion for young women: Effects of low income and living with a single parent. *Journal of Family Issues, 3,* 147–163.

Shedler, J., & Block, J. (1990). Adolescent drug use and psychological health: A longitudinal inquiry. *American Psychologist, 45*(5), 612–630.

Simmons, R. G., & Blyth, D. A. (1987). *Moving into adolescence.* Hawthorne, NY: Aldine.

Simons, R., & Whitbeck, L. (1991). Sexual abuse as a precursor to prostitution and victimization among adolescent and adult homeless women. *Journal of Family Issues, 12*(3), 361–379.

Smith, J. C., Mercy, J. A., & Warren, C. W. (1985). Comparison of suicides among Anglos and Hispanics in five southwestern states. *Suicide and Life-Threatening Behavior, 15*(1), 14–26.

Smith, K., & Crawford, S. (1986). Suicidal behavior among "normal" high school students. *Suicidal and Life-Threatening Behavior, 16,* 313–325.

Spirito, A., Brown, L., Overholser, J., & Fritz, G. (1989). Attempted suicide in adolescence: A review and critique of the literature. *Clinical Psychology Review, 9,* 335–363.

Spirito, A., Stark, L. J., Fristad, M., Hart, K., & Owens-Stively, J. (1987). Adolescent suicide attempters hospitalized on a general pediatrics floor. *Journal of Pediatric Psychology, 12,* 171–189.

Strunin, L., & Hingson, R. (1987). Acquired immunodeficiency syndrome and adolescents: Knowledge, beliefs, and attitudes and behaviors. *Pediatrics, 79,* 825–828.

Strunin, L., & Hingson, R. (1992). Alcohol, drugs, and adolescent sexual behavior. *International Journal of the Addictions, 27*(2), 129–146.

Sullivan, H. S. (1953). *The interpersonal theory of psychiatry.* New York: W. W. Norton.

Svec, H. (1987, April–May). Youth advocacy and high school dropouts. *High School Journal,* pp. 185–192.

Tanner, J. M. (1962). *Growth at adolescence*. Springfield, IL: Charles C Thomas.

Tanner, J. M. (1972). Sequence, tempo, and individual variation in growth and development of boys and girls aged twelve to sixteen. In J. Kagan & R. Coles (Eds.), *Twelve to sixteen: Early adolescence.* New York: W. W. Norton.

Tanner, J. M. (1990). Reluctant rebels: A case study of Edmonton high school dropouts. *Canadian Review of Sociology and Anthropology, 27,* 74–93.

Tidwell, R. (1988). Dropouts speak out; qualitative data on early school departures. *Adolescence, 92,* 939–954.

Tishler, C. L., McKenry, P. C., & Morgan, K. C. (1981). Adolescent suicide attempts: Some significant factors. *Suicide and Life-Threatening Behavior, 11*, 86–92.

Toolan, J. M. (1975). Suicide in children and adolescents. *American Journal of Psychotherapy, 29*(3), 339–344.

Turiel, E. (1974). Conflict and transition in adolescent moral development. *Child Development, 45,* 14–29.

U.S. Bureau of the Census. (1992). *1990 census of the population: Vol. 1. Characteristics of the population.* Washington, DC: U.S. Government Printing Office.

U.S. Department of Education. (1992a). *The condition of education.* Washington, DC: National Center for Education Statistics.

U.S. Department of Education. (1992b). *Digest of education.* Washington, DC: National Center for Education Statistics.

U.S. Department of Health and Human Services. (1983). *Runaway and homeless youth: National program inspection.* Washington, DC: Author.

U.S. Department of Health and Human Services. (1989a). *HIV/AIDS surveillance report.* Washington, DC: U.S. Department of Health and Human Services, Public Health Service, Centers for Disease Control.

U.S. Department of Health and Human Services. (1989b). *Vital statistics of the United States, 1989: Vol. 1. Natality.* Washington, DC: Author.

U.S. Department of Health and Human Services. (1991). *HIV/AIDS surveillance report.* Washington, DC: U.S. Department of Health and Human Services, Public Health Service, Centers for Disease Control.

U.S. Department of Health and Human Services. (1993). *National household survey on drug abuse.* Washington, DC: Substance Abuse and Mental Health Service Administration.

U.S. Department of Health and Human Services. (1994, midyear edition). *HIV/AIDS surveillance report.* Washington, DC: U.S. Department of Health and Human Services, Public Health Service, Centers for Disease Control.

U.S. General Accounting Office. (1989). *Homelessness: Homeless and runaway youth receiving services at federally funded shelters.* Washington, DC: U.S. Government Printing Office.

Valles, E., & Oddy, M. (1984). The influence of a return to school on the long-term adjustment of school refusers. *Journal of Adolescence, 7,* 35–44.

Ventura, S. (1982). Births of Hispanic parentage, 1979. *Monthly Vital Statistics Report, 31,* 1–11.

Ventura, S., & Heuser, R. (1981). Births of Hispanic parentage, 1978. *Monthly Vital Statistics Report, 29*(Suppl.), 1–11.

Weatherley, D. (1964). Self-perceived rate of physical maturation and personality in late adolescence. *Child Development, 35,* 1197–1210.

Whitbeck, L., & Simons, R. (1990). Life on the streets: The victimization of runaway and homeless adolescents. *Youth and Society, 22*(1), 108–125.

Withers, L. E., & Kaplan, D. W. (1987). Adolescents who attempt suicide: A retrospective clinical chart review of hospitalized patients. *Professional Psychology: Research and Practice, 18,* 391–393.

Yates, G. L., MacKenzie, R., Pennbridge, J., & Cohen, E. (1986). A risk profile comparison of runaway and non-runaway youth. *American Journal of Public Health, 78*(7), 820–821.

Zelnik, M., & Shah, F. (1983). First intercourse among young Americans. *Family Planning Perspectives, 15,* 64–70.

Zide, M. R., & Cherry, A. L. (1992). A typology of runaway youths: An empirically-based definition. *Child and Adolescent Social Work Journal, 9*(2), 155–168.

Zimbardo, P. G. (1971). The social bases of behavior. In F. L. Ruch & P. G. Zimbardo (Eds.), *Psychology and life* (10th ed.). Glenview, IL: Scott, Foresman.

**Diane de Anda, PhD,** is associate professor, Department of Social Welfare, School of Public Policy and Social Research, University of California, Los Angeles, 405 N. Hilgard Avenue, Los Angeles, CA 90024.

### For further information see

Adolescent Pregnancy; Adolescents: Direct Practice; Alcohol Abuse; Child Welfare Overview; Childhood; Drug Abuse; Families Overview; HIV/AIDS Overview; Homelessness; Human Development; Human Sexuality; Juvenile Corrections; Mental Health Overview; Primary Prevention Overview; Runaways and Homeless Youths; School-Linked Services; School Social Work; Substance Abuse: Direct Practice; Suicide; Youth Services.

**Key Words**

adolescents
childhood
developmental stages

READER'S GUIDE

## Adolescents

*The following entries contain information on this general topic:*

Adolescence Overview
Adolescent Pregnancy
Adolescents: Direct Practice
Gay and Lesbian Adolescents
Runaways and Homeless Youths

# Adolescent Pregnancy

**Constance W. Williams**

Adolescent pregnancy in the United States gained prominence as a social problem in the 1970s when the overall birthrate (that is the number of births per 1,000 females) among teenagers was declining. Although the birthrate declined, the number of births to teenagers rose. At the same time, the birthrate among older women declined, thus increasing the proportion of births to adolescents. Approximately 1 million teenagers became pregnant every year during the 1970s. More than half of those teenagers gave birth. In 1970, the birthrate among teenagers was 68.3, and the number of births to teenagers was 656,460 (Moore, Snyder, & Malla, 1993). This bulge in teenage births, which brought teenage childbearing to public attention, is attributable partly to the existence of more than 10 million teenagers in the population during the early 1970s (Becerra & Fielder, 1987).

FIGURE 1

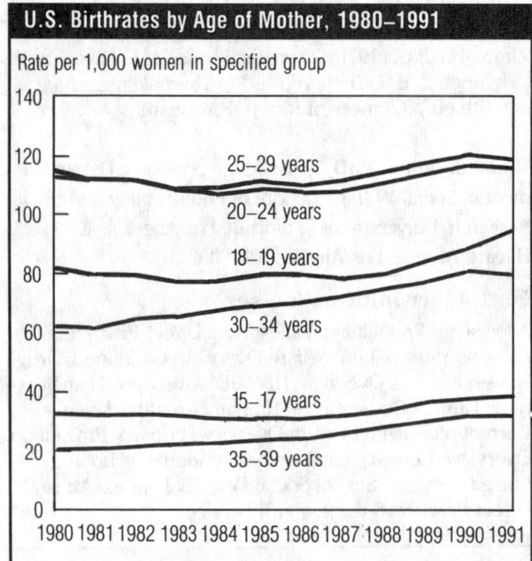


SOURCE: Ventura, S. J., & Martin, J. A. (1993b). National Center for Health Statistics. *Advance report of final natality statistics*, 1991 (Monthly Vital Statistics Rep. Vol. 42, No. 3, Suppl.). Hyattsville, MD: U.S. Public Health Service.

## Demographics

Age specific birthrates between 1980 and 1990 increased for all age groups (Figure 1). From 1980 to 1988, the birthrate for older teenagers aged 18 to 19 years and younger teenagers aged 15 to 17 years remained relatively stable, but increased annually between 1988 and 1991. The birthrate for women between ages 18 and 19 years rose from 79.9 in 1988 to 94.4 in 1991, whereas the birthrate for younger teenagers increased less, from 33.6 in 1988 to 38.7 in 1990. During this growth in teenage birthrates, the number of teenagers in the population decreased from 9.2 million in 1986 to 8.4 million in 1991 (Ventura & Martin, 1993b). Until 1986, when teenage birthrates began to climb, women in their thirties were the only age group for whom birthrates had steadily increased since 1980.

In the 1980s two trends were evident among women younger than age 20 years (Table 1). During the first half of the 1980s, their birthrates declined from 53 in 1980 to 51 in 1985 when the number of women between ages 15 and 19 years who gave birth fell below the half million mark to 477,705 (Moore, et al., 1993). During the second half of the 1980s, birthrates steadily rose from 50 in 1986 to 57 in 1989. The number stayed below a half million until 1989, when females younger than age 20 years had 517,989 births (Moore, et al., 1993). Births to women younger than age 20 years continued to climb until teenagers accounted for 533,483 (13 percent of the 4,158,212 births that occurred in the United States in 1990 (Moore & Snyder, 1994). Because most of the childbearing women younger than age 20 years were unmarried, their climbing birthrate is reflected in the number of births to unmarried women younger than age 20 years, which nearly doubled between 1970 and 1990, from 199,900 to 360,645.

Birthrates for unmarried women aged 15 to 44 years increased from 29.4 per 1,000 in 1980 to 43.8 in 1990 and climbed again to 45.2 in 1991 (Table 2). The rate for unmarried white women between ages 18 and 19 years more than doubled, rising from 24.1 per 1,000 in 1980 to 49.6 in 1991. In 1980, unmarried black women aged 18 to 19 years had a birthrate of 118.2 per 1,000 that climbed to 148.7 by 1991. The high nonmarital births among black and white older (ages 18 to 19 years) teenage women reflect a societal trend. For example, the number of births to unmarried white women in 1991 was 707,502, more than double the 328,924 births to unmarried white women in 1980; the number of births to unmarried black women in 1991 was 463,750, 45 percent higher than the 318,799 births to unmarried black women in 1980 (Ventura & Martin, 1993b).

TABLE 1

**Fertility of U.S. Women Younger than Age 29 Years, 1970, 1980, 1985, 1989, 1990**

| Age | 1970 | 1980 | 1985 | 1989 | 1990 |
|---|---|---|---|---|---|
| | | Number of births | | | |
| Under 15 years | 11,752 | 10,169 | 10,220 | 11,486 | 11,657 |
| 15–17 years | 223,590 | 198,222 | 167,789 | 181,044 | 183,327 |
| 18–19 years | 421,118 | 353,939 | 299,696 | 325,459 | 338,499 |
| Under 20 years | 656,460 | 562,330 | 477,705 | 517,989 | 533,483 |
| | | Number of nonmarital births | | | |
| Under 15 years | 9,500 | 9,024 | 9,386 | 10,612 | 10,675 |
| 15–17 years | 96,100 | 121,900 | 118,931 | 140,686 | 142,398 |
| 18–19 years | 94,300 | 140,877 | 151,991 | 196,582 | 207,572 |
| Under 20 years | 199,900 | 271,801 | 280,308 | 347,880 | 360,645 |
| | | Nonmarital births per 1,000 unmarried women | | | |
| 15–19 years | 22.4 | 27.6 | 31.6 | 40.1 | 42.5 |

SOURCE: Becerra, R. M., & Fielder, E. P. (1987). Adolescent pregnancy. In A. Minahan (Ed.-in-Chief), *Encyclopedia of social work* (18th ed., Vol. 1, pp. 40–51). Silver Spring, MD: National Association of Social Workers.
National Center for Health Statistics. (1987). *Advance report of final natality statistics, 1985* (Monthly Vital Statistics Rep., Vol. 36, No. 4, Suppl.). Hyattsville, MD: U.S. Public Health Service.
Ventura, S. J., & Martin, J. A. (1993a). National Center for Health Statistics. *Advance report of final natality statistics, 1990* (Monthly Vital Statistics Rep., Vol. 41, No. 9, Suppl.). Hyattsville, MD: U.S. Public Health Service.
Ventura, S. J., & Martin, J. A. (1993b). National Center for Health Statistics. *Advance report of final natality statistics, 1991* (Monthly Vital Statistics Rep., Vol. 42, No. 3, Suppl.). Hyattsville, MD: U.S. Public Health Service.
NOTE: *Fertility* is defined as the number of live births.

TABLE 2

**Birthrates for Unmarried U.S. Women by Age and Race of Mother, 1980, 1990, 1991**

| Mother's Race and Age | 1980 | 1990 | 1991 |
|---|---|---|---|
| All races | | | |
| 15–44 years | 29.4 | 43.8 | 45.2 |
| 15–17 years | 20.6 | 29.6 | 30.9 |
| 18–19 years | 39.0 | 60.7 | 65.7 |
| Under 20 years | 27.6 | 42.5 | 44.8 |
| White | | | |
| 15–44 years | 18.1 | 32.9 | 34.6 |
| 15–17 years | 12.0 | 20.4 | 21.8 |
| 18–19 years | 24.1 | 44.9 | 49.6 |
| Under 20 years | 16.5 | 30.6 | 32.8 |
| Black | | | |
| 15–44 years | 81.1 | 90.5 | 89.5 |
| 15–17 years | 68.8 | 78.8 | 80.4 |
| 18–19 years | 118.2 | 143.7 | 148.7 |
| Under 20 years | 87.9 | 106.0 | 108.5 |

SOURCE: Ventura, S. J., Martin, J. A., Taffel, S. M., Mathews, T. J., & Clarke, S. C. (1994). National Center for Health Statistics. *Advance report of final natality statistics, 1992* (Monthly Vital Statistics Rep., Vol. 43, No. 5, Suppl.). Hyattsville, MD: U.S. Public Health Service.
NOTE: Rates are live births per 1,000 unmarried women in specified group.

FIGURE 2

**U.S. Birthrates for Unmarried Women Ages 15–17 Years and 18–19 Years by Race of Mother, 1980–1991**

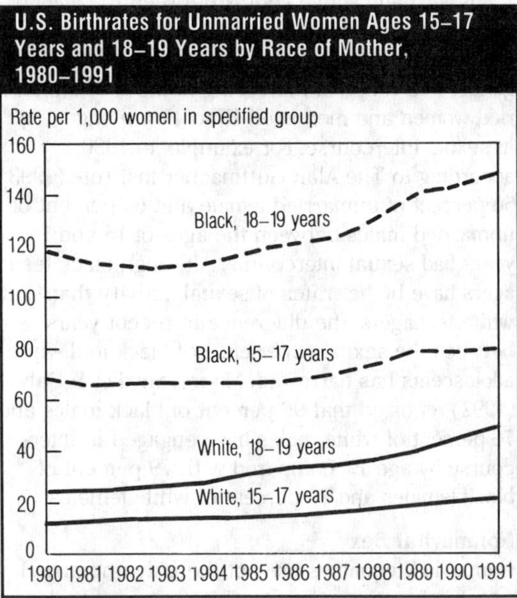


SOURCE: Ventura, S. J., Martin, J. A., Taffel, S. M., Mathews, T. J., & Clarke, S. C. (1994). National Center for Health Statistics. *Advance report of final natality statistics, 1992* (Monthly Vital Statistics Rep., Vol. 43, No. 5, Suppl.). Hyattsville, MD: U.S. Public Health Service.

Since 1986, the increase in the birthrate for unmarried black and unmarried white women aged 18 to 19 years was more substantial than the increase for teenagers age 15 to 17 years (Figure 2). The birthrate for unmarried white women aged 18 to 19 years increased from 24.1 in 1980 to 49.6 in 1991 compared with an increase from 118.2 in 1980 to 148.7 in 1991 for black unmarried women aged 18 to 19 (Table 2). Birthrates for white and black unmarried teenagers between ages 15 and 17 remained steady between 1980 and 1985 and increased between 1986 and 1991. The birthrate for white unmarried teenagers aged 15 to 17 years increased from 14.9 in 1986 to 21.8 in 1991, whereas the birthrate for black unmarried teenagers aged 15 to 17 years increased from 67 in 1986 to 80 in 1991 (Ventura et al., 1994). According to 1991 final natality statistics (Ventura & Martin, 1993b), women younger than age 20 years accounted for a disproportionate share of Hispanic births, and one out of five American Indian births was to a woman in this age group.

## Factors Related to Adolescent Pregnancy

Adolescent pregnancy and birthrates are affected by trends in sexual experience and premarital sex among teenagers, access to family planning and abortion services, socioeconomic status, and race and ethnicity (Spitz et al., 1993).

### Sexual Experience

Trends in sexual experience are closely related to an increasing acceptance of premarital sex, cohabitation, and changes in standards of sexual behavior in the general population. National surveys conducted during the 1970s documented rising levels of sexual activity among teenagers (Vinovskis, 1988). Dryfoos (1990) estimated that, in the 1980s, sexually active youths between the ages of 10 and 19 years numbered 13.5 million.

Sexual experience among teenagers varies by gender and race. An increasing number of unmarried women and men aged 15 to 19 are engaging in sexual intercourse. For example, in 1990, according to The Alan Guttmacher Institute (1993) 50 percent of unmarried female and 60 percent of unmarried males between the ages of 15 and 19 years had sexual intercourse. Although black teenagers have higher rates of sexual activity than white teenagers, the difference in recent years between the sexual experience of black and white adolescents has narrowed. Moore, Snyder, & Daly (1992) reported that 96 percent of black males and 76 percent of white males have engaged in intercourse by age 19, compared with 79 percent of black females and 76 percent of white females.

### Nonmarital Sex

Unmarried teenagers are not the only unmarried people who engage in sexual intercourse. Rather, the uncoupling of sex, marriage, and childbearing is evident in the increase in births to unmarried women of all ages. According to Ventura and Martin (1993b), the number of births to unmarried mothers in 1991 was 1,213,769, the highest ever reported in U.S. history. The proportion of all births that were to unmarried women was 29.5 percent, whereas the percentage of all births to unmarried women was 21.8 for white women and 67.9 for black women. Nonmarital births increased 6 percent for white women compared with 2 percent for black women.

A significant proportion of teenagers who give birth are unmarried. In 1990, 68 percent of all births to women aged 15 to 19 years were to unmarried mothers whereas 92 percent of black babies and 57 percent of white babies born to teenagers were born to unmarried mothers (AGI, 1993). Still, the highest birthrates for unmarried women are not among teenagers. For example, in 1991, birthrates for unmarried women of all races were highest for women aged 20 to 24 years, at 68 per 1,000 followed by aged 18 to 19 years at 65.7 per 1,000 (Ventura & Martin, 1993b).

### Access to Family Planning and Abortion Services

According to data compiled by Moore & Snyder (1994), Medicaid replaced Title X as the primary funding source for contraceptive services. Public expenditures for contraception services declined by 27 percent between 1980 and 1992. In response to reduced funding, family planning agencies have cut back services including outreach and education and some clinics have closed (Moore & Snyder, 1994). Since the 1970s, teenagers have used family planning clinics in increasing numbers. Annually, 1.5 million teenagers depend on family planning clinics to obtain medically prescribed contraception (Dryfoos, 1990). Consequently, a decline in publicly supported family planning services increases the risks of unwanted pregnancies and births among teenagers.

Following the legalization of abortion in 1973, teenage pregnancies terminated by abortion doubled from 20.1 percent in 1972 to 40 percent in 1982 (Hardy & Zabin, 1991). Between 1980 and 1990, abortion rates for women aged 15 to 19 years declined by more than 10 percent in 26 states and the District of Columbia (Spitz et al., 1993). Declines in abortion rates were greater than declines in pregnancy rates, which contributed to the rise in birthrates among teenagers in 29 states and in Washington, DC (Spitz et al., 1993). Thus, teenage sexual activity has increased whereas contraceptive services and abortion have become less available. Consequently, the risk of pregnancy among teenagers is greater. These conditions have contributed to increasing birthrates among teenage women.

### Socioeconomic Status

Unmarried teenage childbearing is associated with poverty, welfare dependence, and residence in female-headed households. In 1990, the proportion of all Aid to Families with Dependent Children (AFDC) recipients who first became mothers at age 19 or younger was estimated at 51 percent. Long-term dependence on AFDC has been linked to becoming a recipient as a teenage mother (Moore et al., 1993). However, according to Hacker (1992), fewer than 10 percent of AFDC recipients have received welfare more than 10 years, and only one-fourth have been recipients for five years or more. Although being an unmarried mother and a welfare recipient usually assures living in poverty, most mothers on welfare were living in poor households before they had children (Bane, 1986). Early childbearing, then, makes it difficult for teenage mothers to complete school and join the labor force; but the single act of becoming a teenage mother does not cause poverty. However, the growing number of poor children in American society and the adverse social outcomes they experience assure continued attention to teenage childbearing despite the knowledge that poverty and welfare are associated with antecedent social and economic conditions.

### Race and Ethnicity

By age 19 years, sexual activity among males of all racial groups is prevalent enough to be considered normative behavior, and "85 percent of black females and 70 percent of all others" are sexually experienced by age 19 years (Dryfoos, 1990, p. 67). Although sexual activity is widespread among adolescents, there are differences between groups in the age at which sexual activity is initiated. Black males and females begin sexual activity earlier than their white or Hispanic counterparts. Also, the risk of unintended pregnancies is increased for young, black, sexually active girls because they rarely use contraception the first time they have intercourse (Dryfoos, 1990).

Until recently, most information about adolescent fertility was reported for black, white, and all other populations. Hispanic adolescents, though, may be white or black. Before 1989, the National Center for Health Statistics tabulated birth data by race of child. Since 1989, the center has tabulated data by race of mother (Ventura & Martin, 1993b). In 1991, 97 percent of Hispanic mothers were reported to be white. Consequently, the change in tabulation of birth data based on the race of the mother rather than the race of the child, as well as a higher fertility rate among Hispanic compared with non-Hispanic white teenagers, have resulted in higher estimates of births to white adolescents. Furthermore, except for teenagers aged 15 to 17 years, Hispanic women have the highest fertility rates of any racial or ethnic group (Ventura & Martin, 1993b).

The use of the racial designations *black* or *white* obscures both regional differences among black and white adolescents within the United States and the cultural orientation of teenagers whose country of origin is not the United States. Similarly, the classification of Hispanic adolescents as either black or white and the use of broad categories such as Asian or Pacific Islanders obscures differences in childbearing patterns between Hispanic and Asian subgroups. The increasing diversity of the U.S. population suggests that adolescent pregnancy and childbearing should be studied in the context of class, race, ethnicity, culture, and each group's particular experience in the United States.

## Consequences of Early Childbearing

Adolescent pregnancy and childbearing, especially for girls younger than 15 years, are associated with adverse outcomes such as miscarriages, stillbirths, premature births, and low birthweight babies (Hayes, 1986). Poverty, poor nutrition, and late or no prenatal care together with age result in the birth of a disproportionate number of low-birthweight babies to teenage mothers. Infants of teenage mothers are vulnerable to adverse effects because of interactions between environmental factors such as poverty and biological vulnerabilities such as low birthweight (Hardy & Zabin, 1991). Low-birthweight babies are at risk for long-term developmental problems that may be further exacerbated by inadequate parenting skills. Furthermore, lower school achievement, behavioral and emotional problems, and the likelihood of becoming a teenage parent are associated with children born to adolescent mothers (Dryfoos, 1990).

In addition, some adolescent girls may leave school as a result of pregnancy, although many girls drop out of school before they become pregnant (Dryfoos, 1990). School failure, poor basic skills, early sexually activity, pregnancy, and early childbearing are complexly interrelated (Dryfoos, 1990). The consequences of early childbearing, then, should not be separated from developmental, economic, environmental, and familial conditions that make some adolescents vulnerable to the early initiation of unprotected sexual intercourse. Early onset of sexual activity increases the risk of conception and exposure to sexually transmitted diseases and infection with acquired immune deficiency syndrome (AIDS) (Dryfoos, 1990).

## Federal Policy

### Office of Adolescent Pregnancy Programs

The Carter administration identified adolescent pregnancy as a serious domestic problem in need of government intervention. Passage of the Adolescent Health, Services, and Pregnancy Prevention and Care Act of 1978, which was the first federal legislation dealing with teen pregnancy, led to the establishment of the Office of Adolescent Pregnancy Programs (Dryfoos, 1990). The focus of this office was to provide services to pregnant and parenting teenagers and their children. The Adolescent Family Life Act of 1981 (Title XX) was passed during the Reagan administration. The act funded programs to encourage teenagers to abstain from sexual activity and to choose adoption rather than keep their babies (Dryfoos, 1990; Vinovskis, 1988).

### AFDC and Welfare Reform

The link between long-term receipt of welfare, teenage motherhood, and high nonmarital birthrates has influenced legislators to include provisions for the prevention of teenage pregnancy in several welfare reform proposals. Underlying the provisions to curb births to adolescents is the assumption that welfare is an incentive for nonmarital childbearing. This assumption is not validated by the data on teenage birthrates in states with high AFDC benefits compared with birthrates in low-benefit states. A literature review of studies that have examined changes in benefit levels over time and changes in out-of-wedlock birthrates indicated no association between the two (Wilson & Neckerman, 1986). Yet, young unmarried mothers are the target of proposals to limit the length of time a person may receive AFDC as a way to decrease births to unmarried women.

***Work and Responsibility.*** A key provision of President Clinton's proposed welfare reform plan—the Work and Responsibility Act of 1994—would restrict most AFDC recipients to a lifetime maximum of 24 months of cash assistance beginning at 18 years. Such arbitrary time limits do not consider individual differences among young unmarried mothers. The NASW (1993) Welfare Reform position paper argued that the diversity of the welfare population requires flexibility, not arbitrary time limits on receipt of benefits. Robert Greenstein, Executive Director of the Center on Budget and Policy Priorities, testifying before the Subcommittee on Human Resources of the Committee on Ways and Means Hearing on Welfare Reform in June 1994, warned that requiring mothers to leave welfare in two years would have the potential to increase child poverty. Further, the imposition of a *family cap,* a provision that allows states to deny benefits to women who bear additional children while receiving AFDC, would have the same potential.

Women who apply for AFDC are expected to cooperate with paternity establishment procedures. A more strict definition of cooperation in the Work and Responsibility Act of 1994 would require mothers who apply to give the name of the father and other information that may be useful in locating the father to enable paternity establishment and the collection of child support. Failure to cooperate could lead to denial of benefits.

In addition, unmarried minor mothers must stay in school and live at home or with a responsible adult. Teenage fathers would be held responsible for child support and may be assigned to a job for the purpose of fulfilling their child support obligation. The proposed Work and Responsibility Act of 1994 provides for the award of demonstration grants to prevent teenage pregnancy in high-risk communities. Demonstrations may include sex education, abstinence education, life skills education, and contraceptive services. Abortion services are not included despite the fact that in 1988, 40 percent of pregnancies to teenagers aged 15 to 19 years ended in induced abortion (Ventura et al., 1992). The emphasis is on delayed sexual activity and adolescent pregnancy prevention before marriage.

***NASW position.*** NASW's (1993) Welfare Reform position paper proposed several objectives to guide the debate on welfare reform:

- Provide real jobs with real pay.
- Strengthen the safety net.
- Increase opportunities, not sanctions.
- Incorporate different strokes for different folks.
- Establish universal benefits and services whenever possible.

The reform of AFDC and child support enforcement could assist teenage mothers and fathers in achieving personal and economic independence. However, such achievement depends on the availability of education, job opportunities, child care, and health care. Thus, the NASW welfare reform objectives must be a part of any effort to change welfare.

## Programs and Services

A comprehensive study of programs for the prevention of adolescent pregnancy is included in Dryfoos's (1990) book *Adolescents at Risk: Prevalence and Prevention.* Her extensive research identified successful models in the categories of "school curricula, special services in schools and communitywide multicomponent programs" (p. 195). Successful models showed an active link between school and health services and used a range of services and approaches that involved collaboration among staff, community workers, parents, and youths. Although programs have been successful in helping students delay initiation of sexual intercourse and improve contraceptive use, Dryfoos concluded that few of those programs have documented reductions in teenage births.

An example of a program with characteristics Dryfoos associated with successful models is the Self Center Program established in 1981 by doctors at Johns Hopkins Hospital in Baltimore. It is a primary pregnancy-prevention research and demonstration project with a school-linked reproductive health clinic and related educational and psychosocial services. Self Center Program participants, compared with nonparticipants, delayed the onset of sexual activity and had reduced rates of abortion, pregnancy, and birth (Hardy & Zabin, 1991). The Self Center Program reached adolescents who were not pregnant, in contrast to the Johns Hopkins Adolescent Pregnancy and Parenting Program that reached adolescents after pregnancy. There is a need for programs that focus on primary prevention such as the Self Center Program as well as programs that serve adolescents who are already parents. Programs that serve adolescent parents may prevent subsequent births, an appropriate goal because second and higher order births occur among the most disadvantaged teenagers (Hardy & Zabin, 1991).

According to Williams (1991), the most significant difference between a group of mothers of one child compared with mothers of similar ages with two children was their educational attainment. Mothers with one child were attending high school or post–high school programs, whereas the majority of mothers with two children were dropouts. The findings indicated the importance of primary prevention programs that may succeed in helping some adolescents avoid premature parenthood and stay in school as well as the necessity for comprehensive programs for teenage parents.

## Conclusion

Services and programs for adolescent mothers are located in schools, health care settings, and a wide range of public and private agencies. Social workers in these settings often provide leadership in program planning and advocacy as well as individual and group counseling. Social work professionals are frequently on multidisciplinary teams of clinicians and researchers who provide services to pregnant adolescents. Social workers are employed in Head Start programs, child care centers, and public schools that serve children of adolescent parents. Consequently, social workers have an opportunity to contribute to the understanding of the developmental and material needs of these children and their parents. Knowledge about the long-term consequences of adolescent childbearing on the children of mothers and fathers aged younger than 20 years is needed for program and policy development.

## References


Adolescent Family Life Act of 1981 (Title XX).

Adolescent Health, Services and Pregnancy Prevention and Care Act of 1978, P.L. No. 95-626, 92 Stat. 3551 (1978).

Alan Guttmacher Institute. (1993). *Facts in brief: Teenage sexual and reproductive behavior.* New York: Alan Guttmacher Institute.

Bane, M. J. (1986). Household composition and poverty. In S. H. Danziger (Ed.), *Fighting poverty: What works and what doesn't* (pp. 209–231). Cambridge, MA: Harvard University Press.

Becerra, R. M., & Fielder, F. P. (1987). Adolescent pregnancy. In A. Minahan (Ed.-in-Chief), *Encyclopedia of social work* (18th ed., Vol. 1, pp. 40–51). Silver Spring, MD: National Association of Social Workers.

Dryfoos, J. G. (1990). *Adolescents at risk: Prevalence and prevention.* New York: Oxford University Press.

Hacker, A. (1992). *Two nations: Black and white, separate, hostile, unequal.* New York: Charles Scribner's Sons.

Hardy, J. B., & Zabin, L. S. (1991). *Adolescent pregnancy in an urban environment: Issues, programs, and evaluation.* Baltimore: Urban & Schwartzenberg; Washington, DC: Urban Institute Press.

Hayes, C. (Ed.) (1987). *Risking the future: Adolescent sexuality, pregnancy, and childbearing.* (Vol. 1). Washington, DC: National Academy Press.

Moore, K. A., & Snyder, N. O. (1994). *Facts at a glance.* Washington, DC: Child Trends.

Moore, K. A., Snyder, N. O., & Daly, M. (1992). *Facts at a glance.* Washington, DC: Child Trends.

Moore, K. A., Snyder, N. O., & Malla, C. (1993). *Facts at a glance.* Washington, DC: Child Trends.

National Association of Social Workers. (1993, October 13). *Welfare reform.* Washington, DC: Author.

National Center for Health Statistics. (1987). *Advance report of final natality statistics, 1985* (Monthly Vital Statistics Rep., Vol. 36, No. 4, Suppl.). Hyattsville, MD: U.S. Public Health Service.

Spitz, A. M., Ventura, S. J., Konin, L. M., Strauss, A., Frye, R. L., Heuser, C., Smith, L., Smith, S., Wingo, P., & Marks, J. S. (1993). Surveillance for pregnancy and birth rates among teenagers, by state–United States, 1980 and 1990. In Centers for Disease Control, *Surveillance Summaries* (Morbidity and Mortality Weekly Report Vol. 42, No. SS-6, pp. 1–27). Atlanta, GA: Centers for Disease Control and Prevention, U.S. Public Health Service.

Ventura, S. J., & Martin, J. A. (1993a). National Center for Health Statistics. *Advance report of final natality statistics, 1990* (Monthly Vital Statistics Report, Vol. 41, No. 9, Suppl.). Hyattsville, MD: U. S. Public Health Service.

Ventura, S. J., & Martin, J. A. (1993b). National Center for Health Statistics. *Advance report of final natality statistics, 1991* (Monthly Vital Statistics Report, Vol. 42, No. 3, Suppl.). Hyattsville, MD: U.S. Public Health Service.

Ventura, S. J., Martin, J. A., Taffel, S. M., Mathews, T. J., & Clarke, S. C. (1994). National Center for Health Statistics. *Advance report of final natality statistics, 1992* (Monthly Vital Statistics Rep., Vol. 43, No. 5, Suppl.). Hyattsville, MD: U.S. Public Health Service.

Ventura, S. J., Taffel, S. M., Mosher, W. D., & Henshaw, S. (1992). National Center for Health Statistics. *Trends in pregnancies and pregnancy rates, United States, 1980–88* (Monthly Vital Statistics Report, Vol. 41, No. 6, Suppl.). Hyattsville, MD: U.S. Public Health Service.

Vinovskis, M. A. (1988). *An "epidemic" of adolescent pregnancy? Some historical and policy considerations.* New York: Oxford University Press.

Williams, C. W. (1991). *Black teenage mothers: Pregnancy and child rearing from their perspective.* Lexington, MA: Lexington Books.

Wilson, W. J., & Neckerman, K. M. (1986). Poverty and family structure: The widening gap between evidence and public policy issues. In S. H. Danziger (Ed.), *Fighting poverty: What works and what doesn't* (pp. 232–259). Cambridge, MA: Harvard University Press.

## Further Reading

Burton, L. M. (1990). Teenage childbearing as an alternative life-course strategy in multigeneration black families. *Human Nature, 1*(2), 123–143.

Furstenberg, F. F., Jr., Brooks-Gunn, J., & Morgan, S. P. (1987). *Adolescent mothers in later life.* New York: Cambridge University Press.

Hofferth, S. L., & Hays, C. D. (1987). *Risking the future: Adolescent sexuality, pregnancy and childbearing.* Vol. II. Washington, DC: National Academy Press.

Jones, E. F., Forrest, J. D., Goldman, N., et al. (1986). *Teenage pregnancy in industrialized countries.* New Haven, CT: Yale University Press.

Ooms, T., (Ed.) (1981). *Teenage pregnancy in a family context: Implications for policy.* Philadelphia: Temple University Press.

**Constance W. Williams, PhD,** is associate professor, Brandeis University, Heller School for Advanced Studies in Social Policy, Waltham, MA 02254.

**For further information see**

Abortion; Adolescence Overview; Adolescents: Direct Practice; Adoption; Child Abuse and Neglect Overview; Child Foster Care; Child Welfare Overview; Families Overview; Family Life Education; Family Planning; Human Sexuality; Maternal and Child Health; Poverty; Primary Prevention Overview; Public Health Services; Single Parents; Women Overview; Women and Health Care; Youth Services.

**Key Words**

adolescent
nonmarital births
pregnancy
teenage birthrates
teenage pregnancy

# Adolescents: Direct Practice

**Mark I. Singer**
**David L. Hussey**

Adolescence is the last stage of childhood. It marks the transition between childhood and adulthood and is a diverse developmental period generally spanning the second decade of life. Adolescence begins with the recognizable physical changes of puberty and concludes with the more socially determined phenomena associated with an individual assuming the cultural role and capacities of adulthood.

Some theorists have divided adolescence into periods such as early and late adolescence (Newman & Newman, 1991). These somewhat arbitrary divisions reflect the enormous diversity of growth and change in youths during this developmental phase. Jerome Kagan (1971) was one of the first to argue for the inclusion of a developmental stage called "early adolescence" in which the new cognitive capabilities of 12-year-olds could be seen in their ability to "examine the logic and consistency of existing beliefs" (p. 998).

## Characteristics of Adolescence

### Physical and Biological Changes

The physical and biological changes of normal adolescence follow a sequential order for males and females that varies considerably in the timing of each event, but usually not in the order of appearance. Pubertal changes specifically measured during adolescence include breast, pubic hair, and male external genitalia changes (Tanner, 1962). Other changes include maturation of the body's motor systems resulting in increased size and strength; development of secondary sex characteristics, particularly the growth of facial and body hair; increasing neuronal complexity of the brain, resulting in the capacity for adult judgment and abstract thinking; menarche in females; and the hormonal shift signaling the acquisition of reproductive capacity. These changes may alter not only individuals' ability to perform physical and cognitive tasks but also the way in which they are perceived by themselves and others. Girls, for example, are generally more dissatisfied than boys with their physical appearance and overall body image (Petersen, Schulenberg, Abramowitz, Offer, & Jarcho, 1984; Rauste-von Wright, 1989).

### Psychosocial Changes

Aside from physical and biological changes, psychosocial transformations also are associated with adolescence. These include the development of intense personal relationships, the primacy of peer-group affiliations, dating, masturbation, and increased sexual experiences. Other psychosocial aspects of the adolescent period include increased introspection and self-absorption, drug and alcohol experimentation, and increased demands for independence.

Adolescents have been characterized for their heightened sensitivity to peer relations and increased conflict with parents (Newman & Newman, 1991; Papini & Sebby, 1988). Empirical research of the 1950s (Bowerman & Kinch, 1959; Douvan & Adelson, 1966) shows a more differentiated picture in which adolescent orientations to parents and peers vary according to issues and family patterns. Strong ties to peers do not necessarily imply weak ties to parents. Important studies (Hunter & Youniss, 1982; Jennings, Allerbeck, & Rosemayr, 1976; Kandel & Lesser, 1972) have consistently documented the central role of family in the lives of young people (Offer & Schonert-Reichl, 1992).

## Theories of Adolescence

Developmental theorists such as Freud, Erikson, and Piaget offered important formulations illuminating the transitions and advancements associated with adolescence. Their stage-theory models outlined the behavioral and cognitive phases of growth through which individuals must progress. According to psychoanalytic theory, the adolescent has a "second chance" to undo any negative effects of events that may have occurred in childhood and restructure his or her personality (Blos, 1962). In adolescents lower ego strength and increased aggressive and libidinal impulses can lead to a disruption in the balance of psychic structure. Freud (1958) postulated that the difference between normal development and psychopathology depends in part on whether the cathectic shifts in adolescence are gradual or sudden and abrupt. When detachment from parents takes place slowly and gradually, the defenses are transitory, less intense and rigid. When the change is abrupt, the sequence of events assumes a more defensive and pathological quality.

### Identity and Role Confusion

Erikson's theory of adolescent identity and role confusion suggests that the psychic state becomes most acute when the adolescent is exposed to a "combination of experiences which demand his simultaneous commitment to physical intimacy (not by any means overtly sexual), to decisive occupational choice, or energetic competition, and to psychosocial self-definition" (Erikson, 1959, p. 123). Psychosocial theory views human development as a product of the interaction between the individual (psycho) needs and abilities and societal (social) expectations and demands. A psychological crisis is a normal set of stresses and strains that arises when a person must make psychological efforts to adjust to the demands of the social environment. Crisis is used, in a developmental sense, as a turning point, a crucial period of increased vulnerability and heightened potential. Tension and conflict are necessary elements in the developmental process because they drive the ego system to develop new capacities. Identity diffusion results when there is turmoil and a lack of understanding about one's sexual, occupational, and self definition. According to Erikson, by the end of adolescence one must accomplish a satisfactory level of self-integration or remain defective or conflict-laden.

### Growth and Maturation

Piaget's theory of development emphasizes growth and maturation reflecting one's increased capacity to abstract and differentiate cognitively. Cognitions help one successfully adapt to and master the environment. Between ages 12 and 15, the last stage of cognitive maturity is reached, leading to the capacity for "formal operational" thinking. During this stage the form of thinking is important, not just the content. Consequently, the adolescent learns to abstract and to recognize underlying connections and relationships. Mental processes allow key elements to be combined, reversed, and examined in such a way as to abstract hypothetical solutions to situations that may never actually occur. This stage of development is the final one in cognitive maturation and is not necessarily reached by everyone (Dilut, 1972).

### Crisis and Turbulence

Aside from Freud's and Erikson's studies, much has been written about adolescence as a period of tremendous crisis and turbulence in Western culture. G. Stanley Hall (1904) used the late 19th-century knowledge of evolution in formulating his developmental concept of adolescence. He introduced the phrase *sturm und drang* (storm and stress) to characterize the psychology of adolescents and their vacillating moods. Yet current empirical findings indicate that only about 20 percent of adolescents have a stormy time, with the same proportion proceeding smoothly into adulthood. The remainder show a more episodic pattern of development and progress, stalled by periods of anxiety and stress (Offer, Howard, Schonert, & Ostrov, 1991).

Daniel Offer (1969) constructed the Offer Self-Image Questionnaire for Adolescents (OSIQ) to explore content areas dealing with impulse control, mood, body image, social relations, morals, sexual attitudes and behavior, family relations, mastery of external world, vocational and educational goals, psychopathology, and coping. Since 1962, the questionnaire has been administered to more than 30,000 teenagers in 11 countries. Offer measured behavioral and emotional responses through interviews with adolescents and their parents, teacher ratings, and analyses of psychological testing on both normal and disturbed teens. Offer's studies did not find turmoil to be prevalent in "normal" (nonclinical) adolescent populations (Offer & Schonert-Reichl, 1992). He found that 80 percent of teenagers did not experience marked or persistent stress and turmoil (Offer et al., 1991). These findings clearly indicate that most young people in the United States enjoy life and are happy with themselves most of the time. Affective responses appeared mild for the most part, easily handled by the adolescent, and only on rare occasions did they reach clinical proportions. In general, however, girls described themselves as sadder, lonelier, and more easily hurt than boys and more sensitive to their internal world. Girls reported they were more empathic than boys and felt more attached to their relatives and friends. Offer's empirical studies indicate that turmoil should be seen as only one route through adolescence, and a route the majority of subjects do not take.

## High-Risk Adolescents

Although most youths are able to negotiate adolescence successfully, adolescents today face many risks that were unknown during the adolescence of their parents or grandparents. Of the 28 million girls and boys ages 10 to 17 in the United States, about seven million (25 percent) are considered to be at high risk for the negative consequences of behaviors such as substance abuse, school failure, and unprotected sexual intercourse (Carnegie Council on Adolescent Development, 1989).

### Pregnancy

Today, youths enter puberty at a significantly younger age than did youths in previous generations. In this country during the early 1800s, the average age of a girl's first menstrual period was 16; today it is 12.5 (Carnegie Council on Adolescent Development, 1989). Almost a million adolescents become pregnant each year in the United States, with teenage women accounting for 13 percent of this country's births and 26 percent of its abortions (Henshaw & Van Vort, 1989; National Academy of Sciences, 1987). From 1973 to 1985, the pregnancy rate for adolescents under 15 years of age increased by 23 percent. During this same time period, the abortion rate for adolescents increased by 62 percent (Gans, 1990). There has also been a steep increase in nonmarital births among adolescents. In 1970, fewer than one-third of births to women under age 20 were nonmarital; by 1987 this percentage jumped to more than two-thirds (Moore, 1988).

### HIV/AIDS and Other STDs

Among the most serious threats facing today's adolescents is the lethal human immunodeficiency virus (HIV), the cause of acquired immune deficiency syndrome (AIDS). Approximately 20 percent of all AIDS cases are diagnosed in people between 20 and 29 years of age (Gans, 1990). Because HIV infection has a latency period from eight to 10 years, many of these individuals were likely to have been infected during adolescence. Other types of sexually transmitted diseases (STDs) are also at high levels among adolescents. During the 1980s, the incidence of gonorrhea decreased in every age cohort except adolescence. Currently, females ages 15 to 19 have the highest age-specific rates of gonorrhea (Kokotailo & Stephenson, 1993). Overall, it is estimated that adolescents account for 30 percent of the 20 million cases of STDs (U.S. Congress, 1991).

### Poverty

Many adolescents seen by social workers come from impoverished backgrounds and have few environmental and family resources. At the end of the 1980s, about 20 percent of American youths were living in poverty. In 1989 the poverty rate for African American children was 44 percent, four times the rate for white children; 38 percent of Hispanic youths were living in poverty (Center for the Study of Social Policy, 1993). Children and adolescents from low-income families are nearly seven times as likely to be in fair or poor health than are children from higher-income families (those with incomes over $35,000). Consequently, youths from low-income families have almost twice as many short-term hospital stays and 1.4 times as many disability days in which they miss school than do youths from higher-income families (Gans, 1990). Children from low-income families compared with youths from higher-income families are more than three times as likely to be physically abused, five times as likely to be sexually abused, and more than four times as likely to be emotionally abused (National Center on Child Abuse and Neglect, 1988).

### School Failure

Educational factors continue to play an important role in the lives of adolescents. Despite the significance of education in securing meaningful employment and ensuring self-sufficiency, only 69 percent of the students who entered ninth grade in 1986 graduated from high school in 1990. This rate is indicative of the downward trend in the proportion of adolescents receiving their high school diploma on time. Between 1985 and 1990, the percentage of students graduating from high school declined by 4 percent (Center for the Study of Social Policy, 1993). The quality of education provided to this country's children and adolescents has come under increased scrutiny and criticism. A national study found that only 11 percent of 13-year-olds were "adept" readers. In tests requiring analytic or persuasive writing, fewer than one in five eighth graders wrote adequate essays. The study concluded that students at all grade levels had deficiencies in higher-order thinking skills (Applebee, Langer, & Mullis, 1986).

## Critical Issues in Direct Practice with Vulnerable Youths

The three leading causes of death among adolescents—accidents, homicides, and suicides—are all largely preventable and directly related to psychosocial and developmental issues. Recognizing and understanding these avenues to mortality are of crucial importance to social workers who work with adolescents.

### Substance Abuse

The use of alcohol and other drugs is a key factor underlying each of the major causes of death among adolescents. Alcohol and other drugs are associated with half of all fatal motor vehicle accidents, 49 percent of murders, and between 20 percent and 35 percent of suicides (Office of Substance Abuse Prevention, 1991). The use of mood-altering substances has also been related to depression (Anglin, 1993; Joshi & Scott, 1988), sexual abuse (Singer, Petchers, & Hussey, 1989), delinquency (Meeks, 1989), and mental illness (Singer & White, 1991).

Since 1975, a survey conducted annually by the University of Michigan's Institute for Social Research has been one of the best sources of data on adolescent substance use. Each year approximately 16,000 high school seniors are surveyed, constituting a representative sample of youths attending public and private high schools in the coterminous United States (National Institute on Drug Abuse, 1992).

***Changes in use of substances.*** This survey has documented a continuous decline in the use of illicit drugs by high school seniors since 1980. The use of cocaine among high school seniors also has declined continuously since 1985. Annual prevalence of marijuana use among seniors continued to decline and fell to its lowest level since the study began (24 percent). Although these trends are encouraging, the use of mood-altering substances among adolescents remains at unacceptably high levels, particularly considering their contribution to mortality and morbidity. For example, in 1991, about 30 percent of high school seniors reported drinking five or more drinks in a row within the last two weeks. In addition, there has been no systematic decline in the use of inhalants, a class of drugs easily obtained and frequently used by younger adolescents.

It should be noted that the High School Seniors Survey obtains information only from students who were in school on the survey date and therefore does not include students who were truant or who dropped out of school. These students are likely to have higher rates of alcohol and drug abuse than their in-school counterparts. Additionally, the survey reports national trends that may not reflect local trends or those occurring in certain economic or ethnic subgroups.

***Screening and assessment techniques.*** Many adolescents whose use of drugs and alcohol is problematic are unlikely to perceive themselves as abusing mood-altering substances. It is therefore imperative that social workers be aware of the signs of substance abuse and knowledgeable about screening and assessment techniques. Such techniques vary from asking a few brief screening questions such as, "Are your friends into drinking or doing drugs?" and "Do any of your friends or family members think you drink too much or do drugs too much?" to more lengthy and in-depth assessments that, in extreme cases, may require hospitalization. (For a thorough discussion of substance abuse screening and assessment techniques specifically used for adolescents, see Anglin, 1993.)

### Violence and Victimization

Another serious problem facing today's adolescents is increasingly frequent exposure to violence in schools, neighborhoods, and homes. Studies of youths exposed to violence document a variety of serious sequelae including depression (Green et al., 1991), anxiety (Garbarino, Dubrow, Kostelny, & Pardo, 1992; Green et al., 1991), posttraumatic stress (Garbarino et al., 1992), and acting-out behaviors (Eth & Pynoos, 1985).

***Victims of abuse.*** Adolescents are more likely than any other age group of children to be the victims of physical, sexual, or emotional abuse (Gans, 1990). The U.S. Department of Health and Human Services (1988) estimated, from the reports it received in 1986, that between 1 million and 1.5 million children and adolescents were maltreated (that is, were victims of neglect or physical, sexual, or emotional abuse). In a national survey, 12 percent of eighth and tenth graders reported that someone raped or tried to rape them, and 18 percent reported that someone tried to force them to have sex against their wishes (American School Health Association, 1989). Compared with children from nonabusing families, maltreated children are twice as likely to live in a single-parent, female-headed household; are four times as likely to be supported by public assistance; and are affected by numerous family stress factors such as health problems, alcohol and drug abuse, and spouse abuse (Russel & Trainor, 1984).

Many adolescents have adopted the abusive thoughts and actions of their adult role models. In a survey of students in the sixth to ninth grades in Rhode Island, 65 percent of the boys and 57 percent of the girls thought it was acceptable for a man to force a woman to have sex if they dated for more than six months. In the same survey, 51 percent of the boys and 31 percent of the girls thought it was permissible for a man to force a woman to have sex with him if he spent a lot of money on her (U.S. Public Health Service, 1989).

***Victims of violent crime.*** Increasingly, adolescents are becoming the victims of violent crimes. In 1933, natural causes accounted for more than twice as many adolescent deaths as did violence or injury, but by 1985 the opposite was true (Fingerhut & Kleinman, 1989). Adolescents are the victims of violent crime and theft at twice the rate of adults over 20 years of age (Bureau of Justice Statistics, 1988). African American males are at particularly high risk of violent death. From 1987 to 1989, the firearm homicide rate among African American males ages 15 to 19 increased by 71 percent (to 85.3 deaths per 100,000), making firearm homicide the leading cause of death among this group. During the same time period, motor vehicle crashes, the second leading cause of death among African American adolescent males, fell 3 percent to 26.5 deaths per 100,000 (Fingerhut, Ingram, & Feldman, 1992).

Studies focusing on inner city populations suggest high rates of exposure to violence among adolescents. A study by the Urban Institute that involved interviews with almost 400 randomly selected ninth- and tenth-grade males from inner city Washington, DC, schools found that 27 percent had been attacked, threatened, or robbed by a person with a weapon, and 12 percent had been badly beaten by a nonhousehold member. Some of these young men also were the perpetrators of violence: 22 percent had been part of a group that attacked or threatened someone; 9 percent had robbed someone; and 4 percent had shot, stabbed, or killed someone (Brounstein, Hatry, Altschuler, & Blair, 1989). A national survey of more than 2,500 students in grades six to nine by pollster Louis Harris revealed that almost 40 percent of the students knew someone who had been killed or injured by a gun, and 15 percent said that they had carried a gun within 30 days of the survey ("Student Poll," 1993).

***Social work intervention.*** Although many professionals who work with adolescents are sensitive to the mental health consequences of sexual and physical abuse and inquire about such maltreatment routinely, far fewer seek to determine the extent to which an adolescent has been exposed to other forms of violence. Given that all forms of violence can adversely affect adolescents, social workers should widen their scope of inquiry to include violence exposure that may have occurred in school or in the neighborhood. Violence exposure should be seen not only as violence that has been directly perpetrated on the adolescent but also as violence that the adolescent has witnessed or that has happened to a family member, friend, or acquaintance. Finally, social workers should ask adolescents directly about violent and predatory acts they have committed, with particular emphasis on their possible involvement in gangs or street clubs.

## Suicide

***Prevalence.*** Surveys and research (Gallup Organization, 1991; Meehan, Lamb, Saltzman, & O'Carroll, 1992; Shaffer, Garland, Vieland, Underwood, & Busner, 1991) estimate that between 6 percent and 13 percent of adolescents attempt suicide at least once in their lives. In 1988, a total of 2,059 adolescents ages 15 to 19 completed suicide, accounting for 11.3 deaths per 100,000 in this age group (National Center for Health Statistics, 1992). Between 1960 and 1988, the rate increased from 3.6 deaths per 100,000 to 11.3 deaths per 100,000. These numbers reflect a 200 percent increase among adolescents, compared with a 17 percent increase for the general population during the same 28-year period. Among adolescents and adults the suicide rate is higher for males than for females, and is higher for whites than other groups (National Center for Health Statistics, 1992). Native Americans, however, appear to have the highest suicide rates of any ethnic group in the United States, depending on tribe (Shaffer, 1988). The most common method of attempted suicide is ingestion or overdose; firearms, followed by hanging and gassing, are the most frequent methods of completed suicide. Males are more likely to choose these more violent and lethal means of suicide (Berman & Jobes, 1991). Biopsychosocial influences contributing to the rise in adolescent suicide are thought to include increased substance abuse, increased use of firearms, increased psychosocial stress among adolescents, and a social imitation effect that may lower taboos against suicide and cause some adolescents to model the behavior (Garland & Zigler, 1993; Gould & Shaffer, 1986; Gould, Wallerstein, & Kleinman, 1990).

***Social work assessment.*** Suicidal adolescents have been shown to exhibit many symptoms of distress including substance abuse, anxiety, obsessive-compulsive behavior, hostility, and antisocial behavior. Depression is the most common pathological symptom of suicidal individuals of all ages (Stillion, McDowell, & May, 1989). Overall, suicidal behavior accounts for 25 percent to 40 percent of adolescent inpatient psychiatric admissions (Stillion et al., 1989).

In assessing suicidal adolescents, professionals use a variety of strategies such as matching social demographics, developing psychological profiles, using psychometric assessments, and identifying specific high-risk groups. Strategies typically include attempting to recognize risk factors identified from studies or psychological autopsies of those who have completed suicide. Risk factors for adolescent suicidal behavior include drug and alcohol abuse; prior suicide attempt; psychiatric disturbance, particularly conduct disorders and affective illnesses; family history of suicidal behavior; and the availability of a lethal method, particularly a firearm (Brent et al., 1993; Shaffer, Garland, Gould, & Trautman, 1988). Antisocial or aggressive behavior is also highly correlated with adolescent suicidal behavior (Brent et al., 1993), and many adolescent suicide attempters and completers have had trouble with the police (Cohen-Sandler, Berman, & King, 1982). Although these risk factors are useful for assessment, they are still somewhat inaccurate in that they yield too many false positives and they are not situation-specific (Rotheram, 1987).

## Problem Clusters and Severely Emotionally Disturbed Youths

Working therapeutically with adolescents usually entails a combination of promoting positive adaptive functioning and preventing or treating maladaptive dysfunction. A wide variety of psychotherapies may be used with adolescents and their families, some of which include cognitive, behavioral, client-centered, psychodynamic, and family therapy approaches. Group modalities are particularly applicable for adolescent treatment because of the developmental importance placed on peer affiliations during adolescence.

Over the past decade there also has been growing recognition among mental health professionals of the need for intensive, multidimensional, and flexible treatment models, particularly with severely emotionally disturbed youths (Knitzer, 1982, 1992). Among severely emotionally disturbed youths, risk factors are often interrelated and many problem behaviors coexist or come in "packages" (for example, early sexual activity, substance abuse, and delinquency) and serve similar functions for the adolescent (for example, peer acceptance) (Jessor & Jessor, 1977; Kazdin, 1993).

As a result of these comorbidities, recent treatment emphasis has shifted to developing a very individualized or "wraparound" approach to serving these multiproblem youths (Van Den Bergh & Minton, 1987). Priority is placed on maintaining and treating adolescents in their community and avoiding restrictive and disruptive interventions such as hospitalization and residential treatment (Kazdin, 1993). Components of this model include identifying and developing the strengths of the child and empowering the family and community to meet treatment needs (Knitzer, 1992). A key element in accomplishing this task is the creation of flexible funding models developed from cross-system collaboration in planning and resource sharing. Coordinated planning can create noncategorical, community-based alternatives to costly, traditional services. Such alternatives can span the child's life domains of school, family, community, and health (Duchnowski, Johnson, Hall, Kutash, & Friedman, 1992). Community-based treatment options should include a range of services such as family preservation treatment, foster care, and intensive case management with mechanisms to ensure that services are linked and well-coordinated, so that children and families can adjust easily from one service to another (Knitzer, 1992).

## Challenges for the 1990s and Beyond

There is little evidence to suggest that many of the serious problems faced by adolescents will subside in the near future. Indeed, much of what we have presented above indicates the opposite trend. The extent of at-risk behaviors, adverse conditions, and dysfunctions prevalent among adolescents is formidable, particularly among minority and low-income youths. The emerging trend of comprehensive community- and home-based services as alternatives to institution-based care may never be fully realized. In some states, despite savings achieved by the downsizing or closing of state psychiatric facilities, a significant proportion of monies that were earmarked for community- and home-based services is being diverted from the mental health system (Hogan, 1992). The U.S. health care system is likely to remain in financial crisis for many years, and adolescents living in poverty do not presently receive adequate services. Within these fiscal contexts, social workers face the serious challenge of being asked to do more with less.

Schools represent one of the most cost-efficient and convenient environments in which to serve adolescents. An array of services should be available in schools, from health and mental health care to job counseling. Although there is little disagreement among youth-serving professionals about the importance of school-based services, the funding mechanisms for these services remain elusive (Carnegie Council on Adolescent Development, 1989). Professionals interested in the health and well-being of adolescents must advocate for expanding services in schools.

Examining the efficacy of social work interventions should also remain a high priority. The enthusiasm generated by new home- and community-based treatment models can be sustained by support from carefully designed outcome studies. Such studies provide an opportunity to compare and improve clinical models, and of course, to develop more efficient services.

The challenges facing adolescents are daunting. Although there have been some creative efforts to address their needs, the agenda remains unfinished. Supporting the well-being of our nation's youths enables us to look toward our own futures with a sense of optimism, security, and purpose.

## References

American School Health Association. (1989). *The national adolescent student health survey: A report on the health of America's youth.* Oakland, CA: Third Party Publishing.

Anglin, T. M. (1993). Psychoactive substance use and abuse. In M. Singer, L. Singer, & T. Anglin (Eds.), *Screening adolescents at psychosocial risk* (pp. 41–83). New York: Lexington.

Applebee, A., Langer, J., & Mullis, I. (1986). *The writing report card: Writing achievement in American schools.* Princeton, NJ: Educational Testing Service.

Berman, A. L., & Jobes, D. A. (1991). *Adolescent suicide: Assessment and intervention.* Washington, DC: American Psychological Association.

Blos, P. (1962). *On adolescence.* New York: Free Press.

Bowerman, C. E., & Kinch, J. W. (1959). Changes in family and peer orientation of children between the fourth and tenth grades. *Social Forces, 57,* 206–211.

Brent, D. A., Perper, J. A., Mortiz, G., Allman, C., Friend, A., Roth, C., Schweers, J., Balach, L., & Baugher, M. (1993). Psychiatric risk factors for adolescent suicide: A case-control study. *Journal of the American Academy of Child Psychiatry, 32,* 521–529.

Brounstein, P. S., Hatry, H. P., Altschuler, D. M., & Blair, L. H. (1989). *Pattern of substance abuse and delinquency among inner city adolescents* (Report to the National Institute of Justice). Washington, DC: Urban Institute.

Bureau of Justice Statistics. (1988). *Bureau of Justice Statistics annual report, fiscal 1987.* Washington, DC: U.S. Government Printing Office.

Carnegie Council on Adolescent Development. (1989). *Turning points: Preparing American youth for the 20th century.* New York: Carnegie Corporation of New York.

Center for the Study of Social Policy. (1993). *Kids count data book: State profiles of child well-being.* Washington, DC: Author.

Cohen-Sandler, R., Berman, A. L., & King, R. A. (1982). Life stress and symptomatology: Determinants of suicidal behavior in children. *Journal of the American Academy of Child Psychiatry, 21,* 178–186.

Dilut, E. (1972). Adolescent thinking a la Piaget: The formal stage. *Journal of Youth and Adolescence, 4,* 281.

Douvan, E., & Adelson, J. (1966). *The adolescent experience.* New York: John Wiley & Sons.

Duchnowski, A. J., Johnson, M. K., Hall, K. S., Kutash, K., & Friedman, R. M. (1992). The alternative to residential treatment study: Initial findings. *Journal of Emotional and Behavioral Disorders, 1,* 17–26.

Erikson, E. (1959). Identity and the life cycle. *Psychological Issues, 1,* 101–164.

Eth, S., & Pynoos, R. S. (1985). Developmental perspective on psychic trauma in childhood. In C. Figled (Ed.), *Trauma and its wake: The study and treatment of post traumatic stress disorder* (pp. 36–52). New York: Brunner/Mazel.

Fingerhut, L. A., Ingram, D. D., & Feldman, J. J. (1992). Firearm homicide among black teenage males in metropolitan counties. *Journal of the American Medical Association, 267,* 3054–3058.

Fingerhut, L. A., & Kleinman, J. C. (1989). *Trends and current status in childhood mortality, United States, 1900–1985* (DHHS Publication No. PHS 89-1410). Hyattsville, MD: National Center on Health Statistics.

Freud, A. (1958). Adolescence. *Psychoanalytic Study of the Child, 13,* 255–278.

Gallup Organization. (1991). *Teenage suicide study: Executive summary.* (Available from the Gallup Organization, Inc., 47 Hulsish Street, Princeton, NJ 08542)

Gans, J. E. (1990). *America's adolescents: How healthy are they?* Chicago: American Medical Association.

Garbarino, J., Dubrow, N., Kostelny, K., & Pardo, C. (1992). *Children in danger: Coping with the consequences of community violence.* San Francisco: Jossey-Bass.

Garland, A. F., & Zigler, E. (1993). Adolescent suicide prevention. *American Psychologist, 48,* 169–182.

Gould, M. S., & Shaffer, D. (1986). The impact of suicide in television movies: Evidence of imitation. *New England Journal of Medicine, 315,* 690–694.

Gould, M. S., Wallerstein, S., & Kleinman, M. (1990). Time-space clustering of teenage suicide. *American Journal of Epidemiology, 131,* 71–78.

Green, B., Korol, M., Grace, M., Vary, M., Leonard, A., Glesser, G., & Smitson-Cohen, S. (1991). Children and disaster: Age, gender, and parental effects of PTSD symptoms. *Journal of the American Academy of Child and Adolescent Psychiatry, 30,* 945–951.

Hall, G. S. (1904). *Adolescence: Its psychology and its relations to physiology, anthropology, sociology, sex, crime, religion, and education.* New York: Appleton.

Henshaw, S. K., & Van Vort, J. (1989). Teenage abortion, birth and pregnancy statistics: An update. *Family Planning Perspectives, 21,* 85.

Hogan, M. F. (1992). New futures for mental health care: The case of Ohio. *Health Affairs, 11,* 69–83.

Hunter, F. T., & Youniss, J. (1982). Changes in functions of three relations during adolescence. *Developmental Psychology, 18,* 806–811.

Jennings, K. M., Allerbeck, K., & Rosemayr, L. (1976, April). *Value orientations and political socialization in five countries.* Paper presented at the Workshop on Political Behavior, Dissatisfaction, and Protest, Louvain-La-Nueve, Belgium.

Jessor, R., & Jessor, S. L. (1977). *Problem behavior and psychological development: A longitudinal study of youth.* San Diego: Academic Press.

Joshi, N. P., & Scott, M. (1988). Drug use, depression and adolescents. *Pediatric Clinics of North America, 35,* 1349–1364.

Kagan, J. (1971). A conception of early adolescence. *Daedalus, 100,* 997–1012.

Kandel, D. B., & Lesser, G. S. (1972). *Youth in two worlds: United States and Denmark.* San Francisco: Jossey-Bass.

Kazdin, A. E. (1993). Adolescent mental health: Prevention and treatment programs. *American Psychologist, 48,* 127–141.

Knitzer, J. (1982). *Unclaimed children: The failure of public responsibility to children and adolescents in need of mental health services.* Washington, DC: Children's Defense Fund.

Knitzer, J. (1992). Children's mental health policy: Challenging the future. *Journal of Emotional and Behavioral Disorders, 1,* 8–16.

Kokotailo, P. K., & Stephenson, J. N. (1993). Sexuality and reproductive health behavior. In M. Singer, L. Singer, & T. Anglin (Eds.), *Screening adolescents at psychosocial risk* (pp. 249–292). New York: Lexington.

Meehan, P. J., Lamb, A., Saltzman, L. E., & O'Carroll, P. W. (1992). Attempted suicide among young adults: Progress toward a meaningful estimate of prevalence. *American Journal of Psychiatry, 149,* 41–44.

Meeks, D. E. (1989). Substance abuse disorders. In F. Turner (Ed.), *Child psychopathology: A social work perspective* (pp. 317–350). New York: Lexington.

Moore, K. A. (1988). *Facts at a glance.* Washington, DC: Child Trends, Inc.

National Academy of Sciences. (1987). Risking the future: A symposium on the National Academy of Science's report on teenage pregnancy. *Family Planning Perspectives, 19,* 119–125.

National Center for Health Statistics. (1992). *Vital statistics of the United States: Vol. 2. Mortality—Part A.* Washington, DC: U.S. Government Printing Office.

National Center on Child Abuse and Neglect. (1988). *Study findings. The study of national incidence and prevention of child abuse and neglect: 1988.* Washington, DC: U.S. Department of Health and Human Services.

National Institute on Drug Abuse. (1992). *National high school senior drug abuse survey 1975–1991.* Monitoring the future survey. Washington, DC: U.S. Department of Health and Human Services.

Newman, B. M., & Newman, P. R. (1991). *Development through life: A psychosocial approach* (5th ed.). Pacific Grove, CA: Brooks/Cole.

Offer, D. (1969). *The psychological world of the teenager—A study of normal adolescent boys.* New York: Basic Books.

Offer, D., Howard, K., Schonert, K., & Ostrov, E. (1991). To whom do adolescents turn for help? Differences between disturbed and nondisturbed adolescents. *Journal of the American Academy of Child and Adolescent Psychiatry, 30,* 623–630.

Offer, D., & Schonert-Reichl, K. A. (1992). Debunking the myths of adolescence: Findings from recent research. *Journal of the American Academy of Child and Adolescent Psychiatry, 31,* 1003–1014.

Office of Substance Abuse Prevention. (1991, Spring). *The fact is. . . .* Washington, DC: U.S. Department of Health and Human Services.

Papini, D. R., & Sebby, R. A. (1988). Variations in conflictual family issues by adolescent pubertal status, gender, and family members. *Journal of Early Adolescence, 8,* 1–15.

Petersen, A. C., Schulenberg, J. E., Abramowitz, R. H., Offer, D., & Jarcho, H. D. (1984). A self-image questionnaire for young adolescents (SIQYA): Reliability and validity studies. *Journal of Youth and Adolescence, 13,* 93–111.

Rauste-von Wright, M. (1989). Body image satisfaction in adolescent girls and boys: A longitudinal study. *Journal of Youth and Adolescence, 18,* 71–83.

Rotheram, M. J. (1987). Evaluation of imminent danger for suicide among youth. *American Journal of Orthopsychiatry, 57,* 102–110.

Russel, A. B., & Trainor, C. M. (1984). *Trends in child abuse and neglect: A national perspective.* Denver: American Humane Association.

Shaffer, D. (1988). The epidemiology of teen suicide: An examination of risk factors. *Journal of Clinical Psychiatry, 49,* 36–41.

Shaffer, D., Garland, A., Gould, M., & Trautman, P. (1988). Preventing teenage suicide: A critical review. *Journal of the American Academy of Child and Adolescent Psychiatry, 27,* 675–687.

Shaffer, D., Garland, A., Vieland, V., Underwood, M., & Busner, C. (1991). The impact of curriculum-based suicide prevention programs for teenagers. *Journal of the American Academy of Child and Adolescent Psychiatry, 30,* 588–596.

Singer, M. I., Petchers, M. K., & Hussey, D. L. (1989). The relationship between sexual abuse and substance abuse among psychiatrically hospitalized adolescents. *Child Abuse and Neglect, 13,* 319–325.

Singer, M. I., & White, W. (1991). Addressing substance abuse among psychiatrically hospitalized adolescents. *Journal of Adolescent Chemical Dependency, 2,* 13–27.

Stillion, J. M., McDowell, E. E., & May, J. H. (1989). *Suicide across the lifespan: Premature exits.* New York: Hemisphere.

Student poll finds wide use of guns. (1993, July 20). *New York Times,* p. A6.

Tanner, J. M. (1962). *Growth at adolescence* (2nd ed.). Oxford, England: Blackwell Scientific Publications.

U.S. Congress, Office of Technology Assessment. (1991). *Adolescent health* (Publication No. AOTA-H-468). Washington, DC: U.S. Government Printing Office.

U.S. Department of Health and Human Services. (1988). *Study findings: Study of national incidence and prevalence of child abuse and neglect.* Washington, DC: U.S. Government Printing Office.

U.S. Public Health Service. (1989). *Promoting health/preventing disease: Year 2000 objectives for the nation* (draft). Washington, DC: U.S. Department of Health and Human Services.

Van Den Bergh, J., & Minton, B. (1987). Alaska native youth: A new approach to serving emotionally disturbed children and youth. *Children Today, 16,* 15–18.

### Further Reading

Kotlowitz, A. (1991). *There are no children here.* New York: Doubleday.

Oster, G. E., & Caro, J. E. (1990). *Understanding and treating depressed adolescents and their families.* New York: John Wiley & Sons.

Reiss, A. J., & Roth, J. A., (Eds.). (1993). *Understanding and preventing violence.* Washington, DC: National Academy Press.

Singer, M. I., Singer, L. T., & Anglin, T. M. (1993). *Screening adolescents at psychosocial risk.* New York: Lexington Books.

Turner, F. J. (1989). *Child psychopathology: A social work perspective.* New York: Free Press.

Walker, C. E., Bonner, B. L., & Kaufman, K. L. (1988). *The physically and sexually abused child.* New York: Pergamon Press.

**Mark I. Singer, PhD, ACSW, LISW,** is associate professor of social work, Mandel School of Applied Social Sciences, Case Western Reserve University, 14055 Euclid Avenue, Cleveland, OH 44106. **David L. Hussey, PhD, ACSW, LISW, CCDCCC,** is Clinical Director, Beech Brook, 3737 Lander Road, Pepper Pike, OH 44124.

### For further information see

Adolescence Overview; Adolescent Pregnancy; Adult Corrections; Alcohol Abuse; Child Abuse and Neglect Overview; Child Sexual Abuse Overview; Child Welfare Overview; Childhood; Children: Direct Practice; Children: Group Care; Children: Mental Health; Children's Rights; Criminal Behavior Overview; Drug Abuse; Eating Disorders and Other Compulsive Behaviors; Families Overview; Families: Demographic Shifts; Families: Direct Practice; Family Life Education; Gang Violence; Group Practice Overview; HIV/AIDS Overview; Homicide; Human Development; Human Sexuality; Juvenile Corrections; Mental Health Overview; Poverty; Runaways and Homeless Youths; School Social Work Overview; School-Linked Services; Sexual Assault; Substance Abuse: Direct Practice; Suicide; Violence Overview; Youth Services.

**Key Words**

| | |
|---|---|
| adolescence | direct practice |
| childhood | human development |

# Adoption

**Richard P. Barth**

Adoption creates a legal family for children when the birth family is unable or unwilling to parent. Yet, adoption is not only a program for children. Adoption creates new families, expands existing families, and engages adoptive parents in the priceless costs and benefits of parenting. Birth parents who voluntarily place their child with adoptive parents may also benefit from adoption because it frees them from the parenting role, which they judge themselves unready to assume. Adoption also offers birth parents the hope for a better life for their child. At its best, adoption meets the hopes of the child, the adoptive parents, and the birth parents. American adoption law and practice have developed to address the needs of this adoption triangle.

Communities also have an interest in the policies and practices of adoption. The future of our communities and society depends on our children, and their future requires an adequate family life. Many communities within our society, especially Native American tribes, ethnic communities, and other self-defined communities such as foster parents and gay men and lesbians are asserting their right to adopt or to have first claim on children available for adoption. Because adoption occurs at the intersection of love and law, it evokes a powerful response from these communities. Adoption is a social and legal institution that reflects the status, interests, and moral views of nearly every social entity.

## History of American Adoption

Early in U.S. history, children were more likely to be indentured than to be adopted. Nonetheless, adoptions date back to the beginning of the republic: The first governor of Massachusetts was an adoptive father of an older child. The end of slavery and indentured servitude resulted in the growth of orphanages, and individual states first began to legislate and regulate adoption practices at that time (Whitmore, 1876). Regulations emerged to protect birth parents' rights to give or withhold permission for the child's adoption, adopting parents' rights not to have their child reclaimed and children's rights to be cared for by suitable adopting parents.

By 1929, every state had adoption statutes. Statutes varied on several accounts, but all reflected concern that adoption promote the welfare of the child. The first regulations required social investigations of prospective adoptive parents and trial placement periods in prospective adoptive homes (Heisterman, 1935). A few states also required home visits by agents of the state child welfare department, although the rationale for the visits was rarely clarified.

Foster care and adoptions were intertwined in the late 19th century. The great expansion of foster care and adoption is often associated with Charles Loring Brace (1859). The middle-class leaders of child care agencies expected to save both souls and money by placing poor children in good homes (Clement, 1979). Placing agencies were concerned less with the needs of the children than with the social and moral problems children might create in the larger community. The most common reason for placement was poverty, not protection from child abuse or abandonment. This rationale for foster and adoptive placements was judged unacceptable by the 1920s.

For most of the 20th century, adoption of older children took a back seat to infant adoption. Adoption of older children began to reemerge after World War II. In 1949 the Children's Home Society began a "new type of child care program in North Carolina to provide ways and means of placing older children in institutions, in family homes for adoption" (Weeks, 1953, p. i). This effort was partly in response to waiting lists to place children in orphanages. Today orphanages are unnecessary, and foster care is the typical setting for older children awaiting adoption.

## Types of Adoption

Adoption occurs through a variety of means involving different types of agencies and auspices, each with unique procedures and requirements. Taken together, approximately 119,000 children were adopted in 1990 (Flango & Flango, 1993). Generally, adoptions are grouped into four categories: stepparent, independent, relinquishment or agency, and intercountry.

### Stepparent Adoptions

Stepparent adoptions refer to the adoption of children by the spouse of a parent. Stepparent adoptions differ from other adoptions because the adoption involves a child who is already legally in the family. In most states, stepparent adoptions are about twice as common as nonstepparent adoptions. Stepparent adoptions are typically administered separately from nonstepparent adoptions and, because of their impact on the distribution of family property, are often overseen in superior court or probate court.

### Independent Adoptions

Independent adoptions occur when parents place children directly with adoptive families of their choice without an agency serving as an intermediary. Intermediaries are most often counselors or attorneys. In the 1950s, agency adoptions and independent adoptions were about equal in number and primarily involved infants. Independent adoptions held steady at about 20 percent of all adoptions in the 1960s and 1970s (Meezan, Katz, & Russo, 1978) but have increased recently to nearly one-third (National Committee for Adoption, 1989). As of 1993, only six states outlawed independent adoptions (McDermott, 1993). Nationally, about 25,000 children are adopted independent of agencies each year (Stolley, 1993).

### Agency or Relinquishment Adoptions

Agency or relinquishment adoptions are those that follow the voluntary or involuntary legal severance of parental rights to the child and are overseen by a public or private agency. The intent of the Adoption Assistance and Child Welfare Act of 1980 was to increase the number of relinquishment adoptions, and this type of adoption appears to have increased in proportion to other forms of adoptions since 1980, although adoption statistics, especially at the national level, are not collected systematically enough to verify this assertion. State data do illustrate these trends, however; in California, relinquishment adoptions increased 88 percent between 1981 and 1992.

Little information is available to compare independent and agency adoptions. Evidence comparing independent and agency adoptions of infants found few differences in outcomes between them (Meezan et al., 1978). Parent satisfaction is high for both (Berry, Barth, & Needell, in press). Efforts to make the infant home-study process more intensive, to screen adoptive families more rigorously, or to require extensive agency review of placements have not been founded on evidence that independent adoptions are less satisfactory than agency adoptions. Although fingerprint checks for felonious criminal behavior and assessments of the safety of the household are undoubtedly warranted to screen adoption applicants, adoption policies must be circumspect about using additional criteria to screen out families seeking to adopt children. These additional criteria add barriers to the recruitment, approval, and retention of adoptive families and may prevent adoptions. Adoption agencies are especially helpful when they focus on assisting applicants to determine the best kind of adoption for them and provide necessary preplacement training and postplacement support for adoptive parents caring for children with special needs (Emery, 1993).

### Intercountry Adoptions

Intercountry adoptions involve the adoption of foreign-born children by adoptive families. In the United States, intercountry adoptions are a small but significant proportion of adoptions. Federal law requires a satisfactory home study. Private adoption agencies assist families by conducting family assessments for Latin American, Pacific Rim, or Eastern European adoptions. Also, children who are adopted must clearly be orphans. These adoptions raise a number of policy issues such as proper safeguarding of birth parent rights, cultural genocide, and resolving citizenship for the child. The nature and use of international adoptions merit careful review and analysis. More than 9,000 foreign-born children were adopted in the United States in 1991 (Immigration and Naturalization Service, 1991), roughly 10 percent of all adoptive placements. Recent trends include new restrictions on Korean adoptions and an expansion in the number of countries from which children are being adopted, including Eastern European countries and China.

### Special-Needs Adoptions

Another conceptual framework for adoption is to contrast special-needs adoptions and non–special-needs adoptions. Federal law describes special-needs adoption as indicating that the child cannot or should not be returned to the home of his or her birth parents and that the child has a specific factor or condition (such as ethnic background; age; membership in a minority or sibling group; or the presence of factors such as medical conditions or physical, mental, or emotional handicaps) that make it reasonable to conclude that the child cannot be placed with adoptive parents without providing adoption assistance or medical assistance. In addition, the state must find that a reasonable but unsuccessful effort has been made to place a child with appropriate adoptive parents without providing adoption or medical assistance. This latter requirement is waived if it would be against the best interests of the child. State regulations vary widely in their interpretations of the Adoption Assistance and Child Welfare Reform Act but generally identify special-needs adoptions as involving the adoption of children age three or older, ethnic children, handicapped children, emotionally or intellectually impaired children, or sibling groups of three or more.

Although disadvantaged and disabled children are adopted under each type of adoption, this categorization allows for a useful public policy focus. Between 1982 and 1986, the number of special-needs adoptions showed little or no growth (National Committee for Adoption, 1989), but the foster care population grew by 7 percent (Tatara, in press). More recent data on adoption are not available, although the growth in the national foster care population since 1986 is estimated at 53 percent and the likelihood that special-needs adoption is growing at that rate is exceedingly small. Special-needs adoption of foster children now appears to account for about 10 percent of all exits from foster care (Barth & Berry, 1988).

## Major Adoption Legislation

### Indian Child Welfare Act

For the first 200 years, American adoption was legislated locally. The first major piece of national legislation influencing adoption was the Indian Child Welfare Act (ICWA) of 1978. The legislation provides legal guidelines to promote the stability and security of Native American tribes and families and to prevent the unwarranted removal of Native American children from their homes. The passage of ICWA was fueled by the recognition that as many as 30 percent of Native American children were not living in their homes but were residing in boarding schools, foster homes, or adoptive homes. Founders of the act asserted that the viability of Native American tribes was dissipating in the face of the removal of its children. The act emphasizes protecting tribal communities and institutions (about half of Native Americans are members of tribes).

Within this broad act are protections specific to adoption. Most notably, termination of a Native American's parental rights requires the highest standard of proof. Child welfare authorities must show beyond a reasonable doubt that the continued custody of the child by the parent or Native American custodian is likely to result in serious emotional or physical damage to the child. Thus, the court must find with virtual certainty that the child will be seriously harmed in the future before he or she is freed for adoption. This high standard protects tribal rights but leaves little latitude for overseeing the child's right to be safe.

Section 1915 of the act legislates the adoptive placements of Native American children after termination of parental rights. Preference is given to placement with a member of the child's extended family, other members of the child's tribe, or other Native American families. The act places the rights of the tribe above those of the birth parent. For example, Native American parents who are tribal members cannot place their children for adoption with non–Native American families off the reservation; placement of tribal children is governed by the tribe.

As a result of these stringent provisions, ICWA is not without controversy. Fischler (1980) argued that the greater sovereignty for Native American adults places Native American children in jeopardy. Further, by regarding children as the property of parents, families, and tribes, ICWA does not protect children adequately. Defenders of ICWA argue that a child's right to a lifelong cultural affiliation deserves at least as much protection as the right to household permanency (Blanchard & Barsh, 1980). They propose that the choice to protect culture is what tribal child welfare professionals have made explicit in their support of ICWA.

The impact of the act has undergone little evaluation. The only assessment of ICWA implementation indicates that, as envisioned by the framers of the act, an increasing proportion of Native American children are being placed in foster and adoptive homes with Native American parents. Yet, Native American children in care are less likely than other children to have a case plan goal of adoption (Plantz, Hubbell, Barrett, & Dobrec, 1989). State and federal courts have yet to achieve a consistent balance between the interests of tribal survival, child welfare, and parental authority. The conflict is especially vexing when the parents of a Native American child want to place the child in a non–Native American family or a tribe seeks to place a child on an unfamiliar reservation in which the child has no close kin (Hollinger, 1989).

**Adoption Assistance and Child Welfare Act of 1980**

The Adoption Assistance and Child Welfare Act was passed in 1980. This broad act mandates that child welfare agencies implement preplacement preventive services, programs to reunify placed children with their biological families, subsidized adoption, and periodic case reviews of children in care.

Permanency planning legislation since 1980 may have resulted in a decrease in the per capita rate of children in nonkinship foster care and has clearly resulted in an increase in the number of children legally freed from their parents for adoption. In 1982 more than 50,000 children were legally free from their parents and waiting to be placed (Maza, 1983). About 17,000 of these children had the specific permanent plan of adoption and approximately 14,400 older children were placed for adoption in the United States (Maximus, 1984). By 1988 roughly 19,000 adoptions were finalized for children from the child welfare system. Despite inadequate data, there is little doubt that the massive increase since 1975 in the placement of older foster children and special-needs children for adoption has greatly changed the historic purpose and scope of adoptions.

The Adoption Assistance and Child Welfare Act encourages states to develop adoption subsidy programs for special-needs adoption and reimburses the state for 50 percent of the subsidy costs. The intent was to ensure that families were not penalized financially for adopting. Reforms to make subsidies available to families that adopt special-needs children passed, over the objections that sentiment should be the only consideration in adoption. Instead, law acknowledged subsidies as a means to facilitate the adoption of special-needs foster children and promote new adoptions. Subsidies are meant to encourage families to adopt. Families that adopt special-needs children are entitled to subsidies without a means test, although their financial condition can be taken into account.

Adoption assistance payments are now provided in all states, and state adoption subsidy programs operate in virtually every state. Nationwide, adoption assistance payments rose from $442,000 in 1981 to an estimated $100 million in 1993 among 40 states (U.S. Senate, 1990). Even after two decades of state subsidies and a decade of federal subsidies, however, policy and practice in this area have not stabilized. Diverse state interpretations of subsidy law continue to emerge.

When they were conceived more than a decade ago, adoption subsidies were a risky and refreshing departure. The absence of strict income requirements was intended to provide support to potential adoptive parents from all social groups. The availability of subsidies makes clear that low income should not be a barrier to adoption. More than half the families adopting older children receive subsidies. The concern among legislators and administrators about "paying people to be parents" has not been vanquished, however, and federal and state lawmakers continue to pursue ways to curtail subsidies. Ironically, the Adoption Assistance and Child Welfare Act, which stipulates that adoption is preferable to long-term foster care, requires that foster parents who decide to adopt receive subsidies no greater than the foster care rate. In practice, subsidies are almost always less than the foster care rate.

Some states have begun to use fixed schedules of payment levels based principally on family income. Others are using the median state income as an eligibility guideline for special care increments. These approaches do not consider the expenses associated with adequate care of children with different needs. Further, they ignore the intent of the subsidies to minimize fiscal penalties for adopting children and to help children tap the vast pools of emotional and material resources that adoptive families provide across the lifespan (Barth, 1993).

### Multiethnic Placement Act

The passage of the Howard M. Metzenbaum Multiethnic Placement Act of 1994 prohibits any agency or entity that receives federal assistance "to categorically deny to any person the opportunity to become an adoptive or a foster parent, solely on the basis of race, color, or national origin of the adoptive or foster parent, or the child, involved; or delay or deny the placement of a child for adoption or into foster care, or otherwise discriminate in making a placement decision, solely on the basis of race, color, or national origin of the adoptive or foster parent, or the child involved" (S. 553(a)1(A&B). Identified as a "permissible consideration" is that agencies may consider the cultural ethnic or racial background of the child and the capacity of the prospective parents to meet the needs of the child as one of a number of factors to determine the best interests of the child. Although there are not penalties to the state for failing to comply with this act, any individual aggrieved by an action in violation of subsection (a) shall have the right to bring an action seeking relief in a U.S. district court and noncompliance is considered a violation of Title VI of the Civil Rights Act of 1964. The act also requires that states provide diligent recruitment of potential adoptive and foster families that reflect the ethnic and racial diversity of children in the state for whom foster and adoptive homes are needed.

The passage of this act may increase the likelihood of adoption for African American children; however, this cannot be assumed to be an inevitable result of the law. Given the discretion that the law allows, unless child welfare workers understand the adverse implication of past practices for the adoption of children of color, they are unlikely to change practices based solely on the new law. The recruitment provision implicitly calls for a maintenance of current minority-focused recruitment efforts and some accelerated efforts for states that are not now doing diligent recruitment. This legislation could be the most significant adoption legislation in U.S. history, or it could have little influence. It is likely to unleash a torrent of lawsuits if states continue current practices of strict racial matching even when unmatched children and families are waiting.

## Current Adoption Practice

Recruitment of adoptive parents for foster children is arguably the most important element of adoption practice because once adoptive placements are made, adoptions generally require few ongoing services. Recruitment is especially critical for African American children because they are strikingly overrepresented in foster care. Although adoption practices vary broadly, practitioners struggle to decide how to keep pace with emerging trends in a way that fits their agency and is in the best interests of children, families, and the community.

### Adoption Planning for the Child

Permanency planning legislation provides grounds to free many children for adoption, but agencies have been slow to implement the specifics of the legislation, and many barriers to placement and permanence remain. Determining a child's eligibility for adoption continues to be a confused mixture of answers to three questions. Is the child (1) easily interested in adoption? (2) likely to be adopted? (3) likely to remain adopted? Some children are never considered for adoption because they seem content in a less permanent situation. Social workers with narrow ideas about "adoptability" continue to reject some children as too severely handicapped or too old to be adopted. Adjusting practice to the needs of these older children includes recognizing that some disruption is inevitable. As Cole (1986) wrote, "The only failed adoption is the one you didn't try" (p. 4). Workers who recognize and accept the possibility of disruption in adoption find creative ways to facilitate adoptions for all waiting children and support the placement in accordance with the risk involved.

Not every child will be better off adopted than in long-term foster care or guardianship. Yet the general evidence of positive adoption outcomes is powerful (Bartholet, 1993). The value of adoption and the relatively modest disruption rates of about 10 percent (Barth, 1988; Festinger, 1986) make adoption the clear and convincingly superior plan over foster care. But many children are casually resigned to foster care, given little encouragement to consider adoption, and their promising tomorrows are readily swapped for a "manageable placement" today.

Speedy efforts to place children while they are young and better able to fit into an adoptive family's home represent the starting point for successful adoption. Adoption delayed is often adoption denied. Efforts to terminate parental rights more quickly when reunification is improbable and to move children into foster-adopt situations deserve full support and dissemination.

Many states require an evidentiary hearing in family or juvenile court to determine that the child should be freed for adoption, followed by a separate civil court hearing to terminate parental rights. This system is triple jeopardy for children. The first jeopardy is that the family court will return them to a situation that is least likely to promote their well-being and allow them to grow unharmed. This jeopardy is the one condoned by public policies that are overly protective of parental rights. The second jeopardy is that the civil court, in its inexperience in these matters, will, after much delay, overturn the family court decision. The third jeopardy is that the child will grow without a plan, without the right to join a family, and without the freedom of permanence.

Practitioners need the tools and the support to work with foster children and parents toward adoption. Younger children are likely to be referred to adoption units, and older foster children are increasingly referred for emancipation services. Agencies continue to neglect latency-age children in care. These are children whose likelihood of adoption into a same-race family is judged to be low and whom agencies are hesitant to free from their birth parents because they will become "legal orphans" unless an adoptive home awaits. These children are thus not transferred to adoption units, entered into adoption books, or referred to adoption fairs. They are denied the opportunity of a lifetime family.

**Recruitment of Adoptive Parents**

Because so many children in foster care would benefit from adoption, adoptive parents are in high demand. Most children who could benefit from adoption will never be freed because no adoptive family is available to encourage the courts to free the child. Among the 17,000 foster children who were freed from their parents and waited to be placed for adoption in 1985, more than two-thirds were six years old or older and 38 percent were black (National Committee for Adoption, 1989). In the same year most of the children adopted were five years old or younger and only 23 percent were black. With the great pressure for racial matching and an increase in the pool of adoptive children, adoption exchanges and networks strive to fill the need for adoptive parents. Exchanges serve as matching resources, listing children waiting for adoption and their special needs and parents seeking to adopt. Nationwide exchange systems, such as the National Adoption Information Exchange System, contribute to the effectiveness of these regional exchanges (U.S. Department of Health and Human Services, 1981).

In addition to exchanges, parent recruitment also occurs through community education. Broad education in the community can reach groups of potential parents that may never have considered adoption. Beginning in 1979, Father George Clements, a priest in Chicago, challenged every African American church in Chicago through the One Church, One Child program to accept the responsibility and opportunity to have one member of each congregation adopt an African American child (Veronico, 1983). Federal and state governments have subsequently provided several years of support to One Church, One Child to encourage its replication. Many states now have a version of One Church, One Child and focus on recruitment of families from other ethnic groups. The program has not yet been evaluated.

Another recruitment strategy that has shown promise involves using special features on television or in newspapers to present a particular child and a description of his or her strengths and needs. These media campaigns are modestly successful and inexpensive. Ethnic adoption fairs also bring interested parents and eligible children together in a picnic situation. Recent efforts focus on retaining potential adoptive parents by improving the speed, quality, and sensitivity of the agency's response to parents once they inquire about adoption.

**Preplacement Services**

Home studies are a nearly 150-year-old tradition and continue to serve the primary function of screening adoptive families to protect children from harmful situations. A well-established but secondary function is to help adoptive families clarify their intentions and flexibility regarding the characteristics of children they seek to adopt. During the past decade there has also been a greater use of the group home-study process for training and support of preadoptive families so they are more able to parent special-needs children successfully. The group approach to preplacement provides particular opportunities for ongoing support. Many of these groups prepare participants to become adoptive or foster parents. Groups may last for as long as 10 sessions and include guest presentations by current foster and adoptive parents. Prospective foster parents are told that they may change their minds and become adoptive parents instead. People who expressly want to adopt (and they usually outnumber those who want only to provide foster care) are oriented to the social services system and the legal and moral responsibility to facilitate the child's reunification with the birth family when that is the case goal. Adoptive families that begin the process in such multifamily groups often maintain contact with peers well beyond their time of contact with the social worker. Although group home studies have not been well evaluated, some evidence suggests that they strengthen high-risk placements (Barth & Berry, 1988).

Social workers try to provide adopting parents with all pertinent information about the child during preplacement services. Because of the inevitable coordination problems and some confidentiality concerns, much valuable background information is not shared. This inefficiency could be redressed by rethinking the type of information that is collected and how it is summarized and transmitted to the families. Even worse, some social workers withhold information to increase the likelihood of adoption.

The strong confirmation by researchers of the importance of information sharing calls for prompt action (Barth, 1988). Better information is associated with better outcomes. Also, the success of a few "wrongful adoption" cases is forcing agencies to change their information-sharing practices and states to change their laws to reduce liability.

**Ethnic and Racial Matching**

Matching between adoptive parent and child is as old as adoption and primarily based on the strictures of social convention rather than the child's psychosocial needs. Matching has been dominated by concerns of religion and race. As recently as 1974, 35 states had "religious protection" statutes (Gollub, 1974) that required agencies to place a child in a family with the same religion as their birth parent(s). Although most professionals agree that the child should be allowed spiritual and ethical development, religious matching is increasingly disfavored (Child Welfare League of America, 1978). Only a few agencies still require that the child and adoptive parent be of the same religion, although many agencies attempt to adhere to birth parents' religious preferences in selecting an adoptive home.

Transracial adoptions are mostly found among older child adoptions. About 8 percent of all adoptions are transracial or transethnic, with about 1 percent being adoptions of African American children by white parents (Stolley, 1993). Transracial adoptive placements are currently used only in exceptional circumstances because of concerns that children will be denied exposure to their own cultural heritage and be less prepared to cope with racism. This position, espoused in 1972 and maintained today by the National Association of Black Social Workers, is accepted in many agencies and has been codified into some state laws. Although a number of special adoption projects have been initiated to help encourage placement of African American children in same-race placements, African American children are far less likely to be adopted than other children of similar age and behavior (Barth, Courtney, & Berry, 1994; Barth, Courtney, & Needell, 1994; Bartholet, 1993).

The expectation of same-race adoption is controversial. Even the National Association for the Advancement of Colored People has disagreed, with its general membership calling for less emphasis on race in placements and its executive council calling for greater emphasis on racial matching. Practitioners generally agree that children benefit from the cultural education provided by members of their own race, but some stress the overriding importance of finding adoptive parents regardless of race. Although the current Child Welfare League of America (1978) policy states that children should not be denied placement if other-race parents are able and willing to adopt, many agencies wait for same-race placements so long that children are never freed for adoption or are so old that prospective parents become unwilling to adopt them.

Case law is raising new concerns about the legality of placement decisions based primarily on race ("Michigan May Limit Race," 1986). In 1991 the U.S. Office for Civil Rights found that criteria for adopting or methods of administration of adoption services that result in the exclusion, limitation, or segregation of ethnic children relative to adoptive placements violate their civil rights (Belloli, 1991). Further, research on the impact of this practice on children does not justify it. It appears that no single factor determines the outcome of an adoption, not even race. Numerous investigators (Feigelman & Silverman, 1983; Grow & Shapiro, 1972; Simon & Alstein, 1987; Vroegh, 1992) have found that children adopted transracially are as well adjusted as other adopted children, and the burden of proof is shifting to the opponents of greater flexibility in placement. The history of adoption in this nation shows a steady trend toward broadened access to adoption for children and parents and away from strict matching criteria. This trend should accelerate with the implementation of the Multiethnic Placement Act.

**Open Adoption**

The practice of open adoption, or the continuance of contact or correspondence between the adopted child and birth parents, is increasingly common. An estimated 55 percent of adoptive families in California during 1988 to 1989 had contact with the birth family in the two years following placement (Berry, 1991). The benefits of open adoption are debatable. On ideological grounds, because outcome data on open adoptions are scarce, Pannor and Baran (1984) called for "an end to all closed adoptions" (p. 245). They view the secrecy of conventional adoptions as an affront to the rights of adopted children. Kraft, Palombo, Woods, Mitchell, and Schmidt (1985a, 1985b) countered that open adoptions interfere with the process of bonding between the adoptive parent and child. Other evidence suggests that the adoptive parents' control over their child's contact with birth parents is critical to the success of the placement (Barth & Berry, 1988) and the parents' comfort with the placement (Berry, 1991).

Open adoptions are gaining increasing support. Whereas most open adoptions continue to be voluntary on the adoptive parents' part, recent case law has added stipulations to adoption decrees that provide birth parents with visitation rights (Hollinger, 1993). A few countries (for instance, New Zealand) have made open adoptions the requirement for all adoptions on the grounds that it is in the child's best interest. These changes are in stark contrast to the historical notion of adoption as a parent–child relationship equivalent to the birth parent–child relationship and without condition. This change occurred despite the absence of noteworthy evidence that children in open adoptions have better outcomes than other children.

The potential benefit of open adoption is that it provides a resource for coping with the typical transitions in the child's understanding about adoption as he or she moves toward adulthood. The danger for older children is that continued contact with birth parents may disrupt the development of the child's relationship with the new family. The older adoptive child and parent are trying to become a family and need a structure to do so. It may seem that the older a child, the less detrimental and more natural it is to retain ties to former caretakers. The danger in this logic is that older children have a more difficult time developing ties to their new family because they are also pushing toward independence and this development may be preempted by contact with birth families. Open adoption can perhaps best be viewed as an enrichment to a stable placement, not a necessity for all placements or, most certainly, a palliative for a troubled one.

**Nontraditional Adoptions**

The traditional requirement that adoptive parents be married couples who own a home with a full-time mother at home severely narrowed the field of possible adoptive parents. Although these requirements might have been helpful in reducing the field of applicants during the infant adoption boom, they were also erroneously promulgated to protect children from unsuitable parents. Instead, they limited the placement of special-needs children. The bigger pool of parents needed for these waiting children is not attainable without flexible requirements. Requirements for adoptive parents have typically been more flexible in public agencies than in private ones. Public agencies supervise adoptions with parents with lower incomes, lower education levels, older ages, and more children in the home than do private agencies (State of California Department of Social Services, 1987).

Agencies are beginning to recognize the potential of unconventional adoptive parents, especially single parents. An early study of single-parent adoptions (Branham, 1970) found that, in general, applicants were emotionally mature, tolerant, and independent and had a supportive network of relatives. Barth and Berry (1988) found that single parents adopted older and more difficult children with no more adoption disruptions than couples.

Adoption of children by kin who cared for them as foster parents has increased in recent years. Kinship foster care has become the most common type of foster care in many urban areas

(Barth, Courtney, Berrick, & Albert, 1994). Kinship adoptions represented 14 percent of all adoptions of foster children in 1992. Although this is generally a more protective legal arrangement for children than foster care, kinship adoptions are more likely to be by older, less educated, poorer, single parents than other adoptions (Magruder, 1994).

**Adoptions by Foster Parents**

Recruitment efforts are eased by the use of foster parents as adoptive parents. Adoptions by foster parents increased in the 1970s as the number of special-needs children freed for adoption increased, without an associated increase in adoptive applicants. Before that, foster parents were considered inappropriate for adoption. Sometimes the foster parents knew at the initial placement that the placement could become an adoptive placement; at other times they decided to adopt after the child had lived with them as a foster child for some time. Some foster parents have felt pressured by an agency to adopt the child (Meezan & Shireman, 1982), although others intended to adopt from the very beginning. More than 80 percent of special-needs adoptions are now by foster parents. Fost-adopt or legal-risk adoptions involve placing a child into a foster home with the plan for adoption, assuming that the child will not go home to birth parents. Although fost-adopt placements are becoming more commonplace and agencies are developing guidelines and administering them, they are surrounded by controversy. The major objection is that foster parents hoping to adopt will not work toward the child's reunification with the biological family, one of the major goals of foster care (Lee & Hull, 1983). The dual goals of reunification with the biological family and the integration of the child into the fost-adopt family impose a strain on foster parents' and children's loyalties. Some professionals believe that beginning an adoption as a foster parent reduces a sense of entitlement to be a parent, resulting in less commitment to parenthood and a weaker parent–child bond (Ward, 1981).

Foster families are also not screened as carefully as adoptive families for compatibility with the child (Meezan & Shireman, 1985). The time constraints involved in foster placements allow little matching or placement preparation, both thought to be important to adoption success. Also, confidentiality is less protected in a foster home adoption, where the foster parents and biological parents have met. Fost-adoptions may be disquieting to other foster children present in the foster home. In addition, adoption by foster families may render these families unavailable for other foster children, draining the already dwindling pool of foster families.

The advantages of fost-adoptions are continuity of home life and a familiar community for the child, the opportunity for ongoing assessment of the placement, and the involvement of the child in the decision to adopt. Fost-adoptions can begin when the children are younger and are more able to bond with a new family, even if custody battles stretch out in the courts for years. Adoptive parents who were previously foster parents are also reported to be more accepting of ongoing contact with the agency, especially when problems arise. Fost-adoptions are gaining wider acceptance among professionals, especially for adoptions of older children, and these placements compare favorably to conventional adoptive placements in terms of continuity for the child and placement stability (Barth & Berry, 1988).

Several situations especially lend themselves to fost-adoption, generally when there is little likelihood of children's reunification with their biological parents. Fost-adoption may be appropriate if the child has been relinquished by the mother (and the father is unknown, absent, or likely to relinquish in the future); if the child has been abandoned; if parental rights have been terminated but are being contested; if the child's birth parents have terminated their rights to the child's siblings; or if the birth parents are unlikely to be able to parent the child (Gill & Amadio, 1983).

**Postplacement Services**

Agency support after placement may be needed for some children. Any placement will have challenges. The goal for the agency is to stay close enough to the family to be aware of these problems and guide the family to resources to aid in their resolution. However, many families are reluctant to seek services until it is too late because they are afraid they will lose their child.

Both the child and the parents have needs in postplacement services. Agencies typically maintain contact with the family during the first three to six months to reassure the child of continuity with his or her past and to enable the family to explore uncertainties without feeling lost (Fitzgerald, Murcer, & Murcer, 1982). The goal is to catch problems early in the placement before they escalate into unsalvageable disasters. The evidence is increasingly clear that three months is far too brief a time (Barth & Berry, 1988). Agencies must establish ways to provide services for high-risk placements throughout adolescence. Postlegalization counseling services may be useful but they are not specifically geared toward preserving placements on the verge of disruption. Rather, they tend to serve adoptees placed as infants, not older child adoptees, and help them reconcile their adoptions, make decisions about searching for birth parents, and deal with their concerns as they become adolescents and young adults.

Many agencies have introduced support groups of adoptive families for parents and children. It is often helpful for new adoptive parents and children to talk to fellow adopters and adoptees about what is normal in adoption and to share realistic expectations and feelings about the process. These groups also facilitate supportive relationships that parents and children can fall back on when they need to. Support groups probably operate best when started during the home study, but successful versions have been developed after placement to support high-risk placements.

There is a clamor for the development of postplacement and postlegalization services that meet the demands of supporting older-child adoptions. The call is for something far more than mandatory visits soon after the adoption and the availability of crisis intervention services. Although the principles underlying this demand are sound, a few concerns arise. First, postadoption services should not be staffed at the expense of recruitment and home study efforts. Resources spent on conventional postplacement services are not as valuable to agencies and families as dollars spent on recruitment because most adoptions succeed with no significant agency effort after placement. Second, although referral to outside services is often useful, social workers or other adoptive families involved with the family should be available to assess the situation and coordinate postplacement services from other providers. Families are less likely to ask the agency for help when they lose contact with the worker who did their home study. The home study is a poignant process that builds strong bonds between the worker and family. The organization of services should facilitate a continuous relationship among the family, social worker, and other adoptive families who can assist in times of duress.

Adjusting to older-child adoptions is often difficult. At times, the future of the adoption may be in doubt. With so much riding on the outcome of such a crisis, it is unwise to rely on conventional social casework counseling or office-based psychotherapy. Intensive in-home adoption preservation services may be needed. Since permanency planning, family preservation services have emerged in most states. They have been used primarily for keeping children out of the child welfare or mental health systems and not to help preserve adoptive placements.

Few adoptive families now have the benefit of intensive home-based, family preservation services to prevent adoption disruption. Iowa, Massachusetts, and Oregon have developed promising programs to support families in times of crisis (Barth, 1991). For families in crisis, in-home interventions reduce the likelihood of alienation that can occur during out-of-home care. The specific presenting problems that precipitate adoption disruptions are those that signal the breakdown of other families, especially assault, running away, and noncompliance of latency and teenage children. Intensive services are costly, but if they are successful, their costs can be favorably weighed against the lifelong benefits that follow adoption.

## Conclusion

Recent changes in adoption jeopardize its place in the child welfare services continuum. The child welfare service "system" is an amalgam of programs. The outcomes of efforts to prevent out-of-home placements, to reunify families, and to provide long-term care all depend on the quality of the programs that have previously worked with the children. Each program must work if the other programs are to do what they are intended for. If older children in the child welfare system are not adopted or able to stay adopted, then the rationale for moving quickly to terminate the rights of birth parents (after a determination that children cannot go home) is weakened. Indeed, even the pressure to leave children in or return them to unsafe birth families is intensified when permanent adoptive homes are unavailable, because social workers fear that children will experience more harm in a lifetime of foster care than at home. Many agencies will not free children from foster care until a stable home is all but guaranteed. Without confidence that terminating parental rights and freeing a child for adoption will ultimately result in an adoption, judges lose their conviction to do so, time limits on foster care are rendered insignificant, and mandates for speedy permanency planning become moot. Successful older-child adoption services may not be the hub of effective child welfare services but they are critical.

Not everyone believes that adoption is of great value to children and American society. Adoption foes are gaining greater attention as they argue that adoption is a cause of trauma to children and birth parents and that both experience irreparable harm from their separation. If adoption is to maintain a powerful role in child welfare services, the arguments for the resilience of children's capacity to make attachments (Eyer, 1992), the benefits to children of adoption (Rutter & Rutter, 1993), and the congruence between adoption and American values need better articulation and dissemination (Bartholet, 1993). Many social workers are not as sure as they once were of adoption's advantages over long-term foster care or guardianship and may fail to make a case about its value to foster families and children. Often, adoption is not viewed as a clear and desirable alternative to foster care.

Adoption is facing increasing scrutiny by all interested adult parties. Birth mothers and fathers, adopting parents, and adoption agencies and centers are developing new and more rigorous procedures for trying to ensure that their needs are met. These efforts may work against the interests of children who need adoptive homes. Despite the general success of adoption for all parties involved, a considerable tightening of adoption regulation and more procedural barriers to adoption may occur in the next decade. These procedures may result in diminished interest on the part of potential adoptive parents who will instead choose to pursue surrogacy arrangements or fertility treatments with lower success rates. Such strategies will not lead to the adoption of children in need of placement. Of the utmost importance is the public policy goal of increasing adoptive placements. In addition, a substantial challenge exists to find ways to make adoption a way to create and affirm family, ethnic, and community relationships in all their manifestations. This involves supporting a range of adoptive arrangements that allow the child to recognize the significance of birth parents and siblings, racial and ethnic make-up, and cultural origins and give the child opportunities to acting on that recognition.

## References


Adoption Assistance and Child Welfare Act of 1980. P.L. 96-272, 94 Stat. 500.

Barth, R. P. (1988). Older child adoption and disruption. *Public Welfare, 46*(1), 23–29.

Barth, R. P. (1991). Adoption preservation services. In E. M. Tracy, D. A. Haapala, J. Kinney, & P. J. Pecora (Eds.), *Intensive family preservation services: An instructional sourcebook* (pp. 237–250). Cleveland: Case Western Reserve University, Mandel School of Applied Social Sciences.

Barth, R. P. (1993). Fiscal issues in adoption. *Public Welfare, 51,* 21–28.

Barth, R. P., & Berry, M. (1988). *Adoption and disruption: Risks, rates, and responses.* Hawthorne, NY: Aldine de Gruyter.

Barth, R. P., Courtney, M., Berrick, J., & Albert, V. (1994). *From child abuse to permanency planning: Pathways through child welfare services.* New York: Aldine de Gruyter.

Barth, R. P., Courtney, M., & Berry, M. (1994). Timing is everything: An analysis of the time to adoption and legalization. *Social Work Research, 18,* 139–148.

Barth, R. P., Courtney, M., & Needell, B. (1994, March 17). *The odds of adoption versus remaining in foster care.* Paper presented at the Second Annual National Child Welfare Conference, Washington, DC.

Bartholet, E. (1993). *Family bonds.* New York: Simon & Schuster.

Belloli, S. G. (1991, June 4). Office of Civil Rights charges MDSS of race matching. *Detroit News,* pp. 1, 13.

Berry, M. (1991). Open adoption in a sample of 1296 families. *Children and Youth Services Review, 13,* 379–396.

Berry, M., Barth, R. P., & Needell, B. (in press). Auspices of adoption. *American Journal of Orthopsychiatry.*

Blanchard, E. L., & Barsh, R. L. (1980). What is best for tribal children: A response to Fischler. *Social Work, 25,* 350–357.

Brace, C. L. (1859). *The best method of disposing of our pauper and vagrant children.* New York: Wynkoop, Hallenbeck & Thomas.

Branham, E. (1970). One parent adoptions. *Children, 17*(3), 103–107.

Child Welfare League of America. (1978). *Adoption guidelines.* New York: Author.

Clement, P. F. (1979). Families and foster care: Philadelphia in the late nineteenth century. *Social Service Review, 53,* 407–420.

Cole, E. S. (1986). Post-legal adoption services: A time for decision. *Permanency Report, 4*(1), 1, 4.

Emery, J. (1993). The cases for agency adoption. *The Future of Children, 3*(1), 139–145.

Eyer, D. E. (1992). *Mother-infant bonding: A scientific fiction.* New Haven: Yale University Press.

Feigelman, W., & Silverman, A. R. (1983). *Chosen children: New patterns of adoptive relationships.* New York: Praeger.

Festinger, T. (1986). *Necessary risk: A study of adoptions and disrupted adoption placements.* New York: Child Welfare League of America.

Fischler, R. S. (1980). Protecting American Indian children. *Social Work, 25,* 341–349.

Fitzgerald, J., Murcer, B., & Murcer, B. (1982). *Building new families through adoption and fostering.* Oxford, England: Basil Blackwell.

Flango, V. E., & Flango, C. R. (1993). Adoption statistics by state. *Child Welfare, 72,* 311–319.

Gill, M. M., & Amadio, C. M. (1983). Social work and law in a foster care/adoption program. *Child Welfare, 62,* 455–467.

Gollub, S. L. (1974). A critical look at religious movements in adoption. *Public Welfare, 32,* 624–636.

Grow, L. J., & Shapiro, D. (1972). *Black children, white parents: A study of transracial adoption.* New York: Child Welfare League of America.

Heisterman, C. A. (1935). A summary of legislation on adoption. *Social Service Review, 9,* 269–293.

Hollinger, J. H. (1989). Beyond the best interests of the tribe: The Indian Child Welfare Act and the adoption of Indian children. *University of Detroit Law Review, 66,* 452–491.

Hollinger, J. (1993). Adoption law. *The Future of Children, 3*(1), 43–62.

Immigration and Naturalization Service, Statistical Analysis Branch. (1991). *Statistical year books.* Washington, DC: U.S. Government Printing Office.

Indian Child Welfare Act of 1978. P.L. 95-608, 92 Stat. 3069.

Kraft, A. D., Palombo, J., Woods, P. K., Mitchell, D., & Schmidt, A. W. (1985a). Some theoretical considerations on confidential adoptions: Part I. The birth mother. *Child and Adolescent Social Work, 2,* 13–21.

Kraft, A. D., Palombo, J., Woods, P. K., Mitchell, D., & Schmidt, A. W. (1985b). Some theoretical considerations on confidential adoptions: Part II. The adoptive parent. *Child and Adolescent Social Work, 2,* 69–82.

Lee, R. E., & Hull, R. K. (1983). Legal, casework, and ethical issues in risk adoption. *Child Welfare, 62,* 450–454.

Magruder, J. (1994). Characteristics of relative and nonrelative adoptions by California public adoption agencies. *Children & Youth Services Review, 16,* 123–131.

Maximus, Inc. (1984). *Child welfare statistical fact book: 1984: Substitute care and adoption.* Washington, DC: Office of Human Development Series.

Maza, P. L. (1983). Characteristics of children free for adoption. *Child Welfare* (Research Notes #2). Washington, DC: Children's Bureau, Administration for Children, Youth and Families.

McDermott, M. (1993). The case for agency adoption. *The Future of Children, 3*(1), 146–152.

Meezan, W., Katz, S., & Russo, E. M. (1978). *Adoptions without agencies: A study of independent adoptions.* New York: Child Welfare League of America.

Meezan, W., & Shireman, J. F. (1982). Foster parent adoption: A literature review. *Child Welfare, 61,* 525–535.

Meezan, W., & Shireman, J. F. (1985). *Care and commitment: Foster parent adoption decisions.* New York: State University of New York Press.

Michigan may limit race as factor in adoptions and foster care. (1986, December). *New York Times.*

National Committee for Adoption. (1989). *Adoption factbook: United States data issues, regulations, and resources.* Washington, DC: Author.

Pannor, R., & Baran, A. (1984). Open adoption as standard practice. *Child Welfare, 63,* 245–250.

Plantz, M. C., Hubbell, B. J., Barrett, B. J., & Dobrec, A. (1989). Indian child welfare: A status report. *Children Today, 18*(1), 24–29.

Rutter, M., & Rutter, M. (1993). *Developing minds: Challenge and continuity across the life span.* New York: Basic Books.

Simon, R. J., & Alstein, H. (1987). *Transracial adoptees and their families: A study of identity and commitment.* New York: Praeger.

State of California Department of Social Services. (1987). *Characteristics of relinquishment adoptions in California, July 1986: June 1987.* Sacramento: Author.

Stolley, K. S. (1993). Statistics on adoption in the United States. *The Future of Children, 3*(1), 26–42.

Tatara, T. (1994). Some additional explanations for the recent rise in the U.S. child substitute care flow data and future research questions. In R. P. Barth, J. D. Berrick, & N. Gilbert (Eds.), *Child welfare research review* (pp. 126–145). New York: Columbia University Press.

U.S. Department of Health and Human Services. (1981). *Study findings: National study of the incidence and severity of child abuse and neglect* (Publication No. OHDS 81-30325). Washington, DC: Author.

U.S. Senate, Committee on Finance. (1990). *Foster care, adoption assistance, and child welfare services.* Washington, DC: U.S. Government Printing Office.

Veronico, A. (1983). One church, one child: Placing children with special needs. *Children Today, 12,* 6–10.

Vroegh, K. S. (1992). *Transracial adoption: How it is 17 years later.* Chicago: Chicago Child Care Society.

Ward, M. (1981). Parental bonding in older-child adoptions. *Child Welfare, 60,* 24–34.

Weeks, N. B. (1953). *Adoption for school-age children in institutions.* New York: Child Welfare League of America.

Whitmore, W. H. (1876). *The law of adoption in the United States.* Albany, NJ: J. Munsell.

**Richard P. Barth, PhD,** is Hutto Patterson professor, School of Social Welfare, University of California at Berkeley, 207 Haviland Hall, Berkeley, CA 94720.

**For further information see**

Adolescent Pregnancy; Child Abuse and Neglect Overview; Child Care Services; Child Foster Care; Child Welfare Overview; Children: Group Care; Children: Mental Health; Children's Rights; Families Overview; Maternal and Child Health; Organizations: Context for Social Services Delivery; Poverty; Public Social Services; Youth Services.

**Key Words**

adoption | foster care
child welfare services | policy

READER'S GUIDE

## Adults

*The following entries contain information on this general topic:*

Adult Corrections
Adult Courts
Adult Day Care
Adult Foster Care
Adult Protective Services
Aging Overview
Aging: Direct Service
Aging: Public Policy Issues and Trends
Aging: Services
Aging: Social Work Practice
Baby Boomers
Elder Abuse
Men Overview
Men: Direct Practice
Women Overview
Women: Direct Practice

# Adult Corrections

C. Aaron McNeece

It is nowadays impossible to say definitely *the precise reason* for punishment.

—Nietzsche, *The Genealogy of Morals, Peoples, and Countries*

Although corrections can be defined in a more comprehensive manner, this entry deals only with jail and prison programs designed primarily to incarcerate adult offenders. According to Sullivan (1990), incarceration was originally a ritual for the redemption of sin through punishment, and its rhetoric often takes on a decidedly theological cast. As an integral part of the justice system, the prison rationalizes revenge through retribution and isolates it in accordance with social demands.

## History

For more than a thousand years the most common punishments for transgressions of moral codes and threats to the social order were death, slavery, maiming, or the payment of fines. However, from the Enlightenment to the late 20th century, the philosophy of utilitarianism dominated penal reform. One of the most influential Enlightenment writers on penal reform, Cesare Beccaria (1819), decreed that punishment should be prescribed according to the gravity of the offense, creating a hierarchy of penalties. Crime would be deterred less by the severity of punishment than by its certainty. Later reformers such as John Howard (1791/1973) translated this theory into specific penal reforms, and it was the driving force behind American penology beginning in the late 18th century.

An opposing philosophy, *deontology,* was articulated by Immanuel Kant in his work, *The Metaphysics of Morals* (1796/1991). Punishment would never be imposed just for the purpose of securing some extrinsic good such as the deterrence of crime; the penal law was to be a categorical imperative. Punishment was imposed because an individual had committed an offense (Heath, 1963). A case could be made that today penology has once more shifted from utilitarianism to retribution, based on the neo-Kantian principle of "just deserts."

The first American prison, opened in 1773, was an old converted copper mine near Simsbury, Connecticut George Washington used as a military prison. A few years later the Quakers created the Philadelphia Society for Alleviating the Miseries of the Public Prisons, with the goal of improving the situation of convicts by substituting imprisonment in solitary confinement for physical torture or the death penalty. The "penitentiary movement" began with the Walnut Street Jail in 1790, and the organization was renamed the Pennsylvania Prison Society in 1887 (Sullivan, 1990).

John Howard (1726–1790) initiated lay visiting in England's jails and prisons. The John Howard Society, a voluntary advocacy and prisoners' rights organization, was established in England in 1866 and in Massachusetts in 1889. The Correctional Association of New York was formed in 1844, and the Prisoners' Aid Association of Maryland was created in 1869 (Fox, 1983).

It is ironic that some writers date the beginning of professional social work to 1893, when settlement house workers lobbied to be placed on the program of the National Conference of Charities and Correction (Fox, 1983), although from the beginning the field of corrections had been anathema to social work. Correctional work had always been a part of philanthropy and preprofessional social work, but as social work became recognized as a profession, the field of corrections came to be viewed as beyond its concern. Part of this division was the result of the social work emphasis on self-determination. By its nature, corrections is coercive and difficult to reconcile with the principle of self-determination (Fox, 1983). By accepting employment in an authoritarian setting with nonvoluntary, unmotivated clients, the social worker in a correctional setting was often considered to be in violation of professional values (Treger, 1983).

The ideology, if not the reality, of correctional rehabilitation in the 1950s was rooted in the practices of therapeutic treatment, either psychotherapy or some form of group treatment. By the end of the 1960s, however, political and social events made rehabilitation in a prison setting seem impossible (Sullivan, 1990). The 1970s began with prison activism and violence on an unprecedented scale at Soledad, California, and Attica, New York, and culminated in the slaughter of 33 inmates in Santa Fe, New Mexico, in 1980. Since then, American prisons have been plagued by overcrowding, violence, inmate abuse, and recidivism. There have been few resources directed at improving treatment or living conditions.

## Functions of Incarceration

### Liberal Ideologies

Liberal ideologies assume that most of the defects of human behavior have their origins in the social environment and that the key to changing offenders lies in learning how to manipulate either these environments or their psychological consequences (Shover & Einstadter, 1988). Liberals assume that incarceration should provide treatment to rehabilitate, reeducate, and reintegrate offenders into the community. Liberals, including some social workers, have been active in the correctional reform movement (Cullen & Gilbert, 1982) as a reaction to the conservative ideologies and punitive strategies popular in the 1970s.

### Conservative Ideologies

According to the conservative view, the primary cause of crime is inadequate control over a fundamentally flawed human nature (Currie, 1985). Conservatives support the notion of retribution or just deserts, not necessarily as vengeance, but because it serves utilitarian purposes as well. Punishment is not only proper, but necessary, because it reinforces the social order. Deterrence is an expected outcome of incarceration, because punishing offenders for their misdeeds will reduce both the probability of their repeating the act (specific deterrence) and the likelihood of others committing criminal acts (general deterrence). The incapacitation function of incarceration reflects an especially pessimistic view of human nature: Offenders probably cannot be rehabilitated, but they cannot commit other crimes against people outside the prison as long as they are incarcerated (Von Hirsch, 1976).

### Radical Ideologies

Radical ideologies are based on the view that the nature and rate of crime in America are inevitable results of the structure and dynamics of the capitalist economic system (Gibbons, 1979). According to Rusche and Kirchheimer (1939), the threat of incarceration was an effective capitalist device for controlling the labor supply. Radicals do not pursue the naive belief that crime can be eradicated, but they do argue that the types and rates of crime could be substantially affected by changes in the political economy. Because of their focus on the larger social environment, radicals have devoted little effort to reforming correctional programs aimed at individual offenders. To the extent that reforms actually are adopted, they only strengthen the ability of the correctional system to control problem populations. According to this view, the only hope for meaningful change is a socialist economy (Schmidt, 1977).

## Jails

Despite having the longest history of any type of penal institution, jails have been studied less than prisons have and are not ordinarily included in a discussion of corrections. Before jails there were unscalable pits, suspended cages, and sturdy trees to which prisoners were chained pending trial (Shover & Einstadter, 1988). Jails are particularly local institutions, the majority of which are dirty and dilapidated and hold only a few prisoners, are located in rural areas, and were built 50 to 80 years ago (Flynn, 1983). A smaller number of jails are newer, are located in urban areas, and may hold several thousand inmates. The latter type of jail currently houses most of the jail population.

Such disparate groups as people awaiting trial, inmates serving misdemeanor sentences, mentally ill people, alleged parole violators, felony prisoners in transit, intoxicated people "drying out," and juveniles may be found in the same jail. Jail inmates are disproportionately people of color, poor people, and disadvantaged people—leading one critic to refer to the jail as "the ultimate ghetto" of the criminal justice system (Goldfarb, 1975). A former inmate, John Irwin (1985), disputed the notion that jails house dangerous criminals. He argued that jail inmates are people who are not well integrated into conventional society; have few ties to social networks; and are perceived by their jailers as irksome, offensive, and threatening rather than dangerous.

Jails are administered by the police, usually the county sheriff. However, a rapidly growing practice is the contracting of local jail services to a private corporation. In 1984, the Corrections Corporation of America opened the first private correctional facility in Houston under contract to the U.S. Immigration and Naturalization Service. By 1991, Texas had 24 for-profit jails and prisons (Bowman, Hakim, & Seidenstat, 1993). Because of the expense of new construction, more jurisdictions have been entering into contracts involving for-profit organizations. Usually, the local government issues bonds to pay for jail construction costs and pledges the revenues generated from the lease of the facility to retire the bonds. However, if revenues are not as high as expected, the county's credit rating may suffer. In addition, several of these "rent-a-cell" arrangements have resulted in lawsuits against the county for escapes, assaults, riots, and fires (Bowman et al., 1993). Privatization also makes accountability more difficult and costly, because it adds at least one more layer of bureaucracy (Keating, 1990).

The number of jail inmates per 100,000 residents ranges from 37 in Iowa to 276 in Georgia (U.S. Department of Justice, 1988). In June 1991, jails held an estimated 426,479 people, an increase of 5.2 percent from the previous year (U.S. Department of Justice, 1992c). In 1992, the jail population had risen another 4.2 percent, to 444,584 (U.S. Department of Justice, 1993b). The average daily population of the nation's jails more than doubled between 1978 and 1988, with the growth rate in the female population exceeding that of males. There were just over 10 million admissions to jails in 1991 and just under 10 million releases (U.S. Department of Justice, 1992c).

Other facts noted in the Annual Survey of Jails conducted by the U.S. Department of Justice (1992c) included the following:

- Males constituted 90.7 percent and females 9.3 percent of all jail inmates. White non-Hispanic people were 41.1 percent of the jail population; black non-Hispanic people, 43.4 percent; Hispanic people, 14.2 percent; and non-Hispanic people of other races, 1.2 percent.
- Unconvicted inmates (awaiting trial or arraignment) constituted 51 percent of the total jail population; convicted inmates (serving a sentence or probation or parole violators) constituted 49 percent.
- Jails were operating at 101 percent of rated capacity in 1991, down from 104 percent in 1990 and 108 percent in 1989.
- Almost half (47 percent) of the jails held inmates because of crowding at other jails or prisons.
- Of the jurisdictions surveyed, 27 percent had at least one jail under court order to limit the population, and 30 percent were under court order to improve one or more conditions of confinement.
- In 1991, 546 inmate deaths were reported in jails, with only 51 percent being for "natural" causes. AIDS-related deaths accounted for 15 percent of all 1991 reported deaths in jail.

### Jail Conditions

Many jails are filthy, dilapidated, unsafe facilities with inadequate food and medical care and weak or absent supervision (Shover & Einstadter, 1988). Among the 508 jails surveyed in 1991 with average daily populations of at least 100 inmates, 136 were under a court order to reduce overcrowding. The courts also had ordered 66 jails to provide recreational facilities, 58 to provide medical services, 50 to provide libraries, 46 to provide more staff, and 37 to appropriately classify and separate inmates. Forty of these largest jails were under court order to improve the "totality of conditions," including such things as eliminating fire hazards and providing educational programs (U.S. Department of Justice, 1992c). Smaller jails sometimes find it even more difficult to provide specialized services or to adequately separate juveniles from adults or convicted inmates from those awaiting trial. Race relations are so strained in some jails that African American, Hispanic, and white inmates are segregated.

Most jails are designed to maximize the smooth, efficient processing of large numbers of inmates, and there is little concern about the nearly total absence of constructive daily activities for inmates (Gibbs, 1983). The daily routine in jail is one of unrelieved idleness. Watching television, playing cards, and making idle conversation are the most common forms of recreation. Only a small proportion of inmates have access to any social or rehabilitative services (Shover & Einstadter, 1988).

Overcrowding remains a critical problem in jails, although rated jail capacity did increase by 9 percent in 1991, primarily because of court-ordered construction. Even so, occupancy in the nation's jails was 101 percent of capacity that year and 107 percent in the larger jails (U.S. Department of Justice, 1992c). Construction of new facilities had reduced occupancy to 99 percent of capacity by 1992, but overcrowding was still a major problem in the nation's largest jails, with occupancy running at 114 percent (U.S. Department of Justice, 1993b). Jails are frequently overcrowded as a direct result of prison overcrowding. Because prison beds were not available for 18,304 convicted offenders in 1991, jails were used for the overflow. Although the national average was 2.1 percent, in Louisiana 25.1 percent of all jail inmates were state prisoners for whom there were no beds (U.S. Department of Justice, 1993a). Although it is difficult to assess the extent of this practice, a number of local jurisdictions are also using jails as an alternative to prison, because they have more control over the type and severity of punishment received at the local level. In certain Florida counties, for example, one offender might receive a maximum one-year jail sentence for a misdemeanor drug offense, whereas a felony drug offender might receive either probation or a 60- to 90-day sentence in the state prison (McNeece, 1992).

By 1992 nine of the largest 503 jurisdictions were operating boot camp programs, which served about 4 percent of the jail population. In these same jurisdictions, 275 jails provided drug treatment; 295, alcohol treatment; 212, psychological counseling; and 350, educational programming. In those jails offering alcohol or drug treatment, the participation rate was less than 10 percent (U.S. Department of Justice, 1993b).

**Juveniles in Jail**

More than 100,000 juveniles were admitted to adult jails each year during the mid-1980s, with the average daily population varying between 1,500 and 1,700 (Schwartz, 1989). Despite two decades of "reform," including a specific amendment to federal law to remove juveniles from jail, the average daily population of juveniles in jail dropped only slightly by 1988, from 1,740 to 1,451 (U.S. Department of Justice, 1992c). Some believe that this is a conservative figure; another official report showed that the average daily juvenile population climbed to 2,250 by 1989 (Flanagan & Maguire, 1990).

Legislation introduced in 1973 would have banned the admission of juveniles to adult jails, but it was eventually changed so that juveniles could still be kept in jail as long as they were separated from adult prisoners. In many cases this legislation actually worsened conditions for juveniles. To comply with the new law, juveniles were locked up in drunk tanks, segregation units, women's cell blocks, abandoned sections of jails, and makeshift units in storage areas (Schwartz, 1989).

**Women in Jail**

Although women compose fewer than 10 percent of the jail population, they experience a number of problems more seriously than men. Jailed women are more likely to have a substance abuse problem, particularly with cocaine, and to be in need of treatment (U.S. Department of Justice, 1992f). Health services in jails are generally inadequate, but women's health problems are even less likely to receive proper attention (McNeece, 1992). It is also estimated that about 80 percent of women offenders are mothers, and two-thirds of all women in jail have children under the age of 18 (U.S. Department of Justice, 1992e). In addition to the trauma of separation from their children while in jail, women inmates also run the risk of having their parental rights terminated (Johnston, 1992). Sexual harassment of female inmates by male guards is another serious issue (Barry, 1990).

## Prisons

The stereotype of the prison as a "big house" holding 2,000 or 3,000 inmates has never been an accurate view of the U.S. prison, and it has become increasingly inaccurate since World War II (Irwin, 1980). Many states have never relied on large institutions to house convicted offenders, preferring to use smaller, decentralized road camps or prison farms. Nonetheless, large prisons do exist. In 1990, California had 17 of the nation's 26 largest prisons, including one with an average daily population of 7,443 inmates. On the other hand, 786 of 1,207 state prisons had fewer than 500 inmates in 1990. About 36.3 percent of all state prisoners resided in maximum security facilities in 1990, with 50.4 percent in medium security and 13.3 percent in minimum security programs (U.S. Department of Justice, 1992a).

**Imprisonment in the United States**

The United States has the highest proportion of its citizens in prison of any major industrialized nation (Selke, 1993). In 1988 the rate was approaching 300 inmates per 100,000 population. Canada, the next most punitive nation, incarcerated about one-third and the Netherlands, about one-tenth as many. There were 803,334 inmates in state prisons on December 31, 1992, and another 80,259 in federal prisons—an increase of 7.2 percent over the previous year's total prison population. Another 18,191 inmates were housed in local jails because of overcrowding in state prisons (U.S. Department of Justice, 1993c).

The number of prisoners in custody per 100,000 population in 1992 ranged from 259 in the Northeast to 355 in the South, whereas the total combined rate for the nation was 329 per 100,000. California (478) and Texas (477) had the highest incarceration rates. A total of 480,000 people were admitted to prison during 1991, and 436,991 were released (U.S. Department of Justice, 1993a). Among those people living in state or federal prisons in 1991 (U.S. Department of Justice, 1993d),

- White people composed 35 percent of the population; black people, 46 percent; and Hispanic people, 17 percent.
- Women accounted for 5.7 percent of the population.
- Sixty-five percent had less than a high school education.
- Sixty-nine percent had never earned more than $15,000 per year.
- Fewer than half were sentenced for a violent crime, about a fourth for a property crime, and a fifth for a drug crime.
- Women were more likely than men to be incarcerated for larceny, fraud, and drug charges.
- Men were more likely than women to be in prison for robbery, assault, and burglary.

- There were 1,856 deaths, of which only 43 percent were from "natural" causes; 26 percent were from acquired immune deficiency syndrome (AIDS).

In one of the earliest attempts to study the factors influencing prison populations, Rusche and Kirchheimer (1939) concluded that the economic system determines both the penal system and the penal population. Society had to keep masses of urban, lower-class workers under control to guarantee their labor; the threat of prison or an almshouse was one way to accomplish this. Rothman's (1971) interpretation of history regarded this conclusion as too simplistic. The invention of the penitentiary was an attempt to stabilize society during a period of tremendous social upheaval. It was "an effort to insure the cohesion of the community in new and changing circumstances" (Rothman, 1971, p. xviii).

Zimring and Hawkins (1991) argued that there is no automatic link between rates of imprisonment and social indicators such as crime rates, unemployment, the age structure of the population, or trends in drug arrests. The authors attributed the growth in prison populations more to "incentives toward crowding and toward overconfinement in the cost structure of imprisonment" (p. 222) than to deliberate legislative policy. They cited as another contributing factor the allocation of responsibility for fiscal matters to levels of government that do not determine levels of imprisonment. Prison populations have increased dramatically in recent years, with state prisons operating at 118 percent of capacity in 1992 and federal prisons at 137 percent of capacity. In 1992, 14 states were operating at 125 percent or more of their highest rated capacity (U.S. Department of Justice, 1993c).

One could easily argue that drug-related crime is a major contributing factor in increasing imprisonment in the United States, with a 281 percent increase in the number of drug offenders represented in the prison population between 1986 and 1991 (U.S. Department of Justice, 1993d). In 1990, drug offenses accounted for about one in three commitments to state prison. Among all inmates in 1991, 62 percent reported being regular users of illicit drugs before their imprisonment.

The mean length of sentence for state inmates in 1991 was 150 months, and the median was 108 months. The mean and median sentences for violent offenses (such as murder, kidnapping, rape, and assault) were 216 and 180 months, respectively; for property offenses, 116 and 60 months; and for drug offenses, 95 and 60 months (U.S. Department of Justice, 1993a).

Time served is a more revealing indicator of correctional policy, however. As many states adopted mandatory sentencing laws and eliminated parole, prison populations swelled dangerously. State prisons, although not as overcrowded as federal prisons, frequently operate under federal court orders to reduce overcrowding and improve other conditions. They have responded by increasing "good time" or "gain time," leading to what some critics call a "revolving door" correctional system (Sullivan, 1990). For all states, in 1991 the average inmate served only 32 percent of the sentence imposed (U.S. Department of Justice, 1992b).

The growth rate in the number of sentenced federal prisoners has increased more than twice as fast as the comparable rate for state prisoners: 15.9 percent versus 6.8 percent for 1992 and 12.5 percent versus 6.4 percent for 1991 (U.S. Department of Justice, 1993a). Both this growth rate and the increasing length of sentences are due in part to the introduction of mandatory minimum sentences for offenders prosecuted under federal law—for example, five years for an offense involving five grams of "crack" cocaine (U.S. Department of Justice, 1992b).

### Privatization

Private, for-profit corporations have a long history of involvement in the provision of correctional services, from laundry and food services, to medical and psychiatric services, to complete prison operation. Kentucky transferred the state prison to private hands in 1825 (Sellin, 1976). In 1851 the California legislature, attempting to avoid the deficits that were common in state-operated prison systems in the East, granted a 10-year lease to two businessmen to provide land, build a prison, and operate it (Durham, 1993). By 1885, 13 states had turned at least a portion of their inmates over to private corporations, but by 1923 not a single state continued this practice. Disclosures and allegations of inmate abuse, opposition from organized labor, disputes with private contractors, and the reform movement had returned corrections to the public sector (McCrie, 1993).

However, private interest and activity in corrections never completely disappeared. The prison population explosion, coupled with increasing demands for cost cutting, led to a revival of privatization. By 1989, eight states were contracting with private companies to build and operate 60 facilities with 10,750 beds. The major incentives for this type of arrangement were speed and cost. In some cases construction time has been cut by 80 percent, and cost savings of 3 percent to 40 percent for private prison operation have been reported (Joel, 1993). Nevertheless, the debate continues over whether the quality of private services is as good and whether inmate rights are as well protected in private prisons (Press, 1990).

**Prison Conditions**

Selke (1993) maintained that four overriding features of prison life must be considered: (1) violence, (2) corruption, (3) racism, and (4) boredom. Violence, always a fact of prison life, has been exacerbated in recent years because of overcrowding. Corruption also has been a historical problem in closed prisons as both inmates and staff attempt to ameliorate the strains of living and working in such an unpleasant atmosphere. Racism has been a commonly recognized fact of prison life since the civil rights movement of the 1960s. According to Irwin (1980), "the hate and distrust between white and black prisoners constitute the most powerful source of divisions" in prison (p. 183).

Boredom is a reflection of the absence of meaningful activities for most inmates. Prisoners are confined to their living and sleeping unit an average of nearly 14 hours per day, 18.5 hours per day for those in maximum security units (U.S. Department of Justice, 1992a). Even in the best correctional programs, the routine that pervades prison life compels some inmates to bizarre and outrageous conduct. An air of distrust permeates most interactions and most relationships in prison. Those who do well on the inside may not be getting the kind of treatment necessary to readjust to life outside prison. Shover and Einstadter (1988) recalled one California inmate who made a "model" adjustment to prison life but turned catatonic while being prepared for release.

Other serious issues for inmates are the lack of autonomy over one's actions, excessive noise, and the lack of privacy (Shover & Einstadter, 1988). State inmates have an average of 56 square feet of living space, and federal inmates have only 44 square feet. Only 31.3 percent of state inmates are housed in one-person sleeping quarters; one in four sleeps in an area shared with 50 or more inmates (U.S. Department of Justice, 1992a).

About one-third of all inmates in state prisons in 1992 had participated in a drug abuse treatment program while incarcerated. However, only 13.4 percent are currently in treatment, and only 22.2 percent of those inmates who were under the influence of a drug at the time of their offense are in treatment. Only 6.2 percent of all inmates were court-ordered to have drug treatment while incarcerated (U.S. Department of Justice, 1993a). Recognizing the severity of the drug problem, 39 states use some type of diagnostic or assessment procedure for all newly sentenced inmates; 44 states allow Alcoholics Anonymous, Narcotics Anonymous, or Cocaine Anonymous groups to meet once or twice per week in prisons; 31 states make individual therapy or counseling available in prison; 36 states have group counseling; 30 states have some type of intensive residential program, frequently based on a therapeutic community model; and 44 states have some type of short-term drug education program for inmates (Lipton, Falkin, & Wexler, 1992).

The reasons inmates enroll in treatment, education, or other types of prison programs may have more to do with boredom and the lack of normal human interaction than with a rational plan for rehabilitation. Inmates often try to convince prison or parole authorities to increase their "good time" and grant them an earlier release by enrolling in every prison program available as a way to appear rehabilitated (McNeece & Lusk, 1979; Schmidt, 1977).

According to a national survey of state prison inmates, 65 percent had less than a high school education, and 31 percent had participated in basic (less than ninth grade) or high school–level educational programs since entering prison. Another 12 percent had participated in college-level programs, and 31 percent, in vocational training. Participation rates were about the same for men and women (U.S. Department of Justice, 1993d). A study by Sarri (1993) indicated that educational offerings to inmates with physical handicaps, developmental disabilities, or problems with the English language are extremely limited.

About seven of 10 inmates have a work assignment in prison, with the two most common being general janitorial (13 percent) and food preparation (13 percent). The mean number of hours worked per week in these assignments was 32. About two-thirds of inmates are paid for their work assignments, at an average wage of $0.56 per hour. Work assignments earn extra privileges or good time credit for 43 percent of inmates (U.S. Department of Justice, 1993d).

**Juveniles in Prison**

Approximately 1.5 percent of all new admissions to state prisons are juveniles (U.S. Department of Justice, 1992d). Between 25 percent and 30 percent of all juveniles in prison are in Florida, where prosecutors as well as judges are granted broad discretion to try them as adults (McNeece, 1994a; Schwartz, 1989). Juveniles are the most likely candidates in prison for sexual abuse, including gang rape (Irwin, 1980). The number of juvenile offenders waived to adult courts increased by about 78 percent between 1985 and 1989, but the waiver of nonwhite male juvenile drug offenders to adult criminal courts increased by an astounding 850 percent (National Center for Juvenile Justice, 1991). This trend has resulted in an increasing number of juveniles being committed to adult prisons, with the majority being youths of color. It is alarming to note that young black men are more likely to be in prison or under some type of justice system supervision than to be enrolled in a college or university (McNeece, 1994b).

### Women in Prison

The rate of incarceration for women has grown much faster than the rate for men (U.S. Department of Justice, 1993c). Women experience many of the same problems in prison as they do in jail, but the problems are exacerbated by longer stays. Problems that are unique to women include pregnancy, childbirth, and the loss of custody of children. More than 76 percent of the women in prison have children, and 88 percent of those women have children under the age of 18 years (U.S. Department of Justice, 1991). Generally, female prisoners are given fewer opportunities than male prisoners for education, training, and other services while in prison, although these disparities have been challenged in the courts (Shover & Einstadter, 1988).

An early study on women's prisons found informal social organizations that differ markedly from men's prisons (Giallombardo, 1966). Psuedo-families sometimes helped ease the burdens of confinement by providing social support for female inmates. Perhaps more relevant issues for today's incarcerated women are drug treatment, health care, education and vocational training, and child rearing.

## Prisoners' Legal Rights

Although inmates in jails and prisons have the same constitutional rights as all other citizens, some disturbing trends have been apparent both in cases that the U.S. Supreme Court has reviewed and those that it has refused to review on appeal. In *McClesky v. Zant* (1991) the Court made it more difficult for an inmate to file a habeas petition in a second or subsequent appeal. During the next term, in a case involving a death row inmate (*Herrara v. Collins,* 1992), the Court stated emphatically that habeas corpus relief in the federal courts is not appropriate when the petitioner's only claim is "actual innocence."

In *Crawford-EL v. Britton* (1992) the Court refused to hear the appeal of an inmate whose papers were seized during pending *pro se* federal litigation. Also in 1992, in *Holt v. Caspari,* the Court refused to hear an appeal from a Missouri inmate who, after pleading "no contest" to a "minor infraction" of prison rules, had the charge changed to a "major violation." The Court ruled that this action did not deprive him of due process. Also in 1992, an appeal was filed on behalf of a pretrial detainee in Georgia who had committed suicide while in the jail's isolation unit. The Court refused to acknowledge in *Boggs v. Jones* that there was a violation of the detainee's legal rights, despite a finding of deliberate indifference to the inmate's medical needs and the jailer's failure to correct a known dangerous condition conducive to suicide. (The detainee had told the jailer that he would kill himself if not removed from isolation. The jailer told him to "go ahead.")

## Future of Incarceration

Corrections in the United States is a growth industry. States and communities do not seem to have the capacity to build jails and prisons fast enough to keep pace with the growing inmate population. The United States may be approaching a crisis that will force a reexamination of certain assumptions about minimum mandatory sentences, the use of parole, and imprisonment for illicit drug use. There is already a dramatic increase in the use of alternatives to jails and prisons—such as pretrial release, electronic monitoring, victim restitution, and community service programs. The cost and relative ineffectiveness of traditional incarceration programs may eventually direct attention to less restrictive, more efficient, and more humane methods of handling adult offenders.

The Violent Crime Control and Law Enforcement Act of 1994, the largest crime bill in the history of the country, emphasizes the construction of new correctional facilities. It provides $9.7 billion for new prisons, boot camps, and "other alternative correctional facilities that free traditional prison and jail space for confinement of violent offenders" (U.S. Department of Justice, 1994). The most highly publicized portion of the act, funding for 100,000 new police officers, will receive $8.8 billion, whereas prevention programs get only $6.1 billion. Although this act may result in higher incarceration rates because of the funding of new facilities and the provisions for mandatory life sentences for certain federal offenders, there may be some relief to this trend because of the "safety valve" clause that exempts other offenders from mandatory minimum drug sentences. The long-range effects of this important legislation may not be known for at least a decade.

## References


Barry, E. (1990). Women in prison. In C. Lefcourt (Ed.), *Women and the law* (pp. 1–35). Deerfield, IL: Clark, Boardman & Callahan.

Beccaria, C. (1819). *An essay on crimes and punishments* (2nd ed.). Philadelphia: Philip H. Nicklin.

Boggs v. Jones, C.A. 11. (1992).

Bowman, G., Hakim, S., & Seidenstat, P. (1993). *Privatizing correctional institutions.* New Brunswick, NJ: Transaction Books.

Crawford-EL v. Britton, C.A. D.C., 951 F2d 1314 (1992).

Cullen, F., & Gilbert, K. (1982). *Reaffirming rehabilitation*. Cincinnati: Anderson.

Currie, E. (1985). *Confronting crime.* New York: Pantheon Books.

Durham, A. (1993). The future of correctional privatization. In G. Bowman, S. Hakim, & P. Seidenstat (Eds.), *Privatizing correctional institutions* (pp. 33–49). New Brunswick, NJ: Transaction Books.

Flanagan, T., & Maguire, K. (1990). *Sourcebook of criminal justice statistics: 1987.* Washington, DC: U.S. Department of Justice, Bureau of Justice Statistics.

Flynn, E. (1983). Jails. In S. H. Kadish (Ed.), *Encyclopedia of crime and justice* (pp. 915–922). New York: Macmillan.

Fox, V. (1983). Foreword. In A. R. Roberts (Ed.), *Social work in juvenile and criminal justice settings* (pp. ix–xxvii). Springfield, IL: Charles C Thomas.

Giallombardo, R. (1966). *Society of women*. New York: John Wiley & Sons.

Gibbons, D. (1979). *The criminological enterprise*. Englewood Cliffs, NJ: Prentice Hall.

Gibbs, J. (1983). Problems and priorities: Perceptions of jail custodians and social service providers. *Journal of Criminal Justice, 11,* 327–338.

Goldfarb, R. (1975). *Jails*. Garden City, NY: Anchor Books.

Heath, J. (1963). *Eighteenth century penal theory*. London: Oxford University Press.

Herrara v. Collins, 113 S. Ct. 858 (1992).

Holt v. Caspari, C.A. 8, 961 F2d 1370 (1992).

Howard, J. (1973). *Prisons and lazarettos*. Montclair, NJ: Patterson Smith. (Original work published 1791)

Irwin, J. (1980). *Prisons in turmoil*. Boston: Little, Brown.

Irwin, J. (1985). *The jail*. Berkeley: University of California Press.

Joel, D. (1993). The privatization of secure adult prisons: Issues and evidence. In G. Bowman, S. Hakim, & P. Seidenstat (Eds.), *Privatizing correctional institutions* (pp. 51–74). New Brunswick, NJ: Transaction Books.

Johnston, D. (1992). *Children of offenders*. Pasadena, CA: Pacific Oaks Center for Children of Incarcerated Parents.

Kant, I. (1991). *The metaphysics of morals*. New York: Cambridge University Press. (Original work published 1796)

Keating, M. (1990). Public over private: Monitoring the performance of privately operated prisons and jails. In D. McDonald (Ed.), *Private prisons and the public interest* (pp. 130–154). New Brunswick, NJ: Rutgers University Press.

Lipton, D., Falkin, G., & Wexler, H. (1992). Correctional drug abuse treatment in the United States: An overview. In C. Leukefeld & F. Tims (Eds.), *Drug abuse treatment in prisons and jails* (pp. 8–30) (NIDA Research Monograph 118). Washington, DC: U.S. Government Printing Office.

McClesky v. Zant, 111 St. Ct. 1454 (1991).

McCrie, R. (1993). Private correction: The delicate balance. In G. Bowman, S. Hakim, & P. Seidenstat (Eds.), *Privatizing correctional institutions* (pp. 19–32). New Brunswick, NJ: Transaction Publishers.

McNeece, C. (1992). *An evaluation of anti-drug abuse act grant-funded substance abuse treatment programs in Florida*. Tallahassee: Florida State University, Institute for Health and Human Services Research.

McNeece, C. (1994a). Juvenile justice in Florida. In A. Imershein, M. Mathis, & C. McNeece (Eds.), *Who cares for the children*? New York: General Hall.

McNeece, C. (1994b). National trends in offenses and case dispositions. In A. Roberts (Ed.), *Critical issues in crime and justice* (pp. 155–168). Newbury Park, CA: Sage Publications.

McNeece, C., & Lusk, M. (1979). A consumer's view of correctional policy: Inmate attitudes regarding determinate sentencing, *Criminal Justice and Behavior, 6,* 383–389.

National Center for Juvenile Justice. (1991). *National estimates of juvenile court delinquency cases: 1985–89* (National Juvenile Court Data Archive). Pittsburgh: Author.

Press, A. (1990). The good, the bad, and the ugly: Private prisons in the 1980s. In D. McDonald (Ed.), *Private prisons and the public interest* (pp. 19–41). New Brunswick, NJ: Rutgers University Press.

Rothman, D. (1971). *The discovery of the asylum: Social order and disorder in the new republic.* Boston: Little, Brown.

Rusche, G., & Kirchheimer, O. (1939). *Punishment and social structure.* New York: Columbia University Press.

Sarri, R. (1993, November). *Educational programs in state departments of corrections: A survey of the states.* Paper presented at the American Society of Criminology, Phoenix, AZ.

Schmidt, J. (1977). *Demystifying parole.* Lexington, MA: D. C. Heath.

Schwartz, I. (1989). *(In)justice for juveniles: Rethinking the best interests of the child.* Lexington, MA: Lexington Books.

Selke, W. (1993). *Prisons in crisis.* Bloomington: Indiana University Press.

Sellin, T. (1976). *Slavery and the penal system.* New York: Elsevier.

Shover, N., & Einstadter, W. (1988). *Analyzing American corrections.* Belmont, CA: Wadsworth.

Sullivan, L. (1990). *The prison reform movement: Forlorn hope.* Boston: Twayne.

Treger, H. (1983). Social work in the justice system: An overview. In A. R. Roberts (Ed.), *Social work in juvenile and criminal justice settings* (pp. 7–17). Springfield, IL: Charles C Thomas.

U.S. Department of Justice, Bureau of Justice Statistics. (1988). *Census of local jails 1988* (NCJ-127101). Washington, DC: U.S. Government Printing Office.

U.S. Department of Justice, Bureau of Justice Statistics. (1991). *Women in prison* (NCJ-127991). Washington, DC: U.S. Government Printing Office.

U.S. Department of Justice, Bureau of Justice Statistics. (1992a). *Census of state and federal correctional facili-*

*ties, 1990*. Washington, DC: U.S. Government Printing Office.

U.S. Department of Justice, Bureau of Justice Statistics. (1992b). *Drugs, crime, and the justice system* (NCJ-133652). Washington, DC: U.S. Government Printing Office.

U.S. Department of Justice, Bureau of Justice Statistics. (1992c). *Jail inmates, 1991* (NCJ-134726). Washington, DC: U.S. Government Printing Office.

U.S. Department of Justice, Bureau of Justice Statistics. (1992d). *National corrections reporting program, 1987* (NCJ-134928). Washington, DC: U.S. Government Printing Office.

U.S. Department of Justice, Bureau of Justice Statistics. (1992e). *Women in jail, 1989* (NCJ-134732). Washington, DC: U.S. Government Printing Office.

U.S. Department of Justice, National Institute of Justice. (1992f). *Drug use forecasting: 1991 annual report.* Washington, DC: U.S. Government Printing Office.

U.S. Department of Justice, Bureau of Justice Statistics. (1993a). *Correctional populations in the United States, 1991* (NCJ-142729). Washington, DC: U.S. Government Printing Office.

U.S. Department of Justice, Bureau of Justice Statistics. (1993b). *Jail inmates, 1992* (NCJ-143284). Washington, DC: U.S. Government Printing Office.

U.S. Department of Justice, Bureau of Justice Statistics. (1993c). *Prisoners in 1992* (NCJ-141874). Washington, DC: U.S. Government Printing Office.

U.S. Department of Justice, Bureau of Justice Statistics. (1993d). *Survey of state prison inmates, 1991* (NCJ-136949). Washington, DC: U.S. Government Printing Office.

U.S. Department of Justice. (1994). *Fact sheet:* Violent Crime Control and Law Enforcement Act of 1994 (NCJ-FS000067). Washington, DC: U.S. Government Printing Office.

Von Hirsch, A. (1976). *Doing justice.* New York: Hill and Wang.

Zimring, F., & Hawkins, G. (1991). *The scale of imprisonment.* Chicago: University of Chicago Press.

## Further Reading

Cromwell, P. F., & Killinger, G. G. (1994). *Community-based corrections.* St. Paul, MN: West.

Fox, V. (1985). *Introduction to corrections.* Englewood Cliffs, NJ: Prentice Hall.

Haas, K. C., & Alpert, G. P. (1991). *The dilemmas of corrections: Contemporary readings* (2nd ed.). Prospect Heights, IL: Waveland Press.

Meninger, K. (1968). *The crime of punishment.* New York: Viking Press.

Snarr, R. W. (1992). *Introduction to corrections* (2nd ed.). Dubuque, IA: William C. Brown.

**C. Aaron McNeece, PhD,** is professor of social work and director, Institute for Health and Human Services Research, Florida State University, 2035 E. Dirac Drive, Tallahassee, FL 32310.

### For further information see

Adult Courts; Criminal Behavior; Criminal Justice: Class, Race, and Gender Issues; Civil Rights; Health Care: Jails and Prisons; Juvenile and Family Courts; Probation and Parole; Rehabilitation of Criminal Offenders; Sentencing of Criminal Offenders.

**Key Words**
adult corrections
criminal justice system
prisoners

# Adult Courts

**Paul M. Isenstadt**

This entry explains the role of social work in the criminal justice system, with a focus on the adult criminal court process. Although a small cadre of social workers have combined law and social work in their professional education, most social workers have little contact with the adult court in serving their clients and lack the knowledge necessary to render that service effectively. Such knowledge, however, is necessary to effect social change.

## Foundation and Structure of the Court System

To understand the court system, one must first understand the building blocks of law: the Constitution; statutes; common law; criminal versus civil law; adversary system; and case law (Berman, 1971).

### Constitution

The federal Constitution is the major component of law with which all other components, including state constitutions—all states maintain their own constitutions—and statutes at the federal, state, and municipal level must be consistent. The U.S. Constitution serves as the framework for the review and interpretation of all statutes. The process of judicial review (*Marbury v. Madison*) culminates in the U.S. Supreme Court as the ultimate authority; the Court reviews less than 300 cases each year.

### Statutes

Statutes are the laws passed by the legislative branch of government, enforced by the executive branch, and interpreted by the judicial branch. Knowledge of the statutes pertaining to various aspects of social work practice, in public welfare, mental health, and the criminal field (or justice system) is indispensable for the social work practitioner.

**Common Law**

The common law is a composite of ancient traditional doctrines and judicial opinions reformulated and accepted as a component of our system of jurisprudence. One can think of it as the distillation of centuries of judicial opinions and analysis. An example would be the doctrine of *parens patriae.* This concept, which goes back to the reign of Edward I in England (1272–1307), allowed the kings of England to stand in the role of parent to members of the nobility found to be "idiots or lunatics" (Stone, 1988, p. 800)—the original intent being to protect property, not people. It is transformed in our legal system such that the state can act in what it takes to be the best interest of a citizen who is mentally incapacitated or a minor. The *parens patriae* doctrine spawned the juvenile court, which was introduced into our legal system in 1899 in Chicago (Platt, 1969). In addition, it formed the basis for our mental health civil commitment laws, which until *O'Connor v. Donaldson* challenged the concept that *parens patriae* could not justify the removal of procedural safeguards to those who evidence symptoms of mental illness. Although deinstitutionalization somewhat contributed to the challenge of *parens patriae,* this common law principle still exists in public welfare, juvenile justice, health care, and other areas of social welfare. The debate regarding the extent of government interest in the lives of citizens remains a source of controversy in both the written and electronic media.

Thus, common law may challenge our philosophy and practice in the field of social work and may force us to examine the level of legal intrusiveness in the lives of those with whom we work (Beis, 1984).

**Criminal versus Civil Law**

The role of civil statutes are often used to enforce the role of government in carrying out its role of *parens patriae.* Accompanying these statutes are the rules for interpretation and enforcement known as "regulations," which guide local, state, and federal agencies. The removal of certain behaviors from the realm of civil law and their assignment to the realm of criminal statutory law was first noted in *Lessard v. Schmidt* (1972). Since then, criminal statutes have proliferated as society continues to attempt to regulate aberrant behavior, especially crime and violence, through the criminal system.

**Adversary System**

Our legal system is based on the idea that the process of argument will ultimately produce the truth. Although the adversarial procedure is often found to be confrontational and even humiliating, we cling to it in preference to the continental inquisitorial system in which the judge not only serves as the ultimate authority, but also conducts a major part of the investigation.

**Case Law**

The basis of case law are decisions made by judges in previous cases. Often noted under the concept *stare decisis* (let the previous decision stand), it is a major influence in our interpretation of the law. Although many citizens may be unable to identify the Bill of Rights or other statutes, they certainly are familiar with the Miranda rights (*Miranda v. Arizona*), which is part of case law. The role of case law in effecting social change is a slow but often effective process.

## Structure of the American Court System

Because the U.S. court system is structured differently among the 50 states and the federal court system, the semantics vary; they are often confusing and in no way maintain consistency across jurisdictions. The system includes the full range of courts, from the local municipal courts to the Supreme Court—the court of last resort. Social work practitioners should become familiar with these courts and their jurisdictions.

The court system is structured in various levels and jurisdictions. In civil matters, for example, courts decide the amount of monetary damages in redress of grievances. In criminal matters, the courts decide guilt and innocence as well as punishment for offenses against the law. The following courts typically can be identified in the court system, as they pertain to adult criminal court.

**Lower Courts**

The lower courts, or lower tribunals, are often referred to as police courts or justices of the peace, whose primary functions are to conduct hearings on probable cause and to arraign. These courts often have jurisdiction over violations committed under municipal ordinances and statutes governing misdemeanors. They are often the enforcement entity for statutes involving victimless crimes. These courts also serve an important role in determining bail. These courts are the entryway into the criminal justice system and are often the first experience that a defendant has with the legal system. For this reason, it is important for social workers to understand their role and focus.

### Trial Courts

Most trial courts, also called *primary courts,* retain both criminal and civil jurisdictions. These courts are commonly known as district, circuit, and superior courts. In criminal matters, the task of these courts is to determine guilt or innocence, starting with the presumption that the defendant is innocent until proven guilty beyond a reasonable doubt.

### Appellate Courts

The function of appellate courts is to determine whether errors in law or procedures had occurred during the course of the trial. This function does not entail retrying the case but only reviewing the records and transcripts of the trial court to make sure that it followed procedures and ruled fairly and equitably. The appellate process is a slow process and may take years. All states maintain appellate systems, usually composed of intermediate courts of appeal and a supreme court. In addition, the federal government maintains 12 circuit courts that serve as appellate courts for the federal district courts, as well as the U.S. Supreme Court.

## Phases of Judicial Processes

Because the focus of this article is the adult criminal court system and the role of social work in it, it is important to understand the various phases of judicial procedure in criminal matters. The court is involved in three phases—pretrial, trial, and sentencing, in addition to appellate review.

### Pretrial

The pretrial process begins on effecting an arrest. The role of arrest is solely to bring an accused individual before the "bar of justice" where a determination is made regarding guilt or innocence. An arrest is effected either through probable cause or through a warrant signed by a judge on the basis of probable cause (that is, facts indicating more likely than not that an act occurred).

***Initial phase.*** The first step after arrest is for the defendant to make an appearance before a magistrate. In cases of misdemeanors, the facts of the case are identified in the form of a complaint brought by the state against the individual. In cases involving felonies, there are normally two options:

1. *Prosecution on the basis of information.* This process (also followed in misdemeanors) involves a review by the district attorney of the facts of the case as presented by law enforcement authorities and an authorization by the prosecutor (if probable cause exists) to proceed with the case toward a trial.
2. *Prosecution on the basis of indictment.* In some jurisdictions, the facts of the case are presented to a grand jury to determine whether the defendant should be brought before the court. Although more jurisdictions now bypass the grand jury in the formalizing of charges, some still use it in cases involving public agencies and government officials.

***Initial appearance.*** On the determination of adequate information an indictment is made, and the individual enters the court system. At the initial appearance (called "arraignment"), the defendant makes a plea regarding guilt or innocence and a determination is made regarding eligibility for counsel. This is also the time during which bail is set. Bail is the opportunity, pursuant to the Constitution, to set the individual free provided that there are sufficient guarantees, monetary or otherwise, that the defendant will appear before the tribunal. Social work is often involved in the bail process; for example, a social worker may be asked to testify as to the probability that an individual will appear. The review of information relevant to support systems in the community, as well as permanency related to job and educational involvement, often are critical in determining bail.

***Preliminary examination.*** In this phase of the judicial proceedings, often referred to as a "probable cause hearing," a determination is made regarding whether there is sufficient evidence to proceed with the case. It is during this phase that attorneys often argue issues of admissibility of evidence (especially in the context of Miranda rights and search and seizure laws). This is also when the process of "discovery" of relevant evidence is undertaken. It should be noted that the preliminary hearing often discloses the information that can then be pursued through discovery to gather a more complete set of facts. Preliminary examination is different from civil proceedings where interrogatories and depositions (sworn statements) are used as major tools of the preliminary process. In particular, it is at this preliminary stage that all material facts are gathered and tested and subsequently reported to the judge who prepares the case for trial. In many cases, the preliminary hearing is held in a lower court, and the record is passed on to the trial court. The social worker's participation in this phase of inquiry may involve presenting information either on behalf of the state or the defense. The social worker should be aware that the determination here is not that of the ultimate decision, but only of whether there is sufficient evidence to take the case to trial.

In summary, the preliminary hearing serves the following purposes:

1. To determine whether the existing evidence is sufficient (that is, there is probable cause) for a warrant of arrest that was issued.
2. To determine the reasonability of the arrest, search, and seizure, and the overall compliance with the conditions of the warrant.
3. To afford the judge who issued the warrant (or whose jurisdiction issued it) the opportunity to hear the accused and the witnesses and to determine whether probable cause still exists.
4. To set bail, if appropriate.

If probable cause exists, the individual will then be referred to the trial court; this process is often referred to as being "bound over for trial."

### Trial Process

Full-fledged trials are the exception, not the rule, in the adult criminal court system. Although long arguments and extensive trials are associated with criminal cases, in reality, the criminal justice system could not possibly afford lengthy trials in all the cases presented to it. Most cases in fact are "pleaded out," a term that refers to the plea bargain process. In most jurisdictions, more than 90 percent of the cases are "pleaded," that is, prosecution and defense negotiate an agreement deemed to serve the best interest of both the people (society) and the defendant. This process of negotiation often results in reducing or dropping certain charges in exchange for an admission of guilt to the reduced charge. Although the court oversees the entering of the guilty plea to ensure that it was arrived at without coercion, the process is in fact executed by the prosecution and the defense. In large cities, less than 1 percent of cases are brought to trial.

The role of social workers in this practice is mostly one of evaluation and assessment and of making recommendations for treatment. Attorneys often call on social workers to make recommendations regarding a treatment plan. A major consideration here is the issue of community safety and whether, in the estimation of the social worker, an individual can be treated on an outpatient basis. As will be discussed later in this entry, this determination becomes a critical role in most criminal prosecutions. If the case does go to trial, the prosecution must prove beyond a reasonable doubt that an act occurred and that the act was committed by the defendant. This process entails the introduction of evidence and questions of law that must be decided by the judge. The case can be tried before either a judge or a jury of 6 or 12 individuals (depending on statute). In summary, the basis for conviction is proof beyond a reasonable doubt and normally consists of the jury's unanimous decision, although in some jurisdictions less than unanimous verdicts are permitted by statute.

### Sentencing

If a conviction is made, then an individual is sentenced pursuant to statute. The sentencing process normally requires a review by the Probation Department in the form of a report called a Pre-Sentence Investigation Report (PSIR). This report is compiled by the Probation Department, often in collaboration with other professionals in the community. Historically, the role of social work in the sentencing process has been an active one. Social workers have been asked to evaluate the merits and risks of keeping an offender in the community. Recently, this has been especially important in cases involving the physical and sexual abuse of children, where the needs of the victims constitute a major factor in the presentence investigation. Such investigation, together with character references, other letters, and even testimony of the presentencing hearing are reviewed by the court before sentence is imposed pursuant to statute.

### Appellate Process

The appellate process affords a review of the trial record to make sure that no error of law or of the rules of admissibility of evidence has been committed. The critical aspect to note here is that the appellate process is a review of the transcript and does not involve actual testimony. The appellate court may order a reversal of a lower court decision and a retrial of the case, or it may affirm it and let it stand. Social workers have participated in the appellate process by assisting in the sifting of information and testimony that were given. It should be noted, however, that the role of social work in the appellate process is generally nominal. Social work has been more actively involved in the appeal of class action suits challenging social welfare and other governmental practices (that is, public welfare, education, or mental health systems).

## Social Work in the Criminal Court Process

The role of social work in the criminal court process takes many forms, some of which have been briefly described. It should be noted that social work's role in court proceedings overall has been rather minimal and often misrepresented as an effort to excuse criminal behavior. In contrast, social work's role in civil proceedings such as child custody cases has been much more extensive and appreciated. Social workers often have not been given enough credit as expert witnesses, allegedly because they lack adequate or sufficient training. However, a review of their role suggests a need for their increased involvement.

**Evaluation of Competency**

The criminal court system has traditionally regarded forensic psychiatry as the primary mental health authority, especially on questions of criminal responsibility and competency to stand trial (Stone, 1988). This field's primary focus has been on the mental state of the defendant at the time that the act occurred and on the defendant's ability to stand trial and to aid counsel. The question of criminal responsibility, which focuses primarily on the *mens rea* (mental state) of the defendant as a legal defense (that is, pleading not guilty by reason of insanity) has received considerable attention. Nonetheless, it remains very controversial in the law. It is noteworthy that since the Hinkley decision (*U.S. v. Hinkley*), the insanity defense has been extremely limited and restricted in the court system. It is therefore critical that an evaluation of responsibility consist of more than merely the mental state; it should include an awareness of the dynamics of complex factors affecting the defendant and influencing his/her actions.

The role of the evaluator is to provide information and documentation that may ultimately be used in court. In some cases, the report may be furnished by a social worker in what is referred to as "attorney work product." This is usually a confidential document prepared at the request of the attorney and falls under the privileged attorney–client relationship. Although theoretically this document could be subpoenaed before the court, in most cases it is not. In many cases, the social worker provides background information about the defendant that is used by the court in the sentencing phase, as previously discussed. The emphasis here is on finding a balance between the rehabilitative potential of the individual and issues of public safety.

The contribution of social work here is to bring to the evaluation process an awareness of the systemic features of the defendant's environment, including racial, ethnic, and cultural variations, rather than merely focusing on mental state. Clinical social work is increasingly being recognized in cases involving potential violence. Although the literature generally supports the notion that the best predictor of violence is past history, social workers often go beyond historical observation to review the full range of background information, including family system, support systems, and community systems that are critical in understanding the defendant's needs. Despite its potential contributions, however, the social work profession has not had a major role in evaluation, perhaps because of reluctance to be forced to defend its clinical work. However, social workers should be prepared to contribute to the evaluation process and to substantiate their reports with relevant research data.

**Expert Witness**

The social worker may also be involved in the court system in what is referred to as an "expert witness status." The expert witness must be qualified by the court on the basis of significant educational credentials and experience. Social workers may provide expert testimony in the course of trial or during sentencing. It should be noted that the credentials of would-be experts are often challenged in an attempt to disqualify them. Social work has received recognition for expertise in the area of child neglect or abuse. For example, the concept of the battered child syndrome originated in social work and was first introduced in 1962 (Kempe, Silverman, Steele, Droegemuelleg, & Silver, 1962). In all cases, it is important for social workers to be clear about their background, knowledge, and experience in the field in which an attorney requests help. Testimony requires not only clarity and brevity in formulating a theoretical frame of reference but also an ability to review and support their findings through the literature. The need to support findings requires social workers to remain current with research in the field in which they are likely to testify. Moreover, social workers should be prepared to be challenged about their knowledge and expertise. They might be asked the following questions:

1. How much are you being paid for your testimony in this case?
2. How are you different from a physician in your training and experience?
3. Is it not true that you have testified on numerous occasions for defendants in similar cases?

These confrontational and intrusive questions are used as an attempt to impeach through cross-examination the credibility of the expert witness. Although many people who specialize in the forensic field are very comfortable in responding to these questions, social workers whose primary arena is not that of a courtroom might feel extremely intimidated. It is important, therefore, that social worker–witnesses receive adequate preparation with counsel and testify assertively. Indeed, responding to questions succinctly and directly and responding only to the question asked remains critical, especially because open-ended answers might leave an expert witness exposed to increased scrutiny and the possible discrediting of their testimony.

Often the court will appoint a social worker as an expert in a particular case. This may involve the testimony of a social worker on a specific issue of matter-of-fact, often without the direct examination of the defendant.

### The Client

Identifying the "client" has always been at the center of the social worker's overall education and training. Whether the client is an individual, a family, a group, or a subsystem of the community is an important factor in the provision of social work services. This is also true from the judicial viewpoint, and social workers must be very clear on who, in fact, their client is. There will be major pressure on the social worker to compromise on this point, especially from the defense counsel, whose role is to present the case with as many facts as possible. However, social workers must avoid participating in the determination of guilt or innocence.

## Social Work and the Process of Change

This entry has attempted to explain the function of the adult criminal court system and the role of social work in it. The major difference between the field of social work and that of the legal system is one of approach. The latter uses an adversarial approach, a confrontive, argumentative one, to determine the truth. Social workers, whose primary commitment is to their clients, cultivate a relationship of trust and may find it difficult to reconcile their values with those of the legal system. Although it is extremely important for social workers to recognize their role and expertise in the legal system, in no way should they compromise their professional values. With the exception of those few people who are comfortable in the court system, it is quite clear that most social work activity takes place outside the courts. Courtroom procedures are formal ones and most factors affecting change occur outside formal processes, through various preliminary and postadjudicatory phases. The following are some areas where social work can be most effective in promoting change affecting the adult criminal court system.

### Alternatives to the Penal System

The challenge for social work at this time is to provide adequate alternatives to the adult criminal system. In view of the proliferation of correctional institutions and prisons under the 1994 crime bill we must become more and more creative with alternatives (probation, halfway houses, electronic monitoring). The expectation that the court system can be innovative and creative in providing a range of opportunities is unrealistic. As a profession, social work must work toward the development of creative alternatives such as early childhood education and job and vocational training, especially for minority and disenfranchised youth. We cannot expect the criminal justice system to be an instrument of social change.

### Education and Training

Social workers have historically avoided working in the fields of corrections and criminal justice systems. They see these fields as alien to their own professional values and feel little ability to effect change in the systems. Unless more social work professionals join these fields and try to change their practices from within, however, change will be very slow in coming. Social work has the capacity to proffer creative alternatives to the formalized legal system managed by the courts.

### Instruments of Social Change

Although in this entry I have attempted to give information about the adult court system, I have also attempted to provide information about the role of the court system as an instrument of social change. The adversarial process will undoubtedly experience change within the context of statutes and case law, but these changes are likely to be slow and reactive to political forces as identified by the media. Social change through class action suits takes extensive time and resources, especially for indigent individuals attempting to redress their grievances through litigation. Thus, social work must effect change in our society by focusing on the range of programs in education, vocational training, and family support because they are likely to be far more effective than the court system.

## References

Beis, E. (1984). *Mental health and the law.* Rockville, MD: Aspen Publishers.

Berman, H. (1971). *Talks on American law* (rev. ed.). New York: Vintage Books.

Kempe, C. H., Silverman, F. N., Steele, B. F., Droegemuelleg, W., & Silver, H. K. (1962). The battered child syndrome. *Journal of the American Medical Association, 181*(1), 17–24.

Lessard v. Schmidt, 346 F. Supp. 1078 (E.D. Wisc. 1972).
Marbury v. Madison, 1 Cr. 138 (1803).
Miranda v. Arizona, 384 U.S. 436 (1966).
Platt, A. (1969). *Child savers.* Chicago: University of Chicago Press.
Stone, A. (1988). Psychiatry and the law. In *The new Harvard guide to psychiatry.* Cambridge, MA: Harvard University Press.
U.S. v. Hinkley, 721 F. Supp. 520 (D.D.C. 1982).

### Further Reading

Craige, H. B., Saur, W. G., & Arcuri, J. B. (1982). The practice of social work in legal services programs. *Journal of Sociology and Social Welfare, 9,* 307–317.
Lloyd, C. (1985). Evaluation and forensic psychiatric occupational therapy. *British Journal of Occupational Therapy, 48*(5), 137–140.
Schroeder, L. O. (1979). Legal liability: A professional concern. *Clinical Social Work Journal, 7*(3), 194–199.
Schroeder, L. O. (in press). *The legal environment of social work* (rev. ed.). Washington, DC: NASW Press.
Whitmer, G. E. (1983). The development of forensic social work. *Social Work, 28,* 217–223.
Zborowsky, E. K. (1985). Developments in protective services: A challenge for social workers. *Journal of Gerontological Social Work, 8*(3–4), 71–83.

**Paul M. Isenstadt, LCSW,** is program director, ComCor, Inc., 3615 Roberts Road, Colorado Springs, CO 80907.

### For further information see

Adult Corrections; Civil Rights; Criminal Behavior Overview; Domestic Violence: Legal Issues; Family Views in Correctional Programs; Female Criminal Offenders; Homicide; Juvenile and Family Courts; Police Social Work; Probation and Parole; Rehabilitation of Criminal Offenders; Sentencing of Criminal Offenders; Substance Abuse: Legal Issues; Violence Overview.

**Key Words**
corrections
courts
criminal justice
sentencing

# Adult Day Care

**Natalie Gordon**

According to the New York State Adult Day Care Services Association (1992), adult day care (ADC) is the provision of community-based services to adults in a congregate setting. These services range from limited direct services to extensive and intensive medical therapeutic services for people with severe medical problems and decreasing functional ability. Professional health, social, and supportive services are delivered by an interdisciplinary team with a holistic approach that recognizes the interrelationship among the physical, social, emotional, and environmental aspects of well-being. ADC is designed not only to benefit clients, but also to give respite to caregivers and to enable them to maintain their elderly relatives in the community (Lawton, Brady, Saperstein, & Grimes, 1989; Retsinas, 1991).

ADC provides social, restorative, and health services to fulfill the following goals:

- to promote an individual's maximum level of independence, enabling him or her to remain in the community and preventing premature placement in a nursing home
- to maintain an individual's present level of functioning and to prevent or delay further deterioration
- to monitor and address an individual's changing needs
- to restore and rehabilitate an individual to his or her highest level of physical, mental, and emotional functioning
- to provide planned and supervised recreational, socialization, and peer-interaction activities in a supportive environment
- to provide respite, support, and education for family caregivers, to protect their own physical and mental health and to enable them to maintain a good level of care
- to serve as an integral part of the community service network and continuum of care and to reduce gaps in services (Chappel, 1984).

### Models of Services

ADC has long struggled with the concept of classifying programs on the basis of models of care. This struggle originated in the early European programs, where models were identified by their major treatment category (for example, social work, psychiatry, or rehabilitation therapies). In the United States such specific models are still in use and are generally reinforced by regulatory agencies, funding sources, and providers of services (National Institute on Adult Day Care [NIADC] 1990b).

**Range of Models**

Conrad, Hanrahan, and Hughes (1990) found that ADC programs range from those that are heavily medical to those that are social and recreational and that the characteristics of ADC vary greatly across the country. In essence, all types share common elements but emphasize different aspects of health and social programming. Weissert et al. (1989) distinguished among three types of ADC: (1) centers affiliated with nursing homes and rehabilitation centers; (2) centers affiliated with general hospitals, social service agencies, and housing; and (3) special-purpose centers. Tate (1988) categorized ADC as "the health or restorative" model (Medicaid reimbursable in 28 states), "the maintenance" model, and "the [psycho] social" model (often supported by Title XX of the Health, Education and Welfare Act [Social Security Act] of 1975).

Although the boundaries are blurred, distinctions can best be made between the social and the medical models of care. Programs that the medical model offer are medical and rehabilitation services, as well as health support services. They are geared toward those who are frail and may otherwise require nursing home placement. These programs are viewed as an alternative when less than 24-hour care is needed or when supplemental care in the home can be provided by the formal or informal systems or a combination of both.

Programs that operate according to the social model are varied. In general, they provide psychosocial services, some health monitoring, and supervised activities. They attempt to prevent deterioration through the regular attendance by and supervision of clients and the provision of respite to caregivers (Tate, 1988). For those who are physically and functionally intact, senior centers offer opportunities for socialization. Although they are expected to reach out to the frail elderly (on the basis of the Rehabilitation Act of 1973 and the 1990 Americans with Disabilities Act, which prohibit discrimination on the basis of handicap), a study of 300 senior citizens centers in New York State found that the directors believed that the centers could not handle more than 10 percent of their members being frail and that the centers were better able to work with the physically impaired than with the mentally frail (Cox & Monk, 1990).

In general, the traditional community clubs for the aged—senior citizens centers and church groups—do not attract frail and disabled clients and are not prepared to serve them. Because of their special needs (which require medical and psychosocial monitoring and an individual level of intervention), these clients are best helped in day care programs with nursing, social services, medical services, and rehabilitation services (Goldstein, 1982). One of the strengths of ADC centers is their ability to accommodate a wide variety of participants who have special needs. The centers are able to meet these needs most effectively when the providers use a holistic approach and exercise a high degree of professionalism in the assessment, development, and implementation of diverse plans of care and documentation (Katz & Maginn, 1989).

Perhaps because of the difficulties inherent in classification, it is commendable that the NIADC standards (1990) emphasize the development of programs that could be expanded or modified according to the needs of the population served, rather than being differentiated on the basis of health or nonhealth services. In short, a continuum of care is needed, so that participants who may not need extensive medical and therapeutical services at one point may receive additional services if they need them in the future.

**Services for Special Populations**

More and more ADC programs are being developed or adapted for clientele with specific types of problems and needs. The most common programs are those serving persons with Alzheimer's disease, acquired immune deficiency syndrome (AIDS), mental illness, visual impairment, hearing loss, or communication disorders. In addition, programs have been developed for people with specific rehabilitative needs, head injuries, or developmental disabilities. It should be noted that although there are benefits to providing specialized programs, many nonspecific ADC programs may also serve these individuals.

***People with Alzheimer's disease.*** The capacity of ADC centers to serve the growing number of people with Alzheimer's disease and their caregivers has been increasing because of the impact of the National Alzheimer's Association and the Federal Administration on Aging. Some centers serve only those with a specific level of dementia, whereas others are more flexible about joint programming with the general ADC group. Conrad and Guttman (1991) suggested that the two groups should be integrated only for those activities that are not overwhelming to the persons with Alzheimer's disease and that do not disturb the entire group.

People with Alzheimer's disease are frequently disturbed when they begin day care. However, after several weeks of attendance, during which they are provided with patterning, sufficient "cueing," and habitual reference points that help in orientation so that the environment becomes familiar, they often become stable and even improve (Baldwin, 1988). For such programs to be successful, however, their staffs must be trained in ways to communicate with and respond to those who have lost the ability to think, act, and convey needs in conventional ways (NIADC, 1990b).

People with Alzheimer's disease participate in a structured program of nonthreatening activities whose aim is to promote dignity and self-esteem. Special recreational and therapeutic programs can stimulate these clients cognitively, reduce their stress and anxiety, and enhance their remaining capabilities. Numerous routine activities and therapies encourage memory and conversation and help overcome loneliness and depression, and specially trained recreational therapists conduct exercise and movement classes. Conrad and Guttman (1991) have found that the most important aspect of Alzheimer's disease centers is the provision of support for families. These centers emphasize therapeutic recreation, assistance with and training in personal care tasks, and entertainment and that rehabilitation services are less important.

Alzheimer's disease centers tend to have longer hours than do general ADC centers and are more likely to provide transportation and to have a carefully designed physical environment that is both safe and supportive. They frequently offer educational and supportive services to caregivers, including support groups to strengthen the caregivers' ability to deal with the illness and with their feelings and to increase coping skills (Conrad & Guttman, 1991; NIADC, 1990b).

***People with AIDS.*** The increase in the number of people with AIDS has greatly influenced the development of resources to meet their specific needs. In some states, Medicaid waivers are the vehicle through which the AIDS centers are created and funded, generally through enhanced fees for services that are provided to this special population. According to Kurland and Dryer (1990), such ADC centers must provide a secure and safe environment for the participants, who may have a range of physical and functional impairments or may be suffering from AIDS-related dementia. In addition to providing services that are comparable to those provided by centers for people with other unique disabilities, ADC centers for AIDS patients must establish infection-control measures, known as "universal precautions," and must handle them with great care and sensitivity. Emotional support, education for at-home care, and strong medical supervision enable clients to remain at home; the warm, accepting environment at the centers counters the suffering that occurs with isolation and the stigma that can lead to loneliness and despair.

Nurses and other providers of direct care are familiar with the progression of AIDS. Therefore, links to services provided by outpatient and residential drug and alcohol treatment centers are established, as are links with child care services, so clients with young children can attend the centers. Kurland and Dryer (1990) recommended that centers should not be specifically identified as AIDS facilities because, with the social stigma attached to AIDS, it is vital to maintain confidentiality. Support groups are another important part of the program, which ultimately must include memorial services and bereavement. Many participants do not have supportive families, and many have lost their friends either to AIDS or because of their fear of the illness.

***People with severe mental illnesses.*** Because individuals with severe mental illnesses may be present in any ADC center, the staff must be able to respond to seriously disturbed persons, acute psychotic behavior, and suicide threats. In programs in non–mental health settings, psychiatric consultation for medication and related issues and professional social work for crisis intervention are necessary. In programs that are designed specifically for this population, all staff must know how to carry out crisis intervention procedures and how to gain access to psychiatric consultation. These programs comply with state regulations for professional staff with appropriate training who must be able to conduct ongoing evaluations of the participants, develop and carry out service plans, and conduct individual and group therapy. Furthermore, because psychotic behaviors, chronic mental health problems, and repeated or lengthy institutionalization often lead to severe strain on or the lack of involvement of family members (Van Buskirk, 1990), staff in centers that serve this population must be skilled in using family therapy techniques. It is important to provide an environment that minimizes distractions for the participants, who may be disturbed by loud noises, the movement of other people in and out of an area, and other activities that take place in an area. Private interviewing areas are necessary because they help protect confidentiality and can be used to calm patients who have become anxious.

The services of such ADC centers include planned and supervised recreation, peer interaction, and assessment for and referral to entitlements. Most mental health agencies communicate regularly with each other, and the ADC facility becomes part of this network (Van Buskirk, 1990).

***People with visual impairments, hearing loss, and communication disorders.*** Vision, hearing, and communication disorders or losses are common problems of elderly participants of ADC centers and affect the vital functions of everyday life. Specialized ADC centers that address the needs of individuals with these impairments have physical facilities and equipment that accommodate the special needs of those with sensory impairments, protect the participants from injury, and enhance their ability to function independently. Consultants are available to work with and advise the staff; coordinate and conduct staff training programs; and provide ongoing advice concerning the assessment of individual participants and on the development, implementation, and evaluation of treatment programs.

Such consultants include orientation and mobility (O&M) instructors, audiologists, and speech-language pathologists. An O&M instructor has a range of functions, from advising on the structural environment to providing the participant who is blind or visually impaired with mobility instruction and orientation to the site and facilitating the overall rehabilitation process. An audiologist identifies and evaluates hearing-impaired participants, determines the need for hearing rehabilitation, and establishes an individual program to help participants make the best use of their hearing. A speech-language pathologist evaluates and diagnoses speech and language disorders and designs and implements appropriate treatment programs. Other services include access and referral to other rehabilitation services, support groups for caregivers, and support groups for participants.

## Profile of Centers

### Clientele

According to the 1989 National Adult Day Center Census (NIADC, 1990a), 75 percent of the ADC centers serve patients with Alzheimer's disease, visual and hearing impairments, physical handicaps, or mental retardation and developmental disabilities; people in wheelchairs who need assistance to transfer to other locations; and the frail aged; 70 percent serve people with frequent (more than weekly) incontinence. Furthermore, 56 percent of all participants in all ADC centers need assistance with or are dependent in two or more activities of daily living. It is conjectured that the ADC centers are treating such a high proportion of people with disabilities because of the preference for and the growing availability of home- or community-based services (Kaye & Kirwin, 1990); hence, fewer elderly people are entering nursing homes. The clients of ADC centers are marginally functioning elderly people who have different needs but share a determination to remain independent in the community (Goldstein, 1982; Griffin, 1993). They include people who are isolated, who will not reach out for services; mentally impaired, for whom there are few services; and medically fragile, who need continuous monitoring. Many are loners; some have a history of depression, paranoia, or schizoid personality; and many have moderate dementia and a myriad of illnesses (Goldstein, 1982). Many of the specific problems of recipients of adult protective services have been handled effectively in ADC centers (Griffin).

Most ADC centers primarily serve an older population with an average age of 76 years, although over one-third also serve participants under age 50. Women generally outnumber men by more than two to one, but centers that serve a distinct subpopulation usually have a higher proportion of nonaged and male participants. On average, almost 75 percent of all participants are white, 16 percent are black, and 6 percent are Native American (Zawadski, 1990). An issue to be examined is the low proportion of participants who are people of color. According to the American Society on Aging (1992), participation is low because services are not located where these elders live and there is a lack of transportation to neighborhoods where services exist. To overcome low enrollment, some centers "reach in" to the community, in addition to doing the more common "outreach" work. Staff who are culturally diverse and in-service programs on cultural diversity also contribute to clients' comfort with services.

### Services

Zawadski's (1990) study of a nationally representative sample of ADC centers identified 40 percent of the centers that responded as "full-service centers" that provided all key long-term-care services—nursing, social work, personal care, and therapy—and 29 percent as "partial-service centers" that provided personal care and at least two of the three other professional services. The remaining 31 percent included specialized centers targeted toward specific populations and offering intensive services in only a few areas.

A nationally representative study (Weissert et al., 1989) indicated that, at a minimum, all centers provided social interaction, exercise, and one hot meal a day and serve an average of 20 participants each day (Weissert et al., 1989). The core services that Tate (1988) deemed essential are transportation, health surveillance, counseling activities, and rest. Additional services that ADC programs often provide include special diets; personal care services; physical, occupational, and speech therapy; training in the use of environmental aids; evaluation of the home setting with suggestions for easing the performance of the tasks of daily living; individual and group counseling for families and caregivers of the frail elderly; nutrition, consumer education, and self-care health skills; skilled nursing and medical specialists; and a variety of peripheral services like shopping, laundry, and barber and other grooming services (Tate, 1988). Figure 1 depicts the key services of the 1,400 ADC centers in 49 states that responded to the National Adult Day Center Census '89 (Zawadski, Outwater, & Stuart, 1990).

### Staffing

The staff of a typical center includes the director (a nurse or a social worker) and an assistant, plus some or all of the following: recreation-activity staff, nursing aides, nurses, social workers, custodial workers, van drivers, case managers, administrative personnel, and office staff. Most staff members are paid employees. Consultants tend to be physicians or various types of therapists, whereas in-kind staffing (that is, free or below-cost goods or services from other programs or organizations) is usually obtained for fiscal management or bookkeeping services (Weissert et al., 1989).

ADC is becoming more professionalized because of demands from funding sources, participants and their families (Baldwin, 1988), and the providers of services who are members of NIADC. Standards that were developed by NIADC in 1984 and updated in 1990 strongly contributed to ADC's professionalization. These standards have influenced state regulations but, according to NIADC (1990b), have failed to make the case for regulations that reflect the changing population that is being served. Therefore, NIADC strongly recommends that state and federal regulatory agencies consider the development of a generic licensing category for *all* ADC centers.

## Financing of Services

Because there is no single funding source for *any* long-term-care program, including ADC, differ-

FIGURE 1

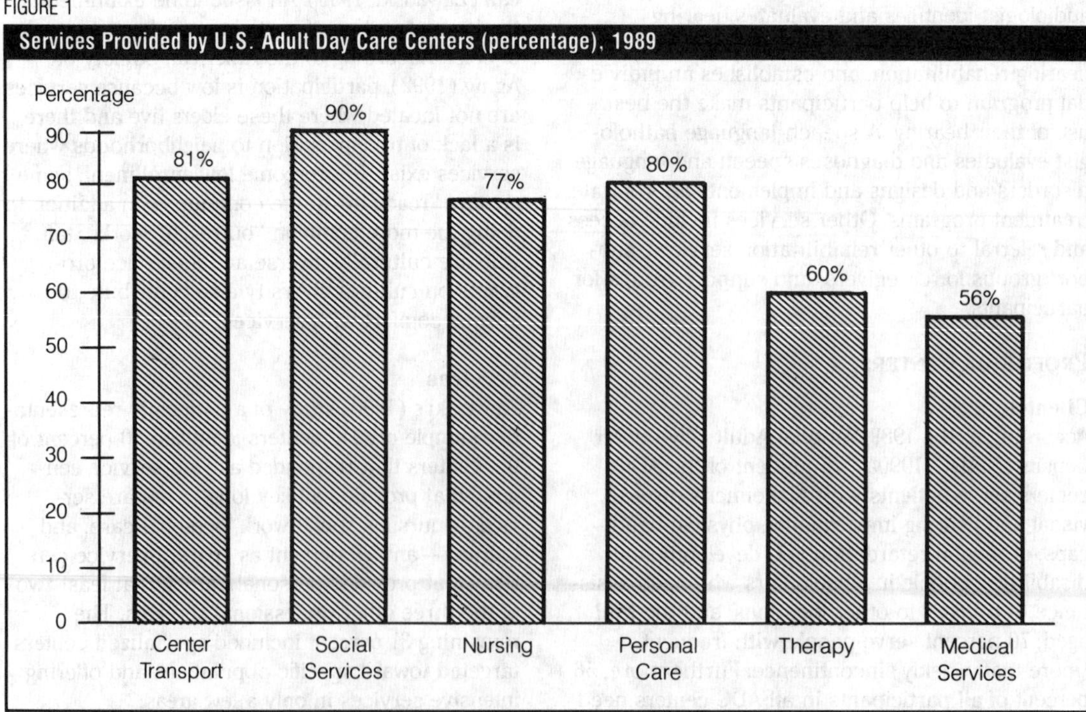


SOURCE: National Adult Day Center Census '89. As represented in Zawadski, R., Outwater, M.A., & Stuart, M. (1990, October 19). Most centers offer key services. *NCOA Networks*, p. 8. Reprinted with permission of The National Council on the Aging.

ences in funding exist from region to region (Baldwin, 1988; Wertheimer, 1992). Even home health care under Medicare is restricted to meeting acute care needs. One hope has been that uniform coverage at a national level via Medicare would include ADC as a waivered service and hence would eliminate uncertainties and inequities (Griffin, 1993; Zawadski, Outwater, & Stuart 1991).

### Funding Mix

ADC is currently supported by public funds; out-of-pocket expenditures of participants; a small amount of demonstration grants; some philanthropic gifts; and, to a lesser but growing degree, private long-term-care insurance. Funds are generally targeted to the characteristics of specific participants (NIADC, 1990a), and there are many restraints on both public and private funding (Asbury & Merrill, 1989). Most of the revenues come from federal sources, of which Medicaid is the largest. Medicaid provides federal and state funds for eligible, low-income participants in some states, and each state decides which programs are funded. Centers that are associated with nursing homes and have religious affiliations rely considerably more on nongovernment funding (Zelman, Elston, & Weissert, 1991). Many centers charge fees but most participants cannot afford to pay the full cost. Fundraising activities become an intricate part of the programs with marketing campaigns to enlist financial aid (Goldston, 1989). Rural senior centers are less likely to expand programs than urban centers because their small size and low density of population cannot support this kind of organizational structure (Krout, 1990).

As Zawadski, Outwater, and Stuart (1990) concluded in the National Adult Day Center Census '89, because of the multiple funding sources and despite the resourcefulness of centers in fundraising and using volunteers, many centers find it difficult to remain financially viable. More than half the 1,400 centers that responded to the census were operating at a deficit. Nevertheless, the number of centers continues to increase, which reflects the fact that ADC is an essential community service (Zawadski, Outwater, & Stuart, 1990).

### Cost-Effectiveness Issues

Some critics have suggested that it is cheaper to institutionalize patients than to provide ADC. This point is debatable. Although it was conjectured that one of the factors that influenced the expansion of day hospitals in Great Britain was that day hospitals were less costly than was in-patient treatment, it became more difficult to defend this position in the 1980s as costs increased (Hildick-Smith, 1984). Thus, although there are savings when ADC is first introduced, they may be compromised later on. Furthermore, because ADC centers serve a different population (Baldwin, 1988), they do not significantly diminish the use of institutions (Harder, Gornick, & Burt, 1986).

The question of cost-effectiveness is important because funding decisions are often based on a comparison between the relative costs and benefits of adult day care centers and nursing homes. However, it is difficult to assign dollar values to the in-kind contributions of the informal support system of relatives who act as caregivers (Von Behren, 1989). As Weissert et al. (1989) stated, for people with severe impairments, community care is not less costly than institutional care, especially when the social, emotional, physical, and financial costs to their caregivers are considered. In sum, although no study shows that ADC costs less or that participants make measurable gains, the support that ADC offers to frail participants and the respite it provides to informal caregivers seem to delay and often to eliminate the need for nursing home placements. In addition, participants and their caregivers are so overwhelmingly satisfied with the care they receive in ADC centers that political support for such programs increases every year. Weissert et al. believe that ADC will probably continue to play an increasingly important role in long-term care.

## Role of Social Workers

### Types of Services

Social work is one of the services that is commonly provided (as opposed to "contracted activities") in ADC centers and is a central component of ADC initiatives, whether such programs are designed according to the medical or social model of care (Kaye & Kirwin, 1990). Among health care professionals, social workers with master's-level training are the best prepared to provide, supervise, and administer needed services.

Beginning with the application and admission process, social workers identify the unmet needs of clients and alert the organization and policymakers to these needs. For individual participants, they assess psychosocial needs, coordinate plans of care, and supervise services. Counseling and treatment to help clients and their families adjust to illness and aging, ensuring compliance with medical treatment, informing clients of options for care, providing emotional support, developing self-help groups, and working on family issues all require social work skills. Social workers provide appropriate counseling that is based on a knowledge of aging, the emotional and social aspects of chronic illness, family dynamics, and additional community and institutional resources that enhance health and help clients to make the maximum use of their capacity to function (Kaye & Kirwin, 1990).

Because social workers design and participate in all types of services, they must be skilled in working both with clients and their families, who may obstruct plans of care, and with staff. The social work connection to caregivers through individual and group counseling reduces stress, enables early intervention, and prevents elder abuse.

**Requisite Knowledge and Skills**

Because social workers are integrated into the primary care team, they expand the medical model that may otherwise insufficiently value the psychosocial issues on which the clients' and families' use of services may depend. Knowing the value of these programs for monitoring social and health well-being and for overcoming isolation, social workers educate physicians and other gatekeepers. They also need knowledge of community-based service, such as adult day health care, because they control entry of frail elderly clients into such programs (Society for Social Work Administrators in Health Care, 1993).

In addition to advocacy, social workers have the responsibility to translate what is known about psychosocial needs and quality-of-life issues into usable standards against which social workers' contributions to long-term care in general and to ADC specifically can be measured. Such standards could be applied to all programs and would enable the federal government to require all programs to function on professionally acceptable levels.

Furthermore, because of their professional education, social workers have skills that include an understanding of organized systems. They and nurses are most often directors of ADC programs (Mace, 1984). They are aware of the need for high-quality, cost-effective services and are active in documenting the need for funding for both individual programs and for the implementation of social policies. In short, social workers contribute at each point of the continuum of long-term care in every professional role.

## Implications for the Future

It has been projected that the number of people age 65 and older in the United States will increase from 12 percent of the population in 1986 to approximately 20 percent of the population by 2030 (Butler, Lewis, & Sunderland, 1991). Of these people, the fastest-growing group will be those age 85 and older. Persily (1988) forecast that declining birthrates, the increasing labor force participation of women, and geographic dispersion of the family will all increase the need for community programs, such as ADC.

Those who care for both their parents and their children (the "sandwich generation") will need these programs. American industry is already obligated by the Family and Medical Leave Act of 1993 to provide help to workers, who would otherwise be forced to leave the work force because of caregiving responsibilities. An increasing number of publications that are targeted to businesses are encouraging businesses to consider ADC an advantage both to employees and to the organizations (Beck, 1990; Erickson, 1992; Gordon, 1993; Henderson, 1991). Two businesses that are supporting ADC in the workplace are Lancaster Laboratories in Lancaster, Pennsylvania, and Stride Rite in Cambridge, Massachusetts (Gillis, 1990; Thornburg, 1993). Businesses may also become more concerned about services for the large number of retirees (Persily, 1988). Given the projected number of elderly people, the predictable health care problems associated with the aging process, and other demographics, it is feasible to assume that many more elderly people will require ADC services (Griffin, 1993).

However, a major barrier to the provision of additional ADC services is funding. At this writing, it is too early to predict the place of ADC in whatever health care reforms are initiated. Among the many plans that have been proposed, a common theme is the need for high-quality care and greater accountability of providers for patients' outcomes.

Managed care seems to be closer to realization with or without health care reforms. Thus, in the future, the successful health care organization will integrate the formal and informal systems to provide the full spectrum of services including at-home services, both medical and personal; ADC; personal services; respite care; short-term and long-term institutional care; and acute care (Persily, 1988).

A growing number of networks are offering a continuum of services, from those based in the community to those provided in institutions. One model is On Lok, which opened one of the nation's first adult day health centers in 1973. Since 1979, On Lok has provided a capitated managed-care program that integrated long-term and acute care and used multipurpose ADC centers, where multidisciplinary teams encourage preventive care in the centers and in the enrollees' homes.

The evolving health care environment is extremely fluid, and the future of ADC is closely connected to the expected restructuring of the health care system. Social workers must anticipate the challenges and contribute to the integration of long-term-care programs, such as ADC, into whatever new systems are instituted for financing and delivering care.

## References


American Society on Aging. (1992). *Serving elders of color: Challenges to providers and the aging network.* San Francisco: Author.

Americans with Disabilities Act of 1990. P.L. 101-336, 104 Stat. 327.

Asbury, C., & Merrill, J. (1989). Dementia long term care services: The emerging role of day centers. *Pride Institute Journal of Long Term Home Health Care, 8*(4), 28–34.

Baldwin, B. A. (1988). Community management of Alzheimer's disease. *Nursing Clinics of North America, 23,* 37–56.

Beck, M. (1990, July 2). A home away from home: Day care offers self-esteem to the elderly and respite to the family. *Newsweek,* p. 56.

Butler, R. N., Lewis, M., & Sunderland, T. (1991). *Aging and mental health* (4th ed.). New York: Macmillan.

Chappel, N. (1984). Who benefits from adult day care? *Canadian Journal on Aging, 2*(1), 9–25.

Conrad, J., Hanrahan, P., & Hughes, S. L. (1990). Survey of adult day care in the United States. *Research on Aging, 12*(1), 36–56.

Conrad, J., & Guttman, R. (1991). Characteristics of Alzheimer's versus non-Alzheimer's adult day care centers. *Research on Aging, 13,* 96–116.

Cox, C., & Monk, A. (1990). Integration of the frail and well elderly. *Journal of Gerontological Social Work, 15,* 131–147.

Erickson, E. (1992, November). Adult day care fills rural need. *Successful Farming,* p. 71.

Family and Medical Leave Act of 1993. P.L. 103-3, 107 Stat. 6.

Gillis, D. (1990). Making ends meet: Innovative care for the young and the elderly. *Atlantic Magazine, 266,* 510.

Goldstein, R. (1982). Adult day care: Expanding options for service. *Journal of Gerontological Social Work, 5,* 157–168.

Goldston, S. M. (1989). *Adult day care: A basic guide.* Owings Mills, MD: National Health Publishing.

Gordon, J. (1993, February). Elder care in Washington. *Washington Business Journal,* pp. 25–27.

Griffin, L. W. (1993). Adult day care services and adult protective services. *Journal of Gerontological Social Work, 20,* 115–131.

Harder, W., Gornick, J., & Burt, M. (1986). Adult day care: Substitute supplement. *Milbank Quarterly, 64,* 414–441.

Health, Education and Welfare Act (Social Security Act) of 1975. P.L. 93-647, 88 Stat. 2337–2360.

Henderson, N. (1991, March). Finding care for your aging parents. *Changing Times,* p. 50.

Hildick-Smith, M. (1984). Geriatric day hospitals: Changing emphasis in costs. *Age and Aging, 13,* 95–100.

Katz, K. S., & Maginn, P. D. (1989). The intake assessment, plan of care, and discharge planning process. In L. C. Webb (Ed.), *Planning and managing adult day care: Pathways to success* (pp. 145–157). Owings Mills, MD: National Health Publishing.

Kaye, L. W., & Kirwin, P. M. (1990). Adult day care services for the elderly and their families. *Journal of Gerontological Social Work, 15,* 167–183.

Kirwin, P. M., & Kaye, L. W. (1991). Services consumption patterns over time among adult day care program participants. *Home Health Care Services Quarterly, 12,* 45–58.

Krout, J. A. (1990). *The organization, operation and programming of senior centers in America: A seven year follow up.* Fredonia: State University of New York.

Kurland, C., & Dryer, E. (1990). Profile of an adult day health center for persons with symptomatic HIV infection. In National Institute on Adult Day Care (Ed.), *Standards and guidelines for adult day care* (pp. 178–191). Washington, DC: National Council on the Aging.

Lawton, M. P., Brody, E. M., Saperstein, A., & Grimes, M. (1989). Respite services for caregivers: Research findings for service planning. *Home Care Services Quarterly, 10,* 5–32.

Mace, N. (1984). Day care for demented clients. *Hospital and Community Psychiatry, 35,* 976–980.

National Institute on Adult Day Care. (1990a). *National adult day center census '89.* Washington, DC: National Council on the Aging.

National Institute on Adult Day Care. (1990b). *Standards and guidelines for adult day care.* Washington, DC: National Council on the Aging.

New York State Adult Day Services Association, Inc. (1992). *Position paper, public policy statement.* Albany, NY: Author.

Omnibus Budget Reconciliation Act of 1986. P.L. 99-509, 100 Stat. 1874.

Persily, N. (1988). 10 years from now: Consumer views. *Provider for long term care professionals.* Washington, DC: American Health Care Association.

Rehabilitation Act of 1973. P.L. 93-112, 87 Stat. 355.

Retsinas, J. (1991). Triggers to nursing home placement. *Geriatric Nursing, 12,* 235–236.

Society for Social Work Administrators in Health Care. (1993). *A Special Report of the Health Care Reform Task Force.* Chicago: American Hospital Association.

Tate, L. A. (1988). Adult day care: A practical guidebook and manual [Special issue]. *Activities, Adaptation and Aging, 11*(2).

Thornburg, L. (1993). Daycare for kids and elders is a natural. *HR Magazine, 38,* 48–50.

Van Buskirk, L. (1990). Adult day care for those with mental health needs. In National Institute on Adult Day Care (Ed.), *Standards and guidelines for adult day care* (pp. 206–210). Washington, DC: National Council on the Aging.

Von Behren, R. (1989). *Adult day care: A program of services for the functionally impaired.* Washington, DC: National Council on the Aging.

Weissert, W. G., Elston, J. M., Bolda, E. J., Cready, C. M., Zelman, W. N., Sloane, P. D., Kalsbeek, W. D., Mutran, E., Rice, T. H., & Kock, G. G. (1989). Models of adult day care: Findings from a national survey. *The Gerontologist, 29,* 640–649.

Wertheimer, J. (1992). Organization of psychogeriatrics in western countries. In M. Bergener, K. Hasegaw, S. Finkel, & T. Nishimurata (Eds.), *Aging and mental disorders: International perspectives* (pp. 298–316). New York: Springer.
Zawadski, R. (1990). ADC growth uneven, but impressive. *NCOA Networks,* p. 9.
Zawadski, R., Outwater, M. A., & Stuart, M. (1990). Most centers offer key services. *NCOA Networks,* p. 8.
Zawadski, R., Outwater, M. A., & Stuart, M. (1991). Financing adult day services varies widely across nation. *NCOA Networks,* p. 7.
Zawadski, R., & Stuart, M. (1990). A "typical" center participant? No way. *NCOA Networks,* p. 8.
Zelman, W. M., Elston, J. M., & Weissert, W. G. (1991). Financial aspect of adult day care: National survey results. *Health Care Financing Review, 12,* 27–36.

## Further Reading

American Association of Homes for the Aging. (1985). *Guide to caring for mentally impaired elderly.* Washington, DC: Author.
Der-McLeod, D., & Chin Hansen, J. (1992). On Lok: The family continuum. *Generations, 17*(3), 71–72.
Goldston, S. M. (1989). *Adult day care: A basic guide.* Owings Mills, MD: National Health Publishing.
Hughes, S. L. (1986). *Long term care: Options in an expanding market.* Rockville, MD: Aspen Publishers.
Levine, G., & Scharf, J. (1987). *Serving persons with Alzheimer's disease: Training manual and managing problem behaviors of persons with Alzheimer's* [Videotape and instructor's guide]. Columbus: Ohio Association of Adult Day Care.
Panella, J. (1987). *Day care programs for Alzheimer's disease and related disorders.* New York: Demos Publications.
Pizzi, M. (1990). Productive living strategies for people with AIDS. *Occupational Therapy in Health Care, 7,* 2–4.
Snyder, A. (1990). Recommendations for adult day care centers serving individuals with visual impairments, hearing loss and communication disorders. In National Institute on Adult Day Care (Ed.), *Standards and guidelines for adult day care* (pp. 192–205). Washington, DC: National Council on the Aging.
Webb, L. C., & Owings, M. (1988). *Planning and managing adult day care: Pathways to success.* Owings Mills, MD: National Health Publishing.
Yeatts, D. E., Crow, T., & Folts, E. (1992). Service use among low-income minority elderly: Strategies for overcoming barriers. *The Gerontologist Society of America, 32*(1), 24–32.

**Natalie Gordon, DSW,** is vice president for social work and community programs, The Jewish Home and Hospital for Aged, 120 West 106th Street, New York, NY 10025.

**For further information see**

Adult Foster Care; Adult Protective Services; Aging Overview; Case Management; Community; Disability; Elder Abuse; Families Overview; Family Caregiving; Health Care: Direct Practice; Homelessness; Income Security Overview; Long-Term Care; Managed Care; Natural Helping Networks; Poverty; Public Social Services; Social Security; Social Welfare Policy.

**Key Words**

| | |
|---|---|
| adult day care | gerontology |
| aged | special populations |

# Adult Foster Care

**Marion L. Beaver**

Foster care for adults is a significant and relatively new addition to the panoply of residential care arrangements for a diverse population of adults who cannot maintain full independence. This form of foster care falls into the category of community-based alternatives to institutional care (Braun & Rose, 1987). These community-based alternatives are frequently referred to as community residential facilities (CRFs), a generic term that includes all nonpublic residential facilities housing adults with a history of developmental disability, mental illness, or problems associated with aging (McCoin, 1987b). A variety of homes are included under the CRF rubric: personal care homes, boarding homes, community care, board and care, domiciliary, congregate care homes, and adult foster care (AFC) homes.

## Overview

Although AFC dates back to the Middle Ages, it still lacks a precise definition (McCoin, 1987a). Generally it refers to a specialized form of sheltered housing in which the resident is placed in a "substitute family setting for a planned period of time" (Newman & Sherman, 1977, p. 436). The placement is usually in the private home of a nonrelative who provides support and supervision for the disabled or dependent adult in return for financial compensation. The money received by the caretaker typically comes to the resident in the form of Supplemental Security Income (SSI), which is supplemented by additional income in most states (McCoin, 1987a).

Foster homes in which adults are placed usually serve one to six residents (Sherman, Newman, & Frenkel, 1984). However, it is not unusual to house up to 20 residents (Oktay, 1987). Most AFC programs try to limit the number of residents in a given home to maintain a familylike environment.

The major purpose of AFC is to enable physically and mentally disabled adults and frail elderly individuals to live in a family setting (Handy, 1968). The natural family is, in most cases, the optimal environment for the promotion of individual function and quality of life. However, some mentally or physically disabled adults are too impaired to be cared for at home; in these cases, the foster family is a viable substitute (Braun & Rose, 1987). AFC offers a less restrictive level of care, allows for more interaction with family members because of the type of living environment, and is preferable to nursing home care when the detrimental effects of institutionalization are considered (Mehrota, 1991).

## Historical Development

AFC has its foundation in the Catholic Church and the family (McCoin, 1987a). Early Catholic ideas of the nature of God and the church, the church's obligation to provide for dependent individuals, and the notion of the communion of saints and devotion to them set the stage historically for AFC (Miller, 1989).

Devotion to Saint Dympna in the 13th century occasioned the taking of mentally ill pilgrims into private homes in Gheel, Belgium (Miller, 1989). Belgium eventually recognized that the care of mentally ill people in the homes of nonrelatives was a humane and practical form of care, and in 1852 made such care an integral component of the country's mental health program (Handy, 1968). Other countries, such as Scotland, France, Germany, and Switzerland, followed Belgium's example.

### Developments in the United States

The first AFC program in the United States was developed in Massachusetts in 1885 (Handy, 1968; McCoin, 1989).

Hospitals in the United States generally took responsibility for working out individualized plans for psychiatric patients who were about to be returned to the community. However, many patients had no place of their own to return to (Handy, 1968). When hospital personnel were able to locate a family willing to take in a patient, they found that many patients not only adjusted to community living but actually improved in settings that encouraged normal living (Handy, 1968).

In spite of the strides in Massachusetts, foster care for adults remained largely dormant as a form of care until the Great Depression, when, for economic reasons, the country was forced to reconsider the use of such care (McCoin, 1987a).

The Social Security Act of 1935 had a great effect on the way sick and dependent adults received care. Before its enactment, the most common form of public support available for impoverished adults was institutional care (Oktay, 1988). However, the Social Security Act prohibited residents from living in publicly financed institutions; as a result, foster care for adults expanded considerably (McCoin, 1989; Oktay, 1987).

### Impact of Deinstitutionalization

The deinstitutionalization and release of mentally ill individuals from state mental hospitals in the 1970s sparked the next period of growth for adult foster care (McCoin, 1987a). This deinstitutionalization resulted in a considerable increase in the number of homeless people because only 10 percent to 30 percent of the deinstitutionalized patients went to live in alternative institutions or in sheltered living arrangements, such as foster care homes, halfway houses, shelter care facilities, supervised hotels, and nursing homes (Segal, 1987). Although AFC was too small a program to accommodate the large number of mentally disabled and elderly patients discharged from state mental hospitals, larger community residential facilities proliferated to help fill the gap in services (Mor, Sherwood, & Gutkin, 1984).

## Programs and Program Sponsors

A variety of programs, all of which use the AFC model, have been established since the late 1970s. The Southwest Denver Community Mental Health Center Host Home program (Polak, 1978) is an example of a program designed to provide care during crises as an alternative to hospital admission.

Another model, the Short Term Bed program, was developed to provide short-term or transitional help while the person's skills are being developed and supports are being organized (Carling, Levine, & Stockdill, 1987). The SERV Centers of New Jersey Home Care program provides a long-term living situation, as well as the full array of community support and rehabilitation services the adult may require (Carling et al., 1987). Catholic Social Services of Miami Valley in Dayton, Ohio, developed a program called the Community Living Project for impaired adults who cannot live independently but do not require nursing care (Eckerle, Fagnani, Foley, & Kautz, 1981).

The Boston Back Bay Aging Concerns Committee, an intergenerational organization, includes housing programs as part of its community planning process. These programs incorporate the concept of shared living arrangements for elderly people who live in the community (Action for Boston Community Development, 1985). The Community Care Program, a foster care program developed in 1979 by Johns Hopkins Hospital, provides care for frail elderly individuals who otherwise would have been discharged to nursing homes (Oktay, 1988). These programs demonstrate the flexibility of the foster family care approach for adults in the United States.

## Policy and Policy Issues

A review of the literature illustrates major enigmas in AFC policy (Blake, 1989). For instance, the 1976 Keys Amendment to the Social Security Act was a federal attempt to establish standards for AFC and other community residences in which a large number of SSI recipients resided (McCoin, 1983). The standards were to be made part of each state's Title XX plan authorizing grants to the states for social services (Oktay, 1987). This designation made it possible for people not receiving cash assistance such as SSI to become recipients of services, because programs under the Title XX block grants were no longer tied to an income criterion (Oktay & Palley, 1988). However, the federal government did not assume responsibility for implementing the standards, but instead left this task to the states.

Concerned about the lack of standards for regulating AFC and similar homes, the American Bar Association's Commission on Legal Problems for the Elderly and the Commission on the Mentally Disabled developed a model act for regulating all community-based residential care facilities that provide lodging, residence, and personal assistance for two or more adults who are unrelated to the caregivers (Beyer, Bulkley, & Hopkins, 1984). Although the act is broad in scope, it provides uniform guidelines by which the states are expected to operate.

Perhaps the greatest merit of the act is that it requires licensure and recommends that no home have more than 30 residents because higher numbers result in an institutional atmosphere (McCoin, 1987b). In compliance with the act, most states provide some form of regulation of foster care homes for adults through licensure or certification (McCoin, 1989). However, in some states many of the smaller AFC homes are still not formally regulated (McCoin, 1987b).

## Characteristics of Caregivers

Which persons are most likely to become foster parents for adults who need this type of care? What factors should be considered in selecting caregivers? Do foster parents enable the disabled frail elderly adults who use their homes to achieve a higher quality of life?

Studies have shown that most of the people who provide care are between the ages of 30 and 50 (Braun, Vandivort, & Kurren, 1985). A social worker's caseload of AFC residents and managers in a rural and small town setting in southern Ohio indicated that the mean age of residents with psychiatric diagnoses was 58. The caregivers were mostly female and took a protective attitude toward the residents, even viewing them as family members (Miller, 1987).

The success of AFC often rests on the quality of care that the caretakers provide. Foster parents must be willing to work with the agency and accept the agency's assistance in dealing with problematic behavior that they are unable to handle. The caretakers must be skilled in working with adults whose minds are impaired. Thus, foster parents must understand the limitations and vagaries of individuals who are placed in their care.

Caring for frail elderly people often puts a tremendous burden on caregivers because of the multiple services that must be furnished by different agencies. Caregivers are frequently expected to make sure the necessary services are provided.

## Financing Options

The funding basis can be private pay, fee for service, Medicaid waiver, demonstration project, or grant (Westbrook, 1986). However, a considerable portion of the money to pay for residents in foster care comes from the federally funded Supplemental Security Income program (McCoin, 1987a). If a veteran is provided a home, the money comes from the veteran's pension. The cost of care for residents with limited incomes is frequently supplemented by the sponsoring agency (Oktay, 1987), which may be a state developmental disability agency, a mental health agency, or an area agency on aging. Funds are also available on a more limited basis through state departments of health and through the Veterans Administration (Gelfand & Olsen, 1980).

## Components of Adult Foster Care

AFC entails more than finding the right foster home for a particular person. The seven components of foster care are (1) recruitment of homes, (2) training of providers, (3) matching clients and providers, (4) supervision, (5) licensing, (6) regulation, and (7) monitoring.

### Recruitment of Homes

Foster homes for adults are frequently selected on the basis of the community in which they are located. The recruiter scrutinizes the community to determine the availability of resources, such as employment and educational opportunities, recreational activities, churches of different faiths, and transportation facilities (Handy, 1968).

Appeals for foster homes can be made through the press, radio, and television (Wymelenberg, 1980). A speaker's bureau can be effective in carrying the campaign to a variety of service groups and social organizations, such as church congregations, social clubs, and parent–teacher associations. Another useful strategy for selecting foster homes is to encourage current providers to recommend foster care to others (Carling et al., 1987). The community's knowledge and understanding of the program are critical factors to the program's success.

### Training of Providers

In the early years of AFC, training for caregivers was mostly limited to an hour-long annual meeting, although additional sponsor training took place in the field on an individual basis as problems arose (Handy, 1968). However, the training of caregivers has been upgraded to include more substantive issues.

The content of training is currently focused on normalization and sensitivity to the need for rehabilitation, rather than on custodial care alone (Carling et al., 1987). Other issues that are incorporated into training programs include nutrition, first aid, medication issues, procedures for sharing information on a regular basis, and advice on how to handle emergencies.

### Matching Clients and Providers

The achievement of a good match between the potential client and the provider of daily care is a complex process that is influenced by the preferences and characteristics of both individuals (Carling et al., 1987). Trial visits to the home and information sharing can help the potential client and caretaker get to know each other. Social workers will want to know how the members of the foster family relate to each other, the division of responsibilities among the family members, the fluidity of roles, and the flexibility of performance (Handy, 1968). The role and place to be assigned to the potential resident must also be taken into consideration.

### Supervision

Supervision is critical in AFC. The resident is the one who needs the services. The caregiver, on the other hand, needs information about how to help the resident. Caregivers should be given as much information about the resident's physical and social functioning as necessary to help them understand and meet the resident's needs. Caregivers should be informed of any special problems the potential resident may have, including mental health problems (Handy, 1968).

The primary social work role with the caregiver is basically educational: teaching and imparting essential information about the resident's physical and mental health, interpreting the agency's rules and regulations, and identifying what resources to use should a need arise.

### Licensing, Regulation, and Monitoring

The laws of most states require the licensing of facilities that provide care to frail elderly, chronically mentally ill, and developmentally disabled adults. However, there is wide variation among states in the character of legislation and in the method of delegating authority to licensing agencies. Foster care programs are administered by a variety of federal, state, and private agencies, each of which sets its own standards (Oktay, 1987). Providers have described the licensing and monitoring systems as a bureaucratic nightmare (Oktay, 1988).

Despite the Keys Amendment to the Social Security Act, which provided for standards to be set by state and local authorities, boarding homes and foster care homes are often not covered by fire safety codes because they are in residential rather than institutional categories (Butler, 1979–1980).

Regulators are frequently frustrated by their lack of effective authority to confront unlicensed and substandard facilities (Oktay, 1988). Thus, regular monitoring of foster care homes for adults is necessary. The essential components of a monitoring program include clear standards for services; scheduled and unscheduled visits; a periodic process of recertification; effective coordination with other agencies using the home; designation of one agency as having primary responsibility for monitoring; and sufficient information to evaluate whether agreed-on services have been provided, received, and evaluated before payment is made (Carling et al., 1987).

## Case Management

The basic form of intervention for residents in foster care homes is case management. Case management is an approach to service delivery that attempts to ensure that residents are receiving all the services to which they are entitled. It is the case manager's responsibility to make certain that residents are linked to an array of needed services and to ascertain whether the service delivery system is responsive to a particular resident's needs.

Generally, case managers negotiate the service delivery system on behalf of the adult residents. They also oversee the type of care that is provided to the resident in the home as well as the number of instrumental activities that the residents are able to perform successfully, such as shopping, cleaning the house, doing the laundry, and managing money and medication (McCoin, 1987a).

Case managers are expected to stay in close contact with the caregivers and to develop an overall plan for each resident that includes the services needed by the resident on a 24-hour basis. In addition, case managers should continuously monitor the services provided to the resident. Thus, case managers are workers who ensure that the service plan is implemented in a timely and appropriate way.

## Social Work Intervention

If social workers are to intervene effectively in AFC programs, they should be knowledgeable about the clients who are served. They should have knowledge of disability, the aging process, and of how best to assist families with their decision to place their older or disabled relatives.

The final decision regarding the selection of an adult for a home should include input from the adult's physician and other members of the health care team and interviews with the adult and members of the family. The social worker should develop a multidimensional functional assessment that takes into consideration the potential resident's social and psychiatric history, personality, present mental status, present physical condition, and attitude toward the foster care program and predisposing and precipitating factors relating to the person's illness. Careful consideration of these factors by the social worker should result in the best possible match between the resident and the caregiver.

## Research in Adult Foster Care

Generally studies that have focused on foster care programs for adults have found them to be cost effective; beneficial to the physical, social, and psychological well-being of the residents; and an acceptable alternative to nursing home care to the residents' relatives. For instance, an evaluation of a Poughkeepsie, New York, foster home program for elderly infirm individuals at the end of the first year indicated that the program was cost-effective; provided satisfactory care; reduced hospital stays; and prevented costly, unnecessary care in health-related or skilled nursing facilities (Talmadge & Murphy, 1983).

In a similar vein, Braun and Rose (1987) compared the outcomes and costs of care for disabled elderly patients in three different long-term-care settings in Honolulu nursing homes, geriatric foster homes, and their own homes. They found that clients in the two community settings exhibited more improvement in self-care and mobility and expressed greater well-being than did equally disabled clients in nursing homes.

Anderson, Lakin, Hill, and Chen (1992) examined the social integration of older persons with developmental disability in four types of residential placements: foster homes, group homes, large private facilities, and state institutions. Primary caregivers completed questionnaires on the residents' activities and relationships that were indicative of social integration for 235 facilities and 370 residents. The findings showed that foster care and group homes offered residents the most opportunities for socializing and that state institutions and large private facilities offered the fewest such opportunities.

In spite of the positive light in which AFC has been described, Dunkle (1982) reported that this form of care is underused by elderly individuals because they do not know about such programs and because the caretakers expect that the older people's dependence will increase. Professionals are urged to view foster care for the elderly as a viable option (Oktay & Volland, 1987) and to take care to match the older people to the home environment (Dunkle, 1982).

## Problems, Issues, and Trends

AFC, like other human services programs, is not problem free, and some problems have been embedded in the programs for years. These problems are troublesome, but if they are to be dealt with effectively, they must be addressed.

### Problems

Some argue that adult residential care has been inadequately developed conceptually and thus has a low profile, lacks a uniform national policy, and has inadequate funding sources even though it is cost-effective (McCoin, 1989). No clear authority has emerged to bring order out of this chaos and improve the delivery of services (Blake, 1989).

Despite Congressional proposals that would have required all states to establish and maintain minimum standards for admission, discharge, transfer policies, life safety, sanitation, nutrition, access to health and social services, emergency services, medication policies, civil and religious liberties, and protection of patients' funds, the problems still exist (U.S. General Accounting Office, 1989). However, there is still concern about the number of suspected and undocumented cases of inadequate medical care, poor nutrition, untrained and unlicensed personnel administering medications, and violations of fire-safety laws in these homes. Additional problems that have been cited are fraud, abuse, and theft of residents' personal funds (Volland, 1988).

In their study of residential care for the elderly, Mor et al. (1984) found that 57 percent of the providers of residential care reported revenues that did not meet costs. However, the providers' most significant complaints concerned regulatory demands.

### Issues

Despite the feasibility of adult foster care as a viable option for disabled adults and the frail elderly, a number of issues are vigorously debated among legislators, health professionals, writers who are knowledgeable about the subject, and those involved in the day-to-day care of adult residents. Most of the issues relate primarily to the operational aspects of AFC.

For instance, what services should be available to AFC residents, and who should provide them? How can a state ensure the enforcement of minimum standards of health, safety, and welfare? How can quality of care standards be improved without adversely affecting family-operated facilities? To what extent does AFC engender feelings of guilt among family members who are unable or unwilling to take adult relatives into their homes? Although standardized training is required for adult foster caregivers, many believe that such training is inadequate. However, there is no consensus on how much training is needed.

Because many nursing and boarding homes do not honor existing fire safety codes, to what extent should the federal government take a more aggressive role in reviewing standards? This is a serious issue when one considers the vulnerable populations that use these facilities. Also, an increasing number of AFC homes are shifting from a custodial to a rehabilitative focus, especially those for developmentally disabled adults (Srole, 1977). McCoin (1987a) questioned how these homes can be rehabilitative if they have limited financial resources and inadequate community supports.

Finally, serious questions can be raised about the issue of termination. For instance, what mechanisms are in place to provide clear evidence for documenting problems? Do workers or other helping personnel have the right to remove residents from the home without warning? If a resident has to be removed from the home, what backup home is available? Another concern is the extent to which workers are able to pay diligent attention to residents' rights and preferences.

### Trends

Particularly noteworthy is the potential AFC has for other target populations, particularly homeless people. From a policy perspective, the primary response to homelessness has been the establishment of short-term facilities such as emergency shelters and bridge housing. However, AFC and other types of residential facilities can play a more meaningful role in providing homeless people with more permanent, secure, and integrated residences and lifestyle (Ginsberg, 1988; Searight & Searight, 1988).

## References


Action for Boston Community Development. (1985). *Shared living: A community planning guide*. Boston: Author.

Anderson, D. J., Lakin, K. C., Hill, B. K., & Chen, T. H. (1992). Social integration of older persons with mental retardation in residential facilities. *American Journal of Mental Retardation, 96*(5), 488–501.

Beyer, J., Bulkley, J., & Hopkins, P. (1984). *A model act regulating board and care homes: Guidelines for states*. Rockville, MD: Project Share.

Blake, R. (1989). The anarchy of adult foster care policy. *Adult Residential Care Journal, 3*(2), 93–106.

Braun, K. L., & Rose, C. L. (1987). Family perceptions of geriatric foster family and nursing home care. *Family Relations, 36*(3), 321–327.

Braun, K., Vandivort, R., & Kurren, G. (1985). Loving families adult frail elderly. *Aging, 339*, 37–38.

Butler, R. N. (1979–1980). Public interest report no. 28: Fires in boarding homes for the elderly. *International Journal of Aging and Human Development, 10*(4), 401–404.

Carling, P. J., Levine, I. S., & Stockdill, J. W. (1987). Foster family care for people with long-term mental health problems: Report of a National Institute of Mental Health sponsored workshop. *Adult Foster Care Journal, 1*(2), 79–88.

Dunkle, R. E. (1982). Problems in utilizing adult foster homes. *Clinical Gerontologist, 1*(2), 74–75.

Eckerle, R., Fagnani, C., Foley, M. J., & Kautz, E. S. (1981). *Community living project: Implementation of contract model of community care for impaired adults: Final report*. Dayton, OH: Catholic Social Services of the Miami Valley.

Gelfand, D. E., & Olsen, J. (1980). *The aging network: Programs and services*. New York: Springer.

Ginsberg, L. (1988). Shelter issues in the 1990's: The potential roles of adult foster care and community residential facilities. *Adult Foster Care Journal, 2*(4), 260–272.

Handy, I. A. (1968). Foster care as a therapeutic program for geriatric psychiatric patients. *Journal of the American Geriatrics Society, 16*(3), 350–358.

McCoin, J. M. (1983). *Adult foster homes: Their managers and residents*. New York: Human Sciences Press.

McCoin, J. M. (1987a). Adult foster care: Old wine in a new glass. *Adult Foster Care Journal, 1*(1), 21–41.

McCoin, J. M. (1987b). *Directory of residential care facilities*. Richmond, VA: National Association of Residential Care Facilities.

McCoin, J. M. (1989). Toward a social movement for adult residential care. *Adult Residential Care Journal, 3*(3), 161–180.

Mehrota, C. M. (1991). Foster care for older adults: Issues and evaluations. *Home Health Care Services Quarterly, 12*(1), 115–136.

Miller, M. C. (1987). Small town streets and country lanes. *Adult Foster Care Journal, 1*(1), 56–65.

Miller, M. C. (1989). Catholicism and early adult foster care. *Adult Residential Care Journal, 3*(1), 6–13.

Mor, V., Sherwood, S., & Gutkin, C. E. (1984). Psychiatric history as a barrier to residential care. *Hospital and Community Psychiatry, 35*, 368–372.

Newman, E. S., & Sherman, S. R. (1977). A survey of caretakers in adult foster homes. *Gerontologist, 17*(6), 436–437.

Oktay, J. S. (1987). Foster care for adults. In A. Minahan (Ed.-in-Chief), *Encyclopedia of social work* (18th ed., Vol. 1, pp. 634–638). Silver Spring, MD: National Association of Social Workers.

Oktay, J. S. (1988). Community care for the frail elderly: The Johns Hopkins Hospital program. *Adult Foster Care Journal, 2*(1), 3–82.

Oktay, J. S., & Palley, H. A. (1988). The frail elderly and the promise of foster care. *Adult Foster Care Journal, 2*(1), 8–25.

Oktay, J. S., & Volland, P. J. (1987). Foster home care for the frail elderly as an alternative to nursing home care: An experimental evaluation. *American Journal of Public Health, 77*(12), 1505–1510.

Polak, P. R. (1978). A comprehensive system of alternatives to psychiatric hospitalization. In L. I. Stein & M. A. Test (Eds.), *Alternatives to mental hospital treatment*. New York: Plenum Press.

Searight, H. R., & Searight, P. R. (1988). The homeless mentally ill: Overview, policy implications, and adult foster care as a neglected resource. *Adult Foster Care Journal, 2*(4), 235–259.

Segal, S. P. (1987). Deinstitutionalization. In A. Minahan (Ed.-in-Chief), *Encyclopedia of social work* (18th ed., Vol. 1, pp. 376–382). Silver Spring, MD: National Association of Social Workers.

Sherman, S. R., Newman, E. S., & Frenkel, E. R. (1984). Community acceptance of the mentally ill in foster family care. *Health and Social Work, 9*, 188–199.

Srole, L. (1977). Gheel, Belgium: The natural therapeutic community. In G. Serban & B. Astrachan (Eds.), *New trends of psychiatry in the community* (pp. 111–129). Cambridge, MA: Ballinger.

Talmadge, H., & Murphy, D. F. (1983). Innovative home care program offers appropriate alternative for elderly. *Hospital Progress, 64*, 50–51.

U.S. General Accounting Office. (1989, November 26). *Entering a nursing home: Costly implications for nursing homes and the elderly*. Report to Congress. Washington, DC: U.S. Government Printing Office.

Volland, P. J. (1988). Foster care for the frail elderly: Implications of the Johns Hopkins experience. *Adult Foster Care Journal, 2*(1), 72–82.

Westbrook, G. J. (1986). Foster families for the frail elderly. *Continuing Care Coordinator, 5*(1), 49.

Wymelenberg, S. (1980). Foster homes: Another link in continuity. *Hospitals, 54*(13), 61–63.

## FURTHER READING

American Association of Retired Persons. (1992). *Staying at home: A guide to long term care and housing*. Washington, DC: Author.

Kane, R. A., & Kane, R. L. (1986). *Long-term care: Principles, programs, and policies*. New York: Springer.

Koff, T. H. (1982). *Long-term care: An approach to serving the frail elderly*. Boston: Little, Brown.

Monk, A. (Ed.). (1985). *Handbook of gerontological services*. New York: Van Nostrand Reinhold.

Peace, S. M. (1984). *Shared living: A viable alternative for the elderly*. Washington, DC: International Federation on Aging.

Sherman, S. R., & Newman, E. S. (1988). *Foster families for adults: A community alternative in long-term care*. New York: Columbia University Press.

Streib, G. F., Folts, W. E., & Hilken, M. A. (1984). *Old homes—New families: Shared living for the elderly*. New York: Columbia University Press.

Zedlewski, S. R., Barnes, R. O., Burt, M. R., McBride, T. D., & Meyer, J. A. (1990). *The needs of the elderly in the 21st century*. Washington, DC: Urban Institute Press.

**Marion L. Beaver, DSW,** is associate professor, University of Pittsburgh, School of Social Work, 2117 Cathedral of Learning, Pittsburgh, PA 15260.

### For further information see

Adult Day Care; Adult Protective Services; Aging Overview; Aging: Services; Case Management; Deinstitutionalization; Developmental Disabilities: Definitions and Policies; Family Caregiving; Health Care Overview; Hospital Social Work; Long-Term Care; Managed Care; Natural Helping Networks; Patient Rights; Poverty; Public Health Services; Public Social Services; Social Security; Social Welfare Policy; Social Work Profession Overview.

**Key Words**

adult foster care    residential care

# Adult Protective Services

Carol D. Austin

*Adult protective services* are the programmatic response to reported cases of elder abuse, neglect, and self-neglect. Burr (1982) defined adult protective services as "a social service with medical and legal components provided to individuals with certain identifiable characteristics who are found in circumstances and situations which are considered to be harmful or dangerous" (p. 2). As such, they reflect the complexity of situations involving elder abuse and deal with its social, legal, and medical aspects. Responsibility for providing adult protective services rests with state and local governments. Such services may be necessary if individuals are in danger of harming themselves or others or no longer have the capacity to act on their own behalf and there are no significant others who can responsibly become involved.

Protective services are designed to ensure that older adults who may be targets of victimization receive the support and assistance they require. The source of this victimization varies and includes family, friends, neighbors, unscrupulous businesspeople, and criminals. Vulnerable older adults frequently experience mental and physical disabilities that limit their ability to take care of their basic needs and put them at higher risk. Protective services clients reside in a variety of living arrangements, from living with relatives, to living alone, to being homeless. In 1986 the most frequently provided adult protective services were case management, homemaker service, legal services, mental health treatment or counseling, and medical treatment and supplies (National Association of State Units on Aging [NASUA] & American Public Welfare Association [APWA], 1988). The common theme in these care plans is the possibility of legal intervention in the client's life.

Legal intervention is called for when individuals are not capable of making personal or business decisions and are dangerous to themselves or others. This guideline has been interpreted to mean that legal involvement is necessary when individuals refuse services identified as necessary to their security or to public safety. A number of legal actions are possible. In the past, they included civil commitment and individual, agency, and public guardianship. Today, legal actions in use include emergency intervention, substitute payee, power of attorney, and the creation of a trust. The use or imposition of these measures directly affects older adults' most fundamental right, the right to self-determination. These legal issues incorporate ethical concerns that are at the heart of social work practice.

Physical or mental vulnerability and abuse produce medical problems addressed by adult protective services programs. Physical abuse involves the premeditated use of physical force that results in injury, pain, or impairment. Psychological abuse is the planned infliction of mental or emotional torment by intimidation and humiliation in both verbal and nonverbal forms. Identification, diagnosis, and treatment of physical or psychological injury are key medical activities in the delivery of adult protective services.

Although states vary in their adult protective services statutes, a number of common themes can be identified. Adults who receive protective services are described as abused, neglected, exploited, and possibly living in locations that are unsafe and unhealthy. They are of concern to local public social services agencies when they are no longer coping well and there is no one willing to assist and supervise them. In such situations, the client's decision-making power may be designated to another on the client's behalf. A balance must be struck between protecting clients' safety and preserving their independence and self-determination.

## Historical Development

In the late 1950s, two groups of social workers, one associated with the National Council on Aging and the other with the Benjamin Rose Institute, came together to focus professional attention on protective services for elderly people. The source of their concern was the increasing number of mentally and physically disabled elderly people who could no longer manage their daily needs and who were easy prey to abuse, neglect, accident, illness, and exploitation.

By the early 1960s, activity had intensified, expanding to include both research and demonstration projects across the nation. The National Council on Aging received a four-year grant to study the comparative effectiveness of three model protective services programs in Houston, San Diego, and Philadelphia. During this period, adult protective services programs were also developed in Washington, DC; rural Colorado; and Chicago. These efforts produced a profile of clients and services.

The Benjamin Rose Institute, with support from the Social Security Administration, conducted a five-year study, Protective Services for Older People, from 1963 to 1968 to evaluate the effectiveness of the demonstration service (Blenkner, Bloom, Nielsen, & Weber, 1974). Referrals for older adults received between June 1964 and June 1965 were randomly assigned to the experimental group (receiving the experimental service) or to the control group (receiving the usual community services). All participants and their identified collaterals were interviewed at regular intervals.

The main hypothesis was that members of the experimental group would report higher levels of contentment and higher survival rates than would members of the control group. The intervention consisted of protective services, including social casework, supported by financial, medical, home aide, social service assistant, placement, fiduciary, and guardianship service. Legal and psychiatric consultation also were provided. Social casework services were based on a psychoanalytic model and were provided by master's-level social workers.

This landmark study produced unexpected results that challenged practitioners' assumptions regarding the positive benefits of adult protective services for vulnerable elderly people. The primary finding was that those who received services failed to demonstrate significantly higher contentment or survival scores than those who did not receive services. In fact, the intensive experimental services appeared to increase the chance of death and the rate of institutionalization. These findings touched off a storm of controversy. Researchers examined the methodology to determine whether sources of systematic bias were somehow introduced into the data, thus producing the negative findings. Practitioners found their confidence in the effectiveness of their work shaken. This study, one of the earliest experimental program evaluations, had a profound impact on the further development of practice research.

Elder abuse and adult protective services have been the focus of intermittent attention from Congress. In 1965 the House Select Committee on Aging released its second report titled *Elder Abuse: A National Disgrace* (U.S. House of Representatives, 1965). While gathering data for the report, "the subcommittee found that only about 4.7% of the average state's total budget for protective services was allocated for the elderly" (Wolf, 1988, p. 9). Early hearings before the Senate Special Committee on Aging in 1978 and 1980 highlighted elder abuse. The visibility of the problem was increased when the committee issued a report titled *Elder Abuse: An Examination of a Hidden Problem* (U.S. Senate, 1979). This report put forward a range of policy options for consideration and possible legislation. The 1984 amendments to the Older Americans Act required the Commissioner on Aging to report on the unmet needs for prevention of elder abuse. In addition, the amendments instituted a state-level requirement to coordinate elder abuse prevention activities with existing adult protective services.

By 1968 fewer than 20 communities in the United States had communitywide protective services for aged people in place. Today all states have an adult protective services statute in place. Expansion of adult protective services programs was stimulated by funding and policy mandates in Title III of the Older Americans Act and Title XX of the Social Security Act (later the Social Services Block Grant Act of 1981). In some states the passage of adult protective services laws was accompanied by a designated budget to support the services. By definition and in operation, elder abuse and adult protective services are inseparable. A study conducted jointly by the National Association of State Units on Aging and the American Public Welfare Association (1988) reported that "in more than three fourths of the states in this country, adult protective service social service agencies serve as lead agencies for elder abuse" (p. 3).

## Population at Risk

Recent projections suggest that as many as 1 million to 2 million older people annually may suffer abuse. Cases of neglect present complex practice challenges. Neglect can be defined by the willful or nonwillful failure of caregivers to fulfill their caregiving obligations. In cases of self-abuse and self-neglect, elderly people increase their own vulnerability by engaging in either willful or nonwillful behaviors that endanger their welfare, health, or safety. Because individuals are more likely to live alone, it is harder to detect the abusive or neglectful behavior, and the risk of self-abuse or self-neglect is even higher.

Cash and Valentine (1987) studied the adult protective services caseload in South Carolina. During the 10-year period from 1974 to 1984, 13,273 cases of substantiated maltreatment were recorded and the victims served. During the same period, 4,082 cases of maltreatment were unsubstantiated. The victim was most likely to be a poor, white woman over the age of 65 who was ambulatory and living with a friend or relative. The substantiated adult protective services clients received casework counseling (70 percent) and mental health services (12.9 percent); 17.7 percent were placed in a protective setting, and 2.2 percent required court action. The majority of clients were able to live at home with such services as health care (30.6 percent), homemaker services (17.3 percent), financial assistance (10.4 percent), housing (9.5 percent), and other supportive and supplemental social services.

In a 1992 study, the Public Policy Institute of the American Association of Retired Persons investigated the characteristics of repeat elder abuse clients (Simon, 1992). Data were gathered from five states: Delaware, Florida, Illinois, Texas, and Wisconsin, all of which varied in their mix of administrative structures and reporting laws. Onsite and telephone interviews were conducted with 50 adult protective services programs from the five states. The major finding was that as many as 20 percent of the program's current clients may have been through the system before. Study respondents reported that repeat clients were more likely to have resisted efforts to provide services or to have suffered mental or physical deterioration.

## Diversity

*Diversity* is described in the adult protective services client population in terms of the various subpopulations requiring oversight—that is, adults who are abused, neglected, or exploited and who have no one willing to intervene responsibly on their behalf. They are also described as "incapacitated"—impaired by reason of mental illness, mental deficiency, physical illness or disability, or advanced age. The most common profile of an individual requiring adult protective services (a poor, white woman over age 65) masks the reality that adults from a variety of racial, ethnic, and cultural groups may also fall into the categories cited above. Unfortunately, data on the adult protective services caseload are not reported by racial or ethnic group. As a result, little is known about the incidence and prevalence of abuse or neglect in minority communities, and one could conclude that these populations have been underserved. The absence of data on minority clients makes it difficult to learn about the dynamics of elder abuse and neglect in these populations. There is some danger that this vacuum will be filled with stereotypes and misconceptions, thus continuing to reinforce inadequate outreach efforts as well as poorly conceived investigative activities.

## Scope of Services

The scope of adult protective services is described in state policy manuals and varies broadly. One jurisdiction may define adult protective services as incorporating whatever services are necessary and appropriate; another jurisdiction will identify a variety of specific services that are available (NASUA & APWA, 1988). For example, the state of Delaware lists the following services: preliminary investigation of medical and psychiatric care, social casework, goods and services that allow the client to remain at home, respite care, emergency care, placement in a rest or residential home, referral to legal assistance (to establish power of attorney or representative payee) or public guardian, referral for medical assessment, transportation, and other services (Delaware Code Ann., 1986).

Where services are not specified or are defined ambiguously, the agency providing adult protective services has wide discretion, potentially unconstrained by specific legal direction. Legal Counsel for the Elderly, Inc. (1987), sponsored by the American Association of Retired Persons, observed that

> since these agencies tend towards intervention, individual personality traits or eccentricities may not be sufficiently protected.... The range of authorized services highlights a key point: the social services agency wields considerable power in determining what kind of intervention is appropriate. In practice, the statutes offer more than they can deliver, since resources to match appropriate services are not available. (p. 88)

The more familiar adult protective services are those that require legal action to change the status of the potential ward or to give specific power and responsibility to designated individuals by court appointment. Perhaps the most familiar of these situations is guardianship, although guardianship and conservatorship are closely linked. Both are court appointed and are designed to assist the abused or neglected incompetent elder by appointing benevolent, conscientious caregivers. Guardians are responsible for the care, comfort, and maintenance of their ward. They can determine the ward's place of residence, can decide what is to be done with the ward's property (furniture, clothing, and vehicles), are responsible for seeing that the ward receives necessary medical treatment and services, and, if there is no conservator appointed, can also manage the ward's financial affairs. In contrast, conservators are appointed specifically to manage the ward's estate and to ensure oversight and accountability. The conservator may also be responsible for compensating the guardian for care provided to the ward. One individual can serve in both capacities.

Although many guardians and conservators are appointed by the court to alleviate an abusive situation, many others are appointed when no abuse or neglect has been substantiated. In these situations, the court has determined that the elder is no longer able to manage her or his affairs and that an alternative decision maker is needed; at this point the elder's self-determination and participation in decision making are severely restricted or totally removed. Once appointed, the guardian or conservator is answerable to the court.

The appointment of a guardian or conservator, however, may not solve the problem. Guardians and conservators may also engage in abusive and neglectful behavior. It is reasonable to ask whether guardians and conservators can be required to provide a higher standard of care than other caregivers. After reviewing state abuse and neglect statutes, Frolik (1990) concluded that "nothing in the statutes suggests or requires that guardians are held to a higher standard than other caregivers" (p. 42).

Over time, a number of reforms to the guardianship and conservatorship system have been advocated. Keith and Wacker (1993) identified problems in guardianship proceedings that must be reformed. Among these are violations of civil rights, involuntary commitment, protection of due process, and procedures for evaluating competency. Keith and Wacker studied the effects of several reforms (specific statement of incapacity on petition, proposed ward at hearing, representation by legal counsel, and recommendation of court visitor and ward) on guardianship rulings. They found that courts overwhelmingly ruled in favor of full power for guardians, even when advocated reforms were in place.

Power of attorney, durable power of attorney, and representative payee systems have been more recently developed and used in adult protective services. *Power of attorney* is a legal measure that authorizes one person to manage the affairs of another, including signing documents and conducting transactions on the other's behalf. Elders can delegate as much or as little of the decision making as they desire. Although this arrangement can be terminated at any time, the elder must be competent to initiate power of attorney—a restriction that clearly limits the utility of the standard power of attorney.

The *durable power of attorney* differs from the power of attorney in that it is not affected by the elder's subsequent incapacity. The arrangement can be terminated at any time, and the elder can decide, before losing capacity, who will manage his or her affairs and what that responsibility will entail. The durable power of attorney enhances autonomy and provides a means for future planning.

*Representative payees* must be identified when clients receive either social security benefits or Supplemental Security Income. Neither power of attorney nor conservatorship is recognized for this purpose. Before the client designates a representative payee, a physician must declare the client incapable of handling his or her own affairs.

## Statutory Authority

Adult protective services are authorized and funded from two primary sources at the federal level, the Social Services Block Grant Act of 1981 and the Older Americans Act. Under the Social Services Block Grant (previously Title XX), states are given discretion to fund services that fall under broadly defined objectives. Adult protective services fall under two of these objectives:

1. preventing or remedying neglect, abuse, or exploitation of children and adults unable to protect their own interests
2. preventing or reducing inappropriate institutional care by providing for community-based care, home-based care, and other forms of less intensive care.

Adult protective services are also authorized in the Older Americans Act under provisions for programs aimed at preventing elder abuse, neglect, and exploitation. More specifically, statutory language speaks to "ensuring the coordination of services provided by area agencies on aging with services instituted under the state adult protective service program."

The contents of adult protective services statutes vary from state to state, although common elements can be identified. These statutes define abuse, neglect, and exploitation, although some exclude cases of self-neglect. A court will intervene and order services only when it has been demonstrated that the adult has been incapacitated or is vulnerable owing to mental or physical disability. In some states, the standard used to intervene under the adult protective services statute is the same as that used to appoint a guardian. Regan (1981) observed that standards for involuntary protective orders have been vague and have frequently included too much or too little. Most state adult protective services statutes cover all adults, although some are restricted to adults over age 60. In these cases, the statute may be identified as the elder abuse law.

The identification and investigation of suspected cases of abuse and neglect can be a difficult and challenging process. Forty-three states mandate reporting of suspected cases of abuse and neglect by specific individuals (NASUA & APWA, 1988), including physicians, health care providers, court-appointed surrogates, police officers, social worker advocates, and administrators of health care facilities or residential homes. Reports are received by the regional or state agency responsible for administering the adult protective services program.

A common problem involves the caregiver who blocks access to the client. State statutes address this problem through several different approaches. Police intervention on probable cause is one possibility, as is court-ordered visitation and access. Search warrants, personal interviews, and subpoenas are used in different jurisdictions. Nineteen state laws, however, do not include any provision designed to improve access to older adults suspected of being victims of abuse or neglect (Legal Counsel for the Elderly, Inc., 1987).

Adult protective services programs often serve involuntary clients who have refused service or are unable to consent owing to impairment or caregiver interference. In such cases, emergency intervention may be necessary. State statutes vary widely regarding the type of emergency intervention that is sanctioned. When court proceedings are initiated in these situations, legal representation for the recipient of the intervention is rare. Usually emergency interventions are time limited, with the goal being to remove the individual from an immediately dangerous situation.

Some states require representation by legal counsel; others provide for the appointment of a guardian *ad litem*. A guardian ad litem may not serve as an advocate but can adopt a neutral stance. Due process concerns abound in these complex practice situations. Client rights will vary widely across jurisdictions: For example, depending on their state of residency, clients may be at their hearing, have the right to trial by jury, or be required to examine the options of the least restrictive environment. Twenty-three states require the placement in the least restrictive environment. In 35 states, guardianship may result from adult protective services intervention (Legal Counsel for the Elderly, Inc., 1987).

Some adult protective services statutes cover residents of long-term-care facilities, although the Older Americans Act also requires each state to have a long-term-care ombudsman who receives complaints and investigates cases of alleged abuse and neglect in institutional settings. The NASUA and APWA study (1988) reported that in 37 states the state protective services agency investigated or provided services in cases of suspected institutional abuse and neglect. Where responsibility for community and institutional oversight are separate, clarity of jurisdiction and authority is necessary for effective service delivery to protect vulnerable adults, regardless of where they live.

## State Administration

Findings from a national study of adult protective service programs provide a comprehensive picture of how programs are administered throughout the country (NASUA & APWA, 1988). They are administered by state adult protective services agencies, state units on aging, or state agencies that combine both programs. Thirty-seven states administer their adult protective services program through a state-administered adult protective services agency. Twenty-seven have separate administrative structures for adult protective services and state units on aging. In 13 states, these programs are combined. In five states, adult protective services are delivered through other organizational arrangements. In states with a state adult protection service, local services are normally provided through county departments of social service. In states where adult protective services are administered by the state unit on aging, area agencies on aging provide information, referral, and support services to adult protective services cases. Effective local-level coordination between these two delivery systems is important for quality service provision.

In 1986 the Social Services Block Grant accounted for 45 percent of total direct expenditures for adult protective services. Other funding sources included state funds (39 percent), county funds (13 percent), Older Americans Act funds (4 percent), and "other" (1 percent). The majority of these funds are administered by the state adult protective services agency. The state unit on aging and the adult protective services agency most frequently collaborate on training and educational activities.

## Practice Issues

Adult protective services programs and the clients they serve present social workers with a daunting set of practice challenges. Serving this vulnerable population raises many of the most basic issues practitioners confront, issues that go to the foundation of social work humanism. These cases often involve legal actions that strip individuals of their rights. In practice, removing or limiting an elder's right to self-determination has repercussions, often creating anguish for the family, the adult protective services worker, and other concerned individuals. Regan (1981) wrote that "depriving clients of their personal liberty, their right to make personal care decisions and their right to control their property for extended periods without an adversary hearing, may violate the due process clause of the fourteenth amendment" (p. 1121).

There is another set of professional values and responsibilities that come into play, those regarding protection for and outreach to individuals who may be at risk. Before it is possible to assess whether adult protective services intervention is required, it is necessary to locate these individuals and gain access. Outreach and case finding have not received sufficient attention. More emphasis has been placed on the provision of services, both social and legal, than on casefinding in the community. One effective outreach model uses gatekeepers to locate and identify high-risk elderly people. Gatekeepers are nontraditional referral sources (meter readers, postal workers, bank personnel, and residential property managers) who are trained to identify high-risk elderly people living in the community and refer them to community services. This approach combines a clinical intervention with a systematic community organization effort (Raschko, 1990). To be proactive in the identification of vulnerable elderly people, it is necessary to develop innovative outreach programs.

A major challenge confronting social workers in adult protective services is inadequate knowledge of the nature and extent of abuse and neglect in minority communities. Outreach and assessment activities are affected by workers' knowledge and awareness of multicultural factors. Culturally appropriate programs are required if adult protective services are to reach vulnerable elders. Workers need sufficient sensitivity to distinguish culture-specific behaviors as they apply to legal definitions and the consideration of appropriate sanctions. The racial and ethnic diversity of the older population must be underscored in the provision of adult protective services. Vulnerable adults are present across population groups. Adult protective programs and services must reflect this diversity in both design and implementation.

Guardianship is a highly restrictive action. Guardians are appointed to manage the affairs of elders who have been judged incompetent. Personal history, values, social class, and ethnicity are important considerations in assessing an older person's capacity to function independently. Once appointed, guardianships are essentially permanent. It is necessary, therefore, to protect the elder and to avoid appointing a guardian in situations where an incapacity is temporary or reversible. The purpose of guardianship is to protect people who require protection, yet some guardians may be abusive. The goal is to create a guardianship system that incorporates multiple safeguards and protections. Guardianship is a very serious, apparently permanent termination of an individual's rights from which there is usually no recourse. It is not an expedient resolution, and it should be used with caution.

Adult protective services programs will become more and more important as the number of older adults grows into the next century. The sheer growth of the population suggests an increased demand for services. Planning for this reality is required. It is necessary to examine structural arrangements to determine which ones facilitate the provision of effective services and the efficient receipt of referrals. Innovative alternatives to standard guardianship should be further developed and evaluated. With the creation of additional options, guardianship may be used only in those cases where it is absolutely necessary.

Greater attention to the needs of elderly people requiring protective services is necessary in public and professional education programs. They are often an invisible population, but they are present nonetheless, and their numbers will increase in the future. It is clear that funding for adult protective services is not sufficient to meet the identified need, much less to serve those individuals who remain isolated. The quality and quantity of current and future service delivery depends to a great extent on the adequacy of funding. As the population of older people grows, there is considerable risk that less and less funding will be available. Adult protective services is one program where doing more with less is a potentially dangerous practice. Planning for the demographic changes to come requires activity on several fronts: legal, programmatic, educational, and fiscal.

## References

Blenkner, M., Bloom, M., Nielsen, M., & Weber, R. (1974). *Final report: Protective services for older people. Findings from the Benjamin Rose Institute Study.* Cleveland: Benjamin Rose Institute.

Burr, J. (1982). *Protective services for adults* (DHHS Publication No. OHDS 82-20505). Washington, DC: U.S. Department of Health and Human Services.

Cash, T., & Valentine, D. (1987). A decade of adult protective services: Case characteristics. *Journal of Gerontological Social Work, 10*(3–4), 47–60.

Delaware Code Ann. Supp. tit. 31, §3904 (1986).

Frolik, L. (1990). Elder abuse and guardians of elderly incompetents. *Journal of Elder Abuse and Neglect, 2*(3–4), 31–56.

Keith, P., & Wacker, R. (1993). Implementation of recommended guardianship practices and outcomes of hearings for older persons. *Gerontologist, 33*(1), 81–87.

Legal Counsel for the Elderly, Inc. (1987). *Decision making, incapacity and the elderly: A protective service practice manual*. Washington, DC: American Association of Retired Persons.

National Association of State Units on Aging & American Public Welfare Association. (1988). *Adult protective services: Programs in state social service agencies and state units on aging*. Washington, DC: Author.

Older Americans Act Amendments of 1984. P.L. 98-459, 98 Stat. 1767.

Raschko, R. (1990). The gatekeeper model for isolated, at-risk elderly. In N. Cohn (Ed.), *Psychiatry takes to the streets*. New York: Guilford Press.

Regan, J. (1981). Protecting the elderly: The new paternalism. *Hastings Legal Journal, 32*, 1111–1123.

Simon, L. M. (1992). *An exploratory study of adult protective service programs' repeat elder abuse clients*. Washington, DC: American Association of Retired Persons, Public Policy Institute.

Social Services Block Grant Act of 1981. P.L. 97-35, 95 Stat. 867–871.

U.S. House of Representatives, Select Committee on Aging. (1965). *Elder abuse: A national disgrace*. Washington, DC: U.S. Government Printing Office.

U.S. Senate, Special Committee on Aging. (1979). *Elder abuse: An examination of a hidden problem*. Washington, DC: U.S. Government Printing Office.

Wolf, R. (1988). The evolution of policy: A ten-year retrospective. *Public Welfare, 46*(2), 5–13.

### Further Reading

American Bar Association, Commission on Legal Problems of the Elderly. (1986). *Statement of recommended judicial practices*. Washington, DC: Author.

American Bar Association, Commission on Legal Problems of the Elderly. (1989). *Guardianship: An agenda for reform*. Washington, DC: Author.

Pilemer, K., & Wolf, R. (Eds.). (1986). Elder abuse: Conflict in the family. Boston: Auburn.

Tatara, T. (1991). *Elder abuse and neglect: A national research agenda*. Washington, DC: National Aging Resource Center on Elder Abuse.

U.S. House of Representatives, Select Committee on Aging. (1987). *Abuses in guardianship of the elderly and infirm: A national disgrace*. Washington, DC: U.S. Government Printing Office.

**Carol D. Austin, PhD,** is assistant dean, Faculty of Social Work, University of Calgary, 2500 University Drive, NW, Calgary, Alberta, Canada T2N 1N4.

### For further information see

Adult Day Care; Adult Foster Care; Advocacy; Aging Overview; Aging: Services; Community; Community Development; Community Needs Assessment; Community Organization; Disability; Ethnic-Sensitive Practice; Families: Demographic Shifts; Family Caregiving; Health Planning; Health Services Systems Policy; Homelessness; Income Security Overview; Long-Term Care; Mental Health Overview; Natural Helping Networks; Patient Rights; Poverty; Public Health Services; Public Social Services; Social Security; Social Welfare Policy; Supplemental Security Income.

**Key Words**

adult protective services
aging services
elder abuse
elder neglect

# Advocacy

**James S. Mickelson**

Advocacy has always been a significant part of the social work profession. Although its prominence has fluctuated over the years, it remains at the core of professional practice. Today, advocacy efforts are becoming increasingly sophisticated as the profession increases its political role to ensure social justice.

### Advocacy Defined

The *Social Work Dictionary* defines advocacy as action that empowers individuals or communities (Barker, 1991). This definition must be qualified, however; although empowerment is viewed as a component of advocacy, some groups (such as children and the severely mentally ill) cannot be empowered. In social work, advocacy can be defined as the act of directly representing, defending, intervening, supporting, or recommending a course of action on behalf of one or more individuals, groups, or communities, with the goal of securing or retaining social justice.

### Components of Advocacy

Before any advocacy efforts are undertaken, it is important to determine that the environment is obstructing a client's self-determination or causing a social injustice. Second, the social worker must determine the degree to which the individual or community can be empowered to confront the problems in the environment that distress them. Even after advocacy action is undertaken, the social worker must reassess the role the individual or community can play in effecting social change or maintaining advancements. Once it is determined that individuals, groups, or communities need intervention to bring about change in the environment, the social worker is obligated to advocate on their behalf, especially for those who cannot be empowered.

Although advocacy is a fundamental component of the profession, it is generally viewed as an element of macro practice, because it is more concentrated and viable in macro-level practice areas. In the course of any practice setting, however, caseworkers or micropractitioners undertake advocacy efforts. Such actions are often referred to by other terms. For example, in a case management setting the worker may seek assurances from a provider that certain services that may be different from the routine will be provided if the client requests them. In other settings, advocacy may be the primary function of social workers employed as community organizers, political aides, lobbyists, or elected officials, whose job is to bring about social change. For example, a social worker who is employed by the Child Welfare League of America may be responsible for developing recommendations for legislation that assists families.

Because social workers practice in numerous settings and with various types of clients, they must use different approaches to champion their clients' rights. To ensure effective outcomes, social workers must possess various advocacy skills and strategies, combined with a thorough understanding of the client's circumstances. The cardinal rule of social work is to start where the client is, and the same principal applies to advocacy.

Consequently, information is essential to any advocacy effort (Richan, 1991). Before taking any action, social workers must understand the situation, policies, public perception, client–environment interaction, and issues relating to the problem. Information about the client's background and presenting problem or the community's problem and demographics must be obtained before any "assessment" can be reached or community-organization strategy developed. Intervention in the political arena involves the same processes and has the same basic requirements as case or community work (Haynes & Mickelson, 1991).

## Interrelatedness of Micro and Macro Advocacy

Like the profession, advocacy can be divided into two general areas: case (micro) and class (macro) advocacy. Case advocacy refers to working with the client's interaction with the environment. Class advocacy refers to intervention to change the environment through social policy. A person-in-environment perspective provides many points of intervention and different forms of advocacy efforts. As Figure 1 illustrates, social workers need both micro and macro skills to work with the environment and the individual, regardless of the point of intervention. To determine which social work setting requires more work with the environment or the individual, follow a point of intervention across the person–environment paradigm. For example, a political aid advocates more on environmental circumstances than on addressing individual problems; whereas the case manager's intervention is more individual than environmental.

Social workers advocate in many arenas, only a few of which are presented in Figure 1. The social worker can practice as a U.S. senator or as a case worker in a family services center. Regardless of the setting, the practitioner continually encounters unmet needs, social problems, social injustice, and gaps in or barriers to service. Irrespective of the form of intervention—community organization, casework, administration, or political activity—the resource most needed for advocacy is information. The following examples of case and class advocacy highlight the interrelatedness of the two.

### Case Advocacy

A case worker in a unit that addresses low-income clients, homelessness, and resettlement encountered several homeless families who could not receive emergency food stamps. After some exploration the social worker discovered that they were being denied services because they had no address (being homeless) and therefore were not considered to be residents. These families needed an advocate to begin the process that would entitle them to receive emergency aid. By advocating for one family the social worker gained data on how poorly the system worked and how many needy families did not receive assistance.

### Class Advocacy

In reviewing state regulations, the social worker found a way to make the system respond to the families' pressing needs. With data on what the "glitch" was, the social worker convened a meeting of area service providers to discuss the withholding of emergency aid from clients who have no address. The worker explained the problem and what had been achieved with the client. Through these meetings and working with local legislators, a state policy was clarified, and the state implemented new regulations that allowed homeless people throughout the state to receive emergency food stamps. The social worker continued with the advocacy efforts and twice testified before the U.S.

FIGURE 1

**Social Worker Role in Advocacy**

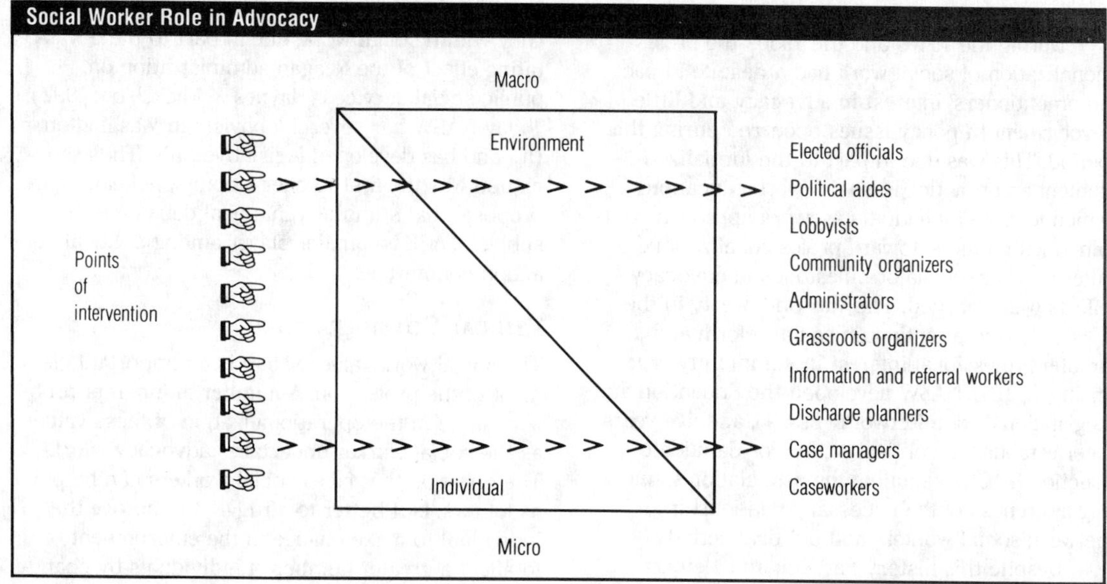


Congress on legislation that resulted in the Hunger Prevention Act of 1988 (P.L. 100-435).

Clearly, the interrelatedness between micro and macro practice is critical for both arenas if the profession is to work effectively for its clientele. The class advocate cannot bring about change without needed data from case advocates who have a clear understanding of the effect of social policy on individual clients. Changing social policy is time consuming and slow. The micro social worker does not always have the time to address policy change and therefore must rely on the macro practitioner to work for social justice.

**Empowerment**

The goal of empowerment is to increase the individual's ability to improve his or her circumstances toward the more critical goal of social justice. "The process of empowerment addresses two objectives: the achievement of the more equitable distribution of resources and non-exploitative relationships between people and the enabling of people to achieve a creative sense of power through enhanced self-respect, confidence, knowledge and skills" (Rees, 1991, p. 66).

Social workers who practice as caseworkers and group workers incorporate the concept of empowerment into the very heart of their work and value orientation. They have come to view client empowerment as central to the overall profession (Simon, 1990).

**Importance to the Profession**

Advocacy on behalf of an individual or a community is at the very core of the social work profession. The *NASW Code of Ethics* (NASW, 1994) clearly states that advocacy is a basic obligation of every professional social worker. Two sections within the code address advocacy:

- Section II-G, The Rights and Perogatives of Clients—The social worker should make every effort to foster maximum self-determination on the part of the client.
- Section VI-P, The Social Worker's Ethical Responsibility to Society—Promoting the General Welfare. Promoting the general welfare includes eliminating discrimination; ensuring access to resources; expanding choice and opportunity; promoting diversity of cultures; providing professional services in emergencies; advocating change in policy and legislation to promote social justice; and encouraging informed public participation in public policy, all of which are clearly within the practice of all social workers. Failure to do so is failure to practice social work ethically.

## Historical Background

Although social work had its beginnings in direct practice, it has always focused on goals related to social justice and equity. It is true that during certain times in its history, the profession turned away from advocacy. Nevertheless, advocacy efforts began with Jane Addams and her Hull House Settlement in Chicago. Jeannette Rankin, a child welfare worker concerned about the plight of children, took her concerns into the elected political arena and became the first woman and the first social worker to serve in Congress in 1917.

During the 1940s and the 1950s the professionalization of social work had a definite impact on practitioners' interest in advocacy, and little involvement in policy issues occurred during this period. This was due in part to the formalized content and practice in social work education, which took an individual casework approach combined with a move toward professionalization. After this period, major milestones in advocacy efforts were reached. The War on Poverty in the 1960s focused attention on social reform and a greater professional interest in community organizing. In 1971 NASW developed the Education and Legislation Action Network (ELAN), and five years later established Political Action for Candidate Election (PACE), signaling the association's emerging awareness of the necessary relationship between social workers and political activity.

Despite this history, Pardeck and Meinert (1994, p. 102) argue that the profession has turned its back on advocacy and state: "Even in the recent times when the country had liberal presidents as in the Kennedy/Johnson and Carter eras, social workers remained distant from the halls of power." Indeed, social action had been deemphasized in social work education. A 1972 study of 51 social work schools found that the majority of graduate students and educators did not consider social action or initiation of social change to be a primary function of the profession (Carlton & Jung, 1972).

By the 1980s, the social work profession did not have many social workers trained or even interested in advocacy, either as a professional career choice or as an adjunct to clinical practice. To help bring about the needed change in social work education, the Council on Social Work Education (CSWE) included the following statement as part of its 1982 *Curriculum Policy Statement:* "The knowledge and skills students accumulate in social welfare policy and services should prepare them to exert leadership and influence as legislative and social advocates, lobbyists, and expert advisors to policy makers and administrators" (CSWE, 1982). This commitment was further strengthened in the 1992 Curriculum Policy Statement: "The pursuit of policies, services and programs through legislative advocacy, lobbying, and other forms of social and political action, including providing expert testimony, participation in local and national coalitions and gaining political office" (CSWE, 1992).

NASW had held several Social Workers in Politics conferences that moved the profession in a more political direction by the end of the 1980s. The early 1990s saw a continued growth of advocacy within social work, due in part to the devastating effect of the Reagan administration on public social services (Haynes & Mickelson, 1992). Today, NASW has several lobbyists in Washington, DC, and has developed legislative bills. The association was the first to offer a complete health care proposal that stimulated national debate on the subject. PACE is a major player among political action committees.

## Ethical Considerations

The social work value system is an important element of the profession. A number of inherent problems arise in the operationalization of these values as the social worker undertakes advocacy efforts. The question that faces social workers can be put as follows: Is it better to struggle to improve the individual to make change in the environment or to affect a greater number of individuals by changing the environment? Success with individuals may be easily and quickly achieved and, consequently, may be more rewarding. "Implicit in this debate are a set of value conflicts that are at the core of the past, present, and future of social work" (Reeser & Epstein, 1990, p. 9). Such ethical conflict has caused social work practice to suffer major reformation several times in its relatively short history, and there has been a clear struggle for decades between clinical practice and social reform (Specht & Courtney, 1994). This conflict is heightened because of ethical dilemmas that practitioners face when they assume the role of advocate.

### Social Work Values and Conflicts

***Self-determination.*** Self-determination, the most important professional value, causes conflict for the social worker undertaking advocacy efforts. Young children, some elderly people, emotionally disturbed clients, and developmentally disabled people are the most obvious examples of client groups for whom self-determination may be irrelevant. Social workers, therefore, must assume an active responsibility for deciding the best advocacy for specific clienteles. Self-determination in these situations just cannot be obtained.

***Impartiality.*** Impartiality is an essential professional value. It is necessary to keep one's personal values out of casework to ensure the client's self-determination. However, impartiality on a macro level supports the status quo, whereas the *NASW Code of Ethics* clearly states that social workers must be concerned with the general welfare. The common phrase used to articulate this is "doing nothing is a political act." The goal of advocacy is to bring about change, which occurs either when individuals who have the power are motivated for the common good or face public pressure. An advocate cannot create public pressure by being impartial.

Additionally, advocacy efforts must be adversarial at some level. The social worker who sees himself or herself as a helping professional or a kind person feels conflicted when using strategies to put pressure on those with power. Social workers struggle to keep in mind who their client is and what is in the client's best interest.

***Funding issues.*** "There is no profession that places a greater value on the individual in his/her social context than does the profession of social work" (Vinic & Lenin, 1991, p. xiii). This belief gives the practitioner a potentially tremendous direct and indirect impact on legislative, administrative, and financial decisions. The practitioner is an ideal conduit between those who have problems and needs and those who are politically active. However, social workers may be reluctant to support public funding for social services because this may be or appear to be self-serving. Most social work programs are publicly funded, and a politically effective social worker can be a positive influence on human-service funding during the budget allocation process. Although this may appear self-serving, one should remember that without sufficient funds to hire professionally trained social workers, human services will be poorly delivered.

## Future Issues

During shifting political and economic trends, social workers will need to compete with many other interests for public and legislative attention. Only the most sophisticated, influential, and committed groups will be successful in long-term advocacy toward social justice. No other profession is better suited to take on this role than social work, and the role of advocacy in the profession is likely to continue.

Some believe that the profession has lost its mission (Specht & Courtney, 1994). Although such debate is healthy, it may widen the gap between the micro and macro practitioners. If the profession does not value advocacy in both the macro and micro practice, social work could lose its uniqueness. This is clearly an issue that will concern the profession for some time. What lies ahead is dependent on the profession's ability not to repeat historical disinterest in advocacy.

Advocacy in the social work profession is now shifting to a more politically sophisticated approach. Today NASW monitors the number of social workers nationwide who hold elected offices and who have entered the political arena. This political advocacy trend is likely to continue, with social work schools placing greater emphasis on political content. Social work schools have offered political curriculum content and political placements, and the Graduate School of Social Work at the University of Houston has established the first concentration in political social work (Fisher, in press). Interestingly, this track prepares students who are interested in both the micro- and macro-level practice.

As the era of high tech has arrived, so has the need for greater individual interaction. Unquestionably, the social work profession will succeed in the interpersonal aspects of political advocacy. However, to really compete the practitioner must use present technology. With the establishment of NASW's Center for Social Policy and Practice in 1986 the profession began to position itself to coordinate and exchange information and influence policy formulation that is pertinent to the practitioner and the general welfare. Although information is important, the use to which it is put is the critical factor in bringing about change. Such advocacy efforts require nurturing from the professional association. Acceptance and formal inclusion of advocacy will ensure that the profession will continue from its historical roots to become a growing force for social justice.

Effective interaction between social workers who work on micro and macro levels has not always occurred. All social workers require a combination of both micro and macro skills. We must use our resources to help groups build a community-based system of social care that leads to healthy communities (Specht & Courtney, 1994). When the combined efforts of both micro and maco practitioners focus on the needs of clients, social justice for all will be achieved.

## References

Barker, R. L. (1991). *Social work dictionary* (2nd ed.). Silver Spring, MD: NASW Press.

Carlton, T. O., & Jung, M. (1972). Adjustment or change: Attitudes among social workers. *Social Work, 17*, 64–71.

Council on Social Work Education. (1982). *Curriculum policy statement.* Washington, DC: Author.

Council on Social Work Education. (1992). *Curriculum policy statement.* Alexandria, VA: Author.

Fisher, R. R., Haynes, K. S., Latting, J. K., & Buffum, W. (in press). Empowerment-based curriculum design: Building a political social work program. In P. Nurius &

L. Gutierrez (Eds.), *Education and research for empowerment practice.* Seattle: University of Washington Press.

Haynes, K. S., & Mickelson, J. S. (1991). *Affecting change: Social workers in the political arena* (2nd ed.). New York: Longman.

Haynes, K. S., & Mickelson, J. S. (1992). Social work and the Reagan era: Challenges to the profession. *Journal of Sociology and Social Welfare, 19*(1), 169–183.

Hunger Prevention Act of 1988. P.L. 100–435, 102 Stat. 1645.

National Association of Social Workers. (1994). *NASW code of ethics.* Washington, DC: Author.

Pardeck, J., & Meinert, R. (1994). Do social workers have a major impact on social policy? In H. J. Karger & J. Midgley (Eds.), *Controversial issues in social policy* (pp. 93–106). Boston: Allyn & Bacon.

Rees, S. (1991). *Achieving power: Practice and policy in social welfare.* North Sydney, Australia: Allen & Unwin.

Reeser, L. C., & Epstein, I. (1990). *Professionalization and activism in social work: The sixties, the eighties, and the future.* New York: Columbia University Press.

Richan, W. C. (1991). *Lobbying for social change.* New York: Haworth Press.

Simon, B. L. (1990). Rethinking empowerment. *Journal of Progressive Human Services, 1*(1) 27–39.

Specht, H., & Courtney, M. E. (1994). *Unfaithful angels: How social work has abandoned its mission.* New York: Free Press.

Vinic, A. & Lenin, M. (Eds.). (1991). *Social action in group work.* Binghamton, NY: Hearth Press.

## Further Reading

Amidei, N. (1991). *So you want to make a difference: Advocacy is the key.* Washington, DC: OMB Watch.

Bobo, K., Kendall, J., & Max, S. (1991). *Organizing for social change: A manual for activists in the 1990's.* Cabin John, MD: Midwest Academy.

Fisher, R. (1984). *Let the people decide: Neighborhood organizing in America.* Boston: Twayne.

Mahaffey, M., & Hanks, J. (Eds.). (1982). *Practical politics.* Washington, DC: National Association of Social Workers.

**James S. Mickelson, MSW, ACSW,** is president and chief executive officer, Children At Risk, 4625 Lillian, Suite 200, Houston, TX 77007.

### For further information see

Charitable Foundations and Social Welfare; Citizen Participation; Civil Rights; Community Organization; Ethics and Values; Federal and Administrative Rule Making; Federal Social Legislation from 1961 to 1994; Fundraising and Philanthropy; Health Services Systems Policy; Human Rights; National Association of Social Workers; Peace and Social Justice; Policy Practice; Progressive Social Work; Social Development; Social Justice in Social Agencies; Social Planning; Social Welfare History; Social Welfare Policy; Social Work Profession Overview; Social Workers in Politics.

**Key Words**

| | |
|---|---|
| advocacy | social justice |
| intervention | social policy |

READER'S GUIDE

## African Americans

*The following entries contain information on this general topic:*

African Americans Overview
African American Pioneers in Social Work
African Americans: Caribbean
African Americans: Immigrants
Haitian Americans

# African Americans Overview

**Bogart R. Leashore**

African Americans are descendants of Africans who have similar physical features, are citizens of the United States, and identify themselves culturally with the continent of Africa. Over time, African Americans have been referred to as "colored," "Negroes," "Afro-Americans," and "blacks" and, in some locales, as "mulattos," "quadroons," and "creoles." The most recent shift in terms, from "blacks" to "African Americans" refers to their national and geographic or regional origin, as well as to the physical feature of skin color (Asamoah, Garcia, Ortiz Hendricks, & Walker, 1991). The African ancestors of African Americans were descendants of ancient civilizations and empires and included kings, queens, and honorable people. Many came to the New World with European explorers long before slavery began in America. For example, when Balboa came upon the Pacific Ocean, there were 30 Africans with him; Africans also accompanied Cortes when he came to Mexico and were part of French explorations of the New World, including Jesuit missionary expeditions into Canada (Franklin, 1969). In 1619, one year before the *Mayflower* landed at Plymouth Rock, 20 Africans were brought to Jamestown, Virginia, by the Dutch (L. Bennett, 1964; Franklin). Subsequently, Africans were involuntarily brought to America in large numbers as slaves who were exploited and oppressed.

## History

### Passage from Africa to Slavery in America

The voyage from Africa to America, known as the "Middle Passage," involved overcrowded ships, harsh conditions, disease, suicides by jumping overboard, and maiming as a consequence of chained hands and feet, one person to another. Including those who died during the passage, it has been estimated that 5 million to 15 million Africans were enslaved in less than four centuries (Franklin, 1969). As an economic institution, the slave trade involved transporting Africans to the Caribbean and Latin America, as well as to North America, essentially to produce sugar, tobacco, cotton, and other crops; slavery meant economic prosperity for its promoters. Thus, specific methods were developed, including the establishment of slave-trading posts on the coast of West Africa and the trading of European goods brought on ships for slaves. Native Africans helped the slave traders obtain slaves by, for example, turning over captives from intertribal wars. The traders often had to remain two or three weeks at one post before enough slaves could be captured and to make stops at several places to get more slaves (Franklin).

Spain brought so many Africans into Cuba that by 1506 the fear of slave uprisings prompted a ban against bringing in more. Africans were also taken to Spanish and Portuguese colonies in what is now Mexico, Panama, Colombia, Peru, Brazil, Argentina, Guatemala, Venezuela, Ecuador, and Chile. In the 18th and 19th centuries, the British took Africans to Belize and to modern-day Honduras and Nicaragua. Slaves were taken to the Caribbean islands, where they frequently outnumbered white people, as in Jamaica. Many were exported from one island to another and to America, for example, to South Carolina, from Antigua, Barbados, Cuba, and Jamaica (Franklin, 1969).

The involuntary removal of millions of Africans from their homeland and the harsh journey to America is one of the most tragic events in the history of humankind. Because slaves meant economic profits, the greater their number, the greater the profits. Therefore, African captives were wedged in together on ships, with no room or freedom to move about, chained together two by two (Franklin, 1969). Resistance and uprisings by the captives before boarding and aboard ship were common, as was "self-imposed starvation.... Despite the most elaborate precautions slave insurrections frequently broke out.... Sometimes weapons would reach the slaves through the female captives who were frequently given comparative freedom on the deck.... Occasionally the slaves were successful in overpowering the crew and escaped by compelling the pilot to direct them homeward" (Wish, 1937, pp. 301–302). Despite such resistance, as the colonization of the New World expanded, slave trading increased.

Laws supporting slavery appeared in colonial America as early as the 1680s and later became more rigid and restrictive (Kolchin & Foner, 1993). As an institution, American slavery was reinforced by laws that were generally referred to as the *Black Codes*, which, among other things, established slaves as property, not people; maintained the dominance of whites; and protected the whites' ownership of slaves. Under these statutes, slaves were denied the basic rights enjoyed by white people. These laws legitimated the racial subordination of African Americans and thus institutionalized racism (Franklin, 1969).

Although some slaves worked as house servants, most slaves worked as agricultural field workers, laboring from sunrise to sunset, with longer hours during harvest time. Punishment by whipping was common, food was rationed, only basic clothing was provided, and housing was poor (Franklin, 1969). There were exceptions to many of the generalizations about slavery and variations over time in the conditions under which slaves lived. For example, some slaves lived in small groups on farms or plantations with close supervision by white owners and others lived in large units with absentee owners. The latter facilitated the emergence of an indigenous African American culture. For example, slaves were able to transform the Christianity of whites into a religion that met their needs and to create families and distinctively African American communities that served as a means of survival (Kolchin & Foner, 1993). Their ability to do so was enhanced by the incorporation and reinterpretation of elements from their African heritage.

The history of slavery and of African Americans has been clouded by historians and narrow assumptions about race, including the assumption that the enslaved Africans only imitated their white owners and did not have traditions, beliefs, and behaviors. The limitations of the many historical studies of slavery and of African Americans indicate the need for further research on the conditions under which slaves lived such as family life and kinship, religion, adaptation, health, and work (Gutman, 1975). We need to investigate traditional interpretations and to use new approaches.

**Survival of African Cultural Characteristics**

Although there is no dispute that slavery separated Africans from their geographic homeland, controversy remains over the survival of elements of the cultural heritage of Africans in America. Despite the contention by social scientists that the slaves did not retain Africanisms, or African survivals, general aspects and subtle survivals may be discerned, even though overt African behaviors, customs, and beliefs may have disappeared. Using their common experiences in the New World, as well as their background of cultures with complex social and economic arrangements, the slaves fashioned a new way of life, with beliefs and behaviors that reflect their African heritage. Today, evidence of African cultures can be found in the language, literature and the arts, religion, social organization, and work and play habits of African Americans. The belief in good and evil forces, a religious life created from a blend of Christianity of whites with the spiritualism and religions of Africa, extended family and kinship patterns, honor of the dead, the role of ancestors, rituals, food, ways of dressing, child-rearing practices, etiquette, child-naming practices, respect for and the role of elders, and aesthetic expressions mirror African traditions (Franklin, 1969; Genovese, 1976; Herskovits, 1958; Turner, 1991).

Mirrored African traditions like baptism by immersion, which was common in Africa among the Yoruba, Ashanti, and Dahomean kingdoms, are particularly noticeable in the religious practices of many African Americans, as well as in general American life. Motor habits, including swaying, clapping, foot patting, and jumping and running during worship, are also part of African traditions, as are emotional displays during worship and full participation, such as shouting and call and response. Beliefs in various forces of the universe, such as good and evil, are integrated into daily life. Beliefs in magic and folklore, for example, in voodoo; hoodoo; omens and superstitions; and the magical powers of roots, herbs, and charms, also exist. Braiding and wrapping hair; codes of polite behavior, such as averting eyes in speaking to elders; a concept of time that relates more to approximation than to punctuality; mutual aid and cooperation through lodges and benevolent societies; the importance of women in the family; informal adoption; women carrying babies on their hips and objects on their heads; and musical and dance forms are elements of African traditions that have survived in this country (Herskovits, 1958).

Ethnographic studies of Africanisms have discovered African religious elements, including songs, as well as elements and patterns of African social organization, such as family, kinship, and marriage, in modern Brazil and Haiti. Herskovits (1958) suggested that there is less reluctance to acknowledge the presence of African elements in the Caribbean and Latin America than in the United States.

Although variations existed among different groups of Africans, some commonalities in values and behaviors may be noted in the context of the Africentric perspective, which includes the following principles. The *interconnectedness of all things* is reflected in the individual's link with people who have died and those who are unborn, as well as in harmony with nature and others. *Oneness* of mind, body, and spirit is reflected in holistic medicine that incorporates physical and spiritual healing. The *collective identity* is stressed, rather than rugged individualism and independence from others. The *consanguineal family structure*, including all relatives connected by blood and by marriage, is maintained. *Analogue thinking,* in which gradations of meaning are seen, is common, in contrast to binary thinking, in which matters are viewed as mutually exclusive or polar opposites such as good or bad, right or wrong. Time is *phenomenological*—oriented to the present, the here and now—as opposed to being a precise mathematical operationalization. Finally, spiritualism is integrated into daily life, and religious worship involves active participation through singing, shouting, testifying, and the power of healing (Turner, 1991).

### Resistance to Slavery

***Insurrections.*** Despite the institutionalization of slavery, there was direct and indirect resistance to it. Slaves' resistance included deliberate slowing of work, destruction of property, indifferent work, feigning illness and pregnancy, self-injury, suicide, and infanticide. It has been suggested that slaves were not cheerful workers and that slave insurrections and revolts occurred frequently, despite elaborate precautions (Bauer & Bauer, 1942). For example, an insurrection was planned in Virginia in 1663, when slaves joined forces with white servants against their masters, but the plans were discovered and the effort thwarted. Insurrections occurred in New York City in 1712 and 1741; in South Carolina in 1720 and subsequent years; and in Georgia, Maryland, and other states. White people sometimes participated in insurrections by providing weapons and even leadership. Some insurrections received national attention: one near Richmond, Virginia, in 1800, led by a young slave named Gabriel Prosser, and an extensive slave revolt that was planned in 1822 in Charlestown, South Carolina, by Denmark Vessey, a carpenter who had bought his freedom. Two of the most noted revolts were one by Nat Turner, a slave, in Virginia in 1831, in which more than 50 white people were killed, and one led by John Brown, a white man, at Harper's Ferry, West Virginia, in 1859 (Wish, 1937).

***Abolition movement.*** Among the many opponents of slavery, or abolitionists, were Sojourner Truth and Harriet Tubman, both of whom were born into slavery (Johnson, 1991). Sojourner Truth, a prominent speaker at antislavery meetings, also advocated temperance, prison reform, better conditions for working people, and women's suffrage. Harriet Tubman made 19 secret trips into the South and led more than 300 slaves to freedom in the North, notably Canada. She was a leader, or "conductor," of what became known as the "Underground Railroad," which had secret stations and hiding places in barns, cellars, churches, and woodsheds, from the South to Canada. Other leaders and conductors of the Underground Railroad included William Still in Philadelphia and Frederick Douglas, an escaped slave who became a famous abolitionist speaker and writer. White participants in the Underground Railroad included John Fairfield, the son of a Virginia slaveholder, who posed as a peddler, a slave trader, or an evangelist, and brought many slaves out of the South; Thomas Garrett, a Quaker, who fed and hid slaves when they reached Wilmington, Delaware; and Susan B. Anthony, a leader in women's suffrage. It should also be noted that runaway slaves frequently found shelter among Native Americans, with whom some intermarried (Hughes & Meltzer, 1963).

By 1831 the power of the antislavery movement had intensified, and there were simultaneous and closely connected movements for women's rights, temperance, and other reforms. Abolitionists argued that slavery was contrary to the beliefs of Christianity, contrary to the fundamentals of freedom as an inalienable right, uncivilized, economically unsound and a waste of human resources, and a menace to the peace and safety of the nation. They formed organizations, such as the New England Anti-Slavery Society in 1831 and the American Anti-Slavery Society in Philadelphia in 1833, and published pamphlets and periodicals to support the movement and held meetings and lectures to rally support for their cause (Franklin, 1969). The Civil War began in 1861, and on January 1, 1863, President Abraham Lincoln issued the Emancipation Proclamation, proclaiming that all slaves would be free. With the defeat of the Confederate army, slavery was ultimately made illegal in 1865 with the adoption of the 13th amendment (Franklin, 1969).

### Reconstruction

***Freedmen's Bureau.*** There was much chaos after the Civil War during the period called Reconstruction. Many freed slaves were homeless and unemployed. In response to this situation, the federal government established the Bureau of Refugees, Freedmen, and Abandoned Land in 1865. The Freedmen's Bureau provided basic supplies and medicine, established schools, supervised work contracts, and administered confiscated or abandoned land, some of which was leased or sold to the former slaves. The Freedmen's Bureau operated in a hostile environment. Northerners viewed it as expensive, and Southerners vehemently objected to federal interference and resented the enfranchisement of the former slaves.

Despite the opposition, the Freedmen's Bureau provided relief to African Americans as well as whites. From 1865 to 1869, it issued food and clothing, established 46 hospitals, provided free transportation for resettling displaced people, distributed land, promoted better working conditions, organized courts and boards of arbitration, lent money, and established and supervised schools at all levels. The Freedmen's Bureau helped establish Howard University, the Hampton Institute, St. Augustine's College, Atlanta University, Fisk University, and Johnson C. Smith University, among others (Franklin, 1969). These and other historically African American colleges and universities continue to provide opportunities for higher education. After President Lincoln's assassination, President Andrew Johnson, a Southerner, voided most land transfers to the freed slaves and returned property to the wealthy whites. It has been suggested that the federal government's failure to undertake needed and massive land redistribution—"40 acres and a mule"—as was hoped by the freed slaves was the primary reason for the failure of Reconstruction (Marable, 1991).

***Rise and decline of civil rights.*** African American churches established many schools during Reconstruction, including 257 schools in North Carolina between 1865 and 1869, that served 15,600 African American students. Passage of the 14th amendment granted civil rights to African Americans, and the 15th amendment granted African American men the right to vote. African Americans were soon elected to office; for example, between 1869 and 1901, 816 African Americans were elected as state and federal legislators. Northern states were forced to amend or repeal laws that discriminated against African Americans; thus, in 1865 Illinois permitted African Americans to testify in courtrooms and city streetcars could no longer be segregated in Philadelphia. Subsequent legislation, such as the Civil Rights Act of 1875, offered further protection of African Americans' civil rights. However, an economic recession and hostility by white Southerners, including organized terrorist and vigilante efforts such as those by the Ku Klux Klan and the Knights of the White Camelia, created a political and social climate of fear and intimidation with a resulting decline in the quality of life for African Americans and the demise of Reconstruction. In 1883 the Supreme Court declared the Civil Rights Act of 1875 unconstitutional, and in 1896 *Plessy v. Ferguson* instituted the principle of "separate but equal." Disenfranchisement became the rule, and lynchings of African Americans became common (Marable, 1991).

### Self-Help and Philanthropy

With the end of Reconstruction, schools and churches were the only major institutions left for improving the social and economic conditions of African Americans. In most states, public agencies discriminated against African Americans in their provision of social services, and many private institutions directed services to poor white people, especially recent immigrants from Europe.

***Church-related organizations.*** Self-help through church-related mutual aid societies and fraternal associations provided various forms of relief. For example, as early as 1787, the Free African Society, a mutual aid society, which was established in Philadelphia by two African American ministers, Absalom Jones and Richard Allen, provided assistance and economic relief during illness or injury. Other mutual aid societies included the Rising Star and Sisters of Love beneficial societies in Atlanta, developed by the Wheat Street Baptist Church, and the Afro-American Benevolent Society of the Shiloh Baptist Church in Cleveland.

Social and charitable groups were established throughout the country. Fraternal associations were formed for mutual aid, economic, and social purposes. For example, the Free Order of Masons was established to promote unity and fellowship and to stimulate cooperative economic activity. The insurance benefit features of many fraternal associations made them increasingly popular; indeed, between 1900 and 1915 most of the insurance held by African Americans was through fraternal associations. In addition to insurance benefits, many associations operated homes for elderly people, newspapers, grocery stores, hotels, banks, and other enterprises that provided important services for African Americans (Davis, 1980).

African American churches served social welfare functions by providing services in poor communities and jails. Some established or supported homes for aged people and for orphans (Carlton La-Ney, 1989). Others created day nurseries, kindergartens, gymnasiums, music schools, employment programs for working girls and women, and boys' and girls' clubs. Charitable organizations included the National Association of Colored Women. African Americans also established hospitals and sanitariums to help less fortunate and poor people (Franklin, 1969).

***Tuskegee Institute.*** Booker T. Washington, born into slavery in 1856, made an outstanding contribution to self-help in 1881 when he established the Tuskegee Institute in Alabama, a prominent African American university that continues to educate large numbers of African Americans. Washington and his students raised funds for land and laid the foundation for the building. Wealthy white philanthropists, including Andrew Carnegie and J. G. Phelps Stokes, later contributed funds to support the institution (Hughes & Meltzer, 1963). In 1900 Washington and others formed the National Negro Business League, which subsequently provided training for African American business leaders and resources to help African American businesses (Davis, 1980).

***The National Association for the Advancement of Colored People.*** NAACP, which is still a major civil rights organization, began in 1909 following a meeting in New York City in response to a lynching in Illinois. Those present included W.E.B. DuBois and Jane Addams. A white Boston lawyer, Moorfield Storey, became the president, and DuBois became director of publicity and research and editor of *The Crisis,* the NAACP's official journal. There were more than 400 branches of the NAACP by 1921 (Hughes & Meltzer, 1963).

***National Urban League.*** The National Urban League was formed in 1911, after a presentation by George Edmund Haynes, a young African American graduate student of social work at Columbia University, about the findings of his extensive study of the social and economic conditions of African Americans in New York City. The league sought, as it does now, to pursue social and economic opportunities for African Americans in urban communities. With the support of leading African Americans, such as Booker T. Washington, and white philanthropists, such as Julius Rosenwald, the league sponsored employment, housing, and other programs and services for African Americans. Its program for preparing professional social workers, which included providing fellowships and internships, supported many outstanding African American social work leaders, such as Garry W. Moore, E. Franklin Frazier, and Forrester B. Washington, who were successive directors of the Atlanta University School of Social Work, and Inabel Burns Lindsay, who became the founding dean of the Howard University School of Social Work (Franklin, 1969; Ross, 1978). Charles S. Johnson, a sociologist, became the league's director of research and investigation in 1921 and started the organization's magazine *Opportunity: A Journal of Negro Life* in 1923; the magazine's motto was "Not Alms, but Opportunity." Branches of the league were established throughout the United States, and social workers from across the nation, regardless of race, participated in the league's annual conferences (Hughes & Meltzer, 1963).

***The Nation of Islam.*** Founded in 1930, the Nation of Islam—the Black Muslims—served as a religious organization with an emphasis on self-help among African Americans. Wallace Fard, its founder, was succeeded by Elijah Muhammad (Davis, 1980). Later, Malcolm X became its most prominent leader.

**The 20th Century**

***Segregation and discrimination.*** Southern disenfranchisement of African Americans was countered by their hope for better employment opportunities, which drew them to cities in the North. However, employment opportunities were limited, and housing was segregated and overcrowded, leading to poor health and high mortality rates. Lynchings and race riots were common. The level of hostility was so great in some cities that African Americans were not allowed to live in them, and other cities did not allow them within their boundaries (Franklin, 1969). In 1913 Woodrow Wilson became the first Southern Democrat president since the Civil War, and half his Cabinet appointees were Southerners. His administration introduced national legislation that sought to disenfranchise African Americans, and Wilson issued executive orders segregating federal employees. African Americans were barred from entering the U.S. Marines, Coast Guard, and Air Force and could serve in the U.S. Navy only as messmen. Although they served in the U.S. Army with distinction during World War I, African Americans were largely segregated (Hughes & Meltzer, 1963).

The Ku Klux Klan flourished throughout the country after World War I. Preaching racial hatred, its members, wearing white hoods to keep them anonymous, lynched, burned, beat, and otherwise threatened African Americans, promoting lawlessness and violence. NAACP actively protested racial bigotry and injustice with crusades against lynching and campaigns to protect African Americans. The Universal Negro Improvement Association was started by Marcus Garvey to promote the interests of African Americans and to plan for a movement to Africa. Garvey, a native of Jamaica, came to the United States in 1916 and made a strong case for racial pride among African Americans. He promoted self-help, self-reliance, and cooperative economic development. He was subsequently imprisoned for mail fraud, pardoned by President Calvin Coolidge, and deported to Jamaica. George Baker, known as "Father Divine," began a Peace Mission movement with large-scale feeding programs and cooperative enterprises, such as grocery stores, barber shops, tailor shops, furriers, hotels, and boardinghouses across the country. Although his followers were primarily African American, later a significant number of white people joined him (Davis, 1980).

***Unionization.*** Efforts to protect African Americans included the unionization of labor. Many unions that were affiliated with the American Federation of Labor excluded African Americans from membership or segregated them in separate union locals. In 1925, under the leadership of A. Philip Randolph, the Brotherhood of Sleeping Car Porters and Maids was organized to obtain better working conditions and wages (Franklin, 1969).

***Prominent artists, scientists, and scholars.*** A literary movement emerged among African American writers and other artists interested in social and economic problems. Because the center of this literary movement was Harlem, New York City, one of the largest African American urban communities in the nation, the movement became known as the "Harlem Renaissance." Among the movement's numerous writers were Claude McKay, Georgia Douglass Johnson, Arna Bontemps, Langston Hughes, Countee Cullen, Alain Locke, Nella Larsen, James Weldon Johnson, and Zora Neale Hurston. There were also many prominent musicians and dancers: Noble Sissle, Florence Mills, Louis Armstrong, Ethel Waters, Eubie Blake, Josephine Baker, Paul Robeson, Duke Ellington, Ella Fitzgerald, Marian Anderson, the Mills Brothers, Lionel Hampton, Bill Robinson, Rose McClendon, Adelaide Hall, and W. C. Handy. Painters included Aaron Douglas, William H. Johnson, Hale Woodruff, Palmer Hayden, E. Simms Campbell, Henry Ossawa Tanner, and Laura Wheeler Waring (Hughes & Meltzer, 1963).

African American scientists and scholars also made many contributions. They included historians Rayford Logan and Carter G. Woodson, who served as editor of the *Journal of Negro History*, which was begun in 1916 by the Association for the Study of Negro Life; biologist Ernest Just; and sociologists Charles Johnson, E. Franklin Frazier, and W.E.B. DuBois, who started the journal *Phylon: A Journal of Race and Culture* in 1940 while he was at Atlanta University. Daniel Hale Williams, a physician, was a pioneer in heart surgery; Charles Drew became an authority on preserving blood plasma, and William A. Hinton originated the Hinton test for syphilis.

***The Great Depression and World War II.*** Cultural programs and services provided by the Works Projects Administration, the National Youth Administration, and the Civilian Conservation Corps during the Great Depression of the 1930s extended many training and employment opportunities to African Americans (Franklin, 1969).

Mary McLeod Bethune, whose parents had been slaves, established a school in Florida that later became the Bethune–Cookman College, which exists today. A friend of President Franklin D. Roosevelt and a member of his "Black Cabinet" of advisers, she became director of Negro Affairs for the National Youth Administration under the New Deal. Bethune was also president of the National Council of Negro Women and became a friend of Eleanor Roosevelt. Other members of the Black Cabinet included William H. Hastie; Robert L. Vann; Robert C. Weaver; Lawrence A. Oxley, a social worker; and William J. Trent. The Black Cabinet promoted social and economic equality and opportunities for African Americans and achieved some success. For example, more African Americans were employed by the federal government, some discriminatory civil service regulations were changed, and most formerly segregated government cafeterias were opened to African Americans. Nevertheless, many of the New Deal programs, especially in the South, discriminated against African Americans (Franklin, 1969).

The "separate but equal" doctrine of *Plessy v. Ferguson* of 1896 had provided a basis for the segregation of African Americans in education, as well as in other areas. The resulting inequality and inadequacy led NAACP to fight its unconstitutionality. In 1945 the U.S. Army integrated its forces to fight in Germany. Distinguished military service was rendered by, among others, Colonel Benjamin O. Davis, Jr., a commanding officer in Europe, and Dorie Miller, a messman in the U.S. Navy who destroyed Japanese planes at Pearl Harbor (Hughes & Meltzer, 1963).

In the meantime, bombings and race riots occurred in major urban areas, where housing discrimination against African Americans had become a serious problem. Segregation in modes of transportation, such as trains, buses, and taxicabs, was another problem. It should be noted that although German prisoners of World War II who were transported to prisons within the United States could eat in the restaurants of railway stations, their African American guards could not. The segregation of African Americans in the South was typified through the institutionalization of Jim Crow regulations manifested by signs, such as "Whites Only" and "Colored," that separated them from whites in designated places like laundries, benches in public parks, water fountains in department stores, theaters, restaurants, and other businesses (Hughes & Meltzer, 1963). Poll taxes and literacy tests were used to exclude African Americans from voting and exerting political power. Even the Social Security Act of 1935 discriminated against large numbers of African Americans because many were in occupations, such as agricultural and domestic work, that were not covered for old age and unemployment benefits (Cates, 1983; Quadagno, 1988).

***The 1950s and 1960s.*** With *Brown v. Board of Education of Topeka* (1954), the Supreme Court banned racial segregation in public schools and the doctrine of "separate but equal." Thurgood Marshall, legal counsel for NAACP at that time, successfully argued the case against racial segregation and later became the first African American justice of the Supreme Court. Despite this decision, there remained a need to enforce it. Segregation continued in the South, with resistance and protests by African Americans, including the Montgomery, Alabama, boycott of public buses, which was precipitated in 1955 by the arrest of Rosa Parks, an African American, for refusing to give up her seat to a white man; the push to admit African American youths to a segregated public high school in Little Rock, Arkansas; sit-ins by African American students at segregated public lunch counters; read-ins to integrate public libraries; boycotts and picketing of businesses that refused to serve African Americans; the "freedom rides" by African Americans and whites throughout the South to integrate interstate transportation and facilities; and the march from Selma to Montgomery, Alabama, for voting rights. NAACP; the Congress of Racial Equality (CORE); the Student Non-Violent Coordinating Committee (SNCC); and the Southern Christian Leadership Conference (SCLC), under the leadership of the Rev. Martin Luther King, Jr., a Nobel Peace Prize winner, were among the organizations that led and supported these and other protests (Hughes & Meltzer, 1963). In 1968 the National Association of Black Social Workers (NABSW) was founded to advance the social welfare of African Americans (Johnson, 1976).

## African Americans in the 1990s

African Americans have fought and endured institutionalized racism, discrimination, and oppression in the United States. Amid inhumane assaults and against great odds, it is remarkable that they have made substantial improvements in advancing the quality of their lives, as well as the lives of Americans in general. However, improvements for African Americans have been uneven, and African Americans continue to differ on many socioeconomic indicators when compared with whites. Nevertheless, they have achieved much in a hostile environment and have made impressive contributions to the development of this country as a democracy and a leading nation of the world.

African Americans represent 12.3 percent of the resident population of the United States, according to the 1990 census, and number about 30 million (E. C. Bennett, 1992). They constitute the largest and most visible racial group in the country. Since the enactment of civil rights legislation in the 1950s and 1960s, the education, income, health, and living conditions of African Americans have generally improved. However, during the 1980s improvements slowed and, in some instances, conditions grew worse. For example, African American infant mortality is twice that of whites, and African American children are more likely to live in poverty than are white children. Compared with white people, African Americans are only half as likely to attend college, and the income of those who do attend is one-third less than that of their white counterparts. The net wealth of African Americans is only one-tenth that of whites, despite a significant increase in the number of affluent African Americans in the 1980s. These disparities have been attributed to the Republican-dominated national politics of the 1980s, which negated civil rights gains and socioeconomic advancements for African Americans and promoted an atmosphere that was antagonistic to people of color. Other disparities point to polarizing factors that have increased the gap between rich and poor people, including more opportunities for educated middle-class African Americans and fewer for urban poor people. The changing economy and demographic factors have also been presented as contributing to the disparities. Furthermore, evidence indicates that racial discrimination continues to be a factor that hinders improvements in the quality of life for African Americans (O'Hare, Pollard, Mann, & Kent, 1991).

### Age and Marital Status

Understanding the circumstances of African Americans and the racial disparities that exist between them and white Americans can be enhanced by examining demographic characteristics. For example, both groups have aged since 1980; the median age of African Americans was 28.0 years in 1991, up from 24.8 years in 1980, and the median age of white people was 33.9 years in 1991, up from 30.8 years in 1980. In 1991, a larger proportion of African Americans (33 percent) than of whites (25 percent) were under age 18, and among those age 65 and over, 8 percent and 13 percent were African Americans and whites, respectively.

With regard to marital status, of the African American women age 15 and over in 1991, 38 percent were married, 11 percent were divorced, 39 percent never married, and 11.9 percent were widowed; of African American men aged 15 and over, 44.8 percent were never married, 43.1 percent were married, 3.3 percent were widowed, and 8.8 percent were divorced. Larger proportions of white men and women were married—62.4 percent and 59 percent, respectively. Among African Americans ages 35 to 44, the majority of men and women were married, as were white people. Differences in the marital status of African Americans and white Americans reflect differences in mortality rates, age distributions, and age at first marriage (E. C. Bennett, 1992). In addition, unemployment, low wages, and limited job security have discouraged many African American men from marriage. The increase in female-headed families has been related to a decrease in the ratio of employed African American men to African American women. Claims that welfare programs have been disincentives for low-income African Americans to marry have not been strongly supported by research (O'Hare et al., 1991).

Since 1950 both African American and white married-couple families have declined. For African Americans, married-couple families decreased from 78 percent in 1950 to 48 percent in 1991; for white Americans the decrease was less dramatic—from 88 percent in 1950 to 83 percent in 1991. Increases in the proportion of never-married women with children and in the rates of marital separation and divorce have contributed to an increase in African American female-headed families. Although there has been a decrease since 1960 in the proportion of children living with two parents for both African Americans and whites, the decrease has been greater for African American children (E. C. Bennett, 1992). African American children are more likely to live with grandparents than are white or Hispanic children; for example, in 1990, 12 percent of African American children, compared with 4 percent of white and 6 percent of Hispanic children, lived in households that included grandparents. Many African American children live with never-married mothers who generally have fewer economic resources than do married-couple families; many are poor and live in central cities and public housing (O'Hare et al., 1991).

## Education and Employment

The gap in the educational status of African Americans and whites has been substantially reduced over time. However, differences remain, especially in rates of high school completion and college enrollment. Attendance at nursery school, Head Start, and kindergarten programs has increased across the country and has often been greater among African Americans (Jaynes & Williams, 1989). In 1991, 82 percent of African Americans ages 25 to 34 had completed at least four years of high school, compared with 87 percent of their white counterparts (E. C. Bennett, 1992). African American children and youths are more likely than are whites to drop out of school. Those who remain in school tend to earn lower grades, score below the national average on standardized tests, and are more likely to be suspended or expelled. According to some educators, these issues are compounded by socioeconomic factors outside the school, such as low income, as well as inside the school, for example, a social climate that discourages academic performance (O'Hare et al., 1991).

***College enrollment.*** There has been a marked decline in college enrollment among African Americans since 1977, when the rate was virtually equal to that of whites. After 1979 college enrollment increased rapidly for whites, but dropped sharply for African Americans. Thus, in 1986, 36.5 percent of African American high school graduates entered college, compared with 57 percent of whites in 1984. The college-completion rate for African Americans is about half that of whites. Although several reasons have been offered for the decline in college enrollment among African Americans, the reduction in financial aid has been considered the most important (Jaynes & Williams, 1989).

***Labor force participation.*** African Americans constitute 10.8 percent of the total labor force, 10.1 percent of employed people, and 19.9 percent of unemployed people. Generally, the labor force participation rate is higher for men than for women; white men have a higher rate than do African American men, who, in turn, have a higher rate than do African American women, who share a rate comparable to that for white women. The employment picture for African Americans has deteriorated since the early 1980s, and the unemployment rate for African Americans was twice that of whites in 1991 (E. C. Bennett, 1992). The reasons for this downturn include difficulty finding jobs; the greater likelihood of being laid off; the decline in stable, higher wage blue-collar jobs in the industrial cities; continued racial discrimination and negative stereotyping with white employers; the dispersion of jobs to the suburbs; and limited education. African Americans remain unemployed for longer periods than do whites; many are underemployed and work fewer hours than they would like, and others are discouraged workers who have given up searching for work (O'Hare et al., 1991).

**Income and Economic Status**

The median family income for African Americans in 1990 was $21,420, or 58 percent of the median family income for whites, which was $36,920. In 1990 African American families were more than three times as likely as were white families to be poor; that is, 29 percent of all African American families were living in poverty, compared with 8 percent of all white families. Furthermore, 75 percent of African American families living in poverty versus 43 percent of such white families were headed by women with no husbands present, and 56 percent of African American families with children under age 18 years that were headed by women were poor in 1990, compared with 38 percent of their white counterparts (E. C. Bennett, 1992).

***Middle class.*** Much less attention has been given to middle-income and affluent African Americans than to those who live in poverty. The income of African American married-couple families increased in the 1970s and 1980s; by 1989 African American families in which both spouses were employed had a median income that was 82 percent of that of their white counterparts. Families of young African Americans, especially of those who completed college, have average incomes nearly equal to the incomes of white families. In married-couple families in which the head of the household is age 25 to 44 and is a college graduate, the median income of African Americans is 93 percent ($54,400) that of whites ($58,800). In 1967 one out of every 17 African American families had an income of $50,000 or more; one out of seven had incomes at this level in 1989. However, among whites, one in six had incomes at this level in 1967 and one in three did so in 1989. Although the increase in the proportion of African Americans with incomes of $50,000 or more may have been the result of economic expansion after the 1981–83 recession, it may also be the result of the civil rights movement of the 1960s, which provided new educational and employment opportunities for African Americans (O'Hare et al., 1991).

***Total wealth.*** A more comprehensive measure of the economic status of the family is its total wealth, which includes accumulated assets. There is a large disparity between the assets of African Americans and whites. For example, in 1988, 16 percent of African American households versus 47 percent of white households had assets of $50,000 or more, and nearly 30 percent of African American households but only 9 percent of white households reported no assets. These differences can be explained in part by the younger age structure of African Americans, as well as by the history of racial oppression. The large number of African American female-headed households may also be responsible for some of the difference. Furthermore, home equity accounts for 43 percent of aggregate wealth in the United States and is the single largest asset for most Americans. The homeownership rate for African Americans is about two-thirds that of the total population, and the equity in homes owned by African Americans is only 60 percent of the national average, primarily because of residential segregation (O'Hare et al., 1991).

**Health Status**

Health status is an important measure of quality of life. As with education and income, there continue to be significant differences between the health status of African Americans and whites across the lifespan. These differences are related to several factors, including poverty and socioeconomic status, access to health services, and representation in health care professions.

***Infant and child mortality.*** Infant mortality, an international measure of general health status, is the rate at which babies die before their first birthday. In 1991 the infant mortality rate in the United States was 8.9 deaths per 1,000 live births—a higher rate than those of many other developed nations, such as Japan, Sweden, Finland, France, and Canada. Over the past 100 years, the infant mortality rate for African Americans has continued to be approximately twice that of whites. For example, in 1991 the infant mortality rates for African Americans and whites were 17.6 and 7.3, respectively (U.S. Department of Health and Human Services, 1993).

Low birthweights are common among African Americans and contribute to infant mortality rates even though normal-weight African American babies also have a higher mortality rate than do white babies. The death rates of African American infants are higher than those of white infants during the neonatal period (first 28 days of life) and during the postneonatal period (28 days to one year after birth). Research has shown that babies are more likely to die in the neonatal period if their mothers did not receive health care during the prenatal period. African American mothers are twice as likely as are white mothers to receive no care or care that does not begin until the last months of pregnancy. Research has shown that many risk factors associated with infant mortality and low birthweight are related to social and economic conditions. These risk factors include low-income and inadequate health insurance, preexisting health conditions, poor nutrition, inadequate and crowded housing, stressful work, and transportation and child care problems that affect the use of services (Office of Minority Health, 1989b).

The death rates for African American children ages five to 14 years are 30 percent to 50 percent higher than those for white children. The leading causes of death of children in this age group are injuries in or near the home as a result of unrepaired stairways, inadequate or absent window screens or guards, missing smoke detectors, defective heaters, lead poisoning, fire hazards, and accidents to pedestrians (Jaynes & Williams, 1989).

***Health of adolescents and young adults.*** Adolescents and young adults ages 15 to 24 are the most medically underserved group in the U.S. population. Adolescent childbearing is a major issue because of health, personal, social, and economic consequences. Although birth rates among African American adolescent females have declined since the 1960s, they are proportionately higher than those for whites; for example, in 1984, 20 percent of all African Americans were born to adolescents, compared with 11.1 percent of white babies. However, it should be noted that the majority of all adolescent births in the United States are to white adolescents. Regardless of race, adolescent motherhood increases the likelihood of a woman's lower educational and occupational achievement, lower wages, and the risk of living in poverty. The early initiation of sexual intercourse increases the risk of contracting sexually transmitted diseases, such as gonorrhea and syphilis, genital herpes, chlamydia, papilloma virus, venereal warts, and acquired immune deficiency syndrome (AIDS) (Jaynes & Williams, 1989).

***Adult mortality.*** Among African American males ages 15 to 44, homicide is the leading cause of death; for those ages 25 to 34, the homicide rate is seven times that of whites. Death rates that are due to homicide are so high in the United States that homicide is recognized as a public health problem, not just a criminal justice problem. Risk factors related to homicide include residence in low-income urban areas with overcrowded and substandard housing, alcohol and drug abuse, and easy access to weapons (Office of Minority Health, 1989a).

Other health problems that differentially affect African Americans are AIDS, substance abuse, hypertension, and cancer (Jaynes & Williams, 1989). In 1991, 29 percent of the reported cases of AIDS were among African Americans; furthermore, 52 percent of children under age 13 with AIDS and 52 percent of women with AIDS were African American (Thomas & Crouse Quinn, 1991). Many African American adults who have AIDS are intravenous drug users who identify themselves as heterosexual (Jaynes & Williams, 1989). Therefore, their sexual partners are at a high risk of contracting AIDS, as are those who may share needles with them. Effective educational and risk-reduction services for AIDS and human immunodeficiency virus (HIV) should recognize that the history of racism and persistent inequality experienced by African Americans in the United States have led many to believe that AIDS involves conspiracies by the government to promote drug use among African Americans and that HIV and AIDS are a form of genocide by whites to eliminate them. Distrust and the fears of some people may be related to the Tuskegee Syphilis study, in which medical treatment was not provided to African American men who had contracted syphilis. The experiment, which Jones (1981) described, was conducted for 40 years (until the early 1970s) by the federal government with an original study population of 399 African American men with syphilis and 201 controls. By failing to provide known and effective medical treatment, the government demonstrated little regard for the lives of the men involved (Thomas & Crouse Quinn, 1991).

The excessive use of tobacco, alcohol, or illegal drugs leads to other health problems for many African Americans. For example, African American men have a higher mortality rate for lung cancer, and deaths related to smoking are high among all African Americans. Alcohol use is related to deaths from cirrhosis of the liver, and African Americans have a higher rate of mortality from this disease than do whites. African Americans also have higher rates of hypertension than do whites; because hypertension is a significant factor for strokes, the age-adjusted death rate from strokes among African Americans is nearly twice that of whites. Similarly, hypertension is related to end-stage renal disease, and the estimated incidence of this disease is three to four times higher among African Americans than among whites (Jaynes & Williams, 1989).

African Americans have a higher incidence of and poorer survival rates for lung cancer, prostate cancer, cancer of the esophagus, and cervical cancer. It has been suggested that although much more research is needed, the higher rates of cancer among African Americans is related to their low socioeconomic status and lack of access to preventive services (Jaynes & Williams, 1989).

Sickle cell anemia is a hereditary disease that affects 7.8 percent of the African American population. It is a complex disease that may cause severe emotional and medical problems. Sickle cell crises involve pains in the chest, legs, and abdomen because of the lack of oxygen. Depending on the type of crisis, pain medications, fluids, antibiotics, blood replacement, folic acid, oxygen therapy, or other treatment may be necessary. Treatment is important, as are testing for the sickle cell trait and counseling before having children with another person with the trait (Alcena, 1992).

***Mental health.*** Mental health data revealed that for all age groups, whites had lower admission rates to state and county mental hospitals than did people of other races. The greatest racial differential was for people ages 25 to 44; white women had the lowest rates and men who are not white had the highest rates. Admission rates were higher for racial and ethnic groups than for whites with regard to schizophrenia, alcoholism, and depression. Furthermore, people of color who had been discharged from psychiatric inpatient units in general hospitals were more likely than were white people to have been diagnosed as schizophrenic, with a reversal of this pattern for affective-depressive disorders. White people were more likely than people of other races to have been diagnosed as depressed (U.S. Department of Health and Human Services, 1986).

***Life expectancy.*** The life expectancy at birth for Americans was at an all-time high of 75.5 years in 1991. The highest life expectancy at birth, 79.6 years, was for white women, followed by African American women (at 73.8 years), white men (at 72.9 years), and African American men (at 64.4 years). Although the life expectancy for African American men increased in 1991, it was below the peak of 65.3 reached in 1984. In 1991 the age-adjusted death rate for African Americans was 1.6 times that for white Americans, the same ratio as in 1987. The leading cause of death for African Americans and white Americans was the same within broad age groups, except for the 15 to 24 and 25 to 44 age groups. For persons ages 15 to 24, accidents and their adverse effects were the leading cause of death for whites, whereas homicides and legal intervention were the leading causes of death for African Americans. For persons ages 25 to 44, the leading causes of death for whites was accidents and their adverse effects, whereas for African Americans, it was HIV infection. In 1991 the mortality rates were higher for African Americans than for whites for most of the leading causes of death. The greatest differential was for homicide and legal intervention, for which the age-adjusted death rate for African Americans was 6.8 times that of whites. The differential was also large for HIV infection (3.4); nephritis, nephrotic syndrome, and nephrosis (2.8); septicemia (2.7); diabetes mellitus (2.4); cerebrovascular diseases (1.9); chronic liver diseases and cirrhosis (1.6); pneumonia and influenza (1.5); and diseases of the heart (1.5). Lower age-adjusted rates for African Americans than for whites were reported for two leading causes of death—chronic obstructive pulmonary diseases and allied conditions and suicide (U.S. Department of Health and Human Services, 1993).

### Current Status in the Criminal Justice System

Throughout their history in the United States, African Americans have experienced great inequalities in the criminal justice system. Data on this system are greatly limited to certain crimes, primarily homicide, assault, rape, robbery, larceny, burglary, and automobile theft. People who are arrested for these crimes are disproportionately of lower socioeconomic status, whereas a disproportionate number of members of the middle and upper classes commit corporate crimes; engage in tax evasion, fraud, and related crimes; and do not receive equal attention. African Americans are overrepresented in the criminal justice system as victims and as offenders (Jaynes & Williams, 1989).

African Americans represent 47 percent of those awaiting trial or serving jail terms, 40 percent of prisoners sentenced to death, and 45 percent of prisoners in state and federal facilities. They are disproportionately represented for every offense except drunk driving, although they are more likely to be stopped and detained for this offense as well than are whites (Hacker, 1992).

Crimes committed by African Americans may be interpreted as revenge against a history of racism, or resistance to laws and how they are enforced, or as a form of rebellion by young and poor African Americans who believe that they have never had a fair chance and are unlikely to get one. The 1991 videotape of a young African American man in Los Angeles being beaten by police demonstrated brutality and continued injustice despite the principle of presumed innocence and constitutional safeguards. Many African Americans have encountered discourteous and hostile treatment by the police, who tend to judge people by their color first. African Americans are three times more likely than are whites to be killed by the police.

Although many police are African Americans, most are white. Victims who are white can expect police to be more solicitous; African American victims tend to receive less attention and interest from the police (Hacker, 1992).

Victims of common crimes, such as robbery and aggravated assault, are twice as likely to be African Americans, particularly people who are concentrated in the lower socioeconomic classes. African Americans are also disproportionately the victims of homicide and lose a proportionately greater amount of their personal wealth and property than do whites; most offenses committed by African Americans are against other African Americans (Jaynes & Williams, 1989).

In prosecuting cases, people of color plea bargain less than do white people, seemingly because of feelings of alienation and suspicion of the justice system. Limited research has suggested that among those who plea bargain, white people receive better deals than do African Americans and people in other racial groups. Racial discrimination in the use of the death penalty is reflected in the disproportionate rates of execution of African Americans; for example, between 1930 and 1962, 54 percent of the executions were of African Americans, and in 1987, 42 percent of the prisoners with death sentences were African American. It has been concluded that African Americans will continue to be disproportionately involved in the criminal justice system as long as great socioeconomic disparities with whites exist. The disproportionate involvement of African Americans in criminal activity perpetuates negative stereotypes and fears of them, especially of young African American men (Jaynes & Williams, 1989).

## Social Work Practice

Both the providers and users of social services are influenced by certain values, norms, beliefs, and traditions. Traditionally, professional social work practice has used the medical model for the delivery of services, with less reliance on the perceptions of the person-in-situation and more on diagnosis and cure. Emphasis has also been given to insight, individual understanding and responsibility, the resolution of dependence, expressiveness, and thinking through as a form of problem solving. Less interest has been given to changing environmental circumstances, working with significant others, and intervening with other systems. These practice approaches, generally used with middle-class whites, may be inappropriate and harmful with others, including African Americans. Therefore, it is important to know and understand the culture of African Americans and to use it to promote their health and well-being. Where services are located, who provides them, and when and how should be consistent with the cultural identity of the recipients (Pinderhughes, 1989).

### Ethnic-Sensitive Practice

Various approaches and models can be used to provide ethnic-sensitive social work practice (Devore & Schlesinger, 1987). There is much diversity among African Americans, as well as many commonalities. Therefore, a range of approaches and models should be considered, including psychosocial, structural, behavioral, systems, task-centered, problem-solving, life model, and ecological. A combination or integration of these or other approaches, specifically family systems, behavioral, and task-centered, which should be adapted to the particular case circumstances, has been recommended for practice with African Americans (Freeman, 1990a). Regardless of which practice approach is used in the provision of social services for African Americans, it may be useful to draw on several concepts and perspectives, specifically the empowerment, worldview, strengths, and Africentric perspectives.

***Empowerment.*** Empowerment counters the negative value or image of African Americans, which has been rendered through a history of racism in the United States and the inability to influence life circumstances, with a positive value or image and the ability to influence the conditions of one's life. It counters powerlessness and hopelessness with the ability to address problems competently, beginning with a positive view of oneself (Solomon, 1976). As a treatment goal and process, it can counter racial oppression and poverty by helping African Americans increase their ability to make and implement basic life decisions (Boyd-Franklin, 1989).

***Worldview.*** Worldview involves one's perceptions of oneself in relation to other people, objects, institutions, and nature. It relates to one's view of the world and one's role and place in it. The worldviews of African Americans are shaped by unique and important experiences, such as racism and discrimination, and involve, in varying degrees, traditional attributes of the African American family and community life, such as strong ties to immediate, extended-family, and fictive kin; a strong religious orientation; a strong achievement orientation; a strong work orientation; and egalitarian role sharing (English, 1991; Hill, 1972). These traditional attributes are consistent with and can be used in combination with the strengths and the Africentric perspectives.

***Strengths perspective.*** The strengths perspective seeks to identify, use, build, and reinforce the strengths and abilities that people have in contrast to the pathological perspective, which focuses on their deficiencies and inabilities. It is useful across the life cycle and throughout the stages of the helping process (assessment, intervention, and evaluation) and emphasizes people's abilities, beliefs, values, interest, aspirations, accomplishments, and resources (Freeman, 1990b; Weick, Rapp, Sullivan, & Kristhardt, 1989).

***Africentric perspective.*** The Africentric perspective acknowledges African culture and expressions of African values, beliefs, institutions, and behaviors. It recognizes that African Americans have retained, to some degree, the elements of African life and values that were previously discussed.

### Use of Services

Broman, Neighbors, and Taylor (1989) found that African Americans ages 31 to 64 are more likely to use the services of social workers than are whites, whereas among those under age 30 the rate of use is the same as for whites. However, white people ages 65 and over are more likely to use social workers than are African Americans in this age group. The low use of community-based services by elderly African Americans suggests the need for greater outreach to them and more African American service providers to serve them (Daly, 1993; Spence & Atherton, 1991). Richardson (1992) found that many older African Americans are unaware of available services, such as senior information and referral services, whereas the most frequently used services were transportation, health, and assistance provided by churches, as well as services that provide help with finances and home maintenance. An evaluation of social services used by African Americans revealed positive responses and satisfaction with the services that were provided (Taylor, Neighbors, & Broman, 1989).

## Conclusion

African American communities in the United States have been described as both weak and enduring amid constant change. Thousands of businesses are owned by African Americans, and there are thousands of churches and more than 100 predominantly African American colleges and universities, fraternal and women's organizations, and political, social, and professional organizations (Billingsley, 1993). Many of the businesses, schools, churches, and organizations have developed social service programs, such as after-school activities, family support services, food and shelter, transportation services, educational and scholarship programs, and mentoring projects. Through individual and organized efforts, the self-help and mutual aid traditions continue. For example, Kessel (1989) found that nearly one-fourth of all African Americans donated all or almost all their charitable contributions to African American organizations and 57 percent indicated that half or more of their total charitable contributions were given to African American organizations that served the needs of African Americans.

The government must contribute to a better quality of life for African Americans that truly rests on equality of opportunity and social justice by establishing public policies and services to enhance the well-being of African Americans and of all Americans. Too many structural barriers that block the entry of African Americans into the socioeconomic mainstream of American society persist. Special attention should be given to policies and services that will improve African Americans' status, employment, education, and income and that will reduce their involvement in the criminal justice system (Leashore, 1994).

## References


Alcena, V. (1992). *The status of health of blacks in the United States of America.* Dubuque, IA: Kendall/Hunt.

Asamoah, Y., Garcia, A, Ortiz Hendricks, C., & Walker, J. (1991). What we call ourselves: Implications for resources, policy, and practice. *Journal of Multicultural Social Work, 1,* 7–22.

Bennett, E. C. (1992). *The Black population in the United States* (Current Population Reports, series P-20, No. 464). Washington, DC: U.S. Government Printing Office.

Bennett, L. Jr. (1964). *Before the Mayflower: A history of the Negro in America.* Chicago: Johnson.

Bauer, R. A., & Bauer, A. H. (1942). Day to day resistance to slavery. *Journal of Negro History, 27,* 338–419.

Billingsley, A. (1993). *Climbing Jacob's ladder: The enduring legacy of African-American families.* New York: Simon & Schuster.

Boyd-Franklin, N. (1989). *Black families in therapy: A multisystems approach.* New York: Free Press.

Broman, C. L., Neighbors, H. W., & Taylor, R. J. (1989). Race differences in seeking help from social workers. *Journal of Sociology and Social Welfare, 16,* 109–123.

Brown v. Board of Education of Topeka, 347 U. S. 483 (1954).

Carlton La-Ney, I. (1989). Old folks' homes for blacks during the progressive era. *Journal of Sociology and Social Welfare, 16,* 43–60.

Cates, J. R. (1983). *Insuring inequality, administrative leadership in social security: 1935–1954.* Ann Arbor: University of Michigan Press.

Daly, A. (1993). African-American and white management styles: A comparison in one agency. *Journal of Community Practice: Organizing, Planning, Development, and Change, 1,* 57–79.

Davis, L. G. (1980). The politics of black self-help in the United States: A historical overview. In L. S. Yearwood

(Ed.), *Black organizations: Issues on survival techniques* (pp. 37–50). Lanham, MD: University Press of America.

Devore, W., & Schlesinger, E. G. (1987). *Ethnic-sensitive social work practice* (2nd ed.). Columbus, OH: Charles E. Merrill.

English, R. A. (1991). Diversity of world views among African-American families. In J. R. Everett, S. Chipungu, & B. R. Leashore (Eds.), *Child welfare: An Africentric perspective* (pp. 19–35). New Brunswick, NJ: Rutgers University Press.

Franklin, J. H. (1969). *From slavery to freedom: A history of Negro Americans* (3rd ed.). New York: Vintage Books.

Freeman, E. M. (1990a). The black family's life cycle: Operationalizing a strengths perspective. In S.M.L. Logan, E. M. Freeman, & R. G. McRoy (Eds.), *Social work practice with black families: A culturally specific perspective* (pp. 55–72). New York: Longman.

Freeman, E. M. (1990b). Theoretical perspectives for practice with black families. In S.M.L. Logan, E. M. Freeman, & R. G. McRoy (Eds.), *Social work practice with black families: A culturally specific perspective* (pp. 38–52). New York: Longman.

Genovese, E. D. (1976). *Roll, Jordan, roll: The world the slaves made.* New York: Vintage Books.

Gutman, H. G. (1975). *Slavery and the numbers game: A critique of time on the cross.* Urbana: University of Illinois Press.

Hacker, A. (1992). *Two nations: Black and white, separate, hostile, unequal.* New York: Ballantine Books.

Herskovits, M. J. (1958). *The myth of the Negro past.* Boston: Beacon Press.

Hill, R. (1972). *The strengths of black families.* New York: Emerson Hall.

Hughes, L., & Meltzer, M. (1963). *A pictorial history of the Negro in America* (new rev. ed.). New York: Crown.

Jaynes, G. D., & Williams, R. M. Jr. (Eds.). (1989). *A common destiny: Blacks and American society.* Washington, DC: National Academy Press.

Johnson, A. E. (1976). The National Association of Black Social Workers, Inc.: A view of the beginning. *Black Caucus Journal of the NABSW, 7,* 13–17.

Johnson, A. E. (1991). The sin of omission: African-American women in social work. *Journal of Multicultural Social Work, 1,* 1–15.

Jones, J. (1981). *Bad blood: The Tuskegee syphilis experiment—A tragedy of race and medicine.* New York: Free Press.

Kessel, F. (1989). Black foundations: Meeting vital needs. *Crisis, 96,* 14–18.

Kolchin, P., & Foner, E. (Consulting Eds). (1993). *American slavery, 1619–1877.* New York: Hill and Wang.

Leashore, B. R. (1994). Social policies, black males, and black families. In R. Staples (Ed.), *The black family: Essays and studies* (5th ed., pp. 334–340). Belmont, CA: Wadsworth.

Marable, M. (1991). *Race, reform, and rebellion: The second reconstruction in black America, 1945–1990* (2nd ed.). Jackson: University of Mississippi Press.

Office of Minority Health, U.S. Department of Health and Human Services. (1989a). *Closing the gap: Homicide, suicide, unintentional injuries, and minorities.* Washington, DC: U.S. Government Printing Office.

Office of Minority Health, U.S. Department of Health and Human Services. (1989b). *Closing the gap: Infant mortality, low birthweight and minorities.* Washington, DC: U.S. Government Printing Office.

O'Hare, W. P., Pollard, K. N., Mann, T. L., & Kent, M. M. (1991). African-Americans in the 1990s. *Population Bulletin, 46*(1), 2–39.

Pinderhughes, E. (1989). *Understanding race, ethnicity, and power.* New York: Free Press.

Plessy v. Ferguson, 163 U.S. 537, 551 (1896).

Quadagno, J. (1988). *The transformation of old age security: Class and politics in the American welfare state.* Chicago: University of Chicago Press.

Richardson, V. (1992). Service use among urban African-American elderly people. *Social Work, 37,* 47–54.

Ross, E. L. (1978). *Black heritage in social welfare, 1860–1930.* Metuchen, NJ: Scarecrow Press.

Solomon, B. B. (1976). *Black empowerment: Social work in oppressed communities.* New York: Columbia University Press.

Spence, S. A., & Atherton, C. R. (1991). The black elderly and the social service delivery system: A study of factors influencing the use of community-based services. *Journal of Gerontological Social Work, 16,* 19–35.

Taylor, R. J., Neighbors, H. W., & Broman, C. L. (1989). Evaluation by black Americans of the social service encounter during a serious personal problem. *Social Work, 34,* 205–211.

Thomas, S. B., & Crouse Quinn, S. (1991). The Tuskegee syphilis study, 1932 to 1972: Implications for HIV education and AIDS risk education programs in the black community. *American Journal of Public Health, 81,* 1498–1505.

Turner, R. J. (1991). Affirming consciousness: the Africentric perspective. In J. R. Everett, S. Chipungu, & B. R. Leashore (Eds.), *Child welfare: An Africentric perspective* (pp. 36–57). New Brunswick, NJ: Rutgers University Press.

U.S. Department of Health and Human Services. (1986). *Health status of the disadvantaged chartbook, 1986.* Washington, DC: U.S. Government Printing Office.

U.S. Department of Health and Human Services (1993). *Advance report of final monthly statistics, 1991. Monthly vital statistics report.* Hyattsville, MD: Public Health Services, National Center for Health Statistics.

Weick, A., Rapp, C., Sullivan, W. P., & Kisthardt, W. (1989). A strengths perspective for social work practice. *Social Work, 34,* 350–354.

Wish, H. (1937). American slave insurrections before 1861. *Journal of Negro History, 22,* 299–320.

## FURTHER READING

Billingsley, A. (1968). *Black families in white America.* Englewood Cliffs, NJ: Prentice Hall.

Everett, J. E., Chipungu, S. S., & Leashore, B. R. (Eds.). (1991). *Child welfare: An Africentric perspective.* New Brunswick, NJ: Rutgers University Press.

Gary, L. E. (Ed.). (1981). *Black men.* Beverly Hills, CA: Sage Publications.

Martin, E., & Martin, J. (1985). *Helping tradition in the black family and community.* Silver Spring, MD: National Association of Social Workers.

McAdoo, H. P. (Ed.). (1981). *Black families.* Beverly Hills, CA: Sage Publications.

National Urban League, Inc. (1994). *The state of black America.* New York: The National Urban League, Inc.

Logan, R. W., & Winston, M. R. (1982). *Dictionary of American Negro biography.* New York: W. W. Norton.
Stack, C. B. (1974). *All our kin.* New York: Harper & Row.
West, C. (1993). *Race matters.* Boston: Beacon Press.
White, B. W. (Ed.). (1981). *Color in a white society.* Silver Spring, MD: National Association of Social Workers.

**Bogart R. Leashore, PhD, ACSW,** is professor and dean, Hunter College, School of Social Work, 129 East 79th Street, New York, NY 10021.

The author acknowledges with appreciation the assistance of Professor Lee Sellers and the staff of the Hunter College School of Social Work Library.

**For further information see**

Advocacy; African American Pioneers in Social Work; African Americans: Caribbean; African Americans: Immigrants; Civil Rights; Community; Ethnic-Sensitive Practice; Families Overview; Federal Social Legislation from 1961 to 1994; Haitian Americans; Human Rights; Income Distribution; Jobs and Earnings; Mutual Aid Societies; Natural Helping Networks; Peace and Social Justice; Poverty; Social Welfare Policy; Social Work Profession Overview.

**Key Words**

African Americans; black Americans; cultural competence; ethnicity

# African American Pioneers in Social Work

**Barbara W. White**
**Dianne M. Hampton**

Historically, leadership has been the paramount source of the success or failure of organized group life. It is well-documented that great leaders have been associated with or involved in great historical movements, events, causes, and issues. Such is the situation in the profession of social work and its antecedents of social movements and events. The history of social work is replete with records of superior, humane leadership that emerged, developed, and blossomed in hostile social environments. However, the role that African American leaders played in social changes and the nature of sociohistorical syndromes of why they have been active participants is often unclear and equivocal.

African Americans have made significant contributions to social work and to the progress the profession claims toward its mission. This is a collective story of these leaders who blazed trails that often led through dangerous social, moral, spiritual, legal, economic, and political wilderness in search of equal citizenship, dignity, and opportunity. Throughout ever-recurring, acute times within this nation, a few courageous and dedicated African American leaders stepped forward to assume the high risks of advocating social reform. The struggle for survival and advancement in American society has been the crucible in which superior African American leadership has been forged. In the context of their times and circumstances, there is a large, rich storehouse of strategies and movements—all focused on their dedication to the belief that the democratic process will triumph over people and nations. Such contributions must be credited in the history of the social welfare institution, because the progress of this nation was the result of the efforts of many racial and ethnic groups.

The lineage of these contributors exceeds the limitations of this entry. African American leaders who are cited here constitute a mere microcosm of those contributors in this category who deserve mention. Because all of these leaders could not be included, the authors have selected 16 profiles to present as demonstrative of African American contributors to the legacy that the social work profession is obligated to follow in contemporary practice. Readers are encouraged to use the references cited here and other sources to obtain additional biographical information. This entry fills in gaps in our history by presenting some examples of noteworthy accomplishments that all social workers can use as role models.

## African American Church as the Social Agency

In filling in these gaps in knowledge, we must understand the role of the African American church. African American people dealt differently with local responsibility. They served those who showed need—whether a fugitive slave or a free African American individual. Need was the only requirement for welfare administered by these churches. This was a different approach from the eligibility focus of white social welfare.

Before the American Revolution, African American churches were established as centers for social welfare, antislavery activity, and leadership development. At the end of the Revolutionary War when the Constitution of the United States was drafted, Richard Allen and Absolom Jones began the first formal social welfare agency, the Free African Society of Philadelphia. The Bureau of Refugees, Freedmen, and Abandoned Lands, better known as the Freedman's Bureau, served former slaves as the first Department of Health and Human Services.

There were other unsung heroines, heroes, caregivers, movers, shakers, and groundbreakers who were on the leading edge—handling individual and institutional responses to human needs. Their African American experiences, values, and visions spanned the free and slave communities.

## Exemplars of African American Leaders

***Catherine (Katy) Ferguson (1774–1854),*** former slave, was one of the first African American women to provide education and welfare services. She began the first Sunday school in New York City. In 1793 her home became a school for the poor. The school later moved to the Murray Street Church. For 40 years she operated the Murray Street Sabbath School. Twenty of her initial group of 48 were white children who came from destitute parents and the almshouse. These efforts established Katy Ferguson as a child welfare social worker who developed secular education for the poor and the African American people.

***Harriet Ross Tubman (1820–1913)*** escaped from slavery in 1849 and became a pillar in the abolition movement and conductor of the Underground Railroad. She risked her life to free over 300 slaves. During the Civil War, she served as a spy and scout for the Union Army and nursed hospitalized soldiers. This humanitarian continued her caregiving mission after the war, although the federal government did not pay her for her work with the Union Army. For over 35 years she fought to attain the widow's pension that was denied her. Finally, in 1898 she received $20 per month for life. These funds were shared with the poor who sought her help.

Tubman dreamed of a home for the aged. This dream was partially realized a few years after 1906 when she deeded her home and 25 acres of land in Auburn, New York, to the African Methodist Episcopal Zion Church. She was a pioneer social worker and a caseworker who helped people improve their life status as well as a community organizer in establishing care of elderly people. Tubman was one of the operators of one of the first Traveler's Aid Societies within her home.

***Ellen Craft (1826–1892)*** was another pillar in the abolitionist movement. This fugitive ex-slave and her husband were celebrated abolitionists who spoke frequently to groups of their daring escape. During the escape, the fair-skinned Craft posed as a sickly, young slave owner traveling to Pennsylvania, with her husband posing as the slave. The publicity of their exploits made them subject to efforts of recapture and forced them to flee to Europe, where they remained from 1851 to 1869. They worked in the abolition movement in England while attending school and later became teachers. After the Civil War, they returned to Georgia, opened a school, and farmed.

Despite Ku Klux Klan activity, Ellen and William Craft offered fair tenant farming privileges to freed slaves. Social action, education, and consultation were a part of their service delivery to the African American community.

***Lugenia Burns Hope (1871–1947) and John Hope (1868–1936)*** were another strong husband and wife alliance in the African American community. Like the Crafts, they were dedicated contributors who met the health, education, and welfare needs of African American individuals and others.

John Hope, president of Morehouse College, Atlanta, Georgia, understood his wife's commitment to community work. Lugenia was one member of a small, closely knit group of elite African American women in the South around the turn of the century. She built her life around organized social and political reform and thoroughly understood the southern network and the power of women's clubs.

In 1903 these clubs evolved into the Neighborhood Union, which addressed the diverse but interrelated issues of sickness, mental illness, poverty, unemployment, truancy, and recreation. The Neighborhood Union became a fountainhead of a remarkable tradition of African American self-help in Atlanta and was supported by community workers. These workers were aware of the endemic problems in communities throughout the city. The Neighborhood Union drew national attention and was emulated in Alabama, Virginia, and Tennessee. Eventually, the Neighborhood Union was selected by the federal government to handle flood and health problems.

In 1920 Lugenia used her position as wife of the president of Morehouse College, as well as the Neighborhood Union's success, to assist in the establishment of the first African American School of Social Work at Atlanta University. She was a civic leader with a vision. Her multifaceted efforts pioneered satellite maternal and child health care clinics, neighborhood schools, adult education classes, and graduate education for African Americans.

***Sarah A. Collins Fernandis (1863–1951),*** a contemporary of Lugenia Burns Hope, had a similar vision. She founded the first African American social settlements in the United States in Washington, DC, and Rhode Island. After receiving her master's degree in social work from New York University, she taught in Baltimore public schools.

On seeing a greater need, she began her lifelong career of organizing social welfare and public health activities in African American communities. By the early 1900s, she organized and presided over the Women's Cooperative Civic League, which worked to improve sanitation and health conditions in African American neighborhoods.

During World War I, Fernandis moved to Pennsylvania and organized a War Camp Community Center. In 1920 she became the first African American social worker employed in the City Venereal Disease Clinic of the Baltimore Health Department (Peebles-Wilkins, 1987a).

***Janie Porter Barrett (1865–1948),*** another contemporary of Hope and Fernandis, was a social welfare activist who made her home into a place for needy people. Using her savings and contacts from the Hampton Institute, her alma mater, Barrett led a successful fundraising campaign to develop the Locust Street Social Settlement. She provided job training for people of all ages who learned to sew, care for children, raise livestock, and cook.

In 1915 Barrett refused an offer from Tuskegee Institute to become its dean of women and instead became superintendent at the Virginia Industrial School for Colored Girls near Richmond. She was convinced the state needed a rehabilitation center for African American girls in legal difficulties. Barrett obtained regular state and philanthropic subsidies and increased the school's enrollment to 100. By the mid-1920s, the Russell Sage Foundation ranked the center among the country's five best institutions of its type.

As a resident among the center's girls, she fostered an atmosphere of community. Each individual's behavior was monitored closely for appropriate treatment. The center was without locks, bars, or physical punishment. The program reflected ideals of progressive reform and set the standard for treatment in which humane social work was becoming increasingly important. Barrett received the William E. Harmon Award for Distinguished Achievement among Negroes in 1929 and participated in the White House Conference on Child Health and Protection in 1930 (Shute, 1985).

***Anita Rose Williams (1891–1983)*** was the first African American Catholic social worker in the United States and the first African American supervisor employed by a Baltimore agency during the early 20th century when child welfare practitioners flourished. Although she had no formal education after high school, she attended sociology lectures at The Johns Hopkins University while volunteering work at family and child welfare agencies.

In 1921 Williams restructured Baltimore's four African American parishes as the Bernard Atkins Organization that promoted economic and social assistance for Catholic youths. An extension of her work with four other social workers at Catholic Charities resulted in the organization of the Baltimore Emergency Relief Commission (Peebles-Wilkins, 1987b).

***Inabel Burns Lindsay (1900–1983),*** an activist, educator, researcher, and administrator, played a vital role in developing policies and programs for the St. Louis public welfare system during the Great Depression. Lindsay introduced social work courses at Howard University's Department of Sociology in Washington, DC. She fought to create a school of social work and to establish a two-year accredited master of social work program.

In 1944 Howard University's Board of Trustees authorized a separate school, and Lindsay was appointed Howard's first female academic dean. She was determined not to establish a "Negro" school of social work but a high-quality professional school open to students of all races. She pioneered work with elderly individuals, especially African American elders. Her research and writing laid the foundation in gerontology studies.

Lindsay was a critical participant in development and implementation of the Older Americans Act of 1965 (P.L. 89-73). In retirement she became a consultant to the White House and the Congress. Today, we still reap the rewards of her life work ("Black History: Inabel Burns Lindsay," 1990).

***Edward Franklin Frazier (1894–1962)*** was an eminent African American sociologist and director of the Atlanta School of Social Work. An ardent supporter of Lugenia Burns Hope's work with the Atlanta Neighborhood Union, he wrote in 1924 that social work held "the greatest promise for improving race relations in the south" (Frazier, 1924, p. 252). He diligently labored to accredit the Atlanta school and to make it a first-class school of professional social work. By 1927 the school had established a reputation as the preeminent voice for African-centric social work issues.

Frazier made important contributions to the African American movement of the 1920s and was outspoken in his denunciation of racism. The wealth of information in his articles contrasts sharply with the paucity of literature about African American people found in social work journals and conferences of the time.

In the five years that Frazier was in Atlanta, he published 29 articles, conducted research, taught classes, and administered the Atlanta School of Social Work. He tirelessly chronicled African American community life and social customs. Drawing on social work's case method, he went to docks, union halls, and saloons to conduct research. Frazier devoted his intellectual and political attention to exposing the socioeconomic roots of racism. Frazier's legacy, which is not covered in most histories of social welfare, is relevant to the crisis confronting social work in the 21st century (Platt & Chandler, 1988).

***Lester Blackwell Granger (1896–1976)*** worked globally to identify the needs of an entire race. He linked the needs of African Americans with the needs of a nation at a point in history when the nation was forced to depend on all its people. He saw the nation as a community, a fact we must promote today.

During World War II he championed a plan to open defense plants to African American workers. He targeted military segregation and helped break down racial barriers in the armed services. Much of the credit for the successful integration of our armed services is attributed to Granger.

Granger headed the National Urban League from 1942 to 1961, during the stormiest time in civil rights in this country. He fought for unionization of African American workers. When all-white unions would not admit African American members, he assisted in the organization of separate locals. During Granger's leadership, the Urban League grew in size and influence and trained and promoted many African American social workers. He also was at the helm of the National Conference of Social Work and was the first American elected president of the International Conference of Social Work.

Granger was a primary figure in bringing about the acceptance of equal opportunity for African Americans as a legitimate goal of society. His application of professional social work methods of group work and community organization as an advocacy tool linked social work practice with industry. He helped plant the seeds for the development of occupational social work ("Black History: Lester Granger," 1991; Brown, 1991; Syers, 1987).

***Whitney Moore Young, Jr. (1921–1971)*** harvested the crop that Granger sowed. Young served in a segregated U.S. Army company in Europe during World War II, where he acted as go-between for white officers and African American enlisted men. He later referred to this experience as the inspiration for his subsequent career as an expert in race relations. With a master's degree in social work from the University of Minnesota, Young worked for the Urban League of St. Paul and later became executive secretary at the branch in Omaha, Nebraska. At age 33 he was named dean of Atlanta University's School of Social Work, where he acquired a formidable reputation as an administrator and fundraiser.

In 1961 Young went to the National Urban League as its executive director. During his 10-year tenure, he successfully secured jobs and training for African Americans in areas traditionally closed to them. Selective placement was the name he gave to this pioneering employment program that was responsible for moving African American professionals into well-paid white-collar jobs in major business and industry. Young's innovative "Marshall Plan" was considered a major inspiration for the "War on Poverty" of the Johnson Administration. He was an advisor on race relations to Presidents Kennedy, Johnson, and Nixon.

Young served as president of NASW from 1969 until his death in 1971. He is considered one of the principal pioneers in community organization, demonstrating the use of community organization in advocacy for oppressed people. Equally important, he pioneered the development of social work in industrial settings with both union and management (Camp, 1985; Peebles-Wilkins, 1987c).

***James Dumpson (1909– )*** straddles the line between social policy practice and education. His contributions to the profession are in the mainstream of both.

Dumpson served as vice president of the New York Community Trust, one of the nation's largest, oldest, and most respected philanthropic organizations and a leader in the community foundation movement. The trust distributes approximately $60 million each year to projects primarily in New York City.

Dumpson made history in 1959 when he was named Commissioner of Welfare for New York City. This was the first time a social worker had held this position, and he was the only African American welfare commissioner in the country at the time. He also served as administrator of the New York City Human Resources Administration. Between administrations in the New York City government, Dumpson was named Dean of the Fordham University School of Social Work. Fordham named an endowed academic chair for Dr. Dumpson when he retired. He was one of the first African Americans appointed dean of a nonblack institution of social work education. He was also the first African American president of the Council on Social Work Education.

As one of the country's leading social workers, Dumpson advised Presidents Kennedy and Johnson on various advisory commissions, including the President's Commission on Narcotics and Drug Abuse. He also was appointed United Nations' advisor to the government of Pakistan, where he assisted in setting up schools of social work after Pakistan's partition from India. Dumpson became, like Lester Granger, a primary representative of this nation in international social work and social welfare (Blythe & Briar, 1987; personal communication with J. Dumpson, December 5, 1994).

***John E. Jacob (1934– )*** served as president and chief executive officer of the National Urban League between 1982 and 1994. His career spanned over 25 years with the Urban League system before his retirement in 1994. He also served as chairman of Howard University's Board of Trustees.

His writings on the American underclass have influenced social thinkers and policymakers in the last decade to establish new approaches to servicing an entire class of a nation's abandoned, oppressed, and ignored people. Jacob wrote "To Be Equal," a weekly news column distributed by Copley News Service to more than 600 newspapers, and his radio editorial "The Commentary" was broadcast by more than 90 radio stations (National Urban League, 1990).

In his role as Urban League president, Jacob produced *The State of Black America,* an annual analysis of key issues by distinguished African American scholars. *The State of Black America* has become must reading for policymakers and commentators. It includes facts and recommendations the nation and our communities should heed to assess society's progress.

The 1994 assessment in *The State of Black America* urged President Clinton to move forward with a "Marshall Plan" approach that invests in the human and physical infrastructure and in the training and creation of jobs now and in the future (Tidwell, 1994). This plan followed the roots of Whitney Young's conceptual framework for employment programs.

***Ronald V. Dellums (1935– )*** was elected to the 92nd Congress, November 1, 1970, and has been re-elected each succeeding Congress to the Democratic seat from the ninth district of Oakland, California. A career as a psychiatric social worker in Berkeley led to Dellums' involvement with community affairs and local politics. He won a seat on the Berkeley City Council in 1967 and emerged as a spokesman for racial and ethnic groups and disadvantaged people. From his seat on the council, Dellums mounted his first campaign for the House of Representatives in 1970 and has been re-elected every two years since.

This policymaker has established himself as a forceful opponent of a growing defense budget. Known as a "fiery liberal activist," he has championed cuts in the defense budget to provide social benefits and employment programs for poor people and the underclass. Before assuming chair of the full Committee on Armed Services in February 1993, he spent a decade as chairman of its various subcommittees. He also chaired and served on the Committee on the District of Columbia. In the 104th Congress, he will be the ranking minority member of the newly proposed Committee on National Defense (personal communication with C. Stephenson, press secretary for Ronald Dellums, December 5, 1994).

Dellums has introduced legislation on a wide variety of issues, including comprehensive health care, housing, the environment, youth employment, and restrictions on nuclear arms deployment. He repeatedly sponsored measures for U.S. support to end apartheid in South Africa. As former chair of the Congressional Black Caucus, the largest body of African Americans elected to Congress in history, his effective voice for domestic programs for underprivileged people rings throughout the U.S. Capitol (Duncan, 1994; Ragsdale & Treese, 1990).

***Edolphus Towns (1934– ),*** a seven-term New York Democratic Representative, was elected in 1982 to the 98th Congress. During his first six terms, he was the representative of the 11th Congressional District. Since 1992 he has represented the 10th Congressional District of Brooklyn, New York. In November 1994, he was re-elected to the 104th Congress. Towns gained stature during the 102nd Congress as chairman of the Congressional Black Caucus and as a member of the powerful Energy and Commerce Committee. He chaired the Human Resources and Intergovernmental Relations Subcommittee of the Government Operations Committee and served as a member of the Health and Environment and Commerce, Consumer Protection, and Competitiveness subcommittees. This former hospital administrator and professor received his master's of social work degree from Adelphi University in New York. He was the first African American deputy borough president in Brooklyn's history, a post in which he served for six years. Towns and Dellums are the only African American professional social workers to have served in Congress (personal communication with K. Munir, press secretary for Edolphus Towns, December 5, 1994).

Towns' legislative agenda reflects his liberal background and activism for social and health reform. He has been a primary player in promoting universal health care. He advocated Medicaid coverage for drug and alcohol treatment for pregnant women and higher reimbursement rates for nonphysicians to improve access to health care in poor communities. His understanding of these issues has been pivotal in identifying the health care needs of women, economically disadvantaged people, elderly people, and other underserved populations. He fought to save the Poison Prevention Control Centers, to improve training opportunities for prospective physicians of color, to equalize the quality of medical service in urban–rural communities, to reform the welfare system, and for passage of the Family and Medical Leave Act of 1993 (P.L. 103-3).

An ardent supporter of accessible health care, Towns passionately protects the nation's nutritional vitality. He has chaired hearings on the implications of eating raw seafood, the efficacy of the U.S. Department of Agriculture's food inspection service, and the link between cancer and diet. The Federal Drug Administration's activities pertaining to licensing and designation of nutritional supplements are under his constant vigilance (Duncan, 1994; Ragsdale & Treese, 1990; "Social Worker Is Elected," 1991).

## Summary

These exemplars of leadership in social work and social welfare express the essential and indispensable roles assumed by women and men of African descent. Each of these people developed into vital instruments in bringing about social changes in their persistent pursuit of equal citizenship, dignity, and opportunity. Such leaders identified needs in their environment and found successful ways to meet them. Their work established models and set standards that were carried out in other communities. They brought the two streams of treatment and reform together in their practice.

When great leadership was demanded, African American leaders emerged. It seems that the greater the leadership challenge, the more positive and effective has been the leadership produced. These African American leaders helped establish social work's principles of social reform and self-determination. Such pioneers unequivocally went beyond the rhetoric and acted on their concern for the welfare of others, learned the applied science of social work practice, found their own contribution, and refused to be defeated. They have demonstrated their full measure of devotion to human service and have enspoused true social work values.

## References


Black history: Inabel Burns Lindsay. (1990, February). *NASW News, 35*(2), 4.

Black history: Lester Granger. (1991, February). *NASW News, 36*(2), 16.

Blythe, B. J., & Briar, S. (1987). Direct practice effectiveness. In A. Minahan (Ed.-in-Chief), *Encyclopedia of social work* (18th ed., Vol. 1, pp. 399–407). Silver Spring, MD: National Association of Social Workers.

Brown, A. W. (1991). A social work leader in the struggle for racial equality: Lester Blackwell Granger. *Social Service Review, 65*(2), 266–280.

Camp, H. C. (1985). Young, Whitney Moore, Jr. In A. Whitman (Ed.), *American reformers* (pp. 913–914). New York: H. W. Wilson.

Duncan, P. (Ed.). (1994). *Politics in America: The 103rd Congress.* Washington, DC: Congressional Quarterly Press.

Family and Medical Leave Act of 1993. P.L. 103-3, 107 Stat. 6.

Frazier, E. F. (1924). Social work in race relations. *Crisis, 27,* 252–254.

National Urban League. (1990). *Biographical sketch: John E. Jacob.* (Available from National Urban League, 500 East 62nd Street, New York, NY 10021)

Older Americans Act of 1965. P.L. 89-73, 79 Stat. 218.

Peebles-Wilkins, W. (1987a). Fernandis, Sarah A. Collins [Biographical sketch]. In A. Minahan (Ed.-in-Chief), *Encyclopedia of social work* (18th ed., Vol. 2, p. 923). Silver Spring, MD: National Association of Social Workers.

Peebles-Wilkins, W. (1987b). Williams, Anita Rose [Biographical sketch]. In A. Minahan (Ed.-in-Chief), *Encyclopedia of social work* (18th ed., Vol. 2, p. 947). Silver Spring, MD: National Association of Social Workers.

Peebles-Wilkins, W. (1987c). Young, Whitney Moore, Jr. [Biographical sketch]. In A. Minahan (Ed.-in-Chief), *Encyclopedia of social work* (18th ed., Vol. 2, pp. 947–948). Silver Spring, MD: National Association of Social Workers.

Platt, T., & Chandler, S. (1988). Constant struggle: E. Franklin Frazier and black social work in the 1920s. *Social Work, 33,* 293–297.

Ragsdale, B. A., & Treese, J. D. (1990). *Black Americans in Congress, 1870–1989.* Washington, DC: U.S. Government Printing Office.

Shute, M. N. (1985). Barrett, Janie Porter. In A. Whitman (Ed.), *American reformers* (pp. 54–55). New York: H. W. Wilson.

Social worker is elected Hill's black caucus chief. (1991, February). *NASW News, 36*(2), 10.

Syers, M. (1987). Granger, Lester Blackwell [Biographical sketch]. In A. Minahan (Ed.-in-Chief), *Encyclopedia of social work* (18th ed., Vol. 2, p. 926). Silver Spring, MD: National Association of Social Workers.

Tidwell, B. (Ed.). (1993). *The state of black America 1994.* New York: National Urban League.

## Further Reading

Battle, M. (1990, February 28). *Contributions of black social workers: A historical perspective.* Paper presented at the University of Missouri, School of Social Work. (Available from National Association of Social Workers, 750 First Street, NE, Suite 700, Washington, DC 20002-4241)

Blockson, C. L. (1991). *Black genealogy.* Baltimore: Black Classic Press.

Hines, D. C. (Ed.). (1993). *Black women in America: An historical encyclopedia* (Vol. 1). Brooklyn, NY: Carlson Publications.

Johnson, A. (1991). The sin of omission: African American women in social work. *Journal of Multicultural Social Work, 1*(2), 1–12.

Logan, R., & Winston, M. (1982). *Dictionary of American Negro biography.* New York: W. W. Norton.

Rouse, J. A. (1989). *Lugenia Burns Hope: Black Southern reformer.* Athens: University of Georgia Press.

**Barbara W. White, PhD, ACSW,** served as president of the National Association of Social Workers from July 1991 to June 1993. She is dean, School of Social Work, University of Texas at Austin, 1925 San Jacinto Boulevard, Austin, TX 78712. **Dianne M. Hampton, BA,** is special assistant to the president's office, National Association of Social Workers, 750 First Street, NE, Suite 700, Washington, DC 20002.

### For further information see

African Americans Overview; Archives of Social Welfare; Social Welfare History; Social Work Practice: History and Evolution; Social Work Profession Overview; Social Work Profession: History.

**Key Words**
African Americans social work history

# African Americans: Caribbean

**Josephine A. Allen**

Caribbean Americans are residents of the United States who arrived from countries that constitute the Caribbean region. They are naturalized citizens or permanent residents who participate in a transnational social system that descriptively defines their bi- or multicultural lifestyles.

Characterized by circular patterns of movement, Caribbean Americans are inextricably tied to the Caribbean region through culture and through family and friendship networks and regularly interact with nationals from their countries of origin in communities within the United States as well as during visits to these countries. A heterogeneous population, Caribbean Americans are racially diverse. However, like other African Americans, Caribbean people who are of African descent are part of that segment of the U.S. population who are racially distinct and frequently marginalized.

## History

### Political and Geographic Definitions

The Caribbean is generally thought of as a group of islands, although it frequently includes the mainland territories of French Guiana, Guyana, Surinam, and Belize. The political status of the Caribbean territories includes independent countries (Cuba, the Dominican Republic, and Haiti); independent members of the British Commonwealth (Jamaica and Trinidad and Tobago); dependencies of France (French Guiana, Guadeloupe, and Martinique), The Netherlands (The Netherlands Dependencies), the United Kingdom (Cayman Islands, Anguilla, Montserrat, and the Turks and Caicos Islands), and the United States (the U.S. Virgin Islands); and finally Puerto Rico in its "commonwealth" association with the United States. The windward islands include Dominica, Grenada, Carriacou (Petit Martinique), St. Lucia, St. Vincent and the Grenadines, Barbados, and Trinidad and Tobago. The leeward islands include Anguilla, Antigua-Barbuda, St. Kitts-Nevis, and Montserrat. The Caribbean also is divided into the Greater and Lesser Antilles. The larger northern islands of Cuba, Jamaica, Haiti, and the Dominican Republic and Puerto Rico constitute the former; the smaller eastern islands, the latter (Table 1).

TABLE 1
**Foreign-Born Caribbean American Population, by Place of Birth, 1980 and 1990, Based on a Sample**

| Place of birth | 1980 (1,000) | 1990 (1,000) | Percentage of distribution |
|---|---|---|---|
| Antigua–Barbuda | 4 | 12 | 0.1 |
| Bahamas | 14 | 22 | 0.1 |
| Barbados | 27 | 43 | 0.2 |
| Cuba | 608 | 737 | 3.7 |
| Dominican Republic | 169 | 348 | 1.8 |
| Grenada | 7 | 18 | 0.1 |
| Haiti | 92 | 225 | 1.1 |
| Jamaica | 197 | 334 | 1.7 |
| Trinidad | 66 | 116 | 0.6 |
| Caribbean[a] | 1,258 | 1,938 | 9.8 |

SOURCE: U.S. Department of Commerce, Bureau of the Census. (1982). *1980 census of the population and housing* (Vol. 1, Chap. C & D). Washington, DC: Government Printing Office; U.S. Department of Commerce, Bureau of the Census. (1992). *1990 census of the population and housing* (Data paper listing CPH-L-98). Washington, DC: Government Printing Office.
[a]Includes other areas not shown separately.

### Plantation System and Slavery

European colonial settlers joined indigenous groups such as the Caribs and Arawaks and began the plantation systems by importing both Africans who were enslaved and indentured and Asian people as indentured servants. By the 18th century, the development of sugar plantations and the production of this commodity together with tobacco, indigo, and cotton led to a flourishing trans-Atlantic slave trade that largely characterized this region. The Caribbean received more than 50 percent of all of the African people brought to the Americas during the 17th century and more than 60 percent of those brought during the 18th century (Knight, 1978).

> The Caribbean region received approximately one half of all Africans brought to the Americas during the nearly 350-year span of the organized trans-Atlantic slave trade. The islands and coastal perimeter of the Caribbean formed the host society for about 5 million Africans.... Given the transportation facilities of the time, this constituted one of the greatest migrations of modern times, although the migrants went unwillingly and with no prospect of ever returning to their homelands. (p. 87)

***Two economies.*** The fully developed and rather complex plantation system created two societies by the late 18th century—one European American and the other African American—as well as two economies. The import of consumer items and the export of plantation products as major activities in each of these countries were important aspects of local economic structures closely related to the local system of distribution and merchandising in which a major sector of the population is involved. Each Caribbean colony traded both within its metropolitan areas and with other colonies. The local market operatives (known as higglers) became adept in domestic and subsequently international trade. The caste and class systems of these plantation societies became well defined and carefully maintained with some built-in flexibility. Note that there also were free African American people in this region.

***Caste system.*** People brought as slaves from Africa, free people of African descent, and white people were subjected to a fairly rigid caste system in which social class and status were rigidly and clearly defined. The planter class formulated laws restricting the economic activities of the nonwhite populace. As a result a pervasive and complex social system existed based on the mutually reinforcing divisions of race, color, and occupation throughout the Caribbean.

> On the plantation as well as in the cities, the color of one's skin fixed both the social position and the occupation of the possessor, with blackness indicating menial and arduous labor and whiteness reflecting superiority and leisure. (Knight, 1978, p. 96)

It was not until the end of the 19th century with the breakdown of plantation society that there was more significant flexibility in this caste–class system.

## Economic and Social Conditions

### Effects of Economic Crisis

With these historically based patterns and structures firmly in place, the current global economic crisis also has had a serious effect on the Caribbean region. Structural adjustment requirements imposed by the International Monetary Fund and the World Bank disproportionately affect women, particularly those of African descent who are in the lower socioeconomic strata, many of whom are heads of households and solely responsible for their children. The required reductions in the range of social welfare expenditures by the governments of this region are noteworthy. This situation in part explains the marginality of Caribbean life.

During the 1980s and 1990s most of this region's nations have had to deal with the debt crisis and structural adjustment, and this has made sustainable economic transformation difficult. Structural adjustment policies have led to cutbacks in government services that are both staffed by and used largely by women (Antrobus, 1989). Increasingly high levels of unemployment, rising food prices, currency devaluations, and reductions in social services have forced women into developing coping strategies to support and protect their families.

### Women's Roles

Women in the Caribbean have higher rates of participation in the labor force than in most other countries in the developing world (Momsen, 1993). Their rates of employment often are even above those of women in many industrialized countries. During the past two decades, there has been both an increase in the proportion of women in the labor force and a significant movement of women from agriculture into the service sector (Momsen, 1993). This high level of economic activity by women is related to several historical factors:

- During slavery, women were expected to perform much of the heaviest field labor alongside men.
- After emancipation, the migration of men left many women alone with the major responsibility of supporting their children. Moreover, this gender-specific pattern of migration encouraged the development of households headed by women, a system of visiting unions, men with responsibilities toward more than one family or household, and difficulties during family reunification attempts.
- Access to land ownership meant that many Caribbean women and their children were able to manage because of their participation in subsistence agricultural production. Momsen (1993) pointed out that "In the Eastern Caribbean women inherited land in their own right or were able to cultivate land belonging to migrant male relatives" (p. 232).
- Women have come to see education as their principal route to economic security and well-being. The trend toward mothers working for their children's school fees on the one hand and the increase in the number of women in the University of the West Indies on the other are major indicators of this belief and pattern of behavior (Ellis, 1986). In reference to Barbados Momsen (1993) noted that the increase in economic activity was greater during the 1970s and 1980s for women than for men as a result of improved female education levels. For women in this country, employment opportunities have been expanding especially rapidly in light industry and tourism. Although men have traditionally sought economic opportunity largely through migration, women have sought it through education.

## Migration Patterns and Experiences

### History of Migration

The systematic study of migration to the United States includes consideration of the society from which individuals leave, the dynamics of transplantation, and the resources and services and perspectives of the society to which they emigrate. Migration to find employment has been a traditional pattern throughout the Caribbean region. The tradition of a plantation system dependent on forced labor through slavery and an indenture system and colonialism is evident. Since the late 19th century, Caribbean people have migrated to the East Coast of the United States. However, there has been a circular movement to and from the North American and other societies. These new immigrants, after arriving, must work out a new way of life that includes residence in the United States or Canada but that also does not cut off effective ties and allegiances to their home countries (Hendricks, 1974).

A history of intra- and extra-Caribbean migration is evident over time. Slavery and the plantation system were supplemented and later replaced in the mid–19th century by indentured or contract workers from West Africa, India, China, and Portugal. Agricultural labor circulated throughout the Caribbean as noted earlier, and several Caribbean nations today simultaneously export numerous skilled and unskilled workers and import labor for seasonal agricultural work or jobs in the tourist industry.

> Approximately 10,000 Anglophone Caribbean workers travel to southern Florida each year to cut sugar cane in the U.S. government's "H-2" program. Jamaicans come to New England for a few weeks each fall to pick apples. Although an unknown number of "H-2" workers simply walk off at the end of their contract periods and join the growing Caribbean communities of New York, Miami, and Hartford, Connecticut, they do not constitute a significant portion of the new immigrants in these communities. (Kasinitz, 1992, p. 23)

High unemployment and limited opportunities lead many citizens of these nations to believe that migration is the only way for young people to become employed, successful adults. These efforts to gain experience and to find employment opportunities have led to an outward-looking culture and a steady stream of migrants. However, these immigrants maintain close ties with their Caribbean nations. The importance of remittances to families and communities that are left behind and the respective Caribbean economies also must be noted.

Connections with family members in their Caribbean home nations in addition to remittances include vacations and other holiday or family emergency and business visits. Many immigrants plan to return to their native country for retirement, and still others find the movement between urban communities of the Caribbean diaspora in the United States and their island homes fluid and culturally consistent.

### Ethnic and Cultural Differences

Increasing public recognition of the problem of undocumented workers in the United States has occurred in recent years. Immigrants who find themselves in this status came to this country perhaps on vacation and decided not to return home. They may live initially with relatives or friends, rely on them for support and acculturation, and eventually develop an independent economic resource base. They also live in fear of being detected and deported. This marginal status has wide implications for understanding some sectors of the immigrant population to this country. As Momsen (1993) noted,

> Despite a commonality based on a long history of colonialism and a location on the periphery of the world economy, Caribbean states have different levels of wealth and nutrition, and of social benefits. Population size and fertility rates vary as does the relative importance of different sectors of the economy. (p. 234)

The importance of recognizing and distinguishing among the diverse experiences and cultures within this region is highlighted in this statement by Momsen. Social workers should keep this in mind when working with Caribbean immigrant individuals, families, and communities. The ethnic diversity of the African American community within the United States is noteworthy and contextualizes this discussion of African Caribbeans. The importance of recognizing the diversity even within this group of immigrant populations can assist in providing appropriate and effective services to members of these communities.

Individuals from every sector of Caribbean society have come to the United States—well-educated members of the urban middle and upper classes who are interested in protecting their economic wealth from the uncertainty of local structural adjustment-related policies and directives, children of the middle class seeking broader opportunities, and people of low income seeking a better quality and a higher standard of life. Economic incentives and broader opportunity in the United States and Europe explain the steady stream of migrants escaping high unemployment rates and persistent poverty.

The emphasis on ethnic and cultural differences does not suggest conflicts or marked divisions between citizens of African heritage in the United States. Instead, it is an acknowledgment of the positive survival of African patterns, practices, and traditions and their common experiences in addition to the historical and cultural similarities of various groups within that larger group. The relations between Caribbean American and African American people have varied over time. Bryce-Laporte (1983) has suggested that these Caribbean immigrants experience contradiction and tensions of identity more intensely than European immigrants. Caribbean immigrants have been largely ambivalent about identifying with African Americans.

> Beyond the normal competition and socialization conflicts between old and new Americans . . . they are torn between their participation . . . in the fight for pluralistic society and racial justice in the United States . . . and the sense of calling to return and share in the fate, life quality and needs of their ancestral homes. (Bryce-Laporte, 1983, p. 197)

### Racism and Racial Distribution in the United States

In addition and perhaps more important, the climate of racism and racial discrimination in this country was not partial to these immigrants and affected them as severely as the larger resident African American population. For both groups it was primarily race that structured their life chances. Thus, a dynamic intertwining of race, class, and ethnicity characterizes the Caribbean immigrant communities in the United States.

Although south Florida, and Miami in particular, are destinations for many immigrants to the United States from the Caribbean, New York City has been the primary point of disembarkation for these immigrants. Considering why Caribbean immigrants in New York City chose to deemphasize their separate ethnic identity and become part of the larger African American community at one point in their early American experience and to emphasize their cultural distinctiveness at another much later and more contemporary point, Kasinitz (1992) suggested that significant growth in the size of the Caribbean community in this city is one of several complex factors. Referencing two major waves of immigrants from the English-speaking Caribbean, Kasinitz noted that the migration of Caribbean people to the United States started in earnest in the first decade of the 20th century and grew steadily until the 1930s and the Great Depression. From then until the mid-1960s there was a significant decrease in this trend.

The Hart–Cellar Immigration Reform Act of 1965 led to another significant increase in the number of immigrants to the United States from this region. More Caribbean people migrated to this country during the late 1960s and 1970s than in the preceding seven decades (Kasinitz, 1992). This trend continues to the present as a result of the Immigration Reform Act as well as the structural adjustment–related economic and government service crises affecting life in these countries.

**Haitian and Cuban Immigrants**

The most-recent wave of Caribbean immigrants has included political and economic refugees from Haiti and Cuba. The economic sanctions imposed on the governments of these countries have been extremely effective.

The plight of Haitian immigrants is noteworthy because of its complexity and because of their flight from political and economic oppression. The differential treatment of these immigrants by American political leaders has been widely documented (Caribbean migration, 1980; Lawyers Committee for Human Rights, 1980; Miller, 1984). In contrast to Bosnian immigrants, other Eastern European immigrants, and immigrants to the United States from Cuba, large numbers of recent Haitian immigrants have been returned to Haiti or isolated in detention camps (for example, Fort Drum in New York and Guantanamo Bay, Cuba). They have not routinely been granted political asylum and readily integrated into American life. President Clinton's decision to retain the policy of the Bush administration in this regard has prolonged this differential treatment. With President Aristide's return to Haiti, the resignation of the military hunta, and the support of American and Caribbean leaders, there is increased optimism about a dramatic decline in the number of Haitian people seeking political asylum and greater economic security in the United States.

**Mutual Aid and Benevolent Associations**

With the first major wave of immigrants from the Caribbean region to the United States came the development of essential coping mechanisms that remain viable today. Maintaining contact with other people of the same ethnic heritage has been successfully managed through the organization of various beneficial, social, and cultural societies; mutual aid societies; and benevolent associations in cities where there are substantial numbers of Caribbean people. Since 1925 these societies have been organized by and assisted immigrant groups from Anguilla, Antigua, Guiana, Dominica, Grenada, Montserrat, Jamaica, St. Lucia, Turks and Caicos Islands, Trinidad and Tobago, and the British Virgin Islands (Jenkins, Sauber, & Friedlander, 1985).

In addition to these benevolent and mutual aid organizations, various social clubs were initiated on the basis of color and class plus status in the United States (Reid, 1969). The range of organizations includes literary clubs, cricket clubs, fraternal orders, and politically motivated groups such as the Council on West Indian Affairs, the Jamaica Progressive League, the United Aid for Persons of African Descent, and the West Indian Federation of America (established in 1933) whose specific objective was facilitating the federation and self-government of the West Indian colonies (Reid, 1969). From promoting the development of supportive communities for new immigrants and established residents of Caribbean origin, these organizations served social, economic, and political functions. They saw their functions as including contributing to the economic welfare of the community through the stimulation of businesses, promoting the housing needs of their constituents, contributing charitable assistance when needed, and assisting their members in securing employment.

## Naturalization and Citizenship

The early Caribbean immigrants had few incentives to become American citizens and often found that they were at a disadvantage when they relinquished citizenship in their country of birth. The race question has been critical in American history and life. To renounce citizenship in a society in which their humanity, accomplishments, and contributions were valued and in which they were majority players with all of the rights and responsibilities of every other citizen was not easily done. These pre-1960 immigrants were more likely to work toward the development and independence of their homelands and the improvement of the political economy of the Caribbean region than pledge allegiance to another flag (Kasinitz, 1992).

Only during the later migratory waves, after the 1960s, have the numbers significantly increased of naturalized Caribbean people of African descent. This trend occurred because the quest for independence was alive and real in several of these island nations. In addition, the changes brought about by the civil rights movement in this country and the expansion of opportunities for those previously disenfranchised and discriminated against in many other ways also contributed to more-frequent naturalization. Changes in the immigration and naturalization legislation also has resulted in the frequent link between naturalized citizenship and access to societal benefits and services. Citizenship has become more attractive as a result of these factors.

## Stages of Adaptation

What have been characterized as stages of adaptation for immigrants may be helpful in working with Caribbean people who have become permanent residents or who desire this status. Cox (1987) maintained that there are stages in the adaptation process that include the period when a decision to migrate is being contemplated, options are weighed, and contacts are made. This is the premigration stage. The stage when a decision to move has been made follows, after which a transition stage ensues and preparations to leave are made and implemented. This is followed by the reception and initial resettlement stage when relocation is complete and housing, employment, child care, and community options are explored. Integration is the final stage when many of the settling-in tasks are completed, but this stage may be an ongoing process.

Cox (1987) and Ross-Sheriff (1990) described four alternative models of adaptation: (1) assimilation, (2) integration, (3) separation, and (4) marginalization. The earlier historical review of the immigration of Caribbean people of African descent to the United States as well as the recent Haitian refugee situation allows for the implementation of each of these models. The use of these models and stages may assist service providers in obtaining knowledge of the experiences, needs, and circumstances of new immigrant individuals and families as well as those who have been naturalized or who are already permanent residents. Cox and Ross-Sheriff also suggested the need to examine the experiences of previous immigrants and to evaluate the service delivery patterns and relate these to current experiences, needs, and program or service responses.

Age; family composition; socioeconomic, educational, and cultural characteristics; occupation; rural or urban backgrounds; belief systems; and social supports are variables that influence the migration process and the experiences of the individuals and families at each stage. The social, political, economic, and cultural responses of the host communities also are critical in determining the experiences of new residents (Bryce-Laporte, 1983; Cox, 1987; Ho, 1993).

## Social Work's Response

As social work practitioners, understanding the complexity of the migration experiences from the perspectives of the immigrants themselves as well as the community's reception or acceptance of Caribbean immigrants is essential. Caribbean migration has largely reflected the export of formerly menial and enslaved labor and now seasonal farm workers, students, and professionals from every field.

### Work with Families

The historical pattern of the male family member migrating first and, after establishing a residence, sponsoring his wife is no longer the case (Ho, 1993). Alternatively, the husband and wife may come together to the community in which they have decided to settle or the wife may come first in cases where her skills are the most marketable or desired by the host country. This is particularly true of nurses and other skilled professionals. Gordon (1990) noted that the constant factor since the acceleration of Caribbean immigration to the United States in the 1960s has been that women form the largest number of immigrants. Gordon further suggested that, rather than dependents, these women have often come as independent workers. Depending on the constellation of skills and family support systems already in place in the host communities, a decision is made about the order in which the family members will migrate.

Once in this country immigrants work to establish an economically stable environment so that the remaining family members may join them. During this period, children often are left behind with grandparents, aunts and uncles, other relatives, or family friends. The demands of becoming economically secure mean working hard on several part-time jobs or on a full-time job and one or more part-time jobs (Drachman, 1992; Gopaul-McNicol, 1993; Ho, 1993).

***Reunification issues.*** On the arrival of the parents, a number of factors may produce anxiety and stress that must be managed if a positive mental health status is to be maintained. Dealing with conflicting values and practices concerning work, child rearing, gender roles, therapy, and the use of counseling or other professional services are only some of the issues that must be addressed. After the children have joined their parents in the new environment, a number of additional stressors may emerge. The reversal of roles; parent–child conflicts; excessive stress occasioned by the process of immigrating; family disruptions; intergenerational conflicts; and the process of settling into a new social, political, economic, and cultural milieu often lead to the need for counseling and other social welfare services (Thrasher & Anderson, 1988). One of the areas of cultural dissonance is in the frequent use of physical punishment with their children by African American parents.

***Issues related to adolescence.*** For children who have made adaptations to the temporary loss of parents during their formative years and must readjust when the family reunites during their adolescence, individual and family counseling services are often needed. The global economic crisis that often precipitated the migration to this country initially leads to families in which both parents are working outside of the home and to there being a lack of or minimally adequate supervision for children. The crisis that is particularly virulent in urban areas with violence, poverty, high unemployment rates, underemployment, and highly visible peer influences produces cultural dissonance and the strong desire to fit in.

America's political and military influence and its popular culture through satellite dishes, the Cable News Network, videocassette recorders, and the tourist industry are absorbed by Caribbean people and by people worldwide, even in the most remote corner of their region. The international pervasiveness of U.S. cultural symbols has not prepared these young people for the changes or for their reactions to the losses they suffer as a direct result of the move to this country. In some instances, the same types of violence that are experienced and expressed in their countries of origin also are experienced in the new environment. Issues such as drug trafficking, youth gangs, and interethnic rivalries are serious and must be dealt with expeditiously (Bryce-Laporte, 1983; Palmer, 1990).

**Work with Communities**

Community development strategies must be sensitive to the historical and contemporary experiences of each immigrant population and to the cultural characteristics that can facilitate or impede the effectiveness of the strategies as they are thoughtfully employed. Together with individual and family counseling, work with communities must be considered and undertaken.

***Education.*** Education is highly valued among Caribbean people across class, race, and ethnicity (Bryce-Laporte, 1983; Palmer, 1990; Sewell-Coker, Hamilton, & Fein, 1985). It is seen as the route to economic well-being, social status, social mobility, and success. In the English-speaking Caribbean countries, the eleven plus or common entrance examination system is used to determine access to college preparatory school placement. The authoritative, structured, and academically rigorous school environments of this region are often significantly different from those found in the United States. The pressure from Caribbean parents to achieve academically is high. The attractiveness of competing social activities and other related peer group activities may therefore result in parent–child conflict, academic underachievement, rebellion, and antisocial behavior. The primacy of the family in all of its forms is one of the strengths of this population.

The disruptions within the family imposed by the migration of one parent and then the other, leaving children for extended periods, can lead to severe problems at home and in school. The pressures imposed by peers and the fragile bond that may exist after the reunification with parents together with a different system of education make life stressful for many children, adolescents, young adults, and their parents (Sewell-Coker, Hamilton, & Fein, 1985). The need for ethnically sensitive practice is clear.

With the increasing numbers of children who are entering the school systems of the United States from families who have migrated to this country, schools are becoming the agencies of choice in terms of the provisions of services and other interventions that facilitate the sociocultural adaptation of children and their families (Vayle, 1992). Consultations by these professionals with schools that have significant numbers of Caribbean families of African descent are often effective. Thrasher and Anderson (1988) noted that although Caribbean families do not usually seek outside assistance with their problems, because education is so highly valued professional help will be sought and accepted if their children are experiencing problems in school.

***Health and human services.*** Special services designed to help new immigrants are rarely available to address problems related to health, mental health, families, children, or elderly individuals from the traditional social institutions and human services organizations. There is a need for social supports that can be made available while these individuals and families are in the process of adapting to and integrating into the host society. Social work intervention is often required to deal with adjustment and adaptation; issues of separation and reattachment; identity issues, especially among children and adolescents; stress; and the clash of cultures.

In the process of assessing needs and delivering services to African Americans from the Caribbean, social work professionals must survey the available community resources. As noted above, immigrants depend for help primarily on earlier arrivals from their ethnic and island group. Assistance from such local resources as self-help ethnic associations, family, and friends may be helpful in a crisis. Emphasizing the use of mutual assistance associations as one component of a viable service plan should be paired with an informed assessment of the strengths of the particular individuals, families, and communities that are in need of assistance so an appropriate service plan or strategy may be employed. The centrality of the extended family in the socialization and care of children is important in this regard.

Spirituality and religion are important in the lives of many Caribbean Americans. The social support gained from members of church and other spiritual groups may be invaluable in finding solutions to problems involving family members and other interpersonal relationships. The significance of reinforcing and interpreting commonly held values in this way must be emphasized.

Social workers are encouraged to recognize and understand the needs and cultural differences of people of African descent who came to this country from the Caribbean. Developing an ethnically sensitive practice and recognizing the value of ethnically based support groups and organizations are essential to effective service delivery in the Caribbean American community.

***Diversity.*** A variety of strategies may be combined to create more-responsive and more-effective service delivery outcomes among Caribbean Americans. The diversity within this community must be appreciated if there are to be effective service outcomes. The hiring of social workers and other human services professionals who are first- or later-generation Caribbean Americans as cultural consultants and the hiring of social workers who are experienced in working with ethnically diverse populations are important.

In addition, a commitment to community outreach efforts geared to overcome the unfamiliarity and distrust that often characterize new immigrants may be positively received. Because studies have shown that most Caribbean immigrants do not rely on formal systems of support or on formal human services organizations, drawing on and working with the strong social networks located in these communities are important strategies.

A final strategy is that of empowerment. Empowerment here is defined by Allen, Barr, Cochran, Greene, and Dean (1989) as

> an intentional, ongoing process centered in the local community, involving mutual respect, critical reflection, caring, and group participation, through which people lacking an equal share of valued resources gain greater access to and control over those resources. (p. 2)

If families gain access to information and other needed resources, if they are involved in an intentional ongoing process that is centered in the local community involving mutual respect, critical reflection, caring and group participation, they will be able to build their communities and care for their families effectively while connecting with communities in the wider society.

## References

Allen, J., Barr, D., Cochran, M., Greene, J., & Dean, C. (1989). *Networking bulletin: Empowerment and family support* (Vol. 1, Issue 1. October 1989). Ithaca, NY: Cornell University; Cornell Empowerment Group.

Antrobus, P. (1989). *Women and planning: The need for an alternative analysis.* Paper presented at the University of the West Indies second Disciplinary Seminar in the Social Sciences on Women, Development Policy and Management of Change, Barbados, April.

Brice, J. (1982). West Indian families. In M. McGoldrick, J. K. Pearce, & J. Giordano (Eds.), *Ethnicity and family therapy* (pp. 123–133). New York: Guilford Press.

Bryce-Laporte, R. (Ed.). (1983). *Caribbean immigration into the United States.* Washington, DC: Research Institute on Immigration and Ethnic Studies. Smithsonian Institution.

*Caribbean migration: Oversight hearing before the Subcommittee on Immigration, Refugees, and International Law, Committee on the Judiciary, House of Representatives,* 96th Cong., 2d Sess. (1980).

Cox, D. (1987). *Migration and welfare: An Australian experience.* Englewood Cliffs, NJ: Prentice Hall.

Drachman, D. (1992). A stage-of-migration framework for service to immigrant populations. *Social Work, 37,* 68–72.

Ellis, P. (1986). *Women of the Caribbean* (pp. 91–100). Atlantic Highlands, NJ: Zed Books.

Gopaul-McNicol, S.-A. (1993). *Working with West Indian families.* New York: Guilford Press.

Gordon, M. H. (1990). Dependents or independent workers?: The status of immigrant women in the United States. In R. W. Palmer (Ed.), *In search of a better life:*

*Perspectives on migration from the Caribbean.* New York: Praeger.

Hart–Cellar Immigration Reform Act of 1965. P.L. 89-236, 79 Stat. 911.

Hendricks, G. (1974). *The Dominican diaspora: From the Dominican Republic to New York City—Villagers in transition.* New York: Teachers' College Press.

Ho, C. (1993). The internationalization of kinship and the feminization of Caribbean immigration: The case of Afro-Trinidadian immigrants in Los Angeles. *Human Organization, 52,* 32–40.

Jenkins, S., Sauber, M., & Friedlander, E. (1985). *Ethnic associations and services to new immigrants in New York City.* New York: Research and Program Planning Information Department, Community Council of Greater New York.

Kasinitz, P. (1992). *Caribbean New York: Black immigrants and the politics of race.* Ithaca, NY: Cornell University Press.

Knight, F. W. (1978). *The Caribbean: The genesis of a fragmented nationalism.* New York: Oxford University Press.

Lawyers Committee for Human Rights. (1980). *Refugee refoulement: The forced return of Haitians under the U.S.–Haitian interdiction agreement.* New York: Author.

Miller, J. C. (1984). *The plight of Haitian refugees.* New York: Praeger.

Momsen, J. H. (1993). *Women and change in the Caribbean: A Pan-Caribbean perspective.* Bloomington: Indiana University Press.

Palmer, R. W. (Ed.). (1990). *In search of a better life: Perspectives on migration from the Caribbean.* New York: Praeger.

Reid, I. (1969). *The Negro immigrant: His background characteristics and social adjustment, 1899–1937.* New York: Arno Press.

Ross-Sheriff, F. (1990). Displaced populations. In L. Ginsberg et al. (Eds.), *Encyclopedia of social work* (18th ed., suppl., pp. 78–93). Silver Spring, MD: NASW Press.

Sewell-Coker, B., Hamilton-Collins, J., & Fein, E. (1985). Social work practice with West Indian immigrants. *Social Casework: Journal of Contemporary Social Work, 66*(9), 563–568.

Simon, J. L. (1984). Immigrants, taxes and welfare in the United States. *Population and Development Review, 10,* 55–70.

Stepik, A., & Portes, A. (1986). Flights of despair: A profile of recent Haitian refugees in South Florida. *International Migration Review, 20,* 329–350.

Thrasher, S., & Anderson, G. (1988). The West Indian family: Treatment challenges. *Social Casework, 69*(3), 171–176.

Vayle, M. R. (1992). International women's group: A bridge to belonging. *Social Work in Education, 14,* 7–14.

## Further Reading

Coppin, A. (1992). Recent US economic policies and the central Caribbean economics. *Review of Black Political Economy, 20,* 55–71.

Dechesnay, M. (1986). Jamaican family structure: The paradox of normalcy. *Family Process, 25,* 293–300.

Elliston, I. (1985). Counseling West Indian immigrants: Issues and answers. In R. Samuda & A. Wolfgang (Eds.), *Intercultural counseling and assessment: Global perspective.* Lewiston, NY: Hogrefe.

Longres, J. F. (1991). Toward a status model of ethnic sensitive practice. *Journal of Multicultural Social Work, 1*(1), 41–56.

McLaughlin, M. (1981). *West Indian immigrants: Their social networks and ethnic identification.* Unpublished doctoral dissertation, Columbia University, New York.

McPherson-Blake, P. C. (1991). *The psychological factors associated with the immigration of Haitians and Jamaicans to South Florida and changes in their parental roles.* Unpublished doctoral dissertation, Barry University, Miami, Florida.

Mortimer, D. M., & Bryce-Laporte, R. (1981). *Female immigration to the United States: Caribbean, Latin American and African experiences.* Washington, DC: Research Institute on Immigration and Ethnic Studies.

Payne, M. A. (1989). Use and abuse of corporal punishment: A Caribbean view. *Child Abuse and Neglect, 13*(3), 389–401.

Pryor, C. B. (1992). Integrating immigrants into American schools. *Social Work in Education, 14,* 153–159.

Stinner, W. F., Bryce-Laporte, R., & De Alberquerque, K. (1982). *Return immigration and remittances: Developing a Caribbean perspective.* Washington, DC: Research Institute on Immigration and Ethnic Studies, Smithsonian Institution.

Watts-Jones, D. (1992). Cultural and integrative therapy issues in the treatment of a Jamaican woman with panic disorder. *Family Process, 31,* 105–113.

**Josephine A. Allen, PhD, ACSW,** is associate professor and director of the baccalaureate social work program, Department of Human Service Studies, Cornell University, N132 Martha Van Rensselaer Hall, Ithaca, NY 14853.

### For further information see

African Americans Overview; African Americans: Immigrants; Community; Community Needs Assessment; Displaced People; Ethnic-Sensitive Practice; Haitian Americans; International Social Welfare: Organizations and Activities; Mutual Aid Societies; Social Welfare Policy.

**Key Words**

| | |
|---|---|
| African Americans | cultural sensitivity |
| Caribbeans | immigrants |

## African Americans: Haitians

*See* Haitian Americans

# African Americans: Immigrants

**Fariyal Ross-Sheriff**

Between 1965 and 1992, 2,275,422 people emigrated from Africa to the United States (USINS, 1992). This number represents only 2 percent to 3 percent of the total number of immigrants to this country, but it is nonetheless a significant number of people to examine in terms of social work implications. This entry explores three groups of African immigrants: legal immigrants, refugees, and illegal migrants. Included in the discussion are characteristics of African immigrants, U.S. policies and practices that affect who immigrates, reasons for African emigration, and patterns of settlement and integration.

Historically, multiple emigration patterns and complex economic, social, and political factors have resulted in the dispersion of Africans to other parts of the world and in the settlement of people from other parts of the world in the African continent. People of African ancestry came to the United States more than a century before the Mayflower arrived in America (Bryce-Laporte, 1972). In the recent past, people with African ancestry, from the West Indies, the Caribbean, and South America, as well as Asians from Africa have immigrated to the United States. (Information about these immigrants is presented elsewhere in this encyclopedia.)

This entry focuses on African immigrants who emigrate directly from the continent of Africa, who have African ancestry, and who have come to the United States since the Immigration Act of 1965 when preference categories were established. Therefore, data and discussions related to citizens of African countries with ancestry other than African, for example, Asian refugees from Uganda, white South Africans, and others are not included in this entry.

Immigrants (including refugees) are people who cross national boundaries to take up permanent residence in countries in which they are not natives. They come to settle, work, and live in a new homeland and usually, but not necessarily, become citizens in due time. A refugee is a person who is outside his or her country, "and who is unwilling to return to, and is unable or unwilling to avail himself or herself of the protection of, that country because of persecution or well-founded fear of persecution on account of race, religion, nationality, membership in a particular social group, or political opinion. . ." (Refugee Act of 1980, P.L. 96-212).

## Africans Who Emigrate

### Immigrants

Before 1965, less than 0.71 percent of immigrants to the United States came from Africa. (See Table 1.) Historically, U.S. immigration laws have excluded certain racial groups, specifically people of color, either by explicitly singling out a nationality to limit their numbers or by opening the doors only for certain others. The Naturalization Act of 1790, for example, limited U.S. citizenship to "free white persons" who resided in the United States for two or more years (Muller, 1993). This law was passed to appease white residents who were concerned that black people coming from the Caribbean would be entitled to citizenship (Muller, 1993).

TABLE 1
**Immigration to the United States from Africa between 1901 and 1965**

| Year | Africa | Total | Percentage of African origin |
|---|---|---|---|
| 1901–1910 | 7,368 | 8,795,386 | .08 |
| 1911–1920 | 8,443 | 5,735,811 | .15 |
| 1921–1930 | 6,286 | 4,107,209 | .15 |
| 1931–1940 | 1,750 | 528,431 | .33 |
| 1941–1950 | 7,367 | 1,035,039 | .71 |
| 1951–1960 | 14,092 | 2,515,479 | .56 |
| 1961–1965 | 9,631 | 1,450,312 | .66 |

Source: Dinnerstein, L. & Reimers, D. (1975). *Ethnic Americans: A history of immigration and assimilation.* New York: Harper & Row.

From the late 1880s to the middle of the 20th century restrictions on the basis of race and country of origin were implemented to exclude Asians, Eastern Europeans, and other people of color, including the Africans. The McCarran-Walter Act of 1952 allegedly reversed racially based quotas, by establishing quotas for immigrants from the "Asian-Pacific Triangle." Nevertheless, it gave preference to northwestern Europeans (Helton, 1992).

***1965 Immigration Act.*** The 1965 Immigration Act, the "Kennedy-Johnson amendment" to the McCarran-Walter Act of 1952, phased out the national origins system, restructured the preference system established in 1952, and developed a process of individual labor certification. The new legislation established ceilings that favored the Western Hemisphere over the Eastern Hemisphere, but it allowed immigrants according to criteria favoring family reunification and needed occupational skills rather than ethnicity (Rockett, 1983).

On the basis of the 1965 act, current U.S. immigration policy allows for four main categories of people:

1. Those reuniting with families of citizens or legal permanent residents
2. Those who are needed (permanently or temporarily) for their work skills
3. Refugees or people seeking asylum who are of interest to the United States for foreign or domestic policy reasons or for humanitarian reasons, that is, those with a well-founded fear of persecution
4. Those seeking temporary stays, including tourists, students, and diplomats (Bean, Vernez, & Keeley, 1989).

Although the 1965 Immigration Act was represented as free of racial or national quotas, a relatively small number of people from Africa can qualify for entry to the United States under its rules. Nonetheless, the Immigration Act of 1965 has opened new opportunities for Africans to enter the United States. In fact, the percentage of immigrants from Africa doubled after the 1965 act. During the period 1955 to 1964, the percentage of immigrants from Africa was 0.7 percent; during the decade after the 1965 Immigration Act, from 1965 to 1974, the percentage of immigrants increased to 1.5 percent. Data from 1983 to 1992 indicate that the percentage increased again to 2.7 percent in 1983 and continues to be over the 2 percent range (see Table 2). Africa continues to be a relatively minor contributor to U.S. immigration.

A very small number of Africans are eligible for immigration under the terms of the preference system, which stresses family reunification and occupational selectivity (Rockett, 1983). However, there was an increase in emigration from Africa in the 1980s, specifically of well-educated persons from sub-Saharan Africa, which Apraku (1991) attributes to poor economic and political conditions in Africa. He notes that during this period sub-Saharan Africa fared worst among developing countries and contributed to an increase in emigration that exceeded Africa as a whole as well as the world. As an example, he noted, "a 9 percent increase [in emigration] for the whole of Africa in 1980 was matched by a 28 percent increase for sub-Saharan Africa" (Apraku, 1991, p. xxi).

***Characteristics of immigrants.*** An analysis of the 1992 immigration statistics shows that the African immigrant population is largely highly skilled and well educated. (See Table 3.) Of the 8,716 immigrants, who were subject to direct numerical limitations (family-sponsored and employment-based preferences), over half (4,967) were admitted for reasons of professional expertise and technical skills. Of this number, only 166 fell into a category of unskilled workers and their families (USINS, 1993). The rest were people with advanced degrees or skilled workers and professionals and their families. The percentage of African immigrants under the employment-based preference category was relatively high (18 percent) compared with the total percentage of immigrants in this category (12 percent). On the other hand, the percentage of immigrants in the family reunification/sponsorship category was relatively low (14 percent) compared with the total percentage in this category (22 percent).

TABLE 2
**Immigration to the United States from Africa between 1983 and 1992**

| Year | Africa | Total | Percentage of African origin |
|---|---|---|---|
| 1983 | 15,084 | 559,763 | 2.7 |
| 1984 | 15,540 | 543,903 | 2.9 |
| 1985 | 17,117 | 570,009 | 3.0 |
| 1986 | 17,463 | 601,708 | 2.9 |
| 1987 | 17,724 | 601,516 | 2.9 |
| 1988 | 18,882 | 643,025 | 2.9 |
| 1989 | 25,166 | 1,090,924 | 2.3 |
| 1990 | 35,893 | 1,536,483 | 2.3 |
| 1991 | 36,179 | 1,827,167 | 2.0 |
| 1992 | 27,086 | 973,977 | 2.8 |

SOURCE: U.S. Immigration and Naturalization Service. (1993). *1992 statistical yearbook of the Immigration and Naturalization Service*. Washington, DC: U.S. Government Printing Office.

## Refugees

Worldwide, Africa has the largest proportion of refugees and internally displaced persons relative to the total population, the most pressing human tragedies, and the hardest-to-solve human problems. Millions of people have left their lands and homes under the threat of starvation and famines caused by drought; millions more have been forced to leave by war, civil unrest, political terror, and bloody ethnic persecution. Military strife between warring factions in Somalia compounded by drought has created hundreds of thousands of refugees in Somalia. According to the Refugee Policy Group (1992), there are 1 million internal refugees in Ethiopia, some 300,000 in Chad, 3 million to

TABLE 3

**Comparison of Immigrants from Africa with Total Number of Immigrants in Two Categories for Admission (FY 1992)**

| Categories | Total | Percentage | Total of African Immigrants | Percentage |
|---|---|---|---|---|
| Family-sponsored | 213,123 | 21.9 | 3,749 | 13.8 |
| Employment-based | 116,198 | 11.9 | 4,967 | 18.3 |

SOURCE: U.S. Immigration and Naturalization Service. (1993). *1992 statistical year book of the Immigration and Naturalization Service.* Washington, DC: U.S. Government Printing Office.
NOTE: Total for all immigrants in 1992 was 973,977.

4 million in Mozambique, approximately 500,000 each in Liberia and Uganda, and 850,000 in Angola, to name just a few. Endemic starvation in parts of Sudan compounded by religious warfare has resulted in an unending flow of an estimated number of 4.5 million internal refugees. The bloody and ethnic civil war in Rwanda that erupted in April 1994 has claimed the lives of thousands and made even more people homeless. In Africa today, an estimated 20 million are refugees and internally displaced.

Most African refugees find their way to neighboring countries. However, the U.S. coordinator for refugee affairs (1992) stated that "despite the usually generous asylum policies found within Africa, there are refugees who must be settled outside the region. They are, generally, either political dissidents who are not welcome in neighboring countries, or urban refugees not easily assimilated into the predominately rural economies of countries of first asylum" (p. 7).

***U.S. refugee policy.*** Despite the massive numbers of uprooted persons on the African continent, African refugees make up only a small percentage of the total that enter the United States. Compared with more than 80 percent of refugees who were admitted from the former Soviet Union and Southeast Asia, African refugee admissions constitute less than 5 percent. A brief historical review of the U.S. refugee policy sheds light on this matter. The Refugee Act of 1980 (P.L. 96-212), which governs the current refugee flow into the United States, was designed to reestablish congressional control over the numbers of refugee arrivals (control that had been in the hands of the executive branch since the Cuban crisis in the 1950s). The law removed ideological and geographical considerations from the definition of "refugee" and adopted the United Nations standard of a refugee as a person with a "well-founded fear of persecution," as stated in the introduction of this entry. This standard was designed to apply equally to all victims of political oppression and to consider individual cases, not mass or group determination of refugee status. The law also established statutory recognition to the principle of asylum and created the Office of Refugee Resettlement under the Department of Health and Human Services to coordinate and implement this new policy (Bean, Vernez, & Keeley, 1989).

***Ceiling and admission statistics.*** Every year Congress sets admission ceilings for refugees from different geographical areas. These ceilings are based on recommendations from the U.S. coordinator for refugee affairs on behalf of the president, and they take into account the nature of the refugee situation, the number of refugees and conditions in the country from which they are coming, and "an analysis of the impact of the participation of the United States in the resettlement of such refugees on the foreign policy interests of the United States" (USCRA, 1992).

The *Proposed Refugee Admissions for Fiscal Year 1993* (USCRA, 1992) does not reveal much about U.S. foreign policy interest in Africa as a region. However, an analysis of ceiling and admission statistics from 1980 to 1988 indicates very small numbers from Africa. (See Table 4.) Additionally, statistics from 1991 to 1993 reflect very small increases in resettled refugees or refugee allocations. For FY 1991, the actual number of resettled refugees constituted 3.9 percent of the total number of refugees (4,424 of 112,811); for FY 1992, it was anticipated that refugees from Africa would be 4.5 percent of the total refugees (6,000 of 131,200); and the ceiling for Africa for FY 1993 was set at 5.3 percent (7,000 of 132,000) (USCRA, 1992, pp. 3–4). Despite known political upheavals and wars in Africa, the refugee ceilings remain consistently low. Ceilings for Asia and Eastern Europe and the former Soviet Union, the same regions that supplied most of the refugees to the United States before the 1980 Refugee Act (when decisions on refugee quota were based on U.S. policy consider-

TABLE 4

**African Refugee Ceilings and Actual Arrivals, 1980 to 1988**

| Year | Total ceiling | Ceiling for Africa | Actual total | Actual from Africa |
|---|---|---|---|---|
| 1980 | 231,700 | 1,500 | 207,116 | 955 |
| 1981 | 217,000 | 3,000 | 159,252 | 2,119 |
| 1982 | 140,000 | 3,500 | 97,355 | 3,326 |
| 1983 | 90,000 | 3,000 | 61,681 | 2,648 |
| 1984 | 72,000 | 2,750 | 71,113 | 2,747 |
| 1985 | 70,000 | 3,000 | 68,045 | 1,453 |
| 1986 | 67,000 | 3,000 | 62,440 | 1,315 |
| 1987 | 70,000 | 2,000 | 64,828 | 1,994 |
| 1988 | 83,000 | 3,000 | 75,754 | 1,588 |

SOURCE: Bean, F. D., Vernez, G., & Keeley, C. B. (1989). *Opening and closing the doors. Evaluating immigration reform and control.* Washington, DC: The Rand Corporation and The Urban Institute.

ations), continue to remain relatively high (Bean et al., 1989).

Refugees have come from all over the African continent. Ethiopians, Liberians, Mozambicans, Somalis, Sudanese, and Zairian refugees were designated for special consideration for fiscal year 1992. Since the early 1980s, there has been a major influx of refugees from Ethiopia. However, African refugees constitute less than 3 percent of all refugees resettled in the United States, and the funding for refugees in Africa, which was lower than funding for refugees in other parts of the world, is falling (Refugee Reports, 1994).

### Illegal Immigrants

The U.S. Immigration and Naturalization Service (INS) estimates that in October 1992 a total of 3.2 million illegal aliens lived in the United States. Illegal immigrants are those who are admitted legally on a temporary basis and do not depart or adjust their status to a legal permanent alien or those who enter the country without inspection. Although it is inherently difficult to estimate the size of this hidden population, INS estimates that approximately 120,000 (4 percent of the total number) of illegal immigrants are from Africa (USINS, 1993).

## Reasons for Emigration

People from developing countries often cite inequalities in economic development, employment opportunities, and better income and living conditions as reasons for migration to the United States. Such explanations represent an oversimplification of the migration process. In the developing countries of Africa, there is a tendency to overproduce highly specialized and skilled workers who in turn cannot be supported materially (that is, with research or equipment) or compensated monetarily. The nonindigenous nature of the African educational and training system "prepares students for foreign-oriented qualifications, relies excessively on expatriate teachers and foreign books, and uses foreign rather than indigenous languages as the medium of instruction. As a result, the education received is often not geared toward Africa's development needs" (Apraku, 1991, p. 10). In a survey of 250 of the 800 randomly selected professionals and highly skilled workers in the United States from 34 African countries, Apraku found that even though skilled African emigrants stated economic considerations in their home country, their earning power, and prospects for professional advancement abroad as important factors in their decision to emigrate, more important and more often cited were political factors such as dictatorship or lack of freedom. More than half of the respondents considered political factors important. Other significant factors included civil wars, tribalism, and family and cultural pressures.

## Patterns of Settlement and Integration

Traditionally, immigrants with African ancestry have settled in New York City; Boston; New Bedford, Massachusetts; and Florida (Farley & Allen, 1983). Immigrants of African ancestry are overrepresented in some of these areas compared with the native African American population (Farley & Allen, 1983). These immigrants are more familiar with the English language than any other immigrant group. More than 65 percent of immigrants of African ancestry speak English, compared with 5 percent of Latinos, 52 percent of non-Latino whites, and 15 percent of other races (Farley & Allen, 1983).

Whereas integration into a society may be measured in various ways (for example, language skills, cultural adaptation, development of organizations, and participation in the political process), few are as important as economic adjustment. In a study of the economic adaptation of Eastern European, Afghan, and Ethiopian refugees, Gozdziak (1989) found that non-Southeast Asian refugees (including Ethiopians) had high labor force participation rates, low unemployment rates, and little reliance on public assistance.

### Example of Ethiopian Refugees

A comparative analysis of Ethiopian refugees with others studied by Gozdziak (1989) sheds light on the settlement, status, and challenges faced by the largest group of African refugees. Most of the refugees start their careers in the United States in entry-level positions. Similarly, Ethiopian refugees began their work history in the United States in service sector jobs. Together with their Afghan counterparts, they were particularly successful at obtaining positions as managers and sometimes owning operations such as parking lots, taxi cabs, gas stations, and convenience stores. With few exceptions, however, Ethiopian refugees showed little upward mobility.

One factor that predicts labor force participation is length of stay. As refugees gain more language and survival skills and acculturate to life in America, they learn job development and social skills. A refugee's education level before arrival together with his or her transferrable skills were the most important predictors of labor force participation. Ethiopians were found to be generally well educated; many had college degrees in technical and financial fields. The tremendous underemployment of Ethiopians clearly suggests racial discrimination for people from Africa.

Levels of self-sufficiency for the Ethiopians were generally low, 55 percent to 333 percent of the federal poverty level (most under 250 percent), even when earned and public assistance sources were combined. The single most important factor in moving out of poverty for all the groups was the ability to use multiple wage earners soon after their arrival. Families with young children or others who because of age or disability could not work had a more difficult time moving up economically. Ethiopian men who lived together and shared rent but not other resources were also in a difficult situation (Gozdziak, 1989; McSpadden, 1991).

### Skilled Immigrants

Unlike the refugees, skilled African immigrants represent a very different population. Apraku (1991) found that the average African immigrant is a highly trained and experienced male at an economically productive age, who is well paid and highly satisfied with his current job. However, this study focused on a sample taken from professional directories and did not address those skilled workers employed outside of their specialization or those working in positions traditionally considered nonprofessional. It is interesting to note that the immigrants maintain close ties with their country, family, and friends through annual remittances for family support, personal investment projects, and frequent home visits. Nearly all the respondents planned to resettle in their home countries in the future (Apraku, 1991).

## Implications for Social Work

The demographic landscape of American society is changing. Immigrants and refugees of color—women, children, and elders—including those from Africa will outnumber white people for the first time in the 21st century (Watson, 1992). The consequences of this increasing diversity are manifested at different levels. Politically, the racial mix can cause tensions and conflicts; economically, it can produce expanded economic opportunities or pockets of poverty; culturally, it can be welcomed as an enrichment or feared as a threat to established systems and values. Social workers and other human services professionals can play a role in policy, administration, and direct service levels to facilitate the settlement of African immigrants and to support their growth opportunities and contribution to American society.

### Policy Issues

In the current politically conservative national climate, there is an anti-immigrant sentiment. Several proposals have been introduced as a part of proposed immigration reform that would reduce federal benefits to legal immigrants. There have been suggestions that immigrants with permanent resident status not be eligible for such federal programs as Social Supplemental Income (SSI), Aid to Families with Dependent Children (AFDC), Medicaid (except for emergency services), food stamps, school lunches, nutritional assistance to elders, and so on.

Refugee and immigrant advocates have expressed concerns that eliminating immigrant eligibility would undermine the hard work of immigrant families and perpetuate unjustified restrictive measures and misinformation about the economic impact of immigrations. Overwhelming evidence demonstrates that immigrants support themselves through participation in the labor force market rather than through welfare. The Urban Institute estimated that immigrants generate $285 billion in income and pay more than $70 billion in taxes, much higher than the $5.7 billion they use in welfare benefits. Use of public benefits by immigrants is substantially lower than it is for those born in this country (Borjas, 1989; Simon, 1989). Because a relatively high number of African immigrants come under the special preference category with skills and professional training, their contributions are likely to be higher than those of other immigrants.

### Discrimination and Cultural Issues

Refugees, immigrants, and illegal migrants enter a culture with a distinct history of discrimination against people of African ancestry. Recent immigrants from Africa not only face discrimination from the majority white American population, but also face prejudices from African Americans. Some African Americans fear being displaced from their housing by immigrants who are moving into inner-city neighborhoods in search of moderate-priced housing (Muller, 1993). Some African Americans also may link unemployment to immigration (Muller, 1993). Cultural, political, and attitudinal differences between African Americans and immigrants with African origins may result in increased tension. Unfortunately, this tension further divides the African American and African communities and may contribute to the exploitation of both groups (Bryce-Laporte, 1972). However, to the benefit of both groups, African immigrants and African Americans have also come together in civil rights protests, labor struggles, and local community and political organizations (Bryce-Laporte, 1972). Social work and human services professionals can play a critical role in serving this population (specifically the refugees) during its resettlement and adaptation to life in America.

Immigrants from African countries may share some similarities, yet they cannot be lumped together because of the many obvious distinctions—culture, language, religion, traditions, and so on. There are wide differences and disparities among conationals from single countries in Africa. For example, in Ethiopia alone there are more than 70 languages, which reflect the diverse cultures. Cultural differences may translate for Ethiopian refugees as having a small support network. Even if an Ethiopian lives in an environment heavily populated with immigrants from Ethiopia, he or she may feel culturally isolated because of cultural and linguistic barriers. Hostilities generated in countries of origin between tribes of different warring factions may be a source of serious tensions. Sensitivity to the historical background and cultural differences of African refugee and immigrant groups will enable social workers to serve this population effectively.

The first-generation professional and highly skilled immigrants may not feel the impact of discrimination as poignantly as those who have witnessed its effects in their grandchildren. Refugees, on the other hand, experience serious problems and discrimination. Immigrants of African ancestry experience "double invisibility" (Bryce-Laporte, 1972), invisibility because of their race and because of their origin. Although immigrants of African ancestry have contributed greatly to American society, their cultural impact has been ignored (Bryce-Laporte, 1972).

**Social Work Roles**

Social workers must find ways to advocate for and serve clients from tremendously varied backgrounds. In working with people from any culture, social workers can empower their clients and help them negotiate their immediate and wider environment within the host culture while preserving and honoring their own cultural ways. For African immigrants to America, there are issues to be addressed at three levels: policy, programs and services, and support for settlement and adaptation to life in this country so that they can contribute to society on a par with other residents.

At the policy level, one major consideration for African immigrants and refugees to the United States should be equitable refugee and immigrant admittance and support in maintaining country and family ties. Africa has not been a major supplier of immigrants to the United States, and we would not wish to advocate greater emigration from any region. Nonetheless, we must advocate equitable and fair laws for all who wish to enter here. At the same time the conditions that force emigration (including dictatorial regimes, human rights abuses, and foreign-based education systems) must be addressed. Our government can be influenced in developing and enforcing policies that advocate human rights and social justice, which in turn will reduce refugee flows to the United States.

On a microlevel, social services must be ready to work with not only the major ethnic groups that reside in a given area but with minority immigrant groups as well. Many immigrant services are well equipped to work with Mexican and other Hispanic groups, and our refugee services are well focused on meeting the needs of Southeast Asians. As the Refugee Policy Group (1989) so aptly stated in a press release for its study on non-Southeast Asian refugees, "Those who are 'making it' are doing so not because of, but rather despite, the resettlement system, which on the whole has not been responsive to the presence of new refugee groups." They call for services to be flexible and efficient in responding to the varied needs of different ethnic groups, refugee households, and skill levels.

Although social workers cannot become knowledgeable about cultural practices and needs of all African immigrants and refugees they encounter in practice, they can learn about general issues that affect African immigrants. Their knowledge about policies and service needs of African refugees and immigrants will help social workers deliver relevant services and influence policies that affect African immigrants.

## References


Apraku, K. K. (1991). *African emigres in the United States: A missing link in Africa's social and economic development*. New York: Praeger.

Bean, F. D., Vernez, G., & Keeley, C. B., (1989). *Opening and closing the doors. Evaluating immigration reform and control*. Washington, DC: The Rand Corporation and The Urban Institute.

Borjas, G. (1989). *Friends or strangers: The impact of immigrants on the U.S. economy*. New York: Basic Books.

Bryce-Laporte, R. S. (1972). Black immigrants: The experience of invisibility and inequality. *Journal of Black Studies*, *3*(1), 29–56.

Dinnerstein, L., & Reimers, D. (1975). *Ethnic Americans: A history of immigration and assimilation*. New York: Harper & Row.

Farley, R., & Allen, W. R. (1983). *The color line and the quality of life in America*. New York: Russell Sage Foundation.

Gozdziak, E. (1989). *New Americans: The economic adaptation of Eastern European, Afghan and Ethiopian refugees*. Washington, DC: Refugee Policy Group.

Helton, A. C. (1992). U.S. refugee policy: African and Caribbean effects. *TransAfrica Forum*, 93–102.

McSpadden, L. (1991). Cross-cultural understanding of independence and dependence: Conflict in the resettlement of single Ethiopian males. *Refuge, 10*(4), 21–25.

Muller, T. (1993). *Immigrants and the American city*. New York: New York University Press.

Refugee Act of 1980. P.L. 96-212, 94 Stat. 102.

Refugee Policy Group. (1989). Press release on issue paper *New Americans: The economic adaptation of Eastern European, Afghan and Ethiopian refugees*. Washington, DC: Author.

Refugee Policy Group. (1992). *Internally displaced in Africa: Assistance, challenges and opportunities*. Washington, DC: Author. (Available from RPG, 1424 16th St. NW, Suite 401, Washington, DC 20036)

Refugee Reports. (February 28, 1994, p. 15). Washington, DC: US Committee for Refugees.

Rockett, I.R.H. (1983). American immigration policy and ethnic selection: an historical overview. *The Journal of Ethnic Studies, 10*, 1–26.

Simon, J. (1989). *The economic consequences of immigration*. Cambridge, MA: Basil Blackwell.

U.S. Coordinator for Refugee Affairs. (1992). *Proposed refugee admissions for fiscal year 1993: Report to Congress*. Washington, DC: Author.

U.S. Immigration and Naturalization Service. (1992). *1991 Statistical year book of the immigration and naturalization service*. Washington, DC: U.S. Government Printing Office.

U.S. Immigration and Naturalization Service. (1993). *1992 Statistical year book of the immigration and naturalization service*. Washington, DC: U.S. Government Printing Office.

Warren, R. *Estimates of the resident illegal alien population by country or area of citizenship and components of change: October 1992* (1992). Statistics on emigration and illegal immigration distributed at the December 7 Carnegie breakfast briefing: "The fiscal year 1992 INS *Statistical Yearbook*: Data and policy issues."

Watson, B. (1992). The demographic revolution: Diversity in 21st century America. In *The state of black America*. New York: National Urban League.


**Fariyal Ross-Sheriff, PhD,** is professor and director of the doctoral program, Howard University, School of Social Work, Washington, DC 20059.

### For further information see

African Americans Overview; African Americans: Caribbean; Community; Displaced People; Ethnic-Sensitive Practice; Haitian Americans; Human Rights; International and Comparative Social Welfare; Mutual Aid Societies; Social Welfare History; Social Welfare Policy.

**Key Words**

| | |
|---|---|
| African Americans | undocumented |
| immigrants | migrants |
| refugees | |

# Aged Adults

*See* Aging *(Reader's Guide)*

# Agency-Based Research

**Eloise Rathbone-McCuan**

Decades of debate over the relationship between social work practice and the effectiveness of the quality of social work research continues to occupy the profession's attention. As Jenkins (1992) noted, "there is no rule book in social work that gives greater honor to a practitioner or a research professional" (p. 263). Likewise, contest judging and ranking the various contributions of social agency researchers and academic researchers are not useful. Distinctions between "pure" and "applied" research, if each is thoughtfully critiqued for its unique contributions, have professional value. If the merit of either is assigned from a positivist hierarchical bias, the debate makes no real professional contribution.

This entry describes the integration of social work practice and research from the standpoint of agency-based research. The discussion focuses on the conduct of research in social services settings by staff social work researchers. Social agencies were the original sites for conducting early social welfare research, which was often funded by wealthy foundations (Reid, 1985). These agencies and their research-minded practitioners produced knowledge that is invaluable to the social work profession.

According to Austin (1992), social work research began in schools of social work in the 1950s and 1960s. This trend, however, did not produce an increased number of social worker researchers with doctorates who pursued agency-based careers. As more social workers trained for and occupied positions in schools of social work, fewer were hired by social agencies. The exodus of researchers from practice agencies has greatly reduced the amount and quality of publication by agency professionals. Today, the agency-based social work researcher is an endangered breed. The small number of these researchers accounts, in part, for the gap between the current pattern of research activities, mainly in academia, and the world of practice and its knowledge (Task Force on Social Work Research, 1991).

The study of social work researchers who pursue a career of agency-based research is limited (Fanshel, 1980). To sharpen understanding of research as practice, the characteristics of agency-based positions are identified in this entry, and the diverse involvement of researchers in the priorities of agency programs is illustrated. The many opportunities for nonagency researchers to connect to service settings indicate benefits from cooperation with community agencies. The key functions of agency research are mentioned to highlight the connections that agency researchers maintain with policy and practice issues. Finally, typical challenges and potential rewards are noted.

## Agency-Based Researchers and Agency-Focused Research

The agency-based researcher is employed by and routinely works within a human services agency and is assigned responsibilities for generating information that is relevant to the organization's human services mission. Information generated by the researcher is used and distributed primarily according to agency priorities, policies, and administrative decisions. Agency-focused research addresses the who, what, when, where, why, and how of service provision and use, translated into questions that are answered through the research process. Any social work researcher has the potential to engage in agency-focused research, but researchers complete too few agency studies while employed by schools of social work. Typically, the major professional identity of the academic researcher is with faculty peers.

### Characteristics of the Position

The 10 characteristics of an agency-based research position are as follows:

1. Research activities are defined as service-related functions, and the relevance of the information product is evaluated by the agency in conjunction with service goals. (For example,evaluation of the discharge-planning function is a quality assurance task.)
2. The quality of research studies is evaluated by measures linked to agency goals and responsibilities. (For example, a "good" study provides clear guidelines for linking informal and referral activities with case management services.)
3. The researcher's professional reference group includes other professionals who are employed by the service organization. (For example, the researcher asks a clinical supervisor in the agency to read and comment on a paper for publication.)
4. The utility of information is judged in connection with the information's immediate applicability to services. (For instance, the researcher is told that the final data analysis must be completed for use in congressional budget hearings.)
5. Administrative factors influencing the researcher's work are similar to those affecting service delivery functions. (For example, budget constraints require that casework aides and research interviewers remain on temporary budget lines.)
6. The researcher's control over the generation of information supports related service objectives. (For example, a random sample pre- and postintervention client satisfaction questionnaire was changed to a follow-up questionnaire given to all clients.)
7. Research activity must contribute to the resources of the agency, such as increasing the effectiveness of services, funding for programs, and creditability in the community. (For example, grant funds to implement and evaluate a gang diversion program are preferred over a grant to study the social factors of gang membership.)
8. Research processes and products are collective activities that are not under the autonomous control of the researcher. (For example, an agency director can establish priorities for

data collection efforts that are separate and unrelated to the researcher's priorities.)

9. The use of research information is the most frequent criterion for measuring a project's worth to the agency. (For example, a manual for training senior citizen peer counselors is developed before an article about the program is written for professional publication.)
10. Rewards from the generation of information that is relevant to broader theory and practice issues are considered of secondary importance to the agency's application of the information. (For example, empirical validation of the strengths model with elderly patients is secondary to analyzing barriers to the agency's implementation of the practice model.)

**Role of the Researcher**

Agency-based researchers are usually geographically accessible to the agency; they often conduct their research within the service delivery environment and give priority to working relationships with practitioners and clients as is necessary for their research. The organizational structures of the agency become familiar to them, and access to information is partly legitimated by their position as employees.

The example of an agency-based researcher who is temporarily relocated to a women's correctional facility from her permanent research office at the state department of corrections is illustrative. Her research activity at the prison is to evaluate the prerelease work training programs available to incarcerated rural women. The researcher conducts interviews with facility staff and inmate representatives and reviews case records of women paroled to rural communities. After completing these activities, the researcher returns to the state office to draw a random sample of previously imprisoned women distributed throughout all rural counties. At the same time, she is analyzing the pilot data on rural parolees who are successfully employed.

The goal of improving services to rural women inmates involves many levels of decision making and numerous providers from different service units. The researcher is required to establish a link between the state department and the local corrections facilities. The collection of information can facilitate input from inmates and facility staff, and the researcher can incorporate their input into a grant-application design. The researcher's proposal is strengthened by the pilot data she gathered and the cooperative relationships that were built to support a future innovative program.

In the foregoing situation, the collection of information, data analysis, and interpretation of findings—all basic components of scientific study—are central to program planning and the resource-acquisition process necessary to create a new program. The researcher also completed the groundwork of building ownership of the program's design among the staff and positive expectations among the women inmates. Ideally, the researcher would play a direct role in helping to bridge communications among federal, state, and local units as the project was implemented and evaluated and the results considered for agency programs and policies.

## Academic Involvement in Agency-Focused Research

In this section the different entry points into agency-focused research are discussed from the vantage point of the social work researcher who maintains a time- and role-limited agency connection. Unlike agency-based researchers, academic investigators usually have specific data collection motives that draw them into the mental health, public welfare, and health care agency sectors. Schilling, Schinke, Kirkham, Meltzer, and Norelius (1988) presented this rationale for participating in agency-focused research:

> Ties to social service, health and educational organizations are necessary if researchers are to test the utility of interventions that show promise. . . . Clinical investigators need access to patients and clients. . . . Researchers testing community-based interventions desire the cooperation of agency practitioners. (p. 76)

**Motives of Researchers**

Some specific conditions and circumstances that encourage the academic researcher to pursue agency research linkages include the following:

- the need to field-test instruments and practice models initially developed in nonagency settings with client caseloads
- the desire to reach a specific client population to generate needed research samples
- the intention to test methodological validity through applications to an existing agency database
- the wish to supplement income through research consultation or contract research
- the search for an agency that is willing to cooperate in a research project or grant application
- an assignment from a school of social work to develop agency connections that will offer research opportunities for students
- the need to reconnect with an agency to update professional knowledge about practice, programs, and policies

- the willingness to gather perspectives from different racial, ethnic, age, and socioeconomic groups who are accessible only in the larger community.

**Cooperative Involvement**

All these situations can serve as incentives for cooperative involvement between an academic researcher and an agency. But even well-intentioned researchers and receptive agencies can find it difficult to develop and maintain working relationships that meet the needs of both parties. Some agencies may face pressure to improve the effectiveness and efficiency of their services and therefore may welcome the opportunity to field-test investigators' practice models. In other agencies, staff may have struggled to reach a consensus about intervention approaches and ways to integrate their clinical orientations. In addition, the increasing caseload demands on staff and the pressures on agencies to do more with less sometimes make it impossible to participate in research. Under these conditions an agency might be less receptive to an offer to field-test a new clinical model.

Many academic social workers obtain doctoral research training long after they have established a practice specialty. By obtaining research skills they are able to pursue areas of interest and concern developed from their previous experience as practitioners (Reid, 1993). For instance, a social worker who is completing a doctorate may have expertise in child protective services. From this expertise, the researcher may develop an interest in investigating the long-range benefits of family preservation programs. When approaching a child welfare agency, the researcher may find that resources rather than interest govern the agency's response. (In other situations, the lack of resources to conduct studies of mutual interest may lead to an agency's and researcher's cooperation in the search for funds for research.)

**Standards of Sample Diversity**

The need to select appropriate samples is one of the greatest motivators for academic researchers to seek entry into community agencies. There are countless examples of research projects in which investigators used only easily accessible agencies, such as religion-connected family and child agencies or private drug and alcohol treatment centers, whose clients and staff are not diverse in terms of race, ethnicity, age, income, and lifestyle. Federal funding agencies recently added more-rigorous standards for gender and racial diversity in the samples used in funded research. This expectation extends across the biomedical and social science disciplines and is helping to reduce the inability to generalize because of the artificial homogeneity of samples. The standards of sample diversity are especially important for social work research intended to increase the quality of life and empowerment of clients.

When academic researchers and agency practitioners work together and achieve a mutually beneficial end, the practice and research sectors of the profession have achieved the desired integration. Perhaps there are many more examples of smaller-scale projects that routinely produce such useful integration. Unfortunately, too few of these efforts are reported in the professional literature.

## Functions Assumed by Agency-Based Researchers

The rewards and obligations of researchers who are committed to agency-based research are often different from those of academic researchers. Some agency-based researchers believe "those who can, do; those who can't, teach"; they think it is a great challenge to conduct good research in an agency environment. Other researchers select the agency environment to avoid the built-in career stress associated with academic social work, such as the requirement to publish and to maintain a teaching load. In any case, responsibilities for generating information that meets an agency's needs and the standards of scientific research can fulfill a researcher's professional agenda.

Once a researcher enters agency-based research, he or she may find that the initial job description has a minimal relationship to the actual responsibilities of the job. The predictability of a position is not necessarily the same as its stability. Predictability relates to the degree to which the functions and tasks undertaken are predetermined or, at least, anticipated. Stability relates to the projected duration of a position; its position in the agency; and the consistency of its salary, as well as its supports. A project-funded research job to evaluate a particular project may be far more predictable yet less stable than a position as resident researcher. If the salary is grant connected, the researcher may feel that the job is unstable. Perhaps the higher the stability of a job, as determined by a fixed salary line, the less frequent are the opportunities and demands for nontraditional roles that can enhance creativity.

**Assignments and Responsibilities**

Many agency-based researchers assume a fairly typical set of assignments and responsibilities that include the following:

***Grant writing.*** Grants that fund service delivery are of greater interest to an agency than are research-only grants. Writing grants for programs will take precedence over more restricted research applications. Service grants require the researcher's involvement with practitioners, for example, to create conceptual service and evaluation frameworks for a proposed service model.

***Database management.*** As agencies have moved into technological information management, there has been an increasing demand for experienced researchers to help practitioners and managers learn and apply the technology. Some staff researchers have moved from a social research function (for example, testing theoretical frameworks or interpreting research findings in relation in social theory) to that of a data manager. The "data cruncher" function can be used creatively to integrate process and outcome research on services into an agency's daily operations. For example, staff can be introduced to computerized client assessment procedures and record-keeping approaches to give them daily information about the status of their caseloads. This information is equally valuable to practitioners and administrators. The translation of information can be a powerful interface among the researcher, the practitioner, and the manager.

***Written products.*** In addition to writing grants, the researcher writes the reports and products that evolve from a project. Practice protocols, such as standardized intake assessments, long-range planning reports, and agency-accreditation documents are only a few examples of written materials that incorporate the results of research.

### Broad Scope

The complexities of quality assurance systems that were instituted in health and mental health care agencies in the mid-1980s demand both the technical and the creative skills of the social work researcher. Public relations functions, often involving all forms of news media, may be dependent on the creation of a statistical document about an agency's productivity or the gaps in funding for certain services. The responsibility for translating data and packaging information may draw the researcher into pivotal points of management—for example, when administrators are engaged in highly competitive win–lose budget negotiations.

In multidisciplinary agency settings, such as teaching and research hospitals or large mental health centers, researchers may be asked to represent the social work department on committees that monitor and review research on human subjects. Participation in these committees can help infuse a social work presence into the agency's broader research decision-making processes that may affect patients as subjects and social workers as data collectors. Through committee assignments, researchers can give voice to the many unpredictable effects of research trials and data collection activities, such as the disruption of services when patients of ambulatory clinics are subjects in studies monitoring cost-efficiency.

The agency-based researcher may become involved in teaching social work staff to evaluate their practice through research methods or in consulting with staff on writing for professional publication. Student interns may occupy a significant amount of the researcher's time when their practicum activities include research projects and assignments. These interactions bring both satisfaction and frustration; they are important and time-consuming activities, even when the administration does not make such activities a priority.

A continuum of activities, both traditional and nontraditional, for the social work researcher are incorporated in the agency position. The social work researcher's participation in the critical and mundane aspects of agency operations is part of the integrative process that prevents the researcher from being perceived as a nonessential professional who is cloistered in the shadows of methodological and statistical abstractions.

## Special Challenges in the Agency Environment

When the researcher enters the agency environment with the expectation of career achievements, he or she must be flexible and adaptable. Because research activities are rarely the norm in the daily schedule of a busy agency, the impressive credentials that the researcher may have accumulated do not automatically make him or her a valued staff member. As with most positions, the researcher undergoes a trial period within the formal and informal structures of the agency. For the researcher, the ability to demonstrate an understanding of the utility of the agency's service mission is an important initial and ongoing challenge.

Even if they are hired on a permanent basis, researchers must be prepared to encounter the stress of acquiring soft money. Although their own salaries may be on a permanent budget line, they must devote much time and energy to maintaining funding for their support staff. The interdisciplinary qualities of a research team are similar to those of a highly specialized clinical treatment team; each member brings a special expertise that contributes to the effectiveness of the team. Therefore, the loss of a qualified and experienced applied statistician from a research team is equivalent to the loss of a geropsychiatrist from a geriatric mental health team.

If the researcher was previously socialized into "the community of scholars," reinforced by the ideals of academic life, it may be necessary to refocus peer relationships and align with practitioner colleagues' expectations. To be involved with an agency is to have the opportunity to participate in a community of doers. This participation may provide exposure to the cutting edge of innovative practice that evolves from the daily human needs of clients rather than from the think-tank world of some academic researchers. Practitioners must give priority to analyses of completed clinical assessments, the rapid development of a complex intervention plan, and the application of new skills when the therapeutic work is unfamiliar. It is with their practitioner peers that agency-based researchers can and should find the colleagues with whom to learn, reflect, plan, and publish.

## Contributions and Rewards

Researchers find that the agency environment gives them the opportunity to participate in the development of practice and the formulation of policies—processes that are central to the social work profession. They use their skills, training, and interest in research to find ways to engage in both the direct and indirect dimensions of social work practice. In the human services agencies, the distinctions between the micro and macro sides of practice are often artificial and meaningless. Thus, researchers can find opportunities to work in either the clinical or policy domain, as well as in numerous integrative areas.

The agency-based researcher functions in an environment in which there are sometimes endless possibilities for generating new information and analyzing untapped caches of data. Access to so much data can be a temptation to "play in the data fields," even though much of the researcher's data analysis is prescribed by the agency's needs and priorities. Therefore, the researcher will benefit from a structured investigation plan if he or she wishes to continue to write for professional publications. Although the agency environment is not necessarily an antipublication environment, administrators and practitioners may not be accustomed to preparing professional publications. The researcher can help familiarize them with this activity through individual and collaborative writing for professional publications.

New national and local agencies and organizations have emerged to address major gaps in advocating for and meeting human needs. These agencies and organizations are giving a new meaning to social investigation. The explosion of consumer and self-help advocacy groups for people with acquired immune deficiency syndrome (AIDS), Alzheimer's disease, or chronic mental illnesses and their families both conduct and fund social research that shows promise of reducing human suffering. Social movements have also challenged the scientific community to give greater attention to the relationship between gender and illness and to the inequities in medical and social care among uninsured people. Applied research has been and will continue to be an important tool of social change for these groups.

Several prestigious human services agencies—for example, the Benjamin Rose Institute in Cleveland, the Menninger Foundation in Topeka, and the Philadelphia Geriatric Center—have long histories of supporting research as part of their clinical care mission. Although these agencies are the exception, there can be a goodness-of-fit between social work researchers and their agency employers because these researchers make a vital contribution to the work of these agencies.

An agency-based researcher is one career profile within the diverse continuum of specialties that define social work and contribute to its significance. As Cheetham (1992) noted, "The challenge for the evaluative researcher is thus [to find] the way and means to assess effectiveness in all the contexts in which social work is seriously practiced" (p. 273). Agency-based researchers and agency-focused investigations will continue to contribute to social work's advancement in the 21st century.

## References

Austin, D. (1992). Findings of the NIMH task force on social work research. *Research on Social Work Practice, 2*(3), 311–322.

Cheetham, J. (1992). Evaluating social work effectiveness. *Research on Social Work Practice, 2*(3), 265–287.

Fanshel, D. (1980). The future of social work research: Strategies for the coming years. In D. Fanshel (Ed.), *Future of social work research* (pp. 3–17). Washington, DC: National Association of Social Workers.

Jenkins, S. (1992). Preface: The conference concept. *Research on Social Work Practice, 2*(3), 263–264.

Reid, W. J. (1985). Research in social work. In A. Minahan (Ed.-in-Chief), *Encyclopedia of social work* (18th ed., Vol. 2, pp. 474–487). Silver Spring, MD: National Association of Social Workers.

Reid, W. J. (1993). Toward a research-oriented profession: An essay review of *Building social work knowledge for effective services and policies: A plan for research development. Research on Social Work Practice, 3*(1), 103–117.

Schilling, R. F., Schinke, S. P., Kirkham, M. A., Meltzer, N. J., & Norelius, K. L. (1988). Social work research in social service agencies: Issues and guidelines. *Journal of Social Service Research, 11*(4), 75–87.

Task Force on Social Work Research. (1991). *Building social work knowledge for effective services and policies: A plan for research development*. Austin: University of Texas School of Social Work.

## Further Reading

Collins, R. L. (1993). Methodological issues in conducting substance abuse research on ethnic minority populations. *Drugs and Society, 6*(1/2), 59–77.

Morgan, D. L. (Ed.). (1993). *Successful focus groups: Advancing the state of the art*. Newbury Park, CA: Sage Publications.

Reid, W. J., & Bailey-Dempsey, C. (1994). Content analysis in design and development. *Research on Social Work Practice, 4*(1), 101–114.

Stanfield, J. H. II, & Rutledge, D. M. (Eds.). (1993). *Race and ethnicity in research methods*. Newbury Park, CA: Sage Publications.

**Eloise Rathbone-McCuan, PhD,** is associate chief, Social Work Service, Colmery–O'Neil Veterans Administration Medical Center, 2200 Gage Boulevard, Topeka, KS 66614.

**For further information see**

Community Needs Assessment; Deinstitutionalization; Direct Practice Overview; Economic Analysis; Ethics and Values; Management Overview; Meta-analysis; Planning and Management Professions; Policy Analysis; Quality Assurance; Recording; Social Planning; Social Welfare Policy; Social Work Practice: Theoretical Base; Social Work Profession Overview; Volunteer Management.

**Key Words**
agency-based research
program evaluation
program planning

READER'S GUIDE

## Aging

*The following entries contain information on this general topic:*

Adult Day Care
Adult Protective Services
Aging Overview
Aging: Direct Practice
Aging: Public Policy Issues and Trends
Aging: Services
Aging: Social Work Practice
Elder Abuse

# Aging Overview

**Ruth E. Dunkle**
**Theresa Norgard**

Most people in the United States now live to old age. Life expectancy at birth was 47 years in 1900, 68 years in 1950, and 75 years in 1987 (National Center for Health Statistics [NCHS], 1990). Overall U.S. mortality rates in this century have decreased 69 percent from 1900, with approximately 92 percent of the change occurring since 1950 (U.S. Bureau of the Census, 1984). Consistent with improved chances of survival, an unprecedented 77 percent of babies born in 1980 are expected to live to age 65 (U.S. Bureau of the Census).

Not only are people living longer, but the number of people age 65 and over—and in particular those over age 85—is growing more rapidly than the rest of the population, (U.S. Department of Health and Human Services [DHHS], 1991). This growth is attributable to the increases in the annual number of births before 1921 and to the greatly improved chance of survival to old age. In the United States the total number of people age 65 and over has more than doubled since 1950 to about 28 million people (Siegel & Taeuber, 1986). In 1990, 32 million elderly people lived in the United States; by the year 2030 that number will be 65 million (DHHS, 1991). In fact, by the year 2030, those age 65 and over will outnumber those under 65.

The increase in life expectancy to age 85 has been especially dramatic. Between 1900 and 1985 the average number of additional years of life for men age 85 rose by 32 percent, from 3.8 years to

5.0 years. The increase for women age 85 was 59 percent, from 4.1 years to 6.5 years. The chances of surviving from age 65 to age 85 also have increased since 1900. In 1985 the probability of living another 20 years beyond age 65 doubled for men and tripled for women. Between 1989 and 2050 the population age 85 and over is expected to climb from about 1 percent to 5 percent of the total population and to increase from 10 percent to 22 percent of the population 65 and over (U.S. Bureau of the Census, 1989).

## Demographic Characteristics

The elderly population is a demographically heterogeneous group. The individual and societal needs that arise from the absolute number of elderly people are easier to identify when the gender, racial, marital, housing, ethnic, socioeconomic, employment, and geographic diversity of this population is considered. The differing types and life situations of older people and their relative proportion in the total population have important implications for social policy, planning, and practice.

### Gender

Men slightly outnumber women in all age groups under age 35, but there are 18.3 million women and only 12.6 million men over age 65. At older ages the disparity between the number of men and women becomes even more dramatic. In 1989 there were 84 men for every 100 women between the ages of 65 and 69. Among people 85 and older, there were only 39 men for every 100 women. Because, on average, women live longer than men, older women face a number of challenges at advanced ages. For example, one-half of older women are widowed, older women tend to be more economically disadvantaged (DHHS, 1991), and older women report higher levels of morbidity and functional limitations (Crimmins & Saito, 1993; Verbrugge, 1989).

### Race

Race and gender are important factors in determining life expectancy. Since the turn of the century, there has been a marked improvement in survival rates to age 65 for all race and gender groups as reported in the census data (U.S. Bureau of the Census, 1989). The survival rate for women of color (78 percent) surpasses that of white men (75 percent), making gender a more important factor than race. Age-adjusted death rates are much higher among black Americans than among white Americans because of two factors: (1) an infant mortality rate for black Americans that is double the rate for white Americans and (2) a greater likelihood for black Americans to die from certain preventable causes of death such as homicides and accidents.

Although life expectancy at birth for black Americans increased during most of this century, it continues to be less than that for white Americans until about age 80. The causes of this reversal at 80 and older are not well understood. It may reflect age misreporting or faulty data collection (Coale & Kisker, 1986) or a greater robustness among black elderly people surviving to advanced age.

There is a less-dramatic difference in life expectancy between black and white Americans when age 65 is used as the point of comparison rather than birth. If black Americans live to age 65, their life expectancy is closer to that of white Americans than it was at birth. In 1987 black Americans at age 65 could expect to live 15.4 more years, roughly 1.6 years less than white Americans of the same age. Despite the narrowing of black–white mortality differentials, black Americans in the 1980s were at the level of life expectancy attained by white Americans in the 1950s (Keith & Smith, 1988).

### Marital Status

Most Americans marry at some point in their lives. In fact, only one in 20 older men and women have never been married, with a similar proportion divorced (U.S. Bureau of the Census, 1990). Most older men remain married and live in nuclear family settings until they die, but nearly half of all older women are widowed. In 1989, 74 percent of all older men were married and living with their spouse, whereas only 40 percent of older women were living with a spouse and 49 percent were widowed (U.S. Bureau of the Census, 1990). The differential between men and women with respect to widowhood increases with age. Whereas 60 percent of women ages 75 to 79 are widowed as compared to 18 percent of men, by age 85, 82 percent of women and 43 percent of men are widowed (Sweet & Bumpass, 1987). In general across all races, 34 percent of older women between the ages of 65 and 69 are widowed; the figure for men is only 7 percent.

These differential rates of widowhood for men and women are attributable mainly to the shorter average life expectancy of men. Furthermore, men tend to marry women who are younger than they are, and men who lose a spouse through divorce or death are more likely to remarry than are women (Uhlenberg, 1980). Because a greater proportion of women are widowed, they are more likely than men to experience the increased risk of depression, mortality, changes in social networks and social participation, and economic hardship associated with widowhood.

**Living Arrangements**

Living arrangements vary considerably by sex. In 1989, about 82 percent of men age 65 and over lived with their spouse or other family members, compared to 57 percent of women in the same age group. Among women 75 and older, fewer than half were living with a spouse or other family member in 1989.

There are striking differences by race and ethnicity in the living arrangements of older people. Older people of color are more likely than white men and women to live with relatives other than a spouse. In 1989, about 26 percent of Hispanic Americans and 24 percent of black Americans were living with other relatives, compared to 12 percent of older white Americans (U.S. Bureau of the Census, 1990).

Although the percentage of elderly people living alone is projected to remain about the same, their numbers will increase substantially. By the year 2050, about 15.2 million older Americans are expected to be living alone.

Living alone can lead to increased vulnerability for older people. Generally, older people who live alone, particularly if they are women, minorities, or 85 or older, have lower incomes than do couples. Many elderly people who live alone are more likely to have chronic health conditions that threaten their independence. Although family and friends provide a great deal of assistance with daily activities for elderly people, many frail, older people who live alone may have no one to help them (Antonucci, 1990). Many older people living alone with little or no help must rely on paid assistance, formal social services programs, or institutionalization.

**Ethnicity**

Although the proportions of older people in the nonwhite and Hispanic populations are smaller than those in the white population, the nonwhite and Hispanic elderly populations are increasing at a faster rate than the white elderly population because of higher fertility rates. In 1989, 13 percent of white Americans were age 65 and over, compared with 8 percent of black Americans, 7 percent of people of other races (primarily Native Americans and Asian/Pacific Islanders), and 5 percent of Hispanic Americans (DHHS, 1991). Although these proportions are expected to remain relatively stable through the end of this century, the older minority population is expected to increase more rapidly than the older white population. Between 1990 and 2030, the older white population is expected to grow by 92 percent, compared with 247 percent for the older black population and people of other races, and 395 percent for the older Hispanic population (DHHS, 1991).

**Socioeconomic Status**

Even though older people are more likely to be poor than are other adults, striking improvements have occurred in levels of income and poverty among older people, especially between 1960 and 1974, when there was a general increase in the standard of living and improvements in social security and employer pension benefits. The poverty rate among people 65 and older was cut nearly in half between 1966 and 1974, declining from approximately 28 percent to 14.6 percent.

In 1989 the median cash income for families in which the head of household was 65 to 74 years old was nearly $24,800, and the median cash income for families in which the head of household was age 85 or older was $17,600. The median income for individuals ages 65 to 74 was about $10,821, and for individuals age 85 and older it was $7,900. The oldest old (85 years and older) were the most likely to live below or near the poverty level. In 1989 the poverty rate for people 85 and older was twice that of people ages 65 to 74 (DHHS, 1991).

Age, gender, race, ethnicity, and marital status all affect the economic well-being of older people. In some instances understanding the economic status of elderly people is difficult because of the different poverty standards used by the U.S. Bureau of the Census for older Americans versus younger ones. For example, in 1989 individuals under age 65 with incomes below $5,947 were "officially" living in poverty, whereas older people were not considered to be impoverished until their income dropped below $6,452. The differential criteria was even greater for married couples, with the cutoff for younger married couples being $7,501 versus $8,343 for older couples.

Very old women are the most likely to live in poverty, with one in five age 85 and older living in poverty in 1989. In general older women, regardless of marital status, have low personal incomes, but the economic status of women living alone is especially low. In 1989 widows had the lowest and divorced women the second lowest median incomes of unmarried women.

Poverty rates are much higher among older individuals and families of color than their white counterparts. In 1989 the poverty rate among black elderly (30.8 percent) was more than triple the rate for white elderly (9.6 percent), and among Hispanic older people (20.6 percent) the rate was more than double that of white elderly. Black and Hispanic elderly people have few assets and smaller pensions and earnings compared to their white counterparts. The net worth (income plus assets) of older Hispanic households is about half that of white households, and the net worth of older black households is only one-quarter that of white households (U.S. Bureau of the Census, 1986). Overall, older people have very few options available for moving out of poverty (Duncan, 1984), so their poverty status is much more likely to be long-term compared to the general population.

**Employment**

Because so many people are living longer, people are spending more time in all aspects of life: family roles, education, work, and retirement (Hagestad, 1981; Livi-Bacci, 1982; Riley, 1983). One major shift has been the increasing amount of time spent in retirement. Older people retire for a variety of reasons, including health, access to social security benefits and private pensions, downturns in the economy that encourage early retirement, and the desire to pursue leisure and volunteer activities. Whereas in 1900 the average man spent only one and one-half years of his 46 years of life in retirement or outside the labor force, by 1980, 13.6 years of a 70-year life span were spent outside the labor force.

Although most workers leave the labor force before age 65, or normal retirement age, many continue to work in retirement. The Social Security Administration estimated that 22 percent of older women and 24 percent of older men were employed for at least two years after receiving their first social security retirement benefits (Iams, 1987).

Labor force participation and retirement vary dramatically by gender and race. Historically, black women over age 65 have worked in the labor force at rates higher than those of white women. More recently the rates have become more similar. In 1989 about 8 percent of older white women and 10 percent of older black women were working outside the home. The labor force participation rate for older black men (14.3 percent) was slightly lower in 1989 than that of older white men (16.8) and has fallen at a more rapid pace since the 1970s than that of older white men. In the future, middle-age and older workers are expected to become a larger part of the labor force. Although older men are projected to increase their labor force participation only marginally, women are expected to increase their rates from 43.5 percent in 1988 to 49 percent in 2000 (Fullerton, 1989).

**Geographic Distribution**

Elderly people are concentrated in various parts of the United States. Eight states accounted for approximately 48.9 percent of the national population of older people in 1986: New York, California, Florida, Pennsylvania, Illinois, Ohio, Michigan, and Texas, all states with a population of 2 million or more. The concentration of elderly is accounted for by one of two factors: (1) the natural growth of the aged population (that is, people have lived in an area and grew old there) or (2) migration to the location.

Overall residential stability is increasing among older people, primarily because of longer moves. Local moves are declining. In the 1980s approximately 75 percent of those over the age of 60 had lived in the same house for the preceding five years (Longino, Soldo, & Manton, 1990).

The elderly who do move are a socially and economically advantaged group by comparison (Longino, Biggar, Flynn, & Wiseman, 1984), moving in the largest numbers to Florida and Arizona (Longino et al., 1990). In fact, Florida has had the largest share of the migrant pool of elderly since 1955. In 1980, for instance, 25.9 percent of the pool moved there (Flynn, Longino, Wiseman, & Biggar, 1985).

Long-distance moves among the elderly are tied to life course events rather than the labor market. Retirement lifestyle, family ties, and health are motivating factors in long-distance moves (Litwak & Longino, 1987). For those who do migrate, there are typically three moves. The first occurs when the person retires, is healthy, has enough retirement income, and is still married. The second move happens when some form of disability occurs and regular activities of daily living, such as cooking and shopping, become difficult. These problems are exacerbated with widowhood. Typically, family members encourage the elderly person to move closer to them so that they can provide care. The third move is usually to an institutional setting when the family no longer is able to provide care.

## Elderly Competence: Physical and Mental Health

**Physical Health**

Reviewing the population trends and demographic characteristics of elderly people provides a context from which to understand who they are. It is important also to view these facts within a social and environmental context to appreciate the interplay that produces behavior and subsequent adjustment to old age.

Competence is a trait that humans strive for in all areas of their lives, whether it is work, family, or basic functional ability. Many older people find various aspects of their daily lives, such as health or mental health, compromised with advancing age and seek ways to adapt to maximize their competence. How the individual interacts with the environment is a critical component in understanding this process, because environments produce behavior and behavior produces environments (Ittelson, 1960).

The major cornerstone of competence for older people is their health status. Since the turn of the century, acute conditions and infectious diseases have mostly been replaced by chronic conditions (McKinlay & McKinlay, 1990). Although most older people are in good health, declines in health and physical functioning tend to become more pronounced with advancing age, with variations due to gender, race, ethnicity, and economic status. Decrements in physical health and functioning can compromise the older person's sense of competence by increasing dependency on others, diminishing economic resources, and restricting the potential for social participation. More than four out of five people age 65 and older have at least one chronic condition, with multiple conditions becoming more common at advanced ages, especially among older women.

The most prevalent chronic conditions for older people are arthritis, hypertension, hearing impairments, and heart disease. In most cases the rates for these diseases increase with age (DHHS, 1991). Diseases of the circulatory, digestive, and respiratory systems and cancer are the leading causes of hospitalization among older people, and chronic conditions (including circulatory, respiratory, nervous system, and musculoskeletal problems) are the leading cause for physician visits. Heart disease, cancer, and stroke are the leading causes of death in the United States, and together they account for seven of every 10 deaths among older people (DHHS, 1991).

The types of conditions older people experience vary by economic status, gender, race, and ethnicity. Older people with higher incomes report their health as being much better than do older people with less income. In 1989, for example, about 26 percent of older people with incomes over $35,000 described their health as excellent compared to others their age, whereas only about 10 percent of those with low incomes reported excellent health (National Center for Health Statistics, 1989). Older men are more likely than women to experience acute illnesses that are life threatening, whereas older women tend to experience more chronic illnesses that cause functional limitations. Arthritis and osteoporosis, for example, are more common among women, and men have higher rates of coronary heart disease.

Data comparing ethnic and racial groups with white Americans are sparse, but the available data suggest that the health of older black Americans is generally poorer than that of white Americans (Jackson & Perry, 1989). In 1989, 45 percent of black elderly people reported their health as fair or poor, whereas only 27 percent of white elderly people reported fair or poor health. Black elderly individuals tend to have higher rates of chronic diseases, including diabetes, hypertension, and arthritis. Elderly Hispanic American individuals rate their health as poorer than that of white Americans but better than that of elderly black Americans (Markides, Coreil, & Rogers, 1989). At least one study reported that Asian American and Pacific Islander elderly people report lower rates of activity limitations and better health status than the general population (Yu, Liu, & Kyrzeja, 1985). Infectious diseases, particularly respiratory disease, are still problematic among older Native Americans, who also suffer from more chronic conditions and functional limitations than the general elderly population (Kunitz & Levy, 1989).

The prevalence of functional limitations in addition to health status is an important indicator of the quality of life and sense of competence among older Americans. Of the 27.9 million noninstitutionalized older people, 12.9 percent reported having difficulty performing the usual activities of daily living (such as bathing, dressing, and walking). Approximately 11.4 percent of the total elderly population had one or more functional limitations, and 47 percent had at least one functional limitation. Of the 3.2 million elderly people experiencing difficulty performing daily activities, 32 percent had difficulty with two to three activities and 21 percent had difficulty with four or more activities (DHHS, 1991).

Functional impairment increases with age. For example, in 1989 about 5.9 percent of older people ages 65 to 69 reported at least some level of functional impairment, whereas 34.5 percent of people age 85 and older were functionally impaired. The proportion of older people with functional limitations was higher among black Americans than among white or Hispanic Americans, with 26.3 percent of black elderly people reporting at least some functional impairments compared with 19 percent of white and 14 percent of Hispanic elderly people (Leon & Lair, 1990).

Some older people do not receive assistance with daily activities despite their difficulties. In 1986, about 1 million older disabled people had incomes below the federal poverty level for one person age 65 and older. About 63 percent of this group received no help. Likewise, about 1 million older disabled people lived barely above the poverty level, and 64 percent of this group received no help with daily activities (DHHS, 1991).

#### Mental Health

Older people generally experience good mental health, despite negative stereotypes and generalizations such as the belief that memory loss and dysphoria are normal expectations in later life. These stereotypes have implications for treatment.

Although national statistics show that 10 percent to 28 percent of community-dwelling elderly people suffer from mental health problems serious enough to warrant professional attention (George, Blazer, Winfield-Laird, Leaf, & Fischback, 1988), these people do not receive their share of mental health services. The elderly constitute 12 percent of the population, but they receive only 6 percent of the psychological services at community mental health centers (Flemming, Buchanan, Santos, & Rickards, 1984) and make only 4 percent of the outpatient visits to private psychiatrists (Schurman, Kramer, & Mitchell, 1985). Nursing homes have become the repositories for mentally ill elderly people (Sherwood & Mor, 1980). With the passage of the Omnibus Budget Reconciliation Act of 1987, mental health services are more likely to be offered to older people who live in nursing homes (Fogel, Gottlieb, & Furino, 1990).

There are several reasons for the low use of mental health services by elderly individuals. First, some service providers underestimate the benefit of psychological treatment for the elderly people, partly because of their negative attitudes about older clients (Dye, 1978; Gatz & Perarson, 1988; Knight, 1986; Setting, 1982). If professionals were trained from a psychoanalytic treatment perspective, they might view older people as mentally recalcitrant. Freud believed that the mental elasticity of older people was limited and that there was too much psychological territory to cover to make treatment productive (Cath, 1965). Moreover, many professionals believe that treating older people does not require the level of treatment they were trained to provide. This view tends to make the professional feel like a caretaker rather than a therapist (U.S. Commission on Civil Rights, 1979). That older people frequently require a higher level of concrete services than do younger people should not preclude the use of psychological services as well (Blum & Tros, 1980).

Older people might tend not to seek services because they believe that only "crazy" people use them (Lazarus & Weinberg, 1980) or because they, like some service providers, feel that older people cannot benefit from such services. The result is that older people present with more serious problems when and if they do seek psychological services (Gallagher & Thompson, 1982; Lowy, 1979). Research shows that elderly people who seek mental health services are more likely to leave treatment without their problems being resolved and are more likely to receive medication for their problems than are other age groups (Goldstrom et al., 1987).

### Vulnerability of the Elderly

Because aging takes place within a social context, older people's health, mental health, and functioning can be dramatically affected by how they feel about growing old and how they are treated by others. Lawton and Nahemow (1973) derived an ecological model of aging based on the concept of a person–environment "fit" that helps to explain the relationship between the social and physical world and the well-being of the older person. In this model behavior is viewed as an interaction of the individual's competence and the demand made by the environment. Competence and demand interact to produce a profile of competencies that may vary over time and in different areas of a person's life (Lawton, 1982). Higher competence is associated with less dependence on the environment, and lower competence is related to greater vulnerability to the environment. Lawton and Nahemow explained that in the demand–competence model, an adaptation level is incorporated that allows the balance between the level of external stimulation and the sensitivity of the individual to be taken into consideration. As Lawton and Nahemow (1973) stated in their environmental docility hypothesis, "As the competence of the individual decreases, the proportion of behavior attributable to environmental, as contrasted with personal, characteristics increases" (p. 658). For example, an elderly person who has hearing and vision deficits and who uses a wheelchair is more dependent on the surrounding environment to maintain social, psychological, and physical functioning than is a healthy older person who is able to draw on personal resources to provide the stimulation to maintain well-being.

Social factors also contribute to incompetence. For example, a widower who never performed certain household tasks like cleaning and cooking may report limitations because he never learned the skills, not because of an inability to perform the function. An older woman may report limitations in shopping because markets are scarce in inner-city neighborhoods, and she lacks transportation to area stores. When the fit between an individual's competence and environment is good, adaptation is positive. When the environmental demands are too great, adaptation is poor and the outcome is likely to be negative.

The concept of social roles describes society's expectations for people in particular social positions. It is these social role expectations that lead to expectations of certain behaviors at various ages. For example, parents are expected to act responsibly in providing care to their young children, and grandparents are expected to live separately from their own children.

These social roles, however, are not carried out in a vacuum; they are defined through interaction with others. Knowledge of social roles allows people to anticipate the behavior of others and respond accordingly. This process becomes problematic at older ages because the behavioral expectations of older people are unclear. Old age has been characterized as a "roleless role." Neugarten (1980) argued that behaviors considered appropriate at given ages have relaxed somewhat in recent years. Karp and Yoels (1982) believed that the relaxation of age norms should not be equated with the absence of age norms, but these norms are not clear in most social arenas. An older person's competence can be compromised because of these ambiguities.

Kuypers and Bengtson (1973) described the process by which social factors affect competence. In their old age vulnerability cycle model they described an adaptation of the social breakdown syndrome to problems of aging. In the model issues such as role loss, ambiguous norms, viewing aging as an inevitable decline, and societal values that emphasize economic productivity can make individuals' competence vulnerable. Following this vulnerability is an increasing demand on the environment to define the situation. Older people face unprecedented dependencies and have more doubts concerning the appropriateness of past coping styles. If this process continues, older people are labeled as incompetent and they ultimately move into dependent roles where they face further atrophy of competence.

## Future Challenges in Aging

### Demographic Trends Affecting Care

Demographic trends in the United States are shifting, primarily because of increasing longevity and the rapidly growing numbers of people over age 85. People over age 65 constituted 12 percent of the population in 1993, will make up 13 percent at the turn of the century, and will represent 21 percent of the population by the year 2010 (Myers, 1990).

Two-thirds of all deaths occur after age 65 and 30 percent after age 80. It is anticipated that the growth of the elderly group will slow down considerably by the middle of the 21st century, after the baby boomers pass through the later stages of life. By the time the baby boomers move into very old age (85 and over), they will represent 5.2 percent of the population (Myers, 1990).

Of increasing concern is whether people are living longer but sicker lives. One rather optimistic scenario suggests that the human life span is fixed at about 85 years or so and that, increasingly, modern societies will be able to postpone the onset of disease and disability until relatively late in life (Fries, 1980). Others have argued that the human life span may not be fixed, that people may increasingly live well beyond the average of 85 years at a faster pace than disease and disability can be postponed (Schneider & Brody, 1983; Verbrugge, 1984). The result will be added years to life during which people will be sick and disabled and in greater need of formal and informal health care resources. Whether or not the onset of disease and disability can ever be postponed remains to be seen. Nonetheless, increasingly large numbers of older people will advance into the 21st century, and some of them will be chronically ill and disabled.

The changing demographic picture of the U.S. population presents many potential problems. The need for long-term care is perhaps the most obvious, with 9 million older people estimated to need such care by the year 2000 and 19 million by 2040 (Rice & Feldman, 1983). As many as 10 percent of the current 27.9 million older people who live in the community may be as functionally impaired as older people who live in institutions (Callahan, Diamond, Giele, & Morris, 1980).

Caregiving is one area that will expand with the increasing number of older people in need of long-term care. Individuals whose functional capacities are chronically impaired require services on a sustained basis to maintain their maximal levels of psychological, physical, and social well-being (Kane & Kane, 1987). Individuals who are served can reside in their own homes or in an institutional facility.

Regardless of where the elderly person lives, most families provide a great amount of care. More than 80 percent of care provided to older people is provided by family members (Brody, 1985). These figures have been scrutinized as more people become concerned with the changing demographic picture and the increased concern over the division of scarce resources. Some believe that the increasing numbers of older people, with their increasing needs, mean fewer resources for younger people. It appears, though, that this intergenerational inequity need not exist. It is not a zero-sum game; resources allocated for one group do not benefit that group alone. For example, although Medicare dollars are used to provide home health care to older people, not only the older person benefits. The help from Medicare may make it possible for a family member who has been providing the care to work outside the home or at least find time to rest from the strain and routine of caring.

Other demographic factors affect family caregiving, too. Increased divorce rates and childbirth outside of marriage result in growing numbers of single-parent households. Increased participation of women in the labor force and a growing preference for smaller or childless families result in fewer children to share caregiving. All of these factors jeopardize family caregiving as a central feature in the care of older people (Brody, 1985).

Motivating factors to provide care include continuity of generations, reciprocity of generations, filial responsibility, and younger people's confronting of their own dependency needs. About 71 percent of the elderly help their children or grandchildren and 46 percent help their great grand-children through gifts, child care, housekeeping, or home repairs. Two-thirds of the elderly report receiving help from their children, mainly task-oriented rather than financial. Only 3 percent of the elderly receive money on a regular basis from their children, and about 14 percent receive money occasionally. In general, more older people give help to their families than receive help from them (Hogan, Clogg, & Eggebeen, 1990). This picture changes, though, with increasing age. The percentage of elderly giving help to their children generally decreases as they get older (Hogan et al., 1990; Troll, Miller, & Atchley, 1979).

### Socioeconomic Factors

Disparities in socioeconomic status and the consequences associated with low economic status will also require greater attention in the future. Despite the often-claimed leveling of economic disparities in old age, analysis of recent census data suggests that economic inequality continues into old age, particularly for women, people of color, and physically impaired people (Crystal & Shea, 1990). Even though average life expectancy has increased, socioeconomic factors affecting mortality and health persist and in some cases have increased (Kitagawa & Hauser, 1973; Williams, 1990). Furthermore, poor people are at a disadvantage regarding many psychosocial and environmental risk factors (for example, health behaviors, acute and chronic stress, sense of self-efficacy and control, social relations and supports, and work-related hazards) associated with the etiology and course of disease and functional limitations. These factors may have additive and cumulative negative effects on health and physical functioning over the life course (House et al., 1990). It may be necessary to focus social policies and programs not on age per se, but increasingly on problems or life conditions that call for intervention (Neugarten, 1980).

### Community and Institutional Caregiving

Caregiving occurs in the community and in institutions. Increasing numbers of elderly people mean that there will be a greater need for acute medical services (hospitals and related medical services and personnel) and for nursing home care. In fact, the number of people needing nursing home care is expected to increase from 1.5 million to 5.2 million between 1980 and 2040 (Rice & Feldman, 1983). In addition, there will be a growing need for a better financed and organized system of community care services. Despite the growth in community care, many older people do not receive needed services and their numbers are expected to grow. Defining, measuring, and ensuring quality care within community settings continue to be areas of paramount importance (Applebaum, 1990).

Another significant problem is the need for more home care workers, particularly paraprofessionals who provide the bulk of care to older disabled people living in the community. Retention and recruitment of home care workers will continue to be a challenge well into the future (Feldman, Sapienza, & Kane, 1990).

## The Future

The main political and social challenge in the coming decade is accepting a multiracial and multigenerational society. Older people represent only one end of the human life span and are clearly affected by the life situations of people younger than 65. Cultural pluralism is a force that will affect the future of the United States as growing numbers of ethnic and "minority" populations become the majority in various regions of the country (Torres-Gil, 1986).

Hispanic Americans expect to be the fastest-growing minority group in the United States

(DHHS, 1991). Although people of color in general are underrepresented in the older age groups, their presence affects the aging society. As Torres-Gil (1986) stated, Hispanic Americans are the only group that has ever had to assimilate into the American culture while the society is aging. Because of the unequal political power between younger Hispanic and older white people that results from fewer numbers of Hispanic voters in combination with their lower registration and voting rates, older white people have a better chance to compete for scarce resources. Furthermore, because Hispanic people are more likely to be poor (twice as likely as the general population, according to Torres-Gil), their access to employment and education, two critical features of assimilation, is limited.

The black population over the age of 65 is growing faster than white Americans in the same age group, but they still represent a smaller percentage of the aged population than do white people (Johnson, Gibson, & Luckey, 1990). As a result, it is likely that white Americans will fare better in the competition for services. Certain factors exacerbate the service implications for black people. Statistics show that black elderly people are at greater risk than white elderly people for morbidity and mortality (Reed, 1990) and, therefore, are physically less able to participate in programs and services outside the home. They need to receive in-home services at ages under 65 (Johnson et al., 1990). In general, however, elderly people of color receive less needed care than do white elderly (Aday & Andersen, 1975; Health Resources Administration, 1977).

The United States needs to prepare for an aging society, and people of color are a critical ingredient in that adjustment. When the baby boom generation ages, younger black and Hispanic people will be the mainstays in the labor force and the military (Torres-Gil, 1986) to support the predominantly white elderly. These young people will need educational support, and the level of support they receive will be determined primarily by white voters.

Social security and retirement and pension plans are the central arenas of policy conflicts in the future (Torres-Gil, 1986). Policy decisions, as well as behaviors of the various racial groups, affect the future of the aging society. For instance, the decision Congress made in 1983 to increase the eligibility age for social security benefits poses problems for groups that tend to have lower life expectancies or have not gained citizenship. Currently, black and Hispanic Americans have lower rates of pension plan coverage than do white Americans because of fewer employment opportunities (Rogers, 1979).

The sheer increase in the numbers of elderly people alone warrants special planning efforts. Of particular concern will be the needs of racial and ethnic subgroups within society as a whole and in the elderly population. Their access to services is inconsistent with their numbers, health status, and economic need (Leutz, Capitman, MacAdam, & Abrahams, 1992). Based on current trends and future projections, many of the elderly who will need care in the future will be 85 and over, female, and of low economic status. Many will have few or inadequate social resources such as family, friends, or organizational affiliations. Whether or not these needs are met will be determined by policy decisions. The diversity, longevity, and political and social generational claims (Torres-Gil, 1992) will all come into play in determining whether the needs of older people are met.

## References


Aday, L., & Andersen, R. (1975). *Development of indices of access to medical care*. Ann Arbor, MI: Health Administration Press.

Antonucci, T. C. (1990). Social supports and social relationships. In R. Binstock & L. George (Eds.), *Handbook of aging and social sciences* (pp. 205–226). New York: Academic Press.

Applebaum, R. (1990). Assuring the quality of in-home care: The "other" challenge for long-term care. *The Gerontologist, 30*(4), 444–450.

Blum, J., & Tros, S. (1980). Psychodynamic treatment of the elderly: A review of issues in theory and practice. In C. Eisdorfer (Ed.), *Annual review of gerontology and geriatrics* (Vol. 1, pp. 204–236). New York: Springer.

Brody, E. (1985). Parent care as a normative family stress. *The Gerontologist, 25,* 19–25.

Callahan, J. J., Jr., Diamond, L., Giele, J., & Morris, R. (1980). Responsibility of families caring for their severely disabled elderly. *Health Care Financing Review, 1,* 29–48.

Cath, S. H. (1965). Some dynamics of middle and later years: A study in depletion and restitution. In M. A. Berezen & S. H. Cath (Eds.), *Geriatric psychiatry: Grief, loss, and emotional disorders in the aging process* (pp. 21–72). New York: International Universities Press.

Coale, A. J., & Kisker, E. E. (1986). Mortality crossover: Reality or bad data. *Population Studies, 40,* 329–401.

Crimmins, E. M., & Saito, Y. (1993). Getting better and getting worse: Transitions in functional status among older Americans. *Journal of Aging and Health, 5*(1), 3–36.

Crystal, S., & Shea, D. (1990). Cumulative advantage, cumulative disadvantage, and inequality among elderly people. *The Gerontologist, 30,* 437–443.

Duncan, G. (1984). *Years of poverty, years of plenty: The changing economic fortunes of American workers and families.* Ann Arbor: University of Michigan, Institute for Social Research.

Dye, C. (1978). Psychologists' role in the provision of mental health care for the elderly. *Professional Psychology, 9,* 38–49.

Feldman, P. H., Sapienza, A. M., & Kane, N. M. (1990) *Who cares for them? Workers in the home care industry.* New York: Greenwood.

Flemming, A., Buchanan, J., Santos, J., & Rickards, L. (1984). *Mental health services for the elderly: Reports on a survey of mental health centers.* Washington, DC: White House Conference on Aging.

Flynn, C., Longino, C., Wiseman, R., & Biggar, J. (1985). The redistribution of America's older population: Major national migration patterns for three census decades, 1960–1980. *The Gerontologist, 25,* 292–296.

Fogel, B., Gottlieb, G., & Furino, A. (1990). In B. Fogel, A. Furino, & G. Gottlieb, *Mental health policy for older Americans: Protecting minds at risk* (pp. 1–22). Washington, DC: American Psychiatric Press.

Fries, J. F. (1980). Aging, natural death, and the compression of morbidity. *New England Journal of Medicine, 330,* 130–135.

Fullerton, H. N. (1989). New labor force projections, spanning 1988 to 2000. *Monthly Labor Review, 112*(11), 3–20.

Gallagher, D., & Thompson, L. (1982). *Elders' maintenance of treatment benefits following individual psychotherapy for depression: Results of a pilot study and preliminary data from an ongoing replicated study.* Paper presented at the 90th Annual Convention of the American Psychological Association, Washington, DC.

Gatz, M., & Perarson, C. (1988). Ageism revised and the provision of psychological services. *American Psychologist, 43,* 184–188.

George, L., Blazer, D., Winfield-Laird, I., Leaf, P. J., & Fischback, R. (1988). Psychiatric disorders and mental health service use in later life: Evidence from the epidemiologic catchment area program. In J. Brody & G. L. Maddox (Eds.), *Epidemiology and aging* (pp. 189–219). New York: Springer.

Goldstrom, I. D., Burns, B. J., Kessler, L., Feurberg, M., Larson, D., Miller, N., & Cromer, W. (1987). Mental health service use by the elderly adults in a primary care setting. *Journal of Gerontology, 42,* 147–153.

Hagestad, G. O. (1981). Problems and promises in the social psychology of intergenerational relations. In R. W. Fogel, E. Hatfield, S. Kiesler, & J. March (Eds.), *Aging: Stability and change in the family* (pp. 11–46). New York: Academic Press.

Health Resources Administration. (1977). *Health of the disadvantaged* (DHEW Publication No. HRA 77-628). Washington, DC: U.S. Department of Health, Education, and Welfare.

Hogan, D. P., Clogg, C. C., & Eggebeen, D. J. (1990, November). *Intergenerational exchanges in American families.* Paper presented at the meeting of the Gerontological Society of America, Boston.

House, J. S., Kessler, R. C., Herzog, R. A., Miro, R. P., Kinney, A. M., & Breslow, M. J. (1990). Age, socioeconomic status, and health. *Milbank Quarterly/Health and Society, 68*(3), 383–411.

Iams, H. (1987). Jobs of persons working after receiving retired worker benefits. *Social Security Bulletin, 50*(11), 4–19.

Ittelson, W. H. (1960). *Visual space perception.* New York: Springer.

Jackson, J. J., & Perry, C. (1989). Physical health conditions of middle-aged and aged blacks. In K. S. Markides (Ed.), *Aging and health: Perspectives on gender, race, ethnicity, and class* (pp. 111–176). London: Sage Publications.

Johnson, H., Gibson, R., & Luckey, I. (1990). Health and social characteristics: Implications for services. In Z. Harel, E. McKinney, & M. Williams (Eds.), *Black aged: Understanding diversity and service needs.* Newbury Park, CA: Sage Publications.

Kane, R., & Kane, R. L. (1987). *Long-term care: Principles, programs, and policies.* New York: Springer.

Karp, D., & Yoels, W. (1982). *Experiencing the life cycle: A social pathology of aging.* Springfield, IL: Charles C Thomas.

Keith, V. M., & Smith, D. P. (1988). The current differential in black and white life expectancy. *Demography, 5*(4), 625–632.

Kitagawa, E. M., & Hauser, P. M. (1973). *Differential mortality in the United States: A study in socioeconomic epidemiology.* Cambridge, MA: Harvard University Press.

Knight, B. (1986). Therapist attitudes as explanations of under service of elderly mental health: Testing an old hypothesis. *International Journal of Mental Health, 22*(4), 261–269.

Kunitz, S. J., & Levy, J. E. (1989). Aging and health among Navajo Indians. In K. S. Markides (Ed.), *Aging and health: Perspectives on gender, race, ethnicity, and class* (pp. 211–245). London: Sage Publications.

Kuypers, J. A., & Bengtson, V. L. (1973). Social breakdown and competence. *Human Development, 16,* 181–201.

Lawton, M. P. (1982). Competence, environmental press, and the adaptation of older people. In M. P. Lawton, P. G. Windley, & T. O. Byerts (Eds.), *Aging and the environment: Theoretical approaches* (pp. 33–59). New York: Springer.

Lawton, M. P., & Nahemow, L. (1973). Ecology and the aging process. In C. Eisdorfer & M. P. Lawton (Eds.), *The psychology of adult development and aging* (pp. 619–674). Washington, DC: American Psychological Association.

Lazarus, L., & Weinberg, J. (1980). Treatment in the ambulatory care setting. In E. W. Busse & D. G. Blazer (Eds.), *Handbook of geriatric psychiatry* (pp. 427–453). New York: Van Nostrand Reinhold.

Leon, J., & Lair, T. (1990). *Functional status of the noninstitutionalized elderly: Estimates of ADL and IADL difficulties.* (Publication No. PHS 90-3462). Washington, DC: U.S. Government Printing Office.

Leutz, W. N., Capitman, J. A., MacAdam, M., & Abrahams, R. (1992). *Care for frail elders: Developing community solutions.* Westport, CT: Auburn House.

Litwak, E., & Longino, C. (1987). The migratory patterns of the elderly: A developmental perspective. *The Gerontologist, 27*(2), 266–272.

Livi-Bacci, M. (1982, December). Social and biological aging: Contradictions of development. *Population and Development Review, 8*(4), 771–781.

Longino, C., Biggar, J., Flynn, C., & Wiseman, R. (1984). *The retirement migration project: A final report to the National Institute on Aging.* Unpublished manuscript, University of Miami, Center for Social Research in Aging, Coral Gables, FL.

Longino, C., Soldo, B., & Manton, K. (1990). Demography of aging in the United Sates. In K. Ferraro (Ed.), *Gerontology: Perspectives and issues* (pp. 19–44). New York: Springer.

Lowy, L. (1979). *Social work with the aging: The challenge and promise of the later years.* New York: Harper & Row.

Markides, K. S., Coreil, J., & Rogers, L. P. (1989). Aging and health among southwestern Hispanics. In K. S. Markides (Ed.), *Aging and health: Perspectives on gender, race, ethnicity, and class* (pp. 177–210). London: Sage Publications.

McKinlay, J. B., & McKinlay, S. M. (1990). Medical measures and the decline of mortality. In P. Conrad & R. Kern (Eds.), *The sociology of health and illness: Critical perspectives* (pp. 10–23). New York: St. Martin's Press.

Myers, G. C. (1990). Demography of aging. In R. Binstock & L. George (Eds.), *Handbook of aging and the social sciences* (pp. 19–44). New York: Academic Press.

National Center for Health Statistics. (1989). Current estimates from the National Health Interview Survey. *Vital and Health Statistics*, 10(176).

National Center for Health Statistics. (1990). Life tables. *Vital Statistics of the United States, 1987* (Vol. 2, pp. 183–204).

Neugarten, B. L. (1980). *Age or need? Public policies for older people.* Beverly Hills, CA: Sage Publications.

Reed, W. (1990). Health care needs and services. In Z. Harel, E. McKinney, & M. Williams (Eds.), *Black aged: Understanding diversity and service needs* (pp. 1–27). Newbury Park, CA: Sage Publications.

Rice, D., & Feldman, J. (1983). Living longer in the United States: Demographic changes and health needs of the elderly. *Milbank Quarterly/Health and Society, 61*(3), 362–397.

Riley, M. W. (1983). The family in an aging society: A matrix of latent relationships. *Journal of Family Issues, 4,* 439–454.

Rogers, G. (1979). *Private pension coverage and vesting by race and Hispanic descent.* Washington, DC: U.S. Government Printing Office.

Schneider, E. L., & Brody, J. A. (1983). Aging, natural death, and the compression of morbidity: Another view. *New England Journal of Medicine, 309,* 854–856.

Schurman, R., Kramer, P., & Mitchell, J. (1985). The hidden mental health network. *Archives of General Psychiatry, 42,* 89–94.

Setting, J. (1982). Clinical judgement in geropsychology practice. *Psychotherapy: Theory, Research and Practice, 19,* 397–404.

Sherwood, S., & Mor, V. (1980). Mental health institutions and the elderly. In J. E. Birren & R. B. Sloane (Eds.), *Handbook of mental health and aging* (pp. 854–884). Englewood Cliffs, NJ: Prentice Hall.

Siegel, J. S., & Taeuber, C. M. (1986). Demographic dimensions of an aging population. In A. Pifer & L. Bronte (Eds.), *Our aging society: Paradox and promise* (pp. 79–110). New York: W. W. Norton.

Sweet, J. A., & Bumpass, L. L. (1987). *American families and households.* New York: Russell Sage Foundation.

Torres-Gil, F. (1986). The Latinization of a multigenerational population: Hispanics in an aging society. *Daedalus, 115*(1), 325–348.

Torres-Gil, F. (1992). *The new aging: Politics and change in America.* Westport, CT: Auburn House.

Troll, L., Miller, S. J., & Atchley, R. C. (1979). *Families in later life.* Belmont, CA: Wadsworth.

Uhlenberg, P. (1980). Death and the family. *Journal of Family History, 5*(3), 313–320.

U.S. Bureau of the Census. (1984). Demographic and socioeconomic aspects of aging in the United States. *Current population reports* (Series P-23, No. 138). Washington, DC: U.S. Government Printing Office.

U.S. Bureau of the Census. (1986). Household wealth and asset ownership: 1988. *Current population reports* (Series P-70, No. 22), and Household wealth and asset ownership: 1984 (Series P-70, No. 7). Washington, DC: U.S. Government Printing Office.

U.S. Bureau of the Census. (1989, January). Projections of the population of the United States, by age, sex, and race: 1988 to 2080. In G. Spencer (Ed.), *Current population reports* (Series P-25, No. 1018). Washington, DC: U.S. Government Printing Office.

U.S. Bureau of the Census (1990, June). Marital status and living arrangements. *Current population reports* (Series P-20, No. 445). Washington, DC: U.S. Government Printing Office.

U.S. Commission on Civil Rights. (1979). *The age discrimination study: A report of the U.S. Commission on Civil Rights (Part 2).* Washington, DC: U.S. Government Printing Office.

U.S. Department of Health and Human Services (1991). *Aging America: Trends and projections* (No. FCoA 91-28001). Washington, DC: U.S. Government Printing Office.

Verbrugge, L. M. (1984). Longer life but worsening health? Trends in health and mortality of middle-aged and older persons. *Milbank Quarterly/Health and Society, 62*(3), 475–519.

Verbrugge, L. M. (1989). The twain meet: Empirical explanations of sex differences in health and mortality. *Journal of Health and Social Behavior, 30,* 282–304.

Williams, D. R. (1990). Socioeconomic differentials in health: A review and redirection. *Social Psychology Quarterly, 53*(2), 81–99.

Yu, E. S., Liu, H., & Kyrzeja, W. T. (1985). Physical and mental health status indicators for Asian-American communities. In *DHHS: Black and minority health: Cross-cutting issues in minority health.* Washington, DC: U.S. Department of Health and Human Services.

**Ruth E. Dunkle, PhD,** is professor, University of Michigan, School of Social Work, 1065 Frieze Building, Ann Arbor, MI 48109. **Theresa Norgard, MA, MSW,** is currently a National Institute on Aging predoctoral trainee at the University of Michigan in social work and sociology.

### For further information see

Adult Day Care; Adult Foster Care; Adult Protective Services; Aging: Direct Practice; Aging: Public Policy Issues and Trends; Aging: Services; Aging: Social Work Practice; Baby Boomers; Deinstitutionalization; Direct Practice Overview; Disability; Ecological Perspective; Ethnic-Sensitive Practice; Families Overview; Family Caregiving; Housing; Income Security Overview; Long-Term Care; Managed Care; Mental Health Overview; Poverty; Primary Prevention Overview; Retirement and Pension Programs; Social Security; Women Overview.

**Key Words**

aged
aging
gerontological social work

# Aging: Direct Practice

**Ronald W. Toseland**

The rapid increase in the number of older adults in the United States and other Western industrialized nations has led to heightened interest in direct practice with this population. It is now possible to specialize in gerontological social work in many schools of social work (Lobenstine, 1991). There has also been a tremendous increase in the number of high-quality texts on social work practice with the elderly (Beaver & Miller, 1992; Greene, 1986; Holosko & Feit, 1991; Lowy, 1985; Monk, 1990; Sherman, 1984, 1991; Silverstone & Burack-Weiss, 1983; Toseland, in press) and an increase in texts designed for gerontological practitioners with diverse professional backgrounds (Brink, 1986; Burnside & Schmidt, 1994; Butler, Lewis, & Sunderland, 1991; Herr & Weakland, 1979; Keller & Hughston, 1981; Knight, 1986; MacLennan, Saul, & Weiner, 1988; Sadavoy & Leszcz, 1987; Waters & Goodman, 1990; Weiner, Brok, & Snadowsky, 1987).

To work effectively with elderly people, social workers must understand and be sensitive to the experience of aging. They can increase their sensitivity by (1) identifying their feelings and attitudes about the elderly, (2) being aware of how membership in a particular age cohort affects elderly individuals, (3) recognizing the tremendous variability among elderly individuals, (4) being aware of how gender and ethnic minority status affect the aging experience, and (5) learning about development in later life. This entry describes the ways in which social work practice can be modified on the basis of an enhanced sensitivity to elderly people and the experience of aging.

## Steps in Increasing Sensitivity

To work effectively with the elderly, it is essential for social workers to understand and be sensitive to the experience of aging. Understanding what it is like to be in the latter years of one's life helps practitioners be empathic, realistic, and effective. When working with individuals who are younger than they are, social workers have the advantage of having experienced similar developmental issues. In contrast, few practitioners have experienced the developmental issues faced by elderly people. To minimize the effect of a lack of personal experience, it is essential for practitioners to be aware of their feelings and attitudes toward elderly people and to sensitize themselves to the issues with which elderly people typically struggle. There are four steps in this process.

*Step 1: Modify stereotypes and negative images.* Stereotypes and negative images can be modified by talking with older adults about their experiences and by reading about and studying what it is like to be elderly. Negative images and stereotypes can be subtle; for example, it has been suggested that practitioners are more likely than are lay helpers to underestimate the capabilities of older clients (Wills, 1978). They may do so because they frequently work with older adults who do not function at optimal levels. Whatever the reason, stereotypes and negative images of aging interfere with effective helping, whereas an awareness of one's stereotypes about older adults promotes effective helping.

*Step 2: Be aware of the effects of membership in a particular cohort.* Consider for example, two older women, one who sought employment during the early 1930s and the other who sought employment during the early 1940s. The first woman sought employment during the Great Depression, when jobs were very scarce. Even with a high level of education and skills, this woman was unlikely to find work. The second woman sought employment during World War II, when there was a great demand for female workers to help out with the war effort. The different experiences of these two women are likely to have profoundly affected their development and the way they react to helping interventions by social workers.

*Step 3: Recognize the tremendous variability among elderly individuals.* Chronological age is often not sufficient for understanding the experience of a particular individual. Although the old-old (over age 85) are often thought to experience limitations in their everyday functioning and the young-old are often thought to be relatively unaffected by age-related changes in physical functioning, health status varies tremendously from person to person. Many individuals in their 70s are in excellent health, whereas many individuals in their 60s are in poor health. Similarly, although it is often said that older adults experience increasing role losses as they age, many assume new roles they were unable to pursue when they were younger. For example, older adults may retire and hence lose the role of worker, but many pursue leisure and volunteer activities that they were unable to engage in while working.

Thus, experienced practitioners have come to recognize that knowledge of adult development is often more helpful than knowledge of chronological age in understanding older adults (Knight, 1986). For example, the theory of adult development proposed by Erikson and his colleagues (Erikson, Erikson, & Kivnick, 1986) suggests that the young-old tend to be vitally involved in valued activities, yet spend more time taking stock of what they have accomplished in their lives and contemplating how to spend their remaining years. The young-old experience "time reversal," that is, they are more concerned about how much time they have left to live and less concerned about how many years they have lived. They also identify more with the older than with the younger generation. Frequently, they experience changes in their body image and increasing feelings of inferiority, and may be more concerned about dying than are the old-old.

In contrast to the young-old, the old-old are more concerned about maintaining and preserving their independence, well-being, and sense of self (Tobin, 1991). They compensate for slower cognitive processes, loss of stamina, and lower energy levels by restricting their social and physical environments to those they can comfortably manage. They maintain their sense of mastery, competence, and independence by taking fewer risks and by limiting their life space to the comfortable and the familiar.

The old-old maintain stability of the self by blending the present and the past and making the past vivid to reaffirm the self. Their reconstruction of the past is not necessarily accurate, however; they frequently use distortions of past events that are based on selective memory, inflated beliefs of mastery and control, magical coping, and myth making to enhance their self-image and to manage stress (Tobin, 1991). Tobin and Lieberman (1976) reported that individuals who were more likely to survive the transition from a community residence to a nursing home were those who asserted that the move was totally voluntary and that the new environment was ideal.

The old-old also tend to be less introspective, spending more time describing their physical functioning than their psychological or social functioning. In addition, they tend to use more emotion-focused coping skills (such as the positive reappraisal of events, distancing, and acceptance) and fewer problem-focused coping skills (including the seeking of emotional support, problem solving, and confrontation) (Folkman, Lazarus, Pimley, & Novacek, 1987; R. Lazarus & DeLongis, 1983).

*Step 4: Learn how gender and ethnic minority status affect the aging experience.* Hooyman and Kiyak (1993) pointed out that older women and older people of color are at a higher risk of being unhealthy, poor, alone, and inadequately housed. Because women live longer than do men, yet frequently marry older men, they are likely to spend some portion of their old age alone. Older widows are also more likely to be poor or near-poor than are their married counterparts. When working with people of color, it is particularly important to keep in mind how cultural traditions and heritage are likely to affect the process of engagement and relationship building, as well as an individual's overall receptivity to receiving health care and social services. Language barriers, the absence of services in their communities, their lack of understanding about how to gain access to services and resources, cultural insensitivity, and a host of other factors often hamper the ability of older people of color to get help. Hooyman and Kiyak (1993) described a number of strategies that social workers can use to increase the responsiveness of health care and social services to the needs of these elderly people.

## Engagement and Relationship Building

A heightened sensitivity to the experience of aging has many implications for engagement and relationship building. For example, clinical practice with older adults may require modifications in the initial contact, the pace and tone of clinical interactions, the helping relationship, and the physical setting.

Membership in a particular cohort has an important influence on older adults' attitudes toward social services and social workers. For example, older adults, especially those who migrated from Europe in the first two decades of the 20th century, tend to have more negative attitudes toward the use of mental health and social services than do younger adults and thus are often reluctant to seek needed services. Therefore, initial contacts with older adults often involve more outreach, more discussion of entitlements, and greater efforts to overcome their reluctance and resistance to using needed services and resources than do initial contacts with younger clients.

Initial contacts may also be complicated by developmental issues. An attitude of acceptance of their circumstances, a positive reappraisal of deteriorating situations, and worries about how the use of services will interfere with their financial and physical independence tend to militate against the old-old reaching out for assistance.

**Physical Functioning Issues**

The pace and tone of clinical work are governed largely by the physical functioning of elderly clients. When working with frail older persons, social work practitioners should consider whether it is necessary to make adjustments for their slowed cognitive processes, lack of stamina, or reduced energy levels. Young, energetic practitioners may have to slow the pace of their communication with elderly clients because elderly clients may not be able to follow rapid speech because of reduced sensory capacity, especially hearing (Kart, Metress, & Metress, 1978). Among elderly people who are well, the inability to follow the social worker's rapid pace may cause embarrassment, reinforce feelings of incompetence, and provoke them to terminate services. Confused older adults may become agitated. Slowing the pace of sessions may not be sufficient for older clients who lack stamina because of acute or chronic health problems. For such clients, social workers should consider holding briefer sessions more frequently.

Frail older adults may present with a lowered energy level and a muted emotional tone (Lakin, Openheimer, & Bremer, 1982). When working with the frail elderly, practitioners will find that it is useful to be more active, taking greater responsibility for structuring sessions and for soliciting input and feedback by paraphrasing, prompting, and questioning. Highlighting the core messages that are communicated and amplifying muted statements of feeling may also be beneficial.

**Relationship Issues**

To engage older adults, social workers should also consider how the helping relationship should be modified. For example, because the old-old are more concerned about preserving their sense of self than about developing new insights, they prefer warm, supportive, nonconfrontational helping relationships (Lakin, Openheimer, & Bremer, 1982). In a study of brief psychotherapy, L. Lazarus and Groves (1987) found that elderly clients used the helping process to restore their self-esteem and sense of mastery, to reestablish a sense of self over time, to consolidate diverse and disparate aspects of the self, and to validate their sense of normalcy. Because of the natural tendency to blend past and present experiences and to make the past vivid to reaffirm the self, the old-old tend to prefer a there-and-then focus to a here-and-now focus in their interactions with practitioners (Lakin et al.; Toseland, in press).

Transference and countertransference issues may also differ in work with some older adults. Social workers report that older clients often perceive them as authority figures (Tobin & Gustafson, 1987), perhaps because the current cohorts of elderly people were socialized to respect those with professional degrees. In addition, social workers often report that older clients relate to them as adult children (Pollock, 1987). This type of transference is sometimes misperceived as an attempt to infantilize the social workers. Rather, experience suggests that it is more often an attempt to place social workers in a comfortable perspective. Thus, older adults can often be overheard saying to one another that "she reminds me of my daughter" or "he's a lot like my son." Social workers should keep in mind that this type of transference offers them a unique opportunity to help older people work through unresolved issues with their children, reappraise their relationship with their children, and perceive their children in new ways.

Countertransference issues may also be different in work with the elderly. Knight (1986) reported that workers have a tendency to relate to elderly clients as parents or grandparents. Countertransference reactions may be triggered by fears of dependence, infirmity, and death that can make some social workers particularly reluctant to work with frail older adults. Conversely, overidentification with a frail elderly client may result in the failure to make appropriate placement decisions.

**Physical Setting Issues**

To engage older adults, social workers may have to ensure that modifications are made in the physical settings in which the clinical work takes place. Ramps for wheelchairs, nonskid carpets, handrails, high-back armchairs that are not too low to the ground, and meeting rooms that are free from background noise are essential. Also, because of the stigma attributed to the use of social services, the auspices under which services are provided and how services are named may be essential to engaging reluctant older adults. For example, a wellness workshop provided under the auspices of a church or a synagogue is likely to be better attended than is a mental health support group sponsored by the county mental health center. Similarly, a seminar called "Preserving Your Financial Security" offered by a senior citizens' center is likely to be received more positively than is a seminar on benefits offered by the local department of social services.

## ASSESSMENT

Sensitivity to the experience of aging may help social workers modify assessment strategies they typically use with clients of other age groups. Most textbooks on social work practice emphasize the importance of a multidimensional assessment for clients of any age. A multidimensional assessment is particularly important when working with elderly clients because these clients' functioning is "usually a product of interacting physical, mental, and social factors, making interpretation of observed or reported behavior difficult" (Kane, 1990, p. 55). At a minimum, a comprehensive multidimensional assessment should consider the physical, psychological, social, and environmental aspects of an older adult's functioning.

### Evaluation of Support Networks

Assessments of elderly clients may require a more intensive evaluation of support networks. As older adults become frail, they tend to rely on a spouse, their adult children, or other family members. If family members are unavailable, frail elderly often rely on friends, neighbors, or members of the clergy for support. Thus, when social workers assess frail elderly clients, they must inquire about the availability of primary and secondary caregivers and gain the clients' permission to interview these caregivers. In addition to providing useful information about the functioning of elderly clients, interviews with caregivers can help social workers determine the burden these caregivers are experiencing in providing care. Helping caregivers reduce the burden of caregiving and work through issues and problems that interfere with their ability to provide care can often be as useful as direct intervention with frail elderly clients.

### Collaborations with Other Professionals

Another adaptation of assessment processes that may be required is the use of a team approach because some elderly people experience complicated interactions between their physical, psychological, and social functioning (Applegate, Deyo, Kramer, & Meehan, 1991; Rubenstein, Stuck, Sui, & Weiland, 1991; Schmitt, Farrell, & Heinemann, 1988). Consultations with specialists may also be warranted in particular situations. For example, it is often helpful to have a geriatrician confirm a diagnosis of dementia because the symptoms of other types of physical problems (an electrolyte imbalance, for instance) and mental problems (such as severe depression) are similar to those experienced by someone with dementia. Similarly, consultation with a physiatrist, a physical therapist, and an occupational therapist is often essential for a comprehensive assessment of an elderly client who is suspected of having had a stroke.

### Specialized Instruments

Still another adaptation that is common when assessing older adults is the use of standardized assessment instruments that have been developed specifically for the elderly. Some instruments measure a single dimension, such as depression, whereas others measure a number of dimensions. Some assessments can be completed in a few minutes, whereas others require much more time. Gerontological social workers should consider developing a file of different instruments they might find useful when working with the range of client problems they are likely to encounter in their particular practice setting. For a description of some commonly used measures, see Israel, Kozerevic, and Sartorius (1984); Kane and Kane (1981); and Mangen and Peterson (1982). For a description of how to use them in clinical settings, see Sherman (1984, 1991).

## INTERVENTION

### Indirect Interventions

Almost any intervention strategy that is useful for helping younger people can be useful for helping elderly people. However, some intervention strategies are used more frequently with elderly clients than with clients of other ages. For example, social work practice with the elderly is often characterized by indirect interventions, where social workers do not intervene directly with older people, but rather are called on by family members and other informal helpers who see older persons experiencing difficulties but do not know how to help.

***Information and referral role.*** As sources of information and referrals, social workers must be familiar with the wide range of community resources and services available to elderly people. At a basic level, they should be able to help elderly adults gain access to local, state, and federal programs that are designed to ensure a basic standard of living by providing for their financial, nutritional, health, and housing needs. In addition, social workers are frequently called on to help frail elderly adults receive health care services that allow them to live independently in the community. Thus, familiarity with how to apply for home care programs, day treatment programs, and outpatient and inpatient services is essential.

Family members sometimes also need assistance in caring for their frail elderly relatives. Knowledge of respite services; adult day care programs; and such services as telephone reassurance, friendly visiting, and emergency response systems can enable them to continue to care for their relatives at home. When family caregivers themselves need services, social workers may suggest counseling programs and support groups in convenient community locations.

***Case manager role.*** Social workers who work with elderly people are likely to fulfill the role of case manager. To live in the community, frail older people often require services that are provided by professional and paraprofessional helpers under the auspices of a number of different organizations. Therefore, social workers are often called on to develop service plans and to set up, coordinate, and monitor the delivery of a set of health and social services. Because chronic conditions change periodically, social workers have to review service plans from time to time, reassess the situations of their elderly clients, and make changes in service plans as needed. The expected increase in the number of frail older people who will live in the community, along with the growing role of single-point-of-entry and managed care systems, suggests that in the future there is likely to be an even greater demand for social workers to act as case managers and supervisors of paraprofessional case managers.

### Direct Interventions

A number of strategies are used frequently when intervening directly with elderly people. The most prominent are techniques to stimulate life review and reminiscence. Sherman (1991) suggested that reminiscence can be both a private and a public experience. Reminiscing involves thinking about; reflecting on; and creating meaning, coherence, and continuity from past experiences. It also often involves telling others about the past. This process affirms older adults' importance and individuality and connects them to their peers. Thus, techniques for reminiscing can be used with individuals and groups to foster mental health and to promote socialization. Reminiscence can also be used in clinical practice situations (Disch, 1988; Sherman, 1984).

Unlike reminiscence and life-review techniques, which can be used with elderly people who reside in the community and in institutions, other strategies are associated with specialized practice in particular settings. For example, sensory training and remotivation techniques are used most frequently with frail elderly people in day treatment and institutional settings (Weiner et al., 1987).

Reality orientation and validation intervention strategies are widely used with elderly adults who are cognitively impaired. Reality orientation techniques may be helpful for those with mild dementia (Burnside & Schmidt, 1994; Toseland, in press; Weiner et al., 1987), but they are not effective for those with moderate or severe dementia, for whom validation techniques are more effective (Feil, 1992, 1993).

Although many different types of interventions are used with elderly adults who live in the community, group work is the preferred modality in many settings because of its socialization and therapeutic benefits. Toseland (in press) developed a typology of five groups for elderly adults: (1) support groups; (2) therapy groups; (3) social, recreational, and educational groups; (4) service and advocacy groups; and (5) family caregiving groups. In addition to an emphasis on support, group work with the elderly is often characterized by the use of program activities where adults might sing songs together, guess the names of popular songs of the past, or share and discuss cherished photographs. Thus, it is helpful for gerontological social workers to develop a repertoire of program activities that can be used for both therapeutic and socialization purposes (Burnside & Schmidt, 1994; Helgeson & Willis, 1987; Toseland).

## Practice Effectiveness

Increasing attention has been paid to the effectiveness of direct practice with the elderly. In addition to specialized publications such as the *Journal of Gerontological Social Work,* articles on practice effectiveness may be found in journals like *Social Work, Families in Society, Journal of the American Geriatrics Society, The Gerontologist, Psychology and Aging,* and *Clinical Gerontologist.* Given the many different intervention strategies that can be used with well and frail elderly persons, no practice modality or theoretical framework can be singled out as most effective for all the concerns that are brought to gerontological social workers. To determine the most effective practice strategy for a particular practice problem, social workers often find it helpful to conduct a literature search using an online service or CD-ROM. Three databases that are particularly relevant to gerontological social workers are *Social Work Abstracts Plus*, PsycLIT, and MEDLINE.

## SUMMARY

Because of the great diversity among older adults and the many different settings in which social workers practice with elderly people, it is difficult to provide a comprehensive overview of direct practice with this population. This entry has attempted to highlight some of the most important ways that direct practice strategies and skills are modified when working with older adults. Clearly, the most important aspect of practice with the elderly is for social workers to sensitize themselves to the experience of aging and to avoid the stereotypes and negative images that interfere with effective helping.

## REFERENCES

Applegate, W., Deyo, R., Kramer, A., & Meehan, S. (1991). Geriatric evaluation and management: Current status and future research directions. *Journal of the American Geriatric Society, 39,* 2S–7S.

Beaver, M. L., & Miller, D. A. (1992). *Clinical social work practice with the elderly* (2nd ed.). Belmont, CA: Wadsworth.

Brink, T. L. (Ed.). (1986). *Clinical gerontology: A guide to assessment and intervention.* New York: Haworth Press.

Burnside, I., & Schmidt, M. (1994). *Working with the elderly: Group process and techniques* (3rd ed.). Boston: Jones & Bartlett.

Butler, R. N., Lewis, M., & Sunderland, T. (1991). *Aging and mental health* (4th ed.). New York: Macmillan.

Disch, R. (Ed.). (1988). *Twenty-five years of the life review: Theoretical and practical considerations.* New York: Haworth Press.

Erikson, E., Erikson, J., & Kivnick, H. (1986). *Vital involvement in old age.* New York: W. W. Norton.

Feil, N. (1992). *The Feil method: How to help disoriented old-old* (rev. ed.). Cleveland: Edward Feil Productions.

Feil, N. (1993). *The validation breakthrough: Simple techniques for communicating with people with "Alzheimer's-type" dementia.* Baltimore: Health Professions Press.

Folkman, S., Lazarus, R., Pimley, S., & Novacek, J. (1987). Age differences in stress and coping processes. *Psychology and Aging, 2,* 171–184.

Greene, R. R. (1986). *Social work with the aged and their families.* New York: Aldine de Gruyter.

Helgeson, E. M., & Willis, S. (Eds.). (1987). *Handbook of group activities for impaired older adults.* New York: Haworth Press.

Herr, J. J., & Weakland, J. H. (1979). *Counseling elders and their families* (Vol. 2). New York: Springer.

Holosko, M. J., & Feit, M. D. (Eds.). (1991). *Social work practice with the elderly.* Toronto: Canadian Scholars' Press.

Hooyman, N., & Kiyak, H. (1993). *Social gerontology: A multidisciplinary perspective.* Needham Heights, MA: Allyn & Bacon.

Israel, L., Kozerevic, D., & Sartorius, N. (1984). *Source book of geriatric assessment.* (A. Gilmore, Ed.). New York: Karger AG.

Kane, R. A. (1990). Assessing the elderly client. In A. Monk (Ed.), *Handbook of gerontological social services* (2nd ed., pp. 55–89). New York: Columbia University Press.

Kane, R. A., & Kane, R. L. (1981). *Assessing the elderly: A practical guide to measurement.* Lexington, MA: D. C. Heath.

Kart, G., Metress, E., & Metress, J. (1978). *Aging and health.* Reading, MA: Addison-Wesley.

Keller, J. F., & Hughston, G. A. (1981). *Counseling the elderly: A systems approach.* New York: Harper & Row.

Knight, B. (1986). *Psychotherapy with older adults.* Beverly Hills, CA: Sage Publications.

Lakin, M., Openheimer, B., & Bremer, J. (1982). A note on old and young in helping groups. *Psychotherapy: Theory, Research and Practice, 19,* 444–452.

Lazarus, L., & Groves, L. (1987). Brief psychotherapy with the elderly: A study of process and outcome. In J. Sadavoy & Leszcz (Eds.), *Treating the elderly with psychotherapy* (pp. 265–293). Madison, CT: International Universities Press.

Lazarus, R., & DeLongis, A. (1983). Psychological stress and coping in aging. *American Psychologist, 38,* 245–254.

Lobenstine, J. C. (Ed.). (1991). *National directory of educational programs in gerontology and geriatrics* (5th ed.). Washington, DC: Association for Gerontology in Higher Education.

Lowy, L. (1985). *Social work with the aging.* New York: Longman.

MacLennan, S., Saul, S., & Weiner, M. (1988). *Group therapies for the elderly.* Madison, CT: International Universities Press.

Mangen, D., & Peterson, W. (1982). *Research instruments in social gerontology* (Vol. 2). Minneapolis: University of Minnesota Press.

Monk, A. (Ed.). (1990). *Handbook of gerontological services* (2nd ed.). New York: Columbia University Press.

Pollock, G. (1987). The mourning-liberation process: Ideas on the inner life of the older adult. In J. Sadavoy & M. Leszcz (Eds.), *Treating the elderly with psychotherapy* (pp. 3–30). Madison, CT: International Universities Press.

Rubenstein, L., Stuck, A., Sui, A., & Weiland, D. (1991). Impacts of geriatric evaluation and management programs on defined outcomes: Overview of the evidence. *Journal of the American Geriatrics Society, 39,* 98–104.

Sadavoy, J., & Leszcz, M. (Eds.). (1987). *Treating the elderly with psychotherapy: The scope for change in later life.* Madison, CT: International Universities Press.

Schmitt, M. H., Farrell, M. P., & Heinemann, G. D. (1988). Conceptual and methodological problems in studying the effects of interdisciplinary geriatric teams. *The Gerontologist, 28,* 753–764.

Sherman, E. (1984). *Working with older persons: Cognitive and phenomenological methods.* Boston: Kluwer-Nijhoff.

Sherman, E. (1991). *Reminiscence and the self in old age.* New York: Springer.

Silverstone, B., & Burack-Weiss, A. (1983). *Social work practice with the frail elderly and their families.* Springfield, IL: Charles C Thomas.

Tobin, S. (1991). *Personhood in advanced old age: Implications for practice*. New York: Springer.

Tobin, S., & Gustafson, J. (1987). What do we do differently with elderly clients? *Journal of Gerontological Social Work, 6*, 29–46.

Tobin, S., & Lieberman, M. (1976). *Last home for the aged: Critical implications of institutionalization*. San Francisco: Jossey-Bass.

Toseland, R. (in press). *Group work with older adults* (2nd ed.). New York: Springer.

Waters, E. B., & Goodman, J. (1990). *Empowering older adults*. San Francisco: Jossey-Bass.

Weiner, M., Brok, A., & Snadowsky, A. (1987). *Working with the aged* (2nd ed.). East Norwalk, CT: Appleton-Century-Crofts.

Wills, T. (1978). Perceptions of clients by professional helpers. *Psychological Bulletin, 85*, 968–1000.

**Ronald W. Toseland, PhD,** is professor and director, Ringel Institute of Gerontology, School of Social Welfare, University at Albany, State University of New York, Albany, NY 12222.

**For further information see**

Adult Day Care; Adult Protective Services; Aging Overview; Aging: Public Policy Issues and Trends; Aging: Services; Aging: Social Work Practice; Bereavement and Loss; Brief Therapies; Clinical Social Work; Direct Practice Overview; Families Overview; Group Practice Overview; Human Development; Interviewing; Mental Health Overview; Natural Helping Networks; Public Social Services; Self-Help Groups; Social Work Practice: Theoretical Base.

**Key Words**

aging
gerontological
direct practice
social work
elderly

# Aging: Public Policy Issues and Trends

**Fernando M. Torres-Gil**
**Michele A. Puccinelli**

A demographic revolution is under way in the United States. The population is aging, a process that fundamentally affects both public and private policy-making and attitudes. In the public arena, population aging has implications for the system of financing and delivering health and social services to elderly people and their families. In the private sector, it affects recruitment and employment policies, as well as the design of benefit and compensation packages. Over the next several decades, old-age benefits and programs will change as the U.S. population continues to age.

At the beginning of the 20th century, fewer than one in 10 Americans was 55 or older, and one in 25 was 65 or older. By 1986, one in five Americans was at least 55 years old, and one in eight was at least 65 (U.S. Senate, 1986). From 1900 to 1986, the percentage of Americans age 65 and older tripled, from 4.1 percent to 12.1 percent, and their number increased more than ninefold, from 3.1 million to 29.2 million (American Association of Retired Persons [AARP], 1987). By 1991, 12.6 percent of the U.S. population was 65 or older, up from 9.2 percent in 1960, and the median age increased from 29.4 to 33 during the same period (U.S. Bureau of the Census, 1989). Furthermore, the rate at which the 65-and-older population is growing has far outpaced that of the rest of the population. Between 1980 and 1990, the number of Americans 65 or older increased 21 percent, compared with 8 percent for the rest of the population (AARP, 1990). The 75-plus population is the fastest-growing age group within the elderly population. Whereas the 65 to 74 age group is eight times larger than it was in 1900, the 74 to 84 group is 12 times larger, and the 85-and-older group is expected to quadruple between 1980 and 2030.

The real increase, however, is yet to come. Although the dramatic growth of the older population during the 1960s and 1970s has slowed during the 1990s because of the relatively smaller number of babies born during the Great Depression, there will be a rapid increase between the years 2010 and 2030, when the baby boomers reach age 65.The projected growth of that population will raise the median age of the U.S. population to 36 by the year 2000 and to 40 by 2020 (U.S. Senate, 1991). The proportion of people age 65 or older will grow from 13 percent in 2000 to 22 percent in 2030, representing approximately 66 million people (AARP, 1992). The maturation of the baby boomers will begin in 2010. By then, more than a quarter of the U.S. population will be at least 55 years old, and one in seven will be at least 65 years old. By 2030, when the baby boom cohort (by then, the "senior boom") enters later life, one in three will be 55 or older, and one in five will be 65 or older (U.S. Senate, 1986).

The demographic drama will not end there. The elderly population will become more diversified because a greater proportion will be nonwhite. Between 1990 and 2030, the older white population will grow 92 percent, compared with 247 percent for the older African American population and people of other races and 395 percent for older Hispanic people (U.S. Senate 1991). In contrast, young people will be fewer in number. The U.S. Bureau of the Census projected that by the year 2030, the number of Americans under 35 will have dropped from 55 percent of the population in 1989 to 41 percent (U.S. Bureau of the Census, 1989). What does this trend mean? In simple terms, the U.S. population will be a nation of older, more diverse, complex groups with a declining proportion of youths.

## Age-Based Public Benefits and Policies

What do these facts mean for social policies for older people? How will population aging affect our values, attitudes, and reactions to the political forces it creates? How will these projections affect our views of providing public benefits and programs to older people?

Increases in longevity and the absolute number of older people mean that more people require assistance and more are without families. To provide older people with a basic level of health, income, and social services, government, the private sector, and families must greatly increase the current level of benefits, services, and programs. Determining the best way to do so and paying for such increases is the challenge of the next 20 years.

The mesh of social policies for older people means many things to many people. To a frail, older person who lives alone, it often is a bewildering set of forms, busy phones, and harried bureaucrats. For many other senior citizens and their families, it is an important source of income, social support, and benefits. For those working in gerontology and social work, it is an expanding and exciting profession. For advocates, liberals, and proponents of big government, it defines a sacred welfare state. To the private sector and voluntary agencies, it often seems a quasi-socialistic intrusion on families and individuals.

All these perceptions contain some element of truth. Existing social policies for older people include a vast array of fragmented but important agencies, services, and benefits. They encompass legislation authorizing a variety of direct and indirect benefits and services, agencies to administer them, a constituency to protect them, and professionals to work with elderly people and their families.

The source of most legislation and the resultant benefits is the federal government. State and local governments provide substantial additional services and are charged with their delivery. Insurance companies and contract agencies handle much of the paperwork associated with reimbursement. Nonprofit and for-profit organizations coordinate and deliver services to the aged.

Existing benefits to older people and their families can be broken down by legislative origin and the specific service provided. Most policies originate with a federal law that authorizes certain services and benefits while outlining eligibility criteria, establishing administrative structure, and appropriating funds. The bulk of benefits and services for older adults is provided by a few major legislative acts and programs: the Social Security Act, Medicare and Medicaid, and the Older Americans Act.

### Social Security

The Social Security Act of 1935 is the cornerstone of legislation for older people. The act sets up three trust funds: Old-Age and Survivors Insurance (OASI), Hospital Insurance (HI), and Disability Insurance (DI). It includes Medicare Part A and Part B, Medicaid (a federal–state partnership), Supplemental Security Income (SSI), and the Social Services Block Grant (Title XX).

It also encompasses the largest portion of the federal budget: Social Security and Medicare paid $417 billion in benefits in 1992, most of it tax-free. That year, 42 million people received monthly checks, and 134 million people paid into the system expecting to receive benefits later (personal communication, Social Security Administration Office of Inquiries, July 20, 1993).

The Social Security Act benefits and programs remain the best known, most expensive, and most diverse of social policies for the elderly. From its beginning as the OASDI (Old-Age and Survivors and Disability Insurance) program, it has expanded to include a greater variety of benefits and protection. To most individuals, however, social security means a monthly check to retirees. To many older people it forms the basis for the "social contract"—an implicit understanding that if a person has made contributions, then he or she will receive social security benefits, and the government will not significantly alter the benefits or manner of funding.

### Medicare and Medicaid

Medicare and Medicaid have been the primary health insurance programs for elderly and poor people. Both are undergoing major reforms and eventually may become part of a national health care system. Medicare, signed into law by President Lyndon Johnson in the Health Insurance for the Aged Act of 1965, is the U.S. version of national health care for the elderly and has become the primary source of publicly funded health care for elderly people. Medicare has an age requirement but does no means-test. Medicare is oriented toward acute care, primarily covering hospital and skilled-nursing facility costs. It also provides substantial home health services. However, it does not cover noninstitutional social services for people who are chronically ill. Medicare is the single largest health-care program for older people in the United States and has greatly improved the availability of hospital care for older people.

Medicare is under great strain, however. Its costs and the imposition of cost-containment features have precipitated more stringent requirements and higher out-of-pocket costs for the elderly. It may face bankruptcy by the year 2000 if physician bills continue to rise as rapidly as they did during the 1980s. In addition, fiscal pressures on Medicare will grow: Today, four workers pay taxes for each Medicare enrollee. By the middle of the next century, the number of taxpayers per enrollee may drop to two (Rosenblatt, 1991).

Medicaid, also enacted in the Health Insurance for the Aged Act of 1965, was intended to provide medical care to poor and medically indigent people. It has become the de facto long-term-care program for the middle-class elderly who have reached poverty level, paying for the bulk of publicly funded nursing home care. Unlike Medicare, Medicaid is a grant in aid to states, which have the option to participate and can choose the types of eligibility and services that are covered and the fees to be charged. Not surprisingly, 50 different state Medicaid arrangements exist. States can choose whether to cover only those people enrolled in welfare programs (for example, Aid to Families with Dependent Children [AFDC] and Supplemental Security Income [SSI]) or to include people who are medically needy (that is, those who might qualify for money payment programs but exceed asset or income limits for eligibility). In recent years, the federal government has required states to expand eligibility and coverage without increasing its funding levels.

Also in contrast to Medicare, Medicaid is a means-tested program. States determine income and asset levels required for eligibility while the federal government categorizes the services that states can offer. States find this program a costly burden even with the federal government picking up 50 percent to 83 percent of the cost, depending on the per capita income of the state.

Medicare and Medicaid have provided important health care benefits to their beneficiaries. However, the large gaps in these systems (for example, limited long-term care), the burdens of escalating costs, and the growing number of Americans without health insurance have created tremendous pressures to create a system that provides comprehensive coverage to all. Current health care reform proposals may fundamentally alter the nature of the Medicare and Medicaid programs. In addition, those programs' biases toward medically oriented and institutional long-term care (for example, hospitals and nursing homes) may also create pressure to develop a continuum of home- and community-based long-term-care services that includes social services. Such a system may well develop to include all people regardless of age.

### Older Americans Act

The Older Americans Act (OAA) also is a primary source of human and social services for the elderly. Enacted in 1965 it has a budget of approximately $1 billion in 1994 and the ambitious goal of "assuring the well-being of the elderly" while serving as the focal point for aging policy within the federal government. The Administration on Aging (AoA), an agency of the U.S. Department of Health and Human Services (DHHS), is responsible for administering the programs funded by the OAA. The act creates an "aging network" of visible, accessible, and popular community programs and services. The network comprises 670 local agencies and 57 state units on aging and uses the services of more than 27,000 providers. Next to the infrastructure of social security district offices, this network is the primary service arm for older people in DHHS.

Notwithstanding its admirable intentions and many accomplishments, the OAA is under constant scrutiny because of its non-means-tested, universal entitlement features. Any person age 60 or older is entitled to its benefits, regardless of income or need. The relatively low level of funding for the act, however, requires it to target services to those with the "greatest economic and social needs." In addition, its position at the bottom of the DHHS bureaucracy has limited its utility. Historically, the act has lacked the political backup to influence aging policy in DHHS and other federal agencies. Its placement has made it difficult to fulfill its legislative mandate to be the federal government's chief advocate on behalf of older people. However, this situation was rectified in 1993 when

President Bill Clinton and DHHS Secretary Donna Shalala elevated the position of commissioner of the Administration on Aging to an assistant secretary level. The assistant secretary for aging is now responsible for overseeing aging policy in DHHS.

These four social programs demonstrate the major role the federal government has played in providing public benefits and services to older people. In addition, other programs aid older people, including subsidized housing, transportation services, and volunteer programs (for example, ACTION and Foster Grandparents). Together these public programs constitute a federal commitment toward older people and their families. However, they also have increasingly raised questions about government's ability to afford them and implement them efficiently. Concerns about the serious problems facing young people, people of color, and the inner cities, as well as other unresolved social issues, have raised some questions about the status of public benefits to older persons relative to the needs of other groups. However, as this issue evolves, the elderly population, a potent political force that can influence public policy and electoral politics, will exert pressure for the retention and expansion of these programs and benefits. Their political clout will likely grow as they double in number over the next century. The politics of aging will be an important consideration in the way we view the New Aging in the 21st century.

## Emergence of a Politics of Aging

Since the Townsend Plan (and subsequent movement) of the 1930s, in which federal payments of $200 per month were advocated for all people older than age 60 who agreed to retire from work, senior citizens have strongly influenced public policies and political decisions. Their activism pressured President Franklin Roosevelt to pass the Social Security Act; their alliance with President John Kennedy, labor unions, and the Democratic party helped establish Medicare and Medicaid. Senior citizens as a group might not always have been principal players, but they have been an important political force.

Today high voting rates and sophisticated old-age organizations give senior citizens a high degree of political visibility and influence with elected officials. However, questions arise about the appropriateness and effectiveness of older people as a political interest group. The politics of aging—participation by and for the elderly in the political process—evoke both positive and negative views.

Regardless of how one views the political participation of older people, their activism since the 1930s demonstrates their importance as a political constituency. Government officials, elected and appointed, carefully avoid alienating them. Organized aging groups have proved that they can force Congress to repeal unpopular legislation (for example, the Medicare Catastrophic Coverage debate of the late 1980s) or alter budget priorities as they did in the budget debates of the early 1990s. Their "old-style" political involvement (based on a propensity to vote in large numbers), an evolving group identity, and a proliferation of aging organizations whose sole purpose is representation have very successfully enabled older citizens to pressure federal and state governments to expand and protect benefits and programs.

More older people vote than people in other age groups. For example, in the 1992 presidential election, 71 percent of those age 60 and older voted, compared with 58 percent of people 25 to 44 and 43 percent of those 18 to 24. This ratio has increased over time. The consistently high registration and voting rates among the elderly of all races remain powerful political tools. The increasing voting rate of older voters compared with that of younger voters does not go unnoticed by politicians.

In addition, the growing identity of the elderly as a politically active group is a phenomenon unique to the 20th century. In the past, there were too few elderly people to form a constituency. Elders were more likely to be part of intergenerational economic and social systems. Today, however, being old constitutes a way of life, a phenomenon promoted through public policy and popular culture. Studies show that one's interest in politics steadily increases with age. People become more attentive to political campaigns and devote more time to news and public affairs as they grow older. This mounting interest fortifies the historical legacy of their generation: the New Deal approach to addressing social issues. The establishment of social security, Medicare, the Older Americans Act, and other public programs gives the elderly an impetus to use their collective political strength to preserve these benefits of old age.

Age-based organizations have become centers of political activity for many senior citizens. Francis Townsend of the Townsend Movement and George McLain of the California Pension Movement crystallized the fear and disenchantment of elderly people during the Great Depression. At their peak, the Townsend Movement had as many as 2 million members and the McLain organization reached about 100,000 (Hudson & Strate, 1985). Today, there are three categories of interest groups representing elders (Ficke, 1985): (1) mass membership organizations representing older people, (2) professional associations representing people who act for or on behalf of elders, and (3) public interest organizations representing the constituent concerns of public and provider groups. These groups provide numerous opportunities for older people, family members, and those working with the elderly to participate in organized activities.

By the beginning of the 1990s, notwithstanding the political battles of the 1980s—or perhaps because of them—the elderly had reached what Day (1990) described as "the pinnacle of their organizational success and [had] achieved Washington insider status" (p. 33). Organizational growth and activity since the 1930s have resulted in a political system that now recognizes the elderly population as a formidable political force. The political backlash generated by their success might have diminished their moral credibility, but they are, nevertheless, more powerful than most other groups. Where they have merged with other groups (for example, civil rights advocates, women, disabled people, and children), they are now the senior partner rather than a peripheral player.

## Politics of the New Aging

In the coming years, the politics of aging will undergo dramatic changes. Longevity, diversity, and generational issues will influence the politics of the New Aging. A new political climate will effect changes in strategies for and approaches to political involvement by other people.

In general, longevity means that aging issues will affect both the old and the young. An increasing life expectancy means an individual can anticipate up to 25 years in retirement—a sufficient cause to worry about pensions and health benefits. Family members such as spouses and children will become concerned about caring for an aging relative and the related costs. Longevity, then, will alter the politics of aging by diminishing the aggregate political influence of the elderly, despite their greater numbers. However, it might create a set of common concerns among older people as time affects their personal and social status. In other words, a longer life span might become the great equalizer.

Increasing diversity among the elderly may serve to broaden further their political effectiveness and cohesiveness. An income gap is one sign of change in the social, economic, and political profile of the older population in the politics of the New Aging. Increasing diversity means augmented complexity and divisiveness. It means intensified competition for scarce public resources (for example, taxes, revenues, services). Diversity means more stratification in age, income, and race where poor elderly and young minority groups might have to compete with affluent elders for public resources and priorities (for example, means-tested benefits versus middle-income tax breaks).

Generational tension may force the young and old populations to compete against each other. A wild card in future generational conflict will be the influence and political activity of the baby boom generation, which will become the nation's largest-ever group of elders. The baby boomers are likely to have greater age-identification and allegiance than today's elderly, giving them tremendous political influence on issues of common interest (for example, protection of pension and retirement plans, implementation of strong law-and-order measures). Financial support for benefits and programs for older people and the increasing cost of entitlement programs are central to the New Aging. Can the country afford the current array of public benefits and services? How will it finance services for an anticipated larger cohort of older people? As the U.S. population ages, tensions and debates escalate over the allocation of public and private resources among generations and within subgroups of the elderly. Are too many resources being spent on today's older population? How do we prepare for more poor and low-income older people?

Generational issues, increasing life expectancies, and diversification of the aged population in the coming decades will directly affect the economics of aging. The economics of the New Aging reflects circumstances now affecting the financial security of individuals as they age; it raises unsettling questions about the financial status of future generations of older people. The economics of the New Aging exposes the fiscal consequences of being unprepared for the demographic revolution. Examining the current economic status of the elderly unveils fiscal pressures that will require significant changes if the nation is to afford programs for future generations of older people. To provide economic security for later generations, policymakers must carry out major reforms and decisions must be made in the 1990s while there is time to prepare for the aging of the baby boomers.

## Aging in the 21st Century

The forces of diversity, longevity, and generational tensions illustrate why public policies of aging require modification and reform. These forces have redefined aging in American society and presage a new set of political and social roles for the elderly of the next century. The premises underlying the programs, benefits, and services that originated since the 1930s may require a reconceptualization. The United States in the 1990s and beyond will differ significantly from the United States of the 1930s to 1960s, when the present approach to serving older people was developed.

The premises for the New Aging include the following:

- reinvolving the family
- relinquishing age-segregated and interest-group politics
- viewing older people as a resource
- responding to a more diverse society
- avoiding policies forcing competition
- preparing younger generations for long life
- renewing activist government while retaining private sector responsibilities.

Much work remains to be done. Responding to aging and other domestic concerns before the political demands of the older baby boomers increase will further complicate matters. Difficult decisions and political trade-offs will be necessary if we are to avoid conflicts among and within generations and diverse populations. Baby boomers, in particular, play a key role. They can either be a selfish political block, protecting age-based benefits, or they can support public policies that invest in the needs of younger groups. But no matter how this cohort responds to the New Aging, every individual, regardless of age, will have a stake in an aging society. By the year 2020, for example, today's elders will require extensive health and long-term care and will be unable to live in areas with poor public transportation or high crime rates. They will depend on an elaborate and expensive social welfare system, and their children and grandchildren will depend on a strong economy to lessen the financial burden of caring for their older relatives.

The decade of the 1990s is a window of opportunity to understand and act on public policy issues and trends affecting an aging society. The existing systems of public benefits and services may evolve into a different approach to aging in the 21st century. Whatever form that approach might take, it will need to account for a different set of circumstances and recognize that aging is not a fixed point in time but an ongoing process. Aging policy promises to be an exciting and important domestic concern well into the 21st century.

## References


American Association of Retired Persons. (1987). *A profile of older Americans: 1987.* Washington, DC: Author.

American Association of Retired Persons. (1990). *A profile of older Americans: 1990.* Washington, DC: Author.

American Association of Retired Persons. (1992). *A profile of older Americans: 1992.* Washington, DC: Author.

Day, C. (1990). *What older Americans think: Interest groups and aging policy.* Princeton, NJ: Princeton University Press.

Ficke, S. (Ed). (1985). *An orientation to the Older Americans Act.* Washington, DC: National Association of State Units on Aging.

Health Insurance for the Aged Act of 1965. P.L. 89-97, 79 Stat. 290.

Hudson, R., & Strate, J. (1985). Aging and political systems. In R. Binstock & E. Shanas (Eds.), *Handbook of aging and the social sciences* (2nd ed., pp. 554–588). New York: Van Nostrand Reinhold.

Older Americans Act of 1965. P.L. 89-73, 79 Stat. 218.

Rosenblatt, R. (1991, May 18). Bankruptcy of part of Medicare feared. *Los Angeles Times.*

Social Security Act of 1935. P.L. 100-360, 49 Stat. 620.

U.S. Bureau of the Census. (1989). *Statistical abstract of the United States* (109th ed.). Washington, DC: U.S. Government Printing Office.

U.S. Senate. (1986). *Aging America: Trends and projections.* Washington, DC: U.S. Government Printing Office.

U.S. Senate. (1991). *Aging America: Trends and projections.* Washington, DC: U.S. Government Printing Office.


## Further Reading


Bass, S., Kutza, E., & Torres-Gil, F. (Eds.). (1990). *Diversity in aging.* Glenview, IL: Scott, Foresman.

Dychtwald, K. (1989). *Age wave.* Los Angeles: Jeremy P. Tarcher.

Gelfand, D. (1988). *The aging network* (3rd ed.). New York: Springer.

Light, P. (1988). *Baby boomers.* New York: W. W. Norton.

Pifer, A., & Bronte, L. (1986). *Our aging society: Paradox and promise.* New York: W. W. Norton.


**Fernando M. Torres-Gil, PhD,** is assistant secretary for aging, Administration on Aging, U.S. Department of Health and Human Services, 200 Independence Avenue, SW, Washington, DC 20201. **Michele A. Puccinelli** is a graduate student of the University of Southern California.

### For further information see

Aging Overview; Families: Demographic Shifts; Family Caregiving; Family Preservation and Home-Based Services; Federal Social Legislation from 1961 to 1994; Long-Term Care; Poverty; Social Security; Social Welfare Policy; Women Overview.

**Key Words**

| | |
|---|---|
| advocacy | legislation |
| aging | policy |

# Aging: Services

**Neal S. Bellos**
**Mary Carmel Ruffolo**

A discussion of social work services for older Americans risks reinforcing ageism (Butler, 1969) or scapegoating elderly people. Because social work's constituency is drawn from people who are poor, sick, emotionally distressed, and oppressed by discrimination, a portrait of how some elderly people are served by social work may extend the "poor, sick, and senile" label to all 31 million older Americans. The description may be qualified by noting that the system has worked quite well for most elderly people, but that qualification supports the stereotype of older people as "greedy geezers" (Fairlie, 1988).

Although 20 years of written comment from different academic disciplines has accentuated the diversity of older Americans (Bass, Kutza, & Torres-Gil, 1990; Binstock, 1983; Kalish, 1979; Neugarten, 1974, 1982; Radner, 1993; Smeeding, 1990; Torres-Gil, 1992), older Americans are persistently subjected to contradictory ageist stereotypes. One brands them as poor, sick, and dependent, a view based on a misery perspective (Tornstam, 1992) that becomes benevolent when used as the rationale for the entitlement of health and social services for the elderly (Binstock, 1983; Kalish, 1979). The second holds older people to be so well off, so powerful, and so selfish that they risk bankrupting the nation (Longman, 1985). Both stereotypes scapegoat elderly people, thereby obscuring an accurate understanding of the needs and interests of the older population.

Older Americans are not a homogeneous group. Chronological age is no longer the indicator of social, economic, or health needs that it may have been in the 1950s and the 1960s (Neugarten, 1982). Age has both positive and negative dimensions (Atchley, 1991). On the positive side more than 70 percent of Americans age 65 or older report themselves to be in good, very good, or excellent health (U.S. Senate, 1992a). As many as 85 percent are healthy and living like other adults (Bronte, 1991). Even though a large majority have one or more chronic illnesses, most elderly people conduct their lives without disability and loss of autonomy (Kermis, 1986b). Mental decline is not an inevitable outcome of old age (Birren, Sloane, & Cohen, 1992), and older people generally have not been abandoned by their children (Shanas, 1979). Significant increases in social security benefits and pension coverage have made the economic situation of the retired similar to that of the rest of America (Schulz, 1992). And the fact that younger people also are healthier bodes well for the future (Palmore, 1986).

On the other hand, some 15 percent to 30 percent of older people experience a negative side of old age. Income gains in recent years have moved older Americans from the category of poor only to near poor (incomes between 10 percent and 20 percent of the poverty line) (Schulz, 1992). Increases in life expectancy have resulted in more years of disability (Schneider, 1990). Older people's risk of mental illness increases because of comorbidity with chronic diseases (Kermis, 1986a; Lebowitz & Niederehe, 1992). The increasing incidence of Alzheimer's disease and the burdens of long-term care are growing concerns for elderly people and their families.

Old age must also be understood as a part of the larger society (Kart, Metress, & Metress, 1988). The social construction of aging into a social problem has obscured the fundamental issues of older Americans (Estes, 1979). The system is not working for everybody (Atchley, 1991) and has disadvantaged poor people, racial and ethnic groups, disabled people, and women. These disadvantages become the vulnerabilities of old age, some of which generate the need for social work services. The elderly and their problems can best be understood by distinguishing their differences in age, gender, race and ethnicity, and income.

## Differences among Older Americans

### Age

Differences within the 65-and-over age group are significant. Neugarten (1974) identified a healthier, better educated, more active, and more affluent "young-old" group, ages 55 to 74, and a frail and vulnerable "old-old" group, ages 75 and over. Moreover, their characteristics do not remain static. Different birth cohorts grow old in different ways, changed by society and in turn changing society (Riley, 1987).

In 1990 some 31 million Americans were age 65 and over, including 18 million ages 65 to 74; 10 million ages 75 to 84; and 3 million 85 and over, including some 35,000 centenarians (Taeuber, 1992). The population of older Americans is expected to double in size by the year 2030, with the 85-and-over age group tripling (U.S. Senate et al., 1991). The 85-and-over age group, which is increasing in number and has a high proportion of economic, health, and mental health problems, constitutes a major constituent for social care. Only 8.4 percent of those ages 65 to 69 were classified as poor in 1990, but 20.2 percent of those 85 and over fell into that category and 39.8 percent fell into the near-poor ranks (Radner, 1993). This income differential is compounded for the 85-and-over age group, whose health expenses are nearly twice those of the young-old (Schulz, 1992).

Alzheimer's disease affects 14 percent of all elderly people, occurring in 3 percent of those ages 65 to 74, 18.7 percent of those ages 75 to 85, and 47.2 percent of those age 85 and over (U.S. Senate et al., 1991). The old-old have a three times greater chance of losing independence, a seven times greater chance of entering a nursing home, and a 2 times greater chance of dying compared with those 65 to 74 years of age (U.S. Senate et al., 1991).

### Gender

Women of all races live longer than their male counterparts, and this longevity is accompanied by vulnerability in income, health, and the quality of life. Currently there are three older women for every two older men. Specifically, there are 84 men for every 100 women in the age group 65 to 69, and 39 men for every 100 women in the 85-and-older age group (U.S. Senate et al., 1991). Three-fourths of men and slightly over one-third of women age 65 and over are married. Men remarry at a ratio eight times higher than that of women (U.S. Senate et al., 1991).

White and African American widows tend to live alone. Hispanic American and Asian American widows tend to live with others, indicating a stronger support system (Stanford & Du Bois, 1992). Women represent 78 percent of all elderly people living alone, and 24 percent of those living alone are below the poverty level, in contrast to 14 percent for elderly people living in family settings (U.S. Senate et al., 1991). The poverty rate for elderly women in 1991 was 16 percent compared with 8 percent for men (American Association of Retired Persons, 1992). Women's income is substantially reduced when they become widowed, with sizable risk of poverty (Schulz, 1992). Older women are disadvantaged by income owing to the economic marginality they experience during their entire adult life (Dressel, 1986; Minkler & Stone, 1985).

Gender has health implications also. In later life men develop diseases that kill, whereas women more often experience chronic disabling diseases (Taeuber, 1992). For example, half of all women age 45 and over and 90 percent 75 and over have osteoporosis. Only 20 percent of those who have the disease are men (U.S. Senate, 1992a). More than 75 percent of nursing home residents are women, and more than one-half of all women are likely to spend some time in a nursing home compared with only one-third of all men (Pepper Commission, 1990).

### Race and Ethnicity

Elderly people in racial and ethnic groups are a constituency for social care services for two reasons. First, they have experienced the damages of discrimination, which may deepen in old age (Markides, Liang, & Jackson, 1990; Markides & Mindel, 1987). Second, these elderly are increasing more rapidly than are white elderly. In 1990 racial and ethnic groups were 10 percent of the elderly population; this proportion will double by 2030, with a growth rate of 92 percent for white, 247 percent for African American, and 395 percent for Hispanic elderly people (Taeuber, 1992). Hispanic Americans may become the largest racial and ethnic group in the next century (Butler, Lewis, & Sutherland, 1991). Among the elderly in 1990, 28 million were white, 2.5 million were African Americans, 1.1 million were Hispanic Americans, 116,000 were Native Americans, and 450,000 were Asians and Pacific Islanders (U.S. Senate et al., 1991).

At about age 80, a mortality crossover takes place in which life expectancy for African Americans exceeds that of white elderly (U.S. Senate et al., 1991). Hooyman and Kiyak (1993) suggested that this crossover is the result of a combination of biological vigor, psychological strength, and sufficient resources for coping with stress.

Lower income for people of color is evident in the elderly population. Ten percent of elderly white Americans, 33 percent of African Americans, and 22.5 percent of Hispanic Americans lived below the poverty line in 1990 (Radner, 1993). Native Americans were among the poorest elderly (Butler et al., 1991). Minority females currently have the lowest income among the elderly, with a poverty rate of 37.9 percent and a 60.1 percent poverty rate for those living alone (Radner, 1993).

The discrimination, racism, exclusion, immigration, and acculturation that have damaged and disadvantaged racial and ethnic groups are evident in the elderly. But it is not clear that these factors interact with the stresses of aging to produce double jeopardy (Markides et al., 1990; Markides & Mindel, 1987). Evidence also has not indicated that older minority elderly have any lower levels of life satisfaction than can be expected for lower socioeconomic status groups in America (Markides & Mindel, 1987). After controlling for income, African American elderly are no more likely to experience depression than are white elderly, and they have higher levels of life satisfaction compared with whites (Stanford & Du Bois, 1992).

Extended and augmented families of African Americans, filial piety toward Asian American elderly, the role of Hispanic American extended families, and the kinship systems of Native Americans provide sources of support that may reduce the use of formal services by these groups (Stanford & Du Bois, 1992). However, traditional support systems are weakened by the social mobility and acculturation of younger ethnic people (Markides & Mindel, 1987). Moreover, Native Americans' kinship tradition may be ineffective because the entire family has few resources for help (Butler et al., 1991). These changes, which potentially reduce family support, call for increased attention by community services. In addition, such factors as cultural isolation and language barriers may impede service delivery.

**Low Income**

Just as wealth determines the capacity to sustain good health by providing the basis for rest, good nutrition, recreation, emotional security, and quality health care (Butler et al., 1991), low income is a basis for poor health, poor nutrition, more stress, and fewer coping resources (Stanford & Du Bois, 1992). The economic problems of old age start with the end of earnings, when retirement places formerly self-sufficient people at economic risk (Schulz, 1992). Reduced income affects widows, people living solely on social security income, couples whose income was wiped out by lending failures, people without vested pensions, people using all their assets to pay for long-term care, people whose pensions had no inflation adjustments, and disabled workers who have no supplements to their disability pensions (Schulz, 1992).

Smeeding (1990) identified "'tweeners" as the elderly group who are the least well-off. Representing about 20 percent of all people age 65 and over and 40.9 percent of elderly single people living alone, 'tweeners have incomes between 100 percent and 200 percent of the poverty line (the near poor). They are neither poor enough to be eligible for assistance through public programs nor well-off enough to maintain themselves. They are particularly at risk in cases of high housing costs, high medical care costs, and the death of a spouse.

**Summary on Differences**

Most older Americans look upon their retirement years with satisfaction (Harris & Associates, 1981). However, a significant minority of elders concentrated among, but not limited to, people who are very old, poor or near poor, members of racial and ethnic groups, and women, are most vulnerable to an old age marred by poor physical and mental health and loss of autonomy. These individuals are the targets of social care.

## AGING SERVICES NETWORK

From the inception of the Social Security Act of 1935, older Americans have become the prime constituents of a huge and complicated services structure that administers a myriad of health and social services programs. Thousands of national, state, and local agencies employing perhaps as many as 2 million people (Morris, 1989) have created an Aging Enterprise (Estes, 1979). Although these resources appear to be substantial, they fall short in meeting the more serious concerns of this group.

The Social Security Act and the Older Americans Act of 1965 (OAA) are the core elements of the vast network providing services to all older Americans. The Social Security Act, along with subsequent amendments for Medicare, Medicaid, and Block Grants, represents the large-scale public spending for income maintenance and health care for elderly people. The OAA, through the Administration on Aging (AoA), initiated a national network of state and local, public and private agencies charged with providing a system of coordinated and comprehensive locally based programs responsive to the needs of older Americans. This network has become the major program for in-home and community-based services. It is composed of 10 regional AoA offices, 57 state units on aging, 670 local area agencies on aging, almost 200 Native American tribal organizations, 15,000 nutrition sites, and 27,000 local services provider agencies (Quirk, 1991; U.S. Senate, 1992b). It provides a wide range of services, including homemaker and chore services, home health assistance, transportation, home-delivered meals, adult day care services, information and referral, protective and legal services, senior center programs, congregate meals, employment counseling, health promotion, friendly visiting, and nursing home ombudsmen. The programs serve the vulnerable and well elderly people. During fiscal year (FY) 1990 (U.S. Senate, 1992b) the network reached 10 million older persons in need of nutrition and supportive services, such as transportation, information and referral, and in-home services. Over 140 million congregate meals were served, more than 100 million meals were delivered, and over 85,000 frail elders received in-home services (U.S. Senate, 1992b).

In FY 1991 AoA initiated the Eldercare Campaign, a multiyear, national effort to assist older people at risk of losing their independence by building public awareness, expanding organizational involvement, and creating community coalitions. The campaign has been implemented by funding national aging and nonaging organizations, creating an Older Americans Act Eldercare Volunteer Corps, developing community coalitions, funding product development to heighten local awareness, providing cooperating organizations with up-to-date information, forming a national center for coalition building, and creating 13 national Eldercare Institutes within national organizations and academic institutions to provide technical assistance and training.

The OAA was reauthorized and signed into law in September 1992, appropriating $846 million for local programs and new activities. In addition to strengthening the Eldercare Campaign, the act contained stronger provisions targeting AoA programs to those in social and economic need for health promotion expansion and support of family caregivers, and it added a new title to help elders strengthen their rights and services.

The new initiatives and increased funding in recent fiscal years are not necessarily indicators of overall expansion of services to older Americans. Binstock (1991) observed that if OAA funds are adjusted for inflation, they have declined substantially since 1981, and Medicare and Social Security expenditures of $343.2 billion in 1990 were 275 times the OAA appropriation of that year. The funds allocated to OAA programs are insufficient (Kutza, 1991) to achieve the broad and comprehensive goals of the act and may be largely symbolic (Binstock, 1991).

Two ongoing issues, targeting and cost sharing, reflect current policy discussions on aging and were important topics during reauthorization of the Older Americans Act (Binstock, 1991; Gelfand & Bechill, 1991; Hudson & Kingson, 1991). First, limited funds and growing numbers of disadvantaged older people make it reasonable to target disadvantaged people for services. Second, because some elders with financial means are interested in these programs, it makes sense to permit these individuals to share in program costs. However, targeting and cost sharing run counter to the original intent of the act to serve all older Americans regardless of income. The network has responded to the realities of limited funding and expanded demand by targeting disadvantaged people and permitting older people to pay part of the costs of some programs on a strictly volunteer basis. Opinion is split on the matter (Gelfand & Bechill, 1991). Some advocates are concerned that the overall program will be stigmatized or exclusionary; some are concerned that programs may lose the support of more well-to-do elders; others believe targeting and cost sharing will improve congressional support because programs and funds are addressed to the most needy older people, avoiding the taint of entitlement.

The debate in public policy reflects the stereotypes about older Americans. The stereotype currently being used in congressional debates is that old people are well off. That view signals budget reductions for programs serving older Americans (Radner, 1993). Other concerns about the services network have been expressed. Estes (1979) proposed that the prime beneficiaries of the Aging Enterprise programs are service providers who gain their livelihood from the programs, which have little impact on the lives of the disadvantaged elderly. Morris (1989) saw serious problems with the entire system. Specialization and fragmentation have made the system so cumbersome that additional and multiplying layers of case management and information and referral networks are necessary adjuncts of services. The system is expensive, with many organizations, many funding patterns, and many eligibility criteria. These dynamics virtually prevent the services system from evolving into a truly comprehensive, coordinated, and effective way of dealing with the major issues facing older Americans.

## Services Social Workers Provide for Older Americans and Their Families

Fragmentation of services for older people, the increasing specialization of services, and the complexity of the service system network make it difficult for older people to gain access to needed services. Social workers who provide services for older people are primarily engaged in working with those experiencing difficulties in the community, in hospitals, and in institutional settings. Maneuvering the network to obtain critical services becomes a major challenge for social workers. The target population for most social work services is older people who are vulnerable because of illness, impairment, or disability; who risk losing their autonomy; who are dependent; who need multiple services over a long period of time; or who are experiencing family protectionism or professional paternalism (approximately 30 percent of all older people).

The majority (69 percent) of older noninstitutionalized people lived in a family setting in 1990, and about 31 percent lived alone (U.S. Senate et al., 1991). In 1984, about 6 million (23 percent) older people had health-related difficulties with one or more personal care activity, and 27 percent had difficulty with one or more home management activity (U.S. Senate et al., 1991). Chronic conditions affect more than 80 percent of the elderly (U.S. Senate et al., 1991). Advancing age increases the probability for multiple illnesses, which in turn makes elders more dependent on assistance.

People 65 and older compose 12 percent of the total U.S. population and account for more than one-third of the nation's personal health care expenditures (U.S. Senate, 1992a). At any given time only 5 percent of the elderly live in nursing homes, although this figure may be misleading (Kastenbaum, 1983) because, of those who turned 65 in 1990, 43 percent will enter a nursing home before they die (U.S. Senate, 1992a). Most older people who are vulnerable and at risk in the community, in hospitals, and in nursing facilities, are part of the oldest-old (85 and over) population (U.S. Senate et al., 1991). Only 20 percent of elderly people who are disabled live in nursing homes, and more than one-half with severe disabilities live at home (Pepper Commission, 1990). The 80 percent of elderly people who are disabled and live at home are dependent on family and friends for their care (Pepper Commission, 1990). Most long-term caregiving is provided by individuals and families from their own resources. Women who provide the majority of caregiving services for older family members (Bass, 1990) face stressful lives (Brody, 1985).

Depression is the most common disorder of older people, which affects 15 percent to 25 percent of those who are not institutionalized (Birren et al., 1992; Lebowitz & Niederehe, 1992). Only 1 percent to 2 percent of people seen by community mental health centers are elderly, and less than 7 percent of the elderly are treated by private psychiatrists (Kermis, 1986a). Alzheimer's disease is the major cause of cognitive impairment, affecting 10 percent of the total aging population and 47 percent of those over 85 (U.S. Senate et al., 1991). The risk of suicide increases with age (Kermis, 1986b). Almost 30 percent of people in treatment for alcoholism are older than 55, and drug abuse and addiction to prescribed medications are serious problems (Kermis, 1986b).

Although public laws call for coordinated, comprehensive, and effective services for older people, in reality these programs cannot serve all who need them because of limited funding and the complexity and diversity of the service needs. Social work services for older people confront system dysfunctions and ensure that older people and their families have the opportunity to meet the challenges of day-to-day living in the least restrictive setting. Kane and Kane (1987) indicated that long-term care presents problems of access, cost, and quality for most older people and their families. Stull, Bowman, Cosbey, McNutt, and Drum (1990) found that lower accessibility of formal long-term care services increases the probability of nursing home placement of older people in need of care services. In addition, ethnic elderly, the fastest growing age group, are less likely to use services (Barresi & Stull, 1993).

Cultural isolation, language barriers, long travel distances to obtain services, and the general lack of services specifically oriented toward and operated by members of respective ethnic groups contribute to low use of services by minority elders (Barresi & Stull, 1993). These barriers have been increased by the lack of knowledge, insensitivity, ageism, sexism, and racism that exists in the health, mental health, and social services systems (Butler et al., 1991; Kermis, 1986b; Lebowitz & Niederehe, 1992; Stanford & Du Bois, 1992).

Social workers enter partnerships with older people and their families to deliver services based on identified needs and available resources. Social workers are primarily involved in generating choices for older people and their families, advocating for quality services, and surmounting the barriers to services.

### Case Management or Care Management Services

One of the primary ways that social work delivers services to older people and their families in need of long-term care is case management or care management. The *NASW Standards for Social Work Case Management* (NASW, 1992) defined social work case management as a method of providing services whereby a professional social worker assesses the needs of the client and the client's family, when appropriate, and arranges, coordinates, monitors, evaluates, and advocates for a package of multiple services to meet the specific client's complex needs. The primary goal of case management is to optimize client functioning by providing quality services in the most efficient and effective manner to individuals with multiple complex needs. Steinberg and Carter (1983) identified 11 functions of most case management programs for older people: case finding, prescreening, intake, assessment, goal setting, care planning, capacity building, care plan implementation, reassessment, termination, and maintaining relationships. Case management programs operate in organizational settings that include hospitals, public agencies, area agencies on aging, senior centers, family services agencies, and nursing facilities.

Several innovative case management programs (Miller, 1991) targeting specialized groups of older people have been successful in helping older people obtain services and maintain optimal levels of functioning in community settings (for example, On Lok Senior Health Services Consolidated Model of Long-Term Care, San Francisco, California; Nursing Home Without Walls, State of New York; PASSPORT, State of Ohio; Rural Elderly Enhancement Program, Montgomery, Alabama; and Robert Wood Johnson Program in Hospital Initiatives in Long-Term Care in 24 sites throughout the country). Although the programs vary in the way services are organized and delivered, they enhance the home care services delivered to older people and create alternatives to traditional services intervention.

### Advocacy Services

Because of shortcomings in the delivery of case management services to older people and their families, social workers need to engage in advocacy efforts for radical changes in the services network. Advocacy services, such as ombudsmen programs and community coalitions, operate on client system change and larger system change levels. Protecting older people's autonomy, providing choices for care for older people and their families, and increasing the accessibility of services that are culturally competent for all groups of older people are part of the advocacy services that social workers provide.

### Direct Services

In addition to case management services and advocacy services, social workers in the community provide a wide array of direct services. These might include individual and family counseling, grief counseling, adult day care, crisis intervention, adult foster care, adult protective services, respite services, support and therapeutic groups, and transportation and housing assistance.

***Individual and family counseling services.*** Older people are emphasized as "focal points"; that is, counseling interventions focus on examination of the older person's needs and strengths, the family's needs and strengths, and the resources available to meet the identified needs. Social workers are challenged to negotiate within the family system structure for appropriate choices that enhance the older person's autonomy.

***Grief counseling services.*** Older people and their families who face role loss (for example, self-sufficiency), loss of significant others (for example, a spouse, adult children, or adult siblings), and loss due to chronic health and mental health conditions are helped by grief counseling services. The services are provided in a variety of organizational settings, including mental health centers, hospice programs, senior centers, family counseling centers, and workplace settings.

***Adult day care services.*** Structured community-based day care services are designed to meet the needs of functionally impaired adults through individual plans of care (National Institute on Adult Daycare, 1984). Day care services focus on providing a variety of health, social, and related support services. Older people who participate in day care services live in the community. Social workers provide individual and family counseling, group work services, outreach and broker services, supportive services, and care planning services for older people enrolled in these programs.

***Crisis intervention services.*** Older people may initiate crisis services involving immediate responses to unsafe situations, but often the request for assistance comes from family members or outside agencies. Social workers who provide crisis intervention services are available 24 hours a day. They work to stabilize the crisis situation and connect the older person and the family to needed supportive services.

***Adult foster care services.*** Older people who participate in adult foster care programs require some assistance in daily living activities but are not in need of 24-hour nursing care. Foster care services are designed to help older people remain in the community. Social workers are involved in recruiting foster care homes, matching foster families with an older person, and monitoring the quality of life for older people in the foster care setting.

***Adult protective services.*** Social workers in protective services determine if adults are at risk for personal injury or harm owing to the actions or inactions of others, such as physical abuse, psychological abuse, material (financial) abuse, active neglect (in which caregivers deliberately withhold medications or nourishment, or fail to provide basic care), or physical neglect by family members or primary caregivers. Social workers are involved in outreach to older people who are vulnerable to such maltreatment, developing resources to stop the maltreatment, and providing ongoing counseling to the older persons and his or her family.

***Respite services.*** When older people require 24-hour at-home care, respite services allow families to keep the older family member in the home while allowing family members time away from caregiving responsibilities. Social workers are involved in the recruitment and training of respite care workers, as well as in identifying families in need of these services.

***Support and therapeutic groups.*** Older people and their families are helped by support groups and therapeutic groups that are formed in the community to assist caregivers; older people who are experiencing major life changes such as retirement, illnesses such as Alzheimer's disease, and alcohol or poly-substance abuse problems; older people and their families who are coping with chronic health or mental health conditions; and families of older people who have a terminal illness. Social workers facilitate the formation of support and therapeutic groups and the development of group themes and conduct the group sessions. The groups may be short term or continuous.

***Transportation and housing assistance.*** The needs of older people who are isolated, live in rural communities, are homeless, or experience problems in their current living situation are met by transportation and housing services. Social workers operate as brokers for transportation services and help find appropriate housing in the community. They also offer supportive counseling and help older people complete applications for assistance.

Case management community services permit many older people with chronic health and mental health problems to live in the community. Although the services are valuable, a majority of eligible older people do not receive them because of access problems, financial problems, lack of knowledge about the programs available, and personal difficulties with accepting help.

***Counseling, therapy, and advocacy services.*** The goal of social work services in institutional settings such as hospitals and nursing facilities is to enhance the quality of life and promote maximum levels of independence for older people. The *NASW Standards for Social Work Services in Long-Term Care Facilities* (NASW, 1981) recommend that social work services in long-term-care facilities include direct services to individuals, families, and significant others; health education for residents and families; advocacy; discharge planning; community liaison; participation in policy and program planning; quality assurance; development of a therapeutic environment in the facility; and consultation with other members of the long-term-care team. Social workers in long-term-care facilities are involved in assisting older people and their families in the transition from the community to long-term-care facilities, maintaining supportive ties for older people in the community, and developing care plans that maximize the older person's potential for independence. Group therapy services provided in many nursing facilities include reality orientation groups and reminiscence groups.

In addition to providing services to older people, social workers are involved in helping informal caregivers and family members meet the needs of elders. They also are involved in the training of informal caregivers and in the support of caregivers over time. Families and informal caregiving networks provide significant services to older people in meeting their daily needs. Social workers engage in delivering caregiving services in such locations as workplace settings and religious or community senior centers.

## Conclusion

Social workers are developing many services in the community and in institutional settings to address the emerging problems faced by older people with acquired immune deficiency syndrome (AIDS) (10 percent of all AIDS cases have involved people age 50 or older) (National Institute on Aging, 1992), older people with severe mental health disorders, older people who are homeless, older people from racial and ethnic groups, and older people who are developmentally disabled. Traditional services do not meet the special needs of these groups.

Currently, social work services constitute a significant component of the aging services network. With the rapid growth of the aging population, the limited resources available for services provision, and the increasing need for long-term care services, social workers are challenged to ensure that services protect the autonomy and choices of older people and their families, are culturally relevant, and enhance quality of life.

## References

American Association of Retired Persons. (1992). *A profile of older Americans.* Washington, DC: Administration on Aging.

Atchley, R. (1991). *Social forces and aging: An introduction to social gerontology.* Belmont, CA: Wadsworth.

Barresi, C., & Stull, D. (1993). Ethnicity and long-term care: An overview. In C. Barresi & D. Stull (Eds.), *Ethnic elderly and long-term care.* New York: Springer.

Bass, D. (1990). *Caring families: Supports and interventions.* Silver Spring, MD: NASW Press.

Bass, S. A., Kutza, E. A., & Torres-Gil, F. M. (1990). *Diversity in aging: Challenges facing planners & policy makers in the 1990s.* Glenview, IL: Scott, Foresman.

Binstock, R. H. (1983). The aged as scapegoat. *The Gerontologist, 23,* 136–143.

Binstock, R. H. (1991). From the great society to the aging society: 25 years of the Older Americans Act. *Generations, 15*(3), 1–18.

Birren, J. E., Sloane, F. B., & Cohen, G. D. (1992). *Handbook of mental health and aging.* San Diego: Academic Press.

Brody, E. M. (1985). Parent care as a normative family stress. *The Gerontologist, 25,* 19–29.

Bronte, L. (1991). The "new" older Americans. In U.S. Senate, Special Committee on Aging, *Lifelong learning for an aging society: An information paper* (pp. 5–11). 102d Congress, 1st session, Report No. 102-58. Washington, DC: U.S. Government Printing Office.

Butler, R. N. (1969). Ageism: Another form of bigotry. *The Gerontologist, 9,* 243–246.

Butler, R. N., Lewis, M. L., & Sutherland, T. (1991). *Aging and mental health: Positive psychosocial and biomedical approaches.* New York: Macmillan.

Dressel, P. (1986). An overview of the issues. *The Gerontologist, 26,* 128–131.

Estes, C. (1979). *The aging enterprise: A critical examination of social policies and services for the aged.* San Francisco: Jossey-Bass.

Fairlie, H. (1988). Talkin' 'bout my generation. *New Republic, 198,* 19–22.

Gelfand, D. E., & Bechill, W. (1991). The evolution of the Older Americans Act: A 25-year review of the legislative changes. *Generations, 15*(3), 19–22.

Harris & Associates. (1981). *Aging in the eighties: America in transition.* Washington, DC: National Council on Aging.

Hooyman, N. R., & Kiyak, H. A. (1993). *Social gerontology: A multidisciplinary perspective.* Boston: Allyn & Bacon.

Hudson, R. B., & Kingson, E. R. (1991). Inclusive & fair: The case for universality in social programs. *Generations, 15*(3), 51–56.

Kalish, R. A. (1979). The new ageism and the failure models: A polemic. *The Gerontologist, 19,* 398–402.

Kane, R. A., & Kane, R. L. (1987). *Long-term care: Principles, programs and policies.* New York: Springer.

Kart, C. S., Metress, E. K., & Metress, S. P. (Eds.). (1988). *Aging, health and society.* Boston: Jones and Bartlett.

Kastenbaum, R. J. (1983). The 4% fallacy: r.i.p. *The International Journal of Aging and Human Development, 17,* 71–74.

Kermis. M. D. (1986a). The epidemiology of mental disorder in the elderly: A response to the Senate/AARP report. *The Gerontologist, 26,* 482–487.

Kermis, M. (1986b). *Mental health in later life: The adaptive process.* Boston: Jones and Bartlett.

Kutza, E. A. (1991). The Older Americans Act of 2000: What should it be? *Generations, 15*(3), 65–69.

Lebowitz, B. D., & Niederehe, G. (1992). Concepts and issues in mental health and aging. In J. E. Birren, R. B. Sloane, and G. D. Cohen (Eds.), *Handbook of mental health and aging* (pp. 1–26). San Diego: Academic Press.

Longman, P. (1985). Justice between generations. *The Atlantic Monthly, 25,* 73–81.

Markides, K. S., Liang, J., & Jackson, J. S. (1990). Race, ethnicity, and aging: Conceptual and methodological issues. In R. H. Binstock & L. K. George (Eds.), *Handbook of aging and the social sciences* (pp. 112–129). San Diego: Academic Press.

Markides, K. S., & Mindel, C. H. (1987). *Aging and ethnicity.* Newbury Park, CA: Sage Publications.

Miller, J. A. (1991). *Community-based long-term care: innovative models.* Newbury Park, CA: Sage Publications.

Minkler, M., & Stone, R. (1985). Feminization of poverty and older women. *The Gerontologist, 25,* 351–357.

Morris, R. (1989). Challenges of aging in tomorrow's world: Will gerontology grow, stagnate, or change? *The Gerontologist, 29,* 494–501.

National Association of Social Workers. (1981). *NASW standards for social work services in long-term care facilities.* Washington, DC: Author.

National Association of Social Workers. (1992). *NASW standards for social work case management.* Washington, DC: Author.

National Institute on Adult Daycare. (1984). *Standards for adult day care.* Washington, DC: National Council on Aging.

National Institute on Aging. (1992). *Bound for health: A collection of age pages.* Washington, DC: U.S. Department of Health and Human Services.

Neugarten, B. L. (1974). Age groups in American society and the rise of the young-old. *Annals of the American Academy of Political and Social Science, 415,* 187–198.

Neugarten, B. L. (Ed.). (1982). *Age or need? Public policies for older people.* Beverly Hills, CA: Sage Publications.

Older Americans Act of 1965. P.L. 89-73, 79 Stat. 218.

Palmore, E. B. (1986). Trends in the health of the aged. *The Gerontologist, 26,* 298–302.

Pepper Commission (U.S. Bipartisan Commission on Comprehensive Health Care). (1990). *A call for action: Final report* (Senate Print No. 101-11). Washington, DC: U.S. Government Printing Office.

Quirk, D. A. (1991). The aging network: An agenda for the nineties & beyond. *Generations, 15*(3), 23–26.

Radner, D. B. (1993). *An assessment of the economic status of the aged. Studies in Income Distribution, 16.* Washington, DC: Social Security Administration.

Riley, M. W. (1987). The significance of age in sociology. *American Sociological Review, 52,* 1–14.

Schneider, E. L. (1990). Interventions in aging. In R. N. Butler, M. R. Oberlink, & M. Schechter (Eds.), *The promise of productive aging: From biology to social policy* (pp. 12–18). New York: Springer.

Schulz, J. H. (1992). *The economics of aging.* Westport, CT: Auburn House.

Shanas, E. (1979). Social myth as hypothesis: The case of the family relations of old people. *The Gerontologist, 24,* 603–607.

Smeeding, T. M. (1990). Economic status of the elderly. In R. H. Binstock & L. K. George (Eds.), *Handbook of aging and the social sciences* (pp. 362–382). San Diego: Academic Press.

Social Security Act of 1935. P.L. 100-360, 49 Stat. 620.

Stanford, E. P., & Du Bois, B. C. (1992). Gender and ethnicity patterns. In J. E. Birren, R. B. Sloane, & G. D. Cohen (Eds.), *Handbook of mental health and aging* (pp. 1–26). San Diego: Academic Press.

Steinberg, R., & Carter, G. W. (1983). *Case management and the elderly.* Lexington, MA: Lexington Books.

Stull, D. E., Bowman, K., Cosbey, J., McNutt, W., & Drum, M. (1990). *A family perspective of the institutionalization of frail elderly.* Paper presented at the 43rd annual meeting of the Gerontological Society of America, Boston.

Taeuber, C. M. (1992). *Sixty-five plus in America: Current population reports, special studies.* Washington, DC: U.S. Bureau of the Census.

Tornstam, L. (1992). The quo vadis of gerontology: On the scientific paradigm of gerontology. *The Gerontologist, 32,* 318–326.

Torres-Gil, F. M. (1992). *The new aging: Politics and change in America.* Westport, CT: Auburn House.

U.S. Senate, Special Committee on Aging. (1992a). *Developments in aging: 1992* (Vol. 1). 103d Congress, 1st Session, Report No. 103-140. Washington, DC: U.S. Government Printing Office.

U.S. Senate, Special Committee on Aging. (1992b). *Developments in aging: 1992* (Vol. 2). 103d Congress, 1st Session, Report No. 103-140. Washington, DC: U.S. Government Printing Office.

U.S. Senate, Special Committee on Aging, the American Association of Retired Persons, the Federal Council on Aging, & the U.S. Administrations on Aging. (1991). *Aging America: Trends and projections* (rev. ed.). Washington, DC: U.S. Department of Health and Human Services.

## Further Reading

Beaver, M. L., & Miller, D. A. (1992). *Clinical social work practice with the elderly: Primary, secondary and tertiary intervention* (2nd ed.). Belmont, CA: Wadsworth.

Bumagin, V. E., & Hirn, K. (1990). *Helping the aging family: A guide for professionals.* New York: Springer.

Cox, E. O., & Parsons, R. J. (1994). *Empowerment-oriented social work practice with the elderly.* Pacific Grove, CA: Brooks/Cole.

Hancock, B. L. (1990). *Social work with older people* (2nd ed.). Englewood Cliffs, NJ: Prentice Hall.

Schneider, R. L., & Kropf, N. (Eds.). (1992). *Gerontological social work: Knowledge service settings and special populations.* Chicago, IL: Nelson-Hall.

**Neal S. Bellos, PhD, ACSW,** is professor, and **Mary Carmel Ruffolo, PhD, ACSW,** is assistant professor, Syracuse University, School of Social Work, Brockway Hall, Syracuse, NY 13244.

### For further information see

Adult Day Care; Adult Foster Care; Advocacy; Aging Overview; Aging: Direct Practice; Aging: Public Policy Issues and Trends; Aging: Social Work Practice; Bereavement and Loss; Community; Community Needs Assessment; Deinstitutionalization; Direct Practice Overview; Disability; Elder Abuse; End-of-Life Decisions; Ethnic-Sensitive Practice; Family Caregiving; Health Care Overview; Hospice; Human Development; Income Security Overview; Long-Term Care; Mental Health Overview; Natural Helping Networks; Organizations: Context for Social Services Delivery; Poverty; Primary Prevention Overview; Public Health Services; Public Social Services; Social Security; Social Welfare Policy.

**Key Words**

aged
elder care
geriatric services
gerontological social work

# Aging: Social Work Practice

**Maria E. Zuniga**

Social work practice with elderly people is complex and demanding, given the range of needs of this population, the various subgroups of at-risk elderly people, and the multiple roles social workers must undertake to address their needs (Maldonado, 1987). Demographic projections forecast that social workers will serve an ever-increasing number of elderly clients. People 85 years or older made up one-tenth of the elderly population in the United States in 1990. By the year 2050, this group, the "oldest-old," are expected to constitute almost one-fourth of the elderly population (65 and older). In the 1980s, while the elderly population grew by 22 percent to more than 31 million people, the 85-plus population surged at a growth rate of 38 percent. In contrast, the under-65 population grew by only 8 percent between 1980 and 1990. This growth of both the old and the old-old population will increasingly affect their families, the health care system, and the social service systems in the United States (U.S. Bureau of the Census, 1989).

As the number of elderly Americans grows, so does the number of elderly people who fall into certain risk categories (U.S. Department of Health and Human Services, 1990). Consider, for instance, the following:

- About 5,841,000 noninstitutionalized elderly people have physical impairments.
- About 3,343,000 noninstitutionalized older people have Alzheimer's disease.
- An estimated 963,000 elderly people are abused.

- Approximately 2,509,000 elderly minority members have incomes less than twice the poverty level.
- More than 9,460,000 noninstitutionalized elderly people live alone.

The complexity of serving elderly people with such diverse needs is exacerbated by the growing number of culturally diverse elderly people. In 1990, about 2.6 million black people were 65 or older. By the year 2020, this group is projected to number more than 5.5 million, or 10.7 percent of the elderly population. Their high-risk status is underscored when one notes that 33.9 percent of the black population age 65 and older are poor (U.S. Senate, 1990). In 1987, about two out of three black women 72 and older who lived alone were living in poverty.

Between 1990 and 2020, the number of Latino elderly people is estimated to quadruple (Poth & Hyde, 1990). In 1988, the Latino population numbered 19.4 million and constituted 8.1 percent of the total U.S. population. Although Latinos tend to be a young population compared to the white population, about 5 percent of all Latinos are 65 or older, and of that number almost 7 percent are 85 or older (U.S. Bureau of the Census, 1988). More than 70 percent of the Latino elderly population live in California, Texas, Florida, and New York, with different subgroups concentrated in different states. Mexican Americans are typically concentrated in California and Texas; most of the Cubans live in Florida; and Puerto Ricans are concentrated largely in New York, which also contains various Latino groups from other Caribbean islands. Central American people are found in California and Texas as well.

The Asian American population appears to be the fastest growing group of elderly. According to the 1990 U.S. Census, Asian Americans are now located in every part of the United States. This group also appears to be the most diverse because it includes many subgroups: Chinese, East Indian, Hawaiian, Japanese, Korean, Malaysian, Southeast Asian, and Thai people. Census data indicate that in the 1980s the Asian American population increased 79.6 percent, from 3.83 million to 6.88 million (Austin, Schoenrock, & Roberts, 1991).

The smallest group of minority elderly people are Native American. The life expectancy for this group has changed dramatically: In the 1940s it was 51.0 years; by 1980 it was 71.1 years. In 1970, 83,000 Native Americans were 60 or older, in 1980 there were 109,000 Native Americans in this age group, and in 1990 the number was 166,000 (U.S. Bureau of the Census, 1994). These Native American elders experience the poverty endemic to the Native American population. The poverty of young Native American families implies that they will continue to be unable to contribute to the financial support of their elders (Red Horse, 1990).

It behooves social workers to develop the knowledge and skills to serve the growing elderly population in the United States, especially those elderly people who belong to various racial and ethnic groups (Manuel, 1982; McNeely & Colen, 1983). Although social workers undertake multiple roles in their work with elderly people, this entry examines only practice themes related to work in the health and mental health arenas, with a focus on long-term-care issues. The unique features of working with minority elderly people are elucidated where possible to underscore cultural and situational perspectives.

## Theoretical Frameworks

Social work is unique in its historical orientation of attending to the person-in-situation context. An ecological approach that builds on this view is viable for work with aged persons because it emphasizes the elder's context, examining the dynamics that occur between elderly persons and the various systems with which they interact, whether family systems, neighborhoods, health or recreational systems, and so on (Germain & Gitterman, 1980). An ecological approach urges the professional to assess the quality of the elder person's interaction, to ask what is needed to enhance the ability of the elder to obtain the best output from that interaction, and to evaluate how the systems in this elder's environment can be changed to best benefit him or her.

Elderly people experience dramatic changes as they age: retirement, widowhood, change of living situation, different economic status, and change in health status, to name a few. The ecological theme of adaptation is the centerpiece for this framework and enables the professional to focus on how the elder adapts to these changes. The elder must learn to cope with the changes, to address the resulting circumstances and the emotional hurdles that accompany the changes. Germain and Gitterman (1980) used the term "adaptation" to refer to the ability of individuals to reach a goodness of fit with their environment or the variety of systems that affect them so that they can survive and, as much as possible, actualize. Adaptation also implies that systems must change as needed to accommodate the individual.

An ecological perspective, then, allows social workers to focus on client strengths, to search for past coping mechanisms, and to help elderly people develop new skills that will enable them to address their new context successfully. The focus on strengths thus enables clients to face problems in living with a sense of optimism and with the social worker's expectations that options can be found for problem solving. This perspective offers positive input to the elder's identity and sense of competence—two related concepts in the ecological frame. Helping elderly people feel capable and consequently feel good about who they are supports two other integral concepts, relatedness and autonomy. The ecological framework incorporates relatedness and autonomy, which revolve around the central theme of adaptation, as a way to allow the social worker to assess how they characterize the elderly client. For example, does the client present with a positive sense of identity? In what ways does this elder feel he or she is capable? Is he or she able to have meaningful and supportive relations with others? Does he or she have the capability and available options to maintain autonomy?

**Positive Identity**

Because American society places a high value on youthfulness, growing old often is experienced as evolving into a life stage that is unimportant and misperceived. As a result, aging can negatively affect the elderly person's positive identity (Ray, Raciti, & Ford, 1985). As elderly people are exposed to ageist views and sentiments, they incorporate these views, which contribute to their devalued status, weakening their sense of self (Berman-Rossi, 1991; Delon & Wenston, 1989). For minority elderly people who spent most of their lives contending with negative expectations and stereotypical perceptions about their ethnicity or race, the added burden of now having to address ageist reactions or behaviors can overwhelm their pursuit of positive identity.

**Competence**

As one's identity is challenged, there is a corresponding attack on one's sense of competence, or one's ability to interact with surrounding systems effectively. White (1974) identified the pursuit of competence as an almost innate drive that urges people to continue to learn, to risk, and to apply themselves to new pursuits as they develop and adapt.

Many non-Western cultures view elderly people as the most competent or wise members of the population because of the difficulties they have experienced during their lives (Sotomayor & Curiel, 1988). People around them seek their knowledge and counsel. In contrast, U.S. culture often devalues the older population, equating aging with senility. It is not unusual for social workers and other professionals to interact with elderly clients in a patronizing manner based on biased assumptions about their competencies (Ebener, 1992). This behavior can cause an elder to introject these perceptions and begin questioning his or her own capabilities (Berman-Rossi, 1991). As these elders begin to feel increasingly bad about themselves, they will be less inclined to feel good in their interactions with people around them; indeed, they might be inclined to forgo social interactions and thus heighten their isolation and alienation.

**Relatedness**

Relatedness is another concept integral to this framework (Germain & Gitterman, 1980). Each human being needs to reach out to others and to be reached in a meaningful way that mediates one's aloneness in this world. One component of successful aging involves social resources. As Solomon (1979) noted, an elderly person must have at least one significant other who offers an exchange of affection. To the extent that these social or emotional resources are available, an elderly client will have more options for facing life's dilemmas.

**Autonomy**

The importance of having options underpins the last concept in this framework, autonomy. All four concepts are interrelated; if one area is enhanced or ignored, the other areas will similarly be enhanced or weakened, and the elderly client's ability to adapt will be stronger or weaker. Adaptation for elderly people often is related directly to having to adjust to being less physically able, feeling weak because of an illness, having to rely on medication for the rest of their life, or having to rely on strangers for daily living needs. Thus, it appears that at every juncture, an elderly person's ability to maintain independence is threatened. Helping elderly clients accept their limitations while negotiating ways to support other areas of autonomy is a core practice need in working with this population.

Consideration of the concepts that revolve around adaptation enables social workers to assess these areas and to plan interventions to ensure that these areas are addressed as needed. For instance, in health and mental health settings, the concern with autonomy is critical: The 71-year-old woman who has broken a hip is not only concerned with the stress of being in a nursing home but will undoubtedly be fearful of her inability to care for herself and the need to rely on others. Thus, the discharge planner must consider various factors such as economic issues and nearness to family to ensure appropriate placement. However, a most important intervention is to help this elder examine her fears and anxieties related to this often-dreaded situation. Acknowledgment of the feelings, reactions, and emotional turmoil related to loss of autonomy is a major intervention that social workers can offer elderly clients in this kind of dilemma. The social worker must also strive to ensure that this elderly woman have as much input as possible to balance out the loss of autonomy in this particular area. Consequently, social workers must consciously consider how their work supports adaptation and whether and how their interventions strengthen the elderly person's identity, competence, relatedness, and sense of autonomy.

## Developmental Frameworks

Social work with elderly clients requires knowledge of what is considered healthy or successful aging. Havighurst (1963) and Neugarten (1964) viewed ongoing involvement with life, as described by activity theory, as healthy aging. Other theorists, such as Cummings, Dean, Newell, and McCaffrey (1960), promoted disengagement theory, which suggests that the aging person and society make a gradual and mutual withdrawal as a means by which society enables large groups of people to leave the work force and other social roles. Social workers must keep in mind that some of these theoretical orientations have been criticized for lack of applicability to elderly people from certain cultural groups (McNeely & Colen, 1983).

Other orientations have noted various qualities associated with successful adjustment to aging (Clark & Anderson, 1967):

- an attitude toward life that is self-accepting and cooperative, with appropriate levels of aspiration
- a realistic value of personal independence (not wanting to burden children or others), yet recognizing the limitations imposed by one's aging
- social acceptance (being congenial and interesting to others)
- resilience (handling losses and illness and accepting life's realities)
- patience with oneself and others.

Many professionals have been trained using Erikson's (1963) stage theory, which delineated one stage, integrity versus despair, as the core theme of old age. In general terms, Erikson's premise for this stage is the acceptance of one's life with all its failures, limitations, and successes as something that has to be and something for which one must take responsibility. Old age is part of the tapestry of life that all people must weave into the pattern of their existence, thereby offering motifs and perspectives from which future generations might benefit (Lowy, 1979).

In other efforts to examine the diversity of human development schemata, some theorists have attempted to specify how the development of intimacy and identity occurs differently for men and women (Jordan, Kaplan, Miller, Stiver, & Surrey, 1991). Questions are also being raised as to whether developmental axioms should rest so heavily on the individuation–separation thesis that underpins many conceptions of healthy development. As theorists undertake cross-cultural work, they acknowledge that many world cultures view healthy development as incorporating the growth of the individual within a collective context, so the range of familial closeness is different and allows for less individuation than that seen as the norm in the United States. This difference in individuation can easily be misunderstood as implying enmeshment and dysfunction. Thus, in old age, minority people who come from traditional cultures like those in Mexico, India, and Japan can have certain expectations of their role in the family and the community, expectations that can be misassessed by a professional trained with a more narrow view of development (Roland, 1988). Many Mexican elders, for example, view their family as being the center of their worldview, with related expectations of frequent contact and involvement, and could be misunderstood as being demanding and narcissistic, given the U.S. culture's clear demarcation between old and other age generations in social, recreational, and living situations.

An important specification has been the differences that elderly people experience depending on whether they are "young" elderly (65 to 84) or "old" elderly (85 and older). Solomon (1979) delineated the different life crises and associated developmental tasks that characterize each group. The life crisis for the young elderly grandmother who is confronting her first major experience with a life-threatening illness has different implications than it does for the 86-year-old great grandmother who has lived through many life-threatening problems. Moreover, the availability of resources for each elderly group will most likely differ. The older elder will probably face long-term-care needs with drained resources and greater financial demands. This awareness of potential differences among older people should push the social work practitioner to consider the special themes of both groups, using assessment as a way for making differentiations that will shape intervention processes.

In an effort to comprehend better the situation of elderly people, social work professionals can view role theory as a framework for examining the implications of the multiple role changes that elderly people experience. Some of the tenets of role theory argue that external influences determine the roles and behaviors a person will learn. Correspondingly, because the development of one's self-concept is related to such role learning, changes in self-concept will also mean changes in roles.

The saliency of this theory for the elderly population is that although older people lose many roles through retirement, widowhood, and deaths of relatives and friends, society constrains the roles they can take on. For example, society might be uncomfortable with the idea of elders taking on the role of sexual partner and expect older people to refrain from sexual behavior (Delon & Wenston, 1989). The danger is that as elderly people lose roles in a natural fashion, ageist attitudes constrain their ability to take on new roles, which affects their sense of identity. Similarly, the lack of role structure constrains social interaction that in turn contributes to isolation. Role theory enables a clinician to assess how a client views his or her status or position in society as defined by his or her roles. Does negative self-perception reflect low status and losses of roles related to old age, or does it reflect problems related to long-standing personality issues? In the former case, intervention goals can focus on new role formulations as one way to address the poor self-concept and the depression that often results (Delon & Wenston, 1989).

This abbreviated review of various theories of aging underscores the fact that the framework one selects informs and guides one's practice. The social worker's job is to become familiar with diverse perspectives for examining aging and to be equipped with theories that contribute to the individualization of each elderly client, considering the implications of gender, cohort, class, and racial–ethnic origins as well as the implications of whether the client is young-old or old-old. Moreover, given the demographic realities of the immigrant elderly population, social workers must understand unique cultural themes of aging and the stressors related to immigration and acculturation to assess the client accurately. For example, immigrant Vietnamese elders may be influenced by the grief of having relatives in their country of origin whom they have not seen in years and may never see again. The unique cultural origins of this context must be considered if intervention for depression is to be viable. Thus, these different views demand the cultivation of a substantive knowledge base if the social worker is to work effectively with elderly clients.

## Countertransference

Professionals working with elderly clients must confront the inevitable losses that accompany aging: the loss of loved ones, of physical prowess, of youthfulness, and so on. Many social workers might want to avoid confronting realities that appear depressing. In particular, the reality that we all must die is especially apparent in working with very old clients. In a culture that tends to avoid the reality (Yalom, 1980), social workers must be prepared to address the reality of death in their own lives. As Monk (1983) underscored, gerontological social work is unique in that social workers must acknowledge the reality of their own aging, the temporality of life, and the reality of death. As Yalom declared, death is a part of living, but in the United States, the tendency is to push it aside and get on with the issues of living. The paradox is that only in facing death can we face life.

Consequently, social workers will experience greater or lesser resistance to working with elderly people depending on their own experiences with death and dying. How has death been a part of their lives? Do they carry unresolved death issues with them? Have they been able to decipher meaning in dying so as to apply meaning to living? Have they examined their filial maturity or filial crisis and the countertransference themes that can be provoked in relation to their own aging parents (Lowy, 1979)? If these questions are not resolved, social workers' work with elderly clients will provoke these themes, raising issues that can be burdensome and can contribute to a reluctance to work with this age group.

Aside from these personal reactions to work with elderly people, professionals are not immune from society's ageism. Some may feel that elderly people are less useful because they no longer work (Ebener, 1992). Others may see elderly clients as less deserving of scarce societal resources as they compete for them with children and adolescents (Zuniga, 1988). Other professionals may hold the pessimistic view of "why bother with this age group; they're so close to dying, anyway." Or they may see elderly people as rigid, set in their ways, and impervious to change and may question why they should bother to work with them, especially in a mental health context (Monk, 1983). Finally, work with elderly people is not viewed as glamorous in this youth-oriented society, and gerontological workers may have low status.

In view of this variety of possible stereotypes, coupled with the stereotypes about diverse racial and cultural groups, it behooves the social worker to seek supervision and consultation to identify any unacceptable attitudes that may exist. This self-examination will need to occur regularly, because different elderly people will provoke different issues.

## Relationship Building

The critical nature of developing relationships with elderly clients sets the stage for the work to follow: conducting the assessment process, formulating the problem to be worked on, developing the treatment strategy, implementing the strategy, and terminating and evaluating the case (Beaver & Miller, 1985). The core social work skills of empathy, warmth, and genuineness (Hepworth & Larsen, 1986) must permeate the initial contact. Many elderly people are extremely distrustful of formal interventions, often fearing that their autonomy will be jeopardized. For minority elders this distrust is exacerbated from the overt discrimination that many of them experienced during the early decades of the 20th century (Zuniga-Martinez, 1980).

If the social worker can undertake some of the work in a client's home, the client's resistance might be lessened, because the professional is on the client's turf and the client is more in command. Moreover, the social worker gets an opportunity to see how the systems in the client's situation function, interact with, and affect the client. Also, working in clients' homes enables the social worker to use household artifacts such as photos and other memorabilia as a way of building a relationship with clients by asking about the celebrations, rituals, or events in their lives that are commemorated in their homes. It is not unusual to see pictures of Martin Luther King, Jr., or President John F. Kennedy in the homes of many minority elders. Asking clients to reflect on these men is an icebreaker that can hasten development of trust. If the social worker has the time, another way to build a relationship is to let the client reminisce (Zuniga, 1989); reminiscence has been especially helpful with elderly Latino people.

For workers who function as discharge planners in a hospital setting, extra time will not be available; they will have to rely on their genuineness and warmth to communicate their sincere desire to be helpful. In these instances the social worker's major contribution is his or her acknowledgment of the client's feelings as legitimate and normal.

## Communication

Relationship building uses the individualizing process as one way to connect with elderly clients. It also demands that the social worker check frequently to see whether the elderly client has really heard or understood the social worker's explanations. Often because of anxiety, hearing impairments, or language barriers, elderly clients, especially immigrants, do not always understand even the most thoroughly explained prescriptions or regimens.

Social workers are wise to use formal names in addressing elders unless an elder has given the worker permission to do otherwise. For minority elders the cultural protocol is always to use formal names because many of these people have endured embarrassing situations in which they received little respect (Zuniga, 1983). For social workers in hospital settings, where interviews often are held at a client's bedside, hovering over a client is threatening. Sitting at the client's bedside to ensure an equal level of interaction is one option. If the elder is so ill, however, that the social worker cannot communicate without leaning over the person, the social worker should ask the client to excuse the behavior and explain that he or she feels it is important to hear everything the client has to say.

Because communication is such a vital issue for elderly people who speak a limited amount of English, social workers must consider how communication channels can be improved. Are there interpreters in the agency setting who understand the intricacies of interpretation so as to ensure that the best interpretation is being made? Are there language needs of clients that are not being met? Can the social worker advocate on behalf of elderly people who could benefit from language services? Hyde (1990) noted the importance of meeting the needs of elderly people with limited English capabilities. Language issues, if unheeded, can inhibit sound health and mental health interventions.

## Mental Health Intervention

Mental health services for elderly people is a complex arena of care, a fact that contributes to underutilization. Mental health services have generally been developed without regard for the unique needs of elderly people, in particular, the need for accessibility. Moreover, many elderly people do not believe in the appropriateness of mental health intervention. Some have misconceptions about mental health care and fear they will be deemed crazy and institutionalized. Others find it difficult to view their problems as psychological in nature (Knight, 1983). Still others are not able to afford the services.

Mental health professionals generally are not trained to work with elderly people and, as already noted, may have ageist attitudes about this group. Mental health assessment and diagnosis for elderly clients require expertise about the physiology of aging as well as particular knowledge about organic diseases that can mimic mental illness processes (Knight, 1983). In addition, elderly people as a group are particularly vulnerable to affective disorders, such as depression, because of negative self-images, isolation, and loss of autonomy associated with age-related changes such as retirement, bereavement, and diminished physical capacity. Mental health professionals might confuse symptoms of depression, such as insomnia, early morning awakening, lack of appetite, and reduced energy levels, with what they interpret as "natural" aging processes (Delon & Wenston, 1989). Or they may not connect with the range of agencies and community contacts that serve elderly people in order to use these agencies for referrals or as sources of educational material that can break down the perceptual barriers surrounding mental health services. Programs such as Ventura, California's Mobile Outreach Team, are needed so that mental health services will be geographically accessible to elderly people, thereby preventing inappropriate institutionalization (Knight, 1983).

Mental health services that can be offered, even partially, in clients' homes provide opportunities for important person-in-situation assessment, giving the mental health professional a realistic view of what is available to the elder and to sort out the ambience of the elder's setting. Home visits can allay the fears of some elderly people about mental health intervention, enabling a social worker to offer services without the threat of the formal agency atmosphere and with a sense of privacy. Programs such as the Outreach Team are now considered part of the continuum of services that should characterize long-term care for elderly people.

## Long-Term Care

Social workers have broadened their view of long-term care, from perceiving it as something limited to nursing home placements to including it in both institutional and community services. In reality, elderly people who are chronically impaired might profit from care in both institutional and community settings, depending on their situation (Silverstone & Burack-Weiss, 1983). Consequently, social work practice has shifted its goals from being institutionally specific to being defined by the client's problem and needs, which can be found on different points along the continuum of care.

The ability of the elderly client to perform activities of daily living such as cooking, bathing, dressing, shopping, and managing their finances is a crucial baseline that helps define functionality and identifies areas requiring intervention by kin, friends, or formal agencies. Typically, the lack of functioning results from diseases such as Alzheimer's disease, cardiovascular conditions, arthritis, osteoporosis, and sensory impairments, to name a few (Silverstone & Burack-Weiss, 1983). Functioning is also challenged by ecological aspects, including poverty, poor housing or housing in high-crime areas, transportation barriers, isolation, depression, or anxiety, and, for culturally diverse elderly people, social and institutional discrimination.

It is not unusual that the presenting problem of an elderly client is an outcome of a cluster of issues that affect functioning and that demand multifaceted interventions. For example, a Filipino elder who is depressed and isolated may not take advantage of the local nutrition program because she lives in a high-crime area and fears for her safety. Family members who do not have the resources to move her to a safer place feel guilty about her situation. Thus, they tend to visit less often, exacerbating her depression and sense of abandonment. The social worker must rule out prior episodes of depression or physical contributions, such as the effects of medication or poor nutrition, and refer the client for a physical examination. Depression demands various intervention points to promote the needed change and to prevent escalation of illness to the level that hospitalization might be needed. Intervention includes talking about the elder's feelings, albeit in a culturally prescribed manner. It would also demand identifying housing resources and undertaking family work to improve communication among family members, thus changing familial behaviors. Intervention is multifaceted and demands not only sound mental health work with both the elder and the family but also knowledge of community resources to address the elder's various needs, for example, housing, companionship, and transportation. Thus, the mental health worker is not just operationalizing the goals of a mental health agency but is addressing the needs of an elderly person.

In addition, the mental health worker must decipher culturally appropriate interventions for this elder Filipino client. Traditional talk therapy must be managed so as to save the elder and her family from feeling ashamed—for the elder, ashamed that her family is not more available; for the family, ashamed that an outsider has to be involved in an intimate family situation. Reframing is a useful device to help clients see their dilemma from a new perspective: "I sense a lot of love in this family because you want to protect each other from hurt feelings." Use of examples of work with other families the social worker has had experience with can also be helpful. The worker can explain how the other family coped and felt, rather than ask the elder and her family to talk directly about their feelings, at least during initial work sessions.

As noted before, for elderly cohorts, mental health and talk therapy have not been part of their experience. For minority elderly people and their families, developing trust with people outside their cultural group can be a barrier to mental health intervention; moreover, talk therapy will be culturally foreign. The social worker's job is to be flexible and creative in offering mental health interventions, always keeping the focus on the particular needs of the elderly client as noted on the continuum of care.

## Health Care

A basic notion in gerontology is that the aging process is characterized by progressive and individualistic deterioration of physical health (Markides & Mindell, 1987). Consequently, aging and health issues go hand in hand. Health care is more acceptable than mental health care to the elderly because it does not carry a stigma. However, how an elder responds to health care will depend on his or her individual health history, coping experiences, and the cultural mind set he or she has toward illness and health care.

The focus here is on pharmacology, which has relevance for all elderly people, and special relevance for elderly people of color. Excessive or improper drug use among the elderly is not new and is a phenomnon that can result in misdiagnosis of symptoms, aggravation of health problems, hospitalization, and even death. People who are 65 and older constitute 12 percent of the U.S. population, yet use 25 percent to 33 percent of prescribed medications (Davison, 1973). At least 75 percent of elderly people take prescribed medication on a regular basis (Penner, 1990). Elderly people misuse drugs frequently. Underuse is a common problem and often occurs because of the prohibitive cost of drugs, the perceived harm they cause, real or imagined side effects that the client deems more unpleasant or debilitating than the original condition, or a perceived lack of benefit from a drug. About 50 percent of elderly people underuse their hypotensive medication, causing inadequate control of hypertension (Penner, 1990).

Fifteen percent of all geriatric hospital admissions can be traced to overuse of drugs or improper prescribing. Although there is a paucity of data when comparisons are made of drug misuse between elders of color and white elders, the variables of low income and lack of formal education, both of which are correlated with people of color, predict misuse (Eve, 1986).

There are multiple reasons for such medication difficulties. As Penner (1990) noted, key issues are the reality that elderly people have a high incidence of chronic disease and that medicine is a means of disease management. Moreover, the physiological decline of elderly people, and the accompanying sensory and cognitive impairments, contribute to drug misuse. For example, explanations about drug regimens are not always correctly heard, adequately explained, or clearly understood. The communication issue regarding drugs is particularly noteworthy for non-English-speaking elderly people or for those who speak only a limited amount of English.

There has been a recent growth in information about the reactions to drugs that are often found among different racial groups. Research is beginning to delineate differences in how drugs are metabolized by different groups, such as Asian Americans (Lin, Poland, & Lesser, 1986) and Latinos (Marcos & Cancro, 1982). To illustrate, Lin et al. compared Asians to Caucasians and found that the drug diazepam metabolized at a significantly slower rate for Asians. Similarly, Puerto Rican patients in another study were found to require less than half the amount of tricyclics that Anglo patients required; also, twice as many Latinos as non-Hispanic whites reported side effects that resulted from the medication (Marcos & Cancro, 1982). Some studies have found that environmental factors such as smoking and alcohol intake, as well as exposure to various drugs and toxins, have been related to faster elimination of some medications (Goth, 1981). The bulk of the studies to date have examined psychotropic medications; other studies are examining pharmacological differences among minority groups for medications used for cardiovascular disease and, specifically, hypertension (Lin et al., 1986).

Social workers must be able to assess prescription and over-the-counter drug use in elderly clients. This assessment should discern whether an elderly client comprehends how the medicine works and its relevance to his or her health. Social workers should also assess the knowledge of caretakers of elderly people. If a caretaker's knowledge about particular drug regimen of an elder is minimal, he or she could unwittingly contribute to drug abuse. An elderly client may need to be taught how to ask physicians about drugs being prescribed and to ask about drug interactions and counterindications for over-the-counter drugs, alcohol, and certain foods.

It also is incumbent on the social worker to determine whether and how an elder informs other physicians or specialists about his or her regimens. One helpful guide is to remind an elder to write out all the prescription names and dosages of the drugs being taken and share this data with his or her new physician. For some elders, it may be easier to place all their medicine bottles in a bag for a new physician to inspect the needed prescription data.

It is important to teach minority elders to ask their doctor whether it is possible to prescribe a lesser dosage level than is generally prescribed. Alternatively, the social worker can teach elderly clients to evaluate how they feel on the new medication and to report immediately any symptoms or side effects to their physicians and caretakers.

When an elder has an array of medication that must be taken daily, the social worker should assess the routine that is used to ensure that the medication regimen is followed. For example, are dosage trays used? Are reminders placed on the bathroom mirror or refrigerator door? One 72-year-old man, concerned about his forgetfulness, decided that to ensure compliance he would take all of his medication at the same time each morning. As his body became more toxic, he began having visual hallucinations. The mental health worker had difficulty making a diagnosis. The social worker's assessment of the man's medication routine revealed the problem. The man was then taught how to use egg trays to establish his weekly medicine routine and to check his tray at breakfast, lunch, and dinner to ensure that he did not forget to take his pills. The residency manager in the senior housing facility was asked to help him establish his pill trays and to monitor pill intake if possible.

The role of the social worker in medication management is a crucial one and should not be limited to medical social workers. Including an assessment of drug regimens for each elderly client will enable the social worker to discern whether this is an area where the elder needs help. The social worker can make appropriate referrals, seek information from physicians with the client's permission, and help inform caregivers or seek the aid of people in the elder's context who could be beneficial in supporting a viable medicine routine for the client. If elderly people of color are resistant to taking medication, the social worker should question whether there might be some sensitivity of the client to dosage levels or whether the client is experiencing other side effects. When the elder does not speak English, it is particularly important to assess his or her comprehension of prescription regimens and to offer educational material or to contact his or her physicians to increase knowledge about drugs and ensure appropriate drug compliance.

For Latino and Asian immigrant elderly people, who may be less acculturated, the social worker is wise to ask any whether herbal remedies are being used or whether teas or other regimens have been prescribed by a cultural specialist. It is important to ensure that nontraditional healing regimens do not conflict with western medicine regimens. Also, for an elder who is reluctant to use prescribed drugs, one device for ensuring compliance is to suggest that a culturally viable herbal tea be used in conjunction with the drug. The caveat in such a case is to seek verification from a pharmacist that no contraindications exist.

## Conclusion

Social workers who serve elderly people have an extensive body of knowledge with which they must become familiar. Working with this population demands that social workers diligently examine their attitudes about the elderly, about dying, and about the diversity they encounter within this group. This diversity implies that the social worker must individualize each elder to ascertain when and how differences should influence how the social worker will use theories and how he or she will formulate interventions. The ecological framework guides the social worker so that he or she is conscious of the theme of adaptation and of how social work interventions support viable adaptation. Adaptation will always address the concern for strengthening the identity of elders, enabling them to feel competent and to use their expertise as needed, and ensuring that they have or can develop the network of supports that will help them feel important and nurtured. Regardless of the setting or the role of the social worker, he or she must consider how social work contributes to the sense of autonomy of elders, however autonomy is culturally defined. These themes help make social work intervention a respectful and humanistic approach, because they illustrate the major strivings that all human beings undertake in their lives, beginning in their early years and lasting until they die.

## References


Austin, B., Schoenrock, S., & Roberts, J. L. (1991). *Developments in aging* (Vol. 1). Washington, DC: U.S. Government Printing Office.

Beaver, M. L., & Miller, D. (1985). *Clinical social work practice with the elderly.* Homewood, IL: Dorsey Press.

Berman-Rossi, T. (1991). Elderly in need of long-term care. In A. Gitterman (Ed.), *Handbook of social work practice with vulnerable populations* (pp. 503–548). New York: Columbia University Press.

Clark, M., & Anderson, B. (1967). *Culture and aging.* Springfield, IL: Charles C Thomas.

Cummings, E., Dean, L., Newell, D., & McCaffrey, J. (1960). Disengagement: A tentative theory of aging. *Sociometry, 23,* 23–35.

Davison, W. D. (1973). The hazards of drug treatment in old age. In J. Brocklehurst (Ed.), *Textbook of geriatric medicine and gerontology* (pp. 632–648). London: Churchill Livingston.

Delon, M., & Wenston, S. (1989). An integrated theoretical guide to intervention with depressed elderly clients. *Journal of Gerontological Social Work, 14,* 131–146.

Ebener, D. (1992). The influence of negative perceptions of aging on the delivery of rehabilitation services: Implications for rehabilitation counselor education. *Rehabilitation Education, 6,* 335–340.

Erikson, E. (1963). *Childhood and society.* New York: W. W. Norton.

Eve, S. (1986). Self-medication among older adults in the U.S. In K. Dean, T. Hickey, & B. Holstein (Eds.), *Self-care and health in old age* (pp. 204–229). London: Croom Helm.

Germain, C., & Gitterman, A. (1980). *The life model of social work practice.* New York: Columbia University Press.

Goth, A. (1981). *Medical pharmacology: Principles and concepts* (10th ed.). St. Louis: C. V. Mosby.

Havighurst, R. (1963). Successful aging. In R. Williams, C. Tibbits, & W. Donahue (Eds.), *Processes of aging* (pp. 299–320). New York: Atherton Press.

Hepworth, D., & Larsen, J. (1986). *Direct social work practice.* Belmont, CA: Wadsworth.

Hyde, J. (1990). *Language barriers and ethnic minority elderly.* San Diego: San Diego State University, University Center on Aging.

Jordan, J., Kaplan, A., Miller, J., Stiver, I., & Surrey, J. L. (1991). *Women's growth in connection: Writings from the Stone Center.* New York: Guilford Press.

Knight, B. (1983). Assessing a mobile outreach team. In M. S. Smyer & M. Gatz (Eds.), *Mental health and aging: Programs and evaluations* (pp. 23–50). Beverly Hills, CA: Sage Publications.

Lin, K., Poland, R. E., & Lesser, I. M. (1986). Ethnicity and psychopharmacology. *Culture, Medicine, and Psychiatry, 10,* 151–165.

Lowy, L. (1979). *Social work with the aging.* New York: Harper & Row.

Maldonado, D. (1987). Aged. In A. Minahan (Ed.-in-Chief), *Encyclopedia of social work* (18th ed., Vol. 1, pp. 95–106). Silver Spring, MD: National Association of Social Workers.

Manuel, R. C. (Ed.). (1982). *Minority aging: Sociological and social psychological issues.* Westport, CT: Greenwood.

Marcos, L. R., & Cancro, R. (1982). Pharmacotherapy of Hispanic depressed patients: Clinical observations. *American Journal of Psychotherapy,* 36, 505–512.

Markides, K., & Mindel, C. (1987). *Aging and ethnicity.* Newbury Park, CA: Sage Publications.

McNeely, R., & Colen, J. (1983). *Aging in minority groups.* Beverly Hills, CA: Sage Publications.

Monk, A. (1983). Social work with the aged: Principles of practice. In F. J. Turner (Ed.), *Differential diagnosis and treatment in social work* (3rd ed., pp. 129–144). New York: Free Press.

Neugarten, B. (1964). *Personality in middle age and late life: Empirical studies.* New York: Atherton.

Penner, M. (1990). Medications and the ethnic minority. In E. Stanford, S. Lockery, and S. Schoenrock (Eds.), *Ethnicity and aging: Mental health issues* (pp. 40–47). San Diego: San Diego State University, University Center on Aging.

Poth, S., & Hyde, J. (1990). *Demographic profile of the Hispanic elderly.* San Diego: San Diego State University, University Center on Aging.

Ray, D., Raciti, M., & Ford, E. (1985). Ageism in psychiatrists: Associations with gender, certification, and theoretical orientation. *The Gerontologist, 25,* 496–500.

Red Horse, J. (1990). American Indian aging: Issues in income, housing, and transportation. In *Aging and old age in diverse populations* (pp. 1–16). Washington, DC: American Association of Retired Persons.

Roland, A. (1988). *In search of self at India and Japan.* Princeton, NJ: Princeton University Press.

Silverstone, B., & Burack-Weiss, A. (1983). The social work function in nursing homes and home care. In G. S. Getzel & M. J. Mellor (Eds.), *Gerontological social work practice in long-term care* (pp. 7–34). New York: Haworth Press.

Solomon, R. (1979). *Curriculum design in aging.* Unpublished doctoral dissertation, Hunter College, School of Social Work, New York.

Sotomayor, M., & Curiel, H. (Eds.). (1988). *Hispanic elderly: A cultural signature.* Edinburg, TX: Pan American University Press.

U.S. Bureau of the Census. (1988). *The Hispanic population in the United States: March 1988* (Population Characteristics Series P-20, No. 431). Washington, DC: U.S. Government Printing Office.

U.S. Bureau of the Census. (1989). *Projections of the population of the United States, by age, sex, and race: 1988–2080* (Current Population Series P-25, No. 1019). Washington, DC: U.S. Government Printing Office.

U.S. Bureau of the Census. (1994). *Characteristics of American Indians by tribe and language.* Washington, DC: U.S. Government Printing Office.

U.S. Department of Health and Human Services. (1990). *Elder facts: The growth of America in the early 1980s.* Washington, DC: U.S. Government Printing Office.

U.S. Senate Special Committee on Aging. (1990). *Developments in aging: 1989* (Vol. 1, Report 101-249). Washington, DC: U.S. Government Printing Office.

White, R. (1974). Strategies of adaptation: An attempt at systematic description. In G. Coelho, D. Hamburg, &

J. Adams (Eds.), *Coping and adaptations* (pp. 47–68). New York: Basic Books.

Yalom, I. (1980). *Existential psychotherapy.* New York: Basic Books.

Zuniga, M. (1983). Social treatment with the minority elderly. In R. L. McNeely & J. Colen (Eds.), *Aging in minority groups* (pp. 260–269). Beverly Hills, CA: Sage Publications.

Zuniga, M. (1988). Latinos and aging policy: Integration perspective. *Generations, 12,* 68–71.

Zuniga, M. (1989). Mexican American elderly and reminiscence: Interventions. *Journal of Gerontological Social Work, 14,* 61–74.

Zuniga-Martinez, M. (1980). *Los ancianos: A study of the attitudes of Mexican Americans regarding support of the elderly.* Unpublished doctoral dissertation, Brandeis University.

## Further Reading

Asante, M. K., & Gudy Kunst, W. B. (Eds.). (1989). *Handbook of international and intercultural communication.* Newbury Park, CA: Sage Publications.

Brislin, R. W., Cushner, K., Cherrie, C., & Mong, M. (1986). *Intercultural interactions: A practical guide.* Beverly Hills, CA: Sage Publications.

Devore, W., & Schlesinger, E. (1987). *Ethnic sensitive social work practice.* Columbus, OH: Charles E. Merrill.

Fawcett, J. T., & Carino, B. V. (Eds.). (1987). *Pacific bridges: The new immigration from Asia and the Pacific Islands.* New York: Center for Migration Studies.

Ho, M. K. (1987). *Family therapy with ethnic minorities.* Beverly Hills, CA: Sage Publications.

Stanford, E. P., & Lockery, S. A. (Eds.). (1983). *Minority aging and long-term care: Proceedings of the 9th Institute on Minority Aging.* San Diego: Campanile Press, San Diego State University.

**Maria E. Zuniga, PhD,** is professor, San Diego State University, School of Social Work, San Diego, CA 92182.

### For further information see

Adult Day Care; Adult Foster Care; Aging Overview; Aging: Direct Practice; Aging: Public Policy Issues and Trends; Aging: Services; Assessment; Ecological Perspective; Elder Abuse; End-of-Life Decisions; Ethnic-Sensitive Practice; Family Caregiving; Long-Term Care; Natural Helping Networks; Poverty; Public Social Services; Social Security; Women Overview.

**Key Words**

aged
ethnic-sensitive practice
social work practice

# Aid to Families with Dependent Children

**Mimi Abramovitz**

During the Great Depression of the 1930s, Congress enacted Aid to Dependent Children (ADC). After rejecting broader proposals that would have covered all poor children, regardless of the structure of the families in which they lived, Congress made ADC part of the Social Security Act of 1935 (Bell, 1965). ADC provided financial assistance to children who lacked support or care because of the absence, incapacity, or, under certain conditions, unemployment of a parent. Renamed Aid to Families with Dependent Children (AFDC) in 1962, the program's goals include strengthening family life and self-support. Although either parent can apply for AFDC, historically the overwhelming majority of adult recipients have been mothers. AFDC began as a program to enable single mothers to remain at home, but the record shows that societal ambivalence about single mothers has resulted in policies that contradict this objective.

## Joint Federal–State Administration

With the passage of the Social Security Act of 1935, the federal government assumed responsibility for providing a minimal level of economic support to many individuals and families in the United States. The landmark legislation contained two approaches to economic security: social insurance and public assistance. The two social insurance programs, Old Age Insurance and Unemployment Compensation, were universal, nonstigmatized, and popular, unlike the original means-tested public assistance programs—Old Age Assistance, Aid to the Blind, ADC, and Aid to the Permanently and Totally Disabled, which was added in 1950. In 1974 all the public assistance titles, except the highly controversial AFDC program, were consolidated into a federal income support program known as Supplemental Security Income (SSI). Although AFDC programs today exist in all 50 states, the District of Columbia, Guam, Puerto Rico, and the Virgin Islands, participation by the states remains voluntary (U.S. House of Representatives, 1992). AFDC is administered at the federal level by the U.S. Department of Health and Human Services (DHHS).

AFDC and other public assistance programs, also called categorical relief or grant-in-aid programs, are jointly administered and funded by the federal government and the states. To receive federal funds, a state must meet the requirements of the Social Security Act. One such requirement is that the state develop a plan that outlines its compliance with federal AFDC standards. This plan becomes a contract between the state and the federal government. Within broad federal guidelines, each state sets its own standards of need, benefit levels, income limits, and administrative patterns. In addition, states can decide whether to assist pregnant women, to condition eligibility on the "suitability" of the home, to count food stamps and housing subsidies as income when calculating the AFDC grant, to require that unmarried parents under age 18 and their children live with a parent or guardian, or to provide aid to children over age 18 who are in school (U.S. Department of Health and Human Services, 1991; U.S. House of Representatives, 1992). To experiment with programs that are not in accordance with federal rules, states must receive a federal waiver. Despite many federal requirements, states have considerable and decisive control over the design of their AFDC programs. With this autonomy comes room for administrative discretion and discrimination (Trattner, 1989). Over the years, states' rights arguments have sometimes given license to antiwelfare and racist social policies.

## Funding and Spending

In 1993 federal and state funding for AFDC totaled $25.2 billion, up from $21.2 billion in 1990 and $16.5 billion in 1985 (U.S. House of Representatives, 1994). The federal share of the 1993 total equaled $14.7 billion, about 1 percent of the total federal budget of $1,408 billion. In 1991 AFDC expenditures, including federal contributions to the states, accounted for 3.4 percent of the average state's total budget. Of the expenditures financed by the average state's revenues, AFDC costs made up only 2 percent of the budget (Center on Budget and Policy Priorities, 1992). Annual increases for AFDC reflect inflation, population growth, programmatic changes, the business cycle, long-term trends in the economy, and the political climate. Although the AFDC program absorbs fewer public dollars than is popularly perceived, its cost has sparked controversy and frequently is a lightning rod for those who are opposed to all social welfare spending.

Except for Guam, Puerto Rico, and the Virgin Islands, the AFDC program is funded through an open-ended federal appropriation to the states that is drawn from income tax dollars. The current reimbursement rate (subject to change every two years) ranges from 50 percent to almost 80 percent of benefit costs and 50 percent for administrative and staff-training costs. Some states require localities to finance some of the nonreimbursed costs. Because federal reimbursement rates vary inversely with the per capita income of the states, poorer states, many of which are in the South, receive proportionately more federal funds than do wealthier states, which tend to be in the North (U.S. House of Representatives, 1992).

The AFDC dollar pays for both benefits and administrative costs. Of the $25.2 billion spent in 1993, 88 percent went for benefits and 12 percent went for administration. This pattern has remained relatively constant since the early 1970s, contrary to the popular belief that administrative costs absorb a disproportionate amount of AFDC expenditures (U.S. House of Representatives, 1994).

## Eligibility

AFDC eligibility rules determine who receives aid. They emphasize family composition, income level, age of the children, and the applicant's willingness to participate in a welfare-to-work program and to cooperate with the welfare department to obtain paternity and child support. To qualify for assistance, a child in a single-parent household must be deprived of support because the parent is deceased, continually absent from the home, or suffering a mental or physical incapacity that is expected to last more than 30 days.

### Unemployed Parent Program

Under certain limited conditions, a two-parent family can receive aid if the principal earner is unemployed. To be classified as unemployed, an AFDC parent must work fewer than 100 hours a month, have a work history, and meet a host of other requirements. Qualifying families receive aid under the smaller Unemployed Parent program (AFDC-UP). Enacted in 1962, AFDC-UP existed in only 28 states until it became mandatory under the 1988 Family Support Act. In 1993 AFDC-UP served 359,000 families and 1.4 million individuals in an average month. As states try out more flexible definitions of unemployment, the AFDC-UP program may grow (U.S. House of Representatives, 1994).

### Means Test

In addition to being without parental support, AFDC applicants must pass two income, or means, tests to qualify for aid. Federal law stipulates that a family's total income before any deductions must be less than 185 percent of the state's need standard and that income after deductions must not exceed 100 percent of the state's need standard (Larin & Porter, 1992). Because need standards are low, only the poorest of poor people become eligible for AFDC.

### Age of Children

The age of children also determines a family's eligibility for AFDC. The program serves children from birth (although many states now assist pregnant mothers) until their 18th birthdays, or, at a state's option, their 19th birthdays for full-time students. When the youngest child reaches age 18 (age 19 if the child is in school), a family's benefits cease. For AFDC mothers who are too young to collect social security or are not eligible for SSI, this juncture can be disruptive because there are no state or federal income support programs for able-bodied adults under age 62 with no children in the home. Only some states offer local assistance, which in most cases is meager. If the AFDC mother is ill or lacks work skills, serious financial hardship can result.

Federal law also requires AFDC mothers to cooperate with the state in establishing the paternity of a nonmarital child, obtaining child support payments, and assigning support rights to the state. Welfare reform proposals by both Democrats and Republicans in late 1994 sought to make child support procedures more stringent. Child support payments that are less than the AFDC grant go directly to the government, and the mother receives $50 in addition to her regular AFDC check (U.S. House of Representatives, 1992).

### Other Requirements

As of October 1, 1990, all nonexempt able-bodied AFDC recipients whose youngest child is at least age three (one year in some states) are required to participate in the Job Opportunity and Basic Skills (JOBS) program established by the 1988 Family Support Act. They must enter an educational, job training, or employment program or face the reduction or loss of benefits. If Congress passes the Democratic or Republican proposals made in late 1994, these work rules may be tightened by the imposition of a lifetime limit on AFDC recipiency. Since the early 1990s, some states have conditioned eligibility on the AFDC applicants' marital, childbearing, and parenting status, as well as work behavior. Similar proposals appear in President Clinton's 1994 welfare reform proposals as well as other bills introduced in Congress.

## Standard of Need

The Social Security Act of 1935 requires each state to establish a standard of need but remains silent on its definition. Although the standard is a benchmark against which the adequacy of state AFDC programs can be measured, federal guidelines stipulate only that a state's standard must be objective, equitable, monetary, and uniformly applied. Federal regulations define the need standard as "the money value assigned by the State to the basic and special needs it recognizes as essential for applicants and recipients [of AFDC benefits]" (quoted in Larin & Porter, 1992, p. 1).

### Basis for Standards

The need standard, which determines both the number of AFDC cases and benefits levels, is central to the AFDC reicipient's quality of life. In most states the need standard includes the cost of all basic needs such as food, clothing, shelter, utilities, personal care items, and household maintenance supplies. Half the states include transportation, and one-quarter include educational expenses, medicine chest supplies, and household equipment. Even fewer include such items as a telephone, insurance premiums, or the repair of household equipment (U.S. Department of Health and Human Services, 1991).

Most states calculate the need standard using the federal poverty line or the results of local market-basket surveys. The states prefer a low standard because it reduces the welfare rolls, benefit levels, and costs. Not all states actually make payments equal to the standard because federal law neither defines the kind or number of items to be used in the calculation of the standard nor requires states to use current prices in setting the standard. The federal government last required states to update their standards in 1969 (U.S. Department of Health and Human Services, 1991).

The standard of need for a three-person family ranges from a high of $1,648 a month in New Hampshire to a low of $320 a month in Indiana (U.S. House of Representatives, 1994). In most states, the standard of need falls far below the cost of living (Larin & Porter, 1992). From July 1970 to January 1992, the median need standard for all states rose from $232 a month to $579 a month, or 149 percent. During the same period, however, the consumer price index (CPI) jumped 275 percent (U.S. House of Representatives, 1994). Although the 1988 Family Support Act called for states to reevaluate their need standards at least once every three years and to report their findings to DHHS, the reporting requirement was subsequently dropped (Larin & Porter, 1992).

## Benefits

In 1993 the average AFDC benefit payment for a three-person family in current dollars (not adjusted for inflation) was $373 per month, up from $178 in 1970. But benefits vary widely by state. The average payment for a family of three ranged from a low of $120 in Mississippi to a high of $762 in Alaska (U.S. House of Representatives, 1994). In all but two states, average benefits for a family of three fell below the nation's median standard of need of $579 per month. This figure falls below the cost of living. AFDC families may also receive Medicaid, food stamps, and housing subsidies, although a few states deduct the value of food stamps and housing grants from AFDC payments.

Despite the increase in average benefits from 1970 to January 1993, benefit levels failed to keep pace with inflation. The purchasing power of the payment actually plummeted 47 percent. Although food stamps offset some of the loss, only in Alaska and Hawaii did the AFDC and food stamp package lift a family of three above the 1993 poverty line. In Mississippi, the lowest benefit state, the package equaled only 43 percent of this measure, which is widely viewed to be understated (U.S. House of Representatives, 1994).

AFDC recipients and supporters have consistently called for a national minimum benefit to eliminate inequities among the states and to make the grant more adequate. This proposal appeared in an early version of the 1988 Family Support Act but did not survive the political process. Welfare rights advocates have also challenged the states in court for the failure of AFDC benefits to match need standards. But even when judges have declared that AFDC or general assistance benefits and need standards are too low, these court victories have not resulted in higher benefits.

## AFDC Caseload

The controversies surrounding AFDC reflect deep concerns about the program's size, composition, and cost. It is widely assumed that the program is constantly growing, and the growth is typically blamed on the work, marital, and childbearing behavior of AFDC recipients. Government data suggest, however, that the AFDC program has expanded and contracted largely in response to the growth in the population (which exerts a constant upward pressure on the program), the condition of the economy, and programmatic changes. The data further suggest that growth is not as rapid or extreme as AFDC debates imply. Other analyses suggest that the AFDC program expands and contracts in response to levels of political pressure and grassroots turbulence (Epsing-Anderson, 1990; Orloff, 1993; Piven & Cloward, 1971).

### Size of Caseload

As an entitlement program, AFDC must serve all eligible people. Thus, the changes in its size reflect a variety of changes that can make more or fewer people eligible for the program. The number of AFDC families rose more than 50 percent from 1971 to 1981, when it reached a high of 3.9 million. But from 1981 to 1989, the number of recipients fell, despite a nearly 30 percent increase in the number of U.S. families and rising rates of poverty, divorce, female-headed families, and births to unmarried mothers (U.S. House of Representatives, 1992). The AFDC rolls were smaller during the 1980s as a result of cuts in benefits, which determined income limits, other program restrictions that countered expansionary pressures, and an anti-AFDC political climate. From 1988 to 1993 AFDC experienced a new growth spurt because of the overall deterioration of the economy, new policies such as the Immigration Reform and Control Act of 1986, and the erosion of unemployment insurance benefits (Congressional Budget Office, 1991). Economists project continued but slower growth for the rest of the 1990s.

The number of AFDC recipients declined as a proportion of the total U.S. population by more than half a percent from the mid-1970s to 1989, when the number reached a low of 4.38 percent. In 1992 the number of AFDC recipients rose to 5.3 percent of the population but remained below the levels of the early 1970s (U.S. House of Representatives, 1994). Whereas 5.3 percent of the population received AFDC benefits, some 49 percent of all people in the United States received some type of direct government payment. In addition, other working and middle-class families claimed indirect governmental subsidies through deductions for dependents, housing, health care, and education that are built into the tax code (Abramovitz, 1983; Wines, 1994).

### Size of Families

Of the 13.6 million AFDC recipients in 1992, more than two-thirds (9.2 million) were children. These children accounted for 14 percent of the U.S. population under age 18 and 63 percent of the children in poverty. In 1970 children on AFDC represented 8.8 percent of all children and 58 percent of all poor children (U.S. House of Representatives, 1994).

Although many observers assume that AFDC encourages childbearing and large families, the average AFDC family consists of three persons, the national average. Welfare families have become smaller, following the national decline in family size. In 1992, 73 percent of AFDC families had two or fewer children compared to 49 percent in 1969. Likewise, only 10 percent had four or more children in 1992, down from 32.5 percent in 1969

(Duvall, 1987; U.S. House of Representatives, 1994). These trends confirm years of empirical research that have found little or no relationship between AFDC benefits and the childbearing decisions of poor women (Moffitt, 1991).

### Nonmarital Births

Critics also attribute the rising rate of nonmarital births to the availability of AFDC. But studies have suggested otherwise. Williams (1992), for example, noted that all the mothers who were surveyed said that the ability to receive AFDC had no effect on their decision to have a child. Studies from the mid-1970s found that women who were on welfare were less likely to refrain from using contraceptives, less likely to desire an additional pregnancy, and less likely to become pregnant than were women who were not on public assistance (Wilson & Neckerman, 1986). Trend data have also tended to confirm that there is no conclusive association between the receipt of welfare and nonmarital births (Jencks & Edin, 1990; Moffitt, 1991; Wilson & Neckerman, 1986).

The rate of births to teenage mothers in the United States, although still high by international standards, fell from 90.3 births per 1,000 women aged 15 to 19 in 1955 to 50.6 in 1986, years that included the greatest increase in AFDC recipients. In contrast, from 1986 to 1990, as the real value of AFDC benefits fell, the rates of births by teenage mothers and the number of mother-only families rose (Moore, 1992). Nor do states with higher benefits have higher nonmarital birthrates or teenage birthrates (Moore, 1992; Shapiro, Gold, Sheft, Strawn, Summer, & Greenstein, 1991; Wilson & Neckerman, 1986). Finally, despite their more generous welfare benefits, European countries have far lower teenage pregnancy rates than does the United States (Smeeding, 1991).

### AFDC and Family Breakup

Studies of welfare and family composition have concluded that AFDC is not a major force in the breakup of U.S. families. Ellwood and Bane (1985) reported that from 1968 to 1980, almost half the AFDC awards started either after married women were separated or widowed—conditions that plunged them into poverty—or after unmarried childless women gave birth. A U.S. Bureau of the Census (1992) report stated that a fall into poverty significantly increases the chances that a two-parent family will break up. Only after the family breaks up is the mother–child unit eligible for AFDC. This report confirmed the results of studies conducted during the 1970s and 1980s, which found that welfare benefits have little or no consistent effect on marital breakup (Moffitt, 1991; Wilson & Neckerman, 1986). Time-series data have also failed to find a fixed relationship between welfare and family structure.

### Trapped on Welfare

The length of time that families stay on welfare is a controversial subject, evoking stereotypic images of the lazy freeloader who consistently chooses welfare over work. But researchers have found that whereas some families spend many years on welfare, others spend only a few (Bane & Ellwood, 1983). Evaluations of time spent on welfare vary with the unit of time used in the research. Looking at the welfare rolls at one moment in time, researchers found that two-thirds of the recipients had been on AFDC for eight or more years. But when these same researchers studied an entire year, they found that 50 percent of the recipients had been on welfare for four or fewer years and that 30 percent had been on welfare for fewer than two years (U.S. House of Representatives, 1994). Another study that used monthly, rather than annual, data found that 70 percent of AFDC recipients received payments for two years or less. Only 7 percent stayed on welfare for more than eight years (Pavetti, 1993).

Research on whether many families stay on the program across generations has been inconclusive. Although daughters of welfare mothers are more likely than are daughters of nonrecipients to use welfare as adults, the findings are mixed as to the number of welfare daughters who turn to AFDC later on. McLanahan and Garfinkel (1989) found one study that reported that as many as 50 percent to 70 percent of welfare daughters used welfare for at least one year within seven years of leaving home; another study found that only 36 percent of welfare daughters did so. The numbers of welfare daughters are higher for African Americans than for white people and higher for unmarried women than for divorced women (McLanahan & Garfinkel, 1989). Because most studies did not control for confounding variables, even when the intergenerational use of welfare is high, it is not clear whether the cause is welfare, poverty, or something else (U.S. House of Representatives, 1993).

### Racial Composition

In 1992, 38.9 percent of all AFDC families were white, 37.2 percent were African American, and 17.8 percent were Latino; the remaining 6.2 percent were Asian, Native American, or other races, or their race was unknown (U.S. House of Representatives, 1994). The racial composition of the AFDC caseload varies widely by state, ranging from 0.8 percent white in Washington, DC, to 98.2 percent white in Maine (U.S. House of Representatives,

1994). In the nine states that serve more than 100,000 AFDC families, the proportion of white families who were AFDC recipients ranged from a low of 18.1 percent in Texas to a high of 58.4 percent in Ohio (Center on Budget and Policy Priorities, 1992).

Because of persistent racial discrimination in all spheres of American life, African Americans are overrepresented among poor people receiving AFDC relative to their number in the total population (Hacker, 1992). In 1990 about 50 percent of African American and Latino female-headed families with children under age 18 received AFDC, compared to about 24 percent of similar white families (Congressional Budget Office, 1991). But from 1983 to 1992, even though the number of African American female-headed families with children grew faster than the number of such white families nationwide, the percentage of the AFDC caseload that was African American dropped from 43.8 percent to 37.2 percent. The percentage that was white fell from 41.8 percent to 38.9 percent. The increase in AFDC families during this period took place among Latinos, Native Americans, and Asians, who still constitute a smaller proportion of AFDC recipients than do African Americans or whites (Duvall, 1987; U.S. House of Representatives, 1994).

## History of AFDC

### Mother's Pensions

The AFDC program dates back to the 1909 White House Conference on the Care of Dependent Children, which recommended that children of "worthy" mothers who were deprived of the support of breadwinners should be kept with their parents and given aid "as may be necessary to maintain suitable homes for the rearing of children" (Abramovitz, 1992, p. 7). The resulting Mother's Pensions were to be a step above relief for widows and their children and a means of reducing the mounting cost of institutionalizing children, many of whom were in orphanages only because their parents could not support them.

From 1911 to 1920, 40 states enacted Mother's Pension laws in a movement spearheaded largely by women reformers. By 1935, all but two states had such laws. But because implementation was optional, fewer than half the counties nationwide actually offered a pension before the passage of the Social Security Act of 1935. Those that did tended to reserve the grants for the "deserving" poor: those who passed a test of moral conduct as well as financial need. As a reflection of prevailing attitudes toward race and gender, most recipients of Mother's Pensions were widowed and white. Only a few states aided deserted, divorced, or unmarried mothers or women of color (Bell, 1965). Despite the program's intent to help mothers stay home, most "pensioned" mothers worked for wages as well because they could not subsist on the meager benefits. Mother's Pensions became the philosophical and operational model for the Aid to Dependent Children program that was added to the Social Security Act of 1935.

### Social Security Act of 1935

The deterioration of the economy, mounting social unrest, and massive unemployment during the Great Depression forced President Franklin Delano Roosevelt and Congress to enact the Social Security Act in 1935—six years after the 1929 stock market crash. The act was part of a larger effort to stimulate purchasing power, stabilize the political economy, mute social unrest, and maintain the legitimacy of the government. By shifting social welfare responsibilities from the states to the federal government, this landmark legislation launched the modern U.S. welfare state, albeit much later than in most other Western industrial nations.

The needs of women were not a high priority for the architects of the Social Security Act. The original act covered only retired workers, most of whom were men. The men's nonemployed wives and children were not insured until the act was amended in 1939 to include benefits for workers' survivors and dependents. Although many African American women worked for wages in 1935, they, along with many African American men, were virtually excluded from the act, which for many years did not cover farm laborers, domestic servants, and those engaged in other occupations that were then filled largely by African American women and men.

An initial version of the legislation had mandated that families should be furnished with subsistence "compatible with health and decency." But Congress struck the language when southern legislators protested that this national criteria would impose northern standards on the South and thus disrupt the latter's lower wage scales for mostly African American tenant farmers (Bell, 1965). Southern legislators also succeeded in defeating provisions that would have required states to provide relief to any citizen who met the criteria of age and need (Abbott, 1938). Policies that similarly excluded disadvantaged African Americans existed in other New Deal programs, such as the National Recovery Act (1933), the Agricultural Adjustment Act (1933), and the Fair Labor Standards Act (1938).

The Social Security Act also categorized some women as deserving of aid and others as undeserving of aid. On the basis of an idealized image of womanhood, the act's programs favored women who were married, previously married, or lacked breadwinners through no fault of their own (for example, through illness, disability, death, or temporary unemployment) over single mothers, abandoned wives, and women whose breadwinners did not provide adequate support. The "undeserving" women tended to be poor, immigrants, or women of color whose poverty and other life circumstances prevented them from following the idealized mainstream version of wives and motherhood (Abramovitz, 1992).

The categorization of women as deserving or undeserving of aid based on standard definitions of women's roles deeply influenced the development of the AFDC program. Were poor women who applied for income support "proper" women who would provide "good" care for their children, or were they "deviants" who should be penalized for violating work and family norms? If not for the women's network (which included Eleanor Roosevelt), AFDC might never have become part of the Social Security Act. Poor mothers were a special concern of this group, which had already fought for and won Mother's Pensions (1911–1920), the Children's Bureau (1912), the Sheppard–Towner Act (1921), and positions in the Roosevelt administration (Muncy, 1991; Ware, 1981; Witte, 1963). Unfortunately, many of the early reformers were products of their times and accepted the prevailing views of "worthy" and "unworthy" women that continue to shape AFDC policy today.

### AFDC: 1935 to 1980

From the start, the AFDC program penalized women for departing from the prescribed roles of wife and mother. The states took longer to implement AFDC than other public assistance programs and set benefits well below those for elderly and blind recipients. The AFDC grant included funds for children but not their mothers until 1950, forcing many women to work outside the home. Beginning in 1939 the survivors' insurance component of the Social Security program absorbed the families of widows and divorced women, leaving AFDC to be used mostly by unmarried women. In the early 1940s many states, mostly in the South, refused to extend aid to African American women, so that employers would be supplied with field hands and domestic workers.

By the 1950s, as a result of a variety of complex social, economic, and demographic changes, never-married mothers and African American women were overrepresented on the AFDC rolls (Trattner, 1989). The African American caseload grew because of poverty, the dislocations following the mechanization of southern agriculture (which forced more than 20 million people off the land between 1940 and 1970), and the subsequent employment discrimination in both the North and the South. In the late 1950s the changing and expanding caseload, combined with McCarthyism, fueled another harsh attack on public welfare, especially AFDC (Axinn & Levin, 1982).

***Behavioral standards.*** Reflecting prevailing views that most African American and many poor families were by definition "immoral," state welfare departments intensified their use of behavioral standards as a condition of aid (Myrdal, 1944). "Man-in-the-house" and "suitable-home" rules, which equated unmarried motherhood with unfit motherhood, were used by about half the states by 1960 to deny AFDC to thousands of poor mother-only families. Under pressure from the civil rights and welfare rights movements in the early 1960s, the federal government eventually limited, but did not disallow, the use of these moral fitness rules. Bell (1965) suggested that the mounting hostility toward AFDC during the years following World War II, and some of its virulence, was partly a backlash against the growing strength of the civil rights movement.

***Services and work incentives.*** The postwar poverty and new social problems increased the demand for welfare (Ehrenreich, 1985). Faced with larger welfare rolls and unable to make "immoral" behavior a condition of aid, the states began to consider work programs and social services as an alternative way to reduce the welfare rolls. The 1956 amendments to the Social Security Act promised new social services in the hope that counseling would help people leave welfare for work, but the funds were not appropriated. The 1962 amendments to the Social Security Act were influenced by the social work profession and came to be called the "social service" amendments because they authorized federal funds for counseling and employment services, created the AFDC-UP program (for a limited group of unemployed fathers), loosened criteria for eligibility, and, for the first time, allowed AFDC recipients to keep a portion of their earned income as a work incentive. The shift to services and work incentives did not redress the "welfare crisis." The rolls continued to grow because of inadequate funding for the promised services, the lack of child care services, administrative barriers, and the serious misdiagnosis of what led to poverty and the use of welfare.

Critics blamed mounting poverty and rising welfare costs on the never fully implemented "soft" social services and the behavior of poor people. The perceived failure of social services to lower the welfare rolls and a growing punitive attitude toward poor people produced new interest in "hard" work requirements. Billed as an innovation, AFDC's low benefits and strict eligibility rules had operated since 1935 as an informal, if unacknowledged, work requirement. In the mid-1960s, Congress began to experiment with formal work rules, such as work incentives and the Community Work Experience Program—a harbinger of "workfare."

***Work Incentive Program.*** By 1967, in the wake of urban uprisings, AFDC policy became more punitive. The 1967 amendments to the Social Security Act reintroduced behavioral standards as a condition of aid by imposing a freeze on the number of deserted and "illegitimate" children who could receive AFDC. The freeze, which covered children of never-married women but not those of deceased or unemployed fathers, was too politically controversial to be implemented. But the amendment's Work Incentive Program (WIN) was put into place.

With WIN, participation in a work program became a condition of aid. Nonexempt welfare mothers were required to enter a job-training or work-placement program with the promise of help with child care, employment, and social services. WIN II, enacted in 1971, added more punitive sanctions for nonparticipation. By all accounts, the WIN program was a dismal failure. It placed too few women in jobs, was too costly, and was plagued by administrative flaws, inadequate child care services, numerous labor market barriers, and a host of other problems similar to those faced today by the 1988 Family Support Act (Rein, 1982). In 1977 President Jimmy Carter unsuccessfully attempted another major welfare reform program—the Program for Better Jobs and Income—which included work incentives, strict work rules, a public works program, and differential treatment for deserving and undeserving poor persons (Handler & Hasenfeld, 1991).

**Welfare Reforms from Reagan to Clinton**

Despite the failure of work programs, work-oriented welfare reform became the hallmark of the Reagan administration, which promoted economic recovery by redistributing income from the have-nots to the haves. Seeking to increase profits by lowering wages, reducing the overall standard of living, and weakening the influence of trade unions, the Reagan administration launched an attack on unions, the minimum wage, and the welfare state. To make sure that people chose low-paid jobs over welfare, it was necessary to lower social benefits. The Omnibus Budget Reconciliation Act of 1981 cut domestic programs, strengthened AFDC work requirements, and encouraged states to bear more responsibility for social welfare. The Deficit Reduction Act of 1984 reversed some of the more restrictive AFDC provisions but left the basic package intact (U.S. House of Representatives, 1992).

***Family Support Act.*** The 1988 Family Support Act, especially JOBS, transformed AFDC from a program to help single mothers stay home with their children into a mandatory work program. Reminiscent of earlier efforts, JOBS requires mothers to go to work or school or to enter a job-training program in exchange for benefits, employment, education, and social services. Welfare mothers who refuse to participate face the reduction or termination of benefits. Like its predecessors, the JOBS program has foundered because of rising unemployment, the proliferation of low-paid jobs, sex and racial discrimination in the labor market, the lack of health benefits, the absence of affordable child care, and too little investment in the program's service component (Riccio & Friedlander, 1992; U.S. General Accounting Office [GAO], 1987, 1991). The JOBS program also suffers from a lack of state funds; a host of other implementation problems (Hagen & Lurie, 1992); and the poor health, limited education, and presence of young children at home that makes employment difficult for many women on welfare (GAO, 1987, 1991).

***Other reforms.*** The 1988 Family Support Act legitimated the use of government funds to leverage behavioral change and paved the way for a second round of welfare reform focused on the marital, childbearing, and parenting behavior of poor women. Arguing that welfare induces irresponsible or deviant behavior, state and federal legislators have supported various initiatives designed to promote "family values" and to get women off welfare by giving them incentives to marry, limit their family size, and improve their parenting. Seemingly benign, the family cap denies aid for children conceived or born while the mother is on AFDC.

Some states reward marriage by overriding existing AFDC rules that deem a stepparent's income as being available to the family. The override granted to stepparents is denied to mothers who marry the biological father of their children on the grounds that fathers, unlike stepparents, are, by definition, responsible for providing support. Other states have considered making the use of Norplant, a long-lasting contraceptive implant, a condition of aid. Two other "reforms"—Learnfare and Healthfare—use government dollars to regulate parenting. An ever-growing number of states across the nation have applied for and secured federal approval to implement Learnfare and Healthfare programs. The idea has also appeared in federal welfare reform bills. Learnfare reduces AFDC benefits for any child who fails to meet specified requirements to attend school, and Healthfare docks the checks of families who fail to immunize their children in a timely fashion. Finally, some states with higher benefits have tried unsuccessfully to deny full benefits to families that have moved from states with low-benefits.

"Reforms" such as these have gained ground despite two decades of programmatic failures (Rein, 1982); 20 years of research showing that the receipt of welfare has little or no relationship to decisions regarding work, marriage, and childbearing (Moffitt, 1991); and evaluations of welfare-to-work programs that have found that such programs result in only modest gains (Riccio & Friedlander, 1992). The 1994 welfare reform proposals made by President Clinton and in the Republican Contract With America intensify existing work rules with limits on welfare uses, strict paternity rules, and severe family caps. The proposals also include plans to decentralize AFDC and a host of other entitlement programs, thereby undermining the underlying principle of the modern welfare state in the United States.

The failure of policymakers to consider either the poor history of coercive measures or the large body of research showing that the configuration of welfare benefits does not shape women's work, marital, or parenting decisions suggests that the current assault on AFDC, like previous ones in the 19th and 20th centuries, may serve political rather than social welfare ends. These include legitimizing the work ethic (Piven & Cloward, 1971), punishing women who are viewed as departing from prescribed wife and mother roles (Abramovitz, 1992), keeping welfare benefits lower than prevailing wages (Cloward & Piven, 1993), creating the impression that the government is doing something about poverty (Handler & Hasenfeld, 1991), and deflecting attention from the underlying causes of the nation's mounting economic distress and the real causes of the frayed social fabric.

## Alternative Approaches

Most of the major welfare reforms since the 1970s have focused on encouraging or forcing AFDC mothers to work. But Congress has periodically considered the negative income tax—a more positive alternative. In 1969 President Richard M. Nixon introduced the Family Assistance Plan, which offered a $1,600 minimum annual income for families of four (about 45 percent of the prevailing poverty level), allowed the recipients to keep other government benefits, and provided some fiscal relief for the states. Proposed by a conservative president and designed for families with children regardless of the family head's employment status, the Family Assistance Plan was ultimately defeated because of liberal opposition to its low minimum grant and conservative fears that a guaranteed income would undercut the supply of low-wage workers and blur the line between the deserving and undeserving poor (Handler & Hasenfeld, 1991).

### Earned Income Tax Credit

In 1975 Congress enacted the earned income tax credit (EITC)—a wage subsidy for the working, not the welfare, poor. The credit, which refunds 10 percent of earned income up to $8,000, was originally proposed as a "work bonus" to offset social security taxes paid by low-wage workers (Handler & Hasenfeld, 1991). Underused for many years, EITC became permanent in 1979 and more generous over time. It gained the attention of advocates in the mid-1980s and was adopted by President Clinton in the early 1990s. The Clinton plan expanded the credit to ensure that a family of four with a full-time minimum-wage worker would be lifted out of poverty by a combination of the EITC and food stamps. The plan also provided a smaller credit to childless workers.

The tax credit is a step toward a more universal and nonstigmatized system of income support. As an employment-based benefit, it has the potential to help the working poor, including welfare mothers who would receive a package of wages and welfare (Spalter-Roth, Hartmann, & Andrews, 1992). But EITC does not cover welfare mothers without income from wages. Because the labor market is absorbing fewer and fewer workers, it may become necessary to develop a comprehensive, universal, nonstigmatized income support system for those who become personally or structurally excluded from paid employment.

### Programs in Other Countries

Effective social programs are not impossible. A study of Canada, Australia, Great Britain, Germany, the Netherlands, France, and Sweden during the 1980s, all with pretransfer (before counting the impact of income support programs) poverty rates similar to that of the United States, found that the income maintenance programs in these countries reduced poverty by an average of 16.5 percent, compared to a reduction of only 6.6 percent in the United States. As for welfare, U.S. programs for poor women lifted less than 5 percent of single mothers with children out of poverty versus 89 percent in the Netherlands, 81 percent in Sweden, 75 percent in Great Britain, 50 percent in France, 33 percent in Germany, and 18.3 percent in Canada. Among children of single parents in the United States, poverty dropped less than 4 percent, whereas it plummeted nearly 30 percent in the other countries (Blank, 1988; Smeeding, 1991). The European programs work better than the U.S. program does because they invest more money, provide higher benefits, pay children's allowances that are not tied to mothers' work efforts, recognize the special needs of single-parent families, and rely on comprehensive programs for all people, rather than income-tested programs just for the poor.

## Potential for Real Reform

If one considers only income support, an agenda for real welfare reform in the United States might include mid-range and long-term goals, as well as the immediate one of assisting families in need. The mid-range goals would be to put an end to welfare cuts, to raise the public assistance grant, to replace mandatory employment with voluntary employment and programs that train welfare mothers for skilled jobs that pay more than the minimum wage, and to implement an effective child support program. The long-term goals would be to establish a national minimum standard of public assistance benefits equal to the official poverty line that is offered to all families regardless of their structure, to develop decent jobs in the public and private sectors, and to provide skill-enhancing educational and employment programs and adequate health care and child care services.

### Universal Family Policy

A more far-reaching change would replace the public assistance programs with a universal family policy for all families, regardless of their structure. This policy would protect individuals and families from the risk of lost income and the reduced capacity to provide care to family members. The Social Security Act programs, both insurance and public assistance, historically have covered the risks of the loss of income as a result of retirement, unemployment, illness, disability, and the absence of support from the breadwinner. Those who crafted the Social Security Act assumed that the income would cover the needs of caretaking as well. But because of massive changes in demographics, family structure, and women's roles, traditional caretakers no longer are available to perform their roles. A growing number of families can no longer provide adequate care for children, ill family members, and elders. Declining or lost wages, the growth of women's participation in the labor force, dual-earner households, single-parent families, and nonsupporting fathers have placed new and multiple demands on caretakers, most of whom are women. This reduced capacity for caretaking is neither a temporary nor an emergency condition. Nor, in most cases, is it a matter of choice. Rather, the need for support for caretaking has become a permanent feature of family life.

If reduced caretaking time was recognized as a normative risk because of events largely beyond an individual's control and was treated like the loss of income for reasons of old age, unemployment, illness, and disability, it could become the basis for a universal family benefit system. This system might include financing for child care; family leave; flextime; elder care; and cash assistance in the form of child support, the EITC, and a family or children's allowance. Some of these programs have already been instituted. By addressing all families, this approach could mainstream poor single mothers into larger, nonstigmatized programs and eliminate the need for AFDC. It would also implicitly acknowledge that unpaid caretaking work in the home, like paid work in the labor market, is both a service and a contribution to society.

### Political Action

To promote any of these agendas for change requires political action by AFDC clients, the social work profession, and many others. The foremothers of social work participated in the reform movements that forced the expansion of the social welfare programs before World War I and again in the 1930s. In the 1960s, poor African American single mothers organized the National Welfare Rights Organization in alliance with professional middle-class reformers and legal service attorneys and won a major expansion of the AFDC program (Brenner, 1989; Davis, 1993; Kotz & Kotz, 1977; West, 1981). Welfare mothers around the country have begun to organize as in years past to improve AFDC, to challenge current welfare reforms, and to create a comprehensive and universal income-support system that recognizes society's responsibility for meeting basic human needs. This organization is critical because the historical record shows that social policy rarely changes in a progressive direction without pressure from below.

## References

Abbott, G. (1938). *The child and the state* (Vol. 2). Chicago: University of Chicago Press.

Abramovitz, M. (1983). Everyone's on welfare: The role of redistribution in social policy revisited. *Social Work, 28*, 440–447.

Abramovitz, M. (1992). *Regulating the lives of women: Social welfare policy from colonial times to the present* (rev. ed.). Boston: South End Press.

Agricultural Adjustment Act of 1933. Ch. 25, title I, 48 Stat. §1.

Axinn, J., & Levin, H. (1982). *Social welfare: A history of the American response to need.* New York: Harper & Row.

Bane, M. J., & Ellwood, D. T. (1983). *The dynamics of dependency: The routes to self-sufficiency.* Washington, DC: U.S. Department of Health and Human Services.

Bell, W. (1965). *Aid to dependent children.* New York: Columbia University Press.

Blank, R. M. (1988). Women's paid work, household income and household well-being. In S. E. Rix (Ed.), *The American woman, 1988–1989: A status report* (pp. 123–161). New York: W. W. Norton.

Brenner, J. (1989). Towards a feminist perspective on welfare reform. *Yale Journal of Law and Feminism, 2,* 99–129.

Center on Budget and Policy Priorities, Center for Law and Social Welfare Policy, & Children's Defense Fund. (1992). *Selected background material on welfare programs.* Washington, DC: Author.

Cloward, R., & Piven, F. F. (1993). A class analysis of welfare. *Monthly Review, 44,* 25–31.

Congressional Budget Office. (1991, December). *CBO staff memorandum: A preliminary analysis of growing caseloads in AFDC.* Washington, DC: Author.

Davis, M. (1993). *Brutal need: Lawyers and the welfare rights movement, 1960–1973.* New Haven, CT: Yale University Press.

Deficit Reduction Act of 1984. P.L. 98-369, 98 Stat. 494.

DeParle, J. (1991, January 10). Fed by more than slump, welfare caseload soars. *New York Times,* pp. A1, A16.

Duvall, H. (1987, August). *Trends in AFDC recipient characteristics, 1967–1986.* Paper presented at the workshop for the National Association for Welfare Research and Statistics.

Ehrenreich, J. H. (1985). *The altruistic imagination: A history of social work and social policy in the United States.* Ithaca, NY: Cornell University Press.

Ellwood, D. T., & Bane, M. J. (1985). The impact of AFDC on family structure and living arrangement. In R. Ehrenberg (Ed.), *Research in labor economics* (Vol. 7). Greenwich, CT: JAI Press.

Epsing-Anderson, G. (1990). *The three worlds of welfare capitalism.* Princeton, NJ: Princeton University Press.

Fair Labor Standards Act of 1938. Ch. 676, 52 Stat. 1060.

Family Support Act of 1988. P.L. 100-485, 102 Stat. 2343.

Hacker, A. (1992). *Two nations: Black and white, separate, hostile, and unequal.* New York: Charles Scribner's Sons.

Hagen, J. L., & Lurie, I. (1992). *Implementing JOBS: Initial state choices* (summary report). New York: Nelson A. Rockefeller Institute of Government, State University of New York.

Handler, J. F., & Hasenfeld, Y. (1991). *The moral construction of poverty: Welfare reform in America.* Newbury Park, CA: Sage Publications.

Immigration Reform and Control Act of 1986. P.L. 99-603, 100 Stat. 3359.

Jencks, C., & Edin, K. (1990). The real welfare problem. *American Prospect, 1,* 31–50.

Kotz, N., & Kotz, M. (1977). *A passion for equality: George Wiley and the movement.* New York: W. W. Norton.

Larin, K. A., & Porter, K. H. (1992). *Enough to live on: Setting an appropriate AFDC need standard.* Washington, DC: Center on Budget and Policy Priorities.

McLanahan, S., & Garfinkel, I. (1989). Single mothers, the underclass and social policy. *Annals of the American Academy of Political and Social Science, 301,* 92–104.

Moffitt, R. (1991). *Incentive effects of the U.S. welfare system* (Special Report Series 48). Madison: Institute for Research on Poverty, University of Wisconsin.

Moore, K. S. (1992, January). Facts at a glance. *Child Trends,* pp. 5, T2.

Muncy, R. (1991). *Creating a female dominion in American reform 1890–1935.* New York: Oxford University Press.

Myrdal, G. (1944). *An American dilemma.* New York: Harper & Bros.

Omnibus Budget Reconciliation Act of 1981. P.L. 97-35, 95 Stat. 357.

Orloff, A. S. (1993). Gender and the social rights of citizenship: The comparative analyses of gender relations and welfare states. *American Sociological Review, 58*(3), 303–328.

Pavetti, L. A. (1993). *The dynamics of welfare and work: Exploring the process by which young women work their way off welfare.* Cambridge, MA: Kennedy School of Government, Harvard University.

Piven, F. F., & Cloward, R. A. (1971). *Regulating the poor: The functions of public welfare.* New York: Pantheon.

Rein, M. (1982). *Dilemmas of welfare policy: Why work strategies haven't worked.* New York: Praeger.

Riccio, J., & Friedlander, D. (1992). *GAIN: Program strategies, participation patterns, and first-year impacts in six counties.* New York: Manpower Demonstration Research Corporation.

Shapiro, I., Gold, S. S., Sheft, M., Strawn, J., Summer, J., & Greenstein, R. (1991). *The states and the poor: How budget decisions in 1991 affected low-income people.* Albany, NY: Center on Budget and Policy Priorities.

Smeeding, T. M. (1991, September 25). *The war on poverty: What worked?* Testimony given before U.S. Joint Economic Committee, Washington, DC.

Social Security Act of 1935. Ch. 531, 49 Stat. 620.

Social Security Act Amendments of 1956. Ch. 836, 70 Stat. 807.

Social Security Act Amendments of 1967. P.L. 90-248, 81 Stat. 821.

Spalter-Roth, R., Hartmann, H. I., & Andrews, L. (1992). *Combining work and welfare: An alternative anti-poverty strategy.* Washington, DC: Institute for Women's Policy Research.

Trattner, W. I. (1989). *From poor law to welfare state: A history of social welfare in America* (4th ed.). New York: Free Press.

U.S. Bureau of the Census. (1992). Studies in household and family formation. *Current population reports* (Series P-23, No. 129). Washington, DC: U.S. Government Printing Office.

U.S. Department of Health and Human Services. (1991). *Characteristics of state plans for Aid to Families with Dependent Children, 1990–1991.* Washington, DC: Author.

U.S. General Accounting Office. (1987). *Work and welfare: Current AFDC work programs and implications for federal policy.* Washington, DC: U.S. Government Printing Office.

U.S. General Accounting Office. (1991). *Welfare to work: States begin JOBS but fiscal and other problems may impede their progress.* Washington, DC: U.S. Government Printing Office.

U.S. House of Representatives, Committee on Ways and Means. (1992, May 15). *1992 green book: Overview of entitlement programs. Background material and data on programs within the jurisdiction of the Committee on Ways and Means.* Washington, DC: U.S. Government Printing Office.

U.S. House of Representatives, Committee on Ways and Means. (1993, July 7). *1993 green book: Overview of entitlement programs. Background material and data on programs within the jurisdiction of the Committee on Ways and Means.* Washington, DC: U.S. Government Printing Office.

U.S. House of Representatives, Committee on Ways and Means. (1994, July 15). *1994 green book: Overview of entitlement programs. Background material and data on programs within the jurisdiction of the Committee on Ways and Means.* Washington, DC: U.S. Government Printing Office.

Ware, S. (1981). *Beyond suffrage: Women in the New Deal.* Cambridge, MA: Harvard University Press.

West, G. (1981). *The National Welfare Rights Organization: The social protest of poor women.* New York: Praeger.

White House Conference on the Care of Dependent Children. (1909). *Proceedings.* Washington, DC: U.S. Government Printing Office.

Williams, L. A. (1992). The ideology of division: Behavior modification welfare reform proposals. *Yale Law Review, 102,* 719–746.

Wilson, W. J., & Neckerman, K. M. (1986). Poverty and family structure: The widening gap between evidence and public policy issues. In S. Danziger & D. H. Weinberg (Eds.), *Fighting poverty: What works and what doesn't* (pp. 232–259). Cambridge, MA: Harvard University Press.

Wines, M. (1994, November 20). Taxpayers are angry. They're expensive, too. *New York Times,* p. E5.

Witte, E. E. (1963). *The development of the Social Security Act.* Madison: University of Wisconsin Press.

**Mimi Abramovitz, DSW,** is professor, Hunter College, School of Social Work, 129 East 79th Street, New York, NY 10021.

### For further information see

Child Support; Families: Demographic Shifts; Federal Social Legislation from 1961 to 1994; Hunger, Nutrition, and Food Programs; Income Security Overview; Jobs and Earnings; JOBS Program; Poverty; Social Planning; Social Security; Social Welfare Policy; Unemployment Compensation and Workers' Compensation; Welfare Employment Programs: Evaluation.

**Key Words**

Aid to Families with Dependent Children
income security
public assistance
welfare

**READER'S GUIDE**

**AIDS/HIV**

*The following entries contain information on this general topic:*

HIV/AIDS Overview
HIV/AIDS: Direct Practice
HIV/AIDS: Men
HIV/AIDS: Pediatric
HIV/AIDS: Women

# Alaska Natives

**Eileen M. Lally**
**Helen Andon Haynes**

Alaska's indigenous peoples have experienced rapid technological and cultural change in just a few short years. As late as 1955, posted signs stated "No Natives and No Dogs Allowed." Schoolchildren were punished for speaking their native languages. A respected elder, Max Dolchok (1993), succinctly stated, "Within a span of 70 years, Alaska Natives have gone from wearing animal skins to three-piece suits. Through all this change, we are still a people of seasons!"

Along with the changes have been major losses. The traditional male role has essentially been lost. "Who needs a hunter when you can go to the store?" (Dolchok, 1993). Women's roles have changed from that of homemaker and fishing and trapping partner to main provider. The few village jobs are in the stores, schools, and health clinics and are filled mostly by women. Vacancies are rare, and the competition for an open position is intense. Many rural men find cash-paying work only during the summer's firefighting and construction seasons. Who, then, are these "people of seasons," and what is social work's relationship to the Alaska Native?

## Alaska Native Defined

### Relationship to Other American Indian Groups

About 2.5 million indigenous people lived in this country before the arrival of Europeans. At the turn of the 20th century, there were only 220,000 American Indians and Alaska Natives in the United States (Fleming, 1992). The diversity that is found in the more than 800 recognized native tribes defies distinct categorization (Manson & Trimble, 1982). Each of these entities is unique. There is tremendous variation, even within the same geographic region, in how Indian and non-Indian cultures find expression in the lifestyles of Indian families, communities, and tribes (Fleming, 1992). Alaska Natives share commonalities with American Indian groups, yet they are geographically and culturally separate and distinct.

In 1871, shortly after the United States purchased Russia's interest in Alaska, Congress ceased making any further treaties with American Indians. The statutes and appropriation legislation that have explicitly included Alaska Natives established that the "unique legal relationship," "trust responsibility," or "guardianship" is not tied to reservation status and the federal government's management in trust of native lands. Furthermore, the legislation explicitly extends to Alaska Natives the same protection and services to which American Indians elsewhere are entitled (Cordes, 1990).

Distinct Alaskan tribal entities include the Aleut, Athabascan, Haida, Inupiat, Tlingit, Tsimshian, and Yup'ik groups. These groups are collectively referred to as "Alaska Natives." This term was popularized and expanded during the formation of the Alaska Native Claims Settlement Act of 1971 to include all of Alaska's indigenous peoples.

### Language Groups

Two major Alaska Native linguistic families, as Langdon (1987) defined them, are the Eska-Aleutian and Na-Dene. The Eska-Aleutian family is separated into Aleuts and Eskimos. The Eskimos are subdivided into Inupiat and Yup'ik, and there are few similarities between the two. Inupiat is spoken across the northern tier of Alaska all the way to Greenland. Yup'ik is subdivided into three major languages—Siberian Yup'ik, Central Yup'ik, and Alutiiq—and is spoken along the southcentral coast as well as in the former Soviet Union.

The Na-Dene language family is made up of the Athabascan languages (Ahtna, Dena'ina, Gwich'in, Han, Holikachuk, Ingalik, Koyukon, Tanana, Tanacross, Upper Kuskokwim, and Upper Tanana), as well as Eyak and Tlingit. Also included are a number of Athabascan languages in northern Canada, British Columbia, and California, as well as the Apache and Navajo languages of the southwest United States. Because of constant contact among Athabascan tribal people, there is mutual comprehensibility among the distinct languages. However, Eyak and Tlingit speakers cannot be understood by speakers of Athabascan languages. Ironically, Alaskan Athabascans can communicate with Arizona Apaches in their own languages, but they must use English to communicate with the Alaskan Tlingit (Engstrom, 1991; Langdon, 1987).

## Legal Status

### Alaska Native Land Claims Settlement

From 1750 to 1800, the Russians colonized the territories of the Aleuts and coastal Indians to exploit the sea otter trade. The southern Eskimos also made contact with Russians during that time and later made contact with American whalers traveling through the Bering Straits in the 1850s. The American whalers were the northern Eskimos' earliest contact with non-natives. However, the most powerful introduction to the technology of the Western world did not occur until the early 1960s. The discovery of oil in the early 1960s and the passage of the Alaska Native Claims Settlement Act (ANCSA) of 1971, which created Alaska Native corporations, brought about rapid cultural change for all Alaska Natives (Fleming, 1992).

### Regional Corporations

The ANCSA settlement, spurred by a worldwide oil embargo, freed the vast Prudhoe Bay oil fields for development. ANCSA provided $962.5 million (about $3 per acre) and title to 44 million acres (10 percent of the state) to state-charted native corporations. It required natives to set up village and regional corporations. The land that ANCSA conveyed does not belong to individual Alaska Natives or tribes but to the corporations. ANCSA extinguished not only aboriginal title to the land, but also aboriginal hunting and fishing rights. State and federal laws conflicted with traditional ways that had the force of law among the native people (Berger, 1985). Additionally, a new structure was added to Alaska Native life—the corporate stockholding company.

### Shareholder Enrollment

With the formation of the regional and village corporations, the Alaska Native people became shareholders. Most natives enrolled both in their village corporation and the regional corporation and were granted 100 shares of each. Natives who did not permanently reside in the state were given a choice to join one of 12 regional corporations in Alaska or a 13th regional corporation, which was based in Seattle. In total, about 80,000 native people who proved they were at least one-quarter Alaska Native became either village or at-large shareholders (Berger, 1985).

The average Alaska Native does not personnaly own land as a result of ANCSA and has received little direct monetary benefit since the act was passed. However, not all corporate benefits can be measured in dividends received. One corporation employed 22 percent of its shareholders. Another developed jobs by entering into a joint venture to operate a zinc mine. Regional corporations account for 5 percent of Alaska's jobs in the private sector and also provide educational scholarships.

### Current Status

*Village Journey* (Berger, 1985) eloquently described the dilemmas facing Alaska Natives. ANCSA imposed a capitalistic, corporate structure without settling the issues of sovereignty and self-determination. Morehouse (1992) gave a clear picture of the Alaska Natives' dual political status and unresolved situations such as tribal courts, subsistence rights, and village governmental structures. Though perhaps not its explicit intention, ANCSA appears to have been designed to speed assimilation. Alaska Natives now question if they got what they bargained for in the settlement (Morehouse, 1992).

## Demographics

### Population Composition

Alaska is a sparsely populated state, with 550,043 people. More than half (56.1 percent) of the Alaska Natives, who make up 15.6 percent of the total population, live in rural areas. The 1990 U.S. Census showed 150 villages of 500 or fewer persons that were mostly native villages (Huskey, 1992). The Anchorage area contains 20 percent of the Alaska Native population, making Alaska's only metropolitan area also the state's largest native "village" (Alaska Department of Labor, 1992a).

Alaska has a youthful population; the median age is 29.8 years. Forty-one percent of the Alaska Native population is under 18 years, and the median age is 24.1 years. The majority (65 percent) of these native children and youths lives in the 209 small (population under 2,500) communities in rural Alaska (Alaska Department of Labor, 1992a).

Although a small proportion of Alaska's population is over age 65, a curious phenomenon is occurring. Alaska has experienced the largest percentage increase in people over age 65 of any state. The Alaska Native over-65 population increased 30 percent between 1980 and 1990. Control of infectious diseases, especially tuberculosis, has increased the Alaska Natives' life expectancy from 35 years in 1940 to 67 years in 1988 (Waring, McNabb, & Elliott, 1988). Generally, the aged dependency rate (people of nonworking ages who must be supported by each person of working age) has also increased, from 4.4 percent in 1980 to 8.7 percent in 1990 (Alaska Department of Labor, 1992b).

### Income

The per capita income for all Alaskans was $17,610 in 1989; the figure for Alaska Natives was $9,140. Although the income of Alaska Natives increased 79.1 percent over a 10-year period, their income level continues to be the lowest of all ethnic groups in Alaska and is only 45.9 percent of white people's per capita income. Similarly, 6.8 percent of Alaskan families live in poverty, yet the family poverty rate of Alaska Natives is 21.5 percent (Williams, 1992). Given that more than half of Alaska Natives live in rural areas, their low income level is exacerbated because of the high cost of living in rural Alaska. One measure of poverty is the use of public assistance programs. Berman and Foster's 1986 study indicated that 40 percent of Aid to Families with Dependent Children, 41 percent of Medicaid, 55 percent of adult public assistance, and 36 percent of food stamps went to Alaska Natives.

### Employment

Alaska Natives have an unemployment rate of 22.1 percent, compared with a statewide rate of 8.8 percent. The unemployment rate for Alaska Native men is 27.3 percent and for women 16.1 percent—considerably higher than the rate for any other ethnic group (Alaska Department of Labor, 1993a). The occupational data indicate that employment is based on gender lines, with fewer opportunities for men's traditional subsistence work (Alaska Department of Labor, 1993b).

**Education**
In the 1960s and 1970s, hundreds of Alaska Native adolescents were sent away to Bureau of Indian Affairs high schools in Oregon, Oklahoma, New Mexico, and southeast Alaska. Many other village students attended religious-affiliated boarding schools throughout Alaska. In 1975, a lawsuit was filed against the state of Alaska for failing to provide village high schools. The lawsuit, popularly referred to as the "Molly Hootch" case, was settled in 1976. It required the state of Alaska to establish a high school program in every village with eight or more high school students, unless the villagers decided against a local program (Cotton, 1984).

With the advent of local high schools, more Alaska Natives have been completing high school. In 1980, only 46.3 percent of the eligible population graduated; in 1990, 63.1 percent graduated. Data from the 1990 Census indicate that the graduation rate for all Alaskans is 86.6 percent (Kleinfeld, 1992). Postsecondary education, however, has had no "Molly Hootch" case to bring baccalaureate education to Alaska Natives. Although the University of Alaska has regional sites, only 10 percent of Alaska Natives have earned bachelor's degrees or higher, compared with 23 percent of the general U.S. population (U.S. Bureau of the Census, 1992). Alaska Natives are taking advantage of preprimary school programs. More than one-fourth of children enrolled in preprimary school in the state are Alaska Natives (Alaska State Data Center, 1992).

**Correctional Institutions**
One-third of the inmates in Alaskan correctional institutions are Alaska Natives, yet Natives constitute only 15.6 percent of the state's population (U.S. Bureau of the Census, 1992). Natives account for 59 percent of all inmates jailed for violent crimes and for 38 percent of all convicted felons for sex-related offenses. Alcohol is a suspected contributing factor in at least 80 percent of violent crimes (Waring et al., 1988).

**Birthrates**
The Alaska Native birthrate is 3.9 percent—higher than that of many developing nations. Alaskan trend analysis estimates that 22 percent of the babies born by 2012 will be Alaska Natives, although Alaska Natives will continue to constitute only 16 percent of the state's population. Similar trend analysis data predict that by 2000, Alaska Natives will make up 21 percent of all Alaskan children under 5 years and 22 percent of all school-age children. The youth dependency rate (the number of people under age 18 who are dependent on people ages 19 to 64) is 74.6 for Alaska Natives versus 43.4 for white people (Alaska Department of Labor 1992b). Almost 25 percent of all Alaska Natives are under age 10, and 40 percent are under 16 (U.S. Department of Health and Human Services, 1993).

**Health Status**
The leading cause of death for Alaska Natives is unintentional injury, followed by cancer, heart disease, suicide, stroke, and cirrhosis. The suicide rate of Alaska Natives is three times that of white people, and the unintentional injury rate is 2.5 times that of white people (Alaska Bureau of Vital Statistics, 1993b). In 1987, 1988, and 1989, the unintentional injury death rates among young people ages 10 to 24 were three times higher for Alaska Natives than for white people. In 1990 and 1991, the rates for white people held steady, and those for Alaska Natives dropped to twice that of white people (Alaska Bureau of Vital Statistics, 1993b). Deaths of Alaska Natives account for 30 percent of all injury deaths, which include drowning, suicide, alcohol, and drugs (Middaugh et al., 1991).

The infant mortality rate for white Alaskans is 8.4 per 1,000 infants; the Alaska Native rate is almost twice that, at 16.3. Postneonatal mortality rates are more than twice those for white people (Alaska Bureau of Vital Statistics, 1993b). Between 1987 and 1991, 47.1 percent of the reported gonorrhea cases were from Alaska Natives. During 1991, this percentage dropped to 38 percent. Type II diabetes has been increasing for the last 20 years in the Alaska Native population, in a pattern similar to that for American Indians, probably because of an increasingly westernized diet and an increasingly sedentary lifestyle (U.S. Department of Health and Human Services, 1993).

In many areas of rural Alaska, the lack of clean water and basic sanitation facilities has reached crisis proportions. Water-borne diseases and hepatitis are increasing. Overall, the health of Alaska Natives has improved—for example, there are now fewer deaths from infectious diseases, longer life expectancies, and prenatal care for pregnant women. Yet, self-inflicted injuries such as suicides, homicides, and alcohol-related deaths have wreaked havoc among the Alaska Native people.

## Cultural Considerations

**Worldview**
Richard Nelson, in his book *Make Prayers to the Raven* (1983), described a cycle of life that is specific to the Koyukon Athabascan ("The People"). Yet one may infer that all Alaska's indigenous peoples follow and revere this cycle of life because

the major components are adhered to by differing tribal groups. When Dolchok (1993) said, "We are still a people of seasons," he referred to Native life being patterned around the changing seasons, the natural cycle of the year. Each season brings change for man, animal, and plant life. In Alaska, seasonal changes are dramatic. "The world is transformed from warm, bright and flowing to cold, dark and frozen" (Nelson, 1983, p. 9). The People must make decisions and preparations for seasonal change. Alaska Natives are particularly sensitive to the need to hunt, fish, gather firewood, and pick berries when they are ripe. Those who work with Alaska Native people must understand each season's tasks. Spring brings light and warmer weather. Hunting and visiting other villages occupy The People. Summer means fish camp and the opportunity to catch a winter's supply of food for both people and sled dogs. Fall is a most important season, for this is when The People hunt for the winter's supply of moose and caribou. The meat is smoked, dried, and frozen for the winter. If men have left the village to obtain work, most will return at this time to ensure that their families have sufficient food supplies for the winter. Without these subsistence activities, many natives would have a difficult time: The cost of groceries is extraordinarily high. A medium-sized jar of mayonnaise cost $6 in 1993, and other food is equally expensive.

### Values and Traditions

In almost any Alaska Native social services organization, one will see posted a listing of the most common Native values: Respect for elders, love for children, respect for others, respect for nature, domestic skills, humility, sharing, cooperation, hard work, hunting skills, family roles, humor, spirituality, knowledge of language, knowledge of family tree, avoidance of conflict, and responsibility to clan or tribe. Although there is no one Alaska Native view and each person must be viewed as an individual, most Alaska Natives share the following sentiments: A love of family, a sense of belonging to the group, and ties to and feelings for the land. The importance of elders to the community is evident: Native social services programs often include elders as helpers and teachers. The Inupiat Spirit Movement emphasizes a return to community and a return to the old ways of sharing and caring. Spirit camps, held away from villages, offer the opportunity to experience community and give a time and place to learn anew traditional ways of coping (Mohatt, McDiarmid, & Montoya, 1988). Maintaining harmony among people, nature, and the spirit world is important (Lenz, 1989). Generally, the more traditional native villages experience less social dysfunction, as evidenced by their lower rates of alcohol use, suicide, and unintentional injuries (Fienup-Riordan, 1992).

### Religion and Spirituality

There are hundreds of belief systems held by American Indians and Alaska Natives. The most common beliefs of indigenous people include belief in a Creator, a connection with the spirit world, a concept of harmony and wellness, and the idea that one is responsible for one's own wellness (Fleming, 1992).

Many Athabascan people are faithful Christians, but they are equally committed to their traditional religion. They have attained a fairly high level of fluency in white culture without losing the vitality of their own Athabascan lifestyle. There is a Native way and a white person's way, and the two can coexist comfortably (Nelson, 1983, p. 235). Although the Koyukon people also express this sentiment, they are acutely conscious of growing social problems in their villages, afflictions centered on the health and well-being of young people. Many of the elders wonder if the recent decline of traditional beliefs and morality might be at fault.

The Inupiat and Yup'ik belief systems appear to have been based on the principle of reincarnation and the recycle of spirit forms from one life to the next. Shamans had a special place as healers in Inupiat society. Today, Christianity and traditional beliefs are practiced side by side (Langdon, 1987). The belief systems of the Tlingit and Haida were linked to the Raven, a trickster whose activities resulted in most of the features of the universe; other mythical beings and spirits have also influenced human affairs. Both cultures had a strong belief in reincarnation. Many contemporary people continue to hold and practice traditional beliefs (Langdon, 1987).

## Social Services System

### Federal Services

***Indian Health Service.*** The Indian Health Service (IHS) was established in 1955. In the 1950s, Alaska experienced a widespread tuberculosis epidemic. There have been no higher tuberculosis death rates in the world than those related to Alaska Native people during that time. The initial work of IHS in reducing tuberculosis death rates and infant mortality was extraordinary (Mohatt et al., 1988).

IHS provides 12 percent of all Alaska's spending ($206 million) for health care services (Institute of Social and Economic Research, 1992).

These include basic health care provided by clinics and small hospitals in regional hub villages as well as a large hospital and outpatient center in Anchorage. An experimental program that uses Native healers is under way in one rural hospital. The program is expected to be a model for other areas of the state that wish to meld traditional healing practices and modern medicine (SouthCentral Foundation, no date).

Since 1968, IHS has funded and trained paraprofessional community health aides to provide basic services in remote villages. These aides often are the villagers' first contact with any health care. The IHS Office of Community Health Services provides a broad range of services: Social services, child protection, mental health, substance abuse, fetal alcohol syndrome prevention, and the special-needs childrens' registry.

***Native corporations and "638" federal contractors.*** With the advent of self-determination policies in the late 1970s, driven by the Indian Self-Determination Act (P.L. 93-638), most direct social service and educational functions of the Bureau of Indian Affairs have been contracted out to Native organizations, referred to as "638s." In addition to the 13 "for-profit" regional corporations established under the ANCSA, there are 12 companion social services corporations. These organizations provide the following types of social services to their regions: Education, employment, health, injury prevention, mental health care, and child welfare and other services. P.L. 93-638 allows the Native corporations to contract for government funds to provide services. For example, some health money slated for the Indian Health Service is distributed among the organizations so that health prevention and treatment needs are provided by the regional organization rather than exclusively by the IHS.

### State Social Services

The Alaska Department of Health and Social Services (Alaska DHSS) houses the divisions of Public Assistance, Public Health, Family and Youth Services, Mental Health and Developmental Disabilities, and Alcohol and Drug Abuse. Alaska DHSS provides some direct services, such as child protective services, the Alaska Psychiatric Institute hospital, and public health nurses.

## Significant Issues for Social Workers

### Substance Abuse

Alcoholism is not unique to Alaska Native people. The entire state experiences a high incidence of alcoholism and alcohol-related problems—domestic violence, child abuse and neglect, unintentional injury, and suicide. Although there is no consensus that Alaska Natives are genetically predisposed to alcoholism (McCarthy, 1993; Napoleon, 1990), there is evidence to illustrate alcohol's devastating effect on their lives. In *Alaska Natives at Risk,* Waring et al. (1988) concluded that "Alcohol is a common contributor to these grim statistics on death and violence" (p. 3).

One of the more positive indicators of the alleviation of substance abuse is the open discussion of alcoholism currently taking place among Alaska Natives. There is a movement to confront the problem, to no longer ignore, deny, or accept it as inevitable (Manson, 1989; Tucker, 1990). The Canadian film *The Honour of All* (Lucas, 1985) and the resulting "New Directions" and "Family Systems" training programs in Alaska resulted in the "Sobriety Movement." Recognizing the need for cultural awareness and specificity (Fleming, 1992; Sullivan, 1991; Tucker, 1990), several Native nonprofit regional corporations have begun reviving traditional approaches to healing and substance abuse treatment. The Tanana Chiefs Conference has three recovery camps in remote sites of interior Alaska. John Titus, a pioneer in the recovery camp treatment, said,

> We came from the woods, and that's where we return when we have problems. We find that has the most healing power. I think that is how to fight alcoholism and drugs, by going back to nature, our healing ground. All the programs started by white men have failed. We do not comprehend them. It is time for Native people to fall back to our Native ways. We did, and it works. (Burko, 1990, p. A-1)

Other Native nonprofit groups in southeast Alaska and the western regions have similar programs, based on the cultural heritage and lifestyle (Sullivan, 1991; Turner, 1990). In addition to these innovative treatment modalities, treatment specialists make use of formal Alcoholics Anonymous groups, support groups, and counseling. To be successful practitioners, social workers in Alaska must have a knowledge of substance abuse and its effects on individuals, families, and communities.

### Fetal Alcohol Syndrome

Preliminary data show that the minimum fetal alcohol syndrome prevalence rate for the state of Alaska was 0.5 cases per 1,000 live births during 1978 to 1990. The rate for Alaska Natives was more than four times that rate, at 2.1 cases per 1,000 live births. Debate surrounds the prevalence rate for natives. Most Alaska Native births occur at Indian Health Service facilities, so the numbers may be indicative of better case-finding and reporting, compared with the less-intensive efforts to identify fetal alcohol syndrome in the non-native population (Alaska DHHS, 1993). An aggressive combined prevention effort to combat the prevalence of fetal alcohol syndrome was begun in the late 1980s by the Indian Health Service, the Alaska Native Health Board, the Alaska Department of Health and Social Services, and native nonprofit organizations (U.S. Department of Health and Human Services, 1993). This joint effort is credited with a 25 percent reduction in fetal alcohol syndrome and fetal alcohol effect in 1990 (Kleinfeld, 1992).

**Teen Pregnancy**

Alaska has the second-highest rate of teen pregnancy in the United States. Only 10 countries worldwide have higher teen pregnancy rates than that of Alaska Natives. Forty-five percent of all Alaskan births in 1989 to women younger than 18 were to Native women (Dick, 1992). From 1988 to 1991, an Alaska Native teenage girl age 15 to 19 was more than twice as likely to give birth as her white counterpart (Alaska Bureau of Vital Statistics, 1993a). Rural teenagers were more likely to give birth than urban teenagers and were also more likely to be Medicaid recipients than mothers who were 20 or older (Alaska Bureau of Vital Statistics, 1993b).

**Suicide**

Suicide is the fourth leading cause of death in Alaska for all young people. Native suicide rates for 10- to 24-year-olds during the period from 1987 to 1991 were consistently three times that of white people of the same age group (Alaska Bureau of Vital Statistics, 1993b). The suicide rates of the 1950s among Alaska Natives were similar to those of the U.S. population at large. During the 1970s, the rate for Alaska Natives increased significantly, peaked in 1976, leveled off until the mid-1980s, and then showed another rapid increase (Hlady & Middaugh, 1988; Kettl & Bixler, 1991; Waring et al., 1988).

Alcohol plays a significant role in suicides. It is estimated that alcohol is involved in 50 percent to 80 percent of suicides (Hlady & Middaugh, 1988; Waring et al., 1988). Kettl and Bixler (1991) used Emile Durkheim's theories of anomie and societal disintegration to explain the high rates of alcoholism and suicide. Not all Alaska Native groups experience devastatingly high rates of suicide; the interior Athabascans and Inupiat appear to be the most ravaged. These two groups, more so than any other Alaska Native group, have experienced the most rapid social and cultural changes, beginning in the late 1960s with oil field development. As with the culture-specific alcohol treatment programs, many regional nonprofit native corporations are developing local suicide prevention programs (Mattaini, no date; Mullin, no date).

**Mental Health**

Given the social problems, poverty, and anomie of the last 30 years, it is no wonder that Nelson, McCoy, Stetter, and Vanderwagen (1992) stated that "Native Americans appear to be at higher risk than other U.S. ethnic groups for mental health problems" (p. 257). This holds true for Alaska Natives as well. Social workers provide a significant portion of the mental health treatment in Alaska, especially in rural areas. Several 638s are now certified as community mental health centers. One 638 developed a "clubhouse" model for seriously mentally ill clients. All regional hubs have community mental health centers.

Alaska Natives do not separate the mind from the body. This mind–body connection is consonant with modern psychiatric practice. As in the area of physical health care, the use of Native healers and traditions in mental health settings is becoming more acceptable. Successful mental health workers use their personal traits to form a relationship with the mental health consumer. The ability to bond in this way has been shown to be the most effective quality a provider can have for work with Alaska Natives (South-Central Foundation, no date).

**Child Welfare**

The Division of Family and Youth Services is charged by the state of Alaska to provide child protective services. Data indicate that Alaska Native children are at risk (Alaska DHSS Division of Family and Youth Services, 1993; Waring et al., 1988). Reports of sexual assault continue to escalate. Twenty percent of Alaska's infants to 19-year-olds are Alaska Natives, yet 30 percent of the assault cases reported in fiscal year 1992 and 35 percent of the assault cases that were substantiated by Child Protective Services involved Alaska Native children. Evidence indicates that much of the abuse and neglect is alcohol-driven (Waring et al., 1988). Twenty-five percent of alleged youth offenders are Alaska Natives, as are 41 percent of the juveniles in detention facilities. Substance abuse appears to be a contributing factor. The state has begun the Alaska Youth Initiative with the intent of providing services for hard-to-serve children so that they can remain at home.

**Indian Child Welfare Act**

In 1976, Alaska Native and American Indian children were found to be placed in out-of-home care at 12 to 18 times the rate of non–American Indian children nationwide, with 85 percent of those Native children placed in non–American Indian homes (Cross, 1986). In 1978, Congress passed the Indian Child Welfare Act (ICWA) to address the need for special attention for American Indian and Alaska Native children and their families. The intent of the law was to compel government child welfare agencies to provide for the cultural as well as the physical needs of children. The act reads: "To protect the best interests of the Indian children; to preserve Tribes, cultures, and families" (Alaska DHSS, 1990). The ICWA requires an active effort on the part of child protection agencies to keep children safely at home whenever possible. If in-home care is not possible, the act requires that a child be placed with a relative or an extended family member and gives the tribe jurisdiction in the placement or adoption of the child (Alaska DHSS, 1993; Costin, Bell, & Downs, 1991; Kessel & Robbins, 1984). The ICWA does not absolve the state from its child welfare obligation; it is a way to protect both the child's and the tribes' interests.

Alaska's Division of Family and Youth Services acknowledges the needs of Alaska Native children and subscribes to the long-term goal of having the tribes assume full responsibility for the welfare of their children (Alaska DHSS, 1990). To that end, Alaska has developed a State–Tribal Indian Child Welfare Act agreement. This agreement, signed by 28 tribes throughout the state, strengthens the intent of the federal ICWA and specifies ICWA day-to-day procedures in Alaska. It also clarifies specific procedures for individual tribes and thus gives more autonomy to the individual Alaska Native entities (Alaska DHSS Division of Family and Youth Services, 1993). One effect of ICWA has been the formalization of "cultural" adoptions of Alaska Native children into a family with at least one Alaska Native adoptive parent. In 1990, 65 cultural adoptions were completed without the formality of a superior court proceeding. This number is slightly more than one-quarter of all Alaska Native children adopted that year (Alaska Bureau of Vital Statistics, 1993a).

### Delivery of Services

Alaska is a rural state comprising many small, isolated villages. It has few roads. Most of its communities can be reached only by aircraft or boat. As a result, few villages have access to professionals for health and social services. The successful community health aide training model has no parallel for paraprofessional mental health providers, although there is an effort under way (currently funded at $1 million) to design training and support for village-based behavioral health counselors similar to the community health aide program.

There is a significant lack of trained professionals, including social workers, to provide health and social services outside the major population centers. The 50 Alaska Native individuals who have earned a bachelor of social work degree from the University of Alaska are in great demand for entry-level positions. However, IHS and other providers require a minimum of a master of social work degree (MSW) for most social services positions. But no MSW program exists in Alaska, and the financial and familial burden of leaving the state for up to two years is often too great. As a result, there are fewer than 10 Alaska natives with an MSW in the entire state.

## Role of Social Work

Social workers must understand and accept Alaska Natives as a people with many strengths and a history of survival in an often harsh and demanding physical environment. To be effective, social workers must become willing learners who are culturally competent and can adapt to ever-changing situations. Social work's emphasis on person-in-environment and respect for diversity gives professionally trained social workers the basis they need to work with Alaska Native people.

Social workers can play an active role in empowering Alaska Native people to design and deliver programs and policies to meet their needs. This goal will be more readily attained when Alaska has an educational avenue by which Alaska Natives can earn the MSW credential that most social services organizations require.

Finally, the social work profession must remain true to its advocacy role, particularly in the political arena. Alaskan citizens have an almost unprecedented relationship with their legislators, one of easy and almost daily access. Social work advocates must avail themselves of this unique opportunity to create responsive social services systems for all Alaskans.

## References


Alaska Bureau of Vital Statistics. (1993a). Vital statistics for young adults in Alaska. *Alaska Vital Signs, 3,* 1–5.

Alaska Bureau of Vital Statistics. (1993b). *1990 Annual Report.* Juneau: Alaska Department of Health and Social Services.

Alaska Department of Health and Social Services. (1993, March). *An interim report on the Alaska FAS prevention project.* Anchorage: Author.

Alaska Department of Health and Social Services, Division of Family and Youth Services. (1990). *Into the 90's: The strategic plan for service to Alaska's families, children and youth.* Juneau: Author.

Alaska Department of Health and Social Services, Division of Family and Youth Services. (1993). *Annual report.* Juneau: Author.

Alaska Department of Labor. (1992a, March). *Alaska population overview: 1990 census and estimates.* Juneau: Author.

Alaska Department of Labor. (1992b, March). *Population projections Alaska: 1990-2010.* Juneau: Author.

Alaska Department of Labor (1993a). *Unemployment Rate (%) by Race, 1990.* U.S. 1990 Census, STF3. Anchorage: Author.

Alaska Department of Labor. (1993b). *Occupation by race and sex. State of Alaska, 1990.* U.S. 1990 Census, Equal Employment Opportunity File for Alaska. Anchorage: Author.

Alaska Native Claims Settlement Act of 1971. P.L. 92-203, 85 Stat. 688.

Alaska State Data Center. (1992). Alaskans outpace U.S. in education. *AKCENS: Bulletin of the Alaska state data center, 9,* 1–3.

Berger, T. (1985). *Village journey: The report of the Alaska native review commission.* New York: Hill and Wang.

Berman, M., & Foster, K. (1986). Poverty among Alaska natives. *Institute of Social and Economic Research Summary No. 31.* Anchorage, AK: Institute of Social and Economic Research.

Burko, C. (1990, April 18). Return to traditional lifestyle touted as new medicine for Native alcoholics. *Anchorage Times,* p. A-1.

Cordes, P. (1990, April-June). The federal government—Native American relationship and the Indian Health Service in Alaska. *Alaska Medicine, 32,* 67–68.

Costin, L. G., Bell, C. J., & Downs, S. W. (1991). *Child welfare: Policies and practice.* (4th ed.). New York: Longman.

Cotton, S: (1984). Alaska's "Molly Hootch case": High schools and the village voice. *Educational Research Quarterly, 8,* 30–43.

Cross, T. L. (1986). Drawing on cultural tradition in Indian child welfare practice. *Social Casework: The Journal of Contemporary Social Work, 67,* 283–288.

Dick, S. E. (1992). *An estimate of the number of children with special care needs in the state of Alaska.* Unpublished master's thesis, University of Illinois at Chicago.

Dolchok, M. (1993, June). *Cross-cultural realities that impact client, clinician and treatment outcome.* (Presentation given to Alaska Chapter of NASW.) Anchorage, AK: South-Central Foundation.

Engstrom, R. (1991, July 21). Native Alaska languages. *Anchorage Daily News.* Sunday supplement, p. 1.

Fienup-Riordan, A. (1992, April). *Cultural change and identity among Alaska natives: Retaining control.* Anchorage, AK: Institute of Social and Economic Research.

Fleming, C. (1992). American Indians and Alaska natives: Changing societies past and present. In M. A. Orlandi (Ed.), *Cultural competence for evaluators* (pp. 147–171). Washington, DC: U.S. Department of Health and Social Services.

Hlady, W. G., & Middaugh, J. P. (1988, February). Suicides in Alaska: Firearms and alcohol. *American Journal of Public Health, 78,* 179–180.

Huskey, L. (1992, March). *The economy of village Alaska.* Anchorage, AK: Institute of Social and Economic Research.

Indian Child Welfare Act of 1978. P.L. 95-608, 92 Stat. 3069.

Indian Self-Determination Act. P.L. 93-638, 88 Stat. 2206.

Institute of Social and Economic Research. (1992, December). The cost of health care in Alaska. *ISER Research Summary No. 53.* Anchorage, AK: Author.

Kessel, J. A., & Robbins, S. P. (1984). The Indian child welfare act: Dilemmas and needs. *Child Welfare, 3,* 225–232.

Kettl, P. A., & Bixler, E. O. (1991). Suicide in Alaska natives, 1979-1984. *Psychiatry, 54,* 55–63.

Kleinfeld, J. (1992, April). *Alaska native education: Issues in the nineties.* Anchorage, AK: Institute of Social and Economic Research.

Langdon, S. J. (1987). *The native people of Alaska.* Anchorage, AK: Greatland Graphics.

Lenz, M. (1989, June 30). Yup'ik teacher gives clues to communicating. *Tundra Drums,* p. 25.

Lucas, P. (Producer and director). (1985). *The honour of all* [video]. Alkali Lake, Canada: Alkali Lake Indian Bank.

Manson, S. M. (Ed.). (1989, Spring). *American Indian and Native Alaska Mental Health Research, 2*(3) [Entire issue].

Manson, S. M., & Trimble, J. E. (1982). American Indian and Alaska native communities: Past efforts, future inquiries. In L. R. Snowden (Ed.), *Reaching the underserved: Mental health needs of neglected populations.* (pp. 143–163). Beverly Hills, CA: Sage Publications.

Mattaini, M. A. (no date). *Village suicide prevention: Empowering for self-help.* Unpublished manuscript.

McCarthy, M. (1993, March 21). The myth of the drunken Indian. *Anchorage, Daily News. We Alaskans Supplement,* pp. G6–7.

Middaugh, J. P., Miller, J., Dunaway, C. E., Jenkerson, S. A., Kelly, T., Ingle, D., Perham, K., Fridley, D., Hlady, W. G., & Hendrickson, V. (1991, August). *Causes of death in Alaska 1950, 1980–89.* Juneau: Alaska Department of Health and Social Services.

Mohatt, G. V., McDiarmid, W., & Montoya, V. (1988). Societies, families, and change: The Alaskan example. In S. M. Manson & N. G. Dinges (Eds.), *Behavioral health issues among American Indians and Alaska natives: Exploration on the frontiers of the biobehavioral sciences* (pp. 325–352). Denver, CO: National Center for American Indian and Alaska Native Mental Health Research.

Molly Hootch v. Alaska State Operated School System, 536 P. 2nd 793 (1975).

Morehouse, T. A. (1992, March). *The dual political status of Alaska natives under U.S. policy.* Anchorage, AK: Institute of Social and Economic Research.

Mullin, C. (no date). *Suicide prevention.* Unpublished manuscript.

Napoleon, H. (1990). *Yu'ya'raq: The way of the human being.* Unpublished manuscript.

Nelson, R. K. (1983). *Make prayers to the raven.* Chicago: University of Chicago Press.

Nelson, S. H., McCoy, G., Stetter, M., & Vanderwagen, W. (1992). An overview of mental health services for American Indians and Alaska natives in the 1990s. *Hospital and Community Psychiatry, 43,* 257–261.

South-Central Foundation (no date). *Traditional native healing practices in Alaska.* Unpublished manuscript.

Sullivan, A. (1991). Elements for building a culturally specific addiction treatment program. *Alaska Medicine, 33,* 154–156.

Tucker, E. (Ed.). (1990). *Report on leadership in sobriety: A conference for rural women on substance abuse.* Anchorage: Alaska Women's Commission.

Turner, E. J. (1990, August 13). Natives caught in time of rapid change. *Tundra Times,* p. 25.

U.S. Bureau of the Census. (1992). *Census of population and housing summary social, economic, and housing characteristics—Alaska.* (Publication No. CPH 5-3). Washington, DC: U.S. Government Printing Office.

U.S. Department of Health and Human Services, Public Health Service, Indian Health Service, Alaska Area Office. (1993). *Office of community health service FY 92 report.* Anchorage, AK: Author.

Waring, K., N. McNabb, S., & Elliott, N. (1988). *Alaska natives at risk: A report prepared for the Alaska Federation of Natives.* Anchorage, AK: Institute of Social and Economic Research.

Williams, G. (1992, July). Income in Alaska: A decade of change. *Alaska Economic Trends,* pp. 3–4.

### Further Reading

Fejes, C. (1981). *Villagers.* New York: Random House.

Morgan, L. (1974). *And the land provides: Alaska natives in a year of transition.* Garden City, NY: Doubleday.

Nelson, R. K. (1969). *Hunters of the northern ice.* Chicago: University of Chicago Press.

Scollon, R., & Scollon, S. B. K. (1980). *Interethnic communication.* Fairbanks: University of Alaska Fairbanks, Alaska Native Language Center.

Wallis, V. (1993). *Two old women.* Fairbanks, AK: Epicenter Press.

**Eileen M. Lally, EdD, ACSW, LCSW,** is professor, University of Alaska, Social Work Department, 3311 Providence Drive, Anchorage, AK 99508. **Helen Andon Haynes, Koyukon Athabascan, CHES, EdM, BSW,** is deputy director, Health Nations Project, National Center for American Indian and Alaska Native Mental Health Research, University of Colorado, Boulder.

### For further information see

American Indians; Community; Ethnic-Sensitive Practice; Health Care: Direct Practice; Mental Health Overview; Rural Social Work Overview.

**Key Words**
Alaska Natives    Native Americans

# Alcohol Abuse

**Sandra C. Anderson**

Although most adult Americans drink alcoholic beverages and 11 million of them suffer from alcoholism or alcohol dependence and 7 million from alcohol abuse (National Institute on Alcohol Abuse and Alcoholism [NIAAA], 1990), there has never been a universally accepted definition of these problems. Keller and Doria (1991) summarized the evolution of definitions from classical times to the present. As early as 1785, Dr. Benjamin Rush called intemperance a disease and addiction, and alcoholism was treated as a disease throughout the 19th century. Although adherents of the moral model of alcoholism have voiced their opposition to the disease model for over 100 years, it has continued to flourish. The majority of health care professionals regard alcoholism as a disease and, as noted by Keller and Doria, the terms "alcoholism," "alcohol addiction," and "alcohol dependence" are identical in meaning within the disease conception of alcoholism.

## Diagnosis of Alcoholism

Most codification schemes of alcoholism are based on several phenomena: tolerance to alcohol and withdrawal when alcohol is not consumed (physical dependence), impaired control of drinking, and psychosocial problems related to the use of alcohol (Beresford, 1991). The two most often used classification systems of alcohol abuse and dependence are the *Diagnostic and Statistical Manual of Mental Disorders* (DSM) and the *International Classification of Diseases* (ICD). This section addresses the most recent revisions of these two systems, the DSM-IV (American Psychiatric Association, 1994) and the ICD-10 (World Health Organization, 1992).

The DSM-IV diagnosis of *alcohol dependence* requires that at least three of the following seven criteria occur at any time in the same 12-month period:

1. tolerance (need for markedly increased amounts of alcohol to achieve intoxication or desired effect, or markedly diminished effect with continued use of the same amount of alcohol)
2. withdrawal (those symptoms experienced when no alcohol is consumed, or a need to take alcohol or closely related substance to relieve or avoid withdrawal symptoms)
3. alcohol often taken in larger amounts or over a longer period than was intended
4. a persistent desire or unsuccessful effort to cut down or control alcohol use

5. a great deal of time spent in activities necessary to obtain alcohol, use alcohol, or recover from its effects
6. important social, occupational, or recreational activities given up or reduced because of alcohol use
7. continued alcohol use despite knowledge of having a persistent or recurrent physical or psychological problem that was likely to have been caused or exacerbated by alcohol.

The clinician must specify if the criteria occur with or without physiological dependence (evidence of tolerance or withdrawal).

A diagnosis of *alcohol abuse* requires that one or more of the following four criteria occur at any time during the same 12-month period:

1. recurrent alcohol use resulting in a failure to fulfill major role obligations at work, school, or home
2. recurrent alcohol use in situations in which it is physically hazardous
3. recurrent alcohol-related legal problems
4. continued alcohol use despite persistent or recurrent social or interpersonal problems caused or exacerbated by the effects of alcohol.

For the clinician to arrive at a diagnosis of alcohol abuse, the client must never have met the criteria for alcohol dependence. Grant and Towle (1991), however, pointed out that the inability to diagnose abuse if a person has ever met the criteria for dependence is a requirement not supported by epidemiological studies. Cahalan and Room (1974) and Clark and Midanik (1982) have shown that many symptoms of alcohol dependence in young adults remit spontaneously later in life, raising questions about the disorder's chronicity.

The ICD-10 classification includes categories for the alcohol dependence syndrome and the harmful use of alcohol. A diagnosis of *alcohol dependence* requires that at least three of the following six criteria be met at some time during the previous year: (1) strong compulsion to drink, (2) impaired capacity to control drinking, (3) withdrawal state or drinking to relieve or avoid withdrawal symptoms, (4) tolerance, (5) progressive neglect of alternative interests, and (6) drinking despite evidence of harmful consequences. A narrowing of drinking patterns is also a characteristic feature. A diagnosis of *harmful use of alcohol* (*alcohol abuse* in the DSM-IV) requires that alcohol abuse be responsible for physical or mental harm to the user.

## Etiology of Alcoholism

Although no single theory adequately explains the etiology of alcoholism, a number of explanations have been advanced. The major explanatory theories can be categorized as moral, psychological, biological, sociocultural, and multivariate.

### Moral Model

The evils of drinking have been written about since the 18th century in England. The view based on Christian morality is that the person with alcoholism is defective in moral character and lacks the strength of will to resist temptation. This model reached its height in the United States in 1917 with the unsuccessful experiment of national prohibition. As noted by Marlatt (1988), many Christian moralists continue to view drinking as sinful, although most scholars have abandoned this model.

### Psychological Theories

This category includes personality theory, psychodynamic theory, and learning theory.

***Personality theory.*** Personality theory assumes that there are certain personality traits that predispose an individual to alcoholism. The term "alcoholic personality" is often used to describe the client who is immature, dependent, impulsive, and easily frustrated. Yet these traits can just as easily be attributed to the effects of alcoholism. In addition, other clinical populations show many of these personality traits but are not alcoholic, and not all people with alcoholism demonstrate the traits (Donovan, 1986). Vaillant (1983) concluded that personality variables are of minimal importance as a cause of alcoholism.

***Psychodynamic theory.*** Adherents of variants of psychoanalytic theory postulate that a structural deficit in object relations leads to ego weaknesses (for example, the inability to manage affect and impulse) sufficient to produce alcoholism. The addiction then inflates the otherwise vulnerable self (Donovan, 1986). This theory is dependent on the retrospective reports of the client. Early childhood deficiencies in object relations are not specific to alcoholism and, in fact, are commonly reported by nonalcoholic adults who have a variety of psychosocial problems.

***Learning theory.*** From a social-learning perspective, addictive behaviors consist of overlearned, maladaptive habit patterns usually followed by some form of immediate gratification. These "bad habits" can lead to disease end states, but this does not mean that the behavior itself is a disease or is constitutionally determined (Marlatt & Gordon, 1985). The tension-reduction hypothesis underlying this theory has not been supported empirically, however. People consuming alcohol actually become *more* anxious and depressed over time.

### Biological Theories

Genetic theories of alcoholism rest on the assumption that alcoholics are constitutionally predisposed to develop physical dependence on alcohol. Kendler, Heath, Neale, Kessler, and Eaves (1992) found that genetics accounted for 50 percent to 61 percent of a woman's tendency to develop alcoholism, and Bohman, Sigvardsson, and Cloninger (1981) found a threefold incidence of alcoholism among adopted-away daughters of alcoholic biological mothers, regardless of the presence or absence of alcoholism in the birth father or in adoptive parents. Monozygotic twins have a significantly higher concordance rate for alcoholism than do dizygotic twins (Murray & Stabenau, 1982), and Goodwin (1979) found that the incidence of alcoholism among sons of alcoholics was four times greater than that among a control group of sons of nonalcoholics, whether the sons were raised by their own alcoholic parents or by nonalcoholic foster parents.

In their review of research on the genetics of alcoholism, Crabbe and Goldman (1992) concluded that whether a person becomes alcoholic is dependent on the interaction of multiple "vulnerability" genes and environmental conditions that decrease or increase the probability of becoming an alcoholic. Alcoholism may be a number of disorders with various combinations of common factors or it may be a single disorder with specific subtypes. For example, Cloninger, Bohman, and Sigvardsson's (1981) subtypes describe alcoholism without (Type I) and alcoholism with (Type II) antisocial personality traits.

Research on potential biological risk markers has been inconclusive. Most studies have not confirmed the report that alcoholics are more likely than nonalcoholic controls to possess a particular gene form ($A_1$) for a receptor of the neurotransmitter dopamine (Blum et al., 1990). Although some researchers (Whipple, Berman, & Noble, 1991) reported attenuated brain wave responses in recovering alcoholics and their young sons who had never tried alcohol, it has not been demonstrated that these children are at greater risk for eventually becoming alcoholic (Crabbe & Goldman, 1992). In summary, although genetic knowledge will help identify individuals who are biologically at risk, the ultimate etiological model must take into account both genetic vulnerability and environmental reactivity.

### Sociocultural Theories

Sociocultural theorists note that societies vary tremendously in the ways they encourage or regulate the use of alcohol. Within the United States, rates of alcoholism vary by age, gender, occupation, social class, ethnicity, religion, and family background (Vaillant, 1983). For example, men have a significantly higher rate of alcoholism than do women, possibly attributable to the extent of social pressure and stigma attached to problem drinking by women. Sociological theory is one of the least developed areas in the field of alcoholism, perhaps because of the difficulty in separating sociocultural variables from constitutional ones.

### Multivariate Causal Model

Because the diverse theoretical hypotheses on the etiology of alcoholism have thus far failed to demonstrate an unequivocal, single cause of the disease, it seems appropriate to view alcoholism as the final product of the interaction of a number of complex variables. In any particular individual, one or more of these etiological variables may predominate.

Donovan (1986) noted that the model of Cloninger, Reich, and Wetzel (1979) best reflects the multifactorial nature of the etiology of alcoholism. Cloninger et al. suggested that heavy drinking is a nongenetic phenomenon associated with gender, sociocultural variables, prealcoholic psychopathology, and stress. Alcohol dependence, on the other hand, is a separate phenomenon, heavily controlled by genetic vulnerability. Thus, they argued, mood disorders and antisocial personality disorders are not directly related to alcohol dependence but may be related to heavy drinking that can trigger the vulnerability in a genetically predisposed individual.

## Development of Alcoholism

When alcohol is ingested, the body begins to metabolize it in the stomach, then in the liver. Alcohol is initially converted to acetaldehyde by the enzyme alcohol dehydrogenase and then is converted to an acetate that is broken down into water, hydrogen, and oxygen. The average adult is able to oxidize slightly less than one "drink" (one-half ounce of ethanol) per hour, but there are significant differences in individual rates of metabolism. Drinking large amounts of alcohol over time results in tolerance, which requires the ingestion of even larger doses of alcohol to get the same psychological effect.

The development of alcohol problems follows variable patterns over time and does not necessarily proceed directly to a severe final stage (Pattison, Sobell, & Sobell, 1977). The development of alcohol dependence occurs as the susceptible individual experiences gratification from alcohol consumption, ingestion becomes more frequent, psychological dependence develops, and ingestion continues to increase until tolerance and physical dependence develop. At this point, withdrawal symptoms act to keep the person drinking. Although this is the essence of the addiction process, most alcoholics experience spontaneous periods of abstinence alternating with periods of prolonged drinking.

## CONSEQUENCES OF ALCOHOLISM

### Physical

Long-term use of substantial amounts of alcohol can result in diarrhea, gastritis, pancreatitis, fatty liver, alcoholic hepatitis, and cirrhosis. Heavy drinking is also related to increased risk of cancer of the mouth, tongue, pharynx, esophagus, stomach, colon, liver, and pancreas. Alcoholics often develop degenerative heart disease, nutritional deficiencies, and acute and chronic brain damage. Alcoholic women often suffer from infertility and a high frequency of gynecologic problems. Drinking during pregnancy can result in harm to the fetus ranging from mild physical and behavioral deficits to fetal alcohol syndrome.

It is increasingly important to consider the relationship between alcohol and HIV (human immunodeficiency virus) and AIDS (acquired immune deficiency syndrome). It is now clear that alcohol impairs the ability of white blood cells to defend against HIV. In addition, some people are more likely to engage in certain high-risk sexual behaviors when drinking as a result of alcohol's disinhibiting effects (National Institute on Alcohol Abuse and Alcoholism, 1992).

Alcohol plays a significant role in trauma, a major cause of morbidity and mortality in the United States. Alcohol is involved in the majority of traffic fatalities, fires and burns, hypothermia cases, falls, and homicides. Alcohol is also associated with at least 20 percent of completed suicides (Lowenfels & Miller, 1984).

### Emotional

Between 6 million and 12 million children live in households with at least one alcoholic parent. Although a large proportion of these children function well and do not develop serious problems (Werner, 1986), they are at risk for alcoholism and a variety of cognitive, emotional, and behavioral difficulties. Children from alcoholic families tend to have lower IQ, verbal, and reading scores, but still perform within normal ranges (Bennett, Wolin, & Reiss, 1988). They report higher levels of depression and anxiety than children from nonalcoholic families (Anderson & Quast, 1983), and are frequently diagnosed as having conduct disorders (West & Prinz, 1987). Despite numerous studies that show an association between alcoholism and violence in the family, causality remains in doubt (Martin, 1992). When compared to nonalcoholic families, families of alcoholics do have lower levels of family cohesion, expressiveness, independence, and intellectual orientation and higher levels of conflict (Clair & Genest, 1986; Filstead, McElfresh, & Anderson, 1981; Moos & Moos, 1984). It should be noted, however, that these problems do not appear to be specific to this population and often occur in other dysfunctional families.

### Financial

Alcohol abuse and alcoholism cost society many billions of dollars each year. Most of the costs result from medical treatment of the consequences of alcoholism; only a minority of health costs are for the treatment of alcoholism itself. Other expenses are related to lost productivity, losses to society from premature deaths, treatment of fetal alcohol syndrome, criminal justice and social welfare administration, and property losses from motor vehicle crashes and fires (Rice, Kelman, & Miller, 1991).

## EPIDEMIOLOGY

The prevalence of alcohol use and abuse in the United States is measured most directly by two national surveys: the National Survey of High School Seniors and the National Household Survey on Drug Abuse. Data for the National Survey of High School Seniors are gathered annually by a self-administered questionnaire given to students in the eighth through 12th grades. The most recent survey indicated that 88 percent of the class of 1992 had used alcohol at least once, 77 percent had used it in the past year (down from 78 percent in 1991), 51 percent had used it in the past month (down from 54 percent in 1991), 3.4 percent had used it daily (equal to the 1991 rate), and 28 percent had consumed five or more drinks in a row in the past two weeks (National Institute on Drug Abuse, 1993). The 1992 follow-up survey of college students indicated that 87 percent had used alcohol in the past year and 71 percent in the past month.

The 1992 National Household Survey on Drug Abuse surveyed the population age 12 and older living in households, college dormitories, and homeless shelters in the United States. Estimates indicate that there were 98 million current (past month) drinkers of alcohol in 1992 compared to 105 million in 1988 and 113 million in 1985. The overall rate for current alcohol use was 48 percent, down slightly from 1990. Current use among 12- to 17-year-olds declined from 20 percent in 1991 to 16 percent in 1992. Rates of alcohol use among 12- to 13-year-olds increased to 26 percent. Of the 133 million people age 12 and older (65 percent of the population) who drank alcohol in the past year, 42 million drank at least once a week (Substance Abuse and Mental Health Services Administration, 1993).

When the demographic correlates of alcohol use are examined, there are significant differences among subgroups. Although the prevalence of alcohol use does not differ among males and females under age 18, differences do occur after age 18, with males significantly more likely to drink. Residents of nonmetropolitan areas were significantly less likely to drink, and the rate of use was lower in the South. People with more years of education were more likely to drink, and those who were unemployed were significantly less likely to drink.

The National Institute on Drug Abuse defines heavy drinkers as those who drank five or more drinks per occasion on five or more days in the past month. Of those age 12 and older, 10 million Americans (5 percent of the population) were heavy drinkers; this number has changed little since 1988. Heavy drinking was most common among those ages 18 to 25. Eleven percent of current alcohol drinkers also used one or more illicit drugs, compared with 2 percent of those who were not current alcohol users (Substance Abuse and Mental Health Services Administration, 1993).

Trends in alcohol use for sociodemographic subgroups are based on findings from the 1985, 1988, 1990, and 1992 National Household Surveys on Drug Abuse. Any use of alcohol decreased slightly between 1985 and 1992 for all subgroups except eighth graders. The most striking differences in trends of heavy alcohol use were for educational attainment, reflected in the steady increase in use by those who had not finished high school (Flewelling, Rachal, & Marsden, 1992). Parker and Harford (1992) reported that although there are more current drinkers among people in white-collar than in blue-collar occupations, those in blue-collar jobs are at greater risk for alcohol dependence. The prevalence of dependence and severe dependence on alcohol is especially high among food service workers (particularly bartenders and waitresses), farmers, fishers, forestry workers, mechanics, construction workers, machine operators, and laborers. In 1992, 66 percent of adults with a college degree were current drinkers, compared with only 36 percent of those having less than a high school education. However, the rate of heavy alcohol use among college graduates was 5.7 percent and the rate among high school dropouts was 10.6 percent (Substance Abuse and Mental Health Services Administration, 1993).

Much of the knowledge of alcoholism is based on studies of male subjects. Studies involving more female subjects reveal significant differences between alcoholic men and women.

**Women**

Williams, Grant, Harford, and Noble (1989) estimated that of the 18 million alcohol-abusing or dependent individuals in the United States, nearly one-third are women. In the general population, 83 percent (87 percent of men and 79 percent of women) have used alcohol at some time in their lives. Seventy percent of men and 60 percent of women have used alcohol in the past year, and 56 percent of men and 40 percent of women are current drinkers. Of the 65 percent of the total population that has used alcohol in the past year, 38 percent (49 percent of men and 27 percent of women) have used alcohol at least 12 times, and 20 percent (30 percent of men and 12 percent of women) drink at least once per week. Men are much more likely than women to be heavy drinkers (8 percent and 2 percent, respectively) (Substance Abuse and Mental Health Services Administration, 1993). In general, women consume less alcohol and have fewer alcohol-related problems than men do, but among the heaviest drinkers, women surpass men in the severity of problems resulting from their drinking. Although women under age 35 report more heavy drinking and higher rates of drinking-related problems than do older women, the incidence of alcohol dependence is greater among women ages 35 to 49 (Williams, Stinson, Parker, Harford, & Noble, 1987).

Overall patterns in women's drinking have remained consistent over the past few decades, but the drinking patterns of employed women are different from those of women not employed outside the home. In reviewing the literature in this area, Shore (1992) noted that there is less abstinence, increased consumption, and greater frequency of drinking occasions among employed women. Given this finding, it is interesting to note that although a majority of women professionals drink, most are light to moderate drinkers and few are heavy drinkers (La Rosa, 1990; Shore 1990). Little is known about women employed in blue-collar and other jobs.

There is no evidence to support the hypothesis that role conflict or role overload increases women's drinking; in fact, alcohol consumption and related negative consequences decrease with increasing numbers of children (Shore, 1990). Hammer and Vaglum (1989) also found that having children correlated with lower levels of alcohol consumption among women employed full-time. Hence, as Shore (1992) pointed out, "role deprivation, defined as the lack of meaningful or life-enriching roles, may be a more significant influence on women's drinking behavior than role conflict or role overload" (p. 162).

Women alcoholics experience greater shame, guilt, and depression over their substance abuse than do alcoholic men (Turnbull, 1989). They frequently also have a history of being overresponsible in their family of origin (Bepko & Krestan, 1990). Because socially unacceptable behavior is more narrowly defined for women than it is for men, immense social stigma leads to low self-esteem. The psychosocial problems of alcoholic women are similar to those of women in the general population and may be more a result of gender than of substance abuse.

The interval between onset of drinking-related problems and entry into treatment is shorter for women than it is for men (Piazza, Vrbka, & Yeager, 1989), and women experience greater physiological impairment earlier in their drinking careers (Hill, 1984). For a number of reasons, women become intoxicated after drinking a smaller quantity of alcohol than that needed to intoxicate men. First, women have less body water than men of comparable size, so women achieve higher concentrations of alcohol in their blood after consuming equivalent amounts of alcohol. Second, because of diminished activity of gastric alcohol dehydrogenase (the primary enzyme involved in the metabolism of alcohol), more alcohol enters the systemic circulation. This "first-pass metabolism" in the stomach is decreased in women compared to men and is virtually nonexistent in alcoholic women (Frezza et al., 1990). Third, fluctuations in gonadal hormone levels during the menstrual cycle may affect the rate of alcohol metabolism, making a woman more susceptible to elevated blood alcohol concentrations just before the beginning of the menstrual flow (Sutker, Goist, & King, 1987).

Chronic heavy drinking is more physically damaging to women than it is to men. Female alcoholics have death rates 50 percent to 100 percent higher than those of male alcoholics and a greater percentage of women die from suicides, alcohol-related accidents, circulatory disorders, and cirrhosis of the liver (Hill, 1982). Menstrual disorders, some of which can have adverse effects on fertility, and early menopause are associated with chronic heavy drinking. Women who have experienced sex abuse and rape are at very high risk of developing both alcoholism and sexual dysfunction (Wilsnack, 1984).

One subgroup of drinkers, pregnant women, are at high risk for having children with abnormalities that fall on a continuum, with complete "fetal alcohol syndrome" (FAS) at one end and subtle cognitive–behavioral deficits at the other (Anderson & Grant, 1984). Alcohol is acutely toxic to the fetus independent of the effects of malnutrition (Phillips, Henderson, & Schenker, 1989), and prenatal alcohol exposure is one of the leading causes of mental retardation in the Western world. Criteria for the diagnosis of FAS are (1) prenatal or postnatal growth retardation (weight or length below the 10th percentile); (2) central nervous system involvement, including neurological abnormalities, developmental delays, behavioral dysfunction, intellectual impairment, and skull or brain malformations; and (3) a characteristic face with short palpebral fissures (eye openings), a thin upper lip, and a flattened midface and philtrum (the groove in the middle of the upper lip) (Sokol & Clarren, 1989).

Although children with FAS are born only to women who consume large amounts of alcohol during pregnancy, neurological and growth deficits have been observed in infants born to moderate drinkers (Russell, 1991). It is probable that each abnormal outcome in brain structure and function has its own dose–response relationship and that vulnerability of individual organ systems may be greatest at the time of their most rapid cell division (Weiner & Morse, 1989). There is evidence that the number of women who drink during pregnancy is declining, but the rates of alcohol consumption among high-risk populations (pregnant smokers, women under the age of 25, and women with the least education) remain unchanged (Serdula, Williamson, Kendrick, Anda, & Byers, 1991).

### Children and Adolescents

Current use of alcohol has dropped for the 12- to 17-year-old cohort, but use has increased slightly for those in the 12- to 13-year-old subgroup. Adolescents who develop alcohol or other drug problems tend to share certain characteristics. They frequently show aggressive behavior in early childhood (Loeber, 1988); experience difficulty in school (Hawkins & Lishner, 1987); experience inadequate parental supervision and parental substance abuse (Johnson, Schoutz, & Locke, 1984);

associate with peers who use drugs (Elliott, Huizinga, & Ageton, 1985); and live in neighborhoods characterized by mobility, poverty, and disorganization (Herting & Guest, 1985).

Most explanatory theories of child and adolescent alcohol abuse are based on experience with adults. The exceptions are "problem behavior" theories that view alcohol abuse in the context of other developmental problems, such as delinquency and teenage pregnancy, which often occur concomitantly (Hawkins, Jenson, Catalano, & Lishner, 1988). These theories suggest that adolescents with poor coping and social skills find interpersonal situations unrewarding, and alternative behaviors lead to delinquency or drug use (Schinke, Botvin, & Orlandi, 1991). Intervention based on these theories takes into account multiple causes of antisocial behavior at the individual, family, school, and community levels.

The lack of a clear definition of alcohol abuse and alcoholism in adolescents often leads to incorrect diagnosis, which can be self-fulfilling or stigmatizing. Although relatively few adolescents evidence physical dependence on alcohol, the consequences of their drinking can be devastating (Henderson & Anderson, 1989). Alcohol is the major cause of all fatal and nonfatal crashes involving adolescent drivers (Long, Brendtro, & Johnson, 1993) and is associated with homicides, suicides, and drownings—the other three leading causes of death among youths (National Commission on Drug-Free Schools, 1990). Among sexually active teens, those who have at least five drinks daily are three times less likely to use condoms, placing them at greater risk for HIV infection (Hingson, Strunin, Berlin, & Heeren, 1990). Finally, those who start using alcohol between ages 13 and 16 are much more likely to develop drug problems than those who wait until after age 19. Most youths who use illegal drugs first used alcohol and continue the regular use of alcohol with other drugs (National Commission on Drug-Free Schools, 1990).

**Elderly People**

Studies of the general population indicate that the elderly consume less alcohol and have less severe alcohol-related problems than do younger people (Smart & Adlaf, 1988). In spite of these findings, around 10 percent of people over age 65 have some kind of drinking problem, with at least 8 percent being alcohol dependent (Bienenfeld, 1987). The elderly among the inpatient medical population have an 18 percent to 21 percent prevalence of alcoholism, whereas those in the inpatient psychiatric population have rates of 44 percent (Curtis, Geller, Stokes, Levine, & Moore, 1989). Alcoholism in the elderly is generally characterized as a lifelong pattern of dependency continued into old age (early onset) or as reactive or geriatric alcoholism (late onset). Atkinson, Turner, Kofoed, and Tolson (1985) estimated that about two-thirds of elderly alcoholics began drinking heavily before age 60 and that elderly women are more likely to be late-onset alcoholics (Holzer et al., 1986). Late-onset problems tend to be less severe and are associated with less family alcoholism and greater psychological stability than early-onset problems (Atkinson, Tolson, & Turner, 1990). Contrary to popular belief, retirement is not associated with changes in alcohol consumption (Ekerdt, De Labry, Glynn, & Davis, 1989), and the overall relationship between life stressors and the onset of alcoholism remains unclear.

The majority of the elderly who take over-the-counter drugs regularly also use alcohol or prescribed medications that interact with alcohol. Alcohol-related brain disease may result in a serious decline in intellect among older alcoholics. Alcoholism is a significant risk factor in suicide among the elderly (Barraclough, Bunch, Nelson, & Sainsbury, 1974) and can mimic and contribute to major depression. Because the size of the elderly population will increase significantly in the future, there will likely be greater numbers of elderly alcohol abusers and alcoholics (Williams et al., 1987).

**Lesbians and Gay Men**

A number of early studies reported higher rates of substance abuse among gay men and lesbians compared with men and women in the general population (see Anderson & Henderson, 1985, for a review of studies focusing on lesbian alcoholics). Most of these studies have serious methodological limitations, and more recent studies indicate that differences in heavy alcohol use may not be as large as previously thought (McKirnan & Peterson, 1989).

The differences that do exist have been explained in a number of ways. No evidence exists that suggests biological differences inordinately predispose lesbian and gay men to develop a physical dependence on alcohol. If they are equally predisposed, however, then oppression of gay men and lesbians and subculture support of drinking could produce higher rates of alcoholism among them. Internalized homophobia results in tremendous anxiety and self-hatred, sometimes assuaged by alcohol. There is little in the literature about alcoholism among gay men and lesbians who are American Indian, African American, Hispanic American, or Asian American.

**People with Mental and Physical Disabilities**
Of all clients with coexisting disabilities, those with mental disorders in conjunction with substance disorders have received the most attention. The National Institute of Mental Health Epidemiological Catchment Area studies indicate that when compared with nonalcoholics, alcoholics are 21 times more likely to also have a diagnosis of antisocial personality disorder, four times more likely to have a diagnosis of drug abuse or schizophrenia, and six times more likely to have a diagnosis of mania (Helzer & Pryzbeck, 1988). Their risk of having a diagnosis of major depression is only slightly increased, and there is no increase in risk of having an anxiety disorder.

No good estimates exist of individuals with mental retardation who have alcohol problems, but a number of studies indicate that those with developmental disabilities are less likely to use or abuse alcohol (Reiss, 1990). One study of people dually diagnosed with mental retardation and substance disorders concluded that their alcohol-related problems were similar to those of alcoholics who were not mentally retarded (Westermeyer, Phaobtong, & Neider, 1988). It was suggested, however, that mentally retarded clients may experience problems at lower doses of alcohol than people who were not mentally retarded.

Significant numbers of spinal cord injuries are alcohol related, and continued use of alcohol following injury can lead to serious complications (Heinemann, Doll, & Schnoll, 1989). Alcohol also is involved in more than half of all traumatic head or brain injuries (Sparadeo, Strauss, & Barth, 1990).

Little information is available on alcoholism in blind or visually impaired people. There is some published material on hearing-impaired people, but it is not known whether rates of alcohol use or dependency among people who are deaf differ from those of the general population.

**Homeless People**
The National Coalition for the Homeless, an advocacy group, claims that over the course of a year, 3 million people are homeless (Hopper & Hamberg, 1984). The rate of alcoholism among this population has remained stable at 30 percent to 33 percent since the turn of the century (Stark, 1987). Even though this rate is at least three times greater than that in the general population, little attention has been directed toward this subgroup of the homeless population (Koroloff & Anderson, 1989). The few completed studies have significant deficiencies, including failure to gather sufficiently detailed information on alcohol use, use of small samples restricted to male shelter users, and lack of testing for reliability and validity of self-report data. The subpopulation of homeless alcoholics is more diverse than it was 40 years ago, containing more adolescents and women (Anderson, 1987; Anderson, Boe, & Smith, 1988; Corrigan & Anderson, 1984). Approximately 15 percent of homeless women and 45 percent of homeless men are alcoholic. The highest rate of alcoholism is found among homeless American Indians, whereas the rate of alcoholism is below average for homeless Hispanics and even lower for homeless Asian Americans (Wright, Knight, Weber-Burdin, & Lam, 1987).

Alcoholic homeless people suffer most medical disorders at much greater rates than those reported by the nonalcoholic homeless population. The major physical health concerns in order of frequency are peripheral vascular disease, hypertension, gastrointestinal disorders, traumas, eye problems, neurological disorders, cardiac problems, tuberculosis, arterial disease, and diabetes. Alcoholic homeless people also show disproportionately high rates of other drug abuse and mental illness. Psychiatric impairment is twice as common among homeless alcoholic women as men (Wright et al., 1987), and individuals with dual diagnoses tend to be younger, never married, and childless (Koegel & Burnam, 1987). Farr, Koegel, and Burnam (1986) found that almost half of the homeless chronically mentally ill people in their study also were chronic substance abusers.

**American Indians and Alaska Natives**
Studies of drinking prevalence among Native Americans indicate that tribes vary widely in alcohol use (May, 1982), but as a whole American Indians have very high mortality rates from alcohol-related causes. At least 80 percent of homicides, suicides, and automobile crashes in the American Indian population are alcohol related (Smith, 1989), and the death rate from cirrhosis is five times higher among American Indians and Native Alaskans ages 25 to 44 than it is for the general population (National Institute on Alcohol Abuse and Alcoholism, 1990).

A number of etiological theories have been advanced about the high prevalence of alcohol use and abuse in this population. American Indians are a severely oppressed group, plagued with poverty, social alienation, and poor access to jobs and education. It has been suggested that they drink to release anger, deal with boredom and depression, and handle pressures from forced acculturation

(Littman, 1970). May (1991) noted that abusive drinking styles and the high-risk environments in which American Indians drink (rural bordertowns) combine to produce high levels of intoxication, arrest, trauma, and mortality. He also pointed out that there is no consistent racially based physiological difference in alcohol metabolism between American Indians, white Americans, and African Americans.

American Indian women drink less than do American Indian men, but are at greater risk for alcohol-related health problems. Their drinking patterns are often bimodal (that is, they drink heavily or abstain) (May, 1991). Women account for nearly half of cirrhosis deaths among American Indians (Indian Health Service, 1988) and have a cirrhosis death rate six times higher than that for white women (National Institute on Alcohol Abuse and Alcoholism, 1985). Fetal alcohol syndrome is 33 times higher in American Indians than it is in white Americans (Chavez, Cordero, & Becerra, 1989).

**African Americans**

The 1992 National Household Survey on Drug Abuse (Substance Abuse and Mental Health Services Administration, 1993) found that white Americans are significantly more likely than African Americans and Hispanics to have consumed alcohol in their lifetime, in the past year, and in the past month. There are very similar rates of heavy alcohol use (around 5 percent) for all groups when taken as a whole. White females are significantly more likely than African American and Hispanic females to have ever consumed alcohol, and equal proportions of white and African American women drink heavily.

**Hispanic Americans**

The Hispanic population of the United States comprises a number of subgroups, but most of the alcoholism research has focused on Mexican Americans. The lack of homogeneity among subgroups makes generalization of the findings risky, but research indicates that the prevalence of alcoholism among Hispanic males is greater than that among the general population (Caetano, 1985). Hispanic women, on the other hand, are much more likely to be abstainers or very light drinkers than their male counterparts or than women in the general population. Although the drinking patterns of Hispanic males have not significantly changed, the proportion of Hispanic women drinkers becomes greater with each generation beyond immigrant status (Gilbert, 1991). Mexican American women report heavy drinking and alcohol-related problems more often than do Cuban American and Puerto Rican women (Caetano, 1988). The disease model of alcoholism is not generally accepted in the Hispanic culture, and chemical dependency tends to be viewed as a moral weakness (Aguilar, DiNitto, Franklin, & Lopez-Pilkinton, 1991).

**Asian Americans**

There are many Asian nationalities, and relatively little is known about their use of alcohol because few studies have identified Asian Americans by subgroup. Although they drink less and have fewer alcohol-related problems than any other major ethnic group in the United States, some see alcoholism among Asian Americans as a growing area of concern (Gordis, 1990). Asians rarely drink alone, strongly encourage moderation (Chi, Lubben, & Kitano, 1989), and tend to handle problems within the family or community rather than turning to public treatment services. Thus, Asian Americans may underreport alcoholism.

Asian American women and youths drink less than their American counterparts (Chi et al., 1989), but drinking patterns among different groups of Asian Americans vary widely (Gordis, 1990). Koreans, both male and female, are most likely to be abstainers (Chi & Kitano, 1989). Among men, 28 percent of Japanese, Koreans, and Filipinos are heavy drinkers. Among women, 12 percent of Japanese, 4 percent of Filipinos, and almost none of the Korean and Chinese are heavy drinkers (Gordis, 1990).

Asians apparently metabolize alcohol more rapidly than whites, and the flushing response (facial flushing, headache, dizziness, rapid heart rate, and itching) is common among some Asian Americans (Gordis, 1990). Although this response may help protect against alcoholism, it alone does not explain lower prevalence because not all Asians have the response and some who do continue to drink over the response.

**Other Ethnic Groups**

Several writers have noted the rise in alcoholism rates in the American Jewish Community (see, for example, Rosen, 1989), in spite of the general belief that rates are low. In terms of cultural heritage, Italians have low rates of alcoholism, whereas the French and Irish have high rates. Most of these differences have been explained by sociocultural factors. Among youths, alcohol use by ethnic group is highest to lowest in this order: American Indian, white, Hispanic American, African American, and Asian American (Wallace & Bachman, 1991).

## Contemporary Debates and Issues

A number of unresolved issues in the alcoholism field have been mentioned here. Controversy continues about the disease concept of alcoholism and the relative roles of biological and psychosocial factors in its etiology. The distinctions between alcohol abuse and dependency are not always clear, and there is debate about the validity of traditional conceptions of the nature and progression of alcoholism. Much more clarity is also needed in defining the dual diagnosis of mental and substance disorders.

The resolution of these issues could have profound implications for the prevention and treatment of alcoholism. It is likely that treatment in the future will make better use of differential diagnosis of abuse–dependence and primary–secondary alcoholism in order to use abstinence and moderation methods in complementary ways. As the overall consumption of alcohol declines, there is a growing demand for more attention to primary prevention. It is incumbent on the social work profession to prepare not only clinicians but also those capable of beginning the arduous task of developing a comprehensive prevention strategy.

## References


Aguilar, M. A., DiNitto, D. M., Franklin, C., & Lopez-Pilkinton, B. (1991). Mexican-American families: A psychoeducational approach for addressing chemical dependency and codependency. *Child & Adolescent Social Work, 8,* 309–326.

American Psychiatric Association. (1994). *Diagnostic and statistical manual of mental disorders* (4th ed.). Washington, DC: Author.

Anderson, S. C. (1987). Alcoholic women on skid row. *Social Work, 32,* 362–365.

Anderson, S. C., Boe, T., & Smith, S. (1988). Homeless women. *Affilia, 3,* 62–70.

Anderson, S. C., & Grant, J. F. (1984). Pregnant women and alcohol: Implications for social work. *Social Casework: The Journal of Contemporary Social Work, 65,* 3–10.

Anderson, S. C., & Henderson, D. C. (1985). Working with lesbian alcoholics. *Social Work, 30,* 518–525.

Anderson, E., & Quast, W. (1983). Young children in alcoholic families: A mental health needs-assessment and an intervention/prevention strategy. *Journal of Primary Prevention, 3,* 174–187.

Atkinson, R. M., Tolson, R. L., & Turner, J. A. (1990). Late versus early onset problem drinking in older men. *Alcoholism: Clinical & Experimental Research, 14,* 574–579.

Atkinson, R. M., Turner, J. A., Kofoed, L. L., & Tolson, R. L. (1985). Early versus late onset alcoholism in older persons: Preliminary findings. *Alcoholism: Clinical & Experimental Research, 9,* 513–515.

Barraclough, B. M., Bunch, J., Nelson, B., & Sainsbury, P. (1974). A hundred cases of suicide. *British Journal of Psychiatry, 125,* 355–373.

Bennett, L. A., Wolin, S. J., & Reiss, D. (1988). Cognitive, behavioral, and emotional problems among school-aged children of alcoholic parents. *American Journal of Psychiatry, 145,* 185–190.

Bepko, C., & Krestan, J. (1990). *Too good for her own good.* New York: Harper & Row.

Beresford, T. P. (1991). The nosology of alcoholism research. *Alcohol Health & Research World, 15,* 260–265.

Bienenfeld, D. (1987). Alcoholism in the elderly. *American Family Physician, 36,* 163–169.

Blum, K., Noble, E., Sheridan, P. J., Montgomery, A., Ritchie, T., Jagadeeswaren, P., Nogomi, H., Briggs, A. H., & Cohn, J. B. (1990). Allelic association of human dopamine D2 receptor gene in alcoholism. *Journal of the American Medical Association, 263,* 2055–2060.

Bohman, M., Sigvardsson, S., & Cloninger, C. R. (1981). Maternal inheritance of alcohol abuse: Cross-fostering analysis of adopted women. *Archives of General Psychiatry, 38,* 965–969.

Caetano, R. (1985). Drinking patterns and alcohol problems in a national sample of U.S. Hispanics. In *Alcohol use among U.S. ethnic minorities* (pp. 147–162). Rockville, MD: U.S. Department of Health and Human Services.

Caetano, R. (1988). Alcohol use among Hispanic groups in the United States. *American Journal of Drug and Alcohol Abuse, 14,* 293–308.

Cahalan, D., & Room, R. (1974). *Problem drinking among American men.* New Brunswick, NJ: Rutgers Center of Alcohol Studies.

Chavez, G. F., Cordero, J. F., & Becerra, J. E. (1989). Leading major congenital malformations among minority groups in the United States, 1981–1986. *Journal of the American Medical Association, 261,* 205–209.

Chi, I., & Kitano, H.H.L. (1989). Asian Americans and alcohol: The Chinese, Japanese, Koreans, and Filipinos in Los Angeles. In *Alcohol use among U.S. ethnic minorities* (Research Monograph 18, p. 376). Washington, DC: National Institute on Alcohol Abuse and Alcoholism.

Chi, I., Lubben, J. E., & Kitano, H.H.L. (1989). Differences in drinking behavior among three Asian-American groups. *Journal of Studies on Alcohol, 50,* 15.

Clair, D., & Genest, M. (1986). Variables associated with the adjustment of offspring of alcoholic fathers. *Journal of Studies on Alcohol, 48,* 345–355.

Clark, W. B., & Midanik, L. (1982). Alcohol use and alcohol problems among U.S. adults: Results of the 1979 national survey. In National Institute on Drug Abuse and Alcoholism, *Alcohol consumption and related problems* (Alcohol and Health Monograph 1, pp. 3–52) (DHHS Publication No. ADM 82-1190). Washington, DC: U.S. Government Printing Office.

Cloninger, C. R., Bohman, M., & Sigvardsson, S. (1981). Inheritance of alcohol abuse: Cross-fostering analysis of adopted men. *Archives of General Psychiatry, 38,* 861–868.

Cloninger, C. R., Reich, T., & Wetzel, R. (1979). Alcoholism and affective disorders: Familial associations and genetic models. In D. W. Goodwin & C. K. Erickson (Eds.), *Alcoholism and affective disorders* (pp. 57–86). New York: Spectrum Publications.

Corrigan, E. M., & Anderson, S. C. (1984). Homeless alcoholic women on skid row. *American Journal of Drug & Alcohol Abuse, 10,* 535–549.

Crabbe, J. C., & Goldman, D. (1992). Alcoholism: A complex genetic disease. *Alcohol Health & Research World, 16,* 297–303.

Curtis, J. R., Geller, G., Stokes, E. J., Levine, D. M., & Moore, R. D. (1989). Characteristics, diagnosis, and treatment of alcoholism in elderly patients. *Journal of the American Geriatrics Society, 37,* 310–316.

Donovan, J. M. (1986). An etiologic model of alcoholism. *American Journal of Psychiatry, 143,* 1–11.

Ekerdt, D. J., De Labry, L. O., Glynn, R. J., & Davis, R. W. (1989). Change in drinking behaviors with retirement: Findings from the normative aging study. *Journal of Studies on Alcohol, 50,* 347–353.

Elliott, D. S., Huizinga, D., & Ageton, S. A. (1985). *Explaining delinquency and drug use.* Beverly Hills, CA: Sage Publications.

Farr, R. K., Koegel, P., & Burnam, A. (1986). *A study of homelessness and mental illness in the skid row area of Los Angeles.* Los Angeles: Los Angeles County Department of Mental Health.

Filstead, W. J., McElfresh, O., & Anderson, C. (1981). Comparing the family environments of alcoholic and "normal" families. *Journal of Alcohol & Drug Education, 26,* 24–31.

Flewelling, R. L., Rachal, J. V., & Marsden, M. E. (1992). *Socioeconomic and demographic correlates of drug and alcohol use* (DHHS Publication No. ADM 92-1906). Washington, DC: U.S. Government Printing Office.

Frezza, M., Di Padova, C., Pozzato, G., Terpin, M., Baraona, E., & Lieber, C. S. (1990). High blood alcohol levels in women: The role of decreased gastric alcohol dehydrogenase and first-pass metabolism. *New England Journal of Medicine, 322,* 95–99.

Gilbert, M. J. (1991). Acculturation and changes in drinking patterns among Mexican-American women. *Alcohol Health & Research World, 15,* 234–238.

Goodwin, D. W. (1979). Alcoholism and heredity. *Archives of General Psychiatry, 36,* 57–61.

Gordis, E. (Ed.). (1990). Epidemiology. In *Alcohol and health: Seventh special report to the U.S. Congress* (p. 35). Washington, DC: U.S. Department of Health and Human Services, National Institute on Alcohol Abuse and Alcoholism.

Grant, B. F., & Towle, L. H. (1991). A comparison of diagnostic criteria. *Alcohol Health & Research World, 15,* 284–292.

Hammer, T., & Vaglum, P. (1989). The increase in alcohol consumption among women: A phenomenon related to accessibility or stress? A general population study. *British Journal of Addiction, 84,* 767–775.

Hawkins, J. D., Jenson, J. M., Catalano, R. F., & Lishner, D. L. (1988). Delinquency and drug abuse: Implications for social services. *Social Service Review, 62,* 258–284.

Hawkins, J. D., & Lishner, D. L. (1987). Schooling and delinquency. In E. H. Johnson (Ed.), *Handbook on crime and delinquency prevention* (pp. 179–221). Westport, CT: Greenwood Press.

Heinemann, A. W., Doll, M., & Schnoll, S. (1989). Treatment of alcohol abuse in persons with recent spinal cord injuries. *Alcohol Health & Research World, 13,* 110–117.

Helzer, J. E., & Pryzbeck, T. R. (1988). The co-occurrence of alcoholism with other psychiatric disorders in the general population and its impact on treatment. *Journal of Studies on Alcohol, 49,* 219–224.

Henderson, D. C., & Anderson, S. C. (1989). Adolescents and chemical dependency. *Social Work in Health Care, 14,* 87–105.

Herting, J. R., & Guest, A. M. (1985). Components of satisfaction with local areas in the metropolis. *Sociological Quarterly, 26,* 99–115.

Hill, S. Y. (1982). Biological consequences of alcoholism and alcohol-related problems among women. In National Institute on Alcohol Abuse, *Special populations issues* (Alcohol and Health Monograph No. 4, pp. 43–73) (DHHS Publication No. ADM 82-1193). Washington, DC: U.S. Government Printing Office.

Hill, S. Y. (1984). Vulnerability to the biomedical consequences of alcoholism and alcohol-related problems among women. In S. C. Wilsnack & L. J. Beckman (Eds.), *Alcohol problems in women: Antecedents, consequences, and intervention* (pp. 121–154). New York: Guilford Press.

Hingson, R. W., Strunin, L., Berlin, B. M., & Heeren, T. (1990). Beliefs about AIDS, use of alcohol and drugs, and unprotected sex among Massachusetts adolescents. *American Journal of Public Health, 80,* 295–299.

Holzer, C. E., Myers, J. K., Weissman, M. W., Tischler, G. L., Leaf, P. J., Anthony, J., & Bednarski, P. B. (1986). Antecedents and correlates of alcohol abuse and dependence in the elderly. In G. Maddox, L. N. Robins, & N. Rosenberg (Eds.), *Nature and extent of alcohol problems among the elderly* (pp. 217–244). New York: Springer.

Hopper, K., & Hamberg, J. (1984). *The making of America's homeless: From skid row to new poor 1945–1984.* New York: Community Service Society of New York.

Indian Health Service. (1988). *Indian Health Service chart series book* (DHHS Publication No. 1988 0-218-547). Washington, DC: U.S. Government Printing Office.

Johnson, G. M., Schoutz, F. C., & Locke, T. P. (1984). Relationships between adolescent drug youth and parental drug behaviors. *Adolescence, 19,* 295–299.

Keller, M., & Doria, J. (1991). On defining alcoholism. *Alcohol Health & Research World, 15,* 253–259.

Kendler, K. S., Heath, A. C., Neale, M. C., Kessler, R. C., & Eaves, L. J. (1992). A population-based twin study of alcoholism in women. *Journal of the American Medical Association, 268,* 1877–1882.

Koegel, P., & Burnam, M. A. (1987). Traditional and nontraditional homeless alcoholics. *Alcohol Health & Research World, 11,* 28–34.

Koroloff, N., & Anderson, S. C. (1989). Alcohol-free living centers: Hope for homeless alcoholics. *Social Work, 34,* 497–504.

La Rosa, J. H. (1990). Executive women and health: Perceptions and practices. *American Journal of Public Health, 80,* 1450–1454.

Littman, G. (1970). Alcoholism, illness, and social pathology among American Indians in transition. *American Journal of Public Health, 60,* 1769–1787.

Loeber, R. (1988). Natural histories of conduct problems, delinquency, and associated substance use: Evidence for developmental progressions. In B. B. Lahey & A. E. Kazdin (Eds.), *Advances in clinical child psychology* (Vol. 11, pp. 73–124). New York: Plenum Press.

Long, N., Brendtro, L., & Johnson, J. (1993). Alcohol and kids: Facing our problem. *Journal of Emotional and Behavioral Problems, 2,* 2–4.

Lowenfels, A., & Miller, T. (1984). Alcohol and trauma. *Annals of Emergency Medicine, 13,* 1056–1060.

Marlatt, G. A. (1988). Matching clients to treatment: Treatment models and stages of change. In D. M. Donovan & G. A. Marlatt (Eds.), *Assessment of addictive behaviors* (pp. 474–483). New York: Guilford Press.

Marlatt, G. A., & Gordon, J. R. (Eds.). (1985). *Relapse prevention: Maintenance strategies in the treatment of addictive behaviors.* New York: Guilford Press.

Martin, S. E. (1992). The epidemiology of alcohol-related interpersonal violence. *Alcohol Health & Research World, 16,* 230–237.

May, P. A. (1982). Substance abuse and American Indians: Prevalence and susceptibility. *International Journal of the Addictions, 17,* 1185–1209.

May, P. A. (1991). Fetal alcohol effects among North American Indians. *Alcohol Health & Research World, 15,* 239–248.

McKirnan, D. J., & Peterson, P. L. (1989). Alcohol and drug use among homosexual men and women: Epidemiology and population characteristics. *Addictive Behaviors, 14,* 545–553.

Moos, R. H., & Moos, B. S. (1984). The process of recovery from alcoholism: Comparing functioning in families of alcoholics and matched control families. *Journal of Studies on Alcohol, 45,* 111–118.

Murray, R. M., & Stabenau, J. R. (1982). Genetic factors in alcoholism predisposition. In E. M. Pattison & E. Kaufman (Eds.), *Encyclopedic handbook of alcoholism* (pp. 135–144). New York: Gardner Press.

National Commission on Drug-Free Schools. (1990). *Toward a drug-free generation: A nation's responsibility.* Washington, DC: U.S. Department of Education.

National Institute on Alcohol Abuse and Alcoholism. (1985). *Alcohol use among U.S. ethnic minorities* (Research Monograph No. 18). Rockville, MD: U.S. Department of Health and Human Services.

National Institute on Alcohol Abuse and Alcoholism. (1990). *Seventh special report to the U.S. Congress on alcohol and health.* Washington, DC: U.S. Department of Health and Human Services.

National Institute on Alcohol Abuse and Alcoholism. (1992). Alcohol and AIDS. *Alcohol Alert, 15,* 1–4.

National Institute on Drug Abuse. (1993). *National survey results on drug use from the Monitoring the Future study, 1975–1992* (NIH Publication No. 93-3597). Rockville, MD: U.S. Department of Health and Human Services.

Parker, D. A., & Harford, T. C. (1992). The epidemiology of alcohol consumption and dependence across occupations in the United States. *Alcohol Health & Research World, 16,* 97–105.

Pattison, E. M., Sobell, M. B., & Sobell, L. C. (1977). *Emerging concepts of alcohol dependence.* New York: Springer.

Phillips, D. K., Henderson, G. I., & Schenker, S. (1989). Pathogenesis of fetal alcohol syndrome: Overview with emphasis on the possible role of nutrition. *Alcohol Health & Research World, 13,* 219–227.

Piazza, N. J., Vrbka, J. L., & Yeager, R. D. (1989). Telescoping of alcoholism in women alcoholics. *International Journal of the Addictions, 24,* 19–28.

Reiss, S. (1990). Prevalence of dual diagnosis in community-based day programs in the Chicago metropolitan area. *American Journal on Mental Retardation, 94,* 578–585.

Rice, D. P., Kelman, S., & Miller, L. S. (1991). The economic cost of alcohol abuse. *Alcohol Health & Research World, 15,* 307–316.

Rosen, I. J. (1989). Substance abuse in the American Jewish community. *Jewish Social Work Forum, 25,* 58–71.

Russell, M. (1991). Clinical implications of recent research on the fetal alcohol syndrome. *Bulletin of the New York Academy of Medicine, 67,* 207–222.

Schinke, S. P., Botvin, G. J., & Orlandi, M. O. (1991). *Substance abuse in children and adolescents: Evaluation and intervention.* Newbury Park, CA: Sage Publications.

Serdula, M., Williamson, D. K., Kendrick, J. S., Anda, R. F., & Byers, T. (1991). Trends in alcohol consumption by pregnant women: 1985 through 1988. *Journal of the American Medical Association, 265,* 876–879.

Shore, E. R. (1990). Business and professional women: Primary prevention for new role incumbents. In P. M. Roman (Ed.), *Alcohol problem intervention in the workplace: Employee assistance programs and strategic alternatives* (pp. 113–124). New York: Quorum.

Shore, E. R. (1992). Drinking patterns and problems among women in paid employment. *Alcohol Health & Research World, 16,* 160–164.

Smart, R., & Adlaf, E. (1988). Alcohol and drug use among the elderly: Trends in use and characteristics of users. *Canadian Journal of Public Health, 79,* 236–242.

Smith, E. M. (1989). Services for Native Americans. *Alcohol Health & Research World, 13,* 94.

Sokol, R. J., & Clarren, S. K. (1989). Guidelines for use of terminology describing the impact of prenatal alcohol on the offspring. *Alcoholism: Clinical & Experimental Research, 13,* 597–598.

Sparadeo, F. R., Strauss, D., & Barth, J. T. (1990). The incidence, impact, and treatment of substance abuse in head trauma rehabilitation. *Journal of Head Trauma Rehabilitation, 5,* 1–8.

Stark, L. (1987). A century of alcohol and homelessness: Demographics and stereotypes. *Alcohol Health & Research World, 11,* 8–13.

Substance Abuse and Mental Health Services Administration. (1993). *National household survey on drug abuse: Population estimates 1992* (DHHS Publication No. SMA 93-2053). Rockville, MD: U.S. Department of Health and Human Services.

Sutker, P. B., Goist, K. C., & King, A. R. (1987). Acute alcohol intoxication in women: Relationship to dose and menstrual cycle phase. *Alcoholism: Clinical & Experimental Research, 11,* 74–79.

Turnbull, J. E. (1989). Treatment issues for alcoholic women. *Social Casework: The Journal of Contemporary Social Work, 70,* 364–369.

Vaillant, G. E. (1983). *The natural history of alcoholism.* Cambridge, MA: Harvard University Press.

Wallace, J. M., & Bachman, J. G. (1991). Explaining racial/ethnic differences in adolescent drug use: The impact of background and lifestyle. *Social Problems, 38,* 333–357.

Weiner, L., & Morse, B. A. (1989). FAS: Clinical perspectives and prevention. In I. J. Chasnoff (Ed.), *Drugs, alcohol, pregnancy, and parenting* (pp. 127–148). Boston: Kluwer Academic Publishers.

Werner, E. E. (1986). Resilient offspring of alcoholics: A longitudinal study from birth to age 18. *Journal of Studies on Alcohol, 47,* 34–40.

West, M. D., & Prinz, R. J. (1987). Parental alcoholism and childhood psychopathology. *Psychological Bulletin, 102,* 204–218.

Westermeyer, J., Phaobtong, T., & Neider, J. (1988). Substance use and abuse among mentally retarded persons: A comparison of patients and a survey population. *American Journal of Drug & Alcohol Abuse, 14,* 109–123.

Whipple, S. C., Berman, S. M., & Noble, E. P. (1991). Event-related potentials in alcoholic fathers and their sons. *Alcohol: An International Biomedical Journal, 8,* 321–327.

Williams, G. D., Grant, B. F., Harford, T. C., & Noble, B. A. (1989). Populations projections using DSM-III criteria: Alcohol abuse and dependence, 1990–2000. *Alcohol Health & Research World, 13,* 366–370.

Williams, G. D., Stinson, F. S., Parker, D. A., Harford, T. C., & Noble, J. (1987). Demographic trends, alcohol abuse, and alcoholism, 1985–1995. *Alcohol Health & Research World, 11,* 80–83, 91.

Wilsnack, S. C. (1984). Drinking, sexuality, and sexual dysfunction in women. In S. C. Wilsnack & L. J. Beckman (Eds.), *Alcohol problems in women* (pp. 189–227). New York: Guilford Press.

World Health Organization. (1992). *The international classification of diseases (ICD-10): Classification of mental and behavioural disorders.* Geneva: Author.

Wright, J. D., Knight, J. W., Weber-Burdin, E., & Lam, J. (1987). Ailments and alcohol: Health status among the drinking homeless. *Alcohol Health & Research World, 11,* 22–27.

## Further Reading

Bepko, C., & Krestan, J. A. (1985). *The responsibility trap: A blueprint for treating the alcoholic family.* New York: Free Press.

Brown, S. (1985). *Treating the alcoholic: A developmental model of recovery.* New York: John Wiley & Sons.

Frances, R. J., & Miller, S. I. (Eds). (1991). *Clinical textbook of addictive disorders.* New York: Guilford Press.

Hester, R. K., & Miller, W. R. (Eds.). (1989). *Handbook of alcoholism treatment approaches: Effective alternatives.* New York: Pergamon Press.

Straussner, S.L.A. (Ed.). (1993). *Clinical work with substance abusing clients.* New York: Guilford Press.

**Sandra C. Anderson, PhD, ACSW, LCSW,** is professor, Portland State University, Graduate School of Social Work, Portland, OR 97207.

### For further information see

Adolescence Overview; Criminal Justice: Class, Race, and Gender Issues; Disability; Drug Abuse; Eating Disorders and Other Compulsive Behaviors; Homelessness; Human Development; Maternal and Child Health; Mental Health Overview; Primary Prevention Overview; Substance Abuse: Direct Practice; Substance Abuse: Federal, State, and Local Policies; Substance Abuse: Legal Issues; Violence Overview.

**Key Words**

addiction
alcoholism
chemical dependency
drug abuse

## Aliens

*See* Displaced People; Migrant Workers

## Altmeyer, Arthur J.

*See* Biographies section, Volume 3

# American Indians

Ronald G. Lewis

The subjects of federal policy and Indian relationships are complex and confusing. There are so many thousands of policies and treaties, along with statutes, executive orders, and bureaucratic memos, that to try to review them all would be analogous to whispering "kitty, kitty" and seeing a tiger step out. From an American Indian[1] perspective, the field of American Indian policy has minimally anything to do with American Indian customs, laws, or the methods Indian people might use to resolve conflict. "Policy," translated to the American Indian people, constitutes a complex, erratic, and at times confusing and contradictory branch of Anglo-American legal thought. American Indian tribes have claims that have validity under federal law, and most individuals have little knowledge of why these "Indian problems" were not resolved decades ago.

The policies are extensive in scope and cover concerns such as property rights, civil cases, constitutional concerns, treaties, water rights, and international law. One cannot present all concerns in one entry; therefore, this entry reviews the demographics of the Indian population, gives an overview of the Indian–federal government relationship through policies, and graphically shows the colonizing effect of the major policies on the Indian people. Federal policy here means all levels of policy, such as basic ideas on long-range policies, including those that influence the action of a government for extended periods; the guiding principles adopted and pursued by the government official in power for a short time; and rules and procedural practices laid down by government administrators to put accepted policy into effect (Taylor, 1973).

## Demographics

There are 323 American Indian tribes in the lower 48 states and 224 in Alaska (personal communication with Branch of Acknowledgment and Research, File of Tribal Services, January 6, 1995). Almost as many tribes existed in 1990 as there were in the 1600s, when the first cultural encounter took place. It has been estimated that in the 1600s there were 240 tribes (North American peoples and cultures, 1984). Fifty or more tribes are known to have since become extinct, but contrary to popular belief, American Indians are not a vanishing people:

> Experts' estimates of precisely how many Indians there were within the territory of the United States when the non-Indian arrived range from a conservative and widely accepted figure of 850,000 up to more than a million. The United States census count for 1980 was 1.4 million, representing 6 percent of the U.S. population. Although this suggests a decline in population, if we look more deeply into the figures, a different view emerges. The Indian populations did indeed decline rapidly from the 1600's through the 1800's. In 1900 it was recorded as 237,196, indicating a nearly 75 percent decline during the previous 200 years. The greatest reduction took place during the 19th Century, and undoubtedly it is that period that gave rise to the stereotype of the Indians as a vanishing race. (Spicer, 1982, p. 1)

By the 1980s, Indian people had gained in numbers of tribes and individuals. Over the last 300 years, growth has accelerated. Three factors have aided this growth: (1) improved census procedures for both the tribes and the United States, (2) a much more tolerant attitude that has allowed individuals to claim their Indian heritage, and (3) a reopening of tribal roles.

The view of most Americans and the federal government is that American Indians are just another minority group. Yet Indian people own more than 50 million acres of land and have more than 200 separate governments and native languages. The American Indian is not just another minority. Indian people possess a unique constitutional right to special recognition that allows them to be separate and apart from the rest of U.S. citizens. Misunderstanding this unique condition undermines the guarantees of all U.S. treaties and of the Constitution.

### Location

The geographic location of contemporary American Indians reflects historical trends, attitudes, and policies of non-Indians. Manifest destiny set

[1]Author's note: Much thought has been given to the terms "Native American," "Indian," and "American Indian." Most American Indians use "Indian" and "Native American" interchangeably. Virtually all laws are written with the term "Indian," and the Bureau of Indian Affairs uses the term "Indian." In addition, the term "Native American" includes other groups, such as Hawaiians, and this entry does not address their needs. For these reasons, the author feels most comfortable with the term "American Indian."

up a system of forced migration. As a testament to that system, the present concentration of the Indian population is in three western states. Oklahoma (once known as Indian territory) maintains the largest population. Arizona represents the second-largest concentration, and California has the third-largest concentration (a testament to relocation policies and other Indian policies). This grouping of Indians reflects themes of forced migration, isolation of Indian people, and a migration from rural reservations to the cities.

## Historical Perspective

American Indians are not immigrants but are the original inhabitants of what is now the United States. Unlike people of Third World countries, who can at least hope to gain control of their countries, the tiny Indian population may have to be content with being a minority population in their own land. In the present, as in the past, Indian people are daily subjected to government policies of forced assimilation, segregation, and cultural pluralism. The form and substance of their relations with federal and state governments are matters of fundamental significance in their everyday lives and future prospects as indigenous people. History, in Indian life, is really describing the complex relationship between the federal government and the Indian people.

Complicating any analysis of American Indian history is the fact that it has been written largely from a non-Indian point of view. This has proved detrimental to the American Indian people because many American Indian people remember and hear customs and traditions that have persisted over many centuries but are not reflected in contemporary policies and law. For many American Indians, this dichotomy has made life difficult because the blending of Indian customs and contemporary policy is not easy; therefore, reflections concerning Indian history must be tempered with an American Indian perspective, which could provide an understanding of the cultural conflict represented by this duality of ideas.

The following historical examination is divided into separate periods of federal Indian policies. Each phase is characterized by the impact of some kind of federal initiative. By approaching the subject in this manner, two themes become apparent: (1) federal Indian law, court decisions, and policies that control the lives of Indian people can be more easily understood within a historical perspective and (2) through an examination of these policies, one can gauge the impact, however small, of the policies on the Indian people themselves.

## Discovery, Subjugation, and Treaty Making (1532 to 1818)

The history of the Americas does not begin in 1492 with the Spanish Conquest or in 1000 with the Viking settlement. Current anthropological studies suggest that Indian people populated the western hemisphere at least 25,000 years ago and that they were the first to do so. The "25,000 years" is a widely used and convenient concept; however, strong evidence suggests that Indian people may have been here 75,000 years ago (Josephy, 1991).

### Cultural Development

The histories of these groups are as exciting and revealing as the histories of Europe or Asia. The Indians developed a great variety of cultures, traditional and religious precepts, lifestyles, and languages. When the Europeans first arrived, there were 240 tribes, with as many languages ("North American Peoples and Cultures," 1984). Each group differed from the others, as exemplified by the variety of government preferences, such as the democracies of the Plains Indians; the confederacies of groups of the Eastern seaboard; and later, the first written constitution, the Great Binding Law of the Five Nations of the Iroquois. There was also a worldview of intellectual and spiritual traits that made the people of the pre-European era a self-sufficient group.

The accomplishments of Indian people in the arts, medicine, agriculture, theology, physics, astronomy, and engineering are brillantly conceived in comparison with the works of their counterparts in the eastern hemisphere. It is only with grief that one can view the destruction of the great Mayan library, which may have contained as many as 1 million volumes on the subjects of law, theology, physics, astronomy, architecture, and engineering.

### Relationships with Other Sovereignties

***Spain.*** In the 16th and 17th centuries, the king of Spain, a devout Roman Catholic following the dictates of his religion, sought the advice of Francisco de Vitoria, a prominent theologian. Vitoria concluded that "the natives were the true owners of the land," "they were entitled to their customs and government" and "might not be enslaved" or "despoiled of their property unless they should be so inconsiderate as to wage war against the Spanish" (Cohen, 1942, p. 44). On further investigation, contemporary writings showed that the relationship between the Spanish and American Indian people was a complicated and complex one in which Spain tended not to recognize tribes as separate governments. Historically, there was a distinction between how the Spanish people treated American Indians as opposed to how the English people treated them.

***Great Britain.*** In the initial stages of its colonization of America, the British Crown dealt with the American Indians as foreign sovereign nations, as manifested by the initiation of the treaty process. Britain and several of its colonies entered into treaties with tribes. The treaties were signed agreements between equal nations offering mutual obligation. As each colonial power grew and the Indians became less of a threat, it became clear that there were signs of encroachment on Indian lands and that Indian people were being treated unfairly or brutally. This brutal treatment was personified by the Dutch, who originated the practice of scalp bounties and skull payments. Thus, to avoid Indian wars, which would be costly, Britain increasingly assumed the role of protectorate over the tribes.

***United States.*** After gaining independence, the United States, faced with the "Indian problem," chose to adopt the British policy of dealing with Indians through treaties. Treaty making became, for the United States, a way of defining both the legal and the political relationships between the two groups. "In 1778, the United States government entered into its first treaty with the Indians—the Delaware tribe. In the course of the next century over six hundred treaties and agreements were made with the nations of North America" (Deloria & Lytle, 1983, p. 4).

The Articles of Confederation, which became effective in 1781, were ambiguous in regard to state and federal power over Indian concerns; however, the federal government had sole and exclusive authority over Indian affairs. After a period of uncertainty, this precept became more solidified with the advent of the U.S. Constitution. Congress was granted powers over American Indian people and exerted its influence by establishing federal Indian laws that regulated large portions of Indian affairs. In the years between 1790 and 1834, the Trade and Intercourse Acts were passed:

> The central policy embodied in the Acts was one of separating Indians and non-Indians and subjecting nearly all interaction between the two groups to federal control. The act established the boundaries of Indian country and protected the incursion by non-Indians.... Non-Indians were prohibited from acquiring Indian land by purchase or treaty. (Canby, 1981, p. 11)

During these years, federal control over American Indians was carefully orchestrated. The fundamental concept giving impetus to the movement was the belief that Indians were culturally inferior and that the American government had a responsibility to raise them to the level of the rest of society, which meant to "Christianize and civilize." "American statesmen, including Washington, Jefferson, and their successors, congratulated themselves on their superior, benevolent system of managing Indian affairs. They felt fully justified in interfering in Indian social, religious and economic practices" (McNickle, Young, & Buffalohead, 1978, p. 1). Federal control was extended through federal agents. Indian agents were appointed as the official liaisons with the tribes. They were not content to aid in negotiating treaties and making payments, but also involved themselves in the private lives of the Indians, eroding the Indian culture.

## Removal (1828 to 1887)

Despite the Trade and Intercourse Acts, friction increased as non-Indians began to covet Indian lands. With the pressures of westward expansion, federal Indian policy began to change. Under the guidance of President Andrew Jackson, what had been an implicit proposition became an articulated policy: the removal of the Indian tribes toward the West. The Indian Removal Act was passed on May 28, 1830. From an Indian perspective, the Indian Removal Act of 1830 was significant because it represented the first clear break with the policy of "good faith" and encouraged racist attitudes that would eventually facilitate the destruction of Indian autonomy and the suppression of Indian values and institutions.

### Cherokee Nation Experience

Before the enactment of the Indian Removal Act of 1830, the Cherokee people had established a well-functioning community that exceeded, in many ways, the surrounding non-Indian communities. The Cherokees had established a school system that encompassed more than 200 schools. In addition, Sequoyah had invented a script specifically adapted to the Cherokee sound system, so the tribe was able to publish a bilingual newspaper and a variety of textbooks. The Cherokee population soon reached a literacy rate, in their own language, of 90 percent. By 1827 the Cherokee nation had adopted a written constitution.

Although the territorial parameters of Cherokee country were well established, the discovery of gold in 1828 led to increasingly frequent border clashes between the Cherokees and the non-Indian residents of Georgia. The State of Georgia refused to recognize Cherokee boundaries and claimed the right to enter Indian territory. The Cherokee nation brought a lawsuit against the state in a case that eventually reached the Supreme Court (*Cherokee Nation v. Georgia,* 1831). The Court ruled that the Cherokee people "had unquestioned rights to the land they occupied." Chief Justice Marshall, moreover, writing for the Court, stated that the Cherokee tribe had succeeded in demonstrating that it was a state, "a distinct political society separated from others, capable of managing its own affairs and governing itself" (*Cherokee Nation v. Georgia,* 1831).

A second important Supreme Court decision (*Worchester v. Georgia,* 1832) involved a missionary who had been apprehended in Indian territory by Georgia officials and was subsequently sentenced to hard labor. Chief Justice Marshall reviewed the history of relations with the Indians and the Trade and Intercourse Acts that "manifestly consider the several Indian Nations as distinct political communities having territorial boundaries, within which their authority is exclusive" (*Worchester v. Georgia,* 1832) and concluded that the powers of the State of Georgia did not extend to the territory of the Cherokee nation. Although the actual decisions were soon shown to be unenforceable and hence were unable to provide any meaningful relief to the Cherokee people against non-Indian intrusions onto their lands, these two cases were destined to become among the most influential in the development of American Indian law. On May 12, 1830, after vigorous debate in which the Eastern senators and representatives stated that they deplored the Indian Removal Act as a violation of American honor, it was nevertheless put into force.

### Abrogation of Indian Sovereignty

Between 1830 and 1840, approximately 70,000 to 100,000 Indians were rounded up and force-marched westward to Oklahoma. Thousands perished as a result of disease, adverse weather, and malnutrition. These marches became a lasting symbol of imposed suffering. The sustenance on the reservations was wholly dependent on assistance from the federal government. Christian missionaries and teachers flooded the reservations in an attempt to "civilize" and "assimilate." The army was there to keep peace, rather than to protect the American Indians.

Although the United States continued to sign treaties with the Indian nations until 1871, Indians were not treated as the citizens of a separate sovereignty. In the 1850s and 1860s, the treaty became a device for undermining the independence of tribal governments; weakening and ultimately destroying Indian spiritual leaders; and legitimating interference by Congress, the U.S. government, and religious groups in the day-to-day management of tribal society. In effect, the U.S. government began dealing with Indian people not as citizens of their own nations but as dependent paupers. Hereafter, Congress dealt with Indians by passing legislation, with or without tribal approval. Significantly, in 1849, when the East had been nearly emptied of Indians, federal administrative responsibility for Indian affairs was moved from the War Department to the Department of the Interior. After 1871, Congress unilaterally ended treaty making as a result of compromises between the Senate and the House. "Agreements" and executive orders, together with legislation of Congress, took the place of treaties. In addition, executive administrative rules and court decisions subsequently became entities that American Indian tribes had to endure. In the 1880s the United States, perhaps developing a conscience, decided that wars were costly, so one alternative was to have the Indians assimilate.

## Allotment and Assimilation (1887 to 1934)

The American Indian systems of common land tenure had never been understood by the Americans, who had been accustomed to private ownership of land. The idea of individualizing American Indian land tenure was distilled from earlier European philosophical writers and biblical texts and had been incorporated into early treaties.

### General Allotment Act of 1887

Congress, responding to people who coveted Indian lands and to various well-intentioned religious groups, proceeded to pass the most important, and, to the Indians, the most devastating piece of Indian legislation in the United States: the Indian General Allotment Act of 1887. This act, also known as the Dawes Act, was designed to provide a solution to the Indian problem by turning Indians away from their past and by fitting them into the American vision of a productive society. This legislative solution, however, underestimated both the American greed for land and the tenacity of American Indian customs and traditions.

Under the General Allotment Act of 1887, 160 acres of land were allotted to each family head; each Indian was to choose his or her own allotment; the allotted land was to be held in trust for 25 years; on expiration of the trust, "good Indians" would receive title to their allotment and would have U.S. citizenship bestowed on them; surplus lands would revert to the government.

The primary effect of the General Allotment Act of 1887 was a precipitous decline in the total amount of Indian-held land, from 138 million acres in 1887 to 48 million acres in 1934. Of the 48 million acres that remained, some 20 million acres were desert or semidesert. Much of the land was lost by sale as tribal surplus; the remainder passed out of the hands of the allottees. Another effect was the "checkerboard" pattern of ownership by tribes, causing many of the serious jurisdictional problems of today. If the 90 million acres of land lost through this process had remained under Indian ownership, the problem of poverty among most tribes could be solved with less difficulty and with more certainty (*Report of the Hoover Commission,* 1948).

**Components of Assimilation**

Assimilation by "appropriate social policy" became a fundamental aspect of Indian policy and consisted of five important components. First, whereas previously a variety of private organizations, church groups, and government agencies had dabbled in "educating" the Indians, this task was now shifted to Bureau of Indian Affairs schools, where Indians were required to abandon their languages, native dress, religious practices, and other traditional customs. Second, traditional leaders and traditional procedures were undermined when the government simply bypassed them when dealing with questions of law and order and with political issues. Third, the exercise of authority by tribal leaders was discouraged, and Bureau of Indian Affairs superintendents became the de facto government of many reservations. Fourth, missionaries were sent to reservations with the implicit mandate to "civilize" the Indians. Fifth, the Major Crimes Act of 1885 ousted the jurisdiction of tribal authorities with respect to a broad range of criminal activity.

A consequence not explicitly envisioned by the Dawes Act followed from the stipulation that all American Indians who were granted title to their land allotments would also be granted U.S. citizenship. Furthermore, when Congress passed a statute in 1924 conferring citizenship on all Indians, the legal foundations were laid for the encroachment of state jurisdiction over Indians and their lands. Each Indian, then, was to be a U.S. citizen, a citizen of the state in which he or she resided, and a member of a tribe; therefore, an Indian could have three separate sets of rights: federal, state, and tribal (but not necessarily in that order).

**Summary of Federal Indian Law**

The basic elements of federal Indian law that daily affect American Indians and are inherent in the treaties are as follows:

- *The trust relationship:* "Indian tribes are not foreign nations but constitute 'distinct political communities' that may, more correctly, perhaps be denominated 'domestic dependent nations'... whose relation to the United States resembles that of a ward to a guardian" (*Cherokee Nation v. Georgia,* 1831, p. 1).
- *Tribal governmental status:* Indian tribes are sovereign—that is, government and state laws do not apply within reservation boundaries without congressional consent (*Worchester v. Georgia,* 1832).
- *Reserved-rights doctrine:* "Tribal rights, including rights to land and to self-government are not granted to the tribe by the United States. Rather, under the reserved-rights doctrine, tribes possessing inherent sovereignty retained ('reserved') such rights as part of their status as prior and continuing sovereigns" (*United States v. Winans,* 1905, p. 371).
- *Canons of construction:* Courts of the common law tradition have evolved general rules and principles that they apply to the interpretation of written documents such as treaties. These rules and principles are known in legal terminology as "canons of construction," and those that pertain specifically to Indian law have generally developed to the benefit of the tribes. These canons of construction require, for instance, that the treaties be construed broadly in determining the continued existence of Indian rights but narrowly when considering the restriction or abrogation of those rights. Most of the special canons of construction that have evolved for the interpretation of treaty rights have also been applied to agreements (*Antoine v. Washington,* 1975), executive orders (*Arizona v. California,* 1963), and statutes (*Squire v. Capoerman,* 1956) dealing with Indians.
- *Congressional plenary power:* Rights established by treaty or by other documents can be abrogated by Congress pursuant to its plenary power (*Lonewolf v. Hitchcock,* 1903).

Although the term "treaty" seems to suggest equal bargaining positions, the Indian tribes were often at a clear disadvantage when negotiating such arrangements. The actual documents were invariably written in English and were generally interpreted and explained by individuals who had a stake in a successful outcome of the proceedings. Hence, the Indians were not always told the truth during the negotiating sessions. Moreover, at the concluding stage of the treaty-making process, when extensive debate on ratification became tedious, the Senate would frequently amend the text of the treaties, completely changing their meaning (Deloria & Lytle, 1983).

## Indian Reorganization Policy (1928 to 1945)

The 1920s saw some abrupt shifts in Indian policy in favor of the Indian people. An attempt was made to improve the quality of administrative personnel in the Bureau of Indian Affairs in Washington, DC. In addition, the now-classic Meriam Report of 1928 (Meriam, 1928) was issued. This report, which denounced the living conditions of Indians on reservations, recommended that Indian health and education receive more funding and encouraged more tribal control of government activities. The report had no immediate impact because the economic collapse in 1929 directed political attention to other matters. However, the outraged Senate began an eight-year study and reached basically the same conclusions as the report had. Moreover, in the early days of his administration, President Franklin D. Roosevelt made clear his intentions to radically alter the administration of Indian affairs and appointed John Collier, a man widely known for his interest in and appreciation of Indian culture, as Indian commissioner.

### Indian Reorganization Act of 1934

On June 18, 1934, Congress passed the Indian Reorganization Act, also known as the Wheeler–Howard Act. The act prohibited the further allotment of tribal lands to individuals and gave each tribe the option of accepting the provisions for reorganization. It established a $10 million revolving credit fund from which loans could be made to incorporated tribes. Furthermore, the 1934 act directed the secretary of the interior to give Indians preference for employment within the Bureau of Indian Affairs. In reality, not all tribal peoples accepted this contemporary form of governance and the ramifications of the 1934 act. Some traditional Indians, even to this day, oppose the new form of government, the bylaws, and the constitutions represented by the 1934 act. Therefore, tension remains between the tribal council and the tribal people and occasionally flares up. The 1934 act itself did not incorporate any ideas or concepts of what the Indians culturally felt about authority or leadership or an American Indian concept of political structures.

## Termination (1953 to 1968)

During the 1950s, Congress introduced policies that brought the Indians to the brink of disaster. The new policies are aptly known as "termination" because their purpose was to terminate federal benefits and services to certain Indian tribes and to force the dissolution of the reservations of these tribes.

### Policy

The termination policy was initiated with Congress's adoption of House Concurrent Resolution No. 108. This resolution called for ending the special relationship between Indian tribes and the federal government as rapidly as possible. In the course of the following decade, Congress terminated federal assistance to more than 100 tribes. Congress then passed P.L. 83-280, which made provision for the extension of state jurisdiction over specified reservations. This statute allowed state governments to assume civil and criminal jurisdiction over reservations in several states: California, Minnesota, Nebraska, Oregon, Wisconsin, and Alaska (a territory at the time). Because the document was assembled so poorly, much litigation between the states and the tribes continues.

### Relocation Program

A measure that complemented the termination policy was the relocation program, which, in principle, encouraged Indians to leave their reservations and seek employment in densely populated urban centers. The Bureau of Indian Affairs planned specifically to separate relocated American Indians from their tribal associations. Therefore, the first urban relocation centers were established in Denver, Chicago, and Los Angeles, with others added later. The term "urban Indians" began to appear around this time. Urban Indians were not just a product of relocation; some had moved on their own at earlier times, and others had always lived in urban areas. Some of the large cities began as Indian villages or as Indian commercial centers. Regardless, in 1956, the Bureau of Indian Affairs recruited and paid the cost of removal for 5,603 wage earners, a total—with their families—of 12,626 American Indians.

The outgrowth of the urban phenomenon is that those groups have formed an American Indian community that interacts socially while forming social and political ties that have evolved into traditions and customs. They have developed creative and adaptive responses to the urban environment, which makes them distinctly American Indian. The urban American Indians have few spokespersons in Washington, DC, and they often do not receive adequate public policy attention. In the 1980 census, almost two-thirds of the 1.4 million people who identified themselves as American Indians did not live on reservations, tribal trust lands, or other

Indian lands. Many urban Indians have low-incomes and are facing dire economic circumstances.

## "Self–Determination" Era (since 1961)

The mistakes of the termination period and their devastating impact on American Indian people led to the political activism of the period from the 1960s to the present. This new phase of Indian policy may be characterized by an expanded recognition of the role of tribal self-government and by the general exclusion of reservations from the scope of state authority.

In July 1970 President Richard M. Nixon specifically rejected the termination policy in his message to Congress and thus formally inaugurated a shift in federal policy. The president stated that "the goal of any new national policy toward the Indian people [is] to strengthen the Indian's sense of autonomy without threatening his sense of community."

### Early Legislation

During the 1960s and 1970s, Congress enacted a number of statutes that endeavored to implement the new policy of self-determination. It passed the Indian Civil Rights Act of 1968, which prohibited the states from acquiring jurisdiction over Indian reservations without the consent of the tribes living there; the Indian Financing Act of 1974; the Native American Programs Act of 1974; and the Indian Self-Determination and Education Assistance Act of 1975.

Even though this period is called "self-determination," "self" has been left out. The 1975 act, in essence, gives tribal governments the authority to assume contractually the responsibility for some government services. However, when one looks at tribal resources, the amount of money appropriated by Congress, and the requirement that tribes ask for administrative permission to engage in contracts, one can readily see that controls remain firmly in non-Indian hands.

### Indian Child Welfare Act

One particularly important act was the Indian Child Welfare Act of 1978. The intent was for the act to become a legal tool to halt the adoption of American Indian children by those in mainstream society, religious groups, and others, thus protecting American Indian families and strengthening the tribes against all kinds of expropriations. The act established standards for the placement of American Indians in foster or adoptive homes to prevent the breakup of American Indian families. It gave Indian tribes jurisdiction over Indian children and took jurisdiction away from the states, transferring it to the tribes and the courts. Nonetheless, the number of adoptions of American Indians continues to be high.

## Colonization as a Theoretical Perspective

A theoretical explanation of the plight of American Indian people within the United States that goes beyond preoccupation with the individual can be found in the socioeconomic theories of colonialism. *Colonialism* may be defined as a situation in which the destiny of a nation or an identifiable group within a state is substantially controlled by external authorities and their agencies. The result of the situation is to make one nation or group dependent on the external authority. The effect of a colonial relationship, whether intended or not, includes the extraction of benefits by the dominant partner in the relationship. It is possible to make a distinction between structural and cultural colonialism (see Kellough, 1980).

### Factors in Structural and Cultural Colonialism

Structural colonialism, which focuses on political control and decision-making powers, is illustrated historically in relation to Indian people in the United States by acts, such as the taking of American Indian lands, decision making for American Indians by non-Indian government agencies, and an imposed economic dependence. Cultural colonialism has as its goal the substitution of the dominant partner's cultural values for those of the colonized people. In the United States, this form of colonialism is exemplified by the use of missionaries who are entrusted with the task of civilizing "savages" and by the imposition of health care or educational programs that tend to destroy the American Indian community's cultural identity.

Some of the factors in the educational areas that have produced and entrenched the colonial situation are boarding schools, military regime, separation from families, suppression of Indian languages, denigration of traditional ways of life, and authoritarian processes generated by Calvinistic philosophy. Factors in the social areas are the high rate of institutionalization of children, rural-urban dichotomy, technology, systematic reduction of the land base, loss of decision-making power, and legal conflicts. Factors in the religious areas are loss of the unity of the Indian worldview, destruction or the forcing underground of traditional spiritual ceremonies, denigration of cosmologically based values, and proliferation of proselytizing religious sects.

American Indians, for the most part, find themselves in the large, impersonal mass that characterizes American society. Because they feel powerless, the unity as a community or group among Indians has produced anomie. An important overall effect of the colonial interference in decision-making processes is an erosion of genuine native leadership; a decay of traditional institutions; and an individual social weakening, which is reflected in high incidences of suicide, alcoholism, and so on. Even more significant, this interference deprives Indians of a direct experience with their environment, be it natural or social, because in all aspects of Indians' lives the external agencies stand between the Indian people and their daily tasks. As a group or community, Indians have little direct experience in dealing with the outside world, nor do individuals have a real understanding of mainstream society, or, for that matter, of the internal dynamics of their own community.

**Lack of Institutional Power**

The acculturating thrust of the colonial situation through education and religious proselytizing and through the promotion of mainstream institutions such as tribal constitutions, governments, and courts administered or supervised by the Bureau of Indian Affairs, has effectively stripped the Indian people of any real institutional power. Furthermore, an acculturation differential has developed, with some individuals absorbing a higher degree of mainstream values and lifestyles. One example are those people referred to by the American Indian people as "wannabes"; these individuals have no biological connection to but have developed a close cultural affinity with Indian people. A second example are those who claim distant lineal connection through a deceased grandmother (usually a Cherokee) and have little relationship with their heritage. A third example are people who are biologically Indian, but who were raised in the mainstream and have thus accepted mainstream values. These individuals may frequently emerge as brokers between the Indian and non-Indian worlds and, being marginal to the more traditional lifestyles, give rise to deep factional rifts within the community. Hence a characteristic consequence of the colonial situation of American Indians is the lack of ritual integration.

American Indian communities, whether urban or on reservations, represent the clustering of individuals into a unit. This unit constitutes a way of life that allows the people to be involved in an intimate association with each other; offers them the ability to form a social cohesion that bonds the community into units; and permits them to live their lives as a unit facing a common milieu (both natural and social) and, through cooperation, develop institutions to deal with everyday life. In urban areas, without the protection of the reservation, the community goes through a process of adaptation to the surrounding social environment, resulting in an acculturation differential that is less than would be the case on a reservation.

**Impact of Assimilation Policy**

Where does this situation leave American Indians today? For better or worse, the assimilationist policies far outweigh all others, and there is little doubt that the trend will continue. However, hopeful signs exist that perhaps Americans are ready to accept a "blip" in their mind-set. For example, historians have begun a form of demythologizing. I am referring to ethnocentric bias, the tendency to interpret another culture using the norm and values of one's own culture as a point of reference. Admittedly, there is nothing "normal" about decrying this tendency among historians, many of whom would doubtless protest that they are faithfully reproducing the literal record of the Indian–white experience. This is fair enough, but we should stop deluding ourselves about the significance and explanatory value of such history, for it is essentially a white history, a white reality, a white thought-world (Martin, 1987). If historians have gained this insight, politicians have not. The Reagan administration continually took the position that tribal governments should be more like state and local governments: They should be taxed and have revenue-raising powers. Thus the government used an assimilationist policy to make tribal governments, under the guise of self-sufficiency, imitate mainstream governments.

The concept of New Federalism for American Indians began during the latter years of the Reagan administration and continued through the Bush era. The plan now appears to be firmly entrenched in President Clinton's plans. "Self-governance" might be a laudable goal, but any such plans should be approached with benevolent skepticism because historically Congress has attempted to terminate federally recognized tribes. In fact, in 1983 the Republican Party of Arizona approved a resolution calling for the termination of tribes and the abrogation of all treaties and agreements. Other groups have followed.

If self-governance is the future, then all American Indians need to be aware of such plans and important issues must be resolved. The federal government must state clearly that federal recognition of tribal sovereignty and the trust and responsibility of the federal government will be carried out in perpetuity. Anything less will leave the American Indian people with the feeling of termination.

**The Future**

Economic, social, and political changes will not occur until there is a solid recognition among policymakers that American Indian people represent a departure from mainstream values and worldviews. The American Indian people have survived in a society whose values and ideas, on the most basic levels, are contradictory to their fundamental worldview. Unless the "primitive" notion is dismissed and American Indian values concerning tribal existence are approached as equal to European concepts and then incorporated into the fabric of social policies, little progress will be made. To have survived surrounded by a society with extremely different values is an accomplishment of no small order.

Outcomes of federal and state policies since the 1800s have demonstrated the futility of the federal and state governments' attempts to determine how American Indians should live. History has shown that American Indians have a remarkable capacity for determining this for themselves. If those rights can be returned to the tribes and Indian communities and Indian people are allowed to hold the dominant society at arm's length, then they can make useful choices within the social environment that encompasses them and hence maintain their sovereignty.

## Implications for Social Workers

If, as recent events have suggested, American Indians are entering a period of self-determination, many of the programs will be the responsibility of the tribes. Although some tribes have only a council and small staff, other tribes have legislative, executive, and judicial branches. It will be their responsibility to resolve the interjurisdictional problems they encounter. Programs for which they will assume responsibility will be those that make use of social workers—for example, social services, child welfare services, and portions of the functions of the Indian Health Services. In the future, social workers will become employees of the tribes, not of the Bureau of Indian Affairs or the Indian Health Service. The tribes will need individuals with the capacity to understand that Indians are not just a "minority" with social problems, but are a group who have a unique traditional special status and who are attempting to disengage and untangle the myriad federal laws that have protected and hurt their people. This process will be difficult because these issues are not just social problems—they involve deeper issues of ideas of a democratic theory; of international law; of consent; of civil rights; and, of utmost importance, cultural survival. The final struggle will be to help the federal government realize the legal and moral rights of tribes and American Indians in regard to self-determination. The government must clearly affirm the special relationship that tribes have as a result of inherent tribal sovereignty. Social workers must have a fundamental knowledge of this struggle.

The social work profession also has more concrete goals. For example, the schools of social work must develop appropriate administration policies to ensure that schools clearly recognize that the social work profession should and must be involved in reducing prejudice and stereotypes of American Indians. The schools must recognize that the cultural and ethnic traits of certain groups affect the way people negotiate with the system. They must enhance the cultural factors that will enrich the larger society. To accomplish these goals, school administrators must be willing to eliminate policies and concepts that do not allow for the free discussion of these ideas.

After schools of social work have changed those policies, they must make an effort to recruit faculty who are competent in areas of cultural sensitivity, recruit students who are committed to practice in areas where cultural competence is needed, and encourage and develop field practicums with American Indian populations.

Finally, all efforts must be made to ensure that schools of social work integrate relevant writings concerning American Indians into all areas of the core curriculum and also integrate the addition of specialized courses that would enrich the curriculum as a whole. Thus, future social work graduates who work on social problems will have the knowledge that they are also involved in the survival of a people who are threatened daily with having their treaties abrogated, their governing power extinguished, and their lands confiscated. It is not an easy task but a worthwhile and essential challenge.

## References


Antoine v. Washington, 420 U.S. 194 (1975).

Arizona v. California, 373 US. 546 (1963).

Canby, W. (1981). *American Indian law in a nutshell.* St. Paul, MN: West Publishing.

Cherokee Nation v. Georgia, 30 U.S. (5 Pet.) 1 (1831).

Cohen, F. (1942). *Handbook of federal Indian law.* Albuquerque: University of New Mexico Press.

Deloria, W., & Lytle, M. C. (1983). *American Indians, American justice.* Austin: University of Texas Press.

Indian Child Welfare Act of 1978. P.L. 95-608, 92 Stat. 3069.

Indian Civil Rights Act of 1968. P.L. 90-284, 82 Stat. 77–80.

Indian Financing Act of 1974. P.L. 93-262, 88 Stat. 77.

Indian General Allotment Act of 1887. Ch. 119, 24 Stat. 388.
Indian Reorganization Act of 1934. Ch. 576, 48 Stat. 984.
Indian Self-Determination and Education Assistance Act. P.L. 93-638, 88 Stat. 2203 (1975).
Josephy, A. (1991). *The Indian heritage of America*. New York: Houghton Mifflin.
Kellough, G. (1980). From colonialism to economic imperialism: The experience of the American Indian. In J. Harp & J. R. Hofley (Eds.), *Structure inequality in Canada* (pp. 343–377). Englewood Cliffs, NJ: Prentice Hall.
Lonewolf v. Hitchcock, 187 U.S. 553 (1903).
Martin, C. (1987). *The American Indian and the problems of history*. New York: Oxford University Press.
McNickle, D., Young, R., & Buffalohead, R. (1978). *Captive nations: A political history of American Indians*. Washington, DC: U.S. Department of Interior, Library of Congress.
Meriam, L. (1928). *The problem of Indian administration*. Baltimore: Johns Hopkins University Press.
*Message from the President of the United States: Recommendations for Indian policy*. (1970, July). Washington, DC: U.S. Government Printing Office.
Native American Programs Act of 1974. P.L. 88-452, 88 Stat. 2324.
North American peoples and cultures. (1984). In *The new encyclopedia Britannica* (Vol. 13, pp. 213–218). Chicago: Encyclopedia Britannica.
*Report of the Hoover Commission*. (1948). Washington, DC: U.S. Government Printing Office.
Spicer, E. (1982). *The American Indians*. Cambridge, MA: Belknap Press.
Squire v. Capoerman, 351 U.S. 76 (1956).
Taylor, L. S. (1973). *A history of Indian policy*. Washington, DC: Bureau of Indian Affairs.
U.S. Bureau of the Census. (1984a). *American Indian areas and Alaska native villages, 1980* (Supplementary Report, No. PC 80-15-13). Washington, DC: U.S. Government Printing Office.
U.S. Bureau of the Census. (1984b). *A statistical profile of the American Indian population: 1980 census*. Washington, DC: U.S. Government Printing Office.
United States v. Winans, 198 U.S. 371 (1905).
Worchester v. Georgia, 31 U.S. (6 Pet.) 515 (1832).

**Ronald G. Lewis, PhD,** is professor, Eastern Michigan University, School of Social Work, Ypsilanti, MI 48197. Dr. Lewis is an enrolled member of the Cherokee Nation and was the first American Indian to receive a PhD in the field of social work.

**For further information see**

Advocacy; Alaska Natives; Civil Rights; Community; Ethnic-Sensitive Practice; Federal Social Legislation from 1961 to 1994; Human Rights; Natural Helping Networks; Peace and Social Justice; Poverty; Rural Social Work Overview; Social Welfare Policy.

**Key Words**
American Indians
Native Americans
Indian policy

## Anorexia

*See* Eating Disorders and Other Compulsive Behaviors

# Archives of Social Welfare

**David J. Klaassen**

The archives of social welfare are, in effect, one of the cumulative by-products of social welfare activities over the years. Of necessity, individuals, organizations, and agencies create records in the process of planning, delivering, or evaluating services to various client groups. By one definition, those records become archives through simple inertia—by surviving beyond the period in which they are needed for their original purpose of informing current, day-to-day affairs. A more rigorous and meaningful definition designates as archives only those noncurrent records that have been consciously selected because of some continuing value and then administered in a manner that ensures their preservation and availability for use.

In the transition to noncurrent, or archival, status, the records themselves do not change, but the perception of them does as they come to possess values for people and purposes often quite different from those for which they were created. Archives provide a tangible as well as an informational link with the past that gives an institution administrative continuity, informs and enriches commemorative celebrations, provides the basis for an appealing promotional or fundraising campaign, and protects legal and property rights. Descendants of people mentioned in archival records find evidence of their family lineage for genealogical, medical, or legal purposes. Scholars and others with an interest in the past examine archives, despite having no personal connection with the individual or institution whose records they seek. The unique relationship—or, often, the very lack of an apparent relationship—between the creators and the users of archives has important implications for archivists and historical researchers.

## Nature of Archives

Relatively few of the correspondence, memoranda, diaries, minutes, reports, speeches, financial records, case files, photographs, and other documents that fill the file cabinets of social welfare agencies and organizations were written or saved with an "external" audience in mind. In most cases they are a part of the action they record and are intended to communicate to a specific recipient. The result is an information source that is qualitatively different from those with which most social work researchers are likely to be more familiar.

When compared with the published books and articles that form the basis for traditional library research, archives are relatively spontaneous and less self-conscious, often affording an unguarded glimpse of intent or controlling values. Published works generally represent finished products, whereas archival materials record, and are a part of, the process (that is, the preparations, the negotiations, the rejected alternatives).

Compared with survey and questionnaire data or participant–observer documentation that support much empirical research, archival sources offer evidence that exists independent of the researcher's bias. Documents whose information content is fixed at the time of their creation eliminate any concern about individuals under study having their responses altered through an awareness of being observed or a desire to give the interviewer a favorable answer.

This "tell-it-like-it-was" integrity has its drawbacks, however. There are no guarantees that the information desired by a particular researcher was ever recorded or, if it was, that it has been preserved and can be located. The available resources may be dauntingly vast, whereas the subset related to a specific topic may be disappointingly limited and fragmentary (Stuart, 1988).

Archival materials are, by definition, unique or nearly so. Correspondence, memoranda, and other records are often prepared with, at most, a single duplicate copy. Even minutes, reports, and conference proceedings that were mimeographed or photocopied for wider distribution are unlikely to have been systematically preserved in many places. Precisely for this reason, archival records are seldom allowed to circulate. Thus, "going to source" often implies just that. Rarely will a single research library or interlibrary loan facility bring together the primary source materials needed for a particular research project.

## Sources of Records

The researcher who effectively exploits archival source materials begins by supposing the existence of a potentially useful source of information—an individual or organization who, as a participant or observer, might have created a useful record. Then he or she sets out to verify the existence and location of the source. To appreciate the diversity of available sources, it is useful to survey the range of institutions whose activities in the field would have resulted in the creation of records.

### National Associations

Organizations whose primary purpose was or is the planning or provision of some kind of social service are the obvious starting point. National associations have long provided leadership in specialized areas, often serving a network of local affiliated agencies but sometimes working directly in communities throughout the country. Researchers have relied heavily on the records of these associations because of their relative convenience. The associations' outlook and activity predisposed them toward careful analysis of existing conditions and appropriate remedial actions. Furthermore, historically there have been relatively few prominent national associations, making the identification and use of their records a manageable proposition.

Records of national associations best document high-level planning and setting of standards. They also often reflect an awareness of conditions and activities in specific locales, but usually only as a secondary or summary account received from a local affiliate. For a more intimate picture of social work as it was actually practiced and of the condition of client populations, it is often necessary to rely on the records of local agencies. Social welfare historians have tended to assume that the prescriptive literature of social work journals and conference proceedings provides an accurate description of practice, in large part because local agency records can be difficult to locate, particularly for more than a case study approach.

### Government Agencies

Many of the same generalizations can be applied to the records of government agencies. Their value for researchers will be shaped by the nature of the agency or department's responsibilities. Since the advent of social security and New Deal–based welfare programs, federal records have documented the lives of individual citizens to a much greater degree than have records of national organizations in the private sector. For pre-1930s topics, researchers interested in local conditions and activities must rely on records of state and local public relief or welfare programs, just as they would with private-sector records. In any case, researchers can expect public records at any level to present considerable bulk and complexity.

### Individuals

The list of potential sources does not end with the organizations and agencies most directly involved in the planning and delivery of services. Personal papers of individuals associated with these institutions often reflect the historical legacy of "taking work home" and provide a valuable supplementary source. Records of social work education—schools of social work, their organizations, and their students and faculty—are particularly appropriate as evidence of social work's aspirations. In some cases, for example, in records related to field placement, they also provide a view of existing patterns in practice.

The field of social welfare is not the exclusive province of the social work profession. Records of business, labor, religion, and health care provide perspectives of their respective contributions toward improvement of the well-being of individuals, groups, and communities.

### Memoirs and Oral Histories

Finally, there is a special category of historical source material that must be distinguished from the preceding materials in that it is a self-conscious effort to re-create or analyze events long after their occurrence. This category would include, along with published and unpublished personal memoirs, oral history interviews designed either to fill the gaps in existing written records or to provide an alternative source in their absence.

NASW sponsored an oral history project in 1980–1981 to record the recollections of pivotal figures in the development of the social work profession. The full set of transcripts of interviews with Harriett Bartlett, Arthur Dunham, Arlien Johnson, Gisela Konopka, Inabel Lindsay, Helen Harris Perlman, Gladys Ryland, and Gertrude Wilson is available at the National Social Work Library at NASW, the University of Minnesota, Columbia University, the University of Washington, and the Library of Congress. Additional social work leaders have been interviewed in other ongoing oral history projects, most notably those at Columbia University, Smith College, and the University of California at Berkeley. All of these interviews provide a type of insight and understanding that written records seldom capture.

## Responsibility for Maintaining Archives

Archives don't just happen. The availability of a documentary base from which to re-create and learn from the past requires a combination of resources, perceived need, and the will to act in selecting, organizing, and preserving records. Surviving archival records fall into two categories: those that have remained in the custody of the institution or individual that created or accumulated them and those for which the responsibility has been transferred to another party. In the United States and Canada, unlike in some European countries, there is no overall plan or policy that prescribes which records will be preserved and by whom. The resulting dispersal reflects a free-market approach to records preservation.

### Government Records

Government records are the most predictable. State and federal laws establish archival agencies at the respective levels with responsibility for the preservation of government records of enduring value. To varying degrees state archives are responsible for records of local government as well. Thus, all surviving records of the U.S. Department of Health and Human Services and its predecessors are the responsibility of the National Archives and Records Administration, whereas the records of, for example, the Minnesota Department of Human Services are a part of the state archives administered by the Minnesota Historical Society. The volume and complexity of government records—particularly those of the post–World War II era—tries the resources of the archiving body. As a result, researchers using these records can expect to find no more than the most rudimentary checklists summarizing records in the condition that the archiving body received them.

### Records of Social Services Institutions

Other institutions and organizations support their own archival programs to the extent that their administrative and informational needs and their sense of historical legacy can be reconciled with budgetary realities. Relatively few social services organizations maintain a full archival program in the sense of systematically selecting, arranging, describing, and preserving their inactive records and providing reference services to researchers. One notable example is the Salvation Army. Other organizations have saved some of their inactive records from destruction but have done little to provide effective access to those records.

Barbeau and Lohmann (1992) argued that the contemporary social administrator has a responsibility, both to the agency and to the social work profession, to maintain and preserve records that can provide the content needed so others may benefit from historical understanding. As a top priority, they urge the development of guidelines for records management procedures that would aid executives and nonpublic social services agencies in identifying what records to retain. Cox (1992) offered detailed guidance for organizations regarding what should be involved in a records management and archives program, including a case study that described how a professional association can effectively manage its own information systems, respond to membership needs, and promote a continued sense of the profession's origins and culture.

## Focus of Archives

Institutional archives normally exist primarily to satisfy the administrative informational needs of the parent institution; secondarily, they accommodate the work of historical researchers. In contrast, a variety of libraries and historical societies collect unpublished materials for cultural, research, and educational purposes. Klaassen (1990) analyzed the circumstances in which it is appropriate for an organization or agency to transfer its records to an outside repository. In instances in which an organization's scale of operation is large enough to generate substantial records but too small to be able to afford specialized staff, collaboration may be the most effective means of meeting administrative needs as well as providing a valuable research resource.

### Geographic Area

Most collecting repositories focus on a defined geographic area. State historical societies have long been the dominant institution of this type; some of them serve the dual role of managing state archives and collecting documents related to general state history. However, there are growing numbers of city historical societies and regional research centers, the latter usually housed in a university library.

### Subject

A number of collecting repositories concentrate on a subject rather than a geographic area. The Social Welfare History Archives at the University of Minnesota is the most relevant example. Other related theme collections include the Schlesinger Library on the History of Women at Radcliffe College; the Sophia Smith Collection (also concentrating on women's history with a subemphasis on social work) at Smith College; the Walter P. Reuther Library of Labor and Urban Affairs at Wayne State University; and the Rockefeller Archives Center, which documents the activities of other philanthropic organizations as well as those established by the Rockefeller family. There are also important collecting emphases within more broadly defined repositories. The State Historical Society of Wisconsin, for example, has acquired the papers of many influential figures from the social security movement and has assembled an outstanding social action collection, particularly for the 1960s and 1970s.

Institutional archives occasionally collect materials to supplement the records of the parent institution. The National Archives and Records Administration administers a network of presidential libraries, each of which seeks to document the activities of a presidential administration (beginning with Herbert Hoover) by bringing together the personal papers of the president and the records and papers of various organizations and individuals associated with that administration. Thus, for example, the Dwight D. Eisenhower Library in Abilene, Kansas, holds the papers of Oveta Culp Hobby, the first secretary of Health, Education, and Welfare. Similarly, college and university archives solicit the papers of notable faculty members and administrators and, occasionally, of prominent alumni.

A particular set of archival records could end up in any of a number of repositories, because areas of collecting interest overlap. To use one example, the papers of a prominent social worker could attract the interest of the college archives of his or her alma mater, the city or state historical society from the area in which he or she lived, any of a number of subject collections, or even the Library of Congress Manuscripts Division.

## Social Welfare Collections

Until about 1960 very little collecting was being done in the area of social services. Most of what was collected was in the form of personal papers of reformers, particularly individuals such as Frances Perkins, Jane Addams, and Lillian Wald, who were significantly involved in public policy debates. Radcliffe College (specifically its Schlesinger Library), Columbia University, the Library of Congress, the New York Public Library, and the State Historical Society of Wisconsin were among the few repositories to show an early interest in the records of social services and social reform.

The rediscovery of poverty in America during the early 1960s and the concomitant expansion of academic historians' interest to embrace social as well as political and economic history created a climate that encouraged the preservation of social welfare records. The Social Welfare History Archives, concentrating primarily on records of national nongovernment organizations in the welfare and service field, was founded at the University of Minnesota in 1964. Represented in its more than 9,000 linear feet of records are national organizations, local agencies and organizations (most of them from the Minneapolis–St. Paul area), and individual social workers. It was soon joined by other university-affiliated urban archives at the University of Pittsburgh, the University of Illinois at Chicago (then Chicago Circle), Temple University, and Case Western Reserve University. These repositories attempt to document the entire range of urban life in their respective cities. In each case the records of organized social reformers and social services agencies represent an important segment of their total holdings.

## Research Use of Archives

Given the variety of institutional settings in which social welfare records may be held (not to mention the possibility of their being in the hands of private individuals) and the lack of an overall system to provide for their preservation, it should come as no surprise that there is no single means of locating a particular set of records. Basically there are three approaches:

1. One can follow the tracks of previous researchers by scrutinizing their footnote citations and source notes. This obviously will produce no previously unused sources, but it may identify some that escape notice in the other approaches.
2. One can rely on the various descriptive finding aids that have been devised to inform the research community of available materials. The effectiveness of this approach is limited primarily to the holdings of professionally staffed repositories.
3. In the absence of specific information, one can draw on either of the two previous approaches to provide the basis for informed speculation about where inquiries about particular records might best be directed. Staff members at repositories with significant social welfare holdings are often good sources of information.

Inadequate resources, variations in practice from one repository to the next, and the complexity of primary sources have combined to limit the effectiveness of efforts at information sharing among repositories. Researchers relying on existing guides and directories have no grounds for confidence that they have identified all relevant sources, but the situation is significantly improved over what it was during the 1970s.

### Impact of Computerization

Computerization is profoundly affecting the way archivists describe their holdings. Published national reference tools that list archival repositories and describe their holdings are rapidly being supplanted by, and merged into, online national bibliographic databases. For example, the *National Union Catalog of Manuscript Collections* (Library of Congress, 1959) has long been the principal source for locating a particular collection. The information contained in it is being added to the Research Libraries Information Network (RLIN), a database that lists the holdings of most of the nation's major research libraries. RLIN includes more than 350,000 entries that describe archives and manuscript collections in those libraries. The advantages of placing this archival descriptive information in a machine-readable database such as RLIN or the Online Computer Library Center, a system that parallels RLIN for smaller college libraries, are the ease of adding new records to keep information current and the greatly enhanced searching capability. Access to these systems is channeled through the member libraries.

Computers have largely replaced typewriters for preparation of the in-house finding aids that provide detailed information about the contents of individual collections, meaning that the resulting machine-readable text files can easily be copied and distributed on a diskette. Some archives have begun to make these finding aids available electronically over the Internet and the World Wide Web, allowing researchers with computer communication capability to learn about the contents of collections without leaving home. Another resource, the *National Inventory of Documentary Sources in the United States* (NIDS) (Chadwyck-Healey, 1984), brings together, through microfiche reproduction, the detailed finding aids (known as inventories or registers) describing the contents of collections in repositories throughout the United States. More than 20,000 collections from more than 200 repositories are included in NIDS, but it is most valuable for its extensive coverage of the holdings of the National Archives, the Library of Congress Manuscripts Division, and the Presidential Libraries system, all of which are important sources for the study of aspects of social welfare history.

## Special Problems

Researchers who rely on archival sources to recreate and analyze social welfare history must come to terms with several problems. One of these has to do with the changing nature of modern records, most notably their sheer volume. Records, particularly of government but also of other entities, accumulate at a nearly unmanageable rate, often exceeding the resources available to institutional archives and leaving collecting repositories reluctant to accept responsibility for massive collections.

**Developments in Technology**

The changes are qualitative as well as quantitative. Complex bureaucratic structures inevitably spawn extensive housekeeping paperwork that offers little of interest to most researchers. Developments in office technology shape the historical record as well. The typewriter, the mimeograph, and the photocopy machine all increased the accumulation of paper by making it easier to create and duplicate documents. Computers are tending to do the same thing. Many important discussions conducted by telephone may never be recorded. The transition to the automated office, which is progressing more slowly in social services organizations and agencies than in the for-profit and education sectors, will profoundly affect the records available to future researchers, but not necessarily by bringing an end to paper records. Electronic mail, for example, is replacing both conventional correspondence and telephone calls to some extent; many individuals print file copies of important messages for future reference. As more data are stored only in machine-readable form, archivists face significant challenges in providing continued access after the hardware and software with which these data were stored have become obsolete.

**Privacy Issues**

Data privacy is another critical issue for social welfare researchers. When a field involves as many shared confidences as does social welfare, access to its records by third parties will inevitably raise difficult questions. Klaassen (1983) traced the historical development of social workers' attitudes toward the confidentiality of case records, showing how the early, relaxed policies were gradually tightened. Current professional standards permit research use, contingent on the informed consent of the client. This does not adequately address the circumstances of historical research in which, years later, scholars rely on information contained in the files to reconstruct the circumstances of the client population or the methods of the helping professional.

Archivists who administer case records have derived their access policies from experience with other sensitive materials such as census records. The key element is the effect of the passage of time, the assumption being that after sufficient time has elapsed—75 years in the case of census manuscripts—the diminished need to protect individual privacy is offset by the societal interest in learning from the lessons of history. Social workers, archivists, and historians must address this issue more satisfactorily. Individual researchers must anticipate the likelihood of their encountering sensitive references in all types of social welfare records—not just in case records but also in correspondence, committee and board proceedings, and other administrative documents as well—and acknowledge their personal responsibility to disguise personal identities in any disclosure of such material.

A final issue has to do with the problem of balance in the documentation provided by the archives of social welfare. Most of the records discussed in this entry were the product of the planners and providers of social services. The fact that much of social welfare history is similarly skewed toward an analysis of social welfare institutions and their professionals is, in part, both a cause and an effect of this situation.

## Conclusion

Chambers (1986) emphasized the need to see welfare history "from the bottom up." Some of the works he cited, together with many subsequent publications, have demonstrated that researchers can study social welfare clients by making effective use of case records, client ombudsman files, and the records of consumer and self-help organizations, where they exist.

Archival source materials mirror the subtleties and ambiguities of the events to which they owe their existence. For precisely that reason, they can be irreplaceably valuable to researchers as well as exasperating. In many ways, however, their complexity is their charm, for much of the fun is in the chase.

## References

Barbeau, E., & Lohmann, R. (1992). The agency executive director as keeper of the past. *Administration in Social Work, 16,* 15–26.

Chadwyck-Healey. (1984). *National inventory of documentary sources in the United States.* Teaneck, NJ: Author.

Chambers, C. (1986). Toward a redefinition of welfare history. *Social Service Review, 61,* 1–33.

Cox, R. (1992). *Managing archival institutions: Foundational principles and practices.* Westport, CT: Greenwood.

Klaassen, D. (1983). The provenance of social work case records: Implications for archival appraisal and access. *Provenance: Journal of the Society of Georgia Archivists, 1,* 5–30.

Klaassen, D. (1990). The archival intersection: Cooperation between collecting repositories and nonprofit organizations. *Midwestern Archivist, 15,* 25–38

Library of Congress. (1959). *National union catalog of manuscript collections.* Washington, DC: Author.

Stuart, P. (1988). Historical research. In R. Grinnell (Ed.), *Social work research and evaluation* (3rd ed., pp. 342–361). Itasca, IL: F. E. Peacock.

**FURTHER READING**

Hinding, A. (Ed.). (1979). *Women's history sources: A guide to archives and manuscript collections in the United States.* New York: R. R. Bowker.

Leashore, B., & Cates, J. (1985). Use of historical methods in social work research. *Social Work Research & Abstracts, 21*(2), 22–27.

National Historical Publications and Records Commission. (1988). *Directory of archives and manuscript repositories in the United States* (2nd ed.). Phoenix: Oryx.

O'Toole, J. (1992). *Understanding archives and manuscripts.* Chicago: Society of American Archivists.

**David J. Klaassen, MA, CA,** is archivist and professor, University of Minnesota, Social Welfare History Archives, 101 Walter Library, Minneapolis, MN 55455.

**For further information see**

Computer Utilization; Historiography; Mass Media; Research Overview; Social Welfare History; Social Work Practice: History and Evolution; Social Work Profession Overview.

**Key Words**

archives
history
research

## Artificial Intelligence

*See* Expert Systems

READER'S GUIDE

### Asian Americans

*The following entries contain information on this general topic:*

Asian Americans Overview
Asian Americans: Chinese
Asian Americans: Japanese
Asian Americans: Southeast Asians
Asian Indians
Pacific Islanders

# Asian Americans Overview

**Pallassana R. Balgopal**

This entry presents an overview of Asian Americans, focusing on the composition of this diverse ethnic group, including a historical analysis, as well as their participation in contemporary America. The term "Asian Americans" encompasses a wide range of peoples and cultures, including people of Chinese, Filipino, Japanese, Asian Indian, Korean, Vietnamese, Cambodian, Hmong, Laotian, Thai, "other Asian," and Pacific Island descent. Under the category "other Asian" are people of Bangladeshi, Burmese, Indonesian, Malaysian, Pakistani, and Sri Lankan descent. People of Hawaiian, Samoan, and Guamanian descent are known as "Pacific Islanders." People of Tongan, Tahitian, Fijian, Northern Mariana Island, and Palauan descent are classified as "other Pacific Islanders" (U.S. Bureau of the Census, 1992).

## Population: Composition and Distribution

The 1990 U.S. census reported the total Asian and Pacific Islander population to be greater than 7 million, of which 95 percent were Asians and 5 percent were Pacific Islanders. People of Chinese, Filipino, Japanese, Asian Indian, and Korean descent constituted a major portion of the total Asian population, followed by people of Cambodian, Hmong, Laotian, and Thai descent. The total "other Asian" population was reported to be 302,209 (see Figure 1). The total Pacific Islander population included people of Hawaiian, Samoan, Guamanian, and other Pacific Island descent (U.S. Bureau of Census, 1992). In 1991, more than 1.8 million immigrants were granted legal permanent resident status. Asia was the leading continent of origin for nonlegalized immigrants, with 43.5 percent of the total entering United States (U.S. Immigration and Naturalization Service, 1991).

## Immigration History

From 1776 until 1882, the United States had no restrictions on immigration. During this period, emigration was mostly from Europe. People began to emigrate from Asia in the mid-19th century. The first to come to the United States were people from China; by 1852, they numbered over 25,000 and had settled primarily in California (Chandrasekhar, 1982). Between 1890 and 1920, immigrants from Japan came to the United States, mostly as contract laborers.

The Philippines became a possession of the United States in 1899, and Filipinos were allowed to enter the United States freely until 1934. The earliest Filipino immigrants came as students or as unskilled laborers. Those who came in the 1960s were mostly professionals (Kitano, 1987). After the 1965 Immigration Act the number of Filipinos who immigrated to the United States steadily increased.

FIGURE 1

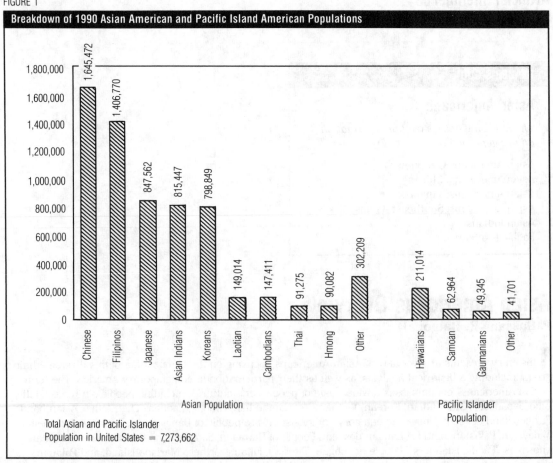

**Breakdown of 1990 Asian American and Pacific Island American Populations**



Source: U.S. Bureau of the Census. (1992). *1990 Census of population—General population characteristics*. Washington, DC: U.S. Government Printing Office.

The majority of Korean immigrants, like the Filipino immigrants, came during the 1960s. About 90 percent of them have been in the United States for fewer than 15 years. Los Angeles has the largest Korean community (Kitano, 1987).

Immigration by people from the Pacific Islands to the United States increased during the 1950s. People from Samoa came in 1951, when the U.S. Navy, which was then the largest employer in Samoa, closed its base there. The immigration of the people from Guam was facilitated by the Organic Act of Guam of 1950. Many Tongans came to this country because of their connection with the Church of Jesus Christ of Latter-day Saints and hence settled in Salt Lake City, Utah (Morales & Sheafor, 1992).

During the initial years of the 20th century, Asian Indians (then called "Hindus") entered the United States. The early immigrants were agricultural workers from northern India, who arrived during a period of general hostility toward Asians that also provoked executive exclusion orders in 1910, 1917, and 1923. The second phase of Asian Indian immigration occurred after 1965. At present, there are more than 1.2 million Asian Indians in the United States.

After the Vietnam War, people from Cambodia, Laos, and Vietnam entered the United States, mostly as refugees. The inflow of Vietnamese refugees into the United States began in 1975 and consisted mostly of professionals. The refugees who have immigrated since then generally have less education than the first group (Morales & Sheafor, 1992).

## Asian Americans in the American Context

### Early Stereotyping

American stereotypes of Asians have changed dramatically over the past several years. In the late 19th and early 20th centuries Asians were considered an inferior race and were subject to discrimination. Although positive and negative stereotypes were perpetuated during this period, the views were mainly negative. Japanese were stereotyped as intelligent, industrious, progressive, shrewd, shy, and quiet. Chinese were stereotyped as superstitious, sly, conservative, and traditional and as having strong loyalties to family (Sue & Kitano, 1973). There were restrictions on immigration and on acquiring U.S. citizenship. Antimiscegenation laws prohibited interracial marriages. Antialien land laws prevented Asian immigrants from buying property. Chinese and Japanese children were segregated in schools (Kitano, 1987; Murase, 1977). Chinese immigrants were perceived as "exotic curiosities," but later this perception was changed to "inassimilable, immoral, treacherous heathens" who deprive white Americans of their jobs (and possibly of their women) (Hurh & Kim, 1989, p. 512).

This early stereotyping of Japanese and Chinese immigrants influenced attitudes toward Asian Indians, who were viewed as superstitious, backward, spineless people with filthy and immodest habits. The anti-Indian feelings were so strong that anti-Indian riots occurred in Seattle, Everett, and Bellingham, Washington, The Asiatic Exclusion League strongly supported limiting the number of immigrants from India. Asians, in general, were subject to humiliating experiences because of the negative image of them held by the majority of white Americans (Hess, 1982).

### 1990s—Myths and Realities

Although negative stereotypes still exist, Asian Americans are currently seen as successful, industrious, intelligent, hardworking, patient, clean, and courteous people (Kitano, 1969; Sue & Kitano, 1973). They are considered a model minority, with low rates of juvenile delinquency, mental illness (Kitano, 1969; Kitano & Sue, 1973), and divorce (Sue & Kitano, 1973). They are considered to have stable close-knit families that "take care of their own," with little need for outside social services (Crystal, 1989). Asian Americans are considered to be high socioeconomic achievers with high levels of education (Hurh & Kim, 1989). Greenwald (1985) reported that they were seen as the most skilled of any immigrant group in the United States. According to Sue and Kitano (1973), Japanese Americans are seen as the most successful minority in an economic sense.

The successful image of this group is also considered to be a myth, however (Crystal, 1989; Hurh & Kim, 1989), because of factors such as longer hours of work and the reporting of household income, rather than the income of individual family members. The 1990 census reported extensively on the economic characteristics of Asians and Pacific Islanders (U.S. Bureau of the Census, 1992):

- The labor force participation rate for Asians and Pacific Islanders (64 percent) was lower than that of whites (66 percent).
- Male Asian and Pacific Islanders who worked year-round, full-time had median earnings ($26,760) that were lower than those of comparable white men ($28,880).
- Female Asian and Pacific Islanders who worked year-round, full-time had higher median earnings ($21,320) than did female white workers ($20,050).

- The median family income of Asians in 1990 was greater ($42,250) than that for white families ($36,920). However, Samoans, Guamanians, and Vietnamese had relatively lower incomes.
- A larger proportion of the Asian and Pacific Islander families had three or more earners than did white families; these additional earners contributed to their higher median family income.
- A larger proportion (11 percent) of Asian and Pacific Islander families than of white families (8 percent) lived below the poverty level.

In reality, Hurh and Kim (1989) observed that Asian Americans earn less than do white Americans despite additional years of schooling and concluded that this inequity in earnings is caused by discrimination in the American labor market. Asian American men have difficulty finding jobs that are commensurate with their education; thus, they work in low-level administrative jobs or low-to-medium levels of employment in professional or service occupations.

The mythical success of Asian Americans results in their exclusion from educational, health, housing, employment, and social welfare programs (Crystal, 1989; Kim, 1973) and a lack of attention to the real problems and needs of this group, such as unemployment, underemployment, poverty among the elderly, and increasing rates of divorce and juvenile delinquency (Hurh & Kim, 1989).

Early Asian immigrants tended to live in large metropolitan areas on the two coasts. Their clustering resulted in specific urban "Chinatowns" that can be found in most U.S. cities. Asian immigrants coming from Korea, the Philippines, Taiwan, India, and other South Asian countries generally have scattered throughout the country. However, Asian Americans in most urban areas have formed new enclaves to help meet the cultural and ethnic needs of new immigrants.

## Unique Characteristics

### Individualism–Collectivism

The individualism–collectivism theory links culture and social behavior. "Individualism" implies an ability to depend on oneself, assuming responsibilities for actions and living styles, and generally not succumbing to social pressures to conform. "Collectivism" implies a greater emphasis on the views, needs, and goals of the group; that is, social norms and duty are defined by the group, and there are higher expectations to integrate and cooperate with members of the group.

The United States has an individualistic culture, with an emphasis on self-reliance, competition, and independence (Triandis, Botempo, & Villareal, 1988). On the other hand, Asians have a collectivist cultural pattern that focuses on the interdependence of members, harmonious relationships, and the preservation of integrity. It is argued that Asians stress collectivism, rather than individualism, because the individual is expected to make sacrifices for the family (Segal, 1991); the needs of the family take precedence over the needs of the individual; and group cooperation, rather than individual competition, is stressed (Mikler, 1993). The emphasis on restraining the expression of emotions and implicit obedience to family authority and elders are other indicators of collectivism (Sue, 1981).

### Family Ties

The family is the fundamental unit for Asians, and there is interdependence among family members. Asian families are generally patriarchal, and in traditional Asian families, age, sex, and generational status determine the roles that members play. The father is the head of the family, and his authority is unquestioned; he is the main disciplinarian and is usually less approachable and more distant than the mother, who is the nurturer and caretaker (Mikler, 1993; Sue, 1981; Sue & Wagner, 1973). The main duty of the son is to be a good son; the son's obligations as a husband and father are secondary. Children are expected to take care of their parents in old age. They usually live with their parents until they get married, and, in many cases, sons continue to live with their parents even after marriage (Mikler, 1993).

Because the family members' roles are explicitly defined, there is little conflict in the family. Family harmony is stressed, and family members are expected to control their emotions to preserve it. The emphasis on controlling emotions has caused Westerners to consider Asians inscrutable (Sue & Wagner, 1973). Problems are kept within the family, and sharing negative information outside the home is discouraged because it would bring disgrace to the family (Lum, 1986). The strong emphasis on obligations to the family and the inculcation of guilt and shame act as social controls (Sue, 1981).

### Marriage and Child Rearing

The traditional custom of arranged marriages is now prevalent mainly among South Asians (Bangladeshi, Indian, Pakistani, and Sri Lankan) families. Asian parents attempt to restrict the choice of their children's mates within their own ethnic groups and influence the selection of mates. However, unlike the past, sons and daughters have increasing control over decisions about whom they will marry (Devore & Schlesinger, 1991; Nambiar, 1993).

Grandparents play a significant role in child rearing in Asian families. Frequently, they move in with their adult children and serve as nurturers and role models, as well as provide child care. The older generation is also instrumental in the preservation of the native language and cultural heritage.

### Religion

The formal religions of Asian Americans are Buddhism, Hinduism, Christianity, and Islam. Many Japanese Americans are of Buddhist background, but may attend an all-Japanese American Christian church (Kitano, 1969). Buddhists are tolerant of other faiths and do not have a rigid institutionalized religion. Ethical behavior with parents, friends, and strangers is the focus of all religious training among them.

For Asian Indians, Hinduism is the main religion. Hindus believe that a person is not a separate individual, but that the self or "Atman" is a part of the cosmic absolute or "Brahman"; that physical satisfaction and knowledge are illusions and that life consists of impermanence, suffering, and the absence of ego; and that one's future is determined by one's deeds in the present. Nirvana—salvation from the cycle of reincarnation and becoming one with Brahman—is seen as the ideal state. Most Asian Indian families have a designated place of worship in their homes, and most major cities in the United States now have Hindu temples.

An increasing number of Korean immigrants and Chinese immigrants from Taiwan, Singapore, and Hong Kong are Christians. Communities with significant Korean and Chinese American populations have built their own churches. Similarly, Asian Indians who are Christians, especially those from the southern state of Kerala, have established Christian churches. Sikhs, who were one of the earliest Asian Indian immigrant groups, came from the northwestern province of Punjab and follow the religion of Sikhism. They, too, have built places of worship, known as Gurudwaras.

Islam is the main religion for immigrants from Pakistan, Malaysia, Indonesia, and Bangladesh. The Quran is the holy book of the Muslims. Many of the immigrant Muslims adhere strictly to their religious practices and visit mosques every Friday to offer prayers. Mosques have been built in a number of American communities through the support of Muslims from all over the world.

### Close Ties with Countries of Origin

Most Asian immigrants maintain close ties with their countries of origin, especially through visits at least once every two or three years. Although visiting is expensive, many continue this practice primarily because of their active participation with their kinship networks. Saran's (1985) study of Asian Indians found that Indian immigrants maintain close ties with India through frequent visits and by subscribing to local Indian newspapers. Asian Americans also keep close ties through visits of their relatives to the United States, overseas telephone calls, ethnic movies, and audiotapes.

## PROBLEMS

### Restrictive Legislation

Because Asian Americans are a distinct ethnic and racial group, they have faced numerous prejudices. It is worthwhile to highlight some of the prohibitive and restrictive legislation and policies that have hampered this ethnic group from sharing the American pie.

From 1776 to 1882, the U.S. government had no policy of control or restriction over immigration. The Burlingame Treaty of 1868 allowed the free immigration of people from China. However, immigrants from Asia were subjected to labor exploitation, blatant discrimination, and social violence. The Chinese Exclusion Act of 1882, the first restrictive legislation, banned Chinese immigration until 1943, when a token quota of 105 Chinese per year was established. Thereafter, federal and local legislation, such as the Asian Land Law of 1913 and the Asians Exclusion Act of 1924, supported legal inequality and the social segregation of these groups until the passage of the Civil Rights Act of 1964 (Lee, Balgopal, & Patchner, 1988).

The Immigration Act of 1907 permitted the entry of parents, wives, or children of Japanese American residents into the United States. The Immigration Act of 1917 added more groups to the category of "inadmissable aliens" and included the provision of a literacy test for prospective immigrants. The Immigration Act of 1924 was enacted to control the flood of immigrants in an already depressed labor market and introduced a quota system that restricted the number of immigrants of each nationality. The Immigration Act of 1946 authorized the admission to the United States of persons of races indigenous to India and to the Philippine Islands and consequently made them eligible for naturalization.

### Different Customs and Value Base

The Immigration and Nationality Act of 1965 revised the quota system and resolved many of the racist features of earlier immigration laws (Chandrasekhar, 1982). That an increasing number of people from different countries in Asia have equal access to the United States is creating problems of different kinds because these immigrants have different lifestyles and value systems. Although Asian Americans are seen as hardworking, immigrants who excel are often viewed as "foreigners" who are taking jobs and other economic opportunities away from "real" Americans. At one time or another, most Asian immigrants and refugees experience a sense of powerlessness because of the language barrier, unfamiliarity with American customs and norms, prejudice, and the loss of social support networks and a sense of belonging that is found in their native environments (Hirayama & Citingok, 1988). Asian Americans experience extreme cultural conflict because of the negative connotation attached to many of their values, which differ from Judeo-Christian values.

Although Asian Americans are seen as well educated and economically comfortable, an increasing number of them are poor and marginally educated and trained. These Asian Americans also face racial discrimination and have language difficulties. Moreover, even those who are well qualified face discrimination in the labor market, and underemployment is a serious occupational problem. Asian Americans are generally excluded from administrative policymaking or decision-making positions (Hurh & Kim, 1989). Interracial tensions and conflicts between Asian Americans and other minorities, especially African Americans (Morales & Sheafor, 1992), have occurred because of Asian Americans' image of success. Thus, Asian Americans who own small businesses in economically depressed areas may be seen by other minority groups as a threat and therefore become targets for violence, as witnessed during the riots in Los Angeles in 1992.

Asian Americans are competitive because they do not want to fail and bring shame to their families. This dynamic can lead to conflict within the family, especially in parent–child relationships. Although juvenile delinquency rates are still low, it is generally recognized that such criminal acts in Asian American communities are underreported and violent activities by Asian youth gangs have increased throughout the country (Morales & Sheafor, 1992). In addition, there seems to be an increase in alcoholism (Chi, Lubben, & Kitano, 1989), and although exact data do not exist, domestic violence in Asian families is being reported in Washington, DC; Los Angeles; Chicago; and New York. Women's shelters that focus on Asian American women who have been abused are being established in these cities (Ho, 1990).

## Implications for Social Work Practice

Although Asian Americans are extremely heterogenous, one can identify certain characteristics that are distinctly different from other ethnic American groups. Social workers need to recognize implications for practice on the basis of these commonalities.

Until recently, Asian Americans were reluctant to seek assistance from the social welfare system because most Asian Americans handle problems within their families, and there is a stigma about and shame in experiencing mental and emotional distress. The pressures experienced by individuals and families are further exacerbated when Asian Americans hide their feelings from members of their ethnic groups. Human services agencies have reported increases in the number of Asian Americans seeking assistance for emotional stress and problems ranging from depression to anxiety. In addition to the establishment of women's shelters for Asian Americans, mental health and other family services agencies are also beginning to get Asian American clients for counseling for marital conflict and parent–child difficulties (Ho, 1990).

Asian Americans, like other people of color, are victimized because of their racial and other ethnic differences and are increasingly the victims of hate crimes that are reported in ethnic newspapers and magazines. Their hard work and pressure to succeed also can draw a negative reaction from institutions, as well as from other ethnic groups.

Social workers must respond to Asian American groups at both the macro and micro levels. At the macro level, institutional and societal discriminatory policies must be eliminated. Community services that are sensitive to the cultural needs of this group is an immediate need.

At the micro level, effective social work intervention must recognize this group's unique values, especially those related to the importance of the family. Daily survival is a crucial issue for many Asian Americans who have had many experiences related to devastating wars, separation from family members, poverty as a result of migration, and humiliation and shame because of the sudden change in their socioeconomic status. Thus, many believe that life is to be endured rather than enjoyed (Berg & Miller, 1992). A brief, task-centered approach focused on problem solving, rather than sustaining insight into problems, is useful (Ramakrishnan & Balgopal, 1986). The emphasis on shame in the Asian culture drives these clients to find amenable solutions quickly (Berg & Miller, 1992). The social worker should be directive and give guidance and advice in the sessions. Until a level of trust is established, it is necessary to focus on external factors and provide concrete help with practical problems and active referrals (Dhooper & Van Tran, 1987).

There is a tendency for Asian Americans to somaticize emotional stress as physical symptoms. Therefore, Dhooper and Van Tran (1987) proposed that social workers must assume multiple helping roles, such as social services worker, health educator, teacher, guide, and family friend and be flexible in their approach.

Because there is a prevailing sense of powerlessness among many Asian Americans, empowerment is an essential issue in intervention. In this regard, the social worker's task is to help clients increase their capacity for connectedness to other social systems to create necessary social networks and resources (Hirayama & Citingok, 1988).

## References


Berg, I. K., & Miller, S. D. (1992). Working with Asian American clients: One person at a time. *Families in Society, 73*(6), 356–363.

Chandrasekhar, S. (1982). *From India to America: A brief history of immigration; problems of discrimination; admission and assimilation.* La Jolla, CA: Population Review Publications.

Chi, J. E., Lubben, E., & Kitano, H. H. (1989). Differences in drinking between three Asian American groups. *Journal of Studies in Alcohol, 50,* 15–23.

Civil Rights Act of 1964. P.L. 88-352, 78 Stat. 241.

Crystal, D. (1989). Asian Americans and the myth of the model minority. *Social Casework, 70*(7), 405–413.

Devore, W., & Schlesinger, E. G. (1991). *Ethnic-sensitive social work practice.* Toronto: Macmillan.

Dhooper, S. S., & Van Tran, T. (1987). Social work with Asian Americans. *Journal of Independent Social Work, 1*(4), 51–62.

Greenwald, J. (1985, July 8). Finding niches in a new land: Industrious arrivals create mini monopolies as they gravitate to familiar fields. *Time,* pp. 72–75.

Hess, G. R. (1982). The Asian Indian immigrants in the United States—The early phase, 1900–65. In S. Chandrasekhar (Ed.), *From India to America* (pp. 113–126). La Jolla, CA: Population Review Publications.

Hirayama, H., & Citingok, M. (1988). Empowerment: A social work approach for Asian immigrants. *Social Casework, 69*(1), 41–47.

Ho, C. K. (1990). An analysis of domestic violence in Asian American communities. A multicultural approach to counseling. *Women and Therapy,* 1–2, 129–150.

Hurh, W. M., & Kim, K. C. (1989). The "success" image of Asian Americans: Its validity and its practical and theoretical implications. *Ethnic and Racial Studies, 12*(4), 512–538.

Immigration Act of 1907. Ch. 1134, 34 Stat. 898.

Immigration Act of 1917. Ch. 29, 39 Stat. 874.

Immigration Act of 1924. Ch. 190, 43 Stat. 153.

Immigration Act of 1946. Ch. 945, 60 Stat. 975.

Immigration and Nationality Act of 1965. P.L. 89-236, 79 Stat. 911.

Kim, B.L.C. (1973). Asian-Americans: No model minority. *Social Work, 18,* 44–53.

Kitano, H.H.L. (1969). *Japanese Americans: The evolution of a subculture.* New York: Prentice Hall.

Kitano, H.H.L. (1987). Asian Americans. In A. Minahan (Ed.-in-Chief), *Encyclopedia of social work* (18th ed., Vol. 1, pp. 159–169). Silver Spring, MD: National Association of Social Workers.

Kitano, H.H.L., & Sue, S. (1973). The model minority. *Journal of Social Issues, 29*(2), 1–9.

Lee, J. J., Balgopal, P. R., & Patchner, M. A. (1988). Citizen participation: An effective dimension for serving the Asian American elderly. In D. S. Sanders & J. Fischer (Eds.), *Visions for the future* (pp. 113–124). Honolulu: University of Hawaii, School of Social Work.

Lum, D. (1986). *Social work practice and people of color: A process-stage approach.* Monterey, CA: Brooks/Cole.

Mikler, S. R. (1993). Asian Indian immigrants in America and sociocultural issues in counseling. *Journal of Multicultural Counseling and Development, 21,* 36–49.

Morales, A. T., & Sheafor, B. W. (1992). *Social work: A profession of many faces.* Needham Heights, MA: Allyn & Bacon.

Murase, K. (1977). Minorities: Asian Americans. In J. Turner (Ed.-in-Chief), *Encyclopedia of social work* (17th ed., pp. 953–960). Washington, DC: National Association of Social Workers.

Nambiar, S. (1993, November 17). Love with a proper stranger. *Washington Post,* pp. C1, C4.

Organic Act of Guam of 1950. Ch. 512, 64 Stat. 384.

Ramakrishnan, K. R., & Balgopal, P. R. (1986). Task centered casework: Intervention strategy for developing societies. *Journal of International and Comparative Social Welfare, 2*(1–2), 21–28.

Saran, P. (1985). *The Asian Indian experience in the United States.* Cambridge, MA: Schenkman.

Segal, U. A. (1991). Cultural variables in Asian Indian families. *Families in Society, 72*(4), 233–241.

Sue, D. W. (1981). *Counseling the culturally different: Theory and practice.* New York: John Wiley & Sons.

Sue, S., & Kitano, H.H.L. (1973). Stereotypes as measures of success. *Journal of Social Issues, 29*(2), 83–98.

Sue, S., & Wagner, N. N. (1973). *Asian-Americans: Psychological perspectives.* Ben Lomond, CA: Science and Behavior Books.

Triandis, H. C., Botempo, R., & Villareal, M. J. (1988). Individualism and collectivism: Cross-cultural perspectives on self-in-group relationships. *Journal of Personality and Social Psychology, 54,* 323–338.

U.S. Bureau of the Census. (1992). *1990 census of population—General population characteristics.* Washington, DC: U.S. Government Printing Office.

U.S. Immigration and Naturalization Service. (1991). *Statistical yearbook of the Immigration and Naturalization Service.* Washington, DC: U.S. Government Printing Office.


**Pallassana R. Balgopal, DSW,** is professor, University of Illinois, School of Social Work, 1207 W. Oregon Street, Urbana, IL 61801.

**For further information see**

Asian Americans: Chinese; Asian Americans: Japanese; Asian Americans: Southeast Asians; Asian Indians; Civil Rights; Direct Practice Overview; Ecological Perspective; Ethnic-Sensitive Practice; Families Overview; Goal Setting and Intervention Planning; Human Rights; Income Distribution; Jobs and Earnings; Pacific Islanders; Social Welfare Policy; Social Work Profession Overview.

**Key Words**

| | |
|---|---|
| Asian Americans | Chinese |
| Asian Indians | Japanese |

# Asian Americans: Chinese

**Doman Lum**

The Chinese came to the United States in the mid-19th century. Between 1850 and 1880 the Chinese population grew from 7,520 to 105,465. By 1870, the Chinese constituted 8.6 percent of California's population and 25 percent of its wage-earning force. They were part of the 1849 California gold rush; worked in the agricultural fields on the West Coast; became the major labor force to build the transcontinental railroad from Sacramento, California, to Promontory Point, Utah; and were enlisted as strike breakers and workers in the industrial Northeast (Takaki, 1990).

Because of economic competition and white racism, the Chinese were stereotyped as "heathen, morally inferior, savage, and childlike" (Takaki, 1990, p. 217). Bret Harte, the 19th-century editor of the *Overland Monthly*, coined the term "the heathen Chinee," which alluded to the imagined barbaric nature of Chinese people. Sociopolitical racism led to the Chinese Exclusion Act of 1882, which prohibited Chinese labor immigration and denied U.S. citizenship to Chinese living in the United States. In 1906, California passed antimiscegenation laws barring marriages between whites and Asians, and in 1921 California denied citizenship to Chinese women who married American citizens.

However, because China was a World War II ally, Congress passed the Magnuson Act of 1943, which repealed the Chinese Exclusion Act of 1882. The 1952 McCarran-Walter Act granted naturalized citizenship to foreign-born Asians, and the 1965 McCarran Immigration Act opened immigration to 20,000 people per year from separate Asian countries.

Consequently, there have been four distinct waves of Chinese entering the United States since 1965: (1) immigrants from mainland China arriving from Hong Kong as a point of departure, (2) immigrants from Taiwan who are Mandarin-speaking Chinese, (3) refugees from Vietnam who are ethnic Chinese, and (4) recent Hong Kong residents who have migrated because of the treaty that returns Hong Kong to the People's Republic of China in 1997.

At present, Chinese Americans comprise Americanized Chinese who have been in the United States for four generations, Cantonese-speaking Hong Kong Chinese, Mandarin-speaking Taiwanese Chinese, and Vietnamese Chinese. Among these groups is a wide range of acculturation, socioeconomic classes, educational background and achievement, and cultural behavior.

The 1990 U.S. Census revealed that the Chinese are the largest Asian group in the United States (population 1,645,472), followed by Filipinos (1,406,770), Japanese (847,562), East Indians (815,447), Koreans (798,849), Vietnamese (614,547), and other Southeast Asians (525,454). The following 10 states have the most Chinese American inhabitants: California (704,850), New York (284,144), Hawaii (68,804), Texas (63,232), New Jersey (59,084), Massachusetts (53,792), Illinois (49,936), Washington (33,962), Maryland (30,868), and Florida (30,737) (U.S. Bureau of the Census, 1992).

## Chinese Cultural Values and Family Structure

Chung (1992) cited a number of Asian cultural commonalities that could be applied to Chinese Americans:

- high cultural context involving interpersonal communication; associations with people; and group-oriented family, cultural, and employment identity
- a worldview emphasizing harmony between people and their environment
- patterns of association highlighting family and group collectivity, strong commitment in social relationships, process-oriented teamwork, centralized hierarchical authority, and conflict avoidance in social participation.

Traditional Chinese American family values center on the patriarchal father as the leader of the family, the mother as the nurturing caregiver, and the sons as more valuable than the daughters. However, economic pressures have forced both parents in many low-income Chinese immigrant and refugee families to work at low-paying jobs to keep the family intact. Moreover, many parents are unable to speak English, have minimal education, are unemployed, and depend on their children who are acculturated and act as translators and links to mainstream American society.

Traditionally, the family relationship was based on filial piety and mutual obligation. The child was expected to obey parents and elders. The interdependent roles of family members were intended to keep the family intact and out of trouble. But with many parents working in two or more jobs and absent from the home, Chinese-speaking adolescents and young adults increasingly have been unable to compete academically and economically with their white counterparts. Some Vietnamese Chinese and Hong Kong–born Chinese who have lived in the inner cities and Chinatowns have turned to peer Asian gangs for identity and economic and social power. Juvenile delinquency and felony crime are common among these groups. Moreover, the Asian "model minority" myth has been discredited by the emerging social, economic, education, and employment problems of Chinese Americans who entered the United States between the mid-1960s and late 1980s. At the same time, most American-born Chinese and Chinese young adult immigrants and refugees from Hong Kong, Vietnam, and Taiwan have been able to overcome language, educational, and cultural barriers; graduate from universities; and enter employment in the technical and human services. The strong traditional family structure and accompanying values have sustained them through their struggle.

Another sustaining force for many Chinese American individuals and families has been the Protestant, Buddhist, and Roman Catholic churches in major metropolitan areas whose members are predominantly ethnic Chinese in language or cultural background. Chinese churches integrate religious faith and cultural values such as respect, obligation, duty, and loyalty to family and others (Lum, 1992).

The values of good performance and achievement are stressed in the home and exercised in school, bringing honor to the family. It is not uncommon for Chinese American students to study constantly in their spare time: Failure in school disgraces the entire family. Likewise, the symbols of adult success are financial security, personal happiness, and family harmony. Many Chinese American adults value a large home, luxury automobile, money, many children, and respect in the Chinese community.

## Social Problems

Chinese Americans cope with a set of problems common to many minority Americans. The Chinese American family is, for its members, a reference point and source of personal identity and emotional security. Because it exerts control over interpersonal conduct, social relations, and occupational and marital selection, it can be a source of stress and conflict for members who react to its structural boundaries. Serious family conflicts emerge in the forms of rejecting ethnic identity, pursuing individual freedom, dropping out of school, running away, and joining peer gangs.

Asian cultures teach self-control as a method of dealing with life's problems; negative feelings are held within. Sue (1981) reported that the restraint of strong feelings and the shame and disgrace associated with psychological problems caused many Asian Americans to express their difficulties through physical complaints, which are an acceptable means of expressing problems. Chinese people tend to somaticize their depressive reactions (Marsella, Kinzie, & Gordon, 1973). Psychosomatic illness is socially acceptable in the Chinese community because one consults a physician rather than a mental health professional.

Along these lines, mental illness and retardation, criminal behavior, job failure, and even poor school grades are kept in the family. To share negative information outside the home is to bring disgrace on the family name. This standard of morality may seem harsh and rigid to the outsider, but to many Chinese Americans it maintains honor and harmony in the family and before the Chinese and American communities (Lum, 1992).

### Social Images

A number of social images characterize the struggle of Chinese immigrant groups who are acculturating in the United States. Lee (1992) identified nine self-images that point to the psychosocial adaptation problems and sociocultural adjustment of recent Chinese arrivals:

1. refugee image—mentally retreating from political oppression and planning to return for revenge and revolution
2. victim image—feeling victimized by events, particularly among women who were deserted as war brides or divorcees and forced to raise a family in this country as a single parent

3. face-saving image—failing in business, marriage, or family in the country of origin and dreaming of rebuilding the business or family in this country
4. sojourner image—suffering from past experiences of family, professional, or business failure and maintaining a neutral stance in the United States
5. betrayed image—feeling cheated by friends and business associates for investing money in the United States because of legal and emotional problems and lack of investment return
6. opportunistic image—maintaining a detached attitude toward social and political changes and being unwilling to commit to the well-being of the American or Chinese community
7. crusader image—glorifying the virtues of Chinese culture or anticommunism and building a psychological defense to justify an existence in this strange land
8. pioneer image—overcoming frustrations and miseries of this adopted country and striving to contribute talents and resources to its well-being
9. participant image—adapting to the American way of life and becoming a part of the American social, economic, and cultural community.

**Family Issues**

Of all the Chinese American subgroups, elderly people pose the most significant challenge for joint community social action. Responsibility for their care tends to fall to elders themselves or their spouses, relatives, or friends. Children provide only limited assistance because of separate living arrangements and geographic distance. Yet children in Chinese families traditionally are taught that they are responsible for their parents, especially in health care crises and in dealing with problems of old age. Because of geographic separation, work schedules, and other lifestyle obstacles, second- or third-generation children may have to rely on ethnic-oriented public services on weekdays and fulfill their obligations to their parents during weekends or evenings (Cheung, Cho, Lum, Tang, & Yau, 1980; Lum, 1983).

There is a need in the Chinese American community for adequate child care for young children whose parents must work to support their families. When grandparents are available to care for their grandchildren, there is an opportunity to expose these youngsters to the Chinese language and culture. This opportunity also gives elderly people a meaningful way to contribute to the family's welfare. In the absence of grandparents, adequate child care facilities in Chinese American churches and social services centers are needed in large metropolitan areas with many young Chinese families.

Increasingly, Chinese American families need effective family counseling and parenting education classes to deal with the social, cultural, and developmental problems of Chinese American youths. It is very important to have qualified bilingual and bicultural Chinese American social services workers who are able to conduct family therapy with a minority perspective. Moreover, agencies should develop community outreach to Chinese churches, family associations, and area schools to teach parenting skills and to facilitate English as a Second Language (ESL) classes, job training, and employment placement services, particularly to Chinese-speaking immigrants and refugees.

There are large-scale macro community problems in the Chinatown area of large cities such as San Francisco, New York, and Los Angeles. Among the major social problems facing Chinatowns are poverty among elderly Chinese and recent refugees, substandard housing, low-paying jobs in restaurants and sewing factories, Asian gangs and protection intimidation, and lack of adequate educational and recreational facilities. Major social, economic, educational, and political commitments are necessary to deal with these issues sufficiently.

## Social Work Implications

It is important for social workers to consult with local Asian American social service centers, particularly those with Chinese American staff members. In many metropolitan regions there are specialized services such as the Asian Pacific Counseling and Treatment Center in Los Angeles, the Asian Community Mental Health Service of Oakland, and On Lok Adult Service Center in San Francisco. It is crucial that social workers gain an Asian perspective on cases involving Chinese clients and use consultation and referral.

A community organizing strategy also is needed to deal with problems facing Chinese Americans. According to Lee (1992), Chinese American communities need program strategies (self-empowerment, self-help, self-development, self-transformation, and self-liberation); diverse resource staffing (community organizers, social workers, community mental health workers, sociocultural experts, educators, political–economic leaders, natural scientists, computer experts, engineers, and restaurant and motel innkeepers); and leadership development (community leaders, professional staff, youths, and women's groups). Lee outlined a specific plan to use these components in a step-by-step action plan that relies on schools of social work to train Chinese American clergy, real estate agents, and community leaders; Chinese ethnic churches to establish specific program services to meet sociocultural needs; and regional community councils to coordinate local service efforts.

## References


Cheung, L.Y.S., Cho, E. R., Lum, D., Tang, T. Y., & Yau, H. B. (1980). The Chinese elderly and family structure: Implications for health care. *Public Health Reports, 95,* 491–495.

Chung, D. K. (1992). Asian cultural commonalities: A comparison with mainstream American culture. In S. M. Furuto, R. Biswas, D. K. Chung, K. Murase, & F. Ross-Sheriff (Eds.), *Social work practice with Asian Americans* (pp. 27–44). Newbury Park, CA: Sage Publications.

Lee, I. C. (1992). The Chinese-American's community organizing strategies and tactics. In F. G. Rivera & J. L. Erlich, (Eds.), *Community organizing in a diverse society* (pp. 133–158). Boston: Allyn & Bacon.

Lum, D. (1983). Asian-Americans and their aged. In R. L. McNeely & J. L. Colen (Eds.), *Aging in minority groups* (pp. 85–94). Beverly Hills, CA: Sage Publications.

Lum, D. (1992). *Social work practice and people of color: A process-stage approach* (2nd ed.). Pacific Grove, CA: Brooks/Cole.

Marsella, A. J., Kinzie, J. D., & Gordon, P. (1973). Ethnocultural variations in the expression of depression. *Journal of Cross-Cultural Psychology, 4,* 435–458.

Sue, D. W. (1981). *Counseling the culturally different: Theory and practice.* New York: John Wiley & Sons.

Takaki, R. (1990). *Iron cages: Race and culture in 19th century America.* New York: Oxford University Press.

U.S. Bureau of the Census (1992). *Censdata.* Washington, DC: U.S. Government Printing Office.


## Further Reading


Furuto, S. M., Biswas, R., Chung, D. K., Murase, K., & Ross-Sheriff, F. (1992). *Social work practice with Asian Americans.* Newbury Park, CA: Sage Publications.

Sue, S., & Morishima, J. K. (1982). *The mental health of Asian Americans.* San Francisco: Jossey-Bass.

Takaki, R. (1989). *Strangers from a different shore.* New York: Penguin.

Takaki, R. (1993). *A different mirror: A history of multicultural America.* Boston: Little, Brown.

Uba, L. (1994). *Asian Americans: Personality patterns, identity, and mental health.* New York: Guilford Press.

Vargas, L. A., & Koss-Chioino, J. (1992). *Working with culture: Psychotherapeutic interventions with ethnic minority children and adolescents.* San Francisco: Jossey-Bass.


**Doman Lum, PhD, ThD,** is professor of social work, California State University, Division of Social Work, 6000 J Street, Sacramento, CA 95819.

**For further information see**

Asian Americans Overview; Community Needs Assessment; Displaced People; Ethnic-Sensitive Practice; Families Overview; Human Rights; International Social Welfare; Mutual Aid Societies.

**Key Words**

Asian Americans
Chinese Americans
culturally competent practice
diversity

# Asian Americans: Japanese

**Kenji Murase**

In the American ethnic landscape, the case of Japanese Americans presents a seeming paradox. Only 50 years ago, they were an undesirable minority perceived as incapable of being assimilated into this society. This view is epitomized by a declaration made on the floor of Congress that people of Japanese ancestry born in this country were "not citizens of the United States and never can be. . . . There is a racial and religious difference they can never overcome. They are pagan in their philosophy, atheistic in their beliefs, alien in their allegiance, and antagonistic to everything for which we stand" (*Congressional Record,* 1942).

These attitudes provided the rationale for anti-Japanese legislation in the early 1900s that prevented Japanese immigrants from owning land, prohibited them from intermarriage, denied them the right to become American citizens, and excluded them from entering the United States. This history of virulent anti-Japanese sentiment peaked after the outbreak of World War II when 120,000 Japanese Americans, of whom two-thirds were American citizens, were removed from the West Coast and interned in concentration camps in the interior (Weglen, 1976). The basis for their incarceration was the belief that Japanese Americans could not be trusted to be loyal to the United States and therefore were to be treated as potential spies and saboteurs.

Consider then the status of Japanese Americans today. In just 50 years, they have been transformed from an undesirable and hated minority to a group that is now often characterized as a model minority. By almost any standard, Japanese Americans are firmly established as middle-class Americans. Their mean income is higher than that of white Americans; they are among the highest educated of all racial and ethnic groups; they are overrepresented in the professions; the vast majority live in white neighborhoods; and currently over half of all new marriages involving Japanese Americans are with white Americans (Kitano, Yeung, Chai, & Hatanaka, 1984).

Japanese Americans also present the paradox of a group that has maintained its ethnic identity while becoming structurally assimilated into the life of the larger society. Their experience can be seen as a departure from the European immigrant experience in which a zero-sum relationship prevails between assimilation and retention of ethnicity—that is, in which ethnic identity weakens as structural assimilation strengthens (Fugita & O'Brien, 1991). By contrast, Japanese Americans have been able to maintain high levels of ethnic consciousness and ethnic community involvement while becoming structurally assimilated into the dominant society. Their ability to maintain ethnic identity despite pressure to assimilate is explained by a cultural legacy and social structure that predate their immigration to this country in the early 1900s. Elements of traditional Japanese culture structure social relationships in such a way that adaptation to changing exigencies occurs without loss of group cohesion.

## Sociodemographic Characteristics

Unlike other Asian Americans, the population of Japanese Americans has remained relatively stable over the past several decades. In the 10-year period from 1980 to 1990, the number of Japanese Americans increased by only 21 percent to a total of 847,562. In the same period, Filipinos increased by 82 percent, Chinese by 104 percent, Koreans by 125 percent, and Vietnamese by 135 percent (U.S. Bureau of the Census, 1991). These differences in population growth rates reflect a marked decline in immigration from Japan at a time of rapidly increasing immigration from other Asian countries.

The 1990 Census reported that the following states had the largest concentration of Japanese Americans: California (312,989), Hawaii (247,486), New York (35,281), Washington (34,366), and Illinois (21,831). Other states with substantial populations of Japanese Americans are New Jersey, Texas, Oregon, and Colorado. In Hawaii, Japanese Americans constitute almost one-fourth of the state population.

Of Asian Americans, Japanese Americans have the highest median age (33.5 years) compared to Asian Indians (30.1 years), Chinese (29.6 years), Filipinos (28.5 years), and Koreans (26.0 years). With an average of 2.7 persons per household, Japanese Americans have the smallest households among Asian Americans compared to Asian Indians (2.9 persons), Chinese (3.1 persons), Koreans (3.4 persons), Filipinos (3.6 persons), and Vietnamese (4.4 persons) (Gardner, Robey, & Smith, 1985).

In the 25 to 29 age group, the 1980 Census reported that Japanese Americans had the highest proportion of high school graduates of Asian Americans, with 96.4 percent high school graduates among men and 96.3 percent high school graduates among women. In comparison, the proportion of high school graduates in the white population was 87.0 percent among men and 87.2 percent among women.

Family poverty levels reported for 1979 reveal that Japanese Americans had the lowest proportion among all major ethnic groups, with 4.2 percent compared to 7.0 percent for white Americans, 26.5 percent for black Americans, and 21.3 percent for Hispanics. The poverty level for other Asian Americans was 6.2 percent for Filipinos, 7.4 percent for Asian Indians, 10.5 percent for Chinese, 13.1 percent for Koreans, and 35.1 percent for Vietnamese (U.S. Bureau of the Census, 1983).

## Japanese Cultural Legacy

Any understanding of the Japanese American experience requires an appreciation of the profound influence of Japanese cultural orientations that were preserved and passed on by immigrant forebears. More than anything else, the survival and achievements of Japanese Americans are tributes to the enduring power of their cultural legacy. Despite the passage of time, traditional cultural values and practices continue to play a significant role in the lives of contemporary Japanese Americans.

Unlike most European groups, whose primary identification was defined by place of birth—the village or provincial region—the Japanese have a long history as a nation–state, which led to an abiding sense of themselves as a people. Within the Japanese concept of peoplehood, all members of their ethnic group—not just those of family, kin, or region—were viewed as quasi-kin. This means that as people move away from their family of origin into schools, factories, or other organizations, they relate to others as if they were kin. Once a person becomes a member of an organization, that person enters into a relationship that is closer to being a relative than to being a party in a limited contract. For Japanese Americans this meant that although they were initially excluded from mainstream economic opportunities, they were able within their institutionalized quasi-kin relationships to develop lasting social and economic relationships that provided the basis for their self-sufficiency and security (O'Brien & Fugita, 1991).

Another important component of the Japanese cultural legacy is an ethical system rooted in Confucian traditions transplanted to Japan from China during the seventh century (Reischauer, 1981). At the center was the notion of obligation and loyalty to one's family. The family, and not the individual, was the basic unit of society. The traditional Japanese family was patrilineal, patriarchal, and patrilocal. The father was the supreme head of the family and the decision maker for all family members. Male children were given preferential treatment over female children and were expected to carry on the family tradition. A woman was expected to be subservient to men throughout her life, first to her father, then to her husband and sons. Each family member was assigned a definite position in a hierarchical scale that bound him or her to others in a network of moral duties and rules for proper conduct (Yanagisako, 1985). Thus, the survival of the family, rather than the fulfillment of an individual member's needs, took precedence in the family system.

The traditional Japanese values and practices were most evident in the immigrant generation (the *Issei*). As succeeding generations of Japanese Americans have become acculturated, there has been a change in the family structure and behavior. The original patriarchal, male-dominated family network has given way among the second generation (the *Nisei*) to an increasingly important role for women in family affairs. The devastating World War II experience of incarceration in concentration camps also took its toll. Many *Nisei* parents tried to dissociate themselves and their children from traditional Japanese culture and become model Americans in the Anglo-Saxon tradition, often at great psychological cost (Nagata, 1991).

Despite the pressures toward acculturation, Japanese Americans are still influenced by traditional Japanese values and behavior (Yanagisako, 1985). Examples of values emphasized in the home are *oyakoko* (filial piety), *on* (a debt of gratitude to be returned in the future), *giri* (an obligation to be fulfilled), *haji* (shame to the family honor), *gaman* (perseverance), and *enryo* (modesty, not to be a burden to others). In addition, Japanese American families place strong emphasis on such values as hard work and academic excellence, virtues that are compatible with the dominant Anglo-Saxon ethos.

Family stability, as reflected in a low divorce rate, is yet another indicator of the persistence of traditional cultural values. Compared with other Western traditions, Japanese American conceptions of marital roles place greater emphasis on family-centered duties and responsibilities, with less emphasis on individualistic views of love and romance. Moreover, the strong network of families in Japanese American communities serves both as a social support for family cohesion by providing a buttress against the stresses found in all marriages and as a barrier against divorce.

An interesting and relatively recent phenomenon is the increasing out-marriage rate. Antimiscegenation laws in California from 1905 to 1948 prohibited Japanese Americans from intermarriage. During the World War II years, the *Nisei*, whose average age was 19, were physically prevented from meeting women from other ethnic groups. The intermarriage rate for *Nisei* of approximately 4 percent was therefore substantially lower than the approximately 20 percent intermarriage rate of second-generation European ethnics. But by the late 1970s, intermarriage among the third-generation *Sansei* had jumped to about 60 percent of all new marriages. Among the fourth-generation *Yonsei*, the intermarriage rate may be expected to be even higher as the acculturation process continues (Iwasaki-Mass, 1992).

## JAPANESE AMERICAN HISTORY

### Origins: The *Issei* Immigrants

The initial period of Japanese immigration to the United States lasted from 1880 to 1924; during this time, some 400,000 Japanese were admitted as an alternative to admitting the Chinese, whose entry was sharply restricted by the Chinese Exclusion Act of 1882. The *Issei* immigrants answered the need for a continuing supply of cheap and reliable labor by the agriculture, railroad, lumber, and mining industries that were flourishing in the American West. It was also a time of political and economic upheaval in Japan, and most of the immigrants were lured by the enticement of fortunes to be made in America. They were the *watari dori* (birds of flight) who would return with riches (Ichioka, 1988).

Despite their significant role in the development of rail transportation, mining, agriculture, lumbering, and other industries, the Japanese, along with other Asian immigrants, were subjected to humiliating acts of racial discrimination and even mob violence. There were, for example, segregated schools for Japanese children in San Francisco, laws prohibiting interracial marriage, anti-alien land laws prohibiting ownership of property, a variety of local trade union restrictions on entry into skilled crafts, and diversion into employment that was noncompetitive with white workers (Daniels, 1988). Moreover, as Asians the *Issei* were barred from U.S. citizenship, which meant that they were excluded from the American political process and left defenseless against discriminatory legislation. In 1924 the U.S. Immigration Act shut the door on Japanese immigration completely.

The racism of the larger society led to the emergence and institutionalization of a parallel community that was in many respects self-contained (Fugita & O'Brien, 1991). There evolved extensive ethnic community infrastructure that comprised protective mutual aid associations, rotating credit unions, religious institutions, newspapers, language schools, and cultural and recreational groups. This community structure continued the socialization of members in traditional Japanese ways and maintained ethnic community cohesiveness in the face of external threats. The community as developed by the immigrant *Issei* remained largely intact and served to nurture the American-born *Nisei* generation until the outbreak of World War II.

The Japanese, like the Chinese and later the Korean immigrants, became predominantly entrepreneurs and proprietors, or "middlemen minorities" (Bonacich & Modell, 1980). Through the development of subeconomies in their communities, they could circumvent to some extent the economic discrimination and color prejudice of white society. A common denominator to their status was the liquidity of their occupations, which provided a portable or easily liquidated livelihood, such as that of the trader; broker; gardener; truck farmer; service worker; and proprietor of small businesses such as barber shops, laundries, groceries, and restaurants. As a result of their occupational concentration and their residential segregation, Japanese Americans were effectively excluded from the larger society.

With the coming of age of the second-generation *Nisei*, there were important changes in the social structure of the Japanese American community. As the *Nisei* matured they found themselves subjected to two competing influences: the desire to preserve their own sense of ethnicity and the pull of socioeconomic advancement made possible by education. Benefiting from their education, the *Nisei* found opportunities for higher occupational status than had been possible for their *Issei* parents. They could be employed outside the ethnic economy that had been limited to small shopkeepers and farmers. As they began to enter the professions and administrative positions in increasing numbers, the social and psychological values and security provided by the ethnic community began to diminish in importance. The benefits of socioeconomic advancement made possible by higher education were viewed as compensation and reward for the long years of struggle and subsistence living endured by their *Issei* parents (Wilson & Hosokawa, 1980).

**Internment**

For Japanese Americans the internment in concentration camps during World War II is without question the one historical event that universally defines and symbolizes the Japanese American experience. When Japanese forces attacked Pearl Harbor in December 1941, some 125,000 people of Japanese ancestry lived along the Pacific Coast. Approximately two-thirds of this population were American citizens. Despite assurances from military intelligence and the Federal Bureau of Investigation that there was no danger of subversion by Japanese Americans, President Franklin Roosevelt acceded to the demands of the military, powerful agricultural and commercial interests, and racial bigots and issued an executive order authorizing the removal of all Japanese Americans from the West Coast. Although the United States was also at war with Germany and Italy, no similar order was applied to German or Italian Americans.

"Internment" is perhaps the one word that best evokes an understanding of what it is to be a Japanese American. Whether internment was personally experienced by the *Issei* and *Nisei* generations or retold and learned by the *Sansei* and *Yonsei* generations, all Japanese Americans have been profoundly affected by what happened to America's Japanese during World War II. The shared experience of being uprooted and removed to concentration camps produced a deep sense of collective identity that persists regardless of their subsequent geographic dispersion to all parts of the country. The kinship of experiencing a common tragedy for an immutable physical trait, that of bearing the face of the enemy, and the humiliation and hardships endured during internment contributed to their everlasting sense of group identity.

The internment of Japanese Americans is perhaps the bitterest national shame of World War II. It represented the mass incarceration on racial grounds alone, on false evidence of military necessity and in contempt of supposedly inalienable rights, of an entire class of American citizens with their parents who were not citizens of the country of their choice, only because that country had denied them the right to become naturalized citizens on the basis of race (U.S. Commission on Wartime Relocation and Internment of Civilians, 1982).

**Rebuilding the Community**

The end of World War II and the closing of the concentration camps in 1945 signaled the beginning of a new era in Japanese American history. On their release Japanese Americans returned to recreate their former communities that had been destroyed by their removal and internment. There followed a difficult process of recovery and rebuilding of their economic base, their social institutions, and their network of relationships for a viable community life (Zich, 1986).

With an economic base reestablished primarily in small businesses, the professions, and service occupations, Japanese American community workers soon were able to address broader community concerns such as poverty, health care, housing, crime, and delinquency. Over time a network of indigenous community-based services and support systems evolved to meet the economic, social, and psychological needs of the community (Murase, 1985). This indigenous community care and support system comprised institutions such as churches, credit unions, prefectural associations, and social and cultural organizations, as well as individuals such as ministers, priests, doctors, lawyers, teachers, shopkeepers, and others who had gained a measure of respect in the community. Their role as community caretakers represented an extension of the traditional attitude and practice of collective responsibility embedded in their cultural legacy.

**Political Participation**

In the post–World War II period, the *Nisei* and *Sansei* generations came into full maturity and took up leadership in community affairs as the aging *Issei* generation withdrew. The most significant activity of Japanese Americans during this period was their national campaign to secure redress and reparations for their internment during World War II. The first stage of this campaign was to bring the issue before the American public, which was largely uninformed about the World War II experience of Japanese Americans. Key players in this educational process were the veterans of the celebrated 442nd Regimental Combat Team composed of Japanese Americans, which was the most decorated unit in World War II. Japanese American members of Congress (Senators Daniel Inouye and Spark Matsunaga and Congressmen Norman Mineta and Robert Matsui) were instrumental in securing legislation to establish a Commission on Wartime Relocation and Internment of Civilians. The commission conducted public hearings to assess whether any wrong was committed by the government in interning Japanese Americans and to recommend remedial action to Congress.

In its final report issued in February 1983, the commission concluded that the internment of Japanese Americans was not justified by military necessity as claimed by the government in 1942 (U.S. Commission on Wartime Relocation and Internment of Civilians, 1982). It recommended to Congress that the government provide a one-time per capita compensatory payment of $20,000 to each of approximately 60,000 surviving internees. Legislation to implement the commission's recommendation took four additional years of sustained effort by the Japanese American community leadership before President Reagan signed the enabling Civil Rights Act of 1988.

## Interethnic Relations

As an outgrowth of the civil rights movement of the 1960s, Japanese Americans—along with Chinese, Filipino, and Korean Americans—began to frame and assert their common identity as Asian Americans. The designation "Asian American" was a convenient political label that reflected their common historical experience of being subjected to exclusionary immigration laws, restrictive naturalization laws, labor market segregation, and patterns of ghettoization by a society that perceived and treated Asians as all alike.

Japanese Americans who were previously self-defined in terms of their specific ethnicity now began to confront their own racial identity and status in a political environment of heightened racial consciousness. Embracing the pan-ethnic concept of "Asian Americans" signified a new direction in which both assimilation and ethnic particularism were supplanted and transformed (Espiritu, 1992). Japanese American activists saw in the Asian American concept a rallying point for raising political consciousness about the problems besetting all Asian American communities and for asserting demands on public institutions for legislative remedies and resources. Among the demands would be bilingual ballots, bilingual education, redistricting of political boundaries to reflect demographic realities, equal employment opportunities, immigration reforms, and economic development (U.S. Commission on Civil Rights, 1992).

In their relationship with other people of color, Japanese Americans face difficult choices in relation to issues that can potentially unite and issues that threaten to divide. With other Asian American and Hispanic American communities, a common agenda would focus on issues of bilingual education, immigration reform, and employer discrimination against foreign-born or non-English-speaking employees. The same issues, however, could generate conflicts with African Americans, especially during periods of declining public resources and private opportunities. On the other hand, a commitment to civil rights legislation and enforcement, equal opportunity in hiring and promotions, and revitalization of inner cities could unite Japanese Americans and other Asian Americans with African Americans, as well as with other people of color (Asian Pacific American Public Policy Institute, 1993).

## Implications for Social Work Practice

Relatively few of the *Issei* immigrant generation remain, and most of their needs are being met within the security of their families. The exceptions are the isolated elderly people whose children have abandoned the cultural tradition of revering and caring for family elders. They are often in need of housing assistance or long-term health care. In working with this group, social workers need to know that the *Issei* are attached to the traditional values of self-restraint and perseverance and that their fierce sense of family honor and esteem makes them resist dependence on outsiders. If they do seek help, acknowledgment of their problems should be subtle and indirect. They tend to be submissive and compliant, and their expression of emotions is tightly controlled. In these cases it is essential to involve as intermediaries other family members, respected elders, religious leaders, or other authority figures.

The Japanese cultural legacy created the severest conflict for the second-generation *Nisei*. At school they were taught the American ideals of freedom, equality, and individuality, but at home they were imbued with the classical Japanese values of restraint, obedience to authority, and subservience to the group. Attempts to reconcile these conflicting values created serious dilemmas in establishing their identity and in coming to terms with their marginal position in the larger society. They clearly see the contradiction between the realities of their own experience with racism and the American ideals of freedom, individuality, and advancement on the basis of merit. To cope with the barbs of racism, some have internalized their rage and frustration. Their psychological defenses are denial, suppression, and repression, which are then expressed behaviorally in either overcompensation in educational achievement and hard work or through psychosomatic symptoms. In many instances, escape from pain and stress takes the form of alcoholism and gambling.

The cultural legacy inherited from the immigrant *Issei* and passed on to the *Nisei* continues to influence the *Sansei* and *Yonsei* generations who are now the likely consumers of social services. The traditional Japanese culture emphasizes the importance of inner discipline and encourages the concealing of frustrations and disappointments. Individual concerns are submerged beneath those of the family and community, filial piety and moral obligations to others transcend personal desires, and tasks are pursued regardless of difficulties or the probability of failure or defeat (True, in press). Under the parental stricture that second best is not good enough, *Sansei* and *Yonsei* youths frequently experience intense feelings of failure about accomplishments that would satisfy their non-Japanese peers.

Outside the home, *Sansei* and *Yonsei* participate freely in mainstream social and recreational activities. However, although they may feel, speak, act, and think American, they can never "look" American. In subtle ways they are made to feel that they are different and therefore not wholly acceptable. Tacit racial prejudice, often unacknowledged and even unperceived, can generate intense confusion and anxiety about one's identity. *Sansei* and especially *Yonsei* youths may need counseling services to sort out and resolve the conflicts arising from pressures from within their families and from the external world (Oishi, 1985).

Given the cultural legacy and life experiences of Japanese Americans, the social worker must be aware of the extraordinary nature of any request for service. The presenting problem is likely to be a severe dysfunction beyond the coping capacity of the individual or his or her family. Whether the request for service is precipitated by severe family breakdown, acute psychopathology, addiction, physical impairment, or stress, the social worker should be alert to the intrusion of cultural factors in the client's situation (Henkin, 1985).

In the initial assessment, it is essential to establish the client's relative degree of acculturation. One indicator is the client's generational status, whether *Nisei, Sansei,* or *Yonsei*. In general the level of acculturation advances with each succeeding generation: A *Yonsei* client would be less subject to traditional Japanese cultural influences than would a *Sansei* or *Nisei* client. Other signs of acculturation are the client's place of residence, whether in a predominantly urban Japanese community or isolated in a predominantly white suburban community; the extent of the client's involvement with ethnic peers; any association with ethnic community institutions and organizations; and the language spoken in the home (Nagata, 1989).

In working with Japanese American families, it is important to reduce or diffuse the client's feelings of guilt and shame by generalizing the problem; to support the fulfillment of family roles and obligations; to focus on interdependence and not individuation; to use family therapy as the treatment of choice; and to set mutually defined goals (Furuta, 1981). Consistent with the Japanese American proclivity for accepting prescribed roles, doing one's duties, conforming to authority, and fulfilling responsibilities, the therapist's approach should be more directive than nondirective and should be professionally authoritative.

## Future Problems and Prospects

Historically, the status of the Japanese in America has been inextricably linked to the changing character of U.S.-Japan relations. For example, the renewal and intensification of anti-Japanese hostility that erupted in the 1930s can be traced to the Great Depression and the deterioration of relations with Japan. The Japanese attack on Pearl Harbor in 1941 and the outbreak of open hostilities between the United States and Japan fueled the fire storm of hate and hysteria that consumed the nation and compelled the incarceration of 120,000 Japanese Americans in concentration camps.

The post–World War II period brought improved relations between the two countries, creating a favorable climate for Japanese Americans to elevate their socioeconomic status and establish their public image as law-abiding, industrious, and loyal Americans. In the late 1960s and 1970s, as the economy flourished and demand for a technically trained labor force increased, Japanese Americans were highly prized for their capabilities in the fields of engineering, electronics, and the health sciences. Then, in the 1980s, Japan achieved its dominance in the world economy as the U.S. economy began to decline. The resulting massive layoffs and contractions in business and industry were blamed on the Japanese (Japanese American Citizens League, 1992). In the current period, as American hostility continues to be directed against Japan, Japanese Americans and other Asian Americans are again the targets of racial slurs, demeaning caricatures in the media, verbal and physical abuse in the streets, vandalism, arson, and even mob killings (Mydans, 1992). Historical precedent suggests that the status of Japanese Americans will continue to be influenced by the nature of U.S.–Japan relations.

In their relationship with other Asian American groups, a potentially divisive issue for Japanese Americans is the frequent perception that Asian Americans are a model minority. This notion relies heavily on the academic and economic success of Japanese Americans, and the model minority image is then extended to all Asian Americans, as if they constitute a single monolithic group (Gould, 1988). The fact is that many Asian American subgroups, such as Southeast Asian refugees, recent immigrants, elders, and single parents are largely subsisting in poverty (Toji & Johnson, 1992).

The perception of the success of Japanese Americans, particularly in higher education, is also linked to the growing anti-Asian sentiment and discriminatory backlash (Orlans, 1992). Perhaps more insidious is the media's practice of denigrating other minorities of color by attributing Japanese American educational achievement and subsequent upward mobility to a family system that emphasizes the virtues of hard work, sacrifice, and reverence for learning. Such praise for the Japanese American family appears to be part of a broader ideological perspective that places the blame for the educational deficits of other minorities on the deterioration of the family. The political implication is that the cultural system of other minorities is somehow "inferior" and that they, and not societal factors, are to blame for their inequality.

The new emerging Japanese American leadership rejects the model-minority myth and views the future of Japanese Americans as bound up with the fortunes of all Asian Americans and other people of color. They recognize that they must move beyond their own community and respond to the problems and issues common to all minority communities (Asian Pacific American Public Policy Institute, 1993).

With their successful national campaign to secure redress and reparations for their internment during World War II, Japanese Americans possess a proven record of legislative and legal capabilities and accomplishments. Their experience and resources can now be directed to influencing the national political and legal process on behalf of other people of color. Such a development would symbolize the political maturity of an ethnic group that was once singled out by the government as potential subversives and confined to concentration camps. Japanese Americans are now presented with an opportunity to justify the trust and faith of their immigrant *Issei* forebears and the sacrifices they made for future generations.

## References


Asian Pacific American Public Policy Institute. (1993). *The state of Asian Pacific America: A public policy report*. Los Angeles: Asian Pacific American Public Policy Institute, Asian American Studies Center, University of California at Los Angeles.

Bonacich, E., & Modell, J. (1980). *The economic base of ethnic solidarity: Small business in the Japanese American community*. Berkeley: University of California Press.

Civil Rights Act of 1988. P.L. 100-430, 102 Stat. 1619 to 1636.

*Congressional Record*. (1942, February 23). pp. A768–A769.

Daniels, R. (1988). *Asian America: Chinese and Japanese in the United States since 1850*. Seattle: University of Washington Press.

Espiritu, Y. L. (1992). *Asian American pan-ethnicity: Bridging institutions and identities*. Philadelphia: Temple University Press.

Fugita, S. S., & O'Brien, D. J. (1991). *Japanese American ethnicity: The persistence of community*. Seattle: University of Washington Press.

Furuta, B. A. (1981). Ethnic identities of Japanese-American families: Implications for counseling. In C. Getty & W. Humphreys (Eds.), *Understanding the family* (pp. 200–231). New York: Appleton.

Gardner, R., Robey, B., & Smith, P. C. (1985, October). Asian Americans: Growth, change and diversity. *Population Bulletin, 40*(4).

Gould, K. (1988). Asian and Pacific Islanders: Myth and reality. *Social Work, 33,* 142–146.

Henkin, W. A. (1985). Toward counseling the Japanese in America. *Journal of Counseling and Development, 63,* 500–503.

Ichioka, Y. (1988). *The Issei: The world of the first generation Japanese immigrants, 1885–1924*. New York: Free Press.

Iwasaki-Mass, A. (1992). Interracial Japanese Americans. In M. Root (Ed.), *Racially mixed people in America* (pp. 265–279). Newbury Park, CA: Sage Publications.

Japanese American Citizens League. (1992). *The impact of Japan bashing and the "Buy American" movement on Japanese Americans*. San Francisco: Author.

Kitano, H.H.L., Yeung, W. T., Chai, L., & Hatanaka, H. (1984). Asian American interracial marriage. *Journal of Marriage and the Family, 46,* 179–190.

Murase, K. (1985). Alternative mental health service models in Asian Pacific communities. In T. C. Owan (Ed.), *Southeast Asian mental health: Treatment, prevention, service, training and research* (pp. 229–260). Washington, DC: U.S. Government Printing Office.

Mydans, S. (1992, March 4). New unease for Japanese Americans. *New York Times,* p. A8.

Nagata, D. K. (1989). Japanese American children and adolescents. In J. T. Gibbs & L. N. Huang (Eds.), *Children of color: Psychological interventions with minority youth* (pp. 67–113). San Francisco: Jossey-Bass.

Nagata, D. K. (1991). Transgenerational impact of the Japanese American internment: Clinical issues in working with children of former internees. *Psychotherapy, 28*(1), 121–128.

O'Brien, D. J., & Fugita, S. E. (1991). *The Japanese American experience*. Indianapolis: Indiana University Press.

Oishi, G. (1985, April 28). The anxiety of being a Japanese American. *New York Times Magazine,* pp. 54, 58–60, 65.

Orlans, H. (1992). Affirmative action in higher education. *Annals of the American Academy of Political and Social Science, 523,* 144–158.

Reischauer, E. O. (1981). *The Japanese*. Cambridge, MA: Harvard University Press.

Toji, D. S., & Johnson, J. H. (1992). Asian and Pacific Islander poverty: The working poor and the jobless poor. *Amerasia Journal, 18*(1), 83–91.

True, R. H. (in press). Treatment considerations with Japanese American families. In E. Lee (Ed.), *Clinical guide to working with Asian Americans*. New York: Guilford Press.

U.S. Bureau of the Census. (1983). *1980 Census of population, detailed population characteristics* (PC80-1-D1-A, Tables 148, 149, 158, 159, 164, 165). Washington, DC: U.S. Government Printing Office.

U.S. Bureau of the Census. (1991, June). Race and Hispanic origin. In *1990 Census Profile,* No. 2. Washington, DC: U.S. Government Printing Office.

U.S. Commission on Civil Rights. (1992). *Civil rights issues facing Asian Americans in the 1990s*. Washington, DC: U.S. Government Printing Office.

U.S. Commission on Wartime Relocation and Internment of Civilians. (1982). *Personal justice denied*. Washington, DC: U.S. Government Printing Office.

Weglen, M. (1976). *Years of infamy: The untold story of America's concentration camps*. New York: William Morrow.

Wilson, R. A., & Hosokawa, B. (1980). *East to America: A history of the Japanese in the United States*. New York: William Morrow.

Yanagisako, S. (1985). *Transforming the past: Traditions and kinship among Japanese Americans*. Stanford, CA: Stanford University Press.

Zich, A. (1986, April). Japanese Americans: Home at last. *National Geographic, 169,* 512–539.


## Further Reading


Bosworth, A. R. (1967). *America's concentration camps*. New York: W. W. Norton.

Daniels, R., Taylor, S. C., and Kitano, H.H.L. (Eds.). (1986). *Japanese Americans: From relocation to redress*. Salt Lake City: University of Utah Press.

Grodzins, M. (1949). *Americans betrayed: Politics and the Japanese evacuation*. Chicago: University of Chicago Press.

Irons, P. (1983). *Justice at war: The story of the Japanese internment cases*. New York: Oxford University Press.

Tateishi, J. (1984). *And justice for all: An oral history of the Japanese American detention camps*. New York: Random House.

Ten-Broek, J., Barnhart, E. N., & Matson, F. W. (1954). *Prejudice, war and the constitution*. Berkeley: University of California Press.

Uchida, Y. (1982). *Desert exile: The uprooting of a Japanese American family*. Seattle: University of Washington Press.

**Kenji Murase, DSW,** is professor emeritus, San Francisco State University, 683 12th Avenue, San Francisco, CA 94118.

**For further information see**
Asian Americans Overview; Civil Rights; Community Needs Assessment; Ethnic-Sensitive Practice; Families Overview; Human Rights; Social Development; Social Welfare Policy.

**Key Words**
Asian Americans  Japanese Americans

# Asian Americans: Southeast Asians

**Quang DuongTran**
**Jon K. Matsuoka**

Southeast Asian refugees come from three countries in the southeast region of Asia, formerly known as colonial Indochina: Cambodia, Laos, and Vietnam. Cambodia and Laos neighbor Thailand to the west and Vietnam to the east, and Vietnam borders the South China Sea to the east. Since the migration of refugees to the United States began in 1975, "Southeast Asian" has been the preferred term, rather than "Indochinese," to describe an immigrant from Cambodia, Laos, or Vietnam. The term Southeast Asian is preferred because it disassociates the people from the oppression of the former French colony and distinguishes the political context of the migration of people from Cambodia, Laos, and Vietnam from that of other people from the Southeast Asian region, such as Thai, Filipino, Indonesian, or Malaysian immigrants.

## U.S. Policy on Southeast Asian Refugees

The bulk of the refugee resettlement to the United States since 1975 has come from Southeast Asia, mainly Vietnam, Cambodia, and Laos (Cravens & Bornemann, 1990). In 1975 Congress enacted the Indochina Migration and Refugee Assistance Act to assist in the relocation to the United States of U.S. government-employed Vietnamese nationals and their families. However, Vietnamese refugees were exiled en masse beyond the expectations of the U.S. government. The large and constant influx of refugees motivated the Refugee Act of 1980 to facilitate the large-scale resettlement of these people. The act established a ceiling for the admission of Southeast Asian refugees that was beyond the quotas, a public assistance package, and cooperative arrangements among the federal government, private agencies, and state governments to assist the newcomers (Kraut, 1990).

The Refugee Act of 1980 (P.L. 96-212) defined a refugee as

> any person who is outside any country of such person's nationality or, in the case of a person having no nationality, is outside any country in which such person last habitually resided, and who is unable or unwilling to return to, and is unable or unwilling to avail himself or herself of the protection of that country because of persecution or a well-founded fear of persecution on account of race, religion, nationality, membership in a particular social group, or political opinion.

Efforts continued into the late 1980s to facilitate the resettlement of Southeast Asian refugees. One major outcome of these efforts was a mutual agreement between the United States and the Socialist Republic of Vietnam to establish the Orderly Departure Program (ODP). The ODP provided a sanctioned departure from Vietnam that was less risky, controlled the number of refugees, and provided relief to countries of first asylum (Cravens & Bornemann, 1990). Other refugee policies were legislated in the 1980s to address the needs of specific groups of refugees from Southeast Asia and to expedite their relocation to the United States. In 1988 the AmerAsian Homecoming Act was initiated to facilitate the reunion of Vietnamese offspring and their families with their American fathers. By 1992 a total of 62,351 Amerasians and their families had resettled in the United States. In 1989 the U.S. Department of State negotiated an agreement with the Vietnamese government to allow the resettlement of approximately 50,000 political prisoners from "reeducation camps" in Vietnam to the United States (Le, 1993).

## Resettlement of Refugees

According to the State Department, Southeast Asians constitute the largest group of refugees admitted to the United States since 1975. These refugees arrived in the United States in various phases under similar political contexts. Vietnamese were the first large wave of refugees to resettle in the United States in the aftermath of the Vietnam War. Between 1975 and 1979, approximately 90 percent of the refugees from Southeast Asia were Vietnamese (Cravens & Bornemann, 1990). In 1976 a small contingent of Laotian refugees—Laotian nationals and other ethnic groups from Laos (such as the Hmong and the Mien)—resettled in the United States to avoid persecution and genocide for their role in assisting U.S. troops during the Vietnam War.

In 1979 the Vietnamese Socialist government directed the expulsion of ethnic Chinese Vietnamese from Vietnam. This policy led to the massive exodus of Chinese Vietnamese people, who came to be known as the "boat people" because they attempted to escape by sea (Cheung, 1985). At the same time, large-scale atrocities were inflicted on the people of Cambodia by Cambodian communists known as the Khmer Rouge. The genocide led to the exodus of thousands of Cambodians to Thailand and neighboring countries. The majority of Laotian and Cambodian refugees began to arrive in the United States after 1980. Almost 30 percent of the Southeast Asians who were resettled in the United States arrived in 1980 and 1981 (Le, 1993).

According to the 1990 U.S. census, more than 1 million Southeast Asian refugees lived in the United States in that year and constituted approximately 13 percent of the Asian American population. Among the Southeast Asian population, 614,547 were Vietnamese, 147,411 were Cambodian, and 239,096 were Laotian. The census data reflect a pattern of mobility by these refugees that is related to economic opportunities, the search for a comfortable climate, and the development of cohesive communities in various metropolitan and geographic regions. According to the 1990 census, 10 states accounted for approximately 76 percent of the Southeast Asians. California and Texas had the largest Southeast Asian populations, slightly more than half a million, or roughly 45 percent of all Cambodians, Laotians, and Vietnamese. Economic prospects, a favorable climate, and ethnic homogeneity are likely reasons for the high concentration of Southeast Asians in these two states. Support for refugee communities may explain the preferred resettlement of Cambodians in Massachusetts, Pennsylvania, Virginia, New York, and Rhode Island (Le, 1993). Similarly, the Midwest, primarily Minnesota, Wisconsin, and Michigan, has the largest concentration of Laotian refugees, and Louisiana and Florida have large contingencies of Vietnamese.

## Social and Cultural Profiles of Southeast Asians

### Laotians

Laos is populated by various tribally distinctive groups in the highland and lowland areas. Its population is estimated at 4.6 million people, half of whom are ethnic Lao and half of whom come from various tribal groups (*Information Please Almanac,* 1994). The Lao, who represent the dominant culture and language, are closely related culturally and linguistically to the people of northeast and northern Thailand, an area that was part of the old Leeway Kingdom of Lan Xang (United States Catholic Conference [USCC], 1984). Their religion is Theravada Buddhism.

Extended families, with grandparents typically sharing a house with their married children or married grandchildren, are the preferred family form among the Lao. The grandparents usually share the household and babysitting tasks while their children or grandchildren work. Although the husband is the breadwinner and has authority over all family members and key decisions, the Lao woman plays a large role in the prosperity, well-being, and development of the family (USCC, 1984).

In general, the Lao prefer to have their social relationships clearly defined, so that each has a distinct status and a prescribed role (USCC, 1984). The rules for social relations between people of different status and rank are specifically prescribed. Like people of other Southeast Asian cultures, the Lao do not express their feelings verbally (Schiff-Ross, 1991). They emphasize the need to "save face," which means that an individual must stay cool or keep quiet in all circumstances. In the Lao culture, it is considered humiliating to point out a person's errors directly (Outsama, 1977).

A number of independent and ethnically distinct highland tribes live in the mountain regions of northern Laos. The three main highland ethnic groups are the Hmong (Meo), the Mien (Yao), and the Leeway Theung (Kha), whose languages, customs, art, and lifestyles are all different. The highland tribes originated from China. The largest highland tribal group, the Hmong, probably migrated to Laos between 2255 B.C. and 2206 B.C. (USCC, 1984). Another highland group that originated in China, the Mien, has two main branches—the lu Mien (Yew Mien) and the Kim Mun. The majority of lu Mien live in northern Laos and Thailand, whereas the Kim Mun clans are found in northern Vietnam.

In the Iu Mien social system, patrilineal clans, subclans, and lineage groups characterize the social structure. The Iu Mien inherit their clan membership for life from their fathers, and the clan name is attached to an individual's name as a surname. Women do not take on their husbands' clan or surname. The Iu Mien's religion is rooted in the belief system of spirits and ancestors and of the Taoist religion (USCC, 1984).

**Vietnamese**

The culture of the Vietnamese is based on Confucian traditions and the country's early history of Chinese domination. In the 19th century Roman Catholicism was introduced by French missionaries and traders and eventually became widespread. The Confucian traditions have profound influences on the structure and role of the Vietnamese family, which is the basic social unit of Vietnamese society. As in Chinese culture, the extended family and family interdependence are espoused. The family hierarchy and the roles and responsibilities of family members are clearly delineated, and filial piety and respect for elders, teachers, and other authority figures are socially expected behaviors (USCC, 1984). Regardless of their social status, children represent the future of the family, and both children and adults feel a sense of inferiority if children do not achieve the goals set by the family.

Shame and loss of face are collectively shared by an individual's family, so avoiding shame and loss of face motivates much of Vietnamese behavior. Stoic attitudes, self-control, and the avoidance of direct expression of emotions are highly valued. Harmony in interpersonal relationships is accomplished through tact, delicacy, and politeness, sometimes at the cost of honesty and forthrightness (Le, 1993). In general, the Vietnamese are family oriented in their approach to labor and social activity. They are more ambitious and status conscious than other Southeast Asian groups and are oriented to long-term goals and planning (Rumbaut & Ima, 1988).

**Cambodians**

Cambodian society was influenced by the teachings of Buddhism (Pham, 1981). The Cambodian people derived a respect for life in all its forms, tolerance, gentleness, honesty, and an indifference to material wealth from Buddhist teachings.

The Cambodian society is patriarchal, but the father's rights over the family are counterbalanced by duties prescribed by Buddhist morality and sanctioned by civil law. In many cases, husbands and wives share authority. The household is the basic economic unit around which the society revolves. Tolerance, gentleness, and a fondness for the simple pleasures of life are characteristic of Cambodian households (Pham, 1981). In contrast to other Asian cultures, the individual in Cambodian society is not necessarily subordinate to the family or social group. Although the extended family is acknowledged, family structure is based more on the couple relationship.

## Social Welfare Concerns

Southeast Asian refugees experienced traumatic life events during their escape from their home countries and chronic psychological and emotional strains resulting from the life-changing circumstances of resettling in the United States (Nguyen, 1983; Nicassio & Pate, 1984; Rumbaut, 1986).

**Premigratory Risks**

Southeast Asian refugees faced continuous life-threatening crises while avoiding deadly persecution in their home countries and in their flight to freedom. Individuals and entire families frequently perished in their attempts to escape to a neighboring country. For example, those making a journey from a Vietnamese seaport across the Gulf of Thailand to Thailand traveled approximately 1,500 nautical miles. Other routes took the refugees across the South China Sea to Malaysia (1,500 nautical miles), farther south to Singapore (1,600 nautical miles) or Indonesia (2,000 nautical miles), east across the South China Sea to the Philippines (900 nautical miles), or north to Korea across the South China Sea, East China Sea, and Yellow Sea (1,100 nautical miles) (Cravens & Bornemann, 1990).

Many refugees encountered piracy by Thai fishermen during their voyage to Thailand or Malaysia. The Thai assailants robbed refugees of any valuables, sexually assaulted women, threw people overboard to drown or to be shot in the water, and kidnapped women and girls (Cravens & Bornemann, 1990). Refugees who survived those attacks at sea faced still other dangers. Many refugee boats were forced back to sea from Thailand or Malaysia. In 1989 at least 3,400 asylum seekers were towed or escorted back to open waters by the Malaysian coastal patrol (U.S. Department of Health and Human Services, 1989).

**Resettlement Difficulties**

The harsh realities of starting a new life and adjusting to a new culture are daunting challenges for recently arrived refugees. Southeast Asian refugees soon become aware that federal refugee-assistance programs are finite resources and that they must face the challenge of finding stable employment to support their families (Boehnlein, 1987). Those who come to the United States without their extended families worry about their loved ones in their homelands. Moreover, many refugees who immigrate to the United States without their extended family members are obligated to provide financial support to their kin in their homelands even as they try to support themselves. One study revealed that 81 percent of Southeast Asian refugees still had serious concerns about being separated from family members back home after five years of living in the United States (Stein, 1981). In the same study, 67 percent reported painful memories of the war and their departure from home, 59 percent said they were homesick, and more than half were worried about difficulties in communicating with friends and family in their home countries.

Families that arrive in the United States with intact kinship networks experience additional challenges. Southeast Asian parents face the challenge of supporting their families and providing a meaningful future for their children. Parents may attempt to address these needs by obtaining menial, low-skill jobs that do not require English proficiency (Nguyen, 1983). Many parents suffer the stress of status inconsistency resulting from their inability to transfer their employable skills (Vignes & Hall, 1979). Meanwhile, their children rapidly learn to speak English and model mainstream behaviors and values they learn from school and television. Within a few years of living in the United States, parents begin to recognize changes in their children's language, behaviors and attitudes, and peer relationships. These changes often cause tension in parent–child relationships (Hunt, 1991; Tobin & Friedman, 1984).

The transitional experience subjects many Southeast Asians to severe physical and mental health risks. For example, psychiatric illnesses, such as depression, anxiety, psychosomatic disease, and psychosis, were identified in various refugee camps in Southeast Asia (Cheung, 1985; Hussain, 1982). Similar psychiatric dysfunctions have been seen among Southeast Asian refugees in mental health centers in the United States (Flaskerud & Nguyen, 1988; Lin, Masuda, & Tazuma, 1982; Mollica, Wyshak, & Lavell, 1987).

#### Financial and Employment Problems

Illiteracy and minimal educational attainment are problems facing Hmong, Cambodians, and Laotians in their quest to learn English and obtain jobs that require high-level skills. The lack of functional English skills hampers a refugee's ability to enroll in vocational training programs or to pursue higher education. Furthermore, high fertility rates compound difficult economic conditions and limit prospects for economic mobility. In his study of a Southeast Asian refugee community in San Diego, Rumbaut (1986) found that Hmong refugee families had the largest households, with an average of 8.8 persons; Cambodian households averaged 8.7 persons; and Vietnamese households averaged 5.5 persons. However, the average size of the Southeast Asian households was larger than the reported nuclear family size (3.4 persons per nuclear Hmong family, 4.0 for a Cambodian nuclear family, and 4.4 for a Vietnamese family). The fact that the household size is larger than the size of the average nuclear family may mean that refugees continue to maintain the traditional extended family structure of multiple generations under one roof or that refugees find it economically necessary to live in multifamily households (Le, 1993).

A significant percentage of Cambodian households (26.6 percent) are headed by women. Among Hmong families 16.7 percent are headed by women, and among Vietnamese families 8.6 percent are headed by women (Rumbaut, 1986). Fifty-five percent of Southeast Asians are male and 45 percent are female (U.S. Department of Health and Human Services, 1991). The median age is 28: 2 percent are preschoolers, 21 percent are ages 6 to 17, 19 percent are 18 to 24, 54.5 percent are 25 to 64, and 3.5 percent are 65 or older.

Close to one-fourth of Southeast Asians are of school age, indicating the tremendous impact this population could have on the educational systems of their communities. Young adults age 18 to 24 may have an additional effect on vocational training or higher education systems. Most Southeast Asians, however, are of working age and are in the U.S. labor force.

### Social Problems

#### Racism and Discrimination

From the time of their arrival, Southeast Asian refugees experienced racism and discrimination similar to that experienced by other Asian American and ethnic groups. These negative experiences were compounded by negative public sentiment about the Vietnam War and the unpopular decision to admit thousands of refugees into the United States. Refugees who displayed Western traits and mannerisms and who spoke English generally were less likely to encounter oppression than those who had been socialized in traditional and rural settings, were less familiar with American culture and its social nuances, or clung to their traditional styles of dress and mannerisms.

This latter group was subjected to acts of oppression and exploitation in housing, education, and employment. Nevertheless, overt racism was perpetrated against all Southeast Asian refugees and their descendants. Random acts of violence committed against Southeast Asians and Asian Americans in general have steadily increased in recent years (Matsuoka & Ryujin, 1989).

**Acculturation**

*Acculturation* is a natural social process that occurs when one group or entity is subsumed by a larger, more influential cultural group or entity. In the case of Southeast Asians, evacuation, immigration, and resettlement in the United States meant that national and cultural ties to their homelands were sundered and socialization occurred according to dual, sometimes antithetical, cultural forces. Colonial Western influences in Southeast Asia inadvertently provided some refugees with skills and knowledge that facilitated their adjustment and accelerated their acculturation in this country. Those who learned English and Western customs and behavior found their adjustment in the United States less difficult (Matsuoka & Ryujin, 1989). On the other hand, those from remote and agrarian backgrounds who had little contact with Western culture before their arrival in the United States found the adjustment and acculturation process slow, confusing, and arduous. Although most Southeast Asians experienced language difficulties, groups like the Hmong from Laos, who had limited written language, encountered severe difficulties; their inability to communicate impeded their understanding and mobility in their new society (Le, 1993).

Family members have different socialization experiences that affect the rates at which they acculturate. One's age upon entry into the United States is a significant determinant of how quickly one assumes American behavioral patterns. This phenomenon creates disunity within a family as younger members adhere to new standards and expectations and older ones cling to traditional roles (Matsuoka & Ryujin, 1989).

The concept of differential acculturation helps explain intergenerational conflict. Adults generally have well-defined identities and are not as open to experiences in a new society, especially those that are antithetical to their established beliefs and values. Younger people, by contrast, have had less time to acquire such patterns and are more easily influenced by the new society. Schools and the mass media are pervasive socialization forces and regulators of behaviors and attitudes.

Inconsistencies between familial and institutional education generate conflicting sets of moral values. The emotional needs of children are prone to change with acculturation, and Indochinese parents may be especially ill prepared to address them, placing their children in high-risk situations. In other immigrant cultures, the transitional generation is the most affected by cultural conflict and shows high degrees of delinquency, mental illness, and anomie (Haskell & Yablonsky, 1974). In a *Los Angeles Times* survey of Vietnamese in Orange County, California, the largest Vietnamese enclave in the United States (Le, 1993), the greatest concern among the respondents (41 percent) was youth gangs and crime in their own communities. Their inability to keep pace with their peers in school and their sense of alienation from their families because of cultural gaps contributed to the rebellious attitudes and behaviors of the Vietnamese youths.

**Mental Health**

In terms of Southeast Asian mental health and psychological status, numerous studies have examined problems associated with the trauma of evacuation, immigration, and adjustment difficulties (Liu, Tazuma, & Matsuda, 1979; Owan et al., 1985; Williams, 1985). The radical shift from one culture to another resulted in tremendous losses for Southeast Asians. For some, the loss of their loved ones, ancestral homes, and countries had profound effects on their mental well-being that were manifest soon after their departure from their homelands and while they were in refugee camps (Liu, Lamanna, & Murata, 1979; Liu & Murata, 1978). Others exhibited emotional reactions to these experiences only after their immediate survival concerns of shelter, clothing, and food had been met; for example, posttraumatic stress disorder was identified among Cambodian refugees during their resettlement (Kinzie, Fredrickson, Ben, Fleck, & Karls, 1984).

Particular models of coping and adaptation became evident as Southeast Asians settled in and formed enclaves. Since the resettlement phase, many refugees have made strong efforts to unify their families, and they have built or gradually repaired their social networks. The creation of enclaves provided a comfortable base for common customs, language, and culture. Tran (1987) found that support from the ethnic community, self-esteem, and income had significant positive effects on the psychological well-being of Vietnamese refugees.

Special populations, such as Amerasians and former political prisoners, have greater needs for mental health services than do other refugee populations. As pariahs in their country of origin,

Amerasians experienced a tremendous amount of discrimination and were often discarded by both parents; for many, their only hope was to gain asylum in the United States. Political prisoners underwent reeducation, indoctrination programs, and torture at the hands of the communists. The combined effects of loss, resettlement, and physical and mental torture predisposed these prisoners to posttraumatic stress disorder.

## Implications for Social Work Policy and Practice

This entry has documented the arduous transition experienced by Southeast Asian refugees moving from their home countries to a new life in the United States. Although mental health research and services have focused predominantly on the refugees' adjustment difficulties, social workers are encouraged to examine the positive characteristics in their individual and collective struggles. Many Southeast Asian refugees have demonstrated a remarkable ability to overcome extreme adversity throughout the transitional period and in the daunting tasks of cultural adjustment in the United States.

Although Southeast Asian refugees share a common experience of forced immigration, they are heterogeneous in their religious beliefs, native languages, previous exposure to Western cultures, socioeconomic status, and propensity for adjusting to the American way of life. Cultural and social adjustment must be examined in the larger social context. In a study of life satisfaction among Vietnamese refugees, Matsuoka and Ryujin (1989) suggested that the formation of ethnic communities to create an environment in which refugees can practice indigenous ways and begin to interrelate new and old cultural values can promote economic development, community organization, and political strength in the larger society.

One important implication for practice is the promotion of individual and family well-being through intervention at various levels as conceptualized by Bronfenbrenner (1979). An important implication for policy development is the need to emphasize long-term adjustment beyond the current federal resettlement policy. Historically, refugees and immigrants to the United States have contributed to the nation's industrial development by providing critical human resources. Similarly, contemporary refugees will also provide important human resources that will foster the nation's development. Therefore, immigration policies must provide adequate supports, including opportunities to learn English and participate in job training programs, to facilitate the positive long-term adjustment of refugees and immigrants.

## References

AmerAsian Homecoming Act of 1987. P.L. 100-200, 101 Stat. 1329.

Boehnlein, J. K. (1987). A review of mental health services for refugees between 1975 and 1985 and a proposal for future services. *Hospital and Community Psychiatry, 38*(7), 764–768.

Bronfenbrenner, U. (1979). *The ecology of human development: Experiments by nature and design*. Cambridge, MA: Harvard University Press.

Cheung, F. K. (1985, December). Life and mental health conditions of boat refugees. *The Bridge,* pp. 2–4.

Cravens, R. B., & Bornemann, T. H. (1990). Refugee camps in countries of first asylum and the North American resettlement process. In W. H. Holtzman & T. H. Bornemann (Eds.), *Mental health of immigrants and refugees: Proceedings of a conference* (pp. 38–50). Austin, TX: Hogg Foundation for Mental Health.

Flaskerud, J. H., & Nguyen, A. T. (1988). Mental health needs of Vietnamese refugees. *Hospital and Community Psychiatry, 39*(4), 435–437.

Haskell, M. R., & Yablonsky, L. (1974). *Juvenile delinquency*. Chicago: Rand McNally.

Hunt, D. J. (1991). Mental health issues among refugees in the U.S.: The case of Southeast Asian children. *Future Choices, 3*(1), 15–27.

Hussain, M. F. (1982). Race-related illness in Vietnamese refugees. *International Journal of Social Psychiatry, 30,* 153–156.

Indochina Migration and Refugee Assistance Act of 1975. P.L. 94-23, 89 Stat. 87.

*Information Please Almanac.* (1994). Boston: Houghton Mifflin.

Kinzie, J. D., Fredrickson, R. H., Ben, R., Fleck, J., & Karls, N. (1984). Post-traumatic stress disorder among survivors of Cambodian concentration camps. *American Journal of Psychiatry, 141,* 645–650.

Kraut, A. (1990). Historical perspective on refugee movements to North America. In W. H. Holtzman & T. H. Bornemann (Eds.), *Mental health of immigrants and refugees: Proceedings of a conference* (pp. 16–37). Austin, TX: Hogg Foundation for Mental Health.

Le, N. (1993). The case of the Southeast Asian refugees: Policy for a community "at-risk." In *The state of Asian and Pacific America: A public policy report—Policy issues to the year 2020* (pp. 167–188). Los Angeles: LEAP Asian Pacific American Public Policy Institute and UCLA Asian American Studies Center.

Lin, K. M., Masuda, M., & Tazuma, L. (1982). Adaptational problems of Vietnamese refugees. Case studies in clinic and field: Adaptive and maladaptive. *Psychiatric Journal of the University of Ottawa, 7,* 173–183.

Liu, K. M., Tazuma, L., & Masuda, M. (1979). Adaptational problems of Vietnamese refugees. *Archives of General Psychiatry, 35,* 955–961.

Liu, W. T., Lamanna, M., & Murata, A. K. (1979). *Transition to nowhere*. Nashville, TN: Charter House Publishers.

Liu, W. T., & Murata, A. K. (1978). The Vietnamese in America, part V: Resettlement of the refugees. *Bridge: An Asian-American Perspective, 6,* 55–60.

Matsuoka, J. K., & Ryujin, D. H. (1989). Vietnamese refugees: An analysis of contemporary adjustment issues. *Journal of Applied Social Sciences, 14*(1), 20–39.

Mollica, R. F., Wyshak, G., & Lavell, J. (1987). The psychosocial impact of war trauma and torture on Southeast Asian refugees. *American Journal of Psychiatry, 144*(2), 1567–1572.

Nguyen, S. D. (1983). The psycho-social adjustment and the mental health needs of Southeast Asian refugees. *Psychiatric Journal of the University of Ottawa, 7,* 26–35.

Nicassio, P. M., & Pate, J. K. (1984). An analysis of problems of resettlement of the Indochinese refugees in the United States. *Social Psychiatry, 19,* 135–141.

Outsama, K. (1977). *Laotian themes*. New York: Center for Bilingual Education.

Owan, T., Bliatout, B., Lin, K. M., Liu, W., Nguyen, T. D., & Wong, H. Z. (Eds.). (1985). *Southeast Asian mental health: Treatment, prevention, services, training, and research.* Bethesda, MD: National Institute of Mental Health.

Pham, M. A. (1981). *Cross-cultural considerations in counseling refugee students.* Unpublished master's thesis, California State University, Sacramento.

Refugee Act of 1980. P.L. 96-212, 94 Stat. 102.

Rumbaut, R., & Ima, K. (1988). *The adaptation of Southeast Asian refugee youth: A comparative study* (Report to the U.S. Department of Health and Human Services, Family Support Administration, Office of Refugee Resettlement). Washington, DC: Office of Refugee Resettlement.

Rumbaut, R. G. (1986). Mental health and the refugee experience: A comparative study of Southeast Asian refugees. In T. C. Owan (Ed.), *Southeast Asian mental health: Treatment, prevention, services, training, and research* (pp. 433–486). Bethesda, MD: National Institute of Mental Health.

Schiff-Ross, I. D. (1991). *Southeast Asian refugee youth runaways*. Unpublished master's thesis, California State University, Sacramento.

Stein, B. N. (1981). Understanding the refugee experience: Foundations of a better resettlement system. *Journal of Refugee Resettlement, 1,* 62–71.

Tobin, J. J., & Friedman, J. (1984). Intercultural and developmental stresses confronting Southeast Asian refugee adolescents. *Journal of Operational Psychiatry, 15,* 39–45.

Tran, T. V. (1987). Alienation among Vietnamese refugees in the United States: A causal approach. *Journal of Social Service Research, 11*(1), 59–75.

United States Catholic Conference. (1984). *Refugees from Laos: A look at history, culture, and the refugee crisis* (Refugee Information series). Washington, DC: Author.

U.S. Department of Health and Human Services. (1989). *Report to Congress, Refugee Resettlement Program.* Washington, DC: Office of Refugee Resettlement, Family Support Administration.

U.S. Department of Health and Human Services. (1991). *Refugee Resettlement Program, Report to the Congress.* Washington, DC: U.S. Government Printing Office.

Vignes, A. J., & Hall, R. C. (1979). Adjustment of a group of Vietnamese people to the United States. *American Journal of Psychiatry, 136,* 442–444.

Williams, C. (1985). The provision of mental health services to the Southeast Asian refugees. *Journal of Community Psychology, 13,* 258–269.

## Further Reading

Dinnerstein, L., Nichols, R. L., & Reimers, D. M. (1990). *Native and strangers: Blacks, Indians, and immigrants in America* (2nd ed.). New York: Oxford University Press.

Freeman, G. P., & Jupp, J. (Eds.). (1993). *Nations of immigrants: Australia, the United States, and international migration*. New York: Oxford University Press.

Kessner, T., & Caroli, B. B. (1981). *Today's immigrants, their stories: A new look at the newest Americans*. New York: Oxford University Press.

Marsella, A. J., Bornemann, T., Ekblad, S., & Orley, J. (Eds.). (1994). *Amidst peril and pain: The mental health and well-being of the world's refugees*. Rockville, MD: National Institute of Mental Health.

Moynihan, D. P. (1993). *Pandemonium: Ethnicity in international politics*. New York: Oxford University Press.

Takaki, R. (Ed.). (1994). *From different shores: Perspectives on race and ethnicity in America* (2nd ed.). Boston: Little, Brown.

Van Esterik, P. (1992). *Taking refuge: Lao Buddhists in North America*. Toronto: York Lanes Press.

Yans-McLaughlin, V. (Ed.). (1990). *Immigration reconsidered: History, sociology, and politics*. New York: Oxford University Press.

**Quang DuongTran, PhD,** is assistant professor and **Jon K. Matsuoka, PhD,** is associate professor, University of Hawaii, School of Social Work, 2500 Campus Road, Honolulu, HI 96822.

### For further information see

Asian Americans Overview; Civil Rights; Community; Displaced People; Ethnic-Sensitive Practice; Families Overview; Housing; Human Rights; Income Security Overview; Jobs and Earnings; Mental Health Overview; Natural Helping Networks; Peace and Social Justice; Poverty; Social Welfare Policy; Social Work Practice: Theoretical Base.

**Key Words**

| | |
|---|---|
| Amerasians | refugees |
| Asian Americans | Southeast Asians |
| immigrants | |

# Asian Indians

**Pallassana R. Balgopal**

Asian Indians are one of the fastest-growing immigrant groups in the United States. According to the 1990 Census (U.S. Bureau of the Census, 1992), they are the fourth-largest Asian American group, numbering 815,447. Although exact figures are not available, it is estimated that the total population of South Asian Americans (people from India, Pakistan, Bangladesh, Sri Lanka, and Nepal) numbers at least 1.2 million. This figure is considerably higher if Asian Indian immigrants from the Caribbean basin are added.

## Immigration Patterns

Although the earliest record of the presence of an Asian Indian in the United States is documented to be in 1790 in Salem, Massachusetts, it was only in the latter part of the 19th century that this group began immigrating in large numbers to North America (Chandrasekhar, 1982). Unlike people of other races who were brought as indentured laborers to solve the labor shortage on the sugar plantations in the former British colonies, Indian immigrants came to the United States and Canada of their own volition. Between 1899 and 1920, about 7,300 Asian Indians arrived on the West Coast and settled mostly in California. Many (2,000 per year) also immigrated to British Columbia in Canada. This migration pattern lasted until 1909. Most of these immigrants, primarily agricultural laborers, came from the northwestern Indian province of Punjab.

Like other Asian immigrants, Asian Indians were subjected to institutional and societal racism and prejudice. Anti-Indian rioting occurred in the Pacific Coast states. In Bellingham, Washington, 600 lumberjacks herded 200 "Hindus" out of town, resulting in serious injuries among the immigrants (Hess, 1982). Overt racism through stereotypes reinforced by the press was frequently evident. A Hearst journal delightfully reported that the Indians were weak and docile as cattle, and an article in *Overland* warned about the inundation of the "Hindus" (Hess, 1982). Canadian newspapers published similar sentiments, with headlines such as "Horde of Hungry Hindoos Invade Vancouver City," "Get Rid of Hindus at Whatever Cost," and "Bar Hindus from Canada" (Indra, 1979).

Asian Indians were subject to such racist practice in the United States as well. Because only male immigrants were allowed into the country and were not permitted to bring their spouses or other family members, most either remained single or married migrant Mexican women, who were close to them in skin color. Between 1923 and 1946, Indians were denied citizenship, and further immigration was prohibited. Only after the passage of the Immigration Act of 1946 were Asian Indians able to immigrate legally to the United States and, even then, at the rate of only 100 per year. Unable to withstand such punitive policies and overt racism, between 1920 and 1940 more than 3,000 Asian Indians returned to India.

The Asian Indian population in the United States boomed after the Immigration and Nationality Act of 1965. The abolition of the national origins quota and the establishment of preference categories for family reunion, skilled professionals, and refugees has been instrumental in the increase in Asian Indian immigration.

Despite their significant numbers and long residence in the United States, Asian Indians and other South Asian Americans remain peripheral to any discussion of American culture, experience, or history. As with many other marginalized groups, they are excluded from the dominant discourse of the United States. They also are frequently excluded from the general category of Asian Americans. Thus, they are not only the marginal minority, but often the forgotten minority (Hess, 1976).

Until the mid-20th century, Asian Indians lived mostly on the West Coast, especially California. They were perceived by the larger society as a deviant ethnic group who lived in overcrowded, unsanitary conditions and who did not want to assimilate into American life and thus avoided social responsibilities (Buchignani, 1979). These stereotypes were perpetuated by the perception of Asian Indians in their country of origin, the land of mystics, maharajas, holy men, snake charmers, sacred cows, poverty, and overpopulation. Such stereotypes continue even today because of the media-biased portrayal of life in India.

It is difficult to generalize or devise a prototype of Asian Indians. Because of linguistic, religious, and other cultural differences, this is a diverse and heterogenous group. Despite their diversity, people from the different South Asian countries are generally grouped together in one category as Asian Indians. The only common denominator is that their parents or grandparents came from the subcontinent of India and they have similar racial characteristics. Although Asian Indians are a diverse group, they share some commonalities:

- The migration of these people began in the latter part of the 19th century.
- The initial migrants were from northern India and settled on the West Coast as farmers.
- Asian Indians have been subjected to many of the racial biases and prejudices that other Asian Americans have.
- The major influx of Asian Indians to the United States started after 1965, and it is increasing rapidly.
- The new immigrants come from all parts of the subcontinent of India and from all walks of life.

## Asian Indian Community

The Asian Indian community in the United States can be grouped into several categories, although the classification is somewhat arbitrary and is based on the immigrants' profile.

### Classifications

***Punjabi farmers.*** The first immigrants from India were farmers from the northern province of Punjab, who came to the United States between 1895 and 1920. The majority of these immigrants settled in California and engaged in farming.

***Scholars.*** Between the time of Indian independence in 1947 and the passage of the Immigration and Nationality Act of 1965, Indian students came to this country for graduate study. They attended prestigious U.S. universities and, after the completion of their studies, took positions in academia, research, and industry. A number of Asian Indians immigrated in this way and hold successful positions in a variety of professions.

***Professionals.*** Professionals in science, medicine and other health fields, engineering, and business were able to immigrate because of their professional and technical expertise and skills. The largest group of Asian Indian Americans, they are scattered all over the country, and a significant number are well established; some own small and large businesses.

***Refugees.*** When Asian Indians who had settled in such African countries as Uganda were suddenly forced to leave these countries, they came to the United States as refugees. This group was composed primarily of people from the northwestern Indian region of Gujarat. Although they were able to bring only limited finances from their homes in Africa, through hard work and tenacity they have established themselves in various businesses.

***Caribbean Island Indians.*** Since 1965 a number of Indians from the Caribbean Islands and Guiana have immigrated to the United States for economic reasons. Because of their marginal educational and technical background, most are employed in low-paying jobs mainly in the hotel and food service industries.

***Extended families.*** Under the family reunification provision of the Immigration and Nationality Act of 1965 (P.L. 89-236), U.S. citizens of Asian Indian origin, as well as permanent residents, can sponsor their immediate family members for immigration. Generally, these immigrants are not as skilled as their sponsoring relatives. The median income of Asian Indians who immigrated between 1987 and 1990 is one-fifth of those who arrived before 1980. Similarly, the unemployment rate of new immigrants is more than twice that of the pre-1980 group (Melwani, 1994). This limited income and day-to-day struggle to survive has affected the new immigrants and their families. The struggle of these immigrants is further compounded by the myth of being the model minority within the American context and their practice of putting up a front as "successful Americans" for relatives and friends in their countries of origin.

### Spiritual and Philosophical Values

To understand the struggles of Asian Indians, it is essential to understand the key philosophical and spiritual dimensions that direct these people's lives. Asian Indians practice a number of different religions, including Hinduism, Islam, Christianity, Sikhism, and Jainism. Their tenacious individualism is derived from Asian Indian philosophy and their diverse religious backgrounds. The result is that individuals strongly uphold their right to choose their own way of thinking and acting. In practice, this individualism leads to a precarious reaction—the almost cynical disregard for anything or anyone outside the narrow interests of themselves and their families.

### Conscience and *Dharma* Systems

Another important feature of the Asian Indian culture is that it distinguishes between conscience and *dharma* (duty). Asian Indians may be distressed because they have left their families (especially aged parents) and their homelands. Saran and Leonhard-Spark (1980) suggested that Asian Indian immigrants may value India and Indian institutional arrangements more highly than American ones, and Balgopal (1988) noted that they view American values—especially those related to parent–child relationships, dating and marriage, and care of the elderly—with considerable internal turmoil and anguish.

**Parent–Child Interactions**

The philosophical and spiritual beliefs of Asian Indian immigrants often make it difficult for them to cope with a different set of values. Thus, the children and the parents are often caught between two cultures. The children live within the Indian cultural environment at home, but they interact within the dominant Anglo-American culture at school, in the neighborhood, and at work. Their world is neither the old nor the new, but both. Parents have difficulty comprehending their children's attitudes toward elders (the children interact more on equal terms with adults, rather than maintain a distance and pay respect to adults), dating and selecting a life companion, choosing their own career goals, and wanting to move out of their parents' home. Children cannot understand why their parents cling to "old country" values.

Adolescents are perhaps the greatest source of anxiety to their immigrant parents. Asian Indian parents who fear that their children may experiment with drugs or sex question whether they should send their children back to India or whether they should return themselves. Dating and the selection of mates is one of the major areas where the parents and children in Asian Indian American households clash frequently. Indian children often insist on the freedom to choose their own spouses. Peer pressure, American norms of dating, movies, and other influences contribute to the rebellion.

The custom of arranged marriage is increasingly becoming the new battleground in Asian Indian families (Nambiar, 1993). Parents sometimes insist on arranging their children's marriages, although the children's input regarding their expectations for a future spouse may be included.

**Cultural Barriers**

Unlike other immigrant groups who formed their own neighborhoods, such as Little Italy, Chinatown, and Little Tokyo, Asian Indians have yet to form a clearly visible residential area of their own (Saran & Eames, 1980). In large cities such as Chicago, Los Angeles, and New York, small retail businesses and restaurants have opened in specific geographic areas in which recent immigrants live. Because slumlords frequently take advantage of these immigrants, a number of the new arrivals live in substandard housing.

Language is another source of conflict for many Asian Indians. Most Asian Indian immigrants spoke English fluently before they immigrated. However, the number of new immigrants who do not demonstrate a proficiency in English is increasing rapidly, especially as professionals and scholars sponsor dependents and other relatives to immigrate.

**Racial Prejudice**

Because of their skin color, Asian Indians have experienced various degrees of racial discrimination in employment and housing in various parts of the United States. Many Americans consider them a threat to their jobs, because Asian Indian immigrants tend to be well educated and hardworking and are often willing to work under adverse conditions and at low wages. Members of anti-Indian organizations called "Dotbusters" (a reference to the red dot, or *bindi,* worn by Indian women on their foreheads) have attacked Asian Indian Americans, their homes, and business establishments primarily in New Jersey and New York. Asian Indians work hard and try to better themselves economically; the local population often responds violently in a manner that the mayor of Jersey City described as "an animalistic approach to territorial domain" (Balgopal, 1988, p. 26). Envy and prejudice result in violent behavior (Mohan, 1989), and the ethnic newspapers are increasingly reporting Asian Indian victims of hate crimes.

## Unique Contributions

Asian Indians continue to make significant contributions to their new homeland, most noticeably in the fields of science, engineering, computer science, and medicine. The more than 25,000 Asian Indian physicians in the United States (Vyas, 1994) are found all over the country and are providing much-needed health care to people in places where other health care providers are unwilling to locate. Similarly, more than 5,000 well-established Asian Indian academics are found in virtually every field in institutions of higher education. Although Asian Indians have not made much impact in the top levels of medium and large U.S. corporations, a number have begun successful engineering and computer software companies. Overall, Asian Indian businesspeople and professionals project a positive image of their community to their new society; among this group are two Nobel laureates—Har Gobind Khorana (for medicine in 1968) and Subrahmanyan Chandrase Khar (for physics in 1983)—and Zubin Mehta, the former conductor of the New York Philharmonic (Abraham, 1990).

The first Asian Indian congressman, Dilip Singh Saund, was elected from California in 1956.

With the growth of the Asian Indian community, the need to participate actively in the political process is being recognized, and an increasing number of Asian Indians have been elected to political offices in cities and local communities. Several Asian Indians have been appointed to important positions at the state and city levels (Abraham, 1990).

## Implications for Social Work

Asian Indians have a distinctly different value system from most Anglo-Americans that emphasizes the virtues of collectivism through loyalty to the family. Recognizing this difference is key to understanding Asian Indians.

Asian Indian families are beginning to express and share their problems and difficulties. Parent–child conflicts, marital conflicts, the emotional distress of individuals, behavioral problems of children, the rebellion of adolescents, and domestic violence are some of the problems for which they have sought help. Saving the family's pride, doing their duty, and adhering to their cultural traditions is important to this ethnic group.

When family members do not adhere to clearly delineated roles and expectations for the different members, the family experiences conflict. In families where such conflict has been left unresolved for a prolonged period, brief family therapy sessions may be beneficial. Hesitancy to reveal personal difficulties and coping struggles should not be viewed as resistance in the traditional sense. Social workers and all mental health professionals should be patient and develop a trusting relationship before suggesting options for behavioral change. Clarification and exploration are useful intervention techniques (Balgopal, 1988).

Asian Indians depend heavily on their kinship networks for emotional, financial, and other assistance. In the absence of such resources, they may feel lost and question their decision to immigrate. To seek assistance from formal human services organizations is an admission of failure, adding further agony to the guilt over having left their homeland and having failed to abide by the *dharma* to be close to their elderly parents. Most Asian Indian immigrants come to the United States so they can excel economically, but when they fail in this pursuit, depression, alcohol abuse, psychosomatic problems, and marital conflicts are the major manifestations of their maladaptation to American culture (Balgopal, 1988).

When these families face economic hardships, they often do not know where to turn for help. Social services and other human services agencies increasingly contact these families through such sources as schools and physicians.

There are scores of failed dreamers who dispel the stereotype of Asian Indians as affluent scientists and professionals. For these people, the great American dream has turned into a nightmare (Melwani, 1994). Social services agencies must aggressively reach out to them.

With the changing role of women in the United States, Asian Indian women also are becoming more assertive. Because many are unwilling to submit to traditional male dominance, marital conflicts result. Marriage enrichment programs designed specifically for Asian Indians may be helpful. However, in organizing such services, social workers should remember that specific, goal-oriented groups, such as task-centered groups, will be more compatible with the cultural norms and expectations of Asian Indians (Ramakrishnan & Balgopal, 1986) than less-structured groups. Because Asian Indian Americans often are reluctant to seek services from any source other than kinship networks, social workers must be creative in developing preventive services. Asian Indian American cultural and social organizations, whose numbers are rapidly increasing, are valuable resources, and involving Asian Indian social workers is a viable option.

## References


Abraham, T. (1990). Indian American community—A perspective. In *Handbook for Indian immigrants* (pp. 57–61). Pittsburgh: Spindle.

Balgopal, P. R. (1988). Social networks and Asian Indian families. In C. Jacobs & D. D. Bowles (Eds.), *Ethnicity and race: Critical concepts in social work* (pp. 18–33). Silver Spring, MD: National Association of Social Workers.

Buchignani, N. (1979). South Asian Canadians and the ethnic mosaic: An overview. *Canadian Ethnic Studies, 1*(1), 48–68.

Chandrasekhar, S. (1982). A history of United States legislation with respect to immigration from India. In S. Chandrasekhar (Ed.), *From India to America* (pp. 11–28). La Jolla, CA: Population Review Publications.

Hess, G. R. (1976). The forgotten Asian Americans: The East Indian community in the United States. In N. Hundley (Ed.), *The Asian American* (pp. 157–158). Santa Barbara, CA: Clio Books.

Hess, G. R. (1982). The Asian Indian immigrants in the United States—The early phase, 1900–1965. In S. Chandrasekhar (Ed.), *From India to America* (pp. 29–34). La Jolla, CA: Population Review Publications.

Immigration Act of 1946. Ch. 945, 60 Stat. 975.

Immigration and Nationality Act of 1965. P.L. 89-236, 79 Stat. 911.

Indra, M. D. (1979). South Asian stereotypes in the Vancouver press. *Ethnic and Racial Studies, 2*(2), 166–188.

Melwani, L. (1994, January 31). Dark side of the moon. *India Today,* pp. 60C–60F.
Mohan, B. (1989). Ethnicity, power and discontent: The problem of identity reconstruction in a pluralist society. *Indian Journal of Social Work, 1,* 199–212.
Nambiar, S. (1993, November 7). Love with a proper stranger. *Washington Post,* pp. C1, C4.
Ramakrishnan, K. R., & Balgopal, P. R. (1986). Task-centered casework: Intervention strategy for developing societies. *Journal of International and Comparative Social Welfare, 2,* 21–28.
Saran, P., & Eames, E. (Eds.). (1980). *The new ethnics.* New York: Praeger.
Saran, P., & Leonhard-Spark, P. J. (1980). Attitudinal and behavioral profile. In P. Saran & E. Eames (Eds.), *The new ethnics* (pp. 163–176). New York: Praeger.
U.S. Bureau of the Census. (1992). *1990 census of the population—General population characteristics.* Washington, DC: U.S. Government Printing Office.
Vyas, C. (1994). Woes of Indian doctors in the U.S. *India Tribune, 18,* 23.

**Pallassana R. Balgopal, DSW,** is professor, University of Illinois, School of Social Work, 1207 W. Oregon Street, Urbana, IL 61801.

**For further information see**

Asian Americans Overview; Civil Rights; Direct Practice Overview; Ecological Perspective; Ethnic-Sensitive Practice; Families Overview; Goal Setting and Intervention Planning; Human Rights; Income Distribution; Jobs and Earnings; Social Welfare Policy; Social Work Profession Overview.

**Key Words**

Asian Americans    Asian Indians

## Assertiveness Training

*See* Social Skills Training

READER'S GUIDE

### Assessment

*The following entries contain information on this general topic:*



# Assessment

**Carol H. Meyer**

*Assessment* can mean knowing, understanding, evaluating, individualizing, or figuring out. It is a process used in all professional disciplines and, in fact, may be the hallmark of all professional (as opposed to lay) activity. Whether in social work, law, medicine, education, architecture, or engineering, the professional practitioner bases his or her interventions on an understanding of the situation, need, or problem to be addressed. If one were to approach a social work case without an assessment of the configuration of relevant factors involved in the situation, need, or problem, the interventions could be routine, hit or miss, arbitrary, or biased in some way by the practitioner's own predilections. In all professions, assessment is the process that ideally controls the nature, direction, and scope of interventions.

## History

In the profession of social work, it was the introduction of the idea of assessment that first defined the method of social casework, although the term used for assessment was "social diagnosis," the title of the first text on social work methods by Mary Richmond (1917). Richmond used the term "diagnosis" because she had been associated with physicians at The Johns Hopkins School of Medicine and recognized the value of understanding what the data in a case indicated before providing medical treatment. She believed that the new term "social diagnosis" would instruct social workers to use the concept of "knowing through" a problem (diagnosis) within a social, rather than a medical, framework. This emphasis is reflected in Richmond's definition of social diagnosis as the

> attempt to arrive at as exact a definition as possible of the social situation and personality of a human being in some social need—in relation to other human beings upon whom he in any way depends or who depends upon him, and in relation also to the social institutions of his community. (p. 357)

Since 1917, through all the historical landmarks that social work practice has passed, the concept of diagnosis has persisted, although what it has been called, the kinds of variables it has focused on, and the forms it has taken have changed with the times. In some ways, the history of assessment in social work practice has paralleled the history of social work itself, just as it has reflected social work's professional purposes, because what a profession chooses to focus on in assessment or what it recognizes as relevant and significant case data will ultimately define what it does.

Until 1917, when Richmond introduced a diagnostic method that included gathering and interpreting the data of a case, friendly visitors used moral judgments to interpret their clients' behavior. Although Richmond's (1917) text *Social Diagnosis* was overly weighted with concrete details, it offered early social caseworkers a more neutral and objective way of understanding their cases. Furthermore, it introduced them to a way of viewing family problems as being embedded in a social context. Richmond's text became the antecedent of what was later called "psychosocial diagnosis" and then "ecosystems assessment." In the early 1920s, on the way to these later formulations, the concept of social diagnosis took a sharp turn "inward" from Richmond's emphasis on the person in his or her social context to a psychoanalytic emphasis on intrapsychic factors. This was the time after World War I, when psychiatric social workers were involved in the treatment of returning veterans suffering from "shell shock." It was also a time when many social workers had become attracted to the work of Sigmund Freud, who had visited the United States a decade earlier. In this era of psychoanalytically tinged social casework, the concept of diagnosis, or understanding, remained the same as it was originally conceived, but it began to take on the encumbrance of the content of a theory. In the 1920s, this content was psychoanalytic theory, with its emphasis on intrapsychic history and its deemphasis on the social context. This new emphasis undoubtedly accounted for the fact that during the 1930s and 1940s the "diagnostic school" of thought was associated with a psychoanalytic orientation—this theoretical emphasis having taken over the intent of the theoretically neutral process of diagnosis or understanding.

When Virginia Robinson (1930) wrote *A Changing Psychology of Social Casework,* the thrust of her critique of (diagnostic) casework was that it focused excessively on the objective understanding of the events in the client's history—a reflection of the Freudian psychoanalytic emphasis. The "functional school" of thought, developed by Jesse Taft (1936) and Robinson, drew from Otto Rank's psychoanalytic ideas. The approach focused on the client's current situation as reflected in the relationship with the social worker, who carried out the function of the agency. Rather than use diagnosis to understand the nature of case problems, the functional school used evaluation to estimate how the client was using the agency. These two processes—the diagnostic, which sought to understand the "what" and "why" of a case, and the evaluative, which focused primarily on "how" the client used the relationship with the social worker—differed. Both used psychoanalytic theory as the knowledge base of their social casework approaches, each was identified with a school of social work (the New York School for diagnostic and the Pennsylvania School for evaluative), and each sought to understand behavior within a particular framework, but they remained separated through their disagreements about the value of diagnosis. Thus, the subsequent theoretical developments in assessment derived from writers associated with the diagnostic school.

Sheffield, a social worker in Boston who was not well known but who had helped Richmond with *Social Diagnosis*, was probably the earliest theorist to use the term *psychosocial* to represent a dual focus on inner and outer factors in social work cases (Sheffield, 1937). In 1938, Lowry, a casework teacher and one of the original theorists, wrote about (psychosocial) diagnosis as the central unifying concept in social work, saying:

> We find that [diagnosis] or the act of deriving meanings, has two connotations ... 1) to describe an act in which we survey what we know and come to a conclusion as to its meaning; and 2) as a process, a series of acts following upon each other, each taking its meaning from its relatedness to the others and resulting in

a continuing process of developing an increasing understanding of the meaning of each new fact. (Lowry, 1938, p. 587)

Despite the changes in social work since Lowry's statement, the description of the process remains applicable today.

Gordon Hamilton was probably the leading casework theorist of the diagnostic school from the mid-1930s to the 1950s, and in her widely read book *Theory and Practice of Social Casework* (1940/1951) she picked up on Sheffield's concept of psychosocial and created a comprehensive theory of casework centered on diagnosis. Perlman's *Social Casework: A Problem-Solving Process* (1957) was written in an effort to bring together the diagnostic and functional theories through an expanded focus on person, problem, place, and process. Perlman was a noted theorist, and this text was influential in broadening the focus of casework practice to include diagnostic and evaluative processes as the bases of interventions. The next leading casework theorist to influence the focus and direction of diagnosis was Hollis (1964), whose book *Casework: A Psycho-Social Therapy* revived the diagnostic focus on intrapsychic factors, so that once again the concept assumed a psychoanalytic hue. The focus of diagnosis had shifted in the almost 50 years of casework's development from a social, to a psychological, then to a psychosocial, and then again to a psychological one. It seems that the term itself, as well as the concepts of understanding, knowing, and individualizing, could not be disassociated from the chosen theoretical focus. Changing ideologies could not be distinguished from the diagnostic process, and in that half-century, social casework theorists were absorbed with refining the casework process.

Change came about in 1970 with the publication of Harriett Bartlett's influential book, *The Common Base of Social Work Practice.* Bartlett identified the knowledge base as fundamental to all social work processes, including practice with individuals, families, groups, and communities. Furthermore, she argued for a changing social work practice from *doing* to a new emphasis on *knowing* as the central professional task. Bartlett used a new term for diagnosis—*"assessment"*—and she defined it as a separate process that was embedded in a base of knowledge. Given the broad scope of social work's activities, diagnosis seemed too narrow a term to account for the repertoire of knowledge necessary to accommodate social work's modern purposes. Thus, the concept of diagnosis–assessment was brought to the forefront of professional activity, viewed now as a cognitive process that can be used separately from any practice ideology. Meyer (1970, 1976), in her formulation of the ecosystems perspective, proposed the use of the terms "exploration," "assessment," and "intervention," to replace the traditional casework terms "study," "diagnosis," and "treatment." This was a further attempt to distinguish social work from medical processes and to accommodate the broadened ecosystems perspective on practice. This change was not merely semantic; it was an epistemological shift. The ecosystems perspective was designed to resolve the 50-year debate between the psychological and social focuses of diagnosis–assessment. By the 1980s, the assessment process was well established as an essential part of social work methodology—a separate cognitive process applicable to all social work problems; useful in all social work processes; and, on the whole, unencumbered by any ideology.

## Practice Approaches and Assessment

Bartlett's (1970) contribution to the recognition of assessment as a separate, nonideological, cognitive process in social work practice made it possible for assessment to be used in all developing practice approaches (Meyer, 1983). Different theories of personality and behavior and the nature of people's interaction with their environments offer different explanations of case phenomena, and all practice approaches naturally focus on selected features of cases to make assessments. The psychosocial approach (Turner, 1974, 1988) evolved from its roots in the works of Richmond, Hamilton, and Hollis to stress the person-in-environment, with special attention to the client's history. An offshoot of this approach is ego psychology, in which the assessment of ego functioning is the basis of ego-oriented interventions (Goldstein, 1984). The cognitive–behavioral approach (Gambrill, 1983; Rose, 1981; Thyer, 1988) emphasizes the client's current behaviors, viewed as being responsive to learning from the social environment. Mattaini (1990) wove behavioral analysis into the ecosystems perspective, offering a contextual model that focuses on the client's connections to his or her social situation.

The ecosystems perspective has generated the systems and the ecological streams of practice, which address the relatedness of psychological and social factors in cases but which are less derivative of personality and behavioral factors than are the psychosocial and behavioral approaches. A seminal article by Auerswald (1968) introduced the use of an ecological-systems way of thinking to shift the assessment of the etiology of problems from the "patient" to the community.

In its use of the ecological metaphor of mutual adaptation of the person and the environment, the life model (Germain & Gitterman, 1980) focuses on transitions, environmental obstacles, and interpersonal processes in assessing life processes. Allen-Meares and Lane (1987) developed an ecosystems framework for a multidimensional assessment of the effects of the home, community, school, and work on the client.

These and other evolving approaches in this vein are beginning to operationalize the assessment process through ecological and systemic thinking, developing social work practice theory based on the interaction of the person and the environment. Again, the choice of which variables of a case to assess is always determined by one's theoretical orientation and what is thought to be essential knowledge for intervention. The assessment process has been incorporated into dozens of practice approaches, each of which has emphasized particular aspects of the person-in-environment configurations.

## Assessment in Specialized Areas

The evolution of assessment as a crucial process in social work practice has paralleled the evolution of social work itself. One of the most significant developments in social work in the 1980s was the increase in specialization in every area—fields of practice, human development, ethnicity and culture, social problems, and clinical processes—a trend that continues today. As specialization has become the hallmark of American professional life, so it has flourished in social work.

The following are some recent examples of ways in which the assessment process has been applied in social work practice in light of this increased specialization. In the field of family and children's services, Hess and Howard (1981) developed ecological models for assessing adoptive families' and children's psychosocial difficulties. In the field of mental health, Gottlieb (1985) wrote about assessing social supports, and Perlmutter and Jones (1985) elaborated on ways to refine assessments in psychiatric emergencies. In the field of health, Coulton (1981) considered the impact of the person–environment fit on health care. In school social work, the National Council of State Consultants for School Social Work (1981) identified the components of assessment that are necessary in schools, and Levine (1984) developed a tool for assessing the etiology of truancy. Every field of practice is concerned with particular field-related issues, and assessment is always the route to learning more about the extent, causes, effects, and scope of these issues.

Social workers are especially interested in the impact of gender, ethnicity, class, and culture on people's functioning in society. Some examples of this aspect of assessment are diagnostic considerations in work with Asian Americans (Chinn, 1983), the identification of cultural factors in health care (Fandetti & Goldmeier, 1988), the influence of class and race on clinical judgments (Franklin, 1985), and the understanding of rituals that reveal group values (Laird, 1984).

There are abundant examples of approaches to family systems assessment because, like the assessment process included in general practice approaches, family assessments are derived from particular family systems theories. Hartman and Laird (1983) presented a framework for assessing families in several dimensions, and Van Treuren (1986) presented a technique for eliciting from family members their own views of their family's problems. Each family treatment theorist addresses the particular elements and processes in families that he or she considers in a theory to be key to understanding the family's behavior and functioning (Minuchin, 1974).

The *Diagnostic and Statistical Manual of Mental Disorders, Fourth Edition* (commonly called DSM-IV) (American Psychiatric Association, 1994), a classification system widely used in clinical practice, has been criticized for being descriptive and nonspecific in its application to interventions (Kutchins & Kirk, 1986). The associated person-in-environment codification system (Karls & Wandrei, 1986), intended for use by social workers, may encounter similar difficulties in its adoption. However, these classification systems are a response to the compelling demands of accountability to insurance companies and public agencies that finance mental health services.

Although it is not possible to cite all specialized approaches to assessment, it should be evident that such approaches are available in whatever area of social work the practitioner may choose. The aim of all professional practice is to know more so that interventions will be effective. This pursuit of knowledge centers on the use of the assessment process, which is shaped by the questions asked. Thus, assessment is always contextual, embedded in a theoretical perspective or in a category that will direct attention to selected variables.

## Tools of Assessment: Diagrams, Scales, and Computers

### Diagrams

Social work practice has become more complicated as it has matured; it now addresses multiple units of attention on many systems levels. Thus, the assessment process has expanded to encompass the many dimensions of a case. This development has made it difficult for the practitioner to maintain a linear perspective or a simple cause-to-effect vision of interacting phenomena. Instead, what the practitioner sees is almost too much to hold in mind, and often words cannot capture the real-life complexity of the case. In response to this shift to a systemic (versus a linear) perspective, there has been significant development in the use of diagrams that can better describe complex phenomena by depicting graphically what was once restricted to words (Mailick & Vigilante, 1987; Mattaini, 1993a; Vigilante & Mailick, 1988).

The Eco-map (Germain & Gitterman, 1986; Hartman, 1978; Meyer, 1976, 1983) was one of the earliest diagrammatic assessment tools devised. Associated with the ecosystems perspective, it was intended to be used to depict the holistic characteristics of social work cases. Through penciled-in arrows and other figures and the use of colors, it shows, within the boundary of a circle, the relations between a person and different variables in his or her social environment (see Figure 1). Many variations of the Eco-map have been developed as practitioners have become accustomed to using it. Today, it is used in practice with individuals, families, groups, and communities.

The genogram (Hartman, 1978; McGoldrick & Gerson, 1985) is a graphic assessment tool used to depict family relationships over time (see Figure 2). Other assessment devices used in family work are family mapping (Hartman & Laird, 1983; Minuchin, 1974), a structural device that depicts family transactions, and the Circumplex Model of Family Functioning (Olson, 1986), which is associated with the Family Adaptability, Cohesion, and Evaluation Scale III, a rapid-assessment instrument for analyzing particular aspects of family functioning. Social network mapping is used to depict the quality and quantity of nurturing supports in a client's life (Cheers, 1987; Streeter & Franklin, 1992; Tracy & Whittaker, 1990). It expands the unit of attention from the family and addresses a similar need to analyze social functioning. In addition, various types of diagrams have been developed to aid practitioners in mapping and monitoring their practice (Bunston, 1985).

### Scales

The newest developments in assessment have been derived from empirical study and the influence of personal computers. This direction was to be expected, given that once the debate about the uses of assessment was resolved, social workers were free to apply the process to all phenomena of concern. Also, since the 1970s, there has been an interest in practice research—both evaluative and substantive—and the assessment process has been the natural locus of the development of instruments of study, which, after all, are about rigorous ways to ask questions and evaluate answers.

The use of rapid-assessment instruments has become increasingly important as brief treatment has become more and more prevalent (Corcoran & Fischer, 1987; Edelson, 1985; Levitt & Reid, 1981; Toseland & Reid, 1985). As social work practitioners have become more sophisticated in the use of measurement scales, these standardized measures have proliferated to such an extent that one should be able to find a scale to evaluate a client's behaviors and functioning in almost any type of case (Hudson, 1982). Examples of such scales include the Beck Depression Inventory (Beck, 1991), the Family Environment Scale (Moos & Moos, 1986), the McMaster Family Assessment Device (Epstein, Baldwin, & Bishop, 1983), and instruments to measure the fit between the person and the environment (Buffum, 1988; Coulton, 1979).

### Computers

Computers are most familiar to social workers as word processors, but they have lately been used in practice, particularly in the assessment process (Mattaini, 1993a). Computerized assessment programs have been evaluated (Hudson, Nurius, & Reisman, 1988) and applied to tracking clients' progress (Hudson, 1984), as well as to the formulation of problems and the specification of goals (Nurius & Hudson, 1988). The recent *Visual Eco-Scan* program has been computerized to highlight clients' interactions with their environment (Mattaini, 1993b). In view of the rapid development of computerization, social workers have developed an interest in examining ethical issues that may arise through this use of technology in social work practice (Erdman & Foster, 1988; Stewart, 1988), as well as in psychiatric diagnoses (Erdman & Foster, 1987).

## Classification

The use of classification systems (or typologies) in the assessment process is being debated in the profession. Some believe that the classification of problems is a necessary adjunct to assessment, whereas others contend that classification too often leads to stereotyping and labeling. According to Meyer (1993), the real problem is that the classification systems in use, such as clinical diagnoses, behavioral categories, and symptoma-

FIGURE 1

## Sample Eco-map

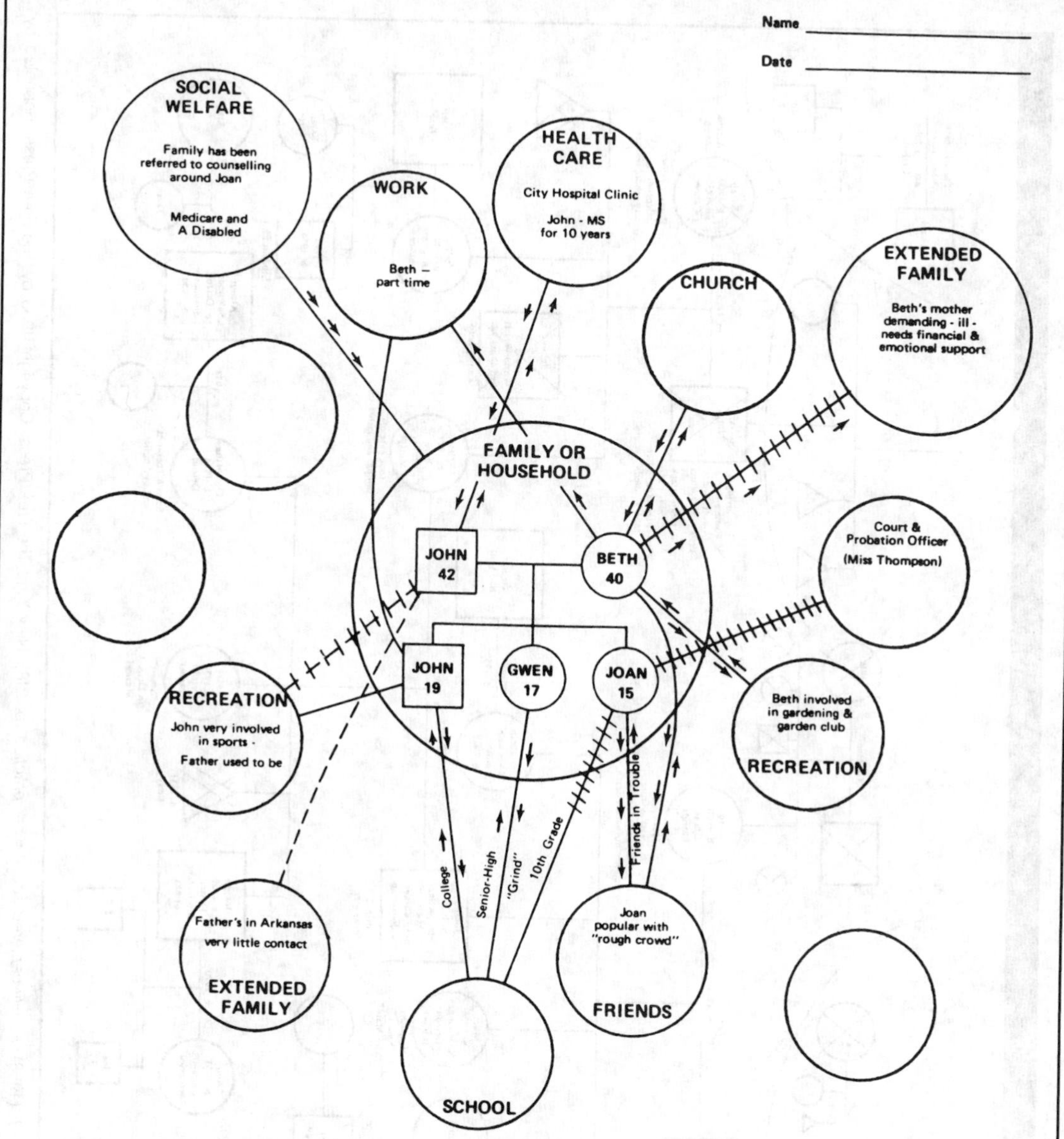

Name ____________________

Date ____________________

SOCIAL WELFARE
Family has been referred to counselling around Joan
Medicare and A Disabled

WORK
Beth – part time

HEALTH CARE
City Hospital Clinic
John - MS for 10 years

CHURCH

EXTENDED FAMILY
Beth's mother demanding - ill - needs financial & emotional support

FAMILY OR HOUSEHOLD
JOHN 42
BETH 40
JOHN 19
GWEN 17
JOAN 15

Court & Probation Officer (Miss Thompson)

RECREATION
John very involved in sports - Father used to be

RECREATION
Beth involved in gardening & garden club

College
Senior-High
"Grind"
10th Grade
Friends in Trouble

EXTENDED FAMILY
Father's in Arkansas very little contact

SCHOOL

FRIENDS
Joan popular with "rough crowd"

Fill in connections where they exist.
Indicate nature of connections with a descriptive word or by drawing different kinds of lines;
——— for strong, – – – – – – for tenuous, +++++++ for stressful.
Draw arrows along lines to signify flow of energy, resources, etc. →→→
Identify significant people and fill in empty circles as needed.

SOURCE: Hartman, A. (1978). Diagrammatic assessment of family relationships. *Social Casework, 59,* pp. 465–476. 

FIGURE 2

## Detailed Genogram

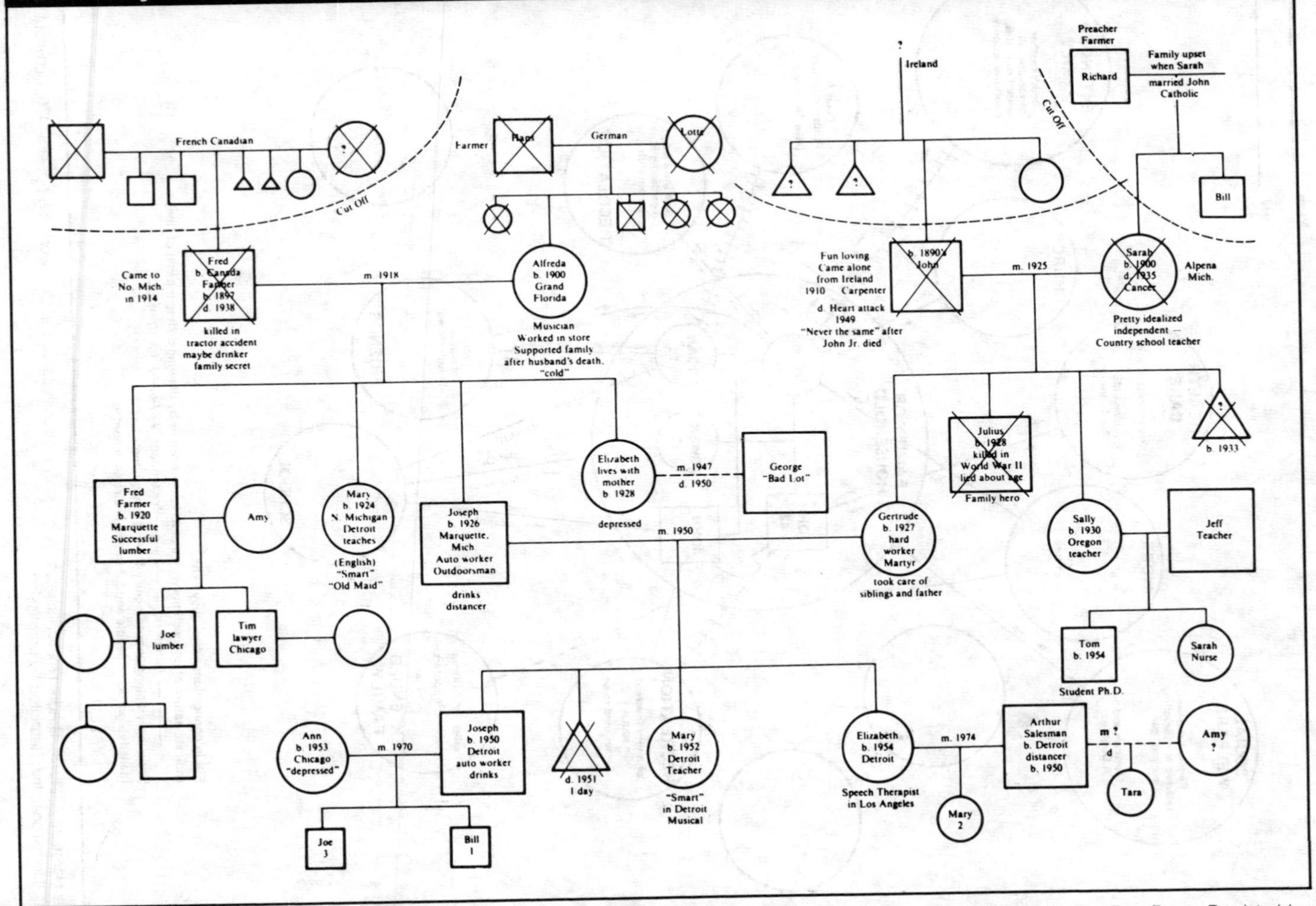

SOURCE: Hartman, A., & Laird, J. (1983). *Family-centered social work practice* (p. 218). New York: The Free Press. Copyright 1983 by The Free Press. Reprinted by permission.

tologies, are all too narrow for the scope of social work assessments. There are as yet no universally recognized classification schemes that encompass psychosocial events—no approaches that would inform social work practitioners about categories of events or processes on which their multilayered practice is based. For example, to identify a schoolchild as a truant does not help a social worker to know what the problem is or to predict outcomes. Research will have to discover empirically the many faces of truancy that could be related to illness, handicap, teachers, parents, friends, or internal conflict. The focus and conceptual boundaries of the prevalent classification approaches (for example, DSM-IV) reflect this dilemma; that is, a system may be descriptively adequate for the clinical purposes of dispensing medications or the administrative purposes of accountability, but too narrowly defined for social work purposes.

Even though the classification schemes available are imperfect for social workers' use, the need for them is not questioned (Mattaini & Kirk, 1991). Assessment is an individualizing process through which the practitioner attends only to the individual, family, or group with whom he or she is working. Although this is the way to know a client, it does not provide for the use of available knowledge to which the practitioner could refer to support his or her understanding of the client. This knowledge is built on grouped data; accumulated experience; and, to the extent possible, classification of problems, events, processes, or persons. The assessment process must draw on a relevant knowledge base, and classification is the most parsimonious way to organize that knowledge for use.

## Content of Assessment

Given the fact that social work is so multilayered in its purpose and focus, the content of assessment is, of course, extremely variable. What is deemed important to know about a client depends largely on the setting in which the client is seen and the presenting request or stated problem. It is neither necessary nor desirable for the practitioner to know "everything" about a client's (individual, family, or group) life to offer services and help. The principles of relevance and salience (Germain, 1968) should govern the pursuit of the content of a case. For example, when a patient needs help in making discharge plans from a hospital, it is obvious that the social worker will need to know about the patient's health care needs, normal lifestyle, support systems, and coping capacity. Yet, in a family services agency, where help with family conflict is the presenting request, the focus of information gathering will be more on the intimate family relationships of the individuals involved.

The narrowing of the content so it becomes more focused has gained significance in recent years because of the redrawing of social services owing to the reduction in economic supports. Managed health care is but one aspect of the national pressure both to reduce services and to make them more focused and thus "effective." Virtually no social work (or health) service today is recompensed for open-ended treatment; the modal time frame is brief, although the needs of chronically ill and disabled people, as well as homeless and anomic people, have required new intermittent (albeit brief) assessments over the life span. Although narrower, more focused assessments have value in that they maintain relevance and salience, there is the danger that they may be superficial and that significant information may be missed.

The emergence of planned short-term treatment has made it necessary for social workers to place greater reliance on the profession's general knowledge base to gain clues about client problems and effective interventions. For example, in planning with a pregnant teenager, it is efficient and appropriate to search the literature for the empirical epidemiological and clinical knowledge about teenage parents. What are these teenagers' ethnic, class, and cultural profiles? What happens to them if a certain intervention is used? What plans are known to have succeeded with one or another type of teenager? What typical resources are useful or not useful? The practitioner still makes an individualized assessment, but calls on his or her knowledge of the repertoire of interventions that may be empirically validated (Tolson, 1988).

## Method of Assessment

Assessment is the crucial professional activity on which all interventions are based, but it cannot be done without the full cognizance and participation of the client (Alcabes & Jones, 1985; Specht & Specht, 1986). Assessment is the process used by social workers (and all other professional helpers) to understand the case, but as both an ethical and a technical consideration, it cannot be carried out detached from the client, that is the individual, family, group, or community. It requires the client's voluntary agreement, input of the data of his or her life story, and a contract for the interventions that are being planned.

The method of assessment is exploratory, similar to methods used in all scientific investigations; it consists of the following steps:

1. Collection and organization of relevant case data. Most agencies provide some kind of outline or instrument for the systematic presentation of this information.
2. Inference, or the interpretation of the case data (or deriving meaning from the interaction of facts, events, relationships, feelings, behaviors, environmental influences, and so forth). The hallmark of professional skill rests in the practitioner's trained judgment (usually theory driven) about what is deemed significant in the client's story. It is in this part of the process that the social worker refers to the profession's knowledge base for help in understanding the client as representative of a classification of people with like problems or circumstances.
3. Evaluation of how the client is functioning, his or her capacities, strengths and weaknesses, and the resources that are available. This part of the process contributes to the individualizing focus of assessment because each client deals in a unique way with problems or circumstances that are defined in general terms in classification systems, for example.
4. Definition of the problem or problems to be addressed. In this part of the process, the practitioner and client together determine what in the situation is "doable" in the particular setting with the resources that are available.
5. Intervention or treatment planning. In this final step of the process, decisions have to be made about the time frame (brief, intermittent, or open ended), the intervention or treatment modality (individual, family, or group), the focus of attention among all the variables in the case, and the expected outcomes.

This process, once called study, diagnosis, and treatment, is now called exploration, assessment, and intervention—concepts that are more in keeping with the demedicalized and broader focus of social work practice (Meyer, 1970). Although it has been described here in steps, in actual practice the process is telescoped, particularly when time pressures require it.

## Conclusion

Assessment is the fundamental process in all professional activity (Abbott, 1988), for it is the way in which a professional person learns to understand the client before taking action. Administrative pressures to act quickly have generated efforts to develop assessment instruments to accelerate the process, and much has been written about rapid assessments. The use of computer systems and pretested instruments undoubtedly will proliferate, but some caution is indicated. When it comes to people working with people, it is never possible to achieve absolute certainty in the assessment process, which is always unfolding and subject to new information and changing circumstances. The process is always constrained by the social worker's skill, biases, judgments, and knowledge (Nurius & Gibson, 1990), as well as by the client's motivation and capacities. Assessment remains a clinical process as long as it is concerned with individualizing a case. Mechanical aids can be useful, but to the extent that they draw on what is generally known, they must always be adapted to the particular case, so that they fulfill the individualizing purposes of assessment.

## References


Abbott, A. (1988). *The system of professions: An essay on the division of expert labor.* Chicago: University of Chicago Press.

Alcabes, A., & Jones, J. (1985). Structural determinants of clienthood. *Social Work, 30,* 49–53.

Allen-Meares, P., & Lane, B. A. (1987). Grounding social work practice in theory: Ecosystems. *Social Casework, 68,* 517–521.

American Psychiatric Association. (1994). *Diagnostic and statistical manual of mental disorders* (4th ed.). Washington, DC: Author.

Auerswald, E. H. (1968). Interdisciplinary vs. ecological approach. *Family Process, 7,* 202–215.

Bartlett, H. (1970). *The common base of social work practice.* Silver Spring, MD: National Association of Social Workers.

Beck, A. (1991). *The Beck Depression Inventory manual.* San Antonio, TX: Psychological Corp.

Buffum, W. E. (1988). Measuring person–environment fit in nursing homes. *Journal of Social Service Research, 11*(2–3), 35–54.

Bunston, T. (1985). Mapping practice: Problem-solving in clinical social work. *Social Casework, 66,* 225–236.

Cheers, B. (1987). The social support network map as an educational tool. *Australian Social Work, 40,* 18–24.

Chinn, J. L. (1983). Diagnostic considerations in working with Asian-Americans. *American Journal of Orthopsychiatry, 53,* 100–109.

Corcoran, K., & Fischer, J. (1987). *Measures for clinical practice: A sourcebook.* New York: Free Press.

Coulton, C. (1979). Developing an instrument to measure person–environment fit. *Journal of Social Service Research, 3,* 159–174.

Coulton, C. (1981). Person–environment fit as the focus in health care. *Social Work, 26,* 26–35.

Edelson, J. L. (1985). Rapid assessment instruments for evaluating practice with children and youth. *Journal of Social Service Research, 8,* 17–31.

Epstein, N. B., Baldwin, L. M., & Bishop, D. S. (1983). The McMaster family assessment device. *Journal of Marital and Family Therapy, 9,* 171–180.

Erdman, H. P., & Foster, S. W. (1987). A review of computer diagnosis in psychiatry with special emphasis on DSM-III. *Computers in Human Services, 2*(1–2), 1–11.

Erdman, H. P., & Foster, S. W. (1988). Ethical issues in the use of computer-based assessment. *Computers in Human Services, 3*(1–2), 71–87.

Fandetti, D. V., & Goldmeier, J. (1988). Social workers as culture mediators in health care settings. *Health & Social Work, 13,* 171–179.

Franklin, D. L. (1985). Differential clinical assessments: The influence of class and race. *Social Service Review, 59,* 44–61.

Gambrill, E. (1983). *Casework: A competency based approach.* Englewood Cliffs, NJ: Prentice Hall.

Germain, C. B. (1968). Social study: Past and future. *Social Casework, 49,* 403–409.

Germain, C. B., & Gitterman, A. (1980). *The life model of social work practice.* New York: Columbia University Press.

Germain, C. B., & Gitterman, A. (1986). The life model approach to social work practice revisited. In F. Turner (Ed.), *Social work treatment* (pp. 618–644). New York: Free Press.

Goldstein, E. (1984). *Ego psychology and social work practice.* New York: Columbia University Press.

Gottlieb, B. H. (1985). Assessing and strengthening the impact of social support on mental health. *Social Work, 30,* 293–300.

Hamilton, G. (1951). *Theory and practice of social casework* (rev. ed.). New York: Columbia University Press. (Original work published 1940)

Hartman, A. (1978). Diagrammatic assessment of family relationships. *Social Casework, 59,* 465–476.

Hartman, A., & Laird, J. (1983). *Family-centered social work practice.* New York: Free Press.

Hess, P., & Howard, T. (1981). An ecological model for assessing psychosocial difficulties in children. *Child Welfare, 60,* 499–523.

Hollis, F. H. (1964). *Casework: A psycho-social therapy.* New York: Random House.

Hudson, W. W. (1982). *The Clinical Measurement Package: A field manual.* Homewood, IL: Dorsey Press.

Hudson, W. W. (1984). *The Clinical Assessment System.* Tallahassee, FL: WALMYR.

Hudson, W. W., Nurius, P. S., & Reisman, S. (1988). Computerized assessment instruments: Their promise and problems. *Computers in Human Services, 3*(1–2), 51–70.

Karls, J. M., & Wandrei, K. (1986, September 12). *Beyond DSM-III: Where psychiatry ends and social work begins.* Paper presented at NASW Clinical Conference, San Francisco.

Kutchins, H., & Kirk, S. A. (1986). The reliability of DSM-III: A critical review. *Social Work Research & Abstracts, 22*(4), 3–12.

Laird, J. (1984). Sorcerers, shamans, and social workers. *Social Work, 29,* 123–129.

Levine, R. S. (1984). An assessment tool for early intervention in cases of truancy. *Social Work in Education, 6,* 133–150.

Levitt, J. L. & Reid, W. J., (1981). Rapid assessment instruments for practice. *Social Work Research & Abstracts, 17*(1), 13–19.

Lowry, F. (1938). Current concepts in social casework practice. *Social Service Review, 12,* 571–597.

Mailick, M., & Vigilante, F. W. (1987). Human behavior and the social environment: A sequence providing the theoretical base for teaching assessment. *Journal of Teaching in Social Work, 1,* 33–47.

Mattaini, M. (1990). Contextual behavior analysis in the assessment process. *Families in Society, 71,* 236–245.

Mattaini, M. (1993a). *More than a thousand words: Graphics for clinical practice.* Washington, DC: NASW Press.

Mattaini, M. (1993b). *Visual EcoScan for clinical practice.* Washington, DC: NASW Press.

Mattaini, M., & Kirk, S. A. (1991). Assessing assessment in social work. *Social Work, 36,* 260–266.

McGoldrick, M., & Gerson, R. (1985). *Genograms in family assessment.* New York: W. W. Norton.

Meyer, C. H. (1970). *Social work practice: A response to the urban crisis.* New York: Free Press.

Meyer, C. H. (1976). *Social work practice: The changing landscape.* New York: Free Press.

Meyer, C. H. (1983). *Clinical social work in an eco-systems perspective.* New York: Columbia University Press.

Meyer, C. H. (1993). *Assessment in social work practice.* New York: Columbia University Press.

Minuchin, S. (1974). *Families and family therapy.* Cambridge, MA: Harvard University Press.

Moos, R., & Moos, B. (1986). *The Family Environment Scale manual.* Palo Alto, CA: Consulting Psychologists Press.

National Council of State Consultants for School Social Work. (1981). That school social work assessment. *School Social Work Journal, 6,* 51–54.

Nurius, P. S., & Gibson, J. (1990). Clinical observation, inference, reasoning, and judgment in social work: An update. *Social Work Research & Abstracts, 26*(2), 18–25.

Nurius, P. S., & Hudson, W. W. (1988). Computer-based practice: Future dream or current technology? *Social Work, 33,* 357–362.

Olson, D. H. (1986). The circumplex model VII: Validation studies and FACES III. *Family Process, 25,* 337–351.

Perlman, H. H. (1957). *Social casework: A problem-solving process.* Chicago: University of Chicago Press.

Perlmutter, R. A., & Jones, J. E. (1985). Assessment of families in psychiatric emergencies. *American Journal of Orthopsychiatry, 55,* 130–139.

Richmond, M. E. (1917). *Social diagnosis.* New York: Russell Sage Foundation.

Robinson, V. (1930). *A changing psychology of social casework.* Chapel Hill: University of North Carolina Press.

Rose, S. D. (1981). Assessment in groups. *Social Work Research & Abstracts, 17*(1), 29–37.

Sheffield, A. (1937). *Social insight in case situations.* New York: D. Appleton-Century.

Specht, H., & Specht, R. (1986). Social work assessment: Route to clienthood. Parts I and II. *Social Casework, 67,* 525–532, 587–593.

Streeter, C. L., & Franklin, C. (1992). Defining and measuring social support: Guidelines for social workers. *Research on Social Work Practice, 2*(1), 81–98.

Stewart, R. P. (1988). Social work practice in a high-tech era. *Computers in Human Services, 3*(1–2), 9–21.

Taft, J. (1936). The relation of function to process in social casework. *Journal of Social Work Process 1,* 1–18.

Thyer, B. (1988). Radical behaviorism and clinical social work. In R. Dorfman (Ed.), *Paradigms of clinical social work* (pp. 123–148). New York: Brunner/Mazel.

Tolson, E. R. (1988). *The meta-model and clinical social work.* New York: Columbia University Press.

Toseland, R. W., & Reid, W. J. (1985). Using rapid assessment instruments in a family service agency. *Social Casework, 66,* 547–555.

Tracy, E. M., & Whittaker, J. K. (1990). The social network map: Assessing social support in clinical practice. *Families in Society, 71*, 461–470.

Turner, F. (1974). Psychosocial therapy. In F. Turner (Ed.), *Social work treatment: Interlocking theoretical approaches* (pp. 84–111). New York: Free Press.

Turner, F. (1988). Psychosocial therapy. In R. Dorfman (Ed.), *Paradigms of clinical social work* (pp. 106–122). New York: Brunner/Mazel.

Van Treuren, R. R. (1986). Self-perception in family systems: A diagrammatic technique. *Social Casework, 67*(9), 299–305.

Vigilante, F. W., & Mailick, M. D. (1988). Needs-resource evaluation in the assessment process. *Social Work, 33,* 101–104.

**Carol H. Meyer, DSW,** is Norman Professor of Family and Child Welfare, Columbia University, School of Social Work, 622 West 113th Street, New York, NY 10025.

## For further information see

Clinical Social Work; Computer Utilization; Diagnostic and Statistical Manual of Mental Disorders; Direct Practice Overview; Ecological Perspective; Expert Systems; Goal Setting and Intervention Planning; Information Systems; Interviewing; Person-in-Environment; Psychometrics; Recording; Research Overview; Single-System Design; Social Work Practice: Theoretical Base; Social Work Profession Overview; Social Work Profession: History.

**Key Words**

assessment
diagnosis
direct practice
ecosystems

# B

## Baby Boomers

**Eric Kingson**

This entry describes the heterogeneity of the baby boom cohorts, the 76 million people born in the United States between 1946 and 1964. The entry distinguishes between cohorts, age groups, and generations and then discusses diverging theories about the origins and implications of the baby boom cohorts. Next, the social and economic characteristics of the baby boom cohorts are reviewed, and challenges for policy and practice in responding to the middle-aging and eventual old-aging of baby boomers are discussed.

Too often, social policies are based on problem definitions or stereotypes that do not acknowledge the diversity of various population groups, resulting in singular approaches to perceived social problems when pluralistic approaches would be more effective. Stereotypic thinking about the baby boom generation provides a case in point. Popular images of baby boomers as privileged "yuppies" or as an entire population at risk of economic calamity in old age overlook the great variety of circumstances among the 76 million people born between 1946 and 1964. There is a danger that policy and social interventions will proceed without adequate attention to the diverse needs and strengths of people among the baby boom cohorts. Of special importance to the social work profession is the possibility that failure to recognize the heterogeneity of the baby boom cohorts will result in less attention being paid to issues of concern to those at greatest risk.

This entry identifies the need for a pluralistic approach to the aging of the baby boom cohorts. Such an approach might best be built on expectations of continuing contribution to family, community, and the economy for the vast majority of boomers as they move through their middle and elder years, taking into account the need to address challenges to health and financial well-being, particularly for people with low incomes or otherwise at risk.

### Definitions

Baby boomers, a group often discussed as a distinct generation, are more appropriately viewed as members of a series of cohorts. Although the demography surrounding the baby boom cohorts has and will continue to have important consequences, many factors must be incorporated into assessments of their present and future well-being.

#### Generations

Because of overlaps in meaning, and because these terms are sometimes used interchangeably, it is important to clarify differences among the terms "generation," "age group," and "birth cohort." The term "generation," as used in literary, popular, and academic discourse, has multiple meanings. It is used variously to mean position of vertical lineage within families (for example, grandparents), people involved (or potentially involved) in a social movement in which age consciousness is important, people currently in a particular age group (for example, elderly people), and people born in a common birth cohort (Bengston, Cutler, Mangen, & Marshall, 1985).The term "generation," as used to define lineage within a family, provides a concept that encourages exploration of relationships within families and how roles, resources, and values are transmitted within the context of families. This concept is sometimes extended as a basis for discussing the "relationships between age groups at the macrosocial level (Bengston et al., 1985, p. 307).

Often, discussions of the baby boomers assume a common identity, shared ideology, or sense of purpose forged by the unique common timing of birth and a common history. In this context, the term "generation" denotes a self-conscious group or subunit of a birth cohort that shares common political concerns or goals (for example, the youthful protesters of the 1960s). A difficulty in applying this concept of generation to the baby boom cohorts is the tendency to assume that all members of this vast group share a common outlook. For instance, in the 1960s and early 1970s, baby boomers were often described as rebellious, although most of them were not involved in the political movements of the times and many were too young to have political involvements of any sort.

**Birth Cohorts and Age Groups**

*Birth cohorts* (also called age cohorts or simply cohorts) consist of people born during roughly the same time period and usually are defined in terms of five or 10 years (Bengston et al., 1985). Members of a cohort move through time together, and as they age they also move through different *age groups*—that is, classifications made according to age at a particular point in time (Daniels, 1988). For instance, today's younger cohorts of baby boomers—people ages 30 to 39 in 1994—are arguably still members of the young adult age group, whereas the older members of the baby boom cohorts—people ages 40 to 48 in 1994—are part of the early-middle-age group. Having been born at roughly the same time, people in the same birth cohort share a common set of early historical circumstances that may shape their attitudes and actions throughout life, although commonality in attitudes and actions may also be a function of aging or of a historical period that affects many birth cohorts in a similar manner (see Bengston et al., 1985).

In this entry, baby boomers are discussed as members of a series of cohorts. It is not appropriate to classify 76 million people as part of a 19-year cohort or to assume commonality of attitudes and goals within this large group. A focus on variations within the baby boomer population as a whole and, more specifically, on intracohort variations leads to more attention being placed on issues of race, ethnicity, gender, and class.

**Baby Boom Phenomenon**

The year 1946 marks the beginning of a 19-year period of high birth rates combined with a large number of annual births. By the end of 1964, the year generally accepted as the end of the trend, some 17 million more people were born than would have been born had the fertility patterns of the early 1940s prevailed (C. Russell, 1987). As the baby boom cohorts moved from the nurseries to the schools and then into the employment and housing markets, the size of these cohorts created strains, opportunities, and adjustments.

**Anticipated Impact**

In recent years, public attention has begun to focus on the implications of the millions of baby boomers that eventually will swell the ranks of the old and the very old segments of the population. After 2010, the first of the baby boomers will reach age 65. Their large numbers, combined with relative declines in the size of the traditional working-age population and with lengthening life expectancies, will bring about a change in the nation's age structure. The U.S. Bureau of the Census has projected that 20.2 percent of the population (69.8 million people) will be age 65 or over by 2030, the year all surviving baby boomers reach ages 66 through 84 (Day, 1992). Perhaps more significant, the bureau has projected that the very old—people 85 and over—will constitute 4.6 percent of the total population (17.7 million people) in 2050, the year in which all surviving baby boomers reach ages 86 through 104. These figures represent roughly a doubling of the projected numbers of the estimated 65-and-over population (33.6 million) in 1995 and almost a fivefold increase in the estimated numbers of people age 85 and over (3.6 million) in 1995. As percentages of the total population, the anticipated increases in the elderly and very old populations from 1990 through 2050 are almost as great.

The middle-aging of the baby boom cohorts seems likely to strain public and private health and disability protection mechanisms and create new pressures with regard to policies affecting older workers and early retirement. Similarly, nearly all analysts agree that the old-aging of baby boomers will strain retirement, health care, and other societal institutions, and some (Moody, 1988) have suggested that baby boomers' old-aging will present new opportunities and needs for lifelong learning and contribution to society. Substantial differences have been expressed, however, about the extent to which the United States will be able to respond to baby boomers' age-related needs while still addressing the needs of other groups.

**Causes of the Phenomenon**

A review of differing explanations about the causes of the baby boom cohorts lends perspective to these differences.

***Demographics.*** The demographic explanations are the most straightforward. The rate at which women of childbearing age have children is primarily responsible for the age structure of society, including the baby boom and the baby bust that followed. Before the late 1930s, birth rates had declined steadily for more than 100 years, from an estimated 55 births per 1,000 population in 1820 to about 19 per 1,000 population in the 1930s (L. B. Russell, 1982). Figure 1 indicates how, after declining steadily, the total fertility rate per thousand women of childbearing age increased suddenly beginning in 1946 and 1947 and remained higher than 3,000 through 1964. Then the total fertility rate fell to a historical low in the late 1970s, with modest increases occurring from 1985 to 1994.

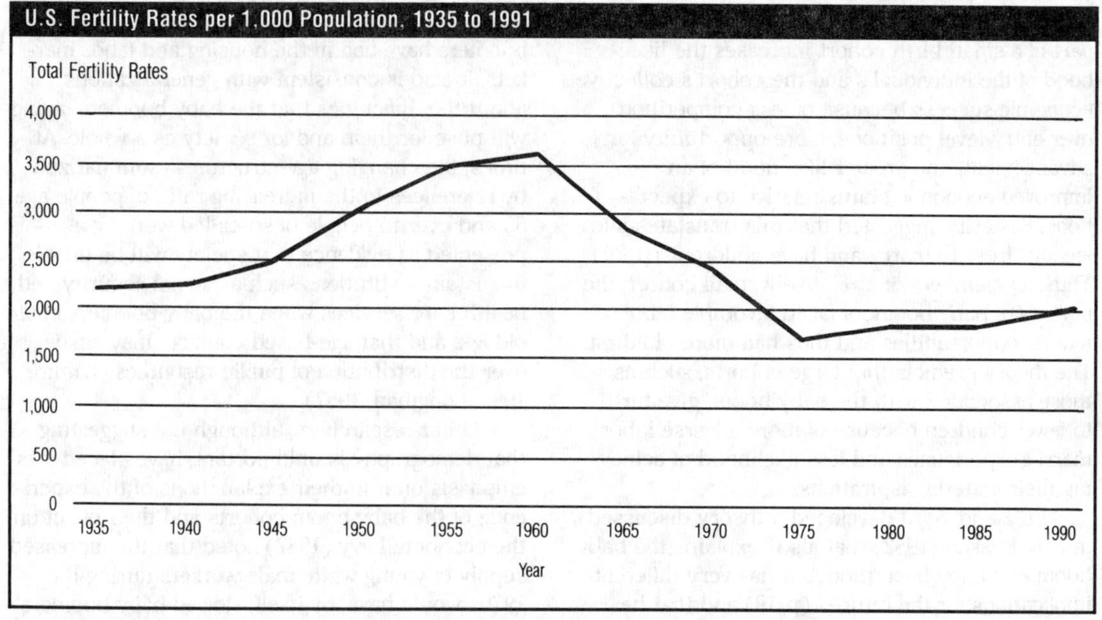


FIGURE 1
U.S. Fertility Rates per 1,000 Population, 1935 to 1991

SOURCE: Social Security Administration, Office of the Actuary. (1990). *Projections: 1989*. Baltimore: Author.

NOTE: The total fertility rate is the average number of children that would be born to a woman if she were to survive the childbearing period and were to experience the age-specific central birth rates for the tabulated year throughout that period.

The demographic explanation for this rise in fertility rates is that more women were marrying and having children, women were having slightly larger families (Bean, 1983), and women were having children earlier. Women born during the later 1920s and 1930s married at a higher rate than did previous cohorts of women; for example, 96 percent of those born in the 1930s married, compared with 92 percent of those born from 1900 through 1909. Moreover, a small percentage of women who married remained childless—7 percent for the 1930s cohort compared with 14 percent for the 1900–1909 cohort (L. B. Russell, 1982). Although the proportion of women who had five or more children declined among the mothers of baby boomers, the average family size actually increased, because proportionally more of these women had two to four children (Bean). Moreover, because the mothers of baby boomers had children earlier than the immediately preceding cohorts, this timing effect contributed to the population bulge (Bean; L. B. Russell).

***Cultural changes.*** No one explanation about the cause of the baby boom phenomenon is sufficient. The initial increase in the fertility rate from 1945 through 1947—which resulted in 1 million more babies being born in 1947 than in 1945—may best be explained by the end of World War II in 1945 and society's ensuing return to normalcy. The end of the war, however, does not account for the continuation of the boom into the 1950s and early 1960s (Light, 1988).

Jones (1980) emphasized cultural changes as contributing to the baby boom, suggesting that "the flush of military victory, the staggering prosperity, the renewed faith in the future—combined in the postwar years to create what can be called the Procreation Ethic" (p. 22), which encouraged marriage and conventionally sized families of two to four children. Child rearing and full-time homemaking were the hallmarks of the socially prescribed feminine role of the 1950s, and financial support was the hallmark of the masculine role. C. Russell (1987) suggested that the "euphoria following World War II, the early marriages, the boom of births, and the beliefs in authority all made domesticity a fad and then fashion of the times" (p. 36). Thus, as Light (1988) suggested, what the war may have started, social conformity and pro-child values continued. Moreover, the economic growth of the postwar years meant that the economic outlook for people contemplating families and children was generally improving.

***Economic influences.*** Easterlin (1987) developed a theory that suggests that, given low levels of immigration, small birth cohorts such as those born in the 1930s generally have larger families and vice versa. According to this theory, being part of a small birth cohort increases the likelihood of the individual's and the cohort's collective economic success because of less competition over entry-level positions, more opportunity for advancement, and greater likelihood of an improved economic status relative to expectations. Easterlin suggested that this translates into feeling "freer to marry and have children" (p. 39). Thus, as members of a relatively small cohort, the parents of baby boomers faced favorable labor market opportunities and thus had more children. The theory predicts that large cohorts, such as those associated with the baby boom, give birth to fewer children because of more adverse labor market experiences and less likelihood of achieving their material aspirations.

Butz and Ward developed a theory discussed in L. B. Russell (1982) that also "explains the baby boom and baby bust, though it has very different implications for the future," (p. 19) and that has stood up to some statistical analysis:

> They argue that a couple will have more children when the husband's income is high, but that decisions about the number and timing of births will also be affected by the wife's earnings. If the wife's earnings are high, the cost of dropping out of the labor market to have and raise children is correspondingly high, and the couple will have fewer children. In the affluent 1950s, when relatively few women held jobs, the effect of husbands' incomes dominated, and couples had larger families and had them sooner. But as rising real wages drew more and more women into the labor market, women's earnings became more important and began to outweigh the effect of husbands' incomes. The birth rate dropped. (pp. 19–20)

### Relationship to Social and Economic Events

Differing views about the origins of the baby boom often lead to different emphases on the extent to which their size versus their historical timing are used to explain their life course experiences and their relationship to social and economic events. These views may color the extent to which the demography of the baby boom cohorts is seen as driving retirement outcomes as well as our understanding of the diversity of these cohorts.

One position, perhaps best exemplified by Easterlin's carefully developed thesis, can be characterized as "demography is destiny." As Easterlin (1987) put it, "for those fortunate enough to be members of a small generation, life is—as a general matter—disproportionately good; the opposite is true for those who are members of a large generation" (p. 39). This view provides a basis for explaining the difficulties that groups of baby boomers have had in the housing and labor markets. It also is consistent with generalizations about the difficulties that the baby boomers' aging will pose for them and for society as a whole. At times, the changing age structure—summarized by references to the increasing ratio of people age 65 and over to people of so-called working age—is presented as evidence that society will be unable to sustain institutions such as social security and health care services when the baby boomers enter old age and that age-based conflicts may ensue over the distribution of public resources (Lamm, 1985; Longman, 1987).

Other researchers, although not suggesting that demography is unimportant, have placed less emphasis on it in their explanations of the experience of the baby boom cohorts and their effect on the economy. Levy (1987) noted that the increased supply of young white male workers during the 1970s would have, by itself, slowed baby boomers' wage progress relative to that experienced by their parents' cohorts. However, he suggested that the economic stagnation from 1973 through 1985 (and possibly beyond) is principally responsible for undermining the progress of these baby boomers, relative to older workers and in absolute terms. Similarly, L. B. Russell (1982) argued that age structure as an explanation for economic and other societal outcomes "has sometimes been important, but, in the postwar years, never dominant" (p. 170). Thus, rather than having fewer opportunities because of potential strains posed by increased numbers, baby boomers in general have had more opportunity for education as well as for a better quality of education. Similarly, Aaron, Bosworth, and Burtless (1989) concluded that the increased cost of social security and Medicare hospital insurance benefits for the baby boom need not create a greater burden on future workers than current ones if a policy is pursued that uses social security surpluses for increased national savings while also reducing deficits in general revenues of the federal government. Plainly, this perspective would discount the extent to which demographic trends by themselves lead to unfortunate retirements for baby boomers and negative economic consequences.

## Diversity of the Baby Boom Cohorts

Although Light (1988) was not the first to distinguish among various groups of baby boomers, his analysis contributed much to an understanding of its diversity. Light identified important cleavages within the baby boom cohorts, including splits by

(1) early versus late boomers, (2) gender, (3) race, (4) amount of education, (5) income position, (6) Vietnam veterans versus protesters, (7) married versus unmarried, (8) working versus not working, and (9) geographic region. Add differences by ethnicity, immigration status, health, pension coverage, religion, and sexual preference, and it becomes clear that baby boomers are not a homogeneous group.

**Age**

Plainly, baby boomers differ by age. For example, some were 17 when the nation lost John F. Kennedy, whereas others had not been born. When the oldest members reach age 65, the youngest will still be in early middle age. As others have also pointed out, new-wave baby boomers are more likely to be at risk during their retirement years than are old-wave boomers (Bouvier & DeVita, 1991; Congressional Budget Office, 1993; Light, 1988). The older ones (born in 1946 to 1954) are more likely to have entered the labor force during favorable periods, to have benefited from relatively low housing costs, to be homeowners, and to have relatively higher rates of private pension coverage and the like (Light, 1988). The new-wave boomers are more likely to be affected by any shrinkage in public and private retirement income systems and are more likely to be paying more for housing (Soldo & Agree, 1988).

**Race and Ethnicity**

About 18 million baby boomers are members of "minorities at risk"—groups that by virtue of their racial or ethnic status experience barriers that significantly restrict their opportunities for social and economic well-being. Most were born in the United States and some have since emigrated to the United States. Approximately 9.5 million African Americans, 6.1 million Hispanics, and 2.8 million people of other races fall into the baby boomer age categories. Because Hispanics are distributed across all racial categories, these three figures are not additive (see Kingson, 1992; Spencer, 1986).

It is important to appreciate the diversity within each of these broad population classifications. For example, among Hispanic baby boomers approximately 60 percent are of Mexican origin (Chicanos), 12.6 percent are of Puerto Rican origin, 4.7 percent are of Cuban origin, 14.1 percent are of Central and South American origin, and 8.6 percent are of other Hispanic origin (DeNavas, 1989). Similarly, Asian Americans trace their origins to many countries, and Native Americans are distributed across 312 federally recognized tribes and more than 200 other identifiable tribes.

In addition to important differences of culture, there are often intergroup differences. As Torres-Gil (1986) pointed out, when ranking Chicanos, Cubans, and Puerto Ricans according to their well-being in terms of education, income position, and unemployment, Puerto Ricans tend to be least well off, Mexican Americans in the middle, and Cubans most well off. There is no doubt that among recent emigres, those from Central American nations—especially those who are undocumented—are among the most vulnerable within the Hispanic baby boom cohorts. It is also important to recognize the vast differences existing within each subclassification of baby boomers who are minorities at risk. Thus, among African Americans ages 25 to 34 in 1988, it is estimated that 13.1 percent had four years of college or more, whereas 19.5 percent had less than four years of high school (Bennett & Cowles, 1989).

The distribution of goods and services varies over the life course by race and minority status. Published data on the poverty rate for people ages 22 to 44 in 1988—a categorization that includes people born from 1944 through 1966—provide a close approximation of the percent of baby boomers below the U.S. poverty threshold. Among African American baby boomers, roughly 23.6 percent had incomes in 1988 that were below the poverty level, compared with approximately 20.6 percent of Hispanic baby boomers and 8.4 percent of white baby boomers (U.S. Bureau of the Census, 1989). Plainly, the implications of such differences in the distribution of resources by race and ethnicity must be taken into account when thinking about the aging of the baby boom cohorts. Similarly, failure to take into account different cultural norms and expectations when planning human services can result in policies and programs that are not acceptable to many groups.

Baby boomers will age as part of a cohort that is more diverse than the current cohort of elderly people with respect to race and ethnicity. As such, their aging will change the demographic composition of elderly populations of the future. As the baby boom cohorts age, the proportion of minority elders will increase from about 14 percent in 1994 to 35 percent in 2050 (Day, 1992), and there will be fewer first- and second-generation European elders relative to 1994. Overall, there will be an increasing need for policymakers to assess how various program and policy changes affect groups differently.

**Family Life**

Diversity and change are the hallmarks of family life for baby boomers. As a group, their family life is characterized by (1) changes in the institution of marriage and the family, (2) diversity of family forms, (3) high likelihood of transition through several forms of family life, (4) fewer children, (5) changing patterns of caregiving to children, and (6) changing and increasingly complex relationships with kin networks. Wattenberg (1986) suggested that baby boomers redefined the traditional family and "set records for a variety of living arrangements that reshaped the definition of families and household composition" (p. 20). It is estimated that a higher proportion (roughly 10 percent, compared with 5 percent of their parents' generation) will never marry (U.S. House of Representatives, 1987). Many members of the baby boom cohorts have postponed having children, had smaller families, divorced more frequently, and raised more children in single-parent households (Saluter, 1989). About half of the marriages of baby boomers are expected to end in divorce, but three-quarters of these people are expected to remarry (Cherlin & Furstenberg, 1982).

Thus, kinship patterns are more complex, and with this complexity come questions of who is responsible for parental and step-parental care (Hagestad, 1986). Fewer children, the increased labor force participation of women, and greater likelihood of parents living longer mean that many baby boomers are likely to have less of a kinship system to rely on for informal support, though this may be partially offset by the presence of more siblings. Again, some will do fine; others—such as divorced single men, who are more likely to become isolated from their children—may be at substantial risk.

Low-income single parents among the baby boom cohorts are likely to be at great risk in the future. The growth of single-parent families is attributable first to divorce and separation and second to births by unmarried parents (Cherlin & Furstenberg, 1982). A small proportion are the result of the death of one parent. Single parenthood has doubled since 1970 to encompass 27 percent of all families with children under age 18 in 1988. Twenty-two percent of white families, 59 percent of African American families, and 34 percent of Hispanic families are headed by a single parent (Saluter, 1989). Seven of eight single parents responsible for young children are women. Single-parent families headed by men have, on average, two-thirds the median income of two-parent families, whereas single-parent families headed by women have, on average, about one-third the median income of two-parent families (Rawlings, 1989). The situation is worse for single-parent families with children under age six; moreover, the child-care responsibilities are obviously much greater (Kamerman & Kahn, 1988; Saluter, 1989).

For baby boomers who are single parents, economic and family responsibilities usually leave little room for employment training and advancement, leisure, or retirement savings (Kamerman & Kahn, 1988). Moreover, the children of such baby boomers are substantially more likely to be at risk of receiving less-than-adequate health care, education, and preparation for productive employment—concerns that have implications for their future productivity as a group and that, on an individual level, may affect their ability to provide care or financial support to baby boomers who may need such support in advanced old age.

**Education**

With respect to education, the baby boom cohorts have already done considerably better than previous generations (C. Russell, 1987; L. B. Russell, 1982; U.S. House of Representatives, 1987), but here, too, there is much diversity. Although nearly one-quarter of baby boomers have completed four years of college, more than three million have not gone beyond the eighth grade (Siegel, 1989). Again, minority and younger baby boomers have generally not done as well (DeNavas, 1989; L. B. Russell, 1982; Siegel, 1989). One implication here may be the need to consider an employment and training strategy for the most vulnerable baby boomers and to seek ways to expand lifelong learning opportunities.

**Employment and Income**

The employment and income story is not simple. On the one hand, baby boomers generally have earnings at least as high as those of nonboomers at similar points in their life course (Congressional Budget Office, 1993; L. B. Russell, 1982), and large numbers of new jobs have been added as they entered the labor force (L. B. Russell). On the other hand, baby boomers' work years have coincided with slowed economic growth, stagnant wages, and the loss of manufacturing jobs, resulting in failed expectations of economic progress (Levy, 1988). From 1965 to 1985, a time during which nearly all baby boomers entered the labor force, the economy was able to absorb most of the new workers. However, the unemployment rates—especially for the youngest baby boomers in the labor force during certain years and for minority baby boomers—were high, and the job advancement prospects were more limited. Young minority members of the baby boom, in particular, experienced extraordinarily high rates of unemployment. For example, in 1983—a year the economy was beginning to recover from a deep recession—the unemployment rate for African Americans ages 16 to 19 was 48.5 percent and for African Americans ages 20 to 24 it was 31.4 percent (Jones, 1980).

Although there is little agreement on the causes of slowed economic and wage growth and increased inequality (Bluestone & Harrison, 1986; Levy, 1987), there is little doubt that these changes have had disproportionate effects on baby boomers as a group and on certain groups of baby boomers. In particular, it appears that female baby boomers heading families with children, African American and Hispanic baby boomers, and baby boomers with limited educations have been particularly disadvantaged by the combined phenomena of slowed wage growth and increased inequality. Stagnant wages seem to have had the greatest effect on men, particularly men without high school diplomas. Levy's (1987) analysis showed that the changes in annual earnings from 1973 to 1986 were felt most by men ages 25 to 34 with four years of high school education who worked full-time year-round. Annual earnings for this group, which consists entirely of people born toward the middle and end of the baby boom, declined on average by 16 percent from 1973 to 1986. This analysis provides a warning that within the baby boom the prospects for men with less education are not as great as they were for the male cohorts who preceded them. Similarly, during this same period, Levy noted that African American women made considerable progress, whereas "black men began to divide, with many doing very well and others dropping out of the labor force altogether, a behavior that in part reflected a developing underclass" (p. 10).

Given that the trend in income distribution since the mid-1970s has been toward greater inequality, it is not surprising that many baby boomers are doing quite well and many others are not. Among the 39.1 million men ages 25 to 44 in 1989, 6.7 million (17.1 percent) reported that they earned less than $10,000 in 1988, whereas 7.2 million (18.3 percent) reported incomes of at least $40,000. In contrast, among the 40 million women in these age groups, 18.5 million (46.4 percent) reported incomes under $10,000, whereas 1.5 million (3.7 percent) reported incomes of at least $40,000. The incomes of people in the older age categories—who are in their prime earning years—are generally higher than those in the younger groups.

It also is not surprising that about 11 percent of all baby boomers had below-poverty incomes in 1991 (see U.S. Bureau of the Census, 1992) and that about 45 percent of the more than 5 million single female baby boomers heading families with children in 1991 had below-poverty incomes.

## Housing

The inequality that exists in the income distribution of baby boomers is being further magnified by the inequality of wealth accumulation opportunities between baby boomers who are household renters and owners and between owners who purchased housing early enough to be on the receiving end of the housing market's appreciation windfalls and those who did not. Review of these patterns suggests greater disparities within the baby boom cohorts as a whole relative to past generations. It also suggests that younger baby boomers are, on average, less advantaged with respect to housing and potential equity than older baby boomers and that large numbers will be entering their retirement years with little or no equity (Sternlieb & Hughes, 1982). In general, the likelihood that economic security will be improved by home-equity accrual is diminished for the members of the baby boom cohorts, especially for the approximately 3.5 million low-income renters (see Apgar, DiPasquale, McArdle, & Olson, 1990).

Baby boomers entered the housing market during a period of rapidly increasing costs for purchases and rentals. Even so, some baby boomers are very well housed, especially the older ones who caught the first wave of appreciation (L. B. Russell, 1982). Over the entire period in which baby boomers entered the housing market, however, homeownership rates fell—primarily from 1980 to 1988—relative to past cohorts in all age categories that include baby boomers (see Apgar et al., 1990). This was true for married and unmarried baby boomers. For 25- to 34-year-old married couples with children, the rate fell from 71.1 percent in 1980 to 62.7 percent in 1988; for young couples without children, the rate fell from 58.3 percent to 53.5 percent (Apgar et al., 1990). The decline was great for nearly all baby boomer age classifications: Homeownership rates dropped from 43.3 percent in 1980 to 36.2 percent in 1988 for people ages 25 to 29, from 61.1 percent to 52.6 percent for people ages 30 to 34, and from 70.8 to 63.2 percent for people ages 35 to 39. On average, the older baby boomers have done better than the younger ones to the extent that they were able to purchase housing at a time when prices and interest rates were both low, and they also caught the wave of appreciation in housing of the late 1970s and 1980s. When the baby boomers are ready to retire, it is likely that the older ones will again be at an advantage, although obviously there is much variance of equity accrual within all baby boom cohorts (Steinlieb & Hughes, 1982). When they retire, many will sell large houses and buy smaller ones. It is possible that this trend will drive down the value of larger houses and will drive up the price of the smaller units just as the younger boomers enter that market.

### Pensions

The value of the private pension system for baby boomers provides yet another important example of the diversity of economic circumstances among the baby boomers. Private pensions and related public-employee pensions are an important part of the retirement income and related disability and survivors' income systems. Unlike the Old-Age and Survivors and Disability Insurance program—social security—which provides widespread protection across all income groups—other employment-related pensions mostly cover workers in the higher-paying sectors of the economy, their benefits falling disproportionately on people in higher-paying positions. Although pension coverage has expanded during the past three decades, in 1990 only 44 percent of "aged units" (defined as either a nonmarried person age 65 or over or a married couple living together in which one person is at least age 65) reported receiving either private or public-employee pension income (U.S. House of Representatives, 1993), with substantial variation by marital status, gender, income, and race (Congressional Budget Office, 1993). Department of Labor data suggest similar bifurcations in coverage for today's workers, with 53 percent of private full-time workers (46 percent of all private workers) covered by at least one plan in 1985 (Beller & Turner, 1989).

The Congressional Budget Office (1993) has suggested that income from "private pensions is likely to remain an important source of the retirement income, particularly for upper income baby boomers, and will gain in importance for women" (p. 39). As is typical of workers earlier in their careers, younger baby boomers have lower coverage rates. In 1988, 41 percent of full-time, year-round private wage and salary male workers ages 25 to 29 were covered by employer-funded pension plans compared with 54 percent of such male workers ages 35 to 39 (Woods, 1989). Comparisons of baby boom cohorts with previous cohorts when they were at similar ages, however, show a trend that does not bode well. There was a decline in coverage between 1979 and 1988 for nearly all age–gender cohort classifications of baby boomers. For example, pension coverage for such workers declined in 1988 in the younger age groups by 12 percent for men ages 25 to 29 and by 14 percent for men ages 30 to 35.

## Implications for Policy and Practice

As the baby boom cohorts move into and through middle age, early old age, and advanced old age, issues of employment, disability, caregiving, life-long learning, retirement income security, health and long-term care, and the role of older people in an aging society will gain in prominence on the national agenda. Whether and how these and other important issues are addressed will depend substantially on the way issues associated with the aging of the baby boom cohorts are defined, for, as social work policy analysts are well aware (see DiNitto, 1991; Jansson, 1994), the agenda-setting and problem-definition stage of the policy process contain the seeds of the policy interventions (or noninterventions) that follow. Consequently, social workers have an important role to play in shaping policy agendas that will emerge as the baby boom cohorts age.

### At-Risk Groups

The problems of those among the baby boom cohorts who have low incomes or who are otherwise at economic risk—for example, those without health insurance—should be of foremost concern to the social work profession and others concerned with preparing for the aging of the baby boom cohorts. Failure to focus on their needs, in both the planning and implementation of policy, will result in poor outcomes for boomers during middle age. Lack of attention is also likely to result in greater inequality of retirement circumstances than is the case for today's elderly people (Palmer, 1989), with single older women at greatest economic risk (Andrews & Chollet, 1988; Hurd, 1988). Social work research can help identify problems concerning those baby boomers at greatest risk, and policy analysis and advocacy can help move such concerns onto the public agenda. There is a need to consider how to intervene before old age to prevent poor economic outcomes, through, for example, efforts directed at expanding affordable housing and homeownership among low-income families. Similarly, to the extent that industrial restructuring has resulted in the loss of higher-paying manufacturing jobs—especially for some baby boomers with limited education—consideration could be given to providing such workers with job training and other advancement opportunities. Similarly, the social work profession's advocacy of universal health care represents an important intervention of potentially substantial assistance to those baby boomers who today are at greatest risk.

### Caregiving

Assuming that age 40 is an acceptable chronological definition of the onset of middle age, then roughly half of the members of the baby boom cohorts are already middle-age. During this period caregiving responsibilities to parents and other older relatives are likely to intensify, with many caregivers simultaneously parenting young or teenage children. The bulk of caregiving to young and old people is provided within the context of the family, primarily by women (Brody, 1978; O'Grady-LeShane, 1993). Although there is much variance in the onset and amount of elder-caregiving responsibilities among family members, caregiving will undoubtedly become an increasingly important concern for large numbers of baby boomers, providing an opportunity for social workers to help define caregiving as a more visible public issue rather than a private concern. The need of elder caregivers for assistance with finding and accessing services also opens opportunities for increased social work interventions in employment and in the more traditional human service settings.

**Aging Work Force**

As the baby boom cohorts age, each year more baby boomers will enter the ranks of "older workers," legislatively defined as beginning at age 40 by the Age Discrimination in Employment Act of 1967. The number of people who will be between the ages of 45 and 64—the age category that includes most middle-aged older workers—is projected to grow from 52 million in 1995 to 79 million by 2010 (Day, 1992). Consequently, we can anticipate that older-worker issues—such as age discrimination, retention, retraining, and early retirement, unemployment, part-time employment, and second and third careers—will grow in importance. Somewhat contradictorily, it is likely that these cohorts will be perceived as placing financial burdens on society in leaving work too early by accepting early retirement benefits and, simultaneously, as blocking pathways to advancement for a younger and, in the aggregate, more diverse workforce by not leaving work soon enough. Serious questions will emerge about the cost of early retirement to the nation's economy.

A related issue, which should be of special concern to the social work profession, concerns involuntary early retirement. Although most early retirements are substantially voluntary, many are due to health limitations, job loss, and lack of employment opportunities—problems that accrue disproportionately to low-income and minority older workers (Atkinson & Sutherland, 1993; Crown, 1990; Gibson, 1993). Whether increases in life expectancy will translate into the ability of baby boomers to work into old age is yet another question. There are different views, though recent research (Manton, 1993; Manton, Corder, & Stallard, 1993) has suggested that there have been measurable improvements in the ability of older populations to work longer, especially among higher-income and more highly educated populations (U.S. House of Representatives, 1987). Even so, much is unknown, and it is reasonable to expect considerable variance in work ability among baby boomers as they age, with the onset of health-related work limitations probably occurring later for higher-income groups, but changing little for lower-income groups (Feldman, 1991). Consequently, policy options must be examined that would increase demand for workers of all ages and potentially encourage work among able baby boomers as they age, without penalizing those who cannot work.

**Disability**

Disability policy is another area of growing concern. The oldest of the baby boomers are entering the age classification—50 through 64—that has the greatest rate of participation in the nation's dominant disability policy, the social security disability insurance program. This program is already large and expensive, and the movement of the baby boom cohorts into prime disability years promises to increase substantially the number of claims, adding additional financing and administrative pressures. In addition to the need to maintain income protection for people who cannot reasonably be expected to find employment, there is also a need to enhance independent living and employment possibilities through programmatic interventions and removal of social and structural barriers to the inclusion of people with disabilities in all aspects of community and economic life.

**Retirement**

Beginning in 2008 the oldest of the baby boom cohorts will reach the age of eligibility for early retirement benefits under social security. There is every reason to believe that social security will remain the most important component of the retirement income system for the baby boom cohorts (Kingson & Berkowitz, 1993; U.S. House of Representatives, 1987). Social security will be most important to those with low and moderate incomes. The best estimates regarding financing are that under present law, social security is adequately funded to meet all benefit obligations until 2028. Large annual surpluses are expected to accrue for roughly 20 years. However, after 2028, yearly deficits are projected in the combined social security (OASDI) trust fund (Board of Trustees, 1994b). As currently projected, there is a 14 percent shortfall over the entire 75-year period for which estimates are made. Deficits could be larger or smaller depending on how actual economic and demographic experiences depart from those used in the cost projections. Some view the projected shortfall as an indication that the program is not sustainable and should be radically restructured. Most analysts believe, however, that although there are real problems on the horizon, these anticipated financing problems can be planned for and responded to, as in the past, by some combination of moderate tax increases, benefit reductions, and investment in the economy.

Many important issues of particular concern to the social work profession will emerge. Issues have been raised about the fairness and adequacy of social security protections for various groups, for example, aged women who are generally at the greatest risk of poverty. Proposed tax and benefit increases must be monitored. Scheduled increases in the age of eligibility for full benefits under social security provide an example of policy changes that may have substantially different effects on minorities. If minority workers, on average, continue to work in more physically arduous labor, or experience higher rates of partially disabling work conditions in late middle age (ages 50 through 64) than white non-Hispanics, then the phasing in of later retirement ages (along with phased-in increases in the actuarial reduction for early retirement) can have a disproportionately negative effect on minority baby boomers. There is also a need to address important issues of public understanding and confidence in social security, because misunderstandings can undermine the consensus that supports this program (Kingson & Berkowitz, 1993). Such an outcome would be unfortunate, especially for those concerned with the well-being of low-income populations, because within the context of a nonstigmatized universal program, social security does more to prevent poverty and to target resources to low-income groups and those otherwise at economic risk than either the welfare or the income tax system (U.S. Bureau of the Census, 1988).

**Health Care**

Health care and long-term care will also grow in importance for the baby boom cohorts. Millions will face considerable income inadequacy because of health care costs in advance of their old age. Currently, the Medicare Hospital Insurance (HI) program faces large projected deficits, and the costs of Medicare's Supplementary Medical Insurance (SMI) program, although funded under the law, are rapidly increasing (Board of Trustees, 1994a; Board of Trustees, 1994c). Although Congress will unquestionably enact financing reforms in advance of the projected depletion in 2001 of the HI trust fund, the magnitude of HI and related SMI financing problems is such that policy reforms may lead to substantial change in the cost and benefits of these programs for baby boomers. Moreover, out-of-pocket costs are growing, and most of today's and tomorrow's elders are not adequately protected against the costs of community-based and institutionally based long-term-care services. In fact, inadequate protection against long-term-care costs represents the single biggest threat to the economic well-being of baby boomers during their retirement years. Perhaps more important, if current patterns persist, limited and differential access to necessary social, health, and rehabilitation services threatens to undermine the well-being and dignity of millions of baby boomers, especially as they move into advanced old age (Kingson & Berkowitz, 1993).

Because these problems are related to the larger crisis of access and financing of health care, they require a comprehensive solution. At a policy level, social work's advocacy of health reform potentially has important consequences for baby boomers. Moreover, there continues to be a need for policy and case advocacy at community levels and for interdisciplinary collaboration to build sound systems of care that seek to serve the whole person.

## Conclusion

The baby boom cohorts will age in an increasingly diverse society in which questions will be raised about the meaning of old age and the distribution of public and private resources across age, racial, and ethnic groups and cohorts. The aging of the baby boom cohorts begins a permanent shift in the age structure, with the U.S. Bureau of the Census projecting that 20.2 percent of the population will be at least age 65 in 2030 and that 20.6 percent will be at least that age in 2050. This change will interact with the projected changing racial and ethnic composition of the nation, especially among young people. The white non-Hispanic population is projected to decline as a percentage of the total U.S. population from about 76 percent in 1990 to 60 percent in 2030 and 53 percent in 2050 (Day, 1992), with the majority of people under age 65 being among what are today termed minority groups. Fernando Torres-Gil's (1992) and Martha Ozawa's (1985) observations of the possibility that a large elderly population composed disproportionately of white non-Hispanics will be forced to compete with a growing young minority population for social resources led each to caution of potential conflicts and to suggest that the pursuit of policies that invest in low-income and minority children is crucial to the well-being of the baby boomers as they age. Attention also must be directed at making investments in the economy, in the continued maintenance of a sound social security program, and in new protections against health and long-term care risks.

The presence of large able-bodied groupings of older baby boomers may lead many, including elderly baby boomers themselves, to focus attention on the potential of most to make social contributions in their old age and on what those who are economically or physically able should return to society during their old age. Similarly, given the importance of social inclusion to the well-being of individuals, and given that the health of most baby boomers will allow participation throughout most if not all of old age, a growing need will exist to expand avenues of social and economic participation. The aging of the baby boom cohorts will provide a potential resource for society that, if well used, will benefit the baby boom cohorts and the cohorts with whom they share time. Questions will emerge about how to use the knowledge and skills of elder baby boomers in the paid labor force. Questions are likely to be raised too about the desirability of providing tax subsidies to firms offering private pension benefits to healthy employees who retire early. As now, there will be much need and opportunity for elders to contribute through employment, community activity, and family life. Arguably, the potential for conflicts over public resources could be reduced by policies that promote burden sharing, greater equity in tax and transfer systems, and expanded employment and community service.

The framing of policy discussions about the aging society in terms of "Can we afford to pay for the retirement years of the baby boom generation?" is an excellent example of the problems inherent in policy discussions that are not based on a full appreciation of the diversity of the baby boom cohorts. This framing encourages dichotomous thinking (for example, we either can or cannot afford baby boom retirees). Also, it may indirectly encourage policy development to proceed with little regard for the great variance of experiences, capacities, and needs among baby boomers during their middle and older years. A danger of particular concern to the social work profession is that policy changes such as reductions in social insurance projections may have irrational and disproportionately harmful effects on different groups of baby boomers—especially the most vulnerable—when their existence as an important part of the baby boom cohorts is not emphasized.

The assumption that the aging of large numbers of baby boomers will inevitably overwhelm the ability of public institutions to respond also is of concern. In reality, the entrance and then movement of the baby boom cohorts through their retirement years will span half a century, potentially allowing for gradual adjustments. To the extent that retirement institutions are strained, some groupings of baby boomers (that is, the younger ones and those who are more dependent on social programs) are more likely to feel the pinch, but there is also the great potential for most aging baby boomers to contribute to society.

Suggesting that policymakers have little choice other than to alter existing public programs may discourage consideration of other options, such as increased investment in the economy, in biomedical research, and in such employment-related strategies as retraining older workers and expansion of part-time employment. It also discourages consideration of strategies that underwrite lifelong learning and encourage lifelong contribution and involvement in the transmission of ideas, values, and culture through crafts, art, and various community activities. The social work profession has an important role to play in injecting an appreciation of this heterogeneity into policy discussions and social work practice.

## References


Age Discrimination in Employment Act of 1967. P.L. 90-202, 81 Stat. 602.

Aaron, H. J., Bosworth, B. P., & Burtless, G. (1989). *Can America afford to grow old? Paying for social security.* Washington, DC: Brookings Institution.

Andrews, E. S., & Chollet, D. (1988). Future sources of retirement income: Whither the baby boom. In S. M. Wachter (Ed.), *Social security and private pensions: Providing for retirement in the twenty-first century* (pp. 71–95). Lexington, MA: Lexington Books.

Apgar, W. C., Jr., DiPasquale, D., McArdle, N., & Olson, J. (1990). *The state of the nation's housing 1989.* Cambridge, MA: Harvard University Press.

Atkinson, A. B., & Sutherland, H. (1993). Two nations in early retirement? The case of Britain. In A. B. Atkinson & M. Rein (Eds.), *Age, work, and social security* (pp. 132–160). New York: St. Martin's Press.

Bean, F. D. (1983). The baby boom and its explanations. *Sociological Quarterly, 24,* 357.

Beller, D. J., & Turner, J. A. (1989). Introduction and summary of major findings. In *Trends in pensions* (pp. 1–14). Washington, DC: U.S. Department of Labor.

Bengston, V. L., Cutler, N. E., Mangen, D. J., & Marshall, V. W. (1985). Generations, cohorts, and relations between age groups. In R. H. Binstock & E. S. Shanas (Eds.),

*Handbook of aging and the social sciences* (pp. 304–308). New York: Van Nostrand Reinhold.

Bennett, C. E., & Cowles, J. H. (1989). The black population of the United States: March 1988. *U. S. Bureau of the Census current population reports* (Series P-20, No. 442). Washington, DC: U.S. Government Printing Office.

Bluestone, B., & Harrison, B. (1986). [The great American job machine: The proliferation of low wage employment in the U.S. economy.] Unpublished raw data.

Board of Trustees, Federal Hospital Insurance Trust Fund. (1994a). *1994 Annual Report of the Board of Trustees of the Federal Hospital Insurance Trust Fund*. Washington, DC: U.S. Government Printing Office.

Board of Trustees, Federal Old-Age and Survivors Insurance and Disability Insurance Trust Funds. (1994b). *1994 Annual Report of the Federal Old-Age and Survivors Insurance and Disability Insurance Trust Funds*. Washington, DC: U.S. Government Printing Office.

Board of Trustees, Federal Supplementary Medical Insurance Trust Fund. (1994c). *1994 Annual Report of the Board of Trustees of the Federal Supplementary Medical Insurance Trust Fund*. Washington, DC: U.S. Government Printing Office.

Bouvier, L. F., & DeVita, C. J. (1991). *The baby boom—Entering midlife*. Washington, DC: Population Reference Bureau.

Brody, E. (1978). Parent care as a normative family stress. *Gerontologist, 18*(1), 19–29.

Cherlin, A., & Furstenberg, F., Jr. (1982). *The shape of the American family in the year 2000*. Washington, DC: American Council of Life Insurance.

Congressional Budget Office. (1993). *Baby boomers in retirement: An early perspective*. Washington, DC: Author.

Crown, W. H. (1990). Economic trends, politics, and employment policy for older workers. *Journal of Aging and Social Policy, 2*(3–4), 131–151.

Daniels, N. (1988). *Am I my parents' keeper? An essay on justice between the young and old*. New York: Oxford University Press.

Day, J. C. (1992). Population projections of the United States by age, sex, race, and Hispanic origin: 1992 to 2050. *Current Population Reports* (Series P-20, No. 438). Washington, DC: U.S. Government Printing Office.

DeNavas, C. (1989). The Hispanic population of the United States: March 1988. *Current Population Reports* (Series P-20, No. 438). Washington, DC: U.S. Government Printing Office.

DiNitto, D. M. (1991). *Social welfare: Politics and public policy*. Englewood Cliffs, NJ: Prentice Hall.

Easterlin, R. A. (1987). *Birth and fortune: The impact of numbers on personal welfare*. Chicago: University of Chicago Press.

Feldman, J. J. (1991). Life expectancy and work capacity. In A. Munnell (Ed.), *Proceedings of the second conference of the National Academy of Social Insurance: Retirement and Public Policy* (pp. 151–157). Washington, DC: National Academy of Social Insurance.

Gibson, R. C. (1993). The black American retirement experience. In J. S. Jackson, L. M. Chatters, & R. J. Taylor (Eds.), *Aging in black America* (pp. 277–300). Newbury Park, CA: Sage Publications.

Hagestad, G. O. (1986). The family: Women and grandparents as kin-keepers. In A. Pifer & L. Bronte (Eds.), *Our aging society: Paradox and promise* (pp. 141–160). New York: W. W. Norton.

Hurd, M. D. (1988). Forecasting the consumption and wealth of the elderly. In S. M. Wachter (Ed.), *Social security and private pensions: Providing for retirement in the twenty-first century* (pp. 47–69). Lexington, MA: Lexington Books.

Jansson, B. S. (1994). *Social policy: From theory to practice*. Monterey, CA: Brooks/Cole.

Jones, L. Y. (1980). *Great expectations: America and the baby boom generation*. New York: Coward, McCann, Geoghegan.

Kamerman, S. B., & Kahn, A. J. (1988). *Mothers alone: Strategies for a time of change*. Dover, MA: Auburn House.

Kingson, E. R. (1992). *The diversity of the baby boom generation: Implications for their retirement years*. Washington, DC: American Association of Retired Persons, Forecasting and Environmental Scanning Division.

Kingson, E. R., & Berkowitz, E. D. (1993). *Social security and Medicare: A policy primer*. Westport, CT: Auburn House.

Lamm, R. D. (1985). *Mega-traumas: America at the year 2000*. Boston: Houghton Mifflin.

Levy, F. (1987). *Dollars and dreams: The changing American income distribution*. New York: Russell Sage Foundation.

Levy, F. (1988). Incomes, families, and living standards. In R. E. Litan, R. Z. Lawrence, & C. L. Schultze (Eds.), *American living standards: Threats and challenges* (pp. 108–153). Washington, DC: Brookings Institution.

Light, P. C. (1988). *Baby boomers*. New York: W. W. Norton.

Longman, P. (1987). *Born to pay: The new politics of aging in America*. Boston: Houghton Mifflin.

Manton, K. G. (1993, October). *Trends for the elderly—Implications for income support, health, and provisions for long-term care*. Paper presented at the Future of Health Care Needs and Resources for the Aged conference, Washington, DC.

Manton, K. G., Corder, L. S., & Stallard, E. (1993). Estimates of change in chronic disability and institutional incidence and prevalence rates in the U.S. elderly population from the 1982, 1984, and 1989 National Long-Term Care Survey. *Journal of Gerontology: Social Sciences, 48,* 5153–5166.

Moody, H. R. (1988). *Abundance of life*. New York: Columbia University Press.

O'Grady-LeShane, R. (1993). Changes in the lives of women and their families: Have old-age pensions kept pace? *Generations, 17*(4), 27–31.

Ozawa, M. (1985, November). *Non-whites and the demographic imperative in social welfare spending*. Paper presented at the National Association of Social Workers Professional Symposium, Chicago.

Palmer, J. L. (1989). Financing health care and retirement for the aged. *Business, work, and benefits: Adjusting to change* (pp. 73–118). Washington, DC: Employee Benefit Research Institute.

Rawlings, S. W. (1989). Household and family characteristics: March 1988. *Current Population Reports* (Series P-20, No. 437). Washington, DC: U.S. Government Printing Office.

Russell, C. (1987). *100 predictions for the baby boom: The next 50 years*. New York: Plenum Press.

Russell, L. B. (1982). *The baby boom generation and economy*. Washington, DC: Brookings Institution.

Saluter, A. F. (1989). Changes in American family life. *Current Population Reports* (Series P-23, No. 163). Washington, DC: U.S. Government Printing Office.

Siegel, P. M. (1989). Educational attainment in the United States: March 1982 to 1985. *Current Population Reports* (Series P-20, No. 415). Washington, DC: U.S. Government Printing Office.

Soldo, B. J., & Agree, E. M. (1988). America's elderly. *Population Bulletin, 43*(3),

Spencer, G. (1986). Projections of the Hispanic population: 1983 to 2080. *Current Population Reports* (Series P-25, No. 995). Washington, DC: U.S. Government Printing Office.

Sternlieb, G., & Hughes, J. W. (1982, June). Running faster to stay in place. *American Demographics*.

Torres-Gil, F. (1986). Hispanics: A special challenge. In A. Pifer & L. Bronte (Eds.), *Our aging society: Paradox and promise* (pp. 219–242). New York: W. W. Norton.

Torres-Gil, F. (1992). *The new aging: Politics and change in America*. Westport, CT: Auburn House.

U.S. Bureau of the Census. (1988). *Measuring the effect of benefits and taxes on income and poverty: 1986*. Washington, DC: U.S. Government Printing Office.

U.S. Bureau of the Census. (1989). Money income and poverty status in the United States: 1988 (Advance data from the March 1989 current population survey). *Current Population Reports* (Series P-60, No. 122). Washington, DC: U.S. Government Printing Office.

U.S. Bureau of the Census. (1992). Poverty in the United States: 1991. *Current Population Reports* (Series P-60, No. 181). Washington, DC: U.S. Government Printing Office.

U.S. House of Representatives, Committee on Ways and Means. (1987). *Retirement income for an aging society*. Washington, DC: U.S. Government Printing Office.

U.S. House of Representatives, Committee on Ways and Means. (1993). *Background material and data on programs within the jurisdiction of the Committee on Ways and Means*. Washington, DC: U.S. Government Printing Office.

Wattenberg, E. (1986). The fate of baby boomers and their children. *Social Work, 31,* 20–28.

Woods, J. R. (1989). Pension coverage among private wage and salary workers: Preliminary findings from the 1988 survey of employee benefits. *Social Security Bulletin, 52*(10), 2–19.

## Further Reading

Cole, T. R., Achenbaum, W. A., Jakobi, P. L., & Kastenbaum, R. (Eds.). (1993). *Voices and visions of aging: Toward a critical gerontology*. New York: Springer.

Kingson, E. R., Hirshorn, B. A., & Cornman, J. M. (1986). *Ties that bind: The interdependence of generations*. Cabin John, MD: Seven Locks Press.

Koff, T. H., & Park, R. W. (1993). *Aging public policy: Bonding the generations*. Amityville, NY: Baywood.

Marmor, T. R., Mashaw, J. L., & Harvey, P. L. (1990). *Misunderstood welfare state: Persistent myths, enduring realities*. New York: Basic Books.

Moon, M. (1993). *Medicare now and in the future*. Washington, DC: Urban Institute Press.

Schultz, J. H. (1992). *The economics of aging*. Westport, CT: Auburn House.

Steuerle, C. E., & Bakija, J. M. (1993). *Retooling social security for the 21st century: Right and wrong approaches to reform*. Washington, DC: Urban Institute Press.

**Eric Kingson, PhD,** is associate professor, Boston College, Graduate School of Social Work, McGuinn Hall, Chestnut Hill, MA 02167.

The author expresses his appreciation to the American Association of Retired Persons for funding and facilitating research that developed into a monograph upon which this entry draws: Kingson, E. (1992, April). *The diversity of the baby boom generation: Implications for their retirement years*. Washington, DC: American Association of Retired Persons, Forecasting and Environmental Scanning Department.

### For further information see

Aging: Public Policy Issues and Trends; Families: Demographic Shifts; Housing; Income Distribution; Income Security Overview; Jobs and Earnings; Long-Term Care; Managed Care; Poverty; Retirement and Pension Programs; Social Planning; Social Security; Social Welfare Policy; Women Overview.

**Key Words**

age cohorts
aging
baby boom

## Barrett, Janie Porter

*See* Biographies section, Volume 3

## Bartlett, Harriett M.

*See* Biographies section, Volume 3

## Barton, Clarissa (Clara) Harlowe

*See* Biographies section, Volume 3

## Battered Women

*See* Domestic Violence

## Beers, Clifford Whittingham

*See* Biographies section, Volume 3

# Bereavement and Loss

**John S. McNeil**

Loss and proper bereavement have been human concerns for hundreds of years. Attitudes toward bereavement have been influenced by multiple variables such as cultural factors, circumstances surrounding the death, and age of the lost one. Scientific study of bereavement, however, did not begin until the 1940s. Numerous grief researchers and theoreticians have proposed varied conceptualizations to explain normal and complicated grief. These formulations have ranged from the disease model, which is formulated on psychoanalytic thinking, to the attachment model, which argues that attachment and loss are typical of human and subhuman species. Another dichotomy is represented in the stage models of grief as opposed to the task model. More recently, attention has been given to the use of the *Diagnostic and Statistical Manual of Mental Disorders* (4th ed.; [DSM-IV]) (American Psychiatric Association, 1994) designation of posttraumatic stress disorder (PTSD) as an additional conceptualization to understand the grief process.

This entry examines bereavement, focusing on these various frameworks. Also discussed are the major intervention strategies used in the treatment of grief, as well as the issues and problems involved in doing bereavement research.

## Definitions

Confusion abounds when attempting to clarify the meanings of terms related to the bereavement process. Agreement is quite consistent regarding loss, whether it refers to a significant other or an object. Loss can be physical or psychosocial. Physical loss is palpable and tangible (for example, loss of a limb, a stolen possession, or a house burned down). Psychosocial loss is intangible and symbolic (for example, retirement, divorce, or development of a chronic illness) (Rando, 1993). In contrast, however, there are almost as many definitions of bereavement, grief, and mourning as there are people writing on the subject.

*Bereavement* has its root in the Old English "beroafian, which means to rob, plunder or to dispossess" (Burnell & Burnell, 1989, p. 29). In current use, it suggests that the survivor has been robbed of a loved one (Burnell & Burnell, 1989). Osterweis, Solomon, and Green (1984) posited that bereavement consists of physiological, psychological, or behavioral responses to the loss. Bereavement has also been defined as the act of separation that results in grief, although another perspective considers bereavement to be a complex series of responses that follows a loss (Dershimer, 1990). This latter definition considers bereavement an umbrella term that encompasses the entire process experienced by the survivor after a significant loss.

Similarly, *grief* has many definitions. The term is derived from the Latin word *gravis* (heavy). Grief can be seen as an intense feeling or emotional suffering caused by a loss (Burnell & Burnell, 1989). This definition also includes the accompanying physiological symptoms (for example, muscular tightness, crying, and sighing) and psychological reactions (for example, sadness, guilt, or anger). Rando (1993) expanded this list to include behavioral and social symptoms as well. Grief is the emotional pain that accompanies loss (Dershimer, 1990). In this sense grief is buffeted by the magnitude of the loss. Sanders (1989) also defined grief in terms of reactions to loss (for example, anger, guilt, physical complaints, illness, or despair). Parkes and Weiss (1983) suggested a more active learning process wherein the survivor proceeds to an inner awareness of an event that has occurred outside the self.

*Mourning* is most often defined as the cultural expression of grief. Averill (cited in Burnell & Burnell, 1989) (p. 29) suggested that mourning is the "conventional behavior established by traditions, customs, and mores of a society." Mourning is the observable underlying process of reaction to the loss (for example, wearing of black) in contrast to the subjective experience of grief (Tallmer, 1987). Tallmer considered bereavement to be a subclass of mourning. In traditional psychoanalytic theory, mourning has been viewed as the detaching of the survivor from the lost love object (Dershimer, 1990)—in other words, decathexis. Rando (1993) accepted the idea of mourning as the cultural and public display of grief but expanded the concept to include the conscious and unconscious processes that occur. Rando viewed grief as the beginning part of mourning and mourning as a much more encompassing term than grief. In fact, in this definition mourning also is more of an umbrella term.

This morass of interchangeability and lack of clarity and specificity has profound implications for research in the field. Replication and comparison of studies are extremely difficult, if not impossible, and clear operationalization of concepts is problematic. In addition to producing conflicting research findings, definitional issues also affect theorizing.

## Theories of Bereavement

Numerous theoretical models have been formulated in an effort to explain the dynamics of bereavement. Raphael (1983) identified six models and their primary contributors:

| *Model* | *Contributor* |
|---|---|
| 1. Psychodynamic | Abraham<br>Fenichel<br>Freud<br>Klein |
| 2. Attachment | Bowlby |
| 3. Changes in the assumptive world, personal constructs, and cognitive | Horowitz<br>Parks, Woodfield, & Viney |
| 4. Stress | Caplan, Maddison, & Walker<br>Raphael |
| 5. Illness and disease | Engel<br>Lindemann |
| 6. Sociobiologic | Averil |

Three of these contributors are discussed in this entry: Freud, Lindemann, and Bowlby. Kübler-Ross is also included because of her special contribution.

### Freud and the Psychodynamic Model

Sigmund Freud's (1917/1957) landmark publication, *Mourning and Melancholia,* provides the theoretical foundation for much of the scientific examination of bereavement. Freud appeared to be interested primarily in melancholia, a pathological condition, and secondarily in mourning, a normal reaction to the loss of a love object. Although Freud's attitudes changed somewhat in later years, he identified the significant features of bereavement and wrote of the grief work that must be done for the survivor to recover from the pain of the loss. He emphasized the need for the bereaved to decathect (that is, withdraw psychic energy) from the deceased and reinvest it into a new relationship. Initially Freud believed the decathexis could occur totally, but he later recognized that the survivor never completely gives up a loved object but instead replaces it. Freud also recognized the necessity of distinguishing between normal and pathological bereavement. This remains a critical thanatological problem because bereavement is highly individual and is influenced by many other variables, such as the mode of death. In keeping with psychoanalytic constructs, considerable attention is paid to intrapsychic factors. Minimal concern is shown for psychosocial variables or a more holistic approach that would guide the work of an ecological practitioner.

### Lindemann and the Illness Model

Erich Lindemann (1944), although trained in the psychoanalytic perspective, made a major contribution in the area of the physiological nature of bereavement. Like Freud, Lindemann was interested in distinguishing normal grief from pathological grief. He was the first bereavement researcher to specify the somatic distresses that are characteristic of acute grief. These include choking, with shortness of breath and tightness in the throat; an empty feeling in the abdomen; a lack of muscular power; and intense distress.

Lindemann had a rather narrow construction of normal grief and considered many people to be suffering from "morbid grief" who would currently be seen as experiencing "normal grief." Nevertheless, Lindemann focused attention on physical symptoms and reinforced the concept of grief work.

In his search to differentiate normal from morbid grief, Lindemann (cited in Rando, 1993), identified nine distortions of the grieving process:

1. overactivity without a sense of loss
2. symptoms of hysteria or hypochondriasis
3. presence of psychosomatic conditions (the most common were ulcerative colitis, rheumatoid arthritis, and asthma)
4. changes in relationships with relatives and friends
5. extreme hostility directed toward specific people
6. struggle against hostility
7. loss of patterns of social interaction
8. engagement in self-destructive (nonsuicidal) activities
9. agitated depression.

Another aspect of Lindemann's work was operationalization of three tasks necessary to complete grief work: (1) emancipation from bondage to the deceased, (2) readjustment to the environment in which the deceased is missing, and (3) the establishment of new relationships.

Lindemann and Freud are the two most frequently quoted early theoreticians in the field of bereavement.

**Bowlby and the Attachment Model**

John Bowlby (1980) is the father of the attachment model. His basic tenet was that individuals are profoundly motivated and affected by attachment and seek to maintain that attachment. Furthermore, this attachment behavior is not only typical of humans but is also seen in subhuman species. Illustrative of the subhuman component is the description of the greylag goose offered by Lorenz (1963):

> The first response to the disappearance of the partner consists in the anxious attempts to find him again. The goose moves about restlessly by day and night, flying great distances and visiting places where the partner might be found, uttering all the time the penetrating trisyllabic long distance call. . . . The searching expeditions are extended farther and farther . . . and quite often the searcher itself gets lost. (p. 40)

Although Bowlby was also interested in distinguishing normal from pathological grief, he found many more features to be representative of normal grieving than have other researchers. For example, anger and the intense effort to recover and reproach the lost one are normal components of the grief process. Both human and subhuman species have a great interest in individual and group safety and security. As a result, when confronted with a loss, all species have a tendency to seek to recover the lost object and then reproach it after recovery, apparently to decrease its likelihood of getting lost again. In his attempt to normalize the grief process, Bowlby (1980) suggested four phases of mourning:

1. numbing that usually lasts from a few hours to a week and may be interrupted by outbursts of extremely intense distress and/or anger
2. yearning and searching for the lost object, which can last for months and sometimes for years
3. disorganization and despair
4. reorganization. (p. 85)

Bowlby observed infants and children and their responses to the loss of the mother or a primary attachment figure. At a descriptive level, he provided evidence that this behavior is essentially the same as that seen in an older child or adult who has suffered the loss of a loved one (Rando, 1993). What makes the bereavement pathological is the type of defense mechanism employed. Typical unhealthy defense mechanisms are repression, fixation, and splitting of the ego. Problematic attachment during childhood does not automatically lead to complicated bereavement later in life.

Documenting the essential role of attachment clarifies the need to understand grief as a type of separation anxiety. Bowlby's formulations challenged some of the earlier truisms of the grief process. Common factors in healthy mourning include anger directed at third parties, the self, and sometimes the deceased person; disbelief that the death has occurred; and a tendency to search for the lost person in hopes of reunion.

**Kübler-Ross**

Elisabeth Kübler-Ross (1969) is best known for her classic *On Death and Dying*. Her work was designed to identify the "phases of dying" and placed an emphasis on the stages a patient passes through in the course of dying. Kübler-Ross delineated five stages—denial and isolation, anger, bargaining, depression, and acceptance—as opposed to the three stages identified by Lindemann (1944) and the 10 identified by Westberg (1971).

Although the stage theory of grief has been questioned, Kübler-Ross's conceptualization created a model for understanding the cognitive and psychological movement of the patient along the death trajectory. This model also has been applied to people suffering losses other than death such as the loss of a body part or a degenerative condition that leads to progressive physical deterioration. Her theory has also been applied to the bereavement experience of the survivor.

## Cultural Influences on Grief

Because it is accepted that grief is a universal experience, discussion regarding the degree to which culture influences the way a person grieves a significant loss has been minimal. Models of bereavement discussed thus far in this entry reflect a predominantly Eurocentric view. Conceptualizing grief and mourning as two separate entities facilitates an understanding of the cultural component, especially if mourning is seen as the cultural manifestation of the grief process. Mourning behavior, therefore, is learned behavior derived from cultural "prescriptions." For example, in Western cultures, because of gender roles, females are permitted more outward expression of their sorrow than are males, who are expected to be more stoic and not succumb to intense grieving. Furthermore, the death of an elderly person warrants less grief than the death of a child, adolescent, or middle-ager.

W. Stroebe and Stroebe (1987) asked, "Is grief universal?" To arrive at an answer, they reviewed the cross-cultural literature and concluded that the answer cannot be a simple yes or no. On the one hand, we have argued that the available evidence supports the view that people in very diverse societies do experience feelings of sadness and despondency on the loss of a person to whom they were close. There are neither reports of indifference . . . nor ones of joy or happiness predominating . . . grief seems to be universally felt. . . . Manifestations of grief in different cultures are extremely varied: Whereas in the West despair and depression and many symptoms of grief last for months and even years, in certain parts of the world any overt sign of grief ceases after a matter of days and there is every indication that the trauma of loss is overcome in the space of a very short time. It appears that symptoms and phases of grief are modified very considerably by cultural factors, and, while no specific examinations exist to test this more closely, systematic variations across groups in social support and social norms, in funeral rites and in meanings assigned to loss can be linked with differences in the emotional reaction to loss. (pp. 54–55)

W. Stroebe and Stroebe (1987) examined factors such as crying, grief symptoms, and duration of grief. In both Western and non-Western cultures they did not find absences of crying but instead found variations in the timing of the crying and the place where crying was acceptable. Symptoms found in non-Western cultures included self-inflicted injury and horror at the sight of the corpse, coupled with fear of the ghost. Duration of grief in some non-Western cultures was limited to specified periods of time. Western cultures also restrict the sanctioned periods of grief through social pressure with comments such as, "It's time to get on with life." In the occupational arena, bereavement is limited by the amount of time one may remain off work, which is regulated largely by the closeness of the blood or marital relationship. Variations may also be influenced by religious beliefs. For example, in Judaism the grief work cycle is delineated in a fairly precise manner that differs from that in most Christian denominations (Moss, 1979).

Cultural influences are important factors in the study of grief models. Much of the research to date has been done by anthropologists. There is a real need for further research on bereavement by social scientists.

## Posttraumatic Stress Disorder

Posttraumatic stress disorder (PTSD), although not considered a theory or model of bereavement, is being discussed in the grief literature more frequently. The DSM-IV (American Psychiatric Association, 1994) states that a diagnosis of PTSD is indicated if a person has experienced an event that is outside the range of usual human experience and that would be markedly distressing to almost anyone. Examples of these events would be a serious threat to one's life or physical well-being; a serious threat or harm to one's children, spouse, or other close relative or friend; sudden destruction of one's home or community; or seeing another person who has been seriously injured or killed as a result of an accident or physical violence. Loss and grief are likely to be greatly affected by the mode of death or loss. Efforts are currently being made to include PTSD as a bereavement model (Sprang, 1991).

## Stage versus Task Theories of Bereavement

Although the stage models of grief have been used widely, they may not address individual idiosyncrasies and other variables that may mitigate passage through the stages of grief. Several researchers have pointed out methodological limitations such as reliance on small clinical samples for generalizations and the lack of comparison groups (Bowman, 1980; Burgess, 1975; Poussaint, 1984). Wortman, Silver, and Kessler (1993) believed the major weakness in stage models is that they do not propose specific mechanisms through which the loss may exert an influence on subsequent mental or physical health.

Although there is general agreement regarding the symptomatology of grief reactions across the models of grief, the conceptualization of the process has been questioned. Worden (1991) criticized the stage models of grief, stating that individuals do not always progress through the grieving process in an orderly fashion and may experience more than one stage at a time. Clinicians and clients may take the stages too literally and inappropriately judge deviations from the model as being pathological. Worden further believed that the stage model implies passivity, an inactive role in which the griever passes through something. The task model, on the other hand, is more congruent with the concept of grief work through its implication that the mourner should take some action. It empowers bereaved people by giving them a task to achieve and provides a sense of leverage. Worden identified four tasks:

1. accepting the reality of the loss
2. working through the pain of the grief
3. adjusting to the environment in which the deceased is missing
4. withdrawing emotional energy from the grieving process and reinvesting it into another relationship.

Several writers have argued that the stage model does not indicate how much time elapses before an individual recovers from the loss (Bornstein & Clayton, 1972; Davidson, 1979; Silver & Wortman, 1980). Charmaz (1980) maintained that the stages of dying may not reflect elements or the sequence of the patient's reactions to death but instead may be a response to institutional demands, staff needs, and cultural values. Kamerman (1988), writing about stage models in general and Kübler-Ross's model in particular, stated that the model has "major flaws" (p. 44).

Although the criticisms seem to view stage and task models as mutually exclusive entities, some overlap appears to be present. In a stage model the bereaved person must accomplish some task, either consciously or unconsciously, to move from one stage to the next. In a task model the individual still moves from one phase to another.

## Bereavement and the Type of Loss

Loss of a significant love object is affected enormously by the type and mode of loss. When a significant person dies, a useful dichotomy is that of "natural" death versus "unnatural" death. A natural death, at best an elusive term, is a death that occurs in the normal sequence of things. For example, an elderly person might die naturally as a consequence of the aging process, following the laws of nature. A death may be considered unnatural if it occurs in a younger person and was caused by something outside the normal progression of life, for example, by accident, homicide, or suicide. Kastenbaum and Aisenberg (1976) suggested that a natural death is one that has not been tainted by human hands. They suggested that society needs a concept such as natural death because it serves a palliative purpose for the following reasons:

- The death of an old person may strike us as natural in that we are not taken by surprise.
- There is nothing else that we might have done or should have done.
- Death of an elder is natural in that it bolsters our faith in the natural order.

In keeping with this perspective one would expect natural death to lead to less-complicated bereavement than unnatural death. To examine this supposition, it is worthwhile to review findings of studies regarding unnatural death.

### Death of a Child

There is widespread agreement that the death of a child is one of the most difficult losses that individuals experience. Osterweis et al. (1984) wrote that any bereavement is painful, but the experience of losing a child is by far the worst. Rando (1986) described the death of a child as being unlike any other loss. Supporting this position is Sanders (1989), who concluded that the death of a child is an "unbearable sorrow," a wound that "cuts deeply, ulcerates, and festers. Scar tissue is slow to form. For some it never heals" (p. 161). Considerable inconsistency exists in the literature regarding many aspects of bereavement, but not in the loss of a child. Death of a child is more likely to be accidental, and it is the suddenness of death that also affects the bereavement process.

### Sudden Death

The effect of a sudden death is considered so devastating that it has been coined the "unexpected loss syndrome" (Parkes & Weiss, 1983, p. 93). An underlying idea is that the bereaved did not have time to prepare for the death or to go through a period of anticipatory grief. Rosen (1990) posited three general categories of sudden death:

1. fatal medical events, such as heart attack, stroke, or death during routine surgery
2. accidental deaths, such as random accidents or catastrophic events such as a natural disaster
3. suicide.

A fourth category might include violent death such as homicide or death by a drunk driver; there is also a need to include miscarriage, stillbirth, perinatal death, or death from sudden infant death syndrome. Although these losses may be categorically similar to fatal medical events, people tend to perceive them as they would perceive losses that stigmatize the grievers, such as deaths resulting from suicide and acquired immune deficiency syndrome (AIDS) (that is, does the individual have a right to openly grieve the loss?).

Another type of sudden death that has received little attention in terms of the grief response is that of violence and urban children. Children may lose a parent, sibling, or significant other and are expected to continue life as if nothing has happened. As a result, the grief may be internalized and expressed through disruptive school behavior, poor academic achievement, or other "acting out" behavior. Doherty (1990) referred to a study of 52 children who had witnessed the murder of a parent. These children suffered severe emotional and learning problems, including depression, short attention spans, violent behavior, nightmares, and memory loss. The tendency of many segments of society to essentially ignore these deaths stigmatizes, or disenfranchises, the grievers.

**Disenfranchised Grief**

Foremost among disenfranchised deaths are those caused by suicide and AIDS. Both have been considered "blemishes of individual character" (Goffman, 1963, p. 4). Both suicide and AIDS survivors are subjected to "courtesy stigma," through which survivors are denied the usual means of bereavement. The loss of social support may force the survivor to grieve silently and alone. Avoidance or a conspiracy of silence creates a situation fraught with potential for complicated grief.

Although not as stigmatized as AIDS-related deaths or suicide, the loss of a lover in an extramarital relationship is also disenfranchised. Even if the relationship was openly known, the surviving partner is not likely to be invited to participate in the mourning rituals, diminishing the opportunity for the partner to bring closure to the loss.

There is also confusion regarding the management of grief after the death of an infant or a loss through miscarriage. A common assumption is that the grief should not be severe because the parents could not have had time to form an attachment to the child. This attitude ignores the possibility that the attachment began with the first signs of pregnancy.

## INTERVENTION

People generally cope with grief in three different ways: (1) some manage their grief alone or with available social support, (2) some use self-help groups, and (3) some seek professional help.

Most bereaved people do a reasonably effective job of dealing with their loss alone or with help from informal support systems. Lund (1989) stated that "many older bereaved spouses do not want or need intervention services" (pp. 218–219). He suggested that many practitioners falsely assume that older bereaved people are socially isolated, incapacitated by the loss, and depressed. Everyone, however, needs support, reassurance, and some education and information after the loss.

**Self-Help Groups**

Many people who encounter difficulties coping with loss find help through self-help groups. Some groups are specific to a particular type of loss, and others are for anyone who is grieving. Among them are

- the Compassionate Friends, a group for parents who have experienced the loss of a child
- SHARE (Source of Help in Airing and Resolving Experiences), a group for parents who have lost an infant
- MADD (Mothers Against Drunk Driving)
- the Samaritans/Safe Place (the Samaritans attempt to prevent suicide, whereas Safe Place helps people who are grieving the loss of someone who died by suicide).

Self-help groups are especially valuable because all members have had a similar common experience. Sharing with someone who has had the same experience can be quite curative and validating.

**Professional Intervention**

Individuals who suffer from complicated grief may require professional intervention. The professional's specific orientation determines the strategies used. Crisis intervention is frequently used during the early period of the grief; these techniques are consistent with the crisis model used in other situations. Raphael (1983) used a cognitive approach, focal psychotherapy, that relies on three types of verbal interaction: (1)discussing the survivor's relationship with the deceased from the beginning, (2) reporting on what has been happening since the loss, and (3) questioning whether the survivor has been through similar hard times in the past.

Volkan (1975) introduced regrief therapy, an approach designed to help the bereaved person remember and reexperience the circumstances surrounding the loss. "Linking objects" (mementos, clothing, photographs, or other special memorabilia) are often used to stimulate memories. A major effort in regrief is to help the bereaved confront the loss, whether through conscious material or dream or fantasy interpretation.

Guided mourning, a cognitive behavioral approach, was developed by Mawson, Marks, Ramm, and Stern (1981). Guided mourning consists of exposure to painful memories or situations, encouragement to visit avoided places and say good-bye to the lost person or object, and exercises such as daily writing and thinking about the death.

Worden (1991), in his model of grief therapy, used four tasks of mourning to assess which of the tasks the bereaved person has not completed. A treatment plan is then developed to help the client complete these tasks.

Psychopharmacological therapy is also widely used, but there is considerable controversy regarding this treatment method. Arguments against medication therapy are similar to those posed in other situations and suggest that any method that protects the person from the pain of the experience is unhealthy and serves to extend the time required for resolution (Dershimer, 1990).

## Bereavement Research

Much of the knowledge regarding bereavement has derived from practice wisdom, the experiences of bereaved people, and beliefs about what constitutes normal bereavement. Until the late 1980s nearly all grief models were designed around the experiences of elderly couples who had suffered the loss of a spouse and any bereavement experience that deviated from this was considered pathological. "Griefologists," if such a term may be used, began to question fundamental assumptions regarding bereavement; pushed for greater clarity of definitions; and expressed a need for research beyond that of measures of central tendency, percentages, and survey data. Although earlier methods of information gathering and development produced valuable data, these questions highlighted the need for improved empirical validation.

In view of the definitional problems regarding grief, mourning, and bereavement constructs, it follows that measurement is a major roadblock in bereavement research. M. S. Stroebe, Hansson, and Stroebe (1993) stated that "currently there is no standard approach to bereavement assessment, in either the clinical or research setting" (p. 460). Validity issues are critical because of the many components of bereavement (for example, cognitive, affective, physiological, and social). These factors appear to change in relative importance over time and are influenced by the focus of the person doing the research. There are no clear boundaries between the construct of grief and other aspects such as depression, state of health, and mood. Sufficiently valid instruments to allow generalization over family systems or cultures do not exist (M. S. Stroebe et al., 1993).

Research design has posed another problem (see Lund, 1989; M. S. Stroebe et al., 1993). Most studies have relied on small samples, which preclude the use of multivariate statistics. Experimental designs using control groups and randomly selected samples are just beginning to be used with any degree of regularity. Longitudinal studies are essentially nonexistent. When such studies have been used, high subject attrition rates have been a matter of great concern. Refusal rates can be a problem, especially among recently bereaved individuals.

Many of these problems, however, can be overcome with improved statistical techniques and the introduction of increasingly sophisticated research designs. In addition, it has been demonstrated that the reluctance of potential study subjects to participate can be conquered (Rando, 1993; Sanders, 1989; M. S. Stroebe et al., 1993; Wallace, 1973). There is still a long way to go, but efforts are headed in the right direction.

## References

Abraham, K. (1924). A short study of the development of the libido, viewed in the light of mental disorders. In *Selected papers on psychoanalysis.* London: Hogarth Press.

American Psychiatric Association. (1994). *Diagnostic and statistical manual of mental disorders* (4th ed.). Washington, DC: Author.

Bornstein, P. E., & Clayton, P. J. (1972). The anniversary reaction. *Diseases of the Nervous System, 33,* 478–482.

Bowlby, J. (1980). *Attachment and loss: Volume III. Loss, sadness and depression.* New York: Basic Books.

Bowman, N. J. (1980). *Differential reactions to dissimilar types of death: Specifically the homicide/murder.* Unpublished doctoral dissertation, United States International University, San Diego.

Burgess, A. W. (1975). Family reaction to suicide. *American Journal of Orthopsychiatry, 45,* 291–298.

Burnell, G., & Burnell, A. (1989). *Clinical management of bereavement: A handbook for health care professionals.* New York: Human Sciences.

Charmaz, K. (1980). *The social reality of death: Death in contemporary America.* Reading, MA: Addison-Wesley.

Davidson, G. (1979). *Understanding: Death of the wished-for child.* Springfield, IL: OGR Service Corporation.

Dershimer, R. A. (1990). *Counseling the bereaved.* New York: Pergamon Press.

Doherty, S. (1990, November 13). Teaching kids how to grieve: In L.A., it's never too early to learn. *Newsweek,* p. 73.

Fenichel, O. (1945). *The psychoanalytic theory of neurosis.* New York: W. W. Norton.

Freud, S. (1957). Mourning and melancholia. In J. Strachey (Ed. and Trans.), *Standard edition of the complete psychological works of Sigmund Freud.* London: Hogarth Press. (Original work published 1917.)

Goffman, E. (1963). *Stigma: Notes on the management of spoiled identity.* New York: Simon & Schuster.

Kamerman, J. B. (1988). *Death in the midst of life.* Englewood Cliffs, NJ: Prentice Hall.

Kastenbaum, R., & Aisenberg, R. (1976). *The psychology of death.* New York: Springer.

Klein, M. (1948). Mourning and its relation to manic-depressive states. In *Contributions to psychoanalysis.* London: Hogarth Press.

Kübler-Ross, E. (1969). *On death and dying.* New York: Macmillan.

Lindemann, E. (1944). Symptomatology and management of acute grief. *American Journal of Psychiatry, 101,* 141–148.

Lorenz, K. (1963). *On aggression.* London: Metheum.

Lund, D. A. (Ed.). (1989). *Bereaved older spouses: Research with practical applications.* New York: Hemisphere Publishing.

Mawson, D., Marks, I., Ramm, L., & Stern, R. (1981). Guided mourning for morbid grief: A controlled study. *British Journal of Psychiatry, 138,* 185–193.

Moss, S. (1979). The grief work cycle in Judaism. In I. Gerber, A. Wiener, A. H. Kutscher, D. Battin, A. Arkin, &

I. K. Goldberg (Eds.), *Perspectives on bereavement* (pp. 170–175). New York: Arno Press.

Osterweis, M., Solomon, F., & Green, M. (Eds.). (1984). *Bereavement: Reactions, consequences, and care.* Washington, DC: National Academy Press.

Parkes, C. M., & Weiss, R. (1983). *Recovery from bereavement.* New York: Basic Books.

Poussaint, A. F. (1984, August). *The grief response following a homicide.* Paper presented at the 92nd annual convention of the American Psychological Association, Toronto.

Rando, T. A. (1986). *Grief, dying, and death.* Champaign, IL: Research Press.

Rando, T. A. (1993). *Treatment of complicated mourning.* Champaign, IL: Research Press.

Raphael, B. (1983). *The anatomy of bereavement.* New York: Basic Books.

Rosen, E. J. (1990). *Families facing death.* Lexington, MA: Lexington Books.

Sanders, C. M. (1989). *Grief: The mourning after.* New York: John Wiley & Sons.

Silver, R. L., & Wortman, C. B. (1980). Coping with undesirable life events. In J. Garber & N.E.P. Eligaman (Eds.), *Human helplessness: Theory and applications* (pp. 279–340). New York: Basic Books.

Sprang, M. V. (1991). *Factors influencing the extent of mourning, the extent of grieving and post-traumatic stress disorder symptomatology in surviving family members after a drunk driving fatality.* Unpublished doctoral dissertation, University of Texas at Arlington.

Stroebe, M. S., Hansson, R. O., & Stroebe, W. (1993). Contemporary themes and controversies in bereavement research. In M. S. Stroebe, W. Stroebe, & R. O. Hansson (Eds.), *Handbook of bereavement* (pp. 457–476). New York: Cambridge University Press.

Stroebe, W., & Stroebe, M. S. (1987). *Bereavement and health: The psychological and physical consequences of partner loss.* New York: Cambridge University Press.

Tallmer, M. (1987). Grief is a normal response to death of a loved one. In A. H. Kutscher, A. C. Carr, & L. G. Kutscher (Eds.), *Principles of thanatology* (pp. 171–185). New York: Columbia University Press.

Volkan, V. D. (1975). Re-grief therapy. In B. Schoenberg, A. Weiner, A. Kutscher, D. Pereta, & A. Carr (Eds.), *Bereavement: Its psychological aspects* (pp. 334–350). New York: Columbia University Press.

Wallace, S. E. (1973). *After suicide.* New York: John Wiley & Sons.

Westberg, G. E. (1971). *Good grief.* Philadelphia: Fortress Press.

Worden, J. W. (1991). *Grief counseling and grief therapy: A handbook for the mental health practitioner.* New York: Springer.

Wortman, C. B., Silver, R. C., & Kessler, R. C. (1993). The meaning of loss and adjustment to bereavement. In M. S. Stroebe, W. Stroebe, & R. O. Hansson (Eds.), *Handbook of bereavement* (pp. 349–366). New York: Cambridge University Press.

### Further Reading

Bloom-Feshbach, J., & Bloom-Feshbach, S. (Eds.). (1987). *The psychology of separation and loss.* San Francisco: Jossey-Bass.

Bowlby, J. (1988). *A secure base: Parent–child attachment and healthy human development.* New York: Basic Books.

Doka, K. (Ed.). (1989). *Disenfranchised grief: Recognizing hidden sorrow.* Lexington, MA: Lexington Books.

Green, B., & Irish, D. (Eds.). (1971). *Death education: Preparation for living.* Cambridge, MA: Schenkman.

Lord, J. (1987). *No time for goodbyes: Coping with sorrow, anger and injustice after a tragic death.* Ventura, CA: Pathfinder.

Schoenberg, B., Gerber, I., Wiener, A., Kutscher, A. H., Peretz, D., & Carr, A. C. (Eds.). (1975). *Bereavement: Its psychosocial aspects.* New York: Columbia University Press.

Simpson, M. (1987). *Dying, death, and grief: A critical bibliography.* Pittsburgh: University of Pittsburgh Press.

Webb, N. B. (1993). *Helping bereaved children: A handbook for practitioners.* New York: Guilford Press.

Zisook, S. (Ed.). (1987). *Biopsychosocial aspects of bereavement.* Washington, DC: American Psychiatric Press.

**John S. McNeil, DSW,** is professor and Louis and Ann Wolens Centennial Chair in Gerontology, School of Social Work, University of Texas at Austin, 2609 University Avenue, Austin, TX 78712.

#### For further information see

Aging: Services; Bioethical Issues; Brief Therapies; Cognitive Treatment; Direct Practice Overview; Disasters and Disaster Aid; End-of-Life Decisions; Ethnic-Sensitive Practice; Family Caregiving; HIV/AIDS Overview; Homicide; Hospice; Hospital Social Work; Interviewing; Natural Helping Networks; Self-Help Groups; Social Work Practice: Theoretical Base; Suicide; Victims of Torture and Trauma; Victim Services and Victim/Witness Assistance Programs.

**Key Words**

bereavement — loss
grief — mourning

## Bethune, Mary McLeod

*See* Biographies section, Volume 3

## Beveridge, Lord William

*See* Biographies section, Volume 3

# Bioethical Issues

**Larry W. Foster**

Bioethics is a multidisciplinary field that encompasses the traditional clinical health care professions and the academic and legal professions. The field of bioethics focuses on ethical issues in health care. Ethics, a branch of philosophy, involves "ought thinking"—what should or should not be done with respect to people. Distinct from but related to professional standards or codes of ethics, philosophic ethics is a systematic discussion of morality, of right and wrong conduct. Bioethics, then, is "the systematic study of human conduct in the area of the life sciences and health care, insofar as this conduct is examined in the light of moral values and principles" (Reich, 1978, p. xix).

Respect for people, preservation of life, and protection of liberty are exemplary moral values. *Autonomy* (the right to freedom in choices or actions), *beneficence* (the duty to benefit others and to maximize good consequences), *nonmaleficence* (the obligation to avoid doing harm to others), and *justice* (the responsibility to allocate benefits and burdens in a fair and equitable manner) are fundamental principles in biomedical ethics (Beauchamp & Childress, 1983). Principles are informed by general ethical theories ranging from deontological theories, which define actions as inherently right as a matter of principle, duty, or right, to teleological theories, which define right actions as those that attain the best outcomes or most desirable consequences.

Bioethics includes biomedical ethics, which is "one type of applied ethics—the application of general ethical theories, principles, and rules to problems of therapeutic practice, health care delivery, and medical and biological research" (Beauchamp & Childress, 1983, pp. ix, x). The scope of topics in bioethics is wide, ranging from the beginning to the end of life and encompassing such issues as sanctity versus quality of life, efficiency versus efficacy of care, justice versus equality in resource allocation, and primacy of the individual versus the common good in biomedical research. Value-laden issues that arise in practice often involve hard choices marked by competing principles, rights, duties, and obligations.

## Reproduction

### Reproductive Technologies

Artificial insemination, in vitro fertilization, and the freezing or transfer of human embryos have increased both options for and complications in family planning for infertile couples and individuals—heterosexual, gay, and lesbian. The right of ex-wives to gestate frozen embryos created with former husbands has been litigated (*Stowe v. Davis,* 1993), as has the priority of genetic rights in claims of parenthood and visitation privileges in surrogacy contracts (*Johnson v. Calvert,* 1993; *Matter Baby M,* 1988). Abramson (1991) asked, "Are infertility and inconvenience sufficient reasons for renting someone else's womb? What makes a mother or father fit and who decides?" (p. 7). Should parents who seek in vitro fertilization and who are at genetic risk be required to undergo genetic testing? Donor selection criteria raise the issue of "worthy" and "unworthy" parents. The potential for selective breeding raises fears of genetic discrimination rooted in racism, sexism, and economics. Should children be viewed as reproductive ends rather than as reproductive means, or as objects to be manipulated in utero to acquire desired offspring by those who can afford such choices (Ryan, 1990)? Potential exploitation of surrogate mothers, especially poor women or those otherwise motivated by financial gain (Parker, 1983)—including the hiring of nonwhite women to gestate embryos from white parents—underscores the imbalance of burdens and benefits associated with costly reproductive technologies. To what extent should privacy rights prevail over community interests in surrogacy contracts? The limits of reproductive freedom also have been challenged by accounts of children being conceived for ulterior motives, such as donation of bone marrow to siblings with terminal cancer ("Conceiving a Child," 1990). To what extent should society protect family procreative rights? Noncoital reproductive decision making in family planning challenges social work to reexamine the limits of procreative liberty. A balance of respect for individual and family autonomy with the welfare and interest of other parties involved is required.

### Prenatal Screening and Diagnosis

Amniocentesis, ultrasound, fetoscopy, and genetic testing and screening have provided a great deal of information for decision making, but not without a corresponding increase in maternal–fetal conflict. The presence of genetic defects such as cystic fibrosis, sickle cell anemia, spina bifida, and Tay-Sachs, or the probability of a future life-shortening disability are examples of pregnancies in which the interests of the mother and the fetus may not coincide. The option of terminating the pregnancy raises the issue not only of the equal and intrinsic value of the fetus and the mother but also of what constitutes a meaningful life and for whom. Who should decide the moral worth and future well-being of a fetus? If fetal surgery is performed, does the fetus have patient rights and thus personhood (Mattingly, 1992)? If a cesarean section is performed on behalf of an unborn fetus against the wishes of a competent patient who is terminally ill, is this an act of beneficence or paternalism (Johnsen, 1986)? Inequities in prenatal care, including cesarean sections (de Regt, Minkoff, Feldman, & Schwarz, 1986), do not favor young, unmarried, and poor and women of color, who are also more likely to have high-risk pregnancies, higher rates of infant mortality, low-birthweight babies, and children with congenital defects and disabilities (Carlton & Poole, 1990). Who should bear the burden of care for disabled newborns? For whom should social work advocate in cases of maternal–fetal conflict—especially when conflicts of interest extend to include the agency and the community?

### Abortion and Fetal Research

Unresolved definitions of when life and personhood begin raise questions: Is abortion killing? When does a woman's right to make decisions about her own body include abortion? Should abortion be an unchallenged right in situations of rape, incest, and significant fetal anomalies? Who or what should determine the assignment of primary and secondary moral worth between a pregnant woman and a fetus?

Society's interest in abortion is relevant. Required waiting periods, parental notification and consent, and the lack of abortion facilities are associated with increases in medical risks—especially for young and poor and women of color (American Medical Association Council on Scientific Affairs, 1992). President Clinton's lifting of the ban on abortion counseling in federally funded clinics and on the use of federal funds for experimental research with fetal tissue from abortions raised both hopes and fears: hopes that people who have incurable diseases such as diabetes, Alzheimer's, Parkinson's, and Huntington's will be helped; fears that unborn fetuses may be harmed by an increase in induced abortions. Fear that "commercial complicity between abortionists and transplanters will be created, and human life will be turned into just another commodity" (Drane, 1991, p. 34) is prevalent. Should justification of fetal tissue transplants hinge on the morality of induced abortions? Does a pregnant woman have the right to decide what will be done with the tissue of an aborted fetus?

The legality of abortion has not resolved the ethical issue of an embryo's personhood or the morality of therapeutic fetal tissue transplants. Social workers in obstetrics and family planning clinics weigh the risks, burdens, and benefits of treatment decisions in the context of sometimes conflicting interests—those of the patient, the family, and the community.

## Adolescent Health

Ethical issues in adolescent health have come into sharp focus with significant increases in adolescent sexual activity, pregnancy, abortion, homelessness, suicide, homicide (Children's Defense Fund, 1990), alcohol and drug abuse (Farrow, 1990), gang-related violence, human immunodeficiency virus infection and acquired immune deficiency syndrome (Bowler, Sheon, D'Angelo, & Vermund, 1992). What is society's responsibility to adolescents who engage in health-compromising behaviors? Many of these youths are homeless or runaways, with multiple health and mental health needs, and are seeking confidential services. When does an adolescent's right to privacy and confidentiality about HIV status give way to the protection of third parties? Does a pregnant teenager's substance abuse constitute fetal abuse?

According to experts in adolescent medicine (Farrow, Deisher, Brown, Kulig, & Kipke, 1991), the problems of these youths "should be viewed as a human rights issue with roots in poverty and victimization" (p. 717). Compared with adults, adolescents are more vulnerable in accessing health care because they are less likely to have health insurance (Office of Technology Assessment, 1991). The legal presumption of a minor's incompetence is also relevant. What is a mature minor? What constitutes decisional capacity? Who decides? On whose behalf does a social worker act—the adolescent in terms of autonomy and the right to informed consent, or the parents or legal guardian?

A strong personal and professional identity is needed to manage conflicting moral claims, rights, and duties in adolescent health. Respect for self-determination is balanced against "protecting [adolescents'] well-being from the harmful consequences of their choices when their decisional capacities are defective" (Buchanan & Brock, 1989, p. 232).

### Organ Transplantation

Altruistic expressions of consent in organ donation have been insufficient in closing the gap between supply and demand for donor organs. Proposals to close the "organ gap" range from presumed and required consent to the use of financial incentives (Barnett & Kaserman, 1993).

Is there a moral obligation to give one's body parts to another person (Murray, 1991)? Are human organs private or public property? Should organ transplantation be based on medical need, merit, ability to pay, or universal entitlement? Ethical issues pertain to informed consent; safety and efficacy of transplantation; donor and recipient selection criteria; risks, burdens, and benefits; compliance with transplant protocols; and resource allocation.

Issues vary depending on whether the donor is living or dead: Living donors are used for skin, blood, kidneys, and bone marrow, whereas deceased donors are used for vital organs such as corneas, heart, liver, kidneys, and lungs. Should living donors risk bodily harm and possibly death for another? Related donors and recipients may be coerced not only by a life-threatening illness but also by family pressure. When, if ever, do family members have a moral right to withhold a life-saving organ? Informed consent is particularly difficult with pediatric donors and recipients because of children's maturity level and decision-making capacity.

In cadaveric donations, defining death is a unique ethical issue. Davis (1993) noted that "cadaveric donors, although legally dead, appear very much alive; thanks to support systems their skin is warm, their color is good, and they continue to digest and eliminate" (p. 119). Should brain-dead patients, either anencephalic infants (born without all or part of brain) or adults in a persistent vegetative state (cortical or higher brain death), be kept on life support so as to be a source of vital organs? Inequities in allocation of organs are evidenced by racial and income disparities in kidney transplants that favor white rather than black people (Kjellstrand, 1988).

As a part of informed consent interviews, social workers explore cultural, religious, and socioeconomic factors in transplantation. Costly organ transplants that are beyond the reach of many people raise another question (Davis, 1992): Should wealthy foreign nationals in need of donor organs receive American cadaver organs? Dhooper (1990) noted "By lobbying and educating the public, social workers can promote practices that encourage equitable organ procurement and allocation policies" (p. 325).

## AIDS

Acquired immune deficiency syndrome (AIDS), a lethal disease caused by the human immunodeficiency virus (HIV), has reached epidemic proportions. This reality, combined with the fact that AIDS is largely preventable, sets the stage for ethical issues related to mandatory HIV testing, disclosure of HIV status to third parties, prevention through lifestyle changes, and participation in randomized clinical trials (Reamer, 1991). Other ethical issues relate to the unique and existential nature of AIDS. The work of Susan Sontag (1990) is relevant. Abramson (1990) aptly summarized her work: "AIDS evokes the most basic human fears and inhibitions through its association with sex, blood, drugs, and death" (p. 171).

Respect for life, people, and the common good are undermined by social stigma, discrimination, neglect, and isolation of people with AIDS or HIV infection. Income and racial disparities exist in HIV status and health care, including increases in HIV infection in mothers and infants, especially for poor women of color (Carlton & Poole, 1990; Kaplan & Krell-Long, 1993). Compared with other infants with problems, infants who are at risk for HIV infection (Levin, Driscoll, & Fleischman, 1991) and AIDS infants, as well as those who have been prenatally exposed to crack cocaine (Bopp & Hall Gardner, 1991), are less likely to receive aggressive care. Does an infant's expected quality of life diminish sanctity of life and the obligation to preserve life? What are the ethical obligations of health care professionals to care for HIV-infected patients and patients who have AIDS? Is there a reasonable level of risk of job-related HIV infection? Should the HIV status of health professionals be disclosed to patients? Can both privacy rights and public health be protected? What are the limits to HIV testing—patients, health care workers, pregnant women, people seeking health insurance, or only those considered at risk for HIV infection? When do a person's rights of privacy and confidentiality about HIV status give way to the protection of third parties? The ethics of secrecy both protects and harms, according to Abramson (1990), who stated that "Decisions to share or protect confidence raise the question of who the client is" (p. 170).

### Death and Dying

#### Definitions of Death

According to the President's Commission for the Study of Ethical Problems in Medicine and

Biomedical and Behavioral Research (1981), "An individual who has sustained either (1) irreversible cessation of circulatory and respiratory functions or (2) irreversible cessation of all functions of the entire brain, including the brain stem, is dead" (p. 2). This recommended definition rules out the higher-brain (cerebral) definition of death, which characterizes people in a persistent vegetative state (PVS). At issue for both advocates and critics of the higher-brain definition of death is the question of personhood: Are human beings who are not conscious (anencephalics and PVS patients) still people? Is a human being with diminished cognitive functions (a senile or developmentally disabled patient) less of a person? Should the definition of death be expanded to include people who have never had or who have lost their capacity to think, know, feel, or be capable of meaningful relations with others? When is life no longer meaningful? Unresolved definitions of death and when personhood ends raise ethical issues in the use of life supports.

**Withholding and Withdrawing Life Support**

To die with dignity is a moral value. To die with unnecessary pain or suffering is a threat to that value. When is the withholding and withdrawing of life support optional or obligatory?

Artificially administered nutrition and hydration are considered forms of life support and can be used to accelerate death, prolong life, and prolong death (Gallagher-Allred, 1991). The symbolism of food and water in artificial nutrition and hydration is central to the ethics of forgoing life support, as is the certainty of definitions of death, medical futility, and patient decisional capacity, especially in cases of progressive dementia and neurological disease. Should neurologically impaired people who find life burdensome and without discernible meaning be kept on life support? Should "do not resuscitate" orders be rescinded without patient-informed consent during palliative surgery or in the emergency room?

The subjective and relative nature of quality of life decisions and the judicious use of resources also are relevant. Accounts of terminally ill patients wanting to live until birthdays, weddings, anniversaries, or maturity of insurance policies are common; these occurrences raise the issue of treatment effect versus benefit. When is treatment that is medically futile but socially beneficial justifiable? Treatments that are palliative or life prolonging are morally defensible if the patient has not expressed wishes to the contrary. Health care professionals and family members have an obligation to honor the withholding or removal of treatment—such as cardiopulmonary resuscitation, ventilation, antibiotics, transfusions, and artificial nutrition and hydration—that does not hold promise for quality of life consistent with a patient's wishes or advanced directives, that is, a living will or durable power of attorney for health care.

**Assisted Suicide and Euthanasia**

Is there a time when being alive no longer means having a life capable of meaning? At that time, is physician-assisted suicide considered death with dignity? Is there a moral difference between killing (active euthanasia) and letting life go by omitting therapeutic treatment (passive euthanasia) (Loewy, 1989)? When, if ever, does a competent patient's right to self-determination include the right to choose death over life?

Increasingly, active killing is being considered a moral option among hopelessly ill people who are dying in pain and distress and in inhumane situations—especially among young people with AIDS (Drane, 1991). Are age and chance of survival—especially among poor and underinsured or uninsured terminally ill people—sufficient criteria for setting limits to care or euthanasia? What is society's responsibility to dying people? Do assisted suicide and euthanasia ever serve the common good? Such a decision evolves from within the community (Dougherty, 1993); its ethos or moral climate is produced by values and moral decisions of community members. An attitude of ambivalence toward active termination of life is prevalent in the helping professions and in the larger community and is reflected in calls for better pain management (Smith, Orlowski, Radey, & Scofield, 1992) and hospice-inspired strategies of caring for terminally ill people (Dougherty, 1993).

## Allocation of Resources

Is health care a right or a privilege? What is a just allocation of resources? Should access to and allocation of health care be based on need, merit, age, or chances for survival? Do individuals who pursue self-destructive lifestyles have a moral claim on health care? Do illegal aliens have a moral claim on health care resources in the United States? Can choice and quality of health care be made available at a reasonable cost to everyone? Such questions are being asked in the context of significant disparities in health status and health care by race, ethnicity, and income. Mortality differences favor white people relative to African Americans (Sorlie, Rogot, Anderson, Johnson, & Backlund, 1992), as do outcomes on 26 other health parameters (for example, low birthweight; heart disease; and, among individuals younger than age 45, hypertension, cancer incidence, and tuberculosis) (Byrd & Clayton, 1992). Disparity in the allocation of health care favors white people relative to African Americans (Council on Ethical and Judicial Affairs, 1990; Weissman, Stern, Fielding, & Epstein, 1991). Elderly people receive significantly more health care than do children (Callahan, 1992), and uninsured newborns in neonatal intensive care receive less care than do infants covered by Medicaid and private insurance (Braverman, Egerter, Bennett, & Showstack, 1991).

The fact that rationing is central to such disparities in health and health care raises the issue of autonomy versus justice and of individual claims in expensive medical care versus societal needs. Brody (1992), commenting on the work of Hadorn and Brook (1991) regarding resource allocation, stated "Rationing occurs only when society tolerates inequities in the distribution of necessary health services" (p. 11). In discussing priorities in mental health services and the lack of support given to these services compared with physical health services, Boyle and Callahan (1993) made the distinction between rationing and setting priorities in services: Setting of priorities is the sorting and ranking of services based on cost, effectiveness, and appropriateness of care, whereas rationing is the "denial of services demonstrated to be beneficial" (p. S6).

Subject to requirements of managed care and organizational–societal mandates to contain costs, social workers ration services on a daily basis through high-risk screening and discharge planning, which often involve counseling patients and families whose access to long-term care, home care services, and medical equipment are rationed by virtue of third-party payers. Such rationing often runs counter to basic tenets of social work practice (Foster, Sharp, Scesny, McLellan, & Cotman, 1993). The extent to which health care decisions are based on costs rather than potential benefit to patients is an ethical dilemma for social workers.

## Biomedical Research

Ethical issues in biomedical research pertain to (1) the freedom of patients or subjects to participate in research without coercion (autonomy), (2) the benefit of the research to present or future patients or subjects and society (beneficence), (3) the risk of harm to patients or subjects (nonmaleficence), (4) the reasonableness of costs to patients or subjects (justice), and (5) the privacy of patient or subject information (confidentiality) (Kanoti, 1983). Participation in biomedical research is viewed as justified when it is in the best interest of the patient or subject, or when the likely benefits outweigh possible risk of harm. However, in whose best interest are randomized clinical trials (Freedman, 1992; Markman, 1992)—the individual patient or future patients?

Commenting on experimental procedures involving individuals as either subjects or controls, Almond (1988) noted that "the patient's autonomy and the need for informed consent may be set against the welfare of future patients—the greatest good of the greatest number" (p. 175). When, if ever, is participation in nontherapeutic research ethically justified? Do AIDS patients have a moral right to participate in clinical trials in which the relative benefits and harms of unapproved drugs are unknown (Levine, 1991)? Should partner notification be a part of research protocols involving AIDS patients? If so, who has this clinical responsibility—research or clinical staff? Are clinical trials that use experimental drugs of unknown risks with incurable cancer patients to prove the efficacy of one treatment protocol over another ethically justified?

In pediatric research, legal presumption of a minor's incompetence raises the question "Are adolescents, ethically speaking, capable of providing their own consent for participation as research subjects?" (Lynch, 1993, p. 127). Whether adolescents should be considered more like children or more like adults depends on their cognitive, emotional, and social maturity. Similar consideration is given to the inclusion of mentally impaired people in nontherapeutic research, but greater safeguards may be necessary because of social worth criteria (Cooke, 1978).

Areas of research that pose ethical issues indirectly related to patients or subjects include finders' fees—or payment to physicians for referral of patients as research subjects—and corporate reimbursement for entering patients into clinical trials that test particular drugs or products (Shimm & Spece, 1991). Research that poses ethical concerns on a more global scale includes the Human Genome Project, which involves mapping the entire gene system to increase the ability to search for and predict, through genetic testing and screening, the future disability of oneself or one's children (McCarrick, 1993). One concern is how society will use this information, particularly law enforcement officials; employers; and insurers of life, health, and disability (Murray, 1993). Reliability and confidentiality of DNA profiles raise fears of genetic discrimination on the basis of cost savings as well as social desirability criteria. Costly genetic testing and screening will compete for scarce societal resources and further challenge social workers and other helping professionals in their efforts to minimize inequities in access to and allocation of health care.

## Conclusion

Like bioethics, social work is inherently normative and a moral enterprise. Social workers, committed to the avoidance of harm and the promotion of good, are vital participants in the discussion of ethical issues in health care. Since Reamer (1985) reviewed the emergence and scope of bioethical issues in social work, the climate of health care has changed and the issues now facing the profession appear more complex and compelling. A dual emphasis on fiscal and ethical accountability in health care reform raises the question of how to both contain costs and ensure equity and equality of care. Ethical concerns include trade-offs between efficiency and equity of care and the uncertainty that surrounds definitions (and quality) of life and death. Patients, families, and legislators question the intent and assumptions that underlie decisions of health care professionals. The questioning serves as a reminder that knowing what one can do clinically is not the same as knowing what one should do ethically or may do legally. An increased awareness of bioethical issues is a first step toward preparing the social work profession to respond to the ethical concerns social workers encounter in health care practice.

## References


Abramson, M. (1990). Keeping secrets: Social workers and AIDS. *Social Work, 35,* 169–173.

Abramson, M. (1991). Ethics and technological advances: Contributions of social work practice. *Social Work in Health Care, 15*(2), 5–17.

Almond, B. (1988). Philosophy and its technologies. *Journal of Medical Ethics, 14,* 173–178.

American Medical Association Council on Scientific Affairs. (1992). Induced termination of pregnancy before and after *Roe v. Wade*: Trends in the mortality and morbidity of women. *Journal of the American Medical Association, 268,* 3231–3239.

Barnett, A. H., & Kaserman, D. L. (1993). The shortage of organs for transplantation: Exploring the alternatives. *Issues in Law & Medicine, 9*(2), 117–137.

Beauchamp, T. L., & Childress, J. F. (1983). *Principles of biomedical ethics* (2nd ed.). New York: Oxford University Press.

Bopp, J., & Hall Gardner, D. (1991). AIDS babies, crack babies: Challenges to the law. *Issues in Law & Medicine, 7,* 3–51.

Bowler, S., Sheon, A., D'Angelo, L., & Vermund, S. (1992). HIV and AIDS among adolescents in the United States: Increasing risk in the 1990s. *Journal of Adolescence, 15,* 345–371.

Boyle, P., & Callahan, D. (1993). Mind and hearts: Priorities in mental health services. *Hastings Center Report, 23*(5), S3–S23.

Braverman, P. A., Egerter, S., Bennett, T., & Showstack, J. (1991). Differences in hospital resource allocation among sick newborns according to insurance coverage. *Journal of the American Medical Association, 266*(23), 3300–3308.

Brody, H. (1992). New definition for rationing. *Ethics in formation, 4*(2), 11.

Buchanan, A. E., & Brock, D. W. (1989). *Deciding for others: The ethics of surrogate decision making*. Cambridge, England: Cambridge University Press.

Byrd, W. M., & Clayton, L. A. (1992). An American health dilemma: A history of blacks in the health system. *Journal of the National Medical Association, 84*(2), 189–200.

Callahan, D. (1992). Reforming the health care system for children and the elderly to balance cure and care. *Academic Medicine, 67*(4), 219–222.

Carlton, T. O., & Poole, D. L. (1990). Trends in maternal and child health care: Implications for research and issues for social work practice. *Social Work in Health Care, 15*(1), 45–61.

Children's Defense Fund. (1990). *S.O.S. America! A children's defense budget*. Washington, DC: Author.

Conceiving a child for "ulterior motive" creates ethics furor. (1990, June). *Medical Ethics Advisor,* pp. 41–43.

Cooke, R. E. (1978). Mentally handicapped. In W. T. Reich (Ed.-in-Chief), *Encyclopedia of Bioethics* (Vols. 3–4, pp. 1108–1114). New York: Free Press.

Council on Ethical and Judicial Affairs. (1990). Black-white disparities in health care. *Journal of the American Medical Association, 263*(17), 2344–2346.

Davis, D. S. (1992). Organ transplants, foreign nationals, and the free rider problem. *Theoretical Medicine, 13,* 337–347.

Davis, D. S. (1993, April). Heartbreak and heart's ease: Thinking about organ donation. *Second Opinion,* 118–120.

de Regt, R. H., Minkoff, H. L., Feldman, J., & Schwarz, R. H. (1986). Relation of private or clinic care to the cesarean birth rate. *New England Journal of Medicine, 315,* 619–624.

Dhooper, S. S. (1990). Organ transplantation: Who decides? *Social Work, 35,* 322–327.

Dougherty, C. J. (1993). The common good, terminal illness, and euthanasia. *Issues in Law & Medicine, 9*(2), 151–166.

Drane, J. F. (1991, September). Medical ethics in the 1990s. *Health Progress,* 29–37.

Farrow, J. A. (1990). Adolescent chemical dependency. *Adolescent Medicine, 74*(5), 1265–1274.

Farrow, J. A., Deisher, R., Brown, R., Kulig, J., & Kipke, M. (1991). Health and health needs of homeless and runaway youth. *Journal of Adolescent Health, 13,* 717–726.

Foster, L. W., Sharp, J., Scesny, A., McLellan, L., & Cotman, K. (1993). Bioethics: Social work's response and training needs. *Social Work in Health Care, 19*(1), 15–38.

Freedman, B. (1992). A response to a purported ethical difficulty with randomized clinical trials involving cancer patients. *Journal of Clinical Ethics, 3*(3), 231–234.

Gallagher-Allred, C. R. (1991). Managing ethical issues in nutrition support of terminally ill patients. *Nutrition in Clinical Practice, 6,* 113–116.

Hadorn, D. C., & Brook, R. H. (1991). The health care resource allocation debate: Defining our terms. *Journal of the American Medical Association, 266,* 3328.

Johnsen, D. (1986). The creation of fetal rights: Conflicts with women's constitutional rights to liberty, privacy and equal protection. *Yale Law Review, 95,* 599–615.

Johnson v. Calvert, 5 Cal. 4th 84 (1993).

Kanoti, G. (1983). Clinical research and ethics. *Cleveland Clinic Quarterly, 50*(12), 28.

Kaplan, M. D., & Krell-Long, L. (1993). AIDS, health policy, and ethics. *Affilia, 8*(2), 157–170.

Kjellstrand, C. M. (1988). Age, sex, and race inequality in renal transplantation. *Archives of Internal Medicine, 148,* 1305–1309.

Levin, B. W., Driscoll, J. M., & Fleischman, A. R. (1991). Treatment choice for infants in the neonatal intensive care unit at risk for AIDS. *Journal of the American Medical Association, 265,* 2976–2981.

Levine, C. (1991). AIDS and the ethics of human subjects research. In F. G. Reamer (Ed.), *AIDS & ethics* (pp. 77–104). New York: Columbia University Press.

Loewy, E. H. (1989). *Textbook of medical ethics.* New York: Plenum Medical.

Lynch, A. (1993). Research involving adolescents: Are they ethically competent to consent/refuse on their own? In G. Koren (Ed.), *Textbook of ethics in pediatric research* (pp. 125–136). Malabar, FL: Krieger.

Markman, M. (1992). Ethical difficulties with randomized clinical trials involving cancer patients: Examples from the field of gynecologic oncology. *Journal of Clinical Ethics, 3*(3), 193–195.

Matter Baby M, 109 N.J. 396, 537A. 2d 1227 (1988).

Mattingly, S. (1992). The maternal–fetal dyad: Exploring the two-patient obstetric model. *Hastings Center Report, 22*(1), 13–18.

McCarrick, P. M. (1993). Genetic testing and screening. *Kennedy Institute of Ethics, 3*(3), 333–354.

Murray, T. H. (1991). Are we morally obligated to make gifts of our bodies? *Health Matrix, 1*(5), 19–27.

Murray, T. H. (1993). Genetics and just health care: A genome task force report. *Kennedy Institutes of Ethics, 3*(3), 327–331.

Office of Technology Assessment. (1991). *Adolescent health: I. Summary and policy options.* Washington, DC: Author.

Parker, P. J. (1983). Motivation of surrogate mothers: Initial findings. *American Journal of Psychology, 140,* 117–118.

President's Commission for the Study of Ethical Problems in Medicine and Biomedical and Behavioral Research. (1981). *Defining death.* Washington, DC: U.S. Government Printing Office.

Reamer, F. G. (1985). The emergence of bioethics in social work. *Health & Social Work, 10,* 271–281.

Reamer, F. G. (1991). *AIDS & ethics.* New York: Columbia University Press.

Reich, W. T. (1978). Introduction. In W. T. Reich (Ed.), *Encyclopedia of bioethics* (p. xix). New York: Free Press.

Ryan, M. (1990). The argument for unlimited procreative liberty: A feminist critique. *Hastings Center Report, 20,* 6–12.

Shimm, D. S., & Spece, R. G., Jr. (1991). Industry reimbursement for entering patients into clinical trials: Legal and ethical issues. *Annals of Internal Medicine, 115*(2), 148–151.

Smith, M. L., Orlowski, J., Radey, C., & Scofield, G. (1992). A good death: Is euthanasia the answer? *Cleveland Clinic Journal of Medicine, 59,* 99–109.

Sontag, S. (1990). *AIDS and its metaphors.* Garden City, NY: Doubleday.

Sorlie, P., Rogot, E., Anderson, R., Johnson, N., & Backlund, E. (1992). Black–white mortality differences by family income. *Lancet, 340,* 346–350.

Stowe v. Davis, 113 S. Ct. 1259 (1993).

Weissman, J. S., Stern, R., Fielding, S., & Epstein, A. (1991). Delayed access to health care: Risk factors, reasons, and consequences. *Annals of Internal Medicine, 114,* 325–331.

## Further Reading

Beauchamp, T. L., & Walters, L. (1994). *Contemporary issues in bioethics* (4th ed.). Belmont, CA: Wadsworth.

Callahan, D. (1990). *What kind of life? The limits of medical progress.* New York: Simon & Schuster.

Friedman, E. (1992). *Choices and conflict: Explorations in health care ethics.* Chicago: American Hospital Publications.

Levine, C. (Ed.). (1993). *Taking sides: Clashing views on controversial bioethical issues.* New York: Duskin.

Monagle, J. F., & Thomasma, L. (1994). *Health care ethics and critical issues.* Gaithersburg, MD: Aspen Publishers.

Pence, G. (1990). *Classic cases in medical ethics.* New York: McGraw-Hill.

Post, S. (1993). *Inquiries in bioethics.* Washington, DC: Georgetown University Press.

Purtilo, R. (1993). *Ethical dimensions in the health professions* (2nd ed.). Philadelphia: W. B. Saunders.

**Larry W. Foster, PhD,** is an ethics consultant and social work educator affiliated with Northeastern Ohio Universities College of Medicine.

## For further information see

Abortion; Aging: Overview; Children's Rights; Ethical Issues in Research; Ethics and Values; Families Overview; Genetics; Health Care Overview; HIV/AIDS: Overview; Hospice; Hospital Social Work; Legal Issues: Low-Income and Dependent People; Managed Care; Maternal and Child Health; Patient Rights; Professional Conduct; Professional Liability and Malpractice.

**Key Words**

bioethics
health care
biomedical ethics

# Biographies

*See* Biographies section, Volume 3

## Birth Control

*See* Abortion; Family Planning

# Bisexuality

**Jean S. Gochros**

As long ago as 1948, Kinsey, Pomeroy, Martin, and Gebhard (1948, 1953) found that the distinction between homosexuality and heterosexuality was not as clear as had been assumed. Since then a wealth of research and anecdotal evidence has supported that revelation. Surprisingly, however, the general public and the helping professions have all but ignored these findings. Bisexual men and women remain largely invisible (Klein & Wolf, 1985; Tielman, Carballo, & Hendriks, 1991). To a large extent this invisibility stems from society's historical tendency to link socially acceptable sexual expression solely with reproduction. The result is a myopic and homophobic view of sexual expression and sexual orientation (Gochros, Gochros, & Fischer, 1986).

The past decade has brought—and the acquired immune deficiency syndrome (AIDS) pandemic has forced—increased awareness of and interest in bisexuality. A rapidly growing body of research and literature is beginning to provide diverse and in-depth discussions of sexual orientation. For example, a 1985 issue of the *Journal of Homosexuality* devoted entirely to bisexuality discussed both theoretical issues and practical concerns of individuals in specific situations (Klein & Wolf, 1985). An international collection of professionals from around the world brought cross-cultural perspectives to bear on bisexuality and the worldwide spread of AIDS (Tielman, Carballo, & Hendriks, 1991).

## Defining and Redefining Bisexuality

What exactly is bisexuality? Popular definitions of "equal" or "some degree of" erotic interest in both genders are both simplistic and misleading. It is helpful to explore differing views of sexual orientation as they have evolved in the 20th century.

Although homosexual and bisexual behaviors have been documented throughout history, labeling, defining, and researching sexual orientation are relatively recent developments. A review of the literature suggests that three major perspectives have evolved sequentially: first, a "pre-Kinsey" perspective, before 1948; second, a "Kinsey" perspective, starting in 1948; and third, a "post-Kinsey" perspective, starting in the 1960s (Boulton, 1991; Klein & Wolf, 1985; Tielman et al., 1991). All three perspectives coexist today.

Each perspective is embraced by many writers and researchers who may disagree with each other on fine points but who share the same general approach. Each perspective provides definitions or descriptions of sexual orientation and suggests causes of homosexuality that form the basis for religious, political, and mental health judgments about sexual orientation and what—if anything—should be done about it.

### Pre-Kinsey Perspective

***Definitions.*** Whether from a religious, political, or mental health perspective, a pre-Kinsey approach sees heterosexuality and homosexuality as bipolar, occurring at opposite ends of a static pole. The two are seen as mutually exclusive: The presence of one rules out the other, for one can no more be "a little bit" homosexual or heterosexual than one can be "a little bit" pregnant. In this view, bisexuality is not a valid concept and does not exist.

***Causative explanations and mental health assessments.*** The pre-Kinsey perspective views heterosexuality as the only possible (hence desirable) norm and sees homosexuality as an abnormal, undesirable deviation from that norm. A fundamentalist clergyman might explain homosexuality as a creation of the devil to be cured through such religious interventions as prayer or exorcism. A mental health professional might explain it as mental illness, neurosis, or a symptom of maladjustment caused by poor parental models, sexual abuse, low self-esteem, compulsivity, or some other emotional disturbance to be cured by some form of psychotherapy. No matter what the rationale, homosexuality is seen as an inability to accept one's true heterosexuality and as an evil to be erased.

### Kinsey Perspective

***Definitions.*** A Kinsey viewpoint sees heterosexuality and homosexuality as often coexisting on a bipolar but nonexclusive continuum ranging from "exclusively heterosexual" to "exclusively homosexual." Kinsey et al. (1948, 1953) defined "sexual orientation" as overt actions and psychological reactions (including fantasy) that result in orgasm and studied how often these actions and reactions had occurred in any three-year period between adolescence and old age in a person's life. Kinsey used a seven-point scale, with individuals' erotic experiences ranging across the scale as follows:

0 = exclusively heterosexual
1 = predominantly heterosexual, incidentally homosexual
2 = predominantly heterosexual, more than incidentally homosexual
3 = equally heterosexual and homosexual
4 = predominantly homosexual, more than incidentally heterosexual
5 = predominantly homosexual, incidentally heterosexual
6 = exclusively homosexual.

Kinsey et al. (1948) found that almost 37 percent of white American men fell somewhere between the two extremes of the scale and that rarely did anyone fall exactly in the middle. Despite attempts to improve it, the Kinsey scale remains a major tool that researchers and clinicians use to assess a person's "degree" of homosexuality.

Kinsey et al. (1948) found that for three years between the ages of 16 and 55, 37 percent of white American men have at least one or two homosexual erotic experiences that lead to orgasm. That number rises to 50 percent when men over age 55 are included. Twenty-five percent have more than incidental homosexual experiences, and 13 percent have predominantly homosexual experiences that lead to orgasm. Moreover, at least 11 percent to 13 percent of white married men have reported homosexual experiences during the course of heterosexual marriage, and 18 percent to 20 percent of self-identified exclusively homosexual men have been married (Gochros, 1989). Yet Kinsey et al. reported that only 8 percent of white American men define themselves as exclusively homosexual later in life. Although the percentages differ for women, the essential findings are the same.

Despite sampling flaws, the Kinsey et al. studies (1948, 1953) are still considered the most comprehensive and generally reliable research available. For the most part, newer research using Kinsey's scale has supported his view that heterosexuality and homosexuality can coexist to varying degrees at various times throughout a person's life (Gochros, 1989; Klein & Wolf, 1985; Tielman et al., 1991).

***Causation and mental health assessments and treatments.*** Although the Kinsey perspective often is more accepting of homosexuality than is the pre-Kinsey view, it divides into two branches. One branch is a "less negative" faction that views homosexuality as variant or learned dysfunctional behavior rather than as sick or pathological. Mental health is more apt to be assessed on an individual basis; attempts are made to "cure" homosexuality only at the patient's request or if the homosexuality is seen as truly dysfunctional for that individual. Nevertheless, this branch often appears as little more than a softening of the pre-Kinsey negative view of homosexuality; it actually depicts an overlap between the pre- and post-Kinsey perspectives.

The true distinction of the Kinsey perspective rests in the second, "completely positive" faction, which views homosexuality purely as a biologically or genetically based variant behavior. Mental health is always assessed on a purely individual basis, and homosexuality itself is never seen as a criterion for such assessment. Indeed, this view remains an essentially bipolar and mutually exclusive view of sexual orientation in which the presence of heterosexuality may be seen as pathology (that is, an inability to accept one's true homosexuality).

This faction also gave rise to a militant gay rights movement and what Klein (1978) saw as an ironic political alliance with militant pre-Kinseys analogous to the clash between white supremicists and African American militants. Just as racial groups with completely opposing stances may both argue that one drop of African American blood in one's history is enough to define a person as African American, so the "religious right" and gay militants may both argue that one "drop" of homosexuality is enough to define a person as homosexual.

Neither faction really accepts the validity of bisexuality, whether the individual scores a 3 on the Kinsey scale or lies somewhere else in the range from 1 to 5. The first faction would argue that the presence of any homosexuality (including fantasies) indicates either pathological denial of one's true heterosexuality or an inability to form satisfying normal relationships. The second faction would see the presence of bisexuality as indicating either political cowardice or pathological denial of one's true homosexuality, at best marking a temporary transition point on the way to acceptance. Each group seeks to "cure" that pathology.

**Post-Kinsey Perspective**

The newest perspective, perhaps beginning with Klein (1978), starts where Kinsey et al. (1953) left off, and it is still evolving. Its proponents are apt to appreciate the concept of bisexuality in that they see both homosexual and bisexual behaviors and lifestyles as valid, viable options. The bipolar continuum of the Kinsey scale implies (and has inadvertently created the popular misconception of) a sharply defined "bisexual" middle category (Ross, 1991). Increasingly, however, theorists have begun to point out flaws in the scale and to debate the concept of a separate, discrete bisexual entity (Hansen & Evans, 1985; Klein, Sepekoff, & Wolf, 1985; Lourea, 1985; Paul, 1985; Ross, 1991; Zinik, 1985).

***Definitions.*** Kinsey used a single dimension—genital erotic behavior, including the psychological component of arousal and orgasm—to define sexual orientation. Post-Kinsey theorists point out that this definition fails to differentiate between behaviors, emotions, and lifestyles. It ignores individual sexual patterns, situational differences, cultural variations, and changes over time. For example, a prisoner may temporarily engage in homosexual behavior because of a lack of heterosexual partners. A woman may have erotic sex with a man but have erotic fantasies about a woman. A man may have a long-term monogamous relationship with a man followed by a similar relationship with a woman, or he may identify himself as heterosexual no matter how many same-sex partners he has had. A woman may enjoy recreational sex and socialization with men yet feel deep emotional attachment to women. In short, a person might have homosexual and heterosexual relationships concurrently, sequentially, or simultaneously (as in "swinging"). An individual might enjoy one aspect of a homosexual relationship and enjoy another aspect of a heterosexual one. Homosexual (or heterosexual) needs might be compelling at one time and weak at another (Klein, 1978).

***Dimensions of sexual orientation.*** Klein, Sepekoff, and Wolf (1985) suggested seven dimensions of sexual orientation: attraction, behavior, fantasy, social preference, emotional preference, self-identification, and lifestyle. Using a modified Kinsey scale, they rated sexual orientation at three periods of a person's life—past, present, and "ideal" future. They reported that regardless of the label people used to define themselves, respondents' self-ratings often varied according to each of the seven dimensions and often changed over time. Both extremes had moved toward bisexuality. Those who had labeled themselves as bisexual at present were most apt to fit their self-labels and to desire little change for the future. Although these researchers warned of limited generalizability because of sampling problems, they presented convincing evidence that sexual orientation is both multivariate and dynamic.

Sexual orientation, then, is a complicated matter with many variations and dimensions. There are wide gaps between people's self-labels and their actual behaviors. Reinisch (1994), for example, noted that 70 percent of self-defined lesbians have had sexual relationships with men and that 15 percent to 26 percent of self-defined exclusively homosexual men have either married or cohabitated with women.

Anecdotal evidence and research tend to support each other. In the area of AIDS, for example, people who test for the human immunodeficiency virus (HIV)—clinicians and epidemiologists—are belatedly realizing that simply asking people to identify themselves as heterosexual, homosexual, or bisexual is both useless and dangerous. To assess degree of risk or source of infection for any individual, people must be asked about specific behaviors with same-sex partners (Gochros, 1991).

***Cultural and cross-cultural perspectives.*** There is evidence that the considerations posed here have universal application and transcend racial, ethnic, national, and religious boundaries (Ross, 1991). At the same time, it is important to recognize that different cultures define and deal with homosexuality and bisexuality in different ways (Tielman et al., 1991). Ross (1991), for example, found that the more homophobic the culture, the more people tend to marry heterosexually to avoid stigma and to "cure" their homosexual desires. Paradoxically, some cultures that are assumed to be homophobic actually focus on behaviors rather than labels, defining a male penetrator in homosexual sex as heterosexual. For some cultures, male hand-holding is simply a sign of friendship. For some, unplanned situational homosexual behavior is considered insignificant as long as one is discreet and does not openly acknowledge it (Gochros, 1989).

Cultural variations are also important in the United States: White people of different ethnic backgrounds, African Americans, Latinos, and Native Americans, for example, may each define sexual orientation differently and hold different values about homosexuality and bisexuality.

A post-Kinsey stance, therefore, is that sexual orientation is too complex and dynamic to justify categorization of people as simply heterosexual, homosexual, or bisexual. Zinik (1985) saw the different views of sexual orientation as fitting into two major models—one a static, rigid model and the other a flexible model. He suggested that the flexible model is the model for the future. Even our terminology suggests the difficulty labels present. The label "bisexual," for example, is actually a misnomer that implies an equal ratio of homosexuality to heterosexuality. Zinik suggested that replacing it with the term "ambisexual," which connotes varying degrees of homosexuality and heterosexuality, would perhaps be useful. Increasingly, however, doing away with all labels is seen as even more useful (Klein & Wolf, 1985; Paul, 1985; Tielman et al., 1991; Zinik, 1985).

## Prevalence of Bisexuality

As suggested by the previous discussion, it is almost impossible to provide a true estimate of the incidence of bisexuality. Research is handicapped by two major problems. First, self-identification and many research designs are still guided by Kinsey and pre-Kinsey views. Many people refuse to participate in research on homosexuality or bisexuality simply because they perceive themselves as heterosexual no matter how many homosexual experiences or fantasies they have had. Conversely, many do not participate in studies on bisexuality or heterosexuality because they consider themselves homosexual and discount any heterosexual experiences or fantasies they may have had. Many research designs have failed to reflect variations over time or in different aspects of participants' lives, and many questionnaires impede honesty rather than promote it. Some research is politically inspired and biased. Hence, some study results may be misleading.

Second, fear of stigma prevents many people from participating in research that could possibly identify them. People in monogamous (usually heterosexual) marriages who have bisexual activities or fantasies—possibly the largest group—remain uncounted and invisible.

The most that can be said, then, is that judging from the various studies, approximately 15 percent of American men and 10 percent of American women—around 25 million altogether and more than the estimated homosexual population—show some degree of homosexual behavior in their sexual history (Zinik, 1985). Data are even more difficult to obtain and interpret in many other countries. Nevertheless, there is evidence that bisexual behavior is common throughout the world (Tielman et al., 1991).

For both men and women, there are wide variations in bisexual behavioral patterns, with changes over time. Less data are available on women than on men, partly because women are apt to recognize homosexual feelings later in life and are less apt to actualize their fantasies. Bisexual women are more apt to be monogamous and to value the emotional intimacy more than erotic sex. Hence they are more likely to have sequential, intense relationships rather than concurrent, casual relationships. It is possible that these facts simply reflect the practices of women in today's society, regardless of sexual orientation (Coleman, 1985a, 1985b; Nichols, 1988).

## Problems Faced by Bisexual Men and Women

Bisexual people and their families face serious problems. Stigma or anticipated stigma from both the heterosexual and homosexual communities, isolation, and lack of adequate responsible role models can lead to confusion, problems in self-identity, low self-esteem, and diminished emotional capacity. Stereotypes based on kernels of truth compound problems. For example, assumptions by one person in a sexual relationship that his or her bisexual partner is going through a phase, is cowardly, has been lying, and so on, add stress and confusion for couples and may indeed contribute to a bisexual partner's secrecy and dishonesty (Gochros, 1989; Lourea, 1985). Biphobia—irrational fear of bisexuality—has been especially destructive for adolescents, who desperately struggle for identity and belonging in society and in their peer groups (Gochros, 1989; Lourea, 1985).

Perhaps the most destructive consequence of homophobia and biphobia occurs when people are forced into unrealistic and untenable lifestyle choices, particularly marriage. When one partner in a marriage begins to face his or her same-sex (or, for homosexual couples, opposite-sex) interests, the problems of loss of self-esteem, isolation, stigmatization, and depression are particularly complex and acute for both partners.

Problems of self-esteem and confusion can exist when any marriage fails to meet the needs of one or both partners or when infidelity comes to light. For most couples there are role models, knowledgeable counselors, literature, and a social support network to help each partner evaluate needs and options. For mixed-orientation couples, however, problems are compounded by the paucity of such supports and by the addition of homophobia, biphobia, and sex-role stereotyping, which interfere with problem solving. Nonetheless, there is evidence that mixed-orientation marriages can be viable and fulfilling for both partners (Gochros, 1989; Matteson, 1985; Wolf, 1985). Convinced by a militant gay support system that bisexuality is simply a cowardly transient stage on the way to accepting homosexuality, however, a bisexual partner may leave a good marriage needlessly. Furthermore, therapists may encourage dysfunctional secrecy or unnecessarily discourage couples who are trying to work out satisfying marital contracts.

Conversely, homophobia prevents many people from acknowledging that they no longer find enough pleasure in a heterosexual relationship to sustain a marriage. Partners who try to sustain the marriage and fail may feel guilt and shame for "not facing reality," when in fact they have not only had little help, but also the reality itself may simply have changed (Gochros, 1989; Lourea, 1985).

Finally, Gochros (1989) noted that, in an ironic twist, sex-role stereotyping has stigmatized the wives of bisexual men even more than it has the men themselves. Interestingly, although research has devoted at least a little attention to such wives, none has focused on the husbands of bisexual or lesbian women. Bisexual people face problems in decisions around the risk of sexually transmitted diseases—particularly AIDS. "To tell or not to tell," to use condoms or not—especially with a spouse—are problems that interfere not only with decisions about health but also with personal relationships.

## Implications for Society

The stigmatization and isolation of bisexual individuals affect society both directly and indirectly. An individual's mental health and his or her personal relationships are hurt by compartmentalization of different facets of personality, secrecy, and dishonesty. Such institutions as marriage and the family cannot help being negatively affected.

A rigid bipolar view of sexual orientation interferes with professional mental health assessments, therapies, and research. This view has hindered safer-sex practices between bisexual men and their often-unaware female sexual or marital partners. Further, a rigid view hampers a professional's ability to provide adequate marital and individual counseling when a secretly bisexual husband has become infected with HIV (Gochros, 1991; Tielman et al., 1991).

Since the 1960s people have been increasingly willing to face and deal with their homosexual desires. Paradoxically, although the AIDS pandemic has helped people recognize and accept homosexuality, it has also served to put many bisexual men even further back in the closet. Such men, trying to wipe out homosexual urges through marriage, are setting the stage for a new crop of marital problems in future generations (Gochros, 1991).

## Implications for Social Work

The growing understanding of bisexuality suggests potential changes for traditional institutions such as monogamous marriage, religious beliefs and doctrines, and traditional sex roles. We can expect difficult ethical and practical issues to emerge in psychology, psychiatry, and social work.

Both partners in a relationship in which one or both people have a bisexual orientation are pioneers in a crisis-prone situation and have few role models. They may need help sorting out conflicting feelings and options while remaining sensitive to each others' needs and rights. Both adolescents and adults may need help in dealing with conflicting sexual feelings, in accepting bisexuality as a valid option, and in "coming out" to others.

Education and social action may be needed to help a school prevent a student from being ostracized. Adults, teenagers, and all other family members (including heterosexual spouses) may need help finding or creating support networks and coping with stigma (Gochros, 1989; Lourea, 1985; Nichols, 1988).

Social workers need to validate the potential viability of mixed-orientation marriages and to be supportive without trying to push people in a particular direction. They also need to guard against hidden sex-role stereotyping by either partner (Gochros, 1989; Lourea, 1985).

With all these tasks, social workers must be able to confront their own value conflicts and be willing to learn from their clients. They also must be creative and courageous in helping clients chart new courses.

In short, social workers will increasingly need to help individuals, couples, families, and communities cope with evolving sexual attitudes and options. The profession will increasingly be asked to help form responsive and responsible social policies that validate bisexual behavior without labeling or stigmatizing those who choose to exercise those options.

## References

Boulton, M. (1991). Review of the literature on bisexuality and HIV transmission. In R. Tielman, M. Carballo, & A. Hendriks (Eds.), *Bisexuality & HIV/AIDS* (pp. 187–209). Buffalo, NY: Prometheus Books.

Coleman, E. (1985a). Bisexual women in marriages. *Bisexualities: Theory and Research, Journal of Homosexuality, 11*(1/2), 87–100.

Coleman, E. (1985b). Integration of male bisexuality and marriage. *Bisexualities: Theory and Research, Journal of Homosexuality, 11*(1/2), 189–208.

Gochros, H., Gochros, J., & Fischer, J. (1986). *Helping the sexually oppressed*. Englewood Cliffs, NJ: Prentice Hall.

Gochros, J. (1989). *When husbands come out of the closet*. New York: Haworth Press.

Gochros, J. (1991). Bisexuality and female partners. In R. Tielman, M. Carballo, & A. Hendriks (Eds.), *Bisexuality & HIV/AIDS* (pp. 175–186). Buffalo, NY: Prometheus Books.

Hansen, C., & Evans, A. (1985). Bisexuality reconsidered: An idea in pursuit of a definition. *Bisexualities: Theory and Research, Journal of Homosexuality, 11*(1/2), 1–6.

Kinsey, A. C., Pomeroy, W. B., Martin, C. E., & Gebhard, P. E. (1948). *Sexual behavior in the human male*. Philadelphia: W. B. Saunders.

Kinsey, A. C., Pomeroy, W. B., Martin, C. E., & Gebhard, P. E. (1953). *Sexual behavior in the human female*. Philadelphia: W. B. Saunders.

Klein, F. (1978). *The bisexual option*. New York: Arbor House.

Klein, F., Sepekoff, B., & Wolf, T. (1985). Sexual orientation: A multivariable dynamic process. *Bisexualities: Theory and Research, Journal of Homosexuality, 11*(1/2), 35–50.

Klein, F., & Wolf, T. (Eds.). (1985). *Bisexualities: Theory and Research, Journal of Homosexuality, 11*(1/2), 135–148.

Lourea, D. (1985). Psycho-social issues related to counseling bisexuals. *Bisexualities: Theory and Research, Journal of Homosexuality, 11*(1/2), 51–62.

Matteson, D. (1985). Bisexual men in marriage: Is a positive homosexual identity and stable marriage possible? *Bisexualities: Theory and Research, Journal of Homosexuality, 11*(1/2), 149–172.

Nichols, M. (1988). Bisexuality in women: Myths, realities, and implications for women. In E. Cole & E. Rothblum (Eds.), *Women and sex therapy* (pp. 235–253). Binghamton, NY: Harrington Press.

Paul, J. (1985). Bisexuality: Reassessing our paradigms of sexuality. *Bisexualities: Theory and Research, Journal of Homosexuality, 11*(1/2), 21–34.

Reinisch, J. (1994). *The new Kinsey report*. New York: St. Martin's Press.

Ross, M. (1991). A taxonomy of "global behavior." In R. Tielman, M. Carballo, & A. Hendriks (Eds.), *Bisexuality & HIV/AIDS* (pp. 21–26). Buffalo, NY: Prometheus Books.

Tielman, R., Carballo, M., & Hendriks, A. (Eds.). (1991). *Bisexuality & HIV/AIDS*. Buffalo, NY: Prometheus Books.

Wolf, T. (1985). Marriages of bisexual men. *Bisexualities: Theory and Research, Journal of Homosexuality, 11*(1/2), 135–148.

Zinik, G. (1985). Identity conflict or adaptive flexibility? Bisexuality reconsidered. *Bisexualities: Theory and Research, Journal of Homosexuality, 11*(1/2), 7–21.

### Further Reading

Bell, A., & Weinberg, M. (1978). *Homosexualities: A study of diversity among men and women*. New York: Simon & Schuster.

Blumstein, P., & Schwartz, P. (1977). Bisexuality: Some social psychological issues. *Journal of Social Issues, 33*(2), 30–45.

Paul, J. (1984). The bisexual identity: An idea without social recognition. *Journal of Homosexuality, 9,* 45–63.

Ross, M. (1983). *The married homosexual man*. London: Routledge & Kegan Paul.

Weinberg, M., Williams, C., & Pryor, D. (1994). *Dual attraction: Bisexuality in the age of AIDS*. Oxford, England: Oxford University Press.

NOTE: Since 1983, the *Journal of Homosexuality* has devoted several issues to bisexuality. A catalog may be obtained and separate issues ordered by writing to Haworth Press, 10 Alice Street, Binghamton, NY 13904.

**Jean S. Gochros, PhD,** is clinical social worker, 1901 Halekoa Drive, Honolulu, HI 96821.

### For further information see

Adolescence Overview; Families: Demographic Shifts; Gay and Lesbian Adolescents; Gay Men Overview; HIV/AIDS Overview; Human Sexuality; Lesbians Overview; Marriage/Partners; Mental Health Overview; Person-in-Environment; Research Overview; Sexual Distress; Social Work Practice: Theoretical Base.

**Key Words**

| | |
|---|---|
| bisexuality | homosexuality |
| heterosexuality | sexuality |

## Black People

*See* African Americans *(Reader's Guide)*

## Blackey, Eileen

*See* Biographies section, Volume 3

## Blindness

*See* Visual Impairment and Blindness

# Boards of Directors

**Sheldon R. Gelman**

From the earliest days of organized philanthropy in the United States, interested and committed individuals have served as trustees, overseers, and board members of charity, social services, and other nonprofit organizations. Although years of experience have provided insight into the functioning of agency boards and all states have passed legislation that guides their operation, there is no unified body of law applicable to nonprofit organizations (Collin, 1987).

No one really knows how many nonprofit organizations exist in the United States (Oleck, 1982). The U.S. Department of Commerce (1993) identified 22,455 nonprofit associations in 1992, of which 1,773 were categorized as social welfare organizations and 2,290 as health related. New York State records list 5,500 registered nonprofit organizations in New York City alone and an additional 2,000 organizations in the city that address health concerns (Macchiarola, 1993).

## Role and Function

Laws relating to the incorporation of nonprofit organizations require that a board of directors be created to ensure basic responsibility for the operation of the corporation. Agency charters and bylaws in turn specify the responsibilities and obligations of boards and their individual members. Whereas boards of public agencies are advisory or administrative and therefore do not have broad powers or responsibilities, boards of directors or trustees of private or voluntary organizations are charged with the general direction and control of those organizations (Mitton, 1974). The board is the policy-making body of the organization, with a legal duty to ensure that the organization's actions are consistent with its goals and objectives. Board members share collective responsibility for the fiscal and programmatic aspects of the organization's performance. The board is responsible to funding sources, the community, governmental and private regulating bodies, and consumers of the agency's services.

Board members of a social services agency thus have a legal and moral obligation to keep themselves fully informed about the agency's operations. Boards typically fulfill the following six functions:

1. maintaining general direction and control of the agency (policy development)
2. directing short- and long-term planning (program development)
3. hiring competent administrative staff (personnel)
4. facilitating access to necessary resources (finance)
5. interpreting the organization to the community at large (public relations)
6. evaluating operations (accountability).

In addition, as stated by Leifer and Glomb (1992), "under well-established principles of nonprofit and corporation law, a board member must meet certain standards of conduct and attention in carrying out his or her responsibilities to the organization. These standards are usually described as the duty of care, the duty of loyalty, and the duty of obedience" (p. 31).

### Legal Obligation

Serving on a board of directors is more than a social experience. The directors of charitable or nonprofit corporations are required to exercise reasonable and ordinary care in the performance of their duties and to exhibit honesty and good faith. They must discharge their duties with the degree of care, skill, and diligence any prudent person would exercise under similar circumstances. The initiation, implementation, and operation of a social services agency is thus the "business" of the board, and according to Weber (1975), board members are expected to approach their responsibilities as they would approach other business transactions. Collin (1987), Pasley (1966), and Streett (1985) noted that the legal standard of care applied to directors of nonprofit organizations is the same as that applied to directors of for-profit corporations, even though the latter receive compensation for their services. This standard of conduct has replaced the more lenient standard that existed for charitable organizations in many states.

Hanson and Marmaduke (1972) indicated that a board of directors as a group manages a nonprofit corporation, delegating responsibilities appropriately but retaining ultimate responsibility for the agency's image and performance. The board of directors is legally and morally accountable to the agency's various constituencies for its actions. A board that fails in its function of both determining policies and evaluating achievement in support of those policies is negligent in performing its mandated functions.

To ensure the well-being of the organization, the board must act prudently and lead the organization in

- developing a mission statement that includes specific goals and a clearly articulated value perspective
- devising a comprehensive plan and strategy for internal development and external service
- compiling a resource base
- developing a viable method for reviewing performance, evaluating achievements, and moving toward goal attainment (Anthes, 1985).

According to Perlmutter (1969, 1973) boards and their members will relate differently to these functions and responsibilities, depending on the agency's stage of evolution and development and its needs at a particular time. Board members must in their fiduciary role be loyal to the organization and act in its best interest.

## Structural Issues

### Who Serves and Why?

Individuals agree to serve as members of an agency board for a variety of reasons. Generally board members are prominent and successful community leaders who donate their time to community service activities. Some have a vested personal interest in a particular cause or issue (for example, a disabled relative). According to Klein (1968), others are motivated because "charitable and related activities are, in our culture, a source of social prestige, and occasionally an auxiliary means of access to the power structure" (p. 194). Although some individuals may be motivated by a quest for prestige or political power or by some other self-interest, Stein (1962) observed that others serve for altruistic reasons. Many individuals serve on boards of charitable or nonprofit agencies as an expression of religious or moral obligation; others do so because of professional commitment. Past or present consumers of an agency's services often serve as board members or in an advisory capacity to the board.

Consumer presence is mandatory on the boards of most public agencies, and consumer representation is increasingly found on the boards of private nonprofit organizations in the health, mental health, and disability fields. The growth of the self-help and self-advocacy movement has contributed to this involvement and has resulted in greater awareness, understanding, and responsiveness by board members to clients' needs and concerns. Regardless of the motivation for serving, acceptance of a board position brings with it an obligation that must be met with care and diligence.

### Board Composition and Selection

In setting up a board, it is crucial to select individuals whose personal commitment, energy, and areas of knowledge are appropriate to the agency's mission and to the specific tasks that need to be performed. Above all, board members must have the time, interest, and willingness to be of service to the agency. Individuals who are overcommitted or who spend much time away from the community tend to slow down the board in carrying out its mandated responsibilities. Unavailable or irresponsible board members force committed members to assume more responsibility than they desire. The lack of regular and consistent attendance at board meetings is one indicator of a board member's failure to meet the required standard of care.

Individuals who serve on boards should be able to work cooperatively and tactfully with one another. Interpersonal skills are critical because board members interact not only with their peers on the board but also with the agency's director and staff, with community leaders and public officials, and with members of the community at large who may also be clients of the agency (Bubis & Dauber, 1987). Members of the board should have legitimacy or standing in the community and be recognized as credible and responsible individuals.

Although the agency's charter may require that the board include bankers, politicians, clergy, and representatives of various professions and designated constituencies, every prospective member should be screened for interest and relevant expertise. It may be advisable to appoint prestigious community leaders as honorary members of the board, thus preventing their potential lack of time, interest, or commitment from hindering the board in the conduct of its business.

All board members should fully understand the nature of the organization and their individual and collective responsibilities as board members. Given the possibility of personal liability, all board members should be involved in an explicit and comprehensive orientation program.

### Board Size

The optimal size of the board of directors of a nonprofit organization is difficult to specify. Often the size and composition are dictated by the agency's charter or bylaws. Although Weber (1975) suggested that boards be composed of 30 to 36 members, this may be too large to permit the development of effective group process. Excessively large boards tend to lack strong feelings of commitment and obligation, resulting in poor or sporadic participation by members. A board that is too small, however, will not have sufficient members to accomplish its work. Sufficient members must regularly be present to ensure a division of labor so that no member or small group has to carry disproportionate responsibility. Size and composition should therefore be related to the agency's goals and objectives. A board of 15 to 18 members usually is sufficient to monitor the six areas of board responsibility previously identified.

A board must have sufficient collective expertise to monitor and evaluate the various elements of the agency's operation. Ideally each member's individual role and unique contribution to the overall effectiveness of the agency should be clear, and the board should take steps to develop into a cohesive work group.

#### Length of Service

Terms of board service should be limited to three years. Reappointment to a second three-year term should be an option for those members who have fulfilled their obligations and functioned effectively. Those who have been unable to meet the expectations set for board members or who can no longer commit themselves to board service should not be recommended for reelection or reappointment. Individuals who fail to meet their obligations should be asked to resign or should not be reappointed (Swanson, 1984).

Board members should serve on a rotating basis, with one-third of the board's positions replaced each year. Such a format promotes continuity, allows ongoing monitoring of the enterprise, and provides for a regular infusion of new talent and the grooming of new leaders. The systematic addition of new members with identified expertise and commitment and the ongoing training of board members help the agency to become self-evaluating. According to many authors (Austin et al., 1982; Blythe & Goodman, 1987; Gelman, 1983; Newman & Van Wijk, 1980; Wildavsky, 1972), the development of a capacity for self-evaluation is the only way that an agency can be responsible and accountable to its goals, mission, and constituencies.

#### Orientation and Training

New board members need orientation, and continuing members need ongoing training. Board members should be fully aware of their roles and responsibilities and the time commitments they are expected to make. All members should be provided with copies of the charter and bylaws and with written descriptions of role expectations and obligations. Members of the board should be familiar with the agency and its facilities, programs, services, and personnel. An orientation manual or board handbook should be developed, disseminated, and periodically revised. Based on member interests and expertise and on the agency's needs, individual board members should be assigned to the six functional areas of board responsibility. Board members need to be familiar with legal standards that should guide their actions, including the business judgment standard (directors are required to act in good faith and exercise their unbiased judgment in conducting the affairs of the organization), the reasonable care standard (the care required of an ordinarily prudent person in conducting their personal affairs), and the trustee or fiduciary rule (a director must exercise the highest level of care, that is, care greater than expected of an ordinarily prudent person).

### Legal Standards

#### Litigation against Nonprofits

Although there may be some disagreement about the threat posed by litigation against nonprofit agencies (Jones & Alcabes, 1989; Whelley, Black, & Whelley, 1989), the management of liability is a growing concern (Antler, 1987; Berliner, 1989; Bernstein, 1981; Besharov, 1985; Gelman, 1988; Reamer, 1989). Unfortunately, research that has been conducted on the liability of social services agencies is flawed by underreporting. Data compiled by the NASW Insurance Trust include only those claims processed for individuals insured by the Trust (NASW, 1989). Only a small percentage of the cases that are initiated actually go to court; most litigation is resolved before the actual trial and therefore does not produce a record.

Gelman (1988) identified six areas in which charges of negligence can involve board members: (1) failure to manage and supervise the activities of the corporation, (2) neglect or waste of corporate assets, (3) conflicts of interest or self-benefit, (4) improper delegation of authority, (5) harm done to third parties through tort (wrongful action) or breach of contract, and (6) offenses against taxing authorities. VanBiervliet and Sheldon-Wildgen (1981) discussed eight potential liability claims that may be brought against human services agencies. Besharov (1985) identified 17 liability pitfalls that may be encountered by social services personnel. The NASW Insurance Trust categorizes its claims by 24 types (NASW, 1989).

Recent revelations about organizational excesses in the nonprofit arena—a lack of board oversight at United Way of America; multiple sets of books at health insurance companies such as Empire Blue Cross/Blue Shield; and compensation levels and overhead charges at several educational institutions—have caused increased scrutiny and raised the potential for litigation. Board members can reduce or limit their potential liability through responsible governance practices, compliance with state volunteer protection laws indemnification, and enrollment in directors' and officers' liability insurance (National Center for Nonprofit Boards, 1992).

In seeking redress for perceived or actual harm, legal counsel usually suggests a "shotgun" approach to identifying potential defendants that not only maximizes the number of defendants but also expands the resource pool that may be available for compensating clients. This strategy differs from the more traditional approach to litigation, which seeks out the "deep pockets" of a corporation. The shotgun approach greatly increases the likelihood that an individual board or staff member will be named as a party in a suit brought on behalf of an agency client (Chute, 1983). The fact or perception that board members or professional staff have insurance coverage may contribute to this practice (Harvey, 1984). The need to incorporate the organization, provide indemnification to board members, and include risk management activities into agency practice is clearly indicated.

### Incorporation

Incorporation is the creation of a legally recognized entity that has an identity separate from the individuals who created it. The new entity (the agency), rather than the individuals involved, contracts for and provides various services. The board of directors becomes the vehicle through which the organization functions and also becomes the employer of a range of personnel (Dimieri & Weiner, 1981).

Under the traditional doctrine of *respondeat superior,* an employer can be held vicariously responsible for harm caused by an employee in the course of his or her employment (Brown, 1977; Chute, 1983; VanBiervliet & Sheldon-Wildgen, 1981). The act of incorporation shields individual board members from harm or damage, real or perceived, that may be attributed to the agency's operations or management. However, the corporate shield does not protect board members who have committed intentional wrongs that result in harm or injury, nor will it provide protection for individual board members named as codefendants in litigation brought against the organization (Harvey, 1984; Jarvis, 1982).

### Indemnification

Most states have passed laws that permit nonprofit organizations to adopt indemnification provisions in their charters or bylaws. *Indemnification* means that the organization will pay, out of its own resources, the cost of litigation and any judgments or settlements awarded against board members. Indemnification laws vary by state, are limited by the resources of the organization or insurance coverage, and may not be applicable if the board member has breached an official duty or acted in bad faith.

### Insurance

Until recently, providers of social services, both governmental and voluntary, were able to purchase reasonably priced insurance to indemnify their organizations in negligence actions brought by injured consumers. In addition to providing personal protection for both staff and board members, insurance coverage minimized the risk to the resources of the organization. However, the insurance crisis of the mid-1980s has left various organizations vulnerable (Shapiro, 1985; "Sorry, your policy," 1986; Wagner, 1986) owing to larger and more frequent damage awards, the erosion of charitable and sovereign immunity, and contingency-fee arrangements that encourage lawyers to file suit (such fees are a percentage of the settlement award; the plaintiff need not have money to bring suit).

The fear of more costly litigation has caused most insurance carriers to raise premiums dramatically or to stop writing liability policies altogether. The crisis has affected municipal governments (which often operate, or are responsible for, social services delivery) and many nonprofit voluntary providers (particularly those involved in child care or residential services), making it necessary for them to self-insure or close their programs. Revelations of physical or sexual abuse and concerns about inadequately trained staff and unsafe physical facilities have resulted in increased consumer demand for satisfaction and monetary compensation. This trend has serious implications for everyone involved in providing services (Davis, 1987).

Organizations must maintain insurance appropriately tailored to the needs of the organization and with levels of coverage sufficient to satisfy potential adverse judgments. Customary coverage for health care, premises, property, and vehicles should also be obtained. In addition, liability coverage for staff, volunteers, and officers should be provided to indemnify them in their official capacities. The level of coverage, which may range from $500,000 to $10 million will correlate with the size of the organization, type of clientele, services provided, and past claims history (Chapman, Lai, & Steinbock, 1984).

Most standard liability policies contain provisions that cover the costs of legal services incurred in defense of a policyholder, as well as coverage in the event of an adverse judgment. Organizations without adequate or appropriate coverage and those unable to secure coverage are in a vulnerable position. The cost of extricating a named party in a lawsuit can run into thousands of dollars.

**Risk Management**

Concerns about agency accountability have grown dramatically as charitable immunity has largely disappeared as a shield against harm caused by agency oversight or actions (Gelman, 1988, 1992; Monagle, 1985; Zelman, 1977). In response, many agencies have developed risk management strategies as a means of limiting their liability exposure (Jennings & Shipper, 1989; Litan & Winston, 1988; Olson, 1988). Risk management involves the ongoing study and assessment of activities and practices that potentially could lead to legal vulnerability (Bryant & Korsak, 1988; Salman, 1986). Risk management is a preventive activity that falls within the fiduciary purview of boards.

One risk management issue that board members should be involved in entails the type of client or service that is to be provided by the agency. One of the board's most important roles is to identify the population served by an agency. Although the agency charter or the original board may have defined the client population, client priorities should be reviewed periodically. A key aspect in deliberations about client population will be the risk factors associated with particular populations. For example, complexity of medical needs, level of aggressiveness, age, psychiatric problems, and location may increase an agency's costs and potential vulnerability. Risk factors will influence both administrative and programmatic issues, such as staffing patterns, level of supervision, training, treatment modalities, and the availability and cost of insurance.

Agencies that provide services to higher-risk populations, such as medically fragile or aggressive clients, are at risk for litigation when staffing patterns provide less coverage than is necessary to meet the identified and documented needs of clients. The more dangerous the situation or the more vulnerable the population served, the greater the need for board oversight. The board must determine what risks are involved in serving a particular population, how and at what cost those risks can be minimized, and whether the agency can or will serve particular populations. An agency's mission, community need, or the level of reimbursement available may influence whether certain risks are assumed by an agency.

## Relationships

**The Executive**

The executive is an employee of the organization and serves at the pleasure of the board. He or she is a professional who is knowledgeable about people, management techniques, service provision, evaluation, fundraising, and conflict resolution and excels as a politician and communicator (Carlton-LaNey, 1987; Gummer, 1984). The executive is a skilled technician who motivates, educates, and trains both lay leaders and staff to act on behalf of the goals of the organization (Glenn, 1985). The executive implements board policy and guides staff in formulating strategies designed to achieve organizational objectives. The executive draws on the energy, expertise, and resources of the board members by involving them and keeping them informed (Blythe & Goodman, 1987; Gelman, 1983).

**Board–Executive Relations**

The literature (Blau & Scott, 1962; Robins & Blackburn, 1974; Senor, 1965; Wiehe, 1978) is filled with contradictory statements about board–executive relations and with cautions about duplication and overlap in roles and functions. A number of authors, recognizing the interdependence of the relationship, view it as a partnership (Bubis & Dauber, 1987; Conrad & Glen, 1976; O'Connell, 1976).

The executive and the board must work together. The board is responsible for evaluating the executive and the agency's operations at regular intervals. Although the executive director is delegated authority for the agency's day-to-day operations and for handling most personnel matters, laws and the agency's charter invest the board with the power and authority to make policy. In other words, the ultimate responsibility for agency functioning and for the performance of the executive and staff resides with the board. Kramer (1985) concluded that most relationships between executives and boards involve elements of power and dependency and may take on a conflictual bent. This creative tension and interdependency can work to the advantage of the organization as long as respect exists and the give-and-take is roughly equal.

Some authors (Tripodi, 1976; Volunteer Bureau of Pasadena, 1972) have suggested that an agency executive must provide leadership for the board in policy-making, but such an arrangement may contradict both the agency's charter and the requirements of law. According to Harris (1977), many formulations that deal with board–executive relations treat the subject as if two separable spheres of activity existed—one occupied by the board and the other by the professional executive. Senor (1965) warned that although the executive may be an ex officio member of the board, granting the executive the right to vote on policy matters creates a potential conflict of interest. It also grants the executive disproportionate power because the executive controls the information the board needs to do its job.

The key, therefore, is the degree to which the board retains its mandated role. Although the board can draw on the executive's expertise and knowledge, it cannot allow its legal responsibility to be diluted or co-opted by overdependence. A collegial working relationship is essential between the board and the executive, but the executive, no matter how seasoned, remains an employee of the organization.

### Board–Staff Relations

According to Trecker (1981), appropriate, effective, and efficient board–staff relations are based on a clear and common understanding of their functions and responsibilities within the organization. The board is responsible for developing and establishing policies that guide the organization, and staff members are responsible for implementing the policies adopted by the board of directors and transmitted through the executive. In implementing and achieving board policy, staff members may choose among several alternatives, but the board is ultimately responsible and therefore must hold staff, including the executive, accountable. Although the evaluation of staff should rest with the designated administrator or supervisory staff, the staff's performance reflects on the agency's goal or mission and on the performance of the board.

This analysis may appear unbalanced in the board's favor. However, ongoing interaction between board and staff is essential to the development of a responsive and accountable agency. It is crucial for staff members to have regular opportunities to report to the board about their experiences in implementing board policies, about obstacles they encounter, and about unmet needs they identify. In this way the board can adjust or modify its policies based on staff experiences. Staff members should know and feel comfortable with members of the board who are assigned to review various programs.

A three-way partnership should thus exist among board, administrator, and staff (Swanson, 1984). Such a partnership is facilitated by clear job descriptions that specify obligations and responsibilities. Personnel standards consistent with those of NASW (1991) help to clarify the rights, responsibilities, and expectations of employees. Similarly, an understanding of the necessity and desirability of creating a self-evaluating agency and a commitment to this objective by all parties are essential to the achievement of agency goals.

## Accountability

The board of directors is ultimately responsible for the performance of the agency it serves. An effective board is critical not only to the efficient operation of an agency but also to meeting identified needs of the community. Board membership in nonprofit organizations requires more than altruism and interest; it requires time, a commitment to the development of expertise, and an understanding of the potential for personal responsibility and liability. The development of an accountable agency requires that the board, in partnership with the executive and staff, continuously monitor and evaluate the agency's finances and programs.

## References

Anthes, E. W. (1985). The board and the life of the organization: An overview. In E. Anthes, J. Cronin, & M. Jackson (Eds.), *The nonprofit board book: Strategies for organizational success* (rev. ed., pp. 1-3). West Memphis and Hampton, AK: Independent Community Consultants.

Antler, S. (1987). Professional liability and malpractice. In A. Minahan (Ed.-in-Chief), *Encyclopedia of social work* (18th ed., Vol. 2, pp. 346–351). Silver Spring, MD: National Association of Social Workers.

Austin, M. J., Cox, G., Gottlieb, N., Hawkins, J. D., Kruzich, J. M., & Rauch, R. (1982). *Evaluating your agency's programs.* Beverly Hills, CA: Sage Publications.

Berliner, A. K. (1989). Misconduct in social work practice. *Social Work, 34,* 69–72.

Bernstein, B. (1981). Malpractice: Future shock of the 1980s. *Social Casework, 62,* 175–181.

Besharov, D. J. (1985). *The vulnerable social worker.* Silver Spring, MD: National Association of Social Workers.

Blau, P. M., & Scott, W. R. (1962). *Formal organizations.* San Francisco: Chandler.

Blythe, B. J., & Goodman, D. R. (1987). Agency board members as research staff. *Social Work, 32,* 544–545.

Brown, K. M. (1977). The not-for-profit corporation director: Legal liabilities and protection. *Federation of Insurance Counsel Quarterly, 28,* 57–87.

Bryant, Y., & Korsak, A. (1988). Who is the risk manager and what does he do? *Hospitals, 52,* 42–43.

Bubis, G. B., & Dauber, J. (1987). The delicate balance—Board–staff relations. *Journal of Jewish Communal Service, 63*(3), 187–196.

Carlton-LaNey, I. (1987). County social services directors' perceptions of their policy boards. *Administration in Social Work, 11*(1), 25–36.

Chapman, T. S., Lai, M. L., & Steinbock, E. L. (1984). *Am I covered for? A guide to insurance for non-profits.* San Jose, CA: Consortium for Human Services.

Chute, C. (1983). Personal liability for director of nonprofit corporations in Wyoming. *Land and Water Review, 28,* 273–311.

Collin, R. W. (1987). Toward a new theory of nonprofit liability. *Administration in Social Work, 11*(1), 15–24.

Conrad, W., & Glen, W. (1976). *The effective voluntary board of directors.* Boulder, CO: National Center for Voluntary Action.

Davis, P. (1987). *Nonprofit organizations and liability insurance: Problems, options, and prospects.* Los Angeles: California Community Foundation.

Dimieri, R., & Weiner, S. (1981). The public interest and governing boards of nonprofit health care institutions. *Vanderbilt Law Review, 34,* 1029–1066.

Feinstein, W. L. (1988). Performing an evolving role: An executive's challenge. *Journal of Jewish Communal Service, 64*(4), 310–315.

Gelman, S. R. (1983). The board of directors and agency accountability. *Social Casework, 64*(2), 83–91.

Gelman, S. R. (1988). Roles, responsibilities, and liabilities of agency boards. In M. Janicki, M. W. Krauss, & M. Seltzer (Eds.), *Community residences for persons with developmental disabilities: Here to stay* (pp. 57–68). Baltimore: Paul H. Brookes.

Gelman, S. R. (1992). Risk management through client access to the case records. *Social Work, 37,* 73–79.

Glenn, W. E. (1985). Board and staff relations. In E. Anthes, J. Cronin, & M. Jackson (Eds.), *The nonprofit board book: Strategies for organizational success* (pp. 87–102). West Memphis and Hampton, AK: Independent Community Consultants.

Gummer, B. (1984). The social administrator as politician. In F. D. Perlmutter (Ed.), *Human services at risk* (pp. 23–36). Lexington, MA: Lexington Books.

Hanson, P. L., & Marmaduke, C. T. (1972). *The board member—Decision maker for the nonprofit corporation.* Sacramento, CA: HAN/MAR Publications.

Harris, J. E. (1977). The internal organization of hospitals. *Bell Journal of Economics, 8*(2), 467–482.

Harvey, B. B. (1984). The public-spirited defendant and others: Liability of directors of not-for-profit corporations. *John Marshall Law Review, 17,* 666–741.

Jarvis, W. F. (1982). The nonprofit director's fiduciary duty: Toward a new theory of the nonprofit sector. *Northwestern University Law Review, 77,* 34–37.

Jennings, M. M., & Shipper, F. (1989). *Avoiding and surviving lawsuits.* San Francisco: Jossey-Bass.

Jones, J. A., & Alcabes, A. (1989). Clients don't sue: The invulnerable social worker. *Social Casework, 70*(7), 414–420.

Klein, P. (1968). *From philanthropy to social welfare.* San Francisco: Jossey-Bass.

Kramer, R. M. (1985). Toward a contingency model of board–executive relations. *Administration in Social Work, 9*(3), 15–33.

Leifer, J. C., & Glomb, M. B. (1992). *The legal obligations of nonprofit boards: A guidebook for board members.* Washington, DC: National Center for Nonprofit Boards.

Litan, R. E., & Winston, C. (Eds.). (1988). *Liability: Perspectives and policy.* Washington, DC: Brookings Institution.

Macchiarola, F. J. (1993). Not-for-profit organizations and the City of New York. *Administrator's Roundtable, 2*(1), 1–2.

Mitton, D. G. (1974). Utilizing the board of trustees: A unique structural design. *Child Welfare, 53*(6), 345–351.

Monagle, J. F. (1985). *Risk management: A guide for health care professionals.* Rockville, MD: Aspen.

National Association of Social Workers. (1989). *Malpractice claims against social workers.* Silver Spring, MD: Author.

National Association of Social Workers. (1991). *Standards for social work personnel practices.* Washington, DC: Author.

National Center for Nonprofit Boards. (1992). Board members and risk: A primer on protection from liability. *Board Member, 1*(6), 1–15.

Newman, H., & Van Wijk, A. (1980). *Self-evaluation for human service organizations.* New York: Greater New York Fund/United Way.

O'Connell, B. (1976). *Effective leadership in voluntary organizations.* New York: Association Press.

Oleck, H. L. (1982). *Nonprofit corporations, organizations and associations.* Englewood Cliffs, NJ: Prentice Hall.

Olson, W. (Ed.). (1988). *New directions in liability law.* New York: Academy of Political Science.

Pasley, R. S. (1966). Non-profit corporations—Accountability of directors and officers. *Business Lawyer, 21*(3), 621–642.

Perlmutter, F. (1969). A theoretical model of social agency development. *Social Casework, 50*(8), 467–473.

Perlmutter, F. (1973). Citizen participation and professionalism: A developmental relationship. *Public Welfare, 31*(3), 25–28.

Reamer, F. G. (1989). Liability issues in social work supervision. *Social Work, 32,* 445–448.

Robins, A. J., & Blackburn, C. (1974, Summer). Governing boards in mental health: Roles and training needs. *Administration in Mental Health,* pp. 37–45.

Salman, S. L. (1986). Risk management process and functions. In G. T. Troyer & S. L. Salman (Eds.), *Handbook of health care management* (pp. 149–182). Rockville, MD: Aspen.

Senor, J. M. (1965). Another look at the executive/board relationship. In M. N. Zald (Ed.), *Social welfare institutions: A sociological reader* (pp. 418–427). New York: John Wiley & Sons.

Shapiro, W. (1985, August 26). The naked cities: Rising insurance rates force officials to pay or pray. *Newsweek,* pp. 22–23.

Sorry, your policy is canceled. (1986, March 24). *Time,* pp. 16–26.

Stein, H. D. (1962). Board, executive and staff. In H. Millman (Ed.), *The social welfare forum* (pp. 215–230). New York: Columbia University Press.

Streett, S. C. (1985). Board powers, responsibilities and liabilities. In E. Anthes, J. Cronin, & M. Jackson (Eds.), *The nonprofit board book: Strategies for organizational success* (pp. 9–22). West Memphis and Hampton, AK: Independent Community Consultants.

Swanson, A. (1984). *Building a better board: A guide to effective leadership.* Washington, DC: Taft Corporation.

Trecker, H. B. (1981). *Boards of human service agencies: Challenges and responsibilities in the 80's.* New York: Federation of Protestant Welfare Agencies.

Tripodi, T. (1976). Social workers as community practitioners, social welfare administrators and social policy developers. In T. Tripodi, P. Fellin, I. Epstein, & R. Lind (Eds.), *Social workers at work* (2nd ed., pp. 162–169). Itasca, IL: F. E. Peacock.

U.S. Bureau of the Census. (1984). *National data book and guide to sources.* Washington, DC: Author.

U.S. Department of Commerce. (1993). *Statistical abstract of the United States 1993* (113th ed., p. 787). Washington, DC: U.S. Government Printing Office.

VanBiervliet, A., & Sheldon-Wildgen, J. (1981). *Liability issues in community based programs.* Baltimore: Paul H. Brookes.

Volunteer Bureau of Pasadena (1972). *So . . . you serve on a board.* Pasadena, CA: Author.

Wagner, L. M. (1986, January). Liability insurance crisis: Coming to grips with long tails and deep pockets. *Illinois Issues,* pp. 8–12.

Weber, J. (1975). *Managing the board of directors.* New York: Greater New York Fund.

Whelley, J., Black, P. N., & Whelley, J. G. (1989, October). *The limits of liability: Social work malpractice on trial.* Paper presented at Social Work '89: NASW's Annual Meeting of the Profession, San Francisco.

Wiehe, V. R. (1978). Role expectations among agency personnel. *Social Work, 23,* 26–30.

Wildavsky, A. (1972). The self-evaluating organization. *Public Administration Review, 32,* 509–520.

Zelman, W. N. (1977). Liability for social agency boards. *Social Work, 22,* 270–274.

## Further Reading

Brilliant, E. L. (1990). *The United Way: Dilemmas of organized charity.* New York: Columbia University Press.

Hopkins, B. R. (1989). *Starting and managing a nonprofit organization: A legal guide.* New York: John Wiley & Sons.

Kurtz, D. L. (1988). *Board liability: Guide for nonprofit directors.* Mt. Kisco, NY: Moyer Bell.

Lai, M. L., Chapman, T. S., & Steinbock, E. L. (1992). *Am I covered for . . . ? A guide to insurance for nonprofits.* San Jose, CA: Consortium for Human Services.

Pollack, D. (1993). Liability insurance for foster parents and agencies: The role of commercial insurers. *Journal of Law and Social Work, 4,* 33–40.

**Sheldon R. Gelman, PhD, ACSW,** is Schachne Dean, Wurzweiler School of Social Work, Yeshiva University, 500 W. 185th Street, New York, NY 10033.

### For further information see

Ethics and Values; Financial Management; Fundraising and Philanthropy; Interdisciplinary and Interorganizational Collaboration; Nonprofit Management Issues; Organizations: Context for Social Services Delivery; Patient Rights; Personnel Management; Planning and Management Professions; Professional Liability and Malpractice; Program Evaluation; Public Services Management; Quality Assurance; Quality Management; Social Work Profession Overview; Strategic Planning; Supervision and Consultation; Voluntarism; Volunteer Management.

**Key Words**
accountability
administration
boards of directors
liability
organization

## Brace, Charles Loring

*See* Biographies section, Volume 3

## Breckinridge, Sophonisba Preston

*See* Biographies section, Volume 3

# Brief Task-Centered Practice

**Laura Epstein**

In 1970 the School of Social Service Administration, University of Chicago, established the Task-Centered Project, which was designed to develop and test a treatment model through empirical research. The task-centered model evolved from the knowledge and techniques that were prevalent at the end of the 1960s: psychodynamic theory, problem-solving and behavioral theories, and outcome research. The action-oriented mood of that time influenced the way the model developed; that is, the model placed high value on action, present-centeredness, and clients' rights to participate freely in their treatment.

Funded originally by a small start-up grant from a private foundation, the research and development later were substantially aided by a grant from the U.S. Department of Health and Human Services. The mission of the Task-Centered Project was twofold: to develop technologies to increase the effectiveness of intervention and to experiment with teaching methods.

The foundational research on the model occurred from 1970 to 1978. During that time, the project enrolled about 125 first-year graduate students who performed the early testing of the model. Doctoral students conducted some studies and supervised all the students, under the general direction of Professors Laura Epstein and William J. Reid. Thirteen social agencies in Chicago, including medical and psychiatric hospitals and clinics, school social work departments in public elementary and high schools, and child welfare agencies, provided the research cases in graduate students' fieldwork placements. Over the eight-year period, the students handled approximately 1,300 cases, using the basic task-centered guidelines.

The first test of task-centered methods involved 32 clients randomly assigned to experimental and control conditions. A year later, the second study, also experimental, had a sample of 87 cases (Reid, 1978). Subsequently, 22 studies were conducted in this country. These were developmental in nature and involved small numbers of clients without the use of control or comparison groups (Reid, 1985). Task-centered treatment of marital and relationship problems received an extensive and rigorous test in a large-scale experiment conducted in England, involving 400 patients allocated to experimental (task-centered) and control (routine service) groups (Gibbons, Butler, & Bow, 1979; Gibbons, Butler, Urwin, & Gibbons, 1978).

With the publication of *Task-Centered Casework* (Reid & Epstein, 1972), the model attracted interest throughout the country and abroad. Practitioners and researchers from many settings studied and used it. Studies in England expanded the development of the model into new problem areas (Gibbons et al., 1978, 1979). A specialized literature began to appear, and various writers developed different versions of the approach, adapting and testing it in different settings and in relation to new problem areas. Reid and his associates conducted ongoing developmental research from the 1980s onward at the State University of New York at Albany (see Reid, 1992). Rooney (1992) extensively elaborated on the model to improve the treatment of involuntary clients, and Epstein (1992) integrated brief treatment and task-centered practices. Twenty years after its development, the task-centered model is a major approach in clinical social work, and its time-limited feature is consistent with the widespread interest in brief treatment.

## Basic Procedures

Task-centered practice is a technology for alleviating specific target problems that clients recognize, understand, acknowledge, and want to attend to. When authorities, such as courts, mandate that problems must be dealt with, it is necessary to manage them in a manner that continually emphasizes the clients' own priorities (Rooney, 1992).

Task-centered practice is planned to be time limited, to take place in eight to 12 interviews over three to four months. These time limits may be altered under particular circumstances to fit the conditions of practice.

Task-centered practice consists of a start-up and four sequential but overlapping steps (see Figure 1). The regularity of the steps induces systematic processes that are most likely to be efficient and to enable clients and practitioners to obtain satisfactory outcomes within the time limits. Under the pressure of problem solving, these steps usually occur somewhat out of sequence; nonetheless, the practitioner should resume the normal sequence as soon as possible.

The basic procedures call for a *case planning phase*, to be accomplished in Steps 1 and 2; the *implementation phase*, to be carried out in Step 3;

FIGURE 1

Map of the Task-Centered Model: Basic Steps

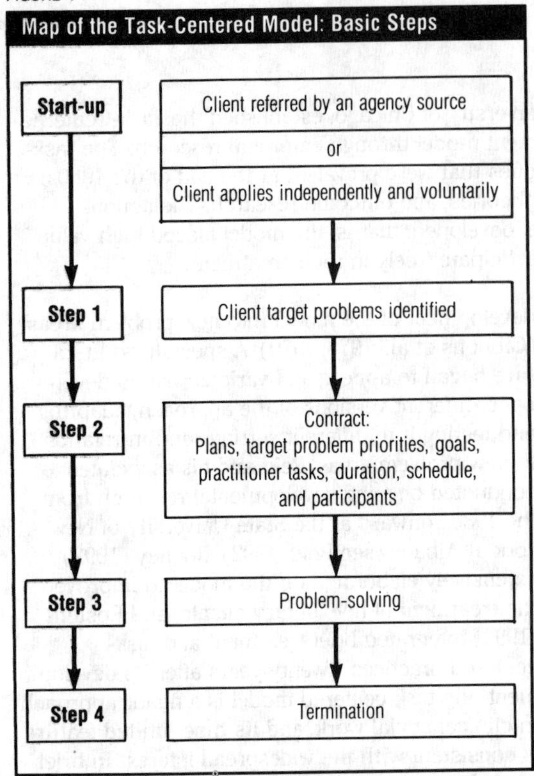


Reprinted with the permission of Macmillan College Publishing Company from *Brief Treatment and a New Look at the Task-Centered Approach* by Laura Epstein. Copyright © 1992 by Macmillan College Publishing Company, Inc.

and the *termination phase*, to be implemented in Step 4. Figure 2 presents a detailed map of the model.

## Case Planning Phase

In this model, the *case plan* is the assessment fitted into a problem-reduction program of action. It organizes the management of referrals, identification of a client's target problems, the making of the contract, and a rapid early assessment.

### Referrals

Many cases start with a referral that may take excessive time if there is conflict between the referring agency and the receiving agency. In the interests of conserving time and in concentrating attention, it is desirable to minimize such conflicts in the start-up step through negotiations. The aim is for the agencies involved to reach as much agreement as possible on what the goals and focus of intervention are to be.

### Identifying Target Problems

Identification of target problems is a prerequisite to implementing the model. Ordinarily, a client experiences distress, uneasiness, upset, turbulence, malfunction, disability, or perplexity or perceives a threat to important goals and expectations. The client knows or believes that a particular event or occurrence is the center of the trouble. Thus, the target problem is the problem that the client thinks should be alleviated and should be worked on.

Clients are generally able to define or describe their perceived target problem. When a client cannot do so, the practitioner helps the client through the process through questions and discussion. Thus, together the client and practitioner develop a statement of the target problem that is as close as possible to the way the client understands the situation. For help in identifying target problems, practitioners sometimes find it useful to consult other people who are involved with the client and who play a part in the problem or its solution.

The target problem is one that the practitioner thinks is appropriate. Therefore, it is crucial in this model that the client's identification of the target problem and the practitioner's determination of the focus be as congruent as possible. Without this congruence, there will be impasses in which the client and the practitioner struggle to avoid or circumvent movement, excessive reluctance, or resistance. When authorities, such as courts or other governmental departments that can exercise sanctions, mandate the target problem to be treated, the formulation of the problem must be modified to take the mandate into account.

The context of the target problem refers to the situation in which the target problem is embedded and the conditions that shape it. These situations or conditions include important interpersonal relations, difficulties in performing roles, economic and financial conditions and difficulties, and other features of the social environment. Influential other people, including professionals, agencies, or other social institutions, may also have opinions that determine the client's situation.

The target problem becomes operational upon the practitioner's explicit willingness to focus on it. If the practitioner judges that the client's selected target problem is wrong or that it is not feasible to work on that problem, then he or she is obligated to state a professional opinion and to help the client explore other options. From a practical standpoint, a single task-centered sequence can manage up to three problems by relating them to one another.

### Making a Contract

The contract represents the case plan—the client's and the worker's agreement to work

FIGURE 2

**Detailed Map of the Task-Centered Model**

**Start-up**

**Client referred by an agency source**

**FIND OUT**
- Source's goals

**NEGOTIATE**
- Source's specific goals
- Source's resources to achieve goals

**Client applies, independently and voluntarily**

Not needed

**Step 1**

**Client target problems identified**

**FIND OUT**
- Problems defined by client
- Client priorities (hold to three)
- Referral source priorities (mandated problems)
- Preliminary rapid early assessment

**Step 2**

**Contract**

**COVER**
- Priority target problems (three maximum)
- Client's specific goals (accepted by practitioner)
- Client's general tasks
- Practitioner's general tasks
- Duration of intervention sequence (time limits)
- Schedule for interviews
- Schedule for interventions
- Parties to be included

**Step 3**

**Problem solving, task achievement, problem reduction. Select as needed**

**DEFINE AND SPECIFY TARGET PROBLEM (THREE MAXIMUM)**
**Restate and name the problem** (the particular conditions and behaviors to be changed)
**Assess** (related to target problem and goal)
- Target problem
  How often it occurs (frequency)
  Where it occurs (site)
  With whom (participants)
  What immediate antecedents (forerunners)
  What consequences (effects)
  What meaning (importance)
- Social context (social conditions precipitating and maintaining the problem)
  Work–school circumstances
  Economic status
  Family organization
  Peer group organization
  Housing state
  Cultural/ethnic background
- Cognitive–affective circumstances
  Client characteristics
  Mode of functioning
  Personal resources
- Other assessments

**GENERATE ALTERNATIVES**
- Find out and identify a feasible range of possible problem-solving actions

**NEGOTIATE SUPPORTIVE AND COLLABORATIVE ACTIONS OF OTHER PERSONS AND AGENCIES**

*continued*

FIGURE 2 (CONTINUED)

**Detailed Map of the Task-Centered Model**

**Step 3 (continued)**

**DECISION MAKING** (confirm goals, select what will be done, and design details of the intervention strategy)
- Re-affirm contract and goals
- Determine basic interventions
- Plan timing and sequence
- Select participants
- Get client agreement and understanding (informed consent)
- Get agreement and understanding of others

**IMPLEMENT** (carry out strategy)

**Develop tasks**
- Formulate tasks
- Get client understanding and agreement to tasks
- Get client understanding of rationale and incentives for tasks
- Summarize tasks
- Review expected difficulties
- Devise plans for client task performance
- Summarize tasks
- Devise plans for client task performance

**Support task performance**
- Review number of sessions outstanding
- Obtain and use resources
- Find out obstacles to resource provision
- Give instruction
- Give guidance
- Do simulations
- Do role plays, simulation, and guided practice
- Accompany client for modeling and/or advocacy
- Other
- Find out obstacles to task performance
  In the social environment: lack of resources, stress, discrimination, structural problems
  In the interpersonal transactions: deficit and conflict, lack of cooperation
  In the psychological state: fears, suspicions, lack of knowledge
- Plan actions to remove, reduce, or alter obstacles
- Remedy practical barriers to task performance, e.g., lack of skills, lack of cooperation and support from others, and lack of resources
- Alleviate cognitive barriers to task performance: discuss fears, suspicions, lack of knowledge, adverse beliefs
- Plan and state practitioner tasks: inform client of practitioner tasks, review implementation of practitioner tasks, review problem state

**Verify** (check, test, confirm, substantiate probable effects of interventions) and
**Monitor** (record problem status regularly—use structured notations, charts, graphs, plus brief, succinct narrative comments)

**Revise contract,** or some parts of it, if:
- Progress unsatisfactory
- Progress exceeds expectations
- New problems emerge
- Problem takes on different characteristics
- Tasks not performed, or poorly performed
- Supports and resources, if ineffective
- Practitioner tasks ineffective or not feasible

**Step 4** — **Termination**

**END**
**EXTEND** on evidence of client commitment
**MONITOR** when mandated by law, court order, or formal agency requirements

toward the reduction of the stated personal problems. The client has a right to participate in the choices made. Such participation pays off in better outcomes because a client who understands the risks and benefits of intervention and the alternatives to treatment is likely to be cooperative.

Two factors direct the selection of intervention activities for inclusion in the contract: (1) the suitability of the proposed interventions for affecting the social situations, problems, and persons involved and (2) the reliability of the information about probable good outcomes. The preferences of the practitioner and the client also influence the selection of interventions, as do the style and requirements of the agency, the limitations and opportunities inherent in the client's situation, and accidental or random occurrences.

Both written and oral contracts can be used. The written contract has the advantage of being explicit and can be used as an instrument of control. Making a contract is a way to achieve clarity between the client and the practitioner. Oral contracts are common, and they can and should be specific.

Involuntary clients pose special problems in the contracting process. They tend to be vulnerable and may agree to a contract that is not realistic. In such cases, they may find themselves punished for failure. When clients who are highly vulnerable are not able to make contracts on their own, practitioners may have to resort to contracts made or underwritten by caretakers.

The contract is not permanent. It can be altered at any time at the discretion of the parties involved. Mutual agreement and continuous work are necessary for it to have any force.

The subjects to cover in the contract include the following:

- major target problems: a maximum of three, stated from the client's perspective, and modified by the mandate, if any.
- specific goals: formulated from the client's point of view, arranged according to the client's priorities, and stated in behavioral or cognitive terms. The goals depict the results the client and practitioner want to achieve.
- client's tasks: statements of exactly what the client is to do in behavioral or cognitive terms. The tasks may be general (relatively comprehensive), partial or unitary, or complex (consisting of several or many parts). They may be changed if necessary.
- practitioner's tasks: activities that the practitioner intends to undertake to support the client's efficient performance of the tasks.
- duration of the intervention: the time limit—approximately how long the process is to last.
- schedule of interventions: an estimate of the order of interventions.
- schedule of interviews: the dates of the interviews and how often they will be conducted.
- participants: who will take part in the interviews.
- location: where the sessions will be held.

**Rapid Early Assessment**

The beginning assessment is what produces the rapid early working assessment, the appraisals and formulations that are the basis for quickly moving into treatment. The six keys to rapid early assessment are as follows:

1. Project an appropriate interviewing atmosphere with a straightforward and responsive manner.
2. Generate significant hypotheses for assessment from the immediate interviewing situation, using observations and impressions formed on the spot in the interview.
3. Constrain information to getting primarily to the target problems and to the present time.
4. Explore selectively; evaluate, on the basis of current information and observations, what appear to be the strengths and weaknesses in the client's personal traits, immediate environment, special features of culture and ethnicity, family and peer relationships, and work and school.
5. Draw full value from immediately available interview data, for example, relationship, attitudinal, and communication behavior shown in or reasonably inferred from the interview and from available collateral information. The purpose is to create a working image of the person.
6. Ensure that the exploration is parsimonious.

In the first step, at the point of identifying the target problem, the generation of rapid early assessment data helps the practitioner evaluate how practical it is to go with the client's early designation of the target problem or to what extent it is advisable to steer the client in a different direction. The initial assessment should be reviewed periodically. The rapid early assessment and its changes constitute the working assessment. In difficult circumstances that are obscure or baffling or when critical issues require considerable study, case planning and contracting may take more time and involve more factors than in the general run of cases.

## Implementation Phase

Implementation refers to the development and use of tasks and the performance of the tasks as best as possible. Goals are most likely to be achieved if the tasks are performed successfully. When the practitioner focuses on the client's identified main issues, he or she is creating conditions that are conducive to problem solving. The practitioner obtains or arranges for the client to have access to needed concrete resources; instructs the client in relevant social skills and helps the client develop an increased capacity for performing them; negotiates resources and favorable attitudes from other agencies and with the client's family members, friends, and other important persons in the client's life, as needed; reviews the client's progress in alleviating the problems; and arranges to terminate, extend, or follow up the original contract.

**Ongoing Assessment**

The ongoing assessment, or reassessment, builds on the original rapid early assessment, making corrections and fine-tuning it. In this assessment, the practitioner looks for errors and omissions in the original assessment, for evidence that the tasks need to be made more "doable," and for obstacles to the performance of the tasks. Barriers are always evident; they indicate the need to revise the tasks, to side-step or overcome the barriers and to alter the circumstances that stand in the way of achieving the tasks.

The task-centered model does not require a psychiatric diagnosis. However, that information is useful as one way to describe the client and to understand the client's traits and abilities. The psychiatric classification, which is always made if the setting is a psychiatric hospital or clinic, is invariably useful when the target problem encompasses a physical disease or neurological condition; when medications or other biological interventions are administered; or when the client is suffering from delusions, hallucinations, or thought disorders.

In normal task-centered work, it is not useful to obtain extensive life-history data for assessing the client because not only is getting the data time-consuming, but the information is usually not needed for the quick reduction of the client's target problem. Although information about a problem's duration and how it has changed or remained constant over time is an aid to full understanding, ordinarily the specific current social and interpersonal situation and the client's reactions and contribution to it often give a good picture of the problems.

The social context refers to the client's work or school activities, health, financial standing, and cultural identification and the makeup of and central relationships in the family. Financial, work, and school data are essential for making judgments because economic status is a strong indicator of all facets of well-being.

The client's history should be explored briefly if the emphasis on the present does not shed enough light to make the situation understandable and to provide levers from which to move the issues in the desired direction. Insights provided by personality and behavioral theories are helpful in putting the accumulated information into manageable frameworks that help the client and practitioner gain a better understanding of the problems and feel secure enough to take the risks needed to bring about change. The task-centered model can be used within any theoretical framework.

**Developing and Using Tasks**

This activity is the major part of the implementation phase. Tasks are particular kinds of problem-solving actions, planned by and agreed on by the practitioner and the client and capable of being worked on by the client and the practitioner outside, as well as inside, the interview. Tasks fit into the problem-solving paradigm in the following manner: (1) problem defined, (2) problem explored, (3) possible tasks developed, (4) tasks tried out, and (5) results tallied.

Tasks are of two broad types—(1) general tasks that state the direction of an action without much detail and (2) operational tasks that state specific actions the client is to take. These are heuristic classifications whose sole purpose is to help one plan in a concrete way. Tasks are related to the client's goals in that they are formulated to affect the problem in such a way that the goal may be realized. Often a general task and a goal are two aspects of the same phenomenon; the statement of the general task indicates what is to be done, and the statement of the goal indicates what the condition ought to be when the task is accomplished. Separate sections of the general task can be thought of as subtasks whose specifics are changed as the client and the practitioner work to complete the general tasks.

There are various types of operational tasks. A *unitary task* is a single action requiring a number of steps. A *complex task* is two or more discrete but closely related actions. *Reciprocal tasks* are separate but related actions worked on by two or more persons. *Cognitive tasks* involve thinking and feeling activities. In real practice these types are fluid, may be combined, and are performed or not performed to fit the circumstances (for a different classification, see Reid, 1992, pp. 36–72).

Task planning consists of a discussion that generates a set of tasks or options for tasks. When the client and the practitioner feel ready, they put together a definite plan of action, or strategy, that summarizes the tasks they have agreed on and how the tasks are to be implemented. The objective is to develop tasks that have a reasonable possibility of being performed.

Task planning starts with the contract and is ongoing; it is done whenever the client or practitioner has to formulate what to do next. To keep from being bogged down, the client and practitioner should plan tasks primarily to take care of major issues; minor or peripheral matters can be handled naturally and informally. The idea of the sequence is to help the client along by formulating the steps in the process. Planning too tightly and being too mechanical, however, will clutter the work and put the emphasis on procedures, rather than on the real nature of the client's situation.

One session may be enough to make a task plan, but it is more usual for tasks to emerge piecemeal during several phases of a single interview or over two or more interviews. Whereas target problems tend to remain stable over the life of the case, tasks change often. Tasks change because they are completed, are not done, or cannot be done. Tasks that are completed are dropped, whereas those that are not done are analyzed to obtain information about the barriers to their achievement and then are revised or dropped.

The sources of information about reasonable tasks to reduce a problem include the client's experience; the practitioner's experience; and expert knowledge about reliable or reasonable problem-solving actions, especially those that have a good track record. Specialized agencies, libraries, journals, consultants and other experts, and data banks are sources of information.

**Achieving the Performance of Tasks**

After alternative tasks have been generated with a client, the next step is to reach an explicit agreement about which ones will be undertaken. Then the details of the implementation (what is to be done, when, with whom, where, under what specific conditions, and how) are discussed and agreed on. The client should emerge with a clear idea—a blueprint—to help him or her accomplish the tasks.

Negotiating and conferring with agency and community officials, neighbors, friends, and family members are the practitioner's chief tasks. Negotiations are conducted to transfer resources, services, and goodwill from the organization to the client and to package or design them in a way that will reduce the client's target problems.

Tasks are used to achieve performance of actions expected to reduce the problem. The achievement of goals and a satisfactory outcome are closely related. A great deal of the implementation phase in this model supports the performance of tasks by (1) obtaining and using resources; (2) skill training, that is, showing the client how to accomplish the tasks; (3) finding out what obstacles are in the way of performing the tasks; (4) removing, reducing, or altering the obstacles; (5) finding remedies for practical barriers to the performance of the tasks; (6) alleviating cognitive barriers through cognitive therapeutic discussions; and (7) judiciously using the practitioner's tasks to move the activity along.

The following are 15 guidelines for increasing the probability that a client will carry out tasks:

1. Allow enough time for discussion to ensure that the client understands and agrees to the tasks.
2. Suggest tasks, but expect that the client will perform best if he or she is committed to the actions.
3. Direct and advise clients when they ask what to do.
4. Establish incentives for completing the tasks, so the client believes that the effort is worthwhile and that it will alleviate the problem.
5. Establish the rationales—compelling reasons—for attempting to perform the tasks.
6. Anticipate expectable difficulties, sift out what is probably real and not real, and give appropriate reassurance.
7. Summarize the tasks at regular intervals, such as at the end of an important discussion or interview.
8. Devise plans for the client's performance of the tasks that are concrete outlines of what the client needs to do and when, where, and with whom. With some clients and some tasks, the client's capability and initiative will make it possible for this step to be brief. However, when the client lacks information and is fearful and inexperienced, the practitioner may have to go into great detail, and the step may be prolonged.
9. Provide resources by locating and selecting the appropriate community services. Describe and explain to the client the characteristics of the resources and how the particular agencies operate. The client should be in a position to make an informed choice among the possible resources and to have some idea of what he or she may reasonably expect. Most often, the client will seek and should get the practitio-

ner's opinion of the usefulness of the resource and the drawbacks to using it. In the event that the client lacks the courage or skills to connect with the resource, and assuming that the client truly needs the resource to make the tasks fully achievable, the practitioner may act for or with the client to achieve a good connection to the resource because the aim is to get the tasks accomplished. The practitioner also may do careful follow-ups to guarantee that a good connection is maintained.

10. Show clients how to do tasks, through instruction, simulation, and guided practice. Instruction is the main technique in this regard and includes imparting information, training the client in skills (or seeing to it that the client gets the instruction in a group or other milieu), and furnishing direction that the client needs to act in an effective manner.

    With role-playing and simulation, the practitioner sets up a situation through which the client rehearses actions to carry out the tasks. Role-playing is a vivid means of learning skills and detecting obstacles to the performance of a task. It is easy to do with children, but more difficult with adults, with whom it should be avoided if either the adult client or practitioner is embarrassed.

    In guided practice, the problem is played out in the session. The practitioner can guide the client by modeling, for example, preferred behavior toward a child, spouse, or relative. When family quarrels occur in an interview, the practitioner can intervene with suggestions and create discussions to clear up misunderstandings and wrongdoing.
11. Work toward the achievement of a task in increments. Break tasks down into parts and attend to the easiest first and the more difficult ones later.
12. Summarize the plans for the performance of a task often, especially when a new phase is entered.
13. Review the performance of a task regularly in a systematic way. Start by inquiring what the client has been able to do since the last session. Complete, substantial, or satisfactory performance should be credited and put aside. Then discuss the circumstances that stood in the way of the client's performance and identify and analyze these barriers.
14. Review the time limits and number of sessions that remain. This is a simple, straightforward matter that causes difficulties only if not done.
15. When difficulties occur, strongly advise the client how to slow down, stay cool, temporize, procrastinate, evade, and avoid unexpected difficulties. Advise the client to take time to think and to consult the practitioner or others.

## Overcoming Obstacles

Because an obstacle is anything that gets in the way of performing the task, there may be many different kinds of obstacles. Usually, scrutinizing the situation will suggest some relatively straightforward, commonsense analysis of what is standing in the way. It is highly advisable to work on the basis of the most obvious, straightforward, and parsimonious explanation of the obstacles, rather than to reach first for a complex, hidden, or obscure obstacle. Thus, it is more feasible, for example, to attribute the client's inability to perform a task to the lack of resources or skills, rather than immediately identify the obstacle as a pathology. One can always move to a more complex analysis if the immediate explanations do not work.

Obstacles to the performance of tasks arise in three overlapping areas: the social environment, interpersonal interactions, and the client's psychological state. In the social environment, obstacles are the lack of resources, stress precipitated by external pressures (including a sudden illness, loss of a job, failure at some undertaking, death of a loved one, or attack), pervasive discrimination, or dysfunctional structural problems (such as an epidemic, the failure of the economic system to provide employment, poor schools, and the like).

In interpersonal transactions, obstacles are relationships that lack intimacy, security, reinforcements, and cooperation. In addition to deficits in relationships, there may be substantial conflict among the persons who are most important to the client. Obstacles to the performance of a task may also reflect the inner psychological state of the individual. Prominent among them are unwarranted fears and suspicions of others that nevertheless have a strong influence on how the client perceives the world.

The following are some reasons for a client's inability to perform a task or inadequate performance of it:

*The client lacks concrete resources* to facilitate the work of the task. Examples of such resources are adequate money; medical and psychiatric care; housing; employment and education; or child care provided by a relative, homemaker, or day care center.

*The client lacks necessary reinforcements* from other persons, such as family members, friends, or authorities. These other important persons may be estranged, uncaring, hostile, oppressive, or exploitative, or they may be unable to help the client because of their own problems.

*The client lacks skills* and does not know how to accomplish the task. The client may be painfully awkward or may have only enough skill to perform the task incompletely or erratically.

*The client has adverse beliefs or unrealistic fears* that lead him or her to think that the tasks have little value or will have negative consequences.

*The client lacks the capacity* to perform the task owing to a disability, incapacity, or serious misunderstanding of the task.

*The practitioner may be biased and unskilled.* The practitioner's personal beliefs and attitudes, as well as a lack of knowledge, can interfere with projecting a hopeful attitude, being appropriately encouraging, and offering relevant suggestions.

To remove, reduce, or alter obstacles such as a lack of skills, cooperation and support of others, or resources, the practitioner should devise a plan. The plan should include the alleviation of cognitive or affective barriers to the performance of tasks through discussion and counseling regarding fears, suspicions, lack of knowledge, and adverse beliefs. The following are some specific explanations of clients' inability to perform tasks, as well as some specific guidelines that are frequently applicable to alleviating these obstacles to performance.

If the necessary *concrete resources* are not available or accessible, the possible remedies are those that lead the client to obtain the resources, if possible. Thus, a client may need help in learning how to withstand the delay in obtaining the resources and how to cope while waiting; during this time, alternative resources should be developed. At the worst—when a genuinely necessary resource is unavailable and no satisfactory substitute is possible—the practitioner should help the client relinquish the expectation that the resource can be obtained. In such a case, the performance of the task is not within the control of the client and probably will not occur. To expect otherwise goes against reality.

Possible remedies for the *lack of reinforcement* are guiding the client in ways to communicate with and behave toward important people (such as a teacher, spouse, parent, child, or relative) to obtain their support, if possible, and approaching these people on the client's behalf. Thus, for example, the practitioner can confer, refer, request, instruct, negotiate, or accompany the client and, if necessary, advocate on the client's behalf.

Possible remedies for the client's *lack of skills* are for the practitioner to work with the client to help him or her acquire skills or to refer the client to experts who can help the client learn these skills.

There are few remedies for changing *adverse beliefs*. The client's experience may have induced beliefs that inhibit the client's performance of tasks. Examples of such beliefs are low self-esteem; awareness of cultural and economic oppression and discrimination; well-established ideas that others view him or her as lowly; and a genuine disregard and disapproval of dominant customs, folkways, ethics, or social conventions. Unrealistically low self-evaluations are learned attitudes that improve with factual, realistic discussions of their inappropriateness, especially if these discussions are supported by experiences with others who like, respect, and appreciate the client. Beliefs based on negative attitudes toward dominant customs, on the other hand, may be intractable, although appeals to basic self-interest and an open discussion of the pros and cons of a particular view may succeed in changing the person's opinion. In any case, the client can at least understand how to protect himself or herself from clashes with normative authorities.

With regard to the client's *lack of capacity,* it is advisable to be cautious not to underrate a client, whether he or she is young, antagonistic, old, or mentally impaired. Obviously, children who are too young to have developed sophisticated verbal and cognitive skills and people whose faculties are seriously deteriorated or who are otherwise ill cannot perform many acts. Those clients need care and protection. The actions that are usually called for are to scale down the tasks to be within the person's capacity and to involve others in doing the tasks for and with the client.

Ideally, the remedy for the *practitioner's bias and lack of skills* is in-service training and professional education.

## Revisions, Terminations, and Extensions

The most important issue in revisions, terminations, and extensions is that they be planned and purposefully related to some demonstrable need or requirement. Plans may be revised and time limits may be extended when there is a clear and mutually understood purpose. Unplanned extensions should be avoided. Actions can be monitored when there is a court order that requires ongoing contact or when some definite professional indication exists.

Planning for termination starts from the beginning of treatment. Early planning forestalls the client's development of dependence on the practitioner and controls the practitioner's tendency to sometimes overinvest in the client. Regular reminders keep the plan in mind and serve to preserve the time-limited structure. The last interview should be a review of what has been accomplished and a look toward the future.

## Effectiveness and Usefulness of the Model

Of the various brief treatment models, the task-centered approach is the one that was designed, developed, and tested by social workers. It was derived from and addresses social work conditions that distinctively interfuse psychotherapy with management of the social environment and the interpersonal field.

Although the task-centered model is fundamentally brief treatment, it is readily adapted as a module of structured treatment and inserted within an ongoing case. As Epstein (1992) noted, the model shares many of the attributes of brief treatment: prompt introduction of intervention, time limits, selected focus on defined problems, relatively specific goals, and emphasis on the present. Third-party payers have a pronounced inclination for the use of brief treatments for conditions covered by medical insurance, and cost-conscious administrators understandably share this preference. Brief treatments have shown generally satisfactory outcomes, although it is not clear that a particular viewpoint, model, or technique will produce a given result (Koss & Butcher, 1986).

The research on the task-centered model that occurred during its initial development indicated that the approach produced good results. Early studies were exploratory. The first controlled test (Reid & Epstein, 1972) consisted of the random assignment of 32 clients (mainly children in a school setting) to experimental and control conditions with the objective of assessing the effectiveness of techniques for planning and carrying out tasks. Independent judges, who did not know which cases were experimental and which were control, ascertained that almost 70 percent of the experimental tasks, in contrast to only 20 percent of the control tasks, had been substantially or completely achieved—a statistically significant difference.

Subsequently, a more sophisticated and extensive study (Reid, 1978) randomly assigned 87 cases to experimental and control conditions: 47 from a public school system, 38 from a psychiatric clinic, and 2 from a youth service agency. The families of the clients in the sample suffered from low income, poor housing, and numerous physical and mental health problems. The problems dealt with were primarily difficulty in performing roles, interpersonal conflict, and dissatisfaction with social relations. It was found that the experimental treatment (the task-centered model) made a distinct contribution to desired changes in the client's target problems. Furthermore, changes occurred (though to a lesser degree) in the client's general problem state that involved difficulties not dealt with in treatment (see Reid, 1978, pp. 225–271).

Studies published thereafter reported on tests, adaptations, and specialized uses of the model (see Diekring, Brown, & Fortune, 1980; Goldberg & Stanley, 1978; Rooney, 1981). On the whole, the outcome research has indicated that the model produces good results with a wide array of targeted problems. The task-centered approach can ordinarily reduce a set of related problems that cluster around the target problem, but it is less effective if the problem is broad in scope or loose in focus. No particular problem area has appeared either specially amenable or, for that matter, typically indifferent to this model.

Continued research and development is necessary to appraise, extend, and discern the differential effectiveness of the task-centered approach. Although the quality and rigor of the numerous studies varied, the model has been useful as a basic set of interventions with many problems in living in ordinary practice. It is easily combined with other approaches and can be adapted to take into account the particular aspects of practice in various settings.

## References


Diekring, B., Brown, M., & Fortune, A. E. (1980). Task-centered treatment in a residential facility for the elderly: A clinical trial. *Journal of Gerontological Social Work, 2,* 225–240.

Epstein, L. (1992). *Brief treatment and a new look at the task-centered approach.* New York: Macmillan.

Gibbons, J., Butler, J., & Bow, I. (1979). Task-centered casework with marital problems. *British Journal of Social Work, 8,* 393–409.

Gibbons, J. S., Butler, J., Urwin, P., & Gibbons, J. L. (1978). Evaluation of a social work service for self-poisoning patients. *British Journal of Psychiatry, 133,* 111–118.

Goldberg, E. M., & Stanley, J. S. (1978). A task-centered approach to probation. In J. King (Ed.), *Pressures and changes in the probation service* (pp. 75–101). Cambridge, England: Institute of Criminology.

Koss, M. P., & Butcher, J. N. (1986). Research on brief psychotherapy. In S. L. Garfield & A. E. Bergin (Eds.), *Handbook of psychotherapy and behavior change* (pp. 627–670). New York: John Wiley & Sons.

Reid, W. J. (1978). *The task-centered system.* New York: Columbia University Press.

Reid, W. J. (1985). *Family problem solving.* New York: Columbia University Press.

Reid, W. J. (1992). *Task strategies: An empirical approach to clinical social work.* New York: Columbia University Press.

Reid, W. J., & Epstein, L. (1972). *Task-centered casework.* New York: Columbia University Press.

Rooney, R. H. (1981). A task-centered reunification model for foster care. In A. A. Maluccio & P. Sinanoglu (Eds.), *Working with biological parents of children in foster care* (pp. 135–150). New York: Child Welfare League of America.

Rooney, R. H. (1992). *Strategies for work with involuntary clients.* New York: Columbia University Press.

## Further Reading

Constable, R., Flynn, J. P., & McDonald, S. (Eds.). (1991). *School social work: Practice and research perspectives* (2nd ed.). Chicago: Lyceum.

Fortune, A. E. (Ed.). (1985). *Task-centered practice with families and groups.* New York: Springer.

Reid, W. J., & Epstein, L. (Eds.). (1977). *Task-centered practice.* New York: Columbia University Press.

Tolson, E. R., Reid, W. J., & Garvin, C. D. (1994). *Task-centered practice within the generalist perspective.* New York: Columbia University Press.

**Laura Epstein, AM,** is professor emeritus, University of Chicago, School of Social Service Administration, Chicago, IL 60637.

### For further information see

Assessment; Brief Therapies; Clinical Social Work; Conflict Resolution; Direct Practice Overview; Diagnostic and Statistical Manual of Mental Disorders; Ecological Perspective; Generalist and Advanced Generalist Practice; Goal Setting and Intervention Planning; Intervention Research; Person-in-Environment; School-Linked Services; School Social Work Overview; Social Work Practice: History and Evolution; Social Work Practice: Theoretical Base; Social Work Profession Overview.

**Key Words**

brief psychotherapy
contracts
goal setting
task-centered treatment

# Brief Therapies

**Margot Taylor Fanger**

Brief therapies are "brief" because they substitute time for timelessness.

—Mardi Horowitz, 1981
*Forms of Brief Therapy*

Planned brief therapy is a specialized field of psychotherapy. Brief, or more accurately, time-effective therapy is not a limited set of methods, but rather a point of view involving the therapist's intention to actively shape well-defined goals with the client and state the goals so that both therapist and client will know when they are achieved. This approach developed in the 1960s from the need to serve more people more effectively in a shorter period of time and expanded with the more recent demands of managed care. Practitioners will continue to develop and practice brief therapy because it offers more treatment opportunities to more people at lower cost, and because it enhances clients' ability to solve their own problems. This entry compares open-ended therapy with brief therapy, cites outcome studies supporting the efficacy of brief therapy, and discusses selection criteria. The author describes specific brief therapy approaches, including psychodynamic, cognitive–behavioral, strategic or solution-oriented, and single session.

## Overview

*Brief therapy* is an umbrella term that includes crisis intervention; therapies that are time-defined by insurance, with approval needed for more sessions; therapies that are somewhat more flexible but are still regulated for a specific number of sessions available per year, such as those in health maintenance organizations; any therapy composed of 20 sessions or fewer; and intermittent therapy with a small number of sessions over a longer period of time. What all these therapies have in common is a small number of actual face-to-face therapeutic encounters. But "the essence of brief therapy lies not in its numerical time characteristics, but in the therapeutic values, attitudes and aims of the therapist" (Budman & Gurman, 1988, p. 9). Therefore, it is most useful to see brief therapy as a particular point of view—a therapy with well-defined goals that are achieved in an efficient manner. These goals, and the length of treatment, are decided in partnership with the client. It is important to note that this entry discusses a *planned* brief therapy, in contrast to many therapies that are brief by default (Bloom, 1992; Budman & Gurman, 1988; Gurman, 1981; Lemon, 1983; L. G. Parad, 1971; Weiss & Jacobson, 1981).

In surveying the numerous brief or time-limited therapeutic approaches, the term "time-effective therapy" is more inconclusive than either "brief therapy" or "time-limited therapy." Although some therapies do specify a particular number of sessions, weeks, or months, others use actual time more flexibly, with a small number of sessions spread over months or even years (Budman & Gurman, 1988; Friedman & Fanger, 1991; Koss & Butcher, 1986; Kreilkamp, 1989). A flexible approach is the key to efficacy; as W. H. O'Hanlon (1990) said, "I begin therapy with new clients assuming that it will be brief, and I let my clients teach me how long it will be. . .the nature of the presenting problem doesn't determine whether therapy is to be brief or not . . . it's the client's response to the therapy that is the determining factor" (p. 49).

**Goal-Focused**

To enhance the efficacy of time-effective therapy, the therapist must take an active role not only initially to help the client define the specific goal of treatment, but also throughout treatment to keep the therapy focused on the goal. The goal must be spelled out in such a way that both client and therapist will know when it has been achieved. For some clients, an agreement or contract concerning the length of treatment can be most useful. The contract not only helps keep the treatment focused, but—perhaps even more important—it conveys to the client the therapist's expectation that desired changes can be achieved in a timely manner. Some therapists use a specific number of sessions (Mann, 1973), whereas others use a more flexible, renewable contract (Friedman & Fanger, 1991). In some treatment settings the number of sessions is mandated by the insurance carrier or administrative structure.

One of the most critical elements for the success of time-effective therapy is the therapist's expectation and intention to help the client achieve his or her goals efficiently (Bloom, 1992; Friedman & Fanger, 1991; Talmon, 1990). Frank (1973) said, "Expectations of patient and therapist seem to affect duration and outcome of treatment, . . .[so] that the more congruent these are, the better the outcome of treatment should be" (p. 159). If therapy is performed without directed expectation and intention, it is less apt to produce the desired results (Weakland, Fisch, Watzlawick, & Bodin, 1974). The time-effective therapist is guided by particular values, such as a belief in using the most economical or parsimonious intervention possible to achieve the client's goal, an assumption that the client has strengths to be used toward this end, and the knowledge that change is ever present in human lives (Budman & Gurman, 1988; Friedman & Fanger, 1991).

**Empowered Client**

Another important aspect of brief therapy is a shift away from the traditional, hierarchical "patient–doctor" relationship toward one of increased partnership with and empowerment of the client. It is essential to increase client participation in shaping the desired goals if the goals are to be reached efficiently. It also follows that the therapist must find ways to identify and increase individual client strengths, including cultural norms, as part of goal attainment. The emphasis shifts from what was wrong in the past to what will be right for an improved future. This shift has strong positive implications for people of color, women, and other members of disempowered segments of society, because it involves moving from helplessness and hopelessness to hopefulness and empowerment through the agency of therapists who actively promote this shift (see Pinderhughes, 1989).

**Comparison of Therapies**

Controversy continues about the comparative merits of brief versus long-term or open-ended therapy (Wylie, 1990). Traditional long-term therapists maintain that brief therapy cannot be as effective as the longer version, that it is a product of bitter practical necessity and therefore is not the treatment of choice if unlimited resources are available. However, long-term therapy has not been proved more effective than brief therapy (Budman & Gurman, 1988; Fisher, 1980, 1984; Frank, 1973; Peake, Borduin, & Archer, 1988; Seeman, Tittler, & Friedman, 1985), and this disagreement may have partially resulted from comparing apples and oranges. Frank (1973) pointed out that

> Psychotherapies can be . . . roughly classified as directive [brief] or evocative [open-ended]. In the former, the therapist tries openly to alleviate specific symptoms or to bring about limited changes in the patient's behavior. In the latter, he tries to evoke and explore a wide range of the patient's feeling and attitudes as a means of promoting personality growth, with the expectation that as he becomes better able to function in general, his symptoms will be resolved. (p. 233)

In other words, although each approach aims to help the client make desired changes, the intended scope of such changes is quite different. Brief therapists aim to solve a problem, and long-term therapists try to change a personality. Moreover, brief therapists often use a developmental model of change wherein the task of therapy is seen as helping clients overcome a particular developmental snag and then resume their lives. Many brief therapists also believe that if the therapist can help clients make even a small change, they may generalize the change to other areas of their lives as well (Bloom, 1992; Budman & Gurman, 1988; Friedman & Fanger, 1991).

In any time-effective therapeutic approach, the first, or evaluation, session is regarded as critical. It is in this session that the therapist first encounters, joins, and begins to understand the client and his or her predicament. More important, the client is helped to specify particular goals to be achieved through therapy, and this in turn sets the stage for the therapeutic action to follow. How these goals are determined and defined reflects the therapist's theories about change. However, it is widely held that client and therapist need to agree about the direction of change and the desired results in the first session (Bloom, 1992; Budman & Gurman, 1988; Budman, Hoyt, & Friedman, 1992; Fisch, Weakland, & Segal, 1982; Friedman & Fanger, 1991; Talmon, 1990).

## History

Many strands have been woven into the fabric of brief psychotherapy as it is practiced today. Psychotherapy per se started in the 19th century, when Sigmund Freud developed his theories and the practice of psychoanalysis. Freud actually conducted brief therapy: He treated the conductor Bruno Walter's right arm cramp in six sessions and composer Gustave Mahler's impotence in a four-hour walk around Leyden in 1908 (Jones, 1955). As psychoanalytic theory and practice expanded to include more elements for analysis, the time required for therapy also increased (Malan, 1963). Accordingly, longer became synonymous with better. This view ultimately penetrated almost the entire field of psychotherapy, and it continues to have a pervasive influence today (Cummings, 1977).

In 1946, psychoanalysts Franz Alexander and Thomas French published a work that applied psychoanalytic principles to a briefer therapy. They challenged some basic psychoanalytic beliefs, especially about the efficacy of therapy being directly proportional to time spent in therapy. They demonstrated that both symptomatic and characterological change could be achieved with short-term techniques (Marmor, 1978). Another such approach was sector therapy, "a goal-limited therapy based directly upon psychoanalytic principles . . . planned to work on unconscious factors that influence the reality situation" and geared especially to briefly treat psychosomatic illness (Deutsch & Murphy, 1955, p. 11).

The Community Mental Health Centers Act of 1963 renewed the exploration of treatment techniques that would serve a greater number of clients with a more diverse presentation of psychological distress than could be treated in either long-term psychodynamic therapy or in psychoanalysis. The ferment in psychotherapeutic practice was well under way; group treatment was gaining more support, and family therapy was developing and being recognized (Sager & Kaplan, 1972). The need for a briefer psychodynamic approach to therapy began to be elaborated and studied (Davanloo, 1978, 1980; Malan, 1963; Mann, 1973; Sifneos, 1972; Wolberg, 1965). During this same period, practitioners also began to investigate and expand both cognitive–behavioral therapies (Beck, Rush, Shaw, & Emery, 1979; Ellis & Grieger, 1977; Phillips & Wiener, 1966) and strategic therapy (Haley, 1963, 1973; Weakland et al., 1974). Also, because crisis-oriented treatment requires interventive techniques that are immediately effective, development of these techniques influenced the unfolding brief therapy practice as well (H. J. Parad, 1968; H. J. Parad & Parad, 1968, 1990; L. G. Parad & Parad, 1968).

Social workers have always been intent on solving specific problems, and many casework settings preclude long-term contact. Furthermore, the essence of social casework is its focused approach (Rapoport, 1967). Social work by nature has contributed to the concepts of time-effective therapy, so these concepts are familiar to many social work practitioners. Social workers were also influenced by the attitudes of psychodynamic therapy, as evidenced by the surprise at the outcome of a long-term–short-term casework study by Reid and Shyne (1969). So imbued were the practitioner–researchers with the idea that "longer is better" that they had difficulty accepting their own results, which showed a reverse outcome. Out of Reid and Shyne's results, however, sprang the task-centered approach to casework, which has been developed and refined into a highly effective brief treatment approach (Reid, 1992).

One social worker unremittingly advocated time limits as a useful part of casework treatment for decades before the present upsurge of interest. Jessie Taft (quoted in L. G. Parad, 1971) said, "Time represents more vividly than any other category the necessity of accepting limitation as well as the inability to do so, and symbolizes therefore the whole problem of living" (p. 125). Taft was influenced by psychoanalyst Otto Rank, and in her Functional School of Social Work at the University of Pennsylvania, she emphasized the use of time-limited casework as a powerful tool that would directly help clients adjust to the vicissitudes of their lives. Taft even applied this perspective to a single interview. The problem-solving approach and elements of the functional approach were integrated in Perlman's (1957) book on social casework, which in turn laid the groundwork for crisis intervention theory, as described by Rapoport in 1967 and 1971 (Lemon, 1983).

By 1980 short-term therapy was sufficiently established to warrant a national conference (sponsored by the Harvard Community Health Plan in Boston). The keynote speaker, Herbert Pardes from the National Institute of Mental Health, summarized developments in the mental health field and society as a whole that had focused attention on brief therapy (Pardes & Pincus, 1981):

- the acceptance of more limited therapeutic goals
- the increasing development of an array of varied treatments along with a rapprochement of different therapeutic approaches
- advances in classification of emotional disorders
- the growing realization that lengthy treatments often do not meet the needs of particular populations
- an increasing concern with the costs of treatment combined with increasing access to treatment
- the growth of prepaid health plans with limited psychiatric benefits. (p. 12)

In the years since that statement, all of these factors have become more clearly important, with a resulting proliferation of approaches and publications. Research on treatment effectiveness has been an integral part of this expansion, but to date no one approach has been demonstrated as more effective than any other (Bloom, 1992; Budman & Gurman, 1988; Koss & Butcher, 1986; Ursano & Hollis, 1986).

## Selection Criteria

The question of which clients are appropriate for time-effective treatment has long been of considerable concern and the focus of research attention (Clarkin & France, 1982). There are two basic approaches to client selection, one that recommends time-effective treatment for all clients and one that has specific criteria for inclusion and exclusion. The most stringent criteria among the latter approach are some of those that were developed from the psychodynamic conceptual frame (for example, Davanloo, 1978; Gustafson, 1986; Malan, 1963; Mann, 1973; Sifneos, 1972). In general, these criteria would also be suitable for long-term therapy clients; for example, the ability to form a relationship, the ability to verbalize feelings and to think psychologically, and a clear motivation to change an identified specific issue. These criteria, which seem mainly aimed at white middle-class clients, exclude much of the increasingly broad spectrum of clients, including people of color, who seek and need effective therapy.

The opposite view—that of at least starting with the expectation of undertaking some form of time-effective therapy with almost all clients—also has early roots (Wolberg, 1965) and appears to be growing. This growth reflects not only the increased and broader demand for therapeutic services but also the growing trend toward an integrative treatment approach that aims to make the therapy fit the particular client rather than the converse. Practitioners from all approaches to time-effective therapy take this inclusive view. Some of the developers of brief treatment with roots in psychodynamic theory took this broad view of client selection from the beginning (Bennett, 1984; Bennett & Wisneski, 1979; Budman & Gurman, 1988; Cummings & VandenBos, 1979; Garfield, 1989; Kreilkamp, 1989; Wolberg, 1965). Budman and Stone (1983) summarized this view: "Patient selection criteria for brief therapy are often rather vague, unclear and contradictory.... We believe that in most circumstances it is unwarranted to exclude patients from brief therapy on the basis of diagnoses, symptoms or apparent motivation" (p. 941).

Cognitive–behavioral therapies, which focus on specific disorders (anxiety, depression, habits, phobias, and so on), use diagnostic categories for selection criteria. Strategic or solution-oriented therapists accept a wide variety of clients wanting to change unsatisfying aspects of their lives. All brief therapists limit their clientele to clients who have the capacity to participate in therapeutic interviews, that is, those who are not actively psychotic or in need of ongoing institutional connection and support in order to function.

## Outcome Studies

As early as 1963, Malan concluded that there was considerable evidence of the effectiveness of brief therapy, and he renewed and reinforced this conclusion in 1976 when he repeated an earlier outcome study of his own. In 1978 Strupp (quoted in Peake et al., 1988) said, "Short-term therapy should be the treatment of choice for practically all patients. On the basis of many reports, about two-thirds of all patients will respond positively to such interventions; the remaining one-third can be continued if this seems indicated, referred elsewhere, or judged to be beyond currently available therapeutic efforts" (p. 37). In general, there are no outcome studies that demonstrate that open-ended therapy has better results than briefer therapies, regardless of the type, severity, or duration of the presenting difficulty (Budman & Gurman, 1988).

Analyses of studies of therapy outcome in relation to the number of sessions have found that the major positive impact of individual therapy occurs in the first six to eight sessions (Koss & Butcher, 1986; Smith, Glass, & Miller, 1980). In one study the authors found that of all mental health clients in 1980, the modal number of visits was one and that 70 percent of clients had six visits or fewer (Taube, Goldman, Burns, & Kessler, 1988). Also, there is a congruence between general client expectations of treatment length, actual time clients stay in therapy, and the time it takes for the major impact of therapy—six to 10 sessions (Garfield, 1971, 1978, 1986, 1989).

Although there is no evidence that long-term therapy is more effective than brief therapy, this conclusion continues to be difficult for many therapists to accept. The idea of "longer is better" has been thoroughly recorded in the annals of therapeutic history. Far from being a sign of either unsuccessful or unsatisfactory treatment, brief therapy—planned or unplanned—is apparently as equally effective as long-term treatment, is more cost-effective, and produces as much client benefit and more client satisfaction than expected (Bloom, 1992; Budman & Gurman, 1988; Koss & Butcher, 1986; Rapoport, 1967; Reid & Shyne, 1969; Smith et al., 1980). "Moreover, a short-term structure tends to mobilize efforts of both the practitioner and the client, to force a focus on attainable goals, and to avoid the dysfunctional relationship complexities often found in long-term treatment" (Bloom, 1992, p. 5).

## Brief Therapy Approaches

Brief therapy approaches fall into three basic categories, according to the view of psychopathology or problem formation that underlies the therapy itself. *Psychodynamic therapy* looks to the past history of the client for the causes of his or her present difficulties with the belief that understanding those causes will change the present emotional state and hence the client's ability to act. *Cognitive–behavioral therapy* looks to the dysfunctional or negative thought patterns or behaviors of the client in the present and seeks to help the client retrain these thought patterns, behaviors, or both to alleviate difficulties. (A subcategory of cognitive–behavioral therapy, described separately, is the "task-centered" approach.) *Strategic* or *solution-oriented* therapy does not see pathology but rather looks at clients' current ineffective patterns that do not reach desired goals. As the attempted solution is noted, specific interventions are designed to interrupt these patterns, to reframe or give new perspective, to help the client achieve the desired results. Multiple-client therapies (couple, family, or group) are oriented broadly under one of these three categories.

### Psychodynamic Approach

Long-term or open-ended psychodynamic psychotherapy grew directly out of a desire to translate the principles of psychoanalysis to a treatment more sparing of time and money. Brief psychodynamic psychotherapy plans to use even fewer resources while still applying some of the original principles. Psychodynamic therapy aims to uncover the causes of the client's present effects or difficulties and so asks "why is a symptom occurring?" Psychodynamic principles include the concepts of early unresolved conflicts, the repression of these conflicts into the unconscious mind, and the need to uncover or perhaps to relive these conflicts, or, through interpretation, to gain insight that allows old responses to change to healthier ones. Transference feelings for the therapist and resistances that need to be worked through and the process of termination are also important.

Malan (1963) believed that long-term psychodynamic therapy had lost its way in terms of achieving directed results and so set out to develop a more active and effective method that still used basic psychodynamic principles. His approach, "focal therapy," consists of working through a specific aspect of psychopathology in a brief amount of time. Davanloo (1978) recommended not only analysis and interpretation of defenses, transference reactions, and resistances, but also an exploration of the libido structure of the patient's conflict. Sifneos (1972) focused on unresolved oedipal issues, especially those played out in the transference with the therapist, and Mann (1973) emphasized the analysis of loss as seen in unresolved separation–individuation issues. The patient selection criteria used in these therapies were relatively narrow and excluded many patients who might have sought help.

By the mid-1980s, psychodynamically oriented therapists began seeking and developing techniques and assumptions that would expand the view of psychodynamic therapy to include broader selection criteria, more flexible uses of duration and spacing of sessions, a view of the client seen in developmental terms, more emphasis on current stressors, and a more eclectic approach. Budman and Gurman (1988) offered a well-explicated version of this modified approach and included a particular way of thinking about clients to help define a workable focal issue. They sought to "capture and understand the core interpersonal life issues that are leading the patient to seek psychotherapy at a given moment in time, and to relate these issues to the patient's stage of life development and to his or her existential concerns" (p. 27) (see also Burke, White, & Havens, 1979; Crits-Christoph & Barber, 1991; Wolberg, 1980).

**Cognitive–Behavioral Approach**

Cognitive–behavioral therapies, by their nature, favor short-term work (Beck & Emery, 1985). They focus on the present and aim to modify or replace distorted cognitions or unwanted behaviors in a discrete and goal-oriented fashion. These therapies tend to focus on specific diagnostic categories, such as phobias, anxiety disorders, obsessive–compulsive disorders, depression, sexual dysfunction, and habit disorders. Cognitive–behavioral therapy is not concerned with *why* a client has certain difficulties but wants to ascertain *what* the dysfunctional cognitive–behavioral pattern is and *how* to change it. Cognitive–behavioral therapists teach cognitive restructuring, problem solving, and behavioral and other coping skills. Although a specific presenting problem is worked on, the ultimate therapeutic goal includes generalization of new skills as well as development of relapse prevention strategies. One of the most widely known of these approaches is Beck's cognitive treatment of depression and anxiety (Beck & Emery, 1985; Beck et al., 1979). In this treatment the therapist teaches the client how to monitor and recognize distorted and automatic thoughts and then to challenge these thoughts with reason, logic, and the empirical testing of homework. The client thus learns to modify distortions and to substitute more appropriate beliefs and ultimately can do this independently (see also Baucom & Epstein, 1990; Ellis & Grieger, 1977; Freeman, Simm, Beutler, & Arkowitz, 1989; Kuehlwein & Rosen, 1993; Peake et al., 1988; Phillips & Wiener, 1966; Young, 1990).

**Task-Centered Approach**

Although many brief therapies include task giving as part of their process, the task-centered approach is organized around this activity and was developed as part of social work practice. As such, it is empirical and integrates concepts and methods from several approaches: cognitive–behavioral, problem solving, cognitive, and structural (Reid, 1992). Practitioners began to formulate the task-centered approach in 1969, after the unexpected results of a controlled study of treatment results that compared a brief service with a continuous service in a family agency. The discovery that "the more active casework techniques. . .[were] more efficacious" (Reid & Shyne, 1969, p. 153) led to a reassessment of method. The emphasis in the task-centered model is on helping the client solve the problems that the client perceives; the client is viewed as resourceful, and the methods used are behavioral instructions to the client, both in the session and between sessions. The social worker may also undertake some specific tasks on the client's behalf. The rationale for this approach underlies most task giving, that is, that actions can change attitudes and thus open new possibilities in the client's life. The contact is usually short in duration, involving six to 12 weekly sessions within a four-month period (Reid, 1992).

**Strategic or Solution-Oriented Approach**

Strategic or solution-oriented therapies ask *what* is happening now and *how* it should be changed—but they do not ask *why*. Cognitive–behavioral approaches also ask what and how, but their emphasis is on what is wrong or problematic, whereas in strategic therapies the question is what is wanted—that is, what is the request. This apparently simple shift from pathology—trying to fix what's wrong—to discovery of the client's request reflects an entirely different set of assumptions about therapy and has a profound effect on the methods used. As Fanger (1993) stated, "learning to be the person you want to be is quite different—and often less time consuming—than learning why you are the way you are" (p. 88).

This approach, built on the work of Milton Erickson, emphasizes interactional skills and aims to develop better ways of dealing with relationships (Fisch, 1982). Erickson was not interested in personal history but was acutely interested in the specific structure of the presenting difficulty, which he explored in detail. He was able to "step into" the client's world and use whatever the client brought, including client individuality (resistance) to help the client make a change. He used tasks liberally, often creating elaborate ones, to produce change. Because of his innovative approach, his therapy was typically brief, but his thinking was not in terms of length of treatment but rather in terms of results achieved (Haley, 1963). To this end, Erickson was active and directive, and he took responsibility for designing strategies to achieve the desired results. Haley (1973) named this model of therapy "strategic." In the past 20 years, there has been a proliferation of Ericksonian therapists who have elaborated and expanded his methods. The description "solution oriented" has increasingly been applied in response to a new understanding that the attempted solution to a problem often *is* the problem (Watzlawick, Weakland, & Fisch, 1974). There are many elaborations of these themes with the constant aim of reframing the original difficulty (see Andreas & Andreas, 1987; Bandler & Grinder, 1979, 1982; Cade & O'Hanlon, 1993; de Shazer, 1982, 1988; Fisch, 1982; Fisch et al., 1982; Friedman, 1993; Friedman & Fanger, 1991; Haley, 1976, 1984; Lankton & Lankton, 1983; W. H. O'Hanlon & Weiner-Davis, 1989; B. O'Hanlon & Wilk, 1987; Walter & Peller, 1992; Watzlawick, 1978; Yapko, 1989; Zeig, 1982; Zeig & Gilligan, 1990).

**Couple, Family, and Group Therapies**

Multiple-client therapies all have versions of brief therapy. As Budman and Gurman (1988) noted,

> Indeed, in sharp contrast to the sorts of philosophical and technical controversies that have characterized the brief therapy movement in traditional individual psychotherapy, marital and family therapists have rarely had to struggle with ways to shorten the treatment process. By the usual standards of traditional individual therapy, marital and family therapy has been overwhelmingly brief. (p. 121)

Couple and family therapists typically need to be more active than do traditional individual therapists, who just get to know how the couple or family functions and then orchestrate their interactions. Because the couple or family interactions are the center of attention, couple and family therapy tends to have a systematic, and often strategic, flavor (see Bandler, Grinder, & Satir, 1976; de Shazer, 1985, 1988; Fisch et al., 1982; Friedman & Fanger, 1991; Friedman & Pettus, 1985; Haley, 1963, 1973; W. H. O'Hanlon & Weiner-Davis, 1989). There are also specific behavioral approaches to marital and family therapy (Baucom & Epstein, 1990; Gurman, 1980; R. B. Stuart, 1980; Weiss & Jacobson, 1981), as well as those that draw on systemic and psychodynamic roots (Bergman, 1985; Gurman, 1981; Gurman & Kniskern, 1981; Kreilkamp, 1989; Sager, 1976). For a comparison of psychodynamic, behavioral, and systemic approaches, see Gurman (1978).

Two family therapy approaches that also encompass time-effective work but do not fit neatly into the categories above are structural family therapy and the Milan school. In the structural family therapy approach, the intent is to diagnose and then restructure a faulty family system, realigning both the family hierarchy and the family boundaries according to a conceptually appropriate model (Aponte, 1992; Minuchin, 1974; Minuchin & Fishman, 1981). The Milan school of family therapy uses a special form of brief therapy in which therapists schedule sessions one month apart for 10 sessions. They aim to interrupt a family's self-destructive sequences of interaction by positively reframing the symptoms and then prescribing them (Palazzoli, Boscolo, Cecchin, & Prata, 1978).

Brief group therapy has roots in the T-group training developed by Kurt Lewin (Sabin, 1981) and has been used increasingly in settings that require cost considerations to be part of treatment planning. Budman and his colleagues have conducted extensive research into the critical elements of effective brief group therapy (see especially Budman & Gurman, 1988, pp. 246–282; see also Budman & Bennett, 1983; Budman, Bennett, & Wisneski, 1981; Budman, Demby, & Randall, 1980; Hoyt, 1993). In these studies, the researchers identified four central aspects most relevant to short-term, time-limited groups—first, establishment and maintenance of a focus in the group; second, pregroup preparation and screening; third, group cohesion; and last, existential factors and the time limit (Budman & Gurman, 1988). One can find a brief group therapy approach in the solution-oriented model in Friedman and Fanger (1991).

**Single-Session and Brief Contact Therapies**

As the interest in and importance of brief therapies have grown, so has the interest in and study of the briefest of therapies, a single session. Although many therapists have had successful single-session therapeutic contacts (see the example of Freud, noted earlier, in Jones, 1955; also see Bloom, 1981, 1992; Hoyt, Rosenbaum, & Talmon, 1992; Rosenbaum, Hoyt, & Talmon, 1990; Talmon, 1990), the formal recognition of such therapy as a viable planned treatment of choice began when Bloom first described it in 1981. Since then, others have experimented with single-session therapy and they seem to agree about the essential basic ingredients for its success. The therapist needs to *expect* to be able to help a client reach a goal in a single session and to convey this expectation to the client in the initial arrangement. The careful identification of a specific client-oriented goal that is small enough in scope to be reached in a brief time is, of course, critical. The therapist must quickly join with the client, encourage the client's expression of affect, look for the client's strengths, and envision this session as the beginning of a process of change that continues afterward, while keeping track of both focus and time. Sessions run from 60 to 90 minutes for individuals and from 90 to 120 minutes for couples and families. Because several of the above-mentioned activities are found in all therapies, the emphasis in single-session therapy is on the therapist's expectation of results and the careful direction and constant attention needed to reach the results in the allotted time (Bloom, 1992; Hoyt et al., 1992; Rockwell & Pinkerton, 1982; Rosenbaum et al., 1990; Talmon, 1990).

The possible viability of contacts briefer than most therapy sessions, that is, 15 or 20 minutes, has also been explored. In some settings, 15 or 20 minutes might be all the time available, but it can still be used effectively (Castelnuovo-Tedesco, 1986; Huber & Backlund, 1993; M. R. Stuart & Lieberman, 1993).

**Family Preservation or Home-Based Services**
Developed in the mid-1970s, family preservation services offer the chance for social workers to go into the homes of families with children at risk for removal to foster homes. The social workers have small caseloads (one or two to five or six) that allow them to spend extended periods of time in the family home where the crisis is actually occurring. The social workers spend from four to six weeks to several months (depending on the program) working with families in this intensive way to help restructure family interactions and provide help with practical problems. Although the work is difficult, the results, in terms of percentage of placements avoided and money saved, are both impressive and heartening (Aponte, Zarski, Bixenstine, & Cibik, 1991; Berg, 1994; Fraser & Leavitt, 1990; Kinney, Haapala, & Booth, 1991; Markowitz, 1992).

## Future of Brief Therapy

The "dramatic resurgence of interest in short-term approaches" that L. G. Parad (1971, p. 145) noted more than 20 years ago not only has continued unabated but is accelerating and expanding. The general health care picture and the delivery of mental health services have become inextricably combined, not only with the surge of managed care and insurance-mandated therapies, but also with the increasing likelihood of a national health care system that includes providing mental health care (Feldman & Fitzpatrick, 1992; Patterson & Sharfstein, 1992; Sabin, 1991). Furthermore, these trends make brief therapies of demonstrated effectiveness the order of the day.

Fortunately, over the past 10 years, methods of time-effective treatment developed into a major treatment modality and will continue to expand in both scope and efficacy. To support this development, more clinical research is needed, not so much to demonstrate again that brief therapy works as well as long-term therapy as to refine and redefine theories about psychotherapeutic change so as to more succinctly reach desired results across many diagnoses. Although many social workers have seen time limits forced by economic necessity as detrimental, ultimately they might inspire the creation of evermore-serviceable therapy.

The trend in the practice of brief therapy itself will become an increasingly integrative one (Budman & Gurman, 1988; Reid, 1992) in which the treatment will be designed to fit the needs of the individual client rather than finding clients to fit a particular therapeutic approach (Friedman & Fanger, 1991; Perlman, 1957). Therapists will need to deemphasize time limits per se while they tailor therapy to individual needs (Bloom, 1992). This integrative therapy will involve a directive therapist who expects to do effective brief work and so helps the client identify and move toward a specific achievable goal in the most parsimonious way. Already, therapists in health maintenance organizations, where time-effective treatment is the order of the day, "tend to shed long-term psychodynamic orientations and to use more eclectic or non-traditional problem-solving short-term therapy models" (Austad, Sherman, & Holstein, 1993, p. 122).

Furthermore, therapists may need to operate differently. As Peake et al. (1988) put it,

> Briefer interventions are imperative . . . [and] they will have their greatest impact delivered intermittently. Therapy can be thought of as a periodic aid to growth, or as something that helps patients through developmental crises and passages. Therapists in this new framework will function like family practitioners, working with individuals and families at symptomatic junctures through their lifespan. This role demands that a therapist's skills encompass timely and accurate developmental diagnoses, and a working knowledge of the forms of brief psychotherapy and of the options available in techniques and strategies. (p. 14)

Because shifting to an intermittent, time-effective approach mobilizes both client and therapist to use available resources more efficiently, there is a growing need for training in the necessary skills for both beginning and advanced practitioners. As Budman (1981) said, "Good brief therapists are made, not born" (p. 465). In the future, part of early therapy training must reflect this increasing need for practitioners familiar with both the philosophy and skills of time-effective therapy, so that they will be equipped to practice in health maintenance organizations and other managed practice systems that will become the standard.

Looking to the future, we need to create a comprehensive and flexible system of mental health care with ongoing support for those who need it but with the great majority of clients seeking help enrolled in some form of time-effective treatment. The goal will be to provide high-quality, efficacious treatment to more people in a shorter amount of time.

## References


Alexander, F., & French, T. M. (1946). *Psychoanalytic therapy, principles and applications*. New York: Ronald Press.

Andreas, S., & Andreas, C. (1987). *Change your mind—And keep the change*. Moab, UT: Real People Press.

Aponte, H. J. (1992). The black sheep of family therapy: A structural approach to brief therapy. In S. Budman, M. Hoyt, & S. Friedman (Eds.), *The first session of brief therapy: A book of cases* (pp. 324–342). New York: Guilford Press.

Aponte, H., Zarski, J., Bixenstine, C., & Cibik, P. (1991). Home/community-based service: A two-tier approach. *American Journal of Orthopsychiatry, 61*(3), 403–408.

Austad, C. S., Sherman, W. O., & Holstein, L. (1993). Psychotherapists in the HMO. *HMO Practice, 7*(3), 122–126.

Bandler, R., & Grinder, J. (1979). *Frogs into princes*. Moab, UT: Real People Press.

Bandler, R., & Grinder, J. (1982). *Reframing: NLP and the transformation of meaning*. Moab, UT: Real People Press.

Bandler, R., Grinder, J., & Satir, V. (1976). *Changing with families*. Palo Alto, CA: Science & Behavior Books.

Baucom, D., & Epstein, N. (1990). *Cognitive behavioral marital therapy*. New York: Brunner/Mazel.

Beck, A. T., & Emery, G. (1985). *Anxiety disorders and phobias*. New York: Basic Books.

Beck, A. T., Rush, A. T., Shaw, B. F., & Emery, G. (1979). *Cognitive therapy of depression*. New York: Guilford Press.

Bennett, M. J. (1984). Brief psychotherapy and adult development. *Psychotherapy: Theory, Research and Practice, 21*, 171–177.

Bennett, M. J., & Wisneski, M. J. (1979). Continuous therapy within an HMO. *American Journal of Psychiatry, 136*, 1283–1287.

Berg, I. K. (1994). *Family-based services: A solution-focused approach*. New York: W. W. Norton.

Bergman, J. S. (1985). *Fishing for barracuda: Pragmatics of brief systemic therapy*. New York: W. W. Norton.

Bloom, B. L. (1981). Focused single-session therapy: Initial development and evaluation. In S. Budman (Ed.), *Forms of brief psychotherapy* (pp. 167–216). New York: Guilford Press.

Bloom, B. L. (1992). *Planned short-term therapy: A clinical handbook*. Boston: Allyn & Bacon.

Budman, S. H. (Ed.). (1981). *Forms of brief psychotherapy*. New York: Guilford Press.

Budman, S. H., & Bennett, M. J. (1983). Short-term group psychotherapy. In H. Kaplan & B. Sadock (Eds.), *Comprehensive group psychotherapy* (rev. ed., pp. 138–144). Baltimore: Williams & Wilkins.

Budman, S. H., Bennett, M. J., & Wisneski, M. J. (1981). An adult developmental model of group psychotherapy. In S. H. Budman (Ed.), *Forms of brief psychotherapy* (pp. 305–342). New York: Guilford Press.

Budman, S. H., Demby, A., & Randall, M. (1980). Short-term group psychotherapy: Who succeeds, who fails? *Group, 4*, 3–16.

Budman, S. H., & Gurman, A. S. (1988). *Theory and practice of brief therapy*. New York: Guilford Press.

Budman, S. H., Hoyt, M. F., & Friedman, S. (Eds.). (1992). *The first session of brief therapy: A book of cases*. New York: Guilford Press.

Budman, S. H., & Stone, J. (1983). Advances in brief psychotherapy: A review of recent literature. *Hospital & Community Psychiatry, 34*, 939–946.

Burke, J. D., White, H. S., & Havens, L. (1979). Which short-term therapy? *Archives of General Psychiatry, 36*, 177–186.

Cade, B., & O'Hanlon, W. H. (1993). *A brief guide to brief therapy*. New York: W. W. Norton.

Castelnuovo-Tedesco, P. (1986). *The twenty-minute hour: A guide to brief psychotherapy for the physician*. Washington, DC: American Psychiatric Press.

Clarkin, J. F., & France, A. (1982). Selection criteria for brief psychotherapies. *American Journal of Psychotherapy, 36*, 166–180.

Community Mental Health Centers Act of 1963. P.L. 88-164, 77 Stat. 290.

Crits-Christoph, P., & Barber, J. P. (Eds.). (1991). *Handbook of short-term dynamic psychotherapy*. New York: Basic Books.

Cummings, N. A. (1977). Prolonged (ideal) versus short-term (realistic) psychotherapy. *Professional Psychology: Research and Practice, 8*, 491–501.

Cummings, N. A., & VandenBos, G. R. (1979). The general practice of psychology. *Professional Psychology: Research and Practice, 10*, 430–440.

Davanloo, H. (Ed.). (1978). *Basic principles and techniques in short-term dynamic psychotherapy*. New York: Spectrum.

Davanloo, H. (Ed.). (1980). *Short-term dynamic psychotherapy*. New York: Jason Aronson.

de Shazer, S. (1982). *Patterns of brief family therapy: An ecosystemic approach*. New York: Guilford Press.

de Shazer, S. (1985). *Keys to solution in brief therapy*. New York: W. W. Norton.

de Shazer, S. (1988). *Clues: Investigating solutions in brief therapy*. New York: W. W. Norton.

Deutsch, F., & Murphy, W. F. (1955). *The clinical interview: Vol. II. Therapy: A method of teaching sector psychotherapy*. New York: International Universities Press.

Ellis, A., & Grieger, R. (Eds.). (1977). *Handbook of rational–emotive therapy*. New York: Springer.

Fanger, M. T. (1993). After the shift: Time-effective treatment in the possibility frame. In S. Friedman (Ed.), *The new language of change: Constructive collaboration in psychotherapy* (pp. 85–106). New York: Guilford Press.

Feldman, J. L., & Fitzpatrick, R. J. (Eds.). (1992). *Managed mental health care: Administrative and clinical issues*. Washington, DC: American Psychiatric Press.

Fisch, R. (1982). Erickson's impact on brief psychotherapy. In J. K. Zeig (Ed.), *Ericksonian approaches to hypnosis and psychotherapy* (pp. 155–162). New York: Brunner/Mazel.

Fisch, R., Weakland, J., & Segal, L. (1982). *The tactics of change: Doing therapy briefly*. San Francisco: Jossey-Bass.

Fisher, S. G. (1980). The use of time limits in brief psychotherapy. *Family Process, 19*(3), 77–92.

Fisher, S. G. (1984). Time-limited brief therapy with families: A one year follow-up study. *Family Process, 23,* 101–106.

Frank, J. D. (1973). *Persuasion and healing: A comparative study of psychotherapy*. Baltimore: Johns Hopkins University Press.

Fraser, M., & Leavitt, S. (Eds.). (1990). *Improving practice technology for work with high risk families: Lessons from the Homebuilders Social Work Education Project*. Hawthorne, NY: Aldine de Gruyter.

Freeman, A., Simm, K., Beutler, L., & Arkowitz, H. (Eds.). (1989). *Comprehensive handbook of cognitive therapy*. New York: Plenum Press.

Friedman, S. (Ed.). (1993). *The new language of change: Constructive collaboration in psychotherapy*. New York: Guilford Press.

Friedman, S., & Fanger, M. T. (1991). *Expanding therapeutic possibilities: Getting results in brief psychotherapy*. New York: Lexington Books.

Friedman, S., & Pettus, S. (1985). Brief strategic interventions with families of adolescents. *Family Therapy, 12,* 197–210.

Garfield, S. L. (1971). Research on client variables in psychotherapy. In A. E. Bergin & S. L. Garfield (Eds.), *Handbook of psychotherapy and behavior change* (pp. 271–298). New York: John Wiley & Sons.

Garfield, S. L. (1978). Research on client variables in psychotherapy. In S. L. Garfield & A. E. Bergin (Eds.), *Handbook of psychotherapy and behavior change* (2nd ed., pp. 191–232). New York: John Wiley & Sons.

Garfield, S. L. (1986). Research on client variables in psychotherapy. In S. L. Garfield & A. E. Bergin (Eds.), *Handbook of psychotherapy and behavior change* (3rd ed., pp. 213–256). New York: John Wiley & Sons.

Garfield, S. L. (1989). *The practice of brief psychotherapy*. Tarrytown, NY: Pergamon Press.

Gurman, A. S. (1978). Contemporary marital therapies: A critique and comparative analysis of psychodynamic, behavioral and systems theory approaches. In T. Paolino & B. McCrady (Eds.), *Marriage and marital therapy* (pp. 445–566). New York: Brunner/Mazel.

Gurman, A. S. (1980). Behavioral marriage therapies in the 1980's: The challenge of integration. *American Journal of Family Therapy, 8,* 86–96.

Gurman, A. S. (1981). Integrative marital therapies: Toward the development of an interpersonal approach. In S. H. Budman (Ed.), *Forms of brief therapy* (pp. 415–457). New York: Guilford Press.

Gurman, A. S., & Kniskern, D. P. (1981). *Handbook of marital therapy*. New York: Brunner/Mazel.

Gustafson, J. P. (1986). *The complex secret of brief psychotherapy*. New York: W. W. Norton.

Haley, J. (1963). *Strategies of psychotherapy*. New York: Grune & Stratton.

Haley, J. (1973). *Uncommon therapy*. New York: W. W. Norton.

Haley, J. (1976). *Problem-solving therapy*. San Francisco: Jossey-Bass.

Haley, J. (1984). *Ordeal therapy*. San Francisco: Jossey-Bass.

Horowitz, M. (1981). Preface. In S. Budman (Ed.), *Forms of brief therapy* (p. v). New York: Guilford Press.

Hoyt, M. F. (1993). Group psychotherapy in an HMO. *HMO Practice, 7*(3), 127–132.

Hoyt, M. F., Rosenbaum, R., & Talmon, M. (1992). Planned single-session psychotherapy. In S. H. Budman, M. F. Hoyt, & S. Friedman (Eds.), *The first session of brief therapy: A book of cases* (pp. 59–86). New York: Guilford Press.

Huber, C. H., & Backlund, B. A. (1993). *The twenty minute counselor: Transforming brief conversations in effective helping experiences*. New York: Continuum.

Jones, E. (1955). *The life and work of Sigmund Freud*. New York: Basic Books.

Kinney, J., Haapala, D., & Booth, C. (1991). *Keeping families together: The homebuilders model*. New York: Aldine de Gruyter.

Koss, M. P., & Butcher, J. N. (1986). Research on brief psychotherapy. In S. L. Garfield & A. E. Bergin (Eds.), *Handbook of psychotherapy and behavior change* (pp. 627–670). New York: John Wiley & Sons.

Kreilkamp, T. (1989). *Time-limited intermittent therapy with children and families*. New York: Brunner/Mazel.

Kuehlwein, K. T., & Rosen, H. (1993). *Cognitive therapies in action*. San Francisco: Jossey-Bass.

Lankton, S. R., & Lankton, C. H. (1983). *The answer within: A clinical framework of Ericksonian hypnotherapy*. New York: Brunner/Mazel.

Lemon, E. C. (1983). Planned brief treatment. In A. Rosenblatt & D. Waldfogel (Eds.), *Handbook of clinical social work* (pp. 401–419). San Francisco: Jossey-Bass.

Malan, D. H. (1963). *A study of brief psychotherapy*. New York: Plenum Press.

Malan, D. H. (1976). *The frontier of brief psychotherapy*. New York: Plenum Press.

Mann, J. (1973). *Time-limited psychotherapy*. Cambridge, MA: Harvard University Press.

Markowitz, L. M. (1992, July/August). Making house calls. *Family Therapy Networker,* pp. 26–37.

Marmor, J. (1978). Current trends in psychotherapy. In H. Davanloo (Ed.), *Basic principles and techniques in short-term dynamic psychotherapy* (pp. 1–7). New York: Spectrum.

Minuchin, S. (1974). *Families and family therapy*. Cambridge: Harvard University Press.

Minuchin, S., & Fishman, H. C. (1981). *Family therapy techniques*. Cambridge, MA: Harvard University Press.

O'Hanlon, B., & Wilk, J. (1987). *Shifting contexts: The generation of effective psychotherapy*. New York: Guilford Press.

O'Hanlon, W. H. (1990, March/April). Debriefing myself: When a brief therapist does long-term work. *Family Therapy Networker,* pp. 48–49, 68–69.

O'Hanlon, W. H., & Weiner-Davis, M. (1989). *In search of solutions: A new direction in psychotherapy*. New York: W. W. Norton.

Palazzoli, M. S., Boscolo, L., Cecchin, G., & Prata, G. (1978). *Paradox and counterparadox*. New York: Jason Aronson.

Parad, H. J. (1968). Crisis intervention. In R. Morris (Ed.-in-Chief) *Encyclopedia of social work* (16th ed., Vol. 1, pp. 196–202). Washington, DC: National Association of Social Workers.

Parad, H. J., & Parad, L. G. (1968). A study of crisis-oriented planned short-term treatment: Part I. *Social Casework, 49,* 346–355.

Parad, H. J., & Parad, L. G. (Eds.). (1990). *Crisis intervention, book 2: The practitioner's sourcebook for brief therapy*. Milwaukee: Family Service America.

Parad, L. G. (1971). Short-term treatment: An overview of historical trends, issues and potentials. *Smith College Studies in Social Work, 41,* 119–146.

Parad, L. G., & Parad, H. J. (1968). A study of crisis-oriented planned short-term treatment: Part II. *Social Casework, 49,* 418–426.

Pardes, H., & Pincus, H. A. (1981). Brief therapy in the context of national mental health issues. In S. H. Budman (Ed.), *Forms of brief psychotherapy* (pp. 7–22). New York: Guilford Press.

Patterson, D. Y., & Sharfstein, S. S. (1992). The future of mental health care. In J. L. Feldman & R. J. Fitzpatrick (Eds.), *Managed mental health care: Administrative and clinical issues* (pp. 335–343). Washington, DC: American Psychiatric Press.

Peake, T. H., Borduin, C. M., & Archer, R. P. (1988). *Brief psychotherapies: Changing frames of mind*. Newbury Park, CA: Sage Publications.

Perlman, H. H. (1957). *Social casework: A problem-solving process*. Chicago: University of Chicago Press.

Phillips, E. L., & Wiener, D. (1966). *Short-term psychotherapy and structured behavior change*. New York: McGraw-Hill.

Pinderhughes, E. (1989). *Understanding race, ethnicity, and power: The key to efficacy in clinical practice*. New York: Free Press.

Rapoport, L. (1967). Crisis-oriented short-term casework. *Social Service Review, 41*(1), 31–43.

Rapoport, L. (1971). Crisis intervention as a mode of brief treatment. In R. E. Roberts & R. E. Nee (Eds.), *Theories of social casework* (pp. 267–311). Chicago: University of Chicago Press.

Reid, W. J. (1992). *Task strategies: An empirical approach to clinical social work*. New York: Columbia University Press.

Reid, W. J., & Shyne, A. W. (1969). *Brief and extended casework*. New York: Columbia University Press.

Rockwell, W. J. K., & Pinkerton, R. S. (1982). Single-session psychotherapy. *American Journal of Psychotherapy, 36,* 32–40.

Rosenbaum, R., Hoyt, M. F., & Talmon, M. (1990). The challenge of single-session therapies: Creating pivotal moments. In R. A. Wells & V. J. Giannetti (Eds.), *Handbook of the brief psychotherapies* (pp. 165–189). New York: Plenum Press.

Sabin, J. E. (1981). Short-term group psychotherapy: Historical antecedents. In S. H. Budman (Ed.), *Forms of brief therapy* (pp. 271–282). New York: Guilford Press.

Sabin, J. E. (1991). Clinical skills for the 1990s: Six lessons from HMO practice. *Hospital and Community Psychiatry, 42,* 605–608.

Sager, C. J. (1976). *Marriage contract and couple therapy*. New York: Brunner/Mazel.

Sager, C. J., & Kaplan, H. S. (Eds.). (1972). *Progress in group and family therapy*. New York: Brunner/Mazel.

Seeman, L., Tittler, B. I., & Friedman, S. (1985). Early interactional change and its relationship to family therapy outcome. *Family Process, 24,* 59–68.

Sifneos, P. (1972). *Short-term psychotherapy and emotional crisis*. Cambridge, MA: Harvard University Press.

Smith, M. L., Glass, G. V., & Miller, T. I. (1980). *The benefits of psychotherapy*. Baltimore: Johns Hopkins University Press.

Stuart, M. R., & Lieberman, J. A. (1993). *The fifteen minute hour: Applied psychotherapy for the primary care physician*. New York: Praeger.

Stuart, R. B. (1980). *Helping couples change: A social learning approach to marital therapy*. New York: Guilford Press.

Taft, J. (1933). *The dynamics of therapy in a controlled relationship*. New York: Macmillan.

Talmon, M. (1990). *Single session therapy*. San Francisco: Jossey-Bass.

Taube, C. A., Goldman, H. H., Burns, B. J., & Kessler, L. G. (1988). High users of outpatient mental health services: I. Definition and characteristics. *American Journal of Psychiatry, 145,* 19–28.

Ursano, R., & Hollis, R. (1986). A review of brief individual psychotherapies. *American Journal of Psychiatry, 143,* 1507–1517.

Walter, J. L., & Peller, J. E. (1992). *Becoming solution-focused in brief therapy*. New York: Brunner/Mazel.

Watzlawick, P. (1978). *The language of change*. New York: Basic Books.

Watzlawick, P., Weakland, J., & Fisch, R. (1974). *Change: Principles of problem formation and problem resolution*. New York: W. W. Norton.

Weakland, J. H., Fisch, R., Watzlawick, P., & Bodin, A. (1974). Brief therapy: Focused problem resolution. *Family Process, 13,* 141–166.

Weiss, R. L., & Jacobson, N. S. (1981). Behavioral marital therapy as brief therapy. In S. H. Budman (Ed.), *Forms of brief therapy* (pp. 387–414). New York: Guilford Press.

Wolberg, L. R. (Ed.). (1965). *Short-term psychotherapy*. New York: Grune & Stratton.

Wolberg, L. R. (1980). *Handbook of short-term psychotherapy*. New York: Thieme-Stratton.

Wylie, M. S. (1990, March/April). Brief therapy on the couch. *Family Therapy Networker,* pp. 26–35, 66.

Yapko, M. D. (Ed.). (1989). *Brief therapy approaches to treating anxiety*. New York: Brunner/Mazel.

Young, J. E. (1990). *Cognitive therapy for personality disorders: A schema-focused approach*. Sarasota, FL: Professional Resource Press.

Zeig, J. K. (Ed.). (1982). *Ericksonian approaches to hypnosis and psychotherapy*. New York: Brunner/Mazel.

Zeig, J. K., & Gilligan, S. G. (Eds.). (1990). *Brief therapy: Myths, methods, and metaphors*. New York: Brunner/Mazel.

## FURTHER READING

Horowitz, M., Marmar, C., Krupnick, J., Wilner, N., Kaltreider, N., & Wallerstein, R. (1984). *Personality styles and brief psychotherapy*. New York: Basic Books.

Katz, S. N. (1975). *Creativity in social work: The selected writings of Lydia Rapoport*. Philadelphia: Temple University Press.
Rabkin, R. (1977). *Strategic psychotherapy: Brief and symptomatic treatment*. New York: Basic Books.
Reid, W. J. (1985). *Family problem solving*. New York: Columbia University Press.
Reid, W. J., & Epstein, L. (1972). *Task-centered casework*. New York: Columbia University Press.
Strupp, H. H., & Binder, J. L. (1984). *Psychotherapy in a new key: A guide to time-limited dynamic psychotherapy*. New York: Basic Books.
Wells, R. A., & Giannetti, V. (1990). *Handbook of the brief psychotherapies*. New York: Plenum Press.

**Margot Taylor Fanger, MSW, ACSW, LICSW,** is clinician, Adult Mental Health, Harvard Community Health Plan, and lecturer, The Cambridge Hospital, Harvard Medical School and Boston College Graduate School of Social Work, 74 Putnam Street, West Newton, MA 02165.

**For further information see**

Brief Task-Centered Practice; Clinical Social Work; Cognitive Treatment; Direct Practice Overview; Ecological Perspective; Ethnic-Sensitive Practice; Family Preservation and Home-Based Services; Family Therapy; Generalist and Advanced Generalist Practice; Goal Setting and Intervention Planning; Group Practice Overview; Interviewing; Managed Care; Mental Health Overview; Psychosocial Approach; Social Work Practice: Theoretical Base.

**Key Words**

brief therapy
time-effective therapy
time-limited therapy

## Brockway, Zebulon Reed

*See* Biographies section, Volume 3

## Bruno, Frank John

*See* Biographies section, Volume 3

READER'S GUIDE

### Budgeting

*The following entries contain information on this general topic:*

Financial Management
Fundraising and Philanthropy
Health Care: Financing
Nonprofit Management Issues
Public Services Management
Public Social Welfare Expenditures

## Buell, Bradley

*See* Biographies section, Volume 3

## Bulimia

*See* Eating Disorders and Other Compulsive Behaviors

## Burns, Eveline Mabel

*See* Biographies section, Volume 3

# C

## Cabot, Richard Clarke

*See* Biographies section, Volume 3

## Cannon, Ida Maud

*See* Biographies section, Volume 3

## Cannon, Mary Antoinette

*See* Biographies section, Volume 3

## Caregiving

*See* Family Caregiving

## Caribbeans

*See* African Americans: Caribbean

## Carlton, Thomas Owen

*See* Biographies section, Volume 3

# Case Management

**Stephen M. Rose**
**Vernon L. Moore**

Since the 1970s, case management has become pervasive in the human services, such as in the areas of mental health, developmental disabilities, services for people with human immunodeficiency virus (HIV) and acquired immune deficiency syndrome (AIDS), long-term care, services for elderly people, immigrant services, and child welfare. The complex set of economic and organizational variables that created case management continue to influence its functioning. These variables are discussed and linked to different case management models and to the way typical case management functions are identified and performed.

Case management has grown dramatically since the early 1980s as an effort to recognize emerging client populations with comprehensive needs for resources from a variety of service sectors. Case management also reflects the shift in national and state social policies and funding priorities from services based in institutions (for example, state psychiatric hospitals, medical hospitals, residential treatment centers, inpatient settings for people with developmental disabilities or multiply handicapped children, youth authorities, or temporary out-of-home placements) to community-based care.

Deinstitutionalization, increasing unemployment rates, and extended poverty contribute to the creation of complex problems. Three populations illustrate this point clearly: (1) homeless people, (2) people with HIV or AIDS, and (3) elderly people who require long-term care. Case management exists for all of them. Case managers' tasks reflect the complex, comprehensive needs of many of their clients. Often these needs include adequate income, affordable housing, insured health care that is both culturally and logistically accessible, job training or placement, and appropriate social supports that require resources or services from service delivery systems that frequently are uncoordinated or fragmented.

### Role of Case Managers

Case managers typically are assigned responsibility for identifying and engaging clients, assessing their needs, locating appropriate services and planning for their use, linking clients to resources, and monitoring the process for targeted or desired outcomes. Most case managers are required to develop an individual service or treatment plan to identify each client's needs and appropriate patterns of the use of resources. These plans become the basis for monitoring clients' use of services and for tracking clients' movement toward the achievement of specified goals, often called outcomes.

Case managers also are supposed to ensure the timely and adequate delivery of appropriate services. However, it is not clear how effective individual case managers or case management programs can be in achieving the outcomes identified in their clients' service plans, especially when many of the resources that clients need may be located in compartmentalized and unresponsive service systems.

Case management usually involves five basic functions: (1) outreach to or the identification of clients (often called engagement); (2) assessment of needs; (3) service or treatment planning; (4) linking or referring clients to appropriate resources; and (5) monitoring cases to ensure that services are delivered and used. Some models of case management add other tasks or specify a practice framework: Clinical case management includes responsibility for therapeutic intervention (Harris & Bergman, 1987; Kanter, 1992; Lamb, 1980). The "strengths perspective" emphasizes that the social worker–client relationship is a collaborative approach based on the assumption that clients are resilient and have the potential for acquiring community-based resources (Kisthardt & Rapp, 1992; Saleeby, 1992; Weick, Rapp, Sullivan, & Kisthardt, 1989). The advocacy–empowerment design links strength-based, partnership–design relationships to critical targets of change in systems that are developed from clients' struggles to live with adequate resources appropriate to their goals (Rose, 1992; Rose & Black, 1985).

Advocacy, another common role that case managers take on, assumes more or less importance depending on the availability of the resources that clients need most, case managers' access to these resources, and the willingness of the case management program to confront other agencies to ensure that clients' needs are met. This latter issue is ubiquitous because case managers are the interface between the client and the service delivery system; it signifies the vital importance of supervisory and agency support to case managers' performance of their jobs and to outcome measures for clients or agencies.

## Development of Case Management

Several historical factors interacted to establish the social context for the development of case management. These factors include the fragmentation in service delivery systems (American Hospital Association [AHA], 1987; Austin, 1992a; Intagliata, 1992; Parrish, 1989; Test, 1979; Turner & TenHoor, 1978; U.S. General Accounting Office [GAO], 1977); severe deficits of resources in such life-sustaining areas as safe affordable housing and continuity of health care (Austin, 1992a, 1992b; Intagliata, 1992; Ryndes, 1989; Wood & Estes, 1988); underdevelopment of appropriate resources to sustain people in their transitions from institutional care to community settings or to reduce recidivism (Austin, 1992a; GAO, 1977; Mechanic & Aiken, 1987; Rose, 1979; Sonsel, 1989; Stroul, 1989); the inability to contain or rationalize the escalating costs of health and mental health care (Capitman, 1986; Rettig et al., 1987; Scull, 1977); and the programmatic limitations found in the normal operations of funding agencies (Parrish, 1989; Rose, 1972; Rose & Black, 1985; Wilson, 1989).

### Funding Issues

Each factor may operate in service delivery systems at federal, state, and local levels. The structure and organization of categorical funding in many service delivery systems support the fragmented delivery of services and significantly shape case management practice (Austin, 1992a; Harris & Bergman, 1988; Intagliata, 1992; Lehman, 1987; Vischi & Stockdill, 1989). Fee-for-service reimbursement in mental health care, for example, often confines case managers and clients to the establishment of service plans based on narrow, allowable costs while denying important needs or services (for example, safe, affordable housing or payment for staff time devoted to building mutual support networks or for advocacy) because these activities are outside the parameters of funding. Lehman (1987), Harris and Bergman (1988), and Mechanic and Aiken (1987) elaborated on this position by advocating for capitated financing as a vehicle for increasing the flexibility of programming for mental health care. The decreased latitude in design and delivery certainly impairs case managers' and their clients' capacities to construct service plans to meet individual goals based on clients' comprehensive needs.

### Coordination Issues

Austin (1992b) systematically analyzed numerous case management delivery systems. She concluded that comprehensiveness of clients' needs often does not serve as the basis for coordination, and that coordination often is restricted only to those services that providers already deliver. "Broker" models of case management, which emphasize referrals and linkage, usually within one service sector, are most common in mental health and long-term-care settings. Within these models, the issues of the comprehensiveness of needs and the effectiveness of case management practice in producing positive outcomes for clients are frequently reduced to the coordination of existing providers and their services and fitting clients' needs or problems to them.

Case coordinators (an early name for case managers) were thought to be a solution to the fragmentation or absence of continuity of care among local providers and between inpatient and community-based mental health and health care. Beginning in 1971, the federal government developed and funded demonstration programs that were designed to effect the coordination of local systems of providers of long-term care. The federal government's intent in these projects, according to Austin (1992a), "was to break down barriers among providers and to create a delivery system that was more responsive to clients' total needs" (p. 202). This goal was not achieved because the case manager's authority was insufficient to produce the intersystem cooperation that was necessary to respond appropriately to clients' needs. Austin concluded that individual case managers had insufficient authority and organizational support to change the behavior of providers in fragmented services systems with fragmented funding.

### Influence of Managed Care

More recently, the concept of managed care (AHA, 1987; Henderson & Collard, 1988) in the health care sector has developed in a manner parallel to case management in the long-term-care arena: Both attempt to reduce the unnecessary use of the more expensive forms of care, especially in institutional settings; both attempt to shift the focus of care from institutions to communities; both struggle to create coordinated service plans among community-based service providers (Capitman, Haskins, & Bernstein, 1986; Phillips, Kemper, & Applebaum, 1988); and both presume that the efficient use of single-system resources can suffice to sustain clients in community settings while reducing the extent of inpatient care. Future evaluative research will have to determine the outcome; it would be premature at this time to differentiate precisely between rationalizing use of services or rationing them.

Each case management policy moves the responsibility for reforming the system from the provider or policy level to the individual case manager–client relationship, or the service-consuming level. Intagliata (1992) addressed this point, discussing the need for supervisory and administrative support for case managers; he concluded that "the effectiveness of the case manager's efforts is constrained by the degree of support provided for case management at higher levels within the system" (pp. 32–33). Obviously, when case management is the central function in a service agency, rather than an ancillary activity, the potential for appropriate levels of supervisory and administrative support increases.

## Case Management Functions

Intagliata (1992) highlighted three basic case management functions: (1) remaining aware of the comprehensive needs of clients, (2) linking clients to resources that are appropriate to their needs, and (3) monitoring services to ensure that they are effective. How these functions are performed can be determined by the priority given to the preset service plan or to the primacy of the client–case manager relationship. Usually, one of these two priorities shapes the definition of each function.

### Focus on the Client

Targeting clients' goals rearranges the typical case management tasks of starting with the identification of clients' problems and the assessment of clients' needs. Goal formulation—identifying clients' strengths and desired outcomes—may begin either with the preset services of providers or with the unique needs and interests of the clients. When clients' goals or desired outcomes shape the practices of case management assessments and steer the definition of the required appropriate resources, clients as whole human beings become the center for systems evaluation. This approach uses a client's individual (and aggregate) goals as the basis for examining the adequacy and appropriateness of services delivered by providers and identifies targets of change in the system to improve the quality of care. Comprehensive human needs—for material resources to live with dignity in a safe and healthy manner, for social resources shaped by the individual's choice, and for emotional validation and support—characterize the goal-formulation process. Clients' individual service or treatment plans, in this formulation, are not confined by a provider's or host agency's services. When broker–model case managers refer clients to existing services and shape assessments of clients' needs from them or their funding regulations, the clients' patterns of usage, measured by clients' consumption of units of service, become the database for most outcome studies.

### Different Models

The impact of the differences in the models of case management practice are outlined in Table 1. In client-driven models, the central determining factor in a client's interactions is the client's relationship with the case manager; in provider-driven models, the service plan is the central factor.

The fundamental difference in primary orientation to the importance and quality of the relationship between the client and social worker or to the primacy of the service plan and its ingredients shapes the approach taken to each area of case management practice. Broker, program-based (attached to a site), and assertive outreach team case manager models usually emphasize the pri-

TABLE 1

**Client-driven versus Provider-driven Case Management Models**

| Case Management Characteristics | Client-Driven Models | Provider-Driven Models |
|---|---|---|
| Fundamental perception of client | Clients as subjects who know and act | Clients as objects who are known and are acted on |
| Case manager sees client's | Strengths to identify and develop | Problems to identify and pathology to manage |
| Case manager seeks | Active participation, reframing deficits, producing direction | Compliance, adaptation to service plans |
| Case management goals | Positive direction, implementation steps, and self-confidence | Improved patterns of service consumption and patient-role behavior |
| Case management needs assessment | Derived directly from client's direction plan and goals | Derived directly from service providers' definitions and outputs |
| Linking | Resources seen as total community, with emphasis on informal social networks | Referrals to existing service providers and use of the formal system |
| Monitoring | Mutual evaluation of process in relation to direction plan | Assures compliance with treatment plan |
| Evaluation | Increasing autonomy, critical assessment of social context, growing self-confidence, involvement with informal networks | Increased units of service consumed, use of fewer inpatient days, improved compliance |
| Focus | Identify strengths and obstacles to the attainment of goals, develop social networks, free the client from clinical judgment and contempt, assess the role of each service system as a support or obstacle | Identify problems, make referrals, and assure the client's compliance with the treatment plan. Keep attention on the client's behavior and functioning, family interaction, keeping appointments |

macy of the service plan; client-driven, strengths-based, and advocacy–empowerment models emphasize the collaborative construction of relationships (the mutual definition of clients' goals), with a derived comprehensive assessment of needs and strengths that leads to individualized strategies of implementation and monitoring (Rose, 1992).

## Common Concerns in the Field

Regardless of the practice area, questions have been generated about the size of caseloads, the advisability of doing case management in teams, the appropriate level of formal education for case management positions, the frequency and duration of contact with clients (often called "intensity"), and the proper location of case management activities (in an office or program site or "in vivo," where the clients live). Also at issue are the appropriateness of case management roles for family members (Seltzer, Ivry, & Litchfield, 1987) and the viability of hiring consumers of services either as members of case management teams or as regular members of the staff, both commonly known in public-sector mental health, to perform case management functions.

Some situations are characterized by intensive case managers—with a master's degree and related work experience; small caseloads (five to 15 cases); and contact with clients as needed, including 24-hour, seven-day-per-week coverage. In other services, case managers have a high school degree, large caseloads (40 to 80 cases), and sporadic contact with clients (rarely more than once a month). Ironically, in many settings, as the complexity of clients' comprehensive needs increases, the size of caseloads also increases, but the educational requirements for employment are lower. Cost cutting takes peculiar turns in these settings.

Research about the efficacy of case management has begun to accumulate, but the results thus far have been restricted to studies done within single service fields, such as mental health (Bond, Miller, Krumwied, & Ward, 1988; Franklin, Solovitz, Mason, Clemons, & Miller, 1987; Goering, Wasylenski, Farkas, Lancee, & Ballantyne, 1988) and long-term care (Austin, 1992b). The debate is complicated by methodological issues related to experimental design factors, to comparable service implementation conditions, and to comparable characteristics of clients (Abrahams & Lamb, 1988; Chamberlain & Rapp, 1991). Over the next several years, outcome studies with adequate controls and comparison groups may emerge to examine case management across and within its many service fields.

## References


Abrahams, R. D., & Lamb, S. (1988). Developing reliable assessment in case-managed geriatric long-term care programs. *Quality Review Bulletin, 14*(6), 179–186.

American Hospital Association, Council on Patient Services. (1987). *Case management: An aid to quality and continuity of care*. Chicago: Author.

Austin, C. B. (1992a). Case management in long-term care: Options and opportunities. In S. M. Rose (Ed.), *Case management and social work practice* (pp. 199–218). New York: Longman.

Austin, C. B. (1992b, February). *When the whole is more than the sum of its parts: Case management issues from a systems perspective*. Paper presented at the First International Long-Term Care Case Management Conference, Seattle, WA.

Bond, G. R., Miller, L. D., Krumwied, R. D., & Ward, R. S. (1988). Assertive case management in three CMHCs: A controlled study. *Hospital & Community Psychiatry, 39*(4), 411–418.

Capitman, J. A. (1986). Community-based long-term care models, target groups and impacts on service use. *The Gerontologist, 26,* 389–397.

Capitman, J. A., Haskins, B., & Bernstein, J. (1986). Case management approaches in coordinated community oriented long-term care demonstrations. *The Gerontologist, 26,* 398–404.

Chamberlain, R., & Rapp, C. A. (1991). A decade of case management: A methodological review of outcome research. *Community Mental Health Journal, 27*(3), 171–188.

Franklin, J. I., Solovitz, B., Mason, M., Clemons, J. R., & Miller, G. E. (1987). An evaluation of case management. *American Journal of Public Health, 7,* 674–678.

Goering, P. N., Wasylenski, D. A., Farkas, M., Lancee, W. J., & Ballantyne, R. (1988). What difference does case management make? *Hospital & Community Psychiatry, 39*(3), 272–276.

Harris, M., & Bergman, H. (1987). Case management with the chronically mentally ill: A clinical perspective. *American Journal of Orthopsychiatry, 57*(2), 296–302.

Harris, M., & Bergman, H. C. (1988). Capitation financing for the chronically mentally ill. *Hospital & Community Psychiatry, 39,* 68–72.

Henderson, M., & Collard, A. (1988). Measuring quality in medical case management programs. *Quality Review Bulletin, 15,* 33–39.

Intagliata, J. (1992). Improving the quality of community care for the chronically mentally disabled: The role of case management. In S. M. Rose (Ed.), *Case management and social work practice* (pp. 25–55). New York: Longman.

Kanter, J. S. (1992). Mental health case management: A professional domain? In S. M. Rose (Ed.), *Case management and social work practice* (pp. 126–130). New York: Longman.

Kisthardt, W., & Rapp, C. (1992). Bridging the gap between principles and practice: Implementing a strengths perspective. In S. M. Rose (Ed.), *Case management and social work* (pp. 112–125). New York: Longman.

Lamb, R. (1980). Therapists–case managers: More than brokers of service. *Hospital & Community Psychiatry, 31,* 762–764.

Lehman, A. F. (1987). Capitation payment and mental health care: A review of the opportunities and risks. *Hospital & Community Psychiatry, 38,* 31–38.

Mechanic, D., & Aiken, L. (1987). Improving the care of patients with chronic mental illness. *New England Journal of Medicine, 317,* 1634–1638.

Parrish, J. (1989). The long journey home: Accomplishing the mission of the community support movement. *Psychosocial Rehabilitation Journal, 12*(3), 107–124.

Phillips, B., Kemper, P., & Applebaum, R. (1988). Case management under channeling. *Health Services Research, 23*(1), 67–81.

Rettig, P. C., et al. (1987). Medicare's prospective payment system: The expectations and the realities. *Inquiry, 24,* 173–188.

Rose, S. M. (1972). *Betrayal of the poor: The transformation of community action*. Cambridge, MA: Schenkman.

Rose, S. M. (1979). Deciphering deinstitutionalization: Complexities in policy and program analysis. *The Milbank Quarterly, 57,* 429–460.

Rose, S. M. (Ed.). (1992). *Case management and social work practice*. New York: Longman.

Rose, S. M., & Black, B. L. (1985). *Advocacy and empowerment: Mental health care in the community*. Boston: Routledge & Kegan Paul.

Ryndes, T. (1989). The coalition model of case management for care of HIV-infected persons. *Quality Review Bulletin, 15*(1), 4–8.

Saleeby, D. (1992). *The strengths perspective in social work practice*. New York: Longman.

Scull, A. (1977). *Decarceration of the mentally ill: A radical view*. Englewood Cliffs, NJ: Prentice Hall.

Seltzer, M. M., Ivry, U., & Litchfield, L. C. (1987). Family members as case managers: Partnership between the formal and informal support networks. *The Gerontologist, 27,* 722–728.

Sonsel, G. E. (1989). Case management in a community-based AIDS agency. *Quality Review Bulletin, 15*(1), 31–36.

Stroul, B. A. (1989). Community support systems for persons with long-term mental illness: A conceptual framework. *Psychosocial Rehabilitation Journal, 12*(3), 9–26.

Test, M. A. (1979). Continuity of care in community treatment. In L. I. Stein (Ed.), *Community support systems for the long-term patient* (pp. 15–23). San Francisco: Jossey-Bass.

Turner, J. C., & TenHoor, W. J. (1978). The NIMH community support program: Pilot approach to a needed social reform. *Schizophrenia Bulletin, 4,* 319–349.

U.S. General Accounting Office. (1977). *Returning the mentally ill to the community: Government needs to do more* (Publication No. HRD-76-152). Washington, DC: Author.

Vischi, T. R., & Stockdill, J. (1989). The financing of comprehensive community support systems: A review of

major strategies. *Psychosocial Rehabilitation Journal, 12*(3), 83–92.
Weick, A., Rapp, C., Sullivan, W. P., & Kisthardt, W. (1989). A strengths perspective for social work practice. *Social Work, 34,* 350–354.
Wilson, S. F. (1989). Implementation of the community support system concept statewide: The Vermont experience. *Psychosocial Rehabilitation Journal, 12*(3), 27–40.
Wood, J. B., & Estes, C. L. (1988). "Medicalization" of community services for the elderly. *Health & Social Work, 13,* 35–42.

## Further Reading

Bowker, J. P. (1985). *Education for practice with the chronically mentally ill: What works?* Washington, DC: Council on Social Work Education.
Moxley, D. P. (1989). *The practice of case management.* Newbury Park, CA: Sage Publications.
Rothman, J. (1992). *Guidelines for case management: Putting research to professional use*. Itasca, IL: F. E. Peacock.
Steinberg, R. M., & Carter, G. W. (1983). *Case management and the elderly*. Lexington, MA: Lexington Books.

**Stephen M. Rose, PhD,** is professor and director, and **Vernon L. Moore, PhD,** is associate professor, University of New England, School of Social Work, Hills Beach Road, Biddeford, ME 04005.

**For further information see**

Advocacy; Agency-Based Research; Child Welfare Overview; Community Needs Assessment; Deinstitutionalization; Direct Practice Overview; Ecological Perspective; Family Preservation and Home-Based Services; Goal Setting and Intervention Planning; Interdisciplinary and Interorganizational Collaboration; Interviewing; Legal Issues: Confidentiality and Privileged Communication; Long-Term Care; Management Overview; Natural Helping Networks; Organizations: Context for Social Services Delivery; Person-in-Environment; Poverty; Public Social Services; Sectarian Agencies; Social Welfare History; Social Work Practice: History and Evolution; Social Work Profession Overview; Supervision and Consultation; Volunteer Management.

**Key Words**

case management
health care
long-term care
mental health care

# Cassidy, Harry

*See* Biographies section, Volume 3

# Certification

*See* Licensing, Regulation, and Certification

# Charitable Foundations and Social Welfare

**Ione D. Vargus**

Foundations, an important source of revenue to social welfare workers, address all kinds of social need. Innovative ideas and new programmatic thrusts have often been implemented only because a foundation was willing to support them. Some foundations have paid special attention to emerging problems and groups that have been underrepresented by service providers. Frequently, the new ideas are institutionalized and incorporated into a government program. At the same time, though, traditional services continue to be the major recipients of foundations.

## Types of Foundations

A *foundation* is a charitable trust or nonprofit corporation that has a principal fund of its own and is organized and operated exclusively to maintain or aid religious, charitable, scientific, literary, or educational activities. Managed by its own trustees or directors, a foundation is part of the system of organized philanthropy as opposed to individual giving. Foundations are extremely diverse; the foundation field comprises independent, community, company, and operating foundations.

### Independent Foundations

The literature usually refers to *independent foundations* as family and private funders. Family foundations represent the largest number of private foundations; they often start out small with no administrative organization. Private and family foundations allow for a high degree of personal control in the giving of grants, generally reflecting the philanthropic interests of the founder. The governance of the foundation may be limited to family members or a close network of friends and associates and the board may be self-perpetuating.

The purpose of a private foundation may be broad or specific. It may have only one or a few areas of interest or it may have general purposes and give grants in a broad range of arenas. The board may establish its own agenda, and it can easily change direction in its funding priorities. In 1992, for instance, the James L. Knight Foundation, which had been awarding about $3 million annually to help liberal arts colleges improve their undergraduate programs, decided to end that effort and give money to local colleges that work with public schools (Nicklin, 1993).

### Community Foundations

A *community foundation,* sometimes called a community trust, charitable trust, or community fund, is a vehicle for administering a number of separate charitable and combined funds in a given geographic area. Whereas banks and trust companies handle fiscal management of funds, a distribution committee handles disbursal of funds. In contrast to a private or family foundation, on which board members may serve for a long time, members of the community foundation distribution committee usually have a time limit for serving and are broadly representative of the locale.

Community foundations can be found in most major cities and focus their giving on the geographic area in which they are based. These foundations often take the name of the locality in which they operate. In contrast to private foundations, community foundations are actually public charities supported by the contributions of a large number of individuals who pool their resources for the common good. These foundations may receive large gifts as well as small gifts; people who are charitably inclined but do not have large amounts of money find community foundations an attractive vehicle for setting up funds. Donors can designate the organization they wish to fund, designate a type of service or a geographic area, or leave an unrestricted gift. An unrestricted gift gives a community foundation much more leeway to respond to emerging community issues and problems. Unlike private foundations, a community foundation must by law and by spirit continually attract new donors to maintain its public charity status. Thus, it is not unusual to see community foundations advertise for donors. A living donor may maintain a role in the grant-making process by using the community foundation staff for professional consultation. With the financial help of private foundations and the support of the Council on Foundations, community foundations expanded rapidly in the 1970s and 1980s. At present, more than 400 community foundations exist.

### Company Foundations

A *company foundation* is set up by a business organization and is a legal entity separate from that company. A company foundation's grant giving is frequently limited to the communities in which the sponsoring company operates. Business cycles affect the amount of corporate giving. Rather than give money, company foundations often offer support by donating equipment and supplies, loaning executives, providing conference and meeting facilities, and extending in-kind services such as printing and management consulting.

### Operating Foundations

*Operating foundations* use their resources to conduct research or provide a direct service. Although designated under the tax law as private foundations, they engage in tax-exempt activities but operate their own programs as determined by their governing bodies. Generally, they do not give grants to outside groups; thus, they are excluded from most directories that provide profiles about foundations. Some foundations have shifted from being a foundation that disburses grants to being only an operating foundation, and vice versa. For instance, the Russell Sage Foundation disbursed funds for its first 40 years, but in 1944 its trustees adopted new policies providing for termination of all grants and devoting the foundation's resources to an operating program (Andrews, 1956).

## History of Foundations

Private philanthropy has a long history and existed even in ancient civilizations. Marts (1961), who traced philanthropic efforts through 40 centuries, identified early efforts such as the Hammurabic code written around 2000 B.C., which directed the Babylonians to relieve the suffering of widows, orphans, and poor people, and the tithe originated by Moses around 1300 B.C., in which people had to give the 10th part of the harvest yield to support religion and poor people. In England, philanthropists developed the charitable trust as the major instrument of their gifts and bequests.

However, philanthropy reached its most extensive development in the United States. Initially, religious organizations were the major channel for support of charitable projects. For African Americans, mutual aid societies such as the African Masonic Lodge in Boston and the Free African Society in Philadelphia, both of which were established in 1787, arose to help free black people and later to help freed slaves (Joseph, 1991). The organizations emerging in the 20th century "distinguished religious from secular purposes; provided greater scope for professional control of medical, educational and social services; and developed funding and coordinating agencies that served the metropolitan community as a whole" (Hammack, 1989, pp. 25–26).

The foundation as an institution is uniquely American in terms of economic and intellectual influence (Fisch, Freed, & Schacter, 1974). Early foundations were financed by large private fortunes and were intended to relieve the suffering of poor and unfortunate populations. George Peabody established the model for the modern foundation when he began his foundation in 1867 with the purpose of discovering and preventing social ills rather than simply alleviating them. Because the Internal Revenue Service did not allow the public to inspect its records before the 1940s, it was difficult to get an accounting of how many foundations actually existed before that time. Some of the best-known established foundations before the Great Depression of the 1930s were the Russell Sage Foundation (established in 1907); the Carnegie Foundation (1911); the Rockefeller Foundation (1913); the Twentieth Century Fund (1919); and the Kresge Foundation (1924) (Kresge Foundation, 1954). Even during the depression (1930 to 1939), some now well-known foundations were created, including the Ford Foundation, the R. W. Johnson Foundation, the W. K. Kellogg Foundation, the Lilly Foundation, and the Alfred P. Sloan Foundation (Andrews, 1973; W. K. Kellogg Foundation, 1955). Community foundations began with the Cleveland Foundation in 1914. The structure that was established—public representation on the board or distribution committee—was a new way to govern a philanthropy.

Richard Eells (1956), who wrote the first comprehensive book on the social, legal, and political implications of corporate philanthropy and conducted a pioneering study of the social and economic aspects of business philanthropy, stimulated a campaign to encourage more corporate charitable giving. Although manuals on how to set up corporate funding had been written before this time, Eells's book took a conceptual approach, emphasizing corporate giving as strengthening a free society.

Of particular importance to the growth and development of the social work profession was the Russell Sage Foundation. In 1917 the foundation published the pioneering textbook on social casework, *Social Diagnosis*, by Mary Richmond, head of the Charity Organization Department (Richmond, 1917). In 1929 it published the first *Social Work Year Book*, and continued publication until the 10th volume in 1949, when the American Association of Social Workers assumed publication (Andrews, 1973). At present, NASW publishes this yearbook, now known as the *Encyclopedia of Social Work*.

## Foundation Giving

Foundation giving can be categorized in the following arenas: education, science, international activities, social welfare, health, humanities and the arts, and religion. Generally, foundations try to keep up with changes in the external environment. Foundations often describe themselves as assisting in the development of new ventures, concepts, and programs; supporting innovative social programs and research; and advocating that some of the ideas from these programs become incorporated into federal grant programs (Jenkins, 1990). A grantseeker of both foundation giving and federal grants often can see the impact of foundations on governmental areas of interest. For example, in social welfare, an approach to a problem funded initially on a demonstration basis by foundations may find its way into a request for proposal by a federal government agency.

Although more than 24,000 grant-making foundations exist (Renz & Lawrence, 1992), it is not easy to secure a foundation grant. There are more applications than grant awards. For instance, according to the *Annual Register of Grant Support* (1993), the Ford Foundation typically receives 30,000 proposals but funds only about 2,000. The Barbara Bush Foundation for Family Literacy typically receives 600 to 700 applications annually but funds only 10 to 20 projects each year (*Foundation Grants Alert,* 1993). Foundation support goes primarily toward conventional charitable activities and established organizations. Social welfare organizations are frequently the beneficiaries of such giving because they have an established service, are problem focused, and are well understood.

However, an entire network of foundations that give to social justice and advocacy has significantly enhanced social reform (Jenkins, 1990). The overwhelming majority of these social justice foundations are private and family foundations concerned with systems change and fundamental improvements. For instance, the Arca Foundation "supports a wide variety of organizations struggling for social and economic justice. It is committed to sustaining these organizations in their different missions of analysis and outreach to a wider public" (Shellow & Stella, 1990, p. 138). The Compton Foundation has as one of its program priorities "social justice, including the provision of adequate social services at the local level with a particular interest in programs directed at youth" (Shellow & Stella, p. 185). "Social change" and "empowerment" have become key terms to these foundations. Furthermore, some foundations have taken risks. The term "venture philanthropy" has arisen to describe this willingness to risk (Reisler, 1988).

### Special-Purpose Foundations

Special-purpose foundations, those that devote efforts entirely to programs within a single field or only a few fields of interest, constitute the most widespread type of giving. Over the past decade, the percentage of special-purpose grant dollars has increased steadily, with children and youths continuing to be the "single largest special beneficiary of foundation grant dollars" (Foundation Center, 1994a, p. xxi).

A number of special-purpose foundations have evolved within the last decade to serve the same kinds of targeted populations that social workers are concerned with: women, homeless people, and people with acquired immune deficiency syndrome. Some funders that fund a target population may serve the national community, whereas others are focused locally. Some may serve long-term needs; others focus on the immediate. Thus, although a group of foundations may limit themselves to a specific population and share the same ultimate goal, there is much diversity in their approach and in their agendas.

Foundations generally do not fund in any significant way minority-controlled social services, although they do fund a number of programs that serve people of color.

### Funding Collaborations

A trend in foundation giving is funding collaborations, that is, partnerships between various entities. Community-based organizations, businesses, universities, and public schools working together to help low-income students gain access to college is a typical example. Public–private partnerships not only increase the dollars available for projects but also increase the community commitment as groups work together. With the goal of decreasing fragmentation, the integration of human services agencies on behalf of children is a funding priority of the Annie E. Casey Foundation (1994). Other foundations have similar goals.

Funding collaborative approaches also is a trend among foundations. For example, the Pew Charitable Trusts, the John D. and Catherine T. MacArthur Foundation, and the Rockefeller Foundation joined to establish the Energy Foundation. The Ford Foundation (1989), which is private, has a national initiative that allocates funds to community foundations to assess the demographic changes occurring in areas that the community foundations serve to determine how the changes may affect their programs, operations, and fundraising efforts. Funders often work together to donate to a particular agency's project, with each funder giving a specific amount that will help meet the budgetary need.

### Social Welfare Funding

Social welfare has always ranked consistently high as a recipient of giving. With the cuts of $50 billion in government social program spending in the 1980s, private, corporate, and community foundations began to reassess their giving. Many decided to increase their funding of social welfare and human services. From 1981 through 1988, social welfare received the largest share of foundation dollars (Foundation Center, 1993). In 1990 foundations awarded more than 12,000 grants to this field, representing 21.5 percent of the giving and constituting the second-largest group of recipients, following education. In addition, health, which includes mental health, received 7,275 grants, representing 12.5 percent of the giving.

As categorized by the Foundation Center (1992), social welfare includes crime, justice, and legal services; employment; food, nutrition, and agriculture; housing and shelter; safety and disaster relief; recreation and sports; youth development; and multipurpose. The multipurpose category includes services to families, individuals, elderly people, children, and other special populations. Other areas of particular interest to social workers also are funded, although they are not categorized as social welfare. These areas include the environment, reproductive rights, community development, peace, and public policy.

Since 1975 there has been a dramatic increase in corporate charitable giving. According to O'Connell (1987), corporate philanthropy grew 10 percent in each of the four years between 1982 and 1985 and 250 percent between 1975 and 1985. During the past several years, corporations have made the largest percentage of their donations to education, with health and human services receiving the second largest amounts (*Annual Register of Grant Support*, 1994).

Although foundations give generously to social welfare activities, boards of foundations often have questions about the effectiveness of their giving. They emphasize evaluation within foundations themselves, as well as assessment to check that the funded project did what it was supposed to do. Furthermore, the boards will question potentially duplicative and overlapping services. Board members are often confused by the number of service providers who spring up when a new problem arises and might not always understand the service distinctions among agencies.

## FOUNDATION RESOURCES

Researching foundations takes work. There may seem to be an abundance of foundations, but many serve only a certain region or city or have a special philosophy or interest.

### Foundation Center

The Foundation Center, which publishes directories, grant indexes, guidebooks, monographs, and bibliographies, offers a wide variety of services and information for grant seekers. The center has regional centers in New York, Washington, DC, Atlanta, Cleveland, and San Francisco and cooperates with public libraries nationally to house its materials. *The Foundation Directory* (Foundation Center, 1994b) provides information on the finances, governance, and giving information of grant-making organizations with assets of $2 million or more. *Foundation Fundamentals: A Guide for Grant Seekers,* also published by the center (1991), is an exceptionally useful book for people who are new to the process of seeking grants. A number of books about how to obtain a grant exist, but the basics for applying for a grant are explained succinctly by the Knight Foundation: "Grant seekers must be credible, explain their needs clearly, have a complete budget and evaluation plan and submit well-written succinct proposals" (*Foundation Grants Alert,* 1992), p. 3).

### National Network of Grantmakers

The National Network of Grantmakers is an association of individual grant makers who are committed to social and economic justice with a strong focus on advocacy. Members often describe their foundations as promoters of social change and as supporters of new approaches. A volunteer organization, the National Network publishes *The Grant Seeker's Guide: Funding Sourcebook* (Shellow & Stella, 1990), which identifies foundations with assets of $1 million or more that address these issues. The guide is designed for the smaller, often grassroots or community-based organization whose fundraising is often limited. The guide has several essential and helpful introductory chapters on grant seeking.

### Council on Foundations

Other resource organizations include the Council on Foundations, which is the national organization to which foundations belong. It publishes the *Foundation News,* which, although geared to foundations, can be helpful to grant seekers who might have interest in the latest concerns in the foundation world. One of the goals of the Council on Foundations is to promote cooperation among grant makers, which appears to be happening to a much greater extent than in the past.

### Independent Sector

The Independent Sector is a nonprofit coalition of more than 800 organizations; its mission is to create a national forum capable of encouraging giving and volunteering. Because its membership has a significant number of foundations, social welfare organizations that belong have an opportunity to interact with foundations and can help keep the foundations current on issues and concerns. The Independent Sector produced the *Non-Profit Almanac 1992–93: Dimensions of the Independent Sector* (Hodgkinson, Weitzman, Toppe, & Noga, 1992), which can serve as an important reference tool for nonprofit managers, grant seekers, and fundraisers.

### Other Resources

Newspapers and newsletters on the workings of foundations include the *Chronicle of Philanthropy,* a national newspaper published twice a month. Annual reports of foundations also serve as an excellent resource, but a major criticism of foundations is that many do not issue annual public reports beyond the form that must go to the Internal Revenue Service (Hanson, 1992; Joseph, 1992).

## ROLE OF SOCIAL WORK

Social workers have been the catalyst for establishing or have actually established private foundations. Two social workers were pioneers in the community foundation field. Frank Loomis was the prime mobilizer of the national movement to establish community foundations, and Wilma Shields shaped the field as the first full-time executive director of the National Council on Community Foundations, later called the Council on Foundations (Newman, 1989).

The number of social workers presently working in the field is unknown. Training in the areas of systems change, advocacy, assessment, and program evaluation, along with a field of service, is particularly helpful for people who wish to be program specialists. People who wish to serve as foundation directors should receive training in these areas as well as in management. Because so many foundations give to social services and other areas of interest to social workers, a person in the profession can also contribute much as a board or trustee member. Social workers are knowledgeable about a number of social and community issues and bring extensive experience on behalf of people—important characteristics for board and distribution committee members.

Social welfare and foundations should be viewed as interdependent. Foundations have played a role in the process of social reform and advocacy, leading to social policy changes. They have sometimes researched social welfare issues in a more comprehensive fashion than the field itself. Believing that U.S. social welfare policy must be fundamentally reformed and modernized, the Ford Foundation initiated a project on social welfare and the American future and published the recommendations in 1989. As part of the overall project, the Ford Foundation financially supported 28 independent research projects on social welfare.

As public funds have been unable to keep up with the pressing social needs, more demands have been made on foundations to help meet basic human needs. Indeed, as state legislatures discuss welfare reform, the suggestion often arises that private funds and foundations should pick up the slack for declining programs. In the past, such a suggestion has prompted foundations to assert, along with social policy advocates, that the government should fund such problems.

Paul Ylvisaker (1989), who was one of the foremost observers of and participants in the foundation world, summed up the importance of foundations. He wrote,

> Modern philanthropy has evolved as America's contribution to the theory and practice of constitutional democracy in an age when complexity and the demand for shared power have outstripped the capacity of governments to handle social problems on their own. Gradually, foundations have emerged from their purely charitable preserve to become an essential and recognized social process—in effect, a set of private legislatures allowing an autonomous determination of public needs and agendas. (p. 52)

## References


Andrews, F. E. (1956). *Philanthropic foundations.* New York: Russell Sage Foundation.

Andrews, F. E. (1973). *Foundation watchers.* Princeton, NJ: Princeton University Press.

Annie E. Casey Foundation. (1994). *Community empowerment, 4*(1).

*Annual register of grant support: A directory of funding sources* (26th ed.). (1993). New York: R. R. Bowker.

*Annual register of grant support: A directory of funding sources.* (27th ed.). (1994). New York: R.R. Bowker.

Eells, R. (1956). *Corporation giving in a free society.* New York: Harper and Brothers.

Fisch, E. L., Freed, D. J., & Schacter, E. B. (1974). *Charities and charitable foundations.* Pomona, NY: Lond Publications.

Ford Foundation. (1989). *The common good: Social welfare and the American future.* New York: Author.

Foundation Center. (1991). *Foundation fundamentals: A guide for grantseekers* (4th ed.). New York: Author.

Foundation Center. (1992). *Foundation giving.* New York: Author.

Foundation Center. (1993). *Foundation grants index* (21st ed.). New York: Author.

Foundation Center. (1994a). *The foundation directory* (16th ed.). New York: Author.

Foundation Center. (1994b). *Foundation grants index* (22nd ed.). New York: Author.

*Foundation Grants Alert.* (1992, October). Alexandria, VA: Capitol Publications.

*Foundation Grants Alert.* (1993, June). Alexandria, VA: Capitol Publications.

Hammack, D. C. (1989). Community foundations: The delicate question of purpose. In R. Magat (Ed.), *An agile servant* (pp. 23–50). New York: Foundation Center.

Hanson, W. (1992). Ethical issues in the philanthropic and nonprofit community. *Leadership IS, 2*(1).

Hodgkinson, V. A., Weitzman, M. S., Toppe, C. M., & Noga, S. M. (1992). *The non-profit almanac, 1992–1993: Dimensions of the independent sector.* San Francisco: Jossey-Bass.

Jenkins, J. C. (1990). Foundation funding of progressive social movements. In J. R. Shellow & N. C. Stella (Eds.), *The grant seeker's guide: Funding sourcebook* (3rd ed., pp. 1–13). Mt. Kisko, NY: Moyer Bell Limited.

Joseph, J. (1991). *Black philanthropy: The potential and limits of private generosity in a civil society.* Washington, DC: Association of Black Foundation Executives.

Joseph, J. (1992, Jul./Aug.). Message from the president. *Foundation News,* pp. 44–45.

Kresge Foundation. (1954). *The first thirty years.* Detroit: Author.

Marts, A. C. (1961). *Man's concern for his fellow man.* New York: W. F. Humphrey Press.

Newman, B. (1989). Pioneers in community foundations. In R. Magat (Ed.), *An agile servant* (pp. 73–88) New York: Foundation Center.

Nicklin, J. L. (February 10, 1993). Philanthropy notes. *Chronicle of Higher Education,* p. A28.

O'Connell, B. (1987). *Corporate Philanthropy* [Entire issue], *7*(4) Washington, DC: Independent Sector.

Reisler, R. F. (1988, Jan./Feb.). Going out on a limb. *Foundation News, 29,* 42–45.

Renz, L., & Lawrence, S. (1992). *Foundation giving: Yearbook of facts and figures on private, corporate and community foundations.* New York: Foundation Center.

Richmond, M. (1917). *Social diagnosis.* New York: Russell Sage Foundation.

Shellow, J. R., & Stella, N. C. (Eds.). (1990). *The grant seeker's guide* (3rd ed.). Mt. Kisko, NY: Moyer Bell Limited.

*Social work year book, 1929.* (1930). New York: Russell Sage Foundation.

W. K. Kellogg Foundation. (1955). *The first twenty-five years.* Battle Creek, MI: Author.

Ylvisaker, P. N. (1989). Community and community foundations in the next century. In R. Magat (Ed.), *An agile servant* (pp. 51–61). New York: Foundation Center.

## FURTHER READING

Gaul, G., & Borowski, N. (April 24, 1993). Foundations build a giant nest egg. *Philadelphia Inquirer,* p. A1, A6–A7.

O'Connell, B. (1986). *Philanthropy in action.* New York: Foundation Center.

Thomas, F. A. (1993). *Our shared future: We must get there together.* Washington, DC: Association of Black Foundation Executives.

**Ione D. Vargus, PhD,** is presidential fellow, Temple University, Ritter Hall Annex, Philadelphia, PA 19122.

**For further information see**

Disasters and Disaster Aid; Fundraising and Philanthropy; Income Distribution; Income Security Overview; International Social Welfare: Organizations and Activities; Nonprofit Management Issues; Organizations: Context for Social Services Delivery; Peace and Social Justice; Poverty; Public Services Management; Public Social Welfare Expenditures; Social Justice in Social Agencies; Social Planning; Social Welfare History; Social Welfare Policy; Voluntarism; Volunteer Management.

**Key Words**

charitable giving
foundations
fundraising
philanthropy
social welfare foundations

## Chavez, Cesar

*See* Biographies section, Volume 3

READER'S GUIDE

### Child Abuse

*The following entries contain information on this general topic:*



# Child Abuse and Neglect Overview

**Susan J. Wells**

There is some disagreement regarding the role of children throughout history and the degree to which they were protected from being harmed by their parents. Many historical accounts have focused on the fact that infanticide was not outlawed by Roman law until 318 A.D. (De Mause, 1976). In these accounts, Western European society's attitude toward children was harsh and cruel: Children were no more than mere chattel of their fathers. These conditions were reported as becoming gradually more civilized through the ages (Stone, 1977). Others have suggested that treatment of children varied more with economic well-being, class, or the circumstances in which they were raised. One argument is that children were regarded by their parents much as they are today. Although children were expected to work and carry responsibilities at an early age and corporal punishment was the norm, there was no lack of compassion and protection for children who were born to loving families (Corby, 1993; Pollock, 1983).

## OVERVIEW

Giovannoni and Becerra (1979) traced the sociolegal history of responsibility for child protection, citing Blackstone's comments in the late 1700s. Blackstone identified maintenance, protection, and education as the duties of parents. In return, the children's duty was to be industrious. Protection was largely thought of as protection from threats outside the family. The parent could lawfully correct the child in a "reasonable manner," and the father had unquestioned right of custody unless parental responsibilities were not met (Abbott, 1938; Ten Broek, 1964–1965).

When the family failed in their responsibilities, particularly in the maintenance of their children, common law supported taking custody from the parent to protect the child. Until the late 1800s, this included taking children from indigent families and placing them elsewhere in an effort to break the cycle of poverty. In 1874 the Society for the Prevention of Cruelty to Children was formed in the United States specifically to protect children from maltreatment. At the same time, states and municipalities passed laws to protect children who were mistreated. These laws varied but focused on the moral behavior of the parents; endangerment of the life or health of a child; deprivation of food, shelter, or clothing; physical cruelty or torture; and exposure to weather (McCrea, 1969, cited in Giovannoni & Becerra, 1979).

In 1909 the White House Conference on Children reinforced efforts to separate poverty from neglect. The participants sought to focus on the quality of a child's care rather than supporting the use of poverty alone as a reason to separate children from their families (U.S. Congress, 1909). Throughout the first half of the 20th century, identification of abuse and neglect was left largely to law enforcement and social work, and case finding rested largely on easily recognizable indicators of abuse or neglect.

In 1962, with the identification of the battered child syndrome, physicians began to identify and describe medical indicators of abuse such as unexplained long bone fractures (Kempe, Silverman, Steele, Droegemueller, & Silver, 1962). Although physicians had long been interested in these puzzling injuries, it was not until 1962 that they were specifically identified as resulting from abuse (DiMaio & DiMaio, 1989; Lazoritz, 1992). In the 20th century there has also been an increasing awareness of the degree to which child deaths are attributable to abuse and neglect (Jason, Carpenter, & Tyler, 1983).

Current trends in the identification of child abuse and neglect include distinguishing poverty from neglect, keeping the family together whenever possible, and eschewing protective intervention solely for reasons of the parents' moral turpitude (National Association of Public Child Welfare Administrators, 1988). In addition there has been a strong emphasis on identification and investigation with less funding and legislation devoted to treatment and prevention (Otto & Melton, 1990). There also has been a great deal of interest in the issue of sexual abuse and in establishing coordinated response teams to these reports (Children's Justice and Assistance Act of 1986; Kaye, Wells, & Sedlak, 1994). The Children's Justice Act allotted funds for the support of grants to states to improve responding to reports of child abuse, particularly, sexual abuse with an emphasis on improving investigation and prosecution.

In 1993 the Omnibus Budget Reconciliation Act (OBRA) added a new program to Title IV-B of the Social Security Act titled Family Preservation and Family Support Services.

## Current Definitions

Child abuse and neglect are legal, social, and cultural constructs that are inextricably linked to time and place. The acceptance of infanticide in ancient times is remarkable to us today, and many practices and conditions currently tolerated will seem barbaric in another time and place. Definitions of abuse and neglect vary not only internationally but also among U.S. states. In addition, definitions mandating legal intervention serve quite a different purpose than social constructions or definitions used in research.

### CAPTA Definitions

The Child Abuse Prevention and Treatment Act (CAPTA) of 1974 was reauthorized and amended by the Child Abuse Prevention, Adoption, and Family Services Act of 1992. As defined by CAPTA, child abuse and neglect

> means the physical or mental injury, sexual abuse or exploitation, negligent treatment, or maltreatment of a child by a person who is responsible for the child's welfare, under circumstances which indicate that the child's health or welfare is harmed or threatened thereby, as determined in accordance with regulations prescribed by the Secretary; the term "person who is responsible for the child's welfare" includes—
>
> (A) any employee of a residential facility; and
>
> (B) any staff person providing out-of-home care; . . . (42 Sec. 5106g)

### Differences in Definitions

States vary from one another in their efforts to specify more closely when the protective services agency should intervene. Some states emphasize that physical abuse or neglect is defined by the presence of serious injury. Other states explicitly include or exclude a variety of conditions, such as a positive drug toxicology in a newborn, truancy or educational neglect, children being left alone, head lice, and parents' behavior not resulting in specific observable harm to the child.

These are relatively identifiable differences in definitions. However, many nuances are not so easily identifiable or debated. When the injury is not permanent or severe, when the abuse is emotional, or when the failure to provide is a result of economic circumstances, it is difficult for the most experienced practitioner or researcher to assign the label of abuse or neglect. Giovannoni and Becerra (1979), in addressing these issues in their classic research on definitions, found that laypersons tended to judge many situations as maltreatment that professionals saw as less serious. Professionals also differed from one another in judgments of seriousness. For example, investigators (protective services workers and law enforcement officers) tended to agree with one another more than they did with attorneys or pediatricians, and they generally rated incidents as more serious. Attorneys most often disagreed with all others and tended to rate incidents as less serious than other professionals.

In addition to areas of disagreement, there are instances of outright confusion. Vague definitions and lack of specific criteria are still rampant in discussions and research (Giovannoni & Becerra, 1979; National Research Council, 1993).

### Westat Study

In one of the most thorough efforts at definition, Westat, Inc., used the definitions listed in Table 1 to count the number of noninstitutionalized children who were abused and neglected by their caretakers in the United States. The study, done for the U.S. Department of Health and Human Services National Center on Child Abuse and Neglect, was of children younger than 18 years. The behavior was nonaccidental or avoidable, and the abuse or neglect resulted in assumed harm (tying or confinement); demonstrable harm (physical abuse); or endangerment (applicable to all types of maltreatment).

Injuries and impairments may be physical, mental, or emotional or include a health condition, impairment, or impaired educational development (including chronic truancy). The forms of suspected maltreatment are listed in Table 2.

One example of differences in definitions is in the failure to provide medical treatment. In the Westat study, endangerment, harm, or probable harm would be counted as abuse or neglect. However, most states have excluded endangerment, harm, or probable harm from their definition of medical neglect. They will not intervene if the condition is not life threatening or likely to cause permanent impairment or if the reason for refusal of treatment is because of religious beliefs or practices (Clearinghouse on Child Abuse and Neglect, 1994).

### Sociocultural Context of Definition

Korbin (1987) succinctly presented the dilemma of cultural context and made the case for cultural competence in evaluating abuse and neglect:

> Failure to allow for a cultural perspective . . . promotes an ethnocentric position in which one's own . . . cultural beliefs and practices are presumed superior to all others. Nevertheless, a stance of extreme cultural relativism, in which all judgments . . . are suspended . . . may justify a lesser standard of care for some children. (p. 25)

By understanding both the viewpoint of the insider and the outsider, one is less likely to jump to unwarranted conclusions. The influx of Vietnamese immigrants, for example, has resulted in child protective services workers becoming more

TABLE 1

**Definitions of Child Abuse and Neglect**

| Severity of Impairment | Description |
|---|---|
| Fatal | Maltreatment (a major contributory cause of death) |
| Serious | Professional treatment or remediation needed to alleviate acute present suffering or to prevent significant long-term impairment |
| Moderate | Behavior problem or physical, mental, or emotional condition with observable symptoms lasting at least 48 hours |
| Probable | No obvious injuries or problems, but in view of extreme or traumatic nature of the maltreatment, it is probable that the child's mental or emotional health or capabilities have been significantly impaired |
| Endangered | Child's health or safety was or is seriously endangered, but child appears not to have been harmed |

Adapted with permission from Westat, Inc. (1987a, 1991a). *Study of the national incidence and prevalence of child abuse and neglect: Report on data collection* (National Center on Child Abuse and Neglect Contract No. 105-85-1702). Rockville, MD: Author.

TABLE 2
**Forms of Child Maltreatment**

| Form | Examples |
|---|---|
| Sexual exploitation | Intrusion (penile penetration)<br>Molestation with genital contact<br>Other fondling<br>Exposure to or lack of supervision of premature sexual activities |
| Other abuse | Physical assault<br>Close confinement (tortuous restriction of movement, e.g., tying or binding or locking in a closet)<br>Verbal or emotional assault (e.g., habitual patterns of threatening, belittling or overly hostile or rejecting treatment)<br>Other overly punitive, exploitative, or abusive treatment (e.g., throwing items at a child; deliberate withholding of food, shelter, sleep or other necessities; or economic exploitation) |
| Inattention to remedial health care needs | Refusal to allow or to provide needed care for diagnosed condition or impairment<br>Unwarranted delay or failure to seek needed care for serious injury, illness, or impairment |
| Inattention to physical needs | Refusal of custody (e.g., abandonment, expulsion, or refusal to accept custody of a runaway)<br>Inadequate supervision<br>Other physical neglect (inadequate nutrition or clothing or unhygienic or dangerous living conditions) |
| Inattention to educational needs | Knowingly permitted chronic truancy (at least five days per month on average)<br>Other (e.g., failed to enroll or repeatedly kept child home) |
| Inattention to developmental and emotional needs | Inadequate nurturance or affection (e.g., failure-to-thrive)<br>Chronic or extreme spouse abuse<br>Knowingly permitted maladaptive behavior (e.g., delinquency, serious drug or alcohol use, etc.)<br>Refusal of psychological care<br>Delay in psychological care |

Adapted with permission from Westat, Inc. (1987b, 1991a). *Study of the national incidence and prevalence of child abuse and neglect: Report on data processing and analysis* (National Center on Child Abuse and Neglect Contract No. 105-85-1702). Rockville, MD: Author.

knowledgeable about the practice of coin rubbing, a healing practice that leaves bruises.

The literature on physical discipline reveals varying levels of tolerance for such discipline. For example, in Sweden, spanking of any type is not sanctioned, whereas in the United States, there is more tolerance of physical discipline. As Korbin (1987) noted, episodes of abuse are often described as discipline that is out of control. Furthermore, at least one study (Dubanoski & Snyder, 1980) comparing two cultures with respect to use of punishment and occurrence of abuse found that endorsement of physical punishment was associated with higher reports of child abuse.

## Incidence and Prevalence of Abuse and Neglect

Several sources suggest trends in maltreatment types and severity of injuries inflicted (American Association for Protecting Children, 1987; National Center on Child Abuse and Neglect, 1993; Straus & Gelles, 1986; Westat, Inc., 1991a). Generally, reports of child abuse and neglect have increased in phenomenal proportions. According to Fontana (1971), in 1962 there were an estimated 10,000 child abuse reports in the United States. In 1992 child protective services agencies responded to nearly 1.9 million reports of abuse to 2.9 million children (National Center on Child Abuse and Neglect, 1994); some reports involved abuse to more than one child. Even after the extraordinary increases in the 1960s and 1970s, reports of abuse more than doubled from 1980 to 1992.

In addition to increases in reports of child abuse to child protective services agencies, Westat, Inc. (1991a), found that reports by community professionals increased from 1980 to 1986. Although the continuing increase in reports of maltreatment may be attributed to increased awareness, perhaps the actual incidences of abuse have increased as well (Daro, Jones, & McCurdy, 1990).

Reports of neglect, however, far outnumber reports of physical abuse. Furthermore, the proportion of reports that allege sexual abuse is increasing. In addition, most reported incidents of child abuse do not involve severe injury or death.

The Second National Incidence Study on Child Abuse and Neglect (Westat, Inc., 1991a), using the definitions presented earlier and including cases of endangerment, documented these trends. In 1986 professionals in the United States recognized 22.6 children per 1,000 as abused or neglected, for a total of 1.4 million children nationwide. Of maltreated children, 64 percent were neglected and 41 percent were abused (some cases involved both types of maltreatment so the figures total more than 100 percent). The most frequent category of abuse was physical abuse (4.9 children per 1,000), followed by emotional abuse (3.0 children per 1,000), and then sexual abuse (2.1 children per 1,000). Physical neglect was the most frequent form of neglect (8.1 children per 1,000), followed by educational neglect (4.5 children per 1,000), and emotional neglect (3.2 children per 1,000). Moderate injuries occurred in 61 percent of the cases, followed by endangerment (18 percent), probable injuries (11 percent), serious injuries (10 percent), and fatalities (0.1 percent).

The study also revealed that females were more likely to be sexually abused than males; however, this finding may reflect that more females than males were *reported* as sexually abused. Abuse increased with increasing age, but neglect did not. Fatalities were more frequent among younger children, and moderate injuries more prevalent among older children. There was a marginal (but not statistically significant) likelihood for African American children to be fatally injured more often than white children and to be recognized more often by professionals as having been abused or neglected. Low income (under $15,000 annually) was a significant risk factor for child maltreatment and injury from maltreatment. Children in families of four or more were more at risk. The child's residence in a metropolitan area was not a significant factor in maltreatment.

Although the number of abuse and neglect cases reported to child protective services has increased by 57 percent since 1980, only 44 percent of the cases known to community professionals were also investigated by child protective services. Of the children known to be abused or neglected in the community, 56 percent were not investigated or served by child protective services, perhaps because of a lack of reporting by community professionals, a screening out of reports before investigation by child protective services, or both.

Straus and Gelles (1986), in examining physical abuse within the family, but asking family members rather than community professionals, found the rate of physical abuse to be 36 children per 1,000. If hitting children with objects, such as a hairbrush, is included, the rate was 140 children per 1,000. Even the more conservative estimate far exceeds the physical abuse known to community professionals that was revealed in the Second National Incidence Study (Westat, Inc., 1991a).

No comparable studies have been done on abuse in out-of-home care. However, data collected by the National Center on Child Abuse and Neglect (1994) from state child protective services agencies suggest the breakdown of cases known to these agencies by type of perpetrator. Forty states reported data, and 692,971 perpetrators were identified. Of these perpetrators, 79 percent were parents, 12 percent were other relatives, 4.6 percent were noncaretakers, 1.4 percent were child care providers, 0.5 percent were foster parents, 0.3 percent were institutional facility staff, and identity was unknown for 2.3 percent. Abuse or abduction by strangers is relatively rare except in the case of gang violence, which results in high homicide and injury rates among children younger than 18.

## Etiology of Abuse and Neglect

It is difficult to talk about etiology of abuse and neglect as one construct. Factors contributing to sexual abuse, physical abuse, and neglect will vary to some degree and be affected by a number of variables. Nevertheless, common threads in research findings have been found. In addition, poverty, drug or alcohol abuse, environment, perceived stress, vulnerability of the child, parent personality, marital status, family history, and knowledge of parenting may play a role. It is most helpful to think of these issues in terms of individual, familial, and socioeconomic factors.

The National Research Council (1993) reported that research on the role of individual factors is contradictory and inconclusive, suggesting that no single factor can explain the occurrence of maltreatment. Giving one example, the council cited alcohol abuse, recommending further research on the unique and immediate effects of alcohol, its co-occurrence with other behaviors such as personality disorders, and the circumstances under which the different types of drinking situations result in child maltreatment.

Familial issues such as single-parent households (Westat, Inc., 1991b), interaction patterns and relationships such as chronic chaotic interactions or lack of sufficient attachment (Maccoby & Martin, 1983), and social isolation (Newberger, Reed, Daniel, Hyde, & Kotelchuck, 1977) appear to be related to inadequate parenting styles that result in abuse or neglect. Egeland's (1988) longitudinal study lends some support to Polansky's (1987) and Helfer's (1987) models of the cycle of neglect and abusive parenting. In Egeland's study, there was a direct relationship between a person's growing up in an emotionally supportive and nonabusive environment and his or her later capacity to parent without maltreating his or her own offspring.

Perhaps the most important factor is a society that supports such intergenerational transfers of trauma and detachment. Poverty is repeatedly identified as a major factor in abuse and neglect. Furthermore, related social stresses such as unemployment and chronically high-risk neighborhoods only exacerbate family problems, childhood deprivation, and lack of hope for a better future (Garbarino & Sherman, 1980; Gil, 1975; Light, 1973; Westat, Inc., 1991b; Whipple & Webster-Stratton, 1991).

## Role of Social Work

### Identification, Assessment, and Treatment

Social workers have long been on the front lines in the identification, assessment, and treatment of child abuse and neglect. Traditionally, child protection agencies hired professionally trained social workers who relied heavily on the casework model to ameliorate family ills and thereby protect children at risk (Stein, Gambrill, & Wiltse, 1978). Since the mid-1970s, there has been much less attention to casework and more emphasis on providing hard services, goal-directed intervention, and case management.

Three separate but parallel trends in service delivery have emerged. First, in case finding, the astronomical increases in reporting have accentuated the importance of investigation and left few resources for treatment in public agencies. At the same time, the management and provision of services have become less the domain of social workers; rather, more professional managers and bachelor's-level caseworkers or technicians manage and provide services, although this trend is not universal.

Second, the lack of services specifically tailored to abused and neglected children and their families and the increasing concern about unnecessary placements have led to the development of home-based and intensive family preservation services. Although these two service approaches are often considered to be one entity, they are clearly distinct. Home-based services grew out of a concern for the development of a holistic service delivery model. Family preservation is more often equated with short-term crisis intervention, the purpose of which is to prevent imminent placement. Family preservation is an attractive approach and is enthusiastically embraced as the answer to some vexing service delivery problems: lack of funding, desire for rapid but effective results, and the promise of a concrete measurable outcome. Although much research has been done on family preservation services, there is more to do before the promise of a measurable outcome is met.

Third, except in the case of sexual abuse, the needs of abused and neglected children are often given short shrift, even though the literature on intervening with all abused and neglected children is minimal. Yet it is abused and neglected children who will transfer what they have learned to their own children. The lack of services and focus is not for want of trying, but is often a result of minimal funding and the emphasis on helping the parent better raise the child.

Social work can provide a leadership role in developing service models that meet the needs of both the family and the child in this population. Social work is uniquely suited to see the multiple roles each profession must play and to construct the means to implement them.

### Interagency Coordination

Child abuse and neglect is an arena in which social work, law enforcement, medicine, education, and psychology uniquely interact to provide services to the child and family. Any profession may be involved in case finding. More child protective services reports are received from schools than from professionals (Westat, Inc., 1991a). Social work, law enforcement, and medicine are often partners in investigation, particularly in response to child deaths and sexual abuse. Law enforcement has worked through probation officers and the courts to respond to complaints of child maltreatment and to use the powers of the state to protect children from harm (Giovannoni & Becerra, 1979). Yet social workers and law enforcement officers have been somewhat suspicious of the other's intentions, whether to save the child or punish the offender. In recent years, new efforts have recognized the legitimate role both play (Besharov, 1990). In addition, federal legislation such as the Children's Justice and Assistance Act of 1986 has promoted coordination through the provision of funding to build multidisciplinary response teams.

### Macrosystems Perspective

Child protection is one of the few arenas in which social work has been the primary profession rather than playing a supporting role. However, with the increased reporting of abuse, child protective services agencies have become less professional and more beleaguered, and now are operating under a constant barrage of public criticism. At the same time, other professions have become more aware of the problem of child abuse and neglect and have joined in the fray.

Since 1962 the medical profession has taken a more assertive role, arguing to its members that physicians have a responsibility to take a leadership role in this field. In the 1980s and early 1990s, the power of the courts over the practice of social work also increased. Since the passage of the Adoption Assistance and Child Welfare Act of 1980, judges who handle cases of neglect and dependency are asked to determine whether the child protection agency has made reasonable efforts to provide services to children in their homes to prevent unnecessary separations. In addition, to prevent "foster care drift," judges also provide monitoring of casework progress for children placed in foster care. As a result of a child death in 1993 in Illinois, there was an unsuccessful movement to mandate that judges also oversee and monitor the provision of these services to children in their own homes.

These developments suggest that social work has a long way to go in providing adequate identification, protection, and treatment to children and families. Perhaps one of its first goals should be to look at the macrosystems that maintain an environment that promotes maltreatment and at the funding, administration, and management of social work agencies that carry such heavy burdens.

## References


Abbott, G. (1938). *The child and the state.* Chicago: University of Chicago Press.

Adoption Assistance and Child Welfare Act of 1980. P.L. 96-272, 94 Stat. 500.

American Association for Protecting Children. (1987). *Highlights of official child neglect and abuse reporting 1985.* Denver: American Humane Association.

Besharov, D. (1990). *Combatting child abuse: Guidelines for cooperation between law enforcement and child protective services.* Washington, DC: American Enterprise Institute.

Child Abuse Prevention, Adoption, and Family Services Act of 1992. P.L. 102-295, 106 Stat. 187.

Child Abuse Prevention and Treatment Act of 1974. P.L. 93-247, 88 Stat. 4.

Children's Justice and Assistance Act of 1986. P.L. 99-401, 100 Stat. 903.

Clearinghouse on Child Abuse and Neglect. (1994). *Ongoing study of state reporting laws.* Washington, DC: Author.

Corby, B. (1993). *Child abuse: Towards a knowledge base.* Bristol, PA: Open University Press.

Daro, D., Jones, E., & McCurdy, K. (1990). *Reliability and validity of the National Incidence Study conducted by Westat Associates in 1988: Methodological review.* Unpublished manuscript. (Available from the National Committee for Prevention of Child Abuse, 332 S. Michigan Avenue, Suite 1600, Chicago, IL 60604.)

De Mause, L. (Ed.). (1976). *The history of childhood.* London: Souvenir Press.

DiMaio, D. J., & DiMaio, V. J. (1989). Neonaticide, infanticide, and child homicide. In D. J. DiMaio & V. J. DiMaio (Eds.), *Forensic pathology* (pp. 299–326). New York: Elsevier.

Dubanoski, R., & Snyder, K. (1980). Patterns of child abuse and neglect in Japanese- and Samoan-Americans. *Child Abuse and Neglect: International Journal, 4,* 217–225.

Egeland, B. (1988). The consequences of physical and emotional neglect on the development of young children. In National Center on Child Abuse and Neglect (Ed.), *Research symposium on child neglect.* Washington, DC: National Center on Child Abuse and Neglect.

Fontana, V. J. (1971). *The maltreated child.* Springfield, IL: Charles C Thomas.

Garbarino, J., & Sherman, D. (1980). High-risk neighborhoods and high-risk families: The human ecology of child maltreatment. *Child Development, 51,* 188–198.

Gil, D. G. (1975). Unraveling child abuse. *American Journal of Orthopsychiatry, 45,* 346–356.

Giovannoni, J., & Becerra, R. (1979). *Defining child abuse.* New York: Free Press.

Helfer, R. E. (1987). The developmental basis of child abuse and neglect: An epidemiological approach. In R. E. Helfer & R. S. Kempe (Eds.), *The battered child* (4th ed., pp. 60–80). Chicago: University of Chicago Press.

Jason, J., Carpenter, M. M., & Tyler, C. W., Jr. (1983). Underrecording of infant homicide in the United States. *American Journal of Public Health, 73,* 195–197.

Kaye, E., Wells, S., & Sedlak, A. (1994). *Justice system processing of child abuse cases: Results of a 42 county survey of interdisciplinary case referral and management.* Unpublished report, Washington, DC.

Kempe, C. H., Silverman, F. N., Steele, B. F., Droegemueller, W., & Silver, H. K. (1962). The battered child. *Journal of the American Medical Association, 181,* 17–24.

Korbin, J. (1987). Child abuse and neglect: The cultural context. In R. E. Helfer & R. S. Kempe (Eds.), *The battered child* (4th ed., pp. 23–41). Chicago: University of Chicago Press.

Lazoritz, S. (1992). Child abuse: An historical perspective. In S. Ludwig & A. E. Kornberg (Eds.), *Child abuse: A medical reference* (pp. 85–90). New York: Churchill Livingstone.

Light, R. (1973). Abused and neglected children in America: A study of alternative policies. *Harvard Educational Review, 43,* 556–598.

Maccoby, E. E., & Martin, J. A. (1983). Socialization in the context of the family: Parent-child interaction. In P. H. Mussen & E. M. Hetherington (Eds.), *Handbook of child psychology: Socialization, personality, and social development* (pp. 1–101). New York: John Wiley & Sons.

McCrea, R. (1969). *The humane movement.* College Park, MD: McGrath Publishing. (Reprinted from Columbia University Press, New York, 1910.)

National Association of Public Child Welfare Administrators. (1988). *Guidelines for a model system of protective services for abused and neglected children and their families.* Washington, DC: American Public Welfare Association.

National Center on Child Abuse and Neglect. (1993). *National child abuse and neglect data system working paper 2: 1991 summary data component.* Washington, DC: U.S. Government Printing Office.

National Center on Child Abuse and Neglect. (1994). *Child maltreatment 1992: Reports from the states to the National Center on Child Abuse and Neglect.* Washington, DC: U.S. Government Printing Office.

National Research Council. (1993). *Understanding child abuse and neglect.* Washington, DC: National Academy Press.

Newberger, E. H., Reed, R. B., Daniel, J. H., Hyde, J. N., Jr., & Kotelchuck, M. (1977). Pediatric social illness: Toward an etiologic classification. *Pediatrics, 60,* 178–185.

Otto, R. K., & Melton, G. B. (1990). Trends in legislation and case law on child abuse and neglect. In R. T. Ammerman & M. Hersen (Eds.), *Children at risk: An evaluation of factors contributing to child abuse and neglect* (pp. 55–84). New York: Plenum Press.

Polansky, N. (1987). *Damaged parents.* Chicago: University of Chicago Press.

Pollock, L. (1983). *Forgotten children: Parent–child relations from 1500 to 1900.* New York: Cambridge University Press.

Stein, T. J., Gambrill, D. E., & Wiltse, K. T. (1978). *Children in foster homes: Achieving continuity of care.* New York: Praeger.

Stone, L. (1977). *The family, sex and marriage in England 1500–1800.* London: Weidenfeld & Nicholson.

Straus, M. A., & Gelles, R. J. (1986). Societal change in family violence from 1975 to 1985 as revealed by two national surveys. *Journal of Marriage and the Family, 48,* 465–479.

Ten Broek, J. (1964–1965). *California's dual system of family law: Its origin, development and present status.* Berkeley: University of California, Department of Political Science.

U.S. Congress. (1909). *Proceedings of the conference on the care of dependent children held at Washington, DC, January 1909.* 60th Cong., 2d session. S. Doc. 721.

Westat, Inc. (1987a). *Study of the national incidence and prevalence of child abuse and neglect: Report on data collection* (National Center on Child Abuse and Neglect Contract No. 105-85-1702). Rockville, MD: Author.

Westat, Inc. (1987b). *Study of the national incidence and prevalence of child abuse and neglect: Report on data processing and analysis* (National Center on Child Abuse and Neglect Contract No. 105-85-1702). Rockville, MD: Author.

Westat, Inc. (1991a). *National incidence and prevalence of child abuse and neglect, 1988. Revised report.* Washington, DC: National Center on Child Abuse and Neglect.

Westat, Inc. (1991b). *Supplementary analyses of data on the national incidence of child abuse and neglect.* Rockville, MD: Author.

Whipple, E. E., & Webster-Stratton, C. (1991). The role of parental stress in physically abusive families. *Child Abuse and Neglect, 15,* 279–291.

**Susan J. Wells, MSW, PhD,** is program director for Child Welfare, Research Triangle Institute, P.O. Box 12194, Research Triangle Park, NC 27709-2194.

**For further information see**

Adolescence Overview; Alcohol Abuse; Child Abuse and Neglect: Direct Practice; Child Foster Care; Child Labor; Child Sexual Abuse Overview; Child Welfare Overview; Childhood; Children: Direct Practice; Children's Rights; Criminal Behavior Overview; Crisis Intervention: Research Needs; Domestic Violence; Drug Abuse; Families Overview; Family Therapy; Legal Issues: Low-Income and Dependent People; Poverty; Runaways and Homeless Youths; School-Linked Services; Substance Abuse: Direct Practice; Victim Services and Victim/Witness Assistance Programs.

**Key Words**

| | |
|---|---|
| child abuse | child protection |
| child neglect | sex abuse |

# Child Abuse and Neglect: Direct Practice

**Sheryl Brissett-Chapman**

Since 1980 reports of alleged child abuse and neglect have more than doubled nationally. When one compares the 1982 data collected by the American Association for Protecting Children of the American Humane Association to data from other national studies, such as those of the National Committee for the Prevention of Child Abuse and the Child Welfare League of America, the escalating increase in concern for vulnerable children is dramatic (Child Welfare League of America, 1986; National Center on Child Abuse & Neglect, 1993; Russell & Trainor, 1984). In 1991, state child protective service agencies received and referred for investigation an estimated 1.8 million reports, involving 2.7 million children (National Center on Child Abuse and Neglect, 1993) compared to 929,000 reports in 1982 (Russell & Trainor, 1984). Reforms in child welfare services, passed as part of the Omnibus Budget Reconciliation Act of 1993, were the result of increasing perceptions that the well-being of more and more American children is threatened by abuse and neglect and family instability.

As if these data were not provocative enough, the mass media now routinely and daily expose the public to various incidents and forms of childhood victimization and exploitation, ranging from physical abuse and neglect to sexual misuse and assault to insidious acts of emotional maltreatment, including parents' abduction of children, custody feuds, and adults' failure to provide appropriate supervision, care, and affection—all of which are requisites for healthy child development. All too often, the most visible consequences of child abuse and neglect are the psychological and emotional impairment or death of children or destabilizing family crises when children are removed by authorities to ensure their safety and protection.

The sheer number of reported cases poses a new challenge to human service systems that are generally ill equipped to tackle all the aspects of intervention in the lives of high-risk families. Most child welfare funds are earmarked for investigations of potential out-of-home placements of children; little is available for families who are in crisis and need services to prevent or reduce the likelihood of their abusing or neglecting their children (Child Welfare League of America, 1986; Metropolitan Washington Council of Governments, 1993).

## History

It is important to note that despite the recent societal preoccupation with and awareness of child maltreatment, the phenomenon is not new. Indeed, adults have attempted to define the concept of child maltreatment, along with the "rights" of children, for many centuries.

### Attitudes toward Children

In earlier times, children were viewed as property; their parents could decide how to care for them and whether they lived or died (Tower, 1989). Ancient societies, such as the German tribes and some Native American tribes, submerged newborns in frigid water to determine their "fitness" (Kempe & Helfer, 1986). Many historical accounts (Breiner, 1990; Giovannoni & Becerra, 1979; Radbill, 1980, Williams, 1980) have associated the prevalence of child maltreatment with societal attitudes that reinforced a hierarchy of adult privileges and rights; in such a hierarchy, the rights of children, particularly those from poor families, were at the bottom.

In the United States, as elsewhere, the corporal punishment of children, legally sanctioned and freely used by adults, both at home and at school, was viewed as a means of shaping children into "moral, God-fearing, respectful human beings" (Tower, 1989, p. 3). An 1854 Massachusetts law, for example, stated that children over age 16 who "shall curse or smite their natural father or mother, . . . shall be put to death" unless the parents were neglectful or cruel to the point of maiming the children (quoted in Bremner, 1970, p. 68).

During the Industrial Revolution, child labor became an increasing problem in this country (Kempe & Helfer, 1980). Children continued to be viewed as property, and parents could treat them as they wished, beating, neglecting, or sending them to work prematurely.

### Efforts to Help Children

By the late 1800s, Jane Addams and her staff at Hull House, a settlement house in the slums of Chicago, had discovered the inhumane working conditions for children who worked in the mills 14 hours a day, many of whom were severely injured or died because of their "carelessness" in handling dangerous equipment (Addams, 1910). Despite Addams's advocacy, it took decades before child labor laws were passed and rigorously enforced.

***Early private agencies.*** Efforts to assist abused and neglected children date back to the 17th century, but were essentially based on the English Poor Law and were directed at poor families. The first Society for the Prevention of Cruelty to Children was established in 1874 as the result of the well-publicized case of Mary Ellen Wilson, a young child who was frequently beaten and inadequately clothed by her caretaker. The child's cries were heard by neighbors, one of whom sought the help of Henry Bergh, founder of the American Society for the Prevention of Cruelty to Animals. The efforts of Bergh and others led to Mary Ellen's protection and to the protection of many other such unfortunate children. Many private societies were formed to provide intervention when children were denied their fundamental rights to adequate care, safety, and protection. Beginning in 1875, states began to authorize social welfare agencies to remove children from parents who could not fulfill the children's basic needs.

***Early government efforts.*** The first White House Conference on Children in 1909 focused on dependent children. In 1912, the U.S. Children's Bureau was created to "investigate and report on all matters relating to the welfare of children and child life among all classes of our people" (Nelson, 1984). In 1935, the Social Security Act placed child protective services within the mandates of public social service agencies. Yet concern for abused and neglected children was relatively mild until the medical profession, represented by Henry Kempe and his colleagues, identified and validated the battered child syndrome in 1962 (Child Welfare League of America, 1989, p. 1).

***Battered child syndrome.*** On the basis of earlier work by Caffey (1946) and others, Kempe, Silverman, Steele, Droegemueller, and Silver (1962) capitalized on the development of radiology as a diagnostic tool to discern the possible basis for what had previously been viewed as "unexplained" fractures or subdural hematomas in children. The concept of inflicted trauma (Caffey, 1946; Silverman, 1953; Woolley & Evans, 1955) became the foundation for understanding and detecting physical abuse in young children. This seminal pediatric discovery generated considerable interest and involvement by many professionals in child-serving disciplines and advocacy groups. With this stimulus came a heightened awareness of the society's inherent responsibility for protecting all its children.

***Children's rights.*** The 1970s witnessed a surge in the debate over children's "rights" or entitlements. These rights tend to be defined by what families, the fundamental social unit responsible for the care and nurture of children, do or not do for their offspring. Goldstein, Freud, and Solnit (1973) identified the basic needs that the family should provide:

> The child's body needs to be tended, nourished and protected. His intellect needs to be stimulated and alerted to the happenings in his environment. He needs help in understanding and organizing his sensations and perceptions. He needs assistance from adults in curbing and modifying his primitive drives (sex and aggression). He needs patterns for identification by the parents, to build up a functioning moral conscience. As much as anything else, he needs to be accepted, valued, and wanted as a member of the family unit consisting of adults as well as other children. (pp. 13–14)

But sheer identification of children's needs does not guarantee that the needs will be provided or considered entitlements. According to the United Nations Declaration of the Rights of the Child (United Nations, 1960), all children are entitled to

1. the enjoyment of the rights mentioned, without any exception, regardless of race, color, sex, religion, or nationality;
2. special protection, opportunities, and facilities to enable them to develop in a healthy and normal manner, in freedom and dignity;
3. a name and a nationality;
4. social security, including adequate nutrition, housing, recreation, and medical services;
5. special treatment, education, and care if handicapped;
6. love and understanding and an atmosphere of affection and security, in the care and under the responsibility of their parents whenever possible;
7. free education and recreation and equal opportunity to develop their individual abilities;
8. prompt protection and relief in times of disaster;
9. protection against all forms of neglect, cruelty, and exploitation;
10. protection from any form of racial, religious or other discrimination, and an upbringing in a spirit of peace and universal brotherhood.

***Legislation.*** Against this backdrop of increasing awareness of children's "rights" to safety and protection, states began to enact legislation that required professionals to report suspicions of child abuse and neglect to local authorities. In addition, several federal laws were subsequently passed to address this increasingly visible and complex problem from a national perspective.

In 1974, the Child Abuse Prevention and Treatment Act (P.L. 93-247) established the National Center on Child Abuse and Neglect to ensure the effective coordination of policies and the development of model programs and services. Established in response to a national groundswell of concern about child abuse, the national center is the primary federal agency responsible for assisting states and communities with the prevention, identification, and treatment of child abuse and neglect through the allocation of funds appropriated by Congress. To receive funds, a state must designate an agency that is responsible for investigating abuse and neglect; establish a reporting system; enact laws that protect children under age 18 from mental injury, physical injury, and sexual abuse; and provide *guardians ad litum* to represent the children's interest in court cases.

The Indian Child Welfare Act of 1978 (P.L. 95-608) addressed the special circumstances of Native American children, who were separated from their families and placed in government schools and other non-Native American settings, sometimes permanently. It provides a better balance between the protection of these children and the need to stabilize and sustain tribes and families.

The Adoption Assistance and Child Welfare Act of 1980 (P.L. 96-272), in response to exposés of "foster care drift" (the numerous children who remain in foster care because of the lack of adequate case planning), focused on the prevention of the removal of children from their families and their placement in out-of-home care, timely reunification of children with their families after they have been removed because of abuse or neglect, and adoption as a permanent plan if the families are not rehabilitated in a reasonable time. The most sweeping legislation since the passage of the Social Security Act of 1935, this act instituted the concept of "reasonable efforts" to keep families together, permanency planning services, and out-of-home placements in the least restrictive setting.

The Omnibus Budget Reconciliation Act of 1993 (Family Preservation and Support Services, P.L. 103-66) complemented the earlier federal legislation by targeting resources for early intervention with families and increasing supports for foster care and adoptive placements. The law provides funding for a comprehensive array of services, as well as for evaluation, resource, training and technical assistance, increasing the effectiveness of state courts, and the development of statewide automated data systems. In combination, these federal laws provide the basis for a community program for child protection. Features of the new legislation included additional funding for family support and, through Title XX social services block grants, free vaccinations for all children who are enrolled in Medicaid, are in health projects for homeless families, or are members of rural or migrant families. The legislation also revamped the Food Stamp Program and expanded the Earned Income Tax Credit to guarantee working parents financial relief (Child Welfare League of America, 1993).

Today, the public is considerably more aware of the problems of child abuse and neglect from reports in the mass media, including newspaper accounts and televised documentaries; the proliferation of local advocacy groups that provide information about prevention and legal reform; and the public disclosures of adult survivors of child abuse and neglect, including those of celebrities. Even adults who alleged that they were victims of child abuse reporting laws have organized nationally and contributed to the prominence of the issues.

Many educators, medical and mental health practitioners, child care workers and counselors, and law enforcement personnel, who are now mandated to report suspected cases of abuse and neglect, participate in numerous specialty conferences and training programs, are involved in multidisciplinary activities, and have access to the rapidly growing literature in the field. Yet the child welfare system and its social workers continue to be the driving force in ensuring that children are protected in the community. With a pressing need to establish effective strategies and programs, the implications for the training, recruitment, and retention of social workers in these highly stressed human services systems are enormous and complex.

## Definitions

Although federal legislation sets forth specific core definitions of child abuse and neglect for states to follow as recipients of federal funding, each state interprets the definitions differently. To compound the problem, each professional discipline has promulgated its own definitions, often, with limited consideration of the federal or state parameters. As a result, there is no universal operational definition of child abuse and neglect. The multiple and overlapping definitions challenge society's ability to understand the prevalence of and trends in child abuse and neglect and to forge an effective national response.

### Neglect

Although child neglect is the most common form of substantiated child maltreatment, representing 44 percent of the cases (National Center on Child Abuse and Neglect, 1993), definitions of neglect have been inconsistent. According to Dubowitz, Black, Starr, and Zuravin (1993) and Zuravin (1991), neglect is a complex phenomenon that must be understood within a continuum ranging from the best possible to grossly inadequate care of children, with less emphasis on parental culpability and more on a shared responsibility that includes parents, families, community, and society. Zuravin (1991) suggested that a definition of neglect, within an ecological context, focuses on what needs of children are not met, rather than the inappropriate intentions or harmful behavior of the parents. Problems with current definitions are related to the following dimensions: consequences of the behavior for the child; subtypes of maltreatment; the identity, intent, and culpability of the perpetrator; the frequency of the behavior; and the age of the child (Zuravin, 1991).

***Types of neglect.*** Kadushin (1988) pointed out that neglect is often considered a low priority in the child protection system. He discussed various types of neglect, such as the deprivation of necessities, inadequate supervision, medical neglect, educational neglect, emotional neglect, failure to protect from injurious circumstances, and community and institutional neglect. Kadushin suggested that the following clusters of variables must be studied to formulate a response to the problem: personality and character factors, family system variables, and social and economic conditions.

***Framework for definition.*** Many writers have argued that neglect is a highly subjective concept and it is framed primarily by the prevailing cultural, economic, political, social, and moral values of the community. Hence, professionals in the field, such as social workers in direct services, health care professionals, and judges and others in the criminal justice system, who have vastly different professional and personal perspectives and experiences, often disagree. Polansky, Hally, and Polansky (1975) attempted to bridge these differences in their definition of neglect:

> Child neglect may be defined as a condition in which a caretaker responsible for the child either deliberately

> or by extraordinary inattentiveness permits the child to experience . . . suffering and/or fails to provide . . . the ingredients generally deemed essential for developing a person's physical, intellectual, and emotional capacities. (p. 5)

***Challenges to social work.*** A number of questions remain: How does the impact of material wealth or deprivation affect the observer? What is the appropriate level of responsibility for the larger community? Whose responsibility is it to confront poverty, social ignorance, and isolation? When is neglect, especially chronic neglect, a response to severe stress, such as poverty, or the result of a parent with an infantile personality who cannot perform his or her parental role? (see Katz, 1971; Nelson, Saunders, & Landsman 1990). What are the implications for prevention and intervention services, given the high levels of clinical depression found in these parents? (see Culp, Culp, Soulis, & Letts, 1989; Zuravin, 1988). It is precisely these questions that challenge contemporary social work practice and provide good reasons to review the current social policy response to the structural, long-standing poverty and pervasive dependence of poor families on debilitating government "benefits" that do not foster competence and self-esteem.

**Physical Abuse**

There is also no agreement on the definition of physical abuse. Unlike neglect, with its focus on acts of omission by caregivers, physical abuse targets acts of aggression against the child, with resultant or potential physical injuries. Yet many local and state jurisdictions document and substantiate physical abuse differentially; some validate a report only when there is demonstrable harm, whereas others validate it when there is a perceived endangerment (when the child is at risk of harm) as well. For example, the study by the National Center on Child Abuse and Neglect (1988, p. 7-1) indicated that in 1986, 1,025,900 children (or 16.3 per 1,000) met the stringent requirement of having experienced demonstrable harm as the result of abuse or neglect. The number increased considerably to 1,584,700 (or 25.2 children per 1,000) when endangered children (who were at risk of harm) were included. The study further noted that

> children who had experienced demonstrable harm . . . were approximately equally divided into those who had been abused and those who had been neglected, with abused children slightly outnumbering those who were neglected. When endangered children were added, . . . neglected children outnumbered abused children by a ratio of 3:2. (p. 7-4)

***Recognition and public awareness.*** The aim of the 1988 study, commonly called the second National Incidence Study (NIS-2), was to assess the incidence of child maltreatment and to determine how the severity, frequency, and character of child maltreatment has changed since NIS-1, which was completed in 1980. NIS-2 addressed five levels of official recognition or public awareness of abuse and neglect:

1. children reported to official child protective services systems
2. children known to other investigatory agencies (the police, courts, and public health departments)
3. children known to schools, hospitals, and day care centers, but who have not been reported for a variety of reasons, including distrust or definitional ambiguities
4. children known to a neighbor, family member, or an involved person (the child or the perpetrator)
5. children who do not realize that they are being maltreated.

Within this matrix of children, NIS-2 concluded that the most frequent type of abuse was physical, followed by emotional and sexual abuse, with incidence rates of 5.7, 3.4, and 2.5 children per 1,000, respectively.

***Identification and documentation.*** In the case of physical abuse, the field is still struggling with issues of accurate identification and documentation. Despite improved medical technology and clinical standards, the ability of medical professionals consistently to detect physical abuse in pediatric settings is hampered by subjective bias, lack of experience, and inadequate training. Wissow and Wilson (1992), for example, found that the ability of physicians to differentiate between intentional and unintentional injury in children by using epidemiological data varied according to their training. Thus, epidemiological data did not consistently influence the physicians' decisions and their conclusions.

The inability to agree on suspected cases of physical abuse is also seen among law enforcement personnel, social workers, and lawyers, who are driven by different ideologies and attitudes toward physical aggression against children. It is no wonder, therefore, that interdisciplinary and interagency collaboration in these cases still remain more of an ideal than a reality in most communities.

Parton (1985) noted that the purposes and ideologies of the legal (penal), scientific (medical), and humanistic (social welfare) disciplines often collide with regard to services to children who are abused. Legal professionals seek punishment of guilt (believing that individuals have free will and children have rights that demand that perpetrators must be held accountable for their actions). Medical professionals view behavior as "determined" and focus on treating dysfunction in their patients. Most social welfare professionals seek to rehabilitate children and their families and to ensure the emotional and physical safety of the children, whereas radical professionals advocate equality and redistribution of concrete resources such as quality services or economic means and accessibility to care on behalf of their clients.

The three disciplines' conceptions of parents also differ. In the penal perspective, parents are viewed as "responsible" for the abuse or neglect; in the medical model, they are considered "irresponsible or not responsible"; and in the social welfare framework, they are thought of as "psychologically, emotionally, and socially inadequate, or socially victimized" (Parton, 1985). The diversity of viewpoints and the complexity entailed in identifying physical abuse in children necessitate less fragmented systems that can facilitate optimal and regular cross-disciplinary investigations and collaboration.

The pediatric community continues to seek more consistent ways to understand and intervene in cases of child physical abuse through the establishment of refined medical evaluations and more reliable, valid diagnostic criteria. Social workers and law enforcement and court personnel often rely on expert medical opinion to guide case management and legal decisions. In the late 1980s and early 1990s, studies attempted to increase clinical competence in this area by focusing on the following:

- expert assessment of suspicious burns, fractures, the "shaken baby syndrome," ocular complications, and other types of physical injuries (Alexander, Sato, Smith, & Bennett, 1990; American Academy of Pediatrics, 1991; Asser, 1992; Brenner, Fischer, & Mann-Gray, 1989; Dalton et al., 1990; Frechette & Rimsza, 1992; Gahagan & Rimsza, 1991; Kelley, 1988; Kessler & Hyden, 1991; Myers & Carter, 1988; Prescott, 1990; Schmitt, 1988; Smith, 1988; Thomas, Rosenfeld, Leventhal, & Markowitz, 1991; Wissow, 1990; Wolff, 1990)
- the occurrence, severity, and frequency of physical abuse during pregnancy (McFarlane, Parker, Soeken, & Bullock, 1992)
- the disclosure of physical abuse among delinquents (Stein & Lewis, 1992)
- the identification and treatment of mental health sequelae as a result of physical abuse (Brown & Anderson, 1991; Cavailoa & Schiff, 1988; Claussen & Crittenden, 1991; Frude, 1989; Herzberger & Tennen, 1988; Kolko, Moser, & Weldy, 1988; Rencken, 1989; Shirk, 1988; Swett, Cohen, Surrey, Compaine, & Chavez, 1991; Walker, Bonner, & Kaufman, 1988).

The definition of intentionality is problematic and is used primarily to separate unintentional injuries from those caused directly by caregivers or that are allowed to occur because of parents' inadequate care. Even when physical abuse results in a child's death, it is difficult to conclude with certainty that the violent act was premeditated or deliberate (Kanda, Orr, Brissett-Chapman, & Lawson, 1993).

Despite these definitional problems, gains have been made in clinical delineations of such injuries as bites; bruises; contact, splatter, and immersion burns; alopecia; skull and extremity fractures; eye, head, and abdominal traumas; and trauma to genitalia. In addition, laboratory and radiographic studies are becoming increasingly sophisticated in providing critical information on which to build a suspicion of physical abuse (Kanda et al., 1993).

## Incidence

The National Center on Child Abuse and Neglect established a national data collection and analysis program and disseminates information to help the states respond to child abuse and neglect. From August to October 1992, the center conducted an exercise of collecting nationwide information on child maltreatment by obtaining data from state child protective agencies. The National Child Abuse and Neglect Data System produced a critical national profile of child abuse and neglect as of 1991 (National Center on Child Abuse and Neglect, 1993). The following sections summarize the profile's findings regarding the increase in reports, the sources and substantiation of reports, and the characteristics of victims.

### Increase in Reports

The number of children reported to state child protective agencies in 1991 increased 2.4 percent from 1990. In 1991, 1.8 million reports of alleged child abuse and neglect were made, involving approximately 2.7 million children. Such reports had more than doubled since 1980.

There is considerable discussion of the basis for the increase in reports of child abuse and neglect since 1980. Some argue that there has been an actual increase in cases, whereas others contend that the growth in the number of reports is the result of the greater ability and willingness of professionals to recognize cases, particularly of physical and sexual abuse. The 1988 NIS-2 report (National Center on Child Abuse and Neglect, 1988), for example, concluded that the second explanation seems likely, because more of the reports are of moderate, less obvious injuries or impairments that may indicate the improved ability to recognize abuse. Mandated reporting and changing professional standards may also be strong factors.

Others contend that the social stressors and difficulties that many families face have actually enhanced the risk of child abuse and neglect and, therefore, that the number of cases is actually increasing. Still others state that poor and ethnic minority children and their families are disproportionately reported, labeled, and routinely mandated into the child welfare system by professionals who are socially and culturally distant from the actual family contexts.

**Sources of Reports and Substantiation Rates**
Educators were the source of 15.6 percent of the reports received by 44 states and the most frequent source in 20 states. Overall, 52 percent of the reports were made by professionals, including social services professionals (12.4 percent) and law enforcement and justice-system personnel (11.5 percent). Anonymous persons made 10.9 percent of the reports, and friends and family members made 28.8 percent.

Forty-nine states provided information on the dispositions of approximately 1.5 million investigations. Because only 41 percent of the cases were substantiated, the majority (59 percent) either were not substantiated or some other disposition was made.

The NIS-2 report (National Center on Child Abuse and Neglect, 1988) generated another interesting observation. Although it confirmed that the number of suspected cases of child maltreatment reported to state child protective services was increasing, it also suggested that many professionals who recognized child maltreatment were *not* reporting it and that many cases that were reported were not substantiated after investigation.

The implications of these findings are numerous. What is the basis for both reporting and screening cases for child protective services? How can universal and culturally competent training be provided to establish a core set of competencies in the area of child abuse and neglect? How do issues of confidentiality and specialization prevent effective multidisciplinary intervention? Have the intake criteria for child protective services narrowed at the very time that professionals, such as teachers, who are exposed to a considerable number of children, have begun to address the problem? (See National Association of Children's Hospitals, 1992, on the increasing national interest in the welfare of children.

**Characteristics of Victims**
Of the substantiated reports from 45 states noted in the 1991 profile, the majority (44 percent) were cases of neglect. The remainder were distributed as follows: physical abuse, 24 percent; sexual abuse, 15 percent; and other forms of child maltreatment, 17 percent. It is important to note that these categories are not exclusive, because some states assign a victim to more than one category if he or she experienced more than one form of maltreatment.

The median age of victims was seven, and the highest percentage of cases for any age, 7.6 percent, was for children under one year. Approximately 53 percent of the victims were female and 46 percent were male.

In the 42 states that reported the racial and ethnic backgrounds of the victims, 55 percent of the children were white, 26 percent were African American, and 9 percent were Hispanic. However, because several states with major Hispanic populations did not specify this group, the number of cases of Hispanic children was probably underestimated.

Forty-five states reported child deaths; their reports indicated that 1,081 children who were known to child protective services died from abuse and neglect. It is assumed that many states may have underreported these cases because a more precise number would require analyses of coroners' reports and studies by child death review teams.

As a result of its studies, the National Center on Child Abuse and Neglect (1993) proposed the following:

- an examination of the impact of educational neglect on the total incidence of child maltreatment and whether there is a correlation between educational neglect and other forms of maltreatment
- an analysis of perpetrators, to develop more precise descriptive predictors of perpetrators
- an analysis of reporting practices, to determine how various groups of mandated reporters are carrying out this responsibility

- clarification of the states' tracking of child placements that result from substantiated/indicated reports
- clarification of the variations in the states' provision of services to child victims and their families, since only 33 percent of families who are investigated receive additional services.

## Contemporary Social Challenges

Despite the progress in recognizing and reporting cases of child neglect and abuse, society faces many challenges. For example, the National Clearinghouse on Child Abuse and Neglect Information (1994) reported the following:

1. The link between substance abuse and child abuse has become stronger; parental substance abuse is highly correlated with child maltreatment and death. Nearly 10 million children under the age of 18 are affected by substance abuse either prenatally through drug exposure or environmentally because the family's ability to nurture and protect the child is impaired.
2. Abused and neglected children frequently experience decreased intellectual functioning, as well as increased disabilities, depression, and drug use.
3. Other effects of child abuse may be long-term and pervasive, impeding the children's mental, physical, and social development. Suicide, violence, and delinquency, as well as other forms of criminality, are frequently related to histories of child abuse.
4. Although child abuse occurs in all racial, ethnic, cultural, and socioeconomic groups, physical abuse and neglect are more likely to occur in poor families. Thus, poor minority communities are disproportionately subjected to interventions by child protective service agencies.

In addition to the obvious and insidious long-term effects of child abuse and neglect and the connection to parents' substance abuse and poverty, other issues hamper society's ability to respond effectively to the epidemic. First, the spiraling number of cases has created a gap between the needs of child victims and their families and the resources to deal with them. In community after community, professionals struggle with unmanagable caseloads and limited treatment services. Second, the widespread lack of effective prevention activities, particularly culturally specific strategies, undermines any ability to curb the escalating incidents of child abuse and neglect.

Other issues include (1) the need for universal and interdisciplinary training of professionals who serve children and families; (2) rigid bureaucratic barriers to coordinated systems intervention; (3) laws on confidentiality that prohibit the necessary professional exchange of information; (4) the due-process rights of adults versus the need to protect children; (5) inadequate incentives for professionals to specialize in the field; (6) nonexistent or limited public, private, and citizen partnerships; (7) the increased identification of children's deaths; and (8) the lack of adequate longitudinal studies. Despite the challenge of these issues, there is optimism that the National Child Abuse and Neglect Data System will be expanded and will eventually be able to document reports of child abuse nationwide. Increasingly, longitudinal studies are focusing on the development of abusive and neglectful parenting practices, and national organizations are taking more responsibility for documenting their efforts to expand preventive services (Daro, 1992; Egeland, 1991).

## Psychosocial Intervention

According to nationally recognized standards of social work practice in the field of child protection (Child Welfare League of America, CWLA, 1989), children need protection from the following forms of maltreatment in addition to physical abuse and neglect: sexual abuse (including forced or coerced sexual contact of any kind by adults with children, exploitation through persistent sexual stimulation, child prostitution, sex rings, or pornography) and emotional maltreatment (such parental behavior as rejecting, terrorizing, berating, ignoring, or isolating a child, which causes or is likely to cause serious impairment to the child's physical, social, mental, or emotional capacities). According to the CWLA's standards,

> a child protective service should be provided to those children whose parents, or other family members, are unwilling or unable to provide the protection children require, and whose condition or situation demonstrates observable evidence of the likelihood or actuality of injurious effects of this failure to meet at least the children's basic minimum needs. (p. 7)

To be effective in a child's behalf, the professional social worker must understand the need for competent psychosocial intervention for both the child and his or her family in a case of suspected child abuse. This intervention is best provided by a trained professional who has special competencies and experience in the subspecialty of child maltreatment.

During the initial evaluation, the social worker should be prepared to (1) interview and observe the child and family for indicators of mental health or clinical problems that suggest child

TABLE 1
**Common Indicators of Sexual, Physical, and Emotional Abuse**

**Sexually Related Behavior**
Sexual victimization of younger children
Overt sexual acting out toward adults
Excessive masturbation
Sex play with others
Knowledge of details of adult sexual activity inappropriate for age or developmental level
Hinting about sexual activity
Promiscuity

**Violence in Behavior**
Combination of violence and sexuality in artwork, written schoolwork, language, or play
Violence against younger children
Fire-setting

**Aberrant Behavior**
Acting-out behavior
Overcompliant behavior
Pseudomature behavior
Repulsion or extreme fear when touched by an adult
Fear of being alone with adults
Excessive bathing
Fear of bathrooms and showers
Sleep disturbances
Encopresis, enuresis
Regressive behavior
Clinical depression
Dissociative disorders
Self-mutilation

**Other Indicators and Associated Factors**
Suicidal ideation or attempts
Psychosomatic complaints
Drug and alcohol abuse
Poor peer relationships
Change in school performance
Problems concentrating in school
Refusal to dress for gym at school
Avoidance of physical or recreational activities
Running away
Delinquency
Developmental delay
Chronic illness
Eating problems

**Parental Behaviors Associated with Risk**
Inappropriate expectations for child, including toilet training
Psychiatric treatment
Substance abuse
Domestic violence

SOURCE: Kanda, M. B., Orr, L. A., Brissett-Chapman, S., & Lawson, T. S. (1993). Intentional injury: Abuse. In M. R. Eichelberger (Ed.), *Pediatric trauma: Prevention, acute care, rehabilitation* (p. 565). St. Louis: C. V. Mosby. Reprinted with permission.

maltreatment (see Table 1); (2) ascertain, perhaps in consultation with a physician or other medical professional, the need to report the situation either to a child protective service agency or to a law enforcement authority; and (3) respond to the emotional needs of the child and the family.

**Assessment of Risks**

The assessment of suspected cases of child abuse has traditionally been an informal process combining broad-based policy and practice guidelines, but based essentially on the expertise of individual workers. Given that personal bias and the quality and presumed relevance of information may lead to faulty decision making, discussions in the field have centered on the need to develop and test risk-assessment models that can be universally applied to improve case monitoring and supervision, the establishment of priorities among cases, and the selection of intervention approaches. It is hoped that such structured risk-assessment models will increase the consistency, timeliness, appropriateness, and quality of decisions and the documentation of cases presented in court, as well as workers' accountability for the actions they take (Cicchinelli, 1991).

***Indicators of risk.*** Although the indicators of risk listed in Table 1 have been well documented as "red flags" for professional concern, no theory of the etiology of abuse and neglect, manifestations of maltreatment, and effective services for either victims or abusers has been universally accepted (Friedrich & Wheeler, 1982; Keller & Erne, 1983; Paluszny, Cullen, Funk, Liu, & Goodhand, 1989) nor empirically demonstrated. Nevertheless, a review of the literature identified the following most frequently agreed-on empirical factors (Herring, 1992):

1. Child previously reported: There have been previous founded or unfounded reports of abuse or neglect of the victim or his or her siblings in the family system.
2. Parent abused as a child: The parent remembers having been abused as a child, or this fact is documented in the parent's history.
3. Age of the parent: The parent was under age 18 at the time of the reported child's or the first child's birth.
4. Age of the child: There are differences in the occurrence and type of abuse of infants, young children, or adolescents.
5. Family composition: This factor generally refers to a single parent raising children alone, including a never-married, separated, or divorced parent and children living in an extended family household.
6. Domestic violence in the home: In a home where violence frequently occurs, a child may be injured accidentally or purposely; emotional abuse is a factor.
7. Separation of a parent or child for a long period: The child may have been raised by a grandmother or other family member or have been in foster care.
8. Parent or caretaker's abuse of substances: The parent or other caretaker may be abusing

drugs or alcohol to the extent that parenting is affected or distributing drugs, both of which affect the child's safety and healthy development.

9. Physical, mental, or emotional impairment of the child: The child has been diagnosed or observed to be mentally retarded, cognitively limited, physically or emotionally handicapped, or chronically ill.
10. Physical, mental, or emotional impairment of the parent or other caretaker: The parent or other caretaker has been diagnosed and treated for mental illness or has a physical or emotional handicap or a chronic physical or mental illness.
11. Low socioeconomic status: The family is dependent on or eligible for public assistance. (Herring, 1992)

In addition to these factors and the indicators noted in Table 1, research has generally found that the probability of abuse increases because of parent and child aggression, harsh disciplinary practices, parental stress and anger, and unrealistic parental expectations (such as for toilet training). In an abusive family, disciplinary issues escalate to the point at which the child is physically abused. Frude (1989) described the progression of events in child abuse incidents as going from situational triggers to parental appraisal to parental anger to parents' reduced inhibitions to parents' habituation to various forms of aggression.

Overall, the literature describes physically abusive parents as needy, impulsive, rigid, and authoritarian; having unrealistic expectations; being unable to delay gratification; and having been exposed to inadequate parental models or supports. In addition, neglectful parents have been described as "infantile personalities" who are burdened with unmet childhood needs (Polansky, Borgman, & DeSaix, 1972) and lack the knowledge, judgment, and motivation to care for their children adequately (Cantwell, 1980).

### Treatment and Services

The social worker, whether in a child protective services agency or in a hospital, must draw on a multidisciplinary, multiagency team to ensure that the identification of cases, planning, treatment, and follow-up are effective. Armed with expert training in social systems theory, the social worker often acts as the liaison among legal, medical, and other community representatives to work in the best interests of the child, the child's family, and the community.

***Initial interview.*** During the initial face-to-face interview with the family, the social worker tries to gain information to build an accurate history of the abusive event, to assess the child's mental health needs, and to make a preliminary determination of the appropriate treatment of both the child and the family members. To establish a basis for suspicion, the social worker should assess not only the status of the child, but the parent-child relationship.

In assessing the situation, the social worker may consider the following questions: Is the abuse condoned because it serves a reportedly higher principle (teaching obedience or teaching about sexuality from one who "loves the child")? Do the parents minimize or deny the incident or have a selective memory? Do they blame the child or shift the blame to others? Are the parents derogatory in attitude or inadequately attached to the child? Do they use verbal insults and put-downs in speaking to the child? What is the level of support provided by the parents, the extended family, and the community?

The social worker may use a structured risk-assessment instrument to help objectify the estimation of the child's safety or the family's ability to ensure the child's protection. The instrument may include the following questions: Are the parents supportive or overwhelmed? Do the adults in the child's life have a clear understanding of what constitutes abuse and of its implications for the child? Are the family members suffering from psychiatric problems or drug addiction? What resources—human and financial—are available for the family? What has been the family's experience with the authorities and with "helping" professionals?

Structured risk-assessment instruments typically focus on child characteristics, parent-related problems, and environmental circumstances. The most common contributing factor appears to be "parent-related" (in 75 percent to 80 percent of all cases involving an out-of-home placement) (Cicchinelli, 1991). A comparison of structural risk-assessment models reveals that most focus on assessing safety, guiding placement decision making, or both. They are often used to determine in-home services, perpetrator removal decisions and reunification decisions and for reasonable efforts documentation. The formats may be matrix, checklists, decision trees, anchored scales, open-ended questions, or weighted items. They may be used in emergencies and nonemergencies (Cicchinelli, 1991).

***Child protective services workers.*** In cases of child abuse and neglect, the primary goal is to protect the children by enabling parents to recognize and correct conditions that are harmful to their children and to fulfill their parenting roles; providing services that stabilize the family situation; and maintaining and supporting the family, when appropriate. With neglectful families, one goal may be to help them function on a day-to-day basis and to establish a coordinated service approach, that may counteract some of the isolation these families experience (Giovannoni, 1988). For abusive parents, the goals may be to help them learn appropriate, nonpunitive methods of discipline; acquire conflict-resolution skills; find more effective ways to interact with the environment; develop the ability to negotiate with social support systems; and gain better knowledge of the developmental needs of children. Family support centers, family preservation programs, in-home parent aides, respite care, Head Start parent-child centers, and family life education all support families with child-rearing duties and may be sources of referral. The challenge for social workers is to ensure the protection of the child with as little intrusion as possible (Child Welfare League of America, 1989).

After the initial services are provided, the social worker must determine whether the family conditions have been alleviated or whether the agency must initiate action, either with the parents' cooperation or through a petition to the court, to mandate additional appropriate services or substitute care for the child. The social worker should also attempt to identify and advocate for ways to overcome the conditions in the community that contribute to or fail to avert the neglect or abuse of children (Child Welfare League of America, 1989, p. 8).

***Social worker in a hospital setting.*** In a hospital setting, the social worker functions as part of a multidisciplinary team and is often exposed to cases of extrafamilial abuse, as well as of parental abuse and neglect. (Other members of the hospital-based team include physicians, nurses, radiologists, psychiatrists, psychologists, and attorneys.) The same procedures are followed for the initial interviews and risk assessments. With regard to intervention, the approach of the entire team, especially of the social worker, is to maintain a careful balance between providing nonjudgmental support and probing for additional relevant psychosocial information. Establishing positive rapport is crucial in this aspect of intervention and requires professional maturity, including the ability to monitor one's emotional responses (anger, repulsion, denial, disbelief, grief, and avoidance) to various forms of child maltreatment. The social worker must pace the intervention and actively assess the concerns and capacities of all who are involved. This wide-angle focus includes professional colleagues on the team, especially in cases of the brutal sexual abuse of young children or severe physical injuries resulting in permanent disfigurement or death.

In addition to assessing the parents' relationship with the child and the risks of current and future abuse, the social worker should determine how the suspicion or disclosure evolved. How are the child and family experiencing the crisis of disclosure? Sometimes families do not appear to be traumatized when, in fact, they are. It is important for the social worker to present a nonjudgmental, open approach to "hearing" the various concerns of various family members. Because the disclosure of suspected abuse or neglect precipitates a crisis for any family, the social worker needs to convey a sensitivity to the difficulties posed; universalize the stress caused to families in similar circumstances; and identify with the families the subsequent needs, issues, and relevant resources to assist the family in addressing concerns for the child.

In many cases, there is a need for additional mental health services for the family, as well as for the child. Typically, these families need assistance in building or rebuilding their coping mechanisms or need to integrate the child's victimization in such a way that the future vulnerability of the victim and his or her siblings is reduced. Mental health resources for these families include parenting education, psychotherapy, and supportive counseling. The social worker makes the appropriate referral of children and families to services, working in concert with the public child welfare system, which is legally responsible for the protection and care of vulnerable children.

## Future Social Policy Concerns

Numerous issues affect the future of all children in this country. First, in 1991, the surgeon general of the United States reported that accidental injuries are the leading cause of disabilities and death among children. Furthermore, the cost of childhood injuries in terms of emotions and money continues to rise. Underage drinking, homicides and assaults, and the use of firearms all are increasing. Indeed, childhood is challenged by avoidable traumas and insults.

Second, as was mentioned earlier, there is no consensus in the field on various aspects of abuse and neglect or caretaker activity that results in intentional injury or deprivation. In this regard, the

U.S. Children's Bureau and the National Center on Child Abuse and Neglect identified the following areas for which further research is needed: (1) the characteristics of those who abuse children fatally, to assist in decisions regarding child removal; (2) examination of the risk of removing children from families who are neglectful because they lack resources for child care; (3) the characteristics of victims who do not grow up to become abusers, to find a way to break the cycle of abuse; (4) ritualistic abuse, as well as multiple personality disorders in children; and (5) ways of disseminating the findings of research to social workers in the field (Stewart, 1990).

Third, from a national leadership perspective, the United States is one of the few democracies that has failed to sign the United Nations Declaration on the Rights of the Child (Child Welfare League of America, 1989). The declaration includes the following:

- Respect for the inalienable rights of children as members of the human community requires protection of their dignity as people.
- Children have a right to protection from all forms of physical or mental violence, injury or abuse, negligent treatment, maltreatment, or exploitation, including sexual abuse, while in the care of parents, legal guardians, or any other person who has the care of the child.
- Children have a right to grow up in a family environment, in an atmosphere of happiness, love, and understanding.
- Children have the right to be heard in any judicial and administrative proceedings affecting them, with ample opportunity for representation and procedures that comport with their sense of dignity.

Other systemic issues that must be addressed in the future include the need for integrated, interagency planning and service delivery approaches; the elimination of bureaucratic regulations and ineffective funding strategies that deter local communities from developing a continuum approach to the prevention and treatment of child abuse and neglect; and the implementation of new strategies to support the retention, development, and protection of social workers in the field, with special emphasis on multidisciplinary training, reduction of paperwork, higher pay, and flexible funds for assisting clients. Finally, consideration must be given to the impact of the family preservation movement on the design of current social services systems; the need to enhance and fund preventive efforts; the examination of institutional abuse and the development of standards that will ensure the protection of children in group and residential care; and the capacity to articulate culturally specific models of service delivery that accommodate and gain the support of indigenous community leaders.

## References


Addams, J. (1910). *Twenty years at Hull-House.* New York: Signet.

Adoption Assistance and Child Welfare Act of 1980, P.L. 96-272, 94 Stat. 500.

Alexander, R., Sato, Y., Smith, W., & Bennett, T. (1990). Incidence of impact trauma with cranial injuries ascribed to shaking. *American Journal of Diseases of Children, 144,* 724–726.

American Academy of Pediatrics. (1991). Diagnostic imaging of child abuse. *Pediatrics, 87,* 262–264.

Asser, S. (1992). Assessment of suspicious burn injuries. *APSAC Advisor, 5*(1), 6.

Breiner, S. J. (1990). *Slaughter of the innocents: Child abuse through the ages and today.* New York: Plenum Press.

Bremner, R. (Ed.). (1970). *Children and youth in America: A documentary history* (Vol. 1). Cambridge, MA: Harvard University Press.

Brenner, S. L., Fischer, H., & Mann-Gray, S. (1989). Race and the shaken baby syndrome: Experience at one hospital. *Journal of the National Medical Association, 81,* 183–184.

Brown, G. R., & Anderson, B. (1991). Psychiatric morbidity in adult inpatients with childhood histories of sexual and physical abuse. *American Journal of Psychiatry, 148,* 55–61.

Caffey, J. (1946). Multiple fractures in long bones of infants suffering from chronic subdural hematoma. *American Journal of Roentgenology, 56,* 163–173.

Cantwell, H. B. (1980). Child neglect. In C. H. Kempe & R. E. Helfer (Eds.), *The battered child* (pp. 183–197). Chicago: University of Chicago Press.

Cavaiola, A. A., & Schiff, M. (1988). Behavioral sequelae of physical and/or sexual abuse in adolescents. *Child Abuse and Neglect, 12,* 181–188.

Child Abuse Prevention and Treatment Act, P.L. 93-247, 88 Stat. 4.

Child Welfare League of America. (1986). *Too young to run: The status of child abuse in America.* Washington, DC: Author.

Child Welfare League of America. (1989). *Standards for services for abused and neglected children and their families.* Washington, DC: Author.

Child Welfare League of America (1993). *Children's Monitor, 6.*

Cicchinelli, L. F. (1991). *Symposium on "Risk" Assessment in Child Protective Services* (proceedings). Washington, DC: National Center for Child Abuse and Neglect.

Claussen, A. H., & Crittenden, P. M. (1991). Physical and psychological maltreatment: Relations among types of maltreatment. *Child Abuse and Neglect, 15* (1–2), 5–18.

Culp, R. E., Culp, A. M., Soulis, J., & Letts, D. (1989). Self-esteem and depression in abusive, neglecting, and nonmaltreating mothers. *Infant Mental Health Journal, 10,* 243–251.

Dalton, H. J., Slovis, T., Helfer, R. E., Comstock, J., et al. (1990). Undiagnosed abuse in children younger than 3 years with femoral fracture. *American Journal of Disease of Children, 144,* 875–878.

Daro, D. (1992). Building a national child welfare data base: Utilizing a variety of sources. *Protecting Children, 8*(3), 4–6, 24–25.

Dubowitz, H., Black, M., Starr, R. H., Jr., Zuravin, S. (1993). A conceptual definition of child abuse. *Criminal Justice and Behavior, 20*(1), 8–26.

Egeland, B. (1991). A longitudinal study of high-risk families: Issues and findings. In R. H., Starr, Jr., & D. A. Wolfe (Eds.), *The effects of child abuse and neglect: Issues and research* (pp. 33–56). New York: Guilford Press.

Frechette, A., & Rimsza, M. E. (1992). Stun gun injury: A new presentation of the battered child syndrome. *Pediatrics, 89,* 898–901.

Friedrich, W. N., & Wheeler, K. K. (1982). The abusing parent revisited: A decade of psychological research. *Journal of Nervous and Mental Disease, 170,* 577–587.

Frude, N. (1989). The physical abuse of children. In K. Howells & C. Hollin (Eds.), *Clinical approaches to violence* (pp. 155–181). New York: John Wiley & Sons.

Gahagan, S., & Rimsza, M. E. (1991). Child abuse or osteogenesis imperfecta: How can we tell? *Pediatrics, 88,* 987–992.

Giovannoni, J. M. (1988). *Overview of issues on child neglect* (proceedings from a symposium, November 10, 1985). Washington, DC: National Clearinghouse on Child Abuse and Neglect Information.

Giovannoni, J. M., & Becerra, R. M. (1979). *Defining child abuse.* New York: Free Press.

Goldstein, J., Freud, A., & Solnit, J. (1973). *Beyond the best interests of the child.* New York: Free Press.

Herring, R. (1992). Unpublished doctoral dissertation. Howard University, Washington, DC.

Herzberger, S. D., & Tennen, H. (1988). Applying the Label of Physical Abuse. In G. T. Hotaling, D. Finkelhor, J. T. Kirkpatrick, and M. A. Strauss (Eds.) (pp. 18–30). *Coping with Family Violence: Research and Policy Perspectives.* Newbury Park, CA: Sage Publications.

Indian Child Welfare Act of 1978, P.L. 95-608, 92 Stat. 3069.

Kadushin, A. (1988). Neglect in Families. In E. W. Nunnally, C. S. Chilman, and F. M. Cox (Eds.), *Mental illness, delinquency, and neglect* (pp. 147–166). Newbury Park, CA: Sage Publications.

Kanda, M. B., Orr, L. A., Brissett-Chapman, S., & Lawson, T. S. (1993). Intentional injury: Abuse. In M. R. Eichelberger (Ed.), *Pediatric trauma: Prevention, acute care, rehabilitation* (pp. 557–567). St. Louis: C.V. Mosby.

Katz, S. N. (1971). *When parents fail.* Boston: Beacon Press.

Keller, H. R., & Erne, D. (1983). Child abuse: Toward a comprehensive model. In A. F. Goldstein (Ed.), *Prevention and control of aggression* (pp. 1–36). New York: Pergamon Press.

Kelley, S. J. (1988). Physical abuse of children: Recognition and reporting. *Journal of Emergency Nursing, 14,* 82–90.

Kempe, C. H., & Helfer, R. (1980). *The battered child* (3rd ed.). Chicago: University of Chicago Press.

Kempe, C. H., Silverman, F. N., Steele, B. F., Droegemueller, W., & Silver, H. K. (1962). The battered child syndrome. *Journal of the American Medical Association, 18,* 17–24.

Kessler, D. B., & Hyden, P. (1991). Physical, sexual, and emotional abuse of children. *Clinical Symposia, 43*(1), 2–32.

Kolko, D. J., Moser, J. T., & Weldy, S. R. (1988). Behavioral-emotional indicators of sexual abuse in child psychiatric inpatients: A controlled comparison with physical abuse. *Child Abuse and Neglect, 12,* 529–541.

McFarlane, J., Parker, B., Soeken, K., & Bullock, L. (1992). Assessing for abuse during pregnancy: Severity and frequency of injuries and associated entry into prenatal care. *Journal of the American Medical Association, 267,* 3176–3178.

Metropolitan Washington Council of Governments. (1993). *Who waits in the shadows? A report on child abuse and neglect.* Washington, DC: Author.

Myers, J.E.B., & Carter, L. E. (1988). Proof of physical child abuse. *Missouri Law Review, 53,* 189–225.

National Association of Children's Hospitals and Related Institutions. (1992). *State of the child.* Alexandria, VA: Author.

National Center on Child Abuse and Neglect. (1988). *Study findings: Study of National Incidence and Prevalence of Child Abuse and Neglect* (DHHS Report No. 105-85-1702). Washington, DC: U.S. Department of Health and Human Services.

National Center on Child Abuse and Neglect. (1993). *National Child Abuse and Data System: Working paper 2—1991 summary data component.* Washington, DC: U.S. Government Printing Office.

National Clearinghouse on Child Abuse and Neglect Information. (1994). *Child abuse and neglect fact sheet.* Washington, DC: Author.

Nelson, B. (1984). *Making an issue of child abuse.* Chicago: University of Chicago Press.

Nelson, K., Saunders, E., & Landsman, M. J. (1990). *Chronic neglect in perspective: A study of chronically neglecting families in a large metropolitan county. Final report.* Oakdale: University of Iowa, National Resource Center on Family Based Services.

Omnibus Budget Reconciliation Act of 1993, P.L. 103-66, 107 Stat. 31.

Paluszny, M. J., Cullen, B. J., Funk, J., Liu, P. Y., & Goodhand, J. (1989). Child abuse disposition: Concurrences and differences between a hospital team, child protection agency and the court. *Child Psychiatry and Human Development, 20,* 25–38.

Parton, N. (1985). *The politics of child abuse.* London: Macmillan.

Polansky, N. A., Borgman, N. D., & DeSaix, C. (1972). *Roots of utility.* San Francisco: Jossey-Bass.

Polansky, N. F., Hally, C., & Polansky, N. A. (1975). *A profile of neglect: A survey of the state of knowledge of child neglect.* Washington, DC: Community Services Administration, U.S. Department of Health, Education, & Welfare.

Prescott, P. R. (1990). Hair dryer burns in children. *Pediatrics, 86,* 692–697.

Radbill, S. X. (1980). Children in a world of violence. In C. H. Kempe & R. E. Helfer (Eds.), *The battered child* (3rd ed., pp. 3–20). Chicago: University of Chicago Press.

Rencken, R. H. (1989). Bodily assault: Physical and sexual abuse. In D. Capuzzi & D. Gross (Eds.), *Youth at risk: A resource for counselors, teachers and parents* (pp. 71–95). Alexandria, VA: American Association for Counseling and Development.

Russell, A. B., & Trainor, C. M. (1984). *Trends in child abuse and neglect: A national perspective.* Denver: American Humane Association.

Schmitt, B. D. (1988). Physical abuse: The medical evaluation. In D. C. Bross, R. Krugman, M. R. Lenherr, D. A. Rosenberg, & B. D. Schmitt (Eds.). *The new child protection team handbook* (pp. 49–65). New York: Garland.

Shirk, S. R. (1988). The interpersonal legacy of physical abuse of children. In M. B. Straus (Ed.), *Abuse and victimization across the life span* (pp. 57–81). Baltimore: Johns Hopkins University Press.

Silverman, F. (1953). The roentgen manifestations of unrecognized skeletal trauma in infants. *American Journal of Roentgenology, 69,* 413–426.

Smith, S. K. (1988). Child abuse and neglect: A diagnostic guide for the optometrist. *Journal of the American Optometric Association, 59,* 760–766.

Stein, A., & Lewis, D. O. (1992). Discovering physical abuse: Insights from a follow-up study of delinquents. *Child Abuse and Neglect, 16,* 523–531.

Stewart, B. (1990). Issues in developing a research agenda for child abuse. In D. J. Besharov (Ed.), *Family violence: Research and public policy issues,* (pp. 146–149). Washington, DC: AEI Press.

Swett, C., Jr., Cohen, C., Surrey, J., Compaine, A., & Chavez, R. (1991). High rates of alcohol use and history of physical and sexual abuse among women outpatients. *American Journal of Drug and Alcohol Abuse, 17*(1), 49–60.

Thomas, S. A., Rosenfield, N. S., Leventhal, J. M., & Markowitz, R. I. (1991). Long-bone fractures in young children: Distinguishing accidental injuries from child abuse. *Pediatrics, 88,* 471–476.

Tower, C. C. (1989). *Understanding child abuse and neglect.* Boston: Allyn & Bacon.

United Nations. (1960). General Assembly resolution 1386 (XIV), November 20, 1959. *Official records of the General Assembly,* (Supplement No. 16). New York: Author.

Walker, C. E., Bonner, B. L., & Kaufman, K. L. (1988). *The physically and sexually abused child: Evaluation and treatment.* New York: Pergamon Press.

Williams, G. J. (1980). Cruelty and kindness to children: Documentary of a century, 1874–1974. In G. J. Williams & J. Money (Eds.), *Traumatic abuse and neglect of children at home* (pp. 66–88). Baltimore: Johns Hopkins University Press.

Wissow, L. S. (1990). The medical history and the physical examination. In L. S. Wissow (Ed.), *Child advocacy for the clinician: An approach to child abuse and neglect* (pp. 49–66). Baltimore: Williams & Wilkins.

Wissow, L. S., & Wilson, M.E.H. (1992). Use of epidemiological data in the diagnosis of physical child abuse: Variations in response to hypothetical cases. *Child Abuse and Neglect, 16*(1), 45–55.

Wolff, J. M. (1990). Bite marks: Recognizing child abuse and identifying abusers. *Families in Society, 71,* 493–499.

Woolley, P. V., Jr., & Evans, W. A., Jr. (1955). Significance of skeletal lesions on infants resembling those of traumatic origin. *Journal of the American Medical Association, 158,* 539–543.

Zuravin, S. J. (1988). Child abuse, child neglect, and maternal depression: Is there a connection? In J. M. Giovannoni (Ed.), *Overview of issues on child neglect* (Proceedings of a symposium, November 10, 1985). Washington, DC: National Clearinghouse on Child Abuse and Neglect Information.

Zuravin, S. J. (1991). Research definitions of child physical abuse and neglect: Current problems. In R. H. Starr, Jr. & D. A. Wolfe (Eds.), *The effects of child abuse and neglect: Issues and research* (pp. 100–128). New York: Guilford Press.

## Further Reading

Kadushin, A., & Martin, J. (1988). *Child welfare services.* New York: Macmillan.

National Association of Social Workers. (1981). *NASW standards for social work practice in child protection.* Silver Spring, MD: Author.

Press, S., Grant, P., Thompson, V. T., & Milles, K. L. (1991). Small bowel evisceration: Unusual manifestation of child abuse. *Pediatrics, 88,* 807–809.

Rush, F. (1980). *The best kept secret: Sexual abuse of children.* New York: McGraw-Hill.

Silverman, F. (1980). Radiologic and specific diagnostic procedures. In C. H. Kempe & R. E. Helfer (Eds.), *The battered child* (3rd ed., pp. 215–240). Chicago: University of Chicago Press.

Thomas, M. P. (1972). Child abuse and neglect, Part I: Historical overview, legal material, and social perspective. *North Carolina Law Review, 50,* 293–349.

Williams, G. J. (1983). Child protection: A journey into history. *Journal of Clinical Child Psychology, 12,* 236–243.

**Sheryl Brissett-Chapman, EdD, ACSW, LCSW,** is executive director, The Baptist Home for Children and Families, 6301 Greentree Road, Bethesda, MD 20817.

### For further information see

Adolescents: Direct Practice; Adult Corrections; Alcohol Abuse; Assessment; Child Abuse and Neglect Overview; Child Care Services; Child Foster Care; Child Sexual Abuse Overview; Child Sexual Abuse: Direct Practice; Child Welfare Overview; Children: Direct Practice; Children: Mental Health; Criminal Behavior Overview; Direct Practice Overview; Domestic Violence; Drug Abuse; Families: Direct Practice; Family Therapy; Female Criminal Offenders; Health Care: Direct Practice; Interdisciplinary and Interorganizational Collaboration; Intervention Research; Interviewing; Legal Issues: Confidentiality and Privileged Communication; Legal Issues: Low-Income and Dependent People; Mental Health Overview; Professional Conduct; Public Social Services; Runaways and Homeless Youths; School Social Work Overview; Social Work Practice: Theoretical Base; Substance Abuse: Direct Practice; Victim Services and Victim/Witness Assistance Programs; Violence Overview.

**Key Words**

child abuse
child protection
neglect
physical abuse
risk assessment

# Child Care Services

Michele J. Vinet

The development of a child care system—composed of family day care homes, child care centers, and Head Start centers—hinges on three interlocking components: quality, equality, and integrity. The low salaries and high turnover of child care workers have hindered the implementation of quality standards. A growth in resource and referral agencies is helping parents find the right care for their children. Social workers are beginning to bring community services to children and their families through child care programs.

Kagan (1990) described the basic issues in early child care and education as a tripod, with each leg—representing quality, equality, and integrity—needing the other to stand. As social need propels the growth in child care services, ensuring that these services are of high quality continues to be the primary concern. Equal access to care is necessary to prevent two tiers of care, with high-quality services available only to parents who can afford them. Furthermore, even with increased funding to raise the standards of quality, the historically disparate variety of providers of services in child care centers, family day care homes, Head Start, or public preschools and the lack of an integrated system of care limit families to the types of care they know about. Despite worries about quality, equality, and the lack of integration of types of providers, there appears to be a consensus that the education of young children is becoming as important as the education of older children.

For almost 50 years, day care and early education have been considered nonessential and distinct entities with different functions. Day care has been viewed as custodial, a social service for the indigent, and part of the welfare system to overcome the negative effects of poverty. Preschools, on the other hand, developed to rescue mothers from the social isolation of the suburbs. They were founded in the private sector to offer mothers and children socialization opportunities. Because there has been no overall vision for early education, programs act as independent entities fighting for survival, not as parts of a coordinated whole. There is still no central federal administration, and federal funding guidelines tend to impede the integration of funding streams.

The lack of superiority of one site over the other, whether in Head Start, schools, family day care, or child care centers, may be leading to new paradigms, however. In the 1990s, there seems to be a movement toward a more seamless system of child care, spurred by new public funding in the late 1980s, the growth of child care resource and referral agencies, the continued involvement by employers, and an increasingly articulate professional cadre of providers. At issue is how individual programs can maintain the benefits of being independent and still reduce "systemic pain" (Kagan, 1990).

## History

Federal involvement in day care has been subject to boom-and-bust cycles, the ebb and flow depending on the crisis of a particular period.[1] In the early 1800s, day nurseries served widows of seamen and other "worthy" women (Beer, 1957). During the Civil War, a federally sponsored day nursery in Philadelphia served children whose mothers worked in clothing factories and hospitals and, later, those whose mothers were war widows. In 1897 the National Federation of Day Nurseries was founded to assist waves of immigrants in preserving their families and in preventing their children from being placed in institutions. The budding field of social work was critical of the group care approach, arguing instead for foster family day care and family services for the deserving poor. During the Great Depression, nurseries were set up through the Works Progress Administration (WPA) for the children of unemployed teachers, nurses, and others who were looking for work. By 1937, 1,900 nurseries cared for 40,000 children. It was the first time that both federal and state funds were spent for day care (Steinfels, 1973). After the Depression, the WPA nurseries were allowed to dwindle. During World War II, with the increased need for women workers, day care centers were provided 50 percent matching grants under the Defense Housing and Community Facilities and Services Act of 1951. Although more than 1,100 of these day care centers were former WPA nurseries, the Federal Works Agency channeled day care funds primarily through local school systems, bypassing social work agencies, day nurseries, and family casework interests and denying funding to family day care. According to Steinfels

[1]The section on history borrows heavily from Emlen (1987).

(1973), more than 1.5 million children were in day care at a cost of nearly $50 million by the end of the war. Yet, when the war was over, federal funds were withdrawn, and few state programs survived.

During the War on Poverty in the 1960s, a new federal expansion of day care occurred. In 1961, amendments to the Social Security Act (P.L. 87-64) authorized grants in aid to state public welfare agencies for day care services. At that time, states began to develop standards for day care. In 1964, under the Economic Opportunity Act (P.L. 88-452), grants for a new program called Head Start were made through community action agencies. In 1965, Title I of the Elementary and Secondary Education Act (P.L. 89-10) authorized preschools, and in 1967, Title IV-A of the Social Security Act (P.L. 90-248) provided for 75 percent matching funds for child care. Numerous work-incentive programs offered child care and social services to parents who were receiving public assistance. However, mothers with children under age six were not required to work, and controversy surrounded compulsory work for other mothers. By the end of the 1960s, annual federal expenditures reached more than $500 million, and more than 200 categorical federal programs affecting child care had been established, including Aid to Families with Dependent Children (AFDC), parent–child centers, assistance for migrant and seasonal farmworkers, assistance for handicapped children, foster grandparents, food services, health services, and child welfare services (Brookings Institution, 1972).

In the 1970s, a standoff occurred in child care between the increasingly articulate day care movement and the beginning of a conservative trend that grew to full force in the 1980s. The women's movement raised day care to a new consciousness as a key factor in women's ability to gain equal opportunity with men in education and employment. Liberal political platforms adopted a comprehensive model of day care, one that was developmental rather than merely custodial and that provided health care, nutrition, education, social services, and parental participation as entitlements for all children. Advocates wanted comprehensive services subsidized and supported by a federal system of high-quality day care services.

In 1971 President Richard M. Nixon vetoed the Comprehensive Child Development Act, refusing to commit the "vast moral authority of the National Government to the side of communal approaches to child rearing" (Roby, 1973, p. 146). Some have argued that this and other defeats in the 1970s reflected a conservative backlash against feminists' demands (Grubb & Lazerson, 1982); however, the potential costs of a day care entitlement loomed as an additional barrier to a national consensus. A hallmark of the 1970s was the concern about the quality of federally supported child care. Numerous studies and policy analyses were devoted to formulating regulatory standards, called the Federal Interagency Day Care Requirements (FIDCR). There was political debate over the cost of meeting these requirements, and active enforcement of day care standards never became federal policy, except for Head Start and Title XX programs. Despite the conservative mood, the 1970s did sustain modest increases in Head Start, Title XX, the U.S. Department of Agriculture's Child Care Food Program, federally supported preschool programs, and work-related income tax deductions for child care (Malone, 1981).

In the eight years of Ronald Reagan's presidency, the federal administration stressed decentralization, deregulation, and privatization (Kahn & Kamerman, 1987), and the private sector was favored for providing child care. Budgetary cuts in all social services came into force, and Title XX funds were converted to social services block grants. Kahn and Kamerman estimated that the true cut in federal child care services in 1986 was about 14 percent. Aspects of privatization were implemented through the dependent care tax credit and dependent care allowance plans, both of which benefited middle- to upper-income families. In 1988 the child and dependent care tax credit paid out $3.4 billion, an amount equal to 52 percent of federal funding for child care (U.S. General Accounting Office [GAO], 1989b). The federal presence in establishing standards was virtually eliminated as the work of the FIDCR was bypassed.

Under the Reagan administration, sharp increases occurred in employer-supported programs, in the use of federal and state tax credits for child care, in child care as an employee benefit, and in employee assistance programs as a vehicle to address the productivity issues affected by maternal employment. Information and referral services also became increasingly widespread as a way to make the child care market more accessible. The modest Dependent Care Development Grants of 1984 provided funds to start information and referral services that offered counseling to parents on child care choices and that documented gaps in care. The National Association of Child Care Resource and Referral Agencies was founded in 1986.

From 1989 to 1992, the U.S. Departments of Education and Health and Human Services conducted three national studies to document the supply of and demand for child care, including the Profile of Child Care Settings, the National Child

Care Survey 1990, and the National Study of Before- and After-School Programs (Seppanen, DeVries, & Seligson, 1993; Willer et al., 1991). In addition, the National Child Care Staffing Study shed light on the working conditions and wages and compensation of child care workers (Whitebook, Phillips, & Howes, 1993). Comparisons of regulatory standards in family day care and child care centers have also aided the development of policy (Children's Foundation, 1993a, 1993b). These studies have been a major boon to understanding developments in child care from the viewpoints of parents, providers of services, and regulatory agencies.

## Current State of Need

In 1965 only 16 percent of four-year-olds were enrolled in early child care and education, compared to 51 percent by 1989 (U.S. Bureau of Labor Statistics, 1990). Although parents are opting for more early education for their children regardless of whether mothers are working, the growth of early child care and education has paralleled the growth of maternal employment. In 1970 only 39 percent of mothers with children under age 18 were in the labor force, compared with 62 percent in 1990 (U.S. Bureau of Labor Statistics, 1990). Willer et al. (1991) documented that in 1990, 7.6 million children were enrolled in child care centers and 4 million were in family day care homes on a regular basis, for a total of 11.6 million children—approximately 25 percent of all children in the United States—in supplemental care.

The average cost of child care varies in different parts of the country. The highest rates are in the Northeast, where care cost an average of $2.18 per hour in 1990, and the lowest rates are in the South, at $1.29 per hour in 1990 (Willer et al., 1991). Approximately 30 percent of the centers and 17 percent of registered family day care homes receive subsidies of some type, whether from public or private funds (Willer et al., 1991). Families with incomes of less than $15,000 spend an average of 23 percent of their income on child care, and 45 percent of them receive public subsidies for care. Families with incomes of no more than $21,000 can receive the earned income tax credit, which supplements income up to $2,000 per year. Parents with incomes over $35,000 spend approximately 7 percent of their income on child care, and 34 percent of them claim the dependent care tax credit (Willer et al., 1991).

Never recorded in the statistics are the wide variety of informal care arrangements parents use to cope with work schedules, from parents alternating shifts to care provided by relatives, older siblings, and unregulated friends and neighbors, to children being left on their own. Parents choose supplemental child care from the formal system, depending on their families' needs and resources and the options they know of in the community. With the enormous amount of variation in supplemental care, however, it is difficult to understand the impact of the choices families make in balancing work and family demands. Surveys of parents have found that parents' primary desire in selecting caregivers for their children is to find people who are warm and loving, who will foster their children's development, and who will prepare their children for school (Willer et al., 1991).

## Current Federal Policies

In 1988 the Family Support Act (P.L. 100-485) established the Job Opportunities and Basic Skills Training (JOBS) program that made training, education, or employment mandatory for families who were receiving public assistance, except when their children were younger than three (or younger than age one for teenage parents). Trainees are provided child care while in training, and child care continues during the transitional year following training, depending on a family's income. In addition to the JOBS program, Title IV-A of the Social Security Act provided $1.5 billion in 1989 for child care for parents in job training and low-income families. Funds from the Elementary and Secondary Education Act were still designated for preschools, and by the end of the 1980s, 32 states had some form of preschool service for three- and four-year-olds (Mitchell, Seligson, & Marx, 1989).

A year after JOBS child care became an entitlement, President George Bush approved landmark child care funding through the Child Care and Development Block Grant (CCDBG) (Blank, 1991). The first authorization of $2.5 billion became available in 1991, with states' shares determined by the number of needy children. In the initial authorization, 75 percent was dedicated to subsidies to make care more affordable, and 25 percent was used to improve the quality and supply of care. Head Start has also received increased funding, and by 1995, $7.6 billion is expected to be allocated to bring the service to full-day, full-year care. The Head Start Improvement Act of 1992 also provided $578 million to purchase buildings, provide health care to siblings, and provide for parents' literacy and education (Children's Defense Fund, 1992). Although the increase in federal dollars has been significant, state revenues have been reduced for child care because of recessions in states in the early 1990s (Blank, 1993).

A cornerstone of the CCDBG is parents' ability to select child care providers, including relatives. Before public funds can be expended, however, any relative or other provider must meet the state's licensing or registration requirements. The Children's Defense Fund, with a long history of monitoring federal funding for child care and other family services, analyzed the impact of the CCDBG in its first two years of operation (Blank, 1993). It found that in the area of improved quality, states have spent considerable funds on regulatory enforcement and monitoring, factors that, it is believed, greatly influence the quality of services. States have helped child care centers to become accredited by the National Academy of Early Childhood Programs, a service of the National Association for the Education of Young Children. The quality of providers of care has been addressed through increased funds for training, especially for providers who serve school-age children, infants, and children with special needs. Funds for training have also been used to help child care providers obtain Child Development Associate credentials. Funds have paid for comprehensive services to families, including health checkups and immunizations, parental education, and social work counseling. In Washington State, child care has been offered to families as a means of preventing intervention from Child Protective Services (Blank, 1993).

The supply of care was enhanced by CCDBG money through start-up funds for infant care, care for children of teenage parents, homeless families, and school-age children. In some states, CCDBG funds were used to extend Head Start programs to full-day, full-year services. States encouraged providers to serve low-income families by raising the reimbursement rates and simplifying contracts and administrative procedures. They also simplified the application process for parents, raised the maximum income for qualification and the income level at which child care subsidies are lost, and reduced parents' copayments for services.

In addition, CCDBG funds have been used to expand resource and referral services to help families gain access to various types of care. Texas has been a notable example in this regard. The Texas Department of Human Services (TDHS) developed the Child Care Management Service (CCMS) to respond to the increased funding for subsidized child care provided by the JOBS program and the CCDBG. In the past, the TDHS contracted directly with approximately 1,100 child care providers. Since the CCMS was started in 1991, the system has grown to include 3,400 providers, and all licensed and registered providers have the opportunity to enter into vendor agreements. Local communities are the focal points for the coordination of services through 27 competitively obtained CCMS contractors. Most of the CCMS contractors are nonprofit community agencies, resource and referral agencies, or child care associations. Backed by a uniform computer system, the CCMS manages nine funding streams for 22 groups of clients. This automated system allows funding searches according to a client's eligibility status and centralizes waiting lists, information on providers of services, billing, and the tracking of data. The CCMS provides parental counseling on child care options, helps families locate services, administers state vouchers, collects data on the supply of and demand for services, trains providers and contracts for other training, and manages grants and loans for start-ups and improvements (Corporate Fund for Children, 1993). The CCMS system in Texas has received national recognition for its innovativeness (Harvard University, 1993).

Although CCDBG funds have opened many avenues for improving the availability and quality of care, these funds are not sustained and thus are only short-term solutions to the larger problem of full subsidization of the cost of care. The accessibility of services has been improved through resource and referral systems, but the reduction in state dollars for child care has meant that the federal matching funds are lower, and states are not drawing down their share on the basis of their population's needs. Long waiting lists exist, and states are able to fulfill only 9 percent to 16 percent of the need (Blank, 1993).

## Current Status of Regulatory Standards

In 1993 the Children's Foundation (1993a) reported that there were 90,558 centers and 273,926 regulated family day care homes. Terminology in child care licensing is defined by the size of the group receiving care. Child care centers are larger than family day care homes, and group day care homes are somewhere between the two. Family day care homes generally can care for up to six children, with the preschool children of the provider considered in the count, but standards for licensing child day care and family day care vary considerably by state. Regulatory standards stress the minimal physical health and safety conditions that must be met to maintain operation. Licensing standards, however, do not address the cognitive, social, physical, or emotional needs of children or the curriculum required to support those needs (Chilman, 1993).

Licensing standards for child care centers may define staff–child ratios; prescreening, training, and minimal qualifications of staff; inspection policies; liability insurance; square footage per child; children's records and immunizations; emergency medical consent; care of sick children; disciplinary policy; transportation; the fire code; and the reporting of child abuse and neglect. Staff may be required to undergo checks for criminal backgrounds, tuberculosis skin tests, chest x-rays, and general medical examinations and to know first aid and cardiopulmonary resuscitation. In most states, however, staff can be hired before the results of the tests are known.

According to the Children's Foundation's (1993b) summary of statistics on the regulation of child care services, 11 states (21 percent) do not require any specific training for providers of family day care, and another 10 require orientation sessions only. Orientations generally cover an introduction to family day care, the state regulations regarding family day care, an overview of how to establish a family day care home, and the responsibilities of providers. In many states, the services of family day care homes have been curtailed because of neighborhood zoning and deed restrictions. Zoning is a form of land-use restriction whose purpose is to protect the value of private property or the characteristics of neighborhoods. Increasingly, it is becoming a barrier to the operation of family day care homes, and some states are working on legislation to enable family day care homes to be a permitted use of residences.

## Employers' Roles in Child Care

Many U.S. businesses that are concerned about their present and future workplaces have established foundations and corporate-giving strategies to support early child care and education. In a handbook for employers based on a survey of Texas employers, the Texas Work and Family Clearinghouse (1992) forecast that, by the year 2000, 75 percent of all children will have wage-earning mothers. Although only 5 percent to 10 percent of workers with children will take advantage of child care benefits at any given time, over time 70 percent to 100 percent will probably use them. Employers have a variety of options to support their employees' child care needs, and they naturally are concerned about liability and cost in considering their options. Flexible scheduling, family leave, and resource and referral services are indirect ways of supporting families' needs. In February 1993, President Bill Clinton signed the Family and Medical Leave Act (FMLA), which requires employers with more than 50 employees to provide up to 12 weeks of unpaid, job-protected leave to eligible employees for certain family and medical reasons, including the care of a newborn or newly adopted child and the care of a seriously ill child, spouse, or parent. On their return from FMLA leaves, most employees must be restored to their original or equivalent positions with equivalent pay, benefits, and other terms of employment (U.S. Department of Labor, 1993). FMLA is a policy triumph in that it enables families to decide to care for family members themselves, when necessary, without losing their jobs.

Employers have also been involved in direct financial assistance for child care through voucher reimbursement systems, dependent care assistance plans, contracts with vendors for specific services like sick child care or evening–weekend shift care, and the operation of on-site or near-site child care centers. Employers, concerned with the supply of well-qualified providers of services for their employees, have supported the training and accreditation of providers. The largest private collaborative effort for child care implemented to date is the American Business Collaboration for Quality Dependent Care. IBM was the catalyst for the collaboration in 1991, and 10 other corporations have since joined it in providing $25.4 million between 1992 and 1994. The purpose of the collaboration is to enhance the quality and increase the supply of child care and elder care. Participating employers have priority in access to specified numbers of slots in communities where services are developed. Projects are managed by Work/Family Directions in Boston, in the areas of care for school-age children; the construction, expansion, or accreditation of centers; and the recruitment, training, and retention of providers of family day care homes (National Report on Work and Family, 1992).

## Developments in the Profession

The National Association for the Education of Young Children (NAEYC), the professional association for the child care field, uses the term *early childhood program* for any program serving young children to age eight. In developing their professional identity, leaders in the field have struggled with celebrating the diversity of settings in which early education occurs while trying to define the profession's unity by a core knowledge, regardless of setting (Bredekamp & Willer, 1992). In 1992 NAEYC created the National Institute for Early Childhood Professional Development to articulate a professional development system. History demonstrates that qualifications and responsibilities have not been translated into requisite compensation. Currently there are many roles and career paths in child care, depending on the age of children served and the care setting. Yet, a core knowledge base has been defined; it includes child development, environmental safety and health, developmentally appropriate activities, the establishment of supportive relationships with and the guidance of children; support for the uniqueness of individual development; the creation of positive, productive relationships with parents; and a basic understanding of the early childhood profession (Bredekamp & Willer, 1992).

NAEYC started a voluntary accreditation procedure through its National Academy of Early Childhood Programs. These high-quality centers adhere to developmentally appropriate practice, low staff–child ratios, and other dimensions of quality care. A developmentally appropriate curriculum balances information on child development and specific tasks at predictable stages for children but allows for individual differences in accomplishing the tasks. For very young children, learning is embedded within the caregiving function, and good programs serve both care and educational functions.

### Wages and Compensation

Salaries in the field have lagged behind expectations of the skills required of professionals. Personnel are generally called *teacher–caregivers* because they provide both education and care to groups of children. Others use the generic term *provider* to refer to an individual who provides child care for payment to unrelated children in his or her own home (Children's Foundation, 1993b). Teacher–caregivers in early childhood programs earned an average of $14,100 in 1991, compared to $28,900 for public school teachers and $27,700 for social workers with a master's degree (Willer, 1990). Although they are better educated than the population as a whole, even teacher–caregivers with bachelor's degrees earned half what other women with bachelor's degrees earned. A study conducted by the Child Care Employee Project (1989) found not only that wages for teacher–caregivers had not risen in real terms since 1976, but that there was a substantial decline in real wages, despite the greater education and training of staff. Furthermore, only 27 percent of teacher–caregivers in centers had health insurance in 1990. In addition, the wages and benefits of assistant teachers and teacher aides were even lower than those for teacher–caregivers, although those were the fastest-growing areas of personnel. Finally, the average annual income of family day care home providers was $11,000 in 1990.

The turnover of staff in 1988 was 40 percent, three times that of the 1970s. In 1992 the turnover was 26 percent, compared to 5.6 percent for public school teachers and 9.6 percent for U.S. companies in general (Whitebook et al., 1993). The high turnover of personnel is a major impediment to implementing developmentally appropriate practice because it means frequent interruptions in children's relationships, which is particularly detrimental to infants and makes it difficult to provide training and to maintain standards of quality (Whitebook et al., 1993).

### Roles for Social Workers

Child care services are constantly changing as the needs of families and children change. High-quality child care services recognize that families are important to the development of healthy children and that children who receive child care or early education must be served in the context of their families and communities. Social workers play significant roles in researching problems and adapting services for families who are culturally and linguistically diverse and for children with congenital and drug-induced disabilities and disabilities related to human immunodeficiency virus. The increased numbers of teenagers who are having babies, "crack" babies, and single-parent families point to the greater need for family support and parenting education—services that are closely aligned with child care and early education.

Services by social workers in child care settings have been increased under the Child Care and Development Block Grant, which has funded demonstration projects of comprehensive services linked with child care that include the early detection of problems, case management, and parenting education. Social workers also intersect with child care as they continually broaden their roles through employee assistance programs. Helping employers respond to the shifting demographics of the work force and calling their attention to employees' needs for child care and elder care are part of this service mission (Googins & Davidson, 1993).

Moving to a universal vision of services for families, social workers and child care professionals need to develop cross-system planning and cross-agency coordination of resources. One-dimensional programs do not serve families; both social work and child care have to think in cross-disciplinary terms to attend to the social, emotional, intellectual, nutritional, and physical needs of the children, their families, and the community. The long-term effects of out-of-home care on infants' attachment and sense of trust should be studied. In addition, models of child care and parenting education for teenage mothers should be examined; for example, advocates are questioning traditional models and proposing alternatives such as "maternal" families for these teenagers. In a "maternal family" a registered family home provider provides child care for the baby of the teenager while the teenager attends school. In addition, the teenager and baby live with the registered family provider in a foster home arrangement. Thus, the teenager is able to learn parenting skills from the provider who is an expert in child development and child rearing. Future social work roles may be defined at this intersection of child and family services (personal communication with L. Parks, editor, *Texas Child Care Magazine* and *Oklahoma Child Care Magazine,* 1993).

## Future Directions

Kagan (1990) stated that it is time to move from the development of programs to reforming the system. Programs have been piloted, developed, and tested, and some model programs have been identified. Now it is time to institutionalize the best models. The field is moving toward a more universal view of care for families that is cross-disciplinary, cross-agency, and cross-system and that allows for the coordination of resources. Society needs to move from a short- to a long-term commitment. Early child care and education are now a permanent part of the social landscape. Opportunities for parenting education must be made universal.

By anticipating and planning for changing family needs, resource and referral agencies can help project future needs and facilitate cross-agency exchanges of information. The National Association of Child Care Resource and Referral Agencies (1992) reported that there were approximately 600 child care resource and referral agencies around the country, many organized into state networks. Almost 70 percent of these services are using Carefinder software and have established standards of service to ensure that they are impartial, serve all types of families, and keep information on all types of services.

The "Nannygate" incident that confronted President Clinton's nominations for U.S. attorney general drew national attention to the plight of working women, both the attorneys and their caregivers. Two nominees were forced to withdraw when it was learned that they had illegally employed undocumented workers as nannies in their homes. Although reported in-home care for children of any age has never exceeded 3 percent of all care, that number had dropped to 1 percent by 1990 (Willer et al., 1991, p. 10). What was at issue, according to women who were interviewed by Wingert (1993), was the double standard of singling out women's child care arrangements and their legality, when men would not have even been asked the question. The incident put a new light on the "mommy trap"—working women must pay other working women to watch their children.

Where will the money come from for higher wages, benefits, and improved job conditions for child care workers? Without better compensation, the recruitment, training, and retention of child care professionals will be seriously undermined. Funds for the reauthorization of Head Start for 1994 mandated a 25 percent "quality enhancement," half of which must be used for salary increases. Advocates have recommended to President Clinton that all funding for child care be earmarked for improvements in the quality of services, specifically salary increases. Raising wages may mean increased fees for parents, as has occurred in employer-supported facilities where comparable-worth studies have been conducted. Some advocate the establishment of private pools of funds to help subsidize child care for low-income parents. Indirect support for teachers may include private scholarships for teacher education, public grants for higher education, and a greater forgiveness of loans for education (Whitebook et al., 1993).

To make the commitment to serving the whole child in the context of the family and the community means that services must be adequately funded and that funding should encourage the integration of services. The debate over funding continues to focus on using the limited dollars to target specific children who need care, with the risk of reinforcing a permanent two-tier system that segregates the poor and reinforces economic segregation, versus spending funds on universal services, thereby fostering integration and generating the broader political appeal of schools as the great social equalizers. Whichever way the debate leans in the next decade, children are important to the nation, and their future will continue to be weighed on a social scale that balances private rights and public responsibility.

## References


Beer, E. (1957). *Working mothers and the day nursery.* New York: Whiteside.

Blank, H. (1991). *The Child Care and Development Block Grant and Child Care Grants to States under Title IV-A of the Social Security Act: A description of major provisions and issues to consider in implementation.* Washington, DC: Children's Defense Fund.

Blank, H. (1993, September). Improving child care quality and supply: The impact of the Child Care and Development Block Grant. *Young Children,* pp. 32–34.

Bredekamp, S., & Willer, B. (1992, March). Of ladders and lattices, cores and cones: Conceptualizing an early childhood professional development system. *Young Children,* pp. 47–50.

Brookings Institution. (1972). *Setting national priorities: The 1973 budget.* Washington, DC: Author.

Child Care Employee Project. (1989). *National Child Care Staffing Study.* Oakland, CA: Author. (6536 Telegraph Avenue A-201, Oakland, CA 94609)

Children's Defense Fund. (1992). *Legislative year in review.* Washington, DC: Author.

Children's Foundation. (1993a). *1993 Child Day Care Licensing Study.* Washington, DC: Author. (725 15th Street, NW, Suite 505, Washington, DC 20005)

Children's Foundation. (1993b). *1993 Family Day Care Licensing Study.* Washington, DC: Author. (725 15th Street, NW, Suite 505, Washington, DC 20005)

Chilman, C. (1993). Parental employment and child care trends: Some critical issues and suggested policy. *Social Work, 38,* 451–460.

Corporate Fund for Children. (1993). *The 1993 best of Texas yearbook.* Austin, TX: Author.

Defense Housing and Community Facilities and Services Act of 1951. Ch. 378, 65 Stat. 293.

Economic Opportunity Act of 1964. P.L. 88-452, 78 Stat. 508.

Elementary and Secondary Education Act of 1965. P.L. 89-10, 79 Stat. 27.

Emlen, A. (1987). Child care services. In A. Minahan (Ed.-in-Chief), *Encyclopedia of social work* (18th ed., Vol. 1, pp. 232–241). Silver Spring, MD: National Association of Social Workers.

Family and Medical Leave Act of 1993. P.L. 103-3, 107 Stat. 6.

Family Support Act of 1988. P.L. 100-485, 102 Stat. 2343.

Googins, B., & Davidson, B. (1993). The organization as client: Broadening the concept of employee assistance programs. *Social Work, 38,* 477–484.

Grubb, W. N., & Lazerson, M. (1982). The frontier of public responsibility: Child care and parent education. In W. N. Grubb & M. Lazerson (Eds.), *Broken promises: How Americans fail their children* (pp. 208–232). New York: Basic Books.

Harvard University. (1993). *Harvard University and Ford Foundation awards for innovations in state and local government.* Cambridge, MA: Author.

Head Start Improvement Act of 1992. P.L. 102-401, 106 Stat. 1956.

Kagan, S. (1990). *Policy perspectives series: Excellence in early childhood education, Defining characteristics and next-decade strategies.* Washington, DC: U.S. Department of Education, Office of Educational Research and Improvement, Information Services.

Kahn, A., & Kamerman, S. (1987). *Child care: Facing the hard choices.* Dover, MA: Auburn House.

Malone, M. (1981). *Child day care: The federal role* (Issue Brief No. 1). Washington, DC: Library of Congress, Congressional Research Service.

Mitchell, A., Seligson, M., & Marx, F. (1989). *Early childhood programs and the public schools: Between promise and practice.* Dover, MA: Auburn House.

National Association of Child Care Resource and Referral Agencies. (1992). *Facts from the field: CCR&R agencies tell us that . . .* Washington, DC: Author.

National Report on Work and Family. (1992, September 15). *Biggest collaborative effort on dependent care kicks off.* Silver Spring, MD: Author.

Roby, P. (1973). *Child care—Who cares?* New York: Basic Books.

Seppanen, P., DeVries, D., & Seligson, M. (1993). *National study of before- and after-school programs, Executive summary.* Portsmouth, NH: RMC Research Corp.

Social Security Act Amendments of 1961. P.L. 87-64, 75 Stat. 131.

Social Security Act Amendments of 1967. P.L. 90-248, 81 Stat. 821.

Steinfels, M. (1973). *Who's minding the children? The history and politics of day care in America.* New York: Simon & Schuster.

Texas Work and Family Clearinghouse. (1992). *Employer-assisted dependent care in Texas: How to choose family-friendly policies to suit your company's needs.* Austin, TX: Author.

U.S. Bureau of Labor Statistics. (1990). *Marital and family characteristics of the labor force from the March 1990 Current Population Survey.* Washington, DC: U.S. Government Printing Office.

U.S. Department of Labor. (1993). *Your rights under the Family and Medical Leave Act of 1993.* Washington, DC: U.S. Government Printing Office.

U.S. General Accounting Office. (1989a). *Child care: Government funding sources, coordination, and service availability.* Washington, DC: U.S. Government Printing Office.

U.S. General Accounting Office. (1989b). *Early childhood education: Information on costs and services at high quality centers.* Washington, DC: U.S. Government Printing Office.

Whitebook, M., Phillips, D., & Howes, C. (1993). *The national child care staffing study revisited: Four years in the life of center-based child care.* Oakland, CA: Child Care Employee Project. (6536 Telegraph Avenue, Suite A-201, Oakland, CA 94609)

Willer, B. (Ed.). (1990). *Reaching the full cost of quality in early childhood programs.* Washington, DC: National Association for the Education of Young Children.

Willer, B., Hofferth, S., Kisker, E., Divine-Hawkins, P., Farquhar, E., & Glantz, F. (1991). *The demand and supply of child care in 1990. Joint findings from the National Child Care Survey 1990 and A Profile of Child Care Settings.* Washington, DC: National Association for the Education of Young Children.

Wingert, P. (1993, February 15). Nannygate II: A women's backlash? *Newsweek,* pp. 20–21.

## Further Reading

Bredekamp, S. (Ed.). (1987). *Developmentally appropriate practice in early childhood programs serving children from birth to age 8.* Washington, DC: National Association for the Education of Young Children.

Hayes, C., Palmer, J., & Zaslow, M. (Eds.). (1990). *Who cares for America's children?* Washington, DC: National Academy Press.

National Association of Child Care Resource and Referral Agencies. (no date). *Summary of standards for CCR&R organizations.* Washington, DC: Author.

Steiner, G. (1976). *The futility of family policy.* Washington, DC: Brookings Institution.

U.S. Bureau of the Census. (1990). *Who's minding the kids? Child care arrangements: Winter 1986–7, Current Population Reports* (Series P-70, No. 20). Washington, DC: U.S. Government Printing Office.

U.S. Department of Education. (1992). *National study of before- and after-school programs* (Prepared by RMC Research Corporation in collaboration with School-Age Child Care Project at Wellesley College and Mathematica Policy Research). Washington, DC: U.S. Government Printing Office.

**Michele J. Vinet, PhD, LMSW-AP,** is the child care specialist for the Austin Independent School District, Division of Community Education and At-Risk Programs, Austin, TX 78703.

**For further information see**

Advocacy; Baby Boomers; Child Support; Child Welfare Overview; Childhood; Families Overview; Families: Demographic Shifts; Family Planning; Income Distribution; Jobs and Earnings; Natural Helping Networks; Poverty; Public Social Services; School-Linked Services; Single Parents; Social Security; Social Welfare Policy; Women Overview.

**Key Words**
child care
early childhood education
family services

# Child Foster Care

**Joyce E. Everett**

Foster care is a publicly funded child welfare system of organized services for full-time residential caregiving of children whose parents' condition or behavior prevents them from discharging their parental responsibilities (Family Impact Seminar, 1990). These services are provided in foster family homes by foster parents, in residential group homes, and in institutions, where the primary adult caretakers may or may not be related to the children in care. This entry focuses specifically on foster family care.

Foster care services operate in all states and are typically administered directly through county social services departments, purchased by the state from a voluntary nonprofit agency foster care program, or both. Children come into foster care for a multitude of reasons and through processes that vary from county to county and state to state (Pecora, Whittaker, Maluccio, Barth, & Plotnick, 1992). Placement may occur as a result of a parent's request for temporary help on a voluntary basis, a court order for removal, or legal actions requiring out-of-home care.

Guided by the principles of permanency in living arrangements and continuity of relationship, foster care services are designed as temporary, comprehensive, and planned supportive services for families with children who cannot be adequately maintained within their own homes. The primary goals for foster care placement are maximum protection of children, permanency, and the preservation of families. Although there is an inherent tension among these goals, the ultimate aim of foster family care is the reunification of children with their biological parents, adoption by foster parents or other families, or preparation for independent living.

## Historical Milestones

Current theory and practice of foster care can be characterized in terms of the historical milestones through which they have evolved. The major turning points in foster care theory and practice emerged from (1) informal placements of children with relatives; (2) the indiscriminate placement of children in almshouses or specialized institutions offering training; (3) foster care as a permanent "rescuing effort"; (4) foster care as a temporary service to families; and (5) the discovery of foster care drift, when a child remains in foster care for a long time, as the impetus toward permanency, placements in the least-restrictive environments, and the provision of preventive and restorative services. Foster care theory and practice are continuing to unfold. As the various layers, textures, and contours of foster care practice reveal themselves, professionals and public policymakers prepare arduous responses to each new wrinkle. Many of these responses represent variations of previous historical themes.

### Informal Placements

Evidence of family foster care, practiced on a limited basis, has been traced back to the ancient Jewish laws and customs of placing orphaned children in the households of other relatives and to the institutional forms of care exemplified in church practices of boarding destitute children (Kadushin & Martin, 1988). Although the history of family foster care in America typically has centered on the experiences of American colonists, this country was originally occupied by Native

American tribes whose history, culture, and societal and family structures included alternative methods of substitute care (Wiltse, 1985). Native Americans were organized into tribes that consisted of confederated extended family units, and children were treated as part of a constellation of people of varying ages and blood relationships. Because the tribe formed a major component of the child-rearing system, a child always had substitute care and was never considered dependent or neglected.

Unlike the response found within Native American traditions, the English Poor-Law tradition influenced the early colonial American response to the needs of destitute, neglected, and orphaned children. Colonists adopted the English practices of indentureship and the binding out of dependent children to a master artisan until the age of 21. These practices served two purposes, namely, to set responsibility for the support and care of the children with a person or family and to offer the rudiments of training for work (Costin & Rapp, 1972). Indenture contracts, used extensively during the colonial period, were accepted as a "business deal from which the person accepting a poor child on indenture was expected to receive from the child, a full equivalent in work for the expenses of his support, care and teaching" (Thurstone, 1930, cited in Costin & Rapp, 1972, p. 331). Children were abused and exploited, but vestiges of indenture continued into the 20th century. Although by today's standards these practices seem harsh, indentureship was considered an efficient and expedient method of care at the time, with the added benefit of providing needy children with some semblance of a familylike environment.

**Almshouses and Training Institutions**

A few private institutions were established for orphans during the colonial period (McGowan & Meezan, 1983); however, in towns with relatively large populations, children were also placed in almshouses, along with other members of the dependent population. These practices were soon subjected to sharp attack in several investigative reports conducted before the Civil War. Considerable criticism was raised about "catch-all almshouses" (Axinn & Levin, 1992), in which there was little or no attempt to provide humane treatment based on a differentiation among the needs of the pauper population. In almshouses, which housed mentally deficient people, families, able-bodied paupers, alcoholics, and others, the education and moral development of children were, according to these reports, wholly neglected.

One response to these reports was the establishment by public and private agencies of "orphan asylums" and other institutions for special classes of children, including blind, delinquent, homeless, "colored" (as they were then called), and deaf children. Motivated by the deplorable conditions of children who lived in nonsegregated almshouses and the developing practice of providing state subsidies to voluntary agencies, many of these institutions were founded under the auspices of various religious denominations in an effort to provide for the children of these denominations. Although institutional care was a viable form of care before 1850, acceptance of institutional care for dependent children waned as the demand increased. Therefore, a new form of child care was required.

**Formal Foster Care Movement**

Charles Loring Brace, secretary of the New York Children's Aid Society, is credited as being the originator of the formal family foster care movement in 1853. Family foster care, as Brace practiced it, began as an effort to "rescue" children whose parents were inadequate or on charity or had abandoned their dependent offspring from the unwholesome influences found in cities (Pecora et al., 1992). Brace began the practice of transporting needy and homeless children by train from large cities to rural areas in the South and West, where they were placed in the homes of farmers or tradespeople to be cared for and were expected to work in exchange for this care. The New York Children's Aid Society retained custody of the children and could remove them at any time; however, it provided limited follow-up after placement. Although estimates of the number of children placed in free foster care vary, numerous historians (for example, Kadushin, 1974; McGowan & Meezan, 1983) have reported that for about 75 years, roughly 100,000 children were transported for placement using these procedures.

Charity workers, the Catholic church and other religious groups, poor families, and the western states opposed Brace's system. Charity workers attacked the methods of selecting free foster homes for children and the lack of supervision following placement (Kadushin, 1974). The Catholic church charged Protestant organizations with attempting to wean children from their Catholic heritage by placing them in non-Catholic homes. Poor families objected to the practice of taking their children away, and the western states objected to the "dumping of dependent children in their area" (Kadushin, 1974, p. 397) out of a concern about regulating interstate placements of children. Although Brace's placement practices suggest that he envisioned placement as long-term substitute care, as early as 1860 the two principles governing the placement of dependent children, namely, free foster care and a preference for care within a family setting, were firmly established.

### Foster Care as a Temporary Service

Charles Birtwell, director of the Boston Children's Aid Society (1886–1911), is credited with carrying these principles one step further by refocusing the questions that are addressed whenever placement of a child is considered. In his view, placement decisions should be guided by a consideration of the child's needs, including the need to focus on reunifying the child with his or her own family, rather than on where the child should be placed. The Boston Children's Aid Society, under Birtwell's leadership, developed systematic procedures for (1) studying the individualized needs of children, (2) studying the prospective foster family, and (3) providing supervision of the home once the child was placed (Kadushin, 1974). On the basis of Birtwell's work, family foster care practice changed from a long-term substitute care service to a temporary and treatment-oriented service (Wiltse, 1985).

Birtwell's vision of family foster care as a temporary service was reaffirmed during the first White House Conference on Children in 1909, when the conference participants declared that every child is entitled to a "secure and loving home." Conferees expressed a clear preference for foster family care for normal children in need of placement with these words: "The carefully selected foster home is, for the normal child, the best substitute for the natural home" (White House Conference, 1909, as cited in Kadushin, 1974, p. 401). Foster care programs, established in each state by Children's Aid Societies, as well as the public sector, subsequently offered a range of foster care options, including receiving homes for emergency placement, boarding homes, and group homes (Pecora et al., 1992).

### Permanency Planning

The incongruencies between statements of foster care policy and the actual practice of foster care placement began to unfold in the latter part of the 1950s with the publication of *Children in Need of Parents* by Maas and Engler (1959). This publication's description of the children in foster care revealed that many such children were destined to grow up in foster care and that only a few would return home or be adopted. Moreover, more than half the parents of children in foster care who participated in the study indicated that they had no relationships or negative ones with the agencies responsible for the children (Maas & Engler, 1959). Foster care, according to this study, had become a "holding tank" for a large number of children (Wiltse, 1985).

Subsequent activity in the 1960s and 1970s came in different forms. In the 1960s, researchers conducted a flurry of descriptive studies of children in care that substantiated the image of foster care as a holding tank and proposed tentative alternatives for practice (Jenkins, 1967; Jenkins & Sauber, 1966; Lawder, 1966; Madison & Shapiro, 1970). In the 1970s, research and demonstration projects identified some of the deficiencies in the ways children were being served, and they developed and tested specific intervention methods for addressing these flaws (Pecora et al., 1992; Wiltse, 1985). For example, federal law required the development of case plans for children in foster care. However, later studies (for instance, Shyne & Schroeder, 1978) indicated that case planning was an exception. The percentages of children with no case plans ranged from a low of 13 percent to a high of 77 percent. Moreover, parents' visits to their children in foster care were not encouraged.

The most widely disseminated results of these demonstration projects in 1973–1974 came from the Oregon Project in Permanency Planning and the Alameda County, California, Project, where such interventions as intensive agency services, goal-oriented casework, deliberate case planning, focused decision making, and outreach efforts were successfully tested. These and other demonstration projects sought to reorient child welfare practice toward ensuring permanency for children in care. By identifying and removing barriers to adoption, offering intensive services to prevent placement, and developing case plans that included the involvement of biological parents, these projects were instrumental in proving that continuity and permanency could be achieved for children in foster care through careful, goal-directed case planning (Wiltse, 1985). In subsequent years, family foster care issues were addressed within the context of permanency planning.

## Policy Framework

The policy framework for foster care is a patchwork of federal and state initiatives that are intended to support and promote the principle of permanence. Permanence for children in substitute care emphasizes the need for placement in a stable, permanent family setting (Family Impact Seminar, 1990). Consequently, in theory and practice, foster care is a temporary service to be discontinued once the parents' condition or behaviors have improved or an alternative plan for permanence, including adoption, long-term foster care, independent living, and guardianship, can be implemented.

Child welfare services for children and their families are administered by individual states, but are regulated and partially funded through a complex array of federal programs authorized under the Social Security Act of 1935 (Takas, 1993). Specifically, the primary sources for federal support of foster care are contained within Title IV-E (P.L. 96-272), Title IV-B (P.L. 96-270), and Title XX (P.L. 97-35) of the Social Security Act of 1935 and the Adoption Assistance and Child Welfare Act of 1980 (P.L. 96-272). Table 1 shows federal appropriations for the primary child welfare programs authorized under the Social Security Act for fiscal years 1990 to 1993.

A review of the major provisions of each of these statutes reveals a tendency to support out-of-home placement rather than programs for reuniting or stabilizing families and their children.

### Title IV-A

The federal government's involvement in foster care began in 1961, when Louisiana denied aid to 22,000 poor African American children who were otherwise eligible for Aid to Families with Dependent Children (AFDC) because their homes were considered unsuitable and their mothers were ineligible for welfare (Bell, 1965). Congress enacted Title IV-A (AFDC–Foster Care Program) of the Social Security Act of 1935 to ensure that these children would receive adequate care outside their homes (General Accounting Office [GAO], 1991). The title required states to provide federally funded foster care as part of the larger AFDC program. Access to these federal funds was limited to children who were removed from their homes as a result of judicial determination and whose parents had previously received or would have become eligible for AFDC payments. Even then, federal funds were available only for the cost of room and board. Because AFDC is an open-ended entitlement program, the federal government was required to pay for as many children as met the eligibility guidelines. Title IV-A funding did not provide for preventive, reunification, or case management services, nor was funding available to children whose parents sought voluntary foster care placement (Burt & Pittman, 1985).The availability of federal funds for foster care under Title IV-A reduced the states' financial responsibilities for providing substitute care. However, the absence of federal funds for reunification and preventive services left states heavily dependent on these funds, with no real incentives to move children out of foster care. The states incurred a loss in federal funding for each child discharged from foster care. Federal audits of the administration of this program have shown that children whose placements were reimbursed under the AFDC–Foster Care Program remained in care longer than did nonfederally reimbursed children and that efforts to reunify families were documented in only a few cases (GAO, 1977). For fiscal year 1991, federal expenditures for benefits of this program were $11.1 billion.

### Title IV-B

Before 1961 only limited federal funds through Title V of the original Social Security Act of 1935 (the Child Welfare Services Program) had been used for foster care (Cox & Cox, 1985). Originally, the intent of the program was to provide aid to homeless, dependent, and neglected children who were living in rural areas. By 1962, with authorization for additional funds, its scope was broadened to include any social services required to promote the well-being of children (Stein, 1987). States were then asked to match federal funding in an effort to provide evidence that child welfare services were being coordinated with other welfare and social services programs. The shift in federal

TABLE 1
**Patchwork Pattern of Federal Foster Care Program Appropriations, Fiscal Years 1990 to 1993 (in millions of dollars)**

| | Fiscal Year | | | |
|---|---|---|---|---|
| Program | 1990 | 1991 | 1992 | 1993 |
| Title IV-B Child Welfare Services | $ 252.6 | $ 245.9 | $ 273.9 | $ 294.6 |
| Title IV-E Foster Care | 1,200.1 | 1,813.2 | 2,039.3 | 2,610.0 |
| IV-E Adoption Assistance | 132.0 | 189.9 | 201.8 | 243.9 |
| IV-E Independent Living | 50.0 | 60.0 | 70.0 | 70.0 |

SOURCE: U.S. House of Representatives, Committee on Ways and Means. (1993). *Overview of entitlement programs: 1993 greenbook.* Washington, DC: U.S. Government Printing Office.

policy at this time was prompted by the increased value and funding of training for social workers who were to provide social services as a means of curbing poverty and the prevalence of foster care drift. In 1967, authorization of this title was changed to Title IV-B.

During the 1970s the federal government assumed a more active role in shaping the nature and quality of child welfare services. Congress authorized an increase in funding for child welfare services under Title IV-B in 1972, 1973, 1976, and thereafter to encourage states to expand and develop supportive, protective, and preventive services. Although Title IV-B makes no direct reference to reunification, the language of the provision encourages states to "establish, extend, and strengthen public social services which supplement parental care and keep families intact" (cited in Burt & Pittman, 1985, p. 29).

Two factors tend to account for the limited impact of Title IV-B. Appropriations for the title have always been far below the authorized levels. For example, the 1973 authorized level of funding was slightly less than $200 million; however, the appropriated funds were reported at $45 million in 1970 and at $56.5 million in fiscal year 1979 (Burt & Pittman, 1985). The federal government was not providing states with the monetary incentives needed to promote the development of preventive and restorative programs at levels sufficient to meet clients' needs. Even though the appropriations were low, the lack of enforceable restrictions on the use of Title IV-B funds also contributed to the legislation's ineffectiveness in reducing inappropriate out-of-home placements. According to one report, most states used Title IV-B funds to pay for out-of-home placements, not preventive services (Children's Defense Fund, 1978). In fiscal year 1991, federal expenditures for Title IV-B were $274 million.

### Title XX

Title XX, enacted in 1974, provides funds to states for an array of social services, including child welfare. Originally, a federal statute mandated that funds were to be allocated to provide social services to people who were receiving AFDC or Supplemental Security Income (SSI) and to specifically defined low-income families (Pecora et al., 1992). This legislation, an amendment to the Social Security Act of 1935, created a new section that allowed states to have more power and discretion in setting priorities for services and funding levels of local programs that were aimed at meeting one of five federally mandated service goals: (1) self-support, (2) self-sufficiency, (3) prevention of abuse and neglect, (4) prevention of inappropriate institutional care, and (5) obtaining appropriate institutional care and services.

In 1981, Title XX was transformed into a block grant as part of the Omnibus Budget Reconciliation Act (P.L. 97-35). This shift brought several important changes, including the elimination of required state matching funds, the merger of separate federal appropriations for social services, and the removal of mandates for the expenditure of funds on welfare recipients and formerly mandated service goals (Kimmich, 1985). On average, states spend about half their funds from social services block grants on child welfare services, including day care, information and referral, protective services, foster care, homemaker assistance, and counseling. About one-third of Title XX recipients are children. However, in the late 1980s, the use of these funds to support child welfare services declined in many states. Nevertheless, Title XX funding has been a major financial source for preventive child welfare services. Unlike the previously described statutes, Title XX is a capped entitlement program. In fiscal year 1991 the entitlement ceiling was $2.8 billion.

## Adoption Assistance and Child Welfare Act

The advocacy momentum in the 1970s ended with the passage of the Adoption Assistance and Child Welfare Act of 1980 (P.L. 96-272), the primary legislative vehicle establishing the current goals and administrative framework for child welfare services and family foster care services in particular (Family Impact Seminar, 1990). In passing the legislation, Congress sought to raise public concern about the rates of admission and discharge of children from foster care. Members of Congress debated the unnecessary removal of children from their homes and their subsequent placement in inappropriate settings, the large number of children who languished in foster care and moved from home to home, ineffective efforts to reunify families, and the absence of provisions for preventive services to avoid or delay placement.

The legislation created a two-tiered funding framework—one for foster care maintenance costs for AFDC- and non-AFDC-eligible children and the other for preventive and restorative services (Pecora et al., 1992). Specifically, the law replaced Title IV-A (AFDC–Foster Care Program) of the Social Security Act with a new subtitle, Title IV-E, and amended Title IV-B, the Child Welfare Services provisions. These provisions in effect changed the federal reimbursement for foster care provided to AFDC-eligible children and increased funding for preventive and reunification services.

### Title IV-E

Title IV-A was transferred to a newly created Title IV-E, a permanently authorized, open-ended entitlement program (Family Impact Seminar, 1990). Under this new Title IV-E program, states are partially reimbursed (1) for monthly payments to foster parents who care for AFDC-eligible children in state custody, (2) for adoption subsidies to parents who adopt children with special needs who are eligible for AFDC and Supplemental Security Income (SSI), and (3) for certain administrative costs of the program. Although states establish their own foster care payment rates and licensing standards, the federal matching rate for foster care maintenance payments is the same as the rate used in AFDC and Medicaid. Federal matching rates vary by states' per capita incomes and range from 50 percent to 83 percent, with the nationwide average about 57 percent (Spar, 1993). The federal share of total foster care spending under Title IV-E was estimated at $2.6 million in fiscal year 1993.

Additional fiscal incentives are included in the program to encourage states to provide child welfare services. These incentives include the imposition of certain ceilings on the use of funds for foster care and encouragements to transfer unused maintenance funds to the states' Title IV-B Child Welfare Services Program. AFDC- and SSI-eligible children who are placed in care are automatically eligible for Medicaid benefits, and their eligibility continues following their adoption until they are 18.

Under the Title IV-E foster care program, states are required in each case to make reasonable efforts either to prevent or to eliminate the need to remove a child from his or her home or to make it possible for a child to return home after placement. When children enter placement as the result of a court proceeding, "the court must determine whether reasonable efforts to prevent placement have been made" (Stein, 1987, p. 644).

As part of the Omnibus Budget Reconciliation Act of 1985, the Independent Living Program, funded under Title IV-E, was established. This capped entitlement authorizes funds to help states provide services—including education, career planning, training in daily living skills, and locating housing—to facilitate the transition of children in foster care to independent living. Appropriations for the program were established at $60 million in 1991 (Spar, 1990).

### Amended Title IV-B

Title IV-B permanently authorizes federal matching grants to states for three types of child welfare services: direct services, training, and research and demonstration programs (Family Impact Seminar, 1990). When the title was enacted, the federal matching rate for IV-B funds was increased, for the first time, to a flat 75 percent. The rate had previously varied from 33 percent to 66 percent. Although Title IV-B authorized funding for general child welfare services in the 1960s, states had been using this funding to pay for maintaining children in foster care. In 1980 one source indicated that as much as 75 percent of the states' Title IV-B funds had been used in this manner (Calhoun, 1980, cited in Stein, 1987). To rectify these practices the amended Title IV-B provisions of P.L. 96-272 limited the funds that could be used for foster care maintenance to the $56.6 million amount spent in fiscal year 1979 (Spar, 1990) and stipulated that funds above this amount must be used for preventive and reunification services. In effect, the law established a cap on federal funds for AFDC foster care when appropriations for Title IV-B reached a specified amount. The intent was simply to provide more money for prevention and reunification services and less for foster care placements.

***New linkages.*** The legislation established a set of fiscal procedures that encourage states to transfer a certain amount of unused Title IV-E foster care funds to the Title IV-B child welfare services program. In short, the legislation created a link between Title IV-E and Title IV-B funding, contingent on two stipulations. The first was that states would be allowed to transfer funds if they capped their federal foster care program and if they implemented protections required by law under the Title IV-B provisions. The second was that if appropriations reached a certain level for two consecutive years ($266 million appropriation level for Title IV-B, the maximum then authorized), states would have to place a cap on their foster care program and implement a preventive preplacement service program to avoid the need for foster care (Spar, 1990). In 1989, legislation increased the authorization of Title IV-B and the amount that would trigger these additional requirements to $325 million (Spar, 1990). The fiscal year 1993 appropriation for child welfare services was $295 million (Spar, 1993).

***Protections for children.*** States are allowed wide discretion in the use of Title IV-B funds, but they must also provide certain protections for all foster children if they are to receive Title IV-B funds (Spar, 1993). These protections and procedures specifically include the following:

- A *detailed written case plan* that describes the appropriateness of the placement, the services provided to the child, and the plan for achieving permanence for each child is required. Placements must be in the least restrictive, most familylike setting available, in close proximity to the biological parents, and consistent with the best interest and special needs of the child.
- *Periodic case review* is required every six months under judicial auspices or through an administrative review procedure. If state agencies use administrative review panels, the panels must consist of at least one person who is not involved in providing case management services or the delivery of services to the child or parents. Dispositional hearings by a court or a court-appointed administrative body are required within 18 months of the child's placement and periodically thereafter.
- A *onetime statewide inventory* of children in care for six months or more must be conducted. In conjunction with the inventory, states must establish statewide information systems that provide data describing the legal status, demographic characteristics, location, and goals for placement of children who are currently in foster care or had been in foster care within the preceding 12 months.
- *Procedural safeguards* regarding removal and placement agreements must be in place, including the participation of parents and children in the development and approval of case plans. Fair hearings must be available for children, parents, or foster parents to appeal the denial of the benefits or services authorized under the act.
- *Reunification or permanent planning services* that include day care, homemaker services, family and individual counseling for parents and children, respite care, parent education, adoptive services, and adoption follow-up must be in place.
- *Voluntary placements* will be eligible for federal reimbursement for the first 180 days if the state meets the foregoing requirements.

**Outcomes**

Evaluations of the extent to which the states have implemented the safeguards and procedural standards mandated by P.L. 96-272 are limited. However, by 1989, 48 states had passed the lowest standard of compliance (case plans and reviews), and 31 of these states had reached the highest levels of compliance (General Accounting Office, 1989). Since the enactment of the Adoption Assistance and Child Welfare Act of 1980, no formal assessments of its impact have been conducted. Nevertheless, the law has been perceived as an effective catalyst for reducing the number of children placed in institutions, shortening the time that children remain in care, and increasing the number of adoptions and reunifications of families with children who were previously placed. An unintended consequence of the law has been an increase in the amount of required paperwork, which is considered a major obstacle for improving the delivery of services (Kamerman & Kahn, 1990).

Although congressional action since 1983 has marginally changed funding levels and administrative procedures, families who are in need of foster care services are more seriously troubled and have multiple problems. The children of these families, many of them adolescents, have dropped out of school, are unable to find jobs, and are having babies themselves; others are medically fragile infants and young children who require more intensive services than are available. In 1987 the National Commission on Children, established by Congress and President Ronald Reagan, was authorized to "assess the status of children and families in the U.S. and propose new directions for policy and program development" (National Commission on Children, 1991, p. viii). The commission's recommendations for child welfare that appear in its final report, *Beyond Rhetoric,* released in 1991, urged a fundamental restructuring of child welfare services and the development of comprehensive community-level supports and services. The framework for the commission's recommendations is "a comprehensive, community-based, family-focused system that will lessen the need to place vulnerable children in substitute care" (p. 293).

A significant component of the commission's recommended service system includes the development of family preservation and family support programs. Bipartisan congressional support of legislation authorizing funding for family preservation in 1991 and 1992 was thwarted by concerns over an adequate financing mechanism. However, in 1993, as part of the Omnibus Budget Reconciliation Act (P.L. 103-66), Title IV-B was amended to provide entitlement matching funds to the states for family preservation and family support services beginning in fiscal year 1994. Total family preservation allocations range from $60 million in 1994 to $255 million in fiscal year 1998. States are authorized to use these funds for community services, such as programs to improve parenting skills, intensive family preservation services for families who are at risk of losing their children to foster care, temporary assistance to parents and other child guardians, and community-based family support services designed to prevent family crises from occurring (Spar, 1993).

Since the 1960s, federal foster care policies have sought to achieve the elusive goal of minimizing the placement of children and increasing services aimed at reunifying and restoring families. Most federal policy for foster care is driven by the need to address special populations of children who are in need of substitute care, such as those needing adoption subsidies and adolescents who benefit from the Independent Living Initiative.

## Children and Their Families

### Sources of Information

Although most states have gradually improved their data-collection systems since 1980, as required by P.L. 96-272, there is no nationally mandated information system for foster care and adoption data, nor are states required to report these data to federal agencies (Family Impact Seminar, 1990). (Federal regulations for the mandatory collection of data for state child welfare agencies were published in 1990 ["Title IV-B and Title IV-E," 1990]; however, it may be years before the system is fully operational and capable of producing valid national profiles.) Consequently, statistics on the children in care or those who have been adopted must be reported with caution because of variations in the definitions of substitute care used by the states, differences in their data-collection methods, gaps in reporting, and inadequate state information systems (Pecora et al., 1992).

Estimates of the number of children in foster care are based primarily on data collected through the American Public Welfare Association's Voluntary Cooperative Information System (VCIS), which was established in 1982. Most states have cooperated with this new data-collection system; however, there are certain limitations in the data. Participation in the survey is voluntary, so not all states report regularly or respond to each item in the same way, which makes it difficult to draw comparisons. It is also important to note that these data focus entirely on out-of-home placements through the child welfare system and neglect to indicate out-of-home placements through the mental health and juvenile justice systems (Pecora et al., 1992). Nevertheless, the VCIS data provide a rough estimate of national trends. The most recent year for which complete data are available is 1990. Some tentative data on the number of children in foster care are available for more recent years.

### Size of the Foster Care Population

According to the VCIS estimates, there were 442,000 children in foster care at the end of fiscal year 1992—a nationwide increase of 5 percent from the last day of 1991. These data indicate that the number of children in foster care has increased over the past several years, reversing the declines reported in the 1970s and early 1980s. According to the National Commission on Children (1991), an estimated 502,000 children were in foster care in 1977; by 1980 this number had dropped to 302,000, and it declined to a low of 275,000 in 1983. However, during the mid-1980s these estimates began to increase substantially. Between 1982 and 1986, there was no appreciable change in the population of children in substitute care, which rose by only 6.9 percent during this period. However, between 1986 and 1990, the substitute care population rose by 45.4 percent. The largest increase occurred between 1987 and 1988 (13.3 percent, compared with an increase of 6.3 percent from 1989 to 1990; Tatara, 1993b). Estimates of the number of children in foster care for 1990 to 1992 suggest smaller growth rates (5.4 percent from 1990 to 1991 and 3.0 percent from 1991 to 1992). The figures for 1991 and 1992 are preliminary estimates and may be higher than the actual number of children in care.

The most common explanation for the increase in the substitute care population is the decline in the rate of discharges from care in the past several years. After a decline of 11,000 foster care children in 1982, from 1983 to 1992 there was a net increase (the number of admissions exceeded the number of discharges), with a substantial increase in 1989 and 1990—40,000 and 43,000, respectively (Tatara, 1993a). In the late 1980s, the discharge rates for foster care were much smaller than the admission rates. In 1990 only 33.2 percent of the children in care left the system, and 40.3 percent were admitted. Comparable data for 1985 show that 40.0 percent were discharged from care and 41.3 percent were admitted (Tatara, 1992).

### Types of Substitute Care

As Table 2 shows, family foster care is the predominant type of foster care placement. Throughout the 1980s, more than two-thirds of children in substitute care resided in foster family homes, including nonfinalized adoptive homes (302,500 children in 1990). Within family foster care living arrangements, an increasing number of children

TABLE 2

**Selected Characteristics of the Foster Care Population in 1982, 1988, and 1990 (percentage)**

| Characteristics | 1982 | 1988 | 1990 |
|---|---|---|---|
| Type of substitute care[a] | | | |
| Family foster home | 72.0 | 71.4 | 74.5 |
| Nonfinalized adoptive home | — | 2.3 | 2.7 |
| Group home | 21.5 | 18.6 | 16.4 |
| Living independently | 0.6 | 0.7 | 0.5 |
| Other | 5.2 | 5.7 | 5.6 |
| Unknown | 0.7 | 1.3 | 0.3 |
| Age[b] | | | |
| Under one year | 2.7 | 5.0 | 4.9 |
| One to five years | 19.8 | 27.4 | 31.1 |
| Six to 12 years | 29.0 | 31.1 | 32.3 |
| 13 to 18 years | 45.3 | 34.1 | 29.7 |
| 19 and over | 2.9 | 2.3 | 1.7 |
| Unknown | 0.4 | 0.1 | 0.3 |
| Race/ethnicity[c] | | | |
| White | 52.7 | 45.5 | 39.3 |
| African American | 34.2 | 36.5 | 40.4 |
| Hispanic | 6.7 | 10.1 | 11.8 |
| Other | 4.6 | 4.2 | 4.3 |
| Unknown | 1.8 | 3.7 | 4.2 |

SOURCE: Tatara, T. (1993). *Characteristics of children in substitute and adoptive care.* Washington, DC: Voluntary Cooperative Information System, American Public Welfare Association.

[a]Data are based on reports from 41 states in 1982, 31 states in 1988, and 28 states in 1990, accounting for 86 percent, 78 percent, and 68 percent of the total substitute care population, respectively.

[b]Data are based on reports from 30 states in 1982, 26 states in 1988, and 23 states in 1990, accounting for 53 percent, 70 percent, and 61 percent of the total substitute care population, respectively.

[c]Data are based on reports from 38 states in 1982, 34 states in 1988, and 31 states in 1990, accounting for 81 percent, 82 percent, and 75 percent of the total substitute care population, respectively.

are placed with relatives, especially in some states. According to data based on information supplied by 25 states to the U.S. Department of Health and Human Services in 1992, the percentage of children placed with relatives grew from 18 percent to 31 percent of the foster care caseload from 1986 through 1990. There was a small decline in the percentage of children residing in group homes, institutions, and emergency care between 1986 and 1990; however, the number of such children rose during that period, from 57,100 (20 percent) in 1986 to 66,000 in 1990, according to reports from 39 states in 1989 for 83 percent of the total substitute care population and 28 states in 1990 for 68 percent of the total population.

### Characteristics of Foster Care Children

Children in care during the late 1980s were considerably younger than were those in care in the early 1980s. The median age of children in care was 12.6 years in 1982, compared to 9.4 years in 1988 and 8.6 years in 1990. There was also an increase in the number of infants in care during this period, from 7,100 infants in 1982 to about 17,000 infants in 1988 to 19,900 in 1990. The drop in the median age of the foster care population is partially attributed to this recent increase in the number of infants admitted to care (see Table 2).

In 1990 girls represented 48.7 percent of the foster care population, and boys represented 51.0 percent, a very slight change from 1982, when girls represented 46.7 percent and boys 52.9 percent. There were slight variations in the racial composition of the substitute care population. Although the percentage of white children in care declined throughout the 1980s, there were more white children in care in 1990 than in 1982 (159,600 and 138,100, respectively). During the same period, the number of African American children in care rose from 89,600 in 1982 to 164,000 in 1990. Among Hispanic children the increase was more significant—from 17,600 in 1982 to 47,900 in 1990. Since 1985, however, the proportion of minority children in care has risen only slightly.

Each year from 1982 to 1988, 75 percent to 78 percent of the children in care did not have any known disabilities, and in 1990 the percentage was 75.6 percent. About one-fifth of the children in care had one or more disabling conditions from 1982 to 1988. On the basis of information from 16 states that provided this information for 38 percent of the total substitute care population, an estimated 52,000 children (13 percent) were reported in 1990 to have one or more disabling conditions (Tatara & Pettiford, 1990).

### Legal Custody of Children in Care

There was no appreciable change in the percentage of children in care whose parental rights were neither terminated nor relinquished between 1983 (85 percent) and 1990 (87.5 percent) or in the percentages of children who were placed in care with a court-ordered termination or relinquishment (a voluntary termination) of parental rights (11 percent in 1983 and 11.8 percent in 1990).

## Dynamics of the Foster Care System

Although descriptive data about the demographic characteristics of children in foster care are important, these data limit understanding of the dynamic flow of children through the system at a given time. Indicators of this dynamic flow include such information as the reasons for placement, the duration of stay, number of placements, and permanency goals for children in care (Family Impact Seminar, 1990).

### Reasons for Placement

VCIS data show that between 1984 and 1990 slightly less than three-fourths of the children in care entered because of parental condition or absence, protective services, or both (see Table 3). Whereas 31,300 children (17.0 percent) were placed in 1984 because of parental condition or absence (for example, economic hardship, substance abuse, homelessness, illness, imprisonment), by 1990, 50,700 (20.7 percent) had been placed for this reason. In addition, 102,500 children (55.7 percent) were placed because of protective service reasons in 1984, compared to 123,000 children (50.2 percent) in 1990.

The percentages of children placed for reasons of status offense or delinquency did not change appreciably in 1984 and 1990 (9.9 percent in 1984 and 11.3 percent in 1990), nor did the percentages of children placed because of the children's disability or hardship (2.3 percent in 1984 and 1.9 percent in 1990). The percentage of children who entered care because parental rights were relinquished or terminated was small each year from 1984 to 1990 (1.4 percent in 1984 and 0.8 percent in 1990).

### Length of Time in Care

Overall, the length of stay for children in care was slightly shorter during the 1980s. In 1982 the median duration in care was 1.7 years; 25 percent of the children had been in care more than 4.3 years, and 10 percent were in care more than 7.4 years. In 1988 the median duration was 1.4 years; 25 percent of the children had been in care more than 2.9 years, and 10 percent were in care longer than 5.0 years (Tatara, 1992).

In 1990, 22 states provided data on the length of time for 58 percent of the population of children in care. According to these data, 18 percent of the children were in care for six or fewer months; 15 percent, for six months to one year; 24 percent, for one to two years; 16 percent, for three to five years; and 10 percent, for five years or more. By comparison, in 1984, 24 percent of the children

TABLE 3

**Selected Characteristics of Dynamic Flow of Children in Substitute Care, 1984 and 1990 (percentage)**

| Characteristics | 1984 | 1990 |
|---|---|---|
| Reason for entry[a] | | |
| Protective service | 55.7 | 50.2 |
| Status offense/delinquency | 9.9 | 11.3 |
| Child disability | 2.3 | 1.9 |
| Parental condition/absence | 17.0 | 20.9 |
| Relinquishment of parental rights | 1.4 | 0.8 |
| Other state-defined reason | 9.3 | 12.5 |
| Unknown | 4.4 | 2.4 |
| Length of time in care[b] | | |
| Zero to six months | 24.3 | 17.8 |
| Six months to one year | 17.1 | 14.8 |
| One to two years | 19.9 | 23.9 |
| Two to three years | 11.6 | 15.8 |
| Three to five years | 11.5 | 16.9 |
| Five years or more | 15.2 | 10.2 |
| Unknown | 0.4 | 0.6 |
| Permanency goals[c] | | |
| Reunify | 50.8 | 57.6 |
| Adoption | 14.1 | 13.8 |
| Independent living | 8.7 | 7.0 |
| Long-term foster care | 16.8 | 12.4 |
| No goal (care/protection) | 6.8 | 2.9 |
| Guardianship | — | 3.0 |
| Unknown | 2.8 | 3.3 |

SOURCE: Tatara, T. (1993). *Characteristics of children in substitute and adoptive care.* Washington, DC: Voluntary Cooperative Information System, American Public Welfare Association.

[a]Data on the reason for entry are based on reports from 25 states in 1984 and 19 states in 1990, accounting for 43 percent and 46 percent of the total substitute care population during those years.

[b]These figures are based on data supplied by 27 states in 1984 and 22 states in 1990, accounting for 58 percent of the total substitute care population in both years.

[c]Data are based on reports from 36 states in 1984 and 26 states in 1990, accounting for 74 percent and 67 percent of the total substitute care population during those years.

had been in care for six or fewer months; 17 percent, for six months to one year; 20 percent, for one to two years; 12 percent, for two to three years; 12 percent for three to five years; and 15 percent, for five or more continuous years (Tatara, 1992). These data also indicate that the length of stay in foster care was shorter in 1984 than in 1990.

### Number of Placements

Overall, nearly a majority of the children in care in 1990 did not experience any change in their living arrangements during their current placements. However, more children were moved from one placement to another in 1990 than in 1982 (54 percent in 1990 and 42.6 percent in 1982). The percentage of children who experienced at least one change in placement during their stay in care rose from 19 percent in 1982 to 27.5 percent in 1990. Likewise, the percentage of children who were moved from one placement to another two to four times increased from 1982 (17.9 percent, or 46,900 children) to 1990 (23.6 percent, or 95,800 children). Only 19 states, accounting for 38 percent of the total substitute care population, provided information on this subject in 1982, whereas 15 states, accounting for 51 percent of the total population, reported this information in 1990 (Tatara, 1993a).

### Permanency Goals

From 1982 to 1988, the percentage of children whose permanency goal was reunification increased from 39.2 percent to 60 percent, whereas the percentage whose permanency goal was adoption remained about the same at 16.5 percent in 1982 and 15 percent in 1990. During this period, there was a decline in the percentage of children with a permanency goal of independent living (from 11 percent in 1982 to 5 percent in 1990) and in long-term foster care (from 18.7 percent in 1982 to 12 percent in 1990).

## Characteristics of Foster Parents

Statistical data about foster parents—the caregivers of service—have become available only recently (Kaye & Cook, 1993). Although these data must be reviewed with caution because of methodological and sampling limitations, they provide estimates of the demographic trends in the population of foster parents. Kaye and Cook's National Survey of Current and Former Foster Parents estimated that there were 131,100 licensed family foster homes, including homes licensed for emergency care, family group care, and specialized foster family care, in 1990. (Homes that are licensed for care by relatives only were excluded from this estimate.) On the basis of the average licensing capacity of the surveyed homes, which was 3.1 children, an estimated 406,400 family foster care beds were officially available. Kaye and Cook noted that "foster homes licensed before 1980 had an average capacity of 3.9 beds per home, whereas bed capacity in homes licensed between 1980 and 1985 had dropped to 2.9 beds, and those licensed after 1985 had an average capacity of 2.6 beds" (p. iv). These data indicate that there will be an even greater shortage of foster family homes in the future.

The supply of foster family homes has not kept pace with the growth of the foster care population. From 1985 to 1990, the number of children in foster care increased by 47 percent, whereas the number of foster family homes declined by 27 percent (Spar, 1993). Several factors are associated with the growing shortage of foster homes, including the increased employment of women who might previously have provided full-time foster care; the low reimbursement rates; inadequate support services, such as respite care; and insufficient preservice and in-service training opportunities for foster parents.

Previous studies of foster parents (Hampson & Tavormina, 1980; Peterson & Pierce, 1974; U.S. Children's Bureau, 1980) were remarkably consistent in their profiles of foster parents. Foster parents tended to be in their mid- to late-40s, to be married, to have a high school education or less, and to have low to lower-middle incomes. Foster mothers were mainly homemakers, although in the 1980s an increasing number were employed either full-time or part-time. Foster fathers were mostly blue-collar or skilled laborers. The majority of foster parents were white, and a significant minority were African American, but few were Hispanic.

Kaye and Cook's (1993) survey of foster parents showed that the percentage of foster mothers with less than a high school education had declined among those licensed after 1980. Among foster mothers licensed after 1985, an increasing percentage were employed (42 percent full-time, 18 percent part-time), and only one-third were homemakers. Although there was a slight increase in the percentage of licensed Hispanic foster parents after 1985, the percentage of African American foster parents declined from 1980 to 1985. Shortages in minority foster parents were most notable in urban areas. Moreover, African American and Hispanic foster parents "were more likely to be caring for children at or above their licensing capacity" (Kaye & Cook, p. 102). The shortage of foster parents occurred at a time when the number of children in foster care increased.

## Foster Care Services

The goals of foster care programs are achieved through the provision of services to children, their biological parents, and foster families. The provision of services is designed to meet the needs and treatment goals established by social workers who carefully develop individualized case plans for each child in care. Children in foster care may require health care services from physicians, educational and psychological testing in schools, and social services as they adjust to new environments. Their biological parents are frequently in need of concrete and professional services, such as substance abuse treatment, parent education, family counseling services, child care, transportation services, housing assistance, and employment services. Foster parents require training in child management; child care as a respite service; direct intervention in the home to resolve difficulties that may emerge between the child and the foster parents; and adoption-related services, if the foster parents plan to adopt children for whom they have provided care (Stein, 1987). Although certainly not an exhaustive description of foster care services, the following sections highlight the range of services that are typically available in foster care programs. The scarcity of community resources restricts the effectiveness of these services and their distribution among the parties involved.

### Case Management

In the child welfare field, the provision of case management services is an essential component of permanency planning. Most families who need foster care services have multiple and diverse problems that require assistance from a wide range of service providers. Case managers perform such tasks and functions as negotiating and coordinating services; referring parents to community resources; planning and managing visiting arrangements; assisting parents, foster parents, and children with the identification, development, and use of their own social networks; monitoring the delivery of services; evaluating the attainment of treatment goals; and collaborating with foster parents (Pecora et al., 1992). Case managers frequently conduct home visits to assess the child's adjustment to a foster care placement and evaluate the attainment of treatment goals.

### Respite Services

Respite services are designed to give caregivers, both biological parents and foster parents, time away from their child care responsibilities. Respite services help reduce stress, which often results from uninterrupted child care responsibilities and personal and family crises, and thus minimize some of the risks of foster care placement. Various forms of respite care are available to parents and foster parents; they include day care services and homemakers who help parents develop new child care skills or assume short-term child care responsibilities to allow parents to take several hours each week away from their routines.

### Training of Foster Parents

As the emphasis on permanency has gained prominence, the idea of viewing foster parents as partners within the team of caretakers has resulted in the movement toward the professionalization of foster parents. This trend has been prompted by (1) the expansion and specialization of foster parents as role models and parent educators; (2) the shift toward more treatment-oriented foster care; (3) the special needs and demands of children in care in such areas as acquired immune deficiency syndrome (AIDS), substance abuse, and family violence; and (4) the complex situations of the children and families involved in the foster care system. Since the mid-1970s, foster care agencies and other child welfare-oriented organizations have invested a great deal of energy in the development of educational curricula and other resources to promote the professionalization of foster parents.

Foster parenting today requires competence and knowledge in many areas: child development; behavior management; cultural diversity; the philosophy and practice of permanency planning; the effects of separation and placement on children and their families; and the needs of children who have experienced physical and sexual abuse, exposure to drugs or AIDS during infancy, and family violence. Other support services that have been found useful are support groups for foster parents, the establishment of "buddy" systems for newly recruited foster parents, and membership in foster parent associations.

### Parent Education

Many of the parents who require foster care services lack basic information and skills in parenting and child care. Instruction in such areas as child-caring skills, child development, and alternative methods for disciplining children is common in foster care programs. The methods used to educate parents vary widely, from those provided in the client's home or within a formal classroom setting to those that involve small-group discussion, video training, or role modeling by foster parents.

**Therapy**

Individual, family, and group clinical services to children and families are provided as one way of resolving the complex problems that lead to placement. Therapy is used to help families alter family dynamics or promote positive parent–child relationships (Pecora et al., 1992).

## Future Issues for Social Workers

The future of social workers in foster care practice is linked to the conditions under which families function and to the societal supports that are available to assist families in their child-rearing functions. The situation is further complicated by the emerging recognition of the importance of racial and cultural diversity in child-rearing practices. The development of ethnic-sensitive clinical services is a challenge for the social work profession as it seeks to protect and provide for the welfare of children and to create a balance between the rights and interests of all parties involved.

**Recruitment and Retention Issues**

Throughout the United States, state and county social services agencies report difficulty recruiting and retaining qualified social work staff. Studies have found that only about 25 percent of the caseworkers who provide direct services in child welfare have social work training and that only 10 percent have graduate degrees in social work. Moreover, about half had no previous experience working with children and families (Family Impact Seminar, 1990).

The reasons most frequently cited for staffing difficulties include (1) high caseloads of clients with complicated and multiple family difficulties; (2) high rates of staff turnover due, in part, to job-related stress, inadequate training, and the lack of public and agency support; (3) increased scrutiny by the media and the courts in the form of class action suits and indiscriminate news exposés and judicial and administrative reviews and dispositions; (4) reduction in required qualifications following the reclassification or declassification of social work positions; and (5) low salaries and insufficient promotional opportunities. Some efforts have been made to address staff shortages and to improve the qualifications of foster care workers. Many of these efforts—the result of adjudication following class action suits filed against the state—have reduced caseloads and improved in-service training and hiring practices. Solutions to these concerns, however, require the systematic compilation of data, leadership by the federal government and the social work field, advocacy by child welfare workers, and a willingness of helping professionals to work in collaboration with other interested groups.

## Future Issues in Foster Care

**Placement with Relatives**

On both a policy and practice level, foster care theory and practice will be shaped by five emerging trends. The first is the increasing percentage of children who are placed not in traditional foster homes but with their own relatives. Placements with relatives are more likely to occur in large urban areas, among economically disadvantaged children of color and their families. Although children have been placed with relatives since the inception of child welfare services, the dramatic increases in such placements raise concern about the boundaries between informal mutual aid systems and the expanding role and responsibility of government for ensuring the protection of children who are living with relatives. These types of placements raise obvious concerns about the equitable distribution of financial support to relatives who care for other children and about regulatory standards for ensuring the children's protection. Equally as important are the other concerns with regard to placing children with relatives: defining the role of such caregivers in the placement process, understanding the impact of the placement of relatives on permanency planning, clarifying the goals for placing children with relatives, and providing adequate services to strengthen both the kinship network and the families of children in care.

**Emphasis on Foster Parents**

Because greater emphasis has been placed on permanency planning since the early 1980s, foster care as a service system has been considered a low priority among child welfare services. However, as professional views about the roles of foster parents shift, foster parents are much more likely to become members of a treatment team and to gain a more prominent voice in case planning and permanency planning. Moreover, the need for specialized foster family homes (those with the capacity to offer therapeutic services) and for training foster parents as a means of ensuring a higher quality of substitute care is likely to increase as the needs of the children entering care change. The projected shortage of foster parents will require state agencies to engage in more aggressive recruitment and retention efforts. Recruiting, training, and supporting foster parents are key issues in the child welfare services that will be necessary in the next 10 years.

### Coordination of Services

As a result of the fragmentation and categorical nature of the service delivery systems for families with children in foster care, there are obvious gaps in services, as well as the duplication and inadequate coordination of services. "Child and family problems do not neatly divide themselves into: foster care, child abuse and neglect, special education, mental health, juvenile justice, developmental disabilities, teen pregnancy, runaways and the rest. The same children appear in different systems at different times or at the same time" (Kamerman & Kahn, 1990, p. 164). Conflicting eligibility requirements, rigidity in funding arrangements, and specialized professional staff have created obstacles to the greater coordination of services across systems. As a result, children and their families have received services for the diagnosed problem or condition that a single system can provide, but their remaining needs have not been treated or otherwise addressed.

Efforts to integrate and "decategorize" children's services are necessary reforms of the child welfare system. These reforms will require the implementation of innovations in the financial, organizational, and managerial supports for foster family care.

### Family Preservation

The development of and reliance on family preservation programs represent the fourth emerging trend in foster family care. Although these programs have many different names, structures, and orientations, they share certain common features, including a focus on the family unit, rather than on individual family members, and provision of home-based, crisis-oriented, short-term intensive services. One essential element of these programs is the relatively small caseloads to which social workers are assigned; these small caseloads are necessary for stabilizing the family, preventing placement, and promoting family reunification. The emergence of family preservation programs may turn foster family care into a temporary service, rather than a long-term substitute care service.

### Amount and Pattern of Funding

Finally, the most important factor in the future of family foster care is the amount and pattern of funding for these services. Budgetary cuts during the 1980s and early 1990s severely undermined the provision of services to reunify families by deemphasizing funding for preventive services. Without sufficient funding for preventive services, permanency as a goal of foster care is an illusion.

## References

Adoption Assistance and Child Welfare Act of 1980, P.L. 96-272, 94 Stat. 500.

Axinn, J., & Levin, H. (1992). *Social welfare: A history of the American response to need* (3rd ed.). New York: Longman.

Bell, W. (1965). *Aid to dependent children*. New York: New York University Press.

Burt, M., & Pittman, K. (1985). *Testing the social safety net*. Washington, DC: Urban Institute Press.

Children's Defense Fund. (1978). *Children without homes*. Washington, DC: Author.

Costin, L., & Rapp, C. (1972). *Child welfare: Policies and practices*. New York: McGraw-Hill.

Cox, M., & Cox, R. (1985). *Foster care: Current issues, policies and practices*. Norwood, NJ: Ablex.

Family Impact Seminar. (1990). *Crisis in foster care: New directions for the 1990s*. Washington, DC: American Association for Marriage and Family Therapy, Research and Education Foundation.

General Accounting Office. (1977). *Children in foster care institutions: Steps government can take to improve their care*. Gaithersburg, MD: Author.

General Accounting Office. (1989, August). *Foster care: Incomplete implementation of the reforms and unknown effectiveness* (Report No. GAO/PEMD-89-17). Gaithersburg, MD: Author.

General Accounting Office. (1991, September). *Foster care: Children's experiences linked to various factors; better data needed* (Report No. GAO/HRD-91-64). Gaithersburg, MD: Author.

Hampson, R., & Tavormina, J. (1980). Feedback from the experts: A study of foster mothers. *Social Work, 25,* 108–113.

Jenkins, S. (1967). Duration of foster care—Some relevant antecedent variables. *Child Welfare, 46,* 450–456.

Jenkins, S., & Sauber, M. (1966). *Paths to child placement*. New York: Community Council of Greater New York.

Kadushin, A. (1974). *Child welfare services* (2nd ed.). New York: Macmillan.

Kadushin, A., & Martin, J. (1988). *Child welfare services* (4th ed.). New York: Columbia University Press.

Kamerman, S., & Kahn, A. (1990). Social services for children, youth and families in the United States. *Children and Youth Services Review* [Special Issue], *12*(1/2).

Kaye, E., & Cook, R. (1993). *National survey of current and former foster parents* (Pub. No. 105-89-1602). Washington, DC: U.S. Department of Health and Human Services, Administration on Children, Youth and Families.

Kimmich, M. (1985). *America's children: Who cares?* Washington, DC: Urban Institute Press.

Lawder, E. (1966). Quasi-adoption. *Children, 13,* 11–12.

Maas, H., & Engler, R. (1959). *Children in need of parents*. New York: Columbia University Press.

Madison, B., & Shapiro, M. (1970). Permanent and long term foster care as a placement service. *Child Welfare, 49,* 131–136.

McGowan, B., & Meezan, W. (1983). *Child welfare: Current dilemmas, future directions*. Itasca, IL: F. E. Peacock.

National Commission on Children. (1991). *Beyond rhetoric: A new American agenda for children and families*. Washington, DC: Author.

Omnibus Budget Reconciliation Act of 1981, P.L. 97-35, 95 Stat. 357.

Omnibus Budget Reconciliation Act of 1983, P.L. 98-270, 98 Stat. 157.

Omnibus Budget Reconciliation Act of 1993, P.L. 103-66.

Pecora, P., Whittaker, J., Maluccio, A., Barth, R., & Plotnick, R. (1992). *Child welfare challenge: Policy, practice and research*. New York: Aldine De Gruyter.

Peterson, J., & Pierce, A. (1974). Socioeconomic characteristics of foster parents. *Child Welfare, 53,* 295–304.

Shyne, A., & Schroeder, A. (1978). *Public social services for children and their families*. Rockville, MD: Westat.

Social Security Act of 1935, Ch. 531, 49 Stat. 620.

Spar, K. (1990, November). *Child welfare and foster care reform: Issues for Congress*. Washington, DC: Congressional Research Service, Education and Public Welfare Division.

Spar, K. (1993, September). *Kinship foster care: An emerging federal issue*. Washington, DC: Congressional Research Service, Education and Public Welfare Division.

Stein, T. (1987). Foster care for children. In A. Minahan (Ed.-in-Chief), *Encyclopedia of social work* (18th ed., Vol. 1, pp. 639–650). Silver Spring, MD: National Association of Social Workers.

Takas, M. (1993). *Kinship care and family preservation*. Washington, DC: Center on Children and the Law, American Bar Association.

Tatara, T. (1992, August). Child substitute care population trends FY82 through FY91. *Research Notes, 6*. Washington, DC: Voluntary Cooperative Information System, American Public Welfare Association.

Tatara, T. (1993a, October). *Characteristics of children in substitute and adoptive care*. Washington, DC: Voluntary Cooperative Information System, American Public Welfare Association.

Tatara, T. (1993b, August). U.S. child substitute care flow data for FY92 and current trends in the state child substitute care populations. *Research Notes, 9*. Washington, DC: Voluntary Cooperative Information System, American Public Welfare Association.

Tatara, T., & Pettiford, E. (1990). *Characteristics of children in substitute and adoptive care*. Washington, DC: Voluntary Cooperative Information System, American Public Welfare Association.

Title IV-B and Title IV-E of the Social Security Act: Data collection for foster care and adoption (1990). *Federal Register, 55*(188), 39540.

U.S. Children's Bureau. (1980). *1980 Foster parent survey*. Washington, DC: Administration for Children, Youth and Families, Division of Program Development and Innovation.

U.S. House of Representatives, Committee on Ways and Means. (1993). *Overview of entitlement programs: 1993 green book*. Washington, DC: U.S. Government Printing Office.

Wiltse, K. (1985). Foster care: An overview. In J. Laird & A. Hartman (Eds.), *A handbook of child welfare: Context, knowledge, and practice* (pp. 565–584). New York: Free Press.


## Further Reading


Algate, J., Maluccio, A., & Reeves, C. (1990). *Adolescents in foster families: Child care policy and practice*. Chicago: Nelson-Hall.

Barth, R., & Barry, M. (1987). Outcomes of child welfare services under permanency planning. *Social Service Review, 61,* 71–89.

Brace, C. L. (1973). The dangerous classes of New York, and twenty years' work among them. Washington, DC: National Association of Social Workers.

Gustavsson, N., & Segal, E. (1994). *Critical issues in child welfare*. Thousand Oaks, CA: Sage Publications.

Wells, K., & D'Angelo, L. (1994). Specialized foster care: Voices from the field. *Social Service Review, 68*(1), 127–144.

Wulczyn, F., & George, R. (1993). Foster care in New York and Illinois: The challenge of rapid change. *Social Service Review, 66*(2), 278–294.


**Joyce E. Everett, PhD,** is associate professor, Smith College School for Social Work, Lilly Hall, Northampton, MA 01063.

## For further information see

Adoption; Advocacy; Child Welfare Overview; Childhood; Children: Mental Health; Conflict Resolution; Crisis Intervention: Research Needs; Deinstitutionalization; Families Overview; Homeless Families; Poverty; Public Social Services; Runaways and Homeless Youths; School-Linked Services; Single Parents; Social Welfare Policy.

**Key Words**

child welfare services
children
family foster care
foster care

# Child Labor

**Jack Otis**

*Child labor* refers to the paid employment of children who are not physically mature or who are below a legally identified age. The minimum age for employment may vary from 14 to 18 years, depending on the nature of the work and the child labor standards of the country in which the work is performed. Most scholars in the field and the International Labour Organization (ILO) sharply distinguish "child labor" from "child work." *Child work*, at whatever age it may begin in primitive or technologically advanced societies, refers to adult-guided activities whose focus is the child's maturation and enculturation into the family and society of which he or she is a part (George, 1990). Although the child's development of educational, cultural, domestic, or vocational skills is often of immediate economic benefit to the child, the family, or society, it need not be. Child work is developmental in nature; it is not driven by the impoverishment of the child and his or her family or by market forces. However, child labor is considered to be synonymous with child exploitation because the activities may be hazardous; interfere with the child's education; or "be harmful to the child's health or physical, mental, spiritual, moral and social development" (*Convention on the Rights of the Child*, 1989, p. 10).

*Child bondage* is the compulsory service of a child to an employer. It is usually the result of a debt owed by or a payment made to impoverished parents. Bondage often becomes the de facto equivalent of slavery because the employer makes every effort to keep the child in debt (*Children in Bondage,* 1991) by nonexistent or inadequate wages and charges for services. The carpet industry in India and the brothels of Thailand rely heavily on bonded labor. As Gargan (1992) noted, as many as 300,000 children are working in bondage in an area around Sewapuri, India. In Third World and developing countries, human bondage, including child bondage, is widespread and often continues from generation to generation ("Slavery," 1992). As Fyfe (1989) pointed out,

> There should be little argument about what constitutes the super exploitation of children through work. Priority ought to go to the targeting and rooting out of child prostitution, child pornography, bonded and tied labor, and work in hazardous occupations, including military service.... We can identify the extremes—children working in slave-like conditions in factories and mines, using dangerous chemicals in pesticide-soaked fields, imprisoned in homes as domestic servants, working as prostitutes, or in guerrilla armies. (p. 4)

Children are considered desirable employees not only because they work for low or no wages, but because they are powerless and docile. These traits make them especially vulnerable to physical, emotional, and sexual abuse. Cesar Chavez and the United Farm Workers Union identified child labor as a form of child abuse ("Child Labor and Child Abuse," 1985). According to the ILO (*IPEC Programme Document,* 1993), "the exploitation and subjugation of children, at and through work, is perhaps the single most common form of child abuse and neglect in much of the world today" (p. 4).

The social work profession and social work education in the United States and internationally, although highly sensitive to problems of child abuse, have shown little awareness that child labor is both a form and a cause of child abuse and neglect. According to the ILO's International Programme on the Elimination of Child Labour (*IPEC Programme Document,* 1993),

> Few human rights abuses are so unanimously condemned, while being so universally practiced, as child labor. By any objective measure this issue should be high on the global agenda, but in practice it is surrounded by a wall of silence and perpetuated by ignorance. (p. 1)

There are a number of reasons for this state of affairs:

*Conceptual.* Opposition to child labor is weakened by the failure to distinguish child work from child labor. Those who are opposed to child labor are not opposed to the development of "world of work" materials or to employment or preemployment programs for disadvantaged teenagers and preteenagers that are designed to overcome attitudinal and educational deficits and to socialize and train these youths for the job market (*Another Ounce of Prevention,* 1988). Opponents of child labor support private and public efforts to expand entry-level jobs and summer job programs. They also believe it is reasonable and desirable for children to do chores at home or to work on farms in support of family values as long as schooling is not impaired and the work is not hazardous. It is not child work but child labor that reformers argue should be prevented or ameliorated, because child labor is, by definition, exploitive and harmful to the healthy maturation of children.

*Economic.* The manufacturing, mining, agricultural, domestic, and service sectors find significant short-term profit in the employment of children at substandard wages and without the benefits normally provided to adults. Impoverished children and their families remain silent about abuses because they fear the loss of any income that is critical to their survival.

*Political.* Financially hard-pressed governments of developing countries often support the immediate economic benefits that are a byproduct of the availability of cheap, docile child labor, and their underpaid officials may be bribed. In addition, in both developing and developed countries, the collection of statistics and labor inspections is greatly impeded by the employment of many children in the informal sectors of economy where they are invisible. For these reasons, official responses may vary from angry denial of the existence of the problem to grudging admission and lax enforcement of child labor legislation.

*Educational.* Most Third World and many developing countries have neither the legislation nor the infrastructure, personnel, and facilities to implement a compulsory, universal educational system. Nations that have such systems are better able to manage, prevent, and ameliorate the development of child labor. Opponents of child labor wage an uphill struggle against the perceived self-interest of the child and the child's family, the profits of agricultural and business enterprises, and the short-term benefits to the economy of the country and to its officials. Supporters of child labor in Third World and developing countries justify it as a means of mitigating extreme poverty. In the industrialized West, child labor is often supported by attributing the beneficial aspects of child work to child labor.

## Historical Development

### Impact of Industrial Revolution

In one form or another, child work, as distinguished from child labor, has existed in various forms in all societies of the world. Hunting and gathering societies and later agrarian ones trained and used children to obtain food and to help in herding, harvesting, and domestic activities. During the Middle Ages, the apprenticing of children to artisans, though at times exploitative and cruel, had a similar socialization function that was of long-term benefit to the vocational development of maturing children. The transition of child work to child labor was a byproduct of the Industrial Revolution that began in 18th-century Britain. In craft guilds in the Middle Ages, a skilled individual worker performed all or most of the operations needed to produce a product. During the Industrial Revolution, however, mechanization simplified production and made it more efficient in the early textile mills and thus made it possible to employ unskilled women and children at reduced wages. "There can be little doubt that the condition of the workers, especially the women and children, in the early textile factories was miserable: 14 to 16 hours per day spent performing repetitive tasks in noisy, smelly, and unsanitary surroundings" ("Work and Employment," 1985, p. 940).

Brutality and long hours were common. In the 1730s, of 17 girls on a work schedule of 4:00 A.M. to 11:00 P.M., five died. Continuing abuses led the British Parliament in 1802 to pass the Health and Morale of Apprentices Act, which banned night work and limited the workday of child apprentices to 12 hours, and in 1833 to pass the Factory Act, which banned the employment of children under age nine in factories. However, in factories and homes, coal had replaced wood in England and northern France, and a British royal commission discovered that children, some as young as age six, were working 14 hours a day in coal mines. This discovery led to the identification of the continuing global problem of lax enforcement of child labor legislation. In the 1870s, legislation in Great Britain requiring compulsory full-time schooling helped reduce the widespread abuse of child labor ("Work and Employment," 1985).

### Industrial Servants

In the 18th century, impoverished children were shipped from the streets of English cities to Virginia and other colonies as indentured servants. The conditions of travel were primitive; many died of hunger and disease on the long ocean crossing, and their bodies were thrown overboard. Those who survived were treated as commodities; they did not have even the meager legal protection provided in England at that time (Zinn, 1980). In the 1700s, the American colonies were also going through an Industrial Revolution that created the need for cheap, tractable, unskilled workers, which led to the significant expansion of child labor. Children who were employed by the mills could earn more money than their entire families could make on the farms. Because girls were less needed on the farms than were boys, they were sent to the mills. As young as 11, they worked six days a week for 12 or more hours a day. In addition to being exploited in the factories, young girls were often victims of sexual abuse (Rosner, 1980).

The Puritan ethic of hard work and the chronic labor shortage in colonial America promoted the growth of child labor, and children as young as three were ordered to be apprentices (Fyfe, 1989). The Horatio Alger stories and the real-life successes of people like John D. Rockefeller; financier Jay Cooke; and Horace Greeley, founder of the *New York Tribune,* all of whom began work in their teens, weakened efforts to legislate against child labor. However, the Puritan belief in literacy as a means of reaching God through Bible study and the view passed on by America's founding fathers that democracy required a literate citizenry led some northeastern states in the early 19th century to pass laws that reduced working hours for children to allow time for schooling. The laws were not always enforced.

**Opposition to Child Labor**

In the 18th and 19th centuries, growing opposition to child labor came from a variety of sources: from labor unions, which were concerned about unemployment and low salaries of adults; from social reformers, who were concerned about the exploitation of children; and, in Prussia, from an army that was concerned about the physical condition of its recruits. Charles Dickens and Karl Marx wrote tellingly about the evils of child labor. Jean Jacques Rousseau, Ralph Waldo Emerson, Henry David Thoreau, and others pronounced children to be innately good and identified society as the source of corruption. Scientific developments were calling attention to the special nature of the child and to childhood as a special period of growth and development. Darwin stressed the power of environment to modify development, and Freud emphasized the importance of personality and character formation in infancy and childhood. G. Stanley Hall's studies of puberty and adolescence profoundly influenced the growth of the child study movement (Trattner, 1984). In the late 19th and early 20th centuries, a driving force in the opposition to child labor by social reformers was the transformed valuation of the child from the economic to the emotional. At the annual meeting of the National Child Labor Committee (NCLC) in 1905, Felix Adler declared that to make a profit out of children was to "touch profanely a sacred thing" (quoted in Zelizer, 1985, p. 6). This "sacralization" of the child gave greater shock value to the conditions that were investigated and exposed by the early social reformers.

In 1900, in a labor force of 29 million, there were about 2 million working children ages 10 to 15 (U.S. Bureau of the Census, 1940). At the turn of the century, the first Child Labor Committee was established in Alabama by Edgar Murphy, an Episcopal clergyman. Murphy's photographs of children in textile mills had a great public impact and influenced child labor legislation in several states. In 1904 the newly organized NCLC investigated children who were employed in Pennsylvania's coal mines and glass factories; in both industries, working conditions were dangerous and child mortality rates were high. NCLC used photographic evidence to raise public awareness of the issue, and in 1911 it hired the noted sociologist–photographer Lewis W. Hine to continue on a more comprehensive basis his exposure of the appalling conditions under which children worked in the United States (Curtis & Mallach, 1984). During that period, Sarah N. Cleghorn wrote the widely read poem (quoted in Cahn & Cahn, 1972, p. 46):

> The golf links lie so near the mill
> That almost every day
> The laboring children can look out
> And see the men at play.

The National Consumer League, led by Florence Kelley, actively opposed child labor, and Mrs. Mary "Mother" Jones, the union organizer, led marches protesting child labor. At that time, child welfare was broadly defined and seen as part of all movements for "social betterment":

> Thus, the fight for the regulation of child labor was part of the child welfare movement. As one reformer put it: "Effective and adequate child-caring work must include the enforcement of proper child labor laws; they are an essential part of the child caring system." (Trattner, 1984, p. 130)

By 1914, almost all states had passed child labor legislation and established minimum ages for leaving school. However, many states did not adequately protect children from dangerous occupations, and enforcement of child labor laws was notoriously lax. For these reasons, social reformers gave priority to the enactment of federal legislation. Between 1916 and 1930, three laws were enacted in Congress but failed in the courts. The first was the Keating–Owen Act of 1916, which attempted to regulate child labor in interstate commerce; the second placed an additional tax on the net profits of manufacturers if they employed children under age 14; the third, in the early 1930s, was the attempt by the National Recovery Administration to prohibit the employment of children below age 16. A determined effort throughout the 1920s to limit child labor through a constitutional amendment was unsuccessful (Postol, 1989).

Grace Abbott, a noted social worker, was especially important in the attempt to strengthen the federal role. As director of the child labor division of the Children's Bureau, she was responsible for administering the Keating–Owen Act. By inserting a child labor clause in war-goods contracts between private industries and the federal government during World War I, she was able to continue Keating–Owen policies after the act was declared unconstitutional by the Supreme Court. While serving as director of the Children's Bureau from 1921 to 1934, she fought for ratification by the states of a constitutional amendment against child labor. She served later as the U.S. delegate to the International Labour Organization.

It was not until 1938 that the Fair Labor Standards Act (FLSA) was passed. Along with establishing uniform federal standards for employees of all ages, it established national standards for child labor. FLSA regulations established a minimum-age requirement for work in certain occupations, limited the hours of employment for 14- and 15-year-olds, and prohibited the employment of youths under age 18 in specific hazardous occupations. However, on family farms, children of any age can work. Child labor legislation is administered and enforced as part of the broader responsibilities of the Wage and Hour Division within the Employment Standards Division of the U.S. Department of Labor. In 1990, there were approximately 1,000 compliance officers to enforce the FLSA, including child labor regulations (*Child Labor: Characteristics of Working Children,* 1991, p. 2). States may not weaken the federal standards, but they can enact, administer, and enforce stricter child labor legislation.

At the international level, the administrative enforcement of ILO conventions and recommendations on member states is weak or nonexistent, but the same laxity occurs in most nations that have adequate laws and regulatory provisions. In the United States, for example, a report by the U.S. General Accounting Office (1992) pointed out that

> Labor's enforcement of federal child labor provisions may be ineffective. The National Child Labor Committee estimates that each year, there are at least 100,000 minors illegally working on farms and 1 million child labor violations. Limited resources and low fines for child labor violations have hampered Labor's child labor enforcement in all industries. During 1989, Labor inspected only 1.5 percent of all workplaces covered by FLSA. In 1990, penalties for child labor violations averaged $212 a violation. Labor acknowledged that its penalties were inadequate to deter violations. As part of the fiscal year 1991 budget legislation, the Congress gave Labor the authority to increase the maximum civil monetary penalty for a nonwillful violation from $1,000 to $10,000 for each child. Despite this new authority, Labor generally has increased assessed penalties by far smaller amounts for violations that do not involve a serious injury. (pp. 22–23)

Since 1990, several states have revised their child labor laws. However, the laws of a number of states have remained unchanged for the past 50 to 80 years. To stimulate change in state laws, to improve enforcement procedures and penalties, and to provide more comprehensive protection to working minors, in 1992 the Child Labor Coalition of the National Consumers League, composed of a broad spectrum of 34 organizational members, published and made available to any "child advocate" a detailed proposal for a model state child labor law. Its adoption would strengthen the laws of most states. In its major provisions, the model law

- significantly revises and updates the list of Hazardous Occupation Orders—those occupations, machines, and worksites that are prohibited for minors under the age of 18
- provides equal protection under the law for migrant and seasonal farm worker children by setting a minimum age of 14 for employment and prohibiting minors from dangerous agricultural occupations and substances
- establishes a linkage between educational fulfillment and continuation of work
- reasonably restricts employment for all minors under the age of 18
- requires work permits as a means to monitor employment and facilitate investigations
- acknowledges the vulnerability and inexperience of working minors through requiring labor education prior to employment, so that minors are knowledgeable about the laws protecting them in the workplace
- provides enhanced enforcement provisions and specific enforcement financing
- establishes stiff penalties for employers who are child labor law violators. (*A Model State Child Labor Law,* 1992, p. 2)

To strengthen child labor legislation on the federal level, bills were introduced in the U.S. House and Senate in 1993.

## International Standards

Since 1919, the International Labour Organization has called for the protection of working children, as well as the eventual abolition of child labor. The most important ILO standards are the Minimum Age Convention, 1973 (No. 138), and the related Minimum Age Recommendation, 1973 (No. 146). These conventions require member states

(a) to specify a minimum age for admission to employment and to raise it progressively to a level consistent with the fullest physical and mental development of young persons
(b) to ensure that the minimum age for admission to employment shall not be less than the age of completion of compulsory schooling and, in any case, shall not be less than 15 years. (*Child Labour,* 1986, p. 17)

However, the minimum is flexible and can be lower or higher, depending on the nature of the work. A country's economy and educational facilities are also taken into consideration. As the ILO's briefing manual (*Child Labour,* 1986) pointed out,

> Conventions are comparable to multilateral international treaties: they are open to ratification by member States and, once ratified, create specific, binding obligations. A State that has ratified a Convention is expected to apply its provisions by legislation or other appropriate means as indicated in the text of the Convention.
>
> Recommendations are intended to offer guide-lines for action by member States.... But no specific substantive obligations are entailed. (p. 15)

On the basis of the 1959 Declaration on the Rights of the Child, the General Assembly of the United Nations adopted the Convention on the Rights of the Child in 1989. According to Article 32 of the convention on child labor:

1. States Parties recognize the right of the child to be protected from economic exploitation and from performing any work that is likely to be hazardous or to interfere with the child's education, or to be harmful to the child's health or physical, mental, spiritual, moral or social development.
2. States Parties shall take legislative, administrative, social and educational measures to ensure the implementation of this article. To this end, and having regard to the relevant provisions of other international instruments, States Parties shall in particular:
   *(a)* provide for a minimum age or minimum ages for admissions to employment;
   *(b)* provide for appropriate regulation of the hours and conditions of employment;
   *(c)* provide for appropriate penalties or other sanctions to ensure the effective enforcement of this article. (*Convention on the Rights of the Child,* 1989, p. 10)

Although most countries of the world have taken legislative action to define, control, and prohibit, under specified circumstances, child labor, national and international enforcement efforts continue to be ineffective. The United Nations Children's Fund (UNICEF), the leading international advocate for the welfare of children, does not give high priority to child labor as a continuing problem. UNICEF prefers to direct its efforts to areas that are less controversial and that may reach more children (Albright, Kunstel, & McKay, 1987). ILO, the most active international organization opposed to child labor, has only moral and persuasive power over its member states. As of 1992, the Minimum Age Convention (No. 138) had been ratified by only 40 member states, including just 12 in the developing world, where the problems tend to be more widespread and more serious for working children, but where child labor is of greater importance to the economy and to the survival of families. In an attempt to overcome these problems, the ILO inaugurated a global initiative, the International Programme on the Elimination of Child Labour (IPEC), in 1990. Six countries that requested the ILO's assistance—Brazil, India, Indonesia, Kenya, Thailand, and Turkey—were considered priorities for action in 1992–93, and several other developing countries have expressed interest in IPEC. IPEC provides technical advisory services for the design and implementation of national programs that meet international standards, with the aims of heightening public consciousness, preventing child labor, and ameliorating abusive conditions under which many children are currently employed (*IPEC Programme Document,* 1993). ILO plans to expand IPEC as funds are made available.

## The Nature and Extent of Child Labor

Although the varied and frequently cruel nature of child labor throughout the world is not in doubt, attempts to quantify the phenomenon are beset by numerous problems. Data collection is unsystematic even in developed countries. In the United States, for example, administration of the Fair Labor Standards Act is dependent on the states, but most states do not have centralized data-gathering systems to document the number and types of work permits issued and the industries in which working children are employed. There is no national comprehensive data-collection system to identify the number and nature of accidents or illnesses suffered by children while employed. More-

TABLE 1
**Number of Children in the United States, by Age and Likely Work Status, 1992**

| Age | Number | Number Who Are Likely To Have Worked | Percent |
|---|---|---|---|
| 12 and 13 | 6,762,450 | 676,245 | 10 |
| 14 | 3,243,107 | 486,466 | 15 |
| 15 | 3,321,609 | 930,050 | 28 |
| 16 | 3,304,890 | 1,685,494 | 51 |
| 17 | 4,410,062 | 1,739,132 | 39 |
| Total | 21,042,118 | 5,517,387 | 26 |
| Total U.S. children Ages 12–16 | 16,632,056 | 3,778,255 | 23 |

SOURCE: *Sacrificing America's Youth* (p. 7). (1992). Chicago: National Safe Workplace Institute. Adapted by permission.

over, virtually every country of the world has an invisible, underground economy that depends on child and other illegal forms of labor. Those who benefit from that economy—employers, parents, children, and government officials—are unwilling to provide accurate information and to incriminate themselves. Typically, estimates are based on expert opinion, census data, and information and projections from surveys, but often the bases for estimates are not provided. For the reasons just noted, estimates of child labor should be viewed with caution.

**United States**

The National Safe Workplace Institute (*Sacrificing America's Youth*, 1992), on the basis of its estimates and those of the Bureau of Labor Statistics and the General Accounting Office (GAO), stated that of the 20 million children ages 12 to 17 in 1992, about 5.5 million were employed. Table 1 presents a breakdown of the number of children by age and those who were "likely to have worked" in that year. Many thousands of children under age 12, who work in their homes, as migrant laborers with their families, in garment industry sweatshops, and as itinerant candy peddlers (Dumaine, 1993) were not included in the totals in Table 1. In addition, there are guesstimates of as many as 1 million child prostitutes (Fyfe, 1989, pp. 67–70).

According to a GAO study (*Child Labor: Characteristics of Working Children*, 1991), not only did the employment of children in the United States increase significantly during the 1980s, but more children under age 18 were working longer hours and getting injured on the job. The findings of the study included the following:

- The number of working children quadrupled, and the number of serious injuries reported annually doubled.
- About 51 percent of 16- to 17-year-olds and 28 percent of 15-year-olds were employed at some time in 1988.
- Children from poor families, defined as having incomes under $20,000, were more likely to work in hazardous industries, such as manufacturing, construction, transportation, and agriculture, than were those from prosperous families with incomes over $60,000. During a year, the former worked fewer weeks, but longer hours per week. White children were more likely to be employed than nonwhite children.
- The U.S. Department of Labor uncovered 1,475 violations that were responsible for serious workplace injuries to children between 1983 and 1990. No employers were cited for willful violations, which may be referred for criminal prosecution and carry a penalty of up to $10,000. Only when a child was seriously injured on the job was the $10,000 maximum fine imposed by the U.S. Department of Labor. Most penalties were in the $200 range, well below the statutory maximums.

The American Academy of Pediatrics (cited in *Child Labor Amendments*, 1991, p. 58) gives a sharply higher estimate—that more than 100,000 children are injured on the job each year.

The U.S. Department of Labor had 1,059 investigators in 1980; in 1993, only 833 agents enforced all its regulations, including those governing child labor. "According to the National Safe Workplace Institute . . . a business can expect a visit by a federal labor inspector once every 50 years" (Dumaine, 1993, p. 87). The staff of state regulatory agencies have also been cut. Because no comprehensive data on work-related injuries and illnesses of minors exist, the true magnitude of the problem is unknown. The little that is known comes from investigative newspaper reports (Stancill, 1993; Wagner & Breton, 1991).

Farm work, the least regulated sector by the Fair Labor Standards Act, is considered to be the most dangerous area for the employment of children. Butterfield (1990) reported that "each year, 300 or more children under the age of 16 are killed while working—run over by tractors or pulled into the whirling blades of wood chippers or suffocated when they fall into grain elevators. Another 23,500 are injured—hundreds in accidents that are leaving them without arms, legs, or fingers" (p. 1). Of all workers in agriculture, five- to 14-year-olds have the highest rate of injury (*Accident Facts*,

1989). From available statistics, Rivera (1985) estimated that of those killed in agriculture, "more than half die without ever reaching a physician; an additional 19.1 percent die in transit to a hospital and only 7.4 live long enough to receive inpatient care" (p. 567). Children who work in the fields along with their families are exposed to toxic pesticides for extended periods (Wagner & Breton, 1991). In addition, the education of children who work on farms is threatened because of the long hours of strenuous work. It has been estimated that the school drop-out rate for the children of migrant workers is 50 percent to 60 percent nationwide (Martin, 1988).

Numerous studies have shown that working in excess of 15 to 20 hours per week during the school year is correlated with lower academic achievement and involvement in school (Steinberg, Fegley, & Dornbusch, 1993). In their longitudinal study of working adolescents from different socioeconomic and ethnic backgrounds and different types of communities, Steinberg et al. concluded that jobs that take up

> more than 20 hours weekly diminish youngsters' investment in school, increase delinquency and drug use, further autonomy from parental control, and diminish feelings of self-reliance. (p. 179)
>
> • • • • •
>
> Across the outcomes studied, inspection of group means indicated that nonworkers generally were better adjusted than adolescents with moderate work hours, who in turn were better adjusted than adolescents with long work hours. (p. 178)

Several factors have influenced the current increase in the employment of children and illegal child labor in the United States:

- Changing demographics have made the employment of adolescents by service industries, such as fast-food chains and supermarkets, more urgent.
- Parents and children often give greater priority to consumption values, such as clothes and cars, than to education.
- Economic pressure is greater on families and children who live below the poverty line; in the past two decades, their numbers have increased.
- The restructuring of the economy in the 1980s, the reduction in defense expenditures, and the recession of the early 1990s placed increased pressure on middle-class families to supplement their incomes.
- In the 1980s and early 1990s, immigration—legal and illegal—surged. Impoverished immigrant parents from Mexico, Central America, and Asia expect their children to work alongside them on farms, in urban sweatshops, and in piecework activities in the home.
- Enforcement efforts have been weakened by cuts in federal and state budgets.

**International**

Child labor is a serious problem in most countries of the world, developing as well as industrialized. On the basis of its 1992 survey, the ILO (*ILO Press Release*, 1992) stated:

> The total number of working children is certainly in the hundreds of millions. And although the condition of child workers has worsened dramatically in recent years, and their number has increased in many countries, few have developed comprehensive plans to deal with this serious and difficult problem. (p. 1)

The ILO survey estimated that in some countries, the majority of children over age 10 are working. In some regions, as many as 25 percent of all children aged 10 to 14 are working, many without education and condemned to lifelong poverty, and many employed illegally and in dangerous circumstances that cripple and kill them. The survey noted that the greatest number of working children live in Asia, where they constitute as much as 11 percent of the total labor force in some countries. According to ILO's Committee of Experts, several million children work as bonded laborers in South Asia; in India, an estimated 1 million or more work in brick kilns, stone quarrying, construction, and carpet weaving. In some African nations, 20 percent of all children work, and children may constitute up to 17 percent of the work force. Because Latin America is the most urbanized region in the developing world, more Latin American children work in cities, and in some countries as many as 26 percent work. In Brazil, 18 percent of all children 10 to 14 work, and in Mexico a similar proportion of children aged 12 to 14 work (*ILO Press Release,* 1992, pp. 1–4).

A study by the Bureau of International Labor Affairs (*Foreign Labor Trends,* 1993) of the U.S. Department of State's Human Rights Reports (HRR) for 1990 and 1991 and the ILO's 1992 survey provided evidence to support the view that child labor is a serious international problem. The HRR study included 170 countries: 47 in Africa, 33 in South and Central America, 28 in East Asia/Pacific, 35 in Europe, and 27 in the Near East and South Asia.

The following examples illustrate the severity of working conditions for many children in the developing world. In Bangladesh, children are employed throughout the booming export garment industry.

> Some of these children are as young as seven. They work on the same schedule as adults at least six days a week, often seven days a week, from 7:00 or 8:00 in the morning until the late afternoon or evening. Occasionally, to fill rush seasonal orders, they work all through the night for as much as 36 hours straight. They help make pajamas, blouses, shirts and other clothes for customers in the United States, Canada and Europe. They earn from $4 to $10 a month. (Senser, 1992, p. 166)

In the gold-mining region of Peru, a journalist reported the discovery of more than 70 common graves containing, for the most part, the bodies of children and youths who worked in the gold mines. Because of ties between elected officials and owners of the mines, no official judicial inquiry was conducted. CODENI, a private Peruvian children's rights coordinating organization, reviewed the circumstances of children working in the mines. It found that both the work and the living conditions were extremely hazardous:

> Housing provided by the employer is also hazardous. Usually on the edge of the river, these unsafe shacks with no walls leave their dwellers defenseless against insects and wild beasts. The most frequent illnesses are anemia, malaria, gastro-intestinal infections, rabies and parasites. Youngsters who are sick do not rest since only actual days worked are paid. Some are forced to wait until the malaria attacks subside to return to the mine. Undernourished and unable to purchase the necessary medicine, they perish in total abandonment. Some youngsters reported to CODENI that those who were bitten by rabid bats had simply been tied to tree trunks and left to die.
>
> In extremely harsh conditions death is commonplace. Clearings near camps are used as secret graves. Deaths go unregistered. These are the cemeteries that were thought to be common graves. ("Life and Death," 1992, p. 10)

A nine-month investigation of child labor by the Cox Newspapers (Albright et al., 1987) detailed the shocking conditions of child labor in India, North Africa, Asia, and South America. It found that girls as young as seven work as rug weavers in Morocco. In the Philippines, children work 90 to 110 hours a week in tiny factories and sleep next to their sewing machines. In India, boys as young as eight, without protective glasses, shoes, or gloves, work with molten glass around crude open furnaces for less than a dollar a day. In Brazil, where there are 7 million abandoned and homeless children, many survive through street crime. In Thailand, girls as young as 13 are sold into prostitution by their debt-ridden families. Child prostitution has become a "scourge on the world's children"; in part because of the fear of AIDS, preteenage children are seen as safer and therefore more desirable (Simons, 1993).

Serious child labor problems also exist in the developed world, for example, in Britain, Italy, and Spain. A 1985 survey showed that 40 percent of the British children who were questioned were working, many illegally. In western Europe, the highest numbers of child workers are probably in Italy and Spain; in Spain, an estimated 100,000 children labor on family farms, and in Italy, reports indicate that the leather industry is a special cause for concern (*World Labour Report,* 1992).

Increasingly, international organizations are viewing child labor as a human rights issue. According to the director general of the ILO (cited in *ILO Press Release,* 1992):

> Child labor is a human rights question. It is just unacceptable that more than a hundred million children are working, that so many children are denied their basic rights. Child labor is the single most important source of child abuse and child exploitation in the world. (p. 4)

In a major study, the U.N. Commission on Human Rights (*Rights of the Child,* 1992) underscored the sale of children, child prostitution, and child pornography as violations of the rights of children.

In Paraguay, work is under way to draft constitutional articles on children's rights ("What about Children's Rights?" 1992). At a 1993 meeting of the European Parliament in Strasbourg, France, women's groups identified child prostitution as a critical human rights issue. In its various forms, child labor is emerging as an important, complex social problem and human rights issue that requires action.

## Policy and Program Implications

Students of child labor agree that it will not be eliminated in the foreseeable future, but that policies and programs can be adopted to reduce and humanize it (Bequele, 1992; *Child Labour,* 1986; Fyfe, 1989; *Humanising Child Labour,* 1985; Mendelievich, 1979; Myers, 1991; Pollock, Landrigan, & Mallino, 1990; *Sacrificing America's Youth,* 1992). Such measures include the following:

### Improved Working Conditions

The highest priority should be given to eliminating or ameliorating hazardous working conditions. Hazardous activities include work in glass factories, mines, construction, and pesticide-laden fields; operating mechanized farm equipment; late-night door-to-door selling; military service; and developmentally destructive work, such as prostitution and pornography. In the United States, the National Consumers League and the National Safe Workplace Institute play leading roles in identifying and opposing hazardous child labor and in advocating for stronger legislation on federal and state levels.

**Universal, Compulsory Education**

All countries should establish policies that call for the promotion and enforcement of universal compulsory education. The historical experience of the industrialized West demonstrates a direct relationship between the establishment and enforcement of compulsory primary school education and the reduction of child labor. For impoverished nations, a formidable obstacle to eliminating or reducing child labor is the dearth of school facilities, educational materials, and teachers. Too often this situation is a consequence of the lack of political will and misplaced priorities. Many Third World African countries, for example, that confront no external threat spend disproportionate amounts on their military. However, African countries such as Botswana, Ghana, Ivory Coast, Madagascar, Rwanda, and Zambia have all significantly expanded primary education despite comparatively low levels of per capita income. The Asian experience is instructive. In 1872, when it was still a poor country, Japan introduced compulsory primary school education. By 1910, almost all of the six-to-13 age group attended school. In the 1950s, both North and South Korea launched successful campaigns to get all primary age children into school. China and Sri Lanka provide similar dramatic examples of governments giving high priority to primary school education (Weiner, 1991).

**Child Labor Laws**

Relevant child labor legislation must be developed or improved and enforced. Historically child labor legislation has been undermined by inadequate administration and enforcement efforts. Strategies for dealing with administrative and enforcement problems need to be devised for each government level by each government level if they are to be effective. Public awareness and action are preconditions. As the Director General of the ILO (*ILO Press Release,* 1992) pointed out,

> You can't rely simply on laws or on a government. Instead, you must create a movement for change, a movement against child labor that would involve governments, but also the media, communities and non-government organizations involved in human rights, women's issues and child issues. (p. 5)

As a result of the growth of the integrated global economy, new program and policy strategies are emerging:

1. International boycotts of products produced by child labor. The boycotting of Indian carpets produced by child labor, which began in Germany in 1991 and then spread to Switzerland, has caused a shortage of orders (*Foreign Labor Trends,* 1993, p. 4). Legislation introduced in the U.S. Senate in 1994, the Child Labor Deterrence Act, bans the import of goods produced by children under age 15.
2. Action by international corporations. In 1992 Levi Strauss and Co. required contractors to certify that they do not employ children (*Foreign Labor Trends,* 1993, p. 4).
3. U.S. federal legislation banning the importation of products produced by child labor. The Child Labor Deterrence Act of 1993 (S. 613 and H.R. 1397) bans the import of products manufactured or mined by underage children (*Child Labor Update,* 1993, p. 7).

**Raising the Public's Consciousness**

It is essential that the public be made aware of the existence of child labor; the various forms that it takes and their consequences; and the necessity for strengthening current laws, regulations, and enforcement procedures. In many countries child labor is an accepted way of life, and no distinction is made between it and child work. The lack of public understanding that child labor is harmful to the physical, emotional, academic, and moral development of children leads to its perpetuation. On the international level, organizations such as the International Labour Organization, UNICEF, and the World Health Organization have an important role and obligation, despite the sensitivities of their member states, to increase awareness of child labor so that relevant action may be taken. Public information campaigns have catalyzed state and federal child labor legislation in the United States, but much more is needed.

**Intragovernment Coordination**

Governments should establish interagency bodies to coordinate the work of national, state, and local levels of departments or ministries that are responsible for labor, health, education, welfare, community development, and income- and employment-generating programs. The function of such interagency coordinating bodies would be to increase the effectiveness of services that attempt to protect working children and to reduce child labor (Fyfe, 1989).

### Informational Campaigns on Rights and Grievances

Public and private organizations should establish programs to alert children and their families to their rights; the mechanisms for redressing grievances; and the physical, maturational, and educational hazards of their employment. Nongovernment organizations can play a significant role by conducting extensive educational and information campaigns, providing needed services to working children and their families, and advocating for the children (*Child Labour,* 1986).

### Self-Advocacy

Mechanisms of self-advocacy should be promoted to unite children with common problems so that they can deal with them more effectively. Limited successes have been achieved by street children in Latin America, child workers in India, child rice farmers in Ghana, and schoolchildren protesting child prostitution in the Philippines (Fyfe, 1989). The empowerment of children and the raising of public consciousness have led to some local changes in working conditions and the provision of social and recreational services. Successes are limited because underlying problems of grinding poverty and high fertility rates are not addressed or, in any case, easily overcome.

### Services for Working Children

Creative services should be developed for children who must work but who need support and protection. Services might include health, recreational, counseling, and nutritional services, as well as nonformal education or vocational training fit in around work schedules, that would permit children to obtain better, less exploitative employment. Children who work in agriculture are educationally at risk because they may need to work before and after school or to miss school; migrant children who must move frequently have even greater educational deficits. To keep children from working in the fields, day care must be provided for the children of hired farm workers; in the United States, the federal Migrant Head Start program does not meet this need (U.S. General Accounting Office, 1992).

### Situation Diagnosis

Situation diagnosis should be the basis for policy and program planning. Because of the differences between countries and within countries, systematic diagnoses of child labor should be carried out on national, state, and local levels, wherever working children are thought to be common (Myers, 1991). Situation diagnosis is field oriented; analysts go into communities to obtain first-hand information and to document both quantitative and qualitative evidence to gain a better understanding of

- the nature, magnitude, and distribution of the problem, with special emphasis on how children are affected by the work they do. Recognising that not all children are significantly at risk, it should identify which most urgently need attention.
- current policy and program responses to the working children problem, assessing the impact of both public and private sector actions on the children involved.
- unmet needs, with an estimate of the minimum additional action that would be required to provide endangered working children a reasonable level of protection. (Myers, 1991, p. 166)

The services developed should be based on subnational planning, especially in countries that contain significant economic, industrial, cultural, and regional diversity, to ensure that programs are relevant to the child labor problems they address.

### Evaluation

Evaluation procedures and findings should be designed and used administratively. The policies and programs that have an impact on the lives of working children and their families should be closely monitored. The individual, familial, economic, and societal factors that produce child labor are complex, and changing them produces consequences that should be identified and evaluated. For example, the elimination of child labor in an exploitive factory may produce street children who are worse off than they were before.

## Role of Social Work

In general, the social work profession and social work education do not consider child labor a serious area of concern. For example, the *Social Work Almanac* (Ginsberg, 1992) included sections on "Special Problems of Children" and "Child Abuse and Neglect," but neither section discussed child labor. Similarly, although the 18th edition of the *Encyclopedia of Social Work* (Minahan, 1987, Vol. 1, pp. 223–265) contained articles on "Child Abuse and Neglect," "Child Care Services," "Children," "Child Sexual Abuse," and "Child Support," none of the articles identified or discussed child labor as a practice or policy issue. And, although the second edition of the *The Social Work Dictionary* (Barker, 1991, p. 34) included an entry for child labor, the entry did not stress the enormity of the problem. Furthermore, an extensive review of social policy and child welfare texts revealed little or no coverage of child labor as a responsibility of social work policy analysts or practitioners (Allen, 1992; Binnicker, 1992).

Currently, as Kadushin (1987) pointed out, laws that affect the general well-being of children are no longer considered part of child welfare practice in social work. The child welfare community is in general agreement that child welfare practice is a "specialized field," defined by legislative enactments administered by the U.S. Department of Health and Human Services and implemented by the states, and includes the services defined by the Child Welfare League of America (CWLA) as "unique and specific" to child welfare social work (Kadushin, 1987, pp. 266–267). Thus, policy and program issues that affect working children and their families are ignored or are explicitly assigned to the U.S. Department of Labor and its corresponding departments in the states. However, the U.S. Department of Labor has no social service mandate and, at best, only a weak enforcement capability. Another factor that may have contributed to the removal of child labor from social work's field of vision has been the increasing emphasis on clinical and private practice in the 1980s and 1990s.

The field of social work is defined by others as it defines itself. In 1987 the secretary of labor established a 21-member Child Labor Advisory Committee that included appointees from the National Consumers League, the National Education Association, the National Parent–Teachers Association, the AFL–CIO, and the National Child Labor Committee, but none from NASW, CWLA, Family Service America, or the Council on Social Work Education. The Child Labor Coalition of the National Consumers League, initiator of *A Model State Child Labor Law* (1992), is composed of 16 diverse organizations. Social work is not represented. Should it be? Are child labor policies and programs an area for social work knowledge building, program development, and practice?

The thoughtful response to this question by the field of social work, practitioners and educators, individuals and organizations, in the United States and internationally, is fundamental to any discussion of the policy and practice roles of social work in preventing and ameliorating child labor. The definition of child advocacy in *The Social Work Dictionary* (Barker, 1991) may point the way to an answer:

> Championing the rights of children to be free from abuse or exploitation by others and to have opportunities in development toward their full potential. Since the beginning of their existence, social workers have led in this effort by fighting for *child labor* laws.... The field distinguishes between case advocacy and policy advocacy. (p. 33)

In the United States and many other countries, social work has become a mature profession. On the international and national levels, social work organizations have the ability to analyze and reflect on policy and program issues and to stimulate changes in curricula and practice in schools of social work and social service agencies. The key U.S. social work organizations that may consider the issue and implications of child labor as a child welfare responsibility are the following:

- *NASW:* a professional membership organization with over 150,000 members in 55 chapters. In November 1994 NASW joined the Child Labor Coalition.
- *Council on Social Work Education:* an educational standard-setting and accrediting organization for undergraduate and graduate social work education programs in the United States. In addition to academic institutions and social work educators, members may be social agencies and professional organizations.
- *Families International:* a national standard-setting organization for privately funded family services agencies. Professionals and private citizens may also be members.
- *Child Welfare League of America:* the major national private organization with an advocacy role for children. It is a federation of voluntary child welfare agencies.
- *American Public Welfare Association:* a voluntary organization whose focus is on the administration and delivery of public welfare services. Its membership consists of individuals and over 1,200 local, state, and federal public welfare organizations.
- *Children's Bureau:* located within the Administration for Children, Youth, and Families of the U.S. Department of Health and Human Services and historically responsible for programs on behalf of children.

Key international social work and social welfare organizations are the following:

- *International Council on Social Welfare:* a membership organization of national committees and other international organizations that provides a forum for the discussion of welfare issues.
- *International Federation of Social Workers:* made up of the national professional social work organizations from every region of the world. Welfare issues are discussed at biennial meetings.

- *International Association of Schools of Social Work:* a worldwide association of individual members and schools of social work whose purpose is to share information and improve standards of training and education in social work.
- *International Union for Child Welfare:* includes public and private organizations that are concerned about child welfare. Its functions are to disseminate information, provide training, and facilitate research.

Should these organizations adopt child labor as an important, continuing concern? Their answers will have a significant impact on millions of children in the United States and throughout the world.

## References


*Accident facts.* (1989) Chicago: National Safety Council.

Albright, J., Kunstel, M., & McKay, R. (1987, June 21–26). Stolen childhood. *Austin American Statesman* [Austin, TX], pp. 1–39.

Allen, K. (1992). *Social welfare, social policy and child labor: An annotated bibliography.* Unpublished manuscript, University of Texas at Austin.

*Another ounce of prevention: Education and employment interventions for 9 to 15 year olds.* (1988). Washington, DC: National Commission for Employment Policy.

Barker, R. L. (1991). *The social work dictionary* (2nd ed.). Silver Spring, MD: National Association of Social Workers.

Bequele, A. (1992). Beyond poverty. *International Children's Rights Monitor, 9*(2).

Binnicker, D. G. (1992). *Child labor: An annotated bibliography.* Unpublished manuscript, University of Texas at Austin.

Butterfield, B. D. (1990, April 22). The tragedy of child labor. *Boston Globe,* p. 1.

Cahn, R., & Cahn, W. (1972). *No time for school no time for play.* New York: Julian Messner.

*Child labor amendments of 1991: Hearings on S.600 before the Subcommittee on Labor and the Subcommittee on Children, Family, Drugs and Alcoholism of the Senate Committee on Labor and Human Resources.* (1991). Washington, DC: U.S. Government Printing Office.

Child labor and child abuse on the farm. (1985). *Food and Justice* (United Farm Workers Union), *2*(2).

*Child labor: Characteristics of working children.* (HRD-91-83BR). (1991). Washington, DC: General Accounting Office.

*Child labor update and recommendations for action.* (1993). Washington, DC: National Consumers League.

*Child labour: A briefing manual.* (1986). Geneva, Switzerland: International Labour Organization.

*Children in bondage, slaves of the subcontinent.* (1991). London: Anti-Slavery International.

*Convention on the Rights of the Child.* (1989). New York: United Nations.

Curtis, V. R., & Mallach, S. (1984). *Photography and reform: Lewis Hine and the National Child Labor Committee.* Milwaukee: Milwaukee Art Museum.

Dumaine, B. (1993, April 5). Illegal child labor comes back. *Fortune,* pp. 86–94.

Fair Labor Standards Act of 1938. P.L. 85-231, 52 Stat. 1060.

*Foreign labor trends: International child labor problems.* (1993). Washington, DC: U.S. Department of Labor, Bureau of International Affairs.

Fyfe, A. (1989). *Child labour.* Cambridge, MA: Polity Press and Basil Blackwell.

Gargan, E. A. (1992, July 9). Bound to looms by poverty and fear, boys in India make a few men rich. *New York Times,* p. A8.

George, I. (1990). *Child labour and child work.* New Delhi, India: Ashish Publishing House.

Ginsberg, L. (1992). *Social work almanac.* Washington, DC: NASW Press.

*Humanising child labour.* (1985). Calcutta, India: Institute of Psychological and Educational Research.

*ILO press release.* (1992, July 21). Washington, DC: International Labour Organization.

*IPEC programme document.* (1993). Geneva: International Labour Office.

Kadushin, A. (1987). Child welfare services. In A. Minahan (Ed.-in-Chief), *Encyclopedia of social work* (18th ed., Vol. 1, pp. 265–275). Silver Spring, MD: National Association of Social Workers.

Life and death of children working in Peruvian gold mines. (1992). *International Children's Rights Monitor, 9*(2).

Martin, P. L. (1988). *Harvest of confusion: Migrant workers in U.S. agriculture.* Boulder, CO: Westview Press.

Mendelievich, E. (1979). *Children at work.* Geneva: International Labour Organization.

Minahan, A. (Ed.-in-Chief). (1987). *Encyclopedia of social work* (18th ed.). Silver Spring, MD: National Association of Social Workers.

*A model state child labor law.* (1992). Washington, DC: National Consumers League.

Myers, W. E. (1991). *Protecting working children.* London: Zed Books.

Pollock, S. H., Landrigan, P. J., & Mallino, D. L. (1990). Child labor in 1990: Prevalence and health hazards. *Annual Review of Public Health, 11,* 359–375.

Postol, T. (1989). Child labor in the U.S.: Its growth and abolition. *American Educator, 3*(2), 30–31.

*Rights of the child.* (1992). New York: U.N. Commission on Human Rights, Economic and Social Council.

Rivera, F. P. (1985). Fatal and nonfatal farm injuries to children in the United States. *Pediatrics, 76,* 567–573.

Rosner, J. (1980). *Emmeline.* New York: Pocket Books.

*Sacrificing America's youth.* (1992). Chicago: National Safe Workplace Institute.

Senser, R. A. (1992, September 19). On their knees. *America,* pp. 166–167, 173.

Simons, M. (1993, April 9). The sex market: Scourge on the world's children. *New York Times,* p. A3.

Slavery. (1992, May 4). *Newsweek,* pp. 30–39.

Stancill, N. (1993, March). Kids on the job. *Houston Chronicle,* pp. 1–8.

Steinberg, L., Fegley, S., & Dornbusch, S. M. (1993). Negative impact of part-time work on adolescent adjustment: Evidence from a longitudinal study. *Developmental Psychology, 29,* 171–179.

Trattner, W. I. (1984). *From poor law to welfare state.* New York: Free Press.

U.S. Bureau of the Census. (1940). *Sixteenth census of the United States.* Washington, DC: U.S. Government Printing Office.

U.S. General Accounting Office. *Hired farmworkers: Health and well-being at risk.* (1992). Washington, DC: Author.

Wagner, M., & Breton, M. (1991, December 8–11). *Fields of pain*. Sacramento: Sacramento Bee.

Weiner, M. (1991, February 7). Suffer the children. *Far Eastern Economic Review*, pp. 26–27.

What about children's rights? (1992). *International Children's Rights Monitor, 9*(2), 16.

Work and employment. (1985). In *Encyclopedia Britannica* (15th ed., Vol. 29, p. 940).

*World labour report 1992.* (1992). Geneva: International Labour Organization.

Zelizer, V. A. (1985). *Pricing the priceless child.* New York: Basic Books.

Zinn, H. (1980). *A people's history of the United States.* New York: Harper & Row.

## Further Reading

Baron, A. (1991). *Work engendered: Toward a new history of American labor.* Ithaca, NY: Cornell University Press.

Boyden, J., & Holden, P. (1991). *Children of the cities.* New Jersey: Zed Books Limited.

Greenberger, E., & Stinberg, L. (1986). *When teenagers work: The psychological and social cost of adolescent employment.* New York: Basic Books.

Greene, L. L. (1992). *Child labor: Then and now.* New York: Franklin Watts.

Hawes, J. M., & Hiner, N. R. (1991). *Children in historical and comparative perspective: An international handbook and research guide.* Westport, CT: Greenwood Press.

Laird, J., & Hartman, A. (1985). *A handbook of child welfare: Contexts, knowledge and practices.* New York: Free Press.

Louv, R. (1990). *Childhood's future.* Boston: Houghton Mifflin.

Nardinelli, C. (1990). *Child labor and the industrial revolution.* Bloomington: Indiana University Press.

Nazario, T. A. (1988). *In defense of children: Understanding the rights, needs and interests of the child.* New York: Charles Scribner's Sons.

Sawyer, R. (1988). *Children enslaved.* London: Routledge.

**Jack Otis, PhD,** is professor of social work, sociology, and education, University of Texas, School of Social Work, 2609 University Avenue, Austin, TX 78712.

### For further information see

Adolescence Overview; Child Abuse and Neglect Overview; Childhood; Children's Rights; Families Overview; Families: Demographic Shifts; Income Security Overview; Jobs and Earnings; Poverty; Runaways and Homeless Youths; Violence Overview.

**Key Words**

child labor | child work
child welfare | employment

# Child Sexual Abuse Overview

**Jon R. Conte**

The study of sexual abuse of children has grown from a somewhat delimited field of professional activity in the late 1970s to a complex, multidimensional, and multidisciplinary field of practice today. Early knowledge dealt with issues such as the incest taboo, characteristics of sexual offenders and child victims, and recognition and identification of child victims. Since the 1970s the research supporting the study of child abuse has blossomed to create a large number of subspecialty areas, including victims (for example, identification, prevalence, effects of abuse, treatment), offenders (for instance, nature of sexual offenses, role of sexual arousal in sexual offenses, effects of treatment), prevention (for example, effectiveness of programs teaching children to prevent, escape, or avoid being abused), and policy research (such as how the justice system responds to cases of child sexual abuse). In a single area of this field, such as the assessment of children who may have been sexually abused, there are diverse research areas informing practice, including research on false reports, anatomical dolls, children as witnesses, validation criteria, and assessment protocols.

## Overview

### Definitions

A general definition of *child sexual abuse* is forced, tricked, or manipulated contact with a child by an older person (generally five or more years older) that has the purpose of the sexual gratification of the older person. These definitional elements are not to be applied in a rigid way when determining whether a specific act constitutes sexual abuse. For example, if contact is forced or tricked (as in the context of wrestling with a child) and the age difference between the older person and the child is only three years or even less, the contact is still likely to be abuse.

For many types of behavior it is difficult to determine whether the behavior has the intent of sexual gratification. For example, a parent may repeatedly enter a bathroom where his 11-year-old child is showering. The repeated nature of this act, its lack of respect for the child's privacy, and the lack of sensitivity to the child should raise concern about the adult's parenting skills; it may or may not also represent an instance of child sexual abuse.

The critical point for social workers is that many behaviors should alert the professional to the fact that the child (or family) may need services. The absence of a clear case of sexual abuse should not result in lack of services if the behavior is of concern for other reasons (for example, it deprives a child of an appropriate sense of control and privacy).

**Characteristics**

The characteristics of childhood sexual abuse may be thought of along a number of dimensions. There has been some tendency in the literature to describe the sexual acts to which children are exposed. As might be expected when dealing with a complex behavior such as sex, there is a wide range of actions. Children are exposed to acts that range from fondling to intercourse. Several investigators have documented that more serious sexual acts (for example, vaginal intercourse) tend to occur in intrafamily (incest) abuse cases rather than in extrafamily cases (see Conte, 1991). Children of virtually all age groups have been identified following victimization, although as might be expected, abuse of preverbal young children and infants is difficult to document. Girls are more likely to be identified for abuse, although current trends seem to indicate that abuse of boys is an underreported but growing problem. Currently, clinical samples consist of about 20 percent male victims. Data on sexual offenders show that adult offenders who abuse boys tend to abuse a much larger number of victims that those who target girls (mean number of victims, 150 versus 19.8, respectively) (Abel, Becker, Mittelman, Cunningham-Rathner, Rouleau, & Murphy, 1987). About 70 percent of victims are abused more than once, and many victims are abused over significant portions of their childhood.

**Risk Factors**

It is generally recognized that among the characteristics of abuse that are important in understanding the nature of the child's experiences and their potential impact are the sexual acts to which the child is exposed, the temporal qualities and nature of those acts (that is, duration, frequency, degree of force, degree of injury), the context in which the abuse takes place (for example, the nature of the relationships between offender and child and the presence of other traumatic or stressful events in the child's life), and the processes used to gain access and control of the child. Other dimensions (often referred to as the "dynamics" of childhood sexual abuse) have received little empirical investigation but are critical to understanding the child's experience of sexual abuse. These dynamics vary across cases but include betrayal, lack of consent, powerlessness, coercion and manipulation, secrecy, isolation, blame, and loss. Clinical treatment of victims rests in part on helping the child describe her or his experience along these dimensions.

There has been relatively little research effort to identify factors that increase the risk for sexual victimization, perhaps because of a historical assumption that all children are at risk. In an early summary of risk factor research, Finkelhor (1986) observed that the strongest associations across studies involved the parents of the abused child. Girls who are abused are more likely to live without their natural fathers, have mothers employed outside the home, have mothers who are disabled or ill, witness violence between their parents, or report a poor relationship with one of their parents.

Although there has been insufficient study of factors that increase risk for sexual victimization, this area of research remains important. Sexual offenders do not abuse every child with whom they come in contact. Several investigators have used sexual offenders as subjects to understand the processes whereby they recruit, abuse, and maintain children in abusive situations. Offenders claim a special ability to identify vulnerable children (for example, children in single-parent families, children who are emotionally needy, children with significant material needs) and use that vulnerability against the child (Conte, Wolf, & Smith, 1989). Although such claims might alert all adults to the potential role of certain characteristics of children and childhood in abuse, it is not clear that offenders have any greater capacity to identify vulnerability than do other adults. The critical issues may have to do more with the willingness of offenders to use those vulnerabilities against the child.

**Prevalence and Incidence**

Understanding the extent of the problem of childhood sexual abuse serves to sensitize the public and policymakers to the magnitude of the problem and alerts professional social workers that they are likely to encounter victims of childhood sexual abuse in virtually every practice setting. Estimates of the prevalence of sexual abuse vary among studies from 6 percent to 62 percent of females and 3 percent to 31 percent of males (Peters, Wyatt, & Finkelhor, 1986). Although some theorize that estimates vary in part because of the methodological differences in studies (for example, the number of questions used to assess sexual abuse experiences and whether subjects are interviewed in person or through mailed questionnaires) and as a result of natural variation in samples drawn from different populations, in fact, there is little research data to support these theories.

What is clear is that the sexual abuse of children is a significant and relatively common problem of childhood. It is associated with a wide range of psychosocial problems in childhood and adulthood (Briere, 1992) and may be an underlying etiological factor in why clients seek social work services. The failure to screen for childhood sexual abuse (and, indeed, family violence in general) may be regarded in the near future as a form of social work malpractice.

An interesting assessment principle learned in the past decade or so is that one of the best ways to identify victims is to ask clients about their experiences. Although not every victimized person will tell the first professional who asks, and many victims (for example, very young children) present special assessment problems for the social worker, many people will report histories of childhood sexual abuse if asked.

### Child Abuse as a Health Problem

The sexual abuse of children is a multidisciplinary problem. It is a crime in every state and, when detected, initiates a law enforcement investigation and involvement of the justice system. The child requires protection, and the child's parent may not have the internal or external resources to care adequately for the child; they may require a range of social services. The psychosocial effects of abuse, the impact of intervention on the child and family, and treatment of the abuser involve a range of mental health services. Concern over the physical trauma resulting from sexual assault, the potential for sexually transmitted diseases, and the potential usefulness of medical evaluations in detecting abuse (especially in young children) involve medical and health services. As a result, many different professions have roles to play in responding to childhood sexual abuse.

The social worker, with a dual interest in helping the abused child and facilitating the response of other professionals, plays an important role in coordinating services, advocating for the abused child, and facilitating effective and humane interventions. Social workers in a wide range of settings (for example, schools, social services departments, sexual assault centers, and mental health agencies) can play this traditional social work role. Social workers in health settings can also serve this function and respond to the unique health-oriented aspects of child sexual abuse.

## ASSESSMENT

The sexual abuse of children triggers strong emotional reactions in parents, loved ones, and professionals who confront a child who may have been sexually abused. Sexual abuse inherently involves dimensions such as sexuality, deviancy, power, control, interpersonal relationships, and gender and ageist politics; consequently, denial, minimization, and rationalization historically have been inherent components of the problem. Although most people intellectually recognize that sexual abuse occurs, it is often difficult for adults to accept the fact of abuse when a specific child has been abused.

### Disclosure and Discovery

There has been little systematic study of the various ways that children disclose abuse or what factors lead to disclosure. Children may not disclose or present "indicators" of abuse at all until asked. Some children disclose abuse in subtle ways through behavioral changes reflecting anxiety or stress (for example, nightmares or fearfulness), through sexual behaviors or statements, or through disguised statements to peers or adults. Some children disclose abuse only when asked about it, whereas others disclose abuse in clear, precise statements after the first incidence.

An adult in the child's life (for example, a teacher, parent, parent of the child's friend) who is concerned about the possibility of abuse can report these concerns to the state child abuse trama agency, which will undertake an assessment to substantiate the abuse allegation. In most cases, there is little doubt about what took place. Children five years and older who make clear disclosures of sexual acts are generally recognized to be describing real events. Although much attention has been given to the concern over false reports of abuse, the current professional literature confirms that such reports are extremely rare. When they do occur, false reports are more likely to be originated by adults rather than children, and they are more often based on misperception than on any villainous motives (Berliner & Conte, 1993).

Currently there is widespread belief that certain characteristics (for example, cases involving young children or allegations arising in the context of divorce or custody disputes) are associated with a decreased likelihood that the allegation of abuse is true. As Berliner and Conte (1993) pointed out, there is no currently available research that supports the idea that these characteristics are associated with a decreased likelihood that the case involves "real" abuse. However, these characteristics may have a powerful effect on the professional's belief about the case.

Young children do present special problems for the assessment of sexual abuse. Language abilities vary, and some young children lack the intellectual or verbal abilities to describe what did or did not happen to them. Others may be so fearful or anxious because of the trauma, coercion, or manipulation to which they were exposed that no amount of reassurance or relationship-building can overcome these feelings.

**Interviewing Young Children**

Interviewing young children about sexual abuse is similar to interviewing adult clients from unfamiliar cultures. The interviewer must have special skills to understand the developmental capabilities of the child (for example, the ability to place events in time), the language of the child (for instance, terms used for various body parts and the ability of the child to understand complex sentences), and the effects of sexual abuse on the child (for example, the impact of offender coercion on a child's willingness to report experiences) (Jones, 1992).

Although skepticism abounds about children as reporters of events, current research on children as witnesses suggests that young children can provide reliable information about experiences. For example, information that children provide during free recall is quite accurate. Children are more likely to make errors of omission than of commission, and young children, like all witnesses, can be misled by suggestive interviewing techniques. (For a summary of child witness research, see Steward, Bussey, Goodman, & Saywitz, 1993.) The trained social worker with special skills in interviewing young children can be a "translator" to help others understand the nature and extent of the child's experiences.

**Validation Criteria**

There has been increasing interest in criteria for discriminating between "true" and "false" cases of abuse. The motivations for seeking such criteria are complex. They rest in the denial that is part of human reactions to abuse and in an awareness of the serious implications that a decision about abuse can have for the child and the adults involved in the case. Decision-making criteria—formal or informal, simple or complex, articulated or not—are an integral part of assessments.

In the early phase of modern awareness of childhood sexual abuse, behaviors (for example, somatic complaints, fearfulness, and behavioral regression) were thought to be diagnostic of abuse. It is currently recognized that childhood behavior indicative of anxiety or stress should alert the professional to assess for the source of anxiety, but not to assume that sexual abuse is the only possible source. Conte, Wolf, and Smith (1989) cautioned against overreliance on a single criterion. In their national survey of validation criteria, medical indicators such as vaginal tears or scarring were rated as the most important criteria for substantiating abuse. Bays and Chadwick (1993) pointed out that most sexually abused children lack clear positive indicators of abuse. Therefore, the absence of medical signs of abuse should not deter professionals from considering abuse as a possibility or from providing appropriate services.

Another popular set of criteria involves comparing the child's description with what is known about sexual abuse. If a child describes a gradual increase in the sexual nature of the abuse (for example, moving from back rubbing to genital fondling to intercourse), this is thought to be indicative of real abuse, because "grooming" the child is frequently a part of sexual abuse. The problem with using such criteria is that many children are raped at the first occurrence of sexual abuse and experience no gradual increase in the intensity of the abuse. Because there is considerable variation in children's experiences with sexual abuse, what sounds like an atypical experience may be just that—not typical—but accurate nonetheless.

**Validation Protocols**

A number of more-structured systems for the validation of allegations of abuse have been disseminated (Berliner & Conte, 1993). All these systems operate on the assumption that some set of criteria discriminates between true and false cases of abuse, but not one of these systems has been substantiated through empirical research; they exist as ideas or theories about the difference between true and false cases. Typical of these systems is the Sexual Abuse Legitimacy Scale (Gardner, 1989), which asks the evaluator to indicate the presence or absence of a series of characteristics. Twenty-six criteria deal with the alleged child victim, 11 deal with the accuser (usually the mother), and 13 deal with the accused (usually the father). Scores in the range of 50 percent of the maximum or more are highly suggestive of bona fide sexual abuse, and those below 10 percent suggest the report is fabricated. Criteria for the child include "very hesitant to divulge the abuse"; for the accuser, "appreciates importance of relationship" between child and father and "initially denies abuse"; and for the accused, "allegation not in the context of divorce" and "career choice involving children."

The Sexual Abuse Legitimacy Scale suffers from many of the problems manifested by all the systems that are based on criteria for discriminating between "true" and "false" cases. It is based entirely on the author's personal observations of an unknown number of cases seen in a specialized forensic practice. No research study has ever determined whether the scale can be coded reliably. Many of the criteria are poorly defined. Conceptually, each criterion said to be indicative of one type of abuse may also be indicative of another. For example, one can imagine that an assertive child raised in a family and school environment that has supported verbalization may disclose abuse without a great deal of hesitancy. There has been no scientific test of the ability of the scale to discriminate among cases, and there is no evidence that the numerical scores have any real meaning. Indeed, the entire scale and the "parent alienation syndrome" on which it is based have never been subjected to peer review or empirical test. In summary, there is no demonstrated ability of this scale or of any other similar device to make valid predictions on the basis of the identified criteria.

### Social Work Assessment of Possible Abuse

The current research literature suggests that what children say about experiences is generally accurate. The social worker who avoids the use of leading and suggestive interviewing techniques and who seeks to facilitate the child's disclosure rather than to get the child to confirm some preexisting idea about what did or did not happen can help the child in reporting his or her experience. The neutral and objective stance of the social worker as operationalized in the assessment interviews helps ensure the accuracy of information obtained from the child and others. (For an excellent discussion of ways to maintain objectivity, see White, 1990.) The application of traditional social work assessment and interviewing skills, informed by specialized knowledge in childhood sexual abuse, is required.

## Effects of Child Sexual Abuse

Concern for the psychosocial effects of childhood sexual abuse has been a part of the field from the early discovery of the extent of the problem. Childhood sexual abuse is associated with problems in childhood and throughout development. Childhood effects include those indicative of stress, trauma, and anxiety (for example, fearfulness, sleep problems, and withdrawal).

### Psychosocial Effects

Studies using measures of child functioning consistently indicate that sexually abused children score between nontraumatized children and children in psychiatric care. For example, Gomes-Schwartz, Horowitz, and Sauzier (1985) compared 156 sexually abused children to the norms provided with the Louisville Behavior Checklist and found that preschool children ($n = 30$) were rated as more pathological than the normative group on 10 of the 16 behavioral dimensions of the checklist (infantile aggression, hyperactivity, antisocial behavior, aggression, social withdrawal, sensitivity, fear, inhibition, academic disability, immaturity, learning disability, normal irritability, neurotic behavior, psychotic behavior, somatic behavior, and prosocial deficits). Comparison of the abused children to the norms for children receiving mental health services revealed that abused children exhibited less overall pathology and fewer specific difficulties. School-age sexually abused children ($n = 58$) exhibited significantly more pathology than nonabused children on every dimension of the checklist, although they exhibited less-problematic functioning on 11 of 16 dimensions than did other children in mental health treatment (that is, compared with clinic norms).

Sexually abused children have also been shown to have significantly lower self-esteem than other children (Tong, Oates, & McDowell, 1987); to be more depressed (Mannarino, Cohen, & Gregor, 1989); and to more often exhibit sexual behavior problems (Friedreich, Urquiza, & Beilke, 1986; White, Halpin, Strom, & Santelli, 1988).

In a comprehensive discussion of the long-term effects of childhood abuse, Briere (1992) reviewed a large body of research and suggested that specific effects can be grouped into major types: posttraumatic behaviors, cognitive distortions, altered emotionality (depression and anxiety), dissociation, impaired self-reference, disturbed relatedness, and avoidance (for example, the use of substances).

### Medical Effects

Koss and Heslet (1992) reviewed research on the medical complications of all forms of violence and noted both acute effects (for example, genital injuries, sexually transmitted diseases, pregnancy) and chronic medical complaints (for example, chronic pelvic pain, gastrointestinal symptoms [irritable bowel], eating disorders, alcohol dependence, and elevated risk of human immunodeficiency virus [HIV]). At least one study with children has documented similar health problems: Rimsza, Berg, and Locke (1988) reported that abused children were more likely than nonabused children to present with symptoms of muscle tension, gastrointestinal and genitourinary difficulties, emotional reactions, runaway behavior, and other behavior problems.

Differences for school problems and early pregnancy were not significant. There is no question that childhood sexual abuse is associated with significant psychosocial and health-related problems for the child victim and for the adult who was victimized in childhood.

## Treatment

Because they traditionally work in social services, health, and mental health agencies accessible to the most vulnerable, powerless, and oppressed populations, social workers are likely to encounter many child victims and adults who were victimized in childhood. The time-honored social work roles of advocate, service broker, case manager, medical social worker, youth and family worker, and psychotherapist are all likely to be needed in responding to the special needs of victims of sexual abuse.

### Crisis Intervention

The disclosure of sexual abuse is a crisis for the child and for those who love the child. The interventions of child protection, health and social services, and law enforcement require the child and loved ones to participate in fact finding, assessment, and case planning. These processes are stressful, but necessary, and the social worker can help the child and loved ones understand why the process is necessary, what to expect, and how to benefit from the interventions of the various systems that respond to sexual abuse. Both child and parent will have many concerns to address, questions to ask, and emotions to process with the social worker's help.

Parents feel a wide range of emotions when a child is abused. Popular views of the effects of abuse (for example, that abuse inevitably leads to sexual offenses, drug addiction, or prostitution) can frighten a parent. The social worker can educate the parent about the importance of treatment in reducing the risk for negative effects of abuse. In an effort to deal with their feelings, some parents deny the impact of the abuse, avoid interacting with the system about the abuse, and refuse to take a child to treatment. Such parents are often "blamed" by the system or labeled as neglectful. The social worker who recognizes that many such parents are dealing with their own emotional issues can approach the parents not as neglectful but as needing support and assistance in doing the right thing for their child. Such an approach will do much to involve the parent in his or her own treatment and in the child's healing.

### Treatment of Long-Term Effects

Currently there is little research on the treatment of the long-term effects of childhood sexual abuse in either child or adult populations. Thus, it is not known whether specialized treatment of childhood victimization can successfully prevent or reduce the risk for long-term impact. Such treatment should be based on emerging ideas about childhood sexual abuse and trauma, and it has been argued that such treatment is a specialization (Herman, 1992). Social workers are likely to need specialized training in the treatment of child victims and adult survivors of childhood sexual abuse.

## Conclusion

Social work can have a unique role in responding to the sexual abuse of children. Because of the profession's focus on community health, mental health, and social services agencies (especially agencies serving the most vulnerable and powerless populations), social workers are in frequent contact with abused children or with adults who were abused in childhood. It is increasingly clear that child abuse is associated with a wide range of childhood and adult problems, such as substance abuse, relationship problems, and emotional difficulties. These problems often bring clients into agencies or other settings where social workers work. Because of the profession's historical interest in both "person-changing" and "context-changing" interventions, social workers bring a time-honored understanding of the importance of contextual interventions for the multifaceted problem of childhood sexual abuse.

## References


Abel, G. G., Becker, J. V., Mittelman, M., Cunningham-Rathner, J., Rouleau, J. L., & Murphy, W. D. (1987). Self-reported sex crimes of nonincarcerated paraphiliacs. *Journal of Interpersonal Violence, 2*(1), 3–26.

Bays, J., & Chadwick, D. (1993). Medical diagnosis of the sexually abused child. *Child Abuse and Neglect, 17*(1), 91–110.

Berliner, L., & Conte, J. R. (1993). Sexual abuse evaluations: Conceptual and empirical obstacles. *Child Abuse and Neglect, 17*(1), 111–126.

Briere, J. N. (1992). *Child abuse trauma: Theory and treatment of the lasting effects.* Newbury Park, CA: Sage Publications.

Conte, J. R. (1991). The therapist in child sexual abuse: The context of helping. In J. Briere (Ed.), *New directions for mental health services: Treating victims of child sexual abuse* (pp. 87–98). San Francisco: Jossey-Bass.

Conte, J. R., Wolf, S., & Smith, T. (1989). What sexual offenders tell us about prevention. *Child Abuse and Neglect, 13,* 293–302.

Finkelhor, D. (Ed.). (1986). *A sourcebook on child sexual abuse.* Newbury Park, CA: Sage Publications.

Friedreich, W., Urquiza, A., & Beilke, R. (1986). Behavior problems in young sexually abused children. *Journal of Pediatric Psychology, 11,* 47–57.

Gardner, R. A. (1989). Differentiating between bona fide and fabricated allegations of sexual abuse of children. *Journal of the American Academy of Matrimonial Lawyers, 5,* 1–26.

Gomes-Schwartz, B., Horowitz, J., & Sauzier, M. (1985). Severity of emotional distress among sexually abused preschool, school-age and adolescent children. *Hospital and Community Psychiatry, 36,* 503–508.

Herman, J. L. (1992). *Trauma and recovery.* New York: Basic Books.

Jones, D.P.H. (1992). *Interviewing the sexually abused child: Investigation of suspected abuse.* London: Gaskell.

Koss, M. P., & Heslet, L. (1992). Somatic consequences of violence against women. *Archives of Family Medicine, 1,* 53–59.

Mannarino, A. P., Cohen, J. A., & Gregor, M. (1989). Emotional and behavioral difficulties in sexually abused girls. *Journal of Interpersonal Violence, 4,* 437–445.

Peters, S. D., Wyatt, G. E., & Finkelhor, D. (1986). Prevalence. In D. Finkelhor (Ed.), *A sourcebook on child sexual abuse* (pp. 15–59). Newbury Park, CA: Sage Publications.

Rimsza, M. E., Berg, M. D., & Locke, C. (1988). Sexual abuse: Somatic and emotional reactions. *Child Abuse and Neglect, 12,* 201–208.

Steward, M. S., Bussey, K., Goodman, G. S., & Saywitz, K. J. (1993). Implications of developmental research for interviewing children. *Child Abuse and Neglect, 17*(1), 25–37.

Tong, L., Oates, K., & McDowell, M. (1987). Personality development following sexual abuse. *Child Abuse and Neglect, 11,* 371–383.

White, S. (1990). The investigatory interview with suspected victims of child sexual abuse. In A. M. LaGreca (Ed.), *Through the eyes of the child: Obtaining self-reports from children and adolescents* (pp. 368–394). Needham Heights, MA: Allyn & Bacon.

White, S., Halpin, B., Strom, G., & Santelli, G. (1988). Behavioral comparisons of young sexually abused, neglected and non-referred children. *Journal of Clinical Child Psychology, 17,* 53–61.

**Jon R. Conte, PhD,** is associate professor, University of Washington, School of Social Work, Seattle, WA 98195.

**For further information see**

Adolescence Overview; Assessment; Child Abuse and Neglect Overview; Child Day Care; Child Foster Care; Child Sexual Abuse: Direct Practice; Children: Direct Practice; Children: Mental Health; Criminal Behavior Overview; Crisis Intervention: Research Needs; Domestic Violence; Families Overview; HIV/AIDS: Pediatric; Interdisciplinary and Interorganizational Collaboration; Interviewing; Legal Issues: Low-Income and Dependent People; Mental Health Overview; Professional Liability and Malpractice; School Social Work Overview; Sexual Assault; Single Parents; Victim Services and Victim/Witness Assistance Programs; Violence Overview.

**Key Words**

| | |
|---|---|
| child abuse | sexual abuse |
| child sexual abuse | trauma |

# Child Sexual Abuse: Direct Practice

**Lucy Berliner**

Child sexual abuse encompasses a broad range of nonconsensual sexual behaviors involving children. It includes all sexual acts accomplished by force or threat of force and sexual activities committed by an adult or a significantly older child or adolescent with a child. Sexual behavior includes penetration, sexual touching, voyeurism, and sexual exposure. The defining characteristic of sexual abuse is that the child does not or cannot give consent because of coercion or significant inequality in age, size, knowledge, or position in the relationship.

The legal definitions of sexual abuse that permit civil or criminal intervention may not include all the circumstances that conform to a clinical description of sexually abusive behavior. Criminal statutes apply to adults and adolescents who commit forced sexual contact or are of a proscribed age differential. Federal and state statutes name and define the particular crime and the applicable penalties. The ages of consent vary but are usually between 14 and 16 years. Civil child abuse statutes generally define the conduct more broadly but limit intervention to cases involving caretaker offenders or situations in which a caretaker fails to protect a child.

## Incidence and Prevalence

General population studies have found that the vast majority of cases of sexual abuse are not reported to authorities. Hence, the annual incidence of sexual abuse is not known. Only a minority of children tell anyone at the time about their abuse experiences (Finkelhor, Hotaling, Lewis, & Smith, 1990), and only 6 percent to 12 percent of cases are reported to law enforcement agencies (Russell, 1984; Saunders, Villeponteaux, Lipovsky, Kilpatrick, & Veronen, 1992). Even for cases that are reported, there are no reliable national statistics. Child abuse definitions and reporting systems vary across states and may include only abuse committed by caretakers. National crime statistics currently do not identify crimes against children.

The prevalence of sexual abuse is determined through retrospective surveys of adults in the general population that ask respondents about their childhood experiences. There is substantial variation in lifetime rates across studies. Different definitions and research methodologies, including the number of screening questions and the method of survey (for example, in-person, telephone, or mail), account for at least some of the differences. In general, studies that use broader definitions, ask more questions, and use in-person interviews reveal higher rates of abuse (Russell, 1984; Wyatt, 1985). Telephone surveys of national samples have revealed that 27 percent of the women and 16 percent of the men had a sexual abuse experience before age 18 (Finkelhor et al., 1990) and that 9 percent of the women had reported a forcible rape by age 18 (Saunders, Kilpatrick, Resnick, Hanson, & Lipovsky, 1992). Although reporting has increased dramatically in recent years, there is little evidence that the rates of sexual abuse have changed significantly (Feldman et al., 1991).

The lack of memory for the experience, a recently identified phenomenon, may obscure the true rates of sexual abuse in survey populations. Studies have shown that a substantial percentage of subjects with documented histories of abuse do not report abuse when questioned many years later (Widom & Morris, 1993; Williams, in press). The explanations for the lack of recall are the subject of current controversy, especially under circumstances in which repression or the complete loss of memory for significant abuse is reported (Loftus, 1993).

## Characteristics

The characteristics of sexual abuse situations vary, depending on whether a clinical or a nonclinical population is described. General population surveys suggest that abuse by parental figures constitutes 6 percent to 16 percent of the cases; by relatives, approximately 25 percent of the cases; and by strangers, 5 percent to 15 percent of the cases. The remainder of cases involve persons known but not related to the child victims (Finkelhor et al., 1990; Saunders, Kilpatrick, et al., 1992). In clinical samples, parental figures and family members constitute a substantially larger proportion of abusers (about one-third and one-half, respectively) (Conte & Schuerman, 1987; Gomes-Schwartz, Horowitz, & Cardarelli, 1990). Offenders are overwhelmingly male in both clinical and nonclinical samples; 95 percent of the girls and 80 percent of the boys were abused by men (Finkelhor & Russell, 1984). In cases of abuse in day care settings, women are represented at a much higher rate (40 percent) (Finkelhor, Williams, & Burns, 1988). Boys are more likely to be abused by nonfamily members and girls by family members (Faller, 1989).

All types of sexual acts occur, with attempted or completed intercourse reported in 20 percent to 40 percent of the nonclinical cases (Finkelhor et al., 1990; Russell, 1984). Multiple episodes of abuse are more common in clinical samples. For example, Conte and Schuerman (1987) found that 25 percent of victims experienced a single incident, 44 percent were abused several times, and 25 percent reported more than 10 occurrences. Child victims range in age from infancy to 18 years. Many offenders are teenagers, and one study reported adolescent offenders in more than 40 percent of the cases (Saunders, Kilpatrick, et al., 1992).

Ethnicity is not necessarily associated with differences in rates of sexual abuse (Wyatt, 1985) but is associated with differences in abusive experiences, offender–victim relationships, and family characteristics in clinical samples (Rao, DiClemente, & Ponton, 1992). Asian children tend to be the oldest at the time of their first victimization, and African American children tend to be the youngest of the ethnic groups. Hispanic and African American victims are more likely than are Asian or white victims to experience penetration offenses. Asian children are most likely to be abused by a male relative, and white children are most likely to be abused by an acquaintance.

Some risk factors for sexual abuse have been identified. Girls are more likely than are boys to be abused. Both boys and girls are at a higher risk if they have lived some part of their childhood without one of their biological parents or if they perceive their families as unhappy (Finkelhor &

Baron, 1986; Finkelhor et al., 1990). The rate of sexual abuse among children with disabilities is 1.75 times higher than that among children without disabilities (National Center on Child Abuse and Neglect, 1993). Socioeconomic status is not associated with sexual abuse in nonclinical samples (Elliott & Briere, 1992; Russell, 1984), although rates of sexual abuse are higher among children of lower socioeconomic status in clinical samples (Sedlack, 1992).

Sexual abuse is accomplished in a variety of ways. Force, threat of force, or the fear of injury or death occurs in a substantial percentage of cases (Gomes-Schwartz et al., 1990; Saunders, Kilpatrick, et al., 1992). However, in other cases, offenders may engage in a process of victimization in which the relationship is gradually sexualized over time (Berliner & Conte, 1990). Offenders report that they use a variety of strategies to involve children, maintain their cooperation, and prevent disclosure (Conte, Wolfe, & Smith, 1989; Lang & Frenzel, 1988).

## Reporting and Disclosure

Commonly, there is a delay between the last episode of abuse and the discovery or report of abuse. Gomes-Schwartz et al. (1990) found that only 24 percent of the cases became known within a week of the episode, and some cases were not reported for more than a year. In half the cases, the children did not initiate the report. Instead, the abuse was uncovered as a result of concern about suspicious or unusual statements, behavior, medical findings, or, in rare cases, because of confession or incriminating evidence (for example, pornographic pictures). Sgroi (1982) described children's disclosures as either purposeful or accidental. When children report abuse, it is most often to a parent, usually their mothers.

### Inconsistent Reports

Children who have been abused sometimes deny the abuse or recant earlier statements. Lawson and Chaffin (1992) found that more than 40 percent of the children with confirmed sexually transmitted disease did not report that they have been abused when questioned by trained interviewers. In another study, almost three-fourths of the children did not reveal their abuse experiences when initially interviewed (Sorensen & Snow, 1991). From 8 percent to 22 percent of abused children recant the allegations (Jones & McGraw, 1987; Sorensen & Snow, 1991). Recantations may occur because the children are threatened or pressured or because they perceive the consequences of reporting to be negative. Many children report regret or fears about reporting (Sauzier, 1990), although the vast majority have retrospectively agreed that reporting was necessary to protect themselves and others and to promote their psychological recovery (Berliner & Conte, in press).

Children's reports of abuse may contain inconsistencies and be accompanied by reactions that seem inconsistent with victimization. The "child sexual abuse accommodation syndrome" (Summit, 1983) identifies the psychological dynamics of sexual abuse situations that may account for this behavior. Children may feel helpless to escape the situation or feel responsible for the abuse or the consequences of disclosure. They may also care for or have positive feelings toward their abusers. As a result, the initial reports may be tentative and elaborated on only over time; in addition, the children may recant their allegations or may fail to exhibit fear or anger toward the offenders. These behaviors are neither diagnostic for the purpose of proving sexual abuse nor present in all cases.

Another explanation for inconsistencies or incompleteness in children's reports is that they may feel embarrassed or distressed about recounting abusive sexual experiences. Sexual abuse is most often aversive or frightening, and unpleasant emotions may be evoked when the experiences are recalled. Avoidance coping strategies may hinder full disclosure or even interfere with normal memory process.

### False Reports

Not all reports of abuse are true, although studies have consistently found that only about 5 percent of reports are fictitious (Jones & McGraw, 1987). Fictitious reports include mistaken interpretations of nonsexual behavior and reports that are the result of psychological disturbance or influence by others. Intentionally false reports are the least common explanation. Fictitious reports are more likely to emanate from adults than from children. The rates of false or uncertain cases are higher in custody or visitation disputes, although a substantial proportion are considered valid (Thoennes & Tjaden, 1990).

A great deal of concern has been raised about the suggestibility of children, especially young children, who may be questioned about possible sexual abuse (Ceci & Bruck, 1993). Laboratory analogue studies have revealed certain characteristics of interview situations that have been associated with increased rates of inaccurate reports, such as repeated, suggestive, or coercive interviewing by influential individuals with preconceived ideas about what may have happened.

Although there is the potential for eliciting false reports through improper interviewing, studies have also shown that children are unlikely to reveal abusive experiences unless they are directly asked (Lanktree, Briere, & Zaidi, 1991).

## Impact of Sexual Abuse

Sexual abuse affects children in a variety of ways; there is no universal or uniform impact (Beitchman, Zucker, Hood, da Costa, & Ackerman, 1991; Kendall-Tackett, Williams, & Finkelhor, 1993). Many different patterns of response are found in clinical samples of abused children, ranging from no discernible negative impact to moderate levels of distress and, in some instances, severe psychiatric disorders. Studies have found that when sexually abused children are compared with nonabused children on parental report measures, they have more emotional and behavioral problems but do not have the level of disturbance found in clinical samples (Gomes-Schwartz et al., 1990). Results based on standardized self-report measures of depression, anxiety, and self-esteem generally reveal few differences between abused and nonabused children (Mannarino, Cohen, & Gregor, 1989) except among adolescents, where significant differences are found (Gidycz & Koss, 1989; Wozencraft, Wagner, & Pellegrin, 1991). Differences have been reported on structured psychiatric interviews (Runyan, Everson, Edelsohn, Hunter, & Coulter, 1988), personality tests (Basta & Peterson, 1990; German, Habernicht, & Futcher, 1990), and projective tests (Stovall & Craig, 1990).

### Emotional and Behavioral Problems

When sexually abused children are compared with children in treatment, they are more likely to be diagnosed with depression and to have suicidal behavior (Lanktree et al., 1991) and to have more anxiety (Kolko, Moser, & Weldy, 1988). When compared with adolescents in inpatient treatment settings, they are more likely to have lower self-esteem (Cavaiola & Schiff, 1989) and more substance abuse problems (Singer, Petchers, & Hussey, 1989). Teenage mothers with histories of sexual abuse are more likely to abuse their children or to have them taken by child protective services (Boyer & Fine, 1991). Even when family dysfunction is taken into account, sexually abused girls have lower self-esteem, more internalized aggression, and poorer relationships with their mothers (Hotte & Rafman, 1992).

Sexually abused children exhibit more sexual behavior than do comparison groups of nonabused, neglected, physically abused, and psychiatrically disturbed children (Gale, Thompson, Moran, & Sack, 1988; Kolko et al., 1988; White, Halpin, Strom, & Santelli, 1988). However, most sexually abused children do not display unusual sexual behavior (Friedrich, 1993), although they are significantly more likely to engage in sexual behavior that is coercive or imitative of adult genital sexual behavior (Friedrich et al., 1992).

Symptoms of anxiety and fear that are consistent with a posttraumatic stress disorder (PTSD) are frequently found in sexually abused children (Wolfe, Gentile, & Wolfe, 1989). Between one-third and one-half of sexually abused children meet the diagnostic criteria for PTSD, and a majority exhibit partial PTSD (McLeer, Deblinger, Atkins, Ralphe, & Foa, 1988; McLeer, Deblinger, Henry, & Orvaschel, 1992). PTSD includes intrusive, unpleasant recollections of the event; hyperarousal; and avoidance and numbing symptoms (American Psychiatric Association, 1994). The abused children who meet these diagnostic criteria, when compared with those who do not, are more likely to be female and older, to have longer histories of sexual abuse, and to have had force used in the abuse. They are also more likely to report feelings of guilt (Wolfe, Sas, & Wekerle, 1994).

### Cognitive Functioning

There appears to be a relationship between sexual abuse and cognitive functioning. Einbender and Friedrich (1989) reported that sexually abused children were cognitively impaired, and higher levels of distress were reported in sexually abused children with higher cognitive functioning (Shapiro, Leifer, Martone, & Kassem, 1992). These findings may indicate that sexual abuse affects cognitive processes or that children who are more able to appreciate the meaning of the abusive behavior are more negatively affected. Children with a global, stable, and internal attributional style (Wolfe et al., 1989) and children who blame themselves (Morrow, 1991) have more symptoms of depression. Abused girls who appraise their experience as threatening and who use wishful thinking as a coping strategy are more distressed than are those who do not (Johnson & Kenkel, 1991).

### Long-Term Impacts

One of the most important research findings on the effects of sexual abuse experiences is that although most children who are assessed do not have significant psychopathology, sexual abuse is a risk factor for subsequent distress. Many of the more serious outcomes are not apparent until adolescence or adulthood. An association with severe depression and suicidality, substance abuse, running away, and self-destructive behavior has been documented (Kendall-Tackett et al.,

1993). Adults in nonclinical samples who have been abused have more symptoms of depression, anxiety, somatization, and dissociation than do adults who have not been abused (Briere & Runtz, 1988), a finding that remains true even in samples of highly functioning women (Elliott & Briere, 1992). Sexual abuse increases the risk of various psychiatric diagnoses, including depression, certain anxiety disorders, and substance abuse (Saunders, Villeponteaux, et al., 1992). Adults with histories of sexual abuse are more likely than are those without such histories to suffer from a variety of physical and somatic complaints (Springs & Friedrich, 1992; Walker, Torkelson, Katon, & Koss, 1993). Interpersonal difficulties, including the greater likelihood of remaining single or, for those who marry, of being divorced (Elliott & Briere, 1992) and of having less satisfaction, greater discomfort and sensitivity, and more maladaptive patterns in relationships, have been reported (Elliott, 1994).

Researchers and clinicians have postulated a "sleeper effect" of sexual abuse experiences (Briere, 1992). In this conceptualization, the ultimate impact of sexual abuse cannot be determined on the basis of initial responses. Some children may successfully resolve the experience relatively quickly. But for others, the expression of negative consequences may be delayed because the coping strategies they use to reduce aversive emotions that are associated with confronting the abusive experience (avoidance, dissociation, forgetting, or denial, for example) may eventually become maladaptive or fail. It may also be the case that certain types of impact are not salient or cannot be effectively addressed until later developmental stages (for example, when they reach an age when they may begin to have sexual relationships).

**Other Factors**

The nature of the abusive experience and its aftermath also affects the level of psychological impact. In general, sexual abuse that involves violence or force, penetration, longer duration, and a closer relationship to the offender usually has a greater negative impact (Conte & Schuerman, 1987). Children with preexisting problems are more negatively affected (Mannarino, Cohen, & Berman, 1994). Characteristics of poor family functioning and the lack of maternal support have consistently been associated with more severe emotional effects (Conte & Schuerman, 1987; Everson, Hunter, Runyan, Edelsohn, & Coulter, 1989; Friedrich, Beilke, & Urquiza, 1987). As understanding of the complex relationships between abusive experiences and subsequent maladjustment has increased (Mullen, 1993), there has been greater interest in the influence of attachment and normal developmental processes on the nature and severity of the consequences over time (Alexander, 1992; Cole & Putnam, 1992).

**Impact of Intervention**

The impact of intervention on sexually abused children has also been investigated. Although relatively few studies have examined the intervention process, the various activities—interviews, placement, and testifying—have not been shown to contribute significantly to the harm done by sexual abuse. The findings with regard to multiple interviews or protracted proceedings are mixed. Placement is associated with greater initial distress but comparable improvement when abused children who are placed are compared with nonplaced abused children (Runyan et al., 1988). This finding may mean that the initial distress is related more to the lack of maternal support—the most significant reason for placement—than to placement per se (Hunter, Coulter, Runyan, & Everson, 1990). Separation of offenders from children is not associated with increased distress (Berliner & Conte, in press).

Runyan et al. (1988) found that although children whose cases did not enter the legal system and those whose cases had been resolved did not differ on measures of distress, children whose cases were pending had more distress. A great deal of concern has been expressed about the impact of testifying in court, although relatively few children actually testify in criminal court trials (Smith, Elstein, Trost, & Bulkley, 1993). Testifying is not always associated with increased psychological distress (Whitcomb et al., 1991). The most rigorous study of the impact of testifying in criminal court found that only children who testified more than once were more distressed and that distress associated with testifying was correlated with the lack of maternal support (Goodman et al., 1992). Comprehensive court-preparation programs have been found to reduce children's fears about testifying and to improve their courtroom performance (Sas, 1991).

## Course of Symptoms and Treatment

Most children's symptoms improve over time, with or without treatment, although 10 percent to 24 percent either do not improve or deteriorate (Kendall-Tackett et al., 1993). In a series of case studies, Friedrich and Reams (1987) found that symptoms tended to fluctuate over time, and Lanktree and Briere (1993) reported that different symptoms subsided differentially. It is possible that certain symptoms decrease more readily than do others, whereas still other symptoms have a delayed onset.

There have been many excellent clinical reports on approaches to the treatment of sexually abused children (Friedrich, 1990; Gil, 1991; James, 1989; Jones, 1986). Group therapy has been the most specifically described therapeutic approach, with numerous published articles (Berman, 1990; Furniss, Bingley-Miller, & van Elberg, 1988; Mandell & Damon, 1989). Groups, which are usually characterized as supportive and psychoeducational, encourage the expression of feelings about the abuse and the offender, supply corrective information about abuse and offenders and information on the prevention of further abuse, identify a support system, and involve victims in self-esteem and skills-enhancing activities.

Although no reports of controlled treatment outcome studies have been published, a number of such studies are being conducted. Reports that are available offer assessments of participants before and after various treatment programs. In general, these studies have found that children improve over the course of intervention (Bentovim, van Elberg, & Boston, 1988; Deblinger, McLeer, & Henry, 1990; Hiebert-Murphy, De Luca, & Runtz, 1992; Nelki & Watters, 1989). However, without comparison groups of children who are not receiving therapy, improvement cannot be attributed to the therapeutic experience. Although they did not use random assignment, Gomes-Schwartz et al. (1990) found that the children who were receiving the specialized crisis response at their clinic showed significant improvement when compared with children who were receiving therapy in the community—a finding that lends some support to the widely accepted notion of abuse-focused therapy.

## Offenders

Sexual offenders are a heterogeneous group and may be of any age, ethnicity, or socioeconomic background; there is not a psychological test or profile that discriminates them (Murphy & Peters, 1992). Although many adult sexual offenders admit to committing other types of crimes (Weinrott & Saylor, 1991), most offenders who come to the attention of authorities do not have criminal records. There is no characteristic or set of characteristics that either confirms or rules out the possibility that an individual has engaged in sexual misconduct with children.

### Characteristics of Offenses

Sexual offenders may engage in a variety of types of sexual misbehavior. In one well-known study (Abel, Becker, Cunningham-Rathner, Mittelman, & Rouleau, 1988) in which subjects were promised confidentiality, about half the offenders who admitted abusing their own daughters also reported abusing nonrelated girls, and 20 percent stated that they had raped women. The usual offender has a few victims, but some, especially those who prefer boy victims, may have scores or hundreds of victims. About half the offenders begin to offend during adolescence. About one-fourth of male offenders were sexually abused as children (Hanson & Slater, 1988). Although less is known about female offenders, there is currently little basis for assuming that they differ significantly from male offenders except that they are more likely to have histories of sexual abuse and to offend in concert with male offenders (Allen, 1990).

The motivations for offending vary among offenders (Quinsey, 1986). Child molesters as a group have greater sexual interest in children (except those who offend only against their biological children). However, most sexual offenders are not exclusively sexually interested in or involved with children; most have adult sexual relationships as well. Most sexual offenses are planned, and offenders describe using elaborate strategies to engage their child victims and to maintain their cooperation (Lang & Frenzel, 1988). There is no particular pattern to offending; some offenders choose victims of only a certain age or gender, and others appear to be more opportunistic or situational in targeting their victims.

### Treatment of Offenders

Sexual offenders remain at risk indefinitely of committing further offenses, which occur as long as 30 years after their initial convictions, although at a relatively low rate (Hanson, Steffy, & Gauthier, 1993). Previous sexual offenses and non-family victims are associated with reoffenses. Some reviews of the available treatment outcome studies have come to optimistic conclusions about the success of treatment programs in reducing recidivism (Becker & Hunter, 1992; Marshall, Jones, Ward, Johnston, & Barbaree, 1991). However, Quinsey, Harris, Rice, and Lalumiere (1993) cautioned that the methodologies used in most studies, especially the lack of random assignment to treatment conditions, preclude assertions about the effectiveness of treatment.

The success of treatment seems to be at least partially related to the type of offense and criminal history. For example, incest offenders reoffend less frequently than do extrafamilial offenders (Lang, Pugh, & Langevin, 1988). Abel, Mittelman, Becker, Rathner, and Rouleau (1988) found that self-reported treatment failure was predicted by a single marital status and a history of more varied deviant behavior and targets (for example, male and female victims, post- and prepubescent victims, hands-on and hands-off offenses). One study in which investigators compared treated and untreated offenders and had access to unofficial reports of recidivism, as well as official records, found that treated offenders had significantly lower rates of reoffending (Marshall & Barbaree, 1988).

Contemporary approaches to treatment that have been widely described are primarily cognitive–behavioral and focus on inappropriate sexual interests, cognitive distortions, and inadequate social skills (Marshall, Laws, & Barbaree, 1990). Most incorporate a relapse-prevention component in which offenders learn to recognize and avert the chain of events that precedes their offenses (Laws, 1989). These programs usually encourage offenders to avoid situations in which there is a high risk of reoffending, such as unsupervised contact with children.

Family reunification is the stated goal of intervention by the child protection system. Current social policy favors children remaining with or returning to homes with offenders as long as their safety is ensured. Clinical approaches to the reunification process have been described (Meinig & Bonner, 1990). However, no research has documented the impact of reunification on children or the effectiveness of interventions that are designed to reunify families.

## Conclusion

Sexual abuse is not uncommon in the lives of children, usually produces at least moderate initial effects, and is a risk factor for the development of serious difficulties. A significant subset of adults who were abused as children will continue to suffer the deleterious impact of these experiences. Fortunately, intervention efforts are not necessarily associated with an increase in the traumatic impact of abuse. Although no published research identifies the kinds of treatment that work best for the various problems that sexually abused children may develop, many efforts are under way to provide this essential information. One of the most important findings of research to date is that the availability of support to children can make a significant difference in mitigating negative outcomes. Little is known about whether, and for which children, family reunification after incest is in the children's best interests.

## References


Abel, G. G., Becker, J. V., Cunningham-Rathner, J., Mittelman, M., & Rouleau, J. L. (1988). Multiple paraphiliac diagnoses among sex offenders. *Bulletin of the American Academy of Psychiatry and the Law, 16,* 153–168.

Abel, G. G., Mittelman, M., Becker, J. V., Rathner, J., & Rouleau, J. L. (1988). Predicting child molesters' response to treatment. In R. A. Prentky & V. L. Quinsey (Eds.), *Human sexual aggression: Current perspective* (pp. 223–234). New York: New York Academy of Sciences.

Alexander, P. C. (1992). Application of attachment theory to the study of sexual abuse. *Journal of Consulting and Clinical Psychology, 60,* 185–195.

Allen, C. M. (1990). *A comparative analysis of women who sexually abuse children* (Project Report 90-CA-1214). Ames: Iowa State University of Science and Technology, Department of Human Development and Family Studies.

American Psychiatric Association. (1994). *Diagnostic and statistical manual of mental disorders* (4th ed.). Washington, DC: Author.

Basta, S. M., & Peterson, R. F. (1990). Perpetrator status and the personality characteristics of molested children. *Child Abuse and Neglect, 14,* 555–566.

Becker, J. V., & Hunter, J. (1992). Evaluation of treatment outcome for adult perpetrators of child sexual abuse. *Criminal Justice and Behavior, 19,* 74–92.

Beitchman, J. H., Zucker, K. J., Hood, J. E., da Costa, G. A., & Ackerman, D. (1991). A review of the short-term effects of child sexual abuse. *Journal of Child Abuse and Neglect, 15,* 537–556.

Bentovim, A., van Elberg, A., & Boston, P. (1988). The result of treatment. In A. Bentovim, A. Elton, J. Hildebrand, M. Tranter, & E. Vizard (Eds.), *Child sexual abuse within the family: Assessment and treatment* (pp. 252–268). London: Wright.

Berliner, L., & Conte, J. R. (1990). The process of victimization: The victim's perspective. *Child Abuse and Neglect, 14,* 29–40.

Berliner, L., & Conte, J. R. (in press). The effects of disclosure and intervention on sexually abused children. *Child Abuse and Neglect.*

Berman, P. (1990). Group therapy techniques for sexually abused preteen girls. *Child Welfare, 69,* 239–252.

Boyer, D., & Fine, D. (1991). Sexual abuse as a factor in adolescent pregnancy and child maltreatment. *Family Planning Perspectives, 24,* 4–19.

Briere, J. (1992). *Child abuse trauma: Theory and treatment of the lasting effects.* Newbury Park, CA: Sage Publications.

Briere, J. N., & Runtz, M. (1988). Symptomatology associated with childhood sexual victimization in a non-clinical sample. *Child Abuse and Neglect, 11,* 51–59.

Cavaiola, A. A., & Schiff, M. (1989). Self-esteem in abused, chemically dependent adolescents. *Child Abuse and Neglect, 13,* 327–334.

Ceci, S. J., & Bruck, M. (1993). Suggestibility of the child witness: A historical review and synthesis. *Psychology Bulletin, 113,* 403–439.

Cole, P. M., & Putnam, F. W. (1992). Effect of incest on self and social functioning: A developmental psychopathology perspective. *Journal of Consulting and Clinical Psychology, 60,* 174–184.

Conte, J. R., & Schuerman, J. R. (1987). Factors associated with an increased impact of sexual abuse. *Child Abuse and Neglect, 11,* 201–212.

Conte, J. R., Wolfe, S., & Smith, T. A. (1989). What sexual offenders tell us about prevention strategies. *Child Abuse and Neglect, 13,* 293–302.

Deblinger, E., McLeer, M. D., & Henry, D. (1990). Cognitive behavioral treatment for sexually abused children suffering post-traumatic stress: Preliminary findings. *Journal of the American Academy of Child and Adolescent Psychiatry, 29,* 747–752.

Einbender, A. J., & Friedrich, W. N. (1989). Psychological functioning and behavior of sexually abused girls. *Journal of Consulting and Clinical Psychology, 57,* 155–157.

Elliott, D. M. (1994). Impaired object relations in professional women molested as children. *Psychotherapy, 31,* 79–86.

Elliott, D. M., & Briere, J. (1992). Sexual abuse trauma among professional women: Validating the Trauma Symptom Checklist–40 (TSC-40). *Child Abuse and Neglect, 16,* 391–398.

Everson, M. D., Hunter, W. M., Runyan, D. K., Edelsohn, G. A., & Coulter, M. L. (1989). Maternal support following disclosure of incest. *American Journal of Orthopsychiatry, 59,* 198–207.

Faller, K. C. (1989). The myths of the "collusive mother": Variability in the functioning of mothers of victims of intrafamilial sexual abuse. *Journal of Interpersonal Violence, 3,* 190–196.

Feldman, W., Feldman, E., Goodman, J. T., McGrath, P. J., Pless, R. P., Corsini, L., & Bennett, S. (1991). Is child sexual abuse increasing in prevalence? Analysis of the evidence. *Pediatrics, 88,* 29–33.

Fineklhor, D., & Baron, L. (1986). High-risk children. In D. Finkelhor (Ed.), *A sourcebook on child sexual abuse* (pp. 60–88). Newbury Park, CA: Sage Publications.

Finkelhor, D., Hotaling, G., Lewis, I. A., & Smith, C. (1990). Sexual abuse in a national survey of adult men and women: Prevalence, characteristics, and risk factors. *Child Abuse and Neglect, 14,* 19–28.

Finkelhor, D., & Russell, D.E.H. (1984). Women as perpetrators: Review of the evidence. In D. Finkelhor (Ed.), *Child sexual abuse: New theory and research* (pp. 171–185). New York: Free Press.

Finkelhor, D., Williams, L. M., & Burns, N. (1988). *Nursery crimes: Sexual abuse in day care.* Newbury Park, CA: Sage Publications.

Friedrich, W. N. (1990). *Psychotherapy of sexually abused children and their families.* New York: W. W. Norton.

Friedrich, W. N. (1993). Sexual victimization and sexual behavior in children: A review of recent literature. *Child Abuse and Neglect, 17,* 59–66.

Friedrich, W. N., Beilke, R. L., & Urquiza, A. J. (1987). Children from sexually abusive families: A behavioral comparison. *Journal of Interpersonal Violence, 2,* 391–402.

Friedrich, W. N., Grambsch, P., Damon, L., Hewitt, S. K., Koverola, C., Lang, R. A., Wolfe, V., & Broughton, D. (1992). Child sexual behavior inventory: Normative and clinical comparisons. *Psychological Assessment, 4,* 303–311.

Friedrich, W. N., & Reams, R. A. (1987). Course of psychological symptoms in sexually abused young children. *Psycotherapy, 24,* 160–170.

Furniss, T., Bingley-Miller, L., & van Elberg, A. (1988). Goal oriented group treatment for sexually abused adolescent girls. *British Journal of Psychiatry, 152,* 97–106.

Gale, J., Thompson, R. J., Moran, T., & Sack, W. H. (1988). Sexual abuse in young children: Its clinical presentation and characteristic patterns. *Child Abuse and Neglect, 12,* 163–171.

German, D. E., Habernicht, D. J., & Futcher, W. G. (1990). Psychological profile of the female adolescent incest victim. *Child Abuse and Neglect, 14,* 429–438.

Gidycz, C. A., & Koss, M. P. (1989). The impact of adolescent sexual victimization: Standardized measures of anxiety, depression and behavioral deviancy. *Violence and Victims, 4,* 139–149.

Gil, E. (1991). *The healing power of play.* New York: Guilford Press.

Gomez-Schwartz, B., Horowitz, J., & Cardarelli, A. (1990). *Child sexual abuse: The initial effects.* Newbury Park, CA: Sage Publications.

Goodman, G. S., Taub, E. P., Jones, D.P.H., England, P., Port, L. K., Rudy, L., & Prado, L. (1992). Emotional effects of criminal court testimony on child sexual assault victims. *Monographs of the Society for Research on Child Development, 57,* 1–163.

Hanson, R. K., & Slater, S. (1988). Sexual victimization history of child sexual abusers: A review. *Annals of Sex Research, 1,* 485–499.

Hanson, R. K., Steffy, R. A., & Gauthier, R. (1993). Long-term recidivism of child molesters. *Journal of Consulting and Clinical Psychology, 61,* 646–652.

Hiebert-Murphy, D., De Luca, R. V., & Runtz, M. (1992). Group treatment for sexually abused girls: Evaluating outcome. *Families in Society: Journal of Contemporary Human Services, 73,* 205–213.

Hotte, J. P., & Rafman, S. (1992). The specific effects of incest on prepubertal girls from dysfunctional families. *Child Abuse and Neglect, 16,* 273–283.

Hunter, W. M., Coulter, M. L., Runyan, D. K., & Everson, M. D. (1990). Determinants of placement for sexually abused children. *Child Abuse and Neglect, 14,* 407–418.

James, B. (1989). *Treating traumatized children.* Lexington, MA: Lexington Books.

Johnson, B. K., & Kenkel, M. B. (1991). Stress, coping and adjustment in female adolescent incest victims. *Child Abuse and Neglect, 15,* 293–305.

Jones, D. P. H. (1986). Individual psychotherapy for the sexually abused child. *Child Abuse and Neglect, 10,* 377–385.

Jones, D. P. H., & McGraw, J. M. (1987). Reliable and fictitious accounts of sexual abuse to children. *Journal of Interpersonal Violence, 2,* 27–45.

Kendall-Tackett, K. A., Williams, L., & Finkelhor, D. (1993). The impact of sexual abuse on children: A review and synthesis of recent empirical studies. *Psychological Bulletin, 113,* 164–180.

Kolko, D. J., Moser, J. T., & Weldy, S. R. (1988). Behavioral/emotional indicators of sexual abuse in psychiatric inpatients: A controlled comparison with physical abuse. *Child Abuse and Neglect, 12,* 529–541.

Lang, R. A., & Frenzel, R. R. (1988). How sex offenders lure children. *Annals of Sex Research, 1,* 303–317.

Lang, R., Pugh, G., & Langevin, R. (1988). Treatment of incest and pedophilic offenders: A pilot study. *Behavioral Sciences and the Law, 6,* 239–255.

Lanktree, C. B., & Briere, J. (1993, August). *Outcome of therapy for sexually abused children: A longitudinal study*. Paper presented at the annual meeting of the American Psychological Association, Toronto.

Lanktree, C., Briere, J., & Zaidi, L. (1991). Incidence and impact of sexual abuse in a child out-patient sample: The role of direct inquiry. *Child Abuse and Neglect, 15,* 447–453.

Laws, D. R. (1989). *Relapse prevention with sex offenders*. New York: Guilford Press.

Lawson, L., & Chaffin, M. (1992). False negatives in sexual abuse disclosure interviews: Incidence and influence of caretaker's belief in abuse in cases of accidental abuse discovery by diagnosis of STD. *Journal of Interpersonal Violence, 7,* 532–542.

Loftus, E. F. (1993). The reality of repressed memories. *American Psychologist, 48,* 518–537.

Mandell, J. G., & Damon, L. (1989). *Group treatment for sexually abused children*. New York: Guilford Press.

Mannarino, A. P., Cohen, J. A., & Berman, S. R. (1994). The relationship between preabuse factors and psychological symptomatology in sexually abused girls. *Child Abuse and Neglect, 18,* 63–72.

Mannarino, A. P., Cohen, J. A., & Gregor, M. (1989). Emotional and behavioral difficulties in sexually abused girls. *Journal of Interpersonal Violence, 4,* 437–451.

Marshall, W., & Barbaree, H. (1988). The long-term evaluation of a behavioral treatment program for child molesters. *Behavior Research and Therapy, 26,* 499–511.

Marshall, W., Jones, R., Ward, T., Johnston, P., & Barbaree, H. (1991). Treatment outcome with sex offenders. *Clinical Psychology Review, 11,* 465–485.

Marshall, W., Laws, D., & Barbaree, H. (1990). *Handbook of sexual assault: Issues, theories, and treatment of the offender.* New York: Plenum Press.

McLeer, S. V., Deblinger, E., Atkins, M. S., Ralphe, D. L., & Foa, E. (1988). Post-traumatic stress disorder in sexually abused children. *Journal of the American Academy of Child and Adolescent Psychiatry, 27,* 650–654.

McLeer, S. V., Deblinger, E., Henry, D., & Orvaschel, H. (1992). Sexually abused children at high risk for post-traumatic stress disorder. *Journal of the American Academy of Child and Adolescent Psychiatry, 31,* 875–879.

Meinig, M., & Bonner, B. L. (1990). Intrafamilial sexual abuse: A structured approach to family intervention. *Violence Update, 11,* 1–11.

Morrow, K. B. (1991). Attributions of female adolescent incest victims regarding their molestation. *Child Abuse and Neglect, 15,* 477–482.

Mullen, P. E. (1993). Child sexual abuse and adult mental health: The development of disorder. *Journal of Interpersonal Violence, 8,* 429–431.

Murphy, W. D., & Peters, J. M. (1992). Profiling child sexual abusers: Psychological considerations. *Criminal Justice and Behavior, 19,* 24–37.

National Center on Child Abuse and Neglect. (1993). *A report on the maltreatment of children with disabilities.* Washington, DC: U.S. Department of Health and Human Services.

Nelki, J. S., & Watters, J. (1989). A group for sexually abused young children: Unraveling the web. *Child Abuse and Neglect, 13,* 369–378.

Quinsey, V. L. (1986). Men who have sex with children. In D. N. Webster (Ed.), *Law & mental health: International perspectives* (Vol. 2, pp. 140–172). Elmsford, NY: Pergamon Press.

Quinsey, V. L., Harris, G. T., Rice, M. E., & Lalumiere, M. L. (1993). Assessing treatment efficacy in outcome studies of sex offenders. *Journal of Interpersonal Violence, 8,* 512–523.

Rao, K., DiClemente, R. J., & Ponton, L. E. (1992). Child sexual abuse of Asians compared with other populations. *Journal of the American Academy of Child and Adolescent Psychiatry, 31,* 880–886.

Runyan, D. K., Everson, M. D., Edelsohn, G. A., Hunter, W. M., & Coulter, M. L. (1988). Impact of intervention on sexually abused children. *Journal of Pediatrics, 113,* 647–653.

Russell, D. E. H. (1984). *Sexual exploitation: Rape, child sexual abuse, and workplace harassment* (Sage Library of Social Research No. 155). Newbury Park, CA: Sage Publications.

Sas, L. (1991). *Reducing the system-induced trauma for child sexual abuse victims through court preparation, assessment and follow-up* (Final Report 4555-1-125). Ontario: London Family Court Clinic.

Saunders, B. E., Kilpatrick, D. G., Resnick, H. S., Hanson, R. A., & Lipovsky, J. A. (1992, January). *Epidemiological characteristics of child sexual abuse: Results from wave II of the National Women's Study*. Paper presented at the San Diego Conference on Responding to Child Maltreatment, San Diego.

Saunders, B. E., Villeponteaux, L. A., Lipovsky, J. A., Kilpatrick, D. G., & Veronen, L. J. (1992). Child sexual assault as a risk factor for mental disorders among women: A community survey. *Journal of Interpersonal Violence, 7,* 189–204.

Sauzier, M. (1990). Disclosure of child sexual abuse: For better or worse. *Psychiatric Clinics of North America, 12,* 455–469.

Sedlack, A. J. (1992, August). *Demographic research and child abuse*. Paper presented at the Centennial Convention of the American Psychological Association, Washington, DC.

Sgroi, S. M. (1982). *Handbook of clinical intervention in child sexual abuse*. Lexington, MA: Lexington Books.

Shapiro, J. P., Leifer, M., Martone, M. W., & Kassem, L. (1992). Cognitive functioning and social competence as predictors of maladjustment in sexually abused girls. *Journal of Interpersonal Violence, 7,* 156–164.

Singer, M. I., Petchers, M. K., & Hussey, D. (1989). The relationship between sexual abuse and substance abuse among psychiatrically hospitalized adolescents. *Child Abuse and Neglect, 13,* 319–325.

Smith, B. E., Elstein, S. G., Trost, T., & Bulkley, J. (1993). *The prosecution of child sexual and physical abuse cases*. Washington, DC: American Bar Association Center on Children and the Law.

Sorensen, T., & Snow, B. (1991). How children tell: The process of disclosure in child sexual abuse. *Child Welfare League of America, 70,* 3–15.

Springs, F. E., & Friedrich, W. N. (1992). Health risk behaviors and medical sequelae of childhood sexual abuse. *Mayo Clinical Procedures, 67,* 527–532.

Stovall, G., & Craig, R. J. (1990). Mental representations of physically and sexually abused latency-aged females. *Child Abuse and Neglect, 11,* 371–383.

Summit, R. C. (1983). The child sexual abuse accommodation syndrome. *Child Abuse and Neglect, 7,* 177–193.

Thoennes, N., & Tjaden, P. G. (1990). The extent, nature and validity of sexual abuse allegations in custody/visitation disputes. *Child Abuse and Neglect, 14,* 151–163.

Walker, E. A., Torkelson, N., Katon, W. J., & Koss, M. P. (1993). The prevalence rate of sexual trauma in a primary care clinic. *Journal of the American Board of Family Practitioners, 6,* 465–471.

Weinrott, M. R., & Saylor, M. (1991). Self-report of crimes committed by sex offenders. *Journal of Interpersonal Violence, 6,* 286–300.

Whitcomb, D., Runyan, D. K., De Vos, E., Hunter, W. M., Cross, T. P., Everson, M. D., Peeler, N. A., Porter, C. Q., Toth, P. A., & Cropper, C. (1991). *Child victim as witness research and development program* (Executive Summary, Grant No. 87-Mc-CX-0026). Washington, DC: U.S. Department of Justice, Office of Justice Programs, Office of Juvenile Justice and Delinquency Prevention.

White, S., Halpin, B. M., Strom, G. A., & Santelli, G. (1988). Behavioral comparisons of young sexually abused, neglected, and nonreferred children. *Journal of Clinical Child Psychology, 17,* 53–61.

Widom, C. S., & Morris, S. (1993, October). *Accuracy of adult memories of earlier childhood sexual victimization: Preliminary findings.* Paper presented at the annual meeting of the American Society of Criminology, Phoenix.

Williams, L. (in press). Recall of childhood trauma: A prospective study of women's memories of child sexual abuse. *Journal of Consulting and Clinical Psychology.*

Wolfe, D. A., Sas, L., & Wekerle, C. (1994). Factors associated with the development of posttraumatic stress disorder among child victims of sexual abuse. *Child Abuse and Neglect, 18,* 37–50.

Wolfe, V. V., Gentile, C., & Wolfe, D. A. (1989). The impact of sexual abuse on children: A PTSD formulation. *Behavior Therapy, 20,* 215–228.

Wozencraft, T., Wagner, W., & Pellegrin, A. (1991). Depression and suicidal ideation in sexually abused children. *Child Abuse and Neglect, 15,* 505–510.

Wyatt, G. E. (1985). The sexual abuse of Afro-American and white women in childhood. *Child Abuse and Neglect, 9,* 507–519.

**Lucy Berliner, MSW,** is director of research, Sexual Assault Center, Harborview Medical Center, 1401 East Jefferson, Seattle, WA 98122.

### For further information see

Adolescence Overview; Assessment; Child Abuse and Neglect Overview; Child Abuse and Neglect: Direct Practice; Child Sexual Abuse Overview; Child Welfare Overview; Direct Practice Overview; Families Overview; Legal Issues: Low-Income and Dependent People; Professional Liability and Malpractice; School Social Work Overview; School-Linked Services; Sexual Assault; Social Work Practice: Theoretical Base.

**Key Words**
child abuse
direct practice
child sexual abuse

# Child Support

**Irwin Garfinkel**

The term "child support" has more than one meaning. At its broadest, it refers to all institutions—public and private, from the family to the school—by which a society supports its children. This entry deals with the narrower meaning of child support: the transfer of income to a child with a living parent, usually the father, who is absent from the home. Divorce, separation, and out-of-wedlock birth all create situations where children may be eligible for child support. The nonresident parent pays private child support; the government pays public child support.

All Western industrialized societies provide a mixture of private and public income transfers to children potentially eligible for child support. The laws and practices that govern both the private and public transfers may be thought of as constituting a child support system.

From colonial days through the 1950s, divorce, separation, and out-of-wedlock births were relatively rare events, whereas widowhood was far more common, and thus the proportion of children who were affected by the U.S. child support system, narrowly defined, was small. During the first half of the 20th century, widowhood became less common, and divorce, separation, and out-of-wedlock births became more common. Until about 1960, the two trends offset one another. During the past 30 years, however, the proportion of children living in single-parent families has increased dramatically. Whereas in 1960 about 8 percent of all children were living with a single parent (mostly their mothers), by 1991 25 percent were doing so (U.S. Bureau of the Census, 1991). According to a leading demographer (Bumpass, 1984), more than half the children born during the 1980s will live with a single parent before they reach adulthood, and nearly all will be eligible for child support. The figures are even more striking for black children, more than half of whom were living in a single-parent family in 1990 and about 80 percent of whom are expected to do so some time in their lives.

Now that half the next generation will be affected by it, the quality of the U.S. child support system has become of vital importance to the nation's future. Social workers are concerned with child support policy because children, along with the aged, the disabled, and the poor, make up a disproportionate share of their clients, and the profession has played a leading role in shaping child welfare policy.

As of the early 1990s, the child support system was in the midst of a profound transformation. This entry describes the traditional child support system, contrasts it with the newly emerging child support assurance system, and considers future directions.

## Traditional System

In the old U.S. child support system, the laws and institutions governing private and public support were separate. Family courts established the nonresident parent's responsibility to pay support, set the amount to be paid, and enforced the parent's obligation to pay. Public assistance, or welfare, departments provided cash and in-kind benefits to poor children and their custodial parents. Because of recent federal initiatives, these two systems are becoming increasingly intertwined.

### Family Law and Private Child Support

Family law has traditionally been a province of the states. Consequently, before 1974, private child support was nearly exclusively a state and local matter. State laws established the duty of nonresident parents to pay child support but left all the details up to the local courts (Krause, 1981). In short, the system was characterized by local judicial discretion.

Judges had the authority to decide whether any child support should be paid, and if so, how much. They also had full authority over the actions that would be taken if nonresident parents failed to pay, imprisonment being the severest punishment.

In a few jurisdictions, judges used a child support obligation schedule, which is similar to a tax table. For example, in the 1970s, most counties in Michigan used only two facts to determine child support: the absent parent's income and the number of children who required support. The state of Delaware used a much more complicated formula designed by Judge Elwood F. Melson (Garfinkel, 1992; General Accounting Office, 1993). But such schedules were the exception rather than the rule.

In the few states that were leaders in the field, such as Michigan and Wisconsin, absent parents had to make all child support payments to a government agency that had the authority to initiate legal action when child support obligations were not met. The Michigan Friend of the Court, founded in 1917, is the oldest such agency. Still, these agencies usually did not use their authority unless they were specifically requested to do so by the custodial parent (Cassetty, 1978; Chambers, 1979). In most cases, the burden of collecting overdue support fell to the custodial parent.

The most effective tool for enforcing child support was wage garnishment—a legal order to the employer of the absent parent to withhold a specified amount from the employee's wages. The ultimate sanction for those who did not pay was imprisonment. In Michigan, for example, as of the 1970s thousands of absent fathers were jailed each year for failing to comply with child support orders (Chambers, 1979, p. 316). Although imprisonment was used throughout the country, there are no data to indicate the total number of absent fathers who were imprisoned.

### Public Assistance

The second part of the child support system—public assistance—dates back to colonial days. The British settlers brought with them the Elizabethan Poor Laws, which required local governments to provide and fund public assistance to their needy residents. Mothers' pensions, enacted by 40 states during the Progressive Era in the first two decades of the 20th century, shifted fiscal responsibility to the states and with the enactment of the Aid to Dependent Children (ADC) program in the Social Security Act of 1935, the federal government assumed about half the cost. (When benefits for the caretakers of dependent children were added in 1951, ADC was changed to Aid to Families with Dependent Children, AFDC.)

Although both mothers' pensions and ADC were designed primarily for children of widows, some states included divorced, separated, and never-married mothers in mothers' pensions and children who lost the earnings of a parent because of disability or absence, as well as death, among those who were eligible for ADC. When ADC was enacted, most of the children who benefited were orphans; in the 1990s, the overwhelming majority of the children's mothers are divorced or separated or have never been married. Widows constitute less than 2 percent of the AFDC caseload (U.S. House of Representatives, 1992).

Although conditions varied over time and place, for the most part the aid provided to poor children of divorce, separation, and out-of-wedlock birth and their mothers was meager. In the decade following President Johnson's declaration of the War on Poverty in 1964, welfare benefits were increased substantially. Congress added Medicaid and food stamps to the welfare-benefit package and allowed mothers on welfare to keep a small portion of their earnings and to continue to receive welfare. Supreme Court decisions expanded the eligibility for welfare by declaring state residency requirements and man-in-the-house rules unconstitutional. States raised AFDC levels.Between 1976 and 1991, however, AFDC plus food stamp benefits declined by 23 percent. In 1992, the median state AFDC-plus-food-stamp benefit for a family of three equaled only 72 percent of the poverty level—only 3.5 percent higher than AFDC alone before the declaration of the War on Poverty (U.S. House of Representatives, 1992).

Public child support transfers to poor children via AFDC and food stamps are substantially larger than are private transfers to children from all income classes—in 1989, $24.7 billion versus $11.2 billion. Counting Medicaid expended on children would add $13.7 billion in public transfers.[1]

## Weaknesses of the Traditional System

The traditional child support system did not work well. Indeed, it fell short at every stage. Only six of 10 mothers who were eligible for child support were awarded it (U.S. Bureau of the Census, 1981). Divorced mothers were the most likely to receive an award—about eight out of 10—and unmarried mothers were the least likely to receive it—only one in 10. The failure to establish paternity underlay the abysmal record of child support for children who were born out of wedlock.

Awards were too low and too infrequently updated to keep pace with either inflation or increases in the nonresident parent's income. According to the child support guidelines that are now used in most states, the awards under the traditional system were only a third to a half of what they should have been (Garfinkel, Oellerich, & Robins, 1991). In addition, they were inequitable, treating equals unequally (White & Stone, 1976; Yee, 1979) and imposing higher burdens in percentage terms on poor than on nonpoor nonresident fathers.

Finally, the system failed to collect all that was owed. Of those with awards, about 50 percent received the full amount to which they were entitled; 25 percent received something, but less than what was owed; and 25 percent received nothing (U.S. Bureau of the Census, 1981).

Many people argued that nonresident fathers did not pay child support because they were too poor. Although there were many poor nonresident fathers, the inability to pay was only part of the problem. On the basis of estimates of the incomes of nonresident fathers and the share of income that should have been devoted to child support according to the two most widely used child support guidelines, in 1983 nonresident fathers should have been paying $25 billion to $32 billion in child support, when, in fact, they owed only $9 billion and paid only $7 billion (Garfinkel & Oellerich, 1989). If the private child support system was perfectly efficient—if all nonresident fathers were obligated to pay support in accordance with modern child support guidelines and all paid the full amount—the poverty gap for children potentially eligible for child support and welfare costs would both drop by a quarter. It is difficult to escape the judgment that a major part of the problem lies with the traditional child support enforcement system that is run by the local judiciary in a highly discretionary manner (Garfinkel, 1992).

Like nearly all social problems, the failures of this country's child support system were more serious for poor people and people of color than for other groups. Only 43.3 percent of poor mothers but 64.5 percent of nonpoor mothers had child support awards; only 34.5 percent of black mothers and 40.6 percent of Hispanic mothers had child support awards. Most of the difference in child support awards for the racial and ethnic groups is attributable to differences in income and the marital status of the mothers. Black people, for example, have lower incomes and a much higher proportion of out-of-wedlock births than do white people. Although minority-group mothers are much less likely than are white mothers to have child support awards, black and Hispanic mothers with awards are only slightly less likely than are white mothers to receive support—69.7 percent and 69.8 percent versus 76.5 percent (U.S. Bureau of the Census, 1991, p. 5).

[1]The amount for AFDC—$17.3 billion—includes funds for AFDC-UP (for unemployed parents) and disabled parents and is therefore an overestimate. The amount for food stamps was calculated using the total $12.5 billion and multiplying it by 0.6 (the proportion of food-stamp households with children). Because households with children are likely to be larger than other households receiving food stamps, this figure is an underestimate. The Medicaid figures include both children and adults on AFDC (U.S. House of Representatives, 1992). The child support figure is from the U.S. Bureau of the Census (1991).

The public part of the child support system is also severely flawed. Unlike children of widows, who are eligible for Survivors Insurance as well as welfare, children who are eligible for child support are aided only by programs for the poor. As a consequence, the system that aids them—popularly known as welfare—does nothing to prevent poverty; provides meager, below-poverty-level benefits; sharply reduces benefits when mothers earn more; and takes away medical care coverage when a mother leaves welfare. For unskilled single mothers who cannot earn much more than welfare and cannot afford to forgo health insurance, the current welfare system is akin to a poverty trap.

Because welfare programs are designed to aid only the poor, benefits are reduced when earnings increase. After four months on a job, a woman on AFDC faces a reduction in benefits of a dollar for every dollar that she earns, in excess of her work expenses. This reduction is equivalent to a 100 percent tax on earnings. Thus, what the government gives with one hand it takes away with the other hand. Yet, because they have little education and experience and would have child care expenses if they worked, most women on AFDC could not earn enough to lift their families out of poverty even if they worked full-time (Michalopoulos & Garfinkel, 1989; Sawhill, 1976). If they also received child support from the children's absent fathers, some but not all of these families would attain an income above the poverty level. Clearly, the only way to alleviate this kind of poverty without creating dependence is to supplement, rather than replace, the earnings of these custodial parents.

## Toward a Child Support Assurance System

As AFDC cases began to reflect the demographic trends of divorce, separation, desertion, and out-of-wedlock births, congressional interest in child support payments grew. In 1950, Congress enacted the first federal child support legislation, which required state welfare agencies to notify law enforcement officials when a child who was receiving AFDC benefits had been abandoned by the father. Other legislation, enacted in 1965 and 1967, required states to enforce child support and establish paternity and allowed them to acquire the addresses of absent parents from the Internal Revenue Service, as well as from the U.S. Department of Health, Education, and Welfare (Garfinkel & McLanahan, 1986).

The most significant legislation was enacted in 1974, when Congress added Part D to Title IV of the Social Security Act, thereby establishing the Child Support Enforcement, or IV-D, program. The legislation created the federal Office of Child Support Enforcement, required all states to establish comparable state offices, and authorized federal funding for three-quarters of the state's expenditures on child support enforcement. Federal funds were made available for all welfare cases and for nonwelfare cases for up to one year. After a series of one-year extensions, in 1980, federal support was extended permanently to all children who were eligible for support, irrespective of income or AFDC status.

The creation of the new child support enforcement program stimulated research and proposals for reform (Cassetty, 1978; Chambers, 1979; Garfinkel & Melli, 1982; Krause, 1981; Sawhill, 1983). The most comprehensive proposal and the model for most recent legislation was the proposal for a new child support assurance system (CSA). CSA would replace the local judicial discretion of the traditional private system with the bureaucratic regularity of the federal social security system and, like Survivors Insurance, simultaneously prevent poverty and reduce dependence on welfare by providing aid to beneficiaries in all income classes.

### Child Support Principles

The basis for child support assurance (CSA) would be a partnership of responsibility between parents and the government. Parents would be responsible for sharing income with their children, and the government would be responsible for enforcing private support and for assuring a steady flow of income to all children with an absent parent.

The essential mechanics of CSA are easy to understand. Child support awards would be set by a legislated formula—based on a percentage of the nonresident parent's income—and payments would be deducted from the absent parent's earnings, just like social security deductions. The government would guarantee a minimum level of child support, an assured benefit. The assured benefit would be financed from welfare savings and from a small addition to the social security payroll tax.

Like Survivors Insurance, CSA would aid children of all income classes who suffered loss of income because of the absence of a parent. The cause of the absence differs, of course. Survivors Insurance compensates for the loss of income arising from widowhood, whereas CSA would compensate for the loss of income arising from divorce, separation, and nonmarriage. Withholding a flat percentage of the nonresident parent's income would make the bulk of the financing of CSA similar to a proportional payroll tax, which is used to finance all the social insurance programs. In the case of CSA, however, the "tax" would apply only to those who were legally liable for child support. The assured-benefit component of CSA makes the benefit structure of the system like all other social insurance programs in that it would provide greater benefits to low-income families than would be justified on the basis of the families' contributions or taxes.

CSA would increase the economic security of all children—rich and poor alike—who live apart from a parent. Withholding a fixed percentage—17 percent, for example—from the paychecks of all nonresident parents would increase the amount and regularity of private payments at all income levels. Even so, private support payments for many poor children would continue to be low and irregular, just as the incomes of the children's fathers often are. The assured benefit would compensate by providing a steady, secure source of income for these children. It would more than double the reduction in poverty and welfare dependence achieved from private support alone.

Increases in private child support redistribute income from men to women and children. Because children on welfare receive only the first $50 per month and the rest offsets the costs of welfare, increases in private support also redistribute income from the mostly poor fathers of children on welfare to the nonpoor. In contrast, the assured benefit would increase taxes and thereby redistribute income from the nonpoor to the poor and near-poor families headed by single mothers. It is estimated that the savings in welfare costs that would be generated by stronger enforcement could offset the costs of a modest assured benefit of $2,000 for the first child, $1,000 each for the second and third children, and $500 each for up to three more children (Garfinkel, 1992).

### Legislation

In 1984 and 1988, Congress enacted major legislation that enticed or required the states to take large strides toward adopting the collection features of CSA and permitted two states to take minor steps toward implementing an assured benefit. The Child Support Enforcement Amendments of 1984 required states to adopt numerical child support guidelines that courts could use to determine child support obligations and required them to withhold child support obligations from the wages and other income of nonresident parents who were one month delinquent in their payments of child support. The bill also encouraged states to develop expedited administrative or bureaucratic, rather than judicial, processes for establishing paternity.

The Family Support Act of 1988 immensely strengthened the 1984 guidelines and the withholding and paternity-establishment provisions. Whereas the 1984 Child Support Amendments allowed the courts to ignore the guidelines, the 1988 legislation made the guidelines the presumptive child support award. Judges may depart from the guidelines only if they construct a written justification that can be reviewed by a higher court. Furthermore, the Family Support Act required that by 1993, states would have to review child support awards of Title IV-D cases (those being handled by the Office of Child Support Enforcement) at least every three years and directed the Department of Health and Human Services (DHHS) to study the impact of a required periodic review of all child support cases. Instead of waiting for fathers to become delinquent in paying for child support before sums would be withheld from their paychecks, the 1988 legislation required withholding the child support obligation from the outset for all Title IV-D cases as of 1990 and for all child support cases as of 1994.

The Family Support Act also had three major paternity provisions: (1) States must either establish paternity in at least half the out-of-wedlock cases on AFDC or increase the proportion of such cases in which they establish paternity by three percentage points each year; (2) states must obtain the social security numbers of both parents in conjunction with the issuance of birth certificates; and (3) all parties in a contested paternity case must take a genetic test upon the request of any party, with the federal government paying 90 percent of the cost of the test.

The 1984 and 1988 legislation also took two cautious steps in the direction of an assured child support benefit by directing the secretary of DHHS to grant Wisconsin (in 1984) and New York (in 1988) waivers that would allow them to use federal AFDC funds to pilot an assured child support benefit. In effect, Wisconsin was to be given a block grant to run both a child support assurance system and the AFDC system at the same cost to the federal government as the old AFDC system alone. Extra costs or savings were to be borne solely by or be of benefit to the state.

Although the guidelines and withholding provisions of the Family Support Act of 1988 are large strides toward establishing the collection portion of a child support assurance system, as of the early 1990s, the nation has only begun the transition from the traditional to a new system. Even though the federal government has offered to reimburse the states for 90 percent of the costs of automating their child support record-keeping systems for over a decade, most states have not yet done so. Most states lack the administrative capacity to receive, monitor, and distribute all child support payments and are therefore unlikely to be able to implement universal income withholding by 1994. Although child support guidelines have been enacted in all the states, the degree to which they are being used, especially in nonwelfare cases, is unclear. Indeed, there is a debate in many states about whether Congress really meant the guidelines and withholding provisions to apply to all cases (Williams, 1994). Demonstrations of periodic updating suggest that until a way is found to routinize updating—for example, by establishing child support orders as a percentage of income—in practice the vast majority of cases will not be updated. All states are a long way from a universal establishment of paternity. Finally, crossing state lines is still an effective way to avoid a child support obligation (Garfinkel, McLanahan, & Robins, 1994; U.S. Commission on Interstate Child Support, 1992).

### Child Support Benefits

That the United States has only begun the transition to a new system is also indicated by statistics on the enforcement of child support awards. Between 1978 and 1989, the proportion of never-married mothers with awards increased from slightly more than one in 10 to nearly three in 10 (Nichols-Casebolt & Garfinkel, 1991). Although this is a respectable rate of improvement, it still leaves over 70 percent of the children who were born out of wedlock with no paternity established and without legal entitlement to private support. Moreover, whereas never-married mothers constituted 19 percent of all mothers who were potentially eligible for support in 1978, by 1989, they accounted for 30 percent of the total. As a consequence, despite progress, the proportion of all eligible mothers who were actually granted awards was still close to 60 percent. Similarly, because of a shift in the demographic composition of children who were potentially eligible for support and, what is even more important, because of the substantial increase over time in the earnings of divorcing women, the real value of awards declined 25 percent between 1978 and 1985 (Beller & Graham, 1991; Garfinkel, 1992; Robins, 1992). The real value of awards increased between 1985 and 1989, perhaps owing to the influence of the child support guidelines. But awards in 1989 remained below what they had been in 1978—$2,873 versus $3,421 (in 1989 dollars). Finally, the percentage of child support due that was actually paid increased 4 percent from 1978 to 1989, 65 percent to 69 percent (U.S. Bureau of the Census, 1991, pp. 5, 9). In sum, like Alice in Wonderland, the child support system has had to run faster just to keep in place.

Moreover, neither the federal government nor any state has adopted an assured child support benefit. Although Wisconsin applied for and received a federal waiver to use federal AFDC funds to help finance an assured benefit, Tommy Thompson, Wisconsin's governor since 1987, blocked the demonstration. New York State is currently conducting such a demonstration, but only mothers who qualify for welfare are eligible to receive the assured benefit. By targeting benefits to poor single mothers, New York is moving away from the principle of universality that sustains the country's social security system.

## Future Directions

As of early 1993, there was strong support for further reforms of the child support system. The National Commission on Children, a bipartisan commission appointed jointly in 1987 by President Reagan and Congress and chaired by U.S. Senator Jay Rockefeller, endorsed federally subsidized state demonstrations of a full-fledged child support assurance system and, provided that the demonstration results were positive, enactment of a national program (National Commission on Children, 1991). The U.S. Commission on Interstate Child Support (1992), although opposing a federal system, advocated a number of measures to strengthen enforcement and endorsed the idea of state experimentation with an assured child support benefit. Most important, though his administration has provided no details as yet, President Clinton has stated his intention both to strengthen the private child support system and dismantle the existing welfare system. Heretofore, leadership on child support has emanated from Congress.

As the provisions of the 1988 Family Support Act are implemented and new legislation is enacted, the traditional U.S. child support system will continue to evolve toward a child support assurance system. Local judicial discretion will increasingly be replaced by the bureaucratic regularity that is characteristic of the social security and income tax systems. At the least, it seems likely that the federal government will provide funding for a number of states to pilot a non-income-tested assured child support benefit.

The precise form the new system will take, however, is an open question. Will there be an assured benefit? If so, how large will it be? Who will be eligible for it—only those with legal entitlement to private support or all children with living absent parents? Will the assured benefit and child support guidelines be established nationally, as in Old-Age Insurance, or by each state, as in Unemployment Insurance and Workers' Compensation? Will the Social Security Administration or Internal Revenue Service replace the local judiciary in enforcing the collection of private child support payments? These issues will be resolved during the 1990s as social workers and other concerned citizens struggle within the political system to achieve a myriad of objectives, including improvement of the lives of children.

## References


Beller, A., & Graham, J. T. (1991). The effect of child support enforcement on child support payments. *Population Research and Policy*, *10*, 91–116.

Bumpass, L. (1984). Children and marital disruption: A replication and update. *Demography*, *21*, 71–82.

Cassetty, J. (1978). *Child support and public policy: Securing support from absent fathers*. Lexington, MA: D. C. Heath.

Chambers, D. (1979). *Making fathers pay: The enforcement of child support*. Chicago: University of Chicago Press.

Child Support Enforcement Amendments of 1984. P.L. 98-378, 98 Stat. 1305.

Family Support Act of 1988. P.L. 100-485, 98 Stat. 1757.

Garfinkel, I. (1992). *Assuring child support: An extension of the social security system*. New York: Russell Sage Foundation.

Garfinkel, I., & McLanahan, S. S. (1986). *Single mothers and their children: A new American dilemma*. Washington, DC: Urban Institute Press.

Garfinkel, I., McLanahan, S. S., & Robins, P. (Eds.). (1994). *Child support and child well-being*. Washington, DC: Urban Institute Press.

Garfinkel, I., & Melli, M. (1982). *Child support: Weaknesses of the old and features of a proposed new system* (Special Report 32A). Madison: Institute for Research on Poverty, University of Wisconsin.

Garfinkel, I., & Oellerich, D. T. (1989). Noncustodial fathers' ability to pay child support. *Demography*, *26*, 219–233.

Garfinkel, I., Oellerich, D., & Robins, P. (1991). Child support guidelines: Will they make a difference? *Journal of Family Issues*, *12*, 404–429.

General Accounting Office. (1993). *Child support assurance: The effect of applying state guidelines to determine fathers' payments*. Washington, DC: U.S. Government Printing Office.

Krause, H. O. (1981). *Child support in America: The legal perspective*. Charlottesville, VA: Michie.

Michalopoulos, C., & Garfinkel, I. (1989, August). *Reducing the welfare dependence and poverty of single mothers by means of earnings and child support: Wishful thinking and realistic possibility* (Discussion Paper 882-89). Madison: Institute for Research on Poverty, University of Wisconsin.

National Commission on Children. (1991). *Beyond rhetoric: A new national agenda for children and families*. Washington, DC: Author.

Nichols-Casebolt, A., & Garfinkel, I. (1991). Trends in paternity adjudications and child support awards. *Social Science Quarterly*, *27*(1), 89.

Robins, P. K. (1992). Why child support payments have declined from 1978 to 1985. *Journal of Human Resources*, *27*, 362–379.

Sawhill, I. V. (1976). Discrimination and poverty among women who head families. *Signs*, *2*, 201–211.

Sawhill, I. V. (1983). Developing normative standards for child support payments. In J. Cassetty (Ed.), *The parental child support obligation* (pp. 79–114). Lexington, MA: D. C. Heath.

Social Security Act of 1935. P.L. 100-360, 49 Stat. 620.

U.S. Bureau of the Census. (1981). Child support and alimony: 1978. In *Current Population Reports* (Series P-23, No. 112). Washington, DC: U.S. Government Printing Office.

U.S. Bureau of the Census. (1991). Child support and alimony: 1989. In *Current population reports* (Series P-60, No. 173). Washington, DC: U.S. Government Printing Office.

U.S. Commission on Interstate Child Support. (1992). *Supporting our children: A blueprint for reform* (Report to Congress). Washington, DC: U.S. Government Printing Office.

U.S. House of Representatives, Committee on Ways and Means. (1992). *1992 green book: Background material and data on programs within the jurisdiction of the Committee on Ways and Means*. Washington, DC: U.S. Government Printing Office.

White, K. R., & Stone, R. T. (1976). A study of alimony and child support rulings with some recommendations. *Family Law Quarterly*, *10*, 75–91.

Williams, R. (1994). Implementation of the child support provisions of the Family Support Act: Child support guidelines, updating awards and routine income withholding. In I. Garfinkel, S. S. McLanahan, & P. Robins (Eds.), *Child support and child well-being*. Washington, DC: Urban Institute Press.

Yee, L. M. (1979). What really happens in child support cases: An empirical study of the establishment and enforcement of child support awards in the Denver District Court. *Denver Law Quarterly*, *57*, 21–70.


## Further Reading


Beller, A. H., & Graham, J. W. (1993). *Small change: The economics of child support*. New Haven, CT: Yale University Press.

Danziger, S. H., Sandefur, G. D., & Weinberg, D. H. (Eds.). (1994). *Poverty and public policy: What do we know? What should we do?* Cambridge, MA: Harvard University Press.

Ellwood, D. (1988). *Poor support*. New York: Basic Books.

Garfinkel, I., McLanahan, S., & Robins, P. (Eds.). (1992). *Child support assurance: Design issues, expected impacts, and political barriers as seen from Wisconsin*. Washington, DC: Urban Institute Press.

Macoby, E., & Mnookin, R. (1992). *Dividing the child: Social and legal dilemmas of custody*. Cambridge, MA: Harvard University Press.

McLanahan, S. S., & Sandefur, G. (1994). *Growing up with a single parent: What hurts, what helps*. Cambridge, MA: Harvard University Press.


**Irwin Garfinkel, PhD,** is Mitchell I. Ginsberg Professor of Contemporary Urban Problems, Columbia University,

School of Social Work, 622 West 113th Street, New York, NY 10025.

**For further information see**

Adult Corrections; Advocacy; Aid to Families with Dependent Children; Child Welfare Overview; Childhood; Families Overview; Families: Demographic Shifts; Federal Social Legislation from 1961 to 1994; Hunger, Nutrition, and Food Programs; Income Security Overview; Legal Issues: Low-Income and Dependent People; Poverty; Single Parents; Social Security; Unemployment Compensation and Workers' Compensation; Welfare Employment Programs: Evaluation.

**Key Words**
child support
child welfare
parental absence

# Child Welfare Overview

**David S. Liederman**

As the United States enters the 21st century, the depth and breadth of society's most insidious ills continue to affect children profoundly. Racism, poverty, violence, and abuse of alcohol and other drugs impinge on the life of every child in the United States. Children are influenced by the society in which they are born and raised; they, in turn, influence society. The degree to which their needs are met is often considered a barometer of society's health. This entry examines the welfare of children in the United States.

It is necessary, but not sufficient, that children's basic survival needs—food, shelter, clothing, and love—are met. Under ordinary conditions, families—the primary resource for children—are able to meet these needs and more. Ideally, families who are sometimes incapable of meeting their children's needs are able to receive assistance to resolve the problems that threaten the well-being of their children. Assistance may come informally from the community through neighbors, religious organizations, and civic associations or formally through government and voluntary agencies. Optimally, the two systems—formal and informal—work together.

Government has organized a formal service delivery system known as child welfare, which is sanctioned by the community and designed to assist children who have been abused or neglected or who are at risk and their families. The government and voluntary agencies that constitute the formal child welfare system are a part of community efforts designed to

- protect and promote the well-being of all children
- support families and seek to prevent problems that may result in neglect, abuse, and exploitation
- promote family stability by assessing and building on family strengths while addressing needs
- support the full array of out-of-home care services for children who require them
- take responsibility for addressing social conditions that negatively affect children and families, such as inadequate housing, poverty, chemical dependence, and lack of access to health care
- support the strengths of families whenever possible
- intervene when necessary to ensure the safety and well-being of children.

## Types of Services

Child welfare policy and practice are subject to political, social, and economic swings and have adapted repeatedly to changing conditions. Since the early 1980s service delivery has shifted from a strict child protection approach, with minimal involvement of the child's family, to a child-centered, family-focused approach. Child-centered, family-focused practice acknowledges not only that most children want to live with their families, but that it is healthier for them to live with their families, with one crucial caveat: Children must be safe from emotional and physical harm. Child-centered, family-focused practice strengthens and supports families and keeps children with their parents whenever possible.

### Family Preservation and Family Support

Family preservation services and family support help parents support and care for their children through (1) family resource, support, and educational services that enhance family functioning; (2) family-focused casework services that address problems as they arise; and (3) intensive family-centered crisis services that seek to stabilize families when there is an imminent risk of separating children from their parents because of abuse or neglect. All three forms of family preservation promote functioning of the family as an interdependent unit by facilitating the development and social functioning of children, supporting parents in their child-rearing role, and improving family and community life.

### Child Protective Services

Child protective services (CPS) respond to the dramatic increase in the number of reports of child abuse and neglect. According to the National Committee to Prevent Child Abuse (1993), in 1993 there were just under 3 million reports of child abuse or neglect, with a substantiation rate of approximately 34 percent. Child protective services traditionally have been undertaken by state or county government agencies that are charged by law with the protection of children. CPS agencies investigate reports of child abuse and neglect, assess the degree of harm and the ongoing risk of harm to the child, determine whether the child can remain safely in the home or should be placed in the custody of the state, and work closely with the family or juvenile court regarding appropriate plans for the child's safety and well-being. Family and juvenile courts, working with CPS agencies, will, as appropriate, declare children in need of protection, remove children from their parents' custody and place them in the custody of CPS agencies, and approve children's placement in out-of-home care. In addition, courts periodically review the progress that is being made toward resolving the problems that led to the child's placement and toward developing permanent plans for children who cannot return home.

### Out-of-Home Care

The American Public Welfare Association (1993) estimated that in 1992 there were 442,000 children in out-of-home care, up from 280,000 children in 1986. Detailed information on children in out-of-home care is currently limited; comprehensive data will be available in the future through the Adoption and Foster Care Analysis System, which is managed by the U.S. Department of Health and Human Services and is designed to collect uniform, reliable information on children in the care of public child welfare agencies (*Federal Register,* 1993). Children in out-of-home care may be in family foster care, kinship care, or residential group care.

***Family foster care.*** This care is a resource for children who have experienced or are at imminent risk of serious physical abuse, sexual abuse, emotional maltreatment, or neglect; have special medical or other needs; require care and protection, on a temporary basis, away from their parents; cannot be adequately protected and nurtured by kin; and can benefit from living in a family setting. Foster care may be provided at different levels. Therapeutic foster care has become important as an intensive level of foster care for children with complex needs. Despite the steady increase in the number of children needing care over the past several years, the number of family foster care homes has decreased. More foster families are needed to provide the nurturing and support these children need.

***Kinship care.*** Kinship care is "the full-time nurturing and protection of children by relatives, members of their tribes or clans, godparents, stepparents or other adults to whom a child, the child's parents, and family members ascribe a family relationship" (Child Welfare League of America, 1994, p. 2). Increasingly, formal kinship care is being used in response to the profound increase in the incidence of child abuse, neglect, and maltreatment and the insufficient number of foster families. Information from 29 states indicates that relatives are currently caring for 83,000 children whom public child welfare agencies have determined cannot remain safely with their parents because of abuse or neglect (U.S. Department of Health and Human Services, 1992a). The majority of children in kinship care are members of racial and ethnic groups, mostly African American (Child Welfare League of America, 1994). Otherwise, the children in family foster care and those in kinship care are similar in terms of mental health, physical health, and educational needs. As kinship care has evolved into an essential child welfare service, agencies have tried to develop policy and practice that respond to the unique family and cultural issues involved in kinship care, including the promotion of informal kinship arrangements as a way of preserving families and avoiding the unnecessary placement of children in the custody of the state.

***Residential group care.*** Care is provided in a variety of settings: community-based group homes, residential treatment centers, and secure facilities. Emphasis traditionally has been on resolving the emotional and behavioral problems of children who need services that cannot be provided in a family setting. Residential group care services have become increasingly diversified to meet the complex needs of children, and they often involve the children's families in care.

### Adoption

Adoption is provided "for children who cannot be cared for by their birthparents and who need and can benefit from new and permanent family ties" (Child Welfare League of America, 1988, p. 9). The purpose of adoption as a child welfare service is to provide a supportive, nurturing family for a child who otherwise might not have one. A legal parent–child relationship between a child and his or her adoptive parents is established, and the parental rights of the birthparents are legally terminated.

In 1990 approximately 119,000 children were adopted in the United States (Flango & Flango, 1993), and each year there are approximately 20,000 children in foster care who are free for adoption but are awaiting adoptive placement (Tatara, 1993). Adoption services are provided through voluntary agencies, public agencies, or private intermediaries such as lawyers and physicians. The adoption field currently faces a number of issues that greatly influence adoption policy and practice:

- the trend toward open adoption and its impact on children, families, and agencies
- the need to recruit families to adopt children who have special needs
- continuing debates over transracial adoptions, as well as gay and lesbian adoptions
- different approaches to adoption by licensed agencies and private intermediaries who facilitate adoption.

### Independent-Living Services

Independent-living services are designed to prepare young people who must leave foster care at age 18 with the skills and competence to function as adults. Approximately one-third of the children in out-of-home care are between the ages of 13 and 18 (DeWoody, Ceja, & Sylvester, 1993). Some 50,000 of these young people were in residential group care in 1989 (U.S. Department of Health and Human Services, 1992a). Young people in out-of-home care, whether in family foster care or group residential care, need preparation in basic living skills. Services that focus on educational attainment, employment, and career preparation are particularly important in preparing youths for independent living, especially in light of research that suggests that young people in out-of-home care are at risk of falling behind educationally; often are not prepared to seek or maintain jobs; need an array of health care services before and after discharge from foster care, including services related to substance abuse, prevention of infection with the human immunodeficiency virus, and prevention of unplanned pregnancy and parenting; and need assistance in locating adequate housing after discharge from care (Barth, 1990).

### Child Day Care

Child day care supports the healthy growth and development of children and families by supplementing parental caregiving and child rearing. The need for high-quality day care will increase as the number of single-parent and two-wage-earner families continues to grow. In 1990 approximately 5.3 million children were enrolled in day care centers, not including unlicensed family day care homes (Mathematica Policy Research, 1991). Child day care may be offered as group care or family care. *Group day care* is care of children in groups in facilities equipped to serve young children, including day care centers, day nurseries, child care centers, play groups, and group day care homes. Family child day care is usually provided by one adult in a private residence, for less than 24 hours a day and for six or fewer children (Child Welfare League of America, 1992b). High-quality child day care providers are crucial to service delivery and children's health. Recruiting and retaining providers when salaries are prohibitively low and benefits are subpar is a significant issue in child day care.

### Adolescent Pregnancy and Parenting Services

Young people in the out-of-home care system tend to be at high risk of engaging in early, unprotected sexual activity, thus increasing their risk of pregnancy and early parenting. Surveys have found that young people in out-of-home care, when compared with young people who are not in care, are more likely to have had sexual intercourse, more likely to become pregnant, and less likely to obtain and use contraceptives (Polit, Morton, & White, 1989). Of particular concern to many child welfare professionals is the development of policies to ensure that adolescent sexuality and family-planning issues are addressed for young people in out-of-home care; that adolescent pregnancy and parenting services are included in case plans for young people in out-of-home care; and that training is provided for caseworkers, foster parents, and administrators on sexuality and family planning services.

## Child Welfare Law

### Adoption Assistance and Child Welfare Act of 1980

The Adoption Assistance and Child Welfare Act of 1980, considered the most important child welfare legislation enacted over the past several decades, is contained in both Title IV-B and Title IV-E of the Social Security Act. Title IV-B is the major source of federal support for protective and preventive services for abused and neglected children and troubled families. Although the protection and care of these children and families are primarily the responsibility of state or county child welfare systems, federal support has been essential to help states fulfill their obligation.

***Title-IV-B.*** The Title IV-B Child Welfare Services Program was originally established to help support initial investigation and law enforcement regarding child abuse or neglect, as well as counseling, parent education, and comprehensive in-home preventive services. The act states that services must be designed to (1) intervene early with problems that might result in abuse, neglect, exploitation, or delinquency; (2) prevent family breakup and the separation of children from their families; (3) secure appropriate out-of-home care for children necessarily separated from their families; (4) reunify children with their families whenever possible after separation; and (5) place children with adoptive families when reunification with their families of origin is not possible.

***Title IV-E.*** Title IV-E, the Federal Foster Care and Adoption Assistance program, is the single most important program of federal support for children who have been separated from families who are unable or unwilling to care for them and who have been placed in out-of-home care—that is, in family foster care, kinship care, group homes, or residential facilities or with adoptive families. Title IV-E is a means-tested entitlement program under which states are partially reimbursed for the costs of caring for children up to age 18 who have been removed from their parents' custody if the children receive (or are eligible to receive) benefits under Aid to Families with Dependent Children or Supplemental Security Income.

Title IV-E requires states to ensure that children who are taken into the custody of the state and placed in foster care have a permanent home within a reasonable period. It also provides a subsidy program to meet the special needs of children who are adopted. The law sets forth certain standards that states must meet to receive federal funds. These standards, which have had a significant impact on the way child welfare services are provided, include reasonable efforts to keep children with their families whenever possible, permanency planning services, and out-of-home placement in the least restrictive setting.

**Omnibus Budget Reconciliation Act of 1985**

The Omnibus Budget Reconciliation Act (OBRA) of 1985 established a new subpart of Title IV-E entitled Independent Living Initiatives. This program funds services for adolescents in out-of-home care who will not be reunited with their families or be adopted and who will leave care at age 18 to live on their own. Services must be designed to teach basic living skills, provide educational and job training opportunities, and assist youths in locating housing. Independent-living services may be made available to young people beginning at age 16 and continue through age 18 or, at the state's option, through age 21. Eligibility for the program is not limited to young people who are Title IV-E–eligible; all adolescents in out-of-home care may receive federally funded independent-living services.

**Omnibus Budget Reconciliation Act of 1993**

The 1993 OBRA established a new subpart of Title IV-B of the Social Security Act, entitled Family Preservation and Support Services. This program provides funding for (1) community-based family support programs that work with families before a crisis occurs to enhance child development and increase family stability; (2) family preservation programs that serve families in crisis or at risk of having their children placed in out-of-home care and provide follow-up services, including family reunification; and (3) evaluation, research, training, and technical assistance in the area of family support and family preservation. The law targeted a total of $1 billion for the five years (1994 through 1998) for which the Family Preservation and Family Support Program was authorized.

**Indian Child Welfare Act of 1978**

The Indian Child Welfare Act responded to the number of Native American children who had been separated from their families and placed in non–Native American foster homes and adoptive homes. The purpose of the act is to protect the best interests of Native American children and to promote the stability and security of tribes and families by requiring the placement of Native American children in foster homes or adoptive homes that reflect the unique values of Native American culture.

**Child Abuse Prevention and Treatment Act of 1974**

The Child Abuse Prevention and Treatment Act (CAPTA) was enacted in response to growing public concern about child abuse and provides financial assistance to states and communities to prevent, identify, and treat child abuse and neglect. To receive funds states must designate an agency responsible for investigating abuse and neglect; establish a reporting system for all known or suspected instances of child abuse and neglect; enact laws that protect all children under age 18 from mental injury, physical injury, and sexual abuse; and develop a system that provides a guardian *ad litem* who represents the interests of abused and neglected children when the children's cases go to court.

**Other Federal Laws**

Two other federal laws influence child welfare practice significantly. The Family Unification Program provides housing assistance in the form of Section 8 rental certificates to eligible families whose children are at imminent risk of placement in foster care or cannot return home from foster care because their families have housing problems. Also, Title XX of the Social Security Act provides federal funding to states to assist children and families in crisis.

**State Laws**

Each state addresses child welfare services in its statutes. In most states the law

- directs that services be available to help strengthen and support families
- defines the conduct that constitutes child abuse and neglect
- identifies the agency responsible for receiving, screening, and investigating reports of child abuse and neglect
- identifies the individuals required to report suspected child abuse and neglect
- provides immunity from liability for making a report of child abuse and neglect
- sets penalties for people who knowingly fail to report child abuse and neglect
- identifies the court that has jurisdiction over child abuse and neglect cases and that has the authority to remove children from the custody of their parents
- specifies the duties of the agency in working to preserve and reunify families
- sets forth the conditions under which parental rights can be terminated and a child freed for adoption
- describes the procedures for adoption.

Although federal and state laws direct that child welfare services be in place to meet the needs of children, these laws have not been fully or consistently implemented. Over the past decade, the American Civil Liberties Union, the National Youth Law Center, and other legal aid organizations and advocacy groups have brought more than 60 cases against the public child welfare agencies of half the states. Many cases have been class action suits based on the provisions of the Adoption Assistance and Child Welfare Act of 1980, alleging violations of the federal operational requirements for states' receipt of federal funds for foster care and adoption assistance. Some cases have been based on the 14th Amendment to the Constitution or Section 1983 of the Civil Rights Act and have claimed that state child welfare agencies have violated children's civil rights or constitutional right to due process. These cases generally claim that the agencies serving children and families have failed to provide the services needed by children who have been abused or neglected. They usually focus on the insufficient number of caseworkers, which results in excessive caseloads; inadequate training and supervision for social workers and foster parents; the dearth of appropriate foster family placements; and the lack of coordinated information services.

## Child Welfare Policy

Child welfare law and judicial decisions are important components of child welfare policy, which, as a whole, is directed toward protecting children, strengthening and preserving families, and ensuring that governmental decision making is based on what children and their families need. For child welfare policy to achieve these goals, child welfare issues must be clearly defined, and various approaches must be analyzed in terms of their ability to protect children and enhance the strengths of children and families. Policymakers continue to debate a number of child welfare policy issues, including the proper role of government in protecting children, the balance between protecting children and preserving families, definitions of when in-home services are most appropriate and when out-of-home care should be used, and the allocation of resources between prevention and treatment services.

## Child Welfare Agencies

Child welfare services in the United States are provided primarily through both public and voluntary agencies. Although the two types of child welfare agencies share the goal of providing high-quality services for children, they differ in their underlying philosophy, the types of children they serve, their sources of authority, and funding.

**Public Agencies**

The public child welfare agency's role is to ensure that child welfare services are made available to the children and families who need them. Agencies are responsible for "providing leadership in community and program planning and in maintaining child welfare services under public, voluntary, and proprietary auspices so that they will be available in every political subdivision for all families and children" (Child Welfare League of America, 1984, p. 93). Specific roles for public child welfare agencies include the provision of direct services, standard setting and licensing, information and data collection for the jurisdiction, and promotion of research and demonstration projects.

**Voluntary Agencies**

In contrast to public agencies, voluntary child welfare agencies receive their authorization from a group of citizens who wish to provide services to children and families in certain communities (Costin, Bell, & Downs, 1991). Voluntary agencies are free to choose their service areas and the geographic location in which services will be provided, although many agencies advocate that voluntary agencies should choose functions and policies that "reflect responsible community planning and the priority needs of all of the community's children" (Costin et al., 1991, p. 23). Specific responsibilities for voluntary agencies include keeping abreast of the changing needs of the community, as well as of new practice knowledge; serving as leaders in their communities and working with others to provide high-quality services; monitoring legislation and understanding its effects on children in their communities; promoting measures that support families and children and opposing those that do not; and, if possible, engaging in research.

Public and private agencies often work together to help children and their families. The United States has a long history of public–private financing in the provision of child welfare services, primarily through public agencies that purchase services from voluntary agencies. Many people believe that purchase of services leads to increased flexibility in the provision of services, more innovative programs, and decreased service costs (Smith, 1989). Others, however, fear that this mixture of funds could promote an inappropriate delegation of authority by the public agency or a loss of autonomy for private agencies (Kettner & Martin, 1994).

**National Organizations**

Several national organizations work with and for public and private nonprofit child welfare agencies. The Children's Bureau is part of the federal Administration for Children and Families of the Department of Health and Human Services. Its mandate, in large part, comes from the Social Security Act of 1935, Title IV-B. Among its other responsibilities, the Children's Bureau administers grant programs to the states, provides states with technical assistance, and advocates for children on a national level.

The Child Welfare League of America (CWLA) is the largest and oldest child welfare membership organization in North America, representing the public and voluntary child welfare sectors. CWLA provides leadership in child welfare public policy and practice, including standard setting, provision of consultation and technical assistance, program expertise in all substantive child welfare areas, advocacy on national children's issues, and information services.

The Children's Defense Fund is a national advocacy group that gathers and disseminates data, monitors the implementation of federal and state policies, provides information and technical assistance, and lobbies Congress on behalf of children.

The American Bar Association Center on Children and the Law is sponsored by the American Bar Association's Young Lawyers Division. The center, established in 1978, addresses child abuse and neglect, civil and criminal court issues, child welfare legal training and curriculum development, and child abduction research. It also provides technical assistance on child maltreatment fatalities.

## CHILD WELFARE SOCIAL WORKERS

**Roles and Responsibilities**

Child welfare social workers play a variety of roles. They provide direct services to children and their families, offering counseling and, through case management, helping families gain access to a range of services, including health care, mental health services, child day care, and housing. They may also facilitate legal intervention when children are abused or neglected and must, for their protection, be separated from their families. Experienced child welfare social workers serve as supervisors to support and guide direct service staff, assist them in providing high-quality service, provide a link between staff and management, and shape policy and practice. Workers with supervisory experience can advance professionally to manage program divisions and departments or the agency as a whole, with responsibilities that include fiscal management, program development and management, community networking, and public relations. Child welfare social workers also help community groups take action on their own behalf through community organizing; work to improve social institutions, systems, laws, and practices through public policy and advocacy; conduct research to support public policy efforts and advance practice; and develop curricula and teach social workers and other professionals about innovations in service delivery, program and practice issues, entitlements, and available resources.

**Education**

The bachelor's degree in social work (BSW) generally is the first level of professional education for entry into child welfare social work. The BSW curriculum is built on a liberal arts foundation and includes the knowledge, values, processes, and skills that have proved essential for the practice of social work. Students who earn a BSW are expected to have the professional judgment and proficiency to apply, with supervision, a consistent approach across various service systems. The master's degree in social work (MSW) prepares students for the advanced practice of professional child welfare social work. Graduates of MSW programs have advanced analytic and practice skills for self-critical, accountable, and ultimately, autonomous practice. An MSW is usually required for employment at supervisory or administrative levels.

#### Licensing

Although provisions vary, social work is legally regulated by licensure, certification, or registration in all 50 states, the District of Columbia, and the territories. In Canada, four provinces—Quebec, New Brunswick, Prince Edward Island, and Newfoundland—require registration of social workers. This legal regulation of the profession is designed to protect the public by identifying social workers who have been professionally educated; have demonstrated a level of practice competence by passing an examination; and, in most cases, have accumulated a defined amount of experience. State licensure or provincial registration regulates the use of the title of social worker and the scope of social work practice.

#### Recruitment and Retention

In recent years the child welfare field has found it difficult to attract and retain a fully trained work force that is adequately large and reflects clients' cultural diversity. As the demand for services has grown, the number of individuals entering the child welfare work force has declined. Professionals have identified a number of steps they believe are essential to the effective recruitment and retention of child welfare staff, including

- creating a positive national image of child welfare
- informing the public of career opportunities in the child welfare field
- funding child welfare scholarships, grants, internships, and work–study programs
- improving professional child welfare education and training programs to ensure that staff members are competent and capable
- advocating for salaries and benefits for child welfare staff commensurate with the required skills and responsibilities
- creating working environments and personnel policies that support staff members.

### Trends

#### Cultural Issues

The child welfare field faces a host of challenges in providing high-quality services to an increasingly multicultural population of children and families. Demographic changes reflect the need for responsive and culturally competent child welfare services. Children who are members of racial and ethnic groups are disproportionately represented in the child welfare system, particularly in out-of-home care and the juvenile justice system, and remain in these systems for longer periods than do white children. The most significant increase in the number of children entering the child welfare system has been from the Latino, African American, and Pacific Asian cultures. A common characteristic of these children—poverty and its associated factors, such as poor education, unemployment, homelessness, and welfare dependence—increases their likelihood of exposure to the child welfare system and entry into out-of-home care. In response to these issues, the child welfare field has been placing particular emphasis on cultural competence; that is, the acceptance and integration of culture and ethnicity as central factors in the planning and provision of services to children and their families in a pluralistic social environment.

#### Substance Abuse

The drug abuse epidemic of recent years has had a profound impact on the safety and protection of children and young people, and it has placed new demands on the child welfare system. An increasing number of women of childbearing age have become involved with alcohol and drugs, prenatal alcohol and drug exposure has affected a growing population of infants, a greater number of young children have been exposed to parental substance abuse, and significant percentages of young people are using and abusing alcohol and other drugs. Alcohol and other drugs have increasingly become factors in child maltreatment and are a primary reason that children and young people enter out-of-home care. Child welfare agencies have focused on

- the prevention of child maltreatment because of parental alcohol and drug abuse
- the need to make accurate and comprehensive child protective services risk assessments when parental alcohol or drug abuse is a factor
- the role of family preservation programs

- decision making about placement and the type of out-of-home care placement that most effectively meets the needs of drug-involved children and young people and their parents
- the importance of providing specialized out-of-home care services for drug- or alcohol-affected children and youths
- permanency planning that appropriately balances family reunification efforts with permanence and stability for drug- or alcohol-involved children and young people outside their birth families.

**HIV/AIDS**

Human immunodeficiency virus (HIV) and acquired immune deficiency syndrome (AIDS) have had a growing impact on the child welfare system as HIV infection has increasingly affected children, young people, and their families. A growing number of children are being diagnosed with AIDS, and an even larger number of children and young people are testing positive for HIV. If current trends continue, AIDS will soon rank among the five highest causes of death for women, children, and adolescents (U.S. Department of Health and Human Services, 1993).

Children who are not infected by HIV may be affected by the epidemic. Michaels and Levine (1992) estimated that by the year 2000, the mothers of approximately 82,000 to 125,000 children will have died from AIDS. Thus, agencies must be prepared to identify both extended and adoptive families to care for children and youths who are orphaned by AIDS. Support services must be available to encourage and ensure permanency for children and youths.

**Increased Court Involvement**

The juvenile court, which has the legal responsibility to determine the validity of allegations of abuse or neglect and to decide whether children should be placed in the custody of the child protective services agency, has become an essential partner of child welfare agencies. Like the child welfare system, the juvenile court system has experienced a caseload crisis and has been under intense pressure in its handling of child abuse and neglect cases. Courts are required to hear an escalating number of cases involving children who have been abused or neglected; the cases involve severe and complex problems, such as drug and alcohol abuse, that severely affect the well-being of children and their families; and court hearings have become more frequent and more complex over the last several years, as the role of the court has grown.

Attorneys, guardians *ad litem,* and court-appointed special advocates (CASAs) who advocate for children's interests assist courts and supplement the work of child welfare agencies in evaluating the needs of an individual child for protection and care. Guardians *ad litem* may be attorneys or other people appointed by a court to represent the interests of children. CASAs, trained lay volunteers who are assigned to represent children who appear before the court, operate in more than 600 jurisdictions throughout the United States. They, like attorneys and guardians *ad litem,* have been given increased responsibility and latitude in representing the needs of abused or neglected children.

Increasingly, child welfare professionals and agencies have become subject to civil liability when, in the course of practice, they have made professional judgments or have provided or failed to provide services to children and their families and harm to a child has resulted. Civil liability has been based on failures to properly investigate reports of child abuse or neglect and on failures to adequately select or monitor foster homes. Child welfare agencies also may face civil liability for the wrongful removal or detention of children, particularly when procedural requirements for taking custody of children are not followed. In a few states, criminal sanctions have been sought for child welfare malpractice, particularly when a child has died. The growing threat of civil or criminal liability has led to a number of efforts in the child welfare field to ensure that standards of practice are consistently met, including the assurance of competent legal representation for children in the child welfare system and the use of child protective teams to ensure agency and professional accountability.

**Management Information Systems**

A management information system is the way an organization collects, stores, and reports data. These procedures need not be computerized although they often are. Technology is less expensive and more refined than ever before, and more and more child welfare agencies are taking advantage of technological advances. Electronic information management can help social workers spend more time with children and families and less time with paperwork.

**Health Care Reform**

Issues related to health care reform are of increasing importance to the delivery of child welfare services. Proposals to reform the U.S. health care system vary widely in their approaches to the accessibility of health care and related social services for highly vulnerable populations, the nature and scope of health care benefit packages, and the organizational and financing structure of the reformed health care system. The focus on managed care as the primary mechanism for the delivery and financing of health services—including mental health care, substance abuse prevention and treatment, and developmental services—is likely to have significant ramifications for the design and delivery of child welfare services in both the public and voluntary sectors. The relationship between health care reform and Medicaid, the major source of federal funding for health care services for low-income individuals and a critical financing resource for a range of services needed by children and families in the child welfare system, is equally important. Providers of child welfare services in numerous states have relied on Medicaid as a key funding source for mental health care, substance abuse prevention and treatment, and developmental services. Health care reform is likely to affect this use of Medicaid, and changes in the funding and delivery of child welfare services are likely to follow.

### Welfare Reform

Since the 1980s increasing attention has been given to the reform of Aid to Families with Dependent Children (AFDC), the primary federal program that supports low-income children with cash assistance. Approximately half of the children in out-of-home care and a large percentage of children who live with their own families are eligible to receive benefits. Reform of the AFDC program has become a highly complex, political issue and will have significant impact on the child welfare system. Proposals for welfare reform include limitations on the period of time that families may remain on welfare; denial of benefits for children born to families already receiving benefits; and elimination of benefits for children born out of wedlock to teenage mothers or for children whose paternity has not been established. Other important issues include the extent to which quality education, training opportunities, full-time jobs, and public-sector work will actually be made available to help AFDC recipients become self-sufficient.

Despite almost unanimous agreement that the current welfare system is not working well for clients, social workers, or administrators, there is no consensus on how to change it. Child welfare advocates generally have focused on reform efforts that promote parenting, encourage self-sufficiency, include child development services and child care, ensure the establishment of paternity and the enforcement of child support, emphasize the prevention of adolescent pregnancy, and provide access to high-quality health care and housing.

## References


Adoption Assistance and Child Welfare Act of 1980. P.L. 96-272, 94 Stat. 500.

American Public Welfare Association. (1993, August). *Voluntary cooperative information system, VCIS Research Notes* (No. 9). Washington, DC: Author.

Barth, R. (1990). On their own: The experiences of youth after foster care. *Child and Adolescent Social Work, 7*(5), 419–440.

Child Abuse Prevention and Treatment Act of 1974. P.L. 93-247, 88 Stat. 4.

Child Welfare League of America. (1984). *Standards for organization and administration for all child welfare services agencies*. Washington, DC: Author.

Child Welfare League of America. (1988). *Standards for adoption service* (rev. ed.). Washington, DC: Author.

Child Welfare League of America. (1992a). *Building partnerships: Schools and agencies advancing child welfare practice*. Washington, DC: Author.

Child Welfare League of America. (1992b). *Standards of excellence for child day care services*. (Rev. ed.). Washington, DC: Author.

Child Welfare League of America. (1994). *Kinship care: A natural bridge*. Washington, DC: Author.

Costin, L. B., Bell, C. J., & Downs, S. W. (1991). *Child welfare: Policies and practice* (4th ed.). New York: Longman.

DeWoody, M., Ceja, K., & Sylvester, M. (1993). *Independent living services for youths in out-of-home care*. Washington, DC: Child Welfare League of America.

*Federal Register.* (1993). *58*, 67912–67947.

Flango, V. E., & Flango, C. R. (1993). Adoption statistics by state. *Child Welfare, 72*, 311–319.

Indian Child Welfare Act of 1978. P.L. 95-608, 92 Stat. 3069.

Kettner, P., & Martin, L. (1994). Purchase of service at 20: Are we using it well? *Public Welfare, 52*(3), 14–20.

Mathematica Policy Research. (1991). *A profile of child care settings: Early education and care in 1990* (Contract No. LC88 090001). Washington, DC: U.S. Department of Health and Human Services and U.S. Department of Education.

Michaels, D., & Levine, C. (1992). Estimates of the number of motherless youth orphaned by AIDS in the United States. *Journal of the American Medical Association, 268*, 3456–3461.

National Committee to Prevent Child Abuse. (1993, April). *Current trends in child abuse reporting and fatalities: The results of the 1993 annual fifty state survey*. Chicago: Author.

Omnibus Budget Reconciliation Act of 1985. P.L. 99-272, 100 Stat. 82.

Omnibus Budget Reconciliation Act of 1993. P.L. 103-66, 107 Stat. 312.

Polit, D., Morton, T., & White, C. (1989). Sex, contraception and pregnancy among adolescents in foster care. *Family Planning Perspectives, 21*, 203–208.

Smith, S. (1989). The changing politics of child welfare services: New roles for the government and the nonprofit sectors. *Child Welfare, 68*, 289–299.

Tatara, T. (1993). *Characteristics of children in substitute and adoptive care, fiscal year 1989*. Washington, DC: American Public Welfare Association.

U.S. Department of Health and Human Services, Centers for Disease Control and Prevention. (1993, May). *HIV/AIDS surveillance report,* Vol. 5, No. 1. Washington, DC: U.S. Government Printing Office.

U.S. Department of Health and Human Services, Office of the Inspector General. (1992a). *Trends in foster care*. Washington, DC: U.S. Government Printing Office.

U.S. Department of Health and Human Services, Office of the Inspector General. (1992b). *Using relatives for foster care* (OEI-06-90-02391). Washington, DC: U.S. Government Printing Office.

## Further Reading

Bremner, R. (Ed.). (1974). *Children and youth in America: A documentary history, Volumes 1–3*. Cambridge, MA: Harvard University Press.

Kadushin, A., & Martin, J. (1988). *Child welfare services*. New York: Macmillan.

Kamerman, S., & Kahn, A. (1976). *Social services in the United States: Policies and programs*. Philadelphia: Temple University Press.

Laird, J., & Hartman, A. (Eds.). (1985). *A handbook of child welfare: Content, knowledge and practice*. New York: Free Press.

Pecora, P., Whittaker, J., & Maluccio, A. (1992). *The child welfare challenge: Policy, practice, and research*. New York: Aldine de Gruyter.

**David S. Liederman, MSW, ACSW,** is executive director, Child Welfare League of America, 440 First Street, NW, Suite 310, Washington, DC 20001.

### For further information see

Adoption; Advocacy; Aid to Families with Dependent Children; Child Abuse and Neglect Overview; Child Foster Care; Child Labor; Child Support; Childhood; Children: Direct Practice; Community; Domestic Violence; Families Overview; Family Preservation and Home-Based Services; Homelessness; Income Security Overview; Juvenile Corrections; Legal Issues: Low-Income and Dependent People; Natural Helping Networks; Poverty; Professional Liability and Malpractice; Public Social Services; Runaways and Homeless Youths; School Social Work Overview; School-Linked Services; Social Welfare Policy; Welfare Evaluation Programs: Evaluation; Youth Services.

**Key Words**
child welfare    children

# Childhood

**Jeanne M. Giovannoni**

Childhood, in a strictly biological sense, demarcates a period in the life cycle between birth and the achievement of full adult physical maturation. From the perspective of human development theory, childhood encompasses not only the process of physical development but also cognitive, emotional, social, and moral development. This developmental perspective is integral to social work theory and practice.

Three tenets are elemental:

1. The various domains of human development are interdependent.
2. Development is a sequential process, with maturation at a given stage dependent on achievement of a previous one.
3. The successful negotiation of the developmental process by individual children is dependent on interaction with their environments.

The human beings who emerge from childhood to adulthood are the embodiment of the interplay of this enormously complex interaction of forces. Each is unique. Each shares commonalities with the others.

The idea of stages of development is integrally linked with environmental influences. Children's needs are differentiated by their particular developmental stages and tasks, which in turn depend on environmental supports for full achievement. Although there may be inherent limitations on each individual's potential, the environment mediates the fulfillment of that potential. Abundant evidence (Germain, 1979) supports the idea that children's development may be enhanced or retarded by environmental experiences, both nurturing and challenging, but these conclusions are imprecise because of the complexity of the interactions that contribute to healthy development. The present state of expertise derived from child development theory and research is more advanced in measuring effects on child development—that is, outcomes—than in explaining causal and contributing factors (Cicchetti, 1984).

Childhood is also a sociologic concept that refers to the particular sets of roles and expectations a society accords its children. Although developmental theories posit or at least seek universals concerning the needs and processes common to all children, as a sociologic concept childhood can be defined only within given social contexts. For example, 19th-century American children were expected to work at a very early age, whereas 20th-century children are forbidden to do so. Even the chronological demarcation of childhood from adulthood varies with the particular privilege or responsibility in question, such as the right to give consent to sexual relations, drive a car, vote, or become emancipated.

In American society, the roles and statuses of children in relation to society are generally mediated by the family, with primary responsibility for children's development assigned to the parents. Children's access to the rights and rewards of society are conditioned not by their status as children but by their parents' status in that society. Although the idealized autonomous family in the United States shares child-rearing responsibilities with a variety of social institutions, it simply is not possible to cite universal rights accruing to all children. Such rights are determined by the accident of their birth and their parents' capacity to purchase developmental supports, to link them with community resources, and to love and cherish them.

This entry gives an overview of the present conditions of childhood in the United States in the major areas affecting development, including living conditions, health, education, and the particular needs arising from special developmental impediments. Because society relies on families to provide for children, the conditions of childhood reflect the inequality that pervades the status of adults in American society. The inextricable relationship between ethnicity and gender and income inequality among adults is mirrored in inequality among children. From a developmental perspective this means that children simply do not have an equal opportunity to develop their optimal potential. The absence of any universal social policies to ensure minimal developmental supports for all children, even those necessary to survive, precludes any assumption of basic minimum standards for the condition of childhood.

## Children's Representation in the Population

In 1990 there were 64 million children under age 18, and 54 million—about one-fifth of the total U.S. population—under age 14. There has been a consistent decline over the past three decades in the fertility rate (the number of births to women of childbearing age at a particular time) worldwide, in both developed and developing countries. In 1988 the U.S. fertility rate was 1.9 births per 1,000 women, below the rate necessary to replace population deaths. The proportion of households with children is declining, with slightly more than a third of all households having at least one child as a member. Also changing is the "dependency ratio," calculated as the number of children under age 14 per 100 people in the "working age" population, ages 15 to 64. In the United States that ratio is now 32.8. In Africa it is 85.4 and in Mexico, 66.8 (U.S. House of Representatives, 1990a). This favorable U.S. ratio is mitigated by the increasing elderly nonworking populations. Still, if children were viewed as a responsibility of the total society, this distribution would be a favorable one. If, on the other hand, the concern for children is reflective only of the immediate self-interests of adults, then as the ratio of children to adults declines, so might the general level of societal concern for children.

## Children in Families

A persistently increasing proportion of American children live with only one parent, almost always their mother. In 1960 slightly less than one in 10 children lived in a single-parent family; by 1990 one in four did so. There are large differences in this proportion across ethnic groups, but the directions of increase are parallel. In 1990 approximately 20 percent of white children, 30 percent of Hispanic children, and half of all African American children lived with only one parent (U.S. House of Representatives, 1992). The likelihood that children will spend at least part of their childhood with only one parent is greater still, and thus increasing numbers of American children will experience changes in their family structure, their most crucial environment.

The effects on children of being raised only by their mother are uncertain. Although the general assumption is that the effects are deleterious, there is little to substantiate this view. The negative consequences for children of single parenthood must be judged in the context of other familial characteristics. A key reason it is difficult to establish these consequences is the inextricable relationship between female heads of household and poverty.

## Children of Working Mothers

The increasing participation of mothers in the labor force is a societal trend of even greater magnitude than that of changing family structures. In 1991, 67 percent of all mothers were in the labor force (defined as working full-time or part-time or actively seeking work). Typical American children, regardless of their age or the marital status of their mothers, will spend a significant proportion of their childhood in a family with a working mother (U.S. House of Representatives, 1992).

The implications of this trend depend on children's stages of development and on the substitute parental care given them. Infants need consistent, nurturing substitute caregivers. In the preschool years the need for such intense caretaker interaction diminishes, and wider contact with both adults and other children can be beneficial. Once they enter school, young children continue to need careful protective supervision until they are in their teens.

Given these minimal parameters of children's developmental needs, family and children's advocates have expressed continuing and mounting concern about the children of working mothers. Despite the growing preponderance of children whose mothers are in the labor force, the continuing social policy response has been a reliance on the family and the marketplace.

## Economic Circumstances of Children

The economic circumstances into which children are born and under which they live are strong determinants of their chances to survive at all, the quality of their lives in childhood, and their ultimate life chances in adulthood. It is impossible to discuss the children's circumstances without accounting for the disparities among them attributable to economic circumstances.

During the 1980s poverty in America increased, but disproportionately among children, especially children of color and very young children. In 1970 about 25 percent of the aged population and about 15 percent of children were considered poor. By 1990 the proportion of poor aged had been reduced by half, to 12 percent, whereas the proportion of poor children under age 18 had increased to 21 percent and of children under six to 23.6 percent—almost one child in four (U.S. House of Representatives, 1992).

The prevalence of poverty among children is related both to their family structure and to their ethnicity. Among African American and Hispanic children in female-headed households in 1990, roughly two out of three were poor (65 percent of African American children and 68.4 percent of Hispanic children), whereas slightly less than half of white children in female-headed families were poor (U.S. House of Representatives, 1992). The assumption that an increase in families headed by women accounts for increases in poverty has dominated public policy debates, but having families headed by men is no insurance against poverty. The rate of poverty among African American children in male-headed families was equal to the overall poverty rate for all children, one in five. Among Hispanic children it was even greater (one in four, or 26.7 percent), and even among white children it was one in 10. Despite the overwhelming vulnerability of children of color, at any given time, three out of four poor children will be white, due to their greater representation in the overall child population (U.S. House of Representatives, 1992).

The above data are based on a definition of poverty in an absolute sense, above or below a given income threshold. Absolute poverty information gives one picture of economic disadvantage, but information across income levels gives a picture of the degree of relative deprivation. Just as absolute poverty in the United States increased during the 1980s, so did the gaps in income distribution, and this was true among households with children as well as the rest of the population. In 1990 the highest-income group among married couples with children received almost seven times the share of income that the lowest-income group did (40.3 percent versus 6.0 percent). This disparity was even more pronounced among the families of single mothers, with the highest-income group receiving 17 times the share of income received by the lowest-income group (50 percent versus 3.2 percent) (U.S. House of Representatives, 1992). This degree of income inequality among children adds to the concern about the most-disadvantaged children and their life chances relative to other, more-advantaged children.

American public social policies that directly or indirectly benefit children augment or supplant family incomes through cash transfers or cash equivalents and in-kind benefits such as food stamps and public housing. Cash transfers include those that either directly distribute cash or permit the retention of income through the tax system.

### Tax System and Social Insurance

Policies executed through the tax system and social insurance programs rely on some degree of parental participation in the labor force. The largest policy in scope is the tax exemption of $2,000 per dependent. In 1985, 73.3 million such exemptions were claimed, making this tax exemption the largest of any income support program. But the exemption benefits only those with enough income to have a tax liability and thus is of the least benefit to the poorest children (U.S. House of Representatives, 1990b, p. 35).

Also tied to labor force participation are the social insurance programs. The two principal ones that affect children are Unemployment Compensation and the dependents' benefits provisions of Old Age and Survivors Insurance and Disability Insurance (OASDI). Reliable data on the actual numbers of children who benefit from unemployment compensation directly (through dependent allowances in about one-third of the states) or indirectly (through participation in the compensation awarded their breadwinner) are not available. Still, unemployment compensation must be considered a safety net for those children whose family's income is jeopardized through the temporary unemployment of an otherwise regularly employed breadwinner. In 1988 about 3.25 million children received OASDI benefits, with outlays estimated at close to $11 billion (U.S. House of Representatives, 1990b).

**Public Assistance**

Unlike the tax and social insurance programs, public assistance programs are not limited by labor force attachment. They are financed out of the general treasury, and eligibility criteria are based on some minimal financial deficit and on type of need. Two public assistance programs address economic dependence of children. One, relatively minor in coverage, is the Supplemental Security Income (SSI) program. Children under age 18 who have a disability that would qualify an adult under the program's requirements may receive benefits, provided their family's incomes and assets meet certain specified limitations. In 1989 about 31.5 million children received SSI benefits (U.S. House of Representatives, 1990b).

The other, and major, public assistance program targeted at needy dependent children is Aid to Families with Dependent Children (AFDC), inaugurated as Title IV-A of the Social Security Act of 1935. At any given time the AFDC recipient child population is over three times that of the OASDI, and, because AFDC is not means-tested, its importance to children who are poor is far greater than OASDI. The federal government shares in costs and has some basic requirements for states' AFDC programs, but the states administer them and determine the benefit levels and income eligibility standards; hence, there is wide variation in both. In 1992 the maximum allowable grant for a family of three ranged from $924 in Alaska to $120 in Mississippi. In no state are either income eligibility or benefit levels established with regard to poverty-level standards (Wald, 1992).

AFDC is virtually synonymous with "welfare" in both the rhetoric of policymakers and in public opinion, and for decades it has been the sole object of welfare reform. Children—the legislatively intended targets and by far the majority of recipients—have hardly been considered in any of the reform measures, proposed or enacted, or in the various rationales divined to support the reforms. Welfare reform has not addressed the facets of AFDC that most directly affect children and their immediate suffering. By any reckoning, AFDC fails to meet policy criteria of either equity or adequacy. State variations in program implementation defy all standards of equity. The efficacy of AFDC as an antipoverty measure has never been ensured because poverty standards are not part of the calculation. Hence, AFDC does not "lift most children out of poverty." Quite the contrary: At present, its antipoverty effectiveness has been eroded over the past several years as the actual dollar value of grants has declined and as eligibility has been constricted. These are the reform issues that most directly affect children, and they simply are not on the policy agenda.

Although poverty may be measured in terms of income, poverty is much more than the mere absence of income. The circumstances of living attendant on poverty status can have a profound effect on the conditions under which children live, the quality of their lives, and their chances for survival. The following sections describe key factors in the conditions of childhood trends that affect all or most children, with particular attention given to the disproportionate burdens that impinge on poor children.

## Geographic Dispersion

American children are becoming increasingly urbanized. Beyond the urban–rural distinction, ethnic differences persist. About half of all white children live outside "central cities," in suburban areas, compared to only one-fourth of African American and about one-third of Hispanic children. A still more-crucial distinction is between nonpoverty areas and poverty areas, those where 20 percent or more of the inhabitants are identified as living below the poverty level. Here differences among children attributable to both ethnic and poverty status are more pronounced. About 19 percent of all children reside in poverty areas, but 47 percent of poor children do. Furthermore, over two-thirds of African American poor children, somewhat more than half of Hispanic poor children, and one-third of white poor children reside in poverty areas (U.S. House of Representatives, 1992). Thus, even among poor children the impact of poverty status on where they live is two times greater among African American children than white children. The conditions of life in poverty areas, especially those in central cities, are well documented and strongly influence the quality of the environments in which these children spend their childhood.

## Housing

Closely linked to the quality of life in the neighborhoods in which children live is the housing in which they reside. The 1980s saw a dramatic decline in the availability of affordable housing for all Americans, but especially for young families with children. Home ownership among this population declined from 39 percent to 29 percent, with no concomitant expansion in affordable rental housing (U.S. House of Representatives, 1989).

The result of this imbalance in housing supply and demand has been an increase in the number of people living in substandard, overcrowded conditions and, worst of all, in homelessness. Calculations of the number of homeless people, including children, vary widely. In 1987 national estimates ranged from 35,000 to 500,000 homeless children (U.S. House of Representatives, 1989). Homeless families typically are headed by women with two or three children under age five.

Although the number of children affected by homelessness may be questioned, the effects on children are indisputable. Their physical health is impaired, their school attendance sporadic, and, in one study by the Institute of Medicine (1988), 43 percent of homeless preschoolers examined manifested serious developmental delays. In the face of the rapidly deteriorating housing situation for both middle- and low-income families, public policy responses have not simply been lacking, they have been negative. According to the House Select Committee on Children, Youth and Families (1989), of all the federal budget cuts in low-income programs during the 1980s, reductions in housing assistance were the most severe, exacerbating family housing problems. Thus, although several public policies are in place to address the housing needs of families with young children, their adequacy is alarmingly insufficient. Six million families with incomes at or below the poverty level receive no federal housing assistance whatsoever.

## Health

Assessing the health status of children is problematic because it is difficult to define "health." The World Health Organization (1978) defined it as "a state of complete physical, mental and social well-being and not merely the absence of disease or infirmity" (p. 7). But measures of health in these terms do not exist, so the conventional measures resort to assessing the absence of health: mortality (death) and morbidity (sickness). These measures have their shortcomings for adults, but they are especially inadequate for assessing the health status of children. Because children are developing, decelerations or even reversals in the growth process may not be immediately manifested by overt pathology. The picture of the health of American children that is presented here, in the traditional terms, is necessarily incomplete.

### Mortality

Mortality among children (both rates and causes) is age-linked. Infant mortality—death in the first year of life—in the United States has been reduced by half since the 1970s, but two factors remain especially problematic. The first is the persistent gap between white infants and others. Despite equal reductions among all groups, the African American infant mortality rate remains double that of white infants (8.2 per 1,000 births among whites, 17.7 among African Americans, and 15.2 among other ethnic groups).

The other source of concern is the lack of progress in the United States relative to other developed countries. Among 27 countries, the U.S. infant mortality rate ranked 13th for whites and 26th for African Americans. The single greatest cause of infant deaths is low birthweight (weight lower than normal for the gestational age, or born prematurely). The low birthweight rate among African American infants is about triple that of white infants (U.S. House of Representatives, 1992).

Notable here is the difference in the infant mortality rates measured at two time periods, from one to 28 days after birth and from 28 days to 11 months. Thirty-eight percent of the infants who die do so on the first day. These differences reflect the strides that have been made in prolonging the lives of infants, especially those of low birthweight, rather than in reducing the incidence of low birthweight (Starfield, 1992).

For children who do survive to their first birthday (the vast majority), the death rate declines dramatically and the causes are not precisely reflective of physical ill health. Among preschoolers, injuries are by far the major cause of death (approximately 20 per 100,000 children). Among children ages five to 14, the death rate declines further and is due mostly to injury (about 10 per 100,000) and, to a lesser degree, cancer (fewer than five per 100,000). At adolescence, however, the death rate rises. Again injuries predominate, the majority caused by motor vehicles (most alcohol-related), followed by homicide and suicide. Here an ethnic difference is observed, especially among males. Among white male adolescents the leading cause of death is motor vehicle accidents (60.3 per 100,000), followed by suicide (23.4 per 100,000) and homicide and "legal intervention" (11.5 per 100,000). In contrast, among African American male adolescents, homicide and legal intervention are the leading causes of death (101.8

per 100,000), followed by motor vehicle accidents (38.0 per 100,000) and suicide (14.5 per 100,000). Among female adolescents the death rate is much lower, but the patterns are the same. Suicide rates among younger children are much lower than among adolescents, but, alarmingly, they are rising (U.S. House of Representatives, 1992).

### Morbidity

Chronic and acute illness among children is not as definitively measured as is mortality, especially acute transitory illness such as colds and ear infections. Still, some general observations can be made. In a given year, about three out of five children are free of transitory illness that interferes with their activity or school attendance, but those children who do have such conditions tend to have more than one. Healthy children tend to be free of health problems, whereas those in poor health have several. The linkage between poverty and health status is pronounced. One estimate is that the frequency of health problems among poor children is two to three times that of other children and that the loss of school days is 40 percent to 50 percent higher (Starfield, 1992).

Chronic disabling conditions afflict far fewer children, especially those conditions that are severe or life-threatening. Still, about 2 million children are estimated to have severe conditions, like asthma, that require extensive health care, with each severe condition afflicting less than 10 percent of children. Each life-threatening condition, such as leukemia, afflicts less than 1 percent of children. It is encouraging that the survival rate among these children is now about 90 percent, indicating the successes of medical advancements. For these children the challenge is less to ensure their survival than to find ways to improve their quality of life (Perrin, Guyer, & Lawrence, 1992).

The 1980s saw the extensive growth of two conditions affecting children. The first was the rapid rise of infants prenatally exposed to drugs. It is estimated that 11 percent of children born in 1989 were so afflicted (Chasnoff, 1989). The other condition was acquired immune deficiency syndrome (AIDS).

In 1992 AIDS was thought to afflict fewer than one in 20,000 children, but expectations are that the incidence will increase, with the most common form of transmission being parent to child. AIDS transmission through blood transfusions is declining with increased efficacy of blood supply screening. Pediatric AIDS is highly concentrated among poor children and ethnic minorities. In 1990 reported pediatric AIDS cases were 55 percent African American, 22 percent Hispanic, and 23 percent white, similar to the distribution of AIDS in the female adult population (U.S. House of Representatives, 1992).

### Health Care for Children

By 1992 lack of accessible health care in the United States had reached crisis proportions and president-elect Clinton made health care reform one of his highest priorities. For children, health care is financed either through private insurance or through the federal–state Medicaid program. Access to private insurance largely depends on the labor force attachment of at least one parent. Medicaid eligibility is linked to AFDC eligibility, and because states determine that eligibility, there is wide variation between states. Only 63 percent of children were covered by employer-based insurance in 1990 (Monheit & Cunningham, 1992). For those who meet the eligibility requirements of Medicaid programs, a large set of health care benefits, many specifically targeted to mothers and children (such as prenatal and well-baby care), are mandated.

At the center of the national health care crisis are the uninsured. Between 1977 and 1987 the proportion of uninsured children rose by 40 percent, from 12.7 percent to 17.8 percent—an increase of 3.1 million children (Monheit & Cunningham, 1992). Rising unemployment, declines in employee benefits, and constricted eligibility for Medicaid were contributing factors, but 87 percent of uninsured children had one employed parent. Medicaid is estimated to reach only half the children living in poverty, and about one-third of all children living below poverty have no insurance of any kind. As might be expected, data on health care use by uninsured children indicate that they receive 40 percent to 50 percent less physician and hospital care than do low-income children with insurance (Monheit & Cunningham, 1992).

Health care reform for all Americans that does not address the many particular health needs of children may still fail them. Reforms predicated solely on the status of children's parents rather than on children's specific universal health care needs, such as prenatal care and immunization, will only perpetuate the current maldistribution of care.

## Education

More than any other nation, the United States has ascribed to a national goal of universal education up to high school completion. Four issues are persistent sources of concern over attaining this goal: overall achievement, discrepancies among groups, unfavorable international comparisons, and less-than-universal high school completion.

Overall achievement, as measured by various national tests in different subjects at successive grade or age levels, reflects a persistently mediocre performance level (U.S. House of Representatives, 1992). Long-range trends indicate veritable stagnation in the test score improvements of white students, but a fairly consistent improvement among African American and Hispanic students that gradually will close the gaps between them. Proficiency scores of white students and of all students in advantaged urban and suburban areas have remained fairly constant (U.S. House of Representatives, 1992). In contrast, steady improvements have been made among students in disadvantaged urban areas as well as among both African American and Hispanic students, although their scores are still consistently lower than those of white students and advantaged students at all ages and in all subjects. Despite improvements, the alarming fact is that over half of African American and Hispanic students in 1990 performed at less than the basic levels.

Concern about the achievement of students who remain in school is matched by concern over those who drop out and fail to complete high school. Between 1973 and 1990 the dropout rate for all students fell. In 1990 about 4 percent of white, 6 percent of African American, and 9 percent of Hispanic students left school. Encouraging data from the National Center for Education Statistics (1990) indicate that in 1986 about half of all white and African American students and about a third of Hispanics who had dropped out returned to school. High school completion rates are less favorable, because they reflect the cumulative effects of dropping out. Still, these figures show a consistent rise in high school completion for African American and white students to 78 percent and 87 percent, respectively, in 1990. Unfortunately, there was little change for Hispanics, with around 60 percent completing high school. College completion rates reflect the distribution of high school completion rates, dropping in the 1980s from a peak in the 1970s. Twenty-two percent of white students, 12 percent of African Americans, and 11 percent of Hispanics completed four years of college in 1990 (U.S. House of Representatives, 1992).

## Children with Special Needs

So far, this discussion has covered the common needs of all children: a nurturing, loving family; a decent place to live; maintenance of their physical health; and an education that develops their intellectual potential. Special needs are those not universally shared by developmental peers. These needs might arise out of particular characteristics of individual children, out of deficits in their social resources, or, most likely, from an interaction between the two. The major systems developed to address the needs of these children affirm the problems they present to society. To a large extent these systems are analogous to those that address categories of adult problems—mental retardation, mental illness, and criminal behavior. Other entries in this encyclopedia deal in depth with the children facing these problems and the systems addressing them. This discussion is limited to nascent ideologies that span the treatment of all special needs.

Categorizing children according to the problems they represent for society rather than in the context of their children's total developmental requirements is deleterious to them in at least three ways:

1. Partializing or compartmentalizing children's total functioning can eclipse attention to the whole person and common childhood needs.
2. Basing service systems on isolated problem categories jeopardizes the recognition of related, multiple problems.
3. Compartmentalizing the theoretical understanding of problems, including etiology and amelioration, obscures the commonalities that may underlie the development of multiple sets of problems, and, most important, their common effects on children's development.

The harmful effects of the categorical approach to children's services have received increasing attention in the past several years. Added to the recognized potential for children to "fall through the cracks" in a disarticulated system is a growing concern over the failure of some systems to address the multiple special needs of children and the failure of all systems to address their common needs as children.

In response to these concerns is a growing movement to "decategorize" services or at least to coordinate service delivery systems in the hope of treating the whole child. Advocacy and implementation of these policy goals are ongoing in both the public and the private sectors. One public sector example is the Child and Adolescent Services Programs model initiated through the National Institute of Mental Health. Programs have been developed in over half the states and are intended to provide an integrated core of services, including health, educational, and social services, for severely emotionally disturbed children and their families. A more-ambitious model developed in California's Ventura County that provides a similar set of core services to children entering child welfare, mental health, juvenile justice, and special education systems. Strong advocacy for these integrated services programs has emanated from several private foundations (Soler & Shauffer, 1991).

Integral to these service integration and coordination goals are accompanying goals to care for children in normal family environments. This ideology is akin to the long-standing goal of deinstitutionalization for adults. Although each categorical service system has its own expression of these goals—"least restrictive" in juvenile justice and mental health, "normalization" for the developmentally disabled, and "family preservation" in child welfare—the basic principles are the same. Children, regardless of their problems, should be provided with environments that most closely resemble natural families and with the least possible extrusion from the community (Knitzer & Cole, 1989).

Although decategorization and deinstitutionalization may represent the dominant ideological thrusts of policies for children with special needs, realization of these goals is far from complete. More progress has been made with respect to deinstitutionalization: Far fewer children are in institutions, or at least they are in smaller ones like group homes. Decategorization, especially of funding, is attenuated at the level of demonstration projects.

Apart from the usual barriers to change presented by organizational entrenchment, there may be deeper, more-profound barriers to overcome. The dominant social value that children's needs are best met through the family and the marketplace persists. However, the social problem categories—delinquency, child abuse, and mental illness—have prompted exceptions to this policy stance by socially providing for the children so categorized. As a result, more fundamental changes in social values may take place and service systems for children may be established on the basis of their needs, not the social problems they represent.

## CONCLUSION

Social work has always been concerned with the well-being of children and with enhancing childhood. Efforts of direct practitioners have focused on children with special needs and on providing socialization and developmental group experiences for children and youths. Organized advocacy of policies and programs to enrich children's lives has paralleled practitioner efforts. Although some progress has been made in enhancing the health and education of children, alarmingly greater proportions of children are becoming enmeshed in the hazards of poverty and the assaults on opportunity inflicted by increasing inequality. The effectiveness of both direct practice and advocacy rests on a full appreciation of and commitment to providing all children with a childhood that can develop their full human potential. As the 21st century approaches, social work, through its dual roles, has a major contribution to make to the maturation of American society through the achievement of such a childhood.

## REFERENCES


Chasnoff, I. J. (1989). Drug use and women: Establishing a standard of care. *Annals of the New York Academy of Science, 52*, 208–210.

Cicchetti, D. (1984). The emergence of developmental psychopathology. *Child Development, 55*, 1–7.

Germain, C. B. (1979). *People and environments.* New York: Columbia University Press.

Institute of Medicine, Committee on Health Care for Homeless People. (1988). *Homelessness, health, and human needs.* Washington, DC: National Academy Press.

Knitzer, J., & Cole, E.S. (1989). *Family preservation services: The program challenge for child welfare and child mental health agencies.* New York: Bank Street College of Education.

Monheit, A. C., & Cunningham, P. J. (1992). Children without health insurance. *The Future of Children, 2*(2), 154–170.

National Center for Education Statistics. (1990). *Dropout rates in the United States: 1989.* Washington, DC: U.S. Department of Education.

Perrin, J., Guyer, B., & Lawrence, J. M. (1992). Health care services for children and adolescents. *The Future of Children, 2*(2), 58–77.

Social Security Act of 1935. P.L. 100-360, 49 Stat. 620.

Soler, M., & Shauffer, C. (1991). Fighting fragmentation: Coordination of services for children and families. *Nebraska Law Review, 69*, 278–297.

Starfield, B. (1992). Child and adolescent health status measures. *The Future of Children, 2*(2), 25–39.

U.S. House of Representatives, Select Committee on Children, Youth and Families. (1989). *Children and families: Key trends in the 1980's.* Washington, DC: U.S. Government Printing Office.

U.S. House of Representatives, Select Committee on Children, Youth and Families. (1990a). *Children's well-being: An international comparison.* Washington, DC: U.S. Government Printing Office.

U.S. House of Representatives, Select Committee on Children, Youth and Families (1990b). *Federal programs affecting children and their families, 1990.* Washington, DC: U.S. Government Printing Office.

U.S. House of Representatives, Committee on Ways and Means (1992). *1992 green book: Overview of entitlement programs.* Washington, DC: U.S. Government Printing Office.

Wald, M.S. (1992). *Welfare reform and children's well-being: An analysis of Proposition 165.* Palo Alto, CA: The Stanford Center for the Study of Families, Children, and Youth.

World Health Organization (1978). *Primary health care: Report of the international conference on primary health care.* Geneva: Author.

## Further Reading

Bremner, R. H. (1971). *Children and youth in America: A documentary history, Vol. 1 and II.* Cambridge, MA: Harvard University Press.

Cherlin, A. J. (1988). *The American family and public policy.* Washington, DC: Urban Institute Press.

Dicker, S. (1990). *Stepping stones: Successful advocacy for children.* New York: Foundation for Child Development.

Erickson, E. H. (1959). *Identity and the life cycle.* New York: International Universities Press.

Hernandez, D. T. (1993). *America's children: Resources from family, government, and the economy.* New York: Russell Sage Foundation.

Huston, A. C. (1991). *Children in poverty: Child development and public policy.* Cambridge, England: Cambridge University Press.

Kotlowitz, A. (1991). *There are no children here.* New York: Anchor.

Levine, M., & Levin, A. (1992). *Helping children as social history.* New York: Oxford University Press.

National Science Foundation. (1993). American childhood [Entire issue]. *Daedulus, 121*(1).

Phinney, J. S., & Rotheram, M. J. (Eds.). (1987). *Children's ethnic socialization: pluralism and development.* Newbury Park, CA: Sage Publications.

**Jeanne M. Giovannoni, PhD, ACSW,** is professor emerita, University of California, Los Angeles, School of Public Policy and Social Research, Department of Social Welfare, 247 Dodd Hall, UCLA 145202, 405 Hilgard Avenue, Los Angeles, CA 90024.

### For further information see

Adolescence Overview; Aid to Families with Dependent Children; Child Abuse and Neglect Overview; Child Foster Care; Child Welfare Overview; Children: Direct Practice; Children: Group Care; Children: Mental Health; Families Overview; Health Care: Direct Practice; HIV/AIDS: Pediatric; Homelessness; Human Development; Hunger, Nutrition, and Food Programs; Maternal and Child Health; Poverty; School-Based Services; Social Security; Welfare Employment Programs: Evaluation.

**Key Words**

child poverty
childhood
child welfare

READER'S GUIDE

## Children and Youths

*The following entries contain information on this general topic:*

Adolescence Overview
Adolescent Pregnancy
Adolescents: Direct Practice
Adoption
Child Abuse and Neglect Overview
Child Abuse and Neglect: Direct Practice
Child Care Services
Child Foster Care
Child Labor
Child Sexual Abuse Overview
Child Sexual Abuse: Direct Practice
Child Support
Child Welfare Overview
Childhood
Children: Direct Practice
Children: Group Care
Children: Mental Health
Children's Rights
Families *(See Reader's Guide)*
Gay and Lesbian Adolescents
Juvenile and Family Courts
Juvenile Corrections
Runaways and Homeless Youths
Youth Services

# Children: Direct Practice

**Anthony N. Maluccio**

Social work has a long tradition of direct work with children in a range of settings, such as child welfare, child guidance, hospitals, schools, and neighborhood centers. This entry focuses on generic principles and strategies for direct social work practice with preadolescents and, to a lesser extent, with their families, within an eclectic conceptual framework. The emphasis is on a social work frame of reference rather than on child psychoanalysis or child psychotherapy. Limited attention is given to a social work focus on advocacy and prevention or to specialized topics such as child abuse and neglect, foster family care, or group treatment, which are covered elsewhere in this encyclopedia. Similarly, parental involvement in social work practice is beyond the scope of this entry, although it is, of course, crucial in work with children.

## Children as Clients

Children are not little adults; rather, they are human beings with unique qualities, characteristics, and needs. As a result, work with children as clients has special features, although it should also be emphasized that there are numerous variations to such work, depending on the children's age, ethnic and racial background, socioeconomic stratum, health, and family structure, among other factors. The following are some special features that should be taken into account when working with children:

First, there is children's fluid ego development. Children are highly susceptible to external influences, both positive and negative, and their defenses are not rigidly set. They have a limited ability to deal with internal impulses and external demands. Psychological conflicts are close to the surface or active and are not necessarily repressed or suppressed, as with adults. Children's behaviors (for example, crying by a two-year-old or fear of leaving parents expressed by a three-year-old) often reflect age-appropriate qualities or typical developmental tasks and are not necessarily symptoms of pathological deviations.

Second, children are characterized by action language; that is, they act out their feelings, are more spontaneous than adults, and view play as real and as work. Third, children experience less-rigid boundaries between reality and fantasy, and their fantasies and dreams are less disguised. Fourth, children are dependent on their parents or other adults; therefore, social work practice with children usually involves work with their parents or other caregivers as an integral part of the service.

Finally, children who come to the attention of social workers are, for all intents and purposes, "involuntary clients," and they need to be approached as such. They are generally brought to an agency because their behavior is troubling to someone in their environment. Depending on the particular setting and the children's presenting problems, social workers are called on to play a variety of roles, the most frequent of which are clinician, advocate, mediator, and educator.

## The Helping Relationship

The principles involved in engaging children in the helping relationship with a social worker are basically the same as those for adults, especially adults who are involuntary clients, but they are applied differentially in response not only to such aspects as a child's age and developmental status but to the objectives of initial sessions.

### Objectives

Typical objectives in early sessions include

- gaining the child's confidence and establishing a trusting relationship
- learning about the child's views on her or his situation, needs, and difficulties
- observing how the child responds to the social worker
- arriving at an initial assessment of the child's functioning, qualities, and coping patterns
- establishing a tentative working agreement or contract.

### Guidelines

There are no clear-cut rules for accomplishing these objectives because each child is unique. There are, however, various guidelines, as delineated by such writers as Barker (1990), Greenspan (1981), Hebert (1989), and Mishne (1983). They include the following:

- Let the child set the stage, choose what to talk about, and have as much control as appropriate.
- Offer a frank yet simple explanation of why the child is there.
- Focus on the child as a person in her or his own right, on what she or he is thinking, feeling, and doing now.

- Be sensitive to issues of cultural, economic, ethnic, and racial diversity, including differences between the child and the practitioner in each area.
- Convey respect for the child and her or his world and excitement about her or his capacity to grow.
- Structure the relationship, through such means as explaining the nature of the child's freedom and responsibility, setting limits (for example, what the child can and cannot do in the office), and establishing the format and extent of confidentiality.
- Convey a sense of hope about the child's situation and potential.
- Avoid the common error of directing the child toward areas of the parent's or another adult's interest or concern before the child is ready.
- Avoid interrogating the child through persistent questions.
- Put aside formal interview procedures and let the session flow naturally, using activities and nonverbal tools.

**Resistance**

In line with the analogy of the involuntary client, one may expect that a child will manifest resistance in the child–worker relationship. It is crucial to perceive such "resistive" behavior within the context of the child's struggle to adapt, rather than to perceive it as a negative phenomenon.

In particular, one should understand that children will typically fight direct efforts to change them, especially because these efforts represent a rejection of who they are, of their identity or self-concept. Children must be accepted and cherished for who they are before they are ready to open themselves to change and thus become more vulnerable. It is not easy to convey such a sense of acceptance, because children generally get to a social worker when parents, teachers, or others are directly or indirectly conveying some complaint against them.

**Transference and Countertransference**

The psychoanalytic concept of transference—that is, the irrational repetition of patterns of behavior originating in early relationships—must be modified in social work practice with children. In particular, one should recognize that a child is realistically dependent on adults and is realistically fearful of the social worker's power or authority. In a setting such as a foster care agency or a residential treatment center, for example, transference reactions are not simply symbolic but reflect a child's feelings toward a social worker who has the authority to move the child from one family or placement to another.

Social workers must also be aware of their own potential countertransference reactions. In child welfare settings, these reactions may include the rescue fantasy common among practitioners who work with children who have been subjected to child abuse or neglect, the tendency of some social workers to identify with parents of demanding adolescents, or the tendency of some social workers to provoke or encourage the acting-out behavior of adolescents.

**Therapeutic Value of the Relationship**

Perhaps more so than in work with adults, the helping relationship is often the chief therapeutic vehicle in direct practice with children. Children in treatment typically view such a relationship as a natural life experience rather than as an artificial event. Thus, in play therapy a child is not engaged in *play* (which is an adult concept), but in *life* itself.

The helping relationship can have tremendous therapeutic value; through it, the child can come to regard herself or himself as important and accepted and can gradually reduce the behaviors that elicit negative feedback from others. To be effective in this way, practitioners need to respond sensitively to children, maintain a sincere belief in children, and emerge as genuine human beings from behind their adult inhibitions and defenses (Moustakas, 1972).

To promote therapeutic relationships with children, social workers also need to pay attention to issues of confidentiality and limit setting. Confidentiality is not absolute; a child needs to be helped to see that what goes on or what is shared is confidential between her or him and the social worker, except when there is a threat that the child may hurt herself or himself. If certain kinds of information must be revealed to someone else, such as the parents, the child should be involved as much as possible in the decision. The parents' understandable need for feedback can be met through joint sessions with children and parents or through sharing overall themes, rather than specific points from sessions with the child.

Setting limits with children in the treatment session can be an important part of a corrective emotional experience. The treatment session may indeed be viewed as a laboratory for life, in which the child can learn and grow. For example, when a child threatens a social worker or someone else with physical harm, it is essential to deal with the child's fear of loss of control by restraining her or him. This action, of course, must be carried out in a way that avoids being punitive, conveying rejection, or displaying one's anger.

## ASSESSMENT

Children who come to the attention of social workers present a wide range of backgrounds, problems, needs, and diagnostic categories. In light of social work's emphasis on the person-in-situation, it is useful to view assessment in cases involving children within an ecological framework that takes into account the children's cultural, socioeconomic, ethnic, and racial diversity; child development theories; and findings of research on coping and adaptation (Garbarino, 1992; Germain, 1991). Such a framework incorporates analyses of three key features:

1. the child's social situation
2. the child's development, including functioning and adaptive patterns
3. the interaction between the child's situation and the child's development and functioning.

### Child's Social Situation

The process of formulating an assessment begins with a broad understanding of the environment that impinges on the child, including the family dynamics and interaction; social context and social systems; ethnic and racial characteristics; and environmental pressures, demands, and opportunities. Because this environment covers a great deal of ground, the social worker selects the most significant factors that are impinging on the child and family, following the concepts of the family as a system of interacting forces and as a system in interaction with other forces or systems in its environment.

The major practice principles flowing from the systems concepts are these:

- "Parents from different ethnic groups employ culturally prescribed strategies to teach children how to cope with anxiety" as well as other challenges to their development (Gibbs, Huang, & Associates, 1989, p. 4).
- Children may be reacting to certain pressures or realities within the family. For instance, parental discord in a family with a child who is about to go to school for the first time may exaggerate the child's fear of separation.
- Children may be the focus of family tension or conflict, and their behavior may reflect the family's problems and patterns of interaction and communication. In some families, for example, children may become scapegoats.
- Children's functioning is influenced by the family's coping patterns and exchange with its environment. For example, a child's fear of interacting with other children may be compounded by the family's realistic concern about living in a neighborhood with a high crime rate.

### Child's Development and Functioning

The purpose of this area of the assessment is to achieve an in-depth understanding of the child's growth and functioning within the impinging social situation. Therefore, the social worker must ask these key questions:

- Where is the child developmentally?
- What is expected of her or him, that is, what are the crucial tasks in that particular life stage?
- How is the child managing these tasks? What are her or his adaptive patterns or typical ways of coping?

Following are three useful principles for addressing the foregoing questions. First, understand where the child is in relation to what is expected in that particular developmental phase. Is the child showing age-appropriate behavior? Where is the child in relation to her or his sexual identity? Is the child retarded in some aspect of development? Is the child regressing in response to some traumatic life event?

In considering these questions, it is important to pay attention to sociocultural and other variations. One should view the stages of child development proposed by various theorists (DiLeo, 1977; Newman & Newman, 1987) as guidelines rather than as fixed traits. As research on human development among diverse ethnic groups has shown, there is a broad range of behaviors that can be considered "normal" (Garbarino, 1992). In this connection, Germain (1991) conceptualized human development, life transitions, and life events as the outcomes of person–environment processes, "rather than as separate segments of life confined to predetermined ages and stages of experience" (p. 141). In addition, Gibbs et al. (1989) presented a conceptual framework for assessing the influence of ethnicity on the development of children of color.

Second, understand the child's unique ways of coping and how they can be strengthened if useful and modified if not. Children use a range of coping techniques (Garmezy & Rutter, 1983; Haggerty et al., 1994). For example, a review of empirical studies identified 15 different strategies that children use to cope with stress (Ryan-Wenger, 1992). In particular, children of color demonstrate diverse coping strengths in the face of oppressive conditions (Pinderhughes, 1989).

Third, analyze what the child is conveying through her or his behavior. What does the behavior indicate about the child's ego functioning and coping? The child's symptoms reflect her or his adaptive mechanisms. Some children in foster care, for instance, express their fears about being removed through anger, withdrawal, or other behaviors that say "I'm afraid to grow up."

In this regard Gibbs et al. (1989) underscored that practitioners "should always use knowledge about a child's ethnic background as a *general* guide to psychosocial assessment but should always be mindful of the individual child's unique characteristics, situation, symptoms, defenses, and coping strategies" (p. 15).

To help analyze a child's behavior and development, social workers use formal evaluations conducted by psychologists, psychiatrists, neurologists, and other specialists. In addition, they may use a variety of diagnostic tools, including drawings, questionnaires, play materials, games, stories, and picture books, that complement direct interviewing and observations of a child.

The choice of diagnostic tools depends on such factors as what the social worker is comfortable with; the appropriateness of the tool in relation to the child's developmental status and other characteristics; and the social worker's primary purpose, which may include obtaining fantasy material, testing the child's ability to concentrate, or eliciting feelings and perceptions of self or family.

Whatever the purpose, the findings should be used as one piece of a puzzle, as part of the overall complex of information that has been gathered, rather than in isolation. Guided by a research perspective, the social worker needs to test any hypothesis or inference derived from the use of a diagnostic tool against the available evidence. Moreover, it is important to analyze the findings within the developmental context of the particular child, to avoid the danger of ascribing pathology when the main issue may be one of immaturity in development.

### Interaction of a Child's Situation and Her or His Development and Functioning

In this part of assessment, the key questions are, What happens when a child with certain qualities and coping patterns meets a particular environmental situation? What must be changed to achieve a more mutually satisfying transaction? Additional questions are these: How are the child and family affecting each other? What resources for growth, or blocks to, are there in the child's and family's impinging environment? What should be added or modified to provide a more nurturing environment that is conducive to the child's natural growth and development?

Practice principles pertaining to these questions include the following:

- Analyze what is happening in the parent–child interaction. The idea of the reciprocal nature of the relationship between a child and her or his parents is especially noteworthy. Children are active participants in interactions with others and initiate behaviors in response to their own needs and traits, as well as in reaction to others. For example, a child who tends to whine is likely to provoke parental frustration and rejection; the parents' response may lead to further negative behaviors by the child and perhaps abuse by the parents, particularly if they are overwhelmed by other problems.
- Understand that parents' capacity to meet a child's needs may vary with each phase of development. Some parents, for example, are much more comfortable or competent with young children than with adolescents.
- Identify resources in the environment that may be helpful for the child. A teacher, for instance, may be supportive to a child whose parents are in the process of divorce.
- Identify blocks in a child's developmental process. In schools, for example, children whose organic impairments, such as hearing loss or visual impairment, are not detected for a while may tend to act out, be withdrawn, or have learning problems.
- Identify the supports that the parents need to be more effective in their roles. For example, research in child welfare agencies has demonstrated that in some families out-of-home placement of children can be prevented by the provision of supports such as day care, self-help groups, and income maintenance (Fraser, Pecora, & Haapala, 1991).

## Approaches to Treatment

On the basis of the analysis and assessment described thus far, a social worker can formulate a treatment that is geared to the unique needs and characteristics of a particular child and his or her family system. Treatment plans and goals may be established through the use of a variety of different approaches that generally include, to one degree or another, working not only with the child but with the parents; the family system; collaterals, such as teachers; and other significant people.

The major approaches social workers use in direct practice with children are psychoanalytically oriented psychotherapy (see Mishne, 1983); behavior modification (see Graziano & Mooney, 1984); and nondirective, client-centered therapy

TABLE 1

## Major Social Work Approaches to Direct Practice with Children

### I. Psychoanalytically Oriented Psychotherapy

A. Unit of Attention

1. The child.
2. The parent–child system.
3. The family.

B. Objects of Help

1. To resolve personal or interpersonal conflicts.
2. To modify internal processes.
3. To achieve individual change in the child.

C. Role of the Helper

1. Primarily a therapist.
2. The client–therapist relationship is largely hierarchical.

D. Helping Processes

1. Study: historical emphasis; clinical observations; focus on child's feelings, defenses, and adaptive patterns; emphasis on child's interaction with significant others, including the therapist; some attention to the environmental situation.
2. Assessment: normative assessment, with an emphasis on diagnosis, psychodynamics, and pathology; focus on ego functioning, unconscious motivation, and link between the past and the present.
3. Treatment: provide treatment within the context of the child–therapist relationship; use of the environment, but emphasis on clinical approaches, such as interview and verbalization; the client's motivation is crucial; emphasis on corrective emotional experience and on gaining self-awareness; intrapsychic, interpersonal focus or both.

E. Structural Arrangements

1. Primarily office interviews.
2. Short-term or open-ended treatment.

F. Critique: It is most effective with a narrow range of people and problems (for example, verbal, motivated, "neurotic" people), limited attention to environmental or systemic change, and a preoccupation with psychopathology.

### II. Behavior Modification

A. Unit of Attention

1. The child in her or his social context.
2. The parents or caregivers.

B. Objects of Help

1. To reshape the child's behavior.
2. To build new modes of interaction between the child and significant others.
3. To reinforce the child's positive coping patterns.

C. Role of the Helper

1. Teacher, guide, and consultant; the relationship may be important (for example, to motivate or support), but is not necessarily viewed as the chief vehicle of help.

D. Helping Processes

1. Study: focus on observable behavior, observation in the child's natural environment as much as possible, keeping records of the child's behavior.
2. Assessment: simple, practical problem definition; focus on behaviors of concern to the client or significant others; effort to understand child in her or his natural surroundings, rather than to test or interview the child in a clinical setting; no assessment of the child's internal states, but behavior analysis—particularly events that lead to learning certain behaviors (reinforcement).
3. Treatment: develop a plan of therapy on the basis of the behavior analysis; motivate the child by involving him or her in programming; emphasis on behavior shaping through incremental changes; control of contingencies reinforcing child's responses; use of environment and training of parents; variety of behavior modification techniques, such as modeling.

E. Structural Arrangements

1. Treatment in the office, as well as in the child's environment.
2. The importance of controlling environmental stimuli or influences is stressed.

F. Critique: Its effectiveness with certain populations (for example, chronic psychiatric patients, autistic children) or children with specific symptoms (such as tics) has been demonstrated empirically, but it is of questionable value with multiproblem situations. It is more effective in closed settings in which there is greater opportunity to control the environment. There are ethical issues in regard to the use of certain techniques (for instance, aversive conditioning). The emphasis on specificity in formulating problems and goals and the need to set gradual expectations of change is especially valuable.

### III. Nondirective, Client-Centered Therapy

A. Unit of Attention

1. The child.
2. The parents or other significant figures.

B. Objects of Help

1. To free up the child's drive toward self-realization.
2. To provide a good "growing ground" for the child's development.

C. Role of the Helper

1. Primarily a counselor to the child, the parents, or both.
2. A consultant to others involved with the child, such as teachers.
3. The client–social worker relationship is symmetrical more than hierarchical.

D. Helping Processes

1. Study: emphasis on the here and now; the child's feelings, reactions, and attitudes; the feelings of significant others.
2. Assessment: no diagnosis per se; sensitivity to the child's expressed feelings and attitudes, rather than underlying feelings and attitudes. Key questions: (1) What is getting in the way of the child's self-realization? (2) How is the child's drive for self-realization being expressed? How does the child deal with frustration resulting from blocks in the drive for self-realization?
3. Treatment: primarily experiential; the child experiences the self as he or she is; extensive emphasis on the client–social worker relationship, which provides an opportunity to express the self freely and thus grow into an accepting, warm, secure adult; the use of play, which is seen as the child's natural medium of expression, is prominent. The overall goal is to help the child develop a consistent philosophy of life, gain strength to be herself or himself, and form honest relationships with others. Reflection and clarification of the client's feelings and attitudes are used extensively. There is also emphasis on helping parents and others to become more understanding of child.

E. Structural Arrangements

1. Office interviews.
2. A well-equipped playroom.
3. Open-ended and usually long-term treatment.

F. Critique: It is more appropriate for young children, especially those who tend to be withdrawn, who have capacity to relate to adults, or both. The child's self-determination or power is overemphasized and inadequate attention is paid to the environment.

(see Moustakas, 1959). Some form of play therapy is generally used within each of these approaches, especially with young children. Other approaches, which are beyond the scope of this entry, include cognitive therapy, family therapy, and psychoeducation. Some social workers consistently use one approach, whereas others draw from various modalities in an eclectic fashion or in response to what seems to work best with each child.

The three approaches are outlined and compared in Table 1, in relation to the following components: unit of attention, object of help, role of helper, helping processes, and structural arrangements. In addition, a brief critique of the effectiveness or appropriateness of each approach with different child populations is presented. It should be noted that this critique is tentative because there has been little research in this area of social work practice. There is, however, extensive research on the effects of child psychotherapy in general, which Weisz and Weiss (1993) reviewed and summarized. It should also be stressed that in the field of social work as a whole, there is a continuing need to develop and refine practice approaches that are more responsive to children and families from different socioeconomic, ethnic, and racial groups.

Finally, all three approaches pay careful attention to the meaning and handling of termination in each case. As much as possible, the decision to end treatment is based not only on evidence of removal of the symptoms or of the pathology but on an appraisal of the child's development and "capacity to handle problematic environmental conditions" (Mishne, 1983, p. 327). The emphasis in the termination phase is on helping the child to consolidate treatment gains and helping parents to strengthen their parenting skills.

## References


Barker, P. (1990). *Clinical interviews with children and adolescents.* New York: W. W. Norton.

DiLeo, J. H. (1977). *Child development: Analysis and synthesis.* New York: Brunner/Mazel.

Fraser, M., Pecora, P., & Haapala, D. (1991). *Families in crisis.* New York: Aldine de Gruyter.

Garbarino, J. (1992). *Children and families in the social environment* (2nd ed.). New York: Aldine de Gruyter.

Garmezy, N., & Rutter, M. (1983). *Stress, coping and development in children.* New York: McGraw-Hill.

Germain, C. B. (1991). *Human behavior in the social environment—An ecological view.* New York: Columbia University Press.

Gibbs, J. T., Huang, L. N., & Associates (1989). *Children of color—Psychological interventions with minority youth.* San Francisco: Jossey-Bass.

Graziano, A. M., & Mooney, K. G. (1984). *Children and behavior therapy.* New York: Aldine de Gruyter.

Greenspan, S. (1981). *The clinical interview of the child—Theory and practice.* New York: McGraw-Hill.

Haggerty, R. J., Sherrod, L. R., Garmezy, N., & Rutter, M. (1994). *Stress, risk, and resilience in children and adolescents.* Cambridge, England: Cambridge University Press.

Hebert, M. (1989). *Working with children and their families.* Chicago: Lyceum Books.

Mishne, J. (1983). *Clinical work with children.* New York: Free Press.

Moustakas, C. E. (1959). *Psychotherapy with children—The living relationship.* New York: Ballantine Books.

Moustakas, C. E. (Ed.). (1972). *The child's discovery of himself.* New York: Ballantine Books.

Newman, B. M., & Newman, P. R. (1987). *Development through life: A psychosocial approach.* Chicago: Dorsey Press.

Pinderhughes, E. (1989). *Understanding race, ethnicity, and power.* New York: Free Press.

Ryan-Wenger, N. M. (1992). A taxonomy of children's coping strategies: A step toward theory development. *American Journal of Orthopsychiatry, 62,* 256–263.

Weisz, J. R., & Weiss, B. (1993). *Effects of psychotherapy with children and adolescents.* Newbury Park, CA: Sage Publications.


## Further Reading


Aldgate, J., & Simmonds, J. (Eds.). (1988). *Direct work with children—A guide for social work practitioners.* London: B. T. Batsford.

Ho, M. H. (1992). *Minority children and adolescents.* Newbury Park, CA: Sage Publications.

Lynch, E. W., & Hanson, M. J. (Eds.). (1992). *Developing cross-cultural competence: A guide for working with young children and their families.* Baltimore: Paul H. Brookes.

Pecora, P. J., Whittaker, J. K., & Maluccio, A. N. (1992). *The child welfare challenge—Policy, practice, and research.* New York: Aldine de Gruyter.

Zigler, E., & Finn-Stevenson, M. S. (1993). *Children in a changing world: Development and social issues.* Monterey, CA: Brooks/Cole.


**Anthony N. Maluccio, DSW, ACSW,** is professor, Boston College, Graduate School of Social Work, Chestnut Hill, MA 02167.

### For further information see

Adolescents: Direct Practice; Child Abuse and Neglect: Direct Practice; Child Sexual Abuse: Direct Practice; Children: Mental Health; Direct Practice Overview; Families Overview; Family Therapy; Goal Setting and Intervention Planning; Human Development; Interviewing; Legal Issues: Low-Income and Dependent People; Psychosocial Approach; Runaways and Homeless Youths; School Social Work Overview; Social Development; Social Work Practice: Theoretical Base.

**Key Words**
children direct practice

# Children: Group Care

**James K. Whittaker**

This entry addresses the question of what constitutes quality group child care services and what their function should be in an overall continuum of services for children, youths, and families. The historical and political context of group child care is reviewed, as are present demographic trends, evaluation research, and practice innovations. The challenges in group child care for social work practice, policy, and evaluation research include an ecological focus in assessment and intervention; greater emphasis on family involvement; a more comprehensive approach to evaluation, including qualitative research and systematic analysis of routinely gathered data; greater attention to prevention of institutional abuse and neglect; a redefinition of the "success" criterion in group child care; greater specification of intervention components; more attention to maintenance and generalization of treatment gains; and a focus on quality assurance.

Social workers play a number of key roles in the delivery of group child care services. Bachelor's-level practitioners frequently function as direct care staff, and master's-level practitioners often provide group and individual treatment as well as family involvement and aftercare services. Social work administrators are involved in program development and policy-level practice in a wide range of agency settings in child welfare, child mental health, and juvenile justice. Master's- and doctoral-level social work researchers are involved in research on the effectiveness of group child care services, and many social workers are involved in advocacy and reform efforts through regional, state, and national associations such as NASW and the Child Welfare League of America.

Group child care is a service in flux. Concerns about effectiveness, cost, and child safety have stimulated much public debate. The redesign of group care services for troubled children and their families will require the talents of social workers at many different levels within the profession. Perhaps the key question for the immediate future is, What defines effective group child care services, and how narrow or wide a role will they play in the overall continuum of social services for children and families?

## Context for Group Child Care

The debate over institutional child care refuses to die. Even when professional views and popular opinion are virtually unanimous about a particular use of institutional care (for example, the undesirability of orphan asylums), counterarguments may still be heard. So strong was the sentiment against the use of group care settings for purely dependent children that by the mid-20th century, less than 10 percent of children in such settings fit the description of true orphans, and by far the greater proportion of purely dependent children were being served in foster family care (Kadushin & Martin, 1988). The "orphan asylum," for all intents and purposes, was out of business and therefore out of public consciousness save for the occasional treatment by social historians or the publicity generated by popular culture, such as the musical *Annie*.

### Practice and Policy Issues

In the 1980s, with the specter of increasing numbers of "crack babies" from "no-parent families," some serious proposals were advanced to reinvent the orphan asylum as a social response to what was perceived to be a growing class of needy and dependent children. These proposals were quickly countered and roundly dismissed by social workers and other advocates of family support and family preservation. It is significant, however, that the proposals surfaced at all, given the overwhelming weight of conventional professional wisdom against the use of group care settings for the purpose of rearing children to maturity (Ford & Kroll, 1990). Were the proposals born of desperation, a quick fix to a problem with staggering implications for social services? Or were they the conscious expression of some long-standing doubt about the adequacy of new service initiatives such as family preservation, specialized foster care, and special-needs adoption to meet the continuing care, treatment, and maturational needs of seriously drug-impaired children? Whatever the particulars, this brief rekindling of interest in orphanages reflects the feelings of ambivalence that surround group child care services. Wolins (1974) put it this way:

> Over the years the full and part time group care programs that have existed in this country have fallen into disuse—an occurrence that most professionals, who saw little good and much evil in their impact on children, greeted with considerable satisfaction. As

> professionals withdrew their approbation the programs deteriorated; innovation ceased, and cycles of predictions of bad results and their fulfillment spiraled the programs downward. (p. 1)

One result of this inattention is what practitioners in one leading residential agency cite as the growing gulf between theory and public policy, on the one hand, and everyday practice reality, on the other (Small, Kennedy, & Bender, 1991). Basic questions of policy and practice about group child care remain unanswered:

- Should group care be seen as a treatment of first or last resort?
- With what types of children is it most and least effective?
- What is the proper relationship of residential group care services, in-home family preservation services, therapeutic foster care, and other community-based alternatives? What relative proportions of each should exist in an overall continuum of care?
- What are the critical ingredients in a successful group care program, and how can they be implemented, monitored, and maintained?
- How should we measure success in residential child care, and what is a proper metric for assessing benefits and costs?

### Issues Related to Residential Services

Residential provision of any kind today is viewed with extreme suspicion and antipathy. It is often seen as part of the problem and not part of the solution. The many reasons for this attitude involve issues of cost, effectiveness, and presumed secondary social and psychological costs of the service. Specific reasons for the relatively low opinion about residential services include

- lack of clear-cut diagnostic indicators for residential placement
- inclination of service systems to use residential placement as a treatment of first rather than last resort
- presumption of intrusiveness, particularly with respect to the youth's biological family, and the resulting disempowerment of families
- potential for a variety of physical and psychological abuses and for institutional neglect
- absence of hard evidence of treatment effectiveness, particularly for long-term outcomes
- difficulty in documenting and agreeing on the critical components of effective residential services and ensuring their presence through quality control procedures
- high cost of residential services for the relatively few youths served, which, some argue, retards the growth of more preventive front-end services.

Underlying these specifics is a deep sense of pessimism about the prospects for change. Social historians such as Rothman (1980) have argued that institutions are essentially unreformable. Others have argued that institutions are flawed either in their original intent (social control) or in their effects—essentially to perpetuate a cycle of placement–replacement. Lost in this argument are distinctions between types of residential provision—public versus voluntary versus proprietary, large versus small, and treatment-oriented versus custodial. This perception is nowhere more evident than in the current antiresidential sentiment engendered by reports in the popular press of scandals in private psychiatric hospitals for youths.

If for no other reason than cost alone, policymakers need a better understanding of what can reasonably be expected from various types of residential care in contrast to nonresidential alternatives. The National Mental Health Association's (NMHA, 1989) estimates of the cost per episode of various types of care for seriously emotionally disturbed children are shown in Table 1. This same report noted that residential care was rising, particularly the placement of youths in private psychiatric facilities and the use of out-of-state placements. The report concluded that the more than $1 billion that states spend each year on out-of-state residential placement might be more properly spent on nonresidential community-based alternatives.

## Historical Highlights

### Milestones

Some of the more important historical milestones for group care and treatment services are the following:

- The Ursuline nuns of New Orleans established an orphanage in 1729 to care for children orphaned by an Indian massacre at Natchez. This was the first children's institution in the present boundaries of the United States (Bremner, 1970; Whittaker, 1971a).
- The House of Refuge, the first institution for juvenile delinquents, was founded in New York City in 1825. Similar institutions were founded in Boston in 1826 and Philadelphia in 1928 (Bremner, 1970).
- The Lyman School, the first state reform school for boys, was founded in Westborough, Massachusetts, in 1847 on the model of the German agricultural reformatory. It is not without irony that the Lyman School was also the first state

TABLE 1

**Types of Care for Seriously Emotionally Disturbed Children and Cost per Episode**

| Type of Care | Description | Cost |
|---|---|---|
| Intensive in-home crisis services | Six weeks of intensive in-home crisis counseling may be offered to prevent removal of children from home and to stabilize the family situation. | $1,100 |
| Day treatment | A year of treatment in a day treatment program may be offered to children who are seriously emotionally disturbed. Often, this treatment has prevented the removal of the child from home. | $15,000–$18,000 |
| State hospital | Nationally, the average daily cost in a state hospital for treatment of adolescents and children is $299. The cost per episode would be $38,272 based on an average length of stay of 128 days. | $38,272 |
| Residential treatment facility | Nationally, the average daily cost in a residential treatment facility is $111.67. Because of incomplete data this rate is considered an underestimate of the actual cost of the service. Based on an average length of stay of 15.4 months, the cost per episode would be $52,300. | $51,592 |

SOURCE: National Mental Health Association. (1989). *Invisible Children Project: Final Report*. Alexandria, VA: Author.

training school to close in the now famous "Massachusetts experiment" in deinstitutionalization in the early 1970s (Bremner, 1970, 1974; see also Coates, Miller, & Ohlin, 1978).

- The New York Children's Aid Society sent its first band of children to the West in 1855. What Charles Loring Brace and others saw as an effort to save children from the evil influences of the city and congregate institutions, others—notably, the Irish Catholic community in New York City, where children were most affected—saw as a nativist plot to separate their children from their culture, families, and religion. One direct outgrowth of this placing-out movement was the rise in Catholic and other denominational institutions to care for destitute, dependent, and neglected children (Bremner, 1970).
- The move in the late 19th century from congregate to cottage-style institutions was an attempt to achieve a more familylike atmosphere (Rothman, 1980).
- The inception and growth of the mental hygiene movement, beginning with the work of William Healy in Chicago, emphasized classification of childhood disorders, differential diagnosis, and treatment (Bremner, 1970; Whittaker, 1971b).
- Many children's institutions in the 1930s, 1940s, and 1950s moved slowly from the care of essentially dependent children to the residential treatment of emotionally disturbed children (Bettelheim & Sylvester, 1949; Bremner, 1974; Mayer & Blum, 1971; Redl & Wineman, 1957).
- Since the early 1970s, exposure of abuse and neglect in residential institutions for disturbed and delinquent children has been coupled with, and in part is responsible for, efforts to deinstitutionalize service programs in mental health, juvenile correction, child welfare, and mental retardation (Blatt, 1992; Child Abuse and Neglect in Residential Institutions, 1978; Coates et al., 1978; Hanson, 1982; National Commission on Children in Need of Parents, 1979; Taylor, 1981; Wolfensberger, 1972; Wooden, 1976).

### Phases in Residential Care

These events in the history of group child care cluster in four phases.

***Physical separation.*** First, the period of physical separation sought to extricate dependent, delinquent, and "defective" children from indiscriminate mixing in almshouses, workhouses, jails, and the like. Instead of housing them with adults, policymakers provided a separate set of institutions specifically for their use (Whittaker, 1971a).

***Cottage movement.*** Then, in the late 19th century, a move began to replace cold, barracks-style institutions with smaller, family-style units staffed by houseparents. Although the resulting "cottages"—which sometimes contained more than 25 children—were often quite large by today's standards, they maintained at least some semblance of a familylike atmosphere.

***Psychological phase.*** In this phase, begun in the early 20th century, reformers sought to transfer the central organizational and treatment concepts of the emergent child guidance movement to the institution (Whittaker, 1971b). These concepts included use of psychological tests, the psychiatric team concept, and the delineation of child care and child treatment functions. The pioneering work in the late 1940s and early 1950s of Hershel Alt, Bruno Bettelheim, Fritz Redl, and others developed various psychoanalytically grounded expressions of the therapeutic milieu, with much more attention to factors such as group dynamics and a much greater focus on child care staff members as the primary agents of treatment.

***Ecological phase.*** Finally, what might be called the ecological or environmental phase was simulated at least in part by an increasing corpus of outcome evaluations that showed that differences in treatment outcome were related more to factors such as the presence or absence of postplacement community supports than to factors such as caseworker judgment, degree of success achieved in a program, treatment model, or severity of presenting problems (Whittaker & Pecora, 1984). These findings, as well as the broader policy thrust toward deinstitutionalization and service normalization, forced the attention of residential programs to shift from an almost total preoccupation with what went on inside the milieu to such external factors as development of community linkages, family work, and aftercare. Also contributing to this trend were natural environment interventions by applied behavior analysts and psychoeducators that boldly moved treatment from the clinic to the client's own milieu (Hawkins, Peterson, Schweid, & Bijou, 1966; Hobbs, 1966; Rhodes, 1967; Risley & Wolf, 1966; Tharp & Wetzel, 1969).

An important question to raise about the historical evolution of group services for children is whether it represents true progress in society's sincere attempts to care for children in need or whether some less obvious purpose is being served through a mechanism (child removal) that despite cosmetic changes remains essentially the same. As noted, some historians, such as Rothman (1980), have argued that social control has always been a major driving force in the creation and maintenance of institutions, whereas others, such as Downs and Sherraden (1983), have illuminated multiple reasons for institutional expression at any particular time. Many reformers in the children's field would argue that the sheer size of the residential budget and the entrenched advocacy of existing programs constitute a powerful force working against innovation and change.

## Varieties of Residential Child Care Services

Residential child care services include many different types of services. For example, child care may be provided in group homes for adolescent status offenders; residential treatment centers for emotionally disturbed children; state training schools for adolescent delinquents; shelter care facilities for street children; respite care group homes for developmentally disabled adolescents; and group residences for "dependent-neglected" children. Each of these types of group child care services shares the common element of caring for groups, however small, of special-needs children, 24 hours a day. The 24-hour care is the most obvious commonality.

National standard-setting associations recognize several different types of group care settings for children who are dependent, who have behavioral and emotional difficulties, or both. These include residential treatment centers, group homes, crisis and shelter care facilities, children's psychiatric facilities, and respite care facilities (Child Welfare League of America, 1984). Depending on state and local jurisdictions, group care services for children might be provided under mental health, juvenile correction, child welfare, or developmental disabilities auspices or under a combination of two or more of these. One must be wary of references to "group and institutional care" as though it were a single entity. This segment of the service continuum contains a range of different kinds of residential placements that overlap considerably in terms of definition, purpose, population served, and bureaucratic responsibility.

Concepts used to describe residential care are not well specified, nor is the implied progression of serving the most "severely disturbed" child in more sophisticated and restricted residential treatment centers empirically borne out in existing programs where severely disturbed children are increasingly being treated in less restrictive, more family-oriented settings (National Mental Health Association [NMHA], 1989). Moreover, Maluccio and Marlow's (1972) observation of two decades ago regarding the placement process in institutional care is still largely correct:

> The decision to place a child in residential treatment is presently a highly individualized matter based on a complex set of idiosyncratic factors defying categorization. The literature does not indicate agreement on consistent criteria or universal guidelines and it is not certain whether institutions diverse in origin, philosophy, policy, and clientele can agree on a basic set of premises. (p. 239)

## Integrated Treatment Approach

*Therapeutic milieu* has been used to describe the process of environmental group treatment. Whittaker (1979) defined it as

> a specifically designed environment in which the events of daily living are used as formats for teaching competence in basic life skills. The living environment

> becomes both a means and a context for growth and change, informed by a culture that stresses learning through living. (p. 36)

*Teaching formats* here include rule structures, daily routines, play, and activities, as well as more individualized education, counseling, and treatment services for children and their parents.

Models of residential treatment so defined typically avoid strictly psychogenic explanations of problem behavior and proceed instead from an essentially developmental–educational base. This typically involves identification of skill deficits and the teaching of social competence in such areas as managing emotionality, developing more effective interpersonal skills, and mastering proximate and distal community environments. Examples of such residential programs include Project RE-ED, developed by Hobbs (1982) in the early 1960s, and the Walker School in Needham, Massachusetts, developed by Trieschman (Small et al., 1991; Trieschman, Whittaker, & Brendtro, 1969; Whittaker, 1979).

Obviously, not all residential treatment centers adopt such an integrated approach to the therapeutic milieu. For example, in recent definitions by the Child Welfare League of America, "treatment services" are listed as separate from work on behalf of or directly with children in a therapeutic milieu. This separation of treatment functions—often along disciplinary lines—has from the beginning been a source of staff conflict and has plagued the development of a unified and consistent total milieu approach to working with children (Piliavin, 1963; Whittaker, 1971b; Whittaker & Trieschman, 1972). Some residential programs, such as Project RE-ED, have attempted to overcome this separation of service by combining educational and treatment functions in a single role: the teacher–counselor (Hobbs, 1982). The teaching family model of group home treatment has similarly combined all significant helping functions in a single pivotal role, the "teaching parent," with auxiliary support services provided by a training consultant (Phillips, Phillips, Fixsen, & Wolf, 1974).

Ultimately, debate on the efficacy of residential treatment and other group care programs will improve with the ability to specify the essential dimensions and components of both kinds of services. Wells (1991b) called for a new partnership between researchers and practitioners, and Curry (1991) delineated the types of studies that must be implemented to determine what critical components any form of residential child care must have.

## Characteristics of Residential Group Care

Analysts have only a partial picture of national trends in group child care. For example, the most recent national systematic and comprehensive census of children and youths specifically in group care settings was completed by Pappenfort and his colleagues at the University of Chicago, for the focal year 1981. This study updates an earlier survey that Pappenfort conducted in 1965 (Dore, Young, & Pappenfort, 1984; Pappenfort, Kilpatrick, & Roberts, 1973; Pappenfort, Young, & Marlow, 1983). Although clearly dated in its aggregate figures, many trends observed continue to hold, for example:

- Although the number of residential group care facilities has increased markedly since 1966, the number of children and youths in care has declined.
- The rate of growth has been concentrated in two areas: facilities for children and youths who are considered either delinquent or status offenders and mental health facilities.
- Facilities in all categories declined in size from 1966 to 1982. In 1966 less than half of the facilities surveyed had fewer than 26 children and youths in residence. Yet the majority of facilities surveyed in 1982 had 26 or fewer children.
- Among the facilities surveyed in 1982, the number of children was almost evenly divided between public and private facilities. Slightly more than one-third of all children were in juvenile justice facilities, one-fourth were in mental health facilities, and about one-fifth were in child welfare facilities.

In certain streams of care, nongovernmental services play a major role. For example, a large portion of services for emotionally disturbed people are provided in voluntary, nonprofit, and proprietary agencies. Some analysts are concerned with what appears to be a shift of youngsters (especially status offenders) from more traditional streams of care (for example, juvenile justice) to private drug rehabilitation and psychiatric residential settings that are often proprietary (Schwartz, Jackson-Beelk, & Anderson, 1983).

### Number of Children in Care

Seen in the aggregate, group care does not seem to be expanding out of control. In fact, children in group care represent the smaller proportion of children in all substitute care who in total make up less than 1 percent of all U.S. children ages 0 to 18. The overwhelming majority of children under 18 live with their families (Whittaker, 1988). Nevertheless, Gershenson (1990) observed that

> about one child enters substitute care every 35 seconds. During the year 750,000 will be admitted to juvenile facilities, 200,000 to child welfare facilities and at least 50,000 to psychiatric hospitals or residential treatment centers. (p. 1)

### Types of Problems

By any measure, a significant and disturbing number of children are removed from their families, albeit temporarily and (for some) voluntarily. These children are being placed without benefit of preventive, intensive in-home services, which may have obviated the need for placement (NMHA, 1989). Children entering group care settings exhibit a range of problems, including serious emotional disturbances, substance abuse, all forms of child abuse and neglect, delinquent behaviors, and learning disabilities. These labels do not give a full picture of the child coming into residential care. A clinical view helps to describe these "children of action and impulse" (Ekstein, 1983):

> Their records are replete with litanies of behavior so dangerous that one marvels that they have so far survived physically intact. These are children who throw chairs at their teachers when asked to sit down; dismantle principals' offices when sent there; and strike out with fists, rocks and teeth at other children, at parents, at grandparents. Their classic response [when asked] what they would do if threatened by a younger child is "get a big stick and beat him to a pulp." These are children who treat their own bodies with total disregard for safety, hurling themselves into busy streets on bicycles without brakes, climbing to dangerous heights in trees and buildings. Many of their families have other equally impulsive and aggressive members who lash out verbally and physically without regard for social consequences.... In one family with two boys in placement, the eight year old had been hit by a car while riding his big wheeled tricycle in a major thoroughfare; the six year old had attempted to throw himself out of a second floor window; and the father was in jail for throwing the two year old out the window in a fit of rage. (Small et al., 1991, pp. 328–329)

### Family Involvement

Intake studies of children entering residential care settings typically show a high percentage coming from families headed by single parents. These families are often faced with a host of psychological, legal, and financial problems. Having a difficult child is but one component of an overall constellation of problems (Fitzharris, 1985; Wells & Whittington, 1993; Whittaker, Fine, & Grasso, 1989). These problems pose a special challenge to policymakers and social work practitioners alike in forging a partnership with "parents as partners" consistent with the family-centered philosophy that characterizes reform thinking in child welfare services in the 1990s.

Consideration of family involvement raises a more fundamental question about residential care: Is it best viewed as a substitute for a family that has failed or as a support for a family in crisis?

## Outcome Research on Residential Child Care

What does the outcome research on residential group child care reveal about the effectiveness of that service in remediating the problems of troubled children and youths? The answer is, of course, "it depends"—on how you read the evidence, when you read the evidence, and how confident you are in the methodological rigor of the various studies. For example, does your analysis include objective indicators of adjustment, such as school performance and contact with police? (Residential care fares rather poorly on these measures.) Or do you include more subjective indicators, such as therapists' judgment of "progress" or parental satisfaction? (Residential care fares better on these indicators.) Do you sample behavior during residential care or at the point of discharge? (Residential care looks reasonably effective here.) Or, do you sample behavior at regular intervals in more distal environments such as school, neighborhood, and family? (The "decay" of treatment effects appears both rapid and progressive when measured in this way.)

### Methodological Issues

The lack of methodological rigor can threaten the reliability and validity of outcome studies. Some of the more prominent methodological problems are the following:

***Absence of controls.*** For ethical and practical reasons, many studies do not use control groups—which are required in the classic experimental design. Although this omission leaves interpretations of the results of such studies open to question—particularly with respect to "success"—troubled children should not be deprived of needed care and treatment for the sake of establishing a control group. To get around this problem, some outcome studies have tended toward a comparison group design, whereby differential approaches to residential and nonresidential treatment are tested on a similar population of referrals.

***Poorly defined service units.*** In such an all-encompassing service strategy as milieu treatment, it is often difficult to specify the exact components of a service unit or to identify which interventions are most potent in changing behavior. Although such questions are not of paramount interest to the clinician concerned primarily with positive movement in an individual case, they are of concern to executives and planners charged with the responsibility for program expansion. An often-heard refrain in the field is, "We know we are doing some things right, but we are not sure which ones."

***Improper selection of outcome criteria.*** All too often, residential programs have been evaluated on a narrow range of criteria—for example, grades in school, recidivism, or absence of police contact—that either are not directly related to services offered or that occur in community environments where the residential program has little involvement, much less control. Such outcome studies typically show discouraging results and lead to the self-defeating conclusion that "nothing works with these kids." The opposite problem is reflected in some outcome studies that have used extremely diffuse and poorly defined measures of community and personal adjustment. These ratings often are based on the clinical judgment of the therapists who provided the services and hence are open to questions of reliability and validity.

***Sample selection.*** Troubled children and youths seldom are randomly assigned to residential programs; instead, placement depends on such factors as severity of problem, prognosis for positive change, and available bed space. These factors can bias sample selection in a number of ways. For example, some programs may "cream off" applicants—accepting only those children with the greatest chance of a positive outcome—to dispose toward program successes. This problem of nonrandom program assignment, particularly when coupled with the absence of a control group, can confound the interpretation of program results particularly for a demonstration project seeking funds for expansion on the basis of a high degree of success in the pilot phase.

***Lack of utility.*** Because many of the studies of residential child care are outcome studies, often conducted by outside researchers, many practitioners doubt the value of the research enterprise and believe that its findings are of little use in shaping day-to-day practice. Almost by definition, outcome research cannot be directly useful because it focuses not on the treatment process as it is occurring but on a "payoff" that occurs long after children have left care, if at all. Moreover, its results are cast in terms of group data—30 percent adjusted "well," 30 percent adjusted "poorly"—and offer little to the practitioner who is looking for help and direction with an individual case (Whittaker, 1979).

To control for some of these methodological problems, some researchers have proposed a multilevel approach to evaluation, in residential child care that includes the use of descriptive case studies, outcome and follow-up studies, process evaluation and system analyses (Curry, 1991; Durkin & Durkin, 1975). Some group care models (such as the teaching family model) have incorporated formative (process) evaluation directly into their training procedures and operational policies so that program staff and supervisors receive continuous feedback on treatment effectiveness (Fixsen, Collins, Phillips, & Thomas, 1982). Other promising developments include more sophisticated assessment measures, such as the Child Behavior Checklist (Achenbach, 1991; Achenbach & McConaughy, 1987), family assessment instruments (Dunst, Trivette, & Deal, 1988; McCubbin & Thompson, 1987), and other practical measures (Hudson, 1982).

Despite these advances, however, many of the extant studies suffer from one or more of the methodological problems noted. (For a detailed review of residential research, see Pecora, Whittaker, & Maluccio, 1992. Other useful perspectives are provided by Dinnage & Pringle, 1967; Prosser, 1976; Kadushin, 1980; Pfeiffer, 1989; Curry, 1991; and Gershenson, 1956.)

**Research Implications**

Although much further research is needed, several tentative generalizations may be drawn from the existing corpus of research on residential child care:

- The quality of supports available in the postdischarge environment (such as family, school, neighborhood, or peer group) appears to be a powerful determining factor of a child's adjustment irrespective of adjustment and progress made in the residential program (Wells, Wyatt, & Hobfoll, 1991).
- Contact and involvement with family appear to be positively correlated with postdischarge adjustment (Wells, Wyatt, & Hobfoll, 1991).
- In general, neither the severity of the child's presenting problems nor the specific treatment method used is strongly associated with postdischarge adjustment.
- Youths with supportive community networks are more likely than those without such networks to maintain their treatment gains.

In sum, the evidence on the effectiveness of residential care and treatment is inconclusive, although the bulk of the studies point out the importance of specifying and operationalizing treatment methods and putting more staff resources to work in the "real world" environments to which most youths eventually return. This follows a general trend in human services to place much greater emphasis on environmental helping and, in particular, on the identification of social supports and life skills as key parts of a complementary professional intervention (Tracy & Whittaker, 1990).

### Need for More Research

Clearly, more research is needed on residential care before definitive conclusions can be drawn as to its efficacy, appropriateness, and contraindications. Curry (1991) detailed an ambitious plan of within-, between-, and across-program studies that, if implemented, would substantially improve current understanding of the types of residential provision that work with particular types of children under particular conditions. Similarly, Wells (1991a) offered a careful and thoughtful analysis of research questions pertaining to residential intake criteria.

In the meantime, policy and program planners should be suspicious of residential programs that purport to obtain extreme results. It is probably true here as elsewhere in social services research that as the results get better, the program design probably is weaker. Similarly, correlation does not equal causation. Many of the findings of residential research are correlational: They show patterns of association, not causal chains. Experiments must prove the efficacy of specific treatment regimes.

Furthermore, a single research strategy cannot be expected to answer all the needs of residential child care. For example, the longitudinal studies of children in care carried out by the Dartington Research Unit in Great Britain (Bullock, 1990) are as essential to planning child and youth policy in Britain as are the similar studies of foster care in the United States (Fanshel, Finch, & Grundy, 1990; Fanshel & Shinn, 1978). Such cohort studies provide answers to five basic questions: (1) Who comes into care? (2) For what reasons? (3) How long do they stay? (4) What factors are associated with their discharge? (5) Where do they go? These basic epidemiological data are essential for planning purposes. They reveal patterns of placement across various systems: social services, mental health, and juvenile corrections.

Not since the Pappenfort study in the early 1980s (Pappenfort, Young, & Marlow, 1983), has there been research specific to group care. It is unfair, however, to expect such studies to provide guidelines for improving residential practice. For this we will need process or formative evaluation and more within-program studies, as Curry (1991) described.

Useful research for residential care need be neither expensive nor complex. For example, Fanshel et al. (1990), Fanshel and Shinn (1978), and Whittaker, Overstreet, Grasso, Tripodi, and Boylan (1988) illustrated how routinely gathered data on family contacts can be monitored in new ways for the purpose of improving practice. For example, Fanshel and Shinn's research shows that visits by parents to a child in foster care is the single best predictor of the child's return home. Fanshel (1982) noted that such data can be routinely monitored—much as vital signs are monitored for a patient in a hospital—and used to guide social work activity. If, as suggested by Pecora, Whittaker, and Maluccio (1992), a supportive community environment—in particular, family support—is correlated with positive outcome, and absence of such support is correlated with negative outcome, valid and reliable measures of such support available to child and family could be gathered at intake and monitored during placement. Instruments for obtaining such information already exist and with only slight modification could be adapted to the residential intake process (Tracy & Whittaker, 1990). Analogously, in the area of child presenting problems, an instrument like Achenbach's child behavior checklist (1982, 1991) could provide staff with a reliable, empirically based system for describing, quantifying, and classifying both adaptive and maladaptive behavior.

Wolins (1974) described residential child and youth treatment as a "powerful environment." It is also an extremely expensive, labor-intensive, radical service intervention. In many social services budgets, for example, it commands the lion's share of the budget and serves the fewest children and youths. In the present move toward in-home services and permanency planning, it is imperative that rigorous evaluation inform the policy recommendation as to what the place and purpose of residential group care should be in an overall continuum of child and youth services.

## Practice Trends

### Ecological Perspective

Success in residential care, however defined, is largely a function of the supports available in the posttreatment community environment and has much less to do with either the presenting problem or the type of treatment offered. Consequently, what has become known as the ecological perspective continues to have profound implications for residential children's services (Wells et al., 1991; Whittaker, 1979). This perspective views the residential environment as a complex interplay of many different elements both within and outside the formal service context. Chief among these is the quality of the linkages between the residential program and the family before, during, and after placement. Also important are the neighborhood, peer group, world of work, and other present and future sources of influence over behavior in the community environment. The Massachusetts "experiment" in deinstitutionalization highlighted the importance of these community linkages as they interact with the formal service program (Coates et al., 1978).

One implication of this trend for professional social workers in residential care is that they will spend less time in direct treatment of children and more time working with and through the environment, particularly in creating and maintaining social support networks for children and their families (Tracy & Whittaker, 1990; Whittaker, 1979; Whittaker, Garbarino, & Associates, 1983). Specifically, this will mean factoring the environment more prominently into the youth service equation, whether that service occurs in a residential treatment center, group home, or the youth's own home. For example, youth care workers will likely

- teach children and families practical skills to cope effectively with their proximate and distal environments.
- work to enhance naturally occurring support networks where they exist and help create them where they do not. (The carefully conducted research of Wahler and others cautions against overreliance on interpersonal skills training as the sole form of intervention [Dumas & Wahler, 1983]).
- operate on the premise that "environmental helping" is not synonymous with "aftercare"; it begins before placement, continues during placement, and lasts as long after placement as it is needed.

These implications regarding postplacement support hold for other forms of out-of-home placement as well. For example, to what extent do foster parents continue to provide important supports to youths once the formal service contact has terminated. One might expect more contact and support than would be provided in shift staff settings, but such an assertion is unsupported by empirical evidence.

**Involvement of Families**

If the group residential center is to be seen as a temporary support for families in crises rather than as a substitute for families that have failed, it must engage families as full and equal partners in the helping process. Traditionally, and for a variety of reasons, parents have been kept at arm's length from the process of treatment in institutional settings. Maluccio and Sinanoglu (1981) documented a variety of ways in which parents of children in foster and residential care can assume a meaningful role in helping. These include participating in parenting skills training, in family support groups, in the life-space of the residential institution, and in family therapy (Jenson & Whittaker, 1987). As in adoption and foster family care, the enormous potential helping power of parents has barely been tapped. Without a strong family intervention component, it is doubtful that any model of out-of-home treatment (including foster-family–based treatment) can improve significantly on the rather meager results emerging from earlier outcome studies with respect to ultimate community reintegration. The study by Wells, Wyatt, and Hobfoll (1991) seems to bear this out. Again, the question of which setting—group care or foster family-based treatment—encourages greater parental involvement remains to be tested empirically.

Group residential treatment, as an intervention, is best viewed as part of an overall continuum of care that includes home-based, family-centered programs designed to prevent unnecessary out-of-home placement, services designed to reunify separated children and families, specialized adoption services, family support and education programs, and various kinds of specialized family foster care. These services are best viewed as complementary, although the precise relationships among them with respect to such matters as criteria for intake are anything but clear at this time. In all areas of youth services, we possess only primitive technologies of change and even more primitive methodologies for measuring their effects. A key practice challenge for social workers involves sorting out what they know about family involvement from all the services to determine which technologies might be transferred to residential group care. A final family work challenge involves the development of family engagement strategies that are relevant and culturally appropriate for children and families of color.

**Comprehensive Evaluation**

Perhaps the greatest single lesson to be learned from the history of group child care is the need to guard against premature enthusiasm and the tendency to generalize and overinterpret from incomplete evaluations. Such lessons should not be lost on advocates of foster family–based treatment and family preservation services. Problems such as maintenance, generalization, and community reintegration will remain for years to come, and they cannot define the entire set of criterion variables against which programs are measured.

The teaching-family model of group home treatment—although somewhat disappointing in its lack of distinctive effects in distal environments—has taught social work practitioners a great deal about the proximate environment, the treatment setting. This model illustrates how a program can document its component parts, how those processes can be tracked and evaluated, and how married couples (teaching parents) can be effectively trained to carry out program objectives. Some model foster care and treatment programs have drawn heavily on portions of the teaching-family technology and used it as a model in other ways, molding it and refashioning it to launch new programs. Their commitment, like that of the earlier pioneers in the teaching family model, is to rigorous evaluation of both processes and outcomes (McSweeney, Fremouw, & Hawkins, 1982). Evaluation of this kind, whatever it ultimately delivers in successful outcomes, will almost certainly provide us with rich, data-based inferences from which to launch the next generation of programs. For the present, social workers would do well to avoid viewing residential group child care and other services as dichotomous. They must instead examine more minutely the treatment process variables involved in each and their relation to desired child and family outcomes.

## Future Challenges

As social work practitioners, program planners, and policymakers assess the history, research base, and current status of residential care, several challenges emerge. Some of these involve long-term research that will benefit children and families in the future. Others have the potential to affect more immediately the lives of children who are now in residential care. Several apply equally to family preservation, family foster care, and other services.

### Prevention of Abuse and Neglect

The Hippocratic oath warns "First, do no harm." With an at-best tentative record of treatment effectiveness, a minimalist approach to policy development suggests that youths removed from their biological caregivers should not be subject to abuse or neglect in their out-of-home placements (Blatt, 1992). The task is to prevent not only physical and psychological abuse but the special kind of institutional neglect that deprives youths of developmental opportunities that challenge their growth. Many resources exist for addressing the special problems of abuse and neglect in out-of-home care settings—screening procedures, case review mechanisms, reporting requirements, training modules—a good many of which were developed by the National Center on Child Abuse and Neglect. The best guarantor of safety, however, remains a high level of program quality throughout the milieu that adheres to the highest level of professional standards and is monitored through citizen review.

### Documentation of Outcomes

A critical challenge for residential services involves specification and documentation of intervention outcomes. Among the many methodological problems that exist in the research base on residential care is the narrow and inconsistent range of outcome indicators, which makes cross-study comparisons extremely difficult. Whittaker et al. (1988) argued that a good criterion for residential provision ought to include multiple time points and multiple measures. A related task involves the presentation and dissemination of this outcome data to a range of consumers: practitioners, board members, policymakers, families, and youths themselves.

### Specifying Intervention Components

Residential services are difficult to specify and to measure. Yet the advent of computerized management information systems holds great promise for the systematic analysis of routinely gathered data. For example, supportive family contact during treatment has been shown to correlate with successful postplacement adjustment. Yet many questions remain unanswered. To what extent does timing (for example, frontloading versus focus on aftercare) make a difference? Does the intensity of family work matter, for example, structural family therapy versus liaison work or even telephone contact? Does it make a difference who initiates the contact? Are there racial or ethnic differences in effective family work? Although these are difficult questions, all are answerable given the capacity to analyze routinely gathered data. Social workers could, for example, empirically determine a minimum threshold amount of contact for any youth entering care and then set in place a tracking system to ensure that the amount of care is actually delivered. Similar questions could be raised for group interventions within the milieu, for special education services, life-space interventions, and more individualized forms of therapy.

**Maintenance and Generalization of Gains**

The real test of change is, of course, in the post-placement environment. How do we design learning experiences that are "portable"? How do we design effective aftercare programs that include work with extended family, friends, and other collateral helpers? To what extent do staff members facilitate the use of self-help? Do some patterns of residential care yield more long-lasting outcomes? Michigan, for example, is experimenting with a short-term, intensive form of residential placement that is followed by extensive community follow-up. Finally, how should the assessment of pluses and minuses in a youth's environment be incorporated into the overall determination of risk and acuity?

**Quality Assurance**

There is enormous variation in residential care in the United States. Licensing standards speak only minimally to quality of care issues, and standards from national professional bodies are only a little better. Because of the huge costs of inpatient psychiatric hospitalization, many insurance companies are instituting "utilization reviews" to help ensure that the appropriate type and length of care is provided. Other remedies include peer review, as pioneered in the California and North Carolina associations of voluntary agencies; more criterion-based training that is actually tied to staff career advancement; and more frequent use of program audits. Also needed are more systematic assessments of "model" service programs and a search for technologies from companion services, such as family preservation, that might have application to residential services.

Finally, it is clear that service agencies themselves cannot address these challenges effectively without help from university professional schools, public-sector services, and private foundations. A partnership among voluntary service agencies, the public sector, and schools of social work holds great promise for the development of quality residential care services for troubled youths and their families.

## References


Achenbach, T. (1982). A normative–descriptive approach to assessment of youth behavior. In A. J. McSweeney, W. J. Fremouw, & R. P. Hawkins (Eds.), *Practical program evaluation in youth treatment* (pp. 24–49). Springfield, IL: Charles C Thomas.

Achenbach, T. A. (1991). *Manual for the Child Behavior Checklist 4-18 and 1991 Profile.* Burlington: University of Vermont, Department of Psychiatry.

Achenbach, T. A., & McConaughy, S. (1987). *Empirically based assessment of child and adolescent psychopathology: Practical applications.* Newbury Park, CA: Sage Publications.

Bettelheim, B., & Sylvester, E. (1949). A therapeutic milieu. *American Journal of Orthopsychiatry, 18,* 191–206.

Blatt, E. R. (1992). Factors associated with child abuse and neglect in residential settings. *Children and Youth Services Review, 14,* 493–517.

Bremner, R. H. (1970). *Children and youth in America: A documentary history* (Vol. 1). Cambridge, MA: Harvard University Press.

Bremner, R. H. (1974). *Children and youth in America: A documentary history* (Vol. 3). Cambridge, MA: Harvard University Press.

Bullock, R. (1990). The implications of recent child care research finding for foster care. *Adoption and Fostering, 14*(3), 43–45.

*Child abuse and neglect in residential institutions.* (1978). (DHEW Publication No. OHDS 78-30160). Washington, DC: U.S. Government Printing Office.

Child Welfare League of America. (1984). *Directory of member agencies.* New York: Author.

Coates, R. B., Miller, A. D., & Ohlin, L. E. (1978). *Diversity in a youth correctional system.* Cambridge, MA: Ballinger.

Curry, J. (1991). Outcome research on residential treatment: Implications and suggested directions. *American Journal of Orthopsychiatry, 61,* 348–358.

Dinnage, R., & Pringle, M. K. (1967). *Residential care: Facts and fallacies.* London: Longman.

Dore, M. M., Young, T. M., & Pappenfort, D. M. (1984). Comparison of basic data for national survey of residential group care facilities: 1966–1982. *Child Welfare, 63,* 485–495.

Downs, S. W., & Sherraden, M. (1983). The orphan asylum in the nineteenth century. *Social Service Review, 57,* 272–290.

Dumas, J. E., & Wahler, R. G. (1983). Predictions of treatment outcome in parent training: Mother insularity and socioeconomic disadvantage. *Behavioral Assessment, 5,* 301–313.

Dunst, C. J., Trivette, C. M., & Deal, A. E. (1988). *Enabling and empowering families.* Cambridge, MA: Brookline Books.

Durkin, R. P., & Durkin, A. B. (1975). Evaluating residential treatment programs for disturbed children. In M. Guttentag & E. Struening (Eds.), *Handbook of evaluative research* (pp. 275–339). Newbury Park, CA: Sage Publications.

Ekstein, R. (Ed.). (1983). *Children of time and space, of action and impulse.* Englewood Cliffs, NJ: Appleton-Century-Crofts.

Fanshel, D. (1982). *On the road to permanency: An expanded data base for children in foster care.* New York: Child Welfare League of America.

Fanshel, D., Finch, S. J., & Grundy, J. F. (1990). *Foster children in life course perspective.* New York: Columbia University Press.

Fanshel, D., & Shinn, E. (1978). *Children in foster care: A longitudinal investigation.* New York: Columbia University Press.

Fitzharris, T. (1985). *The foster children of California: Profiles of 10,000 children in residential care.* Sacramento, CA: Children Services Foundation.

Fixsen, D. L., Collins, L. B., Phillips, E. L., & Thomas, D. L. (1982). Institutional indicators in evaluation: An example from Boys Town. In A. J. McSweeney, W. J. Fremouw, & R. P. Hawkins (Eds.), *Practical program evaluation in youth treatment* (pp. 203–230). Springfield, IL: Charles C Thomas.

Ford, M., & Kroll, J. (1990). *Challenges to child welfare: Countering the call for return to orphanages.* St. Paul, MN: North American Council on Adoptable Children.

Gershenson, C. P. (1956). Residential treatment of children: Research problems and possibilities. *Social Service Review, 30*(3), 268–275.

Gershenson, C. P. (1990). *Preparing for the future backwards: Characteristics of the ecology for children and youth in long term out of home care.* Unpublished manuscript.

Hanson, R. (Ed.). (1982). *Institutional abuse of children and youth.* New York: Haworth Press.

Hawkins, R. P., Peterson, R. F., Schweid, E., & Bijou, S. W. (1966). Behavior therapy in the home: Amelioration of problem parent–child relations with the parent in a therapeutic role. *Journal of Experimental Child Psychology, 4,* 99–107.

Hobbs, N. (1966). Helping disturbed children: Psychological and ecological strategies. *American Psychologist, 21,* 1105–1151.

Hobbs, N. (1982). *The troubled and troubling child.* San Francisco: Jossey-Bass.

Hudson, W. (1982). *The clinical measurement package: A field manual.* Homewood, IL: Dorsey Press.

Jenson, J. M., & Whittaker, J. K. (1987). Parental involvement in children's residential treatment: From preplacement to aftercare. *Children & Youth Services Review, 9,* 81–100.

Kadushin, A. (1980). *Child welfare services* (3rd ed.). New York: Macmillan.

Kadushin, A., & Martin, J. (1988). *Child welfare services* (4th ed.). New York: Macmillan.

Maluccio, A. N., & Marlow, W. D. (1972). Residential treatment of emotionally disturbed children: A review of the literature. *Social Service Review, 46,* 230–251.

Maluccio, A. N., & Sinanoglu, P. A. (Eds.). (1981). *The challenge of partnership: Working with parents of children in foster care.* New York: Child Welfare League of America.

Mayer, M. F., & Blum, A. (Eds.). (1971). *Healing through living: A symposium on residential treatment.* Springfield, IL: Charles C Thomas.

McCubbin, H. L., & Thompson, A. J. (Eds.). (1987). *Family assessment inventories for research and practice.* Madison: University of Wisconsin Press.

McSweeney, A. J., Fremouw, W. J., & Hawkins, R. P. (Eds.). (1982). *Practical program evaluation methods in youth treatment.* Springfield, IL: Charles C Thomas.

National Commission on Children in Need of Parents. (1979). *Final report.* New York: Author.

National Mental Health Association. (1989). *Invisible children project: Final report.* Alexandria, VA: Author.

Pappenfort, D. M., Kilpatrick, D. M., & Roberts, R. W. (Eds.). (1973). *Child care: Social policy and the institution.* Chicago: Aldine.

Pappenfort, D. M., Young, T. M., & Marlow, C. R. (1983). *Residential group care: 1981*. Chicago: University of Chicago, School of Social Service Administration.

Pecora, P. J., Whittaker, J. K., & Maluccio, A. N. (1992). *The child welfare challenge: Policy, practice, and research.* New York: Aldine de Gruyter.

Pfeiffer, S. (1989). Follow-up of children and adolescents treated in psychiatric facilities: A methodological review. *The Psychiatric Hospital, 20,* 15–20.

Phillips, E. L., Phillips, E. A., Fixsen, D. L., & Wolf, M. M. (1974). *The teaching family handbook*. Lawrence: University of Kansas, Bureau of Child Research.

Piliavin, I. (1963). Conflict between cottage parents and caseworkers. *Social Service Review, 37,* 17–25.

Prosser, H. (1976). *Perspective and residential child care: An annotated bibliography.* New Jersey: Humanities Press.

Redl, F., & Wineman, D. (1957). *The aggressive child.* New York: Free Press.

Reeder, R. R. (1925). Our orphaned asylums. *Survey, 54,* 283–287.

Rhodes, W. C. (1967). The disturbing child: A problem of ecological management. *Exceptional Children, 33,* 449–455.

Risley, J. R., & Wolf, M. M. (1966). Experimental manipulation of autistic behaviors and generalization into the home. In R. Ulrich, J. Stachnik, & J. Mabry (Eds.), *Control of human behavior* (Vol. 1, pp. 193–198). Glenview, IL: Scott, Foresman.

Rothman, D. J. (1980). *Conscience and convenience: The asylum and its alternatives in progressive America.* Boston: Little, Brown.

Schwartz, I. M., Jackson-Beelk, M., & Anderson, R. (1983). *Minnesota's "hidden" juvenile control system: Inpatient psychiatric and chemical dependency treatment.* Unpublished manuscript, University of Minnesota, Hubert H. Humphrey Institute of Public Affairs.

Small, R., Kennedy, K., & Bender, B. (1991). Critical issues for practice in residential treatment: The view from within. *American Journal of Orthopsychiatry, 61,* 327–335.

Taylor, R. B. (1981). *The kid business.* Boston: Houghton Mifflin.

Tharp, R. G., & Wetzel, R. J. (1969). *Behavior modification in the natural environment.* New York: Academic Press.

Tracy, E. M., & Whittaker, J. K. (1990). The social network map: Assessing social support in clinical social work practice. *Families in Society, 71,* 461–470.

Trieschman, A. E., Whittaker, J. K., & Brendtro, L. K. (1969). *The other 23 hours: Child care work in a therapeutic milieu.* New York: Aldine.

Wells, K. (1991a). Placement of emotionally disturbed children in residential treatment: A review of placement criteria. *American Journal of Orthopsychiatry, 61,* 335–348.

Wells, K. W. (1991b). Long term residential treatment for children: Introduction. *American Journal of Orthopsychiatry, 61,* 324–327.

Wells, K., & Whittington, D. (1993). Characteristics of youth referral to residential treatment: Implications for program design. *Children and Youth Services Review, 15,* 195–217.

Wells, K., Wyatt, E., & Hobfoll, S. (1991). Factors associated with adaptation of youths discharged from residential treatment. *Children and Youth Services Review, 13,* 199–217.

Whittaker, J. K. (1971a). Colonial child care institutions: Our heritage of care. *Child Welfare, 50,* 396–400.

Whittaker, J. K. (1971b). Mental hygiene influences in children's institutions: Organization and technology for treatment. *Mental Hygiene, 55,* 444–450.

Whittaker, J. K. (1979). *Caring for troubled children: Residential treatment in a community context.* San Francisco: Jossey-Bass.

Whittaker, J. K. (1988). Family support and group child care. In G. Carmen & R. Small (Eds.), *Permanency planning: Reforming group child care* (pp. 29–61). Washington, DC: Child Welfare League of America.

Whittaker, J. K., Fine, D., & Grasso, A. (1989). Characteristics of adolescents and their families in residential treatment intake: An exploratory study. In E. Balcerzak (Ed.), *Group care of children: Transition towards the Year 2000* (pp. 67–87). Washington, DC: Child Welfare League of America.

Whittaker, J. K., Garbarino, J., & Associates. (1983). *Social support networks: Informal helping in the human services.* New York: Aldine.

Whittaker, J. K., Overstreet, E. J., Grasso, A., Tripodi, T., & Boylan, F. (1988). Multiple indicators of success in residential youth care and treatment. *American Journal of Orthopsychiatry, 58,* 143–147.

Whittaker, J. K., & Pecora, P. J. (1984). A research agenda for residential care. In J. Philpot (Ed.), *Group care practice: The challenge of the next decade* (pp. 71–87). Surrey, England: Community Care/Business Press International.

Whittaker, J. K., & Trieschman, A. E. (Eds.). (1972). *Children away from home: A sourcebook of residential treatment.* New York: Aldine.

Wolfensberger, W. (1972). *Normalization.* New York: National Institute on Mental Retardation.

Wolins, M. (1974). *Group care: Explorations in the powerful environment.* New York: Aldine.

Wooden, K. (1976). *Weeping in the playtime of others: The plight of incarcerated children.* New York: McGraw-Hill.

### Further Reading

Barth, R. P., Courtney, M., Bellick, J. D., & Albert, V. (1994). *From child abuse to permanency planning: Child welfare services, pathways and placements.* New York: Aldine de Gruyter.

Colton, M. J., & Hellinckx, W. (Eds.). (1993). *Child care in the EC.* Aldershot, England: Ashgate.

Lyman, R. D., Prentice-Dunn, S., & Gabel, S. (1989). *Residential and inpatient treatment of children and adolescents.* New York: Plenum Press.

Pine, B. A., Warsh, R., & Maluccio, A. N. (1993). *Together again: Family reunification in foster care.* Washington, DC: Child Welfare League of America.

Schwartz, I. M., & Beker, J. (1994). Does institutional care do more harm than good? In E. Gambrill & T. J. Stein (Eds.), *Controversial issues in child welfare* (pp. 275–290). Boston: Allyn & Brown.

Whittaker, J. K., & Pfeiffer, S. I. (in press). Research priorities for residential group child care. *Child Welfare.*

**James K. Whittaker, PhD, ACSW,** is professor, University of Washington, School of Social Work, 4101 Fifteenth Avenue, NE, Seattle, WA 98195.

### For further information see

Adolescence Overview; Adoption; Case Management; Child Abuse and Neglect Overview; Child Care Services; Child Foster Care; Child Welfare Overview; Children's Rights; Deinstitutionalization; Domestic Violence; Families Overview; Homelessness; Juvenile Corrections; Program Evaluation; Quality Assurance; Runaways and Homeless Youths; Social Planning; Social Welfare Policy; Youth Services.

**Key Words**
group care
orphanages
residential treatment

# Children: Mental Health

**Paula Allen-Meares**

The social work profession has historically been concerned with the interactions of people with environments and the consequences of these interactions for health and mental health over the life span. Social workers know that the early life experiences of infants, children, and adolescents have much to do with the adaptations that are required for successful functioning as adults. They also know that too few of the children and adolescents who need mental health services receive them.

Isolation and loneliness are significant problems for many of this country's youths (Christopher, Kurtz, & Howing, 1989). At the community level there are insufficient services to address such needs, and the services that do exist are often fragmented and poorly coordinated. Perhaps the increase in suicide, drug abuse, and violence among youths is an expression of dysfunctional transactions between them and their environments (home, school, and community) and the lack of services to meet their emotional needs.

Evidence suggests that suicide is the third leading cause of death among adolescents (Christopher et al., 1989). Suicide attempts often correlate with loss and separation (the death of a parent or the divorce of parents, for example), abuse and neglect, and the use of drugs. The use of drugs, especially alcohol—the "gateway drug"—has increased steadily; 70 percent of high school seniors consume alcohol at least occasionally (Wallach & Corbett, 1990). Antecedents to the use of alcohol include peer pressure to drink, to be nonconformist, and to be independent of parental figures; poor academic performance; and various antisocial behaviors. There is considerable national concern about the drug epidemic. Millions of dollars are being spent on law enforcement strategies to reduce the use and spread of drugs and the proliferation of violence, but far fewer dollars are being spent on prevention and treatment that target the roots of these problems.

The mental disorders of children and adolescents vary in the age at which they can first be recognized as problems (National Advisory Mental Health Council, 1990). These disorders can be divided into three major areas: (1) emotional disturbance, such as depression and eating disorders; (2) behavioral problems, such as conduct disorders and antisocial acting out; and (3) developmental delays or impairments, such as attention-deficit disorders, that limit or curtail the ability to communicate effectively. These areas are not mutually exclusive, and a child or adolescent often has two disorders at the same time. The term that characterizes the presence of two or more disorders is *comorbidity*.

## National Policy

National policy on the care of mentally ill people is embodied in the 1963 Mental Retardation Facilities and Community Mental Health Centers Construction Act—called the Community Mental Health Centers Act (CMHCA) or the Community Mental Health Services Act (CMHSA)—and its amendments and in the 1980 Mental Health Systems Act that amended the CMHCA. Also, mental health policy is embodied in the 1965 legislative titles to the Social Security Act, Title XVIII (Medicare) and Title XIX (Medicaid); the Education for All Handicapped Children Act of 1975; the Individuals with Disabilities Education Act of 1990; and the various yearly budget reconciliation acts. This fragmentation of mental health policy in the United States has led to conflicting priorities among public agencies for services to low-income people and an uncoordinated service delivery system. It appears that people who have funds or appropriate insurance coverage have an array of mental health services and providers from which to select, whereas low-income people have limited options (National Association of Social Workers, 1994).

The neglect of the mental health needs of children and adolescents has historical roots. Services to children were virtually ignored in the 1963 act, and state mental health agencies continue to spend most of their funds on mental hospitals that serve predominantly adults. The major federal policy response has been the Child and Adolescent Service Program, which has identified seriously emotionally disturbed children as a major target group (Friedman, 1986), but these children are only one group among the many who need mental health services.

Other legislation, such as the Education of the Handicapped Amendments of 1986 and Title I, authorizes early intervention programs that target infants and toddlers who are developmentally disabled or at risk of disabilities. The aim of this legislation is to address the mental health needs of infants and their families and to intervene at the earliest point of development.

## Family, Life Events, and Community Conditions

The roots of many of the emotional problems experienced by children and adolescents are found within their immediate environment. It is well known that environmental conditions in the family and community; economic level; and such stresses as the death of a parent, parental divorce, or a parent with impaired mental health functioning can affect the developmental outcome of youths (Goodyear, 1990). The economic circumstances of children are proscribed by the economic and living conditions of their parents. Children and adolescents in single-parent and ethnic minority families are the most likely to be poor. Poverty continues to be the dominant factor shaping people's lives and is often intertwined with racism and sexism.

There is a strong association between the employment status of fathers and the mental health problems of children. Dew, Penkower, and Bromet (1991) found that children whose fathers were unemployed were two times as likely to commit suicide as were others. They also reported an established association between unemployment and child abuse and found that children whose parents were unemployed suffered developmental delays, rejection by peers, behavioral problems, retarded social skills, and increased depression. Such findings confirm the at-risk circumstances that many children are in and the consequences of these circumstances for the children's functioning.

Some communities are plagued with impoverished conditions, the absence of informal and formal support systems (mental health services, child care, and the like), low social integration, and factors that undermine a sense of belonging.

Many youths are alienated and lack emotional support, especially after puberty, when feelings of isolation become more pronounced. The violence, gangs, and cult worship that are prevalent among young people are expressions of needs that are not being met in their daily lives. According to Christopher et al. (1989), adolescents indicate that they have more problems and fewer close friends than did their parents.

Access to vital mental health services is inadequate in rural communities. Some reasons for the dearth of services include the great distances between communities, the lack of qualified professionals, the poor economy, few specialized services for children (although 33 percent of the nation's youths reside in rural communities, only 3 percent of mental health programs for them are found in rural areas), and the scarcity of other support services (Petti & Leviton, 1986).

Different ethnic and racial groups also experience a number of mental health problems that social workers are only beginning to learn about. Too few cross-cultural comparative studies have addressed the mental health needs of youths of different racial or ethnic groups. For example, the suicide rates of Native American adolescents are three to 10 times higher than those of other groups (McShane, 1988). Furthermore, developmental disabilities, school-related problems, depression, and drug addiction are common problems among Native American youths that are not attended to by the mental health system. Some of these same problems are found in African American and Latino youths. A culturally sensitive perspective is important to the identification of mental health problems and the use of appropriate assessment and intervention procedures in the populations.

## Prevalence

The prevalence of mental health problems in childhood and adolescence has been inadequately studied, yet the number of children and adolescents who experience emotional and mental health problems is escalating (Christopher et al., 1989). According to the most recent data available, approximately 12 percent, or 7.5 million, of the youths in the United States suffer from an emotional or mental health disorder, but less than 28 percent of this group, or 2.1 million youths, receive treatment. Thus, over 70 percent of the youths who need mental health services do not receive them (National Association of Social Workers, 1991). Furthermore, the specific mental health problems of children and adolescents appear to be neglected. For example, depression in childhood and adolescence has only recently been recognized as a legitimate emotional disorder (Allen-Meares, 1987). According to epidemiological studies on children and adolescents, the prevalence of depression ranges from 2 percent to 33 percent in select populations (Kashani & Simonds, 1979). Rates among clinical populations vary, with the highest estimates ranging well over 50 percent (Reynolds, 1984). The problem of identifying and determining depression in this group can be attributed to denial that it could exist and the lack of adequate diagnostic criteria and suitable instruments for assessments. Efforts to unveil this disorder in children and adolescents have been spearheaded by developmental psychopathologists.

Child and adolescent psychiatry has lagged behind adult psychiatry in developing instruments that identify and diagnose affective disorders in children and youths (Anderson, Williams, McGee, & Silva, 1987). The *Diagnostic and Statistical Manual of Mental Disorders*, third edition (American Psychiatric Association, 1980), commonly known as DSM-III, has been adapted over the years (APA, 1987, 1994) to improve its diagnostic capability to identify emotional problems in children and adolescents and now includes five areas that provide more information on prevailing strengths and stresses. Nevertheless, many mental health practitioners rely primarily on only one or two areas (Lieberman, 1987). DSM-III was criticized for the low reliability of some of the newer categories, poorly validated categories, and the overproliferation of subcategories (Anderson et al., 1987). Yet, given all its shortcomings, DSM is one of the most widely relied-on instruments in mental health settings and one about which practitioners need to be informed.

In addition to DSM-IV, new points of view that more fully embrace the important role of the environment in the development of mental disorders have appeared in the literature. For example, the transactional view suggests that rather than focusing on the development of the "child" or "adolescent," it is important to look at the familial, societal, biological, and environmental factors that could contribute to certain mental disorders (Cicchetti & Schneider-Rosen, 1984). Moreover, a youth's developmental outcome has many historical and causal determinants. For example, depression could be attributed to a dysfunctional relationship between the child's coping abilities and developmental stage and the resources in the immediate environment. If the environment is supportive and provides the resources needed for the child to develop the necessary skills, it can offset or buffer developmental difficulties (Allen-Meares,

1987). In other words, the environment can act to reduce the child's emotional vulnerability and decrease the probability of depression. However, an environment that lacks adequate resources and is stressful, disorganized, and unresponsive can contribute to and exacerbate problems in functioning. The adoption of the transactional perspective requires one to assess more broadly in the determination of the adolescent's difficulties.

## New Concepts and Trends

New concepts that appear to be gaining attention in the area of child and adolescent mental health are resilient children, modifiers of risk factors, "mattering," and prevention. Resilient children are defined as those who do not develop mental health problems despite unfavorable environmental and family conditions, such as a schizophrenic or affective disorder in a parent, chronic poverty, problems in mother–infant attachment, abuse and emotional neglect, and a high level of stress, that put children at high risk of mental health problems (O'Grady & Metz, 1986). Research is under way to learn more about how these children survive and what protects them from a host of mental health problems.

The notion of resilient children has led to research on the concept of modifiers of risk factors, that is, factors that interact to buffer and prevent high-risk conditions from resulting in devastating outcomes for children. Several modifiers of risk factors have received considerable attention in the literature: greater social support from extended family members and friends, an internal locus of control, and a lower frequency of stress (O'Grady & Metz, 1986).

*Mattering*, the degree to which a person believes he or she is important to others—the opposite concept of significant others—is gaining importance in the field of adolescent mental health. Rosenberg and McCollough (1981) identified three important aspects of mattering: (1) feeling that you command attention from others, (2) feeling that you are important to others, and (3) feeling that others depend on you. This concept is independent of approval. Rosenberg and McCollough found that adolescents who feel that they do not matter to their parents are more likely to suffer mental health problems, such as low self-esteem, depression, anxiety, and delinquency. As many families struggle to meet the requirements of daily living, the attention and time devoted to the development of mattering in children could be threatened.

Practitioners who work with children and adolescents who seem to be in situations that could lead to mental health problems or who are further along the continuum of dysfunction should pay close attention to the literature and research on such concepts as resilient children, modifiers of risk factors, and mattering. Such concepts are important for the development of assessment procedures and preventive strategies and offer new direction for a more comprehensive understanding of cause and effect.

Bloom (1987) stated that primary prevention refers to "practices aimed at . . . *preventing* predictable physical, psychological, or sociocultural problems for individuals or populations at risk . . . protecting current strengths; . . . and *promoting* desired goals" (p. 303). It is a relatively new concept that is concerned with emphasizing and reinforcing the strengths of the individual, rather than being preoccupied with blaming the victim. Several assumptions undergird prevention: (1) there are multiple causes for problems in functioning; (2) populations, such as children and adolescents, who are at risk because of specific characteristics can be identified before pathology or difficulties in functioning become evident; and (3) select interventions can result in the reduction of risk factors and their effects when the intervention takes place before problems occur.

## Web of Services

Some families with private health insurance can choose to place their children with mental health problems in private psychiatric hospitals. Children and adolescents from low-income families that lack insurance coverage often have fewer options and must rely on public mental health services with long waiting lists and insufficient personnel. However, even those families with private insurance coverage find it is not enough.

Public mental health services have often been provided through a web of social institutions that spans the mental health, health, social welfare, educational, and juvenile justice systems. Despite efforts to improve services in these systems, far more work is urgently needed (National Advisory Mental Health Council, 1990). Fragmentation still characterizes this so-called web of services. A strong network of organizations that includes such systems is urgently needed to advocate on behalf of low-income children with mental health problems.

Positive developments in this area include the trends toward integrating child–youth services with mental health services and establishing community-based systems of services that prevent and treat emotional disturbances in children. Some states are moving to operationalize the continua of care and services at the community level while retaining fiscal responsibility at the state level and encouraging partnerships between the public and private sectors (Friedman, 1986). The bottom line is that we need a comprehensive approach that takes into account the various agencies whose primary responsibilities are the provision of services to children and adolescents and their families. Collaboration and interagency agreements can ensure that adequate and appropriate services are being provided (Knitzer & Yelton, 1990). A strong case management system must undergird such arrangements.

## Conclusion

The too little, too late approach must be replaced because the future of this country's children and society depends on it. Social workers play a variety of roles in the provision of services. They can and should continue to advocate at every level of society for greater attention to all services that impinge on children and their families. Adequate health and child care, programs that provide youths with constructive leisure-time activities, services that support the family's role as primary caretaker, and school programs that address both the cognitive and mental health needs of children and adolescents could offset the consequences of other crippling conditions. Social workers need to be active in lobbying at the national and state levels of government and working cooperatively with related professional associations and groups. As case managers, providers of direct services, and diagnosticians, social workers bring a unique perspective to the interdisciplinary mental health system.

## References


Allen-Meares, P. (1987). Depression in childhood and adolescence. *Social Work, 32,* 512–516.

American Psychiatric Association. (1980). *Diagnostic and statistical manual of mental disorders* (3rd ed.). Washington, DC: Author.

American Psychiatric Association. (1987). *Diagnostic and statistical manual of mental disorders* (3rd ed., rev.). Washington, DC: Author.

American Psychiatric Association. (1994). *Diagnostic and statistical manual of mental disorders* (4th ed.). Washington, DC: Author.

Anderson, J. C., Williams, S., McGee, R., & Silva, P. A. (1987). DSM-III disorders in preadolescent children. *Archives of General Psychiatry, 44,* 69–76.

Bloom, M. (1987). Prevention. In A. Minahan (Ed.-in-Chief), *Encyclopedia of social work* (18th ed., Vol. 2, pp. 303–315). Silver Spring, MD: National Association of Social Workers.

Christopher, G. M., Kurtz, D., & Howing, P. T. (1989). Status of mental health services for youth in school and community. *Children and Youth Services Review, 11,* 159–174.

Cicchetti, O., & Schneider-Rosen, R. (Eds.). (1984). *New directions for child development—Childhood depression.* San Francisco: Jossey-Bass.

Dew, M. A., Penkower, L., & Bromet, E. J. (1991). Effects of unemployment on mental health in the contemporary family. *Behavior Modification, 15,* 501–544.

Education for All Handicapped Children Act of 1975. P.L. 94-142, 89. Stat. 773.

Education of the Handicapped Act Amendments of 1986. P. L. 99-457, 100 Stat. 1145.

Friedman, R. (1986). Major issues in mental health services for children. *Administration in Mental Health, 14,* 6–13.

Goodyear, I. M. (1990). Family relationships, life events and child psychopathology. *Journal of Child Psychology and Psychiatry, 31,* 191–192.

Individuals with Disabilities Education Act of 1990. P.L. 101-476, 104 Stat. 1142.

Kashani, J., & Simonds, J. F. (1979). The incidence of depression in children. *American Journal of Psychiatry, 136,* 1203–1205.

Knitzer, J., & Yelton, S. (1990). Collaborations between child welfare and mental health. *Public Welfare, 48,* 24–33.

Lieberman, F. (1987). Mental health and illness in children. In A. Minahan (Ed.-in-Chief), *Encyclopedia of social work* (18th ed., Vol. 2, pp. 111–123). Silver Spring, MD: National Association of Social Workers.

McShane, D. (1988). An analysis of mental health research with American Indian youth. *Journal of Adolescence, 11,* 87–116.

Mental Health Systems Act of 1980. P.L. 96-398, 94 Stat. 1564.

Mental Retardation Facilities and Community Mental Health Centers Construction Act of 1963. P.L. 88-164, 77 Stat. 282.

National Advisory Mental Health Council. (1990). *National plan for research on child and adolescent mental disorders.* Rockville, MD: U.S. Department of Health and Human Services.

National Association of Social Workers. (1994). Mental health. In *Social work speaks: NASW policy statements* (3rd ed., pp. 176–180). Washington, DC: Author.

O'Grady, D., & Metz, J. R. (1986). Resilience in children at high risk for psychological disorder. *Journal of Pediatric Psychology, 12,* 3–23.

Petti, T. A., & Leviton, L. C. (1986, Spring). Rethinking rural mental health services for children and adolescents. *Journal of Public Health Policy,* 58–77.

Reynolds, W. M. (1984). Depression in childhood and adolescence: Phenomenology, evaluation and treatment. *School Psychology Review, 13,* 171–182.

Rosenberg, M., & McCollough, B. C. (1981). Mattering: Inferred significance and mental health among adolescents. *Research in Community and Mental Health, 2,* 163–182.

Wallach, P., & Corbett, K. (1990). Illicit drug, tobacco, and alcohol use among youth: Trends and promising approaches in prevention. In H. Resnik (Ed.), *Youth and drugs: Society's mixed messages* (pp. 5–23). Rockville, MD: U.S. Department of Health and Human Services.

## Further Reading

Kernberg, P., & Chazan, S. (1991). *Children with conduct disorders.* New York: Basic Books.

McCubbin, H., & Thompson, A. (Eds.). (1991). *Family assessment inventories for research and practice.* Madison: University of Wisconsin.

Munger, R. (1991). *Child mental health practice from the ecological perspective.* Lanham, MD: University Press of America.

Rose, S., & Edelson, J. (1987). *Working with children and adolescents in groups.* San Francisco: Jossey-Bass.

Salizinger, S., Antrobus, J., & Glick, J. (Eds.). (1980). *The ecosystem of the sick child: Implications for disturbed and mentally retarded children.* New York: Academic Press.

Siepker, B., & Kandaras, C. (Eds.). (1985). *Group therapy and adolescents: A treatment manual.* New York: Human Sciences Press.

Sileveira, W., & Trafford, G. (1988). *Children need groups: A practical manual for group work with young children.* Aberdeen, England: The University Press.

Tindale, J., & Gray, D. (1989). *Peer counseling: An in-depth look at training peer helpers.* Muncie, IN: Accultured Development.

Weiner, I. (Ed.). (1987). *Behavior therapy in children and adolescents: A clinical approach.* New York: John Wiley & Sons.

**Paula Allen-Meares, PhD, LCSW,** is dean and professor, University of Michigan, School of Social Work, 1065 Frieze Building, Ann Arbor, MI 48109.

**For further information see**

Adolescence Overview; Adolescents: Direct Practice; Advocacy; Alcohol Abuse; Assessment; Child Abuse and Neglect; Child Foster Care; Child Welfare Services; Childhood; Children: Direct Practice; Children: Group Care; Drug Abuse: Eating Disorders and Other Compulsive Behaviors; Families Overview: Families: Direct Practice; Family Therapy; Federal Social Legislation from 1961 to 1994; Human Development; Mental Health Overview; Person-in-Environment; Poverty; Primary Prevention Overview; Runaways and Homeless Youths; School-Based Services; Social Welfare Policy; Substance Abuse: Direct Practice; Suicide; Violence Overview; Youth Services.

**Key Words**

| | |
|---|---|
| adolescents | mental health |
| children | school social work |

# Children's Rights

**David Wineman**

Children, strangely, have both more and fewer rights than adults. Because of their perceived immaturity and vulnerability, more laws protect children against harm than protect adults. But because children are also perceived both as incompetent to act reasonably in their own self-interest and in need of guidance and control, they historically have had less constitutional protection against arbitrary interference with fundamental freedoms and civil liberties by state authority and their own parents. However, since the mid-1960s the courts in a number of cases (and with a certain cautious ambivalence) have held that children are persons for constitutional purposes and are entitled to a certain measure of protection against state and parental contravention of their civil liberties. This entry addresses how these constitutional guarantees and other protections and rights provided in state and federal statutes affect the lives of children in schools, the parent–child relationship, foster care, and adoption and in instances of neglect and abuse.

## Public Schools

### Constitutional Rights

Beyond the right to a free public education, available to all children in the United States, including illegal aliens, the U.S. Supreme Court has established in several cases that public school students retain their rights to freedom of expression, fair disciplinary procedures, equal treatment, and personal privacy beyond the schoolhouse gate.

***Freedom of expression.*** In its landmark 1969 decision, *Tinker v. Des Moines Independent Community School District,* the U.S. Supreme Court reversed the suspension of students for the peaceful wearing of black armbands to protest the Vietnam War. In this vigorous endorsement of academia as a free marketplace of ideas, the Court established the standard that student expression is fully protected so long as it does not substantially violate others' rights or materially disrupt the educational environment.

Almost 20 years later, however, in two separate decisions, a more conservative Supreme Court expressed a stronger concern with the school as a civilizing and protective environment than as the free marketplace of ideas. In *Bethel School District No. 403 v. Fraser* (1986), the Court, without discarding *Tinker,* upheld the suspension of a student for his use of "elaborate, graphic and explicit sexual metaphor" in a nominating speech at an election assembly. In so ruling, the Court observed that the rights of students in schools "are not automatically coextensive with the rights of adults in other settings," and that such rights may be appropriately balanced against "society's countervailing interest in teaching students the boundaries of socially appropriate behavior."

Within two years of *Bethel,* in *Hazelwood School District v. Kuhlmeier* (1988), the Supreme Court upheld the right of school officials to excise two pages from the official school newspaper dealing with student pregnancy, sexual activity, and birth control. Observing that the paper was part of the journalism course and reiterating the special character of the school environment expressed in *Bethel,* the Court held that official control of speech related to legitimate pedagogical concerns did not "offend the First Amendment" and deemed such control necessary "to assure . . . that readers or listeners are not exposed to material . . . inappropriate to their level of maturity" (p. 271).

The long reach of these two decisions into First amendment activity in high schools is illustrated in a 1991 federal court unpublished decision (*Paye v. Gibralter School District*) in the Eastern District of Michigan upholding prepublication review and censorship of a student literary magazine. The magazine was published under the supervision of two English teachers, leaders of a special project in creative writing financed by non–school district funds. The district superintendent, reacting to board member complaints that certain pieces promoted satanic worship, drinking, and killing, confiscated 51 undistributed magazines. Even though the teachers were doing this on their own time, and no class, credit, or official curriculum was involved, the federal court ruled that school-sponsored expression existed, essentially by virtue of faculty leadership of a "supervised learning experience."

Still another form of expression, personal appearance as manifested in hairstyle or dress, remains a perennial source of controversy. Although clearly not school sponsored and just as clearly a fundamental form of personal expression protected by the constitutional guarantees of privacy and free speech, not all courts have agreed that students can groom and dress themselves as they please.

***Discipline, due process, and freedom from cruel and unusual punishment.*** In *Goss v. Lopez* (1975), the Supreme Court for the first time considered the degree of constitutional protection due to students facing school suspension. Finding that students have both liberty and property interests in their education, the Court set forth the precise procedure under the due process clause of the 14th amendment. Before a suspension of up to 10 days (the punishment of the students in the case before it), the Court held that a student must be afforded oral or written notice of charges and, if denied, an opportunity to rebut. When, because of emergencies or because a student poses a danger to persons or property, prior notice of charge and hearing was impossible, such notice, the Court said, "should follow as soon as practicable" (p. 583). The *Goss* Court noted that longer suspensions or expulsions may require more formal procedures but set forth no guidelines. Since *Goss,* many states have enacted statutes providing due process protections for both short- and long-term suspensions.

Two years after *Goss,* the Court considered in *Ingraham v. Wright* (1977) whether corporal punishment in public schools violated the Eighth amendment's prohibition of cruel and unusual punishment and whether advance notice and hearing was required by the due process clause before it could be administered. Ingraham, a junior high student in Dade County, Florida, had been beaten so severely (for failure to cooperate in a reading task) that he was confined to bed with a rectal hematoma for 10 days.

In a narrow ruling a 5 to 4 majority found that the Eighth amendment had been historically construed as applying to punishment of convicted felons in prisons and that no basis existed for applying it to discipline in public schools. Justice Byron White's words on this reasoning in his stinging dissent from this decision are as follows:

> The Eighth Amendment places a flat prohibition against the infliction of "cruel and unusual punishments." This reflects a societal judgment that there are some punishments that are so barbaric and inhumane that we will not permit them to be imposed on anyone, no matter how opprobrious the offense. . . . If there are some punishments that are so barbaric that they may not be imposed for the commission of crimes, designated by our social system as the most thoroughly reprehensible acts an individual can commit, then, *a fortiori,* similar punishments may not be imposed on persons for less culpable acts, such as breaches of school discipline. (*Ingraham v. Wright,* 1977, p. 685)

The *Ingraham* Court also ruled that no advance notice or hearing is required *before* the administration of corporal punishment. Although conceding that corporal punishment inflicted by public officials implicated an interest protected by the due process clause—the student's liberty interest to be free from bodily restraint and punishment involving appreciable physical pain—the majority said that the right to sue for damages or press criminal assault charges for excessive punishment *after* it was inflicted is adequate procedural due process.

Although *Ingraham* constitutionally *permits* corporal punishment in schools, it does not *require* it. Nothing in this decision prevents states, municipalities, or school districts from banning corporal punishment by statute, regulation, or written policy and a number have done so. At this writing, corporal punishment in schools has been abolished by statute in 26 states, and in the remaining states it is forbidden by regulation in most major cities (A. Maurer, executive director, End Violence against Next Generation, Berkeley, CA, personal communication, March 14, 1994).

***Law enforcement and searches.*** School officials may allow police into school to question or arrest students, but no one can require a student to talk to the police. The constitutional right to remain silent, as in any interaction with the police outside school, remains in place. In some school districts, principals must advise a student of the right to remain silent and to be represented by a lawyer if the student is a suspect in a crime, especially if the parents cannot be reached (Price, Levine, & Carey, 1988).

Students may be searched by police only on possession of a warrant based on probable cause to believe they have committed a crime; principals cannot permit the removal of students from school by police unless they are placed under arrest. Searches by school officials follow a more lenient standard than that applied to police. In *New Jersey v. T.L.O.* (1985), the Supreme Court found that Fourth amendment protections against unreasonable searches and seizures do apply to student searches by public school officials. However, a majority of the justices feared that the time required to obtain a probable cause warrant from a judge would "unduly interfere with the maintenance of the swift and informal disciplinary procedures needed in schools." Influenced also by its belief that lowered protection may reasonably apply to minors instead of that required for adults, the Court applied the lesser standard of *reasonable suspicion,* ruling that school officials can search a student

> when there are reasonable grounds for suspecting that the student has violated or is violating either the law or the rules of the school. Such a search will be permissible in its scope when the measures adopted are reasonably related to the objectives of the search and are not excessively intrusive in the light of the age and sex of the student and the nature of the infraction. (p. 342)

This imposes two tests on school officials. First, there must be some fact or facts providing a reasonable basis to believe that evidence of wrongdoing will be found on the suspected student. Second, the search must be appropriate to the maturity level and gender of the student and not be more intrusive than necessary to find the specific thing being sought.

***Tracking.*** *Tracking*—the test-balanced placement of children into ability groups—is ubiquitous among school districts in the United States. Although no court has found tracking unconstitutional in itself, particular instances have been found to be unconstitutionally discriminatory and in violation of the equal protection clause of the 14th amendment. The words of one judge who ruled against the tracking system in Washington, DC, highlight the most common fallacies and dangers of tracking that give rise to unlawful discrimination:

> Because these tests are standardized primarily on and are relevant to a white middle-class group of students, they produce inaccurate and misleading test scores when given to lower class and Negro students. As a result, rather than being classified according to ability to learn, these students are in reality being classified according to their socioeconomic or racial status, or—more precisely—according to environmental and psychological factors which have nothing to do with innate ability. (*Hobson v. Hanson, 1967*)

***Race and gender discrimination.*** Since the Supreme Court's landmark 1954 ruling in the case of *Brown v. Board of Education,* which declared racially segregated public schools to be a violation of the equal protection clause of the 14th amendment, hundreds of cases have been litigated involving different aspects of school segregation: de facto segregation, racial imbalance, freedom of choice, busing, token integration, and housing patterns.

Discrimination on the basis of gender in public schools is prohibited by the 14th amendment as well as by various state and federal statutes. Thus, no public school can have fixed quotas for girls and boys; prohibit girls from taking courses that are traditionally taught to boys, such as shop (and vice versa); or constitutionally maintain a competitive sports program for boys in a particular sport in the absence of an alternate opportunity in the same sport for girls. When this is not the case and the girls in question could compete effectively on the boys' team, they cannot be prohibited from doing so on the basis of gender (Price et al., 1988). On the issue of all-male or all-female public schools, it is clear that a school cannot, on both constitutional and statutory grounds, exclude one gender from a special program that is not available to the excluded gender in another school (*Garrett v. Detroit Board of Education,* 1991).

Female students are the most frequent targets of another widespread practice: removal from school or extracurricular activities for becoming pregnant, becoming a parent, or getting married. Almost without exception, the courts have found rules under which this practice is carried out to be in violation of the 14th amendment or Title IX of the Education Amendments of 1972.

**Statutory Rights**

The rights in this section are basically statutory. They are based in law enacted separately from the U.S. or state constitutions.

***Diplomas and grades.*** Students have a substantial right to receive a diploma given the successful completion of academic requirements for graduation. Although few court precedents exist in this area, higher-educational officials have tended to recognize this on their own. A decision of the New York City chancellor is instructive on this point. The case involved the withholding of a diploma by a school principal from a student whom he considered a "poor citizen." The chancellor ruled that the diploma must be issued:

> Students who violate rules of conduct are subject to disciplinary measures, but the manipulation of a diploma is not a proper or legitimate disciplinary tool in view of the inherent difficulty in defining "citizenship" and the clear danger and impropriety of labelling students as "good" or "bad" citizens. The school system should award the diploma on the basis of carefully defined educational criteria, and not deny or delay the diploma on other than educational grounds or as a means of discipline. In brief, the school is empowered to grant diplomas, not citizenship. (Price et al., 1988, p. 141)

Unlike diplomas, policies on the use of grades as punishment, particularly for absences, vary widely between the states. The use of academic penalties (lowering of grades or withholding credit) as a means of discipline has been widely challenged as a violation of a student's right to both substantive and procedural due process. Allegations charging violations of substantive due process typically challenge the fundamental right of the school to use grades as discipline for misconduct; those alleging violations of procedural due process relate to the procedure involved in enforcement of school rules, for example, notice and hearings.

An analysis of court responses in substantive due process challenges to school district authority to adopt rules allowing academic punishment for attendance violations has indicated that decisions are basically determined by particular statutes in each state. State statutes prescribing penalties for truancy and regulating student conduct will determine the district's ability to adopt local rules calling for additional sanctions when students miss school (Bruin, 1989).

However, several state courts have found that counting suspension days as unexcused absences is illegal even when the policy for academic sanctions for nonattendance is validly based. Thus, if a student is suspended for misconduct other than violation of purely academic rules directly related to learning, such as cheating, added academic punishment is prohibited (Bruin, 1989).

A second kind of substantive due process issue occurs when the basic fairness or reasonableness of a penalty is challenged—not the rule itself. A Mississippi school board adopted a rule prohibiting students from using or possessing alcohol while at school and while traveling to and from school. When an honor student admitted having two or three sips of beer at home before coming to school, she was denied all credit for her second-semester work. The Mississippi Supreme Court ruled that the punishment was unreasonable when compared with other offenses forbidden by school rules (Bruin, 1989).

***School records.*** From kindergarten through the 12th grade, a great deal of personal information steadily builds up in the so-called cumulative file of every student in American education. This record, by the best professional standard, exists purely to protect the quality of the student's educational development.

In 1974 Congress passed an amendment to the Family Educational Rights and Privacy Act (Buckley Amendment) that guarantees parents or students age 18 years or older the right to examine the student file in all schools receiving federal funds. Virtually every public school, and private schools receiving federal funding, are affected by this law. Students younger than 18 may view their record if the school allows access to it or if the parent requests so in writing.

The Buckley Amendment also bars access to the record by outsiders, absent the written consent of the parent or a student 18 or older. Records can be sent to a school to which a student is being transferred only after the parent has been given a chance to request a copy and challenge anything deemed improper. Even surrender of records in compliance with a lawful court order or subpoena must be preceded by a reasonable effort to notify parents. Release of records without consent may occur only in an emergency if the information in the records is strictly necessary to protect the health and safety of the students or others. The control of record information by parent or child 18 or older extends to being able, against school wishes, to require school release of information to third parties.

***Students with handicapping conditions.*** Three important federal laws guarantee every student's right to a free and appropriate public education regardless of handicap:

1. The Education for All Handicapped Children Act of 1975 provides federal funds to school districts that agree to follow specified procedures.
2. Section 504 of the Rehabilitation Act of 1973 requires that treatment of handicapped individuals be equal with nonhandicapped individuals, whether in regular or special education classes.
3. Title II of the Americans with Disabilities Act of 1990 requires public entities (units of state and local governments) to make their programs and services accessible to qualified persons with disabilities.

Under the Education for All Handicapped Children Act, *handicapped children* includes children who are mentally retarded; hard-of-hearing or deaf; blind or visually impaired; speech impaired; seriously emotionally disturbed; or orthopedically impaired (preventing movement) and children with specific learning disabilities or impairments in strength, vitality, or alertness as a result of a chronic or acute health problem. Both Section 504 of the Rehabilitation Act and the Americans with Disabilities Act define a *handicapped person* as anyone who has a physical or mental impairment that limits at least one major life activity.

These statutes can combine to provide extremely powerful civil rights protection for handicapped children's educational needs. A 1993 Michigan case in which the U.S. Department of Education Office for Civil Rights ruled that part of a collective bargaining agreement was in violation of Section 504 of the Rehabilitation Act and Title II of the Americans with Disabilities Act is illustrative in this regard. The Office for Civil Rights report made the following conclusions:

> The District is violating Section 504 and Title II by subjecting students with disabilities to a different treatment on the basis of disability. Specifically, students with disabilities have been denied enrollment in their neighborhood schools and have been denied the opportunity to participate in regular education classes because they are counted differently than are students without disabilities for the purpose of determining maximum class sizes. Through the application of the provisions, the District also failed to educate students with disabilities with students without disabilities to the maximum extent appropriate to their individual needs. Finally, the District failed to provide appropriate education services because of the provisions. (Burkhour, 1993, pp. 1, 7)

A student falling within diagnostic categories of the Education for All Handicapped Children Act is entitled to an education "reasonably calculated to enable the child to receive passing marks and advance from grade to grade" (*Board of Education of the Hendrick Hudson School District v. Rowley,* 1982, p. 204). The range of services required under this standard must be determined on a case-by-case basis pursuant to an evaluation conducted by the school with the parents' written consent. By law, within a maximum of 30 days after the completion of the evaluation, an individualized education program must be prepared in a meeting including one or both parents along with a team of educational professionals.

Once in an individualized education program for a handicapping condition, a student cannot legally be suspended for more than 10 days for behavior related to that handicap. Shorter, emergency suspensions can occur, and if the behavior in question is not related to the handicap, a district may proceed as it would with any nonhandicapped student (Beekman, 1989).

## Parent–Child Relationship

Whoever legally provides a physical habitat for a minor child and has primary responsibility for his or her upbringing is said to have custody of the child. Status of custodians may range from biological parents through adoptive parents, foster parents, guardians, relatives, or institutional personnel. Nothing casts a more revealing light on the powerlessness of children and their status as mere property or chattel than the laws of custody.

Parents and children have a fundamental right to live together without state interference, absent a judicial determination of neglect or abuse. However, children do not have a right to remain with their parents over their parents' objections. Parents may voluntarily surrender their right to their children and give their custody to third parties, whether or not the children agree with that decision. Legally, within the family system, a child holds only the right to be supported and nurtured until the age of majority. The parental right to nonabusive control and discipline over the child is absolute. Conversely, the law is directly involved in the increased autonomy of minors on another level. Until the age of majority, children have been regarded as legally incompetent to consent to their own medical treatment, but in recent decades this has begun to change. Most states now recognize special circumstances that permit adolescent minors to obtain, and physicians to provide, certain medical services without the consent of a parent or guardian. This is particularly the case for special types of medical care, such as treatment of drug or alcohol abuse, venereal disease, or prenatal care. Also, minors have the right to obtain over-the-counter birth control devices without parental consent (Guggenheim & Sussman, 1985).

A minor may obtain an abortion without the knowledge or consent of a parent in about one-third of the states. In the other states, she has a right to a judicial "bypass" hearing in which she either is found sufficiently mature to make this decision independently or, if not, will be found in need of an abortion on a best-interest basis.

**Custody**

Parents involved in separation or divorce may privately decide with whom the child will reside; if they cannot decide, a judge who has the power to grant custody to either parent or order joint custody will do so. Normally, the "losing" parent is not stripped of all the rights and duties of parenthood. Financial support of the child may still be required and visitation rights are usually granted. Judges are expected to base their decision in contested custody cases on a "best interest of the child" standard (statutory or otherwise). In practice, however, it is seldom the case that a child is either seriously consulted or represented when his or her "best interest" is being decided. Although a handful of states are legally required to consider and give weight to the preference of a child old enough to form an intelligent opinion, the most that can be said is that most American courts follow the rule that in custody matters a child's preference *may* be considered but is inconclusive.

With respect to representation, every court that determines child custody has the inherent power to appoint an attorney to represent a child's interest; in practice this rarely happens. In fewer than five states, an attorney is *required* to be appointed to represent the child in every contested custody case. In a rare and remarkable statement of principle in one case, the Supreme Court of Wisconsin said that legal representation "is due children who are not to be buffeted around as mere chattels in a divorce controversy, but rather are to be treated as interested and affected parties whose welfare should be the prime concern of the court in its custody determination" (Guggenheim & Sussman, 1985, pp. 136–137).

Court-ordered visitation of the noncustodial parent is regarded as a recognition of the child's right of association with both parents. Only on a determination of negligence or unfitness during such visitation could this right be abrogated. The right to visitation with a noncustodial parent does not translate, however, into the child's right to refuse to visit when ordered by the court. Unless there are truly extraordinary circumstances, the court will protect the noncustodial parent's right to visit his or her children even over their objection. Although a clear right to remain with siblings does not exist, most courts will consider the effect of custody decisions on all the children of a family and deal sensitively with the desirability of their sharing the same custodial setting.

**Abuse**

Apart from criminal assault laws that protect people of all ages, every state, since the medical discovery of the battered child syndrome in the early 1960s, has rewritten child abuse and neglect laws to more fully protect the right of a child (usually until age 18) to be raised by one's parents free from substantial harm. The courts have interpreted such laws as also applying to nonparental adults, in any custodial setting, acting in the role of the parent. This right is complicated by a network of rights accorded to parents to raise their children relatively free from coercive state intervention into the family. It is important to understand the tension between these two sets of rights as well as the operations of the law in one of the most awesome powers of the state: the permanent dissolution of the parent–child relationship. Although varying between states, *abuse* is typically coupled with serious physical injury, sexual intercourse, or sexual molestation. Some states define abuse more broadly to include conditions in which parents create a risk of serious injury or inflict psychological abuse.

**Neglect**

*Neglect* is more loosely defined and is typically associated with the failure of parents to provide adequate shelter, food, clothing, and medical care. *Abandonment* (leaving a child without adequate supervision for a certain length of time) is also considered an act of neglect in most states. Commonly, the failure to send a child to school is treated as a form of neglect, although it can also result in criminal charges.

More than one-third of the states have statutes identifying "immorality" as constituting child neglect. None of the states has a clear or consistent interpretation of how the particular behavior that is considered immoral (for example, alcoholism, promiscuity, or drug use) actually perpetrates, or in itself constitutes, child neglect. Since the 1960s the courts have shown increasing resistance to consider so-called immorality an equivalent with neglect unless it creates deficiencies in child care that require separating the child from the parent (Guggenheim & Sussman, 1985). Anyone may report suspected neglect or abuse, including the victim, to the local police or social welfare department of the county or state. Names of reporting individuals are not generally revealed to families. When individuals are identified, good faith reporting usually immunizes them from civil liability.

Certain categories of human services providers are required by law to report suspected child abuse. Doctors and hospitals in all states must report suspected abuse, and in many states, school teachers, social workers, dentists, and nurses must report suspected abuse. Failure on the part of individuals in these roles to report suspected child abuse is punishable in most states as a misdemeanor.

A report typically leads to home investigation by a department of social welfare caseworker, or, less often, by police. If, on investigation, there is credible evidence to believe that maltreatment is occurring, the following options are open to the investigating agency: It may file a petition in the appropriate court to have the child declared abused or neglected; it may try to encourage the parents to participate in an educational, training, or rehabilitative program under threat of a court petition; it may, in less-severe instances, merely encourage the family to accept voluntary help; or it may refer the family or the child to another family agency.

**Removal from Home**

A child can be taken from the parental home only with court approval. Emergent circumstances—conditions in the home constituting an extreme danger to the health and safety of the child—are the only exception to this rule. In such cases a hearing must be scheduled at the earliest time possible for a judicial determination as to whether continued separation from the home is necessary. In making a judicial determination of abuse or neglect, the evidentiary standard that must be met is either proof that is "clear and convincing" or supported by a "preponderance of evidence." In most states, children in neglect and abuse proceedings are assigned an attorney to represent them, as are parents who cannot afford their own attorneys. After a judicial determination of neglect or abuse of sufficient severity, the court may order a child to be taken from parents and placed in foster care with a licensed foster parent, a relative, or in an institution that provides care for neglected and abused children. Usually such children become court wards.

Once a child has been in state foster care for some time and after parents have failed to respond to rehabilitative assistance, or on the occurrence of some grave and compelling event affecting a child still in the parental home, the state may seek to involuntarily terminate parental rights. Because parents have a fundamental right to raise their children, the state can deprive them of this right only under compelling circumstances. Grounds for involuntary termination cannot be minor or defined with such overbreadth as to sanction termination for less-than-compelling reasons.

The first major test of overly vague and broad termination statutes was brought in *Alsager v. District Court* (1975/1976) by parents who challenged an Iowa law that authorized termination for "refusal to give a child necessary parental care and protection" (quoted in Guggenheim & Sussman, 1985, p. 122) or for parental conduct "likely to be detrimental to the physical or mental health and morals of a child" (p. 123). Based on this language, rights to four of five children were terminated because the home was unkempt and the children were often dirty and unruly, although there was no evidence or judicial finding that the children were harmed in any way. On appeal, a federal court reversed, finding unconstitutional vagueness in the law because it did not give fair warning of what parental conduct is proscribed, it permitted arbitrary and discriminatory termination, and it inhibited the exercise of the fundamental right to family integrity (Guggenheim & Sussman, 1985).

Three years later, the Arkansas Supreme Court found unconstitutionally vague a statute permitting termination if parents failed to provide a child with "a proper home." The court's language is instructive:

> Using any of [the possible] meanings does little to make the words, "a proper home," clearly understandable so that it doesn't mean one thing to one judge,

> something else to another, and something yet different to still another. What is a proper home? A correct home? A suitable home? A fit home? Is propriety to be determined ethically, socially, or economically? Or on the basis of morality? Or prosperity? Is the standard a maximum, a minimum, a mean or an average? (Guggenheim & Sussman, 1985, p. 123)

**Foster Care**

*Foster care* is a nonparental custodial relationship between a child and an adult, of a noninstitutional form, usually for a limited time during which natural parents are unable to provide care. It may be established voluntarily by agreement between the natural parents and foster parents, between natural parents and a public or private child care agency, or involuntarily due to a finding of abuse or neglect by a state department of social welfare or a court (in which case the supervising agency could be public or private). Whereas in separation or divorce custody proceedings a child may have some input, however meager, regarding with whom the child will live, in foster placement the child has no input at all.

**Termination of Parental Rights**

Although intended to be temporary, foster care may extend for long periods during which the child and foster parents form attachments, and resistance to a return to natural parents may occur. In some states, foster parents may prevail if they can show courts that it is in the "best interest" of the child to remain with them (Guggenheim & Sussman, 1985). In recent years the theory of "psychological parenthood" has bolstered court decisions along these lines. But in other states, courts require proof that a child will be harmed by the natural parents before foster parents will be granted long-range or permanent custody (Guggenheim & Sussman).

Although becoming a foster parent does not create a right to adoption or a guarantee of success, foster parents may attempt to adopt a foster child. Of course, without involuntary termination of parental rights or the parent's permission, no adoption can occur, and generally the legal standard for involuntary termination of parental rights is severe because of the fundamental right of family integrity.

Nonetheless, in some states there is a trend toward allowing termination of parental rights and adoption when persuasive proof is presented that the best interests of the child would be served. What has arisen with this trend has been described as no-fault termination of parental rights. These trends have occurred mainly when children and foster parents have been together for a long time and the child considers the foster parent to be his or her "real" parent. Obviously, in jurisdictions in which no-fault theory has gained a foothold, the longer foster parents retain custody, the stronger their chance becomes to adopt the child (Guggenheim & Sussman, 1985). However, an influential factor in such cases is the supervising agency's recommendation to the court. When an agency having legal custody of a child opposes adoption, a court, even in no-fault jurisdictions, is hesitant to overrule it.

A new development in the foster parent–biological parent sector, prodigiously reported in the media, is the rare instance in which children have been provided access to the court to proceed as party plaintiffs to present their own view of what is in their best interest. It is far too early to tell whether this signifies a trend toward a radical transformation of children's rights law or will remain without precedential or growth potential as aberrational blips in legal history.

**Goals and Standards**

Although the laws just discussed do affect family reunification, extended foster care, and adoption, they shed little light on what has been happening to foster children for several decades in the real world, particularly among those children in involuntary state care. Every state has a government-operated child welfare system regulated by federal and state laws and funded by public money. By current standards, a system that is functioning properly should be offering the following services:

- preventive services to families designed to avert the need for foster care
- adequate protection of children in their homes
- reasonable foster placement procedures
- adequate placement resources and supports
- family reunification services
- special treatment for children with special needs
- access to permanent adoption for children who cannot be returned to their homes
- management structure and resources to provide responsible monitoring and accountability.

The rarity with which these goals and standards are met in these frequently underfunded, understaffed, and mismanaged systems has made the children enmeshed in state foster care one of the most at-risk populations in the United States. For instance, thousands of children placed in foster care programs are shuttled from one home to another, causing their education and emotional development to be disrupted. Children are often placed in homes with untrained and poorly supported foster parents, under the supervision of poorly trained and enormously overworked social workers. Some children eligible for adoption must wait years for an adoptive family, or are never adopted at all, often simply because administrators have failed to do the paperwork (Bond, 1993).

### Reforms

So far only litigation or threat of litigation has been able to bring about positive change in these delinquent bureaucracies. A major player on this scene has been the Children's Rights Project of the national American Civil Liberties Union. Replicating a litigative model used earlier to reform other public institutions such as prisons, psychiatric hospitals, and schools, the project commenced lawsuits in the early 1980s to reform child welfare systems around the country.

The constitutional principles of individuals' rights to due process and equal protection under the law and their right not to be harmed while under the care of the state provided a basic foundation for these challenges. The primary statutory basis was provided by the Adoption Assistance and Child Welfare Act of 1980, which was replaced by child welfare, foster care, and adoption assistance provisions contained in the Omnibus Budget Reconciliation Act of 1993. The basic thrust of the act deemphasizes foster care in favor of increased services to children's biological families and speedier adoption procedures to facilitate either return to the original family or adoption in a timely fashion. The pivotal change in the law is a new permanent entitlement program capped at $895 million over five years. Funds are to be used to create or expand family support and family preservation services such as respite care, in-home visits and drop-in centers, services to improve parenting skills, developmental screening for children, information and referral to other community services, reunification and preplacement preventive services such as intensive family preservation, and follow-up reunification services and permanency planning. Foster, adoptive, and biological families will be eligible for all these services. A related provision of the act is health care coverage for adoptees. Group health care plans must now cover children placed for adoption, regardless of whether the adoption is final. Additionally, coverage may not be denied to an adoptee on the basis of a preexisting condition prior to adoption. Clearly this act is a plus to litigative attempts at reform of malfunctioning child welfare systems.

Through these efforts, the Children's Rights Project has succeeded in obtaining either court orders mandating systemwide reform or consent decrees, the equivalent of court-approved and court-monitored promises by child welfare systems to change their practices and procedures. At the time of this writing, the project has sued 10 states or local governments: Connecticut; District of Columbia; Kansas; Kansas City, Missouri; Louisiana; Louisville, Kentucky; Milwaukee, Wisconsin; New Mexico; New York City; and Philadelphia.

## Adoption

*Adoption* is the permanent legal termination of the relationship between a child and his or her natural parent or parents and the establishment of a new parent–child relationship with all the legal and other characteristics of the natural relationship. The necessary prior step to any adoption is the voluntary or involuntary termination of parental rights. Subsequent to this step, the child becomes a ward of the state or of a licensed child care agency until an adoption occurs. Although children do not have a constitutional right to be adopted, most states have a statutory duty to search for adoptive homes for children in long-term state foster care.

### State Laws

In a number of states and in the District of Columbia, minors who are parents may surrender their child for adoption without parental consent, whereas in other states consent of one or both parents is required. In most states, parental consent is not required of married minors who mutually agree to adoption. In every state, however, if the unmarried father is available he must be notified and provided a chance to appear at a hearing before an adoption (*Stanley v. Illinois*, 1972). Whether his consent will be required will depend on the extent and quality of his relationship with the potential adoptee.

Natural parents do not have an unfettered right to choose prospective adoptive parents, particularly if their rights have been terminated involuntarily. The agency or court, as surrogate parent, will usually decide on a best-interest basis which adoptive family is most suited. Even when parents have proceeded on a totally private voluntary basis and have placed the child with the prospective adoptive parents, the last word is still the state's, by means of a court that must give final approval on a best-interest basis.

Once a child has been surrendered for adoption, there is a six- to nine-month waiting period (varying among the states) during which parents may reclaim the child before the final adoption decree. After this point, the natural parent can regain custody only if he or she can show that the surrender occurred as a result of a complete lack of understanding or some form of coercion (Guggenheim & Sussman, 1985).

**Rights of Children**

A child would have a right to appeal an adverse decision in an adoption proceeding in states where the child is recognized as a party to, as opposed to the subject of, the proceedings. Because children are rarely appointed counsel in adoption proceedings to begin with, and if so mainly in the status of subject, such appeals are rare.

In most states, adoption records are sealed and can be opened, if at all, only by a court order on a showing of "good cause," a standard of which interpretation differs widely, depending on the severity and subjective judgment of judges. The dominant view among adoption professionals is that sealed records best protect the interests of adoptive families and birth parents against violations of privacy from each other or outsiders who might gain access to open records.

Court challenges to the constitutionality of confidentiality statutes have consistently failed because legislatures have been able to convince courts that sealed adoption statutes serve rational state interests in promoting adoptions (Guggenheim & Sussman, 1985). Such rulings do not imply, however, a constitutional duty to seal records, leaving this decision up to each state. Thus, in Alabama, Kansas, Montana, Pennsylvania, and South Dakota, adult adoptees have access to birth records and related court documents without court permission. Moreover, for the past several years, even in states with confidentiality statutes, so-called open adoptions have been approved by courts when all parties consent. This alternative allows an adopted child to retain a relationship with the natural parents, including visitation rights.

## Commentary

The children's rights movement is a history of emergent recognition of children as existentially separate beings from their adult caretakers and controllers and as possessing independent interests and rights of their own. Child protection law concretizes this adult–child separateness. It establishes that the welfare of the custodial child's body and mind has a unique value to the state against which the countervailing values of family privacy and the fundamental rights of parents are to be balanced. But child protection in the lawbooks and child protection in reality can and do differ radically. Hundreds of thousands of children are "saved" by the state from the "bad" parent only to be equally harmed by the state, the "good" parent. In this regard the growing recognition of the child as a person for constitutional purposes in the cumulative case law since the mid-1950s has come dramatically into play. It has enabled massive class action reform litigation using the constitutional principles of due process and equal protection, combined with federal statutes, to challenge state welfare bureaucratic neglect.

Yet it is children who, without access to the courts, may be legally beaten by a parent short of medically significant physical harm, when similar spousal maltreatment would constitute a criminal assault. It is children who, in 24 states, can be assaulted by a teacher, having been denied by the Supreme Court the protection accorded a convicted felon in prison. It is foster children, the poorest and most disadvantaged in the land, who need to be rescued from developmental damage by state neglect. It is the postpubescent adolescent girl unable to safely communicate with parents who must, in two-thirds of our states, face the unjustified burden of a judicial hearing to realize her constitutional right to an abortion. In this century children have made dramatic gains and come within striking distance of some adult rights. Nonetheless, it is still children who most strongly bring to mind George Orwell's (1946) dictum in the political satire *Animal Farm* that all animals are created equal but some are more equal than others.

## References


Adoption Assistance and Child Welfare Act of 1980. P.L. 96-272, 94 Stat. 500.

Alsager v. District Court, 406 F. Supp. 10 (S.D. Iowa 1975), *aff'd*, 545 F.2d. 1137 (8th Cir. 1976).

Americans with Disabilities Act of 1990. P.L. 101-336, 104 Stat. 327.

Beekman, L. E. (1989). Discipline and the special education student. In C. B. Vargon (Ed.), *School discipline: Contemporary issues in law and policy* (pp. 52–55). Ann Arbor: University of Michigan, School of Education.

Bethel School District No. 403 v. Fraser, 478 U.S. 675 (1986).

Board of Education of the Hendrick Hudson School District v. Rowley, 458 U.S. 176 (1982).

Bond, J. C. (1993). *A source for change.* New York: ACLU Public Education Department.

Brown v. Board of Education, 344 U.S. 1 (1954).

Bruin, L. (1989). Student attendance and academic sanctions. In C. B. Vargon (Ed.), *School discipline: Contemporary issues in law and policy* (pp. 84–86). Ann Arbor: University of Michigan, School of Education.

Burkhour, H. (1993). Agreement discriminates against special education student. *Exchange, 14*(2), 1, 7.

Education for All Handicapped Children Act of 1975. P.L. 94-142, 89 Stat. 773.

Family Educational Rights and Privacy Act of 1974. P.L. 93-380, 88 Stat. 571.

Garrett v. Detroit Board of Education, 775 F. Supp. 1004 (E.D. Mich. 1991).

Goss v. Lopez, 419 U.S. 565 (1975).

Guggenheim, M., & Sussman, A. (1985). *The rights of young people.* New York: Bantam Books.

Hazelwood School District v. Kuhlmeier, 484 U.S. 260 (1988).

Hobson v. Hansen, 269 F. Supp. 401 (D.D.C. 1967).

Ingraham v. Wright, 430 U.S. 651 (1977).

New Jersey v. T.L.O., 469 U.S. 325 (1985).

Omnibus Budget Reconciliation Act of 1993. P.L. 103-66, 107 Stat. 31.

Orwell, G. (1946). *Animal farm.* New York: New American Library.

Paye v. Gibralter School District. Lexis 16480 (unpublished opinion, E.D. Mich., Aug. 6, 1991).

Price, J. R., Levine, A. H., & Carey, E. (1988). *The rights of students.* Carbondale: Southern Illinois University Press.

Rehabilitation Act of 1973. P.L. 93-112, 87 Stat. 355.

Stanley v. Illinois, 405 U.S. 645 (1972).

Tinker v. Des Moines Independent Community School District, 393 U.S. 503 (1969).

Title IX, Education Amendments of 1972. 20 U.S.C. 1681.

### Further Reading

Besharov, D. J. (1990). *Recognizing child abuse.* New York: Free Press.

Curwin, R. L., & Mendler, A. N. (1988). *Discipline with dignity: Problems and solutions.* Alexandria, VA: Association for Supervision and Curriculum Development.

Garbarino, J., Brookhouser, P. E., & Authier, K. J. (1987). *Special children—Special risks: The maltreatment of children with disabilities.* New York: Aldine de Gruyter.

Hardin, M. (Ed.). (1983). *Foster children in the courts.* Boston, MA: Butterworth Legal Publishers.

Jonas, F. H. (1987). *Positive classroom discipline.* New York: McGraw-Hill.

Oakes, J. (1985). *Keeping track: How schools structure inequality.* New Haven, CT: Yale University Press.

**David Wineman, MSW,** is professor emeritus, Wayne State University, School of Social Work, Detroit, MI 48202.

### For further information see

Adolescence Overview; Adoption; Advocacy; Bioethical Issues; Child Abuse and Neglect Overview; Child Foster Care; Child Labor; Child Sexual Abuse Overview; Child Support; Child Welfare Overview; Childhood; Civil Rights; Cults; Domestic Violence; Ethics and Values; Families Overview; Human Rights; Juvenile and Family Courts; Juvenile Corrections; Legal Issues: Low-Income and Dependent People; Patient Rights; Runaways and Homeless Youths; School Social Work Overview; Single Parents; Social Welfare Policy; Youth Services.

**Key Words**

adoption
children's rights
foster placement
parental responsibility
schools

## Chinese

*See* Asian Americans: Chinese

# Church Social Work

**Diana R. Garland**

The roots of almost all modern social services are in religious organizations; hence the church can be considered the "mother of social work" (Johnson, 1941, p. 404). Churches continue to serve as prominent contexts for social work practice; more than 12 percent of the social workers who responded to a 1991 survey of NASW members reported that they practiced in sectarian settings (Gibelman & Schervish, 1993). Furthermore, churches play a crucial role in social welfare in the United States; in 1991 they gave an estimated $6.6 billion to social causes (Filteau, 1993). This entry defines church social work and describes its historical development, the organizational and cultural characteristics of the church, role expectations and constraints of church social workers, and the current settings of church social work practice.

### Definitions of Church Social Work

Simply stated, church social work is social work that takes place under the auspices of a church organization. Churches are organizations that seek to develop, renew, and guide peoples' religious lives in accord with Christian principles and traditions. Like other social organizations, they have structures based on a division of responsibility and privilege among people; tasks to be performed; and defined processes, rules, and norms for performing them. They have bodies of beliefs, codified in creeds and doctrines, that define the organization's culture in distinctive ways.

Churches have histories that link them with a long heritage and contribute in significant ways to their identity and organizational mission. They are participants in an ideal, the Church, to which all followers of Jesus Christ in the past, present, and future belong. The apostle Paul instructed Christians to consider themselves part of one body, the body of Christ, each with an indispensable function (Romans 12:3–8; 1 Corinthians 12). In another image, all Christians are members of the "household of God" who, with Christ as the cornerstone, grow into a holy temple, a dwelling place for God in the Spirit (Ephesians 2:19–22). These ideals, the teachings of Christ and other holy scriptures, and historical traditions motivate and guide the self-critique, continuous modifications, and development of church organizations. However, actual groups and organizations of Christians vary dramatically in the ways they understand and strive to achieve the ideals of the Christian faith.

### Settings

The church social worker practices in this context much as the medical social worker practices in a hospital or the school social worker practices in a school, although church social work is practiced in an array of organizational settings, including congregations and parishes, denominational organizations, and ecumenical organizations. A *congregation* refers to a group of persons who band together for religious purposes and have a shared group identity; they often have a central meeting place. A *parish* is the community that the congregation serves.

A *denomination* refers to an organization of many congregations (such as United Methodists or Presbyterians USA) that share certain beliefs and practices and choose to cooperate with each other to achieve what they could not achieve individually. Denominations sponsor various social services and social action agencies and projects; publication houses that produce journals, newsletters, and educational materials for member congregations; colleges and seminaries for general education and the education of clergy; and national and international mission projects. Denominations organize themselves into overlapping levels, such as local, state, and national bodies.

*Ecumenical organizations* are organizations of churches, denominations, or both that choose to cooperate in activities and goals through which they transcend theological, ecclesiological, and historical differences. Ecumenical activities occur at several levels, from community ministries composed of churches of various denominations that are located in the same neighborhood or community to the World Council of Churches and other national and international organizations.

### Social Ministries

Within the various levels of church structure, church social workers often provide leadership in *Christian social ministries,* activities carried out by Christians to help people with special needs and to bring about social justice. These activities are considered the central responsibilities of the church and of individual Christians. Christian social ministries grow out of Jesus' teaching that neighbors are to be loved as we love ourselves and that all persons are neighbors, that responding to the needs of others is the way to respond faithfully to God's love, and that God is less concerned with religious ritual than with social justice. The social worker who is employed by a congregation helps members understand community needs, defines those needs as a challenge central to the mission of the church, and equips church members for effective service and social action. Christian social ministries may be led by people other than professional social workers, however; church leaders may have varying professional and nonprofessional backgrounds.

Church social workers and Christian social workers are not equivalent categories (see Loewenberg's, 1988, extensive discussion of the role of the professional social worker's personal religious beliefs and values; see also Marty, 1980). The personal faith of the social worker does not define church social work; rather, church social work is defined by the context in which the social worker practices. Although many social workers who work in church settings believe that their practice is based primarily on their faith and use their professional social work knowledge and skills as they fit, many others integrate their personal faith with their professional practice, both drawing from and struggling with the tensions that sometimes are created. Still others separate faith from practice: Some church social workers are not Christians, and others view their personal faith and church membership as distinct from their professional practice. Church social work is a practice specialization—a context for practice—not a value and belief system of the professional.

## Historical Development

Long before the birth of the social work profession, the church was concerned with human needs, particularly those of poor, oppressed, and marginalized people. In the first three centuries of the Christian era, Christians amazed the world around them with the extent to which they ministered to the needs of others. Hippolytus (A.D. 217) considered the care of widows a test for baptism. Early Christians assumed the major task of caring for abandoned and orphaned children, taking them into their own homes or creating foundling homes. They also sought to ransom slaves, even by voluntarily placing themselves in bondage. Converts (such as gladiators, actors, and prostitutes) who had to leave their occupations to join the fellowship were given work by wealthy members or support from a common fund (Hinson, 1988).

### Early Institutions

From the beginning, Christians also created institutions to meet human needs. The *agape,* a fellowship meal to feed the poor and hungry, began as a part of the Eucharist. With Constantine's conversion to Christianity came major support for a wide range of church ministries, especially those targeting orphans, foundlings, and poor people. Churches and individual church members established hospitals. Monasteries gave employment to many people, more for the purpose of giving aid than for the work the people could do. During the medieval period social service was left, for the most part, in the hands of the church. Monasteries continued to serve as centers of charity and fed the hungry during famine and war (Hinson, 1988).

Throughout the Reformation and the modern period (1500 to the present), the church concerned itself with the issues of poverty, social welfare, and family life. The early English Puritans frequently criticized the social and economic abuses of the 17th century, condemning landlords who charged excessive rents and wealthy people who ignored the needs of the poor. The Quakers' egalitarianism supported pacifism, care for the poor, prison reform, reforms in care for the mentally ill and disabled, and opposition to slavery. For example, in the 1700s John Woolman traveled throughout the American South, convincing Quakers to free their slaves, to work toward legislation banning the further importation of slaves, and to boycott the products of slave labor (Leonard, 1988).

### Voluntary Societies

During the 18th and 19th centuries, church groups and individuals formed voluntary societies, and denominations established agencies to which they assigned various social ministries. These societies and agencies addressed the problems of hunger, slum life, unemployment, workers' rights, mental illness, disabilities, prison reform, and the care of widows and orphans. With the founding in 1850 of the Five Points Mission in New York City by Phoebe Palmer, a holiness evangelist, Protestant institutional ministries in the slums of the nation began (T. Smith, 1976)—the seedbed for the development of the social work profession. The term "social gospel," first used in 1886 by Iowa Congregationalist minister Charles O. Brown (Leonard, 1988), became the label for that era's efforts to Christianize the social order. Walter Rauschenbusch, a 19th century German Baptist pastor and leader of the social gospel movement, despaired of individualized attempts at social service because he saw that they perpetuated the corrupt social system. The social gospel movement provided a Christian theological basis for social concern and social action and was the impetus for the development of the extensive structure of sectarian agencies that still exists.

### Professional Social Work

In the midst of this ferment, the social work profession was developing. Some Christians chose social work as the expression of their faith. Owen R. Lovejoy started his career as a minister and later became a leading social work executive and social reformer. Jane Addams rejected a foreign missionary career to become a pioneer social worker in the settlement house movement. Many people attempted to hold church and social work together. For example, Maud Reynolds McClure started a settlement house in Louisville, Kentucky, and in 1912 began teaching social work courses in the Baptist Woman's Missionary Union Training School, which later became the Carver School of Church Social Work of the Southern Baptist Theological Seminary.

Since those early years of the social work profession, the relationship between the church and social work has been dramatically uneven, ranging from collaboration to mutual disinterest or disdain. With the secularization of society and social services, the church has moved from being the primary host setting to being one of many host and primary settings in which social workers practice.

## Organizational Characteristics of the Church

The church functions as a host setting for church social work much like the hospital and school are the settings for medical social work and school social work. In host contexts, the social worker provides services that enable the organization to pursue its primary functions more effectively.

Social ministry and social action are central functions of the church, along with worship, fellowship, and evangelism.

The church context is, foundationally, a voluntary organization with multiple structural layers. Social workers often relate not only to the church organization that employs them but also to other organizational levels. For example, the social worker in a denomination-sponsored child welfare agency often spends significant time consulting, speaking, and developing resources in local congregations. Social workers who are employed in a congregation must deal with denominational policies and programs that affect their work and the social issues of the community. In all church settings for social work practice, social workers must respond to a constituency of small voluntary groups wielding power that can be both supportive and oppressive. It has been suggested that religious organizations are "different enough from other forms of organizational participation to make the religious context indecipherable to the traditionally trained organizational analyst" (Braskamp, Brandenburg, & Ory, 1987, p. 79).

### Church Governance

Church polity directly affects the choices a church social worker makes in seeking to influence decisions and programs. The three basic types of church governance—episcopal, presbyterian, and congregational—roughly correspond to political monarchies, aristocracies, and democracies, respectively (Moberg, 1984). Episcopal polity (Roman Catholic, Episcopal, and Lutheran) invests authority in an ecclesiastical hierarchy. Authority flows from the central church government down, so that clergy can operate independently of local congregations.

Presbyterian polity (Presbyterian and Methodist) theoretically gives local congregations decision-making authority, but the clergy who control the middle levels of church organization and the elders in local congregations tend to operate as an aristocracy. Clergy are subject to control by both the congregation—operating through its elders—and the middle levels of church organization, the presbytery. Churches with congregational polity (Baptists) loosely organize themselves as democracies. Local churches retain their autonomy and their right to choose and control the clergy. Even in the denominations just named, however, these types of government are often mixed. Democratic tendencies are increasingly apparent in episcopal and presbyterian churches, and congregational churches increasingly vest power in their centralized governments (Moberg, 1984).

### Impact of Structure

Polity has significant ramifications for church social work. Episcopal polity allows the church leader to use the power of a secure office to take a stand on social issues and to develop programs that may not receive the required majority vote in a locally autonomous congregational church. In addition, denominational levels of church government develop policy statements on social issues, provide materials, and develop programs that have a significant impact on the social ministries of many local congregations. On the other hand, locally autonomous congregational churches may be able to develop creative services to meet particular local needs or innovative social service programs that can serve as models for other churches because they are not required to receive the sanction or follow the direction of any central denominational government. They also may be involved in activities that would not be endorsed by a central denominational government, such as advocacy on behalf of migrant farmworkers or participation in the sanctuary movement by harboring illegal aliens.

Within these formal structures, churches vary in the actual informal structures through which they operate. A congregational church with a highly charismatic leader, for example, may be authoritarian in its decision making. In the same way, episcopal structures are often bureaucratic and democratic, with decisions made by rules, regulations, and general consensus. Nevertheless, this typology of church organizations can help social workers assess a particular church organization's formal and informal decision-making and organizational processes.

Variations in church organizational structures are not simply the outgrowth of organizational development processes; they also reflect different beliefs about the nature and mission of the church. The church is a mission-driven organization. The mission of the church is to tell the story of its faith and to serve as a living witness to the love of God, as shown in the life, death, and resurrection of Jesus Christ. Church social workers must articulate the relationship between their professional practice and this overarching mission of the church community, both in the local congregation and in denominational and ecumenical organizations.

## Cultural Characteristics of the Church

Churches have their own languages, nonverbal symbols, codes, norms, and patterns of relationships—their own culture. They also have historical identities that shape their current understanding of themselves and reflect not only an overarching denominational heritage, but the unique histories of particular communities and the interweaving of the church with the events and development of the church's surrounding social and physical environment. Like families, churches develop over time and go through organizational stages that partially shape their current response to the human needs and resources within and outside themselves (Moberg, 1984). Understanding code phrases and religious symbols requires an understanding of this cultural context, which may include latent and subconscious, as well as overt, meanings (Carroll, Dudley, & McKinney, 1986; Garland, 1993; Moberg, 1984).

Church social workers operate within and use the language and cultural patterns of the church community; the Bible, theology, and Christian values are keys to understanding and working effectively in this setting. For example, social workers can use biblical concepts of conflict management, confession, and repentance to help Christian families and groups work through conflict. The concepts of the "family of God" and Christian hospitality are the bases for social action on behalf of homeless and isolated people and social ministry programs that strive to include them in the life of the community. Biblical teachings on the value and role of children provide impetus for child welfare services.

Understanding these distinctive characteristics of the church context is just as important for effective social work practice as is understanding the culture, history, and current life experiences of an ethnic family that requests family services. Church social workers must have at least a rudimentary understanding of biblical studies, theology, church history, Christian ethics, denominational and congregational development, and current religious issues and concerns.

Often, social workers will find not only commonalities but basic conflicts between the values and knowledge of social work and a congregation or a denomination's beliefs and practices. Midgley and Sanzenbach (1989) identified basic conflicts between social work practice and fundamentalist religious teaching in the major areas of values (for example, the idea of individual worth and dignity versus the idea of individual sinfulness and worthlessness), knowledge base (for instance, scientific knowledge versus biblical interpretation), and practice approaches (such as professional intervention versus divine salvation). Church social workers must find ways to live with or challenge the contradictions inherent in their dual roles as social workers and church leaders when such conflicts exist. Such conflicts between the host setting and professional values and practices are not unique to church social work, however; for example, social workers in health care and mental health services must confront value conflicts with host medical organizations.

## Role Expectations and Constraints of Church Social Workers

Church social workers serve, at least in part, as leaders of the church, especially with respect to the church's social ministries. Those who are on the staffs of congregations serve directly in leadership roles. Even social workers who are employed to provide direct clinical services to clients in specialized agencies carry at least a minor responsibility for providing church leadership. Christian faith requires a lifestyle of service, and church employees are responsible for providing leadership by linking church members with opportunities to express this lifestyle and by preparing them to serve effectively.

As Hessel (1992) concluded, "The primary role of professional church workers is to equip a faithful *community* to intervene compassionately in the social system and to enhance caring interpersonal relations in ways that are consistent with Christian maturity" (p. 125). For example, social workers who provide family therapy services for children in a denominationally sponsored residential care facility may link members of supporting congregations in caring ways with the families being served by the agency. That linkage may be one of supportive friendship for a family that is isolated in its crisis, of respite care for family members who have no one to help them with the daily responsibility of a child with special needs, or of material assistance during a time of family crisis. The volunteer service of church members is a tremendous resource to social services: In 1991 churchgoers donated an estimated 1.8 billion hours of service in the United States (Filteau, 1993).

Social ministry often leads to attempts to bring about social change. For example, many community-based church agencies help poor families pay high winter utility bills. In one community, social workers in these agencies led their supporting congregations to lobby for local and state legislation to limit utility bills to a fixed percentage of income and to require landlords to weatherize low-income rental properties.

Church organizations often expect their social workers to be members of the denominations and congregations they serve because of their roles as church leaders. Professional relationships with clients sometimes originate in shared church functions, such as church committees, groups, or educational and other social ministry programs led by social workers (Taggart, 1962). Boundaries of client–professional relationships and between professional and private life are therefore much less well defined than in other professional contexts (Ferguson, 1992; Wikler, 1986, 1990) and at times may be virtually absent. These flexible boundaries allow clients and church members greater access, both formally and informally, to church social workers than is possible in other social services settings. Social workers also have greater potential knowledge of clients' and members' social networks and other resources and barriers to intervention. Often, however, social workers have to cope with personal or organizational confusion of roles and the result of being almost constantly, if informally, "on duty."

## Settings for Social Work Practice

### Congregational Staff

More and more church congregations—particularly large congregations in urban areas—are employing social workers to carry out a variety of responsibilities, such as developing and directing social ministries in the surrounding community, directing youth and family service programs, leading social action and advocacy programs, and providing counseling services for church and community members. Social workers also are called on to function as members of the clergy, for example, by leading worship and Bible study as well as in the social ministries of the congregation. They may be ordained or in other ways recognized by the church congregation as spiritual leaders.

Examples of services and programs developed and provided by church social workers in congregational contexts include educational and action groups that study key social issues, day care and respite care services for children, after-school tutoring and activity programs, adult day care and respite care for frail elderly adults and their caregivers, shelter and feeding programs for homeless families, transportation services to medical care in rural communities for elderly and poor families, job placement and training programs, self-help and educational groups and programs, emergency assistance, material and social support for clients of public child protective services and family preservation programs, support and sponsorship programs for immigrants and refugees, building and repairing homes for poor families, friendship and mentoring programs for teenage parents and others with special needs, activity programs for residents of juvenile detention centers and prisons, and foster care and adoption support programs (Bailey, 1993; Ferguson, 1992; Garland, 1987, 1993; Johns, 1988; B. Smith, 1989). Often, service programs grow to include advocacy components, through which churches become voices on behalf of those they serve with local, regional, and national organizations and governments.

### Community Agencies and Service Programs

A major function of a denomination is to provide ways in which congregations can pool their resources for ministry. Denominationally sponsored social services agencies and boards are considered ministries of the local churches that support them in areas remote from the supporting churches or in response to needs that require professional competence beyond the resources and capabilities of church congregations. They also develop and publish materials that churches can use in their ministries, such as study guides on key social issues (including poverty, homelessness, and child abuse) and resources for educational programs (such as workshop guides for marriage and parent education). Church social workers are most commonly employed in these settings. Examples of denominational social ministry and social action organizations include residential child care and treatment programs; shelters for homeless people and families, pregnant teenagers, and abused family members; community-based family service agencies; professional lobbying and governmental legislation "watch" committees; housing, nutrition, home care, and socialization programs for aging families; adoption and foster care agencies; hospitals; refugee resettlement programs; and disaster and world hunger relief agencies.

Ecumenical agencies and organizations resemble denominational agencies and organizations in that they represent the cooperation and coordination of various congregations to provide ministry, develop resources, and influence social policy beyond what any one local congregation could do. Their goal, however, is to bridge denominational differences that may otherwise divide participants to achieve their shared mission and goals. In a local community, a cluster of churches may unite to assess the community's needs and to provide services such as emergency assistance, nutrition programs, senior adult programs, child care centers and after-school clubs, single-parent groups, self-help groups, counseling, and advocacy efforts (Bailey, 1988, 1992). These various programs may be housed in one community location or dispersed among the buildings of participating community churches, with the day care center in one church, emergency assistance in another, and senior citizens programs in yet another. Louisville, Kentucky, has seven of these ecumenical community ministries; each involves 20 to 25 churches, employs six to 10 staff members, and has an army of volunteers. Cross-Lines Cooperative Council in Kansas City, Kansas, involves 40 denominations and 600 cooperating churches and, in addition to the services offered by most community ministries, teaches job skills and develops businesses staffed by former welfare recipients and retired volunteers (Bakeley, 1986).

Over time, many of these church-sponsored denominational and ecumenical organizations may become increasingly independent of the original supporting religious groups; the growing dependence on fees from clients, governmental grants and service contracts, and other funding sources can accelerate the process of secularization. A social worker in such a setting may be aware of the historical mission of the agency but not experience any current shaping of his or her professional social work role by the agency's church roots. Some agencies, however, retain their religious mission and identity even when they diversify their funding support; these agencies usually expect professional staff members to be active church members and to play key leadership roles in both local churches and denominational and ecumenical organizations.

#### Mission Programs

Church congregations identify many of their community service programs as "missions" of the church. Missionaries are people who are sent from the church to serve people who are geographically or culturally distant from the congregation, as were the early missionaries—Paul, Silas, Barnabus, and Timothy—whose journeys are recorded in the Book of Acts. Church social workers often may be identified as missionaries, especially when they are working with specific cultural groups (such as Native Americans, immigrants, and refugees) either in this country or abroad. In these settings, social workers lead one or more of the community services identified above. In international settings they may also be involved in community development, agricultural consultation, schools, health services, and hunger and disaster-relief programs.

#### Consultation

Social workers in nonsectarian settings may serve as consultants with churches. The One Church–One Child program, for example, was begun by a social worker in a public child welfare agency who was concerned about the increasing number of African American children on waiting lists for adoption. She contacted an African American priest and, in turn, pastors of other African American congregations. Together they developed a program that encourages church families to adopt children and provides a variety of congregational supports to the adoptive families (Lakin & Hargett, 1986).

Social workers who work as consultants from outside the organization help churches identify their resources and needs for ministry, the needs of individuals and families in their communities, and the ways in which churches can respond to those needs. For example, ChildServ, a United Methodist child welfare agency in Chicago, helps churches conduct assessments of the needs of children in their communities and of the resources they have to respond to those needs and then works with churches to focus their efforts, develop new services, and evaluate those services. Consultants have helped churches develop child care services, child abuse prevention programs, programs to prevent teenage pregnancy, and alternative programs for youths at risk of involvement in gangs (Friedrich, 1990). Consultants also may make guest presentations in churches and religious groups, ranging from preaching Sunday morning sermons to leading workshops and retreats, and may offer assistance in program development and management, training and consulting with volunteers, or developing evaluative methods that are congruent with the church's objectives in ministry.

### Development of the Field

Social workers in church agencies have defined their practice on the basis of the practice features and concerns that they share with social workers in similar agency contexts. For example, social workers who are involved in community ministries have used the work of community organizing as a reference, and those in children's services of the church have looked to and been incorporated into the social work specialization of child welfare.

Social workers in prominent church leadership positions, however, such as members of congregational staffs, have often embraced a dual professional identity, which they have reinforced by pursuing a divinity or Christian education degree from seminaries that offer social work courses. They then complete a master's of social work degree at a university that accepts the seminary course work toward their degree requirements. With the two degrees come two professional identities, which the social worker–church leader is left to integrate or hold in tension with one another.

Social work is beginning to recognize practice in churches and church agencies as a unique context for practice. For example, church social work gained recognition in social work and in theological education with the establishment of the Carver School of Church Social Work of the Southern Baptist Theological Seminary in 1984 and the accreditation of its master of social work degree in 1987 by the Commission on Accreditation of the Council on Social Work Education. These developments signal the profession's increased attention to this challenging context for social work practice.

## References


Bailey, P. L. (1988). Southern Baptist programs of church social work. *Review and Expositor, 85*(2), 285–290.

Bailey, P. L. (1992). Social work practice in community ministries. In D. R. Garland (Ed.), *Church social work* (pp. 58–65). St. Davids, PA: North American Association of Christians in Social Work.

Bailey, P. L. (1993). Social work practice with groups in the church context: A family life ministry model in an inner-city church. *Social Work with Groups, 16*(1–2), 55–67.

Bakeley, D. (1986, May). *Cross-lines.* Paper presented at Building Family Strengths: Ninth National Symposium, Lincoln, Nebraska.

Braskamp, L. A., Brandenburg, D. C., & Ory, J. C. (1987). Lessons about clients' expectations. In J. Nowakowski (Ed.), *The client perspective on evaluation.* San Francisco: Jossey-Bass.

Carroll, J. W., Dudley, C. S., & McKinney, W. (Eds.). (1986). *Handbook for congregational studies.* Nashville, TN: Abingdon.

Ferguson, J. (1992). The congregation as context for social work practice. In D. R. Garland (Ed.), *Church social work* (pp. 36–57). St. Davids, PA: North American Association of Christians in Social Work.

Filteau, J. (1993, June–July). Churches play critical role in national social welfare. *Intercom*, 5.

Friedrich, L.D.F. (1990). Serving children and families through agency consultation. In D. R. Garland & D. L. Pancoast (Eds.), *The church's ministry with families: A practical guide* (pp. 155–170). Dallas: Word.

Garland, D.S.R. (1987). *Social workers on church staffs.* Louisville, KY: Paul Adkins Institute, Carver School of Church Social Work, Southern Baptist Theological Seminary.

Garland, D.S.R. (1993). *Church agencies: Caring for children and families in crisis.* New York: Child Welfare League of America.

Gibelman, M., & Schervish, P. H. (1993). *Who we are: The social work labor force as reflected in the NASW membership.* Washington, DC: NASW Press.

Hessel, D. T. (1992). *Social ministry* (rev. ed.). Philadelphia: Westminster Press.

Hinson, E. G. (1988). The historical involvement of the church in social ministries and social action. *Review and Expositor, 85*(2), 233–241.

Johns, M. L. (1988). *Developing church programs to prevent child abuse.* Austin: Texas Conference of Churches.

Johnson, F. E. (1941). Protestant social work. In R. H. Kurtz (Ed.), *Social work year book* (pp. 403–412). New York: Russell Sage Foundation.

Lakin, D., & Hargett, J. (1986, September). *The role of the black church in the adoption of black children with developmental disabilities.* Paper presented at Social Work '86: NASW's Annual Meeting of the Profession, San Francisco.

Leonard, B. J. (1988). The modern church and social action. *Review and Expositor, 85*(2), 243–253.

Loewenberg, F. M. (1988). *Religion and social work practice in contemporary American society.* New York: Columbia University Press.

Marty, M. E. (1980). Social services: Godly and godless. *Social Service Review, 54,* 463–481.

Midgley, J., & Sanzenbach, P. (1989). Social work, religion and the global challenge of fundamentalism. *International Social Work, 32,* 273–287.

Moberg, D. O. (1984). *The church as a social institution.* Grand Rapids, MI: Baker Book House.

Smith, B. (1989). Families at risk: Programs that work. *Family Resource Coalition Report, 8,* 3–5.

Smith, T. (1976). *Revivalism and social reform: American Protestantism on the eve of the Civil War.* Gloucester, MA: Peter Smith.

Taggart, A. D. (1962). The caseworker as parish assistant. *Social Casework, 43,* 75–79.

Wikler, M. (1986). Pathways to treatment: How orthodox Jews enter therapy. *Social Casework, 67*(2), 113–118.

Wikler, M. (1990). "Fishbowl therapy": Hazards of orthodox therapists treating orthodox patients. *Journal of Psychology and Judaism, 14*(4), 201–212.


## Further Reading


Bos, D. (1993). *A practical guide to community ministry.* Louisville, KY: Westminster/John Knox Press.

*Church social work.* (1988). [Special issue]. *Review and Expositor, 85*(2).

Garland, D.S.R. (1988). The church as a context for social work practice. *Review and Expositor, 85*(2), 255–265.

Garland, D.S.R. (Ed.). (1992). *Church social work: Helping the whole person in the context of the church.* St. Davids, PA: North American Association of Christians in Social Work.

Garland, D.S.R. (1993). *Precious in his sight: A guide to child advocacy.* Birmingham, AL: New Hope.

Garland, D.S.R. (1994). *Church agencies: Caring for children and families in crisis.* New York: Child Welfare League of America.

Garland, D.S.R., & Pancoast, D. L. (1990). *The church's ministry with families: A practical guide.* Dallas: Word.

Joseph, M. V. (1982, Spring). The developmental process of parish social ministries: A decade of experience. *Social Thought,* 22–35.

Joseph, M. V., & Conrad, A. P. (1988). *The parish as a ministering community: Social ministries in the local church community.* Hyattsville, MD: Pen Press.

Morris, R. (1986). *Rethinking social welfare: Why care for the stranger?* New York: Longman.

Peeler, A. (1985). *Parish social ministry: A vision and resource.* Washington, DC: National Conference of Catholic Charities.

**Diana R. Garland, PhD, ACSW, BCD, CFLE,** is dean, Carver School of Church Social Work, The Southern Baptist Theological Seminary, 2825 Lexington Road, Louisville, KY 40280.

**For further information see**
Advocacy; Child Welfare Overview; Citizen Participation; Community; Community Practice Models; Direct Practice Overview; Ethics and Values; Families Overview; Family Life Education; Homelessness; Hospice; Hospital Social Work; Human Rights; Interdisciplinary and Interorganizational Collaboration; Mutual Aid Societies; Natural Helping Networks; Organizations: Context for Social Services Delivery; Peace and Social Justice; Poverty; Public Social Services; Rural Social Work; School-Linked Services; School Social Work Overview; Sectarian Agencies; Settlements and Neighborhood Centers; Social Welfare History; Social Work Practice: History and Evolution; Voluntarism; Volunteer Management.

**Key Words**
church social work    sectarian agencies

# Citizen Participation

**Dorothy N. Gamble**
**Marie Overby Weil**

Citizen participation embodies the basic social work values of human liberation and empowerment of the dispossessed. Community practice is the primary vehicle for building citizen participation through social and economic development, organizing, planning, advocacy, and social change efforts. For social workers, even the conceptualization of clients as citizens can be critical in framing a more liberating, less paternalistic practice. Every day, social workers increase the capacity of individuals to engage in democratic processes by informing service consumers of their rights, helping them make decisions and take responsibility for those decisions, teaching social technologies necessary for groups to form effective organizations for social change, and advocating for consumer organizations. These actions are central to social workers' belief in the worth and dignity of individuals.

## Definition

*Citizen participation* as it relates to social work practice is the active, voluntary engagement of individuals and groups to change problematic conditions and to influence policies and programs that affect the quality of their lives or the lives of others. Citizen participation, the hallmark of a democratic society, takes place primarily through two types of structures: citizen-initiated groups that engage in a full range of social and economic problem areas, and government-initiated advisory and policy-setting bodies.

Table 1 outlines the range of citizen participation activities generally observed in the United States. Social workers may be involved with the whole range of activities as described, but this entry relates primarily to the first two areas—citizen-initiated and government-initiated involvement.

Citizen-initiated groups that work voluntarily on complex social problems are the heart of a democratic, pluralistic society. They are also the means through which oppressed groups, which are often marginalized by government structures, can affect positive change in their communities and can provide a vehicle for local, regional, and national action on issues of social concern. Government-initiated groups, such as planning boards, recreation commissions, or health and welfare boards, open public processes to community involvement and allow greater public scrutiny. These organizations can be impotent or influential, depending on their legal responsibility and the local community culture.

## Importance for Social Work Practice

### Empowerment and Skills Development

As society becomes more complex, people struggle to understand and influence the systems that affect their lives. When voluntary engagement with community systems enables individuals to make better use of community resources and to shape the character of those resources, these individuals have an increased sense of personal power. In the last decade, social workers have enlarged the meaning of empowerment as a goal of their practice (Rappaport, Swift, & Hess, 1984; Solomon, 1976, 1985; Staples, 1990). Social workers who engage in empowerment-focused practice seek to develop the capacity of individuals to understand their environment, make choices, take responsibility for their choices, and influence their life situations through organization and advocacy.

Empowerment-focused social workers also seek to gain a more equitable distribution of

TABLE 1
## Types of Citizen Involvement

**Citizen-Initiated Involvement**
- Neighborhood organizations concerned with economic development, controlled development, improved public services
- Communities of interest (functional communities), such as feminist interests, anti-violence, worker safety, AARP, NAACP, La Raza, gay and lesbian groups
- Nonprofit service boards such as United Way, ARC, battered women's services, Meals on Wheels, hospice boards
- Client organizations such as associations for the mentally ill, legal services consumers, or persons with AIDS
- Public interest groups such as MADD, Common Cause, Public Citizen, and RESULTS
- Consumer and membership groups such as NASW, AMA, state employee associations

**Government-Initiated Citizen Involvement**
- Local and regional health and social service boards, human services planning commissions, recreation commissions, and aging advisory boards
- Local planning boards, water pollution control boards, and agriculture stabilization boards
- Block grant advisory boards and Head Start policy councils

**Coalitions**
Time-limited association of organizations such as local and regional environmental, economic development, health access, or social justice coalitions

**Social Movements**
Organized effort to promote social goals that touch a wide spectrum of social institutions, such as the civil rights movement, women's movement, American Indian movement, and disabilities movement

**Electoral–Political Participation**
- Voting
- Working for a political party or candidate
- Running for office

**Obligatory Participation**
- Taxes
- Jury duty
- Military service

Adapted and expanded from Langton, S. (1978). What is citizen participation? In S. Langton (Ed.), *Citizen participation in America: Essays on the state of the art.* Lexington, MA: Lexington Books.

resources and power among different groups in society. This focus on equity and social justice has been a hallmark of the social work profession since its beginning, through activities of the early settlement workers such as Jane Addams, Julia Lathrop, and Grace Abbott (Costin, 1983). Citizen participation can be a key activity both for developing the capacity of individuals to understand and influence their environment and for acquiring more equitable resource distribution in a democratic society.

Through citizen participation activities, people can develop personal, interpersonal, and intergroup knowledge and skills that improve both their self-concepts and their day-to-day functioning (Adams, 1975; Freire, 1985; Gamble, 1978; Kieffer, 1984). It is also generally accepted that some forms of citizen participation can increase both the sense of control and the development of social and economic support for individuals in complex societies (Berry, Portney, & Thomson, 1993; Biddle & Biddle, 1979; Florin & Wandersman, 1984; Hall, 1988; Rappaport et al., 1984; Rohe, 1985). These benefits can accrue to the clients of human services when social workers facilitate the clients' active participation in organizations that affect the quality of the clients' lives.

### Participatory Democracy

Although considerable debate continues concerning the effect of degree and type of citizen participation on the condition of democracy, supporters of participatory democracy continue to draw lessons from John Stuart Mill and Jean-Jacques Rousseau on the limits of representative government and the necessity for the citizenry to be engaged in active participation. In recent years, societies across the globe have regained or seized the opportunity for active participation as totalitarian governments lose their means of control. In the United States, although voting for elected officials has been declining, grassroots organizations and voluntary activity have continued to thrive (Berry et al., 1993). Although the growing number of grassroots organizations makes use of a variety of generalist organizers and facilitators, social work organizers bring to this role a well-developed understanding of the human condition, group process skills, and guidance for ethical practice.

## Place of Participation in U.S. History and Culture

The framers of our Constitution provided in the First amendment the right of citizens to participate in government by ensuring the right to free speech, the right to assemble peaceably, and the right to petition the government for redress of grievances. Tocqueville (1835/1969) provided a classical perspective on the value of participation and its significance in American society. In his view, the small New England town meetings were an ideal means for face-to-face discussions that culminated in shared values, joint decisions, and strong communities. The original freedoms to participate in government were not extended to African Americans or women until later in our history, through the abolition of slavery with the 13th, 14th, and 15th amendments (ratified in 1865, 1868, and 1870, respectively) and voting rights guarantees in the 19th and 24th amendments (ratified in 1920 and 1964, respectively).

Although the Constitution guarantees the right of citizens to organize and petition to influence government policies, U.S. citizens have traditionally also organized to create their own programs, services, and social supports. Voluntary associations and intentional communities throughout our history have contributed to the knowledge and experience of participatory democracy. Voluntary associations not only provide individuals with a source of social support, they also provide an organizational arena in which to practice democracy and to influence representative government. Some intentional communities have been organized as cooperatives wherein each individual is required to participate in significant ways to help the community function.

**Civil Rights Movement**

In recent years, some major movements and legislative initiatives have significantly shaped the arguments for and against strong participatory democracy. The most recent civil rights movement for African Americans began in the late 1950s, as black Americans—disenfranchised by segregation laws and de facto segregation practices of public schools, voter registration structures, and public conveniences—organized to increase the opportunities available to them and to extend their rights. Their voice struck a chord in American political history, and although there was also an organized effort to maintain the bonds of oppression, black and white organizations across the country engaged in civil disobedience to demonstrate the need for change.

The Southern Christian Leadership Conference, led by the Rev. Martin Luther King, Jr., joined local community and church groups, the Student Non-Violent Coordinating Committee, and other groups to implement nonviolent strategies that led to federal legislation and protection of voting and civil rights for African Americans (Branch, 1988). Dr. King was markedly influenced by the life and writings of Mahatma Gandhi, who was committed to empowerment of the peoples of India and to social development. From Gandhi's examples and from his own study of Christian theology Dr. King developed the philosophy and practice of nonviolent protest and resistance that eventually led to major legislative changes for racial minorities and women. From 1954 to 1968, major legislation was passed in support of the civil rights of African Americans.

Other groups who participated in and learned from the civil rights movement benefited from its momentum and strategies. The women's movement, the American Indian movement, the anti–Vietnam War movement, and the disability rights movement followed in the late 1960s and early 1970s. The women's movement sought political and social equality for all women. It built an alternative system of services for women, exemplified by rape crisis centers, domestic violence shelters, and women's health clinics. This movement provided the opportunity for many women to practice a range of feminist leadership, research, and decision-making styles grounded in egalitarian decision making (Bricker-Jenkins & Hooyman, 1986; Cummerton, 1986; Weil, 1986).

**War on Poverty**

In 1964, the Economic Opportunity Act, which was designed to eliminate the causes of poverty, required local antipoverty organizations to develop, conduct, and administer their programs "with the maximum feasible participation of residents of the areas and members of the groups served." Although programs for poor people had been established in 1932 during the Great Depression, this War on Poverty was the first time in U.S. history that the federal government provided resources for community structures in which poor people were actively involved in local decision making. New organizations were created to recruit and train low-income citizens for a variety of leadership roles in the community. Many low-income citizens were employed as paraprofessionals to reach out to every block and into every hollow of urban neighborhoods and rural communities. The Model Cities program, which followed in 1966, also called for citizen involvement on the part of service recipients. Although the War on Poverty promised more than it was able to deliver, it challenged the traditional policy- and decision-making bodies in most communities. The challenge was more than the political system was willing to accept, and soon the "maximum feasible participation" requirement was dismantled, except in a few programs, such as the early education program Head Start.

The participation and empowerment lessons learned in this brief period, however, have been used effectively in many low-income communities. The current wide use of participation techniques by middle-class groups demonstrates the value of these lessons. Since then, wisdom gained from the research and development arm of the Office of Economic Opportunity has been used to build strong participatory organizations. Mainstream groups concerned with the environment, educational reform, peace, and community redevelopment all make use of grassroots and decision-making strategies learned during the War on Poverty.

**Volunteers**

In his inaugural speech in 1989, George Bush spoke of "a thousand points of light," referring to the possibility of thousands of community volunteers working to transform the conditions of poor, elderly, and developmentally delayed people and to reduce drug abuse and provide for other community needs. Bush presented a classic conservative viewpoint: Use volunteers to help poor people in order to reduce public social spending. Bush's speech continued the philosophy, already established by the Reagan administration, to refocus the strategy for mitigating oppressive conditions. The strategy was based on helping poor people as individuals through face-to-face volunteer involvement rather than by involving poor and oppressed people in policy and program decisions, which had sometimes resulted in structural changes.

The campaign to recruit more volunteers resulted in some increased voluntary service, especially on the part of businesses and religious organizations. Religious organizations contributed significant time and resources to the resettlement of large numbers of southeast Asian refugees and to the building of new housing for homeless people through Habitat for Humanity. Although this volunteer spirit grew in the late 1980s (Gallup Organization, 1990), social problems such as drug abuse, child abuse, domestic violence, rape, teen pregnancy, infant mortality, and teen homicide persisted or grew a significant amount despite volunteer efforts to curb them.

**Community-Owned Government**

In the 1990s the phrase "reinventing government," popularized by Osborne and Gaebler (1992) through their book by the same name, conveyed a perspective that the Clinton–Gore administration has adopted. Osborne and Gaebler made a distinction between clients and citizens and described a community-owned government in which families and communities, rather than professionals, solve problems. "We let the police, the doctors, the teachers and the social workers have all the control," they suggested, "while the people they are serving have none" (p. 51). Although the idea sounds similar to "maximum feasible participation," it is based on the notion that professionals become the facilitators and community organizers for local problem solving and that existing resources in the public, private, and voluntary sectors of the community could creatively—and more effectively—mobilize to respond to community problems.

Rather than establishing a new structure of organizations and employees to facilitate participation, as was done during the War on Poverty, community-owned government requires new thinking and collective behavior on the part of service providers and citizens and no significant new resources or a requirement that poor people be part of the planning. If this idea is to be successful, it will require considerable reformulation in the education and training of professionals. Professional service providers of all kinds will have to learn skills that will empower community residents to participate in solutions to community problems. Such skills require an understanding of the processes for human organization and use of techniques for building the leadership capacity of people. Because the past two decades of professional education for social workers, police, teachers, and health providers have been focused on personal outcome measures, the new education must have an equal focus on group processes and organizational outcomes. Social work education has an advantage, because human processes are traditionally part of the educational foundation, and because some advanced curricula enable students to gain more knowledge and skills in how to effectively open community problem solving and social planning to the consumers of their services.

## Social Workers' Roles and Responsibilities

Citizen participation is an essential element in all forms of community practice, including organizing, political empowerment, planning, program development, social and economic development, and social change. Table 2 presents the central roles that social workers take in building citizen participation in many types of organizations. Social workers may be involved in citizens' organizations and social movements as professionals or as volunteers. As direct community organizers, social workers may be working for citizens' groups that focus on issues such as housing, the environment, human services, and social justice. In political empowerment efforts social workers will focus on

TABLE 2
**Social Work Roles in Building Citizen Participation**

| | |
|---|---|
| • Organizer | • Planner |
| • Community educator | • Facilitator |
| • Empowerment strategist | • Coach |
| • Coalition builder | • Trainer |
| • Volunteer coordinator | • Advocate |
| • Leadership developer | • Policy analyst |
| • Program coordinator | • Community liaison |
| • Advocate researcher | • Board developer |
| • Economic developer | • Recruiter |

strategies to increase participation and to improve needed services, programs, and policies. Building on the strengths of citizens to advocate for needs and issues in a pluralistic political arena is a key role for social workers (Fisher, 1984; Grosser & Mondros, 1984; Rubin & Rubin, 1992). Both alternative agencies and mainstream programs increasingly use citizen participation strategies to strengthen their planning and program development processes.

**Building Coordinated Services**

Many social and economic development organizations have evolved from citizen participation activities. Examples of community-based organizations that combine economic and social services development are Bethel New Life in Chicago and Chicanos por la Causa in Phoenix, in which social service and program development are connected to the overall neighborhood economic development effort (National Congress for Community Economic Development, 1990). Citizen participation is a critical element in both social and economic community development. Community development directors find themselves in foundation board rooms as frequently as they do in neighborhood living rooms. Although there are real tensions between the need to meet proposal and negotiation deadlines and the need for broad community involvement, a balance of these activities is necessary to sustain any community development project.

The effort to build a coordinated, comprehensive, community-based child and family services system—including social services, child mental health, juvenile justice, and public health—is a major task that demonstration programs throughout the nation are undertaking. These system reform efforts, which often are funded by private foundations, are increasingly grounded in citizen participation and community development models. Planners, managers, and direct service workers are engaged in citizen participation activities by facilitating the design of programs for a particular community, implementing the programs, troubleshooting, and evaluating family and community outcomes. Foundations such as Annie E. Casey, Kellogg, Robert Wood Johnson, and Pew have greatly increased their focus on citizen participation and often encourage or require their grantees—whether citizens' groups or public agencies—to ensure broader participation in reviewing and implementing programs.

Social workers, therefore, are involved in the encouragement of citizen participation in a variety of ways and through a number of organizational roles. Program managers and agency administrators in the nonprofit sector work with their boards of directors and their advisory boards to develop and implement policies and program directions. Leaders in state and county human services programs also work with citizen participation through commissions, advisory groups, consumer committees, and advocacy groups. As citizens increase their knowledge and understanding of agency missions and strategies, their public knowledge and commitment to social programs in both the public and voluntary sectors make them critical actors in support of human services.

**Planning**

Earlier writings have viewed social planning as a community practice activity that depends less on citizen participation than on other methods of community practice (Brager & Specht, 1973; Rothman & Zald, 1985). Increasingly, however, both government and private funders of community-based human services expect planners to be heavily engaged in citizen participation, with individuals and groups involved from the beginning of planning through implementation and monitoring. Social planning is once again being greatly emphasized at the community level (Lauffer, 1978; Weil, 1994). Therefore, social workers engaged in planning not only need the technical skills typically required for planning but also the process and facilitation skills for working with individuals and groups in the planning process.

**Conducting Research**

Researchers also engage citizens in community-based investigations for social problems and community issues. Community-based research that involves the residents of a geographic location or members of a community of interest has an illustrious history in social work. Jane Addams and the women of Hull House published the first community study to identify community problems and map the area's populations, in *Hull-House Maps and Papers* (1895). Immigrants from Italy, Germany, and Bulgaria were among the Hull House neighbors who participated in the research, analysis of problems, social intervention plans, and public action to solve local problems (Deegan, 1990). Current researchers are again involving community members in research that enables them to use investigative and analytic processes in development and action projects (Daley & Wong, 1994; Gaventa, 1981; Johnson, 1994).

As an advocate researcher, a social worker is engaged in a process of collaborative research and evaluation with a community group. The researcher's responsibility is to facilitate the groups' involvement in research activities and to help group members analyze and present the research findings as information critical to decision making in community or public issues (Johnson, 1994; Weiler & Sherraden, 1994).

**Meeting the Needs of Underserved Groups**

Since the 1970s, small alternative agencies and programs that serve the needs of underserved groups such as women, Asian Americans, African Americans, and Native Americans have burgeoned. These programs grew out of participatory planning and citizen action strategies. These community-based programs, which serve ethnic and racial neighborhoods and rural areas, range from direct service provision such as church-based tutoring to the United Black Fund, which is designed to provide a funding mechanism for programs and services targeted to African American communities (Perlmutter, 1988; Rodgers & Tartaglia, 1990). In many communities women have built entire service networks to serve women's needs. Examples include the nationwide network of domestic violence coalitions and shelters, rape crisis centers, and programs serving women that are empowerment focused to build employment skills and self-sufficiency (Mauney, Williams, & Weil, 1993). In building these programs, activist volunteers frequently are the program initiators. They often begin with community meetings about problems and engage in a community action process to call attention to the issues. Volunteers who receive support and legitimation from the community frequently become staff members. As programs develop, they increase the range of citizen participation through boards and consumer feedback structures. In the battered women's movement, women have ensured the involvement of battered and formerly battered women in volunteer and staff leadership.

**Facilitating Citizen Involvement**

Volunteer service providers and board members of nonprofit organizations engage in citizen involvement in many of their policy-making and direct service activities. There is a significant amount of literature on working with boards and building leadership for policy engagement in the nonprofit sector, but the literature relating to direct service volunteers focuses primarily on their recruitment, training, motivation, and organizational use. This focus overlooks volunteers as a potential resource for public education, social policy analysis, and community change and may also fail to recognize the empowering personal change often experienced by individual volunteers. Empowerment is an educational, consciousness-raising process, which enables volunteers to deal with obstacles and problems, to exert leadership, and to increase decision-making power in their own lives and communities (Solomon, 1976, 1985).

Social work in citizen participation efforts may involve primary activities such as organizing, facilitating, community education, liaison, program coordination, planning, building coalitions, or doing advocate research. As an organizer and facilitator, the social worker focuses on helping individuals and groups define issues for action; analyzing the issues; developing appropriate action strategies; carrying out action strategies; and working with the group in evaluating outcomes, revising strategies, and moving on to other issues.

The role of community educator and liaison is similar; however, more time and resources are devoted to developing the capacity of individuals to sustain organizations. Community-development projects often engage people who have had little history in organizing for change. The role of facilitator therefore is expanded to work in adult education and collaborative research models to help people analyze the conditions that affect their lives and to plan strategies for change. Highlander Center in New Market, Tennessee, is a model for this kind of work (Horton, Kohl, & Kohl, 1992). The social worker, as a liaison, connects the grassroots group to other groups engaged in similar endeavors and to community resources. A central part of this role is the training and supporting of group members so that they can carry forward these liaison and communication roles themselves to represent their interests in the larger community.

As coalition builders, social workers may be involved in bringing together a range of diverse groups that have enough shared concern around a particular issue to join forces to implement change (Mizrahi & Rosenthal, 1992). Such coalitions may be composed of citizens' groups or combinations of citizens' groups, advocacy organizations, human services professionals, and for-profit interests.

## INFLUENCING THE PUBLIC AGENDA

In addition to voting or running for office, people try to influence government in a democracy in two major ways: One is by trying to get certain issues adopted as part of the public agenda; the second is by trying to influence the direction of public problem solving once the issue is under debate. Research indicates that public agendas are most often set by elected officials, by energetic groups who have a special concern, or by traditional business-based groups, rather than by specific structures designed for participatory democracy, such as neighborhood organizations (Berry et al., 1993;

Gaventa, 1980). Once an issue has been opened for public debate, however, both neighborhood organizations and energetic organizations with special concerns can be effective in influencing the outcome.

Citizen access to public debate of issues can occur through government-initiated structures, in which citizens speak at public hearings, participate in regular public meetings, join task forces, or become part of advisory committees or policymaking boards. Citizen-initiated efforts to influence debate occur through letters, telephone calls, meetings with officials, and other lobbying activities directed toward elected officials. These efforts often are coordinated by the staff of coalitions with a particular focus, including political action committees and movements (Mahaffey & Hanks, 1982). Whether or not public bodies respond to the advice and comments of citizens has been the subject of a number of studies. These studies have provided better understanding of the nature of public decision making (Hall, 1988; Morrison, 1984; Rich, 1982; Rosener, 1982). In some cases, elected officials who have little information on or interest in a particular policy can be influenced by a small number of letters or calls. For highly controversial issues, such as gun control or the location of a toxic waste dump, massive contacts of elected officials and long hours of public hearings are often the norm.

NASW established its own Political Action for Candidate Election (PACE) committee in 1976, and although its direct financial contribution to political campaigns is small in comparison with those of the medical, insurance, or banking political action committees, it has been active and successful in supporting progressive candidates at the national and state levels. NASW also plays a key role in influencing progressive social legislation at the national level. For example, NASW was the first professional organization to offer a specific health care reform proposal, which was introduced in Congress in 1992.

## Building Organizations for Democratic Participation

Involving people in citizen participation to enlarge democratic processes, social and economic development, and quality-of-life decisions involves working with individuals, groups, and communities to define and achieve common goals. The community worker initially must engage members of the community or work with existing indigenous leadership in the community to enlarge the interest and refine the focus of the social concern. The engagement process builds from where people are with their concerns to clarifying their problem identification. This process may involve numerous individual and group meetings to clarify concerns, to define common ground, and to define issues for action. To facilitate awareness, the social worker may do research with group members on their selected issue, locate sources of information, launch a needs assessment, or conceptualize a basic action plan.

### Capacity Building

The social worker may teach members about group process and assist the group in deciding on its own decision-making structure. Helping the group to welcome diversity and to ensure open access to new members is a critical part of the early work with organizations. Facilitating awareness relates to learning about the context and causes of problems and an analysis of political and power issues that relate to that issue.

To increase the capacity of people to organize, social workers and leaders need to help group members research and analyze issues and to develop skills in presenting what they have learned to their own group and to community leaders and media representatives. In capacity-building activities, group members learn process and task skills. They must also learn leadership abilities as well as content knowledge and the ability to speak out for their group.

Group members need to learn how to share leadership in functional ways and to work effectively with each other and, often, with members of other groups. Clearly articulating issues, motivating participation, and implementing a strategy for change are all activities that build capacity (Kahn, 1991; Kettner, Daley, & Nichols, 1985; Rubin & Rubin, 1992).

### Strategies and Action Plans

Community workers frequently facilitate group organization by helping members determine activities and roles, develop action strategies, and carry out planned actions. A principal responsibility is to help leaders and members attend appropriately to issues of both process and task accomplishment. The community worker typically spends a considerable amount of time working with group leaders on plans, activities, and agendas and may often work with subcommittees on particular aspects of group organizing and action tasks. The social worker may also initially help group members connect with other citizens' groups and confront opposing forces. In an empowerment model, the social worker is concerned with developing skills and capacities so that the group members are secure in their own skills and are able to carry out the group's action agenda.

Social workers frequently link groups to needed resources, whether assisting in applying for funding or connecting with coalitions to strengthen their skills and abilities for public action. Typically, most of the work with leaders to set goals, design strategies and action plans, and consider how to gain the resources needed to carry out plans will be done in small groups. The social worker with an empowerment focus also helps groups work toward independence and deal with the resulting transformation of the social worker's role, which may be disengagement or change to an occasional consultation.

## Methods and Techniques for Increasing Participation

People cannot participate in decision making unless there are structures in the state or the community that allow access to agenda-setting and policy-making processes. Some local government councils and boards have barriers such as inaccessible agendas and extremely formal citizen comment rules that limit citizen input in the decisions made by local boards. Some communities, however, have elaborate lists of citizen advisory boards with specific guidelines that direct the selection process to ensure broad and diverse community representation. Still others have paid staff to facilitate input of neighborhood organizations in municipal decision making (Berry et al., 1993).

### Asking Questions

As the staff of both public and voluntary social planning efforts, social workers have an excellent opportunity to help develop both the structures and processes for citizen involvement. Asking the right questions can be the most useful exercise to ensure the broadest possible citizen involvement in any community-planning activity (Rosener, 1978). The following four questions are basic to planning for such involvement:

1. *Who* should be involved in the planning exercise? This question helps planners remember all the possible different ethnic, geographic, gender, age, service, socioeconomic, powerful, powerless, religious, business, education, social, and special interest groups or leaders in a community that might be part of the planning process. Listing the key power brokers in a community is a lot easier than identifying stakeholders who are powerless. Planners often avoid involving powerless groups because they worry about who would "represent" poor people or ethnic minorities, as though a person or even a few people could collectively represent such groups. In identifying possible representatives from different groups, it is particularly important to remember that individuals usually represent one perspective of the group with whom they are identified and rarely represent the collective group perspective.
2. *Why* should people who represent different group perspectives be involved? In affirming why the groups should or should not be involved, the planners are more likely not to deceive themselves or the groups they hope to engage. Being able to answer why adolescents should be involved in plans for decreasing violence in the schools, for example, affirms a partnership with youths in the community-planning process.
3. *When* should the different groups be involved in the process? Clearly, not all the stakeholders must be involved from the beginning. Often some preliminary assessment work must be undertaken to provide a rationale for the planning process. Also, a basic structure often is necessary to engage the citizen stakeholders. Planners should not, however, believe that their work is somehow objective and value-free. Every question posed or goal established is wrapped in a particular value perspective. The process itself should allow for the reformulation of questions and goals as new perspectives are identified. Some groups can be permanently alienated from the planning process if they are not part of framing the earliest questions about the community problem or issue.
4. *How* should the different groups be involved in the process? An identified structure for involving different groups early in the planning process helps the process become more inclusive. Without a plan, the centripetal momentum of any planning process can rapidly become exclusive. Tested technologies, such as the nominal group technique, make it possible to engage people with different perspectives and different socioeconomic status at the same time. Also, to avoid token representation, planners should consider a degree of depth in seeking the inclusion of any group.

### Building Structures

Social workers often play a key role in building structures for participation as community organizers. Organizations with structures that make it easy for new members to join and to develop their citizenship and leadership capacities through participation serve as models for democracy (Mondros & Wilson, 1993). Chavis, Florin, and Felix (1993) described a meta-level structure, the enabling system, which "nurtures the development and maintenance of a grassroots community development process through the provision of resources, incentives and education" (p. 48). These enabling systems may be as traditional as the United Way of America and the agricultural extension services, or they may be new regional and statewide resource centers that focus on domestic violence, health promotion, or urban or rural economic development. These structures promote the emergence of partnerships among the public, private, and voluntary sectors of communities. They also have the potential to increase the level of citizen participation by enabling the development of new grassroots organizations around issues previously ignored in the public agenda.

### Facilitating Inclusion

Although structure is critical to the development of participatory democracy, the processes used in organizations are equally important. During the War on Poverty, some participatory and decision-making techniques were tested, especially for their effectiveness in facilitating the inclusion of poor and disenfranchised people. A particularly enduring example is the nominal group technique (NGT) process, which was researched and developed by Delbecq and Van de Ven (1976). The NGT process, which was designed for face-to-face priority setting, can be modified for a mail-out response, a process called the Delphi technique. Although NGT does require that citizens be able to read in order to participate, its rules level the playing field for participation, so that a mother receiving public assistance sitting in the same group as a local banker has the same capacity to suggest ideas and influence decisions. Although the nominal group technique requires trained facilitators, volunteers from the local community can be trained to facilitate the groups effectively. Social work students have served as effective facilitators of NGT for community meetings all across the country.

In recent years, a variety of manuals have appeared to facilitate the participation of citizens in solving community problems (Brody, 1982; Creighton, 1992; Kahn, 1991). Many of the manuals emphasize techniques for consensus building and collaboration, to bring a wide variety of stakeholders in a community together to solve problems. Fisher and Ury (1991) generated popular interest in developing negotiation skills with their publication *Getting to Yes: Negotiating Agreement Without Giving In*. Dispute resolution centers are growing across our nation as more people become trained in mediation skills, training that is reaching all the way down into the elementary schools. In our haste to arbitrate, negotiate, and mediate community conflicts, it would be well to remember the lessons of Lewis Coser (1956) regarding the value of nonviolent conflict in our communities. It is often through nonviolent conflict that we are able to see a perspective on community issues to which we had been formerly blind. Nonviolent conflict often helps us discover the diversity we must be able to incorporate to achieve more lasting community solutions.

### Using New Technology

Modern community organization will always depend on a range of process skills, but new technology opens a whole new resource arena for citizens. The revolution in communication technology in recent years has enormous implications for citizen participation. Now many people can watch town meetings as well as the U.S. Congress on cable television. The ability to communicate one's views to an elected official becomes easier with fax machines and opiniongrams.

Citizens' groups are connected to information networks such as Helpnet, and they are learning to gather and use information available through new "information highways." Some grassroots organizations with statewide or nationwide boards already use electronic mail for regular communication by sending newsletters and resource information to each other on computers purchased through foundation grants (Downing, Fasano, Friedland, & McCullough, 1991). Inevitably, some groups will always be excluded from the new technology because of its cost. Cooperative ownership of some new technology, located in regional "enabling systems" that nurture the development and maintenance of grassroots groups (Chavis et al., 1993), could be the answer to making these technologies more widely available.

Although new technology has made communication easier, the range and depth of issues have become more complex. Getting access to critical information and being able to meet with an issue's critical actors will continue to be the important knowledge and skill areas for people working in citizen participation. Some of the most valuable people to the citizen participation process will be local community organizers and state and national public interest lobbyists.

## Essential Component of Democratic Societies

We hear the heaves and sighs of democracy in the making all across the globe. This energetic impulse for democratic institutions, though not without its setbacks, pushes the social work profession to reexamine its relationship with the ideals of democratic participation. Because we work directly with people who are often vulnerable and marginalized in societies, we are often acutely aware of their inability to obtain access to decision-making structures and power. In some countries, social workers have been imprisoned and tortured for helping marginalized people have greater roles in the decisions that affect their social and economic existence. In the United States, although social workers are not always in official leadership roles, they can be found in national and state associations, developing policies committed to the common good and supporting a political economy focused on social justice.

The widening gaps in income and opportunity in our nation sharply illustrate Dahl's (1985) articulation of competing visions for American society. One vision is congruent with the value perspective and goals of community practice: "A vision of the world's first and grandest attempt to realize democracy, political equality, and political liberty on a continental scale" (p. 162); the other is a vision in which the unrestricted pursuit of wealth can produce the world's most prosperous society. The second view that has held sway in recent years centers on the protection of property and the pursuit of wealth. Uninhibited license to pursue this wealth has placed American society in a perilous position, a position that is increasingly questioned even by those who have benefited from it. Fragile prosperity must give way to clear and democratic means to define and pursue the common good. What is needed is a truly inclusive vision of the common good for a vast and diverse nation focused on "the achievement of democracy, political equality, and the fundamental rights of all citizens" (Dahl, pp. 162–163). Social work is part of this effort.

## References


Adams, F. (1975). *Unearthing seeds of fire: The idea of Highlander*. Winston-Salem, NC: John Blair.

Berry, J. M., Portney, K. E., & Thomson, K. (1993). *The rebirth of urban democracy*. Washington, DC: Brookings Institution.

Biddle, W., & Biddle, L. (1979). *The community development process: The rediscovery of local initiative*. New York: Holt, Rinehart & Winston.

Brager, G., & Specht, H. (1973). *Community organizing* (2nd ed.). New York: Columbia University Press.

Branch, T. (1988). *Parting the waters: America in the King years, 1954–63*. New York: Simon & Schuster.

Bricker-Jenkins, M., & Hooyman, N. R. (Eds.). (1986). *Not for women only: Social work practice for a feminist future*. Silver Spring, MD: National Association of Social Workers.

Brody, R. (1982). *Problem solving: Concepts and methods for community organizations*. New York: Human Sciences Press.

Chavis, D. M., Florin, P., & Felix, M. R. J. (1993). Nurturing grassroots initiatives for community development: The role of enabling systems. In T. Mizrahi & J. D. Morrison (Eds.), *Community organization and social administration* (pp. 41–67). New York: Haworth Press.

Coser, L. A. (1956). *The functions of social conflict*. New York: Free Press.

Costin, L. B. (1983). *Two sisters for social justice: A biography of Grace and Edith Abbott*. Champaign: University of Illinois Press.

Creighton, J. L. (1992). *Involving citizens in community decision making: A guidebook*. Washington, DC: Program for Community Problem Solving.

Cummerton, J. M. (1986). A feminist perspective on research: What does it help us see? In N. Van Den Bergh & L. B. Cooper (Eds.), *Feminist visions for social work* (pp. 80–100). Silver Spring, MD: National Association of Social Workers.

Dahl, R. (1985). *A preface to economic democracy*. Los Angeles: University of California Press.

Daley, J. M., & Wong, P. (1994) Community development with emerging ethnic communities. *Journal of Community Practice, 1*(1), 9–24.

Deegan, M. J. (1990). *Jane Addams and the men of the Chicago School, 1892–1918*. New Brunswick, NJ: Transaction Books.

Delbecq, A. L., & Van de Ven, A. H. (1976). *Group techniques for program planning*. Glenview, IL: Scott, Foresman.

Downing, J., Fasano, R., Friedland, P., McCullough, M., Mizrahi, T., & Shapiro, J. (Eds.). (1991). *Computers for social change and community organizing*. New York: Haworth Press.

Economic Opportunity Act of 1964. P.L. 88-452, 78 Stat. 508.

Fisher, R. (1984). *Let the people decide: Neighborhood organizing in America*. Boston: G. K. Hall.

Fisher, R., & Ury, W. (1991). *Getting to yes: Negotiating agreement without giving in* (2nd ed.). New York: Penguin Books.

Florin, P., & Wandersman, A. (1984). Cognitive social learning and participation in community development. *American Journal of Community Psychology, 12*, 689–708.

Freire, P. (1985). *The politics of education: Culture, power, and liberation*. South Hadley, MA: Bergin & Garvey.

Gallup Organization. (1990). *Giving and volunteering in the United States, 1990*. Washington, DC: Author.

Gamble, D. N. (1978). Dignity and success: The experience of welfare rights members. In J. W. Hanks (Ed.), *Toward human dignity: Social work in practice* (pp. 133–145). Washington, DC: National Association of Social Workers.

Gaventa, J. (1980). *Power and powerlessness: Quiescence and rebellion in an Appalachian valley*. Champaign: University of Illinois Press.

Gaventa, J. (1981). Land ownership in Appalachia, USA: A citizens' research project. In F. Dubell (Ed.), *Research for the people: Research by the people* (pp. 118–130).

Linkoping, Sweden: Linkoping University Department of Education.

Gottlieb, N. (1987). *Alternative social services for women*. New York: Columbia University Press.

Grosser, C., & Mondros, J. (1984). Pluralism and participation: The political action approach. In R. Roberts & S. Taylor (Eds.), *Theory and practice of community social work* (pp. 154–178). New York: Columbia University Press.

Hall, B. (Ed.). (1988). *Environmental politics: Lessons from the grassroots*. Durham, NC: Institute for Southern Studies.

Horton, M., Kohl, J., & Kohl, H. (1992). *The long haul: An autobiography*. New York: Doubleday.

*Hull House maps and papers*. (1895). New York: Crowell.

Johnson, A. K. (1994). Linking professionalism and community organization: A scholar/advocate approach. *Journal of Community Practice, 1*(2), 65–86.

Kahn, S. (1991). *Organizing: A guide for grassroots leadership*. Silver Spring, MD: NASW Press.

Kettner, P., Daley, J. M., & Nichols, A. W. (1985). *Initiating change in organizations and communities*. Monterey, CA: Brooks/Cole.

Kieffer, C. H. (1984). Citizen empowerment: A developmental perspective. In J. Rappaport, C. Swift, & R. Hess (Eds.), *Studies in empowerment: Steps toward understanding and action* (pp. 9–36). New York: Haworth Press.

Langton, S. (1978). What is citizen participation? In S. Langton (Ed.), *Citizen participation in America: Essays on the state of the art* (pp. 13–24). Lexington, MA: Lexington Books.

Lauffer, A. (1978). *Social planning at the community level*. Englewood Cliffs, NJ: Prentice Hall.

Mahaffey, M., & Hanks, J. (Eds.). (1982). *Practical politics*. Washington, DC: National Association of Social Workers.

Mauney, R., Williams, E., & Weil, M. (1993). *Beyond crisis: Developing comprehensive services for battered women in North Carolina*. Winston-Salem, NC: Z. Smith Reynolds Foundation.

Mizrahi, T., & Rosenthal, B. B. (1992). Managing dynamic tensions in social change coalitions. In T. Mizrahi & J. D. Morrison (Eds.), *Community organization and social administration* (pp. 11–40). New York: Haworth Press.

Mondros, J. B., & Wilson, S. M. (1993). Building high access community organizations: Structures as strategy. In T. Mizrahi & J. D. Morrison (Eds.), *Community organization and social administration* (pp. 69–85). New York: Haworth Press.

Morrison, J. D. (1984). Can organizing tenants improve housing? *Social Development Issues, 8*, 103–115.

National Congress for Community Economic Development. (1990). *Human investment . . . community profits*. Report and recommendations of the Social Services and Economic Development Task Force. Washington, DC: Author.

Osborne, D., & Gaebler, T. (1992). *Reinventing government: How the entrepreneurial spirit is transforming the public sector*. Reading, MA: Addison-Wesley.

Perlmutter, F. D. (1988). Alternative federated funds: Resourcing for change. In F. D. Perlmutter (Ed.), *Alternative social agencies: Administrative strategies* (pp. 95–108). New York: Haworth Press.

Rappaport, J., Swift, C., & Hess, R. (1984). *Studies in empowerment: Steps toward understanding and action*. New York: Haworth Press.

Rich, R. C. (Ed.). (1982). *The politics of urban public services*. Lexington, MA: Lexington Books.

Rodgers, A., & Tartaglia, L. J. (1990). Constricting resources: A black self-help initiative. *Administration in Social Work, 14*, 125–137.

Rohe, W. (1985). Urban planning and mental health. In A. Wandersman & R. Hess (Eds.), *Beyond the individual: Environmental approaches and prevention* (pp. 79–110). New York: Haworth Press.

Rosener, J. B. (1978). Matching method to purpose: The challenges of planning citizen participation activities. In S. Langton (Ed.), *Citizen participation in America: Essays on the state of the art* (pp. 109–123). Lexington, MA: Lexington Books.

Rosener, J. B. (1982). Making bureaucrats responsive: A study of the impact of citizen participation and staff recommendations on regulatory decision making. *Public Administration Review, 42*, 339–345.

Rothman, J., & Zald, M. (1985). Planning theory in social work community practice. In S. H. Taylor & R. W. Roberts (Eds.), *Theory and practice of community social work* (pp. 125–153). New York: Columbia University Press.

Rubin, H. J., & Rubin, I. S. (1992). *Community organizing and development* (2nd ed.). New York: Macmillan.

Solomon, B. B. (1976). *Black empowerment: Social work in oppressed communities*. New York: Columbia University Press.

Solomon, B. B. (1985). Community social work practice in oppressed minority communities. In S. H. Taylor & R. W. Roberts (Eds.), *Theory and practice of community social work* (pp. 217–257). New York: Columbia University Press.

Staples, L. (1990). Powerful ideas about empowerment. *Administration in Social Work, 14*, 29–42.

Tocqueville, A. de. (1969). *Democracy in America* (G. Lawrence, Trans.). New York: Doubleday. (Original work published 1835)

Weil, M. (1986). Women, community, and organizing. In N. Van Den Bergh & L. B. Cooper (Eds.), *Feminist visions for social work* (pp. 187–210). Silver Spring, MD: National Association of Social Workers.

Weil, M. (1994). Introduction. In A. Faulkner, M. Roberts-DeGennaro, & M. Weil (Eds.), *Diversity and development in community practice* (pp. xi–ixx). New York: Haworth Press.

Weiler, M. T., & Sherraden, M. (1994). Classroom and advocacy: A project on the working poor in St. Louis. *Journal of Community Practice, 1*(1), 99–105.

## Further Reading

Amidei, N. (1994). *So you want to make a difference: Advocacy is the key* (7th ed.). Washington, DC: OMB Watch.

Bobo, K., Kendall, J., & Max, S. (1991). *Organize: Organizing for social change, a manual for activists in the 1990s.* Cabin John, MD: Seven Locks Press.

Bryson, J. M., & Crosby, B. C. (1992). *Leadership for the common good: Tackling public problems in a shared-power world.* San Francisco: Jossey-Bass.

Delgado, G. (1994). *Beyond the politics of place: New directions in community organizing in the 1990s.* Oakland, CA: Applied Research Center.

Hanna, M. G., & Robinson, B. (1994). *Strategies for community empowerment: Direct-action and transformative approaches to social change practice.* Lewiston, NY: Edwin Mellen Press.

Haynes, K. S., & Mickelson, J. S. (1991). *Affecting change: Social workers in the political arena* (2nd ed.). New York: Longman.

Mondros, J. B., & Wilson, S. M. (1994). *Organizing for power and empowerment.* New York: Columbia University Press.

Simon, B. Levy. (1994). *The empowerment tradition in American social work history.* New York: Columbia University Press.

Zander, A. (1990). *Effective social action by community groups.* San Francisco: Jossey-Bass.

**Dorothy N. Gamble, MSW, ACSW,** is clinical assistant professor and director of admissions, and **Marie Overby Weil, DSW, ACSW,** is professor and director, Community Social Work Program, University of North Carolina at Chapel Hill, School of Social Work, 223 E. Franklin St., Chapel Hill, NC 27599.

**For further information see**

Advocacy; Civil Rights; Community; Community Development; Community Needs Assessment; Community Organization; Community Practice Models; Computer Utilization; Fundraising and Philanthropy; Interdisciplinary and Interorganizational Collaboration; International and Comparative Social Welfare; Mutual Aid Societies; Natural Helping Networks; Organizations: Context for Social Services Delivery; Peace and Social Justice; Sectarian Agencies; Settlements and Neighborhood Centers; Social Planning; Social Work Education; Social Work Profession Overview; Social Workers in Politics; Voter Registration.

**Key Words**
citizen participation
community development
community organization

# Civil Rights

**William L. Pollard**

Civil rights protect the individual from arbitrary abuses by the state or other people. Basic rights of citizens are identified in the Bill of Rights of the Constitution of the United States. During the past 200 years, the passage of several amendments has enabled a greater number of individuals previously not considered to be full members of the society to share in the advantages of citizenship, a privilege previously reserved for white men. The history of the United States and the subsequent expansion of civil rights reflect a number of efforts to extend civil liberties to several oppressed groups: women, African Americans, Hispanics, American Indians, other people of color, gay men, lesbians, people with disabilities, unborn children, and others.

Civil rights are intended to act as a protection to ensure that people—regardless of race, creed, color, physical limitations, or gender or other characteristics—are treated fairly and are not discriminated against. In addition, civil rights have also protected individuals from artificially established forms of discrimination that prevent access to opportunities to meet the basic needs and privileges offered to others in society.

## Background

The story of civil rights in the United States reflects forces that have given impetus to changes attempting to ensure that all people are treated fairly in their normal intercourse with other citizens and with government. The early history of the United States is marked by several notable examples of resistance to infringement on the rights of the individual. Mayflower passengers and later the victims of the Bunker Hill massacre were among the earliest advocates of civil rights. Eventually, the American War of Independence led to the establishment of strong principles, which were to provide a springboard for the attainment of civil rights for classes of citizens who had been ignored by the founding fathers, who enslaved people; denied women rights; and advocated for the killing of American Indian men, women, and children.

### Origins in English Laws

The concept of civil rights in the United States has its origins in English laws that concern the protection of the individual from abuses by the state. These laws have given the United States background and tradition that have emphasized protecting the rights of the individual from the actions of any force attempting to discriminate against or oppress citizens. The idea of individual rights helped to force the development of the Magna Carta of England under King John in 1215 (Burns, Ralph, Lerner, & Meacham, 1986). Under its provisions,

> No freeman shall be taken or imprisoned or disseised [dispossessed] or exiled or in any way destroyed, nor

> will we go upon nor send upon him, except by the lawful judgment of his peers or by the law of the land.... To no one will we sell, to no one will we refuse or delay, rights or justice.

The Magna Carta determined that no individual could be imprisoned or have property taken without legal sanction.

In 1689 the English Parliament adopted the Declaration of Rights and Liberties, which extended rights to protect the individual. The act prohibited excessive fines and cruel or unusual punishment, guaranteed the right to a jury trial with impartial jurors, prohibited fines or forfeiture of liberties unless an individual was convicted, guaranteed rights to petition the king and speak freely, and denied the king the right to suspend or levy taxes without approval of Parliament. In 1694 these rights were extended to subjects in British colonies.

The principles enunciated in the Magna Carta provided the foundation of the legal system that currently operates in the United States and in England, and they provided the foundation on which U.S. civil rights are founded. The English people who founded the original 13 colonies did so as an act of protest against the capricious behavior of the King of England, but they did not fare so well as colonists either. Not only were the colonists taxed without representation, but limits were placed on their right to free speech, their right to bear arms, and their right to elect people of their choice to represent them. These conditions led to the fight to independence. But they were so powerful that they fostered principles adopted by the men and women enslaved by the colonists and generations of their descendants who even today resist efforts to limit individual freedom.

## Civil Rights in the United States

Civil rights laws in the United States have been created and revised as a means of protecting citizens from the abuses of government and people who regard themselves as superior because of their race, gender, class, or other ascribed indicator of privilege. Civil rights are expected to protect citizens from biased treatment under the law, regardless of race, gender, age, national origin, or religion. It is generally agreed that basic civil rights include voting, equal employment opportunities, equal education, and equal treatment in the acquisition of housing and the use of public accommodations. Although these principles seem rather simple on the surface, they have been difficult to implement. During the past 200 years, history in the United States has been dominated by the civil rights issues shaping the thinking and behavior of citizens. Following the American Revolution, a young United States was forced to make major decisions about who were citizens and what protections and privileges they should have. These civil rights have continued to be at the forefront of American political thought, encompassing not only race and gender, but also sexual orientation, physical conditions, language, and other concerns.

### Liberty and Equality

Principles of liberty and equality were among the many revolutionary ideals that shaped the philosophy of the early Americans and their struggle for independence. These same ideals were later to revisit the founders as they grappled with the question of slavery and later generations as they grappled with the question of rights of women.

Before the revolutionary war could be concluded, leaders had to make decisions about slavery. The men who signed the Declaration of Independence and framed the Constitution were forced to confront the contradictions imposed by owning slaves at the same time they espoused language and values in support of freedom, democracy, and the pursuit of happiness. Eventually, the men who had the greatest influence were those who convinced others that slavery was necessary. This decision meant that freedom and rights enjoyed by white men were not to be extended to the enslaved men, women, and children of African descent. These sentiments were to guide the laws and practices of the United States until well into the 20th century. Racist, sexist, and homophobic policies and practices were the result of this legacy of the subordination of others until abolitionists protested the civil rights issues in the 19th century and advocates of women's rights did so in the dawn of the 20th century.

### Fundamental Human Rights

The individual's claim to privacy and the right to bear arms were also protected by civil rights enunciated in the Constitution. Constitutional rights also ensure the individual's authority to vote and to have access to public accommodations. For many groups the civil rights struggle has emerged more as a conflict over fundamental human rights, rather than the legal authority granted to all citizens. Such was the case of African Americans, who were victimized by their enslavement before the Emancipation Proclamation and the Jim Crow era that defined black and white relations following Reconstruction and beyond. The idea of the civil rights struggle being a fight for human rights also seems true for American Indians, who were victimized by genocide efforts before, during, and after the American War of Independence. The massacres at Sand Creek and Wounded Knee (Brown, 1971) indicate the atrocities that native people had to face in a nation that has since become an advocate of human rights throughout the world. Further, the idea of a struggle for human rights is reflected in the ongoing efforts of women to be recognized as people who should be judged by their character and productivity, rather than by their gender. This concept is also shared by proponents of the civil rights of gay men and lesbians, as well as people with disabilities.

## 18th and 19th Centuries

In the 18th and 19th centuries, civil rights were privileges accorded only to white men. During these years, some of the most infamous atrocities in the history of the United States occurred. People of color throughout the United States experienced all kinds of abuse. In addition to the violence and physical abuse suffered by African Americans, Native Americans suffered death and genocide in massacres by American troops in the West (Brown, 1971), and Asian immigrants from China and Japan suffered abuse as they provided the backbone for the labor that helped build the West (Kitano, 1980).

### American Indians

For American Indians the 19th century was a period in which their civil rights struggle consisted primarily of staying alive. The years following the Civil War in the United States were tragic ones for the Indians of the Plains as they were systematically removed from their lands either by treaties or by war. The Sand Creek Massacre and Wounded Knee demonstrated how the people suffered genocide that was implemented to make the West safe for "civilized" people. Like other oppressed groups in the United States, Native Americans can question the nature of justice, as well as law and order. Their civil rights were violated by genocide, their forced adaptation of a strange way of life, and their isolation on reservations, not unlike the homelands where black South Africans were forced to live under apartheid. For American Indians the matter of civil rights was one of no rights respected by white men. Their struggle in the 19th century and even today has been a struggle for the right to be recognized as human beings and accorded the rights and privileges due them as citizens.

Late in the 1840s, gold was discovered in California, and thousands of fortune seekers from the East headed for the territories that the United States had recently acquired from the defeated Mexican government. This transition occurred as the people in the eastern United States were beginning to have strong debates over the question of slavery. The discovery of gold encouraged the rapid migration of Americans to "golden opportunities" in the West. Washington policymakers justified the "permanent Indian frontier" as manifest destiny. This concept of destiny assigned to Europeans and their offspring the responsibility of ruling everything within the United States, including the Indians, their land, and the wealth it contained. The inevitable conflicts with the Indians of the Plains led to several broken treaties and countless armed conflicts. The epitome of the civil rights struggles for Native Americans was the 14th amendment to the Constitution, which granted equal rights to all people, *except Indians*. This deliberate exclusion, the decision to deny liberty and equality to the native people of America, implied a refusal to recognize the humanity of America's original people.

### African Americans

Because millions of people of African descent were forced into slavery in the United States, slavery has been a major civil rights issue for the country. Following their war of independence, the 13 original colonies entered an uneasy peace that was shattered by the emergence of an abolitionist movement that set the stage for organized protest against the institution of slavery. After the war, several states discontinued slavery for people who had served in the Continental Army, and other states ended involuntary servitude regardless of prior service. These acts formed the foundation for what was to become the movement to abolish slavery.

***Abolitionist movement and the Civil War.*** The abolitionist movement was the genesis of the American civil rights movement. Frederick Douglass and Harriet Beecher Stowe were among the people who most vividly expressed protestations against slavery, and Stowe's *Uncle Tom's Cabin* (1851) was among other forces that contributed to an escalation in sentiment against slavery. Early civil rights protesters were joined by underground railroad conductors and the radical challenges of John Brown and others. No factor, however, had a more profound impact on relationships between the North and South than the Dred Scott decision in 1857 (Lipsitz & Speak, 1989). This Supreme Court ruling declared that the Missouri Compromise, which banned slavery in certain territories, was unconstitutional; the decision favored slaveholding interests by suggesting that the Missouri Compromise would deprive citizens of their property—slaves—without due process of law. The

14th amendment in 1866 eventually overturned the Dred Scott decision, but not before a civil war tore the country apart in a bloody four-year conflict.

On January 1, 1863, President Abraham Lincoln declared the enslaved people residing in the rebellious states of the South to be free. Although the Emancipation Proclamation can be seen as only a war measure, it called attention to the need for additional legislation to ensure the civil rights of African Americans. In 1865 the 13th amendment, which prohibited slavery, was passed.

***Post–Civil War.*** In subsequent civil rights legislation, all African Americans were freed from their enforced servitude by the passage of the 14th amendment, the Civil Rights Act of 1866. Enactment of the 14th amendment ensured that most citizens (Indians were excluded from the act) were allowed equal protection under the law by preventing states from establishing laws that would deprive any person the right of citizenship without due process of law. The 14th amendment has the reputation of being the most frequently challenged amendment because it was the catalyst for using the Bill of Rights as protection against state action. Until passage of the Civil Rights Act in 1964, the matter of state's rights was often used by states in the South as a means to restrict liberties that had been promised to African Americans by the 14th amendment. The 15th amendment, passed in 1870, extended the right to vote to African Americans; however, this right was to be short-lived because of changes in voting eligibility in many southern states that were intended to minimize the effect of the mandate.

In the years following the Civil War, in spite of the 13th, 14th, and 15th amendments, southern states continued to develop procedures and, in some instances, laws that restricted the citizenship of black people. Before the Civil War, all of the southern states had enacted codes that were designed to control and discipline enslaved people. These slave codes, as they were called in some places, became black codes in the years following the Civil War, designed to restrict the freedom of African Americans and regulate their relationships with white people. In many ways these practices became the foundation on which Jim Crow laws were established to regulate the social, political, and economic life of African Americans. Jim Crow laws continued well into the 20th century until the Civil Rights Act was passed in 1964.

Black codes paved the way for the Jim Crow laws, and the *Plessy v. Ferguson* decision in 1896 firmly entrenched laws that severely restricted the civil rights of African Americans. In upholding *Plessy v. Ferguson,* the U.S. Supreme Court established the idea that the doctrine of separate but equal accommodations was justifiable use of state power (Lipsitz & Speak, 1989). This "separate but equal" doctrine established a heritage that, in practice, resulted in poor services and less-than-adequate opportunities for education and employment for all Americans.

**Mexican Americans**

Among other groups in the United States who were victimized by discriminatory practices are men and women of Mexican descent. Mexicans, who had a long history of residence in what is now the southwest part of the United States, were among this country's earliest citizens. In February 1848 the Treaty of Guadalupe Hidalgo ended the Mexican–United States War (McLemore, 1980). This treaty, ratified in October 1848, forced Mexico to give to the United States approximately one-half of Mexico's land, including what is now the states of Arizona, California, Nevada, New Mexico, Texas, and Utah, as well as parts of Colorado and Wyoming (Graebner, 1984). Texas had gained its own independence in 1836 but was then annexed to the United States by the 1848 treaty.

Mexican Americans are one of the oldest and largest racial and ethnic groups in the United States. As non-Hispanic U.S. citizens began to settle in the lands acquired from Mexico, conflicts emerged with the former citizens of Mexico and as a result, these "new" U.S. citizens lost their land in American courts. Although the Treaty of Guadalupe Hidalgo had ensured that land ownership would be respected for Mexicans remaining on the conquered lands, American courts found Mexican titles and Spanish land grants worthless and allowed others to acquire the land. This support of racism by the American legal system resulted in the denial of due process and fundamental civil rights to another group of early Americans.

## 20th Century

The 20th century began with continued efforts at improving conditions and opportunities for previously disenfranchised people—women as well as people of color. In 1920 the 19th amendment granted women the right to vote. However, the struggle for civil rights for all citizens continued.

**Specific Populations**

***African Americans.*** African Americans fought courageously in segregated units during World War I, as they continued to fight for civil rights. Not until 1923 did the Supreme Court use its authority to interpret the Constitution to enforce the civil rights amendments and the statutes passed after the Civil War. *Moore v. Dempsey* involved black sharecroppers in Phillips County, Arkansas, who had tried to improve their economic condition by organizing; frightened white people reacted violently and more than 200 people were killed. Twelve black people were accused of murder. In determining that their civil rights to a fair trial had been violated, the Supreme Court initiated an era in which de facto realities were to be more important than de jure laws in considering civil rights cases.

The National Association for the Advancement of Colored People (NAACP), the most active ally of black citizens at the time, was a powerful force in supporting the defendants. This civil rights organization found much work to be done for civil rights, in spite of modest gains.

***Japanese Americans.*** Another area of discriminatory practice was heightened by the U.S. entry into World War II following the Japanese bombing of Pearl Harbor. After the United States entered the war, over 110,000 Japanese American citizens, who were determined to be security risks, were incarcerated (McLemore, 1980). They were forced to abandon their homes and sell their farms before being sent to concentration camps. In spite of this denial of rights, some Japanese Americans fought and died in the European Theater. Senator Daniel Inouye from Hawaii, who lost an arm in battle, was one of these soldiers. The denial of civil rights to the Japanese Americans during World War II illustrates the ease with which civil rights can be eliminated or restricted.

***Mexican Americans.*** By 1910, in spite of being unwanted and mistreated, Mexicans began a significant movement north to the United States. Upheaval during the Mexican Revolutionary War (1910–1920) was a contributing factor to this movement. However, even before their migration began to become visible, Mexicans' civil rights were retarded by the same forces that exhibited ethnic antipathies toward African Americans and American Indians. De facto segregation in schools, housing, and employment emerged as Mexican Americans settled in barrios and worked at the menial jobs many were forced to take. During the Great Depression of the 1930s, there were massive deportations of over 400,000 people—many of these citizens were blamed for the economic hardship brought on by the stagnation of the economy and deported as scapegoats. Some of those deported had been U.S. residents for over 10 years, and the forced repatriation included their children, who had been born as citizens in the United States. These violations of civil rights reflected the deep sentiments that have continued to make the struggle for civil rights an ongoing concern for other population groups.

Although there were some modest gains for Mexican Americans, in the 1960s Cesar Chavez became a force for civil rights for Mexican Americans and others as he provided leadership on behalf of migrant workers. His organizational skills and nonviolent approach to civil rights made him a hero and role model to many. During this period, legislation provided new tools. In 1968 the Bilingual Education Act was passed to provide federal aid for bilingual instruction. Bilingual instruction was not new to the United States, as it had begun in the 1840s in Cincinnati, New York City, and other places. The Bilingual Education Act probably gave impetus to a decision by José Angel Gutierrez, president of the Crystal City, Texas, School Board. In the early 1970s, Gutierrez ordered elementary school classes in that city to be taught in both English and Spanish (Rivera, 1984). His decision was supported in 1974, when the U.S. Supreme Court unanimously ruled in the case of *Lau v. Nichols* that public schools must provide specially designed programs for students who speak little or no English. Gutierrez was a founding member of the La Raza Unida Party, a political party established to enfranchise Mexican Americans.

**Court Decisions**

In the latter half of the 20th century, there have been many Supreme Court decisions related to civil rights. The following are among some of the key decisions.

***Education.*** In 1954 the Supreme Court's decision on *Brown v. Board of Education* overruled the "separate but equal" doctrine that had been valid since 1896. The court ruled that segregation of school children on the basis of race was unconstitutional even if the facilities were of equal quality. This decision resulted in elimination of overt racial discrimination in public areas of transportation, hotel and restaurant accommodations, theaters and auditoriums, parks, recreational areas, even barber shops. However, it took years of activism to implement the full implications of the decision.

***Health.*** In 1973 the Court's decision in *Roe v. Wade* gave women the right to abortion and what many believe to be control over their own bodies. Almost simultaneously, however, as a spin-off from the "moral majority" movement, "right-to-life" groups began to mount an offensive against the decision. This "civil rights" movement on behalf of fetuses continues in the 1990s and has culminated in the deaths of at least two doctors who provided abortions.

***Housing.*** In *Shelly v. Kraemer* in 1948, the Court held that private arrangements to maintain racial segregation in housing patterns could not be recognized.

***Justice.*** In *Gideon v. Wainwright* in 1963, the Court determined that indigent accused have the right to secure appointment of legal defense at the government's expense. *Miranda v. Arizona* in 1966 established the Fifth amendment privilege against self-incrimination. The decision required that police inform a person taken into custody of the right to remain silent and the right to legal counsel. Since 1966 the Supreme Court has modified this decision in a number of ways. With the *In re Gault* decision in 1967, the Court established protections for juveniles including the right to representation by legal counsel, right to timely notice, right to confront and cross-examine complainants, and right to protection against self-incrimination.

**Civil Rights Legislation**

The first civil rights act since 1875, the Civil Rights Act of 1957 (P.L. 85-315), established the Commission on Civil Rights and strengthened federal enforcement powers. In the early 1960s, a number of events including the assassination of President John F. Kennedy, protest actions by civil rights groups, and the civil rights conversion of President Lyndon B. Johnson established a climate for advanced civil rights legislation. The result was the Civil Rights Act of 1964 (P.L. 88-352).

The act strengthened voting rights and mandated equal access in a number of key areas. Any program receiving federal funding was forbidden to discriminate on the basis of race, color, religion, or national origin. Victims of discrimination on the basis of race, color, religion, or national origin in cases that involved interstate commerce were granted injunctive relief; that is, the court has the power to order certain acts to be done. The U.S. Department of Education was authorized to desegregate public education. The Civil Rights Commission was given expanded investigative power. The Equal Employment Opportunity Commission was established to oversee civil rights in employment. To help communities resolve problems involving discrimination, the act set up a Community Relations Service in the U.S. Department of Commerce.

The Education for All Handicapped Children Act of 1975 (P.L. 94-142) extended national public education policy to mandate free public education for all children with disabilities. In 1986 the Education of the Handicapped Act Amendment (P.L. 99-457) expanded services to children with disabilities from birth through age five years. Passage of the Americans with Disabilities Act in 1990 gave the United States an opportunity to remove yet another deterrent to full citizenship for another class of U.S. citizens. The implementation of the Americans with Disabilities Act took a significant step not only toward making the workplace more accessible to people with disabilities, but to ensuring that the world is more open and receptive to all people, including those who were prevented from obtaining services because they were not sighted or because they were dependent on a wheelchair for transportation.

The Civil Rights Act of 1991 (P.L. 102-166) reversed a set of Supreme Court decisions that had eroded protection of women and people of color in the workplace. The act mandates monetary damages for victims of intentional discrimination based on race, gender, disability, or religion. Age, however, was not included as a discriminating factor.

**Other Struggles for Civil Rights**

On an August afternoon in 1963, Dr. Martin Luther King, Jr., shared his dream of a United States free of the racial bigotry that had been so carefully preserved by the authors of the Jim Crow legislation that governed black and white relationships in the South. Although Dr. King's enduring words motivated change for some, the struggle has continued for disenfranchised groups.

Almost 30 years after Dr. King's address, gay men, lesbians, and bisexuals filled the streets of Washington, DC, to demonstrate for civil rights. The importance of this large demonstration lies in the fact that U.S. citizens witnessed another 20th-century milestone in its history of human rights. The 1993 March on Washington called attention to the fact that millions of Americans were being dehumanized and discriminated against, not because of the quality of their character, but because of their sexual orientation.

The years between the two demonstrations reflect the transformation that is taking place in the United States as the matter of civil rights has become more inclusive and as the legal claims and privileges of a greater number of people are being protected. Diverse groups now call attention to the manner in which established customs and laws have deprived citizens of fundamental rights. For example, people have challenged the insensitivities that denied people access to facilities because they could not manipulate a wheelchair in a bathroom or use an elevator that gave directions only for sighted people. In Michigan an individual's right to assisted suicide was challenged by conflicts between those who believe it imperative to maintain life and those who believe the individual has a right to end his or her own life under special circumstances. Elsewhere, proponents of the rights of the unborn child have taken their struggle to such extremes that violence and death have occurred.

## The Social Work Profession and Civil Rights

Social work has its origins in the turbulent years of the Progressive Era. Those were years of constant change as the United States experienced rapid growth resulting from the immigration of Eastern Europeans and other populations seeking opportunities in the land of democracy. During those years large numbers of African Americans migrated north to flee the racial antipathies of the southern Jim Crow policies. Although they were not always in the forefront of civil rights and social justice, the leading social reformers eventually developed a stance consistent with democratic values and a belief in the rights of all people regardless of race, color, or creed. As a founding member of NAACP, Jane Addams was one of the social reformers who joined with W.E.B. DuBois to establish this early civil rights organization. Such action set the standard for what has become the social work profession's commitment to civil rights.

The advocacy role of social work forces the continuation of behavior that is supportive of civil and human rights. The settlement house movement from which social work originated supported actions that increase the diversity of the profession. This diversity is reflected not only by the people who deliver services, but by the profession's willingness to offer services that are sensitive to people's differences. Now that social work comprises individuals who are of diverse backgrounds, the profession should be increasingly closer to the forefront in advocating for human rights. The struggle for civil rights should continue as long as any group of people is oppressed and not permitted the opportunity to achieve.

During the past several years, the major social work organizations have taken steps to ensure that all of their members have an opportunity to participate fully in the management of those organizations. They have achieved this goal by developing standards and organizational bylaws that value the diversity of their memberships and by establishing mechanisms that ensure the widest possibility for participation of individual members.

For several years, NASW has worked with a number of civil rights groups. In addition, NASW has made elimination of racism, sexism, homophobia, and poverty major national priorities. The NASW Delegate Assembly, the organization's governing body, has developed public policy statements relating to disabilities, gay men and lesbians, women, abortion, people with acquired immune deficiency syndrome (AIDS), people of color, and other civil rights issues. Similarly, the Council on Social Work Education, which accredits schools of social work, has expressed a strong commitment to addressing concerns related to oppressed groups in its curriculum policy statement and accreditation standards. Thus, cultural diversity, women, and sexual orientation are mandated areas for curricula of accredited social work programs.

## Future Issues

The arrival of the 21st century should find social workers faced with a new set of civil rights issues. Among them will be the question of how immigrants to the United States will be treated. With civil wars in Eastern Europe and poverty in the Caribbean and in Central and Latin America, the plight of immigrants—who they are, who they should be—will be a subject of debate. Unlike the immigrants of the last century, many of the current ones are people of color. During the 1994 general election, Californians voted overwhelmingly to deny basic services to many immigrants. This action and other treatment call to question the changing nature of racism as we struggle to understand why the new immigrants are not as welcome as the "huddled masses struggling to breathe free" were in the waning years of the 19th century. On the other hand, the previous history of the civil rights struggle in the United States may offer some clues as to how the nation may extend and protect these rights in the next century.

Another civil rights focus is end-of-life decisions. Until the late 20th century, it was presumed that people should not have decision-making authority over how their lives may end. However, activists are suggesting changes. Choice in Dying promotes living wills, the use of other advance directives, and attention to civil rights for people who face the end of their lives. Other groups also address rights in dying, and a physician promotes the right to die by offering aid to people who want to end their lives.

The 20th century began with attention to the civil rights problems of African Americans who were forced by law into a condition of second-class citizenship. As the United States has matured, its citizens have become less tolerant of some forms of discrimination and have expanded this nation's capacity to extend and promote civil rights to a larger group of citizens.

Since the 1963 March on Washington, there have been renewed efforts to break down the formal and informal barriers that disadvantage women. Equity in pay and employment benefits still remain key concerns of women. In addition, women still must deal with the hostility that is manifested in violence by men who consider women property, a situation not unlike the slavery that existed before the U.S. Civil War. Shelters provide a refuge for women who are the victims of violence, just as the underground railroad provided refuge for African Americans fleeing the bondage of slavery. Yet more remains to be done so that women have the legal means to shelter themselves from the violence of men that often ends in a woman's death, because current laws do not provide adequate protection from abuse.

The 20th century has witnessed civil rights transformed from a focus on African Americans in the early 1900s to an enlarged perspective that is more inclusive. The citizens of the United States are now more aware of their diversity and diverse needs. The founders of this country were white men who, in the early years, served their own needs well. Now that the citizenry is represented by elected officials who more accurately reflect that citizenry, those officials have brought focus to issues that reflect their differences. Today's elected officials are not all white men. They are women, and they are Americans of African, Puerto Rican, Cuban, Mexican, Native American, and Asian descent. Elected officials today may be gay or lesbian. They may be people with disabilities. The diversity this country has begun to embrace has led to a greater awareness of the need for legislation that will ensure that all people are valued and that all have equal protection under the law.

Since it became a nation, the United States has struggled with how to reduce the arbitrary discrimination faced by people who suffer persecution because they are members of an oppressed group. The civil rights struggle continues today because this nation has not found ways to ensure that all people have equal access to the right of citizenry. The process to include different populations under the civil rights umbrella has been incremental and dependent on the identification of oppressed groups. The struggle continues because, as one group—be it disabled people or gay men and lesbians—advances, another oppressed group finds both the courage and the support to mount its own struggle for civil rights.

Finally, the struggle for civil rights continues because obstacles such as bigotry in diverse forms still pose threats to equal opportunity for all citizens. Although these threats may seem small, represented by fringe groups such as the Ku Klux Klan or the Aryan Nation, they serve as reminders of the diversity of this nation. And they reinforce the idea that civil rights have been granted to those who have fought for them, rather than having them awarded as a birthright of a privileged class.

## References


Americans with Disabilities Act of 1990. P.L. 101-336, 104 Stat. 327.

Bilingual Education Act of 1968. P.L. 89-10.

Brown, D. (1971). *Bury my heart at Wounded Knee.* New York: Holt, Rinehart & Winston.

Brown v. Board of Education of Topeka, Kansas, 347 U.S. 483, 74 S. Ct. 686 (1954).

Burns, E. M., Ralph, P. E., Lerner, R. E., & Meacham, S. (1986). *World civilizations.* New York: W. W. Norton.

Civil Rights Act of 1866. Ch. 31, 14 Stat. 27.

Civil Rights Act of 1957. P.L. 85-315, 71 Stat. 634.

Civil Rights Act of 1964. P.L. 88-352, 78 Stat. 241.

Civil Rights Act of 1991. P.L. 102-166, 105 Stat. 1071.

Education for All Handicapped Children Act of 1975. P.L. 94-142, 89 Stat. 773.

Education of the Handicapped Act Amendment. P.L. 99-457, 100 Stat. 1145.

Gideon v. Wainwright, 83 S. Ct. 792 (1963).

Graebner, N. A. (1984). Mexican War. In *World book encyclopedia* (Vol. 13, pp. 369–371). Chicago: World Book Encyclopedia.

In re Gault, 387 U.S. 1 (1967).

Kitano, H. L. (1980). *Race relations.* Englewood Cliffs, NJ: Prentice Hall.

Lau v. Nichols, 414 U.S. 563, 94 S. Ct. 786 (1974).

Lipsitz, L., & Speak, D. M. (1989). *American democracy.* New York: St. Martin's Press.

McLemore, S. D. (1980). *Racial and ethnic relations in America.* Boston: Allyn & Bacon.

Miranda v. Arizona, 384 U.S. 436 (1966).

Moore v. Dempsey, 43 S. Ct. 265 (1923).

Plessy v. Ferguson, 163 U.S. 537 (1896).

Rivera, F. (1984). José Angel Gutierrez. In *World book encyclopedia* (Vol. 8, p. 428). Chicago: World Book Encyclopedia.

Roe v. Wade, 93 S. Ct. 705 (1973).

Shelly v. Kraemer, 68 S. Ct. 836 (1948).

Stowe, H. B. (1851). *Uncle Tom's cabin.* New York: National.


## Further Reading


Baker, R. S. (1964). *Following the color line.* New York: Harper & Row.

Branch, T. (1988). *Parting the waters: America in the King years 1954–63.* New York: Simon & Schuster.

Compton, B. (1980). *Introduction to social welfare and social work.* Homewood, IL: Dorsey Press.
DuBois, W.E.B. (1983). *Black reconstruction in America.* West Hanover, MA: Halliday Lithograph.
Franklin, J. H. (1947). *From slavery to freedom.* New York: Alfred A. Knopf.
Higginbotham, A. L. (1980). *In the matter of color.* New York: Oxford University Press.
Meier, A., & Rudwick, E. M. (1966). *From plantation to ghetto.* New York: Hill & Wang.
Myrdal, G. (1944). *An American dilemma.* New York: Harper & Row.
Woodward, C. V. (1966). *The strange career of Jim Crow.* London: Oxford University Press.

**William L. Pollard, PhD,** is dean, Syracuse University, School of Social Work, Brockway Hall, Syracuse, NY 13244.

**For further information see**

Abortion; Advocacy; African Americans Overview; American Indians; Asian Americans Overview; Children's Rights; Citizen Participation; Developmental Disabilities; Definitions and Policies; Disability; End-of-Life Decisions; Ethics and Values; Federal Social Legislation from 1961 to 1994; Gay Men Overview; Hispanics Overview; HIV/AIDS Overview; Homelessness; Human Rights; Lesbians Overview; Patient Rights; Peace and Social Justice; Policy Practice; Progressive Social Work; Social Welfare History; Social Work Practice: History and Evolution; Social Work Profession Overview; Women Overview.

**Key Words**
civil rights
discrimination
diversity
equality
social justice

READER'S GUIDE

## Clinical Social Work

*The following entries contain information on this general topic:*

Assessment
Brief Task-Centered Practice
Brief Therapies
Clinical Social Work
Cognition and Social Cognitive Theory
Cognitive Treatment
Crisis Intervention: Research Needs
Diagnostic and Statistical Manual of Mental Disorders
Direct Practice Overview
Ecological Perspective
Ethnic-Sensitive Practice
Generalist and Advanced Generalist Practice
Gestalt
Goal Setting and Intervention Planning
Group Practice Overview
Interviewing
Licensing, Regulation, and Certification
Managed Care
Person-in-Environment
Psychosocial Approach
Recording
Termination in Direct Practice
Transactional Analysis

# Clinical Social Work

**Carol R. Swenson**

Since the 1960s, there have been substantial developments in knowledge and changes in contexts of social work practice. These changes have challenged prior distinctions about practice based on method (casework, group work, community organization) and setting (medical, psychiatric, family, and children's services). Social work has sought new role definitions and new language to describe those practitioners whose primary focus is on individuals, families, and small groups in their transactions with environments. One of the newer role definitions is "clinical social work," about which there is no consensus of opinion but multiple voices. Included are the public voices of NASW; the National Federation of Societies of Clinical Social Work; schools of social work; prominent social workers; and, increasingly, regulatory and credentialing organizations. More privately, individual social workers, other professionals, and many members of the public have their own unique understandings.

In this entry, *clinical social work* means practice primarily with and on behalf of individuals, families, and groups, by social workers trained in this specialization. Clinical social workers work with clients to bring about social and psychological change and to increase access to social and economic resources. They also join with other social workers in other forms of social work practice, such as social action, bringing their unique perspective gained from direct knowledge of client experience. This definition is intended to be a broad and inclusive one, while emphasizing that clinical social work is a specialization and, consequently, requires at least master's level training.

"Clinical social work" is, for many social workers, the best of the alternative terms rather than a clear-cut preference. These social workers find "direct practice" mystifying to other professionals and the public, and "social work" not specific enough. "Clinical" comes from the Greek word *kline*, meaning "bed," and by extension, "at the bedside." Although this word has been criticized for possibly conveying pathology, the term includes many positive connotations. It emphasizes a living person who can be helped (rather than a dead one who can only be studied), observation (rather than controlled experiment), and unique instances (rather than statistical aggregates or general theory). Most of all, it emphasizes *being with* people in their struggles. These are all values espoused by clinical social workers. "At the bedside" is a location in people's ordinary life space (as opposed to institutions or laboratories, for instance), and thus "clinical" has potential for incorporating a destigmatizing, normalizing perspective. Furthermore, the lay public and other professionals recognize that clinicians work compassionately with people seeking change—as contrasted with research or influencing broad societal conditions. "Clinical" is also the language used by NASW, the National Federation of Societies of Clinical Social Work, and many state regulatory boards.

## Clinical Social Work Today

As a specialization of social work, clinical practice shares the values, history, and purposes of social work. It affirms person–environment transactions as the focus of attention. It uses the common social work processes of engagement, assessment/formulation, intervention, evaluation, and prevention (Council on Social Work Education, 1982).

Clinical social workers draw from the common social work knowledge base of social and individual theories, social policy, and research methodology. They also draw from specialized theories of human behavior and change that describe individuals, families, and small groups, and interventions at those levels. In addition, clinical social workers trained since the 1970s incorporate general systems and ecological perspectives in conceptualizing their practice (Chetkow-Yanoov, 1992; Germain, 1978; Gordon, 1969; Meyer, 1993). They value these perspectives for bringing coherence to the multiple levels of social work assessment and intervention, and for providing a unifying force within the profession (De Hoyos, 1989). Further, they have been trained more broadly in intervention skills at various systems levels, including social change (Germain & Gitterman, 1980; Lee, 1994; Lister, 1987; Weissman, Epstein, & Savage, 1987).

Clinical social workers work with the whole range of human pain and suffering, from acquired immune deficiency syndrome (AIDS) to xenophobia. They work with survivors of physical and mental illness, of deprivation and neglect, and of a society rife with oppression and violence. They work with refugees and with unemployed, frail elderly, and homeless people. They work with troubled marriages, family conflict, and lack of social connection. They work with children with learning difficulties, adolescents struggling with sexuality and sexual identity issues, and adults trying to make meaning of their lives. They work with substance abusers, perpetrators of violence and abuse, and criminal offenders. And, in some instances, they work with people with no identifiable problems in living to provide a facilitative and supportive environment for successful development and socialization.

Clinical social work draws from multiple theoretical frameworks. Some practitioners espouse a single perspective, while others draw from multiple ways of thinking. The small group is seen as a central vehicle of change in many of these approaches. There are several key streams of thought: ecological/strengths/ethnic-sensitive/empowerment perspectives; cognitive/behavioral/problem-solving approaches; psychodynamic approaches; family systems perspectives. More detail is provided on these various approaches elsewhere in this volume. There are also specialized theoretical perspectives that have arisen around particular problem areas, such as alcoholism. Recently, narrative and social constructionist approaches have been generating great interest. New metatheoretical developments such as postmodernism (Gergen, 1985) are leading to increasing comfort with holding multiple perspectives, which are viewed as "lenses" for understanding complex phenomena such as client troubles and social problems.

Interventions with individuals, families, and groups are all by clinical social workers, with some practitioners preferring one modality and others using all of them. Clinical social workers also intervene with other service providers to arrange services, to coordinate their work, and to advocate for clients. Many if not most client situations will include both types of interventions, especially for the clinician who remains mindful of the "dual focus" (Wood & Middleman, 1989). Both direct work with clients and work on clients' behalf have a host of linguistic complexities. Is direct work called "therapy," "treatment," "counseling," "work"? Clinicians wishing to stress the uniqueness of social work or the strengths perspective may prefer the latter; clinicians who work in multidisciplinary settings may prefer the former. Likewise, many terms have been used for work with other service providers: "resource development and mobilization," "indirect work," "advocacy, brokerage, and mediation," "service provision." A tentative solution to the linguistic form for direct work is "therapeutic conversations," which conveys the ideas of healing change but is compatible with a strengths perspective and reduces the power differential between client and clinician. It also connotes that the clinician as well as the client may be positively changed through the process. It can be applied equally well to work with individuals, families, and groups. The most comprehensive current language for work on behalf of clients seems to be "case management" (Roberts-DeGennaro, 1987), though that term carries connotations of standardization and disempowerment that some find distasteful.

In addition to work with and on behalf of specific clients, clinical social workers also engage in practice with and on behalf of populations to bring about social change. In this arena, they join with their colleagues who are specialists in larger systems work, bringing their own unique contribution of intimate knowledge of client experiences and perspectives. This work includes prevention and education programs to address specific issues (alcohol and drug abuse, teenage pregnancy, AIDS, violence, and so forth) and also broad goals of developing healthy communities and families (Germain, 1982; Homonoff & Martin, 1994). Clinical social workers, with and for their clients, influence the political process through social action, legislative testimony, public speaking, and use of the media (Stein, 1994). They initiate class advocacy efforts in relation to injustices and problems they identify (Landers, 1993). They influence organizations to be more responsive to client needs (Anonymous, 1989; Gitterman & Miller, 1989). They develop new services and programs (Lee, 1986) and new conceptualizations of problems and solutions (Anderson, Reiss, & Hogarty, 1986) that are consistent with social work values. Some clinical social workers emphasize working with members of oppressed groups toward removing internal and external power blocks to liberation (Lee, 1994; Mancoske & Hunzkler, 1989; Solomon, 1976). And some confront the beneficiaries of privilege and domination (White, 1986).

Nationally, clinical social workers make up the largest proportion of social workers. About 70 percent of the master's-level and 40 percent of the doctoral-level NASW members describe direct services as their primary function (Gibelman & Schervish, 1993). When secondary function is considered, 33 percent of master's and 30 percent of doctoral members indicate direct service. There have also been substantial increases in the proportion of students who indicate direct practice or clinical practice as their primary field of interest. There are approximately 10,000 members of the National Federation of Societies of Clinical Social Work. About 20,000 clinical social workers hold Diplomates. The Diplomate credential is offered through both NASW and the American Board of Examiners. Although the two credentials differ somewhat, Diplomate certificates offered by both organizations recognize clinical experience and advanced training and supervision beyond the master's level.

Clinical social workers work in a variety of settings, including, but by no means limited to, health and mental agencies, schools, family and child welfare agencies, elder services, work sites, corrections, shelters, and community centers. Some of these settings are quite specialized, such as tertiary care hospitals, and others are broader, such as family and children's services and community centers. Some settings focus on people with identified problems, and others offer programs for the whole community and see primary prevention and community education as key functions. Some settings focus on the most oppressed and stigmatized, such as corrections and shelters, while others, such as hospitals, include a complete cross-section of the community. Even with these latter settings, however, social workers are likely to focus on high-risk groups.

Some settings are developed and staffed primarily by social workers, especially family and children's services and community centers. Some settings are controlled by other disciplines, such as schools and hospitals, and others are fully interdisciplinary. In some of these latter settings, social workers may be quite influential and may occupy key administrative positions; in others, they may be relatively less visible and less powerful. Settings also cover a range from those that are relatively small, informal, and collegial to others that are large, complex, formal, and hierarchical.

Clinical social workers work in both public and private nonprofit agencies. Historically, these were the primary ways services were organized, and jobs were primarily salaried and full time. Increasingly, clinical social workers function in the private and for-profit sectors: They are employed by corporations in employee assistance programs; they work in for-profit nursing homes and hospitals; and they are in group or solo private practices. With "privatization," vendorship, third-party reimbursement, health maintenance organizations, and the advent of managed care, the landscape of service delivery arrangements and career patterns is in flux (Strom & Gingerich, 1993). Many valuable social work services that agencies had discretion about providing, such as home visits, community education, and developmental/socialization activities, may not be reimbursable under new funding patterns, and decisions are often made by nonprofessionals whose bottom line is profit. Clinicians may piece together a variety of part-time jobs, with tenuous connections to multiple organizations and with uncertainty about their career path or income level.

The picture also varies by geography. In different parts of the country, different service arrangements are dominant. For example, in some areas, public social services may offer more extensive and more professional services. Private practice may be more prominent in other locales. Preferred approaches to practice vary, as do availability and kinds of advanced training, degree and type of specialized professional organizations and licensing, and even whether the term "clinical social work" is preferred.

## Historical Development

Clinical social work arose in part from the appreciation that there were many similarities of direct practice in different settings and among the modalities of individual, family, and group work. Developments in practice, in organizational arrangements, and in theory reciprocally influenced one another.

Beginning in the 1950s, numerous professional organizations and educational specializations were slowly integrated. The National Association of Social Workers was formed in 1955, out of seven different associations representing medical, school, and psychiatric social work; group work; community organization; and research; as well as an association with a broad social work membership (Battle, 1987). At the same time, agencies seeking to respond to client needs increasingly found that specialization as casework or group-work agencies was not effective. They began to seek social workers trained to work in multiple modalities. Methods specializations began to give way, and schools of social work experimented with varied curricular arrangements.

Practice theories began to proliferate (Germain, 1983). The psychosocial approach, drawing from psychodynamic theory as well as social role theory and other cultural perspectives, was dominant in casework, with small pockets of enthusiasm for the more humanistic functional approach. The problem-solving approach attempted to integrate the precise knowledge of individual ego functioning from the psychosocial approach with the ideas of focus and time limits from the functional approach. It provided a haven of appreciation of social support, cognitive processes, and participatory democracy and could be used with individuals, families, and groups. Other group approaches continued to support healthy development and socialization. The advent of family systems theory in the 1950s began to provide a theoretical bridge between casework and group work. This was followed by general systems theory and cybernetics in the 1960s. By offering concepts that could be applied to systems of any size, from atoms to societies, and by emphasizing transactional rather than linear ideas of cause and effect, these theories opened whole new ways of thinking about social problems, human development, and clinical interventions.

The emergence of clinical social work also was influenced by the social and professional struggles of the 1960s. During this period, a profound and sustained criticism was aimed at direct practice, which was still generally called casework. The critique included two components: first, that casework was acquiescing in, or perhaps even contributing to, the oppression of the poor and other disadvantaged people (Alinsky, 1965; Piven & Cloward, 1972). According to the critics, social work needed to reemphasize that part of its mission that had to do with social action and social change, with the goal of greater social and economic justice. Working with individuals, families, and groups was often described as a "cop-out," "Band-Aid," or as "cooling the mark"; it was seen as reducing motivation of the oppressed to engage in social protest. The atmosphere became decidedly chilly for caseworkers/clinicians who tried to stand with troubled individuals in a social change era. They would find themselves and their concerns ignored in professional meetings; occasionally they were verbally assaulted.

The other criticism was that casework was methodologically inadequate and not scientifically rigorous. Critics pointed to studies that showed imprecise understanding of problems, lack of agreement between clients and clinicians, unclear intervention "technologies," and questionable outcomes, and demanded greater accountability (Fischer, 1978; Wood, 1978). These criticisms occurred at the time doctoral-level education in social work greatly expanded. During the 1960s, people came to believe the university could help preserve and strengthen the knowledge base about direct practice roles and functions. In addition, research methodologies and ways of thinking, developed in the university, were increasingly applied to practice. Demonstration projects on new practice technologies were undertaken, with more-rigorous specification of problems and interventions and more-rigorous evaluation of outcomes (Reid & Epstein, 1977). A body of empirically supported practice principles and a methodology of expanding these at the level of the single case were developed (Fischer, 1978; Jayaratne & Levy, 1979). The model of the "scientist-practitioner" was proposed. And more sophisticated outcome studies began to produce positive findings of effectiveness (Reid & Hanrahan, 1982; Rubin, 1984, 1985).

For these various conceptual, practical, and political reasons, beginning in the late 1960s, groups calling themselves clinical social workers began to gather at the state and local levels. They organized more broadly in 1971, becoming the National Federation of Societies of Clinical Social Work. The federation has been particularly concerned about developing credentialing at an advanced level, expanding clinical social work vendorship, mentoring young clinical social workers, and influencing clinical practice curricula in schools of social work.

**Developments in Practice**

A brief review of the many developments in practice theory during the 1970s and 1980s would emphasize three trends. First, older theoretical perspectives, such as family systems, cognitive–behavioral, and psychosocial approaches continued to be elaborated, often with a proliferation of subtypes emerging. For overviews of many of these perspectives, see Dorfman (1988) and Turner (1986). For example, object relations and self-psychological approaches joined ego psychology and psychoanalytic drive theory as underpinnings of the psychosocial approach; family approaches expanded to include structural, strategic, systemic, communications, narrative, psychoeducational, and so forth. Second, some new perspectives emerged, particularly the ecological and life model approaches, ethnic-sensitive practice, and empirically based practice. The ecological approaches emphasized offering a broad array of growth-enhancing, strengths-focused services, located in people's life space, and drawing from a transactional, cybernetic epistemology (Germain & Gitterman, 1980). As described above, empirically based approaches emphasized clear specification of problems, goals, and interventions, and practice based on research findings. Ethnic-sensitive and culturally competent practice (Devore & Schlesinger, 1981, 1991; Lum, 1986) began to supplant earlier approaches that were blind to cultural diversity and its significance. And finally, some key concepts from the 1960s such as empowerment and liberation were incorporated into direct practice with oppressed groups (Bricker-Jenkins & Hooyman, 1986; Pinderhughes, 1983; Solomon, 1976; Van Den Bergh & Cooper, 1986), even as the community-organizing and social action arenas from which these concepts sprang were disappearing as separate entities.

During the late 1970s and the 1980s, there were additional elements that shaped the development of clinical social work. Central to all of these, perhaps, was the conservative onslaught on the values and programs of the earlier "Great Society." Public sector jobs and training grants were cut back, the "age of narcissism" took over, and the poor and afflicted were either ignored or blamed for their problems. Public service became unfashionable, while clinical social work services became acceptable to the middle class. The pool of applicants for schools of social work shrank, and applicants became increasingly young, female, middle class, and clinically oriented (Rubin & Johnson, 1984; Walz & Groze, 1991).

There was major change in service delivery arrangements. As an outgrowth of the conservative ethos, services were privatized. Formerly public agencies became vendors, competing in the market for government contracts. Programs such as Medicare and Medicaid purchased services from agencies and sometimes private practitioners. Insurance companies, health maintenance organizations, and preferred provider plans began to offer mental health coverage as part of their benefits, albeit within the profit-making rubric. Clinical work in nontraditional agencies serving the poor and oppressed also took root, seeded by a small number of clinical social workers.

**Increasing Independence**
All of these factors led to a different relationship of the clinical social worker to clients and to the society. Previously, agencies had been a primary means of accountability: Most social work clinicians worked under agency auspices, and training and supervision were provided. Now, many agencies hired fee-for-service workers who might receive little supervision or training; increasing numbers of social workers established independent practices, either solo or in groups; and interdisciplinary group practices tended to rely on professional credentialing rather than supervision. These changes increased the need for mechanisms of accountability and ensuring levels of competence of individual practitioners, a function previously carried out primarily by agencies.

A more independent relationship of the clinical social worker to the society took three forms: regulation, vendorship, and private practice. Regulation can mean simply title protection (only those who meet certain criteria may use the title) or licensing, which includes more stringent examination of a professional's training, experience, and knowledge. The first state to have a social work-licensing or title protection law was California, which had some regulation as far back as 1929. However, regulation did not really develop until the 1960s. During that era, seven other states developed some type of regulation. In the 1970s, 14 other states followed suit, and today there is some form of regulation in all states (Thyer & Biggerstaff, 1989). A related issue is vendorship, or being among those mental health professionals who are reimbursable for services by insurance companies and governmental programs. In 1984, NASW made vendorship its highest priority, and by 1989, 22 states and Washington, DC, included clinical social workers in vendorship laws.

Private practice has also increased dramatically in clinical social work. There had been a few independent practitioners for a long time, but it was not until 1956 that private practice was officially sanctioned by NASW for members with appropriate training and experience. By 1991, 63 percent of NASW members reported some independent practice. However, many clinical social workers have very small private practices; in one state survey, about 30 percent reported a private practice of 10 or fewer hours a week (Frost, 1991).

Clinicians report many reasons for private practice: flexibility and independence, ability to exercise their professional judgment, and supplementing inadequate agency income. Some describe it as offering enrichment to their agency work by providing a different group of clients (Barker, 1991; Biggerstaff, 1992; Frost, 1991). Some of these criteria may be essential in order for clinicians, who are predominantly female, to meet family responsibilities (Biggerstaff, 1992). Additional reasons derive from the current service delivery context. As long as agencies offer career advancement primarily through administrative positions and make part-time work difficult or unremunerative, significant numbers of clinicians will engage in private practice because they see no other alternative. When positions in public and nonprofit agencies are eliminated and working conditions deteriorate, the situation is exacerbated.

**Definitions**
Part of the process of regulation and credentialing is specification of a professional service. Definitions both codify what "is" and provide a vision of "what might be." In addition, they reflect the environmental context in which definitions are being developed. A brief examination of several definitions of clinical social work illuminates some issues and changes over time.

One of the early definitions of clinical social work was commissioned by NASW, which established a Task Force on Clinical Social Work Practice in 1978. This definition is noteworthy in several ways. Patricia Ewalt, convener of the task force, pointed out that the "person-in-situation" perspective common to social work as a whole was affirmed, that "psychotherapeutic activity [was] deemed to be a part but not the whole of clinical social work practice," that assessment ("biopsychosocial") was emphasized, and that clinical social work was placed within the mission of social work (Cohen, 1979, p. 23). The task force added: "At this early stage it was intended that there be a lack of specificity in this statement regarding the technical interventive strategies of clinical social work" (p. 26). The authors emphasized the high value given to interventions in the "social situation."

In 1984, NASW adopted a definition that read:

> Clinical social work shares with all social work practice the goal of enhancement and maintenance of psychosocial functioning of individuals, families, and small groups. Clinical social work practice is the professional application of social work theory and methods to the treatment and prevention of psychosocial dysfunction, disability, or impairment, including emotional and mental disorders. It is based on knowledge of one or more theories of human development within a psychosocial context.

> The perspective of person-in-situation is central to clinical social work practice. Clinical social work includes interventions directed to interpersonal interactions, intrapsychic dynamics, and life-support and management issues. Clinical social work services consist of assessment, diagnosis and treatment, including psychotherapy and counseling, client-centered advocacy, consultation, and evaluation. (Minahan, 1987, pp. 965–966)

This definition moves beyond the 1979 definition in placing clinical social work even more solidly within the social work profession and in specifying interventions more fully and more broadly. An evaluative component is added. There is medical language used ("diagnosis," "treatment," "dysfunction," "disorder") and also strengths-focused language ("enhancement," "prevention," "life support," "counseling").

The National Federation of Societies of Clinical Social Work and the American Board of Examiners in Clinical Social Work have also developed definitions—most recently, jointly (American Board of Examiners in Clinical Social Work, 1993). Their definitions are quite similar to those of NASW but tend to be more elaborate. The definition developed in 1993 shows less use of language modeled on medicine and more specification of social work purpose and values than the 1991 definition. It elaborates the knowledge base and the types of problems toward which intervention is directed. The definition emphatically affirms clinical social work as a part of the profession of social work and refers to ethical, philosophical, artistic, and theoretical realms of knowledge. Variation in explanatory theories is mentioned, as is the value of self-determination and mutually determined goals.

## Toward the Year 2000: Challenges and Controversies

In the realm of theory, there are important new developments. Modern awareness of the limitations of the search for a single "truth" or explanatory system has led to a new appreciation of the necessity of multiple perspectives (McNamee & Gergen, 1992). This has led to comfort with various theoretical "lenses" and especially to a greater attentiveness to the client's perspective (Anderson & Goolishian, 1988; Hoffman, 1990; Maluccio, 1980). Strengths are the focus rather than pathology (Goldstein, 1990b; Saleeby, 1992). Trauma theory provides a buttress for the strengths perspective (Herman, 1992). Individualistic conceptions of the self are being challenged (Swenson, 1993, 1994, in press). A multiplicity of roles and intervention strategies are valued, with environmental interventions as well as interventions directly with clients accorded status and efficacy (Germain & Gitterman, 1980). Sociopolitical aspects of problems and the necessity of social as well as individual solutions are emphasized (Morell, 1987; Sessions, 1994; White, 1986). Groups are viewed as a pivotal modality, since they are a part of ordinary, successful living and hold the potential for integrating individual growth, mutual aid, and action for social change (Lee & Swenson, 1986; Northen, 1988).

Ecological, life model, and community- and family-based approaches have emphasized a broad array of services and programs particularly suited to poor and disadvantaged populations (Adams & Nelson, in press; Germain & Gitterman, 1980; Lee & Swenson, 1978; Nelson & Landsman, 1992; Smale, Tuson, Cooper, Wardle, & Crosbie, 1988). The concepts of social care and community social work are being elaborated with a particular focus on vulnerable and deprived groups (Challis & Hugman, 1993; Harrison, 1991). Empowerment strategies are particularly advocated for work with poor and oppressed groups (Gutierrez, 1990; Lee, 1994; Solomon, 1976).

Narrative and social constructionist approaches to therapeutic conversations with individuals and families have developed techniques for significantly different kinds of therapeutic interventions (Borden, 1992; Dean, 1993; Holland, 1991; Laird, 1984; Saari, 1991). Brief, solution-focused interventions are being developed (Fanger, 1990). Particularly important new stances are reducing the power differential of clinician and client, addressing the client's participation in a community of relationships and confronting the privileged with their participation in systems of oppression (Garcia & Swenson, 1992; Swenson, 1993; White, 1986).

At the same time, there are changes in practice evaluation technology. New methods, drawn from the interpretive social sciences (Riessman, 1993; Scott, 1989), naturalistic inquiry (Rodwell, 1990), qualitative research (Ruckdeschel, 1985), and heuristics (Tyson, 1992), are more congruent with clinical experience and are supplementing earlier approaches. Millstein (1994) offers a comprehensive integration at the level of single cases (or "small *N*s"). Salience is being given to mixed qualitative and quantitative designs in program evaluation as well (Allen-Meares & Lane, 1990; Vera, 1990). These new developments offer opportunities to bridge the often-bitter debates between researcher and clinician, "scientists" and "artisans," and empiricists and social constructionists (Atherton, 1993; Goldstein, 1981, 1990a).

These theoretical developments have room for advanced levels of skill and knowledge and are also accessible to less-advanced practitioners, thus providing bridges between levels of training. They find resonance in other disciplines and are therefore useful to clinicians in interdisciplinary settings. They are simultaneously more congruent with historic social work purposes and values than some other theories that previously have been embraced by clinical social workers. The fate of these newer perspectives, as clinical social work moves toward the year 2000, remains to be seen.

The service delivery picture is in considerable flux. The trend toward "medicalizing" many problems may continue, as the health–mental health sector grows and changes. However, there are suggestions that managed care may move the health fields toward a wellness and prevention model more congruent with social work values. There are strong pressures toward case management and time-sensitive practice. The demand for accountability and outcome research increases the importance of supporting interventions empirically. Funding patterns will probably continue to diversify, with distinctions between public, private nonprofit, and private for-profit entities becoming more and more blurred. Clinical social workers are established as licensed service providers in all but one state and are increasingly becoming vendors; ironically, under managed care, solo private practice in all health and mental health disciplines may wither away.

The fate of comprehensive community-based services or a flowering of social care seems much less certain. There are some vigorous efforts under way, such as family-based services (Nelson & Landsman, 1992), various AIDS education and prevention programs (De La Cancela, 1989), community-based demonstration grants (Adams, in press; Krauth, in press), and a variety of programs for the chronically mentally and physically ill (Paradis, 1987; Rubin, 1984). However, there are far from enough programs to meet the need, and continuing voter revolt against taxes and public support of services bodes ill for expansion.

The relationship of clinical social work to the rest of the profession remains a somewhat uneasy one. Some of the criticisms of the 1960s can be heard again today (Specht & Courtney, 1994). There is fertile theory building taking place to support practice that is communitarian, strengths focused, normative, comprehensive, and liberatory. However, there are serious obstacles to these forms of practice: Too little funding and too few programs mean lack of access for potential clients and lack of jobs for clinicians. In addition, there are ideological impediments: Social problems are being redefined as medical problems with medical solutions; individualism and "blaming the victim" are prevalent within the larger society; and a level of cynicism exists about achieving a "good society." These are issues for the whole profession to address, rather than scapegoating clinical social workers.

There are many important, unanswered questions about clinical social work. We do not even know what language is preferred by master's-level direct practitioners and why. We do not know if there are variations by geography, practice setting, years of practice experience, and other characteristics. We do not have comprehensive data about what practice looks like in terms of client demographics, problems addressed, theories preferred, and intervention skills and roles utilized. We do not know how clinicians' ideals of practice compare with the actual and what factors influence any discrepancies. We cannot determine whether there are differences in values and the nature of practice relating to preferred professional identification. Under what auspices do practitioners work, with what financial arrangements? If they engage in private practice, is it full- or part-time practice and for what reasons? And finally, do social workers whose primary work is directly with individuals, families, and groups hold different values than those who choose policy, planning, administrative, and research roles?

In the absence of comprehensive, national answers to these questions, the studies available (Abell & McDonell, 1990; Bogo, Raphael, & Roberts, 1991; Butler, 1990; Frost, 1991; Rubin & Johnson, 1984; Seiz & Schwab, 1992; Walz & Groze, 1991) suggest a mixed picture. Many master's students describe preferences for fewer disadvantaged clients and more "therapeutic" roles and prefer these more strongly if they choose "therapist" or "clinical social work" terms over more generic ones. However, there are still large numbers of students who show interest in poor and vulnerable groups and a broader range of roles: They may be the majority, their numbers may be underestimated, and they may be increasing as we move out of the Reagan–Bush years.

In addition, there are some data about value orientations of more senior social workers. For example, Seiz and Schwab (1992) studied social workers with at least five years' experience in Texas. They found marked values differences in individuals with agency-only practice, combined agency and private practice, and private practice only. While the latter two groups listed "helping the poor" as the lowest of eight values, and "promoting social justice" fared only somewhat better, the 45 percent of the sample in agency-only practice listed these values as first and second, respectively. Frost (1991) found that private practitioners engaged in a broad array of interventions with their clients in addition to "therapy"; they utilized diverse theoretical frameworks; they saw diverse caseloads in terms of ethnicity, socioeconomic status, and sexual orientation, taking these differences into account in their interventions; and they adjusted fees frequently.

The struggle over the term "clinical social work" reflects the enduring tension within social work between its social change and its individual-family change dimensions. Addressing social problems such as poverty and oppression has proved to be much more difficult than we thought in the heady times of the 1960s. There has been a general societal breakdown in a sense of community and responsibility. One outcome is apparently fewer jobs in agencies serving poor and oppressed populations, while opportunities with middle-class clients and traditional therapeutic roles seem less threatened. Hard data are lacking, but positions seem particularly limited that enable a focus on developmental-socialization or class advocacy and empowerment practice.

Efforts to integrate the individual-family level and the social level continue. Morrell asserted in 1987 that "cause" *is* "function," and Hartman reiterated in 1993: "The professional is political." Walz and Groze (1991) suggested a new model of clinician–activist in which clinical work is essential. This model offers services preferentially to the most oppressed and needy and the "client" is seen as a special instance of a wider social problem. The social problem is "researched" through understanding the wisdom and experiential knowledge of the client, while the client's concern is addressed clinically. The knowledge collected by the clinician is used to inform advocacy and social action efforts. Walz and Groze suggested that a closer operational link between clinicians and advocates needs to be forged and that social work needs to aggressively recruit "people who have a strong identification with the plight of poor people who view themselves as capable of influencing social change" (p. 503). Lee (1994) proposes that clinicians must be advocates with their clients for change in the structural arrangements of society and against oppressive and crippling forces.

The clinician–activist approach is reminiscent of Schwartz's emphasis (1969) on "private troubles" as unique expressions of "public issues" and his belief that the social work "mediating function" was uniquely suited to address both the individual and the social dimensions of problems. It is congruent with the newer approaches to clinical practice identified above. Perhaps these new theoretical developments and the changed sociopolitical climate of the Clinton era will enable all social workers to join with their clients in more effectively addressing major social problems and providing services to individuals, families, and groups.

## References

Abell, N., & McDonell, J. (1990, March). *Why social work? Contrasting graduate faculty and student views on preparation for professional practice.* Paper presented at the Annual Program Meeting of the Council on Social Work Education, Reno.

Adams, P. (in press). Community-based practice with families. In P. Adams & K. Nelson (Eds.), *Reinventing human services: Community- and family-centered practice.* New York: Aldine de Gruyter.

Adams, P., & Nelson, K. (Eds.). (in press). *Reinventing human services: Community- and family-centered practice.* New York: Aldine de Gruyter.

Alinsky, S. (1965). The war on poverty—Political pornography. *Journal of Social Issues, 21*(1), 41–47.

Allen-Meares, P., & Lane, B. (1990). Social work practice: Integrating qualitative and quantitative data collection techniques. *Social Work, 35,* 452–458.

American Board of Examiners in Clinical Social Work. (1993). Clinical social work definition updated. *Diplomate, 6*(3), 6–7.

Anderson, C., Reiss, D., & Hogarty, G. (1986). *Schizophrenia and the family.* New York: Guilford Press.

Anderson, H., & Goolishian, H. (1988). Human systems as linguistic systems: Preliminary and evolving ideas about the implications for clinical theory. *Family Process, 27*(4), 371–394.

Anonymous. (1989). *Blaming the victim: A strategy to address post-traumatic stress disorder with in-patient psychiatric staff.* Unpublished manuscript, Simmons College School of Social Work, Boston.

Atherton, C. (1993). Empiricists versus social constructionists: Time for a cease-fire. *Families in Society, 74*(10), 617–624.

Barker, R. (1991). *Social work in private practice* (2nd ed.). Silver Spring, MD: NASW Press.

Battle, M. (1987). Professional associations: National Association of Social Workers. In A. Minahan (Ed.-in-Chief), *Encyclopedia of social work* (18th ed., Vol. 2, pp. 333–341). Silver Spring, MD: National Association of Social Workers.

Biggerstaff, M. (February 27–March 2, 1992). *Survey of private practitioners.* Paper presented at the Annual Program Meeting of the Council on Social Work Education, Kansas City.

Bogo, M., Raphael, D., & Roberts, R. (1991). Interests, activities, and self-identification among social work students: Toward a definition of social work identity. *Journal of Social Work Education, 29*(3), 279–292.

Borden, W. (1992). Narrative perspectives in psychosocial intervention following adverse life events. *Social Work, 37,* 135–141.

Bricker-Jenkins, M., & Hooyman, N. (Eds.). (1986). *Not for women only: Social work practice for a feminist future.* Silver Spring, MD: National Association of Social Workers.

Butler, A. (1990, March). *Who chooses private practice and why?* Paper presented at the Annual Program Meeting of the Council on Social Work Education, Reno.

Challis, D., & Hugman, R. (1993). Editorial: Community care, social work, and social care. *British Journal of Social Work, 23,* 319–328.

Chetkow-Yanoov, B. (1992). *Social work practice: A systems approach.* New York: Haworth Press.

Cohen, J. (1979). Nature of clinical social work. In P. Ewalt (Ed.), *Toward a definition of clinical social work* (pp. 23–31). Washington, DC: National Association of Social Workers.

Council on Social Work Education. (1982). *Curriculum policy statement for baccalaureate and master's degree programs in social work education.* Alexandria, VA: Author.

Dean, R. (1993). Constructivism: An approach to clinical practice. *Smith Studies in Social Work, 63*(3), 127–146.

De Hoyos, G. (1989). Person-in-environment: A tri-level practice model. *Social Casework, 70*(3), 131–138.

De La Cancela, V. (1989). Minority AIDS prevention: Moving beyond cultural perspectives towards sociopolitical empowerment. *AIDS Education and Prevention, 1*(2), 141–155.

Devore, W., & Schlesinger, E. (1981). *Ethnic sensitive social work practice.* St. Louis: C. V. Mosby.

Devore, W., & Schlesinger, E. (1991). *Ethnic sensitive social work practice* (3rd ed.). New York: Macmillan.

Dorfman, R. (1988). *Paradigms of clinical social work.* New York: Brunner/Mazel.

Fanger, M. (1990). *Heightened health for patient and therapist: The use of strategic brief therapy in health care.* Unpublished manuscript, Harvard University Community Health Plan, Cambridge, MA.

Fischer, J. (1978). *Effective casework practice: An eclectic approach.* New York: McGraw-Hill.

Frost, A. (1991). *Private practice in Eastern Massachusetts: Preliminary findings.* Unpublished manuscript, Simmons College School of Social Work, Boston.

Garcia, B., & Swenson, C. (1992). Writing the stories of white racism. *Journal of Teaching in Social Work, 6*(2), 3–17.

Gergen, K. (1985). The social constructionist movement in modern psychology. *American Psychologist, 40*(3), 266–275.

Germain, C. (1978). General systems theory and ego psychology: An ecological perspective. *Social Service Review, 52*(4), 535–550.

Germain, C. (Ed.). (1979). *Social work practice: People and environments.* New York: Columbia University Press.

Germain, C. (1982). Teaching primary prevention in social work: An ecological perspective. *Journal of Education for Social Work, 18*(1), 20–28.

Germain, C. (1983). Technological advances. In A. Rosenblatt & D. Waldfogel (Eds.), *Handbook of clinical social work* (pp. 26–57). San Francisco: Jossey-Bass.

Germain, C., & Gitterman, A. (1980). *The life model of social work practice.* New York: Columbia University Press.

Gibelman, M., & Schervish, P. (1993). *Who we are: The social work labor force as reflected in the NASW membership.* Washington, DC: NASW Press.

Gitterman, A., & Miller, I. (1989). The influence of the organization on clinical practice. *Clinical Social Work Journal, 17*(2), 151–164.

Goldstein, H. (1981). Qualitative research and social work practice: Partners in discovery. *Journal of Sociology and Social Welfare, 18,* 101–121.

Goldstein, H. (1990a). The knowledge base of social work practice: Theory, wisdom, analogue, or art? *Social Casework, 71*(1), 32–43.

Goldstein, H. (1990b). Strength or pathology: Ethical and rhetorical contrasts in approaches to practice. *Families in Society, 71*(5), 267–275.

Gordon, W. (1969). Basic constructs for an integrative and generative conception of social work. In G. Hearn (Ed.), *The general systems approach: Contributions toward a holistic conception of social work* (pp. 5–11). New York: Council on Social Work Education.

Gutierrez, L. (1990). Working with women of color: An empowerment perspective. *Social Work, 35,* 149–153.

Harrison, D. (1991). *Seeking common ground.* Hampshire, England: Avebury Press.

Hartman, A. (1993). The professional is political. *Social Work, 38,* 365–366, 504.

Herman, J. (1992). *Trauma and recovery.* New York: Basic Books.

Hoffman, L. (1990). Constructing realities: An art of lenses. *Family Process, 29*(1), 1–12.

Holland, T. (1991). Narrative, knowledge, and professional practice. *Social Thought, 17*(1), 32–40.

Homonoff, E., & Martin, J. (1994, March). *It takes a village to raise a child: Introduction into the social work curriculum of a community education model for prevention.* Paper presented at the Annual Program Meeting of the Council on Social Work Education, Atlanta.

Jayaratne, S., & Levy, R. (1979). *Empirical clinical practice.* New York: Columbia University Press.

Krauth, K. (in press). The making of a patch team. In P. Adams & K. Nelson (Eds.), *Reinventing human services: Community- and family-centered practice.* Manuscript submitted for publication.

Laird, J. (1984). Sorcerers, shamans, and social workers: The use of ritual in social work practice. *Social Work, 29,* 123–129.

Landers, S. (1993, January). Concern for patients sparks probe. *NASW News,* pp. 1, 16.

Lee, J. (1986). No place to go: Homeless women. In A. Gitterman & L. Shulman (Eds.), *Mutual aid and the life cycle* (pp. 245–262). Itasca, IL: F. E. Peacock.

Lee, J. (1994). *The empowerment approach to social work practice.* New York: Columbia University Press.

Lee, J., & Swenson, C. (1978). Theory in action. *Social Casework, 59,* 359–370.

Lee, J., & Swenson, C. (1986). The concept of mutual aid. In A. Gitterman & L. Shulman (Eds.), *Mutual aid and the life cycle* (pp. 361–380). Itasca, IL: F. E. Peacock.

Lister, L. (1987). Contemporary direct practice roles. *Social Work, 32,* 384–391.

Lum, D. (1986). *Social work practice and people of color: A process-stage approach.* Monterey, CA: Brooks/Cole.

Maluccio, A. (1980). *Learning from clients.* New York: Free Press.
Mancoske, R., & Hunzkler, J. (1989). *Empowerment based generalist practice.* New York: Cummings & Hathaway Press.
McNamee, S., & Gergen, K. (1992). *Therapy as social construction.* Newbury Park, CA: Sage Publications.
Meyer, C. (1993). *Assessment in social work practice.* New York: Columbia University Press.
Millstein, K. (1994). Building knowledge from the study of cases: A reflective model for practitioner self-evaluation. *Journal of Teaching in Social Work, 8*(1–2), 255–280.
Minahan, A. (Ed.-in-Chief). (1987). *Encyclopedia of social work* (18th ed., Vol. 2). Silver Spring, MD: National Association of Social Workers.
Morell, C. (1987). Cause *is* function: Toward a feminist model of integration for social work. *Social Service Review, 61*(1), 144–155.
Nelson, K., & Landsman, J. (1992). *Alternative models of family preservation: Family-based services in context.* Springfield, IL: Charles C Thomas.
Northen, H. (1988). *Social work with groups.* New York: Columbia University Press.
Paradis, B. (1987). An integrated team approach to community mental health. *Social Work, 32,* 101–104.
Pinderhughes, E. (1983). Empowerment for our clients and for ourselves. *Social Casework, 64,* 331–338.
Piven, F., & Cloward, R. (1972). *Regulating the poor: The functions of public welfare.* London: Tavistock.
Reid, W., & Epstein, L. (1977). *Task-centered practice.* New York: Columbia University Press.
Reid, W., & Hanrahan, P. (1982). Recent evaluations of social work: Grounds for optimism. *Social Work, 27,* 328–340.
Riessman, C. (1993). *Narrative analysis.* Newbury Park, CA: Sage Publications.
Roberts-DeGennaro, M. (1987). Developing case management as a practice model. *Social Work, 32,* 466–470.
Rodwell, M. (1990, March). *Naturalistic inquiry: The research link to social work practice?* Paper presented at the Annual Program Meeting of the Council on Social Work Education, Reno.
Rubin, A. (1984). Community-based care of the mentally ill: A research review. *Health & Social Work, 9,* 165–177.
Rubin, A. (1985). Social work practice effectiveness: More grounds for optimism. *Social Work, 30,* 469–476.
Rubin, A., & Johnson, P. (1984). Direct practice interests of entering MSW students. *Journal of Education for Social Work, 20*(1), 5–16.
Ruckdeschel, R. (1985). Qualitative research as a perspective. *Social Work Research & Abstracts, 21*(2), 17–21.
Saari, C. (1991). *The creation of meaning in clinical social work.* New York: Guilford Press.
Saleeby, D. (Ed.). (1992). *The strengths perspective.* New York: Longman.
Schwartz, W. (1969). Public needs and private troubles—One job or two? *Social welfare forum, 1969.* New York: Columbia University Press.
Scott, D. (1989). Meaning construction and social work practice. *Social Service Review, 63*(1), 39–51.
Seiz, R., & Schwab, A. (1992). Value orientations of clinical social work practitioners. *Clinical Social Work Journal, 20*(3), 323–335.
Sessions, P. (1994). Private troubles and public issues: The social construction of assessment. *Journal of Teaching in Social Work, 8*(1–2), 111–128.
Smale, G., Tuson, G., Cooper, M., Wardle, M., & Crosbie, D. (1988). *Community social work: A paradigm for change.* London: National Institute for Social Work.
Solomon, B. (1976). *Black empowerment: Social work in oppressed communities.* New York: Columbia University Press.
Specht, H., & Courtney, M. (1994). *Unfaithful angels: How social work has abandoned its mission.* New York: Free Press.
Stein, M. (1994, January). Can social workers influence the public debate about human services? *Social Work Focus* (Massachusetts NASW newsletter), p. 2.
Strom, K., & Gingerich, W. (1993). Educating students for new market realities. *Journal of Social Work Education, 29*(1), 78–87.
Swenson, C. (1993). *Clinical constructions of community.* Unpublished manuscript, Simmons College, Boston.
Swenson, C. (1994). Clinical practice and the decline of community. *Journal of Teaching in Social Work, 10*(1/2), 195–212.
Swenson, C. (in press). Professional understandings of community: At a loss for words? In P. Adams & K. Nelson (Eds.), *Reinventing human services: Community- and family-centered practice.* New York: Aldine de Gruyter.
Thyer, B., & Biggerstaff, M. (1989). *Professional social work credentialing and legal regulation.* Springfield, IL: Charles C Thomas.
Turner, F. (1986). *Social work treatment: Interlocking theoretical approaches.* New York: Free Press.
Tyson, K. (1992). A new approach to relevant scientific research for practitioners. *Social Work, 37,* 541–556.
Van Den Bergh, N., & Cooper, L. (Eds.). (1986). *Feminist visions for social work.* Silver Spring, MD: National Association of Social Workers.
Vera, M. (1990). Effects of divorce groups on individual adjustment: A multiple methodology approach. *Social Work Research & Abstracts, 26*(3), 11–20.
Walz, T., & Groze, V. (1991). The mission of social work revisited: An agenda for the 1990s. *Social Work, 36,* 500–504.
Weissman, H., Epstein, I., & Savage, A. (1987). Expanding the role repertoire of clinicians. *Social Casework, 68*(2), 150–155.
White, M. (1986, Spring). On the conjoint therapy of men who are violent and the women with whom they live. *Dulwich Centre Newsletter,* Adelaide, New Zealand, pp. 12–16.
Wood, G., & Middleman, R. (1989). *The structural approach to social work practice.* New York: Columbia University Press.
Wood, K. (1978). Casework effectiveness: A new look at the research evidence. *Social Work, 23,* 437–458.

**Carol R. Swenson, DSW, ACSW, LICSW,** is associate professor, Simmons College, School of Social Work, 51 Commonwealth Avenue, Boston, MA 02116.

**For further information see**

Assessment; Case Management; Direct Practice Overview; Ethics and Values; Goal Setting and Intervention

Planning; Interviewing; Licensing, Regulation, and Certification; Mental Health Overview; National Association of Social Workers; Person-in-Environment; Private Practice; Professional Conduct; Social Work Education; Social Work Practice: Theoretical Base; Social Work Profession Overview; Supervision and Consultation; Vendorship.

**Key Words**

case management | direct practice
clinical social work | theories of practice

# Cognition and Social Cognitive Theory

**Paula S. Nurius**
**Sharon B. Berlin**

Although the helping professions have long been concerned with how people use information to bring meaning and organization to their lives, recent social cognitive theory has provided significant refinements to our understanding. Social cognition refers to the ways that people perceive, interpret, remember, and apply information about themselves and the social world. One of the principal benefits of social cognition for social work practice is its empirically supported and practically useful framework for explaining how the person–environment interaction unfolds and how it might be altered in the service of solving clients' problems and helping them achieve positive goals. This entry focuses on the core features of the social–psychological study of social cognition: identifying and describing key concepts and processes; describing ways in which social cognition is related to problems in living and to practice interventions; and discussing the role of emotion in cognition and the art of clinical reasoning. The entry further addresses new frontiers related to human memory, information processing, and the social construction of reality. Cognitive theories focus on how individuals use information to construct meaning. The key feature of a cognitive perspective is the understanding that people bring meaning and organization to their encounters in the physical and social world (Singer & Salovey, 1991; Wyer & Srull, 1984).

Each of us is an active participant in creating the meaning of our lives, but we are not the sole participants. Meaning-making involves complex interactions between the individual and the environment. The meanings we assign cannot be independent of the linguistic categories, rules, values, and goals of our culture. In addition, environmental events that threaten survival have similar meanings across cultures. Finally, the families, communities, and opportunity structures we are born into and grow up in provide us with a foundation of memories that we use to shape and understand the ongoing flow of information and experience.

It is this focus on the person–environment interplay that makes cognitive theory of special interest to social work. Several streams of investigation occurring within social and personality psychology, most notably in the area of social cognition, show promise of contributing to an empirically supported and practically useful conceptual framework for explaining how this interaction unfolds and how it might be altered to help clients solve problems and achieve goals. In general terms, the study of social cognition reflects an appreciation for the dynamic, reciprocal relationship between people and their environments and the ways this relationship shapes perception, interpretation, feeling, motivation, and action.

## Key Concepts and Processes of Social Cognition

Social cognition is the study of how people interpret, analyze, remember, and use information about themselves and the social world. We are continuously bombarded with far more information than we can possibly handle. Moreover, much of this information is complex, ambiguous, and provocative. To avoid paralyzing overload and to allow us to functionally navigate through our social world, we must rely on numerous information processing shortcuts or aids to screen, sort, interpret, manage, store, and recall information that seems relevant. Considerable study on how information gets processed has identified many of these cognitive aids and their effects.

Research on how the brain interacts with our sensory–perceptual system and long- and short-term memory has provided the basis of an information-processing paradigm (for example, Anderson, 1983). This paradigm has proved useful in identifying the ways people perceive and encode social information; pull information together to form inferences and conclusions; and store, edit, and retrieve information about themselves and the social world. Social cognition builds on earlier social learning theory by adding an understanding that input from the environment is mediated or filtered. That is, rather than having a direct stimulus effect, input must be perceived and interpreted, and there is important individual variability in these perceptual and interpretive processes. Because social cognition is concerned with how people form meaning from social information in their environment, influences such as prior expectations, goals, and feelings must be taken into account.

**Intellectual Context**

The past three decades have witnessed extraordinary gains in the psychological study of mind and meaning. Some view this attention to the role of cognition in human functioning as an extension or evolution of behavioral theory and emphasize the ways that cognitive mediational processes adhere to traditional rules of learning (see Arnkoff & Glass, 1992; Mahoney, 1980). Others take the position that, beyond evolution within one particular school of thought, this focus on cognition constitutes a revolution in modern psychology, one that has altered all of the theories of human behavior and behavior change (Arnkoff & Glass, 1992; Sperry, 1993).

Strengthened by the more general emphasis of postmodernism on constructivism and deconstruction, cognitive concepts clearly have insinuated themselves into psychodynamic, behavioral, family systems, and ecological systems of theory. At the same time, more purely cognitive clinical theories also draw on concepts from a variety of perspectives. Cognitive theories are essentially integrative (Arnkoff & Glass, 1992). Depending on which other perspectives are enjoined, different versions of cognitive therapy tend to give varying emphasis to the roles of behaviors, emotions, rationality, interpersonal influence, early history, and broader social context in influencing experience.

**Schemas**

Although there are many important elements in information processing, schemas, or knowledge representations, and heuristics, or information-processing shortcuts, play central roles. *Schemas* (also called "schemata") are the cognitive structures or memory representations that contain our experiences and learning (for example, about ourselves, other people, attitudes, social roles, norms, and events). Schemas are the backlog of classifications or conceptions that we repeatedly draw on to make sense of our experience. In our ongoing effort to form meaning, we draw on our knowledge of past situations to guide us in what to look for and pay attention to, what interpretations to make, and how to respond. Findings from each new experience then become recorded as updates to our existing network of schemas.

Schemas are critically important in providing the preconceptions that make information processing more rapid, efficient, and automatic. They help us anticipate, search for, and recognize aspects of a stimulus or situation that are important, and they help us make sense of them. Schemas help us fill in the gaps when information is missing and are helpful in interpreting new experiences (see Fiske & Taylor, 1991, and Markus & Zajonc, 1986, for reviews).

At the same time, schemas incline us to confirm our understanding of reality, to be highly biased toward information that fits our expectations, to overlook or discount confusing or contradictory information, and to rely on relatively stereotypic images and habitual modes of social interaction. Depending on the particular circumstances, this tendency toward simplicity and stability can work as an asset or a liability. It can, for example, contribute to the tenacity with which both the well-adjusted optimistic person and the clinically depressed person seek out, find, and build on expectation-confirming input from their experiences and their environment.

Schemas do not simply reside in memory as isolated bits of stored information. Rather, they are part of a memory structure that organizes concepts into hierarchical clusters and networks of related knowledge. "Nodes" of knowledge linked to one another form networks of ideas, and when nodes are activated they enter consciousness (short-term memory). There are a number of models regarding the specific ways in which knowledge is stored, interrelated, and retrieved from long-term memory (Anderson, 1990; Ashcraft, 1989; and Fiske & Taylor, 1991, provide overviews).

Social cognition research has been influenced by the view that memory nodes are linked to one another on the basis of association (for example, they may produce the same kind of affect or sensation) and that linkages among nodes are strengthened by repeated activation. Thus, once we come to think of certain attributes as meaningfully related (as with stereotypes), it is very difficult to *not* think in terms of these clusters. When we are experiencing a certain emotional or physiological feeling, we are far more inclined to think about and be able to retrieve information consistent with that feeling than information that is contradictory to it.

As we encounter stimuli, we draw on our fund of schemas to help us make sense of what we are experiencing. Although individuals can amass a tremendous array of schemas over time, we cannot access them all, all at once. In fact, people are greatly limited in the number of schemas they can access and draw on at any given moment. Because we are actually working with only a tiny portion of our total store of information at any given moment, the presently activated subset of schemas is called our "working knowledge" (Markus & Nurius, 1986; Nurius & Markus, 1991). Among the forces that influence what information we draw on at any given moment are heuristics.

### Heuristics

*Heuristics* are information-processing strategies that are essentially mental shortcuts. Because we cannot constantly gather all possible data and consider all possibilities of meaning and response, we rely on rules of thumb to reduce complex problem solving to seemingly simple judgments. Heuristics are the recall strategies that determine which schemas get activated to process the information we encounter at any given moment.

Like schemas, heuristics are double-edged. These thinking processes are quick, automatic, and often reasonably accurate. They also lead to systematic biases and, sometimes, errors. Under routine and low-risk circumstances, which make up much of our lives, the biases or consistencies of heuristics may be both safe and helpful. In social work, however, situations are often unclear and unique, and the consequences of judgment errors can be quite costly. There are both benefits and risks for social workers using heuristics as we draw on our repertoires of knowledge in inferring the meaning of clients' expressions, in interpreting the intentions of their actions, and in assuming the causes of events in their lives.

***Interpretive strategies.*** Space does not permit a complete discussion of heuristics, but the following interpretive strategies illustrate how heuristics are used in social work. Social workers may at times

- base inferences and judgments on how easily and quickly information comes to mind (the availability heuristic)
- decide how to categorize a particular person or event on the basis of how much it resembles their preexisting notions—their schemas—of types of people and events (the representativeness heuristic)
- estimate the likely outcome of a situation based on how easily a given outcome can be envisioned and the emotional intensity of the envisioned outcome (the simulation heuristic)
- establish a reference point of comparison early in the process of forming a judgment when the information is ambiguous (anchoring effects).

***Information-processing strategies.*** Social workers also use heuristics when they engage in information-processing strategies such as the following:

- relying on preconceptions to classify people and events as having or not having certain attributes or as being or not being members of certain groups (social categorization)
- attributing people's behavior to their individual characteristics such as personality traits, rather than to external factors (the fundamental attribution bias)
- anticipating a relationship between two variables, leading them to overestimate the degree of relationship or to impose a nonexistent one (covariation estimation and illusory correlation).

(For a more thorough discussion of heuristics and interpretive strategies, see Bandura, 1986; Baron & Byrne, 1987; Berlin & Marsh, 1993; Fiske & Taylor, 1991; Kahneman, Slovic, & Tversky, 1982; Nisbett & Ross, 1980; Nurius & Gibson, 1990; Turk & Salovey, 1988.)

### Interdisciplinary Intersections Connecting Mind and Body

Although the focus here is on social cognitive theory, it is important to note that advances are increasingly stemming from convergence and synthesis across several domains of research and practice. Work from the memory system, for example, helps tie together how knowledge structure (for instance, schemas) and information processing strategies (for example, heuristics) develop and function interdependently. One important development from this arena has been the distinction between declarative and procedural knowledge (Anderson, 1983; for a different—although less influential—model of information processing and memory functioning known as "connectionism" or "parallel distributed processing," see McClelland, Rumelhart, & Hinton, 1986). *Declarative knowledge* is the cumulative information we have amassed about people, objects, and events of the world and includes information about concepts, facts (or presumed facts), attitudes, relationships, and beliefs. *Procedural knowledge* can be thought of more as "knowing how" information. It includes the rules, strategies, and skills involved in doing things. Even more fundamentally, it involves the how-to information for acquiring, manipulating, storing, retrieving, and acting on declarative knowledge (Cantor & Kihlstrom, 1989; Linville & Clark, 1989a,b)—that is, knowledge of the cognitive operations for perceiving, remembering, and thinking as well as acting in context-specific conditions.

Procedural knowledge can also be thought of as including the cognitive heuristics discussed earlier as well as higher-order metarules involved in strategizing (for example, planning, monitoring, and making decisions about what problems and goals are higher priority and how best to deal with them; see Ashcraft, 1989; Baron, 1982). We draw more fully on these distinctions in types of knowledge and memories later in the entry.

Study of the relationships between the brain, the mind, and the complex processes of assigning and constructing meaning have become increasingly sophisticated and multidisciplinary and have yielded a new field of cognitive neuroscience. Some of this work has attempted to better integrate a biological base, synthesizing neurophysiology, neuropsychology, and computational science with models of cognition. One focus has been to better specify the ways in which sensory perception and language serve as media for these relationships (see Kosslyn & Koenig, 1992, for an overview written for the nonspecialist reader with an emphasis on visual perception). Other work has examined the intersections between cognitive science and clinical phenomena (cognitive science here is understood to encompass not only cognitive psychology but also artificial intelligence, neuroscience, linguistics, philosophy, and anthropology). For example, examination of interrelations among social cognitive processes such as those described in this entry, neurological mechanisms, and medication effects adds a cutting-edge dimension to understanding normative functioning, clinical dysfunction, and treatment considerations (D. J. Stein & Young, 1992). In short, future work will likely further bridge interrelated yet relatively independently pursued areas of study regarding how people perceive, interpret, use, and act on information about themselves and the world around them.

### Conscious and Automatic Modes of Information Processing

From an information-processing perspective, it is impossible to pay full and complete attention for long periods of time, especially when trying to attend to multiple things at once. Although it is relatively easy to focus on a few stimuli or tasks, being vigilant to all the social stimuli around us is exhausting and approaches the experience of paranoia. In some situations, such as a new environment, we are more aware of our thinking and reactions as we carefully observe our surroundings and monitor ourselves. However, most of the time people are unaware of their own cognitive processes and are distinctly miserly with their cognitive effort. That is, we construct an understanding of reality as quickly as possible, relate to this construction as patent reality, and tenaciously resist challenge and change.

Part of what accounts for this relative lack of awareness are differences in our modes of processing. Memory and information processing function in both conscious and automatic modes. To use a similar concept, we operate with varying degrees of "mindfulness" versus "mindlessness" (Langer, 1989; Langer & Piper, 1987), or varying degrees of attentiveness or alertness at the moment. The negative colloquial connotations of the term "mindlessness" belie the importance of this state of functioning. With increasing familiarity, practice, and a sense that something is known, the studied concentration and introspection that accompany highly mindful states are no longer necessary and begin to wane.

The capacity to treat some stimuli in a more automatic, efficient, and familiar manner protects us from becoming overwhelmed by the enormity of information available in the environment. (For a discussion of the broader notions of automatic and controlled processes, including distinctions of intentionality and levels of consciousness, see Bargh, 1984, 1989; Kihlstrom, 1987, 1990; Loftus, 1992; Schneider & Shiffrin, 1977.) On the downside, being on autopilot entails a degree of insensitivity to the environment, a heavy reliance on past constructs stored in memory, and thus a lesser likelihood of making cognitive distinctions and generating creative responses.

Social work practice often involves helping clients accomplish personal change by shifting from more mindless modes of processing (associated with the problem) to awkward-feeling mindful modes (associated with new patterns) to more natural-feeling new mindless modes (associated with incorporation of new patterns into one's self-concept and social niche). Social workers also try to teach clients to notice or self-observe subsequent problematic forms of mindlessness (see Brower & Nurius, 1993; Nurius, 1994).

### Social Product and Social Force

Theories of social cognition pivot around the notion of the self–society interface. On the one hand, individuals' schemas and their ongoing thoughts, feelings, and actions are products of social forces such as messages from family, community, media, and so forth, as well as intrapersonal influences such as personality, beliefs, and mood: "Our meanings derive from our interactions with the world and with one another" (Hare-Mustin & Marecek, 1990, p. 1; see also Hewitt, 1991, and Mead, 1934, for extended discussions).

This interface is, however, a two-way street: People are not only social products or passive receptors of stimuli that emanate from their surroundings. People are also social forces who strive to affect their physical and social environments to achieve their aims and meet their needs. We not only manipulate and interact with our environments but also imbue them with personal meaning (Brower, 1989, 1990). This social product–social force duality is readily evident in the development and functioning of the self-concept: Input from the social environment significantly influences an individual's self-definition and self-evaluation, and that individual's prevailing view of self colors and directs subsequent transactions and social functioning, which in turn provide more self-relevant feedback, and so on (Nurius, 1989, 1991). Better understanding of the specific mechanisms of a client's social–cognitive interplay allows social workers to target more precise preventive and remedial interventions.

**Constructivism: Individual as Agent**

Some aspects of learning can be understood as responses to positive and negative reinforcement. Yet knowledge can also be gained through observation and imagination, which do not involve direct interaction or reinforcement. Individuals receive and process input, but constructivism holds that they also creatively generate knowledge. We form mental representations in the form of schemas and scripts (even of phenomena we have never experienced) that influence the way we act and the results we hope to achieve. We also take considerable (albeit often unconscious) license in editing our memory-based knowledge. Thus, learning is to some extent an effort of will or motivation (for example, to achieve a goal, to experience a pleasure) and is fundamentally built on and guided by mental representations.

Although we speak of information processing, the constructivist aspect of the social–cognitive perspective suggests that we do not simply process information by "reading" our environments—that there is an objective reality waiting to be apprehended. Rather, humans are active participants in their own experiences (Bandura, 1989; Mahoney, 1991); defining situations is a process in which we create meaning according to our expectations and intentions (Cantor & Kihlstrom, 1987; Hewitt, 1991). The limits to our creativity, which prevent us from living exclusively in an invented reality, are the boundaries imposed by our social and material worlds. As the person–environment concept suggests, we are constructors of our personal realities.

Importantly, we all transform our learning into tacit knowledge. That is, we come to take for granted that what we "know" (about people, situations, explanations) is literally what has happened, is now, and will take place. Theories and guesses become simple realities that we no longer question and that we use without awareness of the part they play in forming impressions and making decisions. Particularly in familiar relationships and situations, we assume that others share our tacit knowledge and our conception of the circumstance that we are in; thus, we rarely check our assumptions. The relevance of this for social work becomes evident in the need for reviewing and checking out our own assumptions, assessing what may be assumed to be obvious or consensual to a client, and assessing the challenges in transferring therapeutic changes into the client's daily routine and relations.

**"The Self" and Motivated Behavior**

Study of the self has been a central element of social cognitive work. Theorists and practitioners have focused on representation of the self in memory and the functional effects of self-representations on information processing, motivation and self-regulation, ways that people present themselves to others and attempt to influence how others view and react to them, and clinical aspects of self-development and change. It is beyond the scope of this entry to fully review this considerable body of work (see Bandura, 1989; Brower & Nurius, 1993; Evans & Hollon, 1988; Higgins, 1989; Kihlstrom et al., 1988; Markus & Wurf, 1987; Nurius, 1994; Nurius & Berlin, 1994; Oosterwegel & Oppenheimer, 1993; Segal & Blatt, 1993, for more detailed discussion). Three social cognitive contributions of particular interest to social work involve the situational responsiveness of the self-concept, the multiple perspectives of the self-concept, and ways through which the self-concept exerts influence on motivated or goal-related behavior.

***Situational responsiveness of the self-concept.*** Rather than having "a" self-concept, recent formulations of the self hold that each individual has multiple concepts about who she or he is, sometimes is, was, should be, or could be. Recent views of the self-concept distinguish between the accumulated repertoire of self-schemas that a person has amassed in memory over a lifetime and the situationally responsive subset of this self-concept repertoire that is actually active and working at any point in time (Markus & Kunda, 1986; Nurius & Markus, 1991). Because working memory is quite constrained in its "cognitive space," only a very limited number of schemas can be activated at any one time. What gets activated tends to be influenced by stimuli that are currently salient. Thus, although we all tend to have some core self-schemas that are frequently active (for example, those that depict status characteristics or attributes that are highly salient or important to us), we tend to experience considerable variability in our prevailing working self-concepts.

The situational variability of the self-concept is important because it influences social functioning, often in ways that are not immediately evident to the individual. Appraisals of self-worth and self-efficacy are likely to reflect the self-schemas that are currently salient. Basic information processing will be biased by the working self-concept—influencing what individuals look for and perceive as well as how they interpret and interact with their immediate environment.

This situated functioning and responsiveness of the self-concept raises important assessment considerations for social work practice. Rather than a global or trait-like approach to self-concept (and related factors such as self-esteem and self-efficacy), a contextually embedded approach to the working self is likely to be more fruitful (Damon & Hart, 1986; Nurius, 1994; Nurius & Berlin, 1994; Wurf & Markus, 1990).

***Multiple perspectives of the self-concept.*** Another aspect of the dynamic nature of the self-concept has to do with the varying perspectives that it contains. Some work has examined distinctions between our actual selves, our ideal selves, and our "ought" selves, including the effects of discrepancies among these types of self-conceptions (Higgins, 1987, 1989). Other research has focused on time perspectives; how past and future views of the self are stored in memory and drawn on (Markus & Nurius, 1986; Markus & Ruvolo, 1989). Future or possible selves have been posited as the concrete representation in knowledge structure form of our goals, plans, aspirations, and fears. These distinctions reflect the understanding that self-conceptions are not just catalogues of recorded events about who we are, what we have done, and how others see us (Hooker, 1992; Ryff, 1991).

In contemplating the future, we are not restricted to being either realistic (for example, we all harbor desires and fears of disaster that may be improbable but are nonetheless compelling) or to being grounded in our own experience (for example, we can all imagine positive and negative possibilities for ourselves rooted in the experience of others). Some possible selves will be relatively fleeting in their development and influence, such as the experience of "trying on" different selves in adolescence. However, as with all schemas, the future selves and situations that we spend most time thinking about and interacting with others about will become increasingly elaborated and interrelated with other aspects of the self and social experience (Greenwald & Banaji, 1989).

***Influence of the self-concept on behavior.*** Assisting clients in formulating and achieving change goals involves developing, elaborating, and routinizing new schemas (of future selves and situations) to the point that these new (or revised) knowledge structures become more salient and influential than current schemas. This process involves change at each level of the memory and at the information-processing level, including

- new declarative knowledge about what desired attributes, competencies, or situations "look like" and consist of
- new procedural knowledge about how one manifests an attribute, enacts a skill, or responds to contingencies (if *X* occurs, then respond *Y* way)
- new sensory–perceptual habits for seeking out information consistent with change goals
- newly configured working knowledge that is biased in the direction of changed and future conceptions of self and social environment (Linville & Clark, 1989; Nurius, 1993, 1994; Nurius & Berlin, 1994).

**Integrative Frameworks**

Efforts have been made to provide integrative frameworks that pull together many of the social cognitive factors described thus far in explaining individual adaptation to the social world. One in particular, Cantor and Kihlstrom's (1987, 1989) depiction of "social intelligence," allows clinicians to integrate general principles of social learning, social cognition, and social interactions into a whole to help individuals enlarge their repertoires of declarative and procedural knowledge and apply those repertoires to derive meaning, solve problems, and accomplish both mundane and significant life tasks. (For additional readings on motivated social cognition, see Showers & Cantor, 1985; Tetlock, 1989; and Wyer & Srull, 1989.)

Social intelligence is directed at the tasks of social life and differs from academic intelligence in the interpersonal and life experience foundation of its knowledge base (Cantor & Kihlstrom, 1989). Integrative work such as this reflects an ecological orientation—an effort to more fully embed the perceptual and interpretive focus of cognitive theory in social life and individual needs—which will continue to be of interest to social work.

## Emotion and Cognition

Are emotions part of social cognition? The answer to this seemingly simple question is actually quite complex. Fundamental questions (and debates) have arisen in efforts to define exactly what emotion is and in examination of the influence of emotion on cognition and cognition on emotion. The directions that have been undertaken in theorizing and investigating the relationship of emotion and cognition are varied and uneven in their level of specification and evidence. In addition, the relevant literature is voluminous and spans a considerable time frame. Rather than attempt to summarize this varigated literature, we identify some of the major issues and directions of current work particularly relevant to social cognition and social work practice. (For useful overviews see Fiske & Taylor, 1991; Frijda, 1993; Izard, Kagan, & Zajonc, 1984; Lewis & Haviland, 1993; Smith & Lazarus, 1990; N. L. Stein & Oatley, 1992.)

It quickly becomes apparent that numerous distinctions are made in discussion of emotion. Quite simply, what is the phenomenon underlying the statement "I *feel* . . ."? In some cases, this statement refers to preferences or evaluations: what we like and do not like, or find pleasant or attractive, unpleasant or unattractive. In some cases it refers to current mood, to a general positivity or negativity in how we are feeling at any given point in time (for example, being in a good or bad mood). Other times the phenomenon is better understood as emotions or affects. In contrast to preferences, evaluations, and moods, emotions refer to more intense, differentiated, and shorter-term affective states (such as love, joy, sadness, fear, and anger, as well as the rich array of degrees and combinations of each).

As important as feelings are to individuals' experiences and well-being, the practice literature has been notably vague about what exactly is being referred to, what factors generated these feeling responses and how any given feeling is expected to positively or negatively influence a client's functioning. Social cognition theory and research offer a potentially useful direction for clarifying these critical questions. One line of work examines the ways in which social cognition helps individuals *interpret* the stimulus they are responding to (perhaps an expression or comment by someone) as well as their own physiological state (heart beating quickly, skin temperature rising) and, based on the *meaning that they give* to these phenomena, assign an emotion label to themselves ("I am feeling very anxious."). Schachter and Singer's (1962) classic research is part of the foundation of this work, which has been advanced in several ways in recent years (see Fiske & Taylor, 1991, for a review).

An underlying premise to this work is that although physiological arousal may occur with little or no cognitive involvement, emotions require a more active role by the individual in interpreting personal meaning (for an opposing perspective, see Zajonc, 1980, 1984). Different people may have different emotional reactions to the same phenomena, depending on how they interpret it and what personal meaning they understand it to hold for them. Some of this work has examined the process of interpretation in terms of cognitive appraisals, based on a view that appraisals serve an important mediational role in linking individual's goals and beliefs with situational cognitive interpretations and emotional responses (see Frijda, 1987; Frijda, Kuipers, & ter Schure, 1989; Lazarus & Smith, 1988; Roseman, 1984; Scherer, Wallbott, & Summerfield, 1986; Smith & Ellsworth, 1985). This research is particularly relevant for social work practice because of its application to questions of coping; of how cognitive interpretations and emotional responses set the stage for subsequent action that may or may not result in effective coping outcomes (see Carver & Scheier, 1983, 1990; Folkman & Lazarus, 1988; Folkman, Lazarus, Dunkel-Schetter, DeLongis, & Gruen, 1986; Smith, Haynes, Lazarus, & Pope, 1993).

Although there are variations in the theoretical models, the process of cognitive mediation is often viewed as beginning with primary appraisals regarding personal relevance and relatively primitive emotional involvement in the form of rudimentary reactions to potential harm or benefit. This is followed by secondary appraisals of how to cope with the situation (Can I handle this? What are my options?) and more specific emotions associated with the answers to these questions. Because some work related to cognitive mediation has not been clear about the nature of emotional involvement, this more recent research contributes to a more complete model of social cognition. In the case of coping, greater attention to the role of emotions has expanded prior attention to approach–avoidance behavior or defensive processes to a richer array of coping strategies that include emotion-regulating as well as more behavioral problem-solving functions and that recognizes ways that emotions affect coping and that coping efforts affect subsequent emotion (Carver & Scheier, 1994; Folkman & Lazarus, 1988; Norris & Nurius, in press).

According to appraisal theory, rudimentary feelings such as alertness to the possibility of harm are transformed into specific emotions as a function of interpretation of meaning, and different emotions are products of certain types of cognitive appraisals (for example, anger resulting from appraisals about someone else being responsible for a personal harm; anxiety resulting from appraisals of low or uncertain coping potential). Complementary to understanding how cognition shapes emotion is how emotion influences cognition. Some of this latter work has built on information processing and memory models. Mood congruence is an example of this. *Mood congruence* means that people can more easily perceive inputs and remember material (for instance, memories, skills) whose emotional nature is consistent with their current mood state (see Blaney, 1986; Fiske & Taylor, 1991; Isen, 1987, for reviews). Thus, when people are happy they tend to more easily recall positive events and views of themselves and others, which subsequently prompts them to search for, notice, interpret, and act on positive input and to be relatively resistant to mood-incongruent input. By contrast, when we are anxious, it may be easier to recall anxiety-related material and more difficult to recall mood-incongruent memories or skills such as those related to confidence and joy.

Findings related to negative mood congruence have been less consistent and robust relative to findings related to positive mood congruence (with the exception of research involving depressed people for whom negative mood–congruent memory tends to be stable [Johnson & Magaro, 1987]). In addition to memory, mood has been found to be associated (generally in a mood-congruent fashion) with people's judgments, their helpfulness or prosocial activity, and their styles of decision making.

Although there is considerable variation in social cognitive approaches to examining emotion and considerable unevenness in the nature of findings to date, it is clear that emotion is increasingly recognized as important in the complex dynamics of people's relationships with their environments and in their efforts to perceive, interpret, and respond to their social world.

## Social Cognition and Problems in Living

### Conditions That Create Problems

Personal psychosocial problems occur under a combination of two main conditions. First, people experience problems when they view themselves, others, and the world in restrictive, inflexible, and outdated ways. As a consequence, they are unable to take advantage of current opportunities and personal strengths to craft solutions to difficult life situations. For example, when memories of personal weaknesses or absence of support from others dominates current assessments of what is possible, individuals are held to a relatively narrow range of functioning. Further, they are often unable to imagine how things could be different; they are not able to recall or create a compelling image or feeling of themselves in improved circumstances or the procedural scripts that would allow them to enact the difference.

The second main condition that promotes personal problems includes environmental deficits such as deprivation, danger, and abandonment or personal inadequacies beyond the individual's control (for example, certain mental and physical health problems). It is not the person's limited fund of knowledge and experience that is blocking adaptation, but rather that circumstances are overwhelming.

Virtually every kind of human problem ultimately comprises both social ingredients and personal ingredients. The relative contributions of these two aspects vary; sometimes problems seem mostly social and sometimes mostly personal. These two broad domains of influence interact; they affect each other.

In many instances the interaction can be understood as an interplay of realistically difficult life circumstances and memory-driven assessments of how they can be managed. People respond to their notions of environmental circumstances, and in the same gesture they act on the environment. When a person sizes up a situation and responds to it, that response—whether it be passivity, aggression, optimism, neglectfulness, persistence, or self-centeredness—influences the ongoing flow of interactions and, thus, the circumstances to which he or she must next respond.

### Conditions That Support Changes

Following the same logic, there are two broad and essential parts to personal change. First, circumstances must allow positive differences (for example, there must be a job for the persistent person to find or a supportive neighbor who will respond to the depressed and withdrawn person's first tentative gesture of sociability). Second, the individual needs to discern the possibility for social opportunities and the possibility for developing the skills and strengths necessary to take advantage of them. Further, he or she needs to reflect on and plan about these possibilities, feel the emotional pull of them, and view these developments as meaningful.

The momentum for positive change is increased through a spiral of person–environment shifts, when, for example, the individual anticipates opportunities, encounters and perceives a real chance to improve a difficult situation, acts on it, receives and perceives feedback that this new response worked, and then continues to act and react on the basis of an emerging, new perspective or self-schema. It does not matter much how the spiral gets started. Sometimes people only need to be persistent and optimistic enough to create opportunities in a relatively responsive environment. Sometimes the possibilities must be located for them (and sometimes wrenched out of a depriving environment) and repeatedly underscored before they can apprehend the novelty and begin to imagine how things could be different.

Developing a new perspective is usually a long-term and incremental task. It requires the ability to hold automatic conclusions in abeyance—to observe them and get distance from them—and then to mindfully and awkwardly look for other cues and practice other cognitive, emotional, and behavioral responses. An elaborate, well-organized, accessible memory network is built from innumerable episodes of reflecting, feeling, behaving, and being responded to that are eventually summarized as tacit, abstract, readily available classifications about oneself in a given domain. Creating such episodes is the main work of personal change.

Theories of social cognition prompt social workers to assess the extent to which personal perspectives and social conditions must be altered to create a spiral of change. On the social side, the task is to find or create clear signals that the client's world will allow and even support what he or she is defining as improvement. On the personal side, work focuses on enlarging the procedural and declarative content of the client's schemas and rehearsing the mindful processing needed to access new frameworks and ignore the old ones that heuristic processing will automatically activate (for related reading, see Abramson, 1988; Berlin, Mann, & Grossman, 1991; Brower & Nurius, 1993; Granvold, 1994; Maddux, Stoltenberg, & Rosenwein, 1987).

## Social Cognition and Clinical Reasoning

Theories of social cognition also prompt social workers to examine their own patterns of drawing conclusions, namely the extent to which their preconceptions and thinking processes lead them to predictable and not always useful clinical judgments (see Berlin & Marsh, 1993; Brower & Nurius, 1993; Gambrill, 1990; Gibbs, 1991; Nurius & Gibson, 1990; Nurius & Hudson, 1993; and Turk & Salovey, 1988, for detailed discussions of clinical decision making).

All of us, clients, social workers, and humanity in general, have limited accessible memory, allocate attention toward what we expect to find, interpret cues according to preconceptions, and question these basic assumptions with varying degrees of discomfort and resistance. As with human reasoning in general, many of the biasing forces (schemas, scripts, heuristics) are extremely valuable yet dangerous in their potential for error. Experience to date suggests that awareness alone of the potential for problems is not sufficient to guard effectively against them (Arkes, 1981; Kleinmuntz, 1990). Social workers are as vulnerable as anyone else to the effects of stereotypes and preconceptions (for example, Cousins, Fischer, Glisson, & Kameoka, 1985; Franklin, 1985; Kurtz, Johnson, & Rice, 1989). Although no panacea, social cognition research can help social workers better understand the dangers buried in the context of interpersonal practice and more effectively manage them.

## Conclusion

Part of the value of social cognition theory is its usefulness in bridging knowledge about human behavior in the social environment (under mundane as well as exceptional circumstances) with theory and strategies for personal change. Many problems in living are at least partly the result of the same processes that explain what are generally considered to be normal, adaptive patterns of functioning. The content of the predominant self- and social schemas for the depressed person and the happy person are likely to be substantially different, but the functional effects of their schemas, their patterned ways of drawing on their self- and social knowledge as they interact with others, and the role of their expectations in shaping their and others' behavior stem from the same social cognitive processes.

The future of social cognition research will likely include an increasing focus on naturalistic settings and questions of real world concern. Controversial questions of interest to social work—like how much we can trust clients' memories of past life events and how we determine the rationality of fear in the face of environmental threats—are now at the forefront of investigation (Loftus, 1993; Wandersman & Hallman, 1993). The future provides opportunity for social work to test the usefulness of findings in practice, to press for extension into heretofore neglected areas, and to actively participate in the generation and application of social cognition work in the service of social welfare.

## References

Abramson, L. Y. (Ed.). (1988). *Social cognition and clinical psychology: A synthesis.* New York: Guilford Press.

Anderson, J. R. (1983). *The architecture of cognition.* Cambridge, MA: Harvard University Press.

Anderson, J. R. (1990). *Cognition psychology and its implications* (3rd ed.). New York: Freeman.

Arkes, H. R. (1981). Impediments to accurate clinical judgment and possible ways to minimize their impact. *Journal of Counseling and Clinical Psychology, 49,* 323–330.

Arnkoff, D. B., & Glass, C. R. (1992). Cognitive therapy and psychotherapy integration. In D. K. Freedheim (Ed.), *History of psychotherapy* (pp. 657–694). Washington, DC: American Psychological Association.

Ashcraft, M. H. (1989). *Human memory and cognition.* Glenview, IL: Scott, Foresman.

Bandura, A. (1986). *Social foundations of thought and action: A social cognitive theory.* Englewood Cliffs, NJ: Prentice Hall.

Bandura, A. (1989). Human agency in social cognitive theory. *American Psychologist, 44,* 1175–1184.

Bargh, J. A. (1984). Automatic and conscious processing of social information. In R. S. Wyer, Jr., & T. K. Srull (Eds.), *Handbook of social cognition* (Vol. 3, pp. 1–44). Hillsdale, NJ: Lawrence Erlbaum.

Bargh, J. A. (1989). Conditional automaticity: Varieties of automation influence in social perception and cognition. In J. S. Uleman & J. A. Bargh (Eds.), *Unintended thought* (pp. 3–51). New York: Guilford Press.

Baron, J. (1982). Personality and intelligence. In R. Sternberg (Ed.), *Handbook of human intelligence* (pp. 308–352). Cambridge, MA: Cambridge University Press.

Baron, R. A., & Byrne, D. (1987). *Social psychology: Understanding human interaction* (5th ed.). Boston: Allyn & Bacon.

Berlin, S. B., Mann, K. B., & Grossman, S. I. (1991). Task analysis of cognitive therapy for depression. *Social Work Research & Abstracts, 27*(2), 3–11.

Berlin, S. B., & Marsh, J. C. (1993). *Informing practice decisions.* New York: Macmillan.

Blaney, P. H. (1986). Affect and memory: A review. *Psychological Bulletin, 99,* 229–246.

Brower, A. M. (1989). Group development as constructed social reality: A social–cognitive understanding of group formation. *Social Work with Groups, 12,* 23–41.

Brower, A. M. (1990). Student perceptions of life task demands as a mediator in the freshman year experience. *Journal of the Freshman Year Experience, 2,* 7–30.

Brower, A. M., & Nurius, P. S. (1993). *Social cognition and individual change: Current theory and counseling guidelines.* Newbury Park, CA: Sage Publications.

Cantor, N., & Kihlstrom, J. F. (1987). *Personality and social intelligence.* Englewood Cliffs, NJ: Prentice Hall.

Cantor, N., & Kihlstrom, J. F. (1989). Social intelligence and cognitive assessments of personality. In R. S. Wyer, Jr., & T. K. Srull (Eds.), *Advances in social cognition* (Vol. 2, pp. 1–59). Hillsdale, NJ: Lawrence Erlbaum.

Carver, C. S., & Scheier, M. F. (1983). A control-theory model of normal behavior and implications for problems in self-management. In P. C. Kendall (Ed.), *Advances in cognitive–behavioral research and therapy* (Vol. 2, pp. 127–194). San Diego: Academic Press.

Carver, C. S., & Scheier, M. F. (1990). Principles of self-regulation: Action and emotion. In E. T. Higgins & R. M. Sorrentino (Eds.), *Handbook of motivation and cognition: Foundations of social behavior* (Vol. 2, pp. 3–52). New York: Guilford Press.

Carver, C. S., & Scheier, M. F. (1994). Situational coping and coping dispositions in a stressful transaction. *Journal of Personality and Social Psychology, 66,* 184–195.

Cousins, P. S., Fischer, J., Glisson, C., & Kameoka, V. (1985). The effects of physical attractiveness and verbal expressiveness on clinical judgments. *Journal of Social Service Research, 8,* 59–74.

Damon, W., & Hart, D. (1986). Stability and change in children's self-understandings. *Social Cognition, 4,* 102–118.

Evans, M. D., & Hollon, S. D. (1988). Patterns of personal and causal inference: Implications for the cognitive theory of depression. In L. B. Alloy (Ed.), *Cognitive processes in depression* (pp. 344–278). New York: Guilford Press.

Fiske, S. T., & Taylor, S. E. (1991). *Social cognition* (2nd ed.). New York: McGraw-Hill.

Folkman, S., & Lazarus, R. S. (1988). Coping as mediator of emotion. *Journal of Personality and Social Psychology, 54,* 466–475.

Folkman, S., Lazarus, R. S., Dunkel-Schetter, C., DeLongis, A., & Gruen, R. (1986). The dynamics of a stressful encounter: Cognitive appraisal, coping, and encounter outcomes. *Journal of Personality and Social Psychology, 50,* 992–1003.

Franklin, D. L. (1985). Differential clinical assessments: The influence of class and race. *Social Service Review, 59,* 44–61.

Frijda, N. H. (1987). Emotion, cognitive structure, and action tendency. *Cognition and Emotion, 1,* 115–143.

Frijda, N. H. (Ed.). (1993). *Appraisal and beyond: The issue of cognitive determinants of emotion.* Hillsdale, NJ: Lawrence Erlbaum.

Frijda, N. H., Kuipers, P., & ter Schure, E. (1989). Relations among emotion, appraisal, and emotional action readiness. *Journal of Personality and Social Psychology, 57,* 212–228.

Gambrill, E. (1990). *Critical thinking in clinical practice.* San Francisco, CA: Jossey-Bass.

Gibbs, L. E. (1991). *Scientific reasoning for social workers: Bridging the gap between research and practice.* New York: Macmillan.

Granvold, D. (Ed.). (1994). *Cognitive and behavioral treatment: Methods and applications.* Pacific Grove, CA: Brooks/Cole.

Greenwald, A. G., & Banaji, M. R. (1989). The self as memory system: Powerful, but ordinary. *Journal of Personality and Social Psychology, 57,* 41–54.

Hare-Mustin, R., & Marecek, J. (Eds.). (1990). *Making a difference: Psychology and the construction of behavior.* New Haven, CT: Yale University Press.

Hewitt, J. P. (1991). *Self & society: A symbolic interactionist social psychology* (5th ed.). Boston: Allyn & Bacon.

Higgins, E. T. (1987). Self-discrepancy: A theory relating self and affect. *Psychological Review, 94,* 319–340.

Higgins, E. T. (1989). Continuities and discontinuities in self-regulatory and self-evaluative processes: A developmental theory relating self and affect. *Journal of Personality, 57,* 407–444.

Hooker, K. (1992). Possible selves and perceived health in older adults and college students. *Journal of Gerontology, 47,* 85–95.

Isen, A. M. (1987). Positive affect, cognitive processes, and social behavior. In L. Berkowitz (Ed.), *Advances in experimental social psychology* (Vol. 20, pp. 203–253). New York: Academic Press.

Izard, C. E., Kagan, J., & Zajonc, R. B. (Eds.). (1984). *Emotions, cognition, and behavior.* New York: Cambridge University Press.

Johnson, M. H., & Magaro, P. A. (1987). Effects of mood and severity on memory processes in depression and mania. *Psychological Bulletin, 101,* 28–40.

Kahneman, D., Slovic, P., & Tversky, A. (Eds.). (1982). *Judgment under uncertainty: Heuristics and biases.* Cambridge, MA: Cambridge University Press.

Kihlstrom, J. F. (1987). The cognitive unconscious. *Science, 237,* 1145–1152.

Kihlstrom, J. F. (1990). The psychological unconscious. In L. A. Pervin (Ed.), *Handbook of personality theory and research.* New York: Guilford Press.

Kihlstrom, J. F., Cantor, N., Albright, J. S., Chew, B. R., Klein, S. B., & Niedenthal, P. M. (1988). Information processing and the study of the self. In L. Berkowitz (Ed.), *Advances in experimental social psychology* (Vol. 21, pp. 145–180). New York: Academic Press.

Kleinmuntz, B. (1990). Why we still use our heads instead of formulas: Toward an integrative approach. *Psychological Bulletin, 107,* 296–310.

Kosslyn, M., & Koenig, O. (1992). *Wet mind: The new cognitive neuroscience.* New York: Free Press.

Kurtz, M. E., Johnson, S. M., & Rice, S. (1989). Students' clinical assessments: Are they affected by stereotyping? *Journal of Social Work Education, 24,* 3–12.

Langer, E. J. (1989). *Mindfulness.* Reading, MA: Addison-Wesley.

Langer, E. J., & Piper, A. I. (1987). The prevention of mindlessness. *Journal of Personality and Social Psychology, 53,* 280–287.

Lazarus, R., & Smith, C. A. (1988). Knowledge and appraisal in the cognition–emotion relationship. *Cognition and Emotion, 2,* 281–300.

Lewis, M., & Haviland, J. (Eds.). (1993). *Handbook of emotions.* New York: Guilford.

Linville, P. W., & Clark, L. R. (1989). Can production systems cope with coping? *Social Cognition, 7,* 195–236.

Loftus, E. F. (Ed.). (1992). Special issue on the unconscious. *American Psychologist, 47*(6).

Loftus, E. F. (1993). The reality of repressed memories. *American Psychologist, 48,* 518–537.

Maddux, J. E., Stoltenberg, C. D., & Rosenwein, S. (Eds.). (1987). *Social processes in clinical and counseling psychology.* New York: Springer-Verlag.

Mahoney, M. J. (1980). *Psychotherapy processes.* New York: Plenum.

Mahoney, M. J. (1991). *Human change processes.* New York: Basic Books.

Markus, H., & Kunda, Z. (1986). Stability and malleability of the self-concept. *Journal of Personality and Social Psychology, 51,* 858–866.

Markus, H., & Nurius, P. S. (1986). Possible selves. *American Psychologist, 41,* 954–969.

Markus, H., & Ruvolo, A. (1989). Possible selves: Personalized representations of goals. In L. A. Pervin (Ed.), *Goal concepts in personality and social psychology* (pp. 211–242). Hillsdale, NJ: Lawrence Erlbaum.

Markus, H., & Wurf, E. (1987). The dynamic self-concept: A social psychological perspective. *Annual Review of Psychology, 38,* 299–337.

Markus, H., & Zajonc, R. B. (1986). The cognitive perspective in social psychology. In G. Lindzey & E. Aronson (Eds.), *Handbook of social psychology* (3rd ed., pp. 137–230) New York: Random House.

McClelland, J. L., Rumelhart, D. E., & Hinton, G. E. (1986). The appeal of parallel distributed processing. In D. E. Rumelhart, J. L. McClelland, & the PDP Research Group, *Parallel distributed processing: Explorations in the microstructure of cognition* (Vol. 1). Cambridge, MA: MIT Press.

McGuire, W. J., & McGuire, C. V. (1988). Content and process in the experience of self. *Advances in Experimental Social Psychology, 21,* 97–144.

Mead, G. H. (1934). *Mind, self, and society.* Chicago: University of Chicago Press.

Nisbett, R. E., & Ross, L. (1980). *Human inferences: Strategies and shortcomings of social judgments.* Englewood Cliffs, NJ: Prentice Hall.

Norris, J., & Nurius, P. S. (in press). A cognitive ecological model of response to sexual coercion in dating. *Journal of Psychology and Human Sexuality.*

Nurius, P. S. (1989). Form and function of the self-concept: A social cognitive update. *Social Casework, 70,* 285–294.

Nurius, P. S. (1991). Possible selves and social support: Social cognitive resources for coping and striving. In J. A. Howard & P. L. Callero (Eds.), *The self–society dynamic: Cognition, emotion, and action* (pp. 239–258). Cambridge, MA: Cambridge University Press.

Nurius, P. S. (1993). Human memory: A basis for better understanding the elusive self-concept. *Social Service Review, 67,* 261–278.

Nurius, P. S. (1994). Assessing and changing self-concept: Guidelines from the memory system. *Social Work, 39,* 221–229.

Nurius, P. S., & Berlin, S. B. (1994). Treatment of negative self-concept and depression. In D. K. Granvold (Ed.), *Cognitive and behavioral treatment: Methods and applications* (pp. 249–271). Pacific Grove, CA: Brooks/Cole.

Nurius, P. S., & Gibson, J. W. (1990). Clinical observation, inference, reasoning, and judgment in social work: An update. *Social Work Research & Abstracts, 26*(2), 18–25.

Nurius, P. S., & Hudson, W. W. (1993). *Practice, evaluation, and computers: Practical guidelines for today and beyond.* Pacific Grove, CA: Brooks/Cole.

Nurius, P. S., & Markus, H. (1991). Situational variability in the self-concept: Appraisals, expectancies, and asymmetries. *Journal of Social and Clinical Psychology, 9,* 316–333.

Oosterwegel, A., & Oppenheimer, L. (1993). *The self-system: Developmental changes between and within self-concepts.* Hillsdale, NJ: Lawrence Erlbaum.

Roseman, J. (1984). Cognitive determinants of emotion: A structural theory. In P. Shaver (Ed.), *Review of personal-*

*ity and social psychology: Emotions, relationships, and health* (Vol. 5, pp. 11–36). Beverly Hills, CA: Sage Publications.

Ryff, C. (1991). Possible selves in adulthood and old age: A tale of shifting horizons. *Psychology and Aging, 6,* 286–295.

Schachter, S., & Singer, J. E. (1962). Cognitive, social, and physiological determinants of emotional state. *Psychological Review, 69,* 379–399.

Schacter, D. L. (1992). Understanding implicit memory: A cognitive neuroscience approach. *American Psychologist, 47,* 559–569.

Scherer, K. R., Wallbott, H. G., & Summerfield, A. B. (Eds.). (1986). *Experiencing emotion: A cross-cultural study*. Cambridge, England: Cambridge University Press.

Schneider, W., & Shiffrin, R. M. (1977). Controlled and automatic human information processing: I. Detection, search, and attention. *Psychological Bulletin, 84,* 1–66.

Segal, Z. V., & Blatt, S. J. (Eds.). (1993). *The self in emotional distress: Cognitive and psychodynamic perspectives.* New York: Guilford Press.

Showers, C., & Cantor, N. (1985). Social cognition: A look at motivated strategies. *Annual Review of Psychology, 36,* 275–305.

Singer, J. L., & Salovey, P. (1991). Organized knowledge structures and personality. In M. J. Horowitz (Ed.), *Person schemas and maladaptive interpersonal patterns* (pp. 33–80). Chicago: University of Chicago Press.

Smith, C. A., & Ellsworth, P. C. (1985). Patterns of cognitive appraisal in emotion. *Journal of Personality and Social Psychology, 48,* 813–838.

Smith, C. A., Haynes, K. N., Lazarus, R. S., & Pope, L. K. (1993). In search of the "hot" cognitions: Attributions, appraisals, and their relation to emotion. *Journal of Personality and Social Psychology, 65,* 916–929.

Smith, C. A., & Lazarus, R. S. (1990). Emotion and adaptation. In L. A. Pervin (Ed.), *Handbook of personality theory and research.* New York: Guilford Press.

Sperry, R. W. (1993). The impact and promise of the cognitive revolution. *American Psychologist, 48,* 878–885.

Stein, D. J., & Young, J. E. (Eds.). (1992). *Thoughtful extensions: Cognitive science.* San Diego: Academic Press.

Stein, N. L., & Oatley, K. (Eds.). (1992). *Basic emotions.* Hillsdale, NJ: Lawrence Erlbaum.

Tetlock, P. E. (1989). Social and cognitive strategies for coping with accountability: Conformity, complexity, and bolstering. *Journal of Personality and Social Psychology, 57,* 632–640.

Turk, D. C., & Salovey, P. (Eds.). (1988). *Reasoning, inference, and judgment in clinical practice.* New York: Free Press.

Wandersman, A. H., & Hallman, W. K. (1993). Are people acting irrationally? Understanding public concerns about environmental threats. *American Psychologist, 48,* 681–686.

Wurf, E., & Markus, H. (1990). Possible selves and the psychology of personal growth. In D. Ozer, A. Stewart, & J. Healey (Eds.), *Perspectives on personality* (Vol. 3, pp. 39–62). Greenwich, CT: JAI Press.

Wyer, R. S., Jr., & Srull, T. K. (1984). *Handbook of social cognition.* Hillsdale, NJ: Lawrence Erlbaum.

Wyer, R. S., Jr., & Srull, T. K. (Eds.). (1989). *Social intelligence and cognitive assessments of personality.* Hillsdale, NJ: Lawrence Erlbaum.

Zajonc, R. B. (1984). On the primacy of affect. *American Psychologist, 39,* 117–123.

Zajonc, R. B. (1980). Feeling and thinking: Preferences need no inferences. *American Psychologist, 35,* 151–175.

## FURTHER READING

Bennett, M. (Ed.). (1993). *The development of social cognition.* New York: Guilford Press.

Lewis, M., & Haviland, J. (Eds.). (1993). *Handbook of emotions.* New York: Guilford Press.

Manstead, A. S. R. (Ed.). (1992). *Emotion in social life.* Hillsdale, NJ: Lawrence Erlbaum.

Safran, J. D., & Greenberg, L. S. (Eds.). (1991). *Emotion, psychotherapy and change.* New York: Guilford Press.

Suls, J. (Ed.). (1993). *Psychological perspectives on the self.* Hillsdale, NJ: Lawrence Erlbaum.

Wyer, R. S., Jr., & Srull, T. K. (1989). *Memory and cognition in social context.* Hillsdale, NJ: Lawrence Erlbaum.

Wyer, R. S., Jr., & Srull, T. K. (Eds.). (1994). *Handbook of social cognition* (2nd ed.). Hillsdale, NJ: Lawrence Erlbaum.

**Paula S. Nurius, PhD, ACSW,** is associate professor, University of Washington, School of Social Work, 4101 15th Avenue, NE, Seattle, WA 98195. **Sharon B. Berlin, PhD, ACSW,** is professor, University of Chicago, School of Social Service Administration, 969 East 60th Street, Chicago, IL 60637.

### For further information see

Assessment; Clinical Social Work; Cognitive Treatment; Direct Practice Overview; Ecological Perspective; Goal Setting and Intervention Planning; Group Practice; Human Development; Person-in-Environment; Psychosocial Approach; Single-System Design; Social Development; Social Work Practice: Theoretical Base.

**Key Words**

cognitive theory
constructivism
memory
perception
psychosocial factors

# Cognitive Treatment

Donald K. Granvold

Cognitive intervention methods, once considered to be revolutionary (Baars, 1986; Dember, 1974; Mahoney, 1977), have been widely accepted by social workers and other mental health practitioners. This acceptance is coincident with the emergence of an empirical practice orientation as the predominant philosophy across disciplines. A mass of findings supports the efficacy of cognitive methods in the treatment of a broad range of emotional disorders and behavioral problems (Brower & Nurius, 1993; Foreyt & Rathjen, 1979; Freeman, Simon, Beutler, & Arkowitz, 1989; Granvold, 1994a; Hollon & Beck, 1986; Vallis, Howes, & Miller, 1991), including affective disorders (Blackburn, 1988; Freeman, 1990; Hollon & Najavits, 1989; Perris, 1989), anxiety disorders (Barlow, 1988; Beck & Emery, 1985; Michelson & Ascher, 1987), personality disorders (Beck & Freeman, 1990; Freeman & Leaf, 1989; Rothstein & Vallis, 1991; Turkat & Maisto, 1985), posttraumatic stress disorder (Dancu & Foa, 1992; Foa, Rothbaum, Riggs, & Murdock, 1991; Parrott & Howes, 1991), child sexual abuse (Deblinger, 1992; Duehn, 1994; Sgroi, 1989), impulse control disorders (Hazaleus & Deffenbacher, 1986; Lochman, Burch, Curry, & Lampron, 1984; Novaco, 1975, 1977a, 1977b), chronic pain (Corey, 1988; Eimer, 1989; P. C. Miller, 1991; Salkovskis, 1989; Turk, Meichenbaum, & Genest, 1983), eating disorders (Edgette & Prout, 1989; Garner, 1992; Garner & Bemis, 1985; Garner, Fairburn, & Davis, 1987), medical disorders (Freeman & Greenwood, 1987; Hibbard, Gordon, Egelko, & Langer, 1986), substance abuse (Beck, Wright, Newman, & Liese, 1993; Oei & Jackson, 1984; Schinke & Singer, 1994; Shorkey, 1994), marital distress (Baucom & Epstein, 1990; Beck, 1988; Dattilio & Padesky, 1990; Ellis, Sichel, Yeager, DiMattia, & DiGiuseppe, 1989; Granvold, 1988; Granvold & Jordan, 1994), and family problems (Epstein, Schlesinger, & Dryden, 1988; Huber & Baruth, 1989; Munson, 1994).

On the strength of such empirical support, cognitive methods have become convincingly established as viable procedures for the treatment of a broad range of populations and problems. However, the application to at-risk populations (for example, elderly, unemployed or underemployed, and physically and mentally disadvantaged individuals and immigrants to the United States) has not been well explored or perhaps has been significantly underreported. Noteworthy exceptions to this trend have been reported by Nurius and Berlin (1994), Richey (1994), and Schinke and his colleagues (Gilchrist, Schinke, Trimble, & Cvetkovich, 1987; Schinke, Schilling, & Gilchrist, 1986; Schinke & Singer, 1994). These authors address, respectively, the incorporation of cognitive methods with behavioral procedures in the enhancement of self-concept, social skills training, and the prevention of health care problems with at-risk clientele. The integration of cognitive methods with other psychosocial–environmental interventions with these populations remains one of several challenging frontiers for cognitive and cognitive–behavioral practitioners. Furthermore, we need additional outcome studies in which cognitive intervention methods are isolated to determine their comparative efficacy in the treatment of various populations and problems. Social workers have a unique opportunity to contribute to the development of knowledge in this area as a result of their access to people individually and collectively in these groups.

This entry covers cognitive assessment and intervention procedures. First, it defines cognition and then describes the features that are commonly embedded in the cognitive approach. Next, it addresses assessment methods, interventions, and treatment procedures.

## Definition of Cognition

Seiler (1984) stated that the term "cognitive" is "probably just as ambiguous as it is popular" (p. 11). Defining cognition is a somewhat confounding task because the term is used as a label for various phenomena. A useful means of clarification is to distinguish among cognitive content, cognitive process, and cognitive structure.

*Cognitive content* (also referred to as *cognitive products)* includes thoughts, self-verbalizations, decisions, accessible beliefs, values, attributions, images, and recognition–detection meanings attached to stimuli (Ingram & Kendall, 1986). These are products of information processing and can be accessed through direct questioning.

*Cognitive process* is the mechanism by which information is selected (input), transformed, and delivered (output). Included are such functions as selective attention, perception, encoding, storage, and retrieval. Errors in information processing, described by Beck, Rush, Shaw, and Emery (1979), are frequent targets of intervention in cognitive therapy.

*Cognitive structure,* defined as the architecture of the system, refers to the way in which information is organized and internally represented (Ingram & Kendall, 1986). Structure is a functional psychological mechanism that serves to store information (iconic–sensory phenomena and beliefs) and comprises associative linkages–networks of meaning and memory nodes. Information processing is guided by these structures.

This tripartite conceptualization of cognition has implications for the etiology of given disorders, assessment strategies, and intervention approaches. Thus, the various meanings and clinical implications of cognitive intervention are contingent on the social worker's conceptual orientation.

## Common Features of Cognitive Treatment

Although there is great variability in the way cognitive treatment is practiced, several features distinguish cognitive intervention from other approaches. The following paragraphs cover the distinguishing features that are generally agreed on by cognitive practitioners.

### Idiosyncratic Subjective Experience

The unique private meanings the client holds in relation to the problem and its context are the focus of the collaborative treatment experience. The social worker seeks to understand (1) the specific meanings of life events and corresponding emotional responses and (2) the perceptual patterns, information-processing patterns, and belief structures that are operative in organizing reality. Attention to these phenomena validates the client and provides the shared awareness and meaning base from which the client and the social worker collaboratively proceed. Self-report data are relied on heavily in establishing the client's problems and their etiology.

### Collaborative Effort

Resolution of the client's problem is a collaborative effort of the client and the social worker. The client provides specific content related to views of self, others, and the world; implements the strategies developed in a session; and reports outcomes of the efforts. The social worker provides structure, assessment measures and guidelines, characteristic information related to the client's problem and its treatment, alternative intervention strategies for selection and implementation, and evaluation tools and procedures for measuring the outcomes. The generation of a treatment strategy is a team effort in which the client and the social worker "join forces" against the problem. Trust, an important ingredient in the therapeutic alliance, is built through the collaborative approach. The objective is not only for the client to trust the social worker (and his or her honesty, caring, and expertise) but for the client to develop and expand trust in self. The collaborative effort may also focus on the client's motivation to change; this is a requirement with involuntary clients and those who are receiving treatment for problems such as addictions (Beck et al., 1993).

### Structured and Directive Approach

Cognitive therapy is focused on a specific problem that may be cognitive, emotional, behavioral, physical–physiological, social–environmental, or a combination of these areas. In whatever way it is conceptualized, the social worker and the client specifically define the problem or problems they have targeted for change. Treatment has direction and prescribed procedures for resolving the problem. The social worker acts to maintain control of the treatment by setting treatment guidelines and limits; maintaining a strategic focus on targeted problems; and managing such issues as noncompliance, power struggles, and preparation to end treatment. Although a pervasive spirit of collaboration is sought with the client, the ultimate responsibility for the conduct of treatment resides with the worker.

### Active Approach

As noted in the section the collaborative nature of cognitive therapy, the client is expected to take an active role both within and outside the treatment setting. Freeman and Dattilio (1992) noted that the client does not come in to be "therapized" but instead actively participates in resolving the problem. After the strategy for change is formulated collaboratively, the client puts the change effort into effect and gathers outcome data. Homework assignments are used to promote the transfer of gains from the treatment setting to the client's natural environment and to produce more resilient change (Granvold & Wodarski, 1994). Homework is graduated in level of demand and is structured to facilitate generalization across populations, settings, and circumstances within given settings. The assessment and outcome data that the client gathers are brought to the social worker for collaborative consideration in evaluating the effectiveness of the treatment strategy and the modification of the change effort.

### Education Model

Cognitive therapy involves didactic instruction, along with such techniques as bibliotherapy, written assignments, the use of audiotapes and videotapes, and attendance at lectures and seminars. Early in treatment, it is necessary to present the cognitive model to the client. The interactive nature of cognitive, emotional, behavioral, physical–physiological, and social–environmental factors and their contribution to emotional disturbance and maladaptive behavior are explained and discussed. The client's misconceptions about the problem and its treatment are addressed early in treatment. The nature of the therapeutic relationship is discussed, with attention focused on the expected collaboration between the social worker and the client. Empirical practice procedures are delineated. Throughout treatment, the social worker educates the client with problem-specific information and content relevant to the treatment process. For example, the concept of relapse prevention is introduced early in treatment, and procedures for the prevention of relapse are presented and discussed at strategic intervals. The development of the client's knowledge of the problem and conceptual grasp of cognitive treatment are critical to the collaborative enterprise between the client and the social worker.

**Socratic Method**

The use of Socratic questioning or guided discovery is one of the key features of cognitive treatment. Far greater results can be expected through the use of the Socratic method than through direct suggestions, explanations, or directives. Skillful questioning facilitates the disclosure of critical cognitive phenomena and leads the client through a process of self-discovery and reasoning. The Socratic method (1) stimulates the client's development of self-awareness and self-observation; (2) facilitates the shift from vague, ill-defined concerns to focused definitions of the problem; (3) gives the social worker access to the client's characteristic patterns of perceiving, reasoning, information processing, and problem solving; (4) exposes the client's belief system; (5) exposes the client's coping mechanisms and tolerance of stress; and (6) is effective in the social worker's modeling of reasoning, the challenging of irrational beliefs, and problem solving (Granvold, 1994b). Questioning also facilitates the client's active participation in the treatment experience, fosters the collaborative effort, and limits the social worker's authoritarian role that is typical of some treatment approaches.

**Empirical Focus**

The client and the social worker embark on an empirical investigation of the client's cognitive functioning as it relates to his or her emotional and behavioral responses. Once precepts, ideas, beliefs, attitudes, and expectations are identified, an attempt is made to validate them in a systematic way. The process involves the generation of hypotheses that, when tested, will "prove" that targeted cognitions are either valid, rational, and adaptive or lack support. These experiments may be in-session exercises in logic, reasoning, or recall of life experiences or may involve homework to be conducted in vivo. Disproved hypotheses are revised on the basis of evidence and then retested. Outcome measures are used to document the cognitive, emotional, and behavioral changes that the client experiences as a result of the process. These measures not only are meaningful in evaluating specific cognitive restructuring but serve to document the success of treatment and the efficacy of the methods that are used.

**Time-Limited Treatment**

The social worker's provision of structure to the treatment experience and the active participation of the client shorten the length of time required for effective results. Cognitive treatment is an efficient approach, and the inherent generalizability of cognitive change promotes lasting effects. The comparative brevity of cognitive treatment methods makes for a comfortable fit with the time limits set by managed care and third-party payer systems.

**Relapse Prevention**

For treatment to be considered successful, the results must be sustained long after treatment is terminated. In the past, change efforts that showed convincing signs of success at the point of termination often failed to be sustained for a significant period after termination. In short, the methods showed short-term efficacy but were not resilient against posttreatment challenges. Rather than discard the proved methods, a series of strategies to prevent relapse were developed and incorporated in treatment along with the original procedures. Marlatt (1985) described relapse prevention as "a self-management program designed to enhance the maintenance stage of the habit-change process" (p. 3). Relapse-prevention strategies are integral parts of cognitive treatment for all categories of problems. Procedures aimed at maintenance and relapse prevention include self-efficacy development, coping skills training, knowledge of and inoculation against relapse, environmental planning (stimulus control procedures), self-monitoring, lifestyle change, social system support, fading, early detection of relapse cues, and follow-up contacts and booster sessions (Granvold & Wodarski, 1994). These and other procedures promote clients' sustained mastery of the cognitive, emotional, and behavioral skills developed in treatment and better prepare clients to cope with future challenges to their well-being.

## Assessment

The assessment of cognitive functioning is not done to the exclusion of other interacting variables, including emotional, behavioral, physical–physiological, and social–environmental factors. It is recognized that cognition is but one ingredient in the dynamic puzzle of human functioning and that, as noted by Meichenbaum and Cameron (1981), cognitive factors are simultaneously both causes and effects. The focus here, however, is on the assessment of cognitive functioning.

As was explained previously, cognition is not a single phenomenon. Therefore, various assessment devices and formats are used depending on the component of cognitive functioning under scrutiny.

### Cognitive Content

The assessment of cognitive content (products) is typically conducted through an interview, with paper and pencil, or with a computer. An extensive array of standardized measures have been developed for problem areas in which clients' self-statements, thoughts, satisfaction, expectations, and beliefs are sought. In addition to standardized measures, forms for monitoring and recording faulty cognitions and associated responses have also been developed (for example, the "Daily Record of Dysfunctional Thoughts" by Beck et al., 1979, and the "Rational–Emotive Therapy Self-Help Form" by Ellis & Dryden, 1987). These forms may be used as homework, thereby producing individualized data that may not be exposed by standardized measures. For additional information on the assessment of cognitive content, see Kendall and Hollon (1981); Kendall and Korgeski (1979); Merluzzi and Boltwood (1989); Merluzzi, Glass, and Genest (1981); Michelson and Ascher (1987); Schwartz and Garamoni (1986); and Segal and Shaw (1988).

### Cognitive Process

The assessment of cognitive-process functions is more difficult to accomplish than is the assessment of cognitive content. The assessment of information processing is most frequently accomplished through interview procedures. Beck et al. (1979) described faulty information processing, such as arbitrary inference, selective abstraction, and overgeneralization, that is characteristic of depressed clients. They detailed the use of Socratic questioning to expose the process and to validate or invalidate the thinking and thus to arrive at specific information-processing errors. The assessment of cognitive process functions through this interview format has been applied to an array of problems, including anxiety (Beck & Emery, 1985; Freeman & Simon, 1989; Guidano & Liotti, 1983), agoraphobia (Michelson, 1987; Thorpe & Burns, 1983), depression (Beck et al., 1979; Freeman, 1990), personality disorders (Beck & Freeman, 1990; Rothstein & Vallis, 1991), anorexia nervosa (Garner & Bemis, 1985), and substance abuse (Beck et al., 1993).

Another cognitive-process assessment procedure, developed by Mahoney (1991), is stream of consciousness, "an exercise in which the client is invited to attend to and, as best one can, report ongoing thoughts, sensations, images, memories, and feelings" (p. 295). Mahoney identified two significant differences between streaming and Freud's "free association." First, the privacy of the client is honored because clients are not asked to share all their awareness. Second, the shared content is less subject to authoritative interpretation than tends to be the practice with free association.

### Cognitive Structure

Consideration of the methods of assessment focused on cognitive structure first requires attention to theory. Many cognitive and cognitive–behavioral practitioners are constructivists. According to this philosophy, there is no fully knowable external reality; the individual is active in the creation of his or her unique reality. Several fundamental implications for assessment are derived from this viewpoint (G. J. Neimeyer & Neimeyer, 1993):

- The primacy of personal meaning is emphasized.
- The individual is recognized as self-organizing developmentally progressive knowledge structures.
- Processes of knowing are emphasized.
- Assessment is oriented toward the viability (utility) as opposed to the validity (truth) of the client's worldview.

For a more thorough discussion of constructivism, see Dowd and Pace (1989), Guidano (1988), Guidano and Liotti (1983), Hayek (1978), Mahoney (1991), G. J. Neimeyer (1993), Polanyi (1958), Popper (1972), and Weimer (1977).

Unlike assessment focused on single cognitions, constructivist assessment is aimed at gaining insight into the client's comprehensive framework of personal knowledge (G. J. Neimeyer & Neimeyer, 1993). In this manner the dynamic interaction among cognitions is sought, along with insight into the core structure. Neimeyer and Neimeyer further explained the procedures for tapping into the core structure as follows:

> Significantly, the more tacit and elusive character of an individual's core structure requires an approach to assessment that is sometimes 'looser,' more evocative, and more symbolic than conventional cognitive–behavioral procedures for both assessment and psychological change, which tend to require relatively 'tight,' articulate, and verbal self-reports (cf. R. A. Neimeyer, 1988). (p. 17)

The result is that constructivist assessment may incorporate the use of idiosyncratic imagery, metaphors, and "vertical exploration" of the client's verbalized constructions. In constructivist assessment, attention is focused on both process and outcome in recognition of their interplay. Here attention will be devoted to structural methods.

There are several methods for the assessment of cognitive structure, including laddering, downward arrow, and repertory grid (see R. A. Neimeyer, 1993, for descriptions of these procedures). With each method, an important schema or personal construct that the client uses to construe the world or his or her existence in it is selected for exploration into higher-order conceptualizations. Structured interview methods or written assignments are used to guide the discovery. An assessment conducted in this manner is a personal construction of the client's assumptive reality. The social worker gains an understanding of the client's personal meaning systems and can then engage the client in modifications that may have cognitive, emotional, or behavioral benefits.

## Targets of Intervention

Most practitioners who use cognitive approaches in their treatment strategies subscribe to a reciprocal determinism model of human functioning (Bandura, 1978b). According to this view, cognitions, behavior, and personal factors (emotion, motivation, physiology, and physical factors) and social–environmental factors are interactive in human functioning. Cognitions, although not singularly causative, are considered to be an intrinsic part of dysfunction (Beck & Weishaar, 1989). On the basis of this view, cognitive therapy is focused on the modification of cognitive factors that are identified as being operative in the client's personal and interpersonal distress. Targets for change include cognitive content (episodic knowledge based on specific life events and accessible beliefs, thoughts, attributions, and decisions), cognitive process (perception and information processing), and cognitive structure (nonconscious schemata that guide the processing of information). It is recognized that there is an interaction among cognitive factors, as well as between cognition and other variables. Hence, isolation of a specific cognitive variable for intervention is done with cognizance of its interrelatedness and, in some instances, inseparability. The following table presents a brief description of cognitive content, process, and structure targets of intervention.

| *Cognitive Content* | *Cognitive Process* | *Cognitive Structure* |
|---|---|---|
| Expectancies | Perception | Schematic functioning |
| Causal attributions | Information-processing errors | |
| Beliefs-schemata (accessible) | | |

### Cognitive Content

***Expectancies.*** An expectancy is the subjective view (self-schema) that one can significantly influence certain outcomes. Expectancies represent the individual's belief in his or her capacity to understand, predict, and control life events (Baucom & Epstein, 1990):

> These expectancies are considered to fulfill an active role in decision making in which the individual selects among response options those viewed as most likely to produce the most desirable effects. Hence, motivation, the selection of behavior to exhibit, and coping efforts are all profoundly influenced by self-expectations. (Granvold, 1994b, p. 13)

The most frequently cited conceptualizations of self-expectancy are locus of control (Rotter, 1954, 1966), learned helplessness (Seligman, 1975), and self-efficacy (Bandura, 1977, 1978a). *Locus of control* relates to the perception of life events as self-controlled or controlled by outside forces. An internal locus of control reflects the view that an event, condition, or circumstance is contingent on one's own behavior, whereas an external locus of control reflects the view that a life event, condition, or circumstance is controlled by external forces (not contingent on one's behavior). *Learned helplessness* is conceptualized as an expectation of self as inept, helpless, and failing. Success and failure are viewed as independent of the individual's own skill and influence. Significant life events are viewed as uncontrollable by the individual, and these people characteristically lack aggressiveness and competitiveness. In his *self-efficacy* model, Bandura conceptualizes two types of expectancies: outcome expectancies and efficacy expectancies.

> An outcome expectancy is the view that a given behavior will produce a specific outcome, and an efficacy expectancy is the conviction that one can effectively behave in a manner to produce the desired outcome. This dichotomy establishes the independence between the judgments of *what* behavior is necessary to produce the desired outcome (as perceived by the individual) and the belief (or lack thereof) in one's *ability* to behave successfully. (Granvold, 1994b, p. 14)

***Causal attributions.*** The view one holds regarding the cause of behavior, feelings, and events is referred to as *attribution.* Recognized as influential in psychological well-being (Metalsky & Abramson, 1981), these causal beliefs may be highly inaccurate. In an attempt to remove causal ambiguity, there is a tendency to reach singular, definitive, simplistic causal explanations (drawn from contextual information or beliefs about oneself, others, and the world) (Granvold, 1994b). Such mental processing is likely to produce inaccurate conclusions, given the complexity of human psychosocial functioning. Many forms of negative attributions have been identified in the literature:

- *Blaming:* "You make me mad."
- *Terminal hypotheses* (Hurvitz, 1975): Interpretations of behavior, meanings, or feelings in such a way that nothing can be done to change the situation. "You're a manic depressive" (psychological classification); "You're a Scorpio; that's why you act the way you do" (pseudoscientific labeling); "He's just like his father" (inappropriate overgeneralization).
- *Coercion or impression management* (Epstein, 1982): "You're talking more to me just because the social worker asked you to."
- *Malevolent intent:* "You failed to call to tell me you were running late *just* so I would worry."

There is much to be learned about the development and maintenance of attributional patterns and the assessment and measurement of attributions. Despite the limitations in professionals' understanding of this cognitive phenomenon, the modification of negative attributions is a viable objective of intervention in the psychosocial treatment of clients.

***Accessible beliefs-schemata.*** Conscious schemata, classified as cognitive content, are beliefs to which one can gain access through thinking, imaging, and direct inquiry. Meanings about the self and the world have been dichotomized into explicit (a part of conscious awareness) and tacit (knowledge of which one has no explicit awareness) meanings (Polanyi, 1966). It is assumed that human behavior is influenced by both tacit and explicit knowledge. Although accessible beliefs that promote maladaptive cognitive, emotional, and behavioral consequences have been isolated for modification by many practitioners, Ellis's and Beck's conceptualizations have been the most influential.

In his rational–emotive behavior therapy, Ellis (1973) focused on the client's "irrational beliefs." He posited that "at the heart of psychological disturbance lies the tendency of humans to make devout, absolutistic evaluations of perceived events in their lives" (Ellis & Dryden, 1987, p. 14). Absolutistic cognitions (in the form of "musts," "shoulds," and "have tos") are commonly considered to interfere with an individual's happiness, relationships with significant others, attainment of short- and long-term goals, and health and survival.

A. T. Beck identified dysfunctional cognitions (automatic thoughts) that operate to promote negative views of the self, the world, and the future. These schemata are defined as inflexible, general rules or silent assumptions (beliefs, attitudes, and concepts) that (1) develop as enduring concepts from past (early) experiences; (2) form the basis for screening, discriminating, weighing, and coding stimuli; and (3) form the basis for categorizing, evaluating experiences, and making judgments and distorting reality situations (Rush & Beck, 1978).

Beliefs isolated for change may be rigid or flexible, durable or fragile, concrete or abstract, active or dormant, broad or narrow, and prominent or relatively inconsequential (Freeman, 1990). Furthermore, under stress and emotional disturbance, dormant maladaptive schemata may become activated. When highly activated, these idiosyncratic, maladaptive schemata probably inhibit other more adaptive or situationally appropriate schemata (Beck & Freeman, 1990). Also, in this active state little stimulation is required to trigger maladaptive schemata.

### Cognitive Process

***Perception.*** Perception is an active process in which knowledge that is stored within the individual converges with external sensation (Neisser, 1967; Roth & Tucker, 1986). Schemata influence perceptual functioning in the areas of selective attention, the meaning of stimuli (including evaluative judgments), and memory. Data are screened in or out, assigned a meaning, weighed more or less heavily, and stored for retrieval or dismissed. Perceptual activity has been identified as operative in maladaptive functioning. For example, depressed individuals have been found to attend selectively to stimuli that support, reinforce, and promote depression (Beck, Rush, et al., 1979). Evidence from the environment that supports the cognitions associated with the depression is screened in, whereas potentially equally meaningful nonsupportive data are screened out. Other factors that influence perception include past and current life experiences in a given stimulus category that result in sensitization or desensitization. Also, physical factors, body chemistry (for example, medications), and emotional arousal states may predispose a client to perceptual error.

***Information-processing errors.*** Cognitive distortions can be made both positively and negatively. Positive distortions result in unreasonable optimism, overconfidence, and insensitivity to threat and vulnerability. Negative distortions support an individual's dim view of himself or herself, the world, and the future (Beck, Rush, et al., 1979). Although these distortions were initially identified in relation to depressed clients, they are present to some degree in all people and are evident in extreme degrees in persons who display various emotional and behavioral problems (Miller & Porter, 1988). As with positive distortions, negative distortions disadvantage the individual in approaching life circumstances, have a detrimental effect on interpersonal relationships, and promote unhappiness. Freeman (1990) noted that distortions in information processing occur in many combinations and permutations. The following is an incomplete list of some typical distortions, taken from the work of Beck, Rush, et al. and Freeman:

- *absolutistic thinking:* all-or-nothing, polarized thinking ("I am totally worthless"; "I'm a total success.")
- *arbitrary inference:* mind reading ("She thinks I'm incapable; I just know it") and negative prediction, or the anticipation that something bad or unpleasant is going to happen without adequate or realistic evidence to support it ("I just know something bad is going to happen on this trip.")
- *overgeneralization:* drawing a general rule or conclusion on the basis of one or more isolated incidents and applying the concept across the board to related and unrelated situations ("Not only does Jane not like me, none of your friends like me.")
- *selective abstraction:* focusing on the negative in a situation, ignoring other positive (sometimes more salient) features, and viewing the entire experience as negative on the basis of the selective view ("That the evening out was enjoyable doesn't matter; it was the 15-minute argument we had that's important.")
- *magnification and minimization:* errors in evaluating the significance or extent of a behavior, condition, or event that are so extreme as to constitute a distortion ("I can't believe you forgot to buy apples; I only asked you to get 15 items at the store!"; "Sure it took 10 years to earn my recent promotion, but anyone could have done it.")
- *personalization:* relating a negative event or situation to oneself without adequate causal evidence to make the connection ("If I had been home with Dad, I don't believe he would have had a heart attack. So it's my fault he's dead"; "There is road construction on the freeway today just because I have to go to a meeting in the city.")
- *perfectionism:* rigidly demanding perfection in one's own or others' behavior ("I must score 100 percent on the examination, or I'm a failure.").

### Cognitive Structure

***Schematic functioning.*** It is assumed that an individual's cognitive structure is hierarchically organized, with sets of schemata operating at the tacit level as rules through which views of self and the world are constructed (Guidano, 1988). It is also assumed that an individual's constructs occupy a more central or a more peripheral role in the person's construct system (Kelly, 1955; R. A. Neimeyer, 1987). Although functioning at a tacit level, these schemata have been influential in the development of the client's dysfunction and may continue to be partly accountable for its maintenance. Cognitive assessment of hierarchically ordered belief structures exposes "associated beliefs and conclusions that the client reaches at progressively lower levels of cognitive awareness" (R. A. Neimeyer, 1993, p. 69). These faulty beliefs and conclusions, identified as the client develops increasing awareness, are targeted for intervention, with the ultimate goal of restructuring deeply held core structures. Also, the thought pattern connecting the surface-awareness cognitions with core structures is pursued for modification. To clarify, consider the following client, Joe. Joe failed a major examination and became extremely depressed. The hierarchy of his beliefs, from higher-level to lower-level awareness, was revealed through Socratic inquiry as follows:

- I'm stupid and incapable.
- I'm a big disappointment to my parents.
- I can't please my parents.

- I'm worthless.
- I don't deserve success and happiness.

Each belief exposes cognitive distortions for restructuring. The core belief, "I don't deserve success and happiness," is assumed to have influenced Joe in other life experiences aside from the failed examination that activated his latest episode of depression. Connections between this core belief and other undesirable outcomes would be sought, and focused attention would be given to the cognitive restructuring of the core belief. For related reading on the exposure and targeting of schematic functioning for cognitive intervention, see Guidano (1988), Guidano and Liotti (1983), Mahoney (1991), R. A. Neimeyer (1993), R. A. Neimeyer and Neimeyer (1987), and Wessler and Hankin-Wessler (1987).

## Cognitive Intervention Methods

Once the social worker has determined that a cognitive intervention strategy is the preferred approach for treating the client, he or she must decide which procedure to select. In making this decision, it is important first to distinguish cognitive therapies from behavioral and insight-oriented therapies, which may also affect and focus on cognitive functioning. Hollon and Beck (1986) described cognitive therapies as "those approaches that attempt to modify existing or anticipated disorders by virtue of altering cognitions or cognitive processes" (p. 443). They further clarified that cognitive interventions use three basic mechanisms of therapeutic change: (1) rational analyses, (2) logical–empirical assessment, and (3) repetition or practice. *Rational analyses* involve the procedures of disconfirmation and reconceptualization, *logical–empirical assessment* procedure focuses on the systematic analysis of evidence that confirms or refutes the client's cognitions, and *repetition* emphasizes practice and the persistent bombardment of faulty cognitions.

Cognitive therapies can be differentiated by the relative emphasis placed on these three mechanisms. For example, Beutler and Guest (1989) noted that "rational–emotive therapy (Ellis, 1962) relies on disconfirmation and rational appeal, whereas Beck, Rush, et al. (1979) emphasize empirical procedures, and self-instruction training (Meichenbaum, 1977) capitalizes on repetition" (p. 128). Beutler and Guest went on to state that rational approaches are aimed at "a relatively high or abstract level of cognitive activity," whereas empirical approaches target "cognitive structures within the lower (specific) and midlevel range of the schematic hierarchy" (p. 129) (and thus are more unique to the individual than the rational approach). Repetition-based interventions "target the bottom-up (from specific data to general knowledge) systematic creation of new structures that are designed to ultimately compete with prior dysfunctional schematic networks" (p. 130). Hence, these interventions are more responsive to individual differences and have less of an effect on higher-order structures.

The selection of the cognitive treatment procedure should be made on the basis of the nature of the specific problem targeted for change, the client's characteristics, and the empirical support for the alternative methods used for that problem with the target client population. There is significant variability within cognitive interventions; therefore, the social worker must discriminate carefully in making the selection. The following is an explication of cognitive restructuring, which is the most frequently used approach to cognitive therapy.

### Cognitive Restructuring

*Cognitive restructuring* is an intervention method that systematically guides the client in (1) the identification of faulty schemata or errors in information processing; (2) the disputation of faulty thinking; and (3) the assumption of alternative cognitions that are determined to produce more adaptive cognitive, emotional, and behavioral functioning. The emphasis placed on rational, empirical, and repetition procedures varies. Rational–emotive therapy (Ellis, 1962), for example, is aimed at irrational ideas, which are assumed to be representative of core cognitive structures. These irrational beliefs and their derivatives are identified, challenged, and replaced by competing rational statements. Approaches emphasizing empirical procedures (such as that of Beck, Rush, et al., 1979) seek to uncover expectations, illusions, beliefs (automatic thoughts), and information-processing functions unique to the individual that are associated with the client's dysfunction. The client is then guided in seeking evidence to validate or invalidate the operative cognitions. This approach is less didactic than is rational–emotive therapy, and clients are encouraged to draw their own conclusions from testing out their cognitions. Repetition-based interventions focus on clients' awareness of negative self-statements and the images they emit, with little attention given to a rational analysis of clients' belief systems (Meichenbaum, 1977). The client is guided in the development of self-instructions as a means of solving problems or managing stress. These self-instructions are repetitiously applied by the client under rehearsed and in vivo circumstances and lead to desired cognitive restructuring. This self-instruction procedure (see Meichenbaum) is highly problem specific and most responsive to individual differences.

One theoretical development that has produced modification in cognitive restructuring procedures is the work of Safran (Safran, 1984a, 1984b, 1988; Safran & Segal, 1990) on cognitive–interpersonal approaches. Arguing that cognitive and interpersonal processes are completely interdependent, Safran and Segal called for an integrative theoretical model with therapeutic interventions aimed at changing core interpersonal schemata. This objective is sought through the use of cognitive–interpersonal interventions that "make explicit both negative self-evaluative activity and guiding dysfunctional attitudes" and produce an awareness "of the complex interconnection between deep structure and surface structure in the moment" (p. 133). The client is encouraged "to 'check out' the veridicality of a particular self-critical thought, perception, or assumption, in context of an appreciation of the way in which the thought being tested fits into the overall cognitive organization" (p. 133), thereby facilitating a change in core cognitive structures. The authors present several procedures to facilitate change in this manner.

A review of the literature revealed more than two dozen approaches or technologies that have been identified with cognitive therapy (Beutler & Guest, 1989). A significant number of these procedures fall under the cognitive restructuring category. Although the term *cognitive restructuring* denotes a systematic intervention focused on the modification of thoughts, perceptions, beliefs, and schematic structures, as the foregoing has shown, there is significant variability among these interventions. Furthermore, cognitive restructuring can be used in conjunction with other cognitive methods (such as thought stopping and covert sensitization) and behavioral methods (such as skills training and deep-muscle relaxation). The integration of these procedures, along with environmental modification efforts, may even more ideally meet the challenges posed by the clients whom social workers often serve.

### Other Cognitive Methods

Several other cognitive intervention procedures have been developed and applied to various problems and populations. Problem solving has been used extensively with both children and adults; it is defined by D'Zurilla (1988) as "a cognitive–affective–behavioral process through which an individual (or group) attempts to identify, discover, or invent effective or adaptive means of coping with problems encountered in everyday living" (p. 86). Support for the use of this procedure lies in the fact that problem-solving deficiencies have been found to be associated with a variety of personal and interpersonal problems (Kazdin, Esveldt-Dawson, French, & Unis, 1987; Nezu & Carnevale, 1987; Weisz, Weiss, Wasserman, & Rintoul, 1987), and training in problem solving has been found to improve the functioning of various clinical populations (Bedell, Archer, & Marlow, 1980; Jannoun, Munby, Catalan, & Gelder, 1980; Nezu, 1986).

Covert-conditioning methods, including systematic desensitization (Wolpe, 1958, 1990), thought stopping (Wolpe, 1958, 1969, 1990; Wolpe & Lazarus, 1966), covert sensitization (Cautela, 1966, 1967), and covert modeling (Cautela, 1971), have been used with varying degrees of success with a wide range of disorders and populations. Furthermore, cognitive therapies, such as coping skills training (Goldfried, 1971, 1973; Meichenbaum, 1977), stress-inoculation training (Jaremko, 1980; Meichenbaum, 1977; Novaco, 1975, 1977a, 1977b), and guided imagery (Beck, 1970; Edwards, 1989; Leuner, 1984), have substantial empirical support for their efficacy.

## Conclusion

Cognitive therapy procedures can be distinguished from other treatments by the extent to which cognitive content, process, and structures are sought for exposure and change. These phenomena have been identified as inherently causally connected with clients' dysfunction and, as such, are viable intervention targets. This attention to the role of cognition in dysfunction and psychosocial change creates a dependence on a scientific understanding of cognition itself (Tataryn, Nadel, & Jacobs, 1989). As greater understanding is generated through further scientific exploration of cognition, a corresponding evolution in treatment procedures can be expected to unfold.

A number of issues are certain to receive attention during the future development of cognitive treatment methods. The relationship between affect and cognition continues to be a subject of lively debate. Does cognition drive emotion, or can an affective response arise independent of cognitive processing? Some have posited that emotional and cognitive processing occur simultaneously and interactively (Guidano, 1988; Guidano & Liotti, 1983; Mahoney, 1988, 1991). Clarification of this relationship has profound implications for treatment.

Another important challenge is the development of cognitive assessment methods in correspondence with the various cognitive models. Valid techniques for the assessment of cognitive processing, content, and structure are necessary to advance the understanding of these phenomena and the development of increasingly efficacious change strategies. Constructivism can also be expected to have a significant effect on the development of cognitive treatment models. This philosophy appears to be gaining increasing acceptance among cognitive and cognitive–behavioral practitioners. Constructivism's assertion "that humans actively create and construe their personal and social realities" (Mahoney, 1988, p. 364) is both ontologically and epistemologically significant. The mind is not viewed only as a receptacle for sensory data but functions generatively in the construction and ordering of reality. The constructivist philosophy promotes an emphasis in practice on developmental history and current developmental processes, content that may receive little or no attention from practitioners who subscribe to a rationalist view. Sharp practice distinctions will be evident between those who do and those who do not subscribe to constructivism.

The future of cognitive treatment appears highly promising, but issues such as those briefly identified here and many others expose the unsettled state of affairs within the ranks of cognitivists. Although the departure from behaviorism may be largely in the past, formidable theoretical and practice challenges remain.

## References


Baars, B. J. (1986). *The cognitive revolution in psychology.* New York: Guilford Press.

Bandura, A. (1977). Self-efficacy: Toward a unifying theory of behavior change. *Psychological Review, 84,* 191–215.

Bandura, A. (1978a). Reflections on self-efficacy. *Advances in Behavior Research and Therapy, 1,* 237–269.

Bandura, A. (1978b). The self system in reciprocal determinism. *American Psychologist, 33,* 344–358.

Barlow, D. N. (1988). *Anxiety and its disorders: The nature and treatment of anxiety and panic.* New York: Guilford Press.

Baucom, D. H., & Epstein, N. (1990). *Cognitive–behavioral marital therapy.* New York: Brunner/Mazel.

Beck, A. T. (1970). The role of fantasies in psychotherapy and psychopathology. *Journal of Nervous and Mental Disease, 150,* 3–17.

Beck, A. T. (1988). *Love is never enough.* New York: Harper & Row.

Beck, A. T., & Emery, G. (1985). *Anxiety disorders and phobias: A cognitive perspective.* New York: Basic Books.

Beck, A. T., & Freeman, A. (1990). *Cognitive therapy of personality disorders.* New York: Guilford Press.

Beck, A. T., Rush, A. J., Shaw, B. F., & Emery, G. (1979). *Cognitive therapy of depression.* New York: Guilford Press.

Beck, A. T., & Weishaar, M. (1989). Cognitive therapy. In A. Freeman, K. M. Simon, L. E. Beutler, & N. Arkowitz (Eds.), *Comprehensive handbook of cognitive therapy* (pp. 21–36). New York: Plenum Press.

Beck, A. T., Wright, F. D., Newman, C. F., & Liese, B. S. (1993). *Cognitive therapy of substance abuse.* New York: Guilford Press.

Bedell, J. R., Archer, R. P., & Marlow, H. A., Jr. (1980). A description and evaluation of a problem solving skills training program. In D. Upper & S. M. Ross (Eds.), *Behavioral group therapy: An annual review.* Champaign, IL: Research Press.

Beutler, L. E., & Guest, P. D. (1989). The role of cognitive change in psychotherapy. In A. Freeman, K. M. Simon, L. E. Beutler, & N. Arkowitz (Eds.), *Comprehensive handbook of cognitive therapy* (pp. 123–142). New York: Plenum Press.

Blackburn, I. M. (1988). An appraisal of cognitive trials of cognitive therapy for depression. In C. Perris, I. M. Blackburn, & H. Perris (Eds.), *Cognitive psychotherapy* (pp. 329–364). New York: Springer.

Brower, A. M., & Nurius, P. S. (1993). *Social cognition and individual change.* Newbury Park, CA: Sage Publications.

Cautela, J. R. (1966). Treatment of compulsive behavior by covert sensitization. *Psychological Record, 16,* 33–41.

Cautela, J. R. (1967). Covert sensitization. *Psychological Reports, 20,* 459–468.

Cautela, J. R. (1971). *Covert modeling.* Paper presented at the meeting of the Association for the Advancement of Behavior Therapy, Washington, DC.

Corey, D. (1988). *Pain: Learning to live without it.* New York: Macmillan.

Dancu, C. F., & Foa, E. G. (1992). Posttraumatic stress disorder. In A. Freeman & F. M. Dattilio (Eds.), *Comprehensive casebook of cognitive therapy* (pp. 79–88). New York: Plenum Press.

Dattilio, F. M., & Padesky, C. A. (1990). *Cognitive therapy with couples.* Sarasota, FL: Professional Resource Exchange.

Deblinger, E. (1992). Child sexual abuse. In A. Freeman & F. M. Dattilio (Eds.), *Comprehensive casebook of cognitive therapy* (pp. 159–167). New York: Plenum Press.

Dember, W. N. (1974). Motivation and the cognitive revolution. *American Psychologist, 29,* 161–168.

Dowd, E. T., & Pace, T. M. (1989). The relativity of reality: Second-order change in psychotherapy. In A. Freeman, K. M. Simon, L. E. Beutler, & H. Arkowitz (Eds.), *Comprehensive handbook of cognitive therapy* (pp. 213–226). New York: Plenum Press.

Duehn, W. D. (1994). Cognitive–behavioral approaches in the treatment of the child sex offender. In D. K. Granvold (Ed.), *Cognitive and behavioral treatment: Methods and applications* (pp. 125–134). Pacific Grove, CA: Brooks/Cole.

D'Zurilla, T. J. (1988). Problem-solving therapies. In K. S. Dobson (Ed.), *Handbook of cognitive–behavioral therapies* (pp. 85–135). New York: Guilford Press.

Edgette, J. S., & Prout, M. F. (1989). Cognitive and behavioral approaches to the treatment of anorexia nervosa. In A. Freeman, K. M. Simon, L. E. Beutler, & H. Arkowitz (Eds.), *Comprehensive handbook of cognitive therapy* (pp. 367–383). New York: Plenum Press.

Edwards, D.J.A. (1989). Cognitive restructuring through guided imagery. In A. Freeman, K. M. Simon, L. E. Beutler, & H. Arkowitz (Eds.), *Comprehensive handbook of cognitive therapy* (pp. 283–297). New York: Plenum Press.

Eimer, B. N. (1989). Psychotherapy for chronic pain: A cognitive approach. In A. Freeman, K. M. Simon, L. E. Beutler, & N. Arkowitz (Eds.), *Comprehensive handbook of cognitive therapy* (pp. 449–465). New York: Plenum Press.

Ellis, A. (1962). *Reason and emotion in psychotherapy.* New York: Lyle Stuart Press.

Ellis, A. (1973). *Humanistic psychotherapy.* New York: McGraw-Hill.

Ellis, A., & Dryden, W. (1987). *The practice of rational–emotive therapy.* New York: Springer.

Ellis, A., Sichel, J. L., Yeager, R. J., DiMattia, D. J., & DiGiuseppe, R. (1989). *Rational–emotive couples therapy.* New York: Pergamon Press.

Epstein, N. (1982). Cognitive therapy with couples. *American Journal of Family Therapy, 10,* 5–16.

Epstein, N., Schlesinger, S. E., & Dryden, W. (Eds.). (1988). *Cognitive–behavioral therapy with families.* New York: Brunner/Mazel.

Foa, E. B., Rothbaum, B. O., Riggs, D., & Murdock, T. (1991). Treatment of PTSD in rape victims: A comparison between cognitive–behavioral procedures and counseling. *Journal of Consulting and Clinical Psychology, 59,* 715–723.

Foreyt, J. P., & Rathjen, D. P. (Eds.). (1979). *Cognitive behavior therapy: Research and applications.* New York: Plenum Press.

Freeman, A. (1990). Cognitive therapy. In A. S. Bellack & M. Hersen (Eds.), *Handbook of comparative treatments for adult disorders* (pp. 64–87). New York: John Wiley & Sons.

Freeman, A., & Dattilio, F. M. (1992). Cognitive therapy in the year 2000. In A. Freeman & F. M. Datillio (Eds.), *Comprehensive casebook of cognitive therapy* (375–379). New York: Plenum Press.

Freeman, A., & Greenwood, V. (Eds.). (1987). *Cognitive therapy: Applications in psychiatric and medical settings.* New York: Human Sciences Press.

Freeman, A., & Leaf, R. C. (1989). Cognitive therapy applied to personality disorders. In A. Freeman, K. M. Simon, L. E. Beutler, & H. Arkowitz (Eds.), *Comprehensive handbook of cognitive therapy* (pp. 403–433). New York: Plenum Press.

Freeman, A., & Simon, K. M. (1989). Cognitive therapy of anxiety. In A. Freeman, K. M. Simon, L. E. Beutler, & H. Arkowitz (Eds.), *Comprehensive handbook of cognitive therapy* (pp. 347–365). New York: Plenum Press.

Freeman, A., Simon, K. M., Beutler, L. E., & Arkowitz, H. (Eds.). (1989). *Comprehensive handbook of cognitive therapy.* New York: Plenum Press.

Garner, D. M. (1992). Bulimia nervosa. In A. Freeman & F. M. Dattilio (Eds.), *Comprehensive casebook of cognitive therapy* (pp. 169–176). New York: Plenum Press.

Garner, D. M., & Bemis, K. M. (1985). Cognitive therapy for anorexia nervosa. In D. M. Garner & P. E. Garfinkel (Eds.), *Handbook of psychotherapy for anorexia nervosa and bulimia* (pp. 107–146). New York: Guilford Press.

Garner, D. M., Fairburn, C. G., & Davis, R. (1987). Cognitive–behavior treatment of bulimia nervosa: A critical appraisal. *Behavior Modification, 11,* 398–431.

Gilchrist, L. D., Schinke, S. P., Trimble, J. E., & Cvetkovich, G. T. (1987). Skills enhancement to prevent substance abuse among American Indian adolescents. *International Journal of the Addictions, 22,* 869–879.

Goldfried, M. R. (1971). Systematic desensitization as training in self-control. *Journal of Consulting and Clinical Psychology, 37,* 228–234.

Goldfried, M. R. (1973). Reduction of generalized anxiety through a variant of systematic desensitization. In M. R. Goldfried & M. Merbaum (Eds.), *Behavior change through self-control* (pp. 297–304). New York: Holt, Rinehart & Winston.

Granvold, D. K. (1988). Treating marital couples in conflict and transition. In J. S. McNeil & S. E. Weinstein (Eds.), *Innovations in health care practice* (pp. 68–90). Silver Spring, MD: National Association of Social Workers.

Granvold, D. K. (Ed.). (1994a). *Cognitive and behavioral treatment: Methods and applications.* Pacific Grove, CA: Brooks/Cole.

Granvold, D. K. (1994b). Concepts and methods of cognitive treatment. In D. K. Granvold (Ed.), *Cognitive and behavioral treatment: Methods and applications* (pp. 3–31). Pacific Grove, CA: Brooks/Cole.

Granvold, D. K., & Jordan, C. (1994). The cognitive–behavioral treatment of marital distress. In D. K. Granvold (Ed.), *Cognitive and behavioral treatment: Methods and applications* (pp. 174–201). Pacific Grove, CA: Brooks/Cole.

Granvold, D. K., & Wodarski, J. S. (1994). Cognitive and behavioral treatment: Clinical issues, transfer of training, and relapse prevention. In D. K. Granvold (Ed.), *Cognitive and behavioral treatment: Methods and applications* (pp. 353–375). Pacific Grove, CA: Brooks/Cole.

Guidano, V. F. (1988). A systems, process-oriented approach to cognitive therapy. In K. S. Dobson (Ed.), *Handbook of cognitive–behavioral therapies* (pp. 307–354). New York: Guilford Press.

Guidano, V. F., & Liotti, G. (1983). *Cognitive processes and emotional disorders.* New York: Guilford Press.

Hayek, F. A. (1978). *New studies in philosophy, politics, economics, and the history of ideas.* Chicago: University of Chicago Press.

Hazaleus, S. L., & Deffenbacher, J. L. (1986). Relaxation and cognitive treatments of anger. *Journal of Consulting and Clinical Psychology, 54,* 222–226.

Hibbard, M. R., Gordon, W. A., Egelko, S., & Langer, K. (1986). Issues in the diagnosis and cognitive therapy of depression in brain damaged individuals. In A. Freeman & V. Greenwood (Eds.), *Cognitive therapy: Applications in psychiatric and medical settings* (pp. 183–198). New York: Human Sciences Press.

Hollon, S. D., & Beck, A. T. (1986). Cognitive and cognitive–behavioral therapies. In S. L. Garfield & A. E. Bergin (Eds.), *Handbook of psychotherapy and behavior change* (3rd ed.). New York: John Wiley & Sons.

Hollon, S. D., & Najavits, L. (1989). Review of empirical studies on cognitive therapy. In A. Frances & R. Hales

(Eds.), *Review of psychiatry* (Vol. 7, pp. 643–667). New York: American Psychiatric Press.

Huber, C. H., & Baruth, L. G. (1989). *Rational–emotive family therapy: A systems perspective.* New York: Springer.

Hurvitz, N. (1975). Interaction of hypotheses in marriage counseling. In A. S. Gurman & D. G. Rice (Eds.), *Couples in conflict* (pp. 225–240). New York: Jason Aronson.

Ingram, R. E., & Kendall, P. C. (1986). Cognitive clinical psychology: Implications of an information processing perspective. In R. E. Ingram (Ed.), *Information processing approaches to clinical psychology* (pp. 4–21). New York: Academic Press.

Jannoun, L., Mumby, M., Catalan, J., & Gelder, M. (1980). A home-based treatment program for agoraphobia: Replication and controlled evaluation. *Behavior Therapy, 11,* 294–305.

Jaremko, M. E. (1980). The use of stress inoculation training in the reduction of public speaking anxiety. *Journal of Clinical Psychology, 36,* 735–738.

Kazdin, A. E., Esveldt-Dawson, K., French, N. H., & Unis, A. S. (1987). Problem-solving skills training and relationship therapy in the treatment of antisocial child behavior. *Journal of Consulting and Clinical Psychology, 55,* 76–85.

Kelly, G. A. (1955). *The psychology of personal constructs* (Vols. 1 & 2). New York: W. W. Norton.

Kendall, P. C., & Hollon, S. D. (1981). *Assessment strategies for cognitive–behavioral interventions.* New York: Academic Press.

Kendall, P. C., & Korgeski, G. P. (1979). Assessment and cognitive–behavioral interventions. *Cognitive Therapy and Research, 3,* 1–21.

Leuner, H. (1984). *Guided affective imagery: Mental imagery in short term psychotherapy.* New York: Thieme-Stratton.

Lochman, J. E., Burch, P. R., Curry, J. F., & Lampron, L. B. (1984). Treatment and generalization effects of cognitive behavioral and goal setting interventions with aggressive boys. *Journal of Consulting and Clinical Psychology, 52,* 915–916.

Mahoney, M. J. (1977). Reflection on the cognitive-learning trend in psychotherapy. *American Psychologist, 32,* 5–13.

Mahoney, M. J. (1988). The cognitive sciences and psychotherapy: Patterns in a developing relationship. In K. S. Dobson (Ed.), *Handbook of cognitive–behavioral therapies* (pp. 357–386). New York: Guilford Press.

Mahoney, M. J. (1991). *Human change processes.* New York: Basic Books.

Marlatt, G. A. (1985). Relapse prevention: Theoretical rationale and overview of the model. In G. A. Marlatt & J. R. Gordon (Eds.), *Relapse prevention* (pp. 3–70). New York: Guilford Press.

Meichenbaum, D. (1977). *Cognitive-behavior modification: An integrative approach.* New York: Plenum Press.

Meichenbaum, D., & Cameron, R. (1981). Issues in cognitive assessment: An overview. In T. V. Merluzzi, C. R. Glass, & M. Genest (Eds.), *Cognitive assessment* (pp. 3–15). New York: Guilford Press.

Merluzzi, T. V., & Boltwood, M. D. (1989). Cognitive assessment. In A. Freeman, K. M. Simon, L. E. Beutler, & H. Arkowitz (Eds.), *Comprehensive handbook of cognitive therapy* (pp. 249–266). New York: Plenum Press.

Merluzzi, T. V., Glass, C. R., & Genest, M. (Eds.). (1981). *Cognitive assessment.* New York: Guilford Press.

Metalsky, G. I., & Abramson, L. Y. (1981). Attributional styles: Toward a framework for conceptualization and assessment. In P. C. Kendall & S. D. Hollon (Eds.), *Assessment strategies for cognitive–behavioral interventions* (pp. 13–58). New York: Academic Press.

Michelson, L. (1987). Cognitive–behavioral assessment and treatment of agoraphobia. In L. Michelson & L. M. Ascher (Eds.), *Anxiety and stress disorders: Cognitive–behavioral assessment and treatment* (pp. 213–279). New York: Guilford Press.

Michelson, L., & Ascher, L. M. (Eds.). (1987). *Anxiety and stress disorders: Cognitive–behavioral assessment and treatment.* New York: Guilford Press.

Miller, D. T., & Porter, C. A. (1988). Errors and biases in the attribution process. In L. Y. Abramson (Ed.), *Social cognition and clinical psychology* (pp. 3–30). New York: Guilford Press.

Miller, P. C. (1991). The application of cognitive therapy to chronic pain. In T. M. Vallis, J. L. Howes, & P. C. Miller (Eds.), *The challenge of cognitive therapy: Applications to nontraditional populations* (pp. 159–182). New York: Plenum Press.

Munson, C. E. (1994). Cognitive family therapy. In D. K. Granvold (Ed.), *Cognitive and behavioral treatment: Methods and applications* (pp. 202–221). Pacific Grove, CA: Brooks/Cole.

Neimeyer, G. J. (Ed.). (1993). *Constructivist assessment: A casebook.* Newbury Park, CA: Sage Publications.

Neimeyer, G. J., & Neimeyer, R. A. (1993). Defining the boundaries of constructivist assessment. In G. J. Neimeyer (Ed.), *Constructivist assessment: A casebook* (pp. 1–30). Newbury Park, CA: Sage Publications.

Neimeyer, R. A. (1987). An orientation to personal construct therapy. In R. A. Neimeyer & G. J. Neimeyer (Eds.), *Personal construct therapy casebook* (pp. 3–19). New York: Springer.

Neimeyer, R. A. (1988). Integrative directions in personal construct therapy. *International Journal of Personal Construct Psychology, 1,* 283–297.

Neimeyer, R. A. (1993). Constructivist approaches to the measurement of meaning. In G. J. Neimeyer (Ed.), *Constructivist assessment: A casebook* (pp. 58–103). Newbury Park, CA: Sage Publications.

Neimeyer, R. A., & Neimeyer, G. J. (Eds.). (1987). *Personal construct therapy casebook.* New York: Springer.

Neisser, U. (1967). *Cognitive psychology.* New York: Appleton-Century-Crofts.

Nezu, A. M. (1986). Efficacy of a social problem solving therapy approach for unipolar depression. *Journal of Consulting and Clinical Psychology, 54,* 196–202.

Nezu, A. M., & Carnevale, G. J. (1987). Interpersonal problem solving and coping reactions of Vietnam veterans with posttraumatic stress syndrome. *Journal of Abnormal Psychology, 96,* 155–157.

Novaco, R. W. (1975). *Anger control: The development and evaluation of an experimental treatment.* Lexington, MA: D. C. Heath.

Novaco, R. W. (1977a). Stress-inoculation: A cognitive therapy for anger and its application to a case of depression. *Journal of Consulting and Clinical Psychology, 45,* 600–608.

Novaco, R. W. (1977b). A stress-inoculation approach to anger management in the training of law enforcement officers. *American Journal of Community Psychology, 5,* 327–346.

Nurius, P. S., & Berlin, S. S. (1994). Treatment of negative self-concept and depression. In D. K. Granvold (Ed.), *Cognitive and behavioral treatment: Methods and applications* (pp. 249–271). Pacific Grove, CA: Brooks/Cole.

Oei, T.P.S., & Jackson, P. R. (1984). Some effective therapeutic factors in group cognitive–behavioral therapy with problem drinkers. *Journal of Studies on Alcohol, 45,* 119–123.

Parrott, C. A., & Howes, J. L. (1991). The application of cognitive therapy to posttraumatic stress disorder. In T. M. Vallis, J. L. Howes, & P. C. Miller (Eds.), *The challenge of cognitive therapy: Applications to nontraditional populations* (pp. 85–109). New York: Plenum Press.

Perris, C. (1989). Cognitive therapy with the adult depressed patient. In A. Freeman, K. M. Simon, L. E. Beutler, & N. Arkowitz (Eds.), *Comprehensive handbook of cognitive therapy* (pp. 299–319). New York: Plenum Press.

Polanyi, M. (1958). *Personal knowledge: Towards a post-critical philosophy.* Chicago: University of Chicago Press.

Polanyi, M. (1966). *The tacit dimension.* Garden City, NY: Doubleday.

Popper, K. R. (1972). *Objective knowledge: An evolutionary approach.* London: Oxford University Press.

Richey, C. A. (1994). Social support skill training. In D. K. Granvold (Ed.), *Cognitive and behavioral treatment: Methods and applications* (pp. 299–338). Pacific Grove, CA: Brooks/Cole.

Roth, D. L., & Tucker, D. M. (1986). Neural systems in the emotional control of information processing. In R. E. Ingram (Ed.), *Information processing approaches to clinical psychology* (pp. 77–94). New York: Academic Press.

Rothstein, M. M., & Vallis, T. M. (1991). The application of cognitive therapy to patients with personality disorders. In T. M. Vallis, J. L. Howes, & P. C. Miller (Eds.), *The challenge of cognitive therapy: Applications to nontraditional populations* (pp. 59–84). New York: Plenum Press.

Rotter, J. B. (1954). *Social learning and clinical psychology.* Englewood Cliffs, NJ: Prentice Hall.

Rotter, J. B. (1966). Generalized expectancies for internal versus external control of reinforcement. *Psychological Monographs, 80*(1, Whole No. 609).

Rush, A. J., & Beck, A. T. (1978). Behavior therapy in adults with affective disorders. In M. Hersen & A. S. Bellack (Eds.), *Behavioral therapy in the psychiatric setting.* Baltimore: Williams & Wilkins.

Safran, J. D. (1984a). Assessing the cognitive–interpersonal cycle. *Cognitive Therapy and Research, 8,* 333–348.

Safran, J. D. (1984b). Some implications of Sullivan's interpersonal theory for cognitive therapy. In M. Reda & M. Mahoney (Eds.), *Cognitive psychotherapies: Recent developments in theory, research and practice.* Cambridge, MA: Ballinger.

Safran, J. D. (1988). *A refinement of cognitive behavioural theory and practise in light of interpersonal theory.* Toronto: Clarke Institute of Psychiatry.

Safran, J. D., & Segal, Z. V. (1990). *Cognitive therapy: An interpersonal process perspective.* New York: Basic Books.

Salkovskis, P. (1989). Somatic problems. In P. Hawton, P. Salkovskis, J. Kirk, & D. Clark (Eds.), *Cognitive behavior therapy for psychiatric problems* (pp. 235–276). New York: Oxford University Press.

Schinke, S. P., Schilling, R. F., & Gilchrist, L. D. (1986). Prevention of drug and alcohol abuse in American Indian youths. *Social Work Research & Abstracts, 22*(4), 18–19.

Schinke, S. P., & Singer, B. R. (1994). Prevention of health care problems. In D. K. Granvold (Ed.), *Cognitive and behavioral treatment: Methods and applications* (pp. 285–298). Pacific Grove, CA: Brooks/Cole.

Schwartz, R. M., & Garamoni, G. L. (1986). A structural model of positive and negative states of mind: Asymmetry in the internal dialogue. In P. C. Kendall (Ed.), *Advances in cognitive behavioral research therapy* (Vol. 5, pp. 1–62). New York: Academic Press.

Segal, Z. V., & Shaw, B. F. (1988). Cognitive assessment: Issues and methods. In K. S. Dobson (Ed.), *Handbook of cognitive–behavioral therapies* (pp. 39–81). New York: Guilford Press.

Seiler, T. B. (1984). Developmental cognitive therapy, personality and therapy. In N. Hoffman (Ed.), *Foundations of cognitive therapy: Theoretical methods and practical applications* (pp. 11–49). New York: Plenum Press.

Seligman, M.E.P. (1975). *Helplessness: On depression, development, and death.* San Francisco: W. H. Freeman.

Sgroi, S. M. (1989). *Sexual abuse treatment for children, adult survivors, offenders and persons with mental retardation: Vol. 2. Vulnerable populations.* Lexington, MA: Lexington Books.

Shorkey, C. T. (1994). Use of behavioral methods with individuals recovering from substance dependence. In D. K. Granvold (Ed.), *Cognitive and behavioral treatment: Methods and applications* (pp. 135–158). Pacific Grove, CA: Brooks/Cole.

Tataryn, D. J., Nadel, L., & Jacobs, W. J. (1989). Cognitive therapy and cognitive science. In A. Freeman, K. M. Simon, L. E. Beutler, & H. Arkowitz (Eds.), *Comprehensive handbook of cognitive therapy* (pp. 83–98). New York: Plenum Press.

Thorpe, G., & Burns, L. (1983). *The agoraphobia syndrome.* New York: John Wiley & Sons.

Turk, D., Meichenbaum, D., & Genest, M. (1983). *Pain and behavioral medicine: A cognitive–behavioral perspective.* New York: Guilford Press.

Turkat, I. D., & Maisto, S. A. (1985). Personality disorders: Application of the experimental method to the formulation and modification of personality disorders. In D. H. Barlow (Ed.), *Clinical handbook of psychological disorders* (pp. 502–570). New York: Guilford Press.

Vallis, T. M., Howes, J. L., & Miller, P. C. (Eds.). (1991). *The challenge of cognitive therapy: Applications to nontraditional populations.* New York: Plenum Press.

Weimer, W. B. (1977). A conceptual framework for cognitive psychology: Motor theories of the mind. In R. Shaw & J. Bransford (Eds.), *Perceiving, acting, and knowing: Toward an ecological psychology* (pp. 267–311). Hillsdale, NJ: Lawrence Erlbaum.

Weisz, J. R., Weiss, B., Wasserman, A. A., & Rintoul, B. (1987). Control-related beliefs and depression among

clinic-referred children and adolescents. *Journal of Abnormal Psychology, 96,* 58–63.
Wessler, R. L., & Hankin-Wessler, S. (1987). Cognitive appraisal therapy. In W. Dryden & W. Golden (Eds.), *Cognitive–behavioral approaches to psychotherapy* (pp. 196–223). New York: Hemisphere.
Wolpe, J. (1958). *Psychotherapy by reciprocal inhibition.* Stanford, CA: Stanford University Press.
Wolpe, J. (1969). *The practice of behavior therapy.* New York: Pergamon Press.
Wolpe, J. (1990). *The practice of behavior therapy* (2nd ed.). New York: Pergamon Press.
Wolpe, J., & Lazarus, A. A. (1966). *Behavior therapy techniques.* New York: Pergamon Press.

## Further Reading

Beck, J. S. (in press). *Cognitive therapy: Basics and beyond.* New York: Guilford Press.
Craighead, L. W., Craighead, E., Kazdin, A. E., & Mahoney, M. J. (Eds.). (1994). *Cognitive and behavioral interventions: An empirical approach to mental health problems.* Needham Heights, MA: Allyn & Bacon.
Dattilio, F. M., & Freeman, A. (Eds.). (1994). *Cognitive–behavioral strategies in crisis intervention.* New York: Guilford Press.
Dobson, K. S. (Ed.). (1987). *Handbook of cognitive–behavioral therapies.* New York: Guilford Press.
D'Zurilla, T. J. (1986). *Problem-solving therapy: A social competence approach to clinical intervention.* New York: Springer.
Finch, A. J., Nelson, W. M., & Ott, E. S. (Eds.). (1993). *Cognitive–behavioral procedures with children and adolescents: A practical guide.* Needham Heights, MA: Allyn & Bacon.
Freeman, A., & Dattilio, F. M. (Eds.). (1992). *Comprehensive casebook of cognitive therapy.* New York: Plenum Press.
Guidano, V. F. (1987). *Complexity of the self.* New York: Guilford Press.
Kingdom, D. G., & Turkington, D. (1994). *Cognitive–behavioral therapy of schizophrenia.* New York: Guilford Press.
Ramirez, M. (1991). *Psychotherapy and counseling with minorities: A cognitive approach to individual and cultural differences.* Needham Heights, MA: Allyn & Bacon.
Wilkes, T.C.R., Belsher, G., Rush, A. J., & Frank, E. (1994). *Cognitive therapy for depressed adolescents.* New York: Guilford Press.

**Donald K. Granvold, PhD, LMSW-ACP,** is professor, University of Texas at Arlington, School of Social Work, Arlington, TX 76019.

**For further information see**

Brief Therapies; Child Sexual Abuse: Direct Practice; Children: Direct Practice; Cognition and Social Cognitive Theory; Direct Practice Overview; Eating Disorders and Other Compulsive Behaviors; Families: Direct Practice; Family Therapy; Goal Setting and Intervention Planning; Human Development; Intervention Research; Mental Health Overview; Person-in-Environment; Social Work Practice: Theoretical Base; Substance Abuse: Direct Practice; Suicide; Torture Victims.

**Key Words**

| | |
|---|---|
| assessment | cognitive treatment |
| cognitive process | intervention |
| cognitive restructuring | |

## Cohen, Wilbur

*See* Biographies section, Volume 3

## Collaboration

*See* Interdisciplinary and Interorganizational Collaboration

READER'S GUIDE

## Community

*The following entries contain information on this general topic:*

# Community

**Emilia E. Martinez-Brawley**

The social relationship, wrote Tönnies in *Community and Society,* is the most general, the simplest, and the deepest social entity or form. It rests on the original and natural conditions of mutual dependence and attachment among people, and consequently it is the most necessary requirement of human beings (Tönnies, 1887/1957).

Association and cooperation among individuals may not be as essential for survival as are food and shelter, but the need for social interaction comes very close to the biological basic needs. As soon as human beings satisfy hunger and gain protection from exposure to the elements, the drive to associate and cooperate to satisfy other needs and to live in fellowship with others gives rise to interdependence and community.

A well-known student of community (Pelly-Effrat, 1974) suggested that the elusive concept of community is like Jello: It is slippery and hard to hold. This has been the case historically and continues to be the case today. The *New English Dictionary on Historical Principles* (Murray, Bradley, Craigh, & Unions, 1988) suggests that the term is derived from the Latin word *communis,* a noun describing quality, implying "fellowship, community of relations or feelings" (p. 702). In medieval Latin, however, *communis* came to be used concretely, in the sense of a "body of fellows or fellow-townsmen" (p. 702). Through the decades, the term has been used in diverse ways and in various contexts. Community is truly a mental construct, a conceptual framework imposed on an associational phenomenon by the participants and the observer.

A review of the myriad works on communities shows that writers, be they social scientists, philosophers, journalists, or literary figures, have struggled with the ramifications of the term. However, for purposes of a social science overview, two relatively comprehensive ways of looking at the concept can be identified. The first broad category is structural, in the sense that it deals with communities in relation to their space, their parameters, and their political identity as entities of the state. The second is sociopsychological, in the sense that it emphasizes meaning, identity, nonanomic relationships, and a sense of belonging. Furthermore, contemporary social theorists range from those who believe that meaningful relationships can be tied only to space to those who believe that space, locality, and proximity are irrelevant to the maintenance of solidarity among people in the associational sense connoted by the term "community."

## Structural Perspective

From the structural perspective, community is often referred to as the mediating structure between the individual and the state (Durkheim, 1893/1960). For Durkheim, the state was too remote from the individual to perform its socializing function successfully without the aid of intermediary units, such as communities, to penetrate individual consciousness and bring them into the torrent of social life. Thus, Durkheim saw community as the link between the individual and the society at large, represented by the state, a link that molded, socialized, and transformed the individual.

The community is often seen as a political entity and is organized as a province, a city, a township, a neighborhood, and so on. These structures carry out many political and social functions and mediate between the state as a central power and the individual. As a mediating unit of influence on the individual, the community also can be analyzed from the perspective of the power that the collective can exert on the individual. Hunter's (1953) famous research in Atlanta used "the concept of community as a frame of reference for the analysis of power relations" (p. 11). Vidich and Bensman (1968), in their work in a small upstate New York town, took a similar path, using the community—in their case the small town—to identify power relationships between it and the society at large.

But as the study of works by Hunter (1953) and Vidich and Bensman (1968) also showed, the mediating role of the community is intertwined with many other social and spatial relationships, resulting in the confluence of the structural and the sociopsychological. Community cannot be looked at unidimensionally. Neither structural nor sociopsychological dimensions alone will suffice.

## Sociopsychological Perspective

Tönnies's (1887/1957) concepts of *gemeinschaft* and *gesellschaft* are critical to our understanding not only the evolution of the concept of community but also of the debate about size and social relationships. Although Tönnies's concept of gemeinschaft was bound to territory, the use of the term in a contemporary context stresses just as much the psychological aspects of the mediating role of communities (Martinez-Brawley, 1990).

Tönnies was primarily concerned with understanding the ways people relate to each other. In gemeinschaft—which translates roughly as "community"—people relate to each other through mutuality, common destiny, close bonds, and personal rewards and obligations derived from the close bonds. In gesellschaft—which translates roughly as "society"—rationality is valued, the market directs trade and exchanges, and self-interest prevails over the sense of common obligations and duties (Warren & Lyon, 1983). For Tönnies, gemeinschaftlich (the adjective form) relationships were prevalent in families, villages, and small geographic units, whereas gesellschaftlich relationships were predominant in larger social units. Bell and Newby (1972) summarized Tönnies's fundamental concepts as being two ends in the continuum of social relationships. For Tönnies, they stated, gesellschaft was the antithesis of gemeinschaft.

> Opposed to the concept of community was *Gesellschaft* (variously translated as "society" or "association") which essentially means everything that community is not. *Gesellschaft* refers to the large scale, impersonal and contractual ties that were seen by the nineteenth century sociologists to be on the increase, at the expense of *Gemeinschaft*. Here is the central idea that runs through so many community studies: social change is conceptualized as a continuum between two polar types: *Gemeinschaft* or community and *Gesellschaft* or society.

Using a stronger psychological approach, Clark (1973) suggested that it was neither territory nor function but psychological elements that kept the notion of community alive. Clark proposed a considerable reorientation of the study of community to free the concept from its strong ties to structural elements, among them "place" and "function." He relied on psychological concepts and proposed that "despite all the potential dangers, what had deprecatingly been termed community-in-the-mind must in fact be the springboard for any realistic examination of the phenomenon" (Clark, 1973, p. 409). Through his detailed discussions of the elements of community, Clark (1973) concluded that "the strength of community within any given group is determined by the degree to which its members experience both a sense of solidarity and a sense of significance" (p. 409). Those essential elements of community flow from MacIver's (1924) early assertions that "life is essentially and always communal life. Every living thing is born into community and owes its life to community" (p. 209). Community is not circumscribed to the sphere of social interactions, but it permeates the visceral and psychological spheres of life (Clark, 1973).

Solidarity, significance, and security are the essential elements of life (Clark, 1973). Although solidarity, that is, cohesiveness or "we-ness," can be found in large and small units, in place and nonplace communities, the degree to which it can be observed justifies the extent to which the term "community" can truly be applied. A sense of significance and security must permeate those manifestations of collective behavior that help perpetuate the idea of community. Significance and security are enhanced by familiarity with the environment, a sense of being known and of orientation, and the affection and support of friends and neighbors (Martinez-Brawley, 1990).

## Community throughout American History

Throughout American history, the emphasis on communal behavior has been cyclical. In contemporary America, many have said that community is often hidden behind essentially individualistic strivings. To Slater (1976), contradictory streaks in the American character have been obvious; individualism has been in constant tug-of-war against the desire for community. The desire for "community," that is, for solidarity, cohesiveness, and the wish to live in a total and visible collective entity, has always been countered by the desire for individual freedom, the enterprising push, the drive to expand and conquer.

American individualism preceded the revolutionary struggle against monarchical and aristocratic authority, but so did the American sense of a supportive collective. Bender (1978) suggested that the English settlers of the early 17th century who came to America, particularly those who came as part of the Puritan migration, carried with them an intense commitment to community. He wrote that John Winthrop, the Puritan leader, expressed strong communal ideals in a sermon he delivered on board the *Arbella* before the main contingent of Puritans landed in Massachusetts Bay in 1630. In this sermon, Winthrop made clear the Puritans' willingness to abridge themselves of "superfluities, for the supply of others' necessities," to "uphold a familiar commerce together," to "delight in each other," and to "make others' conditions" their own (Bender, 1978, p. 63).

The covenanted community, wrote Smith (1966), existed under God's tutelage. It was

> composed of individuals bound in a special compact with God and with each other. The ties extended vertically within the society, uniting the classes and the society to God. . . . It found an ideal social form in the township, modeled on the English original . . . and it became the matrix into which innumerable communities were poured. . . . Indeed, one of the most important attributes of the covenanted community was that it could reproduce itself almost to infinity once its essential form had become fixed. (pp. 6–7)

And reproduce itself it did through the new and emerging colonies where small towns, both in the American mind and in reality, began to represent the true spirit of cooperation and community. Late into the 1800s, as far west as Iowa, the language of 19th-century evangelical Protestantism sounded much like John Winthrop's. In *Iowa, the Promised Land of the Prophets,* Brown (1884) criticized the evils of capitalism, which he saw as associated with large cities that were in his mind the essence of greed and decline:

> Cooperative farms and cooperative factories were the expression of "a willingness to be equal with our neighbor, and not above him." The unions and the Grange organizations were engaged in educating the people "up to a higher and truer love and brotherhood. . . . Societies and lodges will be merged into the great society—the State—of which all are members, and brethren: a society of mutual helpfulness, of mutual benefits, of mutual love and good will, wherein my neighbor's child will be as dear to me as my own." (Brown, 1884, as cited in Smith, 1966, pp. 204–205)

But class struggles and the fight for capital and wealth, all rooted in individualistic strivings, grew side by side in the American reality. The Puritan covenanted community of the New England Pilgrims was a different type of community from that of Jamestown, Virginia, where planters fashioned their own gentry based on slavery and race and class exploitation. The New England communities had been founded on God's guidance, whereas the Virginia ones were based on a plantation economy, servile labor, and the tutelage of money (Smith, 1966). Class, property ownership, and money played a central role outside the covenanted community tradition:

> The New World provided opportunities for making money; some had come with money and as such had a head start; others, even the indentured servants or their sons and daughters, rose in the world. Their prosperity was hardly scorned; it was indeed considered praiseworthy. And so the wealth was put to work creating and displaying a commensurate life-style, and political and economic power. (Lingeman, 1980, p. 398)

The frontier provided an escape hatch for many landless farmers and migrants and, after the Civil War, even for a few slaves (Bender, 1978). Although ostensibly communal and classless, those who went West found that the ideals of equality were soon overshadowed by the fact that the various settlers had not, in fact, arrived as equals. Some had more skills and education and were able to set up as tradespeople and professionals; others had more money and were able to speculate with land. In the early settlements all people fought against similar odds, but soon the communal spirit began to subside in favor of more individualistic or even anticommunal pursuits. Furthermore, as peoples from all over the world began to arrive in America, communities became ethnic enclaves in which the patterns the migrants had brought with them were reproduced. Concentrated efforts at amalgamation did not break the spirit of the new citizens, and large cities became a conglomeration of neighborhoods that often duplicated the European villages or ethnic gemeinschaften (the plural form) from which their inhabitants had originated with their varied communal patterns and distinctive levels of collective ethos.

Although the westward movement is often depicted as an individualistic effort of rugged pioneers or pioneering families, as Bender (1978) pointed out, community efforts were essential to survival in the West.

> Men and women moved west in the company of kin or friends; they were also quick to form a network of community relations in the new localities where they settled. The like-minded tended to find each other. Sometimes this like-mindedness was founded on common origins. . . ; more often, membership in national institutions, whether churches or voluntary associations, facilitated the development of new bonds of community. (p. 96)

Thus, ties began to shape the integration of people in their daily lives. Churches, for example, provided codes of behavior and fellowship in the daily interaction of many western communities. Vertical ties to national or translocal institutions (Warren, 1963) shaped not only the way in which complete strangers could become integrated into local communities but also the number of spheres of action in which citizens could participate. By the time Tocqueville visited America in 1835, he found that Americans belonged to two distinct political systems: one local, or in contemporary terms, horizontal, fulfilling the daily, ordinary duties of citizenship; and one translocal, or vertical, wherein the general interests of the country prevailed (Tocqueville, 1835/1945).

Higham's (1974) thesis that "Americans have commonly been enmeshed in divergent systems of integration" (p. 7)—that many forces shaped the American communal experience at the same time—provides an excellent explanation for our concern over the dichotomous communal and individualistic forces that shape life in American society. Bellah, Madsen, Sullivan, Swiddler, and Tipton (1985) described this push of contradictory forces:

> The inner tensions of American individualism add up to a classic case of ambivalence. We strongly assert the value of our self-reliance and autonomy. We deeply feel the emptiness of a life without sustaining social commitments. Yet, we are hesitant to articulate our sense that we need one another as much as we need to stand alone, for fear that if we did we would lose our independence altogether." (pp. 150-151)

## Community Continuum

Community historians have referred to the last decade of the 19th century and the first decade of the 20th century as the "Age of Confidence" (Canby, 1934). These were years when people felt confidently secure in their destinies as Americans and when traditional small-town values were still uncontroversially seen as the epitome of community (Lingeman, 1980). Writers in literature and popular works of the period perceived the rural small town or village (the gemeinschaft) as the only community and the city (the gesellschaft) as anticommunity. Although many literary works and popular magazines of the period had begun to report about small-town dwellers who took lucrative positions in the cities (Lingeman, 1980), the overall American attitude was squarely on the side of Booth Tarkington (1899), who, "with the languid scorn a permanent fixture always has for the transient and the pity an American feels for a fellow being who does not live in his town" (p. 4), wrote about city people whizzing by in big trains through the villages.

During the 1920s and 1930s the view of the small town began to shift, and by the 1940s and 1950s it had changed altogether. Lewis's (1920) *Main Street* depicted the suffocation a young city college graduate experiences after she marries a provincial doctor and arrives in Gopher Prairie, a rural Minnesota town. Small towns were by then perceived as provincial and binding for the individual, and the city was viewed as the only truly liberating unit of social interaction.

During the decades following the 1950s, the pendulum swung again, and the small town, village, and other manageable geographic locales were placed in the position of redeemers of anomie. Although advances in technology, transportation, and mass communication might account for some of the popular shift of sentiments, explanations of these pendulum-like mood swings are likely to be less rational and have more to do with the cyclical nature of fashion and cultural preferences (Martinez-Brawley, 1990).

Similar shifts to those registered in literature were apparent in the social sciences. During the first three decades of the 20th century, students of the community assumed that gemeinschaft, at that time only identified with the rural towns or villages, was a good thing and that its integrity was to be guarded and its passing deplored. Until the 1950s, the prevalent social science concept was that community was found only in nonurban environments. Urbanism was perceived to destroy cohesiveness and mutuality. The notion that gemeinschaft was also found in the urban neighborhoods did not emerge until later and still is debated. Only during the 1940s, 1950s, and 1960s did social scientists turn to the city to scrutinize its nature and see if elements of gemeinschaft were found within it. Hillery (1969) proposed that the village could axiomatically be labeled "community" and proceeded to compare it to the city. He concluded that the city contained "variations of the same type of thing as the folk village. The two models are best to be viewed as varying from each other in degree, that is, as an existing continua" (p. 61). This same hypothesis was proposed by Rivera and Erlich (1981), who analyzed the flourishing ethnic and minority communities of the inner city. Rivera and Erlich's use of the term "neo-gemeinschaft" to describe cohesive ethnic and minority metropolitan pockets is accurate, because the nature of people's interaction in those units is similar to the interaction of people in small towns.

### Utopian and Therapeutic Communities

The modern world is plagued by anomie and disorientation. Having lost much of the feeling of control over their destinies, people are struggling with their sense of selfhood. They turn to community because the family is perceived to be weakening and becoming more remote. Because of the processes of civilization and industrialization, the family is growing smaller, less orthodox, less encompassing, and less capable of satisfying individual needs (Martinez-Brawley, 1990; Roszak, 1978).

The idea of utopias is not new. The American utopians had their antecedents in Europe. Darley (1978) recognized the difficulties and failures experienced by many Britons in their quest for the perfect community, but she also recognized that, within limitations, many of these quixotic seekers of community fulfilled their dreams and provided realizable blueprints not only for architectural but also for sociopsychological communities.

Kanter (1972), a student of visionary communal movements in the United States, suggested that utopian communities have been the response to three forces: religious, political–economic, and psychosocial. Religious communities often emerged when separatist and pietist sects sought closer contact with God and each other. Another type of utopian community emerged out of political–economic concerns because of increasing dislocation and poverty in the wake of the Industrial Revolution. Like the religious communes, this type of community was inspired by the social creed of reformers who sought "in the small socialist community a refuge from the evils of the factory system" (Kanter, 1972, p. 5). Many modern communes are the result of psychosocial forces. These communities reject society's emphasis on achievement and material gains and seek to provide their members with a place to grow, experience intimacy, and realize their potential. For the truly utopian groups, all modern institutions are considered "sick" and "are felt to be instrumental in promoting the neurotic behavior at the root of our most pressing social problems" (Kanter, 1972, p. 7).

Initially successful but rather short-lived communal settlement efforts became part of the widespread American quest for community as the personal solution of the 1970s and 1980s. These alternative communities, or neo-gemeinschaften, are perceived by their proponents as the solution to today's problems of belonging and as performing functions once carried out not just by communities but by families.

Although the modern search for community as a personal solution often shares many of the characteristics of the utopian movements described by Kanter (1972) and Darley (1978), the search involves not only communes or utopias but also ordinary towns and villages across the United States. People joining the search for personal community include intellectuals, social philosophers, utopian thinkers, and religious mystics as well as average citizens—insurance salespeople, entrepreneurs, teachers, farmers, and civil servants—who join clubs or settle in villagelike developments and retirement communities that offer total care. An article in the *Atlanta Constitution* mentioned interest clubs as a way to help "people cope with the largeness of city life by providing smaller, more human-sized community" (Long, 1987, p. 38).

But the search has also touched more-dangerous extremists, who often end up threatening the liberty and well-being of those who flock to them. For example, followers of the Bhagwan Shree Ragneesh, an Indian sect that settled in the village of Antelope, Oregon, offended many of the long-time residents of the town and had difficulties patching up relationships with the locals after their leader encountered serious trouble in 1985 and emigrated to escape legal entanglements in the United States. Another example of abuses of this search for community was the Reverend Jim Jones's community in Georgetown, Guyana, where fanaticism led to the suicide–massacre of hundreds in 1978 (Martinez-Brawley, 1990). A similar incident took place in Waco, Texas, in 1993 when the followers of a religious cult led by David Koresh refused to surrender to federal authorities and perished in a tragic fire (Pressley, 1993).

Alternative arrangements that take the place of family and gemeinschaft have been flourishing for many people. For many of the old and the young in search of community, shopping malls have become the community. Individuals often find that a variety of "contrived" environments become their community and fulfill a need where family might not exist or might have failed. In our contemporary world, the smaller the family becomes, the more individuals search for purpose and meaning in the larger collective, in contrived groups, and in artificial or utopian communities.

**Occupational–Professional Communities**

People partially satisfy their need for identity and significance in their occupation–profession or community of interest. A professional community, according to Goode (1957), is a "community without physical locus, and like other communities with heavy in-migration, one whose founding fathers are linked rarely by blood with the present generation" (p. 194).

For many people in modern society, occupational or professional communities constitute an important source of identity and significance. Many observers have viewed community of interest as a poor substitute for other forms of communities; however, these other communal units can be viewed in a positive light. They offer rewards that differ from those of the intimate gemeinschaft. Generally, most members of a group or an occupational–professional body identify with an affilia-tional community on a national or even worldwide basis (for example, the legal, medical, or social work communities); yet professional or occupational communities offer much at the level of the region or the immediate locale. They offer themes, justification, and ways and means for people of like mind to gather and pursue collective goals.

### Racial–Ethnic Communities

Through the decades, membership in racial or ethnic communities has been another way in which citizens have sought the support of communal grouping. The notion of membership in an ethnic community is more than mere inclusion in an ethnic category. Although in the ethnic category only objective criteria related to background are considered, "the ethnic community has two additional characteristics: identity or self-consciousness and organization" (Martiniello, 1993, p. 240). Racial or ethnic communities perform many of the socialization functions in this pluralistic society. Tradition, language, creed, and other elements of heritage are maintained through ties to racial and ethnic communities. Ethnic–racial communities also have been the way groups of citizens have faced, in solidarity, oppressive power and class struggles. Through racial–ethnic community building, leaders have often counteracted the political powerlessness of the group, maintained the support of the members, and reaffirmed the existence of the community.

The ties that bind members of racial and ethnic communities are vertical and horizontal. People identify with a group in terms of national or even international agendas and as local points of contact and support. Often, racial and ethnic ties transcend national boundaries and provide the means through which groups find identity and meaning in global ways.

## Power, Influence, and Leadership in the Community

Power, influence, and leadership are important concepts in understanding communities or, perhaps more importantly, in understanding who benefits from community policies (Lyon, 1977; Walton, 1976). A distinction should be drawn between *power,* the abstract potential to affect the course of events in particular communities, and *influence,* the concrete operational capability of actually swaying the course of specific actions. Magill and Clark (1975) asserted that "power refers to potential but not necessarily exerted influence. Influence is conceived as the making of decisions that cause change" (p. 35). According to Freeman, Fararo, Bloomberg, and Sunshine (1968), "*leadership* refers to a complex process whereby a relatively small number of individuals in a collectivity behave in such a way that they effect (or effectively prevent) a change in the lives of a relatively large number" (p. 189). "Powerful actors" are people who have the potential to exert influence, "influentials" are people who do exert influence, and "leaders" are people who exert influence by mobilizing others to join in their causes. Although powerful actors, influentials, and leaders can be the same people, the attributes of power, influence, and leadership are not necessarily embodied in the same individuals. Whether the same people are identified as powerful and influential and carry out the charismatic leadership role in a given instance indicates the degree of elitism or pluralism in a particular community.

According to Wilson (1973), the influence or active power of one group over another is not simply the result of the overt efforts of the influential (superordinate) over the subordinate or controlled group. The behavior of subordinates (whether individuals or groups) is modified by what they perceive to be the influential's power ability or command of power resources. These properties could include high social status, reputation for power, capability of bearing arms, control of political office, control of mass media, or wealth and land ownership. Inducement and persuasion, two more subtle ways of exercising power and influence, are applied by groups who wish to influence another group without resorting to threats or penalties. Furthermore, power and influence are affected by public perceptions. A group can have influence because it is perceived to have power or access to power resources.

Although power is distinct from influence, and leadership is a corollary of influence, the three are interactive in the reality of community events. Although these concepts (particularly power and influence) often, at least for study purposes, are considered separately, practitioners must consider their complementary nature in affecting community outcomes (Martinez-Brawley, 1990).

Many models explain how power, influence, and leadership are distributed in communities. Two explanatory models, elitism and pluralism, provide a basic framework for understanding.

### Elitism

In the elitist model, power and influence are highly centralized in communities (Hunter, 1953; Lynd & Lynd, 1929, 1937; Michels, 1962; Mosca, 1939; Pareto, 1935; Piven & Cloward, 1977; Vidich & Bensman, 1968). Power resides in the hands of a few individuals or groups who are directly or indirectly involved in decisions simply because the scope of their personal or group interest is so pervasive that it is almost impossible for them to be indifferent to any decision. According to Olsen (1970), theorists who see communities as primarily elitist "offer a broader explanation of the underlying bases of social power than that proposed by Marx. . . . For them, control of the means of economic production is just one possible resource for exercising power, rather than the only one" (p. 187). Elitist theorists and Marxists agree that there is a two-class arrangement in society. The elite exercise power; the masses do not. For the Marxists, the elite can be overthrown by the masses; for the elitists, emerging challenges to the elite are always, in the end, absorbed into the ruling classes.

Although contemporary elitism might be slightly more participatory than classic elitism (with a larger number of leaders or with a cluster of corporate leaders), chances are it will still resemble a pyramidal structure. The broad base of the pyramid symbolizes the larger participation of community members at the lowest levels of the decision-making process; the narrower top of the pyramid represents the decision-making elite. Until recently, the literature often suggested that two types of elites existed in communities, one based on wealth and one on the consequences of the electoral process. Currently, researchers are less prone to separate the two, because they often are found in close interaction at the upper levels of the pyramid, particularly in small communities where elitism often prevails (Piven & Cloward, 1977). The degree of interaction of the power actors has been found to be related to the size of the communities. Comparative studies have found that smaller towns tend to have more centralized patterns of decision making. Thus, the smaller the town, the fewer "the leaders, who are more often in agreement with each other" (Magill & Clark, 1975, p. 38).

### Pluralism

In the pluralist model, such as in modern democratic societies, power tends to be relatively decentralized. Pluralist theorists disagree about the degree of decentralization that exists, but they believe the elitist model does not reflect the contemporary power distribution reality. They propose that the decentralization of power is a prerequisite for effective political democracy (Olsen, 1970).

Pluralism can be visualized as a circle within which a number of small circles, representing the loci of decision making, are found. Thus, pluralist thinkers do not speak of a single community power structure but rather various loci of decisional control. As Polsby (1960) pointed out,

> The first and perhaps most basic presupposition of the pluralist approach is that nothing can be assumed about power in any community. If anything, there seems to be an unspoken notion among pluralist researchers that at bottom nobody dominates in a town so that their first question to a local informant is not likely to be, "Who runs this community?" but rather "Does anyone at all run this community?" (p. 474)

Power is tied to issues, and "issues can be fleeting or persistent, provoking coalitions among interest groups and citizens, ranging in their duration from momentary to semi-permanent" (p. 476). In very heterogeneous communities, which prevail in the United States, issue politics provide a reasonable illustration of how decisions are made. Rule by coalitions, rather than by small power groups, occurs more often in real contemporary communities when the interests of citizens are diverse. Manipulation of constituencies, rather than command or even subtle persuasion, is central to community decision making.

## Social Work Practice in the Community

Knowledge of community variables is an important component of the social worker's armamentarium. Historically, social workers have always worked in the context of communities. The very raison d'être of social work was to bridge the gap between an increasingly mobile and industrialized society and the support needs of individuals that had been typically met in gemeinschaft. The early social work pioneers worked out of settlement houses, where the emphasis was on the incorporation of new immigrants into the community and the alleviation of the causes of pauperism. Jane Addams, Edith and Grace Abbott, Florence Kelly, and Julia Lathrop, to name but a few, all worked within the context of community. Among the activities at Hull House, the famous Chicago settlement house, were plays, concerts, a community kitchen, a club for working women, and other similar activities. In many ways, social work as a profession became the institutional response to caring within the context of the industrial world, its purpose being to address the breakdown of natural communities.

In spite of the influences of the scientific charity movement of the early 20th century and of Freudian psychology and its intrapsychic corollaries, social work never totally removed itself from its early roots in the community. Social work practice, regardless of the context or specialty, requires an understanding of the ties that bind the individual, the family, or the group to larger societal networks. Furthermore, as resources for professional practice interventions dwindle, social workers increasingly fill the role of mobilizer of community resources to resolve personal problems or address public issues.

Traditional models of community work typically have identified locality or community development, social planning, and social action as the three modalities for community intervention. However, new ways of looking at community practice hold promise for social work.

According to Rothman and Tropman (1987), *locality or community development* attempts to create social conditions of economic and social progress, preferably with the participation of the whole community. *Social planning* usually addresses long-term goals of the community; process is important because the community planner and social workers tend to function in interdisciplinary teams to accomplish social planning goals. *Social action* has social change as an overarching goal, and social action practitioners see their role as promoting change in the context of communities, often challenging the existing power arrangements and structures. Descriptions of these three approaches constitute the bulk of the literature in social work in the community.

An additional modality has recently gained an audience in the United States. The concept of community social work or community-oriented social work, which captured center stage in the United Kingdom in the past decade, offers a way of expanding existing paradigms of practice.

Community social work, according to the 1980 Barclay Working Party, which was set up in Britain by the Secretary of State for Social Services to study the role and tasks of social workers, "rests upon our understanding of the nature of community and the meaning of social care" (National Institute for Social Work, 1982, p. 199). The Working Party's report defined *community* "as a network, or informal relationships between people connected with each other by kinship, common interest, geographical proximity, friendship, occupation, or the giving and receiving of services—or various combinations of these" (p. 199). The Working Party defined *social care* as "the sum of helping (and when need be, controlling) resources available to people in adversity, whether provided informally by community networks or formally by the public services" (p. 199); in the United States, such resources would be provided by the formal services—public, voluntary, or private—or by other informal networks of family and friends.

The Working Party further suggested not so much that community social work was a specific technique or method but, rather, that it depended on "an attitude of mind in all social workers, from the director of the department or agency to front-line workers, which regards members of the public as partners in the provision of social care" (National Institute for Social Work, 1982, p. 198). Community-oriented social work requires the practitioner see community as a potentially nourishing and important source of support and identity to its members.

Although community-oriented social work is important, there is no single recipe that those involved in using and providing social care should follow. A growing body of literature related to community-oriented social work was developed in the past decade (Hadley, Dale, & Sills, 1984; Hadley & Hatch, 1981; Hadley & Young, 1990; Smale, Tuson, Cooper, Wardle, & Crosbie, 1988). The intensity of community problems in such areas as child welfare, youth services, and elderly care has stirred a great deal of interest in innovating and discovering new approaches that enhance community participation (Martinez-Brawley, 1990; Martinez-Brawley with Delevan, 1993).

Most social workers are accustomed to practicing within the confines of bureaucratic agencies, whether those agencies are governmental, part of the traditional voluntary sector, grassroots, or even private and for profit. Community-oriented social work is predicated on a different understanding of the community, particularly at the local level. It requires the interweaving of the formal and informal systems of care. It is based on the notion that caring for people is the common task of professionals and laypeople in their roles as friends and neighbors, and it requires the development of a truly cooperative and egalitarian relationship among all caring systems in the community. Thus, community-oriented social work presupposes a power shift in the professional relationship (Darvill & Smale, 1990). Community-oriented social work also presupposes that the professional is open to different ways of accomplishing goals while recognizing that the professional is often constricted by standards and particular techniques of helping and the layperson is not. From the interweaving of different ways of doing things, new approaches emerge.

Community-oriented social work emphasizes the creation of an egalitarian environment in which local people participate in the caring of community members. Such an environment might open professionals and agencies to closer scrutiny and, potentially, criticism, but it might also open them to the possibility of attaining the local support they never had before. Community-oriented services are as much an attitude as a collection of techniques. Because communities and local people vary, community-oriented social services will have unique aspects in each local community (Martinez-Brawley, 1990).

Although community-oriented social work might appear to distance the professionals from their peers or to put greater reliability on informal sources of support than on formal ones, the fact is that community social work emphasizes the complementarity of professional networks and knowledge with community networks of care and with collective wisdom.

Community-oriented social work must be evaluated in terms of its own goals and objectives. Several goals have been articulated in most community social work projects: early warnings of cases at risk, better access to care, responses to needs that are negotiated with the community, local participation in defining social services, locally managed resources, and coordinated planning (Smale et al., 1988). But community-oriented social work also has the characteristics of a social movement; it implies an art of working in an egalitarian fashion with the local community collectively and with its members individually; it implies a high level of respect for what laypeople can do in the community and the recognition that the answers to our social ills are truly complex. As a result of conservative times and cuts in resources, social workers have had to be more proactive in defining their role, more assertive in attempting to prevent rather than solve problems, and more oriented toward teamwork with a variety of disciplines. In short, by becoming actively engaged with informal community resources, social workers have developed a new way of functioning and thinking about the community, partly because a positive relationship between social agencies and the community often is the most powerful argument and provides the most convincing evidence in favor of preserving a given service. The new community-oriented practitioner is committed to knowing the community and therefore can achieve the most successful interweaving of formal and informal energy and creativity on behalf of the consumers of social services.

## References


Bell, C., & Newby, H. (1972). *Community studies: An introduction to the sociology of the local community.* New York: Praeger.

Bellah, R. N., Madsen, R., Sullivan, W. M., Swiddler, A., & Tipton, S. M. (1985). *Habits of the heart: Individualism and commitment in American life.* Berkeley: University of California Press.

Bender, T. (1978). *Community and social change in America.* New Brunswick, NJ: Rutgers University Press.

Brown, L. (1884). *Iowa, the promised land of the prophets.* Des Moines, IA: Central.

Canby, H. S. (1934). *The age of confidence.* New York: Farrar & Rinehart.

Clark, D. C. (1973). The concept of community: A reexamination. *Sociological Review, 21,* 397–416.

Darley, G. (1978). *Villages of vision.* London: Granada.

Darvill, G., & Smale, G. (1990). Introduction: The face of community social work. In G. Darvill & G. Smale (Eds.), *Partners in empowerment: Networks of innovation in social work* (pp. 11–28). London: National Institute for Social Work.

Durkheim, E. (1960). *The division of labor in society.* Glencoe, IL: Free Press. (Original work published 1893)

Freeman, L. C., Fararo, T. J., Bloomberg, W., & Sunshine, H. (1968). Locating leaders in local communities: A comparison of some alternative approaches. In W. D. Hawley & F. M. Wirt (Eds.), *The search for community power* (pp. 189–199). Englewood Cliffs, NJ: Prentice Hall.

Goode, W. J. (1957). Community within a community: The professions. *American Sociological Review, 22,* 194–200.

Hadley, R., Dale, P., & Sills, P. (1984). *Decentralising social services: A model for change.* London: Bedford Square Press/National Council for Voluntary Organisations.

Hadley, R., & Hatch, S. (1981). *Social welfare and the failure of the state: Centralised social services and participatory alternatives.* London: Allen & Unwin.

Hadley, R., & Young, K. (1990). *Creating a responsive public service.* London: Harvester Wheatsheaf.

Higham, J. (1974). Hanging together: Divergent unities in American history. *Journal of American History, 61*(1), 5–28.

Hillery, G. A. (1969). *Communal organizations: A study of local societies.* Chicago: University of Chicago Press.

Hunter, F. (1953). *Community power structure: A study of decision makers.* Chapel Hill: University of North Carolina Press.

Kanter, R. M. (1972). *Commitment and community: Communes and utopians in sociological perspective.* Cambridge, MA: Harvard University Press.

Lewis, S. (1920). *Main street.* New York: P. F. Collier.

Lingeman, R. (1980). *Small town in America: A narrative history, 1620–the present.* New York: Putnam.

Long, K. (1987, November 20). Clubs: Small communities in the big city. *Atlanta Constitution,* p. 38.

Lynd, R. S., & Lynd, H. M. (1929). *Middletown.* New York: Harcourt Brace Jovanovich.

Lynd, R. S., & Lynd, H. M. (1937). *Middletown in transition: A study in cultural conflicts.* New York: Harcourt Brace Jovanovich.

Lyon, L. (1977). Community power and policy outputs: A question of relevance. In R. Warren (Ed.), *New perspectives on the American community* (pp. 2–6). Chicago: Rand McNally.

MacIver, R. M. (1924). *Community.* New York: Macmillan.

Magill, R. S., & Clark, T. N. (1975). Community power and decision making: Recent research and its policy implications. *Social Service Review, 49,* 33–45.

Martinez-Brawley, E. (1990). *Perspectives on the small community: Humanistic views for practitioners.* Silver Spring, MD: NASW Press.

Martinez-Brawley, E., with Delevan, S. M. (1993). *Transferring technology in the personal social services.* Washington, DC: NASW Press.

Martiniello, M. (1993). Ethnic leadership: Ethnic communities' political powerlessness and the state in Belgium. *Ethnic and Racial Studies, 16*(2), 236–255.

Michels, R. (1962). *Political parties* (Eden and Cedar Paul, Trans.). New York: Free Press.

Mosca, G. (1939). *The ruling class.* New York: McGraw-Hill.

Murray, A. H., Bradley, H., Craigh, W. A., & Unions, C. T. (Eds.). (1988). *New English dictionary on historical principles.* Oxford: Clarendon Press.

National Institute for Social Work. (1982). *Social workers: Their roles and tasks* (Barclay Report). London: Bedford Square Press.

Olsen, M. E. (1970). Social pluralism as a basis for democracy. In M. E. Olsen (Ed.), *Power in societies* (pp. 182–187). New York: Macmillan.

Pareto, V. (1935). *The mind and society* (A. Bongiorno & A. Livingston, Trans.; A. Livingston, Ed.). New York: Harcourt, Brace.

Pelly-Effrat, M. (1974). Approaches to community: Conflicts and complementarities. In M. P. Effrat (Ed.), *The community: Approaches and applications* (pp. 1–32) New York: Free Press.

Piven, F. F., & Cloward, R. A. (1977). *Poor people's movements: Why they succeed, how they fail.* New York: Random House.

Polsby, N. W. (1960). How to study community power: The pluralist alternative. *Journal of Politics, 22,* 474–484.

Pressley, S. A. (1993, April 27). Cultists started fire in Waco, probers say. *Washington Post,* p. A-1.

Rivera, F. G, & Erlich, J. L. (1981). Neo-gemeinschaft minority communities: Implications for community organization in the United States. *Community Development Journal, 3,* 189–200.

Roszak, T. (1978). *Person/planet: The creative disintegration of industrial society.* Garden City, NJ: Anchor Press/ Doubleday.

Rothman, J., & Tropman, J. E. (1987). Models of community organization and macro practice perspectives: Their mixing and phasing. In F. M. Cox, J. L. Erlich, J. Rothman, & J. E. Tropman (Eds.), *Strategies of community organization: Macro practice* (pp. 3–26). Itasca, IL: F. E. Peacock.

Slater, P. (1976). *Pursuit of loneliness: American culture at the breaking point.* Boston: Beacon Press.

Smale, G., Tuson, G., Cooper, M., Wardle, M., & Crosbie, D. (1988). *Community social work: A paradigm for change.* London: NASW/PADE Publications.

Smith, P. (1966). *As a city upon a hill: The town in American history.* New York: Knopf.

Tarkington, B. (1899). *The gentleman from Indiana.* New York: Doubleday & McClure.

Tocqueville, A. De. (1945). *Democracy in America* (Vol. 1, H. Reeve, Trans., P. Bradley, Ed.). New York: Knopf. (Original work published in 1835)

Tönnies, F. (1957). *Community and society* (Gemeinschaft und Gesellschaft) (C. P. Loomis, Trans., Ed.). East Lansing: Michigan State University Press. (Original work published 1887)

Vidich, A. J., & Bensman, J. (1968). *Small town in mass society: Class, power and religion in a rural community.* Garden City, NJ: Anchor Books.

Walton, J. (1976). Community power and the retreat from politics: Full circle after twenty years? *Social Problems, 23*(3), 292–303.

Warren, R. L. (1963). *The community in America* (3rd ed.). Chicago: Rand McNally.

Warren, R. L. & Lyon, L. (1983). Introduction. In R. Warren & L. Lyon (Eds.), *New perspectives on the American community* (pp. 2–6). Homewood, IL: Dorsey Press.

Wilson, W. J. (1973). *Power, racism and privilege: Race relations in theoretical and sociohistorical perspectives.* New York: Free Press.

## Further Reading

Abrams, P. (1980). Social change, social networks and neighborhood care. *Social Work Service, 22,* 12–23.

Bachrach, P., & Baratz, M. (1970) *Power and poverty: Theory and practice.* New York: Oxford University Press.

Curtis, R. F., & Jackson, E. F. (1966). *Inequality in American communities.* New York: Academic Press.

Hadley, R., & McGrath, M. (1980). *Going local: Neighborhood social services.* London: Bedford Square Press.

Harrison, W. D. (1989). Social work and the search for postindustrial community. *Social Work, 34,* 73–75.

Jacobson, M. G. (1988). Working with communities. In H. W. Johnson (Ed.), *The social services: An introduction* (pp. 308–323). Itasca, IL: Peacock.

Ross, M. G. (1955). *Community organization: Theory and principles.* New York: Harper & Brothers.

Weinbach, R. W. (1990). *The social worker as manager: Theory and practice.* New York: Longman.

Wellstone, P. (1978). *How the rural poor got power: Narrative of a grass-roots organizer.* Amherst: University of Massachusetts Press.

Zablocki, B. (1971). *The joyful community.* Baltimore: Penguin Books.

Zinsmeister, K. (1987). The revolt against alienation. *Policy Review, 2,* 60–68.

**Emilia E. Martinez-Brawley, EdD, ACSW, LSW,** is dean and professor, Arizona State University, School of Social Work, Tempe, AZ 85287.

### For further information see

Community Development; Community Needs Assessment; Community Organization; Community Practice Models; Cults; Ethnic-Sensitive Practice; Families Overview; Families: Demographic Shifts; International and Comparative Social Welfare; Mutual Aid Societies; Natural Helping Networks; Rural Social Work; Self-Help Groups; Settlements and Neighborhood Centers; Social Development; Social Welfare History; Social Work Profession: History.

**Key Words**

community
community social work
ethnic groups
identity
leadership
power
social groupings

# Community-Based Corrections

Jeffrey A. Butts

Community-based corrections programs have become an essential component of both the juvenile and adult justice systems. The best-known community corrections programs are probation and parole. In 1990 state and federal agencies supervised 2.7 million adults on probation and more than 500,000 on parole. Three percent of the adult male population was on either probation or parole in 1990 (Jankowski, 1991). Other widely used community corrections programs include restitution, in which the offender repays or repairs the damages resulting from his or her crime; house arrest, in which the offender may not leave home except for work or other approved activities; and community service, in which the offender is ordered to perform unpaid work as repayment to the general community.

## Definitions

To understand the role of community corrections programs, it is necessary to differentiate the functions of punishment and corrections. *Punishment* is a retributive reaction to an offender's violation of the law. Through punishment, society indicates its disapproval of certain forms of behavior such as violence, theft, and the use of illicit drugs. A secondary goal of punishment may be to deter future violations by the offender (specific deterrence) or similar violations by other potential offenders (general deterrence). Punishment, however, primarily is social retribution for a wrongful act.

*Corrections,* on the other hand, is primarily an effort to influence or correct unlawful behavior. Corrections programs seek to reduce future law violations by teaching offenders that certain behaviors are wrong and will result in negative consequences and that other types of behavior may be substituted for illegal acts. Whereas punishment is simply an event, corrections is a process through which behavioral outcomes are achieved. Community corrections programs can involve elements of punishment as well as corrections.

Community corrections offers an alternative to incarcerating adjudicated juveniles and convicted adults. If well managed, such programs can be a more cost-effective method of achieving the goals of rehabilitation, control, and punishment. Offenders who remain in their own communities avoid the negative effects of imprisonment, potentially enhancing their rehabilitation. Supervision in the community enables offenders to repay damages directly to the community rather than simply "doing time" in a state-operated facility. Community corrections advocates argue that because the vast majority of incarcerated offenders eventually return to the community, providing punishment and supervision in the community allows them to work and receive treatment in the same social context in which they must live after their release from the justice system. In other words, community corrections can greatly enhance an offender's adjustment to society after release from supervision, and this is thought to reduce the likelihood of recidivism.

## Structures and Functions

Community corrections are administered under a variety of organizational and governmental structures. In some jurisdictions either the state or the local government has complete responsibility for community corrections. In other jurisdictions the state and local governments share this responsibility. Increasingly, community corrections programs are operated by private companies under contract to a state or local government.

Community corrections programs can be used at either the "front end" or the "back end" of the justice system. In other words, they can be used for first-time, low-risk offenders who have not been incarcerated (sometimes not even convicted) or for more serious offenders as an alternative to incarceration and a means to supervise those being released, or paroled, to the community from correctional institutions.

With the exception of those who commit federal crimes, offenders are tried and sentenced by state or county courts. (Technically, juveniles receive adjudications and dispositions rather than convictions and sentences.) In criminal or juvenile court cases that do not involve a period of confinement, the responsibility for carrying out the community-based sentence usually remains with the court that imposed the sentence. One jurisdiction may use only a rudimentary form of community corrections, such as traditional probation and fines, whereas another jurisdiction may have an elaborate array of programs that offer various levels of punitiveness and offender control.

A court decision to impose a term of community corrections is based largely on the degree to which the offender is thought to present a risk to the public safety. In other words, the court must assess the likelihood that the offender will commit new crimes if allowed to remain in the community. The court is also likely to consider whether available programs will be able to address the offender's rehabilitation needs. Often, the decision must also take into consideration the seriousness of the criminal act and the public's attitude toward the offender. In highly visible or notorious cases, a court may be reluctant to sentence an offender to a community-based program even if the probability of rearrest appears to be low.

## Origins of Community Corrections

Interest in community-based corrections is as old as prisons themselves. Prisons were introduced in the United States in the late 1700s, although the use of physical confinement as a form of punishment had already existed for centuries. Although prisons were initially welcomed as a "cure" for crime, it soon became apparent they could never accomplish this unrealistic goal. As Morris (1974) observed, "prisons have few friends" (p. ix). Almost as soon as the first prisons were completed, reform movements began to call for their improvement or abolition. Dissatisfaction with the ineffectiveness of prisons and their generally inhumane conditions became widespread. During the mid-1800s, prison reformers argued that community settings would be more effective for offender rehabilitation and that the treatment of offenders should be individually designed, an approach that was impossible in the prisons of the 19th century. A community corrections movement began to flourish in the United States during the late 19th century, along with other social reform efforts.

The oldest and most widely used community corrections program is probation. The first use of formal probation in the United States occurred in Boston in the 1840s, when a shoemaker named John Augustus became concerned that drunkards and vagrants were receiving inadequate care and were too often imprisoned inappropriately. He proposed to the court that it release such offenders to his custody, and he would attempt to reform them and help them find employment. Augustus reportedly performed this service for hundreds of people and eventually attracted the attention of other communities and courts. In 1878 Massachusetts became the first state to have paid probation officers, and by 1915, 33 states had passed laws authorizing the use of paid probation officers. Probation was initially far more popular for juvenile offenders, but by the mid-1950s adult probation programs had been established in every state.

## Programs and Services

Community corrections includes a wide range of programs and services to divert prison-bound offenders, control and supervise offenders who have been given community-based sentences, and supervise offenders at the end of their prison terms. Because offenders sentenced to community corrections remain in the community, they can live in their own homes and maintain access to employment opportunities. They must meet regularly with a supervisor, who closely monitors their activities and associations. Frequently, courts impose a number of conditions that offenders must meet to continue in community-based programs. For example, a court may require a convicted drug offender to submit to random drug tests or order a suspected gang member to stay away from other gang members and certain neighborhoods. Offenders may be ordered to maintain employment or engage in a job search or, in the case of a juvenile offender, to attend school regularly. If the offender violates any of these conditions, the court can revoke the community-based sentence and subject the offender to more severe controls or immediate incarceration.

Although they have been granted a community-based sentence rather than imprisonment, offenders in a community corrections program are not "free." Each program model involves various degrees of control on the movements and activities of offenders. The essence of community corrections, however, is that these restrictions do not prevent offenders from realizing the benefits of living in their own homes and communities. Locked detention facilities and jails, even those located in or near residential areas, are not community-based programs. Similarly, boot camps are not considered community corrections programs, although they are often promoted as alternatives to incarceration. If a locked facility or boot camp is operated as a day program, however, and offenders are able to return to their own homes at night, such a program might be considered a community corrections program. As in all criminal justice policy, the use of community corrections is most appropriate when it offers an effective balance between protecting the public and controlling or rehabilitating the offender.

Community corrections programs can be placed on a continuum of severity. At one end of the continuum are the least punitive, least expensive, and most widely used correctional sanctions, such as fines and traditional probation supervision. On the other end of the continuum are more punitive, control-oriented, and costly programs, such as intensive supervision and electronic surveillance. Many of the following community corrections programs are also called "intermediate sanctions," because on a continuum of severity they would fall somewhere between traditional probation and prison.

**Informal Diversion**

Many courts have found that diverting first-time offenders and those who have committed minor crimes from formal court processing can be a cost-effective alternative to formal conviction and sentencing (Baker & Sadd, 1981). In the adult justice system, "pretrial diversion" or "deferred prosecution" programs became popular during the 1980s for their potential to reduce the administrative and financial burdens of prosecution and trial while effectively intervening in relatively minor cases. In such cases, a prosecutor, intake worker, or other screening officer is authorized to handle the case informally before formal charges are filed. In lieu of prosecution, the offender agrees to some type of service or sanction, often a term of community service, restitution, or informal probation. The offender avoids the stigma of a formal trial and possible conviction, and the court benefits by providing some sanction for cases that might otherwise end in dismissal. Diverted or deferred cases also move quickly through the system because they do not involve protracted courtroom procedures.

Informal processing is particularly widespread in the juvenile justice system. In the early 1990s one-half of all delinquency cases referred to juvenile courts across the country were handled informally without the filing of a petition or a formal adjudication hearing (Butts et al., 1993).

**Suspended Sentence**

One of the most basic community corrections programs is the suspended sentence. An offender who is convicted of a relatively minor offense and sentenced to a period of supervision or confinement is granted a suspension of the sentence pending the satisfaction of other conditions. For example, an offender who is convicted of theft and sentenced to six months in jail may be granted a suspended sentence provided that he or she completes the terms of restitution imposed by the court. Suspended sentences, in fact, are often the legal basis for the existence of community corrections programs. Instead of ordering the offender to pay restitution or serve time in jail, the court is actually permitting the offender to earn the right to avoid incarceration.

**Victim–Offender Mediation**

Victim–offender mediation programs are also known as dispute resolution, arbitration, and conciliation programs. The idea behind this program model is to avoid the formal court process by informally mediating the "disputes" between offenders and victims. The aim of victim–offender mediation is to restore the losses incurred by victims and, just as important, to involve offenders in a face-to-face confrontation with the consequences of their behavior.

Technically, the court does not impose a solution in mediated cases. Instead, a mediator assists the involved parties in reaching their own resolution. For instance, under a mediator's supervision, a youth accused of vandalism or theft would engage in a discussion with the victim to arrive at an acceptable method of repairing damages or replacing stolen property. Through the mediation process the youth might agree to repaint a wall that he or she marred with graffiti, for example, or to pay for damages to a car that he or she stole. Programs may also involve "indirect mediation" if offenders and victims do not wish to meet. In these cases the mediator functions as a go-between to arrange a mutually agreeable method of resolution and restitution.

**Restitution**

Both the adult and juvenile justice systems increasingly require offenders to compensate victims for losses resulting from their offenses. The use of restitution has been advocated as a way to move the entire justice system away from retributive justice and toward a restorative justice model. Under the restorative justice concept, the mission of law enforcement, the courts, and corrections is not simply to punish offenders but to restore losses to victims and peace to the community. In this view, one of the basic aims of any corrections program is to hold offenders accountable for their actions.

Restitution programs involve actual cash payments to victims of crime, usually property crime, which accounts for the vast majority of all crimes committed. Payments to victims are sometimes made directly by offenders, or they can be made by the court after the offender has first paid the court. Offenders lacking the financial resources to pay restitution are sometimes provided with work to earn restitution money. Restitution appears to achieve public safety goals as well as rehabilitative goals and is at least as effective as more traditional dispositions such as probation (Galaway & Hudson, 1990).

**Community Service**

Offenders in community service programs are closely supervised as they perform socially useful, unpaid labor: road repair and cleanup, gardening and landscaping of public spaces, working in a local food bank, or any number of other specialized tasks that take advantage of the offender's skills and employment background. Proceeds from community service work are often diverted as restitution payments to victims or are used to pay the costs of the offender's supervision. Unlike victim restitution programs, community service can also be used for cases that do not involve an individual victim (for example, drug possession). Community service programs are proving to be especially popular, as they encourage the community to become more aware and involved with the justice system.

**Traditional Probation**

Traditional probation, the most widely used community corrections program, involves the suspension of a more restrictive sentence for a defined period of supervision in the community. During this period the offender is free to remain in the community, to work, and to attend school. In exchange for this freedom, the offender must agree to specific behavioral conditions through a formal agreement or contract with the court. Typically, probation agreements incorporate conditions meant to control as well as rehabilitate the offender. For example, a contract may require an offender to meet regularly with a probation supervisor and adhere to a strict curfew.

Probation contracts include provisions for the revocation of probation should the offender violate the conditions stipulated in the contract. If probation is revoked, the court reinstates the offender's suspended sentence and incarcerates him or her for the remainder of the sentence. To ensure the offender's understanding of the importance of the probation contract, some jurisdictions use "shock probation" programs in which offenders begin their sentences with a brief period of incarceration before being released to community supervision.

**Intensive Probation**

Intensive probation is similar to traditional probation but involves closer supervision and a greater degree of control over the offender's behavior. Offenders must agree to more rigorous supervision contracts and meet with their probation worker several times a week or, in some cases, several times a day. Probation supervisors have much smaller caseloads than their counterparts in traditional probation programs. One survey of probation programs found that the average intensive probation caseload was 22 clients per worker, whereas workers in a traditional probation program supervised an average of 120 offenders (Byrne, Lurigio, & Baird, 1989).

Although many believe that intensive supervision is what all probation programs should provide, public agencies do not always have the funds to deliver on such a promise. Most jurisdictions use intensive probation only for low-risk offenders who would otherwise be incarcerated and for offenders with special needs or risk factors such as chronic drug abuse. Intensive probation programs proliferated in the United States during the 1980s, when many state and local governments simultaneously faced growing correctional caseloads and contracting budgets that made incarceration an avenue of last resort. In response, there was an increased willingness to experiment with supervising larger numbers of offenders in the community. Intensive probation programs are currently the most widely used community corrections program after traditional probation (U.S. General Accounting Office, 1990).

**House Arrest and Electronic Surveillance**

Electronic monitoring or in-home surveillance is an increasingly popular community corrections program, as it offers a high degree of offender control yet avoids most of the costs of confinement. Electronic monitoring is primarily a punishment program in which surveillance and control are the primary objectives. An offender sentenced to a period of electronic monitoring is confined to the home, and electronic equipment is used to enforce this order. In many such programs the offender wears a nonremovable wrist or ankle bracelet that sends a signal confirming the offender's presence via a customized phone whenever the probation officer places a call to the offender's home. Other programs use equipment that can detect whether the offender is within a prescribed distance of a specialized phone. If the offender attempts to leave the defined area, the phone automatically places a warning call to the probation office. Any violation of these conditions constitutes an infraction of the probation contract and can result in the offender's incarceration.

These programs are sometimes called "house arrest plus" because the offender is usually subjected to regular face-to-face or telephone contact with probation officers as well as electronic surveillance (Dilulio, 1989). Although offenders sentenced to electronic monitoring have more freedom than they would in prison, a period of house arrest and intensive probation supervision can often be more onerous.

## Growth of Community-Based Corrections

During the 1980s and early 1990s, many state and local policymakers began to reconsider the importance of community corrections. Several factors combined to make the limited choice of incarceration versus traditional probation appear insufficient: a growing prison population, rapidly increasing costs of building and operating prisons, a greater need for effective supervision of more serious offenders, high rates of recidivism for offenders placed on traditional probation, and increased public demand for accountability from law enforcement and the courts.

The use of community corrections programs increased dramatically during the 1980s and early 1990s. The Bureau of Justice Statistics reported that the number of adults supervised by state or federal probation agencies increased 126 percent between 1980 and 1989 (Greenfield, 1992). Of the 4.3 million adults under correctional supervision in 1990, 74 percent were being supervised in the community; 61 percent were under some form of probation (Jankowski, 1991).

The increased use of community corrections, however, did not reduce the growth of the U.S. prison population. The number of state and federal prisoners grew 168 percent between 1980 and 1992, from 329,821 to 883,593 (Gilliard, 1993). From the 1930s through the 1970s, the per capita rate of state and federal prisoners remained relatively constant at between 100 and 150 prisoners per 100,000 U.S. residents (Greenfield, 1992). Between 1980 and 1992, the U.S. imprisonment rate grew 137 percent, from 139 to 329 prisoners per 100,000 residents (Gilliard, 1993). Throughout the 1980s and early 1990s, the rate of imprisonment in the United States set a new record every year. By the early 1990s the United States had earned the dubious distinction of having the highest per capita imprisonment rate in the world, surpassing the previous leaders, the former Soviet Union and South Africa.

## Effectiveness of Community-Based Corrections

From the beginning of the community corrections movement, many people were skeptical about the effectiveness of any criminal justice program that did not rely on incarceration. However, quality evaluations of correctional effectiveness were rare until the 1980s. Lipton, Martinson, and Wilks (1975) surveyed much of the existing research evidence on correctional effectiveness. The authors studied more than 200 separate evaluations of correctional treatment programs and found the results less than impressive. The news media summarized their conclusions as "nothing works." Although the phrase was greatly misleading, it influenced numerous policymakers.

### Current Studies

More recent studies have found evidence that community corrections programs such as intensive probation, restitution, and electronic monitoring can be effective for some offenders (Andrews et al., 1990; Barton & Butts, 1990; Gendreau & Ross, 1987; Greenwood & Zimring, 1985; McCarthy, 1987; Petersilia, 1987). No single program model, however, is effective in every case and every jurisdiction. The effectiveness of a corrections program is closely related to its initial conceptualization, the extent of its political support, and the skill with which it is implemented (Petersilia, 1990a). The poor reputation of community-based corrections often is the result of inadequate funding and poor implementation. The caseloads of probation officers, for example, have increased to impossible levels in many large cities. In 1990 one-half of all probationers in Los Angeles County were being supervised by a probation officer with a caseload of at least 1,000 other offenders (McShane & Krause, 1993).

### Issues in Evaluations

Some of the continuing political problems with community corrections may result from the fact that such programs are often described and evaluated as alternatives to incarceration. Researchers typically evaluate community corrections programs by comparing their effects on recidivism with those of incarceration. In reality, however, community corrections programs often serve as an alternative to doing nothing. Community corrections are often used for offenders charged with misdemeanors, minor drug offenses, lesser property crimes, and other offenses that do not usually result in incarceration.

Conversely, community corrections programs are also criticized for contributing to a problem known as "net widening"—the tendency of the justice system to use alternative programs as supplements to rather than substitutes for incarceration (for example, Ezell, 1989). Many of the benefits of community corrections programs can be reaped only if such programs draw their clientele from the offender population most likely to be incarcerated. When they draw instead from those likely to be outside the "net" of the corrections system (that is, offenders not likely to be incarcerated), the existence of community corrections programs does nothing to reduce, and may even increase, the scope and costs of the justice system.

## PUBLIC PERCEPTIONS

The criminal justice system receives a great deal of media attention, yet it is often difficult for the public to discern the various levels of punishment and control provided by correctional programs. In popular discourse, anything less than incarceration is dismissed as a "slap on the wrist," suggesting that confinement is the only just response to crime. Offenders sentenced to community-based corrections, however, can receive highly punitive dispositions, as they are often subject to more than one sanction. An offender may be ordered to pay fines and court costs in addition to victim restitution; he or she may also be ordered to perform several weeks or months of community service work and to submit to long periods of probation supervision. In some states the courts impose "combined sanctions" that involve a relatively brief period of incarceration followed by an extended term of probation, community service, or other community-based sanctions. Some researchers have found that serious and repeat offenders may actually prefer a short stay in prison to an extended sentence of intensive probation (Petersilia, 1990b).

### Public Support

Public support for community corrections often surprises policymakers who assume that their constituents favor high rates of imprisonment and would disapprove of sentencing offenders in the community. However, researchers have found that the public supports the use of community corrections provided that the programs are operated safely, incorporate some elements of punishment (for example, restrictions on freedom of movement, unpaid labor, or victim restitution), encourage offenders to develop useful skills and new ways of controlling their behavior, and offer treatment to offenders who need it (for example, drug abusers).

Gottfredson and Taylor (1984) found that state legislators in Maryland believed that the public wanted the predominant response to crime to involve state-operated prisons. When surveyed, however, a sample of Maryland residents actually supported the use of community-based probation and parole. Although state lawmakers predicted that nearly two-thirds of their constituents would agree to ending parole, only 29 percent actually did. The legislators also predicted that less than 40 percent of the public would favor the use of community rehabilitation centers, whereas 73 percent indicated such support in the survey.

### Critical Factors

Bennett (1991) also found high levels of public support for community corrections. The critical factor in the public's support for community-based corrections seemed to be awareness of the programs as well as confidence that the programs would be well managed and would exercise close control of offenders. Bennett's study asked each respondent to indicate whether prison was the most appropriate response to a series of crimes. Initially, prison was the preferred response of 63 percent of respondents. After being introduced to the idea of community corrections and listening to a description of restitution and intensive supervision programs, however, only 27 percent of the respondents preferred prison. Even for cases involving serious felonies, most respondents supported community-based corrections. Bennett concluded that the public does not favor imprisonment for its own sake, but rather expects a corrections system that is accountable and demonstrates an active concern for public safety. Thus, the public's demand for prisons may be due more to frustration with the management of the criminal justice system than to an emotional desire for vengeance and retribution.

## CONCLUSION

The use of community corrections programs is critical to the effectiveness and fiscal stability of the criminal justice system. Without access to a full range of community-based alternatives, the corrections system would be able to offer only incarceration as a serious sanction for convicted offenders and adjudicated delinquents. From a public safety perspective, the vast majority of offenders do not require incarceration. Community corrections are absolutely necessary for the courts to provide control, supervision, and treatment for many offenders. If community corrections programs are adequately funded and competently managed, effective supervision of even greater numbers of offenders might be possible. Society would be well served by any reductions in imprisonment made possible by the judicious use of community corrections programs.

## REFERENCES


Andrews, D. A., Zinger, I., Hoge, R. D., Bonta, J., Gendreau, P., & Cullen, F. T. (1990). Does correctional treatment work? A clinically relevant and psychologically informed meta-analysis. *Criminology, 28*, 369–404.

Baker, S. H., & Sadd, S. (1981). *Diversion of felony arrests: An experiment in pretrial diversion*. Washington, DC: U.S. Government Printing Office.

Barton, W. H., & Butts, J. A. (1990). Viable options: Intensive supervision programs for juvenile delinquents. *Crime & Delinquency, 36*, 238–256.

Bennett, L. (1991). The public wants accountability. *Corrections Today, 53,* 92, 94–95.

Butts, J. A., Snyder, H. N., Finnegan, T. A., Aughenbaugh, A. L., Tierney, N., Sullivan, D. P., Poole, R. S., Sickmund, M., & Poe, E. (1993). *Juvenile Court Statistics 1991*. Washington, DC: U.S. Department of Justice, Office of Juvenile Justice and Delinquency Prevention.

Byrne, J., Lurigio, A., & Baird, C. (1989). The effectiveness of the new intensive supervision programs. *Research in Corrections, 2,* 1–48.

DiIulio, J. J., Jr. (1989). Punishing smarter: Penal reforms for the 1990s. *Brookings Review, 7,* 3–12.

Ezell, M. (1989). Juvenile arbitration: Net widening and other unintended consequences. *Journal of Research in Crime and Delinquency, 26,* 358–377.

Galaway, B., & Hudson, J. (1990). *Criminal justice, restitution, and reconciliation*. Monsey, NY: Criminal Justice Press.

Gendreau, P., & Ross, R. R. (1987). Revivification of rehabilitation: Evidence from the 1980s. *Justice Quarterly, 4,* 349–407.

Gilliard, D. K. (1993). *Prisoners in 1992*. Washington, DC: U.S. Department of Justice, Bureau of Justice Statistics.

Gottfredson, S., & Taylor, R. (1984). Public policy and prison population: Measuring opinions about reform. *Judicature, 68,* 190–201.

Greenfield, L. A. (1992). *Prisons and prisoners in the United States.* Washington, DC: U.S. Department of Justice, Bureau of Justice Statistics.

Greenwood, P., & Zimring, F. (1985). *One more chance: The pursuit of promising intervention strategies for chronic juvenile offenders* (R-3214-OJJDP). Santa Monica, CA: Rand.

Jankowski, L. (1991). *Probation and parole 1990*. Washington, DC: U.S. Department of Justice, Bureau of Justice Statistics.

Lipton, D., Martinson, R., & Wilks, J. (1975). *The effectiveness of correctional treatment: A survey of treatment evaluation studies.* New York: Praeger.

McCarthy, B. R. (1987). *Intermediate punishments: Intensive supervision, home confinement and electronic surveillance.* Monsey, NY: Criminal Justice Press.

McShane, M. D., & Krause, W. (1993). *Community corrections*. New York: Macmillan.

Morris, N. (1974). *The future of imprisonment.* Chicago: University of Chicago Press.

Petersilia, J. (1987). *Expanding options for criminal sentencing* (R-3544-EMC). Santa Monica, CA: Rand.

Petersilia, J. (1990a). Conditions that permit intensive supervision programs to survive. *Crime and Delinquency, 36,* 126–145.

Petersilia, J. (1990b). When probation becomes more dreaded than prison. *Federal Probation, 54,* 23–27.

U.S. General Accounting Office. (1990). *International sanctions: Their impacts on prison crowding, costs, and recidivism are still unclear.* Washington, DC: U.S. Government Printing Office.

## Further Reading

Cromwell, P. F., & Killinger, G. G. (1994). *Community-based corrections: Probation, parole, and intermediate sanctions* (3rd ed.). St. Paul, MN: West.

Duffee, D., & McGarrell, E. (1990). *Community corrections: A community field approach.* Cincinnati: Anderson.

McCarthy, B. R., & McCarthy, B. J., Jr. (1991). *Community-based corrections* (2nd ed.). Belmont, CA: Wadsworth.

**Jeffrey A. Butts, PhD,** is senior research associate, National Center for Juvenile Justice, 710 Fifth Avenue, Pittsburgh, PA 15219.

**For further information see**

Adult Corrections; Conflict Resolution; Criminal Behavior Overview; Deinstitutionalization; Juvenile and Family Courts; Legal Issues: Low-Income and Dependent People; Peace and Social Justice; Police Social Work; Probation and Parole; Rehabilitation of Criminal Offenders; Social Planning; Substance Abuse: Legal Issues; Victim Services and Victim/Witness Assistance Programs.

**Key Words**

community-based corrections
criminal justice
incarceration
probation

# Community Development

**W. David Harrison**

The term "community development" has many different meanings, but all revolve around the notion of taking planned action to address the common concerns of people who share a geographic locality, cultural and philosophical solidarity, or essential social and economic relations. Development involves growth, maturation, and strengthening. It also implies a movement from simpler to more complex forms of organization. Deliberate community development efforts aim to improve people's lives by improving important aspects of the life that they have in common. The aims of development are to enhance the effective structure and functioning of social networks, new technologies, and the economic arrangements that are important to identified communities.

Community development practice often begins with helping communities realize that they can plan to make things better. The next step, after this realization, involves negotiating a joint vision about preferred outcomes and methods of reaching them. Thus, community development practice is the process of working with communities to help them recognize how they can improve community life and welfare both in the present and in the future. It is axiomatic in social work that a well-developed community is a desirable state of affairs and that community development is a desirable activity.

Community development practice involves planned change. For social workers, planned change focuses not only on the use of professional expertise to enhance the interwoven fabric of social life but on enhancing the abilities (capacity building) of community members and including these people as participants in community development activities. Thus, community development emphasizes both the achievement of specific goals and the development of less tangible qualitative aspects of social life in a community, such as the improvement of the capabilities—especially the leadership capabilities—of the residents.

## Different Perspectives on Community Development

### Geographic Locality

To understand community development, it is important to consider the component terms, "community" and "development." Conventionally, community has implied a definable geographic area. Thus, the fundamental idea of a locality, in the sense of physical proximity, is important in much community development thinking and activity. Barker's (1991) definition reflects the locality approach. It refers to community development as "efforts made by professionals and community residents to enhance the social bonds among members of the community, motivate the citizens for self-help, develop responsible local leadership, and create or revitalize local institutions" (p. 43). People's lives are shaped through local social interactions. This traditional cornerstone of sociology has become a natural component of social work practice.

### Social Work Views

From a social work perspective, community development advances people's well-being through enhancing the social environment they share. Social workers and other professionals have always done much of their work on an interpersonal basis to address shared local concerns for promoting people's well-being (Lappin, 1985). Social workers have attempted to maintain imperiled community bonds or to build new ones (Harrison, 1991). They also have negotiated ways to understand the common bonds of social life while maintaining divergent interests.

One of the most important sociological ideas about community came from the sociological perspective of functionalism (not to be confused with the functional approach to social work practice). This outlook stems from the idea that to maintain itself, a society must fulfill certain social functions, such as nurturance of the young and the distribution of food and other essential resources. Functionalism regards social structures (definable social entities that exist in relationship to other structures) and social functions (the roles, purposes, and uses of the entities) in a given social system as inextricably intertwined. It is often taken for granted that the social institution of the community, like the social institution of the family, provides many of these essential structures. However, in contemporary life many of these functions are no longer fulfilled locally through enduring roles that include a common identity and relationship. Thus, modern-day community development is often concerned with ensuring the provision of these functions and maintaining their quality. Social work has adopted many of the ideas of functionalism, especially through its applications of systems theory (for example, Compton & Galaway, 1989).

Today's community structures range from voluntary associations of individuals who are concerned about specific issues, such as Neighborhood Watch groups to prevent crime, to highly bureaucratized structures, such as school boards and child protection agencies. These structures fulfill a variety of functions, some that are obvious and others that can be understood only after intensive systematic analysis. For example, an industrial development board may encourage employers to locate their businesses in a certain area, thus serving an obvious economic function; however, it may be less apparent that the same board serves environmental protection functions through its latent tax and zoning practices. Social workers must be able to use the logic of research, the observations of community members, and their own experiential knowledge to ascertain the relationships between elements of community systems.

### Cultural Views

An anthropological understanding of the term community is also important to practitioners. *Culture*, the collective conventions and practices that describe a way of life, and *ethnicity*, the groupings of people according to these shared practices, are vitally important dimensions of community. Although culture and ethnicity are characteristic of all human civilizations, they are especially important in contemporary community development efforts around the world.

Modern communications, as well as migrations for economic and political reasons, appears to be hastening the disintegration of communities in many parts of the world. Communities experiencing the disruption of conventional community relations may respond by trying to reinforce or impose the maintenance of cultural and ethnic practices. French authorities, for instance, have tried to ban the use of common English words to describe new technology. Still, the traditional ethnic and cultural bases of common self-interest, grounded in geographic proximity, may become less important. Emerging forms of community are based on a common consciousness of interaction or a shared situation and new, drastically enhanced forms of communication.

In short, social workers recognize that community involves a sense of well-being and integration that comes from belonging to a functional social group. The importance of community life to the well-being of most people cannot be overstated. This fundamental aspect of the relationship of the individual and the community holds tremendous motivational power that can be directed toward community development.

## Historical Themes

### Loss of Community

The question of whether there is a loss of community ties and a consequent need to develop new communities is not new. It goes back at least to the industrialization of Europe, when serious concerns were expressed about whether the profound shift from agrarian and local social organization to urban industrial forms was weakening essential community bonds (Harrison, 1991). In the United States, this shift paralleled the philosophy of individualism, which remains so fundamental as to be a tacit assumption in most social discourse.

Nearly a century ago, in *Community and Society,* the German social philosopher Ferdinand Tönnies (1887/1957) clarified two useful concepts to understanding changes in community life: *gemeinschaft,* an outlook characterized by local, communal, intimate relations between people, and *gesellschaft,* societal, self-interested, surface-level relations without a common sense of emotional partnership. Both concepts describe phenomena that are identified today. Therefore, one way to examine the question of whether there is a loss of community is to ask to what degree has there been a movement from gemeinschaft to gesellschaft.

Wirth's (1938) article "Urbanism as a Way of Life" was another significant work in that it framed most of today's questions about the nature of social change in communities. Evidence for and against the decline of communities is contradictory because there are so many different types of communities with different dynamics.

### U.S. Communitarian Experiments

Although the ideology of individualism is widely accepted as a central motif in U.S. history, this country has also had a history of organized community development. Often the community projects have been referred to as communitarian experiments, whether they have involved the religious and secular communes of the 19th and 20th centuries or the attempts to develop new towns and "enterprise zones" in impoverished areas in recent years. For social work, notable historical themes in community development are found in the history of the settlement houses that served immigrant communities from the 1800s to well into the 1900s. Many elements of contemporary community development practice were apparent in these institutions. These settlements, as precursors of today's community development activities, focused largely on people with common ethnic and geographic bonds. After the turn of the century, however, social reforms and Progressive efforts became much more prominent in the discourse of the rapidly professionalizing fields of social work and public health.

### Rise of Professionalism

Community organizing flourished again after World War I as the practice of social work professionalized and legislation institutionalized social services as a governmental function (Austin & Betten, 1990). Social agencies and professional practice became more bureaucratic. By the 1960s, competing professional ideologies and technologies led to clashes in perspective between "professional experts," who were interested in psychosocial and behavioral change and had specific conceptions of community well-being, and community members, who were interested in self-determination and the provision of concrete resources (for example, welfare rights). The urban disturbances of the 1960s and an increasing sense of Black Community that was tied to a shared perception that the community's development was tied to Black Power forced a reexamination of the relationship between liberal community development practitioners and members of communities.

### International "Decolonizing Efforts"

Social work is but one of several fields involved in community development. Particularly important to community development have been educational efforts, economic development efforts, and public health efforts. Community development can be thought of as a way to improve national strength and well-being. Thus, in many areas around the world, political and community development efforts are and have been inseparable.

After World War II, the attempt to make orderly transitions from exploitive colonial relations between countries to relations between independent nations caused a wave of community development initiatives by Western countries (United Nations, 1955). International efforts to decolonize the "developing" world began with experts attempting to organize indigenous people, an approach that has rarely led to efficient or sustained development. As local people began to insist on assuming control over their own collective destiny, community development efforts tended to focus on developing an infrastructure to provide administrative and economic justice. It is particularly important to recognize that in many parts of the world, women have been first excluded from development efforts, then marginally included, and in some cases eventually recognized as central members of the communities of which men have so often been the formal leaders. The marginal-inclusion phase has been referred to in terms of the "pseudo-feminist myth" of integrating women into development (Anand, 1984).

### From External Expertise to Local Control

The pattern of shifting from external expertise to local control can be seen in many well-intentioned, but externally initiated, community development projects of the past. A dramatic example is the changes in the efforts of some Native American tribes to develop as communities. Some tribes have developed the ability to go beyond the externally generated, often patronizing approaches to community development under the powerful influence of the Bureau of Indian Affairs (Cornell, 1988). From the implementation of special Native American child welfare laws at the local level to the reaping of economic profits from casino gambling, these projects seek to make use of the unique status of collective, indigenous residential communities with deeply rooted values and social structures.

A similar process of moving toward increased community self-determination and participation appears to be occurring now as Western social workers and other professionals try to facilitate community development in former Soviet Bloc countries. The aim of these initiatives is to provide for the well-being of people whose way of life had been based on central directives and mass bureaucracies rather than on locally responsive services and community awareness. Many Eastern European communities are eager for Western social technology and are attempting to learn Western models of delivering social services and community development. It appears likely that Eastern European communities will benefit by learning models of community development that stress local control and participation. In the coming years, it will be a matter of extraordinary practical and theoretical interest to determine the extent to which the Western community development influence has been a beneficial force.

## Contemporary Social Context

The most fundamental question about community development today is whether there has been a loss of community in recent years. Western societies clearly have become more complex and more specialization of functions has occurred. Thus, the family and the community no longer fulfill many of the functions they once did. The question about the loss of community applies not only to Western societies but to the former Communist countries and to other parts of the world as well.

Many social phenomena have led to the widespread concern about the loss of community. People are distressed about the disintegration of neighborhoods, the rising crime rate, the geographic dispersion of families, and the extraordinary migration and mobility of members of most social classes and ethnic groups. Some experts (for example, Etzioni, 1993) believe that drug use has so altered social relations that community development is all but impossible in some localities, whereas others contend that it is only through community development work that the demand for drugs will be stemmed. Even the tendencies toward chaos in some parts of post-Communist Eastern Europe and Eurasia and toward authoritarian or fundamentalist regimes in other areas can be interpreted in terms of contemporary fears about the breakdown of community. New forms of social organization to develop community are needed and may evolve in those regions.

## Contemporary Communitarian and Postmodernist Perspectives

### Communitarian Movement

A new version of the communitarian commitment has recently emerged. Communitarianism has assumed the proportions of a movement for community development, although it tends to focus more on the redevelopment of social relations in economically developed areas than on the development of poor localities. The movement is the product of the ideas of academics, professionals, and members of the public who are concerned about the weakening of community as a fundamental characteristic of American society.

One of the most interesting aspects of contemporary communitarian thinking is its appeal to people of diverse political orientations. For example, the conservative Senator Sam Nunn (D-GA) and the liberal Senator Barbara A. Mikulski (D-MD), a social worker, were both strong advocates for the National and Community Service Act of 1990. Although the act provides funds to states, tribes, and educational institutions to improve communities at the local level, its implicit goal is to strengthen the nation. In addition, although it is not limited to young people, the act is intended both to foster a long-term commitment to a collective, community spirit among the young and to benefit them directly through opportunities for occupational and personal improvement by providing community-based services to address serious unmet human needs, including many that are attributable to poverty. It is too early to evaluate the effects of this legislation. However, the alleviation of poverty does not seem to be the criterion of primary interest. Instead, the specific number of participants and projects engaged, as well as the qualitative considerations of "whether the programs do, in fact, foster a community service ethic" (Byron, 1992, p. 7) appear to be the most important criteria. In keeping with the impulse that led to the National and Community Service Act, the 1992 Democratic national ticket embraced many communitarian ideals in its campaign. Community service is being realized as a matter of long-term national interest as it becomes institutionalized as a method of paying back to the government some of the costs of higher education. The extraordinary success of conservative Republican candidates in the 1994 elections produced a significant change in governmental ideology that may have dramatic effects on the focus and the forms of community development. However, because of the paradoxical usage by politicians of such terms as community empowerment, self-determination, and revitalization, the specific implications of the 1992 and 1994 elections for community development are debatable.

Going beyond social analysis and longing for a revitalization of earlier forms of community, Bellah, Madsen, Sullivan, and Tipton (1985), Etzioni (1993), and Taylor (1992) have combined practical concerns and a moral dimension. They advocate a community development movement that would involve the fundamental reorientation of many social practices and institutions to advance the common good. Many different principles are involved in contemporary communitarian thinking and related proposals for community development. Most of the implications for community development stem from the principle that "Each member of the community owes something to all the rest, and the community owes something to each of its members. Justice requires responsible individuals in a responsive community" (Etzioni, 1993, p. 263).

Communitarians have developed a number of specific ideas for putting principles into practice. Many ideas concern social policies and how they reflect the rights and responsibilities of individuals in relation to the communities in which individuals reside. They often involve how people would best provide for the care and nurture of one another, both in periods of natural dependence (such as childhood and old age) and in situations that require extraordinary care (for example, severe and persistent mental illness). Although these ideas have been widely discussed, it is unclear whether communitarian ideas can compete with the ethics of individualism as a basis for either the behavior of individuals or for the development of social policies.

**Postmodernism**

Another influence on community development thinking has been the notion of postmodernism. This collection of ideas is based on the belief that new forms of communication and social organization are replacing the familiar modern (in the sense of scientific, rational, analytic) ones. Postmodernists assert that a new interpretive consciousness is evolving to deal with the effects of modernism and its technologies on social relations and identity (Gergen, 1991). Drastically innovative technologies make the social relations that were formerly dependent on local proximity less and less central to life's experience and the interdependence that community implies. For example, telephones are widely used to maintain emotional bonds, although the nature of the relationship is altered in the process.

Postmodernism is difficult to define because it is based on the belief that life is different because the social and technological environments are changing rapidly, that the nature of the bonds between people and how people perceive reality have changed drastically and rapidly. The shape of the changes is not unified or clear, except that there is a tendency to consider the "death" of many modern social institutions, such as community life as it has evolved in our cultural consciousness, and how we live as a result. Community development activities increasingly will take the form of addressing new ways to form and carry out community functions in the context of the many social and technical changes that are occurring.

**Relevance for Social Work**

Social workers often function to supplement the caring functions of communities. However, a significant professional issue is whether social workers simultaneously function to develop communities based on care and contribute to the decline of communities by providing impersonal services such as case management. Similarly, the question of whether social workers function best as individual professionals, especially in therapeutic and protective roles, or as agents of community development is hard to resolve, because few would deny the need for both functions but there is seldom agreement on the best ways to provide the functions.

This discussion has progressed further in Great Britain than in the United States. There has been a vigorous debate over the merits of "community social work" as a form of practice that integrates both individual care services and community developmental functions (Harrison & Hoshino, 1984; Smale, Tuson, Cooper, Wardle, & Crosbie, 1988). Among the most interesting dimensions of this discussion of social work's community development functions have been those concerning "patches," or geographic, community areas, in which social workers are partners with others in performing a variety of care-organizing, developmental, and social change work (see, for example, Hadley, Dale, & Sills, 1984). Tasker (1988), Smale and Bennett (1989), and Darvill and Smale (1990) presented excellent examples of the integration of community development work and the delivery of specific social services.

## Emerging Forms of Community

Earlier community development themes are evident in the form of new collective identities and the related implementation of functional relations in community groups. For example, in many regards there are "gay communities" and "military communities" that have discernible structures and functions and that share many cultural and psychological characteristics, if not always the locality that has traditionally been associated with community life.

Similar developments have occurred with regard to organizations and informal groups of people who seek to support one another. People may come together because of ethnicity, illness, bereavement, or other life situations. These quasi-communities are based less on locality than on a shared awareness of a common life situation and the related provision of mutual support and often advocacy for the group. Whether these are communities or will become so is unclear, although they certainly fulfill certain social functions that have traditionally been located in the community.

There are examples, however, of community development activities of an altered form. Consider the development of self-help projects, such as "buddy" programs, that began in the mid-1980s to care for people with AIDS (Kayal, 1993; Schmalz, 1993). These projects, which contributed significantly to the movement to advocate for better services and more specific rights, include wide-area telephone and computer networks that allow support and other functions. They show that community development activities in the realm of social care are being carried out not just where there is a geographic community, but where there is a more broadly defined community with shared stakes in its relations with other social institutions. Perhaps the most dramatic example has been the development of "deafness as culture" (Dolnick, 1993), which has little to do with destigmatizing people who are deaf and much to do with developing a comprehensive community of socioeconomic and cultural intimacy. The increasing flexibility of social work roles has, in many cases, led to new ways that professionals have worked to develop these newly defined community bonds, often moving from the "case" to a more collective definition of the situation as one that might be developed into a community. However, the pace of development from within these newly defined cultural communities challenges social work not to perpetuate outdated, externally imposed assumptions about dependence, community development, and disability.

## Characteristics of Community Development Practice

Because it varies so widely, community development practice is best understood in terms of flexible applications of general planned-change models. Community development practice has focused largely on the goal of citizen participation. Thus, enhancing the functioning of communities, rather than the reform of major social structures, is the central principle of practice. The practical activity involves developing a representation of the community situation as perceived by the members of the community, articulating goals and actions to achieve the goals, and consolidating the skills and capacities that have evolved. The practitioner must be able to function with the tension generated by working toward these general a priori goals while emphasizing self-determination. The skills required are largely motivational and organizational, mobilizing and enabling people to make choices about whether and how they want to work to enhance community functioning. Frequently this process is referred to as empowerment (see, for example, Darvill & Smale, 1990; Rubin & Rubin, 1986).

Community development work involves finding common goals in the community. Goals often emerge as alternatives to an unsatisfactory state of affairs. Frequently, the process of finding common beliefs and goals begins from the auspices of an existing agency or program that is familiar in the community. As it evolves, the dilemma of the worker being external to the community often dissipates. Organization and action to achieve goals may involve advocacy and political work, and thus the early focus of community development work is frequently on how community members perceive the functioning of the agency from which the worker operates. Often these relations have to do with social services, particularly those that involve the care and well-being of the very young and the aged or that involve health or social protection. This focus may lead to a concern for the relations between agencies and other community structures and eventually move to more general or diverse community concerns.

Community development work almost always involves organizations, and relates especially to helping community members develop new ways to keep organizations functional (Selsky, 1991). Examples include using research as a tool to advocate for community goals (Graham & Jones, 1992), developing and maintaining leadership structures and community representation on decision-making boards, and hiring specialists to achieve specific goals, such as marketing the community for potential economic development. Often, community development expertise is required to take advantage of opportunities that have been made available through laws and policies but that are highly technical and perhaps inaccessible.

One such opportunity was the Community Reinvestment Act of 1977 (CRA), which sought to eliminate racial and economic discrimination in banks' lending decisions. In reviewing the act, the U.S. Senate Committee on Banking, Housing, and Urban Affairs (1992) concluded that community organizations had been "central to the success of CRA" (p. 59) and that a much more active approach to community engagement was required if CRA was to fulfill its promise. The committee report emphasized community development goals and specified a number of criteria to be used to evaluate banks. The criteria explicitly included requirements that financial institutions demonstrate how their efforts contribute to community-based development initiatives. The technical nature of the subject made it essential that specialists and community members work together.

## Conclusion

Although the breadth and inherent vagueness of community development as an entity have been noted for some time (Khinduka, 1987), interest in the topic has been accelerating. This increased interest may reflect a cycle of concern for community-level social organization that is played out in the frame of economic uncertainty, persistent ethnic segregation, increasingly divergent senses of the common good, and the new communitarian and postmodern sensibilities, as well as the tendency to develop new forms of quasi-community social relations made possible by technological advances. Marris (1987) framed these uncertainties by stating that deliberate community development initiatives are best understood as efforts to make sense of the large-scale social changes that are occurring. Thus, the ideas of community and community development can be understood most fundamentally in terms of the constructions of social reality that they represent and the practical benefits that can be made of them.

## References

Anand, A. (1984). Rethinking women and development. In ISIS Women's International Information & Communication Service, *Women in development* (pp. 5–9). Philadelphia: New Society Publishers.

Austin, M. J., & Betten, N. (1990) The roots of community organizing: An introduction. In N. Betten & M. J. Austin (Eds.), *The roots of community organizing, 1917–1939* (pp. 3–31). Philadelphia: Temple University Press.

Barker, R. L. (1991). *The social work dictionary* (2nd ed.). Silver Spring, MD: NASW Press.

Bellah, R. N., Madsen, R., Sullivan, W. M., & Tipton, S. M. (1985). *Habits of the heart: Individualism and commitment in American life*. Berkeley: University of California Press.

Byron, W. J. (1992). Renewing community: When Congress does it right. *Commonweal*, 119(8), 6–9.

Community Reinvestment Act of 1977. P.L. 95-128, 91 Stat. 1147.

Compton, B. R., & Galaway, B. (1989). *Social work processes* (4th ed.). Belmont, CA: Wadsworth.

Cornell, S. (1988). *The return of the native: American Indian political resurgence.* New York: Oxford University Press.

Darvill, G., & Smale, G. (1990). *Pictures of practice: Vol. 2. Partners in empowerment: Networks of innovation in social work*. London: National Institute for Social Work.

Dolnick, E. (1993). Deafness as culture. *Atlantic, 272*(3), 37–53.

Etzioni, A. (1993). *The spirit of community: Rights, responsibilities, and the communitarian agenda*. New York: Crown.

Gergen, K. J. (1991). *The saturated self: Dilemmas of identity in contemporary life.* New York: Basic Books.

Graham, H., & Jones, J. (1992). Community development and research. *Community Development Journal, 27,* 235–241.

Hadley, R., Dale, P., & Sills, P. (1984). *Decentralising social services*. London: Bedford Square Press.

Harrison, W. D. (1991). *Seeking common ground: A theory of social work in social care*. Aldershot, England: Avebury.

Harrison, W. D., & Hoshino, G. (1984). Britain's Barclay Report: Lessons for the United States. *Social Work, 29,* 213–218.

Kayal, P. M. (1993). *Bearing witness: Gay Men's Health Crisis and the politics of AIDS.* Boulder, CO: Westview.

Khinduka, S. K. (1987). Community development: Potentials and limitations. In F. M. Cox, J. L. Erlich, J. Rothman, & J. E. Tropman (Eds.), *Strategies of community organization: Macro practice* (pp. 353–362). Itasca, IL: F. E. Peacock.

Lappin, B. (1985). Community development: Beginnings in social work enabling. In S. H. Taylor & R. W. Roberts (Eds.), *Theory and practice of community social work* (pp. 59–94). New York: Columbia University Press.

Marris, P. (1987). *Meaning and action: Community planning and conceptions of change*. London: Routledge & Kegan Paul.

National and Community Service Act of 1990. P.L. 101-610, 104 Stat. 312.

Rubin, H. J., & Rubin, I. (1986). *Community organizing and development*. Columbus, OH: Bobbs-Merrill.

Schmalz, J. (1993, November 28). Whatever happened to AIDS? *New York Times Magazine,* pp. 56–61, 81, 85–86.

Selsky, J. W. (1991). Lessons in community development: An activist approach to stimulating interorganizational collaboration. *Journal of Applied Behavioral Science, 27,* 91–115.

Smale, G., & Bennett, W. (1989). *Pictures of practice: Volume 1. Community social work in Scotland*. London: National Institute for Social Work.

Smale, G., Tuson, G., Cooper, M., Wardle, M., & Crosbie, D. (1988). *Community social work: A paradigm for change.* London: National Institute for Social Work.

Tasker, L. (1988). Community work and community social work. *Community Development Journal, 23,* 100–106.

Taylor, C. (1992). *The ethics of authenticity*. Cambridge, MA: Harvard University Press.

Tönnies, F. (1957). *Community and society (gemeinschaft und gesellschaft)* (C. P. Loomis, Trans.). East Lansing: Michigan State University Press. (Original work published 1887)

United Nations. (1955). *Social progress through community development.* New York: Author.

U.S. Senate Committee on Banking, Housing, and Urban Affairs. (1992). *Report on the status of the Community Reinvestment Act* (S. Prt. 102–121, Vol. 1). Washington, DC: U.S. Government Printing Office.

Wirth, L. (1938). Urbanism as a way of life. *American Journal of Sociology, 44,* 1–24.

## Further Reading

Bulmer, M. (1987). *The social basis of community care.* London: Allen & Unwin.

Dalley, G. (1988). *Ideologies of caring: Rethinking community and collectivism.* London: Macmillan Education.

Fisher, R., & King, J. (Eds.). (1993). *Mobilizing the community: Local politics in the era of the global city.* Newbury Park, CA: Sage Publications.

Friere, P. (1984). *Pedagogy of the oppressed.* New York: Continuum.

Hatry, H. P. (1991). *Excellence in managing: Practical experiences from community development agencies.* Washington, DC: Urban Institute Press.

Kahn, S. (1991). *Organizing: A guide for grassroots leaders* (rev. ed.). Silver Spring, MD: NASW Press.

Martinez-Brawley, E. E. (1990). *Perspectives on the small community: Humanistic views for practitioners.* Silver Spring, MD: NASW Press.

Netting, F. E., Kettner, P. M., & McMurtry, S. L. (1993). *Social work macro practice.* New York: Longman.

Parker, E. B., & Hudson, H. E. (1992). *Electronic byways: State policies for rural development through telecommunications.* Boulder, CO: Westview Press.

Potter, R. B., & Salua, A. T. (Eds.). (1990). *Cities and development in the Third World.* New York: Mansell.

**W. David Harrison, PhD, ACSW, CCSW,** is professor, University of Alabama, School of Social Work, Tuscaloosa, AL 35487.

### For further information see

Citizen Participation; Community; Community Needs Assessment; Community Organization; Community Practice Models; Families Overview; Families: Demographic Shifts; International and Comparative Social Welfare; Mutual Aid Societies; Natural Helping Networks; Rural Social Work; Settlements and Neighborhood Centers; Social Development; Social Planning; Technology Transfer.

**Key Words**

community development

international social work

# Community Needs Assessment

John E. Tropman

Long before the social work profession was organized, issues were raised about what communities and their members "need," including protection from the elements, from illness and disease, from attack, and from hunger and want. Throughout history, the division of resources among the haves and the have nots, which is a major issue today, has been of concern. In early Judaism, members of the community were entitled to some of the fruits of that community; "social welfare" was not something special but a legitimate claim on the community's help and resources. Christianity and modern Judaism share much of this orientation. Especially over the past 150 years, as the concept of society replaced that of community, the social welfare enterprise expanded, and there have been increased social and administrative pressures to develop measures and procedures for defining and assessing community needs and their correlates.

Needs assessment must begin with a focus on a group, which is usually some kind of community, although large-scale assessments may involve an entire society. This entry uses a "triple-community" approach; that is, *community* can be defined as a common location (geographic community), a common activity (work location), or a common belief and commitment (identification) (Fellin, in press; Garvin & Tropman, 1992). Thus, assessments can be made about needs in St. Paul, Minnesota (geographic community), at a social agency (a work location), or in a Roman Catholic or Asian community (a community of identification). Because these three communities may overlap, social workers usually focus on one of them in needs assessments.

*Need* has been defined as "the gap between what is viewed as a necessary level or condition *by those responsible* for this determination and what actually exists" [italics added] (Siegel, Attkisson, & Carson, 1987/1995, p. 11). It has been further defined as *normative need,* which refers to an accepted standard; *comparative need,* which refers to an individual's position vis-à-vis others; *felt need,* which refers to a person's or a subgroup's perceptions; and *expressed need,* which refers to the articulation of one of the other needs, often through demands for better treatment and better wages (Chambers, Wedel, & Rodwell, 1992). These definitions do not incorporate distinctions between need and want (for distinctions between them, see McKillip, 1987). A community needs assessment explores and attempts to accommodate different values.

Assessment refers to both the identification of ways to measure, count, estimate, and appraise conditions of need and the establishment of priorities among needs because not all needs can be met in a given situation. Much of the discussion of needs assessments centers on these two themes (Chambers et al., 1992; Cheung, 1993; Harlow & Turner, 1993; McKillip, 1987; Siegel et al., 1987/1995). The United Way of America's (1982) definition incorporates these themes:

> Needs assessment is a systematic process of data collection and analysis as inputs into resource allocation with a view to discovering and identifying goods and services the community is lacking in relation to the generally accepted standards, and for which there exists some consensus as to the community's responsibility for their provision. (p. 10)

## Historical Background

### Early Assessments

Needs assessments have been made throughout history. In the United States, muckrakers called attention to such problems as conditions in the meat-packing industry in the early 1900s (Sinclair, 1906). Scientific philanthropy, which was an attempt to conduct organized needs assessments, also began at that time (Axinn & Levin, 1975). The first Pittsburgh Survey (1909–1911) was one example of this attempt to do needs assessments, in this case, of an entire city (Trattner, 1984). During the Great Depression of the 1930s, the social science community was asked to look at the social conditions of the country, and the President's Research Committee on Social Trends (1933) put together the book *Recent Social Trends in the United States*. In addition, another survey of Pittsburgh was completed in the late 1930s (Klein, 1938). World War II accelerated the development of social science investigations and survey research.

### New Areas of Assessment

After 1950, community needs assessment expanded into new areas. A landmark study of St. Paul, Minnesota, was *Community Planning for Human Services* (Buell, 1952), which concluded that "in every community there are a relatively small group of families in which . . . agencies concentrate whatever is being done about dependency, chronic illness ... and ... those who are in trouble" (p. 414). By the 1960s the number of federal and state social welfare programs had greatly increased and there were more and more demands to know facts about need and about the distribution of resources and to use "rational, analytical approaches for greater cost effectiveness in resource allocation" (Chambers et al., 1992, p. 103). The inclusion of a needs assessment in the requirements for applying for federal funds was an important driving force. Warheit, Bell, and Schwab (1977) maintained that the government's focus on needs assessment was indicative of a broader societal recognition of complex social and personal needs. One result was the rising expectation that human services agencies would address these needs in well-defined and effective service programs.

An important and controversial needs-assessment tool—the measure of poverty—was developed in the 1960s by Molly Orshansky of the Social Security Administration. The controversy over its definition illustrates the interplay of technical and political elements in the field of community needs assessments. The first point of controversy was the nature of the food budget that was initially established to meet the basic nutritional requirements to sustain a family of four in the short run. Although the cost of a food basket consistent with American eating habits was priced by expert shoppers, many professional social workers thought that the minimum basic level was too low.

The second point of controversy was how the cost of the food basket was computed, to determine how much of its budget a family spends on food. Some said 25 percent, others said 33 percent, and still others argued that for poor people, it was about 50 percent (on the grounds that families with low incomes spend proportionately more on food). Analysts also had to make adjustments for different-size families and for urban or rural residence (Orshansky, 1993).

These controversies over the measure of poverty remain today. They illustrate not only the complexity of the calculation of needs, but the nature of the decisions and the political considerations that are behind these commonly used figures.

In the 1980s, community analysis and comparison grew in importance. The United Way of America (1986) developed *Quest,* a stand-alone software package that was designed to assist, support, and enable communities to aggregate individual opinions about assessments and to develop community-specific reports. This software also drives a process called Compass, which involves people from a broad range of local organizations in needs assessment efforts.

## Critical Perspectives

Community needs assessment incorporates several important perspectives. One perspective, the cycle of assessment and evaluation, stresses the connection between needs assessment and program evaluation: Needs assessments direct programs toward appropriate targets, whereas program evaluations determine whether the targets have been met. In assessing needs, the question, What conditions exist? leads to the broader question, What should be done about these conditions? In program evaluation, the questions asked are, What was done? and Was it efficient and effective? From this perspective, assessment and evaluation are part of an ongoing process of continuous improvement (Kaufman, 1991).

Other perspectives concern how the needs of people are known. Some diagnoses of needs are within the province of experts, but individuals (customers, clients, or patients) also have much to say about their needs and what affects them. Both experts and individuals may differ over definitions of needs versus wants. This issue raises the important political matter of who defines needs. Most of those involved in defining poverty, for example, would not have to live under the conditions they propose.

Further complexities arise when questions of need are addressed at the community level. Although individuals may perceive their own needs, they may have little knowledge about or interest in the needs of the larger community, especially if that community includes people with whom they do not identify. And even if they are aware, they may be unwilling to support the allocation of resources that the recognition of needs implies.

## Political and Technical Methods of Assessment

Community needs assessment must involve both political and technical elements. With regard to the political elements, a needs assessment must be perceived as fair if it is to be accepted. The establishment of a fair perception requires the involvement of those who are affected. Typically, participation is the process through which both information on needs is obtained and legitimation is established. It generally involves a wide range of stakeholders and the use of their perspectives. Stakeholders have been defined as people who are affected by the programs or service(s) being planned or evaluated and include (a) those who make decisions about programs or funding, (b) those who provide the service, (c) those who receive the service, (d) the community at large that provides the funding for and receives general benefit from social programs, and (e) the social science research community that is involved in developing methods and knowledge to apply. (Innes & Heflinger, 1989, p. 227)

If relevant stakeholders are appropriately involved and differences among them are managed, the technical elements of needs assessment come into play. The major technical methods can be broadly divided into quantitative methods (in which numerical indicators and rates are developed) and qualitative methods (by which in-depth information is obtained). Both types of methods have their strengths and weaknesses, and each tends to supplement the other. Politics (values) may enter the technical elements, as when differences among stakeholder groups extend to arguments about which method produces the most useful information. As in any research, the information sought by technical methods must be reliable (accurate) and valid (measuring something useful or important).

**Quantitative Measures**

In quantitative measures, heavy emphasis is placed on the development of numerical indicators of social conditions and problems. Siegel et al. (1987/1995) divided quantitative techniques into three main categories: (1) indicator methods, (2) social survey methods, and (3) community group approaches. Distinctions within each category are presented in Table 1.

The most general quantitative approach is the social and health indicators approach, which builds a profile of a particular community from existing data. Often census data are the main ingredients, but other kinds of data, including those collected by states and localities, are used. According to Warheit et al. (1977), "the underlying assumption of this approach is that it is possible to make useful estimates of the need and social well-being of those in a community by analyzing statistics on factors found to be highly correlated with persons in need" (p. 30). Measures of this kind are indirect and must be used with care.

Social survey methods include various kinds of analyses of the demand for services. Agencies compile information on unmet needs in a community through a variety of means, including telephone surveys, face-to-face interviews, and letters from clients and professionals. The existence tallies and assays (inventories of resources and services) and user tallies and assays (measures of utilization) that are developed usually indicate deficiencies in or demands for services. Inventories of services are hampered by the lack of an accepted taxonomy of human services organizations; thus, each tally is, in effect, a research project in its own right, and agencies must be queried about the nature of the specific services they provide. User measures and assays compile, for example, rates of use, rates under treatment, and users per thousand. These measures are useful in setting acceptable standards of service and in comparing the measures of a specific community to national and regional measures.

Social or citizen survey methods are among the most popular and frequently used needs-assessment approaches (Chambers et al., 1992). If the sampling is done randomly, the results have scientific reliability. The techniques (the personal interview, the mailed questionnaire, and the telephone interview) can be used with an entire community or with a subcommunity, such as the African American community or people over age 60. Among the problems with the survey techniques are the costliness of large-scale interview methods and the low rates of return associated with mailed questionnaires.

Specially designed surveys within scientific sampling frameworks must not be confused with consumer surveys that ask consumers to rate services they did or did not receive. Such consumer surveys are important and appropriate, but do not have the scientific reliability of a sampling frame. Consumer surveys are problematic for some kinds of needs assessments: They tell an agency or a planning body what needs are present for those receiving a service but often tell nothing about the needs of those who are not receiving the service.

**Qualitative Measures**

Qualitative measures focus on the development of in-depth information about problems and conditions. The scope and breadth of quantitative measures are often criticized for lacking the richness and fullness that can come from interaction with the system. Qualitative researchers assess community needs through focus groups, participant observation, and discussions with key informants. Because of the heavy involvement of community members in the development of information for needs assessments, qualitative methods also serve some of the political functions mentioned before. Qualitative researchers must determine whether to look toward the elites of a community or the persons in the street for information. Usually, input from each is important to obtain a balance.

TABLE 1

**Quantitative and Qualitative Needs Assessment Methods**

| Methods and Method Families | | Characteristics and Technical Considerations: Perspective Represented | Optimal Sponsor | Source of Information | Information-Processing Function | Measurement Expertise Needed | Time and Resources Needed |
|---|---|---|---|---|---|---|---|
| Indicator approaches | 1. Social and health indicator analyses | Government and private agencies | Local, state, regional, or federal planners | Public archives, planning agencies | Compilation of existing data | Moderate to high | Moderate to extensive |
| Social survey approaches | 2. Demands for services | Service agencies and consumers | Community agencies, along with above | Information systems | Compilation | Moderate | Moderate |
| | 3. Analyses of service providers and resources | Planners | Local and regional planners | Local records and surveys | Compilation and development of new data | Low | Moderate |
| | 4. Citizen surveys | Private citizens | Regional, state, or federal planners | Face-to-face, telephone, or mailed surveys | Development of new data | High | Extensive |
| Community group approaches | 5. Community forums | Private citizens and consumers | Community agencies | Public meetings | Integration of existing and new data | Low | Moderate |
| | 6. Nominal group techniques | Planners, service providers, citizens | All levels | Specific projects | Development of new data | Moderate | Minimal |
| | 7. Delphi technique | Planners, service providers, experts | All levels | Specific projects | Development and integration | Moderate | Moderate |
| | 8. Community impressions | Citizens, key informants, consumers, providers | Community agencies, regional planners | Specific projects | Development, compilation, and integration | Moderate | Minimal |

SOURCE: Siegel, L. M., Attkisson, C. C., & Carlson, L. G. (1995). Need identification and program planning in the community context. In J. E. Tropman, J. Erlich, & J. Rothman (Eds.), *Tactics and techniques of community intervention* (3rd ed., p. 16). Itasca, IL: F. E. Peacock. Reprinted by permission of C. Clifford Attkisson.

***Public meeting.*** In the needs assessment process, three kinds of groups are among the most popular: (1) the public meeting (or community forum); (2) the focus group; and (3) the representative, or special-purpose, group. The public meeting or forum is an open meeting at which anyone who is interested can present views. Public forums are often large and are run by organizers who state problems, present options, suggest preliminary solutions, and ask for opinions. Often a great range of views is presented. Because those members of the community who feel most strongly and have the most suspicions about an issue are likely to attend a public meeting, an assessor is often the subject of personal attack and must exert control.

***Focus group.*** The focus group is a specially assembled collection of people who can respond, through a semistructured or structured discussion, to the concerns and interests of the assessor. Members of the group are invited and encouraged to bring up their own ideas and issues. Often the focus group is asked to test reactions to alternative approaches to an issue. When the discussion of an issue is well advanced, these groups are sometimes called briefing groups. The focus group tends to yield mass approaches; however, it is possible to have a focus group composed of key informants and other elites.

***Representative group.*** The representative group is a version of the focus group. Its strength is that its members have been selected specifically to represent different perspectives and points of view in the community. Social scientists call this type of group a "purposive" sample. At its best, the representative group is a focus group that reflects the cleavages in the community and seeks to bring the diverse views to the table; at its worst, it is a front group manipulated by schemers to make the community think that it has been involved (Vinter & Tropman, 1970).

***Techniques.*** Community groups can be structured, semistructured, or unstructured. The difference lies in how much control the assessor asserts on the process. In an unstructured group, members approach issues any way they wish. In a structured group, members provide information on community needs by addressing objectives outlined by the assessor (Chambers et al., 1992). Sometimes it is appropriate to add structure through the nominal group technique or the delphi technique as a way to help a group see its underlying preference structure. With the delphi technique, all members of a group are asked to rate, rank, or assess some event independently. The results from the entire group are tabulated and fed back to all participants, so they know where the group stands and where their response fits with respect to the group. The participants are then asked if they wish to modify their answers. This process is completed several times until consensus is reached.

With the nominal group technique, each participant lists issues or problems independently; these lists are then collated and put up around a room. Each participant has a short time to argue for or against any issue listed. Finally, the group votes to establish the priorities among the issues.

Sometimes additional individual efforts are required to assess community needs. The *key informant* technique uses elites to identify knowledgeable persons (opinion leaders, influential individuals) in the community and invites these people to share their views about community needs. Advantages of this approach include a greater depth of information and the fact that the individuals' importance may carry some weight in the presentation of the results. However, these individuals' views may not be representative of the community.

Another technique, *participant observation,* allows the assessor of community needs to get information by "hanging around," seeking to join ongoing activities, and asking questions. The purpose is immersion in the community and getting the feel of what is going on. In organizational needs assessments, participant observation can involve line workers as well as executives. In the community arena, the weaknesses of this technique are its heavy reliance on the assessor to pull together information in a fair and unbiased manner and the possibility that the assessor has biases of omission; that is, by looking at one small area intensively, the assessor may miss other areas of potential importance.

## Issues

### Role of the Assessor

Among the issues that crop up regularly in doing community needs assessments are the need to define community and needs, to identify the relevant targets of activities, and to decide who should be included in the assessments. Because what is a need to one is a want to another, the assessor may be involved in making value judgments. The role of the assessor is always somewhat uncertain: On the one hand, he or she may be a skilled researcher–statistician who is developing information by numerical means but is emotionally distant from the problems in question; on the other hand, the assessor may be an impassioned advocate who is attempting to demonstrate pressing needs. Maintaining a balance between involvement and distance is always difficult; the assessor must not be compromised by the selective organization of material and presentation of data to bolster a specific case, attitude, or viewpoint. Tension between seeking information and providing validation may surface.

Because the assessor engages in judgments that are close to evaluations, he or she may be a target of suspicion. Any needs assessment involves making some judgments about the adequacy (or inadequacy) of existing institutional and organizational arrangements. Such judgments can be threatening to the guardians of those institutions and may lead to inappropriate criticism of the assessor.

There is also the potential for conflict between seeking information and undertaking action. An assessor may be moved to act to resolve a community problem before the full range of data is collected and analyzed. Even under the best of circumstances, communities are loosely coupled systems, and getting information from them can be difficult. How wide and deep should an assessment go? How much money is available for assessment?

To avoid the need to conduct a major study every time community needs must be assessed, an assessor must have two simultaneous goals: (1) to do the immediate needs assessment and (2) to use that assessment to lay the groundwork for establishing an ongoing system of collecting and analyzing information. To some extent, these two goals work against one another. The first is a short-term goal that serves a program–operation function, whereas the second is a long-term goal that serves a program–development function.

### Oversight and Community Participation

Among other issues, management of the community committee is one of the most complex. Often an oversight group is formed to assist the assessor by providing direction and requesting, overseeing, and releasing the report. The assessor must keep this group informed and incorporate its interests and perspectives into the needs assessment (Tropman, 1977).

Still another issue is the management of stakeholders' involvement in community needs assessments. The exact role of stakeholders must be made clear. Stakeholders should not think they are making decisions when they are only advising. The dangers here are dishonesty on the part of the assessor and angry reactions on the part of the stakeholders when they find they have been "used." Issues of stakeholder management also arise because stakeholders may disagree with one another. As a community seeks to come to decisions about what its needs are and what should be done about them, different criteria for decision making are brought to bear. Among them are the breadth of preference in the community, accommodation of those who feel deeply, the advice of experts, and the interests of the powerful and of those who may carry out the changed programs. The conflicts arising from the different criteria must be carefully managed.

### Implementation

Issues of implementation also surface. Needs assessments often generate great interest at the beginning, but once information is in hand, interest wanes. Workers must be aware of this possibility and make plans for implementation even before assessment technically begins. Implementation is one of the concerns of the community committee, which can oversee implementation after the assessor's work is done. Without implementation, there will be little change and improvement in community needs, and there may be considerable disaffection in the community itself.

## Conclusion

Needs assessment is one of the important techniques used in social work to determine when gaps in service exist, when people's basic requirements are not being addressed, and when certain groups are experiencing special disadvantages. The technical and political problems in carrying out needs assessment are substantial, and the problems of implementation may be even greater. Four basic aspects of needs assessment are important. First, the involvement of those affected is a central principle of needs assessment, not only because involvement is a central value but because those affected often provide information and implement changes. Second, several methods of assessment should be used. Each method has its orientations and biases that can be overcome to some extent through the use of crosscutting methodologies. Third, a balance must be maintained between the technical and the political elements of community needs assessment. And fourth, a balance must be kept between the requisites of assessment and those of implementation. A modest assessment that brings about community betterment is preferable to a premier assessment that gets filed away.

## References

Axinn, J., & Levin, H. (1975). *Social welfare: A history of the American response to needs.* New York: Dodd, Mead.

Buell, B. (1952). *Community planning for human services.* New York: Columbia University Press.

Chambers, D. E., Wedel, K. R., & Rodwell, M. K. (1992). *Evaluating social programs.* Needham Heights, MA: Allyn & Bacon.

Cheung, K. M. (1993). Needs assessment experience among area agencies on aging. *Journal of Gerontology, 19*(3–4), 77–91.

Fellin, P. (in press). *The community and the social worker.* Itasca, IL: F. E. Peacock.

Garvin, C., & Tropman, J. E. (1992). *Social work in contemporary society.* Englewood Cliffs, NJ: Prentice Hall.

Harlow, K. S., & Turner, M. J. (1993). State units and convergence models: Needs assessment revisited. *The Gerontologist, 33,* 190–191.

Innes, R. B., & Heflinger, C. A. (1989). An expanded model of community assessment: A case study. *Journal of Community Psychology, 17,* 225–235.

Kaufman, R. (1991, December). Toward total quality "plus." *Training,* pp. 50–54.

Klein, P. (1938). *A social study of Pittsburgh.* New York: Columbia University Press.

McKillip, J. (1987). *Need analysis: Tools for the human services and education.* Newbury Park, CA: Sage Publications.

Orshansky, M. (1993). Measuring poverty. *Public Welfare, 51*(1), 27–28.

President's Research Committee on Social Trends. (1933). *Recent social trends in the United States: Report of the President's Research Committee on Social Trends.* New York: McGraw-Hill.

Siegel, L. M., Attkisson, C. C., & Carson, L. G. (1995). Need identification and program planning in the community context. In J. E. Tropman, J. Erlich, & J. Rothman (Eds.), *Tactics and techniques of community intervention* (3rd ed., pp. 10–34). Itasca, IL: F. E. Peacock. (Original work published 1987)

Sinclair, U. (1906). *The jungle.* New York: Doubleday, Page.

Trattner, I. (1984). *From poor law to welfare state: A history of social welfare in America.* New York: Free Press.

Tropman, E. J. (1977). Staffing committees and studies. In F. J. Cox, J. L. Erlich, J. Rothman, & J. E. Tropman (Eds.), *Tactics and techniques of community practice* (pp. 105–111). Itasca, IL: F. E. Peacock.

United Way of America. (1982). *Needs assessment: The state of the art.* Alexandria, VA: Author.

United Way of America. (1986). *Quest* [computer software]. Alexandria, VA: Author.

Vinter, R. D., & Tropman, J. E. (1970). The causes and consequences of community studies. In F. M. Cox, J. L. Erlich, J. Rothman, & J. E. Tropman (Eds.), *Strategies of community organization* (1st ed., pp. 315–323). Itasca, IL: F. E. Peacock.

Warheit, G. J., Bell, R. A., & Schwab, J. J. (1977). *Needs assessment approaches: Concepts and methods.* Washington, DC: U.S. Government Printing Office.

**John E. Tropman, PhD,** is professor, University of Michigan, School of Social Work, 1065 Frieze Building, Ann Arbor, MI 48109.

The author wishes to express deep appreciation to Beverly Bagozzi for her invaluable assistance in preparing this entry.

**For further information see**

Advocacy; Citizen Participation; Community; Community Development; Community Organization; Community Practice Models; Interdisciplinary and Interorganizational Collaboration; Management Overview; Mass Media; Natural Helping Networks; Organizations: Context for Social Services Delivery; Planning and Management Professions; Policy Analysis; Public Social Services; Research Overview; Rural Social Work; Social Planning; Social Welfare Policy; Social Work Profession Overview; Volunteer Management.

**Key Words**

community
methods
needs assessment
program evaluation

# Community Organization

**Si Kahn**

Community organizing is a tool that is used in all cultures and societies to redress the classic imbalance between the powerless and the powerful. It relies on the force of numbers—of many people thinking, working, and acting together—to counterbalance wealthy and powerful groups and the means they have to protect and extend themselves: constitutions, governments, bureaucracies, police forces, tax collectors, armies, corporations, caste and class systems, religious institutions, gendered and racialized violence, ownership and control of resources, educational establishments, and communications systems. Whatever the specific issue around which communities organize, their implicit demand is democratization—the redistribution of resources from the few to the many, including both wealth and power.

However carefully community organizing may be publicly described—whether as a search for acceptability and respectability or for simple safety and security—it is intrinsically radical. It is a demand for fundamental change, for reapportioning, for restructuring. It is by nature a critique of and a confrontation with the existing economic and political establishment. For this reason, community organizing represents a set of potential problems from the viewpoint of any establishment. Establishments that tend toward the authoritarian, whose long-term power is always at risk, work aggressively to restrict community organizing (Fanon, 1968; Memmi, 1967). Their intellectual justifications range from a desire to maintain "law and order" to an effort to protect "management rights." Their techniques range from anti-union media campaigns to arresting or murdering their own citizens for assembling in groups of more than two or, in some cases, for speaking to another person without official permission.

Establishments that tend toward the democratic have a more-complex intellectual relationship to community organizing. Democratic ideology presumes and advocates not just the consent of the governed, but their informed and active participation in that consent. For any constituency to give its informed consent to being governed, whether in the community or in the workplace, it must first be organized. To deny the right to organize is also to deny the basis on which democratic regimes claim authority—the right to govern (Boyte, 1989).

Democratic establishments therefore tend to recognize and institutionalize community organizing, at least initially. The Constitution of the United States, for example, states in the first amendment of the Bill of Rights that "Congress shall make no law respecting . . . the right of the people peaceably to assemble, and to petition the Government for a redress of grievances." Such language in democratic constitutions provides a legal basis and protection for community organizing. Such protections, however, may or may not be reflected in the ongoing realities and dynamics of power and politics.

## History

The history of community organizing in the United States is closely tied to the development of social work as both a theory and a practice. Both community organizing and social work were and are responses to the multiple forces that combined to create American society, with all its strengths and weaknesses. Democratic theory and authoritarian institutions, great wealth and dire poverty, personal freedom and chattel slavery, open elections and disenfranchisement of all but property-owning white males, isolationism and imperialism, pacifism and militarism, communitarianism and capitalism, town meetings and political machines—these are only some of the many complexities and contradictions that shaped American civil society.

The United States then can be seen as a renewed society drawing on many cultures, including, particularly in its early history, Native American, African, and European cultures. The evolving order embodied in the Declaration of Independence and the Constitution, for example, is indebted to the political theory of the Iroquois Confederation as well as to emerging European ideas of emancipation and communalism. Certainly the New England town meeting, at least in its early form, owes more to the traditions of tribal councils than to those of European councils of state. African cultural and political traditions underpin and inform the development of resistance to chattel slavery by the slaves themselves (Harding, 1981).

All these ideas find expression in early community organizing efforts. The years leading up to the American Revolution, and particularly the work of the Committees of Correspondence, can be treated as a classic study in community organizing methodology, including recruitment, communication, direct action, coalition building, fundraising, cultural empowerment, and public relations (Boyte, 1989). The underground railroad of Civil War times is a remarkable study in how those who are most oppressed can organize themselves, develop private and public allies, create secure systems of internal communication, develop leadership with the capacity to take risks, and hold it accountable (Harding, 1981). Abolitionism depended on a remarkable national network of women who circulated petitions and mobilized their local communities into the movement (Lerner, 1979). Other 19th-century movements such as suffrage, populism, anarchism, craft unionism, and pacifism further developed and refined these techniques, as well as their relationship to issues of race, gender, and class.

These 19th-century community organizing movements all have their 20th-century equivalents and parallels, practitioners and theoreticians, although these links are often little known or misunderstood. For example, Saul Alinsky is often claimed as the founder of community organizing, particularly and understandably by members of the Industrial Areas Foundation, which he founded to continue his work (Alinsky, 1946, 1969). Alinsky's own background, however, draws far more both on social work, especially the work of Jane Addams and Hull House, and on earlier community organizing efforts than this claim would suggest: as a criminology student at the University of Chicago, as a youth worker with Chicago gang members, as the biographer of industrial union leader John L. Lewis. Alinsky is an important codifier of and creative contributor to the tradition of community organizing, but he is hardly its inventor (Fink, 1984).

Similarly, other key social movements of our time, which are often thought of as unique, are in fact rooted in and shaped by their own historical ancestors. The civil rights movement of the 1960s owes a great deal not only to Rosa Parks, Dr. Martin Luther King, Jr., and Malcolm X, but also to Nat Turner, Denmark Vesey, Harriet Tubman, Sojourner Truth, Frederick Douglass, Marcus Garvey, and W.E.B. Dubois (Harding, 1981; Morris, 1984).

As with Addams and Alinsky, the relationship and parallels between the development of community organizing movements and the development of social work are often overlooked. It is too easy to see Hull House and the other founding settlement houses as a type of late 19th-century community development corporation or multipurpose neighborhood center. The settlement houses were, however, far more radical and far more committed to community organizing than some of their surface resemblances to today's government-sponsored community service centers would suggest. Jane Addams herself, one of the founders of social work as a profession, was a radical, a feminist, a trade unionist, a pacifist, a socialist, an agitator, and an organizer (Evans, 1989). It is interesting to speculate as to how many social work agencies today would be willing to hire her to direct their social change programs.

## Social Change Methods

Community organizing is only one of a number of well-established methods for encouraging and promoting social change. Any analysis of the occasionally vexed relationship between social work and community organizing depends on an understanding of these four methods: service, advocacy, mobilizing, and organizing (Kahn, 1991).

### Service

Service attempts to provide people with the basics they need to survive, subsist, develop, and even flourish within society. Essentially an individualized and personalized approach to social change, it rarely challenges the root causes of the issues addressed. Service therefore can address a problem in the short run but not solve it in the long run. A soup kitchen, for example, is a service approach to the problem of hunger. It can ensure that, on a given day, a given number of people are fed. But it cannot and does not address the question of why these people are hungry. If the soup kitchen closes, the people it serves will again be hungry.

Most of the publicly supported programs that address social issues take a service approach. For example, food stamps, job training, public housing, literacy programs, and public assistance are all service programs. In a society in which many people do without the basics of life, service programs at their best offer humane relief from suffering. But they are at their core helping individuals adjust as best they can to the immediate realities of society, rather than demanding that society change to meet the needs of its individual and collective members. Individuals may be fed, clothed, and housed, but they are not empowered. Service programs may not go as far as directly blaming the victim, but they do begin with the assumption that it is the victim who needs to be fixed, not society.

### Advocacy

Advocacy begins with the assumption that if a society includes large numbers of individuals who are suffering, there must be something wrong not just with those individuals but with society as well; therefore society as well as individuals must be changed. Social workers who lobby either individually or through organizations such as NASW for legislative or administrative changes in programs that affect poor people are practicing advocacy. Legal action to challenge unjust laws and administrative practices is another common advocacy method.

Advocacy does begin to demand changes in society that will benefit its members and, in so doing, begins to raise issues of power and policy. However, in advocacy these issues are usually raised *on behalf of* those who are affected by the policies and practices in question, not by *those who are affected.* Advocates, however effective, are representing someone else. Thus, although advocacy can change relationships of power within society, because it does not involve people acting on their own behalf, it does not simultaneously empower the disempowered.

### Mobilizing

Mobilizing begins the process of empowerment by asking people to stand up for themselves. When people show up at a city council meeting to protest the closing of a neighborhood clinic, pass petitions around, picket in front of the clinic, or hold a press conference to denounce the mayor, they are mobilizing. In mobilizing, people who have been disempowered and dispossessed begin to find their voices, to discover confidence, to feel that they actually have a chance of changing the conditions of their lives and communities.

Because mobilizing is usually a direct response to an immediate situation, it is also limited in what it can accomplish. Mobilizing sometimes leads to such success (or such frustration) that those involved decide to extend the process and go on to build a community organization. But mobilizing far more often is limited to the immediate situation and therefore is also limited in both time and scope. It does challenge and sometimes change relations of power but usually only in the short run.

### Organizing

Organizing as a social change process creates and sustains an ongoing challenge to relationships of power within society (Kahn, 1994). Unlike mobilizing, which takes place within a relatively short time frame and therefore is unequipped to address systemic and structural issues, organizing aims to build permanent community organizations that can address and advance the needs of their members. These community organizations then offer a safe space and a separate base of power for those who constitute the organization and whom they represent. Within this space, people who have been disempowered and dispossessed can begin to practice the democratic skills of citizenship and leadership. Through this process they become empowered not just individually but collectively (Evans & Boyte, 1986), and they are then able to mount a consistent challenge to the power of established institutions within society.

Such a theory and practice, of course, is far more popular with those who lack power than with those who already have power. Organizing implies a radical critique (from any political point of view) of those in power and of the institutions that they control, including government at all levels (Fink, 1984). Such a critique is rarely welcomed by those in power, who tend to use their position and power to discourage organizing as a social change method, in favor of service or, at worst from their point of view, advocacy.

## Social Work and Social Change

Most institutions and individuals who exercise real power are less than enthusiastic about a philosophy of social change that, from their point of view, can best be described as "biting the hand that feeds you." This dynamic creates many levels of tension for social work and social workers who, on the one hand, are deeply aware of society's inequities and, on the other, depend heavily on public employment and funding for their own well-being. A social worker may believe that an independent community organization of public housing tenants is the best hope for improving conditions in a particular housing project. But if that social worker is employed by the public housing authority, he or she is not exactly in a position to encourage and assist that organizing process.

This situation creates a double bind for many social workers. To the extent that they identify and work with people who are organizing for power, they run the risk of being monitored, mistrusted, restricted, and even disciplined by their employing agency. To the extent that they are seen as representatives of the agency, they may be monitored and mistrusted by those they are trying to help.

Part of the reason for this double bind comes from the extent to which successful programs developed through independent community organizing efforts are eventually institutionalized and bureaucratized by the public and private sectors. For example, a major response by government to the U.S. civil rights movement of the 1960s was the War on Poverty. The local "community action agencies" established across the nation adopted the civil rights movement's emphasis on "participatory democracy" and called for "maximum feasible participation" of the poor. However, the federal guidelines established for funding meant that poor people could never have more than one-third of the seats on the governing bodies of these agencies, with two-thirds of the seats reserved for those in power. Ironically, many of the poor people who held these seats and who were hired by these agencies as "community organizers" believed that what they were doing was real community organizing—at least until they attempted to challenge community power, when all too often they found themselves not only powerless but unemployed.

Although the "community action agency" case is specific to the late 1960s and early 1970s, the principle operates broadly today. Institutions and individuals who hold power attempt to undercut and conservatize community organizing by incorporating it into ongoing public programs and agencies. In fact, agency regulations limit many people who hold the job title of "community organizer," social workers among them, to service work.

This situation not only frustrates these individuals; it also misleads people in the community at large about the nature of community organizing. The base for community organizing, as Jane Addams understood, can exist only *outside* the established institutions of society, whether public or private. Because the purpose of community organizations is to change the relationships of power within society, they cannot themselves operate from *within* the power structure. People do occasionally bite the hand that feeds them, but hardly anyone ever bites his or her own hand.

## Constituencies

Although community organizing is inherently radical, the techniques and processes known generically as "organizing" are themselves essentially neutral and value free. The powerful as well as the powerless organize; in fact, effective organizing by the former group is one of the reasons there is such a disparity in power and wealth in so many societies. Right-wingers and fascists as well as progressives and populists adopt and adapt the processes and techniques of organizing to their various ends (Hallie, 1979). Organizing can be an authoritarian as well as a democratic technique; organizations can be constructed from the top down as well as from the bottom up.

The term "community organizing," however, as opposed to simply "organizing," has usually but not always been used to refer to situations in which a relatively powerless constituency uses democratic means to achieve progressive ends. The goals people are working toward, how they are doing that work, and who they are as a group of individuals are therefore critical to a definition and exploration of community organizing (Boyte, 1984).

### Defining Constituencies

In the language of community organizing, "who people are" is the constituency question. Constituency can be defined by issue (people working toward a particular shared goal or goals), community (people living or working in a particular place) or identity (people sharing race, class, gender, sexual orientation, religion, ethnicity, age, physical ability, language, or tribe). These may of course overlap and intersect: People living in a neighborhood, for example, often share a racial or ethnic identity and a common set of issues, which may be the result of both where they live and who they are.

One particular community, the workplace, is often excluded from discussions of constituency. "That's labor organizing, not community organizing" is a common statement. This response is ironic, because for many people the workplace is not only where they spend the greatest part of their public time but, given the degree of alienation and rootlessness in modern industrial societies, one of their few consistent communities. This peculiar exclusion reflects both class bias and the degree to which unions threaten the power of modern industrial establishments. Union organizing is in fact as much community organizing as, for example, neighborhood organizing. Particularly when it takes gender and race into account, union organizing is critical to a broad and interdependent approach to social change in any culture, society, or nation (Brecher, 1972; Fantasia, 1988).

Constituency as identity is often defined by race, gender, or class. Race, gender, and class can be thought of as three lenses, three different but interacting ways of looking at the world and how it works. Viewing the world through any particular lens produces different theories and practices of social change. Looking at the world through the lens of race produces, for example, black nationalism and "negritude" as theory and African national liberation movements and the southern civil rights movement as practice. Looking at the world through the lens of gender produces feminism as theory and the international women's movement as practice. Looking at the world through the lens of class produces different economic-based theories of change as theory, including both capitalism and Marxism, and the trade union movement and multinational corporations as practice.

Although activists and theorists have long argued about which of these three forces is the most important, the central factor in determining which position a person takes is usually who he or she is: a person of color, a woman, a worker. Of course, many people fit into not just one but two or three of these categories; for example, an Asian woman, a working-class woman, an Asian working-class woman (Davis, 1983). When two or three of these categories are involved at the same time, it is often hard to figure out how they are combining. For example, if an African American woman loses her job, one might ask, did she lose the job because she is a woman, because she is an African American, or both?

### Building Constituency Power

What is important to community organizing is to accept people's way of looking at themselves and the world and to help them build power based on their own analysis. This means that race, gender, and class are not just issues of identity. They are also political forces, rooted in who people believe they are but also affecting who they believe they could and should be and become (Minnich, 1990). Such dreaming produces powerful momentum, especially when people's identities and sense of themselves have been denied and suppressed both individually and collectively by racism, sexism, or classism. This sense of personal and collective possibility—who people come to believe through the process of community organizing that they could and should be, not just as individuals but as a group, as an organization, as a movement—is one of the phenomena that make radical and profound social change possible.

## Separatist Community Organizing

People who have been exploited and oppressed often need to build a separate base of power for themselves before they can confront their opposition, the people, and the systems that are the cause of their problems (Evans & Boyte, 1986). Because their base of power is developed separately, this type of community organizing is called "separatism." It is also sometimes referred to as "single-constituency organizing." What is important is to recognize separatism not just as a social phenomenon—people wanting to be with others like them—but as a strategic technique for building power.

Many classic forms of community organizing are based on a separatist strategy. Separatism based on class explains why workers do not want management sitting in on the union meeting or joining the union. Separatism based on race explains why people of color may want to join organizations that do not include white people. Separatism based on gender explains why women sometimes want to build organizations that exclude men.

Because people may have two or three identities, these "separatist" categories can also be combined. Within a local or national union, for example, there might be many "caucuses," or separatist communities, within the larger community organization. There might be one caucus for Latinos, another caucus for women, and a third for Latinas. Furthermore, one caucus could make demands on another caucus as well as on the larger organization. The women's caucus might have within it a separate Latina caucus whose goal is to make sure that the particular needs of Latinas are taken into account in the process of advocating within the union for women.

## COALITIONS

Although separatist community organizing can be critically important as a social change process, over the long run many people and organizations that began with separatism will also begin to see a need to work together across the lines that divide them, including but not limited to race, gender, and class. One reason for this development is that although in many cases critical issues cross these and other dividing lines, the people whose lives these issues affect do not initially see the overlaps.

Toxic wastes are a good example of this phenomenon. When toxic wastes affect the people working in a factory, the problem is considered a "workplace health and safety issue." When these same toxic wastes are trucked to a poor or working-class community and dumped into a leaking landfill, the problem is described as a "neighborhood issue" or, if the neighborhood residents are mostly people of color, as a "racial issue." When children start getting sick from the toxic wastes, the problem is a "women's and children's issue" or a "health issue." And when the toxic waste seeps into the nearby streams and fish start dying, the problem becomes an "environmental issue."

Although the name of the issue may change along the way, the heart of the issue is the same barrel of poison that never should have been there in the first place. The people are different, the communities are different, and the issue is given a different name. But it is the same fight, with the potential to unite people across lines that would otherwise divide them.

Although some issues are common across race, gender, and class lines, other issues are very different and often in conflict with each other, even between and among so-called progressive community organizations (Bulkin, Pratt, & Smith, 1984; Evans, 1979). For example, there is a real conflict between established systems of seniority, a principle central to working-class organizations (trade unions), and affirmative action, a principle equally central to organizations of women and of people of color. For community organizers to pretend that these differences and conflicts do not exist—to say, "it's all the same struggle" or, "we're all in this together"—is asking one group or the other to give up something that is central to its organization, issue, and identity. In both the short and the long run, this is asking for trouble.

However, it is also true that those who are in power usually oppose both affirmative action and seniority. And with remarkable consistency, people who are against the rights of people of color also oppose the rights of women and the rights of working people. There are some exceptions, such as some labor and civil rights supporters who are against reproductive rights. But generally, an important reason to build organizations that cross race, gender, and class lines is that even where the issues of the various groups really are different, two things are the same: the opposition and a broad vision of a different, better world.

Although people and communities may not always agree on the most important issue to work on at a particular time, they can often agree that the ways in which power is exercised and the people who hold the power must be changed before they or anyone else can win on their issues. Power—and the questions of who has it and how it can be transferred and transformed by a positive, affirming vision of a world in which people and communities are valued and respected because of, not in spite of, who they are and can be—is one great issue that can unite across race, gender, and class lines (Kaye-Kantrowitz, 1992).

## Organizations and Movements

Within community organizing, a saying exists: Organizers organize organizations. This is not just a definition but a prescription. It is generally considered practical and reasonable for a community organizer or a team of organizers to decide to build a new organization from the ground up (Kahn, 1994). If their analysis of conditions is reasonably accurate, if their strategy and tactics are sound, if they do their job conscientiously and well, then that organization will most probably be built.

But community organizers are only rarely able to organize movements, periods of rapid and profound transformation that are essential to an ongoing process of social change. Movements depend on the convergence of the right economic, political, and social conditions (Bloom, 1987). Even the most skilled community organizers are usually unsuccessful in deliberately organizing movements. In fact, it is hard even to predict movements. Very few people predicted the great anticolonial movements in Africa beginning in the 1950s, the civil rights movement in the southern United States during the 1960s, or the international women's movements of the 1970s.

Yet major social change movements occur with some regularity, and it is likely that the 1990s and 2000s will see many such movements throughout the world. The success of any particular movement will have much to do with the skills and abilities of the people involved. Success will depend on how clearly they can see what to do and on their abilities to mobilize, organize, strategize, and publicize. The movement will also be influenced by the degree to which the people who are involved have learned to understand, work with, and trust each other. Because any movement's future depends heavily on leaders, organizers, organizations, networks, and coalitions, community organizers must work in nonmovement periods to create the conditions and resources that will make a movement most effective once it begins.

As any movement reaches its peak and begins to ebb, it must find ways to consolidate and protect the gains it has won. By building community organizations that can outlast the waning of the movement, community organizers can ensure that the movement's work will be carried on and that its new leaders will continue to grow.

## Power and Culture

Successful community organizing changes more than power. It also changes the relationship that the people being organized have to power. To do this, community organizing must change how people think about and relate to themselves and others (Minnich, 1990).

Although people and communities may win on the issues, they do not necessarily develop new understandings of how and why they won, of power and how it is exercised, or of difference and how it is exploited. They may experience the power of numbers, but they may not gain the concurrent power of knowledge and understanding. And although some of the conditions of their lives may change, they will not necessarily transform their relationships to others (particularly their relationships to those different from themselves), to themselves, and to power itself (Minnich, 1990).

Political education makes these transformations possible. Yet traditional educational methods, which are fundamentally intellectual, are often inadequate to deal with a transformative process, particularly one that challenges racism, sexism, homophobia, anti-Semitism, and other barriers that divide people from each other. Breaking through such barriers is a visceral and emotional as well as an intellectual process.

Culture—poems, songs, paintings, murals, chants, sermons, quilts, stories, rhythms, weavings, pots, and dances—can make such emotional and visceral breakthroughs and lift people out of themselves. Culture can transform consciousness and can perform the acts of political education that, combined with community organizing, make social change transformative rather than merely instrumental. Yet within the world of community organizing, culture is too often merely an "add-on" and an afterthought. Cultural workers and cultural work itself are often minor adjuncts to the community organizing process: a quilt at an auction, a song or two at a rally, a chant on a picket line. Many community organizers have yet to recognize fully and incorporate into their lives and work the lessons of culture and cultural work, to draw on the full power that culture can provide. Community organizing must draw on and incorporate the full variety of traditional and nontraditional forms from many cultures: oral poetry, storytelling, *midrash,* meditation, quilting, theater, preaching, drumming, unaccompanied song, and silence.

This is the critical challenge to community organizers and social workers today: to reach, teach, and organize people in ways that transform their understanding of power and their relationship to power—not just individually, but collectively. It is at this intersection of culture and power that the future of community organizing, of social change, and of social work must be found.

## References


Alinsky, S. D. (1946). *Reveille for radicals.* New York: Vintage Books.

Alinsky, S. D. (1969). *Rules for radicals: A pragmatic primer for realistic radicals.* New York: Vintage Books.

Bloom, J. (1987). *Class, race and the civil rights movement.* Bloomington: Indiana University Press.

Boyte, H. C. (1984). *Community is possible: Repairing America's roots.* New York: Harper & Row.

Boyte, H. C. (1989). *Commonwealth: A return to citizen politics.* New York: Free Press.

Brecher, J. (1972). *Strike!* San Francisco: Straight Arrow Books.

Bulkin, E., Pratt, M. B., & Smith, B. (1984). *Yours in struggle: Three feminist perspectives on anti-Semitism and racism.* Ithaca, NY: Firebrand Books.

Davis, A. (1983). *Women, race and class.* New York: Vintage Books.

Evans, S. M. (1979). *Personal politics: The roots of women's liberation in the civil rights movement and the New Left.* New York: Alfred A. Knopf.

Evans, S. M. (1989). *Born for liberty: A history of women in America.* New York: Free Press.

Evans, S. M., & Boyte, H. C. (1986). *Free space: The sources of democratic change in America.* New York: Harper & Row.

Fanon, F. (1968). *The wretched of the earth.* New York: Evergreen.

Fantasia, R. (1988). *Cultures of solidarity: Consciousness, action and contemporary American workers.* Berkeley: University of California Press.

Fink, D. (1984). *The radical vision of Saul Alinsky.* Maryknoll, NY: Orbis Books.

Hallie, P. (1979). *Lest innocent blood be shed: The story of the village of Le Chambon and how goodness happened there.* New York: Harper & Row.

Harding, V. (1981). *There is a river: The black struggle for freedom in America.* New York: Harcourt Brace Jovanovich.

Kahn, S. (1991). *Organizing: A guide for grassroots leaders* (rev. ed.). Silver Spring, MD: NASW Press.

Kahn, S. (1994). *How people get power* (rev. ed.). Washington, DC: NASW Press.

Kaye-Kantrowitz, M. (1992). *The issue is power: Essays on women, Jews, violence and resistance.* San Francisco: Aunt Lute Books.

Lerner, G. (1979). *The majority finds its past: Placing women in history.* New York: Oxford University Press.

Memmi, A. (1967). *The colonizer and the colonized.* Boston: Beacon Press.

Minnich, E. K. (1990). *Transforming knowledge.* Philadelphia: Temple University Press.

Morris, A. (1984). *Origins of the civil rights movement.* New York: Free Press.


## Further Reading


Bobo, K., Kendall, J., & Max, S. (1991). *Organizing for social change: A manual for activists in the 1990s.* Cabin John, MD: Seven Locks Press.

Brager, G., & Sprecht, H. (1973). *Community organizing.* New York: Columbia University Press.

Burghardt, S. (1982). *Organizing for community action.* Beverly Hills, CA: Sage Publications.

Burghardt, S. (1982). *The other side of organizing.* Cambridge, MA: Schenkman Publishing.

Cox, F. (1975). *Strategies of community organization.* Itasca, IL: F. E. Peacock Publishers.

Delgado, G. (1986). *Organizing the movement: The roots and growth of ACORN.* Philadelphia: Temple University Press.

Ecklein, J. (1984). *Community organizing.* New York: Free Press.

Kramer, R. M., & Specht, H. (1975). *Readings in community organization.* Englewood Cliffs, NJ: Prentice Hall.

Perlman, R., & Gurin, A. (1972). *Community organization and social planning.* New York: John Wiley & Sons.

Pharr, S. (1988). *Homophobia: A weapon of sexism.* Inverness, CA: Chardon Press.

Rotman, J. (1974). *Planning and organizing for social change.* New York: Columbia University Press.

Staples, L. (1984). *Roots to power: A manual for grassroots organizing.* Westport, CT: Praeger.


**Si Kahn, PhD,** is executive director, Grassroots Leadership, 1300 Baxter Street, Suite 200, Charlotte, NC 28236.

### For further information see

Advocacy; Citizen Participation; Civil Rights; Community; Community Development; Community Needs Assessment; Community Practice Models; Ethics and Values; Fundraising and Philanthropy; Human Rights; Interdisciplinary and Interorganizational Collaboration; Management Overview; Mass Media; Music and Social Work; Mutual Aid Societies; Natural Helping Networks; Peace and Social Justice; Poverty; Rural Social Work Overview; Settlements and Neighborhood Centers; Social Planning; Social Welfare; Social Workers in Politics; Unions; Volunteer Management.

**Key Words**

advocacy
community organization
grassroots leadership
political power

# Community Practice Models

**Marie Overby Weil**
**Dorothy N. Gamble**

Community practice has been an essential element in social work from its earliest beginnings. It encompasses a wide scope of practice, ranging from grassroots organization and development to human services planning and coordination. Community practice uses multiple methods of empowerment-based interventions to strengthen participation in democratic processes, assist groups and communities in advocating for their needs and organizing for social justice, and improve the effectiveness and responsiveness of human services systems. Community practice focuses on work with individual community leaders, elected officials, and professionals, as well as with task groups made up of combinations of these people. The objectives of community practice are to

- develop the organizing skills and abilities of citizens and citizen groups
- make social planning more accessible and inclusive in a community
- connect social and economic investments to grassroots community groups
- advocate for broad coalitions in solving community problems
- infuse the social planning process with a concern for social justice.

Community practice encompasses a variety of models and methods of intervention that seek to improve the social and economic quality of life for vulnerable populations and communities. This entry focuses on eight current models of community practice that have grown out of the earliest traditions of social work in America. The roots of community practice from which these traditions come are in the Settlement House movement, the Charity Organization Societies movement, grassroots organization, the organizing and development histories of diverse ethnic and racial groups, and the rural development movement. These movements, along with the ethnic and racial organizational activities, are the taproots of community practice as it has evolved in community development, social planning, and social action in the United States (Betten & Austin, 1990b; Rivera & Erlich, 1992; Rubin & Rubin, 1992). Each of these areas and each of these groups has its own complex history; examples are provided in this entry.

## Roots of Community Practice

### Settlement Movement

The settlement houses, as exemplified by the work of Jane Addams and her colleagues at Hull House in Chicago, concentrated on social research and community change through the use of information from house-to-house surveys to build programs and seek more just and inclusive services and social policies (Addams, 1960). Members of the Hull House community were deeply involved not only in local program development but also in the design and implementation of the juvenile court in Illinois and the national Children's Bureau, a major force in policy setting for the nation's children and families. Settlement residents at Hull House used research and developed methodologies for community study that focused on engaging residents and neighborhood citizens in community problem solving (Deegan, 1990). This pioneering work set a standard for community research as well as for community involvement in social planning and development practice. Settlement members were also involved in social action at local, national, and international levels. Jane Addams's work in the international peace movement was recognized with the award of the Nobel Prize for Peace in 1931.

Major models of community work in organizing, planning, and development evolved from the settlement movement and have had incalculable impact on community practice and services in the nonprofit sector. At their best, the settlements engaged and continue to engage neighborhood residents in educational reform, environmental actions, program development, intergroup relations, and broad arenas of social and economic development.

### Charity Organization Movement

The Charity Organization Societies focused on coordination of human services and on finding ways for different programs to collaborate effectively to meet recognized social needs. Its central mission was connecting services, increasing communication across agencies, and integrating services to see that needy people received services. The vision of the Charity Organization Societies was to assure that charitable work was carried forward in an effective and efficient way. It focused on service development, community service planning, resource development for human services, and coordination. Its focus was typically on the town or city, as evidenced in the broad national network of Health and Welfare Planning Councils that were once a central part of social services planning in many urban areas of the United States.

At citywide levels, Health and Welfare Planning Councils have dealt with social program planning and resource allocation. With the expansion and increasing complexity of the voluntary human services sector, a greater focus on resource development and federated funding evolved into the establishment of Community Chests, the United Way, and Jewish Federations, all of which continue to focus on resource development and allocation.

**Grassroots Organizing**

Grassroots organizing grows from two streams: the Settlement House movement and the Labor movement. Historically, settlement workers assisted in the development of community groups to improve the quality of life in their neighborhoods, to achieve access to political power, to seek redress of problems, and to pursue social justice. Saul Alinsky, whose work in the Back of the Yards area in Chicago spawned numerous organizations, adapted his methods of grassroots organizing from the labor movement, in which he had experience as an organizer for the Congress of Industrial Organizations (Alinsky, 1971; Betten & Austin, 1990a).

**Race and Ethnicity in Community Practice**

The roots of community practice cannot be discussed without recognition of the influences of racism and prejudice. The history of racism and the exclusion of some groups—especially groups of color—from full participation as citizens bears on an important aspect of the history of community organization and social development in North America. Racism and prejudice in American society have made it essential for ethnic and racial groups to build their own survival, self-help, and community-change organizations throughout our history.

***Native Americans.*** The historical survival strategies, community and environmental foci, and development efforts of Native Americans are instructive for community practice. To rebuild their communities and tribal institutions, Native Americans have had to reestablish their governance systems and foster economic and social development (Edwards & Egbert-Edwards, 1992). Currently, a wide variety of social planning and program, community, and economic development efforts are taking place all across North America. The Inuit people of Alaska are renowned for art-and-craft cooperatives. The Navajo nation, in addition to being involved in crafts, is engaged in various economic development activities, including housing and commercial enterprises that range from construction of shopping centers to light industrial production of circuit boards. The Hopi people, in keeping with their traditions, engage in physical planning for environmental protections with a multigenerational, multidecade focus (Weil, 1990). The Cherokee nation in Oklahoma, under Wilma Mankiller's leadership, has invested heavily in housing and economic development, and the Eastern Band of the Cherokee in North Carolina adapt service systems models in child welfare and juvenile services for their communities. On the West Coast and East Coast and in Canada, as well as in the Southwest, tribal groups are engaged in environmental development and tourism.

Throughout Indian country, efforts to connect social and economic development have been receiving increasing emphasis. Native American tribes are also deeply involved in implementation of the Indian Child Welfare Act of 1978 in planning for development of family support and family preservation programs under the Family Support Act of 1993, and in strengthening tribal-based service systems.

***African Americans.*** Equally instructive for community practice is the long history of African Americans in developing community institutions, establishing civil rights, and seeking equality of opportunity. Many European immigrant groups initially formed their own burial societies, mutual aid associations, child welfare programs, social agencies, religious institutions, and other self-help groups as basic means of group support and advancement. For African Americans, that same group support was often their key to basic survival. During slavery and after emancipation, many African Americans organized mutual aid societies and later formed agencies and programs to serve their community. The Anti-Slavery Societies were instrumental in providing safety and support for fugitives escaping slavery in the South.

Throughout U.S. history, many support and aid groups and community development projects have been formed through the African American church. Ministers and church members from early history through the civil rights movement and to the present have promoted citizen participation and have served as community organizers and developers. The civil rights movement, which grew from earlier struggles for liberation articulated in part by Frederick Douglass and W.E.B. DuBois, is yet a more recent example of the continuous indigenous movement for liberation and rights for African Americans (Branch, 1988; Foner, 1970; Williams, 1987).

African American organizers and community leaders have promoted participation in life-saving and liberty-producing projects, from the Underground Railroad to the civil rights movement of the 1950s and 1960s (Williams, 1987). William Still, for example, worked for the Anti-Slavery Society, offering support, counseling, and resettlement assistance to fugitives who had escaped slavery, and documented their experiences in his 1872 book, *The Underground Railroad* (Johnson 1977; Still, 1872/1970). He was also committed to organizing in the African American community, to fundraising for the Anti-Slavery Society, and to engaging in political participation and change activities. Lugenia Burns Hope, who organized the Neighborhood Union in Atlanta in 1908 for development of community-based planning and service provision, was another early role model for community practice in the African American community (Johnson, 1991).

African Americans not only founded their own organizations but also contributed a great deal to work in settlements and other community-focused work. For example, George Edmund Haynes was a cofounder of the National League on Urban Conditions Among Negroes (later renamed the National Urban League), and his sister, Birdye Henrietta Haynes, pioneered in settlement work—working to establish community-relevant programs in Chicago and New York (Carlton-LaNey, 1994). Much of the focus on empowerment strategies has grown from work in African American communities (Simon, 1994; Solomon, 1986).

***Hispanic populations.*** Similar historical models for community development can be found among the early peoples of the Southwest with successive populations of tribal groups and later mestizo settlements considerably before the arrival of Northern Europeans in that region. Various Latino organizations have worked together in La Raza and have been engaged in many organizing and development projects. Chicanos in the South and Southwest have been engaged in community change in San Antonio and other cities; Puerto Ricans in the Northeast have been involved in educational, development, and organizing projects; and direct organizing is in progress among Central American immigrant and refugee groups (Cordoba, 1992; Montiel & Ortego y Gasca, 1992; Morales, 1992).

***Asian Americans.*** Each successive group of Asians who settled in North America had to organize for mutual support because of widespread discrimination and oppressive labor conditions. Currently organizing and development within and among the various Asian American communities is strongest on the West Coast. Chinese Americans have worked actively to develop service systems, particularly for seniors in Seattle, San Francisco, and Los Angeles (Lee, 1992). In 1988 Japanese Americans won a long struggle to gain government reparations for losses suffered during internment. The Japanese American Citizens League, among other organizations, has been a strong force in the community and in external relations; Murase (1992) pointed out that "the concept of Asian American was a unifying force among Japanese, Chinese, Korean, and Filipino Americans. It provided the basis for an alliance with Black, Hispanic, and Native American groups for collective action against the forces of oppression" (p. 175). Much organizing and development work is taking place within the Southeast Asian refugee communities (Asian American Mental Health Training Center, 1981; Vuong & Huynh, 1992). The Asian American Mental Health Training Center in Los Angeles is one example of a highly successful Pan-Asian program planning, service implementation, and training project.

**Rural Community Organization**

As Settlements and Charity Organization Societies were taking shape in the cities, rural America experienced another type of community practice. Rural community development efforts can be traced deep into American history. In *Democracy in America,* Alexis de Tocqueville (1835/1956) observed that any group of five or more Americans would almost inevitably organize themselves to create some project or association. Rural survival often demanded cooperation, and many efforts in rural development have been related to electrification; access to clean water, livestock, and crop cooperatives; and the development of basic services, from schools to volunteer fire brigades. Rural community councils were formed in some areas, and in the 1930s there was a strong farming cooperative movement (Austin & Betten, 1990). The Highlander Center in New Market, Tennessee, which began organizing the rural poor people of the Appalachian region, has since the 1930s remained a major training ground for both rural and urban citizen-participation activists (Horton, Kohl, & Kohl, 1992). Today it organizes for economic and environmental justice in rural America and around the globe.

***Agricultural extension agents.*** Agricultural extension agents working out of land-grant agricultural and technical colleges have developed citizen participation programs for rural development, technical assistance, and organization of social support systems. Programs for the organization of social support systems were a particular focus of home demonstration agents, who worked primarily with farm women. The agents, trained in the same land-grant colleges as the agricultural agents, worked with farm women in groups called home demonstration clubs. In these clubs, women learned to improve their canning, sewing, and home decorating skills, but they also learned leadership skills and developed important social support networks. Unlike the Settlements and Charity Organization Societies, the major impetus for rural development resulted from legislation and federal funding to develop more-efficient agricultural technology (Austin & Betten, 1990). Although agents entered rural areas as experts, they learned to use a low-key "discussion method" in leadership development. Grassroots organizers, armed with knowledge and new approaches to issues ranging from cultivation methods to development of cooperatives, worked on local projects and facilitated collaboration between farmers and extension agents (Lord, 1939).

Historically, African American colleges have provided their own agricultural and home demonstration agents to serve African American farming families and to work with them in rural collaborative organization and community support. Although the Cooperative Extension Service is now integrated, the efforts of these agents, especially those in the rural southeastern United States, continue to provide significant social and development support for African American families in rural development through home demonstration clubs and, more recently, through specific economic development projects for African American women (Carlton-LaNey, 1992; Johnson & Jennings, 1994). Eventually the Cooperative Extension Service programs also developed 4-H Clubs for rural youths, which provide economic development as well as agricultural training programs. Although a massive population shift has now placed the majority of Americans in urban areas, these services continue apace in rural and exurban American communities. Indeed, the population shifts and persistence of rural poverty render organizing and development—both social and economic—critical current concerns for rural America (Christenson & Robinson, 1989; Duncan, 1992).

***Organization of farm workers.*** Another side of rural community practice relates to the organization of farm workers. The organization of grape pickers in California by Cesar Chavez grew into a nationwide organization of crop harvesters called the United Farm Workers Union. They are still active and are sometimes assisted in their organizing efforts by La Raza.

The various roots of community practice have shaped the way community practice has emerged in the 1990s. There is a strong literature regarding community organization and social planning with many major works appearing in the late 1960s and 1970s; a resurgence is now occurring. Models guide teaching and community practice. Rothman (1995) developed a taxonomy of three models of community organization in 1976 and recently revised and elaborated the connections among locality development, social action, and social planning. In 1985 Taylor and Roberts edited a volume that presented five models of community social work. The following section describes current models of practice found in a range of communities. The models presented are developed by the authors from history, from the practice literature, and from research on current practice. They relate to the objectives of community practice: to develop the organizing skills and abilities of citizen groups, to make social planning more accessible and inclusive in a community, to connect social and economic investments to grassroots groups, to advocate for broad coalitions in solving community problems, and to infuse the social planning process with a concern for social justice. The characteristics of each model are described with a focus on their relevance for social work and social workers' practice roles.

## Current Models of Community Practice

The current realities of practice reveal a complex and interconnected set of models for community practice. Surveys of the literature and research on current practice provide the basis for a new constellation of eight basic models of community practice: (1) neighborhood and community organizing, (2) organizing functional communities, (3) community social and economic development, (4) social planning, (5) program development and community liaison, (6) political and social action, (7) coalitions, and (8) social movements (Table 1). The models illustrate the kinds of organizations that exist in the 1990s and that are expected to persist. Each model is analyzed in terms of desired outcome, system targeted for change, primary constituency, scope of concern, and primary social work roles (Weil & Gamble, 1993).

TABLE 1

**Current Models of Community Practice for Social Work**

| Comparative Characteristics | Models | | | | | | | |
|---|---|---|---|---|---|---|---|---|
| | Neighborhood and Community Organizing | Organizing Functional Communities | Community Social and Economic Development | Social Planning | Program Development and Community Liaison | Political and Social Action | Coalitions | Social Movements |
| Desired outcome | Develop capacity of members to organize; change the impact of citywide planning and external development | Action for social justice focused on advocacy and on changing behaviors and attitudes; may also provide service | Initiate development plans from a grassroots perspective; prepare citizens to make use of social and economic investments | Citywide or regional proposals for action by elected body or human services planning councils | Expansion or redirection of agency program to improve community service effectiveness; organize new service | Action for social justice focused on changing policy or policy makers | Build a multiorganizational power base large enough to influence program direction or draw down resources | Action for social justice that provides a new paradigm for a particular population group or issue |
| System targeted for change | Municipal government; external developers; community members | General public; government institutions | Banks; foundations; external developers; community citizens | Perspectives of community leaders; perspectives of human services leaders | Funders of agency programs; beneficiaries of agency services | Voting public; elected officials; inactive/ potential participants | Elected officials; foundations; government institutions | General public; political systems |
| Primary constituency | Residents of neighborhood, parish, or rural county | Like-minded people in a community, region, nation, or across the globe | Low-income, marginalized, or oppressed population groups in a city or region | Elected officials; social agencies and interagency organizations | Agency board or administrators; community representatives | Citizens in a particular political jurisdiction | Organizations that have a stake in the particular issue | Leaders and organizations able to create new visions and images |
| Scope of concern | Quality of life in the geographic area | Advocacy for particular issue or population | Income, resource, and social support development; improved basic education and leadership skills | Integration of social needs into geographic planning in public arena; human services network coordination | Service development for a specific population | Building political power; institutional change | Specified issue related to social need or concern | Social justice within society |
| Social work roles | Organizer<br>Teacher<br>Coach<br>Facilitator | Organizer<br>Advocate<br>Writer/ communicator<br>Facilitator | Negotiator<br>Promoter<br>Teacher<br>Planner<br>Manager | Researcher<br>Proposal writer<br>Communicator<br>Manager | Spokesperson<br>Planner<br>Manager<br>Proposal writer | Advocate<br>Organizer<br>Researcher<br>Candidate | Mediator<br>Negotiator<br>Spokesperson | Advocate<br>Facilitator |

Chart compiled by M. Weil and D. Gamble (1994).

Policy analysis and policy practice in research, action, and program implementation should be viewed as activities that undergrid each model. The need for policies, programs, and political and organizational processes that encourage citizen participation and support long-term goals for social justice is a major raison d'être of each model. The development or change of policies at local, state, regional, national, and global levels is an essential element of organizing, service reform, political action, and social change. These models are described as discrete forms in Table 1 but are often observed in interaction as more complex and overlapping organizations and processes that change to respond to new challenges or shifts in the environment.

The rationale and organizing principles that guide this conceptual framework are grounded in place, purpose, and values. Community practice occurs on an intersecting continuum from local to global. The local place is necessary because human societies require some face-to-face interaction. The world as "place" is possible because of available communication technology.

**Purposes of Community Organizations**

The reasons community organizations exist vary widely, and often the structures reflect the particular purpose of the organized effort. Community practice efforts will focus primarily on one or more of the following issues:

***Improving the quality of life.*** Community practice efforts will improve the quality of life from a single local issue, such as securing a railroad crossing gate in a rural community, to complex social issues, such as devising strategies to improve education and opportunities for African American youth, to the design and implementation of global strategies for sustainable development.

***Advocacy.*** Community organizations will advocate for a community of interest, such as children with severe emotional or behavioral problems; for a specific issue, such as human rights for gays and lesbians; for resource attainment, such as efforts to fund minority economic development projects through the 1977 Community Reinvestment Act (P.L. 95-128); or for establishment of political and social rights for women worldwide.

***Human social and economic development.*** Strategies to build human social and economic development will ensure social support and economic viability and sustainability, expand participation, and build grassroots leadership locally, regionally, and globally. These strategies include cooperative and business development for Native Americans, reestablishment of a greenbelt in Kenya by African women, and implementation of the United Nation's Agenda 21 blueprint for sustainable social and economic development.

***Service and program planning.*** Community practice efforts will involve service and program planning for a newly recognized or a reconceptualized need or for an emerging population. Efforts include health and social services for people with acquired immune deficiency syndrome (AIDS) and human immunodeficiency virus (HIV); development of alternative services for battered women; and development of adoption, foster care, and juvenile services within Native American communities.

***Service integration.*** Community practice efforts also will involve service integration that will develop local, national, and international means of coordinating human services for populations in need—for example, building the continuum of family support, preservation, and child welfare services; building a network of well-connected services for healthy and frail senior citizens; or providing food and protection, relocation opportunities, and services for new starts for refugees from national or international conflicts.

***Political and social action.*** Political and social action will build political power for economically marginalized people; protect weak and poor people; foster institutional change for inclusion and equity; and increase participatory democracy and equality of access and opportunity in local, regional, and international efforts, such as political organizing in communities of color; Children's Defense Fund's work in national research and organizing for the rights, protection, and welfare of children (1994); and Amnesty International's efforts to prevent torture and secure release of political prisoners worldwide.

***Social justice.*** Social justice will build toward human equality and opportunity across race, ethnicity, gender, and nationality—for example, in securing voting rights for women, making reparations to Japanese Americans for internment during World War II, and building the fabric of civil and human rights laws nationally and globally.

The value base that supports community practice is grounded in respect for both the dignity of the individual and the interdependence of families and communities and in the development of social, political, and distributive justice. One of the central tasks for social workers is to engage the inevitable tensions between the individual and the community, including competing views of issues, and divergent strategies to solve problems.

**Neighborhood and Community Organizing**
This model of community practice focuses on work and geographic neighborhoods and communities. Although such geographic organizations may be founded on the basis of one issue or critical incident, many evolve to deal with the full range of community social, political, and environmental issues. Leaders from local community organizations may often represent their community in the larger political life of a city, county, or region.

Neighborhood and community organizing has a dual focus: capacity building and task accomplishment. As citizens become involved in organizing activities, they develop skills in organizing, problem analysis, planning, and leadership. They also seek to accomplish a series of specific tasks related to improving social and economic conditions in their own community and to shape the direction of city or regional planning and external development. This type of organizing occurs when citizens band together to strengthen their community and improve the quality of their lives and opportunities in dense urban communities, in suburban neighborhoods, and in rural areas.

Often the external target for change is municipal or county government and sometimes it is companies that plan to establish a development or downsize a source of employment. Internal development focuses on capacity building and leadership development to aid the group as it seeks to make needed changes in its political, social, and physical environments. The neighborhood, parish, or community typically forms the primary constituency, and the scope of concern broadly focuses on the quality of life in the geographic area.

Social workers' roles in neighborhood and community organizing include organizer, educator and teacher, coach, and facilitator. The organizer will often work with neighborhood residents to establish an organization and may later become staff for the group, offering assistance in both process and technical skill development. When formal leadership is established in the group, the social worker will typically function as a staffperson, working with officers and committee members to plan meetings, set goals, locate resources, plan and carry out strategies, and evaluate task and process efforts.

An important part of this group development process is the clarification of group leadership and staff facilitation roles. The social worker will more often be involved in leadership development within the group rather than directly take on leadership roles. In organizing, the social worker assists group members in defining issues for action, developing strategies for recruiting members, teaching techniques for doing background research and needs assessments, and planning strategies for action. As an educator and teacher, the social worker uses adult education models in consciousness raising and issue examination and serves as a formal or informal teacher of leadership skills, group facilitation skills, research skills, and action skills.

Current examples of neighborhood organizations include Communities Organized for Public Service of San Antonio, a broad-based Industrial Areas Foundation–developed organization in Texas; Project MASH (Make Something Happen) in the Stowe Village Housing Project of Hartford, Connecticut, which engages in community organization and job, neighborhood, and service development; the organizing and service development for Central American immigrants and refugees in the Palms district of Los Angeles; and CARE (the Community and Resource Exchange) of Minneapolis and Hennepin County, Minnesota, which was established to fight drugs and crime.

**Functional Community Organizing**
The salient distinction of this model is its focus on a functional rather than a geographic community. A functional community is a community of interest. People may or may not live in close proximity, but they share a concern about a common issue, which can range from advocacy for the needs of children with disabling conditions to environmental protection. The central focus and desired outcome in organizing functional communities is action for social justice focused on advocacy and on changing policies, behaviors, and attitudes in relation to their chosen issue. In their efforts to seek social justice, functional communities may also develop services for their specific population that have not been addressed or, if so, inadequately addressed in the mainstream service system.

***Types of communities.*** One example of service development by a functional community is the development of service systems for women, evolving from feminist organizing and consisting of rape crisis centers and domestic violence programs, and more recently expanding to deal with women's employment and economic development issues (Gottlieb, 1980; Gutierrez & Lewis, 1994; Hooyman & Bricker-Jenkins, 1985; Mauney, Williams, & Weil, 1993).

Functional communities often are engaged in community education about their chosen issue. An example is the gay and lesbian communities' work to educate others about AIDS and to press for appropriate health care, supportive health policy, and the social, economic, and civil rights of people who have tested HIV-positive. Members of functional communities may work to establish particular services and may also seek specific new policies or policy changes with government institutions. For example, Vietnam veterans groups have worked to obtain access to treatment and disability payments related to Agent Orange; social workers have organized to attain professional licensure.

As functional communities organize, they also engage in internal capacity building, increasing knowledge about their issue, and leadership development. At times, new members of functional communities may first be drawn to support groups and, with increased knowledge and skills, move into organizing, case advocacy, and policy advocacy. Parents of children who have severe emotional disturbances, for example, may initially seek out support groups and evolve into advocacy leaders in the Alliance for Mentally Ill Children and Adolescents, or the Federation of Families. Strength within the group, clarity of mission, and the ability to recruit members and sustain leadership to support the group's issues are central factors for success for organizations that are formed from a community of interest. Members may be people who are directly affected by a problematic issue, such as toxic waste dumps, or people who may not be directly affected but who support the goals of the group. The primary constituency of a functional community is like-minded people in a community, region, nation, or international organization. The scope of concern is advocacy for the chosen issue or population. This advocacy can take the form of education, research, public action, policy development, lobbying, and service development.

Other examples of functional communities include the Association of Retarded Citizens, which functions at the local and national levels to improve services and advocate for the rights of children and adults with developmental disabilities; many women's organizations; environmental organizations; and groups such as Amnesty International, which documents human-rights violations and seeks protection and justice for political prisoners worldwide through the organization of local advocacy groups.

The feminist model of community practice can be viewed as one example of organizing by a functional community; however, the wide range of organizing, planning, service development and coordination, social action, and change undertaken by women for women argues for its identification also as a specific model grounded in particular theoretical perspectives and values (Gutierrez & Lewis, 1994; Hooyman & Bricker-Jenkins, 1985; Van Den Bergh & Cooper, 1986; Weick & Vandiver, 1982; Weil, 1986).

***Social work roles.*** As in neighborhood organizing, a social work organizer may engage with the community-of-interest group as a facilitator who assists the group in recruiting members, defining problems, and determining advocacy strategies and tactics. The social worker may also teach research and analysis techniques, as has been the case for more than 50 years at the Highlander Center, New Market, Tennessee, where generations of people have been educated in research related to a variety of issues, including labor rights, civil rights, and environmental protection (Gaventa, 1980). The social worker will assist the group in developing process, decision making, and technical skills. Because there is often greater geographic dispersion of a community-of-interest organization, the social worker may also take on more responsibility in writing and communication, such as helping the group to develop a newsletter, communication trees, computer bulletin boards, and reports that will be used in lobbying and public education efforts.

In functional communities the ability of the group to articulate and educate about its issues is of critical importance. The organizer and leaders of the group may spend much time in public, government, and media relations in efforts to get the group's message across. A social worker may spend considerable time with members rehearsing these skills and helping the group prepare documents and reports that can be used to further their cause. Communication within the group and to its various audiences is a major means of working toward the goals of social justice and changing policies and societal behaviors.

**Community Social and Economic Development**

This model is closely related to earlier models of social or locality development as articulated by Ross (1955), Rothman (1979), and Lappin (1985). In this new typology, however, the model merges social and economic development in recognition that for effectiveness in low-income and oppressed communities, social development must accompany economic development for either type of development to be successful (National Congress for Community Economic Development, 1991). The goal of this merged model of community development is to improve the quality of life and opportunities for citizens in low-income or oppressed communities. In some earlier models the focus was almost exclusively on process goals of helping citizens in such communities come together and determine what they wished to pursue. The current model moves beyond that process goal to recognition of the need for development of technical, political, and process skills so that citizens can actually achieve their community goals, not just formulate them. In the community-development model, the focus and desired outcome are to initiate plans and development from a grassroots perspective, prepare citizens to make use of social and economic investments, and develop and use internal and external resources to make those investments.

***Dual focus.*** There is a clear and continuous dual focus in the community development model on strengthening the capacity of citizens and communities to develop and implement plans for social and economic development and resource development and enlisting the resources available through city and county governments, banks, foundations, and external developers. The goal in relation to external systems targeted for change is to persuade those with resources to invest in the social and economic development of the community in ways that ensure a high degree of community determination. Some of the more narrowly designed development efforts have not allowed the profits of development to remain in the community. Experience with such programs has caused community leaders and program staff to stress community reinvestment and to avoid collaboration with external funders who are not committed to this same goal.

Successful social and economic community efforts have combined development of housing, community-owned small businesses, cooperatives or employee-owned businesses, and support services such as day care for children and seniors. Increasingly, more sophisticated economic development groups are incorporating major social and service development components into their missions. For example, the Bethel New Life Corporation in Chicago initially focused on housing development, expanded to job training and business development, and more recently added day care centers for children and elderly people as a social service to enable community members to work, create jobs, train for work, and support further economic development. Economic development corporations may choose to establish some services as economic development opportunities and others as a basic service with no expectation of profit but as a necessary aspect of infrastructure development for a community (National Congress for Community Economic Development, 1991).

***Constituencies.*** The primary constituencies in social and economic development are low-income, marginalized, or oppressed groups in an urban or rural area. In this model, development groups or corporations will seek to meet the needs of a particular population, such as Chicanos por la Causa in Phoenix, which is engaged in housing, job development and training, day care, and support and educational and training services for adolescent parents and disadvantaged youths. The needs of low-income populations in more widely dispersed rural areas are the concern of organizations such as Community Action Programs, established by the federal government in 1965. Native American groups are increasingly engaged in combined social and economic development: The Zuni sponsor a large crafts cooperative, and the Navajo have invested heavily in small businesses that interface with high-tech development industries, as well as in housing, tourism, and crafts production. Another example is the Rural Economic Development Center of North Carolina, which seeks to encourage economic and social development in one of the nation's most rural states.

***Scope.*** The scope of concern in social and economic development will be a balance of investment in both the social and economic areas as well as the improvement of the educational level and leadership skills of the citizens. Internally, for the nascent community development corporation, there will be serious attention to capacity building—particularly in technical and management skills—to develop services and economic development projects. These efforts will be linked with improving basic education and technical and leadership skills within the targeted community. The emerging corporation will focus on developing economic growth projects that can produce income for individuals and groups, and social support and service programs to create the infrastructure to build a more functional and self-sufficient community.

***Social work roles.*** In economic and social development activities, a social worker often will become a staff member of the corporation or staff the group in its early organizational stages. Social workers should be skilled in needs assessment and research to determine realistic development goals and to identify needed community skills and resources. The ability to organize and do training is also necessary in developing community leadership and technical skills. Planning, managing, and negotiating are essential roles for social workers involved in economic and social development. The social worker in social and economic development is likely to be intensively engaged with participants in many aspects of development and therefore needs high-level skills in both process and task and technical areas.

Social and economic citizen participation are critical elements of community development. Although there are tensions between the need to meet proposal and negotiation deadlines and the need for broad involvement, these projects do not sustain community support without active citizen participation. In America and throughout the world, there is increased interest in designing economic development that is sustainable for the community and the environment (Estes, 1993).

**Social Planning**

Social planning can be conducted at the individual agency level, by a consortium of human services agencies, or by a regional human services planning council. Elected bodies and government bureaus at city, county, and regional levels also engage in social planning. Often social planning is done by a task force that combines the private and public interests and resources in the planning process. "Social planning refers to the development, expansion, and coordination of social services and social policies" and is a method of practice and application of rational problem solving that occurs organizationally on a continuum from local to societal (Lauffer, 1981, p. 583). It may focus specifically on coordinating human services for a given area or look more broadly at social and economic issues. Lauffer (1978) identified roles for planners at four levels: (1) direct service agencies, (2) service sectors, (3) comprehensive local planning structure, and (4) regional or intersectorial—or intergovernmental—planning structures. Current examples include the reemergence of local planning councils in Kansas, West Virginia, and Massachusetts; Area Agencies on Aging; sectarian federations; specialized funding federations (such as Women's Way or the United Black Fund); and the United Way, community action agencies, and community mental health boards and human resource commissions.

***Focus.*** In all these settings, the central task of planners is to bring rationality to the human services, social planning, and service integration processes. From the earliest efforts of the Charity Organization Societies, to current efforts to integrate services across systems, planners have sought to make better use of resources and determine what resources are needed in the human services to enable the system to serve those in need. Planners need specific technical skills and are often charged, whether by elected bodies or by human services planning councils, with developing citywide or regional proposals for development and action. Although planners also seek to educate the public about directions for services and development, they chiefly seek to influence the perspectives of community leaders and human services leaders to develop, fund, evaluate, merge, or change particular programs. Increasingly, however, there has been pressure and a variety of efforts to open up planning processes and make strong consumer and community participation the norm. The Our Children Today and Tomorrow planning project in the seven westernmost counties of North Carolina, for example, engaged parents and children intensively in its three-year process to plan appropriate and family-friendly services for children.

***Constituencies.*** The primary constituency for planning can consist of elected officials, leaders of social agencies, interagency organizations, or a combination of these. The scope of concern for planners will be either human services network planning and coordination or integration of social needs into geographic planning in the public arena. The essential skills of planners are technical; they include research, needs assessments, evaluation, proposal development, and analysis. Because planners engage with such a wide variety of individuals and groups, they need excellent communication and management skills. The Community Planning Council of West Virginia, for example, recently led a major multicounty effort to plan, coordinate, and integrate services for children. The Phoenix Futures Forum engaged in a broad-based long-range planning and community-building process that involved hundreds of residents during a period of rapid population and economic growth with outcomes of 21 major new initiatives and eventual involvement of many forum participants on city boards and commissions (Plotz, 1992).

**Program Development and Community Liaison**

This model combines the aspects of two kinds of organizational efforts that were previously articulated by Kurzman (1985) and Taylor (1985). The merger of these models seems warranted in that community liaison activities are an essential aspect of program development. The central goal and desired outcome of this model is to design and implement a new or improved service that has been assessed as needed by a community population. It also involves the expansion or redirection of agency programs to improve community service effectiveness. Interaction among citizens, potential clients, and agency staff is critical in the conception of this model. The interaction between the community and service programs can be strengthened in a variety of ways. Among them are the involvement of potential consumers and citizens in the needs-assessment process; use of focus groups of potential consumers, related agency staff, or both; development of advisory bodies; and involvement of potential consumers and community leaders in policy-making boards. As the program is designed and implemented, mechanisms for feedback to and from the community are valuable in keeping new programs on target.

***Constituencies.*** Systems that are targeted for change are the potential beneficiaries of the new or redesigned service and those who pay for such services. Program designers, planners, and staff will also experience change and shifts in perspective when they are able to develop effective mutual planning strategies with community members. In a parallel to the change pattern, the primary constituencies for the program development model are the agency board (as the group responsible for the agency's direction) and the community representatives involved in the planned change and program development process.

***Scope.*** The scope of concern is service development for a particular population or geographic area. Roles likely to be taken on by a social worker include planner, proposal writer, spokesperson, mediator, and facilitator in the interaction process with constituent groups and external supporters. As the program becomes established, a social worker will often take on roles of manager, monitor, and evaluator to assure that the program stays on track, meets its goals for service and change, and remains responsive to the community and changing environment. The intensive work to develop the family preservation and support models of the Children's Bureau of Los Angeles presents one model of program development and community liaison that also stressed development of strong outcome evaluations of new programs (McCroskey & Meezan, 1992).

**Political and Social Action**

This model draws clearly from practice reality and earlier articulation by Rothman (1979), Grosser and Mondros (1985), Reisch and Wenocur (1986), Rubin and Rubin (1992), and Hanna and Robinson (1994). Social and political action efforts challenge inequalities that limit opportunities, confront decision makers who have ignored community needs, dispute unjust decisions, and empower people through strengthening their belief in their own efficacy and developing their skills to change unjust conditions (Rubin & Rubin, 1992; Staples, 1990). As Rubin and Rubin (1992) noted, "Social action campaigns document a problem, choose as a target those who can effect a solution, symbolize the issue, take pressureful actions and try to ensure the implementation of promised changes" (p. 245). The central focus and desired outcome for this model is action for social, political, and economic justice focused on changing policy or policymakers or changing actions of corporations that disadvantage low-income groups. The goal of social and political action is to shift the balance of power so that those who have been excluded in earlier decision-making processes become players in future decisions. This goal is grounded in strengthening participatory democracy and building social justice.

***Scope.*** The first targets for change are the potential participants in the social and political change effort; the first objective may be capacity building in organizing and leadership skills. A major part of this effort may be in investigative research to determine the scope and seriousness of problems, such as the dumping of toxic wastes or dysfunctional construction patterns of some developers. Political and social action involves the examination of options for action and selection of appropriate tactics. Social action groups are involved in educating their community or constituencies about their issue, recruiting members for a variety of roles, and taking direct action. Members must be confident of their skills to plan actions and convinced of the legitimacy of their cause and tactics.

Public elected and administrative officials are often targets for change in social and political action. Elected and appointed officials are the targets of change, for example, when the change effort is designed to prevent a highway from cutting a minority community in half, or when a redevelopment plan removes low-income and people of color to gentrify a neighborhood, or when public schools are asked to be more accountable.

Other targets of change may be major corporations or businesses that have been engaged in activities that are damaging to the community, such as pollution of the environment or endangerment of the health and livelihood of workers.

Organization of low-income workers or work with labor groups often relates to social and political action. Action groups also want to educate the public to understand their cause, and the mobilization of public opinion can become a major part of an action campaign.

The primary constituents of a political and social action group are citizens in a particular political jurisdiction, or citizens or workers who are committed to a particular case. Although there is great diversity in the causes that will be pursued through direct action, the scope of concern of all will be building political power and promoting institutional change toward greater social justice.

***Social work roles.*** Roles for social workers in political and social action will include those of advocate, educator, organizer, and researcher. Internally, the organizer will be engaged in capacity building, both in terms of internal group process and decision-making skills and in externally focused skills in direct action, public and media relations, and investigative research. Although the organizer may serve directly as an advocate in some instances, it is much more important that the organizer assist group members in becoming their own advocates. Much of the organizer's work is in facilitative leadership and capacity building.

In a direct way, social workers might be involved in political and social action by entering politics and running for office. They might also lead social policy change activities within a reform administration. NASW has been directly involved in political action, most recently in its research, plan development, and lobbying for national health reform. The organization's increasing emphasis on government and legislative relations and lobbying has strengthened the social work profession's position as a player in political and policy change.

Social action is about positive change. In describing the fundamentals of social action, Bobo, Kendall, and Max (1991) noted three principles: "(1) win real, immediate, concrete improvements in people's lives; (2) give people a sense of their own power; and (3) alter the relations of power" (pp. 7–8). Grassroots organizing for political and social action requires not only skills in organizing but also increasingly requires skills in research, computer use, media and public relations, and fundraising for long-term projects that may grow out of the action process. Grosser and Mondros (1985) noted that social action groups may decide to develop their own programs and services so that models will be appropriate and empowering. When such programs are implemented, groups must also master fundraising, communication, and management skills needed for nonprofit administration.

**Coalitions**

Coalitions make it possible for separate groups to work together for collective social change. A *social change coalition,* as defined by Mizrahi and Rosenthal (1993), is "a group of diverse organizational representatives who join forces to influence external institutions on one or more issues affecting their constituencies while maintaining their own autonomy" (p. 14). They further characterized coalitions as having a time-limited life span that typically is filled with dynamic tensions resulting from the simultaneous demands on organizational representatives to remain autonomous while building a new organization from the compatible interests of the diverse members.

***Scope.*** In this model the desired outcome would be to build a multiorganizational power base that is large enough to influence social program direction, including the potential to draw down resources to respond to the common interests of the coalition. The systems most often targeted for change are elected officials who might approve new policies, foundations that may be encouraged to fund new or expanding service programs, and government institutions that may have the authority to respond to a particular social concern but not the readiness to do so.

Generally, because coalition building requires an enormous time commitment, only organizations that have a stake in the particular issues will participate. Examples of coalitions found in many communities are those organized for affordable housing, against the increase in teenage pregnancy and teenage violence, against domestic violence, for service programs for elderly people, and for environmentally safe economic development.

The scope of concern for social change coalitions is the specific issue or issues that member groups can agree to support. Over the past few years, a coalition of major human services, child advocacy, and professional groups have successfully lobbied for federal articulation and legislation to support family-centered, community-based services. This coalition, with leadership from the Children's Defense Fund, the Child Welfare League, Family Impact Seminar, and NASW, among others, successfully lobbied for implementation of the 1993 Family Support Act. Coalitions are likely to have a significant impact on the health care reform process. Coalitions for homeless people have been successful in many urban areas in establishing shelters and services, and some are also concerned with development of low-income housing. To stay together, coalitions develop complex exchange relations and find ways to balance their commitment to the issues that hold them together with the individual agendas and perspectives of member groups (Roberts-DeGennaro, 1986, 1987).

***Social work roles.*** Social workers are likely to be leaders and spokespersons in professional or human services coalitions. To build and maintain the coalition, mediation and negotiation skills are often critical to balance tensions and maintain the coalition's focus. In coalitions of advocacy groups focused on alternative services, such as Coalitions Against Domestic Violence, social workers will also have roles that emphasize group and organization facilitation, teaching and coaching, leadership development, conflict negotiation, and skills in interorganizational relations and planning.

### Social Movements

Social movements occur in all kinds of arenas and have been evident throughout history. Wood and Jackson (1982) described *social movements* as "groups that have varying degrees of formal organization and that attempt to produce or prevent radical or reformist type of change" (p. 3). Generally, social work efforts do not create movements, but the activities of social workers are influenced by current social movements. Sometimes progress toward a just and caring society is assisted by social movements, as in the case of the civil rights movement, and at other times it may be impeded, as in the case of movements spawned as the result of homophobia. Social workers, in keeping with the values of their profession, will be allied with social movements that support democracy, individual dignity, the rights of people of color, the needs of poor people, sustainable development, and activities that support broad goals of human development and liberation.

The desired outcome of social movements is to stimulate action for social change that provides a new paradigm for the way society and social organizations respond to a particular population group or social issue. The systems targeted for change are the general public, and especially political systems. In the United States, the civil rights movement is perhaps the best-known and most far-reaching recent example of a social movement. Over time, its leaders balanced coalitions and managed social change in policies, laws, organizations, institutions, attitudes, and behaviors. In many ways, the civil rights movement gave birth to civil and social rights activities in La Raza, the women's movement, and the subsequent disabilities rights movement. In each of these movements, new paradigms about these groups emerged with the success of the movement. Legislation and attitudes have begun to focus more on abilities than disabilities; women increasingly exercise equal rights and move into leadership positions; and although racism and prejudice have not disappeared, Latinos, African Americans, and Native Americans have established civil rights and continue to work toward social and economic equality. Many social workers have been involved in each of these movements as volunteers and as organizational staff. Their roles often were those of advocate and facilitator.

Social movements often occur when protest erupts as the result of a buildup of oppression or when great and inequitable changes in the political/social system occur. Localized protests may call attention to widespread oppression; when those protests engender widespread support and mass empathy, a social movement emerges. Piven and Cloward (1979) analyzed four different American social movements and concluded that "both the limitations and opportunities for mass protest are shaped by social conditions" (p. 36) and not necessarily by the efforts of organizers and leaders. There may be only a small window of opportunity for change provided by the temporary relaxation of the social order brought about by widespread social protest. Piven and Cloward suggested that the best strategy to achieve sought-for change through social movements is to extend that window of opportunity.

Social movements that can maintain momentum can achieve significant change. The election of Nelson Mandela as president of South Africa is the outcome of a social movement and long-term struggle to end the system of apartheid and establish civil and social rights for all South Africans. The efforts toward human rights in Latin America and many other parts of the world continue. As a social movement succeeds, the ideals that it has advanced are accepted as new, legitimized political and social norms.

## Conclusion

The models presented in this entry illustrate the current range and major models of community practice. As Rothman (1979) noted, actual practice may combine aspects of various models and may be phased sequentially over time as a neighborhood organization grows into intensive work in economic or social development, or as a community of interest builds a needed alternative service system. Local groups increasingly see and act on their connections to global issues and actions. Models can guide practice, but they are not static rubrics. Practice will continue to change in response to local and international issues and internal and external environmental influences.

While practice realities shift, much of the value base for community practice remains constant. In addition to individual dignity and human interdependence, social workers involved in this arena will abide by guiding values that focus on support for those people with the least resources and skills for participation in decision making; target developing skills and reorganizing resources to improve the lives of the poorest or most disenfranchised groups; use strategies and tactics that do not cause physical harm to other groups and individuals; and emphasize civil, social, and distributive justice.

**Trends**

Rubin and Rubin (1992) identified the following four trends in community organization and development practice that occurred from the 1970s into the 1990s: (1) increased attention to issue-based organization; (2) increased emphasis on community-based economic development; (3) community organizations becoming permanent political actors; and (4) new emphases on both neopopulist and feminist ideologies and practice strategies (pp. 26–29). During this same period, the trends in social planning, program development, and human services policy development have emphasized the dysfunction of categorical, separatist programs and have designed interventions to strengthen and unify practice and service delivery. In the 1990s a major reform movement, fostered by foundations, government bodies, and local programs, aims to build strong family-centered, community-based continua of services that focus on appropriate responses to unique needs and on service integration. As we move into the 21st century, community practice will continue to evolve to meet changing needs. The following trends in practice strategies for these models are expected.

***Neighborhood and community organizing.*** As communication technology links increasing numbers of people from distant locations, individuals are able to spend more of their time with their associations of interest, and they may therefore give less time to organizations in their geographic community. Humans, however, require face-to-face encounters and support so the significance of neighborhood, parish, or rural crossroads will prevail. Political, social, and economic problems are still experienced most acutely at the local level. The geographic community is, after all, "where we live" and it will continue to be a powerful force in human life. The incursions of unmanaged development will continue to be a great motivation for the people in any place to protect the communities in which they live. It is not yet clear how the possibility of increased high-tech communication among grassroots groups in different communities, regions, or nations will impact community organization. In neighborhood and community organizing, social workers have a role to facilitate the involvement of neighbors in setting priorities for development and in participating in environmental and social impact studies. Social workers may also provide the technical assistance needed to link communities concerned about similar issues in coalitions or cooperative action.

***Functional communities.*** Communities of interest will continue to grow as communication technologies available to link like-minded individuals increase. Social workers will focus on the needs of groups that have been underrepresented and underserved, helping them develop social action and service strategies. This work will require efforts to develop the leadership capacity and political empowerment of such groups, with the result of improving existing services or developing new services for special needs.

***Community development.*** There will be a continuing need to combine economic and social development strategies to respond to the comprehensive needs of urban and rural communities. Social workers will be required to facilitate broad-based citizen participation, building the leadership, technical, and planning skills among individuals and organizations so that the broadest range of community members and organizations can be part of the development activity. The value of development outcomes will be measured by their social, economic, and environmental sustainability.

***Social planning.*** Successful planning will combine social and physical planning efforts to create more humane service systems, community structures, and environments. The resurgence of local planning efforts and organizations will continue. Social workers will increasingly emphasize participatory planning and efforts to involve consumer groups seriously in planning processes, the use of more-sophisticated technologies to improve interagency planning, and the creation of effective partnerships among nonprofit, for-profit, and public service sectors.

***Program development, community liaison, and service coordination.*** Identifying and responding to the needs of vulnerable populations created by demographic, environmental, economic, and political forces will be emphasized. The focus will be on programs and service integration to meet the needs of the most disadvantaged people and of families and groups facing multiple social problems. These complex needs will require social workers to revitalize consumer participation and communitywide service integration. The most valuable skills for social workers in this area will be the ability to work with consumer groups, effectively educate and relate to the public, and facilitate collaborative planning and coordination.

***Political and social action.*** The focus of social work will be the empowerment of oppressed and marginalized groups. Increased attention will be given to coalition building and the expansion of democracy, with a renewed focus on the common good. On the one hand, this work requires building new and expanded structures for participation that emphasize social justice and multicultural equality. On the other hand, it also requires work to promote educational and economic opportunities for individuals and groups so that they will be able to fulfill their roles in a democracy.

***Coalitions.*** Coalitions will continue to be an essential structure for social change, priority setting, and social action in local, regional, and international arenas. Effective social workers will be skilled in building broad-based multicultural coalitions and human services coalitions, mediating the factors that undermine them and facilitating the factors that bind them, and moving them toward goals for social justice.

***Social movements.*** Social movements will continue to evolve and embed democratic principles and practice in local, national, and international arenas. Social work will connect with and facilitate the enlargement of movements that strengthen democratic structures and processes and that emphasize human rights. Successful change that results from such movements will be measured by economic, social, and cultural sustainability as well as by global environmental rehabilitation and protection.

**Changing Practice**

Ideologies, theories, and practice methods that support these trends will expand, with particular focus on applied democratic development, consumer participation, neopopulist ideology, feminist theory and practice, and theory and practice for sustainable development. The knowledge and research base for community practice will continue to grow and use more-sophisticated quantitative and qualitative methodologies to assess the outcomes of service reforms and planning and development efforts. New knowledge will be used to update models and practice strategies.

Each of these models can enrich and expand citizen participation and community practice in the future. The value base of respect for the individual and recognition of human interdependence that is founded in democratic decision making and participation should be clear. New understandings of diversity and oppression argue eloquently for commitment to social and economic empowerment for poor people, for communities of color, and for marginalized groups; for stronger multicultural consciousness; and for a commitment to equality and opportunity for all members of society. The opportunity to take part in, provide knowledge to, and develop leadership for the further transformation of democracy is at hand (Dahl, 1989). In the United States and abroad, the 1990s and the 21st century will witness a resurgence of community practice, with major opportunities for social work involvement.

The work in each of these models requires high levels of interpersonal, process, task, and technical skills. Community practitioners must recognize that social and human services change is a complex and sometimes arduous process. Most important, however, community practice requires commitment and vision for long-term change. Adopting the idea of abolitionist Theodore Parker, Martin Luther King, Jr., powerfully and frequently evoked the vision for social justice: "The arc of the moral universe is long—but it bends toward justice" (cited in Branch, 1988, p. 197). A central responsibility of the social work profession, and of all social workers, is to support, build, and accelerate that long arc toward social justice.

## References


Addams, J. (1960). *A centennial reader.* New York: Macmillan.

Alinsky, S. (1971). *Rules for radicals.* New York: Random House.

Asian American Mental Health Training Center. (1981). *Bridging cultures: Social work with Southeast Asian refugees.* Los Angeles: Author and Special Services for Groups.

Austin, M. J., & Betten, N. (1990). Rural organizing and the agricultural extension service. In N. Betten & M. J. Austin (Eds.), *The roots of community organizing, 1917–1939* (pp. 94–105). Philadelphia: Temple University Press.

Betten, N., & Austin, M. J. (1990a). The conflict approach to community organizing: Saul Alinsky and the CIO. In N. Betten & M. J. Austin (Eds.), *The roots of community organizing, 1917–1939* (pp. 152–161). Philadelphia: Temple University Press.

Betten, N., & Austin, M. J. (Eds.). (1990b). *The roots of community organizing, 1917–1939.* Philadelphia: Temple University Press.

Bobo, K., Kendall, J., & Max, S. (1991). *Organizing for social change: A manual for activists in the 1990's.* Cabin John, MD: Seven Locks Press.

Branch, T. (1988). *Parting the waters: America in the King years, 1954–63.* New York: Simon & Schuster.

Carlton-LaNey, I. (1992). Elderly black farm women: A population at risk. *Social Work, 37,* 517–523.

Carlton-LaNey, I. (1994). The career of Birdye Henrietta Haynes, a pioneer settlement house worker. *Social Service Review, 68*(2), 254–273.

Childrens' Defense Fund. (1994). *The state of America's children, yearbook 1994.* Washington, DC: Children's Defense Fund.

Christenson, J. A., & Robinson, J. W., Jr. (1989). *Community development in perspective.* Ames: Iowa State University Press.

Community Reinvestment Act of 1977. P.L. 95-128, 91 Stat. 1147.

Cordoba, C. (1992). Organizing in Central American immigrant communities in the United States. In F. G. Rivera & J. L. Erlich (Eds.), *Community organizing in a diverse society* (pp. 181–200). Needham Heights, MA: Allyn & Bacon.

Dahl, R. (1989). *Democracy and its critics.* New Haven, CT: Yale University Press.

Deegan, M. J. (1990). *Jane Addams and the men of the Chicago School, 1892–1918.* New Brunswick, NJ: Transaction Books.

Duncan, C. M. (1992). *Rural poverty in America.* New York: Auburn House.

Edwards, E. D., & Egbert-Edwards, M. (1992). Native American community development. In F. G. Rivera & J. L. Erlich (Eds.), *Community organizing in a diverse society* (pp. 27–48). Needham Heights, MA: Allyn & Bacon.

Estes, R. J. (1993). Toward sustainable development: From theory to praxis. *Social Development Issues, 15*(3), 1–29.

Family Support Act of 1993. P.L. 103-66.

Foner, P. S. (Ed.). (1970). *W.E.B. DuBois speaks: Speeches and addresses 1890–1919.* New York: Pathfinder Press.

Gaventa, J. (1980). *Power and powerlessness: Quiescence and rebellion in an Appalachian valley.* Champaign: University of Illinois Press.

Gottlieb, N. (Ed.). (1980). *Alternative social services for women.* New York: Columbia University Press.

Grosser, C. F., & Mondros, J. (1985). Pluralism and participation: The political action approach. In S. H. Taylor & R. W. Roberts (Eds.), *Theory and practice of community social work* (pp. 154–178). New York: Columbia University Press.

Gutierrez, L. M., & Lewis, E. A. (1994). Community organizing with women of color: A feminist approach. *Journal of Community Practice, 1*(2), 23–44.

Hanna, M., & Robinson, B. (1994). *Strategies for community empowerment.* Lewiston, NY: Edwin Melton Press.

Hooyman, N. R., & Bricker-Jenkins, M. (1985). *Not for women only: Models of feminist practice.* Silver Spring, MD: National Association of Social Workers.

Horton, M., Kohl, J., & Kohl, H. (1992). *The long haul: An autobiography.* Garden City, NY: Doubleday.

Indian Child Welfare Act of 1978. P.L. 95-608, 92 Stat. 3069.

Johnson, A. E. (1977, Spring). William Still—A black social worker: 1821–1902. *Black Caucus Journal,* pp. 14–19.

Johnson, A. E. (1991). The sin of omission: History of African-American women in social work. *Journal of Multicultural Social Work, 1*(2), 1–15.

Johnson, C. E., & Jennings, H. (1994, June). *Economic development for women: Project report.* Raleigh: North Carolina Cooperative Extension Service, North Carolina State University.

Kurzman, P. (1985). Program development and service coordination as components of community practice. In S. H. Taylor & R. W. Roberts (Eds.), *Theory and practice of community social work* (pp. 95–124). New York: Columbia University Press.

Lappin, B. (1985). Community development: Beginnings in social work enabling. In S. H. Taylor & R. W. Roberts (Eds.), *Theory and practice of community social work* (pp. 59–94). New York: Columbia University Press.

Lauffer, A. (1978). *Social planning at the community level.* Englewood Cliffs, NJ: Prentice Hall.

Lauffer, A. (1981). The practice of social planning. In N. Gilbert & H. Specht (Eds.), *Handbook of the social services* (pp. 583–597). Englewood Cliffs, NJ: Prentice Hall.

Lee, I. (1992). The Chinese-American community organizing strategies and tactics. In F. G. Rivera & J. L. Erlich (Eds.), *Community organizing in a diverse society* (pp. 133–158). Needham Heights, MA: Allyn & Bacon.

Lord, R. (1939). *The agrarian revival.* New York: George Grady Press and American Association for Adult Education.

Mauney, R., Williams, E., & Weil, M. (1993). *Beyond crisis: Developing comprehensive services for battered women in North Carolina.* Winston-Salem, NC: Z. Smith Reynolds Foundation.

McCroskey, J., & Meezan, W. (1992). Social work research in family and children's services. In J. Brown & M. Weil (Eds.), *Family practice* (pp. 199–213). Washington, DC: Child Welfare League of America.

Mizrahi, T., & Rosenthal, B. (1993). Managing dynamic tensions in social change coalitions. In T. Mizrahi & J. D. Morrison (Eds.), *Community organization and social administration* (pp. 11–40). New York: Haworth Press.

Montiel, M., & Ortego y Gasca, F. (1992). Chicanos, communities and change. In F. G. Rivera & J. L. Erlich (Eds.), *Community organizing in a diverse society* (pp. 49–66). Needham Heights, MA: Allyn & Bacon.

Morales, J. (1992). Community social work with Puerto Rican communities in the United States: One organizer's perspective. In F. G. Rivera & J. L. Erlich (Eds.), *Community organizing in a diverse society* (pp. 91–112). Needham Heights, MA: Allyn & Bacon.

Murase, K. (1992). Organizing in the Japanese American community. In F. G. Rivera & J. L. Erlich (Eds.), *Community organizing in a diverse society* (pp. 159–180). Needham Heights, MA: Allyn & Bacon.

National Congress for Community Economic Development. (1991). *Human investment—Community profits* (Report and Recommendations of the Social Services and Economic Development Task Force). Washington, DC: Author.

Piven, F. F., & Cloward, R. S. (1979). *Poor people's movements: Why they succeed, how they fail.* New York: Vintage Vooks.

Plotz, D. A. (1992). *Community problem solving case summaries* (Vol. 3). Washington, DC: Program for Community Problem Solving.

Reisch, M., & Wenocur, S. (1986). The future of community organization in social work: Social activism and the politics of profession building. *Social Service Review, 60*(1), 70–93.

Rivera, F. G., & Erlich, J. L. (Eds.). (1992). *Community organizing in a diverse society.* Needham Heights, MA: Allyn & Bacon.

Roberts-DeGennaro, M. (1986). Factors contributing to coalition maintenance. *Journal of Sociology and Social Welfare, 13,* 248–264.

Roberts-DeGennaro, M. (1987). Patterns of exchange relationships in building a coalition. *Administration in Social Work, 11,* 59–67.

Ross, M. G. (1955). *Community organization: Theory and principles.* New York: Harper & Brothers.

Rothman, J. (1979). Three models of community organization practice: Their mixing and phasing. In F. Cox, J. L. Erlich, J. Rothman, & J. E. Tropman (Eds.), *Strategies of community organization* (4th ed., pp. 25–45). Itasca, IL: F. E. Peacock.

Rothman, J. (1995). Approaches to community intervention. In J. Rothman, J. Erlich, J. E. Tropman, with F. M. Cox (Eds.), *Strategies of community intervention: Macro practice* (5th ed., pp. 26–63). Itasca, IL: F. E. Peacock.

Rubin, H. J., & Rubin, I. S. (1992). *Community organizing and development* (2nd ed.). New York: Macmillan.

Simon, B. L. (1994). *The empowerment tradition in American social work: A history.* New York: Columbia University Press.

Solomon, B. B. (1986). *Black empowerment: Social work in oppressed communities.* New York: Columbia University Press.

Staples, L. (1990). Powerful ideas about empowerment. *Administration in Social Work, 14*(2), 29–42.

Still, W. (1872/1970). *The underground railroad.* Chicago: Johnson.

Taylor, S. H. (1985). Community work and social work: The community liaison approach. In S. H. Taylor & R. W. Roberts (Eds.), *Theory and practice of community social work* (pp. 179–214). New York: Columbia University Press.

Taylor, S. H., & Roberts, R. W. (Eds.). (1985). *Theory and practice of community social work.* New York: Columbia University Press.

Tocqueville, A. de (1835/1956). Township and municipal bodies. In R. D. Heffner (Ed.), *Democracy in America* (pp. 61–101). New York: Mentor Books.

Van Den Bergh, N., & Cooper, L. B. (Eds.). (1986). *Feminist visions for social work.* Silver Spring, MD: National Association of Social Workers.

Vuong, V., & Huynh, J. D. (1992). South East Asians in the United States: A strategy for accelerated and balanced integration. In F. G. Rivera & J. L. Erlich (Eds.), *Community organizing in a diverse society* (pp. 201–222). Needham Heights, MA: Allyn & Bacon.

Weick, A., & Vandiver, S. T. (Eds.). (1982). *Women, power and change.* Washington, DC: National Association of Social Workers.

Weil, M. (1986). Women, community and organizing. In N. Van Den Bergh & L. B. Cooper (Eds.), *Feminist visions for social work* (pp. 187–210). Silver Spring, MD: National Association of Social Workers.

Weil, M. (1990). *Social and economic development in Native American communities.* Unpublished manuscript.

Weil, M., & Gamble, D. N. (1993). *Current models of community practice for social work.* Unpublished raw data.

Williams, J. (1987). *Eyes on the prize: America's civil rights years—1954–1965.* New York: Viking Press.

Wood, J. L., & Jackson, M. (1982). *Social movements: Development, participation, and dynamics.* Belmont, CA: Wadsworth.


## Further Reading


Chavis, D. M., Florin, P., & Felix, M.R.J. (1993). Nurturing grassroots initiatives for community development: The role of enabling systems. In T. Mizrahi & J. D. Morrison (Eds.), *Community organization and social administration* (pp. 41–67). New York: Haworth Press.

Daley, J. M., & Wong, P. (1994). Community development with emerging ethnic communities. *Journal of Community Practice: Organizing, Planning, Development & Change, 1*(1), 9–24.

Faulkner, A., Roberts-DeGennaro, M., & Weil, M. (1994). *Diversity and development in community practice.* New York: Haworth Press.

Fisher, R. (1994). *Let the people decide: Neighborhood organizing in America* (rev. ed.). New York: Twayne.

Homan, M. S. (1994). *Promoting community change: Making it happen in the real world.* Pacific Grove, CA: Brooks/Cole.

Kahn, S. (1991). *Organizing: A guide for grassroots leaders* (rev. ed.). Silver Spring, MD: NASW Press.

Kahn, S. (1994). *How people get power.* Washington, DC: NASW Press.

Mondros, J. B., & Wilson, S. M. (1994). *Organizing for power and empowerment.* New York: Columbia University Press.

Rivera, F. G., & Erlich, J. L. (1992). Introduction: Prospects and challenges. In F. G. Rivera & J. L. Erlich (Eds.), *Community organizing in a diverse society.* Needham Heights, MA: Allyn & Bacon.

Ross, M. G. (1958). *Case histories in community organization.* New York: Harper & Row.

Rothman, J., & Zald, M. N. (1985). Planning theory in social work community practice. In S. H. Taylor & R. W. Roberts (Eds.), *Theory and practice of community social work* (pp. 125–153). New York: Columbia University Press.

Rubin, H. J. (1990). Working in a turbulent environment: Perceptions of urban economic development practitioners. *Economic Development Quarterly, 4*(2), 113–127.



**Marie Overby Weil, DSW, ACSW,** is professor and director, and **Dorothy N. Gamble, MSW, ACSW,** is clinical assistant professor and director of admissions, Community Social Work Program, University of North Carolina at Chapel Hill, School of Social Work, 223 E. Franklin Street, Chapel Hill, NC 27599.

**For further information see**

Advocacy; Case Management; Citizen Participation; Community; Community Needs Assessment; Community Organization; Deinstitutionalization; Direct Practice Overview; Goal Setting and Intervention Planning; Interdisciplinary and Interorganizational Collaboration; Mutual Aid Societies; Natural Helping Networks; Peace and Social Justice; Person-in-Environment; Policy Analysis; Poverty; Program Evaluation; Progressive Social Work; Rural Social Work; Settlements and Neighborhood Centers; Social Planning; Social Welfare History; Social Work Practice: History and Evolution; Social Work Practice: Theoretical Base; Technology Transfer; Voluntarism.

**Key Words**

community organization
community practice
economic development
social change
social development

## Compulsive Behaviors

*See* Eating Disorders and Other Compulsive Behaviors

READER'S GUIDE

### Computer Use

*The following entries contain information on this general topic:*

Archives of Social Welfare
Computer Utilization
Continuing Education
Expert Systems
Information Systems
Recording

# Computer Utilization

**William H. Butterfield**

Most social services agencies use computers for managerial activities. Nurius, Hooyman, and Nicoll (1991) reported that only 11.4 percent of the agencies they surveyed were using computers for clinical assessment. Several other surveys (Farrell, 1989; Finn, 1987; Lockshin & Harrison, 1991; Matheson, 1993) have supported that conclusion. However, the use of computers for clinical purposes is rapidly increasing (personal communication, P. Nurius, associate professor, University of Washington, School of Social Work) and is likely to become a major component of agencies' computer usage over the next few years.

Management's major use of computers is for management information systems. Because information systems are covered elsewhere in this encyclopedia, this entry focuses on other areas of computer utilization in social work. These areas are (1) data collection and assessment, (2) interviewing, (3) applications for people with disabilities, (4) bulletin boards, (5) community-based networks, (6) modification of workers' and agencies' behavior, (7) policy development and advocacy, and (8) online and compact disk-read only memory (CD-ROM) databases. Policy and value issues and a number of managerial and implementation issues are also discussed.

## History and Current Status

It is difficult to comprehend how rapidly the use of computers in social work has grown. Volume 17 of the *Encyclopedia of Social Work*, published in 1977, had no entry for computers. Nonetheless, many large private and public agencies were using computers for managerial tasks in the 1960s and 1970s. For example, computers were used to collect data on mental health in the early 1960s (P. Binner & Gaviria, 1963; R. Binner, 1993), and more than three-fourths of all community mental health centers were using computers for managerial purposes by 1980 (Gorodezky & Hedlund, 1982). But computers were expensive and required a specialized staff to make them work, so their adoption by social services agencies was limited to a narrow range of applications.

**Small Computers**

Advancing technology, which improved the capabilities of computers while driving down their cost, and better software programs set the stage for the third event that led to the exponential growth of computer usage: the introduction of small computers with plug-in cards that allowed end users to reconfigure their computers. The introduction of these computers, which are referred to as open-architecture computers, set off an explosion of innovation. It is sometimes difficult to realize that the personal computer (PC) revolution is less than 20 years old. Apple computers, introduced in 1976 (Rebello, Mitchell, & Schwartz, 1993), were among the first to gain public acceptance. But it was only after IBM introduced its IBM PC in 1981 (*Bloomberg Business News*, 1993) and Compaq introduced a portable computer in 1982 (Pope, 1993) that the PC revolution took off. The IBM PC was not the first, and perhaps not even the best, small computer on the market. But the fact that IBM entered the small-computer market gave small computers the legitimacy they needed to be widely adopted by businesses.

By 1993, IBM computers or IBM clones accounted for 90 percent of the sales of PCs, and Apple computers constituted virtually all the remaining 10 percent (*Bloomberg Business News*, 1993). Many writers believe that small powerful computers will displace large mainframe computers and minicomputers. Although it is true that the use of these large computers is rapidly decreasing, it is unlikely that mainframes and minicomputers will be totally displaced by PCs (Goldberg, 1993).

**Networks**

The increase in the use of PCs has been due, in part, to the growth of local and wide-area networks. Networks connect computers together so they can share data, programs, and other resources like printers and scanners. When all computers are located in the same general area (for example, in the same building), the network is commonly called a LAN (local area network). When the connected computers are located at more remote locations, the network is commonly called a WAN (wide-area network). Networking is still in its infancy, but its adoption is highly significant. Networks enable people to use computer resources located in different physical locations, thus making it possible for any location to have access to whatever programs or data resources it needs, regardless of where these programs and resources are physically located.

**New Developments**

Two other developments have promise: electronic document management and the virtual office. Several large companies are already converting all their documents into electronic images that can be accessed regardless of location. The move to the electronic storage of data makes it possible for organizations to be more responsive to their customers while reducing staff and processing costs (Gleckman, Cary, Mitchell, Smart, & Rousch, 1993). These new methods of storing and processing documents create many legal issues (Farber, 1993). For example, the Veterans Administration had to develop procedures that permit physicians to sign medical documents legally on computers (Kolodner, 1992). Many of the legal problems posed by electronic document processing are being overcome, but others, such as issues of privacy, confidentiality, and data security, are far from being resolved (Casmier, 1993; Danca, 1993; L. Smith, 1993a, 1993b; Sullivan, 1993; Woo, 1993).

The advent of small portable computers and WANs has made it possible for many employees to spend much more of their time with clients. Companies are equipping workers with computers with built-in fax and communication capability; computerized information on policies, rules, and services; data-entry forms; and the capability to submit orders and reports and to send and receive electronic mail (E-mail). With this capability, some companies are eliminating assigned offices for many employees. When an employee needs space at the office, he or she calls the office and makes an appointment to use it. Employees who work in this manner are said to have virtual offices (Tilsner, 1993). This trend is new, and its long-term viability has yet to be established. But because it lowers costs, reduces travel, and increases the time spent with clients, there is a good chance it will prove irresistible. The application of this technology to human services agencies and workers is readily apparent.

**Uses in Human Services Agencies**

During the 1970s and 1980s, PCs were not powerful. However, they still gave end users the tools they needed to do many tasks that, heretofore, had been beyond their capacity or were too costly to undertake. The lowered cost and increased availability of small computers, spurred by businesses' extensive investment in information processing, has accelerated the use of computers by human services agencies. Separate figures are not available, but the trend is clear: Computer usage is increasing rapidly, and information processing has become a significant part of the budgets of human services agencies. Nurius et al.'s (1991) survey of 183 social services agencies in the Seattle area found that 92 percent of the 103 agencies responding used personal computers. The median number of computers in an agency was two, and the range was one to 450; 78 percent had fewer than six computers on site, and about 46 percent used mainframes or minicomputers. Virtually all the agencies in the survey reported that they expected to increase the extent to which they were computerized.

> When asked whether they foresaw any barriers that might prevent the agency from reaching its computerization goals within the next five years, 56.6% responded yes. This was felt most acutely by public agencies, with nearly 62% foreseeing significant barriers. The most prevalent identified barrier clearly related to funding problems. This was most pronounced for public (61.8%) versus private (50.0%) and for larger (60.9%) relative to smaller (50.0%) agencies. The second most prominent theme also involved a lack of resources—the inadequacy of needed staff, time, and initiative to "run with the ball." (Nurius et al., 1991, p. 146)

Even though agencies experienced concerns about the costs of computerization, they reported high expectations from their investments in computers. They expected that the computers would improve such factors as decision making, report writing, research and evaluation, and time and cost efficiency.

One reason for the concern reported by these agencies is that the useful life of computers and their software is short. Some agencies in the St. Louis area are replacing their computers after three to five years and updating the computers' software yearly. As people become aware of what computers can do, they want the latest software, much of which will work only in newer, more powerful machines. Agencies are often tempted to retain the old equipment, but the newer equipment is often easier to use and more efficient, so that purchasing new equipment is often cost-effective. The addition of new equipment and software, the upgrading of existing resources, and the hiring and training of staff that use them are major items in the budgets of many social services agencies.

## Computerized Data-Collection and Assessment Procedures

The collection and assessment of data and the selection of goals are necessary precursors to intervention. Computers are used to collect, aggregate, order, and evaluate information.

### Types of Questions Asked

Computers can be used to ask closed questions, quantitative questions, and open-ended questions. A few examples may make it easier to understand the differences.

*Closed questions* are largely yes–no or categorical questions. Their form makes them easy to program and evaluate using a computer. Examples of such questions include these:

- Do you have headaches?
- Do you believe that premarital sex is acceptable?
- From the following list, select all categories that apply to you.
- Select your race from the following list.

*Quantitative questions* measure magnitudes, durations, latencies, or frequencies. Because numbers are used to express the quantities, quantitative questions are also easy to program and evaluate using computers. The following are some examples:

- How old are you?
- How often do you and your spouse engage in sexual activity?
- How often do you drink alcohol?
- How long have you been consuming alcohol?
- On the following scale, using 7 as strongly and 1 as little, tell me how strongly you feel about each of the following statements.

*Open-ended questions* are sometimes referred to as free-form questions. They are designed to let the person answering the questions choose the form and content of the answer. Although they can be evaluated on computers, they are not easily evaluated and thus are used less often on computers. The irony of this situation is that in courses on interviewing, students are encouraged to use open-ended questions, whereas in courses on computerized assessment, students are discouraged from using them. Examples of open-ended questions are as follows:

- Tell me your views on sex.
- What is your race or ethnic identification?
- Tell me about your use of alcohol.

There is some evidence that closed-ended questions yield more information in less time than do open-ended questions (Stuckle, 1989). However, open questions can also be analyzed. The computer can do word counts, look at syntax or word order, or evaluate a client's written responses in many other ways. Gilgun and Connor (1988), for example, conducted a 12-hour open-ended interview with sexual offenders and then used a computer to analyze the content of the interviews.

**Computerized Interviews**

Critics of computerized interviewing are concerned about the use of structured questions and the "mechanistic" nature of such interviews. However, computerized data-collection methods have been found superior to in-person interviews in the following eight areas:

1. acceptability of the interviews and assessment devices by clients
2. range of information gathered
3. completeness of information gathered
4. honesty of clients' responses
5. cost of collecting and analyzing the data
6. presentation of data in graphic form
7. monitoring and tracking of clients
8. collection of sensitive data (for example, on drug usage or sexual practices).

***Quality of information.*** Clients appear to prefer computerized interviews to interviews by professionals (Simmons & Miller, 1971; Weitzel, Morgan, & Guyden, 1973). Angle, Johnsen, Grebenkemper, and Ellinwood (1979) found that computer interviews yielded more complete information than did interviews by clinicians. Lockshin and Harrison (1991) reported that

> clinicians failed to identify (as measured by lack of documentation) 76% of 20 critical problems that a group of 55 patients revealed in the computer interview and that experts believed were important patient findings. The results of investigations examining the ability of clinicians to obtain important clinical information via unstructured interviews are consistent with these findings ([A.] Carr, Ghosh, & Ancil, 1983; Simmons and Miller, 1971; Weitzel, Morgan, & Guyden, 1973).... Evans and Miller (1969)... in a between-group comparison in which subjects completed a questionnaire administered either by a computer or in a conventional paper-and-pencil format, found that subjects in the computer group admitted more symptoms of manifest anxiety, told fewer lies, and demonstrated a greater willingness to agree to socially undesirable statements than did subjects in the paper-and-pencil group. (p. 50)

Ferriter (1993), citing Quintanar, Crowell, and Prior (1982), reported that when the degree of "humanness of an interview was varied, the more mechanistic the language of the computer dialog, the more honest the results obtained, and, conversely, the more human the language of the computer dialog, the more dishonest the answers received" (p. 60). He also found, in his own research, that subjects were more honest and gave more information when they received a structured interview by computer, rather than from a person. He stated: "In computer interviews, no subjects had previous experience with computers and all were over the age of forty. Even so none of them found any problem in using the computer" (p. 65). T. Carr (1991) cited many other studies that found that computerized interviews produce superior outcomes, particularly in such areas as sex, drugs, suicide, smoking, and alcohol consumption.

***Cost-effectiveness.*** There is substantial evidence that computerized data collection is cost-effective. Yokley, Coleman, and Yates (1990) compared the cost of three methods of collecting information: a clinician's interview, a fill-in-the-blank form, and a computer-administered assessment device. The computer-administered interview was at least as effective and as acceptable to clients as were the other formats and was less than half as expensive to the agency. Comparing paper-and-pencil surveys to computerized surveys, Rosenfeld, Doherty, Vicino, Kantor, and Greaves (1989) reported similar results. Hudson (1990) wrote that computerized data collection saves professional staff time, can be designed to check clients' answers for consistency and completeness, and can be designed to ask additional questions to clarify client answers.

Schneider, Taylor, Prater, and Wright (1992) found computerized interviews effective in letting subjects do confidential screening of their risk for infection with the human immunodeficiency virus (HIV). In one trial, the computerized interview correctly identified all people known to be HIV positive in the sample who took the interview. In another group of 55 college students whose HIV status was unknown, seven people were identified as being at risk. Of the seven, three agreed to be tested for the HIV virus; none proved to be HIV positive.

There is also substantial evidence that computers are effective in scoring closed or quantitative information and in giving clinicians the results in a form that helps them evaluate clients' progress (Alexander & Davidoff, 1990; Brand & Houx, 1992; Farrell, 1991; Snyder, Lacher, & Willis, 1988; Warzecha, 1991). The computer can also plot graphs of the results of multiple administrations of an assessment instrument. (Benbenishty & Ben-Zaken, 1988; Hudson, 1990; Nurius & Hudson, 1993). Nurius and Hudson and Schoech (1990) discussed other benefits of using computers to collect and assess data and examined a number of related issues.

***Concerns.*** Several authors have raised concerns about computerized interviews or assessments. For example, Groth and Schumaker (1988) pointed out that the reports generated by computerized information-gathering programs may give a false sense of objectivity and accuracy, particularly if they are interpretive. Others have raised a variety of issues related to the mechanistic nature of computers (Ager & Bendall, 1991; Murphy & Pardek, 1986; Siegal, 1990). Most of these concerns have not been supported when tested experimentally; the overwhelming preponderance of evidence suggests that collecting information with computers is at least as effective as, and in several ways is superior to, other methods of information gathering.

For the most part, these tools have been devised in academic settings or by individuals, rather than in agencies. A notable exception is the Veterans Administration, which continues to develop a systemwide set of applications for clinical use, ranging from an automated *Diagnostic and Statistical Manual of Mental Disorders, Third Edition–Revised* (American Psychiatric Association, 1987) to 44 computerized psychological tests and 33 different types of interviews. Most of these tests and interviews are for direct use by the client; that is, the clients, not the clinicians, enter the data into the computer (Kolodner, 1992). It is not clear how widely these instruments are used by social workers. The author's telephone calls to several Veterans Administration hospitals produced mixed reports of the usage of the applications. There are many sources of information on data collection and assessment. An excellent source is COMPSYCH, a computerized software service and bulletin board for psychologists.

## Computerized Therapy

Many experimental computerized therapy programs were developed in the 1970s and 1980s. Selmi, Klein, Greist, Johnson, and Harris (1982), for example, reported that a computerized program for the behavioral treatment of depression was as effective as treatment by therapists. Greist et al. (1973) devised a program to predict the risk of suicide. Ghosh and Marks (1987) used a computer to administer programs for the self-treatment of agoraphobia. Goodman, Gingerich, and de Shazar (1989) developed a prototype program, BRIEFER, designed to advise family therapists on possible interventions with clients. Finally, Colby (1980) developed a commercial computerized program for treating depression that is reported to be as effective as therapists' interventions when measured after six weeks. Many other such programs have been reported in the literature (see Schoech, 1990, for a discussion of several of them).

Many commercial computerized therapy programs are of dubious value. They have not been experimentally evaluated or validated, and there is little evidence that they are effective. Furthermore, some are promoted as being as capable as, or more capable than, human therapists; one such program even tells users that they can learn to read their opponents' minds.

Progress in developing therapeutic uses for computers has been painfully slow, and few articles describing computerized therapy programs have appeared since the late 1980s. Overall, it is fair to say that therapeutic applications are still in the experimental stage. Dissemination is also a problem; that is, even well-developed programs may not be widely used because most people do not know they exist.

## Computers for People with Disabilities

Social workers are often involved with people who have temporary or permanent disabilities, many of which make it difficult to do the things others take for granted. Computers or devices based on computer technology have made it possible for people with disabilities to do many things that formerly were impossible. Larry Scadden, director, Rehabilitation Engineering Center, Electronic Industries Foundation, in an interview with Kerr (1988), said that "Computers are the best thing that has happened to disabled people in history.... While computers will not provide equality, they will provide independence" (p. 39).

For many severely disabled people, the computer has made it possible to communicate with others for the first time. Computers can be used to turn almost any body movement into a means of communication. A toe wiggle, a puff of air, an eye blink, a slight movement of the head, and many other body movements have been used to communicate with the computer, which translates these efforts into written or spoken communication or operates other devices needed by the user.

The range of available devices is truly astonishing. The Adaptive Equipment Resource Library, operated by the University of Wisconsin, has a list (available on CD-ROM) of over 16,000 products and operates a bulletin board. Another source is C-CAD ONLINE. Conferences on bulletin boards also discuss current issues, legislative initiatives, financing, and funding, among a broad variety of issues. Still another resource is the National Information Clearinghouse, which is jointly operated by the Center for Developmental Disabilities of the University of South Carolina and the Association for the Care of Children's Health. It offers information and referral services on a wide variety of issues related to people with disabilities and has an extensive computerized database of resources and bibliographic citations. It also has a referral service for Vietnam veterans and their families.

Casali and Williges (1990) and Enders (1990) listed other sources of accommodative aids for computer users with disabilities. Koenig (1992) discussed the impact of the Americans with Disabilities Act on the need for adaptive devices and listed several other sources of discussions on people with disabilities.

## Bulletin Board Systems

Bulletin boards have become an important part of computing in the human services. The concept of a bulletin board is simple. A computer is set up so that people at remote sites can call in to a computer and use one of five basic services. They can (1) copy files that have been stored on the host computer and transfer the copies to their own computer or (2) send copies of files that are on their computer to the host computer and store them there. These first two services are often called *file transfer services*. Users can also (3) leave messages on the host computer that will be forwarded to an addressee at some other location or be temporarily stored on the host computer awaiting the addressee's call, or they can (4) pick up messages left by others. In addition, they can (5) gain access to an extensive database that contains information on a variety of topics.

The messages on these bulletin boards may be private (only the sender and the receiver can read them), in which case the computer functions as an E-mail system that allows people to communicate rapidly with others who may be thousands of miles away, or they may be public, in which case the computer is used as a remote conferencing device. Public messages related to a specific topic are stored in areas dedicated to the topic being discussed. Anyone who calls the computer and joins the particular conference can read messages left by others. Several public message areas are usually set up on each bulletin board. Some areas are open to anyone, but others are restricted to people who have declared that they want to participate in a conference.

The following index, taken from a social services bulletin board in the St. Louis area, shows the range of conferences and information available on a single bulletin board:

| Conference Number | Subject |
|---|---|
| 1 | Recovering from child abuse |
| 2 | Breaking the smoking habit |
| 3 | Recovery talk on where to go |
| 4 | Rape survivors |
| 5 | Alcoholism and recovery |
| 6 | Sexual addiction |
| 7 | The help center |
| 8 | Families in recovery |
| 9 | We have a problem |
| 10 | Emotional abuse |
| 11 | Physical abuse |
| 12 | Pack-rats anonymous |
| 13 | Suicide survey |
| 14 | Breaking the sugar addiction |
| 15 | Bereavement of spouse and recovery |
| 16 | When your child is not perfect |
| 17 | Surviving the death of a child |
| 18 | Overcoming overeating |

Another partial listing, from the Project ENABLE bulletin board at the University of Wisconsin, shows the range of topics available on that bulletin board for professionals, clients, and others who are interested in issues related to disabilities:

| Conference Number | Subject |
|---|---|
| 6 | Visual impairments and blindness |
| 7 | Hearing impairments and deafness |
| 8 | Mobility impairments |
| 9 | Employment issues |
| 10 | Education issues |
| 11 | Legal issues |
| 12 | Marketplace: Commercial demonstrations of software products |
| 13 | Graphics and images related to disabilities |
| 14 | Rehabilitation information and software |
| 15 | Psychiatric rehabilitation: Directory of resources |
| 16 | Miscellaneous files relating to disability and rehabilitation |
| 17 | Documents from federal agencies, proposed regulations |
| 18 | Americans with Disabilities Act (ADA) |
| 19 | Rehabilitation Act of 1973, 1992 |
| 20 | Randolph-Sheppard Act |
| 21 | Individuals with Disabilities Act (P.L. 99-142) |
| 22 | Chronic fatigue syndrome |
| 23 | ADA net File/*Newsletter Distribution Directory* |
| 24 | *On Line*, the newsletter of the Rehabilitation Technology Association |
| 25 | *Blind News Digest* |
| 26 | *Handicap Digest* |

Similar bulletin boards exist in many parts of the country (for descriptions, see Landers, 1993; M. Miller, 1992; Steinberg, 1987).

**Conferences as Self-Help**

Bulletin boards are used by both professionals and the general public. Many of the conferences on bulletin boards are used extensively by people who are experiencing the problems being discussed by the conference or by people who have successfully overcome the problems. When used this way, a conference often serves as a self-help group for its members. Some conferences have much in common with the advice columns in newspapers. They differ in that the conversations are ongoing dialogues, as opposed to one-way communications. Some conferences resemble therapy sessions and may represent an emerging form of helping in which the problems of an anonymous person are aired in public and an ongoing dialogue ensues that may help the anonymous client deal with his or her problems. The ethical and legal issues involved in this quasi-therapy are many and will probably take some time to sort out. Furthermore, as far as can be determined, no one has formally studied the usefulness or effectiveness of bulletin boards for either self-help or "therapeutic" purposes.

**Uses by Public Agencies**

Public agencies are also making use of bulletin boards. For example, the White House has a bulletin board that is accessible through many of the major commercial bulletin boards (Grimes, 1993; Manning, 1993). The June 21, 1993, edition of *Infoworld* carried an announcement that the U.S. Department of Labor and several private donors have set up a bulletin board through which shelters for homeless people across the country can share information on veterans, education, and job training opportunities. Similar bulletin boards are available in many other areas of federal and state governments (M. Miller, 1993; Stoll, 1988). The computer program SoapBox allows

> users to quickly compose correspondence to governmental agencies and lawmakers. The database provides flow charts of who's who in the federal government and descriptions of [agency] jurisdictions for more than 600 offices. It also offers staff listings including address, committee assignments and phone and fax numbers.... The program also allows users to create mass [mailings]. (Busse, 1992, p. 16)

Busse reported that there are plans to develop state versions of the program.

A few other examples are TNC Information, developed by J. Schwab at the University of Texas at Austin, which is a database of Texas-based residential programs and facilities for children. NASW has a bulletin board service that Jerry Vest developed for the New Mexico chapter. Many other bulletin board services that are relevant to social work can be found in most metropolitan areas.

## COMMUNITY-BASED APPLICATIONS

Several participants at the Information Technology and Social Work Practice Conference, held in 1984 (Geiss & Viswanathan, 1986), predicted that bulletin board systems would be used by social services agencies to provide information on community resources that clients could reach by using computer terminals located at public sites.

**MORE System**

The Grace Hill Neighborhood Center in St. Louis developed and is testing such a system, known as the Member Organized Resource Exchange (MORE). According to unpublished, untitled documents, the center began MORE, a self-help system that creates solutions for neighbors' problems through neighbors exchanging various resources and skills, in 1982. Networked computers provide linkage services and contain a community resource bank. Residents who need services can use computers located in public facilities, such as libraries, social services agencies, and police substations, to gain access to the MORE computer on which the community resource bank is located. They can earn credits by providing services to other residents in the neighborhood and can use these credits to "buy" services from other neighbors. In addition to the service resource bank, MORE also has a database to help residents find housing, child care, and other services and to learn about the primary health care services offered by the center. Finally, the system is also used to help the community provide protection and support for elderly neighborhood residents.

Residents designed the program so that they can use it themselves and developed a program to train neighborhood teams to use it. Each neighborhood team serves about 1,000 households and operates two MORE computer units. Roughly 20 to 25 members on a team go through 40 hours of training. The center's documents report that evaluations of the program show that neighbors respond well to it and that there is wide acceptance of the role of neighbors within the MORE system.

**MORE Cache Card**

In addition to the MORE community network, the Grace Hill Neighborhood Center is now testing a new technology that is similar to the AT&T Smart Card, which is used mainly for storing medical information. The card contains a simple computer that can do such things as verify passwords and interact with a larger computer. Smart Cards resemble credit cards in size and shape, but they are capable of storing a vast amount of data. The AT&T Smart Card, for example, can hold up to 4 million characters of information (about 2,000 typewritten pages) (Langreth, 1993). The MORE Cache Card has more-modest storage capabilities—about four pages of material—and is manufactured by the National Cache Card Company in St. Louis.

According to the center's documents, the MORE Cache Card can be used for any of the following purposes:

A. electronic deposit of public fund payments including
   1. food vouchers from social services agencies
   2. Aid to Families with Dependent Children (AFDC) payments
   3. social security payments
B. electronic deposit of funds from private sources including
   1. paychecks
   2. service credits for MORE services the neighbor has performed
C. electronic withdrawals or disbursements including
   1. electronic purchases from participating local merchants
   2. cash withdrawals
   3. petty cash purchases
   4. MORE service credits to pay for work performed by MORE members.

Some of the public funds credited to the MORE Cache Card are segregated in special accounts that can be used only for designated purchases (for example, only food can be purchased with food stamp funds). Unrestricted funds are deposited in electronic checking accounts; non-interest-bearing electronic savings accounts; or the petty cash fund, to which small sums can be transferred. The transferred funds in the petty cash account are available without the use of a personal identification number (PIN) so that the owner of a card can, for example, send someone to a store to make small purchases without that person knowing the owner's PIN. The card keeps track of the amount in each account; transactions are recorded and transmitted to a central location by a card attached to each MORE computer. In addition to account balances, a record of the last 10 transactions is kept in the card itself.

In the future, the MORE Cache Card may be used to hold medical information, such as the following, on all family members: (1) Medicaid identification number, (2) information on members (names, blood types, allergies, prescriptions, name of pharmacy, name of insurer, and names of physicians), (3) immunization records, (4) electronic claims data, (5) members' medical records, and (6) members' eligibility for benefits.

The use of the Smart Card represents a major jump in the use of computer technology. If this approach is successful, it may revolutionize the way funds and payments are made in poor areas and the way in which social and medical records are maintained.

The National Electronic Archive of Advance Directives is using the Smart Card technology in its PrepCard to store information on a person's living will. "Using the Social Security and personal ID numbers on [the card]... doctors and family members can get instant access to the patient's living will anywhere in the U.S. at any hour with a touch-tone phone" (E. Smith, 1993, p. 55).

### Modifying Workers' and Agencies' Behavior

Another class of programs, aimed at changing the behavior of workers and agencies, has been developed by L. Miller, Pruger, and their colleagues at the University of California at Berkeley. Their work, which has been under way since 1981, has involved at least two approaches to changing workers' behavior:

1. Increasing the consensus among workers on the extent of a client's disability and on the services to be awarded for that disability. In this approach, no attempt is made to ascertain whether consistent, equitable behavior maximizes the outcomes for clients.
2. Improving outcomes for clients. This is an extension of the first approach. The characteristics of clients' and workers' awards of benefits continue to be important, but added to the data collected on clients' and on workers' behavior are data on the costs of a particular type of service and the availability of different classes of services: (1) those provided by family and friends (informal in-home services), (2) those provided by agencies and other groups (referred in-home services), and (3) those paid for with state or county funds (purchased in-home services). The goal of this approach is to ensure that interventions lead to optimal outcomes for clients as measured by the degree to which the clients remain in the least-restrictive environment (ranging from the community to a permanent nursing home) and the clients' expected level of frailty (the likelihood that the clients will die or enter nursing homes).

**Equity in Assessment**

Pruger (1986) described the first approach in his article on a project designed to improve the level of consensus among workers in three county welfare departments in the San Francisco Bay area. The project helped workers develop behaviorally specific descriptions of the degree of clients' impairment and then used the computer to give workers feedback on how their pattern of assessment compared to that of other workers. The computer was also used to give workers feedback on how their awards compared to the awards given by other workers to clients with similar levels of disability. If the awards deviated too much from the awards given to other similar clients, the workers were asked to enter their explanations. These explanations were used to refine the basis on which decisions were made. In the beginning, the computer allowed for a wide range of acceptable awards, but later the range of unchallenged decisions was narrowed. "When the project began, 60% of the variance in service awards was explained by the variance in client characteristics. When the project ended, the figure was between 85% and 90%" (Pruger, 1986, p. 221). The range was from roughly 15 percent improvement to over 30 percent improvement (Rimmer, 1986).

**Redistribution of Budgets**

The second approach is illustrated by the Multipurpose Senior Services Project (MSSP), a $40-million-dollar experiment funded by the state of California. MSSP was designed to "construct minimum-cost service bundles . . . [and] maintain each client in the most appropriate residence" (Pruger, 1986, p. 222). The project, described in detail by L. Miller (1993), used similar procedures to the In-Home Health Services (IHHS) project to develop equity in assessment. However, the target was not simple equity of awards, but "the redistribution of existing budgets among clients" (L. Miller, 1993, pp. 131–132) so that the funds available were maximally effective in producing the desired outcomes of reducing clients' frailty and increasing the number of clients who remained in noninstitutional settings. As implemented, the program was capable of monitoring and modifying workers' behavior and gave the state the ability to transfer funds to more "efficient" agencies, that is, agencies that were making the best use of the available dollars to produce the desired outcomes. L. Miller estimated that the MSSP program improved outcomes by about 15 percent and saved the state about $3.5 million per year in service costs.

## Policy Development and Advocacy

It is nearly impossible to understand fully the many ways in which computers are used for policy development and advocacy. The use of computers in this area is so widespread that it has become part of the operating fabric of many policy, political, and advocacy groups. Typical uses include the following:

- maintaining mailing and membership lists
- publishing pamphlets and newsletters
- managing fundraising projects
- targeting individuals, groups, or agencies that may be sources of funds, might be helpful, or may be in need of services
- monitoring legislation
- using bulletin boards to report on public hearings
- holding public hearings via computer
- producing mass mailings to legislatures or policy-making bodies
- analyzing legislation
- teleconferencing
- identifying voters who are likely to support a particular advocacy group's positions and encouraging them to register to vote
- monitoring community risk factors (for example, the risk of arson or of drug-related problems)
- monitoring governmental contracts and awards
- using mapping programs to illustrate the impact of current or proposed policies
- maintaining data banks of resources or of services that are available to members of a group or to residents of a community
- presenting computerized educational materials.

Earlier writers thought that computers would be a boon to grassroots movements (see Butterfield, 1986). They were partially right, but they did not fully anticipate that the gains made by the small advocacy-oriented agencies and groups would be offset by the immense increase in computing power of the groups and organizations they sought to influence. This situation was particularly true before the cost of computing power was reduced by the introduction of personal computers. For example, McCullough (1991), citing Danziger, Dutton, Kling, and Kraemer (1982), concluded that until the early 1980s "computers helped reinforce the power of the dominant coalitions in local communities" (p. 9) rather than empower those who were trying to alter those coalitions. However, with the proliferation of personal computers, it is clear that even small and resource-poor organizations can afford and are using computers and that they are using them effectively. In the end, however, "anyone who wants to be an effective player in the game of high technology still had best have plenty of resources. Whatever advances activists make in the computer realm do not even faintly match advances simultaneously made by organizations which wield power in society" (McCullough, p. 10).

## Online and CD-ROM Databases

Two major sources of information for policy-making and advocacy organizations are the various online and CD-ROM databases. These sources do not appear to have been used to any great degree by operating agencies. However, they contain a great deal of information that is useful at the agency level, as well as sources and types of interventions that are useful for individual practitioners.

### Services Online

Several sources of online information were identified earlier. These services, together with INTERNET, available at many universities and colleges (Kantrowitz et al., 1993; Penn, 1993), and the commercial services, such as America On Line, CompuServe, GEnie, and Prodigy Services, represent a radical change in how information is stored and used. The range of information is vast. An individual or agency using these services can tap into virtually almost any type of information it may need. Full texts of many national and international papers and magazines are available, as are some professional journals and many abstracts, from such sources as *Social Work Abstracts,* PsycLIT, and the Social Sciences Citation Index. Some are available online and on CD-ROM, whereas others are restricted to one or the other medium.

There are also many specialized services, such as Dialog, News Net, Dow Jones News/Retrieval, and Lexis/Nexis. One source of information on these more specialized services is McGraw-Hill Publications Online, which makes many of its publications available on these services; for another list, see Mendelsohn and Jacobson (1993). Another resource, published quarterly, is *Online Access,* which reports on lesser-known, but useful, online services.

The U.S. census data, down to the block level, are also available, as are mapping programs (S. Miller, 1992; Schine, 1993). Social services agencies should find these programs useful for locating and tracking clients or identifying targeted populations. Mapping programs often show relationships in data that may not be apparent when the data are viewed in other ways (Butterfield, 1993). Various kinds of marketing and financial data, as well as the full texts of the *Federal Register,* the *Congressional Record,* and many other federal publications, are also available.

In addition to the online databases, the various online services provide all the services found on bulletin boards, including E-mail, file downloading and uploading, and the numbers of computer conferences on almost any topic one can imagine. The services and resources run to thousands of entries (CompuServe's index of available services is, by itself, over five pages). Many local online services are also in operation; for example, many United Ways have online databases of local agencies' services and missions.

### CD-ROMs

The tendency to use online databases and CD-ROM technology will accelerate as the cost of hardware and software comes down. Many businesses are using CD-ROM technology to store regulations, policy manuals, product catalogs, and even insurance claims (Gleckman et al., 1993). It is already much less expensive for large agencies to store policy manuals on CD-ROM than to update and store the same information in printed form. It is now possible, for example, to buy a drive and the software used to create CD-ROMs for a few thousand dollars, and the drives needed to read the CD-ROMS can be purchased for $200 to $300. Such costs are well within the range of many human services agencies. Use of this technology may make it financially possible within the next few years for an agency to provide workers with full sets of records on clients, agency forms and regulations, and a database of community referral sources and services that they can take with them as they work with clients in the field.

CD-ROM technology is changing rapidly. One of the better sources of the latest CD-ROM software and hardware is the Bureau of Electronic Publishing in Parsippany, New Jersey.

## Policy and Value Issues

Many writers have been concerned about the impact of computer technology on clients, social workers, social services agencies, and the culture. The ideas of L. Miller (1993), Pruger (1986), and Rimmer (1986) represent an emerging view of what should drive the delivery of services in human services agencies. This work is important for three major reasons. First, it is based on an economic model of measuring and evaluating outcomes. Second, its focus is on outcomes as opposed to process. Third, it provides clear and comprehensive examples of the use of computers to modify the behavior of professional workers directly.

### Economic Models of Decision Making

Computers are well suited to making judgments on the basis of economic measures. Economic models assume that the best programs are those that are the most efficient, that is, that maximize outcomes while minimizing costs. (See Volume 15 of *Administration in Social Work* for several articles related to this topic.) This assumption is often treated as self-evident or beyond question. Although it is beyond the scope of this entry, it is clear that this assumption is, in fact, challengeable.

Important decisions are not based on economics alone. Tradition, community expectations, moral values and beliefs, and even pragmatic issues like what is politically possible are all routinely invoked when policy issues are considered. A careful reading of L. Miller (1993), Pruger (1986), and Rimmer (1986) reveals that many noneconomic issues were involved in the decision making on their projects. This entry is not the forum for an extensive discussion of such issues, but it is clear that the profession will struggle for some time about the place of economic models in human service decision making. Substantial bodies of literature debate the desirability of using purely economic indicators to measure a program's success (McClintock, 1990).

The fact that computers are involved is really secondary to the main issue. Computers have made possible levels of monitoring and control that were not possible before, but the issues existed before computers were a major force in the social services, and it is unlikely that they will ever be fully resolved. What will happen is that political decisions will lead to legislation that places limits on the way new technology can be used, and those political decisions will consider many issues besides equity and efficiency (for recent examples of efforts to place such limits on technology, see Casmier, 1993; Danca, 1993; L. Smith, 1993a, 1993b; Sullivan, 1993).

**Outcomes versus Process-Based Evaluation**

Computers shape the information that people collect (Murphy & Pardek, 1986). They are excellent at counting, doing mathematical operations, and sorting and organizing data. To be useful to a computer, data must be converted into a form that the computer can use. Therefore, agencies often count discrete events that are easy to measure. For example, an agency may count the number of phone calls or home visits a worker makes in a given period or the number of meetings or classes a client attends. Although there is a long history of using these process measures to judge an agency's or a professional's effort, there has been a substantial movement toward outcome-based measures. For example, as R. Binner (1993) noted:

> How well an information system performs is not just a function of the design of the information system. The design of the service program itself also has an impact on the job information systems can do. . . . If the design of the mental health service system is such that it is largely blind to its results [the question of what was the outcome] can be a very difficult question to answer. . . . This can happen when a service system is designed around the activities of the providers, rather than around clients and their problems. . . . Perhaps the most common way of measuring the product of a mental health service provider is in units of service produced. [For example] an inpatient service provides so many days of care. . . . However, if the providing of a service is seen not as the product of that service but as a means for achieving the product, an entirely different measure of productivity becomes appropriate. If the aim of providing the service is to improve the condition of the client in some way, the product of the service becomes a measure of that client's condition. . . . Information system designers [need] to press program managers and clinicians to identify measures of product that reflect improvement in the lives of their clients. (pp. 49–50)

The focus on outcome versus the focus on effort raises all sorts of issues about what outcomes should be expected. For instance, should a shelter for homeless people be judged by the extent to which its clients are able to avoid homelessness or on the clients' satisfaction with the services or on the clients' increased earning power or on some other basis? The temptation is to use process types of measures or easily measured outcome measures. The issue of appropriate outcome measures is difficult, and even though legions of academics have struggled with how to evaluate outcomes, there is little consensus about what constitutes good outcome measures. What is clear is that federal, state, and private funding sources are pushing for outcome-based evaluations and that agencies will have to respond to maintain their funding base.

**Modifying Workers' Behavior**

There are some who view efforts to modify workers' behavior as inappropriate. However, it is clear that society supports the view that it is legitimate to try to do so. The establishment of regulations and rules and of training efforts are examples of culturally sanctioned methods of bringing about change.

Training is usually designed to reduce the variability of responses. The presumption is that well-trained workers will use the facts and their judgment to make informed decisions that are consistent with the facts.

One factor that seems to improve performance is feedback. Computers can provide feedback not usually given in more traditional means of instruction. In the L. Miller (1993) and Pruger (1986) projects, feedback was used to let workers know how they were doing in comparison to other workers. But L. Miller and his colleagues went beyond simply giving feedback; they systematically altered the feedback, so that they shaped the workers' behavior over time. In terms of the goals they set, the results were what they expected: The equity of awards increased, and funds were redistributed so that the funds maximized the outcomes for the clients and for the agency.

The issue that bothers some commentators is not whether clients or workers should be changed, but how much control is enough (Mandall, 1989). It is clear that if control is absolute, the need to hire professional workers who are thought to be necessary for dealing with situations that require judgment and flexibility may be sharply reduced and even eliminated. It may be that paraprofessional workers who are trained as skilled observers can become the eyes and ears of the computer and that the computer will do the decision making about the allocation of resources. This possibility has led "opponents [to] argue that computerization reinforces the worst, most punitive aspects of bureaucracy for workers and clients and trivializes professional practice" (Grasso & Epstein, 1993, pp. 373–374). Others have talked about the dehumanization of clients and workers (Bowes, Kenney, & Pearson, 1993; Murphy & Pardek, 1986; Pardek & Schulte, 1990; Turem, 1986).

It is possible that these issues are of less concern to clients and workers than some writers think. Monnickendam and Eaglstein (1993) are among the few who have attempted to understand how social workers feel about the introduction and use of computers in social services agencies. They collected data from 47 social workers two months after a computer system was installed in a social services agency in Israel. Among other things, Monnickendam and Eaglstein concluded that social workers do not believe that computers infringe on worker–client relationships "and do not fear the dehumanization and depersonalization of clients" (p. 422). Most likely, further research will show that people's reactions to attempts to control them depend on several factors, including (1) the level of control attempted, (2) the legitimacy of the control as seen by society and the targeted group, (3) the targeted population, (4) the method used to establish control, (5) the timetable for compliance, and (6) the focus of control (self-control or agency control). In the end, the constraints put on the level of control will be based on values and political concerns, rather than on efficiency and cost alone.

## Management Issues

### Implementation

The successful introduction of computers into an organization depends on several factors. For example, Monnickendam and Eaglstein (1993) found that the implementation team has to listen to social workers and that organization-level variables are more important to the acceptance of a computer system than are intrinsic variables, that is, personal values and ethics. R. Binner (1993) endorsed this view, noting that "the information designer will have to be increasingly sensitive to the organizational context and use of the information system. The information system can either become the battleground of a power struggle between ... management and staff or it [can] be a unifying force that moves these groups from an adversarial to a cooperative relationship" (p. 51).

Tigh (1993) suggested that the organization needs to make someone responsible for the computer operation. Fasano and Shapiro (1991) went even further. They endorsed the following statement by a consultant who has experienced both success and failure in introducing computerization into agencies: "I don't even take jobs now unless an organization has one person who is the computer champion/guru. And if an organization can't come up with that person, then I tell them they're not ready to install a database system" (p. 132). Matheson (1993) also supported this view. In a study of agencies that had succeeded in implementing computerization, he reported that

> the only clear evidence of organizational receptiveness to change was the presence of innovative individuals. Every organization in the study had a computer champion—someone considered primarily responsible for the current level of computer usage in strategic planning. Even in the largest organizations, one person was singled out for his or her ability to apply the technology to agency problem solving. Ironically, none of these people were computer programmers or technicians and few of them had formal training in the use of technology. (p. 391)

Kolodner (1992) offered additional advice about what makes for successful introductions and applications: (1) "Clinicians appear to more readily accept applications with little or no required data entry" (p. 6) by them. (2) Data-entry stations must be available when the clinicians want to enter the data. (3) The computer system must respond quickly; clinicians will not tolerate waiting. (4) Data-entry time is an important factor; "in general, the use of the computer must take less time than the manual method unless the perceived benefit" (p. 14) outweighs the time needed to enter the data. (5) Simple applications "have a much higher chance of gaining acceptance than a complicated application" (p. 14). This last point was also endorsed by Tigh (1993), who suggested that agencies should design for the big picture but proceed in small steps.

### Training

The greatest mistake that managers make is expecting that the requirements for training staff in the use of computers are similar to those for other types of office equipment, such as typewriters and copiers. The literature suggests otherwise. Some estimates put training costs at nearly 60 percent of the total cost of introducing computers. Most human services organizations budget small amounts for initial training or for ongoing training. The result is predictable: Many staff do not know how to fully use the software the agency purchases. A further complication is that new versions of old programs arrive on the scene regularly. Each new version differs in both subtle and major ways from preceding versions and imposes a new demand for training on the organization. Therefore, training must be included as an ongoing budget item.

## Security and Integrity of Data

The security and integrity of data are ignored by many small human services agencies. Larger agencies have learned that data constitute a valuable commodity, and many have developed appropriate safeguards. The following sections review several issues that agencies need to consider in developing a plan to ensure the security and integrity of data.

### Controlled Access and Confidentiality

In the early days of the PC revolution, individual computers were dedicated to specific tasks. It was not uncommon to have a database computer, a financial computer, and several computers for word processing. Access and security were handled mainly by locking doors or computers. These methods were not adequate, but they sufficed in many agencies. With the advent of networks and computers with large storage capacities, the single-function computer is becoming the exception. Therefore, controlled access (setting limits on who may use computers and for what purposes) and confidentiality (limiting access to sensitive material to those who have a need to know) become more important issues.

The first level of security is to control who can operate the computer. Most new PCs have optional password-protection schemes that prevent unauthorized individuals from even starting them. The second level of security is to control who can use individual programs on the computer, including who can gain control of the computer's operating system. The third level of security is to control who can gain access to or change or add specific data to a program's data. Many database programs now allow control down to a single item of data; that is, one person may be able to read a person's social security number, and another may be denied access to it.

The fourth level of security is to provide a means of removing the computer's hard disk and locking it in a secure safe. This level has been traditionally used by sensitive areas of the federal government but rarely elsewhere. It is now available for personal computers. With the advent of networks that operate 24 hours a day, this level of security is problematic and is used for only the most sensitive data. The fifth level of security is data encryption. Only a few human services programs, such as Computer Assisted Social Services, produced by WALMYR Publishing Company and included in Nurius and Hudson's (1993) book, offer this level of protection. The use of encryption is increasing as issues surrounding the privacy of computerized records become more urgent (Preston, 1993; Schwartau, 1993; L. Smith, 1993a, 1993b).

Most human services agencies should implement at least the first three levels of control, but many do not. This level of security is usually sufficient to satisfy the legal and ethical standards for protecting the security of data. At least two people must have access to any specific item of data on the computer. Otherwise, data are inaccessible if the password is unavailable because the password holder becomes ill or dies, leaves the agency, or just forgets it.

### Dynamic Nature of Computerized Data

The integrity of data can also be threatened by the changing nature of the data stored on computers. Before computers, documents were stored in filing cabinets and could be retrieved. The advent of computers has greatly altered how records are kept. Because many records no longer exist in paper form and are stored solely in the computer, several problems arise for people who are responsible for maintaining agency records. Three major problems are (1) the dynamic nature of computer records and the programs used to create them, (2) the dynamic nature of agency coding systems, and (3) the volatility of computer records.

Computer records are always changing. Records can be updated, erased from, or added to the computer instantly. As soon as the data in the computer are changed, the exact data that existed when previous reports were generated no longer exist. This situation presents problems if reports need to be rerun or if the contents of a report need to be verified.

Not only do the records in the computer change, but the meaning of data or the codes used to classify data change over time. Two examples from agencies illustrate this issue. One agency used a category called incidental services that included any assistance that did not involve the disbursement of funds, food, or clothing. Later the agency created many more categories, such as group counseling, drug counseling, and individual counseling, and the definition of incidental services was narrowed considerably. Another agency modified its coding system. At one time the agency assigned a code of 1 to single persons and a code of 2 to a married couple. When couples who were not married became common, the categories were expanded to include categories for nonmarried couples, friends living together, and same-sex couples. The order of the codes was also changed, so that a code of 1 meant a married couple and a code of 2 meant an unmarried couple.

Neither agency kept records of when the changes were made. As a result, when they wanted summaries of services and characteristics of clients, they were not aware that the meaning of the data had changed over time. When reports were produced, it became clear that something was wrong with the data. Both agencies spent many hours trying to figure out what had happened. Fortunately, they were able finally to find documents that showed the approximate dates the definitions were changed and thus were able to make valid comparisons of their services and clients over a period of several years. Anyone who has worked with national census files can tell similar tales; for example, the 1990 census did not include Hispanic as a racial category, as earlier censuses had done.

Friedland and Carney (1992) discussed issues of this type in the context of maintaining records of research projects, but the issues they raised are relevant to any computerized data-collection activity. The four major conclusions to be drawn from their article and from my own experience follow.

1. Computer-readable copies of data should regularly be made to preserve the state of the data at a given time.
2. The copies must be treated as permanent records and should be labeled with the date of the copy, the title, the version of the program with which the data were used, and the title and version of the program used to back up the data.
3. A permanent log must be maintained to record any changes in the data-collection procedures, changes in the definitions of codes assigned to categories, and anything else that changes the meaning of the collected data. Some agencies have developed formal review procedures to ensure which changes are approved and recorded.
4. When programs used to collect or back up the data are superseded by new versions, the date of the conversion should be recorded in a log and the old versions retained because the new versions may not be able to use data collected by earlier versions of the programs.

### Validity of Data-Collection, Assessment, and Report-Generation Programs

One dilemma facing anyone who is considering the use of computers in an organization is whether the results obtained from the computer are dependable. Researchers use the terms "validity" and "reliability" to address this issue. *Validity* refers to the accuracy with which an instrument measures some characteristic, whereas *reliability* refers to how reproducible the measurement is (that is, if used more than once, would the measure give the same result). There are sophisticated methods for assessing validity and reliability. Nurius and Hudson (1993) presented a brief, excellent discussion of these issues. As Finnegan, Ivanoff, and Smyth (1991) noted, there is

> little evidence available on the validity of computer based programs for practitioners (Moreland, 1985). The interpretations generated are usually based on amalgamated clinical wisdom. These interpretations are most frequently prepared by the software developer, who may or may not be an expert in the use of the particular instrument. No computer based tests report reliability across subjects or across time. (p. 17)

The situation is not much different today. Some companies and individuals have spent the time and money needed to establish estimates of validity and reliability (Snyder et al., 1988), but most have not. Even when these estimates have been established, they may not be the same in a new setting because validity and reliability are determined by the variables of a particular setting, by the response of the population, by the training of people who use the device, and by how the device is administered or used.

These issues are important from both a legal and a clinical perspective. An agency that uses a new computerized instrument needs to establish its own measures of validity and reliability, both for instruments designed to collect information and for programs needed to produce reports.

There are numerous examples of agencies that have been harmed by inadequately validated and tested computer systems. One of the more dramatic occurred in Vermont (Scheier, 1989):

> When a PC was stolen from the Blue Cross and Blue Shield of Vermont, the thief left a ransom note saying, in effect, "You'll get your PC when I get my insurance claim check." . . . Insiders say Blue Cross's troubles began when it trusted a larger, more experienced company far too much, failing to assign enough inside staff to check the work until the project was hopelessly behind schedule. . . . At its peak, the backlog totaled 238,000 claims in a state with a population of 500,000. (pp. 1, 6)

Two important lessons can be learned from this story: First, keep the old system working until you are sure the new system is doing its job. Second, test and retest to establish validity and reliability. Testing should include using dummy data sets, so the results can be determined independently of the results generated by the computer. Even this level of testing will not reveal all the problems inherent in a system because thoroughly tested programs may still have bugs in them. For an extended discussion of these issues, see Finnegan et al. (1991) and Littlewood & Strigini (1992).

***Quality of technology.*** A related problem is the quality of the technology used to produce the programs. Computer programming technology changes so rapidly that something considered the state of the art today may well be outdated in a year or two. Sometimes programs that use old technology are well done, valid, and reliable and thus warrant continued use. Others should be discarded in favor of programs that use newer technology that makes them easier to use. For example, a well-established, commercial management information system (MIS) program used by several social services agencies does not allow users to make ad hoc queries. Every time users want new information or reports, they have to pay the developers to write a new program. Programs without the capacity to make queries were common in the early to mid-1980s, but today an MIS without this capacity is inadequate and not cost-effective. In another case, a teaching program designed to teach clinical skills does not provide any way for users to update it by adding new information or new questions; again, such a program was acceptable in the early 1980s but not today.

***Viability of vendor.*** The viability of the vendor is yet another problem that agencies rarely address. The computer industry is highly volatile. Hardware and software vendors come and go, and even when they stay in business, they must always be changing their products to keep up with the competition. For this reason, proprietary hardware systems should be avoided. If something fails and proprietary hardware is being used, a replacement may not be available or may be available only at a high cost. The use of such hardware cannot always be avoided, but whenever possible, commonly available hardware should be used. Similar rules hold for software but are harder to implement because most software is proprietary. It is wise to use off-the-shelf software when possible because it is always less expensive to use a commercial product than to develop a new product.

Whenever custom applications are developed, the user needs to have access to the source code (lines of computer code that contain the instructions that tell the computer what to do). The source code can be changed and is understood by anyone who is versed in the computer programming language in which the program is written. Without the source code, it is nearly impossible to modify a program. Many vendors will agree to provide the source code. If the vendor is unwilling to do so, two options are available. The first is to ask the vendor to place the source code in escrow, which means that the code is kept by an acceptable third party who will release the code to the purchaser if the vendor goes out of business or is unable to make the changes needed by the user. Escrowing is a common procedure and is acceptable to many vendors. The second option is to negotiate a performance bond (a bond that will pay the agency a specified sum if the vendor does not meet contractual obligations). This is the least acceptable approach because there can often be substantial delays in converting to other software and in testing new software.

**Emergency Plans and Disk Backups**

Social services agencies often do not have emergency plans. They tend to forget that computers go bad and that nature can do some nasty things to computers. Some agencies and companies have been disabled because of theft or sabotage of data, flooding, rain, earthquakes, fire, bombs, mechanical failure, human error, or electrical outages. Such problems can be costly in time and money. Depending on the amount of data stored, the costs and delays can range from a few hundred dollars to thousands of dollars, and from several hours to several months. Such delays have cost staff and managers their jobs and, in a few cases, have been beyond the capacity of the agencies to handle. When the World Trade Center in New York City was bombed in 1993, many companies that had well-developed emergency procedures were operating at other sites the day after the bombing, but others that had not planned as well were out of business until they could reconstruct their records or gain entrance to the building to get their computerized records. A well-developed emergency plan and timely backups of data can prevent many problems.

***Importance of backups.*** At a minimum, the agency should make arrangements for an alternative work site, for rental or access to computers, for the training of alternate operators, and for adequate backups of computer-readable copies of programs and data. Backups are essential because without them the agency's data-keeping system is at a great risk. The experience of a national human services agency illustrates this problem well. The organization had all its records of donors and fundraising activities and all its financial records on a single computer. The computer's hard drive malfunctioned, and there were no backups. The agency paid over a thousand dollars to have a data-recovery company take the disk apart and recover the data and several hundred dollars more to have a computer consultant reload the programs and data on the computer. The agency was lucky. The recovery was successful. Its management estimated that it would have taken six months and several thousand dollars to reenter the data in the computer. Even so, the organization was without financial records for almost two weeks and believes that it may have lost track of some donations.

To prevent this sort of problem, agencies should back up their programs and data often enough so that if their computers fail, they will only have to reenter a limited amount of data. Many agencies back up daily, others back up weekly, and some back up only monthly. If an agency backs up daily, it will have to replace only a day's data if its computer fails, whereas if it backs up weekly or monthly, a week's or a month's data may have to be reentered. There should be at least three backup copies; one copy should be kept off-site, preferably in a bank vault or in a computer data-storage vault, and rotated with the onsite copies on a regular basis.

***Viruses.*** Viruses are another reason for doing backups. My experience at Washington University and at a number of nonprofit agencies in the St. Louis area has led me to conclude that viruses represent a major threat to the integrity of data. Viruses, as applied to computers, are programs that someone has designed to change data or programs in a computer in ways that the owner or user did not authorize. They are called viruses because they have the ability to copy themselves onto a computer disk or to propagate themselves over networked computers without human knowledge or intervention. The most common way in which a virus "infects" a computer is by copying itself onto a floppy disk that is inserted into a computer and then copying itself back to another computer's hard disk when that floppy disk is used in the second computer. Some viruses are relatively benign. The first virus experienced at Washington University would cause words to start cascading off the screen, in the fashion of water falling over a waterfall, until all the words had fallen off the screen. It did nothing else, and although it was annoying to the user, it was not much more than a temporary inconvenience. Other viruses are severely destructive; they can randomly erase files and have destroyed all the data stored in some agencies' computers. If a single computer in an organization is infected, it is only a matter of time until every computer is infected. When an infection occurs, the agency has to shut off all its computers and begin a deinfection procedure that may sometimes take days. If the agency fails to check every computer disk and every computer it has, the probability is that all its computers will be reinfected ("Viruses," 1993). A few agencies have suffered significant losses of data; most have found the viruses before they did significant damage.

Once the machines and disks have been cleaned and are virus free, the only way to prevent reinfection is to install virus-checking software on all computers and to check all disks that are inserted into the machines. In my experience, even with this level of vigilance, an occasional reinfection will recur, but usually the recurrence will be detected before the virus has done permanent harm. Many software programs are available for checking and cleaning machines; they must be constantly updated because new viruses are being produced daily. Using a good virus-checking program is a must-do activity. The existence of viruses also underlines the need to do backups because the backups may be the only source of data destroyed by a virus infection.

### Verification of Data

The final area to be addressed is the need to "safeguard the integrity of the information system [by implementing] a system of information checks and balances" (R. Binner, 1993, p. 56). The verification of data is an important managerial task. Few agencies can boast of errorless data entry, regardless of who provides the information and who enters it into the computer. However, few human services agencies have established data verification procedures. Common problems are the failure to enter data or the entrance of incomplete or incorrect data.

Computers can be used to do many verification tests. The format and ranges of data can be checked at the point of entry, users can select the correct value from pop-up menus, and the computer can check for duplicate entries and produce reports that make it easy to spot many errors. Each of these approaches to the verification of data has merit and should be used when possible. But the agency needs to have an ongoing data-audit procedure that compares samples of the data in the computer with data in source documents.

The failure to have an ongoing data-audit procedure may have serious consequences. For example, one local agency did not apply for a federal grant when it discovered that follow-up data on clients' outcomes had not been entered for nearly two years. When the staff member who was assigned that task left the agency, the management forgot to assign the task to another person. Another local agency lost over $300,000 in state reimbursements when a state data audit showed that the data stored in the agency's computer had data-entry errors in 3 percent to 5 percent of the cases that were entered. Such rates are not high, but the state agency insisted on error rates of less than 0.3 percent. Because of the serious financial consequences for exceeding that error rate, the local agency now spends over $50,000 a year to train and retrain staff on data-entry procedures and to do ongoing weekly audits of samples taken from the agency's database.

## Conclusion

Computers have had a substantial impact on social work since the 1980s. The use of some applications, such as computerized assessment, computerized interviewing, computer services for people with disabilities, bulletin boards, online information services, and CD-ROMs, seems to be growing, and the usefulness of these applications appears to be established. Other applications, such as using computers to modify workers' and agencies' behavior and Smart Cards, are evolving. Some applications, such as using computers to deliver therapy, have not proved to be as useful as was once predicted.

Overall, computer applications are effective and cost-efficient tools for social workers. The debate is no longer whether computers will be used by social workers, but how they will be used. Although computers will continue to be used primarily for managerial purposes, many of the other uses described here are becoming routine.

## References

Ager, A., & Bendall, S. (Eds.) (1991). *Microcomputers and clinical psychology: Issues, applications, and future developments.* New York: John Wiley & Sons.

Alexander, J., & Davidoff, D. (1990). Psychological testing, computers and aging. *International Journal of Technology and Aging, 3,* 47–56.

American Psychiatric Association. (1987). *Diagnostic and statistical manual of mental disorders* (3rd ed. rev.). Washington, DC: Author.

Angle, H., Johnsen, T., Grebenkemper, N., & Ellinwood, C. (1979). Computer interview support for clinicians. *Professional Psychology, 10,* 49–51.

Benbenishty, R., & Ben-Zaken, A. (1988). Computer-aided process of monitoring task-centered family interventions. *Social Work Research & Abstracts, 24*(1), 7–9.

Binner, P., & Gaviria, B. (1963). The Fort Logan record system. *Journal of the Fort Logan Mental Health Center, 1.*

Binner, R. (1993). Information systems and mental health services: Issues for the 90's. *Computers in the Human Services, 9,* 47–58.

Bloomberg Business News. (1993, June 27). Apple, Compaq CEOs could be twins. *St. Louis Post Dispatch,* pp. 115, 178, 8E.

Bowes, N., Kenney, J., & Pearson, C. (1993). The impact of automation on attitudes and productivity in a human services agency: An emerging issue for employee assistance program managers. *Computers in the Human Services, 9,* 75–96.

Brand, N., & Houx, P. (1992). MINDS: Toward a computerized test battery for use in health psychological and neuropsychological assessment. *Behavior Research Methods, Instruments, and Computers, 24,* 385–389.

Busse, T. (1992, November 23). SoapBox puts you in touch with the government. *Infoworld,* p. 16.

Butterfield, W. (1986). Computers in social work and social welfare: Issues and perspective. *Journal of Sociology and Social Welfare, 9,* 5–26.

Butterfield, W. (1993). Graphics. In L. Beebe (Ed.), *Professional writing for the human services* (pp. 105–150). Washington, DC: NASW Press.

Carr, A., Ghosh, A., & Ancil, R. (1983). Can a computer take a psychiatric history? *Psychological Medicine, 13,* 151–158.

Carr, T. (1991). Microcomputers and psychological treatment. In A. Ager (Ed.), *Microcomputers and clinical psychology: Issues, applications, and future developments.* New York: John Wiley & Sons.

Casali, S., & Williges, R. (1990). Data bases of accommodative aids for computer users with disabilities. *Human Factors, 32,* 407–432.

Casmier, S. (1993, June 23). Simon pushes ban on workplace snooping. *St. Louis Post Dispatch,* pp. 115, 174, 1C.

Colby, K. (1980). Computer psychotherapists. In J. Sidowsky, J. Johnson, & T. Williams (Eds.), *Technology in mental health care delivery systems* (pp. 109–117). Norwood, NJ: Ablex.

Danca, R. (1993, June 28). Privacy act would force firms to inform their employees about E-mail monitoring. *PC Week, 10,* 203.

Danziger, J., Dutton, W., Kling, R., & Kraemer, K. (1982). *Computers and politics: High technology in American local politics.* New York: Columbia University Press.

Enders, A. (1990). *Assisted technology source book.* (Available from Resna, 1100 Connecticut Avenue, NW, Suite 700, Washington, DC, 20036)

Evans, W., & Miller, J. (1969). Differential effects on response bias of computer versus conventional administration of a social science questionnaire. *Behavioral Science, 14,* 216–227.

Farber, D. (1993, Summer). Cyberspace, the Constitution and the electronic frontier foundation. *Educators TECH Exchange,* pp. 21–27.

Farrell, A. (1989). Impact of computers on professional practice: A survey of current practices and attitudes. *Professional Psychology: Research and Practice, 20,* 172–178.

Farrell, A. (1991). Computers and behavioral assessment: Current applications, future possibilities and obstacles to routine use. *Behavioral Assessment, 13,* 159–179.

Fasano, R., & Shapiro, J. (1991). Computerizing the small non-profit: Computer consultants' perspective. *Computers in the Human Services, 8,* 129–145.

Ferriter, M. (1993). Computer aided interviewing in psychiatric social work. *Computers in the Human Services, 9,* 59–68.

Finn, J. (1987, September). *Microcomputers in nonprofit agencies: Utilization trends and training requirements.* Paper presented at the First International Human Service Information Technology Applications Conference, Birmingham, England.

Finnegan, D., Ivanoff, A., & Smyth, N. (1991). Computer applications explosion: What practitioners and clinical managers need to know. *Computers in the Human Services, 8,* 1–19.

Friedland, K., & Carney, R. (1992). Data management and accountability in behavioral and biomedical research. *American Psychologist, 47,* 640–645.

Geiss, G., & Viswanathan, N. (Eds.). (1986). *The human edge: Information technology and helping people.* New York: Haworth Press.

Ghosh, A., & Marks, I. (1987). Self treatment of agoraphobia by exposure. *Behavior Therapy, 18,* 3–16.

Gilgun, J., & Connor, T. (1988). How perpetrators view sexual abuse. *Social Work, 34,* 248–251.

Gleckman, H., Cary, J., Mitchell, R., Smart, T., & Rousch, C. (1993, June). The technology payoff. *Business Week, 3323,* 57–68.

Goldberg, A. (1993, June 28). Why mainframes aren't extinct. *PC Week, 10,* 224.

Goodman H., Gingerich, W., & de Shazar, S. (1989). BRIEFER: An expect system for clinical practice. *Computers in the Human Services, 5,* 53–68.

Gorodezky, M., & Hedlund, J. (1982). The developing role of computers in community mental health centers: Past experience and future trends. *Journal of Operational Psychiatry, 13,* 94–99.

Grasso, A., & Epstein, E. (1993). Computer technology and the human services: Does it make a difference? *Computers in the Human Services, 9,* 373–382.

Greist, J. H., Gustafson, D. H., Stauss, F., Rowse, G., Laughren, T., & Chiles, J. (1973). A computer interview for suicide-risk prediction. *American Journal of Psychiatry, 130,* 1327–1332.

Grimes, B. (1993, June 29). Packages help you write to Congress. *PC Magazine, 12,* 31.

Groth, M., & Schumaker, J. (1988). Psychological testing: Issues and guidelines. *American Journal of Orthopsychiatry, 59,* 256–263.

Hudson, W. (1990). Computer-based clinical practice: Status and future possibilities. In L. Videka-Sherman & W. J. Reid (Eds.), *Advances in clinical social work research* (pp. 105–117). Silver Spring, MD: NASW Press.

Kantrowitz, B., Springen, K., King, P., Rosenberg, D., Hamilton, K., Cohn, B., & Ramo, J. (1993, September 6). Live wires. *Newsweek, 122,* 42–49.

Kerr, S. (1988). For people with handicaps, computers = independence. *Datamation, 34,* 39–44.

Koenig, D. (1992, November 23). Look on the Disabilities Act as an opportunity rather than a burden. *Infoworld,* p. 39.

Kolodner, R. (1992). Mental health clinical computer applications which succeed: The VA experience. *Computers in the Human Services, 8,* 1–15.

Landers, S. (1993, January). Colleagues connect for high-tech talks. *NASW News,* p. 45.

Langreth, R. (1993, July). Medical records in your wallet. *Popular Science,* p. 46.

Littlewood, B., & Strigini, L. (1992). The risks of software. *Scientific American, 265,* 62–75.

Lockshin, S., & Harrison, K. (1991). Computer assisted assessment of psychological problems. In A. Ager & S. Bendall (Eds.), *Microcomputers and clinical psychology: Issues, applications, and future developments* (pp. 47–63). New York: John Wiley & Sons.

Mandall, S. (1989). Resistance and power: The perceived effect which computerization has on a social agency's power relationships. *Computers in the Human Services, 4,* 29–40.

Manning, R. (1993, July). In line with America Online. *Mobile Office,* pp. 133–134.

Matheson, A. (1993). Innovative use of computers for planning in human service organizations. *Computers in the Human Services, 9,* 383–396.

McClintock, C. (1990). Caring vs. cash flow: Using computers to explore dilemmas in human services. *Computers in the Human Services, 7,* 327–353.

McCullough, M. (1991). Democratic questions for the computer age. *Computers in the Human Services, 8,* 9–18.

Mendelsohn, H., & Jacobson, T. (1993). The library literature search. In L. Beebe (Ed.), *Professional writing for the human services* (pp. 31–61). Washington, DC: NASW Press.

Miller, L. (1993). The optimum allocation of in-home supportive type services in the multipurpose senior services program. *Computers in the Human Services, 9,* 111–136.

Miller, M. (1992). Obtaining mental health software by telephone from a computerized bulletin board system. *Computers in the Human Services, 8,* 119–129.

Miller, M. (1993, August 27). U.S. public records going online. *Wall Street Journal, 524,* 239, B1.

Miller, S. (1992, December 7). Streetinfo upgrade taps new census data. *PC Week, 19,* 48.

Monnickendam, M., & Eaglstein, A. (1993). Computer acceptance by social workers: Some unexpected research findings. *Computers in the Human Services, 9,* 409–424.

Moreland, K. (1985). Validation of computer based interpretations: Problems and prospects. *Journal of Consulting and Clinical Psychology, 53,* 816–825.

Murphy J., & Pardek, J. (1986). Technologically mediated therapy: A critique. *Social Casework, 67,* 605–612.

Nurius, P., Hooyman, N., & Nicoll, A. (1991). Computers in agencies: A survey baseline and planning implications. *Journal of Social Service Research, 14,* 141–155.

Nurius, P., & Hudson, W. (1993). *Human services practice, evaluation, and computers.* Pacific Grove, CA: Brooks/Cole.

Pardek, J., & Schulte, R. (1990). Computers in social intervention: Implications for professional social work practice and education. *Family Therapy, 17,* 109–121.

Penn, J. (1993, September). INTERNET:PRESIDENT@WHITEHOUSE.GOV. *PC Computing, 6,* 450.

Pope, K. (1993, July 2). For Compaq and Dell, accent is on personal in the computer wars. *Wall Street Journal, 524,* 183, 1.

Preston, A. (1993, June 28). Encryption technology is on the rise in the private sector. *PC Week, 10,* 207.

Pruger, R. (1986). Information technology in support of service delivery systems. In G. Geiss & N. Viswanathan (Eds.), *The human edge: Information technology and helping people* (pp. 212–227). New York: Haworth Press.

Quintanar, L., Crowell, C., & Prior, J. (1982). Human-computer interaction: A preliminary social psychology analysis. *Behavior Research Methods and Instrumentation, 14,* 210–220.

Rebello, K., Mitchell, R., & Schwartz, E. (1993, July 5). Apple's future. *Business Week, 3326,* 22–28.

Rimmer, E. (1986). Implementing computer technology in human service agencies: The experience of two California counties. *New England Journal of Human Services, 6,* 25–29.

Rosenfeld, P., Doherty, L., Vicino, S., Kantor, J., & Greaves, J. (1989). Attitude assessment in organizations: Testing three microcomputer-based survey systems. *Journal of General Psychology, 116,* 145–154.

Scheier, R. (1989, September 4). Botched system transplant induces Green Mountain blues. *PC Week, 3,* 1, 6.

Schine, E. (1993, July 26). Computer maps pop up all over the map. *Business Week, 3329,* 75–76.

Schneider, D., Taylor, E., Prater, L., & Wright, M. (1992). Risk assessment for HIV infection: Validation study of a computer assisted preliminary screen. *AIDS, 3,* 215–229.

Schoech, D. (1990). *Human services computing: Concepts and applications.* Binghamton, NY: Haworth Press.

Schwartau, W. (1993, June 28). Crypto policy and business privacy. *PC Week, 10,* 207.

Selmi, P., Klein, M., Greist, J., Johnson, J., & Harris, W. (1982). An investigation of computer-assisted cognitive-behavior therapy in the treatment of depression. *Behavior Research Methods and Instrumentation, 14,* 181–185.

Siegal, D. (1990). Computer based clinical practice: An asset or pie in the sky? In L. Videka-Sherman & W. J. Reid (Eds.), *Advances in clinical social work practice* (pp. 118–122). Silver Spring, MD: NASW Press.

Simmons, E., & Miller, O. (1971). Automated patient-history taking. *Hospitals, 45,* 56–59.

Smith, E. (1993, July 19). A "living will" network helps the dying to speak for themselves. *Business Week, 3328,* 55.

Smith, L. (1993a, June 28). Electronic monitoring raises legal and societal questions. *PC Week, 10,* 204.

Smith, L. (1993b, June 28). Encryption, monitoring and E-mail spur the privacy debate. *PC Week, 10,* 202.

Snyder, D., Lacher, D., & Willis, R. (1988). Computer based interpretation of the Marital Satisfaction Inventory: Use in treatment planning. *Journal of Marital and Family Therapy, 14,* 397–409.

Steinberg, D. (1987, November 10). Networks link human-service agencies. *PC Week, 4,* C8.

Stoll, M. (1988, May 3). Instant feedback on what people really think. *PC Week, 5,* 55.

Stuckle, M. (1989). A comparison of clinicians and computer conducted closed ended and open ended interviews. *Dissertation Abstracts International, 50*(12), 4105A.

Sullivan, K. (1993, June 28). Some companies spell it right out: We will be watching you. *PC Week, 10,* 203.

Tigh, R. (1993). Organizational development and information systems: A case study. *Computers in the Human Services, 9,* 145–152.

Tilsner, J. (1993, July 19). But will they get their own water coolers? *Business Week, 3328,* 32.

Turem, J. (1986). Social work administration and modern management technology. *Administration in Social Work, 10,* 15–24.

Viruses: How big? How bad? (1993, July 19). *Information Week,* p. 25.

Warzecha, G. (1991). The challenge to psychological assessment from modern computer technology. *European Review of Applied Psychology, 41,* 213–220.

Weitzel, W., Morgan, D., & Guyden, T. (1973). Towards a more efficient mental status examination. *Archives of Psychiatry, 28,* 215–218.

Woo, J. (1993, January 4). E-mail archives provide windfall for lawyers seeking evidence. *Wall Street Journal, 524,* 4, B6.

Yokley, J., Coleman, D., & Yates, B. (1990). Cost effectiveness of three child mental health assessment methods. *Journal of Mental Health Administration, 17,* 99–107.


## Further Reading


Blythe, B., & Tripodi, T. (1989). *Measurement in direct social work practice.* Newbury Park, CA: Sage Publications.

Cnaan, R. (1989). Social work education and direct practice in the computer age. *Journal of Social Work Education, 25,* 235–243.

Cohen, C., Nizza, A., Rock, B., & Smith, M. (1990). The evolution of a social work information system. *Computers in the Human Services, 4,* 259–274.

Eraut, M., & Hoyles, C. (1989). Groupwork with computers. *Journal of Computer Assisted Learning, 5,* 12–24.

Exell, M., Nurius, P., & Balassone, M. (1991). Preparing computer literate social workers: An integrative approach. *Journal of Teaching in Social Work, 5,* 81–99.

Flynn, J. (1990). Using computers to teach and learn social policy: A report from the classroom and the field. *Computers in the Human Services, 7,* 199–209.

Parsloe, P. (1989). An example of serendipity: The unintended impact of computers on social work practice. *Computers in the Human Services, 5,* 169–185.

Semke, J., & Nurius, P. (1991). Information structure, information technology, and the human services environment. *Social Work, 36,* 353–358.

Smart, S. (1988). Computers as treatment: The use of the computer as an occupational therapy medium. *Clinical Rehabilitation, 2,* 61–69.

**William H. Butterfield, PhD,** is associate professor, Washington University, George Warren Brown School of Social Work, One Brookings Drive, St. Louis, MO 63130.

**For further information see**

Expert Systems; Information Systems; Recording; Research Overview: Survey Research.

**Key Words**

computers

information management

## Confidentiality

*See* Legal Issues: Confidentiality and Privileged Communication

# Conflict Resolution

**Bernard S. Mayer**

An essential part of the task social workers face in most of the settings in which they work is handling conflict in a productive manner. Whether advocating for clients, dealing with conflict within organizations, or helping people learn more-effective ways of coping with conflict in their lives, social workers contend with conflict on a daily basis. Yet aside from some generalized statements about the mediative or advocacy role that social workers play, social work education and social work theory did not embrace this challenge until recently. The field of conflict resolution has grown both conceptually and in practice, and the use of mediation in particular has increased in many of the arenas in which social workers practice. Consequently, there has been a gradual increase in awareness of the relevance of this area to social work and a significant growth in the number of social workers who identify themselves as mediators.

The purpose of this entry is to review the conceptual frameworks that guide the practice of conflict resolution, to examine the various roles that social workers play in conflict resolution and the types of conflict-resolution procedures they use, and to look more specifically at the application of mediation to various fields of practice. As mediation attracts the interest of social workers, it is particularly important to understand it within the context of conflict resolution as a conceptual framework and a field of practice.

### Background

Conflict-resolution procedures have been formally and informally applied to most of the major fields of practice in social work. In 1991 NASW adopted a set of practice standards for social work mediators in recognition of the growing role of mediation in social work practice (NASW, 1991).

Frequently social workers who identify themselves as case managers, counselors, or caseworkers are also performing a number of different conflict-intervention roles. For example, when a child protection worker deals with a parent who has been reported for abuse or neglect, he or she is often acting as an advocate of the interests of the child and the state, a negotiator who is trying to work out a voluntary intervention plan with the parent, an authority figure who will have to decide what action to take, an adviser who is trying to help the parent understand his or her choices and make a good decision, and a substantive expert who will have to make a report to a legal entity. It is the confusion of these roles and the inaccurate message that is often delivered to clients about which role the social worker is playing that so often breed distrust and alienation in the client–worker relationship, especially with involuntary clients.

By understanding the actual nature of the conflict-resolution role that they play at any given time, social workers can clarify their roles and effectively apply a significant body of intervention skills. For example, if child protection workers consider themselves to be negotiators whose job is to try to arrive at a mutually acceptable intervention plan with families—one that protects the children, adheres to the relevant policies and laws, and respects the importance of the family—then they can bring a whole set of powerful collaborative negotiation tools to bear on the problem (Cingolani, 1984; Mayer, 1987b; Murdach, 1986). When negotiations break down or are difficult to initiate, as in other settings, the introduction of a neutral third party may be useful.

This way of looking at the interaction process between the social worker and the client is relevant to arenas as diverse as special education, care of elderly people, mental health, and adoption. Before social workers can adequately benefit from the conceptual and practical tools that the field of conflict resolution offers, however, they must understand the nature of conflict more fully and must overcome the stereotypes that are so often attached to the concepts of negotiation, mediation, and advocacy. For example, it is important to understand that there is no necessary contradiction between approaching a family interaction as a negotiator and acting zealously to protect a child.

## Conceptual Framework

### Definitions of Conflict

*Conflict* can be defined as a state that occurs when "two or more parties believe they have incompatible objectives" (Kriesberg, 1982, p. 17). This definition implies two essential elements of conflict: (1) the perception people have that they are in conflict and the feelings that go along with that perception and (2) the objective differences in the outcomes that people are seeking. Coser (1956) and Kriesberg described this distinction as the realistic and nonrealistic elements of conflict. According to Coser, the realistic element of conflict is based on the issues, problems, interests, and needs of the parties, whereas the nonrealistic element stems from the emotions and tensions that parties to a conflict experience. The realistic element of conflict requires an outcome that satisfactorily addresses the issues and interests of the parties. The nonrealistic element requires some sort of discharge of emotions or energy.

The value of this concept of conflict is that it helps one identify what parties to a conflict need at any given time. There is a natural tendency in many situations to try to resolve a conflict by working on an effective solution. If the person who is in conflict is caught up in the nonrealistic element of conflict, any attempt to arrive at a solution may be resisted, or the conflict will persist even though solutions are found. Thus, a parent who deals with the anger and tears of a child who is in conflict with peers by proposing rational solutions to the stated problem is probably not addressing the child's needs to vent anger, to be heard, and to be validated. Similarly, a marital therapist who directs a couple who disagree about whether to have a child to focus on the pain or upset that they are feeling may also be misdirected. In the first case, the child is dealing with the nonrealistic elements of conflict, whereas the parent is focused on the realistic components. In the second case, the therapist is asking a couple who may want to work on the realistic component of their dispute to focus on the nonrealistic elements.

### Causal Elements

Moore (1986) outlined five causal elements in social conflict: (1) relationship issues (for example, emotions, perceptions and stereotyping, communication, and repetitive negative behavior), (2) value conflicts, (3) inconsistencies in data, (4) structural problems, and (5) conflicts about interests. In any conflict situation, some or all of these elements may be present. It is useful to understand which aspect of conflict the parties are struggling with at any time and in what areas progress in the constructive handling of conflict may be made.

To the extent that the parties may be stuck in the relationship aspect of conflict, a better communication process is generally necessary, the parties need to feel heard and acknowledged by each other, stereotypes must be uncovered and addressed, and behavioral patterns that are escalating the conflict should be examined. To the extent that the parties have inconsistent data, they should be provided with credible objective information on which to base their decisions, and inconsistencies in data need to be cleared up or accepted. If the parties are struggling with differences in values, a values-clarification process is needed, and an attempt to identify underlying value congruencies or to help the parties accept their differences in values so they can proceed with a resolution process should be made. Structural conflict requires either a plan for changing the structure or an acceptance of the limits of resolution that are possible within the current structural framework. Conflicts about interests require an effective collaborative problem-solving process in which interests are identified, creative solutions for meeting interests are sought, and compromises are identified.

This framework can be applied to any conflict and can provide a powerful guide to the intervenor in the conflict. Consider a dispute between an adult child and an elderly parent about the appropriate place for the parent to live at a time in his or her life when considerable care and assistance are needed. To understand the conflict, the intervenor must take into account relationship issues. A whole lifetime of communication patterns, power struggles, behavioral irritations, and unresolved feelings may form the background of an attempt to look at any issue. It may be necessary to acknowledge or at least account for these issues in any attempt to deal with the problem constructively.

Many cultural, generational, or other value issues may be involved. The parent may value independence and autonomy far more than security or comfort, whereas the child may place a higher value on comprehensive medical care and personal security. If the conflict evolves into a dispute over which value is "correct" or more important, it is likely that little will be accomplished. Structural conflict may be generated by the geographic distance between the parent and child or the limited resources that are available, narrowing the possible solutions to the conflict. Conflict caused by inconsistent data could occur in relation to the minimum care necessary for the parent or the prognosis of a particular medical condition. The parent may well believe that he or she could regain a level of health and physical capacity beyond what the adult child thinks is possible. If these data are critical to an outcome, both parties will either have to obtain information that they believe is credible, or they will have to find a solution that works regardless of whose information is accurate. All these aspects of conflict are obstacles to be overcome on the road to the actual problem solving that normally occurs in the area of conflicts about interests.

***Types of interests.*** Interests may be defined as the needs of parties that must be met if the parties are to be satisfied with the outcome. They are of three types: psychological, substantive, and procedural. Psychological interests have to do with people's concerns about how they are treated and relate to the need to be treated with dignity and to have their feelings taken seriously. For instance, the parent in the foregoing example may have an interest in not being patronized or controlled by his or her adult child, whereas the adult child may have an interest in being appreciated for the efforts he or she is making on behalf of the parent.

Procedural interests have to do with people's needs or concerns about how the decision-making or conflict-resolution process is conducted; these concerns can be related to such issues as participation, input, information sharing, and timing. Thus, the parent may have a procedural need to be the decision maker or to be informed fully about medical issues, and the adult child may have a procedural need to be consulted by the parent before important medical decisions are made or expenses are incurred.

Substantive interests have to do with the tangible outcomes, goods, services, or behaviors that people need. For example, the adult child may need an outcome that maximizes the parent's safety and minimizes the amount of time or resources that he or she will have to put into the parent's care, whereas the parent may need to be in his or her own home or community, to maintain ownership of important possessions, or to be in contact with friends and other family members.

Frequently, in problem-solving or conflict-resolution situations, even if people succeed in focusing on their genuine interests, they are preoccupied with substantive interests and are not aware of or do not deal with procedural or psychological interests. Yet these interests are often paramount to the disputants. If these interests are addressed, there is a much greater likelihood that the parties will deal with substantive interests flexibly and creatively. If the parent and adult child can acknowledge and accommodate each other's need for information, respect, and appreciation, their ability to work together on solving the issues related to the care of the parent will be significantly enhanced.

**Intervention**

The intervention of social workers in conflicts like the one just described can occur through the framework of counseling, case management, mediation, or advocacy. Regardless of the framework of intervention, if social workers can understand the nature of the conflict and the tasks that need to be accomplished to reach a collaborative solution, their ability to work with the family will be significantly enhanced.

In accordance with this model of conflict, the task of the intervenor is to help participants deal with the nonessential elements of conflict at least enough so that they can focus on the necessary elements. To do so, the intervenor has to consider which aspect of the conflict the disputants need to work on to move toward an interest-based focus and to obtain enough understanding of the nature of the interests involved in the dispute to promote a creative problem-solving process.

## Obstacles to Resolving Conflict

There are a number of common obstacles to achieving a constructive problem-solving approach to the resolution of conflict.

### Positionality and Premature Problem Solving

When people are faced with conflicts, they often resort to taking positions about what they believe must happen. Sometimes these positions are extreme and rigid. Even if they are taken with the best of problem-solving intentions, they are often problematic because they are premature. If these positions (which are actually proposed solutions to a conflict) are to be productive, it is often necessary to develop an educational process, to repair or establish relationships, to open or improve communications, and to undertake other activities that allow the parties to consider solutions in a constructive, interest-based manner. The essence of what has come to be called "interest-based negotiations" (Fisher & Ury, 1981) is a focus on interests, rather than on positions, outcomes, solutions, or proposals. In practice, establishing such a focus often means finding a means of accepting stated positions as one possible outcome to a dispute and then eliciting from these positions the underlying interests that they represent.

### Distributional Focus in Negotiations

There are two primary dimensions to bargaining or negotiations: the distributional and the integrative (Lax & Sebenius, 1986; Walton & McKersie, 1965). The distributional dimension in bargaining involves a focus on how to divide the existing benefits or utilities among the parties involved in a negotiation. To the extent that people are operating along this dimension, they assume that a fixed amount of benefits is available and that what will accrue to one party will not be available to the others. In other words, the parties assume that the benefits are like a pie that is to be distributed among them and that the pieces that one party eats will no longer be available to the other parties. People often view conflict as occurring along a distributional, fixed-sum, win–lose line. This view encourages positional, manipulative, power-oriented, withholding, and adversarial tactics.

On the other hand, the integrative dimension focuses on how to increase the amount of utilities available to be divided among the disputants—to make the pie larger. To the extent that people operate along this dimension, they assume that cooperation and creativity will result in more benefits. The tactics that are more likely to be used along this dimension are information sharing, cooperation, creative problem solving, brainstorming, and risk taking.

In a labor–management negotiation, for example, distributional negotiations occur when the parties are fighting about what proportion of available resources should go into employee benefits versus other organizational needs. Integrative negotiations occur when joint efforts are made to obtain more resources for the organization or to use available resources more creatively and efficiently. Of course, almost all serious negotiations involve both aspects of bargaining, but the integrative dimension is often not sufficiently engaged.

### Nonconstructive Uses of Power

The way in which power is applied in conflict situations has a lot to do with the degree to which a problem can be resolved constructively. The application of power can range from highly destructive and dangerous (as in situations of domestic violence) to productive and necessary (for example, persuasion based on sharing information and resources).

The problem social workers must face in conflict-resolution situations is how to promote the constructive application of power and to ensure that disempowered parties gain access to available legitimate sources of power. It is not so much that a balance of power must be achieved because such a balance is an elusive goal that an intervenor usually cannot attain. Instead, it is important that the parties to a conflict be helped to obtain access to information, advocates, resources, and support systems so they can be effective in mobilizing and bringing to bear the legitimate sources of power that are available to them. Likewise, it is important that intervenors try to prevent or minimize the use of nonconstructive forms of power. Often the act of supporting people in obtaining access to constructive sources of power will also help them cease using destructive sources. What is constructive and what is destructive depend on the situation, but as a general rule, the kinds of power that are coercive are less conducive to the constructive resolution of conflict, whereas power based on normative or utilitarian appeals is more likely to be constructive (Etzioni, 1975; Gamson, 1968; Hasenfeld, 1978; Mayer, 1987a).

### Design Problems in Conflict-Resolution Procedures

Often, the best intentions and even a high level of communication and conflict-resolution skills do not lead to productive outcomes because of the procedures within which conflict resolution must occur. Conflicts in the child protection system, for example, are often exacerbated by the pressure under which investigations take place and the conflicting roles of the child protection worker who is asked to act as an authority figure and a support person simultaneously. Likewise an employee's grievance negotiation can be exacerbated by procedures that require the filing of a clearly stated complaint, within a set amount of time from the incident, on forms that are designed to be the basis for investigation and litigation. A similar problem exists in efforts to deal with a client's complaints about a therapist's violation of ethical standards. The successful intervention in conflicts, particularly in an organizational context, often requires a consideration of these design issues and efforts to redesign the conflict-resolution process itself (Ury, Brett, & Goldberg, 1988).

#### Inadequately Framed Conflict

One of the subtlest and most powerful ways in which conflict can be exacerbated or reduced is in the framing of the conflict itself. If a parent and an adolescent are in conflict about the adolescent's curfews, chores, and behavior in the house, there are many potential framings for the issue. One framing that people frequently adopt is based on communication and values: "We have to learn to understand each other better and respect each other's values." As nice as it would be for adolescents and parents to do so, such a framing is likely to prove too nebulous, global, and out of touch with the realities of adolescents' developmental issues.

Alternatively, the issue can be framed in terms of power: "You've got to learn that in this house, I am the boss, and you can either follow my rules or leave." This framing invites a power struggle and a win–lose orientation. A third framing may be more interest based: "We have different needs about chores, curfews, and so on, but we also want to find a way to live together. What are the options for how we can meet my needs for assistance, consistency, and reasonable limits and your needs for flexibility, free time, and opportunity to be with your friends?" This framing can promote a negotiation process. It is not that one approach is always better than the others, but it is clear that some framings promote the resolution of conflict and others promote the escalation of it.

#### Power- or Rights-Based Orientation

Under circumstances of stress or tension, people tend to believe that conflict will be solved by the application of power or by the assertion of legal rights. Settling conflict on the basis of an outcome of a power struggle or on who would prevail in a legal situation leads to less-collaborative outcomes than trying to settle conflict on the basis of how to meet the interests of the different parties involved (Ury et al., 1988). It is often particularly hard for people to change from a rights-based approach to an interest-based approach. This change does not imply sacrificing one's rights or giving up the ability to enforce rights through a legal procedure; rather, it requires a different way of thinking about how to achieve a reasonable outcome. Instead of arguing about what a judge might order if a situation were litigated, parties who use an interest-based approach attempt to look at their different interests to identify outcomes that may satisfy these interests. Rights-based approaches are appropriate in conflict situations if interest-based approaches are impossible or unsuccessful, but they are problematic if applied instead of or before an interest-based attempt to solve a problem.

#### Cross-Cultural Problems

Perhaps the greatest challenge in preserving or promoting world peace is how to deal with interethnic conflict. Different cultural attitudes about conflict and its resolution often contribute to the exacerbation of disputes. The circumspect or indirect approach to conflict that is appropriate for people from one culture will appear manipulative and "sneaky" to those from a culture that values directness. Direct eye contact—a sign of sincerity, respect, and attention in some groups—is considered a challenge or a sign of disrespect in others. The awareness of cultural differences is certainly the first step toward surmounting the obstacles to resolving conflicts among people from different cultures, but even with awareness, it is often difficult to communicate across cultural lines when the issues are large or tensions are high.

### Continuum of Conflict-Resolution Procedures

Because of the difficulties people face in overcoming these and other obstacles to the resolution of conflict, appropriate dispute-resolution procedures should be introduced into social work–related activities, and social workers should develop the necessary skills to implement them. It is possible to conceptualize the elements of what has come to be called the alternative dispute- resolution field along a continuum that is defined by the degree to which disputants handle their own disputes—from procedures that involve the unassisted resolution of conflict, to procedures in which third parties help disputants solve their own conflicts, to procedures in which third parties are used to make decisions about the appropriate outcomes for conflicts.

**Unassisted Procedures**

Unassisted procedures are those in which parties to a conflict handle their own disputes. These procedures include negotiation, conciliation, rapport-building activities, information-exchange procedures, collaborative problem solving, and consensus decision making in group settings. Social workers may participate in these unassisted procedures when they are, in effect, parties to the conflict or issue to be resolved. It is often useful for social workers who are involved in dealings with involuntary clients to view themselves as negotiators. By truly understanding this role and by developing the skills necessary to fulfill it effectively, social workers can often promote more-collaborative approaches to handling situations in which they are structurally set up to be in conflict with clients. In addition, whenever social workers are acting as advocates—whether for clients, groups, organizations, or themselves—an understanding of this role will be critical to their success. A second way in which social workers may participate in unassisted procedures is as coaches or teachers for others who will be conducting their own negotiations.

**Nonbinding Assistance**

There are many ways in which social workers act to help others resolve their conflicts. Whether they work as marital counselors with couples in conflict, family therapists intervening in parent–adolescent conflicts, or case managers trying to help clients who are in conflict with a variety of systems, social workers often act as intermediaries of some sort. The effectiveness with which this role is played is often hampered by the fact that it is mixed into many other roles and diluted by contradictory expectations and tasks. Furthermore, it is only recently that social workers have consciously viewed their role in relation to their part in the conflict-resolution process and have received training specifically geared toward this role. As this awareness grows, social workers are defining their roles in the conflict-resolution process more precisely. This change is part of the growing trend to formalize and institutionalize the role of mediator and to apply it in creative ways to an increasingly wide array of social work–related settings.

From a conflict-intervention perspective, the family counselor often acts as a neutral third party whose focus is on the psychological dimension of conflict, whereas the mediator's role is to focus on the procedural aspects and to help parties engage in a constructive and effective negotiation or collaborative problem-solving process. Another process-focused role is that of a facilitator, a person who is responsible for helping groups engage in dialogue, decision making, and problem-solving activities. This role is increasingly in demand for public-input procedures, organizational strategic planning processes, or community problem-solving forums.

Social workers also provide substantive assistance as neutral third parties to those who are in conflict. This role can take the form of evaluating children's needs in a divorce situation, fact finding in disputes involving the allocation of scarce resources, or acting as an expert consultant in a variety of situations involving the care of people with chronic mental illness or developmental disabilities.

**Binding Assistance**

Social workers often find themselves acting as decision makers in conflict situations. A foster care worker who decides how a conflict between a birth parent and a foster parent should be handled, a child protection worker or a child custody evaluator whose decisions are ratified by a court, and a supervisor who decides how disagreements between different workers should be handled are all providing binding assistance in conflict situations. Social workers are less likely to act in the formal role of arbitrators, but informally they are arbitrators all the time.

**Design of a Dispute System**

As organizers and administrators, social workers play an increasingly important role as designers of dispute systems. The purpose of this systems intervention role is to design a system for the constructive handling of disputes that are likely to arise in a system. Whether it involves developing an equal employment opportunity complaint system, a mediation process for handling disputes that arise under the Americans with Disabilities Act of 1990, or a conflict manager's program for playgrounds, the design role is critical to helping construct more-positive approaches to managing conflict. The goal of designing dispute systems is usually to emphasize an interest-based process, an integrative approach to conflict resolution, and the resolution of conflicts at the level at which they occur (Ury et al., 1988).

## Mediation and Social Work Practice

The role of mediation has been of particular interest to many social workers, and the participation of social workers in this growing field has been widespread, especially in the arena of divorce and child custody mediation. Mediation is a powerful intervention tool when used in appropriate circumstances. It is valuable to consider it both as a formal role and as a set of intervention techniques that can be used within other roles. According to the *Standards of Practice for Social Work Mediators* (NASW, 1991):

> Mediation is an approach to conflict resolution in which a mutually acceptable, impartial third party helps the participants negotiate a consensual and informed settlement. In mediation, decision making rests with the parties. Reducing the obstacles to communication, maximizing the exploration of alternatives, and addressing the needs of those who are involved or affected by the issues under discussion are among the mediator's responsibilities. (pp. 1–2)

Mediation is the natural outgrowth of social work practice because its goal is to help parties solve their own problems and to empower people in conflict and because it builds on natural social work skills, such as problem analysis, communication, and systems intervention. However, mediation is not just another application of core social work skills. It draws on many other professional disciplines as well, including sociology, political science, law, and organizational development. Furthermore, as the field of conflict resolution has grown and matured, the conceptual frameworks that inform mediation practice also have developed.

Mediation as a formal practice requires special training and supervision. Nonetheless, with appropriate training and supervision, it is a natural step for social workers to take on this new role, and it is a valuable addition to the services that can be offered to the clients social workers serve.

**Applications of Mediation**

Since the early 1980s, there has been a creative leap in the application of mediation to areas that have traditionally been associated with social work practice.

***Child custody and divorce disputes.*** One impetus for the growth of this approach has been the considerable dissatisfaction of professionals and families with the adversarial nature of decision making on divorce-related issues. The litigation process often exacerbates the already serious problems that divorcing parents have in arriving at a collaborative approach to parenting. It is critical to find a problem-solving process that helps both parents play a significant role in a child's upbringing; that minimizes the likelihood that a child will be caught in the middle of intense parental conflict; and that helps parents proceed through the legal, logistical, and psychological aspects of divorce in a constructive manner. In many circumstances, mediation is the best way to encourage such a process.

***Child welfare.*** Mediation has been successfully applied to adoption disputes and proceedings, child-protection conflicts, conflicts between adolescents and their families—particularly in runaway situations—and permanency planning processes (Mayer, 1985, 1987b; Shaw, 1985). In many of these situations, mediation allows the parties to assert their own needs and concerns in a protected and empowering setting without sacrificing their focus on the key interests of the children. Mediation can help maximize the degree to which both the integrity of the family and the well-being of children can be fostered, and it can significantly decrease the alienation that often exists among parents, adolescents, and intervening agencies.

In child welfare settings, it is often the limited focus of mediation, as opposed to the broader focus of counseling, that makes it valuable. The focus in mediation is on arriving at mutually acceptable solutions to issues about which the parties are in conflict, whereas in counseling, the emphasis is on helping parties change their dynamics, increase their self-awareness, and improve their interpersonal skills. Although the goals of counseling are critical to the long-term improvement of family functioning, the limited focus of mediation can often help families overcome an immediate crisis and take an important first step. Mediation is also often less threatening to family members, particularly teenagers, who are determined to protect their autonomy.

***Care of elderly people.*** Mediation has been used to help families make difficult decisions about the care of their elders. Decisions about living arrangements, special care, the division of responsibilities among family members, and difficult medical decisions are often assisted by a third party acting either formally or informally in the role of mediator (Lemmon, 1985).

***Education.*** Mediation has been used in many ways in the educational system (see, for example, CDR Associates, 1993; Gallant, 1982; Johnson, Johnson, & Dudley, 1992). Disputes about appropriate special education services are often handled through mediation, and a number of states have established mediation programs specifically for this purpose. The use of mediation to handle disputes between students, particularly with the rise of violence in schools, has become increasingly prevalent. Training students to be mediators and providing the structure and support to allow them to intervene in conflicts among students has proved to be an effective intervention tool. Many schools have incorporated mediation into the process for handling disputes about disciplinary actions. With the promotion of site-based management as a tool for reforming schools, the mediation of conflicts within collaborative decision-making bodies in schools has been increasingly sought.

***Equal employment opportunity (EEO) disputes.*** As the right of Americans not to be discriminated against in employment has become more established and institutionalized, so, too, has the need to find methods of addressing complaints of discrimination in a constructive manner. Because important working relationships can be permanently impaired, once a complaint has been filed it is important to develop procedures that protect both the rights of the grievant and the target of the grievance and that constructively address the problems raised in the grievance. Even when there is no legitimate cause for an EEO complaint, there is often a real problem that must be addressed. Many organizations and government agencies have instituted mediation procedures as part of the EEO process (U.S. Army Corps of Engineers, 1993).

***Victim–offender situations.*** In many situations in which nonviolent offenses have occurred, the use of mediation to help the victim and the offender work out appropriate restitution has proved valuable (Umbreit, 1992). Mediation provides a vehicle for offenders to confront the actual effects of what they have done and compels them to deal directly with their victims in setting things right; this is often a more powerful corrective experience than is a court-imposed punishment. Furthermore, mediation can give victims a more direct and powerful say in the outcome and can lead to a healing that court interventions seldom do.

***Health care.*** Health care is a fertile field for the use of mediation to resolve conflicts, and the advent of managed care has increased the need for effective procedures to resolve conflicts among health care providers, professionals, patients, and funders. Health care contracts have increasingly called for mediation to be used to resolve disputes between providers and patients. Health care institutions are also finding that mediation is useful when disputes arise with health care professionals (Gibson & West, 1991).

***Public policy.*** Facilitated approaches to resolving disputes over policies or to making decisions about policies are increasingly common. Conflicts about the location and nature of public housing or group homes in communities, about policies for dealing with homeless people, and about allocating scarce resources among competing needs have all been effectively handled through mediation (Carpenter & Kennedy, 1988). The use of third-party neutrals to bring together various interest groups and policymakers is a powerful tool for moving policy-making out of an adversarial, distributive context and into a collaborative problem-solving arena.

***Mental health.*** Effective programs for dealing with chronic mental health issues require an alliance among service providers, clients and their advocates, and families, yet the relationship among these groups is often extremely conflictual. Mediation has been used as an effective tool for handling conflicts among or between these participants in the mental health system. The California Department of Mental Health conducted a three-year program to initiate conflict-resolution procedures in the state mental health system. Providers, families, and clients were trained in conflict-resolution skills and in mediation, and a select group of clients, family members, and mental health professionals became trainers in conflict-resolution skills. Participants in this program reported that it had a powerful and positive impact on their involvement with the mental health system (CDR Associates, 1991–1993).

Many other applications of mediation are relevant to social work, from collective bargaining to professional malpractice. The applications are growing, and the importance of mediation as a field of practice for social workers is clearly increasing. This area of social work practice has enormous potential that is just beginning to be realized.

## Where To Go from Here

Conflict resolution as a field of social work practice has much to offer, but it is still underdeveloped. Social workers are naturally situated to be involved in a constructive way in helping work on serious social and interpersonal conflicts. For this potential to be realized, social work will have to promote several developments.

First, schools of social work will have to teach conflict-resolution theory and practice more widely. Although more and more schools are offering isolated courses, conflict resolution is seldom presented as a key social work skill or field of practice, and there are few fieldwork placements in conflict-resolution settings.

Second, the conceptual framework that guides conflict resolution will have to be more closely integrated with social work theory and practice. Each field has much to offer the other, but so far little work has been done to apply conflict theory to issues of concern to social workers.

Third, social agencies and other institutions within which social workers work must become more creative in using conflict-resolution procedures. Mediating a dispute over the termination of parental rights is inexpensive compared to the cost of litigating in this arena, but few child welfare agencies have wholeheartedly supported such an approach. Without institutional support, it is unlikely that the potential of mediation in the different arenas that have been discussed will be realized.

Despite the lack of institutional support, mediation and other intentional conflict-resolution procedures are an expanding part of social work practice and agency functioning. The need is great, and the potential is large. The issue is not whether conflict resolution has an important future in social work practice, but of how consciously and proactively the profession will use its potential and guide its development.

## References


Americans with Disabilities Act of 1990. P.L. 101-336, 104 Stat. 327.

Carpenter, S., & Kennedy, W. J. D. (1988). *Managing public disputes.* San Francisco: Jossey-Bass.

CDR Associates. (1991–1993). Internal documents from the California Conflict Resolution in Mental Health Project. Boulder, CO: Author.

CDR Associates. (1993). *Dispute resolution and school restructuring: Final report to the National Institute for Dispute Resolution.* Boulder, CO: Author.

Cingolani, J. (1984). Social conflict perspectives on work with involuntary clients. *Social Work, 29,* 442–446.

Coser, L. (1956). *The functions of social conflict.* New York: Free Press.

Etzioni, A. (1975). *A comparative analysis of complex organizations.* New York: Free Press.

Fisher, R., & Ury, W. L. (1981). *Getting to yes: Negotiating agreement without giving in.* Boston: Houghton Mifflin.

Gallant, C. (1982). *Mediation in special education disputes.* Washington, DC: National Association of Social Workers.

Gamson, W. A. (1968). *Power and discontent.* Homewood, IL: Dorsey Press.

Gibson, J. M., & West, M. B. (1991, Summer–Fall). Hospital ethics committees: Mediation and case review. *NIDR Forum,* pp. 22–23.

Hasenfeld, Y. (1978). Client–organization relations: A systems perspective. In R. C. Sarri & Y. Hasenfeld (Eds.), *The management of human services* (pp. 184–203). New York: Columbia University Press.

Johnson, D., Johnson, R., & Dudley, B. (1992). Effects of peer mediation training on elementary school students. *Mediation Quarterly, 10,* 89–100.

Kriesberg, L. (1982). *Social conflicts.* Englewood Cliffs, NJ: Prentice Hall.

Lax, D. A., & Sebenius, J. K. (1986). *The manager as negotiator: Bargaining for cooperative and competitive gain.* New York: Free Press.

Lemmon, J. A. (1985, Spring). The mediation method throughout the family life cycle. *Mediation Quarterly* (No. 7), 5–22.

Mayer, B. (1985, Spring). Conflict resolution in child protection and adoption. *Mediation Quarterly* (No. 7), 69–82.

Mayer, B. (1987a). The dynamics of power in mediation and negotiation. *Mediation Quarterly* (No. 24), 75–86.

Mayer, B. (1987b). *Mediation and compliance in child protection.* Unpublished doctoral dissertation, University of Denver.

Moore, C. W. (1986). *The mediation process: Practical strategies for resolving conflict.* San Francisco: Jossey-Bass.

Murdach, A. (1986). Bargaining and persuasion with nonvoluntary clients. *Social Work, 31,* 458–461.

National Association of Social Workers. (1991). *Standards of practice for social work mediators.* Silver Spring, MD: Author.

Shaw, M. (1985, Spring). Parent–child mediation: A challenge and a promise. *Mediation Quarterly* (No. 7), 23–24.

Umbreit, M. (1992). The impact of mediating victim/offender conflict: An analysis of programs in three states. *Juvenile and Family Court Journal, 43*(1).

Ury, W. L., Brett, J. M., & Goldberg, S. (1988). *Getting disputes resolved: Designing systems to cut the cost of conflict.* San Francisco: Jossey-Bass.

U.S. Army Corps of Engineers. (1993, July 1). *Corps of Engineers early resolution program* (Circular No. 690-1-690). Washington, DC: Department of the Army.

Walton, R. E., & McKersie, R. B. (1965). *A behavioral theory of labor negotiations.* New York: McGraw-Hill.


**Bernard S. Mayer, PhD, ACSW, LCSW,** is partner, CDR Associates, 100 Arapahoe Avenue, Suite 12, Boulder, CO 80302.

### For further information see

Adoption; Adult Corrections; Advocacy; Aging Overview; Bioethical Issues; Case Management; Child Welfare Overview; Civil Rights; Clinical Social Work; Criminal Behavior Overview; Direct Practice Overview; Disability; Domestic Violence; Employee Assistance Programs; Ethics and Values;

Families Overview; Goal Setting and Intervention Planning; Housing; Human Rights; Intervention Research; Legal Issues: Confidentiality and Privileged Communication; Occupational Social Work; Patient Rights; Professional Liability and Malpractice; Single Parents; Social Work Practice: Theoretical Base; Social Work Profession Overview.

**Key Words**

conflict resolution
dispute resolution
mediation
negotiation

## Consultation

*See* Supervision and Consultation

# Continuing Education

**Kimberly Strom**
**Ronald Green**

The definition of continuing social work education has been subject to a considerable amount of debate over the past 20 years. At the core of the debate is the concept of continuing social work education and whether it applies only to professional development activities for those who have completed their baccalaureate or master's studies in social work, or whether it includes a full range of professional development activities aimed at improving social workers' practice, regardless of how much or what type of formal academic social work study they have completed.

Before the 1960s, when NASW recognized the bachelor of social work degree as the entry-level degree for professional social work practice, and before the 1970s, when a significant number of schools of social work became involved in providing staff development assistance to public human services agencies, continuing social work education tended to be viewed as a post–master of social work, nondegree-granting professional development activity. With the advent of the bachelor of social work degree and the significant increase in staff development work by social work educators, the broader definition of continuing education gained support. A. Lauffer and Sturdevant-Reed (1978) wrote, "We do not distinguish between continuing education and staff development or between the continuing educator and the staff developer" (p. 3). After considerable debate, the Council on Social Work Education (CSWE) convened a national task force of social work continuing educators to develop standards for social work continuing education programs. The task force adopted the broader version, concluding that social work continuing education clearly included both post–professional degree activity and a full range of staff development activities aimed at improving the professional competence of social workers, regardless of professional degree (CSWE, 1980). Subsequently there has been no additional work at the national level, and this definition still stands as the most definitive statement regarding the scope of continuing social work education.

Reflecting a more narrow definition of continuing education, *The Social Work Dictionary* (Barker, 1991) describes *continuing education* as "training taken by social workers and other professionals who have already completed formal education requirements to enter their field" (p. 49). The term *continuing education* in social work refers to a range of educational approaches occurring outside the traditional baccalaureate and master's degree programs. Continuing education can refer to seminars or in-service education programs designed to bolster the skills and knowledge of staff. It can refer to certificate programs, accredited courses, or workshops and conferences that social workers attend to keep abreast of changes in the field. It can also refer to self-study, individual scholarship, and small-group learning processes.

Now that licensure or certification requirements exist for social workers in all 50 states, the issue of assuring professional competency has become increasingly critical. Thirty-two states require evidence of participation in continuing education as a criterion for license renewal. An example of the rationale for continuing education put forth by one licensure board is as follows: "The goals of the Board's continuing professional education requirements are to: enable licensees to maintain and/or expand professional expertise; become aware of new professional developments; and provide responsible and quality service to clients and community" (Ohio Counselor and Social Worker Board, 1990, p. 31). This board clarified that "sources of continuing professional education shall be formally organized learning experiences with education as their explicit principal intent and which are oriented toward the enhancement of counselor and social worker practice" (p. 33).

## Historical Developments

The growth and development of social work continuing education have tended to be cyclical rather than linear. The degree to which continuing education has been significantly represented in social work higher education has been driven by the availability of fee, grant, or contract funding. Before 1976 and the advent of protected Title XX social services training entitlement funding, most programs depended on workshop or institute fee income. Programs reflected the definition of continuing education as a postgraduate activity offered in short-term programs for alumni or other practitioners. A number of schools of social work offered residential summer block programs of one or two weeks. These programs often were staffed by regular faculty members and were provided, at least in part, as a service to alumni.

### 1970s Expansion

During the 1970s, schools began to develop or expand programs by securing federal grant funding and staff development contracts from state and county human services agencies. A few programs made use of multiple funding streams to develop the organizational capacity to offer a broad range of professional development services to large agencies. The focus of this development shifted away from professional development of individual practitioners to strengthening the total organizational capacity of large service organizations to provide quality service. Thus, the client of a continuing education program shifted from the individual social worker's (or his or her agency) purchasing a specific workshop or institute to an agency's contracting for a set of training activities for staff who often were not given a choice about participating. This development initiated a role shift for the continuing educator from "educator" to "organizational developer."

With the development of this broader role, there evolved in the mid-1970s a considerable amount of conflict between individual social work continuing educators and also between continuing educators, deans, and teaching faculty about the proper role of social work continuing education. This was evident in the work of the National Continuing Education Project advisory committee of the Council on Social Work Education, as reported by Loavenbruck (1981). It resulted in articles that argued two sides of what the social work continuing education "vision" should be. On the one hand, Gibelman and Humphreys (1982) asserted that there is a difference between training and education, and that there is an inherent danger in a school developing too close a link to a social agency that is not perceived as always practicing in the most professional manner. On the other hand, Green and Edwards (1982) argued that the best teachers never isolate themselves from real practice, that these relationships can breed research and demonstration opportunities, and that such collaborations could result in agency staff becoming social work students.

### Shift in Locus

In a few instances, this conflict resulted in the exodus of major continuing education programs from schools of social work. At California State University, Sacramento, the program followed the director to the University of California at Davis, Extension Division. Subsequently the program became the largest single provider of continuing education services to county human services agencies in California. At Temple University in Philadelphia, the Center for Social Policy and Community Development was transferred from the School of Social Work to the School of Business, and it continues to be a major provider of continuing education services to city and county human services agencies in Pennsylvania. In a number of other instances, such as at the University of Michigan and the University of Georgia, the conflict resulted in major program downsizing when the original continuing education directors left. Despite this conflict, the stimulus of Title XX in the mid-1970s produced at least a doubling of social work continuing education programs to well over 100 by 1978 (Loavenbruck, 1981). This growth produced a new journal, the *Journal of Continuing Social Work Education,* started by the Continuing Education Program of the School of Social Welfare at the State University of New York at Albany; several attempts to establish a national organization of social work continuing educators and the organization of several annual conferences.

### Funding Issues in the 1980s

This significant growth in social work continuing education activity ceased with the end of protected Title XX training entitlements in the early 1980s. Because many social work education programs had built their continuing education staffs with Title XX contract funding, the end of this funding precipitated the demise of many fully staffed programs. In addition, during the early 1980s there was a significant increase in competition for fee-based continuing education workshops. Rather than social work education programs operating the only workshops or institute programming available, NASW chapters, other professional groups, agencies, and proprietary individuals and organizations began to offer continuing education workshops to the professional community. Increasingly this made it difficult for social work education programs to support full-time staffing for their continuing education efforts. Those programs that sustained themselves during this period developed a broad mixture of programming sustained by federal grants, public agency contracts, and fee-based activity.

In 1982 the NASW Board of Directors approved the adoption of Standards for Continuing Professional Education (NASW, 1982). These standards, which remain in effect today, are targeted at individual social workers and providers of continuing education programs. They set forth the expectations that social workers maintain responsibility for their ongoing practice competence, be active learners, and participate in a minimum of 90 hours of continuing education, selected from a range of learning opportunities, during each three-year period. Continuing education providers and administrators are expected to have programs and policies that reflect the values of the profession, and they must engage in collaborative efforts with NASW to ensure qualified instruction and program evaluation. Although there is little evidence that these standards have had a major effect on the field, their passage reflected the growth of continuing education, its perceived importance, and the recognition that the profession itself had responsibility for ensuring ongoing practitioner proficiency.

### Impact of Legal Regulation

During the late 1980s and early 1990s, the end result of two decades of advocacy for the legal regulation of social work was the initiation of mandatory continuing education for licensure renewal in a number of states. This development in licensure occurred after NASW backed away from mandating continuing education for maintenance of the ACSW (Academy of Certified Social Workers) credential in the mid-1980s (Edwards & Green, 1983). The impact of the state-mandated continuing education requirements brought a renewal of short-term workshop programming in a large number of social work education programs.

Consequently, there appears to be a resurgence of interest in postgraduate certificate programming resulting from the CWSE task force report on post-master's education, which recommended an accreditation process for post-master's continuing education programs (CSWE, 1991). By the mid-1990s mature social work continuing education programs reflected a mix of fee-based short-term offerings for individual graduates and longer term grant- and contract-supported professional and organizational development interventions for large (generally public) agencies.

## Theoretical Underpinnings

Andragogy is generally recognized as the theoretical base that guides the mission and structure of continuing education. As coined by Knowles (1980), *andragogy* refers to processes for the education of adults (in contrast to *pedagogy,* the education of children). The principles of andragogy reflect the view that an adult learner is a voluntary learner who brings a range of experiences and abilities to the educational process. In response to these capacities, then, adult education becomes a more mutual process in which responsibilities for learning are shared between teacher and student. Andragogical educational processes require that a learner assume an active role as a seeker of knowledge; that content be relevant and transferable; and that multiple, nontraditional rewards for learners be used. Creative teaching methodologies, the general absence of formal assignments or grades, and the overall emphasis on relevant applicable content in continuing education all reflect the andragogical orientation.

Davenport and Davenport (1986) reported that some authors have taken issue with the tenets of andragogy, suggesting that it presents a false dichotomy, that its principles do not differ greatly from accepted teaching strategies for children or adults, and that it lacks sufficient empirical testing to be considered a theory. Educators should take such debate into account when using andragogy as a guide. Nevertheless, inasmuch as it provides a framework for teaching adult professionals and preprofessionals, andragogy and the associated techniques remain useful for continuing education delivery.

## Research on Social Work Continuing Education

The literature on social work continuing education abounds with descriptive accounts of various facets of continuing education programming. Yet relatively few empirical studies have been conducted; thus, the body of knowledge in this area is not well developed. The existing scholarship generally addresses the characteristics of social work continuing education, rationales for continuing education and staff development activities, issues in administering continuing education programs, and the evaluation of various facets of continuing education.

**National Studies**

Since 1969 there have been several national studies of varying scope that have described aspects of social work continuing education (Knox, 1979; A. Lauffer & Sturdevant-Reed, 1978; Loavenbruck, 1981; Miller, 1969; Southwick, 1976). The most current efforts of this nature are studies by Boston University (1991, 1992). Its 1991 survey of continuing education programs located in schools of social work throughout the country included information on the structure, funding sources, marketing strategies, and target audiences of continuing education programs. The findings indicated diversity and range in all of these features. A follow-up study in 1992 examined the challenges identified by continuing education administrators. The issues identified included (in order) funding and economic survival, new program development, increasing faculty participation, joint programming with agencies, increasing participant involvement, competition from other providers, and marketing and space (Boston University, 1992).

**The Literature**

Related to the studies on continuing education are published reports on various facets of continuing education administration and training delivery. Knox (1981) addressed the major proficiency areas needed for administrators of continuing professional education. These included a perspective on the broad field of continuing education, an understanding of adults as learners, personal qualities such as innovativeness and interpersonal skills, program development and other administrative abilities, and facility in the incorporation of new ideas from research or other sources. Dane (1985) discussed the internal and external relationships needed to sustain a continuing education program and recommended the use of a "loose coupling" management strategy to address the unique needs and position of continuing education programs.

Others have addressed the question of whether continuing education instruction is the domain of academicians or practitioner–trainers. Weinbach and Kuehner (1981) examined the factors involved in selecting continuing education instructors and recommended that the outcomes desired, fiscal considerations, and the type of program (education versus training) be considered in addition to an instructor's knowledge and teaching ability.

Some authors have addressed the challenges inherent in continuing education delivery to rural areas, noting that logistical barriers must be overcome, that local input is necessary for effective programming, and that multiple benefits can accrue from well-delivered programs (Pippard & Bates, 1983; Rosen & Meddin, 1984). Others have sought to substantiate the need for continuing education, and scholars have noted its benefits for linking social work practice and education (Gullerud & Itzin, 1979), its association with employee job satisfaction (Z. Lauffer & Sharon, 1985), and its capacity to facilitate personal development through transformation (Karpiak, 1992). Such research indicates the many latent benefits of continuing education for individuals, organizations, and the profession as a whole. The CSWE task force report on post–master's education (CSWE, 1991) stated that for professional social work organizations, a related objective of continuing education is "to increase public recognition and status for the profession. Organizational needs met through this function include attracting members, meeting the educational expectations of members and providing revenues for the organization" (p. 10). Such writings cast continuing education in a broad light and address the many functions it serves in the profession.

**Program Effectiveness Evaluations**

By far the greatest amount of empirical research on social work continuing education has been in the area of evaluating program effectiveness. A variety of studies have been conducted to determine the capacity of continuing education programs to produce increased or improved knowledge, skills, and attitudes in their participants or to evaluate the effectiveness of new models of training delivery. Studies of continuing education outcomes have indicated that participants' existing dispositions toward continuing education, and their expectations of such an event, influence the ways in which social workers evaluate their continuing education experiences (Zimmerman, 1981); that agency-based training can yield positive results in teaching social workers single-case evaluation techniques (Doueck, 1993); and that teleconferencing techniques can yield positive change in workers' knowledge skills and attitudes (Barber, Goldberg, Savage, & Fisher, 1983).

***Problems in evaluation.*** Davenport (1992) reviewed eight studies that evaluated continuing education programs and concluded that, although their findings may support the efficacy of continuing education, the methodology used leaves each open to scrutiny. For example, the reliance on participants' self-reports about their skill development makes it difficult to determine if true skill change occurred. Other sources of bias include the lack of pretest and posttest measures, the absence of control groups, and the use of small population samples. Despite these methodological shortcomings, Davenport presented a set of recommendations for continuing education programming on the basis of the available research base. The recommendations affirm the need for precise learning goals and scientific evaluation strategies, opportunities for continuing education participants to apply their newly found knowledge at the training site or with subsequent follow-up, and the importance of programs that use a range of instructional methods and materials that actively involve the learner in the educational process. Davenport's recommendations again reinforce the importance of andragogical approaches in continuing education.

Smith and Schinke (1985), like Davenport, acknowledged practical barriers to scientific evaluation but noted that evaluation is important in substantiating the value of continuing education. Asserting that many continuing education evaluation surveys only identify participants' satisfaction or evaluate only what is taught, not what is learned, the authors offered a single-system evaluation model, assessment measures, and guidelines for its use.

***Needed research.*** The agenda for future research must build on the existing body of knowledge regarding effective and efficient models for continuing education organization and delivery. Specifically, studies must address methods for ensuring substantive skill or knowledge development among participants and cost-effective methods of training delivery. Evaluation studies should be conducted to measure the controlled effect of various instructional approaches. In addition, other research should regularly explore the state of the art in social work continuing education, particularly what kinds of program and organizational designs lead to the most cost-effective educational outcomes.

## Models for Providing Continuing Education

Models that have emerged for developing, organizing, and funding continuing education are as varied as the missions and institutions that have spawned them. As noted by CSWE (1991), "Diversity in both format and content is a major characteristic of continuing education" (p. 6). As such, a number of variables must be considered in the creation or evaluation of any continuing education model. These include

- auspices under which the program operates
- organizational arrangement used to deliver the program
- content and format of instruction
- selection of faculty
- target populations and marketing strategies
- credentials or recognition to be awarded to the continuing education participants.

### Auspices

Social work continuing education is offered through a range of auspices, including universities (through schools of social work, central continuing education departments, or central university extension programs); professional associations (such as NASW and the American Association of Marriage and Family Therapists); social services agencies (that may offer programs for their employees or sponsor them for attendance by the wider community); and freestanding nonprofit or commercial providers, such as corporations for national professional training or smaller groups of private practitioners who offer continuing education to supplement their clinical or consulting efforts.

### Organizational Arrangement

Nonuniversity continuing education programs generally have a clear administrative staffing and policy structure similar to other nonprofit and profit-making organizations. In an organization whose sole purpose is continuing education, the administrator of the continuing education program may report to a board of directors, which is responsible for overall organizational policy. In a multiple function organization, such as a professional association, the continuing education administrator generally reports to a higher executive level and may have an oversight committee of the board of directors or a community advisory group.

In a university setting the range of organizational relationships becomes more complicated because of the unique role relationships of staff to faculty in an academic setting. More often than not, the university-based administrator of social work continuing education will have a faculty appointment, but this is not necessarily so. The administrator may report to the administration staff of the social work educational program, the administration staff of the central university continuing education/extension program, or both.

The policy-making structure of university-based programs varies. In some universities a faculty committee is responsible for administrative policy, program policy, or both. In other situations faculty advisory committees or community advisory committees, and sometimes a mix of faculty and community advisers, have the responsibility. Some universities have no formal policy or advisory governance structure involving faculty, and policy development is purely administrative.

**Content and Format of Offerings**

The full range of information needed by social workers is reflected in the content available through continuing education. Programs may focus on practice techniques, such as brief treatment and imagery; populations, such as sexual abuse survivors and the elderly; problem areas, such as personality disorders and poverty; emerging issues, such as mental health care financing and children infected with human immunodeficiency virus or acquired immune deficiency syndrome; and topics reflective of the core curriculum for social work preparation, such as social policy, research, and ethics. Research among practitioners has found the greatest interest in the areas of clinical practice, supervision, and administration (CSWE, 1991). A survey of continuing education directors in schools of social work revealed that the three most popular topics for 1990–91 were issues related to working with families and children, substance abuse, and gerontology (Boston University, 1991).

As with the content areas of continuing education, formats for delivery also are varied. Information can be conveyed through brief programs (one-hour in-services offered individually or "bundled" around a topic or skill development area); informally organized study groups (for case discussion or review of journal articles); local, regional, or national conferences for training or research dissemination; workshops (typically three-, six-, or 12-hour programs organized around a specific topic); credit or noncredit courses that meet regularly over a specified period of time; certificate programs, in which substantive knowledge is developed in an area through participation in a succession of courses or programs; and institutes that participants might attend for one- or two-week periods for intensive or specialized training.

**Forms of Recognition**

Credentials awarded for continuing education vary with the type of program. They range from continuing education units/credits (CEUs or CECs, which are typically calculated on the basis of one CEU/CEC for each 10 contact hours of training), to tuition-based university course credits, to specialized certificates of completion, which generally are not transferable for university course credits.

**Faculty**

Continuing educators may be individuals from social work practice, social work education, or related fields and professions. Credentialing organizations, however, seek to ensure that instructors, whatever their background, demonstrate expertise in their subject area, have well-developed instructional skills, and are sufficiently familiar with social work to apply their material to the foundation and rigors of contemporary social work practice.

**Funding Arrangements**

A range of strategies is used to fund continuing education programs. Smaller, less-formal types of continuing education typically cost less to develop, market, and implement than do larger events such as conferences. However, the budget for any program must take into account fundamental expenses such as honoraria, facilities, promotional costs, and administrative staffing. Income sources can include registration fees (paid by individuals or employers), training grants, in-kind or donated facilities or services, and sponsorships (for example, by vendors, corporations, or other organizations).

**Populations Served**

Because continuing education serves the range of populations involved in social work, volunteers, paraprofessional staff, direct and indirect service providers, and social work degree graduates and postgraduates all need and participate in supplemental educational programs. Most programs, however, are targeted toward degreed professionals. Educational programs and conferences are marketed in a variety of ways, including individual program brochures and mailings, advertisements in professional journals and newsletters, public service announcements, topical newspaper articles, and periodic catalogs of educational offerings. Mailing lists are available through credentialing organizations, licensure boards, professional organizations, and agency staff listings for dissemination of promotional materials.

Continuing education in social work is characterized by its diversity. Depending on the auspices, audience, and topical focus, myriad models exist for continuing education programming.

## Technological Innovations in Continuing Education

Although in numerous instances newer instructional technologies have been used to support contractual training initiatives, the preponderance of social work continuing education continues to be delivered by an instructor to a group in a classroom setting. This situation appears to be a combination of tradition, the time and interest required to learn new instructional technologies, and the cost of securing the required hardware and software supports. These newer technologies include individualized computer-based interactive training programs, distance learning approaches, and laboratory simulations or virtual reality approaches.

**Individualized Interactive Technologies**

Interactive technologies focus on self-paced individual training and include interactive videodisk (IVD), digital video interactive (DVI), compact disk-interactive (CD-I), and interactive television (ITV).

***IVD.*** IVD involves the use of a 12-inch laser disk player connected to a television monitor and a personal computer. It was first used in social work continuing education in the 1970s to support income maintenance worker training. In the late 1980s and early 1990s, multimedia titles were developed to support child abuse and child sexual abuse training. The use of interactive videodisks never gained wide acceptance, either in the consumer market or in social work continuing education, because of expensive and cumbersome playback equipment and also because a very costly and lengthy process (six to 24 months) is required to produce a single training title.

***DVI.*** DVI, which requires a personal computer with massive hard disk storage capacity and other multimedia add-ons, evolved in the early 1990s as a result of the improvement in digital compression technology. Although this technology has been used in the industrial training area, it has not been used to any degree in social work continuing education. Similar to the interactive videodisk, this technology requires a trainee to have direct access to relatively expensive computer equipment. It also has high initial costs for development.

***CD–I.*** A more promising technology for individualized interactive training is CD–I, a technology developed by the mid-1990s. Based on the compact disk, which gained wide acceptance for audio use in the late 1980s and early 1990s, it has been developed to support full motion video and full interactivity. The advantage to a trainee is that it can be used on a small portable player no larger than a notebook computer, or a player the size and cost of a videocassette recorder (VCR), which attaches to a television set. More important, the development of CD-I for the consumer market encourages active competition in the development and pricing of playback equipment, which in turn creates the capacity for social work agencies and even individual social workers to purchase such equipment.

***ITV.*** ITV is still evolving in the mid-1990s. This technology provides individuals with the capacity to use cable television in an interactive mode and could enable social work continuing educators to develop interactive training programs that could be accessed from home, office, or training room. Although development costs would be high, the potential of reaching a significant proportion of the continuing education client base makes this medium potentially cost-effective. Under this system, social workers will have the capacity to select an interactive training program of their choice at any time they desire. Such programs allow users to practice interviewing, critical thinking, and time management skills, and to further their knowledge in areas such as cultural diversity and stress management.

**Distance Learning Technologies**

The use of distance learning in social work continuing education has, for the most part, been limited to contract training situations. Large public human services agencies have used state-supported television networks for this training, which is conducted via satellite in conjunction with university-based continuing education programs. Over the past several decades, there have been many instances of satellite video transmission of special meetings or conference activities, but these uses have clearly been the exception rather than the rule. Again, it would appear that the infrastructure costs, coupled with the need for most social work continuing education programs to pay their own way, contribute to the overwhelming choice of traditional instructional methods for social work continuing education.

With the advances made in digital compression technologies in the early 1990s, the concomitant shift from analog to digital television as a national standard, and the development of full fiber optic transmission capacities, the capacity for cost-effective distance delivery of social work continuing education offerings should emerge in the mid-1990s. The capacity to use two-way video enables an instructor to view and directly interact with a distant student. This capacity is greatly enhanced when a continuing education program can transmit this information over fiber optic networks, instead of purchasing access to satellites and time for program broadcast and transmittal.

### Lab Simulations and Virtual Reality

The use of laboratory simulations at all levels of social work education has been extremely limited. Simulations have been used in management training under contract with state human services agencies, but the cost of developing and using realistic, controlled simulations in continuing education has impeded the use of this educational technology in social work arenas. It is clear that certain skill training can best be taught in a tightly controlled learning environment and that emerging virtual reality technologies represent the potential capacity for controlled, but extremely lifelike, training experiences. The combination of the power of experiential learning and the capacity to construct realistic, controlled learning experiences presents social work continuing educators with an extremely powerful educational tool waiting to be exploited.

Advances in technology offer social workers, employers, and educators individualized, cost-effective, and convenient methods for acquiring new knowledge or establishing new skills. As yet, however, their capacity has not been fully tapped.

## Emerging Issues

A number of emerging issues confront continuing education as the field moves into the 21st century. Although not limited to social work continuing education specifically, the adequacy of continuing education, programmatic fiscal viability, and mechanisms for quality assurance have all been sources of attention and concern in the profession.

### Adequacy

As social workers strive for recognition and parity with other professionals, the educational preparation of practitioners remains a primary concern. Similarly, substantial discourse has already taken place about the amount and types of continuing education that should be required to ensure ongoing professional competency. Some have argued that continuing education requirements place an onerous burden on social workers, and that the costs (in time and money) of obtaining such training are excessive for individuals and their employing organizations (personal communication with Nancy Graf, continuing education director, Mandel School of Applied Social Sciences, Case Western Reserve University, Cleveland, Ohio). Others have questioned the usefulness of requiring social workers to just accumulate a certain number of continuing education units without tying them to any outcome or competency-based measures (Edwards & Green, 1983).

***Lack of criteria.*** The CSWE (1991) task force on post-master's education further questioned that few, if any, criteria are placed on the type of training or content social workers must receive through continuing education. However, the task force also noted the complexities inherent in mandating continuing education content. For example, some professionals, left to their own devices, might choose to attend continuing education that merely repeats earlier training, is not challenging or of sufficient length or depth to enhance practice adequately, or requires no active participant involvement or demonstrable acquisition of skills or knowledge. Or, people seeking continuing education may avoid topics they do not see as highly interesting, such as those on current research developments, ethics, or social policy, despite the fact that such areas are highly valued by the profession and considered important to quality practice.

***Barriers to prescribing content.*** Efforts to mandate that social workers take continuing education in certain prescribed areas confront a number of barriers. The range of domains in which social workers practice and the number of roles they assume make it difficult to determine educational areas that would be relevant to all members of the profession. Similarly, consumers of continuing education, the organizations that employ them, and the agencies that regulate them all have differing expectations about what social workers need to maintain their competence as practicing professionals. Developing national consensus on required continuing education content would thus be difficult. Coupled with this problem is resistance to regulation on the part of social workers who feel that they are best suited to determine their own developmental needs, particularly if they assume the cost.

In addition, certain fields of social work, and some geographic areas of the country, may find a limited range of available continuing education programs or topics. Groups so affected argue that they must have flexibility in developing or selecting their educational programming. An additional difficulty in mandating content is that of developing universal standards that would be used by the range of continuing education providers across the country.

***Transferability of skills.*** Another concern regarding the adequacy of continuing education has to do with the degree to which skills and knowledge are transferred into enhanced practice or improved outcomes for clients. This issue is especially important to organizations purchasing continuing education services for their staff. Agency administrators and public policy leaders ask, "What are we really getting for our money?" The bottom line is whether the continuing education provided for their staff will make any difference in the quality and quantity of service provided to agency clients. This question is especially important with regard to the capacity to distinguish professional development needs in an organization from other types of organizational needs. It also requires clarity about what can feasibly be affected in terms of client outcomes by the quality and quantity of service provided. For example, regardless of the quality or quantity of continuing education provided to a social worker responsible for helping clients become employed, if no jobs are available the client will not find work.

### Quality Assurance

Although schools of social work constituted the bulk of providers throughout the history of social work continuing education, the 1980s brought a proliferation of providers as professional organizations expanded their educational programming through conferences, institutes, and revenue-generating workshops and as for-profit training groups emerged with local, regional, or nationally delivered programs. The variety among these providers and the diversity in their structures, criteria for instructors, and choices of appropriate content have led to concerns that

> there is no overall system of determining the efficacy or often even the objectives of these programs. Other than a general approval of providers by some state licensing boards, continuing education programs in social work are not subject to either standards or mechanisms of quality control by a certifying body. (CSWE, 1991, p. 13)

There are three essential methods of quality control: (1) screening the resources of the program (such as abilities and credentials of instructors); (2) focusing on the content of the curriculum; and (3) analyzing outcomes through a "criterion referenced" approach that examines the extent to which those completing a program meet certain criteria or performance standards (CSWE, 1991). Any or all of these may be used on a local or regional basis to approve continuing education providers or to evaluate the worth of training programs for an agency's employees.

However, given the range of auspices offering continuing education for social workers, the lack of consensus about the appropriate qualifications of continuing education instructors, the tremendous differences among state licensure laws, and the diversity of outcomes expected from continuing education, nationwide credentialing of continuing education providers is likely to be difficult to implement. In the meantime, credentialing boards, social work educators, employing organizations, and professional organizations must work to develop consensus about the characteristics of quality continuing education and implement those characteristics within each of their domains. And, ultimately, individual consumers of continuing education must be relied on to select carefully the programs and providers they will use in enhancing their existing knowledge and skill bases.

### Fiscal Stability

The issue of securing a stable funding base for social work continuing education remains an ongoing problem. To break even, most fee-based programs require some type of subsidy, in terms of either staff supports or direct funding. As yet, social workers in general do not appear to have accepted responsibility for personally paying for continuing education at a rate sufficiently high for programs to expect to meet actual costs over the long run. There has been a long tradition of offering subsidized continuing education events (supported by partial funding by agencies, foundations, government, or the host organization), and there is a general lack of understanding in the profession in terms of the real costs of quality continuing education. A reality of the profession is that average salaries are not high, and it may be difficult to see how participating in a continuing education event will increase one's income. At the same time, as agencies are pushed to become more efficient, there has been a shift away from agencies granting time and providing support to their staff to participate in general continuing education events outside the agency. A creative tension exists between the real costs of providing quality continuing education, the pressure of mandatory continuing education requirements, and the reluctance of social workers to pay the true cost of continuing education.

Because of these problems, many continuing education programs have expanded beyond fee-based programming to the use of multiple funding support sources. These sources include sales of training services under contract, federal grants, and foundation grants, as well as sales of training materials. Managing the resource development to support continuing education programs in the 1990s requires strategic thinking, a marketing orientation, and the willingness to create and reshape continuing education offerings based on the needs and interests of the marketplace.

## Future Trends

Given the trends toward increased certification for social workers and societal insistence on high-quality professional practice, further development of continuing professional education for social workers is assured. With this development will likely come a greater number of providers, increased efforts to certify continuing education programs, and demands from social workers for relevant content and high-quality instruction.

Shrinking staff development dollars in the voluntary sector and increased scrutiny over use of training funds in the public sector should stimulate the development of more cost-effective forms of continuing education delivery. As technological enhancements allow for distance education, individualized interactive learning processes, and other cost-effective teaching methods that eliminate the need for an instructor for every learning group, there will be a need for a major reorientation for both current instructors and continuing education participants. There will be an even higher level of self-responsibility required of the adult learner and a higher level of proficiency required of those developing or using these approaches.

Creative ways of assessing participation in, and results from, this type of continuing education need to be developed. No longer should a participant simply be able to clock hours without demonstrating that something was gained in the process. No longer will an instructor be able to get away with entertaining a small group behind closed doors, for instruction will be open for all to view and will be measured not by participant happiness ratings but by the difference it makes in participants' capacity to do their jobs.

The pressure for efficiency, effectiveness, and accountability, combined with significant advances in instructional technology, should provide the stimulus for significant advances in social work continuing education in the last decade of the 20th century.

## References

Barber, G., Goldberg, G., Savage, R., & Fisher, S. (1983). A comparison of knowledge and attitude change using teleconferencing and programmed instruction. *Journal of Continuing Social Work Education, 2*(2), 36–39.

Barker, R. L. (1991). *The social work dictionary* (2nd ed.). Silver Spring, MD: NASW Press.

Boston University. (1991). *1991 survey results.* Unpublished research findings.

Boston University. (1992). *1992 survey results.* Unpublished research findings.

Council on Social Work Education. (1980). *Manual of proposed standards and guidelines for social work continuing education programs.* New York: Author.

Council on Social Work Education. (1991). *Post master's education in social work: Report and recommendations.* Alexandria, VA: Author.

Dane, E. (1985). Managing organizational relationships in continuing education programs: Is loose coupling the answer? *Administration in Social Work, 9*(3), 83–92.

Davenport, J., III. (1992). Continuing social work education: The empirical base and practice guidelines. *Journal of Continuing Social Work Education, 5*(3), 27–30.

Davenport, J., III, & Davenport, J. A. (1986). Andragogy: Another bandwagon or legitimate tool in the continuing education armamentarium? *Journal of Continuing Social Work Education, 3*(4), 33–39.

Doueck, H. (1993). Enhancing family-centered practice: A training program for agency-based social workers. *Journal of Continuing Social Work Education, 5*(4), 11–15.

Edwards, R. L., & Green, R. K. (1983). Mandatory continuing education: Time for reevaluating. *Social Work, 28,* 43–48.

Gibelman, M., & Humphreys, N. (1982). Contracting for educational services: The impact on schools of social work. *Journal of Continuing Social Work Education, 2*(1), 3–6.

Green, R. K., & Edwards, R. L. (1982). Contracting between schools of social work and social welfare agencies: A controversial issue. *Journal of Continuing Social Work Education, 2*(1), 7–10.

Gullerud, E. N., & Itzin, F. H. (1979). Continuing education as an effective linkage between schools of social work and the practice community. *Journal of Education for Social Work, 15*(3), 81–87.

Karpiak, I. (1992). Continuing social work education: Simply a matter of rearing silkworms. *Journal of Continuing Social Work Education, 5*(3), 9–14.

Knowles, M. S. (1980). *The modern practice of adult education* (rev. ed.). Chicago: Follett.

Knox, A. (1979). *Enhancing proficiencies of continuing educators.* San Francisco: Jossey-Bass.

Knox, A. B. (1981). Proficiencies needed to administer continuing social work education. *Journal of Continuing Social Work Education, 1*(1), 3–6, 19–21.

Lauffer, A., & Sturdevant-Reed, C. (1978). *Doing continuing education and staff development.* New York: McGraw-Hill.

Lauffer, Z., & Sharon, N. (1985). Social work job satisfaction and participation in continuing education: Implication for administrators of social services. *Journal of Continuing Social Work Education, 3*(3), 3–7.

Loavenbruck, G. (1981). *Continuing social work education provision, trends and future developments.* New York: Council on Social Work Education.

Miller, D. (1969). *Continuing education programs in schools of social work: Report of a survey.* New York: Council on Social Work Education.

National Association of Social Workers. (1982). *NASW standards for continuing professional education.* Washington, DC: Author.

Ohio Counselor and Social Worker Board. (1990). *Laws and regulations governing the practice of counseling and social work.* Columbus, OH: Author.

Pippard, J. L., & Bates, J. E. (1983). The care and feeding of CE programs in rural areas. *Journal of Continuing Social Work Education, 2*(3), 4–8.

Rosen, A. L., & Meddin, B. J. (1984). Some considerations for providing continuing education to rural social service practitioners. *Journal of Continuing Social Work Education, 2*(4), 8–11.

Smith, T. E., & Schinke, S. P. (1985). Designing evaluations of continuing education workshops. *Journal of Continuing Social Work Education, 3*(3), 24–29.

Southwick, P. C. (1976). Social work continuing education: A survey of administrative structure and programming in graduate schools of social work, 1974 (Doctoral dissertation, Graduate School of Social Work, University of Utah). *Dissertation Abstracts International, 37,* 3914A.

Weinbach, R. W., & Kuehner, K. M. (1981). Trainer or academician—Who shall provide? *Journal of Continuing Social Work Education, 1*(3), 3–32.

Zimmerman, S. L. (1981). Continuing education in social work: An evaluation of a summer program. *Journal of Continuing Social Work Education, 1*(3), 15–21, 25–26.

## Further Reading

Association for Continuing Higher Education. *The journal of continuing higher education.* University Park, PA: Author.

Beder, H. (1986). *New directions for continuing education: Marketing continuing education.* San Francisco: Jossey-Bass.

Davis, L. N., & McCallon, E. (1974). *Planning, conducting, and evaluating workshops.* Austin, TX: Learning Concepts.

Goldstein, I. L., & Associates (1989). *Training and development in organizations.* San Francisco: Jossey-Bass.

Matkin, G. W. (1985). *Effective budgeting in continuing education: A comprehensive guide to improving program planning and organization performance.* San Francisco: Jossey-Bass.

Merriam, S. B., & Cunningham, P. M. (Eds.). (1989). *Handbook of adult and continuing education.* San Francisco: Jossey-Bass.

Orem, S. D., & Bruce, D. F. (Eds.). (1991). *Practical programming in continuing professional education: Examples for understanding and improving practice.* Washington, DC: American Association for Adult and Continuing Education.

Pearce, S. D. (1992). Survival of continuing higher education: Dean's perceptions of external threats. *Journal of Continuing Higher Education, 40*(2), 2–7.

Simerly, R. G., & Simerly, A. (1989). *Handbook of marketing for continuing education.* San Francisco: Jossey-Bass.

**Kimberly Strom, PhD,** is assistant professor, the University at Albany, State University of New York, 135 Western Avenue, Albany, NY 12222, and **Ronald Green, JD,** is assistant dean, Case Western Reserve University, Mandel School of Applied Social Sciences, 10900 Euclid Avenue, Cleveland, OH 44106.

### For further information see

Clinical Social Work; Computer Utilization; Council on Social Work Education; International Social Work Education; Licensing, Regulation, and Certification; Management Overview; National Association of Social Workers; Professional Conduct; Professional Liability and Malpractice; Quality Assurance; Social Work Education; Social Work Profession Overview; Special-Interest Professional Associations; Supervision and Consultation; Vendorship.

**Key Words**

certification
continuing education
licensing
professional development
training

# Continuous Quality Improvement

*See* Quality Management

# Contracting

*See* Purchasing Social Services

# Corrections

*See* Courts and Corrections

# Council on Social Work Education

**Donald W. Beless**

The purpose of the Council on Social Work Education (CSWE) is to "provide national leadership and collective action designed to ensure the preparation of competent and committed social work professionals. This includes promoting and maintaining the quality of social work education programs. It also includes stimulating the development of knowledge, practice, and service effectiveness designed to promote social justice and further community and individual well-being" (CSWE, 1993, p. 1).

Working closely with other national and international organizations, CSWE seeks to ensure an adequate supply of competent social work professionals capable of addressing present and future social needs. CSWE helps academic institutions offer new and broadened courses in areas of concern to society by providing leadership in curriculum and educational policy formulation, standard setting, faculty development, information exchange, publications, training, and research.

To achieve its purpose, CSWE administers services and programs in four major areas: accreditation and educational policy, faculty development and knowledge dissemination, external relations and public support, and public policy. The scope and priority of the programs and services in each of these areas are specified in CSWE's strategic plan. The strategic plan was developed and is periodically revised by the CSWE board of directors in consultation with the social work education community.

## Accreditation and Educational Policy

### Accreditation

CSWE is officially recognized by the Commission on Recognition of Postsecondary Accreditation as the sole accrediting body for baccalaureate and master's degree social work programs in the United States. As of January 1994, there were 111 accredited master's degree programs, with an additional eight programs in candidacy status, and 382 accredited baccalaureate programs, with an additional 35 programs in candidacy. Master's and baccalaureate degree programs were combined under the same administrative structure in 80 institutions; in three institutions both degree programs existed but were separately administered. Thirty-six institutions had master's degree programs only, and 334 had baccalaureate programs only.

To receive and maintain accreditation, social work education programs must adhere to the accreditation standards developed by CSWE's Commission on Accreditation and approved by the board of directors. These standards specify criteria regarding the sponsoring educational institution, the autonomy of the program within that institution, personnel policies, financial and educational resources, qualifications of the program administrator and faculty, recruitment and admission policies, governance, curriculum and educational outcomes, advising and grading policies, and physical facilities, including library facilities (CSWE, 1991). Accredited programs are systematically reviewed every eight years by the CSWE Commission on Accreditation.

The primary value of accreditation is that it ensures programs have met the minimum standards considered necessary to provide adequate professional social work education at the baccalaureate and master's degree levels. Beyond meeting the minimum accreditation standards, many programs develop innovative and creative approaches in response to their particular mission, interests, and resources. Graduation from a CSWE-accredited baccalaureate or master's degree program is required to become a member of NASW. State licensing and certification laws for social work also require applicants to possess a degree from a CSWE-accredited institution.

### Educational Policy

Curriculum standards are based on the board-approved curriculum policy statement (CPS). The CPS specifies the purpose of social work education and the essential knowledge, skills, and values expected of its graduates. "It is designed to promote coherence, but not uniformity, balance and scope in fundamental objectives, but not rigidity in the forms in which these objectives are carried out" (Stein, 1963, p. 47).

The Commission on Educational Policy reviews the CPS every seven to 10 years to reflect new developments and changes in social work education. An essential element of the CPS revision process is systematic input from the social work education and practice communities. This input is obtained through a series of national and regional forums, written communications, and focus groups. The most recent CPS was approved by the board in July 1992 (CSWE, 1992) and is incorporated into a revised version of the accreditation standards that will go into effect in June 1995.

## Faculty Development and Knowledge Dissemination

CSWE's faculty development and knowledge dissemination activities are designed to "stimulate and support the systematic development and advancement of knowledge essential for social work research, education, and practice; and to plan and implement an ongoing program of faculty development" (CSWE, 1989, p. 14). These activities include publications, conferences and workshops, and special projects.

### Publications

CSWE's publications program provides information and commentary on a broad range of topics and issues relevant to social work education. The *Journal of Social Work Education* focuses on professional social work education, the practice–

education partnership, and developments in research and theory. The *Social Work Education Reporter* is a news magazine that includes articles about CSWE and member activities as well as items of general interest to social work educators. CSWE also publishes *Statistics on Social Work Education in the United States, Summary Information on Master of Social Work Programs,* and the *Directory of Colleges and Universities with Accredited Social Work Degree Programs* annually, along with various monographs, bibliographies, special reports, and teaching materials. Grant-funded project reports are disseminated to all member programs and organizations.

### Conferences and Workshops

The major CSWE conference is the Annual Program Meeting, which brings together more than 2,000 social work educators, practitioners, officials from public and private human services organizations, and exhibitors. The conference provides a national forum for the exchange and dissemination of knowledge, ideas, technology, and skills and the exploration of issues in social work research, education, and practice. Central features of the annual program meeting include faculty development institutes, invitational papers, competitive paper sessions and symposia covering a wide variety of topics, a media/technology center, a curriculum resource center, a bibliography and syllabi exchange, free literature searches, and exhibits. CSWE also sponsors workshops; satellite video seminars; and, in collaboration with other professional organizations, international and regional conferences.

### Special Projects

With the support of external grants and contracts, CSWE conducts and collaborates in special projects aimed at enhancing the capacity of social work education programs to prepare students for emerging and changing areas of practice. Past projects have included curriculum development in gerontology, women's issues, chronic mental illness, acquired immune deficiency syndrome (AIDS), substance abuse, psychopharmacology, rural mental health, poverty, child welfare, and public human services.

Federally funded minority fellowship programs provide tuition and stipend support for people of color engaged in doctoral study in preparation for clinical or research careers in mental health. Since the inception of these programs (the research program began in 1975 and the clinical program in 1978), more than 300 doctoral students who are people of color have received support. Minority fellowship program graduates are making major contributions to social work education, research, and practice throughout the world.

The teacher's registry and employment information service coordinates the exchange of information between applicants for faculty positions and social work programs with employment vacancies. Since 1990 more than 200 faculty vacancies in schools and departments of social work have been listed annually.

## External Relations and Public Support

CSWE cooperates and collaborates with numerous national and international organizations in the fields of social work and social welfare, human services, and higher education. Activities include interorganizational conferences and seminars, curriculum development projects, research, and dissemination of information about the goals and functions of social work education to related professions and disciplines and to the general public. CSWE represents accredited U.S. schools and departments of social work on the board of the International Association of Schools of Social Work.

The foreign equivalency determination service evaluates foreign academic credentials in social work to determine their equivalency to degrees granted by CSWE-accredited programs. Determination of degree equivalency is required for foreign-educated social workers who wish to establish qualifications in the United States for employment, graduate school admission, NASW membership, and state licensing.

## Public Policy

CSWE, often in collaboration with other professional organizations, initiates, monitors, and advocates for national legislation and administrative policies that have implications for social work education. CSWE issues occasional reports on proposed federal legislation and regulations and aspects of federal budget proposals that are relevant to social work education. The Social Work Congressional Fellows Program—cosponsored by CSWE, the Association of Baccalaureate Social Work Program Directors, the National Association of Deans and Directors of Schools of Social Work, and NASW—provides fellowships for social workers to serve as special assistants on the staffs of members of Congress and congressional committees. The program is intended to encourage more-effective use of social work knowledge in government and to exemplify the value of interaction between social work and government.

## Governance and Membership

CSWE is governed by a national board of directors consisting of three officers and 24 members representing graduate and undergraduate programs, graduate and undergraduate faculty, people of color, practice professionals, and the public at large. The chairs of the Commission on Educational Policy and the Commission on Accreditation are ex-officio members of the board. Officers and members of the board are elected for three-year terms by vote of the full members of CSWE.

The board develops policy as needed to manage CSWE affairs. It meets at least three times a year to review and approve CSWE's policies, programs, plans, and budgets; establish membership dues; and consider changes in the bylaws.

CSWE programs and activities are guided by 12 standing commissions: Accreditation, Education Policy, Field Education, Gay Men/Lesbian Women, Minority Group Concerns, National Legislation and Administrative Policy, Women, Social Work Practice, Faculty Development and Program Planning, International, Program Research (Statistics), and Publications and Media. Commissioners are appointed by the president for three-year terms. The commissions make policy and program recommendations to the board and, under the board's direction, develop and implement plans.

The nominating committee is elected by the full members of CSWE. The nine members, representing the same constituencies represented on the board, meet annually to devise a double slate of candidates for the election of officers and directors.

As of July 1993, CSWE had 3,583 members, 2,552 of whom were distributed among the following full-membership categories: graduate programs, 119; accredited baccalaureate programs, 412; faculty and administrative staff in accredited programs, 1,920; practitioners who carry educational responsibilities for social work students, 99; and agencies, 2. The 1,031 associate members were distributed among the following categories: students, 323; practitioners and other interested individuals, 58; nonaccredited social work education programs, 140; and professional libraries and library associations, 510.

## History

Social work education in the United States traces its roots to 1898, when the New York Charity Organization Society offered a summer training course for charity workers. During the next two decades, social work education became more formal and systematic. By 1919, 17 schools of social work in the United States and Canada had organized the Association of Training Schools for Professional Social Work. Soon thereafter the association changed its name to the American Association of Schools of Social Work (AASSW) and by 1927 had developed educational requirements for membership in the organization. These quickly evolved into a set of academic and organizational requirements designed to ensure that students were adequately prepared for professional practice. By 1935 schools of social work were required to be affiliated with universities, and by 1939 only schools offering two years of graduate study were eligible for membership (Kendall, 1994).

In 1942, as a result of dissatisfaction with the AASSW requirement that social work education be offered exclusively at the graduate level and the desire to prepare undergraduate students for public welfare practice, several baccalaureate programs established the National Association of Schools of Social Administration (NASSA). NASSA members consisted of land grant colleges, private schools, and state universities offering a baccalaureate social work degree and, in a few cases, an additional year leading to a master's degree. In 1943 NASSA was recognized as the official accrediting body for baccalaureate programs.

The existence of two national accrediting organizations purporting to represent social work education was confusing and problematic for students, educators, practitioners, employers, and the public. As a result, in 1946 a coordinating group known as the National Council on Social Work Education (NCSWE) was established to work out a solution. NCSWE consisted of representatives from 13 professional social work associations and government and voluntary agencies. Supported by a grant from the Carnegie Foundation, NCSWE conducted a comprehensive study of social work education. The resulting report recommended that the profession come together to develop and support a single organization that would be responsible for educational and accreditation policies and procedures (Hollis & Taylor, 1951). The collaborative work of the NCSWE and the study report led, in 1952, to the creation of the Council on Social Work Education as a successor to AASSW and NASSA.

The new association was given the responsibility for setting standards for social work education and accrediting master's degree programs. At that time, CSWE viewed baccalaureate programs as preprofessional, and they were not offered accreditation. "A first step in the direction of [establishing CSWE] standards for baccalaureate programs was taken in 1962 when criteria were developed to govern the admission of undergraduate social work departments to constituent membership in [CSWE]" (Kendall, 1994, p. 21). In 1967 additional criteria were developed, including one on preparing students for beginning practice. Three years later CSWE issued new criteria and began a system of official approval of baccalaureate programs. In 1974 accreditation was made available to baccalaureate programs.

## Current Trends

Social work education has demonstrated strong growth since the late 1980s. Between 1988 and 1992, the number of accredited baccalaureate programs increased by 6 percent and the number of accredited master's programs by more than 10 percent. In 1992 more than 41,000 students were enrolled in baccalaureate programs, representing a 25 percent increase since 1988 in full-time students and a 32 percent increase in part-time students. During the same period, enrollment in master's degree programs increased to approximately 32,000, a 27 percent rise in full-time students and a 20 percent rise in part-time students. Applications for admission to the first year of master's programs increased by 60 percent, and applications for advanced standing rose by 68 percent. Presumably as a result of the dramatic increase in applications, the rate of acceptance to first-year master's programs dropped from 61 percent to 52 percent. To the extent that greater selectivity in admissions is an indicator of academic quality, this is an encouraging trend (Lennon, 1993).

The proportions of women and people of color receiving baccalaureate and master's degrees have remained essentially unchanged since the late 1980s. Women received approximately 87 percent of the baccalaureate degrees and 84 percent of the master's degrees awarded in 1992. In the same year, 23 percent of baccalaureate degrees and 17 percent of master's degrees went to people of color (Lennon, 1993).

The number of women faculty members continues to increase. In 1992 women represented about 60 percent of the faculties of both baccalaureate and master's degree programs (Lennon, 1993).

The proportion of minority faculty in master's programs has held steady at about 22 percent. In baccalaureate programs the percentage has risen slightly since 1988, from 24 percent to 27 percent (Lennon, 1993).

## References

Council on Social Work Education. (1989). *Strategic plan*. Alexandria, VA: Author.

Council on Social Work Education. (1991). *Handbook of accreditation standards and procedures*. Alexandria, VA: Author.

Council on Social Work Education. (1992). *Curriculum policy statement*. Alexandria, VA: Author.

Council on Social Work Education. (1993). *Bylaws*. Alexandria, VA: Author.

Hollis, E. V., & Taylor, A. L. (1951). *Social work education in the United States: The report of a study made for the National Council on Social Work Education*. New York: Columbia University Press.

Kendall, K. A. (1994). *The Council on Social Work Education: A history 1952–1988*. Unpublished manuscript.

Lennon, T. M. (1993). *Statistics on social work education in the United States: 1992*. Alexandria, VA: Council on Social Work Education.

Stein, H. D. (1963). Observations on the 1962 curriculum policy statement. In *Education for social work: Proceedings of the eleventh annual program meeting*. Alexandria, VA: Council on Social Work Education.

## Further Reading

Berengarten, S. (1986). *The nature and objectives of accreditation and social work education* (Social Work Education Monograph Series, No. 2). Austin: University of Texas School of Social Work.

Council on Social Work Education. (1994). *Directory of colleges and universities with accredited social work degree programs*. Alexandria, VA: Author.

Council on Social Work Education. (1994). *Summary information on master of social work programs*. Alexandria, VA: Author.

Lennon, T. (1994). *Statistics on social work education*. Alexandria, VA: Council on Social Work Education. In addition, see the *Journal of Social Work Education* (published since 1965) and the *Social Work Education Reporter* (published since 1953).

**Donald W. Beless, PhD, ACSW,** is executive director, Council on Social Work Education, 1600 Duke Street, Alexandria, VA 22314.

### For further information see

Continuing Education; International Social Work Education; Licensing, Regulation, and Certification; Management Overview; National Association of Social Workers; Organizations: Context for Social Services Delivery; Planning and Management Professions; Quality Assurance; Research Overview; Social Work Education; Special-Interest Professional Associations; Social Work Profession Overview; Vendorship.

**Key Words**

accreditation
Council on Social Work Education
management
professional associations
social work education

READER'S GUIDE

## Courts and Corrections

*The following entries contain information on this general topic:*



## Coyle, Grace Longwell

*See* Biographies section, Volume 3

# Criminal Behavior Overview

**Rosemary C. Sarri**

There is far too much crime in the United States for the well-being of the society, more than is ever reported and far more than is ever solved. Therefore, it is not surprising that crime is consistently identified as a social problem of major concern, and one for which billions of dollars are expended each year in crime control even though the interventions appear to have few positive outcomes. Criminal behavior is legally defined as behavior and acts for which a society provides formal sanctions for the violations of social norms. However, the definitions vary significantly among countries, states, and local jurisdictions.

Defining crime as legally proscribed behavior is both a political and a cultural act, as Durkheim (1951) noted in his discussions of the functions of deviance in the social integration of society. Crime is defined as such not only by those with the power to legislate, but by law enforcement officials who exercise considerable discretion at the time of arrest, trial, conviction, and sentencing. In the United States, behaviors that are formally identified as crime are committed primarily in urban areas by young men under age 25 (Gibbs, 1988). Civil infractions, which are more widespread among the population, fall under the civil, not the criminal, code of law. Wilson and Herrnstein (1985) limited their definition to predatory street crime, which they contended is of the greatest concern to the public. However, they failed to consider the extent to which powerful interests conceal corporate and environmental crime, whose actual public health and monetary costs to the public may be far greater. In contrast to Wilson and Herrnstein, Quinney (1974) theorized that in advanced capitalist societies, such as the United States, criminal law is an instrument of the state and ruling classes to maintain and perpetuate the existing social and economic order.

The decision of the police to arrest varies with the seriousness of the offense that is to be charged, the extenuating circumstances of the situation, the police officer's knowledge and experience, the risk to the safety of the police and the observing public, and so forth. Some authors have suggested that the broadest discretion in the entire justice system resides with the police (Quinney & Wildman, 1991). However, prosecutors also have substantial discretion in decisions regarding prosecution, as do judges at various points in the judicial processing of cases.

## History

Since the beginning of recorded history, violations of the social and legal code by individuals or groups have been formally proscribed. Proscriptions can be found in the Code of Hammurabi, in the law codes of ancient Palestine, and the Twelve Tables of Roman Law. For thousands of years, these proscriptions were confined to individuals and groups, although occasionally collective action was taken by the ruler or the state against selected communities for their violations of laws. For thousands of years, laws governing criminal behavior were unwritten, but enforced nonetheless. One such example is English common law, which had many proscriptions governing the behavior of poor people or persons of lesser status, such as women and children. Behaviors, such as child or spouse abuse, were not considered punishable by law enforcement officials because wives and children were considered to be chattel of the husbands or fathers.

The concept of crime was recognized in English law in the reign of Henry II (1154–1189). Gradually, crime came to be defined in criminal codes as a legal category, and responsibility for its control was assigned to agents of the state (Quinney & Wildeman, 1991). However, some behavior was socially proscribed even when it did not involve the violation of criminal law or the application of a legal category to the behavior. For example, violence in the family was socially proscribed, but legal action was seldom taken until laws were passed in the latter half of the 20th century.

Among the many writers of the classical school of criminology in the 18th and 19th centuries, Beccaria (1764/1963) stood out for his progressive reform proposals. Beccaria attempted to construct the criminal code in accordance with the natural rights of persons—rights that individuals have independent of the state (Foucault, 1977). He also became a leader in the penal reform movement to eliminate public torture and execution.

In their studies of primitive societies, Malinowski (1926/1984) and Radcliffe-Brown (1952/1965) proposed anthropological definitions of crime. In his study of the Trobriands, Malinowski proposed the following definition:

> The rules of law stand out from the rest in that they are felt and regarded as the obligations of one person and the rightful claims of another. They are sanctioned not by a mere psychological motive, but by a definite social machinery or binding force, based as we know, upon mutual dependence, and realized in the equivalent arrangement of reciprocal services. . . . The ceremonial manner in which most transactions are carried out, which entails public control and criticism, adds still more to their binding force. (p. 55)

In the 20th century, the definitions of crime and criminal law have been broadened to include both human rights violations by the state and deliberate environmental damage. However, the machinery for implementing international codes of conduct is incomplete and often reflects only the authority of powerful states over those who are less powerful (Walker, 1987).

## Defining Crime

Criminal law defines conduct that is believed to be against the interests of society, whereas civil law refers to conduct against the interests of specific individuals. The kind, type, and frequency of behavior that is proscribed by criminal law are functions of the social systems that authorize and enforce legal and social norms. The parameters for socially permissible behavior, as well as the degree and severity of punishment, are established in the criminal law and by the goals and authority of those who are responsible for the formal enforcement of the law (Walker, 1987). Crime may be defined as illegal behavior in terms of property, in terms of interpersonal behavior, or even in terms of one's own behavior (such as gambling).

Criminologists have developed many theories of criminal behavior and elaborate systems for classifying crimes. An adequate theory of criminal behavior needs to apply to all crimes, to specific modifications that are necessary for the description of various types of crimes, and to the changes in the criminalization and decriminalization of behavior that occur over time and in different jurisdictions. Clinard (1973) pointed out that the most common classifications of crime have been legalistic, individualistic, and social.

### Legalistic Definitions

Legalistic definitions of criminal behavior are the oldest and most frequently used forms of classification of crimes, which may be categorized according to the seriousness of offenses, the types and degree of punishment, and the persons who are affected by the offenses. The definition of what constitutes a felony as opposed to a misdemeanor or a status offense is to be found in criminal law statutes. Legal definitions vary with time and location, so that comparative analyses of trends are often difficult to conduct. In much of the risk-prediction research, the formal systems of classification used by corrections departments are based on categories derived from legal definitions, rather than on systematic epidemiological research.

**Individualistic Definitions**

In contrast to legalistic definitions, individualistic explanations and classifications emphasize the attributes of people who commit crimes, as well as their behavior. Italian criminologists in the 19th century rejected legal definitions and attempted to classify criminals according to the physical and mental characteristics of people who committed specific deviant acts (Beccaria, 1764/1963). They paid little attention to analyzing how society came to label certain behaviors as criminal, rather than as some other type of deviance. Offenders also have been classified by race, age, sex, family background, personality traits, and ethnicity.

All the individualistic approaches to criminal classification are vulnerable because they assume that individuals with specific attributes will commit certain types of crimes. Since 1980 there has been an increased interest in identifying biological-genetic characteristics of offenders that predispose them to crime (Kamin, 1986). Research has demonstrated that approaches that focus on individual characteristics result, in many cases, in the over- and underprediction of actual behavior. Wilson and Herrnstein (1985) exemplify the individualistic approach in their emphasis on biological and psychological explanations of criminal behavior.

**Social Definitions**

The social-behavior classification of crime consists of the construction of a pattern of variables that are linked in specified ways. Crime is assumed to be a social phenomenon, so there must be a delineation of the social context of the act as well as of the offender. Clinard (1973) suggested that although there is a heuristic value in the development of typologies of criminal behavior, these typologies have limitations, and no single typology is likely to be acceptable to everyone. Typologies may differ in terms of their purposes, their adaptability over time, and situational variations.

***Criminal behavior typology.*** One typology developed by Clinard and Quinney (1967) appears to have utility today for both practitioners and researchers. This typology is based on four factors: (1) the criminal career of the offender, (2) the extent to which the behavior has group support, (3) the correspondence between criminal and legitimate behavioral patterns, and (4) societal reaction. The eight types of criminal behavior in the typology are these:

1. violent personal behavior, such as murder or rape
2. occasional property crime, such as auto theft or shoplifting
3. occupational crime, such as embezzlement or false advertising, including "white-collar" crime
4. political crime, such as treason, espionage, or military violations
5. public-order crime, such as vagrancy, addiction, or prostitution
6. conventional crime, such as robbery, larceny, or burglary
7. organized crime, such as racketeering, organized gambling, and drug trafficking
8. professional crime, such as shoplifting, counterfeiting, or forgery.

Clinard and Quinney (1967) did not order their typology according to the seriousness of the offenses with respect to public safety or perceptions of crime. Neither did Gibbons (1979), who constructed a typology of criminal offenders in terms of patterns of offenses, self-image, normative orientation, and other sociopsychological characteristics. Gibbons referred to types of offenders as role careers in which identifiable changes occur. His formulation included 15 adult criminal types and nine juvenile types.

***Public perceptions.*** Public perceptions of crime often differ from perceptions of criminologists. They may define it in terms of the type of victim (for example, child abuse), the type of offender (such as white-collar crime), the object of the crime (for instance, property crime), or the method of criminal behavior (such as organized crime). Public perceptions of the seriousness of crime generally conform to the classifications used by the criminal justice system, but there are some notable exceptions. Miller, Rossi, and Simpson (1986, 1991) emphasized the similarities and differences in the public's perceptions of justice. The National Crime Survey (U.S. Department of Justice, 1986) has also investigated the public's perception of the seriousness of various criminal behaviors. These works have noted that there are wide differences in public perceptions, so that it is difficult to draw specific conclusions about lay persons' views of crime. Moreover, these views fluctuate because of differential information available to the public through the media.

The types of behaviors that are considered to be crimes change over time, although some behaviors, such as homicide, robbery, and burglary, have been considered crimes for centuries, and in most societies. On the one hand, many behaviors, such as family violence and child neglect, may be considered deviant, but not criminal. On the other hand, behaviors that were once defined as criminal, such as public drunkenness, have been decriminalized in most jurisdictions. At the same time, laws governing the operation of vehicles while intoxicated have been tightened because of the risk of harm to victims. The use and abuse of alcohol and drugs have been and are still defined in myriad ways with respect to criminal violations. In the United States, drugs other than alcohol are illegal, whereas in many countries of the world, the use of these drugs may not be considered illegal and is handled as a public health problem or is ignored.

## Measurement of Crime

Because there is no way to know the "true" rate of crime in a society, measurement is typically approached in three different but complementary ways.

### Reports by Law Enforcement Agencies

Crime is officially measured by law enforcement agencies in terms of the total volume of crime reported to and the arrests made by the police. These reports are generated from local police departments to the central state agencies and then to the Federal Bureau of Investigation (FBI), which is part of the U.S. Department of Justice. Although they rely on voluntary reporting by police, these reports cover 95 percent of the U.S. population (U.S. Department of Justice, 1993b), and are published annually by the FBI.

### Reports of Victimization

Crime is measured annually in the National Crime Victimization Survey (NCVS), which includes a stratified random sample of 49,000 households with approximately 101,000 individuals over age 12. NCVS measures most of the crimes reported to the police, except murder, arson, and commercial crime, and crimes that have not been reported. It provides detailed information about the age, sex, education, and income of the victims, whereas the police reports seldom contain such information about persons who have been arrested. Because of the survey methodology and approach in studying victims, NCVS is only partially comparable to police reports to the FBI.

### Self-Reports and Other Means

Crime is measured through self-reports obtained from interviews or other types of surveys of selected population groups. Because of their selective sampling and because they promise confidentiality, self-reports are difficult to corroborate independently. Thus, the validity and reliability of these data cannot be determined. The samples that are usually surveyed contain nonoffenders and often do not adequately represent or include known populations of offenders (Johnston, O'Malley, & Bachman, 1994). Another weakness of self-report surveys is that they usually report a larger proportion of minor or petty offenses than of serious crimes. Chaiken and Chaiken (1982), however, used a combination of self-reports and official data to analyze the behavior of 2,200 jail and prison inmates in California, Michigan, and Texas. They showed that criminal behavior can be classified into 10 different types and that self-report data are often better predictors of subsequent behavior than are official data.

### Direct Observation of People Committing Crimes

Such observations are occasionally possible, but they are usually done by undercover law enforcement officials. As such, they selectively represent only a minute sample of selected types of crimes, for example, drug violations.

## Index of Crime

The total volume of crime known to the police in the United States is referred to as the index of crime and is reported for the nation each year (U.S. Department of Justice, 1993b). These data, reported by local police to state and federal agencies, are only as accurate as the reports that are submitted to the respective bodies. In 1992 the total volume of crime known to the police included 14,438,200 incidents, whereas the total number of persons arrested for those crimes was 11,877,802 (U.S. Department of Justice, 1988, 1993b). Crimes are classified as index (serious person and property violations) and nonindex (property and other) crimes.

The discrepancy between offenses known to the police and arrests occurs because there are many crimes for which a perpetrator cannot be identified. Typically, the more serious and violent the crime, the more likely it is that the police will be able to make an arrest. It is often not possible to determine the perpetrators or victims specifically in many of the reported crimes, and therefore, an arrest cannot be made. The largest discrepancies between reported crimes and

TABLE 1

**Index of Crime, Rate per 100,000 Population, Selected Years, 1960–1992**

| Year | Violent Crime | Property Crime | Total |
|---|---|---|---|
| 1960 | 160.9 | 1,726.3 | 1,887.2 |
| 1965 | 200.2 | 2,248.8 | 2,449.0 |
| 1970 | 363.5 | 3,621.0 | 3,984.5 |
| 1975 | 487.8 | 4,810.7 | 5,298.5 |
| 1980 | 596.6 | 5,353.3 | 5,950.0 |
| 1985 | 556.6 | 4,650.5 | 5,207.1 |
| 1990 | 731.8 | 5,088.5 | 5,820.3 |
| 1992 | 757.5 | 4,902.7 | 5,660.2 |

SOURCE: U.S. Department of Justice, Federal Bureau of Investigation. (1993b). *Crime in the United States: 1992* (Table 1). Washington, DC: U.S. Government Printing Office.

arrests for felonies occur for offenses, such as rape and robbery, when reports often do not result in arrests because of the victims' hesitancy to prosecute. In the case of property crime, the large discrepancies for burglary and larceny reflect the inability to locate the offenders in most instances. However, community tolerance levels, as well as variations in police coverage, are also factors in the discrepancy between the commission of crimes and the arrest of perpetrators. In the case of nonindex felonies and misdemeanors, it is often difficult to determine the perpetrators, as well as the victims. In these instances, there may well be large discrepancies. The NCVS information can shed some light on unreported crimes, but that, too, does not include all crimes.

### Trends in Crime

Table 1 reports the trends in reported crime between 1960 and 1992. As can be observed, there was more than a 300 percent increase in reported crimes between 1960 and 1970, followed by another peak in 1980. From 1980 to 1992, the volume of reported crime declined, albeit unevenly (U.S. Department of Justice, 1993b). Violent crime increased and stabilized after 1980, although between 1990 and 1993 there was a marked increase in violent crime by young adolescents. Much of this crime is attributed to youths being recruited for organized drug rings as distributors and to the increase in youth gangs. A variety of explanations have also been offered with respect to this increase: the greater availability of guns and illegal drugs, the rise in unemployment, and the deterioration of inner-city neighborhoods in metropolitan areas (DeFrancis & Smith, 1994).

Property crime is the dominant pattern. Over half of all crimes known to the police in 1992 were larceny thefts (54.8 percent); 20.6 percent were burglaries, and 11.1 percent were motor vehicle thefts. Among the crimes against persons in 1992, assault was the most frequent at 7.8 percent, followed by robbery, 4.8 percent; rape, 0.8 percent, and murder 0.2 percent (U.S. Department of Justice, 1993b). These patterns contrast with popular perceptions that violent interpersonal crime is the dominant pattern.

## ARRESTS

For the total volume of crimes reported to the police in 1992, 11,877,802 persons were arrested, but adequate information for analysis was available for only 9.6 million individuals in 1992 (see Table 2). The total number of arrests, 14.1 million, is a substantially larger number because some people are arrested several times within a year. The rate of arrests for the total population was 5,566 per 100,000 population, one of the highest in the world for which information is available (Mauer, 1994; U.S. Department of Justice, 1994b).

Arrests are a measure of the response of law enforcement to crime, not a measure of the total volume of criminal behavior. They provide important information because the age, race, location of arrest, and sex of the offenders are identified. Thus, at least on an aggregate level, some comparisons can be made with victimization surveys and self-reports by samples of the larger population.

### Patterns of Arrest

Overall, 45 percent of those arrested in 1992 were less than 25 years old, and larceny theft was the offense for which those under age 18 were most frequently arrested. For the period 1988 to 1992, total arrests were up 7 percent, and the rate of increase in juvenile arrests exceeded that of adults. During that period, arrests for violent crime rose by 23 percent, with arrests for robbery and aggravated assault showing the greatest increase. The increase in arrests for violent crimes reflects a trend noted since 1980 in the total volume of reported crime (see Table 1).

In 1992 there were substantial differences in the patterns of arrests among cities and by regions of the country, as Table 3 indicates. Large cities had the highest rates of arrest, at 7,203 per 100,000 population, whereas rural areas had the lowest rates, at 4,063 per 100,000. Among the regions, the South led with 5,781 arrests per 100,000 population, followed by the West, Northeast, and Midwest. These regional and urban–rural differences reflect differential law enforcement responses, as well as cultural variations in responses to crime.

TABLE 2
**Arrest Trends: 1988 and 1992 (in thousands)**

| Offense | Total Arrests | | Arrests of People under Age 18 | | Arrests of People Age 18 and Older | |
|---|---|---|---|---|---|---|
| | 1988 | 1992 | 1988 | 1992 | 1988 | 1992 |
| Index crime | 1,892 | 2,030 | 531 | 596 | 1,361 | 1,434 |
| Murder | 14.6 | 16.5 | 1.6 | 2.5 | 12.9 | 14.1 |
| Rape | 25.7 | 26.9 | 3.8 | 4.5 | 21.8 | 22.5 |
| Robbery | 105.8 | 128.1 | 22.7 | 34.0 | 83.1 | 94.1 |
| Aggravated assault | 272.9 | 343.9 | 34.4 | 51.3 | 238.4 | 292.6 |
| Burglary | 299.2 | 295.0 | 98.2 | 99.7 | 200.9 | 195.3 |
| Larceny theft | 1,018.8 | 1,062.4 | 307.8 | 331.9 | 710.9 | 728.5 |
| Motor vehicle theft | 141.7 | 143.8 | 56.6 | 63.2 | 85.1 | 80.5 |
| Arson | 12.9 | 13.9 | 5.5 | 6.9 | 7.4 | 6.9 |
| Nonindex crime[a] | 7,103 | 7,381 | 924 | 1,025 | 6,180 | 6,555 |
| Total | 8,995 | 9,411 | 1,455 | 1,621 | 7,541 | 7,989 |

SOURCE: U.S. Department of Justice, Federal Bureau of Investigation. (1993b). *Crime in the United States: 1992*. Washington, DC: U.S. Government Printing Office.

[a]Nonindex crime includes less serious felonies, misdemeanors, and status offenses, such as other assaults, forgery, fraud, embezzlement, receiving or selling stolen goods, vandalism, possessing or carrying weapons, prostitution and other sex offenses, gambling, child abuse, unauthorized driving away of an automobile, liquor law violations, vagrancy, curfew violations, loitering, and running away.

TABLE 3
**Arrest Rate, by City and Region: 1992 (per 100,000 population)**

| Size of City | Rate | Region | Rate |
|---|---|---|---|
| 250,00 or more | 7,203 | South | 5,781 |
| 25,000 or less | 5,386 | West | 5,763 |
| Suburbs | 4,138 | Northeast | 5,476 |
| Rural areas | 4,063 | Midwest | 5,004 |

SOURCE: U.S. Department of Justice, Federal Bureau of Investigation. (1993b). *Crime in the United States: 1992*. Washington, DC: U.S. Government Printing Office.

### Social Class and Race

Arrests vary among people of color and social class; however, information is less complete than is necessary for a careful analysis. Of all people arrested in 1992, 69 percent were white, 29 percent were African American, and 2 percent were Native American or Asian. Information on Hispanics was not available, but, nonetheless, it is clear that people of color were overrepresented among those who were arrested (see Gibbs, 1988, for a discussion of the overrepresentation of these groups). With regard to serious and violent crimes, this overrepresentation occurs for murder, rape, robbery, aggravated assault, and burglary. Persons with low incomes and unemployed people are also overrepresented among those who are arrested (U.S. Department of Justice, 1993b).

### Gender

An important differentiating variable in criminal behavior is gender. Females constituted 19 percent of all people arrested in 1992, although they are more than half the total population. With respect to age, there are few differences in the types of offenses, but young women under age 18 constituted 20 percent of all women who were arrested, a higher percentage than their proportion in the overall female population. In addition, it is young women for whom there has been a greater increase in crime and arrests since 1980.

There are significant differences in the offenses committed by males and females. Females predominate in crimes of larceny theft and in misdemeanors, such as prostitution and running away. That difference is caused by the application of a double standard with respect to males and females, not because males are less likely to run away from home or to engage in sexual behavior. Although the index crimes committed by females increased between 1983 and 1992, arrests of females for murder and other violent crimes actually declined. For murder, rape, robbery, and burglary, more than 90 percent of all arrests were of males.

## VICTIMS OF CRIMES

The annual NCVS provides extensive information about who is affected by criminal behavior. It measures crimes involving violence or personal theft, as well as household crimes, both those that are reported to the police and those that are not. Table 4 presents a summary of national victimization data for the years 1976 to 1992.

**Reported Versus Unreported Crimes**

According to NCVS, nearly 19 million people age 12 or older were victims of crime in 1992, and 14.8 million household crimes were committed (Bastian, 1993). The importance of this survey, however, is the information it provides about unreported crimes. Thus, the 1992 survey revealed that 50 percent of violent crimes and 60 percent of all crimes were not reported to the police. From 1981 to 1992, there was a decline in victims' reports of crimes, similar to crimes reported to the police. That is, the total number of victimizations reported in 1992 was 33,649, compared to 41,454 in 1981. The largest decreases in reports occurred for household burglaries, larcenies, and thefts of motor vehicles; reports of violent crimes were relatively stable from 1976 to 1990, but increased slightly from 1990 to 1992, particularly for assaults and robberies. It is significant that violent crimes decreased for male victims until 1992, but did not for females, for whom the rate was 22.9 per 100,000 population (Bachman, 1994a). However, male homicides outnumbered female homicides by a ratio of nine to one.

**Risk of Becoming a Victim**

Fear of crime affects most people, whether or not they have ever been a victim. Only one in three persons reported that they felt safe in their homes or neighborhoods, a far higher proportion than the number of actual victimizations would justify (DeFrancis & Smith, 1994). However, it is estimated that five out of six U.S. residents can expect to be victims of attempted or completed crimes in their lifetimes. The risk of almost all types of victimization is far greater for poor persons, African Americans or Hispanics, youths, males, those with less education, and unmarried persons (Bachman, 1994a; Bastian, 1993).

***Area of residence and race.*** Residents of central cities are more than three times as likely to be robbed as are residents of nonmetropolitan areas. Although 25 percent of the population are residents of rural areas, they are only 16 percent of violent victimizations and have low rates of victimization for property crimes. African American households are most likely to be victims and to identify crime as a serious neighborhood problem (DeFrancis & Smith, 1994). Overall, there is an increasing perception that neighborhood crime is a serious problem.

***Gender.*** Although males are victimized more frequently than are females, the victimization of females differs in that crimes against women are likely to be committed by intimates, such as husbands and boyfriends, rather than by strangers, which is more typical for males. Injuries to women occur almost twice as often when the perpetrators

TABLE 4

**Number and Rate of Victimizations in the United States, Selected Years, 1976–1992 (in thousands)**

| Category and Type of Crime | 1976 | 1978 | 1980 | 1982 | 1984 | 1986 | 1988 | 1990 | 1992 |
|---|---|---|---|---|---|---|---|---|---|
| Crimes of violence | 5,599 (36.6) | 5,941 (33.7) | 6,130 (33.3) | 6,459 (34.3) | 6,021 (31.4) | 5,515 (28.1) | 5,910 (29.6) | 6,009 (29.6) | 6,621 (32.1) |
| Rape | 145 (0.8) | 171 (1.0) | 174 (0.9) | 153 (0.8) | 180 (0.9) | 130 (0.7) | 127 (0.6) | 130 (0.8) | 141 (0.7) |
| Robbery | 1,111 (6.5) | 1,038 (5.9) | 1,209 (6.5) | 1,334 (7.1) | 1,097 (5.7) | 1,009 (5.1) | 1,048 (5.3) | 1,150 (5.7) | 1,226 (5.9) |
| Assault | 4,344 (25.3) | 4,732 (26.9) | 4,747 (25.8) | 4,973 (26.4) | 4,744 (24.7) | 4,376 (22.3) | 4,734 (23.7) | 4,729 (23.3) | 5,255 (25.5) |
| Theft | 16,519 (96.1) | 17,050 (96.8) | 15,300 (83.0) | 15,553 (82.5) | 13,789 (71.8) | 13,235 (67.5) | 14,056 (70.5) | 12,975 (63.8) | 12,111 (59.2) |
| Household crimes | | | | | | | | | |
| Burglary | 6,663 (88.9) | 6,704 (86.0) | 6,973 (84.3) | 6,663 (78.2) | 5,643 (64.1) | 5,557 (61.5) | 5,777 (61.9) | 5,148 (53.8) | 4,757 (48.9) |
| Larceny | 9,301 (124) | 9,352 (119) | 10,468 (127) | 9,705 (114) | 8,750 (99.4) | 8,455 (93.5) | 8,419 (90.2) | 8,304 (86.7) | 8,101 (83.2) |
| Motor vehicle theft | 1,235 (16.5) | 1,365 (17.5) | 1,381 (16.7) | 1,377 (16.2) | 1,340 (15.2) | 1,356 (15.0) | 1,634 (17.5) | 1,968 (20.5) | 1,959 (20.1) |

SOURCE: Bastian, L. J. (1993, March). *Criminal victimization, 1992* (Report of the U.S. Department of Justice, Bureau of Justice Statistics, Table 1, p. 2). Washington, DC: U.S. Government Printing Office.

NOTE: The rates are calculated per 100,000 in the United States and are presented in parentheses.

are known to the victim rather than strangers (Bachman, 1994a). Women are less likely to report victimizations committed by intimates. Victims and offenders are known to each other in about 40 percent of the reports. Although more than half a million cases of family violence were reported, it is recognized that many cases of family abuse and violence are not reported in NCVS (Bachman, 1994a).

***Age.*** The NCVS survey includes people ages 65 and older in its national sample, and its results challenge some popular stereotypes. Although older people constitute 14 percent of the sample, they reported less than 2 percent of all victimizations in 1992, and the number of victims in this age group steadily declined from its peak in 1980 to 1992 (U.S. Department of Justice, 1994a). Those who were most likely to be victims of crimes were 12- to 24-year-old African American youths, and in general, criminal victimization of all types declined with increasing age during the period under question. The violent crime rate was nearly 16 times as high for people under age 25 as it was for those over age 65. Elderly African Americans were more likely to be victimized than were elderly white people, especially those with lower incomes and those residing in rental properties.

### Other Factors

***Crime in the workplace.*** Crime victimization in the workplace affects nearly 3 million people each year and results in an average loss of 3.5 days per crime (Bachman, 1994b). Six in 10 victimizations occurred in private companies, with men more likely to sustain injury than women. Less than half the victims in the workplace reported the crime to the police, and when asked why, most reported that they either believed the incident to be minor or reported it to a private security guard.

***Use of handguns.*** Offenders with handguns committed 931,000 violent crimes in 1992 (Rand, 1994). This number brought the rate of nonfatal handgun victimizations to 4.5 crimes per 1,000 population aged 12 years or older. The victims also used handguns to defend themselves against the perpetrators and when they did, 20 percent were injured in the incidents. Victims generally used firearms to defend themselves when the offenders were unarmed or armed with weapons other than guns.

## Juvenile Crime

Although crimes reported to the police and those reported to NCVS include age as a variable in their reports, juvenile crime deserves special attention because some behaviors, such as truancy, curfew violations, running away, and incorrigibility, are considered crimes for juveniles but not for adults. These are commonly referred to as status offenses. Moreover, juveniles can be labeled and processed by non–law enforcement agencies in the community.

Of the 1.2 million juveniles taken into custody in 1991, 28 percent were handled by police departments and released; 64 percent were referred to juvenile courts, 6 percent were referred to other police agencies or to adult courts, and 2 percent were referred to a welfare agency (U.S. Department of Justice, 1993a). With regard to the trends from 1972 to 1992, the proportion of juveniles who were warned and released by the police declined from 46 percent to 28 percent. The proportion referred to juvenile courts increased from 30 percent to 64 percent, and waivers to adult courts for processing also increased, even for children as young as age 13.

These changes were associated with increasingly violent and drug-related crimes by juveniles, as well as by less opportunity for employment and the assumption of legitimate adult roles (Currie, 1985; Ohlin & Cloward, 1960). Another important factor affecting referrals to courts was the reduction in funding at all levels for diversion and prevention programs. Nonetheless, the overall rate of juvenile arrests declined from 6,938 per 100,000 in 1979 to 6,434 in 1990 (U.S. Department of Justice, 1993a). An increase in violent assaultive crimes by juveniles occurred in a limited number of central cities. Overall, as was noted earlier, African American and Hispanic juveniles are at particular risk for involvement in violent crimes. Much of that crime includes perpetrators and victims of the same age, sex, residential area, race, and class. Of particular concern is the dramatic increase in homicide rates for males aged 15 to 24. The rate for African American males was 160 per 100,000 population versus 16 per 100,000 population for white males (Center for Health Statistics, 1992). Homicide by youths as young as 10 was reported in several cities and is being addressed by the Centers for Disease Control as a major public health problem (Center for Health Statistics).

## Social Justice and Intervention

An examination of criminal behavior in the United States in the 1990s indicates that it is a pervasive and serious problem that is becoming increasingly resistant to policies and programs aimed at its reduction. The reliance on law enforcement and punishment, rather than on more basic social policies to alleviate poverty, racism, sexism, ageism, unemployment, family and neighborhood violence, the availability of guns, the distribution and abuse of drugs, as well as poor housing and urban deterioration, is probably the principal reason for the failure of criminal justice policies and programs to reduce crime (Christie, 1993; Quinney & Wildman, 1991).

**Effects of Current Policies**

The entire legal and correctional system, as well as various crime prevention programs, all can be viewed as interventions to reduce criminal behavior. Numerous theories of intervention focus on prevention, punishment, deterrence, rehabilitation, and treatment, but few have been adequate for the design and implementation of effective interventions to reduce criminal behavior. Moreover, most of the vast expenditures of the criminal justice system are used for law enforcement, punishment, and custody, not for prevention, rehabilitation, treatment, or education (Currie, 1985).

It is often asked whether this country's response to crime exacerbates the problems it seeks to solve. Incarceration is assumed to reduce crime, both for the offenders and as a deterrent to others who wish to avoid going to prison. The most recent changes in federal and state criminal laws have greatly increased the incarceration of offenders with such provisions as automatic life imprisonment after conviction for three felonies, "consecutive sentences," and "truth in sentencing." In addition, there are more and more crimes for which capital punishment is the prescribed solution and hence more and more executions.

If one examines the developments since the formation of the Law Enforcement Assistance Administration in 1966, one observes that there has been a tremendous increase in the prison population, but that the crime rate, especially for violent crimes, has declined relatively little (U.S. Department of Justice, 1993a). Moreover, if statistical controls are used in analyzing the decline in the population groups that are likely to be incarcerated (for example, those aged 15 to 30), the decrease in the size of the young adult cohort is considered by most to be the key factor in the reduction in crime. Moreover, the costs of prisons and incarceration far outweigh any benefits from incapacitation.

**Comparison with Other Countries**

In a study of crime in Japan, Bayley (1976) noted that Japan has a fairly stable crime rate, that there is minimal use of formal criminal justice sanctions, and that there is strong control of deviant behavior by the community and the family. Bayley also suggested that the low crime rate reflects a society with less income inequality and the relative absence of a severely deprived underclass. The case of Japan shows that there are alternative ways that a society can be constructed and that crime is not an inevitable consequence of urbanization and industrialization. Similar observations would apply to many European countries, particularly the Netherlands and those in Scandinavia (Christie, 1993). The United States now has the second highest rate of incarceration of any country in the world, but incarceration has had little impact on reducing criminal behavior (Mauer, 1994). As Downs (1977) noted, variables, such as per capita income, educational achievement, and racial composition, are related more to incarceration than is the crime rate.

## Conclusion

Social work has not played an active role in the criminal justice systems in recent decades. Given the seriousness of the problem, the amount of resources consumed in this system, and the need for more effective policies and programs, there is an urgent need for the profession to be more actively involved in the design and implementation of solutions. If criminal behavior is to be reduced and controlled, the solutions are likely to be found in interventions to improve family and neighborhood life, eliminate poverty, promote education, and provide greater opportunities for employment, rather than in stronger law enforcement.

## References


Bachman, R. (1994a, March). *Violence against women* (Report of the U.S. Department of Justice, Office of Justice Programs). Washington, DC: U.S. Government Printing Office.

Bachman, R. (1994b, July). *Violence and theft in the workplace* (Report of the U.S. Department of Justice, Office of Justice Programs). Washington, DC: U.S. Government Printing Office.

Bastian, L. J. (1993, March). *Criminal victimization, 1992* (Report of the U.S. Department of Justice, Bureau of Justice Statistics). Washington, DC: U.S. Government Printing Office.

Bayley, D. H. (1976, Summer). Learning about crime: The Japanese experience. *Public Interest*, p. 68.

Beccaria, C. (1963). *On crimes and punishment* (H. Paolucci, Trans.). Indianapolis: Bobbs Merrill. (Original work published 1764)

Center for Health Statistics. (1992). *Homicide rates: 1950–1992.* Atlanta: Centers for Disease Control.

Chaiken, J. M., & Chaiken, M. (1982). *Varieties of criminal behavior.* Santa Monica, CA: Rand Corporation.

Christie, N. (1993). *Crime control as industry.* London: Routledge & Kegan Paul.

Clinard, M. (1973). *Criminal behavior systems.* New York: Holt, Rinehart & Winston.

Clinard, M., & Quinney, R. (1967). *Criminal behavior systems: A typology.* New York: Holt, Rinehart & Winston.

Currie, E. (1985). *Confronting crime: An American challenge.* New York: Pantheon.

DeFrancis, C., & Smith, S. K. (1994, June). *Neighborhoods and crime: Crime data brief* (U.S. Department of Justice, Bureau of Justice Statistics). Washington, DC: U.S. Government Printing Office.

Downs, G. (1977). *Bureaucracy, innovation and social policy.* Lexington, MA: Lexington Books.

Durkheim, E. (1951). *Suicide: A sociological study.* Glencoe, IL: Free Press.

Foucault, M. (1977). *Discipline and punish.* New York: Pantheon.

Gibbons, D. C. (1979). *The criminological enterprise: Theories and perspectives.* Englewood Cliffs, NJ: Prentice Hall.

Gibbs, J. T. (Ed.). (1988). *Young, black and male in America: An endangered species.* Dover, MA: Auburn.

Johnston, L., O'Malley, P., & Bachman, J. (1994). *Natural survey results on drug use from the monitoring the future 1975–1983.* Washington, DC: U.S. Department of Health and Human Services, National Institute on Drug Abuse.

Kamin, L. (1986). Is crime in the genes? The answer may depend on who chooses the evidence. *Scientific American, 254,* 22–27.

Malinowski, B. (1984). *Crime and custom in savage society* (reprint ed.). Westport, CT: Greenwood Press. (Original work published 1926)

Mauer, M. (1994). *Americans behind bars: The international use of incarceration, 1992–93.* Washington, DC: The Sentencing Project.

Miller, J. L., Rossi, P. H., & Simpson, J. E. (1986). Perceptions of justice: Race and gender differences in judges of appropriate prison sentences. *Law and Society, 20*(3), 313–334.

Miller, J. L., Rossi, P. H., & Simpson, J. E. (1991, Summer). Felony punishments: A factorial study of perceived justice in criminal sentencing. *Journal of Criminal Law and Criminology, 82,* 396–422.

Ohlin, L., & Cloward, R. (1960). *Delinquency and opportunity.* Glencoe, IL: Free Press.

Quinney, R. (1974). *Critique of the legal order.* Boston: Little, Brown.

Quinney, R., & Wildeman, J. (1991). *The problem of crime.* Mountain View, CA: Mayfield.

Radcliffe-Brown, A. R. (1965). *Structure and function in primitive society.* New York: Free Press. (Original work published 1952)

Rand, M. J. (1994, April). *Guns and Crime: Crime data brief* (U.S. Department of Justice, Bureau of Justice Statistics). Washington, DC: U.S. Government Printing Office.

U.S. Department of Justice, Bureau of Justice Statistics. (1986). *Criminal victimization in the United States: 1984.* Washington, DC: U.S. Government Printing Office.

U.S. Department of Justice, Bureau of Justice Statistics. (1988). *Report to the nation on crime and justice* (2nd ed.). Washington, DC: U.S. Government Printing Office.

U.S. Department of Justice, Bureau of Justice Statistics. (1993a). *Sourcebook of criminal justice statistics, 1992.* Washington, DC: U.S. Government Printing Office.

U.S. Department of Justice, Federal Bureau of Investigation. (1993b). *Crime in the United States: 1992.* Washington, DC: U.S. Government Printing Office.

U.S. Department of Justice, Bureau of Justice Statistics. (1994a, March). *Elderly crime victims: Selected findings from BJS.* Washington, DC: U.S. Government Printing Office.

U.S. Department of Justice, Bureau of Justice Statistics. (1994b, March). *The severity of crime.* Washington, DC: U.S. Government Printing Office.

Walker, N. (1987). *Crime and criminology: A critical introduction.* New York: Oxford University Press.

Wilson, J. Q., & Herrnstein, R. (1985). *Crime and human nature.* New York: Simon & Schuster.

## Further Reading

Gabor, T. (1994). *Everybody does it! Crime by the public.* Toronto: University of Toronto Press.

Gibbons, D. (1994). *Talking about crime and criminals: Problems and issues in theory development in criminology.* Englewood Cliffs, NJ: Prentice Hall.

Krisberg, B., & Austin, J. (1993). *Rethinking juvenile justice.* Newbury Park, CA: Sage Publications.

Miethe, T. (1994). *Crime and its social control: Toward an integrated theory of offenders, victims and situations.* Albany: State University of New York Press.

Palmer, T. (1994). *A profile of correctional effectiveness and new directions for research.* Albany: State University of New York Press.

Tonry, M. (1991). *Human development and criminal behavior: New ways of advancing knowledge.* New York: Springer-Verlag.

**Rosemary C. Sarri, PhD,** is professor, School of Social Work, and faculty associate, Institute for Social Research, University of Michigan, 1065 Frieze Building, Ann Arbor, MI 48106.

### For further information see

Adult Corrections; Alcohol Abuse; Conflict Resolution; Criminal Justice: Class, Race, and Gender Issues; Criminal Justice: Social Work Roles; Domestic Violence; Drug Abuse; Female Criminal Offenders; Gang Violence; Homicide; Juvenile Corrections; Police Social Work; Poverty; Probation and Parole; Rehabilitation of Criminal Offenders; Sentencing of Criminal Offenders; Sexual Assault; Victim Services and Victim/Witness Assistance Programs; Violence Overview.

**Key Words**

arrests
criminal behavior
index crime
nonindex crime
victimization

# Criminal Justice

*See* Courts and Corrections *(Reader's Guide)*

# Criminal Justice: Class, Race, and Gender Issues

Alfreda P. Iglehart

Historically, people of color, particularly African Americans, have been overrepresented in all phases of the criminal justice system. They are more likely than other people to be stopped by police, arrested, charged, tried, convicted, sentenced, and incarcerated (Johnson & Schwartz, 1991). Indeed, African Americans in particular have been found to face different processes than white Americans at numerous stages of the criminal justice system (Farnworth & Horan, 1980). Historically, people in lower economic groups also have fared less well throughout the criminal justice system compared with people in more affluent groups (Johnson & Schwartz, 1991).

This entry probes the manner in which race and ethnicity, regionalism, gender, and social class are associated with criminal justice processing. Unless mentioned otherwise, all statistics are from the National Criminal Justice Information and Statistics Service (1992) *Sourcebook of Criminal Justice Statistics.* This entry also addresses theoretical perspectives and social work perspectives on criminal justice processing.

## Racial and Ethnic Groups and the Criminal Justice System

Although in 1991 African Americans totaled only 12 percent of the U.S. population, they represented 29 percent of all arrests; 45 percent of arrests for violent crimes (murder, rape, robbery, and aggravated assault); 31 percent of the arrests for property crimes (burglary, larceny and theft, motor vehicle theft, and arson); and 44 percent of all jail inmates. American jails are institutions of color because African Americans total from one-quarter to one-half of the jail population in all regions of the country.

In all phases of the criminal justice system, the presence and processing of people of color have received considerable attention. For example, Petersilia (1985) studied the California, Michigan, and Texas criminal justice systems and concluded that, controlling for offense committed and criminal records, African Americans and Hispanic individuals received longer minimum sentences and served more time than did white individuals. Bynum and Paternoster (1984) found that, although Native Americans did not appear to be treated differentially during sentencing, they were less likely to receive parole than non–Native Americans.

### State Systems

Ethnic minorities are overrepresented among state prison populations. For example, in 1991 46 percent of state prison inmates were African Americans and 17 percent were Hispanic Americans. The incarceration rate for African Americans and Hispanic Americans has historically been higher than that for white Americans. For example, in 1904 African Americans had a state prison incarceration rate of 268 per 100,000, Mexican Americans had a rate of 469 per 100,000, and white Americans had a rate of 187 per 100,000 (Work, 1913). In 1973 the incarceration rate was 368 per 100,000 for African Americans and 46 per 100,000 for white Americans. By 1979 the rate had risen to 544 per 100,000 for African Americans and 65 per 100,000 for white Americans (Christianson, 1981). By 1991 the state prison incarceration rate had risen to 1,081 per 100,000 for African Americans, 530 per 100,000 for Hispanic Americans, and 300 per 100,000 for white Americans.

U.S. district court decisions provide further evidence of the overrepresentation of racial and ethnic groups at various stages of processing. For example, pretrial detention hearings are often used to determine the dangerousness of a defendant and whether police should release the defendant from custody before the trial. According to U.S. Bureau of Justice Statistics (U.S. Department of Justice, 1993), detention was ordered with more than average frequency for African Americans, Hispanic Americans, and other ethnic groups during these hearings in 1990. This is not a surprising revelation. In 1978 Lizotte reported that offenders from racial and ethnic groups were twice as likely as white offenders to be incarcerated between arrest and final disposition.

### Federal Systems

In the federal prison system in 1991, 32 percent of the inmates were African Americans and 27 percent were Hispanic individuals. In 1989 African Americans represented 26 percent of all federal convictions and 27 percent of all defendants sentenced to prison. Hispanic people represented 19 percent of the defendants convicted and 22 percent of those sentenced to prison. According to U.S. Bureau of Justice Statistics (U.S. Department of Justice, 1993), Hispanic offenders are more likely to be incarcerated than non-Hispanic offenders with the same category of convictions.

The 1989 federal sentencing figures reflect the longer sentences received by African Americans compared to white Americans. African Americans received an average of 65 months in contrast to the 52 months received by white Americans. In cases involving violent offenses, African Americans received an average sentence of 98 months and white Americans, 88 months (U.S. Department of Justice, 1992a). African Americans released from federal prisons in 1990 served an average of 61 months for assault, whereas white Americans released in 1990 for the same offense served an average of 37 months (U.S. Department of Justice, 1992b). This 24-month difference in time served can be attributed to the higher percentage of African Americans (55 percent) receiving a sentence of 10 or more years in comparison with white Americans receiving the same sentence (29 percent) (U.S. Department of Justice, 1992b). For individuals released in 1990 for serving a robbery conviction, African Americans served an average of 65 months, whereas white Americans served an average of 56 months.

## Race, Ethnicity, and Regionalism

In states with a high percentage of African Americans or Hispanic Americans, these groups are significantly more likely to be in jail than are white Americans. In comparison with other regions, the South has a larger African American population and a higher percentage of African Americans in its jails. In 11 southern states, African American males outnumber white males in jail. These observations suggest that African Americans in the South are at greater risk of incarceration.

However, some states in other regions also have large African American jail populations, even though they have a smaller percentage of African Americans in the general population. In New Jersey, New York, and Illinois, African American males outnumber white males in jail. In 1988 New York had an African American population of 16 percent, but about one-half (49 percent) of its jail population was African American. A similar situation was true for Illinois, which had an African American population of 15 percent and an African American jail population of 59 percent. Thus, some non-southern states may also pose a higher risk of incarceration for African Americans.

In general, western states have lower percentages of African American populations and lower percentages of African American jail inmates. In the West, however, Hispanic people are at greater risk of incarceration. Again, this may be related to the higher percentage of Hispanic people in these states. For example, in 1988 in New Mexico 38 percent of the population was Hispanic, and more than one-half (54 percent) of the jail inmates were of this ethnic group. In Arizona, California, and Colorado, Hispanic individuals represented one-quarter to one-third of the jail populations. The extent of the minority presence in the jails seems related to the extent of the minority presence in the general population.

## Race, Ethnicity, and Gender

At the intersection of race and gender, females of color are overrepresented in the criminal justice system in comparison with their white counterparts. For example, there are 96.4 million non-Hispanic white females, 15.8 million African American females, and 10.9 million Hispanic females in the country according to the 1990 census (U.S. Bureau of the Census, 1992). However, 58 percent of all women in U.S. jails in 1988 were women of color, and 64 percent of women in state prisons in 1991 were women of color.

Women of color are also more likely to be arrested for more serious offenses than their white counterparts. For example, in 1990 in 75 of the country's largest counties, 908 African American women and 389 white women were reported to have committed violent crimes. Among violent crimes, 595 African American women and 238 white women were arrested for assault.

In 1950 Pollak summarized two major opinions on the race factor in female crime: (1) African American women had a much higher reported rate of criminality than did white women, and (2) African American women surpassed the criminality of white women to a greater degree than African American men surpassed the criminality of white men. Contemporary processing of African American women appears to further support these views.

## Education, Employment, and Crime

The relationship between offender economic level and criminal justice processing has received a great deal of attention. Do people of higher social class manage to escape the iron arm of law and punishment? In 1989, 42 percent of jail inmates had a prearrest monthly income of less than $500, 25 percent had a monthly income between $500 and $999, and 33 percent had a monthly income of $1,000 or more. In that same year, 54 percent of the male jail inmates and 50 percent of the female jail inmates had less than a high school education. Thirty-three percent of the male inmates were high school graduates, and 35 percent of the female inmates were high school graduates. Only 13 percent of the males and 15 percent of the females in jail had some college education.

Among state inmates in 1991, 41 percent did not have a high school diploma, 46 percent were high school graduates, and 13 percent had at least some college education. Also in 1991, 46 percent of the federal prisoners did not have a high school diploma, 50 percent had graduated from high school, and 4 percent had at least some college education. Clearly these figures indicate that those individuals with some college education are less likely to be incarcerated.

An overview of the federal process also reveals differential treatment according to education and employment status at time of arrest. For example, in 1990 pretrial detention hearings, unemployed or poorly educated people were more likely to be detained (U.S. Department of Justice, 1993). Furthermore, U.S. Bureau of Justice Statistics (U.S. Department of Justice, 1992a) 1989 profile of federal defendants indicated that 50 percent of those convicted had less than a high school education, 14 percent were high school graduates, 25 percent had some college education, and 11 percent were college graduates. Of those sentenced to prison in 1989, 55 percent had not graduated from high school, 14 percent were high school graduates, 22 percent had some college education, and 9 percent were college graduates. Thus, the relationship between conviction, prison, and education is evident.

College graduates, in general, received shorter sentences than those defendants with other levels of education. In 1989 the average sentence for defendants with a college degree was 42 months compared with the 57 months received by defendants without a high school education, 63 months received by high school graduates, and 53 months received by defendants with some college education. These differences disappear when the average sentence for violent offenses is compared across educational levels. In this case, college graduates who are sentenced to prison for violent offenses receive a longer average sentence compared with defendants with other levels of education.

Employed people are actually more likely to enter the criminal justice system, but unemployed people are more likely to remain in the system for a longer period. In 1989, 40 percent of federal defendants convicted and 45 percent of defendants sentenced to prison were unemployed. Although the majority of defendants at each stage were employed, longer average sentences were associated with unemployment. Unemployed people received an average sentence of 56 months compared with the 51 months for employed people. In addition, the average sentence for violent offenses was 87 months for unemployed people and 66 months for employed people.

## Perspectives on Criminal Justice Processing

Two major views have emerged to explain the overrepresentation of people of color and people in the lower social classes in the criminal justice system: (1) differential involvement of minority and poor people in the commission of crime and (2) differential processing of minority and poor people in the criminal justice system.

### Differential Involvement

Researchers have identified and used indicators of differential criminal involvement. Hindelang (1978) used victimization survey data and found that, according to victim reports, African Americans were more likely than white Americans to commit rape, robbery, and assault. In addition, Hindelang (1981) found that the highest rate of involvement in personal crimes was associated with African American males between the ages of 18 and 20 years. The California Commission on the Status of Women (1993) also used victimization data to report on women and violence in the state. These data revealed that victims reported the offender of violent crimes to be African American in 28 percent of the victimizations and in 58 percent of single-offender robberies.

Lichtenstein (1982) further noted that differential criminal involvement may also account for differences in sentences received by African Americans and white Americans. Her research showed that the harsher sentences African Americans received for drug crimes could be explained by their more frequent convictions for narcotics violations, whereas white Americans had more frequent marijuana violations.

### Differential Processing

The differential processing approach includes two explanations: (1) the labeling, or interactionist, perspective and (2) the conflict perspective (Farnworth & Horan, 1980). The *labeling perspective* emphasizes the manner in which resources assist groups and individuals in resisting the application of a deviant label. Ethnic minority group members, therefore, would be less likely to resist the application of such a label because of their overrepresentation among the lower classes and their lack of resources. Resource deficits could lead to minority group members and poor individuals having inadequate legal representation and insufficient funds for posting bail.

The *conflict perspective* is derived from the Marxian position that political and economic power is amassed by particular groups in society and, in American society, ethnic minorities and poor people are typically identified as the deprived groups (Farnworth & Horan, 1980). In this approach, the criminal justice system becomes a vehicle for the social control of minority and other deprived groups. For example, Christianson (1981) asserted that the state prison system arose in part as a replacement for slavery to control the newly freed African Americans. He further offered the example of New York, which legislated the emancipation of slaves and the establishment of its first state prison on the same day.

Christianson (1981) also cited the significant correlation between a state's racial composition and its incarceration rate as further proof of the social control function of the criminal justice system. Thus, the percentage of African Americans and Hispanic people in a state's jails may be explained by increased law enforcement and criminal justice efforts to control these populations when they begin to reach a certain percentage of the population. California's incarceration rate is the highest in the nation. According to the 1990 census, California also has a 43 percent minority group population (Usdansky, 1992). In 51 of the nation's largest cities—with a population of at least 100,000—people of color compose more than half of the population; 19 of these cities are in California (Usdansky, 1992).

### Racial and Ethnic Biases

Staples (1975) observed that political and economic oppression leads to differential access to society's resources. He further noted that those crimes associated with poverty and differential access to resources—crimes most likely to be committed by African Americans—are defined by the larger society as a significant threat, whereas those crimes likely to be committed by white Americans are not targeted for harsh punishment. Guy (1984) argued that unemployment and underemployment of African Americans resulting from inferior education gives rise to the overrepresentation of African Americans in the criminal justice system. In addition, the larger society perpetuates myths about this group that continue to reinforce violence against them. One of these myths, according to Guy, is that African Americans are genetically prone to violence.

Zatz (1987) reviewed findings from four historical waves of research on racial and ethnic bias in sentencing as one aspect of criminal justice processing. She examined the change from findings of overt discrimination to more subtle institutionalized biases. She concluded that "in part, this bias results from socially conditioned fears and prejudices that have become institutionalized in the very nature of who and what are defined as harmful; definitions that arise within a social context in which resources are unequally distributed across social groups" (p. 86). This observation is not new or surprising. The Ninth Conference for the Study of Negro Problems, held in 1904 and sponsored by Atlanta University (DuBois, 1904), identified several causes of crime among African Americans: prejudice that limited the opportunities of African Americans; less legal protection of African Americans; laws that are drawn to ensnare ignorant, unfortunate, and careless African Americans; courts that administer one type of justice for white Americans and another for African Americans; punishment that does not distinguish the young African American from the old or the male from the female; and punishment that breeds crime rather than halts it.

## Social Work Perspectives on Justice

Social work's voice in the debate on the causes of the overrepresentation of people of color in the criminal justice system has been relatively quiet. As a knowledge-use profession, social work has relied on the discipline of sociology to articulate positions on this issue. Although the debate has risen and subsided over the decades, the presence of social work researchers has generally not been felt in this body of work.

### Soft Determinism

Social work, however, does appear to espouse the middle road on the issue of the criminal justice processing of minority and disenfranchised groups. This middle road can be described as one of *soft determinism,* defined by Reamer (1983) as follows:

> There is considerable evidence that the doctrine of soft determinism is relatively prominent in the profession of social work. In general, both the profession's literature and conventional practice wisdom embrace the view that the problems under which clients labor are frequently the products of circumstances beyond their control, *to varying degrees,* and that clients themselves are at times partly responsible for their difficulties and are—again, *to varying degrees*—capable of making thoughtful, rational, and voluntary decisions to alter the course of their lives [italics added]. (p. 631)

When applied to criminal behavior and criminal justice processing, this doctrine would suggest that forces beyond as well as within the group's control contribute to minority overrepresentation in the criminal justice system.

This middle course may seem realistic in light of historical documentation of African Americans' recognition of the presence of both external and internal forces contributing to their criminality. For example, the 1904 Ninth Conference for the Study of Negro Problems identified some of the "faults" of African Americans that contributed to criminality (DuBois, 1904), including lack of thrift, substance abuse, unreliability, a tendency toward idleness and vagrancy, and waywardness. The conference also highlighted the role of prejudice and differential processing in contributing to the high rate of African American crime. It appears that the conference attempted to identify all those factors, both internal and external, contributing to African American crime.

Johnson and Schwartz (1991) mirrored the doctrine of soft determinism when they described the multiple causation theory of crime:

> Currently, crime and criminal behavior are not attributed to a single source but to a multiplicity of factors. This has been referred to as the *multiple causation theory,* which combines biological, social, psychological, economic, and environmental factors in explaining why crime and criminal behavior exist.... Social, economic, and environmental factors, including *poverty, racism,* child abuse and neglect, socialization in criminal attitudes by family or peers, lack of educational achievement, and family breakup, may also be involved [italics added]. (p. 253)

With this multiple causation theory, everything seems thrown into the equation and all bases are covered. This theory also recognizes the role of so many different factors that it is difficult to determine how and when they operate.

### Lack of Attention to Differential Processing

The profession, however, has not devoted equal time or attention to all aspects of the theory. Although Johnson and Schwartz (1991) noted several pages later that the disproportionate presence of African Americans in corrections facilities is the result of racial discrimination, the social work profession has not forcefully addressed or attacked this discrimination. The profession seems to give a passing nod to the existence of differential processing while continuing with business as usual. Thus, social work concerns itself with the "back end" of the criminal justice system—those processes occurring after individuals have moved through the system—rather than to the "front end" of the system—those processes determining who enters the system and the extent to which they penetrate it.

### Emphasis on Treatment and Rehabilitation

The treatment and rehabilitation of offenders have dominated the social work profession's interest in the criminal justice system. This focus reflects the historical dominance of direct practice over social reform and social change in the development of social work as a profession. In this development, individual responsibility came to have prominence over social reform and Freudian approaches began to be accepted as a technology for the social diagnosis of individuals (Borenzweig, 1971). In 1935 Grace Coyle wrote, "As case work has 'gone psychiatric' it has not only concentrated upon the individual, it has further centered upon his emotional life, giving decreasing attention to environmental factors social and economic" (p. 100). In addition, the environment became another avenue for advancing direct practice. Jansson (1994) observed the following:

> As Mary Richmond advocated decades earlier, emphasizing the environment encourages social workers to gather information about clients' living conditions. In this way, social workers need not try to change environmental conditions themselves, but can use conditions as aids to clinical work. (p. 20)

Thus, social work's ideology reflects a psychological orientation to social problems (Gummer, 1979). Furthermore, the way in which a problem is defined is used to help identify a solution to the problem. A psychological orientation to social problems suggests that individuals are responsible for the circumstances in which they find themselves and that interventions with individuals have priority over other types of interventions. Structural, institutional underpinnings of problems are overlooked as individuals are treated or rehabilitated. In this view, the criminal justice system, as a structural system, is then perceived as fair and just, whereas the offenders are the ones who need to be "corrected." The orientation and ideology of the profession have often been used to pinpoint the conservative nature of social work (Gil, 1990; Levin, 1982).

## Conclusion

If the criminal justice system differentially administers justice to minority and poor people, then other interventions are needed to supplement individual treatment. For example, Headley (1989) noted that "when political considerations call for more law and order and as the society increasingly shifts toward emphasis on a 'lock-'em-up-

and-throw-away-the-key' mentality" (pp. 4–5), poor African Americans and Latino Americans are the ones most likely to be incarcerated. Morris (1988) suggested that changes in the criminal justice system alone may not resolve the problem of crime because the larger social problem of a structurally isolated underclass and antiminority attitudes reflective in law and order movements must also be addressed.

In addition to the rehabilitation of offenders, social workers must engage in locality development, social action, and policy practice as methods for ensuring the equitable distribution of justice in American society. Rothman with Tropman (1987) provided definitions of these methods of practice. *Locality development* is a process through which community members actively participate in defining their goals and strategies for achieving economic and social progress. The social worker functions as a catalyst, enabler, facilitator, coordinator, or teacher of skills.

With *social action,* disadvantaged groups are organized to make demands of the larger society for needed resources and "treatment more in accordance with social justice" (Rothman with Tropman, 1987, p. 6). This method targets structures and institutions for change, including the criminal justice system, using social protest and other forms of confrontation. The social worker functions as an advocate, agitator, or negotiator. With *policy practice,* the social worker seeks to develop and implement public and social policies, including criminal justice policies, that determine how institutions of society actually operate.

The profession must also acknowledge and respect the unique histories of racial and ethnic groups as they relate to the criminal justice system. This acknowledgment and respect would cause the profession to examine its perspective on criminal justice and to examine critically how this system interfaces with racial and ethnic minority groups. For social work to espouse different roles in this arena, locality development, social action, and policy practice will have to take on larger significance in the profession. As the profession seeks to enhance its relevance in a changing society and as society becomes more diverse, direct practice may have to share the spotlight with other practice methods. When this happens, social work may rediscover its other voices and use them to influence the internal and external forces of the criminal justice system that govern the administration of justice.

## References


Borenzweig, H. (1971). Social work and psychoanalytic theory: A historical analysis. *Social Work, 16,* 7–16.

Bynum, T., & Paternoster, R. (1984). Discrimination revisited: An exploration of frontstage and backstage criminal justice decision making. *Sociology and Social Research, 69,* 90–108.

California Commission on the Status of Women. (1993). *A profile of California women: Violence.* Sacramento, CA: Author.

Christianson, S. (1981). Our black prisons. *Crime and Delinquency, 27,* 364–375.

Coyle, G. (1935). The limitations of social work in relation to social reorganization. *Social Forces, 14,* 94–102.

DuBois, W.E.B. (1904). *Some notes of Negro crime.* Atlanta: Atlanta University Press.

Farnworth, M., & Horan, P. (1980). Separate justice: An analysis of differences in court processes. *Social Science Research, 9,* 381–399.

Gil, D. (1990). Implications of conservative tendencies for practice and education in social welfare. *Journal of Sociology and Social Welfare, 17,* 5–27.

Gummer, B. (1979). On helping and helplessness: The structure of discretion in the American welfare system. *Social Service Review, 53,* 214–228.

Guy, A. (1984). Is the criminal justice system fair to minorities? *Howard Law Journal, 27,* 1115–1129.

Headley, B. (1989). Introduction: Crime, justice, and powerless racial groups. *Social Justice, 16,* 1–9.

Hindelang, M. (1978). Race and involvement in common law personal crimes. *American Sociological Review, 43,* 93–109.

Hindelang, M. (1981). Variations in sex-race-age-specific incidence rates of offending. *American Sociological Review, 46,* 461–474.

Jansson, B. (1994). *Social policy: From theory to policy practice* (2nd ed.). Pacific Grove, CA: Brooks/Cole.

Johnson, L., & Schwartz, C. (1991). *Social welfare—A response to human need* (2nd ed.). Boston: Allyn & Bacon.

Levin, H. (1982). Conservatism of social work. *Social Service Review, 56,* 605–615.

Lichtenstein, K. (1982). Extra-legal variables affecting sentencing decisions. *Psychological Reports, 50,* 611–619.

Lizotte, A. (1978). Extra-legal factors in Chicago's criminal courts: Testing the conflict model of criminal justice. *Social Problems, 25,* 564–580.

Morris, N. (1988). Race and crime: What evidence is there that race influences results in the criminal justice system? *Judicature, 72,* 111–113.

National Criminal Justice Information and Statistics Service. (1992). *Sourcebook of criminal justice statistics.* Washington, DC: U.S. Government Printing Office.

Petersilia, J. (1985). Racial disparities in the criminal justice system: A summary. *Crime and Delinquency, 31,* 15–34.

Pollak, O. (1950). *Criminality of women.* New York: Perpetua.

Reamer, F. (1983). The free will–determinism debate in social work. *Social Service Review, 57,* 626–644.

Rothman, J., with Tropman, J. (1987). Models of community organization and macro practice perspectives: Their mixing and phasing. In F. Cox, J. Erlich, J. Rothman, & J. Tropman (Eds.), *Strategies of community organization* (pp. 3–26). Itasca, IL: F. E. Peacock.

Staples, R. (1975). White racism, black crime, and American justice: An application of the colonial model to explain crime and race. *Phylon, 36,* 14–22.

U.S. Bureau of the Census. (1992). *General population characteristics: 1990 census of the population.* Washington, DC: U.S. Government Printing Office.

Usdansky, M. (1992, December 4). Minorities in majority. *USA Today,* p. 8A.

U.S. Department of Justice, Bureau of Justice Statistics. (1992a). *Compendium of federal justice statistics.* Washington, DC: U.S. Government Printing Office.

U.S. Department of Justice, Bureau of Justice Statistics. (1992b). *Federal sentencing in transition, 1986–90.* Washington, DC: U.S. Government Printing Office.

U.S. Department of Justice, Bureau of Justice Statistics. (1993). *Compendium of federal justice statistics.* Washington, DC: U.S. Government Printing Office.

Work, M. (1913). Negro criminality in the south. *Annals of the American Academy of Political and Social Science, 49,* 74–80.

Zatz, M. (1987). The changing forms of racial/ethnic biases in sentencing. *Journal of Research in Crime and Delinquency, 24,* 69–92.

## Further Reading

Bridges, G., & Crutchfield, R. (1988). Law, social standing, and racial disparities in imprisonment. *Social Forces, 66,* 699–724.

Douyon, E., & Normandeau, A. (1990). Justice and ethnic minorities: An international selective bibliography. *Canadian Journal of Criminology, 32,* 661–668.

Jackson, P. (1989). *Minority group threat, crime, and policing: Social context and social control.* New York: Praeger.

Kramer, J., & Steffensmeier, D. (1993). Race and imprisonment decisions. *Sociological Quarterly, 34,* 357–376.

McNeely, R., & Pope, C. (Eds.). (1981). *Race, crime, and criminal justice.* Newbury Park, CA: Sage Publications.

Simms, M., & Myers, S., Jr. (Eds.). (1988). *The economics of race and crime.* New Brunswick, NJ: Transaction Books.

Stern, S. (Compiler). (1988). *Discrimination in the criminal justice system, 1910–1955* (Papers of the NAACP, Part 8). Frederick, MD: University Publications of America.

Taub, R., Taylor, D., & Dunham, J. (1984). *Paths of neighborhood change: Race and crime in urban America.* Chicago: University of Chicago Press.

**Alfreda P. Iglehart, PhD,** is associate professor, University of California, Los Angeles, School of Public Policy and Social Research, Department of Social Welfare, 405 Hilgard Avenue, Los Angeles, CA 90024-1452.

### For further information see

Adult Corrections; Civil Rights; Community-Based Corrections; Criminal Behavior Overview; Criminal Justice: Social Work Roles; Domestic Violence; Family Views in Correctional Programs; Female Criminal Offenders; Homicide; Human Rights; Juvenile Corrections; Legal Issues: Low-Income and Dependent People; Police Social Work; Poverty; Probation and Parole; Rehabilitation of Criminal Offenders; Runaways and Homeless Youths; Sentencing of Criminal Offenders; Substance Abuse: Federal, State, and Local Policies; Victim Services and Victim/Witness Assistance Programs; Women Overview.

**Key Words**
classism
criminal justice
discrimination
racism
sentencing

# Criminal Justice: Social Work Roles

**Jerome G. Miller**

Until the late 1870s social work in the United States was undifferentiated from the so-called social science movement, which included economics, history, political science, statistics, and sociology. However, as these burgeoning disciplines focused on theory and research, culminating in the establishment of the American Social Science Association, those disciplines that had been involved in direct social work services moved to create an independent body that they dubbed The National Conference of Charities and Correction (Hollis & Taylor, 1951). In these early years, those who saw themselves as "social workers" were often intimately involved with the criminal justice system and with juveniles sentenced to the reform schools and youth facilities of the times.

The name of this new organization betrayed the fact that until the mid-1920s, a substantial amount of social work effort was directed at institutional "wards"—individuals confined to prisons, reform schools, state schools for the "feeble-minded," and state mental hospitals. The efforts of social workers relative to delinquents were predominantly directed at moving them from almshouses to appropriate institutional care (Hollis & Taylor, 1951).

In the early years of the 20th century, social work was largely grounded in the social traditions of the time—that is, sustaining and running a system of institutions reserved mostly for the socialization or exile of indigent individuals and those viewed as socially deviant, usually immigrants and black Americans. However, as social workers took on the mantle of professionalism in the 1920s and 1930s, they moved away from many of their earlier ties to these institutions.

As Willard (1925) summarized matters,

> Social work no longer attends chiefly to the confinement and management of state wards, but derives its

> problems from community processes far beyond state institutions.... On account of the necessary reference to social ends involved in social work thus broadly conceived, those ends must be fixed through appreciation of the social processes themselves in any state, and their merits defined in terms of social values. (pp. 55–56)

The changes that occurred in the field were dramatically illustrated in the themes around which social workers organized their national conferences. Following is the nine-item agenda for the 1893 National Conference of Charities and Correction (Rush, 1978):

1. State Boards of Charities
2. Charity Organizations
3. Indoor and Outdoor Relief
4. Immigration
5. Child-Saving
6. Reformatories
7. The Prison Question
8. The Feeble-Minded
9. The Insane. (p. 42)

Over the subsequent three decades, there was a marked shift away from work with captive and quasicaptive populations. With professionalization, the rehabilitative ethic soon took root in American social work practice, bolstered initially by Freudian and Rankian psychiatric theory and later absorbing elements of ego psychology and behaviorist clinical psychology. The National Conference of Charities and Corrections became the National Conference of Social Work. As the following 12-item agenda for the 1928 National Conference of Social Work indicated, social workers were leaving institutional management concerns to take up such new matters as adequate family support systems, the provision of casework services, community organizations, and policy formulation (Rush, 1978):

1. Children
2. Delinquents and Correction
3. Health
4. The Family
5. Industrial and Economic Problems
6. Neighborhood and Community Life
7. Mental Hygiene
8. Organization of Social Forces
9. Public Officials and Administration
10. The Immigrant
11. Professional Standards in Education
12. Educational Publicity. (p. 43)

## Establishment of the Juvenile Court

In the early years of the emerging profession, social workers such as Jane Addams, Sophonisba Breckenridge, Louise Bowen, and Amelia Sears were especially crucial to juvenile justice reform, particularly in helping establish the juvenile court, a development that had implications well beyond the simple matter of technique or social work practice. Indeed, the American psychologist and social theorist George Herbert Mead found something quite grand in the conception of the juvenile court, which contained within it the potential to challenge the basic principles around which society had organized itself. Mead saw the juvenile court as potentially ushering in a new stage in the evolution of American society, a process which had begun centuries earlier when the criminal court replaced tribal blood vengeance. Through the establishment of criminal courts, tribal societies were stopped from killing each other, although the criminal courts nevertheless retained the need to see vengeance enacted. The major problem became that of fitting the punishment of the crime. According to Mead (1964), this approach was doomed to failure. As he put it, the court

> becomes established, acquires a dogmatic structure, holds on to motives which belonged to the earlier situation. But finally we see the situation as one in which we try to do with self-consciousness what took place by a process of evolution. That is, we try to state the problem with reference to a particular child.... the juvenile court represents a self-conscious application of the very process of evolution out of which the courts themselves arose. (p. 30)

With the invention of the juvenile court, Mead saw societies as becoming less prone to organize themselves around hostility, turning instead to the more productive tasks of identifying and addressing those personal, familial, and social factors that have since been called the "root causes" of antisocial behavior. Ideally, with its emphasis on problem solving rather than punishing, the juvenile court would help society redefine the very elements around which it had organized itself, with less need to find social cohesion in mutual hostility toward outsiders.

Indeed, the juvenile court had the potential to undo the basic premises of the criminal justice procedure itself. As recently as 1950, the eminent Harvard Law School professor Roscoe Pound remarked that the creation of the juvenile court was as potentially great an event in the history of western jurisprudence as the signing of the Magna Carta. By allowing into the legal arena consideration of such things as social histories, individual differences, sociological studies, and environmental considerations and economic factors, the newly established juvenile court had opened the door to all the gray, hazy, nondichotomous, and difficult considerations that characterize human motivation and behavior and that had been mostly ruled out in formal adult criminal justice procedure.

The task, then, would be less that of identifying the criminal "enemy" than of carefully evaluating the social and personal correlates and contributions in each individual case of delinquency, with an eye as much toward solving these problems as toward seeking retribution. Unlike any other court in history, the juvenile court would have a decidedly social work emphasis, encouraging sophisticated study of the young offender to formulate a treatment plan and providing an educative function for society as a whole as it addressed human social problems.

## Role of Social Workers in Juvenile Justice

Mead saw the social worker in the court as central to this socially evolutionary task. For example, introducing the narrative "social history" into the court would challenge the precisely defined categories called for by the strict formalities of the criminal justice process. Comparing the lawyer with the social worker in a court setting, Mead (1917) wrote, "The social worker in the court is the sentimentalist, (but) the legalist in the social settlement in spite of his learned doctrine is the ignoramus" (p. 592).

### Reform Issues

Unfortunately, the social reformers who created the juvenile court, the social workers who staffed it, and the juvenile judges who directed it did not appear to grasp the broad vision for societal reform that lay dormant in their work. By the 1960s the juvenile courts had fallen to mimicking the worst of the adult criminal courts while providing few of the civil rights guarantees of the adult criminal justice procedure—in effect, denying youthful defendants legal protection while sending them off to "treatment" regimens and institutions that were as onerous as any adult correctional facility. This was reflected in the U.S. Supreme Court decision *In re Gault,* which established the rights of juveniles to due process (with legal representation). The Court concluded that many of the rehabilitative programs (for example, reform schools) were in fact punitive and nonrehabilitative. Why did this happen? Unfortunately, as Platt discovered, much of the responsibility must be laid at the foot of "helpers" who staffed the juvenile courts and were often supervised by professional social workers (Platt, 1969).

Historically, because a large percentage of the clients of social workers had been in some sense captive, there had always been a seductive tendency to justify coercion in social work practice. Indeed, coercion appears at times to be a natural process that afflicts helping professionals no matter what the setting. This was best described by Trilling (1978) when he wrote, "Some paradox in our nature leads us, once we have made our fellow men the objects of our enlightened interest, to go on to make them the objects of our pity, then of our wisdom, ultimately of our coercion" (p. 124).

Trilling's warning went to the heart of the ambiguity that has plagued professional social work practice in criminal justice and juvenile justice settings from the beginning. Indeed, former University of Chicago School of Social Service Administration Field Supervisor Charlotte Towle was reputed to have occasionally expressed her concern over whether professional social workers should associate themselves at all with the juvenile or adult criminal justice systems (personal communication, 1957).

### Representation

This matter of the use of authority by professional social workers became an increasingly crucial one. Although those who identified themselves as social workers continued to work in "authoritative" settings (that is, court and correctional practice), the percentage of professionally trained social workers diminished. A 1951 survey of social work practitioners revealed that about 12 percent were engaged in work with some element of the justice system—juvenile or adult probation, parole, or the courts. However, only 2.6 percent of those most likely to identify themselves as professionals (that is, belonging to the American Association of Social Workers) worked in criminal justice, juvenile justice, or correctional programs (Hollis & Taylor, 1951). Some attributed this poor representation of social workers in the justice arena to ambivalence in the profession regarding issues of authority:

> The field of delinquency and crime, particularly in regard to probation and parole work and work with the courts has not attracted social workers as practitioners or researchers to any significant degree. In part, the explanation appears to have been in a belief which some held that social work could not be practiced in an authoritarian setting. There are signs that this position is undergoing a change, and that social work will again come to play a large role in one of its traditional areas of activity. (Hollis & Taylor, 1951, p. 149)

However, these predictions turned out to be incorrect. Gibelman & Schervish (1993) found that of 87,265 NASW members surveyed in 1991, only 1,025 (1.2 percent) were working in the justice area. Of the 37,222 respondents who listed a "secondary" practice area (usually part-time), 500 (1.3 percent) were engaged in work in the justice area. This finding suggests that the percentage of professional social workers in the formal adult or juvenile justice systems has declined since the 1980s. Based on my observations in the field, it is my impression that there are relatively few social workers in corrections who have been trained as such. Instead, the workers tend to have a college degree with occasional graduate courses in counseling. The master's level professional social workers are slightly more numerous in the juvenile justice system, where they tend to be in administrative positions.

## Changes in Philosophy

### Problem Solving and Empowerment

Because juvenile justice and adult criminal justice agencies usually hire a limited number of professional staff (psychiatrists, psychologists, and social workers), most professional social workers tend to be used as managers, supervisors, and clinicians. The principles and ethics that motivate and direct social workers in justice settings theoretically should differ little from those used in social work practice with troubled individuals in a variety of other noncoercive settings. As Kahn (1958) wrote,

> Social work methods aim to strengthen individuals and groups so that they can make their own choices. The caseworker does not press upon the client a particular solution to the client's problem. His aim is to help the client make a free choice within the realm of possible alternatives. He seeks to create ability within the client to solve his own problems.
>
> To say that the practitioner of these social work methods does not aim to superimpose his judgments does not, of course, mean that he has no opinions or that he never expresses them. It means that his major emphasis and goal are to increase the inner-directedness of the individual, group, or community. Nor does the failure of the practitioner to superimpose judgment mean that he is a party to any direction defined by those with whom he works. The community organizer would not ardently advocate a specific solution to juvenile delinquency, but neither would he serve a group of individuals concerned with stimulating delinquency. Social work methods are always allied with the goals and values of the profession. (p. 14)

### Increasing Conservatism and Decline in Principles

As American society in the 1990s has grown more conservative on matters of crime and punishment, many social work professionals in justice appear to have fallen in step with prevailing ideology. In the process, those basic principles that at one time were seen as integral to professional social work practice have quietly slipped away. Principles such as individualization, nonjudgmental attitude, confidentiality, and client self-determination that once defined the casework relationship (Biestek, 1957) are currently out of touch with contemporary professional social work as practiced in most criminal justice and juvenile justice settings. The effects are not inconsequential. For example, approximately 48,000 of the 120,000 inmates in California's state prisons in 1994 had been put there by their "helpers"—that is, probation officers largely supervised and managed by professional social workers. These inmates were imprisoned for "technically violating" the conditions of their help—for example, missing appointments, not attending Alcoholics Anonymous meetings, being unemployed, moving or marrying without permission, failing a urine test, and a host of similar reasons.

### Probation and Parole Issues

Between 1977 and 1991 the percentage of individuals returned to prison as technical violators of conditions of probation or parole more than doubled, from 14.5 percent to 30.5 percent of all prison admissions (U.S. Department of Justice, 1991). For the most part these individuals had not engaged in illegal behavior sufficient to warrant an arrest or criminal charge, but instead had aggravated their helpers. Furthermore, a study of more than 7,000 persons terminated from probation—a fourth of whom had violated conditions of their probation—revealed that applying the most severe sanctions (that is, return to prison) "was no more likely to affect the seriousness of chronic violators' subsequent misbehaviors than application of more lenient ones" (Clear, Harris, & Baird, 1992, p. 1).

These developments have brought a change in the philosophy of probation and parole since 1980. Probation was invented by a Boston shoemaker as an alternative to jail, prison, or reform school. The role of probation officers in the early juvenile courts (and, later, in adult courts) was to propose, find, and advocate employment, treatment, and educational alternatives for offenders to keep offenders functioning within the law and to keep families together. There are many indications that this philosophy no longer prevails.

Currently probation officers in most states and virtually all federal jurisdictions sit with the prosecution at sentencing and are seen as an arm of the state, readily arguing for incarceration or institutionalization. Indeed, Andrew Rutherford (1994), the head of a British correction reform group, the John Howard Society, has referred to the U.S. probation system as "attack probation" in which "helping professionals" provide clinical validity to a criminal justice system that appears to be inspired by a melange of political considerations.

## Impact of Disease Models on Criminal Justice

The dramatic turn in the field of psychiatry toward organic conceptions of behavior and away from developmental, family, and societal concerns has compounded the problem of authoritarian approaches. The disease models advanced in contemporary psychiatry relative to juveniles and adults who break the law have had a particularly devastating impact on social work practice. The social history, which had hitherto been a mainstay of professional social work practice, has deteriorated in content and sophistication. Traditional social work conceptions of the causes and treatment of delinquents have been too quickly and easily replaced by the static conceptions of the medical profession (for example, the *Diagnostic and Statistical Manual of Mental Disorders* [DSM]).

### Labeling

As a result, many social workers in justice settings have fallen in line with diagnostic approaches and treatment philosophies that ignore or gloss over developmental stages, family interactions, and personal history. This situation has frequently been a prescription for social disaster. For example, in 1984 Harvard law professor and psychiatrist Alan Stone warned his profession about the "invidious aspect" implicit in the diagnosis of the so-called sociopath as defined by the third edition of the DSM (DSM-III) of the American Psychiatric Association (APA, 1980). He suggested that the wide-ranging criteria for this label, which includes truancy, delinquency, running away from home, theft, vandalism, poor grades, and repeated sexual intercourse in a casual relationship, could be applied to a large percentage of inner-city black males. As Stone pointed out, "The existence of only three of these factors (before age 15) is sufficient to establish the disorder in this age group [according to the DSM-III]." If a male older than 18 is unemployed, is defined as not being a responsible parent, refuses to accept social norms, fails to maintain attachments to a sexual partner, fails to meet financial obligations, does not plan ahead, or shows a disregard for the truth or exhibits "recklessness," he is diagnosed as a sociopath. As Stone concluded, "whatever scientific value the diagnosis of sociopath may have, there can be little question that the urban poor and racial minorities will be swept into this diagnostic category." He then added, "... the DSM-III may well introduce ... racism." The problem appears to have been compounded in the fourth edition of the DSM in which "repeatedly performing acts that are grounds for arrest," "failure to plan ahead," "use of aliases," and "failure to sustain consistent work behavior" are added to the list. With recent studies showing that 70 percent of African American males can anticipate being arrested by age 35 (Miller, 1993; Tillman, 1987) and with unemployment rampant, it would not be difficult to acquire the "antisocial personality" label.

### Life-or-Death Consequences

However, these approaches appear to be increasingly enshrined in social work education and practice. It is not a small matter. These kinds of differences in diagnostic approaches carry life-or-death implications for certain clients. For example, a diagnosis of "sociopath" or "antisocial personality" in Texas is an aggravating factor that must be weighed by the jury in deciding whether a murder defendant deserves the death penalty. Indeed, a friendly middle-aged white Texas physician earned himself the title "Dr. Death" for his ability to convince juries that certain defendants diagnosed as incorrigible sociopaths may be considered incurable and therefore suitable for execution. On occasion, he rendered his diagnosis without ever having met or interviewed the accused—relying instead on observing the defendant's demeanor in the courtroom during the trial.

## Current Trends

Because many social workers have succumbed to a philosophy rooted in the justice system, those who work in justice settings have increasingly come to see themselves as covert agents of law enforcement. A large segment of helping professionals currently view themselves as benign agents of a criminal justice endeavor.

### Authoritarian Philosophies and Practices

These unanticipated consequences of tying help to the authority of the justice system have made eminently sensible the advice of civil libertarian Ira Glasser (1978), who recommended that clients treat their helpers—psychologists, counselors, or social workers—as they would a policeman: with respect and civility, but saying nothing, because anything they say can and will be used against them.

In the world of contemporary American juvenile and criminal justice, professional social workers are expected to deliver one basic commodity—what the British social anthropologist Sir Edmund Leach (1967) called "treatment" when applied to delinquents: "the imposition of discipline by force—the maintenance of the existing order against threats which might arise from its own internal contradictions" (p. 134).

The hostile philosophy that this system engenders and the dichotomous categories into which it sorts complex human behavior has affected other elements of social work practice as well. As a result, the clear distinction between social workers who work in "justice" settings and those in other areas of endeavor is no longer easily made. Although the percentage of social workers who work for courts, prisons, reform schools, detention centers, or probation and parole agencies is falling, it appears that a much larger segment of the profession has come to implicitly adopt the authoritarian philosophy and practices of the justice system. The implications for the profession are ominous.

For example, some child protective workers are indistinguishable from police investigators. Child protective services have so much accepted the criminal justice model that they have come to embody what some have called family dismemberment services. With shrinking budgets for family support programs, abused children are removed from families and sent into the labyrinth of state-supervised foster care and institutionalization while family "perpetrators" are sent off to prison, with no outcome evidence that it does anyone much good.

**Increasing Use of Institutions**

Currently less is heard about the need for family support services and alternatives to long-term institutionalization. Instead, many call for the return of the orphanage on the basis that the underfunded foster care system has failed children. If $150 to $250 per day (the cost of most contemporary childrens' institutions) were spent on temporary foster care or support services for the natural or extended family, the system would probably work fairly well. However, in the wake of such retributive attitudes in the profession, family members are more subject to being prosecuted and children "placed." The search is for a "perpetrator"—someone who can be identified, labeled, punished, and exiled. Such is the quality of "help" for those who wander into the criminal justice and, increasingly, the juvenile justice systems.

It is my opinion, based on 35 years in the field, that national anticrime policy in the 1980s and 1990s developed into a simple axiom: "If you can't understand it, threaten it. If you can't make it go away, jail it." Formal justice procedure has become the *deus ex machina*—that is, the easy solution to problems too daunting to consider seriously.

William Dickey (1992), a University of Wisconsin law professor and former Wisconsin Director of Corrections, has summarized the problem succinctly:

> Parole board members, parole agents, and prison social workers read the newspapers. They do not see anything but "get tough" proclaimed there and see the same thing in the policy statements and actions of political leaders. They have no desire to be "on front street" when the system misfires, as it inevitably must in the complex world of corrections. The messages from leaders and the public are clear: When in doubt, do not grant parole; when in doubt, revoke parole; when in doubt, do not approve a person's furlough or other off-grounds leave. One way these messages are translated within the bureaucracies is, above all, to make sure all the procedures are followed to avoid "blame" for system misfires. *As a result, there is now a bureaucratic culture that reinforces in the world of unwritten rules the same culture that is reflected in the press, in politics, and in academic writing* [italics added]. (p. 43)

The justice system has provided social work a false reassurance that it can solve the problems with difficult individuals, families, and situations; if social work accepts the falsehood, the result can only be professional incompetence.

Some criminologists predict that, if state legislatures follow, the current federal anticrime legislation will result in the imprisonment of 4 to 6 million individuals, most of them members of racial and ethnic groups, by the end of the 1990s. The United States, in the words of Norwegian criminologist Nils Christie (1993, p. 163), will then have become a "gulag society," primarily for young minority males.

## Conclusion

Earlier in the 20th century, before social work was a profession, social workers attempted to bring thought, hope, and a promise of progress to one element of criminal justice: the handling of juveniles. In the 1990s, the moral and ethical strength those early social workers demonstrated is needed more than ever before, as we have witnessed the replacement of the social safety net with the drag-net and as the country is on the verge of incarcerating the absolute majority of the nation's young males of color at some point in their lives. Social work must offer more than the prospect of better management—it must advocate strongly for fundamental change.

## References


American Psychiatric Association. (1980). *Diagnostic and statistical manual of mental disorders* (3rd ed.). Washington, DC: Author.

American Psychiatric Association. (1994). *Diagnostic and statistical manual of mental disorders* (4th ed.). Washington, DC: Author.

Biestek, F. P. (1957). *The casework relationship.* London: Unwin Books.

Christie, N. (1993). *Crime control as industry*. London: Routledge & Kegan Paul.

Clear, T. R., Harris, P. M., & Baird, S. C. (1992). Probationer violations and officer response. *Journal of Criminal Justice, 20,* 1.

Dickey, W. (1992). Reflections of a former corrections director: Are offenders tougher today? *Federal Probation, 56*(2), 43.

Gibelman, M., & Schervish, P. H. (1993). *Who we are: The social work labor force as reflected in NASW membership*. Washington, DC: NASW Press.

Glasser, I. (1978). Prisoners of benevolence: Power versus liberty in the welfare state. In W. Gaylin, I. Glasser, S. Marcus, & D. Rothman (Eds.), *Doing good: The limits of benevolence*. New York: Pantheon Books.

Hollis, E., & Taylor, A. (1951). An expanded role for social work. In E. Hollis & A. Taylor (Eds.), *Social work education in the United States: The report of a study made for the National Council on Social Work Education*. New York: Columbia University Press.

In re Gault, 387 U.S. I, 18 L. Ed. 2d 527, 87 S. Ct. 1428 (1967).

Irwin, J., & Ruslin, J. (1993). *It's about time: America's imprisonment binge.* Belmont, CA: Wadsworth.

Kahn, A. J. (1958). The untried weapon against delinquency. *Federal Probation, 22*(3), 14.

Leach, E. (1967). *A runaway world: The BBC Reith Lectures.* London: British Broadcasting Company.

Mead, G. H. (1917). The psychology of punitive justice. *The American Journal of Sociology, 23,* 577–602.

Mead, G. H. (1964). The problem of society: How we become selves. In G. H. Mead (Ed.), *George Herbert Mead: On social psychology*. Chicago: University of Chicago Press. (Original work published 1934)

Miller, J. (1993). *Duval County jail report* (Report to Federal Court of Middle District of Florida). Alexandria, VA: NCIA.

Platt, A. M. (1969). *The child savers: The invention of delinquency.* Chicago: University of Chicago Press.

Pound, R. (1950). Address to annual meeting of the National Council of Juvenile Court Judges.

Rush, F. M., Jr. (1978). *Social and historical factors in the development of total institutions: Their relevance for the discipline of public administration*. Unpublished manuscript, George Washington University.

Rutherford, A. (1994, March). *Probation practice in the United Kingdom and the U.S.: Cross-cultural trends.* Presentation at the National Center on Institutions and Alternatives, Washington, DC.

Stone, A. A. (1984). *Law, psychiatry and morality: Essays and analysis.* Washington, DC: American Psychiatric Press.

Tillman, R. (1987). The size of the "criminal population": The prevalence and incidence of adult arrest. *Criminology, 25,* 561.

Trilling, L. (1978). Prisoners of benevolence: Power versus liberty in the welfare state. In W. Gaylin, I. Glasser, S. Marcus, & D. Rothman (Eds.), *Doing good: The limits of benevolence.* New York: Pantheon Books.

U.S. Department of Justice. (1991). *Correctional populations in the United States* (NCJ-142729). Washington, DC: Author.

Willard, D. (1925). Form, function, and objectives. In H. W. Odum & D. Willard (Eds.), *Systems of public welfare*. Chapel Hill: University of North Carolina Press.


## Further Reading


Christie, N. (1993). *Crime control as industry.* London: Routledge & Kegan Paul.

Erikson, K. (1966). *Wayward puritans.* New York: John Wiley & Sons.

Konopka, G. (1988). *Courage and love.* Edina, MN: Burgess.

Miller, J. G. (1991). *Last one over the wall: The Massachusetts experiment in closing reform schools.* Columbus: Ohio State University Press.

Rutherford, A. (1993). *Criminal justice and the pursuit of decency.* Oxford, England: Oxford University Press.

Schwartz, I. (1989). *(In)justice for juveniles: Rethinking the best interests of the child.* Lexington, MA: Lexington Books.


**Jerome G. Miller, DSW,** is president, National Center on Institutions and Alternatives, 635 Slaters Lane, Alexandria, VA 22314.

### For further information see

Adult Corrections; Advocacy; Child Abuse and Neglect; Child Foster Care; Child Welfare Services; Civil Rights; Community Needs Assessment; Criminal Behavior Overview; Domestic Violence; Families Overview; Gang Violence; Homelessness; Homicide; Juvenile Corrections; Peace and Social Justice; Runaways and Homeless Youths; Social Justice in Social Agencies; Social Welfare Policy; Social Work Practice; Social Work Profession Overview; Substance Abuse: Legal Issues.

**Key Words**

corrections
criminal justice
juvenile justice

READER'S GUIDE

**Crisis Intervention**

*The following entries contain information on this general topic:*

Brief Task-Centered Practice
Brief Therapies
Crisis Intervention: Research Needs
Managed Care

# Crisis Intervention: Research Needs

**Kathleen Ell**

Crisis intervention theory has grown out of concern for people who experience temporary feelings of severe acute distress and of being overwhelmed or unable to cope with developmental life transitions and major stressful events. Immediate psychological aid, or crisis intervention, is viewed as the best way to prevent more serious psychological breakdown after acute distress. Grounded in the seminal work of Lindemann (1944) on acute grief reactions and the preventive psychiatry research program of Caplan (1964) and colleagues (Parad, 1971; Parad & Parad, 1990), crisis intervention theory and practice grew rapidly during the 1950s and 1960s.

Caplan's research (1964, 1974) emphasized the critical role of environmental resources (particularly the community services system) in crisis resolution and subsequent adaptation; however, the early development of crisis intervention theory emphasized individual- and family-focused clinical approaches (Parad, 1971). Current practice suggests a need for further development of crisis intervention theory as it applies to the social–structural and social systems dimensions of human crises.

Crisis intervention will continue to be a primary mode of psychosocial intervention, particularly in light of ongoing economic constraints on human services systems coupled with increased demands by policymakers for systematically obtained cost-effectiveness outcome data. For example, crisis intervention and other brief psychosocial interventions are likely to be included in emerging managed care and comprehensive health care services packages, particularly if they are found to be both effective and cost-effective. The need also exists to help people whose crises arise within the context of severe and chronic environmental stress. Providing appropriate interventions for people undergoing severe distress is part of everyday practice for most practitioners.

## Psychological Conceptualizations of Crisis

Because crisis theory is based primarily on a synthesis of ego and cognitive psychology and individual stress theories, attention has been focused on the explication of crisis theory as it pertains to the emotional life of individuals. From this psychological perspective, the theory is based on seven primary assumptions (Golan, 1987; Slaikeu, 1990):

1. It is not uncommon for individuals to experience a state of acute emotional disequilibrium and social disorganization in the presence of immediate situational stress or hazardous life events.
2. Acute situational distress is a normative life experience, an upset in a normally steady emotional state that is not pathological, can happen to anyone, and indeed is likely to happen to most if not all people at some time in their lives. Some life events will be universally devastating, whereas others will trigger a crisis depending on the meaning of the event within the overall context of the person's life.
3. Individuals undergoing emotional disequilibrium inherently strive to regain emotional balance within their lives.
4. While struggling to regain emotional equilibrium, the individual is in an intense, time-limited state of psychological vulnerability.

5. During this heightened state of vulnerability, the individual is amenable to psychological intervention.
6. The ensuing emotional response can be characterized by universally common stages of crisis reaction that all individuals experience, regardless of the nature of the precipitating event.
7. Crises afford the opportunity for growth and development, as well as for negative outcomes.

Arguing that acute psychological upsets were frequently triggered by external events, early formulators of crisis theory moved beyond the psychoanalytic tradition that addressed human crisis as solely an intrapsychic experience (Hobfoll, 1988). As a result, ongoing explication of the theory has emphasized the characteristics of the precipitant external events, the psychological crisis, and the coping tasks involved in individuals' resolution of and adaptation to the crisis.

## Precipitant Events

From its inception, crisis theory has attempted to delineate and categorize life events that are likely to precipitate a state of crisis (Baldwin, 1978; Slaikeu, 1990). These efforts have resulted in distinguishing acute situational events, such as serious illness or trauma, death of a loved one, natural and manmade disasters (for example, fire, flood, war), and violent crimes (rape, mugging) from developmental and transitional precipitating events, such as passage from one developmental life stage to another (for example, adolescence, marriage, divorce, parenthood, retirement). The social work and psychological literature includes descriptions of a broad range of precipitating events, thereby attesting to the ubiquitous nature of human stress experience (Lukton, 1982).

## Crisis State

Characterization of the crisis state has been a second primary focus of the literature. Efforts at characterization have resulted in strikingly similar descriptions. A state of crisis is commonly described as a severe emotional upset, frequently accompanied by feelings of confusion, anxiety, depression, anger, and disorganization in usual relationships and social functioning (Halpern, 1973; Parad & Parad, 1990). Individuals in crisis experience heightened psychological vulnerability, reduced defensiveness, and a severe breakdown in coping and problem-solving ability (Slaikeu, 1990). The acute crisis state is generally thought to be time limited, although more-recent research indicates that the duration, originally thought to be six to eight weeks, can be considerably longer and is likely to vary depending on the nature of the precipitating event and the life circumstances of the individual or family (Slaikeu, 1990).

## Resolution and Adaptation

The crisis literature also describes similar sequelae of crises, frequently characterized as phases or stages from the acute onset of the crisis state through its eventual resolution and adaptation. Developmental and coping tasks specific to the precipitant event are delineated (Lukton, 1982). The outcome includes a reduction in the intensity of the psychological upset and a renewed state of emotional equilibrium over a relatively short time. The hallmark of crisis theory is its emphasis that crises have inherent potential to enhance people's ability to cope with events (resulting in emotional growth and positive adaptation), as well as opportunity (through intervention) to reduce the risk that a negative psychological outcome or poor social adaptation will follow a crisis (Danish & D'Augelli, 1980; Golan, 1987; Parad & Parad, 1990). This element of the theory calls for both primary and secondary prevention (Slaikeu, 1990).

## Psychologically Focused Crisis Intervention Practice

### Historical Perspective

The early crisis intervention literature was characterized by extensive conceptual, definitional, and practice debates that attempted to answer the following questions (Parad & Parad, 1990):

- What constitutes a crisis (as distinct from life stress)?
- What is a time-limited crisis?
- What are the unique components of crisis intervention?
- What distinguishes crisis intervention from other forms of brief treatment?
- Is crisis intervention a legitimate practice approach or a poor substitute for more effective, longer-term approaches?
- Who is qualified to provide crisis intervention services?

Since the early 1980s, however, there has been less evidence of the stimulating intellectual climate that characterized the early explication of the theory. Instead, the literature indicates that remarkably similar practice principles have been developed to help a broad range of people experiencing distress and that these principles have been widely accepted and applied.

A burgeoning application of crisis principles and theory in practice has been spurred by cost concerns and declining mental health and social services resources, which have resulted in increased attempts to provide psychosocial services through brief interventions (Parad & Parad, 1990). Reference to the application of crisis theory is so frequent within the social work practice literature that it is often difficult to distinguish the unique components of crisis intervention from those of other social work interventions.

Psychologically focused crisis intervention is distinguished from other forms of psychologically focused brief treatments in the extent to which the intervention focuses on individual or family coping breakdown in the presence of a distinguishable precipitant event. The distinction between crisis intervention and other interventions for individuals experiencing chronic stressors and inadequate environmental resources has received less attention in the literature. In general, crisis intervention focuses on the emotional components of the crisis, whereas other interventions target the environmental resource components.

Consistent with crisis intervention's strong practice roots, an extensive literature delineates its practice principles and applications across a broad spectrum of human services agencies (Golan, 1978, 1987; Parad & Parad, 1990; VandenBos & Bryant, 1987). These practice guidelines generally are targeted for specific popu[illegible]tions (Smith, 1978, 1979) and include specific phases, strategies, and techniques (Golan, 19[illegible]). Crisis intervention incorporates a range of therapies, including psychodynamic, behavioral, cognitive–behavioral, supportive, and family therapies. Practice guidelines have also been formulated for other professionals who are likely to encounter people in crisis (for example, the clergy, lawyers, police, teachers, and nurses) (Hendricks, 1991; Slaikeu, 1990).

The early development of crisis theory and practice was well grounded in basic and applied research (Lindemann, 1944; Parad & Parad, 1990). During the 1970s crisis intervention program evaluations provided evidence of the utility of this approach as well as of other short-term therapies (Parad & Parad, 1990). However, the 1980s produced only a few methodologically rigorous studies of the efficacy of different types of crisis intervention (Slaikeu, 1990).

**Need for Outcome Research**

The need for studies of the effectiveness of crisis intervention in relation to its costs is underscored in current deliberations on what mental health services will be provided by health care and other service systems. Comparative outcome studies using different crisis intervention methodologies are needed (Eggert, Friedman, & Zimmer, 1990; Nelson, Landsman, & Deutelbaum, 1990), along with other research to address critical questions as to what type of crisis intervention (for example, individually focused, family based, or environmentally targeted) is most effective for which groups of clients experiencing which types of crises. Both the short- and the long-term effects of crisis intervention must be examined (Viney, Clarke, Bunn, & Benjamin, 1985).

Outcome research is also needed to advance the scientific knowledge base for crisis intervention practice with socioculturally diverse populations (Bromley, 1987; Weiss & Parish, 1989). It is imperative that studies of effectiveness be conducted in light of research indicating that crisis intervention may not be effective in all cases. For example, it is not known whether crisis intervention in family preservation programs is effective with families under extreme chronic environmental stress (Rossi, 1992). Adverse effects on outcomes among men were found when gender was not considered in the design of the crisis intervention (Viney, Benjamin, Clarke, & Bunn, 1985). Furthermore, even when under presumed severe stress, such as when facing life-threatening illness, people of color and those with lower socioeconomic status are less likely to participate in crisis support groups (Taylor, Folkes, Mazel, & Hilsberg, 1988).

The following questions require a program of practice research:

- For whom is psychologically focused crisis intervention effective, and under what circumstances is this approach ineffective?
- Under what circumstances is family-focused intervention effective?
- Under what circumstances are multimodal and multitargeted interventions effective?
- For whom is group crisis intervention the method of choice?
- What is the cost of crisis intervention versus its benefits, and what costs are associated with failure to provide intervention?
- What assessment tools and taxonomies are needed to better assess the environmental dimensions of severe human distress and explicate appropriate practice guidelines?
- Do practice principles of crisis intervention theory need revision with respect to the ecological dimensions of human crises? For example, how might practice guidelines vary with respect to environmental issues?

- In what ways should crisis intervention be tailored with respect to gender, age, socioeconomic status, and racial/ethnic status?
- In what ways should crisis intervention be adapted for use with clients who live in impoverished, crime-ridden communities with inadequate human services systems?

## Ecological Dimensions of Crisis Practice and Theory

Since the 1970s the quality of social environments has been severely eroded for a rapidly growing portion of the U.S. population. Principally as a result of poverty, the lives of increasing numbers of children and adults are characterized by poor physical and mental health; community and family violence; repeated exposure to class, racial, and ethnic discrimination; and increasing weaknesses and deficiencies in social and human services systems (including child welfare, education, health and mental health, and the justice system) (Mirowski & Ross, 1989; National Research Council, 1993).

A review of the practice literature since the mid-1980s attests to the continued widespread clinical application of psychologically focused crisis intervention theory in practice with individuals and families. However, when social workers encounter people in crisis whose lives are characterized by chronically stressful environments, they must provide interventions that target the socioenvironmental context surrounding individual crises.

## Current Practice: Focus on the Environment

The degree to which environmental factors are the target of crisis intervention is based on an assessment of the available environmental resources. At one end of the environmental resource continuum are people with readily accessible social and community services resources. For these individuals, psychologically focused intervention that supports intrapersonal resources and helps individuals activate external resources remains the intervention of choice. Environmentally focused interventions are used increasingly to address interpersonal components of the crisis and to enhance social support to meet the crisis (Maguire, 1991). Support groups consisting of people undergoing similar crises are widely used across practice settings (Gambe & Getzel, 1989; Gilbar, 1991; Haran, 1988; Northen, 1989; Schopler & Galinsky, 1993), and practice to enhance the support available to families undergoing crises is increasing (Gutstein, 1987; Halpern, 1986; Holmes-Garrett, 1989; Kilpatrick & Pippin, 1987; McPeak, 1989; Silverman, 1986; Taylor, 1986; Van Hook, 1987).

At the other end of the environmental resource continuum are individuals and families whose crises arise within a social context characterized by severely impaired or nonexistent environmental coping resources. For example, an individual or family crisis may emerge as a result of a severe breakdown in the social environment; this includes crises precipitated by repeated domestic and neighborhood violence, homelessness, and chronic unemployment. Similarly, "normative" crises arise for people whose daily lives are characterized by poverty, exposure to discrimination, impaired physical and mental health, and inadequate community services systems.

In these circumstances, clinically focused crisis intervention is provided as only one component within multimodal and multitargeted service models for individuals, families, groups, and communities (Hunner, 1986; Paschal & Schwahn, 1986; Reece, 1986). Multimodal service models emphasize immediate interventions designed primarily to enhance environmental resources to reduce the crisis. For example, communitywide intervention models are used after natural disasters because personal and community resources are impaired at such times (Kaniasty & Norris, 1993; Wright, Ursano, Bartone, & Ingraham, 1990). Residential treatment programs use both structural environmental interventions and intensive crisis therapy (Weisman, 1985). Community programs for severely and persistently mentally ill people provide 24-hour crisis intervention in addition to environmental resources (Kerson, 1989). In response to gang violence and teenage offenders, crisis intervention has been combined with street surveillance (Spergel, 1986) and other services (Stewart, Vockell, & Ray, 1986). In the presence of imminent family breakdown, multiple interventions are aimed at activating or creating social system resources to ameliorate contextual elements of the crisis that impair or preclude an adaptive crisis resolution (Michael, Lurie, Russell, & Unger, 1985; Reece, 1986).

## Conceptualizing the Ecological Dimensions of Crisis Theory

Although the term "theory" is used throughout this discussion and is widely used in the crisis literature, the predictive elements of crisis theory are untested. Research on the role of environmental factors in predicting who will experience a crisis and the course and outcome of a crisis has been particularly sparse (Slaikeu, 1990).

Crisis theory has been strongly influenced by the large body of research on human stress (Golan, 1987; Parad, 1971). For example, the assumption regarding homeostasis is attributable to general systems theory (Bertalanffy, 1968) and more specifically to the seminal work of the physiologist and stress theorist Hans Selye (1976). The emphasis on cognition and coping in crisis theory is based on the seminal work of Lazarus (1966).

Current practice, reflecting the human problems that result from deteriorating social and physical environments, suggests that sociological and ecological conceptualizations of crisis (specifically the interpersonal, interactional, cultural, social–structural, and community dimensions of coping with crises) require further development and research. Although crisis theory is frequently cited as the basis for the broad range of environmental interventions and strategies widely used by social workers, there are important gaps in the knowledge base for practice. Integration of knowledge from research on the interactional, social–structural, and ecological dimensions of stress, social support, and coping is likely to advance the utility of crisis intervention as a broadly targeted practice theory (Coyne, Ellard, & Smith, 1990; Eckenrode, 1991; Hobfoll, 1988; Moos, 1976; Mor-Barak, 1988).

**Hill's Theoretical Model**

Early sociological constructions of family stress based on the seminal work of Hill (1949) closely paralleled and influenced the development of crisis theory. Hill's theoretical model of family crisis was originally based on observations of family responses to war-induced separation and reunion. Briefly stated, Hill's (1958) model proposed the following: **A** (the event) interacts with **B** (the family's crisis-meeting resources) and **C** (the definition the family makes of the event) to produce **X** (the crisis). Determinants **B** and **C**—the family resources and definitions of the event—lie within the family itself and must be seen in terms of the family's structures and values. The hardships of the event, which go to make up the first determinant, lie outside the family and are an attribute of the event itself.

On the basis of the general systems paradigm, Hill's formulations of family stress theory continue to underpin contemporary family stress literature and family crisis intervention (Boss, 1988; McCubbin & Patterson, 1982). Hill's work on family stress spawned decades of research on family stress response, including attempts to explain and predict dysfunctional family behavior in response to stress (McCubbin & McCubbin, 1992).

**Other Conceptualizations**

An emerging body of research is beginning to explain why some families successfully cope with life stress and tragedies, whereas others break down; for example, there is evidence that some family types are balanced, resilient, regenerative, and rhythmic (McCubbin, Thompson, Pirner, & McCubbin, 1988). McCubbin and McCubbin (1992) have also extended Hill's (1958) original family crisis model to include both an adjustment and an adaptation phase that involves consideration of resource factors such as families' vulnerability, typology, and problem-solving repertoire.

Other sociological conceptualizations of stress (Aneshensel, 1992; Pearlin, 1989) have had less influence on the development of crisis theory. Least understood are the effects of social structure and chronically stressful social environments on an individual's vulnerability to crisis and on the outcome of the crisis (Mechanic, 1974). For example, there has been little attention to the ways in which situational crises vary depending on people's social position (Aneshensel, 1992; Pearlin, 1989).

**Need for Theoretical Research**

Research on the psychologically tempered theoretical tenets of crisis theory is sparse (Hobfoll & Shlomo, 1986), but research on the validity of theoretical assumptions and practice principles with respect to diverse sociocultural groups is particularly scant. As a result, questions remain about the ways in which crises, as well as practice guidelines and principles, might vary with respect to gender, socioeconomic status, age, and racial or ethnic status.

Also disturbing is the lack of theoretical development related to the ecological components of individual crises and the failure to examine closely the influence of social systems on crisis experience (Hobfoll, 1988; Moos, 1976). Therefore, little is known about the ways in which crises are precipitated, mediated, or exacerbated by social systems or by the absence of adequate community services systems. For example, community settings such as churches, mutual help groups, and senior centers have been found to buffer life stress (Maton, 1989), whereas chronically stressful environments have been shown to erode supportive resources (Lepore, Evans, & Schneider, 1991). Research is also needed to examine potential links between social–structural and ecological forces and individual coping resources such as self-efficacy and personal sense of control (Aneshensel, 1992).

The following are suggested questions to be addressed in future theoretical research on human crises:

- How might human crises be modeled within an ecological frame?
- Why do some, but not other, individuals and families experience a crisis in the presence of stressful events? For example, what person-in-environment factors predict crises?
- In what ways do environmental factors influence the course of crisis resolution and adaptation?
- To what extent are the basic assumptions and tenets of crisis theory both applicable across diverse populations and ecologically sensitive?
- What are the interpersonal and interactive components of coping tasks and crisis resolution? How do these vary by cultural group?
- What is the meaning of time-limited crises—for example, for those living in chronically stressful environments?
- What is the meaning of homeostasis in the context of the chronic stress that prevails in impoverished communities?
- In what way is crisis response culturally bound? For example, how are maturational crises influenced by culture?

## Conclusion

Crisis intervention will continue to be a primary social work intervention. The utility of providing immediate aid to people under severe disabling distress is unquestioned. Advanced knowledge through the research suggested here is needed to enhance practice with such people.

## References


Aneshensel, C. S. (1992). Social stress: Theory and research. *Annual Review of Sociology, 18,* 15–38.

Baldwin, B. A. (1978). A paradigm for the classification of emotional crises: Implications for crisis intervention. *American Journal of Orthopsychiatry, 48*(3), 538–551.

Bertalanffy, L. von. (1968). *General system theory: Foundations, development, applications*. New York: George Braziller.

Boss, P. (1988). *Family stress management*. Newbury Park, CA: Sage Publications.

Bromley, M. A. (1987). New beginnings for Cambodian refugees—or further disruptions? *Social Work, 32,* 236–239.

Caplan, G. (1964). *Principles of preventive psychiatry.* New York: Basic Books.

Caplan, G. (1974). *Support systems and community mental health*. New York: Basic Books.

Coyne, J. C., Ellard, J. H., & Smith, D. (1990). Social support, interdependence, and the dilemmas of helping. In B. R. Sarason, E. N. Shearin, G. Pierce, & I. G. Sarason (Eds.), *Social support: An interactional view*. New York: John Wiley & Sons.

Danish, S. J., & D'Augelli, A. R. (1980). Promoting competence and enhancing development through life development intervention. In L. A. Bond & J. C. Rosen (Eds.), *Competence and coping during adulthood*. Hanover, NH: University Press of New England.

Eckenrode, J. (Ed.). (1991). *The social context of coping*. New York: Plenum Press.

Eggert, G. M., Friedman, B., & Zimmer, J. G. (1990). Models of intensive case management. *Journal of Gerontological Social Work, 15*(3/4), 75–101.

Gambe, R., & Getzel, G. S. (1989). Group work with gay men with AIDS. *Social Casework, 70*(3), 172–179.

Gilbar, O. (1991). Model for crisis intervention through group therapy for women with breast cancer. *Clinical Social Work Journal, 19*(3), 293–304.

Golan, N. (1978). *Treatment in crisis situations*. New York: Free Press.

Golan, N. (1987). Crisis intervention. In A. Minahan (Ed.-in-Chief), *Encyclopedia of social work* (18th ed., Vol. 1, pp. 360–372). Silver Spring, MD: National Association of Social Workers.

Gutstein, S. (1987). Family reconciliation as a response to adolescent crises. *Family Process, 26,* 475–491.

Halpern, H. A. (1973). Crisis theory: A definitional study. *Community Mental Health Journal, 9,* 342–349.

Halpern, R. (1986). Home-based early intervention: Dimensions of current practice. *Child Welfare, 115*(4), 387–398.

Haran, J. (1988). Use of group work to help children cope with the violent death of a classmate. *Social Work with Groups, 11,* 79–92.

Hendricks, J. E. (Ed.). (1991). *Crisis intervention in criminal justice/social service*. Springfield, IL: Charles C Thomas.

Hill, R. (1949). *Families under stress*. New York: Harper and Brothers.

Hill, R. (1958). Social stresses on the family: Generic features of families under stress. *Social Casework, 39,* 139–150.

Hobfoll, S. (1988). *The ecology of stress*. New York: Hemisphere.

Hobfoll, S. E., & Shlomo, W. (1986). Stressful events, mastery, and depression: An evaluation of crisis theory. *Journal of Community Psychology, 14,* 183–195.

Holmes-Garrett, C. (1989). The crisis of the forgotten family: A single session group in the ICU waiting room. *Social Work with Groups, 12,* 141–157.

Hunner, R. J. (1986). Reasonable efforts to prevent placement and preserve families: Defining active and reasonable efforts to preserve families. *Children Today, 15*(6), 27–30.

Kaniasty, K., & Norris, F. H. (1993). A test of the social support deterioration model in the context of natural disaster. *Journal of Personality and Social Psychology, 64*(3), 395–408.

Kerson, T. S. (1989). Community housing for chronically mentally ill people. *Health & Social Work, 14,* 293–294.

Kilpatrick, A. C., & Pippin, J. A. (1987). Families in crisis: A structured mediation method for peaceful solutions. *International Social Work, 30,* 159–169.

Lazarus, R. S. (1966). *Psychological stress and the coping process*. New York: McGraw-Hill.

Lepore, S. J., Evans, G. W., & Schneider, M. L. (1991). Dynamic role of social support in the link between chronic stress and psychological distress. *Journal of Personality and Social Psychology, 61*(6), 899–909.

Lindemann, E. (1944). Symptomatology and management of acute grief. *American Journal of Psychiatry, 101,* 141–148.

Lukton, R. C. (1982). Myths and realities of crisis intervention. *Social Casework: The Journal of Contemporary Social Work, 63,* 276–284.

Maguire, L. (1991). *Social support systems in practice*. Silver Spring, MD: NASW Press.

Maton, K. I. (1989). Community settings as buffers of life stress? Highly supportive churches, mutual help groups, and senior centers. *American Journal of Community Psychology, 17*(2), 203–232.

McCubbin, H., & McCubbin, M. (1992). Research utilization in social work practice of family treatment. In A. J. Grasso & I. Epstein (Eds.), *Research utilization in the social services: Innovations for practice and administration* (pp. 149–192). New York: Haworth Press.

McCubbin, H., & Patterson, J. M. (1982). Family adaptation to crisis. In H. I. McCubbin, A. E. Cauble, & J. M. Patterson (Eds.), *Family stress, coping, and social support* (pp. 26–47). Springfield, IL: Charles C Thomas.

McCubbin, H., Thompson, A., Pirner, P., & McCubbin, M. (1988). *Family types and family strengths: A life-span and ecological perspective*. Edina, MN: Burgess International.

McPeak, W. R. (1989). Family intervention models and chronic mental illness: New implications from family systems theory. *Community Alternatives: International Journal of Family Care, 1*(2), 53–63.

Mechanic, D. (1974). Social structure and personal adaptation: Some neglected dimensions. In G. Coelho, D. Hamburg, & J. Adams (Eds.), *Coping and adaptation* (pp. 32–44). New York: Basic Books.

Michael, S., Lurie, E., Russell, N., & Unger, L. (1985). Rapid response mutual aid groups: A new response to social crises and natural disasters. *Social Work, 30,* 245–252.

Mirowsky, J., & Ross, C. E. (1989). *Social causes of psychological distress*. New York: Aldine de Gruyter.

Moos, R. H. (Ed.). (1976). *Human adaptation: Coping with life crises*. Lexington, MA: D. C. Heath.

Mor-Barak, M. E. (1988). Support systems intervention in crisis situations: Theory, strategies and a case illustration. *International Social Work, 31*(4), 285–304.

National Research Council. (1993). *Losing generations: Adolescents in high-risk settings*. Washington, DC: National Academy Press.

Nelson, K. E., Landsman, M. J., & Deutelbaum, W. (1990). Three models of family-centered placement prevention services. *Child Welfare, 69*(1), 3–21.

Northen, H. (1989). Social work practice with groups in health care. *Social Work with Groups, 12*(4), 7–26.

Parad, H. J. (1971). Crisis intervention. In R. Morris (Ed.), *Encyclopedia of social work* (16th ed., Vol. 1, pp. 196–202). New York: National Association of Social Workers.

Parad, H. J. & Parad, L. G. (1990). *Crisis intervention*. Milwaukee: Families International.

Paschal, J. H., & Schwahn, L. (1986). Intensive crisis counseling in Florida. *Children Today, 15*(6), 12–16.

Pearlin, L. I. (1989, September). The sociological study of stress. *Journal of Health and Social Behavior, 30,* 241–256.

Reece, C. (1986). Children in shelters. *Children Today, 15*(2), 6–25.

Rossi, P. H. (1992). Assessing family preservation programs. *Children and Youth Services Review, 14,* 77–92.

Schopler, J. H., & Galinsky, M. J. (1993). Support groups as open systems: A model for practice and research. *Health & Social Work, 18,* 195–207.

Selye, H. (1976). *The stress of life*. New York: McGraw-Hill.

Silverman, E. (1986). The social worker's role in shock-trauma units. *Social Work, 31,* 311–313.

Slaikeu, K. A. (1990). *Crisis intervention: A handbook for practice and research* (2nd ed.). Boston: Allyn & Bacon.

Smith, L. L. (1978). A review of crisis intervention theory. *Social Casework, 59,* 396–405.

Smith, L. L. (1979). Crisis intervention in practice. *Social Casework, 60,* 81–88.

Spergel, I. A. (1986). The violent gang problem in Chicago: A local community approach. *Social Service Review, 60,* 94–113.

Stewart, M. J., Vockell, E. L., & Ray, R. E. (1986). Decreasing court appearances of juvenile status offenders. *Social Casework, 67,* 74–79.

Taylor, J. W. (1986). Social casework and the multimodal treatment of incest. *Social Casework, 67,* 451–459.

Taylor, S. E., Folkes, R. L., Mazel, R. M., & Hilsberg, B. L. (1988). Sources of satisfaction and dissatisfaction among members of cancer groups. In B. Gottlieb (Ed.), *Creating support groups: Formats, processes, and effects* (pp. 187–208). Newbury Park, CA: Sage Publications.

VandenBos, G. R., & Bryant, B. K. (Eds.). (1987). *Cataclysms, crises and catastrophes: Psychology in action*. Washington, DC: American Psychological Association.

Van Hook, M. P. (1987). Harvest of despair: Using the ABCX model for farm families in crisis. *Social Casework, 68,* 273–278.

Viney, L. L., Benjamin, Y. N., Clarke, A. M., & Bunn, T. A. (1985). Sex differences in the psychological reaction of medical and surgical patients to crisis intervention and counseling: Sauce for the goose may not be sauce for the gander. *Social Science and Medicine, 20,* 1199–1205.

Viney, L. L., Clarke, A. M., Bunn, T. A., & Benjamin, Y. N. (1985). Crisis-intervention counseling: An evaluation of long- and short-term effects. *Journal of Counseling Psychology, 32*(1), 29–39.

Weisman, G. K. (1985). Crisis-oriented residential treatment as an alternative to hospitalization. *Hospital and Community Psychiatry, 36*(12), 1302–1305.

Weiss, B. S., & Parish, B. (1989). Culturally appropriate crisis counseling: Adapting an American method for use with Indochinese refugees. *Social Work, 34,* 252–254.

Wright, K. M., Ursano, R. J., Bartone, P. T., & Ingraham, L. H. (1990). The shared experience of catastrophe: An expanded classification of the disaster community. *American Journal of Orthopsychiatry, 60,* 35–42.

**Kathleen Ell, DSW,** is professor, University of Southern California, School of Social Work, Montgomery Ross Fisher Building, Los Angeles, CA 90089.

## For further information see

Bereavement and Loss; Brief Therapies; Clinical Social Work; Conflict Resolution; Direct Practice Overview; Families: Direct Practice; Goal Setting and Intervention Planning; Health Care Overview; Homelessness; Hospice;

Hospital Social Work; Interdisciplinary and Interorganizational Collaboration; Intervention Research; Natural Helping Networks; Occupational Social Work; Person-in-Environment; Social Work Practice: Theoretical Base; Social Work Profession Overview; Substance Abuse: Direct Practice; Suicide; Torture Victims.

**Key Words**
crisis intervention intervention research

## Cubans

*See* Hispanics: Cubans

# Cults

**Susan P. Robbins**

Interest in and concern about cults have been typified by controversy since cults first emerged in the late 1960s and early 1970s. The relatively new, small, nontraditional religious groups that proliferated during this period rapidly began to attract the attention of the public and the media (Beckford, 1985; Robbins, 1992). The 1993 armed confrontation in Waco, Texas, between the Branch Davidians and the Bureau of Alcohol, Tobacco, and Firearms generated new public concern about cults. As Beckford (1985) observed, the term "cult" is controversial, and its popular use usually carries pejorative connotations. Cults generally are portrayed as small, unorthodox, possibly dangerous fringe groups whose members are influenced by a charismatic leader (Woodward, Fleming, Reiss, Rafshoon, & Leonard, 1993).

A basic dilemma in examining the phenomenon of cults is that of definition. Traditional distinctions between churches, denominations, sects, and cults have proved problematic in the recent study of new religions, because scholars often disagree about appropriate designations for various groups. Although numerous typologies have been proposed (Anthony & Ecker, 1987; Bird, 1979; Stark & Bainbridge, 1985; Tipton, 1982; Wallis, 1984; Wilber, 1983), there is no single framework for analysis that is currently accepted (Robbins, 1992). Despite varying definitions and typologies, cults are seen as essentially deviant and controversial because of their unconventional beliefs and often total separatism from traditional lifestyles (Beckford, 1985; Robbins, 1992; Shupe & Bromley, 1991).

The new forms of religious consciousness that grew out of the counterculture of the 1960s spawned a wide variety of groups and philosophies. Most scholars now refer to these as "new religious movements" (NRMs) to avoid the pejorative connotation of the term "cult." However, as Beckford (1985) and Robbins (1992) observed, there are no universally accepted distinctions between NRMs and other religious groups.

Although many NRMs are rooted in traditional Western religions, the influence of Hinduism, Buddhism, and other Eastern religions all provided impetus for the formation of new groups such as the Divine Light Mission, the Unification Church, the Rajneesh Foundation, the International Society for Krishna Consciousness, the Children of God, and the Satanic Church. Other groups, such as the Human Potential Movement, Synanon, and the Church of Scientology are less explicitly religious and were derived instead from developments in modern secular culture (Glock & Bellah, 1976). The terms "cult" and "NRM" are usually applied to controversial groups that have attracted publicity and notoriety (Beckford, 1985).

Because of the problem in defining which groups qualify as cults, it is difficult to obtain accurate information about their prevalence. Estimates of the number of NRM groups reported in the media range from 700 to 5,000 (Woodward et al., 1993). The reliability of these estimates is questionable because they are most often provided by cult-watch organizations that are hostile to NRMs. Estimates of the number of people involved in NRMs are conflictual as well. There have never been reliable data on the actual number of recruits, despite assertions about a massive recruitment effort (Beckford, 1985). According to West and Singer (1980), between 2 million and 3 million Americans are involved in cults. In contrast, Shupe and Bromley (1991) contended that the number of communal NRM members has never exceeded 25,000 at any given time. They argued that the expansion in the definition of the term "cult" to include quasi-therapeutic groups, independent fundamentalist churches, and militant political movements has contributed to misleading estimates.

Although estimates vary, most researchers agree that only a very small portion of the young adult population becomes seriously involved in NRMs (Beckford, 1985; Robbins, 1992). Furthermore, NRMs have been found to have low recruitment and high defection rates. Approximately 75 percent of new converts defect within the first year. Studies have shown that those who do join are typically Caucasian, middle-class, young adults in their late teens and early twenties, and approximately 65 percent to 75 percent are male (Barker, 1984; Beckford, 1985; Galanter, 1989; Shupe & Bromley, 1991; Wright, 1987).

Negative stereotypes of cults as dangerous, extreme, and destructive began to emerge in the mid-1970s. The rise of new religions led to the formation of anticult groups, composed initially of parents concerned about their children's NRM affiliations (Robbins, 1992; Shupe & Bromley, 1991; Victor, 1993). The Jonestown, Guyana, tragedy of 1978, in which charismatic leader Reverend Jim Jones led his devout followers to death by murder or suicide, is widely cited as a turning point in the consolidation of anticult sentiment. Cults, from that point on, were seen "through the lens of Jonestown" as groups of people that were brainwashed into submission and led by a manipulative fanatic (Victor, 1993, p. 9). Public tolerance for NRMs quickly vanished once they were labeled as authoritarian, totalistic, dangerous, destructive, fanatic, and violent.

Religious upheavals in society are not new. When viewed from a historical perspective, negative sentiment about NRMs parallels earlier concerns about religious groups such as Mormons, Roman Catholics, and Christian Scientists. Thus, any meaningful analysis of NRMs and the opposition to them must include an understanding of their cultural, structural, and political contexts (Beckford, 1985; Glock & Bellah, 1976; Jenkins, 1992; Wright & D'Antonio, 1993).

## Contemporary Knowledge Base

The cult controversy today is embodied by a polemical debate involving social and behavioral scientists, cult members, former cult members, anticult organizations, therapists, police, and the media. Contemporary knowledge about cults is derived from these often diverse points of view.

The controversy originated in conflicts between cult members and their distraught families who became alarmed about the theologies, practices, and often communal lifestyles of these new religious groups. Even though most converts were legal adults who claimed that their participation was based on free choice, family members levied charges of kidnapping and brainwashing. Police, legislators, psychiatrists, and clergy were unable to offer concrete assistance because of issues of religious freedom (Barker, 1984; Beckford, 1985; Shupe & Bromley, 1991).

### Anticult Organizations

As media reports drew national attention to the emerging NRMs, parental concerns and anticult sentiment coalesced into a grassroots anticult movement (ACM). Anticult groups began to coordinate local and regional activities and, by the 1980s, the movement achieved greater organizational stability. Several predominant organizations such as the American Family Foundation, the Citizens Freedom Foundation, and the Cult Awareness Network emerged as ACM leaders.

ACM organizations in the United States have been expressly organized to combat the destructive influence of NRMs and assist those who are adversely affected by them. In addition to monitoring and exposing NRMs as dangerous and destructive, ACM groups actively lobby against NRMs and provide family members with information and services such as counseling, deprogramming, and forums in which family members are able to express their feelings and concerns (Beckford, 1985; Shupe & Bromley, 1991). According to Beckford, ACM organizations "present the most hostile and damaging image of NRMs... [and] actively exploit opportunities to publicize their case against cults" (p. 116).

Early ACM groups relied heavily on the services of "deprogrammers" who, for a fee, would forcibly abduct, restrain, and deprogram cult members at the request of their families. *Deprogramming* was invented by Theodore Patrick, Jr., a community action worker with no formal professional training or academic credentials (Bromley, 1988). Alleging that cult members were victims of brainwashing achieved through the use of drugs, hypnotism, and other forms of coercive mind control, deprogrammers claimed to be able to break cult-induced trances (Shupe & Bromley, 1991). Deprogrammers use a wide variety of techniques, methods, and behaviors. Some rely on coercive, traumatic, vigilante-style operations and engage in marathon confrontations, whereas others use relatively innocuous, noncoercive techniques. The use of noncoercive techniques led to a more current practice termed "exit counseling" (Robbins, 1992; Shupe & Bromley, 1991; Wright & Ebaugh, 1993). As the ACM grew and became more sophisticated, the use of deprogrammers gave way to the new and growing authority of credentialed mental health professionals.

There is now an alliance among established ACM groups and sympathetic social workers, psychologists, psychiatrists, social scientists, lawyers, and police. The resulting proliferation of professional newsletters, journals, monographs, and seminars on destructive cultism has given greater credibility to ACM ideology.

### Therapist and Client Reports

The prevalent view of mental health professionals who treat former cult members parallels the negative stereotypes espoused in ACM ideology. Clients are labeled "cult victims" or "cult survivors," and therapists rely heavily on psychiatric terminology and diagnoses such as dissociative states, post-traumatic stress syndrome, multiple personality disorder, and cult-imposed personality syndrome to explain the causes, processes, and effects of NRM membership (Mulhern, 1991; Shupe & Bromley, 1991; Victor, 1993). There is also a growing concern among therapists that sexual abuse and exploitation of women and children are central features of most cult environments (Jacobs, 1984; Jenkins, 1992; Victor, 1993). Clinical reports of persistent psychological problems caused by previous cult involvement include depression, loneliness, dissociated states, obsessive review, and uncritical passivity (Galper, 1982; Goldberg & Goldberg, 1982; Ross & Langone, 1988; Singer, 1979). These problems are generally attributed to the effects of brainwashing, coercion, or high-pressure recruitment tactics (Addis, Schulman-Miller, & Lightman 1984; Clark, Langone, Schacter, & Daly 1981; Singer, 1979). Recovery is presumed to be a lengthy process, requiring the assistance of trained professionals. Beckford (1985) and Robbins (1992) have pointed out, however, that not all clinicians agree with these views (see Galanter, 1980; Galanter, Rabkin, Rabkin, & Deutsch, 1979; Gordon, 1988; Kuner, 1983; Ungerleider & Wellisch, 1979).

Client reports about horrifying cult experiences originally came from people who were removed from cults against their will and subjected to coercive deprogramming (Beckford, 1985; Bromley, 1988; Wright & Ebaugh, 1993). Although deprogramming continues to be used, contemporary therapeutic techniques rely on more professional methods such as rehabilitation, reentry counseling, and exit therapies, such as promoting voluntary reevaluation and exit counseling. In contrast to deprogramming, these methods are assumed to be noncoercive and voluntary. However, as Wright and Ebaugh (1993) suggested, they may or may not be coercive, depending on the willingness of the client and the orientation of the therapist. Although they use a wide variety of techniques and methods, most exit therapies parallel anticult ideology in their stereotypical portrayal of cults as destructive (Robbins, 1992; Wright & Ebaugh, 1993).

Critics have suggested that public concern about destructive cultism has created an opportunity for mental health professionals to impose a medical model that defines unconventional religiosity as pathology. It has also allowed therapists to develop prestigious roles as cult experts (Robbins, 1992; Shupe & Bromley, 1991).

### Media Portrayals

The news media play a seminal role in the general public's understanding and perception of cults. As Beckford (1985) reported, the media have depicted cults as problematic, controversial, and threatening from the beginning. Far from being unbiased, the media tend to favor sensationalistic stories over balanced public debates (Beckford, 1985; Richardson, Best, & Bromley, 1991; Victor, 1993). Rowe and Cavender (1991) found that the choice of sources determines the perspective that the media presents.

Newspaper and magazine reports on cults rely heavily on police officials and cult "experts" who portray cult activity as dangerous and destructive. National television talk shows typically feature cult survivors who give terrifying accounts of their victimization (Richardson et al., 1991; Rowe & Cavender, 1991; Victor, 1993). When divergent views are presented, they are often seen as less credible and are overshadowed by horrific stories of ritualistic torture, sexual abuse, and mind control. Furthermore, unfounded allegations, when proved untrue, receive little or no media attention. Thus, negative stereotypes of cults are perpetuated through uncritical and sensationalized reporting (Bromley, 1991; Wright, 1991).

### Empirical Studies

A growing body of literature suggests that NRMs are characterized by an "impressive diversity" that has been "consistently denied or ignored in anti-cult sentiment" (Beckford, 1985, p. 7). Studies of NRMs have shown that their metaphysical assumptions, ideological views, doctrines, organizational structures, range of social relationships, and material resources are quite varied (see Beckford, 1985; Bromley & Hadden, 1993; Glock & Bellah, 1976; Jenkins, 1992). Research on religious conversion has a long history and has produced a wealth of data. Studies on the process of defection and disaffiliation, however, are relatively new (Wright & Ebaugh, 1993).

In contrast to the view that brainwashing and coercive tactics are routinely used and are necessary for indoctrination, the literature suggests that affiliation and conversion are based on complex social and psychological processes and factors (Barker, 1984; Bromley & Richardson, 1983; Lofland, 1977; Lofland & Stark, 1965; Lofland & Skovnid, 1981, 1983; Long & Hadden, 1983; Snow et al., 1980; Snow & Machalek, 1984; Stark & Bainbridge, 1980). It has been widely acknowledged that some NRM groups use coercive, manipulative, and deceptive tactics. However, coercion models provide a limited explanation and are not well supported by the numerous studies on affiliation and conversion (Barker, 1984; Bromley & Richardson, 1983; Robbins, 1992).

Researchers have distinguished among recruitment, conversion, and commitment. *Recruitment* entails joining a group, whereas *conversion* is a radical transformation of identity and belief. *Commitment* may vary in intensity, even among those who are converted (Balch, 1985; Greil & Rudy, 1984b; Robbins, 1992). Wright (1991) pointed out that some groups demand higher levels of commitment than do others.

Among the various factors related to conversion are

- an openness to accepting new ideology
- a pattern of seeking (spiritual, religious, philosophical, or self-fulfillment)
- a "turning point" that coincides with group contact
- forming affective bonds within the group
- neutralizing affective ties outside the group
- interacting intensively with group members.

Conversion is also aided by *encapsulation* (physical, social, or ideological), a process that draws clear boundaries between members and nonmembers and aids in neutralizing bonds with nonmembers (Greil & Rudy, 1984a, 1984b). Research on the role of social networks has also shown interpersonal ties to NRM group members and the absence of countervailing networks to be important factors. The consensus of the numerous studies on conversion is that most recruits voluntarily join NRMs.

Disaffiliation from an NRM may involve one of several processes. It may be initiated by the member (exiting); the group (expulsion); or external agents such as relatives, friends, or counselors (extraction) (Richardson, van der Lans, & Derks, 1986). Wright and Ebaugh (1993) observed that disaffiliation, like conversion, involves complex, multidimensional processes and dramatic shifts of identity.

Research has consistently shown a high rate of turnover and voluntary defection among members of NRMs. In fact, voluntary exit is the most common form of disaffiliation (Barker, 1984; Beckford, 1985; Jacobs, 1984; Robbins, 1992; Wright, 1984). These data have raised serious questions about claims of brainwashing, psychological coercion, and the popular belief that converts need to be deprogrammed. Wright (1991) found that the full range of psychological problems attributed to NRM involvement (depression, dissociated states, obsessive review, and so forth) is also found in the literature on marital dissolution.

Studies on voluntary exits have shown a wide variety of exiting patterns (Beckford, 1985; Robbins, 1992; Wright, 1987). Deterioration of affective bonds within the group, disillusionment with the group's ideology or leadership, dissatisfaction with imposed social restrictions, and family disapproval are important factors in voluntary disaffiliation (Jacobs, 1984; Wright & Ebaugh, 1993; Wright & Piper, 1986).

Differences have been found between members who exit voluntarily and those who have been coercively extracted and deprogrammed. Voluntary defectors are more likely to view their involvement positively, report pleasant memories and rewarding experiences, and feel wiser for the experience. Some experience ambivalence, but few claim they were brainwashed. In contrast, ex-members who have been deprogrammed are more likely to report feelings of alienation, anger, and hostility toward their former groups, and claims of brainwashing are common (Beckford, 1985; Lewis, 1986; Solomon, 1981; Wright, 1988; Wright & Ebaugh, 1993). Several researchers have concluded that stereotypical anticult attitudes are a result of deprogramming rather than negative cult experiences. Some have even suggested that forced intervention and deprogramming may be harmful (see Galanter, 1989; Levine, 1984; Wright & Ebaugh, 1993). (See Robbins, 1992, and Bromley & Hadden, 1993, for a complete discussion and critique of the literature on conversion and disaffiliation.)

**Methodological Issues**

Research on NRMs has been criticized for numerous methodological problems. The use of ambiguous terminology is prevalent, as are problems involving sampling biases, the use of small samples, a lack of control groups, overgeneralization, and unwarranted causal inferences (Balch, 1985; Robbins, 1992). Two distinct sources of bias permeate most NRM research. First, there are the problems inherent in retrospective interpretation. Because most studies rely on retrospective reports from converts or ex-members, these accounts are likely to reflect thoughts and feelings about the current situation as well. Given the dramatic shift in identity that occurs during conversion and disaffiliation, biographic reconstruction raises serious questions about validity. Client reports are generally regarded by researchers as being unreliable, because successful treatment entails acceptance of the idea that clients have been victimized through brainwashing, trauma, conditioning, and mind control. Wright and Ebaugh (1993) have cautioned that retrospective accounts should be treated as "topics of analysis, not just objective data of past events" (p. 121).

The second type of bias is linked to the interpretive framework used by the researcher. Shupe and Bromley (1991) observed that the medicalization of religious conflict has led to a countermobilization of social science and religion scholars who are sympathetic to NRMs. Much of the research centers around attempts either to prove or to debunk allegations of brainwashing and destructive cults. In this regard Stone (1978) noted that reports of NRMs "may tell us more about the observers than about the observed" (p. 143).

## Satanic Cults and Ritual Abuse

Perhaps the most controversial issue arising from the cult debate is that of satanic, ritual abuse. Reports of widespread, organized satanic cults engaging in horrifying rituals began to emerge in the early 1980s. A secret underground cult network was purportedly sponsoring satanic activities that included, among other things, ritualistic torture, sexual abuse, and human sacrifice (Bromley, 1991). Firsthand accounts of satanic ritual abuse came from two primary groups: (1) adults in psychotherapy who claim to have "recovered" previously dissociated memories of being abused in transgenerational cults and (2) young children who were allegedly victims of satanic abuse while in day care (Jenkins, 1992; Jenkins & Maier-Katkin, 1991; Mulhern, 1991; Victor, 1993). Although accounts of transgenerational cult abuse vary, most share common themes and are based on recollections of sexual abuse during early childhood by parents or caretakers. Recovered memories typically include being drugged, brainwashed, and forced to watch or participate in satanic rituals, and this early abuse is alleged to be preparation for a later role in young adulthood as a "devil's bride" or "breeder" who delivers babies solely for the purpose of satanic sacrifice.

By the late 1980s reports of a new crime wave that linked violent crimes to occult practices and satanic worship became common (see Larson, 1989; Raschke, 1990; Schwarz & Empey, 1988). Religions with African and Hispanic origins such as voodoo, Santeria, and Brujeria became linked to satanism because of their use of ritualistic magic and animal sacrifice (Kahaner, 1988).

In an action similar to the response to the religious cult scare of the 1970s, small subgroups of conservative religious leaders, members of family-based groups, mental health professionals, and local law enforcement officers formed a coalition to confront the threat of satanic cults. Claims of ritualistic abuse and kidnapping were disseminated through police and mental health conferences and literature; fundamentalist books, articles, and radio programs; and the mass media (Bromley, 1991; Crouch & Damphouse, 1991; Jenkins, 1992; Victor, 1993).

*Satanism,* as defined by these groups and portrayed in the media, includes a variety of diverse practices such as kidnappings, ritual sexual abuse, sacrifice of children, cannibalism, blood drinking, animal mutilations, and grave desecrations. In addition, a causal link is proposed between teenage murder and suicide and interest in occult symbols, clothing, and books; heavy metal music; and fantasy games such as Dungeons & Dragons (Bromley, 1991; Lyons, 1988; Victor, 1993). Teenage occult involvement is portrayed as being progressive, beginning with music and fantasy games and leading to satanic graffiti, cemetery vandalism, robbery, animal killing, and murder of humans (see Pulling, 1989).

Four levels of satanic involvement are commonly identified in workshops and literature disseminated by local police and mental health professionals:

1. *Dabblers* are typically teenagers or young adults who listen to heavy metal music and are interested in occult or satanic games and imagery.
2. *Self-styled satanists* are criminals who explain or justify their crimes with satanic themes or rationales.
3. *Organized satanists* are members of organized satanic churches such as the Temple of Set or the Church of Satan.
4. *Covert satanists* are part of an international network of multigenerational satanists who engage in kidnapping, child abuse, and human sacrifice (Blimling, 1991; Bromley, 1991; Hicks, 1991).

Despite widespread allegations of organized satanic crime, there is no corroborating evidence that such crime exists (Blimling, 1991; Bromley,

1991; Jenkins, 1992; Lyons, 1988; Melton, 1986a; Richardson, et al., 1991; Victor, 1993). Reports of organized satanic ritual abuse, abductions, murders, and animal mutilations have resulted in numerous and extensive police and FBI investigations, all of which have consistently failed to discover conclusive physical evidence to support these claims (see Bromley, 1991; Lyons, 1988; Victor, 1993).

Charges of satanic child abuse made by children, their parents, and ritual abuse experts are often bolstered by testimony from physicians. Current research has shown, however, that many of the alleged physical "symptoms" of ritual abuse are present in nonabused children as well (Nathan, 1989, 1991a). Police investigations and subsequent court proceedings have failed to find any evidence to support charges of satanic abuse in day care settings (Bromley, 1991; Lyons, 1988; Nathan, 1991b; Victor, 1993). Similarly, no physical evidence has ever been found to support the claims of ritual abuse survivors who have "recovered" memories of satanic murder and ritualistic human sacrifice. To date, neither the FBI nor the police have been able to document even one organized satanic cult murder in the United States (Lanning, 1989a, 1989b; Lyons, 1988).

In a survey of existing evidence, Melton (1986b) concluded that contemporary satanism takes two forms: (1) open satanic groups that pose no public threat and (2) small ephemeral groups that are transitory and that are composed primarily of teenagers and young adults. The latter are often involved in crimes such as murder, rape, and drug trafficking. Authorities point out, however, that the causal link between crimes committed by self-proclaimed satanists and ceremonial satanic worship is tenuous at best (see Lyons, 1988; Ofshe, 1986; Victor, 1993).

Bromley (1991) observed that proponents of satanic conspiracy theory pose an argument that is virtually irrefutable. The lack of evidence is seen as proof of the successful clandestine operation of the cult. Thus, "sensational claims" of cult survivors are transformed into irrefutable "truths" (Victor, 1993, p. 129). Because of lack of verifiable evidence, the current satanism scare has been dubbed by researchers to be a myth, the result of panic and contemporary legend, and numerous authors have directly compared it to the witch hunts of earlier eras (Bromley, 1991; Jenkins, 1992; Jenkins & Maier-Katkin, 1991; Rowe & Cavender, 1991; Victor, 1993). Ritual abuse experts, however, eschew the need for concrete evidence and firmly believe in the existence of a conspiratorial organized underground satanic network (see Beere, 1989; Braun, 1989; Braun et al., 1989; Kaye & Kline, 1987).

## Recovered Memories

The issue of satanic ritual abuse is embedded in an even more controversial debate about the nature, validity, and accuracy of memories involving traumatic events. Adult clients who have "recovered" previously amnesic memories of ritual abuse in their childhood are a primary source of reports. This controversy, in turn, is part of a larger debate about recovered memories of incest and sexual abuse in general.

Recovered memories typically involve terrifying flashbacks, body memories, and images that some therapists believe are real, if not exact, memories of abuse that occurred years or decades earlier. Unhappy adults, mostly women, report memories that surface during therapy while attending self-help conferences or while reading popular books about incest recovery. Some memories surface spontaneously with no apparent stimulus. Contemporary explanations of repressed memory rely heavily on current psychiatric theory that attributes such phenomena to trauma-related and dissociative disorders. Some contend that different physiological processes are involved in encoding traumatic memory and regular memory (see Wylie, 1993b). Both the clinical and social scientific research communities remain divided on this issue.

### Professional Debate

Proponents strongly believe in the veracity, if not the accuracy, of recovered memories. Although specific details may be vague or contradictory, therapists note that the emotional anguish expressed by their clients is real. They argue that society is just now discovering the true extent of childhood sexual trauma, reports of which had historically been attributed to irrational, hysterical women who could not separate fact from fantasy (Wylie, 1993a). A growing body of professionals now believes that childhood sexual abuse underlies much contemporary psychopathology (Ellenson, 1989; Rose, Peabody, & Stratigeas, 1991; van der Kolk, Brown, & van der Hart, 1989).

Failure to believe reports of ritual abuse has been compared to earlier professional skepticism about child sexual abuse (Sexton, 1989). Cult therapists contend that recovered memories of ritual abuse should be believed because they remain unchanged while the client is under hypnosis and the memories are internally consistent. They note that survivors who have never met give similar accounts of satanic abuse (Mulhern, 1991).

However, not all clinicians who accept the theory of dissociated sexual trauma believe satanic ritual abuse allegations. Skeptics cite extensive research demonstrating that memory is reconstructed and is often subject to inaccuracy, alteration, distortion, and fabrication (Cole & Loftus, 1987; Lindsay & Read, in press; Loftus, 1993; Zaragoza, 1987). Controlled studies on hypnotic age regression have shown that memories evoked under hypnosis can be erroneous. Furthermore, people who meet the diagnostic criteria for multiple personality disorder have been found to be easily hypnotized and highly suggestible while in a trance state (Mulhern, 1991).

Critics contend that therapists, either consciously or unknowingly, evoke false memories of abuse through their therapeutic techniques (see Wylie, 1993a). These critics assert that it is the therapists, rather than the alleged abusers, who are victimizing their clients with unsubstantiated theories and personal agendas. They note that there is little or no evidence that sex abuse causes the array of psychiatric symptoms attributed to it. Additionally, the empirical evidence on posttraumatic stress does not support the theory of repressed or dissociated memory. In a thorough review of 60 years of research on repression, Holmes (1990) concluded that the concept of repression is not supported by reliable evidence. Critics fear that uncritical acceptance of recovered memories may result in societal disbelief in genuine cases of abuse (Loftus, 1993; Mulhern, 1991; Wylie, 1993a; Yapko, 1993).

Mulhern (1991) observed that "cultified" therapy sets up a preexisting belief filter that interprets all client responses as evidence of ritual abuse. In this context, recovered memories depend more on the beliefs of the therapist than on the history of the client. Similarities in ritual abuse stories have been attributed to a "rumor panic" involving a cross-contamination of ideas spread by fundamentalist groups, the media, ritual abuse training seminars, and therapists and clients themselves (Bromley, 1991; Jenkins & Maier-Katkin, 1991; Lyons, 1988; Mulhern, 1991; Victor, 1993).

In the absence of corroboration it remains difficult, if not impossible, to determine the validity of recovered memories. According to Wylie (1993a), the truth lies "all across the spectrum, from one extreme to the other" (p. 73). It is possible that some abuse allegations are fully accurate, some are partly accurate, and some are totally false. Currently there are no widely accepted standards for determining the circumstances or conditions for accepting reports of abuse that are based solely on recovered memories. Professional associations such as NASW and the American Psychological Association are now examining repressed memory to develop future guidelines for practitioners (Landers, 1994). The American Medical Association (AMA) has already developed policies related to the use of hypnosis and memory enhancement techniques to recover memories of childhood sexual abuse. In June 1994 the AMA Council on Scientific Affairs recommended amending a policy on memory enhancement to state that "The AMA considers recovered memories of childhood sexual abuse to be of uncertain authenticity, which should be subject to external verification. The use of recovered memories is fraught with problems of potential misapplication." (AMA, 1994, p. 4).

### False Memory Syndrome

Further complicating this debate are criminal and civil charges that clients are often encouraged to file against family members as part of their recovery process. In response, families who contend that they have been falsely accused have joined together with professionals to form the False Memory Syndrome Foundation, a support and advocacy organization. The foundation also promotes and sponsors scientific and medical research on memory, suggestibility, and repression and disseminates the results to the legal and mental health professions and the general public. Members charge that parents and children have become innocent pawns in a profit-oriented sex abuse industry. Their position is bolstered by people who have recanted abuse accusations, claiming that their therapists pressured them into telling melodramatic stories of ritual abuse that never happened (Jaroff, 1993; Ofshe & Watters, 1993).

Wylie (1993a) observed that the polarization of professional opinion makes it unlikely that this controversy will be settled by research or discourse. In-depth discussions of this debate can be found in Calof (1993), Loftus (1993), Mulhern (1991), Wylie (1993a, 1993b), and Yapko (1993).

## Implications for Social Work Practice

Social workers who work with either cult members or their concerned families should first become acquainted with the full range of clinical and social scientific literature on the topic. Too often, clinicians receive training or information that only stereotypes cults as destructive and supports the prevalent anticult movement ideology. The scant social work literature on this topic reflects these negative cult stereotypes (see Addis et al., 1984; Bloch & Shor, 1989; Goldberg & Goldberg, 1982). Because of the polemical debate that has shaped research and practice, social workers must be fully informed to evaluate critically these disparate ideological positions and the adequacy of the research that supports them.

Practice should always be guided by a commitment to social work values and ethics. Specifically, the affirmation of client dignity and individuality and the right to self-determination are essential. Weick and Pope (1988) suggested that self-determination entails a belief in people's inner capacities to know what they need to fully live and grow. Thus, an appreciation of individuality must concomitantly include a respect for diversity in lifestyles, cultures, and religions.

In addition, social workers need to be fully aware of their own biases about NRMs to prevent them from interfering with treatment. A priori assumptions about the destructive nature of cults may lead to an ideological stance that devalues diversity. The imposition of one's personal values and beliefs is antithetical to self-determination and may engender resentment from clients (Hepworth & Larson, 1993).

Because most new converts are young adults, it is not uncommon for NRMs to recruit on college campuses. Students who are considering joining such groups should be encouraged to learn about the group's beliefs and the degree of commitment required. Some groups require converts to sever ties with friends and family members and may require substantial donations of money or possessions. Blimling (1990) suggested that soapbox forums be used to provide an opportunity for NRMs to express their beliefs in a setting in which their views can be openly debated and challenged.

Social work practice with cult members or their families may entail a variety of social work roles including consultant, counselor, therapist, advocate, mediator, and educator. It is important to recognize that the goals and desires of families seeking assistance often conflict with those of their children, who may wish to maintain their cult affiliations.

Bloch and Shor (1989) suggested that in working with concerned families, the initial role should be one of consultation. Given the diversity that characterizes NRMs, the social worker should have specific knowledge about the group involved. Parents of cult members often hold stereotypical images of cults and need accurate information about the beliefs, practices, and structure of the group their child has joined. Thus, the educational component should be an explicit part of consultation.

Most NRM groups frequently rely on various forms of encapsulation to weaken bonds between members and nonmembers, and families often feel confused, afraid, and helpless when the cult member begins to sever family ties. In addition, parents may overtly disapprove of the specific religious beliefs, practices, and lifestyle their child has chosen. A counseling or therapeutic role may be necessary to aid parents in coping with their feelings about their child's cult involvement. Bloch and Shor (1989) stressed the importance of receptivity and flexibility in reaching out to an estranged child.

Most cult members defect on their own; few seek professional help in severing cult ties. More commonly, parents, friends, and anticult groups attempt to pressure cult members into reevaluating their cult involvement. Sometimes exit counseling occurs after a member has already defected (Wright & Ebaugh, 1993).

When working with either current or former cult members, the label of "cult victim" should be avoided because it engenders a predisposition to view the cult experience in a negative light and will likely set up a barrier to effective and accurate assessment. It is especially important to be sensitive to the client's own perceptions about his or her cult involvement. Because some groups do use manipulative and deceptive recruitment techniques, it may be necessary to explore feelings of betrayal or disillusionment. Assessment should include not only the extent of involvement, but the degree of commitment as well (Wright, 1991). Intervention strategies should be based on mutually negotiated goals and should not be coercive.

Finally, as Mason (1991) cautioned, social workers should be careful not to assume dual roles of investigator and therapist. If allegations of child abuse, ritual abuse, or cultic crime surface, they should be referred to the proper authorities for investigation.

## References


Addis, M., Schulman-Miller, J., & Lightman, M. (1984). The cult clinic helps families in crisis. *Social Casework, 64*(9), 515–522.

American Medical Association. (1994, July 14). *Report of the Council on Scientific Affairs* (CSA Report 5-A-94). Chicago: Author.

Anthony, D., & Ecker, B. (1987). The Anthony typology: A framework for assessing spiritual and consciousness groups. In D. Anthony, B. Ecker, & K. Wilber (Eds.), *Spiritual choices: The problem of recognizing authentic paths to inner transformation* (pp. 35–106). New York: Paragon.

Balch, R. W. (1985). What's wrong with the study of new religions and what can we do about it? In B. K. Kilbourne (Ed.), *Scientific research of new religions: Diver-*

gent perspectives (pp. 24–39). Proceedings of the annual meeting of the Pacific Division of the American Association for the Advancement of Science, San Francisco.

Barker, E. (1984). *The making of a Moonie: Choice or brainwashing*? Oxford England: Blackwell.

Beckford, J. A. (1985). *Cult controversies: The societal response to new religious movements*. London: Tavistock.

Beere, D. B. (1989). *Satanic programming designed to undercut therapy*. Paper presented at the Sixth Annual Conference on Multiple Personality/Dissociative States, Alexandria, VA.

Bird, F. (1979). The pursuit of innocence: New religious movements and moral accountability. *Sociological Analysis, 40*(4), 335–346.

Blimling, G. S. (1990, March). The involvement of college students in totalist groups: Causes, concerns, legal issues, and policy considerations. *Cultic Studies Journal*, *7*(1), 41–68.

Blimling, G. S. (1991, March). *Youth and the occult*. Paper presented at the annual program meeting of the Council on Social Work Education, New Orleans.

Bloch, A. C., & Shor, R. (1989). From consultation to therapy in group work with parents of cultists. *Social Casework*, *70*(4), 231–236.

Braun, B. G. (1989). *Ritualistic abuse and dissociation: Believing the unbelievable*. Paper presented at the Orange County Conference on Multiple Personality and Dissociation, Garden Grove, CA.

Braun, B. G., Goodwin, J., Gould, K., Hammond, D. C., Kluft, R. P., Sachs, R. G., Summit, R. C., & Young, W. C. (1989). *Ritual child abuse: A professional overview*. Ukiah, CA: Cavalcade Productions.

Bromley, D. G. (1988). Deprogramming as a mode of exit from new religious movements: The case of the Unificationist movement. In D. G. Bromley (Ed.), *Falling from the faith: Causes and consequences of religious apostasy* (pp. 185–204). Newbury Park, CA: Sage Publications.

Bromley, D. G. (1991). Satanism: The new cult scare. In J. T. Richardson, J. Best, & D. G. Bromley (Eds.), *The satanism scare* (pp. 49–72). Hawthorne, NY: Aldine de Gruyter.

Bromley, D. G., & Hadden, J. K. (Eds.). (1993). *Religion and the social order*. Greenwich, CT: JAI Press.

Bromley, D. G., & Richardson, J. T. (Eds.). (1983). *The brain-washing/deprogramming controversy: Sociological, psychological, legal and historical perspectives*. Lewiston, NY: Edwin Mellen Press.

Calof, D. (1993, September/October). Facing the truth about false memory. *Family Therapy Networker*, pp. 39–45.

Clark, J., Langone, M. D., Schacter, R., & Daly, R. (1981). *Destructive cult conversion: Theory, research, and practice*. Weston, MA: American Family Foundation.

Cole, C. B., & Loftus, E. F. (1987). The memory of children. In S. J. Ceci, M. D. Toglia, & D. F. Ross (Eds.), *Children's eyewitness memory*. New York: Springer-Verlag.

Crouch, B. E., & Damphouse, K. (1991). Law enforcement and the satanism–crime connection: A survey of "cult cops." In J. T. Richardson, J. Best, & D. G. Bromley (Eds.), *The satanism scare* (pp. 191–217). Hawthorne, NY: Aldine de Gruyter.

Ellenson, G. S. (1989). Horror, rage, and defenses in the symptoms of female sexual abuse survivors. *Social Casework, 70*(10), 589–596.

Galanter, M. (1980). Psychological induction into the larger group: Findings from a modern religious sect. *American Journal of Psychiatry*, *135*(12), 588–591.

Galanter, M. (1989). *Cults, faith, healing and coercion*. New York: Oxford University Press.

Galanter, M., Rabkin, R., Rabkin, J., & Deutsch, A. (1979). "The Moonies," a psychological study. *American Journal of Psychiatry, 136*(2), 165–170.

Galper, M. (1982). The cult phenomenon: Behavioral science perspectives applied to therapy. In F. Kaslow & M. B. Sussman (Eds.), *Cults and family* (pp. 141–150). New York: Haworth Press.

Glock, C. Y., & Bellah, R. N. (Eds.). (1976). *The new religious consciousness*. Berkeley: University of California Press.

Goldberg, L., & Goldberg, W. (1982). Group work with former cultists. *Social Work, 27,* 165–170.

Gordon, D. F. (1988). Psychiatry and Krishna consciousness. In D. G. Bromley & L. Shinn (Eds.), *Krishna consciousness in the west*. Lewisburg, PA: Bucknell University Press.

Griel, A. L., & Rudy, D. R. (1984a). Social cocoons: Encapsulation and identity transformation organizations. *Sociological Inquiry, 54*(3), 260–278.

Greil, A. L., & Rudy, D. R. (1984b). What have we learned from process models of conversion? An examination of ten studies. *Sociological Focus, 17*(4), 306–323.

Hepworth, D. H., & Larson, J. A. (1993). *Direct social work practice: Theory and skills* (4th ed.). Belmont, CA: Wadsworth.

Hicks, R. D. (1991). *In pursuit of Satan: The police and the occult*. Buffalo, NY: Prometheus Books.

Holmes, D. S. (1990). The evidence for repression: An examination of sixty years of research. In J. L. Singer (Ed.), *Repression and dissociation* (pp. 85–102). Chicago: University of Chicago Press.

Jacobs, J. (1984). The economy of love in religious commitment: The deconversion of women from nontraditional religious movements. *Journal for the Scientific Study of Religion*, *23*(2), 155–171.

Jaroff, L. (1993, November 29). Lies of the mind. *Time*, pp. 52, 55–56, 59.

Jenkins, P. (1992). *Intimate enemies*. Hawthorne, NY: Aldine de Gruyter.

Jenkins, P., & Maier-Katkin, D. (1991). Occult survivors: The making of a myth. In J. T. Richardson, J. Best, & D. G. Bromley (Eds.), *The satanism scare* (pp. 127–144). Hawthorne, NY: Aldine de Gruyter.

Kahaner, L. (1988). *Cults that kill*. New York: Warner Books.

Kaye, M., & Kline, L. (1987). *Clinical indicators of satanic cult victimization*. Paper presented at the Sixth International Conference on Multiple Personality and Dissociative States, Alexandria, VA.

Kuner, W. (1983). New religious movements and mental health. In E. Barker (Ed.), *Of gods and men: New religious movements in the West* (pp. 255–264). Macon, GA: Mercer University Press.

Landers, S. (1994, January). Walking the fine line of abuse recall. *NASW News*, p. 3.

Lanning, K. V. (1989a) *Child sex rings: A behavioral analysis*. Washington, DC: National Center for Missing and Exploited Children.

Lanning, K. V. (1989b). Satanic, occult, and ritualistic crime: A law enforcement perspective. *Police Chief, 56*, 62–83.

Larson, B. (1989). *Satanism: The seduction of America's youth*. Nashville, TN: Thomas Nelson Press.

Levine, S. (1984). *Radical departures: Desperate detours to growing up*. New York: Harcourt Brace Jovanovich.

Lewis, J. R. (1986). Reconstructing the cult experience: Post-involvement attitudes as a function of mode of exit and post-involvement socialization. *Sociological Analysis, 47*(2), 151–159.

Lindsay, D. S., & Read, J. D. (in press). Psychotherapy and memories of childhood sexual abuse: A cognitive perspective. *Applied Cognitive Psychology*.

Lofland, J. (1977). *Doomsday cult: A study of conversion, proselytization, and maintenance of faith* (rev. ed.). New York: Irvington.

Lofland, J., & Skovnid, N. L. (1981). Conversion motifs. *Journal for the Scientific Study of Religion, 20*(4), 373–385.

Lofland, J., & Skovnid, N. L. (1983). Patterns of conversion. In E. Barker (Ed.), *Of gods and men: New religious movements in the west* (pp. 1–24). Macon, GA: Mercer University Press.

Lofland, J., & Stark, R. (1965). Becoming a world saver: A theory of conversion to a deviant perspective. *American Sociological Review, 30*, 862–875.

Loftus, E. F. (1993). The reality of repressed memories. *American Psychologist, 48*(5), 518–537.

Long, T. E., & Hadden, J. K. (1983). Religious conversion and the concept of socialization: Integrating the brainwashing and drift models. *Journal for the Scientific Study of Religion, 22*(1), 1–14.

Lyons, A. (1988). *Satan wants you: The cult of devil worship in America*. New York: Mysterious Press.

Mason, M. A. (1991). The McMartin case revisited: The conflict between social work and criminal justice. *Social Work, 36*(5), 391–399.

Melton, J. G. (1986a). *Encyclopedic handbook of cults in America*. New York: Garland.

Melton, J. G. (1986b, March). *Evidences of Satan in contemporary America: A survey*. Paper presented at the Pacific Division of the American Philosophical Association, Los Angeles.

Mulhern, S. (1991). Satanism and psychotherapy. In J. T. Richardson, J. Best, & D. G. Bromley (Eds.), *The satanism scare* (pp. 145–172). Hawthorne, NY: Aldine de Gruyter.

Nathan, D. (1989, April 7–13). False evidence: How bad science fueled the hysteria over child abuse. *Los Angeles Weekly*, pp. 15–19.

Nathan, D. (1991a). The ritual sex abuse hoax. In D. Nathan (Ed.), *Women and other aliens* (pp. 148–167). El Paso, TX: Cinco Puntas Press.

Nathan, D. (1991b). Satanism and child molestation: Constructing the ritual abuse scare. In J. T. Richardson, J. Best, & D. J. Bromley (Eds.), *The satanism scare* (pp. 75–94). Hawthorne, NY: Aldine de Gruyter.

Ofshe, R. (1986, September 2). Satanism: Overtones in other slayings. *Los Angeles Times*, pp. 1–2.

Ofshe, R., & Watters, E. (1993). Making monsters. *Society, 30*(3), 4–16.

Pulling, P. (1989). *The devil's web*. Lafayette, LA: Huntington House.

Raschke, C. A. (1990). *Painted black: From drug killings to heavy metal—How satanism is besieging our culture and our communities*. San Francisco: Harper & Row.

Richardson, J. T., Best, J., & Bromley, D. G. (Eds.). (1991). *The satanism scare*. Hawthorne, NY: Aldine de Gruyter.

Richardson, J. T., van der Lans, J., & Derks, F. (1986). Leaving and labeling: Voluntary and coerced disaffiliation from religious social movements. *Research in Social Movements, 9*, 97–126.

Robbins, T. (1992). *Cults, converts and charisma*. Newbury Park, CA: Sage Publications.

Robbins, T., & Anthony, D. (Eds.). (1981). *In gods we trust: New patterns of religious pluralism in America*. New Brunswick, NJ: Transaction.

Rose, S. M., Peabody, C. G., & Stratigeas, B. (1991). Responding to hidden abuse: A role for social work in reforming mental health systems. *Social Work, 36*, 408–413.

Ross, J. C., & Langone, M. D. (1988). *Cults: What parents should know*. Weston, MA: American Family Foundation.

Rowe, L., & Cavender, G. (1991). Caldrons bubble, Satan's trouble, but witches are okay: Media constructions of Satanism and witchcraft. In J. T. Richardson, J. Best, & D. G. Bromley (Eds.), *The satanism scare* (pp. 263–275). Hawthorne, NY: Aldine de Gruyter.

Schwarz, T., & Empey, D. (1988). *Satanism: Is your family safe?* Grand Rapids, MI: Zondervan.

Sexton, D. (1989). *Gaining insights into the complexity of ritualistic abuse*. Paper presented at the Eighth National Conference on Child Abuse and Neglect.

Shupe, A., & Bromley, D. G. (1991, August). *The modern American anti-cult movement: A twenty-year retrospective*. Paper presented at the annual meeting of the Association for the Sociology of Religion, Cincinnati.

Singer, M. T. (1979, January). Coming out of the cults. *Psychology Today*, pp. 72–82.

Snow, D. A., & Machalek, R. (1984). The sociology of conversion. *Annual Review of Sociology, 10*, 167–190.

Snow, D. A., Zurcher, L. A., & Ekland-Olson, S. (1980). Social networks and social movements: A microstructural approach to differential recruitment. *American Sociological Review, 45*, 787–801.

Solomon, T. (1981). Integrating the "Moonie" experience: A survey of ex-members of the Unification Church. In T. Robbins & D. Anthony (Eds.), *In gods we trust: New patterns of religious pluralism in America* (pp. 275–295). New Brunswick, NJ: Transaction.

Stark, R., & Bainbridge, W. S. (1980). Networks of faith: Inter-personal bonds and recruitment to cults and sects. *American Journal of Sociology, 85*(6), 1376–1395.

Stark, R., & Bainbridge, W. S. (1985). *The future of religion: Secularization, revival, and cult formation*. Berkeley: University of California.

Stone, D. (1978). On knowing what we know about new religions. In J. L. Needleman & G. Baker (Eds.), *Understanding the new religions* (pp. 141–152). New York: Seabury.

Tipton, S. M. (1982). *Getting saved from the sixties: Moral meaning in conversion and cultural change*. Berkeley: University of California.

Ungerleider, J. T., & Wellisch, D. K. (1979). Coercive persuasion (brainwashing), religious cults, and deprogramming. *American Journal of Psychiatry, 136*, 279–282.

van der Kolk, B. A., Brown, P., & van der Hart, O. (1989). Pierre Janet on post-traumatic stress. *Journal of Traumatic Stress, 2*, 365–379.

Victor, J. S. (1993). *Satanic panic: The creation of a contemporary legend*. Chicago: Open Court Publishing.

Wallis, R. (1984). *The elementary forms of the new religious life*. London: Routledge & Kegan Paul.
Weick, A., & Pope, L. (1988). Knowing what's best: A new look at self-determination. *Social Casework, 69*(1), 10–16.
West, L., & Singer, M. T. (1980). Cults, quacks, and nonprofessional psychotherapists. In H. I. Kaplan, A. M. Freedman & B. J. Sadock (Eds.), *Comprehensive textbook of psychiatry III* (pp. 32–48). Baltimore: Williams & Wilkins.
Wilber, K. (1983). *A sociable God*. New York: McGraw-Hill.
Woodward, K. W., Fleming, C., Reiss, S., Rafshoon, S., & Leonard, E. A. (1993, March 15). Cultic America: A tower of babel. *Newsweek*, pp. 60–61.
Wright, S. A. (1984). Post-involvement attitudes of voluntary defectors from controversial new religious movements. *Journal for the Scientific Study of Religion, 23*(2), 172–182.
Wright, S. A. (1987). *Leaving cults: The dynamics of defection*. Washington, DC: Society for the Scientific Study of Religion.
Wright, S. A. (1988). Leaving new religious movements: Issues, theory and research. In D. G. Bromley (Ed.), *Falling from the faith: Causes and consequences of religious apostasy* (pp. 143–165). Newbury Park, CA: Sage Publications.
Wright, S. A. (1991). Reconceptualizing cult coercion and withdrawal: A comparative analysis of divorce and apostasy. *Social Forces, 70*(1), 125–145.
Wright, S. A., & D'Antonio, W. V. (1993). Families and new religions. In D. G. Bromley & J. K. Hadden (Eds.), *Religion and the social order* (Vol. 3, Part A, pp. 219–240). Greenwich, CT: JAI Press.
Wright, S. A., & Ebaugh, H. R. (1993). Leaving new religions. In D. G. Bromley & J. K. Hadden (Eds.), *Religion and the social order* (Vol. 3, Part B, pp. 117–138). Greenwich, CT: JAI Press.
Wright, S. A., & Piper, E. S. (1986). Families and cults: Familial factors related to youth leaving or remaining in deviant religious groups. *Journal of Marriage and the Family, 48*, 15–25.
Wylie, M. S. (1993a, September/October). The shadow of a doubt. *Family Therapy Networker*, pp. 18–29, 70, 73.
Wylie, M. S. (1993b, September/October). Trauma and memory. *Family Therapy Networker*, pp. 42–43.
Yapko, M. (1993, September/October). The seductions of memory. *Family Therapy Networker*, pp. 31–37.
Zaragoza, M. D. (1987). Memory, suggestibility, and eyewitness testimony in children and adults. In S. J. Ceci, M. D. Toglia, & D. F. Ross (Eds.), *Children's eyewitness memory* (p. 53–78). New York: Springer-Verlag.

## Further Reading

Beckford, J. A. (Ed.). (1986). *New religious movements and rapid social change*. London: Sage Publications.
Choquette, D. (1985). *New religious movements in America: An annotated bibliography*. Westport, CT: Greenwood.
Richardson, J. T. (Ed.). (1988). *Money and power in new religious movements*. New York: Edwin Mellen.
Shupe, A. D., & Bromley, D. G. (1985). *A documentary history of the anti-cult movement*. New York: Edwin Mellen.
Terr, L. (1994). *Unchained memories: True stories of traumatic memories, lost and found*. New York: Basic Books.
Wright, L. (1994). *Remembering Satan*. New York: Alfred A. Knopf.
Yapko, M. D. (1994). *Suggestions of abuse: True and false memories of childhood sexual trauma*. New York: Simon & Schuster.

**Susan P. Robbins, DSW,** is associate professor, University of Houston, Graduate School of Social Work, Houston, TX 77204-4492.

### For further information see

Adolescence Overview; Child Abuse and Neglect Overview; Child Sexual Abuse Overview; Clinical Social Work; Cognition and Social Cognitive Theory; Conflict Resolution; Ecological Perspective; Ethnic-Sensitive Practice; Families: Direct Practice; Goal Setting and Intervention Planning; Interviewing; Intervention Research; Mass Media; Sectarian Agencies; Social Work Profession Overview; Victims of Torture and Trauma.

**Key Words**

cults
new religious movements
recovered memory
satanic ritual abuse

READER'S GUIDE

## Cultural Competence

*The following entries contain information on this general topic:*

African Americans (*See Reader's Guide*)
Alaska Natives
American Indians
Asian Americans (*See Reader's Guide*)
Deaf Community
Deafness
Ethnic-Sensitive Practice
Management: Diverse Workplaces
National Origin Groups (*See Reader's Guide*)
People of Color (*See Reader's Guide*)
Racial and Ethnic Groups (*See Reader's Guide*)
Special Populations (*See Reader's Guide*)
Visual Impairment and Blindness
White Ethnic Groups

# D

## Day Care

*See* Adult Day Care; Child Care Services

## Day, Dorothy

*See* Biographies section, Volume 3

# Deaf Community

**Tovah M. Wax**

Throughout history the deaf community has evolved into a multifaceted and organic complex with recognizable boundaries and an identifiable sociocultural anthropology that distinguishes it both from the larger mainstream hearing society and from ethnic minority communities. This entry examines the multifaceted nature of deafness, including historical perspectives on deafness. Furthermore, it describes the deaf community and factors that have contributed to deaf culture. Finally, suggestions are offered for social work intervention with the deaf community.

To appreciate the unique complexity of the deaf community, deafness itself must be understood as a multifaceted concept. As succinctly discussed by Lane (1984), deafness is regarded as both a disability and a sociocultural phenomenon. Until recently, membership in the deaf community was ascribed to individuals almost exclusively on the basis of audiological definitions related to hearing loss and functional definitions related to speech ability and communication (Baker & Cokely, 1980; Schroedel, 1984). As Higgins (1980) elaborated, however, there are political, linguistic, and social avenues to membership in the deaf community; for example, shared use of sign language, participation in certain activities (such as attending residential schools for deaf people), and other sociologically circumscribed factors are typically expected or required for acceptance by deaf community members.

### Background

Several global shifts in perspectives about deafness occurred throughout history, starting as early as biblical times (Table 1). Understanding these perspectives will have an impact on the nature and type of social work interventions used with this population.

#### Infirmity Models

At one time deafness was considered a message from God or Satan, conferred as punishment for sin or fall from grace. Deaf people, therefore, were probably regarded with some fear or awe. During the Greco–Roman era, Aristotle was a key proponent of the relationship between thinking and language: Muteness or lack of voice was associated with lack of sense or mind. Deaf people—or, more precisely, those who were mute—were considered incapable of reason and thus unable to conduct most adult transactions such as marriage, property ownership, or voting. The concept of deafness as a deficit was reinforced by medical researchers and practitioners who discovered the physical etiologies of hearing impairment and subscribed to what Lane (1990) called the infirmity model of deafness.

As it became clear that many forms of deafness could not be cured, the focus shifted to rehabilitation, or attempts to compensate for hearing impairment. Audiology became a key component of rehabilitation programs, which had the ultimate goal of helping individuals live independently in the community. However well intentioned these programs or services were, the concept of compensation still assumes deafness is a deficit that requires fixing or making whole.

#### Cultural Model

During the years of civil rights unrest (1960 to 1980), a movement among grassroots deaf people attempting to gain more respect for the deaf com-

TABLE 1

**Perspectives on Deaf People throughout History**

| Historical perspective | Working assumptions |
|---|---|
| Biblical view<br>Sign of disgrace, fall from grace<br>Punishable sin<br>Message from God or Satan | Moral hypothesis |
| Aristotelian view<br>Muteness = Senselessness<br>Nonuse/loss of voice = Lack of mind | Deficit hypothesis |
| Medical view<br>Recognize/discover ear pathology<br>Attempts at cure for deafness | Infirmity model |
| Rehabilitation view<br>Audiology<br>Restoration of hearing function<br>Early goal: Employment<br>Later goal: Independent living | Compensation hypothesis |
| Cultural minority view<br>Deaf culture as sociopolitical reality<br>Oppression, victimization | Cultural model |
| Cultural diversity view<br>Deaf culture as one of many<br>E pluribus pluribus | Difference hypothesis |

NOTE: This table was formulated substantively from the historical reviews offered by Lane, H. (1984). *When the mind hears.* New York: Random House; and Lane, H. (1990). Cultural and infirmity models of Deaf Americans. *Journal of the American Rehabilitation Association, 28,* 11–26.

munity and deaf culture began to crystallize as what Lane (1990) elaborated as a cultural model of deafness. In this model deaf people compose a cultural minority in addition to, beyond, or apart from a medical or rehabilitation perspective. Increasing recognition of American Sign Language and of contributions made by deaf people to science, art, education, and politics (Gannon, 1981) have contributed to what is described as a difference hypothesis. From this perspective, deaf people do not consider themselves disabled or in need of fixing. The prevailing view today thus seems to be one of recognizing and accepting deaf culture as one of many cultures and understanding the unique characteristics of a diverse deaf community (Dolnick, 1993).

The distinction between the infirmity and cultural models of deafness also leads to a distinction in social work intervention approaches. Lane (1990) argued that the infirmity model—or the "medicalization" of deafness—reflects a paternalistic view by keeping deaf people in the dependent role of patient or client. Accordingly, social workers who view deafness as a medical and psychosocial disability are more likely to view deaf people as clientele who need rehabilitative or psychological help. In contrast, the cultural model recognizes that the deaf culture has characteristics that distinguish it from other mainstream cultures, such as a different language; unique educational and social experiences; and a distinct set of values, mores, and folkways. From this perspective, social work intervention is not substantively different from the kind of intervention required with people from other cultural minority groups. Techniques of cross-cultural counseling, advocacy, and empowerment are more likely to be found among social workers adopting this perspective (Wax, 1993).

## Deaf Community

Borrowing from Becker's (1963) deviancy theory, Higgins (1980) described how deaf people—"outsiders" with respect to a larger hearing society—have responded to outsider status by developing into a community. Membership in the deaf community is achieved not only by the shared experience of deafness but also by identification with the world of deaf people and participation in activities or events with others who are deaf. Given a definition based primarily on the common function of deafness, the deaf community appears to conform to the functional and action process perspectives of community (that is, a community developed to serve a particular function or common interest/action) (Rothman, 1987).

### Definitions

Of the factors affecting social organization of the deaf community, communication preference and skill are the most persistent. Deaf people are typically differentiated by two basic modes of communication: oralism and manualism. Some deaf people who are mostly or exclusively oralist (that is, who rely on speaking and speechreading for communication) may not even consider themselves part of the deaf community. Many others belong to organizations for oral deaf people (such as the Alexander Graham Bell Association and the Oral Deaf Adults Society) and may also participate in events with deaf people who sign. Within the signing or manualist deaf community, there are a variety of sign languages, ranging from American Sign Language (the "purest" form of sign language) (Kannapell, 1993; Stokoe, 1960) to signed forms of the English language. Regional and ethnic differences exist in sign language throughout the United States; deaf people can often identify where others learned sign language the same way hearing people can identify where others grew up by listening to their accents (Higgins, 1980).

Although there is still debate about the composition of the deaf community, many people acknowledge distinctions among a deaf population, a deaf community, and a deaf culture (Schroedel, 1984). According to Schroedel, the *deaf population* includes all deaf people and those associated with them, such as professionals specializing in services to deaf people. The *deaf community,* including oralist and manualist deaf people as well as others such as hearing relatives or sign language interpreters, comprises those who are active in the formal social, civic, and religious organizations at the community's core (Higgins, 1980; Schroedel). The *deaf culture* defines more specifically those who adopt American Sign Language (and some of its variants) as a primary means of communication and who share a set of beliefs and values distinguishable from those of the larger deaf community or society at large (Padden & Humphries, 1988). Some people differentiate between people who are culturally Deaf (spelled with an uppercase D) and those who are deaf (spelled with a lowercase d) members of the larger deaf community (Padden & Humphries). Some deaf professionals, however, have commented that this distinction was contrived to justify a perception of political integrity or to embellish ethnic pride (Stewart, 1992) or as a reaction against *audism,* defined by Humphries (1977) as hearing domination over the deaf community.

### Differences from Ethnic Communities

One way in which the deaf community differs from ethnic communities is that most deaf people (90 percent to 95 percent) are born to hearing parents (Schein & Delk, 1974). Consequently, a significant avenue of socialization into the deaf community is through educational institutions such as residential schools and colleges for deaf people and organizations such as the National Association of the Deaf (Van Cleve & Crouch, 1989). Enculturation into the deaf community is more frequently a horizontal than a vertical process, as would be the transmission between deaf parents and their children (Cagle & Pollard, 1987; Higgins, 1980).

Although the deaf community is not geographically circumscribed as are many ethnic communities, a strong sense of community is nevertheless maintained through an extensive and cohesive network of contacts that range from local to international. With the technological advancement of increasingly affordable and available devices now called text telephones (still known popularly as TTYs, TDDs, or TTs), telephone relay systems, and computer electronic mail networks, deaf people have been able to maintain strong connections with each other. Other popular mechanisms for maintaining a viable deaf community have been social clubs, a growing number of political and professional organizations such as the American Deafness and Rehabilitation Association, newspapers and newsletters, and sports tournaments. Consistent with the action process perspective on community (Rothman, 1987), local, regional, and national events offer significant avenues for fostering a sense of community among deaf people. A recent example at the national and even the international level was the Deaf President Now movement in 1987, which culminated in the installation of the first deaf president at Gallaudet University in Washington, DC, a world-recognized liberal arts institution for deaf people. As Higgins (1980) noted, these mechanisms help maintain a cohesive community but do have some drawbacks, including difficulty controlling one's privacy or escaping one's past.

## Deaf Culture

Among the factors that have contributed to the uniqueness of the deaf culture are experiences with residential schools for the deaf, interactions between deaf and hearing people, and a different worldview, or what Padden and Humphries (1988) called a different "center." Deaf children generally left home at an early age to attend a residential school for deaf people, and the experience was emotionally memorable for many families. Because they spent part of the year at school and went home for holidays and summers, many of these children developed a bicultural and bilingual orientation to their hearing families and to the deaf school communities (Lane & Grosjean, 1980). As more hearing family members learn and use sign language, it is more likely that parents, siblings, and extended relatives will become involved in the deaf community.

The interactions between deaf and hearing people are part of the legend and folklore of the deaf culture (Holcomb, 1977; Rutherford, 1993), along with a growing body of artistic, literary, scientific, and other contributions made by deaf people that reflect the experience of being deaf in a hearing world (Gannon, 1981; Lang & Meath-Lang, in press). One frequently shared experience among deaf adults is the "discovery" of deafness as a product of interaction with a larger hearing world (Padden & Humphries, 1988). For example, a child from a deaf family eventually learns that most families are hearing and that his or her family is perceived as different or strange. This shift in perspective sometimes creates a feeling of discomfort or embarrassment that is handled through individual and collective exposures to models of interactions between deaf and hearing individuals. These common experiences illustrate characteristics of the deaf community consistent with the social–psychological perspective of community discussed by Rothman (1987).

Of growing interest is a cultural–anthropological view that understands the deaf culture and the experience of deaf people independently of the larger hearing context (Rothman, 1987). Padden and Humphries (1988) illustrated ways in which deaf people operate from different frames of reference from hearing people. Among hearing people, those who are hard of hearing (who can speak and use the telephone) are perceived as better off than those who are deaf, but the opposite is considered true among deaf people. Deaf people who are born to deaf parents, who have attended or graduated from schools for deaf people, and who are active in the deaf community are perceived as having higher status in the deaf culture than those who do not have these characteristics (Kannapell, 1993). Deafness is valued highly among deaf people in ways that are not generally true among hearing or even some nonculturally deaf people (Kannapell, 1993). From the sociopolitical–structural point of view (Rothman, 1987), the question of who is "authentically" deaf remains a significant issue in the deaf culture today (Dolnick, 1993).

## Social Work Intervention and the Deaf Community

Because deaf people are described both as a disability group and as a cultural community, deaf people face a dilemma. As a disability group, they are recipients of a substantial array of government benefits (vocational rehabilitation, Supplemental Security Income), legal safeguards (Rehabilitation Act of 1973 [P.L. 93-112]; Americans with Disabilities Act of 1990 [P.L. 101-336]), and other social services; as an ethnic minority group, they would not be eligible for most or all of these benefits. Although many deaf people do not view themselves as physically disabled in the same fashion as people who are blind or mobility impaired, they still experience educational, occupational, and social disadvantages as a result of communication and attitudinal barriers (Lane, 1990). Consequently, there is a certain amount of confusion among deaf people about which political agendas to pursue. One way of resolving the dilemma has been to recognize different contexts for action (MacDougall, 1991): At some times sociolinguistic issues are paramount (bilingual education); at other times disability issues become salient (accessibility); and at still other times social and disability issues are concurrently important (cochlear implantation controversy).

### Theory and Research

From the theoretical point of view, the deaf community, including the deaf culture, shares many characteristics with other communities, such as definable boundaries (social systems approach); social stratification (structural); shared experiences and interests (social–psychological); distinctive demographic characteristics (people and territory); and shared sociopolitical purposes (functional and action processes). It follows, therefore, that similar research and intervention strategies are applicable (Rothman, 1987). To the extent that at least some research in the deaf community is cross-cultural, consideration of cross-cultural ethics is obligatory, not only to ensure accurate and appropriately obtained data but also to conduct analyses and interpretations of data that ultimately lead to appropriate intervention strategies (Pollard, 1992). For example, given the relative lack of interest in medical–audiological procedures within the deaf culture, it would be inappropriate, if not offensive, for deaf people to be the objects of attempted social work intervention aimed at compliance with treatments that will prevent or mitigate deafness.

### Cross-Cultural Approaches

Wax (1993) explored evolving perspectives of people with disabilities as consumers in a "disability marketplace." The different consumer perspectives identifiable among segments of the deaf community and appropriate social work intervention strategies applicable to each are summarized in Table 2. People who are members of the deaf culture will tend to have values and perspectives that are significantly different from those of the larger hearing society; consequently, cross-cultural social work intervention strategies are most applicable to this group.

Using strategies similar to those used in working with members of ethnic minority groups, social workers will need to be educated about characteristics of deaf culture and the larger deaf community. Among the most salient characteristics are the primacy of sign language and the need for skills in both signed and spoken communication methods, including effective use of sign language interpreters and technological equipment such as the TTY, visual signaling, and auditory amplification devices. In addition, social workers need to know about language and communication

TABLE 2
**Ethos of Social Work Intervention with the Deaf Community**

| | Deaf consumer context | | | |
|---|---|---|---|---|
| | Segregation | Assimilation | Bicultural | Marginal |
| Cultural perspective | Conflict of values | Congruence of values | Selective congruence of values | Uncertain or unclear values |
| Attitude of social worker (perceived or actual) | Paternalistic and/or patronizing | Therapeutic and/or misguided | Advocate and/or adversary | Therapeutic and/or intrusive |
| Predicted consumer behavior | Refusal or rejection | Acceptance or compliance | Flexible and/or idiographic | Reluctance or resistance |
| Implied social work intervention strategy | Cross cultural | Traditional | Eclectic | Broad spectrum |

issues (oralism versus manualism), cognitive and educational options (mainstream versus residential school), and identity and occupational and lifestyle developmental issues of importance to deaf people. Although their work is focused on education of deaf people who are also from different ethnic backgrounds, Christiansen and Delgado (1993) offered suggestions for understanding and working with multicultural issues in the deaf community. In particular, it is important to recognize that deaf people live primarily in the visual–kinesthetic mode, rather than in the auditory–visual mode typical of hearing communities. Also, power differentials and issues of equity and equality will be magnified beyond what is typically encountered in social worker–client interactions in which the two parties are from different communities or cultures.

**Coevolutionary Approach**

Ultimately, social workers who work with deaf communities will need to adopt what might be called a reconstructionist (Ivey, 1993) or coevolutionary (Harvey & Dym, 1988) approach: Practitioners and community members alike need to minimize assumptions about each other and negotiate a consensus of values or meanings as groundwork for intervention. Skills most helpful to this process include flexibility, negotiation, problem solving, and mutual (as opposed to unidirectional) accommodation. Social workers who have these skills can, for example, serve as mediators, consultants, or advocates in situations in which local deaf communities seek better access to local social services resources.

Members of the deaf community who have been, and want to remain, assimilated into the larger hearing world—mostly people who lost their hearing as adults or older adults—are likely to continue sharing mainstream values and perspectives and are also likely to accept social work intervention geared toward compensating for hearing loss. Many people in this group are likely to accept adaptive technologies that will facilitate mainstreaming. Scherer (1993) offered a model for enhancing "goodness of fit" between consumers and technological equipment. As an example, social workers might work with hard-of-hearing organizations to help secure cost-effective auditory amplification loops. Nonetheless, social workers also must be able to discuss all the options available to people who lose their hearing—including a change of orientation to a more culturally deaf lifestyle within the deaf community—and to facilitate that change process.

A large segment of the deaf community is bicultural and bilingual. Many deaf people, usually college educated, have been pioneers in careers requiring sustained interactions with hearing people; their after-work hours, however, are typically lived within the deaf community. Social work intervention with this group will require a somewhat more existential approach, in that the particular mix of bicultural and bilingual emphasis will vary significantly and uniquely among individuals.

Finally, even within a heterogeneous deaf community, there is a group of individuals who do not easily fit within the norms of that community (Higgins, 1980). A number of people who suddenly become deaf later in life may go through a period of trauma and confusion in which they are not clear about their values and affiliations. In these cases, a broad spectrum of social work services may be applicable, ranging from mental health counseling services to networking to cross-cultural intervention. Social work intervention with deaf community members depends to a large extent on understanding the consumer context of deaf clientele and being able to negotiate mutually agreed-on goals for appropriate changes, depending on which aspect of functioning vis-à-vis the deaf community is of particular salience at the time.

## References


Americans with Disabilities Act of 1990. P.L. 101-336, 104 Stat. 327.

Baker, C., & Cokely, D. (1980). *American Sign Language: A teacher's resource text on grammar and culture.* Silver Spring, MD: T. J. Publishers.

Becker, H. (1963). *Outsiders: Studies in the sociology of deviance.* London: Free Press of Glencoe.

Cagle, K., & Pollard, R. (1987, July). *Culture and conflict in deaf/hearing relations: A discovery process.* Paper presented at the DeafWay International Meeting, Gallaudet University, Washington, DC.

Christiansen, K., & Delgado, G. (1993). *Multicultural issues in deafness.* New York: Longman.

Dolnick, E. (1993, September). Deafness as culture. *Atlantic Monthly,* pp. 37–53.

Gannon, J. (1981). *Deaf heritage.* Silver Spring, MD: National Association of the Deaf.

Harvey, M., & Dym, B. (1988). An ecological perspective on deafness. *Journal of Rehabilitation of the Deaf, 21,* 12–20.

Higgins, P. (1980). *Outsiders in a hearing world.* Newbury Park, CA: Sage Publications.

Holcomb, R. (1977). *Hazards of deafness.* Northridge, CA: Joyce Media.

Humphries, T. (1977). *Communicating across cultures (deaf/hearing) and language learning.* Doctoral dissertation, Union Graduate School, Cincinnati, OH.

Ivey, A. (1993). On the need for reconstruction of our present practice of counseling and psychotherapy. *Counseling Psychologist, 21,* 225–228.

Kannapell, B. (1993). *Language choice—Identity choice.* Burtonsville, MD: Linstock Press.

Lane, H. (1984). *When the mind hears.* New York: Random House.

Lane, H. (1990). Cultural and infirmity models of Deaf Americans. *Journal of the American Rehabilitation Association, 28,* 11–26.

Lane, H., & Grosjean, F. (1980). *Recent perspectives on ASL.* Hillsdale, NJ: Lawrence Erlbaum.

Lang, H., & Meath-Lang, B. (in press). *Deaf persons in the arts and sciences: A biographical dictionary.* Westport, CT: Greenwood Press.

MacDougall, J. (1991). Current issues in deafness: A psychological perspective. *Canadian Psychology, 32,* 612–627.

Padden, C., & Humphries, T. (1988). *Deaf in America: Voices from a culture.* Cambridge, MA: Harvard University Press.

Pollard, R. (1992). Cross-cultural ethics in the conduct of deafness research. *Rehabilitation Psychology, 37,* 87–101.

Rehabilitation Act of 1973. P.L. 93-112, 87 Stat. 355.

Rothman, J. (1987). Community theory and research. In A. Minahan (Ed.-in-Chief), *Encyclopedia of social work* (18th ed., Vol. 1, pp. 308–316). Silver Spring, MD: National Association of Social Workers.

Rutherford, S. (1993). *A study of American deaf folklore.* Burtonsville, MD: Linstock Press.

Schein, J., & Delk, M. (1974). *The deaf population in the USA.* Silver Spring, MD: National Association of the Deaf.

Scherer, M. (1993). *Living in the state of stuck.* Cambridge, MA: Brookline Books.

Schroedel, J. (1984). Analyzing surveys of deaf adults: Implications for survey research on persons with disabilities. *Social Science Medicine, 19,* 619–627.

Stewart, L. (1992). Debunking the bilingual/bicultural snow job in the American deaf community. In M. Garretson (Ed.), *Viewpoints on deafness: A deaf American monograph* (Vol. 42, pp. 129–142). Silver Spring, MD: National Association of the Deaf.

Stokoe, W. (1960). Sign language structure: An outline of the visual communication system of the American deaf. *Studies in Linguistics* (Occasional paper). Buffalo, NY.

Van Cleve, J., & Crouch, B. (1989). *A place of their own.* Washington, DC: Gallaudet University Press.

Wax, T. (1993). Matchmaking among cultures: Disability culture and the larger marketplace. In R. Glueckhauf, L. Sechrest, G. Bond, & E. McDonel (Eds.), *Improving assessment in rehabilitation and health* (pp. 156–175). Newbury Park, CA: Sage Publications.


## Further Reading


Higgins, P., & Nash, J. (1987). *Understanding deafness socially.* Springfield, IL: Charles C Thomas.

Lane, H. (1992). *The mask of benevolence: Disabling the deaf community.* New York: Alfred A. Knopf.

Lucas, C., & Valli, C. (1993). *Language contact in the American deaf community.* San Diego: Academic Press.

Scheetz, N. (1993). *Orientation to deafness.* Needham Heights, MA: Allyn & Bacon.


**Tovah M. Wax, PhD, CSW,** is associate professor and chair, Psychological Services, National Technical Institute for the Deaf, Rochester Institute of Technology, Rochester, NY 14623.

### For further information see

Advocacy; Citizen Participation; Civil Rights; Community; Deafness; Deinstitutionalization; Disability; Ethics and Values; Human Rights; Information Systems; Natural Helping Networks; Social Work Profession Overview.

**Key Words**
deaf community
deaf culture
deafness

# Deafness

K. Dean Santos

The quest to cure or compensate for hearing impairment to educate people who are deaf started as early as the 16th century (DiCarlo, 1964; Moores, 1987). Since the 1970s, the concept of deafness has been evolving from a focus primarily on the disability toward a focus on the significance of the unique social and anthropological phenomena in the lives of people who are deaf. With this shift in focus, deafness is no longer the exclusive province of the medical and rehabilitation fields. Rather, the psychosocial development, mental health, family dynamics, and sociocultural environments of people in the deaf population have been studied and addressed by social scientists and human services professionals. This cultural model of deafness has significant implications for social work practice.

## Deaf Population

Methodological problems, including communication complications and the lack of a consistent definition of deafness (Schein, 1968), prevented accurate estimates of the deaf population before the landmark National Census of the Deaf Population in 1970 (Schein & Delk, 1974). The survey estimated prevalence rates for the following levels of hearing impairment:

- *Hearing impaired:* having a deviation of any kind from normal hearing, including deafness
- *Significant bilateral:* having significant hearing loss in both ears, with some difficulty understanding speech in the better ear
- *Deaf:* unable to hear and understand speech
- *Prevocationally deaf:* onset of deafness before age 19
- *Prelingually deaf:* onset before age three, before the acquisition of language. (Schein & Delk, 1974)

The resulting rates of prevalence (number per 100,000) are routinely applied to local census data to calculate baseline estimates for a specified area. Table 1 represents the rates for each category and a calculated projection of the deaf population in the United States in 1990. Significant variations may result from socioeconomic differences, climate conditions, health care, specialized schools, human services, and other influences. Further variations are found when differentiations are made for age and sex (Ries, 1982) and race or color (Schein, 1987). Of growing concern is the increasing number of persons over age 65 who have hearing impairments (Schein, 1987).

TABLE 1

**Prevalence Rates for Hearing Impairments in the Civilian Noninstitutionalized Population and Estimated Prevalence in the United States, 1990**

| Type of impairment | Rate per 100,000 | Projected number, 1990 |
|---|---|---|
| All hearing impairment | 6,603 | 16,442,313 |
| Significant bilateral | 3,236 | 8,048,251 |
| Deaf | 873 | 2,171,237 |
| Prevocational deaf | 203 | 504,881 |
| Prelingual deaf | 100 | 248,710 |

SOURCE: Adapted from Schein, J. D., & Delk, M. T. (1971). *The deaf population in the United States* (p. 16). Silver Spring, MD: National Association of the Deaf. Calculated on the basis of the total U.S. population of 248,709,873, according to the 1990 U.S. Census [U.S. Bureau of the Census. (1993). *1990 Census of population and housing: Tabulation and publication program.* Washington, DC: U.S. Department of Commerce, Bureau of the Census].

## Nature of Deafness

The technical context for understanding the nature of deafness begins with the nature of sound itself. The physiological aspects of hearing and hearing impairment, audiological variations among individuals, and the ramifications of the age of onset of deafness are also important for understanding the etiology of deafness, communication, and the various implications of deafness for social workers.

### Transmission of Sound

The creation of a sound begins with vibrations that are initiated by some force and are carried through some medium of gas, liquid, or solid. As the vibration forces molecules of the medium against each other, alternating phases of compressed and rarified molecular density are formed. A wavelike pattern is created by the cycle of alternating phases. The time between each alternating cycle determines what is called the "frequency" of the sound wave. The perception of a sound's pitch is related to its frequency, which is identified as hertz (Hz) and is a measure of the number of sound vibrations per second. The perception of loudness is related to its intensity, which is identified as decibels (dB), and is a measure of the sound pressure level (SPL). On a musical scale, for example, bass tones have low frequencies and treble tones have higher frequencies, but the tone at any frequency can be played loudly or softly.

## Physiology of Hearing and Hearing Impairment

Sound is perceived when vibrations from sound waves are successfully transmitted through a series of membrane, bone, and nerve mechanisms until they finally reach the brain, where the signals are decoded into meaningful information (see Figure 1). The outer ear is designed to capture and funnel incoming sound waves, carried by air (air conduction), into the external auditory canal. The vibrations are then received by the tympanic membrane (eardrum), which marks the beginning of the middle ear. Three tiny bones (the ossicles) now become the medium, and the transmission of sound waves continues by bone conduction. Individually known as the malleus (hammer), the incus (anvil), and the stapes (stirrup), these three bones make up the ossicular chain. Vibrations are transferred from the stapes to the inner ear through an entry called the oval window. The inner ear consists of two fluid-filled cavities—one containing the essential organ of hearing, the cochlea, and the other containing the sensory organ for balance and equilibrium, the semicircular canals. The cochlea contains a complex system of sensors that differentiate the various sound frequencies and transmit signals to the brain through the auditory nerve. The signals are received by the auditory center of the brain, where they are processed and translated into meaningful information.

Any interruption in the path of transmission just described can result in some kind of hearing impairment. Physical aberrations may occur in the outer, middle, or inner ear, creating conductive or sensorineural dysfunctions (Pickles, 1988). However, hearing loss may also result from damage to the central nervous system or nonorganic causes (such as psychological disorders that are due to stress or emotional trauma) (Scheetz, 1993). Table 2 presents an overview of organic hearing

FIGURE 1

The Auditory Apparatus

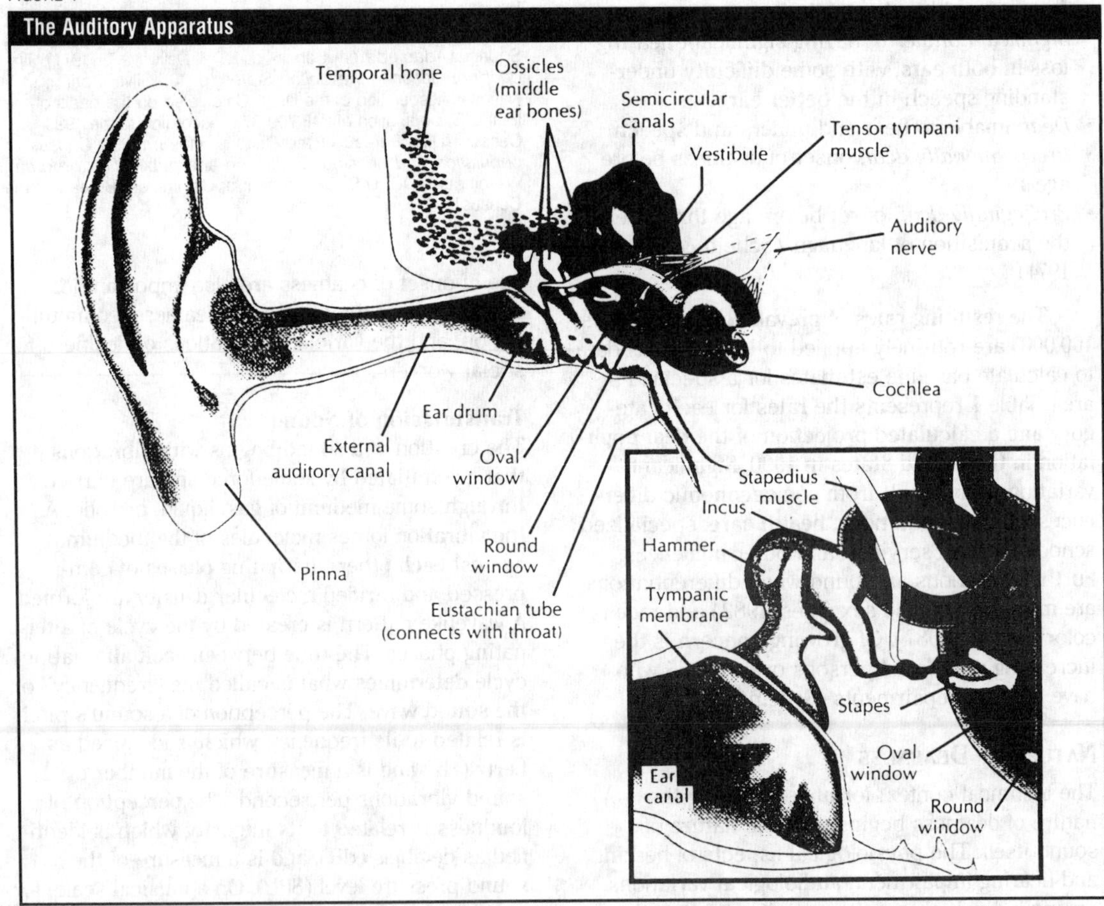


SOURCE: Carlson, N. R. (1991). *Physiology of behavior* (4th ed., p. 193). Needham Heights, MA: Allyn & Bacon. Copyright 1991 by Allyn & Bacon. Reprinted with permission.

TABLE 2

**Types of Organic Hearing Loss: Characteristics, Causes, and Approaches to Treatment**

| Type of hearing loss | Common causes | Medical and audiological approaches |
|---|---|---|
| Conductive hearing loss<br>Dysfunction that occurs in the outer or middle ear in the presence of a normal inner ear<br>• Likened to wearing earplugs | Ear canal<br>• Excessive accumulation of cerumen (ear wax)<br>• Atresia (absence or closure) or occlusion (blockage)<br>Middle ear<br>• Anomaly: missing or malfunctioning ossicles (middle-ear bones) or tympanic membrane (eardrum)<br>• Otitis media: infection in the middle ear<br>• Otosclerosis: abnormal formation of spongy bone tissue, restricting movement of the ossicles. | Medical<br>• Removal of obstruction<br>• Antibiotic therapy<br>• Repair of damaged eardrum or damaged middle-ear parts<br>• Freeing of immobilized bones of the middle ear (stapedectomy)<br>Audiological<br>• Amplification may be useful<br>• Assistive listening devices |
| Sensorineural hearing loss<br>Dysfunction that occurs in the inner ear or along the nerve pathway from the inner ear to the brain stem<br>• Different degrees of hearing loss at various sound frequencies<br>• Range of hearing limited or narrow<br>• Buzzing or ringing in the ears and dizziness may accompany sensorineural hearing loss | Congenital: hearing loss present at birth:<br>• Genetic conditions<br>• Nongenetic factors: prenatal infections, damage to the embryo from diseases such as rubella and cytomegalovirus.<br>Acquired: hearing losses that develop any time after birth (also known as adventitious deafness):<br>• Trauma: bone damage from head injury or exposure to intense noise<br>• Meningitis: an inflammation of the coverings (meninges) of the brain and cerebrospinal fluid<br>• Meniere's disease, caused by increased fluid pressure in the membranous labyrinth of the inner ear<br>• Drugs whose side effects can harm the cochlea or auditory nerve<br>• Presbycusis: hearing loss that is due to the aging process. | Medical<br>• Cochlear implants (prosthetic) in selected patients<br>• Preventive: rubella vaccine, genetic research<br>Audiological<br>• Amplification targeted at frequency ranges where some hearing exists<br>• Functional utility highly dependent on individual circumstances, needs, and desires |
| Central Deafness<br>Dysfunction that is due to anomalies related to the brain stem or cerebral cortex, not attributable to the ear itself<br>• Normal transmission of sounds without amplification through and beyond the auditory nerve<br>• Inability to process (decode) the auditory message | Damage or injury to the brain<br>• Tumor<br>• Abscess or lesion<br>• Head trauma<br>• Mother-child blood incompatibility (Rh-factor)<br>• Aging and loss of brain function | Medical<br>• Treatment focused on the reduction or elimination of a tumor, abscess, or lesion; may or may not restore hearing functions<br>Audiological<br>• Since losses of this nature are not auditorily based, audiological approaches are not indicated |

SOURCE: Adapted from Scheetz, N. A. (1993). *Orientation to deafness* (pp. 37–43). Needham Heights, MA: Allyn & Bacon.

impairments, categorized as conductive loss, sensorineural loss, or central deafness. The table describes the key elements of hearing impairment, common causes related to each category, and some medical and audiological approaches to treatment.

**Audiological Aspects**

Hearing impairment is typically characterized by two audiological dimensions: the severity of the hearing loss and the range of sound frequencies where hearing impairment occurs. The severity of hearing impairments is customarily reported in dB loss and is determined by measuring the minimum intensity (volume) required for a tone to be heard by a person at various points on the scale of frequencies: the higher (louder) the intensity required, the more severe the hearing impairment. Conversational speech usually occurs at an average of 50 to 65 dB, whereas a whisper is at 15 to 25 dB (Higgins, 1980). One classification scheme (Mindel & Vernon, 1971) categorized hearing loss as slight (25 to 40 dB), mild to moderate (40 to 55 dB), moderately severe (55 to 70 dB), severe (70 to 90 dB), and profound (90 dB and above).

Speech tones range in frequency from about 250 to 4,000 Hz. A hearing loss within that range will generally impair a person's ability to understand speech. Because the components of spoken language, such as consonants and vowels, occur at different frequencies, the location of a hearing loss on the scale of frequencies is a primary determinant of the ability to discriminate among the sounds of speech. However, people who are unable to understand speech may perceive sounds at other frequencies, perhaps even musical tones.

The functional hearing of an individual for communication purposes is measured in three ways. First, a profile of the range of frequencies and the severity of a person's hearing impairment is customarily reported on an *audiogram,* a chart that displays the dB loss at various frequencies for each ear. The "puretone average" is the average threshold (dB loss) of three frequencies across the speech range. Second, a person's speech recognition ability is reported on a speech audiometry scale, which gives a percentage score of the number of words a person can identify by hearing alone (without lipreading). More than a measure of whether sound is received, this scale measures to what degree the sounds are processed and understood as speech. For individuals whose hearing loss is severe or profound, a third measure is speech recognition with lipreading, which will give a more complete characterization of the individual's ability to communicate for school, work, or social purposes.

### Onset of Deafness

The age at which the hearing loss occurs strongly influences human communication and all aspects of life that stem from it. The onset variable is designated at one level by the terms "congenital" and "adventitious" deafness, which broadly differentiate those who were born deaf from those who lost their hearing later in life. Specific modifiers mark the onset of deafness in relation to key developmental milestones: "prelingual" deafness (onset before the acquisition of language at ages three to four), "childhood" deafness (onset before adolescence), and "prevocational" deafness (onset before employability at about age 19) (Schein, 1989; Schein & Delk, 1974).

## Etiology of Deafness

Although there is general agreement on the major etiological factors that are responsible for most childhood deafness in the United States, there are significant gaps in knowledge, as well as considerable diversity of opinion, about the proportion of childhood deafness that is attributable to each cause. Ries (1973), for example, found that the etiology could not be identified for nearly half the 1971–72 population of 41,109 students in programs for the deaf. Since the early 1970s, an annual survey of hearing impaired students has been conducted by the Center for Assessment and Demographic Studies at Gallaudet University (see Holt & Hotto, 1994; Hotchkiss, 1989).

According to the 1992–93 survey (Holt & Hotto, 1994), the causes of 52.5 percent of the 48,300 cases of hearing impairments were unknown or unreported, 13.2 percent were due to pregnancy or birth complications, and 13 percent were due to hereditary factors. The remaining 21.3 percent were due to various factors: maternal rubella, meningitis, otitis media, other causes after birth (such as measles and mumps), and congenital cytomegalovirus (CMV). These causes are essentially the same as those reported in several studies in the late 1960s and the 1970s (see Moores, 1987, p. 98).

### Heredity

About half of all cases of childhood deafness are presumed to be hereditary, including a large proportion of cases where specific etiology is unknown (Moores, 1987; Shaver & Vernon, 1978). Whereas about 10 percent of the cases of early childhood deafness and about 20 percent of the cases of hereditary deafness are transmitted by parents at least one of whom has a dominant gene for deafness, approximately 40 percent of early profound deafness and 80 percent of genetic deafness is transmitted by parents who have only recessive genes and no hearing loss (Konigsmark, 1972; Moores, 1987). These estimates are consistent with Schein and Delk's (1974) finding that most deaf children are born to hearing parents. In summarizing a series of complex studies of the hereditary transmission of deafness, Moores (1987) concluded that hereditary deafness of a recessive nature will continue to be a major etiological factor, with a high proportion of hearing individuals being carriers of recessive genes.

### Complications of Pregnancy and Birth

***Maternal rubella.*** Deafness is one of several congenital conditions that can result from the infection of pregnant women by the rubella virus (German measles), particularly during the first trimester of gestation (Moores, 1987). An estimated 8,000 deaf children whose mothers had rubella while pregnant were born in 1964 and 1965, accounting for about half of the children who were born deaf during those years (Stuckless, 1984, 1986). The use of an effective vaccine given to pregnant women since 1969 has been associated with the vast decline in the number of children who are deaf from this cause—from more than 9,000 of school age in 1982–83 to fewer than 1,000 in 1992–93 (Holt & Hotto, 1994). Constituents of the "rubella bulge" (those whose deafness resulted from the 1964 to 1965 rubella epidemic) were counted among school-age children in the 1982–83 survey, will be counted among deaf adults aged 29 to 31 in 1995, and will swell the population of each age group through which they pass for decades to come. Many will have disabling conditions in addition to a hearing impairment.

***CMV.*** Levin and Romero (1995) estimated that the proportion of infants born with CMV, a herpes virus, is 0.5 percent to 1.5 percent—20,000 to 60,000 children, based on the 4 million live births reported in 1993 (*World Almanac and Book of Facts,* 1994). Moores (1987) projected that of the 30,000 infants with CMV estimated by Pappas (1985), 4,000 (13 percent) would have mild to profound hearing loss accompanied in more-severe cases by additional symptoms with serious developmental implications. CMV was not reported on the annual survey (Hotchkiss, 1989) until the early 1990s but was reported as the etiology for 1.3 percent of the cases in the 1992–93 survey (Holt & Hotto, 1994). Although blood tests for the disease are economical and practical, many cases go undiagnosed unless symptoms signal the need for testing, particularly among poor children.

***Other complications.*** Since the 1970s, 11 percent to 14 percent of the cases of childhood deafness have been due to the combined effects of prematurity, birth trauma, pregnancy complications, and Rh incompatibility (Holt & Hotto, 1994; Hotchkiss, 1989). It is difficult to isolate the effects of prematurity from those of birth trauma and other complications at birth. Furthermore, Moores (1987) speculated that the incidence of severe impairments related to prematurity may actually be increased by improved medical techniques that save more premature babies.

#### Meningitis

Meningitis is an inflammation of the coverings of the brain (meninges) and the cerebrospinal fluid, which can lead to the damage of other organs, including the brain and the ear. Although the incidence of deafness caused by meningitis has dropped considerably from the 1920s to the 1990s (Best, 1943; Moores, 1987), the 1992–93 survey estimated the incidence at about 8 percent, which makes meningitis the leading cause of nonhereditary deafness. Moores noted that those who are deaf because of meningitis tend to have severe neurological handicaps as well. Unfortunately, unlike the vaccine for rubella, vaccines for meningitis have not been associated with a reduction in the incidence of deafness (Holt & Hotto, 1994).

#### Other Causes after Birth

Otitis media (an infection of the middle ear) accounted for 3.7 percent of the cases of deafness reported in 1992–93. Other causes of acquired deafness (when the onset is after birth) include high fever, infection, trauma, measles, and mumps. These causes accounted for 6.1 percent of the cases of deafness in 1992–93, down from 9.9 percent and 15.8 percent in 1972–73 and 1982–83, respectively (Holt & Hotto, 1994; Hotchkiss, 1989).

In sum, it appears that heredity will remain an important factor in about half the incidences of early childhood deafness. Medical advances will allow much greater control of environmental causes, but may also result in a higher percentage of individuals with multiple disabling conditions among those who are affected. The emergence of infectious agents, such as CMV, signals the potential for sudden and dramatic increases in early childhood deafness.

## Prominent Issues for Social Work Practice

In addition to the diversity of characteristics inherent in the general population, differences in etiological, physiological, and audiological features distinguish individuals who are deaf from one another, dispelling the image of "the deaf" as a homogeneous population and raising numerous professional issues for social work with people who are deaf.

#### Medical and Audiological Perspectives

Treatment options depend largely on whether hearing loss is conductive, sensorineural, or rooted in the central functions of the brain. The nature and location of abnormalities partially determine to what degree medication, surgery, or prosthetic implants can restore hearing; whether assistive listening devices and other technological aids can be effective for the individual (Epstein, 1987; Pickles, 1988); and whether the condition is even treatable. Knowledge of etiology is important for addressing existing conditions, for recognizing multiple disabling or degenerative conditions, and for determining appropriate strategies for treatment and prevention.

The implications of the etiology and physiology of hearing impairments extend beyond medical and rehabilitative concerns. First, neurological and other organic conditions associated with deafness may have significant behavioral implications (Vernon & Andrews, 1990). Second, audiological features of an individual's hearing profile—the frequency range and severity of the impairment—influence social, psychological, and educational functioning. Third, the age of onset of deafness has a critical impact on the developmental process of each person. Therefore, the professional's understanding of physiological factors and their implications for communication, education, social interaction, and psychosocial development is essential to comprehending the vast array of individual needs, desires, goals, and approaches to be considered in working with people who are deaf.

In working with families who have deaf children, social workers may team with physicians and audiologists to help weigh complicated and value-laden choices or to help adults who become deaf later in life face complex decisions related to communication and social interaction. Scheetz (1993) cautioned against labeling people on the basis of audiological profiles. She noted that other factors to be considered in individual functioning may include the auditory environment, the person's desire and ability to use residual hearing, secondary handicapping conditions, educational and occupational background, lifestyle preferences, and psychological adjustment to the hearing loss.

## Communication

On the discovery of a child's deafness, among the first decisions that parents must make are those related to communication and language development as fundamental tools in preparation for education. A debate between the proponents of oral-aural systems of communication (speech and amplification) and the proponents of manual systems (sign language) has raged for more than two centuries. The history and arguments on each side of this controversy have been abundantly documented in the literature on deaf education (see summaries by Mindel & Vernon, 1971; Moores, 1987; Scheetz, 1993; Vernon & Andrews, 1990).

***Sign language.*** During the early and mid-1800s, most educators of the deaf emphasized manual communication. However, the proponents of manual language even then disagreed about the type of manual system to be used. Some favored a system of "methodical signs" that followed English word order, and others supported "natural sign language" with a word order different from English. A smaller third group relied on a manual alphabet by which exact English could be produced letter by letter (Moores, 1987).

***Oral–aural.*** An emphasis on articulation and speech began to take root in the mid-1800s, eventually leading to a resolution by the 1880 International Congress on Deafness stating that manual communication restricts or prevents speech and language development in deaf children (Moores, 1987). Proponents of the oral–aural communication method emphasize the development of the deaf child's auditory and visual senses, incorporating the early use of amplification and auditory training, as well as speechreading skills (Sanders, 1982; Scheetz, 1993). In another method, known as cued speech, that is used with some deaf children, lip movements are supplemented by coded hand shapes to distinguish speech sounds that otherwise appear similar on the lips (Martin, 1987; Scheetz, 1993).

***Total communication.*** In the early 1970s, a method known as "total communication" was conceived, in which speech is combined with signs (Mindel & Vernon, 1971). It evolved not only as a method of instruction, but as a philosophy of education that "endorses the right of every hearing impaired child to communicate by whether means are found beneficial" (Moores, 1987, p. 11). Attempts to bridge opposing positions between spoken English and American Sign Language (ASL) have spawned a continuum of sign communication modes (see Table 3).

***Continuing debate.*** Total communication has been criticized by those on both sides of the controversy. Oral purists argue that any use of sign language inhibits the development of speech (Moores, 1987) and consider total communication to be essentially a manual method. In contrast, proponents of ASL contend that the attempt to use manual and spoken language simultaneously "subordinates manual language to the spoken one" (Lane, 1992, p. 135). In other words, Signed English and other alternate signing systems incorporate ASL vocabulary into a language structure that resembles English to varying degrees (see Table 3). Yet these systems typically sacrifice unique linguistic and cultural features present in true ASL, which is not merely a visual representation of the spoken language, but a separate language in itself. Some ASL users have expressed strong resistance to "language use policies aimed at shifting them to English" (Nash, 1987, p. 81).

Although the middle ground between the two extremes is vast, the array of methods and systems, with the emotional and political energy generated around them, has created a confusing labyrinth of choices for parents, teachers, and professionals. Furthermore, because communication is also essential for social and psychological health, options must be considered in the context not only of their efficacy for learning and education, but of overall personal and social development (Schlesinger & Meadow, 1972).

TABLE 3
**Modes of Communication: A Continuum**

| Spoken English | Total Communication More English < ---------- > More American Sign Language (ASL) | | | Manual language |
|---|---|---|---|---|
| Aural-oral communication<br>Cued speech | Seeing Essential English (SEE I)<br>Signing Exact English (SEE II) | Signed English (SE) | Pidgin Sign English (PSE)<br>• Ameslish<br>• Siglish<br>• Manual English | ASL |
| Emphasizes auditory and visual senses and amplification and auditory training; cued speech hand shapes distinguish visually similar words. | Represents English in as nearly pure a form as is visually possible, including indicators for verb tense and parts of speech. | Uses the ASL vocabulary in English word order; drops grammatical indicators; English language structure is dominant. | Blends standard English and ASL in a variety of forms; ASL structure is dominant in varying degrees. | Separate language from English; the "native language" of deaf people. |

SOURCE: Adapted from Scheetz, N. A. (1993). *Orientation to deafness* (pp. 73–75). Needham Heights, MA: Allyn & Bacon.

**Cognitive Functioning**

Moores (1987) traced the evolution of views regarding deaf people's ability to think and to learn, describing the three stages of the relationship of thought, language, and deafness that underlie the evolving debate:

1. *The deaf as inferior:* The conclusion that deaf people lag behind hearing children and have lower intelligence, advanced by Pintner and Patterson (1917) and reaffirmed by Pintner, Eisenson, and Stanton (1941).
2. *The deaf as concrete:* The recognition that deaf children's intelligence is not quantitatively inferior but that a qualitative inferiority stems from deaf children's restriction to a world of concrete objects and things and their consequent inability to function abstractly (Myklebust & Brutton, 1953).
3. *The deaf as intellectually normal:* Evidence that no difference in conceptual performance or intelligence exists between deaf and hearing children when the items tested are within the language experience of the deaf children (Rosenstein, 1961; Vernon, 1967).

By 1960 leading researchers no longer considered deaf people to be intellectually deficient but sustained the consensus that they were linguistically impoverished based on their poor standard English skills (Moores, 1987). The issue of language deficiency and its effect on deaf people's ability to develop thought beyond the formal operative level was studied extensively by Furth between 1964 and 1974. Drawing on the theories of Piaget and Inhelder (Piaget, 1926, 1952, 1970; Piaget & Inhelder, 1969) that intelligence is not based on language, Furth (1971) stated that *learning to think* is more important than language instruction. Additional challenges to the assumption of the language deficiency of deaf children included Suppes's (1972) assertion that deaf children do use some internal language (sign language), even if it is different from that of the society in which they live. Liben (1978) argued that limited interaction with the external environment is the primary encumbrance to cognitive development and suggested that the social and educational environments should be examined for overprotectiveness or restrictiveness. Recognition of the "normal intellectual capacity" of deaf people signaled the beginning of a significant ideological shift:

> Furth, among others, contributed to a movement away from the tendency to view deafness and deaf individuals on the basis of deviancy, deficiency, or pathology, substituting the much healthier and more positive approach of searching for strengths and fostering optimal development. (Moores, 1987, p. 158)

On the basis of evidence summarized by Moores (1987), the condition of deafness imposes no limitation on native intelligence, cognitive capability, or sophistication of intellectual functioning. However, deafness may inhibit participation in the communication, interactions, and activities that are part of the informal learning of most children. Concerns about "experiential deficits" as a major contributor to differences in performance and achievement suggest the need to consider carefully the communication, social, and cultural characteristics of the child's home, school, and community. Interventions focused on expanding experiential learning opportunities and interaction with the environment may significantly enhance the performance and achievement potential of young people who are deaf.

## Social Development and the Family

Mindel and Vernon (1971) examined the development of deaf children and their families from the parents' initial suspicion of disability to the diagnosis of deafness and adjustment and life decisions affecting the children, the parents, and the family as a whole. Individual personalities and attitudes, as well as parental relationships, may influence parents' initial perception of a child's deafness and subsequent decisions on behalf of the child. Vocal signals of affection or direction from the parent may fail to evoke the reciprocal responses typically vocalized by hearing children, altering (perhaps in subtle ways) the nature of the parent-child relationship.

The child's reliance on nonconventional communication (primarily nonverbal) typically forces his or her inordinate dependence on a few persons, especially the mother, imposing additional frustrations on the mother, who cannot extricate herself from the care of the child through outside activities. Ambiguity of communication may affect both the explicit and implicit transmission of social sanctions (see Becker, 1987; Meadow-Orlans, 1987); simply stated, the child may not understand the rules well enough to follow them, which leads to adults' perceptions and treatment of the child as "willful." The child's subsequent inability to divert anger and frustration to constructive verbal expression may lead to impulsive, nonconstructive aggression (Mindel & Vernon, 1971).

The literature on deafness and child development emphasizes that early communication, particularly between parents and children, is the key to a healthy developmental process. However, clashing views about the appropriateness of different communication methods often give rise to confusion, indecision, and emotional and psychological turmoil for parents and children. Schlesinger and Meadow (1972) regarded the polarization and conflict to be detrimental to the mental health of deaf children and advocated a combination of oral and manual communication in addition to training in residual hearing, speech, and lipreading.

Meadow (1980) attempted to cut through the emotional involvement of clashing positions among professionals and laypeople with a comprehensive study of linguistic, cognitive, social, and psychological development. She cited studies that found that the incidence of emotional or behavioral disturbance among children who are deaf is three to 10 times that of children with normal hearing. Although Meadow strongly cautioned against the dangers of labeling and stereotyping deaf children, she stressed the importance of viewing behavior in the context of environmental influences that may lead to differences in emotional development. These environmental influences may include the individuals and institutions that affect a deaf child's development, as well as those that are affected by the child's inadequate auditory contact within the social environment.

## Education and the School Environment

Educational issues of communication, language, cognition, and intellectual functioning of deaf children have been treated extensively by Moores (1987) and are the topics of much of the literature on deafness. In recent years, the environment in which education of children who are deaf takes place has been an increasingly prominent focus. Scheetz (1993) began her discussion of the educational environment by broadening the role of education:

> Education assumes the guise of informal as well as formal instruction. In many instances, wisdom acquired outside the classroom is commensurate with learning that occurs in the formal setting. Parents, family members, teachers, and peers all function in an educational capacity. They provide the source through which a lifetime of learning occurs. (p. 73)

The cast of actors and the variety of educational settings, then, suggest the relevance of a psychosocial and cultural perspective, in which self-concept and identity, socialization and social interaction, mental and emotional health, and understanding and respect for diverse value systems are important in creating and maintaining the educational environment.

Scheetz (1993) identified four key decisions that parents must make in selecting the most beneficial learning environment for their child:

1. mode of communication
2. residential versus day programs
3. self-contained versus mainstream settings
4. facilities and activities that emphasize Deaf culture versus integration into activities revolving around hearing students.

***Deaf culture.*** The use of the uppercase "D," as in "Deaf culture" or "Deaf community," was introduced by Woodward (1972) to denote the cultural identity of a people for whom sign language is the language of choice.

The choice between deaf culture and integration with hearing peers is related to decisions regarding communication, program, and setting. The preferred communication mode is the first indicator of whether the individual aligns with deaf culture or the hearing world. The choice between a residential and a day program relates to the balance between the home and school environments, with the residential school for the deaf representing the child's total emersion in the deaf world. The difference between self-contained and mainstream settings is largely one of group composition: a homogeneous class of "all-deaf" children versus a class in which deaf and hearing children are mixed. At the extremes, an oral or Signed English communication philosophy in a mainstream day school would be the most likely to integrate deaf students into the existing (hearing) environment, whereas a residential school using ASL would be the most likely to emphasize deaf culture.

***Differences in environments.*** Sheetz (1993) addressed a number of additional issues related to the social-educational environment. The positive learning environment created by using total communication in direct instruction, the presence of deaf peers, and the opportunity to have deaf teachers as role models are among the advantages of residential schools. However, living in dormitories isolates children from their homes and families and the larger community and fosters the assumption of surrogate roles by houseparents and peers, the process of institutional socialization, rigid external controls on individual flexibility and internal control, and excessive dependence (Becker, 1987; Scheetz, 1993).

Mainstream education, on the other hand, offers the opportunity for students to reside at home and benefit from living with their families; to compete with hearing students; and to receive instruction through some form of total communication, usually with the support of an interpreter (Scheetz, 1993). Differences, such as distorted speech and difficulty communicating with hearing peers, however, often cause deaf children to be excluded and even ridiculed by other children. Deaf students in primarily oral situations may feel isolated, inferior, and frustrated at being deprived of an effective avenue of communication.

***Effects of legislation.*** The nature of educational environments for deaf children has undergone significant change since the passage of The Education for All Handicapped Children Act of 1975. Enrollments in private residential schools dropped 65 percent from 1973 to 1984; as of 1984, 67 percent of deaf students were either partially or fully mainstreamed in public day school programs (Lowenbraun & Thompson, 1989). In 1991, 71 percent of deaf students were mainstreamed (U.S. Department of Education, 1992). The mandate to provide a free and appropriate education for all handicapped children has resulted in new and expanded programs and support services to satisfy the individualized educational program (IEP) of deaf children with diverse characteristics and needs (Moores, 1987). Therefore, the inclusion of deaf students in regular local schools and classes is supported by the law. However, the recent introduction of the concept of "full inclusion"—the enrollment of *all* deaf students in regular classes with hearing peers in local schools—has raised a controversy over the potential elimination of the *choice* between regular and special education environments (Corson & Stuckless, 1994).

***Continuing debate.*** The debate over the best way to educate children who are deaf is far from settled. The Commission on Education of the Deaf (Bowe, 1988, 1991), established by Congress in 1986 to study the quality of education of deaf people, argued that despite the laws, the mandates, and the creation of programs and services, deaf education has failed its students. Lane (1992) suggested that mainstreaming has actually obstructed the education of deaf children. He stated that educational, medical, and rehabilitation specialists wear a "mask of benevolence," depriving deaf children of their natural channels of communication and their cultural environment, while reaping the benefits of the increasing value of their own services. However, one prominent deaf professional (Stewart, 1992) refuted the arguments of such critics of deaf education as unfounded and uninformed and rejected the proposed bilingual-bicultural alternatives as speculative and short-sighted:

> Today our world is far too complex and too demanding, and we simply no longer can afford needless "us" vs. "them" feelings that serve to splinter the community—ASL proponents vs. Signed English proponents, deaf people vs. hard of hearing people, deaf people vs. other disabled people, or deaf people vs. hearing people. (p. 142)

It is not likely that any single approach to education can satisfy the diverse needs and ideologies of this heterogeneous population. Therefore, cooperation and open-mindedness by professionals and laypeople are critical to continuing progress in this field. Sensitivity and respect for cultural values and manifestations and attention to matching individual needs with the appropriate socioeducational environment will require the skills of well-prepared helping professionals.

### Personal Identities

When audiological variables are combined with age of onset and social and cultural factors, a number of group identities become evident among people who are deaf or hearing impaired. From an audiological perspective, the term "hearing impaired" identifies people within all categories of hearing disability, including those people who are deaf or hard of hearing. Audiologically, the degree of hearing loss is one basis for separating persons who identify themselves as "deaf" from those who identify themselves as "hard of hearing," a term that denotes a less severe hearing loss.

***Social and cultural factors.*** From a social and cultural perspective, other factors may have a more significant influence on individual identities than the audiological variables. Age of onset, cultural background, and preference of communication mode are closely interrelated with the social identities of people who have hearing impairments. For a person who has been deaf since birth, prelingual onset of deafness may limit the acquisition of spoken language, increasing the likelihood that sign language will become his or her "first language" and leading to affiliation with the deaf community for support in a world dominated by hearing and speaking people.

A person of the same age and audiological profile who became deaf later in life and is not culturally deaf faces challenges that are quite different, including social marginality between the deaf and hearing worlds and the dilemma of finding an identity. People oriented to oral–aural communication (speech and amplification) may identify themselves as "hard of hearing," "hearing impaired," "oral deaf," or "late-deafened."

People whose communication is primarily manual may identify themselves as "deaf" or as "Deaf" (the uppercase "D" denoting cultural affiliation with the Deaf community, usually based on use of ASL). Although the deaf community is not universally embraced by all who are deaf or hearing impaired, the widespread awareness of its presence and the influence of deaf culture establish it as a reference point for people who have hearing impairments. Even many people who define themselves as "outsiders" to the deaf community may be acknowledging the community's influence by being aware of their rejection of it or exclusion from it.

***Ethnicity, gender, and sexual orientation.*** Cutting across the degree of deafness and the age of onset are the following affiliations within the deaf population that have been asserted since the 1980s: the black deaf, the Hispanic deaf, the Asian deaf, deaf women, and gay and lesbian deaf people (Hairston & Smith, 1983; Holcomb & Wood, 1989; Luczak, 1993; Vernon & Andrews, 1990). The presence of deaf ethnic minority populations has received considerable attention. Delgado (1984), for example, found that about 7 percent of the total deaf school-age population and 51 percent of those with impairments in addition to deafness were black, Asian, Hispanic, Native American, or members of other ethnic minority groups. Fischgrund, Cohen, and Clarkson (1987) noted that nearly one-third of hearing impaired children in the United States are either black or Hispanic. Nash (1992) projected that although the overall population of deaf 18 to 21 year olds will decline, the percentage of ethnic minorities among that age group of deaf persons will increase from 29 percent in 1982 to 39 percent in 2000.

In short, as Stewart (1992) noted, the population of people who are deaf is "a highly representative cross-section of the American population, . . . the only built-in, forced upon us characteristic—not one of us had any say in the matter, whether we end up liking it or not—is the working, or actually the "not working" of our hearing equipment" (p. 139–140). Although the needs and social agenda of the groups may overlap to various degrees, consideration of group differences is a step toward recognizing the vast array of the individual needs of people who are deaf.

### Marriage and Family

In adulthood, deaf individuals and their families are likely to experience a range of life stresses and crises similar to that of their hearing counterparts, as well as some situations that are specific to people who are deaf. Knowledge about unique influences of deafness related to marriage, relationships, family planning, and other aspects of family life may yield important insights into families with deaf members. Although research on the marital patterns of deaf adults has been limited, Schein and Delk (1974) examined the family composition and fertility of the deaf population, including the hearing status of the respondents' parents and spouses, marital status by sex and race, marital status of the deaf population versus the general population, the hearing status of the children of deaf mothers, the age at onset of deafness, and the educational background of the respondents' spouses. They found that among deaf people who marry, the overwhelming majority (85 percent to 95 percent) choose deaf spouses (see also Vernon & Andrews, 1990) and that marriages between deaf people are about as stable as those between hearing couples. They also found that the divorce rate among deaf-hearing couples is higher than the rate for couples in which both partners are deaf, perhaps because cross-cultural issues that parallel those related to interracial marriages may be raised in deaf-hearing marriages and both marital relationships and parenting may be affected by the differences in the partners' communication and educational backgrounds.

***Family planning.*** Issues related to fertility and family planning may also arise. Deaf women marry later than do hearing women and tend to have fewer children (Vernon & Andrews, 1990). Schein and Delk (1974) found that childbearing rates for deaf women were lower than those for the general population, "suggesting some restriction in family size, conscious or unconscious, by the deaf population" (p. 43). Although 92 percent of the deaf respondents in Schein and Delk's study had two normally hearing parents and 88 percent of the children with at least one deaf parent had normal hearing, genetics and heredity pose complex questions involving value-laden alternatives from which to choose.

***Family issues.*** Other family issues that social workers might address include the emotional trauma experienced by parents when the deafness of a child is diagnosed, parenting and behavior management, family communication and interaction, sibling relationships, the stress of ongoing negotiation and advocacy, and the effects on the marital relationship when frustrations and preoccupations dominate family life. Family communication and interaction patterns are influenced by a variety of factors, including the number of family members who are deaf and the nature and severity of their hearing impairment, their relative position in the family, the history of deafness in the family, the educational environments of the children, affiliation of the family and its members with the Deaf community, and many other variables that create a unique constellation in each family.

***Parenting.*** Parenthood as an issue for deaf adults was not prominent in the literature until the late 1980s, when a number of studies appeared on parenting effectiveness, child-rearing skills, and resources in support of deaf parents (Jones, Strom, & Daniels, 1989; Mallory, Schein, & Zingle, 1992; Strom, Daniels, & Jones, 1988). Issues of communication and language skill, development of self-concept, and role reversal of hearing children who have deaf parents were also studied (Buchino, 1990, 1993; Pecora, Despain, & Loveland, 1986; Searls, 1993). In the late 1980s the need to share experiences and express self-conflicting emotions motivated a group of hearing adults who have deaf parents to organize the Children of Deaf Adults (CODA). Participants and speakers from across the country convened periodically to take part in dialogue about their experiences (see Aheroni, 1994). Walker (1986) and Preston (1994) have described life experiences of CODAs from an autobiographical perspective and offered unique insights about the impact of deafness on the family system.

Effective social work practice with the family systems of clients who are deaf requires a whole-family perspective and an overarching sensitivity to the values and culture of the clients and their families. Knowledge of how the etiological and physiological realities interact with social and cultural influences is a key to helping each family function with understanding of the implications of deafness and develop an environment conducive to meeting the needs of all of its members.

### Occupation

Schein and Delk (1974) found that deaf people were working in jobs that were not commensurate with their qualifications and were disproportionately clustered in a limited array of occupations. In addition, the earnings of their deaf respondents were 72 percent of those for individuals in the general population, and the median incomes of the respondents ranged from 62 percent to 76 percent of those of their peers in the general population. It is notable that despite their disproportionate clustering in certain occupations, even the low representation of the deaf respondents over the full range of occupations indicates that deafness does not need to be an absolute barrier to most occupations.

***Effects of legislation.*** Since the 1970s, significant changes have resulted from the Rehabilitation Act of 1973 (P.L. 93-112) and subsequent legislation, as well as from increased access to vocational training centers and postsecondary institutions. Stewart (1992) described the growth of postsecondary educational opportunities as "an amazing explosion." The 1994 Survey on Deaf and Hard of Hearing Students in Postsecondary Education, conducted for the U.S. Department of Education (Lewis & Feris, 1994), estimated that 20,040 deaf and hard-of-hearing students were enrolled in two-year and four-year postsecondary institutions in 1992–93, representing an increase of approximately 3,000 students since 1989–90. Special support services (such as interpreters, tutors, notetakers, counselors, and assistive listening devices) were provided to 4,120 deaf students, 5,270 hard-of-hearing students, and 6,720 students whom the institution did not distinguish as deaf or hard of hearing. In that academic year, an additional 2,900 deaf students, not counted in the survey, attended Gallaudet University (Office of Enrollment Services, 1993) and the National Technical Institute for the Deaf at the Rochester Institute of Technology (1993), the two largest federally funded programs for deaf persons.

***Changes in status and income.*** The greater educational opportunities for deaf people have resulted in the increased occupational status and income levels of those with higher educational attainments. Welsh and McLeod-Gallinger (1992) reported that both the unemployment rates and the occupational status of deaf adults improve markedly as educational levels increase. They also noted that the earnings of deaf people rise dramatically and the discrepancy between the earnings of deaf workers and their hearing counterparts decreases the higher the degree earned.

Nevertheless, Welsh and McLeod-Gallinger (1992) found that the overall employment rates and occupational distribution of deaf people have not improved appreciably since the 1960s. In 1990, the unemployment rate for deaf adults aged 35 to 44 was double that of their hearing counterparts (8 percent versus 4 percent). Among those under age 35, the rate was three to four times the rate for comparable hearing persons. Furthermore, deaf people were still greatly underrepresented in managerial and professional occupations and overrepresented in less skilled areas.

Welsh and McLeod-Gallinger (1992) concluded that the lack of significant overall improvement in the basic academic skills of young deaf adults since the 1960s is a primary limitation on their ability to take advantage of higher educational opportunities that developed during that period.

***Ethnicity.*** One particular challenge is the growing percentage of college-age ethnic-minority deaf persons (Nash, 1992). If this trend continues, this population will remain at high risk of not achieving a postsecondary education unless significant improvements in their academic preparedness are effected. The absence of valid assessment tools, insufficient awareness of services, cultural confusion and value conflicts, and the lack of ethnic minority teachers as role models are among the factors contributing to late intervention (Cohen, Fischgrund, & Redding, 1990; Maestas y Moores & Moores, 1984; Vernon & Andrews, 1990).

Cohen et al. (1990) noted the tendency of educators of the deaf to accept the erroneous proposition that needs related to deafness preclude those related to racial and ethnic group membership and status. Cohen (1991) described as "at-risk" a population of predominantly black and Hispanic students living in a multicultural world of overlapping minority status. They are members of an ethnic and racial culture, the culture of the Deaf community, and the predominant white culture and are confronted by stereotyping, divergent norms and values, and identity confusion. The support systems that instill values, attitudes, and motivations must recognize and address the unique developmental elements of ethnic-minority students who are deaf (Anderson & Grace, 1991; Cohen, 1991; Page, 1993).

***Attitudes and conditions.*** Attitudes and conditions in the work environment continue to be a barrier to employment opportunities. Convincing employers of deaf individuals' capabilities is an ongoing challenge. Scheetz (1993) described the progression of employers' attitudes as follows:

1. *Resistive:* unwilling to consider employing a deaf person
2. *Permissive:* willing to consider employing a deaf person who can function independently and in standard ways, but unwilling to make any accommodations
3. *Accommodative:* willing to restructure a job and to provide necessary accommodations for a qualified deaf individual
4. *Facilitative:* willing to hire a potentially qualified deaf person and to initiate special programs to augment accommodations.

Accommodative or facilitative employers provide deaf people with the opportunity to use their skills. However, appropriate training, effective communication skills, and the ability to engage in interpersonal relations are the necessary characteristics of employees who have successful employment experiences (Scheetz, 1993).

Individual counseling or job coaching may help deaf employees respond to difficult people, situations, or conditions in the workplace. In a study of 25 deaf adults and their responses to difficult employment situations, Foster (1988) concluded that although "no single strategy is universally or consistently better than the others, interactive strategies which have as their goal conflict management or resolution are generally preferred to those which focus on conflict avoidance" (p. 17).

Social workers may also play a role in informing, educating, and assisting employers to see the wisdom of employing deaf people. Social workers in educational systems or in direct practice may help shape environments that build self-esteem, expose deaf youngsters to workplace behaviors, provide information and role models, and are healthy testing grounds for interpersonal communication skills.

## Mental Health

Focusing on the differences of a deaf person's experience in a hearing world could prompt one to expect a high incidence of mental health problems among deaf people. Moores (1987) stated that the deviance model, from which the functioning and development of deaf individuals has traditionally been viewed, "has been the basis for various 'psychologies of deafness.' . . . Implicit in the term 'psychology of deafness' is a belief that the impact of deafness is so overwhelming that general psychological principles are inadequate to deal with the condition" (166–167). Equating "difference" with "deviance" and "deviance" with "deficiency" places deaf people in an impossible position: To be "sufficient" or "nondeviant," they must eliminate what makes them "different," that is, they must hear normally. Moores (1987) observed a trend toward

> a more positive model of human nature [in which the emphasis is placed] on the conditions necessary for a healthy, whole, well integrated person. . . . Implicit in this approach is the assumption that the basic needs of all human beings, hearing or deaf, are essentially similar, and that the development of a healthy personality is based on meeting those needs satisfactorily. (p. 167)

***Mental health resources.*** Demographic data on the relationship of deafness to mental illness has been elusive at best for two overriding reasons: the difficulty in assessing "personality" and in isolating the specific impact of deafness on an individual's mental condition (Moores, 1987). Although there is no conclusive evidence that deaf people have a higher likelihood of mental illness, there is also no evidence that they are any less at risk than is the general population. Yet Robinson's (1978) study found that only 2 percent of the 43,000 deaf people who needed mental health services were receiving them. In a more recent study of a mid-sized city, 5.5 percent of whose population was deaf or hard of hearing, Pollard (1994) reported that from a pool of 84,437 public health case records, only 544 (0.64 percent) pertained to deaf or hard-of-hearing patients.

However, justification of the need for additional resources need not be dependent on some measure of higher risk for the target population when those who are affected are grossly underserved. Schlesinger (1977) noted that there was much progress in the establishment of psychiatric and mental health services for deaf people from 1955 to 1970 but that most services were supported by soft money and became stepchildren in the psychiatric and mental health fields. Rainer and Altschuler (1970) presented a comprehensive set of recommendations, but Moores (1987) noted that most have yet to be systematically applied. Vernon and Andrews (1990) stated that understaffing and the lack of staff with appropriate professional qualifications was widespread, and Dickert (1988) found bias by mental health professionals in evaluations of deaf patients compared with those of hearing patients. Vernon and Andrews (1990) stated that only 13 of 50 states had any hospital programs for serving people who are deaf. In its 1994 listing of regional and national programs, the *American Annals of the Deaf* listed psychiatric services in only 17 states ("Supportive and Rehabilitative Programs," 1994).

***Types and prevalence of disorders.*** Vernon and Andrews (1990) have described nonpsychotic and psychotic disorders, compared patterns of incidence between hearing and deaf people, and outlined key issues in diagnosis and treatment of and services for deaf people. They found that some differences appear between deaf and hearing people in behavioral disorders of less severity than psychosis but that the results of research on the relationship of deafness to psychotic disturbances are somewhat contradictory. In some categories of nonpsychotic disorders, such as mental retardation, attention deficit disorder, and impulse control disorders, differences in the prevalence between deaf and hearing may be related to some organic base separate from deafness such as brain damage associated with the various etiologies of childhood deafness. Communication difficulties between clinicians and deaf patients have frequently led to misdiagnoses of retardation, schizophrenia, and other disorders, yielding erroneous data about prevalence rates. Some disorders such as substance use, anxiety, and impulse control disorders may be influenced by conditions within the social environment (including societal response to deafness) rather than by deafness per se. Vernon and Andrews (1990) pointed out that although some deaf people may have a reality-based suspicion of hearing people by whom they may have been exploited, there is no evidence to support the label of the "paranoid deaf."

Although some patterns have been observed among deaf people who have been treated clinically, conclusive causal relationships between deafness and mental illness or significant differences between deaf and hearing have not been established (Knutsen & Lansing, 1990; Nickless, 1994; Schlesinger, 1977; Schlesinger & Meadow, 1972; Vacola, 1987; Vernon & Andrews, 1990). Much of the literature on mental health and deafness in the late 1980s and early 1990s has shifted to a focus on cultural aspects of mental health and effectiveness of methodologies that are sensitive to the communication and cultural characteristics of deaf people (Cook, Kozlowski-Graham, & Razzano, 1993; Guthman, Lybarger, & Sandberg, 1993; Steinberg, 1991). There has been movement away from studies reflecting the infirmity model (Lane, 1992) to greater emphasis on empowerment and self-advocacy, community and political action, community education, and broad-based planning as the means of meeting the needs of the deaf community (McDougall, 1991; Myers & Danek, 1989; Myers, 1993; Rizzo, Zipple, Pisciotta, & Bycoff, 1992; Wax, 1990).

***Professional skills.*** The preparation of professionals with the special skills for working with deaf people continues to be a key to appropriate and effective mental health services provision to people who are deaf (Critchfield, 1992; Weaver & Bradley-Johnson, 1993; Wyatt & White, 1993). A study of the perspectives of deaf therapists and hearing therapists on the qualifications essential for working with deaf clients (Langholz & Heller, 1988) found that both groups of clinicians rated strong clinical training as the most important qualification. Hearing therapists considered development of communication skills important; however, their deaf counterparts emphasized that it is essential to have the communication skills from the start. The two groups agreed that an understanding of developmental, educational, and linguistic dynamics of deafness and an understanding of the cultural context in which the individual's experience occurs are important qualifications for effective assessment and treatment.

**Deafness in Later Life**

Hearing impairment is expected to be a major concern of the fastest growing segment of the American population—people who are elderly (Weinstein, 1994). Hull (1994) estimated that presbycusis, a deterioration of auditory functions caused by aging, affects as many as 60 percent of people over age 65; that proportion increases with age (Weinstein, 1994). Among the causes of deafness for elderly people are metabolic disorders such as renal disease, diabetes mellitus, and hypertension; ototoxicity, including adverse reactions to medications, which can result in sensory neural hearing loss; degeneration of hearing from exposure to excessive noise; and hearing dysfunctions connected with senile dementia (Weinstein, 1994).

***Psychosocial ramifications.*** The loss of hearing has a multitude of psychosocial ramifications for elderly people (Weinstein, 1994). Loss of hearing in the high-frequency ranges, typically the first to be affected by presbycusis, results in progressive difficulty understanding speech, especially in the presence of competing noises (Gelfand, Ross, & Miller, 1988; Helfer & Huntley, 1991; Helfer & Wilber, 1990). Speechreading becomes increasingly difficult with the reduced vision that also accompanies the aging process (Thorn & Thorn, 1989). The results of such impediments to communication frequently include loneliness, detachment, anxiety, social isolation, and withdrawal (Christian, Dluhy, & O'Neill, 1989; Tidball, 1990). Sensory deprivation (particularly the loss of hearing and vision) has been related to psychopathologies, including visual and auditory hallucinations, depression, and paranoia (Cordiero, 1989; Falconer, 1986; Podoll, Thilman, & North, 1991; Ronnberg, 1990). In addition, elderly people face negative myths and stereotypes about aging and stigmatization and treatment as a minority group (Hudson, Dancer, Patterson, & Reynolds, 1990; Levy & Langer, 1994; Tidball, 1990).

***Interventive approaches.*** Surgery to improve hearing may be effective for some people (Podoll, Thilman, & North, 1991). However, aural rehabilitation is more commonly recommended and may range from the fitting of hearing aids or the use of other assistive listening devices to counseling for the development of coping strategies in difficult listening situations (Hull, 1994). Patterson and Dancer (1981) proposed an educational model of aural rehabilitation services that trained agency staff to educate clients about the advantages of aural rehabilitation, to desensitize those who had negative attitudes and self-perceptions, and to empower clients to take responsibility for coping with the challenges of living with impaired hearing. Empathy and encouragement by professionals, peers (especially in group counseling), and family members are considered key factors for motivating elderly clients to try new coping measures (Falconer, 1986; Hull, 1994; Tidball, 1990).

Becker (1980) revealed the assets and strengths of the deaf community for its lifelong members who grow old. People who become deaf as a result of aging lack the skills and strategies to maintain interpersonal contact without the ability to hear and therefore face detachment and isolation. In contrast, an aging deaf adult is likely to have an established network of friends, a communication style for dealing with diverse communication needs, and a lifetime of experience in finding strategies for human interaction. Elderly deaf community members, therefore, can be an important resource for finding creative ways of helping other elderly people face the challenges of a hearing impairment acquired in later life (Vernon & Andrews, 1990).

### Sociopolitical Influences

Since the mid-1960s, stimulated, in part, by civil rights legislation for people who are disabled, social activism has become prominent within the Deaf community. The Vocational Rehabilitation Act of 1954 (P.L. 88-565) addressed the rehabilitation needs of people with handicaps by establishing the vocational rehabilitation system. The Civil Rights Act of 1964 (P.L. 88-352) legislated nondiscrimination, but did not include people with disabilities among the protected (Myers, 1971). The "bill of rights" for disabled people finally was established in the Rehabilitation Act of 1973, mandating the accessibility of employment, education, health, welfare, and social services to disabled people (DuBow, Geer, & Strauss, 1992) and included such accommodations for deaf people as interpreters and certain technological aids to facilitate access to programs. The Education of All Handicapped Children Act, renamed the Individuals with Disabilities Education Act in 1990, guaranteed free appropriate public school education to all children, regardless of their disabilities (Dubow, Geer, & Strauss). Finally, in 1990, the Americans with Disabilities Act extended antidiscrimination mandates beyond federally funded agencies to include a broad spectrum of public and private entities.

The evolution of legal rights for deaf people has been both a catalyst for social and political activism among deaf people and a product of it. It has given cause for interactions among groups of citizens with disabling conditions, as well as with the general citizenry, raising awareness of the life experiences of people with disabilities and unifying disabled people under a common cause. For deaf people, the culmination of pride, solidarity, and self-empowerment took place in March 1988, when deaf students and their supporters from all over the country conducted an eight-day demonstration at Gallaudet University, demanding that a newly appointed hearing president be replaced by one who was deaf (Gannon, 1989). With the appointment of a deaf president of the university, activism in the deaf community gained impetus, and, since then, the general public has grown more aware of the unique characteristics of the deaf population, including its language and culture.

### Technology and Ethical Considerations

Complex cultural issues must not be overlooked as rapid advances in technology are applied. The Human Genome Project of the National Institutes of Health and the Department of Energy is advancing research on hereditary disorders (Arnos, 1994), and specific genes linked to deafness have been isolated (Couke et al., 1994). However, those for whom deafness itself is a central component of their cultural integrity and values may view these "miracles of science" as a threat to the life of their community, representing a desire by the medical community to eliminate deafness (Arnos). Fears about the proliferation of hereditary deafness, which once spawned the now discredited eugenics movement to control reproduction by deaf people (Lane, 1992; Moores, 1987), have been diminished by findings that more than 90 percent of deaf children are born to hearing couples and that less than 5 percent are born of couples one or both of whom are (Schein & Delk, 1974). Yet, the very premise of deafness as a defect to be avoided has been challenged by many deaf parents who consider their deaf children "normal" (Moore & Levitan, 1992) and would even prefer to have deaf rather than hearing children (Bougham & Shaver, 1982). Moores (1987) expressed his concerns about counseling on these sensitive issues as follows: "It is not the role of the counselor to be directive or to tell prospective parents what they should do. This is especially true in dealing with deaf clients, many of whom are aware of past attempts to limit their choices with respect to reproduction" (p. 107).

These and other ethical and cultural issues must be addressed by multidisciplinary teams, including social workers with knowledge and skills in cross-cultural practice. Counseling or intervention requires the sensitivity and skill to engage deaf clients in context of their own value system and to mediate transactions that cross the boundaries between deaf and hearing cultures.

## Social Work Practice with Deaf People

The infirmity model of deafness, which focuses on eliminating, ameliorating, or compensating for a deficiency, is giving way to a view of people who are deaf as individuals who function without hearing in a social environment that is oriented to sound. The shift has philosophical, ethical, and practical implications for social work. Although rapid advancements in the detection, prevention, and treatment of genetic disorders are creating a revolution in the field of medicine (Vernon & Andrews, 1990), solutions ranging from sterilization and abortion to genetic engineering present a multitude of ethical dilemmas. Approaches involving genetic manipulation, medical treatments, and prosthetic devices (such as cochlear implants) have physical, social, cultural, and ethical implications.

Successful social work assessment and interventions with deaf people require an understanding of the physiology and etiology of deafness, psychosocial development, language and cognition, family dynamics, and cultural variables in the deaf population (Santos, 1988), combined with an ecological perspective (Germain & Gitterman, 1987) and a sensitivity to the cultural context of practice with deaf people. Recognition of and respect for the indigenous support systems within the deaf community (Zieziula, 1980) may result in rich interventive resources. A unique combination of cultural and professional perspectives is emerging among the growing number of deaf social workers who graduate each year from accredited social work programs at institutions, such as Gallaudet University, the Rochester Institute of Technology (home of the National Technical Institute for the Deaf), along with schools of social work that provide appropriate support services for deaf students who are pursuing master's degrees.

While carrying out their professional responsibility to support self-empowerment of the deaf community, social workers and other professionals who are hearing occasionally find themselves among the "targets" of the community's social action. Lane's (1992) indictment of professionals who wear the "mask of benevolence" while perpetuating paternalism toward a population that is dependent on their services gives cause for introspection by each professional. An open mind, a spirit of cooperation, and a commitment to the value of self-determination are essential qualities for reaching solutions that accommodate the people and the cultures of those who are deaf and hearing impaired.

## References


Aheroni, E. (1994). The president's forum. *CODA Connections, 11*(3), 3. (Available from Children of Deaf Adults, P.O. Box 30715, Santa Barbara, CA 93130-0715)

Americans with Disabilities Act of 1990. P.L. 101-336, 104 Stat. 327.

Anderson, G. B., & Grace, C. A. (1991). Black deaf adolescents: A diverse and underserved population. *Volta Review, 93*(5), 73–86.

Arnos, K. S. (1994). Hereditary hearing loss. *New England Journal of Medicine, 331*(7), 469–470.

Becker, G. (1980). *Growing old in silence: Deaf people in old age.* Berkeley: University of California Press.

Becker, G. (1987). Lifelong socialization and adaptive behavior in deaf people. In P. C. Higgins & J. E. Nash (Eds.), *Understanding deafness socially* (pp. 59–79). Springfield, IL: Charles C Thomas.

Best, H. (1943). *Deafness and the deaf in the United States.* New York: Macmillan.

Bougham, J., & Shaver, K. (1982). Genetic aspects of deafness. *American Annals of the Deaf, 127*(3), 393–400.

Bowe, F. (1988, February). *Toward equality—Education of the deaf—A report to the President and the Congress of the United States.* Washington, DC: U.S. Government Printing Office.

Bowe, F. (1991). *Approaching equality: Education of the deaf* (A report on the implementation status of the 52 recommendations presented to the Congress and the President by the Commission on Education of the Deaf). Silver Spring, MD: T. J. Publishers.

Buchino, M. (1990). Hearing children of deaf parents: A counseling challenge. *Elementary School Guidance and Counseling, 24*(3), 207–212.

Buchino, M. (1993). Perceptions of the oldest hearing child of deaf parents: On interpreting, communication, feelings, and role reversal. *American Annals of the Deaf, 138*(1), 40–45.

Christian, E., Dluhy, N., & O'Neill, R. (1989). Sounds of silence: Coping with hearing loss and loneliness. *Journal of Gerontological Nursing, 15*(11), 4–9.

Civil Rights Act of 1964. P.L. 88-352, 78 Stat. 241.

Cohen, O. P. (1991). "At-risk" deaf adolescents. *Volta Review, 93*(5), 57–72.

Cohen, O. P., Fischgrund, J. E., & Redding, R. (1990). Deaf children from racial, ethnic, and minority backgrounds: An overview. *American Annals of the Deaf, 135*(2), 67–73.

Cook, J. A., Kozlowski-Graham, K., & Razzano, L. A. (1993). Psychosocial rehabilitation of deaf persons with severe mental illness: A multivariate model of residential outcomes. *Rehabilitation Psychology, 38*(4), 261–274.

Cordiero, J. P. (1989). Les conduites delirantes chez l'age [Delusional states in the elderly]. *Psychologie Medicale, 21*(8), 1125–1131.

Corson, H., & Stuckless, R. (Guest Eds.). (1994). Special programs, full inclusion, and choices for students who are deaf. *American Annals of the Deaf, 139*(4), 148–171.

Couke, P., Van Camp, G., Djoyodiharjo, B., Smith, S. D., Frants, R. R., Padberg, G., Darby, J. K., Huizing, E. H., Cremers, C.W.R.J., Kimberling, W. J., Oostra, B. A., Van de Heyning, P. H., & Willems, P. J. (1994). Linkage of autosomal dominant hearing loss to the short arm of chromosome 1 in two families. *New England Journal of Medicine, 331*(7), 425–431.

Critchfield, A. B. (1992). Improving training approaches. *Journal of the American Deafness and Rehabilitation Association, 25*(4), 15–20.

Delgado, G. L. (1984). Hearing impaired children from non-native language homes. In G. Delgado (Ed.), *The*

*Hispanic deaf: Issues and challenges for bi-lingual education* (pp. 28–37). Washington, DC: Gallaudet College Press.

DiCarlo, L. M. (1964). *The deaf.* Englewood Cliffs, NJ: Prentice Hall.

Dickert, J. (1988). Examination of bias in mental health evaluation of deaf patients. *Social Work, 33,* 273–274.

DuBow, S., Geer, S., Strauss, K. P. (1992). *Legal rights: The guide for deaf and hard of hearing people.* Washington, DC: National Center for Law and the Deaf, Gallaudet University.

Education for All Handicapped Children Act of 1975. P.L. 94-142, 89 Stat. 773.

Epstein, S. (1987). A medical approach to hearing loss. In S. Schwartz (Ed.), *Choices in deafness: A parents' guide* (pp. 1–14). Kensington, MD: Woodbine House.

Falconer, J. (1986). Aging and hearing. *Physical and Occupational Therapy in Geriatrics, 4*(2), 3–20.

Fischgrund, J. E., Cohen, O. P., & Clarkson, R. L. (1987). Hearing-impaired children in black and Hispanic families. *Volta Review, 89*(5), 59–67.

Foster, S. (1988, October 9–12). *Dealing with barriers in the workplace: Strategies used by deaf people in response to difficult situations at work.* Paper presented at the 18th Southeast Regional Institute on Deafness, Memphis, TN.

Furth, H. G. (1971). Education for thinking. *Journal of Rehabilitation of the Deaf, 5*(1), 7–71.

Gannon, J. R. (1989). *The week the world heard Gallaudet.* Washington, DC: Gallaudet University Press.

Gelfand, S. A., Ross, L., & Miller, S. (1988). Sentence reception in noise from one versus two sources: Effects of aging and hearing loss. *Journal of the Acoustical Society of America, 83*(1), 248–256.

Germain, C. B., & Gitterman, A. (1987). Ecological perspective. In A. Minahan (Ed.-in-Chief), *Encyclopedia of social work* (18th ed., Vol. 1, pp. 488–499). Silver Spring, MD: National Association of Social Workers.

Guthman, D., Lybarger, R., & Sandberg, K. (1993). Providing chemical dependency treatment to the deaf or hard of hearing mentally ill client. *Journal of the American Deafness and Rehabilitation Association, 27*(1), 1–15.

Hairston, E., & Smith, L. (1983). *Black and deaf in America: Are we that different?* Silver Spring, MD: T. J. Publishers.

Helfer, K. S., & Huntley, R. A. (1991). Aging and consonant errors in reverberation and noise. *Journal of the Acoustical Society of America, 90*(4, Pt. 1), 1786–1796.

Helfer, K. S., & Wilber, L. A. (1990). Hearing loss, aging and speech perception in reverberation and noise. *Journal of Speech and Hearing Research, 33*(1), 149–155.

Higgins, P. C. (1980). *Outsiders in a hearing world: A sociology of deafness.* Beverly Hills, CA: Sage Publications.

Holcomb, M., & Wood, S. (1989). *Deaf women: A parade through the decades.* Berkeley, CA: Dawn Sign Press.

Holt, J., & Hotto, S. (1994). *Demographic aspects of hearing impairment: Questions and answers* (3rd ed.). Washington, DC: Gallaudet Research Institute.

Hotchkiss, D. (1989). *Demographic aspects of hearing impairments: Questions and answers.* Washington, DC: Center for Assessment and Demographic Studies, Gallaudet University.

Hudson, M. J., Dancer, J., Patterson, K., & Reynolds, B. (1990). Hearing and vision loss in an aging population: Myths and realities. *Education Gerontology, 16*(1), 87–96.

Hull, R. H. (1994). Assisting the older client. In J. Katz (Ed.), *Handbook of clinical audiology* (4th ed., pp. 793–801). Baltimore: Williams & Wilkins.

Individuals with Disabilities Education Act. P.L. 101-476, 104 Stat. 1142 (1990).

Jones, E., Strom, R., & Daniels, S. (1989). Evaluating the success of deaf parents. *American Annals of the Deaf, 134*(5), 312–316.

Knutsen, J. F., & Lansing, C. R. (1990). The relationship between communication problems and psychological difficulties in persons with profound acquired hearing loss. *Journal of Speech and Hearing Disorders, 55*(4), 656–664.

Konigsmark, B. (1972). *Genetic hearing loss with no associated abnormalities* (Vol. 11, Report 6). Chicago: Maico Audiological Library Series.

Lane, H. (1992). *The mask of benevolence.* New York: Alfred A. Knopf.

Langholz, D., & Heller, B. (1988). Effective psychotherapy with deaf persons: Therapists' perspectives. In D. Watson, G. Long, M. Taff-Watson, & M. Harvey (Eds.), *Two decades of excellence: A foundation for the future* (pp. 54–68). Little Rock, AR: American Deafness and Rehabilitation Association.

Levin, M. J., & Romero, J. R. (1995). Infection: Viral and rickettsial. In W. W. Hay, Jr., J. R. Groothuis, A. R. Hayward, & M. J. Levin (Eds.), *Current pediatric diagnosis and treatment* (12th ed., pp. 1020–1053). Norwalk, CT: Appleton & Lange.

Levy, B., & Langer, E. (1994). Aging free from negative stereotypes: Successful memory in China among the American deaf. *Journal of Personality and Social Psychology, 66*(6), 989–987.

Lewis, L., & Feris, E. (1994). *Deaf and hard of hearing students in postsecondary education.* Washington, DC: National Center for Education Statistics, U.S. Department of Education.

Liben, L. (1978). *Deaf children: Developmental perspectives.* New York: Academic Press.

Lowenbraun, S., & Thompson, M. (1989). Environments and strategies for learning and teaching. In M. C. Wang, M. C. Reynolds, & H. J. Walberg (Eds.), *Handbook of special education research and practice, Vol. 3: Low incidence conditions* (pp. 47–69). Elmsford, NY: Pergamon Press.

Luczak, R. (1993). *Eyes of desire: A deaf gay and lesbian reader.* Boston: Alyson Publications.

Maestes y Moores, J., & Moores, D. (1984). The status of Hispanics in special education. In G. Delgado (Ed.), *The Hispanic deaf: Issues and challenges for bi-lingual education* (pp. 14–77). Washington, DC: Gallaudet College Press.

Mallory, M., Schein, J. D., & Zingle, H. W. (1992). Parenting resources of deaf parents with hearing children. *Journal of the American Deafness and Rehabilitation Association, 25*(3), 16–30.

Martin, F. (1987). *Hearing disorders in children: Pediatric audiology.* Austin, TX: Pro-Ed.

McDougall, J. C. (1991). Current issues in deafness: A psychological perspective. *Canadian Psychology, 32*(4), 612–627.

Meadow, K. P. (1980). *Deafness and child development.* Berkeley: University of California Press.

Meadow-Orlans, K. P. (1987). Understanding deafness: Socialization of children and youth. In P. C. Higgins & J. E. Nash (Eds.), *Understanding deafness socially* (pp. 29–57). Springfield, IL: Charles C Thomas.

Mindel, E., & Vernon, M. (1971). *They grow in silence: The deaf child and his family.* Silver Spring, MD: National Association for the Deaf.

Moore, M., & Levitan, L. (1992). *For hearing people only.* Rochester, NY: Deaf Life Press.

Moores, D. F. (1978). *Educating the deaf: Psychology, principles, and practices.* Boston: Houghton Mifflin.

Moores, D. F. (1982). *Educating the deaf: Psychology, principles, and practices* (2nd ed.). Boston: Houghton Mifflin.

Moores, D. F. (1987). *Educating the deaf: Psychology, principles, and practices* (3rd ed.). Boston: Houghton Mifflin.

Myers, L. J. (1971). *The law and the deaf.* Washington, DC: U.S. Department of Health, Education & Welfare, Social and Rehabilitation Service.

Myers, P., & Danek, M. M. (1989). Deafness mental health needs assessment: A model. *Journal of the American Deafness and Rehabilitation Association, 22*(4), 72–78.

Myers, R. R. (1993). Model mental health state plan (MMHSP) of services for persons who are deaf or hard of hearing. *Journal of the American Deafness and Rehabilitation Association, 26*(4), 19–28.

Myklebust, H., & Brutton, M. (1953). A study of visual perception in deaf children. *Acta Oto-laryngologica* (Suppl.), 105.

Nash, J. E. (1987). Who signs to whom? In P. C. Higgins & J. E. Nash (Eds.), *Understanding deafness socially* (pp. 81–99). Springfield, IL: Charles C Thomas.

Nash, K. (1992). The changing population: A challenge for postsecondary education. In S. B. Foster & G. G. Walter (Eds.), *Deaf students in postsecondary education* (pp. 3–20). New York: Routledge.

National Technical Institute for the Deaf. (1993). *Expanding career horizons for deaf people* (Annual report: The National Technical Institute for the Deaf, October 1, 1992 to September 30, 1993). Rochester, NY: Rochester Institute of Technology.

Nickless, C. (1994). Program outcome research in residential programs for deaf mentally ill adults. *Journal of the American Deafness and Rehabilitation Association, 27*(3), 42–48.

Office of Enrollment Services (1993). *Gallaudet University 1992 enrollment report.* Washington, DC: Gallaudet University.

Page, J. M. (1993). Ethnic identity in deaf Hispanics of New Mexico. *Sign Language Studies, 80,* 185–222.

Pappas, D. (1985). *Diagnosis and treatment of hearing impairment in children.* San Diego: College Hill Press.

Patterson, K., & Dancer, J. (1981). An alternative to aural rehabilitation for the older hearing-aid user: An educational model using supportive services. *Educational Gerontology, 13*(5), 411–413.

Pecora, P. J., Despain, C. L., & Loveland, E. J. (1986). Adult children of deaf parents: A psychosocial perspective. *Social Casework, 67*(1), 12–19.

Piaget, J. (1926). *The language and thought of the child.* New York: Harcourt, Brace, Jovanovich.

Piaget, J. (1952). *The origins of intelligence in children.* New York: International Universities Press.

Piaget, J. (1970). Piaget's theory. In P. Mussen (Ed.), *Charmichael's manual of child psychology.* New York: John Wiley & Sons.

Piaget, J., & Inhelder, B. (1969). *The psychology of the child.* New York: Basic Books.

Pickles, J. O. (1988). *An introduction to the physiology of hearing.* London: Academic Press.

Pintner, R., Eisenson, J., & Stanton, M. (1941). *The psychology of the physically handicapped.* New York: Crofts & Company.

Pintner, R., & Patterson, D. (1917). A comparison of deaf and hearing children in visual memory span for digits. *Journal of Experimental Psychology, 2*(2), 76–88.

Podoll, K., Thilman, A. F., & North, J. (1991). Musikalische halluzinaitonen bei schwerhorigkeit im alter [Musical hallucinations in an elderly patient with acquired deafness]. *Nervenarzt, 62*(7), 451–453.

Pollard, R. (1994). Public mental health service and diagnostic trends regarding individuals who are deaf or hard of hearing. *Rehabilitation Psychology, 39*(3), 3–14.

Preston, P. (1994). *Mother father deaf: Living between sound and silence.* Cambridge, MA: Harvard University Press.

Rainer, J., & Altschuler, K. (1970). *Expanded mental health for the deaf.* Washington, DC: U.S. Department of Health, Education & Welfare, Social and Rehabilitation Service.

Rehabilitation Act of 1973. P.L. 93-112, 87 Stat. 355.

Ries, P. (1973). *Reported causes of hearing loss for hearing impaired students, 1970–71* (Series D, No. 11). Washington, DC: Gallaudet College Office of Demographic Studies.

Ries, P. W. (1982). Hearing ability of persons by sociodemographic and health characteristics, United States. In *Vital and health statistics* (Series 10, No. 140). Washington, DC: U.S. Government Printing Office.

Rizzo, A. M., Zipple, A. M., Pisciotta, J., & Bycoff, S. (1992). Strategies for responding to community opposition in an existing group home. *Psychosocial Rehabilitation Journal, 15*(3), 85–95.

Robinson, L. D. (1978). *Sound minds in a soundless world.* (DHEW Publication No. ADM 77-560). Washington, DC: U.S. Government Printing Office.

Ronnberg, Y. (1990). Cognitive and communicative function: The effects of chronological age and "handicap age" [Special issue: Cognitive gerontology]. *European Journal of Cognitive Psychology, 2*(3), 253–273.

Rosenstein, J. (1961). Perception, cognition, and language in deaf children. *Exceptional Children, 27*(3), 276–284.

Sanders, D. (1982). *Aural rehabilitation: A management model* (2nd ed.). Englewood Cliffs, NJ: Prentice Hall.

Santos, K. D. (1988). Social work assessment with hearing impaired individuals: An applied conceptual framework. In D. Watson, G. Long, M. Taff-Watson, & M. Harvey (Eds.), *Two decades of excellence: A foundation for the future* (pp. 144–161). Little Rock, AR: American Deafness and Rehabilitation Association.

Scheetz, N. A. (1993). *Orientation to deafness.* Needham Heights, MA: Allyn & Bacon.

Schein, J. D. (1968). *The deaf community: Studies in the social psychology of deafness.* Washington, DC: Gallaudet College Press.

Schein, J. D. (1987). The demography of deafness. In P. C. Higgins & J. E. Nash (Eds.), *Understanding deafness socially* (pp. 3–27). Springfield, IL: Charles C Thomas.

Schein, J. D. (1989). *At home among strangers.* Washington, DC: Gallaudet University Press.

Schein, J. D., & Delk, M. T. (1974). *The deaf population of the United States.* Silver Spring, MD: National Association of the Deaf.

Schlesinger, H. (1977). Treatment of the deaf child in the school setting. *Mental Health in Deafness, 1,* 96–105.

Schlesinger, H. S., & Meadow, K. P. (1972). *Sound and sign.* Berkeley: University of California Press.

Searls, M. (1993). Self-concept among deaf and hearing children of deaf parents. *Journal of the American Deafness and Rehabilitation Association, 27*(1), 25–37.

Shaver, K., & Vernon, M. (1978). Genetics and hearing loss: An overview for professionals. *American Rehabilitation, 4*(2), 6–10.

Steinberg, A. (1991). Issues in providing mental health services to hearing-impaired persons. *Hospital and Community Psychiatry, 42*(4), 380–389.

Stewart, L. G. (1992). Debunking the bilingual/bicultural snow job in the American Deaf community. In M. Garretson (Ed.), *Viewpoints on deafness: A deaf American monograph* (pp. 129–142). Silver Spring, MD: National Association of the Deaf.

Strom, R., Daniels, S., & Jones, E. (1988). Parent education for the deaf. *Educational and Psychological Research, 8*(2), 117–128.

Stuckless, E. R. (1984). *Impact of congenital rubella infection on the educational system.* Paper presented at the International Symposium on Prevention of Rubella Infection, World Health Organization, Washington, DC.

Stuckless, E. R. (1986). Rubella and the human burden. In E. R. Greenberg, M. Gruenberg, C. Lewis, & S. Goldston (Eds.), *Monographs in epidemiology and biostatistics: Vaccinating against brain syndromes: The campaign against measles and rubella* (pp. 70–79). New York: Oxford University Press.

Suppes, P. (1972). *A survey of cognition in handicapped children.* Stanford, CA: Stanford University, Institute for Mathematical Studies in the Social Sciences.

Supportive and rehabilitative programs: Regional and local programs. (1994). *American Annals of the Deaf, 139*(2), 286–300.

Thorn, F., & Thorn, S. (1989). Speechreading with reduced vision: A problem of aging. *Journal of the Optical Society of America, 6*(4), 491–499.

Tidball, K. (1990). Applications of coping strategies developed by older deaf adults to the aging process. *American Annals of the Deaf, 135*(1), 33–40.

U.S. Bureau of the Census. (1993). *1990 census of population and housing: Tabulation and publication program.* Washington, DC: U.S. Department of Commerce, Bureau of the Census.

U.S. Department of Education. (1992). *Fourteenth annual report to Congress on the implementation of the Individuals with Disabilities Act.* Washington, DC: U.S. Government Printing Office.

Vacola, G. (1987). Un langage pour des sourds psychotiques et leur famille [A language for deaf psychotics and their families]. *Annales Medico Psychologiques, 145*(4), 372–378.

Vernon, M. (1967). Relationship of language to the thinking process. *Archives of Genetic Psychiatry, 16*(3), 325–333.

Vernon, M., & Andrews, J. F. (1990). *The psychology of deafness: Understanding deaf and hard of hearing people.* White Plains, NY: Longman.

Vocational Rehabilitation Act of 1954. P.L. 88-565, 68 Stat. 662.

Walker, L. A. (1986). *A loss for words: The story of deafness in a family.* New York: Harper & Row.

Wang, M. C., Reynolds, M. C., & Walberg, H. J. (Eds.). (1989). *Handbook of special education research and practice. Vol. 3: Low incidence conditions.* Elmsford, NY: Pergamon Press.

Wax, T. M. (1990). Deaf community leaders as liaisons between mental health and deaf cultures. *Journal of the American Deafness and Rehabilitation Association, 24*(2), 33–40.

Weaver, C. B., & Bradley-Johnson, S. (1993). A national survey of school psychological services for deaf and hard of hearing students. *American Annals of the Deaf, 138*(3), 267–274.

Weinstein, B. E. (1994). Presbycusis. In J. Katz (Ed.), *Handbook of clinical audiology* (4th ed., pp. 568–584). Baltimore: Williams & Wilkins.

Welsh, W. A., & McCleod-Gallinger, J. (1992). Effect of college on employment and earnings. In S. B. Foster & G. G. Walter (Eds.), *Deaf students in postsecondary education* (pp. 185–202). New York: Routledge.

Woodward, J. (1972). Implications of sociolinguistic research among the deaf. *Sign Language Studies, 1,* 1–7.

*World almanac and book of facts.* (1994). New York: Press Publishing.

Wyatt, T. L., & White, L. (1993). Counseling services for the deaf adult: Much demand, little supply. *Journal of the American Deafness and Rehabilitation Association, 27*(2), 8–12.

Zieziula, F. (1980). An alternative approach in service to deaf individuals: Community counseling. *Journals of Rehabilitation of the Deaf, 14*(1), 3–7.


## Further Reading


Anderson, G. B., & Watson, D. (1985). *Counseling deaf people: Research and practice.* Little Rock: Rehabilitation Research and Training Center on Deafness and Hearing Impairment, University of Arkansas.

Baker, C., & Cokely, D. (1980). *American Sign Language: A teacher's resource text on grammar and culture.* Silver Spring, MD: T. J. Publishers.

David, M., & Trehub, S. (1989). Perspectives on deafened adults. *American Annals of the Deaf, 134*(3), 200–204.

Dolnick, E. (1993, September). Deafness as culture. *Atlantic Monthly,* pp. 37–53.

Furth, H. G. (1973). *Deafness and learning: A psychosocial approach.* Belmont, CA: Wadsworth.

Glickman, N. (1986). Cultural identity, deafness, and mental health. *Journal of Rehabilitation for the Deaf, 20*(2), 1–10.

Higgins, P. C., & Nash, J. E. (1987). *Understanding deafness socially.* Springfield, IL: Charles C Thomas.

Kannapell, B. (1993). *Language choice—Identity choice.* Silver Spring, MD: Linstock Press.

Marschark, M. (1993). *Psychological development of deaf children.* New York: Oxford University Press.

Neisser, A. (1983). *The other side of silence: Sign language and the Deaf community in America.* New York: Alfred A. Knopf.

Schildroth, A. N., & Karchmer, M. A. (Eds.). (1986). *Deaf children in America.* San Diego: College Hill Press.
Schwartz, S. (Ed.). (1987). *Choices in deafness: A parents guide.* Kensington, MD: Woodbine House.
Strong, M. (1988). *Language learning and deafness.* New York: Cambridge University Press.
Watson, D., Long, G., Taff-Watson, M., & Harvey, M. (Eds.). (1988). *Two decades of excellence: A foundation for the future.* Little Rock, AR: American Deafness and Rehabilitation Association.

**K. Dean Santos, MSW,** is associate professor, Rochester Institute of Technology, National Technical Institute for the Deaf, Social Work Support, George Eastman Building, Room 3260, One Lomb Memorial Drive, Rochester, NY 14623.

**For further information see**

Aging Overview; Civil Rights; Deaf Community; Developmental Disabilities: Definitions and Policies; Disability; Genetics; Health Care: Direct Practice; Health Services Systems Policy; Human Development; Long-Term Care; Managed Care; Maternal and Child Health; Mental Health Overview; Natural Helping Networks; Organizations: Context for Social Services Delivery; Primary Health Care; Social Work Profession Overview; Visual Impairment.

**Key Words**

communicative disorder
cultural minority
deaf community
disability
hearing impairment

READER'S GUIDE

## Death and Dying

*The following entries contain information on this general topic:*

Bereavement and Loss
End-of-Life Decisions
Hospice
Sentencing of Criminal Offenders
Suicide
Victims of Torture and Trauma

## De Forest, Robert Weeks

*See* Biographies section, Volume 3

# Deinstitutionalization

**Steven P. Segal**

Since the early 1950s, national policy has gradually come to reflect the search for an alternative to institutional care and control as the preferred solution to social problems. Deinstitutionalization, as the policy has become known, developed along different lines among populations that were traditionally subject to care and control in large institutions: elderly people, children, people with mental illness or developmental disabilities, and criminal offenders. As it pertains to each of these groups, *deinstitutionalization* is best defined by a 1977 U.S. General Accounting Office (GAO) report:

> the process of (1) preventing both unnecessary admission to and retention in institutions; (2) finding and developing appropriate alternatives in the community for housing, treatment, training, education, and rehabilitation of [persons] who do not need to be in institutions, and (3) improving conditions, care, and treatment for those who need to have institutional care. This approach is based on the principle that . . . persons are entitled to live in the least restrictive environment necessary and lead lives as normally and independently as they can. (p. 1)

Although this definition reflects the broad aims of the policy of deinstitutionalization, the most discernible consequence of the policy has been the reduction of the average daily census of a select group of large institutions—state and county mental hospitals and children's homes—and the transfer of their resident populations to other supervised living arrangements. These alternative living arrangements, though often smaller, differ little from the institutional character of mental hospitals and children's homes. Thus, many analysts describe the results of deinstitutionalization as transinstitutionalization. The resident population of institutions in the United States actually increased from 1,887,000 (1,052 people per 100,000 population) in 1960, to 2,127,000 (1,046 per 100,000) in 1970, to 2,492,000 (1,100 per 100,000) in 1980, to 3,334,000 (1,340 per 100,000) in 1990. Between 1960 and 1980 this increase amounted to 4.5 percent. Since the mid-1980s, however, there has been an increase of 21 percent. Thus, describing deinstitutionalization as transinstitutionalization has become most appropriate during this time. This entry discusses reasons why the deinstitutionalization movement took hold and the consequences of deinstitutionalization for various populations.

## Origins of Deinstitutionalization

Concern regarding the condition of mental institutions dates back to the last quarter of the 19th century. The situation captured public attention in the late 1940s with the publication of Maisel's (1946) exposé in *Life* magazine, Ward's (1946) book *The Snake Pit*, and Deutch's (1948) book *The Shame of the States*. The United States was ready to take on new challenges after World War II, and coping with the problems of people with mental disabilities—conditions responsible for the rejection of 37 percent of military inductees and for 38 percent of military disability discharges—became a priority.

In addition to improving the condition of people in institutions, policymakers sought alternatives to institutionalization. The concept of community care was an old one. It was reintroduced in the early 1930s as an adjunct of state hospital care. During the late 1950s and early 1960s, innovative state hospital programs demonstrated the utility of such programs. During the 1960s and early 1970s the goal of providing supervised care became confused with the policy of deinstitutionalization, which emphasized moving people out of institutions. With the publication of books like Goffman's (1961) *Asylums*, the negative effect of institutional care was separated from the problems of mentally ill people. The institution had its own negative effects and these were to be avoided.

The policy of deinstitutionalization was aggressively implemented for many reasons. The following five influences combined to make deinstitutionalization seem attractive and feasible: (1) the negative effects of institutionalization documented by journalists and social scientists; (2) the growing costs of institutional care relative to its alternatives; (3) advances in social, psychological, and medical sciences that were thought to make the confinement and isolation functions of the institution obsolete; (4) the development of the civil rights movement, which emphasized the protection of individuals' due process rights and the necessity to approach care and treatment in the least restrictive manner; and (5) the development of an extensive system of public aid that allowed the maintenance function of institutions (in-kind room and board) to be replaced by a system of cash grants to clients. This last development, in particular, created a state-subsidized market for the local provision of care by the private sector.

These trends were created and supported by a unique coalition that spanned the political spectrum. Conservatives viewed the reduction of institutional censuses as a means of saving money, and liberals supported the standards of professional groups who saw in deinstitutionalization the most humane and effective care. There was little political opposition to deinstitutionalization, except by groups like the California State Employees' Association, which was interested primarily in maintaining its members' jobs in state institutions. Without organized political opposition, and with many groups in the political community viewing deinstitutionalization as a means to an end, the policy gained momentum.

In general, efforts to improve institutional conditions have been linked with an increase in the cost of institutional care. In various right-to-treatment decisions in the mental health, child welfare, and developmental disability fields, the courts have specified the types of treatment to which involuntarily detained patients have a right and the types of treatment they may refuse. The courts have also specified patient-to-staff ratios and have defined parameters of overcrowding (*Bartley v. Kremens*, 1975; *Donaldson v. O'Connor*, 1974; *Wyatt v. Stickney*, 1972). The expense of carrying out these orders has often prompted institution officials to reduce patient or inmate loads rather than increase staff or construct new facilities.

Because it is estimated that 20 percent to 60 percent of homeless people are deinstitutionalized

(Torrey, 1988), many have condemned the policy. Yet there are more people in institutions now than at the outset of the policy's implementation. It is therefore important to understand how the policy was implemented in relation to each of its target populations to fully understand its effect.

## Deinstitutionalizing Five Populations

The major effort of the deinstitutionalization movement has been to prevent unnecessary admissions to institutions and to reduce individuals' length of stay. The abandonment of broader deinstitutionalization goals for specific groups as well as the relationship between these goals and the development of appropriate community-based alternatives is explored with respect to five populations: mentally ill people, developmentally disabled people, criminal offenders, children, and elderly people.

### People with Mental Illness

In 1950 the most prevalent form of institutionalization was admission to a state or county mental hospital. These institutions were therefore the most affected by the deinstitutionalization movement. The census of state and county mental hospitals plummeted 84 percent, from a high of 558,922 in 1955 to a low of 88,571 in 1991. The number of such institutions fell from 310 in 1970, to 290 in 1989, to 274 in 1993 (Manderscheid & Sonnenschein, 1992, and personal communication with R. W. Manderscheid, National Institute of Mental Health, Summer 1993).

Although the resident population fell drastically, admissions to state and county mental hospitals increased between 1950 and 1969, reaching a peak of 486,661 in 1969. Admissions steadily declined after 1969, reaching 255,185 in 1991. In 1950 there were 152,186 admissions and 512,501 residents—a ratio of 0.297 admissions for every resident. In contrast, by 1970 there were 348,511 admissions and 330,619 residents—a ratio of 1.05 admissions for every resident. In 1991 this ratio had increased to 2.88 admissions for every resident. Thus, in the mental health field, a revolving-door process of brief hospitalization had led to increasingly higher admission rates and short periods of retention.

This revolving-door pattern also describes the care provided in nonfederal general hospitals with psychiatric services. These facilities, along with nursing homes, have become the new primary service institutions for people with mental illness. The number of nonfederal general hospitals with psychiatric services increased from 166 in 1970 to 332 in 1988. The resident population of these hospitals almost doubled in this time period, from 17,808 to 34,858, and their admissions (technically additions) increased from 478,000 to 877,398. These figures support a revolving-door pattern of care adopted for people with mental illness.

***Alternative facilities.*** The major shift in long-term care for adults, especially elderly people, involved their relocation or the retargeting of their initial placements to nursing homes and board-and-care facilities. Both settings have been described as the new "back wards" in the community. Because Medicaid programs disallowed services in nursing homes considered institutions for mental disease—a classification made when more than 50 percent of the patients have mental illnesses that require inpatient treatment according to their medical records (Jazwieck & Press, 1986)—nursing facilities became increasingly reluctant to acknowledge their patients' mental disorders for fear of losing Medicaid support. This led to an underground system of long-term care for people with mental illness.

Few statistics are available on the prevalence of mental illness among nursing home patients. Estimates vary from 30 percent to more than 85 percent, with the higher estimates being more common (Linn & Stein, 1981). Studies have further shown that approximately two-thirds of patients are suffering from senile dementia (a diagnosis excluded in 1983 from the 50 percent reclassification rule). Using the 85 percent prevalence figure as a benchmark and assuming that two-thirds of these individuals are suffering from senile dementia, one can estimate that 28 percent of those in nursing homes have a major mental disorder exclusive of senile dementia; one-third of these also have a physical illness. In 1990 the number of individuals in nursing homes was 1,772,032. Given the above reasoning, 496,169 would have a diagnosis of a major mental disorder exclusive of senile dementia. A total of 11.6 percent of the nursing home population is under 65 years of age (U.S. House of Representatives, 1992). Among these individuals the prevalence of mental disorder is much higher than among elderly people (Linn & Stein, 1981).

The board-and-care home is a residential facility that provides 24-hour supervision as a nonmedical facility for disabled individuals. These facilities are not part of the formal mental health system, they vary in size from one to more than 500 beds, and they are usually financed on a fee-for-service basis. The disabled individual usually pays for his or her board and care with a Supplemental Security Income (SSI) check. Only a few states license these homes, and licensing is often done through the social services rather than the health or mental health department. This licensing policy takes these disabled individuals out of the formal mental health arena and adds them to the underground system of long-term care for people with mental illness. It is estimated that 300,000 to 400,000 people with serious mental illness live in this system of care.

***Impetus for deinstitutionalization.*** Justification for the deinstitutionalization policy came from several points of view. Studies that compared short- and long-term treatment in mental institutions were unable to demonstrate the effectiveness of the latter. Studies that compared hospital treatment to community treatment combined with psychoactive medications supported the community-based approach. The first major clinical trials were used to convince the public that psychoactive medications were a solution to the control of mental health symptomatology, thus serving as justification for trusting patients outside the confines of mental institutions. Patients were to use the hospital merely to have their medication adjusted over a period of time (see Pasamanick, Scarpitic, & Dinitz, 1967).

A major factor in the reduction of the patient population of state mental hospitals was the 1962 decision of the U.S. Department of Health, Education, and Welfare (DHEW) to revise its policies to allow federal matching funds to be used by state public assistance programs to support individuals released from mental hospitals. The reinterpretation made aid available to former mental patients through the Aid to the Permanently and Totally Disabled program, now the Supplemental Security Income program of the Social Security Act. This action provided support to maintain mental patients in local communities, substituting cash assistance for institutional confinement and simultaneously providing an economic stimulus for the development of community-based residential care.

In addition to providing support to maintain former patients in the community, SSI provides automatic Medicaid eligibility for recipients unless states choose to adopt more stringent standards (Harrington, Newcomer, & Estes, 1985). This provision allows states a cost sharing of 50 percent to 80 percent for the medical care of patients transferred to the community.

Aside from individual support for people outside institutions, the financing of the institutions themselves became another key factor in the demise of the state mental hospital. Before the passage of Medicaid legislation in 1965, state mental hospitals were supported in full by state general funds. Medicaid, or Title XIX of the Social Security Act, allowed states to receive 50 percent or more in federal funds for the cost of patient care by transferring the patient to a nursing home. This cost-shifting incentive was further enhanced because the cost of patient care in the nursing home was less than two-thirds that of the mental hospital.

Ultimately, the civil rights movement put an end to long-term hospitalization. Long-term residence in mental hospitals effectively ceased with elimination of indefinite commitments to state mental hospitals and the restriction of involuntary detention to brief periods of time.

The political coalition that engineered the demise of state mental institutions did not survive to foster the development of alternative care for those who required supportive living arrangements. Most individuals were returned to the community to live either on their own or with their families. Between 10 percent and 30 percent went to live in alternative institutions or in sheltered living arrangements, including foster or family care homes, board-and-care homes, supervised hotels, and halfway houses (Segal & Aviram, 1978). A large proportion of these supervised living arrangements were similar to large mental institutions in character and environment. However, they functioned as smaller administrative entities within local communities.

**People with Developmental Disabilities**

People with developmental disabilities were deinstitutionalized in large part because they lived in the same institutions as people with mental illness. In 1950 state and county mental hospitals housed 48,000 people with developmental disabilities—27 percent of all developmentally disabled residents in public institutions. In 1989 this population had declined 97 percent, to only 1,605 individuals, just 1.7 percent of the developmentally disabled individuals in publicly operated facilities.

However, between 1970 and 1989 the number of public residential facilities serving this population rose from 190 to 1,305. The resident population of these facilities did not rise monotonically with the number of facilities. Between 1950 and 1967 the population rose from 176,000 to 193,000, where it peaked. It then declined to 94,268 by 1989 (U.S. Department of Commerce, 1992).

The recent decline in the population of people with developmental disabilities in publicly operated facilities has been more than compensated for in the increase in both the number and resident population of private facilities catering to this population. Such facilities numbered 10,219 in 1977; in 1989 38,657 facilities included intermediate-care facilities, foster homes, and group residences that provide 24-hour, 7-day-a-week responsibility for room, board, and supervision. (These private facilities exclude single-family homes providing services to a relative and nursing homes, foster homes, and boarding homes not formerly contracted or licensed as mental retardation service providers.) The population of these facilities increased during this same period from 89,120 to 180,023 (U.S. Department of Commerce, 1992). By 1986, 51.9 percent of the beds available in both public and private facilities were located in facilities where the average number of residents was no more than 35, indicating that consistent with deinstitutionalization ideology, small was considered better.

The deinstitutionalization of people with developmental disabilities was prodded by landmark decisions such as *Wyatt v. Stickney* (1972), which dealt with the right to treatment, and decisions related to housing individuals in the least restrictive environments. The movement into the community was also fostered by the increasing costs of improving institutions, combined with the advent of new technologies, communications, and the concept of normalization (the treatment of people in an environment most closely approximating a "normal" situation).

Like people with mental illness, most people with developmental disabilities go on to live with their families or on their own. However, a significant proportion reside in smaller community-based facilities, foster homes, board-and-care homes, and some large group homes that begin to approximate the formal character that is typical of many large institutions. These facilities housed 148,082 residents in 1987, 51 percent of whom lived in organizations with fewer than 100 beds (U.S. Department of Commerce, 1992).

**Criminal Offenders**

On December 31, 1989, 1.6 percent (or 1,630 per 100,000) of the adult population in the United States was under correctional supervision (U.S. Department of Commerce, 1992). The scale of community-based supervision of offenders was also greater than at any other time in history. In 1989 there were 2,520,500 adults on probation in the United States. This figure represents an increase of 236 percent in the probation population in 10 years. Further, the number of adult offenders on parole reached 456,800 by 1989, an increase of 210 percent in the same 10-year period (Bureau of Justice Statistics, 1984a, 1990b).

Although the use of community-based supervision designed to reduce the potential population of prisons has come to characterize the criminal justice system, the national prison census continues to grow, spawning controversial measures to finance the construction of new county jails and state prisons. The increase in the number of individuals with probation or parole status has been matched by an increase in the number of individuals in state and federal prisons. The populations of these facilities rose from 212,953 in 1960 to 315,974 in 1980 to 738,894 in 1990—an increase of 133 percent between 1980 and 1990. Similarly, the population of county jails grew from 203,000 in 1980 to 405,320 in 1990, up almost 100 percent (Bureau of Justice Statistics, 1984a, 1984b, 1990a, 1990b).

These trends are only partially attributable to increases in drug-related and violent crimes between 1980 and 1990. Violent crime rates increased only 35.3 percent and total crime rates only 8 percent in the decade. Drug-related arrest rates have increased 206 percent. Thus, increased law enforcement activity accompanied by an ideological shift away from the justification of rehabilitation to an emphasis on punishment seems to account for the increase in the criminal justice population.

Although alternatives to institutionalization have proliferated, the pressure on the correctional system to confine large numbers of people has increased dramatically. Offenders spend less time in prison and receive shorter sentences, but the number of times they return to custody, through parole revocations, has increased greatly. Cuts in probation and parole budgets have confined community-based supervision to the desk drawer. Like the mentally ill population, the offender population is increasingly subject to the revolving-door phenomenon with little effort invested in real community programming.

**Children**

According to the American Public Welfare Association (APWA), 71.4 percent of children living outside their homes in 24-hour supervised residential care are in foster homes; 18.6 percent are in group homes, residential treatment facilities, and emergency shelters; and 10 percent are in other settings (U.S. House of Representatives, 1992). In 1988 the 452,381 children were in 24-hour care. These figures do not include the number of children living in homeless shelters, estimated at 40,000 to 220,000 in 1988 (U.S. House of Representatives, 1992), nor those in the custody of the correctional system, estimated at 93,945 and growing in 1989

(U.S. Office of Juvenile Justice and Delinquency Prevention, 1990).

The shift to community-based foster home care for dependent and neglected youths dates back to the early part of the 20th century and represents the first departure from the principle of institutional care. The shift from institutional care to foster care since 1980 has been accompanied by a national drive to find permanent homes for foster children. Unfortunately, the effort to find permanent placement for such children seems to have foundered. The population curve describing the number of residents in foster care looks more like a roller coaster than the slide that would characterize the diminishing numbers of a truly deinstitutionalized population. In 1962 the number of children in foster care was 272,000 (3.9 per 1,000 in the U.S. population). By 1972 this number reached 319,800, and in 1977 the population peaked at 500,000 ("A Place," 1984). By 1983 it dropped to 269,500, but by 1991 it had increased to 429,000 (Tatara, 1992).

The post-1983 increase, which is attributed to the crack cocaine epidemic that began in the mid-1980s, continues even though, or perhaps because, family reunification continues to be the major permanency planning goal for children in foster care. Family reunification was reported as the goal for 46.6 percent of the children in care in 1983 and for 57.6 percent in 1988, when the foster care population reached 323,000. Further, the number of children in foster care available for adoption has steadily decreased from 102,000 in 1977 to 50,000 in 1982 ("A Place," 1984) and 35,000 in 1988 (18,000 if children living in nonfinalized adoption homes are excluded).

Foster care seems to be further plagued by an increase in the "churning" of children within the system. In 1982, 43 percent of children in care had experienced more than one placement; by 1988, 54 percent had experienced more than one placement (U.S. House of Representatives, 1992). Data on entering and leaving the system can be interpreted to indicate an increase in children's length of stay in the system—they show relatively stable numbers entering and leaving care with a continuing increase in the population size (Tatara, 1992). Again, it is possible that an unrealistic emphasis on family reunification, given the difficulty of the family problems and the lack of investment in reunification services, may account for these system characteristics (U.S. House of Representatives, 1992). Yet a comparison of results shows that family reunification actually increased from 49.7 percent in 1982 to 61.9 percent in 1988. Also, data on the length of stay of children remaining in care at the end of the fiscal year show that the percentage of children in care for five or more years decreased from 18.2 percent in 1982 to 11.6 percent in 1988 and that the percentage of children in care for less than six months remained stable at 21.7 percent (U.S. House of Representatives, 1992). Given the revolving-door phenomenon and the fact that 15 percent of children entering care in 1988 were reentering the system, it would appear that the system was characterized by the same features of mental hospitals in the mid-20th century. The system problems were aptly illustrated by the woman who was cured of her mental illness 30 times, with each release from the hospital counted as an independent cure, only to die in the same hospital that took credit for each of her cures. Family reunification is not necessarily a successful outcome, and as a goal it may compromise a more important need in the child's life—stability of upbringing. Such stability was often achieved in the now-absent children's institution or children's home.

For the population of youths under age 18, the rate of use of child welfare institutions between 1933 and 1973 decreased 48 percent (Lerman, 1982). In 1980 the U.S. Bureau of the Census indicated that there were 167,306 institutional residents under age 18. By 1988 this figure was estimated at 178,088 (U.S. Department of Commerce, 1992; U.S. House of Representatives, 1992)—similar to the number of beds in such facilities in 1966 (171,222). More important, continuing a trend of the last 20 years, child welfare institutions now focus on children with special problems rather than on the more general functions of the children's home. Of particular note is the increasing use of residential treatment centers for emotionally disturbed children and juvenile justice facilities for juvenile offenders (such as detention centers, reception and diagnostic centers, training schools, and halfway houses). The number and capacity of residential treatment centers for emotionally disturbed children increased from 261 facilities housing 5,270 patients in 1970 to 501 facilities housing 27,781 children in 1990 (Substance Abuse and Mental Health Services Administration, 1990, unpublished provisional data). The number of juvenile justice facilities increased from 647 in 1965 to 2,576 in 1979 to 3,267 in 1989. Between 1979 and 1989 the population of these facilities increased from 74,113 to 93,945. Other facilities, such as those serving pregnant adolescents, have decreased in number from 212 in 1965 to 115 in 1981. By 1990 such facilities were no longer separately identified. Some institutions have engaged merely in relabeling processes that are often spurred by the availability of categorical payments. For instance, children's institutions have often become treatment centers for emotionally disturbed children. This phenomenon may partially account for the relative stability of the number of children in institutions, excluding correctional facilities.

**Elderly People**

Since the early 1900s there has been a steady growth in the institutionalization of older people in the United States. The elderly population residing in group quarters of one type or another increased 267 percent between 1910 and 1970. In 1940, census data showed that 4.1 percent of the total elderly population was institutionalized: 40.5 percent of these were in noninstitutional group quarters such as hotels and boarding houses; 33 percent were in nursing homes, personal care homes, and residential homes; and 23 percent were in mental institutions (Estes & Harrington, 1981).

Between 1960 and 1980, however, there was a 71 percent decrease in the proportion of elderly people living in mental institutions; a 13 percent decrease in the proportion of older residents of noninstitutional group quarters; and a 318 percent increase in the proportion of elderly individuals living in nursing homes, personal care homes, and residential care homes.

By 1990, 1,883,178 elderly people, or 5.9 percent of the elderly population, lived in institutions (Price, Rimkunas, & O'Shaughnessy, 1990). Of those, 94 percent resided in nursing homes, 5 percent in other institutional group quarters, and 1 percent in psychiatric inpatient services. This increase is largely explained by the growth of the nursing home industry. In 1982 a Senate special committee projected that the population of nursing homes will grow to 1,952,000 by the year 2000 and to 2,952,000 by the year 2030 (U.S. Senate, 1982).

Three major federal programs have had a direct effect on the private nursing home and residential care industry: the Social Security Act of 1935 and the Medicare and Medicaid additions to the act. The Social Security Act provided a cash income to retired elderly people so they could live by themselves and to purchase boarding home care. By the late 1950s, shortages of beds in general hospitals created pressure to move chronic patients into nursing homes to make room for acute cases. Medicaid legislation of 1965 had the most dramatic effect on institutional care for older people. For low-income individuals with severe long-term chronic illnesses, nursing-home care services are primarily available through federal and state Medicaid (public assistance) programs designed for the indigent. In 1987 federal and state programs paid for 41.4 percent of all nursing-home care, thus functioning as a major resource for the private nursing-home industry (Estes & Harrington, 1981; Gibson, 1980). From its inception, Medicare has been oriented toward acute care services. In 1987 Medicare provided 93 percent of its funds to hospitals and physicians and only 0.8 percent to nursing homes.

Deinstitutionalization primarily affected elderly individuals who were confined to state and county mental hospitals. They were often moved directly out of hospitals into nursing homes. However, in many cases they were not moved at all; the building names were changed and most of the population stayed in place. As noted previously, it is estimated that 85 percent of those 65 and older who live in nursing and personal care homes have some degree of mental impairment. Given the large-scale and institutional character of today's nursing homes, emphasis is being placed on the need for the deinstitutionalization of nursing home residents and the provision of more home-based care. This emphasis is primarily a product of the extensive costs of the Medicare and Medicaid systems.

## Evaluating Trends in Deinstitutionalization

At its best, deinstitutionalization has succeeded in promoting community care that is more humane and effective than care provided in large institutions. At its worst, deinstitutionalization has resulted in both the forced homelessness of former residents of state institutions and an accumulation of individuals in community-based facilities that are no better than their antecedents. Unfortunately, the second situation occurs more frequently.

For the most part, the problems of deinstitutionalization derive not from the concept itself but from its naive implementation. The array of community-based services necessary to support community care is costly, and as inflation became a severe problem in the 1970s, the political coalition that had forged the deinstitutionalization movement fell apart. The fiscal retrenchment of government has left community care ominously incomplete, and the fate of a noble idea hinges on a poorly designed experiment that is woefully short of resources.

As a result, many residential community care facilities have abandoned the "small is beautiful" philosophy that provided a marked contrast to the operations of large institutions. Capitalizing on economies of scale, many nursing homes and group homes that cater to various populations have come to resemble the institutions they were intended to replace. The term "transinstitutionalization" has been coined to describe this lateral movement of individuals from one dominant institutional form to another. It may also describe the replacement of one type of institution with another as the primary service site for new admissions.

There is ample evidence that deinstitutionalization can work. However, insofar as it demands both the improvement of necessary large institutions and the provision of community-based care, deinstitutionalization remains the expensive creation of a frugal era.

## References


Bartley v. Kremens, 402 F. Supp. 1039 (E.D. Pa. 1975).

Bureau of Justice Statistics. (1984a). *1983 Jail census.* Washington, DC: U.S. Department of Justice.

Bureau of Justice Statistics. (1984b). *Prisoners in 1983.* Washington, DC: U.S. Department of Justice.

Bureau of Justice Statistics. (1984c). *Probation and parole 1983.* Washington, DC: U.S. Department of Justice.

Bureau of Justice Statistics. (1990a). *Jail census.* Washington, DC: Author.

Bureau of Justice Statistics. (1990b). *Prisoners in 1990.* Washington, DC: Author.

Deutch, A. (1948). *The shame of the states.* New York: Harcourt Brace.

Donaldson v. O'Connor, 493 F. 2nd 507 (5th Cir. 1974).

Estes, C., & Harrington, C. (1981). Fiscal crisis, deinstitutionalization and the elderly. *American Behavioral Scientist, 24*(6), 811–826.

Gibson, R. M. (1980). National health expenditures, 1979. *Health Care Financing Review, 2*(1), 1–36.

Goffman, E. (1961). *Asylums: Essays on the social situation of mental patients and other inmates.* New York: Doubleday.

Harrington, C., Newcomer, R. J., & Estes, C. L. (1985). *Long-term care of the elderly: Public policy issues.* Beverly Hills, CA: Sage Publications.

Jazwieck, T., & Press, S. (1986). Federal reimbursement for long-term care of the mentally ill. In M. S. Harper & B. D. Lebowitz (Eds.), *Mental illness in nursing homes: Agenda for research.* Rockville, MD: National Institute of Mental Health.

Lerman, P. (1982). *Deinstitutionalization.* New Brunswick, NJ: Rutgers University Press.

Linn, M. W., & Stein, S. (1981). Chronic adult mental illness. *Health & Social Work, 6*(4, Suppl.), 54S–61S.

Maisel, A. Q. (1946, May 6). Bedlam 1946: Most U.S. mental hospitals are a shame and a disgrace. *Life,* pp. 102–110.

Manderscheid, R., & Sonnenschein, M. A. (Eds.). (1992). *Mental health, United States, 1992.* Rockville, MD: National Institute of Mental Health.

National Institute of Mental Health. (1985). *Patients in state and county mental hospitals.* Rockville, MD: Author.

Pasamanick, B., Scarpitic, F., & Dinitz, S. (1967). *Schizophrenics in the community: An experimental study of the prevention of hospitalization.* New York: Appleton-Century-Crofts.

A place for foster children. (1984, June 27). *New York Times,* p. C15.

Price, R., Rimkunas, R., & O'Shaughnessy, C. (1990, September 24). *Characteristics of nursing home residents and proposals for reforming nursing home care* (Report No. 90-471). Washington, DC: Congressional Research Service.

Segal, S. P., & Aviram, U. (1978). *The mentally ill in community-based sheltered care.* New York: John Wiley & Sons.

Tatara, T. (1992). *Characteristics of children in substitute and adoptive care: A statistical summary of the VCIS national child welfare base.* Washington, DC: American Public Welfare Association.

Torrey, E. F. (1988). *Nowhere to go.* New York: Harper & Row.

U.S. Bureau of the Census. (1980). *United States census of the population 1980: Vol. 1. characteristics of the population: Part 1. Detailed population characteristics, United States summary.* Washington, DC: U.S. Government Printing Office.

U.S. Department of Commerce. (1992). *Statistical abstract of the United States, 1992.* Washington, DC: U.S. Government Printing Office.

U.S. General Accounting Office. (1977). *Returning the mentally disabled to the community: Government needs to do more.* Washington, DC: U.S. Government Printing Office.

U.S. House of Representatives, Committee on Ways and Means. (1992). *1992 green book.* Washington, DC: U.S. Government Printing Office.

U.S. Office of Juvenile Justice and Delinquency Prevention. (1990). *1987 and 1989 census of public and private juvenile custody facilities.* Washington, DC: U.S. Bureau of Justice Statistics.

U.S. Senate, Special Committee on Aging. (1982). *Developments in aging, 1981.* Washington, DC: U.S. Government Printing Office.

Ward, M. J. (1946). *The snake pit.* New York: Random House.

Wyatt v. Stickney, 493 F. Supp. 521, 522 (1972).


## Further Reading


Brown, P. (1985). *The transfer of care: Psychiatric deinstitutionalization and its aftermath.* Boston: Routledge & Kegan Paul.

Dear, M., & Wolch, J. (1987). *From deinstitutionalization to homelessness.* Princeton, NJ: Princeton University Press.

Knitzer, J. (1982). *The failure of public responsibility to children and adolescents in need of mental health services.* Washington, DC: Children's Defense Fund.

Lerman, P. (1982). *Deinstitutionalization and the welfare state.* New Brunswick, NJ: Rutgers University Press.

Stroul, B. A., & Friedman, R. M. (1986). *A system of care for severely emotionally disturbed children and youth.* Washington, DC: Georgetown University Child Development Center.


**Steven P. Segal, PhD,** is professor and director, Mental Health and Social Welfare Research Group, University of

California at Berkeley, School of Social Welfare, 120 Haviland Hall, Berkeley, CA 94720.

**For further information see**

Adult Foster Care; Aging: Public Policy Issues and Trends; Child Welfare Overview; Criminal Justice Overview; Developmental Disabilities: Definitions and Policies; Family Caregiving; Health Care: Reform Initiatives; Health Services Systems Policy; Homelessness; Long-Term Care; Managed Care; Mental Health Overview; Patient Rights; Psychosocial Rehabilitation; Runaways and Homeless Youths; Settlements and Neighborhood Centers; Social Security; Social Welfare History; Social Welfare Policy; Supplemental Security Income.

**Key Words**
community care
deinstitutionalization
transinstitutionalization

## Delinquency

*See* Juvenile and Family Courts; Juvenile Corrections

## Demographics

*See* Families: Demographic Shifts

# Developmental Disabilities: Definitions and Policies

**Kevin L. DeWeaver**

The theoretical concept of developmental disabilities can be confusing to or misunderstood by social workers and other professionals because the intent of the various definitions that have been used over time has differed. The concept of developmental disabilities was developed in the late 1960s by workers who wished to stress the functional needs of people with disabilities. According to Summers (1981), the coalition that aided in the development of the definition was "determined to introduce a law to address the service needs of persons with severe problems related to, but not necessarily caused by, mental retardation" (p. 259).

The original definition of developmental disabilities appeared in the Developmental Disabilities Services and Facilities Construction Amendments of 1970. Despite the functional aspect of the definition, three disabilities—mental retardation, cerebral palsy, and epilepsy—received most of the attention at the state level. In 1975 the Developmentally Disabled Assistance and Bill of Rights Act added autism and some forms of dyslexia while rejecting other learning disabilities as inappropriate to the definition. In the Rehabilitation, Comprehensive Services, and Developmental Disabilities Amendments of 1978, no diagnostic labels or categories were used; instead, the emphasis was clearly on the needs of persons. Two other amendments, the Developmental Disabilities Act of 1984 and the Developmental Disabilities Assistance and Bill of Rights Act Amendments of 1987, continued to hone the definitions in the 1980s.

The Developmental Disabilities Assistance and Bill of Rights Act of 1990 (P.L. 101-496) further amended previous legislation, authorized additional funding, and modified the definition of developmentally disabled once more. The following is the current definition from P.L. 101-496, with the changes in italics:

> Developmental disability means a severe, chronic disability of a person *5 years of age or older* that
>
> A. is attributable to a mental or physical impairment or combination of mental and physical impairments
> B. is manifested before the person attains age 22
> C. is likely to continue indefinitely
> D. results in substantial functional limitations in three or more of the following areas of major life activity: (i) self-care, (ii) receptive and expressive language, (iii) learning, (iv) mobility, (v) self-direction, (vi) capacity for independent living, and (vii) economic self-sufficiency
> E. reflects the person's need for a combination and sequence of special, interdisciplinary, or generic care, treatment, or other services which are of lifelong or extended duration and are individually planned and coordinated; *except that such term,*

> *when applied to infants and young children means individuals from birth to age 5, inclusive, who have substantial developmental delay or specific congenital or acquired conditions with a high probability of resulting in developmental disabilities if services are not provided.*

The definition of developmental disabilities is therefore nondiagnostic and functional, focusing on what the person can do and what skill development steps are needed. The seven major life activities listed in section D of the 1990 act, which McDonald-Wikler (1987) explicated, remain intact. Proponents of the definition consider it less stigmatizing than categorical labels. Furthermore, the definition moves away from the traditional organic model and is more in line with the social systems perspective (Mercer, 1973), with which most social workers are familiar.

Other professionals have identified several issues in relation to the definition. First, because it is not a clinical definition and leaves room for interpretation, inaccuracies in identifying people with developmental disabilities may occur. Second, the definition clearly focuses on people with severe disabilities and services for them, and thus many people with mild disabilities, including many economically disadvantaged persons and people of color, may not receive adequate services in the future (Summers, 1981). Third, Hobbs (1975) was concerned that, without categories, legislators may fail to recognize the problems of persons with developmental disabilities and may limit or discontinue funding for services. Fourth, Summers (1981) called the requirement that the disability be evident before age 22 "a relic of the old categorical definition" (p. 263).

## Major Types of Developmental Disabilities

Although the current definition of developmental disabilities is meant to be functional, it is important to examine various conditions that fit into this evolving definition. The high-risk factors for developmental disabilities remain as cited in McDonald-Wikler (1987). Although many of the etiologies are unknown, examples of specific causes of several major conditions are

- mental retardation—biological (for example, damage to the brain or chromosomal abnormalities) or psychosocial (for example, poverty related)
- cerebral palsy—the result of brain lesions
- epilepsy—genetic component or brain abnormalities
- autism—some form of organic brain abnormality (Baroff, 1991).

### Mental Retardation

In 1983 the American Association on Mental Deficiency (AAMD) released an updated definition: "Mental retardation refers to significantly subaverage general intellectual functioning existing concurrently with deficits in adaptive behavior and manifested during the developmental period" (Grossman, 1983, p. 1). This definition maintained the four levels of retardation (mild, moderate, severe, and profound). In 1987 AAMD changed its name to the American Association on Mental Retardation (AAMR) to reflect a less-stigmatized image of the condition. Also in 1992 AAMR released the current definition of mental retardation:

> Mental retardation refers to substantial limitations in present functioning. It is characterized by significantly subaverage intellectual functioning, existing concurrently with related limitations in two or more of the following applicable adaptive skill areas: communication, self-care, home living, social skills, community use, self-direction, health and safety, functional academics, leisure, and work. Mental retardation manifests before age 18. (p. 1)

In developing this new definition, AAMR sought to express the changing understanding of mental retardation and to describe the system of supports that an individual would need. It replaced adaptive behaviors with 10 adaptive skill areas, emphasizing the person and his or her interaction with the environment. Finally, it replaced the four levels of retardation in the previous definition with a description of the patterns of support systems and their required intensities (intermittent, limited, extensive, and pervasive).

This new definition is congruent with the trends in social work practice today. It (1) continues to move away from labeling and highlights both an individual's strengths and his or her functional limitations; (2) deemphasizes the medical aspects of disabilities and puts them in the proper perspective as only one area of concern; (3) focuses on adaptive skills, not IQ; (4) provides for cultural and linguistic diversity in the assessment process; and (5) reflects the person-in-environment paradigm that social workers have used for many years.

Social workers have made important contributions (such as individual and group counseling, development of alternative living arrangements, and case management activities) to this area (Horejsi, 1979). DeWeaver and Kropf (1992) suggested that "mental retardation has evolved as a legitimate field of practice in social work, as is evidenced in the Fields of Practice Series in which Dickerson's (1981) *Social Work Practice with the Mentally Retarded* was the first text" (p. 36). In addition, Brantley (1988) provides an excellent review of 23 syndromes of mental retardation.

A team of social workers (Ehlers, Krishef, & Prothero, 1977) suggested that up to 3 percent of the U.S. population may be labeled mentally retarded sometime in their lives. However, it is important to keep in mind that although 2.5 percent to 3 percent of the population may be classified as mentally retarded, only 0.9 percent would be considered developmentally disabled (Baroff, 1991).

### Cerebral Palsy

Cerebral palsy is a neuromuscular disorder of balance and movement. "Its symptoms do not reflect an active illness but rather are the residual effects of damage to brain cells in the cortex and cerebellum, usually occurring prenatally or at birth" (Baroff, 1991, p. 158). The three types of cerebral palsy are (1) dyskinesia, in which movements are uncontrolled and purposeless; (2) spasticity, the most common type, in which movement can be slow and restricted; and (3) ataxia, in which balance and gait are affected. The prevalence rate is approximately 0.4 percent of the general population (Baroff, p. 162).

### Epilepsy

Epilepsy, which was the third main category in the 1970 law on developmental disabilities, is primarily a medical condition that "refers to an abnormality in the electrical activity of the brain that causes recurrent seizures" (Baroff, 1991, p. 196) or convulsions that may be classified as grand mal, petit mal, or psychomotor. Males are at a greater risk of epilepsy than are females, and a conservative estimate is that 0.5 of the population is under active treatment for this condition (Baroff, p. 201).

### Autism

Autism is characterized by three factors: (1) an impairment in reciprocal social interactions, (2) an impairment in nonverbal and verbal communication and imaginative activity, and (3) a markedly restricted repertoire of activities and interests (Mesibov & Bourgondien, 1992, p. 79). This disorder is usually recognized early in life (before age 2 1/2) and affects three to four times as many boys as girls. However, the prevalence rate is low; about one in 2,000 have this disorder (Baroff, 1991, p. 126).

### Other Conditions

Dyslexia was added to the 1975 definition of developmental disabilities. Today this condition is also known as developmental reading disorder or specific reading disability (Stanovich, 1992). Because reading affects the ability to learn, this condition has received considerable attention since the mid-1970s. Estimates of the prevalence of dyslexia range from 2 percent to 8 percent (Stanovich, 1992, p. 175).

Another set of conditions is orthopedic problems that involve difficulties in the functioning of muscles, bones, and joints. One such problem, spina bifida, has received recent national attention. For instance, P.L. 102-309, a joint resolution, designated September 1992 National Spina Bifida Awareness Month. Although the prevalence of spina bifida is less than one in 1,000, some researchers have suggested the use of folic acid to reduce the number of cases each year.

People with a hearing loss or deafness may also be considered developmentally disabled. Because hearing loss or deafness can affect speech, language, and learning, it can have a tremendous effect on a person. Visual impairment, which can include blindness, is another important condition and affects more than 1.4 million Americans (Kirchner, 1985). Another added category is deaf–blindness, which affects more than 45,000 people in the United States (Konar, 1984). Head injuries that lead to permanent impairment can be considered another developmental disability; estimates are that 50,000 to 90,000 persons in the United States are affected (Baroff, 1991, p. 3).

Finally, a person may have multiple disabilities at the same time. Developmental disorders can sometimes be traced to problems before birth, at birth, or after birth, or they can be a result of problems at all three times.

Note that the terms used in this field are constantly changing. Today such terms as "retarded," "handicapped," and "disabled" people are no longer appropriate. The preferred terminology is "persons with" whatever condition, to emphasize the people, rather than the conditions. In addition, some agencies have been asked to change the term "client" to "consumer" and the term "problems" to "challenges." Although the terminology will continue to change, one thing is constant: This is a vulnerable group of people who can benefit from various services by professional social workers.

## Historical Overview

Basically, the history of services to people with mental retardation has lugubrious overtones because there were no organized efforts to shelter, protect, or educate these individuals before the 19th century (Davies & Ecob, 1959). Mentally "defective" children often were killed or abandoned by the ancient Greeks and Romans. Other cruelties, such as whippings, were the "treatment" prescribed during the Protestant Reformation in Europe. Many of the myths and superstitions about mental retardation (such as the hopelessness of the condition) that were prevalent in Europe were imported to North America. Dunn (1961) captured the essence of this period, when he stated that "prior to the year 1800, society's record was one of the most pathetic chapters in the history of man" (p. 14).

The 19th century proved to be an age of individual pioneers, such as Henry B. Wilbur, and the development of institutional programs in the United States. In 1848 the first institution for children with mental retardation, the Perkins Institute in Boston, was opened with the goal of curing the condition (Davies & Ecob, 1959). By the 1870s, institutions were viewed as places to protect people with mental retardation from society. Within 10 years, the pendulum had swung, and institutions were used to "protect" society from this population via segregation, sterilization, and other punitive measures.

The so-called Progressive Era in the United States (1900–1919) was not progressive for everyone: People with mental retardation did not prosper at that time (Axinn & Levin, 1975). The "service" of the time was to warehouse inexpensively as many people with mental retardation as possible while sterilization programs continued. Most of these institutions were built in rural areas to remove this population further from the mainstream of society. Social work and the developing field of mental retardation seemed to intersect briefly because this was the era of the children's movement, as witnessed by the White House Conference in 1909 and the development of the Children's Bureau in 1912. Further intersections remained minimal from the 1920s through the 1940s. Leiby (1978) offered some insight into this development:

> The competence of the professionals was in casework, group work, and community organization, and they found their main interest in what came to be called "direct services," in which personal relationships and helpfulness were somewhat central. The idea of direct service in social welfare did not usually include institutions for education and medical care, which had their own sovereign professions. (p. 271)

In 1950 a new organization—the National Association of Retarded Children (later changed to the National Association of Retarded Citizens)—began to advocate the development of community services. This major advancement was brought about by parents and families of persons with mental retardation, who were frustrated by the overall lack of services. In the late 1950s, there was a shift from devaluing people with mental retardation toward maximizing their potential, and efforts were made to coordinate services and to engage in community planning (Doll, 1962).

With the election of John F. Kennedy—whose sister is a person with mental retardation—as president in 1960, the entire field of mental retardation gained a valued ally, who called for research and reform. Kennedy assembled the President's Panel on Mental Retardation, which recommended a national plan of action in 1962. The panel's report contained 95 recommendations for programs and services for this group.

Institutions came under further attack during the early 1960s; Goffman's (1961) book, *Asylums,* for example, became a classic. The President's Committee on Mental Retardation, formed after the panel study, took note of the dehumanizing conditions that existed in many of these institutions. In response, many professionals, parents, and citizens began to lobby for institutional reform.

The events of the 1950s and early 1960s began the convergence of the parallel development of social work and the field of mental retardation, partly because of social workers' planning and policy-making activities that led to jobs as state developmental disabilities planners. This convergence continued for another two decades.

## Public Policy since the 1960s

The public laws that were passed in the 1960s and 1970s provided funding for many professional positions for social workers in this field. These social workers provided direct service, planning, administration, and case management services, which were useful in aiding the transfer of persons with developmental disabilities from institutions to community residences (commonly called the deinstitutionalization movement) (DeWeaver, 1983a). The 1980s ushered in a different approach to legislation and funding patterns.

### Major Public Laws

An outgrowth of the President's Panel on Mental Retardation was the passage of the Maternal and Child Health and Mental Retardation Planning Amendments in 1963, which authorized funding for preventive programs. Also in 1963, the Mental Retardation Facilities and Community Mental Health Centers Construction Act was passed. Two major contributions of this law were the development of a mental retardation branch at the National Institute of Child Health and Human Development and approved funding to build university-affiliated facilities. The 1967 amendments to the Social Security Act were important because they provided for the early screening, diagnosis, and treatment of young poor children (Braddock, 1987). Many federal laws on special education, including the 1975 Education for All Handicapped Children Act, were passed during this period.

Besides defining developmental disabilities initially in 1970, the Developmental Disabilities Services and Facilities Construction Amendments required the establishment of state councils, which would integrate the activities of various agencies of the state governments. The Rehabilitation Act of 1973 (P.L. 93-112) included Section 504, which required all federal agencies to establish regulations to prevent discrimination against persons with various disabilities. Two major areas of discrimination that the act targeted were the denial of participation in any program or activity that received federal assistance and discrimination in employment.

In 1974 the amendments to the Social Security Act consolidated the social services titles into a new Title XX, which grew to $3.3 billion in 1980 (Braddock, 1987). Subsequent amendments raised the authorization levels for people with developmental disabilities. The Supplemental Security Income program provides incomes to a substantial number of people with developmental disabilities, including over half a million people with mental retardation. The Rehabilitation, Comprehensive Services, and Developmental Disabilities Amendments of 1978 revised the definition of mental retardation and instituted priority areas (such as case management, child development, alternative community living, and nonvocational social–developmental services) that were of interest to social workers, who filled some of the important positions funded by the federal government.

The election of Ronald Reagan precipitated a new shift in funding that would include large block grants, cuts in social programs, and increases in spending for defense. In 1981 the Omnibus Budget Reconciliation Act reduced authorization levels for many domestic programs, including Title XX. The focus of the Developmental Disabilities Act Amendments of 1984 was on achieving maximum potential, productivity, and integration into the community; these "amendments redefined priority services to include employment-related activities and deleted nonvocational social–developmental services as a priority" (Braddock, 1987, p. 26). Boggs (1988) summarized the trend in funding patterns as follows:

> There was an eight-fold increase in expenditures as a percentage of GNP [gross national product] from 1962 (0.025%) to 1981 (0.21%), the peak year to date, but the era of easy escalation has passed. Already the struggle is on just to maintain this advance when measured in real dollars. (p. 312)

In the Developmental Disabilities Assistance and Bill of Rights Act Amendments of 1987, the state planning councils were encouraged to accept more of an advocacy role. Attention was also to be paid to the members of racial and ethnic minorities with developmental disabilities, especially to such underserved groups as Native Americans and Native Hawaiians. In addition, professionals were encouraged to seek competitive work for people with developmental disabilities when possible, and university-affiliated facilities were renamed university-affiliated programs, which reflects a more normalized name and a broader scope of services.

In the 1990s two laws stand out. The first, the Americans with Disabilities Act of 1990 is not specific to developmental disabilities but broadens opportunities for competitive work and increases access to transportation and other services in the community (Baroff, 1991). The second, the Developmental Disabilities Assistance and Bill of Rights Act of 1990, refined the concept of developmental disabilities once again. This law renewed funds for the four basic programs: (1) the basic state grant program, (2) the protection and advocacy system, (3) the university-affiliated programs, and (4) projects of national significance. It also increased the estimate of the number of people with developmental disabilities from 2 million to over 3 million and indicated that a substantial portion of people with developmental disabilities remained unserved or underserved. Finally, the law added a purpose that social workers could readily support:

> to advocate for public policy change and community acceptance to enable all people with developmental disabilities to receive the services, supports and other assistance and opportunities necessary to enable such persons to achieve their maximum potential through increased independence, productivity and integration into the community.

As the funding decreased in the early 1980s, the convergence of social work and the field of developmental disabilities may have slowed dramatically. P.L. 101-496 authorized $3,650,000 for fiscal years 1991 to 1993, the same amount as for fiscal years 1988 to 1990, which meant fewer new jobs in the field. The failure to increase the appropriations may be one reason that the membership of the Social Work Division of AAMR dropped from over 900 members in 1979 to approximately 700 in 1994. Another issue is low salaries. A survey of NASW members found that people working in the field of developmental disabilities were the second-lowest-paid group (Gibelman & Schervish, 1993).

### Major Court Cases

Another way to change policy is through the judicial system. The field of developmental disabilities has a rich history of court cases. In *Wyatt v. Stickney* (1972) in Alabama, the court held that "there was a constitutional right to treatment applicable to mentally retarded people in institutions" (Castellani, 1987, p. 18). *ARC v. Rockefeller* (1972) and *Halderman v. Pennhurst State School and Hospital* (1977) contributed to institutional reforms and the development of appropriate community resources (Castellani, 1987).

Several other cases deserve mention. In the *City of Cleburne Tex v. Cleburne Living Center* (1985), the rights of people with mental retardation to live in residences in the community surprisingly had to be reaffirmed. In *Penry v. Lynaugh, Director, Texas Department of Corrections* (1989), partial relief was granted from the death penalty under some circumstances because of evidence of mental retardation and child abuse. This information must now be given to juries on request.

## Concepts of Services

From federal laws and court cases, several important concepts were developed and implemented in the provision of services to people with developmental disabilities. One such concept, least-restrictive environment, became an important force in developing community services and residences. This concept had legal precedents in two important court cases—*Covington v. Harris* (1969) and *Wyatt v. Stickney* (1972). Lakin and Bruininks (1985) defined the concept as follows:

> The policy of placing handicapped persons in the least restrictive environment means that developmentally appropriate care, training, and support based on an individual's needs should be, to the maximum extent possible, provided in the types of community settings that are used by nonhandicapped persons. (p. 13)

Least-restrictive environment is congruent with the concept of normalization, which Nirje (1976) defined as "making available to all mentally retarded people patterns of life and conditions of everyday life which are as close as possible to the regular circumstances and ways of life of society" (p. 181). Normalization supports the integration of all people with developmental disabilities in everyday events and the chance to engage in age-appropriate activities. Wolfensberger (1972) elaborated on this concept and how it is compatible with the delivery of human services.

Another concept with which school social workers are familiar is mainstreaming and its effect on pupils with developmental disabilities (DeWeaver & Rose, 1987). According to this concept, pupils with developmental disabilities are to be integrated into regular educational programs and classes when possible. Dickerson (1981) described the philosophy of mainstreaming this way:

> Mainstreaming is based on the assumption that all children will be accepted into the school system because they are people. It assumes that all children will be included in all the plans designed by school personnel. (p. 15)

Another concept, deinstitutionalization, was implemented in the early 1970s, when the shift from large facilities to residences in the community began (Bradley, 1978). One of the pioneers of the practice, Scheerenberger (1976), suggested that two other components must be addressed for deinstitutionalization to be successful—(1) the prevention of inappropriate institutional admissions and (2) institutional reform. Many positive changes have occurred since the early 1960s. For example, institutions are now more rehabilitation oriented and are viewed as one service—not *the* service—in a continuum of care.

Some critics of mainstreaming argue that the inclusion of children with mental retardation in the regular classroom will distract teachers and the other children and that less will be accomplished. Regarding deinstitutionalization, concerns have been raised about inappropriate discharges, too many discharges, and community services being overrun with the demands of these clients.

## Service Delivery System

The service delivery system in this field is complex and interdisciplinary. Although professionals may view the array of services as rational and planned, consumers and their families may view the system as a web or complex maze (Rubin, 1987). One of the most useful tasks that social workers can perform as part of case management is to link clients and their families to appropriate services (DeWeaver & Johnson, 1983). They can find these services in directories or lists of services that are available from university-affiliated programs in many urban areas; however, in sparsely populated rural areas, social workers have to locate or even assist in the development of needed services (DeWeaver, 1983b).

The service delivery system is further complicated by the bifurcation of services into generic services, which are available to everyone (such as routine dental checkups), and specialized services, which are available primarily to people with developmental disabilities (for example, specific community residences, formerly called group homes). Making these options known to clients and their families is an important duty of social workers in the field.

Using the field-of-practice concept in social work, DeWeaver and Kropf (1992) suggested that it is useful to distinguish the locus of service—community or institution—and various types of agencies—public or private—or other mechanisms for delivering services. The opportunities for service in this field are varied. Many social workers are employed by public (governmental) institutions, called intermediate-care facilities, where they perform a host of duties, including participating in evaluations of clients, counseling parents of clients, and planning discharges. Some social workers are employed in private institutions (such as the Elwyn Corporation).

In the community, social workers are employed as planners, advocates, and protection professionals in public agencies or as providers of direct services and case managers in nonprofit private agencies, such as community mental health centers, that rely on federal, state, and local funds to conduct programs for people with developmental disabilities. Social workers also act as consultants to self-help and advocacy groups of people with developmental disabilities and their families that are located in institutions or in the community (Browning, Thorin, & Rhoades, 1984). In addition, some social workers in private practice do counseling, identify services, and provide follow-up services to people with developmental disabilities.

Not all social workers in this field are readily identified as social workers. Some social workers are no longer considered social workers when they move up the career ladder and become planners, managers, or high-level administrators. Although many may still identify with the profession, their new roles and titles do not reflect what many people perceive to be the functions of social work.

## NASW Standards and Policy Statements

The section on standards for social work in developmental disabilities in the *NASW Standards for Social Work in Health Care Settings* (NASW, 1987) has not changed since they first were published in 1982 and were further explicated by McDonald-Wikler (1987). The *NASW Standards for Social Work Case Management* (1992) includes standards that are germane to practice with people with developmental disabilities. Because there was growing resistance to calling people "cases" and to "managing" them, case management was renamed systems coordination and community education in P.L. 101-496 in 1990.

Finally, a revised policy statement in *Social Work Speaks: NASW Policy Statements* (NASW, 1994)—"People with Disabilities"—is particularly relevant for social workers in the field of developmental disabilities.

## Other Professional Issues

Surveys of social workers in the field of mental retardation indicate that their level of job satisfaction is high; moreover, over 75 percent said they intended to remain in this field. However, about 46 percent of those who worked in institutions wanted to move to community settings (DeWeaver, 1980, 1992). Therefore, one issue is how best to communicate this surprisingly positive information to social work students and practitioners who are looking for career changes.

Another issue is the necessity to have funding follow the clients from the institution to the community (DeWeaver, 1983a). This has been a problem since the early 1970s, when the deinstitutionalization movement began. Social workers need to use their advocacy skills and knowledge of lobbying to effect this important change.

In social work education, faculty need to make students aware of the opportunities for research and practice in the field of developmental disabilities. In the 1980s, although there were some doctoral dissertations on developmental disabilities, many topics were not studied, and at the master's level, the appeal of developmental disabilities or case management to students was low (Rubin, Johnson, & DeWeaver, 1986). Bachelor's-level students seem to have been more open to developmental disabilities and case management and often explored this field when they were informed of it (Rubin & Johnson, 1984). Furthermore, the infusion model of curriculum development—in which content on developmental disabilities is included in required foundation courses—is recommended (DeWeaver & Kropf, 1992), and more specialized concentrations should be offered nationally. Also, schools of social work should continue to work with university-affiliated programs on their campuses and in their regions and hire more social workers who are AAMR members to teach students about developmental disabilities.

The social work profession has increased its efforts to network with AAMR and others in the field of developmental disabilities, but additional networking by social workers and social work organizations would be useful. Furthermore, social work must foster the building of coalitions of social work practitioners, educators, and other professionals in the field of developmental disabilities. By implementing these strategies and addressing these issues, the profession should be able to provide an ample supply of qualified social workers to deliver and administer high-quality services to people with developmental disabilities and their families.

## References


American Association on Mental Retardation. (1992). *Mental retardation: Definition, classification, and systems of supports* (9th ed.). Washington, DC: Author.

Americans with Disabilities Act of 1990. P.L. 101-336, 104 Stat. 327.

Axinn, J., & Levin, H. (1975). *Social welfare: A history of the American response to need.* New York: Harper & Row.

Baroff, G. S. (1991). *Developmental disabilities: Psychosocial aspects.* Austin, TX: Pro-Ed.

Boggs, E. M. (1988). The changing role of the federal government. In M. D. Powers (Ed.), *Expanding systems of service for persons with developmental disabilities* (pp. 289–316). Baltimore: Paul H. Brookes.

Braddock, D. (1987). *Federal policy toward mental retardation and developmental disabilities.* Baltimore: Paul H. Brookes.

Bradley, V. J. (1978). *Deinstitutionalization of developmentally disabled persons: A conceptual analysis and guide.* Baltimore: University Park Press.

Brantley, D. (1988). *Understanding mental retardation: A guide for social workers.* Springfield, IL: Charles C Thomas.

Browning, P., Thorin, E., & Rhoades, C. (1984). A national profile of self-help/self-advocacy groups of people with mental retardation. *Mental Retardation, 22,* 226–230.

Castellani, P. J. (1987). *The political economy of developmental disabilities.* Baltimore: Paul H. Brookes.

City of Cleburne Tex v. Cleburne Living Center, 473 U.S. 432, 105 S. Ct. 3249, 87 L. Ed. 2d 313 (1985).

Covington v. Harris, 325 F. Supp. 325 (1969).

Davies, S. P., & Ecob, K. (1959). *The mentally retarded in society.* New York: Columbia University Press.

Developmental Disabilities Act of 1984. P.L. 98-527, 98 Stat. 2662.

Developmental Disabilities Assistance and Bill of Rights Act Amendments of 1987. P.L. 100-146, 101 Stat. 840.

Developmental Disabilities Assistance and Bill of Rights Act of 1990. P.L. 101-496, 104 Stat. 1191.

Developmental Disabilities Services and Facilities Construction Amendments of 1970. P.L. 91-517, 84 Stat. 1316.

Developmentally Disabled Assistance and Bill of Rights Act of 1975. P.L. 94-103, 89 Stat. 486.

DeWeaver, K. L. (1980). An empirical analysis of social workers in the field of mental retardation. *Dissertation Abstracts International, 41,* 1214A–1215A. (University Microfilms No. 8020351)

DeWeaver, K. L. (1983a). Deinstitutionalization of the developmentally disabled. *Social Work, 28,* 435–439.

DeWeaver, K. L. (1983b). Delivering rural services for developmentally disabled individuals and their families: Changing scenes. In R. Coward & W. Smith (Eds.), *Serving families in contemporary rural America: Issues and opportunities* (pp. 150–170). Lincoln: University of Nebraska Press.

DeWeaver, K. L. (1992, May). *An empirical analysis of AAMR social workers: Ten years after.* Paper presented at the 116th annual meeting of the American Association on Mental Retardation, New Orleans.

DeWeaver, K. L., & Johnson, P. L. (1983). Case management in rural areas for the developmentally disabled. *Human Services in the Rural Environment, 8*(4), 23–31.

DeWeaver, K. L., & Kropf, N. P. (1992). Persons with mental retardation: A forgotten minority in education. *Journal of Social Work Education, 28*(1), 36–46.

DeWeaver, K. L., & Rose, S. R. (1987). School of social work with developmentally disabled pupils: Past, present, and future. *School Social Work Journal, 11*, 45–58.

Dickerson, M. U. (1981). *Social work practice with the mentally retarded.* New York: Free Press.

Doll, E. E. (1962). A historical survey of research and management of mental retardation in the United States. In E. P. Trapp & P. Himelstein (Eds.), *Readings on the exceptional child* (pp. 21–67). Englewood Cliffs, NJ: Appleton-Century-Crofts.

Dunn, L. M. (1961). A historical review of the treatment of the retarded. In J. H. Rothstein (Ed.), *Mental retardation: Readings and resources* (pp. 13–19). New York: Holt, Rinehart & Winston.

Education for All Handicapped Children Act of 1975. P.L. 94-142, 89 Stat. 773.

Ehlers, W. H., Krishef, C. H., & Prothero, J. C. (1977). *An introduction to mental retardation: A programmed text* (2nd ed.). Columbus, OH: Charles E. Merrill.

Gibelman, M., & Schervish, P. (1993). *Who are we: The social work labor force as reflected in the NASW membership.* Washington, DC: NASW Press.

Goffman, E. (1961). *Asylums.* New York: Anchor Books.

Grossman, H. J. (Ed.). (1983). *Classification in mental retardation.* Washington, DC: American Association on Mental Deficiency.

Halderman v. Pennhurst State School and Hospital, 446 F. Supp. 1295 (1977).

Hobbs, N. (Ed.). (1975). Introduction. In *The classification of exceptional children* (pp. 1–9). San Francisco: Jossey-Bass.

Horejsi, C. R. (1979). Developmental disabilities: Opportunities for social workers. *Social Work, 24,* 40–43.

Kirchner, C. (1985). *Data on blindness and visual impairment in the U.S.: A resource manual.* New York: American Foundation for the Blind.

Konar, V. (1984). *Strategies for serving deaf-blind clients.* Hot Springs: Arkansas Research and Training Center.

Lakin, K. C., & Bruininks, R. H. (1985). Contemporary services for handicapped children and youth. In R. H. Bruininks & K. C. Lakin (Eds.), *Living and learning in the least restrictive environment* (pp. 3–22). Baltimore: Paul H. Brookes.

Leiby, J. (1978). *A history of social welfare and social work.* New York: Columbia University Press.
Maternal and Child Health and Mental Retardation Planning Amendments of 1963. P.L. 88-156, 77 Stat. 273.
McDonald-Wikler, L. (1987). Disabilities: Developmental. In A. Minahan (Ed.-in-Chief), *Encyclopedia of social work* (18th ed., Vol. 1, pp. 422–434). Silver Spring, MD: National Association of Social Workers.
Mental Retardation Facilities and Community Mental Health Centers Construction Act of 1963. P.L. 88-164, 77 Stat. 282.
Mercer, J. R. (1973). *Labeling the mentally retarded.* Berkeley: University of California Press.
Mesibov, G. B., & Bourgondien, M. E. V. (1992). Autism. In S. R. Hooper, G. W. Hynd, & R. E. Mattison (Eds.), *Developmental disorders: Diagnostic criteria and clinical assessment* (pp. 69–95). Hillsdale, NJ: Lawrence Erlbaum.
National Association of Social Workers. (1987). Standards for social work in developmental disabilities. In *NASW standards for social work in health care settings* (pp. 15–21). Silver Spring, MD: Author.
National Association of Social Workers. (1992). *NASW standards for social work case management.* Washington, DC: Author.
National Association of Social Workers. (1994). *Social work speaks: NASW policy statements* (3rd ed.). Washington, DC: NASW Press.
New York State Association for Retarded Children and Parisi v. Rockefeller, 72 Civ. 356 (E.D.N.Y. 1972).
Nirje, B. (1976). The normalization principle. In R. B. Kugel & A. Sheerer (Eds.), *Changing patterns in residential services for the mentally retarded* (pp. 179–195). Washington, DC: President's Committee on Mental Retardation.
Omnibus Budget Reconciliation Act of 1981. P.L. 97-35, 95 Stat. 357.
President's Panel on Mental Retardation. (1962). *A proposed program for national action to combat mental retardation.* Washington, DC: U.S. Government Printing Office.
Rehabilitation Act of 1973. P.L. 93-112, 87 Stat. 355.
Rehabilitation, Comprehensive Services, and Developmental Disabilities Amendments of 1978. P.L. 95-602, 92 Stat. 2955.
Rubin, A. (1987). Case management. In A. Minahan (Ed.-in-Chief), *Encyclopedia of social work* (18th ed., Vol. 1, pp. 212–222). Silver Spring, MD: National Association of Social Workers.
Rubin, A., & Johnson, P. J. (1984). Direct practice interests of entering MSW students. *Journal of Education for Social Work, 20*(2), 5–16.
Rubin, A., Johnson, P. J., & DeWeaver, K. L. (1986). Direct practice interests of MSW students: Changes from entry to graduation. *Journal of Social Work Education, 22*(2), 98–108.
Scheerenberger, R. C. (1976). *Deinstitutionalization and institutional reform.* Springfield, IL: Charles C Thomas.
Social Security Amendments of 1967. P.L. 90-248, 81 Stat. 821.
Social Security Amendments of 1974. P.L. 93-647, 88 Stat. 2337.
Stanovich, K. E. (1992). Developmental reading disorder. In S. R. Hooper, G. W. Hynd, & R. E. Mattison (Eds.), *Developmental disorders: Diagnostic criteria and clinical assessment* (pp. 173–208). Hillsdale, NJ: Lawrence Erlbaum Associates.
Summers, J. A. (1981). The definition of developmental disabilities: A concept in transition. *Mental Retardation, 19,* 259–265.
Wyatt v. Stickney, 344 F. Supp. 387 (M.D. Ala 1972).
Wolfensberger, W. (Ed.). (1972). *The principle of normalization in human services.* Toronto: National Institute on Mental Retardation.

## Further Reading

Adams, M. (1971). *Mental retardation and its social dimensions.* New York: Columbia University Press.
Hanley, C. (1981). *Social work with mentally handicapped people.* London: Heinemann.
Schreiber, M. (Ed.). (1970). *Social work and mental retardation.* New York: John Day.
Wikler, L., & Keenan, M. P. (Eds.). (1983). *Developmental disabilities: No longer a private tragedy.* Washington, DC: National Association of Social Workers.

**Kevin L. DeWeaver, PhD,** is associate professor, University of Georgia, School of Social Work, Tucker Hall, Athens, GA 30602.

### For further information see

Case Management; Children: Direct Practice; Children: Mental Health; Deinstitutionalization; Developmental Disabilities: Direct Practice; Disability; Family Caregiving; Health Care: Direct Practice; Human Development; Long-Term Care; Managed Care; Maternal and Child Health; Primary Prevention Overview.

**Key Words**

developmental disabilities
mental retardation
people with disabilities
policy

# Developmental Disabilities: Direct Practice

**Ruth I. Freedman**

Developmental disabilities, as defined by the Developmental Disabilities Assistance and Bill of Rights Act of 1990 (P.L. 101-496), are severe, chronic conditions that

- are attributable to mental or physical impairments or a combination of both
- are manifested before age 22
- are likely to continue indefinitely
- result in substantial limitations in three or more major life activity areas (self-care, receptive and expressive language, learning, mobility, self-direction, capacity for independent living, and economic self-sufficiency)
- require a combination and sequence of special, interdisciplinary, or generic care, treatment, or other services that are of extended or lifelong duration and are individually planned and coordinated.

This definition is based on the severity and chronicity of the person's functional limitations, not on the specific diagnoses or nature of the disabling conditions. People with developmental disabilities may have a variety of conditions that cause their disabilities, including mental retardation, cerebral palsy, autism, epilepsy, childhood psychiatric disorders, communicative disorders, and specific learning disabilities. There is considerable overlap among many of these conditions; for example, people with mental retardation may also have epilepsy, cerebral palsy, or other related developmental disabilities.

## Prevalence

The Administration on Developmental Disabilities (1992) estimated that nationally 3 million individuals have developmental disabilities. Approximately 1.2 million will require an intensive array of services throughout their life (Assistant Secretary for Planning and Evaluation, 1988). Others may require intensive services on an intermittent basis or more minimal services on an ongoing basis.

People with mental retardation make up the largest segment of the population with developmental disabilities and are most likely to be served by state developmental disabilities agencies. Estimates of the prevalence of mental retardation range from 1 percent to 3 percent of the population. The most conservative estimate is that there are at least 2.5 million children and adults with mental retardation in the United States. However, not all people with mental retardation are necessarily developmentally disabled; that is, they may not meet the functional or severity criteria set forth in the federal definition of developmental disabilities. Estimates of the proportion of people with mental retardation within the broader category of people with developmental disabilities range from 35 percent to 90 percent or higher (Amado, Lakin, & Menke, 1990).

Although people with developmental disabilities are a heterogeneous population with a broad range of capabilities and impairments, they share many characteristics and needs:

- significant, ongoing functional limitations in major daily life activities
- functional limitations related to environmental contexts and supports
- the need for services and supports on an extended or lifelong basis
- the need for multiple, complex, interdisciplinary services in the areas of health care, social supports, education, employment, housing, and income support.

It is now reasonable to assume that children with developmental disabilities will outlive their parents (Janicki & Wisniewski, 1985). Furthermore, because of improved habilitation and medical care, an increasing number of people with developmental disabilities are living into old age. Estimates of the size of the population of people aged 65 and over with developmental disabilities range from 200,000 to 500,000, depending on the specific definition and age cutoff used (Gibson, Rabkin, & Munson, 1992). Many of these older people require services from specialized developmental disabilities agencies and from generic programs for all elderly people. Therefore, social workers will increasingly be involved in planning for and providing services to these elders and their families.

Many people with developmental disabilities are poor and rely on governmental assistance from a vast and complex network of agencies. Moreover, poverty and related socioeconomic problems, such as malnutrition, alcohol and drug abuse, teenage pregnancy, lead poisoning, and child abuse and neglect, are widely recognized as significant environmental and biological risks for developmental disabilities (Baumeister, Dockecki, & Kupstas, 1988; Begab, Haywood, & Garber, 1981; Blackman, 1986; Wikler & Keenan, 1983). Socioeconomic conditions, according to many sources, may account for as much as 75 percent of all mental retardation (Brantley, 1988).

Although people with developmental disabilities come from all racial, ethnic, and socioeconomic backgrounds, few data exist, nationwide, about the prevalence and distribution of disabilities among ethnic and linguistic minority populations (Massachusetts Developmental Disabilities Council, 1993). A survey of people of color with disabilities in Massachusetts found that most respondents encountered linguistic, transportation, and accessibility barriers to receiving services or to living independently and had experienced insensitivity and discrimination based on race and disability (Action for Boston Community Development, 1990). In a national study of differences in the use of rehabilitation services by African Americans and white Americans, African Americans reported lower use of physical therapy, counseling, and social services than did the white Americans (Belgrave & Walker, 1991).

## Trends in Services

The service system for people with developmental disabilities has changed profoundly since the 1960s, and programmatic models and practice concepts continue to evolve. The service system has moved from a primarily institution-based model of care (before the late 1960s) to a model of community-based services in the 1970s and 1980s. This shift from an "era of institutionalization and segregation" to an "era of deinstitutionalization and community development" (Bradley & Knoll, 1990, p. 2) involved changes across a variety of programmatic dimensions:

- from segregation and isolation of people in institutions to integration and normalization in less-restrictive community settings
- from a medical model of service delivery to a developmental–educational model
- from a custodial care approach to an emphasis on habilitation–rehabilitation training.

These profound shifts in the philosophy of programs were accompanied by major changes in the administration and financing of services. Before the 1970s, public services for people with developmental disabilities were delivered primarily in state institutions where all care and services (however inadequate) were centralized and provided under one roof. With the shift to community-based treatment, however, services were decentralized and provided by a complex and often fragmented set of local and state agencies and providers offering specialized and generic services under public and private auspices.

In the 1990s the focus on specialized treatment and training programs has been replaced by a concern for individualized supports. Referred to as a "paradigm of individual supports" (Smull & Bellamy, 1991) and the "functional support model" (Bradley & Knoll, 1990), this approach to serving people with developmental disabilities "begins with the individual, looks to the resources of the individual's community, and then develops flexible supports that allow participation in the community" (Smull & Bellamy, 1991, p. 528). According to this model, the facility-based and professionally directed continuum of services is replaced by consumer-driven, highly individualized supports (Smith, 1990).

Some of the key values and principles underlying this new paradigm are empowerment of consumers of services, opportunities for full inclusion in the community, and an enhanced quality of life. The goal is to enable people with developmental disabilities to have real opportunities and exercise real choices regarding their life decisions, such as where to live, work, and socialize. The goal of moving from a service-system approach to a functional supports model is to "coordinate and develop supports to enable the person to exercise a reasonable array of choices" (Smull, 1989, p. 18), recognizing that choices and supports need to change as the person changes.

## Social Work Practice

There is a good fit between the principles of social work practice and the service needs and characteristics of people with developmental disabilities and their families. First, social work practice is based on an ecological approach, in which the individual is viewed within the context of the social system. Recent definitions of mental retardation and developmental disabilities and trends in programming in the disability field stress the reciprocal relationship between the individual and his or her environmental context and supports. The American Association on Mental Retardation's (1992) definition and classification scheme emphasizes that functioning can be influenced as much by the nature of a person's environment as by the person's capabilities. Desirable environments for people with developmental disabilities have three major characteristics: (1) They provide opportunities for fulfilling the person's needs; (2) they foster the person's well-being in physical, social, material, and cognitive areas; and (3) they promote the person's sense of stability, predictability, and control (Schalock & Kiernan, 1990). Social workers may intervene at various levels of the social system (individual, family, group, and community) to promote supportive environments for individuals with developmental disabilities and their families.

Much of social work practice focuses on modifying the way in which one system interacts with other systems. Horejsi (1979) discussed the role of social workers in "boundary work," or intervention at the interface of social systems. People with developmental disabilities and their families need extensive services and supports that involve various health, educational, and social services systems. Therefore, boundary work in the developmental disabilities field may include linking the individual and his or her family with these various systems and may involve case management, information and referral, social brokerage, mediation, and advocacy.

Because of the multiple and complex needs of people with developmental disabilities, an interdisciplinary approach is a critical element of programming. Typically, a number of professionals representing a wide variety of clinical disciplines (including medicine, psychology, neurology, social work, special education, and vocational rehabilitation) are involved in the assessment, planning, and provision of services. "Social workers historically have served to coordinate those perspectives, as well as to function as a member of the team" (NASW, 1987). Thus, social workers may be in a unique position to assess and plan for the service needs of individuals within the context of their families and communities, identifying and mobilizing both informal and formal supports.

Case management, another service concept central to developmental disabilities services and to social work practice, is used to provide services to "clients with complex, severe, long-term (and often life-long) needs that affect many, if not all, aspects of their lives and cut across service delivery systems" (Baerwald, 1983, p. 220). Case management services are designated as a program priority in the federal Rehabilitation, Comprehensive Services, and Developmental Disabilities Amendments of 1978 (P.L. 95-602), as well as by numerous state educational, vocational, and social services agencies serving people with developmental disabilities. Baerwald stressed that social workers are well suited to undertake case management, given their skills in identifying and mobilizing resources.

Finally, in both social work practice and the field of developmental disabilities, prevention efforts play a critical role. It is necessary to address the problems of poverty and the sequelae of poverty—poor health care, inadequate housing, alcohol and substance abuse, child abuse and maltreatment, and violence—to prevent developmental disabilities or to minimize their negative consequences. Efforts to eradicate poverty and adverse socioeconomic conditions are clearly elements of sound social work practice.

Although there is a good fit, in theory, between the principles of social work practice and services for people with developmental disabilities and their families, historically the social work profession has demonstrated little concern with the field of developmental disabilities, "allowing itself to be represented by a relatively small number of standard-bearers" (Horejsi, 1979, p. 40). Proctor (1983), noting that most advances in this field have been made by other specialists, such as teachers and behavioral psychologists, cited the need for new directions in social work in the field of developmental disabilities, marked by "knowledge of current behavior change methodologies, new attitudes toward retardation, and new skills to be made available as training for parents" (p. 122). Specifically, she recommended that social workers "adopt and then instill in parents new, healthier expectations" for their children and "equip parents with more effective skills for working with their children" (p. 123). Proctor suggested that social workers encourage parents to develop realistic positive attitudes toward their children with developmental disabilities that focus on the development of one skill or behavior at a time. Through behavioral training, parents can help their children acquire adaptive behavioral skills, particularly in the areas of self-help and socialization. In addition, social workers can counsel parents on more general problems of behavioral management, such as discipline and parent–child communication.

## NASW Standards for Practice

Since the mid-1980s there has been increased professional interest in and contribution by social workers to the field of developmental disabilities. Most notably, in 1982 NASW and the American Association on Mental Deficiency developed professional standards for social workers who are employed in settings serving people with developmental disabilities (NASW, 1987). These standards, representing a nationwide consensus of current social work opinion, are as follows:

- *Standard 1: All social workers working with developmentally disabled clients shall possess or acquire and develop knowledge about developmental disabilities* (p. 18). Basic knowledge includes information on etiology, diagnosis, assessment, intervention with individuals over the life span, and the availability of appropriate community resources.
- *Standard 2: All social workers shall subscribe to a set of principles regarding developmental disabilities which should underlie their practice* (p. 19). These principles include maintaining clients in least-restrictive environments, providing supports to clients and their families over the life span, maximizing the potential of clients, and ensuring their individual rights and personal dignity.
- *Standard 3: Social work practice and research shall seek to prevent or reduce the incidence of developmental disabilities* (p. 19). Social workers should be aware of the biopsychosocial factors correlated with developmental disabilities, especially those related to poverty, and the appropriateness of primary, secondary, and tertiary prevention techniques.
- *Standard 4: All social workers shall participate in an interdisciplinary approach to serving the needs of developmentally disabled people* (p. 20). An interdisciplinary approach emphasizes the multidimensionality of a client's needs and the importance of integrating the perspectives of the various disciplines into a single plan or set of recommendations for the client or the program.
- *Standard 5: The functions of the social work program shall include specific services to the client population and the community* (p. 20). These functions are delineated in the core standards presented in *NASW Standards for Social Work in Health Care Settings* (NASW, 1987). Specific services to this population of clients include assessment, planning, outreach, advocacy, prevention, and provision of continuity of care. The standards also identify specific services to the community, including the identification of unmet needs, services to at-risk populations, community liaison services, and community planning and coordination.

It was anticipated that these standards for social workers in developmental disabilities would serve as a benchmark of acceptable professional practice and provide practitioners with guidelines for action and with a means of evaluating professional performance (Keenan, 1983). Although the primary intent of the standards was to establish a baseline for the delivery of exemplary services to people with developmental disabilities and their families, most social workers do not know about them, and few demonstrate adequate knowledge, competencies, and skills in this area of practice (Cole, Pearl, and Welsch, 1989).

Cole et al. (1989, p. 334) identified four areas of competence that social workers should master to work with children with developmental disabilities and their families: (1) awareness of common conditions that cause delays in early development, (2) awareness of the impact that the identification of developmental delays may have on the family unit, (3) awareness of community resources that may provide services to children with developmental delays and their families, and (4) awareness of the roles that a social worker can fulfill in assisting families with young children with developmental delays. To have a positive impact on the lives of families with children with developmental disabilities, Cole et al. suggested that social workers should function as case managers, enablers–facilitators, and resource brokers and advocates.

## Life Span Perspective

There is emerging interest within the field of developmental disabilities in the changing needs of people with disabilities and their families across the life span (Seltzer, Krauss, & Heller, 1990). Life span developmental theory looks at changes in the family life cycle, experienced either by the family as a whole or by individual family members. Turnbull, Summers, and Brotherson (1986) identified the following developmental stages and transitions that families in general face, based on the family systems research of Olson et al. (1984): couple, childbearing, school age, adolescence, launching, postparental, and aging. For each stage, Turnbull et al. presented examples of stressors for families with children with mental retardation arising from the various developmental stages and transitions. For example, in the launching stage, families adjust emotionally to the implications of the disability for their adult children, deal with issues of sexuality, decide on an appropriate residence, initiate vocational involvement, recognize the need for continuing family responsibility, deal with the ongoing financial implications of dependence, and plan for guardianship.

Specific stressors at each stage are related to the additional roles and responsibilities faced by these families and the long-term nature of the families' responsibilities. For example, Suelzle and Keenan (1981) noted heightened levels of family stress during points of transition in the life of a child with mental retardation, particularly when beginning and completing school. Olshansky (1962) coined the term "chronic sorrow" to describe the long-term emotional stresses faced by these families.

Wikler (1981) described various family stresses that emerge and reemerge over time owing to the discrepancies between expectations and the performance of the child with developmental disabilities. These stresses include stigmatized social interactions, the prolonged burden of care, the lack of information about the disability and behavioral management issues, and grieving. She suggested that clinicians who understand these chronic stresses can serve these families better and can anticipate periods of difficulty and thus perhaps ameliorate some of those stresses.

Parents with children who do not have disabilities ordinarily expect that parental responsibility will diminish over time as their children mature and become more independent. Parents of children with significant developmental disabilities, however, anticipate the need to continue to assume a substantial degree of responsibility for their children, even in adulthood. Transitional periods become more complex for these families, and the content and timing of milestones often differ from those of families with nondisabled children.

As the person with developmental disabilities changes throughout his or her life, so, too, do the person's parents and siblings. Other family members have their own developmental needs to consider. For example, at the same time that the person with developmental disabilities may be transitioning from school to adult services, parents may face critical decisions about their own jobs and careers, personal and social relationships, and health and well-being. Also, parents may have primary caregiving responsibilities for younger children or their own parents.

As the parents enter middle age, they need to plan for their own future needs, as well as their children's. Because the various family members are likely to be at different stages or developmental milestones, addressing their various sets of needs is a complex and, at times, conflicting task. For example, parents who are approaching retirement may be wrapping up loose ends at home and at work, at the very time that their adult child with developmental disabilities is just transitioning to adulthood and requiring significant emotional, social, and financial support during this stage. The adult child's primary goal at this stage may be to gain increased independence or opportunities for socialization, whereas the parents' primary concern may be for increased economic security and peace of mind.

## Meeting the Needs of Families

Marsh (1992) identified the following central needs of families with a member with mental retardation that are applicable to other developmental disabilities as well: a comprehensive system of care for their relative; information about the disability, interventions, and services and resources; skills to cope with the mental retardation and its sequelae for the family; support; meaningful involvement in intervention; help in managing the process of individual and familial adaptation; contact with other families; and assistance in handling problems in the larger society. Marsh stressed that the relative importance of these needs varies greatly within and across families, as do attempts to achieve a balance that meets the needs of all family members at different stages of the life span.

Families of children with disabilities face many obstacles as they strive to achieve a normalized lifestyle (Seligman & Darling, 1989), including the continuing medical needs of children with disabilities, inappropriate educational programs, behavioral management problems, continuing dependence, financial burden, stigma and its consequences, and physical barriers in the environment. Seligman and Darling stressed that the achievement of a normalized family lifestyle may be related less to the degree of the child's disability or the parents' coping abilities than to the family's access to opportunities for normalization, such as access to satisfactory medical care, appropriate educational programs, and respite care and day care, if needed, and the presence of supportive friends and relatives for the family and of friends and social opportunities for the child. Similarly, Wikler (1981) stated that the extent to which families experience crisis is mediated by the family's interpretation of the stressor event and the familial resources available for managing the stressor. For example, a strong extended family network, a supportive marital partner, contact with another parent with a disabled child, nonjudgmental professionals, and a tolerant community are potential mediators or buffers of the family's stressful events.

## Emphasizing the Family's Strengths and Resources

Early research in the field of developmental disabilities tended to focus exclusively on the subjective and objective burdens experienced by families. More-recent literature has examined the benefits and opportunities expressed by families who care for relatives with developmental disabilities. The benefits expressed by families include satisfaction with the accomplishments of their family members, a strengthened and more cohesive family system, increased tolerance and understanding, opportunities for personal growth and fulfillment, and a greater awareness and appreciation of life (Marsh, 1992; Seligman & Darling, 1989).

There is an emerging recognition in the field of developmental disabilities that researchers and practitioners should examine the positive effects of caregiving and the strengths and coping resources of families, instead of focusing exclusively on the pathology of families or the burdens and negative stresses that the families may experience (Turnbull et al., 1993; Wikler, Wasow, & Hatfield, 1983). Families with a family member with developmental disabilities use a variety of coping styles and adaptations. Turnbull et al. (1993) discussed cognitive coping strategies that enhance family members' self-esteem, sense of control, personal meaning, and well-being. Dunst, Trivette, and Deal (1988) outlined assessment and intervention techniques to enable and empower families to cope more effectively on their own.

## Models of Family Intervention and Practice

Current theories of practice in the field of developmental disabilities emphasize the importance of family-based interventions that incorporate the strengths and coping resources of families. According to Dunst et al. (1988), professionals need to "rethink" intervention practices with families in the following ways:

- adoption of a social system perspective of families that suggests a new and expanded definition of intervention
- movement beyond the child as the sole focus of intervention toward the family as the unit of intervention
- major emphasis upon empowerment of families as the goal of intervention practices
- a proactive stance toward families that places major emphasis upon promotion of growth-producing behavior rather than treatment of problems or prevention of negative outcomes
- focus on family and not professionally identified needs and aspirations as the primary targets of intervention
- major emphasis on identifying and building upon family capabilities as a way of strengthening families
- major emphasis upon strengthening the family's personal social network and utilizing this network as a primary source of support and resources for meeting needs
- a shift and expansion in the roles professionals play and the ways in which these roles are performed. (p. 5)

Schilling (1988) identified a variety of interventions that have been used in helping families with children with disabilities, including individual and group counseling; parent training groups; parent-to-parent programs; counseling and support groups for siblings; and other supportive services, such as respite care and specialized day care. Although all these services have merit, Schilling stressed that no single approach is ideally suited to the needs of this population because of variations in the children's disabilities, the families' coping patterns, and available resources. Schilling described promising new multicomponent interventions that provide (1) therapeutic interventions that combine traditional psychotherapeutic methods with interventions designed to enhance social and community supports; (2) instrumental services that help parents in some material or facilitative manner to obtain supports and resources; and (3) skill-based training models that provide parents and other providers of care with a repertoire of skills to enable them to develop their own personal coping strategies, social support networks, and institutional and community supports.

Some family intervention programs draw on cognitive behavior therapy in the development and enhancement of coping strategies of parents of children with disabilities (Singer, 1993). Cognitive therapy involves teaching people to examine their own patterns of thought and to identify automatic modes of interpreting situations that may be dysfunctional. According to Singer, the cognitive and behavioral skills taught in these interventions include self-monitoring of stressors, progressive muscle relaxation, monitoring and expansion of social support, use of relaxation in natural settings, covert rehearsal for stressful situations, cognitive reframing, an increase in pleasant activities, and time management. Although these strategies have been found useful for some parents of children with disabilities, Singer cautioned that they may not be sufficient by themselves when families encounter a number of challenges, such as severe depression in parents, severe marital discord, severe problem behaviors in children, and abuse and neglect of children in multiproblem families. He suggested that cognitive interventions be included as part of a comprehensive intervention package that attends to environmental and social, as well as cognitive, interventions.

Seligman and Darling (1989) proposed a family practice model consisting of three types of counseling interventions: educational, facilitative, and personal advocacy. In educational counseling the professional gives family members information about the child's disability and about available services and resources. In facilitative counseling, the professional helps family members deal with their feelings, attitudes, and expectations toward the child with disabilities and their caregiving roles and responsibilities. In personal advocacy counseling the professional assists family members in assessing their needs and developing a plan of action for obtaining services and supports. Seligman and Darling also noted the importance and effectiveness of behavioral training programs that are designed to provide parents with skills and techniques to manage disruptive behaviors and to promote adaptive behaviors in the home. Parents are trained to teach their children chewing and feeding skills, motor imitation, self-help skills, appropriate play behaviors and social interaction with parents, articulation and vocabulary skills, and compliance behavior.

For each type of counseling and behavioral training, individual and group formats have been used. The choice of the method or format of intervention depends on the family's preference and needs and the family's and the practitioner's assessments of the appropriateness of various models. Many of these interventions have been practiced with families of children with various types of disabilities, including mental retardation, autism, severe learning disabilities, and chronic illnesses. However, no systematic research has been conducted on the relative effectiveness of these different interventions for families of children with various types of disabilities.

## Family–Professional Collaboration

There has been a dramatic shift in how professionals, including social workers, view and treat families with a member with developmental disabilities and in the nature of the relationships established between families and professionals. One of the problems confronting family–professional relationships is the legacy of such relationships—the tendency of professionals

> to assume that parents are emotionally disturbed and in need of counseling; to view the goal of counseling as assisting parents in accepting and adjusting to a permanent and static condition in their child; to view parents as causing or contributing to their child's problems; to assume an authoritarian professional stance; and to apply conceptual models that have emphasized pathology and fostered passivity among families. (Marsh, 1992, p. 42)

The current family system perspective emphasizes the strengths and coping resources of people with developmental disabilities and their families and the need to support, not supplant, them. Marsh (1992) discussed this shift from a pathology, or medical, paradigm to a competence, or empowerment, paradigm for professional practice. In this new model, families are viewed as basically competent, so the role of professionals is to assist families and consumers of services to meet the goals they have set for themselves.

To implement new models of family-centered practice, social workers and other professionals will need to rethink the nature of their professional relationships with families. Family–professional collaboration, a key element of the new paradigm, will involve shifts in the roles of families and professionals. Bishop, Woll, and Arango (1993) identified seven principles that are crucial to the success of a collaborative relationship between professionals and families with children with special health needs that are equally relevant for families with children with developmental disabilities. According to these principles, both the professional and the family should

1. promote an environment in which they work together to ensure the best services for the child and the family
2. recognize and respect the knowledge, skills, and experience that each brings to the relationship
3. acknowledge that the development of trust is an integral part of a collaborative relationship
4. facilitate open communication, so they both feel free to express themselves
5. create an atmosphere in which the cultural traditions, values, and diversity of families are acknowledged and honored
6. recognize that negotiation is essential in a collaborative relationship
7. commit themselves and their communities to meeting the needs of children with special health needs and their families.

Social workers can play a strong and central role in these models of family-centered practice and collaboration. Slater and Wikler (1986) suggested that social workers take on the new roles of "systems convener, systems activator, systems trainer, and family therapist" (p. 388). As a systems convener, the social worker helps families identify external informal sources of support. As a systems activator, the social worker mobilizes the resources of the extended family members to fulfill a number of functions, including assistance with daily care, planning, and advocacy. Social workers provide systems training by giving families specific information and training about developmental disabilities. These roles reflect a shift in emphasis from planning, providing, and managing services for consumers of services to brokering, enabling, and facilitating supports that are determined by individuals with developmental disabilities and their families.

In addition to developing new ways of collaborating with families, social workers and other professionals are also rethinking the nature of their relationships with the primary consumer of services: people with developmental disabilities. There is a strong push in the field by advocates, families, and professionals to involve people with developmental disabilities in determining their own preferences for housing, work, and social lives. Social workers can facilitate self-advocacy and self-determination by involving and supporting the consumers of services in decision making and planning.

## References


Action for Boston Community Development. (1990). *Summary of ABCD's minority disabled survey project.* Boston: Author.

Administration on Developmental Disabilities. (1992). *Selected program facts.* Washington, DC: U.S. Department of Health and Human Services.

Amado, A. N., Lakin, K. C., & Menke, J. M. (1990). *1990 Chartbook on services for people with developmental disabilities.* Minneapolis: University of Minnesota, Center for Residential and Community Services.

American Association on Mental Retardation. (1992). *Mental retardation: Definition, classification, and systems of support* (9th ed.). Washington, DC: Author.

Assistant Secretary for Planning and Evaluation, Department of Health and Human Services. (1988, December). *Report from the Working Group on Improving Public Policies and Programs Affecting Persons with Mental Retardation and Other Developmental Disabilities.* Washington, DC: Author.

Baerwald, A. (1983). Case management: Defining a concept. In L. Wikler & M. P. Keenan (Eds.), *Developmental disabilities: No longer a private tragedy* (pp. 219–223). Silver Spring, MD and Washington, DC: National Association of Social Workers and American Association on Mental Deficiency.

Baumeister, A. A., Dockecki, P. R., & Kupstas, F. D. (1988). *Preventing the new morbidity: A guide for state planning for the prevention of mental retardation and related disabilities associated with socioeconomic conditions.* Washington, DC: President's Committee on Mental Retardation.

Begab, M., Haywood, C., & Garber, H. (1981). *Psychosocial aspects of mental retardation theory* (Vol. 1). Baltimore: University Park Press.

Belgrave, F. Z., & Walker, S. (1991). Differences in rehabilitation service utilization patterns of African Americans and white Americans with disabilities. In *Future frontiers in the employment of minority persons with disabilities.* Washington, DC: National Conference Proceedings.

Bishop, K. K., Woll, J., & Arango, P. (1993). *Family/professional collaboration for children with special health needs and their families.* Burlington: University of Vermont, Department of Social Work.

Blackman, J. (1986). *Warning signals: Basic criteria for tracking at-risk infants and toddlers.* Washington, DC: National Center for Clinical Infant Programs.

Bradley, V. J., & Knoll, J. (1990). *Shifting paradigms in services to people with developmental disabilities.* Cambridge, MA: Human Services Research Institute.

Brantley, D. (1988). *Understanding mental retardation: A guide for social workers.* Springfield, IL: Charles C Thomas.

Cole, B. S., Pearl, L. F., & Welsch, M. J. (1989). Education of social workers for intervention with families of children with special needs. *Child and Adolescent Social Work, 6,* 327–339.

Developmental Disabilities Assistance and Bill of Rights Act of 1990. P.L. 101-496, 104 Stat. 1191.

Dunst, C., Trivette, C., & Deal, A. (1988). *Enabling and empowering families: Principles and guidelines for practice.* Cambridge, MA: Brookline Books.

Gibson, J. W., Rabkin, J., & Munson, R. (1992). Critical issues in serving the developmentally disabled elderly. *Journal of Gerontological Social Work, 19*(1), 35–49.

Horejsi, C. R. (1979). Developmental disabilities: Opportunities for social workers. *Social Work, 24,* 40–43.

Janicki, M. P., & Wisniewski, H. M. (1985). *Aging and developmental disabilities: Issues and approaches.* Baltimore: Paul H. Brookes.

Keenan, M. P. (1983). Standards for social workers in developmental disabilities: An overview. In L. Wikler & M. P. Keenan (Eds.), *Developmental disabilities: No longer a private tragedy* (pp. 41–44). Silver Spring, MD and Washington, DC: National Association of Social Workers and American Association on Mental Deficiency.

Marsh, D. T. (1992). *Families and mental retardation: New directions in professional practice.* New York: Praeger.

Massachusetts Developmental Disabilities Council. (1993). *1993 MDDC state plan.* Boston: Author.

National Association of Social Workers. (1987). *NASW standards for social work in health care settings.* Washington, DC: Author.

Olshansky, S. (1962). Chronic sorrow: A response to having a mentally defective child. *Social Casework, 43,* 190–193.

Olson, D. H., McCubbin, H. I., Barnes, H., Larsen, A., Muxen, M., & Wilson, M. (1984). *One thousand families: A national survey.* Beverly Hills, CA: Sage Publications.

Proctor, E. K. (1983). New directions for work with parents of retarded children. In L. Wikler & M. P. Keenan (Eds.), *Developmental disabilities: No longer a private tragedy* (pp. 121–126). Silver Spring, MD: National Association of Social Workers and American Association on Mental Deficiency.

Rehabilitation, Comprehensive Services, and Developmental Disabilities Amendments of 1978. P.L. 95-602, 92 Stat. 2955.

Schalock, R. L., & Kiernan, W. E. (1990). *Habilitation planning for adults with developmental disabilities.* New York: Springer-Verlag.

Schilling, R. F. (1988). Helping families with developmentally disabled members. In C. S. Chilman, E. W. Nunnally, & F. M. Cox (Eds.), *Chronic illness and disability* (pp. 171–192). Newbury Park, CA: Sage Publications.

Seligman, M., & Darling, R. B. (1989). *Ordinary families, special children: A systems approach to childhood disability.* New York: Guilford Press.

Seltzer, M. M., Krauss, M. W., & Heller, T. (1990). *Family caregiving over the life course.* Paper presented at the Roundtable on Aging and Developmental Disabilities, Boston.

Singer, G. H. S. (1993). When it's not so easy to change your mind: Some reflections on cognitive interventions for parents of children with disabilities. In A. P. Turnbull, J. M. Patterson, S. K. Behr, D. L. Murphy, J. G. Marquis, & M. J. Blue-Banning (Eds.), *Cognitive coping, families, & disability* (pp. 207–220). Baltimore: Paul H. Brookes.

Slater, M. A., & Wikler, L. (1986). "Normalized" family resources for families with a developmentally disabled child. *Social Work, 31,* 385–390.

Smith, G. (1990). *Supported living: New directions in services to people with developmental disabilities.* Alexandria, VA: National Association of State Mental Retardation Program Directors.

Smull, M. N. (1989). *Crisis in the community.* Baltimore: University of Maryland, Applied Research and Evaluation Unit, Department of Pediatrics.

Smull, M. W., & Bellamy, G. T. (1991). Community services for adults with disabilities: Policy challenges in the emerging support paradigm. In L. H. Meyer, C. A. Pack, & L. Brown (Eds.), *Critical issues in the lives of people with severe disabilities* (pp. 527–536). Baltimore: Paul H. Brookes.

Suelzle, M., & Keenan, V. (1981). Changes in family support networks over the life cycle of mentally retarded persons. *American Journal of Mental Retardation, 86,* 267–274.

Turnbull, A. P., Patterson, J. M., Behr, S. K., Murphy, D. L., Marquis, J. G., & Blue-Banning, M. J. (1993). *Cognitive coping, families, and disability.* Baltimore: Paul H. Brookes.

Turnbull, A. P., Summers, J. A., & Brotherson, M. J. (1986). Family life cycle: Theoretical and empirical implications and future directions for families with mentally retarded members. In J. J. Gallagher & P. M. Vietze (Eds.), *Families of handicapped persons: Research, programs, and policy issues* (pp. 45–65). Baltimore: Paul H. Brookes.

Wikler, L. (1981). Chronic stresses of families of mentally retarded children. *Family Relations, 30,* 281–288.

Wikler, L., & Keenan, M. P. (Eds.). (1983). *Developmental disabilities: No longer a private tragedy.* Silver Spring, MD: National Association of Social Workers and American Association on Mental Deficiency.

Wikler, L., Wasow, M., & Hatfield, E. (1983). Seeking strengths in families of developmentally disabled children. In L. Wikler & M. P. Keenan (Eds.), *Developmental disabilities: No longer a private tragedy* (pp. 111–114). Silver Spring, MD and Washington, DC: National Association of Social Workers and American Association on Mental Deficiency.

**Ruth I. Freedman, PhD,** is assistant professor, Boston University, School of Social Work, 264 Bay State Road, Boston, MA 02215.

**For further information see**

Assessment; Case Management; Childhood; Children: Direct Practice; Children: Mental Health; Deinstitutionalization; Developmental Disabilities: Definitions and Policies; Direct Practice Overview; Disability; Families: Direct Practice; Human Development; Long-Term Care; Mental Health Overview; Primary Prevention Overview; School-Linked Services; School Social Work Overview.

**Key Words**

developmental disabilities

direct practice

## Devine, Edward Thomas

*See* Biographies section, Volume 3

# Diagnostic and Statistical Manual of Mental Disorders

**Janet B. W. Williams**

DSM-IV is the informal name of the fourth edition of the *Diagnostic and Statistical Manual of Mental Disorders* of the American Psychiatric Association (APA, 1994). DSM-IV's predecessor, DSM-III (APA, 1980), differed considerably from the first two editions (APA, 1952, 1968). Its innovative incorporation of specified diagnostic criteria and a multiaxial system for evaluation caused it to have a major impact on the field of mental health (Spitzer, Williams, & Skodol, 1980).

DSM-IV contains a classification that lists all the mental disorders, as well as certain conditions that are not mental disorders but may be a focus of clinical attention. In addition, it includes a detailed description of each diagnostic category and specified diagnostic criteria for each mental disorder to help clinicians make reliable diagnoses. The specific diagnostic categories are grouped into the 17 major diagnostic classes listed in Table 1. Each category is assigned a code number that can be recorded for statistical and record-keeping purposes.

DSM-III was revised in 1985, culminating in the publication of DSM-III-R (APA, 1987). The work of revising DSM-III-R began in 1988 with the appointment of Allen Frances, MD, as chair of the APA DSM-IV Task Force. APA selected the 25 members of the task force and appointed many of them to chair work groups on particular aspects of the classification or the manual. Each of the 13 work groups had five to 16 members and consulted an extensive list of advisers and consultants in the United States and abroad. The task force also established liaisons with many organizations that were interested in DSM-IV, including NASW and other major professional organizations.

Work on DSM-IV proceeded in three major phases (Widiger, Frances, Pincus, & Davis, 1990). First, each work group developed systematic and comprehensive literature reviews focusing on the most pertinent issues in their area, to inform their final decisions and to document the process and the reasons for those decisions. Second, the John D. and Catherine T. MacArthur Foundation funded a series of analyses of data from completed studies or studies in progress to answer specific nosologic questions. Finally, the National Institute of Mental Health, the National Institute on Drug Abuse, and the National Institute on Alcohol Abuse and Alcoholism funded 12 field trials to study the effects of the changes that were being considered. The literature reviews and reports on the data reanalyses and the field trials are being published in a series of volumes called the *DSM-IV Source Book* (Widiger, Frances, Pincus, First, & Davis, 1994).

## Multiaxial System

An important and unique feature of DSM-IV of special interest to social workers is the inclusion of a multiaxial system for evaluation (Williams, 1981, 1985a, 1985b; Williams, Goldman, Gruenberg, Mezzich, & Skodol, 1990). The system is similar to the one inaugurated in DSM-III, which incorporated a multiaxial system into an official classification system for the first time in the United States. With the use of a multiaxial system, psychological, biological, and social aspects of an individual's functioning are evaluated, and the results are recorded on different axes. The DSM-IV system includes the five axes listed in Table 2; each axis requires the evaluation of a different domain of information that may

TABLE 1
**The Major Diagnostic Classes of DSM-IV**

Disorders Usually First Diagnosed in Infancy, Childhood, or Adolescence
Delirium, Dementia, and Amnestic and Other Cognitive Disorders
Mental Disorders Due to a General Medical Condition Not Elsewhere Classified
Substance-Related Disorders
Schizophrenia and Other Psychotic Disorders
Mood Disorders
Anxiety Disorders
Somatoform Disorders
Factitious Disorders
Dissociative Disorders
Sexual and Gender Identity Disorders
Eating Disorders
Sleep Disorders
Impulse-Control Disorders Not Elsewhere Classified
Adjustment Disorders
Personality Disorders
Other Conditions That May Be a Focus of Clinical Attention

Source: American Psychiatric Association. (1994). *Diagnostic and statistical manual of mental disorders, fourth edition* (p. 26). Washington, DC: Author. Reprinted by permission.

TABLE 2
**The DSM-IV Multiaxial System**

| | |
|---|---|
| Axis I | Clinical Disorders<br>Other Conditions That May Be a Focus of Clinical Attention |
| Axis II | Personality Disorders<br>Mental Retardation |
| Axis III | General Medical Conditions |
| Axis IV | Psychosocial and Environmental Problems |
| Axis V | Global Assessment of Functioning |

SOURCE: American Psychiatric Association. (1994). *Diagnostic and statistical manual of mental disorders, fourth edition* (p. 25). Washington, DC: Author. Reprinted by permission.

help the practitioner plan treatment and predict outcome. Axes I and II contain all the mental disorders, and Axis III lists general medical disorders. Axis IV provides a checklist for recording psychosocial and environmental problems that may affect the diagnosis, treatment planning, and prognosis of an individual's mental disorders. Finally, Axis V includes a rating scale to indicate a person's overall level of functioning. Figure 1 presents a form for recording the results of a multiaxial evaluation.

The use of the multiaxial system facilitates comprehensive evaluation with attention to different types of disorders, aspects of the environment, and areas of functioning that may be overlooked if the focus were limited to the assessment of a single presenting problem. Personality disorders and mental retardation are listed on a separate axis from the other mental disorders because they tend to be overlooked, in that their symptomatology is generally chronic and mild relative to the Axis I disorders.

DSM-IV's multiaxial system emphasizes areas of information that have traditionally been considered highly important in social work evaluations: psychosocial and environmental problems and adaptive functioning. It is these areas that are the focus of the Person-in-Environment System (Karls & Wandrei, 1992, 1994; Williams, Karls, & Wandrei, 1989). The inclusion of these areas in the official multiaxial evaluation system of DSM-IV (as of DSM-III) encourages a more comprehensive evaluation of an individual than did DSM-I and DSM-II, which were limited to brief descriptions of the mental disorders and did not include diagnostic criteria or a multiaxial system.

## Other Important Features

DSM-IV differs in other important ways from earlier diagnostic schemes. First, it takes a generally atheoretical approach to the classification of mental disorders, as did DSM-III and DSM-III-R. In other words, it describes the manifestations of the various mental disorders and only rarely attempts to account for the causes of the disturbances, unless the mechanism is included in the definition of the disorder (as in the disorders that are due to general medical conditions). This approach permits clinicians of various theoretical orientations to use the specified criteria to make diagnoses while retaining their diverse theories about the causes of the various disorders.

Second, the inclusion since DSM-III of specified diagnostic criteria as guides for making a diagnosis has enhanced the reliability with which a diagnosis can be made (see, for example, the DSM-IV diagnostic criteria for a major depressive episode in Table 3). With diagnostic criteria, clinicians are better able to agree about the presence or absence of a condition when they evaluate a patient or client. However, although diagnostic reliability is essential for effective communication among mental health professionals, even high reliability does not necessarily indicate high validity or accuracy of the diagnostic definitions.

A word of caution: As noted in the introduction to DSM-IV, it is necessary to obtain much more information beyond a DSM-IV diagnosis before an adequate treatment plan can be formulated for any individual. A DSM-IV diagnosis represents only the initial step in a comprehensive evaluation that leads to a treatment plan. Of course, the additional information that is necessary will be determined, in part, by the theoretical orientation of the clinician and may emphasize the psychological, biological, or social aspects of the functioning of the individual being evaluated.

### Cross-Cultural Considerations

DSM-III was translated into many languages and has been widely used in other parts of the world.

FIGURE 1

**DSM-IV Multiaxial Evaluation Report Form**

The following form is offered as one possibility for reporting multiaxial evaluations. In some settings, this form may be used exactly as is; in other settings, the form may be adapted to satisfy special needs.

***AXIS I: Clinical Disorders***
***Other Conditions That May Be a Focus of Clinical Attention***

Diagnostic code ___ ___ ___.___ ___ DSM-IV name ______________________

___ ___ ___.___ ___ ______________________

___ ___ ___.___ ___ ______________________

***AXIS II: Personality Disorders***
***Mental Retardation***

Diagnostic code ___ ___ ___.___ ___ DSM-IV name ______________________

___ ___ ___.___ ___ ______________________

***AXIS III: General Medical Conditions***

ICD-9-CM code ___ ___ ___.___ ___ ICD-9-CM name ______________________

___ ___ ___.___ ___ ______________________

___ ___ ___.___ ___ ______________________

***AXIS IV: Psychosocial and Environmental Problems***

*Check:*

- ☐ **Problems with primary support group** *Specify:* ______________________
- ☐ **Problems related to the social environment** *Specify:* ______________________
- ☐ **Educational problems** *Specify:* ______________________
- ☐ **Occupational problems** *Specify:* ______________________
- ☐ **Housing problems** *Specify:* ______________________
- ☐ **Economic problems** *Specify:* ______________________
- ☐ **Problems with access to health care services** *Specify:* ______________________
- ☐ **Problems related to interaction with the legal system/crime** *Specify:* ______________________
- ☐ **Other psychosocial and environmental problems** *Specify:* ______________________

***AXIS V: Global Assessment of Functioning Scale*** ***Score:*** ___ ___ ___

***Time frame:*** ______________________

SOURCE: American Psychiatric Association. (1994). *Diagnostic and statistical manual of mental disorders, fourth edition* (p. 34). Washington, DC: Author. Reprinted by permission.

TABLE 3
## DSM-IV Diagnostic Criteria for Major Depressive Episode

A. Five (or more) of the following symptoms have been present during the same 2-week period and represent a change from previous functioning; at least one of the symptoms is either (1) depressed mood or (2) loss of interest or pleasure.

**Note:** Do not include symptoms that are clearly due to a general medical condition, or mood-incongruent delusions or hallucinations.

(1) depressed mood most of the day, nearly every day, as indicated by either subjective report (e.g., feels sad or empty) or observation made by others (e.g., appears tearful). **Note:** In children and adolescents, can be irritable mood.
(2) markedly diminished interest or pleasure in all, or almost all, activities most of the day, nearly every day (as indicated by either subjective account or observation made by others)
(3) significant weight loss when not dieting or weight gain (e.g., a change of more than 5% of body weight in a month), or decrease or increase in appetite nearly every day. **Note:** In children, consider failure to make expected weight gains.
(4) insomnia or hypersomnia nearly every day
(5) psychomotor agitation or retardation nearly every day (observable by others, not merely subjective feelings of restlessness or being slowed down)
(6) fatigue or loss of energy nearly every day
(7) feelings of worthlessness or excessive or inappropriate guilt (which may be delusional) nearly every day (not merely self-reproach or guilt about being sick)
(8) diminished ability to think or concentrate, or indecisiveness, nearly every day (either by subjective account or as observed by others)
(9) recurrent thoughts of death (not just fear of dying), recurrent suicidal ideation without a specific plan, or a suicide attempt or a specific plan for committing suicide

B. The symptoms do not meet criteria for a Mixed Episode (see p. 335).

C. The symptoms cause clinically significant distress or impairment in social, occupational, or other important areas of functioning.

D. The symptoms are not due to the direct physiological effects of a substance (e.g., a drug of abuse, a medication) or a general medical condition (e.g., hypothyroidism).

E. The symptoms are not better accounted for by Bereavement, i.e., after the loss of a loved one, the symptoms persist for longer than 2 months or are characterized by marked functional impairment, morbid preoccupation with worthlessness, suicidal ideation, psychotic symptoms, or psychomotor retardation.

SOURCE: American Psychiatric Association. (1994). *Diagnostic and statistical manual of mental disorders, fourth edition* (p. 327). Washington, DC: Author. Reprinted by permission.

Surprisingly, its use in cultures that were vastly different from those of most of the people who were responsible for developing it was generally successful (Spitzer, Williams, & Skodol, 1983). During the development of DSM-III-R, some improvements were made in the classification and criteria to increase the value of the manual in other cultures, and the introduction discussed its use in different cultures.

This issue received even more attention in DSM-IV, supported by the Conference on Culture and DSM-IV (Mezzich, Kleinman, Fabrega, & Parron, in press), held in Pittsburgh in April 1993 and sponsored jointly by APA and the National Institute of Mental Health. The conference specifically addressed needed changes in the text and criteria that would make them more useful and accurate across cultures. In addition, three innovative features were included in DSM-IV. First, a new section describing culturally related features was added to the text of many disorders because of evidence that the symptoms and course of a number of DSM-IV disorders are influenced by cultural factors. Second, descriptions of some "culture-bound syndromes" were added as examples in some of the residual categories (for instance, "possession" is listed as an example of a dissociative disorder not otherwise specified). Third, an outline for cultural formulation and a glossary of culture-bound syndromes were included in Appendix I.

**Relational Disturbances**

A frequent criticism of DSM-III was that it included only mental disorders that occur in individuals, which restricted its usefulness in the diagnosis and treatment of problems that occur in the family and other relational units (Wynne, 1987). Early in the development of DSM-IV, the Coalition on Family Diagnosis was formed by professional groups that deal with these issues to consider possible changes that might be made in DSM-IV. The result was several new features, including the addition to the section on Other Conditions That May Be a Focus of Clinical Attention of a group of relational problems—relational problem related to a mental disorder or general medical condition, parent–child relational problem, partner relational problem, and sibling relational problem. Furthermore, an optional axis, the Global Assessment of Relational Functioning Scale, was inserted in Appendix B.

**Criteria Sets and Axes Provided for Further Study (Appendix B)**

During the development of DSM-IV, there were many proposals for new categories. The advisory committees that worked on the definitions of disorders and the APA DSM-IV Task Force believed that there was sufficient research and clinical evidence of the validity of each of these categories to justify their inclusion in the revised manual, although not as full-fledged disorders and axes. Table 4 lists the categories for which criteria sets are included in DSM-IV's Appendix B. Also listed are three optional axes that may be useful to clinicians and researchers.

**DSM-IV as an Educational Tool**

Certain features of DSM-IV make it a useful tool for teaching students about basic psychopathology (Skodol, Spitzer, & Williams, 1981). The chapter entitled "Use of the Manual" explains the diagnostic criteria, the organization of the text descriptions of the disorders, and the terms and conventions used throughout the manual. A separate chapter describes the multiaxial system in detail. The manual also contains several appendixes that are useful in teaching. First, a small forest of "decision trees" are provided in Appendix A to make the differential diagnostic process easier by helping clinicians understand the organization and hierarchical structure of the classification. A clinician can use a tree to follow a series of questions to rule in or out various disorders. The decision tree for mood disturbances is presented in Figure 2. The Glossary of Technical Terms (Appendix C) defines technical terms that are included in the diagnostic criteria of DSM-IV. To highlight the differences between DSM-III-R and DSM-IV, the Annotated Listing of Changes lists the corresponding categories in DSM-III-R and DSM-IV, with a brief discussion of the reasons for the major changes. Published with DSM-IV is the "Mini-D," a pocket-sized quick-reference guide containing the diagnostic criteria. Another useful teaching tool is the *DSM-IV Case Book* (Spitzer, Gibbon, Skodol, First, & Williams, 1994), which presents many case vignettes, each with a discussion of the DSM-IV differential diagnosis.

The text for each specific mental disorder includes information under each of the following headings: diagnostic features; subtypes and/or specifiers; recording procedures; associated features and disorders; specific culture, age, or gender features; prevalence; course; complications; familial pattern; and differential diagnosis. Care was taken in the text and criteria of DSM-IV (as in DSM-III and DSM-III-R) to avoid the use of such phrases as a "schizophrenic" or "an alcoholic" because the classification and descriptions are of mental disorders that people have, rather than of the people themselves (Spitzer & Williams, 1979). Instead, the manual refers to "a person with

TABLE 4

## DSM-IV Appendix B: Criteria Sets and Axes Provided for Further Study

This appendix contains a number of proposals for new categories and axes that were suggested for possible inclusion in DSM-IV. The DSM-IV Task Force and Work Groups subjected each of these proposals to a careful empirical review and invited wide commentary from the field. The Task Force determined that there was insufficient information to warrant inclusion of these proposals as official categories or axes in DSM-IV.

The items, thresholds, and durations contained in the research criteria sets are intended to provide a common language for researchers and clinicians who are interested in studying these disorders. It is hoped that such research will help to determine the possible utility of these proposed categories and will result in refinement of the criteria sets. The specific thresholds and durations were set by expert consensus (informed by literature review, data reanalysis, and field-trial results when such information was available) and, as such, should be considered tentative. It would be highly desirable for researchers to study alternative items, thresholds, or durations whenever this is possible.

The following proposals are included in this appendix:

- Postconcussional disorder
- Mild neurocognitive disorder
- Caffeine withdrawal
- Alternative dimensional descriptors for Schizophrenia
- Postpsychotic depressive disorder of Schizophrenia
- Simple deteriorative disorder (simple Schizophrenia)
- Premenstrual dysphoric disorder
- Alternative Criterion B for Dysthymic Disorder
- Minor depressive disorder
- Recurrent brief depressive disorder
- Mixed anxiety-depressive disorder
- Factitious disorder by proxy
- Dissociative trance disorder
- Binge-eating disorder
- Depressive personality disorder
- Passive-aggressive personality disorder (negativistic personality disorder)
- Medication-Induced Movement Disorders
    - Neuroleptic-Induced Parkinsonism
    - Neuroleptic Malignant Syndrome
    - Neuroleptic-Induced Acute Dystonia
    - Neuroleptic-Induced Acute Akathisia
    - Neuroleptic-Induced Tardive Dyskinesia
    - Medication-Induced Postural Tremor
    - Medication-Induced Movement Disorder Not Otherwise Specified

    (**Note:** These categories are included in the "Other Conditions That May Be a Focus of Clinical Attention" section. Text and research criteria sets for these conditions are included here.)

- Defensive Functioning Scale
- Global Assessment of Relational Functioning (GARF) Scale
- Social and Occupational Functioning Assessment Scale (SOFAS)

SOURCE: American Psychiatric Association. (1994). *Diagnostic and statistical manual of mental disorders, fourth edition* (pp. 703–704). Washington, DC: Author. Reprinted by permission.

FIGURE 2

**DSM-IV Differential Diagnosis of Mood Disorders**

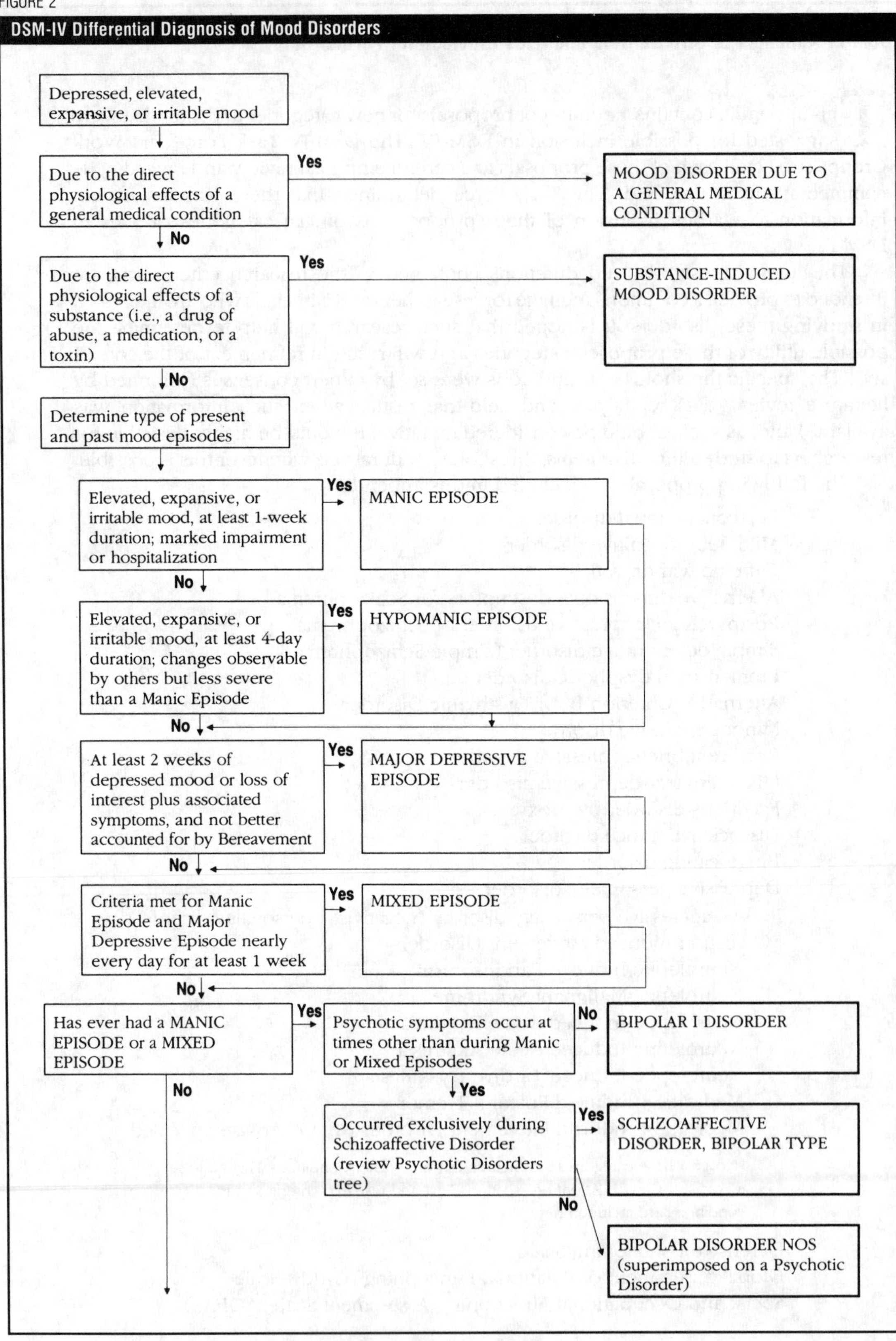

FIGURE 2 (CONTINUED)

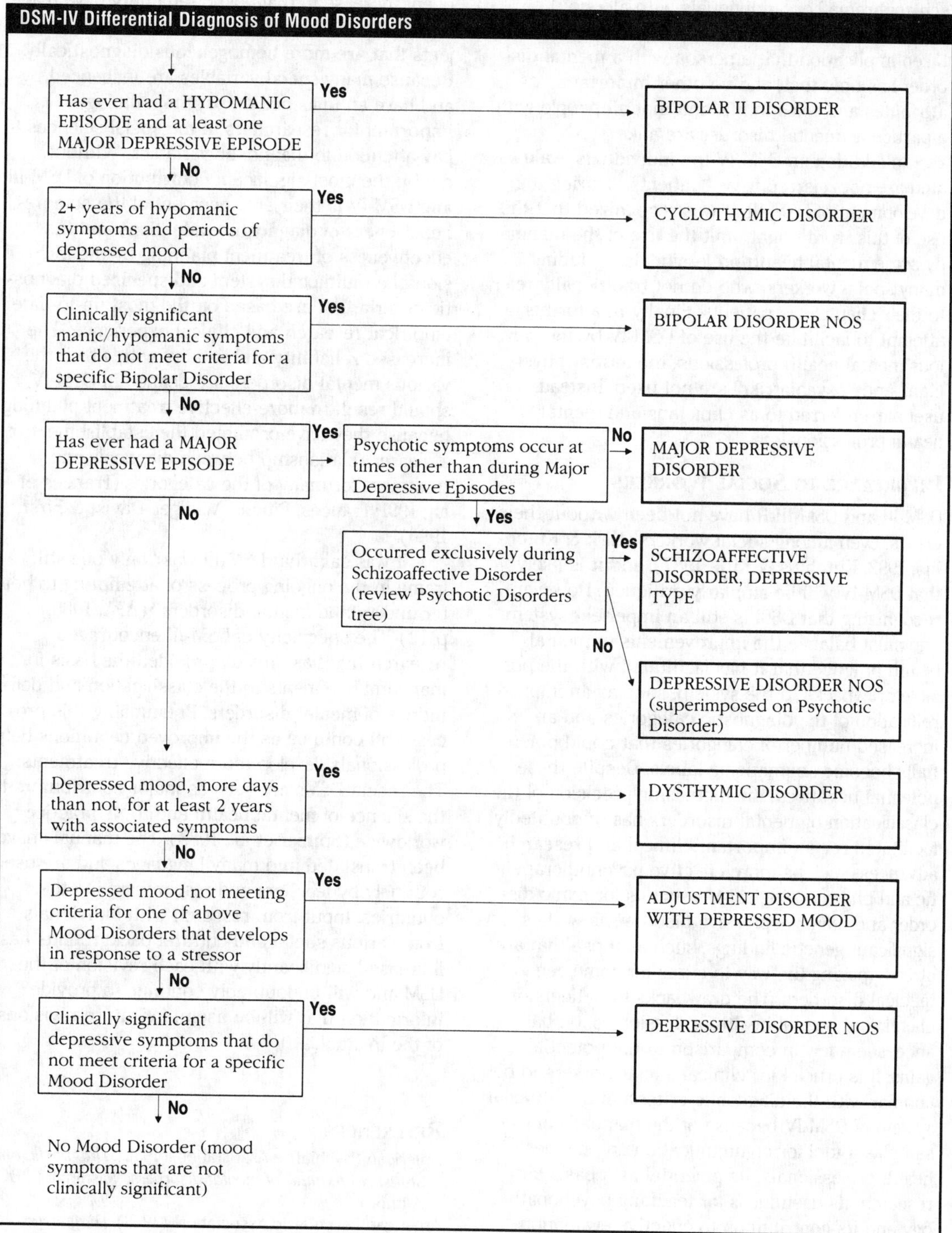


SOURCE: American Psychiatric Association. (1994). *Diagnostic and statistical manual of mental disorders, fourth edition* (pp. 696–697). Washington, DC: Author. Reprinted by permission.

schizophrenia" or "individuals with alcohol dependence." This terminology avoids the mistaken implication that a person with a mental disorder has only that, and no other important attributes and roles in life, and that all people with a particular mental disorder are alike.

In addition, in DSM-IV the individuals evaluated are not referred to as "patients." During the development of DSM-III, it was recognized that the use of this word might limit the use of the manual by some mental health professionals, including many social workers, who do not traditionally refer to their clientele as patients. Finally, in a further attempt to facilitate the use of DSM-IV by the various mental health professions, the terms "physician" and "psychiatrist" are not used. Instead, users are referred to as clinicians and mental health professionals.

## Importance to Social Workers

DSM-III and DSM-III-R have not been without their critics, even among social workers (Kirk & Kutchins, 1992; Kutchins & Kirk, 1987), and it is likely that DSM-IV will be similarly critiqued. However, recognizing that DSM is still an imperfect system, one must balance the improvements in mental health practice that it has facilitated with the possible drawbacks to the system, such as an implied reification of the diagnostic categories and an increased number of categories that could potentially become stigmatizing labels. Despite these potential negatives, the increasing precision of the classification of mental disorders has undoubtedly facilitated recent important clinical and research advances, such as more effective psychotherapeutic and pharmacological treatments for panic disorder and major depressive disorder, as well as significant genetic findings, such as those that are already paving the way to cures for some general medical disorders. The drawbacks to patients or clients and mental health professionals, on balance, seem few in comparison to the potential gains. It is crucial for clinical social workers to be familiar with the diagnostic criteria and multiaxial system of DSM-IV because of the manual's universality as a tool for communication among mental health professionals, its potential as a basis for research, its usefulness for teaching psychopathology, and its contribution to effective evaluation and treatment planning.

In most psychiatric treatment facilities, the language of DSM-IV is the standard terminology used in diagnostic case discussions. Therefore, familiarity with DSM-IV is often required for participation in such discussions. The specificity of the diagnostic criteria in DSM-IV and the consequent increase in diagnostic reliability have made it possible for researchers to select groups of subjects that are more homogeneous diagnostically. Because many social variables are influenced by and have an influence on psychopathology, it is important for researchers in the social sciences to pay attention to diagnostic variables. Without doubt, the most significant contribution of DSM-III and DSM-IV is their enhancement of the comprehensiveness of diagnostic evaluations and the effectiveness of treatment planning by the inclusion of a multiaxial system and specified diagnostic criteria that are based on the most up-to-date empirical research and clinical experience. The increased reliability and validity with which the various mental disorders are defined in DSM-IV should result in more-effective treatment planning because they have promoted the establishment of a clearer relationship between diagnosis and treatment for many of the categories (Frances et al., 1991; Frances, Pincus, Widiger, Davis, & First, 1990).

It was said that DSM-III was "only one still frame in the ongoing process of attempting to better understand mental disorders" (APA, 1980, p. 12). The specificity of DSM-III encouraged research that has already provided the basis for many improvements in the classification and definitions of mental disorders. Presumably, this process will continue as the improved definitions help professionals develop more-effective treatments. The recent DSMs are seen as major contributors to the science of mental health and to its practice worldwide (Spitzer et al., 1983). The manuals have been translated into many languages and are used routinely by teachers and researchers in other countries. Input from research with individuals from various social and cultural backgrounds has increased significantly with each revision of the DSM and will undoubtedly continue to provide information that will be useful for future revisions of the manual.

## References

American Psychiatric Association. (1952). *Diagnostic and statistical manual of mental disorders*. Washington, DC: Author.

American Psychiatric Association. (1968). *Diagnostic and statistical manual of mental disorders* (2nd ed.). Washington, DC: Author.

American Psychiatric Association. (1980). *Diagnostic and statistical manual of mental disorders* (3rd ed.). Washington, DC: Author.

American Psychiatric Association. (1987). *Diagnostic and statistical manual of mental disorders* (3rd ed., rev.). Washington, DC: Author.

American Psychiatric Association. (1994). *Diagnostic and statistical manual of mental disorders* (4th ed.). Washington, DC: Author.

Frances, A., Pincus, H., Davis, W. W., Kline, M., First, M., & Widiger, T. (1991). The DSM-IV field trials: Moving towards an empirically derived classification. *European Psychiatry, 6,* 307–314.

Frances, A., Pincus, H. A., Widiger, T. A., Davis, W. W., & First, M. B. (1990). DSM-IV: Work in progress. *American Journal of Psychiatry, 147,* 1439–1448.

Karls, J., & Wandrei, K. (1992). PIE: A new language for social work. *Social Work, 37,* 80–85.

Karls, J. M., & Wandrei, K. E. (1994). *Person in environment system: The PIE classification system for social functioning problems.* Washington, DC: NASW Press.

Kirk, S. A., & Kutchins, H. (1992). *The selling of DSM: The rhetoric of science in psychiatry.* New York: Aldine de Gruyer.

Kutchins, H., & Kirk, S. A. (1987). DSM-III and social work malpractice. *Social Work, 32,* 205–211.

Mezzich, J. E., Kleinman, A., Fabrega, H., & Parron, D. (in press). *Culture and psychiatric diagnosis.* Washington, DC: American Psychiatric Press.

Skodol, A. E., Spitzer, R. L., & Williams, J.B.W. (1981). Teaching and learning DSM-III. *American Journal of Psychiatry, 138,* 243–244.

Spitzer, R. L., Gibbon, M., Skodol, A. E., First, M. B., & Williams, J.B.W. (1994). *DSM-IV case book.* Washington, DC: American Psychiatric Press.

Spitzer, R. L., & Williams, J.B.W. (1979). Dehumanizing descriptors? [Letter to the Editor]. *American Journal of Psychiatry, 136,* 1481.

Spitzer, R. L., Williams, J.B.W., & Skodol, A. E. (1980). DSM-III: The major achievements and an overview. *American Journal of Psychiatry, 137,* 151–164.

Spitzer, R. L., Williams, J.B.W., & Skodol, A. E. (Eds.). (1983). *International perspectives on DSM-III.* Washington, DC: American Psychiatric Press.

Widiger, T. A., Frances, A. J., Pincus, H. A., & Davis, W. W. (1990). DSM-IV literature reviews: Rationale, process, and limitations. *Journal of Psychopathology and Behavioral Assessment, 12,* 189–202.

Widiger, T. A., Frances, A. J., Pincus, H. A., First, M. B. & Davis, W. W. (1994). *DSM-IV source book,* Vol 1. Washington, DC: American Psychiatric Press, Inc.

Williams, J.B.W. (1981). DSM-III: A comprehensive approach to diagnosis. *Social Work, 26,* 101–106.

Williams, J.B.W. (1985a). The multiaxial system of DSM-III: Where did it come from and where should it go? I. Its origin and critiques. *Archives of General Psychiatry, 42,* 175–180.

Williams, J.B.W. (1985b). The multiaxial system of DSM-III: Where did it come from and where should it go? II. Empirical studies, innovations, recommendations. *Archives of General Psychiatry, 42,* 181–186.

Williams, J.B.W., Goldman, H., Gruenberg, A., Mezzich, J. E., & Skodol, A. E. (1990). DSM-IV in progress: The multiaxial system. *Hospital & Community Psychiatry, 41,* 1181–1182.

Williams, J.B.W., Karls, J. M., & Wandrei, K. (1989). Social work update: The person-in-environment (PIE) system for describing problems of social functioning. *Hospital & Community Psychiatry, 40,* 1125–1127.

Wynne, L. C. (1987). A preliminary proposal for strengthening the multiaxial approach of DSM-III: Possible family-oriented revisions. In G. L. Tischler (Ed.), *Diagnosis and classification in psychiatry: A critical appraisal of DSM-III* (pp. 477–488). Cambridge, England: Cambridge University Press.

## Further Reading

American Psychiatric Association. (1994). *Electronic DSM-IV.* Washington, DC: American Psychiatric Association, Inc.

Fauman, M. A. (1994). *Study guide to DSM-IV.* Washington, DC: American Psychiatric Press, Inc.

Othmer, E., & Othmer, S. C. (1994). *The clinical interview using DSM-IV. Volume I: Fundamentals.* Washington, DC: American Psychiatric Press, Inc.

**Janet B. W. Williams, DSW,** is professor of clinical psychiatric social work, College of Physicians and Surgeons of Columbia University, Unit 74, 722 West 168th Street, New York, NY 10032.

## For further information see

Assessment; Clinical Social Work; Mental Health Overview; Person-in-Environment; Research Overview; Social Work Practice: History and Evolution; Social Work Practice: Theoretical Base.

**Key Words**

assessment
diagnoses
DSM
mental illness

READER'S GUIDE

## Direct Practice

*The following entries contain information on this general topic:*



# Direct Practice Overview

**Elaine Pinderhughes**

Direct practice has traditionally referred to work with people who are experiencing or who are at risk of experiencing social problems. Known as micro or clinical practice and identified as work with individuals, couples, families, and small groups, *direct practice* consists of helping or social treatment through services such as therapy, counseling, education, advocacy, provision of information, referral, and certain aspects of community organization such as social action and mediation. Indirect or macro practice has referred to activities by professionals that focus on the structures through which services are provided: planning, policy analysis, program development, administration, and program evaluation (Connaway & Gentry, 1988; Meyer, 1987; Specht, 1988).

The purposes of both direct and indirect social work practice are to bring about the best possible adaptation among individuals, families, and groups and their environments; to set in motion a change process that will enhance people's problem-solving, coping, and developmental capacities; to link people with systems that provide resources, services, and opportunities; and to promote the effectiveness and humane operation of these systems (National Association of Social Workers, 1981).

Social workers in direct practice are trained on three educational levels to work with people of all age ranges, geographic locations, cultural backgrounds, and economic conditions in any and every setting in which people seek assistance for social problems. These settings include social agencies, clinics, hospitals, day care centers, schools, businesses and corporations, rehabilitative centers, courts, prisons, private settings, government agencies, and legislative institutions. The social problems that are the targets of social work practice and its purposes run the gamut from seeking employment or housing; attending school for the first time; caring for a child or elderly relative; the need for child placement or parenting skills; coping with physical, emotional, and mental illness or hospitalization; coping with depression or boredom that is due to inactivity; poor work performance; out-of-wedlock pregnancy; marital conflict; family dysfunction; poor social relationships; substance abuse; and violence or other problems in the neighborhood (Compton & Galway, 1994; Meyer, 1987).

## Nature of Direct Practice: Complexity and Diversity

The boundaries of practice are continually shifting. As social work's knowledge base grows and its practitioners respond to changing social problems, practitioners are called in ever-increasing numbers to serve society's public and private institutions and are required to move to new arenas and to shape and reshape their practices to meet burgeoning human needs.

The constancy and flexibility needed to facilitate such responsiveness have been provided by social work's person-in-environment perspective, which is sustained by its common base of history, purpose, sanction, knowledge, and skills—attributes that distinguish social work from other professions and mold its identity. This person-in-environment perspective and the primacy of the practitioner–client relationship are constructs that have continually evolved over the years to direct the work of all practitioners, regardless of method, theoretical orientation, problem orientation, or field of practice.

Social work's values have been especially integral to its definition and identity. Belief in the unique and inherent dignity of the individual and in self-determination as a right of all clients has served as a guide for the entire social work process, including the way in which services are organized; the manner of engaging, relating to, and communicating with clients; how their circumstances are evaluated; what goals are set; and what change strategies are implemented and how.

## Context of Practice: A Shifting Landscape

Social work practice is a 20th-century response to the problems caused by industrialization and urbanization and has always been shaped by its environmental context as well as by practitioners' efforts to hone it for greater effectiveness. This context has been characterized by rapid change on many levels.

### Changes in the 1980s and 1990s

New technologies have created massive shifts in social values, lifestyles, and behavior, resulting in consumerism and a "commodity identity" that emphasize buying things, achieving sensations, and passive viewing while simultaneously deemphasizing relationships, participation, imagination, and introspection (Hopps & Pinderhughes, 1987; Specht, 1988). The resultant alienation and anomie, along with shifting sex roles, increasing fragmentation—even atomization—of the family, and the breakdown in supportive, cohesive neighborhoods have created enormous problems, which are reflected in the rapid increase in crime, violence, sexual abuse, teenage pregnancy, and the acquired immune deficiency syndrome (AIDS) epidemic. These changes have been accompanied by rampant disrespect for authority, due process, structure, privacy, and individual rights.

Moreover, the rise in unemployment and cutbacks in taxation policy, budgets, and allocations for the services that could help people cope with these stressful problems have instead compounded them and at the same time have created a major escalation in poverty, an ongoing societal concern. Poverty is an inevitable contributor to family dysfunction and fragmentation; it has steadily increased since the early 1980s and in the mid-1990s is higher than at any time since the 1970s. In addition, escalation in immigrant and minority populations, along with associated issues of dislocation, culture shock, adaptation, assimilation, and system insufficiency at a variety of levels, provide a formidable context within which direct practitioners are called on to function.

### Social Work Response

To meet human needs and the multitude of problems created by societal forces such as these, social work has fashioned a vast array of roles, methods, and skills that constitute an elaborate intervention technology. Informed by an extensive knowledge base that consists of multiple theories, this technology is being increasingly refined in a veritable explosion of new models now arriving on the scene. Compounding these dynamics is the newest contextual determinant, managed care, which expects results that require the least expenditure of time, money, and effort and demands short-term models of intervention that set specific, easily operationalized, and measurable goals.

## A Practice Imperative: Flexibility, Brevity, Breadth, Depth, and Specificity

Practitioners are constantly pressed on all sides to develop explanatory models and practice technology that will accurately reflect what social workers do and will help them function with ever greater brevity, flexibility, breadth, depth, and specificity. Much attention has been devoted to identifying and defining the expected competencies. The rapid proliferation of knowledge about human behavior, practice process, and outcomes, which does not necessarily build on, expand, or exist compatibly with old theory, means that the latter is being replaced, creating tension and some challenging dilemmas in both education and practice (Hepworth & Larsen, 1990). Reflecting the social scene and the ebb and flow that characterize knowledge generally, practice knowledge refinement has been spurred by criticism in these areas: (1) its fragmented nature, (2) inadequate conceptualization of the environment aspect of the person-in-environment mandate, and (3) failure of models of practice to be sufficiently prescriptive for action.

**Multiple Theories and Techniques**

In response to these criticisms and to contextual demand, social work practice has become a complex mosaic, the diversity of which has persistently threatened the profession with fragmentation, conflict, and confusion. For some, this mosaic is seen as willy-nilly growth into a grab bag of diverse (and, in many instances, incompatible) theories, methods, techniques, needs, schools, and specializations that lack a coherent knowledge base and fit poorly with the purposes and intent of social work (Goldstein, 1990). Over the years such criticisms have set in motion enormous activity in the search for a cohesive element. A unifying theory was sought first in the conceptualization of a common base and later in the search for a comprehensive theory that would guide practice and bring cohesion to the social work profession. Some people believed that such a theory or perspective would address the profession's long-time dependence on borrowed theory, as well as the identity struggles with which it has been plagued because of its responsive stance to diverse proliferating social needs and problems. Such a goal, however, has remained elusive. Moreover, a single holistic theory, others insist, is inadequate to explain in depth and in a practical way what social workers actually do. They maintain that the tensions that grow out of the use of a plethora of theories and practice approaches are still best addressed by commitment to the social work's common base, which has served as the identified unifying element for the last 25 years. Still others, rather than focusing on developing a single theory of practice or practice approach, speak of using theory *in* practice (Specht, 1988), using a range of theories and approaches, and practicing "systematic eclectism" (Fischer, 1978; Hartman, 1988; Hepworth & Larsen, 1990).

## Roots to the Present: Casework to Clinical

Use of the terms "direct" or "clinical" to refer to an aspect of practice is the result of many hard-fought battles to bring order and unity to the social work profession and at the same time to respond to changing times, particularly new knowledge and new client groups. Before 1970, practice was defined by methodology (casework, group work, and community organization) or by setting (child welfare, family services, medical social work, psychiatric social work, or corrections). Societal upheaval and the need for more attention to the environment as a factor in the problems being brought by clients, who increasingly are African American, Latino, and poor, prompted awareness of the structural limitation inherent in practice that is based on the method orientation and of its failure to provide guidelines for case workers and group workers to fulfill the person-in-situation mandate of the profession (Meyer, 1987). Moreover, this conception of practice kept alive the divisions that had historically plagued the profession relative to the primacy of environmental reform versus individual change, or social treatment versus direct service.

**Roots in Casework**

Before the redefinition of practice, casework, a term for work with an individual, was the predominant social work practice method. Most prominent among its approaches were the psychosocial, functional, problem-solving, sociobehavioral, and crisis intervention models, all of which are visible in models currently used. Although the psychosocial approach gave some attention to the situation as well as the person in the person-in-environment equation, and although it rejected the medical metaphor as a use base (Hamilton, 1940), that metaphor continued to appear influential, as reflected in the terminology delineating the social work process: study, diagnosis, and treatment. The psychosocial approach is largely based on psychodynamic theory, particularly ego psychology, and was reconceptualized over the years to incorporate concepts of learning theory, family theory, ecological theory, and crisis theory (Woods & Hollis, 1990). Its capacity for openness to development and change "makes it considerably broader than its origins would indicate and vastly richer" (Turner, 1986, p. 486).

**Casework Approaches**

***Functional.*** The functional approach used the significance of the agency, authority, and the time phases of the social work process, along with the fee charged for service, as structural determinants of the intervention episode. Based on work by Jessie Taft and Virginia Robinson, who were influenced by Herbert Mead, John Dewey, and particularly Otto Rank, the functional approach emphasizes self-determination and choice, the human potential for growth, and resistance and termination as aspects of the helping situation that are necessary for movement and growth. These concepts have found wide applicability in the numerous models that have evolved since this approach's conception (Meyer, 1987; Yelaja, 1986) and many find particular utility in the construction of short-term models that are currently in great demand.

***Problem solving.*** The problem-solving approach (Perlman, 1957) incorporates ideas of the psychodynamic and functional orientations, borrowed theory from the learning concepts of John Dancy and the competence concepts of Robert White, thus using person, place, problem, action, and process as central constructs. This approach emphasizes the "here and now," the uses of the casework relationship, and the technique of partialization. The problem-solving approach can be seen as a contributor to later developments such as crisis intervention, work with hard-to-reach clients, use of contracts, and planned short-term treatment (Perlman, 1986).

***Psychobehavioral.*** The psychobehavioral model (Thomas, 1967) uses systematic techniques to facilitate behavior change. The approach draws on the conditioning theory of learning, which was developed by Thorndike, Watson, Skinner, and others, and derives practice principles from concepts that explain the interaction of behavior with previous and consequent events. It also incorporates cognitive theory, which had emerged in tandem with behavior theory and was an outgrowth. Indeed, cognitive behavior therapists have identified specific cognitive elements in behavior change. This approach is particularly preferred by practice researchers (Thyer, 1986) and has been widely integrated into newer models. It is seen by its proponents as "the most advisable therapeutic option," and "its place within eclectic social work practice has been assured" (Tomlison, 1986, p.149).

***Crisis intervention.*** Another significant casework approach that originated before the shift was crisis intervention, which emphasized concepts and principles for work with clients in situations of stress. Too broad and too amorphous to be considered a theory, it nevertheless did offer a framework that distinguished between crisis and other forms of stress, offering guidelines for examining and intervening in stressful situations (Golan, 1986). As much as any approach in practice, the evolution of crisis intervention illustrates the way in which theories and even models that have been borrowed and adapted for practice then recursively influence their root sources while also continuing to expand and then embrace newer developments. Originally developed by psychiatrists Erich Lindeman and Gerald Caplan from several disparate bodies of theory and practice, crisis intervention was adapted and expanded by a number of social workers, including Lydia Rapoport, Howard Parad, and Naomi Golan. The early models for practice incorporated concepts from ego psychology, learning theory, stress theory, life-span developmental psychology, and a variety of other fields. Currently, systems theory, role theory, cognitive theory, and gratification theory also contribute to the theory and models in use. At present there is a trend of applying crisis theory to a given field of practice through the development of different kinds of models for intervention in different settings. It is particularly suitable for clients who experience a high level of pain or anxiety in connection with a clear-cut hazardous event and a recent breakdown in coping and problem-solving capacity (Golan, 1986) (for example, rape victims, battered wives, and victims of violence). Crisis concepts have also been integrated into task-centered problem-solving approaches and a variety of short-term models.

Despite the efforts of other theorists, most notably Bertha Reynolds (1951), to conceptualize more usefully the environment aspect of the person-in-situation equation, the linear perspective of all these approaches provided no guidance for work beyond the individual level and no assistance to practitioners for working directly with the person's environment as well as with the person (Meyer, 1987). It was precisely this deficit along with the search for a common base that led to the shift.

### Group Work and Group Therapy

Group work, a method that is separate from casework, had its origin in the social reform movement, in which it was used for socialization, skills-building, education, and recreation. By the 1960s the varying models that had emerged focused on social goals (citizenship, social action, reform, and environmental change), remediation (rehabilitation and treatment in one's own environment), and growth and support (socialization, education, and therapy) (Rothman & Papell, 1986).

Group work approaches mirror those of case work, are derived from many of the same theories, and also draw from the same theoretical perspectives, borrowing in addition from sociology and social psychology. Meyer (1987) identified five approaches: psychosocial (Northen, 1969), developmental (Tropp, 1971), organizational (Glasser, Sarri, & Vinter, 1967), functional (Phillips, 1974) and mediating (Schwartz & Zalba, 1972).

The mainstream model was developed in answer to a call to cull from the diversity of therapeutic models those characteristics that were common to all. Defining the social worker's roles as those of enabler, facilitator, and teacher, this model emphasizes mutual aid and responsibility, spontaneously and collaboratively chosen activities, and differences among members as sources of strength. It also supports extension of group relationships beyond the group's boundaries. This model serves the definitive social work functions of enhancement, prevention, and empowerment and prescribes—irrespective of the group's level of dysfunction—pleasurable, growth-producing, and creative activities (Rothman & Papell, 1986).

### Family Work and Family Therapy

Joining the interdisciplinary thrust by professionals to incorporate social science systems concepts into their work, social workers helped in the evolution of family theory and therapy. Satir (1967) and Sherz (1970) were among the early theorists who, in embracing this nonlinear, systemic orientation, facilitated considerations of context and meaning as well as relationship, addressing somewhat more accurately the person-in-situation. Direct practitioners enthusiastically welcomed formal family therapy techniques as well as a general family-centered orientation, because much of their practice involved attention to family interactions. In a landmark volume, Hartman and Laird (1983) examined the plethora of family-centered and formal family therapy approaches that social workers use. Additional theorists and their contributions include Walsh (1982), on normal families; Papp (1977, 1983), on strategic models; Carter and McGoldrick (1988), on the life cycle; McGoldrick and Gerson (1985), on genograms; McGoldrick, Pearce, and Giordano (1983), Aponte (1985), and Ho (1987), on culturally specific populations; and McGoldrick, Anderson, and Walsh (1989) and Walters, Carter, Papp, and Silverstein (1988), on women.

## Paradigm Shift

This examination of direct practice approaches that evolved under the old methods' definitions of practice and their present-day utility underscores the enormous effort invested by theoreticians, practitioners, and researchers to define and devise guides for practice that would effectively address what social workers do. It also delineates how wide the range of knowledge that practitioners have borrowed and how overlapping and interlocking the nature of the theories and models they devised to meet escalating demands in the field.

The shift that occurred in practice in the 1970s was highly influenced by the social unrest of the 1960s and the emergence of the systemic paradigm in the social services. The human rights movement increased awareness of the significance of race and ethnicity in people's lives. The consequent press for social equality included all relatively powerless groups, including not only racial minorities but also poor people, prisoners and released offenders, students, and others. Critics, identifying the human rights movement's strong preoccupation with clinical and therapeutic matters, claimed that social work had failed to address poverty and discrimination, and they underscored yet again social work's failure to fulfill its mandate for environmental change. They charged that social work compounded the problems of disempowered people by blaming them for the social conditions from which they suffered instead of eliminating the conditions. Social work responded to this criticism with a reaffirmation of its commitment to social change and to its function of advocacy.

### Common Base: A More Holistic View

Movement of the conception of practice away from the linear to the more systemic paradigm needed to more closely actualize social work's commitment was made possible by the growing popularity of systems concepts in the sciences. Borrowing from systems theory, ecology, and cybernetics, new thinking—already being used by the small number of social workers in family therapy—was then made possible for all practitioners.

Gordon's (1965) and Bartlett's (1970) formulations of a framework emphasized the common base of all social work practice (its purpose, values, sanction, knowledge, and skills) and began the paradigm shift expanding the methods boundary of practice. Identification of the common base, a hoped-for cohesive force in the profession, permitted a holistic view of clients' situations and allowed practitioners to step away from a solitary method approach to see the client situation holistically and, because they were no longer tied to a predetermined method, allowed them to be free to use the common knowledge base for understanding. It also allowed them to choose, from a wide array, those skills appropriate to the assessment of a case (Meyer, 1987). Many theorists expanded this perspective, converting the medical construct of treatment process to the social work process of engagement, assessment, intervention planning, implementation, evaluation, and termination: Meyer (1970, 1976), Pincus and Minahan (1973), Goldstein (1973), Middeman and Goldberg (1974), Siporin (1975), and Nelson (1988). Incorporating planned change concepts, these theorists used a situational or transactional perspective that offered practitioners the language and skills to focus more effectively on the person-in-environment as the unit of attention.

Three trends then followed that have shaped direct practice in its current form, bringing it ever closer to fulfilling its environmental mandate and inspiring in some the hope that cohesion is possible: (1) the development of the ecological perspective with principles and concepts that explain the dynamic interaction between people and their environments, (2) the increasing salience of empirically based practice, and (3) the growth of the generalist model.

**Ecological Perspective**

The advent of ecological concepts and principles facilitated social work's reaffirmation of its historical concern with the social and psychological aspects of people's problems. Refinement of ecological theory by Germain (1976, 1978) and development of ecological models of practice by Germain and Gitterman (1980) (Life Model of Social Work Practice), Meyer (1983), and others facilitated a more manageable perspective on the complexities practitioners struggle with, bringing some order to their intended multilevel efforts at change. Use of an ecological perspective requires a focus not only on the system in question—whether it be an individual, family, or small group—but also on its adaptation to the environment, and it forces a focus on the surrounding environment itself and on the interaction between the system and the environment. Understanding, explaining, predicting, and engineering change in systems seeking assistance, then, required a focus on dynamic rather than static processes (Connaway & Gentry, 1988). This circular, as opposed to linear, perspective permitted a look at the interaction among many variables in a client's situation and provided understanding of the diversity and complexity within systems, in their contexts, and in the interactive processes of both. Currently it is safe to say that nearly every theory and model in use incorporates the ecological perspective as context. Although this perspective is not prescriptive vis-à-vis techniques and strategies, it does permit eclectic choice in terms of those that are appropriate to a given case situation.

***Holistic theory.*** Seen as putting the "social" back in social work (Shulman, 1992; Whitaker & Tracy, 1989), the ecological perspective was also viewed as a promising trend toward the development of a holistic practice theory. Current application of the perspective conceptualizes achievement of the best possible adaptation among individuals, families, small groups, and their environments in a variety of ways: through a focus on socialization (Specht, 1988), on person and environment (Woods & Hollis, 1990), on interaction (Compton & Galway, 1994; Specht, 1988), or on humanizing systems (Schatz, Jenkins, & Shaefer, 1990). The significance of an environmental focus is such that Whitaker and Tracy (1989) were prompted to view their interpersonal model of social treatment as stopping just short of intervention at the macro, societal level. Including the environmental context in understanding the client means including "both the proximate environment of a family, neighborhood, and peer group and the more distal environment of workplace, formal organization and community . . . (and) changing the environment at ANY of these levels is a central and historically legitimate component of compassionate and effective micro level social work practice" (1989, p. 2). Such an expanded conception of practice, in which the environment becomes part of the central focus of the work, means that the emphasis on the psychological view in the change process is currently giving way to the social aspects.

***Culturally appropriate frameworks.*** This heightened focus on environment, which began in the 1970s and extends into the present, has sparked efforts to understand culturally specific populations and to create appropriate frameworks for practice (Devore & Schlesinger, 1991; Lum, 1986). Recognition of the way in which the status assignment of cultural groups influenced their life chances and lifestyles, including the impact of minority status, stratification, stereotyping, and systemic entrapment, has brought forth new conceptualization about social work with a variety of populations, including ethnic minorities and people of color (Chestang, 1972, 1976; Hopps, 1982, 1987; Longres, 1991; Pinderhughes, 1989; Logan, Freeman, & McRoy, 1990; Solomon, 1976), women (Bricker-Jenkins, Hooyman, & Gottlieb, 1991; Dominelli & McCleod, 1989; Weick & Vandiver, 1982), and gay men and lesbians (Cummerton, 1980; Hidalgo, Peterson, & Woodman, 1985; Shernoff, 1984).

**Empirically Based Practice**

Research-based practice also emerged in the late 1970s with the questioning of practice effectiveness (Briar, 1974; Fischer, 1978) and development of Fischer's (1978) empirically based practice formulation, along with Reid and Epstein's (1972, 1977) task-centered practice and models for incorporating research into education for practice (Briar, 1979). The empirical foundation grew out of dissatisfaction with the abstract nature of the practice theories in use and their perceived failure to delineate specificity for practitioner interventions. These newer research-based approaches used feedback from clients to develop pragmatic techniques rather than using current theoretical framework or expanding and reconceptualizing them on the basis of practice wisdom. Task-centered treatment was an influential action-oriented short-term model that emphasized tasks and the alteration of internal psychological processes in instances when these had constituted impediments to action.

Since its inception the interest in using research information not merely for understanding practice (Witkin & Gottschalk, 1988), but also for ensuring accountability has grown exponentially. Proof is seen in the present requirement by the Commission on Accreditation of the Council on Social Work Education that all training social workers develop skills in research consumption and evaluation of one's own practice. The incorporation of research into practice has occupied many educators (Briar, 1974). Much activity has been directed to building practice models that are based on observation, proposition building, application, and testing. Among important developments are the social research and development models (Rothman, 1980; Thomas, 1978, 1984). Single-subject design models for measuring outcomes have been developed by Bloom and Fisher (1982), Nelson (1988), Gingerich (1990), and Collins and Kayser (1992). Some critics caution that the absolute position taken by enthusiasts for a theory development research agenda devalues the importance of other approaches to building knowledge (Hepworth & Larsen, 1990). However, proponents hail these models' capacity to advance practice specificity and "how-to" understanding as limitless, provided all evaluative efforts are criterion oriented and goal centered, simple and parsimonious, invite client participation in the design and implementation, are based on careful preplanning, and are compatible with agency goals and purposes (Whitaker & Tracy, 1989).

## Practice in the Present

### Multiple Practice Foci, Theories, and Approaches

More than ever, the current state of social work practice illustrates the systemic nature of practice itself and the way in which the ever-increasing differentiation that characterizes the evolving theories and models is consistent with "how open systems respond to multiple inputs of energy and information from the environment" (Hartman, 1988, p. ix). Thus, the process of defining practice and its components is constantly in transition as the search continues for explanations of professional endeavors that are sufficiently prescriptive and transferable. Old theories are being expanded and readapted for the multiplicity of new models that are emerging. Practice, no longer based on a single theory or approach, currently is multitheory as well as multimethod and multilevel based. The rapidly increasing number of theoretical perspectives that are used to inform intervention approaches in current use is staggering: Turner (1986) identified 26, Whitaker and Tracy (1989) listed 28, and Zastrow (1992) located 49!

Thus, the specialized nature of knowledge has compounded as practice has become more differentiated. Moving from a simple conception of specialization in terms of method or field, direct-practice knowledge has grown to include special knowledge for work with specific populations, such as poor people, specific cultural groups, and women; work with people at different life-cycle stages, such as children, adolescents, and elderly people; work in special locations, such as rural or urban areas; and work with specific problems, such as substance abuse, sexual abuse, and divorce. Models can be chosen or developed on the basis of this multiplicity of practice foci. Indeed, social workers currently are expected to master a number of theories and practice techniques and possess the capacity to select the interventions and techniques that fit the particular client, problem, situation, and time (Rosen, 1988), a skill that requires great flexibility in thinking and behavior.

### Complex Choices in Rigorous Selection of Models and Theories

Eclectic choice—a rigorous approach to social work practice—must be governed by a number of considerations, including appropriate matching of theory and intervention with client, situation, and problem, and also must give the highest priority to techniques that have been empirically demonstrated to be effective and efficient. Models must be prescriptive for intervention and require the least expenditure of time, money, and effort, and they must be consistent with social work values. Interventions must preserve the dignity and confidentiality of the client and not subject him or her to emotional trauma or humiliation or conflict with the profession's code of ethics. Practitioners are required to be well grounded in the rationale for the use of the intervention, its indications and contraindications for use, cautions to be observed, guidelines for appropriate timing, and specific procedures for implementation (Hepworth & Larsen, 1990).

An example of the multitheory approach currently used in many models is Hepworth and Larsen's (1990) model, which explicates a systematic eclectic problem-solving approach that integrates a task-centered system, cognitive therapy, behavior modification, client-centered therapy, ego psychology, role theory, social learning theory, and several models of family therapy. Theories that supply understanding and guide practice must focus on strengths and incorporate concepts explaining the dynamics of power (Pinderhughes, 1983), diversity, and difference that provide applicability to all populations, particularly disempowered groups (Compton & Galway, 1994). Emphasis currently is placed on

- client collaboration at every stage of practice, including the research process (Tidwell, 1990)
- reciprocity in the practitioner–client relationship
- the ethical imperative that practitioners must monitor both the value assumptions implicit in the intervention or theory base and their own values relative to their influence or understanding the client
- development of an intervention plan that reflects the client's understanding of the problem (Compton & Galway, 1994; Pinderhughes, 1989).

In addition to the approaches already discussed, which have survived the shift from the linear conception of practice and have become incorporated into practice technology either intact, expanded, or in fragments, newer approaches and models have evolved that are based on the use of symbolic interaction theory and existential theory. The interpersonal models, which refine concepts that explain social worker–nonclient interactions and the management of interactions not only with clients but also on their behalf with colleagues, collaterals, administrators, policymakers, consultants, and other professionals, are illustrative of the attempt to further refine concepts that guide the environmental aspect of practice. These models are based on symbolic interactionism, social exchange theory, and social network analysis and focus on correcting problems in social role functioning that are due to social contextual interference (Specht, 1988). Shulman's (1991) interactionist model, which also uses the social interactionist framework and was tested in a specific child welfare setting with involuntary clients, has an empirical base. Representing a beginning effort to develop and test a grounded theory of practice that is holistically conceived, the model tested propositions related to "persons in interaction in context over time" and is based on an effort to examine the core issues in all direct practice (Shulman, 1992).

Somewhat in counterpoint to the strongly entrenched empirically based theory and model building occurring in practice is the revival of interest in phenomenological approaches. These approaches represent a retreat in the dominance of logical positions and empirical models and focus on the person's experience of living and on understanding others' perceptions of the world. They thus emphasize regard for clients' belief systems, spirituality, and faith (Goldstein, 1992). Among the newer theories that focus on subjective reality are narrative theory (Laird, 1993, 1989), which emphasizes the connections among dialogue, relationship, meaning, and purpose; social constructivist theory (Fisher, 1991), which posits that reality and understanding of the world are not absolute but instead are a personally constructed experience; and feminist theory (Davis, 1993; Gutierrez, 1990).

## Generalist and Advanced Generalist Practice

As the conceptualization of direct practice continues to broaden and deepen, the boundaries realign. Seen more and more to extend beyond the level of group into community (and even beyond), not merely in the understanding of a client's situation but also in terms of coping actions engaged in by a practitioner and client, theory and model building for implementation continue apace. In this continuing refinement, a generalist trend in practice has emerged. Using the various perspectives and approaches already described, and various combinations of others to build new models, generalist practice is pushing social work to increasingly define practice more broadly by encompassing the situational context and to connect practice purposes to strategies; it is currently viewed as more consistent with social work's mandate.

### Definitions and Social Work Roles

Like general practice in medicine, generalist social work practice involves work with a wide variety of problems in various settings, with referral to specialists who work in greater depth and specificity and who use more-complex knowledge and more-advanced skills. Explanatory theory and expository model building are well under way (Allen-Meares & Lane, 1987; Schatz, Jenkins, & Shaefer, 1990). Conceptualized originally as role sets designed to respond inclusively and flexibly to a broad range of client systems and consistent with the purposes and function of the profession, generalist practice relies on general problem-solving activities and receives its structure from the social context in which practice occurs (Compton & Galway, 1994; Connaway & Gentry, 1988).

Social work roles are identified as: (1) face-to-face caseworker, counselor, enabler, or educator for individuals, family, and groups; (2) system linking, including broker, case manager, or coordinator, (3) mediator–arbitrator or advocate; (4) system maintaining, including administrator, facilitator, expediter, consultant, and team member; and (5) researcher consumer (Gibbs, Locke, & Lohmann, 1990; Hepworth & Larsen, 1990; Whitaker & Tracy, 1989; Zastrow, 1992). Most models incorporate at least several roles, particularly the first two, with great variation in the emphasis on system-maintaining roles that explicate the process of intervening at the level of agency policy and that function on behalf of clients. The system-maintaining roles, such as mediator, and the system-linking roles, such as case management, continue to be refined—a function of increasing importance in complex delivery networks that require a timely orchestration of service delivery.

**Potential Uses**

Despite promises to truly meet practice needs for brevity, flexibility, and breadth, however, generalist practice approaches are criticized as being more clear about ways to think about practice than about "how to's" (Specht, 1988). Some advocates justify this by pointing to the capacity of generalist practice for producing self-directed, flexible, responsive workers (Connaway & Gentry, 1988), whereas others have redoubled efforts to delineate "how to do the decided" (Compton & Galway, 1994). Generalist practice is particularly suited for small towns and rural areas in the United States, and its applicability to inner city and international—especially Third World—contexts has been enthusiastically proclaimed (Gibbs, Locke, & Lohmann, 1990). Its capacity for response to context means that in work with disempowered groups, such as those based on race, age, gender, sexual orientation, or rural residence, the practitioner can respond to immediate need growing out of contextual reality. For example, creating a solution for inadequate housing means working with conditions in the community and society that present barriers to housing availability. Thus, work with the individual is enhanced by work with other agencies, organizations, institutions, and the community to remove the obstacles that are creating the need.

Theories that explain socialization processes and behavior in context such as symbolic interactionism, along with learning theories and problem-solving approaches that direct work in helping individuals grow and develop competencies (Maluccio, 1981), link clients with supportive resources and facilitate work to humanize systems and influence policy are popular as guides. The emerging models, some of which incorporate existential theory and social constructivism (Goldstein, 1992), take a strongly humanistic stance and also embrace concepts of empowerment, membership, collaboration, regeneration, synergy, dialogue, and discourse. Examples include the strengths models (Saleeby, 1992; Weick, Rapp, Sullivan, & Kisthardt, 1989), empowerment models (Cox & Parsons, 1993; Galper, 1980; Pinderhughes & Pittman, 1985), home-based family preservation models (Tracy, Haapola, Kinney, & Pecora, 1991), and feminist models (Gutierrez, 1990; McGoldrick, Walsh, & Anderson, 1989). Many of these newer models are empirically based.

**Specialization: Advanced Generalist Practice**

Perhaps as a response to criticism concerning the lack of specificity in generalist practice approaches—and thus their lack of utility for the well-entrenched specialized practice found in many agencies—a new trend is occurring in education: that of specialization in generalist practice. A seeming contradiction, this specialization is designed to require the practitioner to use the advanced curriculum content at multiple intervention levels. Advanced social work practice with a generalist orientation offers specialized depth in an area of specialty, such as child welfare, using multimethod, multilevel approaches to practice. It is somewhat predictable that as theories and models are adopted, there will be pressure for the advanced generalist paradigm to constitute the defining framework for all graduate training. Proponents of this thrust see it as an antidote to the prevailing trend in specialized practice toward private practice and avoidance of public social work and practice with oppressed populations.

## Conclusion

As social workers develop new models that are based on research and are characterized by greater intervention specificity, practice continues to evolve both in depth and breadth. Its openness to theory and method multiplicity requires that all practitioners remain flexible in approach; skilled in case-specific ethical choices of theory, model, and technique; and personally committed to the ongoing development of these. There is hope that a holistic theory is not far off and conviction that the capacity to address the situation in person-in-situation is rapidly emerging. Indeed, social work is alive and well.

## References


Allen-Meares, P., & Lane, B. (1987). Grounding social work practice in theory: Ecosystems. *Social Casework, 68,* 515–521.

Aponte, H. (1985). The negotiation of values in therapy. *Family Process, 24,* 323–338.

Aponte, H., Zarski, J., Bixenstine, C., & Cibik, P. (1991). Home/community-based services: A two-tiered approach. *American Journal of Orthopsychiatry, 61*(3), 403–409.

Bartlett, A. (1970). *The common base of social work practice.* New York: National Association of Social Workers.

Bloom, M., & Fisher, J. (1982). *Evaluating practice: Guidelines for the accountable professional.* Englewood Cliffs, NJ: Prentice Hall.

Briar, S. (1974). A new look at social casework. *Social Work, 19*(2), 130.

Briar, S. (1979). Incorporating research into education for clinical practice in social work: Toward a clinical science in social work. In A. Ruhn & A. Rosenblatt (Eds.), *Sourcebook on research utilization* (pp. 132–140). New York: Council on Social Work Education.

Bricker-Jenkins, M., Hooyman, N. R., & Gottlieb, N. (1991). *Feminist social work practice in clinical settings.* Newbury Park, CA: Sage Publications.

Carter, E., & McGoldrich, M. (1988). *The changing family life cycle: A framework for family therapy.* New York: Gardner Press.

Chestang, L. (1972). *Character development in a hostile environment* (Occasional Paper #2). Chicago: University of Chicago School of Social Service Administration.

Chestang, L. (1976). Environmental influences on social functioning: The black experience. In P. Cafferty & L. Chestang (Eds.), *The diverse society: Implications for social policy* (pp. 59–74). Washington, DC: National Association of Social Workers.

Collins, P., & Kayser, K. (1992). *Clinical practice evaluation: Essentials for social work educators.* Boston: Boston College Graduate School of Social Work.

Compton, B., & Galway, B. (1994). *Social work processes.* Monterey, CA: Brooks/Cole.

Connaway, R., & Gentry, M. (1988). *Social work practice.* Englewood Cliffs, NJ: Prentice Hall.

Cox, E., & Parsons, R. (1993). *Empowerment-oriented social work practice with the elderly.* Monterey, CA: Brooks/Cole.

Cummerton, J. (1980). Homophobia and social work practice with lesbians. In A. Weick & S. Vandiver (Eds.), *Women, power and change* (pp. 104–113). Washington, DC: National Association of Social Workers.

Davis, L. (1993). Feminism and constructionism: Teaching social work practice with women. *Journal of Teaching in Social Work, 8*(1/2), 147–164.

Devore, W., & Schlesinger, E. G. (1991). *Ethnic-sensitive social work practice* (3rd ed.). New York: Merrill.

Dominelli, L., & McCleod, E. (1989). *Feminist social work.* New York: Macmillan.

Fischer, J. (1978). *Effective casework practice: An eclectic approach.* New York: McGraw-Hill.

Fisher, D. (1991). *An introduction to constructivism for social workers.* New York: Praeger.

Galper, J. (1980). *Social work practice: A radical perspective.* Englewood Cliffs, NJ: Prentice Hall.

Germain, C. (1976). Time: An ecological variable in social work practice. *Social Casework, 57*(7), 419–426.

Germain, C. (1978). Space: An ecological variable in social work practice. *Social Casework, 59*(9), 515–522.

Germain, C., & Gitterman, A. (1980). *The life model of social work practice.* New York: Columbia University Press.

Gibbs, P., Locke, B., & Lohmann, R. (1990, Fall). Paradigm for the generalist–advanced generalist continuum. *Journal of Social Work Education, 26*(3), 232–243.

Gingerich, W. (1990). Rethinking single-case evaluation. In L. Videka-Sherman & W. Reid (Eds.), *Advances in clinical social work research* (pp. 11–24). Silver Spring, MD: NASW Press.

Glasser, P., Sarri, R., & Vinter, R. (1967). *Individual change through small groups.* New York: Free Press.

Golan, N. (1986). Crisis theory. In F. Turner (Ed.), *Social work treatment: Interlocking theoretical approaches* (pp. 296–340). New York: Free Press.

Goldstein, H. (1973). *Social work practice: A unitary approach.* Columbia: University of South Carolina Press.

Goldstein, H. (1990). The knowledge base of social work practice: Theory, wisdom, analogue, or art? *Families in Society, 71,* 32–42.

Goldstein, H. (1992). If social work hasn't made progress as a science, might it be an art? *Families in Society, 73*(1), 48–55.

Gordon, W. (1965). Toward a social work frame of reference. *Journal of Education for Social Work, 1*(2), 19–26.

Gutierrez, L. (1990). Working with women of color: An empowerment perspective. *Social Work, 35,* 149–153.

Hamilton, G. (1940). *Theory and practice of social casework.* New York: Columbia University Press.

Hartman, A. (1988). Foreword. In B. Dorfman (Ed.), *Paradigms of clinical social work.* New York: Brunner/Mazel.

Hartman, A., & Laird, J. (1983). *Family-centered social work practice.* New York: Free Press.

Hepworth, D., & Larsen, J. (1990). *Direct social work practice: Theory and skills* (3rd ed.). Monterey, CA: Brooks/Cole.

Hidalgo, H., Peterson, T. L., & Woodman, N. J. (1985). *Lesbian and gay issues: A resource manual for social workers.* Silver Spring, MD: National Association of Social Workers.

Ho, M. (1987). *Family therapy with ethnic minorities.* Newbury Park, CA: Sage Publications.

Hopps, J. (1982). Oppression based on color. *Social Work, 27,* 3–5.

Hopps, J. (1987). Minorities of color. In A. Minahan (Ed.-in-Chief), *Encyclopedia of social work* (18th ed., Vol. 2, pp. 161–171). Silver Spring, MD: National Association of Social Workers.

Hopps, J., & Pinderhughes, E. (1987). Profession of social work: Contemporary characteristics. In A. Minahan (Ed.-in-Chief), *Encyclopedia of social work* (18th ed., Vol. 2, pp. 351–366). Silver Spring, MD: National Association of Social Workers.

Laird, J. (1989). Women and stories: Restorying a woman's self-constructions. In M. McGoldrick, F. Walsh, & C. Anderson (Eds.), *Women in families* (pp. 427–450). New York: W. W. Norton.

Laird, J. (1993). Family-centered practice: Cultural and constructionist reflections. *Journal of Teaching in Social Work, 8*(1/2), 77–110.

Logan, S., Freeman, E., & McRoy, E. (1990). *Social work practice with black families.* New York: Longman.

Longres, J. (1991). Toward a status model of ethnic-sensitive practice. *Journal of Multicultural Social Work, 1*(1), 41–56.

Lum, D. (1986). *Social work practice and people of color: A process stage approach.* Monterey, CA: Brooks/Cole.

Maluccio, A. (1981). *Promoting competence in clients: A new/old approach to social work practice.* New York: Free Press.

McGoldrick, M., Anderson, C., & Walsh, F. (1989). *Women in families: A framework for family therapy.* New York: W. W. Norton.

McGoldrick, M., & Gerson, R. (1985). *Genograms and family assessment.* New York: W. W. Norton.

McGoldrick, M., Pearce, J., & Giordano, J. (1983). *Ethnicity and family therapy.* New York: Guilford Press.

Meyer, C. (1970). *Social work practice: A response to the urban crisis.* New York: Free Press.

Meyer, C. (1976). *Social work practice: The changing landscape.* New York: Free Press.

Meyer, C. (1987). Direct practice in social work: Overview. In A. Minahan (Ed.-in-Chief), *Encyclopedia of social work* (18th ed., Vol. 1, pp. 409–422). Silver Spring, MD: National Association of Social Workers.

Meyer, C. H. (Ed.). (1983). *Clinical social work in an eco-systems perspective.* New York: Columbia University Press.

Middleman, R., & Goldberg, G. (1974). *Social service delivery: A structural approach to social work practice.* New York: Columbia University Press.

National Association of Social Workers. (1981). *NASW standards for the classification of social work practice.* Washington, DC: Author.

Nelson, J. (1988). Single subject research. In R. Grinnell (Ed.), *Social work research and evaluation* (3rd ed., pp. 362–400). Itasca, IL: F. E. Peacock.

Northen, H. (1969). *Social work with groups.* New York: Columbia University Press.

Papp, P. (1977). *Family therapy: Full-length case studies.* New York: Gardner Press.

Papp, P. (1983). *The process of change.* New York: Guilford Press.

Perlman, H. (1957). *Social casework: A problem solving process.* Chicago: University of Chicago Press.

Perlman, H. (1986). The problem solving model. In F. Turner (Ed.), *Social work treatment: Interlocking theoretical approaches* (pp. 245–266). New York: Free Press.

Phillips, H. (1974). The essentials of group work skill. Folcroft, PA: Folcroft Press.

Pincus, A., & Minahan, A. (1973). *Social work practice: Method and model.* Itasca, IL: F. E. Peacock.

Pinderhughes, E. (1983). Empowerment for our clients and for ourselves. *Social Casework, 64*(6), 331–338.

Pinderhughes, E. (1989). *Understanding race, ethnicity and power: Key to efficacy in clinical practice.* New York: Free Press.

Pinderhughes, E., & Pittman, A. (1985). A socio-cultural treatment model: Empowerment of worker and client. In M. Day (Ed.), *The socio-cultural dimensions of community mental health* (pp. 82–114). New York: Vantage Press.

Reid, W., & Epstein, L. (1972). *Task-centered casework.* New York: Columbia University Press.

Reid, W., & Epstein, L. (1977). *Task-centered practice.* New York: Columbia University Press.

Reynolds, B. C. (1951). *Social work and social living.* New York: Citadel.

Roberts, R., & Nee, R. (1970). *Theories of social casework.* Chicago: University of Chicago Press.

Rosen, H. (1988). The constructivist–developmental paradigm. In R. Dorfman (Ed.), *Paradigms of clinical social work* (pp. 317–355). New York: Brunner/Mazel.

Rothman, J. (1980). *Social r & d: Research and development in the human services.* Englewood Cliffs, NJ: Prentice Hall.

Rothman, B., & Papell, C. (1986). Social group work as a clinical paradigm. In R. Dorfman (Ed.), *Paradigms in clinical social work* (pp. 149–178). New York: Brunner/Mazel.

Saleeby, D. (1992). *The strengths perspective in social work practice.* New York: Longman.

Satir, V. (1967). *Conjoint family therapy.* Palo Alto, CA: Science and Behavior Books.

Schatz, M., Jenkins, L., & Shaefer, B. (1990). Milford redefined: A model of initial and advanced generalist social work. *Journal of Social Work Education, 3,* 217–231.

Schwartz, W., & Zalba, S. (Eds.). (1972). *Practice of group work.* New York: Columbia University Press.

Shernoff, B. (1984). Family therapy for lesbian and gay clients. *Social Work, 29,* 393–396.

Sherz, F. (1970). Theory and practice of family therapy. In R. Roberts & R. Nee (Eds.), *Theories of social casework.* Chicago: University of Chicago Press.

Shulman, L. (1992). *Interactional social work practice: Toward an empirical theory.* Itasca, IL: F. E. Peacock.

Siporin, M. (1975). *Introduction to social work practice.* New York: Macmillan.

Solomon, B. (1976). *Black empowerment: Social work in oppressed communities.* New York: Columbia University Press.

Specht, H. (1988). *New directions for social work.* Englewood Cliffs, NJ: Prentice Hall.

Thomas, E. J. (Ed.). (1967). *The socio-behavioral approach and applications to social work.* New York: Council on Social Work Education.

Thomas, E. (1978). Mousetraps, developmental research and social work education. *Social Service Review, 52,* 468–483.

Thomas, E. (1984). *Designing interventions for the helping professions.* Beverly Hills, CA: Sage Publications.

Thyer, B. (1986). Radical behaviors in clinical social work. In R. Dorfman (Ed.), *Paradigms of clinical social work* (pp. 123–148). New York: Brunner/Mazel.

Tidwell, B. (1990). Research and practice issues with black families. In S. Logan, E. Freeman, & R. McRoy (Eds.), *Social work practice with black families* (pp. 259–272). New York: Longman.

Tomlison, R. (1986). Behavior therapy in social work practice. In F. Turner (Ed.), *Social work treatment: Interlocking theoretical approaches* (pp. 131–154). New York: Free Press.

Tracy, E., Haapola, D., Kinney, J., Pecora, P. (1991). *Intensive family preservation services.* Cleveland, OH: Case Western Reserve University, Mandel School of Applied Social Sciences.

Tropp, E. (1971). *A humanistic foundation for group work practice* (2nd ed.). New York: Selected Academic Readings.

Turner, F. (1986). *Social work treatment: Interlocking theoretical approaches.* New York: Free Press.

Walsh, F. (1982). *Normal family processes.* New York: Guilford Press.

Walters, M., Carter, E., Papp, P., & Silverstein, O. (1988). *The invisible web: Gender patterns in family relationships.* New York: Longman.

Weick, A., Rapp, C., Sullivan, W. P., & Kisthardt, W. (1989). A strengths perspective for social work practice. *Social Work, 34,* 350–354.

Weick, A., & Vandiver, S. T. (1982). Women, power, and change: Selected papers from social work practice in sexist society. In *First NASW Conference on Social Work Practice with Women.* Washington, DC: National Association of Social Workers.

Whitaker, J., & Tracy, E. (1989). *Social treatment: An introduction to interpersonal helping in social work practice* (2nd ed.). New York: Aldine de Gruyter.

Witkin, S. L., & Gottschalk, S. (1988). Alternative criteria for theory evaluation. *Social Service Review, 62,* 211–224.

Woods, M. E., & Hollis, F. (1990). *Casework, a psychosocial therapy.* New York: McGraw-Hill.

Yelaja, S. (1986). Functional theory for social work practice. In F. Turner (Ed.), *Social work treatment: Interlocking theoretical approaches* (pp. 46–68). New York: Columbia University Press.

Zastrow, C. (1992). *The practice of social work.* Belmont, CA: Wadsworth.

## Further Reading

Davis, L. E., & Proctor, E. K. (1989). *Race, gender and class: Guidelines for practice with individuals, families and groups.* Englewood Cliffs, NJ: Prentice Hall.

Hartman, A. (1994). Reframing the epistemological debate. In E. Sherman & W. J. Reid (Eds.), *Qualitative research in social work* (pp. 464–481). New York: Columbia University Press.

Hopps, J., Pinderhughes, E., & Shankar, R. (1994). *The power to care: Clinical practice effectiveness with clients overwhelmed by persistent poverty.* New York: Free Press.

Imber-Black, E. (1990). Multiple embedded systems. In M. Mirkin (Ed.), *The social and political contexts of family therapy* (pp. 3–18). New York: Allyn & Bacon.

Maluccio, A., Washitz, S., & Libassi, M. (1992). Ecologically-oriented competence centered social work practice. In A. LeCroy (Ed.), *Case studies in social work practice.* Belmont, CA: Wadsworth.

Meyer, C. (1993). *Assessment in social work practice.* New York: Columbia University Press.

Reamer, F. (1990). *Ethical dilemmas in social service* (2nd ed.). New York: Columbia University Press.

Reamer, F. (1994). *The foundations of social worker knowledge.* New York: Columbia University Press.

Videka-Sherman, L., & Reid, W. J. (Eds.). (1990). *Advances in clinical social work research.* Silver Spring, MD: NASW Press.

**Elaine Pinderhughes, PhD,** is professor, Boston College, Graduate School of Social Work, Chestnut Hill, MA 02167.

### For further information see

Assessment; Case Management; Clinical Social Work; Ethics and Values; Generalist and Advanced Generalist Practice; Goal Setting and Intervention Planning; Group Practice Overview; Intervention Research; Interviewing; Mental Health Overview; Person-in-Environment; Program Evaluation; Social Work Practice: Theoretical Base; Social Work Profession Overview.

**Key Words**
clinical social work
direct practice
practice methods

READER'S GUIDE

## Disabilities

*The following entries contain information on this general topic:*

Deafness
Deinstitutionalization
Developmental Disabilities: Definitions and Policies
Developmental Disabilities: Direct Practice
Disability
Visual Impairment and Blindness

# Disability

**Adrienne Asch**
**Nancy R. Mudrick**

For as long as there has been an organized social work profession, social workers have been involved with people with a wide range of conditions defined as disabilities. Clients have included, for example, a family in which a teenage girl diagnosed with schizophrenia required inpatient hospitalization; a 50-year-old husband and father who left construction work after a back injury and was unemployed for more than one year; and a family that sought help when a widowed 75-year-old mother became aphasic after a stroke. Sometimes a worker has discovered that a client who was referred to social services by a school or the court had a drug problem. Social workers have also worked with clients and families dealing with the human immunodeficiency virus (HIV).

Whether working in a hospital social work department, an employee assistance program, a multiservice community mental health program, or a resettlement center for refugees, social workers find that physical, emotional, or cognitive disabilities in some way affect the lives of many of their clients. Often the discovery of disability in themselves or in someone they love brings individuals to the attention of a social worker, either for counseling or for referral to benefits, services, and support groups.

## Background

Individuals, organizations, and government agencies define disability in various ways. For some, disability refers exclusively to a chronic medical condition or physical or mental impairment; for others, disability is the functional consequence of chronic mental or physical conditions; and for still others, disability is the by-product of social and physical environments that do not accommodate people with different functional abilities. Despite these various definitions of disability, there appears to be some consensus that a person with a disability can have either a permanent physical or mental impairment or a chronic health or mental health condition. The health condition or impairment may be visible or invisible to others, and it may be present at birth or begin at any age. Disabilities vary in severity; some people find it extremely difficult to participate in a wide range of employment and recreational activities, especially when the social and physical environment is inaccessible or discriminates against them, whereas others' lives are affected in a single area.

Because many social workers learn about disability at times when their clients are just beginning to learn about it themselves, they have come to view disability as a deeply distressing factor in which a sudden crisis gives way to protracted, irremediable problems, strains, and disappointments. Most of the professional literature about disability focuses on the emotional and social difficulties that often accompany someone's physical impairments. Along with other professionals who work to alleviate social problems and helping people improve their capacity to manage day-to-day life, social workers generally have been aware of disability only when it has compounded existing difficulties or created new ones.

Unfortunately, most research on people with disabilities and their families, and much of the clinical literature on disability reviewed by Asch and Rousso (1985) and Fine and Asch (1988) draws on the early months or years in which an individual or family is dealing with the effects that the impairment will have on someone's life. It is during this time of adjustment and adaptation that a person with a disability most resembles a person who has experienced an acute illness or a sudden injury (for example, a heart attack or a broken leg). It is often necessary for an individual with an acute illness to halt typical school, work, and recreational activities; seek medical advice; and concentrate on getting well. This individual may be quite content to let physicians, friends, and family members make most decisions that affect his or her life, knowing that such "time out" is temporary and that he or she will return to typical roles and relationships after recovery. This "sick role" (Parsons, 1951), however, does not typify the lives of people with long-term conditions (that is, chronic illnesses or disabilities), who report that despite the physical, economic, and social problems of disability, they are generally satisfied with much about their lives (Louis Harris & Associates, 1986; Schultz & Decker, 1985).

Exacerbating the likelihood that physical disability will appear to be inevitably detrimental to life satisfaction and productivity is the social devaluation and stigma pervading most discussions of disability in the popular literature and films. People with disabilities are usually depicted as either courageous heroes or bitter, angry misanthropes who require the salvation of someone's love or a miracle cure. As Goffman (1963, p. 5) noted in his classic discussion of how society views those with characteristics that it dislikes, people with disabilities are stigmatized and often treated as "not quite human," not "normal." Research on attitudes of nondisabled people toward people with disabilities (Antonak & Livneh, 1988; Wright, 1988) shows that the fear of and aversion to disability and illness often leads to fear and rejection of people who have disability and illness. Social workers may have to recognize their own apprehensions of impairment to become effective change agents of the attitudes of people with and without disabilities.

## Disability Rights Movement and the Minority Group Model

Since the late 1960s, people with disabilities—along with friends, families, and professionals—have worked to change the dominant view, shared by bureaucrats and professionals, that chronic illness and disability should be equated with permanent sickness and helplessness and a global incapacity to handle ordinary life. This changed view of disability, although acknowledging the problems that physical limitation imposes, argues that the isolation and poverty often associated with disability can be attributed to institutions, practices, and physical environments that exclude full participation of disabled people in society. This new perspective has substantial implications for the organization of services provided to disabled people and for the social work profession.

As long as disability is understood as a problem requiring exclusively medical and rehabilitation services, the services are based on diagnosis. For example, professionals deliver services for people with multiple sclerosis, muscular dystrophy, cerebral palsy, and spinal cord injury without acknowledging that many difficulties faced by all individuals with mobility impairments stem from the architectural inaccessibility of buildings and transportation. Similarly, services for people with sensory, emotional, and cognitive impairments are often offered by private and public agencies serving only one subgroup of the disabled population. Despite the need for particular and specialized treatments and services based on types of impairment, the movement view contends that people with all kinds of disabilities—motor or sensory; cognitive, emotional, or physical; visible or invisible; acquired early in childhood or later in life—face similar experiences of stigma, isolation, rejection, and discrimination that require similar legal and political remedies.

The disability rights movement argues that, like many other minorities, people with disabilities are disadvantaged as much or more by discrimination as by their physical limitations (Gliedman & Roth, 1980; Hahn, 1983; Scotch, 1988). The movement aims to speak for the needs and rights of those with all types of impairments (Asch, 1986). Also included within the scope of the disability rights movement are people who experience disability-related discrimination because they have a history of chronic disease or impairment or are perceived to be impaired or disabled. This movement has won a partial victory in changing society's perception of disability by the passage of major civil rights legislation in the Americans with Disabilities Act of 1990. This act mandates that society end discrimination in employment, public services, and public accommodations for people with impairments that substantially limit one or more daily life activities, who have a record of such impairments, or who are regarded by others as having such impairments.

## Demography of Disability

Because different government agencies and programs define disability in different ways, the estimates of the number of disabled people in the population also differ. The 1990 U.S. census estimated that 22.4 million people in the United States age 16 and older have a disability—that is, a work disability, a mobility limitation, or a self-care limitation (McNeil, 1993). Data from the 1990 National Health Interview Survey (NHIS) of people living in U.S. households suggested that there are about 33.8 million people with disabilities that impose major limitations on activities or limited an important activity (LaPlante, 1992). If the estimated 2.3 million people with disabilities who are living in institutions were included, the total number of people with disabilities reported by the NHIS would increase to 36.1 million, or approximately 14.5 percent of the U.S. population (LaPlante, 1992).

The 1990–1991 Survey of Income and Program Participation (SIPP) estimated that there are 50 million people with disabilities in the United States, based on respondents' answers to a series of questions about impairments and activity limitation (McNeil, 1993). Perhaps the best-known estimate of the size of the U.S. disabled population is the figure of 43 million cited in the Americans with Disabilities Act of 1990. Tables 1, 2, and 3 display the distribution of disability within various

TABLE 1

**Demographic Characteristics of People with Disabilities**

| Characteristic | % with a disability (NHIS) | % with a disability (SIPP) |
|---|---|---|
| Gender | | |
| Male | 13.7 | 18.7 |
| Female | 14.4 | 20.2 |
| Race | | |
| White | 14.2 | 19.7 |
| Black | 14.9 | 20.0 |
| Other (including unknown) | 8.3 | — |
| Native American, Eskimo, Aleut | — | 21.9 |
| Asian or Pacific Islander | — | 9.9 |
| Hispanic | — | 15.3 |

SOURCE: NHIS data: LaPlante, M. P., Rice, D. P., & Kraus, L. E. (1991). People with activity limitation in the U.S. *Disability Statistics Abstract No. 2*. San Francisco: Disability Statistics Program, University of California. SIPP data: McNeil, J. (1993, June). Census Bureau data on persons with disabilities: New results and old questions about validity and reliability. Presented at the annual meeting of the Society for Disability Studies, Seattle, WA.

NOTE: NHIS = National Health Interview Survey, 1989; SIPP = Survey of Income and Program Participation, 1990/1991. — = data not collected using this category.

TABLE 2

**Age and Income of People with Disabilities, 1989**

| | % with a disability |
|---|---|
| Age | |
| Under 18 | 5.3 |
| 18–44 | 9.0 |
| 45–64 | 22.2 |
| 65–69 | 36.9 |
| 70 and older | 39.0 |
| Household income | |
| Under $10,000 | 26.8 |
| $10,000–19,999 | 19.4 |
| $20,000–34,999 | 11.9 |
| $35,000 or more | 8.2 |

SOURCE: LaPlante, M. P., Rice, D. P., & Kraus, L. E. (1991). People with activity limitation in the U.S. *Disability Statistics Abstract No. 2*. San Francisco: Disability Statistics Program, University of California.

subgroups of the population using data from the NHIS and the SIPP.

Data consistently show that disability is more prevalent among people with low levels of income and education and among those who are not married. This distribution can be partly accounted for by the fact that disability may limit or preclude higher levels of education and the employment opportunities associated with higher income. Unmarried women with disabilities have a high probability of living in poverty (Mudrick, 1988). African Americans have a consistently higher prevalence of disability than do other racial groups in the United States, although this gap appears to be diminishing (Pope & Tarlov, 1991). The probability of disability increases with age, with a noticeable increase in prevalence after age 50. The most prevalent disabling impairments are orthopedic impairments, arthritis, and heart disease, all of which are associated with an onset in midlife or later (Table 4).

Finally, it is not uncommon for an individual to experience more than one impairment. For example, people with cerebral palsy may experience motor, sensory, and cognitive impairments. An additional risk faced by people with a disability is the onset of a secondary disability as a consequence of or related to the primary condition (Pope & Tarlov, 1991). For example, individuals who have paralysis in their lower extremities and require the use of wheelchairs may develop pressure sores.

## SERVICE SYSTEM

Although social workers are likely to meet disabled people as clients and colleagues in any setting, many social workers are employed in the specialized system of for-profit, nonprofit, and public programs intended to serve people with disabilities. In this specialized system they perform multiple roles. As direct service providers, social workers are clinicians, facilitators, educators, advocates, and members of the rehabilitation team, both in hospitals and in community agencies. Direct services may include problem-oriented interaction with individuals with disabilities or with the entire family (Romano, 1981). Social workers also engage in therapy groups, social support groups, case management, and assessment and referral. In addition, social workers in the disability service system also develop programs, administer agencies or parts of agencies, evaluate programs, and design other outcome research.

TABLE 3

**Percentage of People in the Labor Force with and without Disabilities and Employed Full-Time by Race and Gender, 1988**

| | White | | Black | | Hispanic Origin (any race) | |
|---|---|---|---|---|---|---|
| Gender and disability status | % in labor force | % employed full-time | % in labor force | % employed full-time | % in labor force | % employed full-time |
| Males, age 16–64 | | | | | | |
| With no work disability | 89.9 | 76.7 | 83.1 | 62.7 | 89.2 | 72.0 |
| With a work disability | 38.9 | 26.2 | 20.6 | 10.8 | 28.2 | 13.9 |
| Females, age 16–64 | | | | | | |
| With no work disability | 69.5 | 46.8 | 70.9 | 50.0 | 59.1 | 40.1 |
| With a work disability | 28.9 | 14.3 | 22.7 | 8.2 | 17.8 | 9.7 |

SOURCE: McNeil, J. M., Franklin, P. A., & Mars, L. I. (1991). Work status, earnings, and rehabilitation of persons with disabilities. In S. Thompson-Hoffman & I. F. Storck (Eds.), *Disability in the United States: A portrait from national data*. New York: Springer. Data from the 1988 Current Population Survey.

TABLE 4

**Twelve Most Prevalent Impairments Causing Activity Limitation, 1990**

| Main cause of limitation | Number of people (in thousands) | % of people limited in activity |
|---|---|---|
| Orthopedic impairments | 5,873 | 17.4 |
| Arthritis | 4,010 | 11.9 |
| Heart disease | 3,430 | 10.2 |
| Intervertebral disk disorders | 1,762 | 5.2 |
| Asthma | 1,710 | 5.1 |
| Nervous disorders | 1,560 | 4.6 |
| Mental disorders | 1,525 | 4.5 |
| Visual impairments | 1,347 | 4.0 |
| Diabetes | 1,069 | 3.2 |
| Hypertension | 837 | 2.5 |
| Cerebrovascular disease | 679 | 2.0 |

SOURCE: LaPlante, M. P. (1992). How many Americans have a disability? *Disability Statistics Abstract No. 5*. San Francisco: Disability Statistics Program, University of California.

In some service settings disability should be viewed simply as one characteristic among a client's many characteristics, much as sex or race are viewed, and should not be the focus of the service. In other settings the impairment—alcoholism, paralysis, or acquired immune deficiency syndrome (AIDS)—may be the primary reason the client has requested help. Social workers must learn to distinguish between situations in which disability is and is not a client's or a family's principal concern. Because people with disabilities seek social services for situations not specific to issues presented by their impairments, a generalist approach to social work practice is most applicable. Regardless of the setting in which they work with disabled clients or their families, however, social workers should stay alert for instances in which appropriate service includes empowering clients to use civil rights laws or engage in social change activities.

Disabled people have been the subject of legislation in three areas: rehabilitation and education, income support, and civil rights. Consequently, at some times in their lives, they are likely to become involved with the specialized systems that assist with these activities. The two older service systems (that is, rehabilitation and education and income support) typically are restricted to the portion of the population designated as disabled; individuals seeking civil rights protection are served by that set of agencies created to handle all types of civil rights violations.

**Rehabilitation Services and Education**

Since the colonial era in the United States, there have been public policies aimed at assisting people with disabilities. During the colonial era and into the early 19th century, public policies were state and local in origin and focused on providing shelter, primarily at almshouses, to people with disabilities. Starting in the 1830s and continuing throughout the 19th century, institutions were built and administered under state or county auspices to care for people with disabilities. These institutions, called insane asylums, principally housed people with mental illness and mental retardation, although people with other disabilities were also served. Inmates were often involuntarily committed to these public institutions by the state or county or by relatives.

***Employment services.*** Publicly delivered or financed services aimed at people with disabilities who were living in their own homes were first authorized at the federal level for veterans as part of the post–World War I Vocational Rehabilitation Act of 1920. This legislation resulted in the development of a system of state and federal agencies that provide counseling and other services to people with disabilities to enable their employment. Consistently passed and broadened by Congress since 1920, the act underwent significant change when Congress reauthorized it in 1973 and added a civil rights provision. As reauthorized in 1992, the services financed under the Rehabilitation Act are aimed at individuals with the most severe disabilities. In addition to providing funds for the traditional rehabilitation areas of job counseling, retraining, and prosthetic and other assistive devices, the legislation authorizes funding for "supported employment"—a service model in which a person with a severe disability works in a private-sector job with a "job coach" who eases the transition to independent employment. The Rehabilitation Act also funds Independent Living Centers, community agencies typically staffed by people with disabilities, who use peer counseling and advocacy to assist others to live on their own.

***Public education.*** U.S. legislation in the area of disability and public education dates from the Education of the Handicapped Act of 1975. This law, reauthorized in 1990 and named the Individuals with Disabilities Education Act, states that children with disabilities are entitled to public elementary and secondary education and requires children and adults with disabilities to be educated in the least restrictive environment, based on an individualized education program. As a result of this law, an increasing number of children with disabilities are being educated in public schools and "mainstreamed" into regular classrooms to the greatest extent possible.

***Psychiatric disabilities.*** Legislation and services for people with psychiatric disabilities traditionally have been separated from those for people with physical disabilities, despite evidence that those with psychiatric impairments also experience difficulties in functioning at home and at work and confront stigma and discrimination in employment, housing, and other areas. The service system for people with psychiatric impairments consists of both inpatient and outpatient treatment and rehabilitation.

As the nation has closed down its large residential institutions for people with mental illness and mental retardation, inpatient services for people with psychiatric impairments have shifted to short-term hospitalization and supervised group homes in community settings. Outpatient psychiatric care and day treatment programs are also used by people with psychiatric disabilities who live in the community but are unable to sustain employment or who otherwise require supervised activities or specialized treatment during the day.

***Social work roles.*** Social workers engage in a wide variety of roles within the service system that are targeted at problems associated with disability. In hospitals and rehabilitation centers, social workers are among the professionals on the medical and rehabilitation team. In this role they usually function as a source of assessment and referral to arrange discharge and community supports. Mudrick and Devore (1993) presented a case study of the many complex roles and activities that social workers may play with newly disabled people and their families. Through their role in employee assistance programs, social workers may help integrate or reintegrate disabled employees into the workplace. In a relatively new role, social workers may also serve as case managers for the disability management of workers with disabilities of recent onset, regardless of whether the disabilities result from work injuries or chronic illness.

Social workers are also playing an increasingly prominent role in employee assistance programs in the assessment, referral, and treatment of individuals for alcohol and drug abuse. In school settings, social workers are key members of the team that develops and implements the individualized education programs required for every child who receives any form of special education services. Finally, social workers are common among the staffs of psychiatric hospitals, outpatient mental health counseling centers, agencies for transitional living services, and residential settings for children with psychiatric disabilities. In these settings the activities of social workers typically include counseling (as primary therapists or as members of mental health teams), assessment and referral, and advocacy.

**Income Support**

Legislation providing for income support to people with disabilities living in their own homes was enacted in the 20th century. Income support is provided both as social insurance and as public assistance. Those with substantial labor force attachment derive income support through social insurance. If the disability resulted from a work-related injury or illness, a social insurance benefit is payable through a state workers' compensation insurance program. The social security Disability Insurance (DI) program provides long-term income support to workers whose disabilities prevent employment, regardless of the cause of their disabilities. Income support for low-income people with disabilities with little or no labor force experience is available through an income-tested public assistance program, Supplemental Security Income (SSI). In general, the social insurance benefits are greater than those from public assistance. Thus, there is a dual system of income support for people with disabilities based on work attachment.

***Disability Insurance.*** People who have contributed to the social security trust funds while employed are eligible for support under the DI program if their disability prevents their continued employment before the age of eligibility for social security retirement. DI claimants must meet the medical disability criteria, must be unable to engage in "substantial gainful activity," and must have worked in social security-covered employment for a specified number of quarters before the onset of their disabilities; the disabilities do not have to be the result of work injuries.

The size of the DI benefit is determined by the level of previous earnings, using a variant of the social security retirement benefit formula. Because DI is a social insurance program rather than a public assistance entitlement program, assets and the earnings of other household members do not influence eligibility for or the amount of the DI benefits. Benefits can be increased up to a specified amount if the beneficiary has dependents. Medicare coverage is available to DI beneficiaries after they have received benefits for two years. Beneficiaries are periodically reassessed to determine whether they have recovered from their disabilities and can return to paid employment. Some beneficiaries are referred to state rehabilitation agencies to facilitate job reentry, and failure to comply with the referral can result in the termination of benefits.

***Workers' compensation.*** Workers' compensation benefits are intended to replace lost earning capacity that results from an injury on the job. People with permanent disabilities arising from work injuries may receive a lump sum or a monthly payment in perpetuity from workers' compensation. Workers' compensation is not a federal program; laws in every state require employers to purchase workers' compensation insurance to cover the claims made by injured workers. Veterans with service-connected disabilities are eligible for a non–income-tested veterans' compensation benefit that is based on the severity of their disabilities.

***Supplemental Security Income.*** The major source of income support for low-income people with disabilities is the SSI program. The definition of disability that SSI uses for adults is similar to that used by DI; however, children with disabilities are also eligible. The disability criteria used for children are based on the limitations that their disabilities impose in the context of the developmental tasks of growing children.

SSI is an income-tested program that includes a limit on assets and is operated at the federal level by the Social Security Administration. Benefits are paid to eligible individuals and couples and are scaled to income. SSI beneficiaries are immediately eligible for Medicaid coverage for health care costs. SSI is financed from general revenues, and states can supplement the federal SSI benefit if they wish. In 1994, 44 states provided optional supplementation to the basic federal SSI benefit (Social Security Administration, 1994). Low-income veterans with non–service-related disabilities also are eligible for income support through the income-tested veterans' pension program.

***Service providers.*** Service providers in the income transfer system that serves individuals with disabilities are primarily the government agencies that process payments and the private insurance companies that offer workers' compensation insurance. If rehabilitation services are deemed appropriate, the individual is referred to the rehabilitation and medical services system, although the services may be funded by workers' compensation or by DI. Although social workers often work with people who receive income support payments because of disabilities, they are not the primary personnel involved in the administration and provision of income support. Social workers do alert clients with disabilities to their potential eligibility for income support and may function as advocates or offer expert opinions regarding the impact of disability in the application process.

## Civil Rights

### History

The first acknowledgment that the civil rights of people with disabilities needed the protection of federal law came in 1968 with the Architectural Barriers Act, which set standards to ensure that buildings constructed with federal funds or leased by the federal government were accessible to people with disabilities. Viewed as even more significant is Title V of the 1973 Rehabilitation Act, which prohibited recipients of federal funds from discriminating in employment, education, or services. Since the passage of this legislation, other federal legislation has expanded the sectors of protection to prohibit discrimination by both the private and the public sector in the areas of employment, education, air travel, ground transportation, public accommodations, public services, and telecommunications (Table 5).

In addition, states either have added disability to the categories covered by their human rights statutes or have passed new legislation protecting the rights of people with disabilities. State laws often cover discrimination in housing, public accommodations, credit, education, and employment. By 1990 nearly every state had a civil rights law that prohibited, to varying degrees, discrimination on the basis of disability.

### Americans with Disabilities Act

With the passage of the Americans with Disabilities Act of 1990 (ADA), people with disabilities won protection against discrimination comparable to that afforded by Title VII of the Civil Rights Act of 1964 for race, sex, national origin, and religion.

***Definitions.*** The ADA defines people with disabilities as those with physical or mental impairments that affect major life activities, those with a record of such conditions, or those who are perceived as having such disabilities. This definition encompasses people with visible conditions, such as paralysis, and invisible conditions, such as epilepsy, psychiatric illnesses, diabetes, and AIDS. It also includes those who have recovered from a disability, such as people with a history of treatment for alcoholism or mental illness, and those who experience discrimination based on an erroneous belief that they have a disability. Thus, people with current psychiatric impairments, as well as those with a history of such impairments, are protected from discrimination in employment as long as they can perform the essential functions of the job. People with psychiatric disabilities or a history of psychiatric disabilities are also protected against discrimination in public accommodations and services under the ADA.

***Employment provisions.*** The ADA made it illegal for an employer of 15 or more employees to discriminate against a person with a disability in hiring, termination, compensation, benefits, or terms and conditions of employment. Employers must make reasonable accommodation to the needs of qualified people with disabilities who can perform the essential functions of their jobs unless they can show that making such an accommodation would impose an undue burden (that is, would be extremely expensive, given the size of the firm, or would require the elimination of essential functions) or that the performance of the job would create a hazard to other people. The employment provisions of ADA are enforced by the federal Equal Employment Opportunity Commission.

***Services.*** The act also outlaws discrimination in the manner in which public agencies or private

TABLE 5
**Civil Rights Protections for People with Disabilities**

| Title of legislation | General provisions |
|---|---|
| P.L. 90-480, Architectural Barriers Act of 1968 | Sets standards requiring that buildings owned or leased by the federal government or built with federal funds be accessible to and safe for people with disabilities. |
| P.L. 93-112, Rehabilitation Act of 1973 | Prohibits employment discrimination on the basis of disability by federal contractors and grantees. |
| P.L. 94-142, Education for All Handicapped Children Act of 1975 | Establishes that children with disabilities are entitled to an appropriate elementary and secondary education. |
| P.L. 99-435, Air Carrier Access Act of 1986 | Prohibits airlines from discriminating against air travelers on the basis of disability. |
| P.L. 101-336, Americans with Disabilities Act of 1990 | Prohibits discrimination in employment, public accommodation, public services, telecommunications, and transportation on the basis of disability by public and private sector employers, businesses, and service providers. |

businesses that serve the public provide their services to the disabled population.

Other sections of the ADA require that private businesses, public agencies, and transportation systems that serve the public must be accessible and nondiscriminatory toward people with disabilities. These organizations must make readily achievable modifications to ensure that people with disabilities can, for example, use their services, shop on their premises, dine at their tables, or sit in their audiences. The U.S. Department of Justice enforces these sections of the ADA.

### Social Work Role

Social workers in the civil rights system serve primarily as advocates, educators, and facilitators. Some social workers are employed in civil rights enforcement, and others work in human resources. However, a more common role for social workers is to engage in advocacy for the rights of their clients with regard to education, employment, housing, and insurance. In work related to this role, social workers may engage in activities to apprise clients of their rights and to facilitate the enjoyment of those rights. The ADA public accommodation requirements explicitly name social services agencies among those organizations whose facilities must be accessible to people with disabilities. Social work agencies may not discriminate against and must be accessible to serve people with disabilities.

## Challenging Issues

Although the rights of people with disabilities have greater protection than ever before and the system of services is more responsive to the wishes and needs of people with disabilities, some important policy issues remain unresolved.

### Health Insurance

High on this list is the provision of health insurance. A large percentage of people with disabilities have no health insurance coverage (Griss, 1988). Among those who do have insurance, the condition that is the source of disability is often excluded from coverage as a preexisting condition. The cost of insurance for people with disabilities is often extremely high, especially when the expenditures for deductibles and coinsurance are also considered. In addition, health insurance often covers only the costs of acute care; the expenditures necessary for the maintenance of functioning with a chronic condition (especially assistive devices that are not viewed as medical but are essential to daily functioning) are often not covered. The structure of both the public and the private health care insurance systems pushes people who require assistance with activities of daily living into nursing homes, because attendant services for people not in institutions are generally not reimbursable.

### Work Disincentives

A second policy issue involves work disincentives that are inherent in the regulations of the income support programs for people with disabilities. DI beneficiaries establish their eligibility, in part, by withdrawing from the labor force. Unlike the social security retirement program (Old-Age and Survivors Insurance), which reduces benefits as claimants' earnings rise, DI beneficiaries lose all benefits once they have earned in excess of approximately $500 per month for a nine-month period. Thus, DI discourages people with disabilities from working to the greatest extent that they can (part-time, for example), unless they are sure they can earn an amount greater than their DI benefit. The SSI program does have a work provision, although it affects far fewer people than does the social security DI program as SSI beneficiaries are generally individuals who have never been able to work.

### Self-Determination and Safety

The increasing focus on the rights of people with disabilities has stimulated discussions of the boundary between the individual's right to self-determination and public obligations for ensuring safety. This issue is especially evident when an individual with a psychiatric disability wishes to live on the street and the state is concerned that this choice may result in harm to the person with the disability (for example, freezing to death in winter) or to others. This issue is also evident in the discussions about whether a person with AIDS can be denied employment in particular situations because of the risk of transmitting the disease to others or contracting a fatal infection in the workplace. The debate also surfaces when an employer wishes to exclude a worker from a job because of a back condition that is not disabling but that the employer fears may make the worker more susceptible to a severe back injury, even though the worker is able to and wants to perform the work.

### Value of Life with a Disability

With the premise that life with a disability can be as worthwhile as life without a disability and that those with disabilities should be entitled to means that enable them to participate in society, people with disabilities have spoken out when the value of disabled life has been questioned (Asch, 1989; *Disability Rag*, 1994; Disability Rights Coordinating Council, 1983). Disability rights groups have argued against abortion after prenatal diagnoses of disabilities, genetic testing, physician-assisted suicide, and denial of health care to people with disabilities whose families seek to halt treatment.

Many medical professionals take the view that disability leads inevitably to a life that burdens families and society and that gives the disabled person little satisfaction. If society, the helping professions, and the general public were truly to embrace the idea that it is acceptable to be disabled, then people might concentrate on reducing the barriers to life with disability, not on shortening or preventing the lives of those who are disabled.

As the United States and other Western countries increasingly struggle with problems of allocating scarce resources, there will probably be increasing controversy about how much should go toward improving life for disabled people and how much should go toward encouraging abortion of fetuses with disabilities or to assisting suicides of adults with quadriplegia, Alzheimer's disease, Huntington's disease, or other severe impairments. Although these questions may at first appear to be medical decisions or the province of individuals and families only, those in the disability rights movement believe that such life-and-death decisions involve fundamental civil rights.

Social workers may be called on to help families think through these critical decisions. Doing so will require social workers to both understand and respect the perhaps divergent desires and beliefs of family members and to be skilled in helping individuals communicate about especially sensitive and painful issues. Finally, social workers who serve people with disabilities will be called on to work with those who are not disabled—individuals, groups, and organizations in the society at large—to reduce the disabling impact of social and physical environments and to increase understanding and respect for the lives of people with disabilities.

## References


Americans with Disabilities Act of 1990. P.L. 101-336, 104 Stat. 327.

Antonak, R., & Livneh, H. (1988). *The measurement of attitudes toward people with disabilities: Methods, psychometrics, and scales*. Springfield, IL: Charles C Thomas.

Architectural Barriers Act of 1968. P.L. 90-480, 82 Stat. 718.

Asch, A. (1986). Will populism empower disabled people? In H. Boyte & F. Riessman (Eds.), *The new populism: The politics of empowerment* (pp. 213–228). Philadelphia: Temple University Press.

Asch, A. (1989). Reproductive technology and disability. In S. Cohen & N. Taub (Eds.), *Reproductive laws for the 1990s* (pp. 69–124). Clifton, NJ: Humana Press.

Asch, A., & Rousso, H. (1985). Therapists with disabilities: Theoretical and clinical issues. *Psychiatry, 48*, 1–12.

Civil Rights Act of 1964. P.L. 88-352, 78 Stat. 241.

*Disability Rag and ReSource.* (1994, January–February). [Entire issue].

Disability Rights Coordinating Council. (1983). *Elizabeth Bouvia vs. County of Riverside (Declaration of Carol Gill).* Los Angeles: Author.

Education of the Handicapped Act of 1975. P.L. 94-142, 89 Stat. 773-795.

Fine, M., & Asch, A. (1988). Disability beyond stigma: Social interaction, discrimination, and activism. *Journal of Social Issues, 44*(1), 3–21.

Gliedman, J., & Roth, W. (1980). *The unexpected minority: Handicapped children in America*. New York: Harcourt, Brace, Jovanovich.

Goffman, E. (1963). *Stigma: Notes on the management of spoiled identity*. Englewood Cliffs, NJ: Prentice Hall.

Griss, B. (1988). Measuring the health insurance needs of persons with disabilities and persons with chronic illness. *Access to Health Care* (Vol. 1, Nos. 1 and 2). Washington, DC: World Institute on Disability.

Hahn, H. (1983, March–April). Paternalism and public policy, *Society, 20*(3), 36–44.

Individuals with Disabilities Education Act of 1990. P.L. 101-476, 104 Stat. 1142.

LaPlante, M. P. (1992). How many Americans have a disability? In *Disability Statistics Abstract No. 5*. San Francisco: Disability Statistics Program, University of California.

LaPlante, M. P., Rice, D. P., & Kraus, L. E. (1991). People with activity limitation in the U.S. In *Disability Statistics Abstract No. 2*. San Francisco: Disability Statistics Program, University of California.

Louis Harris & Associates. (1986). *The ICD survey of disabled Americans: Bringing disabled Americans into the mainstream*. New York: International Center for the Disabled.

McNeil, J. (1993, June). *Census Bureau data on persons with disabilities: New results and old questions about validity and reliability.* Paper presented at the annual meeting of the Society for Disability Studies, Seattle.

McNeil, J. M., Franklin, P. A., & Mars, L. I. (1991). Work status, earnings, and rehabilitation of persons with disabilities. In S. Thompson-Hoffman & I. F. Storck (Eds.), *Disability in the United States: A portrait from national data* (pp. 133–160). New York: Springer.

Mudrick, N. R. (1988). Disabled women and public policies for income support. In M. Fine & A. Asch (Eds.), *Women with disabilities: Essays in psychology, culture, and politics* (pp. 245–268). Philadelphia: Temple University Press.

Mudrick, N. R., & Devore, W. (1993). Michael Grimes. In E. Tomaszewski (Ed.), *Disabilities awareness curriculum for graduate schools of social work* (pp. 128–137). Washington, DC: National Association of Social Workers, National Center for Social Policy and Practice.

Parsons, T. (1951). *The social system.* New York: Free Press.

Pope, A. M., & Tarlov, A. R. (1991). *Disability in America: Toward a national agenda for prevention*. Washington, DC: National Academy Press.

Rehabilitation Act of 1973. P.L. 93-112, 87 Stat. 355.

Romano, M. D. (1981). Social worker's role in rehabilitation: A review of the literature. In J. A. Browne, B. A. Kirlin, & S. Watt (Eds.), *Rehabilitation services and the social work role: Challenge for change* (pp. 13–21). Baltimore: Williams & Wilkins.

Schultz, R., & Decker, S. (1985). Long-term adjustment to physical disability: The role of social support, perceived control, and self-blame. *Journal of Personality and Social Psychology, 48,* 1162–1172.

Scotch, R. (1988). Disability as the basis for a social movement: Politics and the advocacy of definition. *Journal of Social Issues, 44*(1), 173–188.

Social Security Administration, Office of Supplemental Security Income. (1994). *State assistance programs for SSI recipients* (SSA Publication No. 17-002, Appendix C). Baltimore: Author.

Vocational Rehabilitation Act of 1920. Ch. 219, 41 Stat. 735.

Wright, B. A. (1988). Attitudes and the fundamental negative bias: Conditions and corrections. In H. E. Yuker (Ed.), *Attitudes toward persons with disabilities* (pp. 3–21). New York: Springer.

### Further Reading

Brickner, R. P. (1976). *My second twenty years: An unexpected life*. New York: Basic Books.

Ferguson, P., Ferguson, D., & Taylor, S. (Eds.). (1992). *Interpreting disability: A qualitative reader*. New York: Teachers College Press.

Gartner, A., & Joe, T. (Eds.). (1987). *Images of the disabled, disabling images*. New York: Praeger.

Nagler, M. (Ed.). (1993). *Perspectives on disability: Text and readings* (2nd ed.). Palo Alto, CA: Health Markets Research.

Scotch, R. (1984). *From good will to civil rights: Transforming federal disability policy*. Philadelphia: Temple University Press.

Watson, S. D. (1994). *Maximizing the effectiveness of social services reform: People with disabilities in AFDC, children and family services, and child care.* (Available from Center for the Study of Social Policy, 1250 Eye St., NW, Suite 503, Washington, DC 20005)

**Adrienne Asch, PhD, LICSW,** is Henry R. Luce Professor of Biology, Ethics, and the Politics of Human Reproduction, Wellesley College, Wellesley, MA 02181. **Nancy R. Mudrick, PhD,** is professor, Syracuse University, School of Social Work, Syracuse, NY 13244.

In memory of Irving Zola for his unparalleled contribution to disability scholarship and disability rights.

### For further information see

Advocacy; Bioethical Issues; Case Management; Child Welfare Services; Civil Rights; Community Needs Assessment; Deaf Community; Deafness; Deinstitutionalization; Developmental Disabilities: Definitions and Policies; End-of-Life Decisions; Ethics and Values; Families Overview; Generalist and Advanced Generalist Practice; Hospice; Hospital Social Work; Income Security Overview; Information and Referral Services; Legal Issues: Low-Income and Dependent People; Long-Term Care; Managed Care; Mental Health Overview; Natural Helping Networks; Occupational Social Work; Patient Rights; Primary Prevention Overview; Social Security; Social Welfare Policy; Supplemental Security Income; Unemployment Compensation and Workers' Compensation; Veterans and Veterans Services; Visual Impairment.

**Key Words**

civil rights
disabilities
impairment
mental retardation

# Disasters and Disaster Aid

**Stephen A. Webster**

Few events stretch human capacity and challenge individuals and communities to adapt to rapidly changing environmental conditions like a major disaster. Disasters require people to cope with chaos and extend themselves and their resources to new limits. Worldwide disasters occur frequently, and our awareness of their consequences is increasing because they are regularly reported in the news.

Many definitions of disaster exist, including the following composite: a naturally caused or human-induced event, occurring without warning or developing over time, which strikes so severely that the affected community must respond with exceptional measures (Carter, 1992). Implicit in this definition are additional characteristics. A disaster typically results in

- significant disruption to normal living patterns, economic activities, communication systems, social customs, and overloaded decision-making capacity
- widespread human, material, and environmental losses usually resulting in death, injury, and damage to buildings and community infrastructure
- extraordinary needs for shelter, food, clothing, medical assistance, and other essential human care services.

## Hazards and Disaster Agents

It is important to distinguish between a disaster and a hazard or disaster agent. A *hazard* is a natural or humanmade phenomenon that *may* result in physical damage or economic losses or threaten human life and well-being if it occurs in a human settlement or an area of agricultural or industrial activity. A potentially hazardous event may and often does occur without resulting in a disaster. For example, an earthquake in an unpopulated area or in the middle of the ocean may be a spectacular natural phenomenon but have no deleterious human or environmental impact.

Natural hazards include geologic hazards such as earthquakes; volcanic eruptions; tsunamis (tidal waves caused by earthquakes or volcanic eruptions in the ocean); and landslides; climatic hazards, for example, severe windstorms including tropical cyclones (also known as typhoons and hurricanes) and tornados, floods, and drought; and biological hazards such as diseases and plagues that may produce epidemics. Human actions usually cause or exacerbate environmental hazards such as pollution, deforestation, desertification, pest infestation, and brush or wildfires. Human error is almost always the cause of chemical and industrial hazards leading to accidents such as the 1986 nuclear reactor meltdown in Chernobyl, Ukraine, and the 1984 chemical plant explosion in Bhopal, India; economic mismanagement; and war and civil strife (Wijkman & Timberlake, 1984).

*Compound disasters* occur when one type of hazard triggers a disaster, which in turn sparks another type of disaster. For example, a drought (hazard) may trigger a famine (disaster), which in turn results in civil conflict over water sources, consequently displacing masses of people (disaster). Recently, world attention has been drawn to another type of disaster: the *complex emergency.* Complex emergencies are a type of humanmade disaster characterized by civil conflict and the collapse of political and social systems in all or part of a country. In such a situation, providing assistance is extremely difficult and dangerous. Vulnerable populations and humanitarian responders may find themselves caught between the warring parties. Examples of complex emergencies are prevalent in Africa, where unstable political conditions in Ethiopia, Eritrea, The Sudan, Somalia, Angola, Liberia, and Rwanda have resulted in widespread human suffering. Conditions in the former Yugoslavia and the former Soviet Union, especially in the Caucasus, have also resulted in complex emergencies and profound human suffering. *Migration emergencies* arise when natural and humanmade hazards force people to flee an area or displace people; these emergencies demand extraordinary humanitarian aid.

## Vulnerability

For a hazardous event to result in a disaster, people, buildings, and community activities must be vulnerable. *Vulnerability,* or the overall potential risk of loss of life and property, is highly relative. In any society, certain groups are likely to be more vulnerable than others. For example, poor people are almost always most vulnerable. Poverty forces people to build and live in unsafe structures on marginal or unsafe land such as floodplains or hillsides subject to landslides. Disaster impact analysis suggests that the wealthiest of the population either survive the disaster unaffected or are able to recover quickly (Blaike, Cannon, Davis, & Wisner, 1994).

In addition to poverty, other factors also contribute to vulnerability. Rapid urbanization, especially in developing countries, often results in crowding on unsafe sites. Well-intended development programs also may contribute to vulnerability. The introduction of a new type of livestock may result in overgrazing, which in turn increases the rate of desertification. A road building project may result in deforestation, leading to increased vulnerability to floods or landslides. Societies are also more or less vulnerable. Although communities in developed countries may be just as prone to a hazard as communities in poorer nations, the wealthier nations are less vulnerable because they can afford to invest in preparedness and mitigation activities.

## Impact of Disasters

History records the devastating impact disasters have had on human settlements. Any listing of major disasters would certainly include events over thousands of years. In recent history, on three separate occasions—the tropical cyclone that struck Bangladesh in 1970; the earthquake in Tangshan, China, in 1976; and the drought and famine in the Sudan in 1988—more than 250,000 people were killed. It is conservatively estimated that in the past 50 years, more than 2 million people have been killed by disasters (not including in war and civil strife). Most of the deaths have occurred in poor countries of Africa, Asia, Latin America, and Oceania. In comparison, in the developed countries of North America, Europe, Japan, and Australia, annual death tolls from disasters rarely exceed a few hundred people (Bernstein & Thompson, 1989; Reed, 1992).

Mortality statistics provide an important measure of the impact of disasters. However, in addition to death and injury, disasters destroy economies and create widespread unemployment, homelessness, and human suffering. Hurricane David in 1979 left 600,000 people homeless in Dominica and the Dominican Republic. More than 300,000 were left homeless by the 1972 earthquake in Managua, Nicaragua. There is no comprehensive compilation of total economic losses globally from disasters, but in any given year losses will be in the billions of dollars. A single disaster may devastate a small country's economy. For instance, Hurricane Allen in 1980 destroyed 90 percent of St. Lucia's banana crop and caused total losses equivalent to 89 percent of the country's gross national product. The 1985 earthquake in Mexico City caused economic losses estimated at 3.5 percent of Mexico's gross national product. Loss statistics also have failed to account for the shifting of resources from development to relief. When resources are allocated for disaster relief, fewer funds are available to build schools or health clinics. The costs of missed opportunities that result from disasters may actually outstrip the actual direct losses (Bernstein & Thompson, 1989; Reed, 1992).

## Disaster Management Cycle

An analysis of the occurrence of these various events indicates that disasters, particularly those caused by natural hazards, are recurring phenomena. It is impossible to predict precisely when a disaster will occur. However, it is possible to determine that a particular community is prone to a particular type of hazard and has a definable probability that during a given period a major event will occur. Hazards are often characterized by their probabilities. For example, a 100-year flood has a 1 percent chance of occurring in any one year (Blaike et al., 1994; Bull, 1992; Stephenson, 1991; Thompson, 1992).

As knowledge of disasters has increased, it has become apparent that communities can plan for disasters. Through various programs and activities, communities may actually decrease the likelihood that a disaster will occur or reduce the consequences of a disaster, even if it proves not to be preventable. Recognition that losses from recurring disasters can be minimized has led to a conceptualization of a disaster management cycle (Blaike et al., 1994; Thompson, 1992).

### Preparedness Plans

Recurring disasters have definable phases of activities either responding to a recent disaster or preparing for the next one (Figure 1). Figure 1 is heuristic; in practice, the phases are not so easily distinguishable and usually overlap. The preparedness stage consists of activities that minimize both loss of life and damage. Activities include public education; training programs and evacuation drills; early warning systems; contingency plans; and standing plans of action for rescue, relief, and rehabilitation. These activities, which ensure a rapid and coordinated response, make possible the evacuation of people and their personal property from threatened areas. Preparedness plans are especially important with disasters for which people typically have advance warning, such as drought, tropical cyclones, and certain types of floods. Sophisticated meteorological assessment and monitoring systems instituted in the past 10 years have demonstrated the ability to provide sufficient warning to dramatically reduce deaths and injuries (Kent, 1994; Reed, 1992).

### Response Plans

The response phase involves search and rescue, evacuation, provision of emergency food and shelter, medical assistance, crisis counseling, and assessment. The response phase is time limited, usually lasting no more than two to three weeks in rapid-onset disasters (such as earthquakes, tsunamis, and cyclones) or several months for slow-onset disasters (such as drought and environmental degradation). Assessment is a critical, often overlooked, and frequently poorly executed activity of the response phase. Without proper assessment and communication of needs, considerable unnecessary aid is likely. Unsolicited inappropriate aid is often rendered by concerned individuals and organizations to disaster victims. Aid should encourage development objectives rather than increase the dependence of survivors (Cuny, 1983). Aid in the form of free food, given when farmers in disaster-struck areas have food to sell on the market, may actually impede recovery and will do nothing to support the stabilization of the community's economy.

### Recovery Plans

Recovery activities may last for many years following a disaster. In its initial phase, recovery focuses on rehabilitation of essential infrastructure: utilities, hospitals, and other lifeline services. Given sufficient will and resources, a community will begin reconstruction in an attempt to attain the previous level of community functioning or in some cases even improve community functioning (Stephenson, 1991; Thompson, 1992).

### Mitigation

Mitigation encompasses all activities and programs designed to reduce long-term risk that are

FIGURE 1
Stages in Preparation of or in Response to Recurring Disasters

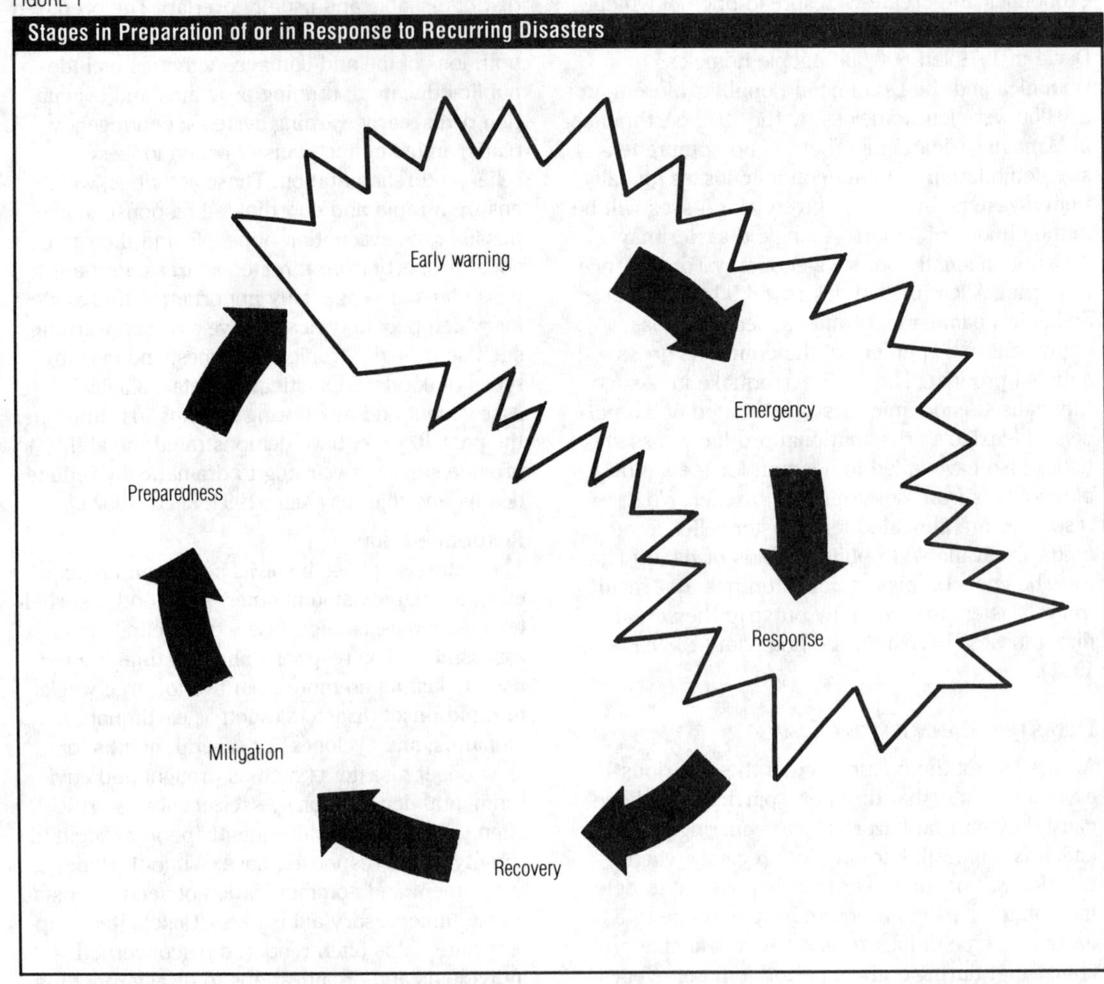


carried out before a disaster occurs and during the recovery stage. Examples of effective mitigation include relocating people from an earthquake fault zone or floodplain; strengthening building codes; improving construction practices; and building a dam, levee, sea wall, or flood catchment basin.

The recurring nature of disasters has proven especially vexing for developing countries. During any given period, millions of dollars invested in development projects are lost because of the destructive forces of disasters. As a result major bilateral donors, the United Nations, nongovernmental organizations, and governments of disaster-prone countries are increasingly targeting interventions in those disaster management cycle phases that reduce the likelihood disasters will occur or reduce the negative consequences should a disaster occur. Therefore, an increased focus has resulted in promoting preparedness and mitigation activities with the expectation that investments made in these areas will, over time, reduce the need for relief (Blaike et al., 1994; Thompson, 1992).

Efforts to promote mitigation are constrained by policymakers' perceptions of risk. If there is a high probability that a similar disaster is unlikely to recur for 20 to 50 years, government authorities may have difficulty justifying major expenditures on mitigation. However, if a river floods a community every three to five years, authorities may more easily justify mitigation expenditures. Given limited resources, government authorities may be reluctant to spend for long-term mitigation because the benefit of expenditures may not be evident for many years. Mitigation is also constrained by cultural attitudes; some cultures reject disaster prevention strategies as interfering with a divine plan (Blaike et al., 1994; Bull, 1994; Thompson, 1992).

## Disaster Responders

The first responders to any disasters are the survivors. In earthquakes, for example, the vast majority of search and rescue efforts are completed by relatives and neighbors. The people offering these mutual aid activities typically include persons from neighboring communities that have escaped the brunt of a disaster (Stephenson, 1992).

To the extent they are capable, local, state, provincial, and national governments provide another source of disaster response services. Most countries that are prone to disasters have created ministries and councils on disasters. These may be units within existing line ministries, dedicated ministries, or coordinating mechanisms within the office of the country's chief executive, that is, the president or prime minister. Most countries also have national Red Cross or Red Crescent societies with disaster-related mandates (Aysan, Clayton, & Davis, 1993; Carter, 1992). In addition, international nongovernmental organizations are an increasingly important source of response services. Many such organizations, including CARE (Cooperative for American Relief Everywhere, Inc.), Save the Children, Medecines Sans Frontiers, OXFAM (Oxford Committee on Famine), and the International Committee of the Red Cross dispatch a relief team to an affected area within days of a disaster.

United Nations agencies have strengthened their role in disaster management. In 1971, the United Nations created a special unit within the secretary general's office to coordinate disaster management efforts. The United Nations General Assembly designated the 1990s as the International Decade for Natural Disaster Reduction, establishing committees in most disaster-prone countries to bring a dedicated focus to reducing losses from natural disasters (Thompson, 1992). The United Nations, in combination with other international governmental and nongovernmental organizations, also has primary responsibility for refugee and complex emergencies.

Countries acting bilaterally regularly respond to disasters, offering financial, personnel, and material resources. For example, the Office of U.S. Foreign Disaster Assistance, United Kingdom Overseas Development Agency, Canada International Development Agency, and Japanese International Cooperation Agency provide direct assistance. The foreign policy agendas of major bilateral donors often influence their response patterns. For instance, the United States is particularly active in Latin America, and Japan focuses aid in the West Pacific and Asia. An emerging trend is the conversion of military and civil defense assets to humanitarian assistance. The U.S. military provided exceptional logistical support following the Bangladesh floods in 1991 and similarly supported Kurdish refugees during the Gulf War. Despite the generosity of donors, the growing number of humanitarian emergencies is outrunning relief budgets, and "compassion fatigue" is increasingly evident (Bailey, 1994).

## U.S. Disasters

The United States is one of the most disaster-prone countries in the world. Hazards routinely causing disasters in the United States include earthquakes, floods, hurricanes, winter storms, droughts, and tornados. The acquired immune deficiency syndrome epidemic is a major disaster. Industrial accidents and environmental degradation are also causing disasters. As a result of its many experiences with disasters, the losses from such disasters, and its generally expansive resource base, the United States over the past 50 years has developed an elaborate resource and response system that is active at all levels of government and also includes numerous private voluntary organizations, particularly the American Red Cross, whose disaster response responsibilities are mandated in federal legislation (Federal Emergency Management Agency [FEMA], 1993).

In the United States, responsibility for disaster response rests first with local and state governments. When a major disaster occurs that is beyond state and local capacity, the governor of the affected state may request a presidential declaration that, when granted, activates a wide range of federal agencies and programs. From 1978 to 1987, there were 262 presidential disaster declarations, 39 lesser "emergencies," and 37 firefighting episodes that generated federal disaster aid. The cost of federal assistance during that period was estimated at more than $2.6 billion in direct grants to states, municipalities, and individual disaster victims. During that period, the government provided another $10.8 million to disaster survivors in the form of highly subsidized loans for home repair and reconstruction and loans to businesses suffering disaster effects (FEMA, 1994).

Federal expenditures have risen significantly during recent years. In fiscal years 1989 to 1994, 216 declarations resulted in federal expenditures estimated at nearly $14 billion. Some particularly

TABLE 1
**Federal Disaster Relief Funds for Recent U.S. Disasters**

| Year | Disaster event | Cost (in billions of dollars) |
|---|---|---|
| 1989 | Hurricane Hugo | 1.4 |
| 1989 | Loma Prieta (CA) Earthquake | .8 |
| 1992 | Hurricane Andrew | 1.9 |
| 1993 | Midwest floods | 1.1 |
| 1994 | Northridge (CA) Earthquake | 4.8 |
| Total | | 10.0 |

SOURCE: Federal Emergency Management Agency. (1994, June). *Fiscal year disaster declarations: Demands on the Disaster Relief Fund* (Report). Washington, DC: Author.
NOTE: Federal obligations constitute only one part of the fiscal resources required to respond to a disaster. These figures do not include expenditures by state and local governments, private insurance companies, the use of personal assets, and private charitable donations.

expensive disasters have occurred recently, evidenced by the federal obligations (Table 1).

## U.S. Assistance Programs

Government roles are well defined in various pieces of federal disaster legislation; such legislation was first created in 1950. As the federal role has expanded, many subsequent amendments and bills have been introduced. Disaster legislation is frequently under congressional review; also Congress and the media scrutinize the legislation and the agencies involved with disaster assistance, given the highly political nature of aid to disaster-affected communities.

### Federal Emergency Management Agency

The most recent disaster legislation is the Robert T. Stafford Disaster Relief and Emergency Assistance Act of 1988 (P.L. 100-707). The 1988 Stafford Act directs FEMA, the lead agency for disaster planning and response, and 27 other federal departments and agencies as well as the American Red Cross to intervene in a disaster. FEMA relates directly to and is integrated into state emergency management and preparedness agencies. After a presidential declaration has been issued, FEMA is authorized to establish disaster assistance centers in affected communities to register individual claims for assistance.

FEMA routinely provides housing assistance in the form of temporary shelters or cash grants for repair, rent, and mortgage assistance to people whose homes are uninhabitable. In cooperation with state social services departments, FEMA provides individual and family grants to lower income people who do not qualify for subsidized loans. In addition, FEMA funds local government and nonprofit organizations for debris cleanup and replacement and return of uninsured infrastructure to its predisaster condition. In partnership with the U.S. Department of Labor, FEMA (1993) provides unemployment compensation to individuals who have lost their jobs as a result of a disaster.

### Small Business Administration

Individuals and businesses affected by a disaster qualify for loans from the Small Business Administration. The amount of Small Business Administration loans is typically for the difference between insurance coverage and the documented loss. Loans may be highly subsidized if individuals can furnish evidence that they cannot qualify for commercial loans. The amount of any loan is limited by the borrower's ability to repay the loan. Such assistance is also limited to the amounts required to replace the lost asset to its predisaster condition. This is an important limiting factor, because federal assistance is conditioned by the proviso that individuals and businesses cannot improve their predisaster condition with disaster-related loans.

### Other Programs

A variety of other disaster assistance is available from federal, state, and local agencies for specific target groups such as farmers, elderly people, or the unemployed population. The assistance programs are substantial but are not routinely activated when a disaster declaration has been issued. Local authorities must creatively seek out possible funding sources and shape funding requests to program guidelines. Under even the best of circumstances, a number of vulnerable people will still be without assistance, and authorities will need to develop creative solutions to meet those people's needs.

Of particular interest to social workers are two types of grants the Center for Mental Health Services (CMHS) of the U.S. Department of Health and Human Services provides through state and local mental health agencies to address mental health problems caused or aggravated by presidentially declared disasters. As part of the Crisis Counseling Assistance and Training Program, an *immediate services grant* typically funds short-term crisis intervention services for up to 90 days after a disaster declaration. If conditions warrant, CMHS will support long-term mental health services for up to 12 months following a presidentially declared disaster through a *regular program grant.* Significant loss of life and property, damage, and injury would be conditions that would promote mental health need and would activate such grants (FEMA, 1993).

### Mitigation Activities

Mitigation activities have been a growing focus of U.S. disaster authorities. Recent earthquakes in California have clearly demonstrated the value of programs that promote earthquake-resistant new construction or involve retrofitting existing buildings to be better able to withstand earthquake stresses. Hazard insurance has also been an effective mitigation tool. Crop, earthquake, flood, and hurricane insurance programs have significantly increased private sector involvement in promoting disaster mitigation. As a result of recent insurance company losses resulting from Hurricanes Hugo and Andrew and the 1994 California earthquake, insurance companies have reevaluated their underwriting policies and may reduce the importance of private insurance as a first line of response for funding disaster recovery and promoting disaster mitigation (Evans, 1992).

## Coping Behaviors

A disaster presents individuals, their support systems, and the community with a set of challenging circumstances requiring exceptional coping skills. The literature on coping behaviors in relation to disaster stress is extensive (Ahearn & Cohen, 1984). The research usually has been based on a case study approach. Indeed, each disaster has its unique evolution depending on a community's experience with disasters and the community's level of social cohesion and competent local institutions.

### Mental Health Issues

In general, the literature has concluded that survivors of disasters experience disorganization but recover reasonably quickly. The speed of recovery is influenced by contextual variables such as the extent of loss, access to personal resources, family and other material and emotional support systems, and personal characteristics such as religious faith. Furthermore, survivors who have valuable and satisfying roles during the response and recovery process enhance their recovery (Dynes & Quarantelli, 1976). Some survivors, though, fail to attain their predisaster level of functioning. They may demonstrate dysfunctional behaviors such as apathy, anger, hostility, and depression and may fail to reintegrate into the community (Titchner, Kapp, & Winget, 1976).

Disaster survivors rarely have prior experience with the mental health and social services system. Disasters do not create mental illness, but they do exacerbate preexisting conditions or at least temporarily disrupt normal functioning. For example, couples experiencing marital tension before a disaster strikes may experience increased tension postdisaster. Because most survivors are unfamiliar with the role of client, they frequently are reluctant to seek counseling from mental health professionals (U.S. Department of Health and Human Services, 1978a, 1978b). Thus, counselors must use creative outreach and provide counseling in natural settings such as churches, homes, and schools as opposed to therapists' offices. Generally, the most effective approaches favor problem solving, sympathetic listening, and benefit advocacy and counseling (which involves explaining to survivors the programs for which they might qualify, helping them apply for such programs, and supporting them through the qualification and review process).

Special attention has been devoted to children's and elderly people's mental health needs. Children may show poststress reactions including fear of separation, difficulty sleeping, bad dreams, and regressive behaviors such as enuresis (Lystad, 1985b). And although elderly people still need information and support, they tend to handle the stress of a disaster more effectively than younger people (Huerta & Horton, 1978). Generally, as for most people, the family is the first line of resource for children and elderly people. Counselors should encourage interventions that use natural helping systems to provide counseling and support before directing survivors to professional sources of assistance.

### Community Phases

***Heroism phase.*** Communities that experience a disaster go through clearly definable phases postdisaster. In general, most communities demonstrate a significant degree of cooperative behavior during the emergency phase. Communities organize themselves, distribute roles, and form loose informal organizations to respond to the crisis. The collective problem solving and shared response to the crisis and a high state of altruism builds bonds among survivors, strengthens their view of the community as a caring place, and result in heightened self-esteem and positive self-image. Positive experiences resulting from this intense period of mutual aid, known as the heroism phase, result in heightened feelings of community pride (Farberow & Gordon, 1981; Lystad, 1985a).

***Honeymoon phase.*** A community then enters the honeymoon phase. During this period, predisaster difficulties in the community (for example, disagreements among business owners or neighbors, dissension related to school curricula) diminish in importance; rather, the future looks bright for most residents as the community grapples with the tasks of rebuilding. A community may adopt slogans such as "We're not giving up—we're going on" to capture optimism for the future. The honeymoon period may be short or relatively long depending on local conditions (Farberow & Gordon, 1981; Lystad, 1985a).

***Disillusionment phase.*** The honeymoon phase inevitably gives way to the disillusionment phase. During this phase, individuals confront the delays resulting from the confusing array of reconstruction programs and the regulations associated with those programs as well as from the sheer effort required to rebuild a community. It is particularly important for mental health workers to anticipate and plan for the disillusionment period because survivors who become depressed will require intervention at both the individual and family levels; the community as a whole also will need mental health intervention. Community events that celebrate progress are especially important as are community meetings that allow people to share their feelings of frustrations and fears that the community may not be able to rebuild. These community meetings also allow for public information sharing and rumor control.

***Reconstruction.*** For most communities, the disillusionment phase eventually ends, and the community then undertakes the long and arduous task of reconstruction (Brenton, 1975; Farberow & Gordon, 1981; Lystad, 1985a). If communities handle the recovery process correctly, they may be able to build development into the recovery (Anderson & Woodrow, 1989). Under these circumstances, communities may actually find they are better off than before the disaster. For example, during reconstruction, unsafe areas are rebuilt in a disaster-resistant manner. In addition, community leaders may revise community land-use patterns depending on their decision whether to rebuild the community as it was or devise a new community land-use plan. New community leaders often emerge in the postdisaster period. Innovative postdisaster recovery programs such as small business revolving loan funds can promote business development and job growth. Self-help housing programs and concessional loan programs may enable lower-income people to improve their skills, as well as result in improved housing for these individuals.

Some communities are unable to cope successfully with the stresses and problems presented by a disaster. One such case, analyzed extensively in the literature, is the 1972 Buffalo Creek flood disaster in the coal mining region of West Virginia. Communities affected by this flood had suffered long-term economic decline and isolation before the disaster; thus, their coping skills already were reduced. Researchers (Gleser, Green, & Winget, 1981) found that almost all survivors were severely traumatized. Even after one year, survivors were coping with anger, alienation, helplessness, and hopelessness, reactions that, in many survivors, became chronic.

## Social Work Roles

### Integral to Preparedness and Mitigation

Social work education programs have not created a specialty focus on disaster programming. Nevertheless, social workers are an important part of the disaster preparedness and response community. Emergency relief has historically been an important function of the social work profession (Devine, 1904). Social workers have important roles in all phases of the disaster management cycle. They need to assist organizations that serve clients in the community to establish preparedness plans. At the first warning of an impending disaster, communities must put these plans into effect. Social workers will need to address the special needs and fears of clients who must evacuate an area. Furthermore, social workers can help disaster management organizations increase their sensitivity to people with special needs. Community organizers can actively build community and neighborhood response teams. In the response and recovery period, social workers will need to provide emergency counseling and assistance. Social work skills in crisis intervention will be especially useful. At the same time, it is important for social workers to know the range of assistance programs that may be available. Benefit counseling will require social workers to function as advocates for disaster survivors.

### Support for Individuals

In a major disaster, different groups and organizations will be involved in the response. These individuals will often confront enormous death, injury, and destruction. Furthermore, they will have extended themselves beyond their normal functioning levels and will require critical incident stress debriefing, an important skill for which social workers are potentially useful (Hartsough & Myers, 1985; U.S. Department of Health and Human Services, 1987).

Social workers will also find that they carry major responsibility for the relief needs of vulnerable groups living either in the community or in institutional settings. People with developmental disabilities or mental illness and elderly people are likely to require special interventions and support. Traditional disaster-response organizations may have little or no skills in supporting people with special needs.

**Support for Recovery**

During the recovery phase, the functions of agencies and institutions will be severely constrained. Community human services facilities (for example, a community center or sheltered workshop) may be destroyed. Hence, social workers must be able to assist agencies in uncovering recovery resources and also the clients of those agencies who will not have normal supports in place. For instance, a family under disaster stress will find it difficult to meet the needs of a child or adult with mental retardation who is normally at school or at work but who now is at home because the school or community employment site has been destroyed or is not open. Social workers skilled in community or organizational development will find their skills in particularly high demand. Organizing a community's recovery, searching out benefit programs, writing grants, and advocating for government programs are all essential activities in the recovery phase.

Social workers who live and work in a community that has experienced a disaster will find their regular work routines and responsibilities significantly affected. They may have to deal with deaths of family members or friends, injured loved ones, or losses of homes and possessions. Even social workers who are not directly affected by a disaster will experience changes in their work responsibilities and patterns. Hospitals will have increased admissions and schools will become an important arena for therapeutic interventions to cope with children's trauma. Telephones may be inoperative, roads closed, and important community facilities destroyed or damaged beyond use.

In international settings, social workers have the potential to provide international humanitarian assistance in disaster conditions. Social workers' skills in conflict resolution may prove to be particularly important in the international arena.

## Conclusion

Many disasters are preventable; for those that are not preventable, at least the consequences can be reduced. Disasters in developing countries have captured the attention of the international humanitarian community from both a prevention and relief point of view. As a result, there has been considerable knowledge growth about disasters, including their causes and effects.

The altruistic and philanthropic response to disasters by survivors and other people, both inside and outside the stricken community, are laudable and hopeful. Indeed, given a strong predisaster community and adequate assistance during recovery, many communities can improve their condition during the reconstruction process.

Social workers have unique disaster mandates to support vulnerable groups such as people with disabilities, children, and elderly people; help prepare agencies and other organizations for effective response; provide therapeutic interventions to survivors and responders; and organize recovery programs that improve the community and address unmet needs. Social workers are increasingly working with international humanitarian aid and development organizations that are active in disaster-prone countries.

However, researchers need to examine the factors leading individuals and governments to choose to invest in preparedness and mitigation. Not enough research exists on disaster preparedness and response for community-based organizations and vulnerable groups living in the community. In addition, researchers must further investigate the factors promoting mutual aid and self-help and how to sustain these orientations throughout the recovery process. More case studies and comparative analyses are required to document the actions communities take to build development into recovery, hence strengthening and improving competence in communities prone to destructive hazards. The social work profession has made and continues to make substantial contributions in the area of disaster management. Overall, the subject should receive increased attention from social work researchers and practitioners.

## References


Ahearn, F. L., & Cohen, R. E. (Eds.). (1984). *Disasters and mental health: An annotated bibliography.* Rockville, MD: National Institute of Mental Health, Center for Mental Health Studies of Emergencies.

Anderson, M. B., & Woodrow, P. J. (1989). *Rising from the ashes: Development strategies in times of disaster.* Boulder, CO: Westview Press and UNESCO.

Aysan, Y., Clayton, A., & Davis, I. (1993). *Disaster management models: Seven country case studies.* (Available from the United Nations Disaster Management Training Programme, Department of Humanitarian Affairs, Palais des Nations, 1211 Geneva, Switzerland)

Bailey, A. L. (1994). Aiming to avoid disaster in disasters. *Chronicle of Philanthropy, 6*(8), 1, 8–11.

Bernstein, A. B., & Thompson, P. (1989). The natural history of natural hazards. In P. S. Auerbach & E. Geehr (Eds.), *The management of wilderness and environmental emergencies* (pp. 389–422). St. Louis: C. V. Mosby.

Blaike, P. N., Cannon, T., Davis, I., & Wisner, B. (1994). *At risk: Natural hazards, people's vulnerability, and disasters.* London: Routledge.

Brenton, M. (1975). Studies in the aftermath. *Human Behavior, 4*(5), 56–61.

Bull, R. (1994). *Disaster economics.* (Available from the United Nations Disaster Management Training Programme, Department of Humanitarian Affairs, Palais des Nations, 1211 Geneva, Switzerland)

Carter, N. C. (1992). *Disaster management: A disaster manager's handbook.* Manila, Philippines: Asian Development Bank.

Cuny, F. C. (1983). *Disasters and development.* New York: Oxford University Press.

Devine, E. T. (1904). *The principles of relief.* New York: Macmillan.

Dynes, R. R., & Quarantelli, E. L. (1976). The family and community context of individual reactions to disaster. In H. Parad, H.L.F. Resnick, & L. G. Parad (Eds.), *Emergency and disaster management* (pp. 231–244). Bowie, MD: Charles Press.

Evans, A. F. (1992). *Proposals to retain reinsurance availability in the Caribbean.* Unpublished manuscript.

Farberow, N. L., & Gordon, N. S. (1981). *Manual for child health workers in major disasters.* Washington, DC: U.S. Government Printing Office.

Federal Emergency Management Agency. (1993, May). *The federal response plan: Executive overview.* [Publication No. FEMA-229(1)]. Washington, DC: Author.

Federal Emergency Management Agency. (1994, June). *Fiscal year disaster declarations: Demands on the Disaster Relief Fund* (Report). Washington, DC: Author.

Gleser, G. C., Green, B. L., & Winget, C. C. (1981). *Prolonged psychosocial effects of disaster: A study of Buffalo Creek.* New York: Academic Press.

Hartsough, D. M., & Myers, D. G. (1985). *Disaster work and mental health: Prevention and control of stress among workers* (DHHS Publication No. 87-1422). Washington, DC: U.S. Government Printing Office.

Huerta, F., & Horton, R. (1978). Coping behavior of elderly flood victims. *Gerontologist, 18,* 541–546.

Kent, R. (1994). *Disaster preparedness* (2nd ed.). (Available from the United Nations Disaster Management Training Programme, Department of Humanitarian Affairs, Palais des Nations, 1211 Geneva, Switzerland)

Lystad, M. (Ed.). (1985a). *Innovations in mental health services to disaster victims* (DHHS Publication No. 85-1390). Washington, DC: U.S. Government Printing Office.

Lystad, M. (1985b). Innovative mental health services for child disaster victims. *Children Today, 14*(1), 13–17.

Reed, S. B. (1992). *Introduction to hazards.* (Available from the United Nations Disaster Management Training Programme, Department of Humanitarian Affairs, Palais des Nations, 1211 Geneva, Switzerland)

Robert T. Stafford Disaster Relief and Emergency Assistance Act. P.L. 100-707, §102(a), 102 Stat. 4689 (1988).

Stephenson, R. S. (1991). *Disasters and development.* (Available from the United Nations Disaster Management Training Programme, Department of Humanitarian Affairs, Palais des Nations, 1211 Geneva, Switzerland)

Stephenson, R. S. (1992). *Disaster assessment.* (Available from the United Nations Disaster Management Training Programme, Department of Humanitarian Affairs, Palais des Nations, 1211 Geneva, Switzerland)

Thompson, P. (1992). *An overview of disaster management* (2nd ed.). (Available from the United Nations Disaster Management Training Programme, Department of Humanitarian Affairs, Palais des Nations, 1211 Geneva, Switzerland)

Titchner, J. L., Kapp, F. T., & Winget, C. (1976). The Buffalo Creek syndrome: Symptoms and character change after a major disaster. In H. Parad, H.L.F. Resnick, & L. G. Parad (Eds.), *Emergency and disaster management* (pp. 283–294). Bowie, MD: Charles Press.

U.S. Department of Health and Human Services. (1978a). *Field manual for human service workers in major disasters* (DHHS Publication No. 87-537). Washington, DC: U.S. Government Printing Office.

U.S. Department of Health and Human Services. (1978b). *Training manual for human service workers in major disasters* (DHHS Publication No. 86-538). Washington, DC: U.S. Government Printing Office.

U.S. Department of Health and Human Services. (1987). *Human problems in major disasters: A training curriculum for emergency medical personnel* (DHHS Publication No. 87-1505). Washington, DC: U.S. Government Printing Office.

Wijkman, A., & Timberlake, W. (1984). *Disasters—Acts of God, acts of man?* Washington, DC: Earthscan International Institute for Environment and Development.


## Further Reading


Barton, A. H. (1969). *Communities in disaster.* Garden City, NY: Doubleday.

Cohen, R. E., & Ahearn, F. L. (1980). *Handbook for mental health care of disaster victims.* Baltimore: Johns Hopkins University Press.

Comfort, L. K. (Ed.). (1988). *Managing disaster: Strategies and policy perspectives.* Chapel Hill, NC: Duke University Press.

Draebeck, T. E., & Hoetmer, G. J. (1991). *Emergency management: Principles and practices for local government.* Washington, DC: International City Management Association.

Dynes, R. R. (1970). *Organized behavior in disaster.* Lexington, MA: D. C. Heath.

Myers, D. (1994, August). *Disaster response and recovery: A handbook for mental health professionals* (DHHS Publication No. SMA94-3010). Washington, DC: U.S. Department of Health and Human Services, Substance Abuse and Mental Health Services Administration.

Parad, H., Resnick, H.L.F., & Parad, L. G. (Eds.). (1976). *Emergency and disaster management.* Bowie, MD: Charles Press.

Quarantelli, E. L. (Ed.). (1978). *Disasters: Theory and research.* Beverly Hills, CA: Sage Publications.

Quarantelli, E. L. (1980). *A 100 item annotated bibliography on disaster and disaster planning.* Columbus: Ohio State University, Disaster Research Center.

Sharma, V. K. (Ed.). (1994). *Disaster management.* New Dehli, India: Indian Institute of Public Administration.

Wright, J. D., & Rossi, P. H. (Eds.). (1981). *Social science and natural hazards.* Cambridge, MA: Abt Books.


**Stephen A. Webster, PhD,** is a private consultant, 1414 Lake View Avenue, Madison, WI 53704.

**For further information see**

Advocacy; Bereavement and Loss; Charitable Foundations and Social Welfare; Community; Crisis Intervention: Research Needs; Displaced People; Ethics and Values; Goal Setting and Intervention Planning; HIV/AIDS Overview; Homelessness; Homicide; Hospital Social Work; Interdisciplinary and Interorganizational Collaboration; Intervention Research; Mass Media; Natural Helping Networks; Organizations: Context for Social Services Delivery; Public Health Services; Public Social Services; Victim Services and Victim/Witness Assistance Programs; Victims of Torture and Trauma; Violence Overview.

**Key Words**

development
disaster
emergency
international
stress

## Discharge Planning

*See* Hospital Social Work

# Displaced People

**Frederick L. Ahearn, Jr.**

Hardly a day goes by without a report of another war, famine, disaster, or catastrophe that causes thousands of individuals, families, and children to flee their homes. The consequence on a global scale is that millions of people are seeking safety and refuge from danger and violence. As the world community responds through the aid of specific countries and the work of the United Nations, an increasing number of social workers are becoming involved in caring for these displaced populations and assisting them in their resettlement and adjustment to their new lives. This entry discusses the nature of this global problem of displacement, defines the various terms used to describe these populations, and examines current U.S. policies pertaining to immigrants, refugees, and illegal aliens. Also, it explores the role of the social work profession in providing the links to the services individuals and families need to be independent; in recognizing the serious psychological dimension of displacement and the value of clinical intervention; and in recognizing the need for social workers to be involved in policy debates about these groups.

## Global Displacement

Millions of people around the world are categorized as displaced people, refugees, immigrants, migrants, and illegal aliens. *Displaced people* are those people who have been uprooted within their own country. *Refugees* are people who have crossed national boundaries in search of refuge. The United Nations defines refugees as people who flee to another country out of a fear of persecution because of religion, political affiliation, race, nationality, or membership in a particular group. *Immigrants* are those individuals who have been granted legal permanent residence in a country not their own. *Migrants* are those people, usually workers, who have temporary permission to live in a country, but plan to return to their country of origin. *Illegal aliens* are people who migrate illegally to another country. Most often the definitions of these categories are political as reflected in international and national policy.

### Displaced People

Because of wars, political oppression, famine, and natural disaster, as of 1993 24.2 million people were displaced around the globe, an increase of 1.2 million since 1992 (U.S. Committee for Refugees, 1993). Of these displaced people, 17.4 million live in Africa (Table 1). There are 5 million in the Sudan, 4.1 million in South Africa, 3.5 million in Mozambique, and 2 million in Somalia. In addition, 3.7 million displaced people are in Asia: 1 million in the Philippines; 600,000 in Sri Lanka; and 550,000 in Afghanistan. The wars in the former

TABLE 1

**People Displaced within Country: A Global Perspective**

| Area of world | Displaced people | % of total |
|---|---|---|
| Africa | 17,395,000 | 72.0 |
| Asia | 3,725,000 | 15.4 |
| The Americas | 1,104,000 | 4.6 |
| Europe | 1,080,000 | 4.5 |
| Middle East | 845,000 | 3.5 |
| Total | 24,149,000 | 100.0 |

SOURCE: U.S. Committee for Refugees. (1993). *1993 world refugee survey*. Washington, DC: Author.

TABLE 2
## Refugees by Region of the World

| Area of world | No. of refugees | % of total |
|---|---|---|
| Africa | 5,698,450 | 32.5 |
| Middle East | 5,586,850 | 31.8 |
| Europe | 3,282,200 | 18.7 |
| Asia | 2,740,300 | 15.6 |
| North America | 141,400 | 0.8 |
| South America | 107,700 | 0.6 |
| Total | 17,556,900 | 100.0 |

SOURCE: U.S. Committee for Refugees. (1993). *1993 World refugee survey*. Washington, DC: Author.

TABLE 3
## U.S. Immigration by Region, 1986 Compared with 1991

| | No. of Immigrants | | |
|---|---|---|---|
| Area of world | 1986 | 1991 | Increase (%) |
| The Americas | 254,078 | 1,297,580 | 410.7 |
| Africa | 15,500 | 33,542 | 116.4 |
| Europe | 69,224 | 146,671 | 111.9 |
| Asia | 258,546 | 342,157 | 32.3 |
| Other | 4,360 | 7,217 | 65.5 |
| Total | 601,708 | 1,827,167 | 203.7 |

SOURCE: U.S. Department of Justice. (1992). *1991 Statistical yearbook of the Immigration and Naturalization Service*. Washington, DC: Author.

Yugoslavia (Bosnia and Herzegovina and Croatia) have uprooted more than 1 million people in Europe. Of the 1.1 million displaced in the Americas, most are accounted for by the political instability in Central America. Furthermore, there are 845,000 displaced Palestinians and Iraqis in the Middle East.

**Refugees**

As of 1993 more than 17.5 million people—an increase of 900,000 since 1992—crossed national borders in search of safety, shelter, and food (U.S. Committee for Refugees, 1993). About one-third of the world's refugees are in the Middle East, and of the 5.7 million refugees in Africa, most fled the violence of the wars in Mozambique, Ethiopia, Eritrea, Liberia, and Somalia (Table 2). The countries with a high percentage of refugees include Malawi, Kenya, Guinea, the Sudan, Zaire, Ethiopia, and Eritrea (U.S. Committee for Refugees, 1993). Most of these refugees are in camps supervised by the United Nations High Commission on Refugees. In these camps, a number of nongovernmental agencies assist in the resettlement of individuals. It is not unusual to find social workers directing these services to assist refugees in the camps.

**Immigrants and Migrants**

Many nations accept for permanent residence in their countries those individuals who voluntarily seek to immigrate for economic reasons, individuals who seek to be with or near family members, or those who were refugees or illegal aliens and now can apply for immigrant status. U.S. law gives preference to refugees, those with strong family ties in the United States, and those with specific job skills.

Annually, the U.S. limit on immigration visas is 366,000 (U.S. Department of Justice, 1993). However, certain groups are excluded from this limit: immediate relatives of U.S. citizens, refugees, Amerasians from Vietnam, certain parolees of the former Soviet Union and Indochina, babies born abroad to legal permanent residents, and aliens eligible under the Immigration and Refugee Control Act of 1986. The United States grants visas following this established list of preferred groups.

Immigration to the United States has been significant in the 1840s, 1880s, from 1900 until World War I, and since 1989. U.S. immigration reached its lowest point during the Great Depression, when, in some years, there were more people leaving the United States than entering. Country-specific immigration quotas were eliminated in 1965, leading to an increase of immigrants from Asia and a decrease from Europe.

More than 1.8 million immigrants—a record number—were granted permanent residence in the United States in 1991 (Table 3). More than 1.1 million of them were illegal aliens living in the United States who were granted legal residence under the Immigration Reform and Control Act of 1986 (IRCA). Since 1989, more than 2.5 million former illegal aliens have been granted permanent status through the legalization provisions of IRCA. In effect, the IRCA legislation came to grips with the reality that millions of illegal aliens resided in the United States: migrant workers, refugees fleeing wars in Central America, tourists and students from other countries who never returned home, and illegal aliens seeking economic opportunity (U.S. Department of Justice, 1993).

A comparison of immigration patterns from 1986 to 1991 reveals that the overall numbers have increased by 203.7 percent, with the largest rise accounted for by the IRCA provisions that benefited many illegal aliens from Mexico and Central America. In 1991 alone, 947,923 Mexicans and 110,820 Central Americans were given permanent residence. Immigrants from the former Soviet Union, Ireland, and Poland account for the increased immigration from Europe in 1991. The largest additions in Asian immigration came from the Philippines and India (U.S. Department of Justice, 1993).

The number of foreign-born people in the United States has increased steadily since 1970. The 1970, 1980, and 1990 census counts revealed the percentage of foreign-born residents to be 4.7 percent, 6.2 percent, and 8.7 percent, respectively. In addition, the 1990 census counted more than 21 million foreign-born Americans (U.S. Department of Commerce, 1992). Immigrants will compose 30 percent of the U.S. population growth in the 1990s. Estimates indicate Hispanics will increase by more than 600,000 in 1996, adding more people than non-Hispanic whites for the first time in U.S. history (The Kiplinger Editors, 1993). These changes toward a more diverse society have fueled the debate about immigration policy and spawned a backlash of resentment toward immigrants, particularly in California, Texas, Florida, New York, Illinois, and New Jersey, where most of the new arrivals settle.

In 1991 there were a total of 19 million migrants to the United States; the majority, 14.7 million, were visitors for pleasure. Another 2.7 million traveled to the United States for business; 282,000 were students; and 161,000 were temporary workers. Slightly more than 18,000 agricultural workers came temporarily to the United States to work; they were mostly from the Caribbean countries and Mexico (U.S. Department of Justice, 1993).

### Illegal Aliens

There is no accurate count of the number of illegal aliens in the United States; estimates range from 1 million to 12 million individuals. Among these individuals are Mexicans and Central Americans who have crossed the Rio Grande or the Arizona and California borders, Chinese brought by boat in exchange for a promise of several years of servitude, and thousands of Irish, Nigerians, and Pakistanis who have entered legally as tourists and have never returned home. Debate on U.S. immigration policy has centered on the impact of undocumented workers on the economy and the extent to which undocumented aliens use social and health services, incurring a cost on society. Studies have demonstrated that illegal aliens take jobs that are not wanted by others (North & LeBel, 1978) and make little use of social and health services (North, 1983).

Since the passage of IRCA, more than 3 million illegal aliens have been given permanent residence (Table 4). The majority—2.3 million—were from Mexico. In addition, 286,000 illegal aliens from Central America and 123,000 from the Caribbean nations were legalized during this period. European illegal aliens consisted mostly of individuals from Poland; undocumented Asians came from the Philippines (29,000), India (22,000), and Pakistan (22,000). The number of illegal aliens processed from Africa arrived mostly from Nigeria (16,000). Colombia, with 35,000 illegal aliens, had the largest number from Latin America (U.S. Department of Justice, 1993).

TABLE 4

**Illegal Aliens who Sought Legalization in the United States, 1986–1992**

| Area of world | No. of Illegal aliens | % of total |
|---|---|---|
| North America | 2,687,568 | 88.7 |
| Asia | 148,086 | 4.9 |
| South America | 103,601 | 3.4 |
| Africa | 44,360 | 1.5 |
| Europe | 40,536 | 1.3 |
| Oceania | 7,413 | 0.2 |
| Total | 3,031,564 | 100.0 |

SOURCE: U.S. Department of Justice. (1992). *1991 Statistical yearbook of the Immigration and Naturalization Service*. Washington, DC: Author.

A key issue is how many illegal aliens remain within U.S. society, have arrived after the deadline for the IRCA provision, or have decided not to apply for residence under the provisions of IRCA. Obviously, the debate about the trade treaty between the United States, Canada, and especially Mexico has focused on the need for economic development elsewhere to stem the tide of illegal immigration.

## SERVICES

### Office of Refugee Settlement

Under the Refugee Act of 1980, a range of services is provided to refugees through the U.S. State Department Bureau of Refugee Programs and the U.S. Department of Health and Human Services Office of Refugee Resettlement. The Bureau of Refugee Programs provides transitional assistance to aid refugees who have received permission to immigrate to the United States. This assistance provides for the movement, reception, assessment, and placement of refugees from abroad. Usually, voluntary agencies known as *volags* receive grants to operate reception centers located in refugee camps where staff evaluate, process, and place refugees. Refugees receive grants for transportation, clothing, housing, and incidentals.

Once they are placed in the United States, refugees receive continued assistance from the Office of Refugee Resettlement. The purpose of this assistance is to promote economic self-sufficiency. For example, refugees are eligible for all the benefits and cash assistance for which citizens qualify, such as Aid to Families with Dependent Children, general assistance in states and localities where the program exists, Supplemental Security Income, and food stamps. The federal government fully reimburses states the expense of these cash assistance programs for the first 18 to 36 months, depending on family composition.

Furthermore, the federal government fully reimburses states the cost of Medicaid assistance for 18 to 36 months to provide health care to eligible immigrants and their families.

In addition, the U.S. government funds states and agencies to deliver a range of services that promotes independence and self-sufficiency. These services include job training and orientation programs, language training, interpreters and translation, counseling and adjustment, parenting skills, and mental health services, as well as services that link immigrants to health programs. Moreover, the U.S. Department of Education gives grants to states that have experienced an influx of refugee children in their local schools.

### Types of Entitlement

When foreign-born populations come to the United States, their status is related to current immigration policy, which indicates the types of entitlement for which an individual or family may be eligible. For example, immigrants who have been granted refugee status are entitled to many of the programs available to citizens. This is also true, with some limitations, for people with the special statuses of *entrant, asylee,* and *parolee,* which grant temporary entrance. Undocumented aliens are ineligible for assistance under the law.

However, some hospitals, schools, and social services agencies provide services without judgment. In many parts of the country, the costs of these services to all types of immigrants have become a divisive political issue. Furthermore, indigenous organizations called mutual assistance programs have been founded in many regions of the United States to provide an array of social and economic services. Some resemble social settlements that served immigrants of the past. The key private agencies involved in the placement of and assistance to immigrants are the U.S. Catholic Conference, World Council of Churches, World Relief Refugee Service, Church World Service, the Lutheran Immigration and Refugee Service, and the Hebrew Immigrant Aid Society.

## Role of Social Work with Displaced Populations

Social workers need to understand the psychological consequences of displacement, and specifically how refugees, immigrants, illegal aliens, and other uprooted populations are at emotional risk from events that compose the migration experience. What happens to a refugee or immigrant under unusual circumstances depends on a number of factors. Social workers must know something about the nature of the migration experience, which may have been rather benign or may have been horrible and traumatic. In addition, social workers must recognize that an individual's reaction depends on when the social worker has entered the individual's life. Behavior changes over time and the displacement experience has definitive phases; reactions vary accordingly. Furthermore, social workers must not view individuals who suffer from the consequences of their migration experience as mental health patients. Although those individuals may exhibit psychological symptoms, in almost all cases they and their families do not consider themselves as suffering from a mental health problem. After all, they were "normal" until they were uprooted, and they will consider the label *mental health patient* as a stigma.

In exploring the psychological effects of displacement, several questions must be considered. Can social workers treat displaced people without understanding their unique experience? How can social workers improve their understanding of refugees and immigrants, improve their ability to help displaced people with their problems, and know what to include in the social work curriculum for training social work students? What type of services can social workers design to address the problems of this group and their families? How might social workers be more effective in helping this population?

### Displacement Experience

Some refugees or immigrants migrate to another country to obtain a better job. Their experience involves displacement, to which they will need to adjust, but in some instances, this displacement may be balanced by the excitement of the move and the prospect of a better life. In contrast, the displacement episode may be horrible. Individuals, families, and children may witness the atrocities of war, see their loved ones murdered, lose their friends, and suffer deprivation as a result of flight. Insufficient food and water, the lack of medical care, inadequate housing, and lack of safety have serious health and mental health implications for all classes of migrants.

The migration experience consists of three phases: (1) premigration, (2) migration, and (3) postmigration. *Premigration,* the time before leaving one's home, may involve a number of traumatic events that produce social, medical, and psychological problems. These events often result from natural disasters such as earthquakes, droughts, famine, or floods, or from humanmade disasters produced by violence and oppression often associated with ethnic, religious, and racial war or revolution; persecution; violence; and unspeakable atrocities (Berry, 1991).

*Migration,* or flight for the refugee or displaced person, is the attempt to escape danger, privation, starvation, harm, and death. Displaced people leave their homes, relatives and friends, familiar surroundings, and work. The process of leaving is fraught with danger and oftentimes involves additional traumatic events. For example, pirates have brutalized, robbed, raped, and killed many boat people from Vietnam and China. Central Americans fleeing war in their country have been exposed to a long, dangerous, and traumatic journey to safety. Somali refugees have left in search for food; many have died of starvation en route.

The process of migration usually means a period of containment in a camp, prison, or detention center. This phase, usually called *first asylum,* may be relatively brief or may last months and even years. Although refugees in asylum are initially relieved that they are safe, fed, and housed, the longer they stay, the more likely they will become uncertain, fearful, and anxious. In many camps, social workers frequently provide a variety of services and programs to assist displaced people with their needs and problems.

After flight and asylum, displaced people may return home or seek settlement in another country—the *postmigration* phase. Families and children returning to El Salvador, for instance, may find their villages destroyed, their families and friends dead, and their fields tainted by war chemicals that make farming impossible. Those who are resettled to other countries may face major problems in adjustment and acculturation. They may have difficulty assimilating into a new society and learning a new language, may not have any support systems, and may lose their cultural identity.

### Model for Understanding Displacement

Over the course of the displacement experience, refugees and immigrants are at particular risk for trauma, loss, and severe deprivation. Although many displaced people are resilient, having tremendous strength to endure great hardship, certain situations and episodes clearly have negative consequences. Individuals who lack the basic social, emotional, and physical requirements of life are at risk for physical and emotional problems. Social workers must grasp the concepts of trauma and stress, loss and bereavement, social and emotional support systems, and coping and adaptation that are useful in understanding how a refugee or immigrant encounters an extraordinary event.

***Trauma and stress.*** The outcome of trauma is stress produced by a perceived threat to life or safety. The outcome of trauma also may be a terrifying, horrible, and emotionally overwhelming event (Bolin, 1985). A *traumatic stressor* is "an overwhelming event resulting in helplessness in the face of danger, anxiety, and instinctual arousal" (Eth & Pynoos, 1985). When refugees and displaced people are exposed to traumatic events, as is common during the migration experience, they are at risk for posttraumatic stress disorder. For example, witnessing violence is a traumatic stressor that oftentimes leads to posttraumatic stress disorder, and seeing a parent or relative murdered—a frequent refugee experience—always leads to psychic trauma, according to Eth and Pynoos. Similar findings by Allodi and Cowgill (1982) have affirmed that torture and the witnessing of torture are psychologically traumatic for children and adults. And Dramen and Cohen (1990) found that children traumatized by terrorism had unresolved psychological problems 10 years later.

A classic study of trauma and children involved the removal of children from London during the blitz of World War II; to guarantee their safety, children were sent to the country (Freud & Burlingham, 1943). Investigators found that children who stayed in London actually suffered less stress than those who were separated from their parents and sent to the countryside. The study identified the family as a buffer to stress and familial separation as a traumatic stressor. Children who have experienced traumatic events are exposed to the potential for social deficits and emotional and developmental delays (Garbarino, 1982).

Stress is cumulative: each traumatic exposure adds to the stress a person must manage. Overall, generalizations about stress are as follows: stress can be viewed as a state within the total organism of the individual, which may be associated with the individual's psychophysical condition; environmental stimuli can produce stress; a refugee, immigrant, or displaced person's response to stress will vary: some are immune, others vulnerable; and reactions of uprooted individuals differ given their health, type of support systems, family network, and patterns of interaction with others.

Trauma and stress produce crisis, a crucial time in one's life, a turning point that has both psychological and physiological consequences. Crisis for displaced people is a time-limited period of psychological disequilibrium, precipitated by the trauma and stress of migration episodes that bring sudden and significant changes in their lives. Crisis, then, is a period that involves danger, change, threat, or challenge that produces a state of personal instability and imbalance. When a person is in this state of disequilibrium, he or she frequently is hopeful and amenable to help and also is susceptible to the influences of outside forces, such as social work clinical intervention.

***Loss and bereavement.*** Another set of concepts that is of help in working with refugees and immigrants and their families consists of loss and bereavement. Following a loss, usually the death of a loved one, a person mourns and grieves for a time. In addition to death, loss may include the destruction of property or things, physical or mental impairment, or separation. Because bereavement is an emotional process emanating from loss, it then follows that displacement victims suffer a variety of losses and experience the process of mourning and grieving.

The work of Kübler-Ross (1976) has gained much recognition. She described a five-stage process of grief and mourning people go through when they lose a loved one. The stages progress from denial, rage and anger, bargaining, and depression, to acceptance. People also may grieve for the loss of their home, neighborhoods, and social attachments, as they did, for example, when the old West End neighborhood of Boston was destroyed through government urban renewal (Fried, 1963). Another example is the Coconut Grove fire: the victims of this nightclub fire suffered physical discomfort, increased susceptibility to illness, withdrawal into apathy, hostility toward others, and a sense of personal isolation, exhibiting a strong sense of denial through it all that anything had happened (Lindemann, 1944). In addition, individuals who lose pets or mementos, such as old family pictures, display a pattern of grief and mourning.

Loss is a defining characteristic of displacement. Children lose parents, relatives, and support systems. For a child, the loss of a parent is an overwhelming disaster. In addition, families lose their homes and neighborhoods, often the locus of geographical identity; they lose their pets and things that they treasure, which cannot be replaced. When individuals lose their homes, they also lose a sense of well-being, safety, and security. The familiarity of place is important to this sense, and without it, many individuals will exhibit fear, nervousness, anxiety, as well as sleep and eating disorders. Furthermore, loss of home is sometimes associated with a child's perception that the adults in their lives did not protect them (Coelho & Ahmed, 1980).

Kenzie, Sack, Angell, Manson, and Rath (1986) studied over time the psychological adjustment of a group of refugee adolescents who had observed the atrocities and genocide of the Khmer Rouge in Cambodia. They had suffered loss, trauma, and deprivation. Four years after their arrival in the United States and with psychological treatment, half of the youths were still encountering symptoms of posttraumatic stress disorder, such as nightmares, recurring dreams, startle reflex, and avoidance behavior. The long-term effects of trauma, loss, and deprivation are intertwined. It is important, therefore, for social workers to establish the specific nature of a displaced person's loss and where in the grieving process he or she may be. This is crucial for any clinical assessment of the individual's situation and any plans for clinical intervention.

***Social and emotional support systems.*** Another important factor in the assessment and treatment of refugees and immigrants is the presence and strength of social and emotional support systems. *Emotional resources* consist of genetic and physiologic endowments and traits, such as psychological skill and capacity, that a person uses to manage stress and resolve problems. *Social resources* are the sum of a person's relations that form networks and linkages of interrelationships.

These supports allow and facilitate a person's management of the trauma and loss that the person has endured. Obviously, the individual with a set of supportive resources will be expected to have greater success in coping with the psychological consequences of displacement trauma and loss. Emotional and social supports may be inherent or acquired. Some people are born innately smarter, have competent and resourceful parents, and have a greater resiliency to stress. Some people who already have experienced trauma and loss acquire support systems that enable them to cope better. Thus, the presence of supportive parents, relatives, and friends is important to the management of refugees' and immigrants' problems. For children who have experienced the trauma of being separated from their parents or families, family networks provide for safety, security, and a sense of self-worth. Resources from outside the family—housing, education, employment and economic opportunities, and availability of and access to health and social services—may or may not be available. Some communities have excellent services and resources that enable families and children to deal with their problems and to maintain their normal daily functioning and independence.

Refugee and migration flight and resettlement not only disrupt family life but bring about the dilemmas of maintaining a person's culture, assimilation, and acculturation. The result may be that parents are no longer able to socialize their children and provide appropriate role models for them. The discontinuity of tradition, values, and expected behaviors becomes apparent between the culture of origin and the culture of settlement. As parents cling to the norms and practices of the past, children more easily adjust and adapt to the new culture. The adjustment of the refugees and immigrant family is disrupted by this differential process of assimilation (Canino, Earley, & Rogler, 1980).

Cultural supports, though, can promote the values and norms of the refugee or immigrant community. Group affiliations such as clubs, mutual assistance associations, and church membership can foster a continued appreciation of language, ritual, custom, and tradition. Schools and churches play a role in supporting refugee and immigrant children. However, the role may be positive or negative. In the country of resettlement, schools—a force in the socialization of children—may actually encourage children to adapt to the new culture and discard the old—its language, customs, and values. Religion is also a transmitter of culture, tradition, and norms, particularly as it inculcates moral values as a guide to behavior. For some people, a belief system provides strength and sustenance; others may reject religion as meaningless in the face of atrocities and hardships. For refugee and immigrant children who lose their cultural supports and thus their cultural identity, the consequences include serious identity problems and delayed development, a process referred to as *cultural bereavement* (Eisenbruck, 1988). It also portends to serious family problems as the old culture clashes with the new culture.

***Coping and adaptation.*** Refugees and immigrants use a number of strategies to manage the stresses they have accumulated. *Coping,* a behavior that protects a person from the effects of internal and external stress (White, 1974), has been defined as efforts "to manage (that is, master, tolerate, reduce, and minimize) environmental and internal demands and the conflicts among them" that tax a person's resources (Lazarus & Launier, 1978, p. 287).

Refugees and immigrants may take three courses in coping with the trauma and stress associated with flight, resettlement, adjustment, and acculturation. They may (1) alter the conditions that produce the stress (most unlikely); redefine the meaning of the displacement episodes and downgrade their significance; or manage the emotional outcomes in such a way as to control them and keep them within bounds (Pearlin & Schooler, 1978). Coping behavior, then, is designed to avoid, prevent, change, manipulate, and manage a person's tensions, problems, and difficult life experiences. Refugees and immigrants learn to cope with the stresses of displacement, and although they will differ in coping styles, they can be expected to follow the patterns of avoidance, prevention, control, alteration, and management. Coping and adaptation are intertwined with the displaced person's systems of social and emotional resources. Strategies to alter, redefine, and manage trauma and stress are helped and made easier or are hampered and prevented by interpersonal relationships and psychological and emotional tools.

Garmezy (1987) has referred to children who successfully cope as "resilient" or "stress resistant." Three factors give such children special protection and enable them to cope better: (1) the child's personality and disposition, (2) his or her environment, and (3) the child's external system of supports. It is these assets that serve as a protective shell against trauma and stress of migration and resettlement. Bronfenbrenner's (1979) work on the understanding of a child's development within the context of family, neighborhood, and community has potential applicability to the study of refugee and immigrant children. The emotional and behavioral reactions of refugee and immigrant children will vary with their developmental tasks and process at particular stages, rather than correspond to the reactions of adults. The trauma and stress of displacement occur at a time when children are vulnerable, on the one hand, and incredibly malleable and adjustable, on the other. Their adjustment and coping will have some advantages as well as disadvantages compared with adult refugees and immigrants (Westermeyer, 1991).

There is still much to learn about how adults and children cope with their refugee or immigrant experiences. How much time does a person need to manage the stresses of migration and adaptation? How are coping strategies interrelated with the type of trauma and stress faced and with the presence or absence of supports? What type of interventions are effective? One thing is sure: research on the resiliency of refugee and immigrant children is a fertile field of inquiry, as is the topic of how coping strategies are differentiated during the various states of development.

## Conclusion

The United States faces a dramatic increase in the number of new arrivals—refugees, immigrants, migrants, and undocumented aliens. Social workers, who play a major role in the resettlement and adjustment of these populations, have much to learn about these groups. For example, knowledge about the concepts of trauma and stress, loss and bereavement, social and emotional resources, and coping and adaptation will lead to a better understanding of the psychological reactions of refugee or immigrant adults and children. Social workers' improved understanding of the phases of the displacement experience; the potential for trauma over time; the degree of loss suffered; the family, neighborhood, and community's role in providing supports; and the various approaches to coping will lead to better assessments of the nature of the problem and give direction for short- and long-term treatment plans.

Only a few years ago, many social workers apparently did not understand the pernicious effects of trauma on people, nor did they believe that traumatized groups could benefit from clinical interventions. Now, it is obvious that social work professionals have an important role to play in assisting refugees and immigrants to manage and resolve the difficulties of their displacement experience and the process of adjustment and acculturation. It is also the professional responsibility of social workers to understand the events and consequences of migration and adaptation so that they can identify the needs of these groups, plan and implement appropriate services for them, and design effective social and clinical services that bring improved functioning and independence. Crucial to this task is the fit between need and service. Undoubtedly, refugees and immigrants may need crisis intervention and, in many cases, long-term clinical treatment. However, there is always a parallel need for additional services, that is, housing, training, language, education, income supports, health care, and other social services. Clinical services must be meshed with social services and the creation of or linkage with mutual assistance associations.

America traditionally has opened its doors to immigrants from around the world, but this is done on a selective and politically motivated basis. Immigration has become an election issue in many states that is dividing and testing many communities. An anti-immigration mood exists: groups of citizens are calling for a reappraisal of existing laws that permit immigrants to enter the United States, cuts in services to this population, and legislation to require the use of English in all official, governmental transactions. Furthermore, in many areas, people are protesting the cost of services to immigrants and refugees. Social workers have much to offer in these debates over immigration and refugee policy. Social workers certainly do not agree with differential treatment of refugees based on race as is evident in the profession's Haitian policy. Who is allowed into the country and the criteria that are used to admit them are of concern to the social work profession. Once here, newcomers should have a right to the services they need to gain economic independence, and the federal government should compensate states and localities that bear the brunt of refugee influx for the extra cost of serving this group. In addition, the social work profession can assist communities in addressing the damaging effects of xenophobia by fostering activities that build understanding and cooperation. NASW has issued a position paper on immigration policy in which it expresses opposition to efforts that would deny health, social services, housing, or education benefits to newcomers.

Serious barriers, however, exist in offering services to refugees and immigrants. In addition to the requirement of relevant service (the fit between need and service), there is the issue of the culture of service and the way in which the service is delivered. Sensitivity to role, status, norms, and customs is essential. Language is a frequent barrier. Should the program use interpreters and train indigenous paraprofessionals? Or is it possible to hire a native who has the requisite professional training?

Clearly, the ideal solution to the problem is primary prevention—prevention of violence, war, civil strife, and all the conditions that produce displacement. This battle must be fought on the political front. It has both international and national aspects. It is important that social workers insist that our professional associations use their influence and weight to change, modify, and create policies that prevent displacement. Furthermore, social workers need to use our voice to advocate for humane laws and regulations that affect immigrants and refugees who come to this country. Social workers must insist that these groups are given the necessary support services they need to adjust to their new reality. When refugees and immigrants are protected by governments and receive appropriate social and emotional assistance, they will develop into competent, secure, and productive U.S. citizens. They will echo the plea of Southeast Asian refugee Arn Chorn:

> I have come to realize that I am alive again. I am not just alive because bullets failed to reach my brain. I am not alive because a stick missed my skull. I am alive because finally and painfully after years, I know that I can love again. I can feel the suffering of others, not just my own. (cited in Crisp, 1988, p. 20)

## References


Allodi, F., & Cowgill, G. (1982). Ethical and psychiatric aspects of torture: A Canadian study. *Canadian Journal of Psychiatry, 27,* 98–102.

Berry, J. W. (1991). Refugee adaptation in settlement countries: An overview with emphasis on primary prevention. In F. L. Ahearn, Jr., & J. L. Athey (Eds.), *Refugee children: Theory, research, and services* (pp. 20–38). Baltimore: Johns Hopkins University Press.

Bolin, R. (1985). Disaster characteristics and psychosocial impacts. In B. J. Sowder (Ed.), *Disasters and mental health: Selected contemporary perspectives.* Washington, DC: U.S. Government Printing Office.

Bronfenbrenner, U. (1979). *The ecology of human development: Experiments by nature and design.* Cambridge, MA: Harvard University Press.

Canino, I. A., Earley, B. F., & Rogler, L. H. (1980). *The Puerto Rican child in New York City: Stress and mental health* (Monograph No. 4). New York: Hispanic Research Center, Fordham University.

Coelho, G. V., & Ahmed, P. I. (Eds.). (1980). *Uprooting and development.* New York: Plenum Press.

Crisp, J. (1988, June). Refugee children: Policy and practice. *Refugees, 54,* p. 20.

Dramen, S., & Cohen, E. (1990). Children of victims of terrorism revisited: Integrating individual and family treatment approaches. *American Journal of Orthopsychiatry, 60*(2), 204–209.

Eisenbruck, M. (1988). The mental health of refugee children and their cultural development. *International Migration Review, 22,* 282–300.

Eth, S., & Pynoos, R. S. (1985). Interaction of trauma and grief in childhood. In S. Eth & R. S. Pynoos (Eds.), *Post-traumatic stress disorder in children* (pp. 168–186). Washington, DC: American Psychiatric Press.

Freud, A., & Burlingham, D. T. (1943). *War and children.* New York: Ernst Willard.

Fried, M. (1963). Grieving for a lost home. In L. Duhl (Ed.), *The urban condition* (pp. 151–171). New York: Basic Books.

Garbarino, J. (1982). *Children and families in the social environment.* New York: Aldine de Gruyter.

Garmezy, N. (1987). Stress, competence, and development: Continuities in the study of schizophrenic adults, children vulnerable to psychopathology, and the search for stress-resistant children. *American Journal of Orthopsychiatry, 57*(2), 159–174.

Immigration Reform and Control Act of 1986. P.L. 99-603, 100 Stat. 3359.

Kenzie, J. D., Sack, W. H., Angell, R. H., Manson, S., & Rath, B. (1986). The psychiatric effects of massive trauma on Cambodian children: 1. The children. *Journal of the American Academy of Child Psychiatry, 25,* 370–376.

The Kiplinger Editors. (1993, September 1). *The Kiplinger Washington Letter,* p. 2.

Kübler-Ross, E. (1976). *On death and dying.* New York: Macmillan.

Lazarus, R. S., & Launier, R. (1978). Stress-related transactions between person and environment. In L. A. Pervin & M. Lewis (Eds.), *Perspectives in international psychology* (pp. 287–327). New York: Plenum Press.

Lindemann, E. (1944). Symptomatology and management of acute grief. *American Journal of Psychiatry, 101,* 141–148.

North, D. S. (1983). Impact of legal, illegal, and refugee migrations on social programs. In M. M. Kritz (Ed.), *U.S. immigration and refugee policy* (pp. 265–285). Lexington, MA: Lexington Books.

North, D. S., & LeBel, A. (1978). *Manpower and immigration policies in the United States* (Special Report No. 20). Washington, DC: Commission for Manpower Policy.

Pearlin, L. I., & Schooler, C. (1978). The structure of coping. *Journal of Health and Social Behavior, 19,* 548–555.

Refugee Act of 1980. P.L. 96-212, 94 Stat. 102.

U.S. Committee for Refugees. (1993). *1993 world refugee survey.* Washington, DC: Author.

U.S. Department of Commerce. (1992). *Statistical abstract of the United States 1992.* Washington, DC: Author.

U.S. Department of Justice. (1993). *1992 statistical yearbook of the Immigration and Naturalization Service.* Washington, DC: Author.

White, R. W. (1974). Strategies of adaptation: An attempt at systematic description. In G. V. Coehlo, D. A. Hamburg, & J. E. Adams (Eds.), *Coping and adaptation* (pp. 47–68). New York: Basic Books.

Westermeyer, J. (1991). Psychiatric services for refugee children. In F. L. Ahearn, Jr., & J. L. Athey (Eds.), *Refugee children: Theory, research, and services* (pp. 127–162). Baltimore: Johns Hopkins University Press.


## Further Reading


Ahearn, F. L., Jr., & Athey, J. L. (Eds.). (1990). *Refugee children: Theory, research, and services.* Baltimore: Johns Hopkins University Press.

Newman, C. J. (1976). Children of disaster: Clinical observations at Buffalo Creek. *American Journal of Psychiatry, 133,* 306–312.

Pynoos, R. S., & Eth, E. (1985). Children traumatized by witnessing acts of personal violence: Homicide, rape, or suicide behavior. In S. Eth & R. S. Pynoos (Eds.),

*Post-traumatic stress disorder in children* (pp. 17–43). Washington, DC: American Psychiatric Press.
Terr, L. C. (1981). Forbidden games. *Journal of the American Academy of Child Psychiatry, 20,* 741–760.

**Frederick L. Ahearn, Jr., DSW,** is dean and professor, National Catholic School of Social Service, The Catholic University of America, Washington, DC 20064.

**For further information see**

Advocacy; African Americans Overview; African Americans: Immigrants; Asian Americans Overview; Civil Rights; Community Needs Assessment; Disasters and Disaster Aid; Ethnic-Sensitive Practice; Haitian Americans; Hispanics Overview; Homelessness; Housing; Human Rights; International Social Welfare: Organizations and Activities; Migrant Workers; Mutual Aid Societies; Peace and Social Justice; Policy Practice; Poverty; Public Social Services; Runaways and Homeless Youths; Rural Poverty; Settlements and Neighborhood Centers; Social Welfare Policy; Victims of Torture and Trauma; White Ethnic Groups.

**Key Words**

| | |
|---|---|
| displaced people | refugees |
| immigrants | undocumented aliens |
| migrants | |

## Dix, Dorothea Lynde

*See* Biographies section, Volume 3

# Domestic Violence

**Liane V. Davis**

Domestic violence, the term that came into common usage in the 1970s to define the problem of wife abuse, has since come to encompass other forms of abuse that occur within families. This entry focuses only on abuse to partners in intimate relationships, with the primary focus on women as the victims.

Labels that are used have vast implications for strategies to ameliorate problems. The term "domestic violence" was intended to bring into public view the violence that occurred to women in the domestic spheres in which they supposedly lived in peace and tranquility. Since then, feminists, who brought the problem originally into public focus, have increasingly used the terms "abuse," "woman abuse," or "battering." Naming the problem in this way redirects the focus from a genderless phenomenon to one that clearly identifies women as its most likely victims. Other terms that have come into use include "partner abuse," "spouse abuse," "intimate violence," and "relationship violence." These labels place the relationship at center stage, minimize the role of gender, and remove the problem from the larger societal arena that sustains it. Each label offers a different lens through which to see the people involved, the nature of the problem, and the possible solutions.

## Historical Overview

Men's right to dominate women has deep roots. Early Roman law gave men *absolute* power over their wives, although whether this power included the right to put their wives to death is not clear (Stedman, 1917). There is no question, however, that husbands could control their wives with physical force. Church doctrine affirmed men's right to control women: "Wives, be subject to your husbands, as to the Lord. . . . As the Church is subject to Christ, so let wives also be subject in everything to their husbands," wrote St. Paul (Ephesians 5:22–24). Friar Cherubino, in his *Rules of Marriage,* advised the good husband to

> take up a stick and beat [your wife] soundly, for it is better to punish the body and correct the soul than to damage the soul and spare the body . . . then readily beat her, not in rage, but out of charity and concern for her soul, so that the beating will redound to your merit and her good. (quoted in Hofeller, 1983, p. 51)

English common law gave men the right to beat their wives as long as the weapon they used was "a rod no bigger than their thumb" (Blackstone, 1979). Thus, the "rule of thumb" was born. The right of men to beat their wives found support in early U.S. judicial decisions as well. For example, in 1864 a North Carolina court ruled

> that the state should not interfere with domestic chastisement unless "some permanent injury be inflicted or there be an excess of violence." Otherwise, the law "will not invade the domestic forum or go behind the curtain," preferring instead to "leave the parties to themselves, as the best mode of inducing them to

make the matter up and live together as man and wife should." (Eisenberg & Micklow, 1977, p. 139)

Such rulings gave legal sanction to husbands' right to control the behavior of their wives and the state's hands-off policy. There were some 19th-century efforts to criminalize wife abuse, and first-wave feminists briefly exposed the problem. By and large, however, men's abuse of their wives occurred with little fear of public sanction until the 1970s, when second-wave feminists once again opened the curtain on the abuse that so many women experienced in their home. The major priorities of what was to become the battered women's movement were to ensure safe, nurturing shelter for all women who were abused and to create a society that no longer tolerated woman abuse.

## Scope of the Problem

### Number of Cases

Abuse of women in their own homes has been well documented. Over 1.5 million married and cohabiting women are severely assaulted each year by their male partners (Straus & Gelles, 1986). From 20 percent to 25 percent of all women have been abused at least once by an intimate male partner (Stark & Flitcraft, 1988), and 22 percent to 35 percent of the women who are treated in hospital emergency rooms are there because of symptoms related to ongoing abuse (Randall, 1990).

Most of the data on spouse abuse come from two National Family Violence Surveys designed to assess how family members deal with conflict (see Straus & Gelles, 1990, for a complete description of the methodology). In 1975 face-to-face interviews were conducted with one adult member from each of a national probability sample of 2,143 households. In 1985 telephone interviews were conducted with a sample of 4,032 households. Participants were asked to think of situations in which they were angry or had a disagreement with a specific family member and to indicate how often they and their partner had engaged in each of 19 specific acts. Of primary interest were the violence tactics—punching, kicking, hitting, threatening with or using a weapon—that family members used against one another. The most startling result of the surveys was that men and women were equally likely to report being violent toward their partners. In the first survey, 12 percent of men and 11 percent of women reported engaging in any of the acts of violence toward their partners, whereas 3.8 percent of men and 4.6 percent of women reported engaging in severely violent acts. From these data, it was estimated that 1.8 million wives and 2.2 million husbands were abused by their partners each year. These results were closely replicated in the second survey, in which it was estimated that 1.6 million women and 2.4 million men were severely abused by their partners annually (Straus & Gelles, 1986).

### Effects and Context of Abuse

If men and women are equally likely to engage in violence toward their partners, why is all the focus on women and so little attention on men? First, the data report *acts* of violence; they do not measure *effects* of the violent acts. The failure to take consequences into account can lead to false conclusions about who is battered. Clearly, there are different effects when a 120-pound woman punches a 200-pound man than when a 200-pound man punches a 120-pound woman. The second survey confirmed other data indicating that there is a greater likelihood for women to be injured as a consequence of assault by their mates than vice versa (Berk, Berk, Loseke, & Rauma, 1983; Brush, 1990; Stets & Straus, 1990).

Second, these data offer no insight into the *context* of the violence. Who initiated it? Was it done in self-defense? Although the second survey suggested that women are about as likely as men to be the initiators (Stets & Straus, 1990), other data conflict. One of the earliest and most widely cited studies found that wives were seven times more likely than were husbands to kill their partners in self-defense (Wolfgang, 1957). Saunders (1988), studying a small sample of battered women, found that among those who used severe violence, only 3 percent reported initiating violence, 40 percent reported always acting in self-defense, and an additional 32 percent said they were always fighting back.

There are other reasons to be skeptical about the claims that men are at a high risk of abuse. First, few abused men seek assistance, in contrast to the millions of women who call the police and appear in emergency rooms, shelters, and courts. Second, studies of different kinds of official records provide consistent findings: 95 percent of those who are assaulted are women, and 5 percent are men (Browne, 1987; Dobash & Dobash, 1979; Schwartz, 1987). Especially compelling was Schwartz's study, which used data from the U.S. Department of Justice's National Crime Survey (NCS), which asks people whether they have been crime victims; Schwartz indicated that women make up 94.1 percent of all spousal assault victims. Furthermore, in instances in which there were injuries, men were *more* likely than women to say that they called the police. Thus, Schwartz concluded that official statistics, if anything, overrepresent the number of battered men. Third, even if men are at serious risk of abuse, they can more easily leave abusive relationships than can women. Considerable evidence indicates that women remain with abusive partners because they are economically dependent on them (Gelles, 1976; Kalmuss & Straus, 1990; Strube & Barbour, 1984). Women's responsibility to provide care for young children further increases their economic dependence; such economic dependence is rare among men.

**Types of Abuse**

There is one additional reason to focus on the abuse of women: The physical violence is only one means by which men control the behavior of women. Schechter (1990) identified three additional ways by which men control their female partners: (1) sexual abuse, (2) economic abuse, and (3) psychological abuse. Studies have found that 10 percent to 14 percent of women have been forced to have sex with their male partners, primarily husbands and ex-husbands (Finkelhor & Yllo, 1985; Russell, 1982). Sexual violence is far greater among battered women, with 33 percent to 59 percent reporting such violations by their abuser (Browne, 1987; Finkelhor & Yllo, 1985). Until recently, however, a woman could not legally accuse her husband of rape because, by law, rape was defined as forced sexual intercourse on "someone other than the wife of the person accused" (Gelles, 1977, p. 339). As of 1988, only one state, Alabama, still prohibited men from being charged with raping their wives (Gelles & Straus, 1988).

Economic abuse occurs when women are denied access to the resources to which they are legally and morally entitled. Women may be prevented from obtaining the education needed to obtain a decent job or be barred from working even if they are well qualified.

Psychological or emotional abuse, which Russell (1982) likened to the brainwashing of prisoners of war, is often the most difficult to document and, therefore, has been the subject of little research. It is through emotional abuse that the batterer undermines, isolates, and terrorizes the abused woman. Schechter (1990) graphically described men who have learned to "terrorize their wives without touching them," thus avoiding the legal consequences of actual physical abuse. She identified five tactics of emotional abuse: (1) isolation, (2) humiliation and degradation, (3) "crazy-making" behavior, (4) threats to harm the woman and those she loves, and (5) suicidal and homicidal threats.

**Risk Factors**

Six variables have been reliably associated with the increased risk of abuse: (1) relationship status, (2) socioeconomic factors, (3) age, (4) childhood experience with violence, (5) alcohol use, and (6) race.

***Relationship status.*** Rates of violence among cohabiting couples are approximately twice as high as among legally married couples (Lane & Gwartney-Gibbs, 1985; Stets & Straus, 1990; Yllo & Straus, 1981). Stets and Straus suggested that cohabiting couples may be more isolated from their social networks, are more likely to struggle over autonomy and control, and may allow conflict to escalate because they are less invested in the relationship.

***Socioeconomic factors.*** Although wife abuse exists across the socioeconomic spectrum, it is more common in families with fewer economic resources. Three specific economic factors have been associated with higher rates of wife abuse: (1) poverty, (2) underemployment and unemployment, and (3) employment in a blue-collar job (Dibble & Straus, 1990; Gelles & Cornell, 1990).

***Age.*** Youth increases a person's risk of being abused and being an abuser (Suitor, Pillemer, & Straus, 1990). For example, there is considerable violence among dating couples (Carlson, 1987). These high rates appear to be caused more by youth than by anything special about dating relationships. Controlling for age, the rate of violence among dating couples actually falls below that of those who are married or cohabiting (Stets & Straus, 1990).

***Childhood experiences with violence.*** Being abused as a child appears to make one more vulnerable to being an abused woman (Gelles, 1976) and being an abusive man (Straus, 1990). The relationship between witnessing parental violence as a child and experiencing violence as an adult is less clear; the data are inconclusive as to whether observing marital violence as a child increases a woman's risk of being battered, but boys who observe marital violence are more likely to become adult abusers (O'Leary, 1988). Strauss, Gelles, and Steinmetz (1980) found that men who observed physical violence between their parents, in comparison to men who did not, were three times more likely to hit their wives. Furthermore, "sons of the most violent parents have a rate of wife beating 1,000 percent greater than that of sons of nonviolent parents" (p. 101).

***Alcohol use.*** Much of the support for the belief that men beat their wives when they are drunk comes from clinical samples in which women are asked to describe their husbands' drinking patterns. These data indicate that anywhere from 35 percent to 93 percent of all batterers are problem drinkers (Leonard & Jacob, 1988). Better-controlled studies also support the relationship between drinking and abuse (see, for example, Leonard, Bromet, Parkinson, Day, & Ryan, 1985). However, Kantor and Straus (1990) found that in only 25 percent of cases was either partner drinking at the time of the abuse.

***Race.*** Research indicates above-average rates of wife abuse among African American and Latino families. Straus et al. (1980) found rates of wife abuse to be twice as high for African American as for other racial minorities and four times as high as for white Americans, and Straus and Smith (1990) found more than twice as many severely abused Latina as non-Latina white women (Straus & Smith, 1990).

On closer examination, these differences are better explained by socioeconomic factors. African Americans actually have lower rates of wife abuse than do white Americans except among those earning $6,000 to $11,999 annually. Because 40 percent of all the African American respondents fell into this income group, they appear more violent than do white Americans (Cazenave & Straus, 1990). Differences between Latina and non-Latina white Americans disappear, too, when economic deprivation, age, and urban residence are controlled for (Straus & Smith, 1990).

## Theories of Battering

Battering has been explained from many different perspectives. Each perspective frames the problem and the solutions differently. Six theories are briefly described in this section.

### Psychoanalytic Theory

Psychoanalytic theorists frame the problem in terms of intrapersonal pathology, emphasizing how early life experiences create the specific pathological personalities seen in abused women and abusing men. Shainess (1979) suggested that childhood experiences with cruel people lead battered women to develop beliefs and behaviors that are dysfunctional when carried into adulthood. These women think of themselves as deserving abuse, fear offending those who are stronger, and submit to rather than resist abuse. Because of deep feelings of unworthiness, they choose abusive men and may even trigger the abusive behavior. The childhood experiences of violent men warp their personalities even more seriously and result in behaviors that are alternately labeled passive–aggressive, psychopathic, obsessive–compulsive, paranoid, and sadistic. Their childhood experiences of abuse, both as victims and observers, have taught these men that violence gets them what they want and allows them to feel good about themselves.

From a psychoanalytic perspective, the solution requires long-term, corrective, individual psychotherapy. Such therapy would enable a battered woman to break the cycle that leads her to choose men who, by their violent treatment, re-create her unhappy, but familiar, childhood.

### Family Systems Theory

Systems theorists, framing the abuse in interactional–systemic terms, see abuse as a characteristic of the relationship. Some completely ignore gender and the power differential between women and men in applying the theory to spouse abuse. While examining the contributions of both partners to developing and maintaining the system, others acknowledge that women tend to be the abused partner (Magill, 1989). Weitzman and Dreen (1982), illustrating this latter perspective, suggested that a battering system develops when two persons, each with a fragile sense of self, merge. The man is "frankly unaware of his own dependency conflicts, intimacy fears, need for control, and social conditions, all of which lead to a certain hunger for power" (p. 260). The woman exhibits many similar underlying psychosocial traits, including a history of violent experiences as a child, dependency conflicts, and a narrow range of coping responses. The rules that govern these relationships ensure the continuation of dysfunctional patterns of interpersonal behavior and prevent change from occurring (Rhodes, 1986). Indeed, it is suggested the violence itself is designed to thwart change.

From a systems perspective, marital counseling is essential to identify dysfunctional patterns and to bring about change in the marital system. Each partner is held responsible for his or her own specific contribution to the violence-producing dysfunction and for changing the way the partners relate to one another.

### Learning Theory

Social-learning theorists stress the opportunities people have to model and be reinforced for abusive behavior. Cognitive–behavioral theorists emphasize how beliefs that support abusive behaviors are internalized. Boys may learn abusive behaviors from their male role models (fathers as well as media stars) while internalizing the belief that they should be in authority. Girls learn to be passive from their role models while internalizing the belief that they are powerless. These behaviors and internalized messages are powerful determinants of subsequent adult actions.

Reinforcement and punishment, key learning theory concepts, are also used to explain how a cycle of violence develops between an individual man and his partner:

> Don grew up seeing his father hit his mother and his mother give in to his father. When he married, he promised himself he would be different. Yet one day he found himself repeating his father's behavior. He had a difficult week at work and stopped at a bar for a few drinks. By the time he got home, Amy was furious and had thrown out his dinner. He screamed at her to fix his dinner and, when she refused, he smacked her. She was so shocked and frightened that she immediately complied. Stunned by his own behavior, he apologized, promising never to hit her again.

With little awareness, Don and Amy had taken the first steps toward developing a cycle of violence. By giving Don what he wanted, Amy rewarded his abusive behavior. At the same time, her own behavior, giving in to Don's demands, was doubly rewarded: Don stopped being violent (negative reinforcement) and became loving and apologetic (positive reinforcement). The rewards they each received increased the likelihood that Don would abuse Amy again and that Amy would respond passively.

From a learning theory perspective, intervention should teach both partners how they have learned and been rewarded for their present behaviors (thus removing it from a pathological framework) and give them opportunities to learn and be rewarded for a new repertoire of actions and supporting beliefs. A number of well-developed cognitive–behavioral models for working both with abusive men as a group and with couples aim to eliminate the violence, teach new behaviors, and change dysfunctional thoughts that serve to maintain the violence in the relationship (see, for example, Edleson & Grusznski, 1988; Faulkner, Stoltenberg, Cogen, Nolder, & Shooter, 1992; Neidig, Friedman, & Collins, 1985).

**Exchange/Social Control Theory**

The most comprehensive approach to the study of family violence was developed by sociologists at the Family Violence Research Laboratory at the University of New Hampshire, who used social exchange and social control theories to explain why people are violent in families. In its simplest form the explanation is that "people hit and abuse family members because *they can*" (Gelles & Cornell, 1990, p. 116). Social exchange theory is also used to explain marital satisfaction and stability, as well as the perceived consequences of the violent resolution of conflicts. Relationships last as long as they are mutually rewarding and end when they are no longer rewarding or when they become too costly. People in all kinds of relationships (for example, husband–wife, parent–child, employer–employee, and friend–friend) experience conflict. The way in which conflict is resolved, however, is affected by the type of relationship: Conflicts involving family members are more difficult to avoid and more costly to walk away from than are those involving friends. In the absence of conflict-resolution skills, anger may escalate and lead to violence, especially when the costs of being violent (such as criminal sanctions or divorce) appear to be less than the rewards (for instance, the release of anger, the gaining of power and control over others) (Gelles & Cornell, 1990; Straus & Gelles, 1990). Social control mechanisms (including criminal sanctions) reduce the likelihood of violence by increasing the costs. Yet, until recently, effective social-control mechanisms were rarely applied when violence occurred in the family. Furthermore, certain social and family structures, such as norms of privacy, family isolation, and women's economic dependence, reduce the effectiveness of such mechanisms.

From this perspective, there are three overarching goals of intervention: (1) to reduce the rewards of being violent, (2) to increase the costs, and (3) to increase the social controls. Interventions may occur at the individual, family, and societal levels and include teaching family members to resolve conflicts nonviolently, working toward full-employment policies and adequate income supports to reduce family stress, and ensuring that women have access to community resources that will enable them to leave men who abuse them.

**Feminist Psychological Theory**

Walker (1979, 1988), a feminist psychologist and one of the most influential theorists to address the problem of wife battering specifically, assumes that "men beat up women in order to keep themselves on the top of this whole messy heap" (1979, p. xi). She differs from the other theorists thus far discussed in her insistence that the behaviors of abused women are actually coping strategies that the women develop as a result of living in a brutalizing environment.

Walker was the first to apply the concept of learned helplessness to the experience of battered women. Like the rats in Seligman's (1975) research, women who are abused discover they can do nothing to stop the violence. What they do learn is how to survive. Survival may be costly, however: Women may distort the reality of their abuse, waiting days until they seek medical care; they may dissociate, becoming observers of their own abuse; and they may passively give in to their abusers. Whatever strategies they use, they have learned how to survive. Although individual women may learn to be helpless within a specific relationship, the society reinforces women's helplessness in many ways; not only does gender role socialization prepare women to respond passively to their abuse, but the poverty, discrimination, and sexism they face as adults combine to undermine their ability to control their lives.

Within individual relationships, a cycle of violence develops. During the first stage, the woman keeps small incidents from escalating by acceding to the batterer's demands. Over time, however, small incidents escalate. As the tension builds, the woman may withdraw, isolating herself from friends and family members because she does not want them to know what is going on. Eventually she realizes that her efforts to prevent a further escalation of the violence are ineffective, and she begins to withdraw from the batterer. Fearing that he is losing control of her, he becomes more and more angry. Finally, during the second stage, he explodes. The third stage, calm and respite, quickly follows. The man is profusely repentant and showers the woman with gifts and promises of change. At this point, he is at his most vulnerable, transformed once again into the man she initially loved.

Walker (1988) developed the construct of the battered women's syndrome, a subset of posttraumatic stress disorder, to describe the behaviors of women who have been repeatedly abused. She suggested that the depression, anxiety, and cognitive distortion of reality that may help women survive the abuse also interfere with women's ability to implement effective strategies to change their life situations.

Walker describes three levels of intervention. Primary prevention (for example, eliminating rigid gender role socialization and reducing overall levels of violence) changes the social conditions that directly and indirectly contribute to the abuse of women. Secondary intervention (including crisis hot lines and financial and legal assistance) may enable women who have just begun to experience abuse to break the cycle of violence and take control over their own lives. Tertiary intervention, for women who are so victimized that they are unable to act on their own, requires a totally supportive environment, such as a shelter, where the women will be safe and where they can slowly regain their ability to make decisions for themselves.

**Feminist Social Work Perspective**

Feminists view the physical violence that occurs in intimate relationships as only one aspect of a pattern of behaviors and policies that are designed to control women and to maintain male hegemony. The cornerstone of feminism rests on the notion that society and all its institutions, including the family, are patriarchal. As Abramovitz (1989) noted,

> Patriarchy is grounded in relations of power as well as in the biological differences between the sexes. It consists of a social system that establishes the shared interests and interdependence among men that enables, if not requires, them to dominate women. . . . Under patriarchy, some men have more power than others and while all men benefit from patriarchy, privileges vary sharply by class and race. (p. 25)

Feminists believe that similar means are used to control women's behavior outside and inside the family. Strict adherence to social norms, the application of deviant labels to women who do not conform, rigid gender role socialization, limited access to economically viable jobs, and violence (both within and outside the home) all combine to constrain what women can be and do. Marriage and the family play central roles in maintaining patriarchal domination. Pleck (1987), in her historical analysis of family violence in the United States, described the importance of the "family ideal" in keeping women in their place. The three key elements of the family ideal are (1) belief in the privacy of the family, (2) belief in conjugal and parental rights, and (3) belief in the preservation of the male-headed two-parent family. Throughout history women have stayed in marriages in which they were at serious risk out of a sense of obligation to their children, to their husbands, and to the family ideal.

Instead of labeling families in which there is abuse as dysfunctional and deviant, feminists see such families as a microcosm of a society that oppresses and keeps women in their place. Feminists do not ask, "Why do women stay in abusive relationships?" Instead they ask, "What are the barriers to women leaving abusive relationships?" The answer is the absence of real options that would enable women to provide for themselves. Jobs cannot keep women out of poverty, Aid to Families with Dependent Children (AFDC) is stigmatizing, many men do not pay child support, and low-income housing and affordable child care are not available. These are not new refrains. In the latter half of the 19th century, antebellum feminists understood that women would escape from violence only if they had equal rights. In writing of these first-wave feminists, Pleck (1987) stated,

> In their minds it was preferable for a mother and her children to live alone rather than to remain bound to the inebriate husband. They reformulated the issue of the drunkard's wife so that it became one of wrongs done to women by men. The very survival of the drunkard's wife, they argued, depended on a woman's rights—her right to custody of her children, her right to her own earnings, and her right to secure a divorce. (pp. 49–50)

One hundred years later the issues are similar. The very survival of the batterer's wife depends on a woman's rights—her right to a job that allows her to support her family, her right to receive adequate child support, and her right to safe and affordable housing.

Feminists acknowledge that women's internalized sense of powerlessness presents a barrier to their ability to escape from victimization. Women's socialization into dependent roles, their acceptance of the message that they are responsible for the success of their marriage and the care of their children, their fear that they will remain alone to care for their children and themselves for the rest of their lives, and their belief that they are not capable of raising children alone combine to create a major psychological barrier for many women.

Intervention requires a continuum of services that abused women need to escape their economic and psychological dependence on abusive men. Shelters offer temporary respite and protection while providing a supportive environment in which women can share their stories with one another and learn that their abuse does not stem from personal but from social pathology. Shelters provide a place in which women become responsible for themselves, learn to trust themselves, and develop confidence in their ability to live apart from their abusers.

Women also need economic support. In the short run, they may turn to AFDC. In the long run, however, they need jobs with salaries and benefits that allow them to support their families, and many need education and training to make a successful transition. Women also need permanent affordable and safe housing and legal assistance to help them successfully negotiate the often-difficult process of separation, divorce, and obtaining child custody and support.

While focusing on the needs of individual battered women, feminists emphasize the need for major social transformation: comparable worth, major transformations in social and family values, respect for diverse family forms, and the achievement of real equality for all women.

## Social Policy and Social Work Practice

Effective social work practice with women who are abused requires social policies that acknowledge the need for a range of concrete resources and long-term social investment to enable all women to escape victimization (Davis & Hagen, 1988). Specifically, we need policies that provide resources to enable battered women to choose whether to stay with their abuser. All women need opportunities (financial assistance, job training, well-paying jobs, assured child support, and affordable child care) to become economically self-sufficient, affordable and safe housing, and supportive counseling to enable them to use services effectively.

Federal policy, thus far, has been restricted to providing support for the emergency and short-term needs of victims and their dependents. The Family Violence Prevention and Services Act of 1984 has provided funds for states to allocate primarily to support temporary shelter for battered women. The Victims of Crime Act (1984) has given priority to victims of spousal abuse for compensation for crime-related costs. The Violence Against Women Act, introduced in 1991 but not yet out of committee, is designed, among other things, to increase substantially the amount of federal funds available for states to support domestic violence programs and to allow federal dollars to support statewide coalitions of organizations for battered women.

The major impetus for policy development has come at the state level. Since the late 1970s, an entire network of services has developed across the country, largely through the committed energy of women, many of them formerly battered, who came together in statewide coalitions to develop services, raise public consciousness, and lobby for governmental funding (Davis, Hagen, & Early, 1994; Schechter, 1982). Many states have been creative in developing their own funding mechanisms and in gaining access to diverse federal funds. As a result, states now directly provide about one-third of the funding for battered women's services and act as brokers for another third from the federal government. States have also begun to ensure the quality of services through some form of regulation of shelters. In addition, states have taken the lead in the development of pro-arrest policies for abusers.

## Roles for Social Workers

Because woman abuse is so widespread, there are few settings in which social workers will not encounter women who are abused. Yet, because of the shame attached to being battered, many women are hesitant to share their secret. Social workers are in key positions to break the silence about the abuse that women experience. Building regular questions about relationships, conflicts, and the ways in which conflicts are resolved into assessments can give women permission to share their stories (Brekke, 1987). A central role for social workers is to link women to the resources they need, for despite all the attention in recent years to services for battered women, a surprising number of women remain unaware of the resources available to them (Davis & Srinivasan, 1992), or if they are aware of resources, they may not know how to gain access to them. Women may also benefit when social workers take on case management roles and hence play a more active role in assisting them to obtain resources (Sullivan, 1991). Even if women seem uninterested in being linked to resources, the provision of information may eventually be fruitful. As NiCarthy, Fuller, and Stoops (1987) observed, many women who repeatedly leave and return to their abusive partners may be learning how to use resources and may be gaining strength to enable them to make major life changes later even if there is no immediate observable change in their behavior.

There is evidence that those giving help in various capacities may minimize or ignore the real abuse in women's lives (Gondolf & Fisher, 1988; Stark, Flitcraft, & Frazier, 1979). Although battered women may require referrals for psychiatric evaluation because of serious depression or anxiety (Rounsaville, Lifton, & Bieber, 1979), suicidal threats (Hoff, 1990; Stark et al., 1979), or substance abuse, social workers should remain involved to mediate and advocate for their clients within these other systems, so that these women are not unnecessarily medicated or labeled or the realities of their lives ignored.

Making decisions, even when not in crisis, may be difficult for women who are used to having little control over their own lives. Yet these women may now be in a position where they have to make a number of major life decisions. Thus, social workers may engage in crisis and longer-term counseling with women who are abused (Roberts, 1984) to help them learn to make and implement these important decisions.

Social workers can also help develop, and perhaps co-lead, support groups for women who are abused. Much of the literature on working with women who are abused, especially to help them counteract the gender role socialization and deal with the psychological sequelae of their abuse, emphasizes the value of support groups (see, for example, Lewis, 1983; NiCarthy, Merriam, & Coffman, 1984; Wood & Middleman, 1992).

Although there is considerable literature on marital therapy as a mode of intervention for women who are abused, such intervention should be offered only when social workers can ensure women's safety. Social workers who wish to undertake family intervention should proceed with caution.

Social work, with its historical focus on the person-in-environment, is in a unique position to frame the problem of woman abuse within the larger social context and to advocate at a national level for policies that truly empower all women.

## References


Abramovitz, M. (1989) *Regulating the lives of women: Social welfare policy from colonial times to the present.* Boston: South End Press.

Berk, R. A., Berk, S. F., Loseke, D. R., & Rauma, D. (1983). Mutual combat and other family violence myths. In D. Finkelhor, R. J. Gelles, G. T. Hotaling, & M. A. Straus (Eds.), *The dark side of families: Current family violence research* (pp. 197–212). Newbury Park, CA: Sage Publications.

Blackstone, W. (1979). *Commentaries on the laws of England,* 444–445 (facsimile of the 1st ed. of 1765–1769).

Brekke, J. S. (1987). Detecting wife and child abuse in clinical settings. *Social Casework, 68,* 332–338.

Browne, A. (1987). *When battered women kill.* New York: Free Press.

Brush, L. D. (1990). Violent acts and injurious outcomes in married couples: Methodological issues in the National Survey of Families and Households. *Gender and Society, 4,* 56–67.

Carlson, B. E. (1987). Dating violence: A research review and comparison with spouse abuse. *Social Casework, 68,* 16–23.

Cazenave, N. A., & Straus, M. A. (1990). Race, class, network embeddedness, and family violence: A search for potent support systems. In M. A. Straus & R. J. Gelles (Eds.), *Physical violence in American families: Risk factors and adaptations to violence in 8,145 families* (pp. 321–339). New Brunswick, NJ: Transaction.

Davis, L. V., & Hagen, J. L. (1988). Services for battered women: The public policy response. *Social Service Review, 62,* 649–667.

Davis, L. V., Hagen, J., & Early, T. (1994). Social services for battered women: Are they adequate, accessible, and appropriate? *Social Work, 39,* 695–704.

Davis, L. V., & Srinivasan, M. (1992, March). *Listening to the voices of battered women: What helps them escape violence.* Paper presented at the 38th Annual Program Meeting of the Council on Social Work Education, Kansas City, MO.

Dibble, U., & Straus, M. E. (1990). Some social structure determinants of inconsistency between attitudes and behaviors: The case of family violence. In M. A. Straus & R. J. Gelles (Eds.), *Physical violence in American families* (pp. 167–180). New Brunswick, NJ: Transaction.

Dobash, R. E., & Dobash, R. (1979). *Violence against wives: A case against the patriarchy*. New York: Free Press.

Edleson, J. L., & Grusznski, R. J. (1988). Treating men who batter. Four years of outcome data from the Domestic Abuse Project. *Journal of Social Service Research, 12,* 3–22.

Eisenberg, S. E., & Micklow, P. L. (1977). The assaulted wife: "Catch 22" revisited. *Women's Rights Law Reporter, 3,* 138–161.

Family Violence Prevention and Services Act of 1984. P.L. 98-457, 98 Stat. 1762.

Faulkner, K., Stoltenberg, C. D., Cogen, R., Nolder, M., & Shooter, E. (1992). Cognitive–behavioral group treatment for male spouse abusers. *Journal of Family Violence, 7,* 37–55.

Finkelhor, D., & Yllo, K. (1985). *License to rape: Sexual abuse of wives*. New York: Holt, Rinehart & Winston.

Gelles, R. J. (1976). Abused wives: Why do they stay? *Journal of Marriage and the Family, 38,* 659–668.

Gelles, R. J. (1977). Power, sex and violence: The case of marital rape. *Family Coordinator, 26,* 339–347.

Gelles, R. J., & Cornell, C. P. (1990). *Intimate violence in families* (2nd ed.). Newbury Park, CA: Sage Publications.

Gelles, R. J., & Straus, M. A. (1988). *Intimate violence*. New York: Simon & Schuster.

Gondolf, E. W., & Fisher, E. R. (1988). *Battered women as survivors: An alternative to treating learned helplessness*. Lexington, MA: Lexington Press.

Hofeller, K. (1983). *Battered women, shattered lives*. Palo Alto, CA: R & E Associates.

Hoff, L. A. (1990). *Battered women as survivors*. London: Routledge & Kegan Paul.

Kalmuss, D. S., & Straus, M. A. (1990). Wife's marital dependency and wife abuse. In M. A. Straus & R. J. Gelles (Eds.), *Physical violence in American families* (pp. 369–382). New Brunswick, NJ: Transaction.

Kantor, G. K., & Straus, M. A. (1990). The "drunken bum" theory of wife battering. In M. A. Straus & R. J. Gelles (Eds.), *Physical violence in American families* (pp. 203–224). New Brunswick, NJ: Transaction.

Lane, K. E., & Gwartney-Gibbs, P. (1985). Violence in the context of dating and sex. *Journal of Family Issues, 6,* 45–59.

Leonard, K. E., Bromet, E. J., Parkinson, D. K., Day, N. L., & Ryan, C. M. (1985). Patterns of alcohol use and physically aggressive behavior. *Journal of Studies on Alcohol, 46,* 279–282.

Leonard, K. E., & Jacob, T. (1988). Alcohol, alcoholism, and family violence. In V. B. Van Hassalt, R. L. Morrison, A. S. Bellack, & M. Hersen (Eds.), *Handbook of family violence* (pp. 383–406). New York: Plenum Press.

Lewis, E. (1983). The group treatment of battered women. *Women and Therapy, 2,* 51–58.

Magill, J. (1989). Family therapy: An approach to the treatment of wife assault. In B. Pressman, G. Cameron, & M. Rothery (Eds.), *Intervening with assaulted women: Current theory, research, and practice* (pp. 47–55). Hillsdale, NJ: Lawrence Erlbaum.

Neidig, P. H., Friedman, D. H., & Collins, B. S. (1985). Domestic conflict containment: A spouse abuse treatment program. *Social Casework, 66,* 195–204.

NiCarthy, G., Fuller, A., & Stoops, N. (1987). Battering and abuse of women in intimate relationships. In D. S. Burden & N. Gottlieb (Eds.), *The woman client: Providing human services in a changing world* (pp. 75–92). New York: Tavistock.

NiCarthy, G., Merriam, K., & Coffman, S. (1984). *Talking it out: A guide to groups for abused women*. Seattle: Seal Press.

O'Leary, K. D. (1988). Physical aggression between spouses: A social learning theory perspective. In V. B. Van Hassalt, R. L. Morrison, A. S. Bellack, & M. Hersen (Eds.), *Handbook of family violence* (pp. 31–55). New York: Plenum Press.

Pleck, E. (1987). *Domestic tyranny: The making of American social policy against family violence from colonial times to the present*. New York: Oxford University Press.

Randall, T. (1990). Domestic violence intervention calls for more than treating injuries. *Journal of the American Medical Association, 264,* 939–940.

Rhodes, S. L. (1986). Family treatment. In F. J. Turner (Ed.), *Social work treatment: Interlocking theoretical perspectives* (3rd ed., pp. 432–453). New York: Free Press.

Roberts, A. R. (1984). Crisis intervention with battered women. In A. Roberts (Ed.), *Battered women and their families: Intervention, strategies, and treatment programs* (pp. 65–83). New York: Springer.

Rounsaville, B., Lifton, N., & Bieber, M. (1979). The natural history of a psychotherapy group for battered women. *Psychiatry, 42,* 63–78.

Russell, D.E.H. (1982). *Rape in marriage*. New York: Macmillan.

Saunders, D. G. (1988). Wife abuse, husband abuse, or mutual combat? A feminist perspective on the empirical findings. In K. Yllo & M. Bograd (Eds.), *Feminist perspective on wife abuse* (pp. 90–113). Newbury Park, CA: Sage Publications.

Schechter, S. (1982). *Women and male violence: The visions and struggles of the battered women's movement*. Boston: South End Press.

Schechter, S. (1990, November). *Women who leave abusive partners and their children: From victim to survivor through support, advocacy, and therapy*. Master class presented at Social Work '90: NASW's Annual Meeting of the Profession, Boston.

Schwartz, M. D. (1987). Gender and injury in spousal assault. *Sociological Focus, 20,* 61–75.

Seligman, M.E.P. (1975). *Helplessness: On depression, development, and death*. San Francisco: W. H. Freeman.

Shainess, N. (1979). Vulnerability to violence: Masochism as process. *American Journal of Psychotherapy, 33,* 174–189.

Stark, E., & Flitcraft, A. (1988). Violence among intimates: An epidemiological review. In V. B. Van Hassalt, R. L. Morrison, A. S. Bellack, & M. Hersen (Eds.), *Handbook of family violence* (pp. 293–317). New York: Plenum Press.

Stark, E., Flitcraft, A., & Frazier, W. (1979). Medicine and patriarchal violence: The social construction of a "private" event. *International Journal of Health Services, 9,* 461–493.

Stedman, B. (1917). Right of husband to chastise wife. *Virginia Law Register, 3,* 241–248.

Stets, J. E., & Straus, M. A. (1990). Gender differences in reporting marital violence and its medical and psychological consequences. In M. A. Straus & R. J. Gelles (Eds.), *Physical violence in American families: Risk factors and adaptations to violence in 8,145 families* (pp. 151–165). New Brunswick, NJ: Transaction.

Straus, M. A. (1990). Ordinary violence, child abuse, and wife-beating: What do they have in common? In M. A. Straus and R. J. Gelles (Eds.), *Physical violence in American families: Risk factors and adaptations to violence in 8,145 families*. New Brunswick, NJ: Transaction.

Straus, M. A., & Gelles, M. A. (1986). Societal change and change in family violence from 1975 to 1985 as revealed by two national surveys. *Journal of Marriage and the Family, 48,* 465–479.

Straus, M. A., & Gelles, R. J. (1990). How violent are American families? Estimates from the National Family Violence Resurvey and other studies. In M. A. Straus & R. J. Gelles (Eds.), *Physical violence in American families: Risk factors and adaptations to violence in 8,145 families* (pp. 95–112). New Brunswick, NJ: Transaction.

Straus, M., Gelles, R., & Steinmetz, S. (1980). *Behind closed doors: Violence in the American family*. Garden City, NY: Doubleday.

Straus, M. A., & Smith, C. (1990). Violence in Hispanic families in the United States: Incidence rates and structural interpretations. In M. A. Straus & R. J. Gelles (Eds.), *Physical violence in American families: Risk factors and adaptations to violence in 8,145 families* (pp. 341–367). New Brunswick, NJ: Transaction.

Strube, M. J., & Barbour, L. S. (1984). Factors related to the decision to leave an abusive relationship. *Journal of Marriage and the Family, 46,* 837–844.

Suitor, J. J., Pillemer, K., & Straus, M. A. (1990). Marital violence in a life course perspective. In M. A. Straus & R. J. Gelles (Eds.), *Physical violence in American families: Risk factors and adaptations to violence in 8,145 families* (pp. 305–317). New Brunswick, NJ: Transaction.

Sullivan, C. M. (1991, August). Battered women as active helpseekers. *Violence Update*, pp. 1, 8, 10.

Victims of Crime Act of 1984. P.L. 98-473, 98 Stat. 2170.

Walker, L. E. (1979). *The battered woman*. New York: Harper Colophon.

Walker, L. E. (1988). The battered woman syndrome. In G. T. Hoteling, D. Finkelhor, J. T. Kirkpatrick, & M. A. Straus (Eds.), *Family abuse and its consequences*. Newbury Park, CA: Sage Publications.

Weitzman, J., & Dreen, K. (1982). Wife beating: A view of the marital dyad. *Social Casework, 63,* 259–265.

Wolfgang, M. E. (1957). Victim-precipitated criminal homicide. *Journal of Criminal Law, Criminology and Police Science, 48,* 1–11.

Wood, G. G., & Middleman, R. R. (1992). Groups to empower battered women. *Affilia, 7,* 82–95.

Yllo, K. A., & Straus, M. A. (1981). Interpersonal violence among marriage and cohabiting couples. *Family Relations, 30,* 339–347.

**Liane V. Davis, PhD, ACSW, LSCSW,** is associate professor, University of Kansas, School of Social Welfare, Twente Hall, Lawrence, KS 66045.

### For further information see

Alcohol Abuse; Conflict Resolution; Drug Abuse; Domestic Violence: Legal Issues; Homicide; Marriage/Partners; Men Overview; Sexual Assault; Substance Abuse: Direct Practice; Victim Services and Victim/Witness Assistance Programs; Violence Overview; Women Overview.

**Key Words**

battered women
domestic violence
spouse abuse

# Domestic Violence: Legal Issues

**Daniel G. Saunders**

Laws and their administration tend to reflect cultural norms. Societies like the United States that derived their laws from British common law once condoned wife beating, at least within certain limits. The phrase "rule of thumb" comes from a British law stating that a man could punish his wife as he would an apprentice or a child with a "rod not thicker than his thumb" (U.S. Commission on Civil Rights, 1982). Social workers who work in a variety of settings and perform various roles need a clear understanding of the history of and recent developments in the legal response to domestic violence and the actions that they can take to fight the problem in the criminal justice arena.

Today, domestic violence is generally defined as a wide range of physical aggression, from pushing and slapping to beating, rape, and assault with a weapon. Threats of violence and stalking are also increasingly being recognized as serious problems that are subject to legal sanctions in nearly every state (Kaysen & Weissman, 1994). Psychological abuse, although not covered under criminal statutes, has severe effects and thus needs to be considered in the treatment of offenders and victims (Follingstad, Rutledge, Berg, Hause, & Polek, 1990). Unlike assaults between strangers, domestic assaults are likely to be repeated (Straus, Gelles, & Steinmetz, 1980). The most affected victims, physically and psychologically, are women, including single and married women and women separated or divorced from their partners (Stets & Straus, 1990a, 1990b).

## History

### Civil Law

In addition to the view of women as property or as children, British common law included the notion that married women did not have a legal identity separate from their husbands and thus could not sue their husbands—a concept known as interspousal tort immunity. Such laws were changed in the 19th century in relation to property, but were slower to change with regard to personal injury (Spector, 1989). Arguments in favor of such laws were that (1) marital harmony would be disrupted if one spouse was allowed to sue another, (2) marital partners might collude in making false claims to defraud insurance companies, and (3) the aggrieved party could use divorce action or criminal prosecution instead of a lawsuit. The evidence goes counter to these arguments: It is violence, not lawsuits, that disrupts marital harmony; there are legal safeguards against fraud, and fraud is rare; and other legal actions do not guarantee that justice will be served.

Even with legal changes, however, battered women may not be treated the same as persons who sue nonintimates because to be held liable, a person must be shown to have caused severe mental distress by "outrageous conduct." Tolman (1992) illustrated this situation by presenting two cases in which battered women were not awarded damages. In one case, the husband was verbally abusive and took control of the family finances after leaving the family. In the second case, an ex-husband frequently drove past his ex-wife's house, embarrassed her publicly, and tried to get her fired from her job. The court ruled that the husband's conduct in the first case was not "outrageous" and that the ex-wife's mental distress was not severe in the second case.

### Criminal Law

Although wife beating was made illegal in most states by 1870 (Pleck, 1987), it took 100 years for the women's movement to push for the consistent enforcement of these laws. Advocates for battered women noted the formal and informal policies that were used to treat wife-assault cases less seriously than other crimes. For example, some police departments had informal "stitch rules" that required a certain number of stitches before an arrest was made (Field & Field, 1973). In addition, before 1970 police department training manuals stated that domestic violence was not serious and that marital privacy should be respected—a notion that often incorporated the patriarchal view that "a man's home is his castle." Furthermore, the police and prosecutors gave a number of reasons that they believed justified nonintervention, for example, the victim would only change her mind later about prosecution, the other segments of the criminal justice system would not follow through, and there would be no witnesses and perhaps the charges had been made vindictively.

Procedures were often put in place to test the determination of the victim to follow through with prosecution. However, arrest and prosecution do not have to be the only goal. Many battered women want their abusers arrested to force them into treatment, rather than to go to prison (Saunders & Size, 1986).

A legal form of assault that only recently has been removed from the books in most states is marital rape (Hart, 1992). Again, this society is influenced by the common law doctrines of the subordination of women and the oneness of husband and wife. The reasoning behind this legal tradition is that rape cannot truly occur in marriage because through the marriage contract, the wife gives consent to sex on demand. Also, if a husband and wife are one, he cannot rape himself. As in the case of tort laws, there is a growing awareness that it is the abuse, not the legal action, that disrupts family life. However, few cases of marital rape have been brought to prosecution, probably because few women know about the new laws.

## Recent Developments

### Arrest

Most reform efforts with regard to domestic violence have focused on changing the behavior of police by changing the policies of police departments and state laws. Several class-action suits in the late 1970s and a successful civil damage suit against a city in the 1980s were filed to force police departments to establish policies that would treat assaults against intimates like any other type of assault. Policy reform was speeded considerably by the attention given to the landmark Minneapolis police experiment, which showed that arrest was the most effective option (Sherman & Berk, 1984); that study, however, was limited to misdemeanor assaults and a six-month follow-up. Five subsequent experiments failed to show that arrest is a deterrent to further violence in all contexts (Sherman, 1992). Advocates for battered women have pointed out that arrest alone may not have much effect; instead, what they believe is needed is a coordinated response among many agencies that includes the prosecution and education of offenders (Zorza & Woods, 1994).

Most of the new policies of preferred arrest or mandatory arrest make it clear that a warrant is not necessary for a misdemeanor assault arrest; that witnesses and injuries do not have to be present; and that domestic violence is a crime against the state, rather than a personal dispute. Most policies explicitly state that a victim's willingness to assist the police and prosecutors with the case should not be considered in the decision to arrest. Often the women are too intimidated or too emotionally attached to the offenders to aid the prosecution. The police must also learn that even if an arrest cannot be made or does not lead to prosecution, investigation and careful record keeping can aid the prosecution later. For abuse of women, unlike child and elder abuse, professionals who *hear* about the abuse are not required by law to report it; only health care workers who *witness* a certain level of injury are required to report it.

It has become clear that more than a change in policies is needed to change attitudes and behavior. In some jurisdictions, a higher arrest rate may be due to the arrests made by only a few police officers (Sherman & Berk, 1984). Police officers may also display their anger over restricted discretion by finding a reason to arrest the victims. For example, if a woman is making a "public disturbance" or used force to defend herself, she may be arrested along with or instead of her partner (Saunders, in press).

**Prosecution**

Because of the likelihood that the victim may be too intimidated to testify against her partner, some prosecutors have "no-drop" policies, whereby they do not usually drop the charges even if the victim wishes to do so. As a result, there is less chance today that victims who refuse to testify will be labeled "hostile" or "uncooperative." Another reason for not dropping charges is that the offender is likely to abuse the woman's children and may leave his current partner only to abuse another (Saunders, 1994). Specially trained prosecutors may be assigned to assist with these cases and may work with police officers, detectives, and victim advocates on "sensitive crimes" task forces.

Some prosecutors' offices have their own victim-support units that are staffed by social workers or other human service workers. These units inform the victims of their rights, gather information for prosecution, refer the victims for services, and support the victims throughout the legal proceedings. In cases in which the offenders are not arrested, these units may send letters to the victims informing them of their legal options and inspect police reports for evidence that could be used in prosecuting the offenders.

In some prosecutors' offices, policies are established to determine when prosecution will be deferred. Typically, prosecution is deferred for first-time, misdemeanor cases, provided the offenders agree to complete a specialized treatment program. Other jurisdictions prefer to obtain a guilty plea or proceed with prosecution and then stay the sentence pending the offenders' successful completion of treatment. The failure to comply with conditions of probation under a stayed sentence leads to swifter and more certain consequences. There is some evidence that a combination of arrest and treatment is effective in lowering the rate of recidivism for domestic violence (Dutton, 1986). However, the results of treatment are not conclusive because well-controlled outcome studies have yet to be conducted (Tolman & Bennett, 1990).

**Restraining Orders**

A restraining order typically orders the assailant to stay away from the victim and may include orders not to contact her by telephone or through the mail. Procedures for obtaining orders of protection are becoming more streamlined in many jurisdictions. Special forms should be readily available and easy to understand. In the past, immediate and inexpensive protection was frequently not available. In most jurisdictions, a temporary restraining order is issued "ex-parte" (without the assailant being present at the hearing).

The failure to comply with restraining orders is now more likely to carry criminal instead of civil penalties (Hart, 1992). A restraining order with civil contempt provisions does not allow police officers to make an immediate arrest; instead, the victim must first inform the judge of the violation and then the offender may be arrested for contempt of court. There is evidence that restraining orders are less effective for those with a history of severe offenses (Elliott, 1989). Thus, battered women should not be lulled into a false sense of security by restraining orders. Among the best protection when the potential for death is high is the woman's relocation in another part of the country with a new identity.

**When Battered Women Kill**

Legal and material resources for battered women appear to be lowering the incidence of wife-to-husband homicide in the United States (Browne & Williams, 1989). However, battered women who kill their partners may find themselves in the midst of another nightmare. Given the bias toward them in the criminal justice system, women who kill could receive a life sentence in prison, even if they killed their partners in self-defense or there were strong mitigating circumstances.

The chances are that the prisons in which these women are incarcerated will be much less adequate than are those for men. Women in prison are sometimes harassed verbally and sexually and are not given the same educational and training opportunities as are men. They may experience nightmares and flashbacks about the past assaults and not receive adequate counseling to handle them. Their children may not be able to visit often, and they may be placed with relatives of their deceased husbands. Many of these women killed their partners in self-defense, but were not acquitted because the proper defense was not provided. The defense attorneys may have too readily plea bargained to a lesser offense or were unable or unwilling to have an expert witness testify.

The defense attorney and expert witness must work together as a team to establish a nonsexist interpretation of the law of self-defense. Advocates for battered women and the woman's personal counselor can also consult for the defense even if they do not testify. Traditionally, self-defense statutes were interpreted by the "reasonable man standard" which asked: What level of force would be justified to repel an attack by one man against another man who was a stranger or acquaintance? This standard ignores two points when applied to battered women: Women usually need to use a weapon to defend themselves successfully, and battered women may realistically fear for their lives on the basis of their history of being abused and threatened and the recent escalation of violence. Men carry lethal weapons with them at all times when they attack women: Choking and beatings with fists are the causes of death about half the time (Chimbos, 1978). The model federal code has now adopted the "subjective standard" for self-defense cases which allows testimony on womens' perceptions of danger (Gibbs, 1993).

An expert witness can be invaluable in helping a judge and jury understand a number of points:

- why the woman stayed in the relationship, including her emotional and material ties and the apathy or hostility of some professionals she may have sought help from
- how events preceding the homicide could reasonably cause the woman to fear that she would be killed
- why the woman may have amnesia for events surrounding the homicide
- why the woman may have a flat affect that makes her appear indifferent to her plight
- why the woman's fear of imminent death could continue even if she was not being attacked at the time she killed her partner.

Because many battered women in prisons were not properly represented at trial, clemency boards have released some of them in recent years. For those who are still in prison, counseling and support groups are slowly being added to prison services (Bauschard, 1986).

**Child Custody Decisions**

Battered women sometimes lose custody of their children because family courts and those who conduct evaluations for them do not fully understand the dynamics of battering relationships (Saunders, 1994). Many do not realize that the male partners' risk of child abuse is about twice as high as that of the battered women (Straus, 1983). Even if the men are not violent toward the children, they have severely emotionally abused them by exposing them to violence against their mothers (Jaffe, Wolfe, & Wilson, 1990). This exposure does not necessarily end when the relationship does. About a fourth of these men continue to threaten and physically abuse their partners after divorce and separation (Saunders, 1994). Some of them find a new partner to batter and may thereby further expose the children to violence.

The courts' and their evaluators' assumptions about these cases are often based on unfounded clinical lore or partial truths. For example, childhood experience with violence is not as strong a predictor of child abuse as was once thought (Kaufman & Zigler, 1987). The results of psychological tests and courtroom demeanor may also be misleading. In these situations, battered women are overwhelmed with multiple traumas: the accumulation of stress from years of physical and emotional abuse, the fear of losing their children, and the fear that their partners will abuse the children. These women often score in the pathological range on psychological tests or appear to be "overly" emotional (angry, tearful, confused, and distraught) to the evaluators or judges. Thus, their evaluations must be placed in the context of past and current stress because the psychological tests usually reflect this stress, rather than a personality trait or chronic mental disorder (Rosewater, 1987).

On the other hand, the problems of men who batter, including alcoholism and psychic wounds from childhood traumas, are usually much more chronic. Yet, these men can be skilled at hiding their problems. Their chronic problems do not often appear as severe mental disorders but as personality disorders, including antisocial, narcissistic, dependent, and borderline personality disorders (Hamberger & Hastings, 1986). Further, the completion of specialized programs for men who batter is not a guarantee that these men will stop their abusive behavior; a substantial minority of them continue to be violent six months to a year after treatment (Saunders & Azar, 1989).

Sole or joint custody should rarely be granted to men who batter because of the risk of continued physical and emotional abuse. Most states have recognized this risk and have passed laws that require that domestic violence be taken into account when decisions about custody are made (Hart, 1992). Such laws may decrease the use of questionable criteria—financial stability and remarriage—that are likely to favor the fathers.

## Social Work Roles

A social work perspective is needed in the legal response to domestic violence because social workers assess people within the social environment and emphasize strengths more than deficits and pathology. Thus, it is possible to place diagnostic labels in a social context and to uncover biases in psychological and psychiatric reports that have a strong impact on legal dispositions. An ecological approach is needed for prevention and intervention that involves many systems. The broadest level of change is the social level.

### Advocating for Social Change

Before one considers steps that can be taken to intervene with current cases, it is important to recognize how social workers can help with primary prevention. Cross-cultural studies have found a clear connection between gender inequality and domestic violence (Levinson, 1989; Yllo, 1983). Thus, social work's continuing struggle against gender inequality will help to reduce domestic violence in the years to come. The profession's struggle against racism and classism is also a form of prevention because there is evidence that racism and classism produce stress and anger that are related to family violence (Cazenave & Straus, 1979; Straus & Smith, 1990).

One of the ironies of family violence is that the offender is often acting out of a sense of powerlessness. Because of this society's hierarchical structures, there is great inequality among men, and men are damaged by sex-role conditioning and sexist norms (Taubman, 1986). Therefore, social workers need to find substitutes for the social messages that push men to be achievement oriented, possessive, and emotionally tough. Programs are needed not only for men who batter, but to help all men adapt to women's increasing status and to loosen the link between men's self-worth and material achievements. Programs are also needed for high-risk groups, for example, the children of battered women and others who witness violence on a daily basis. As Attorney General Janet Reno has said repeatedly, the prevention of violent crime begins with interventions in homes where children experience violence (Brownstein, 1993).

### Advocating for Systems Change

Social workers have been instrumental in creating new federal, state, and local laws and policies like those described here. They have also been involved in helping to ensure that these laws and policies are implemented, for example, by developing and conducting training workshops for police. One type of law that was not described is the expansion in some states of laws that provide compensation for crime victims to include medical and mental health care for battered women.

A large percentage of the staffs of domestic violence organizations, such as battered women's shelters (44 percent of staff, 65 percent of advisory boards) (Roberts, 1981) and offender treatment programs (61 percent) (Pirog-Good & Stets-Kealey, 1985), are social workers. Most programs that provide direct service are also committed to social change and system change, although funding for such efforts is usually meager.

### Advocating for Individuals and Families

Social workers become involved in advocating directly for battered women in a number of ways. Within the criminal justice system, they may provide advocacy in prosecutors' offices. Outside the criminal justice system, they may work for shelter programs as advocates who explain legal rights to victims and help victims through the legal process of obtaining a restraining order or testifying in criminal proceedings and preparing victim-impact statements. In some shelters and medical settings, advocates work with victims' children, to decide if official reports of child abuse and neglect, including emotional abuse, should be made and to make recommendations to the courts about custody and visitation. Social workers also work on legal advocacy projects to ensure equal rights for women in prison and on clemency projects to help some imprisoned women gain freedom.

### Direct Practice

Social workers are involved in a number of direct service functions. For example, they provide supportive counseling to help battered women feel comfortable testifying in court proceedings and to help battered women who killed their partners remember more accurately the events surrounding the homicides. Much of the "counseling" for battered women, their partners, and their children is psychoeducational in that it teaches them about domestic violence laws and changing social norms. Some writers, such as Pence (1989), consider the treatment of men who batter a monitoring function, closely tied to the criminal justice system. In all direct practice work, thorough documentation by the social worker can make the difference between a successful and unsuccessful legal case. If a client chooses to invoke the privilege of worker-client confidentiality, some state laws now include shelter workers.

**Expert Testimony**

Social workers are increasingly being asked to testify as experts in court proceedings because of their extensive practice or research knowledge in the area. They may testify in cases involving battered women who kill or in disputes over child custody, as described earlier. They may also be asked to testify for the prosecution when assailants are on trial.

**Developing a Coordinated Community Response**

Perhaps because of their ecological perspective, social workers have been leaders in the development of coordinated community-response models for stopping domestic violence (see, for example, Brygger & Edleson, 1987). These models usually evolved from task forces with several key agencies: battered women's shelters, prosecutors' offices, police and sheriffs' departments, and programs for men who batter. The goal of coordinating groups is to strive to establish a consistent philosophy and set of policies. Workers from representative agencies may have to overcome mistrust and educate each other about their roles. They usually have to struggle to develop a new set of policies for their community. Recently, many communities have begun to improve their coordination of services by including child protection and health care workers. Often, a coordinating council or a task force sponsors public awareness campaigns or primary prevention programs in the schools. These groups realize that the best hope of solving the problem of domestic violence lies in their attempts to keep it from occurring in the first place.

## References


Bauschard, L. (1986). *Voices set free: Battered women speak from prison.* St. Louis: Women's Self-Help Center.

Browne, A., & Williams, K. R. (1989). Exploring the effect of resource availability and the likelihood of female-perpetrated homicides. *Law and Society Review, 23*(1), 75–94.

Brownstein, R. (1993, July 11). Atty. Gen. Reno calls on U.S. to 'invest in children.' *Los Angeles Times,* p. A4.

Brygger, M. P., & Edelson, J. (1987). The domestic abuse project: A multisystems intervention in woman battering. *Journal of Interpersonal Violence, 2,* 324–336.

Cazenave, N. A., & Straus, M. A. (1979). Race, class, network embeddedness, and family violence. *Journal of Comparative Family Studies, 10,* 280–299.

Chimbos, P. D. (1978). *Marital violence: A study of interspousal homicide.* San Francisco: R & E Associates.

Dutton, D. (1986). The outcome of court-mandated treatment for wife assault: A quasi-experimental evaluation. *Violence and Victims, 1,* 163–176.

Elliott, D. (1989). Criminal justice procedures in family violence crimes. In L. Ohlin & M. Tonry (Eds.), *Family violence* (pp. 427–480). Chicago: University of Chicago.

Field, H., & Field, M. (1973). Marital violence and the criminal process. Neither justice nor peace. *Social Service Review, 47,* 221–240.

Follingstad, D. R., Rutledge, L. L., Berg, B. J., Hause, E. S., & Polek D. S. (1990). The role of emotional abuse in physically abusive relationships. *Journal of Family Violence, 5,* 107–119.

Gibbs, N. (1993, January 18). 'Til death do us part.' *Time, 141*(3), 38–45.

Hamberger, L. K., & Hastings, J. E. (1986). Personality correlates of men who abuse their partners: A cross-validation study. *Journal of Family Violence, 1,* 323–341.

Hart, B. J. (1992). *State codes on domestic violence: Analysis, commentary, and recommendations.* (Available from National Council of Juvenile and Family Court Judges, University of Nevada, P.O. Box 8970, Reno, NV 89507)

Jaffe, P. G., Wolfe, D. A., & Wilson, S. K. (1990). *Children of battered women.* Newbury Park, CA: Sage Publications.

Kaufman, J., & Zigler, E. (1987). Do abused children become abusive parents? *American Journal of Orthopsychiatry, 57,* 186–198.

Kaysen, G., & Weissman, J. (1994). Stalking laws enacted to protect women. *National NOW Times, 27*(1), 14.

Levinson, D. (1989). *Family violence in cross-cultural perspective.* Newbury Park, CA: Sage Publications.

Pence, E. (1989). Batterer programs: Shifting from community collusion to community confrontation. In P. L. Caesar & L. K. Hamberger (Eds.), *Treating men who batter* (pp. 24–50). New York: Springer.

Pirog-Good, M., & Stets-Kealey, J. (1985). Male batterers and battering prevention programs: A national survey. *Response, 8,* 8–12.

Pleck, E. (1987). *Domestic tyranny: The making of social policy against family violence from colonial times to the present.* New York: Oxford University Press.

Roberts, A. R. (1981). *Sheltering battered women: A national study and service guide.* New York: Springer.

Rosewater, L. B. (1987). The clinical and courtroom application of battered women's personality assessments. In D. Sonkin (Ed.), *Domestic violence on trial* (pp. 86–96). New York: Springer.

Saunders, D. G. (1994). Child custody decisions in families experiencing woman abuse. *Social Work, 39,* 51–59.

Saunders, D. G. (in press). The tendency to arrest victims of domestic violence: A preliminary analysis of officer characteristics. *Journal of Interpersonal Violence.*

Saunders, D. G., & Azar, S. T. (1989). Treatment programs for family violence. In L. Ohlin & M. Tonry (Eds.), *Family violence: Crime and justice, A review of research* (Vol. 11, pp. 481–546). Chicago: University of Chicago Press.

Saunders, D. G., & Size, P. B. (1986). Attitudes about woman abuse among police officers, victims, and victim advocates. *Journal of Interpersonal Violence, 1,* 25–42.

Sherman, L. W. (1992). *Policing domestic violence: Experiments and dilemmas.* New York: Free Press.

Sherman, L. W., & Berk, R. A. (1984). The specific deterrent effects of arrest for domestic assault. *American Psychological Review, 49,* 261–272.

Spector, R. G. (1989). Marital torts. *Family Law Reporter, 15,* 3023.

Stets, J. E., & Straus, M. A. (1990a). Gender differences in reporting marital violence and its medical and psychological consequences. In M. A. Strauss & R. J. Gelles (Eds.), *Physical violence in American families.* New Brunswick, NJ: Transaction.

Stets, J. E., & Straus, M. A. (1990b). The marriage license as a hitting license: A comparison of dating, cohabiting, and married couples. In M. A. Straus & R. J. Gelles (Eds.), *Physical violence in American families.* New Brunswick, NJ: Transaction.

Straus, M. A. (1983). Ordinary violence, child abuse, and wife beating: What do they have in common? In D. Finkelhor, R. J. Gelles, G. T. Hotaling, & M. A. Straus (Eds.), *The dark side of families: Current family violence research* (pp. 213–234). Newbury Park, CA: Sage Publications.

Straus, M. A., Gelles, R. J., & Steinmetz, S. K. (1980). *Behind closed doors: Violence in the American family.* New York: Doubleday/Anchor.

Straus, M. A., & Smith, C. (1990). Violence in Hispanic families in the United States: Incidence rates and structural interpretations. In M. A. Straus & R. J. Gelles (Eds.), *Physical violence in American families.* New Brunswick, NJ: Transaction.

Taubman, S. (1986). Beyond the bravado: Sex roles and the exploitive male. *Social Work, 31,* 12–18.

Tolman, R. M. (1992). Psychological abuse of women. In R. T. Ammerman & M. Hersen (Eds.), *Assessment of family violence: A clinical and legal sourcebook* (pp. 291–312). New York: John Wiley & Sons.

Tolman, R. M., & Bennett, L. W. (1990). A review of research on men who batter. *Journal of Interpersonal Violence, 5,* 87–118.

U.S. Commission on Civil Rights. (1982). *Under the rule of thumb: Battered women and the administration of justice.* Washington, DC: U.S. Government Printing Office.

Yllo, K. (1983). Sexuality inequality and violence against wives in American states. *Journal of Comparative Family Studies, 14,* 67–86.

Zorza, J., & Woods, L. (1994). *Analysis and policy implications of the new domestic violence police studies.* New York: National Center on Women and Family Law.

**Daniel G. Saunders, PhD,** is associate professor, University of Michigan, School of Social Work, 1065 Frieze Building, Ann Arbor, MI 48109.

### For further information see

Conflict Resolution; Domestic Violence; Ethics and Values; Families Overview; Homicide; Interdisciplinary and Interorganizational Collaboration; Legal Issues: Confidentiality and Privileged Communication; Legal Issues: Low-Income and Dependent People; Marriage/Partners; Professional Conduct; Professional Liability and Malpractice; Victim Services and Victim/Witness Assistance Programs; Violence Overview; Women Overview.

**Key Words**

| | |
|---|---|
| domestic violence | wife assault |
| legal perspectives | woman abuse |

# Drug Abuse

**Muriel C. Gray**

The National Institute on Drug Abuse (NIDA, 1992) estimates that 85 percent of the general population uses drugs in one form or another. Therefore, a large percentage of social work clients probably use or abuse drugs. Furthermore, drug abuse tends to be masked by various problems that are often the result, rather than the cause, of the drug abuse (Doweiko, 1993).

Given the prevalence of drug use, the potential for drug abuse, the dangers of drug dependence, and the relationship of drugs to a myriad of social problems, most social workers work directly or indirectly with the consequences of drug abuse. Directly, they work with clients who use and abuse drugs or in organizations that address the consequences of drug abuse. Indirectly, they work with clients who have friends and family members with drug problems or in workplaces or communities that deal with the effects of the drug culture. Drug abuse exacerbates most social problems.

## Definitions

Because the terms and concepts used to describe various drug-related phenomena vary widely, depending on the culture in which they are being used and who is using them (Ray & Ksir, 1992), this terminology is often confusing. In general, three frameworks have been used for defining terms and understanding phenomena associated with drug use. First, social norms, cultural values, and legal regulations provide a framework for defining terms and understanding social phenomena associated with drug use (Doweiko, 1993; Mieczkowski, 1992; Ray & Ksir, 1992). Second, drug actions and physiological effects provide a framework for understanding pharmacological phenomena (Doweiko, 1993; Palfai & Jankiewicz, 1991). Third, a framework advanced by the American Psychiatric Association (APA, 1994) in the *Diagnostic and Statistical Manual of Mental Disorders, Fourth Edition* (hereinafter called DSM-IV) offers definitions in the form of standardized diagnostic criteria that take into account the social context, physiological effects, and behavioral consequences of specific drug use.

**Social Framework**

The social standards governing drug use and the way that drugs and drug-use disorders are defined have changed over time and vary among communities and cultures. The resulting ambiguity of terms and concepts requires contextual definitions. The social context in which drug use and abuse occur and the mental disorders frameworks are important, especially to social workers; however, the pharmacological framework, which is usually not included in social work education, is equally important.

**Pharmacological Framework**

Numerous textbooks have provided standard pharmacological definitions for terms and concepts used in discussions about drugs (Abadinsky, 1993; Doweiko, 1993; Freeman, 1992; Galizio & Maistro, 1985; Julien, 1992; Palfai & Jankiewicz, 1991; Payne, Hahn, & Pinger, 1991; Schuckit, 1989). According to the pharmacological framework, the term *drug* refers to any chemical substance entering the body that alters the body's functioning. Although food fits this definition, and many foods have properties similar to some drugs (Carper, 1993), food is usually not considered a drug. *Psychoactive drugs* (also referred to as *mood-altering drugs*) describe drugs that alter sensory perceptions, mood, thought processes, or behavior by acting on the nervous system, especially the central nervous system.

A person's relationship with drugs may be conceptualized along a continuum of nonuse, experimental use, recreational use, and compulsive use, all of which have accompanying behavioral patterns. However, most of what is known about the use of psychoactive drugs focuses on compulsive use. Whereas *drug use* is a general term that includes all drug taking, *drug misuse* usually refers to the inappropriate use of medication.

*Drug abuse* is often used interchangeably with *substance abuse*. These terms usually refer to the use of any drug (legal or illegal) when it is detrimental to the user's physical, emotional, social, intellectual, or spiritual well-being. The concept of substance abuse is far more complex and includes two major phenomena: a pattern of pathological use and social or occupational impairment that occurs over a specified time (APA, 1994). It also refers to the use of a drug when there is no legitimate medical need for it or when it is used in a way that exceeds acceptable social standards.

*Addiction* is both a term and a concept. As a term, it has a narrow focus that refers to dependence on a drug. A social definition of addiction refers to a preoccupation with the acquisition and compulsive use of drugs despite negative consequences. The dependence may be psychological, physical, or both. As a concept, addiction has a broader focus that also takes into account social and behavioral functioning over time. Within this context, Freeman (1992) referred to Bratter and Forrest's conceptualization of addiction as "a continuum of involvement" with a drug. Therefore, according to Peele (1985), the concept of addiction "is best understood as an individual's adjustment, albeit a self-defeating one, to his or her environment" (p. 2). Thus, *psychological dependence* refers to a process of habituation in which the drive to continue to take a drug is emotional or psychological. This type of dependence is often implied by the presence of drug-seeking behavior, especially in the absence of withdrawal illness. On the other hand, *physical dependence* refers to a condition in which the body needs the drug for certain body processes, and when the drug is absent from the body, clinical signs and symptoms of illness result. This illness is also referred to as *withdrawal illness* or *abstinence syndrome*. *Tolerance,* another term often associated with drug dependence, describes the body's ability to adjust to the continued use of a drug.

**Mental Disorders Framework**

DSM-IV (APA, 1994) presents diagnostic criteria that are designed to improve the reliability of clinicians' diagnostic decisions. It introduces the term *substance-related disorders,* which include substance-use disorders and substance-induced disorders. *Substance-use disorders* are conceptualized in terms of physical and social consequences of drug use. *Substance-induced disorders* are conceptualized as other phenomenological disorders induced from the use or abrupt withdrawal of the substance. This schema does not include the term "addiction." Instead, DSM-IV uses the term *psychoactive substance dependence,* which includes many of the behavioral, physiological, and psychological components associated with the concept of addiction. It is critical that social workers be able to distinguish among abuse, dependence, and substance use and between psychiatric disorders and organic disorders associated with substance use in a standardized manner.

## Classifications of Drugs

The several systems by which drugs are classified generally reflect the purpose of such classifications and how the classifications will be used. Classification systems are generally developed for purposes of legal regulation and law enforcement or for understanding the physiological, psychological, and behavioral effects of drug use on users.

The setting and mission of the setting in which social workers practice often determine the classification system or systems that will be most appropriate. However, because social work practice uses a systems perspective, social workers often interface with other social systems that may use a variety of classificatory schemata. Therefore, an understanding of these various schemata may aid in interprofessional collaboration.

### Drug Effects: Law Enforcement

In the broadest sense, drugs may be classified as legal (licit) or illegal (illicit). Legal drugs may be further classified as social, nonprescription, or prescription drugs. *Social drugs,* such as alcohol, nicotine, and caffeine, are an integral part of this culture. Although legal, they may be abused and may cause dependence. *Nonprescription drugs,* also known as over-the-counter drugs, may be purchased without a physician's prescription. *Prescription drugs,* on the other hand, may be purchased only with a physician's prescription; to this end, the distribution of prescription drugs is controlled.

From a legal and drug-enforcement standpoint, the most widely used classification system is one developed as part of the Comprehensive Drug Abuse Prevention and Control Act of 1970 (also referred to as the Controlled Substances Act of 1970). This system classifies drugs on the basis of the extent to which their production and distribution are controlled and regulated. Hence, the Drug Enforcement Agency imposes legal sanctions on the illegal manufacturing and possession of drugs classified as *controlled substances.* The degree of control is determined by the relationship between a drug's medicinal benefit, addictive potential, and potential for abuse. Thus, drugs with a high potential for abuse and addiction and no medical use are more strictly controlled (especially their production) than are drugs with a low potential for abuse and addiction that have medical benefits. These controlled substances are further classified into Schedules I through V, with legal penalties for each schedule reflecting the degree of control. Schedule I drugs carry the most severe penalties.

### Drug Effects: Physiological and Psychological

Drugs may also be classified according to their effects on the user. Because effects may be physiological, psychological, or both, there are several classification systems (Inaba & Cohen, 1990; Julien, 1992; Palfai & Jankiewicz, 1991; Ray & Ksir, 1992). In a general sense, psychoactive drugs may be classified according to their effect on the central nervous system (brain and spinal cord). In this system, drugs are classified as stimulants or depressants. *Depressants* are drugs that inhibit or depress the central nervous system, such as barbiturates, other sleeping pills, benzodiazepines, chloral hydrate, alcohol, and other sedatives. *Stimulants,* including caffeine, cocaine, and amphetamines, are drugs that excite the central nervous system. However, classifying drugs in this manner is complicated because each drug may have different effects depending on the dosage and the neurotransmitters affected by that drug.

### Drug Effects: Behavioral

Some systems classify drugs according to the behavioral effect, they may have on the user. In such systems drugs are identified as sedatives, anxiolytics, neuroleptics, antidepressants, stimulants, narcotic analgesics, or hallucinogens.

*Sedatives,* also known as depressants or downers, cause drowsiness, sleep, and sedation. *Anxiolytics,* also called antianxiety drugs and minor tranquilizers, relieve anxiety without producing drowsiness. *Neuroleptics,* also referred to as antipsychotics and major tranquilizers, relieve hallucinations and symptoms of mania and have a more calming effect than do minor tranquilizers. Although *antidepressants* elevate mood, from a behavioral classification perspective, they are not stimulants; they relieve depression in people who are depressed. Similarly, *stimulants,* which are also called uppers, cause excitation. *Narcotic analgesics,* also known as opioids, may be natural or synthetic. As a classification, they include heroin, methadone, meperidine (Demerol), morphine, and other drugs that relieve pain. *Hallucinogens,* also referred to as psychodelics and psychotogens, cause psychosis-like effects and distort perceptions.

Because drugs may be classified in various ways, a drug-classification system is only a rough cross-referencing system that provides a general profile of expected effects. The decision to use any given classification system is best determined by how it will be used.

**Drug Effects: Social**

A drug may sometimes be classified according to the level of involvement the user has with the drug or how the individual uses it. To this end, drug use may be classified along a continuum.

A drug may be considered *experimental* when a nonuser tries a drug out of curiosity. Drugs such as alcohol, caffeine, and nicotine are classified as *social drugs* because their use is legal and is deeply entrenched in this culture. These drugs, along with marijuana, are typically used by teenagers who are experimenting; they are also referred to as *gateway drugs* because they open the way to the use of other drugs.

Drug use may be considered *recreational* when the drug is used rarely, is used in socially acceptable settings, and is used within a socially prescribed manner without negative consequences. *Heavy social use* or *problem use* may also be referred to as *abuse* when the social consequences of a drug's use are negative (the individual has personal problems, job problems, or family problems related to drug use) or the drug use is clearly above the norm for the person's social group, but the person continues to use the drug.

It is not easy to classify drugs on the basis of social reactions and impact on social life because the acceptance of drug use and the appropriate use of drugs are culturally defined. Therefore, social workers often have the difficult task of classifying patterns and effects of use according to several frameworks that may be incongruent with the users' social culture, drug culture, or both, while taking into account the user's culture and the context in which the drug use and behavior may be better understood.

## Psychopharmacology and Drug Actions

The effects of a drug may mimic or mask psychological or medical conditions. Therefore, it is important to be able to distinguish between drug-induced conditions and conditions with other etiologies. An understanding of basic pharmacological terms and principles helps one make this distinction.

*Psychopharmacology* refers to the study of psychoactive drugs and how they change behavior. The primary focus is on chemical or physiological changes in tissues or organisms. These changes are also known as the *drug effect.* The drug effect is a complex phenomenon that includes such variables as dosage (the amount taken), route of administration (how a drug is taken), individual response curve (determined by age, gender, body weight, physical health, genetics, biorhythms, and the like), setting (where a drug is taken), and mindset (the user's expectations of the effect).

Drug users may also have different expectations depending on the route of administration: ingestion, injection, inhalation, or absorption. *Ingestion* is the entry of a drug (mostly pills) through the mouth into the digestive tract. *Injection* is the use of a needle to insert a drug (typically heroin) into the body. The needle may be inserted in several ways: intravenously (into a vein), intramuscularly (into a muscle), or subcutaneously (into the tissue immediately under the skin). Gases, smoke, and drug particles, such as hardened cocaine ("crack"), may be *inhaled* through the nose and then absorbed through the lungs. In *absorption* a substance enters the body through the mucous membrane, such as the nose (sniffing cocaine powder) or the mouth (chewing nicotine gum).

The preferred route of administration often depends on the characteristics of a particular drug in that some drugs are effective only when administered by certain routes (Payne et al., 1991). Different routes also allow different response times. For instance, inhalation is a rapid method of introducing a drug into the body, whereas absorption through the skin is slower.

Social workers see the behavioral changes that follow drug usage; however, it is important to understand there is a complex chain of events that is out of the user's control once the drug has entered the body. In spite of the social situations and psychological expectations that influence the observed behavioral changes following drug use, these changes result primarily from the mechanism by which the drug is able to act (also known as *drug action*). Thus, drug action refers to the interaction of drug molecules with living tissue (Palfai & Jankiewicz, 1991). This chain of events occurs between the time a drug is taken and the time the response is observed and can be understood using the basic principles of neuroscience or brain neurochemistry.

**Principles of Brain Neurochemistry**

Payne et al. (1991) presented an overview of the basic process by which psychoactive drugs work. In general, the major effects of psychoactive drugs are produced by their action on the central nervous system, which receives messages from the autonomic and peripheral nervous systems, analyzes these messages, and then sends the response to the appropriate system of the body. For this chain of events to take place, the body must accept and receive a drug at *drug receptors*. The interaction of the drug with the receptors produces changes in the nerve cells, which communicate with each other through the release of neurotransmitters. Psychoactive drugs disrupt the individual's "normal" functioning of neurotransmitters. Because these neurotransmitters are located in the brain and because the brain is the primary site of action of psychoactive drugs, addiction has been called a brain disorder. Thus, the brain of an addict has also been referred to as "the addictive brain" (Blum & Payne, 1991). Specific neurotransmitters have different functions and effects and respond to specific types of drugs. In general, a particular neurotransmitter can transmit only one specific message: either to stimulate or to inhibit. However, users often use different types of drugs simultaneously; therefore, the brain may receive and transmit several messages.

## Epidemiology

### Measures

Drug abuse permeates all aspects of this society. It cuts across all ages, racial and ethnic groups, and occupations. It afflicts women and men—both heterosexual and lesbian and gay. It is found among people with mental illnesses and among those with physical illnesses. However, because of social, legal, and political factors, it is difficult to obtain data on the abuse of and dependence on drugs—especially illicit drugs. Therefore, most statistics on the prevalence and incidence of drug use and trends in drug use focus on substance abuse in general, and alcohol in particular. Epidemiological data on drug use are collected from many sources. The U.S. government is probably the most widely used source in that it collects nationwide data from a variety of sources.

NIDA collects data through the National Survey on Drug Abuse (commonly called the National Household Survey), the Drug Abuse Warning Network (DAWN), and the High School Senior Survey. The National Household Survey collects data from members of American households over age 12 every three years. DAWN collects information on admissions to hospital emergency rooms in which drugs are "mentioned." The High School Senior Survey is an annual assessment of substance use among high school seniors; therefore, its statistics may underestimate the magnitude of the problem among adolescents because it does not survey dropouts (Schinke, Botvin, & Orlandi, 1991).

Drug Use Forecasting, a project of the National Institute on Justice, collects data from voluntary interviews and urine samples from individuals who are arrested for nondrug offenses. In addition to these nationwide surveys, the National Institute of Mental Health's Epidemiologic Catchment Area (ECA) Program was carried out in five major U.S. cities to determine the prevalence of diagnoses of alcohol and drug dependence according to DSM-III-R (APA, 1987) criteria based on age, race, and gender (Miller, Belkin, & Gold, 1991). The Narcotics Intelligence Estimates is a report on the worldwide illicit drug situation by the National Narcotics Intelligence Consumers Committee, which is a federal interagency mechanism for coordinating information and estimates from sample surveys, drug seizures, data on drug prices and purity, and other sources. Because of its focus on illicit drugs, estimates of the availability and consumption of drugs are difficult to obtain.

### Age

According to the results of the most recent (1992) National Household Survey (NIDA, 1993), 36 percent of all Americans ages 12 and over have tried illicit drugs, and drug taking was most prevalent for those ages 18 to 25. Alcohol and tobacco were the most popular drugs, but when alcohol and tobacco were not considered, 33 percent of the population still indicated that they had tried marijuana, and nearly 11 percent had tried cocaine. Because most drug users use multiple drugs and many drug users never participate in surveys, it is difficult to determine exactly how many Americans use drugs, especially illicit drugs.

The ECA Program, which studied actual diagnoses and the rates of lifetime and recent prevalence of dependence on alcohol and other drugs, found that the lifetime prevalence rates for illicit drug dependence according to age were 17 percent for those aged 18 to 29, 4 percent for those ages 30 to 59, and less than 1 percent for those aged 60 and over. With regard to the use of licit drugs (prescription or over-the-counter), the study estimated that 25 percent of the population over age 55 use prescribed psychoactive drugs and are at risk of abuse or dependence and 69 percent of the population over age 60 use over-the-counter drugs (Miller et al., 1991). The DAWN data showing trends in drug-related emergency room admissions from 1988 to 1991 indicated that most psychoactive illicit drug use increased and that illicit drug use was most prevalent among individuals under age 35 (NIDA, 1992).

**Racial and Ethnic Groups**

Neither race nor ethnicity alone has been found to correlate with drug use. Rather, research has shown that the economic, physical, and social environment may encourage the greater use of drugs in that drug use is intensified when high unemployment, poverty, and poor health exist (U.S. Department of Health and Human Services [DHHS], 1990a).

In general, fewer African Americans than Latino Americans and white Americans use drugs, but most drug users are poor or people of color. Fewer African American youths use drugs than do youths of other ethnic groups, but of the drug-using population over age 35, African American people are more likely than are Latino or white people to use illicit drugs (NIDA, 1992). In this regard, drug use is among the leading health and social problems in African American communities throughout the country (DHHS, 1990a).

Latino people are a heterogeneous population from different countries of origin who live in various areas of the country (DHHS, 1990b). Because Mexican Americans, Puerto Rican Americans, and Cuban Americans constitute 85 percent of the Latino population in the United States (La Rosa, Khalsa, & Rouse, 1990), more is known about their drug use than about the drug use of other Latino groups. However, as is true for all populations, but especially for Latino groups, it is difficult to determine the actual prevalence of drug use in that reported use by new immigrants may negatively affect the naturalization process. What is known is derived primarily from data from the Hispanic Health and Nutrition Examination Survey, the Hispanic Research Center at Fordham University, and NIDA's National Household Survey.

There are different patterns and trends of drug use and abuse among Latino groups according to the type of drugs that are used, the level of use, age, gender, and degree of acculturation (La Rosa et al., 1990). In general, Latino men tend to use all types of illegal drugs more frequently than do Latina women. However, this trend appears to be changing as Latinas become acculturated and achieve more years of education.

Some natural drugs are a part of the traditional Native American culture. For instance, the Native American Church continues to use mescaline (a hallucinogen found in peyote cactus) in religious ceremonies and has been exempted from certain provisions of the Controlled Substances Act of 1970 in 23 states. Furthermore, Young (1987) found that the use of inhalants (most commonly gasoline) is more prevalent among Native American youths than among other youths and that Native American youths are more likely to continue to use inhalants than are other youths.

Whatever is known about the incidence and prevalence of drug use among the many different groups of Asian Americans is focused on alcohol use. Although Chinese Americans used opium earlier in U.S. history, little is known about the prevalence of contemporary drug use among any group of Asian Americans.

**Elderly People**

Using data from the ECA Program, Miller et al. (1991) reported that people age 60 and over were not likely to use illicit drugs but that the use of illicit drugs was positively related to dependence on alcohol; hence, 60 percent of the elderly who were alcoholics also used illicit drugs. Narcotic and similar drugs used by elderly people are usually obtained through prescription (Iber, 1991); in this regard, the elderly are the largest users of legal drugs in the United States. Furthermore, the use of tranquilizers and over-the-counter medication by the elderly is disproportionate to their numbers. Because the elderly primarily use legal prescription or over-the-counter medications that are socially acceptable, it is not surprising that there are fewer diagnoses of alcohol and drug dependence in the elderly than the actual prevalence rates determined by the ECA Program. Drug reactions in elderly people often are confused with dementia and other disorders of aging. Therefore, social workers must be sensitive to the presence of medical and psychiatric conditions in older people that may be drug induced.

**Sexual Orientation**

It is difficult to determine the prevalence of drug abuse by sexual orientation because most surveys of drug use do not ask about sexual orientation. Although neither homosexuality nor homophobia cause drug addiction (Mosbacher, 1988), it is believed that gay men and lesbians may be at a high risk for substance abuse because of general psychosocial factors as well as culturally specific factors. A national survey of a large homosexual community conducted by McKirnan and Peterson (1989) found that fewer gay men and lesbians abstained from alcohol and other drugs than was estimated in the general population and that within the homosexual population studied, there was a much greater incidence of drug use among lesbians and older people. Furthermore, role status, social settings, the frequenting of homosexual bars, and discrimination were identified as psychosocial factors that contribute to the use and abuse of drugs.

### Gender

Addiction in women is often unrecognized, yet women are as directly involved with drug use as are men (Doweiko, 1993). It has long been recognized that women use more prescription medications and that they are prescribed more psychoactive drugs than are men (Peluso & Peluso, 1988). However, only recently has the literature shown that women use other drugs and that their patterns of use often differ from those of men (Griffin, Weiss, Mirin, & Lang, 1989; Pape, 1988).

### Occupations

There is conflicting data on whether drug use is more prevalent in some occupations than in others. For instance, using data from NIDA and the Employee Assistance Professionals Association, Payne et al. (1991) stated that "drug abuse in the workplace appears to be distributed across occupations and industries, and no correlation between drug abuse and type of work has been demonstrated" (p. 13). On the other hand, Anthony, Eaton, Mandell, and Garrison (1992), using data from the National Institute of Mental Health's ECA Program, found that the prevalence of psychoactive drug disorders was greater among people in the construction trades, waiters and waitresses, and those in the transportation and moving occupations and lower among clinical laboratory technologists and technicians, other health professionals, and secondary and elementary school teachers.

### Mental Disorders

Sciacca (1991) found that almost 50 percent of psychiatric patients who are severely mentally ill abuse drugs. These coexisting conditions (also called dual diagnoses) present a dilemma for social workers, who must determine if a client is primarily a mentally ill individual who is using drugs in response to mental discomfort or a substance abuser whose psychiatric symptoms are in response to or exacerbated by substance use. Thus, social workers must determine if such symptoms as depression, anxiety, paranoia, and hallucinations were triggered by a psychiatric condition or by drug use. This diagnostic dilemma is compounded by the fact that the symptoms of, for instance, crack use and schizophrenia are similar (Orlin & Davis, 1993).

### Homeless People

Although there is a high correlation among homelessness, mental illness, and substance abuse, many people who are homeless are neither mentally ill nor substance abusers. Because the homeless population is hard to identify, identifying drug use and abuse among homeless people is especially difficult. Nevertheless, social workers must determine if there is a relationship between a client's homeless status and his or her substance abuse: Is the homelessness a consequence of drug abuse, or is drug abuse a response to being homeless? Of course, social workers must also be cognizant of the high prevalence of coexisting psychiatric and substance use disorders in this population.

## Models and Theories of Drug Addiction

Models and theories of addiction do not generally distinguish the specific drugs that are used. Most have been derived from observations of and research on alcohol addiction. In general, models provide a framework for understanding the addictive process by describing what happens and how it happens from specific perspectives. On the other hand, theories offer an explanation of why addiction occurs (Freeman, 1992). Using the requirements of a comprehensive model and theory set forth by Peele (1985), one sees that no model incorporates pharmacological, personal experience, situational, and personality components in its description of the addiction process. Similarly, no theory adequately answers the fundamental question of why some drug users become addicted and others do not.

For the most part, these theories are "explanations," rather than developed "theories." These explanations may be categorized as physiological, psychological, and sociological. For instance, the "Bolus theory" (Payne et al., 1991), which is advanced as a physiological and psychological theory of nicotine addiction, states that each inhalation releases a concentration of nicotine into the blood that reaches the brain and results in neurohormonal excitement that a smoker perceives as pleasurable; thus, a smoker attempts to re-create the pleasurable feeling by continuing to inhale. A similar pleasure theory has been posited for the continued use of other drugs.

## Biopsychosocial Consequences

Drugs are not inherently bad. On the one hand, they have been found to enhance quality of life by offering relief for a variety of medical and psychiatric conditions. On the other hand, their abuse has serious consequences, most of which include problems in living that are part of the purview of social work practice.

From a physical standpoint, the consequences of drug abuse vary depending on the specific drugs used, how the drugs are taken into the body, the duration and frequency of use, the amount used, and the overall state of health and state of mind of the user. The physical effects of drug abuse often carry acute and chronic consequences that may include such medical conditions as high blood pressure; gastritis; pancreatitis; liver disease; oral, esophageal, and kidney cancer; spontaneous abortion; premature deliveries; sudden infant death; and cardiac and respiratory arrest. Depending on the nature of drug-seeking behavior and the involvement of the user in criminal behavior, injury or death may result directly from violence, but indirectly from drug use. Of course, not all people who have certain medical conditions are using or abusing drugs, but the presence of these conditions may alert social workers to the need for proper screening to rule out clients' involvement with drugs.

The psychological consequences of drug abuse also vary, depending on the user, the specific drug or drugs used, and the setting. For many people who abuse drugs, psychological dependence on the effect of the drug is a serious consequence. Other effects, either acute or chronic, may include paranoia, psychosis, depression, and anxiety.

The social consequences of drug abuse are borne by individual users, their families, and society at large. Drug abuse/addiction has been called a "disease of the spirit" (Doweiko, 1993, p. 167) in that individual users appear to value their relationship with drugs over their relationships with family members and friends and will go to great lengths to continue to use drugs. Doweiko also observed that once addicted, users tend to view people as either useful in maintaining their addiction or as possible threats to their use of drugs. Therefore, it may be difficult for social workers to enter a helping relationship with drug-addicted clients, who may perceive them as threats to further drug use.

## Role of Social Workers

In the past, social workers avoided helping individuals with substance abuse problems (Googins, 1984). Consequently, social workers today are not viewed as professionals with expertise in working with individuals who abuse drugs. In fact, many social workers indicate that they do not work with substance abusers, when, ironically, many of the people they serve are using and abusing substances. Because most individuals who abuse drugs have myriad problems in living, social workers are often the first human services professionals they meet when they enter various service delivery systems. It is at this juncture that social workers need the expertise to develop appropriate programs and interventions for directly addressing drug abuse as a major social problem.

## References


Abadinsky, H. (1993). *Drug abuse: An introduction*. Chicago: Nelson-Hall.

American Psychiatric Association. (1987). *Diagnostic and statistical manual of mental disorders* (3rd ed., rev.). Washington, DC: Author.

American Psychiatric Association. (1994). *Diagnostic and statistical manual of mental disorders* (4th ed.). Washington, DC: Author.

Anthony, J., Eaton, W., Mandell, W., & Garrison, R. (1992). Psychoactive drug dependence and abuse: More common in some occupations than others? *Journal of Employee Assistance Research, 1*, 148–186.

Blum, K., & Payne, J. (1991). *Alcohol and the addictive brain*. New York: Free Press.

Carper, J. (1993). *Food—Your miracle medicine*. New York: HarperCollins.

Comprehensive Drug Abuse Prevention and Control Act of 1970. P.L. 91-513, 84 Stat. 1236.

Controlled Substances Act of 1970. P.L. 91-513, 84 Stat. 1242.

Doweiko, H. (1993). *Concepts of chemical dependency*. Pacific Grove, CA: Brooks/Cole.

Freeman, E. (1992). *The addiction process: Effective social work approaches*. White Plains, NY: Longman.

Galizio, M., & Maistro, S. (1985). *Determinants of substance abuse*. New York: Plenum Press.

Googins, B. (1984). Avoidance of the alcoholic client. *Social Work, 29*, 161–166.

Griffin, M., Weiss, R., Mirin, S., & Lang, U. (1989). A comparison of male and female cocaine abusers. *Archives of General Psychiatry, 46*, 122–126.

Iber, F. (1991). *Alcohol and drug abuse as encountered in office practice*. Boca Raton, FL: CRC Press.

Inaba, D., & Cohen, W. (1990). *Uppers, downers, all arounders*. Ashland, OR: Cinemed.

Julien, R. (1992). *A primer of drug action*. San Francisco: W. H. Freeman.

La Rosa, M., Khalsa, J., & Rouse, B. (1990). Hispanics and illicit drug use: A review of recent findings. *International Journal of the Addictions, 25*, 665–691.

McKirnan, D., & Peterson, P. (1989). Psychological and cultural factors in alcohol and drug abuse: An analysis of a homosexual community. *Addictive Behaviors, 14*, 555–563.

Mieczkowski, T. (Ed). (1992). *Drugs, crime, and social policy*. Needham Heights, MA: Allyn & Bacon.

Miller, N., Belkin, B., & Gold, M. (1991). Alcohol and drug dependence among the elderly: Epidemiology, diagnosis, and treatment. *Comprehensive Psychiatry, 32*, 153–165.

Mosbacher, D. (1988). Lesbian alcohol and substance abuse. *Psychiatric Annals, 16*(1), 47–50.

National Institute on Drug Abuse. (1992). *Annual emergency room data: Data from the Drug Abuse Warning Network*. Rockville, MD: U.S. Department of Health and Human Services.

National Institute on Drug Abuse. (1993). *National Household Survey on Drug Abuse: Population estimates 1992*.

Washington, DC: U.S. Department of Health and Human Services.

Orlin, L., & Davis, J. (1993). Assessment and intervention with drug and alcohol abusers in psychiatric settings. In L. Straussner (Ed.), *Clinical work with substance abusing clients* (pp. 50–68). New York: Guilford Press.

Palfai, T., & Jankiewicz, H. (1991), *Drugs and human behavior*. Dubuque, IA: William C. Brown.

Pape, P. (1988). EAPs and chemically dependent women. *Alcoholism & Addiction, 8*(6), 43–44.

Payne, W., Hahn, D., & Pinger, R. (1991). *Drugs: Issues for today*. St. Louis: C. V. Mosby–Year Book.

Peele, S. (1985). *The meaning of addiction*. Lexington, MA: Lexington Books.

Peluso, E., & Peluso, L. (1988). *Women and drugs*. Minneapolis: Compcare.

Ray, O., & Ksir, C. (1992). *Drugs, society, and human behavior*. St. Louis: Times Mirror/Mosby.

Schinke, S., Botvin, G., & Orlandi, M. (1991). *Substance abuse in children and adolescents: Evaluation and intervention*. Newbury Park, CA: Sage Publications.

Schuckit, M. (1989). *Drug and alcohol abuse: A clinical guide to diagnosis and treatment* (3rd ed.). New York: Plenum Press.

Sciacca, K. (1991). An integrated treatment approach for severely mentally ill individuals with substance disorders. *New Directions for Mental Health Services, 50*, 69–83.

U.S. Department of Health and Human Services. (1990a, August). Alcohol and other drug use is a special concern for African American families and communities. In *The fact is. . . .* Washington, DC: Author.

U.S. Department of Health and Human Services. (1990b, September). Reaching Hispanic/Latino audiences requires cultural sensitivity. In *The fact is. . . .* Washington, DC: Author.

Young, T. (1987). Inhalant use among American Indian youth. *Child Psychiatry and Human Development, 18*(1), 37–46.

## Further Reading

Galanter, M., & Kleber, H. (Eds.). (1994). *Textbook of substance abuse treatment*. Washington, DC: American Psychiatric Press, Inc.

Landry, M. (1993). *Understanding drugs of abuse*. Washington, DC: American Psychiatric Press, Inc.

Langton, P. (1991). *Drug use and the alcohol dilemma*. Needham Heights, MA: Allyn & Bacon.

Lewis, J., et al. (1988). *Substance abuse counseling: An individualized approach*. Belmont, CA: Brooks/Cole.

McNeece, C., & DiNitto, D. (1994). *Chemical dependency: A systems approach*. Englewood Cliffs, NJ: Prentice Hall.

Miller, N. (Ed.). (1991). *Comprehensive handbook of drug and alcohol addiction*. New York: Marcel Dekker.

Musto, D. (1987). *The American disease: Origins of narcotic control*. New York: Oxford University Press.

Schlaadt, R., & Shannon, P. (1994). *Drugs: Use, misuse and abuse*. Englewood Cliffs, NJ: Prentice Hall.

Venturelli, P. (Ed.). (1994). *Drug use in America: Social, cultural and political perspectives*. Boston: Jones and Bartlett.

Witters, W., et al. (1992). *Drugs and society* (3rd ed.). Boston: Jones and Bartlett.

**Muriel C. Gray, PhD, LCSW, CEAP, CADAC,** is associate professor, University of Maryland at Baltimore School of Social Work, 525 W. Redwood Street, Baltimore, MD 21201.

### For further information see

Adolescence Overview; Adult Corrections; Adult Courts; Alcohol Abuse; Criminal Behavior Overview; Direct Practice Overview; Families Overview; Goal Setting and Intervention Planning; Mental Health Overview; Primary Prevention Overview; Runaways and Homeless Youths; Self-Help Groups; Substance Abuse: Direct Practice; Substance Abuse: Federal, State, and Local Policies; Substance Abuse: Legal Issues.

**Key Words**
addiction
drug abuse
substance abuse

## DSM

*See* Diagnostic and Statistical Manual of Mental Disorders

## DuBois, William Edward Burghardt

*See* Biographies section, Volume 3

## Dunham, Arthur

*See* Biographies section, Volume 3

## Dybwad, Rosemary Ferguson

*See* Biographies section, Volume 3

# E

## EAP

*See* Employee Assistance Programs

# Eating Disorders and Other Compulsive Behaviors

**Sadye L. Logan**

Since the late 1970s, critical attention has focused on the apparent increase in the incidence of such eating disorders as anorexia nervosa, self-starvation, bulimia nervosa, bingeing, purging, compulsive overeating, and obesity and on such compulsive behaviors as addiction to love and sex, gambling, and smoking. In some ways each of these conditions is concerned not only with psychological or physical dependence on a substance, an activity, or a relationship, but with the inability to abstain despite the threat of serious physical, emotional, social, and legal consequences. These disorders and behaviors can extract a high cost from both individuals and their families and are associated with the erosion of self-worth, self-efficacy, and overall productivity. Despite advances in understanding and treating these conditions, it is not clear to what extent ritualistic and repetitive behaviors (such as excessive handwashing, self-abuse, hoarding, and overwork) should be defined as addictions.

## Definitions

### Anorexia Nervosa

According to the fourth edition of the *Diagnostic and Statistical Manual of Mental Disorders,* (DSM-IV) (American Psychiatric Association [APA], 1994), anorexia nervosa is a psychopathogenic condition, usually seen in girls and young women, that is characterized by spontaneous or induced vomiting, extreme emaciation, amenorrhea (loss or irregularity of menstrual functions), and other biological changes. People who suffer from anorexia nervosa experience other psychological and physical conditions, among them a distorted body image, slowing of the heartbeat, loss of normal blood pressure, cardiac arrest, hypothermia, lethargy, dehydration, skin abnormalities, kidney malfunctions, constipation, potassium deficiency, the growth of fine silky hair on the body (laguno), and difficulty conserving body heat (U.S. Department of Health and Human Services [DHHS], 1988b).

The amount of weight loss is an important factor in determining whether an individual is anorexic. To be diagnosed as having anorexia nervosa, a person's weight must usually be less than 99 pounds. To calculate body weight, two methods are frequently used. The first applies the weight-for-height formula used by insurance companies to calculate a person's ideal or desirable body weight (Abraham & Llewellyn-Jones, 1992). With this calculation, an individual is diagnosed as having anorexia nervosa if at least 25 percent of his or her average body weight has been lost. The second method uses the average body weight (ABW) table of women ages 15 to 69, which takes into account a person's weight and height as well as age. With the second calculation, people may be diagnosed as having anorexia nervosa if their weight is less than 75 percent of the ABW.

The essential features of the anorexia nervosa syndrome are as follows (APA, 1994):

- intense fear of becoming obese, even when underweight
- disturbed perception of one's body weight, size, or shape
- refusal to maintain body weight above the minimal normal weight for one's age and height—that is, weight loss leading to maintenance of body weight 15 percent or more below the norm or failure to make an expected weight gain, leading to body weight 15 percent below the norm
- in females, the absence of at least three consecutive menstrual cycles.

### Bulimia Nervosa

Bulimia nervosa refers to episodes of binge eating followed by vomiting, abdominal pain, laxative use, or sleep. Bulimics, like anorexics, are concerned with body weight and have a morbid fear of becoming fat, but most tend to keep nearly normal weight, although some may be underweight and a few may be obese. Binges usually occur in secret, may last as long as eight hours, and may result in an intake of up to 20,000 calories (Abraham & Llewellyn-Jones, 1992). The food that is selected is highly caloric and easily ingested, like ice cream (Conners, 1992).

The binge–purge cycle experienced by bulimics can be devastating to health. It can upset the body's balance of electrolytes (such as sodium, magnesium, potassium, and calcium), causing fatigue, seizures, muscle cramps, irregular heartbeat, and decreased bone density. Repeated vomiting can damage the esophagus and stomach, cause salivary glands to swell, make the gums recede, and erode tooth enamel. Other effects may be rashes; broken blood vessels in the cheeks; and swelling around the eyes, ankles, and feet (DHHS, 1988a).

The essential features of bulimia nervosa syndrome are as follows (APA, 1994):

- recurrent episodes of binge eating, averaging two episodes per week for at least three months, with lack of control over eating behavior
- regular self-induced vomiting, use of laxatives, or rigorous dieting or fasting to counteract binge eating.

**Obesity**

Obesity may be the most prevalent and serious nutritional problem in the United States (Dietz, 1983). It is defined as having excess weight that is 20 percent or more above the ideal or desirable weight for the individual (Stunkard & Wadden, 1992). When the height and body weight of individuals are taken into consideration, obesity can be grouped into three indexes: grossly obese, obese, and overweight. Generally, overweight and obese persons are defined as having an excess of body fat, frequently resulting in significant impairment of health (Stunkard & Wadden, 1992). Obese people tend to die young, to have an increased chance of becoming ill, and to be at risk for disabling diseases and common conditions, such as diabetes, hypertension, and menstrual irregularities (Abraham & Llewellyn-Jones, 1992).

Some believe that attempts to define obesity precisely are not useful (Stunkard & Wadden, 1992) and that emphasis should be placed instead on recognizing the factors that are likely to be involved in the development of obesity, including genetic and environmental factors, excessive caloric intake, decreased physical activity, and metabolic and endocrine abnormalities.

**Compulsive Overeating**

Compulsive overeating is generally described as uncontrollable binge eating that is not accompanied by extreme weight-control behavior, such as starving or purging. It has been found among individuals of normal weight. Research suggests that 20 percent to 40 percent of obese persons have significant problems with compulsive binge eating (Marcus & Wing, 1987). The compulsive overeater recognizes that binge eating is abnormal and experiences negative effects after bingeing that may precipitate further bingeing (Williamson, 1990).

The following diagnostic criteria for compulsive overeating have been suggested (Williamson, 1990):

- recurrent episodes of binge eating at least twice a week for three months
- at least three of the following: consumption of high-caloric, easily ingested food during a binge; inconspicuous eating during a binge; repeated attempts at dieting; negative affect (such as guilt) as the occasion for binge eating; frequent weight fluctuations greater than 10 pounds because of alternating bingeing and dieting
- the nonuse of extreme methods to lose or control weight
- awareness that the eating pattern is abnormal and fear of being unable to stop eating voluntarily
- depression and self-deprecating thoughts following eating binges
- dissatisfaction with body size, but no evidence of other body image disturbance
- episodes of overeating that are not due to anorexia nervosa, bulimia nervosa, or any known physical disorder.

**Atypical Eating Disorders**

Atypical eating disorders are a complex condition that may also be accompanied by other clinical problems, such as depression.

DSM-IV (APA, 1994) pays little attention to these disorders. Among the criteria it lists are these:

- The person has all the criteria for anorexia nervosa and may engage in frequent self-induced vomiting, but despite significant weight loss, his or her weight is in the normal range.
- The person has all the criteria for bulimia nervosa except that binge eating and fasting or excessive exercising occur less than twice a week or for less than three months, the person repeatedly chews and spits out large amounts of

food without swallowing, or the person has recurrent episodes of binge eating but does not regularly fast or engage in excessive exercising.

**Love and Sex Addiction**

During the so-called sexual revolution of the 1970s, love and sex addiction surfaced as psychological problems (Logan, 1992; Summers, 1989). These conditions are viewed as progressive illnesses that cannot be cured but can be arrested (Nakken, 1988; Peele, 1975; Quadland, 1985). Characteristically, they may take several forms, including a compulsive need for sex or sexual gratification, extreme interpersonal dependence, and chronic preoccupation with romantic and related fantasies. According to Hunter (1988), Peele (1985), and *Sex and Love Addicts Anonymous* (1986), the person who is addicted experiences these conditions as

- unacceptable and uncontrollable
- disgusting, demeaning, and against his or her better judgment
- ritualized, obsessive, and the cause of great distress if interrupted
- joyless and pleasureless, without true intimacy or individual growth.

**Compulsive Gambling**

The definition of compulsive gambling is controversial. Because of the lack of knowledge about compulsive gambling, some social services professionals deny that it exists; others argue that the reported number of gamblers is exaggerated and reflects mostly undisciplined gamblers (Rosenthal, 1989). APA (1994) conceptualized compulsive gambling as an addictive disease whose criteria are similar to those for alcohol and drug dependence.

Compulsive gambling is an invisible, progressive illness that according to Gamblers Anonymous can never be cured but can be arrested. Compulsive gamblers have been viewed as moving through three phases of chronicity: (1) the winning phase, in which gambling is experienced as enjoyable, stimulating, and pleasurable; (2) the losing phase, characterized by increased risk taking and increased betting; and (3) the desperate phase, during which a gambler continues to bet with total disregard for the consequences (Custer & Milt, 1985). Rosenthal (1989) identified progression, intolerance of losing, preoccupation, and disregard for consequences as four characteristics of compulsive gambling. These characteristics parallel Custer and Milt's (1985) phases.

APA (1994) criteria for compulsive gambling are

- frequent preoccupation with gambling or with obtaining money to gamble
- frequent gambling of increasingly larger amounts of money or gambling over a longer period than intended
- the need to increase the size or frequency of bets to achieve the desired excitement
- restlessness or irritability if unable to gamble
- repeated loss of money by gambling and returning another day to win back losses ("chasing")
- repeated efforts to reduce or stop gambling
- frequent gambling as a way of escaping from problems or of relieving feelings of helplessness, guilt, anxiety, or depression
- lies to family members, therapists, or others to conceal the extent of involvement in gambling
- illegal acts, such as forgery, fraud, theft, or embezzlement, to finance gambling
- reliance on others to provide money to relieve a desperate financial situation caused by gambling.

**Smoking**

Smoking involves the use of both smoked and smokeless tobacco. (Smokeless tobacco is either sniffed, chewed, or held in the cheek pouch.) The use of tobacco may result in a dependence on nicotine that is similar to the dependence on such substances as alcohol, amphetamines, cocaine, or sedatives, although some of the generic criteria of dependence may not apply to nicotine (APA, 1994).

Over 80 percent of the people who smoke express a desire to stop smoking, and 35 percent try to stop each year, but less than 5 percent are successful in unaided attempts to stop. This dependence can develop with all forms of tobacco and with prescription medication, such as nicotine gum. The most common signs of nicotine dependence are tobacco odor, cough, chronic lung disease, and excessive skin wrinkling (APA, 1994).

The excessive use of nicotine occurs when individuals take nicotine to relieve or avoid withdrawal symptoms after a period of nonuse, such as when they awake in the morning or have been in a smoke-free environment for a number of hours. The essential feature of nicotine withdrawal is a characteristic withdrawal syndrome that develops after the abrupt cessation or reduction in the use of nicotine-containing products following at least several weeks of daily use. The withdrawal syndrome includes four or more of the following symptoms:

- dysphoric or depressed mood
- insomnia
- irritability, frustration, or anger

- anxiety
- difficulty concentrating
- restlessness or impatience
- increased appetite or weight gain.

These symptoms cause clinically significant distress or impairment in social, occupational, or other important areas of functioning and are not due to general medical conditions or better accounted for by another mental disorder (APA, 1994).

## Demographic and Family Characteristics

Age, gender, and ethnicity have a direct impact on how disorders are perceived and responded to both by the individuals who are addicted and by those who provide services to them. Helping professionals must be sensitive to particular cultural, ethnic, social, and environmental factors that affect their clients.

Society sends conflicting and ambiguous messages regarding eating disorders and compulsive behaviors. On the one hand, being fit and slim, sexually active, a social gambler, and a social smoker are depicted as positive personality attributes. These images are reinforced by the media, federal and local governments, and businesses. Evidence suggests that the pressure on adolescents and young adults to maintain an image of glamor and success is increasing (Abraham & Llewellyn-Jones, 1992; Farley, 1994).

### Age of Onset, Gender, and Ethnicity

***Eating disorders.*** Most eating disorders and compulsive behaviors begin in adolescence. Individuals are generally ages 12 to 18 at the onset of anorexia. From 90 percent to 95 percent of anorexics are female (APA, 1994). The disorder is more common among sisters and mothers of individuals who have the disorder than among the general population; most males who exhibit the symptoms are athletes (Andersen, 1990; Greenfeld, 1984). Bulimics begin to binge in their late teens; 18 is cited as the most frequent age of onset, and it is rare for the problem to begin after age 30 (Abraham & Llewellyn-Jones, 1992). Generally, the ages of onset of overeating and of vomiting are different. Bulimia is thought to be more common in women than in men.

Most patients with anorexia and bulimia are white, which may reflect socioeconomic factors or help-seeking patterns rather than an ethnically biased incidence of disorders. Studies have found, however, that a growing number of African American women suffer from eating disorders (Browne, 1993).

***Obesity.*** It is difficult to determine how many people suffer from obesity. The National Institutes of Health (NIH) reported that an estimated 20 percent of adults in the United States and 35 percent of those ages 40 and over were obese (*Facts about Obesity,* 1976). Furthermore, according to the NIH report, children ages six to 11 and adolescents constituted a large proportion of the estimated number of obese people. Stuart and Davis (1972) estimated the number of obese people as 40 million to 60 million, and Harlan (1993) reported that females are more likely than males to be overweight. Despite the national commitment to reducing obesity, the National Health and Nutrition Examination Survey reported the continuing trend for adolescents and adults to be overweight (*Healthy People 2000,* 1991).

Stunkard and Wadden (1992) stressed the importance of acknowledging cultural beliefs in assessing and treating obesity, and there has been substantial research on social and cultural factors related to obesity among Hispanic Americans and African Americans. According to Brown (1992), for example, there are high rates of overweight and obesity among Hispanic Americans and Native Americans, and African American women have a great risk of becoming overweight. Furthermore, the stigma attached to overweight and obesity in the dominant culture is absent in ethnic groups of color.

***Sex and love addiction.*** Sex and love addiction affect both men and women. Statistical profiles are difficult to obtain, however, because Sex and Love Addicts Anonymous, in protecting the anonymity of its members, does not reveal demographic variables and because individuals whose addiction is out of control are often isolated because they tend not to discuss it with anyone.

***Gambling.*** It has been estimated that approximately 7 million adults in the United States are problem gamblers (Volberg & Steadman, 1989). A survey of adolescents across the United States found that they often began to gamble long before they reached high school age (Jacobs, 1989). Custer and Milt (1985) estimated that there is one female to every 10 male compulsive gamblers. Some research suggests that personality factors, such as sensation seeking, may be more significant than gender in the attraction to gambling (Wolfgang, 1988).

Sociocultural factors may have important implications for differences between social gamblers and addicted gamblers. Survey data suggest that African Americans and Hispanic Americans are more likely to have gambling problems than are other ethnic groups (Rosenthal, 1989). Lesuir (1984), however, found that Jews, Italians, and the Irish are overrepresented among members of Gamblers Anonymous.

***Smoking.*** Although there has been a decline in smoking rates, Schwartz (1987) reported that 27 percent of all females and 32 percent of all males smoke tobacco and that more than eight out of 10 smokers began smoking before age 21. Evidence suggests that adolescent girls are the fastest-growing population of smokers and that the proportion of heavy smokers has been increasing within the smoking population even as the total number of smokers decreases (Schwartz).

Ethnic variations in tobacco use are evident in the United States. African American men and women smoke at higher rates than do white Americans, and African American women under age 23 are the fastest-growing population of smokers. Hispanic American men have higher rates of smoking and Hispanic women have lower rates than African American men and women, respectively. Among Native Americans, smoking rates are higher in northern plains populations than in the Southwest. A trend toward a high incidence of the use of smokeless tobacco has been reported (Moncher, Schinke, & Holden, 1992), with a higher lifetime prevalence among white Americans than among African Americans and Hispanic Americans.

### Family Characteristics and Issues

People who suffer from eating disorders and compulsive behaviors typically come from families in which there is a high degree of conflict; control is an issue; and children are deprived of a strong sense of autonomy, identity, and confidence (Minuchin, Rosman, & Baker, 1978). Case studies have revealed that parental attitudes and the home atmosphere are common factors in addiction (Humphrey, 1989; Straber, Salkion, & Burroughs, 1982). In addicts' families, boundaries and structure are overcontrolling, overprotective, and rigid; problem solving is poor; conflict-resolution skills are lacking; patterns of communication are unclear; and family members are overinvolved with each other. Other family factors to be considered are childhood trauma (such as death, divorce, and sexual and other forms of abuse), neglect, ethnicity, affective disorders, sibling rivalries, and the parents' special treatment of one child over others.

Family dynamics and interactional styles vary with the disorder or behavior in question. For example, there is greater disturbance in interactional styles in families of bulimics than in families of anorexics (Mirkin, 1990). Bulimics view their families as discouraging the open expression of feelings and lacking in parental warmth, trust, affirmation, and nurturance. Without professional intervention, such interactional patterns are perpetuated in the families of the symptom bearers. Research suggests that a severe level of pathology exists in the children of compulsive gamblers, as well as in the parent, and that the spouse or partner of a compulsive gambler goes through stages of denial, stress, and exhaustion (Lesuir, 1984). However, eating disorders and compulsive behaviors also function to preserve family equilibrium. The symptom bearer obtains a sense of identity, approval, and control through the special attention the disorder requires, and other family members are able to function in their roles without undue conflict, thus the family's mutual dependencies are reinforced and the underlying conflicts are hidden.

## Etiology and Maintenance

A combination of factors may contribute to the development of eating disorders and compulsive behaviors (Minuchin et al., 1978; Mirkin, 1990). Theoretical perspectives explaining these illnesses differ primarily in their emphases. There is a consensus that these illnesses serve a variety of sociocultural, biological, cognitive–behavioral, psychodynamic, and developmental functions. These factors, in combination with early development, contribute to individual character structure and development and best account for variations in individuals with eating disorders and compulsive behavior (see Figures 1 and 2). However, there is dissension regarding gender issues (Mirkin, 1990). For example, some theories suggest that individual women are to be blamed for their eating disorders, whereas others have proposed that such disorders should be viewed as a tragic response to the unrealistic and contradictory expectations of women by a society that devalues women.

### Sociocultural Factors

Common to all eating disorders and compulsive behaviors are feelings of anxiety, helplessness, and inadequacy (Schaeffer, 1985). Some theoreticians believe that these feelings are based in sociocultural factors and view anxiety as ontological in nature, stemming from individuals' questions about the meaning of life and feelings of being incomplete (Laing, 1965); others consider anxiety to be related to faulty upbringing; and still others think it is a result of both factors (Peele, 1975). It is proposed that in their search for meaning, wholeness, and identity, young people have embraced the notion that their ultimate identity is with their bodies or with an activity, such as gam-

FIGURE 1

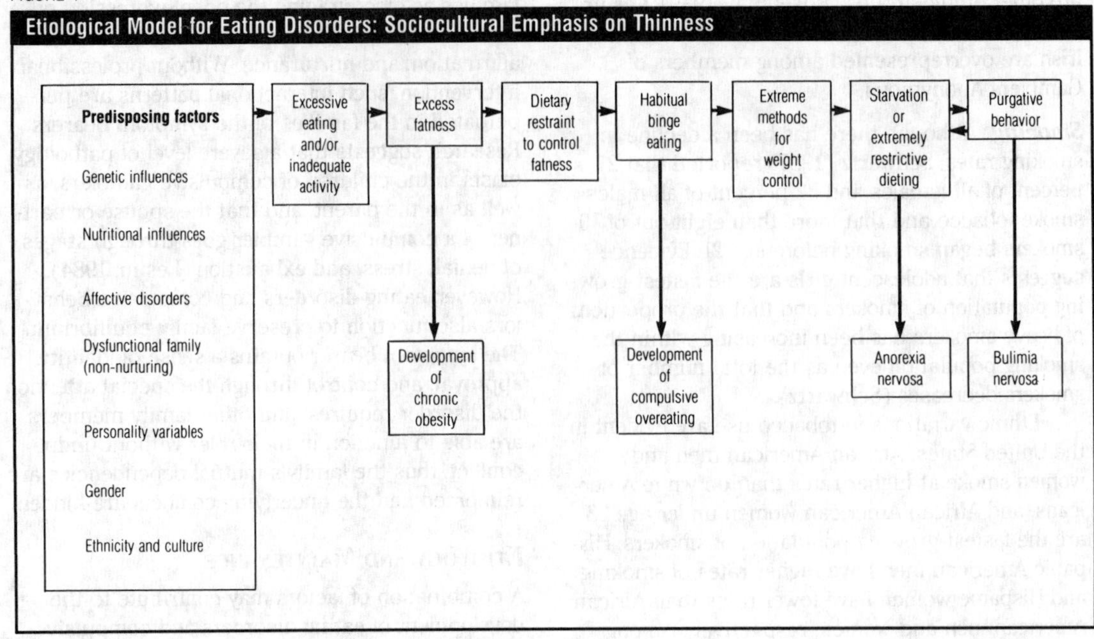


SOURCE: Williamson, D. A. (1990). *Assessment of Eating Disorders, Obesity, Anorexia, and Bulimia Nervosa*. Tarrytown, NY: Pergamon Press. Copyright © 1990 by Allyn and Bacon. Adapted by permission.

FIGURE 2

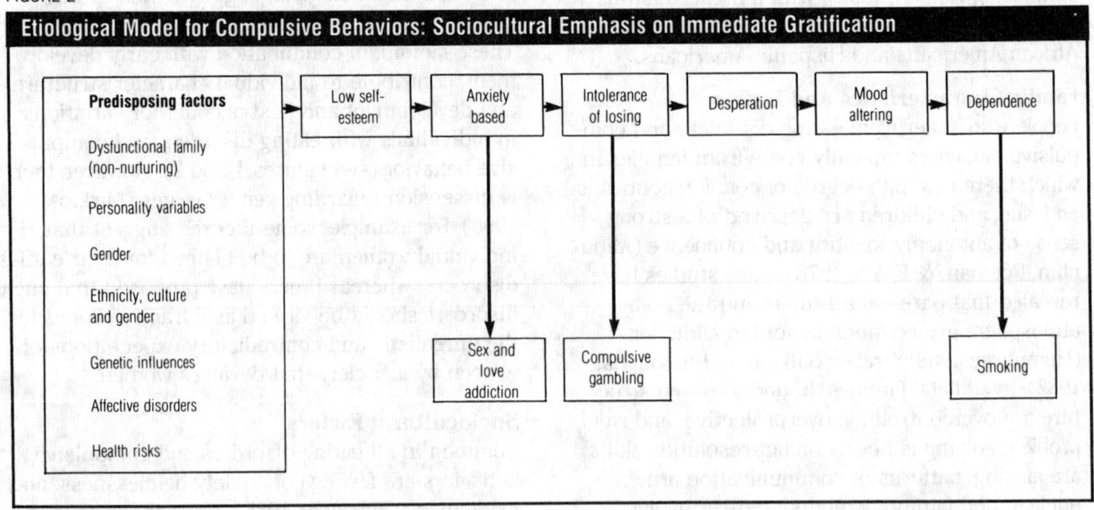


bling or smoking, and that in attempting to eliminate anxiety and conflict, some people develop eating disorders or compulsions.

**Biological Factors**

Research has shown that there is a large genetic component to obesity and that biological factors influence binge eating and compulsive behavior (Stunkard & Wadden, 1992). Furthermore, high rates of major depressive disorders (Herzog, 1984) and of substance abuse and affective disorders have been reported in bulimics and anorexics (Bulich, 1987; Hudson, Pope, & Jonas, 1983). Moreover, a disturbance of the hypothalamus, the master control for all glandular secretions, may be the cause of anorexia and bulimia (Farley, 1994).

Researchers have also tested the use of drugs such as insulin, thyroid, anabolic steroids, psychotropics, and opiods to treat anorexics (Bruch,

1973; Pope & Hudson, 1984). Anorexics responded to antidepressants with minor weight changes and slight overall improvement, but further research is needed, with better controls, to determine which medications work best with various types of clients (Johnson & Conners, 1987).

### Cognitive–Behavioral Factors

Cognitive–behavioral theories on how eating disorders and compulsive behaviors are developed and maintained view eating and compulsive behaviors as a means of coping with stressful life events and unmanageable feelings. Environmental (overt) cues and cognitive (covert) cues are seen as triggering eating binges and acting-out behavior. Binge eating and compulsive behavior are maintained because their highly negative consequences (feeling of fullness, guilt, and weight gain) may overwhelm the positive consequences (Loro, 1984).

### Psychodynamic and Developmental Factors

Psychodynamic explanations for eating disorders and compulsive behaviors attribute repetitive, excessive behavior to the unconscious. Nonnurturing early relationships, inconsistency in parenting, and lack of bonding, it is believed, result in consistent frustration, conflict during the attachment and separation–individuation phases, and serious emotional damage to the individual (Mahler, 1968; Mahler, Pine, & Berman, 1975; Selvini-Palazzoli, 1985). Thus, the individual is at risk of affective instability in adolescence and adulthood, a process that results in an ongoing unconscious search for the ultimate need-gratifying object.

Anorexics and bulimics are especially vulnerable to separation experiences and the accompanying feelings of helplessness and depression (Selvini-Palazzoli, 1985). For them, food becomes the object of gratification and the means of avoiding anxiety and other feelings; for the sexually addicted, love and sex are the objects; for gamblers, gambling; and for smokers, smoking.

## Diagnosis and Assessment

Differentiating eating disorders and compulsive behaviors can be difficult because the symptoms of anorexia nervosa, bulimia nervosa, compulsive overeating, obesity, and compulsive behaviors are similar.

### Eating Disorders

Differential diagnoses of persons with eating disorders can be made through structured clinical interviews and self-report instruments (Williamson, 1990). Structured interviews are designed to assess the core psychopathology of the disorders. Self-report inventories have been criticized for not addressing the bingeing, purging, and avoidance-of-eating behaviors that characterize eating disorders (Schlundt, 1989). In response to such criticism, a variety of behavioral assessment approaches have been developed, including assessment of eating during test meals, measurement of weight and body composition, and assessment of eating and purgative habits via self-monitoring (Williamson, 1990).

Clinicians must also be concerned with assessing the common secondary psychopathology of eating disorders, such as family and interpersonal problems, personality disorders, substance abuse, and depression; numerous instruments and procedures are available for doing so (Williamson, 1990). The highest levels of secondary psychopathology have been found in anorexics, followed by bulimics, compulsive overeaters, and abuse groups.

Assessment of eating disorders in noncompliant individuals, who usually require inpatient care, may best be accomplished in hospitals. Perhaps most challenging is the assessment of atypical eating disorders, whose symptoms or level of severity do not warrant more-specific diagnoses. In such cases, clinicians who are familiar with both eating disorders and other medical or psychiatric disorders are best prepared to conduct such assessments.

### Sex and Love Addiction

The diagnosis and assessment of sex and love addiction require a simultaneous focus on addicted individuals and their environments, including the family system, other intimate relationships, the quality of the individual's environment, and the nurturing and nonnurturing aspects of the individual's life (Logan, 1992). Useful assessment tools include a genogram to explore family dynamics (McGoldrick & Gerson, 1985); a written autobiography, detailing experiences with the addiction; and an ecomap, to examine the individual's sociocultural, physical, and social networks (Hartman, 1979). Through structured questions and basic interviews, together with other criteria such as the intensity of an individual's relationship, ineffectual excuses for continuing the relationship, and the individual's feeling of estrangement when a relationship ends, the clinician may assess whether relationships are addictive (Logan, 1992).

### Gambling

Gambling is among the most popular social activities in the United States. States encourage this trend through legalized lotteries, as a means of increasing revenues (Gaudia, 1992). Despite the recognition that the availability of gambling opportunities encourages abuse, multi-million-dollar lottery wins and huge state lottery prizes are perpetuated through major advertising campaigns (Kaplan, 1984).

Clinicians use a variety of assessment tools for completing a thorough gambling history of an individual (Rosenthal, 1989). More specifically, practitioners tend to use a "damage-and-disability" inventory to elicit information about gambling problems. This tool, along with Gamblers Anonymous's 20 questions, provides information about the various areas of functioning to see how gambling has affected the person's career, family life, and so on. It is like an informal application of the DSM-IV (APA, 1994) criteria for determining the individual's preoccupation with gambling (Rosenthal).

### Smoking

For smoking, a three-stage assessment typology is provided by a sequential assessment model (Moncher et al., 1992). In the first stage, known as a "broad base," the focus is on identification of an individual's general problem areas. If an addictive problem is identified, then in the second, or "basic-assessment" stage, the problem behavior is described in functional and diagnostic terms; tentative decisions are made about the treatment or type of intervention; treatment programs are identified; and inferences are made regarding social, biological, and psychological factors that may foster the addictive behavior, as well as factors that serve as barriers to overcoming the problem. During the third stage, "specialized assessment," a more specific and detailed assessment is made and intervention is begun.

## Treatment and Management

### Anorexia, Bulimia, and Compulsive Overeating

For eating disorders, the trend in treatment and management has been toward a multidisciplinary, multimodal approach. Comprehensive treatment programs use teams that include social workers, physicians, nutritionists, and other professionals. Most treatment programs for anorexics focus on the psychological as well as the physical aspects of the disorder. Both anorexics and bulimics are usually first treated for physical symptoms to ensure medical stability and then receive supportive therapy to address the underlying causes of their disorders. Recent trends in treatment, however, suggest individually oriented intensive long-term care that focuses attention simultaneously on the physicial and psychological symptoms. The aim is to establish a bond of trust with the anorexic person, to change the person's negative mind-set about their self-worth, and to recapture their desire to live (Sherr, 1994).

Strategies of intervention for eating disorders range from prevention to treatment. Most successful treatment programs combine individual and family treatment and may involve multifamily groups. The core elements of three modes of treatment can be summarized as follows (see Forext, 1977; Harper-Giuffre & Mackenzie, 1992; Hornyak & Baker, 1989; Minuchin et al., 1978; Vandereycken, Kog, & Vanderlinden, 1989; Wilson, Hogan, & Mintz, 1992; Yager, Gwirtsman, & Edelstein, 1991):

1. *individual treatment:* journal keeping, modeling, nutritional intervention, cognitive–behavioral techniques, manipulating consequences, and eliciting support from family and friends
2. *family treatment:* designing tasks for each family member, providing alternative ways to respond to the illness, modeling, establishing rules of eating conduct, meeting members' emotional needs, looking for abusive or addictive patterns in family members, and identifying maladaptive communication patterns
3. *group treatment:* education on family dynamics, dependence, stress management, nutrition, distorted self-perceptions, and other factors and the use of a mix of therapeutic devices, such as creative art therapies, rational–emotive techniques, gestalt and process techniques, spiritual counseling, neurolinguistic programming, behavioral modification, and desensitization and confrontation.

Most anorexics can be safely treated as outpatients, although hospitalization, including intravenous feeding, may be needed in severe cases. Early identification and treatment of anorexia and bulimia are key to a successful outcome. According to Herbert (1987), 63 percent to 80 percent of bulimics become binge- and purge-free, and among anorexics, 50 percent regain normal weight and eating habits, 25 percent improve but develop other weight or eating problems, and 25 percent are resistant to intervention.

### Obesity

The primary goal in the treatment of obese persons is to help them adopt permanent changes in eating habits—that is, to eat less, to eat fewer fatty foods, and to engage in more physical exercise. A triage approach to obesity is the most effective for both children and adults. This approach requires a clear definition of the problem with regard to medical and psychological issues, followed by a determination of the severity of the condition and the establishment of a treatment regimen specific to the condition. Dieting is generally an ineffective means of losing weight for an extended period; a high percentage of individuals who lose weight by dieting soon gain it back.

Other treatments for obesity are being explored, including several kinds of surgery that may be performed on the morbidly obese (Abraham & Llewellyn-Jones, 1992; Stunkard & Wadden, 1992). Surgical procedures include gastric restriction, which reduces the amount of food that can be consumed at one time; an intestinal bypass, which permits unlimited consumption, although the individual is subject to diarrhea immediately following eating; and insertion of an intragestive balloon, which by occupying space in the stomach (during inflation) reduces the appetite. Evidence suggests that these procedures are effective for the severely obese (DHHS, 1988a).

Prevention is considered the most-effective approach to the problem of obesity. Preventive programs may be presented at all levels of schooling. Parents, teachers, and other significant persons should model what they teach and become advocates for healthier foods.

### Love and Sex Addiction

Given the range and complexity of patterns in love- and sex-addictive relationships, a multimodal approach is indicated. The aim of treatment is to interrupt or end the circular pattern of interaction. The most-effective approaches to working with this compulsive behavior are modeled after effective drug and food addiction therapies (Peele, 1976). Preventive activities are geared toward individual change, as well as toward changes in major institutions in the society, both educational and recreational.

### Compulsive Gambling

Again, treatment programs for compulsive gamblers are modeled after effective food- and drug-addiction therapies. Treatment may be on an outpatient or inpatient basis and may include lectures, group discussions, attendance at Gamblers Anonymous meetings, and the use of creative devices (such as writing an autobiography) to provide insight into the disorder. The aim of treatment is total abstinence.

### Smoking

The aim of treatment is smoking cessation (Schwartz, 1987). Combinations of treatments tend to be more effective over longer periods than do single interventions. Several interventions hold promise (DHHS, 1988b): low-aversion, directed smoking strategies, such as nicotine fading and the use of nicotine gum; skills training; enhancement of self-attribution of success in treatment; and training to obtain and use social supports. Also effective are postintervention booster sessions, during which obstacles to the application of skills are discussed and potential solutions are practiced. Prevention strategies include social inoculation training (Flay, 1985), life-skills training, values-clarification exercises, self-management procedures, breathing and muscle relaxation exercises, problem-solving and decision-making techniques, and assertion–refusal skills. Families and significant others play an important role in successful prevention programs (Moncher et al., 1992).

## Conclusion

An increase in the incidence of eating disorders and compulsive behaviors in the general population is reflected in the caseloads of social work practitioners and in the increasing body of professional literature by social workers and other helping professionals. This literature explores the similarities between eating disorders and compulsive behavior and their impact on families and society and identifies effective social work approaches to prevention, treatment, and policy issues (Freeman, 1992). Current research and practice reveal that social work is an essential component of comprehensive treatment programs for eating disorders and compulsive behaviors.

## References


Abraham, S., & Llewellyn-Jones, D. (1992). *Eating disorders: The facts* (3rd ed.). Oxford, England: Oxford University Press.

American Psychiatric Association. (1994). *Diagnostic and statistical manual of mental disorders* (4th ed.). Washington, DC: Author.

Andersen, A. E. (Ed.). (1990). *Males with eating disorders.* New York: Brunner/Mazel.

Brown, P. J. (1992). Cultural perspectives on etiology and treatment of obesity. In A. J. Stunkard & T. A. Wadden (Eds.), *Obesity: Theory and therapy* (pp. 179–193). New York: Raven Press.

Browne, M. (1993). Dying to be thin. *Essence, 24*(6), 86–87, 124–128.

Bruch, H. (1973). *Eating disorders: Anorexia nervosa, obesity, and the person within.* New York: Basic Books.

Bulich, C. M. (1987). Drug and alcohol abuse by bulimic women and their families. *American Journal of Psychiatry, 144,* 1604–1606.

Conners, M. E. (1992). Bulimia: Interdisciplinary team practice from a normative and developmental perspective. In E. M. Freeman (Ed.), *The addiction process: Effective social work approaches* (pp. 192–203). New York: Longman.

Custer, R., & Milt, H. (1985). *When luck runs out.* New York: Facts on File Publications.

Dietz, W. H. (1983). Childhood obesity: Susceptibility, cause, and management. *Journal of Pediatrics, 103,* 676–686.

*Facts about obesity.* (1976). (NIH Publication No. 76-974). Washington, DC: U.S. Government Printing Office.

Farley, D. (1994). Eating disorders: When thinness becomes an obsession. In *Current issues in women's health* (2nd ed., pp. 33–37). Rockville, MD: U.S. Department of Health and Human Services.

Flay, D. R. (1985). What we know about the social influences approach to smoking prevention: Review and recommendations. In C. S. Bell & R. J. Battjes (Eds.), *Prevention research deterring drug abuse among children and adolescents* (NIDA Research Monograph No. 63, pp. 67–112). Washington, DC: U.S. Government Printing Office.

Forext, J. P. (Ed.). (1977). *Behavioral treatment of obesity.* New York: Pergamon Press.

Freeman, E. M. (Ed.). (1992). *The addiction process: Effective social work approaches.* New York: Longman.

Gaudia, R. (1992). Compulsive gambling: Reframing issues of control. In E. M. Freeman (Ed.), *The addiction process: Effective social work approaches* (pp. 237–247). New York: Longman.

Greenfeld, D. (1984, July 9). Eating disorders: The price of a society's desire to be thin. *Medical World News, 25*(13), 38–50.

Harlan, W. R. (1993). Epidemiology of childhood obesity: A national perspective. In C. L. Williams & S.Y.S. Kimm (Eds.), *Prevention and treatment of childhood obesity* (pp. 1–5). New York: New York Academy of Sciences.

Harper-Giuffre, H., & Mackenzie, R. R. (Eds.). (1992). *Group psychotherapy for eating disorders.* Washington, DC: American Psychiatric Press.

Hartman, A. (1979). Diagrammatic of family relationships. In B. Compton & B. Galaway (Eds.), *Social work processes* (pp. 209–309). New York: Free Press.

*Healthy people 2000.* (1991). Washington, DC: U.S. Government Printing Office.

Herbert, D. (1987). *Eating disorders: Counseling issues.* Ann Arbor, MI: ERIC Clearinghouse and Counseling Services.

Herzog, D. B. (1984). Are anorexic and bulimic patients depressed? *American Journal of Psychiatry, 141,* 1594–1638.

Hornyak, L. M., & Baker, E. K. (Eds.). (1989). *Experiential therapies for eating disorders.* New York: Guilford Press.

Hudson, J. I., Pope, H. G., & Jonas, J. M. (1983). Family history study of anorexia nervosa and bulimia. *British Journal of Psychiatry, 142,* 133–138.

Humphrey, L. L. (1989). Observed family interactions among subtypes of eating disorders using the structural analysis of social behavior. *Journal of Consulting and Clinical Psychology, 57,* 206–214.

Hunter, M. (1988). *What is sex addiction?* Center City, MN: Hazelden Foundation.

Jacobs, D. F. (1989). Illegal and undocumented: A review of teenage gambling and the plight of children of problem gamblers. In H. J. Shaffer, S. A. Stein, B. Gambino, & T. N. Cummings (Eds.), *Compulsive gambling: Theory, research and practice* (pp. 249–292). Lexington, MA: Lexington Books.

Johnson, C., & Conners, M. (1987). *The etiology and treatment of bulimia nervosa: A biopsychological perspective.* New York: Basic Books.

Kaplan, H. R. (1984). The social and economic impact of state lotteries. *Annals of the American Academy of Political and Social Sciences, 474,* 91–106.

Laing, R. D. (1965). *The divided self.* Middlesex, England: Penguin Books.

Lesuir, H. (1984). *The chase.* Cambridge, MA: Shenkman.

Logan, S. L. (1992). Overcoming sex and love addiction: An expanded perspective. In E. M. Freeman (Ed.), *The addiction process: Effective social work approaches* (pp. 207–221). New York: Longman.

Loro, A. D. (1984). Binge-eating: A cognitive behavioral treatment approach. In R. C. Hawkins, W. J. Fremouw, & P. F. Clements (Eds.), *The binge–purge syndrome: Diagnosis, treatment, and research* (pp. 183–210). New York: Springer.

Mahler, M. (1968). *On human symbiosis and the vicissitudes of individuation: Infantile psychosis.* New York: International Universities Press.

Mahler, M., Pine, F., & Berman, A. (1975). *The psychological birth of the human infant: Symbiosis and individuation.* New York: Basic Books.

Marcus, M. D., & Wing, R. R. (1987). Binge eating among the obese. *Annals of Behavioral Medicine, 9,* 23–27.

McGoldrick, M., & Gerson, R. (1985). *Genograms in family assessment.* New York: W. W. Norton.

Minuchin, S., Rosman, B., & Baker, L. (1978). *Psychosomatic families: Anorexia nervosa in context.* Cambridge, MA: Harvard University Press.

Mirkin, M. P. (1990). Eating disorders: A feminist structural family therapy perspective. In M. P. Mirkin (Ed.), *The social and political contexts of family therapy* (pp. 89–119). Needham Heights, MA: Allyn & Bacon.

Moncher, M. S., Schinke, S. P., & Holden, G. W. (1992). Tobacco addiction: Correlates, prevention, and treatment. In E. M. Freeman (Ed.), *The addiction process: Effective social work approaches* (pp. 222–236). New York: Longman.

Nakken, C. (1988). *The addictive personality: Roots, ritual and recovery.* Center City, MN: Hazelden Foundation.

Peele, S. (1975). *Love and addiction.* New York: Taplinger.

Peele, S. (1976). *Love and addiction.* New York: Signet.

Peele, S. (1985). *The meaning of addiction: Compulsive experience and its interpretation.* Lexington, MA: Lexington Books.

Pope, H. G., & Hudson, J. I. (1984). *New hope for binge eaters: Advances in understanding and treatment for bulimia.* New York: Harper & Row.

Quadland, M. C. (1985). Compulsive sexual behavior: Definition of a problem and an approach to treatment. *Journal of Sex and Marital Therapy, 11,* 121–132.

Rosenthal, R. (1989). Pathological gambling and problem gambling: Problems of definition and diagnosis. In H. J. Shaffer, S. A. Stein, B. Gambino, & T. N. Cummings (Eds.), *Compulsive gambling: Theory, research and practice* (pp. 101–125). Lexington, MA: Lexington Books.

Schaeffer, B. (1985). *Is it love or is it addiction?* Center City, MN: Hazelden Foundation.

Schlundt, D. G. (1989). Assessment of eating behavior in bulimia nervosa. The self-monitoring analysis system. In W. G. Johnson (Ed.), *Advances in eating disorders* (Vol. 2, pp. 1–44). Greenwich, CT: JAI Press.

Schwartz, J. L. (1987). *Review of smoking cessation methods: The United States and Canada 1975–1985* (NIH Publication No. 872940). Washington, DC: National Cancer Institute.

Selvini-Palazzoli, M. (1985). *Self-starvation.* London: Jason Aronson.

*Sex and Love Addicts Anonymous: The basic text for the Augustine Fellowship.* (1986). Boston: Augustine Fellowship, Sex and Love Addicts Anonymous, Fellowship-Wide Services.

Sherr, L. (1994, December 2). The hunger inside. In *20/20.* New York: American Broadcasting Company.

Straber, M., Salkion, B., & Burroughs, J. (1982). Validity of bulimia-restricter distinction in anorexia nervosa parental personality characteristics and family psychiatric morbidity. *Journal of Nervous and Mental Disease, 170,* 345–351.

Stuart, R. B., & Davis, B. (1972). *Slim chance in a fat world: Behavioral control of obesity.* Champaign, IL: Research Press.

Stunkard, A. J., & Wadden, T. A. (Eds.). (1992). *Obesity: Theory and therapy.* New York: Raven Press.

Summers, A. (Ed.). (1989, May). The heat is on. Cover stories: Sexual pursuit. *MS, 17,* 39–56.

U.S. Department of Health and Human Services. (1988a). *Eating disorders: The impact on children and families.* Washington, DC: U.S. Government Printing Office.

U.S. Department of Health and Human Services. (1988b). *The health consequences of smoking: Nicotine addiction. A report of the surgeon general* (Publication No. CDC 88-8406). Washington, DC: U.S. Government Printing Office.

Vandereycken, W., Kog, E., & Vanderlinden, J. (Eds.). (1989). *The family approach to eating disorders: Assessment and treatment of anorexia nervosa and bulimia.* New York: PMA Publishing.

Volberg, R. A., & Steadman, H. J. (1989). Policy implication of prevalence estimates of pathological gambling. In H. J. Shaffer, S. A. Stein, B. Gambino, & T. N. Cummings (Eds.), *Compulsive gambling: Theory, research and practice* (pp. 163–186). Lexington, MA: Lexington Books.

Williamson, D. A. (1990). *Assessment of eating disorders: obesity, anorexia and bulimia nervosa.* Tarrytown, NY: Pergamon Press.

Wilson, C. P., Hogan, C. C., & Mintz, I. R. (Eds.). (1992). *Psychodynamic technique in the treatment of eating disorders.* Northvale, NJ: Jason Aronson.

Wolfgang, A. K. (1988). Gambling as a function of gender and sensation seeking. *Journal of Gambling Behavior, 4,* 71–77.

Yager, J., Gwirtsman, H. E., & Edelstein, C. K. (Eds.). (1991). *Special problems in managing eating disorders.* Washington, DC: American Psychiatric Press.

## Further Reading

Brown, C., & Jasper, K. (1993). *Consuming passions: Feminist approaches to weight preoccupation and eating disorders.* Toronto: Second Storey Press.

Eadington, W. E., & Cornelius, J. A. (Eds.). (1993). *Gambling behavior and problem gambling.* Reno, NV: University of Nevada Press.

Fallon, P., Katzman, M. A., & Wooley, S. C. (1994). *Feminist perspectives on eating disorders.* New York: Guilford Press.

Farley, D. (1983). *Eating disorders require medical attention.* Rockville, MD: U.S. Department of Health and Human Services, Food and Drug Administration, Office of Public Affairs.

Garner, D. M., & Garfinkle, P. E. (1979). The eating attitude test: An index of the symptoms of anorexia nervosa. *Psychological Medicine, 9,* 273–279.

Garner, D. M., & Olmstead, M. P. (1984). *Manual for the eating attitude test.* Odessa, FL: Psychological Assessment Resources.

Hollis, J. (1986). *Fat is a family affair.* New York: Harper & Row.

Lask, B., & Bryant-Waugh, R. (1993). *Childhood onset anorexia nervosa and related eating disorders.* Hillsdale, NJ: Lawrence Erlbaum.

LeBow, M. D. (1983). *Child obesity: A new frontier of behavior therapy.* New York: Springer.

**Sadye L. Logan, DSW, ACSW, LSCSW,** is associate professor, University of Kansas, School of Social Welfare, 204 Twente Hall, Lawrence, KS 66045.

### For further information see

Adolescence Overview; Child Abuse and Neglect Overview; Child Sexual Abuse Overview; Childhood; Direct Practice Overview; Families Overview; Group Practice; Human Development; Human Sexuality; Mental Health Overview; Primary Prevention Overview; School-Linked Services; Self-Help Groups; Sexual Distress; Substance Abuse: Direct Practice.

**Key Words**

| | |
|---|---|
| addictions | eating disorders |
| compulsive behavior | obesity |

# Ecological Perspective

**Carel B. Germain**
**Alex Gitterman**

Germain (1973) introduced an ecological metaphor as a perspective for practice in social casework more than 20 years ago. Despite social work's historical commitment to the person-in-environment, most direct practice had not gone beyond the individual's internal processes and the family's interpersonal processes. Attention to physical and social environments and culture, and to their reciprocal relationships with people, was rare. This inattention was due mainly to the lack of available concepts about environments and culture and how they affect and are affected by human development and functioning.

Most if not all work with the environment had been limited to securing information about clients from family members, landlords, former employers, friends, and neighbors and to providing financial aid and services such as foster care. As important as social provision is, physical and social environments also must be understood and worked with as people interact with them. (Stein and Cloward, 1959, made a notable early effort to fill the environment gap.) Earth Day 1965 highlighted the environment as more than a static setting in which people's lives are played out, and concepts from ecology gradually came to the fore, supplementing the related work of Bartlett (1970) and Gordon (1969).

Ecology, the biological science that studies organism–environment relations, offered concepts of these relations that were less abstract than those offered by systems theories and closer to common human experience. Used metaphorically, the concepts could enable a practitioner and a client to keep a simultaneous focus on person and environment and on their reciprocal relationship. Hence, certain concepts have been singled out as appropriate for social work and congruent with its purpose. They hold the promise of extending social workers' understanding of the interacting personal, environmental, and cultural factors involved in complicated troubled situations and of increasing the quality of help offered to clients to modify their situations. Practice principles derived from the concepts are aimed at promoting individual and family health, growth, and satisfying social functioning.

The conceptual framework of the ecological perspective (Germain, 1979) was later elaborated and refined (Germain & Gitterman, 1987). As time passed, it became clear that the capacity of ecological concepts to implement social work's commitment to the person and the environment was helpful not only in practice with individuals, families, groups, and organizations but also with communities and in political advocacy (Germain & Gitterman, in press). The first part of this entry reviews the original concepts and their further refinement and describes in detail newly added concepts of coercive power, exploitative power, and "life courses." The second part briefly describes the Life Model practice approach that is derived from the ecological concepts.

## Theoretical Foundations

The ecological perspective makes clear the need to view people and environments as a unitary system within a particular cultural and historic context. Both person and environment can be fully understood only in terms of their relationship, in which each continually influences the other within a particular context. Hence, all concepts derived from the ecological metaphor refer not to environment alone or person alone; rather, each concept expresses a particular person:environment relationship, whether it is positive, negative, or neutral. (In accord with the unitary view, person:environment relationships are designated by a colon, replacing the traditional hyphen, which visually fractures their connection.)

Another aspect of the ecological perspective is "ecological thinking," a mode of thought that differs markedly from linear thinking. The latter can explain some simple phenomena (for example, John drops a glass on a tile floor, causing it to break, while he remains unchanged). Ecological thinking can explain complex human phenomena, such as those that enter the social work domain. Ecological thinking examines exchanges between A and B, for example, that shape, influence, or change both over time. A acts, which leads to a change in B, whereupon the change in B elicits a change in A that in turn changes B, which then changes or otherwise influences A, and so on. The process is further complicated by the fact that other variables are usually operating at the same time.

In contrast, linear thinking emphasizes that A causes an effect that changes B at a certain point in time, while A remains unchanged. Ecological thinking is less concerned with cause and more concerned with the consequences of exchanges between A and B and how to help modify maladaptive exchanges. Instead of valuing prediction based on simplistic cause and effect, ecological thinking embraces indeterminacy in complex human phenomena. The original ecological concepts, now refined, include the following.

***Person:environment fit*** is the actual fit between an individual's or a collective group's needs, rights, goals, and capacities and the qualities and operations of their physical and social environments within particular cultural and historical contexts. Hence, for the person and environment, the fit might be favorable, minimally adequate, or unfavorable. When it is favorable or even minimally adequate, it represents a state of relative "adaptedness" (Dubos, 1978), which promotes continued development and satisfying social functioning and sustains or enhances the environment. Adaptedness reflects generally positive person:environment exchanges over time. It is never fixed but shifts in accord with shifts in reciprocal exchanges. When exchanges over time are generally negative, development, health, and social functioning might be impaired and the environment could be damaged.

***Adaptations*** are continuous, change-oriented, cognitive, sensory–perceptual, and behavioral processes people use to sustain or raise the level of fit between themselves and their environment. Adaptations include actions to change the environment (including moving to new environments), or people themselves, or both, and then adapting to those changes and changes made by the environment (such as natural disasters or new social expectations) in a never-ending process.

***Life stressors*** are generated by critical life issues that people perceive as exceeding their personal and environmental resources for managing them. Life stressors include difficult social or developmental transitions, traumatic life events, and any other life issues that disturb the existing fit. Poverty and oppression are among critical life issues that not only make other life stressors difficult to manage but often create more stressors than are suffered by other groups.

Life stressors and challenges differ in meaning and emotional tone. A stressor represents serious harm or loss and is associated with a sense of being in jeopardy. A challenge is experienced as an opportunity for growth and is associated with positive feelings of anticipated mastery and zestful struggle (Lazarus, 1980; Lazarus & Folkman, 1984). Depending on personal, environmental, and cultural differences, some people might experience a disruptive life issue as a stressor, whereas others experience the same issue as a challenge. This latter group is not likely to seek social work services unless anticipated mastery fails to materialize.

***Stress*** is the internal response to a life stressor and is characterized by troubled emotional or physiological states, or both. Associated negative feelings may include anxiety, guilt, anger, fear, depression, helplessness, or despair and are usually accompanied by lowered levels of relatedness, sense of competence, self-esteem, and self-direction. On the one hand, prolonged stress, together with ineffective coping and personal vulnerability, can lead to physiological, emotional, or social dysfunction. On the other hand, challenge may stir up periodic anxiety, but the person continues to feel hopeful and confident and maintains relatedness, a sense of competence, self-esteem, and self-direction.

***Coping measures*** are special behaviors, often novel, that are devised to handle the demands posed by the life stressor. They include efforts to regulate immobilizing, negative feelings and to engage in effective problem solving as required by the particular life stressor. Successful coping depends on various environmental and personal resources. It frequently raises the level of fit by improving the quality of person:environment exchanges and attaining higher levels of relatedness, competence, self-esteem, and self-direction.

The last four attributes are outcomes of adaptive exchanges between the person and past and current environments. They are relatively free of cultural bias, although each may be expressed differently in different cultures.

***Relatedness*** refers to attachments, friendships, positive kin relationships, and a sense of belonging to a supportive social network. The concept of relatedness is based in part on Bowlby's (1973) attachment theory, which states that attachment is an innate capacity of human beings. It was built into the genetic structure of humans because of its survival value in the evolutionary environment. Relatedness is also based on ideas about emotional and social loneliness and isolation (Weiss, 1973, 1982), social network theory (for example, Gottleib, 1986), mutual aid groups (Gitterman & Shulman, 1993), and ideas about relatedness to the natural world (for example, Searles, 1960), including responsible stewardship and the use of pets, gardening, camping, and wilderness experiences (for example, Germain, 1991).

***Competence*** assumes that all organisms are innately motivated to affect their environment in order to survive (White, 1959). This motivation, most highly developed in human beings, is termed "effectance." Opportunities for effective action must be available in the environment from infancy to old age for the development and sustainment of a sense of one's efficacy. Accumulated experiences of efficacy lead to a sense of competence. This is an important hypothesis for social workers, because it suggests that motivation to be effective in the environment can be mobilized even if life circumstances have dampened this motivation. Although we do not yet have the knowledge and skills to help all individuals in all situations to mobilize their competence motivation, it is nevertheless possible in many situations for social workers and clients to devise opportunities for purposive and effective action to improve elements of environments or the person's exchanges with them, however modest.

***Self-esteem*** is the most important part of self-concept; it represents the extent to which one feels competent, respected, and worthy. Hence, it significantly influences human thinking and behavior. A high level of self-esteem is intrinsically satisfying and pleasurable. It is particularly important in childhood and adolescence but continues to develop and even to change in adulthood. Low self-esteem reflects a lack of respect for oneself and feelings that one is inadequate, inferior, unlovable, and unworthy. It is often associated with depression.

***Self-direction*** is the capacity to take some degree of control over one's life and to accept responsibility for one's decisions and actions while simultaneously respecting the rights and needs of others. This capacity must be supported from infancy to old age through opportunities from the environment that enable a person to make age- and health-appropriate decisions and take purposive action. Issues of power and powerlessness are critical to self-direction. People's life circumstances may be such that few options exist in their environment, so personal choice and decisions are meaningless. If people have no control over undesirable life events or financial security (this is most common among poor and oppressed people), then self-direction is threatened. Powerlessness is a cruel and inhumane life condition, because people who are powerless are apt to suffer many more disruptive life stressors with long-term consequences than the rest of the population.

***Habitat and niche*** further delineate the nature of physical and social environments and are particularly helpful ideas in work with communities (Germain, 1985). In ecology, *habitat* refers to places where the organism can be found, such as nesting places, home ranges, and territories. Metaphorically, people's habitats include dwelling places; physical layouts of urban and rural communities; physical settings of schools, workplaces, hospitals, social agencies, shopping areas, and religious structures; and parks and other amenities. Human habitats evoke spatial and temporal behaviors (Germain, 1976, 1978) that help shape and color social environments, and are also patterned by personality, culture, age, gender, socioeconomic status, and experience. Such behaviors serve to regulate social distance, intimacy, privacy, and other interpersonal processes in family, group, community, and organizational life.

In ecology, *niche* refers to the position occupied by a species within a biotic community—the species's place in the web of life. Used metaphorically, niche refers to the status occupied by an individual or family in the social structure of a community. In the United States alone, millions of children and adults are forced to occupy community niches that do not support human rights, needs, and aspirations—often because of color, ethnicity, gender, age, poverty, sexual orientation, or physical or mental states. Many communities are studded with marginal, stigmatized, and destructive niches that denigrate human beings, such as "homeless," "old woman," "gay" or "lesbian," "project tenant," "school dropout," "person with AIDS," "migrant worker," "welfare mother," "hard-core unemployed," "addict" or "ex-addict," "mentally retarded," "mentally ill," "physically disabled," and so on. The existence of oppressive niches is related to issues of power.

In addition to social workers in the areas cited in the 1987 *Encyclopedia of Social Work* (Minahan, 1987), the following social workers are among those who have applied an ecological perspective in certain areas: social work research (Carlson, 1991; Coulton, 1981; Patterson, Memmott, Brennan, & Germain, 1992), social work education (Libassi & Maluccio, 1982), human development (Germain, 1991), and practice issues (Allen-Meares, Washington, & Welsh, 1986; Coulton, 1981; Cox, 1992; Early, 1992; Freeman, 1984; Gitterman, 1991; Guterman & Blythe, 1986; Howard & Johnson, 1985; James & Studs, 1988; Kelley, McKay, & Nelson, 1985; Lee, 1989, 1994; Milner, 1987; Rothman, 1994; Simon, 1994; Wells, Singer, & Polgar, 1986).

## Newly Added Ecological Concepts

***Coercive power*** is the withholding of power from vulnerable groups on the basis of a group's personal or cultural characteristics. The result is oppression of vulnerable populations that renders them powerless (Gitterman, 1991). Despite new laws, coercive power creates and maintains such "social pollutions" as poverty; institutional racism and sexism; oppressive gendered roles in family, work, and community life; homophobia; and physical and social barriers to community participation by people who have severe, chronic physical or mental conditions. Other social pollutions include poor schools and chronic unemployment of people whom the schools have failed to educate; homelessness and lack of affordable housing; and higher rates of infant mortality and chronic illnesses among people of color than among white people.

***Exploitative power*** of dominant groups leads to technological pollution of our air, food, water, soils, and oceans and the increasing presence of toxic chemicals and hazardous wastes in dwellings, schools, workplaces, and communities. Exploitative and coercive power and technological and social pollutions are major stressors that afflict the entire U.S. population, but their burden rests most heavily on vulnerable and powerless groups. Abuses of power express negative person: environment relationships in which the social order permits some people to inflict grave injustices and suffering on others.

***Life course*** conceives biopsychosocial development as consisting of nonuniform, indeterminate pathways of development from birth to old age within diverse environments, cultures, and historical eras. It supplants traditional life cycle models in which so-called life stages are assumed to be universal, fixed, sequential, and predictable. However, stage models ignore the fact that the stages and their tasks originated in the social norms of a particular society at a particular time and therefore are culture-bound and time-bound. Longitudinal studies of children's development (for example, Offer, Ostrov, Howard, & Atkinson, 1988; Rutter, 1979; Thomas, 1975, 1981) reveal the flexibility of development and the potential for change, even in children faced with severe physical challenges (for example, Chess, Fernandez, & Korn, 1980). These researchers and others believe that stage models overlook the complex interplay of maturation, individual potential and resilience, changing environmental constraints and opportunities, and cultural differences. Hence, the models do not incorporate differences related to new family forms; multicultural aspects of American society; gender roles in family and work life; issues of power, oppression, and poverty; and the limitless diversity of individual life experience. The life course conception incorporates difference because it conceives of individual lifelong development as varying with social change—not only with the changing nature of the family, school, workplace, and community, but also with changing ideas, values, and beliefs (Riley, 1978). Development is also considered in terms of individual, historical, and social time (Hareven, 1982).

***Individual time*** refers to the continuity and meaning of individual life experience over the life course. Both are reflected in life stories that we all construct and tell to ourselves and others. Life stories are apparently a part of all societies and cultures and people of all ages. They are our human way of finding meaning and continuity in life events across individual time. "One's identity, then, is built upon the sense one can make of one's own life story" (Laird, 1989, pp. 430–431). The "truth" of life stories lies in their ability to bring out the connections among life events and to lend a sense of coherence to individual and family life (Spence, 1982). Despite their subjectivity, life stories nonetheless exhibit integrity throughout individual time and lend coherence to a life course that is inherently unpredictable (Cohler, 1982). With the empathic, active listening of the social worker, a life story gains increased intelligibility, consistency, and continuity. The teller of the story reinterprets and reconstructs the narrative, which ultimately will contain new conceptions of the self and of one's relationships with others (Stern, 1985).

Overlapping with life stories and related to individual time and perhaps to social and historical time are oral history (for example, Coles, 1967–1977); reminiscence in old age (Butler, 1963); family genealogy (Pinderhughes, 1982); and illness narratives (for example, Kleinman, 1988), including AIDS stories (for example, Monette, 1988).

***Historical time*** refers to the impact of historical and social change on the developmental pathways of a birth cohort (all people born in the same time period, such as a particular decade). Cohort members are exposed to the same sequences of social and historical changes over their life course. Hence, one cohort's experience of growing up and growing older is different from that of another cohort's (Elder, 1984; Riley, 1978, 1985). Several cohorts may experience the same forces, but at different ages, and therefore may experience different effects. The collective lives of a cohort's members press for further social change, which then influences the developmental context of cohorts that follow. For example, issues raised by recent cohorts of women (for example, Van Den Bergh & Cooper, 1986; Weick & Vandiver, 1982) and men (for example, O'Neil, 1982; Pleck, 1981) led to pressure for and achievement of social change that affects all existing cohorts, although differently in terms of cohort age. Although individual and cultural differences are more forceful influences on development than are cohort effects, the cohort concept adds important social and historical dimensions to individual phenomena.

***Social time*** refers to the timing of individual and family transitions and life events as influenced by changing biological, economic, social, demographic, and cultural factors. The term *age crossovers* refers to the changing timetables of many life transitions through which they become independent of age (Neugarten, 1979). For example, no longer is there a fixed, age-connected time for learning, selecting sexual partners, marrying or remarrying, first-time parenting, changing one's career, retiring, becoming an elected official or a college president, or moving into other new statuses and roles. The term *gender crossovers* refers to the transcendence of traditional gender roles—formerly considered unchangeable (Giele, 1980). Such crossovers are reflected in the exchange of traditional gender roles in some families, solo parenting by fathers, and the entry of women into previously male-dominated occupations and of some men into previously female-dominated occupations. Expanded options provided by age and gender crossovers are reshaping the developmental pathways of children and adults.

Individual developmental, behavioral, and narrative processes also merge over social time into collective processes (Hareven, 1982) through which families, groups, and communities are transformed. *Family transformation,* for example, refers to the development of the family over its life course in response to critical life issues and the changes these issues may impose rather than develop through traditional, universal stages (Reiss, 1981). To cope with a grave life stressor, the family may need to modify its structure of roles, tasks, rules, and members' worldview (their shared, often implicit beliefs about themselves and their environment). At first, the family may try to cope using its usual methods. When these fail, the family may experience confusion, upsets in relationships, negative feelings and irritation, and contradictory communications. Increasingly rigid controls may be applied. At that point, the family is likely to be suffering acute stress. In response, it works on restructuring its worldview; reshaping its roles, rules, and routines; and integrating the life issue into the new reality. If the family fails to achieve a new structure, it might break down.

Terkelsen (1980) made a useful distinction between first-order and second-order life issues. A first-order issue may simply require deleting some behaviors and inserting new ones in order to cope effectively with the issue's demands—for example, a status transition, such as school entry—but the family's structure and worldview do not require change. By such "a spontaneous evolutionary leap to a new integration . . . a set of new patterns appears that could not have been predicted from past functioning and that deal better with the new conditions" (Hoffman, 1980, p. 56). First-order life issues such as transitions occur frequently over the life course, leading a family to experience itself as living in a state of flux.

Second-order life issues, such as wrenching harms and losses, require a family to become something new because of the altered reality that affects the family's relationships, communication, roles, exchanges with the environment, and worldview. While needed changes are going on, family members also must manage the attendant pain, anxiety, ambiguity, and disruption that often accompanies change. Second-order life issues occur infrequently, so that the family experiences itself as living in a state of constancy. Reiss's (1981) concept of transformation is similar to the desired outcome of second-order change, and Hoffman's (1980) evolutionary leap is similar to first-order change. Terkelsen (1980) concluded that flux and constancy proceed together—a family continually evolves through first-order changes and episodically restructures itself through second-order changes, thereby transforming itself over its life course.

Most first-order life events, such as developmental and some status transitions, are expectable and predictable. Most second-order events, such as a sudden job loss, death of a loved one, or severe permanent injury, are neither expectable nor predictable. Their effects on family life are different from the effects of expectable and predictable life events, requiring as they do a changed worldview to integrate a new and different reality.

Terkelsen (1980) also declared, "Developmental particulars of each family member are shaped by, and in turn shape, the particulars of each other member's development. Each member's growth is a stimulus in present time for growth in each other member" (p. 42). Life course theorists "take into account the merging of individual pathways into collective configurations—be they families, age groups, or occupational groups" (Hareven, 1982, p. xiii). Hence, it seems that the process of transformation also applies to groups and communities.

The life course conception, with its capacity for incorporating all ecological concepts and the foregoing factors, offers an integrated segment of theory for an ethical and empowering practice with individuals and collectivities that is sensitive not only to ethnicity but to all differences.

## Life Model of Social Work Practice

Two issues raised concern among many sectors of the profession in the 1970s: (1) resistance in direct services to the historical commitment of social work to needed social change and (2) the spread of generalist practice (developed to meet increasingly complex practice situations but thought by some to be superficial because it added together bits from casework, group work, and community modalities). In response to the two concerns, Germain and Gitterman (1980) proposed a practice derived from ecological concepts. The proposed practice offered a reconceived, integrated modality of practice with individuals, families, groups, and organizations. It was later expanded to include community practice and participation in political advocacy (Germain & Gitterman, in press).

The "life model" of social work practice departs from approaches based on clinical processes that are directed to the remedial treatment of personal deficits. Instead, it is patterned on life processes, directed to (1) people's strengths, their innate push toward health, continued growth, and release of potential; (2) modification of environments, as needed, so that they sustain and promote well-being to the maximum degree possible; and (3) raising of the level of person:environment fit for individuals, families, groups, and communities. Although called the life model, it was not intended as a model in the technical sense. Rather, it was a practice modeled on life processes. Hence, the older term is now interchangeable with a more accurate term, "life-modeled practice" (Germain & Gitterman, in press).

Earlier concepts of life space and problems in living are supplanted by the more encompassing paradigm of life stressors–stress–coping within a particular cultural context (recognizing that few people present their predicaments in terms of stressors and stress). All of the concepts presented in this entry express particular person:environment relations and are embodied in life-modeled practice. For example, continuous attention to the level of fit, including personal biopsychosocial features and environmental properties, ecological thinking, and the stressors–stress–coping paradigm are all basic to assessment and intervention. Restored or enhanced relatedness, competence, self-esteem, and self-direction (which apply to collectivities as well as to individuals) are desired outcomes in all practice situations, in addition to agreed-on goals specific to each situation. Life-modeled practice uses practice principles such as empowerment (for example, Lee, 1994; Simon, 1994; Solomon, 1976, 1982) and sensitivity to ethnicity, race, gender, sexual orientation, physical and mental states, and other differences between clients and practitioners. In addition, current portraits of life-modeled practice, ethical concepts, and dilemmas are made explicit, and unethical behaviors are noted (for example, Germain & Gitterman, in press; Reamer, 1992). Life-modeled practice calls on general and differentiated social work knowledge and skills in practice with individuals, families, groups, and communities; in planning and carrying out growth-promoting and preventive services; and in political advocacy.

Empowering aspects of life-modeled practice include a client–social worker relationship conceived as a partnership in which the client and the social worker bring important but differing knowledge and experience to their joint work. Clients are the experts on their own lives. Power differences between social worker and client arising from the social worker's professional status, agency affiliation, race, and educational level are purposively reduced except in certain fields of practice. For example, social work authority is often called on in child welfare and criminal justice issues. From time to time, the client must test the social worker's power and authority, and the social worker in turn must reach for client concern about power and authority vested in the social worker (Gitterman, 1989).

Empowerment results from successful social action carried out jointly by clients and social workers (or by clients alone, when they are ready and interested) and is emphasized in life-modeled practice. Efforts to build or enhance personal power in people who are powerless also is a part of empowerment. These efforts can take the form of

- enhancing relatedness by connecting to informal support systems, such as social networks (for example, Gottleib, 1986) and support, mutual aid, and task groups (for example, Gitterman & Shulman, 1993)

- enhancing competence by providing opportunities for successful action
- enhancing self-esteem through the caring and respect of the practitioner
- enhancing self-direction through encouraging active decision making and techniques such as consciousness-raising, visiting legislators or city or village officials or inviting them to group sessions, participating together in organized peaceful protests, and so on. (Lee, 1994)

As an evolving practice modality, the life model continues to be open to newly developed ideas and knowledge, newly articulated skills, emerging professional issues, and ever-changing social and cultural forces.

## References


Allen-Meares, P., Washington, R. O., & Welsh, B. L. (1986). *Social work services in schools.* Englewood Cliffs, NJ: Prentice Hall.

Bartlett, H. M. (1970). *The common base of social work practice.* New York: National Association of Social Workers.

Bowlby, J. (1973). Affectional bonds: Their nature and origin. In R. S. Weiss (Ed.), *Loneliness: The experience of emotional and social isolation* (pp. 38–52). Cambridge, MA: MIT Press.

Butler, R. (1963). The life review. *Psychiatry, 26,* 65–76.

Carlson, B. E. (1991). Causes and maintenance of domestic violence: An ecological analysis. *Social Service Review, 58,* 569–587.

Chess, S., Fernandez, P., & Korn, S. (1980). The handicapped child and his family: Consonance and dissonance. *Journal of the American Academy of Child Psychiatry, 19,* 56–67.

Cohler, B. J. (1982). Personal narrative and life course. In P. B. Baltes & O. G. Brim, Jr. (Eds.), *Life-span development and behavior* (Vol. 4, pp. 205–241). San Diego, CA: Academic Press.

Coles, R. (1967–1977). *Children in crisis* (Vol. 1–4). Boston: Little, Brown.

Coulton, C. (1981). Person-environment fit as the focus in health care. *Social Work, 26,* 26–35.

Cox, C. (1992). Expanding social work's role in home care: An ecological perspective. *Social Work, 37,* 179–183.

Dubos, R. (1978). Health and creative adaptation. *Human Nature, 1,* 74–82.

Early, B. P. (1992). An ecological–exchange model of social work consultation within the work group of the school. *Social Work in Education, 14,* 207–214.

Elder, G. H., Jr. (1984). Families, kin, and the life course: A sociological perspective. In R. D. Parke (Ed.), *Review of child development research* (Vol. 7, pp. 80–136). Chicago: University of Chicago Press.

Freeman, E. (1984). Multiple losses in the elderly: An ecological approach. *Social Casework, 65,* 287–296.

Germain, C. B. (1973). An ecological perspective in casework practice. *Social Casework, 54,* 323–330.

Germain, C. B. (1976). Time: An ecological variable in social work practice. *Social Casework, 57,* 419–426.

Germain, C. B. (1978). Space: An ecological variable in social work practice. *Social Casework, 59,* 512–522.

Germain, C. B. (1979). Introduction: Ecology and social work. In C. B. Germain (Ed.), *Social work practice: People and environments* (pp. 1–22). New York: Columbia University Press.

Germain, C. B. (1985). The place of community work within an ecological approach to social work practice. In S. H. Taylor & R. W. Roberts (Eds.), *Theory and practice of community social work* (pp. 30–55). New York: Columbia University Press.

Germain, C. B. (1991). *Human behavior in the social environment: An ecological view.* New York: Columbia University Press.

Germain, C. B., & Gitterman, A. (1980). *The life model of social work practice.* New York: Columbia University Press.

Germain, C. B., & Gitterman, A. (1987). Ecological perspective. In A. Minahan (Ed.-in-Chief), *Encyclopedia of Social Work* (18th ed., Vol. 1, pp. 488–499). Silver Spring, MD: National Association of Social Workers.

Germain, C. B., & Gitterman, A. (in press). *The life model of social work practice* (rev. ed). New York: Columbia University Press.

Giele, J. Z. (1980). Adulthood as transcendence of age and sex. In N. J. Smelser & E. Erikson (Eds.), *Themes of work and love in adulthood* (pp. 151–173). Cambridge, MA: Harvard University Press.

Gitterman, A. (1989). Testing professional authority and boundaries. *Social Casework, 70,* 165–170.

Gitterman, A. (1991). Introduction to social work practice with vulnerable populations. In A. Gitterman (Ed.), *Handbook of social work practice with vulnerable populations* (pp. 1–34). New York: Columbia University Press.

Gitterman, A., & Shulman, L. (1993). *Mutual aid groups, vulnerable populations and the life cycle.* New York: Columbia University Press.

Gordon, W. E. (1969). Basic constructs for an integrative and generative conception of social work. In G. Hearn (Ed.), *The general systems approach: Contributions toward an holistic conception of social work* (pp. 5–12). New York: Council on Social Work Education.

Gottlieb, B. (Ed.). (1986). *Marshalling social support: Formats, processes, and effects.* Newbury Park, CA: Sage Publications.

Guterman, N., & Blythe, B. (1986). Toward ecologically based intervention in residential treatment for children. *Social Service Review, 60,* 633–643.

Hareven, T. K. (1982). Preface. In T. K. Hareven & K. J. Adams (Eds.), *Aging and life course transitions: An interdisciplinary perspective* (pp. xiii–xvi). New York: Guilford Press.

Hoffman, L. (1980). The family life cycle and discontinuous change. In E. A. Carter & M. McGoldrick (Eds.), *The family life cycle: A framework for family therapy* (pp. 53–68). New York: Gardner Press.

Howard, T. U., & Johnson, F. C. (1985). An ecological approach to practice with single-parent families. *Social Casework, 66,* 482–489.

James, C. S., & Studs, D. S. (1988). An ecological approach to defining discharge planning in social work. *Social Work in Health Care, 12,* 47–59.

Kelley, M. L., McKay, S., & Nelson, C. H. (1985). Indian agency development: An ecological approach. *Social Casework, 66,* 594–602.

Kleinman, A. (1988). *The illness narratives: Suffering, healing, and the human condition.* New York: Basic Books.

Laird, J. (1989). Women and stories: Restorying women's reconstructions. In M. McGoldrick, S. M. Anderson, & F. Walsh (Eds.), *Women in families* (pp. 427–450). New York: W. W. Norton.

Lazarus, R. S. (1980). The stress and coping paradigm. In L. A. Bond & J. C. Rosen (Eds.), *Competence and coping during adulthood* (pp. 28–74). Hanover, NH: University Press of New England.

Lazarus, R. S., & Folkman, S. (1984). *Stress, appraisal and coping.* New York: Springer.

Lee, J. B. (Ed.). (1989). *Group work with the poor and oppressed.* New York: Haworth Press.

Lee, J. B. (1994). *Empowerment practice in social work.* New York: Columbia University Press.

Libassi, M. F., & Maluccio, A. N. (1982). Teaching the use of ecological perspective in community mental health. *Journal of Education for Social Work, 18,* 94–100.

Milner, J. L. (1987). An ecological perspective on duration of foster care. *Child Welfare, 66,* 113–123.

Minahan, A. (Ed.-in-Chief). (1987). *Encyclopedia of social work* (18th ed.). Silver Spring, MD: National Association of Social Workers.

Monette, P. (1988). *Borrowed time, an AIDS memoir.* San Diego: Harcourt Brace Jovanovich.

Neugarten, B. L. (1979). Time, age, and the life cycle. *American Journal of Psychiatry, 136,* 887–894.

Offer, D., Ostrov, E., Howard, K. I., & Atkinson, R. (1988). *The teenage world: Adolescents' self-image in ten countries.* New York: Plenum Press.

O'Neil, J. M. (1982). Gender-role conflict and stress in men's lives: Implications for psychiatrists, psychologists, and other human-service professionals. In K. Solomon & N. Levy (Eds.), *Man and transition* (pp. 5–44). New York: Plenum Press.

Patterson, S., Memmott, J., Brennan, E., & Germain, C. B. (1992). Patterns of natural helping in rural areas: Implications for social work research. *Social Work Research and Abstracts, 28*(3), 22–26.

Pinderhughes, E. (1982). Black genealogy: Self-liberator and therapeutic tool. *Smith College Studies in Social Work, 52,* 93–106.

Pleck, J. H. (1981). *The myth of masculinity.* Cambridge, MA: MIT Press.

Reamer, F. G. (1992). *Ethical dilemmas in social service* (2nd ed.). New York: Columbia University Press.

Reiss, D. (1981). *The family's construction of reality.* Cambridge, MA: Harvard University Press.

Riley, M. W. (1978). Aging, social change and the power of ideas. *Daedalus, 107,* 39–52.

Riley, M. W. (1985). Women, men, and the lengthening life course. In A. S. Rossi (Ed.), *Aging and the life course* (pp. 333–347). New York: Aldine.

Rothman, J. (1994). *Case management: Integration of individual and community practice.* Englewood Cliffs, NJ: Prentice Hall.

Rutter, M. (1979). Protective factors in children's responses to stress and disadvantage. In M. W. Kent & J. E. Rolf (Eds.), *Primary prevention of psychopathology* (pp. 49–74). Hanover, NH: University Press of New England.

Searles, H. F. (1960). *The non-human environment.* New York: International Universities Press.

Simon, B. L. (1994). *The empowerment tradition in American social work: A history.* New York: Columbia University Press.

Solomon, B. (1976). *Black empowerment: Social work in oppressed communities.* New York: Columbia University Press.

Solomon, B. (1982). Social work values and skills to empower women. In A. Weick & S. T. Vandiver (Eds.), *Women, power, and change* (pp. 206–214). Washington, DC: National Association of Social Workers.

Spence, D. P. (1982). *Narrative truth and historical truth: Meaning and interpretation in psychoanalysis.* New York: W. W. Norton.

Stein, H., & Cloward, R. (Eds.). (1959). *Social perspectives on behavior.* New York: Free Press.

Stern, D. (1985). *The interpersonal world of the infant.* New York: Basic Books.

Terkelsen, K. G. (1980). Toward a theory of the family life cycle. In E. A. Carter & M. McGoldrick (Eds.), *The family life cycle: A framework for family therapy* (pp. 21–52). New York: Gardner Press.

Thomas, A. (1975). A longitudinal study of three brain-damaged children. *Archives of General Psychiatry, 32,* 457–465.

Thomas, A. (1981). Current trends in developmental theory. *American Journal of Orthopsychiatry, 51,* 580–609.

Van Den Bergh, N., & Cooper, L. B. (Eds.). (1986). *Feminist visions for social work.* Silver Spring, MD: National Association of Social Workers.

Weick, A., & Vandiver, S. T. (Eds.). (1982). *Women, power, and change.* Washington, DC: National Association of Social Workers.

Weiss, R. S. (Ed.). (1973). *Loneliness: The experience of emotional and social isolation.* Cambridge, MA: MIT Press.

Weiss, R. S. (1982). Attachment in adult life. In C. M. Parkes & J. Stevenson-Hinde (Eds.), *The place of attachment in adult life* (pp. 171–183). New York: Basic Books.

Wells, L. M., Singer, C., & Polgar, A. T. (1986). *To enhance quality of life in institutions. An empowerment model in long term care: A partnership of residents, staff and families.* Toronto: University of Toronto Press.

White, R. (1959). Motivation reconsidered: The concept of competence. *Psychological Review, 66,* 297–333.

## Further Reading

Coelho, G. V., Hamburg, D. A., & Adams, J. E. (Eds.). (1974). *Coping and adaptation.* New York: Basic Books.

Germain, C. B. (1984). *Social work practice in health care: An ecological perspective.* New York: Free Press.

Germain, C. B. (Ed.). (1979). *Social work practice: People and environments.* New York: Columbia University Press.

Hartman, A. (1994). *Reflection and controversy: Essays on social work.* Washington, DC: NASW Press.

Hartman, A., & Laird, J. (1983). *Family-centered social work practice.* New York: Free Press.

Middleman, R. R., & Wood, G. G. (1990). *Skills for direct practice in social work.* New York: Columbia University Press.
Middleman, R. R., & Wood, G. G. (1989). *The structural approach to social work.* New York: Columbia University Press.
Pinderhughes, E. (1989). *Understanding race, ethnicity, and power.* New York: Free Press.
Reynolds, B. (1982). *Between client and community: A study in responsibility in social case work.* Silver Spring, MD: National Association of Social Workers. (Originally published 1934)

**Carel B. Germain, DSW, ACSW,** is emerita professor of social work, University of Connecticut, School of Social Work, 1798 Asylum Avenue, West Hartford, CT 06117. **Alex Gitterman, EdD,** is professor, Columbia University, School of Social Work, 622 W. 113th Street, New York, NY 10025.

**For further information see**

Assessment Process; Clinical Social Work; Cognitive and Social Theory; Direct Practice Overview; Families Overview; Human Development; Natural Helping Networks; Person-in-Environment; Psychosocial Approach; Social Work Practice: Theoretical Base.

**Key Words**
ecological approach
environmental stress
life changes
person-in-environment
person–situation configuration

# Economic Analysis

**Donald E. Chambers**

On one level, *economic analysis* is simply the use of economic concepts to understand the way the world works. Many of these concepts are familiar: supply, demand, markets, and profit, for example. *Economics* is mainly concerned with commodities and resources that are in scarce supply. Economic concepts were developed to analyze how a society allocates such scarce commodities and resources. Social policies and social programs are also concerned with allocating scarce resources among clients. The fit is inexact but close enough to be useful.

Social workers are familiar with these concepts. Any social worker—as practitioner or policymaker—knows firsthand that resources for target populations are never in infinite supply. The operating policies of social policies and programs are therefore as much about rationing benefits and services as they are about providing them to people who need them. Often economic concepts are not used to understand social welfare policies because economists built their models around the idea that price is the major device for rationing scarce resources: Under conditions of short supply, prices increase until demand falls. A price higher than what consumers are willing to pay tends to ration the commodity, restricting it to those people who are willing to pay more for it than others. But some economists study social problems and public policies by making certain modifications in that idea.

With regard to social policies, the rationing device is not profit but policy statements or administrative regulations stating who gets what, how much, and under which conditions. Consumers of social welfare benefits and services can act in ways similar to buyers of household goods or groceries in a price- or profit-driven system. In this way, economic concepts can illustrate how welfare benefit systems and welfare consumers interact. The consequences of this interaction is discussed in this entry. Testing the validity of how economic concepts model the world involves highly technical issues that this entry cannot consider in depth. Instead, this entry applies economic concepts to one small aspect of the social welfare world to illustrate how that aspect shapes perspectives and directs attention to certain features and not others. In addition, the entry provides examples of relevant social work and social welfare problems researchers have investigated using the methodological tools of economics.

## Applying Economic Concepts to a Social Policy or Program: Child Adoption

Macroeconomics and microeconomics are the two major branches of economics. Microeconomics is particularly relevant to social work and social welfare. It is concerned with the behavior of individual consumers, firms, or markets, and explains, for example, the differences between markets. Microeconomic explanations take as a given certain variables that macroeconomics considers problematic: national income, for example (Varian, 1990).

### Supply and Demand in Child Adoption

Social workers do not usually consider adoption in economic terms. Social workers have viewed adoption in ways that are directly relevant to practice realities as they are traditionally understood: as a psychological event with profound implications for a child's personal and social identity, and as a decision-making event regarding which family best suits the child's needs. To consider adoption in economic terms, children who need parents would be seen not as people in need but as the scarce goods at issue, and adoptive applicants not as people with parenting potential but as the ultimate consumers of this scarce good. This is not the only choice, however. Economic analysis could consider parents the commodity and children the consumers, an interesting exercise. Economic analysis never assists a person in specifying which choices should be made. These choices are part of the fundamental assumptions that the analyst must supply. Results can vary radically depending on the assumptions chosen. Economic analysis then directs one to examine changes in the relationship between the supply of children, the demand for them from people who want to adopt, the rationing mechanisms used to distribute the scarce commodity of children to be adopted, and the unanticipated side effects and possible unwanted consequences of the process. Again, in an economic analysis, children are a scarce commodity, not fundamentally different from other goods. Although this viewpoint may offend sensibilities, it might also lead to interesting conclusions about how to create a better world for children.

### Child Adoption: A Reflection of Supply–Demand Relationships over Time

***Early 20th century—oversupply.*** Through the 1940s, the supply of children relative to that of adults wanting to adopt them was tipped toward an oversupply of children for several reasons. Around the turn of the century, family size was large, multigeneration households were decreasing under industrialization, and immigration was strong. Life expectancy for parents was also much lower, largely because of uncontrolled communicable diseases and poor medical care. All these factors led to a surplus of children whose birth parents could not be caretakers. One societal response to this problem was to create large congregate total institutions, or orphanages. The expectation was that children would grow up there. Although foster family care emerged shortly thereafter, it was not as massive a program as institutional care. Adoption also was not popular, partly because adoption practices (and adoption law) were essentially alien to British and thus to U.S. common law—and, in any case, late to be enacted (Chambers, 1969). Little wonder that children who needed families were in oversupply in the first 30 years of the 20th century.

***Late 20th century—reduced supply.*** After World War II, circumstances changed. The postwar baby boom was in full swing; larger families became the norm. Studies of the negative effects of maternal deprivation put orphanages out of fashion. The emerging consensus created a motive for child care agencies to move children (especially infants) quickly out of institutional care and into permanent adoptive families. Childless families were anxious to have them. Mainstream society was largely unaccepting and inhospitable toward unmarried women rearing children born out of wedlock. Thus, adoption became a widespread and well-accepted practice in the United States. It became the socially expected solution to the problem of childless parents.

The social revolution of the 1960s and 1970s had a strong effect on adoption. One consequence accompanying the radical change in sexual mores and the feminist consciousness of the time was a new social acceptance of unmarried women rearing children. More women were rearing their own out-of-wedlock children, and fewer were born to white middle-class women as better birth control led to fewer unwanted pregnancies. These major factors resulted in a marked reduction in the supply of children readily available for adoption. Recent data on infertility have documented a 50 percent decline in male sperm count from the years 1938 to 1994. This decline is associated with increases in chemical pollutants in water and food, which mimic the presence of estrogen in the human body and "trick the body into changing certain biochemical processes" (Begley & Glick, 1994, p. 76). There is no hard evidence on whether chemicals are directly affecting fertility, but this possibility has been discussed. Keep in mind, though, that it is female fertility, not male fertility, that best predicts population change.

***Unstable demand.*** The demand side of the adoption market was unstable. Infertility is ordinarily a stable constant in a human population, and there is a built-in demand from childless adults wanting children to adopt. In the 1970s and 1980s, the childbearing population increased as the baby boom generation came of age. These factors created an increase in childlessness and thus in the demand for children to be adopted. That demand has been magnified in the late 20th century. Although the data are thin, the accepted wisdom is that infertility has increased dramatically: It may affect nearly 20 percent of couples of child-bearing years. The reasons are not well understood. The response of many adoption agencies to the declining supply–rising demand equation has been to increase the focus of their adoption policies and practices on screening out adoptive applicants—an obviously functional move from the agencies' point of view, because they had more applicants than children. Although practitioners and agency administrators never described it this way, economic analysis would use the term *rationing mechanisms* to describe various adoption policies and procedures such as "securing the best parents available," "matching" children with parents on various characteristics, limiting applicants to one or two children, and making long waiting lists. Such administrative constraints served to deal with the imbalance of supply and demand in adoption with which agencies were struggling. Few of these practices had much grounding in empirical research, but they did serve an important rationing function. One hypothesis is that the more scarce the children became and the more demand increased, the tighter, more arbitrary, and more "theoretical" became formal adoption agency practices with regard to choosing parents. Thus, for most formal, licensed adoptive agencies, entitlement rules, regulations, and practices—not price—were the rationing devices.

But such agencies were not the only players in this drama. The Law of Demand asserts that there is an inverse relation between supply and demand: When supply is tight and demand is strong (surely the case in the adoption market by the 1980s), prices will rise, and vice versa. Price is an element in the adoption market, because private, profit-driven professional practitioners have become the most frequent child placers. They are not only lawyers and physicians. In many places, nearly all human services professionals are represented, including social workers, registered nurses, and psychologists. These private practitioners usually charge fees (sometimes hefty ones) for their services. Economic analysis, even at the most simple level, would hypothesize that such fees constantly rise if supply decreases and demand increases (assuming that, in general, the professionals' price responds to market demand just as any other entrepreneur's).

### Child Adoption Market

These expectations are conditioned in part by the type of market under consideration. An analysis using economic concepts would lead to the following question: Of what type is the market for children in adoption? It is certainly not what is sometimes called a "perfectly competitive market" (Heilbroner & Thurow, 1994). Although it meets the requirement that there are many *firms* (that is, individual entrepreneurs or groups placing children in adoption) who can easily enter or exit the business, neither consumers (adoptive applicants) nor firms have complete information about prices and products, nor do all firms provide a "homogenous product." At least since the 1980s, the types of children available for adoption through adoption placers have varied widely. The important difference was that private adoption placement makers generally placed white, healthy, nondisabled infants, whereas public child welfare or adoption agencies had few such children available for adoption. On the contrary, the children available for them to place in adoption were largely children of color; older than age five years; or with significant physical, emotional, or intellectual disabilities. Many state child welfare agencies closed applications for healthy white infants (and still do), simply because it is unlikely they will have more such children than they can place in adoption from their very long applicant waiting list. However social workers might wish it were different, clearly the type of child considered most desirable by adoptive applicants is not the kind that public child welfare agencies have available. There are, of course, licensed adoption placement agencies who do place both the most desirable kind of child and place children in adoption who are older, who are children of color, or who have significant disabilities. But, despite noble efforts, such agencies have not been able to find enough permanent placements for all the children who need them.

Public child welfare and adoption agencies are thus not in a position to compete with private entrepreneurs for adoptive applications. Their "product" is unpopular. There is an important consequence to this observation: The children who most need adoptive parents are not even in the right line to get them. Furthermore and immediate to the purpose of this analysis, it is an instance of a market in disarray. The public child welfare agency has the legal responsibility to provide for such children. State laws mandate that public child welfare agencies serve the needs of children who are older, disabled, abused, or neglected and who cannot remain with their birth parents. Yet the public agency is systematically excluded from screening all potential adoptive applicants by the way in which the adoption market is structured. No one knows how many adoptive applicants might be willing to adopt children who are considered less than "ideal," but the adoption market prevents anyone from determining certain facts. This simple economic analysis raises the possibility that the public sector, which has a legally assigned responsibility for children who need parents, might require a type of monopoly over adoption placement to perform the important social function of redistributing unparented children into childless families effectively. But, of course, that is not the only problem-solving strategy—and there may be significant reasons against it.

One response to the imbalance in the supply of and the demand for children has been the increase in alien children adopted by American citizens—from a global point of view, the massive enlargement of an international adoption market. Data from the United Nations and the U.S. Immigration and Naturalization Service show with certainty that the number of alien children coming to the United States for adoption has increased substantially (that is, by orders of magnitude) (Lewin, 1990). This should not be surprising; even basic economic concepts would predict that when supply is short and demand strong, entrepreneurs would widen their search for children to place in adoption.

**Concept of Externalities and the Adoption Market**

Another concept economists are fond of using is that of *externalities*, or effects of one sector of a private market on other buyers, users, or sellers. In the international adoption market, the concept of externalities would focus on unintended effects (either positive or negative) on families, children, and nations as a result of adoption market operation.

The following are speculations about externalities regarding the emigration of Central American children for adoption in Europe and the United States. Because Central America has large numbers of desperately poor people and has undergone years of civil war, there are many children deprived of birth parents in Guatemala, El Salvador, Nicaragua, and Honduras. Costa Rica has not had a civil war but is affected because refugees have fled such strife elsewhere. For some, the adoption of Central American infants and young children in other countries creates an externality, a positive one with a real (albeit unintended) fiscal benefit to the nations from which these children come—fewer children will have to be reared at state expense in public institutions.

Speculation might also focus on negative externalities. Possibly the most dramatic externality is the rise in child stealing in Central America. In the 1950s and 1960s, child stealing in Guatemala, for example, was almost unheard of. It is now an everyday fact of life. Local officials have strong evidence for the existence of organized child stealing for the purpose of selling children for importation to the United States and Europe for adoption. Not all child stealing provides children for the adoption market, but rather for the pornography, prostitution, and organ donation markets (Adoptions in Costa Rica, 1988; Fraser, 1994; Marcucci, 1991). When the supply, demand, and price relationships are right, such a state of affairs is entirely predictable from the analysis of adoption market economics. Illegal markets will arise to supply a deficient market supply in ways not very different from those of drug, alcohol, or technology smuggling. That is not an intended effect of the way the U.S. adoption market operates, but it is one that is directly attributable to its present structure in the United States. Thus, child stealing is a negative externality.

As I found in my recent research, many Central Americans are not at all enthusiastic about having their children exported for adoption in other countries, even when the children's natural parents relinquish them for that purpose. Central Americans argue that their children will lose the language and culture of their native lands and that this is a loss of national human capital as well as of the adopted children's personal identity.

**Efficiency of the Adoption Market**

Economic analysis suggests a number of ways to increase the efficiency of the adoption market. It does not do very well what markets are intended to do—in this case, distribute children who need parents to people who want those children. Many American children are going without permanent parents and not all adoptive applicants are getting children. Some adoptive applicants do not have the knowledge or the money to enter the international market (where fees can range from $15,000 to $25,000 per child). Of course, child stealing and other externalities for foreign children, parents, and nations are sometimes negative. With respect to remedies, two respected economists have pointed out a direction:

> The market system (sometimes) has weak spots or ineffective areas peculiar to its institutional nature. The remedy requires political intervention of one kind or another—regulation, taxation or subsidy—for there is no recourse other than political action when the

self-regulating economic mechanism fails. (Heilbroner & Thurow, 1994, pp. 193–194)

Clearly, the adoption market has failed in important respects. It is not self-regulating and is in serious need of intervention. Heilbroner and Thurow's economic analysis suggests that the whole adoption market be made a public-sector monopoly. Scandinavian countries follow that model and, in some countries, maintain national child welfare representatives whose job is to enable legally secure international adoptions that look to the needs and rights of both families and nations. In the United States, that proposal has a downside: Politically, it has formidable opponents, because there are so many economic, personal, and professional interests at stake. Of equal importance is that legislating the private market out of existence (by, for example, restricting all child adoption to nonprofit public agencies) does nothing to alter the market forces at work. Such legislating might only increase the unit profitability of what would then be a totally illegal national and international adoption market. Rendering a practice totally illegal may only substantially increase unit price (as it did with both prohibition and hard drugs) and actually increase the incidence of child stealing.

### Intervention in the Adoption Market

***Subsidization.*** Heilbroner and Thurow's (1994) economic analysis suggests two other strategies. The problem of concern is that older children are often left without adoptive parents. A form of subsidization is embedded in the following example. Although the international adoption of Costa Rican infants is illegal in part, these infants do cross international borders for adoption in the following way: When an infant is part of a sibling group, the infant is adopted along with the rest of his or her brothers and sisters. In most Spanish-speaking countries, the sibling tie is fervently observed, and adoption policies to promote that are very popular. One way such a policy could work is to place children by constructing family groups, sometimes groups that are not related by blood but that include both an infant and perhaps a child of early school age. (One form of family group is called "false twinning.") Adoptions in some countries in Central America other than in Costa Rica may happen in this way. The value served is the adoptive placement of an older child who might not otherwise find an adoptive family. What actually is happening is a form of subsidization: The adoption of the older child is "subsidized" by the inclusion of a younger one or an infant. To object that the kinship is fictional might not be a persuasive argument. Anthropologists the world over have commonly observed fictional kinships serving all sorts of functions. In the United States in particular, the law specifically intends adoptions to be fictional kinships—to mimic the legal status of consanguineous children exactly and erasing all traces of blood ties.

***Privatization.*** Heilbroner and Thurow's (1994) analysis suggests a second kind of market intervention: The adoption market could be totally privatized. Under this proposal, all children in need of parents would become the responsibility of the private sector, including adoption placements. That could take the form of adoption placements through private professional practitioners or of placements through private, nonprofit organizations. An expected advantage is price reduction as an effect of competition, although leaving the fate of children to an unmonitored or regulated profit-driven market gives one pause.

## Examples of Research Methods to Test Hypotheses Derived from Economic Analysis

***Econometrics.*** The branch of economics concerned with research methods is almost but not quite circumscribed by what is called *econometrics*—the application of statistical and mathematical methods to the analysis of economic data to verify or refute economic theories (Maddala, 1992). The formulation of a theoretical model is the first step. In practice, "we include in our model all the variables (factors) we think are relevant for our purpose and dump the rest" (Maddala, 1992, p. 3). The model expresses the theory and the interrelationships between the selected variables in a set of mathematical equations. For example,

$$D = a + Bp + u$$

where $D$ is the quantity of some commodity demanded; $a$, the factor that the model constructor thinks makes most of the difference in determining quantity of demand other than price; $B$, a number that describes how much change in units of demand is produced by a unit change in price; $p$, the price; and $u$, a term that signifies all the other factors that determine quantity other than price. The next step is to bring data from the real world to test whether the predictions of this equation hold true.

Ordinarily the researcher would take into account much more than a single variable. For example, suppose the commodity in question were popular movies. What would affect price? Important factors would include income of potential consumers, the current social acceptability or status of the commodity, and the price and availability of competing commodities such as television; even the weather and season would be important factors. This is significant because should those important factors be left out of the theory and the equation, predictions of type and quantity demanded could be completely wrong. A person in the film business planning next year's production could find it very costly to overestimate demand and produce too much. It could be just as costly to underestimate demand and then have to forgo large profits because the movies wanted were not supplied. The same issue is involved if one considers how costly it is to not understand common social problems. If explanatory models are too simple and overlook crucial factors, society incurs huge losses in human lives and the need for immense capital expenditures for remedial health care and social services.

Because econometrics is an attempt to model life and its complexities, its research methods must take into account many variables operating simultaneously or in time sequence. Regression is a statistical technique used to deal with that reality. Regression techniques are basically elegant correlational methods that quantify the extent to which one variable or many variables are associated with others. In that form, they can be turned into statements that predict the appearance of variables together or in sequence. Regression is important when applied to social welfare problems because it has the potential to answer serious questions and to shape public policy.

Because regression methods of analysis are often used with historical data, one should not conclude that economic theories are never tested by experiments (that is, where data on variables in a theory are collected in the present as they are consciously manipulated). Another research method developed in economics is that of cost-benefit analysis and cost-effectiveness studies. Because those methods are the subject of other entries in the *Encyclopedia of Social Work*, they are not discussed in this entry.

### Negative Income Tax Experiments: Do People Stop Working When They Can Depend on Welfare?

The following is a short account of one of the largest and most costly social experiments ever made.

Economists are concerned with what they call the *labor–leisure choice*: When faced with a choice of spending time earning money or being at leisure, what determines the choice? Indeed, it is an everyday issue. People do decide to take voluntary overtime offered at work, moonlight at a part-time job, look for a better-paying job even if it requires more hours per week, and so on.

Welfare benefits from the public treasury generate somewhat the same kind of labor supply questions. What is their effect on work effort? If welfare benefits are supplied, to what extent do workers substitute the leisure (nonwork time) that results for the opportunity to work for wages? The typical economic model of labor supply decisions generates the sort of theoretical expectations one might expect. In general, workers will forgo work in favor of welfare when welfare produces as much spendable income as work.

***Guaranteed income experiment.*** An example of research methods used to test hypotheses flowing from economic analysis and econometric modeling is the guaranteed income experiments of the 1960s and 1970s, which involved a kind of welfare benefit scheme called the *negative income tax*. Often proposed as a way of folding all income maintenance programs (including Aid to Families with Dependent Children, food stamps, and so on) into a single, easily administered type, a negative income tax would supply income to a worker when, for example, his or her quarterly or monthly income tax statement showed an income below the official poverty line. For example, if it were the public policy of the United States to ensure that all worker families had incomes above the poverty line, the Internal Revenue Service would send a check representing the difference between actual earnings and the official poverty line income for that period. This negative income tax has been called the guaranteed annual income (GAI), and is not a fantasy; it was actually proposed in the 1970s under the Nixon administration and failed to become law by only a single vote.

The GAI experiments were elaborate and extended over nearly 10 years (Skidmore, 1975). Basically, they involved offering carefully chosen samples of low-income workers the chance to participate in an experiment guaranteeing them a certain income whether or not they worked. Researchers were interested in testing hypotheses about the effects of welfare benefit levels on work effort. They believed, however, that the amount of benefit was an important determinant, so participants were placed in one of eight experimental groups. Some were guaranteed incomes equal to the poverty level, one at more than the poverty level (125 percent), and two at less than the poverty level (50 percent and 75 percent). A control group comprised people who had no guaranteed income at all.

The theoretical model developed by the researchers also took into account a common welfare policy allowing recipients to receive public benefits and to also work for wages, but with a proportional reduction in benefits. An example is social security retirement beneficiaries who earn wages and receive benefits. After they reach a certain income and meet other conditions, benefits are reduced by $1 for every $3 earned. Such benefits are said to be "taxed" at a 33⅓ percent level. Thus, in the GAI experiments, experimental groups also varied by the rate at which their benefits were "taxed"—that is, reduced if they worked for wages. For some experimental groups, benefits were thus reduced by 30 percent, some by 50 percent, some by 70 percent, and some not at all. In this way, the data could reveal the extent to which workers would still work for wages and increase income even though their total income was being reduced by this graduated "tax" on their GAI benefits.

This clearly was a type of experimental design: The independent variable (work effort) was consciously manipulated (across groups) in an effort to observe how it was affected by the major dependent variable (welfare benefits). There were random elements in subject selection, although not strictly a random assignment procedure. It was a complex design because it involved so many different groups, each corresponding to a set of conditions about which the researchers hypothesized.

***Research design.*** The research design expended effort to anticipate many variables that the researchers had to control for to produce clean and unambiguous results. Examples include worker age, education, family size, ethnicity, prior earnings, and prior work history (each of which has an independent effect on work effort). Some of these effects were controlled for (that is, eliminated from affecting the conclusions) by allocating worker-participants randomly among strata so that, at that level, groups were rendered roughly equivalent on these factors. If work effort differed across strata, then a separate analysis was done to search for possible differences in association with these control variables. These and many other factors were built into the econometric equations and by which predictions were made about the work effort changes that were expected to occur when GAI benefits were given to subjects. Here is how one economist explained the theory and constructed equations with regard to the GAI experiments:

> I propose a theory along the following lines. Suppose 0 is an index of family attitudes about work and abilities to work. Everything else held constant, families with low values of 0 choose to work more than those with high values. . . . In the absence of the negative income tax (GAI) there will be a critical value of 0, say 0(n) such that families with 0 exceeding 0(n) will not work at all. . . . Note that 0(n) depends on the observable characteristics of the family, especially its wage and nonlabor income. Similarly among families participating in the program there is a threshold 0(p) beyond which they will not work. Because I assume that labor supply is inversely related to 0, it is evident that 0(p) is less than 0(n)—some families would choose to work if the program were not available but would choose not to work if they participated. No family would do the opposite; working under the program but not working otherwise. . . . A negative income tax is inherently more attractive to families that are less willing or less able to work. In terms of an indirect utility function now considered as a function of 0 as well a w and Y, say g(w,Y,0), the threshold 0* is defined succinctly by:
>
> $$T(w,Yo,0^*) = T[(1-T)w, B(o) + (1-T)Yo,0^*],$$
>
> where T is the indirect utility function, w is each hour of work, Y(o) is income from sources other than earnings, B(o) is the coefficient and 0* is an index of family attitudes about work and abilities to work. (Hall, 1975, p. 135)

The findings of the GAI experiments are quite interesting. In general, they supported the direction of the theoretical expectations. Workers did reduce work effort on average and overall; but the amount of the reduction and its wide variability among primary and secondary wage earners in families (generally working wives) were a surprise. For example, primary wage earners reduced work effort only 6 percent to 7 percent on average (that is, only a few hours a week). That finding, although consistent with the general theoretical expectations, does not support either the notion that low-income or poor people will systematically avoid work when given the opportunity to do so at no cost to themselves or the belief that welfare benefits themselves "destroy" work incentives. Of equal interest is that secondary wage earners (female spouses with children, for the most part) reduced work effort by 17 percent, nearly three times that of primary wage earners. Some observers suggest that, not surprisingly, mothers with young children chose to stay home when total family income was ensured (Chambers, 1993). Female heads of households reduced work effort by only 2 percent. One interpretation of these findings is that it shows how low-income people will stay in the workplace as long as that choice presents itself (only a 7 percent work effort reduction) and makes it possible to earn an income above the poverty level. Some people will find reason to choose leisure—but apparently not many.

Of course, the experiments were by no means perfect—there were "contaminating factors": selective attrition, short duration of some subexperiments, contaminating changes in welfare policy during the experiments, and so on (indeed, some economists attacked any interpretation of the findings) (Aaron, 1975). The criticisms should not be surprising; the experiments were on a grand scale, and even small-scale social experiments are difficult to keep free of contamination. All the same, GAI is an example of economic analysis creating hypotheses that were tested by actual experimentation as a research method and that generated useful if controversial findings. However, experimental designs are not the most common method for testing the hypotheses generated by econometric modeling. Research methods in economics generally take the form of multiple regression analysis using already existing data. The following is an example.

### The "Welfare Magnet" Issue: Do Poor People Migrate to States with High Welfare Benefits?

An enduring social welfare issue is whether poor people or welfare beneficiaries migrate to states with the highest welfare benefits. Perhaps this issue endures because this seems such a reasonable thing to expect people (poor or otherwise) to do. After all, why wouldn't a sensible person do so, especially if it involved a short move, such as from Chicago, Illinois, to Kenosha, Wisconsin, or from Kansas City, Missouri, to Kansas City, Kansas—where the states of previous residence are low-benefit and the states of new residence relatively high-benefit states? It is an important social welfare issue because of the immense interstate variability in state-administered benefits for programs such as Aid to Families with Dependent Children and Medicaid.

***Wisconsin study.*** Welfare policy became a central issue in Wisconsin in the mid-1980s during several heated gubernatorial election campaigns. The state legislature, concerned over what came to be called the "welfare magnet" issue, commissioned several studies. One of these legislative studies found that, indeed, 10 percent of recipients of Aid to Families with Dependent Children who had recently moved to Wisconsin said that higher benefits there did play "some role" in their decision (Wisconsin Expenditure Commission as cited in Peterson & Rom, 1990). A Brookings Institution study by Peterson and Rom (1990) developed theoretical models to study and test this theory. Specifically, what they wished to find out is whether the size of the population most likely to be affected by welfare policy in any state changed simply because of the attractiveness of relatively higher welfare benefits. The researchers took a state's poverty rate (based on the U.S. official poverty line) to be an adequate measure of "the size of the population most likely to be affected by welfare policy" (p. 62).

***Research design.*** One of the difficult problems was to measure the net change in poverty rate, independent of the changes in the characteristics of the poor population in the state and of their economic environment. To generate these data, Peterson and Rom also included in their theoretical models such variables as employment opportunities and earnings levels (Figure 1).

This theory and its model consider individual economic conditions to better a worker's employment possibilities: The higher the wage levels are likely to be, the lower the unemployment rate and the lower the poverty rate in the state. In the long term, however, such a state of affairs may induce poor people to stay but also induces poor people in other states with lower wages to move to that state. A larger pool of low-wage workers increases the size of the population most likely to be affected by welfare policy, Peterson and Rom's independent variable. They considered the factor they call "economic conditions" to be measured, in the short term, by changes in the number of workers employed and changes in per capita income. In the long term, they measured economic conditions as wage (earnings) levels:

> We hypothesized that as employment opportunities and per capita income increased, the immediate effect would be a decline in the poverty rate [but] . . . if a state's wages were high, poorer citizens will be both retained and attracted into the state at a rate higher than the nonpoor, increasing its poverty rate over time. (Peterson & Rom, 1990, pp. 71–72)

Therefore, controlling for economic change and other factors, states with higher population growth would attract more low-income people because they have "lower opportunity costs" (Peterson & Rom, 1990). Peterson and Rom did not explain, but could they mean that it costs the poor less to move because they have less property and fewer job or career interests at stake (not necessarily an uncontroversial explanation)? The authors included population growth as an important explanatory variable and also included the level of welfare benefits as a variable, because that lies at the heart of their theoretical explanation of in what states they expect poverty rates to rise

FIGURE 1
Theoretical Model of the Welfare Magnet Effect

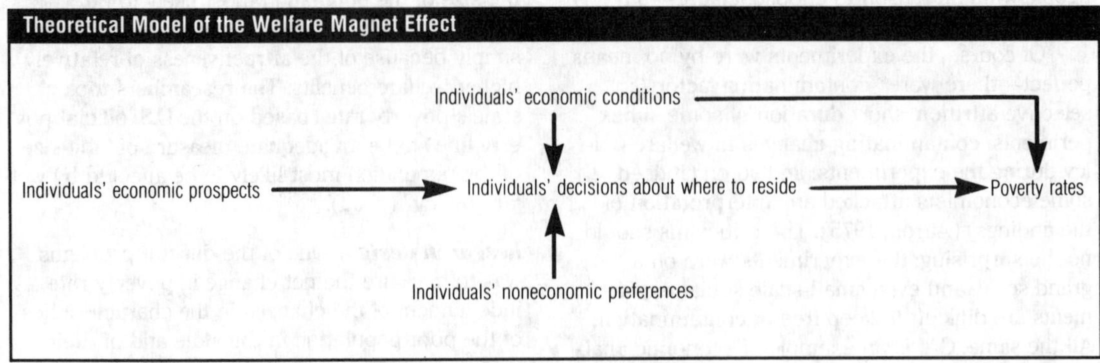


most. The equation expressing the empirical expectations derived from Peterson and Rom's theoretical model appears as follows:

$$P = b(o) + B + W + E + I + N$$

where P represents the change in number in poverty, B represents the change in welfare benefits, W represents the change in wages, E represents the change in employment, I represents the change in per capita income, N represents the change in population, and b(o) represents the coefficient.

Peterson and Rom collected data for three separate five-year periods, because sizable change occurred in poverty rates from 1970 to 1985, rising in one period and falling in two others. The researchers used a multiple regression technique (two-stage, least squares analysis) to examine the simultaneous effects of all these variables on changes in poverty levels in 52 states and other jurisdictions.

***Findings.*** The finding from the study was that, controlling for wage and employment levels, population, and the like, "states offering high welfare benefits have a poverty rate 0.9% higher than states providing low benefits" (Peterson & Rom, 1990, p. 79). Surprisingly, Peterson and Rom concluded, "These differences in poverty rates are most probably due to migration [of poor people to high benefit states]" (p. 79).

***Issues.*** Interpretation of data from such studies is as controversial as the interpretation of data from the negative income tax (GAI) experiments. Peterson and Rom apparently believed that because they controlled for variables such as wage and employment rates and population change, they were entitled to attribute the "leftover" changes in poverty rates to the migration of poor people to high-benefit states. In fact, the implicit claim is that because they controlled for everything that was important in determining poverty rates, the only possibility remaining was the migration of poor people. This sizable claim is unsupported in their presentation. What users of this type of research must do is consider what explanations other than the ones given are possible.

Consider the following example: For certain states (not a small number), the size of the population most likely to be affected by welfare policy (and an increase in poverty rates) is substantially altered by the migration of illegal aliens. California, Texas, Arizona, Florida, and New York are the historical examples. Clearly, aliens are now more sophisticated; almost every coastal state is experiencing significant in-migration not only from Mexico but also from the Caribbean, Central and South America, and many Asian countries, including China and Korea.

There are other plausible scenarios to think about when considering the interpretation of Peterson and Rom's data. The most typical pattern of welfare recipiency is for short periods, often two years on, a year off, another year on, then off forever. No wonder that not many welfare recipients are found to be moving to another state for the precise purpose of obtaining higher benefits—in the main, they do not intend to be on welfare for long. Furthermore, interpreting the study findings is not straightforward, because the standards for deciding whether or how much of a difference or a change is important remains a big—and controversial—issue.

Peterson and Rom interpreted their findings as supporting the notion that high welfare benefits produce a "welfare magnet" effect. However, quite the opposite conclusion could be argued: that it is relatively benign, accounting for only 1 percent of the difference in poverty rates and is therefore relatively unimportant. Thus (Peterson and Rom notwithstanding), these data could be seen as a good example of research methods testing out an economic analysis that appears to lay an old myth to rest. Although it seems obvious that some poor people move from low-benefit to high-benefit states to take advantage of the benefits, the best evidence from the Peterson and Rom study is that the total effect seems very small.

Peterson and Rom's research suggests that perhaps the question ought to be reframed to focus on what is probably more surprising: Why don't masses of welfare recipients move to high-benefit states? The standard assumption in economic analysis is that people are rational about their decisions. But the more interesting possibility is that with regard to geographic location, welfare recipients are not strictly economically rational about where they live. Rather than consider the issue of how poor people take advantage of the welfare system, consider that they do not take advantage of the system as a curious example of economic irrationality that needs explaining. Middle- and upper-class citizens expect to take advantage of as many benefits as the tax code allows—the courts have always held that this is a citizen's right. Why, then, should it be surprising that poor people do the same with welfare benefits? Research should dignify one's consideration of people in poverty. If it does, chances are it will reveal some of the complexity entailed in the lives of low-income workers and welfare recipients living below the poverty level.

## References

Aaron, H. J. (1975). Cautionary notes on the experiment. In J. A. Pechman & P. M. Timpane (Eds.), *Work incentives and income guarantees* (p. 168–189). Washington, DC: Brookings Institution.

Adoptions in Costa Rica. (1988, April 22). *La Nacion* [San Jose, Costa Rica], p. 12.

Begley, S., & Glick, D. (1994, March 21). The estrogen complex. *Newsweek*, pp. 76–77.

Chambers, D. E. (1969). Residence requirements for welfare benefits: Consequences of their unconstitutionality. *Social Work, 14*, 28–37.

Chambers, D. E. (1993). Social policy and social programs. New York: Macmillan.

Fraser, S. (1994, Summer). Searching for the niños. *World View*, p. 15.

Hall, R. E. (1975). Effects of the experimental negative income tax on labor supply. In J. A. Pechman & P. M. Timpane (Eds.), *Work incentives and income guarantees* (pp. 115–156). Washington, DC: Brookings Institution.

Heilbroner, R., & Thurow, L. (1994). *Economics explained* (revised and updated). New York: Touchstone Books, Simon & Schuster.

Lewin, T. (1990, February 12). South Korea slows export of babies for adoption. *New York Times*, pp. A1, A6.

Maddala, G. S. (1992). *Introduction to econometrics*. New York: Macmillan.

Marcucci, I. (1991, March). *Closing session remarks*. Presented at the Central American Conference on Abandonment and Adoption, Tegucigalpa, Honduras.

Peterson, P. E., & Rom, M. C. (1990). *Welfare magnets: A new case for a national welfare standard*. Washington, DC: Brookings Institution.

Skidmore, F. (1975). Operational design of the experiment. In J. A. Pechman & P. M. Timpane (Eds.), *Work incentives and income guarantees* (pp. 36–78). Washington, DC: Brookings Institution.

Varian, H. R. (1990). *Intermediate microeconomics*. New York: W. W. Norton.

**Donald E. Chambers, DSW,** is professor, University of Kansas, School of Social Welfare, 315 Twente Hall, Lawrence, KS 66046.

### For further information see

Community Needs Assessment; Employment and Unemployment Measurement; Income Distribution; Income Security Overview; Jobs and Earnings; Policy Analysis; Poverty; Program Evaluation; Social Planning; Strategic Planning; Welfare Employment Programs: Evaluation.

**Key Words**

adoption
econometric modeling
externalities
negative income tax
social policy

READER'S GUIDE

## Education

*The following entries contain information on this general topic:*

CSWE Curriculum Policy Statements (Appendix 3)
Continuing Education
Council on Social Work Education
Epistemology
Family Life Education
School Social Work Overview
School-Linked Services
Settlements and Neighborhood Centers
Social Work Education
Social Work Practice: History and Evolution
Social Work Practice: Theoretical Base
Supervision and Consultation

## Egypt, Ophelia Settle

*See* Biographies section, Volume 3

# Elder Abuse

**Toshio Tatara**

The late U.S. Representative Claude Pepper once called elder abuse a "national disgrace" (U.S. House of Representatives, 1985). Most Americans might find it hard to believe that the problem even exists and that people in this country are maltreating their elders as well as their children. Studies have revealed, however, that elder abuse, like child abuse, is widespread and that probably hundreds of thousands of the nation's elderly people are being victimized each year. Yet because it is still mostly hidden under a shroud of family secrecy, elder abuse is difficult to combat. Furthermore, most members of the public are not well informed of the problem and are not familiar with ways to bring cases of elder abuse to the fore and to use available protective and treatment services.

## Definitions of Elder Abuse

There are as many definitions of elder abuse as there are elder abuse laws, programs, and research practices. For example, federal definitions of elder abuse are included in the amended (1992) Older Americans Act of 1965, and states have created their own elder abuse definitions in their adult protective service or elder abuse statutes. In addition, researchers have used their own definitions of different types of elder maltreatment for their studies. For a social problem like elder abuse, definitions potentially affect reporting behaviors, incidence, program budgets, service delivery, professional practice, and research. However, only a few studies of elder abuse definitions have been conducted to date.

### Federal Definitions

In 1987 Congress authorized, but did not fund, a federal program entitled "Prevention of Abuse, Neglect, and Exploitation of Older Individuals" as a part of the Older Americans Act (Part G, Title III). Thus, Section 102 of the act now includes the definitions of three major types of elder maltreatment: abuse, neglect, and exploitation. In 1990 Congress appropriated funds for the program, but the Administration on Aging (AoA) has yet to develop federal regulations, so federal elder abuse definitions have not yet been enforced.

Section 102 of the Older Americans Act (OAA) defines *abuse* as "the willful infliction of injury, unreasonable confinement, intimidation, or cruel punishment with resulting physical harm or pain or mental anguish; or deprivation by a caretaker of goods or services which are necessary to avoid physical harm, mental anguish, or mental illness." *Neglect* is defined as "the failure to provide for oneself the goods or services which are necessary to avoid physical harm, mental anguish, or mental illness or the failure of a caretaker to provide such goods or services." Finally, the OAA defines *exploitation* as "the illegal or improper act or process of a caretaker using the resources of an older individual for monetary or personal benefit, profit, or gain."

By including "failure to provide for oneself" in the definition of neglect, Congress recognized self-neglect. Tatara (1993b) showed that in 1991 most of the substantiated elder abuse cases were self-neglect cases. Furthermore, Section 102 does not specify the ages of older people to be protected by the federal elder abuse prevention program. However, given that most other provisions of the OAA deem eligible anyone who is 60 or older, it is assumed that Congress also intended the federal elder abuse program to cover this age group. Additionally, although this is not mentioned in Section 102, one can assume that both domestic and institutional forms of elder abuse are addressed by the federal definitions.

### State Definitions

A great deal of similarity exists among the state definitions of elder abuse, particularly among those that pertain to domestic elder abuse. For example, a recent national survey found that all 46 responding jurisdictions (including the District of Columbia) included two categories of maltreatment in their definitions of domestic elder abuse: physical abuse and neglect (Tatara, 1993b). All but one state recognized financial or material exploitation as a form of elder maltreatment. Self-neglect was also addressed by nearly all the states that participated in the survey. A smaller number of states addressed other types of maltreatment, such as sexual abuse and psychological or emotional abuse.

Despite these general similarities, there still are many differences in the specific terminologies of various elder abuse definitions among the states (American Public Welfare Association and National Association of State Units on Aging, 1986; Thobaben, 1989). For example, some states distinguish *active neglect* (the willful failure of a caregiver to provide services or care) from *passive neglect* (the nonwillful failure of a caregiver to provide services or care). Furthermore, in many states, "exploitation" refers to the unauthorized or improper use of an older person's money or property, but in some states it also includes the exploitation of the person (for example, sexual abuse; Tatara, 1990c).

### Definitions Used by Researchers

Johnson (1986) examined 21 survey research studies of elder abuse conducted between 1979 and 1985 in the United States and found that the types and definitions of maltreatment these studies addressed varied greatly among studies. The researchers used a wide variety of definitions and terminologies to specify different forms of elder abuse, and there was little consensus regarding what components should be included in the standard elder abuse definitions. Not all the researchers recognized such well-accepted abuse categories as "physical abuse," "neglect," and "exploitation." For example, of the 33 different types of maltreatment Johnson's analysis identified, 17 of the studies addressed physical abuse, nine addressed neglect, and only six included exploitation. Nevertheless, these different types of elder abuse studies have contributed to an increased understanding of elder abuse problems. In addition, they undoubtedly have influenced policymakers and professionals in a number of states in their development of formal elder abuse definitions.

### Definitions Used by the National Aging Resource Center on Elder Abuse

Recognizing the importance of using standard definitions of elder abuse for compiling national data, the National Aging Resource Center on Elder Abuse (NARCEA) developed and used its definitions of domestic elder abuse for several survey studies (Tatara, 1990b). Funded by AoA, NARCEA was operated from 1988 to 1992 by a consortium of the American Public Welfare Association, the National Association of State Units on Aging, and the University of Delaware. The seven categories of domestic elder maltreatment NARCEA developed are

1. physical abuse: nonaccidental use of physical force that results in bodily injury, pain, or impairment
2. sexual abuse: nonconsensual sexual contact of any kind with an older person
3. emotional or psychological abuse: willful infliction of mental or emotional anguish by threat, humiliation, intimidation, or other verbal or nonverbal abusive conduct
4. neglect: willful or nonwillful failure by the caregiver to fulfill his or her caregiving obligation or duty
5. financial or material exploitation: unauthorized use of funds, property, or any resources of an older person
6. self-abuse and neglect: abusive or neglectful conduct of an older person directed at himself or herself that threatens his or her health or safety
7. all other types: all other types of domestic elder abuse that do not belong to the first six categories.

NARCEA's definitions of domestic elder abuse are similar to the federal definitions of elder abuse in the OAA. Because they have been widely disseminated through NARCEA's publications and technical assistance activities, these elder abuse definitions are well known and well accepted by the professional community (Tatara, 1990b).

## Extent and Nature of the Problem

### Incidence and Prevalence

The true incidence and prevalence of elder abuse in the United States is not known. Given the nature of the problem, knowing exactly how many older people are victimized each year is probably impossible. Furthermore, incidence and prevalence research in the field of elder abuse is still an emerging discipline, and only a small number of studies have been conducted (Block & Sinnott, 1979; Douglass, Hickey, & Noel, 1980; Lau & Kosberg, 1979; Pillemer & Finkelhor, 1988; Poertner, 1986; Tatara, 1989, 1990c, 1993b). Of these studies, two are of current significance.

First, after interviewing a nationally representative sample of more than 2,000 elderly people, Pillemer and Finkelhor (1988) found that the prevalence of domestic elder abuse, excluding self-neglect, was 32 of every 1,000 older people, or 3.2 percent. Based on this finding, these researchers estimated that there were between 701,000 and 1,093,560 abused elders in the United States. Second, using the data on domestic elder abuse collected from his national survey of states, Tatara (1993b) estimated that nationwide, 1.57 million elderly people became the victims of various types of domestic elder abuse during 1991. This estimate included self-neglect cases because states generally include these in counting elder abuse victims. Finally, no studies have been conducted to determine the incidence or prevalence of institutional elder abuse, and thus the extent of this problem in the United States is not currently known (Pillemer & Moore, 1989; Tatara, 1992; U.S. General Accounting Office, 1989; U.S. House of Representatives, 1989).

### Reported Cases of Domestic Elder Abuse

All U.S. states and territories except Puerto Rico have established state laws that address the reporting of suspected domestic elder abuse cases to designated authorities such as state adult protective service or aging agencies. Most states mandate certain professionals (human services workers, law enforcement personnel, or physicians) to report suspected incidents of domestic elder abuse, but several states make such reporting voluntary. States regularly compile elder abuse statistics on the basis of these reports for various purposes, including policy planning, program development, and research. Researchers often collect these state statistics to generate national information about domestic elder abuse. For example, Tatara (1990c, 1993b) developed estimates of domestic elder abuse reports received nationwide for the past several years: 117,000 reports for 1986, 128,000 for 1987, 140,000 for 1988, 211,000 for 1990, and 227,000 for 1991 (the estimate for 1989 is not available). As these estimates indicate, the number of domestic elder abuse reports that were made to authorities across the country rose a substantial 94 percent from 1986 to 1991. Experts agree, however, that these reports represent only a small portion of the actual incidents of domestic elder abuse, because most domestic elder abuse cases are never reported (Pillemer & Finkelhor, 1988). Also, only about half of the reported elder abuse cases are substantiated each year after investigations (Tatara, 1993b). Clearly, the current elder abuse reporting system and the way it is operated must be improved so that the system can identify cases requiring agency intervention (Faulkner, 1982; Fredriksen, 1989; Salend, Kane, Satz, & Pynoos, 1984; U.S. General Accounting Office, 1991).

### Types and Frequencies of Domestic Elder Abuse

Table 1 displays the results of Tatara's (1993b) recent survey of data from 30 states.

TABLE 1
**Type and Frequency of Domestic Elder Abuse**

| Type of abuse | Percent occurrence |
|---|---|
| Neglect | 45.2 |
| Physical abuse | 19.1 |
| Financial and material exploitation | 17.1 |
| Psychological and emotional abuse | 13.8 |
| Sexual abuse | 0.6 |
| All others | 4.0 |

SOURCE: Tatara, T. (1993). *Summaries of the statistical data on elder abuse in domestic settings for FY 90 and FY 91*. Washington, DC: National Aging Resource Center on Elder Abuse.
NOTE: Data are from 30 states surveyed.

### Characteristics of Abusers and Victims

The abusers in domestic elder abuse cases are more likely to be men. For example, Tatara's (1993b) study of state data found that in 1991, 51.8 percent of all abusers in 18 states were men. Table 2 shows the types of abusers.

The victims of domestic abuse are more likely to be women than men. After analyzing data collected from 29 states, Tatara (1993b) found that during 1991 about two-thirds (67.8 percent) of all domestic abuse victims were females. He also found that in the 52 states he studied in 1991, the median age of elder abuse victims was 78.8 years. Little is known about the racial or ethnic characteristics of elder abuse victims or abusers, because only a few studies on this topic have been conducted to date (Cazenave, 1979, 1983; Longres, 1992).

## CAUSAL EXPLANATIONS OF ELDER ABUSE

Elder abuse, like any other type of domestic violence, is extremely complex, and many different factors cause a single incident. Experts generally agree that each incident is unique and must be

TABLE 2
**Types of Abusers of Elderly People**

| Type | Percentage[a] |
|---|---|
| Adult children of victims | 32.5 |
| Spouses (of both sexes) | 14.4 |
| Other relatives | 12.5 |
| Friends or neighbors | 7.5 |
| Service providers | 6.3 |
| Grandchildren | 4.2 |
| Siblings | 2.5 |
| Others | 18.2 |

SOURCE: Tatara, T. (1993). *Summaries of the statistical data on elder abuse in domestic settings for FY 90 and FY 91*. Washington, DC: National Aging Resource Center on Elder Abuse.
[a]Total does not equal 100 because of missing data.

explained by a combination of psychological, social, and economic factors, along with the mental and physical conditions of the elderly victim and the abuser (Quinn & Tomita, 1986; Sellers, Folts, & Logan, 1992). Researchers have generated a number of theories and hypotheses concerning the reasons that certain types of elder maltreatment occur (Phillips, 1986), but four causal theories of elder abuse are gaining prominence: (1) stress of caregivers; (2) cycle of violence; (3) personal problems of abusers; and (4) impairment of dependent elders. These causal theories of elder abuse are concerned mostly with domestic elder abuse, because only a few researchers have explored the causes of institutional elder abuse to date (Pillemer & Moore, 1989).

**Stress of Caregivers**

Caring for older people is difficult and stressful, particularly true when the elder is mentally or physically impaired, when the caregiver is ill-prepared for the task because of inadequate training and knowledge, or when the needed resources for eldercare are lacking. One theory holds that abuse or willful neglect will occur as a result of increased levels of stress and frustration among caregivers. Over the years, this theory has gained popularity among researchers and professionals who work with elderly people, and a considerable amount of information is available about the negative effect of caregiver stress on elders (Bendik, 1992; Cantor, 1983; George, 1986; Pillemer & Finkelhor, 1989; Poulschock & Diemling, 1984).

**Cycle of Violence**

The cycle of violence theory holds that some families are more prone to violent behavior than others because violence is a learned behavior and is transmitted from one generation to another. Researchers have found that in some families abusive behavior is a normative response to tension or conflict because members of these families have been exposed only to such behavior and have not learned any other way to respond (Fulmer & O'Mallery, 1987; Steinmetz, 1977).

**Personal Problems of Abusers**

More than 30 percent of abusers are adult children of the victims (Tatara, 1993b). Researchers have found that these adult children tend to have more personal problems than do nonabusers (Anetzberger, 1987). Problems such as alcoholism, drug addiction, mental and emotional disorders, and financial difficulty are common. As a result, these adult children become dependent on their elderly parents for their support, and they frequently resort to violence when the support is not provided (Greenberg, McKibben, & Raymond, 1990). This theory postulates that the abusive behavior of these adult children toward their elderly parents is an inappropriate response to the sense of their own inadequacies.

**Impairment of Dependent Elders**

Increased dependency of elderly people on caregivers is theorized to be a major contributing factor to the occurrence of elder abuse (Pillemer, 1985). Researchers have found that older people in poor physical or mental health are more likely to be abused than those who are in good health (George, 1986; Pillemer, 1986). Researchers also have found that abuse tends to occur when the stress level of caregivers is heightened as a result of the worsening of an elder's impairment. Child abuse professionals also are familiar with similar explanations of child abuse, in which the physical or mental disability of children increases the likelihood of abuse.

## Federal Concerns about Elder Abuse

Elder abuse is not new in the United States, but its recognition as a major social problem is recent. Congress first heard the term "elder abuse" in the late 1970s, during a hearing on spousal abuse, which, along with child abuse, was already well known to most Americans. One of the witnesses at the hearing reported her study of the battering of older people and stated that the 1980s would be an era in which elder abuse would become recognized as a serious social problem in the United States (Steinmetz, 1978).

This testimony had considerable impact on federal lawmakers. Congress, under the leadership of Claude Pepper, soon began holding a series of hearings across the country to investigate the problem. Shortly thereafter, the nation's first federal elder abuse legislation, the Prevention, Identification and Treatment of Elder Abuse Act of 1981 (H.R. 769), was introduced, and intensive investigative work by the staff of the House Select Committee on Aging resulted in the publication of a landmark report entitled "Elder Abuse: An Examination of a Hidden Problem" (U.S. House of Representatives, 1981). The federal legislation on elder abuse was modeled after the existing Child Abuse Prevention and Treatment Act of 1974, because federal lawmakers thought that the child abuse legislation had been successful in establishing the leadership role of the federal government to combat that problem. However, the appropriateness of applying the child abuse prevention approach to elder abuse was later questioned, even within Congress (U.S. Senate, 1991).

### Federal Elder Abuse Prevention Program

Throughout the 1980s various subcommittees of the House Select Committee on Aging continued to advocate the creation of a federal program to protect vulnerable elders from abuse, neglect, and exploitation, and for additional studies. In response, AoA funded a variety of research and demonstration projects on elder abuse from its discretionary grants program. Thus, the 1980s generated numerous federal activities designed to gain greater understanding of elder abuse, to support existing efforts by states and localities to reduce the incidence of elder abuse, and to enact federal elder abuse legislation (Wolf, 1988). These federal activities resulted in three tangible outcomes that helped further the elder abuse cause in this country, including (1) the 1990 congressional appropriation of funding for the federal elder abuse prevention program, (2) the 1990 formation of a departmental task force on elder abuse in the U.S. Department of Health and Human Services (DHHS), and (3) federal support of the creation and operation of two national resource centers on elder abuse.

In early 1990 the U.S. House of Representatives, Subcommittee on Health and Long-Term Care, Select Committee on Aging, issued a report, "Elder Abuse: A Decade of Shame and Inaction," which severely criticized Congress for not having taken any decisive action on elder abuse. This report, along with the heightened pressures coming from advocates, influenced Congress in late 1990 to finally appropriate $2.9 million for the OAA's federal elder abuse prevention program. These funds were to be distributed to all states to support a wide variety of activities aimed at strengthening the existing state and local programs for the prevention and treatment of elder abuse (Tatara, 1991). Given the broad scope of federal requirements, the amount of federal funding for the new program was small and largely symbolic. Nonetheless, this congressional decision was an epoch-making event for advocates and professionals concerned with elder abuse who worked hard throughout the 1980s to help enact federal elder abuse legislation. In 1994, with the congressional appropriation of $4.4 million per year, the federal elder abuse prevention program represents a federal commitment to assuming leadership in the nation's efforts to combat elder abuse. However, the funds appropriated are for less than the authorization level. Because the federal program currently is authorized for $15 million a year, the advocacy community continues to exert pressures on Congress to raise the level of federal funding for the program.

### Task Force on Elder Abuse

In May 1990 the secretary of DHHS (1992) established the Task Force on Elder Abuse to develop departmental strategies for addressing elder abuse. The final report of this task force, released in spring 1992, outlined the new DHHS strategies for elder abuse, which included three major federal initiatives directed to (1) improving the quality and availability of data on elder abuse; (2) strengthening technical assistance and training designed to enhance skills and knowledge of professionals working in the elder abuse and neglect network; and (3) improving education of professionals in law enforcement, medicine, and other professional disciplines.

Although the DHHS task force officially ended its activities on January 20, 1993, with the change in the federal administration, some of the efforts to implement its recommendations continue and are expected to bring about positive outcomes. These include an extensive study on the training and technical assistance needs of elder abuse professionals.

### Other Initiatives

AoA also provided funding to establish and operate two national centers specializing in elder abuse: (1) the National Aging Resource Center on Elder Abuse, from 1988 to 1992, and (2) the National Eldercare Institute on Elder Abuse and State Long-Term Care Ombudsman Services, from 1991 to 1993. These centers, staffed by experts, conducted a wide range of activities intended to create greater awareness of elder abuse, improve the delivery of services to victims and their families, and enhance the knowledge of causes of elder abuse.

In addition, AoA is responsible for administering the Long-Term Care Ombudsman Program. This program investigates and provides solutions for "complaints" (which may include abuse, neglect, or exploitation) received from or on behalf of nursing home residents. Besides AoA, several other federal agencies are concerned with the protection of older people (particularly those who are institutionalized) from abuse. For example, the Health Care Financing Administration tries to ensure the health and safety of patients and residents in various health and eldercare facilities that participate in Medicare and Medicaid, and it enforces federal requirements with which these facilities must comply. Also, the DHHS Office of Inspector General oversees the administration of the Medicaid Fraud Control Units program, which investigates patient abuse at the state level as well as fraud and abuse cases in facilities that use Medicaid funds (Office of Inspector General, 1990).

## Efforts to Address Elder Abuse

### State Laws and Agencies

State involvement with elder abuse precedes federal initiatives, dating back to the early 1970s, when several states (Nebraska, North Carolina, South Carolina, and Virginia) enacted adult protective service (APS) laws to create APS programs. These programs generally served people between 19 and 59 and elderly people needing protection or treatment. Typically, these early state APS laws were modeled after state child protective service statutes, which had existed in most states since the 1960s.

In the ensuing 20 years, nearly all states and U.S. territories established some form of law addressing both domestic and institutional elder abuse, although the exact features of these laws vary considerably among the jurisdictions. Almost without exception, however, the state APS laws designate the state APS agency or the state unit on aging as the principal state agency responsible for receiving reports of elder abuse, investigating these reports, providing victims and their families with treatment and protective services, and conducting appropriate activities to prevent and reduce the incidence of elder abuse.

In more than 30 states, the state APS agency is lodged within the state human services or social services agency; it is located within the state unit on aging in the remaining states (Tatara, 1990a). Because states undergo frequent organizational changes, however, the location of the APS agency also changes frequently.

The actual delivery of treatment or protective services is carried out by local departments of the state APS agency or the area agencies on aging, which are accountable to the state units on aging. Because the OAA designates the state units on aging as the administering agencies for its provisions, the federal elder abuse prevention program is implemented through the existing network of state and local aging agencies in each state, and APS agencies in many states do not receive federal funds or are not directly involved with the federal program (Tatara, 1992). However, given that the OAA stresses the importance of coordination between aging agencies and APS agencies, these agencies are expected to develop closer working relationships in the future.

Elder abuse is a multidimensional problem that requires broad expertise and a variety of resources. The APS agency, therefore, works cooperatively with other agencies and programs in the community to ensure maximum benefit of all available resources for clients. A wide range of social, medical, mental health, legal, and advocacy services are available to elder abuse victims and their families in most communities across the country, and professionals from different disciplines participate in providing these services. In many localities four types of services are provided, with varying degrees of emphasis, to vulnerable elders at risk of abuse and to victims and their families: (1) elder abuse treatment, (2) protective services, (3) prevention services, and (4) support services (Tatara, 1993a).

### Elder Abuse Treatment

The medical profession plays a key role in diagnosing problems and in providing clinical treatment for elder abuse. A number of major hospitals and medical centers across the country, particularly those that specialize in geriatrics, operate some type of program for victims of elder abuse and neglect. Typically, emergency and trauma physicians, assisted by a host of other specialists (such as psychiatrists, geriatricians, enterostomal therapists, psychologists, medical social workers, and geriatric nurses), provide leadership in many of these programs. Given that almost two-thirds of elder abuse victims are physically abused or neglected and that the average age of these victims is nearly 80 years (Tatara, 1993b), the role of medical professionals is critical. Recognizing this, the American Medical Association (1992), with assistance from a multidisciplinary panel of experts, compiled a resource guide for physicians entitled "Diagnostic and Treatment Guidelines on Elder Abuse and Neglect."

### Protective Services

Protective services for elderly people are generally the responsibility of APS agencies at the state and local levels (American Public Welfare Association and National Association of State Units on Aging, 1988). In addition, state long-term-care ombudsman offices and state health departments also provide protective services, particularly when institutional elder abuse is involved. In most communities these public agencies work collaboratively with many other public and private agencies (such as the police, prosecutor's office, the courts, client advocacy groups, hospitals and practicing physicians, and social service providers) to ensure the protection of vulnerable elders.

Some legal scholars are critical of adult protective services as being intrusive and neglectful of the rights of clients to self-determination (Regan, 1981). Although state APS laws prohibit involuntary intervention, the issue of ensuring maximum client autonomy remains controversial, particularly because a large portion of APS cases are self-neglect cases.

**Prevention Services**

The most common approach to preventing elder abuse is to provide professional and public education programs at the community level. For example, APS agencies frequently collaborate with other agencies in conducting programs aimed at raising professional and public awareness of elder abuse. These programs generally focus on teaching participants the scope of the problem, state elder abuse laws, and ways to identify abuse and neglect indicators and warning signs. Many states also provide informal caregivers and interested citizens with training related to eldercare. These programs help prevent the potential maltreatment of elderly people and lead to the early identification and appropriate reporting of elder abuse cases.

**Support Services**

Both public and private agencies provide support services, which generally include the guardianship program, the guardian *ad litem,* legal advocacy, financial planning, victim support groups and self-help groups, respite care, foster care and group homes, transportation, and socialization services, to name only a few.

## Conclusion

The United States is becoming an aging society. The U.S. Bureau of the Census predicts that, if the current trends continue, by 2020 the number of people age 60 and older will increase from the current 42 million to 72 million. There is little doubt that elder abuse will be among the most difficult problems facing us. Because of extensive efforts by policymakers and advocates during the past decade, the United States has established laws and programs to address elder abuse at the national and local level. Research studies have helped professionals and the public gain an understanding of the causes and dynamics of the problem and of the needed intervention and treatment services. As a result, a wide range of programs is available to elder abuse victims and their families in most communities across the nation. Yet, compared with other problems of family violence, such as child abuse and spousal abuse, elder abuse still is not well recognized. Only a small portion of the incidents comes to the attention of authorities, and financial resources and technical expertise to support existing programs are grossly inadequate. Additionally, the effectiveness of the current policies and programs and the basic assumptions on which they are based remain controversial. It is clear that the time is now to evaluate critically what exists and to formulate new elder abuse prevention and intervention strategies, when the number of reported cases is still somewhat manageable.

## References

American Medical Association. (1992). *Diagnostic and treatment guidelines on elder abuse and neglect.* Chicago: Author.

American Public Welfare Association and National Association of State Units on Aging. (1986). *A comprehensive analysis of state policy and practice related to elder abuse* (Vol. 1). Washington, DC: Authors.

American Public Welfare Association and National Association of State Units on Aging. (1988). *Adult protective services: Programs in state social service agencies and state units on aging.* Washington, DC: Authors.

Anetzberger, G. J. (1987). *The etiology of elder abuse by adult offspring.* Springfield, IL: Charles C Thomas.

Bendik, M. F. (1992). Reaching the breaking point: Dangers of mistreatment in elder caregiving situations. *Journal of Elder Abuse and Neglect, 4,* 39–59.

Block, M. R., & Sinnott, J. D. (1979). *The battered elder syndrome: An exploratory study.* College Park: University of Maryland Center for Aging.

Cantor, M. H. (1983). Strain among caregivers: A study of experience in the United States. *The Gerontologist, 23,* 597–604.

Cazenave, N. A. (1979). Family violence and aging blacks: Theoretical perspectives and research possibilities. *Journal of Minority Aging, 4,* 99–108.

Cazenave, N. A. (1983). Elder abuse and black Americans: Incidence, correlates, treatment, and prevention. In J. I. Kosberg (Ed.), *Abuse and maltreatment of the elderly* (pp. 187–203). Boston: John Wright.

Child Abuse Prevention and Treatment Act of 1974. P.L. 93-247, 88 Stat. 4.

Douglass, R. C., Hickey, T., & Noel, C. (1980). *A study of maltreatment of the elderly and other vulnerable adults.* Ann Arbor, MI: Institute of Gerontology.

Faulkner, L. P. (1982). Mandating the reporting of suspected cases of older adults. *Family Law Quarterly, 16,* 69–91.

Fredriksen, K. (1989). Adult protective services: Changes with the introduction of mandatory reporting. *Journal of Elder Abuse and Neglect, 122,* 59–70.

Fulmer, T., & O'Mallery, T. (1987). *Inadequate care of the elderly: A health perspective on abuse and neglect.* New York: Springer.

George, L. G. (1986). Caregiver burden: Conflict between norms of reciprocity and solidarity. In K. Pillemer & R. Wolf (Eds.), *Elder abuse: Conflict in the family* (pp. 67–92). Dover, MA: Auburn House.

Greenberg, J. R., McKibben, M., & Raymond, J. A. (1990). Dependent adult children and elder abuse. *Journal of Elder Abuse and Neglect, 2,* 73–86.

Johnson, T. (1986). Critical issues in the definition of elder mistreatment. In K. Pillemer & R. Wolf (Eds.), *Elder abuse: Conflict in the family* (pp. 170–181). Dover, MA: Auburn House.

Lau, E., & Kosberg, J. I. (1979). Abuse of the elderly by information care providers. *Aging, 299,* 11–15.

Longres, J. F. (1992). Race and type of maltreatment in an elder abuse system. *Journal of Elder Abuse and Neglect, 4,* 61–83.

Office of Inspector General. (1990). *Resident abuse in nursing homes: Understanding and preventing abuse* (OEI 06-88-00361). Washington, DC: U.S. Department of Health and Human Services.

Older Americans Act Amendments of 1987. P.L. 100-175, 101 Stat. 926.

Older Americans Act Amendments of 1992. P.L. 102-375, 106 Stat. 1195.

Phillips, L. R. (1986). Theoretical explanations of elder abuse: Competing hypotheses and unresolved issues. In K. Pillemer & R. Wolf (Eds.), *Elder abuse: Conflict in the family* (pp. 197–217). Dover, MA: Auburn House.

Pillemer, K. (1985). The dangers of dependency: New findings on domestic violence against the elderly. *Social Problems, 33,* 146–158.

Pillemer, K. (1986). Risk factors in elder abuse: Results from a case control study. In K. Pillemer & R. Wolf (Eds.), *Elder abuse: Conflict in the family* (pp. 239–263). Dover, MA: Auburn House.

Pillemer, K., & Finkelhor, D. (1988). The prevalence of elder abuse: A random sample survey. *The Gerontologist, 28,* 51–57.

Pillemer, K., & Finkelhor, D. (1989). Causes of elder abuse: Caregiver stress versus problem relations. *American Journal of Orthopsychology, 59,* 179–187.

Pillemer, K., & Moore, D. W. (1989). Abuse of patients in nursing homes: Findings from a survey of staff. *The Gerontologist, 29,* 314–320.

Poertner, J. (1986). Estimating the incidence of abused older persons. *Journal of Gerontological Social Work, 9,* 3–15.

Poulschock, S. W., & Diemling, G. T. (1984). Families caring for elders in residences: Issues in the measurement of burden. *Journal of Gerontology, 39,* 230–239.

Quinn, M., & Tomita, S. (1986). *Elder abuse and neglect: Causes, diagnosis, and intervention strategies.* New York: Springer.

Regan, J. (1981). Protecting the elderly: The new paternalism. *Hastings Law Journal, 32,* 1113–1114.

Salend, E., Kane, R. A., Satz, M., & Pynoos, J. (1984). Elder abuse reporting: Limitations of statutes. *The Gerontologist, 244,* 61–69.

Sellers, C. S., Folts, W. E., & Logan, K. M. (1992). Elder mistreatment: A multidimensional problem. *Journal of Elder Abuse and Neglect, 4,* 5–23.

Steinmetz, S. K. (1977). *The cycle of violence: Assertive, aggressive, and abusive family interaction.* New York: Praeger.

Steinmetz, S. K. (1978). Overlooked aspect of family violence: Battered husbands, battered siblings, and battered elderly. In U.S. House of Representatives, Committee on Science and Technology, *Research into violent behavior: Domestic violence* (pp. 105–164). Washington, DC: U.S. Government Printing Office.

Tatara, T. (1989). Toward the development of estimates of the national incidence of reports of elder abuse based on currently available state data: An exploratory study. In R. Filinson & S. Ingman (Eds.), *Elder abuse: Practice and policy* (pp. 153–165). New York: Human Sciences Press.

Tatara, T. (1990a). *Elder abuse in the United States: An issue paper.* Washington, DC: National Aging Resource Center on Elder Abuse.

Tatara T. (1990b). *NARCEA's suggested state guidelines for gathering and reporting domestic elder abuse statistics for compiling national data.* Washington, DC: National Aging Resource Center on Elder Abuse.

Tatara, T. (1990c). *Summaries of national elder abuse data: An exploratory study of state statistics.* Washington, DC: National Aging Resource Center on Elder Abuse.

Tatara, T. (1991). *The implementation status of the new federal elder abuse prevention program in states.* Washington, DC: National Aging Resource Center on Elder Abuse.

Tatara, T. (1992). *Institutional elder abuse: A summary of data gathered from state units on aging, state APS agencies, and state long-term care ombudsman programs.* Washington, DC: National Aging Resource Center on Elder Abuse.

Tatara, T. (1993a). *Elder abuse: Questions and answers—An information guide for professionals and concerned citizens.* Washington, DC: National Aging Resource Center on Elder Abuse.

Tatara, T. (1993b). *Summaries of the statistical data on elder abuse in domestic settings for FY 90 and FY 91.* Washington, DC: National Aging Resource Center on Elder Abuse.

Thobaben, M. (1989). State elder/adult abuse and protection laws. In R. Filinson & S. Ingman (Eds.), *Elder abuse: Practice and policy* (pp. 138–152). New York: Human Sciences Press.

U.S. Department of Health and Human Services. (1992). *Report from the secretary's task force on elder abuse.* Washington, DC: Author.

U.S. General Accounting Office. (1989). *Board and care: Insufficient assurances that residents' needs are identified and met* (GAO/HRD 89-50). Washington, DC: U.S. Government Printing Office.

U.S. General Accounting Office. (1991). *Elder abuse: Effectiveness of reporting laws and other factors* (GAO/HRD 91-74). Washington, DC: U.S. Government Printing Office.

U.S. House of Representatives, Subcommittee on Health and Long-Term Care, Select Committee on Aging. (1981). *Elder abuse: An examination of a hidden problem* (Publication No. 97-277). Washington, DC: U.S. Government Printing Office.

U.S. House of Representatives, Subcommittee on Health and Long-Term Care, Select Committee on Aging. (1985). *Elder abuse: A national disgrace* (Publication No. 99-502). Washington, DC: U.S. Government Printing Office.

U.S. House of Representatives, Subcommittee on Health and Long-Term Care, Select Committee on Aging. (1989). *Board and care homes in America: A national tragedy* (Publication No. 101-711). Washington, DC: U.S. Government Printing Office.

U.S. House of Representatives, Subcommittee on Health and Long-Term Care, Select Committee on Aging. (1990). *Elder abuse: A decade of shame and inaction* (Publication No. 101-752). Washington, DC: U.S. Government Printing Office.

U.S. Senate, Special Committee on Aging. (1991). *An advocate's guide to laws and programs addressing elder abuse* (Publication No. 102-I). Washington, DC: U.S. Government Printing Office.

Wolf, R. (1988). The evolution of policy: A 10-year perspective. *Public Welfare, 46,* 5–13.

## Further Reading

Anetzberger, G. J. (1987). *The etiology of elder abuse by adult offspring.* Springfield, IL: Charles C Thomas.

Johnson, T. F. (1991). *Elder mistreatment: Deciding who is at risk.* Westport, CT: Greenwood Press.

Lucas, E. T. (1991). *Elder abuse and its recognition among health service professionals.* New York: Garland Publishing.

Rathbone-McCuan, E., & Fabian, D. R. (Eds.). (1992). *Self-neglecting elders: A clinical dilemma.* Westport, CT: Auburn House.

Wolf, R. S., & Pillemer, K. A. (1989). *Helping elderly victims: The reality of elder abuse.* New York: Columbia University Press.

**Toshio Tatara, PhD,** is director, Research and Demonstration Department, American Public Welfare Association, 810 First Street, NE, Washington, DC 20002, and director, National Center on Elder Abuse.

**For further information see:**

Adult Foster Care; Adult Protective Services; Aging Overview; Aging: Direct Practice; Aging: Public Policy Issues and Trends; Aging: Services; Aging: Social Work Practice; Long-Term Care; Patient Rights; Violence Overview.

**Key Words**

aging
prevention
elder abuse

## Elderly People

*See* Aging *(Reader's Guide)*

## Eliot, Martha May

*See* Biographies section, Volume 3

# Employee Assistance Programs

**Nan Van Den Bergh**

*Employee assistance programs* (EAPs) focus on helping to prevent and remediate personal, work, or family problems that interfere with employees' optimal productivity (Kurzman, 1993). Although the term dates only to the early 1970s, social workers began assisting troubled employees at the end of the 19th century, when the changing demography of the work force created a need for workplace interventions.

The workplace of the late 1980s and early 1990s witnessed a similar demographic change. The majority of new entrants to the work force were women and ethnic minorities (Van Den Bergh, 1990). This change in the makeup of the work force has contributed to the prevalence of EAPs. A study by the American Society for Personnel Administrators (ASPA, 1989) found that 79 percent of the respondent organizations had EAPs and that 55 percent of those with no programs intended to launch them within two years; similarly, 60 percent of Fortune 500 firms had EAPs in 1984. EAPs are mandated in federal government agencies and are provided by most state governments and many city and county governments, as well as by the military; there are also over 150 EAPs in higher education.

The Employee Assistance Professionals Association (EAPA) counted 20,000 EAP programs, 7,000 EAPA members, and 80 EAPA chapters in 1991 (EAPA, 1992). In contrast, in 1981 EAPA's predecessor organization, the Association of Labor and Management Consultants on Alcoholism, had counted only 8,000 EAPs and had only 2,800 members (EAPA, 1992, p. i). It began credentialing EAP professionals in 1987 and by 1990 had certified 4,037 employee assistance professionals (Bickerton, 1990).

Social work practitioners hold leadership positions and are the primary professional group in EAP associations, such as the EAPA, the Employee Assistance Society of North America, and the International Association of Individual Social Workers.

## History

### Welfare Capitalism

Changing demographics of the work force in the 1870s, particularly the influx of immigrants and women, caused employers to recognize the need for programs to help "socialize" workers to be productive and loyal. On-the-job drinking, although commonplace, was viewed by early industrialists as antithetical to the development of workplace norms that stressed efficiency and productivity. Employers also were also concerned about unionization and the organized labor movement. The latter part of the 19th century was a period rife with labor agitation; from 1880 to 1900 alone, there were 23,000 strikes in 117,000 businesses (Googins & Godfrey, 1987, p. 19). Prompted by these concerns, employers offered a variety of services to employees. These early services, which were later dubbed "welfare capitalism," included seven elements: (1) company-sponsored housing, (2) medical care, (3) schools and churches, (4) company stores, (5) pension funds, (6) profit sharing and stock ownership, and (7) assistance in case of illness or accidents (Straussner, 1989).

The personnel who performed these services were referred to as welfare secretaries, social secretaries, or welfare workers. The first such provider was Aggie Dunn, who was hired in 1875 by the H. J. Heinz Company of Pittsburgh (Straussner, 1989). Welfare capitalism programs spread rapidly. Jane Addams supported the workplace welfare movement and used her influence to promote welfare programs in a variety of industries (Googins, 1987). A 1919 U.S. Bureau of Labor Statistics survey of the 431 largest U.S. companies found that 141 employed full-time welfare secretaries and 154 contracted with outside agencies for those services. By 1926, 80 percent of the 1,500 largest U.S. firms had some type of welfare program. Social work professionals were actively involved in these early programs. In 1920 more graduates of the New York School of Social Work were employed in industrial settings than in any other area of social work (Popple, 1981).

**20th-Century Movements**

Welfare capitalism programs dwindled during the 1920s, with the rise of organized labor, which decried workplace social services as paternalistic and based on an innate distrust of workers. In addition, the temperance aspects of these programs may have been viewed by the labor movement as intrusive and controlling. Henry Ford, for example, had a corps of investigators who visited workers' homes every six months, scrutinizing employees' lives and alcohol consumption. Another reason for the demise of welfare capitalism in the 1920s was the disdain for Taylorism, which stressed efficiency, discipline, self-reliance, speed, and competitiveness among employees, who were subjected to time-and-motion studies (Googins & Godfrey, 1987).

Several additional phenomena in the mid-20th century contributed to the demise of welfare capitalism programs. First, as the organized labor movement grew, unions took over the job of providing social services at the workplace. Second, the development of the Human Relations Movement in the 1930s and 1940s legitimated the provision of fringe benefits to satisfy employees' security needs. Third, the field of personnel management, whose philosophy was that how employees felt about their jobs influenced their workplace behavior, began during this period. Finally, in the 1930s there emerged government and nonprofit community organizations that were capable of offering social services, lessening the need for the kinds of social services that were typically provided by welfare capitalism programs.

**Workplace Alcoholism Programs**

The creation of Alcoholics Anonymous in 1935 set the stage for the development of EAPs. Workplace alcoholism programs—operated by employees who were recovering alcoholics—were created at companies such as Eastman Kodak, Dupont, Caterpillar Tractor, and Kemper Insurance. These services, whose primary goal was to help alcoholic employees maintain sobriety, were typically affiliated with the companies' medical departments (Bickerton, 1990).

Interest in studying the impact of alcoholism, in general and at the workplace, spawned the founding of the Yale Center for Alcohol Studies in the 1940s. The center's National Committee for Education on Alcoholism became the National Council on Alcoholism, which began working with industries to design model occupational programs. The center was also instrumental in validating empirically that although alcoholism has a negative effect on job performance, rehabilitated alcoholics could be reintegrated into the work force. This research helped influence perceptions of alcoholism as a treatable "disease" and encouraged companies to adopt policies and create programs that would educate employees about alcoholism and allow for any needed treatment. Partly because of the Yale center's research, the American Medical Association in 1956 called alcoholism a disease, an action that contributed to the greater acceptance and understanding of people with drinking problems (Bickerton, 1990).

**Groundwork for EAPs**

Concurrent with the growing interest in and concern about the impact of alcoholism on the workplace, several developments in the 1940s and

1950s laid the groundwork for the EAP service delivery model. First, the demands on industry to produce the weaponry and equipment that the military needed in World War II created the need for "occupational programming" to help employees handle the stresses associated with shiftwork and to maintain safe working conditions, on-the-job discipline, and high productivity. Industry realized that employees could be advantaged, and hence more productive, if they received services that would alleviate their work-related problems (Bickerton, 1990).

Second, Lewis Presnall, of Kennecott Copper Company, who became the first director of the National Council of Alcoholism's labor–management services division in 1959, developed a troubled employee case-finding model based on supervisory observation of deteriorating job performance. Presnall's model was the forerunner of the troubled-employee referrals by supervisors, stewards, coworkers, and family members that are a key element of EAPs today (Bickerton, 1988, 1990). In addition to defining the referral process, Presnall's model allowed for intervention with employees on the basis of their deteriorating job performance that was not necessarily alcohol-related. Furthermore, Presnall believed in the value of referring troubled employees to community resources, another practice of today's EAPs.

**Federal Action**

The development of EAPs was spurred by the passage in 1970 of the Comprehensive Alcohol Abuse and Alcoholism Prevention, Treatment, and Rehabilitation Act (P.L. 91-616), which established the National Institute on Alcoholism and Alcohol Abuse (NIAAA) and mandated the provision of alcoholism programs in all federal agencies and military installations; this act was amended in 1972 to include drug abuse treatment. NIAAA established an occupational program branch, which provided funding for each state ($50,000 per year) to hire two occupational consultants to assist private- and public-sector firms in developing occupational alcoholism programs. The growth in the number of these programs was phenomenal—from 500 in 1973 to 4,000 by 1980 (Googins, 1987).

The professionalism of occupational alcoholism programs was heightened as a result of a grant that NIAAA awarded in 1971 to establish the Association of Labor and Management Consultants on Alcoholism (ALMACA). ALMACA was charged with gathering and disseminating information on occupational alcoholism, as well as with conducting research, developing standards for occupational programs, and serving as an advocacy group for occupational programming. ALMACA, which was later renamed the Employee Assistance Professionals Association, began credentialing occupational consultants in 1987 using the Certified Employee Assistance Program examination.

**Shift from Alcohol Focus**

A shift from a focus on alcohol and drug problems began in the late 1970s as a result of several factors. First, it was generally recognized that even employees in "recovery" had other life problems (marital, family, legal, and financial) that warranted short-term intervention. Second, convincing employees to use occupational programs that focused specifically on addictions proved difficult because of the stigma associated with alcoholism and the psychological denial that is endemic to the disease. Third, the community mental health movement's focus on prevention and early intervention suggested that a broad-brush approach offering assistance for the range of problems that deter employees' productivity might be more effective than a more narrowly focused effort.

In 1978 the NIAAA occupational branch survey of 300 companies with policies on occupational alcoholism found that the most successful programs offered assistance to employees on a broad range of problems (Bickerton, 1990). As a result NIAAA coined the term "employee assistance program" and promoted that concept, rather than that of occupational alcoholism programs. Interventions to assist workers whose job performance was impaired, regardless of the cause, were encouraged, thereby institutionalizing a broad-brush approach to employee assistance. Employees with addictions would be addressed via a "constructive confrontation" model; those without addictions would first be assessed and then referred to the human resources departments or community mental health and social services agencies.

The Wingspread Conference, held in April 1979, which included representatives from social services, management, and labor interests, legitimated the involvement of professional social workers in workplace-based programs. Businesses and labor organizations, the conference participants decided, were "communities" that served as natural environments for social work activities. Appropriate activities for social workers in the workplace could include direct counseling and consultation services, as well as linking these services with community services (Bickerton, 1989). In essence, the conference concluded that the EAP assessment and referral functions were conceptually congruent with the roles that were appropriately performed by occupational social workers.

The extraordinary growth of EAPS—from about 50 in the late 1960s to more than 20,000 in 1991 (EAPA, 1992; Googins, 1987)—can be attributed to several factors: (1) increasing societal awareness of the costs associated with addictions, alcoholism, mental illness, and stress; (2) the increasing costs associated with health care and employers' desires to reduce costly health care claims; (3) growing societal acceptance of alcoholism as a disease and the willingness of alcohol-impaired workers to engage in sobriety–recovery; and (4) the changing demography of the workplace, including the burgeoning number of women and ethnic minorities, who historically have had a greater need for social services programs, particularly to balance work and family demands.

## Costs of Workers' Impairment

Alcohol abuse is a more significant problem than all other forms of drug abuse combined. One in seven adults either abuses or is dependent on alcohol (Masi, 1984). The nation's number one public health problem, alcoholism cost the United States an estimated $142 billion in 1986 (Masi, 1984; Royce, 1989). In addition, the National Institute on Drug Abuse estimated in 1987 that $80 billion in productivity was lost as a result of the misuse of illegal drugs, on which Americans spent $140 billion in 1988 (Royce, 1989).

The costs associated with mental illness are also high: Lost workplace productivity cost $17 billion (Brody, 1988). Furthermore, 85 percent of industrial accidents are believed to be stress induced (Brody, 1988), and industrial stress accounts for an estimated $32 billion in work-related accidents and heart attacks each year (McClellan, 1985).

Unmitigated stress and untreated mental disorders and addictions not only lead to reduced employee productivity, absenteeism, excessive use of sick leave, accidents, and disability payments, but they result in costly health care claims as well. Health care consumes $1 out of every $10 that the United States spends. It costs approximately $1 billion a day—more than the cost of national defense—and represents the largest unmanaged cost to industry (McClellan, 1985).

## Effectiveness of EAPs

EAPs can reduce these costs dramatically. The General Accounting Office (Brody, 1988) estimated that alcoholic employees cost taxpayers $694 million each year; that cost could be cut in half by effective EAPs. The following are examples of the savings that some companies have realized from their EAPs:

- Kennecott Copper Corporation estimated a 6:1 benefit–cost ratio from employees' use of its EAP (Brody, 1988).
- Equitable Life Assurance found a $3 return for every $1 invested in its EAPs; the absenteeism of alcoholic employees dropped from 8 percent to 4 percent after EAP referral to and treatment by alcohol programs (Brody, 1988).
- 3M Company data suggested that 80 percent of the employees who used the EAP showed improved attendance, greater productivity, and enhanced family and community relations (Brody, 1988).
- Illinois Telephone realized savings of $1.2 million over a nine-year period as a result of its employees' use of the company's EAP (Googins & Godfrey, 1987).

It could also be argued that by establishing an EAP, a company reduces the costs it could face by not being in compliance with federal mandates regarding the treatment of employees with disabilities. The Rehabilitation Act of 1973 (P.L. 93-112) requires that employers "reasonably accommodate" alcoholic or addicted employees who desire treatment. Such employees must be given the opportunity to be treated, although employers do not have to pay for the treatment. The Occupational Safety and Health Administration requires that employees experience a "safe" workplace, and alcohol- and drug-dependent employees are significantly more likely to cause workplace accidents than nonaddicted employees. The Drug-Free Workplace Act of 1988 (P.L. 100-690) requires companies of a certain size to assess drug-dependent employees and refer them for treatment. Similarly, the Drug-Free Schools and Communities Act of 1986 requires educational institutions to offer alcoholism and addiction prevention and intervention programs for students and employees.

Other benefits companies realize by establishing EAPs are an improved corporate image and enhanced employee morale. In a survey by the American Society for Personnel Administrators (1989) of 409 firms with EAPs, 98 percent of the respondents said that the benefits of their EAPs outweighed the costs, and 46 percent said that their EAPs had improved the employees' morale.

## Program Design

There are four primary designs for the delivery of EAP services: internal, external, consortium, and association. An internal program is one in which the EAP staff are employees of the organization. In the 1970s most EAPs were of this type, located in large industrial settings. According to practice wisdom, an employer must have at least 2,000 employees to justify one full-time EAP professional, plus the support staff who are allocated to provide secretarial and administrative assistance. In this model, services are usually provided on site or in close proximity to the workplace. The advantages include the EAP staff's greater sensitivity to the organizational culture and dynamics; hence, EAP staff might become more involved in organizational interventions, policy-making, and employee advocacy.

In the external model, services are provided to employees by a contractor, typically in an off-site office. In the past 10 years, this model has seen the most growth (Spitzer & Favorini, 1993). The growth in the number of external programs is primarily explained by their suitability for smaller organizations and the preponderance of small firms in the United States. Eighty percent of non-government workers are employed in work sites with fewer than 100 employees (McClellan, 1985). An additional benefit is that employees may view an external program as offering greater confidentiality than an internal program.

In the consortium model, several employers pool resources to acquire "group coverage." This model is appropriate for organizations, such as chambers of commerce, that have logical connection to or affiliation with each other. Some government grants have been made for EAP demonstration programs based on the consortium concept. The major advantage of this model is cost savings for firms that are members of the consortium.

An association EAP is appropriate for occupational membership groups, such as the Association of Airline Pilots, or state or national professional associations like state bar associations, the American Medical Association, or NASW, for example. The benefits of this model include the EAP staff's sensitivity to the unique professional and occupational issues of the individuals they serve, the ability to accommodate a geographically dispersed group, and the lower stigma associated with the use of the service because of the geographic distance and the lack of connection to employers among those who are served.

## Program Components

A successful employee assistance program usually has 11 components (Masi, 1984):

1. *Top-level management support and adequate funding for its operation.* The organizational placement of the EAP has both political and symbolic significance. Typically, the EAP staff report to a human resources officer or personnel administrator. In a unionized work site, the support of both organized labor and management is critical for program success.
2. *An advisory board.* The board should include representatives of constituent groups (members of the staff association), management, labor, human resources–personnel (or labor relations), a company ombudsperson, community services providers, and EAP staff. Such a group can suggest policy and program directions and serve as an advocate for the EAP with top administrators.
3. *A policy or mission statement.* The statement should that articulate the EAP's purpose, processes (such as eligibility and confidentiality protocols), and procedures, and sanction the use of EAP services by employees.
4. *A program plan.* This plan, evaluated and updated yearly, articulates the EAP's objectives and the services it will provide to achieve those objectives. It is frequently tied to an annual budgetary proposal.
5. *A data-collection mechanism that facilitates program evaluation.* Data should be collected regularly on the services provided (for example, the number of intakes, the number of EAP sessions provided to employees, the number of training sessions offered). Outcome data that measure employees' satisfaction with EAP services and referrals, as well as changes in the presenting problems, should also be collected.
6. *Outreach, development, and marketing.* An ongoing effort must be made to publicize and promote the EAP's services to employees, supervisors, and managers. The program should be modified and expanded as necessary to meet the changing needs of both the employees and the organization.
7. *Supervisor training and employee education.* Supervisors must be skilled in recognizing and intervening with troubled employees. Wellness programs for employees provide an effective complement to EAP activities. The topics of such programs typically include balancing work and career, handling stress, managing change, coping with crises, and building productive relationships.
8. *Confidential and secure records.* Without a guarantee of confidentiality, many employees would never agree to use EAP services. For this reason, information about an employee's contact with the EAP should be carefully protected

and never provided to another person without the employee's written approval.

9. *Ongoing resource development in the organization and the community.* An internal EAP must establish a wide range of relationships with company personnel, including the human resources and affirmative action officer, occupational health and safety employees, and vocational rehabilitation staff, as well as with employee organizations and self-help groups. Relationships must be established with community agencies and groups, so that appropriate referrals can be made for treatment and social services.
10. *The ability to provide assistance to groups of employees or to the entire company in special circumstances in which crisis intervention is called for.* Traumas associated with violence and severe accidents in the workplace, layoffs, or departmental reorganizations may require intervention by the EAP staff.
11. *Competent assessment and appropriate referral.* Following assessment, the EAP staff must be prepared to refer employees to a wide range of services if the problem cannot be resolved quickly.

## Services

The occupational social worker who works as an EAP practitioner is called on to fulfill many roles: counselor, resource broker, teacher, mediator, and program advocate. These roles are addressed in the discussion of direct and indirect services that follows.

### Direct Services

The primary direct service that practitioners offer EAP clients is assessment-and-referral counseling sessions. Typically, an EAP offers as many as three sessions per presenting problem. The common view is that providing an employee with more than three sessions for a particular problem moves beyond assistance and into actual treatment. In the first session, the practitioner works to establish a relationship of trust with the employee and to assess the problem. A referral is typically made when the problem cannot be remediated quickly, for example, if the client has an addictive or mental health disorder. Referrals are frequently made for concrete social services in the community (such as legal assistance or credit-counseling programs) or to community-based support groups (for instance, 12-step programs, Parents without Partners, and Parents and Friends of Lesbians and Gays).

Along with providing individual sessions for employees, EAPs convene peer support groups for employees with similar problems. In an era of managed mental health care and reduced access to services, workplace-based support groups can be a valuable direct service (Van Den Bergh, 1991). Support, assistance, information, and fellowship are offered in these group sessions. These groups take various forms and remain active for varying lengths of time. A support group for HIV-positive employees would be an ongoing group with an open membership. A grief-support group would be time-limited and closed. The EAP practitioner serves as a facilitator at these sessions and is typically more involved and directive with a short-term group than with a long-term group.

EAPs also provide interventions for distressed work groups, including crisis management services. In the early 1990s there was an increase in workplace violence and stress associated with organizational change and downsizing. EAP practitioners use critical incident stress debriefings to help employees affected by such events (Van Den Bergh, 1992). The purpose of these sessions is to prevent or reduce physical and psychological symptoms that could decrease the employees' productivity. Employees are assigned to groups of no more than 12 people and are asked to share their thoughts, feelings, and reactions to the crisis event with the practitioner and other group members. The practitioner also provides information about self-care stress management to the group.

### Indirect Services

Lunchtime lectures or workshops for employees and training for supervisors on topics related to troubled employees are examples of indirect EAP services. The goal of supervisory training is to help supervisors acquire skills to identify, confront, and intervene with impaired workers. Employee educational offerings are designed to enhance employees' personal well-being and thus have a positive impact on productivity. Many of the topics addressed in employee workshops relate to personal and family life because these problems can affect on-the-job performance and productivity as much as can problems in the workplace. By offering tools to manage these normative stresses better, the EAP helps ensure employees' optimal work performance.

It is common for EAP professionals who are associated with internal EAPs to be included on company task forces or committees that address issues that relate to the welfare of employees. Committees that are charged with the design and implementation of workplace, family, or dependent-care policies typically include representatives of EAPs, as do task forces that are involved in generating organizational disaster plans, workplace diversity councils, and groups that draft protocols related to employees who have acquired immune deficiency syndrome (AIDS) or disabilities. And in this era of increased workplace violence, EAP professionals are usually included in efforts to prevent and respond to threats or incidents of violence.

## Future Trends

Perhaps the primary factor that will have an impact on EAPs in the last half of the 1990s will be managed mental health care. Internal EAPs are likely to be affected by this phenomenon more than other types of EAPs because many managed health care firms offer EAPs as part of their services. Companies that are concerned with reducing costs could decide to eliminate their internal EAPs and provide EAP services as part of a managed health care program. Those internal EAPs that remain may turn their focus to wellness and health-promotion programming. Workplace initiatives to educate employees on health and well-being topics would complement the movement toward a national health care policy that emphasizes prevention.

The growth of EAP programs overseas seems likely in view of the relatively lax attitudes of some cultures toward alcohol abuse. European firms in particular have lagged behind U.S. companies in taking an assertive stance toward employees' alcohol consumption. External and consortium EAP models may be put in place to address this problem.

The trends toward greater diversity in the workplace and downsizing and corporate reorganization will continue to challenge EAP practitioners to help employees manage change, handle crises, and accept differences in the workplace.

## References


American Society for Personnel Administrators. (1989, April). The resource survey: Your responses. *Resource*, p. 2.

Bickerton, R. (1988). EAPs: Notes for a history in progress. *Alcohol Health and Research World, 12*(4), 316–321.

Bickerton, R. (1989, September). The EAP agenda and the industrial social worker. *The Almacan*, pp. 20–21.

Bickerton, R. (1990, November–December). Employee assistance: A history in progress. *EAP Digest*, pp. 34–42, 82–84, 91.

Brody, B. (1988, Winter). Employee assistance programs: An historical and literature review. *American Journal of Health Promotion*, pp. 13-19.

Comprehensive Alcohol Abuse and Alcoholism Prevention, Treatment, and Rehabilitation Act of 1970. P.L. 91-616, 84 Stat. 1848.

Drug-Free Schools and Communities Act of 1986. P.L. 89-10, 102 Stat. 252.

Drug-Free Workplace Act of 1988. P.L. 100-690, 102 Stat. 4304.

Employee Assistance Professionals Association. (1992). *EAPA standards for employee assistance professionals*. Arlington, VA: Author.

Googins, B. (1987). Occupational social work: A developmental perspective. *Employee Assistance Quarterly, 2*(3), 37–53.

Googins, B., & Godfrey, J. (1987). Occupational social work: History, development and definition. In B. Googins & J. Godfrey (Eds.), *Occupational social work* (pp. 18–43). Englewood Cliffs, NJ: Prentice Hall.

Kurzman, P. (1993). Employee assistance programs: Toward a comprehensive model. In P. Kurzman & S. Akabas (Eds.), *Work and well-being: The occupational social work advantage* (pp. 26–45). Washington, DC: NASW Press.

Masi, D. (1984). *Designing employee assistance programs*. New York: American Management Association Publications Group.

McClellan, K. (1985). The changing nature of EAP practice. *Personnel Administrator, 30*(8), 29–37.

Popple, P. R. (1981). Social work practice in business and industry: 1875–1930. *Social Service Review, 55*(2), 257–269.

Rehabilitation Act of 1973. P.L. 93-112, 87 Stat. 355.

Royce, J. (1989). *Alcohol problems and alcoholism*. New York: Free Press.

Spitzer, K., & Favorini, A. (1993). The emergence of external employee assistance programs. In P. Kurzman & S. Akabas (Eds.), *Work and well-being: The occupational social work advantage* (pp. 350–371). Washington, DC: NASW Press.

Straussner, S. (1989). Occupational social work today: An overview. *Employee Assistance Quarterly, 5*(1), 1–18.

Van Den Bergh, N. (1990). Managing biculturalism at the workplace: A groups approach. *Social Work with Groups, 13*(4), 71–84.

Van Den Bergh, N. (1991). Workplace mutual aid and self-help: Invaluable resources for EAPs. *Employee Assistance Quarterly, 6*(3), 1–20.

Van Den Bergh, N. (1992). Using critical incident stress debriefing to mediate organizational crisis, change and loss. *Employee Assistance Quarterly, 8*(2), 35–56.


## Further Reading


Akabas, S., & Kurzman, P. (Eds.). (1982). *Work, workers and work organizations: A view from social work*. Englewood Cliffs, NJ: Prentice Hall.

Dickman, F., & Challenger, R. (1988). Employee assistance programs: An historical sketch. In F. Dickman, R. Challenger, W. Emener, & W. Hutchison (Eds.), *Employee assistance programs* (pp. 48–53). Springfield, IL: Charles C Thomas.

Masi, D. (1993). Occupational social work today. *Employee Assistance, 5*(8), 42–44.

Van Den Bergh, N. (1991). Workplace diversity: Challenges and opportunities for employee assistance programs. *Employee Assistance Quarterly, 6*(4), 41–58.

Wrich, J. (1980). *The employee assistance program.* Chicago, IL: Author.

**Nan Van Den Bergh, PhD, ACSW,** is director, Doctoral Program, and associate professor, Tulane University, School of Social Work, New Orleans, LA 70118.

**For further information see**

Alcohol Abuse; Community; Crisis Intervention: Research Needs; Conflict Resolution; Direct Practice Overview; Drug Abuse; Ethics and Values; Families Overview; Family Life Education; Goal Setting and Intervention Planning; Information and Referral Services; Interdisciplinary and Interorganizational Collaboration; Jobs and Earnings; Legal Issues: Confidentiality and Privileged Communication; Managed Care; Management Overview; Natural Helping Networks; Occupational Social Work; Organizations: Context for Social Services Delivery; Person-in-Environment; Primary Prevention Overview; Research Overview; Self-Help Groups; Social Work Practice: History and Evolution; Substance Abuse: Direct Practice; Supervision and Consultation; Unions.

**Key Words**
employee assistance programs
industrial social work
occupational social work

READER'S GUIDE

## Employment

*The following entries contain information on this general topic:*

Employee Assistance Programs
Employment and Unemployment Measurement
Jobs and Earnings
JOBS Program
Occupational Social Work
Personnel Management
Unemployment Compensation and Workers' Compensation
Welfare Employment Programs: Evaluation

# Employment and Unemployment Measurement

**Sar A. Levitan**

The United States is served by a comprehensive labor force reporting system that has been adapted as a model by other nations. Buttressed by technological advances, the Bureau of Labor Statistics (BLS) and the U.S. Bureau of the Census have continued to expand and improve the quality and coverage of labor force data. They have, however, displayed a reluctance to alter or modify the concepts and definitions underlying the measurements that have been developed since the federal government started to keep monthly labor force statistics in 1940.

Labor market statistics have become key guides to the formation and operation of government activities and in the decision processes of the private sector. Few statistical measures are so intimately linked with policy as these indexes. Economic courses of action—and inaction—increasingly are based on the employment and unemployment measurements. The Congressional Budget Office (1993) estimated that a 1 percent rise in unemployment increases the federal deficit by $55 billion owing to declining revenue and increasing transfers in aid of the unemployed. Numerous programs—unemployment benefits, training efforts, aid to blighted areas—are tied to national, state, or local unemployment rates.

Given the role labor force statistics play as a barometer of the nation's economic health and in guiding economic decisions, the system should be flexible enough to meet day-to-day and long-term needs to keep pace with the constantly changing economy or face obsolescence. The labor force count should meet the needs of diverse users, but some issues deserve priority. The problems of unemployment and poverty should command the nation's attention.

Quality statistics are necessary not only to understand the causes and consequences of labor market malfunctions, but also to ameliorate labor market–related economic hardship and promote more equitable, efficient operations. This entry discusses the data sources for measuring labor force operations with emphasis on the information available from the Current Population Survey (CPS), the prime source of information about the nation's work force.

## Data Sources

The major sources for labor force statistics are the decennial census, the Current Employment Statistics (CES) survey, the Income and Program Participation survey, longitudinal surveys, unemployment insurance records, and, most important, the Current Population Survey (Levitan & Gallo, 1989).

The decennial census is the only attempt to count the entire population. Other surveys use it as a base from which to select stratified samples that represent the population in question.

The CES survey produces national employment estimates. It is a cooperative federal–state effort dating back to 1915. The present survey samples some 330,000 establishments employing more than 44 million workers. Employers report the number of employees (specifying the number of women as well as the number of production or nonsupervisory workers) and payroll data, including paid hours of production or nonsupervisory workers. Manufacturing establishments also report overtime hours. The establishment survey has some advantages over the CPS. A larger sample size permits more detailed disaggregation of employment, hours, and wages by industry. The data, however, do not include self-employed, farm, and unpaid family workers, and they count separately each job that moonlighters hold.

The newest major labor force survey, the Survey of Income and Program Participation (SIPP), is designed to obtain extensive information on income and participation in government programs. SIPP is potentially capable of providing comprehensive insights into the interaction of work conditions, including information on health, family structure, and income sources.

Whereas most surveys present a snapshot of the labor force at a specific point in time, of great importance is a longitudinal perspective for better understanding labor market activities and for policy formulation. The national longitudinal surveys of labor market behavior (NLS) and the panel study of income dynamics (PSID) are the major sources for longitudinal labor market analyses. Both date back to the 1960s. NLS includes separate panels for youths, middle-age women, and older men whereas the PSID tracks behavior of families. Longitudinal surveys have provided insights otherwise unavailable about work and other activities that may affect it. However, an inherent shortcoming of longitudinal surveys is the difficulty of ensuring that the sample continues to be representative of the population.

The unemployment insurance administrative records cover 97 percent of total employees and their wages and constitute a valuable source of work force information. Unemployment insurance records are updated continually and can potentially, subject to privacy concerns, be used to track individuals and establishments over time. The data also provide geographic detail not possible from sample surveys.

The Current Population Survey is the most important tool for assessing work-related behavior. It provides data on labor force status, education, earnings, type of industry and occupation, hours worked, reasons for not working, past work history and future work intentions if not working, and union status, along with various demographic characteristics. Supplementary survey questions augment the knowledge derived from the monthly CPS. Regular annual surveys include data about sources of income, work experiences, current educational enrollment, health insurance, and geographic mobility. The relatively large sample size of 60,000 households and diverse inquiries of the CPS render it immensely useful for measuring work force behavior and the interaction between work and family status, poverty, education, and health. But no single survey can meet all of the nation's needs and insatiable curiosity. CPS sample size has been deemed adequate to produce statistically valid monthly national and state estimates for the 11 states with the largest populations and New York City and the Los Angeles–Long Beach metropolitan area, but only annual estimates for other states and larger localities.

## Changing Labor Force Data Needs

Data needs are not immutable. As reality, application, and theory change, measures must be adjusted or added if the labor force statistics are to remain useful and accurate. The concepts of employment, unemployment, and labor force participation that were formed when the social security system was in its infancy do not have the same meaning in a mature welfare system because of massive income support payments, different social mores, and changing economic conditions. For example, until the current measurement was adopted in 1940, the Census Bureau counted only gainfully employed people, treating unemployment as a temporary phenomenon. This approach was in line with the prevailing view that truly unemployed people would reduce their wage demands until some employer would find it profitable to hire them.

It took the massive dislocations of the 1930s to upset these notions and to move the government into adopting measures to count the unemployed. With one of every four labor force participants unable to find a job in 1933—most of them previously stable workers—unemployment could not be written off as a temporary aberration. Yet during most of the Great Depression, there were no reliable joblessness measures. This situation prompted the establishment of a monthly labor force count—the Current Population Survey. The U.S. Bureau of the Census collects the data and the U.S. Bureau of Labor Statistics (BLS) analyzes and disseminates the information. BLS categorizes people into one of the following three groups:

1. *Employed workers* are defined as all those who during the survey week did any work at all (even one hour) as paid employees, or who worked 15 hours or more as unpaid workers in a family enterprise. Also counted as employed are all those not working but who had jobs from which they were temporarily absent because of illness, bad weather, vacation, or strike.
2. *Unemployed persons* are defined as all those who did not work during the survey week but who had made specific efforts to find a job within the past four weeks and who were available for work during the week in question. Also included as unemployed are all those waiting to be called back to a job from which they were laid off.

   The *labor force* is then defined as the sum of employed and unemployed people, and the unemployment rate is the number of unemployed divided by the labor force.
3. If a person is not defined as either employed or unemployed, then the individual is considered "not in the labor force."

Leaving aside the major impact of government spending programs, these labor force definitions have lost a good part of their precision because of dramatic changes in social mores. For example, during the 1930s it was considered proper for a wife to stay home and take care of the children, not only because of the dearth of jobs but because of the prevailing social values. Currently, nearly two of every three wives with husbands present, to use the census language, are in the labor force. In nearly half of the families there are at least two wage earners, and if one happens to lose employment the family exchequer is not automatically exhausted, especially when unemployment insurance continues to supplement the other member's earnings.

The transformation of the economy raises some issues about the rules governing the labor force count (Levitan, 1990). First, the Bureau of Labor Statistics counts a 16-year-old youngster looking for work as unemployed. Even a teenager looking for a few hours of baby-sitting or for an occasional lawn-mowing job is included in the ranks of the unemployed. Until the 1930s, the Census Bureau included individuals 10 years and older in the gainfully employed count. By the time CPS was designed, most states had enacted compulsory education until age 14, and, therefore, CPS raised the labor force participation threshold to age 14. Twenty-seven years later, compulsory education had risen to age 16 and BLS once again raised the labor force threshold.

Considering that nine of every 10 16- and 17-year-olds today are presumably fully occupied in school, a strong case can be made for excluding youngsters and even adults seeking only a few hours of work from the overall labor force, employment, and unemployment measurements, perhaps counting them separately but not as a part of the regular work force. Alternatively, a minimum number of hours of employment or of time spent seeking work might be a useful criterion for determining labor force participation and attachment. This step would both refine the unemployment rate as a measure of labor use and still include part-time workers, some of whom are self-supporting or responsible for the support of others. These numbers have increased significantly since the 1960s.

*Discouraged workers*, defined by BLS as people who fail to seek jobs during the four weeks prior to enumeration because they believe that no jobs are available, represent another controversial aspect of labor force count. Discouraged workers are not included in the monthly report of overall labor force participation either as employed or unemployed. Instead they are counted separately as being outside the labor force, a practice in line with the long-standing criterion for labor force participation status: People must display some tangible effort to find a job, not merely be interested in working.

Clearly, it would be improper to count as unemployed an individual who has not displayed any effort to look for a job, say, for a year or more. On the other hand, the current definition of unemployment excludes hundreds of thousands of people who apparently are ready and would like to work if jobs were available for them. Indeed, people able to work who have given up hope should be considered a prime concern of labor use policy. The fact is that the number of discouraged workers moves in tandem with the unemployment rate. When employment prospects improve, many of these workers counted as discouraged are likely to reenter the work force.

Seasonal adjustments present a third issue controlling the employment and unemployment counts. Currently the adjustments are based on the seasonal fluctuations over the past five years. But abnormal weather conditions or other unusual factors may distort the labor force count during any given period. BLS technicians are cognizant of the distortions caused by unusual events. For example, BLS reported that in May 1993, seasonally adjusted employment rose by 857,000 compared with an average of 31,000 during the preceding four months. BLS was aware that unusual seasonal patterns accounted for the sudden rise in employment, but the agency was obligated to follow its rules and report the numbers as they came out of the preprogrammed computer.

Political considerations frequently intervene in designing and reporting social and economic statistics. Trying to avoid even the slightest suspicion of data manipulation, BLS has adhered to its decision to announce the seasonal adjustment computations at least six months in advance, even though the results might be questioned. Without passing judgment on the methodology, more frequent adjustments in the seasonal adjustment factors might have yielded more-accurate results, but no doubt at the expense of questioning the statisticians' objectivity. For example, in 1992 and other election years, there was reason to believe that a month or two before the election unemployment was actually declining, but the established seasonal adjustments precluded BLS from making the necessary changes. If different seasonal adjustments had been applied to the labor force data—and with wisdom of hindsight it appears that such adjustments would have been perfectly justifiable—then the reported unemployment rates for September and October before elections would have been different from the rates that were officially published. The statistician faces a difficult trade-off between maintaining a credible image of integrity and achieving greater precision in reporting through frequent changes in methodology.

Occasionally, BLS is responsive to social changes. The count of military personnel in the labor force offers a significant illustration. Until 1983, military personnel were not included in the labor force count because during the first 33 years of the CPS the United States had a conscripted military force. The compensation offered, particularly to recruits, was not competitive with prevailing rates paid to the civilian labor force for comparable work, so it was perfectly justifiable to exclude the military from the civilian work force.

But since 1973, the voluntary armed forces have competed with civilian employers for the same workers, most of whom are new entrants into the labor market. In 1983, after 10 years, BLS decided to include military personnel located within the country as part of an alternative labor force estimate. The inclusion of the military in the labor force raised total employment by about 1.5 percent but reduced unemployment by only about one-tenth of a percentage point. Now, largely because of difficulties in determining what proportion of the armed forces was located within this country during the Persian Gulf conflict, BLS is reverting to the old practice of focusing only on the civilian labor force.

## Employment in the Welfare System

During the past 50 years, the United States has developed a major income support—or transfer payment—system. In 1992 these outlays carried a price tag of $866 billion, or 19.5 percent of the total disposable personal income of the American people. Despite public outcry over the "welfare mess," most transfer payments benefit people who are not commonly associated with welfare. In fact, spending for public assistance accounts for less than one-fifth of the income and in-kind support that is currently distributed to roughly one-third of the population.

It follows that the optimal level of employment and unemployment is elusive. To reach full employment we need to understand the implications of this massive transfer system for people's behavior in the labor market and their decisions to look for jobs and to work or not to work.

Under the American welfare system, people increasingly have the option to work or not to work (National Commission on Employment and Unemployment Statistics, 1979). The latter choice may not offer a life of wine and roses, but it is still an existence sustaining body and soul. In addition, forced idleness does not have the same bite in the welfare state as it did in years past. Although the benefits may be relatively low compared to those of other advanced industrialized nations, unemployment insurance still serves as a cushion, but only for a minority of unemployed people. Related to the unemployment insurance system is Old-Age Insurance under social security, which has enabled millions of people to retire at age 65, or at age 62 at actuarially reduced benefits.

A more recent development is the food stamp program, which has vastly reduced hunger in the United States. Having started as a pilot program over three decades ago, in 1993 it provided funds to help feed some 27 million people—more than one of every 10 Americans.

Transfer payments have an impact on almost all classes in society, including the middle class and the affluent. Transfer payments have reached a point where they affect even the labor market decisions of individuals with incomes well above the median level in the United States.

There is another side to the coin. For millions of Americans, employment—even a full-time job—does not offer an escape from poverty. As noted, the underlying notion of the current labor force count is that workers in the labor market are either employed, seeking work, or not included in the work force. This concept may have been adequate during the waning years of the Great Depression when the state, local, or philanthropic support systems in aid of the indigent had broken down, leaving people to work or starve. Since World War II, however, the federal government has developed a comprehensive welfare system that has rendered the labor force count inadequate for public policy formulation. Given the concern about the declining earnings of unskilled and deficiently educated workers, public policy requires reliable estimates of individuals and households that remain poor while people are working or seeking jobs. The lack of such measurements is probably the most serious flaw in our labor force reporting system. For policy formulation, a labor force statistics system should include a measurement of how well the economy is providing for those who are in the labor force.

This is no idle concern. In 1991 nearly 9 million workers, including 2 million people who worked full-time year-round lived below the official poverty threshold. In 1989, during the final year of the most prolonged peacetime economic expansion, a total of 8.4 million workers lived in poverty, including 1.9 million who worked full-time year-round. A number of efforts have been made to develop a labor market–related subemployment, or hardship, index. As long as we lack such a measure, there remains a gaping hole in labor force statistics. Congress has expressed an interest in such an index on several occasions. Specifically, in 1976 Congress mandated the National Commission on Employment and Unemployment Statistics (1976, §13[d][2]I) to explore "the need for the methods to obtain data related employment status and earnings, economic hardship, and family support obligations." Underlying the congressional quest for a labor market–related hardship measurement is the recognition that indexes generated by the data may yield a better understanding of labor market performance and serve as a guide for the allocation of public resources.

Critics have opposed the adoption of a hardship index because it necessarily involves normative judgments, ignoring the fact that the same criticisms have been and still can be made about the current employment and unemployment counts. Others may have been concerned that a hardship index would point to failures of the labor market and generate the demand for measures to aid the working poor. Academics and other consumers of labor force data have been reluctant to adopt new reporting measurements that would involve modifying established concepts and definitions. Whatever the reason, a labor market hardship index is not available.

The Clinton administration emphasized this point by arguing that if the American economy is to prosper and expand, it is not enough to create any job; the goal should be to help a full-time year-round worker garner sufficient income to raise a family of four above the poverty threshold. Given current labor market conditions and government transfer payments, there is a need to fashion policies that deal with the labor market pathologies of the 1990s. Instead of having a monthly sample that counts only people working or not working, policymakers should also have access to the number of people who are unable to attain an adequate standard of living through work.

The labor market–related measurement would not only count employment and unemployment, it would also consider earnings and time worked. Policy could be based on a new index designed to gauge economic hardship. This kind of index can be derived from existing data, but it is not regularly published by government agencies.

In 1979 the National Commission on Employment and Unemployment Statistics urged BLS to develop new measures to assess the degree of economic hardship due to unemployment, involuntary part-time employment, and low earnings. BLS responded by producing such reports for six years before deciding to replace the series with a new one in late 1989. The new report analyzes the labor market problems of poor people rather than examining the economic consequences of labor market pathologies.

Assessments of labor market–related hardship should measure at least three elements (National Council on Employment Policy, 1982):

1. *inadequate individual earnings*—the number of individuals in the labor force who do not earn at least the equivalent of the minimum wage (adjusted for inflation or wage growth) for the number of hours they work, or are able to work

but do not because of unemployment or the unavailability of full-time work

2. *inadequate family income*—the number of labor force participants in families with total *incomes* below the poverty threshold
3. *inadequate family earnings*—the number of labor force participants in families with total *earnings* below the poverty threshold.

The development and annual publication of a labor market–related hardship measure would provide a critical indicator of how far short the economy falls in providing a minimally acceptable family living standard derived from earnings.

The BLS could, with the consultation of outside experts, produce a composite indicator of labor market hardship analogous to the poverty rate. In time, such an indicator might become as accepted as the government poverty line or unemployment count. Indeed, half a century ago a prime designer of CPS wondered whether a phenomenon as complex as unemployment could be expressed in a single number, but respectability and acceptance came with age.

## State and Local Estimates

So far the discussion has considered national data. But businesses and state and local policymakers also need data to plan their operations. The national labor force estimates are based on a monthly survey of 60,000 households, or barely one in every 1,700 households. This survey results in a national estimate that would be quite close to the results obtained from a national census of every member of the population. When the government reports that the national unemployment rate is 7 percent, it can be stated with great confidence (in 95 of 100 cases) that, given the accepted definitions, the true rate of unemployment would range from 6.8 percent to 7.2 percent.

However, a national sample of 60,000 households is not large enough to produce accurate estimates for most local areas. In response to congressional mandates, the BLS currently produces unemployment estimates for about 6,100 state, local, and regional areas. BLS officials recognize that the accuracy of the local estimates—which are the indexes used for numerous allocations of federal grants—leaves much to be desired. The bureau prints a caveat as part of the introductory material to most of its local estimates that warns consumers to use the data with caution. In the absence of more-accurate data, federal officials have to use the BLS estimates; indeed, they are required to use them.

There is a clear need to obtain reliable labor force estimates for local areas. Although the best way to do this is to expand the national survey to local areas, this is not likely. Congress has shown an almost insatiable appetite for increasingly detailed demographic statistics about the labor force and has sought to apply these statistics to ever-smaller areas. Recent legislation intended to provide assistance to 104 blighted communities includes the need to develop labor force and income data for areas covering a few square blocks in a city (Levitan & Miller, 1992). Congress apparently assumed these data could be obtained at zero cost. An apt description of the congressional appropriations for labor force statistics would be billions for the unemployed but not a penny for the bureaucrats. This may be good politics, but it is certainly not conducive to collecting reliable statistics or to carrying out the intent of Congress in targeting the funds to aid the areas in need.

The fact is that the collection of uniform and reasonably reliable data for each of the 50 states and the District of Columbia would require a monthly sample of 377,400 households, or 7,400 per state. Such a sample would cost more than $200 million per year (in 1992 dollars), or more than five times the cost of the current national survey. To collect similar data for all the counties would multiply the cost by a factor of 20. And all these vast expenditure estimates fail to even consider the bother to the citizens who would cooperate in supplying the information to the government enumerators. The household survey clearly is too costly an instrument to use in obtaining state and local employment and unemployment data. For the time being, therefore, we will have to live with the present ways of estimating state and local data, despite all their failings.

Despite the government statisticians' best efforts, the quality of state and local statistics lags behind congressional and executive inclination to base policy decisions on such estimates. Because government officials lack data to allocate the funds properly, the billions may not reach those who need help most.

## Needed Reforms

BLS and the Census Bureau have tried continuously to critically examine and improve their operations. The latest major redesign of the CPS is reflected beginning with the January 1994 monthly report. The changes were based on continuing testing of responses to revised survey questions over a seven-year period and earlier recommendations of the National Commission on Employment and Unemployment Statistics. The new questionnaire sharpened and clarified the definitions relating to discouraged workers, unpaid family workers, and job-seeking efforts and therefore may result in an increased estimate of unemployment. Despite the risk of using more precise reporting instruments and thereby incurring the political flack resulting from a probable boost of the unemployment rate, BLS opted for integrity in reporting the findings.

Nonetheless, to enhance public confidence in the reported data, periodic outside reviews are desirable to suggest new directions and to examine proposed changes. Congress mandated the most recent commission on labor force statistics in 1976, and President Kennedy appointed the previous commission in 1961. The rapidly changing economy necessitates a thorough review of the nation's work force statistics by a new congressionally mandated commission that would consider the following issues:

- An annual labor force–related economic hardship indicator could better illuminate the connection between labor market participation and economic hardship. The commission should consider having BLS publish hardship data based on CPS findings, explore the feasibility of designing a composite annual index of labor market–related economic hardship, and analyze the relationship between family earnings and poverty.
- Gradually expanding the CPS sample size to 120,000 households would significantly increase the reliability of information for smaller states; major labor markets; and subgroups, including youths, people of color, and, union members. Such an expansion would provide a clearer picture of the occupational distribution of the work force.
- Continuing interest in a presumably growing underclass and the preparedness of the work force emphasizes the importance of information about the long-term behavior of individuals. Is the proportion of adults with prolonged forced idleness and below-poverty earnings growing? How frequently do individuals change careers? How strong is the connection between educational specialization and subsequent occupation? Careful longitudinal studies could illuminate public knowledge about those vexing issues.
- The growth in international trade and U.S. trade deficits has heightened interest in comparative international labor force statistics. BLS, the International Labor Organization, the Organization for Economic Cooperation and Development, and the Luxembourg Income Study have taken steps toward improving the comparability in international labor force statistics. But sustained leadership and commitment are imperative if adequate progress is to be achieved.

## References


Congressional Budget Office. (1993). *Economic and budget outlook: Fiscal 1994–1998*. Washington, DC: U.S. Government Printing Office.

Levitan, S. A. (1990). *Programs in aid of the poor* (6th ed.). Baltimore: Johns Hopkins University Press.

Levitan, S. A., & Gallo, F. (1989, December). *Workforce statistics: Do we know what we think we know—And what should we know?* [Testimony presented to U.S. Congress Joint Economic Committee.]

Levitan, S. A., & Miller, E. I. (1992). *Enterprise zones: A promise based on rhetoric*. Washington, DC: George Washington University.

National Commission on Employment and Unemployment Statistics. (1976). P.L. 94-444.

National Commission on Employment and Unemployment Statistics. (1979). *Counting the labor force*. Washington, DC: U.S. Government Printing Office.

National Council on Employment Policy. (1982). *Labor force and productivity measurements: Danger ahead*. Washington, DC: Author.


## Further Reading


Bawden, D. L., & Skidmore, F. (1989). *Rethinking employment policy*. Washington, DC: Urban Institute Press.

Bowen, W. G., & Finegan, T. A. (1969). *The economics of labor force participation*. Princeton, NJ: Princeton University Press.

Fosler, R. S., Alonso, W., Meyer, J. A., & Kern, R. (1990). *Demographic change and the American future*. Pittsburgh: University of Pittsburgh Press.

Ginzberg, E. (1980). *Employing the unemployed*. New York: Basic Books.

Levitan, S. A., Gallo, F., & Shapiro, I. (1993). *Working but poor* (rev. ed.). Baltimore: Johns Hopkins University Press.

Taggart, R. (1982). *Hardship: The welfare consequence of labor market problems*. Kalamazoo, MI: Upjohn Institute for Employment Research.

U.S. Congress, Office of Technology Assessment. (1989, September). *Statistical needs for a changing U.S. economy* (OTA-BP-E-58).Washington, DC: U.S. Government Printing Office.


**Sar A. Levitan, PhD,** was director, Center for Social Policy Studies, George Washington University, 1717 K Street, NW, Suite 1200, Washington, DC 20006. He died in 1994.

### For further information see

Income Distribution; Income Security Overview; Jobs and Earnings; Poverty; Public Social Welfare Expenditures; Social Security; Unemployment Compensation and Workers' Compensation.

**Key Words**

economic hardship
employment
labor force
low income
unemployment

# End-of-Life Decisions

**Karen Orloff Kaplan**

Death and this country's attitudes toward this major life-cycle event have undergone profound changes in recent decades. These changes represent a significant evolution in the understanding and practice of one of social work's fundamental principles: self-determination. Each person must make momentous decisions alone and with loved ones about how to live the latter part of life and about how and sometimes even when to die. Within the context of today's highly complex and technologically sophisticated society, these end-of-life decisions can become torturously difficult, especially because there are few cultural, ethical, or technical guidelines or procedures to ease the decision-making process. Perhaps what is most troublesome is that there are no guarantees that once an individual makes the decisions, the health care system will honor them. However, there are several meaningful ways in which social workers can help remedy these difficulties.

There also are ways that the social work profession can respond proactively and constructively to emerging policy and practice issues in relation to end-of-life decision making. The development of effective social work policy and practice in this area will be based on a careful understanding of the choices that individuals must make and on an appreciation of society's evolving approach to death and to the dying.

Since 1940, national policy and custom related to death have changed profoundly. Before 1940, decisions about how and where people lived the final chapter of their lives traditionally rested with their physicians and family members or close friends. Families generally cared for their ill or elderly members at home; thus, not many decisions were needed about where to spend one's last days. Furthermore, because not many curative medical interventions were available, the choices for medical treatment were few, and the decisions were not complicated.

However, since 1940, as the family structure changed, medical technology advanced, and longevity increased, these decisions have become significantly more intricate. Gradually, responsibility for the decisions and the decision-making process moved from individuals and their families to health care providers (personal communication with A. Fade, JD, associate executive director for program, Choice In Dying, New York, August 1993). Now, society is moving to wrest decisions about death from the control of the health care system and to achieve a better balance by encouraging joint end-of-life decisions by physicians and patients.

This entry reviews the history of the U.S. approach to death and dying and the evolution of the patients' rights and right-to-die movements. It also discusses the current status of issues related to death and dying within psychosocial, legal, and ethical contexts and the role of social workers from policy and practice perspectives.

## End-of-Life Decisions

End-of-life decisions encompass a broad range of medical and psychosocial determinations that each individual must make before the end of his or her life. Where one plans to spend the final months before death; the degree of self-sufficiency one wishes at that time; the use of personal, family, and societal resources to attain these goals; and the extent to which these decisions may change, depending on the course of a particular illness, are among the most important decisions, as is the type and extent of medical treatment one wishes at that time. The formal expression of these decisions through advance directives, such as living wills and durable powers of attorney for health care (also known as health care agents or health care proxies), involve still more decisions, including the selection of a health care agent and the preparation of that person to fulfill the role.

Ideally, individuals will begin thinking about end-of-life decisions early and will review their decisions from time to time throughout their lives. Also, ideally, people will make these decisions on the basis of sufficient information about options and after careful discussions with their loved ones and health care providers. Unfortunately, in this less-than-ideal world, most people are reluctant to face end-of-life considerations, and many lack knowledge about their options and about how to discuss those options with friends and relatives. Many people relinquish their rights to make these decisions for themselves. They either face such decisions only in emergencies, when careful consideration is not possible, or leave the difficult decisions to be made, in anguish, by family members and friends who are ill prepared to decide what their loved ones might have wanted.

As with all psychosocial aspects of life-cycle events and issues of individual empowerment, social workers play an essential role by facilitating and improving the way individuals make end-of-life decisions. From a policy perspective, the profession's formal policies and advocacy for their widespread implementation are also vital. For example, NASW's (1994) policy on end-of-life decisions and its continued advocacy of individual choice within reforms of the health care system are important contributions. The profession's educational responsibility is also significant. Social work can ensure that its practitioners and students are knowledgeable about the ethical and legal frameworks for making valid end-of-life decisions and are comfortable working with clients and other health care providers on these issues.

## Patients' Rights and Right-to-Die Movements

The patients' rights and right-to-die movements evolved in the wake of dramatic strides in medical technology and concomitant social and ethical developments focusing on the empowerment of individuals. The patients' rights movement addresses the need for patients to be well-informed, active participants in medical decisions for themselves, including the decision to refuse treatment. The more radical elements of the right-to-die movement focus on the rights of patients not only to refuse treatment, but to end their lives if the suffering and indignity of the dying process becomes too much to bear. Although these movements began decades ago, the organizations and individuals committed to them continue to influence state and federal legislation and the education and practice of health care professionals.

By the mid-1970s, the activities of the patients' rights and right-to-die movements and the actions of the courts clearly affirmed that all patients have the right to information that will enable them to make an informed decision to consent to or to refuse medical treatment. This right is extended to all competent adults in all but emergency situations (when consent to treatment is assumed for the duration of the emergency). However, the affirmation of this right was hard won.

### Right to Refuse Treatment

***Pre-1960s situation.*** Two common-law traditions—bodily integrity and informed consent—are antecedents to the patients' rights and right-to-die movements in this country (Hill & Shirley, 1992). In 1914 the *principle* of the rights of patients to control their health care was assured by law. As Benjamin Cardozo, Justice of the New York Court of Appeals, wrote in the case of *Schloendorff v. Society of New York Hospital,* "every human being of adult years and sound mind has a right to determine what shall be done with his own body; and a surgeon who performs an operation without his patient's consent commits an assault, for which he is liable in damages (quoted in Hill & Shirley, p. 6). Although the findings in this case were binding only in New York, the decision expressed a principle that was applicable to all states.

Before the 1940s, the right to control one's health care rarely came into question because little could be done medically for life-threatening illnesses. Physicians, frequently with the support and assistance of the patients' friends and family members, were present simply to make the terminally ill persons as comfortable as possible by protecting them from unnecessary physical suffering and emotional distress. Death usually occurred at home with loved ones present. Furthermore, with the support of the patients' relatives and friends, physicians frequently did not tell their patients that the patients were terminally ill, largely because of their untested belief that if they told them, the patients would lose all hope and die quickly and in despair.

The end of World War II heralded the beginning of spectacular advances in health care. Strides in pharmacology, such as the development of antibiotics, and technological progress, such as the maturation of mechanical ventilation, dialysis machines, cardiopulmonary resuscitation, organ transplantation, and artificial nutrition and hydration, are examples of the sophisticated care that became available to cure illnesses, alleviate suffering, and extend life. Americans began to believe that rather than being a natural process, death was an enemy that could and should be conquered, regardless of the cost in dollars or human suffering (Quill, 1993).

***Post-1960s situation.*** As the patients' rights movement gathered momentum in the 1960s and 1970s, a number of patients successfully sued their physicians for not disclosing their diagnoses and for not providing information about treatment options. These suits had two primary results: they provided vital support for the legal principle of informed consent and stimulated a shift in physicians' attitudes toward patients' participation in the medical decision-making process. Although this shift in attitudes is not yet as complete and widespread as it should be, the findings of two often-quoted surveys demonstrate its significant scope. Whereas 90 percent of the physicians surveyed in the 1950s routinely kept terminal diagnoses from their cancer patients, 97 percent of the physicians who were polled in 1978 routinely informed their cancer patients of terminal diagnoses (see President's Commission, 1983).

By the late 1980s, the right of competent adults to refuse treatment was well established. As far as competent adults are concerned, the basic difficulty lies not with the law, but with the gap between the law and the reality of Americans' decision-making behavior. Surveys and polls (for example, Gallup & Newport, 1991) have found that no more than 20 percent of Americans have prepared advance directives.

This attitude toward death still prevails in the 1990s; consequently, the human and financial costs attached to this attitude are enormous (Callahan, 1987; Emanuel & Emanuel, 1994). In a vast number of cases, health care providers use medical technology to heal and to extend and improve life. However, for a number of reasons, physicians are increasingly using the same technology to prolong the dying process. The fear of malpractice suits, training that emphasizes fighting death at all costs, financial pressures, and pressure from families are among the reasons for this overuse of technology (personal communication with M. Meyer, coordinator, educational program, Choice In Dying, August 1993). Regardless of the reasons for prolonging the dying process, as dying is extended, so, too, is the suffering and indignity attached to it. By supporting and condoning this use of technology *if* it disregards individuals' wishes, society runs the risk of stripping patients of their right to make informed choices.

### Rights of Incompetent Patients

Many of the laws and policies concerning end-of-life decisions came about as a result of questions raised since the 1970s relating to competence. By law, adults are considered competent to make such decisions if they can demonstrate an understanding of their conditions and the probable outcomes of treatment and nontreatment (Hill & Shirley, 1992). The two central questions with which patients' rights advocates continue to wrestle are, How can end-of-life decisions be made for individuals who were once competent, but have become incompetent for some medical reason (for example, an accident that results in a persistent vegetative state)? and How are end-of-life decisions made for individuals (including infants and minor children and persons with profound developmental disabilities) who have never been competent? Two much-publicized court battles, the Karen Ann Quinlin case in 1976 and the Nancy Cruzan case in 1990, defined the parameters of current thinking and law about how incompetent individuals' end-of-life wishes can be adequately determined and who should make these determinations.

***Quinlin case.*** The first broad public debate about end-of-life decisions began in relation to the Quinlin case in 1976. Karen Ann, aged 21, who was in a New Jersey hospital in an irreversible coma, became dependent on mechanical respiration and artificial nutrition and hydration. Her father, believing that she would not want to continue living in this condition, petitioned the court to appoint him her legal guardian for the purpose of removing the respirator. The physicians and the state attorney general opposed Mr. and Mrs. Quinlin, and the court denied Mr. Quinlin's request. When the New Jersey Supreme Court overturned this decision in May 1976, physicians removed Karen Ann from the respirator (Choice In Dying, 1993a).

The New Jersey Supreme Court's decision in this case was the first state supreme court decision concerning a right-to-die matter and was critical for the patients' rights and right-to-die movements for two primary reasons. First, it was the first judicial decision to enunciate a *constitutional* right to refuse treatment. The courts again confirmed that individuals had a right to make decisions to refuse medical treatment even though the refusal might hasten the end of their lives. Second, the courts set a precedent by affirming that in the absence of formal advance directives, a patient's family could provide effective *substituted judgment* and, in consultation with a physician, make end-of-life decisions without resorting to the courts (Choice In Dying, 1993a).

***Cruzan case.*** In 1983, physicians diagnosed Nancy Cruzan, aged 24, as being in a permanent and irreversible vegetative state as a result of an automobile accident. Nancy continued in that state, maintained with artificial nutrition and hydration, for seven years. After watching her condition worsen for three years, her family fought, first in the Missouri courts and later in the U.S. Supreme Court, for permission to have the artificial nutrition and hydration withdrawn.

The Missouri courts denied the Cruzans' request on the basis that they did not have "clear and convincing evidence" that Nancy would have wished to have artificial nutrition and hydration removed. Although a state may choose not to impose a "clear and convincing" evidence standard, the U.S. Supreme Court affirmed Missouri's right to do so (Choice In Dying, 1993a).

The importance of this decision for the patients' rights and right-to-die movements is threefold. It not only recognized a constitutional right to refuse medical treatment, but treated artificial nutrition and hydration as a medical procedure that could be refused and underscored the validity of advance directives. Opinion written in conjunction with the Court's decision was that had Nancy Cruzan prepared a living will and appointed a health care agent, her parents could have satisfactorily demonstrated her wishes to the courts (Choice In Dying, 1993a).

In addition to its support of advance directives, the U.S. Supreme Court spoke to decision making on behalf of incompetent patients. As Fade (1993) pointed out, in her concurring opinion, Justice Sandra Day O'Connor "expressly encouraged states to continue as a 'laboratory' for innovative approaches to medical decision making on behalf of incompetent patients" (p. 35).

Individual states began to pass laws about end-of-life decision making in 1976. That year California passed the California Natural Death Act, which allowed individuals, in certain carefully defined circumstances, to plan, *in advance,* for the kind of treatment they would receive at the end of life. Other states followed and, by 1992, all 50 states and the District of Columbia had legislation recognizing some form of advance directive (Fade, 1993).

## Vehicles for Making End-of-Life Decisions

"Advance directive" is a general term that applies to two kinds of legal documents that permit one to specify, in writing, instructions about future medical care. These documents go into effect in the event that a person becomes unable to speak for himself or herself because of a serious illness or incapacity. Each state regulates the use of advance directives differently, but in general, individuals may change their advance directives as frequently as they wish, and the documents become *legally valid* as soon as they are signed in front of the required witnesses (Choice In Dying, 1993b).

A durable power of attorney may go into effect when an individual is temporarily incapacitated, but usually a living will goes into effect *only* when two circumstances exist: (1) it must be determined that the individual is at the end of life and will die regardless of which interventions are used, so that intervention would only prolong the dying process, and (2) the person must be unable to speak for herself or himself. Furthermore, in contrast to a popular misconception that advance directives are used only to limit care, these documents can also be used to specify the types of care an individual wishes to receive and how long that care should continue.

### Living Wills and Durable Powers of Attorney

***Description of documents.*** The two types of advance directives that are used most commonly are the living will and the durable power of attorney for health care (sometimes referred to as a health care proxy or health care agent). In general, people use living wills to document the types of care they would like either to receive or not to receive if, at the end of life, they cannot speak for themselves. For example, many documents specify not only the individual's general wishes about death-prolonging interventions, but also specific wishes with regard to artificial respiration, hydration, and nutrition; they may also indicate the level of pain medication that is preferred.

In the durable power of attorney, the individual specifies a spokesperson and decision maker who will act in the event that he or she is unable to communicate. This agent has authority to make all medical decisions for the patient, ranging from hiring or firing physicians to stopping life support. Many experts believe that the strongest possible statement of one's end-of-life decisions is made through the preparation of *both* a living will and the appointment of a durable power of attorney for health care (personal communication with the staff and Board of Directors, Choice In Dying, September 1994).

***Barriers to use.*** There are three major concerns associated with the use of living wills and durable powers of attorney for health care. One concern, as was mentioned earlier, is that few people actually prepare advance directives. The results of polls (for example, Gallup & Newport, 1991) suggest that only a small number (about 20 percent) of individuals who could have advance directives actually do, although this percentage is slowly increasing.

Part of the problem is simply the lack of awareness of the importance of advance directives. However, polls suggest that there is increasing awareness of the availability of these documents, owing to the highly publicized legal cases, the Patient Self-Determination Act, and the work of several national organizations whose programs are focused in this area.

Another reason that people do not have advance directives is that there is some confusion about how to obtain them. Although many attorneys prepare advance directives for their clients, free or low-cost forms and instructions for preparing living wills and durable powers of attorney for health care are available from a number of sources, such as state health departments, hospitals, and national organizations like the American Association of Retired Persons and Choice In Dying. Choice In Dying's public services also include a toll-free telephone line staffed by professionals who counsel individuals about preparing the forms and ensuring that the forms will be honored.

The second major area of concern is societal and emotional barriers to confronting mortality. People who find it hard to face death find it difficult to make the decisions required to prepare a living will, appoint a health care agent, or even discuss the issues with loved ones and health care providers (Callahan, 1993). Because physicians find it just as difficult or more difficult to confront their patient's mortality, the medical profession as a whole, as well as many individual physicians, have not been leaders in teaching about or encouraging the use of advance directives.

The third major area of concern is that the health care system does not consistently honor the advance directives that patients provide. One problem is that people frequently file their advance directives with other important papers, in essence, making them unavailable. In the absence of the actual documents, the wishes documented in them may not be clearly communicated to providers. Public education efforts have begun to focus heavily on the importance of giving physicians, health care agents, and loved ones copies of these documents and discussing wishes with them.

Once the contents of advance directives are known by physicians and health care facilities, patient's wishes are honored in the majority of cases. Most of the situations in which providers are reluctant to honor requests to withdraw or withhold treatment occur when there were no advance directives, and the patient's wishes were not expressed clearly by any other means; there was disagreement about whether the patient's condition truly was terminal; or the patient's wishes and the provider's values or beliefs did not agree.

Changes are occurring, however. Patient advocacy organizations and the mass media are providing significantly more public education. Because the states all adopted legislation concerning advance directives, physicians are less likely to resist following them. Efforts also are under way to improve the ways that medical students are taught to deal with end-of-life issues. All these efforts are beginning to lower the barriers to the use of advance directives (personal communication with Mathey Mezey, Independence Foundation Professor of Nursing Education, New York University Division of Nursing, and Michael Mulvihill, professor, Albert Einstein College of Medicine). Because social work practice focuses on helping clients take more control of their lives, if social workers are educated about the use of advance directives, they can encourage their clients to prepare and use them.

### "Do Not Resuscitate" (DNR) Orders

A DNR order is an additional way in which end-of-life decisions can be made known. In inpatient settings, it is becoming common for physicians to reach an agreement with terminally ill patients that if the patients' hearts stop, no cardiopulmonary resuscitation will be provided. A DNR order is signed by a physician and placed on a patient's medical chart. If a patient is incompetent, the health care proxy or agent is a party to the decision, basing his or her permission on the patient's living will or previously stated wishes. DNRs are being written more frequently as research findings about the limitations of cardiopulmonary resuscitation are being disseminated more widely (Bonnin, Pepe, Kimball, & Clark, 1993; Murphy et al., 1994).

Nonhospital DNRs are yet another means of making one's end-of-life wishes known. As more and more people are choosing to spend their final days at home, it has become apparent that some type of a formal "do not treat" instruction is needed for emergency medical personnel. Without such instructions, emergency medical personnel generally are required to provide cardiopulmonary resuscitation (Kavolius & Amon, 1994).

Nonhospital DNRs are usually physicians' orders that must be prepared and signed by patients' physicians. They are relatively new arrivals in the field of advance directives. Laws governing them differ substantially from state to state, emergency medical personnel and physicians still have limited knowledge about them, and their usefulness has not been clearly documented (Kavolius & Amon, 1994). Until this area is better defined and understood, experts who provide advice or care for patients who wish to die at home are likely to advise simply that emergency assistance *not* be sought when patients' hearts stop.

### Surrogate Decision Making

Surrogate decision making is a legislatively authorized means of allowing families or close friends to make treatment decisions for patients who either have not prepared a living will or appointed a durable power of attorney for health care (Fade,

1993). As was suggested by the discussion of the Quinlin and Cruzan cases, much of the legal debate and proceedings concerning end-of-life decision making has centered on the wishes of patients who are unable to speak for themselves *and* do not have advance directives.

Traditionally, next of kin or close friends played an important role by helping physicians determine what end-of-life treatment decisions to make for incompetent patients. However, as the practice of medicine became increasingly regulated and as physicians became more vulnerable to and concerned about malpractice litigation, physicians were less willing to rely on this informal method of decision making. In response to the breakdown in informal decision making, states have passed statutes governing surrogate decision making (personal communication with Peter Tuteur, MD, and Bry Benjamin, MD, board members, Choice In Dying). By 1994, 24 states and the District of Columbia had enacted statutes authorizing surrogate decision making in the absence of advance directives that take into consideration the following issues: Can what the patient would have wanted be adequately determined? If so, who should make the decision, and what constraints or supervision should be imposed on the decision making? (Choice In Dying, 1994).

To address these issues, the statutes generally specify the order in which family members and close friends can be called on to serve as surrogate decision makers. They also specify that in the absence of reasonable knowledge about a patient's wishes, the surrogate is required to consider the patient's personal, moral, and religious beliefs when making decisions or if these beliefs are not known, to consider the patient's best interests.

These statutes usually specify that decisions about withholding or withdrawing life-sustaining treatments are enforceable only if incompetent patients are in a terminal condition that can reasonably be expected to cause death within a short time (usually six months) or are in a permanently unconscious or persistent vegetative state. Finally, the statutes generally specify that at least one physician must concur with the attending physician's diagnosis of a patient's condition.

As of 1994, 26 states had not enacted surrogate decision-making statutes. In addition, most individuals and health care providers believe that it is preferable for patients to speak for themselves, at least by means of advance directives (Choice In Dying, 1994). Therefore, even in the presence of surrogate decision-making statutes, experts continue to recommend that people should prepare both a living will and a durable power of attorney. The living will permits a person to specify his or her preferred end-of-life treatment, and a health care agent who has direct knowledge of these wishes can be a powerful advocate. In contrast, a court-appointed surrogate may or may not vigorously represent the individual's wishes and may not be the person the patient would have wanted to make the decisions.

## Legislative Issues

### State Laws

Only two types of advance directives—the living will and the durable power of attorney for health care—are relevant for all competent adults. However, decision making about end-of-life treatments is complex because the laws governing the use of these documents vary from state to state (see Table 1). Although all the states and the District of Columbia have legislative provisions authorizing some form of end-of-life decision making, the differences have significant implications for the ways in which the documents should be prepared.

Although the differences among state laws make it particularly important that individuals have access to documents specific to the states in which they live, there are some features that are common to most state statutes. First, all statutes include the concept that the advance directive becomes effective only when the patient is unable to make and communicate his or her wishes for treatment. Second, most statutes include three conditions that are generally associated with patients who cannot make or communicate their treatment wishes: terminal illness, permanent unconsciousness, or a persistent vegetative state. The definition of "terminal" (that death would occur without the use of life support) in many statutes is broad enough that the statutes cover patients with some form of dementia like Alzheimer's disease or other progressive debilitating conditions, such as amyotrophic lateral sclerosis (Lou Gehrig's disease).

Most of the state statutes protect health care providers from civil and criminal liability related to withdrawing or withholding treatment. They also may provide a "conscience" clause for facilities that, for religious or moral reasons, do not permit withdrawing or withholding treatment.

State legislation has been evolving as medical technology continues to develop and as the public debate about the ethical and social policy aspects of end-of-life decision making proceeds. In 1993, 11 states either passed new statutes or changed their existing statutes, and 18 did so in 1992 (Choice In Dying, 1994). The purpose of many of these changes was to remove restrictions. To deal

TABLE 1
**Major Variations in State Legislation on End-of-Life Decision Making**

| Provision | Number of states with a statute |
|---|---|
| Authorizes both a living will and durable power of attorney | 45 states and the District of Columbia |
| Authorizes only a living will | 2 states |
| Authorizes only a durable power of attorney | 3 states |
| Authorizes surrogate decision making | 24 states and the District of Columbia |
| Authorizes nonhospital do-not-resuscitate orders | 24 states |
| Authorizes the explicit refusal of nutrition and hydration in living wills | 34 states |
| Requires nutrition and hydration in all but limited cases (in living wills) | 1 state |
| Explicitly authorizes a health care agent to order the withdrawal of nutrition and hydration | 32 states |
| Explicitly or implicitly defines some form of permanent unconsciousness as a qualifying condition in living-will statutes | 38 states |
| Explicitly or implicitly defines some form of permanent unconsciousness as a qualifying condition in durable power of attorney statutes | 48 states |
| Has pregnancy restrictions in living-will statutes | 34 states |
| Has preganancy restrictions in statutes on health care agents | 14 states |
| Criminalizes assisted suicide by common law | 10 states and the District of Columbia |
| Criminalizes assisted suicide by statute | 34 states |

SOURCE: Choice In Dying. (1994). *Right-to-Die Law Digest*. New York: Author.

with state-to-state differences, many state statutes explicitly recognize advance directives from other jurisdictions as long as they conform to the statutes' provisions. There is, therefore, incremental movement toward what many experts now believe would be the ideal legislation, which would allow for the broadest possible individual decision making; would be either uniform across states or allow reciprocity among the states' documents; and would authorize living wills, durable powers of attorney, and surrogate decision making. An example is the proposed Uniform Health Care Decisions Act, approved by the national Conference of Commissioners on Uniform State Law in 1993 and the American Bar Association in 1994.

**Federal Legislation**

Expressing concern about how infrequently competent adults were preparing advance directives, Congress enacted legislation in 1990 proposed by Senators John C. Danforth and Daniel Patrick Moynihan. Implemented in 1991, this legislation, known as the Patient Self-Determination Act (P.L. 101-508), requires inpatient health care facilities that receive federal reimbursements to tell all adult patients, on admission, about their right, under state law, to have advance directives and to indicate on patients' charts if the patients have advance directives. The law also requires facilities to have a formal, written policy about advance directives and to educate their staffs and the public about these documents. It contains a "conscience clause" that authorizes state laws on advance directives to permit facilities to refuse, on moral or religious grounds, to honor advance directives if they inform patients of this fact and provide, if requested, a referral to another facility.

Implementation of the act has been flawed. According to a survey by the Joint Commission on Accreditation of Health Care Facilities (Alcenius, 1993), many facilities either do not have a policy or implement an existing one only minimally. In addition, the law has serious defects as a vehicle for stimulating the preparation and use of advance directives.

These defects involve the time at which conversations about advance directives are begun, and the lack of required follow-up. The point of admission to a hospital is one of the least advantageous times to ask patients to consider executing advance directives because they are ill, anxious, and generally not prepared to make significant life decisions. Furthermore, there are no requirements that a patient's actual advance directives must be placed in the medical chart (rather than just a notation that they exist) or that discussions, past the time of admission, must be held with patients who have no directives.

Although the Patient Self-Determination Act has had some influence on increasing the number of persons who have advance directives, Senators Danforth and Moynihan recognized that the law could be amended to correct its defects. Therefore, they proposed amendments that they plan to attach to whatever health care reform bill is proposed in 1995 (personal communication with Senator Danforth, June 1994).

## Use of Advance Directives by Special Groups

### Special Communities

Historically, the academic and public debates about right-to-die issues have taken place among generally well-educated, Caucasian, middle-aged and older middle-class individuals. Repeated surveys have suggested that the majority of those who seek specific information about advance directives also come from these demographic groups. In addition, it appears that more women than men request such information (data collected from membership surveys conducted in 1992 and 1993 by Choice In Dying). For a variety of reasons, special population groups (people of color, people with disabilities, and people with the acquired immune deficiency syndrome [AIDS]) are not well represented either in the debate about end-of-life decisions or among those who have prepared advance directives.

Although spokespersons for various special communities may articulate the arguments in slightly different ways, there are three primary reasons why special population groups have not embraced the concept of advance directives. First, these groups encounter enormous barriers to obtaining equitable access to the health care system. The purpose of advance directives is to document and ensure an individual's participation in his or her own treatment decisions. However, living wills have been associated with limiting care, and as was noted earlier, there is a widespread misperception that living wills are synonymous with stopping treatment. Many people who have difficulty obtaining care are uncomfortable with the notion of stopping what they have worked so hard to obtain. Many experts in the field believe that when living wills are understood as tools to empower, rather than to deprive, their use will become more widespread by special populations.

Second, there is an ostensible antithesis between focusing on living the best life possible and focusing on preparing for death. For example, although people with AIDS clearly face premature death, one of the major convictions within the AIDS community is the importance of *living* with AIDS; thus, people with AIDS, particularly those who have been newly diagnosed, have been reluctant to deal with end-of-life decision making (personal communication with Florent Morellet, board member, Choice In Dying, and the staff of the Gay Men's Health Crisis, August 1994). People in other special communities also focus on leading productive lives in the face of many hurdles. As public attitudes toward death continue to shift from avoidance to acceptance of it as a life-cycle event, the use of advance directives by special populations may become more widespread.

Third, people of different ethnic groups, particularly people of color, confront death and dying in different ways. The results of anthropological studies have suggested that no single theory of grief or approach to death and dying is applicable to everyone (Rosenblatt, 1993). Because the concepts underlying the development and use of advance directives emerged in the United States, these directives may not be compatible—at least as used now—with the beliefs and practices of individuals from other cultures. Studies of the applicability and use of advance directives by minority groups have begun only recently, and the results are still pending (presentation by Sean Morrison, MD, fellow in Geriatric Medicine, Mt. Sinai Medical Center, at Choice In Dying, May 4, 1994).

### Minors

With only certain well-defined exceptions, courts consider minor children legally incompetent to make decisions about medical treatment (Fade, 1994). However, such decision making is complex and emotionally laden and thus is frequently subject to resolution in the courts.

Although the courts generally look to parents to make these decisions, a parent's right to do so is not absolute. With regard to terminating treatment for a child, a court may overrule a parent's decision to stop treatment if physicians believe that treatment should be continued, particularly if it clearly would be beneficial. If the outcome of treatment is not clear, a court tries to take into consideration such factors as what is known about the child's preferences, the risks associated with treatment, and the community's medical standards of practice. Another factor that affects a court's decision is the nature of the child's illness and his or her age; for example, treatment for newborns is governed by a federal law that favors continuation of treatment (Fade, 1994).

The situation is more complex when parents wish to continue treatment in the face of health care providers' arguments that treatment is futile. At least one high-visibility case—Baby "K"—is now in the courts, and its outcome is not yet clear (*New York Times,* February 20, 1994).

Decision makers are beginning to treat a special category of minor children differently. In discussing the situation of "the mature minor," Fade (1994) noted that "children who are able to appreciate the consequences of accepting or refusing medical treatments are [now being] given the right to make decisions for themselves." An example of this trend, Fade stated, was the well-publicized case in which a Florida judge upheld the right of a 15-year old to refuse to take life-sustaining medication following the failure of a liver transplant. Older children, those who are married but less than age 18, and some chronically ill children who may be more mature than their age would fall into this category.

## Emerging Trends and Issues

As most of the previous discussion suggested, there is much flux in the area of end-of-life decision making. Public and professional perceptions and attitudes toward death and dying are shifting, the empowerment of patients to make end-of-life decisions is steadily gaining credence, and the law is evolving to support such empowerment. In the wake of these changes, certain issues will receive greater attention. Because public policy and law on these issues have not yet been determined, social work will have the opportunity to provide leadership based on the profession's long-held values. Among the most important of the emerging issues are assisted suicide (and alternative options), medical futility, health care reform, and special concerns of women.

### Assisted Suicide

This subject has been discussed in various arenas for many years. However, in June 1990, when Dr. Jack Kevorkian assisted a 54-year-old woman with Alzheimer's disease to take her own life, the media brought the public debate about physician-assisted suicide to the forefront. Because of Kevorkian's high visibility, the emotionally charged nature of the issues, and the volume of his well-publicized activities, few groups or individuals do not have strong opinions about physician-assisted suicide. On one end of the spectrum are those who argue that under no circumstances is it defensible to take one's own life or help another commit suicide. At the other end of the spectrum are those who believe that both suicide and assisted suicide are personal decisions with which society should never interfere.

The debate tends to be confused, particularly because important distinctions among terms are blurred. Specifically, *suicide* is the active, unassisted taking of one's life, whereas *physician-assisted suicide* is the act of making the means of suicide, such as a lethal dose of a drug, available to a patient who can then commit suicide. In contrast, *euthanasia* (both active and passive) is the act of taking another's life, presumably one who is suffering from an incurable, intolerable condition or disease. Finally, a distinction is made between *voluntary euthanasia,* when a patient explicitly requests such an action, and *involuntary euthanasia,* when someone else makes the decision on behalf of the patient (Meier, 1994).

***Legal issues.*** As Table 1 indicates, by virtue of statute or common law, assisted suicide is illegal in most jurisdictions. The medical profession has actively rejected making physician-assisted suicide legal. However, the profession's spokespersons, such as representatives of the American Medical Association, acknowledge that many physicians quietly assist patients to end their lives when they are clearly terminal and experiencing uncontrollable pain and intolerable suffering. Both physicians and many laypersons argue that legalizing physician-assisted suicide is risky because it is difficult to build in appropriate safeguards against abuse. Other professional organizations, such as NASW (1994) have enacted policy positions that, on the basis of current law, strongly caution members not to "deliver, supply, or personally participate in the commission of an act of assisted suicide when acting in their professional role" (p. 60). NASW policy states, however, that a social worker may accompany a client who is taking his or her own life and distinguishes "being with" a client from participating in the commission of an act of assisted suicide.

Similarly, although many people believe that physicians should be free to assist those who are suffering, cannot take their own lives, and expressly request assistance (Taylor, 1993), voters have rejected initiatives to legalize physician-assisted suicide in Washington State and California and only narrowly approved a limited measure in Oregon (November 1994).

***Public awareness and education.*** The debate continues to rage, and the public is clearly ambivalent about physician-assisted suicide. However, nurse-attorneys and social workers at Choice In Dying who work with people about issues of death and dying have noted that those who come for referral for help with a suicide frequently are responding from desperation and the lack of knowledge about options. Counselors who deal with end-of-life decisions indicate that many clients move quickly away from the notion of suicide when they are given information about hospices and other resources to support dying at home and are given assistance in negotiating with providers about adequate pain control. Thus, much more public awareness and professional education about end-of-life options would make a significant contribution to the end-of-life decision-making process and, perhaps, clarify the parameters of the debate about assisted suicide.

**Medical Futility**

Much of the public discussion about end-of-life decisions, as well as patients' private conversations with their physicians, concern the determination of medical futility. In most situations, when patients' conditions are such that further treatment would produce negligible or no benefits and would serve primarily to prolong the dying process, further treatment is deemed "medically futile." Most individuals who prepare advance directives indicate that when further treatment is futile, they want all but comfort care to be withdrawn or withheld. Most of the time, these individuals, their loved ones, and their physicians are comfortable with this instruction.

However, the actual situation is often far more complex than the foregoing description of medical futility would suggest. First, in many medical situations, it is difficult to determine clearly when further treatment would be medically futile. Indeed, the state of medicine is such that physicians may disagree about such determinations. In addition, continuing treatment that is not life sustaining may be important to patients, their families, and loved ones for a variety of religious, moral, and ethical reasons.

Therefore, the concept of medical futility and its definition are the subjects of increasing professional and public debate. This country has not resolved even the most basic issues, such as who should define medical futility (the physician, the patient, family members, or others), what the criteria for the definition should be (medical, religious, or ethical), and additional issues, such as how scarce health care resources should be allocated particularly in medically futile situations.

**Economic Concerns and Health Care Reform**

Much of the debate about health care reform has turned on the issue of cost containment. Health care costs in the United States have spiraled out of control in recent decades, and a variety of attempts to control the speed of this growth have failed. When President Bill Clinton was elected in 1992, major, meaningful health care reform was an important part of his agenda.

One issue that is frequently addressed by health care and economic experts in the debate on cost containment is the enormous contribution of medical care at the end of life to total health care expenditures. In this regard, some experts have assumed that people who prepare advance directives are likely to choose less expensive, less technologically dependent care at the end of life (see Weeks, Kofoed, Wallace, & Welch, 1994). If this assumption is correct, it would be logical to assume that if every adult prepared an advance directive, costs associated with terminal care would drop.

The first problem with these assumptions is that preparation of an advance directive is not a guarantee that less care is requested. An advance directive can indicate an individual's wish to be kept alive as long as possible, just as easily as it can reflect the wish to limit care, although no studies have examined the proportion of individuals whose living wills request ongoing care.

In addition, only a few studies have tested the second assumption—that advance directives serve to contain end-of-life health care costs. The findings of the two major studies on this issue (Schneiderman, Kronick, Kaplan, Anderson, & Langer, 1992; Weeks et al., 1994) differed substantially, and no definitive answers to the questions are available.

However, the relationship of advance directives to the containment of health care costs raises serious concerns. On the one hand, if advance directives are meant to reflect individual choice and self-determination, pressure on people to limit treatment at the end of their lives may be problematic. What may save dollars for society may not be in an individual's best interest. On the other hand, it can be argued that health care resources are scarce and that society may have come to some consensus about allocating resources for other than end-of-life care. Before a well-informed position can be taken on this issue, more data are needed at least about what instructions people include in their advance directives and how these instructions actually affect the costs of terminal care.

**Women's Issues**

Miles and August (1990) expressed concern about whether there are systematic biases against honoring women's preferences about medical treatment at the end of life. There is at least anecdotal evidence to suggest that there may be.

As was indicated earlier, 34 states include some pregnancy restrictions in their statutes on living wills, and 14 states include restrictions in their statutes on health care agents. These restrictions generally indicate that a woman's wishes to limit medical treatment at the end-of-life can be ignored if she is pregnant. Although the issue of the rights of women versus the rights of fetuses is too complex to be summarized here, it is worth noting that the issue is being debated and that the courts are slowly making some changes.

With regard to the extent to which women's end-of-life decisions are honored, Miles and August's (1990) study suggested that the courts tend to view a woman's decision about end-of-life treatment as more emotionally derived than a man's. However, this was the only study of its type, and although anecdotal evidence of this bias appears relatively frequently, no conclusive data are available.

## Role of Social Work

### Complexity of Issues

End-of-life decision making is a health care matter. It is an ethical, religious, cultural, and emotional matter. It concerns the allocation of individual, family, and societal resources. It concerns individuals' deepest and most dearly held fears, values, and beliefs. In short, it is complex, delicate, and often controversial. Modern society ill prepares people to face the profound challenge of preparing to die.

As Callahan (1987) noted, "Death, we are told, is no longer a hidden subject. That is at best a half-truth." In fact, the continued masking of death and end-of-life decisions is sustained by the absence of a consensus and social policy on such issues as the allocation of health care resources, assisted suicide, and medical futility; the absence of social, ethical, religious, and cultural supports that encourage accepting and planning for death as a life-cycle event; and the absence of professionals who are trained and comfortable in helping people and organizations deal with these issues.

However, there is increasing agreement that coming to terms with end-of-life issues, making informed decisions, and ensuring that loved ones are untroubled by these decisions and that society honors them are vital life tasks for everyone. It is with just such a constellation of responsibilities that social work's values and skills can make a significant contribution.

### Policy and Practice Directions

Aging and health care are emphasized in the social work curricula, and practice opportunities with older and seriously ill individuals abound. However, a review of the curricula of schools of social work, discussions with students and faculty, and an examination of papers presented at professional meetings suggest that there is, as yet, little sustained or in-depth social work focus on the enormously difficult subjects of end-of-life planning and decision making.

Nevertheless, the profession's commitment to clients' self-determination and empowerment and its skills in working with individuals, families, and communities make social work practitioners and policymakers ideal groups to demonstrate leadership in developing policy and working with individuals to make end-of-life decisions. If the profession is to fulfill these roles, shifts in the profession's focus in the educational, research, practice, and policy arenas must take place.

The first important shift should be educationally based and concentrate on both students and current practitioners. Social work programs and professional meetings already cover a vast amount of content. However, additional content is needed on empowering individuals and families to confront death as a life-cycle event and to prepare for death by taking more control over their health care at the end of life and on preparing social workers to act as mediators when individuals and health care providers are in conflict about specific end-of-life decisions. In addition, students and practitioners need actual practice opportunities to work with clients and health care providers to encourage appropriate, effective end-of-life decision making.

In the practice arena, as solo practitioners and in interdisciplinary settings, social workers can provide leadership by demonstrating how to assist people to make end-of-life decisions and to ensure that such decisions are honored. Particularly in the practice arena, social workers can be instrumental in increasing the number of people who are informed about end-of-life decisions, have thought through these difficult decisions, and have prepared advance directives.

Applied research about end-of-life decision making is sadly lacking from any professional perspective. However, because of the myriad settings in which social workers practice, from community agencies, workplaces, and health care facilities to private offices and clients' homes, professionals encounter multiple opportunities to look systematically at how individuals go about end-of-life decision making and what barriers they encounter. Social work would add much to the nation's knowledge base in this important area if it would sponsor applicable research.

Finally, from a policy perspective, social work has long been a champion of the values and ethics underlying end-of-life decision making. By being one of the first professional organizations to implement a formal policy in this area, NASW (1994) has highlighted its capacity to lead the public debate and response to this highly emotional, but critical, issue. By developing additional policies on end-of-life decision making and minors, women, and ethnic minorities and on such end-of-life issues as medical futility and the allocation of health care resources, NASW can further its significant role in this area.

## Conclusion

In 1975 Butler published a seminal book about aging entitled *Why Survive? Being Old in America.* In an oft-quoted passage, Butler described what many believe is one of the sanest and most humane approaches to the fear of death:

> What can be done about humankind's uneasy knowledge that life is brief and death inevitable? There is no way to avoid our ultimate destiny. But we can struggle to give each human the chance to be born safely, to be loved and cared for in childhood, to taste everything the life cycle has to offer, including adolescence, middle age, perhaps parenthood and certainly a secure old age; to learn to balance love and sex and aggression in a way that is satisfying to the person and those around him; to push outward without a sense of limits; to explore the possibilities of human existence through the senses, intelligence and creativity; and most of all, to be healthy enough to enjoy the love of others and a love for oneself. After one has lived a life of meaning, death may lose much of its terror. For what we fear most is not really death but a meaningless and absurd life. (p. 421)

Social work is pertinent at all parts of the life cycle, but particularly when life is difficult. If the profession chooses to help society deal better with death—one of the most difficult parts of life—it will have made yet another pivotal contribution to humankind. An awareness of the complexities and means of end-of-life planning and decision making; knowledge of the legal, ethical, cultural, religious, and health care elements of the process; and comfort with the techniques to empower those in the process are essential to making this contribution.

## References


Alcenius, M. (1993, June 17). *Regulation and end of life decisions in acute care.* Paper presented at a meeting of the Hastings Center Task Force on Law and Clinical Care, New York.

Bonnin, M. J., Pepe, P. E., Kimball, K. T., & Clark, P. S. (1993, September). Distinct criteria for termination of resuscitation in the out-of-hospital setting, in concepts in emergency and critical care. *Journal of the American Medical Association, 270*(12), 1457–1462.

Butler, R. N. (1975). *Why survive? Being old in America.* New York: Harper & Row.

Callahan, D. (1987). *Setting limits: Medical goals in an aging society.* New York: Simon & Schuster.

Callahan, D. (1993). *The troubled dream of life: Living with mortality.* New York: Simon & Schuster.

Choice In Dying. (1993a). *Case review.* New York: Author.

Choice In Dying. (1993b). *Questions and answers: Advance directives and end-of-life decisions.* New York: Author.

Choice In Dying. (1994). *The right-to-die law digest.* New York: Author.

Emanuel, E. G., & Emanuel, L. L. (1994). The economics of dying: The illusion of cost savings at the end of life. *New England Journal of Medicine, 330,* 540–544.

Fade, A. (1993, Fall). A right-to-die update: The states expand and refine advance directives. *Experience: The magazine of the Senior Lawyers Division, American Bar Association.*

Fade, A. (1994). Tipping the scales. *Choices: The newsletter of Choice In Dying, 3*(3).

Gallup, G., & Newport, F. (1991, January 6). *Mirror of America: Fear of dying.* Report of a Gallup poll conducted in November 1990 and reported by the Gallup Poll News Service.

Hill, T. P., & Shirley, D. (1992). *A good death: Taking more control at the end of your life.* Reading, MA: Addison-Wesley.

Kavolius, A., & Amon, M. (1994). *Survey of emergency medical personnel understanding of non-hospital do not resuscitate orders* (study in progress). New York: Choice In Dying.

Meier, D. E. (1994). Doctor's attitudes and experiences with physician-assisted death: Review of the literature. In J. M. Humber, R. F. Almeder, & G. A. Kasting (Eds.), *Physician assisted death: Biomedical ethics review 1993* (pp. 5–24). Totowa, NJ: Humana Press.

Miles, S., & August, A. (1990). Courts, gender, and "right to die." *Law, Medicine & Health Care, 18*(1–2), 85–95.

Murphy, D. J., Burrows, M. D., Santilli, S., Kemp, A. W., Tenner, S., Kreling, B., & Teno, J. (1994, February 24). The influence of the probability of survival on patients' preferences regarding cardiopulmonary resuscitation. *New England Journal of Medicine, 330*(8), 545–549.

National Association of Social Workers. (1994). Client self-determination in end-of-life decisions. In *Social work speaks: NASW policy statements* (3rd ed., pp. 58–61). Washington, DC: NASW Press.

Patient Self-Determination Act of 1990. P.L. 101-508, 104 Stat. 1388.

President's Commission for the Study of Ethical Problems in Medicine and Biomedical Research. (1983). *Deciding to forgo life-threatening sustaining treatment.* Washington, DC: U.S. Government Printing Office.

Quill, T. E. (1993). *Death and dignity: Making choices and taking charge.* New York: W. W. Norton.

Rosenblatt, P. (1993). Cross-cultural variation in the experience, expression, and understanding of grief. In D. P. Irish, K. F. Lundquist, & V. J. Taylor (Eds.), *Ethnic variations in dying, death, and grief* (pp. 13–19). Washington, DC: Taylor & Francis.

Schloendorff v. Society of New York Hospital, 211 N.Y. 125, 129–130.

Schneiderman, L., Kronick, R., Kaplan, R., Anderson, J., & Langer, R. (1992). Effects of offering advance directives on medical treatment costs. *Annals of Internal Medicine, 117,* 599–606.

Taylor, H. (1993, December 6). Majority support for euthanasia and Dr. Kevorkian increases. *The Harris Poll.* New York: Louis Harris Associates.

Weeks, W. M., Kofoed, L. L., Wallace, A. E., & Welch, H. G. (1994). Advance directives and the cost of terminal hospitalization. *Archives of Internal Medicine, 154,* 2077–2083.

**Karen Orloff Kaplan, ScD,** is executive director, Choice In Dying, Inc., 200 Varick Street, New York, NY 10014.

**For further information see**

Advocacy; Aging Overview; Bereavement and Loss; Bioethical Issues; Civil Rights; Direct Practice Overview; Ethics and Values; Families: Direct Practice; Family Caregiving; Health Care: Direct Practice; Health Care: Reform Initiatives; HIV/AIDS: Direct Practice; Hospice; Hospital Social Work; Human Rights; Legal Issues: Confidentiality and Privileged Communication; Long-Term Care; Managed Care; Patient Rights; Person-in-Environment; Policy Practice; Professional Conduct; Professional Liability and Malpractice; Social Welfare Policy; Social Work Practice: Theoretical Base; Social Work Profession Overview; Suicide.

**Key Words**

advance directives
assisted suicide
end-of-life decisions
health care proxy
living wills

# Environmental Health: Race and Socioeconomic Factors

**Kevin M. Gorey**

The professional discipline of social work concerns itself with the health of individuals and the health of the environments in which they live because of its person-in-environment philosophy. Typically, the most appropriate target for the assessment of and work with clients on an array of problems in living is at their environmental interactions. Compton and Galaway (1989) noted that social work's theoretical framework is based on the relative equilibrium–disequilibrium between people and their environments or the person–situation model. There seems to be a rather close fit between this social work perspective, particularly as it applies to what has come to be called *macro* or *indirect practice,* and the primarily preventive discipline of public health, which concerns itself with the maintenance and improvement of the health of populations through collective or social actions (Last, 1988).

The health issues the author has considered are the following:

- family health (child abuse and neglect, teenage pregnancy)
- social health (crime perpetration and victimization, housing problems)
- mental health (depression, substance abuse)
- physical health (acquired immune deficiency syndrome [AIDS], cancer).

These problems were selected because of their importance and exemplary value across a range of social work content areas, such as children and families, health and disabilities, life-span development, and social work settings. This entry examines the association of socioeconomic-related risks for these health problems among black and white populations in North America. The entry also considers the usefulness of specific analytic epidemiologic methods, which are useful tools in public health as well as in general social work practice.

## Socioeconomic Environment and Health Problems

Socioeconomic conditions, a particularly salient aspect of the physical–social–cultural environment, may be a potentially unifying construct in the observation of an array of health problems. Social class or socioeconomic status (SES) has been found to be associated with a variety of health outcomes, from infant mortality to the diverse health problems experienced by frail elders (Gorey, Cryns, Choi, & Zwana, 1990; Marmot, Kogevinas, & Elston, 1987; Polednak, 1991).

The importance of the socioeconomic environment and the implications of its strong associations with individual as well as social health problems has been underscored by the changing economic climate of the 1980s and early 1990s. During this period in the United States, for example, the poorest quintile lost 20 percent of their relative wealth, whereas the richest quintile gained 10 percent. As a result, the proportion of the nation's population that is poor increased by 41 percent (U.S. House of Representatives, Committee on Ways and Means, 1992).

Another issue of import is racial and ethnic group status. Race in the United States is highly associated with the continuum of health problems from infancy to later years, and it is also highly associated with SES. As the gap between the wealthiest and poorest Americans has widened in the 1980s and early 1990s, so has the black–white socioeconomic gap. For example, in New York State, which has the largest population of black people in the United States (slightly more than 10 percent of the black population in the entire country), the SES of black people relative to white people diminished approximately 20 percent between 1980 and 1990 (Gorey, 1994).

It has been suggested that adjustment for SES may nearly abolish any observed black–white racial group health problem differences. Such an analytic strategy as adjusting for the "cofounder" SES in racial group comparative analyses may be misleading from a preventive public health perspective. In the real world, differences exist between races in terms of living conditions. For example, the prevalence of poverty among black people in the United States has been estimated to be three to eight times the rate for white people, depending on the operational measure of impoverishment used (Gorey, 1994; Gorey & Vena, 1994). Although these differences may be controlled for in the abstract world of statistical constructs, such strategies may result in the loss of useful information.

## New York State Study

Gorey (1994) conducted a study of SES and health problems in New York State. The study constructed an ecological census tract or neighborhood-based measure of socioeconomic inequality that was computed as a function of prevalent impoverishment (the proportion of tract residents below 200 percent of the federally established poverty criterion, which is a function of annual income and household size) and accumulated material resources (home value and car ownership) (U.S. Bureau of the Census, 1992). Black tracts, that is, census tracts in which 400 or more black people resided in 1990, were compared with other tracts on socioeconomic inequality in the upstate region of New York, which included Buffalo, Rochester, Syracuse, and Albany.

### Socioeconomic Inequality

The study resulted in much convergent and divergent validation of the operational definitions of socioeconomic inequality and of the black tract. The index of socioeconomic inequality was found to be highly associated with prevalent impoverishment, unemployment, receipt of public assistance, employment in low-paying service occupations, and housing vacancies, among others. In upstate New York, 81.9 percent of black people were found to live in black tracts, the vast majority adjacent to each other in central inner-city areas. Nearly 20 percent of the New York tracts were so categorized: They generally have 10 percent or greater black representation, and on average the majority of their populations (55.2 percent) are black.

Approximately two-thirds (64.6 percent) of the black census tracts were categorized as high on socioeconomic inequality, that is, low SES, whereas less than 10 percent (7.9 percent) of the other or predominantly white tracts were so categorized. Black people were observed to experience an eight-fold greater exposure to low SES.

### Health Problems Caused by Low SES

The population-attributed risk (PAR) percentage or etiologic fraction was used as a summary measure to describe more fully the SES–problem relationship among black people and white people. The PAR percentage is defined as a fraction of disease (or problem) experience in a population that would not have occurred if the effect associated with the exposure of interest (for example, low SES) were absent (Miettinen, 1974). The PAR percentage is calculated as follows: $[P(RR-1)/P(RR-1) + 1] \times 100$ (Cole & MacMahon, 1971). As the PAR percentage is a function of both the strength of the association of a given risk factor (RR) with disease and the prevalence of the risk factor (P) among the population at risk, it has implications for disease prevention and public health planning.

The average rate ratio findings on SES–problem associations across problem domains (black, RR = 1.86; white, RR = 1.98) and the SES prevalence estimates (high socioeconomic inequality prevalence among black people, 64.6 percent, and among white people, 7.9 percent) were entered into the PAR percentage algorithm. The result was an estimate that the average problem PAR percentage due to low SES among black people is five times that for white people (35.7 percent versus 7.2 percent). Thus, more than one-third of the health problems experienced of black people may be accounted for by socioeconomic factors, whereas less than one-tenth of the similar problems among white people may be accounted for by such phenomena.

## Health Trends

The author has observed the following trends that may be of particular import and interest to social work and public health practitioners alike:

1. Black people in North America experience a diverse range of family, social, mental health, and physical health problems at rates that are threefold those of white rates.

2. The magnitude of the associations between SES and health problems generally are similar for black and white people.
3. Prevalent exposure to low SES-related risks among black people is eight times greater than that observed among white people.
4. The gross attribution of health problem risk due to low SES exposure estimated across the problems of child abuse and neglect, teenage pregnancy, crime perpetration and victimization, depression, substance abuse, AIDS, and cancer is perhaps five times greater among black people.

### Genetic versus Environment Causation

Gorey (1994) offered a socioeconomic explanation for health problems, which is an alternative to the more typical genetic explanation for these observed racial group differences. In another study (1994, unpublished), Gorey found that, when genetic versus environmental causation was discussed in the literature, more than 75 percent favored inheritance. Rushton (1988) offered an exclusively genetic explanation for racial group differences across a range of behaviors from intelligence to temperament and sexual behaviors. However, when Gorey and Cryns (in press) conducted a secondary analysis of the 100 studies in Rushton's review, they found that less than 1 percent of the behavioral variability could be accounted for by race.

Reviewing the discussion sections of articles in this field, one repetitively reads the genetic–environmental point–counterpoint arguments. After observing the stark black–white differences across such a wide array of biological and psychological phenomena, nearly exclusively demonstrating the relatively poorer health status of black people, there are two possible general conclusions: (1) Either black people are an innately inferior race, or (2) the environment operates on black people in a different and relatively discriminatory manner as compared to white people. The author's findings support the latter conclusion.

The finding that SES seems to have a similar impact on black and white people leads to the inference that observed racial group health problem differences are not an effect of race per se. However, that is not to say that race does not matter. In the United States, and in New York State in particular, race matters very much: Prevalent exposure to socioeconomic inequality—or poverty—is eight times more likely among black people as compared to white people; therefore, the proportion of health problems attributable to low SES is probably five times greater among black people.

### Genetic Inheritance

It should be noted that this conclusion does not minimize the importance of genetic inheritance. It is a commonly accepted epidemiologic principle that 100 percent of any disease is environmentally caused and at the same time 100 percent inherited as well (Rothman, 1986). This author's central findings are consistent with this principle as it may apply to a broad array of health problems and behaviors. Simply put, there is probably some genetic component of nearly all diseases; however, whatever genetic factors may be involved are likely to be equally salient among white and black people.

## Implications for Social Work Practice

### Changes in Social Work Education

The *NASW Code of Ethics* (NASW, 1994) refers four times to the profession's responsibility to engage in problem-solving work with those who are politically disenfranchised or discriminated against on the basis of race. Given this expressed commitment and the profession's person–situation practice framework, one would expect social workers to be leaders in building the knowledge base for inquiry into the interrelationship of socioeconomic factors, race, and health problems. Yet very little of the empirical research has been reported in the social work literature. It may be imagined that literally tens of thousands of social workers are currently working in relevant agencies, that the information for perhaps hundreds of potentially important articles is extant in file drawers across the nation. Disseminating information through the professional literature is one more way of sharing our experiences with each other. This critical step in our work with any client system should be taught at graduate schools of social work as a central element of the generalist model, rather than an optional one.

### Macro Interventions

The author's findings also imply clearly the need for macro social interventions in solving, or better yet preventing, problems that are related to disparate economic conditions experienced by differential racial and ethnic groups. Those in positions of economic power typically attempt to explain away social problems by pointing to the "defectiveness of the victims" (Joffe & Albee, 1988). Social workers, who are committed to advocating for those who are relatively powerless—which usually means poor—ought to lead the way in not blaming the victims. Such a mission is probably not possible without a concomitant commitment to systematic empirical research. Again, it is the graduate schools of social work that are ultimately responsible for attracting and effectively training a significant number of social workers as macro advocates and research practitioners.

### Epidemiologic Methods

The usefulness of the general epidemiologic model for preventive social work practice has been discussed at length elsewhere (Siefert, 1983, for example). Some specific epidemiologic analytic methods are extremely helpful, particularly in evaluating the clinical or policy significance of research practice findings. For example, traditional epidemiologic measures of effect size such as the prevalence ratio are useful in cross-sectional or prevalence surveys, and risk ratio (RR) is useful in longitudinal, incidence, or treatment and intervention studies. They have, I think, great practical and intuitive appeal for social workers who are often called on to evaluate the size of a problem in the community or the effect of their intervention.

For example, a researcher might conduct a quasi-experiment to evaluate the effectiveness of group work intervention with adult female survivors of childhood sexual abuse. The findings—that the incidence of problem improvement among women who participated in group work was twice that of women on an agency waiting list—could be interpreted and reported in several ways:

1. RR = 2.00 (95% confidence interval: 1.75, 2.25)
2. $\chi^2 = 5.69, p < .05$
3. $F = 6.68, p < .05$
4. $p < .05$

Which outcome would be most readily explainable at a staff meeting, to a scientifically naive colleague, or even to the reader of a social work journal? I believe that it would be the risk ratio described in item 1.

In addition, in my experience, such measures are effective aids in teaching social work research courses. They tend to facilitate the mutual interpretation of clinical and statistical significance, and in so doing they provide students with a satisfactory answer to their oft-asked question: "I'm going into direct practice, so why do I have to take this 'Scientific Methods in Social Work' course?"

## Conclusion

It is likely that such SES correlates as access to preventive health care over the life course or lack thereof, socioecological stress (Gorey, 1994; Harburg et al., 1973a, 1973b), behavioral and lifestyle risks associated with impoverished environments, and the like are primarily responsible for health problems. The specific pathogenesis or causal pathways for most health problems and particularly those of a social nature, such as child abuse and violent crime, remain unknown.

It is important to note that knowledge of causation is not necessarily required to prevent a problem. For example, cholera was effectively prevented long before its specific causation was well understood (Snow, 1855). Strong associations allow for predictions that can be empirically tested in the field. However, given the strong observed SES–health problem associations, as well as their remarkable consistency across a broad range of reviewed problems, it seems plausible to argue that some factors highly associated with low SES or impoverishment are causally related to family, social, mental health, and physical health problems. Therefore, addressing the problem of severe economic impoverishment, targeting, for example, pockets of vulnerability such as inner-city areas where a large number of people in racial and ethnic groups live, will prevent a large number of health problems among the entire population.

## References


Cole, P., & MacMahon, B. (1971). Attributable risk percent in case-control studies. *British Journal of Preventive Social Medicine, 25,* 242–244.

Compton, B. R., & Galaway, B. (1989). *Social work processes* (4th ed.). Belmont, CA: Wadsworth.

Gorey, K. M. (1994). *The association of socioeconomic inequality with cancer incidence: An explanation for racial group cancer differentials.* Doctoral dissertation, State University of New York at Buffalo.

Gorey, K. M., & Cryns, A. G. (in press). Race differences in behavior: A quantitative replication of Rushton's (1988) review and an independent meta-analysis. *Personality and Individual Differences.*

Gorey, K. M., Cryns, A. G., Choi, N. E., & Zwana, J. M. (1990). Long-term care service use by black and white vulnerable elders: A comparative analysis. *Journal of Minority Aging, 11,* 39–60.

Gorey, K. M., & Vena, J. E. (1994). Cancer differentials among United States blacks and whites: Quantitative estimates of socioeconomic-related risks. *Journal of the National Medical Association, 86,* 209–215.

Harburg, E., Erfurt, J. C., Hauenstein, L. S., Chape, C., Schull, J. W., & Schork, M. A. (1973a). Socioecological stress, suppressed hostility, skin color, and black–white male blood pressure: Detroit. *Psychosomatic Medicine, 35,* 276–96.

Harburg, E., Erfurt, J. C., Hauenstein, L. S., Chape, C., Schull, J. W., & Schork, M. A. (1973b). Socioecological stressor areas and black-white male blood pressure: Detroit. *Journal of Chronic Disease, 26,* 595–611.

Joffe, J. M., & Albee, G. W. (1988). Powerlessness and psychopathology. In G. W. Albee, J. M. Joffe, & L. A. Dusenberg (Eds.), *Prevention, powerlessness, and politics: Readings on social change* (pp. 53–56). Newbury Park, CA: Sage Publications.

Last, J. M. (Ed.). (1988). *A dictionary of epidemiology* (2nd ed.). New York: Oxford University Press.

Marmot, M. G., Kogevinas, M., & Elston, M. A. (1987). Social/economic status and disease. *Annual Review of Public Health, 8,* 111–135.

Miettinen, O. S. (1974). Proportion of disease caused or prevented by a given exposure, trait, or intervention. *American Journal of Epidemiology, 99,* 325–332.

National Association of Social Workers. (1994). *NASW code of ethics.* Washington, DC: Author.

Polednak, A. P. (1991). Black–white differences in infant mortality in 38 standard metropolitan statistical areas. *American Journal of Public Health, 81,* 1480–1482.

Rothman, K. J. (1986). *Modern epidemiology.* Boston: Little, Brown.

Rushton, J. P. (1988). Race differences in behavior: A review and revolutionary analysis. *Personality and Individual Differences, 9,* 1009–1024.

Siefert, K. (1983). Using concepts from epidemiology to teach prevention. In J. P. Bowker (Ed.), *Education for primary prevention in social work* (pp. 54–74). New York: Council on Social Work Education.

Snow, J. (1855). *On the mode of communication of cholera* (2nd ed.). London: Churchill.

U.S. Bureau of the Census. (1992). *1990 census of housing and population: Census tracts, New York State.* Washington, DC: U.S. Government Printing Office.

U.S. House of Representatives, Committee on Ways and Means (1992). *Overview of entitlement programs: 1992 green book.* Washington, DC: U.S. Government Printing Office.

### Further Reading

Barr, K.E.M., Farrell, M. P., Barnes, G. M., & Welte, J. W. (1993). Race, class, and gender differences in substance abuse: Evidence of middle class–underclass polarization among black males. *Social Problems, 40,* 314–327.

Geronimus, A. T., & Korenman, S. (1993). Maternal youth or family background? On the health disadvantages of infants with teenage mothers. *American Journal of Epidemiology, 137,* 213–252.

Gladstein, J., Slater-Rusonis, E. J., & Heald, F. P. (1992). A comparison of inner-city and upper-middle class youths' exposure to violence. *Journal of Adolescent Health, 13,* 275–280.

Jones-Webb, R. J., & Snowden, L. R. (1993). Symptoms of depression among blacks and whites. *American Journal of Public Health, 83,* 240–244.

Lillie-Blanton, M., Anthony, J. C., & Schuster, C. R. (1993). Probing the meaning of racial–ethnic group comparisons in crack cocaine smoking. *Journal of the American Medical Association, 269,* 993–997.

Osmond, M. W., Wambach, K. G., Harrison, D. F., Levine, P., Imershein, A., & Quadagno, D. M. (1993). The multiple jeopardy of race, class, and gender for AIDS risk among women. *Gender & Society, 7,* 99–120.

Saunders, E. J., Nelson, K., & Landsman, M. J. (1993). Racial inequality and child neglect: Findings in a metropolitan area. *Child Welfare,* 72, 341–354.

Wolfner, G. D., & Gelles, R. J. (1993). A profile of violence toward children: A National study. *Child Abuse & Neglect, 17,* 197–212.

**Kevin M. Gorey, PhD,** is assistant professor, University of Windsor, School of Social Work, 401 Sunset, Windsor, Ontario, N9B 3P4, Canada.

### For further information see

Adolescent Pregnancy; Child Abuse and Neglect Overview; Community Needs Assessment; Criminal Justice: Class, Race, and Gender Issues; Ecological Perspective; Ethics and Values; Genetics; Health Services Systems Policy; HIV/AIDS Overview; Housing; Income Distribution; Income Security Overview; Legal Issues: Low-Income and Dependent People; Mental Health Overview; Person-in-Environment; Policy Analysis; Poverty; Primary Health Care; Psychosocial Approach; Public Health Services; Public Social Services; Social Planning; Social Welfare Policy.

**Key Words**

environmental health
health
mental health
race
socioeconomic factors

# Epistemology

**Leon F. Williams**

In recent years, social work scholars have been preoccupied with philosophical issues that call into question the foundation of knowledge on which social work is built. This entry examines some of the philosophical issues that have been raised, especially those having to do with social work epistemology.

*Epistemology* (from the Greek *epistēmē*, "knowledge") is understood as the study of the nature and validity of knowledge, or knowledge of knowledge ("Epistemology," 1986). Typically, epistemologists examine the degrees of certainty and probability and the differences between knowing (with certainty) and believing (without being certain). Their concern is primarily human knowledge—not that it is certain that knowledge is the primary province of humans.

In all inquiries—philosophical, religious, psychological, and scientific—there are common epistemological problems. The social and behavioral sciences, including social work, have generally been plagued by problems of methodology because they glean only proximate truth from their efforts. They must infer a great deal from their methodologies, hoping that their measures accurately reflect what exists in reality. The quality of the knowledge on which such inferences are made is the subject of this entry.

This entry does not present a chronology of the study of the theory of knowledge throughout the ages; rather, it focuses on the main currents of thought that appear to have relevance to social work knowledge. The subject matter of epistemology is vast, and an enormous number of books by numerous individuals of various disciplines and from several nations have been written on the subject. Furthermore, such a brief format precludes the coverage of the main currents in non-Western philosophy bearing on the subject, so that only the major ideas and major contributors in Western philosophy are summarized in this entry.

## Epistemology as a Discipline

On the premise that "the proper study of mankind is man" (as Alexander Pope noted in *An Essay on Man*), epistemology deals with every aspect of human life that is of fundamental importance. The cardinal premise of epistemology is the assumption that to act wisely in the world, it is necessary to know the world and understand it. This is not to say that if a person knows, he or she will inevitably use the knowledge wisely. It is a fact that the past several centuries have witnessed rapid advances in knowledge that have made possible higher standards of life, but it is equally a fact that this knowledge has often increased human misery. New knowledge has been known to provoke a sense of insecurity, even a loss of morale. The universe has been shown to be comparably more vast and the role of humans in it less significant than had once been assumed. Advances in the basic sciences have been disturbing to many people—the manufacture of babies in test tubes, the potential of producing genetically perfect people, the proliferation of nuclear waste as a byproduct of nuclear science, and the possibility that science may be able to look back to the very beginning of the universe. If the world now seems less cozy than it used to be, if its very vastness is forbidding, it is human beings themselves who have discovered the truth about the world—if it is the truth—and who are equally uneasy about their liability to err. Men and women assert confidently what they take to be the truth, only to find later that their assertions are false—hence people's great need to know not only the world around them but themselves, particularly the character and reliability of their own cognitive powers ("Epistemology," 1986, p. 601).

The roots of the current argument over the epistemological basis of social work can be traced back to the classic disciplines of metaphysics, psychology, the philosophy of the mind, and logic. In fact, metaphysics, the study of the nature of existence, is divided into three parts: ontology, cosmology, and epistemology. Epistemology is also associated with a number of subdisciplines that either directly or indirectly influence the knowledge base of social work, one being psychology and another being sociology (although sociology is not thought of as part of the original metaphysics).

Initially, psychology (the science of the mind) and epistemology were closely related branches of philosophy because both were concerned with the genesis of knowledge. In fact, both used the analytic processes or methods of logic. Psychology broke from philosophy, and thus from metaphysics, logic, and epistemology, when it adopted the standard of empiricism early in the 20th century. Sociology (the study of society), on the other hand, fashioned its own quasi-epistemology, known generally as the sociology of knowledge. These two sources forge a link between the philosophical concerns of epistemology and the philosophical systems in social work having to do with individual functioning and cognitive activity and with social organization.

## Certain Truth and Valid Truth

Knowledge or knowing, especially knowing that something is the case (is, in fact, true), is central to epistemology. Epistemology draws a line between *knowing that* and other forms of knowing (*knowing why, knowing how,* and *knowing where,* for example). *Knowing that,* is a statement signifying that something has the value of *truth*. However, before one can know, a crucial aspect of human activity must come into play—the act of *perception;* that is, the person must be in sensory contact with the world to perceive it. Epistemology in most forms treats the link between the individual and objects perceived in the real world as distinct, a function of perception in which the table one sees is only a *representation* of the characteristics of the true table. So the epistemologist is concerned, then, with factual knowledge of the world that is the consequence of material objects in that world and human beings' consciousness of that world. It is a duality. Material objects exist in space and time; have substance; are solid; and can affect other objects, including the human body. The observer gains knowledge of the world through his or her sensory organs. He or she registers those objects through his or her senses, acquiring *sense data* (or *sensa*).

**Fallibility of Human Senses**

However, it is not quite that simple because human senses are notoriously fallible. Take, for example, optical illusions, in which the mind can be tricked into seeing things that are not really there. According to the epistemologist, the fact that a person experiences sense data does not allow her or him to assert that physical objects exist in reality. *Phenomenologists,* representing another branch of epistemology, argue that inferring the existence of physical objects on the basis of experiencing sense data is wholly unnecessary. The observer is sure only of the phenomenon—of what appears. This is a kind of conditional knowing; when the observer says, "I see a table here," all that is meant is, under certain conditions, "If I look in the right direction, if there is sufficient light, and so forth, I shall see a brown rectangular figure" (or whatever). In essence, the phenomenalist doctrine suggests that without loss of meaning, one can always reduce a *physical-object sentence* into a *sense-data sentence* and use that transformation to attain truth about the world (Becker & Dahlke, 1942). Neither sense-data theory nor phenomenalism resolves the basic problem of perception in knowing—the former, because it does not resolve the issue of the existence of the real world (because our perception of it is wholly representational), and the latter, because it produces a series of reductive statements based on the act of perception that can continue ad infinitum.

**Rationalism**

The main doctrines of epistemology are associated in one way or another with theories of knowledge that emphasize (1) reason, (2) sense experience, or (3) concept and language. Reason as a basis for deriving knowledge of the world is most closely associated with the rationalist school, or *rationalism,* which began in ancient Greece and survives in one form or another today. Beginning with Plato and medieval scholasticism and continuing in the work of Thomas Aquinas, the history of rationalism can be traced through the philosophies of René Descartes (1576–1650), Benedict de Spinoza (1632–1677), Gottfried Leibniz (1646–1716), Immanuel Kant (1724–1804), and Georg Hegel (1770–1831) and through the intellectual ferment of the 17th and 18th centuries. Rationalists reject the idea of sense experience, feeling that rational knowledge is distinct from sensory awareness. In fact, the rationalist doctrine suggests, in Descartes's (1637/1960) words, that he who would seek truth must not hope to find it in sensory impressions; he must "detach his mind" from the senses—"nor again in blundering imagination but in pure intellectual apprehension of truth resistant to doubt." Descartes's famous dictum, *"Cogito, ergo sum"* ("I think, therefore I am"), is familiar to all.

The method most closely associated with the process of pure reasoning is mathematics, and Leibniz (1675/1991), the father of symbolic logic, sought to wed the two disciplines. Kant (1781/1990), himself a rationalist, rejected dogmatic rationalism of the type associated with Descartes by denying that rational analysis alone could provide new knowledge. He argued, as did other critics, that pure thought *and* sensory impressions were the sources of representation of the world that could supply objective and valid judgments of things. Hegel (1817/1991), on the other hand, admitted no distinction between thinking about the world and knowing the world; he believed that the fundamental reality is not *matter,* but the *mind.* His was an extreme or ideal form of rationalism that averred that "what is rational is real and what is real is rational"; that the mind in perception undergoes a dialectical process of *thesis, antithesis,* and finally *synthesis,* the latter state occurring when others, using rational methods, arrive at similar conclusions.

Various branches of rationalism sought either to enhance rationalist doctrines or to transcend them. Spinoza (1675/1949), for example, sought to classify the stages of rationalism. His highest and most ideal stage was called *scientific intuition.* In other words, the highest form of rationalism is a sort of intuitive phase that is also almost antirational—a form of pure perception, existing outside rational boundaries. Bergson (1919/1965) argued similarly that intellectual understanding needs to be augmented and corrected by *pure intuition*.

Among the many critics of rationalism, the most strident was Kierkegaard (1844/1985), who argued that the life of reason dehumanizes; the intellectual fails to commit himself or herself, so that, in a sense, he or she never exists; for to *be,* one has to choose, to take sides. The rational versus intuitive arguments and the existential stance of Kierkegaard are reflected in the current debate over epistemologies in social work. Some have argued for the rational underpinnings of the field; others have contended that practice and its intricacies are beyond rationalist tenets and can best be understood on an intuitive level, without biasing presuppositions; and still others have argued, as did Kierkegaard, for greater commitment and activism and against dehumanizing objectivity.

## Empiricism and Certainty

Empiricism is both contemporaneous with and encompassing of the historical developments in rational philosophy. Empiricists differ, however, because they set for themselves the task of understanding the role not only of reason, but also of the senses and the function and use of concepts and language in the production of knowledge. Modern empiricists appear to proceed from the premise that the sense-data argument is limiting because it begins at the point where sensory data are acquired. They argue that the material world preexisted and that sensing it confirms its existence and only demonstrates what is already known.

Of critical importance to empiricist philosophy is the a priori assurance of the existence of a physical world. The *quality* of that assurance is a basic problem. A person may be certain of the existence of an external world containing objects but not certain that that world is exactly as it appears to his or her senses. She can undertake tests and check to determine the quality and relationship of objects. She may even be doubtful about the existence of an object before her because it is either an optical illusion or a hallucination. Nevertheless, she would feel certain that the physical world exists, that she herself exists, that other people exist, that two plus two make four, and that no two objects can occupy the same space at the same time. These would be called *certainties.* Ultimately, the challenge to the empirical epistemology is to discern the nature of certainty.

Rationalists would argue that a person gains complete certainty through the exercise of *reason,* which can provide him or her with absolute truth ("knowing that" truth), at least in those areas of inquiry in which reason is free to function. Reason, according to them, cannot or does not mislead, as do the senses. Reason is *positive* because it contains no hypothetical elements and no inference is involved; reason is intuitive and direct, providing *infallible knowledge,* or the knowledge of what is necessary. As was mentioned, critics of rationalism are legion, and most focus their criticism on the rationalists' claim that infallible knowledge is an outcome of pure reasoning. The fact is that people often think they know something is true when it is essentially false and can have that falsity confirmed by others. Most philosophers would accept a distinction between infallible knowledge and certain but fallible knowledge. No one would contend that one cannot know anything. People can be certain in their knowledge of where they live, how much they earn, their social security number, and the like. What lies beyond their ability, according to empiricists, is having infallible knowledge of *absolute truth.* This argument permits the discipline to accept less than absolute or valid truth as a foundation for the knowledge in the discipline.

## Belief and Truth

Generally, all epistemological schools would agree that *belief* is not the same thing as knowledge. Belief is emotional, signifying a trust in or an esteem for something. Beliefs are formed from sense perceptions—touching, feeling, smelling, seeing, hearing, and tasting—and memories of them, as well as from the inferences drawn from them. In addition, the observer is a person with sensations: pleasure, love, joy, pain, sorrow, and the like. From these sources and from *hearsay knowledge* (knowledge gained from others), the person acquires a body of information that he or she uses as evidence to check whether certain statements are acceptable or not. This process yields *justified belief,* or *justified true belief,* one that has been subjected to exhaustive testing of the senses, of the state of the observer, and of hearsay. Justified belief approaches at least the level of certain knowledge in a hierarchy of knowledge that includes (1) probable knowledge, (2) certain knowledge—not knowledge of absolute truth, and (3) infallible knowledge of absolute truth (Cornman, 1981; Williams & Hopps, 1988).

## Empiricism and Concept Formation

Aside from knowledge, the empiricist is also interested in language and the part it plays in human thinking. In fact, it has been argued that without language there can be no thinking. The basis of language is the *concept;* however, there is no unity of thinking regarding the nature of concepts. What modern empiricism appears to have done is wed the idea of the *concept* to thinking and communication and to a scientific method or process. Thus, naming and classifying objects (in reality) is a major element in empirical methods. The empiricist presumes a direct link between the senses and the real world—that sensory data can be refined into symbols of the real world called *concepts* and that concepts can be further ordered as systems of classification of real-world objects that can be communicated to others through language and can be operationalized and used as tests of the existence of that world.

The most important function of the concept is its use in the hypothetico-deductive method of logic. Social workers know the process as hypothesis testing, in which concepts associated with a theory are converted into variables that can be manipulated experimentally, with the result that the scientist either confirms or disconfirms the original hypothesis (Hoover, 1984; Singleton, Straits, Straits, & McAllister, 1988). The level of knowledge sought by the empiricists is "certain knowledge," ruling out the possibility of infallible knowledge or knowledge of true cause-and-effect relationships. Using these methods the empiricist finds associations between variables in controlled tests that are used to infer the relationship between objects or things as they may exist in the real world. For example, sets of variables making up hypothetical models of gravity, of rocket-engine thrust, of interplanetary distances, and so on were tested in the laboratory, and the results were used to send a rocket to the moon, although no person had been on the moon. By inference, it was assumed that the moon had mass; was a certain distance from the earth; and could be reached using certain fuels, involving certain telemetry. The assumptions or hypotheses about the moon were confirmed by the astronauts' successful landing on the moon.

## Positivist and Social Laws

A branch of empiricism that deserves attention because it appears frequently in the debate over social work epistemologies is *positivism*. Associated primarily with the philosophy of Comte (1830–42/1980), positivism sought to establish a classification scheme for the sciences. Comte claimed that the mind of humans was characterized by three progressive stages of knowledge (also known as the law of three stages): theological, metaphysical, and positivistic (scientific). He argued that a society passes through these three levels of knowledge as well, arriving at the highest stage, which is the scientific. From this vantage point, a society is then capable of undertaking rational planning for the purposes of fashioning the ideal society. Comte argued strenuously for applying the methods of the natural sciences to the problems of society to discover sociological laws established by scientific means—like laws of physics—that remained unquestioned. Comte's critics (Ewing, 1940/1985; Mach, 1906/1975; Scheler, 1923/1972) attacked his position, pointing out that theology, metaphysics, and science are not a continuum but exist as permanent attitudes of the mind; that they are forms of knowledge characteristic of the mind; and that the three are distinct ways of knowing, and none can substitute for the other.

A more radical form of positivism than Comte's is *logical positivism,* which holds that factual statements about objects beyond experience (meaning not based on empirical or substantive reality), such as the metaphysical and the theological, cannot be held to have meaning and are not to be taken seriously (Ayers, 1936). Critics have countered that according to the positivistic definition, any philosophical statement would be meaningless, including the statement of logical positivism.

## Social Construction of Knowledge

It is important to give at least brief attention to philosophical sociology as one of the disciplines that have influenced social work theory and philosophy. Sociology is a relatively new discipline and is still in the process of defining itself. Sociologists did, however, move to stake out the one area of philosophy that is logically associated with their discipline and have, as a result, effectively broadened the debate over the origins of knowledge. Because sociology is the study of the development of relationships in society, it follows that sociologists would entertain epistemological-like theories about the influence of the group or society on the mental perspectives of individuals. The study of how the sociocultural environment influences thinking is called the *sociology of knowledge*. This subdiscipline is not entirely epistemological in that it rests on a single principle that the sociocultural environment influences individual perceptions of the real world. It entertains aspects of rational, empirical, phenomenological, and sense-data theory and philosophy to build a case for such a relationship.

The earliest statement of the sociology of knowledge appeared in Bacon's (1620/1990) *Novum Organum.* In his thesis, Bacon discussed the idols that rule people's minds. According to him the "raw data" (sensory data taken in by observation) are filtered through the psychological framework of the individual. This framework, in turn, is shaped by the various "idols" that are characteristic of the sociocultural environment, including "idols of the tribe," the characteristics inherent in a species; "idols of the den," characteristics associated with the psychological makeup of the individual; and "idols of the theater," or idols that form the foundation of philosophical systems. Most important, Bacon's work established the relationship between the mind and the sociocultural environment.

The sociology of knowledge appears to have two main currents: (1) *strict determinism,* that *all* ideas held by an individual are the product of the larger society, and (2) *interdependence,* that the production of consciousness is a function of both the society and individual traits and characteristics acting on one another. The strict determinists are represented in the thinking of Marx and Engels (1894/1972) (economic determinism), Mannheim (1936), and Durkheim (1915) and the social–behavioral school of psychology represented by James (1907/1974; 1909/1975), Cooley (1902/1956), and Skinner (1953). Pareto (1935), Scheler (1923/1972), and Dewey (1910/1933), on the other hand, argued that although there are indeed environmental influences on individual perceptions, they are modified by the individual's traits, characteristics, culture, ethnicity, and so forth in a state of reciprocity, or interdependence, with the environment. The major contribution of the sociology of knowledge was to introduce the concept of *paradigms,* points of departure in the conceptual universe that transform our way of thinking about ourselves and the environment. One example is atomic theory, or the theory of relativity. Berger and Luckman (1966) and Kuhn (1970) are the major proponents of this dynamic and engaging theorem. It may be safe to say that the concept of paradigm now exists as a paradigm in that it gave social work theorists a new way of looking at the basic philosophical ideas and theories undergirding the profession.

## Empirical Psychology and Social Work

Psychology, especially the subdiscipline *behaviorism*, presents social work with an ongoing dilemma—in that it has demonstrated that empirically derived theory can be allied with practice. Social work (which borrows heavily from psychological theory) was weaned on psychodynamic, psychological perspectives. In contrast to psychology, social work relies on case and descriptive approaches to the development of knowledge and for the validation of theories. The field's theories of knowledge depend on creative uses of analogies and metaphors to describe complex worker–client interactions and the attributes of the client that lie beneath the surface in the unconscious. Thus, some social work theorists would argue that nothing objective can be observed in a relationship that takes place primarily within the realm of the unconscious. Behaviorism, in particular, rejects the existence of the unconscious and focuses instead on the objectifiable behaviors that create conflicts between the individual and the social environment. Using empirical methods, behaviorally oriented psychologists have shown remarkable success in altering the negative behaviors of autistic and self-mutilating children, stopping bed-wetting, and working with a variety of phobias (Bergin, 1971). Documented successes such as these have evaded social work's interventions. In these proscribed areas, psychologists have demonstrated the efficacy of empirical and quantitative methods to direct practice. Social work seems generally ambivalent about empirically based practice because such practice runs counter to the reigning ideal of psychological determinism at the level of the unconscious.

## Social Work Debate

The current debate over epistemology in social work can be traced to the seminal article by Fischer (1973), which asked, "Is casework effective?" Fischer concluded that on any grounds accepted by the methods of scientific investigation, casework is not effective and could be harmful in some instances. His article elicited a series of public and private debates both for and against the effectiveness of casework and even attacks on the veracity of the author (Falck, 1978). Although the conflict was not resolved, a compromise of sorts seems to have been struck. Casework no longer is considered the primary method in social work, having been replaced, in many cases, by clinical methods and psychotherapy or the integrated methods of generalist practice. Moreover, few, if any, studies have been conducted to examine the effectiveness of social work interventions, and such studies that have been done have been challenged on methodological or philosophical grounds (Reid, 1987).

### Nature of Research

Much of the debate over the theory of knowledge in the profession has generally focused on the nature of research. In fact, it is rare to witness a debate of the epistemological basis of any practice technique or theory. This entry is, of necessity, slanted toward research, although epistemology is not just about research. In most disciplines, methods for testing theories (Kuhn's, 1970 puzzle solving) emerge after philosophical debates have created a general consensus on the nature of *valid truth* in those disciplines—whether the discipline can achieve probable knowledge, certain knowledge, or infallible knowledge with their methods. In social work, the process seems reversed. The focus has been on research and evaluation that generally are not associated with the quality of knowledge expected of the discipline.

The philosophical and methodological foundations of social work *research* have been questioned by a number of critics (Dean & Fenby, 1989; Goldstein, 1990; Haworth, 1984; Heineman, 1981;

Krager, 1983; Rein & White, 1981; Ruckdeschel & Farris, 1981). Common themes in the critics' arguments are related to the inadequacy of the "paradigms" that are commonly taught, used, and accepted by social work researchers. Conventional research methodology has been criticized for placing too much value on quantitative methods, experimental designs, objective measurement, and statistical analysis. Critics suggest that social work research, like much social science research, has borrowed methodologies from the physical sciences that are often ill suited to the study of the ever-changing and illusive complexities of social phenomena.

Some critics who admit that there is a place for "hard-science" methodology in social work nonetheless argue that it has been erroneously equated with "good science" (Reid, 1987, p. 479). They propose instead new "paradigms" that are based on different assumptions about what constitutes valid research (Haworth, 1984). These criticisms and proposals have been vigorously disputed (Geismar, 1982; Hudson, 1982; Ivanoff & Blythe, 1989; Lindsey & Kirk, 1992; Thyer, 1989).

These new paradigms lean heavily on the tradition of qualitative methodology that is equated with such disciplines as social psychology and anthropology (Filstead, 1970; Glasser & Strauss, 1967). In that tradition, the researcher's firsthand knowledge of the phenomena under investigation has essential validity (practice wisdom). Moreover, it is assumed that complex social phenomena can best be understood through careful analysis of the configuration of events in which words (analogies and metaphors), rather than numbers and conceptual categories, are the primary tools of analysis. The advocates of the new paradigm also appear to be calling for a more fundamental reorientation to the nature of knowledge and the means of acquiring it in social work (Reason & Rowan, 1981). However, the methodology (and philosophy) for putting these ideas into practice has not been developed in any detail (Krager, 1983). The philosophical methods of deconstruction and critical philosophy, which will not be gone into here, have a small following, but thus far their contribution to social work philosophy has been negligible.

**Qualitative versus Quantitative Debate**

Although most social work researchers acknowledge that good results can come from qualitative research methods, there is little doubt that many researchers are oriented to an implicit hierarchy of methodologies and give qualitative research a lower place in the methodological hierarchy than quantitative research. The critics would like to see this hierarchy eliminated or, as Haworth (1984) suggested, reversed. In a profession without a clearly developed epistemology, the claims of these critics can be entertained and even embraced without the critics having to demonstrate the relevance of these methods to the profession or its consumers (Thyer, 1989). The arguments for and against quantitative research methods appear to represent ideological poles, rather than the systematic and evolutionary theorizing associated with epistemological inquiries. Thus, a text in social work research can attempt to make a distinction between "positivistic" and "naturalistic" research as the politically correct designation of two broad areas of research that may or may not be opposites or within the same order of classification. However, this type of conceptual device conforms to a history in social work of creating simple dichotomies for the purposes of debate (Grinnell, 1993; Hartman, 1990b).

The stridency of the debate and the quality of the reasoning suggest that factors other than philosophical ones may be contributing to the differences of opinion. Critics have charged that the social work research establishment is captured by an obsolescent philosophy of science, namely, logical positivism (Vigilante, 1974) or logical empiricism (Heineman, 1981). Conventional research approaches are rooted in principles that antedate and transcend these philosophical movements. Given the developmental history of the ideas entertained in the philosophy of science and epistemology, it would seem that modern science is a synthesis of a number of epistemological positions going back to antiquity. No single era or theory is sufficient to describe how science is practiced in the present. No researcher has advocated a pure form of logical positivism or positivism or has staked out a claim for a methodology that is based on strict rationalist principles. Empiricism, or science, appears to combine aspects of logic, rationalism, and positivism.

**Differing Ideologies**

What is most obvious is that social work research, and thus its science, has been generally marginal to the main thrust of the profession, which is individualistic qua psychodynamic (Task Force on Social Work Research, 1991). Psychodynamic principles exist in a social context of least accountability and greater subjectivity, as contrasted with the social group and social accounting approach of most researchers. It is normal for science-trained social work researchers to respect theory and to seek its objective validation through group means using controls. The competition between the two poles is illuminated by the furor over the effectiveness of casework and the emergence of at least two discernible ideological camps, the "naturalists" and the "social advocates." In the near past the split was between advocates of individual change and advocates of social change—the same division but with new terminology. The former ideology is dominated by the clinical movement and private for-profit practice.

The clinical movement that emerged in the 1980s appears to be threatening to undermine the professional character of social work, if not its mission. Because clinical methods (or techniques) are widely associated with the movement to private, entrepreneurial practice, the professing, or vocational (altruistic), aspects of the field are weakened. Every profession relies on vocational motives—commitment to common aims, creativity in the pursuit of professional goals, the diligence of individual professionals, self-monitoring and improvement, a common philosophy, language and knowledge, and professional cooperation in a stable peer-oriented environment—to maintain group cohesion. Kuttner (1993) noted that professions such as medicine, law, education, and the ministry can be debased when individual practitioners think of themselves primarily as entrepreneurs—as private people who are selling their skills to the highest bidder in the market (Kuttner, 1993; Walz & Groze, 1991; Wencour & Reisch, 1989).

### Beliefs versus Logic

If epistemology is a philosophical attempt to discover the origins and validity of knowledge, then little of the debate in social work is epistemological in nature. The debate appears to be mainly influenced by beliefs or belief–value systems or preferred ways of behaving. In a discipline, epistemological arguments, which are based not on beliefs but on logical systems, are offered by their originators, fully and specifically, as to the nature of the knowledge (*probable, certain, infallible,* or *valid knowledge*) that will be found acceptable to that discipline; these original arguments are then extended, elaborated on, critiqued, and revised by succeeding scholars. Eventually, a kind of consensus arises that enables the discipline to advance, to treat certain assumptions as givens, and to lay down general principles for its continued work on the basis of the quality of knowledge that can be derived from its methods. Empiricists, for example, agree that the most one can hope to attain in social science research is *certain* knowledge. Hartman's (1990a) jeremiad would suggest that this level of consensus has not been achieved by social work. People on both sides of the debate argue as though hardened positions have been taken, as if the positions are irreconcilable.

## Can the Issues Be Resolved?

The eminent sociometrician Blalock (1964) wrote, in relation to the problem of inferring causality from research, that reality, or at least our perception of reality, consists of ongoing processes. No two events are ever exactly repeated, nor does any object or organism remain precisely the same from one moment to the next. And yet, as scientists, if we are ever to understand the nature of the real world, we must act and think as though events are repeated and as if objects do have properties that remain constant for some period. Unless we allow ourselves to make such simple types of assumptions, we shall never be able to generalize beyond the simple and unique event. As Hoover (1984) stated, the intricate task of getting people to bridge the differences that arise from the singularity of their experience requires a more disciplined approach to knowledge. Knowledge is socially powerful only if it is knowledge that can be put to use. Social knowledge, if it is to be useful, must be communicable, valid, and compelling.

The most valid and compelling knowledge in social work has been and continues to be knowledge derived from empirical methods. In fact, in their summary of research on social work practice, Reid and Hanrahan (1982) noted that improvements in research methodology, including structured experiments, were at least partly responsible for their optimism for the efficacy of clinical social work methods. Still, a standard of practice based on absolutely rational and objective science could stunt and foreshorten much of the work of the field because little is understood of the natural and intuitive processes in social work or in human interaction. On the other hand, a social work that is free of all expectations of being systematic, accountable, and empirical would leave its clients and the public vulnerable to half-baked theories and techniques imposed by charlatans, quacks, or the simply misguided.

## Sociology of Social Work

The sociology of social work would have us note that within that ideology constituting social work's generally accepted belief about itself is a social mandate. The founders of the profession and a succession of scholars since then have affirmed the social dimension of social work. A social work profession that no longer accepts this mandate would no longer be called social work but something else. If, for example, the field existed as an entirely clinical profession, directing its energies toward intervention with troubled individuals within a limited theoretical framework and without curiosity about the social context of those individuals' lives, could one call it social work?

**Clinical–Individual View**

Within the American culture, social work accepts and supports a dualistic view of people: People are authors of their own destiny, and people are influenced by forces outside themselves. Out of the former stance has developed a clinical–individual enterprise that seeks to treat individuals as givens, as bundles of inherited characteristics who are troubled. The stance that views people as social victims requires that the social worker adopt the stance of an advocate of social change, and through the medium of the individual or the group, try to change oppressive social structures, such as families, organizations, communities, governments, policies, and laws. A profession given only to social change could not long sustain itself (Specht, 1972).

The study of epistemology suggests that the clinical–individual stance has much in common with the philosophies of Kant and Hegel, both of whom assumed that any kind of presuppositions about humans can neither be changed by decision nor refuted by experience—that these presuppositions are above and beyond empirical methods of testing theories (Popper, 1972). There are also overtones of idealistic rationalism insofar as the mind is the author of reality and no other reality is acceptable. Higher intuition is the ultimate measure of this form of rationalism.

**Pragmatism and Progressivism**

Some researchers and social activists seem to be captives of the American philosophical ideal of pragmatism and progressivism (Dewey, 1910/1933) and the philosophical school associated with social behaviorism in psychology—in essence, saying that nothing is meaningful unless it can be validated by experience using the methods now associated with science and empiricism. Another way of putting it is that the truth of our ideas means their power to work (James, 1909/1975). This stance is often misconstrued as positivistic when it is only pragmatic.

Popper (1972) noted that there is a tendency in a group of modern philosophies to unveil hidden motives behind people's actions. The popularity of these views lies in the ease with which they can be applied and in the satisfaction that they confer on those who see through things and through the follies of the unenlightened. This pleasure would be harmless were it not that all these ideas are liable to destroy the intellectual basis of any discussion by establishing a kind of reinforced dogmatism. Psychoanalysis, for example, can always explain away any objections by showing that they are due to the repressions of the critic (in modern parlance, the critic's "denial") (Popper, 1972, p. 652). Many of the discussions of social work epistemology deal in argumentative categories (dogmas) that destroy the basis of rational discussion, and they can ultimately lead to antirationalism and mysticism. Later-day Hegelians in the profession, for example, would argue that all knowledge is relative in the sense that all knowledge is uniquely determined by individual or group history or the uniqueness of each experience. Because knowledge is relative, it cannot be understood by any methodology. Taken to this extreme, there is nothing that need be understood about human beings, thus stifling imagination and curiosity—the stuff that makes one human and creates disciplines.

## Public Character of the Scientific Method

Popper (1972), noting that it is not possible for the individual scientist to be objective, argued that science is misunderstood. Science depends for its validity on its public character, which is intersubjective in nature. *Intersubjectivity* means that humans can perceive reality through their senses and communicate that experience to others. In science, intersubjectivity fosters an atmosphere that corrects for individual fallibility. First, there is something approaching free criticism in science. A scientist may offer his or her theory with the full conviction that it is truth, but this stance will not impress fellow scientists and peers; rather it challenges them: They know the scientific attitude means criticizing everything, and they are not deterred by authorities. Second, scientists try to avoid talking at cross-purposes. They try seriously to speak the same language, even if they use different native languages (Popper, 1972, p. 654).

The modern methods of scientific investigation are the result of historical development. They are not bound to any particular philosophical system but have been worked out through trial and error and in open and public dialogue with other scientists and laypeople. This science is understood by both natural and social and behavioral scientists, and that is a remarkable feat in itself—that people in such divergent fields could find a common ground in a language and methodology that evolved within separate disciplines. The paradigm of which the critics speak is the scientific paradigm, which is so influential that there are no other systems to take its place; even critics must use the language of the scientific paradigm to refute it. It has sustained itself because of its utility in explaining phenomena as divergent as microorganisms, human behavior, and the behavior of solar systems. This is not to say that it is flawless. The critics are partially right. The method does lack sensitivity to the specific instance and the individual case; in its technical–statistical posture, it often ignores the intuitive, judgmental, and metaphorical aspects of practice that constitute the art of social work. Kuhn (1970) was instructive in this regard: He observed that no paradigm is fully explanatory of current reality (p. 23). Paradigms are, by nature, incomplete, explaining only a limited number of phenomena well. Once a paradigm has been established, a host of scientists are kept busy trying to fit the paradigm to current or emerging reality (Popper's "mopping up"). *Normal science* is the routine science carried on between paradigms or scientific revolutions. If the profession determines that the dominant paradigm lacks elements that are essential to it, then the principles of normal science allow for revision and innovation.

## The Compleat Researcher

If one assumes that social work has not fully used or adopted scientific methods (research) to understand and test its theories and methodologies (Lindsey & Kirk, 1992; Wencour & Reisch, 1989; Zimbalist, 1977), then one can accept either that the scientific paradigm is in its infancy in the field and thus has fewer adherents than detractors or that the scientific paradigm is of little value. It is obvious from the literature that the latter choice, the scientific–empirical paradigm, has enjoyed enormous practical success. It has enabled scientists to place astronauts on the moon; to model the building blocks of life in human DNA; to manage whole economies; to find cures for syphilis, diphtheria, and typhoid fever; to increase crop yields; to build technologies; to understand human potential through intelligence, aptitude, and other standardized means; and to discover pharmaceutical products that allow mentally ill people to resume normal lives outside institutions.

None of the foregoing is an argument for any school of thought. However, the nature of paradigms, as defined by Kuhn (1970), is that they are ignored at the peril of the investigator or discipline. One cannot return to the pre-Columbian period in history, although there is an organization dedicated to the 15th-century belief in a "flat earth." The Flat Earth Society is a joke, has few adherents, and has no scientific influence. Paradigms represent sea changes in culture, values, perception, theory, knowledge, and technology. Some groups adapt slower than do others, depending on their starting position. Scientific social work is in its infancy.

### Certain Knowledge

Social work must assume, for the sake of epistemology, that the field can attain certain, if not valid, knowledge about the human condition. To settle for something equal to or less than probable knowledge of the human condition is to settle for knowledge dictated by dogma and naive belief, and that appears untenable in an applied discipline. The profession must also assume that one can have knowledge of and insights into the motives of human beings singly or collectively, through sensory experiences grounded in shared humanity. Given the pubic mandate and philosophy espoused by social work, it would be equally remiss to hold a view that celebrates individuals at the expense of the society of which they are a part. If experience is a necessary ingredient of social work methods, then one must find means of discovering whether that experience is valid; whether the interaction with another did, in fact, lead to desired changes in that person's behavior, attitudes, and so forth; whether the methods are sound; and whether the theories that inform the methods are sound.

### Methods of Validation

One may argue over methods of validation, but, at a minimum, such methods should be communicable, based on shared meaning and similar and familiar units of attention (concepts, or sense data). The results of any chosen method must have the weight of truth; must be believable; must be workable; and, therefore, must achieve at least the level of certain truth before they can widely influence practice or theory. Even if the so-called naturalistic orientation to science prevails, researchers will need to produce the studies (however conceived) or demonstration projects that will provide compelling evidence of the validity of such approaches. Because many of the basic elements in the scientific paradigm have not been adopted by the field, the time does not seem ripe for such a fundamental shift in orientation.

Bearing in mind Blalock's (1964) admonition that a discipline must accept certain assumptions to proceed with its intellectual work, theoretical social work has, instead, staked out positions relative to "styles" of research and not according to the goals of the discipline. Why not, one might ask, use both quantitative and qualitative methods, if doing so will move the discipline forward?

There is nothing in the canon that says that either must be practiced exclusively. If the limitation to quantitative studies is their technical and antihumanistic orientation, why not add a qualitative component to enhance the knowledge furnished by statistical tables? In fact, this may be the future direction of empirical research (Allen-Meares & Lane, 1990).

**Critical Juncture**

The profession of social work is at a critical juncture in its history (Walz & Groze, 1991). It must choose between science and nonscience in the middle of the so-called scientific revolution. The battleground that various protagonists have chosen is research. It seems premature to critique the end product of a discipline without knowing the quality of the knowledge sought. Epistemology comes before investigation. The profession needs to answer fundamental questions about the nature of its knowledge, its discipline, before it can know whether that knowledge is valid (Hartman, 1990a). It needs to determine how much truth it is willing to live with and the quality of that truth. The options for an epistemology of social work are many if one recalls rationalism, phenomenalism, logical positivism, empiricism, pragmatism, existentialism, and a host of lesser currents in epistemology. Fundamental to that epistemology are such issues as these: Can one perceive the unconscious motivations of another? Is the knowledge attained in interpersonal transactions valid (truthful)? Can people communicate such knowledge to each other accurately? Is the knowledge subject to objectification? Is individual knowledge socially conditioned or idiosyncratic? Can the individual influence the pool of socially shared knowledge? Until these and other related questions are answered, much of the social work debate will be stalemated.

## References


Allen-Meares, P., & Lane, B. A. (1990). Social work practice: Integrating qualitative and quantitative data collection techniques. *Social Work, 35,* 452–458.

Ayers, A. J. (1936). *Language, truth and logic.* New York: Dover Publications.

Bacon, F. (1990). *Novum organum*. Chicago: Encyclopedia Britannica. (Original work published 1620)

Becker, H., & Dahlke, H. O. (1942). *Max Scheler's sociology of knowledge. Philosophy and Phenomenological Research, 2,* 310–322.

Berger, P. L., & Luckman, T. (1966). *The social construction of knowledge*. Garden City, NY: Doubleday.

Bergin, A. E. (1971). The evaluation of therapeutic outcome. In A. E. Bergin & S. Garfield (Eds.), *Handbook of psychotherapy and behavior change* (pp. 217–270). New York: John Wiley & Sons.

Bergson, H. (1965). *An introduction to metaphysics: The creative mind*. Totowana, NJ: Littlefield, Adams. (Original work published 1919)

Blalock, H. M., Jr. (1964). Bridging the gap between the languages of theory and research. In H. M. Blalock, Jr. (Ed.), *Causal inferences in nonexperimental research* (pp. 172–173). Chapel Hill: University of North Carolina Press.

Comte, A. (1980). *Cours de philosophie positive*. Indianapolis: Hackett. (Original work published 1830)

Cornman, J. W. (1981). Epistemology. In *The encyclopedia Americana*. (Vol. 10, pp. 517–522). Danbury, CT: Grolier.

Cooley, C. H. (1956). *Human nature and social order*. Glencoe, IL: Free Press. (Original work published 1902)

Dean, R. G., & Fenby, B. L. (1989). Exploring epistemologies: Social work action as a reflection of philosophical assumptions. *Journal of Social Work Education, 25*(1), 46–54.

Descartes, R. (1960). *Discourse on method.* Baltimore: Penguin. (Original work published 1637)

Dewey, J. (1933). *How we think.* Boston: D. C. Heath. (Original work published 1910)

Durkheim, E. (1915). *Elementary forms of religious life*. New York: Macmillan.

Epistemology. (1986). *Encyclopedia Britannica* (15th ed., Vol. 18, pp. 601–623). Chicago: University of Chicago Press.

Ewing, A. C. (1985). *The fundamental questions of philosophy*. London: Routledge & Kegan Paul. (Original work published 1940)

Falck, H. S. (1978). The effectiveness of casework practice by Joel Fischer [book review.] *Journal of Education for Social Work, 14,* 121–123.

Filstead, W. J. (Ed.). (1970). *Qualitative methodology: Firsthand involvement with the social world*. Chicago: Aldine.

Fischer, J. (1973). Is casework effective? A review. *Social Work, 18,* 5–20.

Geismar, L. L. (1982). Comments on the "obsolete scientific imperative in social work research." *Social Service Review, 56,* 311–312.

Glasser, B. G., & Strauss, A. L. (1967). *The discovery of grounded theory: Strategies for qualitative research*. Chicago: Aldine.

Goldstein, H. (1990). The knowledge base of social work practice: Theory, wisdom, analogue, or art? *Families in Society, 71,* 32–43.

Grinnell, R. M., Jr. (1993). *Social work research and evaluation*. Itasca, IL: F. E. Peacock.

Hartman, A. (1990a). Many ways of knowing. *Social Work, 35,* 3–4.

Hartman, A. (1990b). A profession chasing its tail—again. *Social Work, 35,* 99–100.

Haworth, G. O. (1984). Social work research, practice and paradigm. *Social Service Review, 58*, 343–357.

Hegel, G. W. F. (1991). *Encyclopedia of the philosophical science in outline*. Indianapolis: Hackett. (Original work published 1817)

Heineman, M. (1981). The obsolete scientific imperative in social work research. *Social Service Review, 55,* 371–397.

Hoover, K. R. (1984). *The elements of social scientific thinking* (3rd ed.). New York: St. Martin's Press.

Hudson, W. H. (1982). Scientific imperatives in social work research and practice. *Social Service Review, 56,* 246–258.

Ivanoff, A., & Blythe, B. J. (1989). Comments on "Exploring epistemologies: Social work action as a reflection of philosophical assumptions." *Journal of Social Work Education, 25,* 176–177.

James, W. (1974). *Pragmatism: A new name for old ways of thinking*. New York: Hafner. (Original work published 1907)

James, W. (1975). *The meaning of truth*. Cambridge, MA: Harvard University Press. (Original work published 1909)

Kant, I. (1990). *Critique of pure reason*. Chicago: Encyclopedia Britannica. (Original work published 1781)

Kierkegaard, S. (1985). *Philosophical fragments*. Princeton, NJ: Princeton University Press. (Original work published 1844)

Krager, H. J. (1983). Science, research and social work: Who controls the profession? *Social Work, 28,* 200–205.

Kuhn, T. S. (1970). *The structure of scientific revolutions.* Chicago: University of Chicago Press.

Kuttner, B. (1993, July 30). The pitfalls of a "virtual corporation" with no permanent workers. *Boston Globe,* p. 15.

Leibniz, G. W. (1991). *Discourse on metaphysics and other essays*. Indianapolis: Hackett. (Original work published 1675)

Lindsey, D., & Kirk, S. A. (1992). The continuing crisis in social work research: Conundrum or solvable problems? An essay review. *Journal of Social Work Education, 28,* 370–382.

Mach, E. (1975). *Knowledge and error: Sketches on the psychology of enquiry*. Boston: D. Reidel. (Original work published 1906)

Mannheim, K. (1936). *Ideology and utopia*. New York: Harcourt, Brace.

Marx, K., & Engels, F. (1972). Concerning the production of consciousness. In J. E. Curtis & J. W. Petras (Eds.), *Sociology of knowledge: A reader* (pp. 97–108). New York: Praeger. (Original work published 1894)

Pareto, V. (1935). *The mind and society*. New York: Harcourt, Brace.

Popper, K. (1972). The sociology of knowledge. In J. E. Curtis & J. W. Petras (Eds.), *Sociology of knowledge: A reader* (pp. 649–660). New York: Praeger.

Reason, P., & Rowan, J. (Eds.). (1981). *Human inquiry: A sourcebook of new paradigm research*. Chichester, England: John Wiley & Sons.

Reid, W. J. (1987). Research in social work. In A. Minahan (Ed.-in-Chief), *Encyclopedia of social work* (18th ed., Vol. 2, pp. 475–487). Silver Spring, MD: National Association of Social Workers.

Reid, W. J., & Hanrahan, P. (1982). Recent evaluations of social work: Grounds for optimism. *Social Work, 27,* 328–340.

Rein, M., & White, S. W. (1981). Knowledge for practice. *Social Service Review, 55,* 1–41.

Ruckdeschel, R. A., & Farris, B. E. (1981). Assessing practice: A critical look at the single case design. *Social Casework, 62,* 413–419.

Scheler, M. (1972). On the positivistic philosophy of the history of ideas and its law of three stages. In J. E. Curtis & J. W. Petras (Eds.), *Sociology of knowledge: A reader* (pp. 161–169). New York: Praeger. (Original work published 1923)

Singleton, R., Jr., Straits, B. C., Straits, M. M., & McAllister, R. J. (1988). *Approaches to social research.* New York: Oxford University Press.

Skinner, B. F. (1953). *Science and human behavior*. New York: Macmillan.

Specht, H. (1972). The deprofessionalization of social work. *Social Work, 17,* 3–15.

Spinoza, B. de (1949). *Ethica inordine geometrico demonstrata Ethics*. (J. Gutman, Ed.). New York: Hafner. (Original work published 1675)

Task Force on Social Work Research. (1991). *Building social work knowledge for effective services and policies: A plan for research and development.* Washington, DC: National Institute of Mental Health, Task Force on Social Work Research.

Thyer, B. A. (1989). To the editor. *Journal of Social Work Education, 25,* 174–176.

Vigilante, J. R. (1974). Between values and science: Education for the profession during a moral crisis, or is proof truth? *Journal of Education for Social Work, 10,* 112–116.

Walz, T., & Groze, V. (1991). The mission of social work revisited: An agenda for the 1990s. *Social Work, 36,* 500–504.

Wencour, S., & Reisch, M. (1989). *From charity to enterprise: The development of American social work in a market economy*. Chicago: University of Illinois Press.

Williams, L. F., & Hopps, J. G. (1988). On the nature of professional communication: Publication for practitioners. *Social Work, 33,* 453–459.

Zimbalist, S. E. (1977). *Historic themes and landmarks in social welfare research*. New York: Harper.

## Further Reading

Aaron, R. I. (1971). *Knowing and the function of reason*. Oxford: Clarendon.

Lewis, H. (1982). *The intellectual base of social work practice*. New York: Haworth.

Marx, K. (1972). *The Marx–Engels reader*. New York: W. W. Norton.

Payne, M. (1990). *Modern social work theory: A critical introduction*. London: Macmillan.

Reid, N. P., & Popple, R. R. (1990). *The moral purposes of social work: The character and intentions of a profession*. Chicago: Nelson-Hall.

Siporin, M. (1982). Moral philosophy in social work. *Social Services Review, 56,* 518–531.

**Leon F. Williams, PhD,** is associate professor, Boston College, Graduate School of Social Work, Chestnut Hill, MA 02167.

**For further information see**

Clinical Social Work; Cognition and Social Cognitive Theory; Ecological Perspective; Generalist and Advanced Generalist Practice; Gestalt; Human Development; Person-in-Environment; Psychosocial Approach; Research Overview; Social Welfare History; Social Work Practice: Theoretical Base.

**Key Words**

epistemology
philosophy
theoretical orientation

## Epstein, Abraham

*See* Biographies section, Volume 3

# Ethical Issues in Research

**David F. Gillespie**

Ethics emerge from value conflicts. In research, these conflicts are expressed in many ways: individuals' rights to privacy versus the undesirability of manipulation, openness and replication versus confidentiality, future welfare versus immediate relief, and others. Each decision made in research involves a potential compromise of one value for another. Researchers must try to minimize risks to participants, colleagues, and society while attempting to maximize the quality of information they produce.

Research ethics are codes or guidelines that help reconcile value conflicts. Although ethical codes provide direction, the decisions made in research must be reached by considering the specific alternatives available. The choices made in each case weigh the potential contribution of the research against the potential risks to the participants. Weighing these alternatives is essentially subjective, entails matters of degree rather than kind, and involves a comparison between the experiences required in the research and those expected in everyday life.

Ethical codes in research stipulate areas of responsibility to participants (subjects, clients, respondents), to colleagues and professional associations, and to sponsoring agencies, the public at large, or society. More discussion has been devoted to the ethics involving participants than to the ethics involving the other groups. The amount of attention given to participants derives historically from biomedical experimentation in which subjects have been exposed to serious risks and irremediable harm. The emphasis on participants in biomedical ethical codes and government regulations has been extended to all types of research. This situation has led to misunderstanding and debate because it blurs the distinctions between biomedical experimentation on human subjects and social science.

Social work researchers and other social scientists, partly because of developments in the medical sciences, have begun to address the particular ethical issues that arise in their work. These issues are summarized in Table 1, which provides an overview of the risks encountered in social research and the steps taken to reduce them. Debates have taken place regarding particular studies that illustrate alternative resolutions of moral dilemmas. Key studies such as Milgram's (1963) research on obedience to authority, Humphreys's (1970) research on homosexuals, and the Project Camelot study aimed at preventing revolutions (Horowitz, 1967) have helped clarify the issues and suggest resolutions.

## Risks in Research

There are three areas of risks in social research. First, participants may be harmed as a result of their involvement. The potential harms include death or injury, stress, guilt, reduction in self-respect or self-esteem, unfair treatment, withheld benefits, and minor discomfort. Second, professional relationships and the knowledge base may be damaged. These risks include falsification of data, plagiarism, abuse of confidentiality, and deliberate violation of regulations. Third, problems for the community or society may result. Societal risks involve the effect of cultural values and beliefs on the knowledge produced and the impact of that knowledge on society. In the following sections, ethical issues are discussed for these three areas of risk.

### Potential Harm to Participants

Although documented cases of death in social research are extremely rare, they do exist (Appell, 1974; Warwick, 1982). Ethical dilemmas may be experienced over the use of placebo therapy when it appears that untreated patients with acquired immune deficiency syndrome (AIDS) will die (Volberding & Abrams, 1985). In the case of terminally ill patients, the treatment may be perceived as their last hope (Vanderpool & Weiss, 1987). Cases of physical abuse or injury are also rare; however, Zimbardo, Haney, Banks, and Jaffe's (1973) simulation of a prison environment was prematurely terminated because volunteer prisoners suffered physical and psychological abuse from participants role-playing as guards.

Psychological harm is more frequently reported. In a study of obedience to authority,

TABLE 1
**Social Research Risks and the Steps Taken to Reduce Them**

| Group | Risk | Risk Minimization Strategy |
|---|---|---|
| Participants | Physical abuse–injury<br>Psychological harm<br>Feelings of guilt<br>Discrimination<br>Denigration of self-respect<br>Social sanctions<br>Economic sanctions<br>Legal sanctions<br>Irritation, frustration, discomfort | Risk–benefit assessment<br>Informed consent<br>Protective research design<br>Screening<br>Pilot studies or diagnostics<br>Outside proposal review |
| Professionals | Falsification of data<br>Plagiarism<br>Abuse of confidentiality<br>Violation of regulations | Professional codes<br>Peer review |
| Society | Harm from deception<br>Undermining of institutional legitimacy<br>Harm to special populations<br>Stereotypes<br>Maintenance of powerful groups | Government regulation<br>Institutional review boards |

Milgram (1963) reported that "subjects were observed to sweat, tremble, stutter, bite their lips, groan, and dig their fingernails into their flesh. These were characteristic rather than exceptional responses to the experiment" (p. 375). Anxiety, depression, and other emotional disturbances also have been reported (Milgram, 1974). Subjects in Humphreys's study of male homosexual activity in public rest rooms revealed apprehensions about being identified.

Another kind of psychological harm involves feelings of guilt. Studies with the potential to create guilt include those that have participants administer electric shocks to fellow participants, beat prisoners while role-playing as guards, fail to help those in obvious need, steal money from a charity box, or participate in illegal acts brought on by experimental entrapment. Murray's (1980) study of helping behavior reported that "virtually every subject who had not responded showed some anxiety to the experimental condition of watching the experimenter drop to the floor after receiving an apparently severe electrical shock" (p. 12).

Safeguarding confidentiality becomes especially difficult in research on people with AIDS (Weitz, 1987) both because of the public fear of the disease and because of discrimination against high-risk populations (Mayer, 1985; Volberding & Abrams, 1985). Fears about relinquishing confidentiality may prevent individuals from participating (Mayer, 1985). Confidentiality is particularly sensitive when the risk to the individual is weighed against the risk to others and to public health (Volberding & Abrams, 1985). Researchers may experience ethical dilemmas in considering their obligation to protect the identity of participants while also considering the implications of participants' human immunodeficiency virus (HIV) status for potential sexual partners or even for members of the research team who may be at some risk of infection. Many claim that prejudice against high-risk groups such as homosexuals and intravenous drug users has slowed progress and reduced needed funding in research on AIDS (Panem, 1985).

Social research has the potential to reduce self-esteem or self-respect. Walster (1965) used a dating ruse to manipulate female participants' feelings of self-worth by giving them a personality test with fixed results. Although the women were debriefed after the study, Diener and Crandall (1978) suggested that participants who received the negative personality reports probably felt bad, and those who received the positive reports may have been angry or embarrassed at having been fooled and perhaps disappointed that the report was not genuine. The dating ruse may have been even more harmful because dating anxiety and low self-esteem due to a lack of dates are frequently mentioned as problems among college students (Jaremko, 1984).

Relationships with others may become damaged through research. Experimental team-building efforts in organizations can disrupt subsequent relationships on the job. When superiors, peers, and subordinates openly exchange feelings and opinions, resentments may linger. Similarly, individuals who volunteer in sex research may find their morality questioned. People serving as informants in studies that become controversial may be subject to sanctions and even ostracized.

Participants in research may suffer career liabilities and other kinds of economic harm. Economic harm occurs when participants earn less money or pay more for things as a result of their involvement. Some participants in public policy experiments may receive less public aid than others, or they may receive unemployment compensation, whereas others do not (Nagel, 1990).

Legal sanctions represent another kind of potential harm. It is not unusual for information about illegal behavior to be collected in research. Except for special legal protection from subpoena, which can be obtained in certain cases by petition, social research does not have legal protection and, because leaks can occur despite safeguards, there is a real potential for harm to some participants. Nagel (1990) conducted a study involving juvenile delinquents who were randomly assigned either to one year of probation or to a one-year jail term. The results showed that the probation group had better subsequent records. It can be argued that those assigned to the jail term condition were harmed even if useful scientific knowledge was gained.

Feelings of irritation, frustration, or discomfort represent minor psychological harm. Respondents can become irritated when an interviewer is abrasive. Frustration or annoyance may result when questionnaires include too many questions or irrelevant questions. Experiments sometimes involve minor physical discomfort, and subjects may be treated in a demeaning or mildly insulting manner.

### Potential Damage to Professional Relationships and the Knowledge Base

Damage to professional relationships occurs when standards of professional behavior are violated. Violations include falsification of data, plagiarism, abuse of confidentiality, and deliberate violation of regulations. Knowledge development depends on accurate and careful data collection, thorough analyses, and unbiased reports. Falsification of data ranges from total fabrication to selective reporting and can be directly harmful to individuals in clinical research.

Sir Cyril Burt claimed to have measured the IQs of more than 50 sets of identical twins separated early in life. A high correlation between the IQs of separated twins suggested a genetic basis for intelligence. After Burt's death, evidence revealed faked data. Coauthors were fictional characters, data were supplied for some of the twins who were never tested, and one set of results was used for more than one publication so that results showed perfect consistency. Eysenck (1977) and Jensen (1977) offered some defense for Burt.

There is evidence that at least mild levels of falsification occur quite often. Azrin, Holz, Ulrich, and Goldiamond (1961) reported that 15 of 16 graduate students indicated successful completion of a study that was impossible to complete. Sometimes good intentions simply become misguided by boredom or the tedious nature of observation. Hyman, Cobb, Feldman, Hart, and Stember (1954) reported a study in which one-fourth of the interviewers fabricated most of the data they collected and all of the interviewers "fudged" some of the data. Smith, Wheeler, and Diener (1975) noted that research assistants view the alteration of data as similar to cheating on classroom tests, a fairly common practice. In laboratory studies and field surveys, researchers can distort findings by the way they give instructions or ask questions. By emphasizing particular words or through body language, an interviewer may bias the information collected.

Research may be carried out with complete objectivity only to have the findings misreported. Findings may be "adjusted" to fit expectations. Several studies may be completed, with only the one supporting a preferred theory being published. McNemar (1960) noted that findings are sometimes discarded as "bad data" when they fail to support hypotheses. A widespread practice is the calculation of numerous statistical tests with only those achieving significance being reported. Wolins (1962) requested original data from 37 studies, and researchers in 21 of these studies replied that the data had been misplaced or destroyed. Of the seven published studies reanalyzed by Wolins, three revealed errors large enough to alter the conclusions drawn from the original data analysis.

Plagiarism is rare because it is usually apparent in the more actively pursued areas of research. Inadequacy of citation and registering of credit to the work of others is a more pervasive problem. The pressure on academics to publish has resulted in some demanding that their names be included on manuscripts written by their graduate students or omitting the names of coworking graduate students from authorship. Fields (1984) reported that the Ethics Committee of the American Psychological Association has received an increasing number of complaints and inquiries from students who believe that "they are being exploited in the process of grinding out publications for academic psychologists" (p. 7).

Taking advantage of privileged information or violating confidentiality is a problem that is difficult to detect. Researchers openly discuss their ideas and share them through proposals. Proposals are reviewed by colleagues, university committees and administrators, and any number of outside researchers and practitioners serving on review panels. Articles prepared for professional journals are also subjected to a review process before publication. There are many opportunities for abuse of confidentiality.

**Potential for Societal Harm**

The research designs and procedures used, topics studied, and results produced can promote harm as well as provide benefit to society. It is curious that researchers list the potential benefits of their study to society while limiting their attention to individual participants when considering the potential harms. The use of deception in research undermines trust by undercutting the expectation that what another person says will be true. Similarly, the willingness of one person to help another in times of need or distress is compromised by studies that use deception to learn about helping behavior.

The ethical balance of knowledge gained versus the potential for social harm from deception has only recently shifted in favor of greater restrictions in the use of deception. Researchers have conducted studies in which stooges fall and release fake blood to test people's reactions to medical emergencies (Piliavin & Piliavin, 1972). Gay (1973) wrote that a number of students did nothing when they saw a student shoot someone because they thought it was a psychology experiment. Reviews indicate that between 19 percent and 44 percent of the research published in psychology includes direct lying to participants (Menges, 1973).

Social research can raise questions about the legitimacy of institutions. Vaughan (1967) reported on the federal hearings of the Wichita jury study in which a senator asked one of the researchers, "Now, do you not realize that to snoop on a jury, and record what they say, does violence to every reason for which we have secret deliberations of a jury?" Similar issues have been raised about the harmful results of biased public opinion polls on the legitimacy of political elections. These biased polls are designed to provide support for a particular candidate or position. The net effect may undermine the legitimacy of the election process and the trustworthiness of the people running for office.

Research may harm special populations such as religious groups, racial or ethnic minorities, and individuals considered deviant. A focus on a category of people as "deviant" or "disadvantaged" highlights the problems of these people. Data may create or reinforce the conditions of victimization or scapegoating. Moynihan (1965) wrote that the Negro family suffered from instability, a propensity to produce illegitimate children, and a matriarchal structure that resulted in harmful effects on children, especially boys. Ryan (1967) disagreed with Moynihan's interpretation, stating that "it draws dangerously inexact conclusions from weak and insufficient data, encourages a new form of subtle racism that might be termed 'savage discovery,' and seduces the reader into believing that it is not racism and discrimination, but the weaknesses and defects of the Negro himself that accounts for the present status of inequality between Negro and white" (p. 463).

Turnbull, Blue-Banning, Behr, and Kerns (1986) reported that families with developmentally disabled children were insulted when they learned of researchers' claims that they were dysfunctional. A group of families organized to protest that researchers neglected to report on positive characteristics of families with developmentally disabled children. They also complained that research was intended to advance researchers, that it was not made available to the families who should be the ones to benefit from it, and that it was not helpful to them. The authors recommended that researchers form partnerships with families being studied and with the organizations that represent them (for example, the Association for Retarded Citizens).

The assumptions underlying interpretations and conclusions drawn in research become fastened to concrete descriptions about who is responsible for existing conditions. The creation of stereotyped images is easy to find in research. Catholics have been portrayed as less hard working than Protestants, as being at a disadvantage because of conformity to an authoritarian church, and as having too many children, which makes it difficult to provide their children with the higher education necessary to compete effectively in contemporary society (Lenski, 1963). Groups may protest a stereotype, as did Lopreato (1967) and others in regard to the image of Italians constructed by Banfield (1958). The weaker the group, however, the less likely they are to protest or even be aware that there is something to protest.

Research may provide information to the more powerful groups in a society that helps maintain their advantage. Project Camelot, a project designed to prevent revolutions, was criticized because it was believed that it would have undermined the political sovereignty of the countries studied. Some believed that the data produced would be fed to the Central Intelligence Agency to control certain affairs in the countries involved. Others drew less pernicious scenarios but still believed that the information would favor the United States in its relationship with these countries. It is important to note that Project Camelot was canceled because of its politically threatening nature rather than as a result of a lack of scientific merit, which provides another illustration of how research may be used at the discretion of those in power.

Rushton's (1990) controversial research in the field of sociobiology has been used to support racist ideology and has led to policies that blame the victim and suggest that society need not take action to overcome the effects of historical discrimination. Fairchild (1991) argued that Rushton's research is based on biased theoretical assumptions and flawed empirical interpretations. Of course, it is equally important to note that research has benefited the poor as well (Lampman, 1985; Macdonald & Sawhill, 1978; Wolf, 1984).

## Minimizing Risk

Individual researchers, professional associations, and the government have taken steps to minimize the risks encountered in research. Most efforts focus on protecting participants. The ratio of risks to benefits is assessed, informed consent is required, research designs and procedures are built to minimize the potential for harm to occur, participants are screened, diagnostic studies are conducted, procedures are designed to assess and deal with potential harms, and proposals are reviewed by others. Each precaution minimizes the risk, and, when taken together, the prospects are good for reducing harm to an occasional occurrence.

### Participant Protections

***Risk–benefit assessment.*** Constructing a risk–benefit ratio for a proposed study is one way to assess its ethical soundness. If the expected benefits exceed the expected risks, the study is presumed ethical. The risk–benefit precaution is a modern version of the end justifying the means. It has its most direct application when those exposed to the risks also receive the benefits. The ratio is more difficult to justify when the participants are subjected to potential harm and the benefits are directed to other individuals or to society.

Risk–benefit ratios have at least four shortcomings. First, it is impossible to predict the benefits and risks of a particular study before its execution. Studies are conducted because the outcome is unknown. Second, the possible risks and benefits are relative, subjectively assessed, and difficult to measure. Third, calculating the ratio is complicated when society benefits at the risk of individual participants. When participants receive no direct benefits, it is imperative that they fully understand and accept whatever risks may exist. Finally, there is a conflict of interest in that the risk–benefit ratio is constructed by the researcher who undoubtedly believes that the research is worth doing.

Even though risk–benefit ratios are insufficient to determine ethical soundness, they provide a useful first step. It may be impossible for a risk–benefit ratio to justify a study, but it can provide enough information to warrant canceling a study.

***Informed consent.*** Informed consent refers to an individual's willingness to participate in a study. Individuals who provide informed consent have been made aware of the design and procedures with enough detail to exercise a rational decision to participate. The provision of informed consent also includes the knowledge that participation is voluntary and that participants can withdraw from the study at any time.

The more dangerous the study, of course, the more important it becomes to obtain informed consent. Informed consent becomes absolutely essential when participants are to be exposed to serious risks or required to suspend their individual rights, as in hypnosis research or drug use studies. Many respondents believe that they do not have a genuine choice, and they may believe that access to services will be blocked unless they participate or that they will receive better treatment if they do. Many people with AIDS, for example, do not want to jeopardize access to the few services they can receive (Weitz, 1987). Prisoners may fear that if they refuse consent they will be penalized by prison officials.

Although informed consent is often desirable and sometimes essential, it is not sufficient by itself to ethically justify a study. Even when researchers make careful efforts to obtain informed consent, participants may maintain misconceptions about the study, believing that the researcher will provide them with the best treatment available (Appelbaum, Roth, Lidz, Benson, & Winslade, 1987). Appelbaum et al. recommended supplementing the researchers' disclosures. For example, a neutral informant can review risks and benefits with participants before they provide informed consent.

***Protective research design.*** Another precaution involves constructing research designs and procedures in such a way as to achieve study goals while maximizing the protection of participants. This process involves estimating the likelihood and severity of harmful effects, the probable duration of these effects, the extent to which any harm incurred can be reversed, the probability of early detection of harm, and the relationship between potential harm from participation in the study and the risks of everyday life. Studies are more ethically justified when the probability of harm is low, when only minor harm is expected, when the harm will be short term if it does occur, when harmful effects can be reversed, when measures for early detection are installed, and when the risks are no greater than one could expect in the normal affairs of one's life.

When the achievement of study goals unavoidably entails risk, researchers can turn to natural field studies so that the research itself does not promote the risks of harm. For example, social work researchers seeking to study the effects of malnutrition can work in areas of poverty where children are experiencing malnutrition (Klein, Habicht, & Yarbrough, 1973).

***Screening.*** Screening provides investigators with an opportunity to select for study only those individuals who show a high tolerance for the potential risks. Zimbardo et al. (1973) administered personality tests to volunteers and selected only those who scored within a normal range. This precaution was believed to reduce the risks involved with the role-playing requirements of the study. Mayer (1985) and Weitz (1987) recommended providing information, counseling, and support services to participants in research on AIDS. Support services are especially important for individuals who obtain information about their HIV status as a result of participating in a study. In excluding individuals from a study, it is important not to convey an impression of deviance, abnormality, or unacceptability.

***Pilot studies.*** When the potential harms are uncertain, a useful precaution involves a pilot study with follow-up diagnostic interviews to assess effects and request advice from participants. Pilot studies typically increase both the scientific rigor of the study and the protections for participants. Including procedures to detect harm and deal with it represents an important precaution in any study in which the potential for harm can be imagined. Many studies, especially experiments, routinely debrief participants to assess and deal with any negative effects. In experiments using treatments that may have possible side effects, arrangements are often made with a clinical practitioner to accept referrals.

***Outside proposal review.*** Requesting others to review research proposals is a helpful precaution in minimizing risks. Different people with various positions and perspectives may identify potential harms and perceive safeguards that the researcher overlooked or could not have known. Of course, for many years proposals for funded research have been required to be reviewed by institutional review boards. Barber (1967) recommended that all research be reviewed by committees that have representatives from outside the profession.

There is little evidence to suggest long-term harm from participation in social research. Neither Milgram (1964) nor Ring, Wallston, and Corey (1970) found any long-term harmful effects from their shock–obedience studies. Zimbardo et al. (1973) also found no subsequent negative effects, even though they prematurely terminated their study because "volunteer prisoners suffered physical and psychological abuse hour after hour for days, while volunteer guards were exposed to the new self-knowledge that they enjoyed being powerful and had abused this power to make other human beings suffer" (p. 243). Clark and Word (1974), in a debriefing conducted after their study of altruism, found that one participant out of the 68 involved continued to be upset but that, after six months, no subjects reported negative aftereffects. Campbell, Sanderson, and Laverty (1964) had difficulty in reversing a conditioned fear, but the evidence leans strongly toward few, if any, long-term negative effects of carefully and ethically constructed studies.

### Professional Codes

Two characteristics of professional codes help to clarify how such codes minimize risks in research. First, professional codes have been developed inductively from the research experiences of professionals. Because the work experience of professionals offers wide variety and because reasonable people differ in the solutions they offer for particular problems, the standards reflected in ethical codes of professional associations tend to be abstract and relative to particular circumstances. Second, professional codes place strong emphasis on researchers' responsibility for their research. These two characteristics distinguish professional codes from laws and government regulations as a means of protecting individuals and society from unnecessary harm.

The two characteristic features of professional codes—abstract relativity and researcher responsibility—are illustrated in the *NASW Code of Ethics* (NASW, 1994):

> *Scholarship and Research*—The social worker engaged in study and research should be guided by the conventions of scholarly inquiry.
>
> 1. The social worker engaged in research should consider carefully its possible consequences for human beings.
>
> 2. The social worker engaged in research should ascertain that the consent of participants in the research is voluntary and informed, without any implied deprivation or penalty for refusal to participate, and with due regard for participants' privacy and dignity.
>
> 3. The social worker engaged in research should protect participants from unwarranted physical or mental discomfort, distress, harm, danger, or deprivation.
>
> 4. The social worker who engages in the evaluation of services or cases should discuss them only for professional purposes and only with persons directly and professionally concerned with them.
>
> 5. Information obtained aboutparticipants in research should betreated as confidential.
>
> 6. The social worker should take credit only for work actually done in connection with scholarly and research endeavors and credit contributions made by others. (p. 4)

Professional codes tend not to specify penalties for violation of principles. The major penalty involves expulsion from the association. Half of the 24 codes reviewed by Reynolds (1975) included a reference to expulsion. Interestingly, none of the codes reviewed by Reynolds specified any benefits for those who complied with the codes. The low level of penalties and rewards suggests that professional codes may not be taken too seriously. The threat of expulsion may carry little significance. It is possible, for example, to achieve a respectable career without being a member of NASW or any other professional association. Professional codes appear to exist as a necessary but not sufficient condition of professional self-regulation.

**Government Regulations**

Government regulations, like state and federal laws, are designed to protect or advance the interests of society and its individuals. Researchers are required to take certain precautions or are prevented from certain activities on the grounds that failure to follow the law or regulations increases the risk of harm to an individual or to society. Regulations tend to be absolute in their requirements.

Government regulations are characterized by what Fletcher (1966) has called "legalism," the assumption that "principles, codified in rules, are not merely guidelines or maxims to illuminate the situation; they are *directives* to be followed" (p. 18).

Government regulations do not invite an evaluation of their moral correctness; they are written to be obeyed (Alexander, 1986). Moreover, obeying a law or regulation does not require individuals to consider underlying ethical issues or moral principles. It is assumed that moral principles were evaluated by those who wrote the law or regulation and that observing the law will result in ethically acceptable behavior (Dokecki & Zaner, 1986).

Laws or regulations can be fallible. The important difference between regulations and professional codes is in the response of their adherents to a law that requires an ethical violation. The professional may violate the law and pay the price, whereas the legalist must obey the law and try to change it. Principle 1.02 of the APA Ethical Principles states that "If psychologists' ethical responsibilities conflict with the law, psychologists make known their commitment to the Ethics Code and take steps to resolve the conflict in a responsible manner" (1992, p. 1600). The term "resolve" is not defined; thus, under certain circumstances, it might be reasonable to go to jail for contempt of court rather than release confidential information.

The development of federal regulations concerning the welfare of human subjects involved in research and the controversies surrounding the regulations have been described by McCarthy (1981) and Gray (1982). Most of the controversy has stemmed from extensions of policies or rulings generated from abuses in biomedical research to social research or similar extensions from specifically funded research projects to all projects under the auspices of institutions receiving federal funding. The debates ensued over a 15-year period from 1966 to 1981, when the current U.S. Department of Health and Human Services (DHHS) regulations were adopted. These regulations, carved out of the controversy and written with the benefit of extensive input from researchers, were designed to end the controversy while not compromising the protection of human subjects.

The regulations apply only to research conducted or funded by DHHS. But individuals who receive funding for research from DHHS must provide a statement showing how the institution they work for protects the rights and welfare of human subjects. The regulations do not require prior approval by an institutional review board for research not funded by DHHS. Institutions are urged, however, to use institutional review boards and other appropriate procedures to protect human subjects in all research conducted under their auspices. Such boards are given wide latitude for the research they review. The regulations specify particular categories of research as being exempt: research conducted in established or commonly accepted educational settings; research involving the anonymous use of educational tests; research involving anonymous survey or interview procedures, except in instances in which risk of criminal or civil liability exists or the research deals with sensitive behavior such as illegal conduct, drug use, or sexual behavior; research involving the observation of public behavior, with the same exceptions noted under survey and interview studies; and research involving the anonymous collection or study of publicly available data, documents, records, pathological specimens, or diagnostic specimens (*Federal Register,* 1981). These exemptions have expanded to cover research and demonstration projects involving social security programs (*Federal Register*, 1983).

The current regulations appear to clarify earlier points of confusion and contention. They indicate that no research involving human subjects should be exempt from federal regulation solely on the basis of belonging to a particular discipline. They also acknowledge that much, if not most, social research involves no more risk than that ordinarily encountered in daily life and that the requirements of participation are sufficiently understood by the public to reduce the need for federal regulations. As a result, research falling in the exempted categories is not required to be reviewed and approved by an institutional review board.

Many federal and state departments have policies regarding the protection of human subjects. The National Commission for the Protection of Human Subjects of Biomedical and Behavioral Research summarized the policies of federal agencies in a report written in 1978. Most governmental regulations are modeled after those issued by the U.S. Department of Health and Human Services. Agency rulings, principally those of DHHS, have been the predominant form of government regulation.

Laws passed to govern social research are neither very restrictive nor very specific. Professionals resist control by laws because laws tend to blur particular circumstances in specific cases. And there is a fear that resolving ethical issues through legal statutes will compromise the quality of knowledge development by exaggerating the potential for risk in social research.

Government regulation should remain relatively stable for a number of years. It is possible that the revolutionary changes in information technology will inspire renewed attempts to promote legalism in government regulation. But today's researchers have learned much from the issues and debates over the past 30 years, and their responsive and sensitive awareness of ethical issues probably will work to maintain a balance among self-imposed constraints, guidance from professional associations, and government regulation.

## References


Alexander, D. (1986). Decision making for research involving persons with severe mental retardation: Guidance from the National Commission for the Protection of Human Subjects of Biomedical and Behavioral Research. In P. R. Dokecki & R. M. Zaner (Eds.), *Ethics of dealing with persons with severe handicaps: Toward a research agenda* (pp. 39–52). Baltimore: Paul H. Brookes.

American Psychological Association (1992). Ethical principles of psychologists and code of conduct. *American Psychologist*, *47*(12), 1597–1611.

Appelbaum, P. S., Roth, L. H., Lidz, C. W., Benson, P., & Winslade, W. (1987). False hopes and best data: Consent to research and the therapeutic misconception. *Hastings Center Report*, *17*(2), 20–24.

Appell, G. N. (1974). Basic issues in the dilemmas and ethical conflicts in anthropological inquiry. *Module*, *19*, 1–28.

Azrin, N. H., Holz, W., Ulrich, R., & Goldiamond, I. (1961). The control of the content of conversation through reinforcement. *Journal of Experimental Analysis of Behavior*, *4*, 25–30.

Banfield, E. (1958). *The moral basis of a backward society*. New York: Free Press.

Barber, B. (1967). Experimenting with humans. *Public Interest*, *6*, 91–102.

Campbell, D., Sanderson, R. E., & Laverty, S. G. (1964). Characteristics of a conditioned response in human subjects during extinction trials following a single traumatic conditioning trial. *Journal of Abnormal and Social Psychology*, *68*, 627–639.

Clark, R. D., & Word, L. E. (1974). Where is the apathetic bystander? Situational characteristics of the emergency. *Journal of Personality and Social Psychology*, *29*, 279–287.

Diener, E., & Crandall, R. (1978). *Ethics in social and behavioral research*. Chicago: University of Chicago Press.

Dokecki, P. R., & Zaner, R. M. (Eds.). (1986). *Ethics of dealing with persons with severe handicaps: Toward a research agenda*. Baltimore: Paul H. Brookes.

Eysenck, H. (1977). The case of Sir Cyril Burt: On fraud and prejudice in a scientific controversy. *Encounter*, *48*, 19–24.

Fairchild, H. H. (1991). Scientific racism: The cloak of objectivity. *Journal of Social Issues, 47*(3), 101–115.
*Federal Register*. (1981, January 26). *46*(16), 8386–8392.
*Federal Register*. (1983, March 4). *48*(9), 9269–9270.
Fields, C. M. (1984). Professors' demands for credit as co-authors of students' research projects may be rising. *Chronicle of Higher Education, 7*, 10.
Fletcher, J. (1966). *Situation ethics.* Philadelphia: Westminster Press.
Gay, C. (1973, November 30). A man collapsed outside a UW building. Others ignore him. What would you do? *University of Washington Daily*, pp. 14–15.
Gray, B. H. (1982). The regulatory context of social and behavioral research. In T. L. Beauchamp, R. R. Thaden, R. J. Wallace, Jr., & L. Walters (Eds.), *Ethical issues in social science research* (pp. 327–344). Baltimore: Johns Hopkins University Press.
Horowitz, I. L. (Ed.). (1967). *The rise and fall of Project Camelot*. Cambridge, MA: MIT Press.
Humphreys, L. (1970). *Tearoom trade: Impersonal sex in public places*. Chicago: Aldine.
Hyman, H. H., Cobb, W. J., Feldman, J. J., Hart, C. W., & Stember, C. W. (1954). *Interviewing in social research*. Chicago: University of Chicago Press.
Jaremko, M. E. (1984). Stress innoculation training for social anxiety, with emphasis on dating anxiety. In D. Meichenbaum & M. E. Jaremko (Eds.), *Stress reduction and prevention* (pp. 419–485). New York: Plenum Press.
Jensen, A. R. (1977). Did Sir Cyril Burt fake his research on heritability of intelligence? *Phi Delta Kappan, 58*, 471–492.
Klein, R. E., Habicht, J. P., & Yarbrough, C. (1973). Some methodological field studies on nutrition and intelligence. In D. J. Kallen (Ed.), *Nutrition, development and social behavior* (pp. 64–83). Washington, DC: U.S. Government Printing Office.
Lampman, R. J. (1985). *Social welfare spending: Accounting for changes from 1950–1978*. San Diego: Academic Press.
Lenski, G. (1963). *The religious factor: A sociologist's inquiry*. Garden City, NY: Doubleday.
Lopreato, J. (1967). *Peasants know more*. San Francisco: Chandler.
Macdonald, M., & Sawhill, I. V. (1978). Welfare policy and the family. *Public Policy, 26*(1), 89–119.
Mayer, K. H. (1985). The epidemiological investigation of AIDS. *Hastings Center Report, 15*(4), 12–15.
McCarthy, C. R. (1981). The development of federal regulations for social science research. In A. J. Kimmel (Ed.), *Ethics of human subject research* (pp. 31–39). San Francisco: Jossey-Bass.
McNemar, Q. (1960). At random: Sense and nonsense. *American Psychologist, 15*, 195–300.
Menges, R. J. (1973). Openness and honesty versus coercion and deception in psychological research. *American Psychologist, 28*, 1030–1034.
Milgram, S. (1963). Behavioral study of obedience. *Journal of Abnormal and Social Psychology, 67*, 371–378.
Milgram, S. (1964). Issues in the study of obedience: A reply to Baumrind. *American Psychologist, 19*, 848–852.
Milgram, S. (1974). *Obedience to authority*. New York: Harper & Row.
Moynihan, D. P. (1965). *The Negro family: The case for national action*. Washington, DC: Office of Planning and Research, U.S. Department of Labor.
Murray, T. (1980). Learning to deceive. *Hastings Center Report, 10*(2), 1–16.
Nagel, S. S. (1990). Professional ethics in policy evaluation: Ends and methods. *Policy Studies Journal, 19*(1), 221–234.
National Association of Social Workers (1994). *NASW code of ethics*. Washington, DC: Author.
Panem, S. (1985). AIDS: Public policy and biomedical research. *Hastings Center Report, 15*(4), 23–26.
Piliavin, J. A., & Piliavin, I. M. (1972). Effect of blood on reactions to a victim. *Journal of Personality and Social Psychology, 23*, 353–361.
Reynolds, P. D. (1975). Ethics and status: Value dilemmas in the professional conduct of social science. *International Social Science Journal, 27*(4), 563–611.
Ring, K., Wallston, K., & Corey, M. (1970). Mode of debriefing as a factor affecting subjective reaction to a Milgram-type obedience experiment and ethical inquiry. *Representative Research in Social Psychology, 1*, 67–88.
Rushton, J. P. (1990). Sir Francis Galton, epigenetic rules, genetic similarity theory, and human life-history analysis. *Journal of Personality, 58*(1), 117–140.
Ryan, W. (1967). Savage discovery: The Moynihan report. In L. Rainwater & W. L. Yancey (Eds.), *The Moynihan Report and the politics of controversy* (pp. 453–478). Cambridge, MA: MIT Press.
Smith, R. E., Wheeler, G., & Diener, E. (1975). Faith without works: Jesus people resistance to temptation and altruism. *Journal of Applied Social Psychology, 5*(4), 320–330.
Turnbull, A. P., Blue-Banning, M., Behr, S., & Kerns, G. (1986). Family research and intervention: A value and ethical examination. In P. R. Dokecki & R. M. Zaner (Eds.), *Ethics of dealing with persons with severe handicaps: Toward a research agenda* (pp. 119–140). Baltimore: Paul H. Brookes.
Vanderpool, H. Y., & Weiss, G. B. (1987). False data and last hopes: Enrolling ineligible patients in clinical trials. *Hastings Center Report, 17*(2), 16–19.
Vaughan, T. R. (1967). Governmental intervention in social research: Political and ethical dimensions in the Wichita jury recordings. In G. Sjoberg (Ed.), *Ethics, politics, and social research* (pp. 50–77). Cambridge, MA: Schenkman.
Volberding, P., & Abrams, D. (1985). Clinical care and research in AIDS. *Hastings Center Report, 15*(4), 16–18.
Walster, E. (1965). The effect of self-esteem on romantic liking. *Journal of Experimental Social Psychology, 1*, 184–197.
Warwick, D. P. (1982). Types of harm in social research. In T. L. Beauchamp, R. R. Faden, R. J. Wallace, Jr., & L. Walters (Eds.), *Ethical issues in social science research* (pp. 101–124). Baltimore: Johns Hopkins University Press.
Weitz, R. (1987). The interview as legacy: A social scientist confronts AIDS. *Hastings Center Report, 17*(3), 21–23.
Wolf, D. A. (1984). Changes in household size and composition due to financial incentives. *Journal of Human Resources, 19*(1), 87–101.
Wolins, L. (1962). Responsibility for raw data. *American Psychologist, 17*, 657–658.
Zimbardo, P. G., Haney, C., Banks, W. C., & Jaffe, D. (1973). The mind is a formidable jailer: The Pirandellian prison. *New York Times Magazine, 122*(8), 38–60.

### Further Reading

American Psychological Association. (1985). *Standards for educational and psychological testing*. Washington, DC: Author.

Bermant, G., Kelman, H. C., & Warwick, D. P. (1978). *The ethics of social intervention*. Washington, DC: Hemisphere.

Carroll, J. D., & Knerr, C. R. (1976, Fall). The APSA Confidentiality in Social Science Research Project: A final report. *P.S.*, pp. 416–419.

Kimmel, A. J. (1988). *Ethics and values in applied social research*. Newbury Park, CA: Sage Publications.

Lee, R. M. (1993). *Doing research on sensitive topics*. Newbury Park, CA: Sage Publications.

Mathews, M. C. (1988). *Strategic intervention in organizations: Resolving ethical dilemmas*. Newbury Park, CA: Sage Publications.

Sieber, J. E. (1992). *Planning ethically responsible research: A guide for students and internal review boards*. Newbury Park, CA: Sage Publications.


**David F. Gillespie, PhD,** is professor, Washington University, George Warren Brown School of Social Work, One Brookings Drive, St. Louis, MO 63130.

### For further information see

Agency-Based Research; Bioethical Issues; Epistemology; Ethics and Values; Intervention Research; Licensing, Regulation, and Certification; Patient Rights; Professional Liability and Malpractice; Qualitative Research; Research Overview; Survey Research.

**Key Words**

ethics
professional liability
social work research

**READER'S GUIDE**

### Ethics

*The following entries contain information on this general topic:*

Bioethical Issues
Civil Rights
End-of-Life Decisions
Ethical Issues in Research
Ethics and Values
Human Rights
*NASW Code of Ethics* (Appendix 1)
Patient Rights
Professional Conduct
Professional Liability and Malpractice

# Ethics and Values

**Frederic G. Reamer**

In the face of significant changes that have taken place in the practice of social work throughout its history, social workers have continued to embrace a set of values central to the profession. There have been both challenges to and constructive changes in the value base of the profession, but the key elements of this foundation have endured.

Although there has been considerable stability in the core values of the profession, it would be a mistake to conclude that the day-to-day ethical issues that social workers encounter have remained static. To the contrary, applications of core values in social work have undergone substantial change over the years in response to social, political, and economic developments.

The subject of ethics and values in social work is broad in scope. In general it encompasses three distinguishable, though related, sets of issues. The first concerns the relevance of the profession's value base to its overall mission, goals, and priorities, especially as reflected in the *NASW Code of Ethics* (NASW, 1994). The second pertains to ethical decisions and dilemmas that social workers encounter as they carry out their professional duties, and the third relates to practitioner misconduct and the enforcement of ethical standards in the profession.

## Value Base of Social Work

The profession of social work historically has been committed to enhancing the welfare of people who encounter problems related to poverty, mental health, health care, employment, shelter and housing, abuse, aging, childhood, hunger, and so on. As the profession has evolved, it has continually stressed the need to attend both to the needs of individual clients and to the ways that the community and society respond to these needs. Thus, there has always been a simultaneous concern in social work for individual well-being and the environmental factors that affect it.

Social workers' appreciation of the complex interaction between individuals and their environment has been grounded in an enduring set of values. As Timms (1983) suggested, discussions of values in social work have been of three types: (1) broad overviews of the profession and social work's mission, which include general references to "value" or "values" (for example, Hamilton, 1940; Younghusband, 1967); (2) critical assessments of social work values or of a particular value (for example, McDermott, 1975); and (3) reports of empirical research on values held by social workers (for example, Varley, 1968).

According to Pumphrey (1959), individuals' values are "formulations of preferred behavior held by individuals or social groups. They imply a usual preference for certain means, ends and conditions of life, often being accompanied by strong feeling" (p. 23). Rokeach (1973) offered what has become a classic definition of value in *The Nature of Human Values*: "an enduring belief that a specific mode or end state of existence is personally or socially preferable to an opposite or converse mode or end state of existence" (p. 5).

From this point of view, one must distinguish among ultimate, proximate, and instrumental values. *Ultimate values* are broadly conceived and provide general guidance to a group's long-term aims. In social work, values such as respect for people, equality, and nondiscrimination might constitute ultimate values. *Proximate values* are more specific and suggest shorter-term goals. In social work they might take the form of policies related to welfare clients' right to health care or affordable housing, or psychiatric patients' right to refuse certain types of treatment. Finally, *instrumental values* specify desirable means to desirable ends. In social work respecting clients' right to confidentiality, self-determination, and informed consent might be considered instrumental values.

## Common Base

Although the core values of the profession identified by different authors vary, there is a common base. Frequently cited values in social work are individual worth and dignity, respect for people, valuing individuals' capacity for change, client self-determination, confidentiality and privacy, providing individuals with opportunity to realize their potential, seeking to meet individuals' common human needs, commitment to social change and social justice, seeking to provide individuals with adequate resources and services to meet their basic needs, client empowerment, equal opportunity, nondiscrimination, respect of diversity, and willingness to transmit professional knowledge and skills to others (Bartlett, 1970; Biestek, 1957; Gordon, 1962; Keith-Lucas, 1977; Levy, 1973; Plant, 1970; Reamer, 1987c, 1990, 1994b, 1995; Teicher, 1967; Timms, 1983).

Pumphrey (1959) offered a comprehensive typology of social work values, placing them into three categories of value-based objectives. The first focuses on the relationship between social work values and values operating in the culture at large with respect to, for example, social justice, social change, and basic human needs. The second category focuses on internal relationships within the professional membership, for example, the ways in which the profession interprets and implements its values and encourages ethical behavior. The final category focuses on social workers' attempts to understand and respond to clients' values.

Levy (1973) also provided an important classification of the profession's values. The first of Levy's three groups includes "preferred conceptions of people," such as the belief in individuals' inherent worth and dignity, capacity and drive toward constructive change, mutual responsibility, need to belong, uniqueness, and common human needs. The second group includes "preferred outcomes for people," such as the belief in society's obligation to provide opportunities for individual growth and development; to provide resources and services to help people meet their needs and to avoid such problems as hunger, inadequate education or housing, illness, and discrimination; and to provide equal opportunity to participate in the molding of society. Levy's third group includes "preferred instrumentalities for dealing with people," such as the belief that people should be treated with respect and dignity, have the right to self-determination, be encouraged to participate in social change, and be recognized as unique individuals.

## Personal Values

A significant portion of social work literature focuses on the need for social workers to clarify their own personal values. Practitioners' personal values influence their views of clients, intervention frameworks and strategies, and definitions of successful and unsuccessful outcomes. Workers' personal values also affect their willingness to endorse and act on the profession's value base. For example, a worker's personal views about the ethics of abortion are likely to have a significant bearing on the worker's response to a pregnant adolescent who is considering abortion. Also, willingness to comply with relevant statutes and agency policy and support of NASW's position on abortion would be affected by the worker's personal views.

The emphasis placed on specific core values has varied considerably throughout social work's history. For example, around the beginning of the 20th century, the emphasis was on ways clients create and contribute to their own problems. Social workers of that era, influenced in part by the methods of the charity organization societies, frequently viewed clients' problems as evidence of character defects rather than as evidence of flawed communities or social policies that did not respond adequately to human needs (Davis, 1967). Thus, the values of concern to social workers at the turn of the century often centered on a client's morality or lack of virtue. A key part of a caseworker's mission was assumed by many to be the inspiration of clients to lead morally upright, prudent lives.

### Environmental Determinants

Social workers gradually became more aware of ways environmental factors shape individuals and limit their opportunities. The Progressive Era, the settlement house movement, and the Great Depression of the 1930s, for example, helped turn social workers' attention to social and economic problems that contributed substantially to the misery suffered by many who lived during those years. As a result of this increased sensitivity, concern about clients' personal morality waned and concern about the need for social change and the enhancement of opportunity increased.

Interest in the environmental determinants of individual problems declined somewhat during the relatively tranquil years immediately following World War II, during which many members of the profession were drawn to the development of psychiatric social work. But widespread concern about large-scale social change emerged once again during the turbulent 1960s. Thus, during the earliest years of the profession, practitioners often focused on the depth and decency of clients' values. Attention gradually shifted to analyses of the broader society's values and commitment to the needs of those who were poor, ill, or otherwise disadvantaged. More recently, especially since the 1970s, there has been increased interest in examining the values of social workers themselves and the ethical aspects of their practice.

### Ethics of Practitioners

The relatively recent surge of interest in the ethics of practitioners is not unique to social work. It is also characteristic of nearly every profession and field, including law, medicine, nursing, dentistry, journalism, engineering, law enforcement, the military, and business. Several reasons account for this growth of interest in professional ethics and values. Technological and other developments have presented professionals with ethical choices that simply were unknown to previous generations of practitioners. Developments in medicine, nuclear power, and computer technology, for example, have been accompanied by enormously complicated issues related to ethics and values. The beginning of the acquired immune deficiency syndrome (AIDS) crisis in the early 1980s, for instance, triggered a series of new and unanticipated ethical questions related to privacy (protection of sexual partners and contact tracing), mandatory testing, the obligation to treat human immunodeficiency virus (HIV)-infected clients, and access to health care (Reamer, 1991). In addition, contemporary professionals have been faced with decisions about the allocation of a growing list of scarce or limited resources, such as food, land, health care, social services, and money, and this has heightened their awareness of ethics and values in professional life. Widely publicized scandals that have taken place in nearly every profession, ranging from mismanagement and fraud to the abuse or exploitation of clients (Reamer & Abramson, 1982), have also contributed to the growing interest in professional ethics.

However, this growth also seems to reflect in large part the maturation of the professions themselves. During its early years, a profession tends to be preoccupied with the technical aspects of its mission. After all, if a profession does not have the capacity to carry out technical tasks skillfully, it has little claim to expertise and to the use of the term "profession." Most professions have focused much greater attention on issues of ethics and values once their reputations for technical expertise have been firmly established. This may explain why the modern or young professions—mainly those other than law and medicine—have recently paid increased attention to ethical issues.

## NASW Code of Ethics

There are several codes of ethics related to social work. Prominent examples include those of NASW, National Association of Black Social Workers, National Federation of Societies for Clinical Social Work, and Canadian Association of Social Workers.

The best-known ethics code to which social workers in the United States subscribe is the *NASW Code of Ethics* (NASW, 1994). The *NASW Code of Ethics* has been a living document, revised periodically to reflect changes in the broader culture and in social work's own standards.

**Historical Development**

The earliest known attempt to formulate a code was an experimental draft code of ethics printed in the 1920s and attributed to Mary Richmond (Pumphrey, 1959). Although several other social work organizations formulated draft codes during the early years of the profession—for example, the American Association for Organizing Family Social Work and several chapters of the American Association of Social Workers—it was not until 1947 that the latter group, the largest organization of social workers of that era, adopted a formal code (Johnson, 1955). In 1960 NASW adopted its first code of ethics, five years after the association was formed.

The 1960 *NASW Code of Ethics* consisted of a series of proclamations concerning, for example, every social worker's duty to give precedence to professional responsibility over personal interests; to respect the privacy of clients; to give appropriate professional service in public emergencies; and to contribute knowledge, skills, and support to programs of human welfare. First-person statements (that is, "I give precedence to my professional responsibility over my personal interests" and "I respect the privacy of the people I serve") were preceded by a preamble that set forth social workers' responsibility to uphold humanitarian ideals, maintain and improve social work service, and develop the philosophy and skills of the profession. In 1967 a principle pledging nondiscrimination was added to the proclamations.

Soon after the adoption of the 1960 code, however, NASW members began to express concern about its level of abstraction, its scope and usefulness for resolving ethical conflicts, and its provisions for handling ethics complaints about practitioners and agencies (McCann & Cutler, 1979). In 1977 the NASW Delegate Assembly established a task force to revise the code and enhance its relevance to practice.

The 1979 code, which formed the foundation of the current code, included six sections of brief, unannotated principles preceded by a preamble setting forth the general purpose of the code, the enduring social work values on which it was based, and a declaration that the code's principles provided standards for the enforcement of ethical practices among social workers. The 1979 code has been revised twice. In 1990 several principles related to solicitation of clients and fee setting were modified following an inquiry into NASW policies by the U.S. Federal Trade Commission, begun in 1986, concerning possible restraint of trade. As a result of the inquiry, principles in the code were revised in order to remove prohibitions concerning solicitation of clients from colleagues or one's agency (original principles II.F.2 and III.K.1) and to modify wording related to accepting compensation for making a referral (principle II.I.1). NASW also entered into a consent agreement with the Federal Trade Commission concerning the issues raised by the inquiry.

In 1993 the NASW Delegate Assembly voted to further amend the code of ethics to include five new principles—three related to the problem of social worker impairment and two related to the problem of dual relationships. The first three principles address instances when social workers' own problems and impairment interfere with their professional functioning, and the latter two address the need to avoid social or nonprofessional relationships with clients. The Delegate Assembly also passed a resolution to establish a task force to review and rewrite the code for submission to the 1996 Delegate Assembly.

**Current Principles**

The sections of the current code set forth principles related to the social worker's general conduct and comportment and ethical responsibilities to clients, colleagues, employers, employing organizations, the social work profession, and society. (The *NASW Code of Ethics* is presented as Appendix 1 of this encyclopedia.) The code's principles are both prescriptive ("The social worker should act to prevent the unauthorized and unqualified practice of social work") and proscriptive ("The social worker should not exploit relationships with clients for personal advantage"). Several of the code's principles are concrete and specific ("The social worker should under no circumstances engage in sexual activities with clients" and "The social worker should respect confidences shared by colleagues in the course of their professional relationships and transactions"), whereas others are more abstract, asserting ethical ideals ("The social worker should promote the general welfare of society" and "The social worker should uphold and advance the values, ethics, knowledge, and mission of the profession").

The wide range of principles in the code indicates that it was designed to serve several purposes. The more abstract, idealistic principles concerning social justice and general welfare provide social workers with important aspirations, as opposed to enforceable standards. Other principles, however, set forth specific rules with which practitioners are expected to comply. Violations provide grounds for the filing of a formal ethics complaint. In addition, a major purpose of the code is to provide social workers with principles to help them resolve ethical dilemmas encountered in practice, a topic that has received considerable attention in recent years.

## Ethical Dilemmas in Social Work

Social workers encounter a wide variety of ethical decisions and dilemmas as a result of their diverse and sometimes conflicting obligations to clients, employers, colleagues, the social work profession, and society at large. Many ethical decisions are routine, such as obtaining clients' consent before releasing confidential information and avoiding sexual contact with clients. In some instances, however, ethical decisions are complex and troubling. Most troubling are decisions that require social workers to choose between two or more conflicting duties or obligations. For example, the *NASW Code of Ethics* (1994) states that the "social worker should not engage in any action that violates or diminishes the civil or legal rights of clients" (p. 6). However, the code also states that the "social worker should adhere to commitments made to the employing organization." It is not difficult to imagine a situation in which these two principles conflict, such as when an agency policy to which a worker is committed results in the violation of a client's civil rights.

Other ethical conflicts that are particularly disquieting include those related to confidentiality and privileged communication; truth-telling; paternalism and self-determination; the obligation to adhere to laws, policies, and agency regulations; whistle-blowing; allocation of limited resources; and the relationship between personal and professional values.

### Confidentiality and Privileged Communication

Social workers assume that information shared by clients should be kept confidential. Although confidentiality certainly is appropriate in nearly every instance, on occasion practitioners need to consider disclosing confidential information, perhaps against a client's wishes, such as when a client seriously threatens to injure a third party or has abused a child or an aged person. In fact, this possibility is recognized by the *NASW Code of Ethics* (1994), which states that social workers may reveal confidential information for "compelling professional reasons." Unfortunately, there is no consensus in the profession about all of the conditions that warrant such disclosure, although there is general agreement that it is appropriate only under extreme circumstances.

Similar problems can arise related to privileged communication. In many states clients of social workers have the right of privileged communication, which provides grounds for social workers to resist disclosure of information about clients in a court of law. However, in states where clients of social workers do not have this right (and occasionally in states where they do), social workers must sometimes choose between a court order to disclose information shared by a client in confidence (for instance, related to a child custody dispute) and a client's right to confidentiality (Wilson, 1978).

### Telling the Truth

Another principle ordinarily embraced in the profession is the client's right to truthful information about matters relevant to his or her care, treatment, and welfare. Yet some social workers argue that in rare instances it may be permissible, or even obligatory, either to withhold the truth from a client or to provide misinformation. Such action is ordinarily defended on grounds that it is sometimes needed to protect a client from harm. Many social workers claim that it is never justifiable for a practitioner to withhold truthful information or provide misinformation to a client, but others point to cases involving, for example, seriously ill clients or children for whom truthful information is considered to be harmful, at least under certain circumstances (Bok, 1978; Gert & Culver, 1976).

### Paternalism and Self-Determination

The tendency to protect clients from harm raises a complex series of issues related to paternalism in social work. Paternalistic action involves interfering with a client's wishes or freedom "for his or her own good." Restraining self-destructive clients or requiring them to receive services against their wishes, withholding information from clients, or providing clients with misinformation are examples of paternalism when these actions are carried out to protect clients from themselves.

Again, however, social workers often disagree about the conditions under which paternalism is justifiable (Reamer, 1983a). There are those who believe that clients have the right to engage in some forms of self-destructive behavior and to take risks, whereas others claim that social workers have a responsibility to protect clients from themselves when they fail to exercise "good" judgment. Debates about these issues frequently revolve around the concepts of self-determination, informed consent, and the extent to which clients are able to exercise sound, informed judgment regarding their own welfare (Culver & Gert, 1982; Dworkin, 1971; McDermott, 1975; Reamer, 1987b).

### Laws, Policies, and Regulations

Another widely held belief in social work is that practitioners should adhere to laws and to agency policies and regulations. On occasion, however, social workers claim that laws, policies, and regulations ought not be obeyed because of the harm that presumably would result. In a number of cases, for example, social workers have chosen not to comply with a local law mandating the reporting of child abuse because of a belief that the child would be exposed to greater risk if the case were reported to the local protective services authority.

Another common example involves social workers' decisions not to report clients' income or assets when doing so would deprive the clients of needed services or benefits. Although the vast majority of social workers do not condone such violations, some defend them, believing that any action to protect a client's welfare is justifiable, even if it violates another ethical principle, law, or policy (Wasserstrom, 1971).

### Whistle-Blowing

Social workers who violate laws or agency regulations place a special burden on colleagues who become aware of these violations. It is tempting to conclude that social workers are always obliged to report such violations, along with instances of fraud, deception, abuse, or exploitation. In practice, however, social workers who have become aware of such transgressions have sometimes found it difficult to blow the whistle.

Friendships, professional loyalties, and the risk to personal job security and reputation have discouraged some practitioners from revealing wrongdoing in the profession. Social workers who obtain evidence of professional indiscretion and misconduct must weigh carefully their obligation to the profession and its clientele, along with competing commitments to colleagues, one's agency, and the risk to one's own career (Reamer & Siegel, 1992; Westin, 1981).

### Distributing Limited Resources

A persistent ethical problem in social work is the need to allocate scarce resources. These resources may include emergency food and shelter, program funds, admission to rehabilitation programs, or a caseworker's time. Social workers use a variety of criteria to distribute limited resources. In some instances they rely on the principle of equality, either by dividing a resource into equally sized portions (for example, money or a worker's time), or by providing clients with equal opportunity to apply or compete for a resource (first come, first served). On occasion a lottery may be used to provide clients with equal opportunity.

Another criterion social workers rely on is need. Many programs have a policy of providing services first to those most in need of them, rather than allocating equal shares or providing equal opportunity to apply for them. Yet another strategy is to give priority to people who have suffered some form of injustice or past discrimination. This principle has formed the basis of affirmative action programs.

Many social workers also allocate limited resources based on a client's ability to pay or to contribute to his or her community in the future. Of course, in many instances those clients who are most persistent, visible, and vocal become recipients of limited social services resources (Reamer, 1990).

### Personal and Professional Values

Conflict between a worker's personal and professional values underlies many ethical decisions and dilemmas (Levy, 1976). In addition, a worker's values may conflict with a client's personal or religious values. For example, a hospital social worker who believes in taking full advantage of the resources of modern medicine may have difficulty respecting the right to self-determination of a patient who refuses a lifesaving blood transfusion for religious reasons. There are no simple answers in these cases, and social workers do not always agree about whether personal or professional values ought to take precedence when they conflict. In each case, workers must weigh the competing obligations of the client, the employer, the profession, and third parties against the requirements of their own conscience. In addition, they must continually examine the nature of their personal values and the ways in which those values influence their understanding of clients' problems, social problems, application of social work knowledge, and strategies of intervention.

## Ethical Decision Making

In the mid-1970s, social workers began to analyze systematically the ways practitioners make ethical decisions and to attempt to resolve ethical dilemmas encountered in practice. Although discussions of ethics and values have taken place since the profession's formal beginning in the late 19th century, the deliberate, systematic study of social workers' ethical conflicts is more recent.

The recent growth of interest in ethical decision making has also occurred in most other professions. Practitioners and scholars in many fields have become interested in examining the ways that principles of ethics and ethical theory—drawn largely from the discipline of moral philosophy and, at times, from theology—can be applied to ethical dilemmas in the professions. Much of the work in this area has focused on two major questions: (1) What are the ethical duties of professionals in relation to clients, colleagues, employers, the profession itself, and the broader society? and (2) What criteria or guidelines can professionals draw on when their ethical duties and responsibilities conflict? (Callahan & Bok, 1980).

Although professionals tend to look to their respective codes of ethics for guidance, most would acknowledge that a code of ethics is limited in its ability to provide full and detailed answers. Codes of ethics are necessarily written in general terms and at a relatively high level of abstraction to address a broad range of issues. Consequently, professionals often will not find specific guidelines in codes that address ethical dilemmas that arise in practice. In addition, as noted earlier, codes of ethics typically contain principles that on occasion may conflict.

To approach the analysis of such ethical dilemmas systematically, social workers and other professionals sometimes draw on theories and principles of ethics. For centuries moral philosophers have been developing a variety of theories and principles related to issues of right and wrong, the nature of duty and obligation, justice, and so on. They have devoted substantial attention to theories of *normative ethics,* or theories intended to guide decisions in ethically complex situations. Although moral philosophers themselves do not agree entirely on ways to distinguish morally right and wrong actions (debates about what is known as *meta-ethics*), there is considerable agreement about major schools of thought that can be applied when faced with ethical dilemmas (Frankena, 1973; Reamer, 1989, 1993, 1995).

For example, the *deontological* point of view claims that certain actions are inherently right or wrong (that is, as a matter of principle). Proponents of this point of view might argue, for instance, that it is inherently wrong for a social worker to lie to a client and, therefore, that no circumstances can possibly justify such deception. Or they might argue that social workers have an inherent obligation to keep information shared by clients confidential, no matter what the extenuating circumstances.

A competing school of thought claims that actions are not inherently right or wrong, but rather that the rightness of an action is determined by the goodness of its consequences. This so-called *consequentialist, utilitarian,* or *teleological* point of view emphasizes the outcome of an action and promotes actions that result in the greatest good. Thus, a strict utilitarian might justify some form of deception, lying, or breach of confidentiality if the good that would likely result would outweigh the harm done (Gorovitz, 1971).

The merits of these points of view have been debated vigorously among philosophers and professionals. Critics of the deontological position have argued that rules and principles may need to be broken in extreme cases, as in an attempt to protect a client or third party from serious harm. To do otherwise, they argue, would be immoral and unprofessional. On the other hand, utilitarianism has been criticized for its impracticality and the difficulty involved in quantifying and weighing possible harmful and beneficial consequences. Perhaps the most serious criticism of utilitarianism is that it may be used to justify acts that violate the rights of a few in order to promote a greater aggregate good. Philosophers continue to disagree about the validity of these different claims. However, such debates and analyses have alerted professionals to critical issues that ought to be considered in ethical dilemmas, especially dilemmas in which professional duties conflict and choices must be made.

## Ethics Enforcement

Sometimes ethics complaints are filed against social workers. Members of NASW, for example, may be named in ethics complaints alleging violation of principles in the association's code of ethics. Over the years there has been a steady increase in the number of ethics complaints filed against social workers, covering a wide range of alleged violations involving social workers' behavior and relationships with clients, colleagues, employers, and the profession (Berliner, 1989).

Ethics complaints filed against NASW members are handled initially by chapter committees on inquiry (COIs), which may accept or reject a complaint on the basis of specific criteria. Using a process of peer review, a chapter COI conducts a hearing during which the complainant, respondent, and witnesses have an opportunity to present testimony. After deliberation and discussion, the COI presents a report to chapter officers summarizing its findings and recommendations. Recommendations may include sanctions or various forms of corrective action, such as suspension from NASW, mandated supervision or consultation, censure in the form of a letter, or instructions to send the complainant a letter of apology. In some cases, the sanction may be publicized. The parties involved in the complaint may appeal the outcome, first to the NASW Committee on Inquiry and then, if necessary, to the executive committee of the NASW Board of Directors.

NASW staff monitor and facilitate ethics adjudication and promote various ethics education activities. In addition to monitoring and facilitating the handling of ethics complaints filed against NASW members, the staff also oversee COIs' handling of complaints filed by social workers against employing organizations alleging violations of an agency's own personnel standards. Furthermore, the NASW staff also oversee COIs' handling of complaints by NASW members when their employers have allegedly restricted their freedom to engage in various forms of professional or social action on behalf of their clients (for example, efforts that seek to eliminate discrimination, enhance access to services, or change policy or legislation). These various activities are designed to enhance, as constructively as possible, the quality of social work services provided to the public (NASW, 1991).

In many instances social workers involved in ethical misconduct are impaired. Professional impairment may involve an inability or unwillingness to comply with professional standards; an inability to develop professional skills or minimal professional competency; or an inability to manage personal stress, psychological dysfunction, or other forms of stress that interfere with professional functioning (Lamb et al., 1987). Impairment and related ethical misconduct may take the form of sexual contact with clients, incompetent delivery of services, financial exploitation of clients, fraudulent activity, or neglect or abandonment of clients.

Impaired social workers also may have a serious substance abuse problem or may be victims of professional burnout. It is essential for social workers to be aware of the warning signs of impairment and be willing to address the problem of impairment whenever it appears in their own or in colleagues' lives. It is also important for social workers to become acquainted with strategies to prevent impairment and the ethics complaints and liability claims that may result from impairments (Reamer, 1992a, 1994b, in press).

## Future of Social Work Ethics

Social workers have been concerned about ethics and values since the profession began. Social work has a long-standing history of commitment to issues of social justice and to the dignified, fair treatment of people in need of assistance. Although many of the ethical issues of current concern in the profession have been the focus of attention for decades, others have emerged only recently. Future changes in the profession will no doubt lead to new ethical issues and questions.

There is no way to know with certainty what issues are likely to emerge in the future, but several trends are worth noting. First, it will be important for social workers to pay close attention to the ethical issues created by technological advances that affect the profession. For example, developments in computer technology will continue to lead to difficult issues related to privacy and confidentiality. Developments in medical technology will raise new questions related to the allocation of health care, the right to life, and the right to die. Developments in industry and the economy will affect employment patterns and thus raise ethical questions about the right to work and to obtain public assistance. In response to these advances, many social work agencies are forming ethics committees to consult on difficult decisions and educate staff members who face difficult ethical choices (Reamer, 1987a).

A second trend worth observing relates to shifts in employment patterns among social workers themselves. In recent years social workers have been entering the mental health field in increasing numbers, many in private practice, whereas the number of social workers in public social services agencies has declined. Such shifts suggest important questions about the mission of social work and its value base (Reamer, 1992b). To what extent should social work place primary emphasis on the poor and oppressed as opposed to more affluent clients? What portion of the profession's resources should be devoted to clinical issues as opposed to social action, such as advocacy on behalf of the least advantaged? How much attention should be paid to those with meager financial resources as opposed to those who have ample assets or insurance coverage to pay for services?

In addition, as social work develops new specialties, novel questions of ethics and values are likely to emerge. For example, as industrial or occupational social work and social workers' involvement in employee assistance programs have grown, so too have problems related to confidentiality, privileged communication, and conflicts between the practitioner's loyalty to the client and employer. Also, as social workers develop increasingly specialized private practices, questions are likely to emerge related to the ethics of advertising, solicitation of clients, and competence.

Finally, the perennial tension between the roles of the public and private sectors in social welfare is likely to continue. The extent to which the public sector has assumed responsibility for social welfare has waxed and waned for decades. In the 1930s and 1960s, there was considerable support for large-scale government involvement in the provision of aid to the poor and oppressed. At other times federal and state officials and the general citizenry have been far less supportive of social welfare underwritten by the public sector. The early 1980s saw the beginning of a significant transfer of responsibility for social services to the for-profit (proprietary) and nonprofit private sector, including private social services agencies, charitable organizations, religious groups, and other voluntary associations. The merits of this shift have been debated widely and will need to be examined continually for their effect on the ability of social workers to fulfill the moral and ethical purposes of the profession (Reamer, 1983b).

The future of social work cannot be predicted with precision, but it is certain that ethical and value issues will continue to permeate the profession. Although some of these issues will change in response to new trends and developments, the fundamental issues related to ethics and values in social work will persist, such as practitioners' moral duty to aid those in need, clients' right to self-determination, and the formulation of criteria for allocating scarce social services resources. Hence, it will always be essential for social workers to examine these issues, which in the end form the very foundation of the profession.

## References


Bartlett, H. M. (1970). *The common base of social work practice*. New York: Columbia University Press.

Berliner, A. K. (1989). Misconduct in social work practice. *Social Work, 34,* 69–72.

Biestek, F. P. (1957). *The casework relationship.* Chicago: Loyola University Press.

Bok, S. (1978). *Lying: Moral choice in public and private life.* New York: Pantheon Books.

Callahan, D., & Bok, S. (Eds.). (1980). *Ethics teaching in higher education.* New York: Plenum Press.

Culver, C. M., & Gert, B. (1982). *Philosophy in medicine: Conceptual and ethical issues in medicine and psychiatry.* New York: Oxford University Press.

Davis, A. F. (1967). *Spearheads for reform.* New York: Oxford University Press.

Dworkin, G. (1971). Paternalism. In R. A. Wasserstrom (Ed.), *Morality and the law* (pp. 107–126). Belmont, CA: Wadsworth.

Frankena, W. K. (1973). *Ethics* (2nd ed.). Englewood Cliffs, NJ: Prentice Hall.

Gert, B., & Culver, C. M. (1976). Paternalistic behavior. *Philosophy and Public Affairs, 6,* 45–57.

Gordon, W. E. (1962). A critique of the working definition. *Social Work, 7,* 6.

Gorovitz, S. (Ed.). (1971). *Mill: Utilitarianism.* Indianapolis: Bobbs-Merrill.

Hamilton, G. (1940). *Theory and practice of social casework.* New York: Columbia University Press.

Johnson, A. (1955). Educating professional social workers for ethical practice. *Social Service Review, 29*(2), 125–136.

Keith-Lucas, A. (1977). Ethics in social work. In J. B. Turner (Ed.-in-Chief), *Encyclopedia of social work* (17th ed., Vol. 1, pp. 350–355). Washington, DC: National Association of Social Workers.

Lamb, D. H., Presser, N. R., Pfost, K. S., Baum, M. C., Jackson, V. R., & Jarvis, P. A. (1987). Confronting professional impairment during the internship: Identification, due process, and remediation. *Professional Psychology: Research and Practice, 18,* 597–603.

Levy, C. S. (1973). The value base of social work. *Journal of Education for Social Work, 9*(1), 34–42.

Levy, C. S. (1976). *Social work ethics.* New York: Human Sciences Press.

McCann, C. W., & Cutler, J. P. (1979). Ethics and the alleged unethical. *Social Work, 24,* 5–8.

McDermott, F. E. (Ed.). (1975). *Self-determination in social work.* London: Routledge & Kegan Paul.

National Association of Social Workers. (1991). *NASW chapter guide for the adjudication of grievances* (rev. ed.). Silver Spring, MD: Author.

National Association of Social Workers. (1994). *NASW code of ethics.* Washington, DC: Author.

Plant, R. (1970). *Social and moral theory in casework.* London: Routledge & Kegan Paul.

Pumphrey, M. W. (1959). *The teaching of values and ethics in social work education.* New York: Council on Social Work Education.

Reamer, F. G. (1983a). The concept of paternalism in social work. *Social Service Review, 57*(2), 254–271.

Reamer, F. G. (1983b). Social services in a conservative era. *Social Casework, 64*(8), 451–458.

Reamer, F. G. (1987a). Ethics committees in social work. *Social Work, 32,* 188–192.

Reamer, F. G. (1987b). Informed consent in social work. *Social Work, 32,* 425–429.

Reamer, F. G. (1987c). Values and ethics. In A. Minahan (Ed.-in-Chief), *Encyclopedia of social work* (18th ed., Vol. 2, pp. 801–809). Silver Spring, MD: National Association of Social Workers.

Reamer, F. G. (1989). Toward ethical practice: The relevance of ethical theory. *Social Thought, 15*(3/4), 67–78.

Reamer, F. G. (1990). *Ethical dilemmas in social service* (2nd ed.). New York: Columbia University Press.

Reamer, F. G. (Ed.). (1991). *AIDS and ethics.* New York: Columbia University Press.

Reamer, F. G. (1992a). The impaired social worker. *Social Work, 37,* 165–170.

Reamer, F. G. (1992b). Social work and the public good: Calling or career? In P. N. Reid & P. R. Popple (Eds.), *The moral purposes of social work.* Chicago: Nelson-Hall.

Reamer, F. G. (1993). *The philosophical foundations of social work.* New York: Columbia University Press.

Reamer, F. G. (1994a). *Social work malpractice and liability.* New York: Columbia University Press.
Reamer, F. G. (1994b). Social work values and ethics. In F. G. Reamer (Ed.), *The foundations of social work knowledge.* New York: Columbia University Press.
Reamer, F. G. (1995). *Social work values and ethics.* New York: Columbia University Press.
Reamer, F. G. (in press). Malpractice and liability claims against social workers: First facts. *Social Work.*
Reamer, F. G., & Abramson, M. (1982). *The teaching of social work ethics.* Hastings-on-Hudson, NY: The Hastings Center.
Reamer, F. G., & Siegel, D. H. (1992). Should social workers blow the whistle on incompetent colleagues? In E. Gambrill & R. Pruger (Eds.), *Controversial issues in social work* (pp. 66–78). Boston: Allyn & Bacon.
Rokeach, M. (1973). *The nature of human values.* New York: Free Press.
Teicher, M. (1967). *Values in social work: A re-examination.* New York: National Association of Social Workers.
Timms, N. (1983). *Social work values: An enquiry.* London: Routledge & Kegan Paul.
Varley, B. (1968). Social work values: Changes in value commitments of students from admission to MSW graduation. *Journal of Education for Social Work, 4,* 67–85.
Wasserstrom, R. A. (Ed.). (1971). *Morality and the law.* Belmont, CA: Wadsworth.
Westin, A. (Ed.). (1981). *Whistle blowing? Loyalty and dissent in the corporation.* New York: McGraw-Hill.
Wilson, S. J. (1978). *Confidentiality in social work.* New York: Free Press.
Younghusband, E. (1967). *Social work and social values.* London: Allen & Unwin.

## Further Reading

Beauchamp, T. L. (1982). *Philosophical ethics: An introduction to moral philosophy.* New York: McGraw-Hill.
Callahan, J. C. (Ed.). (1988). *Ethical issues in professional life.* New York: Oxford University Press.
Emmet, D. (1962). Ethics and the social worker. *British Journal of Psychiatric Social Work, 6*(6), 165–172.
Joseph, M. V. (1989). Social work ethics: Historical and contemporary perspectives. *Social Thought, 15*(3/4), 4–17.
Levy, C. S. (1972). The context of social work ethics. *Social Work, 17,* 95–101.
Loewenberg, F., & Dolgoff, R. (1992). *Ethical decisions for social work practice* (4th ed.). Itasca, IL: F. E. Peacock.
Reamer, F. G. (1982). Conflicts of professional duty in social work. *Social Casework, 63*(10), 579–585.
Reamer, F. G. (1983). Ethical dilemmas in social work practice. *Social Work, 28,* 31–35.
Reamer, F. G. (1985). The emergence of bioethics in social work. *Health & Social Work, 10,* 271–281.
Rhodes, M. L. (1986). *Ethical dilemmas in social work practice.* London: Routledge & Kegan Paul.
Siporin, M. (1982). Moral philosophy in social work today. *Social Service Review, 56*(4), 516–538.
Siporin, M. (1989). Morality and immorality in working with clients. *Social Thought, 15*(3/4), 42–52.

**Frederic G. Reamer, PhD,** is professor, Rhode Island College, School of Social Work, Providence, RI 02908.

**For further information see**

Abortion; Advocacy; Bioethical Issues; Children's Rights; Civil Rights; Clinical Social Work; Direct Practice Overview; Ethical Issues in Research; Ethnic-Sensitive Practice; Health Care: Direct Practice; HIV/AIDS Overview; Human Rights; Legal Issues: Confidentiality and Privileged Communication; Licensing, Regulation, and Certification; National Association of Social Workers; Patient Rights; Peace and Social Justice; Person-in-Environment; Professional Conduct; Professional Liability and Malpractice; Quality Assurance; Social Justice in Social Agencies; Social Work Practice: History and Evolution; Social Work Practice: Theoretical Base; Social Work Profession Overview.

**Key Words**
ethics
values
professional conduct

# Ethnic-Sensitive Practice

**Elfriede G. Schlesinger**
**Wynetta Devore**

Efforts to incorporate understanding of diverse ethnic, minority, and cultural groups into the theories and principles that guide social work practice have been long-standing and persistent. Before World War II, the social work profession, along with others in society, was concerned with the process of absorbing immigrants of diverse cultural backgrounds. Much attention was paid to the cultures of immigrants, although the prevailing "melting-pot" ideology presumed that cultural differences were transient. This emphasis on diversity persisted until the Supreme Court's decision in *Brown v. Board of Education of Topeka* (1954). As a result of that decision, cultural uniqueness was de-emphasized and the integration of diverse groups into the mainstream was encouraged (Schlesinger & Devore, 1979).

Egalitarian motives led many social workers to conclude that attention to differences in lifestyles that are related to ethnicity, social class, race, and minority status were incongruent with the profession's commitment to equality and the uniqueness of each individual. It was not until the 1960s, following the emerging militancy of segments of the African American community, that there was an extensive effort to deal with these issues. In 1973 the Council on Social Work Education (CSWE, 1973) mandated that instruction in diverse ethnic and minority groups must be an integral part of social work education. CSWE's subsequent curriculum policy statements (1984, 1992) reiterated and expanded on this position: Special attention was to be paid to the oppression experienced by minority groups. As a result of these efforts, there has been a greater focus on ethnic issues and on the development of practice-related theories and principles since the mid-1970s (see especially Davis & Proctor, 1989; Devore & Schlesinger, 1981, 1987a, 1987b, 1991; Green, 1982; Lum, 1986, 1992; Pinderhughes, 1989; see also the *Journal of Multicultural Issues in Social Work*).

## Definitions

### Ethnic-Sensitive Practice

*Ethnic-sensitive practice* is based on the view that practice must be attuned to the values and dispositions related to clients' ethnic group membership and social-class position. Attention to the oppression of members of racial and ethnic groups is an essential component of ethnic-sensitive practice and guides the identification of practice models that are thought to be the most consonant with the approach developed (Devore & Schlesinger, 1981, 1987a, 1987b, 1991). Devore and Schlesinger (1991) suggested that

> as various groups send their children to school, become ill, encounter marital difficulties, and generally live their lives, they bring with them a unique ethnic and class tradition. . . . As they confront "helpers" or "caretakers" they expect . . . that these aspects of their being . . . will be understood [whether or not they are aware that] some of their strengths and tensions are related to this aspect of their lives.
>
> Those charged with the responsibility of . . . helping have the obligation to be sensitive to that possibility. (pp. 52–53)

A number of conceptual formulations shed light on how simultaneous membership in the core society and in the ethnic or minority group affects people's behaviors and attitudes. One is the concept of the "dual perspective"—a "conscious and systematic process of perceiving, understanding, and comparing simultaneously the values, attitudes and behaviors of the larger societal system with those of the client's immediate family and community system" (Norton, 1978, p. 3). The concept is derived from the view that all people are a part of two systems: (1) the dominant system, referred to as the sustaining system, which is the source of power and economic resources, and (2) the nurturing system, composed of the physical and social environment of family and community. A closely related perspective is biculturalism, developed by Ho (1987), who suggested that minority-group persons are inevitably part of two cultures:

> Biculturalism demands the bilateral bringing together of items, values and behaviors. It signifies participation in two cultural systems and often requires two sets of behavior . . . but does not mean dual personality; rather it involves two distinct ways of coping with tasks, expectations and behaviors. (pp. 15–16)

Another important perspective is the concept of ethnic reality, developed by Devore and Schlesinger (1981) and discussed briefly in the subsection "Relationship between Social Class and Ethnicity."

### Ethnic Groups and Ethnicity

Most definitions of ethnic groups converge around a number of themes, including the view that ethnic groups share elements of religion, culture, physical appearance, history, or some combination of these characteristics. Alba (1985) proposed this definition: "An ethnic group is a human group that entertains a 'subjective belief' in its common descent because of similarities of physical type or of customs or both or because of memories of colonization and migration" (p. 27).

***Culture and ethnicity.*** A number of analysts use the terms "culture" and "multiculturalism" to address phenomena that are similar to those of interest in ethnic-sensitive practice. In this entry, we use "ethnicity" and related terms because we believe that cultural phenomena are an integral but not the only component of the ethnic experience. As members of an ethnic group, people experience a sense of peoplehood and have a common history. Culture or way of life is one of the components of that experience; other critical elements of that experience are social-class status and minority status. "Culture" is variously defined. It often refers to the fact that human groups differ in how they structure their behavior, their worldview, their perspectives on the rhythms and patterns of life, and their concept of the essential nature of the human condition. More than culture, the terms "ethnicity" and "ethnic group" connote the dynamic interplay among these various factors. Brookins (1993) made this point well:

> Ethnicity refers to group membership in which the defining feature is the characteristic of shared unique cultural traditions and a heritage that spans across generations. Membership in an ethnic group provides the cultural identity and lens through which the developing child comes to understand and act upon prescribed values, norms and social behavior. (p. 1057)

***Minorities of color versus ethnic groups.*** As interest in the areas of ethnicity and culture has increased, analysts have struggled to find appropriate language to describe and discuss relevant phenomena. A number of terms have come under considerable scrutiny. Two terms that are used to refer to members of a minority group or people of color are "minority" and "ethnic group."

For some time, the term "minority group" has been used for people who are "at the lowest end of the spectrum of power and advantage" (Hopps, 1983, p. 77) and are, in large measure, set apart by racism and poverty. Most analysts include in this group African Americans, Native Americans, Native Alaskans, Mexican Americans, and Puerto Ricans, and some also include Asian Americans. In the view of some analysts, the term "minority group" refers to people other than members of ethnic groups who are especially oppressed. Hopps (1982) and others have suggested that the people identified in the past as "racial minorities" should be referred to as "people of color" or "minorities of color."

Use of the term "ethnic group" to refer to members of minority groups or people of color has been questioned. Jaynes and Williams (1989), for example, rejected the idea that African Americans constitute an ethnic group in the same way as do people of European origin. Rather, they suggested that the category "black" should be treated as a "social reality that combines class, ethnicity, cultural heritage, political interest and self-definition" (p. 565).

### Relationship between Social Class and Ethnicity

Many people, including ourselves, believe that membership in a social class is a major determinant of a person's life chances and lifestyle. Nevertheless, major differences in the behavior, attitudes, and life chances between people of the same social class are apparent. Gordon (1964) proposed that ethnic-group membership accounts for some of these differences. He suggested that the point at which social class and ethnic-group membership intersect (which he termed "ethclass") generates identifiable dispositions and behaviors. Devore and Schlesinger (1991) called these dispositions the "ethnic reality," which is characterized by deeply ingrained feelings and actions on such matters as appropriate child-rearing practices or proper care for the aged or dispositions that derive from oppression. Indeed, oppression, in the present or the past, or both, is part of the ethnic reality of many groups. This definition is similar to that of Jaynes and Williams's (1989) definition of social reality.

## Components of Ethnic-Sensitive Practice

Ethnic-sensitive social work practice builds on (1) the components of a professional perspective conceptualized as the "layers of understanding"; (2) a series of assumptions; and (3) prevailing practice principles, skills, and strategies. The approach introduces no new practice principles or approaches; rather, it involves the adaptation of prevailing social work principles and skills to take account of the ethnic reality. It is based on the view that social workers must be attuned to the special dispositions of all ethnic groups and have a special obligation to be aware of and to seek to redress the oppression experienced by members of minority groups.

### Layers of Understanding

The values, knowledge, and skills that are the essential ingredients of professional practice in social work have been conceptualized as the layers of understanding.

***Social work values.*** According to Levy (1973), values are (1) preferred outcomes for people, (2) preferred conceptions of people, and (3) instrumentalities for dealing with people. Emphasis is placed on recognizing the importance of the relationship between people and their environments, of the quality of life and of the importance of social policies in enhancing the quality of life, and views on how people ought to be treated.

***Knowledge of human behavior.*** Familiarity with the range of theories that attempt to explain individual, institutional, community, and organizational behavior is essential if social workers are to take account of the unique ways in which members of diverse ethnic and minority groups encounter various systems and problems.

***Knowledge of social welfare policies and services.*** A core social work function is to help people learn about, gain access to, and use a range of social services. To carry out this function in a sensitive manner requires knowledge of how these services are structured and organized, as well as their basic premises. It is crucial to recognize that barriers to the delivery of ethnic-sensitive services are often built into the very structures that are presumed to serve people.

***Self-awareness.*** The disciplined aware self remains one of the professional's major tools. Development of self-awareness involves the process of discovering "me—not always nice, sometimes judgmental, prejudiced and noncaring" (Devore & Schlesinger, 1981, p. 83) and makes use of this to further empathic skills. In ethnic-sensitive practice, the process is expanded to include the question, "Who am I in the ethnic sense?" Thinking through and feeling the impact of one's ethnicity on one's perception of self and others enhances the capacity to "tune in" to the ethnic reality.

***Knowledge of the impact of the ethnic reality.*** The ethnic reality seeps into the substance of psychological and social being in myriad ways. Ingrained views about the capacity to master nature or to succumb to uncontrollable forces may manifest themselves in divergent responses to family crises, illness, and death. The professional helper may be viewed as one who is appropriately called on to aid in problem solving or as an intruder who has no business interfering with intimate matters that had better remain within the family.

Members of ethnic groups who are particular victims of racism and poverty experience persistent barriers as they struggle to achieve minimal standards of living and to enlarge the range of opportunities that are open to them. Whatever their level of oppression or opportunity, individuals draw on the sustenance and comfort of shared traditions, exemplified by the psychic bonds of a common language, history, and shared rituals and celebrations.

***The route to the social worker.*** The paths to social work services have been conceptualized on a continuum ranging from totally coercive to totally voluntary (Devore & Schlesinger, 1991). Members of oppressed minority groups are likely to be coerced into receiving social work services by the schools, the courts, or other authoritative institutions, whereas those with greater resources are likely to be voluntary clients.

There are clear-cut differences in the initial approach to the client–worker encounter depending on whether clients request social work intervention or intervention is mandated by a legal authority or "encouraged" or required by the client's employer or by one of a number of social institutions, such as a hospital, nursing home, school, or the client's family.

The different routes to the social worker affect the degree to which it is possible for clients to maintain self-direction. How clients define problems affects their readiness and willingness to engage in problem solving. However the client gets to the social worker, it is essential for the social worker to approach problems in the way in which they are defined by the client.

The initial social worker–client encounter, wherever it falls on the voluntary–coercive continuum, must focus on efforts to help the client formulate problems in terms that are manageable to the client. Although this dictum is true for all persons, it is especially important for oppressed, powerless, minority people. The very act of engaging the client in formulating his or her problems can contribute to the client's sense of empowerment.

***Adaptation and modification of strategies and skills.*** Classic and emerging strategies of practice require rethinking and adaptation if the goals of ethnic-sensitive practice are to be achieved. For example, such seemingly clear-cut engagement procedures as establishing eye contact, generating an atmosphere of informality, and encouraging self-disclosure on intimate and troubling matters go counter to the established interactional habits of many groups. Devore and Schlesinger (1991) suggested a series of procedures to show how these adaptations can be made while maintaining the integrity of basic social work approaches. Similar adaptations have been proposed for macro practice. At the administrative level, attention must be paid to the ethnic reality of staff, as well as of client groups. Models of planning must pay particular attention to the dynamics and demographics of populations in the community.

### Assumptions of Ethnic-Sensitive Practice

The following assumptions are drawn from an examination of the ways in which an ethnic group's history, values, and perspectives affect individuals and the group as a whole: (1) Individual and collective history have a bearing on the generation and solution of problems; (2) the present is the most important; (3) nonconscious phenomena affect individual functioning; and (4) ethnicity is a source of cohesion, identity, and strengths, as well as of strain, discordance, and strife.

Each ethnic group and its members have an ethnic history with roots in the past that may affect the members' perceptions of current problems. For example, in the absence of expected intergenerational support, elderly Slavic people may feel ill at ease or, in extreme cases, devastated (Stein, 1976). The individual and collective history of many African Americans leads to the expectation that family resources will be available in times of trouble (Hines & Boyd-Franklin, 1982); yet the younger generation's movement into the middle class may inhibit these young people's capacity to act in accord with this powerful tradition because their family units are smaller and they have greater mobility (Devore & Schlesinger, 1991).

The present, however, is most important. For example, it is in response to current pressures that some Irish people and some Native American people resort to the excessive use of alcohol (Attneave, 1982; McGoldrick, 1982). Similarly, some Native American and African American youths respond to their present oppression by committing suicide and homicide. Likewise, many Mexican American and Puerto Rican women feel tension as they attempt to move beyond traditionally defined gender roles into the mainstream as students and paid employees (Devore & Schlesinger, 1991).

## Practice Principles

### Simultaneous Attention to Individual and Systemic Concerns

The history and traditions of ethnic groups and social class highlight the fact that extensive institutional oppression exists. For this reason it is important that social work be viewed as a problem-solving endeavor that must simultaneously address individual and systemic concerns. The practice models that are the most consonant with the principles of ethnic-sensitive practice are the problem-solving models (Perlman, 1957, 1986), the structural model (Wood & Middleman, 1989), select segments of task-centered practice (Reid, 1978; Reid & Epstein, 1972), ecological models (Germain & Gitterman, 1980, 1986), and institutional change models (Netting, Kettner, & McMurtry, 1993; Rivera & Erlich, 1992).

### Cognitive, Affective, and Behavioral Skills

Ethnic-sensitive practice involves the capacity to adapt the cognitive, affective, and behavioral skills of social work in keeping with an understanding of clients' ethnic reality.

***Cognitive skills.*** At the cognitive level, ethnic-sensitive practice involves knowledge of the rationale behind the stages of the helping process that are characteristic of most models of practice. The preparatory work involved in identifying the characteristics of the community, the agency context, and the nature of the ethnic populations who tend to be served is crucial. Social workers should make efforts to know something about indigenous helping networks, the use of formally organized helping systems, and the ways in which members of various ethnic groups are likely to define and cope with problems.

Attention to such matters as whether there are ethnic-based traditions about discussing intimate concerns with strangers (even professionals) or about avoiding eye contact with strangers is also essential. In addition, it is important to know how to adapt strategies, such as launching the interaction process; setting the stage; tuning in; and displaying warmth, empathy, and genuineness, in keeping with clients' ethnic reality.

***Affective skills.*** Social workers should continually seek to enhance their emotional appreciation of such matters as ethnic-based dispositions and fears associated with seeking or receiving help. The fact that so many people—especially members of minority groups—have not sought services voluntarily calls for ongoing efforts by social workers to sharpen ethnic self-awareness and develop the capacity to respond to others' sense of self.

***Behavioral skills.*** Ethnic-sensitive practice is manifested at the level of daily practice behavior. It represents the capacity to draw on assumptions and facts about diverse ethnic groups in problem solving. Social workers should demonstrate the capacity to move with each client at a pace and in a direction determined by the client's perception of the problem, with an understanding that perception is likely to be affected by the client's ethnicity. In some situations, the process may involve giving up cherished notions about the value of the verbal expression of tension-laden emotions or about the superiority of modern psychiatry over the ministrations of the folk healer. The worker must learn to respect the view of many Native Americans, Asian Americans, or people from Eastern Europe and others that to express negative feelings may be more painful than the trauma evoked by those feelings. The folk healer's capacity to smooth troubled family situations or to alleviate symptoms that do not respond to conventional medical treatment may never cease to surprise. Finally, ethnic-sensitive practice means vigilant attention to systemic sources of oppression that would deny minorities and others access to the goods, services, work, and esteem that are consonant with professional social work values.

***Adaptation of practice skills and strategies.*** Throughout this entry the importance of adapting practice strategies and modalities to be congruent with the coping and behavioral styles of different peoples has been mentioned. The needed adaptations have been delineated by Devore and Schlesinger (1991). Lum (1992) suggested that in paying attention to the special needs and dispositions of members of minority groups to overcome the obstacles that accompany oppression, the social worker should distinguish between "etic" and "emic" goals. Etic goals are derived from the assumption that all human beings are alike in some important respects, whereas emic goals are derived from the unique culture under study. Lum suggested that social workers need to "discover the etic and emic characteristics of the client and cultural background during contact and relationship building" (p. 90). Green (1982) proposed that social workers should focus on culturally based criteria of defining problems, recognize group-specific linguistic categories involved in labeling problems, and incorporate lay strategies into the resolution of problems.

## Ethnic-Sensitive Practice: Present Status

Interest in developing perspectives and practice approaches that would ensure that social workers respond with sensitivity to the diverse ethnic, racial, and class groups that constitute this society has accelerated since the emergence of the liberation movements of the 1960s and the dramatic increase in immigration to the United States since the enactment of major changes in immigration law in 1965. Increasing ethnic diversity, coupled with a growing sense that ethnic and cultural identification add to life's richness and opportunities, makes it imperative that social work refine and expand its knowledge and skill bases in this area.

A number of works have made significant contributions to the profession's ability to achieve the goals of ethnic-sensitive practice. They include (1) the conceptualization of the "dual perspective," introduced by Norton (1978) and CSWE (1973); (2) the concept of and term "ethnic-sensitive social work practice," introduced by Devore and Schlesinger in 1981 and expanded in several subsequent works (Devore & Schlesinger, 1981, 1987a, 1987b, 1991; see also Devore, 1983, 1991); (3) Green's (1982) focus on cultural awareness in the human services; and (4) Lum's (1986, 1992) introduction of the concept of minority social work practice and its focus on work with members of minority communities who have historically been oppressed.

Considerable related work has also emerged. McGoldrick, Pearce, and Giordano's (1982) work on ethnicity and family therapy showed how behaviors and dispositions that are derived from membership in an ethnic group help to shape the response to marital problems and need to be taken into consideration by marriage and family therapists. Ho (1987) discussed family therapy with ethnic minority groups, and Boyd-Franklin (1989) wrote about therapy with African American families. Pinderhughes (1989) brought an understanding of these issues to bear on the principles and process of clinical practice, and Davis and Proctor (1989) focused on how race, gender, and class affect the worker–client relationship.

Each of these works approaches related issues from a different conceptual or practice perspective. Nevertheless, there is substantial congruence between the model of ethnic-sensitive practice discussed here and the perspectives of the other writers on this subject. All would share Green's (1982) contention that services should be provided in a culturally acceptable manner that enhances the "sense of ethnic group participation and power" and that human services systems are obliged to meet the client "not only in terms of the specific problem presented but in terms of the client's cultural and community background" (p. 4). The term "ethnic competence," which Green introduced, requires the social worker to be aware of his or her own ethnic and cultural identification, to be open to differences in this area, and to use the client's cultural resources and acknowledge the client's cultural integrity.

In conclusion, it is important to reiterate that if social workers are to be responsive to special needs and dispositions that derive from ethnic group membership and minority status, they must adapt the prevailing social work knowledge and skills to take account of a group's history, preferred coping styles, stance on developing and using professional services, and level of oppression it has experienced.

## References


Alba, R. D. (1985). *Italian-Americans: Into the twilight of ethnicity*. Englewood Cliffs, NJ: Prentice Hall.

Attneave, C. (1982). American Indians and Alaska native families: Emigrants in their own homeland. In M. McGoldrick, J. K. Pearce, & J. Giordano (Eds.), *Ethnicity and family therapy* (pp. 55–83). New York: Guilford Press.

Boyd-Franklin, N. (1989). *Black families in therapy*. New York: Guilford Press.

Brookins, G. K. (1993). Culture, ethnicity and bicultural competence: Implications for children with chronic illness and disability. *Pediatrics, 91,* 1056–1062.

Brown v. Board of Education of Topeka, 347 U.S. 483, 74 S. Ct. 686 (1954).

Council on Social Work Education. (1973). *Handbook of accreditation standards and procedures.* New York: Author.

Council on Social Work Education. (1984). *Handbook of accreditation standards and procedures* (rev. ed.). New York: Author.

Council on Social Work Education. (1992). *Curriculum policy statement for the master's and baccalaureate social work programs*. Alexandria, VA: Author.

Davis, L. E., & Proctor, E. K. (1989). *Race, gender and class*. Englewood Cliffs, NJ: Prentice Hall.

Devore, W. (1983). Ethnic reality: The life model and work with black families. *Social Casework, 64,* 525–531.

Devore, W. (1991). An ethnic sensitive approach to supervision and staff development: Part I and II. *Social Work Education, 10,* 33–50.

Devore, W., & Schlesinger, E. G. (1981). *Ethnic-sensitive social work practice*. St. Louis: C. V. Mosby.

Devore, W., & Schlesinger, E. G. (1987a). Ethnic-sensitive practice. In A. Minahan (Ed.-in-Chief), *Encyclopedia of social work* (18th ed., Vol. 1, pp. 512–516). Silver Spring, MD: National Association of Social Workers.

Devore, W., & Schlesinger, E. G. (1987b). *Ethnic-sensitive social work practice* (2nd ed.). Columbus, OH: Charles E. Merrill.

Devore, W., & Schlesinger, E. G. (1991). *Ethnic-sensitive social work practice* (3rd ed.). New York: Macmillan.

Germain, C. B., & Gitterman, A. (1980). *The life model of social work practice*. New York: Columbia University Press.

Germain, C. B., & Gitterman, A. (1986). The life model of social work practice revisited. In J. Turner (Ed.), *Social work treatment* (pp. 618–644). New York: Free Press.

Gordon, M. M. (1964). *Assimilation in American life*. New York: Oxford University Press.

Green, J. W. (1982). *Cultural awareness in the human services*. Englewood Cliffs, NJ: Prentice Hall.

Hines, P. M., & Boyd-Franklin, N. (1982). Black families. In M. McGoldrick, J. K. Pearce, & J. Giordano (Eds.), *Ethnicity and family therapy* (pp. 84–107). New York: Guilford Press.

Ho, M. K. (1987). *Family therapy with ethnic minorities*. Newbury Park, CA: Sage Publications.

Hopps, J. G. (1982). Oppression based on color. *Social Work, 27,* 3–5.

Hopps, J. G. (1983). Minorities: People of color. In *Encyclopedia of social work* (17th ed., 1983–1984 suppl., pp. 76–83). Silver Spring, MD: National Association of Social Workers.

Jaynes, G. D., & Williams, R. M., Jr. (1989). *A common destiny: Blacks and American society*. Washington, DC: National Academy Press.

Levy, C. (1973). The value base for social work. *Journal of Education for Social Work, 9,* 34–42.

Lum, D. (1986). *Social work practice and people of color: A process-stage approach*. Monterey, CA: Brooks/Cole.

Lum, D. (1992). *Social work practice and people of color: A process-stage approach* (2nd ed.). Pacific Grove, CA: Brooks/Cole.

McGoldrick, M. (1982). Irish families. In M. McGoldrick, J. K. Pearce, & J. Giordano (Eds.), *Ethnicity and family therapy* (pp. 310–339). New York: Guilford Press.

McGoldrick, M., Pearce, J. K., & Giordano, J. (Eds.). (1982). *Ethnicity and family therapy*. New York: Guilford Press.

Netting, F. E., Kettner, P. M., & McMurtry, S. L. (1993). *Social work macro practice*. New York: Longman.

Norton, D. G. (1978). *The dual perspective: Inclusion of ethnic minority content in the social work curriculum*. New York: Council on Social Work Education.

Perlman, H. H. (1957). *Social casework*. Chicago: University of Chicago Press.

Perlman, H. H. (1986). The problem solving model. In J. Turner (Ed.), *Social work treatment* (pp. 245–266). New York: Free Press.

Pinderhughes, E. (1989). *Understanding race, ethnicity and power: The key to efficacy in clinical practice*. New York: Free Press.

Reid, W. J. (1978). *The task-centered system*. New York: Columbia University Press.

Reid, W. J., & Epstein, L. (1972). *Task centered casework*. New York: Columbia University Press.

Rivera, F. G., & Erlich, J. L. (1992). *Community organizing in a diverse society*. Boston: Allyn & Bacon.

Schlesinger, E. G., & Devore, W. (1979). Social workers view ethnic minority teaching. *Journal of Education for Social Work, 15,* 20–27.

Stein, H. F. (1976). A dialectical model of health and illness: Attitudes and behavior among Slovac-Americans. *International Journal of Mental Health, 5*(2), 117–137.

Wood, G. G., & Middleman, R. (1989). *The structural approach to direct practice in social work*. New York: Columbia University Press.


## Further Reading


Bean, F. D., & Tienda, M. (1987). *The Hispanic population of the United States*. New York: Russell Sage Foundation.

Billingsley, A. (1968). *Black families in white America*. Englewood Cliffs, NJ: Prentice Hall.

Gordon, M. M. (1988). *The scope of sociology*. New York: Oxford University Press.

Jacobs, C., & Bowles, D. D. (Eds.). (1988). *Ethnicity and race: Critical concepts in social work*. Silver Spring, MD: National Association of Social Workers.

Jenkins, S. (1981). *The ethnic dilemma in social services*. New York: Free Press.

Jenkins, S. (1988). *Ethnic associations and the welfare state*. New York: Columbia University Press.

Mindel, C. H., & Habenstein, R. W. (1976). *Ethnic families in America*. New York: Elsevier.

Takaki, R. (1993). *A different mirror: A history of multicultural America*. Boston: Little, Brown.



**Elfriede G. Schlesinger, PhD,** is professor, Rutgers University, School of Social Work, 536 George Street, New Brunswick, NJ 08903. **Wynetta Devore, EdD,** is professor, Syracuse University, School of Social Work, Brockway Hall, Syracuse, NY 13244-6350.


## For further information see


Clinical Social Work; Cognition and Social Cognitive Theory; Direct Practice Overview; Ecological Perspective; Goal Setting and Intervention Planning; Interviewing; Person-in-Environment; Social Work Practice: Theoretical Base; Social Work Profession Overview.



**Key Words**

cultural awareness
ethnic-sensitive practice
multiculturalism

## Evaluation

*See* Program Evaluation; Single-System Design

# Experimental and Quasi-Experimental Design

**Ann E. MacEachron**

Advocacy for scientific methods, especially for experimental and quasi-experimental group designs, persists in social work because of the potential of these methods to enhance the credibility of the profession's knowledge base and to demonstrate the accountability and effectiveness of social work practice (Epstein, 1990; Franklin, 1986; Fraser, Taylor, Jackson, & O'Jack, 1991; S. Kirk, 1991; Lindsey & Kirk, 1992; Reid, 1987; Reid & Hanrahan, 1984; Rubin, 1985; Sheldon, 1986; Task Force on Social Work Research, 1991; Tripodi, 1987; Zimbalist, 1977). This entry defines group designs and reviews their prevalence in social work research, describes four principles that guide the use and choice of group-design methods, and highlights issues in using the principles of group design within the applied context of social work research.

### Definition

Scientific research designs are strategic plans that define systematic methods to study research hypotheses or questions derived from theory or practice. Although the purposes of research designs are multiple, the purpose of experimental and quasi-experimental group designs is to investigate cause-and-effect relationships between interventions and outcomes empirically (see, for example, Brown & Melamed, 1990; Campbell & Stanley, 1963; Cook & Campbell, 1979; Dooley, 1990; Grinnell & Stothers, 1988; R. E. Kirk, 1968; Meehl, 1963; Rubin & Babbie, 1989; Spector, 1981; Tripodi, 1981). The demonstration of causality requires, at a minimum, that the intervention be associated with an outcome, that the intervention precede the outcome, and that no plausible rival or alternative explanations can explain the relationship between the intervention and the outcome.

Group designs vary substantially in the extent to which they support inferences of causality: true experimental designs offer strong inferences, pre-experiments offer very weak inferences, whereas the intermediate quasi-experimental designs may provide strong to very weak inferences of causality (Campbell & Stanley, 1963; Cook & Campbell, 1979).

True experiments tend to be strong because they require randomization procedures to assure that each subject has an equal chance of being assigned to either the experimental or the control group. Randomization procedures strengthen causal conclusions because the characteristics of groups are likely to be equivalent so that the groups may be legitimately compared and so that statistical tests of the experimental effect may be easily interpreted. Quasi-experiments lack randomization. Instead, experimenters compare groups that are likely to have nonequivalent characteristics or examine multiple observations of a single group over time (interrupted time-series designs); hence, there is always some degree of doubt about the comparability of group characteristics and the interpretability of statistical tests of significance. Very weak quasi-experiments (one-group pretest–posttest designs or static-group comparison designs) do not include randomization or other design procedures to support valid causal conclusions. Recent examples of these three levels of designs in the social work research literature are as follows: experimental designs with randomization (Edleson & Syers, 1990; Halpern, 1992; Kirkham & Schilling, 1990), quasi-experimental nonequivalent control group designs (Hepler & Rose, 1988; J. A. Rosenthal & Glass, 1990), time-series designs (Bowen, Farkas, & Neenan, 1991; Jones, 1989; Tucker & Hurl, 1992), and pre-experimental designs (Green & Vosler, 1992; Saunders & Parker, 1989).

### Prevalence

The first group design with a control group in social work was done by Powers and Whitmer in 1951 (cited in Lindsey & Kirk, 1992). Since that time, a substantial number of social work studies have used group designs, as noted by social work scholars who have examined the prevalence of group designs in the social work literature. By extending a previous review of four major social work journals (Weinberger & Tripodi, 1969), Tripodi (1984) examined the prevalence of broadly defined "experimental" articles in journals from 1956 through 1980. He found that before 1960, less than 1 percent of the authors of journal articles reported that they used experimental designs, whereas from 1961 to 1980, the percentage of articles with reports of experimental designs had increased substantially, with an annual range of 3.2 percent to 5.8 percent. Tripodi also found a similiar percentage of experimental studies in the two new social work journals that focused on social work research.

Glisson (1990) reviewed articles in five major social work journals from 1977 to 1988. He found that the overall percentage of experimental designs was 8.6 percent, with true experimental designs at 2.5 percent and all quasi-experimental designs at 6.1 percent. When Fraser and Taylor (1990) reviewed 10 additional social work journals from 1985 to 1988, they found that the overall percentage of experimental designs was 4.2 percent, with true experimental designs at about 1 percent and all quasi-experimental designs at about 3.2 percent.

Even though the publication of experimental and quasi-experimental studies in social work journals has been modest, the relative rate has remained steady since the 1960s. Within the larger context of quantitative social work research, this rate of publication may be viewed as an emergent "crisis" (Task Force on Social Work Research, 1991), a persistent and "perennial situation" (Lindsey & Kirk, 1992) for those who advocate for a broad empirical foundation in social work knowledge, or even as "no crisis" for those who do not believe that a rigorous empirical foundation is essential (see, for example, Heineman, 1981; Mahrer, 1988; Raynor, 1984).

This variety of perspectives is not unique to social work (Fraser et al., 1991); indeed, multiple perspectives exist in education (Campbell & Stanley, 1963), public administration (Houston & Delevan, 1990), and other related professions and disciplines. Such debates may be a perennial characteristic of applied professions because, as in social work, "the possession of a scientific knowledge base does not assure that social work will be able to solve the problems placed at the profession's doorstep.... Thus, social work will always be limited in what it can accomplish" (Lindsey & Kirk, 1992, p. 381).

The limits of our empirically based professional knowledge, however, are not necessarily bounded by research published in social work journals or by social workers. Because social work has a multidisciplinary knowledge base, it may and does rely on much empirical and experimental knowledge derived from other disciplines and related professions. Thomlison (1984), for example, provided empirically based answers about four areas of social work practice based on research from related professional fields. Giannetti and Wells's (1985) literature review indicated the equality of psychotherapeutic outcomes across psychiatry, psychology, and social work. In addition, Cheung's (1990) citation analysis indicated that there is a substantial exchange of ideas and research among social work and other disciplines and related professions.

This exchange of ideas and research becomes obvious in research reviews on social problems, which usually cross disciplinary boundaries: child maltreatment (Berrick & Barth, 1992; Howing, Wodarski, Gaudin, & Kurtz, 1989), children's mental health (LeCroy & Ashford, 1992), mental health services (Hogarty, 1989; Videka-Sherman, 1988), family preservation (Rossi, 1992; Wells & Biegel, 1992), and health care (Ivanoff & Stern, 1992; Rutchick, 1990). In a sense, then, the scientific foundation of social work knowledge and effectiveness resembles a rubber band: If research only by social workers published in social work journals defines social work knowledge and effectiveness, it is limited and small, but if multidisciplinary research on the same problems and issues is included, as social workers typically do, then the range of social work's empirical foundation is stretched and becomes substantially larger.

Therefore, empirical social work knowledge and accountability are dependent on the quality not only of social work research but also of research that social workers incorporate from other disciplines and professions. The quality of both sources of research is directly related to the type of research design that is used. In terms of research using group designs, it is necessary to evaluate the strength of each group design on the basis of four conceptual principles.

## Four Principles Concerning Validity

Although true experiments and quasi-experiments may be differentiated by the presence or absence of randomization, randomization itself does not solve all matters of causal inference (Cook & Campbell, 1979). The evaluation of the causal strength of group designs requires equal consideration of how well researchers control for all threats to a design's internal validity, external validity, construct validity of both the cause and effect, and statistical conclusion validity.

### Internal Validity

Internal validity refers to how well the design allows for a statement that only the experimental treatment is responsible for the observed changes in the outcome variables as measured. Stronger causal inferences may be made if experimenters control for alternative explanations or rival hypotheses to the causal hypothesis. Alternative explanations to the causal hypothesis include the history of events other than the treatment that occurred between the pretest and posttest, the maturation of the subjects, the effects of pretesting on posttests, the quality of measuring instruments, statistical regression to the mean when subjects are chosen by extreme scores, selection bias between the groups, differential loss of subjects from groups, and selection–maturation interaction (Campbell & Stanley, 1963).

Some ways that experimenters may increase a design's internal validity are by randomly assigning subjects to experimental and control or comparison groups (randomization), limiting the time between the intervention and measurement of outcomes, and avoiding subjects who are in a period of rapid maturation. Other ways include using reliable and valid measures that have been standardized, omitting the pretest or using an unobtrusive pretest, and checking pretest equivalency of scores for experimental and comparison groups (Campbell & Stanley, 1963; Dooley, 1990).

**External Validity**

External validity, or generalizability, refers to the extent to which experimental results may be generalized "to particular target persons, settings, and times" and especially "across types of persons, settings, and times" (Cook & Campbell, 1979, p. 71). If the treatment effects are limited to certain specified persons, settings, or times, the generality of the results, and hence the external validity of the study, is lessened (Campbell & Stanley, 1963, p. 16). Because the use of randomly selected samples for generalizing "to" larger populations is rare in experimental studies, Cook and Campbell (1979) and others have focused primarily on how researchers may generalize "across" persons, settings, and times. External validity of group designs may be increased by maximizing the similarity between the experimental treatment setting and the settings that are targeted for generalization, using multiple control groups, using samples representative of different populations, and doing multiple replication studies in different settings with different populations at different historical times (Campbell & Stanley, 1963; Cook & Campbell, 1979; Dooley, 1990).

**Construct Validity**

Construct validity of the cause, the effect, and their conceptual relationship refers to the theoretical and operational definitions of treatments, control conditions, outcomes, and their interrelationships. These definitions specify and "reflect the supposed causal construct" between treatments and outcomes (Dooley, 1990, p. 203; see also Cook & Campbell, 1979). Obviously, construct validity increases with the preciseness of theoretical and operational definitions and with the use of multiple definitions of both the causal treatment and the effected outcome to "triangulate on the referent" (Cook & Campbell, 1979, p. 65).

Given precise definitions, the researcher must also deal with additional concerns about experimental group contamination, control group contamination, and experimental group failure.

*Experimental group contamination* may occur from demand characteristics of the experiment, that is, characteristics of the treatment setting that influence subjects' perception and understanding of the goals of the study. A placebo control group may be warranted here so that the subjects are "blind" to whether they are receiving the treatment. The experimenter's expectancies about the outcomes may also bias the results toward desired responses in a self-fulfilling manner (M. J. Rosenthal, 1976). Thus, the design may call for a "naive" experimenter, who provides the intervention but does not know the purpose of the experiment; a "blind" experimenter, who is unaware of which subjects are assigned to experimental and control groups; a "standardized" experimenter, who has scripted words and behaviors to follow exactly; or a "canned" experimenter, who delivers the intervention by videotape or other such means (Dooley, 1990). A "double-blind" experiment minimizes both the demand characteristics and the experimenter's expectancies because both the subjects and experimenter are "blind" to the subjects' assignment to experimental, placebo, and control groups (Dooley, 1990).

*Control group contamination* occurs when subjects in the control group receive unplanned treatments that could affect the outcome but are not analyzed because no one asked about them. Therefore, it is important for researchers to inquire about such unplanned possibilities and, if they are present, to analyze their impact on the outcomes.

*Experimental group failure* occurs when the experiment fails to demonstrate the effectiveness of the intervention (Cook & Campbell, 1979). The likelihood of such failure decreases if the researcher first does a pilot test of the "treatment integrity" of the intervention and then, during the experiment, checks to ensure the appropriate implementation of the intervention. Without such safeguards, it will remain unclear whether a failed intervention resulted from a truly ineffective intervention or only a poorly administered one (Dooley, 1990; Proctor, 1990; Yeaton & Sechrest, 1981).

### Statistical Conclusion Validity

Statistical conclusion, or inference, validity refers to the evaluation of the statistical significance and strength of relationship between the treatment and outcome measures. Two important issues here are choice of inferential statistics and practical significance.

The choice of appropriate inferential statistical tests depends in part on the type of experimental design that is used (see, for example, Campbell & Stanley, 1963; Cook & Campbell, 1979; Keppel, 1973). The use of quasi-experimental designs, rather than true experimental designs, for example, often necessitates the use of more complex statistical tests that may limit the researcher's conclusions about the strength of a causal relationship between the treatment and the outcome (Achen, 1986; Cappelleri, Trochim, & Reichardt, 1991; Cook & Campbell, 1979; Moffitt, 1991; Stanley, 1991; Vooijs & van der Kamp, 1991).

The choice of appropriate inferential statistical tests also depends on the precision of measurement (nominal, ordinal, interval) of treatment and outcome measures as well as their reliability (consistency) and validity (congruence between the measure and concept of interest) and on the statistical test's robustness in estimating correct statistical decisions even when the assumptions underlying the test are violated by the researcher (see, for example, Craft, 1990; Dooley, 1990; Keppel, 1973; MacEachron, 1982; Tabachnick & Fidell, 1983).

Another consideration is the power of a statistical test or its ability to reject a null hypothesis when it is wrong or, in other words, to indicate statistical significance when there is a "true" relationship between the treatment and the outcome. The power of statistical tests decreases as the experiment's sample size becomes smaller, which, unfortunately, is often the case in experimental studies and hence is often a vexing problem (for example, Cohen, 1977; Kazdin, Bass, Ayers, & Rodgers, 1990). Beyond increasing the size of the sample where possible, Cook and Campbell (1979) recommended the concurrent use of estimates of magnitude effects that are bounded by confidence intervals: "With small samples, power analyses should be reported to illustrate the magnitude of the effect that could have been detected given the sample size, the variances obtained in the study, and the chosen significance level" (p. 41).

The practical or social significance of a study's results are tied to the demonstration of statistical significance. However, because group designs often involve only a small number of subjects that may adversely affect the probability of observing statistical significance, it is important to assess the magnitude of the effect—regardless of statistical significance—in terms of practical importance and social values. The assessment of statistically insignificant magnitude effects is ultimately subjective, but it may be done reasonably in light of the guidelines recommended by Cohen (1977) and Smith, Glass, and Miller (1980).

Given internal, external, construct, and statistical conclusion validity, the question of how to optimize all principles together often arises. One frequently mentioned group design to optimize overall scientific validity is the double-blind, randomized clinical experiment, which includes placebo and "no treatment" control groups and has multiple measures (reliable, valid, and observable) of the intervention and its outcomes. Extension to nonclinical populations requires, of course, a sufficiently large random selection of subjects from the population intended for future generalization. Compromises and trade-offs in overall scientific validity are frequent and often necessary, however. Although theoretical and applied research share an equal concern for issues of internal validity, Cook and Campbell (1979, p. 83) suggested that the priorities for theory-building research are experimental construct validity of the cause and the effect, statistical conclusion validity, and then external validity. In contrast, Cook and Campbell (1979) suggested that the priorities for applied or evaluative research are external validity, construct validity of the effect, statistical conclusion validity, and then construct validity of the cause. The focus of social work research has generally been applied research, which is concerned with intervention effectiveness.

## Applied Issues

### Randomization

The issue of randomization and, consequently, the broader issue of internal validity continues to be a problem in all types of research involving human subjects. As Rivlin (1971) noted, randomization is seldom readily accepted by practitioners because it means that some clients will not receive the intervention services. Heckman, Hotz, and Dabos (1987) summarized a number of specific problems in implementing randomization procedures across both clients and manpower training programs:

> Individuals assigned to treatments often do not show up. Individuals randomized out of a program at one trial may subsequently cross over and become program participants ... randomization may alter the program being evaluated. The impact estimated from an

> experiment may bear little resemblance to the true program in the absence of an experiment. For example, a 50–50 randomization of applicants may require an enlargement of, and possible degradation of, the quality of the accepted applicant pool. In addition, more risk-averse persons may not apply to train in sites in which there is randomization.... Experimental advocates ignore the fact that training centers cannot be forced to participate in experiments but rather must agree to participate in them. This creates a center self-selection problem that may make the experimental evidence unrepresentative of the general population of training centers. (p. 422)

Given these and other difficulties, quasi-experimental designs continue to predominate in social work research using group designs, even in such identified exemplars of research as family preservation (Task Force on Social Work Research, 1991). Yet without randomization, some researchers (see, for example, Metcalf & Thornton, 1992; Rossi, 1992) argue that there are still too many potential threats to internal validity to evaluate the general impact of family preservation programs. Indeed, reviews of family preservation programs (Rossi, 1992; Schuerman, Rzepnicki, Littell, & Budde, 1992; Wells & Biegel, 1992) have indicated that as evaluative research designs become more rigorous and include randomization, the impact of such programs becomes negligible. The challenge is to find the balance (1) between large-scale social experimentation and local innovative research on programs (Rivlin, 1971) or between national "grand strategies" and local "site strategies" (Rossi, 1992), (2) between conditions supportive of randomization and conditions limiting its applicability in implementation (Bawden & Sonenstein, 1992; Metcalf & Thornton, 1992), (3) between use of only one design and either the joint use of mutually supportive experimental and quasi-experimental designs within an evaluation (Heckman et al., 1987) or the use of a "multiplist" strategy involving several complementary quasi-experimental designs to address specific threats to internal validity (Fraser et al., 1991; Neenan & Bowen, 1991; Reynolds & West, 1987), and (4) between group designs and other ways of knowing (Tyson, 1992; Vera, 1990).

**Generalizability**

There has been little emphasis on the external validity or generalizability of experimental and quasi-experimental research in social work. Nurius and Tripodi (1985), for example, reviewed 23 experimental studies in two social work research journals from 1979 through 1983 to examine the frequency with which experimental researchers used 10 potential methods of evaluating generalizability. They found not only a "relative paucity of efforts toward evaluating and enhancing generality" (p. 251) but also virtually no use of random sampling and, more important, no use of replications among experimental studies. In addition, few group designs implemented in social work research per se are of sufficient length to allow for the long-term follow-up to asess the long-term gains of intervention. Lack of time perspective further undermines the generalizability of the intervention's efficacy (Rzepnicki, 1991).

The lack of attention to generalizability, especially across people, settings, and time, is puzzling because of the profession's emphasis on sensitivity to such issues as community, poverty, culture, ethnicity, race, gender, social class, age, sexual orientation, and disability. Of issue here is the pragmatic trade-off that researchers often make between generalizability and statistical conclusion validity. Planning for generalizability requires the inclusion of large and heterogeneous samples of individuals, programs, and communities to test for differences in effects of interventions (Rossi, 1992); yet, constraints on implementation and funding often limit sample size and location of samples such that few valid statistical tests of generalizability are possible (Sheldon, 1986).

Perhaps a more important aspect of generalizability, however, is the conceptual articulation of how diversity interacts with interventions in regard to specified outcomes. Such articulation requires a focus on the elaboration of theory that includes aspects of diversity as concepts that necessitate conceptual explanation and on the presentation of clear rationales for choosing target populations for specific services (Rossi, 1992). When successful, "the demonstration of predicted interaction effects is highly regarded as evidence of complex and refined theorizing, of a more mature and successful science. And, from the standpoint of application such research successes increase the likelihood that eventual helping interventions will be successful, because they are directed to appropriate persons and environments" (Koeske, 1992, p. 161). A common but unfortunate practice, however, is to assume that theories and services are universal and hence to pay little or no attention to diversity.

Generalizability, like statistical conclusion validity, is largely dependent on the construct validity of the treatment, the outcome, and the presumed relationship between aspects of the treatment and the outcome. For example, in light of recent experimental research that has demonstrated that family preservation services have little impact on the prevention of placement, a major effort is under way to improve the construct validity of such research (Lamb & Sternberg, 1992; Rossi, 1992; Wells & Biegel, 1992). This effort includes the development of specific, rather than "fuzzy," definitions of family preservation services, program contexts, and target populations; the use of multiple family and child outcomes to evaluate success; the use of behavioral and standardized measures of treatment and outcome; and the development of explicit theoretical assumptions that underlie family preservation. Indeed, as Lamb and Sternberg (1992) pointed out, these issues are common to most evaluations of public policy because "(a) the goals are neither clear nor universally agreed upon, (b) the outcomes are not readily quantifiable in monetary terms, (c) we do not have simple concrete indices of effectiveness, and (d) the biases of evaluators and policy makers persistently threaten to compromise the evaluation" (p. 158). To succeed, therefore, researchers must negotiate the political and contextual constraints surrounding the implementation of maximally feasible group designs (Moran, 1987; Rossi & Freeman, 1985; Thomas, 1989).

Although it is certainly necessary to demonstrate causal inference, statistical conclusion validity does not determine causality or generalizability. It is possible that statistical analysis of data from the same group design, as illustrated by the debate between Thyer and Nugent (Nugent, 1987, 1988; Thyer, 1987; Thyer & Curtis, 1984), may support alternative conclusions. Only replication of the design and additional analysis tend to resolve such debates by providing substantive evidence that supports a specific approach and its generalizability across people, settings, and time.

Another issue related to generalizability is the specification of the role of social workers in the delivery of services. Critical reviews of the research literature (see, for example, Epstein, 1990; Hogarty, 1989; LeCroy & Ashford, 1992) have consistently highlighted the difficulty of attributing any treatment effect to social workers or the services they provide. This occurs because authors do not describe who provides the service or because social workers are part of multidisciplinary teams that provide services. Therefore, it becomes even more difficult to learn about the effectiveness of social work practice.

## Conclusion

For some time, it has been difficult to demonstrate the effectiveness of social work, in part because of the multiple inadequacies of the group designs that are used (Epstein, 1990; Fischer, 1973; Sheldon, 1986). Although this situation may lead to "disillusionment," Campbell and Stanley (1963) argued that "we must increase our time perspective, and recognize that continuous, multiple experimentation is more typical of science than once-and-for-all definitive experiments" (pp. 2–3). Indeed, despite many environmental constraints (see, for example, Task Force on Social Work Research, 1991; Epstein, 1990; Halpern, 1992; Zimbalist, 1977), there has been a consistent but modest use of group designs in social work research that has augmented and been augmented by research in related disciplinary and professional areas. Given substantial political and fiscal constraints, improvements in the quality of group-design research in social work require attention not only to the fundamental principles underlying group designs but also to the types of trade-offs made in establishing priorities among these principles. Moreover, because social work is clearly preparadigmatic (Glisson & Gillespie, 1992), there will continue to be controversies among social workers and others over such fundamental first principles, as well as what constitutes "legitimate scientific problems and methods" (Kuhn, 1970, p. viii). Nonetheless, it is probable that the elegance of randomized controlled experiments that optimize design principles and hence offer support of causal inferences based on group designs will remain sufficiently enchanting to entice some social work researchers to persist. What remains unknown is whether their efforts will be sufficiently timely and adequate to substantiate the claims that social work has an empirically supported knowledge base and demonstrated practice efficacy.

## References

Achen, C. H. (1986). *The statistical analysis of quasi-experiments*. Berkeley: University of California Press.

Bawden, D. L., & Sonenstein, F. L. (1992). Quasi-experimental designs. *Children and Youth Services Review*, *14*(1–2), 137–144.

Berrick, J. D., & Barth, R. P. (1992). Child sexual abuse prevention: Research review and recommendations. *Social Work Research & Abstracts*, *28*(4), 6–15.

Bowen, G. L., Farkas, G., & Neenan, P. A. (1991). Application of time-series designs to the evaluation of social services program initiatives: The recycling fund concept. *Social Work Research & Abstracts*, *27*(3), 9–15.

Brown, S. R., & Melamed, L. E. (1990). *Experimental design and analysis*. Newbury Park, CA: Sage Publications.

Campbell, D. T., & Stanley, J. C. (1963). *Experimental and quasi-experimental designs for research*. Chicago: Rand McNally.

Cappelleri, J. C., Trochim, T. D., & Reichardt, C. S. (1991). Random measurement error does not bias the treatment effect estimate in the regression–discontinuity design. *Evaluation Review*, *15*, 395–419.

Cheung, K. M. (1990). Interdisciplinary relationships between social work and other disciplines: A citation study. *Social Work Research & Abstracts*, *26*(3), 23–29.

Cohen, J. (1977). *Statistical power analysis for the behavioral sciences (rev. ed.)*. New York: Academic Press.

Cook, T. D., & Campbell, D. T. (1979). *Quasi-experimentation: Design and analysis issues for field settings*. Chicago: Rand McNally.

Craft, J. L. (1990). *Statistics and data analysis for social workers* (2nd ed.). Itasca, IL: F. E. Peacock.

Dooley, D. (1990). *Social research methods* (2nd ed.). Englewood Cliffs, NJ: Prentice Hall.

Edleson, J. L., & Syers, M. (1990). Relative effectiveness of group treatments for men who batter. *Social Work Research & Abstracts*, *26*(2), 10–17.

Epstein, W. M. (1990). Rational claims to effectiveness in social work's critical literature. *Social Science Journal*, *27*, 129–145.

Fischer, J. (1973). Has mighty casework struck out? *Social Work*, *18*, 107–110.

Franklin, D. L. (1986). Mary Richmond and Jane Addams: From moral certainty to rational inquiry in social work practice. *Social Service Review*, *60*, 504–525.

Fraser, M., & Taylor, M. J. (1990). *An assessment of the literature in social work: A report to the NIMH task force on social work research, Part I*. Salt Lake City: University of Utah Graduate School of Social Work.

Fraser, M., Taylor, M. J., Jackson, R., & O'Jack, J. (1991). Social work and science: Many ways of knowing? *Social Work Research & Abstracts*, *27*(4), 5–15.

Giannetti, V. J., & Wells, R. A. (1985). Psychotherapeutic outcome and professional affiliation. *Social Service Review*, *59*, 32–43.

Glisson, C. (1990). *A systematic assessment of the social work literature: Trends in social work research: A report to the NIMH task force on social work research, Part II*. Knoxville: College of Social Work, University of Tennessee at Knoxville.

Glisson, C., & Gillespie, D. F. (1992). Toward the development of quantitative methods in social work research. *Journal of Social Service Research*, *16*(1–2), 1–10.

Green, R., & Vosler, N. R. (1992). Issues in the assessment of family practice: An empirical study. *Journal of Social Service Research*, *15*(3–4), 1–20.

Grinnell, R. M., Jr., & Stothers, M. (1988). Utilizing research designs. In R. M. Grinnell, Jr. (Ed.), *Social work research and evaluation* (3rd ed., pp. 199–239). Itasca, IL: F. E. Peacock.

Halpern, R. (1992). Challenges in evaluating community-based health and social intervention: The case of prenatal care outreach. *Journal of Social Service Research*, *16*(3–4), 117–131.

Heckman, J. J., Hotz, V. J., & Dabos, M. (1987). Do we need experimental data to evaluate the impact of manpower training on earnings? *Evaluation Review*, *11*, 395–427.

Heineman, M. (1981). The obsolete scientific imperative in social work research. *Social Service Review*, *55*, 371–397.

Hepler, J. B., & Rose, S. F. (1988). Evaluation of a multicomponent group approach for improving the social skill of elementary school children. *Journal of Social Service Research*, *11*(4), 1–18.

Hogarty, G. E. (1989). Metaanalysis of the effects of practice with the chronically mentally ill: A critique and reappraisal of the literature. *Social Work*, *34*, 363–374.

Houston, D. J., & Delevan, S. M. (1990). Public administration research: An assessment of journal publications. *Public Administration Review*, *50*, 674–682.

Howing, P. T., Wodarski, J. S., Gaudin, J. M., Jr., & Kurtz, P. D. (1989). Effective interventions to ameliorate the incidence of child maltreatment: The empirical base. *Social Work*, *34*, 330–338.

Ivanoff, A., & Stern, S. B. (1992). Self-management interventions in health and mental health settings: Evidence of maintenance and generalization. *Social Work Research & Abstracts*, *28*(4), 32–38.

Jones, M. B. (1989). Crisis of the American orphanage: 1931–1940. *Social Service Review*, *63*, 613–629.

Kazdin, A. E., Bass, D., Ayers, W. A., & Rodgers, A. (1990). Empirical and clinical focus of child and adolescent psychotherapy research. *Journal of Consulting Psychology*, *58*, 729–740.

Keppel, G. (1973). *Design and analysis: A researcher's handbook*. Englewood Cliffs, NJ: Prentice Hall.

Kirk, R. E. (1968). *Experimental design: Procedures for the behavioral sciences*. Monterey, CA: Brooks/Cole.

Kirk, S. (1991). Scholarship and the professional school [Editorial]. *Social Work Research & Abstracts*, *27*(1), 3–5.

Kirkham, M. A., & Schilling, R. F. II. (1990). Life skills training with mothers of handicapped children. *Journal of Social Service Research*, *13*(2), 67–88.

Koeske, G. F. (1992). Moderator variables in social work research. *Journal of Social Service Research*, *16*(1–2), 159–178.

Kuhn, T. S. (1970). *The structure of scientific revolutions* (2nd ed.). Chicago: University of Chicago Press.

Lamb, M. E., & Sternberg, K. J. (1992). Establishing the design. *Children and Youth Services Review*, *14*(1–2), 157–165.

LeCroy, C. W., & Ashford, J. B. (1992). Children's mental health: Current findings and research directions. *Social Work Research & Abstracts*, *28*(1), 13–20.

Lindsey, D., & Kirk, S. A. (1992). The continuing crisis in social work research: Conundrum or solvable problem? An essay review. *Journal of Social Work Education*, *28*, 370–382.

MacEachron, A. E. (1982). *Basic statistics in the human services: An applied approach*. Baltimore: University Park Press.

Mahrer, A. R. (1988). Discovery-oriented psychotherapy research: Rationale, aims, and methods. *American Psychologist*, *43*, 694–702.

Meehl, P. E. (1963). *Clinical vs. statistical prediction: A theoretical analysis and a review of the evidence*. Minneapolis: University of Minnesota Press.

Metcalf, C. E., & Thornton, C. (1992). Random assignment. *Children and Youth Services Review*, *14*(1–2), 145–156.

Moffitt, R. (1991). Program evaluation with nonexperimental data. *Evaluation Review*, *15*, 291–314.

Moran, T. K. (1987). Research and managerial strategies for integrating evaluation research into agency decision making. *Evaluation Review*, *11*, 612–630.

Neenan, P. A., & Bowen, G. L. (1991). Multimethod assessment of a child-care demonstration project for AFDC recipient families. *Evaluation Review*, *15*, 219–232.

Nugent, W. R. (1987). Information gain through integrated research approaches. *Social Service Review*, *61*, 337–364.

Nugent, W. R. (1988). Author's reply. *Social Service Review*, *62*, 532–534.

Nurius, P. S., & Tripodi, T. (1985). Methods of generalization used in empirical social work literature. *Social Service Review*, *59*, 239–257.

Proctor, E. K. (1990). Evaluating clinical practice: Issues of purpose and design. *Social Work Research & Abstracts, 26*(1), 32–40.

Raynor, P. (1984). Evaluation with one eye closed: The empiricist agenda in social work research. *British Journal of Social Work, 14*, 1–10.

Reid, W. J. (1987). Research in social work. In A. Minahan (Ed.-in-Chief), *Encyclopedia of social work* (18th ed., Vol. 2, pp. 474–487). Silver Spring, MD: National Association of Social Workers.

Reid, W. J., & Hanrahan, P. (1984). Recent evaluation of social work: Grounds for optimism. *Social Work, 27*, 328–340.

Reynolds, K. D., & West, S. G. (1987). A multiplist strategy for strengthening nonequivalent control group designs. *Evaluation Review, 11*, 691–714.

Rivlin, A. M. (1971). *Systematic thinking for social action*. Washington, DC: Brookings Institution.

Rosenthal, J. A., & Glass, G. V. (1990). Comparative impacts of alternatives to adolescent placement. *Journal of Social Service Research, 13*(3), 19–37.

Rosenthal, M. J. (1976). *Experimenter effects in behavioral research*. New York: Irvington.

Rossi, P. H. (1992). Strategies for evaluation. *Children and Youth Services Review, 14*, 167–191.

Rossi, P. H., & Freeman, H. E. (1985). *Evaluation: A systematic approach*. Beverly Hills, CA: Sage Publications.

Rubin, A. (1985). Practice effectiveness: More grounds for optimism. *Social Work, 30*, 469–476.

Rubin, A., & Babbie, E. (1989). The logic of research design. In *Research methods for social work* (pp. 186–236). Belmont, CA: Wadsworth.

Rutchick, I. E. (1990). Research on practice with groups in health care settings. *Social Work in Health Care, 15*, 97–114.

Rzepnicki, T. L. (1991). Enhancing the durability of intervention gains: A challenge for the 1990s. *Social Service Review, 65*, 93–111.

Saunders, D. G., & Parker, J. (1989). Legal sanctions and treatment follow-through among men who batter: A multivariate analysis. *Social Work Research & Abstracts, 25*(3), 21–29.

Schuerman, J. R., Rzepnicki, T. L., Littell, J. H., & Budde, S. (1992). Implementation issues. *Children and Youth Services Review, 14*(1–2), 193–206.

Sheldon, B. (1986). Social work effectiveness experiments: Review and implications. *British Journal of Social Work, 16*, 223–242.

Smith, M. L., Glass, G. V., & Miller, T. I. (1980). *The benefits of psychotherapy*. Baltimore: Johns Hopkins University Press.

Spector, P. E. (1981). *Research designs*. Newbury Park, CA: Sage Publications.

Stanley, T. D. (1991). "Regression-discontinuity design" by any other name might be less problematic. *Evaluation Review, 15*, 605–624.

Tabachnick, B. G., & Fidell, L. S. (1983). *Using multivariate statistics*. New York: Harper & Row.

Task Force on Social Work Research. (1991). *Building social work knowledge for effective services and policies: A plan for research development*. Washington, DC: National Institute of Mental Health, Task Force on Social Work Research.

Thomas, E. J. (1989). Advances in developmental research. *Social Service Review, 63*, 578–597.

Thomlison, R. J. (1984). Something works: Evidence from practice effectiveness studies. *Social Work, 29*, 51–56.

Thyer, B. (1987). Comments on "Information gain through integrated research approaches." *Social Service Review, 61*, 670–672.

Thyer, B., & Curtis, G. (1984). The effects of ethanol intoxication on phobic anxiety. *Behavior Research and Therapy, 22*, 599–610.

Tripodi, T. (1981). The logic of research design. In R. M. Grinnell, Jr. (Ed.), *Social work research and evaluation* (pp. 198–225). Itasca, IL: F. E. Peacock.

Tripodi, T. (1984). Trends in research publication: A study of social work journals from 1956 to 1980. *Social Work, 29*, 353–359.

Tripodi, T. (1987). Program evaluation. In A. Minahan (Ed.-in-Chief), *Encyclopedia of social work* (18th ed., Vol. 2, pp. 366–379). Silver Spring, MD: National Association of Social Workers.

Tucker, D. J., & Hurl, L. F. (1992). An ecological study of the dynamics of foster home placement. *Social Service Review, 66*, 617–641.

Tyson, K. B. (1992). A new approach to relevant scientific research for practitioners: The heuristic paradigm. *Social Work, 37*, 521–533.

Vera, M. I. (1990). Effects of divorce groups on individual adjustment: A multiple methodology approach. *Social Work Research & Abstracts, 26*(3), 11–20.

Videka-Sherman, L. (1988). Metaanalysis of research on social work practice in mental health. *Social Work, 33*, 325–338.

Vooijs, M. W., & van der Kamp, L. J. Th. (1991). Linear versus nonlinear analysis in the measurement of effects in a quasi-experimental design. *Evaluation Review, 15*(5), 625–638.

Weinberger, R., & Tripodi, T. (1969). Trends in types of research reported in selected social work journals. *Social Service Review, 43*(4), 439–447.

Wells, K., & Biegel, D. E. (1992). Intensive family preservation services research: Current status and future agenda. *Social Work Research & Abstracts, 28*(1), 21–27.

Yeaton, W. H., & Sechrest, L. (1981). Critical dimensions in the choice and maintenance of successful treatments: Strength, integrity, and effectiveness. *Journal of Consulting and Clinical Psychology, 49*(2), 156–167.

Zimbalist, S. E. (1977). *Historic themes and landmarks in social welfare research*. New York: Harper.

**Ann E. MacEachron, PhD, ACSW, CISW,** is professor of human development and research, Arizona State University, School of Social Work, Tempe, AZ 85287.

## For further information see

Agency-Based Research; Intervention Research; Meta-analysis; Program Evaluation; Psychometrics; Qualitative Research; Recording; Research Overview; Single-System Design; Survey Research.

**Key Words**

experimental designs research
group designs

# Expert Systems

**Wallace J. Gingerich**

Expert systems are interactive computer programs designed to function much like human consultants, providing expert consultation to the user in a specific problem area. In practice, the computer asks the user a series of questions about the situation at hand and then offers its conclusions and recommendations. Most expert systems allow the user to ask for clarification during the process and for an explanation of the conclusions and recommendations. As with a human consultant, the user is responsible for deciding whether and how to use the advice and recommendations offered by the expert system.

Expert systems originated within the field of artificial intelligence, the branch of computer science that seeks to apply technology to problem solving in ways that would be considered intelligent if done by humans. The first expert system was developed in the late 1960s to help organic chemists describe organic molecular structures (Buchanan & Shortliffe, 1984). The next applications were in the natural sciences, engineering, and medicine. Today, expert systems are routinely used in manufacturing, accounting, and medicine for, among other things, diagnosing robot malfunctions, assessing loan applications, and advising on medical diagnosis and treatment (Waterman, 1986).

Expert systems technology was not applied in the human services arena until relatively recently. Systems have been developed to provide therapy for depressed patients (Mulsant & Servan-Schreiber, 1984) and clients with sexual dysfunction (Binik, Servan-Schreiber, Friewald, & Hall, 1988), to classify learning-disabled students (Ferrara, Parry, & Lubke, 1985), to recommend behavioral intervention strategies in the classroom (Serna, Baer, & Ferrara, 1986), and to advise on the treatment of emotional emergencies in remote areas (Hedlund, Vieweg, & Cho, 1987). Some of these expert systems are regularly used on a day-to-day basis. In addition to these applications, several expert systems have been developed for use specifically in social services applications. They will be discussed later in this entry.

Although these programs are commonly referred to as "expert systems," they would more accurately be described as rule-based (or knowledge-based) consultation systems. The first expert systems were intended to perform at a level comparable to that of human experts; however, as the technology has matured, many of the current systems function more as assistants or colleagues than as true experts.

## Characteristics of Expert Systems

Expert systems are distinguished by several characteristics: the representation of knowledge in the form of if-then rules, the ability to use heuristic reasoning, tolerance for uncertainty and incomplete information, and the capability to explain their reasoning. These unique characteristics make expert systems potentially useful in social work settings.

### If–Then Rules

At the center of an expert system is the knowledge or expertise it contains about the domain. This knowledge is usually represented in the form of if-then rules expressed in natural language, that is, ordinary English as opposed to machine language. The complete set of rules is referred to as the knowledge base for the expert system (Waterman, 1986).

Rules are a simple and intuitively meaningful way of representing expert knowledge about a problem area. Each rule embodies a single, modular chunk of knowledge, stated essentially in the way the human expert would describe it (Davis, Buchanan, & Shortliffe, 1977). For example, a rule in a child protection risk assessment expert system states,

> IF there is physical evidence of abuse or neglect, and
> IF the caretaker is responsible for the injury or neglect, and
> IF the child is under two years old,
> THEN the risk of harm is high. (Stagner & Johnson, 1994)

In most expert systems the rules form a treelike structure such that the consequents inferred by some rules are used to establish the antecedents of other rules. Thus, a chaining process takes place during the consultation in which the intermediate conclusions inferred by some rules are used to reach a final conclusion. In the example above, other rules are invoked to make the determination that there is physical evidence of abuse or neglect. Useful expert systems may consist of as few as eight or 10 rules or as many as hundreds or even thousands of rules. The fully developed set of rules, or knowledge base, offers an accessible and intuitively meaningful representation of expert knowledge in the given domain.

### Heuristic Reasoning

*Heuristics* are rules of thumb that limit the search for solutions in domains that are difficult and poorly understood or that do not lend themselves to procedural description (Waterman, 1986). For example, in chess a commonly accepted heuristic states that in the early part of the game one should develop the middle of the board. Similarly, much of the knowledge of social work practice can be described in if-then rules incorporating heuristics.

Heuristic knowledge contrasts with traditional programming techniques, which use algorithms to apply finite step-by-step procedures that always produce the same result. The algorithmic approach is illustrated by statistical programs that use mathematical formulas to produce the same statistic given the same set of data. Such procedural techniques work well when the knowledge in an area is well defined and highly reliable, such as mathematics or accounting. But because much of social work knowledge is not so concrete, the heuristic approach seems to have more value.

### Tolerance for Uncertainty and Incomplete Information

The rules in expert systems are designed to accommodate uncertainty and incomplete information in a way that mirrors the human decision-making process. Incomplete information may reduce certainty regarding a recommendation, or perhaps alternative recommendations cannot be ruled out. If information is too incomplete, perhaps no recommendation can be made at all.

Social work knowledge is often characterized by uncertainty and incompleteness. For example, the worker might not be completely certain that a caretaker was responsible for injury to a child. Or the information might be incomplete. For example, the worker cannot locate the caretaker and it is not possible to assess whether he or she understands the consequences to the child of his or her behavior. In social work practice, one must sometimes intervene even in the face of uncertainty and incomplete information. Because expert systems can tolerate uncertainty, they have potential value as an aid to practice.

## Explanation Capability

A hallmark of expert systems is their capacity to explain their reasoning. At a minimum this is accomplished by displaying the rules used to reach a conclusion. If intermediate conclusions or subgoals were derived, the system also displays the rules that led to those conclusions. Because the rules are written in the language and terminology of the human expert, displaying the rules that led to the conclusion corresponds roughly to the explanation a human expert would give during a consultation. Some of the more-sophisticated systems may also be able to cite research studies, statutes, policies, diagnostic criteria, or other facts or rules of thumb that were used to arrive at the conclusion.

The capability to explain a conclusion is an important requirement for expert systems. Consultation is inherently interactive, and consultees frequently question the expert to learn the reasoning underlying his or her advice. Questioning helps assure users that the advice is sound and also allows them to incorporate the new knowledge into their own knowledge of the domain. Erdman (1985), for example, found that physicians were more likely to have positive attitudes toward an expert system if the system was able to explain its reasoning.

## Developing an Expert System

The process of developing an expert system is sometimes referred to as "knowledge engineering," reflecting the emphasis on developing the knowledge base as opposed to the actual computer programming itself. A general understanding of the knowledge engineering process will aid in understanding what expert systems are and how they might be used in social work practice.

### Definition of the Knowledge Domain

The first step in developing an expert system is to select a suitable problem—one for which expert knowledge exists (experts perform better than nonexperts) and expertise is needed to arrive at a useful recommendation (Schuerman, 1987). The problem should not be too difficult or too easy; as a general rule, it should be something that a human expert can perform in 10 to 30 minutes. Both of these criteria, expertise and manageable size, are critical to the success of the system. Finally, the problem should be one in which the knowledge is fairly stable over time. If this condition is not met, it will be necessary to update the system constantly.

It is often not easy to know if a problem area lends itself to the development of an expert system. Thus, a common step early in the process is to develop a limited prototype of the system to test the feasibility of the project.

### Knowledge Acquisition and Representation

The process for acquiring and representing knowledge involves a knowledge engineer and a domain expert (Gingerich, 1990; Hart, 1992; Stagner & Johnson, 1994; Waterman, 1986). The knowledge engineer is a computer professional responsible for eliciting knowledge from the domain expert, organizing and representing this knowledge, and programming it into the computer. The domain expert is a recognized expert in the field who is available to describe his or her knowledge about the problem and is committed to the project.

The knowledge acquisition process is interactive and iterative, following what Waterman (1986) called a describe–analyze–refine cycle. The process typically begins with regular meetings in which the knowledge engineer interviews the domain expert to elicit the facts and rules relevant to the domain. Eventually, a prototype of the rule base is used on test cases to identify additional gaps and errors in the knowledge base.

The knowledge acquisition process normally extends over a period of months, or perhaps even years, for larger domains. There comes a time, however, when few additions or refinements to the knowledge base are being made and performance on test cases seems satisfactory. The system then is ready for formal evaluation.

#### Formal Validation

The knowledge base should be evaluated in terms of whether the advice produced by the expert system is accurate and valid and whether the system uses correct reasoning (Buchanan & Shortliffe, 1984; O'Keefe, Balci, & Smith, 1987). Other experts typically are used as the standard of advice; the advice given by the expert system is usually compared with the advice given by human experts on a series of test cases. Validation studies have shown, however, that human experts may not give consistent advice or agree among themselves (Martindale, Ferrara, & Campbell, 1987; Parry & Hofmeister, 1986; Yu et al., 1984). Thus, one must exercise caution when operationalizing the standard of valid advice and the level of performance that can reasonably be expected.

#### Development Tools

Although the first expert systems had to be programmed completely in high-level languages such as Lisp or Prolog, expert system shells that greatly facilitate the development and implementation process are now available (Harmon & King, 1985). These development systems include a user-friendly interface and menus and help systems that make it possible for nonprogrammers to design and implement useful expert systems. The shell provides the basic expert system capabilities, such as the inferencing mechanism and the procedures for handling uncertainty, and the user adds the rules. Expert system shells are analogous to database development systems, which provide data definition and file management capabilities, but the user determines what information is entered and what reports are generated. Commercially available expert system shells cost from several hundred dollars to several thousand dollars.

A full discussion of the development of expert systems is beyond the scope of this entry. However, when building an expert system, it is essential that one follow the general steps outlined in this entry and discussed in detail elsewhere (Buchanan & Shortliffe, 1984; Gingerich, 1990; Hayes-Roth, Waterman, & Lenat, 1983; Pedersen, 1989; Waterman, 1986). Particular attention should be paid to evaluating the correctness and completeness of the knowledge base and the validity of the conclusions, so that the user has a clear idea of the problems for which the expert system is and is not useful.

### Potential Uses of Expert Systems in Social Work

Because expert systems technology is relatively new and largely untried, its actual impact on social work practice has yet to be determined. Accordingly, the following discussion only suggests ways in which expert systems might be used creatively and productively in social work.

#### Making Scarce Expertise More Widely Available

Expert systems have been promoted mainly as a way to capture scarce expertise and distribute it to less-skilled or less-experienced practitioners (Waterman, 1986). For example, many child protective services workers are too inexperienced to have developed the full expertise needed to make accurate assessments of risks of child abuse (Schoech, Jennings, Schkade, & Hooper-Russell, 1985; Stagner & Johnson, 1994). If a fully developed and validated expert system were available to advise on risk assessment, however, perhaps the quality of decisions would be improved.

Expert systems may also be a useful medium for disseminating practice innovations. For an innovation to be adopted, it must be packaged in such a way that practitioners can readily develop the skills to use it (Backer, Liberman, & Kuehnel, 1986; Robinson, Bronson, & Blythe, 1988). Furthermore, there should be some means for determining the consistency with which the intervention is implemented. If social workers find expert systems to be convenient and useful, and if the systems incorporate sufficient tutoring capability, then they may be an effective way to disseminate innovations. For example, changes in eligibility requirements or modifications in criteria for psychiatric diagnoses could be incorporated into a revised version of an expert system and then disseminated simply by mailing updated versions of the software to practitioners.

Research has demonstrated that well-developed expert systems can indeed perform on a par with competent human experts (Parry & Hofmeister, 1986; Yu et al., 1984). In the field of special education, for example, Martindale et al. (1987) evaluated the performance of an expert system that can identify students as learning disabled. The recommendations of the expert system regarding a set of difficult cases were in general agreement with those of a panel of expert reviewers and in some cases conformed more closely with state requirements.

**Training and Tutoring**

In addition to their role as advising tools, expert systems are widely acknowledged to have value as training tools (Buchanan & Shortliffe, 1984; Harmon & King, 1985). Expert systems are interactive and can explain their reasoning. They can provide justification for their conclusions, including references to research literature or to organizational regulations. They may recommend new actions the practitioner would otherwise not have considered. Thus, the inquiring user not only may learn about new actions or decisions but may develop the understanding necessary to reach those same conclusions independently in the future.

**Enhancing Treatment Integrity**

Expert systems that advise on intervention can be used to guide and monitor the implementation of an intervention, specifically, the degree to which the intervention is delivered as intended (Yeaton & Seechrest, 1981). A log of the consultations for each case could be kept to document the pertinent information about the case and the recommended intervention. The practitioner would then document whether or not the intervention was carried out as recommended. This type of documentation would be particularly useful when an intervention is new and practitioners are inexperienced in its use, or when an intervention is being formally evaluated.

Although treatment integrity is required in evaluation research, it almost always is taken for granted and not directly examined. In their systematic review of program evaluation studies, Lipsey, Crosse, Dunkle, Pollard, and Stobart (1987) found that most studies did not report adequate information on implementation of treatment. Furthermore, when complex treatments were evaluated, there was no differentiation made of the actual amount of treatment given. Routine use of an expert consulting system could provide improved assurance that the intervention strategy or approach was being applied consistently with all clients, even though the particular intervention was individualized to fit each case.

**Describing and Refining Practice Wisdom**

During their careers social work practitioners develop proficiency and expertise. Yet as Bloom (1975) noted, most of this practice wisdom is lost because practitioners lack the means to elicit and describe it. The knowledge acquisition, representation, and validation processes required for building an expert system may provide a useful methodology for describing and refining practice wisdom in social work (Mullen & Schuerman, 1990). Indeed, this seems to have been a major contribution of expert systems to social work practice to date.

The extraction of expertise from domain experts, however, has proved a very difficult task (Hoffman, 1987), owing in part to the nature of human expertise. Drawing on the Dreyfus and Dreyfus model of skill acquisition (Benner, 1982; Dreyfus & Dreyfus, 1986), Benner and Tanner (1987) theorized that practitioners who become true experts no longer rely on analytical principles or rules for performing tasks. Instead, they use intuition, a blend of pattern recognition in which the current case is compared with prior situations in the practitioner's experience, commonsense understanding, and skilled know-how. Experts frequently are not able to explicate the formal steps they follow in reaching their decisions, whereas competent nonexperts, who use rules explicitly, can more readily provide justification for their decisions.

Although acquisition of expert knowledge is difficult, it is frequently achievable. A number of useful methods for extracting knowledge from experts have been described (Benbenishty, 1992; Hart, 1992; Hoffman, 1987; Stagner & Johnson, 1994; Waterman, 1986). Unstructured interviews in which the expert is asked to explain his or her reasoning are commonly used. Focused interviews can then be conducted to fill in gaps and clarify inconsistencies. Observing experts while they solve problems, having them talk out loud while doing so, also is a useful technique. Analysis of "tough cases" is useful for revealing some of the more-subtle or refined aspects of the expert's knowledge. The continual process of refining and developing the rule base to provide useful advice across all possible scenarios produces an accessible description of expertise in the domain.

Those who have developed expert systems have frequently noted a somewhat serendipitous benefit. Mulsant and Servan-Schreiber (1984) reported that medical residents found the knowledge engineering process a useful and rewarding way to formalize, test, and refine their knowledge. Furthermore, because the knowledge base could be developed in modules, Mulsant and Servan-Schreiber found it made the formalization process easier than did conventional methods, such as writing a text. Gingerich and de Shazer (1991) observed that building an expert system helped them develop more fully their theory of intervention design, resulting in a flow chart that clarifies how to conduct an assessment interview. Likewise, Stagner and Johnson (1994) report that the knowledge engineering process aided child protection caseworkers in articulating the more-intuitive aspects of risk assessment.

### Developing Theory

According to Winston (1984), the knowledge base should make the important features of the domain explicit, and it should be complete, concise, and understandable. The rules should be stated at a level comparable to the conceptual units the human expert uses, and the underlying logic should map closely the decision rules or rules of thumb the expert uses. In other words, the knowledge base should be a logical, complete, concise, and understandable representation of the expert's problem-solving knowledge about the domain.

The successive refinement, modification, and testing of the rule base required by the knowledge acquisition process often helps identify gaps and inconsistencies in the practice theory. Sometimes these gaps reflect an incomplete description of expertise, but sometimes they represent real gaps in the theory of practice (Gingerich & de Shazer, 1991). As the rule base is elaborated to correct these deficiencies, the theory of practice becomes more developed and refined. This rule base then serves as a concise statement of the theory in a form that makes it readily subject to empirical verification.

## Illustrative Applications

Several expert systems have been developed or are under development for use in social work settings. The first large-scale expert system to be implemented in a social services agency began development in 1988. The Merced County (California) Human Services Agency contracted with Anderson Consulting to develop an expert system to determine client eligibility for public assistance and to calculate benefits (Kidd & Carlson, 1992). The system, known as Merced Automated Global Information Control (MAGIC), incorporates 5,700 rules in its knowledge base, some of which represent written eligibility regulations and others that represent the heuristics that workers use in applying these regulations. In addition to its expert system advising function, MAGIC also assists workers in a variety of case-management tasks. Since the implementation of MAGIC in 1991, a number of benefits have been reported. Delays in seeing clients have dropped from three to five weeks to only 24 to 72 hours. Clients now are given immediate notice about their eligibility and the benefits due to them on completion of the intake interview, rather than days or weeks later. The system has eliminated the need for caseworkers to fill out a myriad of paper forms. With MAGIC, the average caseload per worker has increased from 180 to 330, and error rates and monthly case maintenance activities have both declined, resulting in significant cost savings. Frequent changes in state regulations (averaging one per day) can be incorporated into the rule base quickly, making it possible for the agency and its staff to respond to changes quickly and consistently.

Schuerman and his colleagues at the University of Chicago (Schuerman, 1987; personal communication with J. R. Schuerman, professor, University of Chicago, February 2, 1993; Stagner & Johnson, 1994) are developing an expert system to advise child protection workers on the risk of harm to children in the settings in which they live. The system is currently undergoing refinement and field testing. It is an excellent example of using expert systems technology to capture scarce expertise and make it widely available to other professionals working in the same knowledge area. As noted earlier, many child protection workers may have insufficient experience to develop the expertise necessary to assess risk and the need to intervene to protect the child. Thus, this application is also important because it is being used in an area in which the consequences of making incorrect judgments could be severe.

Mendall Associates is working with the Texas Mental Health and Mental Retardation Department to develop an Automated Screening and Assessment Package (ASAP) that will assist staff in screening individuals for services ("Automated Case Management," 1992; personal communication with M. A. Mendall, knowledge engineer, Mendall Associates, February 2, 1993). ASAP interacts with workers to conduct a global assessment of a client's needs, then consults its knowledge base and makes recommendations about the client's needs, which services should be provided, and any additional assessments needed. This expert system is currently undergoing pilot testing to validate its knowledge base and to assess its utility to practitioners. Once development is completed, the system is expected to be made available to case managers throughout the state of Texas. ASAP is expected to improve the comprehensiveness and accuracy of assessments, to enhance the equity of service delivery, and to reduce paperwork.

Ferns (1992) developed an expert system called Lifenet to advise paraprofessionals on the risk of teenage suicide. The system assists the caseworker in carrying out an interview with an adolescent and assessing whether he or she is in imminent danger of self-harm. Although Lifenet has undergone systematic evaluation and has been found to generally improve caseworker performance, it has not been made available for public use pending further testing and validation.

Finally, a group at the Brief Family Therapy Center in Milwaukee (Gingerich & de Shazer, 1991; Goodman, Gingerich, & de Shazer, 1989) has developed several expert systems designed to advise the solution-focused practitioner on the type of intervention to give at the conclusion of the first therapy session. Both of these expert systems, known as BRIEFER I and BRIEFER II, were developed primarily for research and training purposes, the goal being to describe the decision rules used by expert practitioners as they construct systemic interventions. Both systems, each using a different inferencing strategy, were useful in describing intervention design rules and in training new professionals in the method. Neither system has been made available for general use, largely because of unresolved issues pertaining to legal liability.

## Considerations in the Use of Expert Systems

Although expert systems are likely to benefit social work practice, their potential is still largely unrealized. Experience gained from applying the technology in other fields as well as in social work suggests that a number of factors should be considered when implementing expert systems in social work.

### Selecting Suitable Problems

Expert systems technology should be considered only when the problem area is appropriate to the technology and when the expected benefits of the system outweigh the costs of development and implementation. Appropriate problem areas are those that are well structured and for which the required expertise is clearly established and can be described. Problems such as determining eligibility for service, conducting systematic assessments, and advising on well-defined clinical decisions are suitable candidates for the development of expert systems. In contrast, when an expert relies more heavily on implicit or intuitive knowledge, and the expertise is more fluid and emergent, an expert system is less likely to be successful. Because the most-successful practice applications are those in which the knowledge is relatively well known, expert systems are more likely to function as assistants or reminders to social workers, rather than as experts that exceed or supplant social workers' own professional judgments.

Expert systems should be developed only if the likely benefits justify the costs of development and implementation. Developing large expert systems can be a costly endeavor in terms of the time and human resources required. Estimates range from person-months to person-years of time needed to develop and validate such systems. For example, the Merced system described earlier employed 12 consultants, two programmers, eight caseworkers, and three state welfare program analysts (Kidd & Carlson, 1992). Obviously, expenditures of this magnitude can be justified only if the promise of success is high and the benefits in terms of quality and efficiency of service are large.

### Evaluating Impact on Practice

Expert systems are usually evaluated narrowly for their performance as compared with human experts. This type of evaluation is necessary because it establishes the functionality of the expert system, but it is not sufficient because it does not assess whether the ultimate impact on the client and the service system is beneficial. Expert systems should be considered interventions much like any other helping strategy or procedure and therefore should be systematically designed, developed, and evaluated.

Thomas (1984) identified a number of questions that might be applied to the evaluation of expert systems. For example, does an expert system produce observable changes in practitioner behavior? Do these changes result in improved client outcomes? What are the direct and indirect costs of building expert systems, and do the benefits outweigh the costs? Are practitioners satisfied with the way expert systems perform and the impact they have on their work? What factors affect whether practitioners will adopt and use expert systems? What are some of the unintended effects of using expert systems in social work practice? The answers to these and other questions will require considerable research, but given the nature of social work practice, they are important questions and must be addressed.

**Limitations of Machine Expertise**

Schuerman (1987) called attention to the differences between machine-based expertise and human expertise. A human consultant may "teach, provide emotional support, console, or affirm the consultee's own competence" (p. 17), whereas computers are not able to provide such personalized and empathic interaction. To the extent that the consultant is expected to be a mentor and a caring human being, computer consultation will obviously be inadequate. However, if consultation is sought purely for informational reasons, the lack of personal interaction is not likely to be a limitation.

A related concern is whether computer-based consultation may someday replace human consultants. Although expert systems will probably become commonplace tools for social workers, in most cases the systems will function as "assistants" that support and enhance the work of professionals, not replace them. As expert systems assume some of the more-routine and detail-oriented tasks, professionals will be freed to work on the more-challenging and nonroutine problems.

**Ethical and Legal Issues**

The use of expert systems in social work practice raises ethical issues (Cwikel & Cnaan, 1991; Schoech et al., 1985). Because of the unique nature and function of expert systems, it is not yet clear how their use will be regulated and what liability developers and users will incur. An expert system could be considered analogous to a textbook in that it contains specialized knowledge thought to be useful in professional practice. On the other hand, to the extent that an expert system functions like a human expert—and the user follows its advice accordingly—it could be viewed as a medical device or a professional service and could be subject to strict liability (Adams & Gray, 1987). Strict liability means that the developer of the expert system would be liable for any injury caused by its use. Until these liability issues are resolved, expert systems are not likely to come into widespread use in routine practice.

Who uses an expert system and how it is used also are important considerations. Adams and Gray (1987) advised that only qualified professionals be given access to bona fide expert systems. The expert system should assist or advise, not replace, the qualified professional. Furthermore, the professional should not suspend his or her judgment in blind deference to the expert system.

Adams and Gray (1987) also stated that expert systems should not be made available to nonprofessionals. Herein lies a difficult dilemma. On the one hand, expert systems may contain highly specialized knowledge and offer specific recommendations for action, yet if they are available only to fully qualified professionals, what advantage has been gained? On the other hand, if highly specific and prescriptive advice is given to unqualified users, they may not be able to judge its appropriateness or relevance, and uselessness or harm could result. In a controlled study of erroneous advice giving by an expert system, Will (1991) found that both experts and novices were fooled by the expert system but that novices showed a disproportionate tendency to depend on the erroneous advice of the computer relative to conventional methods. This finding suggests that care must be exercised in how expert systems are used and who is allowed to use them.

**Limitations of Procedural Knowledge**

Expert systems technology requires the extraction and representation of knowledge in the form of if-then rules. This approach appears to be quite useful for knowledge that is well defined and procedural in nature, but it may not be the best fit for more advanced levels of expertise. Although it is possible to extract—or construct—a set of rules and an inferencing system that reproduces an expert's decisions, it is not clear that human expertise in its native state is always linear and rule based. Some expert knowledge may be more implicit or tacit (Schon, 1983).

As our understanding of professional expertise grows and our ability to model it with computer technology improves, it is likely that we will begin to see other theories and methods for representing professional knowledge. One of the more promising emerging technologies is that of neural networks, computer architecture that resembles the structure of the human brain. Neural networks are nonlinear dynamic systems based on fuzzy set theory (Kosko, 1993). Neural systems are well suited to processes such as pattern recognition (visual and language processing) or distinguishing between classes of events, such as discriminating suicidal from nonsuicidal people.

Rather than being programmed deductively with rules and procedures, neural systems are "trained" inductively by being shown many examples over a period of time (Eberhart & Dobbins, 1990). Once a system has been adequately trained, it can then perform the task it was trained to do, that is, recognize new instances and classify them appropriately. For example, when it has been shown enough photographs of a particular individual, a neural network will be able to recognize a new photo of that person even though it has never seen that photograph before. Because of their ability to learn from experience, neural systems have the potential to elucidate the weights or factors that go into human professional assessing and decision making. This and other technologies being developed in the fields of artificial intelligence and cognitive science are likely to have an increasing impact on social work practice in the future.

## Conclusion

Although we are in the very early stages of using expert systems technology in social work practice, such systems will likely come to play an increasingly important role in social work settings. Their chief benefit will probably be to increase the consistency and reliability of decision making in circumscribed areas and to enhance the efficiency with which services are delivered. In the process of developing and validating expert systems, social workers might also increase their understanding of expert social work practice itself and thereby add to the practice knowledge base and enhance their ability to pass knowledge on to others. Ethical and legal issues related to the development and use of expert systems, however, remain to be resolved.

## References


Adams, E. S., & Gray, M. W. (1987). Strict liability for the malfunction of a medical expert system. In W. W. Stead (Ed.), *Proceedings of the 11th annual symposium on computer applications in medical care* (pp. 93–97). New York: Institute of Electrical and Electronics Engineers.

Automated case management system promotes consistent assessments of client needs. (1992). *Case Management Advisor, 3,* 97–98.

Backer, T. E., Liberman, R. P., & Kuehnel, T. G. (1986). Dissemination and adoption of innovative psychosocial interventions. *Journal of Consulting and Clinical Psychology, 54,* 111–118.

Benbenishty, R. (1992). An overview of methods to elicit and model expert clinical judgment and decision making. *Social Service Review, 66,* 598–616.

Benner, P. (1982). From novice to expert. *American Journal of Nursing, 82,* 402–407.

Benner, P., & Tanner, C. (1987). Clinical judgment: How expert nurses use intuition. *American Journal of Nursing, 87,* 23–31.

Binik, Y. M., Servan-Schreiber, D., Friewald, S., & Hall, K. S. (1988). Intelligent computer-based assessment and psychotherapy: An expert system for sexual dysfunction. *Journal of Nervous and Mental Disease, 176,* 387–400.

Bloom, M. (1975). *The paradox of helping.* New York: John Wiley & Sons.

Buchanan, B. G., & Shortliffe, E. H. (Eds.). (1984). *Rule-based expert systems.* Reading, MA: Addison-Wesley.

Cwikel, J. G., & Cnaan, R. A. (1991). Ethical dilemmas in applying second-wave information technology to social work practice. *Social Work, 36,* 114–120.

Davis, R., Buchanan, B., & Shortliffe, E. (1977). Production rules as a representation for a knowledge-based consultation program. *Artificial Intelligence, 8,* 15–45.

Dreyfus, H. L., & Dreyfus, S. E. (1986). *Mind over machine.* New York: Free Press.

Eberhart, R. C., & Dobbins, R. W. (1990). *Neural network PC tools: A practical guide.* San Diego: Academic Press.

Erdman, H. P. (1985). The impact of an explanation capability for a computer consultation system. *Methods of Information in Medicine, 24,* 181–191.

Ferns, W. J. (1992). *The impact of expert system technology on the delivery of social services.* Unpublished doctoral dissertation, City University of New York.

Ferrara, J. M., Parry, J. D., & Lubke, M. M. (1985). *CLASS.1: An expert system for student classification* [technical paper]. Logan: Utah State University.

Gingerich, W. J. (1990). Developing expert systems. *Computers in Human Services, 6,* 251–263.

Gingerich, W. J., & de Shazer, S. (1991). The BRIEFER project: Using expert systems as theory construction tools. *Family Process, 30,* 241–250.

Goodman, H., Gingerich, W. J., & de Shazer, S. (1989). BRIEFER: An expert system for clinical practice. *Computers in Human Services, 5,* 53–68.

Harmon, P., & King, D. (1985). *Expert systems: Artificial intelligence in business.* New York: Wiley.

Hart, A. (1992). *Knowledge acquisition for expert systems.* New York: McGraw-Hill.

Hayes-Roth, B., Waterman, D. A., & Lenat, D. (Eds.). (1983). *Building expert systems.* Reading, MA: Addison-Wesley.

Hedlund, J. L., Vieweg, B. W., & Cho, D. W. (1987). Computer consultation for emotional crises: An expert system for "non-experts." *Computers in Human Behavior, 3,* 109–127.

Hoffman, R. R. (1987). The problem of extracting the knowledge of experts from the perspective of experimental psychology. *AI Magazine, 8,* 53–66.

Kidd, R. C., & Carlson, R. J. (1992). A truly MAGIC solution. In A. C. Scott & P. Klahr (Eds.), *Innovative applications of artificial intelligence* (Vol. 4, pp. 237–247). Menlo Park, CA: American Association for Artificial Intelligence.

Kosko, B. (1993). *Fuzzy thinking: The new science of fuzzy logic.* New York: Hyperion.

Lipsey, M. W., Crosse, S., Dunkle, J., Pollard, J., & Stobart, G. (1987). Evaluation: The state of the art and the sorry state of the science. In D. S. Cordray & M. W. Lipsey (Eds.), *Evaluation studies review annual* (Vol. 11, pp. 153–173). Newbury Park, CA: Sage Publications.

Martindale, E. S., Ferrara, J. M., & Campbell, B. W. (1987). A preliminary report on the performance of Class.LD2. *Computers in Human Behavior, 3,* 263–272.

Mullen, E. J., & Schuerman, J. R. (1990). Expert systems and the development of knowledge in social welfare. In

L. Videka-Sherman & W. J. Reid (Eds.), *Advances in clinical social work research* (pp. 67–83). Silver Spring, MD: NASW Press.

Mulsant, B., & Servan-Schreiber, D. (1984). Knowledge engineering: A daily activity on a hospital ward. *Computers and Biomedical Research, 17,* 71–91.

O'Keefe, R. M., Balci, O., & Smith, E. P. (1987). Validating expert systems. *IEEE Expert, 2,* 81–89.

Parry, J. D., & Hofmeister, A. M. (1986). Development and validation of an expert system for special educators. *Learning Disability Quarterly, 9,* 124–132.

Pedersen, K. (1989). *Expert systems programming: Practical techniques for rule-based systems.* New York: John Wiley & Sons.

Robinson, E.A.R., Bronson, D. E., & Blythe, B. J. (1988). An analysis of the implementation of single-case evaluation by practitioners. *Social Service Review, 62,* 285–301.

Schoech, D., Jennings, H., Schkade, L. L., & Hooper-Russell, C. (1985). Expert systems: Artificial intelligence for professional decisions. *Computers in Human Services, 1,* 81–115.

Schon, D. (1983). *The reflective practitioner: How professionals think in action.* New York: Basic Books.

Schuerman, J. R. (1987). Expert consulting systems in social welfare. *Social Work Research & Abstracts, 23*(3), 14–18.

Serna, R. W., Baer, R. D., & Ferrara, J. M. (1986, May). *An expert system for behavior analysis.* Paper presented at the meeting of the Association for Behavior Analysis, Milwaukee, WI.

Stagner, M., & Johnson, P. (1994). Understanding and representing human services knowledge: The process of developing expert systems. *Journal of Social Service Research, 19,* 115–137.

Thomas, E. J. (1984). *Designing interventions for the helping professions.* Beverly Hills, CA: Sage Publications.

Waterman, D. A. (1986). *A guide to expert systems.* Reading, MA: Addison-Wesley.

Will, R. P. (1991). True and false dependence on technology: Evaluation with an expert system. *Computers in Human Behavior, 7,* 171–183.

Winston, P. H. (1984). *Artificial intelligence.* Reading, MA: Addison-Wesley.

Yeaton, W. H., & Seechrest, L. (1981). Critical dimensions in the choice and maintenance of successful treatments: Strength, integrity, and effectiveness. *Journal of Consulting and Clinical Psychology, 49,* 156–167.

Yu, V. L., Fagan, L. M., Bennett, S. W., Clancey, W. J., Scott, A. C., Hannigan, J. F., Blum, R. L., Buchanan, B. G., & Cohen, S. N. (1984). An evaluation of MYCIN's advice. In B. G. Buchanan & E. H. Shortliffe (Eds.), *Rule-based expert systems* (pp. 589–596). Reading, MA: Addison-Wesley.

**Wallace J. Gingerich, PhD, LISW,** is professor, Case Western Reserve University, Mandel School of Applied Social Sciences, 10900 Euclid Avenue, Cleveland, OH 44106.

## For further information see

Assessment; Computer Utilization; Direct Practice Overview; Goal Setting and Intervention Planning; Information Systems; Professional Liability and Malpractice; Quality Assurance; Recording; Research Overview; Social Work Practice: Theoretical Base.

**Key Words**

artificial intelligence
computer applications
expert systems

# Index

(Note: References to entire entries are in **boldface**)

## B

## O

## R

## U

## Y



## Z